I0796039

מחזור קורן לסוכות • נוסח אשכנז

The Koren Sukkot Maḥzor • Nusaḥ Ashkenaz

קורן ירושלים

THE GROSS FAMILY EDITION

מחזור קורן לסוכות
THE KOREN SUKKOT MAHẒOR

חג הסכת תעשה לך

WITH INTRODUCTION, TRANSLATION AND COMMENTARY BY

Rabbi Lord Jonathan Sacks שליט״א

FOREWORD BY

Rabbi Elazar Muskin שליט״א

•

KOREN PUBLISHERS JERUSALEM

The Koren Sukkot Maḥzor, Nusaḥ Ashkenaz
The Gross Family Edition
Second North American Hebrew/English Edition, 2018

Koren Publishers Jerusalem Ltd.
POB 4044, Jerusalem 91040, ISRAEL
POB 8531, New Milford, CT 06776, USA

www.korenpub.com

Koren Tanakh Font © 1962, 2018 Koren Publishers Jerusalem Ltd.
Koren Siddur Font and text design © 1981, 2018 Koren Publishers Jerusalem Ltd.
English translation and commentary © 2006, 2015 Jonathan Sacks.

Considerable research and expense have gone into the creation of this publication.
Unauthorized copying may be considered *geneivat da'at* and breach of copyright law.
No part of this publication (content or design, including use of the Koren fonts) may be reproduced, stored in a retrieval system or transmitted in any form or by any means electronic, mechanical, photocopying or otherwise, without the prior written permission of the publisher, except in the case of brief quotations embedded in critical articles or reviews.

The creation of this Maḥzor was made possible with the generous support of Torah Education in Israel.

Standard Size, Hardcover, ISBN 978-965-301-659-0
Compact Size, Hardcover, ISBN 978-965-301-800-6

SUA4

DEDICATION

It has been both my pleasure and privilege to dedicate a large number of religious books of which the *Koren Sukkot Maḥzor* is the latest.

I dedicate it to four generations of my family:
My grandparents Hugo and Aranka Gross
and Gershon and Julia Danzig
my parents Paul and Marta Gross
my wife Danielle Gross
and her parents, David and Edith Beissah
and our children and grandchildren
David, Melanie and Shalom Pesach,
Benjamin, Juliet and Miriam Adi, and Samuel

The Torah frequently mentions "many generations" and I used to wonder why. The answer lies in the fact that we are the product of those who precede us. Our lives are largely dependent on our life partners and we devote ourselves and have our existence validated by our children, and our grandchildren. I am in no doubt that the generations that preceded me, together with my wife Danielle and my own children have been the defining influences in my life. Three of my four grandparents were martyrs of the Holocaust and the knowledge that they gave their lives because of their Jewish identity has been the single greatest influence in my approach to life.

I landed in Israel for the first time, in the middle of the night before Pesaḥ, in 1952 at the age of six. As he bent to kiss the ground, my father burst into uncontrollable tears, a traumatic experience for me as a child. When I asked my mother why Dad was so upset, she gently explained that my father's parents and her own mother had always talked of their desire to visit *Eretz Yisrael* but had been murdered by the Nazis only a few years before. My parents had fulfilled that burning ambition in their stead and that had moved my father to such emotion. This was the moment in which I first became conscious of who I am and where I had come from. Imbued with this realization, I was determined to do whatever I could to advance the spiritual and physical welfare of my fellow Jews both "in the Land which the Almighty swore unto our Fathers Abraham, Isaac and Jacob to give us" and in the Diaspora. In this mission, I have been blessed in many ways:

First, by the example of my own dear parents of blessed memory. I had

◂ the good

the good fortune to grow up in a happy, loving and united home based on the two foundations of Judaism and Zionism, both of which I inherited from my mother's milk.

Second, the Almighty blessed me with a wife who has been pivotal in every aspect of my life. We have grown together and she has been the greatest source of strength in ensuring that our children were nurtured in the way that we hoped. Truly the phrase *eishet ḥayyil*, "a woman of worth," could have been written for her.

Finally, both Danielle and I have been blessed with three sons, together with our daughters-in-law and grandchildren, who have exceeded our wildest expectations in terms of character, academic accomplishment and spiritual direction. With the benefit of a far higher level of *limmudei kodesh* than we had, they have not only received the baton of our values and ambitions but they have run further and faster with it than we ever could. All this in the spirit of love and respect to us as their parents, and with the greatest affection and unity with each other.

I have concluded that there is relatively little which any generation can do by itself to validate its own existence. Any such validation must come from the next and subsequent generations.

Many years ago, in a cemetery on the Slovak/Hungarian border, I stumbled across the graves of my great- and great-great-grandparents who died long before the Second World War and whom I therefore never knew. After paying my respects by reciting the *Kaddish* and other relevant prayers in their memory, I metaphorically addressed them and said that I could, so to speak, look them in the face because the four next generations of their family, whom I am honoring with this volume, had all validated their existence by inheriting and then passing on their faith and their values and would do so for the foreseeable future.

The certainty that our children, and with the grace of the Almighty, and theirs, will do the same for us is my greatest satisfaction because it assures the fulfillment of our primary aspiration as both individual Jews and as a People, namely, that we devote ourselves to aspiration —

Out of Zion shall come the Law
and the Word of the LORD from Jerusalem.

Nothing else really matters.

Michael Gross
Herzliya Pituaḥ, 5778 (2018)

CONTENTS

SIMḤAT TORAH — שמחת תורה

PREFACE

זמן שמחתנו
Our time of rejoicing...

We are commanded to rejoice and we are commanded to dwell in fragile huts. Rabbi Sacks has written that this "is spiritual courage of a high order. I have often argued that faith is not certainty: faith is the courage to live with uncertainty. That is what Sukkot represents if what we celebrate is *Sukkot mamash,* not the clouds of glory but the vulnerability of actual huts, open to the wind, the rain and the cold." On Sukkot we celebrate that throughout the year, throughout the Days of Awe which precede it, we continue to flourish as a people, dedicated to service to God, despite that fragility against which life throws its challenges, however deadly.

The *Koren Sukkot Maḥzor* is a project of such scope, that it would have been virtually impossible without the partnership of Danielle and Michael Gross MBE, formerly of London, and now of Herzliya. A founding governor of the Ben Gurion University, a key supporter of Soroka Medical Center, a funder of numerous scholarships of higher education, Chairman of the Yisrael Youth Award, a former honorary officer of the United Synagogue, and a supporter of countless publications, Michael has a long history of leadership, activism and philanthropy both in Israel and the Diaspora, and a reputation for scrupulous integrity and upholding the highest standards. We are privileged to have the Gross Family as a partner and friend of Koren. On behalf of the scholars, editors, and designers of this volume, we thank you; on behalf of the users and readers of this Maḥzor, we are forever in your debt.

We could not have embarked on this project without the moral leadership and intellectual spark of Rabbi Lord Jonathan Sacks. Rabbi Sacks provides an invaluable guide to the liturgy through his remarkable introduction, translation, and commentary. His work not only clarifies the text and explains the teachings of our sages, but uniquely and seamlessly weaves profound concepts of Judaism into the reality of contemporary life. It was our distinct privilege to work with Rabbi Sacks to create a Maḥzor that we believe appropriately reflects the complexity and depth of Jewish prayer.

We only hope that Rabbi Sacks' contribution is matched by the scholarship, design, and typography that have been hallmarks of Koren Publishers Jerusalem for more than fifty years. Rabbi David Fuchs supervised the textual aspects of the work. Rachel Meghnagi edited the English texts and Efrat Gross the Hebrew texts. Jessica Sacks supplied the superb translations of *Kohelet*, Torah readings, and many of the *piyutim*. Thanks also to Lauren Gordon for additional translations. The text for *Mishnayot Sukka* was taken from the Noé edition of the *Koren Talmud Bavli*, with commentary and elucidation by Rav Adin Steinsaltz (Even Israel). Rabbi Eli Clark contributed the informative and useful Halakha Guide. We thank Esther Be'er for assembling and typesetting the texts. Koren is privileged to have a small, but remarkably talented team of consummate and dedicated professionals.

This new edition of the Koren Maḥzor continues the Koren tradition of making the language of prayer more accessible, thus enhancing the prayer experience. One of the unique features of the Maḥzor is the use of typesetting to break up a prayer phrase-by-phrase – rather than using a block paragraph format – so that the reader will naturally pause at the correct places. No commas appear in the Hebrew text at the end of lines, but in the English translation, where linguistic clarity requires, we have retained the use of commas at the end of lines. Unlike other Hebrew/English *maḥzorim*, the Hebrew text is on the left-hand page and the English on the right. This arrangement preserves the distinctive "fanning out" effect of the Koren text and the beauty of the Koren layout.

We hope and pray that this Maḥzor, like all our publications, extends the vision of Koren's founder, Eliyahu Koren, to a new generation, to further *Avodat HaShem* for Jews everywhere.

Matthew Miller, Publisher
Jerusalem, 5775 (2015)

FOREWORD

Walter Isaacson, the famous author who wrote the bestselling biography, *Steve Jobs*, published another work called *The Innovators*. Isaacson's major thesis in this book is that the best innovations do not happen in a "light bulb moment" in someone's garage or attic; rather, they are products of collective efforts.

Isaacson uses the modern computer as a prime example. There is a lingering historic debate over who deserves to be dubbed the inventor. Was it John Atanasoff, who toiled as a lone dreamer in a basement at Iowa State in the late 1930s; or John Mauchly, who led a multi-talented team at the University of Pennsylvania? Mauchly gathered a large team that included dozens of engineers and mechanics. The result was Mauchly's machine was the world's first fully functional, general-purpose electronic computer. Atanasoff's machine, however, was built first but it never worked, partly because he had no one helping him figure out how to make his punched-card burner operate. In the end, it was consigned to a basement at Iowa State and almost forgotten forever.

Perhaps this historic tidbit can help us understand a famous debate in the Talmud (*Sotah* 11b) between two of the greatest Talmudic rabbis, Rabbi Akiva and Rabbi Eliezer, about what Sukkot actually commemorates. The Torah states (Leviticus 23:43) that we are commanded to dwell in booths each year, because, "I [God] settled the children of Israel in booths when I brought them out of the land of Egypt…"

Wondering what the Torah means by "booths," Rabbi Eliezer suggests that it refers to the great miracle of the "Clouds of Glory" that accompanied the Jews for their forty years in the desert, while Rabbi Akiva argues that it means the actual booths they lived in during their wandering in the desert.

On the surface, one can clearly understand Rabbi Eliezer's explanation. According to his approach, the holiday of Sukkot resembles the other two pilgrimage holidays, Pesaḥ and Shavuot, both of which mark miracles that happened to the Jewish people. Likewise, Rabbi Eliezer suggests, Sukkot is intended to arouse in our memory God's supernatural protection of the Jewish people throughout their travels in the desert.

According to Rabbi Akiva, however, what is the purpose of commemorating the booths that the Jewish people built with their own hands in the desert? They weren't miracles at all, they were only a natural result of people building necessary shelter in which to live.

Upon closer analysis, Rabbi Akiva is suggesting a profound insight. Sukkot, he proffers, highlights the Jewish people's dedication and loyalty to and their partnering with God. When the Jewish people built their own huts in the desert, they did so with the belief and prayer that their efforts would be accompanied by God's blessings. How else could they wander in a desert for forty years, surviving the elements, without believing that God would protect them once they did their part?

For Rabbi Akiva, Sukkot and its message are eternally important. Sukkot isn't just a commemoration of some historical moment; it is suffused with the idea that we are partners with God in this world, and that without God we cannot succeed.

As one lifts this Maḥzor and prays during this holiday, it is essential to remember why we pray and for what are we praying. We ask God to partner with us in all our endeavors. The words found in this Maḥzor reminds us of the words of the Psalmist who wrote, "If God will not build the house, in vain do its builders labor on it; if God will not guard the city, in vain is the watchman vigilant" (Psalm 127:1). When man thinks he can build alone, that is when he makes his biggest mistake. Like John Atanasoff, when we do it alone we end up consigned to the basement of life, forgotten forever.

The rabbis of the Rabbinical Council of America are honored to partner with Koren Publishers and Matthew Miller in offering the community this magnificent Maḥzor. It is our hope that as you use the Maḥzor, it will enhance your praying experience and appreciation for the celebration of Sukkot.

Rabbi Elazar Muskin
Senior Rabbi, Young Israel of Century City
Los Angeles, California

INTRODUCTION

SEASON OF JOY:

Essays on the themes and concepts of Sukkot

by

RABBI LORD

JONATHAN SACKS

INTRODUCTION

Season of Joy

It was a sight that, once seen, was never forgotten. Jerusalem was thronged with pilgrims. For days there had been a noise and energy about the streets and arcades you never felt at other times of the year. People were busy constructing their sukkot in courtyards and on the level roofs of their houses, and bringing foliage for the covering through which they would see the stars and which, some said, were reminders of the clouds of glory that accompanied their ancestors on their epic trek through the desert. In the markets people had been busy buying the palm branches, citrons, and twigs of myrtle and willow, examining each for perfection of form so that they could celebrate the festival with what King David had called *hadrat kodesh*, the beauty of holiness (Ps. 29:2).

The courtyard of the Temple was more crowded than at any other time of the year. People were excited. You could feel the anticipation, the barely suppressed exuberance. It was an emotion woven of many strands. The great Days of Awe, with their intense solemnity, were over. The great shofar had sounded, heralding the New Year. On Yom Kippur the High Priest had officiated, confessing the sins of the people and symbolically laying them on one of two goats, chosen by lot, that was then sent out into the desert, a visible symbol of guilt being carried away. The High Priest had atoned for the people. The slate had been wiped clean. Now, less than a week later, there was a palpable feeling of release and a new beginning.

Then there was the mood of thanksgiving. The harvest had been gathered. The fields and groves and vineyards had yielded their produce. It was a time to thank God for His many blessings: the land, the earth, the sun, the rain, the fields and yields, the freedom. People recalled the words of Moses even before they had entered the land: If you love the LORD your God and worship Him with all your heart and soul, then He would send rain in its due season, in autumn and spring, and they would gather in grain, grapes for wine, and olives for oil. There would be grass in the fields for the cattle. "You will eat and be satisfied." So he had said (Deut. 8:10), and so it had been. In Israel you could never take rain for granted. When it came it felt like a blessing from heaven.

◂ The stalls

The stalls were overflowing with produce. The rabbis had specifically ordained that those who lived within a day's distance from Jerusalem should bring to the city the fruit of the fourth year and the produce set aside for the second tithe, and not redeem it for money, so that "the markets of Jerusalem would be decorated with fruit" (*Beitza* 5a).

The Temple courtyard was packed with people who had come from all parts of the land to be here for these holy days. This was the sight that made the sages say that it was one of the miracles that happened regularly at the Temple that though "the people stood crowded together, yet there was ample space when they prostrated themselves" (*Avot* 5:7). There were processions round the altar all seven days of the festival, with people carrying their palm branches, citrons, myrtle and willows. The atmosphere rose to a crescendo when the Levites sang the Hallel and the entire crowd, waving their palm branches, roared their responses: "His loving-kindness is forever," and "Lord, please save us." It was this litany, with its repeated refrain *Hosha na*, "Please save," that gave the western world the word *hosanna* for a shout of jubilation.

There were aspects of the Temple service on Sukkot that happened at no other time of the year. There were processions around the altar, not just with the four kinds but also with branches of willow, *arava*. Accompanying the sacrifices was not just the usual libation of wine but also a special water libation. Every morning at dawn, in a special ceremony, priests and Levites would leave the Temple courtyard and walk south to the Shiloaḥ stream from which they drew water, which was then placed into a golden bowl. As they entered the Temple, shofar blasts were sounded.

So significant was this entire ceremony that, at night on the intermediate days of the festival, in preparation for the next morning's events, a celebration took place in the Temple courtyard known as *Simḥat Beit HaSho'eva*, "rejoicing in the house of the water drawing." So euphoric was the mood on those nights that the sages said, "One who did not see the Celebration of the Place of the Drawing [*Simḥat Beit HaSho'eva*] never saw celebration in his days" (Mishna, *Sukka* 5:1).

The mood was like a wedding. Some played the flute, others harps, lutes and cymbals. People sang, danced and clapped. The leading religious figures in the land, sages, heads of yeshivot, members of the high court, the pious, elders, and men of renown all joined the celebrations.

◂ It was said

It was said that the *Nasi*, Rabban Shimon ben Gamliel, used to juggle with flaming torches (*Sukka* 53a). Sages became acrobats. Scholars did somersaults. They considered it the ultimate dignity to sacrifice your dignity in the sacred cause of joy. So lighthearted and exuberant were the celebrations that people began to be concerned that they might turn into the kind of revelry associated with the Greek Dionysia and the Roman Bacchanalia, where a combination of drink and mixing of the sexes led to the kind of debauchery alien to Judaism, all the more so in the precincts of the Temple. So to prevent the mixing of the sexes, a ladies' gallery was erected in the Temple, the first of its kind, so that the women could watch and see the dancing below. The celebrations went on throughout the night, and there were sages who said that during Sukkot they never slept, so continuous were the celebrations.

To illuminate the Temple at night, three giant candelabra were lit, each with four gold basins and multiple wicks, filled with oil by young men from priestly families. They used to say that the whole of Jerusalem was lit by the radiance that emanated from these lamps (Mishna, 5:3). The singing and dancing went on until dawn, when the shofar was blown to signal that the time had come for the procession to collect the water from the Shiloaḥ spring to begin (Mishna, 5:4).

There was no other moment in the Jewish year quite like Sukkot. Even before the building of the Temple, we read of an annual "festival for God at Shilo" at which young women danced in the vineyards (Judges 21:19–20). Some scholars surmise that it was this festival on which Elkana would go each year to the sanctuary at Shilo, and it was for this reason – Sukkot being among other things a festival celebrating the wine vintage – that Eli the priest, seeing Hannah praying, thought she was drunk (1 Sam. 1:3–18).

The harvest had been gathered, work in the field was for the time-being over, and people had both reason and time to celebrate. This meant that the crowds were larger at this festival than at any other time of the year, even Pesaḥ. During the Roman campaign against Israel in the Great Revolt of 66–70 CE, Cestius Gallus approached the city of Lydda, only to find it almost completely deserted because virtually the whole town had traveled to Jerusalem to celebrate Sukkot there (Wars of the Jews, II:19:1).

It was the obvious time to choose for great national ceremonies. The Torah states that every seven years, at the end of the year of release, the king must convene a national assembly and read Torah to the people (Deut. 31:10–13). This was, in effect, a covenant renewal ceremony, reminding the people of their past, their collective raison d'être, and their commitments to God. The Torah specifies that this was a family celebration to which men, women and children should come. It was a solemn reminder of who the people were, and why.

For the same reason, Solomon chose this time for the consecration of the Temple: the project his father David had conceived, but had been told by God that it would not be he, but his son, who would do it. The task was immense and deeply symbolic. The book of Kings tells us that the work was begun "in the four hundred and eightieth year after the Israelites left Egypt" (1 Kings 6:1), the only event in post-Mosaic history to be dated by reference to the exodus. The number (forty, the number of the wilderness years, multiplied by twelve, the number of the tribes) is itself symbolic. It had taken centuries to settle the land, build towns, unite the tribes into a single kingdom under a single king, and establish Jerusalem as the nation's capital. The building took seven years, and required vast amounts of quarried stone (shaped into blocks at the quarry so that no sound of hammer or chisel would be heard in the sacred precincts of the Temple itself) together with cedar- and pine-wood imported from Lebanon.

The celebrations were launched by a historic speech from Solomon, and went on for two weeks, the second of which was Sukkot. On the eighth day, Solomon told the people that on the morrow they were to return home. The people "blessed the king, going back to their tents happy and buoyant of heart over all the goodness that the Lord had performed for His servant, David, and for His people, Israel" (1 Kings 8:66).

Centuries later, in a much more low-key ceremony, the Second Temple was also dedicated on Sukkot, the celebrations led by the governor Zerubavel and the High Priest Joshua (Ezra 3:1–6). Work on the Temple was desultory because of active opposition on the part of the Samaritans. The entire project lapsed for some seventeen years. Eventually, Jewish life, and with it the restoration of the Temple as the spiritual heart of the nation, was re-energized by two remarkable leaders who had recently arrived from Babylon: Ezra and Nehemiah. Together they convened a new national assembly, one of the most important in Jewish history.

It began on the first of Tishrei, on the day we now know as Rosh

HaShana. In a conscious echo of the septennial address by the king, Ezra stood on a wooden platform in front of the Water Gate in Jerusalem and read the Torah to the assembly, having positioned Levites throughout the crowd to explain to the people what was being said. As they heard the holy words recited, the people started weeping, as it slowly dawned on them how far they had drifted from the covenant their ancestors had made with God. Ezra and Nehemiah, however, stilled the crowd, saying: "Go and enjoy choice food and sweet drinks, and send some to those who have nothing prepared. This day is holy to our Lord. Do not grieve, for the joy of the Lord is your strength" (Neh. 8:10).

The next day they returned and Ezra read further from the Torah. In the course of the reading, the people heard the command to celebrate Sukkot, a practice that had evidently been neglected for generations. Word spread throughout the crowd, and within days it had been carried throughout the country. Everywhere, people could be seen collecting branches from olive trees, palms and myrtles to make coverings for the sukkot that they proceeded to build locally and in Jerusalem itself by two of its gates. The book of Nehemiah records that "the whole company that had returned from exile built temporary shelters and lived in them. From the days of Joshua son of Nun until that day, the Israelites had not celebrated it like this. And their joy was very great" (8:17). The celebrations lasted seven days and "on the eighth day, in accordance with the law, there was an assembly" (8:18), in other words they celebrated Shemini Atzeret.

That moment was a turning point in Jewish history, the start of a long revolution in Jewish life, in which a vision intimated long before by Moses began to become real in the life of the nation. The nation had become, in effect, the People of the Book, whose citadels were houses of study, whose heroes were teachers and scribes, and whose passion was learning and the life of the mind. What Ezra and Nehemiah understood, and would be proved true many times in the following centuries, was that the real battle faced by Israel was less military than spiritual. Jews might lose everything else, but if they kept their identity, they would outlive the mightiest of empires.

Sukkot became not just the festival of ingathering, but also the great moment of national rededication. So it is not surprising that when, several centuries later, the Maccabees celebrated their victory over the Seleucid

Greeks and their Hellenized Jewish sympathizers, and reconsecrated the Temple, they modeled their celebrations on Sukkot, in the form of the festival we now call Ḥanukka. Despite the fact it takes place at a quite different time of the year, beginning on 25 Kislev, the letter they sent to the Jews of Egypt requests them to celebrate at that time "the festival of Sukkot and the festival of the fire given when Nehemiah, who built the Temple and the altar, offered sacrifices" (II Macc. 1:18).

The same book later describes the first time Ḥanukka was observed by the Maccabees, the year they defeated the Greeks: "They celebrated it for eight days with rejoicing in the manner of Sukkot, remembering how not long before, during the festival of Sukkot, they had been wandering in the mountains and caves like wild beasts" (II Macc. 10:6). In other words, they had been unable to celebrate Sukkot properly that year while they were in hiding during the war itself. "Therefore, carrying ivy-wreathed wands and beautiful branches, and also fronds of palms, they offered hymns of thanksgiving to Him who had given success to the purifying of His own holy place" (ibid. 10:7). In other words, Ḥanukka itself was modeled on Sukkot, which had become not only the festival of joy, but supremely the festival of the Temple and national rededication.

Already in Leviticus and Deuteronomy, Sukkot had been singled out for special celebration. "And you shall rejoice on your festival," said Moses in connection with Sukkot, "and you will be truly joyful" (Deut. 16:14–15). So it seemed natural to call these days *zeman simḥateinu*, "our time of rejoicing."

Joy is at the heart of Judaism. "Serve the Lord with joy," said the psalm (100:2), "come before Him with jubilation." Israel would come to know more than its share of sufferings, defeats, destructions and exiles. Yet what sustained it was not sadness but gladness, a deep religious joy. In the last month of his life, Moses had warned the people not to take the land, its freedoms or its produce for granted, nor to forget their origins. The land was not theirs but God's, and therefore the right way to celebrate it was by gratitude. Bad things would happen, he warned, if people ever lost their capacity for joy. Curses would strike the nation, "Because you did not serve the Lord your God with joy and gladness of heart out of the abundance of all good things" (Deut. 28:47).

The one defense against national entropy – the loss of collective energy over time – would be joy itself, a combination of thanksgiving, humility, gratitude, and memories of the suffering that had to be endured in the course of arriving at this place and this estate. Judaism is not a religion of austerity, self-denial and stoic endurance. It is not a faith that allowed itself to be overwhelmed by tragedy. Time and again it arose, phoenix like, from catastrophe, demoralization, and defeat, and each time renewed itself, gathering ever greater strength in the process. True faith, in Judaism, is marked by the capacity for joy.

That, however, is only the first and outermost layer of a festival of unusual complexity and depth. In the following chapters I want to explore the meaning of Sukkot at deeper levels, for it will turn out to be, perhaps more than any other, the festival that tells us what it is to be a Jew, and what difference faith makes to the human condition itself. Our journey begins with one of the last voices of the great tradition of Israel's prophets, the man we know as Zechariah.

The Dual Festival

The defeat of the southern kingdom by the Babylonians in the sixth century BCE was the deepest, most defining trauma of the biblical age. We can still feel the overpowering grief of the book of Lamentations, its raw pain undiminished by the intervening millennia, as the prophet sees the defeat of his people and the ruins of the Temple. We can still hear the despair of the exiles who, "By the rivers of Babylon," sat and wept as they remembered Zion (Ps. 137:1). Yet, as the two great prophets of exile, Jeremiah and Ezekiel, had promised, the people did return. The Babylonian empire was defeated by a newer superpower, Persia, under whose enlightened leader, Cyrus, Jews were given permission to return.

The situation they found in the Holy Land was devastating. The people had lost almost all contact with their religious heritage. As Nehemiah later wrote, they no longer observed the Sabbath. They had intermarried with neighboring people. They no longer knew how to speak Hebrew: "Half of their children spoke the language of Ashdod, or they spoke the language of one of the other nations" (Neh. 13:24). Work had begun on rebuilding the Temple, but it hit a series of difficulties, and the returning exiles turned instead to rebuilding their homes and farms. The unfinished Temple was a visual reminder of Israel's broken state, politically, culturally and religiously.

◂ One prophet

One prophet who undertook the task of kindling a spark of hope from the dying embers of national identity was Zechariah. His message, astonishing in the circumstances, was that despite its forlorn state, the people of the covenant would revive, and then inspire not only themselves, but the world. The day would come when "ten people from all languages and nations will take firm hold of one Jew by the hem of his robe and say, 'Let us go with you, because we have heard that God is with you'" (Zech. 8:23). Zechariah also gave expression to one of the briefest and best summaries ever given of Jewish history: "'Not by might nor by power, but by My Spirit,' says the LORD Almighty" (4:6).

All the prophets had foreseen that the nation would be punished for its sins but would eventually return to God. Beginning with Ezekiel in exile in Babylon, prophecy now took on a darker complexion, as if the road from here to the Messianic Age could no longer pass through the normal processes of history. Israel's glory would be restored, but this would happen only through Divine intervention into the human script, shaking the foundations of the world. Eschatology, *Aḥarit HaYamim*, the vision of the End of Days, began to grow more disturbing.

Zechariah was the first prophet to say that even after Jews returned to their land, this would not be the end of their troubles. The nations of the world would form an alliance and wage war against the Jewish people in Jerusalem. God Himself would be forced to intervene to defend His people and defeat their enemies. The earth would shake. God would crush the Mount of Olives and flatten the surrounding countryside. Mount Zion would tower alone, streams of waters issuing from it, and bringing fertility to the land. After these momentous events, the nations would come to acknowledge that there is only one God: "Then the LORD shall be King over all the earth: on that day the LORD shall be One and His name One" (14:9) – a verse now one of the best-known lines of Jewish prayer.

It was in the course of this prophecy that Zechariah made a unique prediction. Not only would Jerusalem be the capital of Israel, it would become the spiritual center of the world. The nations would gather there once a year on Sukkot:

> And it will be: those remaining from all the nations who came up against Jerusalem will go up year upon year to bow down to the King,

> Lord of hosts, and to celebrate the Festival of Sukkot. And it will be: those from the earth's families who do not go up to Jerusalem and bow down to the King, Lord of hosts – rain shall not fall for them; and if the family of Egypt does not go up, does not come – they will have no [overflow]. This will be the plague that the Lord will bring upon the nations who do not go up to celebrate the Festival of Sukkot; such will be the punishment of Egypt and the punishment of all the nations who do not come up to celebrate the Festival of Sukkot. (14:16–19)

There is no other prophecy quite like this anywhere else in Tanakh: none that says that a Jewish festival will one day be global, observed by all the nations. The pilgrimage festivals were part of Israel's unique heritage, not its universal truths. They are about Israel and its seasons, and about the formative moments of Jewish history: the exodus from Egypt, the giving of the Torah at Mount Sinai and, in the case of Sukkot, the forty years of wandering in the desert without a permanent home. Zechariah was thus making an unprecedented assertion when he spoke of Sukkot as a festival not just for Israel but for everyone.

What led him to do so? There was one unusual feature of the Sukkot sacrifices that might have inspired this thought. Whereas in the case of the other seven-day festival, Pesaḥ, the offerings were the same each day, on Sukkot they were different. On the first day, thirteen young bulls were offered, on the second twelve, and so on until on the seventh day, when there were seven – making a total of seventy in all (Num. 29:12–34). Seventy in the Torah corresponds to the number of nations into which humanity was divided according to Genesis 10. The sages drew the conclusion that in making an offering of seventy young bulls on Sukkot, the Israelites were in effect sacrificing and praying on behalf of humanity as a whole (*Sukka* 55b.) Zechariah may thus have been inspired by an idea implicit in the Torah itself.

Hence the paradox: Sukkot is the most universalistic of the festivals, the only one that will one day be celebrated by all humanity. As Zechariah makes clear, this has to do with its association with rain, and there is nothing distinctively Jewish about the need for rain. All countries, especially in the Middle East, need it. At the same time it is also the most particularist of festivals. No other nation took as a symbol not a castle, a fortress or a

◂ triumphal

triumphal arch, but a fragile tabernacle. No other nation was born, not in its land, but in the desert. Far from being universal, Sukkot seems intensely particularistic, the festival of a people like no other, whose only protection was its faith in the sheltering wings of the Divine Presence.

There are other unusual features of Sukkot. In the list of holy days in Deuteronomy 16, rejoicing is not mentioned in connection with Pesaḥ. It is mentioned once in connection with Shavuot, but twice in the context of Sukkot:

> You shall rejoice [*vesamaḥta*] on your festival.... You shall celebrate for seven days for the LORD your God in the place which the LORD shall choose, for the LORD your God shall bless you in all of your produce and all that you do; and you will be truly joyful [*vehayita akh same'aḥ*]. (Deut. 16:14–15)

It was this that led to the description of Sukkot as *zeman simḥateinu*, "our time of rejoicing." But why a double joy?

Turning to the account of the festivals in Leviticus 23, we notice something else unusual about Sukkot. It is defined not in terms of *one* overriding symbol, but *two*. The first is the command to take the "four kinds" of fruit and foliage:

> On the first day, you shall take for yourselves a fruit of the citron tree, palm fronds, myrtle branches and willows of the brook, and be joyous in the presence of the LORD your God for seven days. (Lev. 23:40)

The second command is quite different:

> You shall dwell in booths for seven days; all those born among Israel shall dwell in booths, so that your descendants will know that I settled the children of Israel in booths when I brought them out of the land of Egypt; I am the LORD your God. (Lev. 23: 42–43)

It was this command – to leave our homes and live in a temporary dwelling – that gave the festival its name.

No other festival has this dual symbolism, and their juxtaposition is curious. Not only are the "four kinds" and the sukka different in character: in a sense they conflict with one another. The "four kinds" are associated with the land of Israel. The sukka is the opposite, a reminder of exodus, exile, the desert, and no-man's-land. In practical terms also they conflicted. The four kinds were, as the sages said, symbols of and a mode of intercession for rain (*Ta'anit* 2b). Indeed the rabbis said that rainfall for the coming year was determined on the first day of Sukkot (Mishna, *Rosh HaShana* 1:2). But the command to live for seven days in a sukka with only leaves for a roof presupposes the absence of rain. If it rains on Sukkot, with the exception of the first night, we are exempt from the command for as long as the rain lasts, if it is heavy enough to spoil the food on the table (Mishna, *Sukka* 2:9).

All this conveys the impression that Sukkot represents two festivals, not one. In fact it does, and therein lies its uniqueness. Though the festivals are often listed together, they represent two quite different cycles of time. First is the annual cycle of the pilgrimage festivals: Pesaḥ, Shavuot and Sukkot. These tell the singular story of Jewish identity and history: the exodus, the revelation at Mount Sinai, and the long journey through the wilderness. Celebrating them, we re-enact what made Israel the particular people it is. The central section of the Amida prayer on these festivals begins with the classic statement of Jewish particularity: "You have chosen us from among all peoples."

There is a second cycle – the festivals of the seventh month, Rosh HaShana, Yom Kippur, and Sukkot. Just as the seventh day, Shabbat, is *zekher lema'aseh bereshit*, a memorial of creation, so is the seventh month. *Hayom harat olam*, "This day is the birth of the world," we say in our prayers on Rosh HaShana. When it comes to Creation, we are all created, and we are all accountable to our Creator, Jew and non-Jew alike. That is why the Mishna says that on Rosh HaShana, "All who have come into this world pass before Him like sheep" (Mishna, *Rosh HaShana* 1:2). All humanity is judged. The language of the prayers on the Days of Awe is markedly more universal than at other times. The central section of the Amida begins by speaking not about Israel, the chosen people, but about humankind as a whole: "And so place the fear of You … over all that You have made." Rosh HaShana and Yom Kippur are about the sovereignty of God over all the world. We reflect on the human, not just the Jewish, condition.

The two cycles reflect two quite different aspects of God as He relates to the world: as Creator and Redeemer. As Creator we relate to God through nature. As Redeemer we relate to God through history. As Creator, God is universal. We are all in God's image, formed in His likeness. We share a covenant of human solidarity, made by God with Noah and through him all humankind after the Flood. We are fellow citizens of the world under the sovereignty of God. As Redeemer, however, God is particularistic. Whatever His relationship with other nations (and He has a relationship with other nations: so the prophets insist), Jews know Him through His saving acts in Israel's past: the exodus, the revelation and the journey to the Promised Land.

It is now obvious what makes Sukkot unique. It is the only festival that is part of both cycles. It belongs to the yearly cycle of Jewish history – Pesaḥ, Shavuot and Sukkot – the year that begins in Nisan, the month of the exodus in which Jewish national history began. But it also belongs to the seventh-month cycle that represents creation and nature: Rosh HaShana, Yom Kippur and Sukkot. The year of nature begins on Rosh HaShana, the anniversary of creation itself. Hence the double joy, and the twofold symbolism.

The "four kinds" represent what is universal about Sukkot. They are about nature. They are the only time we do a mitzva with natural objects: a lulav, etrog, and myrtle and willow leaves. They are about humanity's dependence on nature, and nature's need for rain. That is why Zechariah foresaw that when all nations acknowledged God, they would come together in the seventh month to pray for rain on Sukkot. The sukka, by contrast, has nothing to do with rain. It has to do with history and what makes Jewish history unique. We have undergone repeated experiences of exile. Too often Jews have known that where they are is only a temporary dwelling. Jewish history has often been a long journey across the wilderness of time.

Something else about Sukkot, in this case common to both the "four kinds" and the sukka, also points to this duality. The "four kinds" are unprocessed products of nature. The covering of the sukka must also be made of materials that were once growing and are now detached but not yet turned into crafted objects of a kind capable of contracting *tum'a*, impurity (Mishna, *Sukka* 1:4). Both the "four kinds" and the sukka covering represent the boundary between nature and culture, what Levi-Strauss called the "raw" and the "cooked." Nature is universal. Culture is not. Once again we feel the tension between our common humanity and our religious specificity, between what makes us the same and what makes us different.

More than any other festival, Sukkot represents the dual character of Jewish faith. We believe in the universality of God, together with the particularity of Jewish history and identity. All nations need rain. We are all part of nature. We are all dependent on the complex ecology of the created world. We are all threatened by climate change, global warming, the destruction of rain forests, the overexploitation of non-renewable energy sources, and the mass extinction of species. But each nation is different. As Jews we are heirs to a history unlike that of any other people: small, vulnerable, suffering repeated exile and defeat, yet surviving and celebrating.

Sukkot thus represents the tension at the heart of Judaism in a way not shared by any other faith. The God of Israel is the God of all humanity. But the religion of Israel is not, and will not be, the religion of all humanity. Even in the Messianic Age, Zechariah tells us, the nations will celebrate only Sukkot together with Israel, not the other festivals – despite the fact that on that day God will be One and His name One.

This is one of the most important truths Judaism offers the world: Humanity is formed out of our commonalities and differences. Our differences shape our identity. Our commonalities form our humanity. We are neither completely different, nor all the same. If we were completely different, we could not communicate. If we were all alike, we would have nothing to say. Our differences matter. But so too does the truth that despite our religious differences, we share a common humanity. Sukkot is thus the festival of a double joy: at being part of this people, yet also participating in the universal fate of humankind.

The Strangest Book of the Bible

Our real journey into the meaning of Sukkot, however, begins with a book that is not merely the strangest in Tanakh, but also one of the most unlikely ever to have been included in a canon of sacred texts: Kohelet, known in English through its Greek translation as Ecclesiastes, meaning "one who addresses an assembly."

◂ Kohelet

Kohelet is a strange, bewildering, and much debated book. It was one of the last to be canonized, though it was widely known and studied long before its status was finalized. It was included in the Septuagint, the first translation of the Hebrew Bible into Greek. It is presupposed by the book known as Ben Sira (also known as Ecclesiasticus), written in the late second century BCE. Fragments of Kohelet were found among the Dead Sea scrolls. Nonetheless, there were rabbis who found it problematic. A minority held that it was not to be included in Tanakh. For them it represented merely the human wisdom of Solomon, not a text inspired by *ruaḥ hakodesh*, the holy spirit, a precondition of being included in the Bible.

A homily in the Talmud (*Shabbat* 30a) tells us some of the problems the sages had with the book. "O Solomon, where is your wisdom? Where is your understanding? Not only do your words contradict those of your father David, but they also contradict themselves. Your father David said, 'It is not the dead who praise the LORD' (Ps. 115:17) but you said, 'I thought the dead more fortunate, who have died already, than the living who yet live' (4:2), and then you said, 'Better to be a living dog than a dead lion' (9:4)." Is it better to be alive than dead? Kohelet answers both Yes and No.

Other rabbis pointed out other contradictions. Ibn Ezra counted nine of them and said that the attentive reader would find more. Kohelet praises joy (8:15) and derides it (2:2). He values wisdom (2:13) and denigrates it (6:8). He says things will go well for those who are God-fearing (8:12) and then says that there are righteous people who suffer the fate of the wicked, and wicked people who receive the reward of the righteous (8:14). Such were the internal contradictions in the book that some sages sought not merely to exclude it from the canon but to have it banned (*Shabbat* 30b).

Kohelet's tendency to say one thing and then the opposite makes the book hard to understand, but this alone would not have justified excluding it from the canon. The sages were adroit in resolving apparent contradictions, of which there are many in the Hebrew Bible. Kohelet uses contradiction the way Socrates used questions, to force his listeners to think beyond conventional wisdom, and understand the complexity and many-sidedness of life. He understood what Niels Bohr famously said, that the opposite of a superficial truth is a falsehood, but the opposite of a profound truth may well be another profound truth. The use of contradiction is common within the wisdom literature. One example comes from the book of Proverbs: "Do not answer a fool according to his folly, or you yourself will be just like him. Do answer a fool according to his folly, or he will be wise in his own eyes" (Prov. 26:4–5). It was not its internal contradictions that made some think Kohelet did not belong in the Hebrew Bible, but something far more consequential.

It was that many of the views expressed by Kohelet seem to verge on heresy (see *Vayikra Raba* 28:1; *Kohelet Raba* 1:4, 11:9; *Midrash Mishlei* 25:1). The same fate, he says, awaits the righteous and the wicked, the pure and impure, the good and the sinner (9:2). There is no correlation between effort and reward. The race is not to the swift, nor bread to the wise, nor grace to the learned: time and chance happen to them all (9:11). Kohelet sees "the victims' tears and none to console them; power at the hands of their oppressors, and none to console them" (4:1). Where then is justice and the Judge?

"The fate of man is the fate of cattle; the same fate awaits them both," hence "the pre-eminence of man over beast is nothing" (3:19). What then becomes of the idea of the uniqueness of the human person made in the image and likeness of God Himself? Don't be too righteous or too wicked, says Kohelet (7:16–17). What then should we do: be a little righteous and a little wicked? "Follow your heart where it leads you, your eyes where they allure you," he says to the young man (11:9). What then happens to the third paragraph of the Shema which tells us not to stray "after your heart and after your eyes" (Num. 15:39)?

Kohelet says not a word about Jewish particularity. Scholars have long noted its similarity to other wisdom literature of the ancient Near East, Egyptian, Mesopotamian, even Canaanite. It would not have been out of place in Greece in the third century BCE: in places it reads like a Stoic or Epicurean text. Though it contains many references to God, it never once uses the four-letter name we refer to as Hashem, that is, God as He relates specifically to the Jewish people. Kohelet speaks only of Elokim, that is, the God of creation, nature and humankind as a whole.

The most important feature of Kohelet that makes it seem so remote from faith is his repeated use of the word *hevel*. It occurs no less than thirty-eight times in the course of the book, more than half of its incidences in Tanakh as a whole. *Hevel* has traditionally been understood to

◂ mean futile

mean futile, meaningless, empty, pointless, "absurd" in the existentialist sense, and most famously in the King James translation: "Vanity of vanities, saith the Preacher, vanity of vanities; all is vanity."

This is what makes the book so challenging. Religion in general, Judaism specifically, is the attempt to find meaning in the cosmos and in human life. Faith is the attempt to hear the music beneath the noise, discern the path amidst the undergrowth, to sense the destination of the long journey of which our lives are a part. Judaism is the bold attempt to address directly what Viktor Frankl called, "Man's Search for Meaning." To see life as meaningless – *hevel* – seems in the most profound sense to part company with Jewish tradition.

Thus Kohelet, despite its invocations of God and its pious ending, reads at first like a subversive book. If there is no justice in history, if the strong crush the weak, and power is in the hands of the oppressor, if the wise man who saves the city is forgotten while evil reigns in place of judgement, why are we here at all? We live, we suffer, then we die. That seems to be Kohelet's philosophy. Homo sapiens, however "noble in reason and infinite in faculty," is ultimately no more than the "quintessence of dust." But this is Hamlet, not Judaism. And even if a case can be made for its inclusion in the library of sacred texts, why, of all the books, was it chosen for Sukkot, *zeman simḥateinu*, "our time of rejoicing"? Of all our holy books it seems the most bleak and depressing.

Kohelet is a puzzle to be solved, a mystery to be decoded. If we do so, we will discover not only that it is a profound statement of faith, one of the deepest in literature, but also that it is the key to understanding Sukkot itself.

Who was Kohelet?

Fortunately, the book gives us the clue that allows us to unpack its meaning in its second word, the one that gives it its title as well as the name of its author: Kohelet. Who was he? There is only one possible answer: Kohelet was Solomon. The opening sentence states: "The sayings of Kohelet son of David, King of Israel in Jerusalem." The only son of David who became king was Solomon. The rest of Kohelet confirms this identification. Solomon was the only king of Israel whose life matches the description in chapter two, of a man who amassed a great estate, built palaces, planted vineyards, orchards and gardens, had vast numbers of slaves and servants, accumulated silver and gold, and had many wives and concubines.

Kohelet's claim to have gathered more wisdom than any other king before him (1:16) parallels the description of Solomon in I Kings 5:9, in which "God gave Solomon wisdom and very great insight, and a breadth of understanding as measureless as the sand on the seashore." The statement at the end of the book, that Kohelet "weighed and explored and assembled many wise sayings" (12:9), matches the statement in the book of Kings that Solomon "spoke three thousand proverbs," and was so famous for his wisdom that "people from all nations came to listen" to him (5:12–14).

If Kohelet was Solomon, why is he not called Solomon? This is the first indication that the book is not a treatise to be read, but an encrypted text to be deciphered. Note that the question is not the historical one: who actually wrote Kohelet? Whoever wrote Kohelet, without a shadow of doubt it is meant to be read as the reflections of the man known as Israel's wisest king. In which case, the book should mention Solomon. That is the case with the two other books traditionally ascribed to him, The Song of Songs and Proverbs. The name Solomon appears nowhere in Kohelet. What is more, the word Kohelet appears nowhere else in Tanakh. This strongly suggests that Kohelet is more than the name of the author. It is a clue to the interpretation of the book.

The point is often missed in translation, because it is difficult to convey in other languages the density of associations often carried by a single Hebrew word. That is clearly the case here. The word Kohelet comes from the root ק-ה-ל, meaning "to gather people together." Thus it is usually translated as "Preacher," "Teacher," or "Convener of an assembly." However, what matters here is not what the word means, but rather the associations it carries with it. As soon as we turn to the other key instances of the verb, a fascinating picture begins to emerge.

The first connection is with the mitzva known as *Hak-hel*: the command that the king was to assemble the people every seven years at a national assembly on Sukkot at the end of a sabbatical year:

> Every seventh year, in the scheduled year of release, during the festival of Sukkot, when all Israel comes to appear before the LORD your God

◂ at the place

> at the place that He will choose, you shall read this law before all Israel in their hearing. Assemble the people – men, women, and children, as well as the aliens residing in your towns – so that they may hear and learn to fear the LORD your God and to observe diligently all the words of this law, and so that their children, who have not known it, may hear and learn to fear the LORD your God, as long as you live in the land that you are crossing over the Jordan to possess. (Deut. 31:10–13)

Here then is an immediate connection between Sukkot, a king, an assembly, an act of teaching, and the verb *hak-hel*, from the same root as the word Kohelet. This connection was not lost on the sages, who explained that Solomon was called Kohelet precisely because of this role, and suggested that the book is based on what Solomon taught at these gatherings (*Kohelet Raba* 1:2). Something of this is hinted at the very end of the book: "Kohelet's wisdom went further than this; he taught the people understanding always, and weighed and explored and assembled many wise sayings" (12:9). We do not find in the story of Solomon that he "taught the people." Hence it was not absurd to suggest that this happened at the septennial gathering of the nation on Sukkot.

There is, as we noted in the first chapter, another connection between Solomon and Sukkot, namely the dedication of the Temple, which took place over a fourteen-day period, the last seven of which coincided with Sukkot. If we turn to 1 Kings 8, the chapter that describes the consecration of the Temple (page 461), we find that the verb ק-ה-ל plays a key role in the text. It appears seven times, and a seven-fold repetition is often used in biblical prose to indicate a key word. The chapter tells how Solomon assembled the elders of Israel and all the heads of the tribes, to bring up the Ark of the Covenant of the LORD out of the city of David, which is Zion. Again we find a connection between a national assembly, the king, and Sukkot.

There is a third connection, more oblique, but one that will eventually prove highly consequential. The Temple was the successor to the *Mishkan*, the Tabernacle or Sanctuary that the Israelites made in the desert, their first collective house of worship. Construction began immediately after Moses descended from Mount Sinai with the second set of tablets, having broken the first after the sin of the Golden Calf. In this narrative, too, the key word is ק-ה-ל. At the making of the Calf we read that "When the people saw that Moses delayed to come down from the mountain, the people gathered themselves together [*vayikahel*] around Aaron, and said to him, 'Come, make gods for us, who shall go before us…'" (Ex. 32:1). After securing atonement for the people, Moses commanded them to build the Sanctuary. The narrative begins, "Moses assembled [*vayak-hel*] all the congregation of the Israelites…" (35:1). Again the key word is ק-ה-ל.

The assembly Moses convened to set in motion the building of the Sanctuary was a *tikun*, a setting-right, of the assembly that had committed the sin in the first place. According to tradition, Moses descended the mountain with the second tablets, the sign that the people had been forgiven and the covenant between them and God was still in place – on Yom Kippur. That is why the anniversary of that day became, throughout the generations, the day of forgiveness and atonement. The next day, work on the Sanctuary began (see Rashi to Ex. 35:1). Still today the custom is to begin making the sukka immediately after Yom Kippur.

So there is a whole series of connections between the word Kohelet, from the root ק-ה-ל, and a king, a national assembly, the Sanctuary in the wilderness, the Temple in Jerusalem, and Sukkot. Indeed the prophet Amos calls the Temple *Sukkat David*, "David's Tabernacle" (Amos 9:11). These echoes and evocations are too strong to be coincidental. The key to understanding Kohelet is Sukkot, and the key to understanding Sukkot is Kohelet. Nor is the root ק-ה-ל the only link between the book and the festival.

Wisdom, the Universal Heritage

Recall Zechariah's prophecy that one day Sukkot would be celebrated by all the nations on earth, and the sages' understanding that the seventy bullocks offered during the festival were on behalf of the seventy nations, that is, on behalf of humanity as a whole. Sukkot is the most universalist of the festivals, and Kohelet is by far the most universalist of the five "scrolls" – the Megillot. Ruth, Esther and Lamentations tell highly particularist narratives about characters and events in Jewish history. The Song of Songs is about the particularity of love: what makes this lover and this beloved unique. But Kohelet is consistently, even surprisingly, universal. The word "Israel" only appears twice, and then in the form of an editorial aside, "I Kohelet was king of Israel in Jerusalem" (1:12, and compare 1:1). The four-letter name of God, Hashem, indicating His specific I-Thou relationship with the people Israel, never appears in the book. Instead, forty-two times the word Elokim is used: that is, God in His relationship with humanity as a whole.

The reason for this is that Kohelet is supremely written in the wisdom voice. There are three primary voices in Tanakh. Each corresponds to a different way in which we encounter God, and each is embodied in a different kind of leadership role. Respectively, they are the king, the priest and the prophet, and they correspond to the three modes of God's relationship with the world: through Creation, Revelation and Redemption.

The priest speaks the language of Revelation, that is, God's word in the form of law. The priest's key roles are *lehavdil*, "to distinguish, separate," and *lehorot*, "to instruct, to give a legal ruling." The priest sees distinctions in the world invisible to the naked eye. They are not part of the physical world as such; they are, rather, part of the sacred ontology, the underlying divine order, of the universe. The key words in the priest's vocabulary are *tahor* and *tameh*, pure and impure, and *kodesh* and *ḥol*, holy and profane. He (priests in Judaism were always male) lives within a structure of time wholly determined by divine service: originally the sacrificial service of the Temple. The priest represents the holy in Jewish life. Halakha, Jewish law, belongs to the priestly voice.

The prophet hears and speaks God's word, not for all time but for this time: this place, this context, this circumstance, the today that is different from yesterday and tomorrow. He or she (prophets could be either) senses the presence of God in history, specifically history as a journey toward redemption, that is to say, a society that honors God by honoring His image, humankind. While the priest looks at the sacred nature of things, the prophet is concerned with relationships between persons, and between the individual and God. His or her key words are *tzedek*, fairness, *mishpat*, retributive justice, *ḥesed*, covenant love, and *raḥamim*, compassion. While the world of the priest never changes, the prophet's world is constantly changing, depending on where the people are and in which direction society is moving. The prophet is concerned with faithfulness in Jewish life: loyalty, integrity, and honesty between the people and God and between one another.

Wisdom in the Hebrew Bible is very different from the worlds of the priest and the prophet. It is almost always associated with kings and royal courts, and it is universal, not specific to Judaism. It is part of the human heritage: it is part of what it means to be created in the image and likeness of God. Thus the sages said: "If you are told that there is wisdom among the nations, believe it. If you are told there is Torah among the nations, do not believe it" (*Eikha Raba* 2:13). The sages coined a blessing on seeing "a great sage from the [other] nations" (*Berakhot* 58a). The wisdom literature of Tanakh – Kohelet, Proverbs, Job, and some Psalms – is recognizably similar to the wisdom literature of the ancient Near East as well as the philosophers and moralists of ancient Greece and Rome. Whereas priestly and prophetic consciousness lives in particularity, the essence of wisdom is universality.

If the priestly voice is about revelation and the prophetic about redemption, wisdom belongs to the realm of creation. It is about what we would nowadays call the natural and social sciences. Wisdom and Torah are very different. Wisdom is about facts, Torah is about laws. Wisdom is about what is, Torah about what ought to be. Wisdom is descriptive while Torah is prescriptive. Wisdom is acquired through observation and reflection. Torah is acquired through revelation and tradition. In relation to wisdom, what matters is the truth of a proposition, not its source. Hence Maimonides' famous axiom: "Accept the truth, whoever says it" (Introduction to *Pirkei Avot*). In the case of Torah, however, source is of the essence. Does it come from the revelation at Sinai, or from the Oral Law, faithfully transmitted? Hence the rabbinic rule: "Whoever reports a saying in the name of the one who said it brings deliverance to the world" (*Avot* 6:6).

The words *ḥakham*, a wise person, and *ḥokhma*, wisdom, appear fifty-three times in Kohelet, as against a mere thirty-three times in the entire Mosaic books, where (with the exception of Deuteronomy) they are almost entirely used in connection with the royal court in Egypt – Pharaoh and his advisers – or the Sanctuary, where *ḥokhma* is used in the sense of craftsmanship.

It is therefore no accident that the most universal of books, Kohelet, is read on the most universal of pilgrimage festivals, Sukkot. Wisdom, the knowledge of God in creation, belongs to the seventh month, the month of creation (Rosh HaShana as the anniversary of the birth of the world and humankind). And just as Zechariah said that there would come a time when "those remaining from all the nations… will go up year upon year to bow down to the King, the Lord of hosts, and to celebrate the Festival of Sukkot" (Zech. 14:16), so the book of Kings says, "From all nations people came to listen to Solomon's wisdom, sent by all the kings of the world, who had heard of his wisdom" (1 Kings 5:14). That is the second connection between Kohelet and Sukkot. But it is the third that is the most surprising.

The Structure of Joy

Kohelet is often seen as a depressing, despairing, almost nihilistic book. The author is old, disillusioned, skeptical about the ability of humans to change the world or institute justice in the affairs of men, disinclined to find any redemptive quality in life itself. So, of all biblical books, it seems the least appropriate to read on Sukkot, "the season of our joy." Yet, counterintuitively, it turns out that this is precisely what Kohelet is about.

The root ש-מ-ח, meaning joy or rejoicing, appears no less than seventeen times in the course of the book. To put this in context, the same root appears only once in each of the first four Mosaic books, Genesis, Exodus, Leviticus and Numbers, and twelve times in Deuteronomy. There are more references to joy in Kohelet than in all the Mosaic books combined.

Nor is this all. The references to joy are carefully structured. The overall development of the book is not clear, but one thing is: seven times, after a sequence of dispiriting reflections, Kohelet interrupts his theme with a reference to joy:

1. There is no good for man to find, but that he eat and drink and show himself some good of all his labor; this I saw to be a gift from God… He gave wisdom and insight and joy to those who are satisfied with what they have. (2:24–26)
2. And so I know that there is no good for them but to be happy and to do what is good in their lifetime. And if any man eats and drinks and sees some good of all his labor – that is a gift from God. (3:12–13)

◂ 3. I saw

3. I saw that there is no good at all but for man to take pleasure in his works; for that is his share. (3:22)
4. This is what I have seen that is good: the beauty of eating and drinking and seeing some good of all the labor one toils over beneath the sun, all the days of the life God has given one – for this is one's share. For if God gives any man wealth and belongings, and grants him the power to eat of them, to take hold of what is his, to take pleasure in his labors – that is a gift from God. For he will not think too much about the days of his life; for God has given him the joy of his heart to be occupied with. (5:17–19)
5. And so I praise joy – for there is no good for man beneath the sun, but to eat and drink and be happy. This is what he has to accompany him in his labors, through that life that God has given him beneath the sun. (8:15)
6. Go, eat your bread in joy, and drink your wine with a joyful heart, for God has accepted your deeds… Live well, with the woman you love, all the days of the shallow breath He has given you here beneath the sun. (9:7–9)
7. There is a sweetness in the light; it is good for the eyes to see the sun. And should a man live many years he should rejoice in all of them, remembering, too, the days of darkness, for there will be many. All that comes is but a breath. (11:7–8)

Then comes the ten-line coda, precisely symmetrical with the ten-line introduction to the book. The closing movement, a long adagio beginning with the words, "Young man, rejoice now in your youth" (11:9), is one of the most moving descriptions of age and physical decline in all literature, comparing it to the darkening of the sun, the slow decay of an old house, a well that no longer yields water, a shattered lamp, a broken pitcher, and dust returning to the earth as it was, ending with the words, "Shallowest breath, said Kohelet, it is all but shallow breath" (12:8). The introduction begins with almost identical words, "Shallowest breath, said Kohelet, the shallowest breath, it is all but breath" (1:2), and then describes the endless cycles of nature in which "One age departs, another comes" (1:4). Between the beginning and the end, we have moved from abstract to concrete, from a general statement about the human condition to the intensely personal pattern as the dying author urges the young man to rejoice while he can.

We see here something fascinating. The main text reads almost like a dialogue between the author's jaded persona and his other voice that keeps saying, "Rejoice." It is no accident that this happens seven times. The number seven is a key figure in relation to Solomon. The building of the Temple took seven years (1 Kings 6:38). The celebrations were in the seventh month (1 Kings 8:2). They lasted for "seven days and another seven days" (1 Kings 8:65). In his prayer at the dedication, Solomon made seven petitions to God (1 Kings 8:30–53). So the sevenfold interruption of joy in Kohelet is not random. It is a feature of the text that the author expects sensitive readers to notice. These seven injunctions to joy coincide with the seven days of the festival of joy.

The coda corresponds to the eighth day, on which Solomon took his leave of the people: "On the eighth day he let the people go. They blessed the king and returned home, joyous and glad of heart for all the good which God had shown his servant David and His people Israel" (1 Kings 8:66). That day was, of course, Shemini Atzeret. Not only, then, is Kohelet the only book of the Hebrew Bible that is a treatise on joy. Even its structure precisely parallels that of Sukkot and Shemini Atzeret, seven days of joy plus one.

We have now established three sets of connection between Kohelet and Sukkot. One is the name Kohelet itself, with its multiple associations with kings, the Temple, the Tabernacle, and Sukkot itself. A second relates to *ḥokhma,* wisdom, its universality and its connection to creation. The third has to do with *simḥa,* joy, the theme both of the festival and the book. We can now hazard a hypothesis: This is the interpretive key that unlocks the book and its teachings.

Kohelet has been analyzed by scholars as an isolated text. As such, we cannot begin to say what it means because of its internal contradictions and because we do not know precisely when it was written and why. Who were the intended audience? What were they expected to draw from the book? Which is the real Kohelet, the voice of despair or the counter-voice of joy? Considered in and of itself the book could mean almost anything.

But placing it within the canon and the calendar, and associating it with Sukkot – an association, we have argued, that is anything but random – it ceases to be a work in and of itself. It is part of a larger pattern. That is what we argued in the Pesaḥ Maḥzor (Introduction, page lxxi) about another perplexing work, *Shir HaShirim*, The Song of Songs. Considered in itself, it reads like a series of secular love songs. But considered in its calendrical and canonical context, it resolves one of the most fundamental questions in Judaism: where is the answering response on the part of the Israelites to God's freely given love? A single verse from Jeremiah makes the connection: "I remember the kindness of your youth, your love when you were a bride, how you walked after Me in the desert, through a land not sown" (Jer. 2:2). Shir HaShirim is the record of that love.

Kohelet has a similar function within the Hebrew Bible. What, though, is the question to which it is an answer?

Breath

The meaning of Kohelet hinges on one word: *hevel*. As we saw, it occurs thirty-eight times, more than half of all its occurrences in Tanakh. No other book announces its theme more emphatically, by using one word five times in a single sentence, the second in the book. "*Hevel* of *hevels*, says Kohelet, *hevel* of *hevels*, all is *hevel*."

The word has been translated many ways: "pointless, meaningless, futile, empty, vapor, smoke, insubstantial, absurd, vanity." There is something to these translations, but they do not represent the word's primary meaning. It means "breath." The Hebrew words for soul – among them *nefesh*, *ruaḥ* and *neshama* – all have to do with the act of breathing. The same is true in other ancient languages. Psyche, as in psychology, also derives from the Greek word for breath. *Hevel* specifically means a shallow breath.

What obsesses Kohelet is that all that separates life from death is a shallow breath. He is obsessed by the fragility and brevity of life, as contrasted with the seeming eternity of the universe. The world endures forever. But we are, as we say in our prayers on Rosh HaShana and Yom Kippur, "like a broken shard, like grass dried up, like a faded flower, like a fleeting shadow, like a passing cloud, like a breath of wind, like whirling dust, like a dream that slips away." Dust we are and to dust we return. Take breath away and a living body becomes a mere corpse. Reading Kohelet reminds us of the scene in Shakespeare's King Lear, when the aged king

◂ holds

holds in his arms the dead body of his daughter Cordelia, the only one who truly loved him, and whose faithfulness he discovered too late, and says, "Why should a dog, a horse, a rat have breath, and thou no breath at all?" Or it recalls the verse of T. S. Eliot: "I will show you something different from either / Your shadow at morning striding behind you / Or your shadow at evening rising to meet you; / I will show you fear in a handful of dust."

Kohelet is a sustained meditation on mortality, one of the most profound in all literature. He is traumatized by the "unbearable lightness of being," the fact that life is lived toward death, that our days are numbered, that like Moses, for each of us there will be a Jordan we will not cross, a fulfillment we will not live to see. We do not, cannot know how long we will live, but life will always seem too short.

This single fact, for Kohelet, overshadows all human existence. It mocks all achievement and aspiration. We may accumulate wealth, but who knows what those who come after us will do with it. We may achieve power, but it will pass, on our demise, to other people – as Solomon's kingdom fell to his son Rehoboam, whose failure to heed his father's advisers caused the kingdom to split into two, a division from which it never fully recovered, and which undid all that his father and grandfather had striven to do.

Who knows how posterity will judge us? Who knows if we will be remembered at all? And if we are not remembered, of what consequence is our life? It is a mere pattern drawn in sand that will be dissolved by the next high tide. Whatever we achieve in this life will not save us from oblivion. Naked we came into the world and naked we will return.

That is the overwhelming fact for Kohelet. That is why he says that there is no ultimate difference between the righteous and the wicked, or between man and the animals. We will all die in the end, and that is the most important fact about us.

We can now state, simply and boldly, the connection between Kohelet and Sukkot. A sukka is a *dirat arai*, a temporary dwelling. Kohelet is about the fact that the human body is a temporary dwelling. Life is a sukka. We are strangers and temporary residents on earth. As Rilke said, "even the noticing beasts are aware that we don't feel very securely at home in this interpreted world" (Duino Elegies, 1). We seek the security of a house, a home, and find there is none to be had. There is no way of making human life everlasting. We cannot banish risk and uncertainty. Time is a desert, a wilderness, and all we have as we journey is a hut, a booth, a tent. Kohelet is a philosophical statement of life seen as a sukka.

As such it is not a unique voice in Tanakh. We find something similar in the book of Psalms:

> You have made my days mere handbreadths;
> the span of my years is as nothing before You.
> Mere breath is each man standing…
> Man walks like a shadow,
> He goes as a breath,
> Storing without knowing who will gather…
> Surely everyone is but a breath…
> I dwell with You as a stranger,
> a temporary resident, like all my fathers. (Ps. 39: 6–13)

Likewise in the book of Job:

> Remember, O God, that my life is but a breath;
> Not again will my eyes see good…
> I despise my life; I will not live forever.
> Let me alone, for my days are mere breath. (Job 7:7, 16)

Kohelet was thus not the first to feel that death cast its shadow over the whole of life. Nor was he the last. In 1879, having reached his fiftieth birthday, Leo Tolstoy had achieved success and acclaim. He had published two of the greatest novels ever written, War and Peace, and Anna Karenina. He owned a vast estate, was married, and had fourteen children. Yet he succumbed to precisely the thoughts that had driven Kohelet to despair.

He recounts his crisis by way of a story. A traveler is crossing the steppes when he encounters a ferocious wild animal. To escape, he hides in an empty well. But at the bottom of the well he sees a dragon, its jaws open, ready to eat him. He cannot leave the well for fear of the beast. He cannot drop to the bottom because of the dragon. He seizes hold of the branch of a bush growing in a crevice in the well's wall. It is all that is saving him from death. His arms are growing weak, but still he holds on. Then he sees two mice, one black, the other white, gnawing at the branch. Soon they will eat through it, and he will fall into the dragon's mouth. He sees some drops of honey on the leaves of the bush and stretches out his tongue to lick them.

That, says Tolstoy, is how his life feels to him. He has almost no strength left, he is about to fall, the black and white mice – nights and days – are gnawing away at his future and even the drops of honey no longer give him pleasure. The question that haunted him was simply this: "Is there any meaning in my life that the inevitable death awaiting me does not destroy?" (Tolstoy, A Confession).

Like Kohelet, Tolstoy searched for an answer in wisdom, that is, in science and philosophy, and like Kohelet he found none. Science could not understand the question, and philosophy could only repeat it. For Tolstoy, like Kohelet, the fundamental human question is simply: Why live?

We now sense the depth of the drama of Sukkot seen through the eyes of Kohelet. For ten days, beginning on Rosh HaShana and reaching a climax on Yom Kippur, we have prayed, "Remember us for life, O King who desires life, and write us in the book of life – for Your sake, O God of life." Now, having survived the trial, comes the deepest question of all. What is life? What is this gift we have been granted? What gives life meaning, purpose, substance? What will redeem us from the shadow of death?

A Critique of Pure Happiness

Kohelet's answer, in a word, is joy. That as we have seen is the repeated refrain of the countervoice within the book. Kohelet's alter ego knows that, yes, life is short, knowledge painful, and the ruling powers corrupt. The righteous sometimes die young, and evildoers sometimes reach old age. If you make justice – visible, manifest justice, down here on earth – your precondition for making a blessing over life, you will wait a long time, and you will die disappointed. Kohelet tells us these truths with brutal honesty. But he has grown older, wiser. He has passed through the valley of disillusion and emerged the other side.

What redeems life and etches it with the charisma of grace is joy: joy in your work ("The sleep of a worker is sweet" – 5:11), joy in your marriage

◂ ("See

("See life with the woman you love" – 9:9), and joy in the simple pleasures of life. Take joy in each day. Above all, rejoice when you are young. Kohelet is an old man. No one has written a more moving description of the dying of the light in old age than does Kohelet in the last chapter of the book. Yet his conclusion yields to neither cynicism nor despair. You do not need to be blind to the imperfections of the human world or the slow ravages of age in order to rejoice. You can know life with all its flaws and still have joy.

Aristotle in the Nicomachean Ethics said that happiness is that at which all people aim. It is the one thing good in itself and not as a means to some other end. Judaism in general, and Kohelet specifically, disagree. Yes happiness – *ashrei* in Hebrew – is a value in Judaism. It is the first word in the book of Psalms. We say the prayer we call *Ashrei* three times each day. Yet it is not the supreme value. *Simḥa*, joy, is. As we noted, it appears twelve times in Deuteronomy, seventeen times in Kohelet. What is the difference?

Happiness in the classic sense, eudaemonia in Greek, felicitas in Latin, and *ashrei* in Hebrew, means doing well and faring well. The good person acts morally and is respected by others for doing so. Barring accidents or misfortune, he or she is blessed with a good marriage, children, a reputation for integrity ("the crown of a good name" – Avot 4:17), an honored place within the community, and the feeling of a life well lived. He or she sleeps well at night, knowing they have done nothing of which to be ashamed. That is the happy individual of Psalm 1. He is like a tree planted by streams of water, that gives forth fruit in its due season, and whose leaves do not wither. Psalm 92, the Psalm of the Sabbath day, deepens the imagery. The wicked are like grass: they grow fast but are soon cut down. The righteous are like a tree, giving fruit and shade like a palm, growing tall like a cedar in Lebanon. Happiness is the outcome of a moral life.

But happiness depends on many external circumstances. What of the poor, the exploited, the unemployed? What, asks the Torah repeatedly, of the orphan, the widow, and the stranger within the gates? What, asks Kohelet, of the tears of the oppressed who have no comforter? What of the wise man who saved the city only to be unthanked, ignored, forgotten? What, we might ask nowadays, of the victims of terror, or those who live under tyranny? To speak of happiness under such circumstances is almost to mock the afflicted.

When the world is in a state of order, when there is peace and good governance and accountability, when there are shared values within a society, and those who are blessed share their blessings with the vulnerable and the destitute, when the great and the good are indeed great and good, yes, one can speak of happiness as a central value. What, though, survives when none of these preconditions are met? What is left when the world we live in looks less like a house than a sukka, open to the wind, the rain and the cold? What remains, other than fear, in a state of radical insecurity?

The answer is *simḥa*, joy. For joy does not involve, as does happiness, a judgement about life as a whole. Joy lives in the moment. It asks no questions about tomorrow. It celebrates the power of now. The Talmud says that each Sunday, Shammai, the great sage of the late Second Temple period, was already preparing for Shabbat. Hillel, however, lived by a different principle: "Blessed be God day by day" (*Beitza* 16a). Joy blesses God day by day. It celebrates the mere fact of being here, now, existing when we might not have done, inhaling to the full this day, this hour, this eternity-in-a-moment that was not before and will not be again. Joy embraces the contingency of life. It knows that yesterday has gone and tomorrow is unknown. It does not ask what was or will be. It makes no calculations. It is a state of radical thankfulness for the gift of being. Even in an age too fraught for happiness, there can still be joy.

Rainer Maria Rilke wrote in one of his letters, "The reality of joy in the world is indescribable; only in joy does creation take place (happiness, on the contrary, is only a promising, intelligible constellation of things already there); joy is a marvelous increasing of what exists, a pure addition out of nothingness." He added, "How superficially must happiness engage us, after all, if it can leave us time to think and worry about how long it will last." What saved Kohelet was his belated realization that joy, not happiness, is what redeems life from the shadow of death. Joy does not ask how long it will last. It discovers epiphany in the here and now.

Joy is the antidote to the sickness we sense in the great autobiographical section of Kohelet chapter two. There is no passage like it anywhere else in Tanakh. Kohelet is speaking about how he acquired houses, vineyards, orchards, male and female servants, silver, gold, wives and concubines. He had everything. Except meaning. Except purpose. Except joy. What makes the text unique is its double use of the first person singular.

◂ "I built

"I built for myself… I planted for myself… I collected for myself… I acquired for myself…" (Eccl. 2:4–8). Kohelet's error was spelled out in the Mishna centuries later by Hillel: "If I am not for myself, who will be for me? And if I am only for myself, what am I?"(*Avot* 1:14).

Happiness is something I can feel on my own. But joy in the Torah is essentially shared. A husband must make his wife rejoice (Deut. 24:5). Festivals were to be occasions of collective rejoicing, "you and your sons and daughters, your male and female slaves, and the Levite, the stranger and orphan and widow that dwell within your gates" (Deut. 16:11). Bringing first-fruits to the Temple involved collective celebration: "you and the Levites and the strangers in your midst shall rejoice in all the good things the Lord your God has given to you and your household" (Deut. 26:11). Unlike happiness, *simḥa* only exists in virtue of being shared. It is a form of social emotion.

It is also a religious one. Kierkegaard once wrote, "It is moral to grieve; it is religious to rejoice." Joy is a form of thanksgiving. It is a way of acknowledging life as a gift – and if it is a gift, there must be a Giver. Joy is King David dancing before God the day the Ark was brought to Jerusalem. It is the "righteous and men of good deeds" doing somersaults and juggling with flaming torches in the Temple courtyard during *Simḥat Beit HaSho'eva*. Joy is a Jewish wedding. It is dancing in the presence of the Divine. There is nothing in it of pride or self-satisfaction. It defeats the fear of death by turning our attention outward. For a moment the "I" is silent and we become part of the celebrating "We," our voice merging with others in the song creation sings to its Creator, the nation to its sovereign God, and we to God for "keeping us alive and sustaining us and bringing us to this day." The *Shekhina*, said the sages, does not live in sadness or depression, but in the joy of fulfilling God's command (*simḥa shel mitzva*).

Unlike happiness, joy is not conditional on things going well. No one put this better than the prophet Habakkuk, in one of the most moving passages in the prophetic literature:

Though the fig tree does not blossom,
  and no fruit is on the vines;
though the produce of the olive fails
  and the fields yield no food;

◂ though the

> though the flock is cut off from the fold
> and there is no herd in the stalls,
> yet I will rejoice in the LORD;
> I will exult in the God of my salvation. (Hab. 3:17–18)

Joy alone, Kohelet realized at the end of a long life, has the power to defeat despair. It does not speak the language of reason. It does not answer the existential questions of a disillusioned philosopher-king. Joy belongs to an older, deeper part of the brain. Like music, it gives expression to the inexpressible. It says, yes, life is sometimes unfair and the world unjust, but the very brevity of life makes each moment precious. It says: stop thinking of tomorrow. Celebrate, sing, join the dance however undignified it makes you look. Joy bathes life with light. It liberates the soul from the prison of the self. Joy is Jerusalem on Sukkot. Joy solves no problems but it gives us the strength to keep searching. It sustains the faith we need if we are, in the year ahead, to face the future without fear and heal some of the fractures of our injured world.

The Limits of Wisdom

Kohelet ends with an epilogue, written as if by another hand. It says: "The final word: it has all been said. Hold God in awe, and heed His commands, for that is all man has." It was this sentence that warranted the book's inclusion in Tanakh. Some of the sages questioned Kohelet's place among the sacred scriptures. They held it should be banned ("hidden") because its teachings could lead to heresy. Those who argued for its inclusion said that it began and ended with words of Torah. So this penultimate sentence of the book can look contrived, as if it were added as an afterthought, the intellectual equivalent of a kashrut certification. But this is to misjudge the book as a whole.

On the surface it reads like a subversive book. It challenges conventional religious faith at many points. It questions whether there is justice in the world, whether there is a real difference between the righteous and the wicked, or even between Homo sapiens and the animals. It hints that there are limits to our freedom: what is crooked can never be straightened (1:15; the source of Kant's famous remark that "out of the crooked timber of humanity no straight thing was ever made"). Nothing is really new, "that which is to be is what has been already" (1:9), and try as we might to change the world, it stays as it always was.

God exists – Kohelet uses the word more than forty times – but in the book He seems a long way away. He is in heaven, we are on earth, and there seems to be no contact between us. But this, to repeat, is on the surface. Kohelet is really subversion of a second order. It undermines those who undermine, critiques the critics, subverts the subversion, and shows how too much reliance on intellect and wisdom can lead to nihilism.

It is one of those rare books that refutes itself. Yehuda HaLevi in the *Kuzari* wrote a critique of philosophy in the language of philosophy. Ludwig Wittgenstein did something similar in his *Tractatus Logico-Philosophicus.* He showed that the ultimate truths of philosophy were inexpressible in philosophy. "Of what we cannot speak, thereof we must be silent." Philosophy is like a ladder on which we climb to a higher plane and then find that we must throw the ladder away. Kohelet is Tanakh's most powerful critique of wisdom spoken in the voice of wisdom itself.

Kohelet is not negative about it. He says that wisdom stands to folly as does light to darkness (2:13). It is a shelter, an estate (7:11–12). It "gives the wise man more power than ten rulers in a city" (7:19). It lights up a person's face (8:1). But it fails to uncover meaning in life. It tells us how but not why. It gives us prudence and pragmatism, not moral passion. If you want this, do that. If you want to avoid this, guard yourself from that. It constantly asks, "What is the *yitaron,* the advantage, the return on investment, the cost-benefit ratio?" It speaks of profits, not prophets. It tells us which pitfalls to stay clear of, but not who we are or why we are here.

Recall what we said about wisdom in Tanakh. It sees God not in revelation or redemption, but in creation. It speaks the truths that are universal, not those that are particular. It relates to Elokim, not Hashem, or as Yehuda HaLevi put it, the God of Aristotle, not the God of Abraham (*Kuzari* 4:16). It belongs not to the priest in the Temple nor the prophet in the town square, but to the court and advisers of the king. It speaks the language of realpolitik. Don't criticize a king. Don't curse a rich man. Diversify your investments. When evil is abroad, stay at home. But it fails to give an answer to the most basic of questions: Why live? The best answer it can come up with is that life is *hevel.* It is empty, meaningless, futile, as pointless as trying to chase and hold the wind, but at least it is short.

◂ If the only

If the only way we seek to encounter God is through creation, we will discover the deep truth embedded in biblical Hebrew, that *olam*, meaning "universe," comes from the same root as *ne'elam*, "hidden." Nature is not transparent to the purposes and presence of God. By and large, and with some notable exceptions, mainstream Judaism did not follow Christianity in predicating faith in the existence of God on natural theology, itself built on the Aristotelian premise that purposes are inherent in nature. In the Hebrew Bible nature does not prove the existence of God. It sings the praises of God, and that is something else altogether. If all we have is universal laws and personal choices – as we have today in our secular, scientific, individualistic culture – we will not discover meaning. We will land up where Kohelet found himself after pursuing possessions, power, and a thousand women: pronouncing life *hevel*, a mere shallow, fleeting, insubstantial breath.

There is a reason for this. The meaning of a system lies outside the system. The meaning of chess is not contained in the rules of chess. You can know all the rules by heart and still have no idea why people play it and are so absorbed by it. The meaning of the universe lies outside the universe. That is why Abrahamic monotheism was so transformative – not because it reduced the many gods of paganism to one, but because it spoke about a God outside nature who created nature, a God beyond the universe who made the universe. For the first time it showed that there is meaning to life, not one we invent but one we discover. It was this that rescued the human condition from the tragic sense of life.

But meaning cannot be accessed by pure reason, by "wisdom." That is because, as Kohelet says no less than thirty-two times, wisdom tells us what exists "under the heavens," or "under the sun." Like science, it establishes connections between different empirical phenomena. If X then Y. It does not, cannot, reach beyond the physical universe to that which lies beyond. Wisdom is neither the revelation of the priest nor the word of the prophet. Wisdom can tell us where, when, and how, but not why. Questions of meaning will systematically elude it. Wisdom will always conclude, in the words of one of the wisest of his generation, the late Sir Bernard Williams, "that the world was not made for us, or we for the world, that our history tells no purposive story, and that there is no position outside the world or outside history from which we might hope to authenticate our activities." In short, all is *hevel.*

Meaning is not engraved in nature. It is not written in the galaxies with their billions of stars, nor is it inscribed in the 3.1 billion letters of the human genome. Meaning is not universal but particular. It lives in stories, memories, rituals, songs, in collective acts of worship, and in communities bound together by shared history and the bonds of collective responsibility. It is something we inherit from our parents and hand on, if we are blessed, to our children.

Meaning is more like music than words, more like poetry than prose, more like home than a hotel. It lives in stories, not scientific formulae. Wisdom can give us stoic acceptance or epicurean pleasure, but not meaning. For meaning, we need the priest and the prophet. We need revelation and redemption. We need the word from beyond the universe that created the universe and is capable of inspiring us to change the universe. We need a sense of the sacred and a feeling, however inchoate, for God's purposes in history. That is why, in ancient Israel, there was not one kind of leader but three, and why Tanakh is written in a multiplicity of voices, each with its own perspective and sensibility.

After Tolstoy had experienced his own dark night of the soul, what restored him was neither philosophy nor science but the faith of the workers on his estate, simple people leading ordinary lives, who suffered without life losing its meaning for them. Tolstoy eventually came to the conclusion that what they had was faith. "If a man lives, he believes in something… If he understands the illusory nature of the finite, he must believe in the infinite. Without faith he cannot live."

That is the meaning of the penultimate sentence of Kohelet. Note that wisdom almost invariably uses the metaphor of seeing. We speak of insight, foresight, hindsight, vision. We make an observation. We adopt a perspective. When we understand, we say, "I see." Kohelet uses the word *ra'iti*, "I saw," eighteen times. But revelation, the source of meaning, is not something we see. It is something we hear. That is why *shema* is the key word of Deuteronomy, where it occurs ninety-two times. As Moses said about the revelation at Mount Sinai, "You heard the sound of words but saw no form; there was only a voice" (Deut. 4:12). That is what the penultimate sentence is saying: "The final word: it has all been said. Hold

God in awe, and heed His commands, for that is all man has." Meaning is what we hear, not see.

The divine word is what links the finite – us – to the Infinite, God. In the beginning was the word: "And God said, Let there be..." And, concludes Kohelet, *sof davar*, "In the end is the word." Seeing makes us wise, but it is listening that gives life meaning.

The Freedom of Insecurity

Kohelet is a commentary, oblique and subtle to be sure, to the life of Solomon. It is an answer to the questions that anyone who reads Solomon's story in the book of Kings must ask. What went wrong? How did the wisest man on earth go so far astray? How did the man who built the Temple become the one who, through his myriad wives from many nations, admitted idolatry into the national life of Israel? How did the king whose name means "peace" and whose reign was marked by peace, become the figure who generated so many tensions within the nation that, shortly after his death, it split into two and never in all the subsequent centuries recovered the greatness it once had?

The story of Solomon is the most perplexing in Tanakh. It starts with immense promise. God, through the prophet Nathan, had told David that he would not build the Temple, but his son would. He would have what David lacked: peace. God said that He would adopt David's son as His own: "I will be to him a Father, and he shall be to Me a son" (II Sam. 7:14). It is a uniquely auspicious beginning.

That mood is maintained when David dies and Solomon inherits his throne. God appears to Solomon in a dream and offers him anything he wishes. Solomon asks for only one thing: "an understanding heart, to judge Your people and discern between good and evil" (I Kings 3:9). Pleased with this reply, God says that He will indeed give him wisdom, but also in addition, "riches and honor, so that no other king shall compare with you, all your days" (v. 13).

So it was. Solomon had, says Kings, "wisdom and understanding beyond measure, and breadth of mind like the sand on the seashore." His acumen surpassed that of "all the people of the east and all the wisdom of Egypt." He composed three thousand proverbs. His fame spread throughout the region and "people of all nations came to hear" his wisdom (5:9–14). No other figure in Tanakh is spoken of in these terms.

When the fall came, therefore, it was serious and surprising. Deuteronomy contains three commands about a king of Israel. He should not "acquire many horses for himself or cause the people to return to Egypt" to buy them. He should not have many wives, nor should he accumulate "excessive silver and gold" (Deut. 17:16–17).

Solomon broke all three. He had twelve thousand horses (I King 10:26). He "exceeded all the kings of the earth in riches" (10:23). He had seven hundred wives and three hundred concubines including, says the text, many from "the nations concerning which the Lord had said to the people of Israel: You shall not enter into marriage with them, neither shall they with you, for surely they will turn away your heart after their gods" (I Kings 11:1–8). The result was that idolatry was introduced into Israel at the highest level.

The Talmud (*Sanhedrin* 21b) is candid. It says that Solomon fell because these commands were given a reason by the Torah itself. The king should not own too many horses because that will cause him to return to Egypt to buy them. He should not have too many wives "lest his heart turn away." Solomon thought he was clever enough to break the law without suffering the consequences: buying horses from Egypt or being led astray by his wives. He was wrong in both cases. Tanakh leaves us in no doubt as to his epitaph: "Solomon did evil in the sight of the Lord" (I Kings 11:6).

Much though the narrative tries to skirt around it, one of the precipitating factors was the building of the Temple itself. In a sentence that proved retrospectively to be deeply ironic, the text says that "In the four hundred and eightieth year after the people of Israel came out of the land of Egypt," Solomon "began to build the house of the Lord" (I Kings 6:1). It was a way of saying that the act of Temple-building was about to bring the long Jewish journey to closure.

The idea that there would one day be a central sanctuary in the Promised Land goes back to the song at the Reed Sea: "You will bring them and plant them on the mountain of Your inheritance – the place, Lord, You made for Your dwelling, the Sanctuary, Lord, Your hands established" (Ex. 15:17). It had taken centuries for the land to be conquered and settled,

◂ the tribes

the tribes united under a single king and Jerusalem made the capital city. Building the House of God was now all that remained to be done.

But there are ominous notes throughout the narrative. The building involved a treaty with Lebanon in exchange for the large amount of cedar wood involved in the construction. A labor force was drafted of thirty thousand men working in monthly shifts for the wood alone, together with eighty thousand stone-cutters, seventy thousand men employed to transport the stone and 3,300 officers to supervise the work (I Kings 5:15–25).

The local non-Israelite population – the remaining Amorites, Hittites, Perizzites, Hivites and Jebusites – were taken as slaves. The text adds that "of the people of Israel Solomon made no slaves" (I Kings 9:22). That this needed to be said is alarming. The entire narrative echoes the experience of the Israelites in Egypt, sometimes using the same words. We now realize the significance of a fact told at the very beginning of the story, that "Solomon made an alliance with Pharaoh King of Egypt and married his daughter" (I Kings 3:1). What was a king of Israel doing by forging an alliance, in the form of a marriage, with the imperial power that had once turned his ancestors into slaves? By turning his own people into a corvee, an unpaid, conscripted labor force, Solomon had in effect transformed Israel into a second Egypt.

The consequences were far reaching. After Solomon's death the people came to his son and successor Rehoboam, complaining, "Your father put a heavy yoke on us, but now lighten the harsh labor and the heavy yoke he put on us and we will serve you" (I Kings 12:4). Rehoboam consulted his father's advisers, who told him in effect: if you serve the people, they will serve you. He did not listen, preferring instead the advice of his own friends who told him to assert his authority by making the burden heavier still. Instead of serving the people, Solomon's son expected them to serve him. This was the single most fateful moment in Israel's history. The people rebelled, the kingdom divided, and the nation never fully recovered.

What went wrong? That is Kohelet's question. To understand his answer we must turn to Sigmund Freud's most brilliant disciple, Otto Rank. Rank's most original contribution to the study of human nature was his insight that we are torn between two fears: the fear of living and the fear of dying.

◂ The fear

The fear of living is what we experience in early childhood, namely separation anxiety. The young child knows how vulnerable and dependent he or she is, especially in relation to the mother. We fear being alone. We need the protective embrace of human others. It is for this reason that we seek to identify with a group, a team, a community, or a nation. We merge our identity in theirs. It is the anxiety about being singular, different, individuated, that Rank called the fear of living.

No sooner do we identify with a group, however, than we fear the opposite: losing our individuality. When the "I" is wholly subordinated to the "We," we feel stifled, submerged, suffocated. This is what Rank called the fear of dying. Rank's view was that it was this second fear that led people with a strong sense of self to seek immortality through heroic acts of death-defying courage, or by creating works of art that will live forever (Shakespeare's "Not marble, nor the gilded monuments / of princes, shall outlive this powerful rhyme"). In ancient times rulers sought immortality by building imperishable monuments – temples, pyramids and palaces that would stand forever. The stronger the "I" and the greater the refusal to merge into the "We," the deeper becomes the fear of death, and the more powerful the temptation to defeat it by a personal immortality project, something that will allow my name to live forever.

That is what Kohelet is telling us about Solomon. As we have already seen, no other book in Tanakh uses the first person singular as often as does Kohelet: "I built for myself… I made for myself… I gathered for myself… I acquired for myself" (Eccl. 2:4–9). These are the words of someone obsessed with I-me-mine. And, as Rank said, one with an exaggerated sense of self supremely fears death. That is Kohelet, telling us thirty-eight times how haunted he is by the realization that life is *hevel*, a mere breath that will one day cease, returning us naked to the grave, and turning our bodies to dust. Kohelet does not speak about the Temple, or how Solomon spent thirteen years – almost twice as long as the seven years it took to build the Temple – building a palace for himself (1 Kings 7:1–12). But these facts hover in the background, unmistakably there.

The rabbis said something very acute about Solomon's Temple. They understood Psalm 24 – "Who may ascend the mountain of the Lord? Who may stand in His holy place?" – as referring to the Temple dedication ceremony. The psalm ends with an odd repetition:

◂ Lift up

> Lift up your heads, O gates; be uplifted, eternal doors,
> So that the King of glory may enter.
> Who is the King of glory? It is the LORD, strong and mighty,
> the LORD mighty in battle.
> Lift up your heads, O gates; be uplifted, eternal doors,
> so that the King of glory may enter.
> Who is He, the King of glory?
> The LORD of hosts, He is the King of glory, Selah. (Ps. 24:7–10)

This is how they interpreted these lines: when Solomon tried to take the Ark into the Holy of Holies, the doors refused to open. Hence his command, "Lift up your heads, O gates." The gates then asked him, "Who is the King of glory?" Solomon replied, "The LORD." Yet the doors still refused to open. So Solomon had to ask again, and still they did not open (*Shabbat* 30a). In other words, the sages attributed to gates the suspicion that Solomon regarded himself, not God, as "the king of glory." A man who spends almost twice as long building a palace for himself as building a house for God lays himself open to the suspicion that the Temple was Solomon's own immortality project, the building he believed would make his name live forever.

Those who fear death spend their lives in a futile quest for security, for something they can attach themselves to that will not die. That, suggests the psalm, is the allure of idols: "They have mouths but cannot speak, eyes but cannot see. They have ears but cannot hear" (Ps. 115:5–6). You know where you are with an idol. It does not move. It does not breathe. It does not change. Hence the sin of the Golden Calf. Recall that it began with the people panicking because of the absence of Moses. They needed a leader. Why did they not do the obvious and turn to Aaron, Moses' brother, his partner, spokesman, colleague and companion? Why an object made of gold? Because they wanted something predictable, something that did not get angry with them, challenge them, urge them to ever-greater heights. Bricks, mortar, stone, marble, cedar, silver, gold: these are things you can safely worship because they make no demands. They are there unchanging forever.

Implicit in Kohelet is a story about Solomon's life as a search for security in terms of what we have, what we own, and what we can control. That is a temptation that has led astray some of the most gifted leaders of all times. But it is a false quest. Sukkot tells us why it is a false quest. Because you can live in a hut with only leaves for a roof, exposed to the wind, the cold and the rain, and still rejoice.

And it is joy, not monumental architecture, that defeats the fear of death, because it lifts us beyond the self, the insistent, interminable "I." Joy is something we share with others. Joy is gratitude for the gift of life that we feel in the presence of the Giver of life. We become eternal not by constructing buildings, but by opening ourselves up, making ourselves vulnerable, to the Eternal, to God Himself.

God brought the Israelites from slavery to freedom. But freedom requires the ability to live with insecurity. It means making space for other people to express their freedom in different, unpredictable ways. It means empowering your children, as God empowered Abraham, saying "Walk on ahead of Me" (Gen. 17:1). It means not seeking to turn those around you into clones of yourself or servants of your will. It means, in Judaism, living with an unpredictable God who, when asked by Moses for His name, said, "I will be what I will be" (Ex. 3:14). It means living with God who made every human being in His image, yet who does not have an image. Without the courage to live with insecurity, even the wisest of men, King Solomon, can go astray.

Sukkot is the festival of insecurity. It is the festival of a people who know they will never be entirely safe, surrounded as they are by larger, stronger nations, assaulted as they have so often been for having the courage to be different. Sitting in the sukka, *betzila de-mehemnuta*, "under the shadow of faith" (*Zohar, Emor* 103a), is all the security we need. As David said in Psalm 27:5, "He will keep me safe in His pavilion [lit. sukka] on the day of trouble." If God is our refuge, who then shall we fear? We do not need what Solomon made for himself: a palace of cedar. A sukka is the polar opposite. It is spiritual security in the midst of physical vulnerability. The most monumental building, even the Temple itself, will not guarantee the safety of the nation, if what matters is the building, not the builders, and if we think we are "the king of glory."

Solomon's Temple, the noblest of projects executed in the wrong way for the wrong reason, did not make the king immortal, or the nation invulnerable. It left Solomon with a terrible epitaph, and divided the nation, leaving it very vulnerable indeed.

◂ *What is*

What is a Sukka?

Now we are in a position to ask, what exactly is a sukka? What does it represent, symbolize, recall? What message is it meant to convey? There is only one passage in the Torah relating to the command, and it is brief to the point of obscurity: "You shall dwell in booths [*sukkot*] for seven days; all those born among Israel shall dwell in booths, so that your descendants will know that I settled the children of Israel in booths when I brought them out of the land of Egypt: I am the Lord your God" (Lev. 23:42–43).

The problems are obvious. First, the word sukka or sukkot is not used at any stage to describe the living conditions of the Israelites during the wilderness years. A sukka is a temporary, portable dwelling, a hut or booth. *Nowhere, except in this verse, were the Israelites in the wilderness spoken of as living in sukkot.* Instead they lived in tents. "How goodly are your tents, O Jacob," said the pagan prophet Balaam (Num. 24:5).

After the revelation at Mount Sinai, God told Moses to tell the people to "return to their tents" (Deut. 5:27). When the people complained about the manna, Moses heard them "weeping at the entrance to their tents" (Num. 11:10). During the Koraḥ rebellion, Moses said to the people, "Move away from the tents of these evil men" (Num. 16:26).

And so on.

Tents are made of fabric or animal skins. They do not have coverings of foliage. Where in any case would the people find vegetation in the desert for forty years? Tents are not booths. Not surprisingly, therefore, a dispute arose among the sages as to what exactly a sukka represents.

The dispute appears both in the halakhic midrash, the *Sifra* (to Lev. 23), and also in the Talmud (*Sukka* 11b), but with the names of the rabbis reversed. According to the *Sifra*, Rabbi Eliezer says it means *sukkot mamash*, booths in the literal sense of the word. A sukka is a sukka is a sukka: nothing more, nothing less. Rabbi Akiva says that the sukka represents the clouds of glory that accompanied the Israelites on their journeys through the desert.

There are obvious difficulties with either interpretation. For the one who says it means literally booths, what then is there to celebrate? There was nothing miraculous, or even out of the ordinary, about a group of people on a journey living in temporary shelter. That is what happens

◄ to many

to many nomadic populations. Booths are still used by some Bedouin today. The exodus from Egypt and the giving of the Torah at Mount Sinai – commemorated respectively on Pesaḥ and Shavuot – were clearly epoch-making events, occurrences out of the ordinary, encounters with the Divine. Not so a shed, a hut, a booth.

No less problematic is the view that the sukka represents the clouds of glory. If so, why not say so? Let the verse say, "so that future generations will know that I surrounded the Israelites with clouds of glory when I brought them out of the land of Egypt." The point is serious and substantive. In general we say that *mitzvot einan tzerikhot kavana*, "the fulfillment of a command is not conditional on specific intention" (*Tosafot, Sukka* 42a). But in this case the intent is written into the text of the command itself. It says, "so that future generations will know." The Talmud tells us that this has halakhic consequences. According to one view a sukka whose roof is higher than twenty cubits from the ground is invalid because at that height you are not conscious of the roof, and therefore the sukka is not fulfilling its function of reminding you, "so that future generations will know" (*Sukka* 2a). *How then can there be a command whose purpose is to remind you of something, if the thing it is supposed to remind you of is not stated in the text, and is not even clear to the sages of the Mishna?*

In any case, what is the connection between a booth and clouds? The one does not naturally evoke thoughts of the other. A booth is a humble, fragile, temporary shelter. The clouds of glory were radiant, majestic, an unmistakable sign of the presence of God. There is an obvious dissonance between the two ideas.

To be sure, Rabbi Akiva bases his interpretation on a text, a messianic vision from the book of Isaiah: "Then the Lord will create over the whole site of Mount Zion and over her assemblies a cloud by day, and smoke and the shining of a flaming fire by night; for over all the glory there will be a canopy. There will be a sukka for shade by day from the heat, and for a refuge and a shelter from the storm and rain" (Isaiah 4:5–6). This passage does indeed bring together the idea of clouds, shelter, glory and sukka. Yet the sukka of which Isaiah speaks belongs to the future, not to the past, of which the festival is a memorial.

Let us therefore recall what we have learned thus far from our study of Kohelet. First we noted that the name *Kohelet* is a key to the decryption

◂ of the

of the book and of the festival itself. We saw that the root of the word, ק-ה-ל, strikes multiple connections between the festival and the nation's collective house of worship, the *Mishkan* in the desert and the Temple in Jerusalem. *Hak-hel* is the command (Deut. 31:10–13) that once every seven years on Sukkot, someone (assumed to be the king) was "to address the nation when all Israel comes to appear before the LORD your God *at the place He will choose*," meaning the Temple. The root ק-ה-ל is the first word the Torah uses when Moses commands the Israelites to build the *Mishkan* (Ex. 35:1) – on the day after Yom Kippur just before Sukkot. It is also a key word in the story of the Golden Calf, for which the *Mishkan* itself was a *tikun*, an act of repair. Also, the root appears seven times in I Kings 8, the account of Solomon dedicating the Temple on Sukkot. All of these suggest a Temple connection.

Now consider the clouds of glory themselves. The actual phrase "clouds of glory" appears nowhere in Tanakh. We hear of a Divine cloud in several contexts. God guided the Israelites through the desert in a pillar of cloud by day and fire by night. (Ex. 13:21). A cloud positioned itself at the Reed Sea between the Israelites and the pursuing Egyptians, to protect the people from Pharaoh's army (Ex. 14:19–20). The glory of God appeared in a cloud when manna fell for the people to eat (Ex. 16:10). A cloud covered the top of Mount Sinai when God revealed Himself to the people (Ex. 19:16).

However the most significant accounts of God's glory appearing in a cloud occur in connection with the *Mishkan* and the Temple. Here is the description of the *Mishkan*:

> Then the cloud covered the tent of meeting, and the glory of the LORD filled the Tabernacle. And Moses was not able to enter the tent of meeting because the cloud settled on it, and the glory of the LORD filled the Tabernacle. (Ex. 40:34–35)

And this is the description of the Temple:

> And when the Priests left the Holy Place, the cloud filled the House of the LORD. And the Priests could not stand up to serve because of the cloud – for the Presence of God filled the House. (I Kings 8:10–11)

◂ We begin

We begin to sense a significant connection. Sukkot, as we noted in the first chapter, was the Temple festival par excellence. It was also the time of the year when the first Temple was consecrated, and also the second. It was the festival celebrated in the days of Ezra and Nehemiah after the people had gathered in the Temple to hear the Torah read in public. Immediately after Sukkot that year, the people renewed their Covenant with God. Even the rededication of the Temple in the days of the Maccabees, though it took place at a different time of the year, was explicitly modeled on Sukkot.

Note also how the Temple connection persisted even after the building itself was destroyed. In this context there is a pointed contrast between Pesaḥ and Sukkot. After the destruction of the Temple, the Seder ritual changed dramatically. No longer was the central act the offering of the Paschal Lamb. Instead the ritual was focused on matza, the unleavened bread. There was almost no attempt to replicate the Temple ritual outside its precincts. In the case of Sukkot however, many customs that were practiced *only* in the Temple when it stood – taking the four kinds on the second and subsequent days of the festival, the circuits around the altar, and the beating of the willow branches – were transferred everywhere after the destruction as *zekher leMikdash*, a "reminder of the Temple" (Mishna, *Rosh HaShana* 4:3).

And so a significance appears. *The connection between Sukkot and the clouds of glory has to do with the Mishkan or the Temple.* There are other connections as well. The verb ס-כ-כ, "to cover," from which *sukka* is derived, and which in rabbinic Hebrew designates the roof the sukka, *appears in the Torah only in connection with the Mishkan.* It says about the Cherubim, the angelic, childlike figures above the Ark, that their wings "overshadowed" it (*sokhekhim*, Ex. 25:20, 37, 9). The same verb is used about the *parokhet*, the veil, curtain or canopy that "covered" the Ark (Ex. 40:3).

Now consider the differences between the Sanctuary in the wilderness and the Temple built by Solomon in Jerusalem. Two are fundamental. The first is that the Sanctuary was built entirely by voluntary contributions of money or materials or time. The text in Exodus emphasizes repeatedly that contributions were to be received from every man and woman "whose heart moved them to give" (Ex. 35:21 et al.). The Temple, by contrast, was built on the basis of conscripted labor. There was nothing voluntary about the efforts of the hundreds of thousands of people involved in the construction.

Second, *the Sanctuary was portable*. It was built of a framework and drapes that could be dismantled and carried by the Levites when the time came for the people to travel onward on the next stage of their journey. The Temple, of course, was not portable. It was built in Jerusalem and could not exist anywhere else.

Now let us go back and revisit the scene that transpired when David first expressed his wish to build the Temple. God sent him the following message via the prophet Nathan:

> Go and tell My servant David, "This is what the LORD says: Are you the one to build Me a house to dwell in? I have not dwelt in a house from the day I brought the Israelites up out of Egypt to this day. I have been moving from place to place with a tent as My dwelling. Wherever I have moved with all the Israelites, did I ever say to any of their rulers whom I commanded to shepherd My people Israel, "Why have you not built Me a house of cedar?" (II Sam. 7:5–7)

Now we can state precisely what a sukka is. *A sukka stands in the same relationship to a house that the Mishkan in the desert did to the Temple in Jerusalem.* A sukka moves. A house does not. Those who live in a sukka are on a journey. Those who live in a house have arrived. A sukka suggests a person or nation on the move. A house is what you build when you have come to the end of your wanderings and you want to settle down.

As long as the Temple stood, and even after it was destroyed, God wanted the people never to forget the original *Mishkan* in the desert. Indeed many English Bibles translate the word *Mishkan* as "Tabernacle" from the Latin *taberna* meaning a hut, a shed, a booth, understanding instinctively that the most important thing about it was temporary, portable, the symbol of a people who had not yet arrived.

More than that: it was the symbol of God Himself. Recall that the first time we hear the word cloud mentioned in connection with God, it is *already the symbol of a journey*: "By day the LORD went ahead of them in a pillar of cloud to guide them on their way, and by night in a pillar of fire to give them light, so that they could travel by day or night" (Ex.

◂ 13:21)

13:21). God does not stand still. The God beyond the universe is not a God confined to one place, even the holiest. He is the God whose *Shekhina*, His immanent Presence, is in every place where His people travel. The *Mishkan* was small, fragile, movable. It was the very opposite of the temples of Egypt and ziggurats of Babylon. *But it was filled with the clouds of glory.*

In the last month of his life, as the new generation was about to cross the Jordan and enter the land he could only see from afar, Moses wanted them to understand one thing above all others. The real trial, he said, was not in the past but in the future; not in the desert but in the Promised Land. The greatest challenge to faith would be not poverty but affluence, not slavery but freedom, not exile but home. People who believe that they have arrived become complacent, self-satisfied, self-congratulatory, and that is the beginning of the end of national greatness:

> Be careful that you do not forget the LORD your God, failing to observe His commands, His laws and His decrees that I am giving you this day. Otherwise, when you eat and are satisfied, when you build fine houses and settle down, and when your herds and flocks grow large and your silver and gold increase and all you have is multiplied, then your heart will become proud and you will forget the LORD your God, who brought you out of Egypt, out of the land of slavery.... You may say to yourself, "My power and the strength of my hands have produced this wealth for me." (Deut. 8:11–17)

God wanted us never to take security for granted. Civilizations, as the historian Giambattista Vico documented in *Scienza Nova* (1725), start by being young and energetic, then become successful and wealthy, then self-indulgent and decadent, and eventually fall to younger, hungrier powers.

The only way to avoid this is, one week in every year, to remind yourself of where you came from and how you once lived. *Those were the days when God Himself lived in your midst in a temporary, portable dwelling.* It was made not of bricks or stone but of hangings and drapes. But it was full of the clouds of glory. The word *Mishkan*, from the root ש-כ-ן, means "to dwell." When God says to Moses, "Make Me a sanctuary that I may dwell

◂ [*shakhanti*]

[*shakhanti*] among them" (Ex. 25:8), this is the first time we have heard the verb in connection with God. It is, in this context, a very odd word. Recall that God told Moses at the burning bush that when the Israelites were about to leave Egypt, each woman should "ask of her neighbor [*mi-shekhenta*]" (Ex. 3:22). A *shakhen* is a neighbor. There were times when God revealed Himself in signs, wonders and miracles. But when the Israelites made the *Mishkan* and God dwelled there in clouds of glory, *He was as close to the people as a next-door neighbor.*

On Sukkot, the Temple festival par excellence, the temptation was at its height to believe that what makes a house of God is architectural magnificence on a monumental scale. *That has been true about virtually every religion, ancient and modern, since the dawn of time. But it is not true of Judaism.* God does not live in buildings but in the open heart, the heart that makes itself vulnerable the way the covering of a sukka is vulnerable. If the covering of the sukka is thick enough to keep out the rain, it is invalid (*Mishna Berura* 631:6). If a human heart is thick enough to keep out the word of God that is like rain (Deut. 32:2), then it too will lose its holiness: "Yeshurun grew fat and kicked; you grew fat, thick, gross; then he forsook God who made him" (Deut. 32:15).

For seven days we are commanded to live in a sukka to remind us that *this is how God lived in our ancestors' midst* when they journeyed from Egypt to the Promised Land. It was not just the Israelites who lived in temporary dwellings when God brought them out of the land of Egypt. So did God Himself. *That was the miracle*: that the Creator of heaven and earth lived among the people so closely that, homeless and vulnerable though they were, they could feel the *Shekhina* in their midst.

So Rabbi Eliezer and Rabbi Akiva were both right. The sukka really was a sukka: a portable shrine, a movable sanctuary, a temporary temple. But it was filled with clouds of glory. Not even Solomon's Temple made the people feel as close to God as did the *Mishkan*. A nation that seeks security in stone eventually grows old. A people that never stops traveling, spiritually if not physically, will never grow old.

There is an extraordinary intimation of all this, early on in the Torah. If we examine Genesis carefully, we will discover that the patriarchs did not live in houses. When the word "house" is used in a patriarchal context, it means not a building but rather "family" or "household." Others lived in houses. The patriarchs lived in tents. The contrast is often striking. In Genesis 18, when angels visit Abraham, he is sitting at the entrance of his *tent*. In the next chapter, they come to his nephew Lot in Sodom and find that he is living in a *house* (Gen. 19:2, 4). The first patriarch described as living in a house is Jacob.

The verse that says so is little short of astonishing. "Jacob went to Sukkot, where he built a house for himself and made sheds [*sukkot*] for his livestock. That is why he called the place Sukkot" (Gen. 33:17). This is the first time one of the patriarchs is spoken of as building a house, yet he does not call the place, "house" (as in Beit-El or Beit-Leḥem for example). Instead he calls it Sukkot *in honor of the sheds he has made for his cattle!* How are we to explain this?

The only plausible explanation is that at the very moment Jacob sought to settle in a permanent home, he wished never to forget that he remained, in some sense, a nomadic as Abraham and Isaac were. He was on a journey. To be a Jew is to be on a journey. Judaism was born in two journeys, Abraham's and Sarah's from Mesopotamia, Moses' and the Israelites' from Egypt. Mesopotamia and Egypt, the world's two first great civilizations, worshiped the gods in monumental buildings, to construct which they turned whole populations into slaves. This, says the Torah, is to betray both God and humanity. God does not need that kind of house. Recall what He said to David: "Wherever I have moved with all the Israelites, did I ever say to any of their rulers… 'Why have you not built Me a house of cedar?'" God moves. Israel moves. God does not seek, nor is Israel called on to build, statements in stone. Other nations may do so. But that, says God, is not who I am, nor is it who I want you to be.

The sentence in the Torah which describes the first house ever built by a Jew is also the first place in which the word Sukkot appears – and it appears not once but three times. If you want to understand Sukkot, meditate on this verse.

Recall too the first time the word "house" is used in connection with God (other than as the place name Beit-El). It happens when Jacob is in the middle of a journey, fleeing home and not yet arrived at his destination. Alone at night, Jacob sleeps and dreams of a ladder connecting earth and heaven. He wakes and says, "How awesome is this place! *This is none other than the house of God*; this is the gate of heaven." (Gen 28:17). There was no house there, only a dream and a vision glimpsed in the midst of a journey. Recall too that as the Israelites began their journey out of Egypt toward the Promised Land, their first stop was at a place called Sukkot (Num. 33:5). Those who live in sukkot are on a journey. God's first words to Abraham were *Lekh Lekha*: Move. The definition of a Jew is: one-who-is-on-a-journey.

However humble our sukka, when we invite guests they turn out to be *Ushpizin* – the heroes of our people – just as Abraham and Sarah welcomed anonymous strangers and discovered they were angels. When we sit in a sukka under the shelter of faith, we find ourselves surrounded by the *Shekhina*, God's clouds of glory. In Judaism, as Rabbi Yoḥanan said about God: greatness is humility (*Megilla* 31a). So it is with buildings when they become symbols. The humblest can be the greatest. That is why on Sukkot, the supreme Temple festival, God wanted us to remember the time He lived in our ancestors' midst in a sukka. Never was He closer to them or they to Him than when, using only materials they had donated, and time and skills they had volunteered, they built the *Mishkan*, the Tabernacle, so that the *Shekhina* could live in their midst.

So on this month of months, Tishrei, we begin with the anniversary of the creation of the universe – the home God made for us. But we then go on to remember the *Mishkan*, the home our ancestors made for God. The Torah spends only thirty-four verses describing the creation of the universe, but almost a third of the book of Exodus describing the building of the *Mishkan*, as if to say that it is easy for an infinite, omnipotent God to make a home for us, but His real pleasure – His *naḥat ruaḥ* – lies in the home we build for Him, with one condition, that it is built with humility – not the hubris that turned the wisest of Israel's kings almost into a pharaoh, and led eventually to the division of the kingdom and the destruction of the Temple itself.

The universe is the space God makes for us. The sukka, with its incomplete roof and its door open to strangers, is the space we make for God.

The Four Kinds

The other major symbol on Sukkot is the "four kinds," defined in the Torah in these words: "And on the first day, you shall take for yourselves a fruit of the citron tree, palm fronds, myrtle branches and willows of the brook, and be joyous in the presence of the LORD your God for seven days" (Lev. 23:40).

Uniquely in the case of symbolic objects, the Torah does not tell us why we are to take these four. It intimates why the matza and the Paschal Lamb on Pesaḥ, and why the sukka itself on Sukkot, but not the four kinds. It is not clear what they are, why we take them, or what we do with them. There is even a tantalizing passage in the book of Nehemiah which seems to suggest that, for some at least, they were understood as materials for use in constructing the sukka:

> And they found written in the law which the LORD had commanded by Moses, that the children of Israel should dwell in booths in the feast of the seventh month: And that they should publish and proclaim in all their cities, and in Jerusalem, saying, Go forth unto the mount, and fetch olive branches, and pine branches, and myrtle branches, and palm branches, and branches of thick trees, to make booths, as it is written. So the people went forth, and brought them, and made themselves booths, every one upon the roof of his house, and in their courts, and in the courts of the house of God, and in the street of the water gate, and in the street of the gate of Ephraim. (Neh. 8:14–16)

To be sure, there are differences between this list and that in Leviticus, which does not mention olive branches and pine branches. But there was at least one sage of the Mishnaic period who held that the covering of the sukka should be made of the same materials as the four kinds (*Sukka* 37a).

It was here that the oral tradition proved vital. The fruit of the citron tree [*hadar* tree in Hebrew] was identified with the etrog; the palm fronds with the lulav. The "leafy tree " [as it is called in the Hebrew] was the myrtle, and the willow was self-explanatory. "You shall take," was understood as holding them in the hand, most importantly during the recital of Hallel. The tension in the verse between "On the first day you shall take," and "You shall rejoice before the LORD for seven days" was easily resolved. In the Temple, that is, "before the LORD," the four kinds were to be taken all seven days, while elsewhere only on the first day. So it

◂ was until

was until the destruction of the Second Temple, when Rabban Yoḥanan ben Zakkai ordained that they be taken on all seven days (except Shabbat) everywhere, "in memory of the Temple" (Mishna, *Rosh HaShana* 4:3).

There was also a procession around the altar holding the four kinds, once each day, seven times on the seventh day. The Book of Jubilees, dating from the second century BCE, even attributes this custom to Abraham: "And Abraham took branches of palm trees and the fruit of hadar trees and every day, going round the altar with the branches seven times in the morning, he praised and gave thanks to God for all things in joy" (Jubilees 16:31). The Talmud also mentions another, more stringent custom: "This was the custom of the men in Jerusalem: when a man left his house he carried his lulav in his hand. When he went to the synagogue, his lulav was in his hand. When he said the Shema and the Amida his lulav was still in his hand… If he went to visit the sick or comfort mourners he would go with his lulav in his hand" (*Sukka* 41b).

Rabbinic sources provided a variety of symbolic explanations. One well known account said that the four kinds represented different kinds of Jews. The etrog has fragrance and fruit; the palm, fruit but no fragrance; the myrtle fragrance but not fruit; and the willow has neither. Fragrance means Torah knowledge. Fruit means good deeds. Some Jews have both, some have one but not the other, and some have neither. God said: in order to make it impossible for Israel to be destroyed, let them be bound together so that the righteous atone for the others. The four kinds thus became a symbol of Jewish unity (*VaYikra Raba* 30:12).

Another source related them to four parts of the body. The lulav was the spine, the myrtle the eyes, the willow leaves the mouth and the etrog the heart. Together they amounted to the statement that we worship God "with all my bones," or alternatively that they atoned for the sins we committed with the different limbs (*VaYikra Raba* 30:14).

However these are secondary elaborations. The Talmud itself says that the four kinds were taken as part of the process of asking God to send rain (*Ta'anit* 2b). That the festival had to do with rain was already clear in Zechariah's prophecy that in the Messianic Age the nations of the world would come to Jerusalem on Sukkot so that their lands would be blessed by rain (see page 459). The Mishna (*Rosh HaShana* 1:2) says that on *Ḥag*, the festival par excellence, the rabbinic name for Sukkot, the

◂ world

world is judged in relation to rain. Essentially, the four kinds are all forms of vegetation that require water. The palm tree is associated with an oasis in a desert. The willow usually signifies that there is running water nearby, and the etrog and myrtle both need significant rainfall. Accordingly, Maimonides gave the following explanation in his Guide for the Perplexed:

> I believe that the four species are a symbolical expression of our rejoicing that the Israelites were taken from the wilderness, "no place of seed, or of figs, or of vines, or of pomegranates, or of water to drink" (Num. 20:5), and brought to a country full of fruit-trees and rivers. In order to remember this we take the fruit which is the most pleasant of the fruit of the land, branches which smell best, most beautiful leaves, and also the best of herbs, that is, the willows of the brook. (Guide, 3:43)

The reason behind these specific plants was straightforward, even prosaic. First, says Maimonides, they were plentiful in Israel in biblical times, so that everyone could easily obtain them. Second, they have a good appearance, they are green, and some have a pleasant smell. Thirdly, they keep fresh for seven days, "which is not the case with peaches, pomegranates, quinces, pears, and the like."

There were other ceremonies performed in the Second Temple that were also related to rain. The first was the water libations. Throughout the year a libation of wine accompanied the sacrifices, but on Sukkot there was a water libation also. Each morning there would be a ceremonial procession from the Temple to the Shiloaḥ pool just outside the city, to collect the water to be used in the libations. So intense was the atmosphere surrounding this practice that, as we noted in the first chapter, all-night celebrations known as *Simḥat Beit HaSho'eva*, "Rejoicing at the place of water drawing," took place on the nights beforehand in the Temple.

Another was the willow ceremony. Each day of the festival except Shabbat, people would go to Motza, a town close to Jerusalem, where they would cut willow branches which they brought to the Temple and stood them around the altar. Some believe there is a reference to this in Hallel itself, in Psalm 118:27 translated as: "Bedeck the festival with branches at the corners of the altar" (see *Sukka* 45a). The processions around the altar reached a crescendo on the seventh day when there were seven circuits with willow branches (some say with the lulav) which were then struck. The day was known as "the day of beating" – a custom we still observe on Hoshana Raba.

Because these additional ceremonies had no explicit source in scripture, they became a source of contention between the Pharisees, who believed in an authoritative Oral Law dating back to Moses, and the Sadducees, who denied the Oral Law, and who were also the group most closely associated with the Temple priesthood. There was an occasion, the Talmud says, when a Sadducee priest decided to pour the water libation on his feet rather than on the altar, apparently as a personal protest against what he saw as an unwarranted practice. This led to a riot in which the outraged crowd pelted the hapless priest with their etrogs, and a section of the altar itself was damaged (*Sukka* 48b).

Rain-making ceremonies are not unusual in religions of the ancient world. What made Israel different, however, was a phenomenon disclosed by Moses only at the end of his life. Until then the land had been described as "flowing with milk and honey." What Moses revealed in the last month of his life was something different and more challenging:

> The land you are entering to take over is not like the land of Egypt, from which you have come, where you planted your seed and irrigated it by foot as in a vegetable garden. But the land you are crossing the Jordan to take possession of is a land of mountains and valleys that drinks rain from heaven. It is a land the LORD your God cares for; the eyes of the LORD your God are continually on it from the beginning of the year to its end. (Deut. 11:10–12)

Israel would not have a regular, predictable water supply like the Tigris-Euphrates valley or the Nile delta. It depends on rain, and in Israel rain is not something that can be taken for granted. Drought and famine led Abraham, Isaac and Jacob into exile at some time in their lives.

The result is the second dimension of insecurity that frames Sukkot as a festival: the uncertainty of rain. This meant that the natural focus of attention for those who live in the land is to look up to the heaven, rather than down to the naturally fertile earth. It meant the strongest possible

◂ connection

connection between faith itself and the rainfall needed for the land to yield its produce, and for the nation to be able to celebrate a harvest of plenty.

This is a central theme of the passage in Deuteronomy that became the second paragraph of the Shema:

> If you indeed heed My commandments with which I charge you today, to love the LORD your God and worship Him with all your heart and with all your soul, I will give rain in your land in its season, the early and late rain; and you shall gather in your grain, wine and oil. I will give grass in your field for your cattle, and you shall eat and be satisfied. Be careful lest your heart be tempted and you go astray and worship other gods, bowing down to them. Then the LORD's anger will flare against you and He will close the heavens so that there will be no rain. The land will not yield its crops, and you will perish swiftly from the good land that the LORD is giving you. (Deut. 11:13–17)

Israel is a land where the very climate itself becomes a commentary on the faithfulness of the nation to God. Israel is the land of promise, but it will always depend on He-who-promises.

In the Holy Land, geography becomes destiny. So argued the great Jewish poet and philosopher Yehuda HaLevi:

> [Israel's] fertility or barrenness, its happiness or misfortune, depend upon the divine influence which your conduct will merit, whilst the rest of the world will continue its natural course. For if the Divine Presence is among you, you will perceive by the fertility of your country, by the regularity with which your rainfalls appear in their due seasons, by your victories over your enemies in spite of your inferior numbers, that your affairs are not managed by simple laws of nature, but by the Divine Will. You will also see that drought, death, and wild beasts pursue you as a result of disobedience, although the whole world lives in peace. This shows you that your concerns are arranged by a higher power than mere nature. (*Kuzari*, 1:109)

Unpacking this in non-mystical terms, HaLevi is saying that the topography and climate of a country affects the culture and ethos of those who live there. In Mesopotamia and Egypt, the most powerful reality was the regularity of nature, the succession of the seasons which seemed to mirror the slow revolution of the stars. The cultures to which these cradles of civilization gave rise was cosmological and their sense of time cyclical. The universe seemed to be ruled by the heavenly bodies whose hierarchy and order was replicated in the hierarchy and order of life on earth.

Israel, by contrast, was a land without regularities. There was no guarantee that next year the rain would fall, the earth yield its crops, and the trees their fruit. So in Israel a new sense of time was born – the time we call historical. Those who lived, or live, in Israel exist in a state of radical contingency. They can never take the future for granted. They depend on something other than nature. Even the secular David Ben Gurion, the State of Israel's first Prime Minister, said: "In Israel, in order to be a realist, you must believe in miracles." In Egypt, where the source of life was the Nile, you looked down. In Israel, where the source of life is rain, you had no choice but to look up.

When Moses told the Israelites the full story about the land, he was telling them that it was a place where, not just wheat and barley, but the human spirit also, grew. It was the land where people are lifted beyond themselves because, time and again, they have to believe in something and some One beyond themselves. Not accidentally but essentially, by its climate, topography and location, Israel is the land where, merely to survive, the human eye must turn to heaven and the human ear to heaven's call.

Shemini Atzeret

In February 1997 the then President of the State of Israel, Ezer Weizman, paid the first, and thus far the only, state visit to Britain as the guest of Her Majesty the Queen. The custom is that on the first night of such a visit the queen hosts a state banquet at Buckingham Palace. It was, for the Jews present, a unique and moving moment to hear *HaTikva* played in the banqueting hall of the palace, and to hear the queen propose a toast to the president with the word *LeḤayyim*.

There is a protocol for such visits. Present are many representative

◂ figures

figures, ambassadors, members of the government, and other members of the royal family. At the end of the evening, after most of the guests have taken their leave, there is a small and intimate gathering for just a few individuals, on that occasion the Queen, Prince Philip, the Queen Mother, the Prime Minister and a few others, for a more relaxed and personal conversation with the guest of honor. It was this kind of occasion with its royal protocol that led the sages to their particular understanding of Shemini Atzeret.

It is a strange, even unique day in the Jewish calendar. It is described as the eighth day, and thus part of Sukkot, but it is also designated by a name, *Atzeret*, of its own. Is it, or is it not, a separate festival in its own right? It seems to be both. How are we to understand this fact?

What guided the sages was the detail that whereas on the seven days of Sukkot seventy young bulls were offered, on Atzeret, the eighth day, there was only one. Connecting this to Zechariah's prophecy that in the Messianic Age all nations would celebrate Sukkot, they concluded that the seventy sacrifices of Sukkot represented the seventy nations of the world as described in Genesis 10. Even though Zechariah's vision had not yet been realized, it was as if all humanity were in some sense present in Jerusalem on the festival, and sacrifices made on their behalf. On the eighth day, as they were leaving, it was as if God were inviting the Jewish people to a small private reception. The word *Atzeret* itself was interpreted to mean, "Stop, stay a while." Shemini Atzeret was private time between God and His people. It was a day of particularity after the universality of the seven days of Sukkot.

In some versions of this narrative the emphasis was on the length of time before the people would return to the Temple, virtually half a year until Pesaḥ. Others stressed the sudden shift from seventy sacrifices to one. The memorable phrase, though, that shines through, is the one mentioned by Rashi (Commentary to Lev. 23:36), in which God says to Israel, "It is hard for Me to see you go." This is the language of intimacy.

As we noted in pages xxv-xxxi, Sukkot represents more clearly than any other festival the dualities of Judaism. The four kinds are a symbol of the land of Israel, while the sukka reminds us of exile. The four kinds are a ritual of rain, while eating in the sukka depends on the absence of rain. Above all, though, there is the tension between the universality of nature

◂ and the

and the particularity of history. There is an aspect of Sukkot – rainfall, harvest, climate – to which everyone can relate, but there is another – the long journey through the wilderness – that speaks to the unique experience of the Jewish people.

This tension between the universal and the particular is unique to Judaism. The God of Israel is the God of all humanity, but the religion of Israel is not the religion of all humanity. It is conspicuous that while the other two Abrahamic monotheisms, Christianity and Islam, borrowed much from Judaism, they did not borrow this. They became universalist faiths, believing that everyone ought to embrace the one true religion, their own, and that those who do not are denied the blessings of eternity. *Extra ecclesiam non est salus*, "Outside the church none is saved."

Judaism disagrees. For this it was derided for many centuries, and to some degree still today. Why, if it represents religious truth, is it not to be shared with everyone? If there is only one God, why is there not only one way to salvation? There is no doubt that if Judaism had become an evangelizing, conversion-driven religion – as it would have had to, had it believed in universalism – there would be many more Jews than there are today. As I write, there are an estimated 2.4 billion Christians, 1.6 billion Muslims, and only 13 million Jews. The disparity is vast.

Judaism is the road less traveled, because it represents a complex truth that could not be expressed in any other way. The Torah tells a simple story. God gave humans the gift of freedom, which they then used not to enhance creation but to endanger it. Adam and Eve broke the first prohibition. Cain, the first human child, became the first murderer. Within a remarkably short space of time, all flesh had corrupted its way on earth, the world was filled with violence, and only one man, Noah, found favor in God's eyes. After the Flood, God made a covenant with Noah, and through him with all humanity, but after the hubris of the builders of the Tower of Babel, God chose another way. Having established a basic threshold in the form of the Noaḥide laws, He then chose one man, one family, and eventually one nation, to become a living example of what it is to exist closely and continuously in the presence of God. There are, in the affairs of humankind, universal laws and specific examples. The Noaḥide covenant constitutes the universal laws. The way of life of Abraham and his descendants are the example.

◂ What this

What this means in Judaism is that the righteous of all the nations have a share in the world to come (*Sanhedrin* 105a). In contemporary terms it means that our common humanity precedes our religious differences. It also means that by creating all humans in His image, God set us the challenge of seeing His image in one who is not in my image: whose color, culture, class and creed are not mine. The ultimate spiritual challenge is to see the trace of God in the face of a stranger.

Zechariah, in the vision we read as the haftara for the first day, puts this precisely. He says that in the end of days, "The Lord shall be King over all the earth; on that day the Lord shall be One and His name One" (1:49), meaning that all the nations will recognize the sovereignty of a single transcendent God. Yet at the same time Zechariah envisages the nations participating only in Sukkot, the most universal of the festivals, and the one in which they have the greatest interest since they all need rain. He does not envisage their becoming Jews, accepting the "yoke of the commands," all 613 of them. He does not speak of their conversion. The practical outcome of this dual theology – the universality of God and the particularity of Torah – is that we are commanded to be true to our faith, and a blessing to others, regardless of their faith. That is the way of Abraham.

Shemini Atzeret reminds us of the intimacy Jews have always felt in the presence of God. The cathedrals of Europe convey a sense of the vastness of God and the smallness of humankind. The small synagogues of Tzefat, where Isaac Luria and Joseph Karo prayed, convey a sense of the closeness of God and the greatness of humankind. Jews, except when they sought to imitate the gentiles, did not build cathedrals. Even the Temple reached its greatest architectural grandeur under Herod, a man better known for his political ruthlessness than his spiritual sensibilities.

So, when all the universality of Judaism has been expressed, there remains something that cannot be universalized: that sense of intimacy with and closeness to God that we feel on Shemini Atzeret, when all the other guests have left. Shemini Atzeret is chamber music, not a symphony. It is quiet time with God. We are reluctant to leave, and we dare to think that He is reluctant to see us go. Justice is universal, love is particular. There are some things we share because we are human. But there are other things, constitutive of our identity, that are uniquely ours – most importantly our relationships to those who form our family. On Sukkot we are among strangers and friends. On Shemini Atzeret we are with family.

So, when the Temple stood, it was as if God had said to His people, Stop. Pause. Stand in My courtyard, in Jerusalem the holy city, and feel My presence in the quiet of the day, the still blue sky, and the breeze gently rustling the trees. And even though the Temple has not been rebuilt, and Israel remains surrounded by enemies, and all we have of the Temple Mount is a wall, the most abstract of all religious symbols, yet still today in Jerusalem you can feel the Divine Presence as nowhere else on earth, a presence that does not have to be announced with clarions, robes and rituals, and we know that though God is God of all the world, to us He is also father, husband, neighbor, shepherd, king, and we are His children, and this is our private time together, breathing each other's being, blessed by the gift of being present to one another.

Simḥat Torah

One of the more amusing scenes in Anglo-Jewish history occurred on 14 October 1663. Seven years had passed since Oliver Cromwell had found no legal bar to Jews living in England (hence the so-called "return" of 1656). A small synagogue was opened in Creechurch Lane in the City of London, forerunner of Bevis Marks (1701), the oldest still-extant place of Jewish worship in Britain.

The famous diarist Samuel Pepys decided to pay a visit to this new curiosity, to see how Jews conducted themselves at prayer. What he saw amazed and scandalized him. As chance or Providence had it, the day of his visit turned out to be Simḥat Torah. This is how he described what he saw:

> And anon their Laws that they take out of the press [i.e., the Ark] are carried by several men, four or five several burthens in all, and they do relieve one another; and whether it is that every one desires to have the carrying of it, I cannot tell, thus they carried it round about the room while such a service is singing.... But, LORD! to see the disorder, laughing, sporting, and no attention, but confusion in all their service, more like brutes than people knowing the true God, would

◂ make a

> make a man forswear ever seeing them more and indeed I never did see so much, or could have imagined there had been any religion in the whole world so absurdly performed as this.

This was not the kind of behavior he was used to in a house of worship. It was conduct unbecoming. It was the kind of joy that does not translate easily into other languages of the spirit. It wasn't English.

Simḥat Torah is unique among festivals. It is not mentioned in the Torah, nor in the Talmud. Unlike Purim and Ḥanukka, it was not formalized by any decision on the part of the religious authorities, nor does it commemorate any historical deliverance. It is the supreme example of what the mystics called an *itaruta deletata,* "an awakening from below." It grew from the grassroots, slowly developing over time. It is the only festival that is celebrated as a distinct day only in the Diaspora: in Israel it is subsumed as part of the celebration of Shemini Atzeret. It affords, in other words, a rare glimpse into the reflexes of the collective Jewish soul.

It was born in Babylon, probably at the end of the period of the Amora'im, the rabbis of the Talmud, in the fifth or sixth century. The Babylonian custom – now universal – was to divide the Torah into fifty-four portions to be read in the course of a year. The *Eretz Yisrael* custom was to divide it into 155, or 175 portions, to be read in a three- or three-and a-half-year cycle. On the second day of Shemini Atzeret in Babylon (there was no second day in Israel) the custom was to read the passage in which King Solomon blesses the people at the end of the Temple consecration ceremony and sends them on their way home. Normally the Torah reading on a festival has to do with the festival itself, but on this day it became a custom to read the last portion of the Torah in which Moses blessed the nation at the end of his life. The day was thus known as *Yom Berakha,* "the day of blessing" (*Siddur Rav Sa'adia Gaon*).

It had long been the custom to make a celebration on completing a section of study, a Talmudic tractate or an order of the Mishna (*Shabbat* 118b). This too was attributed to Solomon, who made a feast after God had granted him wisdom (I Kings 3:15). Thus the custom evolved to make a celebration at the completion of the Mosaic books, and it was considered a great honor to be called to the Torah for this last portion.

◂ The celebration

The celebration became known as *Simḥat Torah,* "rejoicing in the Torah," though this was not yet the name given to the day.

No sooner had this custom developed than there was a feeling that it would be wrong to conclude the Torah without also immediately beginning it again. This was expressed in the form of the idea that Satan (prosecuting counsel in the heavenly court) might bring an accusation against the Jewish people that having reached the end of the book, they stopped at that point (*Seder Trois,* 4). Thus it became the norm to begin again with the opening of *Bereshit.* How this was to be done became the subject of many different customs. Some said the Genesis passage by heart. Others read it from a second *Sefer Torah.* In some places only one person was called to the two readings; in others two were called, one for the end, the other for the beginning, but without a blessing in between. The first said the blessing before reading, the second the blessing after. Eventually a consensus emerged. There would be two separate *aliyot,* one for the close of Deuteronomy, the other for the opening of Genesis.

Meanwhile other customs developed in the spirit of the day. The first was to call up many more people to the Torah than on usual occasions. Soon all men in the synagogue received *aliyot,* the portion being read multiple times. Then by the eleventh century the custom appeared of calling up *kol hane'arim,* all the children, with an adult saying the blessing, and the children gathered together under a *tallit* spread over them like a wedding canopy.

Only in the twelfth century do we find the two key honors, being called to the end and the beginning, being described as *Ḥatan Torah,* bridegroom of the law, and *Ḥatan Bereshit,* bridegroom of the beginning. Abraham Yaari, who has written the standard history of Simḥat Torah, speculates the original title was *Ḥatam* or *Ḥotem Torah,* literally the one who "seals" or "concludes" the Torah. Nonetheless, once the word *Ḥatan,* bridegroom, appeared, it soon won universal approval. As early as the eighth century in Babylon the custom had been that on this day people adorned the Torah scroll with women's scarves and ornaments. Thus the Torah had long been treated as a bride, and it became logical to describe those who honored it as bridegrooms. Only much later, under the influence of the mystics in Tzefat associated with Rabbi Isaac Luria, did the custom evolve to do *Hakafot,* circuits around the *bima,* with multiple Torah scrolls.

◂ Simḥat

Simḥat Torah did not develop in Israel, firstly because there was no second day of Shemini Atzeret, secondly and more importantly because they did not complete the Torah reading in a single year. The Jewish community in Israel was devastated by the Crusades. In 1099, virtually the entire community in Jerusalem was massacred by the Christians. The city, said some observers, was knee-deep in blood. It was this almost total destruction of Israeli Jewry that finally brought the three-year cycle to an end. Nonetheless, even in the twelfth century, when Moses Maimonides was living in Fostat near Cairo, there were two synagogues, one of which followed the Babylonian custom, the other of which still maintained the Israeli one of a triennial lection. Despite this split, which Maimonides lamented, the traveler Benjamin of Tudela tells us that the members of the Israeli synagogue joined the Babylonian-oriented community to celebrate the ending of the Torah, so unity prevailed at least one day a year.

Thus far, history. But the very emergence of Simḥat Torah signals something remarkable. Recall that Sukkot and Shemini Atzeret are both described as *zeman simḥateinu*, the season of our joy. The nature of that joy was clear, and signaled in different ways both by the sukka and by the four kinds. The sukka reminded the people how blessed they were to be living in Israel when they recalled how their ancestors had to live for forty years without a land or a permanent home. The lulav, etrog, myrtle and willows were a vivid demonstration of the fruitfulness of the land under the divine blessing of rain. The joy of Sukkot was the joy of living in the Promised Land.

But by the time Simḥat Torah had spread throughout the Jewish world, Jews had lost virtually everything: their land, their home, their freedom and independence, the Temple, the priesthood, the sacrificial order – all that had once been their source of joy. A single devastating sentence, in one of the piyutim of Ne'ila at the close of Yom Kippur, summed up their situation: *Ein shiur rak haTorah hazot.* "Nothing remains but this Torah." All that remained was a book.

Sa'adia Gaon, writing in the tenth century, asked a simple question. In virtue of what was the Jewish people still a nation? It had none of the normal preconditions of a nation. Jews were scattered throughout the world. They did not live in the same territory. They were not part of a single economic or political order. They did not share the same circumambient culture. They did not speak the same language of everyday speech. Rashi spoke French, Maimonides Arabic. Yet they were, and were seen to be, one nation, bound by a bond of collective destiny and responsibility. Hence Sa'adia concluded: our people is a people only in virtue of our Torah (*Beliefs and Opinions*, 3). In the lovely rabbinic phrase about the Ark, that contained the tablets, "It carried those who carried it" (*Sota* 35a). More than the Jewish people preserved the Torah, the Torah preserved the Jewish people.

It was, as we say in our prayers, "our life and the length of our days." Heinrich Heine famously called it the "portable homeland of the Jew." It was their extraterritorial country. It was the legacy of their past and the promise of their future. It was their marriage contract with God, the record of the Covenant that bound them unbreakably together. They had lost their world but they still had God's word, and it was enough.

More than enough. On Simḥat Torah, without their being commanded by any verse in the Torah or any decree of the rabbis, Jews throughout the world sang and danced and recited poems in honor of the Torah, exactly as if they were the "men of renown" dancing in the courtyard of the Temple at the *Simḥat Beit HaSho'eva*, or as if they were King David bringing the Ark to Jerusalem. They were determined to show God, and the world, that they could still be *akh same'aḥ*, as the Torah said about Sukkot: wholly, totally, given over to joy. It would be hard to find a parallel in the entire history of the human spirit of a people capable of such joy at a time when they were being massacred by Christians in the name of the God of love, or brutalized by Muslim radicals like the Almohades in the name of the God of compassion.

A people that can walk through the valley of the shadow of death and still rejoice is a people that cannot be defeated by any force or any fear. King David was despised by his wife, Saul's daughter, Michal, for abandoning his dignity as a king when he danced and leaped with all his might before the LORD (II Sam. 6:14–16). The Spanish and Portuguese Jews of the Creechurch Lane synagogue in 1663 were equally looked down on by Samuel Pepys, who thought their conduct unbecoming in a house of God. Maimonides, however, writes (*Hilkhot Shofar* 8:15) that to experience joy in the fulfillment of a mitzva out of the love of God is to touch the spiritual heights. Whoever stands on his dignity and regards such things as beneath him is, he says, a sinner and a fool, and whoever abandons his dignity for the sake of joy is thereby elevated "because there is no greatness or honor higher than celebrating before God."

Simḥat Torah was born when Jews had lost everything else, but they never lost their capacity to rejoice. Nehemiah was right when he said to the people weeping as they listened to the Torah, realizing how far they had drifted from it: "Do not grieve, for the joy of the LORD is your strength" (Neh. 8:10). A people whose capacity for joy cannot be destroyed is itself indestructible. Zechariah was right: "'Not by might nor by power, but by My Spirit,' says the LORD Almighty" (Zech. 4:6).

Sukkot for Our Time

Of all the festivals, Sukkot is surely the one that speaks most powerfully to our time. Kohelet could almost have been written in the twenty-first century. Here is the ultimate success, the man who has it all – the houses, the cars, the clothes, the adoring women, the envy of all men – who has pursued everything this world can offer from pleasure to possessions to power to wisdom, and yet who, surveying the totality of his life, can only say, in effect, "Meaningless, meaningless, everything is meaningless."

Kohelet's failure to find meaning is directly related to his obsession with the "I" and the "Me": "I built for myself. I gathered for myself. I acquired for myself." The more he pursues his desires, the emptier his life becomes. There is no more powerful critique of the consumer society, whose idol is the self, whose icon is the "selfie" and whose moral code is "Whatever works for you." This is the society that achieved unprecedented affluence, giving people more choices than they have ever known, and yet at same time saw an unprecedented rise in alcohol and drug abuse, eating disorders, stress related syndromes, depression, attempted suicide and actual suicide. A society of tourists, not pilgrims, is not one that will yield the sense of a life worth living. Of all things people have chosen to worship, the self is the least fulfilling. A culture of narcissism quickly gives way to loneliness and despair.

Kohelet was also, of course, a cosmopolitan: a man at home everywhere and therefore nowhere. This is the man who had seven hundred wives and three hundred concubines but in the end could only say, "Woman is more bitter than death" (7:26). It should be clear to anyone

◄ who reads

who reads this in the context of the life of Solomon, that Kohelet is not really talking about women but about himself.

In the end Kohelet finds meaning in simple things. Sweet is the sleep of a laboring man. Enjoy life with the woman you love. Eat, drink and enjoy the sun. That ultimately is the meaning of Sukkot as a whole. It is a festival of simple things. It is, Jewishly, the time we come closer to nature than any other, sitting in a hut with only leaves for a roof, and taking in our hands the unprocessed fruits and foliage of the palm branch, the citron, twigs of myrtle and leaves of willow. It is a time when we briefly liberate ourselves from the sophisticated pleasures of the city and the processed artefacts of a technological age, and recapture some of the innocence we had when we were young, when the world still had the radiance of wonder.

The power of Sukkot is that it takes us back to the most elemental roots of our being. You don't need to live in a palace to be surrounded by clouds of glory. You don't need to be rich to buy yourself the same leaves and fruit that a billionaire uses in worshiping God. Living in the sukka and inviting guests to your meal, you discover – such is the premise of *Ushpizin*, the mystical guests – that the people who have come to visit you are none other than Abraham, Isaac, and Jacob, and their wives. What makes a hut more beautiful than a home is that when it comes to Sukkot there is no difference between the richest of the rich and the poorest of the poor. We are all strangers on earth, temporary residents in God's almost eternal universe. And whether or not we are capable of pleasure, whether or not we have found happiness, nonetheless we can all feel joy.

Sukkot is the time we ask the most profound question of what makes a life worth living. Having prayed on Rosh HaShana and Yom Kippur to be written in the Book of Life, Kohelet forces us to remember how brief life actually is, and how vulnerable. "Teach us rightly to number our days, that we may gain a heart of wisdom" (Ps. 90:12). What matters is not how long we live, but how intensely we feel that life is a gift we repay by giving to others. Joy, the overwhelming theme of the festival, is what we feel when we know that it is a privilege simply to be alive, inhaling the intoxicating beauty of this moment amidst the profusion of nature, the teeming diversity of life, and the sense of communion with those many others with whom we share a history and a hope.

Most majestically of all, Sukkot is the festival of insecurity. It is the candid acknowledgment that there is no life without risk, yet we can face the future without fear when we know we are not alone. God is with us, in the rain that brings blessings to the earth, in the love that brought the universe and us into being, and in the resilience of spirit that allowed a small and vulnerable people to outlive the greatest empires the world has ever known. Sukkot reminds us that God's glory was present in the small, portable Tabernacle Moses and the Israelites built in the desert even more emphatically than in Solomon's Temple with all its grandeur. A Temple can be destroyed. But a sukka, broken, can be rebuilt tomorrow. Security is not something we can achieve physically but it is something we can acquire mentally, psychologically, spiritually. All it needs is the courage and willingness to sit under the shadow of God's sheltering wings.

The sukka became in the course of time a symbol, not only of forty years in the wilderness, but of centuries of exile and dispersion. In the Middle Ages alone, Jews were expelled from England in 1290, from France several times (1182, 1322, 1394), from Vienna in 1421, Cologne in 1424, Bavaria in 1442, Milan in 1489, and most traumatically from Spain in 1492. In the 1880s a wave of pogroms in Eastern Europe sent millions of Jews into flight to the West, and these migrations continue even today. Jewish history reads like a vast continuation of the stages of the Israelites' journey in the thirty-second chapter of the book of Numbers: "They traveled… and they encamped… They traveled… and they encamped." Too often, home turned out to be no more than a temporary dwelling, a sukka. More than most, whether in the Land of Israel or elsewhere, Jews have known the full force of insecurity.

Yet with its genius for the unexpected and its ability to rescue hope from tragedy, Judaism declared this festival of insecurity to be *zeman simḥateinu*, the season of our rejoicing. For the sukka, that quintessential symbol of vulnerability, turns out to be the embodiment of faith, the faith of a people who forty centuries ago set out on a risk-laden journey across a wilderness of space and time, with no more protection than the sheltering presence of the *Shekhina*. Sitting in the sukka under its canopy of leaves, I often think of my ancestors and their wanderings across Europe in search of safety, and I begin to understand how faith was their only home. It was fragile, chillingly exposed to the storms of prejudice and hate. But it proved stronger than superpowers and outlived them all.

◄ Toward

Toward the end of his great *History of the Jews,* Paul Johnson wrote:

> The Jews were not just innovators. They were also exemplars and epitomizers of the human condition. They seemed to present all the inescapable dilemmas of man in a heightened and clarified form.... The Jews were the emblem of homeless and vulnerable humanity. But is not the whole earth no more than a temporary transit camp?

Those words go to the heart of Sukkot. To know that life is full of risk and yet to affirm it, to sense the full insecurity of the human situation and yet to rejoice: this, for me, is the essence of faith. Judaism is no comforting illusion that all is well in this dark world. It is instead the courage to celebrate in the midst of uncertainty, and to rejoice even in the transitory shelter of the tabernacle, the Jewish symbol of home.

Acknowledgments

A work of this scope and complexity is a team enterprise, and it has been a privilege to work with some of the most wonderful colleagues anyone could ask for. The team at Koren is outstanding: Matthew Miller, its tireless and visionary driving force, together with Rachel Meghnagi, Jessica Sacks, Rabbi David Fuchs, Efrat Gross, Rabbi Eli Clark and Esther Be'er, each of whom has contributed massively to this work.

Particular thanks are due to Michael Gross and his family for recognizing the importance of this project.

I owe a huge debt to Dayan Ivan Binstock, responsible for the Minhag Anglia version of the Maḥzor, lending it his unique erudition and eye for detail.

My deepest thanks, as always, are to my wife Elaine, the inspiration of my life, and the human Thou who has taught me to be open to the ultimate Divine Thou.

Ultimately, though, all thanks belong to God who has sheltered us under the sukka of His protection. May He spread over us, all Israel and all humanity, the Tabernacle of His peace, speedily in our days, Amen.

Rabbi Lord Jonathan Sacks
London, 5775 (2015)

מחזור קורן לסוכות

THE KOREN SUKKOT MAḤZOR

Erev Shabbat and Yom Tov

EIRUV TEḤUMIN

On Shabbat and Yom Tov it is forbidden to walk more than 2000 cubits (about 3000 feet) beyond the boundary (teḥum) of the town where you live or are staying when the day begins. By placing food sufficient for two meals, before nightfall, at a point within 2000 cubits from the town limits, you confer on that place the status of a dwelling for the next day, and are then permitted to walk 2000 cubits from there.

בָּרוּךְ Blessed are You, Lord our God, King of the Universe,
who has made us holy through His commandments,
and has commanded us about the mitzva of Eiruv.

By this Eiruv may we be permitted to walk from this place,
two thousand cubits in any direction.

EIRUV ḤATZEROT

On Shabbat it is forbidden to carry objects from one private domain to another, or from a private domain into space shared by others, such as a communal staircase, corridor or courtyard. An Eiruv Ḥatzerot is created when each of the Jewish households in a court or apartment block, before Shabbat, places a piece of bread in one of the homes. The entire court or block then becomes a single private domain within which it is permitted to carry.

בָּרוּךְ Blessed are You, Lord our God, King of the Universe,
who has made us holy through His commandments,
and has commanded us about the mitzva of Eiruv.

By this Eiruv may we be permitted to move,
carry out and carry in from the houses to the courtyard,
or from the courtyard to the houses, or from house to house,
for all the houses within the courtyard.

---

persons in a bond of shared responsibility, and *arev*, "pleasant," the mood that prevails when people join in friendship. An *eiruv* softens the sharp divide of boundaries.

An *eiruv teḥumin* is a device that allows us to walk for up to two thousand cubits beyond the two-thousand-cubit boundary that marks how far we may walk outside the limits of a town. An *eiruv ḥatzerot* joins multiple homes into a single private domain for the purpose of carrying between them on

ערב שבת ויום טוב

עירוב תחומין

On שבת and יום טוב it is forbidden to walk more than 2000 cubits (about 3000 feet) beyond the boundary (תחום) of the town where you live or are staying when the day begins. By placing food sufficient for two meals, before nightfall, at a point within 2000 cubits from the town limits, you confer on that place the status of a dwelling for the next day, and are then permitted to walk 2000 cubits from there.

בָּרוּךְ אַתָּה יהוה אֱלֹהֵינוּ מֶלֶךְ הָעוֹלָם
אֲשֶׁר קִדְּשָׁנוּ בְּמִצְוֹתָיו וְצִוָּנוּ עַל מִצְוַת עֵרוּב.

בְּדֵין עֵרוּבָא יְהֵא שְׁרֵא לִי לְמֵיזַל מֵאַתְרָא
הָדֵין תְּרֵין אַלְפִּין אַמִּין לְכָל רוּחָא.

עירוב חצרות

On שבת it is forbidden to carry objects from one private domain to another, or from a private domain into space shared by others, such as a communal staircase, corridor or courtyard. An עירוב חצרות is created when each of the Jewish households in a court or apartment block, before שבת, places a piece of bread in one of the homes. The entire court or block then becomes a single private domain within which it is permitted to carry.

בָּרוּךְ אַתָּה יהוה אֱלֹהֵינוּ מֶלֶךְ הָעוֹלָם
אֲשֶׁר קִדְּשָׁנוּ בְּמִצְוֹתָיו וְצִוָּנוּ עַל מִצְוַת עֵרוּב.

בְּדֵין עֵרוּבָא יְהֵא שְׁרֵא לַנָא לְטַלְטוּלֵי וּלְאַפּוּקֵי וּלְעַיּוּלֵי
מִן הַבָּתִּים לֶחָצֵר וּמִן הֶחָצֵר לַבָּתִּים
וּמִבַּיִת לְבַיִת לְכָל הַבָּתִּים שֶׁבֶּחָצֵר.

EIRUVIN

Eiruvin are halakhic devices relating to Shabbat and the festivals by which the sages "joined" different domains of space and time. *Eiruv* comes from the same root (ע-ר-ב, literally: combine or join) as *erev*, "evening," the time that joins day and night; *arev*, "a guarantor," who joins another person or

EIRUV TAVSHILIN

It is not permitted to cook for Shabbat on a Yom Tov that falls on Thursday and Friday unless an Eiruv Tavshilin has been made prior to the Yom Tov. This is done by taking a loaf or piece of matza together with a boiled egg, or a piece of cooked fish or meat to be used on Shabbat. While holding them, say the following:

בָּרוּךְ Blessed are You, LORD our God, King of the Universe,
who has made us holy through His commandments,
and has commanded us about the mitzva of Eiruv.

By this Eiruv may we be permitted to bake, cook, insulate food, light a flame and do everything necessary on the festival for the sake of Shabbat, for us and for all Jews living in this city.

CANDLE LIGHTING

On Erev Yom Tov, say the following blessing and then light the candles from an existing flame. If also Shabbat, cover the eyes with the hands after lighting the candles and say the following blessing, adding the words in parentheses.

בָּרוּךְ Blessed are You, LORD our God, King of the Universe,
who has made us holy through His commandments,
and has commanded us to light (the Sabbath light and)
the festival light.

בָּרוּךְ Blessed are You, LORD our God, King of the Universe,
who has given us life, sustained us, and brought us to this time.

On Erev Shabbat Ḥol HaMo'ed that is not a Yom Tov, cover the eyes with the hands after lighting the candles, and say:

בָּרוּךְ Blessed are You, LORD our God, King of the Universe,
who has made us holy through His commandments,
and has commanded us to light the Sabbath light.

---

essential structure of Jewish law that surrounds and protects the holiness of space and time.

CANDLE LIGHTING

Candle lighting on Shabbat and festivals represents *shelom bayit*, "peace in the home." The sages say that Adam and Eve were created on the eve of

עירוב תבשילין

It is not permitted to cook for שבת *on a* יום טוב *that falls on Thursday and Friday unless an* עירוב תבשלין *has been made prior to the* יום טוב*. This is done by taking a loaf or piece of matza together with a boiled egg, or a piece of cooked fish or meat to be used on* שבת*. While holding them, say the following:*

בָּרוּךְ אַתָּה יהוה אֱלֹהֵינוּ מֶלֶךְ הָעוֹלָם
אֲשֶׁר קִדְּשָׁנוּ בְּמִצְוֹתָיו וְצִוָּנוּ עַל מִצְוַת עֵרוּב.

בְּדֵין עֵרוּבָא יְהֵא שָׁרֵא לָנָא לְמֵיפָא וּלְבַשָּׁלָא וּלְאַטְמָנָא וּלְאַדְלָקָא שְׁרָגָא
וּלְמֶעְבַּד כָּל צָרְכָּנָא מִיּוֹמָא טָבָא לְשַׁבְּתָא
לָנוּ וּלְכָל יִשְׂרָאֵל הַדָּרִים בָּעִיר הַזֹּאת.

הדלקת נרות

On ערב יום טוב*, say the following blessing and then light the candles from an existing flame. If also* שבת*, cover the eyes with the hands after lighting the candles and say the following blessing, adding the words in parentheses.*

בָּרוּךְ אַתָּה יהוה אֱלֹהֵינוּ מֶלֶךְ הָעוֹלָם
אֲשֶׁר קִדְּשָׁנוּ בְּמִצְוֹתָיו
וְצִוָּנוּ לְהַדְלִיק נֵר שֶׁל (שַׁבָּת וְשֶׁל) יוֹם טוֹב.

בָּרוּךְ אַתָּה יהוה אֱלֹהֵינוּ מֶלֶךְ הָעוֹלָם
שֶׁהֶחֱיָנוּ וְקִיְּמָנוּ, וְהִגִּיעָנוּ לַזְּמַן הַזֶּה.

On ערב שבת חול המועד *that is not a* יום טוב*, cover the eyes with the hands after lighting the candles, and say:*

בָּרוּךְ אַתָּה יהוה אֱלֹהֵינוּ מֶלֶךְ הָעוֹלָם
אֲשֶׁר קִדְּשָׁנוּ בְּמִצְוֹתָיו וְצִוָּנוּ לְהַדְלִיק נֵר שֶׁל שַׁבָּת.

Shabbat. An *eiruv tavshilin* permits us to prepare food for Shabbat on a festival that immediately precedes Shabbat. All three were instituted to enhance the joy of the festival and the delight of Shabbat without weakening the

Some add:

יְהִי רָצוֹן May it be Your will, Lord our God and God of our ancestors, that the Temple be speedily rebuilt in our days, and grant us our share in Your Torah. And may we serve You there *Mal. 3*
in reverence, as in the days of old and as in former years.

Prayer after candlelighting
(add the words in parentheses as appropriate):

יְהִי רָצוֹן May it be Your will, Lord my God and God of my forebears, that You give me grace – me (and my husband/and my father/and my mother/and my sons and my daughters) and all those close to me, and give us and all Israel good and long lives. And remember us with a memory that brings goodness and blessing; come to us with compassion and bless us with great blessings. Build our homes until they are complete, and allow Your Presence to live among us. And may I merit to raise children and grandchildren, each one wise and understanding, loving the Lord and in awe of God, people of truth, holy children, who will cling on to the Lord and light up the world with Torah and with good actions, and with all the kinds of work that serve the Creator. Please, hear my pleading at this time, by the merit of Sarah and Rebecca, Rachel and Leah our mothers, and light our candle that it should never go out, and light up Your face, so that we shall be saved, Amen.

---

the festivals when in the soft light of the flickering flames, the jagged edges of the week lose their sharpness and we begin to feel the unity of all things in the sensed presence of their Creator.

יְהִי רָצוֹן *May it be Your will.* A beautiful prayer usually said by the woman of the house, invoking the merits and enduring influence of the matriarchs of our people – Sarah, Rebecca, Rachel and Leah – and the courage and devotion of their steadfast love for God and their families. It is a touching summary of the values by which Jewish women through the millennia lived and taught their children.

Some add:

יְהִי רָצוֹן מִלְּפָנֶיךָ יהוה אֱלֹהֵינוּ וֵאלֹהֵי אֲבוֹתֵינוּ, שֶׁיִּבָּנֶה בֵּית הַמִּקְדָּשׁ בִּמְהֵרָה בְיָמֵינוּ, וְתֵן חֶלְקֵנוּ בְּתוֹרָתֶךָ, וְשָׁם נַעֲבָדְךָ בְּיִרְאָה כִּימֵי עוֹלָם וּכְשָׁנִים קַדְמֹנִיּוֹת. וְעָרְבָה לַיהוה מִנְחַת יְהוּדָה וִירוּשָׁלָםִ כִּימֵי עוֹלָם וּכְשָׁנִים קַדְמֹנִיּוֹת: מלאכי ג

Prayer after candlelighting
(add the words in parentheses as appropriate):

יְהִי רָצוֹן מִלְּפָנֶיךָ יהוה אֱלֹהַי וֵאלֹהֵי אֲבוֹתַי, שֶׁתְּחוֹנֵן אוֹתִי (וְאֶת אִישִׁי/ וְאֶת אָבִי/ וְאֶת אִמִּי/ וְאֶת בָּנַי וְאֶת בְּנוֹתַי) וְאֶת כָּל קְרוֹבַי, וְתִתֶּן לָנוּ וּלְכָל יִשְׂרָאֵל חַיִּים טוֹבִים וַאֲרֻכִּים, וְתִזְכְּרֵנוּ בְּזִכְרוֹן טוֹבָה וּבְרָכָה, וְתִפְקְדֵנוּ בִּפְקֻדַּת יְשׁוּעָה וְרַחֲמִים, וּתְבָרְכֵנוּ בְּרָכוֹת גְּדוֹלוֹת, וְתַשְׁלִים בָּתֵּינוּ וְתַשְׁכֵּן שְׁכִינָתְךָ בֵּינֵינוּ. וְזַכֵּנִי לְגַדֵּל בָּנִים וּבְנֵי בָנִים חֲכָמִים וּנְבוֹנִים, אוֹהֲבֵי יהוה יִרְאֵי אֱלֹהִים, אַנְשֵׁי אֱמֶת זֶרַע קֹדֶשׁ, בַּיהוה דְּבֵקִים וּמְאִירִים אֶת הָעוֹלָם בַּתּוֹרָה וּבְמַעֲשִׂים טוֹבִים וּבְכָל מְלֶאכֶת עֲבוֹדַת הַבּוֹרֵא. אָנָּא שְׁמַע אֶת תְּחִנָּתִי בָּעֵת הַזֹּאת בִּזְכוּת שָׂרָה וְרִבְקָה וְרָחֵל וְלֵאָה אִמּוֹתֵינוּ, וְהָאֵר נֵרֵנוּ שֶׁלֹּא יִכְבֶּה לְעוֹלָם וָעֶד, וְהָאֵר פָּנֶיךָ וְנִוָּשֵׁעָה. אָמֵן.

Shabbat, the sixth day, and sinned and were sentenced to exile from Eden on the same day (*Avot deRabbi Natan* 1). God took pity on them and delayed the start of their exile by a day so that they were able to spend one day, Shabbat, in paradise. On that day, said the sages, the sun did not set. It was a day of light, physical and spiritual, in which the first man and woman experienced the harmony of the universe and of their relationship. The candles of Shabbat – customarily two, though Jewish law requires minimally one – symbolize the two aspects of holy time: *zakhor*, "remember" (Ex. 20:8) and *shamor* "guard" (Deut. 5:12). They also symbolize man and woman, humanity and God, heaven and earth, united on this day. Though, since the first humans, we no longer inhabit paradise, we capture something of it on Shabbat and

Minḥa for Weekdays

אַשְׁרֵי Happy are those who dwell in Your House; Ps. 84
they shall continue to praise You, Selah!
Happy are the people for whom this is so; Ps. 144
happy are the people whose God is the LORD.

A song of praise by David. Ps. 145

I will exalt You, my God, the King, and bless Your name for ever and all time. Every day I will bless You, and praise Your name for ever and all time. Great is the LORD and greatly to be praised; His greatness is unfathomable. One generation will praise Your works to the next, and tell of Your mighty deeds. On the glorious splendor of Your majesty I will meditate, and on the acts of Your wonders. They shall talk of the power of Your awesome deeds, and I will tell of Your greatness. They shall recite the record of Your great goodness, and sing with joy of Your righteousness. The LORD is gracious and compassionate, slow to anger and great in loving-kindness. The LORD is good to all,

---

through many streets and across the marketplace throughout the day. He almost forgets that there is a Maker of the world. Only when the time for the afternoon prayer comes, does he remember, 'I must pray.' And then, from the bottom of his heart, he heaves a sigh of regret that he has spent his day on idle matters, and he runs into a side street and stands there and prays. God holds him dear, very dear, and his prayer pierces the heavens."

אַשְׁרֵי *Psalm 145. Ashrei,* at the beginning of Minḥa, is an abridged form of the more extended *Pesukei DeZimra,* the Verses of Praise, of the morning service. It is a meditation prior to the Amida. The Amida is prayer in its purest form, and it requires *kavana,* a direction of the mind, a focusing of our thoughts. *Kavana* involves "clearing your mind of all extraneous thoughts, and seeing yourself as if you are standing before the Divine Presence. Therefore it is necessary to sit for a while before prayer in order to direct your mind, and then pray gently and pleadingly, not like one who prays as if he were carrying a burden which he is keen to unload and leave" (Maimonides,

מנחה לחול

אַשְׁרֵי יוֹשְׁבֵי בֵיתֶךָ, עוֹד יְהַלְלוּךָ סֶּלָה: תהלים פד

אַשְׁרֵי הָעָם שֶׁכָּכָה לּוֹ, אַשְׁרֵי הָעָם שֶׁיהוה אֱלֹהָיו: תהלים קמד

תְּהִלָּה לְדָוִד תהלים קמה

אֲרוֹמִמְךָ אֱלוֹהַי הַמֶּלֶךְ, וַאֲבָרְכָה שִׁמְךָ לְעוֹלָם וָעֶד:

בְּכָל־יוֹם אֲבָרְכֶךָּ, וַאֲהַלְלָה שִׁמְךָ לְעוֹלָם וָעֶד:

גָּדוֹל יהוה וּמְהֻלָּל מְאֹד, וְלִגְדֻלָּתוֹ אֵין חֵקֶר:

דּוֹר לְדוֹר יְשַׁבַּח מַעֲשֶׂיךָ, וּגְבוּרֹתֶיךָ יַגִּידוּ:

הֲדַר כְּבוֹד הוֹדֶךָ, וְדִבְרֵי נִפְלְאוֹתֶיךָ אָשִׂיחָה:

וֶעֱזוּז נוֹרְאוֹתֶיךָ יֹאמֵרוּ, וּגְדוּלָּתְךָ אֲסַפְּרֶנָּה:

זֵכֶר רַב־טוּבְךָ יַבִּיעוּ, וְצִדְקָתְךָ יְרַנֵּנוּ:

חַנּוּן וְרַחוּם יהוה, אֶרֶךְ אַפַּיִם וּגְדָל־חָסֶד:

MINḤA – AFTERNOON SERVICE

The Afternoon Service corresponds to the daily afternoon sacrifice (*Berakhot* 26b). The *Minḥa,* or "meal-offering," was not unique to the afternoon sacrifice. The afternoon service may have become known as Minḥa because of the verse in Psalms (141:2): "May my prayer be like incense before You, the lifting up of my hands like the afternoon offering [*minḥat arev*]."

The sages (*Berakhot* 6b) attached special significance to the afternoon prayer, noting that Elijah's prayer was answered at this time (1 Kings 18:36). It is easier to pray in the morning and evening as we are about to begin or end our engagement with the world for the day. Minḥa is more demanding. It means that we are turning to God in the midst of our distractions. We are bringing Him into our life when it is maximally preoccupied with other things. Minḥa is the triumph of the important over the urgent, of what matters ultimately over what matters immediately. That is why prayer in the midst of the day has a special transformative power.

The Ba'al Shem Tov said: "Imagine a man whose business hounds him

and His compassion extends to all His works. All Your works shall thank You, Lord, and Your devoted ones shall bless You. They shall talk of the glory of Your kingship, and speak of Your might. To make known to mankind His mighty deeds and the glorious majesty of His kingship. Your kingdom is an everlasting kingdom, and Your reign is for all generations. The Lord supports all who fall, and raises all who are bowed down. All raise their eyes to You in hope, and You give them their food in due season. You open Your hand, and satisfy every living thing with favor. The Lord is righteous in all His ways, and kind in all He does. The Lord is close to all who call on Him, to all who call on Him in truth. He fulfills the will of those who revere Him; He hears their cry and saves them. The Lord guards all who love Him, but all the wicked He will destroy. ▸ My mouth shall speak the praise of the Lord, and all creatures shall bless His holy name for ever and all time.

We will bless the Lord now and for ever. Halleluya! *Ps. 115*

---

which include three times the word *Ashrei* ("happy"), the first word of the book of Psalms; and one at the end, which ends with *Halleluya*, the last word of the book of Psalms. Thus *Ashrei* is a miniature version of the book of Psalms as a whole.

Ashrei means "happy, blessed, fruitful, flourishing." It refers not to a temporary emotional state but to a life as a whole. One who is *ashrei* does well and fares well, living uprightly and honestly, respected by those worthy of respect. The word is in the plural construct, literally "the *happinesses* of," as if to say that happiness is not one thing but a harmonious blend of many things that make up a good life. Psalm 1 gives a vivid picture of such a life:

> Happy is one who does not walk in step with the wicked, or stand in the place of sinners, or sit in the company of mockers, but whose delight is in the Torah of the Lord, and who meditates on His Torah day and night. He is like a tree planted by streams of water that yields its fruit in season and whose leaf does not wither – whatever he does prospers. (Verses 1–3)

טוֹב־יהוה לַכֹּל, וְרַחֲמָיו עַל־כָּל־מַעֲשָׂיו:
יוֹדוּךָ יהוה כָּל־מַעֲשֶׂיךָ, וַחֲסִידֶיךָ יְבָרְכוּכָה:
כְּבוֹד מַלְכוּתְךָ יֹאמֵרוּ, וּגְבוּרָתְךָ יְדַבֵּרוּ:
לְהוֹדִיעַ לִבְנֵי הָאָדָם גְּבוּרֹתָיו, וּכְבוֹד הֲדַר מַלְכוּתוֹ:
מַלְכוּתְךָ מַלְכוּת כָּל־עֹלָמִים, וּמֶמְשַׁלְתְּךָ בְּכָל־דּוֹר וָדֹר:
סוֹמֵךְ יהוה לְכָל־הַנֹּפְלִים, וְזוֹקֵף לְכָל־הַכְּפוּפִים:
עֵינֵי־כֹל אֵלֶיךָ יְשַׂבֵּרוּ, וְאַתָּה נוֹתֵן־לָהֶם אֶת־אָכְלָם בְּעִתּוֹ:
פּוֹתֵחַ אֶת־יָדֶךָ, וּמַשְׂבִּיעַ לְכָל־חַי רָצוֹן:
צַדִּיק יהוה בְּכָל־דְּרָכָיו, וְחָסִיד בְּכָל־מַעֲשָׂיו:
קָרוֹב יהוה לְכָל־קֹרְאָיו, לְכֹל אֲשֶׁר יִקְרָאֻהוּ בֶאֱמֶת:
רְצוֹן־יְרֵאָיו יַעֲשֶׂה, וְאֶת־שַׁוְעָתָם יִשְׁמַע, וְיוֹשִׁיעֵם:
שׁוֹמֵר יהוה אֶת־כָּל־אֹהֲבָיו, וְאֵת כָּל־הָרְשָׁעִים יַשְׁמִיד:
‹ תְּהִלַּת יהוה יְדַבֶּר פִּי, וִיבָרֵךְ כָּל־בָּשָׂר שֵׁם קָדְשׁוֹ לְעוֹלָם וָעֶד:
תהלים קטו וַאֲנַחְנוּ נְבָרֵךְ יָהּ מֵעַתָּה וְעַד־עוֹלָם, הַלְלוּיָהּ:

Laws of Prayer 4:16). *Ashrei* is the way we "sit for a while before prayer" in order to direct our mind (*Berakhot* 32b). Therefore, though it may be said standing or sitting, the custom is to say it sitting.

It consists of Psalm 145, chosen for three reasons: (1) It is an alphabetical acrostic, praising God with every letter of the alphabet (except *nun*, missing lest it refer to a verse that speaks about the fall, *nefila*, of Israel). (2) It contains the verse, "You open Your hand, and satisfy every living thing with favor," regarded by the sages as one of the essential features of prayer, namely recognition of our complete dependence on God (*Berakhot* 4b). (3) As the psalm speaks of the joy and serenity of those who trust in God, it fulfills the requirement to pray joyfully (see Rashi, *Berakhot* 31a). Psalm 145 is also the only one of the 150 psalms to be called a psalm (*tehilla*) in its superscription.

Added to Psalm 145 are verses from other psalms: two at the beginning,

HALF KADDISH

Leader: יִתְגַּדַּל Magnified and sanctified may His great name be,
in the world He created by His will.
May He establish His kingdom
in your lifetime and in your days,
and in the lifetime of all the house of Israel,
swiftly and soon –
and say: Amen.

All: May His great name be blessed for ever and all time.

Leader: Blessed and praised, glorified and exalted,
raised and honored, uplifted and lauded
be the name of the Holy One, blessed be He,
beyond any blessing,
song, praise and consolation
uttered in the world –
and say: Amen.

THE AMIDA

The following prayer, until "in former years" on page 30, is said silently, standing with feet together. If there is a minyan, the Amida is repeated aloud by the Leader. Take three steps forward and at the points indicated by ▾, bend the knees at the first word, bow at the second, and stand straight before saying God's name.

When I proclaim the LORD's name, give glory to our God. *Deut. 32*
O LORD, open my lips, so that my mouth may declare Your praise. *Ps. 51*

PATRIARCHS

▾בָּרוּךְ Blessed are You, LORD our God and God of our fathers,
God of Abraham, God of Isaac and God of Jacob;
the great, mighty and awesome God, God Most High,

---

represents the dawn of Jewish faith, and Jacob the nighttime of exile, Isaac represents the afternoon joining of past and future, the unspectacular heroism of Jewish continuity. We are each a link in the chain of generations, heirs

חצי קדיש

ש״ץ: יִתְגַּדַּל וְיִתְקַדַּשׁ שְׁמֵהּ רַבָּא (קהל: אָמֵן)
בְּעָלְמָא דִּי בְרָא כִרְעוּתֵהּ
וְיַמְלִיךְ מַלְכוּתֵהּ
בְּחַיֵּיכוֹן וּבְיוֹמֵיכוֹן וּבְחַיֵּי דְכָל בֵּית יִשְׂרָאֵל
בַּעֲגָלָא וּבִזְמַן קָרִיב, וְאִמְרוּ אָמֵן. (קהל: אָמֵן)

קהל וש״ץ: יְהֵא שְׁמֵהּ רַבָּא מְבָרַךְ לְעָלַם וּלְעָלְמֵי עָלְמַיָּא.

ש״ץ: יִתְבָּרַךְ וְיִשְׁתַּבַּח וְיִתְפָּאַר וְיִתְרוֹמַם וְיִתְנַשֵּׂא
וְיִתְהַדָּר וְיִתְעַלֶּה וְיִתְהַלָּל
שְׁמֵהּ דְּקֻדְשָׁא בְּרִיךְ הוּא (קהל: בְּרִיךְ הוּא)
לְעֵלָּא מִן כָּל בִּרְכָתָא וְשִׁירָתָא, תֻּשְׁבְּחָתָא וְנֶחֱמָתָא
דַּאֲמִירָן בְּעָלְמָא, וְאִמְרוּ אָמֵן. (קהל: אָמֵן)

עמידה

The following prayer, until קַדְמֹנִיּוֹת *on page 31, is said silently, standing with feet together. If there is a* מנין*, the* עמידה *is repeated aloud by the* שליח ציבור*. Take three steps forward and at the points indicated by* ˚*, bend the knees at the first word, bow at the second, and stand straight before saying God's name.*

דברים לב — כִּי שֵׁם יהוה אֶקְרָא, הָבוּ גֹדֶל לֵאלֹהֵינוּ:
תהלים נא — אֲדֹנָי, שְׂפָתַי תִּפְתָּח, וּפִי יַגִּיד תְּהִלָּתֶךָ:

אבות

˚בָּרוּךְ אַתָּה יהוה, אֱלֹהֵינוּ וֵאלֹהֵי אֲבוֹתֵינוּ
אֱלֹהֵי אַבְרָהָם, אֱלֹהֵי יִצְחָק, וֵאלֹהֵי יַעֲקֹב
הָאֵל הַגָּדוֹל הַגִּבּוֹר וְהַנּוֹרָא, אֵל עֶלְיוֹן

THE AFTERNOON AMIDA

The sages (*Berakhot* 26b) associated the afternoon Amida with Isaac, who "went out to meditate in the field toward evening" (Gen. 24:63). If Abraham

who bestows acts of loving-kindness and creates all,
who remembers the loving-kindness of the fathers
and will bring a Redeemer to their children's children
for the sake of His name, in love.
King, Helper, Savior, Shield:
▾Blessed are You, LORD,
Shield of Abraham.

DIVINE MIGHT

אַתָּה גִּבּוֹר You are eternally mighty, LORD.
You give life to the dead
and have great power to save.

In Israel:
He causes the dew to fall.

He sustains the living with loving-kindness,
and with great compassion revives the dead.
He supports the fallen, heals the sick, sets captives free,
and keeps His faith with those who sleep in the dust.
Who is like You, Master of might,
and who can compare to You,
O King who brings death and gives life,
and makes salvation grow?
Faithful are You to revive the dead.
Blessed are You, LORD,
who revives the dead.

When saying the Amida silently, continue with "You are holy" on the next page.

---

requests: for redemption, healing and prosperity, (3) collective material-political requests: for the ingathering of exiles, the restoration of sovereignty, and the removal of enemies, and (4) collective spiritual requests: for the righteous, the rebuilding of Jerusalem, and the restoration of the kingdom of David. The thirteenth blessing is all-embracing, asking God to hear and heed our prayer.

גּוֹמֵל חֲסָדִים טוֹבִים, וְקֹנֵה הַכֹּל
וְזוֹכֵר חַסְדֵי אָבוֹת
וּמֵבִיא גוֹאֵל לִבְנֵי בְנֵיהֶם לְמַעַן שְׁמוֹ בְּאַהֲבָה.
מֶלֶךְ עוֹזֵר וּמוֹשִׁיעַ וּמָגֵן.
ׄבָּרוּךְ אַתָּה יהוה, מָגֵן אַבְרָהָם.

גבורות

אַתָּה גִּבּוֹר לְעוֹלָם, אֲדֹנָי
מְחַיֵּה מֵתִים אַתָּה, רַב לְהוֹשִׁיעַ

In ארץ ישראל:

מוֹרִיד הַטָּל

מְכַלְכֵּל חַיִּים בְּחֶסֶד, מְחַיֵּה מֵתִים בְּרַחֲמִים רַבִּים
סוֹמֵךְ נוֹפְלִים, וְרוֹפֵא חוֹלִים, וּמַתִּיר אֲסוּרִים
וּמְקַיֵּם אֱמוּנָתוֹ לִישֵׁנֵי עָפָר.
מִי כָמוֹךָ, בַּעַל גְּבוּרוֹת
וּמִי דּוֹמֶה לָּךְ
מֶלֶךְ, מֵמִית וּמְחַיֶּה וּמַצְמִיחַ יְשׁוּעָה.
וְנֶאֱמָן אַתָּה לְהַחֲיוֹת מֵתִים.
בָּרוּךְ אַתָּה יהוה, מְחַיֵּה הַמֵּתִים.

When saying the עמידה *silently, continue with* אַתָּה קָדוֹשׁ *on the next page.*

---

of our ancestors, guardians of our children's future, remembering God in the midst of time and placing our destiny in His hands.

The Central Blessings. There are thirteen central blessings in the weekday Amida and they are grouped into four sets of three: (1) personal spiritual requests: for knowledge, repentance and forgiveness, (2) personal material

KEDUSHA

During the Leader's Repetition, the following is said standing with feet together, rising on the toes at the words indicated by ▴.

Cong. then Leader: נְקַדֵּשׁ We will sanctify Your name on earth,
as they sanctify it in the highest heavens,
as is written by Your prophet,
"And they [the angels] call to one another saying: *Is. 6*

Cong. then Leader: ▴Holy, ▴holy, ▴holy is the LORD of hosts;
the whole world is filled with His glory."
Those facing them say "Blessed –"

Cong. then Leader: ▴"Blessed is the LORD's glory from His place." *Ezek. 3*
And in Your holy Writings it is written thus:

Cong. then Leader: ▴"The LORD shall reign for ever. *Ps. 146*
He is your God, Zion,
from generation to generation, Halleluya!"

Leader: From generation to generation
we will declare Your greatness, and we will proclaim Your holiness for evermore.
Your praise, our God, shall not leave our mouth forever,
for You, God, are a great and holy King.
Blessed are You, LORD,
the holy God.

The Leader continues with "You grace humanity" on the next page.

HOLINESS

אַתָּה קָדוֹשׁ You are holy and Your name is holy,
and holy ones praise You daily, Selah!
Blessed are You, LORD,
the holy God.

KNOWLEDGE

אַתָּה חוֹנֵן You grace humanity with knowledge
and teach mortals understanding.

קדושה

During the חזרת הש״ץ, *the following is said standing with feet together, rising on the toes at the words indicated by* ˄.

קהל then ש״ץ: נְקַדֵּשׁ אֶת שִׁמְךָ בָּעוֹלָם, כְּשֵׁם שֶׁמַּקְדִּישִׁים אוֹתוֹ בִּשְׁמֵי מָרוֹם
כַּכָּתוּב עַל יַד נְבִיאֶךָ:
וְקָרָא זֶה אֶל־זֶה וְאָמַר ישעיה ו

קהל then ש״ץ: ˄קָדוֹשׁ, ˄קָדוֹשׁ, ˄קָדוֹשׁ, יהוה צְבָאוֹת, מְלֹא כָל־הָאָרֶץ כְּבוֹדוֹ:
לְעֻמָּתָם בָּרוּךְ יֹאמֵרוּ

קהל then ש״ץ: ˄בָּרוּךְ כְּבוֹד־יהוה מִמְּקוֹמוֹ: יחזקאל ג
וּבְדִבְרֵי קָדְשְׁךָ כָּתוּב לֵאמֹר

קהל then ש״ץ: ˄יִמְלֹךְ יהוה לְעוֹלָם, אֱלֹהַיִךְ צִיּוֹן לְדֹר וָדֹר, הַלְלוּיָהּ: תהלים קמו

ש״ץ: לְדוֹר וָדוֹר נַגִּיד גָּדְלֶךָ, וּלְנֵצַח נְצָחִים קְדֻשָּׁתְךָ נַקְדִּישׁ
וְשִׁבְחֲךָ אֱלֹהֵינוּ מִפִּינוּ לֹא יָמוּשׁ לְעוֹלָם וָעֶד
כִּי אֵל מֶלֶךְ גָּדוֹל וְקָדוֹשׁ אָתָּה.
בָּרוּךְ אַתָּה יהוה, הָאֵל הַקָּדוֹשׁ.

The שליח ציבור *continues with* אַתָּה חוֹנֵן *on the next page.*

קדושת השם

אַתָּה קָדוֹשׁ וְשִׁמְךָ קָדוֹשׁ
וּקְדוֹשִׁים בְּכָל יוֹם יְהַלְלוּךָ סֶּלָה.
בָּרוּךְ אַתָּה יהוה, הָאֵל הַקָּדוֹשׁ.

דעת

אַתָּה חוֹנֵן לְאָדָם דַּעַת
וּמְלַמֵּד לֶאֱנוֹשׁ בִּינָה.

דֵּעָה בִּינָה וְהַשְׂכֵּל *Knowledge, Repentance and Forgiveness.* Note the sequence.

Grace us with the knowledge, understanding
and discernment that come from You.
Blessed are You, Lord,
who graciously grants knowledge.

REPENTANCE

הֲשִׁיבֵנוּ Bring us back, our Father, to Your Torah.
Draw us near, our King, to Your service.
Lead us back to You in perfect repentance.
Blessed are You, Lord,
who desires repentance.

FORGIVENESS

Strike the left side of the chest at °.

סְלַח לָנוּ Forgive us, our Father, for we have °sinned.
Pardon us, our King, for we have °transgressed;
for You pardon and forgive.
Blessed are You, Lord,
the gracious One who repeatedly forgives.

REDEMPTION

רְאֵה Look on our affliction,
plead our cause,
and redeem us soon for Your name's sake,
for You are a powerful Redeemer.
Blessed are You, Lord,
the Redeemer of Israel.

---

short, and this brings us to repentance. Only then do we ask for forgiveness. We must put in the work of self-understanding and self-judgment before we can ask God to excuse our lapses.

חָנֵּנוּ מֵאִתְּךָ דֵּעָה בִּינָה וְהַשְׂכֵּל.
בָּרוּךְ אַתָּה יהוה, חוֹנֵן הַדָּעַת.

תשובה

הֲשִׁיבֵנוּ אָבִינוּ לְתוֹרָתֶךָ
וְקָרְבֵנוּ מַלְכֵּנוּ לַעֲבוֹדָתֶךָ
וְהַחֲזִירֵנוּ בִּתְשׁוּבָה שְׁלֵמָה לְפָנֶיךָ.
בָּרוּךְ אַתָּה יהוה, הָרוֹצֶה בִּתְשׁוּבָה.

סליחה

Strike the left side of the chest at °.

סְלַח לָנוּ אָבִינוּ כִּי °חָטָאנוּ
מְחַל לָנוּ מַלְכֵּנוּ כִּי °פָשָׁעְנוּ
כִּי מוֹחֵל וְסוֹלֵחַ אָתָּה.
בָּרוּךְ אַתָּה יהוה, חַנּוּן הַמַּרְבֶּה לִסְלֹחַ.

גאולה

רְאֵה בְעָנְיֵנוּ
וְרִיבָה רִיבֵנוּ
וּגְאָלֵנוּ מְהֵרָה לְמַעַן שְׁמֶךָ
כִּי גּוֹאֵל חָזָק אָתָּה.
בָּרוּךְ אַתָּה יהוה, גּוֹאֵל יִשְׂרָאֵל.

First we pray for knowledge and understanding. Without these it is as if we travel blind. Judaism is a religion of emotion, but emotion instructed by the mind. Second, understanding should lead us not to intellectual arrogance but humility. Knowing how we should live, we come to realize how we fall

HEALING

רְפָאֵנוּ Heal us, LORD, and we shall be healed.
Save us and we shall be saved,
for You are our praise.
Bring complete recovery for all our ailments,

The following prayer for a sick person may be said here:
May it be Your will, O LORD my God and God of my ancestors, that You speedily send a complete recovery from heaven, a healing of both soul and body, to the patient (*name*), son/daughter of (*mother's name*) among the other afflicted of Israel.

---

for You, God, King, are a faithful and compassionate Healer.
Blessed are You, LORD,
Healer of the sick of His people Israel.

PROSPERITY

בָּרֵךְ Bless this year for us, LORD our God,
and all its types of produce for good.
Grant blessing on the face of the earth,
and from its goodness satisfy us,
blessing our year as the best of years.
Blessed are You, LORD,
who blesses the years.

INGATHERING OF EXILES

תְּקַע Sound the great shofar for our freedom,
raise high the banner to gather our exiles,
and gather us together
from the four quarters of the earth.
Blessed are You, LORD,
who gathers the dispersed of His people Israel.

רפואה

רְפָאֵנוּ יהוה וְנֵרָפֵא
הוֹשִׁיעֵנוּ וְנִוָּשֵׁעָה, כִּי תְהִלָּתֵנוּ אָתָּה
וְהַעֲלֵה רְפוּאָה שְׁלֵמָה לְכָל מַכּוֹתֵינוּ

The following prayer for a sick person may be said here:

יְהִי רָצוֹן מִלְּפָנֶיךָ יהוה אֱלֹהַי וֵאלֹהֵי אֲבוֹתַי, שֶׁתִּשְׁלַח מְהֵרָה רְפוּאָה שְׁלֵמָה מִן הַשָּׁמַיִם רְפוּאַת הַנֶּפֶשׁ וּרְפוּאַת הַגּוּף לַחוֹלֶה/לַחוֹלָה *name of patient* בֶּן/בַּת *mother's name* בְּתוֹךְ שְׁאָר חוֹלֵי יִשְׂרָאֵל.

כִּי אֵל מֶלֶךְ רוֹפֵא נֶאֱמָן וְרַחֲמָן אָתָּה.
בָּרוּךְ אַתָּה יהוה, רוֹפֵא חוֹלֵי עַמּוֹ יִשְׂרָאֵל.

ברכת השנים

בָּרֵךְ עָלֵינוּ יהוה אֱלֹהֵינוּ אֶת הַשָּׁנָה הַזֹּאת
וְאֶת כָּל מִינֵי תְבוּאָתָהּ לְטוֹבָה
וְתֵן בְּרָכָה עַל פְּנֵי הָאֲדָמָה
וְשַׂבְּעֵנוּ מִטּוּבָהּ
וּבָרֵךְ שְׁנָתֵנוּ כַּשָּׁנִים הַטּוֹבוֹת.
בָּרוּךְ אַתָּה יהוה, מְבָרֵךְ הַשָּׁנִים.

קבוץ גלויות

תְּקַע בְּשׁוֹפָר גָּדוֹל לְחֵרוּתֵנוּ
וְשָׂא נֵס לְקַבֵּץ גָּלֻיּוֹתֵינוּ
וְקַבְּצֵנוּ יַחַד מֵאַרְבַּע כַּנְפוֹת הָאָרֶץ.
בָּרוּךְ אַתָּה יהוה, מְקַבֵּץ נִדְחֵי עַמּוֹ יִשְׂרָאֵל.

JUSTICE

הָשִׁיבָה Restore our judges as at first,
and our counselors as at the beginning,
and remove from us sorrow and sighing.
May You alone, LORD,
reign over us with loving-kindness and compassion,
and vindicate us in justice.
Blessed are You, LORD,
the King who loves righteousness and justice.

AGAINST INFORMERS

וְלַמַּלְשִׁינִים For the slanderers let there be no hope,
and may all wickedness perish in an instant.
May all Your people's enemies swiftly be cut down.
May You swiftly uproot, crush, cast down
and humble the arrogant swiftly in our days.
Blessed are You, LORD,
who destroys enemies and humbles the arrogant.

THE RIGHTEOUS

עַל הַצַּדִּיקִים To the righteous, the pious,
the elders of Your people the house of Israel,
the remnant of their scholars,
the righteous converts, and to us,
may Your compassion be aroused, LORD our God.
Grant a good reward to all who sincerely trust in Your name.
Set our lot with them,
so that we may never be ashamed,
for in You we trust.
Blessed are You, LORD,
who is the support and trust of the righteous.

השבת המשפט

הָשִׁיבָה שׁוֹפְטֵינוּ כְּבָרִאשׁוֹנָה וְיוֹעֲצֵינוּ כְּבַתְּחִלָּה,
וְהָסֵר מִמֶּנּוּ יָגוֹן וַאֲנָחָה
וּמְלֹךְ עָלֵינוּ אַתָּה יהוה לְבַדְּךָ בְּחֶסֶד וּבְרַחֲמִים
וְצַדְּקֵנוּ בַּמִּשְׁפָּט.
בָּרוּךְ אַתָּה יהוה, מֶלֶךְ אוֹהֵב צְדָקָה וּמִשְׁפָּט.

ברכת המינים

וְלַמַּלְשִׁינִים אַל תְּהִי תִקְוָה
וְכָל הָרִשְׁעָה כְּרֶגַע תֹּאבֵד
וְכָל אוֹיְבֵי עַמְּךָ מְהֵרָה יִכָּרֵתוּ
וְהַזֵּדִים מְהֵרָה תְעַקֵּר וּתְשַׁבֵּר וּתְמַגֵּר וְתַכְנִיעַ
בִּמְהֵרָה בְיָמֵינוּ.
בָּרוּךְ אַתָּה יהוה, שׁוֹבֵר אוֹיְבִים וּמַכְנִיעַ זֵדִים.

על הצדיקים

עַל הַצַּדִּיקִים וְעַל הַחֲסִידִים
וְעַל זִקְנֵי עַמְּךָ בֵּית יִשְׂרָאֵל
וְעַל פְּלֵיטַת סוֹפְרֵיהֶם
וְעַל גֵּרֵי הַצֶּדֶק, וְעָלֵינוּ
יֶהֱמוּ רַחֲמֶיךָ יהוה אֱלֹהֵינוּ
וְתֵן שָׂכָר טוֹב לְכָל הַבּוֹטְחִים בְּשִׁמְךָ בֶּאֱמֶת
וְשִׂים חֶלְקֵנוּ עִמָּהֶם
וּלְעוֹלָם לֹא נֵבוֹשׁ כִּי בְךָ בָּטָחְנוּ.
בָּרוּךְ אַתָּה יהוה, מִשְׁעָן וּמִבְטָח לַצַּדִּיקִים.

REBUILDING JERUSALEM

וְלִירוּשָׁלַיִם To Jerusalem, Your city,
may You return in compassion,
and may You dwell in it as You promised.
May You rebuild it rapidly in our days
as an everlasting structure,
and install within it soon the throne of David.
Blessed are You, LORD,
who builds Jerusalem.

KINGDOM OF DAVID

אֶת צֶמַח May the offshoot
of Your servant David soon flower,
and may his pride
be raised high by Your salvation,
for we wait for Your salvation all day.
Blessed are You, LORD,
who makes the glory of salvation flourish.

RESPONSE TO PRAYER

שְׁמַע קוֹלֵנוּ Listen to our voice, LORD our God.
Spare us and have compassion on us,
and in compassion and favor accept our prayer,
for You, God, listen to prayers and pleas.
Do not turn us away, O our King,
empty-handed from Your presence,
for You listen with compassion
to the prayer of Your people Israel.
Blessed are You, LORD,
who listens to prayer.

בניין ירושלים

וְלִירוּשָׁלַיִם עִירְךָ בְּרַחֲמִים תָּשׁוּב
וְתִשְׁכֹּן בְּתוֹכָהּ כַּאֲשֶׁר דִּבַּרְתָּ
וּבְנֵה אוֹתָהּ בְּקָרוֹב בְּיָמֵינוּ בִּנְיַן עוֹלָם
וְכִסֵּא דָוִד מְהֵרָה לְתוֹכָהּ תָּכִין.
בָּרוּךְ אַתָּה יהוה
בּוֹנֵה יְרוּשָׁלָיִם.

משיח בן דוד

אֶת צֶמַח דָּוִד עַבְדְּךָ מְהֵרָה תַצְמִיחַ
וְקַרְנוֹ תָּרוּם בִּישׁוּעָתֶךָ
כִּי לִישׁוּעָתְךָ קִוִּינוּ כָּל הַיּוֹם.
בָּרוּךְ אַתָּה יהוה
מַצְמִיחַ קֶרֶן יְשׁוּעָה.

שומע תפלה

שְׁמַע קוֹלֵנוּ יהוה אֱלֹהֵינוּ
חוּס וְרַחֵם עָלֵינוּ
וְקַבֵּל בְּרַחֲמִים וּבְרָצוֹן אֶת תְּפִלָּתֵנוּ
כִּי אֵל שׁוֹמֵעַ תְּפִלּוֹת וְתַחֲנוּנִים אָתָּה
וּמִלְּפָנֶיךָ מַלְכֵּנוּ רֵיקָם אַל תְּשִׁיבֵנוּ
כִּי אַתָּה שׁוֹמֵעַ תְּפִלַּת עַמְּךָ יִשְׂרָאֵל בְּרַחֲמִים.
בָּרוּךְ אַתָּה יהוה
שׁוֹמֵעַ תְּפִלָּה.

TEMPLE SERVICE

רְצֵה Find favor, LORD our God,
in Your people Israel and their prayer.
Restore the service to Your most holy House,
and accept in love and favor
the fire-offerings of Israel and their prayer.
May the service of Your people Israel always find favor with You.

On Erev Succot, continue with "And may our eyes" on the next page.

On Ḥol HaMo'ed:

אֱלֹהֵינוּ Our God and God of our ancestors,
may there rise, come, reach, appear, be favored, heard,
regarded and remembered before You,
our recollection and remembrance,
as well as the remembrance of our ancestors,
and of the Messiah son of David Your servant,
and of Jerusalem Your holy city,
and of all Your people the house of Israel –
for deliverance and well-being,
grace, loving-kindness and compassion, life and peace,
on this day of the Festival of Sukkot.
On it remember us, LORD our God, for good;
recollect us for blessing, and deliver us for life.
In accord with Your promise of salvation and compassion,
spare us and be gracious to us;
have compassion on us and deliver us,
for our eyes are turned to You
because You, God, are a gracious and compassionate King.

HaLevi (*Kuzari* 3:19) highlights that at this juncture in the Amida we are praying for the *Shekhina* to return to Jerusalem. We must therefore bow at *Modim* as if we were standing in the presence of the restored *Shekhina*." (Rabbi Joseph Soloveitchik)

עבודה

רְצֵה יהוה אֱלֹהֵינוּ בְּעַמְּךָ יִשְׂרָאֵל, וּבִתְפִלָּתָם
וְהָשֵׁב אֶת הָעֲבוֹדָה לִדְבִיר בֵּיתֶךָ
וְאִשֵּׁי יִשְׂרָאֵל וּתְפִלָּתָם בְּאַהֲבָה תְקַבֵּל בְּרָצוֹן
וּתְהִי לְרָצוֹן תָּמִיד עֲבוֹדַת יִשְׂרָאֵל עַמֶּךָ.

On ערב סוכות*, continue with "*וְתֶחֱזֶינָה*" on the next page.*

On חול המועד*:*

אֱלֹהֵינוּ וֵאלֹהֵי אֲבוֹתֵינוּ
יַעֲלֶה וְיָבוֹא וְיַגִּיעַ, וְיֵרָאֶה וְיֵרָצֶה וְיִשָּׁמַע
וְיִפָּקֵד וְיִזָּכֵר זִכְרוֹנֵנוּ וּפִקְדוֹנֵנוּ וְזִכְרוֹן אֲבוֹתֵינוּ
וְזִכְרוֹן מָשִׁיחַ בֶּן דָּוִד עַבְדֶּךָ
וְזִכְרוֹן יְרוּשָׁלַיִם עִיר קָדְשֶׁךָ
וְזִכְרוֹן כָּל עַמְּךָ בֵּית יִשְׂרָאֵל, לְפָנֶיךָ
לִפְלֵיטָה לְטוֹבָה, לְחֵן וּלְחֶסֶד וּלְרַחֲמִים, לְחַיִּים וּלְשָׁלוֹם
בְּיוֹם חַג הַסֻּכּוֹת הַזֶּה.
זָכְרֵנוּ יהוה אֱלֹהֵינוּ בּוֹ לְטוֹבָה
וּפָקְדֵנוּ בוֹ לִבְרָכָה, וְהוֹשִׁיעֵנוּ בוֹ לְחַיִּים.
וּבִדְבַר יְשׁוּעָה וְרַחֲמִים
חוּס וְחָנֵּנוּ, וְרַחֵם עָלֵינוּ וְהוֹשִׁיעֵנוּ
כִּי אֵלֶיךָ עֵינֵינוּ, כִּי אֵל מֶלֶךְ חַנּוּן וְרַחוּם אָתָּה.

Temple Service and Thanksgiving. "As the Jew recites *Retzeh* and beseeches God to accept his sacrifices, he is no longer praying in his local synagogue in Warsaw, Vilna or New York. He is suddenly transported to Jerusalem, and his prayer is transformed into an offering in the Temple. Rabbi Judah

וְתֶחֱזֶינָה And may our eyes witness Your return
to Zion in compassion.
Blessed are You, LORD, who restores His Presence to Zion.

THANKSGIVING

Bow at the first nine words.

מוֹדִים We give thanks to You,
for You are the LORD our God
and God of our ancestors
for ever and all time.
You are the Rock of our lives,
Shield of our salvation
from generation to generation.
We will thank You and
declare Your praise for our lives,
which are entrusted into Your hand;
for our souls,
which are placed in Your charge;
for Your miracles
which are with us every day;
and for Your wonders and favors
at all times, evening,
morning and midday.
You are good –
for Your compassion never fails.
You are compassionate –
for Your loving-kindnesses never cease.
We have always placed our hope in You.

During the Leader's Repetition, the congregation says quietly:

מוֹדִים We give thanks to You,
for You are the LORD our God
and God of our ancestors,
God of all flesh,
who formed us
and formed the universe.
Blessings and thanks
are due to Your great
and holy name
for giving us life
and sustaining us.
May You continue
to give us life
and sustain us;
and may You gather our
exiles to Your holy courts,
to keep Your decrees,
do Your will and serve You
with a perfect heart,
for it is for us
to give You thanks.
Blessed be God to whom
thanksgiving is due.

וְעַל כֻּלָּם For all these things may Your name be blessed and exalted,
our King, continually, for ever and all time.
Let all that lives thank You, Selah! and praise Your name in truth,
God, our Savior and Help, Selah!
Blessed are You, LORD, whose name is "the Good"
and to whom thanks are due.

וְתֶחֱזֶינָה עֵינֵינוּ בְּשׁוּבְךָ לְצִיּוֹן בְּרַחֲמִים.
בָּרוּךְ אַתָּה יהוה, הַמַּחֲזִיר שְׁכִינָתוֹ לְצִיּוֹן.

הודאה

Bow at the first five words.

°מוֹדִים אֲנַחְנוּ לָךְ
שָׁאַתָּה הוּא יהוה אֱלֹהֵינוּ
וֵאלֹהֵי אֲבוֹתֵינוּ לְעוֹלָם וָעֶד.
צוּר חַיֵּינוּ, מָגֵן יִשְׁעֵנוּ
אַתָּה הוּא לְדוֹר וָדוֹר.
נוֹדֶה לְּךָ וּנְסַפֵּר תְּהִלָּתֶךָ
עַל חַיֵּינוּ הַמְּסוּרִים בְּיָדֶךָ
וְעַל נִשְׁמוֹתֵינוּ הַפְּקוּדוֹת לָךְ
וְעַל נִסֶּיךָ שֶׁבְּכָל יוֹם עִמָּנוּ
וְעַל נִפְלְאוֹתֶיךָ וְטוֹבוֹתֶיךָ
שֶׁבְּכָל עֵת
עֶרֶב וָבֹקֶר וְצָהֳרָיִם.
הַטּוֹב, כִּי לֹא כָלוּ רַחֲמֶיךָ
וְהַמְרַחֵם, כִּי לֹא תַמּוּ חֲסָדֶיךָ
מֵעוֹלָם קִוִּינוּ לָךְ.

During the חזרת הש״ץ, *the* קהל *says quietly:*

°מוֹדִים אֲנַחְנוּ לָךְ
שָׁאַתָּה הוּא יהוה אֱלֹהֵינוּ
וֵאלֹהֵי אֲבוֹתֵינוּ
אֱלֹהֵי כָל בָּשָׂר
יוֹצְרֵנוּ, יוֹצֵר בְּרֵאשִׁית.
בְּרָכוֹת וְהוֹדָאוֹת
לְשִׁמְךָ הַגָּדוֹל וְהַקָּדוֹשׁ
עַל שֶׁהֶחֱיִיתָנוּ וְקִיַּמְתָּנוּ.
כֵּן תְּחַיֵּנוּ וּתְקַיְּמֵנוּ
וְתֶאֱסֹף גָּלֻיּוֹתֵינוּ
לְחַצְרוֹת קָדְשֶׁךָ
לִשְׁמֹר חֻקֶּיךָ
וְלַעֲשׂוֹת רְצוֹנֶךָ וּלְעָבְדְּךָ
בְּלֵבָב שָׁלֵם
עַל שֶׁאֲנַחְנוּ מוֹדִים לָךְ.
בָּרוּךְ אֵל הַהוֹדָאוֹת.

וְעַל כֻּלָּם יִתְבָּרַךְ וְיִתְרוֹמַם שִׁמְךָ מַלְכֵּנוּ תָּמִיד לְעוֹלָם וָעֶד.
וְכֹל הַחַיִּים יוֹדוּךָ סֶּלָה, וִיהַלְלוּ אֶת שִׁמְךָ בֶּאֱמֶת
הָאֵל יְשׁוּעָתֵנוּ וְעֶזְרָתֵנוּ סֶלָה.
°בָּרוּךְ אַתָּה יהוה, הַטּוֹב שִׁמְךָ וּלְךָ נָאֶה לְהוֹדוֹת.

PEACE

שָׁלוֹם רָב Grant great peace to Your people Israel for ever,
for You are the sovereign LORD of all peace;
and may it be good in Your eyes
to bless Your people Israel
at every time, at every hour, with Your peace.
Blessed are You, LORD, who blesses His people Israel with peace.

The following verse concludes the Leader's Repetition of the Amida.
Some also say it here as part of the silent Amida.

May the words of my mouth and the meditation of my heart *Ps. 19*
find favor before You, LORD, my Rock and Redeemer.

אֱלֹהַי My God, *Berakhot 17a*
guard my tongue from evil and my lips from deceitful speech.
To those who curse me, let my soul be silent;
may my soul be to all like the dust.
Open my heart to Your Torah and let my soul
pursue Your commandments. As for all who plan evil against me,
swiftly thwart their counsel and frustrate their plans.
Act for the sake of Your name; act for the sake of Your right hand;
act for the sake of Your holiness; act for the sake of Your Torah.
That Your beloved ones may be delivered, *Ps. 60*
save with Your right hand and answer me.
May the words of my mouth and the meditation of my heart *Ps. 19*
find favor before You, LORD, my Rock and Redeemer.

Bow, take three steps back, then bow, first left, then right, then center, while saying:

May He who makes peace in His high places,
make peace for us and all Israel – and say: Amen.

יְהִי רָצוֹן May it be Your will, LORD our God and God of our ancestors,
that the Temple be rebuilt speedily in our days,
and grant us a share in Your Torah.
And there we will serve You with reverence,
as in the days of old and as in former years.
Then the offering of Judah and Jerusalem will be pleasing to the LORD *Mal. 3*
as in the days of old and as in former years.

ברכת שלום

שָׁלוֹם רָב עַל יִשְׂרָאֵל עַמְּךָ תָּשִׂים לְעוֹלָם
כִּי אַתָּה הוּא מֶלֶךְ אָדוֹן לְכָל הַשָּׁלוֹם.
וְטוֹב בְּעֵינֶיךָ לְבָרֵךְ אֶת עַמְּךָ יִשְׂרָאֵל
בְּכָל עֵת וּבְכָל שָׁעָה בִּשְׁלוֹמֶךָ.
בָּרוּךְ אַתָּה יהוה, הַמְבָרֵךְ אֶת עַמּוֹ יִשְׂרָאֵל בַּשָּׁלוֹם.

The following verse concludes the חזרת הש״ץ.
Some also say it here as part of the silent עמידה.

תהלים יט יִהְיוּ לְרָצוֹן אִמְרֵי־פִי וְהֶגְיוֹן לִבִּי לְפָנֶיךָ, יהוה צוּרִי וְגֹאֲלִי:

ברכות יז. אֱלֹהַי
נְצֹר לְשׁוֹנִי מֵרָע וּשְׂפָתַי מִדַּבֵּר מִרְמָה
וְלִמְקַלְלַי נַפְשִׁי תִדֹּם, וְנַפְשִׁי כֶּעָפָר לַכֹּל תִּהְיֶה.
פְּתַח לִבִּי בְּתוֹרָתֶךָ, וּבְמִצְוֹתֶיךָ תִּרְדֹּף נַפְשִׁי.
וְכָל הַחוֹשְׁבִים עָלַי רָעָה
מְהֵרָה הָפֵר עֲצָתָם וְקַלְקֵל מַחֲשַׁבְתָּם.
עֲשֵׂה לְמַעַן שְׁמֶךָ, עֲשֵׂה לְמַעַן יְמִינֶךָ
עֲשֵׂה לְמַעַן קְדֻשָּׁתֶךָ, עֲשֵׂה לְמַעַן תּוֹרָתֶךָ.
תהלים ס לְמַעַן יֵחָלְצוּן יְדִידֶיךָ, הוֹשִׁיעָה יְמִינְךָ וַעֲנֵנִי:
תהלים יט יִהְיוּ לְרָצוֹן אִמְרֵי־פִי וְהֶגְיוֹן לִבִּי לְפָנֶיךָ, יהוה צוּרִי וְגֹאֲלִי:

Bow, take three steps back, then bow, first left, then right, then center, while saying:

עֹשֶׂה שָׁלוֹם בִּמְרוֹמָיו
הוּא יַעֲשֶׂה שָׁלוֹם עָלֵינוּ וְעַל כָּל יִשְׂרָאֵל, וְאִמְרוּ אָמֵן.

יְהִי רָצוֹן מִלְּפָנֶיךָ יהוה אֱלֹהֵינוּ וֵאלֹהֵי אֲבוֹתֵינוּ
שֶׁיִּבָּנֶה בֵּית הַמִּקְדָּשׁ בִּמְהֵרָה בְיָמֵינוּ, וְתֵן חֶלְקֵנוּ בְּתוֹרָתֶךָ
וְשָׁם נַעֲבָדְךָ בְּיִרְאָה כִּימֵי עוֹלָם וּכְשָׁנִים קַדְמוֹנִיּוֹת.
מלאכי ג וְעָרְבָה לַיהוה מִנְחַת יְהוּדָה וִירוּשָׁלָםִ כִּימֵי עוֹלָם וּכְשָׁנִים קַדְמֹנִיּוֹת:

FULL KADDISH

Some have the custom to include additional responses in Full Kaddish. *They can be found in the version on page 1464.*

Leader: יִתְגַּדַּל Magnified and sanctified
may His great name be,
in the world He created by His will.
May He establish His kingdom
in your lifetime and in your days,
and in the lifetime of all the house of Israel,
swiftly and soon –
and say: Amen.

All: May His great name be blessed
for ever and all time.

Leader: Blessed and praised,
glorified and exalted,
raised and honored,
uplifted and lauded be
the name of the Holy One, blessed be He,
beyond any blessing,
song, praise and consolation
uttered in the world –
and say: Amen.

May the prayers and pleas of all Israel
be accepted by their Father in heaven –
and say: Amen.

May there be great peace from heaven,
and life for us and all Israel –
and say: Amen.

Bow, take three steps back, as if taking leave of the Divine Presence, then bow, first left, then right, then center, while saying:

May He who makes peace in His high places,
make peace for us and all Israel –
and say: Amen.

קדיש שלם

Some have the custom to include additional responses in קדיש שלם*.*
They can be found in the version on page 1465.

ש״ץ: יִתְגַּדַּל וְיִתְקַדַּשׁ שְׁמֵהּ רַבָּא (קהל: אָמֵן)
בְּעָלְמָא דִּי בְרָא כִרְעוּתֵהּ
וְיַמְלִיךְ מַלְכוּתֵהּ
בְּחַיֵּיכוֹן וּבְיוֹמֵיכוֹן וּבְחַיֵּי דְכָל בֵּית יִשְׂרָאֵל
בַּעֲגָלָא וּבִזְמַן קָרִיב
וְאִמְרוּ אָמֵן. (קהל: אָמֵן)

קהל וש״ץ: יְהֵא שְׁמֵהּ רַבָּא מְבָרַךְ לְעָלַם וּלְעָלְמֵי עָלְמַיָּא.

ש״ץ: יִתְבָּרַךְ וְיִשְׁתַּבַּח וְיִתְפָּאַר
וְיִתְרוֹמַם וְיִתְנַשֵּׂא וְיִתְהַדָּר וְיִתְעַלֶּה וְיִתְהַלָּל
שְׁמֵהּ דְּקֻדְשָׁא בְּרִיךְ הוּא (קהל: בְּרִיךְ הוּא)
לְעֵלָּא מִן כָּל בִּרְכָתָא וְשִׁירָתָא, תֻּשְׁבְּחָתָא וְנֶחֱמָתָא
דַּאֲמִירָן בְּעָלְמָא
וְאִמְרוּ אָמֵן. (קהל: אָמֵן)

תִּתְקַבַּל צְלוֹתְהוֹן וּבָעוּתְהוֹן דְּכָל יִשְׂרָאֵל
קֳדָם אֲבוּהוֹן דִּי בִשְׁמַיָּא
וְאִמְרוּ אָמֵן. (קהל: אָמֵן)

יְהֵא שְׁלָמָא רַבָּא מִן שְׁמַיָּא
וְחַיִּים, עָלֵינוּ וְעַל כָּל יִשְׂרָאֵל
וְאִמְרוּ אָמֵן. (קהל: אָמֵן)

Bow, take three steps back, as if taking leave of the Divine Presence,
then bow, first left, then right, then center, while saying:

עֹשֶׂה שָׁלוֹם בִּמְרוֹמָיו
הוּא יַעֲשֶׂה שָׁלוֹם עָלֵינוּ וְעַל כָּל יִשְׂרָאֵל
וְאִמְרוּ אָמֵן. (קהל: אָמֵן)

Stand while saying Aleinu. Bow at ▾.

עָלֵינוּ It is our duty to praise the Master of all,
and ascribe greatness to the Author of creation,
who has not made us like the nations of the lands
nor placed us like the families of the earth;
who has not made our portion like theirs,
nor our destiny like all their multitudes.
(For they worship vanity and emptiness,
and pray to a god who cannot save.)
▾But we bow in worship
and thank the Supreme King of kings,
the Holy One, blessed be He,
who extends the heavens and establishes the earth,
whose throne of glory is in the heavens above,
and whose power's Presence is in the highest of heights.
He is our God; there is no other.
Truly He is our King, there is none else,
as it is written in His Torah:
"You shall know and take to heart this day *Deut. 4*
that the LORD is God,
in heaven above and on earth below.
There is no other."

Note the contrast between the first and second paragraphs. The first is a statement of Jewish particularity. We thank God for the uniqueness of the Jewish people and its vocation. We are different. It is not our highest aspiration to be like everyone else. We have been singled out for a sacred mission, to be God's ambassadors, His witnesses, part of a nation that in itself testifies to something larger than itself, to a divine presence in history.

The second paragraph is a no less emphatic prayer for universality, for the day when all humanity will recognize the sovereignty of God. All humans are in God's image, part of God's world, heirs to God's covenant with Noah,

Stand while saying עָלֵינוּ. *Bow at* ᵛ.

עָלֵינוּ לְשַׁבֵּחַ לַאֲדוֹן הַכֹּל
לָתֵת גְּדֻלָּה לְיוֹצֵר בְּרֵאשִׁית
שֶׁלֹּא עָשָׂנוּ כְּגוֹיֵי הָאֲרָצוֹת
וְלֹא שָׂמָנוּ כְּמִשְׁפְּחוֹת הָאֲדָמָה
שֶׁלֹּא שָׂם חֶלְקֵנוּ כָּהֶם וְגוֹרָלֵנוּ כְּכָל הֲמוֹנָם.
(שֶׁהֵם מִשְׁתַּחֲוִים לְהֶבֶל וָרִיק
וּמִתְפַּלְּלִים אֶל אֵל לֹא יוֹשִׁיעַ.)
ᵛוַאֲנַחְנוּ כּוֹרְעִים וּמִשְׁתַּחֲוִים וּמוֹדִים
לִפְנֵי מֶלֶךְ מַלְכֵי הַמְּלָכִים, הַקָּדוֹשׁ בָּרוּךְ הוּא
שֶׁהוּא נוֹטֶה שָׁמַיִם וְיוֹסֵד אָרֶץ
וּמוֹשַׁב יְקָרוֹ בַּשָּׁמַיִם מִמַּעַל
וּשְׁכִינַת עֻזּוֹ בְּגָבְהֵי מְרוֹמִים.
הוּא אֱלֹהֵינוּ, אֵין עוֹד.
אֱמֶת מַלְכֵּנוּ, אֶפֶס זוּלָתוֹ
כַּכָּתוּב בְּתוֹרָתוֹ
וְיָדַעְתָּ הַיּוֹם וַהֲשֵׁבֹתָ אֶל־לְבָבֶךָ דברים ד
כִּי יהוה הוּא הָאֱלֹהִים בַּשָּׁמַיִם מִמַּעַל וְעַל־הָאָרֶץ מִתָּחַת
אֵין עוֹד:

ALEINU

Aleinu, one of Judaism's great affirmations of faith, is an ancient prayer, originally composed as the prelude to *Malkhiyot*, the verses relating to God's kingship in the Musaf Amida of Rosh HaShana. Only in the twelfth century did it begin to be said daily at the conclusion of each service.

Therefore, we place our hope in You, LORD our God,
that we may soon see the glory of Your power,
when You will remove abominations from the earth,
and idols will be utterly destroyed,
when the world will be perfected
under the sovereignty of the Almighty,
when all humanity will call on Your name,
to turn all the earth's wicked toward You.
All the world's inhabitants will realize and know
that to You every knee must bow
and every tongue swear loyalty.
Before You, LORD our God,
they will kneel and bow down
and give honor to Your glorious name.
They will all accept the yoke of Your kingdom,
and You will reign over them soon and for ever.
For the kingdom is Yours,
and to all eternity You will reign in glory,
as it is written in Your Torah:
"The LORD will reign for ever and ever." *Ex. 15*
▸ And it is said:
"Then the LORD shall be King over all the earth; *Zech. 14*
on that day the LORD shall be One and His name One."

Some add:
Have no fear of sudden terror or of the ruin when it overtakes the wicked. *Prov. 3*
Devise your strategy, but it will be thwarted; propose your plan, *Is. 8*
but it will not stand, for God is with us.
When you grow old, I will still be the same. *Is. 46*
When your hair turns gray, I will still carry you.
I made you, I will bear you, I will carry you, and I will rescue you.

There is no contradiction between particularity and universality. Only by being what we uniquely are, do we contribute to humanity as a whole what only we can give.

עַל כֵּן נְקַוֶּה לְּךָ יהוה אֱלֹהֵינוּ, לִרְאוֹת מְהֵרָה בְּתִפְאֶרֶת עֻזֶּךָ
לְהַעֲבִיר גִּלּוּלִים מִן הָאָרֶץ
וְהָאֱלִילִים כָּרוֹת יִכָּרֵתוּן
לְתַקֵּן עוֹלָם בְּמַלְכוּת שַׁדַּי.
וְכָל בְּנֵי בָשָׂר יִקְרְאוּ בִשְׁמֶךָ
לְהַפְנוֹת אֵלֶיךָ כָּל רִשְׁעֵי אָרֶץ.
יַכִּירוּ וְיֵדְעוּ כָּל יוֹשְׁבֵי תֵבֵל
כִּי לְךָ תִּכְרַע כָּל בֶּרֶךְ, תִּשָּׁבַע כָּל לָשׁוֹן.
לְפָנֶיךָ יהוה אֱלֹהֵינוּ יִכְרְעוּ וְיִפֹּלוּ
וְלִכְבוֹד שִׁמְךָ יְקָר יִתֵּנוּ
וִיקַבְּלוּ כֻלָּם אֶת עֹל מַלְכוּתֶךָ
וְתִמְלֹךְ עֲלֵיהֶם מְהֵרָה לְעוֹלָם וָעֶד.
כִּי הַמַּלְכוּת שֶׁלְּךָ הִיא וּלְעוֹלְמֵי עַד תִּמְלֹךְ בְּכָבוֹד
כַּכָּתוּב בְּתוֹרָתֶךָ
שמות טו יהוה יִמְלֹךְ לְעֹלָם וָעֶד:
זכריה יד ◂ וְנֶאֱמַר, וְהָיָה יהוה לְמֶלֶךְ עַל־כָּל־הָאָרֶץ
בַּיּוֹם הַהוּא יִהְיֶה יהוה אֶחָד וּשְׁמוֹ אֶחָד:

Some add:

משלי ג אַל־תִּירָא מִפַּחַד פִּתְאֹם וּמִשֹּׁאַת רְשָׁעִים כִּי תָבֹא:
ישעיה ח עֻצוּ עֵצָה וְתֻפָר, דַּבְּרוּ דָבָר וְלֹא יָקוּם, כִּי עִמָּנוּ אֵל:
ישעיה מו וְעַד־זִקְנָה אֲנִי הוּא, וְעַד־שֵׂיבָה אֲנִי אֶסְבֹּל
אֲנִי עָשִׂיתִי וַאֲנִי אֶשָּׂא וַאֲנִי אֶסְבֹּל וַאֲמַלֵּט:

---

and in the future, as polytheism and atheism reveal themselves to be empty creeds, all humanity will turn to the One God.

MOURNER'S KADDISH

The following prayer, said by mourners, requires the presence of a minyan. A transliteration can be found on page 1467.

Mourner: יִתְגַּדַּל Magnified and sanctified may His great name be,
in the world He created by His will.
May He establish His kingdom
in your lifetime and in your days,
and in the lifetime of all the house of Israel,
swiftly and soon – and say: Amen.

All: May His great name be blessed for ever and all time.

Mourner: Blessed and praised,
glorified and exalted,
raised and honored,
uplifted and lauded
be the name of the Holy One, blessed be He,
beyond any blessing,
song, praise and consolation
uttered in the world – and say: Amen.

May there be great peace from heaven,
and life for us and all Israel – and say: Amen.

Bow, take three steps back, as if taking leave of the Divine Presence, then bow, first left, then right, then center, while saying:

May He who makes peace in His high places,
make peace for us and all Israel – and say: Amen.

On Erev Yom Tov, if a weekday continue on page 44, if Erev Shabbat on the next page. On Ḥol HaMo'ed on page 1336; on Shabbat Ḥol HaMo'ed on page 740.

---

for ever and all time." According to the Talmud, whenever Jews enter a synagogue or a house of study and say "May His great name be blessed," the Holy One, blessed be He, nods His head and says: "Happy is the King who is thus praised in this house" (*Berakhot* 3a). Note that Kaddish speaks neither of death nor of the past. It speaks about the future and about peace. We honor the dead by the way we live. We honor the past by the future we create.

קדיש יתום

The following prayer, said by mourners, requires the presence of a מנין*.*
A transliteration can be found on page 1467.

אבל: יִתְגַּדַּל וְיִתְקַדַּשׁ שְׁמֵהּ רַבָּא (קהל: אָמֵן)
בְּעָלְמָא דִּי בְרָא כִרְעוּתֵהּ
וְיַמְלִיךְ מַלְכוּתֵהּ
בְּחַיֵּיכוֹן וּבְיוֹמֵיכוֹן וּבְחַיֵּי דְכָל בֵּית יִשְׂרָאֵל
בַּעֲגָלָא וּבִזְמַן קָרִיב, וְאִמְרוּ אָמֵן. (קהל: אָמֵן)

קהל ואבל: יְהֵא שְׁמֵהּ רַבָּא מְבָרַךְ לְעָלַם וּלְעָלְמֵי עָלְמַיָּא.

אבל: יִתְבָּרַךְ וְיִשְׁתַּבַּח וְיִתְפָּאַר
וְיִתְרוֹמַם וְיִתְנַשֵּׂא וְיִתְהַדָּר וְיִתְעַלֶּה וְיִתְהַלָּל
שְׁמֵהּ דְּקֻדְשָׁא בְּרִיךְ הוּא (קהל: בְּרִיךְ הוּא)
לְעֵלָּא מִן כָּל בִּרְכָתָא וְשִׁירָתָא, תֻּשְׁבְּחָתָא וְנֶחֱמָתָא
דַּאֲמִירָן בְּעָלְמָא, וְאִמְרוּ אָמֵן. (קהל: אָמֵן)

יְהֵא שְׁלָמָא רַבָּא מִן שְׁמַיָּא
וְחַיִּים, עָלֵינוּ וְעַל כָּל יִשְׂרָאֵל, וְאִמְרוּ אָמֵן. (קהל: אָמֵן)

Bow, take three steps back, as if taking leave of the Divine Presence, then bow, first left, then right, then center, while saying:

עֹשֶׂה שָׁלוֹם בִּמְרוֹמָיו
הוּא יַעֲשֶׂה שָׁלוֹם עָלֵינוּ וְעַל כָּל יִשְׂרָאֵל, וְאִמְרוּ אָמֵן. (קהל: אָמֵן)

On ערב יום טוב*, if a weekday continue on page 45, if* ערב שבת *on the next page.*
On חול המועד *on page 1337; on* שבת חול המועד *on page 741.*

MOURNER'S KADDISH

We bring credit to the memory of the dead by doing acts that confer merit on the living. This especially applies to the saying of Kaddish, since it causes the congregation to praise God by saying, "May His great name be blessed

Erev Yom Tov

KABBALAT SHABBAT

On weekdays, Ma'ariv begins on page 44.
On Shabbat begin here (commentary on page 741):

מִזְמוֹר A psalm. A song for the Sabbath day. *Ps. 92*
It is good to thank the LORD
and sing psalms to Your name, Most High –
to tell of Your loving-kindness in the morning
and Your faithfulness at night,
to the music of the ten-stringed lyre and the melody of the harp.
For You have made me rejoice by Your work, O LORD;
I sing for joy at the deeds of Your hands.
How great are Your deeds, LORD, and how very deep Your thoughts.
A boor cannot know, nor can a fool understand,
that though the wicked spring up like grass and all evildoers flourish,
it is only that they may be destroyed for ever.
But You, LORD, are eternally exalted.
For behold Your enemies, LORD, behold Your enemies will perish;
all evildoers will be scattered.
You have raised my pride like that of a wild ox;
I am anointed with fresh oil.
My eyes shall look in triumph on my adversaries,
my ears shall hear the downfall of the wicked who rise against me.
▸ The righteous will flourish like a palm tree
and grow tall like a cedar in Lebanon.
Planted in the LORD's House, blossoming in our God's courtyards,
they will still bear fruit in old age, and stay vigorous and fresh,
proclaiming that the LORD is upright:
He is my Rock, in whom there is no wrong.

יהוה מָלָךְ The LORD reigns. He is robed in majesty. *Ps. 93*
The LORD is robed, girded with strength.
The world is firmly established; it cannot be moved.

ערב יום טוב

קבלת שבת

On weekdays, מעריב *begins on page 45.*
On שבת *begin here (commentary on page 741):*

תהלים צב

מִזְמוֹר שִׁיר לְיוֹם הַשַּׁבָּת:
טוֹב לְהֹדוֹת לַיהוה, וּלְזַמֵּר לְשִׁמְךָ עֶלְיוֹן:
לְהַגִּיד בַּבֹּקֶר חַסְדֶּךָ, וֶאֱמוּנָתְךָ בַּלֵּילוֹת:
עֲלֵי־עָשׂוֹר וַעֲלֵי־נָבֶל, עֲלֵי הִגָּיוֹן בְּכִנּוֹר:
כִּי שִׂמַּחְתַּנִי יהוה בְּפָעֳלֶךָ, בְּמַעֲשֵׂי יָדֶיךָ אֲרַנֵּן:
מַה־גָּדְלוּ מַעֲשֶׂיךָ יהוה, מְאֹד עָמְקוּ מַחְשְׁבֹתֶיךָ:
אִישׁ־בַּעַר לֹא יֵדָע, וּכְסִיל לֹא־יָבִין אֶת־זֹאת:
בִּפְרֹחַ רְשָׁעִים כְּמוֹ עֵשֶׂב, וַיָּצִיצוּ כָּל־פֹּעֲלֵי אָוֶן
לְהִשָּׁמְדָם עֲדֵי־עַד:
וְאַתָּה מָרוֹם לְעֹלָם יהוה:
כִּי הִנֵּה אֹיְבֶיךָ יהוה, כִּי־הִנֵּה אֹיְבֶיךָ יֹאבֵדוּ
יִתְפָּרְדוּ כָּל־פֹּעֲלֵי אָוֶן:
וַתָּרֶם כִּרְאֵים קַרְנִי, בַּלֹּתִי בְּשֶׁמֶן רַעֲנָן:
וַתַּבֵּט עֵינִי בְּשׁוּרָי, בַּקָּמִים עָלַי מְרֵעִים תִּשְׁמַעְנָה אָזְנָי:
◂ צַדִּיק כַּתָּמָר יִפְרָח, כְּאֶרֶז בַּלְּבָנוֹן יִשְׂגֶּה:
שְׁתוּלִים בְּבֵית יהוה, בְּחַצְרוֹת אֱלֹהֵינוּ יַפְרִיחוּ:
עוֹד יְנוּבוּן בְּשֵׂיבָה, דְּשֵׁנִים וְרַעֲנַנִּים יִהְיוּ:
לְהַגִּיד כִּי־יָשָׁר יהוה, צוּרִי, וְלֹא־עַוְלָתָה בּוֹ:

תהלים צג

יהוה מָלָךְ, גֵּאוּת לָבֵשׁ
לָבֵשׁ יהוה עֹז הִתְאַזָּר, אַף־תִּכּוֹן תֵּבֵל בַּל־תִּמּוֹט:

Your throne stands firm as of old; You are eternal.
Rivers lift up, LORD, rivers lift up their voice,
rivers lift up their crashing waves.
▸ Mightier than the noise of many waters,
than the mighty waves of the sea is the LORD on high.
Your testimonies are very sure;
holiness adorns Your House, LORD, for evermore.

MOURNER'S KADDISH

The following prayer, said by mourners, requires the presence of a minyan.
A transliteration can be found on page 1467.

Mourner: יִתְגַּדַּל Magnified and sanctified may His great name be,
in the world He created by His will.
May He establish His kingdom
in your lifetime and in your days,
and in the lifetime of all the house of Israel,
swiftly and soon –
and say: Amen.

All: May His great name be blessed for ever and all time.

Mourner: Blessed and praised, glorified and exalted,
raised and honored, uplifted and lauded
be the name of the Holy One, blessed be He,
beyond any blessing, song, praise and consolation
uttered in the world –
and say: Amen.

May there be great peace from heaven,
and life for us and all Israel –
and say: Amen.

Bow, take three steps back, as if taking leave of the Divine Presence,
then bow, first left, then right, then center, while saying:

May He who makes peace in His high places,
make peace for us and all Israel –
and say: Amen.

נָכוֹן כִּסְאֲךָ מֵאָז, מֵעוֹלָם אָתָּה:
נָשְׂאוּ נְהָרוֹת יהוה, נָשְׂאוּ נְהָרוֹת קוֹלָם, יִשְׂאוּ נְהָרוֹת דָּכְיָם:
◂ מִקֹּלוֹת מַיִם רַבִּים, אַדִּירִים מִשְׁבְּרֵי־יָם, אַדִּיר בַּמָּרוֹם יהוה:
עֵדֹתֶיךָ נֶאֶמְנוּ מְאֹד, לְבֵיתְךָ נַאֲוָה־קֹדֶשׁ, יהוה לְאֹרֶךְ יָמִים:

קדיש יתום

The following prayer, said by mourners, requires the presence of a מנין*.*
A transliteration can be found on page 1467.

אבל: יִתְגַּדַּל וְיִתְקַדַּשׁ שְׁמֵהּ רַבָּא (קהל: אָמֵן)
בְּעָלְמָא דִּי בְרָא כִרְעוּתֵהּ
וְיַמְלִיךְ מַלְכוּתֵהּ
בְּחַיֵּיכוֹן וּבְיוֹמֵיכוֹן וּבְחַיֵּי דְכָל בֵּית יִשְׂרָאֵל
בַּעֲגָלָא וּבִזְמַן קָרִיב, וְאִמְרוּ אָמֵן. (קהל: אָמֵן)

קהל ואבל: יְהֵא שְׁמֵהּ רַבָּא מְבָרַךְ לְעָלַם וּלְעָלְמֵי עָלְמַיָּא.

אבל: יִתְבָּרַךְ וְיִשְׁתַּבַּח וְיִתְפָּאַר
וְיִתְרוֹמַם וְיִתְנַשֵּׂא וְיִתְהַדָּר וְיִתְעַלֶּה וְיִתְהַלָּל
שְׁמֵהּ דְּקֻדְשָׁא בְּרִיךְ הוּא (קהל: בְּרִיךְ הוּא)
לְעֵלָּא מִן כָּל בִּרְכָתָא וְשִׁירָתָא, תֻּשְׁבְּחָתָא וְנֶחֱמָתָא
דַּאֲמִירָן בְּעָלְמָא, וְאִמְרוּ אָמֵן. (קהל: אָמֵן)

יְהֵא שְׁלָמָא רַבָּא מִן שְׁמַיָּא
וְחַיִּים, עָלֵינוּ וְעַל כָּל יִשְׂרָאֵל, וְאִמְרוּ אָמֵן. (קהל: אָמֵן)

Bow, take three steps back, as if taking leave of the Divine Presence, then bow, first left, then right, then center, while saying:

עֹשֶׂה שָׁלוֹם בִּמְרוֹמָיו
הוּא יַעֲשֶׂה שָׁלוֹם עָלֵינוּ וְעַל כָּל יִשְׂרָאֵל
וְאִמְרוּ אָמֵן. (קהל: אָמֵן)

Ma'ariv for Yom Tov

BLESSINGS OF THE SHEMA

The Leader says the following, bowing at "Bless," standing straight at "the LORD." The congregation, followed by the Leader, responds, bowing at "Bless," standing straight at "the LORD."

Leader: **BLESS**
the LORD, the blessed One.

Congregation: Bless the LORD, the blessed One,
for ever and all time.

Leader: Bless the LORD, the blessed One,
for ever and all time.

On weekdays, some congregations follow the ancient custom of saying piyutim here.
The piyutim for Ma'ariv, commonly known as Ma'aravot,
are interweaved in the blessings of the Shema.
For Ma'aravot for the first night of Sukkot, turn to page 116;
for Ma'aravot for the second night of Sukkot, turn to page 134;
for Ma'aravot for the night of Shemini Atzeret, turn to page 150;
for Ma'aravot for the night of Simḥat Torah, turn to page 166.

On Shabbat, Ma'aravot are not recited. When the first day of Sukkot is Shabbat the Ma'aravot for the first night are said on the second night and the Ma'aravot of Shemini Atzeret are said on Simḥat Torah.

---

nights. Night is when we take with us the spirit of Jacob, a man who knew fear but was never defeated by it.

בָּרְכוּ אֶת יהוה *Bless the LORD.* A call by the leader of prayer to the community to join him in praising God, in the spirit of the verse, "Magnify the LORD with me, and let us exalt His name together" (Ps. 34:4). This is a formal summons to public prayer in the presence of a *minyan.*

בָּרְכוּ *Bless.* We do not bless God; God blesses us. To speak of blessing God as we do in this prayer means (1) we acknowledge Him as the source of all our blessings, (2) we humble ourselves in this acknowledgment, (3) we seek to be vehicles of His blessings by creating the space for them to fill. That space – humility, self effacement, an opening of the soul to the presence of God – is what we seek to achieve in prayer.

מעריב ליום טוב

קריאת שמע וברכותיה

The שליח ציבור *says the following, bowing at* בָּרְכוּ*, standing straight at* ה׳.
The קהל*, followed by the* שליח ציבור*, responds, bowing at* בָּרוּךְ*, standing straight at* ה׳.

ש״ץ: **בָּרְכוּ**
אֶת יהוה הַמְבֹרָךְ.

קהל: בָּרוּךְ יהוה הַמְבֹרָךְ לְעוֹלָם וָעֶד.

ש״ץ: בָּרוּךְ יהוה הַמְבֹרָךְ לְעוֹלָם וָעֶד.

On weekdays, some congregations follow the ancient custom of saying piyutim here.
The piyutim for מעריב*, commonly known as* מערבות*,*
are interweaved in the blessings of the שמע*.*
For מערבות *for the first night of* סוכות*, turn to page 117;*
for מערבות *for the second night of* סוכות*, turn to page 135;*
for מערבות *for the night of* שמיני עצרת*, turn to page 151;*
for מערבות *for the night of* שמחת תורה*, turn to page 167.*

On שבת*,* מערבות *are not recited. When the first day of* סוכות *is* שבת
the מערבות *for the first night are said on the second night and*
the מערבות *of* שמיני עצרת *are said on* שמחת תורה*.*

EVENING SERVICE

Ma'ariv is the prayer associated with Jacob, the man whose greatest encounters with God were at night. At night he had a vision, symbolic of prayer itself, of a ladder stretching from earth to heaven. Awakening from that vision he gave the most profound description of the effect of prayer: "Surely God was in this place and I did not know it" (Gen. 28:16). At night he wrestled with an angel and was given the name Israel, one who "struggles with God and with men and prevails" (Gen. 32:28).

Judaism has known its dawns, its ages of new hope, associated with Abraham. It has known the full brightness of day, its ages of peace and continuity, associated with Isaac's life after the binding. But it has also known its

בָּרוּךְ Blessed are You, Lord our God, King of the Universe,
who by His word brings on evenings,
by His wisdom opens the gates of heaven,
with understanding makes time change and the seasons rotate,
and by His will orders the stars in their constellations in the sky.
He creates day and night,
rolling away the light before the darkness,
and darkness before the light.
▸ He makes the day pass and brings on night,
distinguishing day from night:
the Lord of hosts is His name.
May the living and forever enduring God rule over us for all time.
Blessed are You, Lord,
who brings on evenings.

אַהֲבַת עוֹלָם With everlasting love
have You loved Your people, the house of Israel.
You have taught us Torah and commandments,
decrees and laws of justice.
Therefore, Lord our God, when we lie down and when we rise up
we will speak of Your decrees, rejoicing in the words of Your Torah
and Your commandments for ever.

---

of the cosmos. Revelation: God has revealed Himself to us in the form of His word, the Torah, the text of our covenant with Him and our constitution as a holy nation. Redemption: God's interventions in history, as when He brought our ancestors from slavery to freedom. These paragraphs are directed to these three ways through which we come to know God: the wonders of the natural universe, the teachings of the Torah, and the miracles of Jewish history.

The Siddur and Maḥzor are the supreme expressions of Jewish faith. For the most part Jews did not write books of theology; they wrote prayers. In Judaism we do not speak *about* God; we speak *to* God. We do not *discuss* faith; we *express* faith. Faith is our relationship with God made articulate in the words of prayer.

אַהֲבַת עוֹלָם *With everlasting love.* Of all the ways in which God has made

בָּרוּךְ אַתָּה יהוה אֱלֹהֵינוּ מֶלֶךְ הָעוֹלָם
אֲשֶׁר בִּדְבָרוֹ מַעֲרִיב עֲרָבִים
בְּחָכְמָה פּוֹתֵחַ שְׁעָרִים
וּבִתְבוּנָה מְשַׁנֶּה עִתִּים וּמַחֲלִיף אֶת הַזְּמַנִּים
וּמְסַדֵּר אֶת הַכּוֹכָבִים בְּמִשְׁמְרוֹתֵיהֶם בָּרָקִיעַ כִּרְצוֹנוֹ.
בּוֹרֵא יוֹם וָלָיְלָה
גּוֹלֵל אוֹר מִפְּנֵי חֹשֶׁךְ וְחֹשֶׁךְ מִפְּנֵי אוֹר
◂ וּמַעֲבִיר יוֹם וּמֵבִיא לָיְלָה
וּמַבְדִּיל בֵּין יוֹם וּבֵין לָיְלָה
יהוה צְבָאוֹת שְׁמוֹ.
אֵל חַי וְקַיָּם תָּמִיד, יִמְלֹךְ עָלֵינוּ לְעוֹלָם וָעֶד.
בָּרוּךְ אַתָּה יהוה, הַמַּעֲרִיב עֲרָבִים.

אַהֲבַת עוֹלָם בֵּית יִשְׂרָאֵל עַמְּךָ אָהָבְתָּ
תּוֹרָה וּמִצְוֹת, חֻקִּים וּמִשְׁפָּטִים, אוֹתָנוּ לִמַּדְתָּ
עַל כֵּן יהוה אֱלֹהֵינוּ בְּשָׁכְבֵנוּ וּבְקוּמֵנוּ נָשִׂיחַ בְּחֻקֶּיךָ
וְנִשְׂמַח בְּדִבְרֵי תוֹרָתֶךָ וּבְמִצְוֹתֶיךָ לְעוֹלָם וָעֶד

We bow, some bending the knee, when we say the word *Barekhu*. The Hebrew word for "knee" is *berekh*. The word for a pool or reservoir of water is *berekha*. Common to them all is a sense of downward movement – of genuflection in the case of the body, of water from a spring to a pool, and of blessing flowing from heaven to earth as we align ourselves with its energies, moving from self-sufficiency and pride to humility in the face of the Infinite.

THE BLESSINGS OF THE SHEMA

The blessings that surround the Shema, evening and morning, are a precisely articulated summary of the three basic elements of Jewish faith: *creation, revelation* and *redemption*. Creation: God is the Author of the universe, Architect

▸ For they are our life and the length of our days;
on them will we meditate day and night.
May You never take away Your love from us.
Blessed are You, Lord,
who loves His people Israel.

The Shema must be said with intense concentration.
When not with a minyan, say:
God, faithful King!

The following verse should be said aloud, while covering the eyes with the right hand:

Listen, Israel: the Lord is our God, the Lord is One. *Deut. 6*

Quietly: Blessed be the name of His glorious kingdom for ever and all time.

וְאָהַבְתָּ Love the Lord your God with all your heart, with all your *Deut. 6*
soul, and with all your might. These words which I command you today shall be on your heart. Teach them repeatedly to your children, speaking of them when you sit at home and when you travel

---

equivalent of our "Amen"). Though we continue to say it in memory of the Temple, we now say it quietly on account of the Temple's destruction and because it is not part of the biblical text (*Pesaḥim* 56a).

וְאָהַבְתָּ אֵת יהוה אֱלֹהֶיךָ *Love the Lord your God.* Judaism was the world's first civilization to place love at the heart of the moral universe. Not abstract or dispassionate love, but "with all your heart, with all your soul, and with all your might," meaning: with the totality of your being, emotion, intellect and will. Love begets love; love reciprocates love; our love for God is the response to God's love for us.

עַל־לְבָבֶךָ *On your heart.* Rabbi Menaḥem Mendel of Kotzk once asked: "Why does the Torah say that these words should be '*on* your heart'? Should it not say, '*in* your heart'?" He answered: "The human heart is not always open. Therefore the Torah commands us to lay these words *on* our heart, so that when it opens, they will be there, ready to enter."

וְשִׁנַּנְתָּם לְבָנֶיךָ *Teach them repeatedly to your children.* Education is the conversation between the generations. In the only place in the Torah to explain why

כִּי הֵם חַיֵּינוּ וְאֹרֶךְ יָמֵינוּ, וּבָהֶם נֶהְגֶּה יוֹמָם וָלָיְלָה.
וְאַהֲבָתְךָ אַל תָּסִיר מִמֶּנּוּ לְעוֹלָמִים.
בָּרוּךְ אַתָּה יהוה, אוֹהֵב עַמּוֹ יִשְׂרָאֵל.

The שמע *must be said with intense concentration.*
When not with a מנין*, say:*

אֵל מֶלֶךְ נֶאֱמָן

The following verse should be said aloud, while covering the eyes with the right hand:

דברים ו שְׁמַע יִשְׂרָאֵל, יהוה אֱלֹהֵינוּ, יהוה | אֶחָד:

Quietly בָּרוּךְ שֵׁם כְּבוֹד מַלְכוּתוֹ לְעוֹלָם וָעֶד.

דברים ו וְאָהַבְתָּ אֵת יהוה אֱלֹהֶיךָ, בְּכָל־לְבָבְךָ וּבְכָל־נַפְשְׁךָ וּבְכָל־
מְאֹדֶךָ: וְהָיוּ הַדְּבָרִים הָאֵלֶּה, אֲשֶׁר אָנֹכִי מְצַוְּךָ הַיּוֹם, עַל־לְבָבֶךָ:
וְשִׁנַּנְתָּם לְבָנֶיךָ וְדִבַּרְתָּ בָּם, בְּשִׁבְתְּךָ בְּבֵיתֶךָ וּבְלֶכְתְּךָ בַדֶּרֶךְ,

---

Himself known to us, the one that is central is revelation: God's word as recorded in Torah. The history of the Jewish mind is the story of a love affair between a people and a book. Heinrich Heine called the Torah "the portable homeland of the Jew." Wherever Jews went they took Torah with them. Where Torah study was strong Jewish life was strong. This paragraph expresses that love.

שְׁמַע יִשְׂרָאֵל *Listen, Israel.* Since God's primary revelation is through words, the highest religious act is the act of listening – creating a silence in the soul in which we hear the call of God.

יהוה אֱלֹהֵינוּ *The Lord is our God.* He alone is our ultimate Sovereign. To be a Jew is to be a citizen in the republic of faith under the sovereignty of God.

יהוה אֶחָד *The Lord is One.* An ultimate unity pervades the diversity of the world. The universe is the expression of a single creative intelligence; therefore its natural state is harmony. We believe that ultimately all humanity will acknowledge the unity of God. Then and only then, will harmony prevail in the affairs of humankind.

בָּרוּךְ שֵׁם *Blessed be the name.* This was the response of the congregation in the Temple when the officiating priest recited the first verse of the Shema (the

on the way, when you lie down and when you rise. Bind them as a sign on your hand, and they shall be an emblem between your eyes. Write them on the doorposts of your house and gates.

וְהָיָה If you indeed heed My commandments with which I charge you today, to love the LORD your God and worship Him with all your heart and with all your soul, I will give rain in your land in its season, the early and late rain; and you shall gather in your grain, wine and oil. I will give grass in your field for your cattle, and you shall eat and be satisfied. Be careful lest your heart be tempted and you go astray and worship other gods, bowing down to them. Then the LORD's anger will flare against you and He will close the heavens so that there will be no rain. The land will not yield its crops, and you will perish swiftly from the good land that the LORD is giving you. Therefore, set these, My words, on your heart and soul. Bind them as a sign on your hand, and they shall be an emblem between your eyes. Teach them to your children, speaking of them when you sit at home and when you travel on the way, when you lie down and when you rise. Write them on the doorposts of your house and gates, so that you and your children may live long in the *Deut. 11*

וְנָתַתִּי מְטַר־אַרְצְכֶם בְּעִתּוֹ *I will give rain in your land in its season.* At the end of his life, Moses told the next generation, those who would enter the land, that they would find it "not like the land of Egypt, from which you have come, where you planted your seed and irrigated it by foot as in a vegetable garden. But the land you are crossing the Jordan to take possession of is a land of mountains and valleys that drinks rain from heaven" (Deut. 11:10–11). Unlike the Nile Valley and Delta, it did not have a constant, regular supply of water. In Egypt, the natural instinct is to look down to the river for sustenance. In Israel, dependent on rain, the natural instinct is to look up to heaven.

הִשָּׁמְרוּ לָכֶם פֶּן־יִפְתֶּה לְבַבְכֶם *Be careful lest your heart be tempted.* Throughout the book of Deuteronomy, from which this paragraph is taken, Moses warns the people that their greatest trial was not the wilderness years when they wandered without a home. It would be when they entered the land and became

וּבְשׇׁכְבְּךָ וּבְקוּמֶךָ: וּקְשַׁרְתָּם לְאוֹת עַל־יָדֶךָ וְהָיוּ לְטֹטָפֹת בֵּין
עֵינֶיךָ: וּכְתַבְתָּם עַל־מְזֻזוֹת בֵּיתֶךָ וּבִשְׁעָרֶיךָ:

דברים יא וְהָיָה אִם־שָׁמֹעַ תִּשְׁמְעוּ אֶל־מִצְוֺתַי אֲשֶׁר אָנֹכִי מְצַוֶּה אֶתְכֶם
הַיּוֹם, לְאַהֲבָה אֶת־יהוה אֱלֹהֵיכֶם וּלְעׇבְדוֹ, בְּכׇל־לְבַבְכֶם וּבְכׇל־
נַפְשְׁכֶם: וְנָתַתִּי מְטַר־אַרְצְכֶם בְּעִתּוֹ, יוֹרֶה וּמַלְקוֹשׁ, וְאָסַפְתָּ
דְגָנֶךָ וְתִירֹשְׁךָ וְיִצְהָרֶךָ: וְנָתַתִּי עֵשֶׂב בְּשָׂדְךָ לִבְהֶמְתֶּךָ, וְאָכַלְתָּ
וְשָׂבָעְתָּ: הִשָּׁמְרוּ לָכֶם פֶּן־יִפְתֶּה לְבַבְכֶם, וְסַרְתֶּם וַעֲבַדְתֶּם
אֱלֹהִים אֲחֵרִים וְהִשְׁתַּחֲוִיתֶם לָהֶם: וְחָרָה אַף־יהוה בָּכֶם, וְעָצַר
אֶת־הַשָּׁמַיִם וְלֹא־יִהְיֶה מָטָר, וְהָאֲדָמָה לֹא תִתֵּן אֶת־יְבוּלָהּ,
וַאֲבַדְתֶּם מְהֵרָה מֵעַל הָאָרֶץ הַטֹּבָה אֲשֶׁר יהוה נֹתֵן לָכֶם:
וְשַׂמְתֶּם אֶת־דְּבָרַי אֵלֶּה עַל־לְבַבְכֶם וְעַל־נַפְשְׁכֶם, וּקְשַׁרְתֶּם
אֹתָם לְאוֹת עַל־יֶדְכֶם, וְהָיוּ לְטוֹטָפֹת בֵּין עֵינֵיכֶם: וְלִמַּדְתֶּם
אֹתָם אֶת־בְּנֵיכֶם לְדַבֵּר בָּם, בְּשִׁבְתְּךָ בְּבֵיתֶךָ וּבְלֶכְתְּךָ בַדֶּרֶךְ,
וּבְשׇׁכְבְּךָ וּבְקוּמֶךָ: וּכְתַבְתָּם עַל־מְזוּזוֹת בֵּיתֶךָ וּבִשְׁעָרֶיךָ: לְמַעַן

God chose Abraham to be the bearer of a new covenant, it says, "For I have singled him out so tht he may instruct his children and his posterity to keep the way of the Lord by doing what is just and right" (Gen. 18:19). Educating our children is the first duty of a Jewish parent.

וּקְשַׁרְתָּם...וּכְתַבְתָּם *Bind them … write them.* Because God is often hidden in this world, we surround ourselves with reminders of His presence.

וְהָיָה אִם־שָׁמֹעַ תִּשְׁמְעוּ *If you indeed heed.* This, the second paragraph of the Shema, was described by the sages as an act of acceptance of the yoke of the commandments, while the first is acceptance of the sovereignty of heaven (Mishna, *Berakhot* 13a). In Judaism, faith is not merely a general state of mind but also and fundamentally a way of life, the life of the commandments. On this, our fate as a nation depends.

land that the LORD swore to your ancestors to give them, for as long as the heavens are above the earth.

וַיֹּאמֶר The LORD spoke to Moses, saying: Speak to the Israelites and tell them to make tassels on the corners of their garments for all generations. They shall attach to the tassel at each corner a thread of blue. This shall be your tassel, and you shall see it and remember all of the LORD's commandments and keep them, not straying after your heart and after your eyes, following your own sinful desires. Thus you will be reminded to keep all My commandments, and be holy to your God. I am the LORD your God, who brought you out of the land of Egypt to be your God. I am the LORD your God. *Num. 15*

True –

The Leader repeats:

▸ The LORD your God is true –

וֶאֱמוּנָה – and faithful is all this,
and firmly established for us
that He is the LORD our God,
and there is none beside Him,
and that we, Israel, are His people.

---

the days of your life" (Deut. 16:3). As we will mention in the Haggada, Ben Zoma interpreted the emphatic word "all" to include not just days but also nights (Mishna, *Berakhot* 12b).

אֱמֶת *True.* The Hebrew word *emet* means more than "truth" in the conventional Western sense of fact as opposed to falsehood. *Emet* also means "being truthful," keeping your word, honoring your commitments. Hence the importance here of connecting past redemption to future deliverance. Indeed the word *emet* itself is composed of the first, middle and last letters of the alphabet, subliminally suggesting a truth continuous through past, present

יִרְבּוּ יְמֵיכֶם וִימֵי בְנֵיכֶם עַל הָאֲדָמָה אֲשֶׁר נִשְׁבַּע יהוה לַאֲבֹתֵיכֶם לָתֵת לָהֶם, כִּימֵי הַשָּׁמַיִם עַל־הָאָרֶץ:

במדבר טו וַיֹּאמֶר יהוה אֶל־מֹשֶׁה לֵּאמֹר: דַּבֵּר אֶל־בְּנֵי יִשְׂרָאֵל וְאָמַרְתָּ אֲלֵהֶם, וְעָשׂוּ לָהֶם צִיצִת עַל־כַּנְפֵי בִגְדֵיהֶם לְדֹרֹתָם, וְנָתְנוּ עַל־צִיצִת הַכָּנָף פְּתִיל תְּכֵלֶת: וְהָיָה לָכֶם לְצִיצִת, וּרְאִיתֶם אֹתוֹ וּזְכַרְתֶּם אֶת־כָּל־מִצְוֹת יהוה וַעֲשִׂיתֶם אֹתָם, וְלֹא תָתֻרוּ אַחֲרֵי לְבַבְכֶם וְאַחֲרֵי עֵינֵיכֶם, אֲשֶׁר־אַתֶּם זֹנִים אַחֲרֵיהֶם: לְמַעַן תִּזְכְּרוּ וַעֲשִׂיתֶם אֶת־כָּל־מִצְוֹתָי, וִהְיִיתֶם קְדֹשִׁים לֵאלֹהֵיכֶם: אֲנִי יהוה אֱלֹהֵיכֶם, אֲשֶׁר הוֹצֵאתִי אֶתְכֶם מֵאֶרֶץ מִצְרַיִם, לִהְיוֹת לָכֶם לֵאלֹהִים, אֲנִי יהוה אֱלֹהֵיכֶם:

אֱמֶת

The שליח ציבור *repeats:*

◂ יהוה אֱלֹהֵיכֶם אֱמֶת

וֶאֱמוּנָה כָּל זֹאת וְקַיָּם עָלֵינוּ
כִּי הוּא יהוה אֱלֹהֵינוּ וְאֵין זוּלָתוֹ
וַאֲנַחְנוּ יִשְׂרָאֵל עַמּוֹ.

---

prosperous. The greatest challenge to faith is not poverty but affluence. It is then we are in danger of becoming complacent, forgetting why we are here.

צִיצִת *Tassels.* The third paragraph of the Shema is largely about the command of *Tzitzit*, one of the perennial reminders of God's presence in our lives. Since *Tzitzit* were not obligatory at night (the command is that "you shall see them" and at night they could not be seen), the primary message of the third paragraph at night is its concluding verse, about the exodus. It fulfills the command "so that you will remember the day you left Egypt all

He is our King,
who redeems us from the hand of kings
and delivers us from the grasp of all tyrants.
He is our God,
who on our behalf repays our foes
and brings just retribution on our mortal enemies;
who performs great deeds
beyond understanding and wonders beyond number;
who kept us alive, not letting our foot slip; *Ps. 66*
who led us on the high places of our enemies,
raising our pride above all our foes;
who did miracles for us
and brought vengeance against Pharaoh;
who performed signs and wonders
in the land of Ham's children;
who smote in His wrath all the firstborn of Egypt,
and brought out His people Israel from their midst
into everlasting freedom;
who led His children
through the divided Reed Sea,
plunging their pursuers and enemies into the depths.
When His children saw His might,
they gave praise and thanks to His name,
▸ and willingly accepted His Sovereignty.
Moses and the children of Israel
then sang a song to You with great joy,
and they all exclaimed:

> "Who is like You, LORD, among the mighty? *Ex. 15*
> Who is like You, majestic in holiness,
> awesome in praises, doing wonders?"

---

past when He brought us out of Egypt as He said He would. God honors His word. His truth is the basis of our hope.

הַפּוֹדֵנוּ מִיַּד מְלָכִים
מַלְכֵּנוּ הַגּוֹאֲלֵנוּ מִכַּף כָּל הֶעָרִיצִים.
הָאֵל הַנִּפְרָע לָנוּ מִצָּרֵינוּ
וְהַמְשַׁלֵּם גְּמוּל לְכָל אוֹיְבֵי נַפְשֵׁנוּ.
הָעוֹשֶׂה גְדוֹלוֹת עַד אֵין חֵקֶר
וְנִפְלָאוֹת עַד אֵין מִסְפָּר
תהלים סו הַשָּׂם נַפְשֵׁנוּ בַּחַיִּים, וְלֹא־נָתַן לַמּוֹט רַגְלֵנוּ:
הַמַּדְרִיכֵנוּ עַל בָּמוֹת אוֹיְבֵינוּ
וַיָּרֶם קַרְנֵנוּ עַל כָּל שׂוֹנְאֵינוּ.
הָעוֹשֶׂה לָּנוּ נִסִּים וּנְקָמָה בְּפַרְעֹה
אוֹתוֹת וּמוֹפְתִים בְּאַדְמַת בְּנֵי חָם.
הַמַּכֶּה בְעֶבְרָתוֹ כָּל בְּכוֹרֵי מִצְרָיִם
וַיּוֹצֵא אֶת עַמּוֹ יִשְׂרָאֵל מִתּוֹכָם לְחֵרוּת עוֹלָם.
הַמַּעֲבִיר בָּנָיו בֵּין גִּזְרֵי יַם סוּף
אֶת רוֹדְפֵיהֶם וְאֶת שׂוֹנְאֵיהֶם בִּתְהוֹמוֹת טִבַּע
וְרָאוּ בָנָיו גְּבוּרָתוֹ, שִׁבְּחוּ וְהוֹדוּ לִשְׁמוֹ
◂ וּמַלְכוּתוֹ בְּרָצוֹן קִבְּלוּ עֲלֵיהֶם.
מֹשֶׁה וּבְנֵי יִשְׂרָאֵל, לְךָ עָנוּ שִׁירָה בְּשִׂמְחָה רַבָּה
וְאָמְרוּ כֻלָּם
שמות טו מִי־כָמֹכָה בָּאֵלִם יהוה
מִי כָּמֹכָה נֶאְדָּר בַּקֹּדֶשׁ
נוֹרָא תְהִלֹּת עֹשֵׂה פֶלֶא:

---

and future. Thus as the Shema segues into the blessing of Redemption, we base our faith in God's future redemption on the basis of the history of the

‣ Your children beheld Your majesty
as You parted the sea before Moses.
"This is my God!" they responded, and then said:
"The LORD shall reign for ever and ever." *Ex. 15*

‣ And it is said,
"For the LORD has redeemed Jacob *Jer. 31*
and rescued him from a power stronger than his own."
Blessed are You, LORD, who redeemed Israel.

הַשְׁכִּיבֵנוּ Help us lie down,
O LORD our God, in peace,
and rise up, O our King, to life.
Spread over us Your canopy of peace.
Direct us with Your good counsel,
and save us for the sake of Your name.
Shield us and remove from us every enemy,
plague, sword, famine and sorrow.
Remove the adversary from before and behind us.
Shelter us in the shadow of Your wings,
for You, God, are our Guardian and Deliverer;
You, God, are a gracious and compassionate King.
‣ Guard our going out and our coming in,
for life and peace, from now and for ever.
Spread over us Your canopy of peace.
Blessed are You, LORD,
who spreads a canopy of peace over us,
over all His people Israel, and over Jerusalem.

---

the previous one (see 4b). It takes the theme of redemption and translates it into the here-and-now of night, a time of vulnerability and danger, especially in the ancient world. We pray for a peaceful night under the protective canopy of God's sheltering presence.

מַלְכוּתְךָ רָאוּ בָנֶיךָ, בּוֹקֵעַ יָם לִפְנֵי מֹשֶׁה
זֶה אֵלִי עָנוּ, וְאָמְרוּ
יהוה יִמְלֹךְ לְעֹלָם וָעֶד: שמות טו

וְנֶאֱמַר
כִּי־פָדָה יהוה אֶת־יַעֲקֹב, וּגְאָלוֹ מִיַּד חָזָק מִמֶּנּוּ: ירמיה לא
בָּרוּךְ אַתָּה יהוה, גָּאַל יִשְׂרָאֵל.

הַשְׁכִּיבֵנוּ יהוה אֱלֹהֵינוּ לְשָׁלוֹם
וְהַעֲמִידֵנוּ מַלְכֵּנוּ לְחַיִּים
וּפְרֹשׂ עָלֵינוּ סֻכַּת שְׁלוֹמֶךָ
וְתַקְּנֵנוּ בְּעֵצָה טוֹבָה מִלְּפָנֶיךָ
וְהוֹשִׁיעֵנוּ לְמַעַן שְׁמֶךָ.
וְהָגֵן בַּעֲדֵנוּ
וְהָסֵר מֵעָלֵינוּ אוֹיֵב, דֶּבֶר וְחֶרֶב וְרָעָב וְיָגוֹן
וְהָסֵר שָׂטָן מִלְּפָנֵינוּ וּמֵאַחֲרֵינוּ, וּבְצֵל כְּנָפֶיךָ תַּסְתִּירֵנוּ
כִּי אֵל שׁוֹמְרֵנוּ וּמַצִּילֵנוּ אָתָּה
כִּי אֵל מֶלֶךְ חַנּוּן וְרַחוּם אָתָּה.
וּשְׁמֹר צֵאתֵנוּ וּבוֹאֵנוּ לְחַיִּים וּלְשָׁלוֹם מֵעַתָּה וְעַד עוֹלָם.
וּפְרֹשׂ עָלֵינוּ סֻכַּת שְׁלוֹמֶךָ.
בָּרוּךְ אַתָּה יהוה
הַפּוֹרֵשׂ סֻכַּת שָׁלוֹם עָלֵינוּ וְעַל כָּל עַמּוֹ יִשְׂרָאֵל וְעַל יְרוּשָׁלָיִם.

הַשְׁכִּיבֵנוּ *Help us lie down.* Since there is supposed to be no interruption between redemption (the paragraph ending "who redeemed Israel") and the formal act of prayer (Amida), this paragraph is regarded as an extension of

On Shabbat, the congregation stands and, together with the Leader, says:

וְשָׁמְרוּ The children of Israel must keep the Sabbath, Ex. 31
observing the Sabbath in every generation
as an everlasting covenant.
It is a sign between Me and the children of Israel for ever,
for in six days God made the heavens and the earth,
but on the seventh day He ceased work
and refreshed Himself.

The congregation, then the Leader:

וַיְדַבֵּר Thus Moses announced the LORD's appointed seasons Lev. 23
to the children of Israel.

HALF KADDISH

Leader: יִתְגַּדַּל Magnified and sanctified
may His great name be,
in the world He created by His will.
May He establish His kingdom
in your lifetime and in your days,
and in the lifetime of all the house of Israel,
swiftly and soon –
and say: Amen.

All: May His great name be blessed for ever and all time.

Leader: Blessed and praised,
glorified and exalted,
raised and honored,
uplifted and lauded
be the name of the Holy One,
blessed be He,
beyond any blessing,
song, praise and consolation
uttered in the world –
and say: Amen.

On שבת, the קהל stands and, together with the שליח ציבור, says:

שמות לא
וְשָׁמְרוּ בְנֵי־יִשְׂרָאֵל אֶת־הַשַּׁבָּת
לַעֲשׂוֹת אֶת־הַשַּׁבָּת לְדֹרֹתָם בְּרִית עוֹלָם:
בֵּינִי וּבֵין בְּנֵי יִשְׂרָאֵל, אוֹת הִוא לְעֹלָם
כִּי־שֵׁשֶׁת יָמִים עָשָׂה יהוה אֶת־הַשָּׁמַיִם וְאֶת־הָאָרֶץ
וּבַיּוֹם הַשְּׁבִיעִי שָׁבַת וַיִּנָּפַשׁ:

The קהל, then the שליח ציבור:

ויקרא כג
וַיְדַבֵּר מֹשֶׁה אֶת־מֹעֲדֵי יהוה אֶל־בְּנֵי יִשְׂרָאֵל:

חצי קדיש

ש״ץ: יִתְגַּדַּל וְיִתְקַדַּשׁ שְׁמֵהּ רַבָּא (קהל: אָמֵן)
בְּעָלְמָא דִּי בְרָא כִרְעוּתֵהּ
וְיַמְלִיךְ מַלְכוּתֵהּ
בְּחַיֵּיכוֹן וּבְיוֹמֵיכוֹן וּבְחַיֵּי דְכָל בֵּית יִשְׂרָאֵל
בַּעֲגָלָא וּבִזְמַן קָרִיב
וְאִמְרוּ אָמֵן. (קהל: אָמֵן)

קהל וש״ץ: יְהֵא שְׁמֵהּ רַבָּא מְבָרַךְ לְעָלַם וּלְעָלְמֵי עָלְמַיָּא.

ש״ץ: יִתְבָּרַךְ וְיִשְׁתַּבַּח וְיִתְפָּאַר וְיִתְרוֹמַם וְיִתְנַשֵּׂא
וְיִתְהַדָּר וְיִתְעַלֶּה וְיִתְהַלָּל
שְׁמֵהּ דְּקֻדְשָׁא בְּרִיךְ הוּא (קהל: בְּרִיךְ הוּא)
לְעֵלָּא מִן כָּל בִּרְכָתָא וְשִׁירָתָא
תֻּשְׁבְּחָתָא וְנֶחֱמָתָא
דַּאֲמִירָן בְּעָלְמָא
וְאִמְרוּ אָמֵן. (קהל: אָמֵן)

THE AMIDA

The following prayer, until "in former years" on page 74, is said silently, standing with feet together. Take three steps forward and at the points indicated by ▾, bend the knees at the first word, bow at the second, and stand straight before saying God's name.

O Lord, open my lips, Ps. 51
so that my mouth may declare Your praise.

PATRIARCHS

▾בָּרוּךְ▾ Blessed are You, Lord our God and God of our fathers,
God of Abraham, God of Isaac and God of Jacob;
the great, mighty and awesome God, God Most High,
who bestows acts of loving-kindness and creates all,
who remembers the loving-kindness of the fathers
and will bring a Redeemer
to their children's children
for the sake of His name, in love.
King, Helper, Savior, Shield:
▾Blessed are You, Lord,
Shield of Abraham.

DIVINE MIGHT

אַתָּה גִּבּוֹר You are eternally mighty, Lord.
You give life to the dead
and have great power to save.

In Israel:
He causes the dew to fall.

On Simḥat Torah outside Israel:
He makes the wind blow and the rain fall.

(Shabbat), the seventh month (Tishrei), the seventh year (*Shemitta*, the year of release), and the Jubilee at the end of seven cycles of seven years. In the case of the festivals, the basic text of the central prayer is ancient, several of its various parts already mentioned in the Talmud (*Berakhot* 33b, *Pesaḥim* 117b, *Yoma* 87b).

עמידה

The following prayer, until קַדְמֹנִיּוֹת *on page 75, is said silently, standing with feet together. Take three steps forward and at the points indicated by* ˚, *bend the knees at the first word, bow at the second, and stand straight before saying God's name.*

אֲדֹנָי, שְׂפָתַי תִּפְתָּח, וּפִי יַגִּיד תְּהִלָּתֶךָ: תהלים נא

אבות

˚בָּרוּךְ אַתָּה יהוה, אֱלֹהֵינוּ וֵאלֹהֵי אֲבוֹתֵינוּ
אֱלֹהֵי אַבְרָהָם, אֱלֹהֵי יִצְחָק, וֵאלֹהֵי יַעֲקֹב
הָאֵל הַגָּדוֹל הַגִּבּוֹר וְהַנּוֹרָא, אֵל עֶלְיוֹן
גּוֹמֵל חֲסָדִים טוֹבִים, וְקֹנֵה הַכֹּל
וְזוֹכֵר חַסְדֵי אָבוֹת
וּמֵבִיא גוֹאֵל לִבְנֵי בְנֵיהֶם לְמַעַן שְׁמוֹ בְּאַהֲבָה.
מֶלֶךְ עוֹזֵר וּמוֹשִׁיעַ וּמָגֵן.
˚בָּרוּךְ אַתָּה יהוה, מָגֵן אַבְרָהָם.

גבורות

אַתָּה גִּבּוֹר לְעוֹלָם, אֲדֹנָי
מְחַיֵּה מֵתִים אַתָּה, רַב לְהוֹשִׁיעַ

In ארץ ישראל*:*

מוֹרִיד הַטָּל

On שמחת תורה *outside Israel:*

מַשִּׁיב הָרוּחַ וּמוֹרִיד הַגֶּשֶׁם

THE AMIDA

On Shabbat and festivals (with the exception of Musaf of Rosh HaShana) the Amida consists of seven blessings. The first three (expressions of praise) and the last three (expressions of thanks) are as for all Amida prayers, while the middle blessing is dedicated to the specific sanctity of the day (*Kedushat HaYom*). Seven is the sign of the sacred – the seventh day

He sustains the living with loving-kindness,
and with great compassion revives the dead.
He supports the fallen, heals the sick, sets captives free,
and keeps His faith with those who sleep in the dust.
Who is like You, Master of might,
and who can compare to You,
O King who brings death and gives life,
and makes salvation grow?
Faithful are You to revive the dead.
Blessed are You, Lord, who revives the dead.

HOLINESS

אַתָּה קָדוֹשׁ You are holy and Your name is holy,
and holy ones praise You daily, Selah!
Blessed are You, Lord, the holy God.

HOLINESS OF THE DAY

אַתָּה בְחַרְתָּנוּ You have chosen us from among all peoples.
You have loved and favored us.

> Ask now about the former days, long before your time, from the day God created human beings on the earth; ask from one end of the heavens to the other. Has anything so great as this ever happened, or has anything like it ever been heard of? Has any other people heard the voice of God speaking out of fire, as you have, and lived? Has any god ever tried to take for himself one nation out of another nation, by tests, by signs and wonders, by war, by a mighty hand and an outstretched arm, or by great and awesome deeds, like all the things the Lord your God did for you in Egypt before your very eyes? (Deuteronomy 4:32–34)

Non-Jewish sages, among them Blaise Pascal, Jean-Jacques Rousseau, Leo Tolstoy and Winston Churchill, wrote about the uniqueness of the history of the Jewish people, its survival against the odds and its continuity in the most varied and adverse circumstances. It is said that King Frederick the Great once asked his physician, Zimmermann of Brugg-in-Aargau, "Zimmermann, can you name me a single proof of the existence of God?" The physician considered the matter, and could think of only one answer not

מְכַלְכֵּל חַיִּים בְּחֶסֶד, מְחַיֵּה מֵתִים בְּרַחֲמִים רַבִּים
סוֹמֵךְ נוֹפְלִים, וְרוֹפֵא חוֹלִים, וּמַתִּיר אֲסוּרִים
וּמְקַיֵּם אֱמוּנָתוֹ לִישֵׁנֵי עָפָר.
מִי כָמְוֹךָ, בַּעַל גְּבוּרוֹת, וּמִי דְּוֹמֶה לָּךְ
מֶלֶךְ, מֵמִית וּמְחַיֶּה וּמַצְמִיחַ יְשׁוּעָה.
וְנֶאֱמָן אַתָּה לְהַחֲיוֹת מֵתִים.
בָּרוּךְ אַתָּה יהוה, מְחַיֵּה הַמֵּתִים.

קדושת השם

אַתָּה קָדוֹשׁ וְשִׁמְךָ קָדוֹשׁ
וּקְדוֹשִׁים בְּכָל יוֹם יְהַלְלְוּךָ סֶּלָה.
בָּרוּךְ אַתָּה יהוה, הָאֵל הַקָּדוֹשׁ.

קדושת היום

אַתָּה בְחַרְתָּנוּ מִכָּל הָעַמִּים
אָהַבְתָּ אוֹתָנוּ וְרָצִיתָ בָּנוּ

The first three paragraphs of prayer represent the three patriarchs. The first is about Abraham, the first to heed God's call to leave his land, birthplace, and father's house and begin the journey of faith. The second with its theme of resurrection is associated with Isaac, the child who unflinchingly faced death but was restored to life, an eternal symbol that life is God's gift. The third, about holiness, represents Jacob whose children all continued the covenant and whose descendants became, at Sinai, "a kingdom of priests and a holy nation" (Ex. 19:6), meaning a people dedicated to God, His ambassadors and witnesses to the world.

אַתָּה בְחַרְתָּנוּ *You have chosen us.* This striking emphasis on Jewish singularity is common to all three pilgrimage festivals, Pesaḥ, Shavuot and Sukkot, for they are all festivals of history. The truths of Judaism are universal; the history of the Jewish people is not.

You have raised us above all tongues.
You have made us holy through Your commandments.
You have brought us near, our King, to Your service,
and have called us by Your great and holy name.

On Motza'ei Shabbat:

וַתּוֹדִיעֵנוּ You have made known to us, LORD our God,
Your righteous laws,
and have taught us to perform Your will's decrees.
You have given us, LORD our God, just laws and true teachings,
good precepts and commandments.
You have given us as our heritage seasons of joy,
holy festivals, and occasions for presenting our freewill offerings.
You have given us as our heritage the holiness of the Sabbath,
the glory of the festival, and the festive offerings of the pilgrimage days.
You have distinguished, LORD our God, between sacred and secular,
between light and darkness, between Israel and the nations,
between the seventh day and the six days of work.
You have distinguished between the holiness of the Sabbath
and the holiness of the festival,
and have made the seventh day holy above the six days of work.
You have distinguished and sanctified Your people Israel
with Your holiness.

---

already mentioned in the Talmud (*Berakhot* 33b). Havdala represents a most beautiful way in which we become "partners with the Holy One, blessed be He, in the work of creation," by beginning the week with a ceremony inviting us to share in a key activity in which God engaged when creating the universe. In Genesis 1 the verb ב-ד-ל, "to distinguish, differentiate, separate" occurs five times. So we, too, begin each week with an act of Havdala, separation. Normally the separation is between Shabbat and secular time (*ḥol*). Here it is between two different forms of holy time, that of Shabbat and that of a festival. The principle, however, remains the same: knowledge ("You have made known to us") is the ability to differentiate one kind of thing from another. The ability to make distinctions is the mark of the educated mind.

וְרוֹמַמְתָּנוּ מִכָּל הַלְּשׁוֹנוֹת
וְקִדַּשְׁתָּנוּ בְּמִצְוֹתֶיךָ
וְקֵרַבְתָּנוּ מַלְכֵּנוּ לַעֲבוֹדָתֶךָ
וְשִׁמְךָ הַגָּדוֹל וְהַקָּדוֹשׁ עָלֵינוּ קָרָאתָ.

On מוצאי שבת:

וַתּוֹדִיעֵנוּ יהוה אֱלֹהֵינוּ אֶת מִשְׁפְּטֵי צִדְקֶךָ
וַתְּלַמְּדֵנוּ לַעֲשׂוֹת חֻקֵּי רְצוֹנֶךָ
וַתִּתֶּן לָנוּ יהוה אֱלֹהֵינוּ מִשְׁפָּטִים יְשָׁרִים וְתוֹרוֹת אֱמֶת
חֻקִּים וּמִצְוֹת טוֹבִים
וַתַּנְחִילֵנוּ זְמַנֵּי שָׂשׂוֹן וּמוֹעֲדֵי קֹדֶשׁ וְחַגֵּי נְדָבָה
וַתּוֹרִישֵׁנוּ קְדֻשַּׁת שַׁבָּת וּכְבוֹד מוֹעֵד וַחֲגִיגַת הָרֶגֶל.
וַתַּבְדֵּל יהוה אֱלֹהֵינוּ בֵּין קֹדֶשׁ לְחֹל, בֵּין אוֹר לְחֹשֶׁךְ
בֵּין יִשְׂרָאֵל לָעַמִּים, בֵּין יוֹם הַשְּׁבִיעִי לְשֵׁשֶׁת יְמֵי הַמַּעֲשֶׂה.
בֵּין קְדֻשַּׁת שַׁבָּת לִקְדֻשַּׁת יוֹם טוֹב הִבְדַּלְתָּ
וְאֶת יוֹם הַשְּׁבִיעִי מִשֵּׁשֶׁת יְמֵי הַמַּעֲשֶׂה קִדַּשְׁתָּ
הִבְדַּלְתָּ וְקִדַּשְׁתָּ אֶת עַמְּךָ יִשְׂרָאֵל בִּקְדֻשָּׁתֶךָ.

---

open to refutation. His reply: "Your majesty, the Jews." Through its history the singular people bears witness to the single God.

וְרוֹמַמְתָּנוּ מִכָּל הַלְּשׁוֹנוֹת *You have raised us above all tongues.* The Hebrew language has a special sanctity. For some this is because it was the language of creation; for others, Maimonides especially, it was because of the modesty of its expressions. Robert Frost said that "poetry is what is lost in translation." Many of the misunderstandings of Judaism have arisen because of the untranslatability of many of its key terms into Western languages, influenced as they were by Greek concepts that are very different from their Judaic counterparts.

וַתּוֹדִיעֵנוּ *You have made known to us.* A form of the Havdala prayer specific to occasions when a festival falls immediately after Shabbat. The text is

On Shabbat, add the words in parentheses:

וַתִּתֶּן לָנוּ And You, LORD our God, have given us in love
(Sabbaths for rest and) festivals for rejoicing,
holy days and seasons for joy,
(this Sabbath day and) this day of:

On Sukkot: the festival of Sukkot, our time of rejoicing

On Shemini Atzeret & Simḥat Torah: the festival of the eighth day, Shemini Atzeret, our time of rejoicing

(with love), a holy assembly in memory of the exodus from Egypt.

---

particular event or idea; Pesaḥ to liberation, Shavuot to revelation, Sukkot to joy. It also conveys the sense of season: Pesaḥ in spring, Shavuot at the time of first-fruits, and Sukkot in the fall. *Mikra kodesh* means a day made holy by declaration, that is, by *Kiddush*, prayer, and the recitation of Hallel. Rabbi Yaakov Tzvi Mecklenburg (Germany, nineteenth century) understands it to mean "a call to holiness." *Mikra* also means sacred Scripture, for these are days of public gathering when the Torah is read.

SHEMINI ATZERET

For an essay on Shemini Atzeret, see Introduction, page lxxiv.

Shemini Atzeret is a festival with a dual aspect. On the one hand, it is a continuation of the "time of our joy." On the other, it is a festival in its own right, with its own name, its own blessing of *sheheḥeyanu*, and its own distinctive sacrifice in Temple times (*Rosh HaShana* 4b). It is essentially a time of leave-taking, after the long sequence of holy days that began with Rosh HaShana. Pilgrims, in Temple times, were aware that they would not be together again in Jerusalem for almost half a year, until Pesaḥ. The day therefore has the "sweet sorrow" of the last day of a reunion. One commentator compared it to a king whose children came to visit him from time to time. On each occasion of parting he would ask them when they were going to return. The first time they said, "In seven weeks" and he bade them farewell. The second time they said, "In four months," and he bade them farewell. The third time they said "In half a year," and he said, "If we are to be parted for so long, please stay an extra day" (Ḥizkuni on Lev. 23:36).

Hence the name of the day. The Torah states: "On the eighth day, it shall be to you an *Atzeret*" (Num. 29:35). Some understood the word to mean a solemn assembly, a sacred gathering (Targum), or a closing ceremony. Others

On שבת*, add the words in parentheses:*

וַתִּתֶּן לָנוּ יהוה אֱלֹהֵינוּ בְּאַהֲבָה
(שַׁבָּתוֹת לִמְנוּחָה וּ)מוֹעֲדִים לְשִׂמְחָה, חַגִּים וּזְמַנִּים לְשָׂשׂוֹן
אֶת יוֹם (הַשַּׁבָּת הַזֶּה וְאֶת יוֹם)

בסוכות: חַג הַסֻּכּוֹת הַזֶּה, זְמַן שִׂמְחָתֵנוּ
בשמע״צ ובש״ת: הַשְּׁמִינִי חַג הָעֲצֶרֶת הַזֶּה, זְמַן שִׂמְחָתֵנוּ

(בְּאַהֲבָה) מִקְרָא קֹדֶשׁ, זֵכֶר לִיצִיאַת מִצְרָיִם.

שַׁבָּתוֹת לִמְנוּחָה וּמוֹעֲדִים לְשִׂמְחָה *Sabbaths for rest and festivals for rejoicing.* There is a significant difference between rest and joy. Rest renews, joy uplifts. There is no exact English equivalent of the word *simḥa* since it essentially means "joy shared" or "collective celebration." *Simḥa* in Judaism, especially in relation to the festivals, is communal. It must involve everyone, even the poorest and loneliest. The Torah is emphatic in insisting that festive celebration should include "you, your sons and daughters, your male and female servants, and the Levites, the foreigners, the fatherless and the widows who live in your towns" (Deut. 16:14). Maimonides writes:

> While eating and drinking [on a festival], it is one's duty to feed the stranger, the orphan, the widow, and other poor and unfortunate people, for he who locks the doors to his courtyard and eats and drinks with his wife and family, without giving anything to eat and drink to the poor and the bitter in soul – his meal is not a rejoicing in a divine commandment, but a rejoicing in his own stomach.... Rejoicing of this kind is a disgrace to those who indulge in it. (Laws of Festival Rest 6:18)

This insistence on the *inclusive* nature of festivity – simultaneously a moral, political, social and spiritual idea – is fundamental to Judaism and to the kind of community and society we are commanded to create.

THE FOUR NAMES FOR "FESTIVAL"

The *Kedushat HaYom* blessing uses four different terms to describe the festivals: *mo'ed, ḥag, zeman,* and *mikra kodesh. Mo'ed* comes from the same root as *ed,* "a witness." The idea that history is itself a witness to divine redemption is thus embedded in the Hebrew language. *Ḥag* alludes to the festival offering (*ḥagiga*) brought at the Temple. *Zeman* indicates a time dedicated to a

אֱלֹהֵינוּ Our God and God of our ancestors,
may there rise, come, reach, appear, be favored, heard,
regarded and remembered before You,
our recollection and remembrance,
as well as the remembrance of our ancestors,
and of the Messiah son of David Your servant,
and of Jerusalem Your holy city,
and of all Your people the house of Israel –
for deliverance and well-being,
grace, loving-kindness and compassion,
life and peace, on this day of:

On Sukkot: the festival of Sukkot.
On Shemini Atzeret & Simḥat Torah: the festival of Shemini Atzeret.

---

appropriate at all, saying simply *Yom Shemini Atzeret* (Rema in the name of *Sefer Minhagim*).

The idea of leave-taking in a religious context is paradoxical. We part because, as humans, we are creatures of time and space. But God is not. We are never separated from Him, nor He from us. Yet precisely because we are human, there always are times and places where we feel the *Shekhina*, the Divine Presence, more intensely. Supremely that was true of the Temple, above all on Sukkot, the festival of joy. The sense of exultation we feel, for example, in Hallel, still echoes back to us something of what the pilgrims felt as they approached the holiest place on earth. We hear it in David's words in psalm 27: "One thing I ask of the Lord, only this do I seek: to live in the House of the Lord all the days of my life, to gaze on the beauty of the Lord and worship in His Temple."

Shemini Atzeret is when we bid farewell to that exalted mood, and prepare to return to the world and its challenges. But it is as if, for a moment, as we take that leave, we stand alone with God. Not in reverence as on Rosh HaShana, not in awe as on Yom Kippur, not even in celebration as on Sukkot, but in a simple one-to-One intimacy, knowing that, though God is God of all the world and all humanity, no nation, no civilization, has ever walked so long a journey with Him or felt so close, and none has risked more on His behalf. In the music of faith, this, the last movement of the symphony of Tishrei, has a lingering beauty all of its own.

יַעֲלֶה וְיָבוֹא וְיַגִּיעַ *Rise, come, reach….* A crescendo of eight verbs, signifying the

אֱלֹהֵינוּ וֵאלֹהֵי אֲבוֹתֵינוּ
יַעֲלֶה וְיָבוֹא וְיַגִּיעַ וְיֵרָאֶה וְיֵרָצֶה וְיִשָּׁמַע
וְיִפָּקֵד וְיִזָּכֵר זִכְרוֹנֵנוּ וּפִקְדוֹנֵנוּ, וְזִכְרוֹן אֲבוֹתֵינוּ
וְזִכְרוֹן מָשִׁיחַ בֶּן דָּוִד עַבְדֶּךָ, וְזִכְרוֹן יְרוּשָׁלַיִם עִיר קָדְשֶׁךָ
וְזִכְרוֹן כָּל עַמְּךָ בֵּית יִשְׂרָאֵל, לְפָנֶיךָ
לִפְלֵיטָה, לְטוֹבָה, לְחֵן וּלְחֶסֶד וּלְרַחֲמִים
לְחַיִּים וּלְשָׁלוֹם בְּיוֹם

בסוכות: חַג הַסֻּכּוֹת הַזֶּה.
בשמע״צ ובש״ת: הַשְּׁמִינִי חַג הָעֲצֶרֶת הַזֶּה.

---

interpreted it to mean the time of leaving the Sukka and going back into one's regular home (Targum Yonatan). Some read it to mean a time of "holding back" from work (Rashi, Ibn Ezra, Radak). But the most powerful interpretation was that it means "delaying departure," staying an extra day in the precincts of the Temple, or in the realm of the holy (see Rashi, Seforno on Lev. 23:36).

In the Diaspora, Shemini Atzeret had another kind of duality since it was also, possibly, the seventh day of Sukkot. This raised questions such as, "do we take the four kinds?" The answer was no, since taking the four kinds on all seven days is only a rabbinic enactment in memory of the Temple (elsewhere in Temple times the four kinds were taken only on the first day). Do we sit in the Sukka? Opinions and customs differed, but the dominant consensus was yes, but without making a blessing. The problem posed by Shemini Atzeret is that the more we respect the possibility that it may be the seventh day of Sukkot, the more we risk detracting from its distinctive character as a festival in its own right.

The way the day should be referred to in the prayers also occasioned debate. Though the words Shemini and Atzeret appear together in Tanakh several times (Num. 29:35, Neh. 8:18, II Chron. 7:9), the use of the two words together as the name of the festival is post-biblical. Most authorities held that we should say *Yom Shemini Ḥag haAtzeret haZeh*, "the eighth day, this festival of Atzeret" (Rashi, Rif, Rambam, Shulḥan Arukh). Others advocated saying *Yom Shemini Atzeret haḤag haZeh*, "the eighth day, the conclusion of this festival" (Rashal, Taz). Yet others doubted whether the word *Ḥag* is

On it remember us, LORD our God, for good;
recollect us for blessing, and deliver us for life.
In accord with Your promise of salvation and compassion,
spare us and be gracious to us;
have compassion on us and deliver us,
for our eyes are turned to You because You, God,
are a gracious and compassionate King.

On Shabbat, add the words in parentheses:

וְהַשִּׂיאֵנוּ Bestow on us, LORD our God,
the blessings of Your festivals
for good life and peace, joy and gladness,
as You desired and promised to bless us.
(Our God and God of our fathers, find favor in our rest.)
Make us holy through Your commandments
and grant us a share in Your Torah.
Satisfy us with Your goodness, gladden us with Your salvation,
and purify our hearts to serve You in truth.
Grant us as our heritage, LORD our God (with love and favor,)
with joy and gladness,
Your holy (Sabbath and) festivals,
and may Israel, who sanctify Your name, rejoice in You.
Blessed are You, LORD,
who sanctifies (the Sabbath and) Israel and the festive seasons.

---

ward to their ancestors" (Edmund Burke). We ask God to remember; God asks us to remember.

וְהַשִּׂיאֵנוּ ... מְקַדֵּשׁ הַשַּׁבָּת וְיִשְׂרָאֵל וְהַזְּמַנִּים *Bestow on us… who sanctifies the Sabbath and Israel and the festive seasons.* The precise order of the conclusion of this blessing is important. "Israel" comes before "seasons" since it is God who sanctifies Israel, and Israel who consecrates times by fixing the calendar, the first command given to us as a people (Ex. 12:2). Shabbat precedes both, since it was consecrated by God on the seventh day of creation (Gen. 2:1–3), before there was an Israel or a calendar of festivals.

זָכְרֵנוּ יהוה אֱלֹהֵינוּ בּוֹ לְטוֹבָה, וּפָקְדֵנוּ בוֹ לִבְרָכָה
וְהוֹשִׁיעֵנוּ בוֹ לְחַיִּים.
וּבִדְבַר יְשׁוּעָה וְרַחֲמִים חוּס וְחָנֵּנוּ
וְרַחֵם עָלֵינוּ וְהוֹשִׁיעֵנוּ
כִּי אֵלֶיךָ עֵינֵינוּ, כִּי אֵל מֶלֶךְ חַנּוּן וְרַחוּם אָתָּה.

On שבת, add the words in parentheses:

וְהַשִּׂיאֵנוּ יהוה אֱלֹהֵינוּ אֶת בִּרְכַּת מוֹעֲדֶיךָ
לְחַיִּים וּלְשָׁלוֹם, לְשִׂמְחָה וּלְשָׂשׂוֹן
כַּאֲשֶׁר רָצִיתָ וְאָמַרְתָּ לְבָרְכֵנוּ.
(אֱלֹהֵינוּ וֵאלֹהֵי אֲבוֹתֵינוּ, רְצֵה בִמְנוּחָתֵנוּ)
קַדְּשֵׁנוּ בְּמִצְוֹתֶיךָ, וְתֵן חֶלְקֵנוּ בְּתוֹרָתֶךָ
שַׂבְּעֵנוּ מִטּוּבֶךָ, וְשַׂמְּחֵנוּ בִּישׁוּעָתֶךָ
וְטַהֵר לִבֵּנוּ לְעָבְדְּךָ בֶּאֱמֶת.
וְהַנְחִילֵנוּ יהוה אֱלֹהֵינוּ (בְּאַהֲבָה וּבְרָצוֹן)
בְּשִׂמְחָה וּבְשָׂשׂוֹן (שַׁבָּת וּ) מוֹעֲדֵי קָדְשֶׁךָ
וְיִשְׂמְחוּ בְךָ יִשְׂרָאֵל מְקַדְּשֵׁי שְׁמֶךָ.
בָּרוּךְ אַתָּה יהוה, מְקַדֵּשׁ (הַשַּׁבָּת וְ) יִשְׂרָאֵל וְהַזְּמַנִּים.

---

seven heavenly realms, with God above them all – a spatial metaphor, meaning, may our prayers reach the innermost heart of God. Note the motif of memory in this paragraph: the root ז-כ-ר appears seven times, and the related verb פ-ק-ד three times. Judaism is a religion of memory, God's and ours. The Egyptians memorialized their history by monuments and inscriptions. Our history is engraved not on walls of stone but on the mind. We live not *in* the past but *with* the past: it is our satellite navigation system as we travel the wilderness of time, reminding us where we have come from and where we seek to go. "People will not look forward to posterity who never look back-

TEMPLE SERVICE

רְצֵה Find favor, LORD our God,
in Your people Israel and their prayer.
Restore the service to Your most holy House,
and accept in love and favor
the fire-offerings of Israel and their prayer.
May the service of Your people Israel always find favor with You.
And may our eyes witness Your return to Zion in compassion.
Blessed are You, LORD,
who restores His Presence to Zion.

THANKSGIVING

Bow at the first nine words.

מוֹדִים We give thanks to You,
for You are the LORD our God and God of our ancestors
for ever and all time.
You are the Rock of our lives,
Shield of our salvation from generation to generation.
We will thank You and declare Your praise for our lives,
which are entrusted into Your hand;
for our souls, which are placed in Your charge;
for Your miracles which are with us every day;
and for Your wonders and favors
at all times, evening, morning and midday.
You are good – for Your compassion never fails.
You are compassionate – for Your loving-kindnesses never cease.
We have always placed our hope in You.
For all these things
may Your name be blessed and exalted, our King,
continually, for ever and all time.
Let all that lives thank You, Selah!
and praise Your name in truth, God, our Savior and Help, Selah!
Blessed are You, LORD,
whose name is "the Good" and to whom thanks are due.

עבודה

רְצֵה יהוה אֱלֹהֵינוּ בְּעַמְּךָ יִשְׂרָאֵל, וּבִתְפִלָּתָם
וְהָשֵׁב אֶת הָעֲבוֹדָה לִדְבִיר בֵּיתֶךָ
וְאִשֵּׁי יִשְׂרָאֵל וּתְפִלָּתָם בְּאַהֲבָה תְקַבֵּל בְּרָצוֹן
וּתְהִי לְרָצוֹן תָּמִיד עֲבוֹדַת יִשְׂרָאֵל עַמֶּךָ.
וְתֶחֱזֶינָה עֵינֵינוּ בְּשׁוּבְךָ לְצִיּוֹן בְּרַחֲמִים.
בָּרוּךְ אַתָּה יהוה, הַמַּחֲזִיר שְׁכִינָתוֹ לְצִיּוֹן.

הודאה

Bow at the first five words.

מוֹדִים אֲנַחְנוּ לָךְ
שָׁאַתָּה הוּא יהוה אֱלֹהֵינוּ וֵאלֹהֵי אֲבוֹתֵינוּ לְעוֹלָם וָעֶד.
צוּר חַיֵּינוּ, מָגֵן יִשְׁעֵנוּ, אַתָּה הוּא לְדוֹר וָדוֹר.
נוֹדֶה לְּךָ וּנְסַפֵּר תְּהִלָּתֶךָ
עַל חַיֵּינוּ הַמְּסוּרִים בְּיָדֶךָ
וְעַל נִשְׁמוֹתֵינוּ הַפְּקוּדוֹת לָךְ
וְעַל נִסֶּיךָ שֶׁבְּכָל יוֹם עִמָּנוּ
וְעַל נִפְלְאוֹתֶיךָ וְטוֹבוֹתֶיךָ שֶׁבְּכָל עֵת, עֶרֶב וָבֹקֶר וְצָהֳרָיִם.
הַטּוֹב, כִּי לֹא כָלוּ רַחֲמֶיךָ
וְהַמְרַחֵם, כִּי לֹא תַמּוּ חֲסָדֶיךָ
מֵעוֹלָם קִוִּינוּ לָךְ.
וְעַל כֻּלָּם יִתְבָּרַךְ וְיִתְרוֹמַם שִׁמְךָ מַלְכֵּנוּ תָּמִיד לְעוֹלָם וָעֶד.
וְכֹל הַחַיִּים יוֹדוּךָ סֶּלָה, וִיהַלְלוּ אֶת שִׁמְךָ בֶּאֱמֶת
הָאֵל יְשׁוּעָתֵנוּ וְעֶזְרָתֵנוּ סֶלָה.
בָּרוּךְ אַתָּה יהוה, הַטּוֹב שִׁמְךָ וּלְךָ נָאֶה לְהוֹדוֹת.

PEACE

שָׁלוֹם רָב Grant great peace to Your people Israel for ever,
for You are the sovereign LORD of all peace;
and may it be good in Your eyes to bless Your people Israel
at every time, at every hour, with Your peace.
Blessed are You, LORD, who blesses His people Israel with peace.

Some say the following verse.

May the words of my mouth and the meditation of my heart *Ps. 19*
find favor before You, LORD, my Rock and Redeemer.

אֱלֹהַי My God, *Berakhot 17a*
guard my tongue from evil and my lips from deceitful speech.
To those who curse me, let my soul be silent;
may my soul be to all like the dust.
Open my heart to Your Torah
and let my soul pursue Your commandments.
As for all who plan evil against me,
swiftly thwart their counsel and frustrate their plans.
Act for the sake of Your name; act for the sake of Your right hand;
act for the sake of Your holiness; act for the sake of Your Torah.
That Your beloved ones may be delivered, *Ps. 60*
save with Your right hand and answer me.
May the words of my mouth and the meditation of my heart *Ps. 19*
find favor before You, LORD, my Rock and Redeemer.

Bow, take three steps back, then bow, first left, then right, then center, while saying:

May He who makes peace in His high places,
make peace for us and all Israel – and say: Amen.

יְהִי רָצוֹן May it be Your will, LORD our God and God of our ancestors,
that the Temple be rebuilt speedily in our days,
and grant us a share in Your Torah.
And there we will serve You with reverence,
as in the days of old and as in former years.
Then the offering of Judah and Jerusalem *Mal. 3*
will be pleasing to the LORD as in the days of old and as in former years.

On Shabbat, continue with "Then the heavens" on the next page.
If Yom Tov falls on a weekday, the service continues with Full Kaddish on page 78.

ברכת שלום

שָׁלוֹם רָב עַל יִשְׂרָאֵל עַמְּךָ תָּשִׂים לְעוֹלָם
כִּי אַתָּה הוּא מֶלֶךְ אָדוֹן לְכָל הַשָּׁלוֹם.
וְטוֹב בְּעֵינֶיךָ לְבָרֵךְ אֶת עַמְּךָ יִשְׂרָאֵל
בְּכָל עֵת וּבְכָל שָׁעָה בִּשְׁלוֹמֶךָ.
בָּרוּךְ אַתָּה יהוה, הַמְבָרֵךְ אֶת עַמּוֹ יִשְׂרָאֵל בַּשָּׁלוֹם.

Some say the following verse.

יִהְיוּ לְרָצוֹן אִמְרֵי־פִי וְהֶגְיוֹן לִבִּי לְפָנֶיךָ, יהוה צוּרִי וְגֹאֲלִי: תהלים יט

ברכות יז. אֱלֹהַי
נְצֹר לְשׁוֹנִי מֵרָע וּשְׂפָתַי מִדַּבֵּר מִרְמָה
וְלִמְקַלְלַי נַפְשִׁי תִדֹּם, וְנַפְשִׁי כֶּעָפָר לַכֹּל תִּהְיֶה.
פְּתַח לִבִּי בְּתוֹרָתֶךָ, וּבְמִצְוֹתֶיךָ תִּרְדֹּף נַפְשִׁי.
וְכָל הַחוֹשְׁבִים עָלַי רָעָה, מְהֵרָה הָפֵר עֲצָתָם וְקַלְקֵל מַחֲשַׁבְתָּם.
עֲשֵׂה לְמַעַן שְׁמֶךָ, עֲשֵׂה לְמַעַן יְמִינֶךָ
עֲשֵׂה לְמַעַן קְדֻשָּׁתֶךָ, עֲשֵׂה לְמַעַן תּוֹרָתֶךָ.
לְמַעַן יֵחָלְצוּן יְדִידֶיךָ, הוֹשִׁיעָה יְמִינְךָ וַעֲנֵנִי: תהלים ס
יִהְיוּ לְרָצוֹן אִמְרֵי־פִי וְהֶגְיוֹן לִבִּי לְפָנֶיךָ, יהוה צוּרִי וְגֹאֲלִי: תהלים יט

Bow, take three steps back, then bow, first left, then right, then center, while saying:

עֹשֶׂה שָׁלוֹם בִּמְרוֹמָיו
הוּא יַעֲשֶׂה שָׁלוֹם עָלֵינוּ וְעַל כָּל יִשְׂרָאֵל, וְאִמְרוּ אָמֵן.

יְהִי רָצוֹן מִלְּפָנֶיךָ יהוה אֱלֹהֵינוּ וֵאלֹהֵי אֲבוֹתֵינוּ
שֶׁיִּבָּנֶה בֵּית הַמִּקְדָּשׁ בִּמְהֵרָה בְיָמֵינוּ, וְתֵן חֶלְקֵנוּ בְּתוֹרָתֶךָ
וְשָׁם נַעֲבָדְךָ בְּיִרְאָה כִּימֵי עוֹלָם וּכְשָׁנִים קַדְמֹנִיּוֹת.
וְעָרְבָה לַיהוה מִנְחַת יְהוּדָה וִירוּשָׁלָםִ כִּימֵי עוֹלָם וּכְשָׁנִים קַדְמֹנִיּוֹת: מלאכי ג

On שבת*, continue with* וַיְכֻלּוּ *on the next page.*
On יום טוב *which falls on a weekday, the service continues with* קדיש שלם *on page 79.*

On Shabbat all stand and say:

וַיְכֻלּוּ Then the heavens and the earth were completed, and all their array. *Gen. 2*
With the seventh day, God completed the work He had done.
He ceased on the seventh day from all the work He had done.
God blessed the seventh day and declared it holy,
because on it He ceased from all His work He had created to do.

The following until "who sanctifies the Sabbath" below,
is omitted when praying with an occasional minyan or alone.
The Leader continues:

ME'EIN SHEVA

בָּרוּךְ Blessed are You, Lord our God and God of our fathers,
God of Abraham, God of Isaac and God of Jacob,
the great, mighty and awesome God,
God Most High, Creator of heaven and earth.

The congregation then the Leader:

מָגֵן אָבוֹת By His word, He was the Shield of our ancestors.
By His promise, He will revive the dead.
There is none like the holy God
who gives rest to His people on His holy Sabbath day,
for He found them worthy of His favor to give them rest.
Before Him we will come in worship with reverence and awe,
giving thanks to His name daily, continually, with due blessings.
He is God to whom thanks are due, the Lord of peace
who sanctifies the Sabbath and blesses the seventh day,
and in holiness gives rest to a people filled with delight,
in remembrance of the work of creation.

The Leader continues:

אֱלֹהֵינוּ Our God and God of our ancestors,
may You find favor in our rest.
Make us holy through Your commandments
and grant us our share in Your Torah.
Satisfy us with Your goodness, grant us joy in Your salvation,
and purify our hearts to serve You in truth.
In love and favor, Lord our God,
grant us as our heritage Your holy Sabbath,
so that Israel who sanctify Your name may find rest on it.
Blessed are You, Lord, who sanctifies the Sabbath.

On שבת *all stand and say:*

וַיְכֻלּוּ הַשָּׁמַיִם וְהָאָרֶץ וְכָל־צְבָאָם: בראשית ב
וַיְכַל אֱלֹהִים בַּיּוֹם הַשְּׁבִיעִי מְלַאכְתּוֹ אֲשֶׁר עָשָׂה
וַיִּשְׁבֹּת בַּיּוֹם הַשְּׁבִיעִי מִכָּל־מְלַאכְתּוֹ אֲשֶׁר עָשָׂה:
וַיְבָרֶךְ אֱלֹהִים אֶת־יוֹם הַשְּׁבִיעִי, וַיְקַדֵּשׁ אֹתוֹ
כִּי בוֹ שָׁבַת מִכָּל־מְלַאכְתּוֹ, אֲשֶׁר־בָּרָא אֱלֹהִים, לַעֲשׂוֹת:

The following until מְקַדֵּשׁ הַשַּׁבָּת *below, is omitted when praying with an occasional* מנין *or alone.*

The שליח ציבור *continues:*

ברכה מעין שבע

בָּרוּךְ אַתָּה יהוה, אֱלֹהֵינוּ וֵאלֹהֵי אֲבוֹתֵינוּ
אֱלֹהֵי אַבְרָהָם, אֱלֹהֵי יִצְחָק, וֵאלֹהֵי יַעֲקֹב
הָאֵל הַגָּדוֹל הַגִּבּוֹר וְהַנּוֹרָא, אֵל עֶלְיוֹן, קֹנֵה שָׁמַיִם וָאָרֶץ.

The קהל *then the* שליח ציבור*:*

מָגֵן אָבוֹת בִּדְבָרוֹ, מְחַיֵּה מֵתִים בְּמַאֲמָרוֹ, הָאֵל הַקָּדוֹשׁ שֶׁאֵין כָּמוֹהוּ
הַמֵּנִיחַ לְעַמּוֹ בְּיוֹם שַׁבַּת קָדְשׁוֹ, כִּי בָם רָצָה לְהָנִיחַ לָהֶם
לְפָנָיו נַעֲבֹד בְּיִרְאָה וָפַחַד
וְנוֹדֶה לִשְׁמוֹ בְּכָל יוֹם תָּמִיד, מֵעֵין הַבְּרָכוֹת
אֵל הַהוֹדָאוֹת, אֲדוֹן הַשָּׁלוֹם, מְקַדֵּשׁ הַשַּׁבָּת וּמְבָרֵךְ שְׁבִיעִי
וּמֵנִיחַ בִּקְדֻשָּׁה לְעַם מְדֻשְּׁנֵי עֹנֶג, זֵכֶר לְמַעֲשֵׂה בְרֵאשִׁית.

The שליח ציבור *continues:*

אֱלֹהֵינוּ וֵאלֹהֵי אֲבוֹתֵינוּ, רְצֵה בִמְנוּחָתֵנוּ.
קַדְּשֵׁנוּ בְּמִצְוֹתֶיךָ וְתֵן חֶלְקֵנוּ בְּתוֹרָתֶךָ
שַׂבְּעֵנוּ מִטּוּבֶךָ וְשַׂמְּחֵנוּ בִּישׁוּעָתֶךָ
וְטַהֵר לִבֵּנוּ לְעָבְדְּךָ בֶּאֱמֶת.
וְהַנְחִילֵנוּ יהוה אֱלֹהֵינוּ בְּאַהֲבָה וּבְרָצוֹן שַׁבַּת קָדְשֶׁךָ
וְיָנוּחוּ בָהּ יִשְׂרָאֵל מְקַדְּשֵׁי שְׁמֶךָ.
בָּרוּךְ אַתָּה יהוה, מְקַדֵּשׁ הַשַּׁבָּת.

FULL KADDISH

Some have the custom to include additional responses in Full Kaddish. They can be found in the version on page 1464.

Leader: יִתְגַּדַּל Magnified and sanctified may His great name be,
in the world He created by His will.
May He establish His kingdom
in your lifetime and in your days,
and in the lifetime of all the house of Israel,
swiftly and soon –
and say: Amen.

All: May His great name be blessed
for ever and all time.

Leader: Blessed and praised, glorified and exalted,
raised and honored,
uplifted and lauded be
the name of the Holy One,
blessed be He,
beyond any blessing,
song, praise and consolation
uttered in the world –
and say: Amen.

May the prayers and pleas of all Israel
be accepted by their Father in heaven –
and say: Amen.

May there be great peace from heaven,
and life for us and all Israel –
and say: Amen.

Bow, take three steps back, as if taking leave of the Divine Presence, then bow, first left, then right, then center, while saying:

May He who makes peace in His high places,
make peace for us and all Israel –
and say: Amen.

On Simḥat Torah continue with the Hakafot on page 92.

קדיש שלם

Some have the custom to include additional responses in קדיש שלם*.*
They can be found in the version on page 1465.

ש״ץ: יִתְגַּדַּל וְיִתְקַדַּשׁ שְׁמֵהּ רַבָּא (קהל: אָמֵן)
בְּעָלְמָא דִּי בְרָא כִרְעוּתֵהּ, וְיַמְלִיךְ מַלְכוּתֵהּ
בְּחַיֵּיכוֹן וּבְיוֹמֵיכוֹן וּבְחַיֵּי דְכָל בֵּית יִשְׂרָאֵל
בַּעֲגָלָא וּבִזְמַן קָרִיב
וְאִמְרוּ אָמֵן. (קהל: אָמֵן)

קהל ושי״ץ: יְהֵא שְׁמֵהּ רַבָּא מְבָרַךְ לְעָלַם וּלְעָלְמֵי עָלְמַיָּא.

ש״ץ: יִתְבָּרַךְ וְיִשְׁתַּבַּח וְיִתְפָּאַר
וְיִתְרוֹמַם וְיִתְנַשֵּׂא וְיִתְהַדָּר וְיִתְעַלֶּה וְיִתְהַלָּל
שְׁמֵהּ דְּקֻדְשָׁא בְּרִיךְ הוּא (קהל: בְּרִיךְ הוּא)
לְעֵלָּא מִן כָּל בִּרְכָתָא וְשִׁירָתָא, תֻּשְׁבְּחָתָא וְנֶחֱמָתָא
דַּאֲמִירָן בְּעָלְמָא
וְאִמְרוּ אָמֵן. (קהל: אָמֵן)

תִּתְקַבַּל צְלוֹתְהוֹן וּבָעוּתְהוֹן דְּכָל יִשְׂרָאֵל
קֳדָם אֲבוּהוֹן דִּי בִשְׁמַיָּא
וְאִמְרוּ אָמֵן. (קהל: אָמֵן)

יְהֵא שְׁלָמָא רַבָּא מִן שְׁמַיָּא
וְחַיִּים, עָלֵינוּ וְעַל כָּל יִשְׂרָאֵל
וְאִמְרוּ אָמֵן. (קהל: אָמֵן)

Bow, take three steps back, as if taking leave of the Divine Presence, then bow, first left, then right, then center, while saying:

עֹשֶׂה שָׁלוֹם בִּמְרוֹמָיו
הוּא יַעֲשֶׂה שָׁלוֹם עָלֵינוּ וְעַל כָּל יִשְׂרָאֵל
וְאִמְרוּ אָמֵן. (קהל: אָמֵן)

On שמחת תורה *continue with the* הקפות *on page 93.*

KIDDUSH IN THE SYNAGOGUE

On Sukkot and Shemini Atzeret (outside Israel) Kiddush is recited in the Sukka.
The Leader raises a cup of wine and says:

Please pay attention, my masters.

בָּרוּךְ Blessed are You, Lord our God, King of the Universe,
who creates the fruit of the vine.

On Shabbat, add the words in parentheses.

בָּרוּךְ Blessed are You, Lord our God, King of the Universe, who has chosen us from among all peoples, raised us above all tongues, and made us holy through His commandments. You have given us, Lord our God, in love (Sabbaths for rest), festivals for rejoicing, holy days and seasons for joy, (this Sabbath day and) this day of:

On Sukkot: the festival of Sukkot, our time of rejoicing
On Shemini Atzeret & Simḥat Torah: the festival of the eighth day, Shemini Atzeret, our time of rejoicing

(with love), a holy assembly in memory of the exodus from Egypt. For You have chosen us and sanctified us above all peoples, and given us as our heritage (Your holy Sabbath in love and favor and) Your holy festivals for joy and gladness. Blessed are you, Lord, who sanctifies (the Sabbath,) Israel and the festivals.

On Motza'ei Shabbat, the following Havdala is added:

בָּרוּךְ Blessed are You, Lord our God, King of the Universe,
who creates the lights of fire.

Blessed are You, Lord our God, King of the Universe, who distinguishes between sacred and secular, between light and darkness, between Israel and the nations, between the seventh day and the six days of work. You have made a distinction between the holiness of the Sabbath and the holiness of festivals, and have sanctified the seventh day above the six days of work. You have distinguished and sanctified Your people Israel with Your holiness. Blessed are You, Lord, who distinguishes between sacred and sacred.

בָּרוּךְ Blessed are You, Lord our God, King of the Universe,
who has given us life, sustained us, and brought us to this time.

On Sukkot and Shemini Atzeret (outside Israel) add.

בָּרוּךְ Blessed are You, Lord our God, King of the Universe,
who has made us holy through His commandments
and has commanded us to dwell in the sukka.

The wine should be drunk by children under the age of Bar/Bat Mitzva or, if there are none, by the Leader.

קידוש בבית הכנסת

On סוכות *and* שמיני עצרת *(outside* ארץ ישראל*)* קידוש *is recited in the* סוכה.
The שליח ציבור *raises a cup of wine and says:*

סַבְרִי מָרָנָן

בָּרוּךְ אַתָּה יהוה אֱלֹהֵינוּ מֶלֶךְ הָעוֹלָם בּוֹרֵא פְּרִי הַגָּפֶן.

On שבת*, add the words in parentheses.*

בָּרוּךְ אַתָּה יהוה אֱלֹהֵינוּ מֶלֶךְ הָעוֹלָם, אֲשֶׁר בָּחַר בָּנוּ מִכָּל עָם, וְרוֹמְמָנוּ מִכָּל לָשׁוֹן, וְקִדְּשָׁנוּ בְּמִצְוֹתָיו, וַתִּתֶּן לָנוּ יהוה אֱלֹהֵינוּ בְּאַהֲבָה, (שַׁבָּתוֹת לִמְנוּחָה וּ) מוֹעֲדִים לְשִׂמְחָה, חַגִּים וּזְמַנִּים לְשָׂשׂוֹן, אֶת יוֹם (הַשַּׁבָּת הַזֶּה וְאֶת יוֹם)

בסוכות: חַג הַסֻּכּוֹת הַזֶּה, זְמַן שִׂמְחָתֵנוּ

בשמע״צ ובש״ת: הַשְּׁמִינִי חַג הָעֲצֶרֶת הַזֶּה, זְמַן שִׂמְחָתֵנוּ

(בְּאַהֲבָה) מִקְרָא קֹדֶשׁ, זֵכֶר לִיצִיאַת מִצְרָיִם. כִּי בָנוּ בָחַרְתָּ וְאוֹתָנוּ קִדַּשְׁתָּ מִכָּל הָעַמִּים (וְשַׁבָּת) וּמוֹעֲדֵי קָדְשֶׁךָ (בְּאַהֲבָה וּבְרָצוֹן) בְּשִׂמְחָה וּבְשָׂשׂוֹן הִנְחַלְתָּנוּ. בָּרוּךְ אַתָּה יהוה, מְקַדֵּשׁ (הַשַּׁבָּת וְ) יִשְׂרָאֵל וְהַזְּמַנִּים.

On מוצאי שבת*, the following* הבדלה *is added:*

בָּרוּךְ אַתָּה יהוה אֱלֹהֵינוּ מֶלֶךְ הָעוֹלָם, בּוֹרֵא מְאוֹרֵי הָאֵשׁ.

בָּרוּךְ אַתָּה יהוה אֱלֹהֵינוּ מֶלֶךְ הָעוֹלָם, הַמַּבְדִּיל בֵּין קֹדֶשׁ לְחֹל, בֵּין אוֹר לְחֹשֶׁךְ, בֵּין יִשְׂרָאֵל לָעַמִּים, בֵּין יוֹם הַשְּׁבִיעִי לְשֵׁשֶׁת יְמֵי הַמַּעֲשֶׂה. בֵּין קְדֻשַּׁת שַׁבָּת לִקְדֻשַּׁת יוֹם טוֹב הִבְדַּלְתָּ, וְאֶת יוֹם הַשְּׁבִיעִי מִשֵּׁשֶׁת יְמֵי הַמַּעֲשֶׂה קִדַּשְׁתָּ, הִבְדַּלְתָּ וְקִדַּשְׁתָּ אֶת עַמְּךָ יִשְׂרָאֵל בִּקְדֻשָּׁתֶךָ. בָּרוּךְ אַתָּה יהוה, הַמַּבְדִּיל בֵּין קֹדֶשׁ לְקֹדֶשׁ.

בָּרוּךְ אַתָּה יהוה אֱלֹהֵינוּ מֶלֶךְ הָעוֹלָם
שֶׁהֶחֱיָנוּ וְקִיְּמָנוּ וְהִגִּיעָנוּ לַזְּמַן הַזֶּה.

On סוכות *and* שמיני עצרת *(outside* ארץ ישראל*) add:*

בָּרוּךְ אַתָּה יהוה אֱלֹהֵינוּ מֶלֶךְ הָעוֹלָם
אֲשֶׁר קִדְּשָׁנוּ בְּמִצְוֹתָיו וְצִוָּנוּ לֵישֵׁב בַּסֻּכָּה.

The wine should be drunk by children under the age of בר מצווה *or* בת מצווה*, or, if there are none, by the* שליח ציבור.

Stand while saying Aleinu. Bow at ▾.

עָלֵינוּ It is our duty to praise the Master of all,
and ascribe greatness to the Author of creation,
who has not made us like the nations of the lands
nor placed us like the families of the earth;
who has not made our portion like theirs,
nor our destiny like all their multitudes.
(For they worship vanity and emptiness,
and pray to a god who cannot save.)
▾But we bow in worship
and thank the Supreme King of kings, the Holy One, blessed be He,
who extends the heavens and establishes the earth,
whose throne of glory is in the heavens above,
and whose power's Presence is in the highest of heights.
He is our God; there is no other.
Truly He is our King, there is none else,
as it is written in His Torah:
"You shall know and take to heart this day *Deut. 4*
that the LORD is God, in heaven above and on earth below.
There is no other."

Therefore, we place our hope in You, LORD our God,
that we may soon see the glory of Your power,
when You will remove abominations from the earth,
and idols will be utterly destroyed,
when the world will be perfected under the sovereignty of the Almighty,
when all humanity will call on Your name,
to turn all the earth's wicked toward You.
All the world's inhabitants will realize and know
that to You every knee must bow and every tongue swear loyalty.
Before You, LORD our God, they will kneel and bow down
and give honor to Your glorious name.
They will all accept the yoke of Your kingdom,
and You will reign over them soon and for ever.
For the kingdom is Yours, and to all eternity You will reign in glory,
as it is written in Your Torah: "The LORD will reign for ever and ever." *Ex. 15*

Stand while saying עָלֵינוּ. *Bow at* ׳.

עָלֵינוּ לְשַׁבֵּחַ לַאֲדוֹן הַכֹּל, לָתֵת גְּדֻלָּה לְיוֹצֵר בְּרֵאשִׁית
שֶׁלֹּא עָשָׂנוּ כְּגוֹיֵי הָאֲרָצוֹת, וְלֹא שָׂמָנוּ כְּמִשְׁפְּחוֹת הָאֲדָמָה
שֶׁלֹּא שָׂם חֶלְקֵנוּ כָּהֶם וְגוֹרָלֵנוּ כְּכָל הֲמוֹנָם.
(שֶׁהֵם מִשְׁתַּחֲוִים לְהֶבֶל וָרִיק וּמִתְפַּלְלִים אֶל אֵל לֹא יוֹשִׁיעַ.)
׳וַאֲנַחְנוּ כּוֹרְעִים וּמִשְׁתַּחֲוִים וּמוֹדִים
לִפְנֵי מֶלֶךְ מַלְכֵי הַמְּלָכִים, הַקָּדוֹשׁ בָּרוּךְ הוּא
שֶׁהוּא נוֹטֶה שָׁמַיִם וְיוֹסֵד אָרֶץ, וּמוֹשַׁב יְקָרוֹ בַּשָּׁמַיִם מִמַּעַל
וּשְׁכִינַת עֻזּוֹ בְּגָבְהֵי מְרוֹמִים.
הוּא אֱלֹהֵינוּ, אֵין עוֹד.
אֱמֶת מַלְכֵּנוּ, אֶפֶס זוּלָתוֹ
כַּכָּתוּב בְּתוֹרָתוֹ, וְיָדַעְתָּ הַיּוֹם וַהֲשֵׁבֹתָ אֶל־לְבָבֶךָ דברים ד
כִּי יהוה הוּא הָאֱלֹהִים בַּשָּׁמַיִם מִמַּעַל וְעַל־הָאָרֶץ מִתָּחַת
אֵין עוֹד:

עַל כֵּן נְקַוֶּה לְּךָ יהוה אֱלֹהֵינוּ, לִרְאוֹת מְהֵרָה בְּתִפְאֶרֶת עֻזֶּךָ
לְהַעֲבִיר גִּלּוּלִים מִן הָאָרֶץ, וְהָאֱלִילִים כָּרוֹת יִכָּרֵתוּן
לְתַקֵּן עוֹלָם בְּמַלְכוּת שַׁדַּי.
וְכָל בְּנֵי בָשָׂר יִקְרְאוּ בִשְׁמֶךָ לְהַפְנוֹת אֵלֶיךָ כָּל רִשְׁעֵי אָרֶץ.
יַכִּירוּ וְיֵדְעוּ כָּל יוֹשְׁבֵי תֵבֵל
כִּי לְךָ תִּכְרַע כָּל בֶּרֶךְ, תִּשָּׁבַע כָּל לָשׁוֹן.
לְפָנֶיךָ יהוה אֱלֹהֵינוּ יִכְרְעוּ וְיִפֹּלוּ, וְלִכְבוֹד שִׁמְךָ יְקָר יִתֵּנוּ
וִיקַבְּלוּ כֻלָּם אֶת עֹל מַלְכוּתֶךָ
וְתִמְלֹךְ עֲלֵיהֶם מְהֵרָה לְעוֹלָם וָעֶד.
כִּי הַמַּלְכוּת שֶׁלְּךָ הִיא וּלְעוֹלְמֵי עַד תִּמְלֹךְ בְּכָבוֹד
כַּכָּתוּב בְּתוֹרָתֶךָ, יהוה יִמְלֹךְ לְעֹלָם וָעֶד: שמות טו

▸ And it is said: "Then the LORD shall be King over all the earth; on that day the LORD shall be One and His name One." *Zech. 14*

Some add:

Have no fear of sudden terror or of the ruin when it overtakes the wicked. *Prov. 3*
Devise your strategy, but it will be thwarted; *Is. 8*
propose your plan, but it will not stand, for God is with us.
When you grow old, I will still be the same. *Is. 46*
When your hair turns gray, I will still carry you.
I made you, I will bear you, I will carry you, and I will rescue you.

MOURNER'S KADDISH

The following prayer, said by mourners, requires the presence of a minyan. A transliteration can be found on page 1467.

Mourner: יִתְגַּדַּל Magnified and sanctified
may His great name be,
in the world He created by His will.
May He establish His kingdom
in your lifetime and in your days,
and in the lifetime of all the house of Israel,
swiftly and soon – and say: Amen.

All: May His great name be blessed for ever and all time.

Mourner: Blessed and praised, glorified and exalted,
raised and honored,
uplifted and lauded
be the name of the Holy One,
blessed be He,
beyond any blessing,
song, praise and consolation
uttered in the world – and say: Amen.

May there be great peace from heaven,
and life for us and all Israel – and say: Amen.

Bow, take three steps back, as if taking leave of the Divine Presence, then bow, first left, then right, then center, while saying:

May He who makes peace in His high places,
make peace for us and all Israel – and say: Amen.

▸ וְנֶאֱמַר, וְהָיָה יהוה לְמֶלֶךְ עַל־כָּל־הָאָרֶץ זכריה יד
בַּיּוֹם הַהוּא יִהְיֶה יהוה אֶחָד וּשְׁמוֹ אֶחָד:

Some add:

אַל־תִּירָא מִפַּחַד פִּתְאֹם וּמִשֹּׁאַת רְשָׁעִים כִּי תָבֹא: משלי ג
עֻצוּ עֵצָה וְתֻפָר, דַּבְּרוּ דָבָר וְלֹא יָקוּם, כִּי עִמָּנוּ אֵל: ישעיה ח
וְעַד־זִקְנָה אֲנִי הוּא, וְעַד־שֵׂיבָה אֲנִי אֶסְבֹּל ישעיה מו
אֲנִי עָשִׂיתִי וַאֲנִי אֶשָּׂא וַאֲנִי אֶסְבֹּל וַאֲמַלֵּט:

קדיש יתום

The following prayer, said by mourners, requires the presence of a מנין.
A transliteration can be found on page 1467.

אבל: יִתְגַּדַּל וְיִתְקַדַּשׁ שְׁמֵהּ רַבָּא (קהל: אָמֵן)
בְּעָלְמָא דִּי בְרָא כִרְעוּתֵהּ
וְיַמְלִיךְ מַלְכוּתֵהּ
בְּחַיֵּיכוֹן וּבְיוֹמֵיכוֹן וּבְחַיֵּי דְכָל בֵּית יִשְׂרָאֵל
בַּעֲגָלָא וּבִזְמַן קָרִיב, וְאִמְרוּ אָמֵן. (קהל: אָמֵן)

קהל ואבל: יְהֵא שְׁמֵהּ רַבָּא מְבָרַךְ לְעָלַם וּלְעָלְמֵי עָלְמַיָּא.

אבל: יִתְבָּרַךְ וְיִשְׁתַּבַּח וְיִתְפָּאַר
וְיִתְרוֹמַם וְיִתְנַשֵּׂא וְיִתְהַדָּר וְיִתְעַלֶּה וְיִתְהַלָּל
שְׁמֵהּ דְּקֻדְשָׁא בְּרִיךְ הוּא (קהל: בְּרִיךְ הוּא)
לְעֵלָּא מִן כָּל בִּרְכָתָא וְשִׁירָתָא, תֻּשְׁבְּחָתָא וְנֶחֱמָתָא
דַּאֲמִירָן בְּעָלְמָא, וְאִמְרוּ אָמֵן. (קהל: אָמֵן)

יְהֵא שְׁלָמָא רַבָּא מִן שְׁמַיָּא
וְחַיִּים, עָלֵינוּ וְעַל כָּל יִשְׂרָאֵל, וְאִמְרוּ אָמֵן. (קהל: אָמֵן)

Bow, take three steps back, as if taking leave of the Divine Presence, then bow, first left, then right, then center, while saying:

עֹשֶׂה שָׁלוֹם בִּמְרוֹמָיו
הוּא יַעֲשֶׂה שָׁלוֹם עָלֵינוּ וְעַל כָּל יִשְׂרָאֵל, וְאִמְרוּ אָמֵן. (קהל: אָמֵן)

On the first two nights of Sukkot, and on Shemini Atzeret outside Israel, the following psalm is said:

לְדָוִד A psalm of David. The Lord is my light and my salvation – whom then shall I fear? The Lord is the stronghold of my life – of whom shall I be afraid? When evil men close in on me to devour my flesh, it is they, my enemies and foes, who stumble and fall. Should an army besiege me, my heart would not fear. Should war break out against me, still I would be confident. One thing I ask of the Lord, only this do I seek: to live in the House of the Lord all the days of my life, to gaze on the beauty of the Lord and worship in His Temple. For He will keep me safe in His pavilion on the day of trouble. He will hide me under the cover of His tent. He will set me high upon a rock. Now my head is high above my enemies who surround me. I will sacrifice in His tent with shouts of joy. I will sing and chant praises to the Lord. Lord, hear my voice when I call. Be gracious to me and answer me. On Your behalf my heart says, "Seek My face." Your face, Lord, will I seek. Do not hide Your face from me. Do not turn Your servant away in anger. You have been my help. Do not reject or forsake me, God, my Savior. Were my father and my mother to forsake me, the Lord would take me in. Teach me Your way, Lord, and lead me on a level path, because of my oppressors. Do not abandon me to the will of my foes, for false witnesses have risen against me, breathing violence. ▸ Were it not for my faith that I shall see the Lord's goodness in the land of the living. Hope in the Lord. Be strong and of good courage, and hope in the Lord! Ps. 27

Mourner's Kaddish (on previous page)

כִּי־אָבִי וְאִמִּי עֲזָבוּנִי *Were my father and my mother to forsake me.* Were they to die (Ibn Ezra), or, when I leave home (Radak).

לוּלֵא הֶאֱמַנְתִּי *Were it not for my faith.* some commentators link this to the previous verse – my foes and false witnesses might have prevailed had it not been for my faith.

קַוֵּה אֶל־יהוה *Hope in the Lord.* Judaism is the voice of hope in the conversation of humankind. Because we are not alone, because there is a God, and because He cares, we have hope. The Jewish people kept hope alive, and hope kept the Jewish people alive.

On the first two nights of סוכות, *and on* שמיני עצרת *outside* ארץ ישראל, *the following psalm is said:*

לְדָוִד, יהוה אוֹרִי וְיִשְׁעִי, מִמִּי אִירָא, יהוה מָעוֹז־חַיַּי, מִמִּי אֶפְחָד: תהלים כז
בִּקְרֹב עָלַי מְרֵעִים לֶאֱכֹל אֶת־בְּשָׂרִי, צָרַי וְאֹיְבַי לִי, הֵמָּה כָשְׁלוּ וְנָפָלוּ: אִם־תַּחֲנֶה עָלַי מַחֲנֶה, לֹא־יִירָא לִבִּי, אִם־תָּקוּם עָלַי מִלְחָמָה, בְּזֹאת אֲנִי בוֹטֵחַ: אַחַת שָׁאַלְתִּי מֵאֵת־יהוה, אוֹתָהּ אֲבַקֵּשׁ, שִׁבְתִּי בְּבֵית־יהוה כָּל־יְמֵי חַיַּי, לַחֲזוֹת בְּנֹעַם־יהוה, וּלְבַקֵּר בְּהֵיכָלוֹ: כִּי יִצְפְּנֵנִי בְּסֻכֹּה בְּיוֹם רָעָה, יַסְתִּרֵנִי בְּסֵתֶר אָהֳלוֹ, בְּצוּר יְרוֹמְמֵנִי: וְעַתָּה יָרוּם רֹאשִׁי עַל אֹיְבַי סְבִיבוֹתַי, וְאֶזְבְּחָה בְאָהֳלוֹ זִבְחֵי תְרוּעָה, אָשִׁירָה וַאֲזַמְּרָה לַיהוה: שְׁמַע־יהוה קוֹלִי אֶקְרָא, וְחָנֵּנִי וַעֲנֵנִי: לְךָ אָמַר לִבִּי בַּקְּשׁוּ פָנָי, אֶת־פָּנֶיךָ יהוה אֲבַקֵּשׁ: אַל־תַּסְתֵּר פָּנֶיךָ מִמֶּנִּי, אַל תַּט־בְּאַף עַבְדֶּךָ, עֶזְרָתִי הָיִיתָ, אַל־תִּטְּשֵׁנִי וְאַל־תַּעַזְבֵנִי, אֱלֹהֵי יִשְׁעִי: כִּי־אָבִי וְאִמִּי עֲזָבוּנִי, וַיהוה יַאַסְפֵנִי: הוֹרֵנִי יהוה דַּרְכֶּךָ, וּנְחֵנִי בְּאֹרַח מִישׁוֹר, לְמַעַן שׁוֹרְרָי: אַל־תִּתְּנֵנִי בְּנֶפֶשׁ צָרָי, כִּי קָמוּ־בִי עֵדֵי־שֶׁקֶר, וִיפֵחַ חָמָס: ◂ לוּלֵא הֶאֱמַנְתִּי לִרְאוֹת בְּטוּב־יהוה בְּאֶרֶץ חַיִּים: קַוֵּה אֶל־יהוה, חֲזַק וְיַאֲמֵץ לִבֶּךָ, וְקַוֵּה אֶל־יהוה:

קדיש יתום (*on previous page*)

לְדָוִד *Psalm 27.* A psalm of surpassing beauty, expressing our faith that those who place their trust in God need fear no enemy. This does not mean that life is free of risk, nor that we have no enemies. It means that those for whom God is a living presence in their lives have access to a source of strength greater than themselves; that faith is the antidote to fear. It is said during the month of Elul and up to the end of Sukkot because of an interpretation given by the sages: *The Lord is my Light* on Rosh HaShana, *and my Salvation* on Yom Kippur. *He will keep me safe in His pavilion* [*besukko*] refers to Sukkot (*Matte Ephraim* 581:6).

לְךָ אָמַר לִבִּי *On Your behalf my heart says.* This is the voice of God within the human heart.

The following poems, on this page and the next, both from the Middle Ages, are summary statements of Jewish faith, orienting us to the spiritual contours of the world that we actualize in the mind by the act of prayer.

Lord of the universe,
who reigned before the birth of any thing –

When by His will all things were made
then was His name proclaimed King.

And when all things shall cease to be
He alone will reign in awe.

He was, He is, and He shall be
glorious for evermore.

He is One, there is none else,
alone, unique, beyond compare;

Without beginning, without end,
His might, His rule are everywhere.

He is my God; my Redeemer lives.
He is the Rock on whom I rely –

My banner and my safe retreat,
my cup, my portion when I cry.

Into His hand my soul I place,
when I awake and when I sleep.

The Lord is with me, I shall not fear;
body and soul from harm will He keep.

---

way it moves seamlessly from God, Creator of the universe, beyond time and space, to God who is close and ever-comforting, each day as I sleep and awake.

It thus beautifully crystallizes the central miracle of faith, that God – vaster than the universe, older than time – is nonetheless closer to us than we are to ourselves. The final verse, "Into His hand my soul I place," explains the difference faith makes to life. Reality is not indifferent to our existence. We are here because God wanted us to be. We are surrounded by His love, protected by His care, held in His everlasting arms. Therefore we can live in trust, not fear.

The following poems, on this page and the next, both from the Middle Ages, are summary statements of Jewish faith, orienting us to the spiritual contours of the world that we actualize in the mind by the act of prayer.

אֲדוֹן עוֹלָם

אֲשֶׁר מָלַךְ בְּטֶֽרֶם כָּל־יְצִיר נִבְרָא.
לְעֵת נַעֲשָׂה בְחֶפְצוֹ כֹּל אֲזַי מֶֽלֶךְ שְׁמוֹ נִקְרָא.
וְאַחֲרֵי כִּכְלוֹת הַכֹּל לְבַדּוֹ יִמְלֹךְ נוֹרָא.
וְהוּא הָיָה וְהוּא הֹוֶה וְהוּא יִהְיֶה בְּתִפְאָרָה.
וְהוּא אֶחָד וְאֵין שֵׁנִי לְהַמְשִׁיל לוֹ לְהַחְבִּֽירָה.
בְּלִי רֵאשִׁית בְּלִי תַכְלִית וְלוֹ הָעֹז וְהַמִּשְׂרָה.
וְהוּא אֵלִי וְחַי גּוֹאֲלִי וְצוּר חֶבְלִי בְּעֵת צָרָה.
וְהוּא נִסִּי וּמָנוֹס לִי מְנָת כּוֹסִי בְּיוֹם אֶקְרָא.
בְּיָדוֹ אַפְקִיד רוּחִי בְּעֵת אִישַׁן וְאָעִֽירָה.
וְעִם רוּחִי גְּוִיָּתִי יהוה לִי וְלֹא אִירָא.

אֲדוֹן עוֹלָם *Adon Olam*. One of the simplest and most beautiful hymn-like celebrations of Jewish faith. It has been attributed to several possible authors, among them Rabbi Sherira Gaon and Rabbi Hai Gaon in the tenth century. Most scholars however believe it was written by the poet and philosopher Rabbi Solomon ibn Gabirol (born Malaga, Spain, c.1021; died Valencia, c.1058). Little is known about Ibn Gabirol's life or death, except that he spent several unsettled years wandering from town to town and that he died comparatively young. He was the author of a philosophical work, *Mekor Ḥayyim* (in Latin, *Fons Vitae*) and was one of the first since Philo ten centuries earlier, to synthesize Judaism with Greek philosophy. Apart from the limpid simplicity, what gives *Adon Olam* its power and enduring popularity is the

Most congregations sing Yigdal at this point.

GREAT

is the living God and praised.
He exists, and His existence is beyond time.

He is One, and there is no unity like His.
Unfathomable, His Oneness is infinite.

He has neither bodily form nor substance;
His holiness is beyond compare.

He preceded all that was created.
He was first: there was no beginning to His beginning.

Behold He is Master of the Universe; every creature
shows His greatness and majesty.

The rich flow of His prophecy He gave
to His treasured people in whom He gloried.

Never in Israel has there arisen another like Moses,
a prophet who beheld God's image.

God gave His people a Torah of truth
by the hand of His prophet, most faithful of His House.

God will not alter or change His law
for any other, for eternity.

He sees and knows our secret thoughts;
as soon as something is begun, He foresees its end.

He rewards people with loving-kindness according to their deeds;
He punishes the wicked according to his wickedness.

At the end of days He will send our Messiah,
to redeem those who await His final salvation.

God will revive the dead in His great loving-kindness.
Blessed for evermore is His glorious name!

---

physicality of God; principles 6–9 are about revelation; principles 10–13 are about divine providence, reward and punishment, and end with faith in the messianic age and the end of days when those who have died will live again.

Most congregations sing יִגְדַּל *at this point.*

יִגְדַּל

אֱלֹהִים חַי וְיִשְׁתַּבַּח, נִמְצָא וְאֵין עֵת אֶל מְצִיאוּתוֹ.
אֶחָד וְאֵין יָחִיד כְּיִחוּדוֹ, נֶעְלָם וְגַם אֵין סוֹף לְאַחְדּוּתוֹ.
אֵין לוֹ דְּמוּת הַגּוּף וְאֵינוֹ גוּף, לֹא נַעֲרֹךְ אֵלָיו קְדֻשָּׁתוֹ.
קַדְמוֹן לְכָל דָּבָר אֲשֶׁר נִבְרָא, רִאשׁוֹן וְאֵין רֵאשִׁית לְרֵאשִׁיתוֹ.
הִנּוֹ אֲדוֹן עוֹלָם, וְכָל נוֹצָר יוֹרֶה גְדֻלָּתוֹ וּמַלְכוּתוֹ.
שֶׁפַע נְבוּאָתוֹ נְתָנוֹ אֶל־אַנְשֵׁי סְגֻלָּתוֹ וְתִפְאַרְתּוֹ.
לֹא קָם בְּיִשְׂרָאֵל כְּמֹשֶׁה עוֹד נָבִיא וּמַבִּיט אֶת תְּמוּנָתוֹ.
תּוֹרַת אֱמֶת נָתַן לְעַמּוֹ אֵל עַל יַד נְבִיאוֹ נֶאֱמַן בֵּיתוֹ.
לֹא יַחֲלִיף הָאֵל וְלֹא יָמִיר דָּתוֹ לְעוֹלָמִים לְזוּלָתוֹ.
צוֹפֶה וְיוֹדֵעַ סְתָרֵינוּ, מַבִּיט לְסוֹף דָּבָר בְּקַדְמָתוֹ.
גּוֹמֵל לְאִישׁ חֶסֶד כְּמִפְעָלוֹ, נוֹתֵן לְרָשָׁע רָע כְּרִשְׁעָתוֹ.
יִשְׁלַח לְקֵץ יָמִין מְשִׁיחֵנוּ לִפְדּוֹת מְחַכֵּי קֵץ יְשׁוּעָתוֹ.
מֵתִים יְחַיֶּה אֵל בְּרֹב חַסְדּוֹ, בָּרוּךְ עֲדֵי עַד שֵׁם תְּהִלָּתוֹ.

יִגְדַּל *Yigdal.* A poetic setting of the most famous "creed" in Judaism: Moses Maimonides' Thirteen Principles of Jewish Faith. Faced with a philosophically sophisticated, contemporary Islamic culture, Maimonides felt the need to set out the principles of Jewish faith in a structured way, which he did in his Commentary to the Mishna to *Sanhedrin* 10. So influential was this account that it was summarized, after his death, in both prose and poetry. The prose form, thirteen paragraphs each beginning, "I believe with perfect faith" (אֲנִי מַאֲמִין בֶּאֱמוּנָה שְׁלֵמָה), is printed in most prayer books. The poetic form is *Yigdal.* The first five principles have to do with the unity, eternity, and non-

HAKAFOT

The following is said after Full Kaddish. For commentary on the Hakafot, see *page 1207; for commentary on the Torah Reading, see page 1233.*

אַתָּה הָרְאֵתָ You have been shown [these things] so that you may know that the LORD is God; besides Him there is no other. *Deut. 4*

To the One who alone does great wonders, His loving-kindness is forever. *Ps. 136*

There is none like You among the heavenly powers, my LORD, and there are no works like Yours. *Ps. 86*

May the LORD's glory be forever; may the LORD rejoice in His works. *Ps. 104*

May the LORD's name be blessed from now and forever. *Ps. 113*

May the LORD our God be with us as He was with our ancestors; may He never leave us or forsake us. *I Kings 8*

Say, "Save us, God our Savior; gather and deliver us from the nations, that we may give thanks to Your holy name, that we may glory in Your praise." *I Chr. 16*

The LORD is King, the LORD was King, the LORD will be King for ever and all time.

The LORD will give strength to His people; the LORD will bless His people with peace. *Ps. 29*

May our words find favor before the LORD of all.

The Ark is opened.

Whenever the Ark set out, Moses would say, "Arise, LORD, and may Your enemies be scattered; may those who hate You flee before You." *Num. 10*

Advance, LORD, to Your resting place, You and Your mighty Ark. *Ps. 132*

Your priests are clothed in righteousness, and Your devoted ones sing for joy.

For the sake of Your servant David, do not reject Your anointed one.

In that day they will say, "This is our God; we trusted in Him, and He saved us. This is the LORD, we trusted in Him; let us rejoice and be glad in His salvation." *Is. 25*

Your kingdom is an eternal kingdom, and Your dominion is for all generations. *Ps. 145*

For the Torah shall come forth from Zion and the word of the LORD from Jerusalem. *Is. 2*

סדר הקפות

The following is said after קדיש שלם*. For commentary on the* הקפות*, see* *page 1207**; for commentary on* קריאת התורה*, see* *page 1233**.*

אַתָּה הָרְאֵתָ לָדַעַת, כִּי יהוה הוּא הָאֱלֹהִים, אֵין עוֹד מִלְּבַדּוֹ: דברים ד
לְעֹשֵׂה נִפְלָאוֹת גְּדֹלוֹת לְבַדּוֹ, כִּי לְעוֹלָם חַסְדּוֹ: תהלים קלו
אֵין־כָּמְוֹךָ בָאֱלֹהִים, אֲדֹנָי, וְאֵין כְּמַעֲשֶׂיךָ: תהלים פו
יְהִי כְבוֹד יהוה לְעוֹלָם, יִשְׂמַח יהוה בְּמַעֲשָׂיו: תהלים קד
יְהִי שֵׁם יהוה מְבֹרָךְ, מֵעַתָּה וְעַד־עוֹלָם: תהלים קיג
יְהִי יהוה אֱלֹהֵינוּ עִמָּנוּ, כַּאֲשֶׁר הָיָה עִם־אֲבֹתֵינוּ מלכים א׳ ח
אַל־יַעַזְבֵנוּ וְאַל־יִטְּשֵׁנוּ:
וְאִמְרוּ, הוֹשִׁיעֵנוּ אֱלֹהֵי יִשְׁעֵנוּ, וְקַבְּצֵנוּ וְהַצִּילֵנוּ מִן־הַגּוֹיִם דברי הימים א׳ טז
לְהֹדוֹת לְשֵׁם קָדְשֶׁךָ, לְהִשְׁתַּבֵּחַ בִּתְהִלָּתֶךָ:
יהוה מֶלֶךְ, יהוה מָלָךְ, יהוה יִמְלֹךְ לְעֹלָם וָעֶד.
יהוה עֹז לְעַמּוֹ יִתֵּן, יהוה יְבָרֵךְ אֶת־עַמּוֹ בַשָּׁלוֹם: תהלים כט
וְיִהְיוּ נָא אֲמָרֵינוּ לְרָצוֹן, לִפְנֵי אֲדוֹן כֹּל.

The ארון קודש *is opened.*

וַיְהִי בִּנְסֹעַ הָאָרֹן וַיֹּאמֶר מֹשֶׁה במדבר י
קוּמָה יהוה וְיָפֻצוּ אֹיְבֶיךָ, וְיָנֻסוּ מְשַׂנְאֶיךָ מִפָּנֶיךָ:
קוּמָה יהוה לִמְנוּחָתֶךָ, אַתָּה וַאֲרוֹן עֻזֶּךָ: תהלים קלב
כֹּהֲנֶיךָ יִלְבְּשׁוּ־צֶדֶק, וַחֲסִידֶיךָ יְרַנֵּנוּ:
בַּעֲבוּר דָּוִד עַבְדֶּךָ, אַל־תָּשֵׁב פְּנֵי מְשִׁיחֶךָ:

וְאָמַר בַּיּוֹם הַהוּא, הִנֵּה אֱלֹהֵינוּ זֶה קִוִּינוּ לוֹ, וְיוֹשִׁיעֵנוּ ישעיה כה
זֶה יהוה קִוִּינוּ לוֹ, נָגִילָה וְנִשְׂמְחָה בִּישׁוּעָתוֹ:
מַלְכוּתְךָ מַלְכוּת כָּל־עֹלָמִים, וּמֶמְשַׁלְתְּךָ בְּכָל־דּוֹר וָדֹר: תהלים קמה
כִּי מִצִּיּוֹן תֵּצֵא תוֹרָה, וּדְבַר־יהוה מִירוּשָׁלָםִ: ישעיה ב

Father of compassion, favor Zion with Your goodness; *Ps. 51*
rebuild the walls of Jerusalem.
For we trust in You alone, King, God, high and exalted, Master of worlds.

All the Torah scrolls are taken from the Ark.

First Hakafa

Lord, please save us. *Ps. 118*
Lord, please grant us success.
Lord, please answer us on the day we cry.

God of spirits, please save us.
Searcher of hearts, please grant us success.
Mighty Redeemer, answer us on the day we cry.

Some add: The Lord's Torah is perfect, refreshing the soul. *Ps. 19*
A psalm of David. Render to the Lord, you angelic powers, *Ps. 29*
render to the Lord glory and might.
Render to the Lord the glory due to His name.
Bow to the Lord in the beauty of holiness.
The Lord's voice echoes over the waters;
the God of glory thunders; the Lord is over the mighty waters.
For the conductor of music. With stringed instruments. *Ps. 67*
A psalm, a song.
May God be gracious to us and bless us.
May He make His face shine upon us, Selah.
Please, by the power of Your great right hand,
set the captive nation free.
For I said, the world is built by loving-kindness. *Ps. 89*

Second Hakafa

Speaker of righteousness, please save us.
Robed in majesty, please grant us success.
Ancient and loving One, answer us on the day we cry.

Some add: The Lord's testimony is faithful, making the simple wise. *Ps. 19*
The Lord's voice in power. *Ps. 29*
Then will Your name be known on earth, *Ps. 67*
Your salvation among the nations.
Accept Your people's prayer.
Strengthen us, purify us, You who are revered.
A strong arm is Yours, might is Yours; *Ps. 89*
Your hand holds its power, Your right hand raised.

אַב הָרַחֲמִים, הֵיטִיבָה בִרְצוֹנְךָ אֶת־צִיּוֹן, תִּבְנֶה חוֹמוֹת יְרוּשָׁלָםִ: תהלים נא
כִּי בְךָ לְבַד בָּטָחְנוּ, מֶלֶךְ אֵל רָם וְנִשָּׂא, אֲדוֹן עוֹלָמִים.

All the ספרי תורה *are taken from the* ארון קודש.

First הקפה

אָנָּא יהוה הוֹשִׁיעָה נָּא, אָנָּא יהוה הַצְלִיחָה נָא: תהלים קיח
אָנָּא יהוה עֲנֵנוּ בְיוֹם קָרְאֵנוּ.
אֱלֹהֵי הָרוּחוֹת הוֹשִׁיעָה נָּא, בּוֹחֵן לְבָבוֹת הַצְלִיחָה נָא
גּוֹאֵל חָזָק עֲנֵנוּ בְיוֹם קָרְאֵנוּ.

Some add תּוֹרַת יהוה תְּמִימָה, מְשִׁיבַת נָפֶשׁ תהלים יט
מִזְמוֹר לְדָוִד תהלים כט
הָבוּ לַיהוה בְּנֵי אֵלִים, הָבוּ לַיהוה כָּבוֹד וָעֹז:
הָבוּ לַיהוה כְּבוֹד שְׁמוֹ, הִשְׁתַּחֲווּ לַיהוה בְּהַדְרַת־קֹדֶשׁ:
קוֹל יהוה עַל־הַמָּיִם, אֵל־הַכָּבוֹד הִרְעִים
יהוה עַל־מַיִם רַבִּים:
לַמְנַצֵּחַ בִּנְגִינֹת, מִזְמוֹר שִׁיר: תהלים סז
אֱלֹהִים יְחָנֵּנוּ וִיבָרְכֵנוּ, יָאֵר פָּנָיו אִתָּנוּ סֶלָה:
אָנָּא, בְּכֹחַ גְּדֻלַּת יְמִינְךָ, תַּתִּיר צְרוּרָה.
כִּי־אָמַרְתִּי עוֹלָם חֶסֶד יִבָּנֶה: תהלים פט

Second הקפה

דּוֹבֵר צְדָקוֹת הוֹשִׁיעָה נָּא, הָדוּר בִּלְבוּשׁוֹ הַצְלִיחָה נָא
וָתִיק וְחָסִיד עֲנֵנוּ בְיוֹם קָרְאֵנוּ.

Some add עֵדוּת יהוה נֶאֱמָנָה, מַחְכִּימַת פֶּתִי: תהלים יט
קוֹל־יהוה בַּכֹּחַ תהלים כט
לָדַעַת בָּאָרֶץ דַּרְכֶּךָ, בְּכָל־גּוֹיִם יְשׁוּעָתֶךָ: תהלים סז
קַבֵּל רִנַּת עַמְּךָ, שַׂגְּבֵנוּ, טַהֲרֵנוּ, נוֹרָא.
לְךָ זְרוֹעַ עִם־גְּבוּרָה, תָּעֹז יָדְךָ תָּרוּם יְמִינֶךָ: תהלים פט

Third Hakafa

Pure and right, please save us.
Gracious and compassionate, please grant us success.
He who is good and does good, answer us on the day we cry.

Some add: The LORD's precepts are just, gladdening the heart. *Ps. 19*
The LORD's voice in beauty. *Ps. 29*
Let the peoples praise You, God; let all peoples praise You. *Ps. 67*
Please, Mighty One, guard like the pupil of the eye
those who seek Your unity.
Grant truth to Jacob, loving-kindness to Abraham. *Mic. 7*

Fourth Hakafa

He who knows thoughts, please save us.
Mighty and resplendent, please grant us success.
Robed in righteousness, answer us on the day we cry.

Some add: The LORD's commandment is radiant, giving light to the eyes. *Ps. 19*
The LORD's voice breaks cedars, *Ps. 29*
the LORD shatters the cedars of Lebanon.
He makes Lebanon skip like a calf, Sirion like a young ox.
Let the nations rejoice and sing for joy, *Ps. 67*
for You judge the peoples with equity,
and guide the nations of the earth, Selah!
Bless them, cleanse them,
grant them the compassion of Your righteousness always.
Goodness is to be found at Your right hand always. *Ps. 16*

אֵין אַדִּיר There is none so majestic as the LORD,
and none so blessed as the son of Amram;
there is no greatness like the Torah,
and none to learn it out like Israel.

Of God's mouth, of God's mouth, shall Israel be blessed.

There is none so glorious as the LORD,
and none so venerable as the son of Amram;
there is none so worthy as the Torah,
nor any who delight in it like Israel.

Of God's mouth, of God's mouth, shall Israel be blessed.

Third הקפה

זַךְ וְיָשָׁר הוֹשִׁיעָה נָּא
חַנּוּן וְרַחוּם הַצְלִיחָה נָא
טוֹב וּמֵטִיב עֲנֵנוּ בְיוֹם קָרְאֵנוּ.

Some add פִּקּוּדֵי יהוה יְשָׁרִים, מְשַׂמְּחֵי־לֵב — תהלים יט
קוֹל יהוה בֶּהָדָר: — תהלים כט
יוֹדוּךָ עַמִּים אֱלֹהִים, יוֹדוּךָ עַמִּים כֻּלָּם: — תהלים סז
נָא גִבּוֹר, דּוֹרְשֵׁי יִחוּדְךָ כְּבָבַת שָׁמְרֵם.
תִּתֵּן אֱמֶת לְיַעֲקֹב, חֶסֶד לְאַבְרָהָם: — מיכה ז

Fourth הקפה

יוֹדֵעַ מַחֲשָׁבוֹת הוֹשִׁיעָה נָּא
כַּבִּיר כֹּחַ הַצְלִיחָה נָא
לוֹבֵשׁ צְדָקוֹת עֲנֵנוּ בְיוֹם קָרְאֵנוּ.

Some add מִצְוַת יהוה בָּרָה, מְאִירַת עֵינָיִם: — תהלים יט
קוֹל יהוה שֹׁבֵר אֲרָזִים, וַיְשַׁבֵּר יהוה אֶת־אַרְזֵי הַלְּבָנוֹן: — תהלים כט
וַיַּרְקִידֵם כְּמוֹ־עֵגֶל, לְבָנוֹן וְשִׂרְיוֹן כְּמוֹ בֶן־רְאֵמִים:
יִשְׂמְחוּ וִירַנְּנוּ לְאֻמִּים, כִּי־תִשְׁפֹּט עַמִּים מִישֹׁר — תהלים סז
וּלְאֻמִּים בָּאָרֶץ תַּנְחֵם סֶלָה:
בָּרְכֵם, טַהֲרֵם, רַחֲמֵי צִדְקָתְךָ תָּמִיד גָּמְלֵם.
נְעִמוֹת בִּימִינְךָ נֶצַח: — תהלים טז

אֵין אַדִּיר כַּיהוה   וְאֵין בָּרוּךְ כְּבֶן עַמְרָם
אֵין גְּדוֹלָה כַּתּוֹרָה   וְאֵין דּוֹרְשָׁהּ כְּיִשְׂרָאֵל
מִפִּי אֵל מִפִּי אֵל, יִתְבָּרַךְ יִשְׂרָאֵל

אֵין הָדוּר כַּיהוה   וְאֵין וָתִיק כְּבֶן עַמְרָם
אֵין זַכָּאָה כַּתּוֹרָה   וְאֵין חוֹמְדָהּ כְּיִשְׂרָאֵל
מִפִּי אֵל מִפִּי אֵל, יִתְבָּרַךְ יִשְׂרָאֵל

There is none so pure as the LORD,
and none so upright as the son of Amram;
there is none so honored as the Torah,
and none who learn it quite like Israel.
Of God's mouth, of God's mouth, shall Israel be blessed.

There is no king like the LORD,
and no prophet like the son of Amram;
nothing is supported like the Torah,
and no one helps it like Israel.
Of God's mouth, of God's mouth, shall Israel be blessed.

There is no savior like the LORD,
and none so righteous as the son of Amram;
there is none so holy as the Torah,
and none who give voice to it like Israel.
Of God's mouth, of God's mouth, shall Israel be blessed.

There is no guardian like the LORD,
and none so whole as the son of Amram;
there is nothing so perfect as the Torah,
and none to support it quite like Israel.
Of God's mouth, of God's mouth, shall Israel be blessed.

Fifth Hakafa

Eternal King, please save us.
Resplendent and mighty, please grant us success.
Supporter and Helper, answer us on the day we cry.

Some add: The fear of the LORD is pure, enduring for ever. *Ps. 19*
The LORD's voice cleaves flames of fire. *Ps. 29*
Let the peoples praise You, God; let all peoples praise You. *Ps. 67*
Mighty One, Holy One,
in Your great goodness guide Your congregation.
LORD our Master, how glorious is Your name throughout the earth, *Ps. 8*
setting Your splendor over the heavens.

אֵין טָהוֹר כַּיהוה וְאֵין יָשָׁר כְּבֶן עַמְרָם
אֵין כְּבוּדָּה כַּתּוֹרָה וְאֵין לוֹמְדָה כְּיִשְׂרָאֵל
מִפִּי אֵל מִפִּי אֵל, יִתְבָּרַךְ יִשְׂרָאֵל

אֵין מֶלֶךְ כַּיהוה וְאֵין נָבִיא כְּבֶן עַמְרָם
אֵין סְמוּכָה כַּתּוֹרָה וְאֵין עוֹזְרָהּ כְּיִשְׂרָאֵל
מִפִּי אֵל מִפִּי אֵל, יִתְבָּרַךְ יִשְׂרָאֵל

אֵין פּוֹדֶה כַּיהוה וְאֵין צַדִּיק כְּבֶן עַמְרָם
אֵין קְדוֹשָׁה כַּתּוֹרָה וְאֵין רוֹחֲשָׁהּ כְּיִשְׂרָאֵל
מִפִּי אֵל מִפִּי אֵל, יִתְבָּרַךְ יִשְׂרָאֵל

אֵין שׁוֹמֵר כַּיהוה וְאֵין שָׁלֵם כְּבֶן עַמְרָם
אֵין תְּמִימָה כַּתּוֹרָה וְאֵין תּוֹמְכָהּ כְּיִשְׂרָאֵל
מִפִּי אֵל מִפִּי אֵל, יִתְבָּרַךְ יִשְׂרָאֵל

Fifth הקפה

מֶלֶךְ עוֹלָמִים הוֹשִׁיעָה נָּא
נָאוֹר וְאַדִּיר הַצְלִיחָה נָא
סוֹמֵךְ וְסוֹעֵד עֲנֵנוּ בְּיוֹם קָרְאֵנוּ.

Some add יִרְאַת יהוה טְהוֹרָה, עוֹמֶדֶת לָעַד תהלים יט
קוֹל־יהוה חֹצֵב לַהֲבוֹת אֵשׁ: תהלים כט
יוֹדוּךָ עַמִּים אֱלֹהִים, יוֹדוּךָ עַמִּים כֻּלָּם: תהלים סז
חֲסִין קָדוֹשׁ, בְּרֹב טוּבְךָ נַהֵל עֲדָתֶךָ.
יהוה אֲדֹנֵינוּ מָה־אַדִּיר שִׁמְךָ בְּכָל־הָאָרֶץ תהלים ח
אֲשֶׁר־תְּנָה הוֹדְךָ עַל־הַשָּׁמָיִם:

Sixth Hakafa

Helper of the poor, please save us.
Redeemer and Rescuer, please grant us success.
Eternal Rock, answer us on the day we cry.

Some add: The LORD's judgments are true, altogether righteous. *Ps. 19*
The LORD's voice makes the desert quake, *Ps. 29*
the LORD shakes the desert of Kadesh.
The earth has yielded its harvest. May God, our God, bless us. *Ps. 67*
Only One, Exalted One,
turn to Your people, who proclaim Your holiness.
The LORD is righteous in all His ways, and kind in all He does. *Ps. 145*

Seventh Hakafa

Holy and awesome, please save us.
Compassionate and gracious, please grant us success.
Dweller in the heavens, answer us on the day we cry.
Supporter of the innocent, please save us.
Eternally powerful, please grant us success.
Perfect in His deeds, answer us on the day we cry.

Some add: More precious than gold, than much fine gold. *Ps. 19*
They are sweeter than honey, than honey from the comb.
The LORD's voice makes hinds calve and strips the forests bare, *Ps. 29*
and in His Temple all say: "Glory!"
The LORD sat enthroned at the Flood;
the LORD sits enthroned as King forever.
The LORD will give strength to His people;
the LORD will bless His people with peace.
God will bless us, and all the ends of the earth will fear Him. *Ps. 67*
Accept our plea and heed our cry, You who know all secret thoughts.
Yours, LORD, are the greatness and the power, *I Chr. 29*
the glory, majesty and splendor,
for everything in heaven and earth is Yours.
Yours, LORD, is the kingdom; You are exalted as Head over all.
Then the LORD shall be King over all the earth; *Zech. 14*
on that day the LORD shall be One and His name One.
And in Your Torah it is written:
Listen, Israel: the LORD is our God, the LORD is One. *Deut. 6*
Blessed be the name of His glorious kingdom for ever and all time.

הקפה *Sixth*

עוֹזֵר דַּלִּים הוֹשִׁיעָה נָא, פּוֹדֶה וּמַצִּיל הַצְלִיחָה נָא
צוּר עוֹלָמִים עֲנֵנוּ בְיוֹם קָרְאֵנוּ.

Some add מִשְׁפְּטֵי־יהוה אֱמֶת, צָדְקוּ יַחְדָּו: תהלים יט
קוֹל יהוה יָחִיל מִדְבָּר, יָחִיל יהוה מִדְבַּר קָדֵשׁ: תהלים כט
אֶרֶץ נָתְנָה יְבוּלָהּ, יְבָרְכֵנוּ אֱלֹהִים אֱלֹהֵינוּ: תהלים סז
יָחִיד גֵּאֶה, לְעַמְּךָ פְנֵה, זוֹכְרֵי קְדֻשָּׁתֶךָ.
צַדִּיק יהוה בְּכָל־דְּרָכָיו, וְחָסִיד בְּכָל־מַעֲשָׂיו: תהלים קמה

הקפה *Seventh*

קָדוֹשׁ וְנוֹרָא הוֹשִׁיעָה נָא, רַחוּם וְחַנּוּן הַצְלִיחָה נָא
שׁוֹכֵן שְׁחָקִים עֲנֵנוּ בְיוֹם קָרְאֵנוּ.
תּוֹמֵךְ תְּמִימִים הוֹשִׁיעָה נָא, תַּקִּיף לָעַד הַצְלִיחָה נָא
תָּמִים בְּמַעֲשָׂיו עֲנֵנוּ בְיוֹם קָרְאֵנוּ.

Some add הַנֶּחֱמָדִים מִזָּהָב וּמִפַּז רָב, וּמְתוּקִים מִדְּבַשׁ וְנֹפֶת צוּפִים: תהלים יט
קוֹל יהוה יְחוֹלֵל אַיָּלוֹת וַיֶּחֱשֹׂף יְעָרוֹת, וּבְהֵיכָלוֹ, כֻּלּוֹ אֹמֵר כָּבוֹד: תהלים כט
יהוה לַמַּבּוּל יָשָׁב, וַיֵּשֶׁב יהוה מֶלֶךְ לְעוֹלָם:
יהוה עֹז לְעַמּוֹ יִתֵּן, יהוה יְבָרֵךְ אֶת־עַמּוֹ בַשָּׁלוֹם:
יְבָרְכֵנוּ אֱלֹהִים, וְיִירְאוּ אוֹתוֹ כָּל־אַפְסֵי־אָרֶץ: תהלים סז
שַׁוְעָתֵנוּ קַבֵּל וּשְׁמַע צַעֲקָתֵנוּ, יוֹדֵעַ תַּעֲלוּמוֹת.
לְךָ יהוה הַגְּדֻלָּה וְהַגְּבוּרָה וְהַתִּפְאֶרֶת וְהַנֵּצַח וְהַהוֹד דברי הימים א׳ כט
כִּי־כֹל בַּשָּׁמַיִם וּבָאָרֶץ
לְךָ יהוה הַמַּמְלָכָה וְהַמִּתְנַשֵּׂא לְכֹל לְרֹאשׁ:
וְהָיָה יהוה לְמֶלֶךְ עַל־כָּל־הָאָרֶץ זכריה יד
בַּיּוֹם הַהוּא יִהְיֶה יהוה אֶחָד וּשְׁמוֹ אֶחָד:
וּבְתוֹרָתְךָ כָּתוּב לֵאמֹר
שְׁמַע יִשְׂרָאֵל, יהוה אֱלֹהֵינוּ יהוה אֶחָד: דברים ו
בָּרוּךְ שֵׁם כְּבוֹד מַלְכוּתוֹ לְעוֹלָם וָעֶד.

יָבוֹא Majestic One, come quickly, / come, chosen God, in our times,
with Elijah bearing tidings; / let our righteous Messiah come, / the son of David to redeem us –

a day of joy, a day of song, a day of rejoicing, a day of happiness, – let it come.

Great One, come quickly, / come, unmistakable God, in our times,
with Elijah bearing tidings; / let our righteous Messiah come, / the son of David to redeem us –

a day of joy, a day of song, a day of rejoicing, a day of happiness, – let it come.

Glorious One, come quickly, / come, venerable God, in our times,
with Elijah bearing tidings; / let our righteous Messiah come, / the son of David to redeem us –

a day of joy, a day of song, a day of rejoicing, a day of happiness, – let it come.

Worthy One, come quickly, / come, our kind God, in our times,
with Elijah bearing tidings; / let our righteous Messiah come, / the son of David to redeem us –

a day of joy, a day of song, a day of rejoicing, a day of happiness, – let it come.

Pure One, come quickly, / come, upright God, in our times,
with Elijah bearing tidings; / let our righteous Messiah come, / the son of David to redeem us –

a day of joy, a day of song, a day of rejoicing, a day of happiness, – let it come.

Mighty One, come quickly, / come, learned God, in our times,
with Elijah bearing tidings; / let our righteous Messiah come, / the son of David to redeem us –

a day of joy, a day of song, a day of rejoicing, a day of happiness, – let it come.

Redeemer, come quickly, / come, awesome God, in our times
with Elijah bearing tidings; / let our righteous Messiah come, / the son of David to redeem us –

a day of joy, a day of song, a day of rejoicing, a day of happiness, – let it come.

Elevated One, come quickly, / come, strong God, in our times,
with Elijah bearing tidings; / let our righteous Messiah come, / the son of David to redeem us –

a day of joy, a day of song, a day of rejoicing, a day of happiness, – let it come.

Savior, come quickly, / come, righteous God, in our times,
with Elijah bearing tidings; / let our righteous Messiah come, / the son of David to redeem us –

a day of joy, a day of song, a day of rejoicing, a day of happiness, – let it come.

יָבוֹא אַדִּיר בִּמְהֵרָה יָבוֹא בָּחוּר בְּיָמֵינוּ
יָבוֹא אֵלִיָּהוּ לְבַשְּׂרֵנוּ יָבוֹא מְשִׁיחַ צִדְקֵנוּ, בֶּן דָּוִד גּוֹאֲלֵנוּ
יוֹם גִּילָה, יוֹם רִנָּה, יוֹם דִּיצָה, יוֹם חֶדְוָה, יָבוֹא אֵלֵינוּ.

יָבוֹא גָּדוֹל בִּמְהֵרָה יָבוֹא דָּגוּל בְּיָמֵינוּ
יָבוֹא אֵלִיָּהוּ לְבַשְּׂרֵנוּ יָבוֹא מְשִׁיחַ צִדְקֵנוּ, בֶּן דָּוִד גּוֹאֲלֵנוּ
יוֹם גִּילָה, יוֹם רִנָּה, יוֹם דִּיצָה, יוֹם חֶדְוָה, יָבוֹא אֵלֵינוּ.

יָבוֹא הָדוּר בִּמְהֵרָה יָבוֹא וָתִיק בְּיָמֵינוּ
יָבוֹא אֵלִיָּהוּ לְבַשְּׂרֵנוּ יָבוֹא מְשִׁיחַ צִדְקֵנוּ, בֶּן דָּוִד גּוֹאֲלֵנוּ
יוֹם גִּילָה, יוֹם רִנָּה, יוֹם דִּיצָה, יוֹם חֶדְוָה, יָבוֹא אֵלֵינוּ.

יָבוֹא זַכַּאי בִּמְהֵרָה יָבוֹא חָסִיד בְּיָמֵינוּ
יָבוֹא אֵלִיָּהוּ לְבַשְּׂרֵנוּ יָבוֹא מְשִׁיחַ צִדְקֵנוּ, בֶּן דָּוִד גּוֹאֲלֵנוּ
יוֹם גִּילָה, יוֹם רִנָּה, יוֹם דִּיצָה, יוֹם חֶדְוָה, יָבוֹא אֵלֵינוּ.

יָבוֹא טָהוֹר בִּמְהֵרָה יָבוֹא יָשָׁר בְּיָמֵינוּ
יָבוֹא אֵלִיָּהוּ לְבַשְּׂרֵנוּ יָבוֹא מְשִׁיחַ צִדְקֵנוּ, בֶּן דָּוִד גּוֹאֲלֵנוּ
יוֹם גִּילָה, יוֹם רִנָּה, יוֹם דִּיצָה, יוֹם חֶדְוָה, יָבוֹא אֵלֵינוּ.

יָבוֹא כַּבִּיר בִּמְהֵרָה יָבוֹא לָמוּד בְּיָמֵינוּ
יָבוֹא אֵלִיָּהוּ לְבַשְּׂרֵנוּ יָבוֹא מְשִׁיחַ צִדְקֵנוּ, בֶּן דָּוִד גּוֹאֲלֵנוּ
יוֹם גִּילָה, יוֹם רִנָּה, יוֹם דִּיצָה, יוֹם חֶדְוָה, יָבוֹא אֵלֵינוּ.

יָבוֹא מוֹשִׁיעַ בִּמְהֵרָה יָבוֹא נוֹרָא בְּיָמֵינוּ
יָבוֹא אֵלִיָּהוּ לְבַשְּׂרֵנוּ יָבוֹא מְשִׁיחַ צִדְקֵנוּ, בֶּן דָּוִד גּוֹאֲלֵנוּ
יוֹם גִּילָה, יוֹם רִנָּה, יוֹם דִּיצָה, יוֹם חֶדְוָה, יָבוֹא אֵלֵינוּ.

יָבוֹא סַגִּיב בִּמְהֵרָה יָבוֹא עִזּוּז בְּיָמֵינוּ
יָבוֹא אֵלִיָּהוּ לְבַשְּׂרֵנוּ יָבוֹא מְשִׁיחַ צִדְקֵנוּ, בֶּן דָּוִד גּוֹאֲלֵנוּ
יוֹם גִּילָה, יוֹם רִנָּה, יוֹם דִּיצָה, יוֹם חֶדְוָה, יָבוֹא אֵלֵינוּ.

יָבוֹא פּוֹדֶה בִּמְהֵרָה יָבוֹא צַדִּיק בְּיָמֵינוּ
יָבוֹא אֵלִיָּהוּ לְבַשְּׂרֵנוּ יָבוֹא מְשִׁיחַ צִדְקֵנוּ, בֶּן דָּוִד גּוֹאֲלֵנוּ
יוֹם גִּילָה, יוֹם רִנָּה, יוֹם דִּיצָה, יוֹם חֶדְוָה, יָבוֹא אֵלֵינוּ.

Holy One, come quickly, / come, compassionate God, in our times,
with Elijah bearing tidings; / let our righteous Messiah come, / the son of David to redeem us –

a day of joy, a day of song, a day of rejoicing, a day of happiness, – let it come.

Almighty One, come quickly, / come, powerful God, in our times,
with Elijah bearing tidings; / let our righteous Messiah come, / the son of David to redeem us –

a day of joy, a day of song, a day of rejoicing, a day of happiness, – let it come.

The Torah scrolls are returned to the Ark except for the one used in the Torah Reading.

The Leader takes one in his right arm and, followed by the congregation, says:

Listen, Israel: the LORD is our God, the LORD is One. Deut. 6

Leader then congregation:

One is our God; great is our Master; holy is His name.

The Leader turns to face the Ark, bows and says:

Magnify the LORD with me, and let us exalt His name together. Ps. 34

The Ark is closed. The Leader carries the Torah scroll to the bima and the congregation says:

לְךָ Yours, LORD, are the greatness and the power, the glory and the majesty and splendor, for everything in heaven and earth is Yours. Yours, LORD, is the kingdom; You are exalted as Head over all. 1 Chr. 29

רוֹמְמוּ Exalt the LORD our God and bow to His footstool; He is holy. Exalt the LORD our God, and bow at His holy mountain, for holy is the LORD our God. Ps. 99

Over all may the name of the Supreme King of kings, the Holy One blessed be He, be magnified and sanctified, praised and glorified, exalted and extolled, in the worlds that He has created – this world and the World to Come – in accordance with His will, and the will of those who fear Him, and the will of the whole house of Israel. He is the Rock of worlds, LORD of all creatures, God of all souls, who dwells in the spacious heights and inhabits the high heavens of old. His holiness is over the Ḥayyot and over the throne of glory. Therefore may Your name, LORD our God, be sanctified among us in the sight of all that lives. Let us sing before Him a new song, as it is written: "Sing to God, make music for His name, extol Him who rides the clouds – the LORD is His name – and exult before Him." And may we see Him eye to eye when He returns to Ps. 68

יָבוֹא קָדוֹשׁ בִּמְהֵרָה יָבוֹא רַחוּם בְּיָמֵינוּ
יָבוֹא אֵלִיָּהוּ לְבַשְּׂרֵנוּ יָבוֹא מְשִׁיחַ צִדְקֵנוּ, בֶּן דָּוִד גּוֹאֲלֵנוּ
יוֹם גִּילָה, יוֹם רִנָּה, יוֹם דִּיצָה, יוֹם חֶדְוָה, יָבוֹא אֵלֵינוּ.

יָבוֹא שַׁדַּי בִּמְהֵרָה יָבוֹא תַּקִּיף בְּיָמֵינוּ
יָבוֹא אֵלִיָּהוּ לְבַשְּׂרֵנוּ יָבוֹא מְשִׁיחַ צִדְקֵנוּ, בֶּן דָּוִד גּוֹאֲלֵנוּ
יוֹם גִּילָה, יוֹם רִנָּה, יוֹם דִּיצָה, יוֹם חֶדְוָה, יָבוֹא אֵלֵינוּ.

The ספרי תורה *are returned to the* ארון קודש
except for the one used in the קריאת התורה.

The שליח צבור *takes the* ספר תורה *in his right arm, and, followed by the* קהל*, says:*

דברים ו
שְׁמַע יִשְׂרָאֵל, יהוה אֱלֹהֵינוּ, יהוה אֶחָד:

קהל *then* שליח ציבור:

אֶחָד אֱלֹהֵינוּ, גָּדוֹל אֲדוֹנֵינוּ, קָדוֹשׁ שְׁמוֹ.

The שליח ציבור *turns to face the* ארון קודש*, bows and says:*

תהלים לד
גַּדְּלוּ לַיהוה אִתִּי וּנְרוֹמְמָה שְׁמוֹ יַחְדָּו:

The ארון קודש *is closed. The* שליח ציבור *carries the* ספר תורה *to the* בימה *and the* קהל *says:*

דברי הימים א׳ כט
לְךָ יהוה הַגְּדֻלָּה וְהַגְּבוּרָה וְהַתִּפְאֶרֶת וְהַנֵּצַח וְהַהוֹד, כִּי־כֹל בַּשָּׁמַיִם וּבָאָרֶץ, לְךָ יהוה הַמַּמְלָכָה וְהַמִּתְנַשֵּׂא לְכֹל לְרֹאשׁ:

תהלים צט
רוֹמְמוּ יהוה אֱלֹהֵינוּ וְהִשְׁתַּחֲווּ לַהֲדֹם רַגְלָיו, קָדוֹשׁ הוּא: רוֹמְמוּ יהוה אֱלֹהֵינוּ וְהִשְׁתַּחֲווּ לְהַר קָדְשׁוֹ, כִּי־קָדוֹשׁ יהוה אֱלֹהֵינוּ:

עַל הַכֹּל יִתְגַּדַּל וְיִתְקַדַּשׁ וְיִשְׁתַּבַּח וְיִתְפָּאַר וְיִתְרוֹמַם וְיִתְנַשֵּׂא שְׁמוֹ שֶׁל מֶלֶךְ מַלְכֵי הַמְּלָכִים הַקָּדוֹשׁ בָּרוּךְ הוּא בָּעוֹלָמוֹת שֶׁבָּרָא, הָעוֹלָם הַזֶּה וְהָעוֹלָם הַבָּא, כִּרְצוֹנוֹ וְכִרְצוֹן יְרֵאָיו וְכִרְצוֹן כָּל בֵּית יִשְׂרָאֵל. צוּר הָעוֹלָמִים, אֲדוֹן כָּל הַבְּרִיּוֹת, אֱלוֹהַּ כָּל הַנְּפָשׁוֹת, הַיּוֹשֵׁב בְּמֶרְחֲבֵי מָרוֹם, הַשּׁוֹכֵן בִּשְׁמֵי שְׁמֵי קֶדֶם, קְדֻשָּׁתוֹ עַל הַחַיּוֹת, וּקְדֻשָּׁתוֹ עַל כִּסֵּא הַכָּבוֹד. וּבְכֵן יִתְקַדַּשׁ שִׁמְךָ בָּנוּ יהוה אֱלֹהֵינוּ לְעֵינֵי כָּל חָי, וְנֹאמַר לְפָנָיו שִׁיר חָדָשׁ, כַּכָּתוּב:
תהלים סח
שִׁירוּ לֵאלֹהִים זַמְּרוּ שְׁמוֹ, סֹלּוּ לָרֹכֵב בָּעֲרָבוֹת, בְּיָהּ שְׁמוֹ, וְעִלְזוּ לְפָנָיו:

His abode as it is written: "For they shall see eye to eye when the LORD returns *Is. 52*
to Zion." And it is said: "Then will the glory of the LORD be revealed, and all *Is. 40*
mankind together shall see that the mouth of the LORD has spoken."

Father of mercy, have compassion on the people borne by Him. May He remember the covenant with the mighty (patriarchs), and deliver us from evil times. May He reproach the evil instinct in the people by Him, and graciously grant that we be an eternal remnant. May He fulfill in good measure our requests for salvation and compassion.

The Torah scroll is placed on the bima and the Gabbai calls a Kohen to the Torah.

וְיַעֲזֹר May He help, shield and save all who seek refuge in Him,
and let us say: Amen. Let us all render greatness to our God
and give honor to the Torah. *Let the Kohen come forward.
Arise (*name* son of *father's name*), the Kohen.

**If no Kohen is present, a Levi or Yisrael is called up as follows:*

/As there is no Kohen, arise (*name* son of *father's name*) in place of a Kohen./

Blessed is He who, in His holiness, gave the Torah to His people Israel.

The congregation followed by the Gabbai:

You who cling to the LORD your God are all alive today. *Deut. 4*

The Torah portion is read.

The Reader shows the oleh the section to be read. The oleh touches the scroll at that place with the tzitzit of his tallit, which he then kisses. Holding the handles of the scroll, he says:

Oleh: Bless the LORD, the blessed One.

Cong: Bless the LORD, the blessed One, for ever and all time.

Oleh: Bless the LORD, the blessed One, for ever and all time.

Blessed are You, LORD our God, King of the Universe,
who has chosen us from all peoples
and has given us His Torah.
Blessed are You, LORD, Giver of the Torah.

After the reading, the oleh says:

Oleh: Blessed are You, LORD our God, King of the Universe,
who has given us the Torah of truth,
planting everlasting life in our midst.
Blessed are You, LORD, Giver of the Torah.

וְנִרְאֵהוּ עַיִן בְּעַיִן בְּשׁוּבוֹ אֶל נָוֵהוּ, כַּכָּתוּב: כִּי עַיִן בְּעַיִן יִרְאוּ בְּשׁוּב יהוה ישעיה נב
צִיּוֹן: וְנֶאֱמַר: וְנִגְלָה כְּבוֹד יהוה, וְרָאוּ כָל־בָּשָׂר יַחְדָּו כִּי פִּי יהוה דִּבֵּר: ישעיה מ
אַב הָרַחֲמִים הוּא יְרַחֵם עַם עֲמוּסִים, וְיִזְכֹּר בְּרִית אֵיתָנִים, וְיַצִּיל נַפְשׁוֹתֵינוּ מִן הַשָּׁעוֹת הָרָעוֹת, וְיִגְעַר בְּיֵצֶר הָרָע מִן הַנְּשׂוּאִים, וְיָחֹן אוֹתָנוּ לִפְלֵיטַת עוֹלָמִים, וִימַלֵּא מִשְׁאֲלוֹתֵינוּ בְּמִדָּה טוֹבָה יְשׁוּעָה וְרַחֲמִים.

The ספר תורה *is placed on the* שולחן *and the* גבאי *calls a* כהן *to the* תורה.

וְיַעֲזֹר וְיָגֵן וְיוֹשִׁיעַ לְכָל הַחוֹסִים בּוֹ, וְנֹאמַר אָמֵן. הַכֹּל הָבוּ גֹדֶל לֵאלֹהֵינוּ וּתְנוּ כָבוֹד לַתּוֹרָה. *כֹּהֵן קְרַב, יַעֲמֹד (פלוני בֶּן פלוני) הַכֹּהֵן.

**If no* כהן *is present, a* לוי *or* ישראל *is called up as follows:*

/אֵין כָּאן כֹּהֵן, יַעֲמֹד (פלוני בֶּן פלוני) בִּמְקוֹם כֹּהֵן./

בָּרוּךְ שֶׁנָּתַן תּוֹרָה לְעַמּוֹ יִשְׂרָאֵל בִּקְדֻשָּׁתוֹ.

The קהל *followed by the* גבאי:

דברים ד וְאַתֶּם הַדְּבֵקִים בַּיהוה אֱלֹהֵיכֶם חַיִּים כֻּלְּכֶם הַיּוֹם:

The תורה *portion is read.*

The קורא *shows the* עולה *the section to be read. The* עולה *touches the scroll at that place with the* ציצית *of his* טלית*, which he then kisses. Holding the handles of the scroll, he says:*

עולה: בָּרְכוּ אֶת יהוה הַמְבֹרָךְ.

קהל: בָּרוּךְ יהוה הַמְבֹרָךְ לְעוֹלָם וָעֶד.

עולה: בָּרוּךְ יהוה הַמְבֹרָךְ לְעוֹלָם וָעֶד.
בָּרוּךְ אַתָּה יהוה, אֱלֹהֵינוּ מֶלֶךְ הָעוֹלָם
אֲשֶׁר בָּחַר בָּנוּ מִכָּל הָעַמִּים וְנָתַן לָנוּ אֶת תּוֹרָתוֹ.
בָּרוּךְ אַתָּה יהוה, נוֹתֵן הַתּוֹרָה.

After the קריאת התורה*, the* עולה *says:*

עולה: בָּרוּךְ אַתָּה יהוה אֱלֹהֵינוּ מֶלֶךְ הָעוֹלָם
אֲשֶׁר נָתַן לָנוּ תּוֹרַת אֱמֶת וְחַיֵּי עוֹלָם נָטַע בְּתוֹכֵנוּ.
בָּרוּךְ אַתָּה יהוה, נוֹתֵן הַתּוֹרָה.

TORAH READING FOR SIMḤAT TORAH

Three Olim (in some congregations, five) are called up and the Reading of "This is the blessing" is read. In some congregations the third aliya ends with "the thousands of Manasseh," in others with "the heavens in His grandeur."

This is the blessing with which Moses, the man of God, blessed the children of Israel before he died. Moses said: "The LORD came to them from Sinai; He shone out from Seir. He appeared over the crest of Paran, and came, among myriad angels, at His right hand a law of fire, for them. And He embraces the tribes, their holy ones all in His hands; they are drawn after Your steps, and carry Your words. Moses gave us a Law, a heritage to the people of Jacob. There is a King in Yeshurun, as the heads of the people are gathered, the tribes of Israel together. *Deut. 33:1–26*

"May Reuben live; let him not die, nor be left slight in number."

And this to Judah: he said, "Heed, LORD, the voice of Judah, and bring him home to his people. His arms alone need fight for him; You are his Support against his foes."

LEVI

To Levi he said, "Your Tumim and Urim are with Your devoted, the one You tested at Masa, and wrestled at Meriva; who said, of his father and mother: I have seen them not; who did not recognize his brothers, nor know his own sons, for he kept Your words, and guarded close Your covenant. They will teach Your laws to Jacob, and Your Torah to Israel. They will place before You the scent of incense, and offerings burnt on Your Altar. LORD, bless his strength, and receive the work of his hands. Those who rise against him – crush their bearing; all his enemies, until they rise no more."

To Benjamin he said, "Beloved of the LORD, he shall rest on Him in safety; and all through the day He shelters him, and rests between his shoulders."

SHELISHI

To Joseph he said, "His land is blessed of the LORD, with the fruit of the skies, of rain, and of the deeps that bide below, and of the fruit of the sun's harvest, all the fruits of the moon's yield, of the heights of primeval mountains, of the fruit of the ancient hills, and the fruit of the world and its fullness – and the favor of that Presence at the Bush. May this come to the head of Joseph, to the crown of one raised above his brothers. His glory is that of a firstborn bull, his horns the grand horns of the oryx. With these he can gore nations; the ends of the earth together – yes, these are the myriads of Ephraim, the thousands of Manasseh."

קריאה ליל שמחת תורה

Three עולים *(in some congregations, five) are called up and the* קריאה *of* וְזֹאת הַבְּרָכָה *is read. In some congregations the third aliya ends with* אַלְפֵי מְנַשֶּׁה, *in others with* וּבְגַאֲוָתוֹ שְׁחָקִים.

דברים לג:א–כו וְזֹאת הַבְּרָכָה אֲשֶׁר בֵּרַךְ מֹשֶׁה אִישׁ הָאֱלֹהִים אֶת־בְּנֵי יִשְׂרָאֵל
לִפְנֵי מוֹתוֹ: וַיֹּאמַר יהוה מִסִּינַי בָּא וְזָרַח מִשֵּׂעִיר לָמוֹ הוֹפִיעַ
מֵהַר פָּארָן וְאָתָה מֵרִבְבֹת קֹדֶשׁ מִימִינוֹ אשדת לָמוֹ: אַף אִ֣ישׁ דָּ֔ת
חֹבֵב עַמִּים כָּל־קְדֹשָׁיו בְּיָדֶךָ וְהֵם תֻּכּוּ לְרַגְלֶךָ יִשָּׂא מִדַּבְּרֹתֶיךָ:
תּוֹרָה צִוָּה־לָנוּ מֹשֶׁה מוֹרָשָׁה קְהִלַּת יַעֲקֹב: וַיְהִי בִישֻׁרוּן מֶלֶךְ
בְּהִתְאַסֵּף רָאשֵׁי עָם יַחַד שִׁבְטֵי יִשְׂרָאֵל: יְחִי רְאוּבֵן וְאַל־
יָמֹת וִיהִי מְתָיו מִסְפָּר: וְזֹאת לִיהוּדָה וַיֹּאמַר שְׁמַע
יהוה קוֹל יְהוּדָה וְאֶל־עַמּוֹ תְּבִיאֶנּוּ יָדָיו רָב לוֹ וְעֵזֶר מִצָּרָיו
תִּהְיֶה:
לוי וּלְלֵוִי אָמַר תֻּמֶּיךָ וְאוּרֶיךָ לְאִישׁ חֲסִידֶךָ אֲשֶׁר נִסִּיתוֹ בְּמַסָּה
תְּרִיבֵהוּ עַל־מֵי מְרִיבָה: הָאֹמֵר לְאָבִיו וּלְאִמּוֹ לֹא רְאִיתִיו וְאֶת־
אֶחָיו לֹא הִכִּיר וְאֶת־בָּנָו לֹא יָדָע כִּי שָׁמְרוּ אִמְרָתֶךָ וּבְרִיתְךָ
יִנְצֹרוּ: יוֹרוּ מִשְׁפָּטֶיךָ לְיַעֲקֹב וְתוֹרָתְךָ לְיִשְׂרָאֵל יָשִׂימוּ קְטוֹרָה
בְּאַפֶּךָ וְכָלִיל עַל־מִזְבְּחֶךָ: בָּרֵךְ יהוה חֵילוֹ וּפֹעַל יָדָיו תִּרְצֶה
מְחַץ מָתְנַיִם קָמָיו וּמְשַׂנְאָיו מִן־יְקוּמוּן: לְבִנְיָמִן
אָמַר יְדִיד יהוה יִשְׁכֹּן לָבֶטַח עָלָיו חֹפֵף עָלָיו כָּל־הַיּוֹם וּבֵין
שלישי כְּתֵפָיו שָׁכֵן: *וּלְיוֹסֵף אָמַר מְבֹרֶכֶת יהוה אַרְצוֹ
מִמֶּגֶד שָׁמַיִם מִטָּל וּמִתְּהוֹם רֹבֶצֶת תָּחַת: וּמִמֶּגֶד תְּבוּאֹת שָׁמֶשׁ
וּמִמֶּגֶד גֶּרֶשׁ יְרָחִים: וּמֵרֹאשׁ הַרְרֵי־קֶדֶם וּמִמֶּגֶד גִּבְעוֹת עוֹלָם:
וּמִמֶּגֶד אֶרֶץ וּמְלֹאָהּ וּרְצוֹן שֹׁכְנִי סְנֶה תָּבוֹאתָה לְרֹאשׁ יוֹסֵף
וּלְקָדְקֹד נְזִיר אֶחָיו: בְּכוֹר שׁוֹרוֹ הָדָר לוֹ וְקַרְנֵי רְאֵם קַרְנָיו
בָּהֶם עַמִּים יְנַגַּח יַחְדָּו אַפְסֵי־אָרֶץ וְהֵם רִבְבוֹת אֶפְרַיִם וְהֵם

And to Zebulun he said, "Find happiness, Zebulun, in your journeys, and Issachar in your tents. Tribes shall be called to the mountain, to bring righteous offerings there. For they will draw of the plenty of oceans, and of the hidden, buried riches of the sands." REVI'I

To Gad he said, "Blessed be the One who broadens Gad's borders; for he crouches like a lioness, to tear arm and head from his prey. He chose the first place for his own, for the grave of a law-giver hides there. He came with the heads of the people; he performed the LORD's righteousness, and dealt uprightly with Israel."

And to Dan he said, "Dan is a lion cub, leaping from Bashan." ḤAMISHI

And to Naftali he said, "Naftali is sated with favor; filled with the LORD's blessing: go and form your inheritance seaward and south."

To Asher he said, "Most blessed of sons is Asher – may he be beloved of his brothers; may his feet be steeped in oil. Your doors are locked with iron and bronze, and your strength is as long as your days.

"There is none like God, Yeshurun, riding the skies to help you, the heavens in His grandeur."

HALF KADDISH

The Reader says Half Kaddish:

Reader: יִתְגַּדַּל Magnified and sanctified may His great name be,
in the world He created by His will.
May He establish His kingdom
in your lifetime and in your days,
and in the lifetime of all the house of Israel,
swiftly and soon – and say: Amen.

All: May His great name be blessed for ever and all time.

Reader: Blessed and praised, glorified and exalted,
raised and honored, uplifted and lauded
be the name of the Holy One, blessed be He,
beyond any blessing,
song, praise and consolation
uttered in the world – and say: Amen.

אַלְפֵי מְנַשֶּׁה: *וְלִזְבוּלֻן אָמַר שְׂמַח זְבוּלֻן בְּצֵאתֶךָ רביעי
וְיִשָּׂשכָר בְּאֹהָלֶיךָ: עַמִּים הַר־יִקְרָאוּ שָׁם יִזְבְּחוּ זִבְחֵי־צֶדֶק כִּי
שֶׁפַע יַמִּים יִינָקוּ וּשְׂפֻנֵי טְמוּנֵי חוֹל: וּלְגָד אָמַר בָּרוּךְ
מַרְחִיב גָּד כְּלָבִיא שָׁכֵן וְטָרַף זְרוֹעַ אַף־קָדְקֹד: וַיַּרְא רֵאשִׁית לוֹ
כִּי־שָׁם חֶלְקַת מְחֹקֵק סָפוּן וַיֵּתֵא רָאשֵׁי עָם צִדְקַת יהוה עָשָׂה
וּמִשְׁפָּטָיו עִם־יִשְׂרָאֵל: *וּלְדָן אָמַר דָּן גּוּר אַרְיֵה חמישי
יְזַנֵּק מִן־הַבָּשָׁן: וּלְנַפְתָּלִי אָמַר נַפְתָּלִי שְׂבַע רָצוֹן וּמָלֵא בִּרְכַּת
יהוה יָם וְדָרוֹם יְרָשָׁה: וּלְאָשֵׁר אָמַר בָּרוּךְ מִבָּנִים
אָשֵׁר יְהִי רְצוּי אֶחָיו וְטֹבֵל בַּשֶּׁמֶן רַגְלוֹ: בַּרְזֶל וּנְחֹשֶׁת מִנְעָלֶךָ
וּכְיָמֶיךָ דָּבְאֶךָ: אֵין כָּאֵל יְשֻׁרוּן רֹכֵב שָׁמַיִם בְּעֶזְרֶךָ וּבְגַאֲוָתוֹ
שְׁחָקִים:

חצי קדיש

The קורא *says* חצי קדיש:

קורא: יִתְגַּדַּל וְיִתְקַדַּשׁ שְׁמֵהּ רַבָּא (קהל: אָמֵן)
בְּעָלְמָא דִּי בְרָא כִרְעוּתֵהּ
וְיַמְלִיךְ מַלְכוּתֵהּ
בְּחַיֵּיכוֹן וּבְיוֹמֵיכוֹן וּבְחַיֵּי דְכָל בֵּית יִשְׂרָאֵל
בַּעֲגָלָא וּבִזְמַן קָרִיב, וְאִמְרוּ אָמֵן. (קהל: אָמֵן)

קהל וקורא: יְהֵא שְׁמֵהּ רַבָּא מְבָרַךְ לְעָלַם וּלְעָלְמֵי עָלְמַיָּא.

קורא: יִתְבָּרַךְ וְיִשְׁתַּבַּח וְיִתְפָּאַר וְיִתְרוֹמַם וְיִתְנַשֵּׂא
וְיִתְהַדָּר וְיִתְעַלֶּה וְיִתְהַלָּל
שְׁמֵהּ דְּקֻדְשָׁא בְּרִיךְ הוּא (קהל: בְּרִיךְ הוּא)
לְעֵלָּא מִן כָּל בִּרְכָתָא וְשִׁירָתָא, תֻּשְׁבְּחָתָא וְנֶחֱמָתָא
דַּאֲמִירָן בְּעָלְמָא, וְאִמְרוּ אָמֵן. (קהל: אָמֵן)

HAGBAHA AND GELILA

The Torah scroll is lifted and the congregation says:

וְזֹאת הַתּוֹרָה This is the Torah Deut. 4
that Moses placed before the children of Israel,
at the LORD's commandment, by the hand of Moses. Num. 9

Some add: It is a tree of life to those who grasp it, Prov. 3
and those who uphold it are happy.
Its ways are ways of pleasantness, and all its paths are peace.
Long life is in its right hand; in its left, riches and honor.
It pleased the LORD for the sake of [Israel's] righteousness, Is. 42
to make the Torah great and glorious.

The Torah scroll is bound and covered.

RETURNING THE TORAH

The Ark is opened.
|The Leader takes the Torah scroll and says:

יְהַלְלוּ Let them praise the name of the LORD, Ps. 148
for His name alone is sublime.

The congregation responds:

הוֹדוֹ His majesty is above earth and heaven.
He has raised the horn of His people,
for the glory of all His devoted ones,
the children of Israel, the people close to Him.
Halleluya!

As the Torah scroll is returned to the Ark say:

לְדָוִד מִזְמוֹר A psalm of David. The earth is the LORD's and all it contains, Ps. 24 the world and all who live in it. For He founded it on the seas and established it on the streams. Who may climb the mountain of the LORD? Who may stand in His holy place? He who has clean hands and a pure heart, who has not taken My name in vain, or sworn deceitfully. He shall receive blessing from the LORD, and just reward from God, his salvation. This is a generation of those who seek Him, the descendants of Jacob who seek Your presence, Selah! Lift up your heads, O

הגבהה וגלילה

The ספר תורה *is lifted and the* קהל *says:*

וְזֹאת הַתּוֹרָה אֲשֶׁר־שָׂם מֹשֶׁה לִפְנֵי בְּנֵי יִשְׂרָאֵל: דברים ד

עַל־פִּי יהוה בְּיַד מֹשֶׁה: במדבר ט

Some add עֵץ־חַיִּים הִיא לַמַּחֲזִיקִים בָּהּ וְתֹמְכֶיהָ מְאֻשָּׁר: משלי ג

דְּרָכֶיהָ דַרְכֵי־נֹעַם וְכָל־נְתִיבֹתֶיהָ שָׁלוֹם:

אֹרֶךְ יָמִים בִּימִינָהּ, בִּשְׂמֹאולָהּ עֹשֶׁר וְכָבוֹד:

יהוה חָפֵץ לְמַעַן צִדְקוֹ יַגְדִּיל תּוֹרָה וְיַאְדִּיר: ישעיה מב

The ספר תורה *is bound and covered.*

הכנסת ספר תורה

The ארון קודש *is opened.*
The שליח ציבור *takes the* ספר תורה *and says:*

יְהַלְלוּ אֶת־שֵׁם יהוה, כִּי־נִשְׂגָּב שְׁמוֹ, לְבַדּוֹ תהלים קמח

The קהל *responds:*

הודו עַל־אֶרֶץ וְשָׁמָיִם:
וַיָּרֶם קֶרֶן לְעַמּוֹ
תְּהִלָּה לְכָל־חֲסִידָיו
לִבְנֵי יִשְׂרָאֵל עַם קְרֹבוֹ
הַלְלוּיָהּ:

As the ספר תורה *is returned to the* ארון קודש*, say:*

לְדָוִד מִזְמוֹר, לַיהוה הָאָרֶץ וּמְלוֹאָהּ, תֵּבֵל וְיֹשְׁבֵי בָהּ: כִּי־הוּא עַל־ תהלים כד
יַמִּים יְסָדָהּ, וְעַל־נְהָרוֹת יְכוֹנְנֶהָ: מִי־יַעֲלֶה בְהַר־יהוה, וּמִי־יָקוּם
בִּמְקוֹם קָדְשׁוֹ: נְקִי כַפַּיִם וּבַר־לֵבָב, אֲשֶׁר לֹא־נָשָׂא לַשָּׁוְא נַפְשִׁי
וְלֹא נִשְׁבַּע לְמִרְמָה: יִשָּׂא בְרָכָה מֵאֵת יהוה, וּצְדָקָה מֵאֱלֹהֵי יִשְׁעוֹ:
זֶה דּוֹר דֹּרְשָׁו, מְבַקְשֵׁי פָנֶיךָ, יַעֲקֹב, סֶלָה: שְׂאוּ שְׁעָרִים רָאשֵׁיכֶם,

gates; be uplifted, eternal doors, so that the King of glory may enter. Who is the King of glory? It is the LORD, strong and mighty, the LORD mighty in battle. Lift up your heads, O gates; be uplifted, eternal doors, so that the King of glory may enter. Who is He, the King of glory? The LORD of hosts, He is the King of glory, Selah!

As the Torah scroll is placed into the Ark, say:

וּבְנֻחֹה יֹאמַר When the Ark came to rest, Moses would say:
"Return, O LORD, to the myriad thousands of Israel." *Num. 10*
Advance, LORD, to Your resting place, You and Your mighty Ark. *Ps. 132*
Your priests are clothed in righteousness,
and Your devoted ones sing in joy.
For the sake of Your servant David, do not reject Your anointed one.
For I give you good instruction; do not forsake My Torah. *Prov. 4*
It is a tree of life to those who grasp it, *Prov. 3*
and those who uphold it are happy.
Its ways are ways of pleasantness, and all its paths are peace.
▸ Turn us back, O LORD, to You, and we will return. *Lam. 5*
Renew our days as of old.

The Ark is closed
and the service continues with "It is our duty" on page 82.

וְהִנָּשְׂאוּ פִּתְחֵי עוֹלָם, וְיָבוֹא מֶלֶךְ הַכָּבוֹד: מִי זֶה מֶלֶךְ הַכָּבוֹד, יהוה עִזּוּז וְגִבּוֹר, יהוה גִּבּוֹר מִלְחָמָה: שְׂאוּ שְׁעָרִים רָאשֵׁיכֶם, וּשְׂאוּ פִּתְחֵי עוֹלָם, וְיָבֹא מֶלֶךְ הַכָּבוֹד: מִי הוּא זֶה מֶלֶךְ הַכָּבוֹד, יהוה צְבָאוֹת הוּא מֶלֶךְ הַכָּבוֹד, סֶלָה:

As the ספר תורה *is placed into the* ארון קודש*, say:*

וּבְנֻחֹה יֹאמַר, שׁוּבָה יהוה רִבֲבוֹת אַלְפֵי יִשְׂרָאֵל: במדבר י

קוּמָה יהוה לִמְנוּחָתֶךָ, אַתָּה וַאֲרוֹן עֻזֶּךָ: תהלים קלב

כֹּהֲנֶיךָ יִלְבְּשׁוּ־צֶדֶק, וַחֲסִידֶיךָ יְרַנֵּנוּ:

בַּעֲבוּר דָּוִד עַבְדֶּךָ אַל־תָּשֵׁב פְּנֵי מְשִׁיחֶךָ:

כִּי לֶקַח טוֹב נָתַתִּי לָכֶם, תּוֹרָתִי אַל־תַּעֲזֹבוּ: משלי ד

עֵץ־חַיִּים הִיא לַמַּחֲזִיקִים בָּהּ, וְתֹמְכֶיהָ מְאֻשָּׁר: משלי ג

דְּרָכֶיהָ דַרְכֵי־נֹעַם וְכָל־נְתִיבוֹתֶיהָ שָׁלוֹם:

◂ **הֲשִׁיבֵנוּ יהוה אֵלֶיךָ וְנָשׁוּבָה, חַדֵּשׁ יָמֵינוּ כְּקֶדֶם:** איכה ה

The ארון קודש *is closed*
and the service continues with עָלֵינוּ *on page 83.*

Ma'aravot

MA'ARIV FOR THE FIRST NIGHT

The recitation of piyutim for Ma'ariv (Ma'aravot) varies among different communities. Many congregations omit Ma'aravot altogether. On Shabbat, Ma'aravot are not recited.

Each set of piyutim is essentially one long piyut divided into six parts, one part recited before each of the four blessings of the Shema, and two before the two verses in the Geula blessing: "Who is like You, LORD, among the mighty," and "The LORD shall reign for ever and ever." In many congregations, an additional piyut is recited following the Ma'aravot, before the concluding blessing, "Who spreads a canopy of peace."

בָּרוּךְ Blessed are You, LORD our God,
King of the Universe,
who by His word brings on evenings,
by His wisdom opens the gates of heaven,
with understanding makes time change and the seasons rotate,
and by His will orders the stars in their constellations in the sky.

---

and sometimes simply to create a mood. It originated in Israel in the third or fourth century CE, and eventually spread to all major centers of Jewish life. Babylon, Spain, Italy, and Northern Europe all contributed richly to the poetry of the synagogue, and different rites reflect that variety.

Piyut grew more or less contemporaneously with the development of *Midrash Aggada*, rabbinic reflection on and commentary to biblical narrative. *Piyut* incorporates much of this material, suggesting that part of its purpose was educational as well as aesthetic. It reminded people of the laws and traditions relating to the day. It may even have been a way of circumventing the bans that occurred from time to time on the public teaching of Judaism.

We do not know the names of the earliest writers of *piyut*. The first we know by name is Yose ben Yose who lived in Israel, probably in the fourth or fifth century. The first great master of the genre, a century later, was Yannai. A century later still came the virtuoso, R. Elazar HaKalir, who brought the art to extreme sophistication, coining new words, developing new literary techniques, and creating, in short phrases and sometimes single words, dense networks of association and allusion. To judge by the complexity and popularity of *piyut*, the communities to which it was addressed were exceptionally

מערבות

מעריב לליל יום טוב ראשון של סוכות

The recitation of piyutim for מעריב (מערבות) *varies among different communities. Many congregations omit* מערבות *altogether. On* שבת, מערבות *are not recited.*

Each set of piyutim is essentially one long piyut divided into six parts, one part recited before each of the four blessings of the שמע, *and two before the two verses in the* גאולה *blessing:* "מִי־כָמֹכָה בָּאֵלִם יהוה," *and* "יהוה יִמְלֹךְ לְעֹלָם וָעֶד." *In many congregations, an additional piyut is recited following the* מערבות, *before the concluding blessing,* "הַפּוֹרֵשׂ סֻכַּת שָׁלוֹם."

בָּרוּךְ אַתָּה יהוה אֱלֹהֵינוּ מֶלֶךְ הָעוֹלָם
אֲשֶׁר בִּדְבָרוֹ מַעֲרִיב עֲרָבִים
בְּחָכְמָה פּוֹתֵחַ שְׁעָרִים
וּבִתְבוּנָה מְשַׁנֶּה עִתִּים וּמַחֲלִיף אֶת הַזְּמַנִּים
וּמְסַדֵּר אֶת הַכּוֹכָבִים בְּמִשְׁמְרוֹתֵיהֶם בָּרָקִיעַ כִּרְצוֹנוֹ.

PIYUT: THE POETRY OF THE PRAYER BOOK

Jewish prayer is structured around the tension between the fixed and the free, the elements that do not change, and those that do. Historically, the first formulation of Jewish prayer goes back to the time of Ezra and the Men of the Great Assembly, in the fifth century BCE. A second major consolidation occurred in the time of Rabban Gamliel II, after the destruction of the Second Temple. In the absence of sacrifices, prayer assumed greater significance, and it was important for the spiritual unity of the people that they pray the same prayers, at the same time, in the same way.

No sooner had the formal structure been completed than a new type of prayer, *piyut* (the word comes from the same root as "poetry"), began to develop. What makes it different from other prayers is that it is non-obligatory, not part of the halakhic requirement of prayer. *Piyut* was created to augment, adorn, beautify; to reflect more deeply on key points of the service; to bring out in greater depth the distinctive character of specific days; to bring variety to the rhythm and pace of prayer; to inform, educate,

He creates day and night,
rolling away the light before the darkness,
and darkness before the light.
▸ He makes the day pass and brings on night,
distinguishing day from night:
the LORD of hosts is His name.
May the living and forever enduring God
rule over us for all time.

> Those who hold the four species in their hands
> come to glorify You with stringed instruments and flutes;
> with rings of gold they bind their lulavim and ready them –
> may their flagged tribes be numbered as the stars of the sky.

Blessed are You, LORD, who brings on evenings.

---

for Shabbat HaGadol, the Shabbat before Pesaḥ, became a major source in its own right for the laws of Passover cleaning.

The *piyut* for the second night was composed by Yeḥiel ben Isaac of Zülpich, Germany (thirteenth century) and is noteworthy for its evocation of the clouds of glory that surrounded the Israelites as they wandered in the desert. This, according to one view in the Talmud (*Sukka* 11b), is what we recall as we sit in the *sukka*.

בְּעֻגָב וּבְמִנִּים *Stringed instruments and flutes.* These instruments were played in the Temple, and are mentioned in the joyous final Psalm (Ps. 150:4). This may also be a reference to the special celebration of the Rejoicing at the Place of Water Drawing (*Simḥat Beit HaSho'eva*) that took place in Temple times on Ḥol HaMo'ed Sukkot, accompanied by instrumental music played by the Levites (Mishna, *Sukka* 5:4).

גְּמוֹנֵי פָז *Rings of gold.* According to the Mishna, some, to celebrate and beautify the command, would ornament the *Lulav* with strands of fine gold (Mishna, *Sukka* 3:8).

כְּכוֹכְבֵי שַׁחַק *As the stars of the sky.* A reference to God's promise to Abraham: "Look up at the sky and count the stars – if indeed you can count them." Then He said to him, "So shall your descendants be" (Gen. 15:5).

בּוֹרֵא יוֹם וָלָיְלָה
גּוֹלֵל אוֹר מִפְּנֵי חֹשֶׁךְ וְחֹשֶׁךְ מִפְּנֵי אוֹר
◂ וּמַעֲבִיר יוֹם וּמֵבִיא לָיְלָה
וּמַבְדִּיל בֵּין יוֹם וּבֵין לָיְלָה
יהוה צְבָאוֹת שְׁמוֹ.
אֵל חַי וְקַיָּם תָּמִיד, יִמְלֹךְ עָלֵינוּ לְעוֹלָם וָעֶד.

אוֹחֲזֵי בְיָדָם אַרְבָּעָה מִינִים
בָּאִים לְסַלְּדָךְ בְּעֻגָּב וּבְמִנִּים
גְּמוּנֵי פָּז אוֹגְדִים וּמְזַמְּנִים
דְּגָלֵימוֹ כְּכוֹכְבֵי שַׁחַק נִמְנִים.

בָּרוּךְ אַתָּה יהוה, הַמַּעֲרִיב עֲרָבִים.

---

literate, testimony to the high levels of education sustained by Jewry even in ages of persecution and poverty.

Not everyone approved of *piyut*. There were notes of dissent from Rav Hai Gaon, Maimonides, Ibn Ezra and others, on a number of grounds: they were unwarranted interruptions; they made the services too long; they are hard to understand; their use of language was uneven and eccentric. Their theology, thought Maimonides, was sometimes suspect. Yet *piyut* survived and thrived. It remains as a magnificent set of solo intervals in the choral symphony Israel has sung to its Maker, King, Judge, and Redeemer. It is prayer as poetry and poetry as prayer, and its sacred beauty still challenges the mind as it lifts the heart.

The *piyut* for the first night was written by Rabbi Joseph Tov Alem ben Samuel Bonfils (eleventh century). Bonfils was born in Narbonne and became rabbi of Limoges in the province of Anjou. A distinguished halakhist, many of his rulings were cited by later authorities. His responsa and bible commentaries are no longer extant, but sixty-two of his piyutim survive, and were widely adopted by the Jews of France, Germany and Poland. Bonfils weaved both halakhic and aggadic traditions into his poetry, and his *piyut*

אַהֲבַת עוֹלָם With everlasting love
have You loved Your people, the house of Israel.
You have taught us Torah and commandments,
decrees and laws of justice.
Therefore, LORD our God,
when we lie down and when we rise up
we will speak of Your decrees,
rejoicing in the words of Your Torah
and Your commandments for ever.
▸ For they are our life and the length of our days;
on them will we meditate day and night.
May You never take away Your love from us.

> Those who speak the words of that Law formed before all,
> who come out and bide seven days in the sukka –
> grant them merit and protect them from the impenetrable thorns,
> and never falter from the love that is their lot.

Blessed are You, LORD, who loves His people Israel.

The Shema must be said with intense concentration.
When not with a minyan, say:

God, faithful King!

The following verse should be said aloud, while covering the eyes with the right hand:

Listen, Israel: the LORD is our God, the LORD is One. Deut. 6

Quietly: Blessed be the name of His glorious kingdom for ever and all time.

וְאָהַבְתָּ Love the LORD your God with all your heart, with all your Deut. 6
soul, and with all your might. These words which I command you

---

וְגוֹנְנֵם מִמְּסוּכָה *Protect them from the impenetrable thorns.* Based on Prov. 15:19, "A hedge of thorns," a reference to the sufferings and privations of exile.

אַהֲבַת עוֹלָם בֵּית יִשְׂרָאֵל עַמְּךָ אָהָבְתָּ
תּוֹרָה וּמִצְוֹת, חֻקִּים וּמִשְׁפָּטִים, אוֹתָנוּ לִמַּדְתָּ
עַל כֵּן יהוה אֱלֹהֵינוּ בְּשָׁכְבֵנוּ וּבְקוּמֵנוּ נָשִׂיחַ בְּחֻקֶּיךָ
וְנִשְׂמַח בְּדִבְרֵי תוֹרָתֶךָ וּבְמִצְוֹתֶיךָ לְעוֹלָם וָעֶד
◂ כִּי הֵם חַיֵּינוּ וְאֹרֶךְ יָמֵינוּ, וּבָהֶם נֶהְגֶּה יוֹמָם וָלָיְלָה.
וְאַהֲבָתְךָ אַל תָּסִיר מִמֶּנּוּ לְעוֹלָמִים.

הוֹגֵי דָּת מֵרֹאשׁ נְסוּכָה
וּבָאִים וְלָנִים שִׁבְעָה בַּסֻּכָּה
זְכוּת הַמְּצִיאָם, וְגוֹנֵן מִמְּסוּכָה
חֹק אַהֲבָתָם בְּלִי לְחָשְׁכָה.

בָּרוּךְ אַתָּה יהוה, אוֹהֵב עַמּוֹ יִשְׂרָאֵל.

The שמע *must be said with intense concentration.*
When not with a מנין*, say:*

אֵל מֶלֶךְ נֶאֱמָן

The following verse should be said aloud, while covering the eyes with the right hand:

דברים ו שְׁמַע יִשְׂרָאֵל, יהוה אֱלֹהֵינוּ, יהוה ׀ אֶחָד:

Quietly בָּרוּךְ שֵׁם כְּבוֹד מַלְכוּתוֹ לְעוֹלָם וָעֶד.

דברים ו וְאָהַבְתָּ אֵת יהוה אֱלֹהֶיךָ, בְּכָל־לְבָבְךָ וּבְכָל־נַפְשְׁךָ וּבְכָל־
מְאֹדֶךָ: וְהָיוּ הַדְּבָרִים הָאֵלֶּה, אֲשֶׁר אָנֹכִי מְצַוְּךָ הַיּוֹם, עַל־לְבָבֶךָ:

מֵרֹאשׁ *Before all.* A reference to Proverbs 8:23: "I [Wisdom, i.e., the Torah] was formed long ages ago, at the very beginning, when the world came to be." This is the source of the idea that the Torah preceded, and is the blueprint of, Creation.

today shall be on your heart. Teach them repeatedly to your children, speaking of them when you sit at home and when you travel on the way, when you lie down and when you rise. Bind them as a sign on your hand, and they shall be an emblem between your eyes. Write them on the doorposts of your house and gates.

וְהָיָה If you indeed heed My commandments with which I charge you today, to love the LORD your God and worship Him with all your heart and with all your soul, I will give rain in your land in its season, the early and late rain; and you shall gather in your grain, wine and oil. I will give grass in your field for your cattle, and you shall eat and be satisfied. Be careful lest your heart be tempted and you go astray and worship other gods, bowing down to them. Then the LORD's anger will flare against you and He will close the heavens so that there will be no rain. The land will not yield its crops, and you will perish swiftly from the good land that the LORD is giving you. Therefore, set these, My words, on your heart and soul. Bind them as a sign on your hand, and they shall be an emblem between your eyes. Teach them to your children, speaking of them when you sit at home and when you travel on the way, when you lie down and when you rise. Write them on the doorposts of your house and gates, so that you and your children may live long in the land that the LORD swore to your ancestors to give them, for as long as the heavens are above the earth. *Deut. 11*

וַיֹּאמֶר The LORD spoke to Moses, saying: Speak to the Israelites and tell them to make tassels on the corners of their garments for all generations. They shall attach to the tassel at each corner a thread of blue. This shall be your tassel, and you shall see it and remember all of the LORD's commandments and keep them, not straying after your heart and after your eyes, following your own sinful desires. Thus you will be reminded to keep all My commandments, and be holy to your God. I am the LORD your *Num. 15*

וְשִׁנַּנְתָּם לְבָנֶיךָ וְדִבַּרְתָּ בָּם, בְּשִׁבְתְּךָ בְּבֵיתֶךָ וּבְלֶכְתְּךָ בַדֶּרֶךְ, וּבְשָׁכְבְּךָ וּבְקוּמֶךָ: וּקְשַׁרְתָּם לְאוֹת עַל־יָדֶךָ וְהָיוּ לְטֹטָפֹת בֵּין עֵינֶיךָ: וּכְתַבְתָּם עַל־מְזֻזוֹת בֵּיתֶךָ וּבִשְׁעָרֶיךָ:

דברים יא וְהָיָה אִם־שָׁמֹעַ תִּשְׁמְעוּ אֶל־מִצְוֺתַי אֲשֶׁר אָנֹכִי מְצַוֶּה אֶתְכֶם הַיּוֹם, לְאַהֲבָה אֶת־יהוה אֱלֹהֵיכֶם וּלְעָבְדוֹ, בְּכָל־לְבַבְכֶם וּבְכָל־נַפְשְׁכֶם: וְנָתַתִּי מְטַר־אַרְצְכֶם בְּעִתּוֹ, יוֹרֶה וּמַלְקוֹשׁ, וְאָסַפְתָּ דְגָנֶךָ וְתִירֹשְׁךָ וְיִצְהָרֶךָ: וְנָתַתִּי עֵשֶׂב בְּשָׂדְךָ לִבְהֶמְתֶּךָ, וְאָכַלְתָּ וְשָׂבָעְתָּ: הִשָּׁמְרוּ לָכֶם פֶּן־יִפְתֶּה לְבַבְכֶם, וְסַרְתֶּם וַעֲבַדְתֶּם אֱלֹהִים אֲחֵרִים וְהִשְׁתַּחֲוִיתֶם לָהֶם: וְחָרָה אַף־יהוה בָּכֶם, וְעָצַר אֶת־הַשָּׁמַיִם וְלֹא־יִהְיֶה מָטָר, וְהָאֲדָמָה לֹא תִתֵּן אֶת־יְבוּלָהּ, וַאֲבַדְתֶּם מְהֵרָה מֵעַל הָאָרֶץ הַטֹּבָה אֲשֶׁר יהוה נֹתֵן לָכֶם: וְשַׂמְתֶּם אֶת־דְּבָרַי אֵלֶּה עַל־לְבַבְכֶם וְעַל־נַפְשְׁכֶם, וּקְשַׁרְתֶּם אֹתָם לְאוֹת עַל־יֶדְכֶם, וְהָיוּ לְטוֹטָפֹת בֵּין עֵינֵיכֶם: וְלִמַּדְתֶּם אֹתָם אֶת־בְּנֵיכֶם לְדַבֵּר בָּם, בְּשִׁבְתְּךָ בְּבֵיתֶךָ וּבְלֶכְתְּךָ בַדֶּרֶךְ, וּבְשָׁכְבְּךָ וּבְקוּמֶךָ: וּכְתַבְתָּם עַל־מְזוּזוֹת בֵּיתֶךָ וּבִשְׁעָרֶיךָ: לְמַעַן יִרְבּוּ יְמֵיכֶם וִימֵי בְנֵיכֶם עַל הָאֲדָמָה אֲשֶׁר נִשְׁבַּע יהוה לַאֲבֹתֵיכֶם לָתֵת לָהֶם, כִּימֵי הַשָּׁמַיִם עַל־הָאָרֶץ:

במדבר טו וַיֹּאמֶר יהוה אֶל־מֹשֶׁה לֵּאמֹר: דַּבֵּר אֶל־בְּנֵי יִשְׂרָאֵל וְאָמַרְתָּ אֲלֵהֶם, וְעָשׂוּ לָהֶם צִיצִת עַל־כַּנְפֵי בִגְדֵיהֶם לְדֹרֹתָם, וְנָתְנוּ עַל־צִיצִת הַכָּנָף פְּתִיל תְּכֵלֶת: וְהָיָה לָכֶם לְצִיצִת, וּרְאִיתֶם אֹתוֹ וּזְכַרְתֶּם אֶת־כָּל־מִצְוֺת יהוה וַעֲשִׂיתֶם אֹתָם, וְלֹא תָתוּרוּ אַחֲרֵי לְבַבְכֶם וְאַחֲרֵי עֵינֵיכֶם, אֲשֶׁר־אַתֶּם זֹנִים אַחֲרֵיהֶם: לְמַעַן תִּזְכְּרוּ וַעֲשִׂיתֶם אֶת־כָּל־מִצְוֺתָי, וִהְיִיתֶם קְדֹשִׁים לֵאלֹהֵיכֶם: אֲנִי יהוה

God, who brought you out of the land of Egypt to be your God.
I am the Lord your God.

True –

The Leader repeats:

▸ The Lord your God is true –

וֶאֱמוּנָה – and faithful is all this, and firmly established for us
that He is the Lord our God,
and there is none beside Him,
and that we, Israel, are His people.
He is our King, who redeems us from the hand of kings
and delivers us from the grasp of all tyrants.
He is our God, who on our behalf repays our foes
and brings just retribution on our mortal enemies;
who performs great deeds beyond understanding
and wonders beyond number;
who kept us alive, not letting our foot slip; *Ps. 66*
who led us on the high places of our enemies,
raising our pride above all our foes;
who did miracles for us
and brought vengeance against Pharaoh;
who performed signs and wonders
in the land of Ham's children;
who smote in His wrath all the firstborn of Egypt,
and brought out His people Israel from their midst
into everlasting freedom;
who led His children through the divided Reed Sea,
plunging their pursuers and enemies into the depths.
When His children saw His might,
they gave praise and thanks to His name,
▸ and willingly accepted His Sovereignty.
Moses and the children of Israel
then sang a song to You with great joy.

אֱלֹהֵיכֶם, אֲשֶׁר הוֹצֵאתִי אֶתְכֶם מֵאֶרֶץ מִצְרַיִם, לִהְיוֹת לָכֶם לֵאלֹהִים, אֲנִי יהוה אֱלֹהֵיכֶם:

אֱמֶת

The שליח ציבור *repeats:*

◂ יהוה אֱלֹהֵיכֶם אֱמֶת

וֶאֱמוּנָה כָּל זֹאת וְקַיָּם עָלֵינוּ

כִּי הוּא יהוה אֱלֹהֵינוּ וְאֵין זוּלָתוֹ, וַאֲנַחְנוּ יִשְׂרָאֵל עַמּוֹ.

הַפּוֹדֵנוּ מִיַּד מְלָכִים

מַלְכֵּנוּ הַגּוֹאֲלֵנוּ מִכַּף כָּל הֶעָרִיצִים.

הָאֵל הַנִּפְרָע לָנוּ מִצָּרֵינוּ

וְהַמְשַׁלֵּם גְּמוּל לְכָל אוֹיְבֵי נַפְשֵׁנוּ.

הָעוֹשֶׂה גְדוֹלוֹת עַד אֵין חֵקֶר, וְנִפְלָאוֹת עַד אֵין מִסְפָּר

תהלים סו הַשָּׂם נַפְשֵׁנוּ בַּחַיִּים, וְלֹא־נָתַן לַמּוֹט רַגְלֵנוּ:

הַמַּדְרִיכֵנוּ עַל בָּמוֹת אוֹיְבֵינוּ

וַיָּרֶם קַרְנֵנוּ עַל כָּל שׂוֹנְאֵינוּ.

הָעוֹשֶׂה לָּנוּ נִסִּים וּנְקָמָה בְּפַרְעֹה

אוֹתוֹת וּמוֹפְתִים בְּאַדְמַת בְּנֵי חָם.

הַמַּכֶּה בְעֶבְרָתוֹ כָּל בְּכוֹרֵי מִצְרָיִם

וַיּוֹצֵא אֶת עַמּוֹ יִשְׂרָאֵל מִתּוֹכָם לְחֵרוּת עוֹלָם.

הַמַּעֲבִיר בָּנָיו בֵּין גִּזְרֵי יַם סוּף

אֶת רוֹדְפֵיהֶם וְאֶת שׂוֹנְאֵיהֶם בִּתְהוֹמוֹת טִבַּע

וְרָאוּ בָנָיו גְּבוּרָתוֹ, שִׁבְּחוּ וְהוֹדוּ לִשְׁמוֹ

◂ וּמַלְכוּתוֹ בְּרָצוֹן קִבְּלוּ עֲלֵיהֶם

מֹשֶׁה וּבְנֵי יִשְׂרָאֵל, לְךָ עָנוּ שִׁירָה.

Those who bear with them these growing shoots – / may they find their fill of joys / on the Festival of Sukkot.
Shelter them in the shadow of Your hand, / for the merit of [Abraham] who believed in You, / and shattered idols.
They call on You in mind and body; / lead them, like [Isaac] the only son who was told what awaited him / [as the ram appeared] in the undergrowth.
Let the sukka be shade, / for the sake of perfect [Jacob] who peeled [stakes for the goats;] / and who encamped at Sukkot.
In Your shadow, shelter the remnant [of Israel], / crowning them with a turban of salvation, / shielding them from weapons of war.
Holy One, make firm Your covenant, / and send the spirit of impurity away, / from all the rocks and shadows it lurks among.

Smash the red head [of our oppressors,] / make Your arrows drunk with the blood / of the nations that rule over us.
(*Some say:* Break the mighty arm of evil, / and send salvation for goodness, / determined courage and support.)
Show compassion for those who celebrate seven days, / who take hold of four choice species; / and listen to their prayer.

Yes, my Salvation, listen to Your people's prayer, / pasture and delight them with the sweetness of Your wisdom.
Elevated One, as You trod down their enemies [*Some say:* as You subjugated the arrogant] in Your rage, / they sang for You, glory and sweet psalms.

With happiness, with song, with great joy,
and they all exclaimed:
"Who is like You, LORD, among the mighty? *Ex. 15*
Who is like You, majestic in holiness,
awesome in praises, doing wonders?"

---

and Jacob, who called the place where he stayed after his encounter with Esau, Sukkot (Gen. 33:17).

מִנֶּשֶׁק *From weapons.* One of the miracles of the Clouds of Glory was that they protected the Israelites from the slings and arrows of their enemies (Rashi on Ex. 19:4).

טוֹעֲנֵי נִטְעֵי צְמָחוֹת / יַשִּׂיגוּ שֹׂבַע שְׂמָחוֹת / בְּחַג הַסֻּכּוֹת
כַּסֵּם בְּצֵל יְמִינֶךָ / לְמַעַן זְכוּת מַאֲמִינֶךָ / נָתַץ מַסֵּכוֹת
מְחַנְּנִים בְּלֵב וּבָשָׂר / נַהֲלֵם כְּיָחִיד נִתְבַּשַּׂר / בַּעֲצֵי הַסְּבָכוֹת
סֻכָּה תִּהְיֶה לְצֵל / עֲבוּר תָּם הַמְפַצֵּל / חָנָה בְּסֻכּוֹת
פְּלִיטִים בְּצִלְּךָ תַּסְתִּירֵם / צְנִיף יֶשַׁע לְהַכְתִּירֵם / מִגֶּשֶׁק לְסַכּוֹת
קָדוֹשׁ, בְּרִית תַּגְבִּיר / רוּחַ טֻמְאָה תַּעֲבִיר / פְּרָעוֹת וּסְכָכוֹת.

שְׁבֹר קָדְקֹד מְאָדָם / שַׁכֵּר חִצֶּיךָ מִדָּם / אֻמּוֹת הַנְּסִיכוֹת
(נ״א: שְׁבֹר זְרוֹעַ רֶשַׁע / שְׁלַח לְצֶדֶק יֶשַׁע / אֹמֶץ וּסְמָכוֹת)
תָּחֹן חוֹגְגֵי שִׁבְעָה / תּוֹפְשֵׂי מְגָדִים אַרְבָּעָה / וְשַׁוְעָתָם סְכוֹת.

יִשְׁעִי סְכוֹת שַׁוְעַת עַמֶּךָ / וּרְעֵם וְעַנְּגֵם בְּטוּב טַעְמֶךָ
סַגִּיב, כְּדָשְׁתָּ צָרֵיהֶם (נ״א: כְּהִכְנַעְתָּ זֵדִים) בְּזַעְמֶךָ
פְּאֵר וָזֶמֶר נָתְנוּ לְהַנְעִימֶךָ.

בְּגִילָה, בְּרִנָּה בְּשִׂמְחָה רַבָּה
וְאָמְרוּ כֻלָּם
שמות טו **מִי־כָמֹכָה בָּאֵלִם יהוה**
מִי כָּמֹכָה נֶאְדָּר בַּקֹּדֶשׁ
נוֹרָא תְהִלֹּת עֹשֵׂה פֶלֶא:

שֹׂבַע שְׂמָחוֹת *Fill of Joys.* A reference to Psalms 16:11, "In Your presence is fullness (*sova*) of joy." The sages, reading *sheva* (seven) for *sova* (fullness), heard in this phrase an intimation of the seven commands of Sukkot: the "four kinds," the sukka, the *Ḥagiga* (festival offering), and *simḥa*, the command to rejoice (*Vayikra Raba* 30:2).

לְמַעַן זְכוּת *For the merit.* This and the next two verses refer, respectively, to Abraham who broke his father's idols, Isaac who was willing to be sacrificed,

▸ Your children beheld Your majesty
as You parted the sea before Moses.

Those who sing a whole Hallel on each of the eight days,
reading the chapter of the offerings in its time;
lead them and settle them in a fertile land,
and they will believe in the eternal Rock of their salvation.

"This is the Rock of our salvation,"
they opened their mouths and said:

"The LORD shall reign for ever and ever." *Ex. 15*

▸ And it is said, "For the LORD has redeemed Jacob *Jer. 31*
and rescued him from a power stronger than his own."

Amid the beauty of holiness they prayed, in His Sanctuary,
moving to call new song, new praises;
Now You shall lay down peace among them, to make them holy
[*Some say:* peace overflowing];
our King [*Some say:* King], Israel's Rock and Holy One.*

Blessed are You, LORD, who redeemed Israel.

**Some end the blessing as follows (see commentary below):*
Blessed are You, LORD, King, Rock and Redeemer of Israel.

---

differences between ancient Israel and ancient Greece. The Greeks believed in the holiness of beauty. Jews believed in the beauty of holiness. In Greece, beauty was revered in its own right. In Judaism, the beautiful is always subordinate to the right, the good, and the holy.

גָּאַל יִשְׂרָאֵל... מֶלֶךְ צוּר יִשְׂרָאֵל וְגוֹאֲלוֹ *Who redeemed Israel... King, Rock and Redeemer of Israel.* The difference between these two endings, "Rock of Israel and its Redeemer" and "who redeemed Israel," reflects an ancient variation between the Jewish communities of Israel and Babylon. The Talmud Yerushalmi (*Berakhot* 1:6) records the first, the Babylonian Talmud (*Pesaḥim* 116b) the second. The reason for the custom of using the Talmud Yerushalmi's

מַלְכוּתְךָ רָאוּ בָנֶיךָ, בּוֹקֵעַ יָם לִפְנֵי מֹשֶׁה

הַלֵּל גּוֹמְרִים כָּל שְׁמוֹנָה
קוֹרְאֵי פָּרָשַׁת קָרְבָּנוֹת בִּזְמַנָּהּ
טָעֵם וְהוֹשִׁיבֵם בְּאֶרֶץ שְׁמֵנָה
נֶצַח צוּר יִשְׁעֵנוּ לְאָמְנָה.

זֶה צוּר יִשְׁעֵנוּ, פָּצוּ פֶה, וְאָמְרוּ
יהוה יִמְלֹךְ לְעֹלָם וָעֶד: שמות טו

וְנֶאֱמַר
כִּי־פָדָה יהוה אֶת־יַעֲקֹב, וּגְאָלוֹ מִיַּד חָזָק מִמֶּנּוּ: ירמיה לא

בְּהַדְרַת קֹדֶשׁ מְחַנְּנִים בְּמִקְדָּשׁוֹ
רוֹחֲשִׁים שִׁיר וָשֶׁבַח לְחַדְּשׁוֹ
שָׁלוֹם תִּשְׁפֹּת לָהֶם לְהַקְדִּישׁוֹ (נ״א: לְהַגְדִּישׁוֹ)
מַלְכֵּנוּ (נ״א: מֶלֶךְ) צוּר יִשְׂרָאֵל וְקְדוֹשׁוֹ.*

בָּרוּךְ אַתָּה יהוה, גָּאַל יִשְׂרָאֵל.

Some end the blessing as follows (see commentary below):

בָּרוּךְ אַתָּה יהוה, מֶלֶךְ צוּר יִשְׂרָאֵל וְגוֹאֲלוֹ.

הַלֵּל גּוֹמְרִים כָּל שְׁמוֹנָה *Whole Hallel on each of the eight days.* Unlike Pesaḥ, when the full Hallel is said only on the first day(s). On Sukkot, each day had a different offering – fourteen on the first, seven on the last, and one on Shemini Atzeret. Therefore each day of Sukkot is regarded as a separate joy, expressed in the full Hallel (*Arakhin* 10b).

בְּהַדְרַת קֹדֶשׁ *The beauty of holiness.* This phrase marks one of the fundamental

הַשְׁכִּיבֵנוּ Help us lie down, O LORD our God, in peace,
and rise up, O our King, to life.
Spread over us Your canopy of peace.
Direct us with Your good counsel,
and save us for the sake of Your name.
Shield us and remove from us every enemy,
plague, sword, famine and sorrow.
Remove the adversary from before and behind us.
Shelter us in the shadow of Your wings,
for You, God, are our Guardian and Deliverer;
You, God, are a gracious and compassionate King.
▸ Guard our going out and our coming in,
for life and peace, from now and for ever.
Spread over us Your canopy of peace.

Venerable God, renew Your Temple Sanctuary;
strengthen the beloved ones You formed in Your own image,
to bless and praise Your name in Your world;
and protect us with Your covenant of peace.

Morning and evening I shall thank You, LORD my God;
with all my heart I shall honor Your name, with my inner being.
Your loving-kindness is very great to me; You have spared my life from the sword.
The Beloved will gather me back from the searing heat to Him;
(*Some say:* The Beloved will gather me back to Him, bringing me close,
and there shall be a canopy, shade all day from the searing heat.) *Is. 4*

The arrogant rise up against me, and set their faces to battle,
snatching and gorging – beat them down, that they fall in their masses.
The Pure One will judge them from the searing second heaven and first,
bringing the sun out of its case to burn through the dwellers of east and of west;
while those who shelter in Him will see [that same sun] and rejoice, and take delight in it, and the great goodness hidden for them,
and never know hunger or thirst, or harm from the summer heat. *Is. 49*

---

ending on festival nights when *piyutim* are said is that most of the early *piyutim* were composed in Israel and were thus incorporated in the Israeli ending.

הַשְׁכִּיבֵנוּ יהוה אֱלֹהֵינוּ לְשָׁלוֹם, וְהַעֲמִידֵנוּ מַלְכֵּנוּ לְחַיִּים
וּפְרֹשׂ עָלֵינוּ סֻכַּת שְׁלוֹמֶךָ, וְתַקְּנֵנוּ בְּעֵצָה טוֹבָה מִלְּפָנֶיךָ
וְהוֹשִׁיעֵנוּ לְמַעַן שְׁמֶךָ.
וְהָגֵן בַּעֲדֵנוּ, וְהָסֵר מֵעָלֵינוּ אוֹיֵב, דֶּבֶר וְחֶרֶב וְרָעָב וְיָגוֹן
וְהָסֵר שָׂטָן מִלְּפָנֵינוּ וּמֵאַחֲרֵינוּ, וּבְצֵל כְּנָפֶיךָ תַּסְתִּירֵנוּ
כִּי אֵל שׁוֹמְרֵנוּ וּמַצִּילֵנוּ אָתָּה
כִּי אֵל מֶלֶךְ חַנּוּן וְרַחוּם אָתָּה.
◄ וּשְׁמֹר צֵאתֵנוּ וּבוֹאֵנוּ לְחַיִּים וּלְשָׁלוֹם מֵעַתָּה וְעַד עוֹלָם.
וּפְרֹשׂ עָלֵינוּ סֻכַּת שְׁלוֹמֶךָ.

וָתִיק חַדֵּשׁ מְכוֹן אוּלַמֶּךָ
אַמֵּץ אֲהוּבִים כּוֹנַנְתָּ בְּצַלְמֶךָ
לְבָרֵךְ וּלְקַדֵּשׁ שִׁמְךָ בְּעוֹלָמֶךָ
תָּגֵן עָלֵינוּ בִּבְרִית שְׁלוֹמֶךָ.

אוֹדְךָ יהוה אֱלֹהַי בֹּקֶר וָעֶרֶב
בְּכָל לְבָבִי אֲכַבְּדָה שִׁמְךָ וּבְקֶרֶב
גָּדוֹל חַסְדְּךָ עָלַי, וְהִצַּלְתָּ נַפְשִׁי מֵחֶרֶב
דּוֹד עוֹד יוֹסִיף אֹתִי אֵלָיו מֵחֹרֶב.
(נ״א: דּוֹד עוֹד יוֹסִיף אֹתִי אֵלָיו לְקָרֵב
וְסֻכָּה תִּהְיֶה לְצֵל־יוֹמָם מֵחֹרֶב:) ישעיה ד

זֵדִים הַקָּמִים עָלַי, וְשָׂמִים פְּנֵיהֶם בִּקְרָב
חוֹטְפִים וְטוֹרְפִים, כַּתְּתֵם וְנָפַל מֵהֶם רָב
טָהוֹר יִפְקֹד עֲלֵיהֶם רִאשׁוֹן וְשֵׁנִי מְחוֹרָב
יוֹצִיא חַמָּה מִנַּרְתִּקָהּ, לְלַהֵט יוֹשְׁבֵי מִזְרָח וּמַעֲרָב
כָּל חוֹסָיו יִרְאוּ וְיִשְׂמָחוּ, וְיִתְעַנְּגוּ בָהּ צָפוּן טוּב רָב
לֹא יִרְעָבוּ וְלֹא יִצְמָאוּ וְלֹא־יַכֵּם שָׁרָב: ישעיה מט

From the light, from flood and from rain, from anguish and trouble,
we shall shelter and abide, hidden beneath Your wings, clinging close,
and You are a wall of fire around, and glory within,
and over all that glorious Presence, a canopy close envelops.
You shall receive Israel – my whole self longs for it –
and Zion will be redeemed by justice, and her captives by righteousness. *Is. 1*

City of the great King – the groans of the dead rise up from the city;
many are the casualties of the LORD, crushed as a wagon crushes one down.
There they shall be gathered together and there they will fall and will rot,
while the innocent people of Yeshurun rejoice in their downfall, leaning upon their Beloved.
They will quench their thirst with the richness of His house, they will suckle from oceans;
Kindness and truth come together; righteousness and peace kiss one another. *Ps. 85*

Blessed are You, LORD,
who spreads a canopy of peace over all His people Israel,
and over Jerusalem.

Continue with "Thus Moses announced" on page 58.

מִנְּגֹהַּ, מִזֶּרֶם וּמִמָּטָר, מִצָּרָה וְצוּקָה
נֶחֱסֶה וְנִתְלוֹנָן, בְּסֵתֶר כְּנָפֶיךָ לְהִדָּבְקָה
סָבִיב לְחוֹמַת אֵשׁ הָיָה לָהּ, לְכָבוֹד בְּחֻקָּהּ
עַל כָּל כָּבוֹד חֻפָּה חֲשׁוּקָה
פָּנֶיךָ יִרְאֶה, כִּי נַפְשִׁי חֲשׁוּקָה
צִיּוֹן בְּמִשְׁפָּט תִּפָּדֶה, וְשָׁבֶיהָ בִּצְדָקָה: ישעיה א

קִרְיַת מֶלֶךְ רָב, מֵעִיר מְתִים יִנְאָקוּ
רַבִּים חַלְלֵי יהוה, כַּאֲשֶׁר תָּעִיק הָעֲגָלָה יָעִיקוּ
שָׁמָּה יִקָּבְצוּ וְשָׁמָּה יִפְלוּ וְיִמָּקוּ
תְּמִימֵי יְשֻׁרוּן יִשְׂמְחוּ בְּמַפַּלְתָּם וְעַל דּוֹדָם יִתְרַפָּקוּ
יִרְוְיֻן מִדֶּשֶׁן בֵּיתוֹ, יַמִּים יִינָקוּ
חֶסֶד־וֶאֱמֶת נִפְגָּשׁוּ, צֶדֶק וְשָׁלוֹם נָשָׁקוּ: תהלים פה

בָּרוּךְ אַתָּה יהוה
הַפּוֹרֵשׂ סֻכַּת שָׁלוֹם עָלֵינוּ
וְעַל כָּל עַמּוֹ יִשְׂרָאֵל וְעַל יְרוּשָׁלָיִם.

Continue with "וַיְדַבֵּר מֹשֶׁה" on page 59.

MA'ARIV FOR THE SECOND NIGHT

If the second night falls on Sunday, say the Ma'aravot on page 116.

בָּרוּךְ Blessed are You, LORD our God,
King of the Universe,
who by His word brings on evenings,
by His wisdom opens the gates of heaven,
with understanding makes time change and the seasons rotate,
and by His will
orders the stars in their constellations in the sky.
He creates day and night, rolling away the light before the darkness,
and darkness before the light.
▸ He makes the day pass and brings on night,
distinguishing day from night:
the LORD of hosts is His name.
May the living and forever enduring God rule over us for all time.

Let the good company of loved ones, [Israel] rejoice
at their festivals,
taking shelter, seven days, in the shade of the sukka,
taking delight therein, with good food of all kinds,
beloved, keeping its commandments by night and by day.

Blessed are You, LORD, who brings on evenings.

אַהֲבַת עוֹלָם With everlasting love
have You loved Your people, the house of Israel.
You have taught us Torah and commandments,
decrees and laws of justice.
Therefore, LORD our God, when we lie down and when we rise up
we will speak of Your decrees,
rejoicing in the words of Your Torah
and Your commandments for ever.
▸ For they are our life and the length of our days;
on them will we meditate day and night.
May You never take away Your love from us.

מעריב לליל יום טוב שני של סוכות

If the second night falls on Sunday, say the מערבות *on page 117.*

בָּרוּךְ אַתָּה יהוה אֱלֹהֵינוּ מֶלֶךְ הָעוֹלָם
אֲשֶׁר בִּדְבָרוֹ מַעֲרִיב עֲרָבִים
בְּחָכְמָה פּוֹתֵחַ שְׁעָרִים
וּבִתְבוּנָה מְשַׁנֶּה עִתִּים וּמַחֲלִיף אֶת הַזְּמַנִּים
וּמְסַדֵּר אֶת הַכּוֹכָבִים בְּמִשְׁמְרוֹתֵיהֶם בָּרָקִיעַ כִּרְצוֹנוֹ.
בּוֹרֵא יוֹם וָלָיְלָה, גּוֹלֵל אוֹר מִפְּנֵי חֹשֶׁךְ וְחֹשֶׁךְ מִפְּנֵי אוֹר
◂ וּמַעֲבִיר יוֹם וּמֵבִיא לָיְלָה
וּמַבְדִּיל בֵּין יוֹם וּבֵין לָיְלָה
יהוה צְבָאוֹת שְׁמוֹ.
אֵל חַי וְקַיָּם תָּמִיד, יִמְלֹךְ עָלֵינוּ לְעוֹלָם וָעֶד.

יִשְׂמְחוּ בְּחַגֵּיהֶם יְדִידִים וּנְעִימִים
חֲסוּת בְּצֵל סֻכָּה שִׁבְעַת יָמִים
יִתְעַנְּגוּ בָהּ בְּמִינֵי מַטְעַמִּים
אֲהוּבִים, מִצְוֹתֶיהָ מְקַיְּמִים לֵילוֹת וְיָמִים.

בָּרוּךְ אַתָּה יהוה, הַמַּעֲרִיב עֲרָבִים.

אַהֲבַת עוֹלָם בֵּית יִשְׂרָאֵל עַמְּךָ אָהָבְתָּ
תּוֹרָה וּמִצְוֹת, חֻקִּים וּמִשְׁפָּטִים, אוֹתָנוּ לִמַּדְתָּ
עַל כֵּן יהוה אֱלֹהֵינוּ בְּשָׁכְבֵנוּ וּבְקוּמֵנוּ נָשִׂיחַ בְּחֻקֶּיךָ
וְנִשְׂמַח בְּדִבְרֵי תוֹרָתֶךָ וּבְמִצְוֹתֶיךָ לְעוֹלָם וָעֶד
◂ כִּי הֵם חַיֵּינוּ וְאֹרֶךְ יָמֵינוּ, וּבָהֶם נֶהְגֶּה יוֹמָם וָלָיְלָה.
וְאַהֲבָתְךָ אַל תָּסִיר מִמֶּנּוּ לְעוֹלָמִים.

With song, with praise, with great joy,
they shall sing out all seven days, as the written Law asks,
as they bring their festival offerings and their peace offerings
and their bulls for sacrifice;
may their sacrifices, their burnt offerings, be accepted
with love.

Blessed are You, Lord,
who loves His people Israel.

The Shema must be said with intense concentration.
When not with a minyan, say:

God, faithful King!

The following verse should be said aloud, while covering the eyes with the right hand:

Listen, Israel: the Lord is our God, the Lord is One. *Deut. 6*

Quietly: Blessed be the name of His glorious kingdom for ever and all time.

וְאָהַבְתָּ Love the Lord your God with all your heart, with all your soul, and with all your might. These words which I command you today shall be on your heart. Teach them repeatedly to your children, speaking of them when you sit at home and when you travel on the way, when you lie down and when you rise. Bind them as a sign on your hand, and they shall be an emblem between your eyes. Write them on the doorposts of your house and gates. *Deut. 6*

וְהָיָה If you indeed heed My commandments with which I charge you today, to love the Lord your God and worship Him with all your heart and with all your soul, I will give rain in your land in its season, the early and late rain; and you shall gather in your grain, wine and oil. I will give grass in your field for your cattle, and you shall eat and be satisfied. Be careful lest your heart be tempted and you go astray and worship other gods, bowing down to them. Then *Deut. 11*

בְּרֹן וְהַלֵּל וְחֶדְוָה רַבָּה
יְצַהֲלוּ כָּל שִׁבְעָה, כַּדָּת הַכְּתוּבָה
חֲגִיגוֹתֵיהֶם וְשַׁלְמֵיהֶם וּפְרֵיהֶם לְקָרְבָה
קָרְבְּנוֹתֵיהֶם וְעוֹלוֹתֵיהֶם יֵרָצוּ בְּאַהֲבָה.

בָּרוּךְ אַתָּה יהוה, אוֹהֵב עַמּוֹ יִשְׂרָאֵל.

The שמע *must be said with intense concentration.*
When not with a מנין*, say:*

אֵל מֶלֶךְ נֶאֱמָן

The following verse should be said aloud, while covering the eyes with the right hand:

דברים ו **שְׁמַע יִשְׂרָאֵל, יהוה אֱלֹהֵינוּ, יהוה ׀ אֶחָד:**

Quietly בָּרוּךְ שֵׁם כְּבוֹד מַלְכוּתוֹ לְעוֹלָם וָעֶד.

דברים ו וְאָהַבְתָּ אֵת יהוה אֱלֹהֶיךָ, בְּכָל־לְבָבְךָ וּבְכָל־נַפְשְׁךָ וּבְכָל־
מְאֹדֶךָ: וְהָיוּ הַדְּבָרִים הָאֵלֶּה, אֲשֶׁר אָנֹכִי מְצַוְּךָ הַיּוֹם, עַל־לְבָבֶךָ:
וְשִׁנַּנְתָּם לְבָנֶיךָ וְדִבַּרְתָּ בָּם, בְּשִׁבְתְּךָ בְּבֵיתֶךָ וּבְלֶכְתְּךָ בַדֶּרֶךְ,
וּבְשָׁכְבְּךָ וּבְקוּמֶךָ: וּקְשַׁרְתָּם לְאוֹת עַל־יָדֶךָ וְהָיוּ לְטֹטָפֹת בֵּין
עֵינֶיךָ: וּכְתַבְתָּם עַל־מְזֻזוֹת בֵּיתֶךָ וּבִשְׁעָרֶיךָ:

דברים יא וְהָיָה אִם־שָׁמֹעַ תִּשְׁמְעוּ אֶל־מִצְוֹתַי אֲשֶׁר אָנֹכִי מְצַוֶּה אֶתְכֶם
הַיּוֹם, לְאַהֲבָה אֶת־יהוה אֱלֹהֵיכֶם וּלְעָבְדוֹ, בְּכָל־לְבַבְכֶם וּבְכָל־
נַפְשְׁכֶם: וְנָתַתִּי מְטַר־אַרְצְכֶם בְּעִתּוֹ, יוֹרֶה וּמַלְקוֹשׁ, וְאָסַפְתָּ דְגָנֶךָ
וְתִירֹשְׁךָ וְיִצְהָרֶךָ: וְנָתַתִּי עֵשֶׂב בְּשָׂדְךָ לִבְהֶמְתֶּךָ, וְאָכַלְתָּ וְשָׂבָעְתָּ:
הִשָּׁמְרוּ לָכֶם פֶּן־יִפְתֶּה לְבַבְכֶם, וְסַרְתֶּם וַעֲבַדְתֶּם אֱלֹהִים אֲחֵרִים
וְהִשְׁתַּחֲוִיתֶם לָהֶם: וְחָרָה אַף־יהוה בָּכֶם, וְעָצַר אֶת־הַשָּׁמַיִם

the LORD's anger will flare against you and He will close the heavens so that there will be no rain. The land will not yield its crops, and you will perish swiftly from the good land that the LORD is giving you. Therefore, set these, My words, on your heart and soul. Bind them as a sign on your hand, and they shall be an emblem between your eyes. Teach them to your children, speaking of them when you sit at home and when you travel on the way, when you lie down and when you rise. Write them on the doorposts of your house and gates, so that you and your children may live long in the land that the LORD swore to your ancestors to give them, for as long as the heavens are above the earth.

וַיֹּאמֶר The LORD spoke to Moses, saying: Speak to the Israelites and tell them to make tassels on the corners of their garments for all generations. They shall attach to the tassel at each corner a thread of blue. This shall be your tassel, and you shall see it and remember all of the LORD's commandments and keep them, not straying after your heart and after your eyes, following your own sinful desires. Thus you will be reminded to keep all My commandments, and be holy to your God. I am the LORD your God, who brought you out of the land of Egypt to be your God. I am the LORD your God. *Num. 15*

True –

The Leader repeats:

▸ The LORD your God is true –

וֶאֱמוּנָה – and faithful is all this,
and firmly established for us
that He is the LORD our God,
and there is none beside Him,
and that we, Israel, are His people.

וְלֹא־יִהְיֶה מָטָר, וְהָאֲדָמָה לֹא תִתֵּן אֶת־יְבוּלָהּ, וַאֲבַדְתֶּם מְהֵרָה מֵעַל הָאָרֶץ הַטֹּבָה אֲשֶׁר יהוה נֹתֵן לָכֶם: וְשַׂמְתֶּם אֶת־דְּבָרַי אֵלֶּה עַל־לְבַבְכֶם וְעַל־נַפְשְׁכֶם, וּקְשַׁרְתֶּם אֹתָם לְאוֹת עַל־יֶדְכֶם, וְהָיוּ לְטוֹטָפֹת בֵּין עֵינֵיכֶם: וְלִמַּדְתֶּם אֹתָם אֶת־בְּנֵיכֶם לְדַבֵּר בָּם, בְּשִׁבְתְּךָ בְּבֵיתֶךָ וּבְלֶכְתְּךָ בַדֶּרֶךְ, וּבְשָׁכְבְּךָ וּבְקוּמֶךָ: וּכְתַבְתָּם עַל־מְזוּזוֹת בֵּיתֶךָ וּבִשְׁעָרֶיךָ: לְמַעַן יִרְבּוּ יְמֵיכֶם וִימֵי בְנֵיכֶם עַל הָאֲדָמָה אֲשֶׁר נִשְׁבַּע יהוה לַאֲבֹתֵיכֶם לָתֵת לָהֶם, כִּימֵי הַשָּׁמַיִם עַל־הָאָרֶץ:

במדבר טו וַיֹּאמֶר יהוה אֶל־מֹשֶׁה לֵּאמֹר: דַּבֵּר אֶל־בְּנֵי יִשְׂרָאֵל וְאָמַרְתָּ אֲלֵהֶם, וְעָשׂוּ לָהֶם צִיצִת עַל־כַּנְפֵי בִגְדֵיהֶם לְדֹרֹתָם, וְנָתְנוּ עַל־צִיצִת הַכָּנָף פְּתִיל תְּכֵלֶת: וְהָיָה לָכֶם לְצִיצִת, וּרְאִיתֶם אֹתוֹ וּזְכַרְתֶּם אֶת־כָּל־מִצְוֹת יהוה וַעֲשִׂיתֶם אֹתָם, וְלֹא תָתֻרוּ אַחֲרֵי לְבַבְכֶם וְאַחֲרֵי עֵינֵיכֶם, אֲשֶׁר־אַתֶּם זֹנִים אַחֲרֵיהֶם: לְמַעַן תִּזְכְּרוּ וַעֲשִׂיתֶם אֶת־כָּל־מִצְוֹתָי, וִהְיִיתֶם קְדֹשִׁים לֵאלֹהֵיכֶם: אֲנִי יהוה אֱלֹהֵיכֶם, אֲשֶׁר הוֹצֵאתִי אֶתְכֶם מֵאֶרֶץ מִצְרַיִם, לִהְיוֹת לָכֶם לֵאלֹהִים, אֲנִי יהוה אֱלֹהֵיכֶם:

אֱמֶת

The שליח ציבור *repeats:*

› יהוה אֱלֹהֵיכֶם אֱמֶת

וֶאֱמוּנָה כָּל זֹאת וְקַיָּם עָלֵינוּ
כִּי הוּא יהוה אֱלֹהֵינוּ וְאֵין זוּלָתוֹ
וַאֲנַחְנוּ יִשְׂרָאֵל עַמּוֹ.

He is our King,
who redeems us from the hand of kings
and delivers us from the grasp of all tyrants.
He is our God,
who on our behalf repays our foes
and brings just retribution on our mortal enemies;
who performs great deeds beyond understanding
and wonders beyond number;
who kept us alive, not letting our foot slip; *Ps. 66*
who led us on the high places of our enemies,
raising our pride above all our foes;
who did miracles for us
and brought vengeance against Pharaoh;
who performed signs and wonders
in the land of Ham's children;
who smote in His wrath all the firstborn of Egypt,
and brought out His people Israel from their midst
into everlasting freedom;
who led His children through the divided Reed Sea,
plunging their pursuers and enemies into the depths.
When His children saw His might,
they gave praise and thanks to His name,
▸ and willingly accepted His Sovereignty.
Moses and the children of Israel then sang a song to You.

Beautify yourselves through the commands, and be
glorious; / bide in the sukka as you live at home at Sukkot.
On the first day, take up the four species, /
to win favor for the water libation, that they fall at Sukkot.

מֵי עֲנָנִים *Water libation [lit. of clouds]*: Throughout Sukkot, in addition to the wine libation accompanying the sacrifices, there was a water libation. Because this is not mentioned explicitly in the Torah, it became a source of contention between the Pharisees who believed in the Oral Torah, and the Sadducees

הַפּוֹדֵנוּ מִיַּד מְלָכִים
מַלְכֵּנוּ הַגּוֹאֲלֵנוּ מִכַּף כָּל הֶעָרִיצִים.
הָאֵל הַנִּפְרָע לָנוּ מִצָּרֵינוּ
וְהַמְשַׁלֵּם גְּמוּל לְכָל אוֹיְבֵי נַפְשֵׁנוּ.
הָעוֹשֶׂה גְדוֹלוֹת עַד אֵין חֵקֶר, וְנִפְלָאוֹת עַד אֵין מִסְפָּר
הַשָּׂם נַפְשֵׁנוּ בַּחַיִּים, וְלֹא־נָתַן לַמּוֹט רַגְלֵנוּ: תהלים סו
הַמַּדְרִיכֵנוּ עַל בָּמוֹת אוֹיְבֵינוּ
וַיָּרֶם קַרְנֵנוּ עַל כָּל שׂוֹנְאֵינוּ.
הָעוֹשֶׂה לָּנוּ נִסִּים וּנְקָמָה בְּפַרְעֹה
אוֹתוֹת וּמוֹפְתִים בְּאַדְמַת בְּנֵי חָם.
הַמַּכֶּה בְעֶבְרָתוֹ כָּל בְּכוֹרֵי מִצְרָיִם
וַיּוֹצֵא אֶת עַמּוֹ יִשְׂרָאֵל מִתּוֹכָם לְחֵרוּת עוֹלָם.
הַמַּעֲבִיר בָּנָיו בֵּין גִּזְרֵי יַם סוּף
אֶת רוֹדְפֵיהֶם וְאֶת שׂוֹנְאֵיהֶם בִּתְהוֹמוֹת טִבַּע
וְרָאוּ בָנָיו גְּבוּרָתוֹ, שִׁבְּחוּ וְהוֹדוּ לִשְׁמוֹ
◂ וּמַלְכוּתוֹ בְּרָצוֹן קִבְּלוּ עֲלֵיהֶם
מֹשֶׁה וּבְנֵי יִשְׂרָאֵל, לְךָ עָנוּ שִׁירָה.

אַנְווּ בְּמִצְוֹת וְאַדְּרוּ / תֵּשְׁבוּ כְּעֵין תְּדוּרוּ בְּחַג הַסֻּכּוֹת.
בָּרִאשׁוֹן תִּקְחוּ אַרְבַּעַת מִינִים / לְרַצּוֹת עַל מֵי עֲנָנִים בְּחַג הַסֻּכּוֹת.

אַנְווּ *Beautify.* From the line "this is my God and I will beautify Him" (Ex. 15:2), the sages inferred that wherever possible a mitzva should be performed in the most beautiful manner (*Shabbat* 133b; *Sukka* 11b). This applies in particular to Sukkot, where the etrog is described by the Torah as "fruit of the citron [lit. beautiful] tree" (Lev. 23:40).

And on the second, with its hint at the libation of water, /
deep calls to deep at Sukkot. *Ps. 42*
From a day's journey distance, ringing with song, bring
the harvest of your trees' fourth year, /
to make the streets of Jerusalem beautiful with fruits at Sukkot.
Multitudes would ascend to Zion with songs of joy, /
at the festival of harvest, the turn of the year at Sukkot;
and it is with great happiness there that they
would celebrate, / Simḥat Beit HaShoeva at Sukkot.
They would send song and music rising up, /
with all instruments of song, with the flute at Sukkot,
rejoicing all together in the music, / with the young boys
among them, the children of the priests at Sukkot.
They took up in their hands, while skipping and jumping, /
jugs of oil thirty logs in size at Sukkot.
And those learned in Torah, the community's scribes /
were there to be seen, bowing straight to the ground at Sukkot.
Priests and Levites played the cymbals, giving thanks; /
the holy men and those of righteous deeds danced at Sukkot.
To separate the men and women, /
a great new structure was added at Sukkot.
And the people made much joy, much noise of the
cymbals; / how lovely are your steps in sandals at Sukkot… *Song. 7*
And now we take the lulav seven days, with Hallel, /
to commemorate the Temple out in the provinces at Sukkot.

---

eaten in Jerusalem, or redeemed for money which was brought in its place. The sages ordained that if it grew within a day's journey from Jerusalem, the fruit itself, not its monetary equivalent, should be taken, "in order to decorate the markets of Jerusalem with fruit" (*Rosh HaShana* 31b; *Beitza* 5a).

הֲמוֹנִים *Multitudes would ascend.* A description of the joyous scene at the "Rejoicing at the Place of the Water Drawing" that began on the second night of the festival (Mishna, *Sukka* 5:2–4).

לְהַפְרִישָׁם *To separate.* A Ladies Gallery was erected in the Temple courtyard to separate the sexes during the Water Drawing festivities, to preserve the sanctity of the celebrations (*Sukka* 51b).

גַּם בַּשֵּׁנִי, רֶמֶז לְנִסּוּךְ הַמַּיִם לְעֵרָה /
תְּהוֹם־אֶל־תְּהוֹם קוֹרֵא: בְּחַג הַסֻּכּוֹת. תהלים מב
דֶּרֶךְ יוֹם, רְבָעִי לְהַעֲלוֹת בְּשִׁירוֹת /
לְעַטֵּר שׁוּקֵי יְרוּשָׁלַיִם בַּפֵּרוֹת בְּחַג הַסֻּכּוֹת.
הֲמוֹנִים הָיוּ עוֹלִים לְצִיּוֹן בְּרִנָּה /
בְּחַג הָאָסִיף, תְּקוּפַת הַשָּׁנָה בְּחַג הַסֻּכּוֹת.
וְשָׁם חוֹגְגִים בְּשִׂמְחָה רַבָּה / שִׂמְחַת בֵּית הַשּׁוֹאֵבָה בְּחַג הַסֻּכּוֹת.
זְמִירוֹת וּנְגִינוֹת לְהַעֲלִיל / בִּכְלֵי שִׁיר וּבֶחָלִיל בְּחַג הַסֻּכּוֹת.
חָדִים כֻּלָּם בִּנְגִינָה / עִם יְלָדִים פִּרְחֵי כְהֻנָּה בְּחַג הַסֻּכּוֹת.
טוֹעֲנִים וּמְקַפְּצִים לְדִלֵּג /
וּבִידֵיהֶם כַּד שֶׁמֶן שֶׁל שְׁלֹשִׁים לֹג בְּחַג הַסֻּכּוֹת.
יוֹדְעֵי דָת וְחַכְמֵי עֵדָה / מַרְאִים לִפְנֵיהֶם קִדָּה בְּחַג הַסֻּכּוֹת.
כֹּהֲנִים וּלְוִיִּם מְצַלְצְלִים וּמוֹדִים /
הַחֲסִידִים וְאַנְשֵׁי מַעֲשֶׂה מְרַקְּדִים בְּחַג הַסֻּכּוֹת.
לַאֲנָשִׁים מִן הַנָּשִׁים לְהַפְרִישָׁם /
מְתַקְּנִים תִּקּוּן גָּדוֹל שָׁם בְּחַג הַסֻּכּוֹת.
מְרַבִּים הָיוּ בְּשִׂמְחָה וּבְצִלְצוּלִים /
מַה־יָּפוּ פְעָמַיִךְ בַּנְּעָלִים: בְּחַג הַסֻּכּוֹת. שיר השירים
נוֹטְלִים לוּלָב שִׁבְעָה בְּהִלּוּלִים /
זֵכֶר לְמִקְדָּשׁ לַעֲשׂוֹת בִּגְבוּלִים בְּחַג הַסֻּכּוֹת.

---

who did not. The sages nonetheless held that that the water libation was hinted at in the Torah by three superfluous letters in the text describing the Sukkot sacrifices, spelling the word *mayim*, "water" (*Shabbat* 103b).

תְּהוֹם־אֶל־תְּהוֹם קוֹרֵא *Deep calls to deep.* A phrase from Psalms 42:8, understood by the sages to be the sound of the upper and lower waters responding to Israel's water libations (*Taanit* 25b).

דֶּרֶךְ יוֹם *From a day's journey.* Fruit of the fourth year was either taken to be

Build the sukka wherever you live, /
so that your generations may know at Sukkot. *Lev. 23*
Seven days in your finery, in the shade of the fresh leaves, /
you form a symbol of the seven clouds of glory at Sukkot.
And the burning coals will be chilled for you in the next world, the scorching air; /
the sukka will shade you all day from the searing heat at Sukkot. *Is. 4*
For her shade will cover you and protect you from the flames; /
all those born among Israel shall dwell in booths at Sukkot. *Lev. 23*
Those who rise against us – [given the rules of Sukkot,]
they would tear up their restrictions before Your eyes, /
and You and Your household will smile at Sukkot. *Deut. 14*
The leaders [of nations] have banded together, so great are their troubles, /
while Israel rejoice in Hallel and happiness at Sukkot.
Seven days we elevate His glorious name, /
with the lulav and the fruit of the citron tree at Sukkot.
And speaking His praises /
we sing a whole Hallel at Sukkot.

How precious is Your loving-kindness, our Maker, we speak of it in the morning,
and tell of Your faithfulness at night, You who are high above all.
You who are strong and staunch, we shall glorify Your name forever,
just as the beloved ones sang, and they all exclaimed –

With happiness, with song, with great joy,
and they all exclaimed:

"Who is like You, LORD, among the mighty? *Ex. 15*
Who is like You, majestic in holiness,
awesome in praises, doing wonders?"

---

one on each of the four sides of the camp, one above, one below, and one that went ahead of the camp – as cloud by day, fire at night – to indicate which way they should travel (see Introduction, page lx).

סֻכָּה לַעֲשׂוֹת בְּכָל מוֹשְׁבֹתֵיכֶם / לְמַעַן יֵדְעוּ דֹרֹתֵיכֶם: בְּחַג הַסֻּכּוֹת. ויקרא כג
עֲדוּיִים לִהְיוֹת שֶׁבַע בְּצֵל רַעֲנָנִים /
סִימָן לְשִׁבְעָה עֲנָנִים בְּחַג הַסֻּכּוֹת.
פַּחִים לְהָצֵן לֶהָבָה וְשָׁרָב /
וְסֻכָּה תִּהְיֶה לְצֵל־יוֹמָם מֵחֹרֶב: בְּחַג הַסֻּכּוֹת. ישעיה ד
צְלָתָהּ לְהָגֵן מִלַּהַט וּלְסַכּוֹת/
כָּל־הָאֶזְרָח בְּיִשְׂרָאֵל יֵשְׁבוּ בַּסֻּכֹּת: בְּחַג הַסֻּכּוֹת. ויקרא כג
קָמִים יְנַתְּקוּ מוֹסֵרוֹת לִרְאִיָּתֶךָ / וְשָׂמַחְתָּ אַתָּה וּבֵיתֶךָ: בְּחַג הַסֻּכּוֹת. דברים יד
רוֹזְנִים נוֹסְדוּ יַחַד מֵרֹב אֲנָחָה
וְכָל יִשְׂרָאֵל יָשִׂישׂוּ בְּהַלֵּל וּבְשִׂמְחָה בְּחַג הַסֻּכּוֹת.
שֵׁם הַנִּכְבָּד שִׁבְעָה לְהַדֵּר / בְּלוּלָב וּפְרִי עֵץ הָדָר בְּחַג הַסֻּכּוֹת.
תִּשְׁבָּחוֹת לוֹ לְמַלֵּל / וְלִגְמֹר בּוֹ אֶת הַהַלֵּל בְּחַג הַסֻּכּוֹת.

יְקַר חַסְדְּךָ יוֹצְרֵנוּ, בַּבֹּקֶר לְמַלְּלָם
אֱמוּנָתְךָ לְסַפֵּר בַּלֵּילוֹת, מֵעֵין כֹּל נֶעְלָם
חָזָק וְאַמִּיץ, נְפָאֵר שִׁמְךָ לְעוֹלָם
כְּשׁוֹרְרוּ אֲהוּבִים וְאָמְרוּ כֻלָּם.

בְּגִילָה, בְּרִנָּה בְּשִׂמְחָה רַבָּה
וְאָמְרוּ כֻלָּם
מִי־כָמֹכָה בָּאֵלִם יהוה שמות טו
מִי כָּמֹכָה נֶאְדָּר בַּקֹּדֶשׁ
נוֹרָא תְהִלֹּת עֹשֵׂה פֶלֶא:

סִימָן לְשִׁבְעָה עֲנָנִים *Symbol of the seven clouds.* According to the view that takes the Sukka as a symbol of the Clouds of Glory that surrounded the Israelites in the wilderness, the seven days of the festival correspond to seven clouds:

▸ Your children beheld Your majesty
as You parted the sea before Moses.

You sheltered Your redeemed ones with Your beautiful clouds,
and spread the canopy of Your glory over them, paving their way.
They evoked Your Oneness and splendor, they who crossed the waves,
and then the angelic powers praised Your name.

He is Our Rock of salvation;
[Israel] opened their mouths and exclaimed:

"The LORD shall reign for ever and ever." *Ex. 15*

▸ And it is said,

"For the LORD has redeemed Jacob *Jer. 31*
and rescued him from a power stronger than his own."

Build Your Tabernacle; restore that which has fallen;
lay again her foundations, rebuild her on her hill.
Pasture Your flock among [Zion's] dwelling places; pass them on for an inheritance.
Desire as You once did, righteous sacrifice, burned offerings.*

Blessed are You, LORD, who redeemed Israel.

**Some end the blessing as follows (see commentary on page 128):*
Blessed are You, LORD, King, Rock and Redeemer of Israel.

---

to Jerusalem to the temple to celebrate Sukkot (Zech. 14:16–19). Ḥanukka, the eight day festival inaugurated by the Maccabees to celebrate the rededication of the Temple after its defilement by the Greeks, was also modeled on Sukkot, though held later in the year (II Maccabees 10:5–8). In the Grace after Meals we use the phrase, "restore… the fallen Tabernacle of David," to refer to the rebuilding of the Temple.

› מַלְכוּתְךָ רָאוּ בָנֶיךָ, בּוֹקֵעַ יָם לִפְנֵי מֹשֶׁה

יְפִי עֲנָנֶיךָ סִכַּכְתָּ עַל גְּאוּלִים
חֻפַּת כְּבוֹדְךָ פָּרַשְׂתָּ עֲלֵיהֶם, לִהְיוֹת סְלוּלִים
יִחֲדוּךָ וּפֵאֲרוּךָ כְּעוֹבְרֵי גַּלִּים
אָז לְשִׁמְךָ שִׁבְּחוּ בְּנֵי אֵלִים.

זֶה צוּר יִשְׁעֵנוּ, פָּצוּ פֶה. וְאָמְרוּ
יהוה יִמְלֹךְ לְעֹלָם וָעֶד: שמות טו

› וְנֶאֱמַר
כִּי־פָדָה יהוה אֶת־יַעֲקֹב ירמיה לא
וּגְאָלוֹ מִיַּד חָזָק מִמֶּנּוּ:

בְּנֵה סֻכָּתְךָ, וְהָקֵם הַנְּפוּלָה
יְסוֹדוֹתֶיהָ לְשַׁתֵּת וְלִבְנוֹתָהּ עַל תִּלָּהּ
צֹאנְךָ לִרְעוֹת עַל מִשְׁכְּנוֹתֶיהָ לְהַנְחִילָהּ
חֲפֹץ כְּמִקֶּדֶם זִבְחֵי צֶדֶק וְעוֹלָה.*

בָּרוּךְ אַתָּה יהוה, גָּאַל יִשְׂרָאֵל.

Some end the blessing as follows (see commentary on page 128):
בָּרוּךְ אַתָּה יהוה, מֶלֶךְ צוּר יִשְׂרָאֵל וְגוֹאֲלוֹ.

וְהָקֵם הַנְּפוּלָה *Restore that which has fallen.* Here the reference is to the Temple. There are strong connections between Sukkot and the temple. King Solomon held the dedication ceremony for the First Temple on Sukkot (I Kings 8:2). The Second Temple was also inaugurated on Sukkot (Ezra 3:2–6). The prophet Zechariah foresees a day when the nations of the world will all come

הַשְׁכִּיבֵנוּ Help us lie down, O Lord our God, in peace,
and rise up, O our King, to life.
Spread over us Your canopy of peace.
Direct us with Your good counsel,
and save us for the sake of Your name.
Shield us and remove from us every enemy,
plague, sword, famine and sorrow.
Remove the adversary
from before and behind us.
Shelter us in the shadow of Your wings,
for You, God, are our Guardian and Deliverer;
You, God, are a gracious and compassionate King.
▸ Guard our going out and our coming in,
for life and peace,
from now and for ever.
Spread over us Your canopy of peace.

> Whoever calls this holy assembly and keeps it,
> will receive his reward on that day that is to come.
> [The Leviathan,] enclosed in the pride of its
> impenetrable scales –
> our Beloved will repay that man in the sukka of its skin.

Blessed are You, Lord,
who spreads a canopy of peace over us,
over all His people Israel, and over Jerusalem.

Continue with "Thus Moses announced" on page 58.

הַשְׁכִּיבֵנוּ יהוה אֱלֹהֵינוּ לְשָׁלוֹם
וְהַעֲמִידֵנוּ מַלְכֵּנוּ לְחַיִּים
וּפְרֹשׂ עָלֵינוּ סֻכַּת שְׁלוֹמֶךָ
וְתַקְּנֵנוּ בְּעֵצָה טוֹבָה מִלְּפָנֶיךָ
וְהוֹשִׁיעֵנוּ לְמַעַן שְׁמֶךָ.
וְהָגֵן בַּעֲדֵנוּ
וְהָסֵר מֵעָלֵינוּ אוֹיֵב, דֶּבֶר וְחֶרֶב וְרָעָב וְיָגוֹן
וְהָסֵר שָׂטָן מִלְּפָנֵינוּ וּמֵאַחֲרֵינוּ, וּבְצֵל כְּנָפֶיךָ תַּסְתִּירֵנוּ
כִּי אֵל שׁוֹמְרֵנוּ וּמַצִּילֵנוּ אָתָּה
כִּי אֵל מֶלֶךְ חַנּוּן וְרַחוּם אָתָּה.
◂ וּשְׁמֹר צֵאתֵנוּ וּבוֹאֵנוּ לְחַיִּים וּלְשָׁלוֹם מֵעַתָּה וְעַד עוֹלָם.
וּפְרֹשׂ עָלֵינוּ סֻכַּת שְׁלוֹמֶךָ.

קוֹרֵא מִקְרָא קֹדֶשׁ וּמְשַׁמְּרוֹ
יְקַבֵּל לַיּוֹם הַבָּא שְׂכָרוֹ
גַּאֲוָה אֲפִיקֵי מָגִנִּים סְגוּרוֹ
דּוֹד לְמַלְאוֹת לוֹ בְּשֻׂכּוֹת עוֹרוֹ.

בָּרוּךְ אַתָּה יהוה
הַפּוֹרֵשׂ סֻכַּת שָׁלוֹם עָלֵינוּ וְעַל כָּל עַמּוֹ יִשְׂרָאֵל וְעַל יְרוּשָׁלָיִם.

Continue with "וַיְדַבֵּר מֹשֶׁה" on page 59.

MA'ARIV FOR SHEMINI ATZERET

בָּרוּךְ Blessed are You, LORD our God, King of the Universe,
who by His word brings on evenings,
by His wisdom opens the gates of heaven,
with understanding makes time change and the seasons rotate,
and by His will
orders the stars in their constellations in the sky.
He creates day and night,
rolling away the light before the darkness,
and darkness before the light.
▸ He makes the day pass and brings on night,
distinguishing day from night:
the LORD of hosts is His name.
May the living and forever enduring God
rule over us for all time.

> Let me ornament You with glory and praise,
> on the eighth day of the assembly, at night.
> I shall tell of Your mighty deeds in the presence of many,
> my Beloved, who makes day pass and brings on night.

Blessed are You, LORD, who brings on evenings.

אַהֲבַת עוֹלָם With everlasting love
have You loved Your people, the house of Israel.
You have taught us Torah and commandments,
decrees and laws of justice.
Therefore, LORD our God, when we lie down and when we rise up
we will speak of Your decrees, rejoicing in the words of Your Torah
and Your commandments for ever.

דוד *Beloved.* A term of endearment for God, drawn from the language of Song of Songs.

מעריב לליל שמיני עצרת

בָּרוּךְ אַתָּה יהוה אֱלֹהֵינוּ מֶלֶךְ הָעוֹלָם
אֲשֶׁר בִּדְבָרוֹ מַעֲרִיב עֲרָבִים
בְּחָכְמָה פּוֹתֵחַ שְׁעָרִים
וּבִתְבוּנָה מְשַׁנֶּה עִתִּים וּמַחֲלִיף אֶת הַזְּמַנִּים
וּמְסַדֵּר אֶת הַכּוֹכָבִים בְּמִשְׁמְרוֹתֵיהֶם בָּרָקִיעַ כִּרְצוֹנוֹ.
בּוֹרֵא יוֹם וָלָיְלָה, גּוֹלֵל אוֹר מִפְּנֵי חֹשֶׁךְ וְחֹשֶׁךְ מִפְּנֵי אוֹר
◂ וּמַעֲבִיר יוֹם וּמֵבִיא לָיְלָה
וּמַבְדִּיל בֵּין יוֹם וּבֵין לָיְלָה
יהוה צְבָאוֹת שְׁמוֹ.
אֵל חַי וְקַיָּם תָּמִיד, יִמְלֹךְ עָלֵינוּ לְעוֹלָם וָעֶד.

אַעֲנִיד לְךָ תִּפְאָרָה וְהַלֵּל
בְּיוֹם שְׁמִינִי בַּעֲצֶרֶת בְּלֵיל
גְּבוּרוֹתֶיךָ בְּרֹב עָם אֲמַלֵּל
דּוֹד, מַעֲבִיר יוֹם וּמֵבִיא לֵיל.

בָּרוּךְ אַתָּה יהוה, הַמַּעֲרִיב עֲרָבִים.

אַהֲבַת עוֹלָם בֵּית יִשְׂרָאֵל עַמְּךָ אָהָבְתָּ
תּוֹרָה וּמִצְוֹת, חֻקִּים וּמִשְׁפָּטִים, אוֹתָנוּ לִמַּדְתָּ
עַל כֵּן יהוה אֱלֹהֵינוּ בְּשָׁכְבֵנוּ וּבְקוּמֵנוּ נָשִׂיחַ בְּחֻקֶּיךָ
וְנִשְׂמַח בְּדִבְרֵי תוֹרָתֶךָ וּבְמִצְוֹתֶיךָ לְעוֹלָם וָעֶד

אַעֲנִיד *Let me ornament.* A poem composed by thirteenth century liturgist R. Daniel ben Jacob.

▸ For they are our life and the length of our days;
on them will we meditate day and night.
May You never take away Your love from us.

> Remember us, to crown us with splendor, with a year of
> Your goodness,
> that we quench our thirst with the richness of Your house.
> Remember for those who seek You, who dwell in Your house,
> the kindness of youth, the bridal time of Your love.

Blessed are You, LORD, who loves His people Israel.

The Shema must be said with intense concentration.
When not with a minyan, say:

God, faithful King!

The following verse should be said aloud, while covering the eyes with the right hand:

Listen, Israel: the LORD is our God, the LORD is One. *Deut. 6*

Quietly: Blessed be the name of His glorious kingdom for ever and all time.

וְאָהַבְתָּ Love the LORD your God with all your heart, with all your soul, and with all your might. These words which I command you today shall be on your heart. Teach them repeatedly to your children, speaking of them when you sit at home and when you travel on the way, when you lie down and when you rise. Bind them as a sign on your hand, and they shall be an emblem between your eyes. Write them on the doorposts of your house and gates. *Deut. 6*

וְהָיָה If you indeed heed My commandments with which I charge you today, to love the LORD your God and worship Him with all your heart and with all your soul, I will give rain in your land in its season, the early and late rain; and you shall gather in your grain, wine and oil. I will give grass in your field for your cattle, and you *Deut. 11*

---

remember of you the kindness of your youth, your love when you were a bride; how you walked after Me in the desert, through a land not sown."

◂ כִּי הֵם חַיֵּינוּ וְאֹרֶךְ יָמֵינוּ, וּבָהֶם נֶהְגֶּה יוֹמָם וָלָיְלָה.
וְאַהֲבָתְךָ אַל תָּסִיר מִמֶּנּוּ לְעוֹלָמִים.

הַזָּכֵר לְעֶטְרֵנוּ בִּשְׁנַת טוֹבוֹתֶיךָ
וְנִרְוֶה מִדֶּשֶׁן בֵּיתֶךָ
זְכֹר לְדוֹרְשֶׁיךָ, יוֹשְׁבֵי בֵיתֶךָ
חֶסֶד נְעוּרִים וְכְלוּל אַהֲבָתֶךָ.

בָּרוּךְ אַתָּה יהוה, אוֹהֵב עַמּוֹ יִשְׂרָאֵל.

The שמע *must be said with intense concentration.*
When not with a מנין*, say:*

אֵל מֶלֶךְ נֶאֱמָן

The following verse should be said aloud, while covering the eyes with the right hand:

דברים ו שְׁמַע יִשְׂרָאֵל, יהוה אֱלֹהֵינוּ, יהוה | אֶחָד:

Quietly בָּרוּךְ שֵׁם כְּבוֹד מַלְכוּתוֹ לְעוֹלָם וָעֶד.

דברים ו וְאָהַבְתָּ אֵת יהוה אֱלֹהֶיךָ, בְּכָל־לְבָבְךָ וּבְכָל־נַפְשְׁךָ וּבְכָל־
מְאֹדֶךָ: וְהָיוּ הַדְּבָרִים הָאֵלֶּה, אֲשֶׁר אָנֹכִי מְצַוְּךָ הַיּוֹם, עַל־לְבָבֶךָ:
וְשִׁנַּנְתָּם לְבָנֶיךָ וְדִבַּרְתָּ בָּם, בְּשִׁבְתְּךָ בְּבֵיתֶךָ וּבְלֶכְתְּךָ בַדֶּרֶךְ,
וּבְשָׁכְבְּךָ וּבְקוּמֶךָ: וּקְשַׁרְתָּם לְאוֹת עַל־יָדֶךָ וְהָיוּ לְטֹטָפֹת בֵּין
עֵינֶיךָ: וּכְתַבְתָּם עַל־מְזֻזוֹת בֵּיתֶךָ וּבִשְׁעָרֶיךָ:

דברים יא וְהָיָה אִם־שָׁמֹעַ תִּשְׁמְעוּ אֶל־מִצְוֺתַי אֲשֶׁר אָנֹכִי מְצַוֶּה אֶתְכֶם
הַיּוֹם, לְאַהֲבָה אֶת־יהוה אֱלֹהֵיכֶם וּלְעָבְדוֹ, בְּכָל־לְבַבְכֶם וּבְכָל־
נַפְשְׁכֶם: וְנָתַתִּי מְטַר־אַרְצְכֶם בְּעִתּוֹ, יוֹרֶה וּמַלְקוֹשׁ, וְאָסַפְתָּ דְגָנֶךָ
וְתִירֹשְׁךָ וְיִצְהָרֶךָ: וְנָתַתִּי עֵשֶׂב בְּשָׂדְךָ לִבְהֶמְתֶּךָ, וְאָכַלְתָּ וְשָׂבָעְתָּ:

חֶסֶד נְעוּרִים *The kindness of youth.* Based on the line in Jeremiah (2:2), "I

shall eat and be satisfied. Be careful lest your heart be tempted and you go astray and worship other gods, bowing down to them. Then the LORD's anger will flare against you and He will close the heavens so that there will be no rain. The land will not yield its crops, and you will perish swiftly from the good land that the LORD is giving you. Therefore, set these, My words, on your heart and soul. Bind them as a sign on your hand, and they shall be an emblem between your eyes. Teach them to your children, speaking of them when you sit at home and when you travel on the way, when you lie down and when you rise. Write them on the doorposts of your house and gates, so that you and your children may live long in the land that the LORD swore to your ancestors to give them, for as long as the heavens are above the earth.

וַיֹּאמֶר The LORD spoke to Moses, saying: Speak to the Israelites *Num. 15* and tell them to make tassels on the corners of their garments for all generations. They shall attach to the tassel at each corner a thread of blue. This shall be your tassel, and you shall see it and remember all of the LORD's commandments and keep them, not straying after your heart and after your eyes, following your own sinful desires. Thus you will be reminded to keep all My commandments, and be holy to your God. I am the LORD your God, who brought you out of the land of Egypt to be your God. I am the LORD your God.

True –

The Leader repeats:

▸ The LORD your God is true –

וֶאֱמוּנָה – and faithful is all this,
and firmly established for us
that He is the LORD our God,
and there is none beside Him,
and that we, Israel, are His people.

הִשָּׁמְרוּ לָכֶם פֶּן־יִפְתֶּה לְבַבְכֶם, וְסַרְתֶּם וַעֲבַדְתֶּם אֱלֹהִים אֲחֵרִים וְהִשְׁתַּחֲוִיתֶם לָהֶם: וְחָרָה אַף־יהוה בָּכֶם, וְעָצַר אֶת־הַשָּׁמַיִם וְלֹא־יִהְיֶה מָטָר, וְהָאֲדָמָה לֹא תִתֵּן אֶת־יְבוּלָהּ, וַאֲבַדְתֶּם מְהֵרָה מֵעַל הָאָרֶץ הַטֹּבָה אֲשֶׁר יהוה נֹתֵן לָכֶם: וְשַׂמְתֶּם אֶת־דְּבָרַי אֵלֶּה עַל־לְבַבְכֶם וְעַל־נַפְשְׁכֶם, וּקְשַׁרְתֶּם אֹתָם לְאוֹת עַל־יֶדְכֶם, וְהָיוּ לְטוֹטָפֹת בֵּין עֵינֵיכֶם: וְלִמַּדְתֶּם אֹתָם אֶת־בְּנֵיכֶם לְדַבֵּר בָּם, בְּשִׁבְתְּךָ בְּבֵיתֶךָ וּבְלֶכְתְּךָ בַדֶּרֶךְ, וּבְשָׁכְבְּךָ וּבְקוּמֶךָ: וּכְתַבְתָּם עַל־מְזוּזוֹת בֵּיתֶךָ וּבִשְׁעָרֶיךָ: לְמַעַן יִרְבּוּ יְמֵיכֶם וִימֵי בְנֵיכֶם עַל הָאֲדָמָה אֲשֶׁר נִשְׁבַּע יהוה לַאֲבֹתֵיכֶם לָתֵת לָהֶם, כִּימֵי הַשָּׁמַיִם עַל־הָאָרֶץ:

במדבר טו
וַיֹּאמֶר יהוה אֶל־מֹשֶׁה לֵּאמֹר: דַּבֵּר אֶל־בְּנֵי יִשְׂרָאֵל וְאָמַרְתָּ אֲלֵהֶם, וְעָשׂוּ לָהֶם צִיצִת עַל־כַּנְפֵי בִגְדֵיהֶם לְדֹרֹתָם, וְנָתְנוּ עַל־צִיצִת הַכָּנָף פְּתִיל תְּכֵלֶת: וְהָיָה לָכֶם לְצִיצִת, וּרְאִיתֶם אֹתוֹ וּזְכַרְתֶּם אֶת־כָּל־מִצְוֺת יהוה וַעֲשִׂיתֶם אֹתָם, וְלֹא תָתֻרוּ אַחֲרֵי לְבַבְכֶם וְאַחֲרֵי עֵינֵיכֶם, אֲשֶׁר־אַתֶּם זֹנִים אַחֲרֵיהֶם: לְמַעַן תִּזְכְּרוּ וַעֲשִׂיתֶם אֶת־כָּל־מִצְוֺתָי, וִהְיִיתֶם קְדֹשִׁים לֵאלֹהֵיכֶם: אֲנִי יהוה אֱלֹהֵיכֶם, אֲשֶׁר הוֹצֵאתִי אֶתְכֶם מֵאֶרֶץ מִצְרַיִם, לִהְיוֹת לָכֶם לֵאלֹהִים, אֲנִי יהוה אֱלֹהֵיכֶם:

אֱמֶת

The שליח ציבור *repeats:*

◂ יהוה אֱלֹהֵיכֶם אֱמֶת

וֶאֱמוּנָה כָּל זֹאת וְקַיָּם עָלֵינוּ
כִּי הוּא יהוה אֱלֹהֵינוּ וְאֵין זוּלָתוֹ
וַאֲנַחְנוּ יִשְׂרָאֵל עַמּוֹ.

He is our King, who redeems us from the hand of kings
and delivers us from the grasp of all tyrants.
He is our God, who on our behalf repays our foes
and brings just retribution on our mortal enemies;
who performs great deeds beyond understanding
and wonders beyond number;
who kept us alive, *Ps. 66*
not letting our foot slip;
who led us on the high places of our enemies,
raising our pride above all our foes;
who did miracles for us
and brought vengeance against Pharaoh;
who performed signs and wonders
in the land of Ham's children;
who smote in His wrath all the firstborn of Egypt,
and brought out His people Israel from their midst
into everlasting freedom;
who led His children through the divided Reed Sea,
plunging their pursuers and enemies into the depths.
When His children saw His might,
they gave praise and thanks to His name,
▸ and willingly accepted His Sovereignty.
Moses and the children of Israel
then sang a song to You.

On the eighth day I shall pour out my heart and soul
like water,
before the One who rides the heavens in His pride on the eighth day.
On the eighth day [of the Tabernacle,] calling the servant
and his descendants to serve,
Moses called upon Aaron and his sons on the eighth day.

לְשָׁרֵת מְשָׁרֵת וְנִינָיו *Calling the servant... to serve*: The service of the sanctuary, led by Aaron, the first High Priest, was inaugurated after seven days of preparation (Lev. 9:1).

הַפּוֹדֵנוּ מִיַּד מְלָכִים
מַלְכֵּנוּ הַגּוֹאֲלֵנוּ מִכַּף כָּל הֶעָרִיצִים.
הָאֵל הַנִּפְרָע לָנוּ מִצָּרֵינוּ
וְהַמְשַׁלֵּם גְּמוּל לְכָל אוֹיְבֵי נַפְשֵׁנוּ.
הָעוֹשֶׂה גְדוֹלוֹת עַד אֵין חֵקֶר
וְנִפְלָאוֹת עַד אֵין מִסְפָּר
תהלים סו הַשָּׂם נַפְשֵׁנוּ בַּחַיִּים, וְלֹא־נָתַן לַמּוֹט רַגְלֵנוּ:
הַמַּדְרִיכֵנוּ עַל בָּמוֹת אוֹיְבֵינוּ
וַיָּרֶם קַרְנֵנוּ עַל כָּל שׂוֹנְאֵינוּ.
הָעוֹשֶׂה לָּנוּ נִסִּים וּנְקָמָה בְּפַרְעֹה
אוֹתוֹת וּמוֹפְתִים בְּאַדְמַת בְּנֵי חָם.
הַמַּכֶּה בְעֶבְרָתוֹ כָּל בְּכוֹרֵי מִצְרָיִם
וַיּוֹצֵא אֶת עַמּוֹ יִשְׂרָאֵל מִתּוֹכָם לְחֵרוּת עוֹלָם.
הַמַּעֲבִיר בָּנָיו בֵּין גִּזְרֵי יַם סוּף
אֶת רוֹדְפֵיהֶם וְאֶת שׂוֹנְאֵיהֶם בִּתְהוֹמוֹת טִבַּע
וְרָאוּ בָנָיו גְּבוּרָתוֹ, שִׁבְּחוּ וְהוֹדוּ לִשְׁמוֹ
◄ וּמַלְכוּתוֹ בְּרָצוֹן קִבְּלוּ עֲלֵיהֶם
מֹשֶׁה וּבְנֵי יִשְׂרָאֵל, לְךָ עָנוּ שִׁירָה.

שְׁמִינִי אֶשְׁפֹּךְ לֵב וָנֶפֶשׁ כַּמַּיִם
לִפְנֵי רוֹכֵב בְּגַאֲוָתוֹ שָׁמַיִם בַּיּוֹם הַשְּׁמִינִי.
שְׁמִינִי בִּכְהֻנָּה לְשָׁרֵת מְשָׁרֵת וְנִינָיו
קָרָא מֹשֶׁה לְאַהֲרֹן וּלְבָנָיו בַּיּוֹם הַשְּׁמִינִי.

בַּיּוֹם הַשְּׁמִינִי *On the eighth day.* A poem weaving together the various commands and occasions on which the number eight played a significant part.

On the eighth day the ruling for the rains
is noted: whether they should be plentiful or scarce on the eighth day.

On the eighth day [of a boy's life] He calls for the sign
of the covenant,
that the remnant [of Israel] be spared all [harm] on the eighth day.

The eighth day is laid out for faithful [Israel]:
"Give of what is yours to seven, to eight…" on the eighth day. *Ecc. 11*

The eighth day He gave to those leaving the sukka
to sit in their houses and in their yards on the eighth day.

The eighth day was fixed for the young of cattle
from then on [for their sacrifice] to be accepted
by the One who dwells on high from the eighth day.

The eighth day He considered and joined on to the seven,
for [delaying the festival to winter] would cause
trouble for [Israel] the mother of seven on the eighth day.

The eighth day [of the Temple's completion] was one
of ceremony, for the gathering to bless their king,
as [Solomon] sent the people on their way on the eighth day.

The eighth day was reserved by the One wrapped in light,
for a much smaller offering, but good on the eighth day.

---

is also known as Atzeret). However, God brought it forward in order not to burden the people with the need to return to Jerusalem in the cold and rain of winter.

יוֹלֶדֶת הַשִּׁבְעָה *The mother of seven.* A description of the people of Israel in Jeremiah (15:9). Radak takes "seven" there not to be understood literally, but rather as a way of saying "many."

לְבָרֵךְ קְהָל מַלְכָּם *To bless their king.* Solomon sent the people home on the eighth day (1 Kings 8:66).

לְקָרְבָּן טוֹב מְעַט *Smaller offering, but good.* On Shemini Atzeret, only one young bull was offered, unlike the other seven days when a total of seventy were sacrificed.

שְׁמִינִי גְּזֻרַת דַּת גְּשָׁמִים
אִם רַב וְאִם מְעַט נִרְשָׁמִים בַּיּוֹם הַשְּׁמִינִי.
שְׁמִינִי דֹּרַשׁ לְאוֹת בְּרִית
לְהִנָּצֵל בּוֹ מֵאַף שְׁאֵרִית בַּיּוֹם הַשְּׁמִינִי.
שְׁמִינִי הוּכַן לְנֶאֱמָנָה
קהלת יא תֶּן־חֵלֶק לְשִׁבְעָה וְגַם לִשְׁמוֹנָה: בַּיּוֹם הַשְּׁמִינִי.
שְׁמִינִי וִתֵּר לְסֻכָּה עוֹצְרִים
לֵישֵׁב בְּבָתִּים וּבַחֲצֵרִים בַּיּוֹם הַשְּׁמִינִי.
שְׁמִינִי זְמַן לִבְהֵמָה
לְהֵרָצוֹת פְּנֵי שׁוֹכֵן רוּמָה בַּיּוֹם הַשְּׁמִינִי.
שְׁמִינִי חָקַר לְאָסְפוֹ עִם שִׁבְעָה
מִפְּנֵי טֹרַח יוֹלֶדֶת הַשִּׁבְעָה בַּיּוֹם הַשְּׁמִינִי.
שְׁמִינִי טְכֵּס לְבָרֵךְ קָהָל מַלְכָּם
בְּשַׁלַּח הָעָם לְדַרְכָּם בַּיּוֹם הַשְּׁמִינִי.
שְׁמִינִי יִחֵד אוֹר עָט
לְקָרְבָּן טוֹב מְעָט בַּיּוֹם הַשְּׁמִינִי.

לְהִנָּצֵל בּוֹ מֵאַף שְׁאֵרִית *That the remnant be spared.* A reference to God's anger at Moses when he delayed circumcising his son (Ex. 4:24).

תֶּן חֵלֶק לְשִׁבְעָה וְגַם לִשְׁמוֹנָה *Give of what is yours to seven, to eight.* A line from Ecclesiastes (11:2), interpreted by the sages as a reference to the seven days of Sukkot followed by the eighth, Shemini Atzeret.

זְמַן לִבְהֵמָה *Fixed for the young of cattle.* Animals had to be at least eight days old to be offered as a sacrifice (Lev. 22:27).

לְהֵרָצוֹת *To be accepted.* This can also be translated as "not to overburden." According to the *Pesikta,* in principle Shemini Atzeret should have been fifty days after Sukkot, as is Shavuot after Pesaḥ (in the rabbinic literature Shavuot

The eighth day [circumcision,] overrides Yom Kippur
and Shabbat,
in fulfillment of the law of the One who wipes
iniquity clean — on the eighth day.
The eighth day points towards the overflow of happiness,
to the eighth string that will play when He
does wonders — on the eighth day.
That eighth string is waiting for the time to come,
to bring joy to the people close to Him — on the eighth day.
The eighth day is called Atzeret –
an assembly of the nation guarded like the shadow
in God's eye — on the eighth day.
The eighth day, [circumcision,] is laid out in all its laws,
and thirteen covenants were forged
with it — on the eighth day.
That eighth day is there to save those marked by it,
to save them, to guard them from Sheol's
gaping mouth — on the eighth day.
The eighth day, lots are cast then [to choose the
serving priests]
to slaughter the offerings and prepare them — on the eighth day.
The eighth day, when we say "[who has... brought us
to this] time:"
a blessing to the faithful God — on the eighth day.
The eighth day, declared a pilgrim festival in itself,
for all the people to rejoice in — on the eighth day.
The eighth day, desired, with the sacrifice all its own,
to the One of whose glory all the earth is filled — on the eighth day.
The eighth day, which has its own psalm by which
to praise,
and on which we sing a whole Hallel — on the eighth day.

---

had seven strings, but in the Messianic age it will have eight (*Arakhin* 13b).

שְׁלֹשׁ עֶשְׂרֵה בְּרִיתוֹת *Thirteen covenants.* The word *brit*, covenant, is mentioned thirteen times in the Torah in connection with circumcision.

פַּיִס *Lots are cast.* On Shemini Atzeret, lots were cast as to which of the

שְׁמִינִי כִּפּוּר וּמָנוֹחַ דּוֹחֶה
לְקַיֵּם צִוּוּי עֲוֹנוֹת מוֹחֶה בַּיּוֹם הַשְּׁמִינִי.
שְׁמִינִי לְעַדֵּף שִׂמְחָה לְרָאוֹת
לְנַעֲנֵעַ שְׁמִינִי בַּעֲשׂוֹתוֹ נוֹרָאוֹת בַּיּוֹם הַשְּׁמִינִי.
שְׁמִינִי מְזֻמָּן לֶעָתִיד לָבוֹא
לְשַׂמֵּחַ בּוֹ עַם קְרוֹבוֹ בַּיּוֹם הַשְּׁמִינִי.
שְׁמִינִי נִקְרָא עֲצֶרֶת
לְאֹם כְּאִישׁוֹן נִנְצֶרֶת בַּיּוֹם הַשְּׁמִינִי.
שְׁמִינִי סְדוּרָה בְּדָתוֹת
וּבוֹ נִכְרְתוּ שְׁלֹשׁ עֶשְׂרֵה בְּרִיתוֹת בַּיּוֹם הַשְּׁמִינִי.
שְׁמִינִי עֵרֶךְ הַחֲתוּמִים בּוֹ לְהַצִּיל
מְפוֹעֶרֶת גָּנוֹן וְהִצִּיל בַּיּוֹם הַשְּׁמִינִי.
שְׁמִינִי פַּיִס בּוֹ לְהִתְכֵּן
לִטְבֹּחַ טֶבַח וְהָכֵן בַּיּוֹם הַשְּׁמִינִי.
שְׁמִינִי צִוּוּי לוֹמַר זְמַן
לְבָרֵךְ הָאֵל הַנֶּאֱמָן בַּיּוֹם הַשְּׁמִינִי.
שְׁמִינִי קָבוּעַ רֶגֶל בִּפְנֵי עַצְמוֹ
לְשַׂמֵּחַ בּוֹ עַמּוֹ בַּיּוֹם הַשְּׁמִינִי.
שְׁמִינִי רָצוּי קָרְבָּן לְהַקְרִיב בּוֹ לְבַדּוֹ
לְמְלֹא כָל הָאָרֶץ כְּבוֹדוֹ בַּיּוֹם הַשְּׁמִינִי.
שְׁמִינִי שִׁיר בּוֹ לְבַד לְהַלֵּל
לִגְמֹר בּוֹ אֶת הַהַלֵּל בַּיּוֹם הַשְּׁמִינִי.

דּוֹחֶה *Overrides.* The performance of a circumcision on the eighth day overrides both Shabbat and Yom Kippur.

שְׁמִינִי מְזֻמָּן *The eighth string.* Psalms 6 and 12 are headed by the superscription that it was to be played on the *Sheminit,* understood by the sages as an eight-stringed harp. They added that in the Temple in the past the harp

The eighth day, with its blessing in its own name,
to the One who gives the weary strength
and power on the eighth day.

The eighth day – those who seek to sing Your Oneness –
please – in Your great loving-kindness they come into
Your house to bow down;
Quickly, send help from the Sanctuary, by the merit of
Your faithful ones,
of those who sang their testimony to You at the sea –

With happiness, with song, with great joy,
and they all exclaimed:

"Who is like You, LORD, among the mighty? Ex. 15
Who is like You, majestic in holiness,
awesome in praises, doing wonders?"

▸ Your children beheld Your majesty
as You parted the sea before Moses.

Those who bear the yoke of the King, the God of truth,
have dwelled in the sukka seven days in their faithfulness;
as they gave of what was theirs to seven, to eight –
send them quickly, this our Saviour, the seven [shepherds],
eight [princes] –

He is Our Rock of salvation;
[Israel] opened their mouths and exclaimed:

"The LORD shall reign for ever and ever." Ex. 15

▸ And it is said, "For the LORD has redeemed Jacob and rescued Jer. 31
him from a power stronger than his own."

שִׁבְעָה וּשְׁמוֹנָה *The seven, eight.* The "seven shepherds and eight princes" mentioned in Micah (5:4), who will defend Israel against its enemies in the great battle before the End of Days.

שְׁמִינִי תֵּת בְּרָכָה בִּפְנֵי עַצְמָהּ
לַנּוֹתֵן לַיָּעֵף כֹּחַ וְעָצְמָה בַּיּוֹם הַשְּׁמִינִי.

שְׁמִינִי דּוֹרְשֵׁי נִצּוּחַ יִחוּדֶךָ
אָנָּא לְהִשְׁתַּחֲווֹת בָּאִים בְּרֹב חֲסָדֶיךָ
יוּחַשׁ עֶזְרָם מִקֹּדֶשׁ בִּזְכוּת חֲסִידֶיךָ
בְּעֶזְרַת שׁוֹרְרוּ עַל הַיָּם סַהֲדֶיךָ

בְּגִילָה, בְּרִנָּה בְּשִׂמְחָה רַבָּה
וְאָמְרוּ כֻלָּם
שמות טו מִי־כָמֹכָה בָּאֵלִם יהוה
מִי כָּמֹכָה נֶאְדָּר בַּקֹּדֶשׁ
נוֹרָא תְהִלֹּת עֹשֵׂה פֶלֶא:

◂ מַלְכוּתְךָ רָאוּ בָנֶיךָ, בּוֹקֵעַ יָם לִפְנֵי מֹשֶׁה

טוֹעֲנֵי עֹל מֶלֶךְ אֵל אֱמוּנָה
יָשְׁבוּ בַּסֻּכָּה שִׁבְעָה בֶּאֱמוּנָה
כְּנָתְנוּ חֵלֶק לְשִׁבְעָה וְגַם לִשְׁמוֹנָה
לִקְרָאתָם זֶה יִשְׁעֵנוּ, לְהָחִישׁ שִׁבְעָה וּשְׁמוֹנָה

זֶה צוּר יִשְׁעֵנוּ, פָּצוּ פֶה. וְאָמְרוּ
שמות טו יהוה יִמְלֹךְ לְעֹלָם וָעֶד:
◂ וְנֶאֱמַר
ירמיה לא כִּי־פָדָה יהוה אֶת־יַעֲקֹב, וּגְאָלוֹ מִיַּד חָזָק מִמֶּנּוּ:

---

twenty-four "watches" of priests would officiate on that day. This is one of the six ways mentioned by the sages in which Shemini Atzeret had the status of a separate festival in its own right (*Sukka* 48a).

They move on from strength to strength;
they have travelled on from the sukka, they are advised and rejoice on the eighth day;
Now they throw the weight of their bundle upon You,
as they crown the One who helps Israel and redeems them.*

Blessed are You, LORD, who redeemed Israel.

**Some end the blessing as follows (see commentary on page 128):*
Blessed are You, LORD, King, Rock and Redeemer of Israel.

הַשְׁכִּיבֵנוּ Help us lie down, O LORD our God, in peace,
and rise up, O our King, to life.
Spread over us Your canopy of peace.
Direct us with Your good counsel,
and save us for the sake of Your name.
Shield us and remove from us every enemy,
plague, sword, famine and sorrow.
Remove the adversary from before and behind us.
Shelter us in the shadow of Your wings,
for You, God, are our Guardian and Deliverer;
You, God, are a gracious and compassionate King.
▸ Guard our going out and our coming in,
for life and peace, from now and for ever.
Spread over us Your canopy of peace.

As they turn back from the sukka to their houses to dwell,
hear the pouring out of their prayers;
they who call upon Your loftiness, who think upon Your name –
spread Your canopy of peace over them, You who are enthroned upon praises.

Blessed are You, LORD, who spreads a canopy of peace over us,
over all His people Israel, and over Jerusalem.

Continue with "Thus Moses announced" on page 58.

---

the crowd growing larger and stronger as they came nearer to the city (Ibn Ezra, Radak). Here it means going from one command (i.e., source of spiritual strength) to another, from sitting in the Sukka to the distinctive commands and customs of the eighth day.

מֵחַיִל אֶל חַיִל הוֹלְכִים
נָסְעוּ מִסֻּכָּה, וְלִשְׂמֹחַ בַּשְּׁמִינִי נִמְלָכִים
סֵבֶר יְהָבָם עָלֶיךָ מַשְׁלִיכִים
עוֹזֵר יִשְׂרָאֵל וְגוֹאֲלוֹ מַמְלִיכִים.*

בָּרוּךְ אַתָּה יהוה, גָּאַל יִשְׂרָאֵל.

Some end the blessing as follows (see commentary on page 128):

בָּרוּךְ אַתָּה יהוה, מֶלֶךְ צוּר יִשְׂרָאֵל וְגוֹאֲלוֹ.

הַשְׁכִּיבֵנוּ יהוה אֱלֹהֵינוּ לְשָׁלוֹם, וְהַעֲמִידֵנוּ מַלְכֵּנוּ לְחַיִּים
וּפְרֹשׂ עָלֵינוּ סֻכַּת שְׁלוֹמֶךָ, וְתַקְּנֵנוּ בְּעֵצָה טוֹבָה מִלְּפָנֶיךָ
וְהוֹשִׁיעֵנוּ לְמַעַן שְׁמֶךָ.
וְהָגֵן בַּעֲדֵנוּ, וְהָסֵר מֵעָלֵינוּ אוֹיֵב, דֶּבֶר וְחֶרֶב וְרָעָב וְיָגוֹן
וְהָסֵר שָׂטָן מִלְּפָנֵינוּ וּמֵאַחֲרֵינוּ, וּבְצֵל כְּנָפֶיךָ תַּסְתִּירֵנוּ
כִּי אֵל שׁוֹמְרֵנוּ וּמַצִּילֵנוּ אָתָּה, כִּי אֵל מֶלֶךְ חַנּוּן וְרַחוּם אָתָּה.
◂ וּשְׁמֹר צֵאתֵנוּ וּבוֹאֵנוּ לְחַיִּים וּלְשָׁלוֹם מֵעַתָּה וְעַד עוֹלָם.
וּפְרֹשׂ עָלֵינוּ סֻכַּת שְׁלוֹמֶךָ.

פּוֹנִים מִסֻּכָּה לְבֵיתָם לֵישֵׁב
צָקוּן לַחֲשָׁם הַקְשֵׁב
קוֹרְאֵי רוֹמְמוֹתֶיךָ, שִׁמְךָ לְחַשֵּׁב
תִּפְרֹשׂ עָלֵימוֹ סֻכַּת שְׁלוֹמֶךָ, תְּהִלּוֹת יוֹשֵׁב.

בָּרוּךְ אַתָּה יהוה
הַפּוֹרֵשׂ סֻכַּת שָׁלוֹם עָלֵינוּ וְעַל כָּל עַמּוֹ יִשְׂרָאֵל וְעַל יְרוּשָׁלָיִם.

Continue with "וַיְדַבֵּר מֹשֶׁה" on page 59.

מֵחַיִל אֶל חַיִל *From strength to strength.* This commonly used phrase from Psalms (84:8) may refer to the experience of pilgrims as they travelled to Jerusalem for the festival. They would meet and join other groups of pilgrims,

MA'ARIV FOR SIMḤAT TORAH

בָּרוּךְ Blessed are You, LORD our God, King of the Universe,
who by His word brings on evenings,
by His wisdom opens the gates of heaven,
with understanding makes time change
and the seasons rotate,
and by His will
orders the stars in their constellations in the sky.
He creates day and night,
rolling away the light before the darkness,
and darkness before the light.
‣ He makes the day pass and brings on night,
distinguishing day from night:
the LORD of hosts is His name.
May the living and forever enduring God rule
over us for all time.

The eighth day / He brings forth for me in goodness.
He will surround me with songs of escape; / He has me rest in His shade as night falls.

Blessed are You, LORD, who brings on evenings.

אַהֲבַת עוֹלָם With everlasting love
have You loved Your people, the house of Israel.
You have taught us Torah and commandments,
decrees and laws of justice.
Therefore, LORD our God, when we lie down and when we rise up
we will speak of Your decrees, rejoicing in the words of Your Torah
and Your commandments for ever.

Atzeret – itself understood as the time when God asks the Jewish people not to leave immediately, but to stay an extra day.

מעריב לליל שמחת תורה

בָּרוּךְ אַתָּה יהוה אֱלֹהֵינוּ מֶלֶךְ הָעוֹלָם
אֲשֶׁר בִּדְבָרוֹ מַעֲרִיב עֲרָבִים
בְּחָכְמָה פּוֹתֵחַ שְׁעָרִים
וּבִתְבוּנָה מְשַׁנֶּה עִתִּים וּמַחֲלִיף אֶת הַזְּמַנִּים
וּמְסַדֵּר אֶת הַכּוֹכָבִים בְּמִשְׁמְרוֹתֵיהֶם בָּרָקִיעַ כִּרְצוֹנוֹ.
בּוֹרֵא יוֹם וָלָיְלָה
גּוֹלֵל אוֹר מִפְּנֵי חֹשֶׁךְ וְחֹשֶׁךְ מִפְּנֵי אוֹר
◂ וּמַעֲבִיר יוֹם וּמֵבִיא לָיְלָה
וּמַבְדִּיל בֵּין יוֹם וּבֵין לָיְלָה
יהוה צְבָאוֹת שְׁמוֹ.
אֵל חַי וְקַיָּם תָּמִיד, יִמְלֹךְ עָלֵינוּ לְעוֹלָם וָעֶד.

אֶת יוֹם הַשְּׁמִינִי / בְּטוֹב יַזְמִינִי
רָנֵּי פַלֵּט יְסוֹבְבֵנִי / לְעֵת עֶרֶב בְּצִלּוֹ יְלוֹנְנִי.

בָּרוּךְ אַתָּה יהוה, הַמַּעֲרִיב עֲרָבִים.

אַהֲבַת עוֹלָם בֵּית יִשְׂרָאֵל עַמְּךָ אָהָבְתָּ
תּוֹרָה וּמִצְוֹת, חֻקִּים וּמִשְׁפָּטִים, אוֹתָנוּ לִמַּדְתָּ
עַל כֵּן יהוה אֱלֹהֵינוּ בְּשָׁכְבֵנוּ וּבְקוּמֵנוּ נָשִׂיחַ בְּחֻקֶּיךָ
וְנִשְׂמַח בְּדִבְרֵי תוֹרָתֶךָ וּבְמִצְוֹתֶיךָ לְעוֹלָם וָעֶד

אֶת יוֹם הַשְּׁמִינִי *The eighth day.* A poem by the liturgist Isaac HaKatan, focusing not on the day as Simḥat Torah, but as the second day of Shemini

▸ For they are our life and the length of our days;
on them will we meditate day and night.
May You never take away Your love from us.

Love the terrifying [people], bless it with great closeness, /
in great measure, yet more than before;
on this Atzeret, festival of harvest, / may God gather in His
loved ones, bring them close.

Blessed are You, LORD,
who loves His people Israel.

The Shema must be said with intense concentration.
When not with a minyan, say:
God, faithful King!

The following verse should be said aloud, while covering the eyes with the right hand:

Listen, Israel: the LORD is our God, the LORD is One. *Deut. 6*

Quietly: Blessed be the name of His glorious kingdom for ever and all time.

וְאָהַבְתָּ Love the LORD your God with all your heart, with all your soul, and with all your might. These words which I command you today shall be on your heart. Teach them repeatedly to your children, speaking of them when you sit at home and when you travel on the way, when you lie down and when you rise. Bind them as a sign on your hand, and they shall be an emblem between your eyes. Write them on the doorposts of your house and gates. *Deut. 6*

וְהָיָה If you indeed heed My commandments with which I charge you today, to love the LORD your God and worship Him with all your heart and with all your soul, I will give rain in your land in its season, the early and late rain; and you shall gather in your grain, wine and oil. I will give grass in your field for your cattle, and you shall eat and be satisfied. Be careful lest your heart be tempted and *Deut. 11*

◄ כִּי הֵם חַיֵּינוּ וְאֹרֶךְ יָמֵינוּ
וּבָהֶם נֶהְגֶּה יוֹמָם וָלָיְלָה.
וְאַהֲבָתְךָ אַל תָּסִיר מִמֶּנּוּ לְעוֹלָמִים.

אֲיֻמָּה אָהֵב, בֵּרַךְ בְּכֶסֶף / בְּמִדָּה מְרֻבָּה מֵרֹאשׁ בְּתֶסֶף
בְּזֶה עֲצֶרֶת חַג אָסֵף / אוֹהֲבָיו יְקָרֵב אֵלָיו לְהֵאָסֵף.

בָּרוּךְ אַתָּה יהוה, אוֹהֵב עַמּוֹ יִשְׂרָאֵל.

The שמע *must be said with intense concentration.*
When not with a מנין*, say:*

אֵל מֶלֶךְ נֶאֱמָן

The following verse should be said aloud, while covering the eyes with the right hand:

דברים ו **שְׁמַע יִשְׂרָאֵל, יהוה אֱלֹהֵינוּ, יהוה ׀ אֶחָד:**

Quietly בָּרוּךְ שֵׁם כְּבוֹד מַלְכוּתוֹ לְעוֹלָם וָעֶד.

דברים ו וְאָהַבְתָּ אֵת יהוה אֱלֹהֶיךָ, בְּכָל־לְבָבְךָ וּבְכָל־נַפְשְׁךָ וּבְכָל־
מְאֹדֶךָ: וְהָיוּ הַדְּבָרִים הָאֵלֶּה, אֲשֶׁר אָנֹכִי מְצַוְּךָ הַיּוֹם, עַל־לְבָבֶךָ:
וְשִׁנַּנְתָּם לְבָנֶיךָ וְדִבַּרְתָּ בָּם, בְּשִׁבְתְּךָ בְּבֵיתֶךָ וּבְלֶכְתְּךָ בַדֶּרֶךְ,
וּבְשָׁכְבְּךָ וּבְקוּמֶךָ: וּקְשַׁרְתָּם לְאוֹת עַל־יָדֶךָ וְהָיוּ לְטֹטָפֹת בֵּין
עֵינֶיךָ: וּכְתַבְתָּם עַל־מְזֻזוֹת בֵּיתֶךָ וּבִשְׁעָרֶיךָ:

דברים יא וְהָיָה אִם־שָׁמֹעַ תִּשְׁמְעוּ אֶל־מִצְוֺתַי אֲשֶׁר אָנֹכִי מְצַוֶּה אֶתְכֶם
הַיּוֹם, לְאַהֲבָה אֶת־יהוה אֱלֹהֵיכֶם וּלְעָבְדוֹ, בְּכָל־לְבַבְכֶם וּבְכָל־
נַפְשְׁכֶם: וְנָתַתִּי מְטַר־אַרְצְכֶם בְּעִתּוֹ, יוֹרֶה וּמַלְקוֹשׁ, וְאָסַפְתָּ דְגָנֶךָ
וְתִירֹשְׁךָ וְיִצְהָרֶךָ: וְנָתַתִּי עֵשֶׂב בְּשָׂדְךָ לִבְהֶמְתֶּךָ, וְאָכַלְתָּ וְשָׂבָעְתָּ:
הִשָּׁמְרוּ לָכֶם פֶּן־יִפְתֶּה לְבַבְכֶם, וְסַרְתֶּם וַעֲבַדְתֶּם אֱלֹהִים אֲחֵרִים

you go astray and worship other gods, bowing down to them. Then the LORD's anger will flare against you and He will close the heavens so that there will be no rain. The land will not yield its crops, and you will perish swiftly from the good land that the LORD is giving you. Therefore, set these, My words, on your heart and soul. Bind them as a sign on your hand, and they shall be an emblem between your eyes. Teach them to your children, speaking of them when you sit at home and when you travel on the way, when you lie down and when you rise. Write them on the doorposts of your house and gates, so that you and your children may live long in the land that the LORD swore to your ancestors to give them, for as long as the heavens are above the earth.

וַיֹּאמֶר The LORD spoke to Moses, saying: Speak to the Israelites *Num. 15*
and tell them to make tassels on the corners of their garments for all generations. They shall attach to the tassel at each corner a thread of blue. This shall be your tassel, and you shall see it and remember all of the LORD's commandments and keep them, not straying after your heart and after your eyes, following your own sinful desires. Thus you will be reminded to keep all My commandments, and be holy to your God. I am the LORD your God, who brought you out of the land of Egypt to be your God. I am the LORD your God.

True –

The Leader repeats:

▸ The LORD your God is true –

וֶאֱמוּנָה – and faithful is all this,
and firmly established for us
that He is the LORD our God,
and there is none beside Him,
and that we, Israel, are His people.

וְהִשְׁתַּחֲוִיתֶם לָהֶם: וְחָרָה אַף־יהוה בָּכֶם, וְעָצַר אֶת־הַשָּׁמַיִם וְלֹא־יִהְיֶה מָטָר, וְהָאֲדָמָה לֹא תִתֵּן אֶת־יְבוּלָהּ, וַאֲבַדְתֶּם מְהֵרָה מֵעַל הָאָרֶץ הַטֹּבָה אֲשֶׁר יהוה נֹתֵן לָכֶם: וְשַׂמְתֶּם אֶת־דְּבָרַי אֵלֶּה עַל־לְבַבְכֶם וְעַל־נַפְשְׁכֶם, וּקְשַׁרְתֶּם אֹתָם לְאוֹת עַל־יֶדְכֶם, וְהָיוּ לְטוֹטָפֹת בֵּין עֵינֵיכֶם: וְלִמַּדְתֶּם אֹתָם אֶת־בְּנֵיכֶם לְדַבֵּר בָּם, בְּשִׁבְתְּךָ בְּבֵיתֶךָ וּבְלֶכְתְּךָ בַדֶּרֶךְ, וּבְשָׁכְבְּךָ וּבְקוּמֶךָ: וּכְתַבְתָּם עַל־מְזוּזוֹת בֵּיתֶךָ וּבִשְׁעָרֶיךָ: לְמַעַן יִרְבּוּ יְמֵיכֶם וִימֵי בְנֵיכֶם עַל הָאֲדָמָה אֲשֶׁר נִשְׁבַּע יהוה לַאֲבֹתֵיכֶם לָתֵת לָהֶם, כִּימֵי הַשָּׁמַיִם עַל־הָאָרֶץ:

וַיֹּאמֶר יהוה אֶל־מֹשֶׁה לֵּאמֹר: דַּבֵּר אֶל־בְּנֵי יִשְׂרָאֵל וְאָמַרְתָּ אֲלֵהֶם, וְעָשׂוּ לָהֶם צִיצִת עַל־כַּנְפֵי בִגְדֵיהֶם לְדֹרֹתָם, וְנָתְנוּ עַל־צִיצִת הַכָּנָף פְּתִיל תְּכֵלֶת: וְהָיָה לָכֶם לְצִיצִת, וּרְאִיתֶם אֹתוֹ וּזְכַרְתֶּם אֶת־כָּל־מִצְוֺת יהוה וַעֲשִׂיתֶם אֹתָם, וְלֹא תָתוּרוּ אַחֲרֵי לְבַבְכֶם וְאַחֲרֵי עֵינֵיכֶם, אֲשֶׁר־אַתֶּם זֹנִים אַחֲרֵיהֶם: לְמַעַן תִּזְכְּרוּ וַעֲשִׂיתֶם אֶת־כָּל־מִצְוֺתָי, וִהְיִיתֶם קְדֹשִׁים לֵאלֹהֵיכֶם: אֲנִי יהוה אֱלֹהֵיכֶם, אֲשֶׁר הוֹצֵאתִי אֶתְכֶם מֵאֶרֶץ מִצְרַיִם, לִהְיוֹת לָכֶם לֵאלֹהִים, אֲנִי יהוה אֱלֹהֵיכֶם: במדבר טו

אֱמֶת

The שליח ציבור *repeats:*

› יהוה אֱלֹהֵיכֶם אֱמֶת

וֶאֱמוּנָה כָּל זֹאת וְקַיָּם עָלֵינוּ
כִּי הוּא יהוה אֱלֹהֵינוּ וְאֵין זוּלָתוֹ
וַאֲנַחְנוּ יִשְׂרָאֵל עַמּוֹ.

He is our King, who redeems us from the hand of kings
and delivers us from the grasp of all tyrants.
He is our God, who on our behalf repays our foes
and brings just retribution on our mortal enemies;
who performs great deeds beyond understanding
and wonders beyond number;
who kept us alive, *Ps. 66*
not letting our foot slip;
who led us on the high places of our enemies,
raising our pride above all our foes;
who did miracles for us
and brought vengeance against Pharaoh;
who performed signs and wonders
in the land of Ham's children;
who smote in His wrath all the firstborn of Egypt,
and brought out His people Israel from their midst
into everlasting freedom;
who led His children through the divided Reed Sea,
plunging their pursuers and enemies into the depths.
When His children saw His might,
they gave praise and thanks to His name,
▸ and willingly accepted His Sovereignty.
Moses and the children of Israel
then sang a song to You.

The eighth day was given its own strength,
with rules all of its own laid out for the eighth day.

The eighth day was completed with its own priests'
lottery, with pilgrimage and blessing,
with its prayer and song and its ordered offering for the eighth day.

בְּפַיִס רֶגֶל *Lottery, pilgrimage etc.* The six ways in which Shemini Atzeret was considered a festival in its own right: [1] Lots were cast as to which priestly

הַפּוֹדֵנוּ מִיַּד מְלָכִים
מַלְכֵּנוּ הַגּוֹאֲלֵנוּ מִכַּף כָּל הֶעָרִיצִים.
הָאֵל הַנִּפְרָע לָנוּ מִצָּרֵינוּ
וְהַמְשַׁלֵּם גְּמוּל לְכָל אוֹיְבֵי נַפְשֵׁנוּ.
הָעוֹשֶׂה גְדוֹלוֹת עַד אֵין חֵקֶר
וְנִפְלָאוֹת עַד אֵין מִסְפָּר
תהלים סו הַשָּׂם נַפְשֵׁנוּ בַּחַיִּים
וְלֹא־נָתַן לַמּוֹט רַגְלֵנוּ:
הַמַּדְרִיכֵנוּ עַל בָּמוֹת אוֹיְבֵינוּ
וַיָּרֶם קַרְנֵנוּ עַל כָּל שׂוֹנְאֵינוּ.
הָעוֹשֶׂה לָּנוּ נִסִּים וּנְקָמָה בְּפַרְעֹה
אוֹתוֹת וּמוֹפְתִים בְּאַדְמַת בְּנֵי חָם.
הַמַּכֶּה בְעֶבְרָתוֹ כָּל בְּכוֹרֵי מִצְרָיִם
וַיּוֹצֵא אֶת עַמּוֹ יִשְׂרָאֵל מִתּוֹכָם לְחֵרוּת עוֹלָם.
הַמַּעֲבִיר בָּנָיו בֵּין גִּזְרֵי יַם סוּף
אֶת רוֹדְפֵיהֶם וְאֶת שׂוֹנְאֵיהֶם בִּתְהוֹמוֹת טִבַּע
וְרָאוּ בָנָיו גְּבוּרָתוֹ, שִׁבְּחוּ וְהוֹדוּ לִשְׁמוֹ
◂ וּמַלְכוּתוֹ בְּרָצוֹן קִבְּלוּ עֲלֵיהֶם
מֹשֶׁה וּבְנֵי יִשְׂרָאֵל, לְךָ עָנוּ שִׁירָה.

שְׁמִינִי אֹמֶץ בִּפְנֵי עַצְמוֹ
בְּחוֹב קָבְוּעַ לִשְׁמוֹ   בַּיּוֹם הַשְּׁמִינִי.
שְׁמִינִי גְּמָרוֹ בְּפַיִס רֶגֶל וּזְמַן
דְּבַר שִׁיר וְקָרְבָּן מְזֻמָּן   בַּיּוֹם הַשְּׁמִינִי.

The eighth day He added, for the glorified people,
itself glorified with additional offerings, holy — to the eighth day.
The eighth day was specified and fixed as the time from
which young animals would be received as offerings — the eighth day.
The eighth day, those who are sealed [in the covenant]
are marked with that seal,
forever, beloved forever because of that wound — on the eighth day.
The eighth day [of the Tabernacle] was crowned with
great rejoicing,
with the offering that initiated the priests — on the eighth day.
The eighth day, from the days that came before it –
is set apart in all its laws — the eighth day.
The eighth day, when King [Solomon] agreed to send
the people home,
[at the Temple opening,] on the day they blessed
their king — on the eighth day.
The eighth day, when [the pilgrims] bide until morning,
righteousness shall abide in His Sanctuary — on the eighth day.
The eighth day, hear this voice lovingly:
the joyous singing of Beit HaShoeva — on the eighth day.
The eighth day – protect the peace of our homes,
all the days of the pilgrimage — on the eighth day.

On the eighth day, may the Holy One charge His kindness to
His people,
and at night may His song be with them.
The King rules in His world,
and may His pleasantness as ever be upon us.

---

[5] The Levites sang a special song in the temple. [6] The sacrifice – one young bull – was significantly different from that of the seven days of Sukkot (*Sukka* 48a).

כָּלוּל לְשִׂמְחָה גְדוֹלָה *Crowned with great rejoicing.* The inauguration of the Sanctuary in the wilderness after seven days of preparation was an occasion of "as much joy before the Holy One, blessed be He, as the day on which the creation of heaven and earth was completed" (*Megilla* 10b).

שְׁמִינִי הוֹסִיף לְגוֹי נִכְבָּד
וּבְמוּסְפֵי קֹדֶשׁ מְכֻבָּד בַּיּוֹם הַשְּׁמִינִי.
שְׁמִינִי זְמַן וְהֻקְבַּע לְרַצּוֹת
חֹק נוֹלַד בּוֹ לְהֵרָצוֹת בַּיּוֹם הַשְּׁמִינִי.
שְׁמִינִי טִבַּע חֲתוּמִים חוֹתָם
יְדִידִים לָעַד לְמִכְתָּם בַּיּוֹם הַשְּׁמִינִי.
שְׁמִינִי כָּלוּל לְשִׂמְחָה גְּדוֹלָה
לִמְכַהֵן בְּחִנּוּךְ עוֹלָה בַּיּוֹם הַשְּׁמִינִי.
שְׁמִינִי מִלִּפְנֵי פְּנֵי פָנָיו
נֶחֱלָק בְּכָל עִנְיָנָיו בַּיּוֹם הַשְּׁמִינִי.
שְׁמִינִי סְכֵּם לְשִׁלּוּחַ מֶלֶךְ
עֵת וַיְבָרְכוּ אֶת הַמֶּלֶךְ בַּיּוֹם הַשְּׁמִינִי.
שְׁמִינִי פְּנוֹת בֹּקֶר הֲלָנָתוֹ
צֶדֶק יָלִין מְעוֹנָתוֹ בַּיּוֹם הַשְּׁמִינִי.
שְׁמִינִי קוֹל שֵׁמַע בְּאַהֲבָה
רִנַּת בֵּית הַשּׁוֹאֵבָה בַּיּוֹם הַשְּׁמִינִי.
שְׁמִינִי שִׁמּוּר שָׁלוֹם אָהֳלוֹ
תּוֹךְ יְמֵי עֲלִיַּת רִגְלוֹ בַּיּוֹם הַשְּׁמִינִי.

שְׁמִינִי יְצַוֶּה חַסְדּוֹ קָדוֹשׁ לְעַמּוֹ
וּבַלַּיְלָה שִׁירֹה עִמּוֹ
מוֹשֵׁל הַשַּׁלִּיט בְּעוֹלָמוֹ
עָלֵינוּ כְּמֵאָז יְהִי נָעֳמוֹ.

watch would officiate. [2] There is no obligation to sit in the sukka (Rashi on *Sukka* 48a). [3] The blessing of Sheheḥeyanu, "Who has kept us alive," is said. [4] The festival has its own name in the liturgy (Rabbenu Tam).

With happiness, with song, with great joy,
and they all exclaimed:

"Who is like You, Lord, among the mighty? *Ex. 15*
Who is like You, majestic in holiness,
awesome in praises, doing wonders?"

▸ Your children beheld Your majesty
as You parted the sea before Moses.

On the eighth day, Lord, perform goodness for the good,
for those who call out to You with these pleasing words.
Have Your loved ones hear good news;
those who would sing of the pleasantness of Your kingship.

He is Our Rock of salvation;
[Israel] opened their mouths
and exclaimed:

"The Lord shall reign for ever and ever." *Ex. 15*

▸ And it is said,

"For the Lord has redeemed Jacob *Jer. 31*
and rescued him from a power stronger than his own."

On the eighth day – what is ours: seven and eight –
we are charged to give of our portion now as well.
On all these days, may He remember the merit of ancestors,
and take possession once more of the congregation that cannot be counted.*

Blessed are You, Lord, who redeemed Israel.

**Some end the blessing as follows (see commentary on page 128):*
Blessed are You, Lord, King, Rock and Redeemer of Israel.

בְּגִילָה, בְּרִנָּה בְּשִׂמְחָה רַבָּה
וְאָמְרוּ כֻלָּם

מִי־כָמֹכָה בָּאֵלִם יהוה שמות טו
מִי כָּמֹכָה נֶאְדָּר בַּקֹּדֶשׁ
נוֹרָא תְהִלֹּת עֹשֵׂה פֶלֶא:

‹ מַלְכוּתְךָ רָאוּ בָנֶיךָ, בּוֹקֵעַ יָם לִפְנֵי מֹשֶׁה

שְׁמִינִי הֵיטִיבָה יהוה לַטּוֹבִים
קוֹרְאֶיךָ בִּדְבָרִים עֲרֵבִים
טוֹבוֹת יַשְׁמִיעַ לַאֲהוּבִים
נֹעַם מַלְכוּתְךָ עֲנוֹת תְּאֵבִים.

זֶה צוּר יִשְׁעֵנוּ, פָּצוּ פֶה. וְאָמְרוּ
יהוה יִמְלֹךְ לְעֹלָם וָעֶד: שמות טו

‹ וְנֶאֱמַר
כִּי־פָדָה יהוה אֶת־יַעֲקֹב, וּגְאָלוֹ מִיַּד חָזָק מִמֶּנּוּ: ירמיה לא

שְׁמִינִי חֵלֶק לְשִׁבְעָה וְגַם לִשְׁמוֹנָה
מִצְוָה עָלֵינוּ לָתֵת מָנָה
זְכוּת אָבוֹת יִזְכֹּר בָּם שׁוֹכֵן מְעוֹנָה
קְנוֹת שֵׁנִית עֲדַת מִי מָנָה.*

בָּרוּךְ אַתָּה יהוה, גָּאַל יִשְׂרָאֵל.

*Some end the blessing as follows (see commentary on page 128):
בָּרוּךְ אַתָּה יהוה, מֶלֶךְ צוּר יִשְׂרָאֵל וְגוֹאֲלוֹ.

הַשְׁכִּיבֵנוּ Help us lie down, O LORD our God, in peace,
and rise up, O our King, to life.
Spread over us Your canopy of peace.
Direct us with Your good counsel,
and save us for the sake of Your name.
Shield us and remove from us every enemy,
plague, sword, famine and sorrow.
Remove the adversary from before and behind us.
Shelter us in the shadow of Your wings,
for You, God, are our Guardian and Deliverer;
You, God, are a gracious and compassionate King.
▸ Guard our going out and our coming in,
for life and peace, from now and for ever.
Blessed are You,
LORD, who guards His people Israel for ever.
Spread over us Your canopy of peace.

On the eighth day, God, be gracious to us;
bless us from Your holy Sanctuary.
May our King fulfill what He promised,
spreading His peace as a canopy over us –

Blessed are You, LORD,
who spreads a canopy of peace over us,
over all His people Israel, and over Jerusalem.

Continue with "Thus Moses announced" on page 58.

הַשְׁכִּיבֵנוּ יהוה אֱלֹהֵינוּ לְשָׁלוֹם, וְהַעֲמִידֵנוּ מַלְכֵּנוּ לְחַיִּים
וּפְרֹשׂ עָלֵינוּ סֻכַּת שְׁלוֹמֶךָ
וְתַקְּנֵנוּ בְּעֵצָה טוֹבָה מִלְּפָנֶיךָ
וְהוֹשִׁיעֵנוּ לְמַעַן שְׁמֶךָ.
וְהָגֵן בַּעֲדֵנוּ
וְהָסֵר מֵעָלֵינוּ אוֹיֵב, דֶּבֶר וְחֶרֶב וְרָעָב וְיָגוֹן
וְהָסֵר שָׂטָן מִלְּפָנֵינוּ וּמֵאַחֲרֵינוּ, וּבְצֵל כְּנָפֶיךָ תַּסְתִּירֵנוּ
כִּי אֵל שׁוֹמְרֵנוּ וּמַצִּילֵנוּ אָתָּה
כִּי אֵל מֶלֶךְ חַנּוּן וְרַחוּם אָתָּה.
◂ וּשְׁמֹר צֵאתֵנוּ וּבוֹאֵנוּ לְחַיִּים וּלְשָׁלוֹם מֵעַתָּה וְעַד עוֹלָם.
וּפְרֹשׂ עָלֵינוּ סֻכַּת שְׁלוֹמֶךָ.

שְׁמִינִי אֱלֹהִים יְחָנֵּנוּ
מִמְּעוֹן קָדְשׁוֹ לְבָרְכֵנוּ
נְאֻמוֹ יָקֵם מַלְכֵּנוּ
בִּפְרִיסַת שְׁלוֹמוֹ לְסוֹכְכֵנוּ.

בָּרוּךְ אַתָּה יהוה
הַפּוֹרֵשׂ סֻכַּת שָׁלוֹם עָלֵינוּ וְעַל כָּל עַמּוֹ יִשְׂרָאֵל וְעַל יְרוּשָׁלָיִם.

Continue with "וַיְדַבֵּר מֹשֶׁה" on page 59.

Meditation in the Sukka

On entering the sukka:

עולו Come, exalted, holy guests; come our exalted, holy fathers, to sit in the shade of the most high faith, in the shade of the Holy One, blessed be He. Come, beloved Abraham, and with him bound Isaac, and with him perfect Jacob, and with him the shepherd, Moses, and with him the priest, Aaron, and with him righteous Joseph, and with him David the anointed king. "You shall live in booths:" sit, exalted guests. Sit, sit, guests in faith, sit.

הֲרֵינִי I am hereby prepared and ready to fulfill the commandment of Sukka, as the Creator, blessed be His name has commanded me: "You shall live *Lev. 23*
in booths for seven days; every citizen in Israel shall live in booths so that future generations will know that I made the Israelites live in booths when I brought them out of Egypt. I am the LORD your God."

Sit, sit, exalted guests. Sit, sit, holy guests. Sit, sit, guests in faith. Sit in the shade of the Holy One, blessed be He. Worthy is the portion of Israel, as is written, "For the LORD's portion is His people, Jacob His allotted *Deut. 32*
inheritance."

---

passed by. He offered them food, drink and the chance to wash and rest. Unbeknown to him, they were angels, bringing news that Sarah would have a child, Isaac, first child of the covenant (Gen. 18:1–14). At the dawn of Jewish time, an association was being struck: God shows kindness to those who show kindness to strangers. The Hebrew letter *Beit*, with which the Torah begins, also means "house." It is open at one side, signaling graphically that a Jewish home is one that is open to visitors and strangers.

Sukkot is *zeman simḥateinu*, "the time of our joy," and the word *simḥa* in biblical Hebrew refers not just to a personal, private emotional state, but also and primarily to collective celebration: "You shall celebrate a Festival of Booths…. you shall rejoice on your festival – you and your sons and daughters, your male and female servants, and the Levite, the stranger and orphan and widow that dwell within your gates." (Deut. 16:14). The emphasis is on *joy shared with others*, especially with those who might otherwise be alone and excluded.

Maimonides rules: "When one eats and drinks, one must also feed the

תפילה כשנכנסין לסוכה

On entering the סוכה*:*

עוּלוּ אוּשְׁפִּיזִין עִלָּאִין קַדִּישִׁין, עוּלוּ אֲבָהָן עִלָּאִין קַדִּישִׁין, לְמֵיתַב בְּצִלָּא דִמְהֵימְנוּתָא עִלָּאָה בְּצִלָּא דְקֻדְשָׁא בְּרִיךְ הוּא. לֵיעוּל אַבְרָהָם רְחִימָא, וְעִמֵּהּ יִצְחָק עֲקֵידָתָא, וְעִמֵּהּ יַעֲקֹב שְׁלֵמְתָא, וְעִמֵּהּ מֹשֶׁה רַעְיָא מְהֵימְנָא, וְעִמֵּהּ אַהֲרֹן כַּהֲנָא קַדִּישָׁא, וְעִמֵּהּ יוֹסֵף צַדִּיקָא, וְעִמֵּהּ דָּוִד מַלְכָּא מְשִׁיחָא. בְּסֻכּוֹת תֵּשְׁבוּ, תִּיבוּ אוּשְׁפִּיזִין עִלָּאִין תִּיבוּ, תִּיבוּ אוּשְׁפִּיזֵי מְהֵימְנוּתָא תִּיבוּ.

הֲרֵינִי מוּכָן וּמְזֻמָּן לְקַיֵּם מִצְוַת סֻכָּה, כַּאֲשֶׁר צִוַּנִי הַבּוֹרֵא יִתְבָּרַךְ שְׁמוֹ:
בַּסֻּכֹּת תֵּשְׁבוּ שִׁבְעַת יָמִים, כָּל־הָאֶזְרָח בְּיִשְׂרָאֵל יֵשְׁבוּ בַּסֻּכֹּת: לְמַעַן ויקרא כג
יֵדְעוּ דֹרֹתֵיכֶם, כִּי בַסֻּכּוֹת הוֹשַׁבְתִּי אֶת־בְּנֵי יִשְׂרָאֵל, בְּהוֹצִיאִי אוֹתָם מֵאֶרֶץ מִצְרָיִם:

תִּיבוּ תִּיבוּ אֻשְׁפִּיזִין עִלָּאִין, תִּיבוּ תִּיבוּ אֻשְׁפִּיזִין קַדִּישִׁין, תִּיבוּ תִּיבוּ
אֻשְׁפִּיזִין דִּמְהֵימְנוּתָא. זַכָּאָה חֻלְקְהוֹן דְּיִשְׂרָאֵל, דִּכְתִיב: כִּי חֵלֶק יהוה דברים לב
עַמּוֹ, יַעֲקֹב חֶבֶל נַחֲלָתוֹ:

USHPIZIN.

The custom of welcoming guests from another world – Abraham, Isaac, Jacob, Joseph, Moses, Aaron and David – was introduced in the sixteenth century by the great Jewish mystic, Isaac Luria, on the basis of a passage in the *Zohar*, the key text of Jewish mysticism. This states that "When a person sits in the abode of the shadow of faith, the Divine Presence spreads Her wings over him from above, and Abraham and five other righteous ones make their abode with him" (*Emor*, 103b). It is said of Rav Hamnuna the elder that when he entered the Sukka, he would stand by the entrance and say, "Let us invite the holy guests and prepare a table." The *Zohar* adds that "he must also gladden the poor, because the portion of those guests whom he invites must go to the poor" (ibid. 104a).

Hospitality is fundamental to Judaism. Abraham, father of our faith, was sitting at the entrance of his tent in the heat of the day when three strangers

May it be Your will, LORD my God and God of my fathers, that You cause Your Divine Presence to rest among us and that You spread over us the tabernacle of Your peace, in the merit of the commandment of Sukka which we are fulfilling to unify the name of the Holy One, blessed be He, and His Divine Presence, in reverence and love, to unify the name *Yod-Heh* with *Vav-Heh*, in perfect unity in the name of all Israel. May You surround it with the radiance of Your holy and pure glory, spread above their heads like an eagle that stirs up its nest, and from there may a rich flow of life stream down on your servant (*name* son of *mother's name*, Your servant). In the merit of leaving my house to go outside, running in the way of Your commandments, may I be considered as if I had wandered far. Cleanse me thoroughly from my iniquity and purify me from my sin. From the exalted guests, the guests in faith, may Your ears attend to much blessing. To the hungry and thirsty grant unfailing food and drink. Grant me the privilege of sitting and taking refuge under the shadow of Your wings when I take leave of this world, taking refuge from stream and rain when You rain fiery coals on the wicked. May this command of Sukka that I am fulfilling be considered by You as if I had fulfilled it in all its specifics, details and conditions, as well as all the commandments dependent on it. May the sealing of our fate be for good, and grant us the merit of living for many years on the soil of the Holy Land, serving You and revering You. Blessed *Ps. 89*
is the LORD forever, Amen and Amen.

Master of all worlds, may it be Your will that this command of sitting in the sukka be considered as if we had fulfilled it correctly and precisely in every detail, with all the six hundred and thirteen commands that depend upon it, as if we had held all the various intentions held in this by the men of the Great Assembly.

---

the Jewish past join us in the Sukka, to confer their blessing on those who continue their legacy into the present. The humblest of dwellings, when it is shared with others, becomes worthy of receiving the most distinguished of guests.

Why these seven? Because the Sukka is a symbol of exile – the years in which the Israelites wandered in the wilderness without a permanent home – and each of these individuals suffered exile: Abraham to Egypt and Isaac to the land of the Philistines at times of famine, Jacob who fled Esau and Laban and ended his life in Egypt, Joseph who was sold into Egypt as a slave, Moses who had to escape to Midian, Aaron who with the rest of his generation spent

יְהִי רָצוֹן מִלְּפָנֶיךָ יהוה אֱלֹהַי וֵאלֹהֵי אֲבוֹתַי, שֶׁתַּשְׁרֶה שְׁכִינָתְךָ בֵּינֵינוּ, וְתִפְרֹס עָלֵינוּ סֻכַּת שְׁלוֹמֶךָ, בִּזְכוּת מִצְוַת סֻכָּה שֶׁאֲנַחְנוּ מְקַיְּמִין לְיַחֲדָא שְׁמָא דְקֻדְשָׁא בְּרִיךְ הוּא וּשְׁכִינְתֵּהּ בִּדְחִילוּ וּרְחִימוּ, לְיַחֲדָא שֵׁם י״ה בו״ה בְּיִחוּדָא שְׁלִים בְּשֵׁם כָּל יִשְׂרָאֵל, וּלְהַקִּיף אוֹתָהּ מִזִּיו כְּבוֹדְךָ הַקָּדוֹשׁ וְהַטָּהוֹר, נָטוּי עַל רָאשֵׁיהֶם מִלְמַעְלָה כְּנֶשֶׁר יָעִיר קִנּוֹ, וּמִשָּׁם יַשְׁפַּע שֶׁפַע הַחַיִּים לְעַבְדְּךָ (פלוני בֶּן פלונית אֲמָתֶךָ). וּבִזְכוּת צֵאתִי מִבֵּיתִי הַחוּצָה וְדֶרֶךְ מִצְוֹתֶיךָ אָרוּצָה, יֵחָשֵׁב לִי זֹאת כְּאִלּוּ הִרְחַקְתִּי נְדוֹד, וְהֶרֶב כַּבְּסֵנִי מֵעֲוֹנִי וּמֵחַטָּאתִי טַהֲרֵנִי, וּמֵאֻשְׁפִּיזִין עִלָּאִין אֻשְׁפִּיזִין דִּמְהֵימְנוּתָא תִּהְיֶינָה אָזְנֶיךָ קַשֻּׁבוֹת רַב בְּרָכוֹת, וְלָרְעֵבִים גַּם צְמֵאִים תֶּן לַחְמָם וּמֵימָם הַנֶּאֱמָנִים, וְתִתֶּן לִי זְכוּת לָשֶׁבֶת וְלַחֲסוֹת בְּסֵתֶר צֵל כְּנָפֶיךָ בְּעֵת פְּטִירָתִי מִן הָעוֹלָם, וְלַחֲסוֹת מִזֶּרֶם וּמִמָּטָר, כִּי תַמְטִיר עַל רְשָׁעִים פַּחִים. וּתְהֵא חֲשׁוּבָה מִצְוַת סֻכָּה זוֹ שֶׁאֲנִי מְקַיֵּם, כְּאִלּוּ קִיַּמְתִּיהָ בְּכָל פְּרָטֶיהָ וְדִקְדּוּקֶיהָ וּתְנָאֶיהָ וְכָל מִצְוֹת הַתְּלוּיוֹת בָּהּ. וְתֵיטִיב לָנוּ הַחֲתִימָה, וּתְזַכֵּנוּ לֵישֵׁב יָמִים רַבִּים עַל
הָאֲדָמָה אַדְמַת קֹדֶשׁ, בַּעֲבוֹדָתְךָ וּבְיִרְאָתֶךָ. בָּרוּךְ יהוה לְעוֹלָם תהלים פט
אָמֵן וְאָמֵן:

רִבּוֹן כָּל הָעוֹלָמִים, יְהִי רָצוֹן מִלְּפָנֶיךָ, שֶׁיְּהֵא חָשׁוּב לְפָנֶיךָ מִצְוַת יְשִׁיבַת סֻכָּה זוֹ, כְּאִלּוּ קִיַּמְתִּיהָ בְּכָל פְּרָטֶיהָ וְדִקְדּוּקֶיהָ וְתַרְיַ״ג מִצְוֹת הַתְּלוּיִים בָּהּ, וּכְאִלּוּ כִּוַּנְתִּי בְּכָל הַכַּוָּנוֹת שֶׁכִּוְּנוּ בָהּ אַנְשֵׁי כְנֶסֶת הַגְּדוֹלָה.

---

stranger, the orphan, the widow, and those who are distressed and poor. But one who locks the doors of his courtyard, and eat and drinks with his children and wife but does not feed the poor and the embittered soul – this is not the joy of a mitzva, but the joy of his belly…" (*Mishneh Torah,* Laws of the Festivals 6:18). Hospitality is essential to all the festivals, especially to Sukkot, where shared joy is not just one element, but the definitive one, of the festival itself.

The rabbis say that "greater is hospitality than welcoming the Divine Presence" (*Shabbat* 127a; *Shevu'ot* 35b). Hence, according to the *Zohar,* when we offer hospitality to strangers on Sukkot, it is as if the great figures of

On entering the sukka and before saying Kiddush, many have the custom to welcome "guests" from the biblical past, who are said to join us as we sit in the sukka:

אֻשְׁפִּיזִין I invite to my meal the exalted guests,
Abraham, Isaac, Jacob, Joseph, Moses, Aaron, and David.

On the first day I pray you, Abraham, exalted guest,
that all the other exalted guests
may sit here with me and you:
Isaac, Jacob, Joseph, Moses, Aaron, and David.

On the second day I pray you, Isaac, exalted guest,
that all the other exalted guests
may sit here with me and you:
Abraham, Jacob, Joseph, Moses, Aaron, and David.

On the third day I pray you, Jacob, exalted guest,
that all the other exalted guests
may sit here with me and you:
Abraham, Isaac, Joseph, Moses, Aaron, and David.

On the fourth day I pray you, Joseph, exalted guest,
that all the other exalted guests
may sit here with me and you:
Abraham, Isaac, Jacob, Moses, Aaron, and David.

On the fifth day I pray you, Moses, exalted guest,
that all the other exalted guests
may sit here with me and you:
Abraham, Isaac, Jacob, Joseph, Aaron, and David.

On the sixth day I pray you, Aaron, exalted guest,
that all the other exalted guests
may sit here with me and you:
Abraham, Isaac, Jacob, Joseph, Moses, and David.

On Hoshana Raba I pray you, David, exalted guest,
that all the other exalted guests
may sit here with me and you:
Abraham, Isaac, Jacob, Joseph, Moses and Aaron.

---

forty years in the desert, and David who had to flee from the wrath of Saul. Each was sustained by faith, and the Sukka is known in the mystical literature as "the shade of faith."

On entering the סוכה *and before saying* קידוש*, many have the custom to welcome "guests" from the biblical past, who are said to join us as we sit in the* סוכה*:*

אֲזַמִּין לִסְעוּדָתִי אֻשְׁפִּיזִין עִלָּאִין
אַבְרָהָם יִצְחָק יַעֲקֹב יוֹסֵף מֹשֶׁה אַהֲרֹן וְדָוִד.

On the first day
בְּמָטוּ מִנָּךְ אַבְרָהָם אֻשְׁפִּיזִי עִלָּאִי דְּיָתְבוּ עִמִּי
וְעִמָּךְ כָּל אֻשְׁפִּיזֵי עִלָּאֵי:
יִצְחָק יַעֲקֹב יוֹסֵף מֹשֶׁה אַהֲרֹן וְדָוִד.

On the second day
בְּמָטוּ מִנָּךְ יִצְחָק אֻשְׁפִּיזִי עִלָּאִי דְּיָתְבוּ עִמִּי
וְעִמָּךְ כָּל אֻשְׁפִּיזֵי עִלָּאֵי:
אַבְרָהָם יַעֲקֹב יוֹסֵף מֹשֶׁה אַהֲרֹן וְדָוִד.

On the third day
בְּמָטוּ מִנָּךְ יַעֲקֹב אֻשְׁפִּיזִי עִלָּאִי דְּיָתְבוּ עִמִּי
וְעִמָּךְ כָּל אֻשְׁפִּיזֵי עִלָּאֵי:
אַבְרָהָם יִצְחָק יוֹסֵף מֹשֶׁה אַהֲרֹן וְדָוִד.

On the fourth day
בְּמָטוּ מִנָּךְ יוֹסֵף אֻשְׁפִּיזִי עִלָּאִי דְּיָתְבוּ עִמִּי
וְעִמָּךְ כָּל אֻשְׁפִּיזֵי עִלָּאֵי:
אַבְרָהָם יִצְחָק יַעֲקֹב מֹשֶׁה אַהֲרֹן וְדָוִד.

On the fifth day
בְּמָטוּ מִנָּךְ מֹשֶׁה אֻשְׁפִּיזִי עִלָּאִי דְּיָתְבוּ עִמִּי
וְעִמָּךְ כָּל אֻשְׁפִּיזֵי עִלָּאֵי:
אַבְרָהָם יִצְחָק יַעֲקֹב יוֹסֵף אַהֲרֹן וְדָוִד.

On the sixth day
בְּמָטוּ מִנָּךְ אַהֲרֹן אֻשְׁפִּיזִי עִלָּאִי דְּיָתְבוּ עִמִּי
וְעִמָּךְ כָּל אֻשְׁפִּיזֵי עִלָּאֵי:
אַבְרָהָם יִצְחָק יַעֲקֹב יוֹסֵף מֹשֶׁה וְדָוִד.

On הושענא רבה
בְּמָטוּ מִנָּךְ דָּוִד אֻשְׁפִּיזִי עִלָּאִי דְּיָתְבוּ עִמִּי
וְעִמָּךְ כָּל אֻשְׁפִּיזֵי עִלָּאֵי:
אַבְרָהָם יִצְחָק יַעֲקֹב יוֹסֵף מֹשֶׁה וְאַהֲרֹן.

LEAVING THE SUKKA

On the afternoon of Shemini Atzeret (in Israel, on Hoshana Raba), on leaving the sukka:

May it be Your will, Lord our God and God of our fathers,
that as I have fulfilled [Your commandment] and sat in this sukka,
so next year may I have the privilege of sitting in the sukka
made of the skin of Leviathan.

Next year in Jerusalem.

Some add:

Master of the universe, may it be Your will that those holy angels
associated with the command of the sukka
and the command of the four species, (lulav, etrog, myrtle and willow)
that we perform on the festival of Sukkot –
should come with us as we leave the sukka
and return to our houses with us for life and for peace.
And let divine protection, from Your holy dwelling place,
guard us always, saving us from sin and iniquity,
and from all kinds of harm, and from all those times of destruction
that trouble the world.
Let a spirit stir over us from above,
and renew our conscience to serve You truly, with love and with awe.
And let it make us ever constant in our study
of the holy Torah, learning and teaching.
And let the merit of the four species and of the sukka stand by us,
that You may hold back Your anger until we have returned to You
in complete repentance, and repaired what we have damaged,
so that we merit two tables
[one laid with wealth and the other with learning,]
without pain or sorrow, I and my family and all my descendants.
And let us all be peaceful and at ease, vigorous and fresh,
serving the Lord in absolute truth, as is Your beneficent will;
together with all the children of Israel: Amen.
May the words of my mouth and the meditation of my heart *Ps. 19*
find favor before You, Lord, my Rock and Redeemer.

---

on the fifth day of creation (*Bava Batra* 74b–75a). This is referred to in the prayer said on leaving the Sukka on the last day of Sukkot.

תפילה כשיוצאים מן הסוכה

On the afternoon of שמיני עצרת (*in Israel, on* הושענא רבה), *on leaving the* סוכה:

יְהִי רָצוֹן מִלְּפָנֶיךָ יהוה אֱלֹהֵינוּ וֵאלֹהֵי אֲבוֹתֵינוּ
כְּשֵׁם שֶׁקִּיַּמְתִּי וְיָשַׁבְתִּי בְּסֻכָּה זוֹ
כֵּן אֶזְכֶּה לַשָּׁנָה הַבָּאָה לֵישֵׁב בְּסֻכַּת עוֹרוֹ שֶׁל לִוְיָתָן.

לַשָּׁנָה הַבָּאָה בִּירוּשָׁלָיִם.

Some add:

רִבּוֹנָא דְעָלְמָא, יְהֵא רַעֲוָה מִן קֳדָמָךְ
שֶׁאוֹתָן מַלְאָכִים הַקְּדוֹשִׁים הַשַּׁיָּכִים לְמִצְוַת סֻכָּה
וּלְמִצְוַת אַרְבָּעָה מִינִים: לוּלָב וְאֶתְרוֹג, הֲדַס וַעֲרָבָה, הַנּוֹהֲגִים בְּחַג הַסֻּכּוֹת
הֵם יִתְלַוּוּ עִמָּנוּ בְּצֵאתֵנוּ מִן הַסֻּכָּה וְיִכָּנְסוּ עִמָּנוּ לְבָתֵּינוּ לְחַיִּים וּלְשָׁלוֹם.
וְלִהְיוֹת תָּמִיד עָלֵינוּ שְׁמִירָה עֶלְיוֹנָה מִמְּעוֹן קָדְשֶׁךָ
וּלְהַצִּילֵנוּ מִכָּל חֵטְא וְעָוֹן, וּמִכָּל פְּגָעִים רָעִים
וּמִכָּל שָׁעוֹת רָעוֹת הַמִּתְרַגְּשׁוֹת לָבוֹא לָעוֹלָם.
וְתַעֲרֶה עָלֵינוּ רוּחַ מִמָּרוֹם
וְחַדֵּשׁ כִּלְיוֹתֵינוּ לְעָבְדְּךָ בֶּאֱמֶת, בְּאַהֲבָה וּבְיִרְאָה
וְנִתְמִיד מְאֹד בְּלִמּוּד תּוֹרָתְךָ הַקְּדוֹשָׁה, לִלְמֹד וּלְלַמֵּד.
וּזְכוּת אַרְבָּעָה מִינִים וּמִצְוַת סֻכָּה תַּעֲמֹד לָנוּ
שֶׁתַּאֲרִיךְ אַפְּךָ עַד שׁוּבֵנוּ אֵלֶיךָ בִּתְשׁוּבָה שְׁלֵמָה לְפָנֶיךָ.
וּנְתַקֵּן כָּל אֲשֶׁר פָּגַמְנוּ
וְנִזְכֶּה לִשְׁנֵי שֻׁלְחָנוֹת, בְּלִי צַעַר וְיָגוֹן, אֲנִי וּבְנֵי בֵיתִי וְיוֹצְאֵי חֲלָצַי
וְנִהְיֶה כֻּלָּנוּ שׁוֹקְטִים וּשְׁלֵוִים, דְּשֵׁנִים וְרַעֲנַנִּים
וְעוֹבְדֵי יהוה בֶּאֱמֶת לַאֲמִתּוֹ כִּרְצוֹנְךָ הַטּוֹב, בִּכְלַל כָּל בְּנֵי יִשְׂרָאֵל, אָמֵן.
יִהְיוּ לְרָצוֹן אִמְרֵי פִי, וְהֶגְיוֹן לִבִּי לְפָנֶיךָ, יהוה צוּרִי וְגֹאֲלִי: תהלים יט

THE SUKKA OF LEVIATHAN
According to rabbinic lore, in the time to come, God will make for the righteous a Sukka fashioned from the skin of Leviathan, a giant creature made

Kiddush for Yom Tov Evening

On Shabbat add:

quietly: And it was evening, and it was morning – Gen. 1
יוֹם הַשִּׁשִּׁי the sixth day.

Then the heavens and the earth were completed, Gen. 2
and all their array.
With the seventh day, God completed the work He had done.
He ceased on the seventh day from all the work He had done.
God blessed the seventh day and declared it holy,
because on it He ceased from all His work He had created to do.

On other evenings Kiddush starts here:

When saying Kiddush for others, add:
Please pay attention, my masters.

Blessed are You, Lord our God, King of the Universe,
who creates the fruit of the vine.

On Shabbat, add the words in parentheses.

בָּרוּךְ Blessed are You, Lord our God,
King of the Universe,
who has chosen us from among all peoples,
raised us above all tongues,
and made us holy through His commandments.
You have given us, Lord our God, in love
(Sabbaths for rest), festivals for rejoicing,
holy days and seasons for joy,
(this Sabbath day and) this day of:

On Sukkot: the festival of Sukkot, our time of rejoicing

On Shemini Atzeret & Simḥat Torah: the festival of the eighth day, Shemini Atzeret,
our time of rejoicing

(with love), a holy assembly in memory of the exodus from Egypt.

קידוש לליל יום טוב

On שבת add:

בראשית א
quietly וַיְהִי־עֶרֶב וַיְהִי־בֹקֶר

יוֹם הַשִּׁשִּׁי:

בראשית ב
וַיְכֻלּוּ הַשָּׁמַיִם וְהָאָרֶץ וְכָל־צְבָאָם:
וַיְכַל אֱלֹהִים בַּיּוֹם הַשְּׁבִיעִי מְלַאכְתּוֹ אֲשֶׁר עָשָׂה
וַיִּשְׁבֹּת בַּיּוֹם הַשְּׁבִיעִי מִכָּל־מְלַאכְתּוֹ אֲשֶׁר עָשָׂה:
וַיְבָרֶךְ אֱלֹהִים אֶת־יוֹם הַשְּׁבִיעִי, וַיְקַדֵּשׁ אֹתוֹ
כִּי בוֹ שָׁבַת מִכָּל־מְלַאכְתּוֹ, אֲשֶׁר־בָּרָא אֱלֹהִים, לַעֲשׂוֹת:

On other evenings the קידוש starts here:

When saying קידוש for others, add:

סַבְרִי מָרָנָן

בָּרוּךְ אַתָּה יהוה אֱלֹהֵינוּ מֶלֶךְ הָעוֹלָם, בּוֹרֵא פְּרִי הַגָּפֶן.

On שבת, add the words in parentheses.

בָּרוּךְ אַתָּה יהוה אֱלֹהֵינוּ מֶלֶךְ הָעוֹלָם
אֲשֶׁר בָּחַר בָּנוּ מִכָּל עָם
וְרוֹמְמָנוּ מִכָּל לָשׁוֹן, וְקִדְּשָׁנוּ בְּמִצְוֹתָיו
וַתִּתֶּן לָנוּ יהוה אֱלֹהֵינוּ בְּאַהֲבָה
(שַׁבָּתוֹת לִמְנוּחָה וּ)מוֹעֲדִים לְשִׂמְחָה
חַגִּים וּזְמַנִּים לְשָׂשׂוֹן
אֶת יוֹם (הַשַּׁבָּת הַזֶּה וְאֶת יוֹם)

בסוכות: חַג הַסֻּכּוֹת הַזֶּה, זְמַן שִׂמְחָתֵנוּ
בשמע״צ ובש״ת: הַשְּׁמִינִי חַג הָעֲצֶרֶת הַזֶּה, זְמַן שִׂמְחָתֵנוּ

(בְּאַהֲבָה) מִקְרָא קֹדֶשׁ, זֵכֶר לִיצִיאַת מִצְרָיִם

For You have chosen us and sanctified us above all peoples,
and given us as our heritage
(Your holy Sabbath in love and favor and)
Your holy festivals for joy and gladness.
Blessed are you, LORD,
who sanctifies (the Sabbath,) Israel and the festivals.

On Motza'ei Shabbat, the following Havdala is added:

בָּרוּךְ Blessed are You, LORD our God, King of the Universe,
who creates the lights of fire.

Blessed are You, LORD our God, King of the Universe, who distinguishes between sacred and secular, between light and darkness, between Israel and the nations, between the seventh day and the six days of work. You have made a distinction between the holiness of the Sabbath and the holiness of festivals, and have sanctified the seventh day above the six days of work. You have distinguished and sanctified Your people Israel with Your holiness. Blessed are You, LORD, who distinguishes between sacred and sacred.

On the first night of Sukkot, the following blessing is said before the blessing "who has given us life"; on the second night, after it (some say it before on both nights).

If one is unable to sit in a sukka this blessing is omitted.

בָּרוּךְ Blessed are You, LORD our God, King of the Universe,
who has made us holy though His commandments,
and has commanded us to dwell in the sukka.

בָּרוּךְ Blessed are You, LORD our God, King of the Universe,
who has given us life, sustained us, and brought us to this time.

It is customary for all present to drink of the wine.

---

the blessing over sitting in the Sukka, because it applies both to the sanctification of the day and to the mitzva of sitting, which we are performing for the first time this year.

שֶׁהֶחֱיָנוּ וְקִיְּמָנוּ *Who has given us life.* A blessing over the passage of time, made

כִּי בָנוּ בָחַרְתָּ וְאוֹתָנוּ קִדַּשְׁתָּ מִכָּל הָעַמִּים (וְשַׁבָּת)
וּמוֹעֲדֵי קָדְשֶׁךָ (בְּאַהֲבָה וּבְרָצוֹן)
בְּשִׂמְחָה וּבְשָׂשׂוֹן הִנְחַלְתָּנוּ.
בָּרוּךְ אַתָּה יהוה, מְקַדֵּשׁ (הַשַּׁבָּת וְ) יִשְׂרָאֵל וְהַזְּמַנִּים.

On מוצאי שבת*, the following* הבדלה *is added:*

בָּרוּךְ אַתָּה יהוה אֱלֹהֵינוּ מֶלֶךְ הָעוֹלָם
בּוֹרֵא מְאוֹרֵי הָאֵשׁ.

בָּרוּךְ אַתָּה יהוה אֱלֹהֵינוּ מֶלֶךְ הָעוֹלָם, הַמַּבְדִּיל בֵּין קֹדֶשׁ לְחֹל, בֵּין אוֹר לְחֹשֶׁךְ, בֵּין יִשְׂרָאֵל לָעַמִּים, בֵּין יוֹם הַשְּׁבִיעִי לְשֵׁשֶׁת יְמֵי הַמַּעֲשֶׂה. בֵּין קְדֻשַּׁת שַׁבָּת לִקְדֻשַּׁת יוֹם טוֹב הִבְדַּלְתָּ, וְאֶת יוֹם הַשְּׁבִיעִי מִשֵּׁשֶׁת יְמֵי הַמַּעֲשֶׂה קִדַּשְׁתָּ, הִבְדַּלְתָּ וְקִדַּשְׁתָּ אֶת עַמְּךָ יִשְׂרָאֵל בִּקְדֻשָּׁתֶךָ. בָּרוּךְ אַתָּה יהוה, הַמַּבְדִּיל בֵּין קֹדֶשׁ לְקֹדֶשׁ.

On the first night of סוכות*, the following blessing it is said before the blessing* שֶׁהֶחֱיָנוּ*; on the second night, after it (some say it before on both nights). If one is unable to sit in a* סוכה *this blessing is omitted.*

בָּרוּךְ אַתָּה יהוה אֱלֹהֵינוּ מֶלֶךְ הָעוֹלָם
אֲשֶׁר קִדְּשָׁנוּ בְּמִצְוֹתָיו וְצִוָּנוּ לֵישֵׁב בַּסֻּכָּה.

בָּרוּךְ אַתָּה יהוה אֱלֹהֵינוּ מֶלֶךְ הָעוֹלָם
שֶׁהֶחֱיָנוּ וְקִיְּמָנוּ, וְהִגִּיעָנוּ לַזְּמַן הַזֶּה.

It is customary for all present to drink of the wine.

KIDDUSH

אֲשֶׁר קִדְּשָׁנוּ בְּמִצְוֹתָיו וְצִוָּנוּ לֵישֵׁב בַּסֻּכָּה *Has commanded us to dwell in the Sukka.* The mitzva is to dwell in the Sukka (Lev. 23:42–43), but since *leishev* in Hebrew means both "to dwell" and "to sit," the custom is to make the blessing while seated. On the first night, the *sheheḥeyanu* blessing is made *after*

had spare wood. Watching him from the window, Rabbi Mordechai was overcome with emotion. He turned his gaze upward and said, "Master of the universe, see how Your people yearn to fulfill Your commands with love. Here is a poor man, hardly able to walk, going from house to house, weeping because he cannot find wood to build a Sukka." Immediately he had said these words, the rabbi turned to his servant and said, "Come, let us take the wood I had set aside for my Sukka and together you and I will build one for this man instead." That year Rabbi Mordechai ate all his meals in the shoemaker's Sukka.

Rabbi Pinḥas of Koretz, famed for his wisdom, was so thronged with people seeking his advice that he found he had no time to study. Determined to rectify matters, he refused to see anyone and spent his days in study and prayer. As sukkot approached, he invited a number of people to be his guests during the festival, but they, angered by his self-imposed solitude, refused. On the first night, as he sat alone in the Sukka, he recited the Ushpizin, inviting Abraham to be his guest. In a vision he saw the patriarch standing outside the Sukka, refusing to enter. "Why will you not enter?" asked the rabbi. Abraham replied: "I will not enter a place where there are no other guests." The rabbi realized his mistake, and once again opened his home to all who sought to enter.

Rabbi Zusya of Hanipol used to invite simple Jews into his Sukka. His disciples asked him why he did not invite more distinguished guests, scholars and people of special piety. He replied, "Because one day I will leave this life, and I will want to enter the heavenly Sukka where the righteous dwell in peace. When they ask me by what right a simple Jew like me, without learning or piety, claims admission to so holy a place, I will reply, because I welcomed simple Jews into my Sukka."

One year during Sukkot, Rav Aryeh Levin, famed in Jerusalem for his piety, was seen in a Sukka far from his house. Asked why, he explained: "I came to visit the widow of Rabbi Reuven Bonzis of blessed memory. While her husband was alive their Sukka was always filled with guests who had come to see the rabbi. It was always lively and crowded. However, now that the rabbi is no longer alive, their home no longer enjoys the many visitors it once had. How lonely his widow must feel! Therefore I made sure to visit her over Sukkot, as well as other widows whose homes are also no longer crowded with visitors as they were in the past."

at moments when we are specifically aware of the passage of time, like festivals, or memorable events like buying a new house. It is at such moments that we cease merely to exist. We feel vividly alive. We are aware of the power of now. Life is God's gift. The breath we breathe is His. To be a Jew is to make a blessing over life. Though we do not say *Sheheḥeyanu* on the last days of Pesaḥ, we do on Shemini Atzeret because the day is a separate festival in its own right, not simply a continuation of Sukkot.

On the second night (outside of Israel), however, *Sheheḥeyanu* applies only to the day, since it is not the first time we are sitting in the Sukka. It is therefore said directly after the sanctification of the day, before the blessing over the Sukka.

In relation to the command to dwell in the Sukka, the Torah says, "so that your descendants will know that I settled the children of Israel in booths when I brought them out of the land of Egypt" (Lev. 23:43). Therefore, even though the fulfillment of commands does not usually require a specific intention, in the case of Sukka it is important to recall the reason for the command – namely, the recollection of our ancestors' experience as they journeyed from slavery to the Promised Land.

There is a difference of opinion among the sages (*Sukka* 11b) as to what exactly the Sukka represents. According to one view it is a reminder of the temporary dwellings in which our ancestors lived during their forty years' of wandering; to the other, it symbolizes the Clouds of Glory that accompanied them, sheltering them from heat during the day, cold at night, and from the weapons of their enemies. Perhaps both are true: a temporary home can be frail and humble, yet those who live there in faith are surrounded by clouds of glory.

It was this faith of which Jeremiah spoke of in God's name, saying, "I remember of you the kindness of your youth, your love when you were a bride; how you walked after Me in the desert, through a land not sown" (Jer. 2:2). Our ancestors had the courage to undertake a journey into the unknown in response to the call of God. Sitting in the Sukka we renew that courage as we face the new year.

It was the custom of Rabbi Mordechai of Lechovitz to buy wood before Sukkot and give it to the poor of his town so they could each build a Sukka. One year, on the eve of Sukkot, a poor, lame shoemaker came to the rabbi asking for wood. Regretfully, the rabbi told him that he had given it all away. The shoemaker, saddened, limped from house to house asking if anyone

On washing hands before eating the Ḥalla:

Blessed are You, Lord our God, King of the Universe,
who has made us holy through His commandments,
and has commanded us about washing hands.

Before eating the Ḥalla:

Blessed are You, Lord our God, King of the Universe,
who brings forth bread from the earth.

Birkat HaMazon / Grace after Meals

שִׁיר הַמַּעֲלוֹת A song of ascents. *Ps. 126*
When the Lord brought back the exiles of Zion
we were like people who dream.
Then were our mouths filled with laughter,
and our tongues with songs of joy.
Then was it said among the nations,
"The Lord has done great things for them."
The Lord did do great things for us and we rejoiced.
Bring back our exiles, Lord, like streams in a dry land.
May those who sowed in tears, reap in joy.
May one who goes out weeping, carrying a bag of seed,
come back with songs of joy, carrying his sheaves.

Some say:

תְּהִלַּת My mouth shall speak the praise of God, *Ps. 145*
and all creatures shall bless His holy name for ever and all time.
We will bless God now and for ever. Halleluya! *Ps. 115*
Thank the Lord for He is good; His loving-kindness is for ever. *Ps. 136*
Who can tell of the Lord's mighty acts *Ps. 106*
and make all His praise be heard?

---

wealth for me'" (ibid, vv. 14–17). Bereft of a sense of gratitude and of a power higher than humans, nations, like individuals, eventually decay.

The original form of Grace consisted of three blessings, which move sequentially from the universal to the particular. In the first, we thank God for sustaining the world and all that lives. The second is national: we thank God for the land of Israel as well as for the other blessings of Jewish life:

On washing hands before eating the חלה:

בָּרוּךְ אַתָּה יהוה אֱלֹהֵינוּ מֶלֶךְ הָעוֹלָם
אֲשֶׁר קִדְּשָׁנוּ בְּמִצְוֹתָיו וְצִוָּנוּ עַל נְטִילַת יָדָיִם.

Before eating the חלה:

בָּרוּךְ אַתָּה יהוה אֱלֹהֵינוּ מֶלֶךְ הָעוֹלָם, הַמּוֹצִיא לֶחֶם מִן הָאָרֶץ.

ברכת המזון

שִׁיר הַמַּעֲלוֹת, בְּשׁוּב יהוה אֶת־שִׁיבַת צִיּוֹן, הָיִינוּ כְּחֹלְמִים: תהלים קכו
אָז יִמָּלֵא שְׂחוֹק פִּינוּ וּלְשׁוֹנֵנוּ רִנָּה
אָז יֹאמְרוּ בַגּוֹיִם הִגְדִּיל יהוה לַעֲשׂוֹת עִם־אֵלֶּה:
הִגְדִּיל יהוה לַעֲשׂוֹת עִמָּנוּ, הָיִינוּ שְׂמֵחִים:
שׁוּבָה יהוה אֶת־שְׁבִיתֵנוּ, כַּאֲפִיקִים בַּנֶּגֶב:
הַזֹּרְעִים בְּדִמְעָה בְּרִנָּה יִקְצֹרוּ:
הָלוֹךְ יֵלֵךְ וּבָכֹה נֹשֵׂא מֶשֶׁךְ־הַזָּרַע
בֹּא־יָבֹא בְרִנָּה נֹשֵׂא אֲלֻמֹּתָיו:

Some say:

תְּהִלַּת יהוה יְדַבֶּר פִּי, וִיבָרֵךְ כָּל־בָּשָׂר שֵׁם קָדְשׁוֹ לְעוֹלָם וָעֶד: תהלים קמה
וַאֲנַחְנוּ נְבָרֵךְ יָהּ מֵעַתָּה וְעַד־עוֹלָם, הַלְלוּיָהּ: תהלים קטו
הוֹדוּ לַיהוה כִּי־טוֹב, כִּי לְעוֹלָם חַסְדּוֹ: תהלים קלו
מִי יְמַלֵּל גְּבוּרוֹת יהוה, יַשְׁמִיעַ כָּל־תְּהִלָּתוֹ: תהלים קו

BIRKAT HAMAZON / GRACE AFTER MEALS

Grace after Meals is specifically mandated by the Torah itself: "You shall eat and be satisfied, then you shall bless the Lord your God" (Deut. 8:10). Thanksgiving, Moses taught the Israelites, is central to Jewish life, "lest your heart grow haughty and you forget the Lord your God…and you say to yourselves, 'My own power and the might of my own hand have won this

ZIMMUN / INVITATION

When three or more men say Birkat HaMazon together, the following zimmun is said. When three or more women say Birkat HaMazon, substitute "Friends" for "Gentlemen." The leader should ask permission from those with precedence to lead the Birkat HaMazon.

Leader Gentlemen, let us say grace.

Others May the name of the LORD be blessed from now and for ever. *Ps. 113*

Leader May the name of the LORD be blessed
from now and for ever.
With your permission,
(my father and teacher / my mother and teacher / the Kohanim present / our teacher the Rabbi / the master of this house / the mistress of this house)
my masters and teachers,
let us bless (*in a minyan:* our God,)
the One from whose food we have eaten.

Others Blessed be (*in a minyan:* our God,) the One from whose food we have eaten, and by whose goodness we live.

**People present who have not taken part in the meal say:*
*Blessed be (*in a minyan:* our God,) the One whose name is continually blessed for ever and all time.

Leader Blessed be (*in a minyan:* our God,) the One from whose food we have eaten, and by whose goodness we live.
Blessed be He, and blessed be His name.

---

longer version is used when at least ten are present. The act of inviting those present to join in the act of praise is similar to the recitation of *Barekhu*, "Bless the LORD," with which morning and evening services begin. It emphasizes the essentially communal nature of prayer in Judaism. In addition to the regular *zimmun* here, there are special forms of *zimmun* for (1) a wedding meal, (2) a meal after a circumcision, and (3) a meal in a house of mourning.

סדר הזימון

When three or more men say ברכת המזון together, the following זימון is said.
When three or more women say ברכת המזון, substitute חֲבֵרוֹתַי for רַבּוֹתַי.
The leader should ask permission from those with precedence to lead the ברכת המזון.

Leader רַבּוֹתַי, נְבָרֵךְ.

Others יְהִי שֵׁם יהוה מְבֹרָךְ מֵעַתָּה וְעַד־עוֹלָם: תהלים קיג

Leader יְהִי שֵׁם יהוה מְבֹרָךְ מֵעַתָּה וְעַד־עוֹלָם:
בִּרְשׁוּת (אָבִי מוֹרִי / אִמִּי מוֹרָתִי /
כֹּהֲנִים / מוֹרֵנוּ הָרַב /
בַּעַל הַבַּיִת הַזֶּה / בַּעֲלַת הַבַּיִת הַזֶּה)
מָרָנָן וְרַבָּנָן וְרַבּוֹתַי
נְבָרֵךְ (במנין: אֱלֹהֵינוּ) שֶׁאָכַלְנוּ מִשֶּׁלּוֹ.

Others בָּרוּךְ (במנין: אֱלֹהֵינוּ) שֶׁאָכַלְנוּ מִשֶּׁלּוֹ וּבְטוּבוֹ חָיִינוּ.

**People present who have not taken part in the meal say:*
*בָּרוּךְ (במנין: אֱלֹהֵינוּ) וּמְבֹרָךְ שְׁמוֹ תָּמִיד לְעוֹלָם וָעֶד.

Leader בָּרוּךְ (במנין: אֱלֹהֵינוּ) שֶׁאָכַלְנוּ מִשֶּׁלּוֹ וּבְטוּבוֹ חָיִינוּ.
בָּרוּךְ הוּא וּבָרוּךְ שְׁמוֹ.

---

the covenant and its sign, circumcision, and the Torah. The third turns to Jerusalem. The fourth paragraph is a later addition: according to the Talmud (*Berakhot* 48b), it was added after the Bar Kokhba rebellion, c. 135 CE. Over the course of time, it has expanded considerably.

ZIMMUN

A meal at which there are three adult males requires a formal invitation, *zimmun*, to say Grace. The Talmud derives this from the verse, "Magnify the LORD with me; let us exalt His name together" (Psalm 34:4). A slightly

BLESSING OF NOURISHMENT

בָּרוּךְ Blessed are You, LORD our God, King of the Universe,
who in His goodness feeds the whole world
with grace, kindness and compassion.
He gives food to all living things,
for His kindness is for ever.
Because of His continual great goodness,
we have never lacked food,
nor may we ever lack it,
for the sake of His great name.
For He is God who feeds and sustains all,
does good to all,
and prepares food for all creatures He has created.
Blessed are You, LORD,
who feeds all.

BLESSING OF LAND

נוֹדֶה We thank You, LORD our God,
for having granted as a heritage to our ancestors
a desirable, good and spacious land;
for bringing us out, LORD our God,
from the land of Egypt,
freeing us from the house of slavery;
for Your covenant which You sealed in our flesh;
for Your Torah which You taught us;
for Your laws which You made known to us;
for the life, grace and kindness You have bestowed on us;
and for the food
by which You continually feed and sustain us,
every day, every season, every hour.

---

the covenant and its sign, circumcision, the giving of the Torah and the commandments.

ברכת הזן

בָּרוּךְ אַתָּה יהוה אֱלֹהֵינוּ מֶלֶךְ הָעוֹלָם
הַזָּן אֶת הָעוֹלָם כֻּלּוֹ בְּטוּבוֹ, בְּחֵן בְּחֶסֶד וּבְרַחֲמִים
הוּא נוֹתֵן לֶחֶם לְכָל בָּשָׂר
כִּי לְעוֹלָם חַסְדּוֹ.
וּבְטוּבוֹ הַגָּדוֹל, תָּמִיד לֹא חָסַר לָנוּ
וְאַל יֶחְסַר לָנוּ מָזוֹן לְעוֹלָם וָעֶד
בַּעֲבוּר שְׁמוֹ הַגָּדוֹל.
כִּי הוּא אֵל זָן וּמְפַרְנֵס לַכֹּל וּמֵטִיב לַכֹּל
וּמֵכִין מָזוֹן לְכָל בְּרִיּוֹתָיו אֲשֶׁר בָּרָא.
בָּרוּךְ אַתָּה יהוה, הַזָּן אֶת הַכֹּל.

ברכת הארץ

נוֹדֶה לְךָ, יהוה אֱלֹהֵינוּ
עַל שֶׁהִנְחַלְתָּ לַאֲבוֹתֵינוּ אֶרֶץ חֶמְדָּה טוֹבָה וּרְחָבָה
וְעַל שֶׁהוֹצֵאתָנוּ יהוה אֱלֹהֵינוּ מֵאֶרֶץ מִצְרַיִם
וּפְדִיתָנוּ מִבֵּית עֲבָדִים
וְעַל בְּרִיתְךָ שֶׁחָתַמְתָּ בִּבְשָׂרֵנוּ
וְעַל תּוֹרָתְךָ שֶׁלִּמַּדְתָּנוּ
וְעַל חֻקֶּיךָ שֶׁהוֹדַעְתָּנוּ
וְעַל חַיִּים חֵן וָחֶסֶד שֶׁחוֹנַנְתָּנוּ
וְעַל אֲכִילַת מָזוֹן שָׁאַתָּה זָן וּמְפַרְנֵס אוֹתָנוּ תָּמִיד
בְּכָל יוֹם וּבְכָל עֵת וּבְכָל שָׁעָה.

נוֹדֶה *We thank.* After thanking God for the land, the paragraph goes on to add thanks for God's other kindnesses to Israel: the exodus from Egypt,

וְעַל הַכֹּל For all this, LORD our God,
we thank and bless You.
May Your name be blessed continually
by the mouth of all that lives, for ever and all time –
for so it is written:
"You will eat and be satisfied, *Deut. 8*
then you shall bless the LORD your God
for the good land He has given you."
Blessed are You, LORD,
for the land and for the food.

BLESSING FOR JERUSALEM

רַחֵם נָא Have compassion, please,
LORD our God,
on Israel Your people,
on Jerusalem Your city,
on Zion the dwelling place of Your glory,
on the royal house of David Your anointed,
and on the great and holy House that bears Your name.
Our God, our Father,
tend us, feed us,
sustain us and support us,
relieve us and send us relief,
LORD our God,
swiftly from all our troubles.
Please, LORD our God,
do not make us dependent
on the gifts or loans of other people,
but only on Your full, open, holy and generous hand
so that we may suffer neither shame nor humiliation
for ever and all time.

וְעַל הַכֹּל, יהוה אֱלֹהֵינוּ
אֲנַחְנוּ מוֹדִים לָךְ וּמְבָרְכִים אוֹתָךְ
יִתְבָּרַךְ שִׁמְךָ בְּפִי כָּל חַי תָּמִיד לְעוֹלָם וָעֶד
כַּכָּתוּב:
וְאָכַלְתָּ וְשָׂבָעְתָּ, וּבֵרַכְתָּ אֶת־יהוה אֱלֹהֶיךָ דברים ח
עַל־הָאָרֶץ הַטֹּבָה אֲשֶׁר נָתַן־לָךְ:
בָּרוּךְ אַתָּה יהוה
עַל הָאָרֶץ וְעַל הַמָּזוֹן.

ברכת ירושלים

רַחֵם נָא, יהוה אֱלֹהֵינוּ
עַל יִשְׂרָאֵל עַמֶּךָ
וְעַל יְרוּשָׁלַיִם עִירֶךָ
וְעַל צִיּוֹן מִשְׁכַּן כְּבוֹדֶךָ
וְעַל מַלְכוּת בֵּית דָּוִד מְשִׁיחֶךָ
וְעַל הַבַּיִת הַגָּדוֹל וְהַקָּדוֹשׁ שֶׁנִּקְרָא שִׁמְךָ עָלָיו.
אֱלֹהֵינוּ, אָבִינוּ
רְעֵנוּ, זוּנֵנוּ, פַּרְנְסֵנוּ וְכַלְכְּלֵנוּ
וְהַרְוִיחֵנוּ, וְהַרְוַח לָנוּ יהוה אֱלֹהֵינוּ מְהֵרָה מִכָּל צָרוֹתֵינוּ.
וְנָא אַל תַּצְרִיכֵנוּ, יהוה אֱלֹהֵינוּ
לֹא לִידֵי מַתְּנַת בָּשָׂר וָדָם
וְלֹא לִידֵי הַלְוָאָתָם
כִּי אִם לְיָדְךָ הַמְּלֵאָה, הַפְּתוּחָה, הַקְּדוֹשָׁה וְהָרְחָבָה
שֶׁלֹּא נֵבוֹשׁ וְלֹא נִכָּלֵם לְעוֹלָם וָעֶד.

On Shabbat, say:

רְצֵה Favor and strengthen us, LORD our God,
through Your commandments,
especially through the commandment of the seventh day,
this great and holy Sabbath.
For it is, for You, a great and holy day.
On it we cease work and rest in love
in accord with Your will's commandment.
May it be Your will, LORD our God,
to grant us rest without distress,
grief, or lament on our day of rest.
May You show us the consolation of Zion Your city,
and the rebuilding of Jerusalem Your holy city,
for You are the Master of salvation and consolation.

אֱלֹהֵינוּ Our God and God of our ancestors,
may there rise, come, reach, appear, be favored, heard, regarded
and remembered before You, our recollection and remembrance,
as well as the remembrance of our ancestors,
and of the Messiah son of David Your servant,
and of Jerusalem Your holy city,
and of all Your people the house of Israel –
for deliverance and well-being,
grace, loving-kindness and compassion,
life and peace, on this day of:

On Sukkot: the Festival of Sukkot.
On Shemini Atzeret & Simḥat Torah: the Festival of Shemini Atzeret.

On it remember us, LORD our God, for good;
recollect us for blessing,
and deliver us for life.
In accord with Your promise of salvation and compassion,
spare us and be gracious to us;
have compassion on us and deliver us,
for our eyes are turned to You because You are God,
gracious and compassionate.

On שבת, say:

רְצֵה וְהַחֲלִיצֵנוּ, יהוה אֱלֹהֵינוּ, בְּמִצְוֹתֶיךָ
וּבְמִצְוַת יוֹם הַשְּׁבִיעִי הַשַּׁבָּת הַגָּדוֹל וְהַקָּדוֹשׁ הַזֶּה
כִּי יוֹם זֶה גָּדוֹל וְקָדוֹשׁ הוּא לְפָנֶיךָ
לִשְׁבָּת בּוֹ, וְלָנְוּחַ בּוֹ בְּאַהֲבָה כְּמִצְוַת רְצוֹנֶךָ
וּבִרְצוֹנְךָ הָנִיחַ לָנוּ, יהוה אֱלֹהֵינוּ
שֶׁלֹּא תְהֵא צָרָה וְיָגוֹן וַאֲנָחָה בְּיוֹם מְנוּחָתֵנוּ
וְהַרְאֵנוּ, יהוה אֱלֹהֵינוּ, בְּנֶחָמַת צִיּוֹן עִירֶךָ
וּבְבִנְיַן יְרוּשָׁלַיִם עִיר קָדְשֶׁךָ
כִּי אַתָּה הוּא בַּעַל הַיְשׁוּעוֹת וּבַעַל הַנֶּחָמוֹת.

אֱלֹהֵינוּ וֵאלֹהֵי אֲבוֹתֵינוּ
יַעֲלֶה וְיָבוֹא וְיַגִּיעַ, וְיֵרָאֶה וְיֵרָצֶה וְיִשָּׁמַע
וְיִפָּקֵד וְיִזָּכֵר זִכְרוֹנֵנוּ וּפִקְדּוֹנֵנוּ, וְזִכְרוֹן אֲבוֹתֵינוּ
וְזִכְרוֹן מָשִׁיחַ בֶּן דָּוִד עַבְדֶּךָ
וְזִכְרוֹן יְרוּשָׁלַיִם עִיר קָדְשֶׁךָ
וְזִכְרוֹן כָּל עַמְּךָ בֵּית יִשְׂרָאֵל
לְפָנֶיךָ, לִפְלֵיטָה לְטוֹבָה, לְחֵן וּלְחֶסֶד וּלְרַחֲמִים
לְחַיִּים וּלְשָׁלוֹם בְּיוֹם

בסוכות: חַג הַסֻּכּוֹת הַזֶּה.

בשמיני עצרת ושמחת תורה: הַשְּׁמִינִי חַג הָעֲצֶרֶת הַזֶּה.

זָכְרֵנוּ יהוה אֱלֹהֵינוּ בּוֹ לְטוֹבָה
וּפָקְדֵנוּ בוֹ לִבְרָכָה
וְהוֹשִׁיעֵנוּ בוֹ לְחַיִּים.
וּבִדְבַר יְשׁוּעָה וְרַחֲמִים, חוּס וְחָנֵּנוּ וְרַחֵם עָלֵינוּ, וְהוֹשִׁיעֵנוּ
כִּי אֵלֶיךָ עֵינֵינוּ, כִּי אֵל חַנּוּן וְרַחוּם אָתָּה.

וּבְנֵה And may Jerusalem the holy city be rebuilt soon, in our time.
Blessed are You, LORD, who in His compassion
will rebuild Jerusalem. Amen.

BLESSING OF GOD'S GOODNESS

בָּרוּךְ Blessed are You, LORD our God, King of the Universe –
God our Father, our King, our Sovereign,
our Creator, our Redeemer, our Maker,
our Holy One, the Holy One of Jacob.
He is our Shepherd, Israel's Shepherd,
the good King who does good to all.
Every day He has done, is doing, and will do good to us.
He has acted, is acting,
and will always act kindly toward us for ever,
granting us grace, kindness and compassion,
relief and rescue,
prosperity, blessing, redemption and comfort,
sustenance and support, compassion, life,
peace and all good things,
and of all good things may He never let us lack.

בָּרוּךְ *Blessed.* A later addition, dated by the Talmud (*Berakhot* 48b) to the period following the Bar Kokhba rebellion when, after a long delay, the Romans gave permission to the Jews to bury their dead. The failure of the Bar Kokhba rebellion was one of the low points of Jewish history. According to the Roman historian Dio, 580,000 Jews died in the fighting and many others by starvation. Nine hundred and eighty-five towns, villages and settlements were destroyed. Jerusalem was leveled to the ground and rebuilt as a Roman city, Aelia Capitolina. The fact that the sages were able to salvage a fragment of consolation from the fact that the dead were not denied the dignity of burial is testimony to an extraordinary ability to survive catastrophe and preserve the lineaments of hope. The passage is built around threefold references to God's kingship, goodness and bestowal of kindness.

וּבְנֵה יְרוּשָׁלַיִם עִיר הַקֹּדֶשׁ בִּמְהֵרָה בְיָמֵינוּ.
בָּרוּךְ אַתָּה יהוה, בּוֹנֶה בְרַחֲמָיו יְרוּשָׁלָיִם, אָמֵן.

ברכת הטוב והמטיב

בָּרוּךְ אַתָּה יהוה אֱלֹהֵינוּ מֶלֶךְ הָעוֹלָם
הָאֵל אָבִינוּ, מַלְכֵּנוּ, אַדִּירֵנוּ
בּוֹרְאֵנוּ, גּוֹאֲלֵנוּ, יוֹצְרֵנוּ, קְדוֹשֵׁנוּ, קְדוֹשׁ יַעֲקֹב
רוֹעֵנוּ, רוֹעֵה יִשְׂרָאֵל, הַמֶּלֶךְ הַטּוֹב וְהַמֵּטִיב לַכֹּל
שֶׁבְּכָל יוֹם וָיוֹם
הוּא הֵיטִיב, הוּא מֵיטִיב, הוּא יֵיטִיב לָנוּ
הוּא גְמָלָנוּ, הוּא גוֹמְלֵנוּ, הוּא יִגְמְלֵנוּ לָעַד
לְחֵן וּלְחֶסֶד וּלְרַחֲמִים, וּלְרֶוַח, הַצָּלָה וְהַצְלָחָה
בְּרָכָה וִישׁוּעָה, נֶחָמָה, פַּרְנָסָה וְכַלְכָּלָה
וְרַחֲמִים וְחַיִּים וְשָׁלוֹם וְכָל טוֹב
וּמִכָּל טוּב לְעוֹלָם אַל יְחַסְּרֵנוּ.

וּבְנֵה יְרוּשָׁלַיִם *And may Jerusalem.* The third blessing speaks of Jerusalem, home of God's glory, as well as the Davidic monarchy and the Temple, for the restoration of which we pray. As is often the case in the siddur, Jerusalem is associated with the divine attribute of compassion, reflecting the words of Zechariah: "Therefore, this is what the LORD says: I will return to Jerusalem with compassion, and there My House will be rebuilt" (1:16). According to tradition, the Divine Presence never left Jerusalem, even when the city lay in ruins (*Shemot Raba* 2:2).

בּוֹנֶה בְרַחֲמָיו יְרוּשָׁלָיִם, אָמֵן *Who in His compassion will rebuild Jerusalem. Amen.* the unusual appearance of the word *Amen* in this passage (normally we do not say it after our own blessings) signals that this was originally the end of Grace.

ADDITIONAL REQUESTS

הָרַחֲמָן May the Compassionate One reign over us
for ever and all time.
May the Compassionate One be blessed
in heaven and on earth.
May the Compassionate One be praised
from generation to generation,
be glorified by us to all eternity,
and honored among us for ever and all time.
May the Compassionate One
grant us an honorable livelihood.
May the Compassionate One break the yoke from our neck
and lead us upright to our land.
May the Compassionate One send us many blessings to this house
and this table at which we have eaten.
May the Compassionate One send us Elijah the prophet –
may he be remembered for good –
to bring us good tidings of salvation and consolation.
May the Compassionate One bless the State of Israel,
first flowering of our redemption.
May the Compassionate One bless
the members of Israel's Defense Forces,
who stand guard over our land.

A guest says:

יְהִי רָצוֹן May it be Your will that the master of this house shall not suffer shame in this world, nor humiliation in the World to Come. May all he owns prosper greatly, and may his and our possessions be successful and close to hand. Let not the Accuser hold sway over his deeds or ours, and may no thought of sin, iniquity or transgression enter him or us from now and for evermore.

---

is striking: we bring redemption by acts of hospitality. This, according to the sages, is how Abraham and Sarah brought monotheism to the world. They would provide hospitality to strangers. When the meal was over, and the guests would begin to thank them, Abraham would reply, "Thank the One from whom all we have enjoyed has come" (*Sota* 10b).

בקשות נוספות

הָרַחֲמָן הוּא יִמְלֹךְ עָלֵינוּ לְעוֹלָם וָעֶד.
הָרַחֲמָן הוּא יִתְבָּרַךְ בַּשָּׁמַיִם וּבָאָרֶץ.
הָרַחֲמָן הוּא יִשְׁתַּבַּח לְדוֹר דּוֹרִים
וְיִתְפָּאַר בָּנוּ לָעַד וּלְנֵצַח נְצָחִים
וְיִתְהַדַּר בָּנוּ לָעַד וּלְעוֹלְמֵי עוֹלָמִים.
הָרַחֲמָן הוּא יְפַרְנְסֵנוּ בְּכָבוֹד.
הָרַחֲמָן הוּא יִשְׁבֹּר עֻלֵּנוּ מֵעַל צַוָּארֵנוּ
וְהוּא יוֹלִיכֵנוּ קוֹמְמִיּוּת לְאַרְצֵנוּ.
הָרַחֲמָן הוּא יִשְׁלַח לָנוּ בְּרָכָה מְרֻבָּה בַּבַּיִת הַזֶּה
וְעַל שֻׁלְחָן זֶה שֶׁאָכַלְנוּ עָלָיו.
הָרַחֲמָן הוּא יִשְׁלַח לָנוּ אֶת אֵלִיָּהוּ הַנָּבִיא זָכוּר לַטּוֹב
וִיבַשֶּׂר לָנוּ בְּשׂוֹרוֹת טוֹבוֹת יְשׁוּעוֹת וְנֶחָמוֹת.
הָרַחֲמָן הוּא יְבָרֵךְ אֶת מְדִינַת יִשְׂרָאֵל
רֵאשִׁית צְמִיחַת גְּאֻלָּתֵנוּ.
הָרַחֲמָן הוּא יְבָרֵךְ אֶת חַיָּלֵי צְבָא הַהֲגָנָה לְיִשְׂרָאֵל
הָעוֹמְדִים עַל מִשְׁמַר אַרְצֵנוּ.

A guest says:

יְהִי רָצוֹן שֶׁלֹּא יֵבוֹשׁ בַּעַל הַבַּיִת בָּעוֹלָם הַזֶּה, וְלֹא יִכָּלֵם לָעוֹלָם הַבָּא, וְיִצְלַח מְאֹד בְּכָל נְכָסָיו, וְיִהְיוּ נְכָסָיו וּנְכָסֵינוּ מֻצְלָחִים וּקְרוֹבִים לָעִיר, וְאַל יִשְׁלוֹט שָׂטָן לֹא בְּמַעֲשֵׂה יָדָיו וְלֹא בְּמַעֲשֵׂה יָדֵינוּ. וְאַל יִזְדַּקֵּק לֹא לְפָנָיו וְלֹא לְפָנֵינוּ שׁוּם דְּבַר הִרְהוּר חֵטְא, עֲבֵירָה וְעָוֹן, מֵעַתָּה וְעַד עוֹלָם.

הָרַחֲמָן *May the Compassionate One.* A series of additional prayers, dating from the Geonic period. The oldest is the one in which a guest invokes blessings on the hosts and their family. This is immediately preceded by a prayer that Elijah may come and announce the coming of the Messiah. The juxtaposition

הָרַחֲמָן May the Compassionate One bless –

When eating at one's own table, say (include the words in parentheses that apply):
me, (my wife/husband, / my father, my teacher / my mother, my teacher/ my children,) and all that is mine,

A guest at someone else's table says (include the words in parentheses that apply):
the master of this house, him (and his wife, the mistress of this house / and his children,) and all that is his,

Children at their parents' table say (include the words in parentheses that apply):
my father, my teacher, (master of this house,) and my mother, my teacher, (mistress of this house,) them, their household, their children, and all that is theirs.

For all other guests, add:
and all the diners here,

together with us and all that is ours.
Just as our forefathers
Abraham, Isaac and Jacob were blessed in all, from all, with all,
so may He bless all of us together
with a complete blessing,
and let us say: Amen.

בַּמָּרוֹם On high, may grace be invoked for them and for us,
as a safeguard of peace.
May we receive a blessing from the LORD
and a just reward from the God of our salvation,
and may we find grace
and good favor in the eyes of God and man.

On Shabbat: May the Compassionate One let us inherit the time, that will be entirely Shabbat and rest for life everlasting.

On Yom Tov: May the Compassionate One let us inherit the day, that is all good.

On Sukkot: May the Compassionate One restore for us, the fallen Tabernacle of David.

הָרַחֲמָן הוּא יְבָרֵךְ

When eating at one's own table, say (include the words in parentheses that apply):

אוֹתִי (וְאֶת אִשְׁתִּי / וְאֶת בַּעֲלִי / וְאֶת אָבִי מוֹרִי /
וְאֶת אִמִּי מוֹרָתִי / וְאֶת זַרְעִי) וְאֶת כָּל אֲשֶׁר לִי.

A guest at someone else's table says (include the words in parentheses that apply):

אֶת בַּעַל הַבַּיִת הַזֶּה, אוֹתוֹ (וְאֶת אִשְׁתּוֹ בַּעֲלַת הַבַּיִת הַזֶּה /
וְאֶת זַרְעוֹ) וְאֶת כָּל אֲשֶׁר לוֹ.

Children at their parents' table say (include the words in parentheses that apply):

אֶת אָבִי מוֹרִי (בַּעַל הַבַּיִת הַזֶּה), וְאֶת אִמִּי מוֹרָתִי (בַּעֲלַת הַבַּיִת
הַזֶּה), אוֹתָם וְאֶת בֵּיתָם וְאֶת זַרְעָם וְאֶת כָּל אֲשֶׁר לָהֶם

For all other guests, add:

וְאֶת כָּל הַמְסֻבִּין כָּאן

אוֹתָנוּ וְאֶת כָּל אֲשֶׁר לָנוּ, כְּמוֹ שֶׁנִּתְבָּרְכוּ אֲבוֹתֵינוּ
אַבְרָהָם יִצְחָק וְיַעֲקֹב, בַּכֹּל, מִכֹּל, כֹּל
כֵּן יְבָרֵךְ אוֹתָנוּ כֻּלָּנוּ יַחַד בִּבְרָכָה שְׁלֵמָה, וְנֹאמַר אָמֵן.

בַּמָּרוֹם יְלַמְּדוּ עֲלֵיהֶם וְעָלֵינוּ זְכוּת שֶׁתְּהֵא לְמִשְׁמֶרֶת שָׁלוֹם
וְנִשָּׂא בְרָכָה מֵאֵת יהוה וּצְדָקָה מֵאֱלֹהֵי יִשְׁעֵנוּ
וְנִמְצָא חֵן וְשֵׂכֶל טוֹב בְּעֵינֵי אֱלֹהִים וְאָדָם.

בשבת: הָרַחֲמָן הוּא יַנְחִילֵנוּ
יוֹם שֶׁכֻּלּוֹ שַׁבָּת וּמְנוּחָה לְחַיֵּי הָעוֹלָמִים.

ביום טוב: הָרַחֲמָן הוּא יַנְחִילֵנוּ יוֹם שֶׁכֻּלּוֹ טוֹב.

בסוכות: הָרַחֲמָן הוּא יָקִים לָנוּ אֶת סֻכַּת דָּוִד הַנּוֹפֶלֶת.

סֻכַּת דָּוִד הַנּוֹפֶלֶת *Fallen Tabernacle of David.* A phrase taken from Amos 9:11:

הָרַחֲמָן May the Compassionate One make us worthy
of the Messianic Age and life in the World to Come.
He is a tower of salvation to His king, *II Sam. 22*
showing kindness to His anointed,
to David and his descendants for ever.
He who makes peace in His high places,
may He make peace for us and all Israel,
and let us say: Amen.

יְראוּ Fear the Lord, you His holy ones; *Ps. 34*
those who fear Him lack nothing.
Young lions may grow weak and hungry,
but those who seek the Lord lack no good thing.
Thank the Lord for He is good; *Ps. 118*
His loving-kindness is for ever.
You open Your hand, *Ps. 145*
and satisfy every living thing with favor.
Blessed is the person who trusts in the Lord, *Jer. 17*
whose trust is in the Lord alone.
Once I was young, and now I am old, *Ps. 37*
yet I have never watched a righteous man forsaken
or his children begging for bread.
The Lord will give His people strength. *Ps. 29*
The Lord will bless His people with peace.

Taken in this sense, Psalm 37:25 should be understood as, "When the righteous was forsaken or his children forced to search for bread, I never merely stood and watched." Understood thus, it is a warning against being a mere bystander while other people suffer. It thus brings the Grace to a symmetrical close: It began by speaking of God's goodness in feeding the hungry and ends with an injunction for us to do likewise. This too is part of "walking in God's ways."

הָרַחֲמָן הוּא יְזַכֵּנוּ לִימוֹת הַמָּשִׁיחַ וּלְחַיֵּי הָעוֹלָם הַבָּא
מִגְדּוֹל יְשׁוּעוֹת מַלְכּוֹ שמואל ב׳ כב
וְעֹשֶׂה־חֶסֶד לִמְשִׁיחוֹ, לְדָוִד וּלְזַרְעוֹ עַד־עוֹלָם:
עֹשֶׂה שָׁלוֹם בִּמְרוֹמָיו
הוּא יַעֲשֶׂה שָׁלוֹם עָלֵינוּ וְעַל כָּל יִשְׂרָאֵל
וְאִמְרוּ אָמֵן.

יְראוּ אֶת־יהוה קְדֹשָׁיו, כִּי־אֵין מַחְסוֹר לִירֵאָיו: תהלים לד
כְּפִירִים רָשׁוּ וְרָעֵבוּ, וְדֹרְשֵׁי יהוה לֹא־יַחְסְרוּ כָל־טוֹב:
הוֹדוּ לַיהוה כִּי־טוֹב, כִּי לְעוֹלָם חַסְדּוֹ: תהלים קיח
פּוֹתֵחַ אֶת־יָדֶךָ, וּמַשְׂבִּיעַ לְכָל־חַי רָצוֹן: תהלים קמה
בָּרוּךְ הַגֶּבֶר אֲשֶׁר יִבְטַח בַּיהוה, וְהָיָה יהוה מִבְטַחוֹ: ירמיה יז
נַעַר הָיִיתִי גַּם־זָקַנְתִּי תהלים לז
וְלֹא־רָאִיתִי צַדִּיק נֶעֱזָב וְזַרְעוֹ מְבַקֶּשׁ־לָחֶם:
יהוה עֹז לְעַמּוֹ יִתֵּן, יהוה יְבָרֵךְ אֶת־עַמּוֹ בַשָּׁלוֹם: תהלים כט

"On that day I will restore David's fallen shelter – I will repair its broken walls and restore its ruins – and will rebuild it as it used to be." In today's context, a prayer for the rebuilding of the Temple.

נַעַר הָיִיתִי *Once I was young.* The standard translation of this verse (Psalm 37:25) is "I was young and now am old and I have not seen the righteous forsaken or his children searching for bread." I have translated it here according to a fine insight, author unknown, suggesting that the verb *ra'iti* should be understood in the sense in which it appears in the book of Esther, when Esther, pleading on behalf of Jewry, says: "For how can I watch the evil that shall come unto my people? Or how can I watch the destruction of my kindred?" (8:6). The verb there means "stand as a passive witness to."

BLESSING AFTER FOOD – AL HAMIḤYA

Grace after eating from the "seven species" of produce with which Israel is blessed: food made from the five grains (but not bread); wine or grape juice; grapes, figs, pomegranates, olives, or dates.

בָּרוּךְ Blessed are You, LORD our God, King of the Universe,

After grain products (but not bread):	*After wine or grape juice:*	*After grapes, figs, olives, pomegranates or dates:*
for the nourishment and sustenance,	for the vine and the fruit of the vine,	for the tree and the fruit of the tree,

After grain products (but not bread), and wine or grape juice:
for the nourishment and sustenance
and for the vine and the fruit of the vine,

and for the produce of the field; for the desirable, good and spacious land that You willingly gave as heritage to our ancestors, that they might eat of its fruit and be satisfied with its goodness. Have compassion, please, LORD our God, on Israel Your people, on Jerusalem, Your city, on Zion the home of Your glory, on Your altar and Your Temple. May You rebuild Jerusalem, the holy city swiftly in our time, and may You bring us back there, rejoicing in its rebuilding, eating from its fruit, satisfied by its goodness, and blessing You for it in holiness and purity.

On Shabbat: Be pleased to refresh us on this Sabbath Day.

On Sukkot: Grant us joy on this Festival of Sukkot.

On Shemini Atzeret & Simḥat Torah: Grant us joy on this Festival of Shemini Atzeret.

For You, God, are good and do good to all and we thank You for the land

(1) food made from wheat, barley, rye, oats or spelt; (2) grape wine or juice; or (3) grapes, figs, pomegranates, olives or dates.

ברכה מעין שלוש

Grace after eating from the "seven species" of produce with which Israel is blessed: food made from the five grains (but not bread); wine or grape juice; grapes, figs, pomegranates, olives, or dates.

בָּרוּךְ אַתָּה יהוה אֱלֹהֵינוּ מֶלֶךְ הָעוֹלָם, עַל

After grain products (but not bread):
הַמִּחְיָה וְעַל הַכַּלְכָּלָה

After wine or grape juice:
הַגֶּפֶן וְעַל פְּרִי הַגֶּפֶן

After grapes, figs, olives, pomegranates or dates:
הָעֵץ וְעַל פְּרִי הָעֵץ

After grain products (but not bread), and wine or grape juice:
הַמִּחְיָה וְעַל הַכַּלְכָּלָה וְעַל הַגֶּפֶן וְעַל פְּרִי הַגֶּפֶן

וְעַל תְּנוּבַת הַשָּׂדֶה וְעַל אֶרֶץ חֶמְדָּה טוֹבָה וּרְחָבָה, שֶׁרָצִיתָ וְהִנְחַלְתָּ לַאֲבוֹתֵינוּ לֶאֱכֹל מִפִּרְיָהּ וְלִשְׂבֹּעַ מִטּוּבָהּ. רַחֶם נָא יהוה אֱלֹהֵינוּ עַל יִשְׂרָאֵל עַמֶּךָ וְעַל יְרוּשָׁלַיִם עִירֶךָ וְעַל צִיּוֹן מִשְׁכַּן כְּבוֹדֶךָ וְעַל מִזְבְּחֶךָ וְעַל הֵיכָלֶךָ. וּבְנֵה יְרוּשָׁלַיִם עִיר הַקֹּדֶשׁ בִּמְהֵרָה בְיָמֵינוּ, וְהַעֲלֵנוּ לְתוֹכָהּ וְשַׂמְּחֵנוּ בְּבִנְיָנָהּ וְנֹאכַל מִפִּרְיָהּ וְנִשְׂבַּע מִטּוּבָהּ, וּנְבָרֶכְךָ עָלֶיהָ בִּקְדֻשָּׁה וּבְטָהֳרָה.

בשבת: וּרְצֵה וְהַחֲלִיצֵנוּ בְּיוֹם הַשַּׁבָּת הַזֶּה
בסוכות: וְשַׂמְּחֵנוּ בְּיוֹם חַג הַסֻּכּוֹת הַזֶּה
בשמיני עצרת ושמחת תורה: וְשַׂמְּחֵנוּ בְּיוֹם הַשְּׁמִינִי חַג הָעֲצֶרֶת הַזֶּה

כִּי אַתָּה יהוה טוֹב וּמֵטִיב לַכֹּל, וְנוֹדֶה לְּךָ עַל הָאָרֶץ

עַל הַמִּחְיָה *A blessing after other food or drink.* Known as the "three-in-one" blessing, this prayer summarizes the first three paragraphs of the Grace after Meals. It is said after consuming any of the "seven kinds" of produce for which Israel is praised in the Torah (Deut. 8:8) other than bread or matza, namely:

After grain products (but not bread):
and for the nourishment. Blessed are You, LORD, for the land and for the nourishment.

After wine or grape juice:
and for the fruit of the vine.* Blessed are You, LORD, for the land and for the fruit of the vine.*

After grapes, figs, olives, pomegranates or dates:
and for the fruit.** Blessed are You, LORD, for the land and for the fruit.**

After grain products (but not bread), and wine or grape juice:
and for the nourishment and for the fruit of the vine.*
Blessed are You, LORD, for the land and for the nourishment
and the fruit of the vine.*

* *If the wine is from Israel, then substitute "her vine" for "the vine."*
** *If the fruit is from Israel, then substitute "her fruit" for "the fruit."*

BLESSING AFTER FOOD – BOREH NEFASHOT

After food or drink that does not require Birkat HaMazon or Al HaMiḥya – such as meat, fish, dairy products, vegetables, beverages, or fruit other than grapes, figs, pomegranates, olives or dates – say:

בָּרוּךְ Blessed are You, LORD our God, King of the Universe,
who creates the many forms of life and their needs.
For all You have created
to sustain the life of all that lives,
blessed be He, Giver of life to the worlds.

On the last day of Sukkot, on leaving the sukka add the prayer on page 186.

After grain products (but not bread):

וְעַל הַמִּחְיָה.

בָּרוּךְ אַתָּה יהוה עַל הָאָרֶץ וְעַל הַמִּחְיָה.

After wine or grape juice:

וְעַל פְּרִי הַגָּפֶן.*

בָּרוּךְ אַתָּה יהוה עַל הָאָרֶץ וְעַל פְּרִי הַגָּפֶן.*

After grapes, figs, olives, pomegranates or dates:

וְעַל הַפֵּרוֹת.**

בָּרוּךְ אַתָּה יהוה עַל הָאָרֶץ וְעַל הַפֵּרוֹת.**

After grain products (but not bread), and wine or grape juice:

וְעַל הַמִּחְיָה וְעַל פְּרִי הַגָּפֶן.*

בָּרוּךְ אַתָּה יהוה, עַל הָאָרֶץ וְעַל הַמִּחְיָה וְעַל פְּרִי הַגָּפֶן.*

**If the wine is from* ארץ ישראל*, then substitute* גַּפְנָהּ *for* הַגָּפֶן*.*

***If the fruit is from* ארץ ישראל*, then substitute* פֵּרוֹתֶיהָ *for* הַפֵּרוֹת*.*

בורא נפשות

After food or drink that does not require ברכת המזון *or* מעין שלוש *– such as meat, fish, dairy products, vegetables, beverages, or fruit other than grapes, figs, pomegranates, olives or dates – say:*

בָּרוּךְ אַתָּה יהוה אֱלֹהֵינוּ מֶלֶךְ הָעוֹלָם
בּוֹרֵא נְפָשׁוֹת רַבּוֹת וְחֶסְרוֹנָן
עַל כָּל מַה שֶּׁבָּרָאתָ
לְהַחֲיוֹת בָּהֶם נֶפֶשׁ כָּל חָי.
בָּרוּךְ חֵי הָעוֹלָמִים.

On the last day of סוכות*, on leaving the* סוכה *add the prayer on page 187.*

מסכת סוכה
MASSEKHET SUKKA

The Mishnayot of Sukka is based upon The Koren Talmud Bavli, with commentary by Rabbi Adin Steinsaltz (Even Israel). The direct translation of the Mishna text appears in bold, while the elucidation and explanatory text by Rabbi Steinsaltz is in the lighter font.

Massekhet Sukka

CHAPTER 1

1 **A *sukka*,** i.e., its roofing, which is the main and most crucial element of the mitzva, **that is more than twenty cubits high is unfit. Rabbi Yehuda deems it fit.** Similarly, a *sukka* **that is not** even **ten handbreadths high, and** one **that does not have three walls, and** one **whose sunlight** that passes through its roofing **is greater than its shade are unfit.** With regard to **an old *sukka*, Beit Shammai deem it unfit** for the mitzva of *sukka* **and Beit Hillel deem it fit. And which is** considered **an old *sukka*?** It is **any** booth **that one established thirty days** or more **prior to the Festival** without expressly designating that it was for the mitzva of *sukka*. In that case, the assumption is that he constructed it for some other purpose. **However, if he established it** expressly **for the sake of the festival** of *Sukkot*, **even** if he constructed it **at the beginning of the** previous **year, it is fit** for use in the fulfillment of the mitzva of *sukka*, even according to Beit Shammai.

2 With regard to **one who establishes his *sukka* beneath a tree,** it is **as though he established it inside the house** and it is unfit. If one established **a *sukka* atop** another ***sukka*, the upper** *sukka* **is fit and the lower** *sukka* **is unfit. Rabbi Yehuda says: If there are no residents in the upper** *sukka*, **the lower** *sukka* **is fit.**

3 If **one spread a sheet over** the roofing as protection for those sitting in the *sukka* **due to the sun, or** if one spread a sheet **beneath** the roofing as protection **due to the falling leaves, or** if **one spread** a sheet as a canopy **over the** frame of **a four-post** [***kinof***] bed, the area in the *sukka* beneath the sheets is **unfit.** In the first two cases, because the sheet is susceptible to ritual impurity, it renders the otherwise fit roofing unfit. In the case of the canopy, one is not sitting under the roofing of the *sukka*; rather, he is sitting inside a tent. **However, one** may **spread** the sheet **over** the frame of **a two-post** [***naklitei***] **bed,** which has one post in the middle of each end of the bed. When spreading the sheet over the posts it forms an inclined rather than a flat roof, and a tent with an inclined roof is not considered a significant structure.

מסכת סוכה

פרק ראשון

א סוּכָּה שֶׁהִיא גְּבוֹהָה לְמַעְלָה מֵעֶשְׂרִים אַמָּה –
פְּסוּלָה
וְרַבִּי יְהוּדָה מַכְשִׁיר.

וְשֶׁאֵינָהּ גְּבוֹהָה עֲשָׂרָה טְפָחִים
וְשֶׁאֵין לָהּ (שְׁלֹשָׁה) דְּפָנוֹת
וְשֶׁחַמָּתָהּ מְרוּבָּה מִצִּלָּתָהּ – פְּסוּלָה.

סוּכָּה יְשָׁנָה
בֵּית שַׁמַּאי פּוֹסְלִין וּבֵית הִלֵּל מַכְשִׁירִין.
וְאֵיזוֹ הִיא סוּכָּה יְשָׁנָה?
כָּל שֶׁעֲשָׂאָהּ קוֹדֶם לֶחָג שְׁלֹשִׁים יוֹם.
אֲבָל אִם עֲשָׂאָהּ לְשֵׁם חַג
אֲפִילוּ מִתְּחִילַּת הַשָּׁנָה – כְּשֵׁרָה.

ב הָעוֹשֶׂה סוּכָּתוֹ תַּחַת הָאִילָן –
כְּאִילּוּ עֲשָׂאָהּ בְּתוֹךְ הַבַּיִת.

סוּכָּה עַל גַּבֵּי סוּכָּה –
הָעֶלְיוֹנָה כְּשֵׁרָה וְהַתַּחְתּוֹנָה פְּסוּלָה.
רַבִּי יְהוּדָה אוֹמֵר:
אִם אֵין דָּיוֹרִין בָּעֶלְיוֹנָה – הַתַּחְתּוֹנָה כְּשֵׁרָה.

ג פֵּירַס עָלֶיהָ סָדִין מִפְּנֵי הַחַמָּה, אוֹ תַּחְתֶּיהָ מִפְּנֵי הַנְּשָׁר
אוֹ שֶׁפֵּירַס עַל גַּבֵּי הַקִּינוּף פְּסוּלָה
אֲבָל פּוֹרֵס הוּא עַל גַּבֵּי נַקְלִיטֵי הַמִּטָּה.

4 If **one trellised** climbing plants such as **a grapevine, or gourd** plant, **or ivy** [***kissos***], **over** a *sukka* while they were still attached to the ground, **and** then added **roofing atop them,** the *sukka* is **unfit. If** the amount of fit **roofing was greater** than the plants attached to the ground, **or if he cut** the climbing plants so that they were no longer attached to the ground, **it is fit. This is the principle** with regard to the roofing of a *sukka*: **Anything that is susceptible to ritual impurity,** e.g., vessels, **or its growth is not from the ground,** e.g., animal hides, **one may not roof** his *sukka* **with it. And anything that is not susceptible to ritual impurity and its growth is from the ground, one may roof** his *sukka* **with it.**

5 **One** may **not roof** a *sukka* **with bundles of straw** tied with rope, **or bundles of wood, or bundles of twigs. And** with regard to **all** of the bundles, **if one untied them,** they are **fit** for use in roofing the *sukka,* as their lack of fitness is due to the fact that the bundles are tied. **And** even when tied, **all of** the bundles are **fit for** use in constructing the **walls** of the *sukka.*

6 **One** may **roof** the *sukka* **with boards** like those used in the ceiling of a house; this is **the statement of Rabbi Yehuda. Rabbi Meir prohibits** their use. **If one placed a board that is four handbreadths wide atop** the *sukka,* the *sukka* **is fit.** He fulfills his obligation, **provided he does not sleep beneath** the board.

7 In the case of **a roof** made of boards that are four handbreadths wide **upon which there is no** coat of **plaster, Rabbi Yehuda says** that Beit Shammai and Beit Hillel disagree with regard to the manner in which to render it fit. **Beit Shammai say: One moves** each board, and then it is considered as though he placed the board there for the sake of the mitzva of *sukka,* **and one** then **removes one** board **from among** the boards and replaces it with fit roofing. **Beit Hillel say:** One need not perform both actions; rather, **one** must either **move** the boards **or remove one from among** them. **Rabbi Meir says: One** only **removes one from among** them **and does not move** the others.

ד הִדְלָה עָלֶיהָ אֶת הַגֶּפֶן וְאֶת הַדְּלַעַת וְאֶת הַקִּיסּוֹס
וְסִיכֵּךְ עַל גַּבָּהּ – פְּסוּלָה.
וְאִם הָיָה סִיכּוּךְ הַרְבֵּה מֵהֶן, אוֹ שֶׁקְּצָצָן – כְּשֵׁרָה.
זֶה הַכְּלָל:
כָּל שֶׁהוּא מְקַבֵּל טוּמְאָה, וְאֵין גִּידּוּלוֹ מִן הָאָרֶץ –
אֵין מְסַכְּכִין בּוֹ.
וְכָל דָּבָר שֶׁאֵינוֹ מְקַבֵּל טוּמְאָה, וְגִידּוּלוֹ מִן הָאָרֶץ –
מְסַכְּכִין בּוֹ.

ה חֲבִילֵי קַשׁ וַחֲבִילֵי עֵצִים וַחֲבִילֵי זְרָדִין
אֵין מְסַכְּכִין בָּהֶן.
וְכוּלָּן שֶׁהִתִּירָן – כְּשֵׁרוֹת
וְכוּלָּן כְּשֵׁרוֹת לְדְפָנוֹת.

ו מְסַכְּכִין בִּנְסָרִים דִּבְרֵי רַבִּי יְהוּדָה
וְרַבִּי מֵאִיר אוֹסֵר.

נָתַן עָלֶיהָ נֶסֶר שֶׁהוּא רָחָב אַרְבָּעָה טְפָחִים – כְּשֵׁרָה
וּבִלְבַד שֶׁלֹּא יִישַׁן תַּחְתָּיו.

ז תִּקְרָה שֶׁאֵין עָלֶיהָ מַעֲזִיבָה
רַבִּי יְהוּדָה אוֹמֵר:
בֵּית שַׁמַּאי אוֹמְרִים:
מְפַקְפֵּק, וְנוֹטֵל אַחַת מִבֵּינְתַיִם
וּבֵית הִלֵּל אוֹמְרִים:
מְפַקְפֵּק אוֹ נוֹטֵל אַחַת מִבֵּינְתַיִם.
רַבִּי מֵאִיר אוֹמֵר:
נוֹטֵל אַחַת מִבֵּינְתַיִם, וְאֵינוֹ מְפַקְפֵּק.

8 In the case of **one who roofs his *sukka* with** metal **skewers or with the long boards of the bed,** which compose its frame, **if there is space between** each one of **them equal to** the width of the skewers or the boards, and if he places fit roofing in those spaces, the *sukka* is **fit.** In the case of **one who hollows out** and creates a space inside **a stack of grain,** it is **not a *sukka*.**

9 **One who lowers the walls** of the *sukka* **from up downward, if** the lower edge of the wall is **three handbreadths above the ground,** the *sukka* is **unfit.** Since animals can enter through that space, it is not the wall of a fit *sukka*. However, if one constructs the wall from **down upward, if** the wall is **ten handbreadths high,** even if it does not reach the roofing, the *sukka* is **fit. Rabbi Yosei says: Just as** a wall built **from down upward** must be **ten handbreadths, so too,** in a case where one lowers the wall **from up downward,** it must be **ten handbreadths** in length. Regardless of its height off the ground, it is the wall of a fit *sukka*, as the legal status of a ten-handbreadth partition is that of a full-fledged partition in all areas of *halakha*. If **one distanced the roofing from the walls** of the *sukka* at **a distance of three handbreadths** the *sukka* is **unfit,** because three handbreadths of open space, even adjacent to the walls, render the *sukka* unfit.

10 In the case of **a house that was breached,** creating a hole in the middle of the roof, **and one roofed over** the breach, **if from the wall to the roofing there are four** or more **cubits** of the remaining original roof, **it is an unfit** *sukka*. If the roofing is less than four cubits from the wall, the *sukka* is fit, based on the principle of curved wall; the remaining intact ceiling is considered an extension of the vertical wall. **And likewise,** in the case of **a courtyard that is surrounded** on three sides **by a portico,** which has a roof but no walls, if one placed roofing over the courtyard between the different sides of the portico and the roof of the portico is four cubits wide, the *sukka* is unfit. Similarly, **a large *sukka* that was surrounded** at the edge of its roofing **with material with which one** may **not roof** a *sukka*, e.g., vessels susceptible to ritual impurity, **if there are four cubits beneath** the unfit roofing, the *sukka* is **unfit.** The principle of curved wall does not apply to unfit roofing that measures four cubits or more.

ח הַמְקָרֶה סוּכָּתוֹ בְּשַׁפּוּדִין אוֹ בַּאֲרוּכוֹת הַמִּטָּה
אִם יֵשׁ רֶיוַח בֵּינֵיהֶן כְּמוֹתָן –
כְּשֵׁרָה.
הַחוֹטֵט בַּגָּדִישׁ לַעֲשׂוֹת לוֹ סוּכָּה –
אֵינָהּ סוּכָּה.

ט הַמְשַׁלְשֵׁל דְּפָנוֹת מִלְּמַעְלָה לְמַטָּה
אִם גָּבוֹהַּ מִן הָאָרֶץ שְׁלֹשָׁה טְפָחִים –
פְּסוּלָה.
מִלְּמַטָּה לְמַעְלָה
אִם גָּבוֹהַּ עֲשָׂרָה טְפָחִים –
כְּשֵׁרָה.
רַבִּי יוֹסֵי אוֹמֵר:
כְּשֵׁם שֶׁמִּלְּמַטָּה לְמַעְלָה עֲשָׂרָה טְפָחִים
כָּךְ מִלְּמַעְלָה לְמַטָּה עֲשָׂרָה טְפָחִים.
הִרְחִיק אֶת הַסִּיכּוּךְ מִן הַדְּפָנוֹת שְׁלֹשָׁה טְפָחִים –
פְּסוּלָה.

י בַּיִת שֶׁנִּפְחַת וְסִיכֵּךְ עַל גַּבָּיו
אִם יֵשׁ מִן הַכּוֹתֶל לַסִּיכּוּךְ אַרְבַּע אַמּוֹת –
פְּסוּלָה.
וְכֵן חָצֵר שֶׁהִיא מוּקֶּפֶת אַכְסַדְרָה.
סוּכָּה גְּדוֹלָה שֶׁהִקִּיפוּהָ בְּדָבָר שֶׁאֵין מְסַכְּכִין בּוֹ
אִם יֵשׁ תַּחְתָּיו אַרְבַּע אַמּוֹת –
פְּסוּלָה.

11 **One who establishes his *sukka* like a type of circular hut,** with no roof whose walls slope down from the center **or who rested** the *sukka* **against the wall,** by taking long branches and placing one end on the ground and leaning the other end against the wall to establish a structure with no roof, **Rabbi Eliezer deems it unfit because it does not have a roof, and the Rabbis deem it fit;** as, in their opinion, the roof and the walls may be a single entity, indistinguishable from each other. In the case of **a large mat of reeds,** if **one** initially **produced it for** the purpose of **lying** upon it, **it is susceptible to ritual impurity** like any other vessel, **and** therefore **one** may **not roof** a *sukka* **with it.** If one initially produced it **for roofing, one** may **roof** a *sukka* **with it, and it is not susceptible to ritual impurity,** as its legal status is not that of a vessel. **Rabbi Eliezer says** that the distinction between mats is based on use, not size. Therefore, with regard to **both a small** mat **and a large** mat, if **one produced it for** the purpose of **lying** upon it, **it is susceptible to ritual impurity and one** may **not roof** a *sukka* **with it.** If one produced it **for roofing, one** may **roof** a *sukka* **with it, and it is not susceptible to ritual impurity.**

CHAPTER 2

1 **One who sleeps beneath the bed in the *sukka* did not fulfill his obligation,** because the bed constitutes a tent that serves as a barrier between him and the roofing of the *sukka*. **Rabbi Yehuda said: It was our custom that we would sleep beneath the bed before the Elders and they did not say anything to us** to the effect that we are not fulfilling our obligation. Apparently, the halakhic status of the bed is not like that of a tent and it does not prevent fulfillment of the mitzva. **Rabbi Shimon said,** contrary to the opinion of Rabbi Yehuda: **There was an incident involving Tavi, the** Canaanite **slave of Rabban Gamliel, who was sleeping beneath the bed, and Rabbi Gamliel** lightheartedly **said to the Elders:** Did **you see my slave Tavi, who is a Torah scholar and**

יא הָעוֹשֶׂה סוּכָּתוֹ כְּמִין צְרִיף, אוֹ שֶׁסְּמָכָהּ לַכּוֹתֶל
רַבִּי אֱלִיעֶזֶר פּוֹסֵל מִפְּנֵי שֶׁאֵין לָהּ גַּג
וַחֲכָמִים מַכְשִׁירִין.
מַחֲצֶלֶת קָנִים גְּדוֹלָה
עֲשָׂאָהּ לִשְׁכִיבָה – מְקַבֶּלֶת טוּמְאָה וְאֵין מְסַכְּכִין בָּהּ
לְסִיכּוּךְ – מְסַכְּכִין בָּהּ וְאֵינָהּ מְקַבֶּלֶת טוּמְאָה.
רַבִּי אֱלִיעֶזֶר אוֹמֵר:
אַחַת קְטַנָּה וְאַחַת גְּדוֹלָה
עֲשָׂאָהּ לִשְׁכִיבָה – מְקַבֶּלֶת טוּמְאָה, וְאֵין מְסַכְּכִין בָּהּ
לְסִיכּוּךְ – מְסַכְּכִין בָּהּ וְאֵינָהּ מְקַבֶּלֶת טוּמְאָה.

פרק שני

א הַיָּשֵׁן תַּחַת הַמִּטָּה בַּסּוּכָּה –
לֹא יָצָא יְדֵי חוֹבָתוֹ.
אָמַר רַבִּי יְהוּדָה:
נוֹהֲגִין הָיִינוּ
שֶׁהָיִינוּ יְשֵׁנִים תַּחַת הַמִּטָּה בִּפְנֵי הַזְּקֵנִים
וְלֹא אָמְרוּ לָנוּ דָּבָר.
אָמַר רַבִּי שִׁמְעוֹן:
מַעֲשֶׂה בְּטָבִי עַבְדּוֹ שֶׁל רַבָּן גַּמְלִיאֵל
שֶׁהָיָה יָשֵׁן תַּחַת הַמִּטָּה
וְאָמַר לָהֶן רַבָּן גַּמְלִיאֵל לַזְּקֵנִים:
רְאִיתֶם טָבִי עַבְדִּי

knows that slaves are exempt from the mitzva of ***sukka*****?** Since it is a positive, time-bound mitzva, Canaanite slaves, whose status with regard to this halakhic category is like that of women, are exempt from the obligation to fulfill the mitzva of *sukka*. **Therefore, he sleeps under the bed.** Rabbi Shimon continued: **And by the way,** as Rabban Gamliel was not issuing a halakhic ruling, **we learned that one who sleeps beneath the bed did not fulfill his obligation.**

2 **One who supports his *sukka* on the legs of the bed,** i.e., he leans the *sukka* roofing on a bed, the *sukka* **is fit. Rabbi Yehuda says: If** the *sukka* **cannot stand in and of itself** without support of the bed, **it is unfit. A *sukka* that is *meduvlelet* and whose shade exceeds its sunlight is fit.** A *sukka* whose roofing **is thick like a house of sorts, even though** it is so thick **that the stars cannot be seen from within it, is fit.**

3 In the case of **one who establishes his *sukka* at the top of the wagon or at the top of the ship,** although it is portable it **is fit,** as it is sufficient for a *sukka* to be a temporary residence. **And one** may **ascend** and enter **it** even **on** the first **Festival** day. In the case of one who establishes his *sukka* **at** the **top of a tree or atop a camel,** the *sukka* **is fit, but one may not ascend** and enter **it on** the first **Festival** day because the Sages prohibit climbing or using trees or animals on the Festival. If **two** of the walls of the *sukka* are **in the tree and one** is established on the ground **by a person,** or if **two** are established on the ground **by a person and one** is **in the tree,** the *sukka* **is fit, but one may not ascend** and enter **it on** the first **Festival** day because it is prohibited to use the tree. However, if **three** of the walls are established on the ground **by a person and one** is **in the tree,** then since it contains the minimum number of walls required, it **is fit, and one may enter it on** the first **Festival** day. The mishna summarizes that **this is the principle: Any** case **where,** were **the tree removed, the** *sukka* would **be able to remain standing in and of itself,** it **is fit, and one may ascend** and enter **it on** the **Festival,** since the tree is not its primary support.

שֶׁהוּא תַּלְמִיד חָכָם וְיוֹדֵעַ שֶׁעֲבָדִים פְּטוּרִין מִן הַסּוּכָּה
לְפִיכָךְ יָשֵׁן הוּא תַּחַת הַמִּטָּה.
וּלְפִי דַּרְכֵּינוּ לָמַדְנוּ
שֶׁהַיָּשֵׁן תַּחַת הַמִּטָּה לֹא יָצָא יְדֵי חוֹבָתוֹ.

ב הַסּוֹמֵךְ סוּכָּתוֹ בְּכַרְעֵי הַמִּטָּה - כְּשֵׁרָה.
רַבִּי יְהוּדָה אוֹמֵר:
אִם אֵינָהּ יְכוֹלָה לַעֲמוֹד בִּפְנֵי עַצְמָהּ - פְּסוּלָה.
סוּכָּה הַמְדוּבְלֶלֶת, וְשֶׁצִּילָּתָהּ מְרוּבָּה מֵחַמָּתָהּ -
כְּשֵׁרָה.
הַמְעוּבָּה כְּמִין בַּיִת
אַף עַל פִּי שֶׁאֵין הַכּוֹכָבִים נִרְאִין מִתּוֹכָהּ -
כְּשֵׁרָה.

ג הָעוֹשֶׂה סוּכָּתוֹ בְּרֹאשׁ הָעֲגָלָה אוֹ בְּרֹאשׁ הַסְּפִינָה -
כְּשֵׁרָה, וְעוֹלִין לָהּ בְּיוֹם טוֹב.
בְּרֹאשׁ הָאִילָן אוֹ עַל גַּבֵּי גָּמָל -
כְּשֵׁרָה, וְאֵין עוֹלִין לָהּ בְּיוֹם טוֹב.
שְׁתַּיִם בָּאִילָן וְאַחַת בִּידֵי אָדָם
אוֹ שְׁתַּיִם בִּידֵי אָדָם וְאַחַת בָּאִילָן -
כְּשֵׁרָה, וְאֵין עוֹלִין לָהּ בְּיוֹם טוֹב.
שָׁלֹשׁ בִּידֵי אָדָם וְאַחַת בָּאִילָן -
כְּשֵׁרָה, וְעוֹלִין לָהּ בְּיוֹם טוֹב.
זֶה הַכְּלָל:
כָּל שֶׁיִּנָּטֵל הָאִילָן וִיכוֹלָה לַעֲמוֹד בִּפְנֵי עַצְמָהּ -
כְּשֵׁרָה, וְעוֹלִין לָהּ בְּיוֹם טוֹב.

4 In the case of **one who establishes his *sukka* between the trees, and the trees** serve as **walls for it,** the *sukka* **is fit. Those on the path** to perform **a mitzva are exempt from the** mitzva of ***sukka.*** The **ill and their caretakers are exempt from the** mitzva of ***sukka.* One** may **eat and drink** in the framework of a **casual** meal **outside the *sukka.***

5 Apropos eating in the *sukka,* which is discussed in the previous mishna, this mishna relates: **An incident** occurred where **they brought a cooked dish to Rabban Yoḥanan ben Zakkai** for him **to taste, and to Rabban Gamliel** they brought **two dates and a bucket of water. And they** each **said: Take them up to the *sukka*** and we will eat them there. In contrast, the mishna relates: **And when they gave Rabbi Tzadok less than an egg-bulk of food, he took** the food **in a cloth** for cleanliness; he did not wash his hands because in his opinion, one is not required to wash his hands before eating less than an egg-bulk. **And he ate it outside the *sukka* and did not recite a blessing after** eating **it.** He holds that one is not required to recite a blessing after eating less than an egg-bulk, as it is not satisfying, and it is written: "And you shall eat and be satisfied and bless the Lord your God" (Deuteronomy 8:10). The Gemara will explain the halakhic rationale for each of these actions described.

6 **Rabbi Eliezer says: A person is obligated to eat fourteen meals in the *sukka*** over the course of the seven days of the festival of *Sukkot,* **one during the day** each day **and one at night** each night. **And the Rabbis say: There is no quota** for the number of meals, and one may choose whether or not to eat any of the meals **except for the** meal on the **evening of the first Festival** day **of *Sukkot,*** which one is required to eat in the *sukka.* **And furthermore, Rabbi Eliezer said: One who did not eat** a meal on the **evening of the first day** of the Festival should **compensate** with a meal on the **evening of the last day of the Festival,** on the Eighth Day of Assembly, despite the fact that he will not eat it in the *sukka.* **And the Rabbis say: There is no compensation for** this **matter, and with regard to** similar cases where it is impossible to rectify failure to fulfill a

ד הָעוֹשֶׂה סוּכָּתוֹ בֵּין הָאִילָנוֹת וְהָאִילָנוֹת דָּפְנוֹת לָהּ –
כְּשֵׁרָה.
שְׁלוּחֵי מִצְוָה פְּטוּרִין מִן הַסּוּכָּה.
חוֹלִין וּמְשַׁמְּשֵׁיהֶן פְּטוּרִין מִן הַסּוּכָּה.
אוֹכְלִין וְשׁוֹתִין עֲרַאי חוּץ לַסּוּכָּה.

ה מַעֲשֶׂה וְהֵבִיאוּ לוֹ לְרַבָּן יוֹחָנָן בֶּן זַכַּאי
לִטְעוֹם אֶת הַתַּבְשִׁיל
וּלְרַבָּן גַּמְלִיאֵל שְׁנֵי כוֹתָבוֹת וּדְלִי שֶׁל מַיִם
וְאָמְרוּ:
הַעֲלוּם לַסּוּכָּה.
וּכְשֶׁנָּתְנוּ לוֹ לְרַבִּי צָדוֹק אוֹכֶל פָּחוֹת מִכַּבֵּיצָה
נְטָלוֹ בְּמַפָּה וַאֲכָלוֹ חוּץ לַסּוּכָּה, וְלֹא בֵּירֵךְ אַחֲרָיו.

ו רַבִּי אֱלִיעֶזֶר אוֹמֵר:
אַרְבַּע עֶשְׂרֵה סְעוּדוֹת חַיָּיב אָדָם לֶאֱכוֹל בַּסּוּכָּה
אַחַת בַּיּוֹם וְאַחַת בַּלַּיְלָה.
וַחֲכָמִים אוֹמְרִים: אֵין לַדָּבָר קִצְבָּה
חוּץ מִלֵּילֵי יוֹם טוֹב רִאשׁוֹן שֶׁל חַג בִּלְבַד.
וְעוֹד אָמַר רַבִּי אֱלִיעֶזֶר:
מִי שֶׁלֹּא אָכַל [לֵילֵי] יוֹם טוֹב הָרִאשׁוֹן –
יַשְׁלִים לֵילֵי יוֹם טוֹב הָאַחֲרוֹן שֶׁל חַג.
וַחֲכָמִים אוֹמְרִים:
אֵין לַדָּבָר תַּשְׁלוּמִין

positive mitzva, **it is stated: "That which is crooked cannot be made straight; and that which is wanting cannot be numbered"** (Ecclesiastes 1:15).

7 In the case of **one whose head and most of his** body **were in the *sukka* and his table was in the house, Beit Shammai deem it unfit, and Beit Hillel deem it fit. Beit Hillel said to Beit Shammai:** And **wasn't there an incident where the Elders of Beit Shammai and the Elders of Beit Hillel went to visit Rabbi Yoḥanan ben HaḤoranit and they found him** such **that he was sitting with his head and most of his** body **in the *sukka* and his table in the house, and they said nothing to him?** Even Beit Shammai did not object. **Beit Shammai said to them:** Is there **proof from there?** That is not what happened; rather, **they said to him: If you were accustomed** to act in **this** manner, **you have never fulfilled the mitzva of *sukka* in your life.**

8 The mishna continues: **Women, slaves, and minors are exempt from the** mitzva of ***sukka*. A minor who does not need his mother** any longer **is obligated** in the mitzva. There was **an incident where the daughter-in-law of Shammai the Elder gave birth** just before *Sukkot*, and Shammai **removed the** coat of **plaster** from the roof, leaving the beams, **and roofed** with the beams **over the bed for the** newborn **minor.**

9 **All seven days** of *Sukkot*, **a person renders his *sukka*** his **permanent** residence **and his house** his **temporary** residence. If **rain fell, from when is it permitted to vacate** the *sukka*? It is permitted **from** the point that it is raining so hard **that the congealed dish will spoil.** The Sages **told a parable: To what is this matter comparable?** It is comparable **to a servant who comes to pour wine for his master, and he pours a jug [*kiton*] of water in his face** to show him that his presence is not desired. So too, in the *sukka*, rain is an indication that the Holy One, Blessed be He, does not want the person to fulfill the mitzva of *sukka*.

וְעַל זֶה נֶאֱמַר:
"מְעֻוָּת לֹא יוּכַל לִתְקֹן וְחֶסְרוֹן לֹא יוּכַל לְהִמָּנוֹת".

ז מִי שֶׁהָיָה רֹאשׁוֹ וְרֻבּוֹ בַּסֻּכָּה וְשֻׁלְחָנוֹ בְּתוֹךְ הַבַּיִת
בֵּית שַׁמַּאי פּוֹסְלִין וּבֵית הִלֵּל מַכְשִׁירִין.
אָמְרוּ לָהֶם בֵּית הִלֵּל לְבֵית שַׁמַּאי:
לֹא כָּךְ הָיָה מַעֲשֶׂה
שֶׁהָלְכוּ זִקְנֵי בֵּית שַׁמַּאי וְזִקְנֵי בֵּית הִלֵּל
לְבַקֵּר אֶת רַבִּי יוֹחָנָן בֶּן הַחוֹרָנִית
וּמְצָאוּהוּ שֶׁהָיָה יוֹשֵׁב רֹאשׁוֹ וְרֻבּוֹ בַּסֻּכָּה
וְשֻׁלְחָנוֹ בְּתוֹךְ הַבַּיִת, וְלֹא אָמְרוּ לוֹ דָּבָר?
אָמְרוּ לָהֶם בֵּית שַׁמַּאי: מִשָּׁם רְאָיָה?!
אַף הֵם אָמְרוּ לוֹ:
אִם כֵּן הָיִיתָ נוֹהֵג – לֹא קִיַּמְתָּ מִצְוַת סֻכָּה מִיָּמֶיךָ.

ח נָשִׁים וַעֲבָדִים וּקְטַנִּים פְּטוּרִין מִן הַסֻּכָּה.
קָטָן שֶׁאֵינוֹ צָרִיךְ לְאִמּוֹ – חַיָּב בַּסֻּכָּה.
מַעֲשֶׂה וְיָלְדָה כַּלָּתוֹ שֶׁל שַׁמַּאי הַזָּקֵן
וּפִיחֵת אֶת הַמַּעֲזִיבָה וְסִיכֵּךְ עַל גַּבֵּי הַמִּטָּה בִּשְׁבִיל קָטָן.

ט כָּל שִׁבְעַת הַיָּמִים אָדָם עוֹשֶׂה סֻכָּתוֹ קֶבַע וּבֵיתוֹ עֲרַאי.
יָרְדוּ גְשָׁמִים, מֵאֵימָתַי מֻתָּר לְפַנּוֹת –
מִשֶּׁתִּסְרַח הַמִּקְפָּה.
מָשְׁלוּ מָשָׁל: לְמָה הַדָּבָר דּוֹמֶה –
לְעֶבֶד שֶׁבָּא לִמְזוֹג כּוֹס לְרַבּוֹ
וְשָׁפַךְ לוֹ קִיתוֹן עַל פָּנָיו.

CHAPTER 3

1 **A *lulav* that was stolen or that is** completely **dry** is **unfit** for use in fulfilling the mitzva of the four species. The *lulav* **of a tree worshipped as idolatry** [*asheira*] **and** a *lulav* **from a city** whose residents were **incited** to idolatry, which must be burned along with all the city's property, are **unfit. If the top** of the *lulav* **was severed or if the** palm **leaves were severed** from the spine of the *lulav*, it is **unfit. If its leaves,** although still attached, **were spread** and are no longer completely joined to the spine, it is **fit. Rabbi Yehuda says:** In that case, **one should bind** the *lulav* **from the top,** to join the leaves that spread to the spine. A *lulav* from the **palms of the Iron Mountain** are **fit** for use, although it differs from one taken from a standard palm tree, in that its leaves are shorter and do not cover the entire spine. **A *lulav* that has three handbreadths** in length, **sufficient** to enable one **to wave with it, is fit** for use in fulfilling the mitzva.

2 **A myrtle branch that was stolen or that is** completely **dry is unfit. A myrtle branch of a tree worshipped as idolatry** [*asheira*] **or** a myrtle branch **from a city** whose residents were **incited** to idolatry **is unfit.** If **the top** of the myrtle branch **was severed,** if **the leaves were severed** completely, or if **its berries were more numerous than its leaves, it is unfit. If one diminished their** number by plucking berries so that they no longer outnumbered the leaves, the myrtle branch is **fit. But one may not diminish** the number **on the Festival** itself.

3 **A willow branch** that was **stolen or is** completely **dry is unfit.** One **from a tree worshipped as idolatry** [*asheira*] **or from a city** whose residents were **incited** to idolatry **is unfit. If the top was severed, or its leaves were severed, or** if it is **the *tzaftzafa*,** a species similar to, but not actually a willow, it **is unfit.** However, a willow branch that is **slightly dried, and one that a minority of its leaves fell, and** a branch from a willow **that** does not grow by the river, but instead **is from a non-irrigated** field, **is fit.**

פרק שלישי

א לוּלָב הַגָּזוּל וְהַיָּבֵשׁ – פָּסוּל.
שֶׁל אֲשֵׁירָה וְשֶׁל עִיר הַנִּדַּחַת – פָּסוּל.
נִקְטַם רֹאשׁוֹ, נִפְרְצוּ עָלָיו – פָּסוּל.
נִפְרְדוּ עָלָיו – כָּשֵׁר
רַבִּי יְהוּדָה אוֹמֵר:
יַאַגְדֶנּוּ מִלְמַעְלָה.
צִינֵי הַר הַבַּרְזֶל כְּשֵׁירוֹת.
לוּלָב שֶׁיֵּשׁ בּוֹ שְׁלֹשָׁה טְפָחִים כְּדֵי לְנַעֲנֵעַ בּוֹ – כָּשֵׁר.

ב הֲדַס הַגָּזוּל וְהַיָּבֵשׁ – פָּסוּל.
שֶׁל אֲשֵׁרָה וְשֶׁל עִיר הַנִּדַּחַת – פָּסוּל.
נִקְטַם רֹאשׁוֹ, נִפְרְצוּ עָלָיו, אוֹ שֶׁהָיוּ עֲנָבָיו מְרוּבּוֹת מֵעָלָיו – פָּסוּל.
וְאִם מִיעֲטָן – כָּשֵׁר.
וְאֵין מְמַעֲטִין בְּיוֹם טוֹב.

ג עֲרָבָה גְּזוּלָה וִיבֵשָׁה – פְּסוּלָה
שֶׁל אֲשֵׁרָה וְשֶׁל עִיר הַנִּדַּחַת – פְּסוּלָה.
נִקְטַם רֹאשָׁהּ, נִפְרְצוּ עָלֶיהָ, וְהַצַּפְצָפָה – פְּסוּלָה.
כְּמוּשָׁה, וְשֶׁנָּשְׁרוּ מִקְצָת עָלֶיהָ, וְשֶׁל בַּעַל – כְּשֵׁרָה.

4 **Rabbi Yishmael says:** The mitzva of the four species is to take **three myrtle branches, and two willow branches, one *lulav*, and one *etrog*.** With regard to the myrtle branches, **even if** the tops of **two are severed and** the top of **one is not severed,** it is fit. **Rabbi Tarfon says: Even if** the tops of **all three are severed,** it is fit. **Rabbi Akiva says** with regard to the number of each of the species: **Just as** there is **one *lulav* and one *etrog*, so too** there is **one myrtle branch and one willow branch.**

5 **An *etrog*** that was **stolen or is** completely **dry is unfit.** One **from a tree worshipped as idolatry** [*asheira*] **or from a city** whose residents were **incited** to idolatry **is unfit.** An *etrog* that is **fruit that grew on a tree during the three years after it was planted** [*orla*] **is unfit,** because it is prohibited to eat and derive benefit from it. An *etrog* **of impure *teruma* is unfit.** With regard to an *etrog* **of pure *teruma*, one may not take it** *ab initio*, **and if one took it, it is fit,** and he fulfilled his obligation after the fact. With regard to an *etrog* of ***demai***, which is produce acquired from an *am ha'aretz*, who does not reliably tithe his produce, **Beit Shammai deem it unfit, and Beit Hillel deem it fit.** With regard to an *etrog* **of second tithe in Jerusalem, one may not take it** *ab initio*; **and if he took it, it is fit.**

6 If **boil-like blemishes arose on** the **majority** of the *etrog*; if **its pestle**-like protuberance on the upper, blossom end **was removed;** if the *etrog* **was peeled, split, or pierced and is missing any amount, it is unfit.** However, if **boil-like blemishes arose** only **on its minority; if its stem,** which connects it to the tree, **was removed; or it was pierced** but **is** not **missing any amount, it is fit. A Cushite *etrog*,** which is black like a Cushite, **is unfit.** And with regard to an *etrog* **that is leek green, Rabbi Meir deems it fit and Rabbi Yehuda deems it unfit.**

ד רַבִּי יִשְׁמָעֵאל אוֹמֵר:
שְׁלֹשָׁה הֲדַסִּים וּשְׁתֵּי עֲרָבוֹת לוּלָב אֶחָד וְאֶתְרוֹג אֶחָד
אֲפִילּוּ שְׁנַיִם קְטוּמִים וְאֶחָד אֵינוֹ קָטוּם.
רַבִּי טַרְפוֹן אוֹמֵר:
אֲפִילּוּ שְׁלָשְׁתָּן קְטוּמִים.
רַבִּי עֲקִיבָא אוֹמֵר:
כְּשֵׁם שֶׁלּוּלָב אֶחָד וְאֶתְרוֹג אֶחָד
כָּךְ הֲדַס אֶחָד וַעֲרָבָה אַחַת.

ה אֶתְרוֹג הַגָּזוּל וְהַיָּבֵשׁ – פָּסוּל.
שֶׁל אֲשֵׁרָה וְשֶׁל עִיר הַנִּדַּחַת – פָּסוּל.
שֶׁל עָרְלָה – פָּסוּל.
שֶׁל תְּרוּמָה טְמֵאָה – פָּסוּל.
שֶׁל תְּרוּמָה טְהוֹרָה – לֹא יִטּוֹל
וְאִם נָטַל – כָּשֵׁר.
שֶׁל דְּמַאי, בֵּית שַׁמַּאי פּוֹסְלִין וּבֵית הִלֵּל מַכְשִׁירִין.
שֶׁל מַעֲשֵׂר שֵׁנִי בִּירוּשָׁלַיִם – לֹא יִטּוֹל
וְאִם נָטַל – כָּשֵׁר.

ו עָלְתָה חֲזָזִית עַל רוּבּוֹ, נִטְּלָה פִּטְמָתוֹ
נִקְלַף, נִסְדַּק, נִיקַּב וְחָסֵר כָּל שֶׁהוּא – פָּסוּל.
עָלְתָה חֲזָזִית עַל מִיעוּטוֹ, נִטַּל עוּקְצוֹ
נִיקַּב וְלֹא חָסַר כָּל שֶׁהוּא – כָּשֵׁר.
אֶתְרוֹג הַכּוּשִׁי פָּסוּל.
וְהַיָּרוֹק כַּכַּרְתִּי, רַבִּי מֵאִיר מַכְשִׁיר וְרַבִּי יְהוּדָה פּוֹסֵל.

7 What is **the** minimum **measure of a small *etrog*? Rabbi Meir says:** It may be no smaller than **a walnut-bulk. Rabbi Yehuda says:** It may be no smaller than **an egg-bulk. And in a large *etrog*,** the maximum measure is **so that one could hold two in his one hand;** this is **the statement of Rabbi Yehuda. Rabbi Yosei says:** It is fit **even** if it is so large that he can hold only **one in his two hands.**

8 **One may bind the *lulav* only with its own species;** i.e., one of the four species taken with the *lulav*. This is **the statement of Rabbi Yehuda. Rabbi Meir says:** One may do so **even with a string** or **with a cord. Rabbi Meir said:** There was **an incident involving the men of Jerusalem who would bind their *lulavim* with gold rings.** The Sages **said to him: They would bind it with its own species beneath** the rings, which serve a merely decorative purpose and not a halakhic one.

9 **And where** in the recitation of *Hallel* **would they wave** the *lulav*? They would do so **at** the verse: **"Thank the Lord,** for He is good" (Psalms 118:1, 29) that appears **at** both **the beginning and the end** of the psalm, **and at** the verse: **"Lord, please save us"** (Psalms 118:25); this is **the statement of Beit Hillel. And Beit Shammai say:** They would wave the *lulav* **even at** the verse: **"Lord, please grant us success"** (Psalms 118:25). **Rabbi Akiva said: I was observing Rabban Gamliel and Rabbi Yehoshua** and saw **that all the people were waving their *lulavim*, and** the two of **them waved** their *lulav* **only at: "Lord, please save us,"** indicating that this is the *halakha*. With regard to **one who was coming** along **the way and did not have a *lulav* in his hand to take** and fulfill the mitzva while traveling, **when he enters his house** to eat, **he** should **take** the *lulav* **at his table.** He interrupts his meal to fulfill the mitzva of *lulav*. **If he did not take** the *lulav* in the **morning, he** should **take it in the afternoon, as the entire day is suited for** fulfilling the mitzva of ***lulav*.**

ז שִׁיעוּר אֶתְרוֹג הַקָּטָן
רַבִּי מֵאִיר אוֹמֵר: כָּאֱגוֹז
רַבִּי יְהוּדָה אוֹמֵר: כַּבֵּיצָה
וּבְגָדוֹל –
כְּדֵי שֶׁיֹּאחֵז שְׁנַיִם בְּיָדוֹ, דִּבְרֵי רַבִּי יְהוּדָה.
וְרַבִּי יוֹסֵי אוֹמֵר: אֲפִילּוּ אֶחָד בִּשְׁתֵּי יָדָיו.

ח אֵין אוֹגְדִין אֶת הַלּוּלָב אֶלָּא בְּמִינוֹ, דִּבְרֵי רַבִּי יְהוּדָה.
רַבִּי מֵאִיר אוֹמֵר: אֲפִילּוּ בְּחוּט בִּמְשִׁיחָה.
אָמַר רַבִּי מֵאִיר: מַעֲשֶׂה בְּאַנְשֵׁי יְרוּשָׁלַיִם
שֶׁהָיוּ אוֹגְדִין אֶת לוּלְבֵיהֶן בְּגִימוֹנִיּוֹת שֶׁל זָהָב.
אָמְרוּ לוֹ: בְּמִינוֹ הָיוּ אוֹגְדִין אוֹתוֹ מִלְּמַטָּה.

ט וְהֵיכָן הָיוּ מְנַעְנְעִין?
בְּ"הוֹדוּ לַה'" תְּחִילָּה וָסוֹף, וּבְ"אָנָּא ה' הוֹשִׁיעָה נָּא"
דִּבְרֵי בֵית הִלֵּל.
וּבֵית שַׁמַּאי אוֹמְרִין:
אַף בְּ"אָנָּא ה' הַצְלִיחָה נָא".
אָמַר רַבִּי עֲקִיבָא:
צוֹפֶה הָיִיתִי בְּרַבָּן גַּמְלִיאֵל וְרַבִּי יְהוֹשֻׁעַ
שֶׁכָּל הָעָם הָיוּ מְנַעְנְעִין אֶת לוּלְבֵיהֶן
וְהֵם לֹא נִעְנְעוּ אֶלָּא בְּ"אָנָּא ה' הוֹשִׁיעָה נָּא".
מִי שֶׁבָּא בַדֶּרֶךְ וְלֹא הָיָה בְיָדוֹ לוּלָב לִיטוֹל –
לִכְשֶׁיִּכָּנֵס לְבֵיתוֹ יִטּוֹל עַל שֻׁלְחָנוֹ.
לֹא נָטַל שַׁחֲרִית – יִטּוֹל בֵּין הָעַרְבַּיִם, שֶׁכָּל הַיּוֹם כָּשֵׁר לַלּוּלָב.

10 With regard to **one for whom a Canaanite slave, a woman, or a minor was reciting** *Hallel,* **he repeats after them what they are saying** word for word. The mishna notes: **And may a curse come to him** for being so ignorant that he needs them to recite it for him. **If an adult male was reciting** *Hallel* **on his** behalf, he need not repeat each word, as the adult male can fulfill the obligation to recite *Hallel* on his behalf. Rather, **he** simply **answers: *Halleluya,*** to each phrase that is recited.

11 In **a place where they were accustomed to repeat** certain verses, **he,** too, should **repeat** them. If the custom is **to** recite them **plainly,** without repetition, **he** should recite them **plainly. In a place where the custom is to recite a blessing** before *Hallel,* **he should recite a blessing. Everything is in accordance with the local custom** in these matters. In the case of **one who purchases a *lulav* from another** who is an *am ha'aretz* **during the Sabbatical Year,** the seller **gives him an *etrog*** along with it **as a gift, as he is not permitted to purchase** the *etrog* **during the Sabbatical Year** because it is prohibited to engage in commerce with Sabbatical-Year produce.

12 **Originally,** during the Temple era, the ***lulav*** **was taken in the Temple** for **seven** days, **and in the** rest of the **country** outside the Temple it was taken for **one day. Once the Temple was destroyed, Rabban Yoḥanan ben Zakkai instituted** an ordinance **that the *lulav*** should **be taken** even **in the** rest of the **country** for **seven** days, in **commemoration of the Temple. And** for similar reasons, he instituted an ordinance **that** for **the entire day of waving** the *omer* offering, **it** should **be prohibited** to eat the grain of the new crop. It is prohibited to eat the grain of the new crop until the *omer* offering is brought and waved in the Temple on the sixteenth of Nisan. The offering was sacrificed in the morning; however, after taking potential delays into consideration, the new crop remained prohibited until it was clear that the offering had been sacrificed. Practically speaking, it was prohibited to eat the new grain until the sixteenth of Nisan was over; it was permitted only on the seventeenth. Once the Temple was destroyed and there was no longer an *omer* offering sacrificed, it was permitted to eat the new crop on the sixteenth. However, Rabban Yoḥanan instituted an ordinance that eating the new grain would remain prohibited until the seventeenth to commemorate the Temple.

י מִי שֶׁהָיָה עֶבֶד אוֹ אִשָּׁה אוֹ קָטָן מַקְרִין אוֹתוֹ –
עוֹנֶה אַחֲרֵיהֶן מַה שֶּׁהֵן אוֹמְרִין.
וְתָבֹא לוֹ מְאֵירָה.
אִם הָיָה גָּדוֹל מַקְרֵא אוֹתוֹ –
עוֹנֶה אַחֲרָיו "הַלְלוּיָהּ".

יא מָקוֹם שֶׁנָּהֲגוּ
לִכְפּוֹל – יִכְפּוֹל
לִפְשׁוֹט – יִפְשׁוֹט
לְבָרֵךְ – יְבָרֵךְ
הַכֹּל כְּמִנְהַג הַמְּדִינָה.
הַלּוֹקֵחַ לוּלָב מֵחֲבֵירוֹ בַּשְּׁבִיעִית –
נוֹתֵן לוֹ אֶתְרוֹג בְּמַתָּנָה
לְפִי שֶׁאֵין רַשַּׁאי לְלוֹקְחוֹ בַּשְּׁבִיעִית.

יב בָּרִאשׁוֹנָה הָיָה לוּלָב נִיטָּל בַּמִּקְדָּשׁ שִׁבְעָה
וּבַמְּדִינָה יוֹם אֶחָד.
מִשֶּׁחָרַב בֵּית הַמִּקְדָּשׁ הִתְקִין רַבָּן יוֹחָנָן בֶּן זַכַּאי
שֶׁיְּהֵא לוּלָב נִיטָּל בַּמְּדִינָה שִׁבְעָה
זֵכֶר לַמִּקְדָּשׁ.
וְשֶׁיְּהֵא יוֹם הָנֵף כּוּלּוֹ אָסוּר.

13 If **the first** day **of the festival of *Sukkot* occurs on Shabbat, all of the people bring their *lulavim* to the synagogue** on Shabbat eve, as it is prohibited to carry in a public domain on Shabbat. **The next day,** on Shabbat, everyone **rises early and comes** to the synagogue. **Each and every person recognizes his** *lulav* **and takes it.** This emphasis that each and every one recognizes his own *lulav* and takes it is **because the Sages said: A person does not fulfill his obligation** to take the *lulav* **on the first day of the Festival with the *lulav* of another, and** on **the rest of the days of the Festival a person fulfills his obligation** even **with the *lulav* of another.**

14 **Rabbi Yosei says:** If **the first day of** the **Festival occurs on Shabbat, and he forgot and carried the *lulav* out into the public domain, he is exempt** from liability to bring a sin-offering for this unwitting transgression **because he carried it out with permission,** i.e., he was preoccupied with the performance of the mitzva and carried it out.

15 **A woman** may **receive** a *lulav* **from her son or from her husband and return it on Shabbat to the water** in which it had been placed. **Rabbi Yehuda says: On Shabbat one may return** the *lulav* to the water; **and on the Festival one may** even **add** fresh water to the vessel so the *lulav* will not wilt; and **during** the intermediate days of **the Festival, one may** even **change** the water. **A minor who knows** how **to wave** the *lulav* **is obligated in** the mitzva of ***lulav*** due to the requirement to train him in the performance of mitzvot.

CHAPTER 4

1 The ***lulav*** is taken **and** the altar is encircled together with the **willow branch** either **six or seven** days, depending on which day of the Festival occurs on Shabbat. The obligation to recite **the** full ***Hallel*** **and the** mitzva of **rejoicing,** i.e., eating the meat of the peace-offering, **is in effect for eight** days, seven days of *Sukkot* and the Eighth Day of Assembly. The mitzva of ***sukka*** **and** the ritual of **the water libation** on the altar **are** in effect for **seven** days. **The flute** is played in the Temple for **five or six** days, depending on which day of the Festival occurs on Shabbat, to enhance the rejoicing on the Festival.

יג יוֹם טוֹב הָרִאשׁוֹן שֶׁל חַג שֶׁחָל לִהְיוֹת בַּשַּׁבָּת
כָּל הָעָם מוֹלִיכִין אֶת לוּלְבֵיהֶן לְבֵית הַכְּנֶסֶת
לַמָּחֳרָת מַשְׁכִּימִין וּבָאִין
כָּל אֶחָד וְאֶחָד מַכִּיר אֶת שֶׁלּוֹ וְנוֹטְלוֹ.
מִפְּנֵי שֶׁאָמְרוּ חֲכָמִים:
אֵין אָדָם יוֹצֵא יְדֵי חוֹבָתוֹ בְּיוֹם טוֹב הָרִאשׁוֹן
בְּלוּלָבוֹ שֶׁל חֲבֵירוֹ
וּשְׁאָר יְמוֹת הֶחָג
אָדָם יוֹצֵא יְדֵי חוֹבָתוֹ בְּלוּלָבוֹ שֶׁל חֲבֵירוֹ.

יד רַבִּי יוֹסֵי אוֹמֵר:
יוֹם טוֹב הָרִאשׁוֹן שֶׁל חַג שֶׁחָל לִהְיוֹת בַּשַּׁבָּת
וְשָׁכַח וְהוֹצִיא אֶת הַלּוּלָב לִרְשׁוּת הָרַבִּים –
פָּטוּר, מִפְּנֵי שֶׁהוֹצִיאוֹ בִּרְשׁוּת.

טו מְקַבֶּלֶת אִשָּׁה מִיַּד בְּנָהּ וּמִיַּד בַּעְלָהּ
וּמַחֲזִירָתוֹ לַמַּיִם בַּשַּׁבָּת
רַבִּי יְהוּדָה אוֹמֵר:
בַּשַּׁבָּת מַחֲזִירִין, בְּיוֹם טוֹב מוֹסִיפִין, וּבַמּוֹעֵד מַחֲלִיפִין.
קָטָן הַיּוֹדֵעַ לְנַעְנֵעַ חַיָּב בְּלוּלָב.

פרק רביעי

א לוּלָב וַעֲרָבָה – שִׁשָּׁה וְשִׁבְעָה.
הַהַלֵּל וְהַשִּׂמְחָה – שְׁמוֹנָה.
סוּכָּה וְנִיסּוּךְ הַמַּיִם – שִׁבְעָה.
הֶחָלִיל – חֲמִשָּׁה וְשִׁשָּׁה.

2 The mishna elaborates: The ***lulav*** is taken for **seven** days. **How** so? If **the first day of the Festival occurs on Shabbat,** since the mitzva to take the *lulav* on the first day is a mitzva by Torah law, it overrides Shabbat and one takes the *lulav* that day. As a result, the ***lulav*** is then taken for **seven** days. **And** if the first day occurs on one of the **rest of the days** of the week and one of the other days of the Festival coincides with Shabbat, the *lulav* is taken only **six** days. Since the mitzva to take the *lulav* is a mitzva by rabbinic law throughout the rest of *Sukkot,* it does not override Shabbat.

3 The altar is encircled with the **willow branch** for **seven** days. **How** so? If **the seventh day of** the mitzva of the **willow branch occurs on Shabbat,** since on that day it is a mitzva by Torah law, it overrides Shabbat and the mitzva of the **willow branch** is then performed for **seven** days. **And** if the seventh day occurs on one of the **rest of the days** of the week, and one of the other days of the Festival coincides with Shabbat, since the mitzva of the willow branch is then by rabbinic law and consequently does not override Shabbat, it is performed for only **six** days.

4 **How is the mitzva of *lulav*** fulfilled in the Temple when the first day of the Festival occurs **on Shabbat? If the first day of the Festival occurs on Shabbat,** all the people **bring their *lulavim* to the Temple Mount** on Friday. **The attendants receive** the *lulavim* **from them and arrange them on a bench [*itztaba*], while the Elders place their** *lulavim* **in the chamber.** They were given permission to do so due to the concern that they would be injured the following morning in the rush of people in search of their *lulavim.* **And** the court **teaches** the people **to say:** With regard to **anyone whom my *lulav* reaches his possession, it is his as a gift.** They did so to avoid the likely situation where people would inadvertently take *lulavim* that did not belong to them, as on the first day of the Festival one does not fulfill his obligation with a *lulav* that does not belong to him. **The next day** everyone **rises early and comes** to the Temple, **and the attendants throw** the *lulavim* **before them. And** in the confusion, the people **snatch** the *lulavim* **and** in the process **strike one another. And when the court saw that they came to** potential **danger, they instituted that each and every** person **will take** his *lulav* **in his house** and fulfill the mitzva there.

ב לוּלָב שִׁבְעָה כֵּיצַד?
יוֹם טוֹב הָרִאשׁוֹן שֶׁל חַג שֶׁחָל לִהְיוֹת בַּשַּׁבָּת –
לוּלָב שִׁבְעָה
וּשְׁאָר כָּל הַיָּמִים שִׁשָּׁה.

ג עֲרָבָה שִׁבְעָה כֵּיצַד?
יוֹם הַשְּׁבִיעִי שֶׁל עֲרָבָה
שֶׁחָל לִהְיוֹת בַּשַּׁבָּת – עֲרָבָה שִׁבְעָה
וּשְׁאָר כָּל הַיָּמִים – שִׁשָּׁה.

ד מִצְוַת לוּלָב כֵּיצַד (בַּשַּׁבָּת)?
יוֹם טוֹב הָרִאשׁוֹן שֶׁל חַג שֶׁחָל לִהְיוֹת בַּשַּׁבָּת
מוֹלִיכִין אֶת לוּלְבֵיהֶן לְהַר הַבַּיִת
וְהַחַזָּנִין מְקַבְּלִין מֵהֶן וְסוֹדְרִין אוֹתָן עַל גַּבֵּי אִיצְטַבָּא
וְהַזְּקֵנִים מַנִּיחִין אֶת שֶׁלָּהֶן בַּלִּשְׁכָּה.
וּמְלַמְּדִין אוֹתָם לוֹמַר:
כָּל מִי שֶׁמַּגִּיעַ לוּלָבִי לְיָדוֹ –
הֲרֵי הוּא לוֹ בְּמַתָּנָה.
לְמָחָר מַשְׁכִּימִין וּבָאִין
וְהַחַזָּנִין זוֹרְקִין אוֹתָם לִפְנֵיהֶם
וְהֵן מְחַטְּפִין וּמַכִּין אִישׁ אֶת חֲבֵירוֹ.
וּכְשֶׁרָאוּ בֵּית דִּין שֶׁבָּאוּ לִידֵי סַכָּנָה –
הִתְקִינוּ שֶׁיְּהֵא כָּל אֶחָד וְאֶחָד נוֹטֵל בְּבֵיתוֹ.

5 **How is the mitzva of** the **willow branch** fulfilled? **There was a place below Jerusalem, and it was called Motza. They** would **descend there and gather willow branches** [*murbiyyot*] **from there. And they** would then **come and stand them upright at the sides of the altar, and** the **tops** of the branches would **be inclined over the top of the altar. They** then **sounded a *tekia*,** a simple uninterrupted blast, **sounded a *terua*,** a broken sound and/or a series of short staccato blasts, **and sounded** another ***tekia*. Each day they** would **circle the altar one time and say: "Lord, please save us. Lord, please grant us success"** (Psalms 118:25). **Rabbi Yehuda says** that they would say: ***Ani vaho*, please save us. And on that day,** the seventh day of *Sukkot*, **they** would **circle the altar seven times. At the time of their departure** at the end of the Festival, **what** would **they say?** It is **beautiful for you,** altar; it is **beautiful for you, altar. Rabbi Elazar said** that they would say: **To the Lord and to you, altar; to the Lord and to you, altar.**

6 The mishna notes: **As its performance during the week, so is its performance on Shabbat; except** for the fact **that they would gather** the branches **from** Shabbat **eve and place them in basins of gold so that they would not dry. Rabbi Yoḥanan ben Beroka says:** There was a unique custom on the seventh day. **They would bring palm branches** to the Temple **and place them on the ground at the sides of the altar, and that** seventh **day** of *Sukkot* **was called:** The day of the **placing of palm branches.**

7 **Immediately** after fulfilling the mitzva of taking the four species on the seventh day of the festival of *Sukkot*, **children remove their *lulavim*** from the binding **and eat their *etrogim*** as an expression of extreme joy.

8 This mishna elaborates upon the first mishna in this chapter. **The** obligation to recite ***Hallel* and the** mitzva of **rejoicing** on the Festival by sacrificing and eating the meat of peace-offerings **are** always for **eight** days. The mishna explains: **How so?** This **teaches**

ה מִצְוַת עֲרָבָה כֵּיצַד?
מָקוֹם הָיָה לְמַטָּה מִירוּשָׁלַיִם וְנִקְרָא מוֹצָא.
יוֹרְדִין לְשָׁם וּמְלַקְּטִין מִשָּׁם מֻרְבִּיּוֹת שֶׁל עֲרָבָה
וּבָאִין וְזוֹקְפִין אוֹתָן בְּצִדֵּי הַמִּזְבֵּחַ
וְרָאשֵׁיהֶן כְּפוּפִין עַל גַּבֵּי הַמִּזְבֵּחַ.
תָּקְעוּ וְהֵרִיעוּ וְתָקְעוּ.
בְּכָל יוֹם מַקִּיפִין אֶת הַמִּזְבֵּחַ פַּעַם אַחַת, וְאוֹמְרִים:
"אָנָּא ה' הוֹשִׁיעָה נָּא, אָנָּא ה' הַצְלִיחָה נָּא".
רַבִּי יְהוּדָה אוֹמֵר: "אֲנִי וָהוֹ הוֹשִׁיעָה נָּא".

וְאוֹתוֹ הַיּוֹם מַקִּיפִין אֶת הַמִּזְבֵּחַ שֶׁבַע פְּעָמִים.
בִּשְׁעַת פְּטִירָתָן מָה הֵן אוֹמְרִים:
"יֹפִי לְךָ מִזְבֵּחַ, יֹפִי לְךָ מִזְבֵּחַ".
רַבִּי אֶלְעָזָר אוֹמֵר: "לְיָהּ וּלְךָ מִזְבֵּחַ, לְיָהּ וּלְךָ מִזְבֵּחַ".

ו כְּמַעֲשֵׂהוּ בַּחוֹל כָּךְ מַעֲשֵׂהוּ בַּשַּׁבָּת;
אֶלָּא שֶׁהָיוּ מְלַקְּטִין אוֹתָן מֵעֶרֶב
וּמַנִּיחִין אוֹתָן בְּגִיגִיּוֹת שֶׁל זָהָב כְּדֵי שֶׁלֹּא יִכְמוֹשׁוּ.

רַבִּי יוֹחָנָן בֶּן בְּרוֹקָה אוֹמֵר:
חֲרָיוֹת שֶׁל דֶּקֶל הָיוּ מְבִיאִין
וְחוֹבְטִין אוֹתָן בַּקַּרְקַע בְּצִדֵּי הַמִּזְבֵּחַ
וְאוֹתוֹ הַיּוֹם נִקְרָא "חִבּוּט חֲרָיוֹת".

ז מִיָּד תִּינוֹקוֹת שׁוֹמְטִין אֶת לוּלְבֵיהֶן, וְאוֹכְלִין אֶתְרוֹגֵיהֶן.

ח הַהַלֵּל וְהַשִּׂמְחָה שְׁמוֹנָה, כֵּיצַד?
מְלַמֵּד

that a person is obligated in ***Hallel*****, and in the** mitzva of **rejoicing, and in reverence for the last day of the Festival like** he is for **all the other days of the Festival.** The mitzva of ***sukka*** is **seven** days. **How** does one fulfill this obligation for seven full days? When **one finished eating** on the seventh day, **he** should **not dismantle his** ***sukka*** immediately, because the obligation continues until the end of the day. **However, he takes the vessels down** from the *sukka* into the house **from** ***minĥa*** time **and onward in deference to the last day of the Festival,** when he will require the vessels in the house.

9 With regard to the rite of **water libation** performed in the Temple during the Festival, **how** was it performed? **One would fill a golden jug with a capacity of three** ***log*** with water **from the Siloam** pool. When those who went to bring the water **reached the Gate of the Water,** so called because the water for the libation was brought through this gate leading to the Temple courtyard, **they sounded a** ***tekia*****, sounded a** ***terua*****, and sounded** another ***tekia*** as an expression of joy. The priest **ascended the ramp** of the altar **and turned to his left. There were two silver basins there** into which he poured the water. **Rabbi Yehuda said: They were limestone** basins, **but they would blacken due to the wine** and therefore looked like silver. The two basins were **perforated** at the bottom with **two thin** perforated **nose-like** protrusions. **One** of the basins, used for the wine libation, had a perforation that was **broad, and one,** used for the water libation, had a perforation that was **thin, so that** the flow of **both** the water and the wine, which do not have the same viscosity, would **conclude simultaneously.** The basin to the **west of** the altar was **for water,** and the basin to the **east of** the altar was **for wine.** However, if **one poured** the contents of the basin **of water into** the basin **of wine, or** the contents of the basin **of wine into** the basin **of water, he fulfilled** his obligation, as failure to pour the libation from the prescribed location does not disqualify the libation after the fact. **Rabbi Yehuda says:** The basin for the water libation was not that large; rather, **one would pour** the water **with** a vessel that had a capacity of **one** ***log*** on **all eight**

שֶׁחַיָּיב אָדָם בַּהַלֵּל וּבְשִׂמְחָה וּבִכְבוֹד
יוֹם טוֹב הָאַחֲרוֹן שֶׁל חַג
כִּשְׁאָר כָּל יְמוֹת הֶחָג.

סוּכָּה שִׁבְעָה, כֵּיצַד?
גָּמַר מִלֶּאֱכוֹל – לֹא יַתִּיר אֶת סוּכָּתוֹ
אֲבָל מוֹרִיד אֶת הַכֵּלִים מִן הַמִּנְחָה וּלְמַעְלָה
מִפְּנֵי כְבוֹד יוֹם טוֹב הָאַחֲרוֹן שֶׁל חַג.

ט נִיסּוּךְ הַמַּיִם, כֵּיצַד?
צְלוֹחִית שֶׁל זָהָב מַחֲזֶקֶת שְׁלֹשָׁה לוּגִּים
הָיָה מְמַלֵּא מִן הַשִּׁילוֹחַ.
הִגִּיעוּ לְשַׁעַר הַמַּיִם, תָּקְעוּ וְהֵרִיעוּ וְתָקְעוּ.
עָלָה בַּכֶּבֶשׁ וּפָנָה לִשְׂמֹאלוֹ.
שְׁנֵי סְפָלִים שֶׁל כֶּסֶף הָיוּ שָׁם.
רַבִּי יְהוּדָה אוֹמֵר: שֶׁל סִיד הָיוּ
אֶלָּא שֶׁהָיוּ מוּשְׁחָרִין פְּנֵיהֶם מִפְּנֵי הַיַּיִן.

וּמְנוּקָּבִין כְּמִין שְׁנֵי חוֹטָמִין דַּקִּין
(וְאֶחָד) מְעוּבֶּה וְאֶחָד דַּק
כְּדֵי שֶׁיְּהוּ שְׁנֵיהֶם כָּלִין בְּבַת אַחַת.

מַעֲרָבוֹ שֶׁל מַיִם, מִזְרָחוֹ שֶׁל יַיִן.
עֵירָה שֶׁל מַיִם לְתוֹךְ שֶׁל יַיִן, וְשֶׁל יַיִן לְתוֹךְ שֶׁל מַיִם –
יָצָא.

רַבִּי יְהוּדָה אוֹמֵר:
בְּלוֹג הָיָה מְנַסֵּךְ כָּל שְׁמוֹנָה.

days of the Festival and not only seven. **And** the appointee **says to the one pouring** the water into the silver basin: **Raise your hand,** so that his actions would be visible, **as one time** a Sadducee priest intentionally **poured** the water **on his feet,** as the Sadducees did not accept the oral tradition requiring water libation, and in their rage **all the people pelted him with their *etrogim*.**

10 Rabbi Yehuda continues: **As its performance during the week, so is its performance on Shabbat, except** that on Shabbat one would not draw water. Instead, **on Shabbat eve, one would fill a golden barrel that was not consecrated** for exclusive use in the Temple **from the Siloam** pool, **and he** would **place it in the** Temple **chamber** and draw water from there on Shabbat. If the water in the barrel **spilled,** or if it **was exposed** overnight, leading to concern that a snake may have deposited poison in the water, **one would fill** the jug with water **from the basin** in the Temple courtyard, **as exposed wine or water is unfit for the altar.** Just as it is prohibited for people to drink them due to the potential danger, so too, they may not be poured on the altar.

CHAPTER 5

1 **The flute** is played on the festival of *Sukkot* for **five** or **six** days. **This is the flute of the Place of the Drawing** of the Water, **whose** playing **overrides neither Shabbat nor** the **Festival.** Therefore, if the first Festival day occurred on Shabbat, they would play the flute for six days that year. However, if Shabbat coincided with one of the intermediate days of the Festival, they would play the flute for only five days. **One who did not see the Celebration of the Place of the Drawing** of the Water **never saw celebration in his days.**

2 This was the sequence of events: **At the conclusion of the first Festival** day the priests and the Levites **descended** from the Israelites' courtyard **to the Women's Courtyard, where they would introduce a significant repair,** as the Gemara will explain. **There were golden candelabra** atop poles **there** in the courtyard.

וְלַמְנַסֵּךְ אוֹמֵר לוֹ: "הַגְבַּה יָדְךָ"
שֶׁפַּעַם אֶחָד נִסֵּךְ אֶחָד עַל גַּבֵּי רַגְלָיו
וּרְגָמוּהוּ כָּל הָעָם בְּאֶתְרוֹגֵיהֶן.

י כְּמַעֲשֵׂהוּ בְּחוֹל כָּךְ מַעֲשֵׂהוּ בַּשַּׁבָּת
אֶלָּא שֶׁהָיָה מְמַלֵּא מֵעֶרֶב שַׁבָּת
חָבִית שֶׁל זָהָב שֶׁאֵינָהּ מְקוּדֶּשֶׁת מִן הַשִּׁילוֹחַ
וּמַנִּיחָהּ בַּלִּשְׁכָּה.
נִשְׁפְּכָה נִתְגַּלְּתָה –
הָיָה מְמַלֵּא מִן הַכִּיּוֹר.
שֶׁהַיַּיִן וְהַמַּיִם מְגוּלִּין פְּסוּלִין לְגַבֵּי מִזְבֵּחַ.

פרק חמישי

א הֶחָלִיל חֲמִשָּׁה וְשִׁשָּׁה
זֶהוּ הֶחָלִיל שֶׁל בֵּית הַשּׁוֹאֵבָה
שֶׁאֵינוֹ דוֹחֶה לֹא אֶת הַשַּׁבָּת וְלֹא אֶת יוֹם טוֹב.
מִי שֶׁלֹּא רָאָה שִׂמְחַת בֵּית הַשּׁוֹאֵבָה
לֹא רָאָה שִׂמְחָה מִיָּמָיו.

ב בְּמוֹצָאֵי יוֹם טוֹב הָרִאשׁוֹן שֶׁל חַג
יָרְדוּ לְעֶזְרַת נָשִׁים וּמְתַקְּנִין שָׁם תִּיקּוּן גָּדוֹל.
מְנוֹרוֹת שֶׁל זָהָב הָיוּ שָׁם

And there were **four basins** made **of gold at the top** of each candelabrum. **And** there were **four ladders for each and every** pole **and** there were **four children from the priesthood trainees, and in their hands** were **pitchers** with a capacity **of 120** *log* of oil **that they would pour into each and every basin.**

3 **From the worn trousers of the priests and their belts they would loosen** and tear strips to use as wicks, **and with them they would light** the candelabra. **And** the light from the candelabra was so bright that **there was not a courtyard in Jerusalem that was not illuminated from the light of the Place of the Drawing** of the Water.

4 The **pious and** the **men of action would dance before** the people who attended the celebration, **with flaming torches** that they would juggle **in their hands, and they would say before them passages of song and praise** to God. **And the Levites** would play **on lyres, harps, cymbals, and trumpets, and countless** other **musical instruments.** The musicians would stand **on the fifteen stairs that descend from the Israelites' courtyard to the Women's Courtyard, corresponding to the fifteen** Songs of the **Ascents in Psalms,** i.e., chapters 120–134, and **upon which** the **Levites stand with musical instruments and recite** their **song. And** this was the ceremony of the Water Libation: **Two priests stood at the Upper Gate that descends from the Israelites' courtyard to the Women's Courtyard, with two trumpets in their hands.** When **the rooster crowed** at dawn, **they sounded a** ***tekia,*** **and sounded a** ***terua,*** **and sounded a** ***tekia.*** When **they** who would draw the water **reached the tenth stair** the trumpeters **sounded a** ***tekia,*** **and sounded a** ***terua,*** **and sounded a** ***tekia,*** to indicate that the time to draw water from the Siloam pool had arrived. When **they reached the** Women's **Courtyard** with the basins of water in their hands, the trumpeters **sounded a** ***tekia,*** **and sounded a** ***terua,*** **and sounded a** ***tekia.*** When **they reached the ground** of the Women's Courtyard, the trumpeters **sounded a** ***tekia,*** **and sounded a** ***terua,*** **and sounded a** ***tekia.***

וְאַרְבָּעָה סְפָלִים שֶׁל זָהָב בְּרָאשֵׁיהֶם
וְאַרְבָּעָה סוּלָּמוֹת לְכָל אֶחָד וְאֶחָד
וְאַרְבָּעָה יְלָדִים מִפִּרְחֵי כְהוּנָּה
וּבִידֵיהֶם כַּדִּים שֶׁל מֵאָה וְעֶשְׂרִים לוֹג
שֶׁהֵן מַטִּילִין לְכָל סֵפֶל וָסֵפֶל.

ג מִבְּלָאֵי מִכְנְסֵי כֹהֲנִים וּמֵהֶמְיָינֵיהֶן
מֵהֶן הָיוּ מַפְקִיעִין, וּבָהֶן הָיוּ מַדְלִיקִין.
וְלֹא הָיָה חָצֵר בִּירוּשָׁלַיִם
שֶׁאֵינָהּ מְאִירָה מֵאוֹר בֵּית הַשּׁוֹאֵבָה.

ד חֲסִידִים וְאַנְשֵׁי מַעֲשֶׂה
הָיוּ מְרַקְּדִין בִּפְנֵיהֶם בַּאֲבוּקוֹת שֶׁל אוֹר שֶׁבִּידֵיהֶן
וְאוֹמְרִים לִפְנֵיהֶם דִּבְרֵי שִׁירוֹת וְתוּשְׁבָּחוֹת
וְהַלְוִיִּם בְּכִנּוֹרוֹת וּבִנְבָלִים וּבִמְצִלְתַּיִם וּבַחֲצוֹצְרוֹת
וּבִכְלֵי שִׁיר בְּלֹא מִסְפָּר
עַל חֲמֵשׁ עֶשְׂרֵה מַעֲלוֹת
הַיּוֹרְדוֹת מֵעֶזְרַת יִשְׂרָאֵל לְעֶזְרַת נָשִׁים
כְּנֶגֶד חֲמֵשׁ עֶשְׂרֵה (מַעֲלוֹת) שֶׁבַּתְּהִלִּים
שֶׁעֲלֵיהֶן לְוִיִּם עוֹמְדִין בִּכְלֵי שִׁיר וְאוֹמְרִים שִׁירָה.
וְעָמְדוּ שְׁנֵי כֹהֲנִים בַּשַּׁעַר הָעֶלְיוֹן
שֶׁיּוֹרֵד מֵעֶזְרַת יִשְׂרָאֵל לְעֶזְרַת נָשִׁים, וּשְׁנֵי חֲצוֹצְרוֹת בִּידֵיהֶן.
קָרָא הַגֶּבֶר, תָּקְעוּ וְהֵרִיעוּ וְתָקְעוּ.
הִגִּיעוּ לְמַעֲלָה עֲשִׂירִית, תָּקְעוּ וְהֵרִיעוּ וְתָקְעוּ.
הִגִּיעוּ לָעֲזָרָה תָּקְעוּ וְהֵרִיעוּ וְתָקְעוּ.
(הִגִּיעוּ לַקַּרְקַע תָּקְעוּ וְהֵרִיעוּ וְתָקְעוּ).

They continued sounding the trumpets **until they reached the gate** through **which** one **exits to the east,** from the Women's Courtyard to the eastern slope of the Temple Mount. When **they reached the gate** through **which** one **exits to the east, they turned from** facing **east to** facing **west,** toward the Holy of Holies, **and said: Our ancestors who were in this place** during the First Temple period who did not conduct themselves appropriately, stood **"with their backs toward the Sanctuary of the Lord, and their faces toward the east; and they worshipped the sun toward the east"** (Ezekiel 8:16), **and we, our eyes are to God. Rabbi Yehuda says** that **they would repeat and say: We are to God, and our eyes are to God.**

5 **One** sounds **no fewer than twenty-one** trumpet **blasts in the Temple, and one** sounds **no more than forty-eight.** The mishna elaborates: **Each day there were twenty-one** trumpet **blasts in the Temple: Three** blasts were sounded **for the opening of the gates** in the morning, **nine for the daily morning offering, and nine for the daily afternoon offering,** totaling twenty-one. **And** on a day when the additional offerings were sacrificed, e.g., the New Moon, **with the additional offerings they would add nine additional blasts. And on Shabbat eve they would add six** blasts sounded adjacent to the onset of Shabbat: **Three to stop the people from** their **labor,** as the blasts inform the people that Shabbat is approaching and they stop working, **and three** at the onset of Shabbat **to demarcate between sacred and profane.** On **Shabbat eve during the festival** of *Sukkot,* **there were forty-eight** blasts. How so? **Three** in the morning **for the opening of the gates; three for the upper gate; and three for the lower gate; and three for the filling of the** vessel with **water,** as described in the sequence of the ritual of drawing the water for the water libation (48b); **and three** when pouring the water libation **upon the altar; nine for the daily morning offering; and nine for the daily afternoon offering; and nine for the additional offerings; three to stop the people from work; and three** more **to demarcate between sacred and profane,** totaling forty-eight blasts.

הָיוּ תוֹקְעִין וְהוֹלְכִין עַד שֶׁמַּגִּיעִין לַשַּׁעַר הַיּוֹצֵא מִמִּזְרָח.
הִגִּיעוּ לַשַּׁעַר הַיּוֹצֵא מִמִּזְרָח, הָפְכוּ פְּנֵיהֶן מִמִּזְרָח לְמַעֲרָב
וְאָמְרוּ:
אֲבוֹתֵינוּ שֶׁהָיוּ בַּמָּקוֹם הַזֶּה
אֲחוֹרֵיהֶם אֶל הַהֵיכָל וּפְנֵיהֶם קֵדְמָה
וּמִשְׁתַּחֲוִים קֵדְמָה לַשֶּׁמֶשׁ, וְאָנוּ לְיָהּ עֵינֵינוּ.
רַבִּי יְהוּדָה אוֹמֵר: הָיוּ שׁוֹנִין וְאוֹמְרִין: "אָנוּ לְיָהּ וּלְיָהּ עֵינֵינוּ".

ה אֵין פּוֹחֲתִין מֵעֶשְׂרִים וְאַחַת תְּקִיעוֹת בַּמִּקְדָּשׁ
וְאֵין מוֹסִיפִין עַל אַרְבָּעִים וּשְׁמֹנֶה.
בְּכָל יוֹם הָיוּ שָׁם עֶשְׂרִים וְאַחַת תְּקִיעוֹת בַּמִּקְדָּשׁ:
שָׁלֹשׁ לִפְתִיחַת שְׁעָרִים
וְתֵשַׁע לְתָמִיד שֶׁל שַׁחַר, וְתֵשַׁע לְתָמִיד שֶׁל בֵּין הָעַרְבַּיִם.
וּבַמּוּסָפִין הָיוּ מוֹסִיפִין עוֹד תֵּשַׁע.
וּבְעֶרֶב שַׁבָּת הָיוּ מוֹסִיפִין שֵׁשׁ:
שָׁלֹשׁ לְהַבְטִיל אֶת הָעָם מִמְּלָאכָה
וְשָׁלֹשׁ לְהַבְדִּיל בֵּין קֹדֶשׁ לְחוֹל.

עֶרֶב שַׁבָּת שֶׁבְּתוֹךְ הֶחָג הָיוּ שָׁם אַרְבָּעִים וּשְׁמֹנֶה:
שָׁלֹשׁ לִפְתִיחַת שְׁעָרִים
שָׁלֹשׁ לַשַּׁעַר הָעֶלְיוֹן, וְשָׁלֹשׁ לַשַּׁעַר הַתַּחְתּוֹן
וְשָׁלֹשׁ לְמִילּוּי הַמַּיִם, וְשָׁלֹשׁ עַל גַּבֵּי מִזְבֵּחַ
תֵּשַׁע לְתָמִיד שֶׁל שַׁחַר, וְתֵשַׁע לְתָמִיד שֶׁל בֵּין הָעַרְבַּיִם
וְתֵשַׁע לְמוּסָפִין
שָׁלֹשׁ לְהַבְטִיל אֶת הָעָם מִן הַמְּלָאכָה
וְשָׁלֹשׁ לְהַבְדִּיל בֵּין קוֹדֶשׁ לְחוֹל.

6 On **the first Festival** day **of *Sukkot* there were thirteen bulls, two rams, and one goat there.** The mishna proceeds to discuss the division of labor for the Festival offerings among the twenty-four priestly watches, all of which serve in the Temple on the pilgrimage Festivals. The sixteen offerings mentioned above were divided among sixteen priestly watches, one offering per watch. **Fourteen sheep remained to** be divided among the **eight** remaining **watches. On the first day** of the Festival, **six** of the eight remaining watches **sacrifice two** sheep **each** for a total of twelve, **and the remaining** two watches sacrifice **one** sheep **each. On the second** day of the Festival, i.e., the first day of the intermediate days, when twelve bulls were sacrificed, fifteen of the priestly watches sacrifice the bulls, rams, and goat, **five** of the remaining watches **sacrifice two** sheep **each, and the remaining** four watches sacrifice **one** sheep **each. On the third** day of the Festival, when eleven bulls were sacrificed, fourteen of the priestly watches sacrifice the bulls, rams, and goat, **four** of the remaining watches **sacrifice two** sheep **each, and the remaining** six watches sacrifice **one** sheep **each. On the fourth** day of the Festival, when ten bulls were sacrificed, thirteen of the priestly watches sacrifice the bulls, rams, and goat, **three** of the remaining watches **sacrifice two** sheep **each, and the remaining** eight watches sacrifice **one** sheep **each. On the fifth** day, when nine bulls were sacrificed, twelve watches sacrifice the bulls, rams, and goat, **two** of the twelve remaining watches **sacrifice two** sheep **each, and the remaining** ten watches sacrifice **one** sheep **each. On the sixth** day, when eight bulls were sacrificed, eleven watches sacrifice the bulls, rams, and goat, **one** of the remaining watches **sacrifices two** sheep, **and the remaining** twelve watches sacrifice **one** sheep **each. On the seventh** day **they are all equal** and bring one offering each. **On the eighth** day, when there was a completely different configuration of offerings, **they returned to the** standard **lottery** system used to determine which of the priestly watches would sacrifice the offerings, as they did **on the other pilgrimage Festivals,** which do not have as many offerings as does *Sukkot*. **They said** about the ordering of the priestly watches: **One who sacrificed bulls today will not sacrifice** bulls **tomorrow; rather,** they will sacrifice one of the other types of offerings. **They rotate,** so that each of the watches will have the opportunity to sacrifice bulls as well as other animals.

ו יוֹם טוֹב הָרִאשׁוֹן שֶׁל חַג
הָיוּ שָׁם שְׁלֹשָׁה עָשָׂר פָּרִים
אֵילִים שְׁנַיִם
וְשָׂעִיר אֶחָד.

נִשְׁתַּיְּירוּ שָׁם אַרְבָּעָה עָשָׂר כְּבָשִׂים לִשְׁמוֹנָה מִשְׁמָרוֹת.
בְּיוֹם רִאשׁוֹן – שִׁשָּׁה מַקְרִיבִין שְׁנַיִם שְׁנַיִם
וְהַשְּׁאָר אֶחָד אֶחָד.
בַּשֵּׁנִי – חֲמִשָּׁה מַקְרִיבִין שְׁנַיִם שְׁנַיִם –
וְהַשְּׁאָר אֶחָד אֶחָד.
בַּשְּׁלִישִׁי – אַרְבָּעָה מַקְרִיבִין שְׁנַיִם שְׁנַיִם
וְהַשְּׁאָר אֶחָד אֶחָד.
בָּרְבִיעִי – שְׁלֹשָׁה מַקְרִיבִין שְׁנַיִם שְׁנַיִם
וְהַשְּׁאָר אֶחָד אֶחָד.
בַּחֲמִישִׁי – שְׁנַיִם מַקְרִיבִין שְׁנַיִם שְׁנַיִם
וְהַשְּׁאָר אֶחָד אֶחָד.
בַּשִּׁשִּׁי – אֶחָד מַקְרִיב שְׁנַיִם
וְהַשְּׁאָר אֶחָד אֶחָד.
בַּשְּׁבִיעִי – כּוּלָּן שָׁוִין.
בַּשְּׁמִינִי – חָזְרוּ לְפַיִיס כְּבָרְגָלִים.

אָמְרוּ –
מִי שֶׁהִקְרִיב פָּרִים הַיּוֹם לֹא יַקְרִיב לְמָחָר
אֶלָּא חוֹזְרִין חֲלִילָה.

7 **At three times during the year, all** twenty-four **priestly watches** have **equal** status, in that all receive a share in the Temple service independent of the standard order of the watches and all receive a share in the accompanying gifts of the priesthood: **In the portions of the offerings of the Festivals** sacrificed on the altar **and in the distribution of the shewbread** on Shabbat during the Festivals. **On *Shavuot*** that coincides with Shabbat, when the two loaves offered on *Shavuot* would be distributed together with the distribution of the shewbread, the priest charged with the distribution **says to** each priest: **Here is *matza*** from the shewbread **for you,** and **here is leavened bread** from the two loaves **for you.** The principle is that **the priestly watch whose time is fixed** during the Festival **sacrifices** the **daily offerings** during the Festival, as well as vow-offerings, **free-will offerings, and all other communal offerings. And** that watch **sacrifices all of them** even during the Festival, when other aspects of the service are shared by all the watches. In the case of **a Festival that** occurs **adjacent to Shabbat, both** when it occurs **preceding it** and when it occurs **following it, all the watches** that arrived early or remained late to serve in the Temple **were** of **equal** status **in the distribution of the shewbread** on that Shabbat.

8 **If one day happened to separate between** the Festival and Shabbat, **the watch whose time was scheduled would take ten** of the twelve **loaves** of shewbread, **and** the watch **that was detained** after the Festival because there was insufficient time to get home before Shabbat **takes two** loaves. **And during the rest of the days of the year,** when the changing of the watches takes place on Shabbat, **the incoming** watch **takes six** loaves **and the outgoing** watch **takes six** loaves. **Rabbi Yehuda says: The incoming** watch **takes seven** loaves **and the outgoing takes five.** The standard procedure was that the members of **the incoming** watch **divide** the shewbread **in the north** section of the courtyard, **and the outgoing** watch **in the south.** However, there was one exception: The watch of **Bilga,** due to a penalty imposed upon it, **always divides** the shewbread to its members **in the south,** even when it is the incoming watch. **And its ring** used to facilitate slaughter of the animals **was fixed** in place, rendering it useless, **and its niche** among the niches in the wall of the Chamber of Knives, where the priests would store their knives and other vessels, was **sealed.**

ז בִּשְׁלֹשָׁה פְּרָקִים בַּשָּׁנָה הָיוּ כָּל מִשְׁמָרוֹת שָׁווֹת:
בְּאֵימוּרֵי הָרְגָלִים, וּבְחִילּוּק לֶחֶם הַפָּנִים.
בַּעֲצֶרֶת אוֹמֵר לוֹ: הֵילָךְ מַצָּה הֵילָךְ חָמֵץ.

מִשְׁמָר שֶׁזְּמַנּוֹ קָבוּעַ
הוּא מַקְרִיב תְּמִידִין נְדָרִים וּנְדָבוֹת וּשְׁאָר קָרְבְּנוֹת צִבּוּר –
וּמַקְרִיב אֶת הַכֹּל.

יוֹם טוֹב הַסָּמוּךְ לַשַּׁבָּת
בֵּין מִלְּפָנֶיהָ בֵּין לְאַחֲרֶיהָ
הָיוּ כָּל הַמִּשְׁמָרוֹת שָׁווֹת בְּחִילּוּק לֶחֶם הַפָּנִים.

ח חָל לִהְיוֹת יוֹם אֶחָד [לְהַפְסִיק] בֵּינְתַיִם
מִשְׁמָר שֶׁזְּמַנּוֹ קָבוּעַ – הָיָה נוֹטֵל עֶשֶׂר חַלּוֹת
וְהַמִּתְעַכֵּב נוֹטֵל שְׁתַּיִם.

וּבִשְׁאָר יְמוֹת הַשָּׁנָה –
הַנִּכְנָס נוֹטֵל שֵׁשׁ וְהַיּוֹצֵא נוֹטֵל שֵׁשׁ.
רַבִּי יְהוּדָה אוֹמֵר:
הַנִּכְנָס נוֹטֵל שֶׁבַע, וְהַיּוֹצֵא נוֹטֵל חָמֵשׁ.

הַנִּכְנָסִין חוֹלְקִין בַּצָּפוֹן וְהַיּוֹצְאִין בַּדָּרוֹם.
בִּילְגָּה לְעוֹלָם חוֹלֶקֶת בַּדָּרוֹם
וְטַבַּעְתָּהּ קְבוּעָה, וְחַלּוֹנָהּ סְתוּמָה.

Shaharit

The following order of prayers and blessings, which departs from that of most prayer books, is based on the consensus of recent halakhic authorities.

ON WAKING

On waking, our first thought should be that we are in the presence of God. Since we are forbidden to speak God's name until we have washed our hands, the following prayer is said, which, without mentioning God's name, acknowledges His presence and gives thanks for a new day and for the gift of life.

מוֹדֶה I thank You, living and eternal King,
for giving me back my soul in mercy.
Great is Your faithfulness.

Wash hands and say the following blessings.
Some have the custom to say "Wisdom begins" on page 264 at this point.

בָּרוּךְ Blessed are You, Lord our God, King of the Universe,
who has made us holy through His commandments,
and has commanded us about washing hands.

בָּרוּךְ Blessed are You, Lord our God, King of the Universe,
who formed man in wisdom
and created in him many orifices and cavities.
It is revealed and known before the throne of Your glory
that were one of them to be ruptured or blocked,
it would be impossible to survive and stand before You.
Blessed are You, Lord,
Healer of all flesh who does wondrous deeds.

---

not contain God's name so that it may be said immediately on waking, even prior to washing hands.

אֲשֶׁר יָצַר אֶת הָאָדָם בְּחָכְמָה *Who formed man in wisdom.* There are a hundred trillion cells in the human body. Within each cell is a nucleus and within each nucleus a double copy of the human genome. Each genome consists of 3.1 billion letters of genetic code, sufficient if transcribed to fill a library of five thousand volumes. Even this is only the beginning of the miracle, for the development of the body is not a matter of simple genetic determinism. It is

שחרית

The following order of prayers and blessings, which departs from that of most prayer books, is based on the consensus of recent halakhic authorities.

השכמת הבוקר

On waking, our first thought should be that we are in the presence of God. Since we are forbidden to speak God's name until we have washed our hands, the following prayer is said, which, without mentioning God's name, acknowledges His presence and gives thanks for a new day and for the gift of life.

מוֹדֶה/women מוֹדָה/ אֲנִי לְפָנֶיךָ מֶלֶךְ חַי וְקַיָּם
שֶׁהֶחֱזַרְתָּ בִּי נִשְׁמָתִי בְּחֶמְלָה
רַבָּה אֱמוּנָתֶךָ.

Wash hands and say the following blessings.
Some have the custom to say רֵאשִׁית חָכְמָה *on page 265 at this point.*

בָּרוּךְ אַתָּה יהוה אֱלֹהֵינוּ מֶלֶךְ הָעוֹלָם
אֲשֶׁר קִדְּשָׁנוּ בְּמִצְוֹתָיו וְצִוָּנוּ עַל נְטִילַת יָדָיִם.

בָּרוּךְ אַתָּה יהוה אֱלֹהֵינוּ מֶלֶךְ הָעוֹלָם
אֲשֶׁר יָצַר אֶת הָאָדָם בְּחָכְמָה
וּבָרָא בוֹ נְקָבִים נְקָבִים, חֲלוּלִים חֲלוּלִים.
גָּלוּי וְיָדוּעַ לִפְנֵי כִסֵּא כְבוֹדֶךָ
שֶׁאִם יִפָּתֵחַ אֶחָד מֵהֶם אוֹ יִסָּתֵם אֶחָד מֵהֶם
אִי אֶפְשָׁר לְהִתְקַיֵּם וְלַעֲמֹד לְפָנֶיךָ.
בָּרוּךְ אַתָּה יהוה, רוֹפֵא כָל בָּשָׂר וּמַפְלִיא לַעֲשׂוֹת.

מוֹדֶה אֲנִי *I thank You.* Sleep, said the sages, is a sixtieth, a foretaste, of death (*Berakhot* 57b). Waking each morning is therefore a miniature resurrection. We are new, the universe is new (we say later in our prayers, "who renews every day the work of creation"), and before us lies an open page of possibilities. In this simple prayer we thank God for giving us back our life. It does

אֱלֹהַי My God,
the soul You placed within me is pure.
You created it, You formed it, You breathed it into me,
and You guard it while it is within me.
One day You will take it from me,
and restore it to me in the time to come.
As long as the soul is within me,
I will thank You,
LORD my God and God of my ancestors,
Master of all works, LORD of all souls.
Blessed are You, LORD,
who restores souls to lifeless bodies.

TZITZIT

The following blessing is said before putting on tzitzit. Neither it nor the subsequent prayer is said by those who wear a tallit. The blessing over the latter exempts the former.

בָּרוּךְ Blessed are You, LORD our God, King of the Universe,
who has made us holy through His commandments,
and has commanded us about the command of tasseled garments.

After putting on tzitzit, say:

יְהִי רָצוֹן May it be Your will, LORD my God and God of my ancestors, that the commandment of the tasseled garment be considered before You as if I had fulfilled it in all its specifics, details and intentions, as well as the 613 commandments dependent on it, Amen, Selah.

נְשָׁמָה שֶׁנָּתַתָּ בִּי טְהוֹרָה הִיא *The soul You placed within me is pure.* Despite the fact that we have genetically encoded instincts and desires, there is nothing predetermined about whether we use them for good or bad.

הַמַּחֲזִיר נְשָׁמוֹת לִפְגָרִים מֵתִים *Who restores souls to lifeless bodies.* Since waking each morning is like a resurrection, it is an intimation of the fact that the dead can be restored to life, as we believe they will be at the end of days. This prayer is a simple, subtle way of making us daily aware of the interplay between mortality and immortality in the human condition. It opens our eyes to the wonder of being, the miracle that we are here at all.

אֱלֹהַי
נְשָׁמָה שֶׁנָּתַתָּ בִּי טְהוֹרָה הִיא.
אַתָּה בְרָאתָהּ, אַתָּה יְצַרְתָּהּ, אַתָּה נְפַחְתָּהּ בִּי
וְאַתָּה מְשַׁמְּרָהּ בְּקִרְבִּי, וְאַתָּה עָתִיד לִטְּלָהּ מִמֶּנִּי
וּלְהַחֲזִירָהּ בִּי לֶעָתִיד לָבוֹא.
כָּל זְמַן שֶׁהַנְּשָׁמָה בְּקִרְבִּי, מוֹדֶה/ *women* מוֹדָה/ אֲנִי לְפָנֶיךָ
יהוה אֱלֹהַי וֵאלֹהֵי אֲבוֹתַי
רִבּוֹן כָּל הַמַּעֲשִׂים, אֲדוֹן כָּל הַנְּשָׁמוֹת.
בָּרוּךְ אַתָּה יהוה, הַמַּחֲזִיר נְשָׁמוֹת לִפְגָרִים מֵתִים.

לבישת ציצית

The following blessing is said before putting on a טלית קטן. *Neither it nor* יְהִי רָצוֹן *is said by those who wear a* טלית. *The blessing over the latter exempts the former.*

בָּרוּךְ אַתָּה יהוה אֱלֹהֵינוּ מֶלֶךְ הָעוֹלָם
אֲשֶׁר קִדְּשָׁנוּ בְּמִצְוֹתָיו וְצִוָּנוּ עַל מִצְוַת צִיצִית.

After putting on the טלית קטן*, say:*

יְהִי רָצוֹן מִלְּפָנֶיךָ, יהוה אֱלֹהַי וֵאלֹהֵי אֲבוֹתַי, שֶׁתְּהֵא חֲשׁוּבָה מִצְוַת צִיצִית לְפָנֶיךָ כְּאִלּוּ קִיַּמְתִּיהָ בְּכָל פְּרָטֶיהָ וְדִקְדּוּקֶיהָ וְכַוָּנוֹתֶיהָ, וְתַרְיַ״ג מִצְוֹת הַתְּלוּיוֹת בָּהּ, אָמֵן סֶלָה.

---

an elaborate process of interaction between genes and environment, nature and nurture, genetic and epigenetic influences. Faith is not opposed to science, nor is science incompatible with faith. Faith is wonder and gratitude. Therefore, said Maimonides, natural science is one of the paths to the love and awe of God, as we realize the vastness of the universe and the complexity of life (Laws of the Foundations of the Torah 2:2). Each new scientific discovery gives added resonance to the words of the psalm: "How numerous are Your works, Lord; You made them all in wisdom; the earth is full of Your creations" (Ps. 104:24).

BLESSINGS OVER THE TORAH

In Judaism, study is greater even than prayer. So, before beginning to pray, we engage in a miniature act of study, preceded by the appropriate blessings. The blessings are followed by brief selections from Scripture, Mishna and Gemara, the three foundational texts of Judaism.

בָּרוּךְ Blessed are You, Lord our God, King of the Universe,
who has made us holy through His commandments,
and has commanded us to engage in study
of the words of Torah.
Please, Lord our God, make the words of Your Torah
sweet in our mouths and in the mouths of Your people,
the house of Israel,
so that we, our descendants (and their descendants)
and the descendants of Your people,
the house of Israel,
may all know Your name and study Your Torah for its own sake.
Blessed are You, Lord,
who teaches Torah to His people Israel.

בָּרוּךְ Blessed are You, Lord our God, King of the Universe,
who has chosen us from all the peoples and given us His Torah.
Blessed are You, Lord,
Giver of the Torah.

בְּמִצְוֹתָיו *Through His commandments.* This blessing, said over commands between us and God, represents the intention to fulfill an act as a command, thus endowing it with holiness. Only commands between us and God require a blessing beforehand. Commands between us and our fellow humans – such as giving charity, visiting the sick, comforting mourners and so on – do not require a blessing beforehand, since in these cases the command has to do with its effect (*nifal*), rather than the act itself (*pe'ula*) or its agent (*po'el*). Since the effect of acts of kindness is independent of the intention of the agent, no preliminary declaration of intent – that is, a blessing – is necessary.

בָּרוּךְ אַתָּה...אֲשֶׁר בָּחַר בָּנוּ *Blessed are You... who has chosen us.* Unlike the previous blessing, which is one of the *birkot hamitzvot*, blessings over a command, this is a *birkat hoda'a*, a blessing of thanks and acknowledgment.

ברכות התורה

In Judaism, study is greater even than prayer. So, before beginning to pray, we engage in a miniature act of study, preceded by the appropriate blessings. The blessings are followed by brief selections from תנ״ך, משנה *and* גמרא, *the three foundational texts of Judaism.*

בָּרוּךְ אַתָּה יהוה אֱלֹהֵינוּ מֶלֶךְ הָעוֹלָם
אֲשֶׁר קִדְּשָׁנוּ בְּמִצְוֹתָיו, וְצִוָּנוּ לַעֲסֹק בְּדִבְרֵי תוֹרָה.
וְהַעֲרֶב נָא יהוה אֱלֹהֵינוּ אֶת דִּבְרֵי תוֹרָתְךָ
בְּפִינוּ וּבְפִי עַמְּךָ בֵּית יִשְׂרָאֵל
וְנִהְיֶה אֲנַחְנוּ וְצֶאֱצָאֵינוּ (וְצֶאֱצָאֵי צֶאֱצָאֵינוּ)
וְצֶאֱצָאֵי עַמְּךָ בֵּית יִשְׂרָאֵל
כֻּלָּנוּ יוֹדְעֵי שְׁמֶךָ וְלוֹמְדֵי תוֹרָתְךָ לִשְׁמָהּ.
בָּרוּךְ אַתָּה יהוה, הַמְלַמֵּד תּוֹרָה לְעַמּוֹ יִשְׂרָאֵל.

בָּרוּךְ אַתָּה יהוה אֱלֹהֵינוּ מֶלֶךְ הָעוֹלָם
אֲשֶׁר בָּחַר בָּנוּ מִכָּל הָעַמִּים, וְנָתַן לָנוּ אֶת תּוֹרָתוֹ.
בָּרוּךְ אַתָּה יהוה, נוֹתֵן הַתּוֹרָה.

BLESSINGS OVER THE TORAH

In Judaism, Torah study is the highest of all spiritual engagements, higher even than prayer (*Shabbat* 10a), for in prayer we speak to God but in Torah study we listen to God speaking to us, through the sacred texts of our tradition. Judaism is supremely a religion of study. Hence we preface prayer with an act of Torah study.

There are three types of Torah study: (1) study in order to know what to do, (2) study as a substitute for rituals that we are unable to perform, most notably the sacrifices, and (3) study as a religious act for its own sake, an aligning of our intellect with the mind of God.

אֲשֶׁר קִדְּשָׁנוּ *Who has made us holy.* Holiness is not a given of birth, a genetic endowment. It is what we become when we submit our will to that of God. We become holy by what we do. The word "holy" means distinctive, set apart. Just as God is holy because He transcends the physical universe, so we become holy by transcending natural impulses and instincts.

יְבָרֶכְךָ May the LORD bless you and protect you. *Num. 6*
May the LORD make His face shine on you
and be gracious to you.
May the LORD turn His face toward you
and grant you peace.

אֵלּוּ These are the things for which there is no fixed measure: *Mishna Pe'ah 1:1*
the corner of the field, first-fruits,
appearances before the LORD [on festivals, with offerings],
acts of kindness and the study of Torah.

אֵלּוּ These are the things whose fruits we eat in this world *Shabbat 127a*
but whose full reward awaits us in the World to Come:
honoring parents; acts of kindness;
arriving early at the house of study morning and evening;
hospitality to strangers; visiting the sick;
helping the needy bride; attending to the dead;
devotion in prayer;
and bringing peace between people –
but the study of Torah is equal to them all.

Some say:

רֵאשִׁית חָכְמָה Wisdom begins in awe of the LORD; *Ps. 111*
all who fulfill [His commandments] gain good understanding;
His praise is ever-lasting.
The Torah Moses commanded us is the heritage of the congregation of Jacob. *Deut. 33*
Listen, my son, to your father's instruction, *Prov. 1*
and do not forsake your mother's teaching.
May the Torah be my faith and Almighty God my help.
Blessed be the name of His glorious kingdom for ever and all time.

So here, "May the LORD bless you" is a passage from the Torah (Num. 6:24–26), "These are the things for which there is no fixed measure" is a passage from the Mishna (*Pe'ah* 1:1), and "These are the things of which a man enjoys the fruits in this life" is a teaching from the Talmud (*Shabbat* 127a).

וְתַלְמוּד תּוֹרָה כְּנֶגֶד כֻּלָּם *The study of the Torah is equal to them all.* There was a debate among the sages as to which is greater, learning or doing? The conclusion was that "Great is learning, for it leads to doing" (*Kiddushin* 40b).

במדבר ו
יְבָרֶכְךָ יהוה וְיִשְׁמְרֶךָ:
יָאֵר יהוה פָּנָיו אֵלֶיךָ וִיחֻנֶּךָּ:
יִשָּׂא יהוה פָּנָיו אֵלֶיךָ וְיָשֵׂם לְךָ שָׁלוֹם:

משנה, פאה א: א
אֵלּוּ דְבָרִים שֶׁאֵין לָהֶם שִׁעוּר
הַפֵּאָה וְהַבִּכּוּרִים וְהָרֵאָיוֹן
וּגְמִילוּת חֲסָדִים וְתַלְמוּד תּוֹרָה.

שבת קכז.
אֵלּוּ דְבָרִים שֶׁאָדָם אוֹכֵל פֵּרוֹתֵיהֶם בָּעוֹלָם הַזֶּה
וְהַקֶּרֶן קַיֶּמֶת לוֹ לָעוֹלָם הַבָּא, וְאֵלּוּ הֵן
כִּבּוּד אָב וָאֵם, וּגְמִילוּת חֲסָדִים
וְהַשְׁכָּמַת בֵּית הַמִּדְרָשׁ שַׁחֲרִית וְעַרְבִית
וְהַכְנָסַת אוֹרְחִים, וּבִקּוּר חוֹלִים
וְהַכְנָסַת כַּלָּה, וּלְוָיַת הַמֵּת
וְעִיּוּן תְּפִלָּה
וַהֲבָאַת שָׁלוֹם בֵּין אָדָם לַחֲבֵרוֹ
וְתַלְמוּד תּוֹרָה כְּנֶגֶד כֻּלָּם.

Some say:

תהלים קיא
רֵאשִׁית חָכְמָה יִרְאַת יהוה, שֵׂכֶל טוֹב לְכָל־עֹשֵׂיהֶם, תְּהִלָּתוֹ עֹמֶדֶת לָעַד:
דברים לג
תּוֹרָה צִוָּה־לָנוּ מֹשֶׁה, מוֹרָשָׁה קְהִלַּת יַעֲקֹב:
משלי א
שְׁמַע בְּנִי מוּסַר אָבִיךָ וְאַל־תִּטֹּשׁ תּוֹרַת אִמֶּךָ:
תּוֹרָה תְּהֵא אֱמוּנָתִי, וְאֵל שַׁדַּי בְּעֶזְרָתִי.
בָּרוּךְ שֵׁם כְּבוֹד מַלְכוּתוֹ לְעוֹלָם וָעֶד.

יְבָרֶכְךָ יהוה *May the* L*ORD* *bless you.* According to the sages (*Kiddushin* 30a), one should divide one's study time into three: (1) *Mikra*, study of the written Torah; (2) *Mishna*, study of the Mishna, primary text of the Oral Torah; (3) *Talmud*, that is, either the Babylonian or Jerusalem Talmud or other parts of the rabbinic literature dedicated to explaining the logic of the Oral Law (Maimonides, Laws of Torah Study 1:11).

TALLIT

Say the following meditation before putting on the tallit. Meditations before the fulfillment of mitzvot are to ensure that we do so with the requisite intention (kavana). This particularly applies to mitzvot whose purpose is to induce in us certain states of mind, as is the case with tallit and tefillin, both of which are external symbols of inward commitment to the life of observance of the mitzvot.

בָּרְכִי נַפְשִׁי Bless the LORD, my soul. LORD, my God, You are very great, *Ps. 104*
clothed in majesty and splendor, wrapped in a robe of light, spreading out the heavens like a tent.

Some say:

For the sake of the unification of the Holy One, blessed be He, and His Divine Presence, in reverence and love, to unify the name *Yod-Heh* with *Vav-Heh* in perfect unity in the name of all Israel.

I am about to wrap myself in this tasseled garment (tallit). So may my soul, my 248 limbs and 365 sinews be wrapped in the light of the tassel (*hatzitzit*) which amounts to 613 [commandments]. And just as I cover myself with a tasseled garment in this world, so may I be worthy of rabbinical dress and a fine garment in the World to Come in the Garden of Eden. Through the commandment of tassels may my life's-breath, spirit, soul and prayer be delivered from external impediments, and may the tallit spread its wings over them like an eagle stirring up its nest, hovering over its young. May the commandment of the tasseled garment be considered before the Holy One, blessed be He, as if I had fulfilled it in all its specifics, details and intentions, as well as the 613 commandments dependent on it, Amen, Selah. *Deut. 32*

Before wrapping oneself in the tallit, say:

בָּרוּךְ Blessed are You, LORD our God, King of the Universe,
who has made us holy through His commandments,
and has commanded us to wrap ourselves in the tasseled garment.

According to the Shela (R. Isaiah Horowitz), one should say these verses after wrapping oneself in the tallit:

מַה־יָּקָר How precious is Your loving-kindness, O God, and the children of men find refuge under the shadow of Your wings. They are filled with the rich plenty of Your House. You give them drink from Your river of delights. For with You is the fountain of life; in Your light, we see light. Continue Your loving-kindness to those who know You, and Your righteousness to the upright in heart. *Ps. 36*

According to Ashkenazi custom, on Ḥol HaMo'ed one puts on tefillin at this point. In some communities, tefillin are not worn on Ḥol HaMo'ed at all. *See commentary on page 599.*

Wrapping oneself in a tallit to pray is already mentioned in the Talmud (*Rosh HaShana* 17b). It symbolizes the idea of being enveloped by holiness. It is said that God "wraps Himself in light as with a garment" (Ps. 104:2). To be wrapped and robed in holiness as we begin to pray is a momentous way of sensing the closeness of God, who bathes the universe in light if we have eyes to see it or a heart to feel it.

עטיפת טלית

Say the following meditation before putting on the טלית. Meditations before the fulfillment of מצוות are to ensure that we do so with the requisite intention (כוונה). This particularly applies to מצוות whose purpose is to induce in us certain states of mind, as is the case with טלית and תפילין, both of which are external symbols of inward commitment to the life of observance of the מצוות.

בָּרְכִי נַפְשִׁי אֶת־יהוה, יהוה אֱלֹהַי גָּדַלְתָּ מְּאֹד, הוֹד וְהָדָר לָבָשְׁתָּ: תהלים קד
עֹטֶה־אוֹר כַּשַּׂלְמָה, נוֹטֶה שָׁמַיִם כַּיְרִיעָה:

Some say:

לְשֵׁם יִחוּד קֻדְשָׁא בְּרִיךְ הוּא וּשְׁכִינְתֵּהּ בִּדְחִילוּ וּרְחִימוּ, לְיַחֵד שֵׁם י״ה בו״ה בְּיִחוּדָא שְׁלִים בְּשֵׁם כָּל יִשְׂרָאֵל.

הֲרֵינִי מִתְעַטֵּף בַּצִּיצִית. כֵּן תִּתְעַטֵּף נִשְׁמָתִי וּרְמַ״ח אֵבָרַי וּשְׁסָ״ה גִידַי בְּאוֹר הַצִּיצִית הָעוֹלָה תַּרְיַ״ג. וּכְשֵׁם שֶׁאֲנִי מִתְכַּסֶּה בְּטַלִּית בָּעוֹלָם הַזֶּה, כָּךְ אֶזְכֶּה לַחֲלוּקָא דְרַבָּנָן וּלְטַלִּית נָאָה לָעוֹלָם הַבָּא בְּגַן עֵדֶן. וְעַל יְדֵי מִצְוַת צִיצִית תִּנָּצֵל נַפְשִׁי רוּחִי וְנִשְׁמָתִי וּתְפִלָּתִי מִן הַחִיצוֹנִים. וְהַטַּלִּית תִּפְרֹשׂ כְּנָפֶיהָ עֲלֵיהֶם וְתַצִּילֵם, כְּנֶשֶׁר יָעִיר קִנּוֹ, עַל גּוֹזָלָיו דברים לב
יְרַחֵף: וּתְהֵא חֲשׁוּבָה מִצְוַת צִיצִית לִפְנֵי הַקָּדוֹשׁ בָּרוּךְ הוּא, כְּאִלּוּ קִיַּמְתִּיהָ בְּכָל פְּרָטֶיהָ וְדִקְדּוּקֶיהָ וְכַוָּנוֹתֶיהָ וְתַרְיַ״ג מִצְוֹת הַתְּלוּיוֹת בָּהּ, אָמֵן סֶלָה.

Before wrapping oneself in the טלית, say:

בָּרוּךְ אַתָּה יהוה אֱלֹהֵינוּ מֶלֶךְ הָעוֹלָם
אֲשֶׁר קִדְּשָׁנוּ בְּמִצְוֹתָיו וְצִוָּנוּ לְהִתְעַטֵּף בַּצִּיצִית.

According to the Shela (R. Isaiah Horowitz), one should say these verses after wrapping oneself in the טלית:

מַה־יָּקָר חַסְדְּךָ אֱלֹהִים, וּבְנֵי אָדָם בְּצֵל כְּנָפֶיךָ יֶחֱסָיוּן: יִרְוְיֻן מִדֶּשֶׁן בֵּיתֶךָ, תהלים לו
וְנַחַל עֲדָנֶיךָ תַשְׁקֵם: כִּי־עִמְּךָ מְקוֹר חַיִּים, בְּאוֹרְךָ נִרְאֶה־אוֹר: מְשֹׁךְ חַסְדְּךָ
לְיֹדְעֶיךָ, וְצִדְקָתְךָ לְיִשְׁרֵי־לֵב:

According to Ashkenazi custom, on חול המועד one puts on תפילין at this point. In some communities, תפילין are not worn on חול המועד at all. See commentary on page 599.

TALLIT

Tallit, which means a cloak or gown, is one of the ways in which we fulfill the mitzva of *tzitzit*, placing tassels on the corners of our garments to recall us constantly to our vocation: "Thus you will be reminded to keep all My commands, and be holy to your God" (Num. 15:39). In the course of time two different fringed garments were worn: the *tallit*, worn as a mantle during prayer, *over* our clothes; and the *tallit katan*, worn as an undergarment *beneath* our outer clothes.

PREPARATION FOR PRAYER

On entering the synagogue:

HOW GOODLY *Num. 24*

are your tents, Jacob, your dwelling places, Israel.
As for me, *Ps. 5*
in Your great loving-kindness,
I will come into Your House.
I will bow down to Your holy Temple
in awe of You.
LORD, I love the habitation of Your House, *Ps. 26*
the place where Your glory dwells.

As for me,
I will bow in worship;
I will bend the knee
before the LORD my Maker.

As for me, *Ps. 69*
may my prayer come to You, LORD,
at a time of favor.
God, in Your great loving-kindness,
answer me with Your faithful salvation.

הכנה לתפילה

On entering the בית כנסת:

במדבר כד

מַה־טֹּבוּ

אֹהָלֶיךָ יַעֲקֹב, מִשְׁכְּנֹתֶיךָ יִשְׂרָאֵל:

תהלים ה וַאֲנִי בְּרֹב חַסְדְּךָ אָבוֹא בֵיתֶךָ

אֶשְׁתַּחֲוֶה אֶל־הֵיכַל־קָדְשְׁךָ

בְּיִרְאָתֶךָ:

תהלים כו יהוה אָהַבְתִּי מְעוֹן בֵּיתֶךָ

וּמְקוֹם מִשְׁכַּן כְּבוֹדֶךָ:

וַאֲנִי אֶשְׁתַּחֲוֶה

וְאֶכְרָעָה

אֶבְרְכָה לִפְנֵי יהוה עֹשִׂי.

תהלים סט וַאֲנִי תְפִלָּתִי־לְךָ יהוה

עֵת רָצוֹן

אֱלֹהִים בְּרָב־חַסְדֶּךָ

עֲנֵנִי בֶּאֱמֶת יִשְׁעֶךָ:

The following poems, on this page and the next, both from the Middle Ages, are summary statements of Jewish faith, orienting us to the spiritual contours of the world that we actualize in the mind by the act of prayer.

LORD OF THE UNIVERSE,
who reigned before the birth of any thing –

When by His will all things were made
then was His name proclaimed King.

And when all things shall cease to be
He alone will reign in awe.

He was, He is, and He shall be
glorious for evermore.

He is One, there is none else,
alone, unique, beyond compare;

Without beginning, without end,
His might, His rule are everywhere.

He is my God; my Redeemer lives.
He is the Rock on whom I rely –

My banner and my safe retreat,
my cup, my portion when I cry.

Into His hand my soul I place,
when I awake and when I sleep.

The LORD is with me, I shall not fear;
body and soul from harm will He keep.

The following poems, on this page and the next, both from the Middle Ages, are summary statements of Jewish faith, orienting us to the spiritual contours of the world that we actualize in the mind by the act of prayer.

אֲדוֹן עוֹלָם

אֲשֶׁר מָלַךְ בְּטֶרֶם כָּל־יְצִיר נִבְרָא.
לְעֵת נַעֲשָׂה בְחֶפְצוֹ כֹּל אֲזַי מֶלֶךְ שְׁמוֹ נִקְרָא.
וְאַחֲרֵי כִּכְלוֹת הַכֹּל לְבַדּוֹ יִמְלֹךְ נוֹרָא.
וְהוּא הָיָה וְהוּא הֹוֶה וְהוּא יִהְיֶה בְּתִפְאָרָה.
וְהוּא אֶחָד וְאֵין שֵׁנִי לְהַמְשִׁיל לוֹ לְהַחְבִּירָה.
בְּלִי רֵאשִׁית בְּלִי תַכְלִית וְלוֹ הָעֹז וְהַמִּשְׂרָה.
וְהוּא אֵלִי וְחַי גּוֹאֲלִי וְצוּר חֶבְלִי בְּעֵת צָרָה.
וְהוּא נִסִּי וּמָנוֹס לִי מְנָת כּוֹסִי בְּיוֹם אֶקְרָא.
בְּיָדוֹ אַפְקִיד רוּחִי בְּעֵת אִישַׁן וְאָעִירָה.
וְעִם רוּחִי גְּוִיָּתִי יהוה לִי וְלֹא אִירָא.

GREAT

is the living God and praised.
He exists, and His existence is beyond time.

He is One, and there is no unity like His.
Unfathomable, His Oneness is infinite.

He has neither bodily form nor substance;
His holiness is beyond compare.

He preceded all that was created.
He was first: there was no beginning to His beginning.

Behold He is Master of the Universe; and every creature
shows His greatness and majesty.

The rich flow of His prophecy He gave
to His treasured people in whom He gloried.

Never in Israel has there arisen another like Moses,
a prophet who beheld God's image.

God gave His people a Torah of truth
by the hand of His prophet, most faithful of His House.

God will not alter or change His law
for any other, for eternity.

He sees and knows our secret thoughts;
as soon as something is begun, He foresees its end.

He rewards people with loving-kindness according to their deeds;
He punishes the wicked according to his wickedness.

At the end of days He will send our Messiah
to redeem those who await His final salvation.

God will revive the dead in His great loving-kindness.
Blessed for evermore is His glorious name!

יִגְדַּל

אֱלֹהִים חַי וְיִשְׁתַּבַּח, נִמְצָא וְאֵין עֵת אֶל מְצִיאוּתוֹ.

אֶחָד וְאֵין יָחִיד כְּיִחוּדוֹ, נֶעְלָם וְגַם אֵין סוֹף לְאַחְדוּתוֹ.

אֵין לוֹ דְּמוּת הַגּוּף וְאֵינוֹ גוּף, לֹא נַעֲרֹךְ אֵלָיו קְדֻשָּׁתוֹ.

קַדְמוֹן לְכָל דָּבָר אֲשֶׁר נִבְרָא, רִאשׁוֹן וְאֵין רֵאשִׁית לְרֵאשִׁיתוֹ.

הִנּוֹ אֲדוֹן עוֹלָם, וְכָל נוֹצָר יוֹרֶה גְדֻלָּתוֹ וּמַלְכוּתוֹ.

שֶׁפַע נְבוּאָתוֹ נְתָנוֹ אֶל־אַנְשֵׁי סְגֻלָּתוֹ וְתִפְאַרְתּוֹ.

לֹא קָם בְּיִשְׂרָאֵל כְּמֹשֶׁה עוֹד נָבִיא וּמַבִּיט אֶת תְּמוּנָתוֹ.

תּוֹרַת אֱמֶת נָתַן לְעַמּוֹ אֵל עַל יַד נְבִיאוֹ נֶאֱמַן בֵּיתוֹ.

לֹא יַחֲלִיף הָאֵל וְלֹא יָמִיר דָּתוֹ לְעוֹלָמִים לְזוּלָתוֹ.

צוֹפֶה וְיוֹדֵעַ סְתָרֵינוּ, מַבִּיט לְסוֹף דָּבָר בְּקַדְמָתוֹ.

גּוֹמֵל לְאִישׁ חֶסֶד כְּמִפְעָלוֹ, נוֹתֵן לְרָשָׁע רָע כְּרִשְׁעָתוֹ.

יִשְׁלַח לְקֵץ יָמִין מְשִׁיחֵנוּ לִפְדּוֹת מְחַכֵּי קֵץ יְשׁוּעָתוֹ.

מֵתִים יְחַיֶּה אֵל בְּרֹב חַסְדּוֹ, בָּרוּךְ עֲדֵי עַד שֵׁם תְּהִלָּתוֹ.

MORNING BLESSINGS

The following blessings are said aloud by the Leader, but each individual should say them quietly as well. It is our custom to say them standing.

בָּרוּךְ Blessed are You, Lord our God,
King of the Universe,
who gives the heart understanding
to distinguish day from night.

Blessed are You, Lord our God,
King of the Universe,
who has not made me a heathen.

Blessed are You, Lord our God,
King of the Universe,
who has not made me a slave.

Blessed are You, Lord our God,
King of the Universe,
men: who has not made me a woman.
women: who has made me according to His will.

Blessed are You, Lord our God,
King of the Universe,
who gives sight to the blind.

שֶׁלֹּא עָשַׂנִי גּוֹי...עָבֶד *Who has not made me a heathen ... a slave.* We each have our part to play in the divine economy. We thank God for ours, for the privilege of being part of "a kingdom of priests and a holy nation" (Ex. 19:6).

פּוֹקֵחַ עִוְרִים *Gives sight to the blind ... etc.* A series of blessings originally said at home, later made part of the synagogue service. They were initially said to accompany the various actions involved in waking and getting up – opening our eyes, putting on clothes, stretching our limbs, setting foot on the ground and so on. Descartes said: I *think* therefore I am. A Jew says: I *thank*

ברכות השחר

The following blessings are said aloud by the שליח ציבור*, but each individual should say them quietly as well. It is our custom to say them standing.*

בָּרוּךְ אַתָּה יהוה אֱלֹהֵינוּ מֶלֶךְ הָעוֹלָם
אֲשֶׁר נָתַן לַשֶּׂכְוִי בִינָה
לְהַבְחִין בֵּין יוֹם וּבֵין לָיְלָה.

בָּרוּךְ אַתָּה יהוה אֱלֹהֵינוּ מֶלֶךְ הָעוֹלָם
שֶׁלֹּא עָשַׂנִי גּוֹי.

בָּרוּךְ אַתָּה יהוה אֱלֹהֵינוּ מֶלֶךְ הָעוֹלָם
שֶׁלֹּא עָשַׂנִי עָבֶד.

בָּרוּךְ אַתָּה יהוה אֱלֹהֵינוּ מֶלֶךְ הָעוֹלָם
men שֶׁלֹּא עָשַׂנִי אִשָּׁה. / *women* שֶׁעָשַׂנִי כִּרְצוֹנוֹ.

בָּרוּךְ אַתָּה יהוה אֱלֹהֵינוּ מֶלֶךְ הָעוֹלָם
פּוֹקֵחַ עִוְרִים.

MORNING BLESSINGS
A series of thanksgivings, designed to open our eyes to the wonders of the world and of existence. The religious sense is not so much a matter of seeing new things but of seeing things anew.

אֲשֶׁר נָתַן לַשֶּׂכְוִי בִינָה *Who gives the heart understanding.* The translation follows the view of Rabbeinu Asher (Rosh). Rashi and Abudarham translate it as "Who gives the cockerel understanding." The blessing, which tells us that understanding begins in the ability to make distinctions, refers to the first distinction mentioned in the Torah, when God divided darkness from light, creating night and day.

Blessed are You, LORD our God,
King of the Universe,
who clothes the naked.

Blessed are You, LORD our God,
King of the Universe,
who sets captives free.

Blessed are You, LORD our God,
King of the Universe,
who raises those bowed down.

Blessed are You, LORD our God,
King of the Universe,
who spreads the earth above the waters.

Blessed are You, LORD our God,
King of the Universe,
who has provided me with all I need.

Blessed are You, LORD our God,
King of the Universe,
who makes firm the steps of man.

Blessed are You, LORD our God,
King of the Universe,
who girds Israel with strength.

Blessed are You, LORD our God,
King of the Universe,
who crowns Israel with glory.

Blessed are You, LORD our God,
King of the Universe,
who gives strength to the weary.

בָּרוּךְ אַתָּה יהוה אֱלֹהֵינוּ מֶלֶךְ הָעוֹלָם
מַלְבִּישׁ עֲרֻמִּים.

בָּרוּךְ אַתָּה יהוה אֱלֹהֵינוּ מֶלֶךְ הָעוֹלָם
מַתִּיר אֲסוּרִים.

בָּרוּךְ אַתָּה יהוה אֱלֹהֵינוּ מֶלֶךְ הָעוֹלָם
זוֹקֵף כְּפוּפִים.

בָּרוּךְ אַתָּה יהוה אֱלֹהֵינוּ מֶלֶךְ הָעוֹלָם
רוֹקַע הָאָרֶץ עַל הַמָּיִם.

בָּרוּךְ אַתָּה יהוה אֱלֹהֵינוּ מֶלֶךְ הָעוֹלָם
שֶׁעָשָׂה לִי כָּל צָרְכִּי.

בָּרוּךְ אַתָּה יהוה אֱלֹהֵינוּ מֶלֶךְ הָעוֹלָם
הַמֵּכִין מִצְעֲדֵי גָבֶר.

בָּרוּךְ אַתָּה יהוה אֱלֹהֵינוּ מֶלֶךְ הָעוֹלָם
אוֹזֵר יִשְׂרָאֵל בִּגְבוּרָה.

בָּרוּךְ אַתָּה יהוה אֱלֹהֵינוּ מֶלֶךְ הָעוֹלָם
עוֹטֵר יִשְׂרָאֵל בְּתִפְאָרָה.

בָּרוּךְ אַתָּה יהוה אֱלֹהֵינוּ מֶלֶךְ הָעוֹלָם
הַנּוֹתֵן לַיָּעֵף כֹּחַ.

---

therefore I am. To stand consciously in the presence of God involves an attitude of gratitude.

בָּרוּךְ Blessed are You, Lord our God, King of the Universe,
who removes sleep from my eyes
and slumber from my eyelids.
And may it be Your will, Lord our God
and God of our ancestors,
to accustom us to Your Torah,
and make us attached to Your commandments.
Lead us not into error, transgression,
iniquity, temptation or disgrace.
Do not let the evil instinct dominate us.
Keep us far from a bad man and a bad companion.
Help us attach ourselves
to the good instinct and to good deeds
and bend our instincts to be subservient to You.
Grant us, this day and every day,
grace, loving-kindness and compassion in Your eyes
and in the eyes of all who see us,
and bestow loving-kindness upon us.
Blessed are You, Lord,
who bestows loving-kindness on His people Israel.

יְהִי רָצוֹן May it be Your will, Lord my God and God of my ancestors, to save me today and every day, from the arrogant and from arrogance itself, from a bad man, a bad friend, a bad neighbor, a bad mishap, a destructive adversary, a harsh trial and a harsh opponent, whether or not he is a son of the covenant. *Berakhot 16b*

---

to act badly if we do so without deliberation and foresight, in the heat of the moment. We are also social animals. Therefore we are influenced by our environment. So we pray to be protected from bad social influences: not only from bad companions but also, in a secular age, from the ambient culture.

בָּרוּךְ אַתָּה יהוה אֱלֹהֵינוּ מֶלֶךְ הָעוֹלָם
הַמַּעֲבִיר שֵׁנָה מֵעֵינַי וּתְנוּמָה מֵעַפְעַפָּי.
וִיהִי רָצוֹן מִלְּפָנֶיךָ יהוה אֱלֹהֵינוּ וֵאלֹהֵי אֲבוֹתֵינוּ
שֶׁתַּרְגִּילֵנוּ בְּתוֹרָתֶךָ
וְדַבְּקֵנוּ בְּמִצְוֹתֶיךָ
וְאַל תְּבִיאֵנוּ לֹא לִידֵי חֵטְא
וְלֹא לִידֵי עֲבֵרָה וְעָוֹן
וְלֹא לִידֵי נִסָּיוֹן וְלֹא לִידֵי בִזָּיוֹן
וְאַל תַּשְׁלֶט בָּנוּ יֵצֶר הָרָע
וְהַרְחִיקֵנוּ מֵאָדָם רָע וּמֵחָבֵר רָע
וְדַבְּקֵנוּ בְּיֵצֶר הַטּוֹב וּבְמַעֲשִׂים טוֹבִים
וְכֹף אֶת יִצְרֵנוּ לְהִשְׁתַּעְבֶּד לָךְ
וּתְנֵנוּ הַיּוֹם וּבְכָל יוֹם לְחֵן וּלְחֶסֶד וּלְרַחֲמִים
בְּעֵינֶיךָ, וּבְעֵינֵי כָל רוֹאֵינוּ
וְתִגְמְלֵנוּ חֲסָדִים טוֹבִים.
בָּרוּךְ אַתָּה יהוה
גּוֹמֵל חֲסָדִים טוֹבִים לְעַמּוֹ יִשְׂרָאֵל.

יְהִי רָצוֹן מִלְּפָנֶיךָ יהוה אֱלֹהַי וֵאלֹהֵי אֲבוֹתַי, שֶׁתַּצִּילֵנִי הַיּוֹם וּבְכָל יוֹם ברכות טז:
מֵעַזֵּי פָנִים וּמֵעַזּוּת פָּנִים, מֵאָדָם רָע, וּמֵחָבֵר רָע, וּמִשָּׁכֵן רָע, וּמִפֶּגַע רָע,
וּמִשָּׂטָן הַמַּשְׁחִית, מִדִּין קָשֶׁה, וּמִבַּעַל דִּין קָשֶׁה בֵּין שֶׁהוּא בֶן בְּרִית וּבֵין
שֶׁאֵינוֹ בֶן בְּרִית.

וִיהִי רָצוֹן *May it be Your will.* We ask for God's help in leading a holy and moral life. We need that help. We have primal instincts that can lead us

THE BINDING OF ISAAC

On the basis of Jewish mystical tradition, some have the custom of saying daily the biblical passage recounting the Binding of Isaac, the supreme trial of faith in which Abraham demonstrated his love of God above all other loves. On Shabbat and Yom Tov, most omit the introductory and concluding prayers, "Our God and God of our ancestors" and "Master of the Universe." Others skip to "A person should" on page 284.

Our God and God of our ancestors, remember us with a favorable memory, and recall us with a remembrance of salvation and compassion from the highest of high heavens. Remember, LORD our God, on our behalf, the love of the ancients, Abraham, Isaac and Yisrael Your servants; the covenant, the loving-kindness, and the oath You swore to Abraham our father on Mount Moriah, and the Binding, when he bound Isaac his son on the altar, as is written in Your Torah:

It happened after these things that God tested Abraham. He said to him, "Abraham!" "Here I am," he replied. He said, "Take your son, your only son, Isaac, whom you love, and go to the land of Moriah and offer him there as a burnt-offering on one of the mountains which I shall say to you." Early the next morning Abraham rose and saddled his donkey and took his two lads with him, and Isaac his son, and he cut wood for the burnt-offering, and he set out for the place of which God had told him. On the third day Abraham looked up and saw the place from afar. Abraham said to his lads, "Stay here with the donkey while I and the boy go on ahead. We will worship and we will return to you." Abraham took the wood for the burnt-offering and placed it on Isaac his son, and he took in his hand the fire and the knife, and the two of them went together. Isaac said to Abraham his father, "Father?" and he said "Here I am, my son." And he said, "Here are the fire and the wood, but where is the sheep for the burnt-offering?" Abraham said, "God will see to the sheep for the burnt-offering, my son." And the two *Gen. 22*

---

contradiction. On the one hand God had told him that it would be Isaac and Isaac's children through whom the covenant would continue and become eternal (Gen. 17:19). On the other, God had now commanded him to take

פרשת העקדה

On the basis of Jewish mystical tradition, some have the custom of saying daily the biblical passage recounting the Binding of Isaac, the supreme trial of faith in which Abraham demonstrated his love of God above all other loves. On שבת *and* יום טוב*, most omit the introductory and concluding prayers,* אֱלֹהֵינוּ וֵאלֹהֵי אֲבוֹתֵינוּ *and* רִבּוֹנוֹ שֶׁל עוֹלָם*. Others skip to* לְעוֹלָם יְהֵא אָדָם *on page 285.*

אֱלֹהֵינוּ וֵאלֹהֵי אֲבוֹתֵינוּ, זׇכְרֵנוּ בְּזִכְרוֹן טוֹב לְפָנֶיךָ, וּפׇקְדֵנוּ בִּפְקֻדַּת יְשׁוּעָה וְרַחֲמִים מִשְּׁמֵי שְׁמֵי קֶדֶם, וּזְכׇר לָנוּ יהוה אֱלֹהֵינוּ, אַהֲבַת הַקַּדְמוֹנִים אַבְרָהָם יִצְחָק וְיִשְׂרָאֵל עֲבָדֶיךָ, אֶת הַבְּרִית וְאֶת הַחֶסֶד וְאֶת הַשְּׁבוּעָה שֶׁנִּשְׁבַּעְתָּ לְאַבְרָהָם אָבִינוּ בְּהַר הַמּוֹרִיָּה, וְאֶת הָעֲקֵדָה שֶׁעָקַד אֶת יִצְחָק בְּנוֹ עַל גַּבֵּי הַמִּזְבֵּחַ, כַּכָּתוּב בְּתוֹרָתֶךָ:

וַיְהִי אַחַר הַדְּבָרִים הָאֵלֶּה, וְהָאֱלֹהִים נִסָּה אֶת־אַבְרָהָם, וַיֹּאמֶר בראשית כב
אֵלָיו אַבְרָהָם, וַיֹּאמֶר הִנֵּנִי: וַיֹּאמֶר קַח־נָא אֶת־בִּנְךָ אֶת־יְחִידְךָ
אֲשֶׁר־אָהַבְתָּ, אֶת־יִצְחָק, וְלֶךְ־לְךָ אֶל־אֶרֶץ הַמֹּרִיָּה, וְהַעֲלֵהוּ
שָׁם לְעֹלָה עַל אַחַד הֶהָרִים אֲשֶׁר אֹמַר אֵלֶיךָ: וַיַּשְׁכֵּם אַבְרָהָם
בַּבֹּקֶר, וַיַּחֲבֹשׁ אֶת־חֲמֹרוֹ, וַיִּקַּח אֶת־שְׁנֵי נְעָרָיו אִתּוֹ וְאֵת יִצְחָק בְּנוֹ,
וַיְבַקַּע עֲצֵי עֹלָה, וַיָּקׇם וַיֵּלֶךְ אֶל־הַמָּקוֹם אֲשֶׁר־אָמַר־לוֹ הָאֱלֹהִים:
בַּיּוֹם הַשְּׁלִישִׁי וַיִּשָּׂא אַבְרָהָם אֶת־עֵינָיו וַיַּרְא אֶת־הַמָּקוֹם מֵרָחֹק:
וַיֹּאמֶר אַבְרָהָם אֶל־נְעָרָיו, שְׁבוּ־לָכֶם פֹּה עִם־הַחֲמוֹר, וַאֲנִי וְהַנַּעַר
נֵלְכָה עַד־כֹּה, וְנִשְׁתַּחֲוֶה וְנָשׁוּבָה אֲלֵיכֶם: וַיִּקַּח אַבְרָהָם אֶת־עֲצֵי
הָעֹלָה וַיָּשֶׂם עַל־יִצְחָק בְּנוֹ, וַיִּקַּח בְּיָדוֹ אֶת־הָאֵשׁ וְאֶת־הַמַּאֲכֶלֶת,
וַיֵּלְכוּ שְׁנֵיהֶם יַחְדָּו: וַיֹּאמֶר יִצְחָק אֶל־אַבְרָהָם אָבִיו, וַיֹּאמֶר אָבִי,
וַיֹּאמֶר הִנֶּנִּי בְנִי, וַיֹּאמֶר, הִנֵּה הָאֵשׁ וְהָעֵצִים, וְאַיֵּה הַשֶּׂה לְעֹלָה:
וַיֹּאמֶר אַבְרָהָם, אֱלֹהִים יִרְאֶה־לּוֹ הַשֶּׂה לְעֹלָה, בְּנִי, וַיֵּלְכוּ שְׁנֵיהֶם

THE BINDING OF ISAAC

This passage, said daily by those whose liturgy follows the Jewish mystical tradition, evokes the supreme moment of sacrifice by the grandfather of Jewish faith, Abraham. Abraham found himself caught within a seeming

of them went together. They came to the place God had told him about, and Abraham built there an altar and arranged the wood and bound Isaac his son and laid him on the altar on top of the wood. He reached out his hand and took the knife to slay his son. Then an angel of the LORD called out to him from heaven, "Abraham! Abraham!" He said, "Here I am." He said, "Do not reach out your hand against the boy; do not do anything to him, for now I know that you fear God, because you have not held back your son, your only son, from Me." Abraham looked up and there he saw a ram caught in a thicket by its horns, and Abraham went and took the ram and offered it as a burnt-offering instead of his son. Abraham called that place "The LORD will see," as is said to this day, "On the mountain of the LORD He will be seen." The angel of the LORD called to Abraham a second time from heaven, and said, "By Myself I swear, declares the LORD, that because you have done this and have not held back your son, your only son, I will greatly bless you and greatly multiply your descendants, as the stars of heaven and the sand of the seashore, and your descendants shall take possession of the gates of their enemies. Through your descendants, all the nations of the earth will be blessed, because you have heeded My voice." Then Abraham returned to his lads, and they rose and went together to Beersheba, and Abraham stayed in Beersheba.

Most omit this passage on Shabbat and Yom Tov.

Master of the Universe, just as Abraham our father suppressed his compassion to do Your will wholeheartedly, so may Your compassion suppress Your anger from us and may Your compassion prevail over Your other attributes. Deal with us, LORD our God, with the attributes of loving-kindness and compassion, and in Your great goodness may Your anger be turned away from Your people, Your city, Your land and Your inheritance. Fulfill in us, LORD our God, the promise You made in Your Torah through the hand of Moses Your servant, as it is said: "I will remember My covenant with Jacob, and also My *Lev. 26*
covenant with Isaac, and also My covenant with Abraham I will remember, and the land I will remember."

יַחְדָּו׃ וַיָּבֹאוּ אֶל־הַמָּקוֹם אֲשֶׁר אָמַר־לוֹ הָאֱלֹהִים, וַיִּבֶן שָׁם אַבְרָהָם
אֶת־הַמִּזְבֵּחַ וַיַּעֲרֹךְ אֶת־הָעֵצִים, וַיַּעֲקֹד אֶת־יִצְחָק בְּנוֹ, וַיָּשֶׂם אֹתוֹ
עַל־הַמִּזְבֵּחַ מִמַּעַל לָעֵצִים׃ וַיִּשְׁלַח אַבְרָהָם אֶת־יָדוֹ, וַיִּקַּח אֶת־
הַמַּאֲכֶלֶת, לִשְׁחֹט אֶת־בְּנוֹ׃ וַיִּקְרָא אֵלָיו מַלְאַךְ יהוה מִן־הַשָּׁמַיִם,
וַיֹּאמֶר אַבְרָהָם אַבְרָהָם, וַיֹּאמֶר הִנֵּנִי׃ וַיֹּאמֶר אַל־תִּשְׁלַח יָדְךָ אֶל־
הַנַּעַר, וְאַל־תַּעַשׂ לוֹ מְאוּמָה, כִּי עַתָּה יָדַעְתִּי כִּי־יְרֵא אֱלֹהִים אַתָּה,
וְלֹא חָשַׂכְתָּ אֶת־בִּנְךָ אֶת־יְחִידְךָ מִמֶּנִּי׃ וַיִּשָּׂא אַבְרָהָם אֶת־עֵינָיו,
וַיַּרְא וְהִנֵּה־אַיִל, אַחַר נֶאֱחַז בַּסְּבַךְ בְּקַרְנָיו, וַיֵּלֶךְ אַבְרָהָם וַיִּקַּח אֶת־
הָאַיִל, וַיַּעֲלֵהוּ לְעֹלָה תַּחַת בְּנוֹ׃ וַיִּקְרָא אַבְרָהָם שֵׁם־הַמָּקוֹם הַהוּא
יהוה יִרְאֶה, אֲשֶׁר יֵאָמֵר הַיּוֹם בְּהַר יהוה יֵרָאֶה׃ וַיִּקְרָא מַלְאַךְ יהוה
אֶל־אַבְרָהָם שֵׁנִית מִן־הַשָּׁמָיִם׃ וַיֹּאמֶר, בִּי נִשְׁבַּעְתִּי נְאֻם־יהוה, כִּי
יַעַן אֲשֶׁר עָשִׂיתָ אֶת־הַדָּבָר הַזֶּה, וְלֹא חָשַׂכְתָּ אֶת־בִּנְךָ אֶת־יְחִידֶךָ׃
כִּי־בָרֵךְ אֲבָרֶכְךָ, וְהַרְבָּה אַרְבֶּה אֶת־זַרְעֲךָ כְּכוֹכְבֵי הַשָּׁמַיִם, וְכַחוֹל
אֲשֶׁר עַל־שְׂפַת הַיָּם, וְיִרַשׁ זַרְעֲךָ אֵת שַׁעַר אֹיְבָיו׃ וְהִתְבָּרְכוּ בְזַרְעֲךָ
כֹּל גּוֹיֵי הָאָרֶץ, עֵקֶב אֲשֶׁר שָׁמַעְתָּ בְּקֹלִי׃ וַיָּשָׁב אַבְרָהָם אֶל־נְעָרָיו,
וַיָּקֻמוּ וַיֵּלְכוּ יַחְדָּו אֶל־בְּאֵר שָׁבַע, וַיֵּשֶׁב אַבְרָהָם בִּבְאֵר שָׁבַע׃

Most omit this passage on שבת and יום טוב.

רִבּוֹנוֹ שֶׁל עוֹלָם, כְּמוֹ שֶׁכָּבַשׁ אַבְרָהָם אָבִינוּ אֶת רַחֲמָיו לַעֲשׂוֹת רְצוֹנְךָ בְּלֵבָב
שָׁלֵם, כֵּן יִכְבְּשׁוּ רַחֲמֶיךָ אֶת כַּעַסְךָ מֵעָלֵינוּ וְיָגֹלּוּ רַחֲמֶיךָ עַל מִדּוֹתֶיךָ. וְתִתְנַהֵג
עִמָּנוּ יהוה אֱלֹהֵינוּ בְּמִדַּת הַחֶסֶד וּבְמִדַּת הָרַחֲמִים, וּבְטוּבְךָ הַגָּדוֹל יָשׁוּב
חֲרוֹן אַפְּךָ מֵעַמְּךָ וּמֵעִירְךָ וּמֵאַרְצְךָ וּמִנַּחֲלָתֶךָ. וְקַיֶּם לָנוּ יהוה אֱלֹהֵינוּ אֶת
הַדָּבָר שֶׁהִבְטַחְתָּנוּ בְּתוֹרָתֶךָ עַל יְדֵי מֹשֶׁה עַבְדֶּךָ, כָּאָמוּר: וְזָכַרְתִּי אֶת־בְּרִיתִי ויקרא כו
יַעֲקוֹב וְאַף אֶת־בְּרִיתִי יִצְחָק, וְאַף אֶת־בְּרִיתִי אַבְרָהָם אֶזְכֹּר, וְהָאָרֶץ אֶזְכֹּר׃

Isaac and offer him as a sacrifice (Gen. 22:2). It was Abraham's willingness, not merely to sacrifice that which was most precious to him, but to live with the contradiction, in the faith that God would resolve it in the course of time, that made him the hero of faith and its role model through the centuries.

ACCEPTING THE SOVEREIGNTY OF HEAVEN

לְעוֹלָם A person should always be God-fearing, privately and publicly, acknowledging the truth and speaking it in his heart. He should rise early and say: *Tanna DeVei Eliyahu, ch. 21*

Master of all worlds,
not because of our righteousness *Dan. 9*
do we lay our pleas before You,
but because of Your great compassion.

What are we? What are our lives?
What is our loving-kindness? What is our righteousness?
What is our salvation? What is our strength?
What is our might? What shall we say before You,
Lord our God and God of our ancestors?
Are not all the mighty like nothing before You,
the men of renown as if they had never been,
the wise as if they know nothing,
and the understanding as if they lack intelligence?
For their many works are in vain,
and the days of their lives like a fleeting breath before You.
The pre-eminence of man over the animals is nothing, *Eccl. 3*
for all is but a fleeting breath.

---

among the multitudes," refers to the martyrdom of those who went to their deaths rather than renounce their faith. Martyrdom is called *Kiddush HaShem*, "sanctifying [God's] name."

רִבּוֹן כָּל הָעוֹלָמִים *Master of all worlds.* This passage expresses the paradox of the human condition in the presence of God. We know how small we are and how brief our lives.

הֶבֶל *Fleeting breath.* The Hebrew word *hevel* – the key word of the opening chapters of Ecclesiastes, from which this line is taken – has been translated as "vain, meaningless, empty, futile." However, it literally means "a short breath." It conveys a sense of the brevity and insubstantiality of life as a physical phenomenon. All that lives soon dies, and is as if it had never been.

קבלת עול מלכות שמים

לְעוֹלָם יְהֵא אָדָם יְרֵא שָׁמַיִם בְּסֵתֶר וּבְגָלוּי תנא דבי אליהו, פרק כא
וּמוֹדֶה עַל הָאֱמֶת, וְדוֹבֵר אֱמֶת בִּלְבָבוֹ
וְיַשְׁכֵּם וְיֹאמַר
רִבּוֹן כָּל הָעוֹלָמִים
לֹא עַל־צִדְקוֹתֵינוּ אֲנַחְנוּ מַפִּילִים תַּחֲנוּנֵינוּ לְפָנֶיךָ דניאל ט
כִּי עַל־רַחֲמֶיךָ הָרַבִּים:

מָה אָנוּ, מֶה חַיֵּינוּ, מֶה חַסְדֵּנוּ, מַה צִּדְקוֹתֵינוּ
מַה יְּשׁוּעָתֵנוּ, מַה כֹּחֵנוּ, מַה גְּבוּרָתֵנוּ
מַה נֹּאמַר לְפָנֶיךָ, יהוה אֱלֹהֵינוּ וֵאלֹהֵי אֲבוֹתֵינוּ
הֲלֹא כָּל הַגִּבּוֹרִים כְּאַיִן לְפָנֶיךָ
וְאַנְשֵׁי הַשֵּׁם כְּלֹא הָיוּ
וַחֲכָמִים כִּבְלִי מַדָּע, וּנְבוֹנִים כִּבְלִי הַשְׂכֵּל
כִּי רֹב מַעֲשֵׂיהֶם תֹּהוּ, וִימֵי חַיֵּיהֶם הֶבֶל לְפָנֶיךָ
וּמוֹתַר הָאָדָם מִן־הַבְּהֵמָה אָיִן קהלת ג
כִּי הַכֹּל הָבֶל:

ACCEPTING THE SOVEREIGNTY OF HEAVEN

לְעוֹלָם יְהֵא אָדָם *A person should always.* This whole section until "Who sanctifies His name among the multitudes" appears in the ninth-century Midrash, *Tanna DeVei Eliyahu* (ch. 21). Some believe that it dates from a period of persecution under the Persian ruler Yazdegerd II who, in 456 CE, forbade the observance of Shabbat and the reading of the Torah. Jews continued to practice their faith in secret, saying prayers at times and in ways that would not be detected by their persecutors. This explains the reference to fearing God "privately" and "speaking truth in the heart" (that is, the secret practice of Judaism) and the recitation here of the first lines of the *Shema*, which could not be said at the normal time. The final blessing, "Who sanctifies His name

אֲבָל Yet we are Your people, the children of Your covenant,
the children of Abraham, Your beloved,
to whom You made a promise on Mount Moriah;
the offspring of Isaac his only one who was bound on the altar;
the congregation of Jacob Your firstborn son
whom – because of the love with which You loved him
and the joy with which You rejoiced in him –
You called Yisrael and Yeshurun.

לְפִיכָךְ Therefore it is our duty
to thank You, and to praise, glorify, bless, sanctify
and give praise and thanks to Your name.
Happy are we, how good is our portion,
how lovely our fate, how beautiful our heritage.

▸ Happy are we who, early and late, evening and morning,
say twice each day –

Listen, Israel: the LORD is our God, the LORD is One. *Deut. 6*

Quietly: Blessed be the name of His glorious kingdom for ever and all time.

Some congregations say the entire first paragraph of the Shema (below) at this point. If there is a concern that the Shema will not be recited within the prescribed time, then all three paragraphs should be said.

Love the LORD your God with all your heart, with all your soul, and with all your might. These words which I command you today shall be on your heart. Teach them repeatedly to your children, speaking of them when you sit at home and when you travel on the way, when you lie down and when you rise. Bind them as a sign on your hand, and they shall be an emblem between your eyes. Write them on the doorposts of your house and gates.

---

descendants of those You singled out to be witnesses to the world of Your existence and majesty.

יַעֲקֹב בִּנְךָ בְּכוֹרֶךָ *Jacob your firstborn son.* Though Jacob was not the biological firstborn of Isaac and Rebecca, God subsequently declared, "My child, My firstborn, Israel" (Ex. 4:22).

אֲבָל אֲנַחְנוּ עַמְּךָ בְּנֵי בְרִיתֶךָ
בְּנֵי אַבְרָהָם אֹהַבְךָ שֶׁנִּשְׁבַּעְתָּ לּוֹ בְּהַר הַמּוֹרִיָּה
זֶרַע יִצְחָק יְחִידוֹ שֶׁנֶּעֱקַד עַל גַּבֵּי הַמִּזְבֵּחַ
עֲדַת יַעֲקֹב בִּנְךָ בְּכוֹרֶךָ
שֶׁמֵּאַהֲבָתְךָ שֶׁאָהַבְתָּ אוֹתוֹ, וּמִשִּׂמְחָתְךָ שֶׁשָּׂמַחְתָּ בּוֹ
קָרָאתָ אֶת שְׁמוֹ יִשְׂרָאֵל וִישֻׁרוּן.

לְפִיכָךְ אֲנַחְנוּ חַיָּבִים
לְהוֹדוֹת לְךָ וּלְשַׁבֵּחֲךָ וּלְפָאֶרְךָ
וּלְבָרֵךְ וּלְקַדֵּשׁ וְלָתֵת שֶׁבַח וְהוֹדָיָה לִשְׁמֶךָ.
אַשְׁרֵינוּ, מַה טּוֹב חֶלְקֵנוּ
וּמַה נָּעִים גּוֹרָלֵנוּ, וּמַה יָּפָה יְרֻשָּׁתֵנוּ.

◂ אַשְׁרֵינוּ, שֶׁאֲנַחְנוּ מַשְׁכִּימִים וּמַעֲרִיבִים עֶרֶב וָבֹקֶר
וְאוֹמְרִים פַּעֲמַיִם בְּכָל יוֹם

שְׁמַע יִשְׂרָאֵל, יהוה אֱלֹהֵינוּ, יהוה אֶחָד: דברים ו

Quietly בָּרוּךְ שֵׁם כְּבוֹד מַלְכוּתוֹ לְעוֹלָם וָעֶד.

Some congregations say the entire first paragraph of the שמע *(below) at this point. If there is a concern that the* שמע *will not be recited within the prescribed time, then all three paragraphs should be said.*

וְאָהַבְתָּ אֵת יהוה אֱלֹהֶיךָ, בְּכָל־לְבָבְךָ, וּבְכָל־נַפְשְׁךָ, וּבְכָל־מְאֹדֶךָ: וְהָיוּ הַדְּבָרִים הָאֵלֶּה, אֲשֶׁר אָנֹכִי מְצַוְּךָ הַיּוֹם, עַל־לְבָבֶךָ: וְשִׁנַּנְתָּם לְבָנֶיךָ, וְדִבַּרְתָּ בָּם, בְּשִׁבְתְּךָ בְּבֵיתֶךָ, וּבְלֶכְתְּךָ בַדֶּרֶךְ, וּבְשָׁכְבְּךָ וּבְקוּמֶךָ: וּקְשַׁרְתָּם לְאוֹת עַל־יָדֶךָ וְהָיוּ לְטֹטָפֹת בֵּין עֵינֶיךָ: וּכְתַבְתָּם עַל־מְזֻזוֹת בֵּיתֶךָ וּבִשְׁעָרֶיךָ:

אֲבָל *Yet.* Though we may be insignificant as individuals, we are part of something momentous, for "we are Your people, the children of Your covenant,"

אַתָּה הוּא It was You who existed before the world was created,
it is You now that the world has been created.
It is You in this world and You in the World to Come.
▸ Sanctify Your name through those who sanctify Your name,
and sanctify Your name throughout Your world.
By Your salvation may our pride be exalted;
raise high our pride.
Blessed are You, LORD,
who sanctifies His name among the multitudes.

אַתָּה הוּא You are the LORD our God
in heaven and on earth, and in the highest heaven of heavens.
Truly, You are the first and You are the last,
and besides You there is no god.
Gather those who hope in You from the four quarters of the earth.
May all mankind recognize and know
that You alone are God over all the kingdoms on earth.

You made the heavens and the earth, the sea and all they contain.
Who among all the works of Your hands, above and below,
can tell You what to do?

Heavenly Father,
deal kindly with us
for the sake of Your great name by which we are called,
and fulfill for us, LORD our God, that which is written:

> "At that time I will bring you home, and at that time I will gather you, for I will give you renown and praise among all the peoples of the earth when I bring back your exiles before your eyes, says the LORD." *Zeph. 3*

His covenant; therefore, we may not renounce our religion or identity: "I, God, do not change; so you, children of Jacob, are not destroyed" (Mal. 3:6).

אַתָּה הוּא יהוה אֱלֹהֵינוּ *You are the LORD our God.* A prayer for the end of exile, culminating with the verse from Zephaniah (3:20) which speaks of the ingathering of Jews and of a time when "I will give you renown and praise

אַתָּה הוּא עַד שֶׁלֹּא נִבְרָא הָעוֹלָם, אַתָּה הוּא מִשֶּׁנִּבְרָא הָעוֹלָם.
אַתָּה הוּא בָּעוֹלָם הַזֶּה, וְאַתָּה הוּא לָעוֹלָם הַבָּא.
◂ קַדֵּשׁ אֶת שִׁמְךָ עַל מַקְדִּישֵׁי שְׁמֶךָ, וְקַדֵּשׁ אֶת שִׁמְךָ בְּעוֹלָמֶךָ
וּבִישׁוּעָתְךָ תָּרוּם וְתַגְבִּיהַּ קַרְנֵנוּ.
בָּרוּךְ אַתָּה יהוה, הַמְקַדֵּשׁ אֶת שִׁמְךָ בָּרַבִּים.

אַתָּה הוּא יהוה אֱלֹהֵינוּ
בַּשָּׁמַיִם וּבָאָרֶץ, וּבִשְׁמֵי הַשָּׁמַיִם הָעֶלְיוֹנִים.
אֱמֶת, אַתָּה הוּא רִאשׁוֹן, וְאַתָּה הוּא אַחֲרוֹן
וּמִבַּלְעָדֶיךָ אֵין אֱלֹהִים.
קַבֵּץ קֹוֶיךָ מֵאַרְבַּע כַּנְפוֹת הָאָרֶץ.
יַכִּירוּ וְיֵדְעוּ כָּל בָּאֵי עוֹלָם
כִּי אַתָּה הוּא הָאֱלֹהִים לְבַדְּךָ לְכֹל מַמְלְכוֹת הָאָרֶץ.

אַתָּה עָשִׂיתָ אֶת הַשָּׁמַיִם וְאֶת הָאָרֶץ
אֶת הַיָּם וְאֶת כָּל אֲשֶׁר בָּם
וּמִי בְּכָל מַעֲשֵׂי יָדֶיךָ בָּעֶלְיוֹנִים אוֹ בַתַּחְתּוֹנִים
שֶׁיֹּאמַר לְךָ מַה תַּעֲשֶׂה.

אָבִינוּ שֶׁבַּשָּׁמַיִם
עֲשֵׂה עִמָּנוּ חֶסֶד בַּעֲבוּר שִׁמְךָ הַגָּדוֹל שֶׁנִּקְרָא עָלֵינוּ
וְקַיֶּם לָנוּ יהוה אֱלֹהֵינוּ מַה שֶּׁכָּתוּב:
צפניה ג בָּעֵת הַהִיא אָבִיא אֶתְכֶם, וּבָעֵת קַבְּצִי אֶתְכֶם
כִּי־אֶתֵּן אֶתְכֶם לְשֵׁם וְלִתְהִלָּה בְּכֹל עַמֵּי הָאָרֶץ
בְּשׁוּבִי אֶת־שְׁבוּתֵיכֶם לְעֵינֵיכֶם, אָמַר יהוה:

אַתָּה הוּא *It was You who existed.* This prayer, with its emphasis on the changelessness of God, may have been incorporated at a time of persecution, expressing the refusal of Jews to abandon their faith. God does not alter or revoke

OFFERINGS

The sages held that, in the absence of the Temple, studying the laws of sacrifices is the equivalent of offering them. Hence the following texts. There are different customs as to how many passages are to be said, and one should follow the custom of one's congregation. The minimum requirement is to say the verses relating to The Daily Sacrifice on the next page.

THE BASIN

The Lord spoke to Moses, saying: Make a bronze basin, with its bronze stand for washing, and place it between the Tent of Meeting and the altar, and put water in it. From it, Aaron and his sons are to wash their hands and feet. When they enter the Tent of Meeting, they shall wash with water so that they will not die; likewise when they approach the altar to minister, presenting a fire-offering to the Lord. They must wash their hands and feet so that they will not die. This shall be an everlasting ordinance for Aaron and his descendants throughout their generations. *Ex. 30*

TAKING OF THE ASHES

The Lord spoke to Moses, saying: Instruct Aaron and his sons, saying, This is the law of the burnt-offering. The burnt-offering shall remain on the altar hearth throughout the night until morning, and the altar fire shall be kept burning on it. The priest shall then put on his linen garments, and linen breeches next to his body, and shall remove the ashes of the burnt-offering that the fire has consumed on the altar and place them beside the altar. Then he shall take off these clothes and put on others, and carry the ashes outside the camp to a clean place. The fire on the altar must be kept burning; it must not go out. Each morning the priest shall burn wood on it, and prepare on it the burnt-offering and burn the fat of the peace-offerings. A perpetual fire must be kept burning on the altar; it must not go out. *Lev. 6*

---

that study of the laws about sacrifice was a substitute for sacrifice itself (*Ta'anit* 27b). The passage from the Mishna (*Zevaḥim* 5) is also about sacrifices, and was chosen because it does not contain any disagreement between the sages, and thus accords with the rule that one should pray "after a decided *halakha*" (*Berakhot* 31a), that is, an item of Jewish law about which there is no debate.

There are different customs about how many and which passages are to be said. The passages in large type represent the text as it exists in the earliest Siddurim, those of Rabbi Amram Gaon and Rabbi Sa'adia Gaon.

סדר הקרבנות

חז״ל held that, in the absence of the Temple, studying the laws of sacrifices is the equivalent of offering them. Hence the following texts. There are different customs as to how many passages are to be said, and one should follow the custom of one's congregation. The minimum requirement is to say the verses relating to the קרבן תמיד on the next page.

פרשת הכיור

וַיְדַבֵּר יהוה אֶל־מֹשֶׁה לֵּאמֹר: וְעָשִׂיתָ כִּיּוֹר נְחֹשֶׁת וְכַנּוֹ נְחֹשֶׁת לְרָחְצָה, שמות ל
וְנָתַתָּ אֹתוֹ בֵּין־אֹהֶל מוֹעֵד וּבֵין הַמִּזְבֵּחַ, וְנָתַתָּ שָׁמָּה מָיִם: וְרָחֲצוּ
אַהֲרֹן וּבָנָיו מִמֶּנּוּ אֶת־יְדֵיהֶם וְאֶת־רַגְלֵיהֶם: בְּבֹאָם אֶל־אֹהֶל מוֹעֵד
יִרְחֲצוּ־מַיִם, וְלֹא יָמֻתוּ, אוֹ בְגִשְׁתָּם אֶל־הַמִּזְבֵּחַ לְשָׁרֵת, לְהַקְטִיר אִשֶּׁה
לַיהוה: וְרָחֲצוּ יְדֵיהֶם וְרַגְלֵיהֶם וְלֹא יָמֻתוּ, וְהָיְתָה לָהֶם חָק־עוֹלָם, לוֹ
וּלְזַרְעוֹ לְדֹרֹתָם:

פרשת תרומת הדשן

וַיְדַבֵּר יהוה אֶל־מֹשֶׁה לֵּאמֹר: צַו אֶת־אַהֲרֹן וְאֶת־בָּנָיו לֵאמֹר, זֹאת ויקרא ו
תּוֹרַת הָעֹלָה, הִוא הָעֹלָה עַל מוֹקְדָה עַל־הַמִּזְבֵּחַ כָּל־הַלַּיְלָה עַד־
הַבֹּקֶר, וְאֵשׁ הַמִּזְבֵּחַ תּוּקַד בּוֹ: וְלָבַשׁ הַכֹּהֵן מִדּוֹ בַד, וּמִכְנְסֵי־בַד יִלְבַּשׁ
עַל־בְּשָׂרוֹ, וְהֵרִים אֶת־הַדֶּשֶׁן אֲשֶׁר תֹּאכַל הָאֵשׁ אֶת־הָעֹלָה, עַל־
הַמִּזְבֵּחַ, וְשָׂמוֹ אֵצֶל הַמִּזְבֵּחַ: וּפָשַׁט אֶת־בְּגָדָיו, וְלָבַשׁ בְּגָדִים אֲחֵרִים,
וְהוֹצִיא אֶת־הַדֶּשֶׁן אֶל־מִחוּץ לַמַּחֲנֶה, אֶל־מָקוֹם טָהוֹר: וְהָאֵשׁ עַל־
הַמִּזְבֵּחַ תּוּקַד־בּוֹ, לֹא תִכְבֶּה, וּבִעֵר עָלֶיהָ הַכֹּהֵן עֵצִים בַּבֹּקֶר בַּבֹּקֶר,
וְעָרַךְ עָלֶיהָ הָעֹלָה, וְהִקְטִיר עָלֶיהָ חֶלְבֵי הַשְּׁלָמִים: אֵשׁ, תָּמִיד תּוּקַד
עַל־הַמִּזְבֵּחַ, לֹא תִכְבֶּה:

---

among all the peoples of the earth." This entire sequence of prayers is eloquent testimony to how Jews sustained faith and hope, dignity and pride, during some of the most prolonged periods of persecution in history.

OFFERINGS

There now follows a second cycle of study, with the same structure as the first, with passages from: (1) the Torah, (2) the Mishna, and (3) the Talmud (see below). The passages from the Torah relate to the daily, weekly and monthly sacrifices because, in the absence of the Temple, the sages held

May it be Your will, LORD our God and God of our ancestors, that You have compassion on us and pardon us all our sins, grant atonement for all our iniquities and forgive all our transgressions. May You rebuild the Temple swiftly in our days so that we may offer You the continual-offering that it may atone for us as You have prescribed for us in Your Torah through Moses Your servant, from the mouthpiece of Your glory, as it is said:

THE DAILY SACRIFICE

וַיְדַבֵּר The LORD said to Moses, "Command the Israelites and tell them: 'Be careful to offer to Me at the appointed time My food-offering consumed by fire, as an aroma pleasing to Me.' Tell them: 'This is the fire-offering you shall offer to the LORD – two lambs a year old without blemish, as a regular burnt-offering each day. Prepare one lamb in the morning and the other toward evening, together with a meal-offering of a tenth of an ephah of fine flour mixed with a quarter of a hin of oil from pressed olives. This is the regular burnt-offering instituted at Mount Sinai as a pleasing aroma, a fire-offering made to the LORD. Its libation is to be a quarter of a hin [of wine] with each lamb, poured in the Sanctuary as a libation of strong drink to the LORD. Prepare the second lamb in the afternoon, along with the same meal-offering and libation as in the morning. This is a fire-offering, an aroma pleasing to the LORD.'" *Num. 28*

וְשָׁחַט He shall slaughter it at the north side of the altar before the LORD, and Aaron's sons the priests shall sprinkle its blood against the altar on all sides. *Lev. 1*

May it be Your will, LORD our God and God of our ancestors, that this recitation be considered accepted and favored before You as if we had offered the daily sacrifice at its appointed time and place, according to its laws.

It is You, LORD our God, to whom our ancestors offered fragrant incense when the Temple stood, as You commanded them through Moses Your prophet, as is written in Your Torah:

THE INCENSE

The LORD said to Moses: Take fragrant spices – balsam, onycha, galbanum and pure frankincense, all in equal amounts – and make a fragrant blend of incense, the work of a perfumer, well mixed, pure and holy. Grind it very finely and place it in front of the [Ark of] Testimony in the Tent of Meeting, where I will meet with you. It shall be most holy to you. *Ex. 30*

יְהִי רָצוֹן מִלְּפָנֶיךָ יהוה אֱלֹהֵינוּ וֵאלֹהֵי אֲבוֹתֵינוּ, שֶׁתְּרַחֵם עָלֵינוּ, וְתִמְחֹל לָנוּ עַל כָּל חַטֹּאתֵינוּ וּתְכַפֵּר לָנוּ עַל כָּל עֲוֹנוֹתֵינוּ וְתִסְלַח לָנוּ עַל כָּל פְּשָׁעֵינוּ, וְתִבְנֶה בֵּית הַמִּקְדָּשׁ בִּמְהֵרָה בְיָמֵינוּ, וְנַקְרִיב לְפָנֶיךָ קָרְבַּן הַתָּמִיד שֶׁיְּכַפֵּר בַּעֲדֵנוּ, כְּמוֹ שֶׁכָּתַבְתָּ עָלֵינוּ בְּתוֹרָתֶךָ עַל יְדֵי מֹשֶׁה עַבְדֶּךָ מִפִּי כְבוֹדֶךָ, כָּאָמוּר:

פרשת קרבן התמיד

וַיְדַבֵּר יהוה אֶל־מֹשֶׁה לֵּאמֹר: צַו אֶת־בְּנֵי יִשְׂרָאֵל וְאָמַרְתָּ במדבר כח
אֲלֵהֶם, אֶת־קָרְבָּנִי לַחְמִי לְאִשַּׁי, רֵיחַ נִיחֹחִי, תִּשְׁמְרוּ לְהַקְרִיב
לִי בְּמוֹעֲדוֹ: וְאָמַרְתָּ לָהֶם, זֶה הָאִשֶּׁה אֲשֶׁר תַּקְרִיבוּ לַיהוה,
כְּבָשִׂים בְּנֵי־שָׁנָה תְמִימִם שְׁנַיִם לַיּוֹם, עֹלָה תָמִיד: אֶת־הַכֶּבֶשׂ
אֶחָד תַּעֲשֶׂה בַבֹּקֶר, וְאֵת הַכֶּבֶשׂ הַשֵּׁנִי תַּעֲשֶׂה בֵּין הָעַרְבָּיִם:
וַעֲשִׂירִית הָאֵיפָה סֹלֶת לְמִנְחָה, בְּלוּלָה בְּשֶׁמֶן כָּתִית רְבִיעִת
הַהִין: עֹלַת תָּמִיד, הָעֲשֻׂיָה בְּהַר סִינַי, לְרֵיחַ נִיחֹחַ אִשֶּׁה לַיהוה:
וְנִסְכּוֹ רְבִיעִת הַהִין לַכֶּבֶשׂ הָאֶחָד, בַּקֹּדֶשׁ הַסֵּךְ נֶסֶךְ שֵׁכָר
לַיהוה: וְאֵת הַכֶּבֶשׂ הַשֵּׁנִי תַּעֲשֶׂה בֵּין הָעַרְבָּיִם, כְּמִנְחַת הַבֹּקֶר
וּכְנִסְכּוֹ תַּעֲשֶׂה, אִשֵּׁה רֵיחַ נִיחֹחַ לַיהוה:

וְשָׁחַט אֹתוֹ עַל יֶרֶךְ הַמִּזְבֵּחַ צָפֹנָה לִפְנֵי יהוה, וְזָרְקוּ בְּנֵי אַהֲרֹן ויקרא א
הַכֹּהֲנִים אֶת־דָּמוֹ עַל־הַמִּזְבֵּחַ, סָבִיב:

יְהִי רָצוֹן מִלְּפָנֶיךָ, יהוה אֱלֹהֵינוּ וֵאלֹהֵי אֲבוֹתֵינוּ, שֶׁתְּהֵא אֲמִירָה זוֹ חֲשׁוּבָה וּמְקֻבֶּלֶת וּמְרֻצָּה לְפָנֶיךָ, כְּאִלּוּ הִקְרַבְנוּ קָרְבַּן הַתָּמִיד בְּמוֹעֲדוֹ וּבִמְקוֹמוֹ וּכְהִלְכָתוֹ.

אַתָּה הוּא יהוה אֱלֹהֵינוּ שֶׁהִקְטִירוּ אֲבוֹתֵינוּ לְפָנֶיךָ אֶת קְטֹרֶת הַסַּמִּים בִּזְמַן שֶׁבֵּית הַמִּקְדָּשׁ הָיָה קַיָּם, כַּאֲשֶׁר צִוִּיתָ אוֹתָם עַל יְדֵי מֹשֶׁה נְבִיאֶךָ, כַּכָּתוּב בְּתוֹרָתֶךָ:

פרשת הקטורת

וַיֹּאמֶר יהוה אֶל־מֹשֶׁה, קַח־לְךָ סַמִּים נָטָף וּשְׁחֵלֶת וְחֶלְבְּנָה, סַמִּים וּלְבֹנָה שמות ל
זַכָּה, בַּד בְּבַד יִהְיֶה: וְעָשִׂיתָ אֹתָהּ קְטֹרֶת, רֹקַח מַעֲשֵׂה רוֹקֵחַ, מְמֻלָּח,
טָהוֹר קֹדֶשׁ: וְשָׁחַקְתָּ מִמֶּנָּה הָדֵק, וְנָתַתָּה מִמֶּנָּה לִפְנֵי הָעֵדֻת בְּאֹהֶל מוֹעֵד
אֲשֶׁר אִוָּעֵד לְךָ שָׁמָּה, קֹדֶשׁ קָדָשִׁים תִּהְיֶה לָכֶם:

And it is said:

> Aaron shall burn fragrant incense on the altar every morning when he cleans the lamps. He shall burn incense again when he lights the lamps toward evening so that there will be incense before the LORD at all times, throughout your generations.

The rabbis taught: How was the incense prepared? It weighed 368 manehs, 365 corresponding to the number of days in a solar year, a maneh for each day, half to be offered in the morning and half in the afternoon, and three additional manehs from which the High Priest took two handfuls on Yom Kippur. These were put back into the mortar on the day before Yom Kippur and ground again very thoroughly so as to be extremely fine. The incense contained eleven kinds of spices: balsam, onycha, galbanum and frankincense, each weighing seventy manehs; myrrh, cassia, spikenard and saffron, each weighing sixteen manehs; twelve manehs of costus, three of aromatic bark; nine of cinnamon; nine kabs of Carsina lye; three seahs and three kabs of Cyprus wine. If Cyprus wine was not available, old white wine might be used. A quarter of a kab of Sodom salt, and a minute amount of a smoke-raising herb. Rabbi Nathan the Babylonian says: also a minute amount of Jordan amber. If one added honey to the mixture, he rendered it unfit for sacred use. If he omitted any one of its ingredients, he is guilty of a capital offense. *Keritot 6a*

Rabban Shimon ben Gamliel says: "Balsam" refers to the sap that drips from the balsam tree. The Carsina lye was used for bleaching the onycha to improve it. The Cyprus wine was used to soak the onycha in it to make it pungent. Though urine is suitable for this purpose, it is not brought into the Temple out of respect.

It was taught, Rabbi Nathan says: While it was being ground, another would say, "Grind well, well grind," because the [rhythmic] sound is good for spices. If it was mixed in half-quantities, it is fit for use, but we have not heard whether this applies to a third or a quarter. Rabbi Judah said: The general rule is that if it was made in the correct proportions, it is fit for use even if made in half-quantity, but if he omitted any one of its ingredients, he is guilty of a capital offense.

It was taught, Bar Kappara says: Once every sixty or seventy years, the accumulated surpluses amounted to half the yearly quantity. Bar Kappara also taught: If a minute quantity of honey had been mixed into the incense, no one could have resisted the scent. Why did they not put honey into it? Because the Torah says, "For you are not to burn any leaven or honey in a fire-offering made to the LORD." *JT Yoma 4:* *Lev. 2*

וְנֶאֱמַר

וְהִקְטִיר עָלָיו אַהֲרֹן קְטֹרֶת סַמִּים, בַּבֹּקֶר בַּבֹּקֶר בְּהֵיטִיבוֹ אֶת־הַנֵּרֹת יַקְטִירֶנָּה: וּבְהַעֲלֹת אַהֲרֹן אֶת־הַנֵּרֹת בֵּין הָעַרְבַּיִם יַקְטִירֶנָּה, קְטֹרֶת תָּמִיד לִפְנֵי יהוה לְדֹרֹתֵיכֶם:

תָּנוּ רַבָּנָן: פִּטּוּם הַקְּטֹרֶת כֵּיצַד, שְׁלֹשׁ מֵאוֹת וְשִׁשִּׁים וּשְׁמוֹנָה מָנִים הָיוּ בָהּ. שְׁלֹשׁ מֵאוֹת וְשִׁשִּׁים וַחֲמִשָּׁה כְּמִנְיַן יְמוֹת הַחַמָּה, מָנֶה לְכָל יוֹם, פְּרַס בְּשַׁחֲרִית וּפְרַס בֵּין הָעַרְבַּיִם, וּשְׁלֹשָׁה מָנִים יְתֵרִים שֶׁמֵּהֶם מַכְנִיס כֹּהֵן גָּדוֹל מְלֹא חָפְנָיו בְּיוֹם הַכִּפּוּרִים, וּמַחֲזִירָן לְמַכְתֶּשֶׁת בְּעֶרֶב יוֹם הַכִּפּוּרִים וְשׁוֹחֲקָן יָפֶה יָפֶה, כְּדֵי שֶׁתְּהֵא דַקָּה מִן הַדַּקָּה. וְאַחַד עָשָׂר סַמָּנִים הָיוּ בָהּ, וְאֵלּוּ הֵן: הַצֳּרִי, וְהַצִּפֹּרֶן, וְהַחֶלְבְּנָה, וְהַלְּבוֹנָה מִשְׁקַל שִׁבְעִים שִׁבְעִים מָנֶה, מֹר, וּקְצִיעָה, שִׁבֹּלֶת נֵרְדְּ, וְכַרְכֹּם מִשְׁקַל שִׁשָּׁה עָשָׂר שִׁשָּׁה עָשָׂר מָנֶה, הַקֹּשְׁטְ שְׁנֵים עָשָׂר, קִלּוּפָה שְׁלֹשָׁה, קִנָּמוֹן תִּשְׁעָה, בֹּרִית כַּרְשִׁינָה תִּשְׁעָה קַבִּין, יֵין קַפְרִיסִין סְאִין תְּלָת וְקַבִּין תְּלָתָא, וְאִם לֹא מָצָא יֵין קַפְרִיסִין, מֵבִיא חֲמַר חִוַּרְיָן עַתִּיק. מֶלַח סְדוֹמִית רֹבַע, מַעֲלֶה עָשָׁן כָּל שֶׁהוּא. רַבִּי נָתָן הַבַּבְלִי אוֹמֵר: אַף כִּפַּת הַיַּרְדֵּן כָּל שֶׁהוּא, וְאִם נָתַן בָּהּ דְּבַשׁ פְּסָלָהּ, וְאִם חִסַּר אֶחָד מִכָּל סַמָּנֶיהָ, חַיָּב מִיתָה. כריתות ו.

רַבָּן שִׁמְעוֹן בֶּן גַּמְלִיאֵל אוֹמֵר: הַצֳּרִי אֵינוֹ אֶלָּא שְׂרָף הַנּוֹטֵף מֵעֲצֵי הַקְּטָף. בֹּרִית כַּרְשִׁינָה שֶׁשָּׁפִין בָּהּ אֶת הַצִּפֹּרֶן כְּדֵי שֶׁתְּהֵא נָאָה, יֵין קַפְרִיסִין שֶׁשּׁוֹרִין בּוֹ אֶת הַצִּפֹּרֶן כְּדֵי שֶׁתְּהֵא עַזָּה, וַהֲלֹא מֵי רַגְלַיִם יָפִין לָהּ, אֶלָּא שֶׁאֵין מַכְנִיסִין מֵי רַגְלַיִם בַּמִּקְדָּשׁ מִפְּנֵי הַכָּבוֹד.

תַּנְיָא, רַבִּי נָתָן אוֹמֵר: כְּשֶׁהוּא שׁוֹחֵק אוֹמֵר, הָדֵק הֵיטֵב הֵיטֵב הָדֵק, מִפְּנֵי שֶׁהַקּוֹל יָפֶה לַבְּשָׂמִים. פִּטְּמָהּ לַחֲצָאִין כְּשֵׁרָה, לִשְׁלִישׁ וְלִרְבִיעַ לֹא שָׁמַעְנוּ. אָמַר רַבִּי יְהוּדָה: זֶה הַכְּלָל, אִם כְּמִדָּתָהּ כְּשֵׁרָה לַחֲצָאִין, וְאִם חִסַּר אֶחָד מִכָּל סַמָּנֶיהָ חַיָּב מִיתָה.

תַּנְיָא, בַּר קַפָּרָא אוֹמֵר: אַחַת לְשִׁשִּׁים אוֹ לְשִׁבְעִים שָׁנָה הָיְתָה בָאָה שֶׁל שִׁירַיִם לַחֲצָאִין. וְעוֹד תָּנֵי בַּר קַפָּרָא: אִלּוּ הָיָה נוֹתֵן בָּהּ קָרְטוֹב שֶׁל דְּבַשׁ אֵין אָדָם יָכוֹל לַעֲמֹד מִפְּנֵי רֵיחָהּ, וְלָמָּה אֵין מְעָרְבִין בָּהּ דְּבַשׁ, מִפְּנֵי שֶׁהַתּוֹרָה אָמְרָה: ירושלמי יומא ד, הלכה ה

כִּי כָל־שְׂאֹר וְכָל־דְּבַשׁ לֹא־תַקְטִירוּ מִמֶּנּוּ אִשֶּׁה לַיהוה: ויקרא ב

The following three verses are each said three times:

The Lord of hosts is with us; the God of Jacob is our stronghold, Selah. *Ps. 46*
Lord of hosts, happy is the one who trusts in You. *Ps. 84*
Lord, save! May the King answer us on the day we call. *Ps. 20*

You are my hiding place; You will protect me from distress and surround me with songs of salvation, Selah. *Ps. 32*
Then the offering of Judah and Jerusalem will be pleasing to the Lord as in the days of old and as in former years. *Mal. 3*

THE ORDER OF THE PRIESTLY FUNCTIONS

Abaye related the order of the daily priestly functions in the name of tradition and in accordance with Abba Shaul: The large pile [of wood] comes before the second pile for the incense; the second pile for the incense precedes the laying in order of the two logs of wood; the laying in order of the two logs of wood comes before the removing of ashes from the inner altar; the removing of ashes from the inner altar precedes the cleaning of the five lamps; the cleaning of the five lamps comes before the blood of the daily offering; the blood of the daily offering precedes the cleaning of the [other] two lamps; the cleaning of the two lamps comes before the incense-offering; the incense-offering precedes the burning of the limbs; the burning of the limbs comes before the meal-offering; the meal-offering precedes the pancakes; the pancakes come before the wine-libations; the wine-libations precede the additional offerings; the additional offerings come before the [frankincense] censers; the censers precede the daily afternoon offering; as it is said, "On it he shall arrange burnt-offerings, and on it he shall burn the fat of the peace-offerings" – "on it" [the daily offering] all the offerings were completed. *Yoma 33a* *Lev. 6*

Please, by the power of Your great right hand, set the captive nation free.
Accept Your people's prayer. Strengthen us, purify us, You who are revered.
Please, Mighty One, guard like the pupil of the eye those who seek Your unity.
Bless them, cleanse them, have compassion on them,
grant them Your righteousness always.
Mighty One, Holy One, in Your great goodness guide Your congregation.
Only One, Exalted One, turn to Your people, who proclaim Your holiness.
Accept our plea and heed our cry, You who know all secret thoughts.
Blessed be the name of His glorious kingdom for ever and all time.

Master of the Universe, You have commanded us to offer the daily sacrifice at its appointed time with the priests at their service, the Levites on their platform, and the Israelites at their post. Now, because of our sins, the Temple is destroyed and the daily sacrifice discontinued, and we have no priest at his service, no Levite

The following three verses are each said three times:

יהוה צְבָאוֹת עִמָּנוּ, מִשְׂגָּב לָנוּ אֱלֹהֵי יַעֲקֹב סֶלָה: תהלים מו

יהוה צְבָאוֹת, אַשְׁרֵי אָדָם בֹּטֵחַ בָּךְ: תהלים פד

יהוה הוֹשִׁיעָה, הַמֶּלֶךְ יַעֲנֵנוּ בְיוֹם־קָרְאֵנוּ: תהלים כ

אַתָּה סֵתֶר לִי, מִצַּר תִּצְּרֵנִי, רָנֵּי פַלֵּט תְּסוֹבְבֵנִי סֶלָה: תהלים לב

וְעָרְבָה לַיהוה מִנְחַת יְהוּדָה וִירוּשָׁלָםִ מלאכי ג

כִּימֵי עוֹלָם וּכְשָׁנִים קַדְמֹנִיּוֹת:

סדר המערכה

אַבַּיֵּי הֲוָה מְסַדֵּר סֵדֶר הַמַּעֲרָכָה מִשְּׁמָא דִגְמָרָא, וְאַלִּבָּא דְאַבָּא שָׁאוּל: יומא לג.
מַעֲרָכָה גְדוֹלָה קוֹדֶמֶת לְמַעֲרָכָה שְׁנִיָּה שֶׁל קְטֹרֶת, וּמַעֲרָכָה שְׁנִיָּה שֶׁל
קְטֹרֶת קוֹדֶמֶת לְסִדּוּר שְׁנֵי גִזְרֵי עֵצִים, וְסִדּוּר שְׁנֵי גִזְרֵי עֵצִים קוֹדֵם לְדִשּׁוּן
מִזְבֵּחַ הַפְּנִימִי, וְדִשּׁוּן מִזְבֵּחַ הַפְּנִימִי קוֹדֵם לַהֲטָבַת חָמֵשׁ נֵרוֹת, וַהֲטָבַת
חָמֵשׁ נֵרוֹת קוֹדֶמֶת לְדַם הַתָּמִיד, וְדַם הַתָּמִיד קוֹדֵם לַהֲטָבַת שְׁתֵּי נֵרוֹת,
וַהֲטָבַת שְׁתֵּי נֵרוֹת קוֹדֶמֶת לִקְטֹרֶת, וּקְטֹרֶת קוֹדֶמֶת לְאֵבָרִים, וְאֵבָרִים
לְמִנְחָה, וּמִנְחָה לַחֲבִתִּין, וַחֲבִתִּין לִנְסָכִין, וּנְסָכִין לְמוּסָפִין, וּמוּסָפִין
לְבָזִיכִין, וּבָזִיכִין קוֹדְמִין לְתָמִיד שֶׁל בֵּין הָעַרְבָּיִם. שֶׁנֶּאֱמַר: וְעָרַךְ עָלֶיהָ ויקרא ו
הָעֹלָה, וְהִקְטִיר עָלֶיהָ חֶלְבֵי הַשְּׁלָמִים: עָלֶיהָ הַשְׁלֵם כָּל הַקָּרְבָּנוֹת כֻּלָּם.

אָנָּא, בְּכֹחַ גְּדֻלַּת יְמִינְךָ, תַּתִּיר צְרוּרָה.
קַבֵּל רִנַּת עַמְּךָ, שַׂגְּבֵנוּ, טַהֲרֵנוּ, נוֹרָא.
נָא גִבּוֹר, דּוֹרְשֵׁי יִחוּדְךָ כְּבָבַת שָׁמְרֵם.
בָּרְכֵם, טַהֲרֵם, רַחֲמֵם, צִדְקָתְךָ תָּמִיד גָּמְלֵם.
חֲסִין קָדוֹשׁ, בְּרֹב טוּבְךָ נַהֵל עֲדָתֶךָ.
יָחִיד גֵּאֶה, לְעַמְּךָ פְּנֵה, זוֹכְרֵי קְדֻשָּׁתֶךָ.
שַׁוְעָתֵנוּ קַבֵּל וּשְׁמַע צַעֲקָתֵנוּ, יוֹדֵעַ תַּעֲלוּמוֹת.
בָּרוּךְ שֵׁם כְּבוֹד מַלְכוּתוֹ לְעוֹלָם וָעֶד.

רִבּוֹן הָעוֹלָמִים, אַתָּה צִוִּיתָנוּ לְהַקְרִיב קָרְבַּן הַתָּמִיד בְּמוֹעֲדוֹ וְלִהְיוֹת כֹּהֲנִים בַּעֲבוֹדָתָם וּלְוִיִּם בְּדוּכָנָם וְיִשְׂרָאֵל בְּמַעֲמָדָם, וְעַתָּה בַּעֲוֹנוֹתֵינוּ חָרַב בֵּית הַמִּקְדָּשׁ וּבָטַל הַתָּמִיד וְאֵין לָנוּ לֹא כֹהֵן בַּעֲבוֹדָתוֹ וְלֹא לֵוִי בְּדוּכָנוֹ וְלֹא יִשְׂרָאֵל

on his platform, no Israelite at his post. But You said: "We will offer in place of bullocks [the prayer of] our lips." Therefore may it be Your will, LORD our God and God of our ancestors, that the prayer of our lips be considered, accepted and favored before You as if we had offered the daily sacrifice at its appointed time and place, according to its laws. *Hos. 14*

On Shabbat: וּבְיוֹם הַשַּׁבָּת On the Shabbat day, *Num. 28*
make an offering of two lambs a year old, without blemish,
together with two-tenths of an ephah of fine flour
mixed with oil as a meal-offering, and its appropriate libation.
This is the burnt-offering for every Shabbat,
in addition to the regular daily burnt-offering and its libation.

LAWS OF OFFERINGS, MISHNA ZEVAḤIM

אֵיזֶהוּ מְקוֹמָן What is the location for sacrifices? The holiest offerings were slaughtered on the north side. The bull and he-goat of Yom Kippur were slaughtered on the north side. Their blood was received in a sacred vessel on the north side, and had to be sprinkled between the poles [of the Ark], toward the veil [screening the Holy of Holies], and on the golden altar. [The omission of] one of these sprinklings invalidated [the atonement ceremony]. The leftover blood was to be poured onto the western base of the outer altar. If this was not done, however, the omission did not invalidate [the ceremony]. *Zevaḥim Ch. 5*

The bulls and he-goats that were completely burnt were slaughtered on the north side, their blood was received in a sacred vessel on the north side, and had to be sprinkled toward the veil and on the golden altar. [The omission of] one of these sprinklings invalidated [the ceremony]. The leftover blood was to be poured onto the western base of the outer altar. If this was not done, however, the omission did not invalidate [the ceremony]. All these offerings were burnt where the altar ashes were deposited.

The communal and individual sin-offerings – these are the communal sin-offerings: the he-goats offered on Rosh Ḥodesh and Festivals were slaughtered on the north side, their blood was received in a sacred vessel on the north side, and required four sprinklings, one on each of the four corners of the altar. How was this done? The priest ascended the ramp and turned [right] onto the surrounding ledge. He came to the southeast corner, then went to the northeast, then to the northwest, then to the southwest. The leftover blood he poured onto the southern base. [The meat of these offerings], prepared in any manner, was eaten within the [courtyard] curtains, by males of the priest-hood, on that day and the following night, until midnight.

בְּמַעֲמָדוֹ, וְאַתָּה אָמַרְתָּ: וּנְשַׁלְּמָה פָרִים שְׂפָתֵינוּ: לָכֵן יְהִי רָצוֹן מִלְּפָנֶיךָ יהוה הושע יד
אֱלֹהֵינוּ וֵאלֹהֵי אֲבוֹתֵינוּ, שֶׁיְּהֵא שִׂיחַ שִׂפְתוֹתֵינוּ חָשׁוּב וּמְקֻבָּל וּמְרֻצֶּה לְפָנֶיךָ,
כְּאִלּוּ הִקְרַבְנוּ קָרְבַּן הַתָּמִיד בְּמוֹעֲדוֹ וּבִמְקוֹמוֹ וּכְהִלְכָתוֹ.

בשבת: וּבְיוֹם הַשַּׁבָּת שְׁנֵי־כְבָשִׂים בְּנֵי־שָׁנָה תְּמִימִם במדבר כח
וּשְׁנֵי עֶשְׂרֹנִים סֹלֶת מִנְחָה בְּלוּלָה בַשֶּׁמֶן, וְנִסְכּוֹ:
עֹלַת שַׁבַּת בְּשַׁבַּתּוֹ, עַל־עֹלַת הַתָּמִיד וְנִסְכָּהּ:

דיני זבחים

אֵיזֶהוּ מְקוֹמָן שֶׁל זְבָחִים. קָדְשֵׁי קָדָשִׁים שְׁחִיטָתָן בַּצָּפוֹן. פַּר וְשָׂעִיר זבחים פרק ה
שֶׁל יוֹם הַכִּפּוּרִים, שְׁחִיטָתָן בַּצָּפוֹן, וְקִבּוּל דָּמָן בִּכְלִי שָׁרֵת בַּצָּפוֹן,
וְדָמָן טָעוּן הַזָּיָה עַל בֵּין הַבַּדִּים, וְעַל הַפָּרֹכֶת, וְעַל מִזְבַּח הַזָּהָב.
מַתָּנָה אַחַת מֵהֶן מְעַכָּבֶת. שְׁיָרֵי הַדָּם הָיָה שׁוֹפֵךְ עַל יְסוֹד מַעֲרָבִי
שֶׁל מִזְבֵּחַ הַחִיצוֹן, אִם לֹא נָתַן לֹא עִכֵּב.

פָּרִים הַנִּשְׂרָפִים וּשְׂעִירִים הַנִּשְׂרָפִים, שְׁחִיטָתָן בַּצָּפוֹן, וְקִבּוּל דָּמָן בִּכְלִי שָׁרֵת בַּצָּפוֹן, וְדָמָן טָעוּן הַזָּיָה עַל הַפָּרֹכֶת וְעַל מִזְבַּח הַזָּהָב. מַתָּנָה אַחַת מֵהֶן מְעַכָּבֶת. שְׁיָרֵי הַדָּם הָיָה שׁוֹפֵךְ עַל יְסוֹד מַעֲרָבִי שֶׁל מִזְבֵּחַ הַחִיצוֹן, אִם לֹא נָתַן לֹא עִכֵּב. אֵלּוּ וָאֵלּוּ נִשְׂרָפִין בְּבֵית הַדָּשֶׁן.

חַטֹּאת הַצִּבּוּר וְהַיָּחִיד. אֵלּוּ הֵן חַטֹּאת הַצִּבּוּר: שְׂעִירֵי רָאשֵׁי חֳדָשִׁים וְשֶׁל מוֹעֲדוֹת. שְׁחִיטָתָן בַּצָּפוֹן, וְקִבּוּל דָּמָן בִּכְלִי שָׁרֵת בַּצָּפוֹן, וְדָמָן טָעוּן אַרְבַּע מַתָּנוֹת עַל אַרְבַּע קְרָנוֹת. כֵּיצַד, עָלָה בַכֶּבֶשׁ, וּפָנָה לַסּוֹבֵב, וּבָא לוֹ לְקֶרֶן דְּרוֹמִית מִזְרָחִית, מִזְרָחִית צְפוֹנִית, צְפוֹנִית מַעֲרָבִית, מַעֲרָבִית דְּרוֹמִית. שְׁיָרֵי הַדָּם הָיָה שׁוֹפֵךְ עַל יְסוֹד דְּרוֹמִי. וְנֶאֱכָלִין לִפְנִים מִן הַקְּלָעִים, לְזִכְרֵי כְהֻנָּה, בְּכָל מַאֲכָל, לְיוֹם וָלַיְלָה עַד חֲצוֹת.

The burnt-offering was among the holiest of sacrifices. It was slaughtered on the north side, its blood was received in a sacred vessel on the north side, and required two sprinklings [at opposite corners of the altar], making four in all. The offering had to be flayed, dismembered and wholly consumed by fire.

The communal peace-offerings and the guilt-offerings – these are the guilt-offerings: the guilt-offering for robbery; the guilt-offering for profane use of a sacred object; the guilt-offering [for violating] a betrothed maidservant; the guilt-offering of a Nazirite [who had become defiled by a corpse]; the guilt-offering of a leper [at his cleansing]; and the guilt-offering in case of doubt. All these were slaughtered on the north side, their blood was received in a sacred vessel on the north side, and required two sprinklings [at opposite corners of the altar], making four in all. [The meat of these offerings], prepared in any manner, was eaten within the [courtyard] curtains, by males of the priesthood, on that day and the following night, until midnight.

The thanksgiving-offering and the ram of a Nazirite were offerings of lesser holiness. They could be slaughtered anywhere in the Temple court, and their blood required two sprinklings [at opposite corners of the altar], making four in all. The meat of these offerings, prepared in any manner, was eaten anywhere within the city [Jerusalem], by anyone during that day and the following night until midnight. This also applied to the portion of these sacrifices [given to the priests], except that the priests' portion was only to be eaten by the priests, their wives, children and servants.

Peace-offerings were [also] of lesser holiness. They could be slaughtered anywhere in the Temple court, and their blood required two sprinklings [at opposite corners of the altar], making four in all. The meat of these offerings, prepared in any manner, was eaten anywhere within the city [Jerusalem], by anyone, for two days and one night. This also applied to the portion of these sacrifices [given to the priests], except that the priests' portion was only to be eaten by the priests, their wives, children and servants.

The firstborn and tithe of cattle and the Pesaḥ lamb were sacrifices of lesser holiness. They could be slaughtered anywhere in the Temple court, and their blood required only one sprinkling, which had to be done at the base of the altar. They differed in their consumption: the firstborn was eaten only by priests, while the tithe could be eaten by anyone. Both could be eaten anywhere within the city, prepared in any manner, during two days and one night. The Pesaḥ lamb had to be eaten that night until midnight. It could only be eaten by those who had been numbered for it, and eaten only roasted.

הָעוֹלָה קֹדֶשׁ קָדָשִׁים. שְׁחִיטָתָהּ בַּצָּפוֹן, וְקִבּוּל דָּמָהּ בִּכְלִי שָׁרֵת בַּצָּפוֹן, וְדָמָהּ טָעוּן שְׁתֵּי מַתָּנוֹת שֶׁהֵן אַרְבַּע, וּטְעוּנָה הֶפְשֵׁט וְנִתּוּחַ, וְכָלִיל לָאִשִּׁים.

זִבְחֵי שַׁלְמֵי צִבּוּר וַאֲשָׁמוֹת. אֵלּוּ הֵן אֲשָׁמוֹת: אֲשַׁם גְּזֵלוֹת, אֲשַׁם מְעִילוֹת, אֲשַׁם שִׁפְחָה חֲרוּפָה, אֲשַׁם נָזִיר, אֲשַׁם מְצֹרָע, אָשָׁם תָּלוּי. שְׁחִיטָתָן בַּצָּפוֹן, וְקִבּוּל דָּמָן בִּכְלִי שָׁרֵת בַּצָּפוֹן, וְדָמָן טָעוּן שְׁתֵּי מַתָּנוֹת שֶׁהֵן אַרְבַּע. וְנֶאֱכָלִין לִפְנִים מִן הַקְּלָעִים, לְזִכְרֵי כְהֻנָּה, בְּכָל מַאֲכָל, לְיוֹם וָלַיְלָה עַד חֲצוֹת.

הַתּוֹדָה וְאֵיל נָזִיר קָדָשִׁים קַלִּים. שְׁחִיטָתָן בְּכָל מָקוֹם בָּעֲזָרָה, וְדָמָן טָעוּן שְׁתֵּי מַתָּנוֹת שֶׁהֵן אַרְבַּע, וְנֶאֱכָלִין בְּכָל הָעִיר, לְכָל אָדָם, בְּכָל מַאֲכָל, לְיוֹם וָלַיְלָה עַד חֲצוֹת. הַמּוּרָם מֵהֶם כַּיּוֹצֵא בָהֶם, אֶלָּא שֶׁהַמּוּרָם נֶאֱכָל לַכֹּהֲנִים, לִנְשֵׁיהֶם, וְלִבְנֵיהֶם וּלְעַבְדֵיהֶם.

שְׁלָמִים קָדָשִׁים קַלִּים. שְׁחִיטָתָן בְּכָל מָקוֹם בָּעֲזָרָה, וְדָמָן טָעוּן שְׁתֵּי מַתָּנוֹת שֶׁהֵן אַרְבַּע, וְנֶאֱכָלִין בְּכָל הָעִיר, לְכָל אָדָם, בְּכָל מַאֲכָל, לִשְׁנֵי יָמִים וְלַיְלָה אֶחָד. הַמּוּרָם מֵהֶם כַּיּוֹצֵא בָהֶם, אֶלָּא שֶׁהַמּוּרָם נֶאֱכָל לַכֹּהֲנִים, לִנְשֵׁיהֶם, וְלִבְנֵיהֶם וּלְעַבְדֵיהֶם.

הַבְּכוֹר וְהַמַּעֲשֵׂר וְהַפֶּסַח קָדָשִׁים קַלִּים. שְׁחִיטָתָן בְּכָל מָקוֹם בָּעֲזָרָה, וְדָמָן טָעוּן מַתָּנָה אֶחָת, וּבִלְבָד שֶׁיִּתֵּן כְּנֶגֶד הַיְסוֹד. שִׁנָּה בַאֲכִילָתָן, הַבְּכוֹר נֶאֱכָל לַכֹּהֲנִים וְהַמַּעֲשֵׂר לְכָל אָדָם, וְנֶאֱכָלִין בְּכָל הָעִיר, בְּכָל מַאֲכָל, לִשְׁנֵי יָמִים וְלַיְלָה אֶחָד. הַפֶּסַח אֵינוֹ נֶאֱכָל אֶלָּא בַלַּיְלָה, וְאֵינוֹ נֶאֱכָל אֶלָּא עַד חֲצוֹת, וְאֵינוֹ נֶאֱכָל אֶלָּא לִמְנוּיָיו, וְאֵינוֹ נֶאֱכָל אֶלָּא צָלִי.

THE INTERPRETIVE PRINCIPLES OF RABBI YISHMAEL

רַבִּי יִשְׁמָעֵאל Rabbi Yishmael says:

The Torah is expounded by thirteen principles:

1. An inference from a lenient law to a strict one, and vice versa.
2. An inference drawn from identical words in two passages.
3. A general principle derived from one text or two related texts.
4. A general law followed by specific examples [where the law applies exclusively to those examples].
5. A specific example followed by a general law [where the law applies to everything implied in the general statement].
6. A general law followed by specific examples and concluding with a general law: here you may infer only cases similar to the examples.
7. When a general statement requires clarification by a specific example, or a specific example requires clarification by a general statement [then rules 4 and 5 do not apply].
8. When a particular case, already included in the general statement, is expressly mentioned to teach something new, that special provision applies to all other cases included in the general statement.
9. When a particular case, though included in the general statement, is expressly mentioned with a provision similar to the general law, such a case is singled out to lessen the severity of the law, not to increase it.
10. When a particular case, though included in the general statement, is explicitly mentioned with a provision differing from the general law, it is singled out to lessen in some respects, and in others to increase, the severity of the law.
11. When a particular case, though included in the general statement, is explicitly mentioned with a new provision, the terms of the general statement no longer apply to it, unless Scripture indicates explicitly that they do apply.
12. A matter elucidated from its context, or from the following passage.
13. ▸ Also, when two passages [seem to] contradict each other, [they are to be elucidated by] a third passage that reconciles them.

May it be Your will, Lord our God and God of our ancestors, that the Temple be speedily rebuilt in our days, and grant us our share in Your Torah. And may we serve You there in reverence, as in the days of old and as in former years.

Torah is interpreted" (Maimonides, *Laws of Torah Study* 1:11). It was chosen because it appears at the beginning of the *Sifra*, the halakhic commentary to Leviticus, which is the source of most of the laws of offerings. It also reminds us of the indissoluble connection between the Written Law (the Mosaic books) and the Oral Law (Mishna, Midrash and Talmud). Rabbi Yishmael's principles show how the latter can be derived from the former.

ברייתא דרבי ישמעאל

רַבִּי יִשְׁמָעֵאל אוֹמֵר: בִּשְׁלֹשׁ עֶשְׂרֵה מִדּוֹת הַתּוֹרָה נִדְרֶשֶׁת

א מִקַּל וָחֹמֶר

ב וּמִגְּזֵרָה שָׁוָה

ג מִבִּנְיַן אָב מִכָּתוּב אֶחָד, וּמִבִּנְיַן אָב מִשְּׁנֵי כְתוּבִים

ד מִכְּלָל וּפְרָט

ה מִפְּרָט וּכְלָל

ו כְּלָל וּפְרָט וּכְלָל, אִי אַתָּה דָן אֶלָּא כְּעֵין הַפְּרָט

ז מִכְּלָל שֶׁהוּא צָרִיךְ לִפְרָט, וּמִפְּרָט שֶׁהוּא צָרִיךְ לִכְלָל

ח כָּל דָּבָר שֶׁהָיָה בִּכְלָל, וְיָצָא מִן הַכְּלָל לְלַמֵּד
לֹא לְלַמֵּד עַל עַצְמוֹ יָצָא, אֶלָּא לְלַמֵּד עַל הַכְּלָל כֻּלּוֹ יָצָא

ט כָּל דָּבָר שֶׁהָיָה בִּכְלָל, וְיָצָא לִטְעֹן טֹעַן אֶחָד שֶׁהוּא כְעִנְיָנוֹ
יָצָא לְהָקֵל וְלֹא לְהַחֲמִיר

י כָּל דָּבָר שֶׁהָיָה בִּכְלָל, וְיָצָא לִטְעֹן טֹעַן אַחֵר שֶׁלֹּא כְעִנְיָנוֹ
יָצָא לְהָקֵל וּלְהַחֲמִיר

יא כָּל דָּבָר שֶׁהָיָה בִּכְלָל, וְיָצָא לִדּוֹן בַּדָּבָר הֶחָדָשׁ
אִי אַתָּה יָכוֹל לְהַחֲזִירוֹ לִכְלָלוֹ
עַד שֶׁיַּחֲזִירֶנּוּ הַכָּתוּב לִכְלָלוֹ בְּפֵרוּשׁ

יב דָּבָר הַלָּמֵד מֵעִנְיָנוֹ, וְדָבָר הַלָּמֵד מִסּוֹפוֹ

◂ יג וְכֵן שְׁנֵי כְתוּבִים הַמַּכְחִישִׁים זֶה אֶת זֶה
עַד שֶׁיָּבוֹא הַכָּתוּב הַשְּׁלִישִׁי וְיַכְרִיעַ בֵּינֵיהֶם.

יְהִי רָצוֹן מִלְּפָנֶיךָ, יהוה אֱלֹהֵינוּ וֵאלֹהֵי אֲבוֹתֵינוּ, שֶׁיִּבָּנֶה בֵּית הַמִּקְדָּשׁ בִּמְהֵרָה בְיָמֵינוּ, וְתֵן חֶלְקֵנוּ בְּתוֹרָתֶךָ, וְשָׁם נַעֲבָדְךָ בְּיִרְאָה כִּימֵי עוֹלָם וּכְשָׁנִים קַדְמוֹנִיּוֹת.

THE INTERPRETIVE PRINCIPLES OF RABBI YISHMAEL

This passage is included as an item of Talmud, defined in its broadest sense as "deducing conclusions from premises, developing implications of statements, comparing dicta, and studying the hermeneutical principles by which the

THE RABBIS' KADDISH

The following prayer, said by mourners, requires the presence of a minyan.
A transliteration can be found on page 1466.

Mourner: יִתְגַּדַּל Magnified and sanctified
may His great name be,
in the world He created by His will.
May He establish His kingdom in your lifetime
and in your days,
and in the lifetime of all the house of Israel,
swiftly and soon – and say: Amen.

All: May His great name be blessed for ever and all time.

Mourner: Blessed and praised, glorified and exalted,
raised and honored, uplifted and lauded
be the name of the Holy One,
blessed be He,
beyond any blessing,
song, praise and consolation
uttered in the world – and say: Amen.

To Israel, to the teachers,
their disciples and their disciples' disciples,
and to all who engage in the study of Torah,
in this (*in Israel add:* holy) place or elsewhere,
may there come to them and you great peace,
grace, kindness and compassion,
long life, ample sustenance and deliverance,
from their Father in Heaven – and say: Amen.

May there be great peace from heaven,
and (good) life for us and all Israel – and say: Amen.

Bow, take three steps back, as if taking leave of the Divine Presence,
then bow, first left, then right, then center, while saying:
May He who makes peace in His high places,
in His compassion make peace
for us and all Israel – and say: Amen.

On Ḥol HaMo'ed weekdays (except for Hoshana Raba), continue Shaḥarit on page 598.
On Yom Tov, Shabbat of Ḥol HaMo'ed and Hoshana Raba continue on the next page.

קדיש דרבנן

The following prayer, said by mourners, requires the presence of a מנין*.*
A transliteration can be found on page 1466.

אבל: יִתְגַּדַּל וְיִתְקַדַּשׁ שְׁמֵהּ רַבָּא (קהל: אָמֵן)
בְּעָלְמָא דִּי בְרָא כִרְעוּתֵהּ, וְיַמְלִיךְ מַלְכוּתֵהּ
בְּחַיֵּיכוֹן וּבְיוֹמֵיכוֹן וּבְחַיֵּי דְכָל בֵּית יִשְׂרָאֵל
בַּעֲגָלָא וּבִזְמַן קָרִיב, וְאִמְרוּ אָמֵן. (קהל: אָמֵן)

קהל ואבל: יְהֵא שְׁמֵהּ רַבָּא מְבָרַךְ לְעָלַם וּלְעָלְמֵי עָלְמַיָּא.

אבל: יִתְבָּרַךְ וְיִשְׁתַּבַּח וְיִתְפָּאַר וְיִתְרוֹמַם וְיִתְנַשֵּׂא
וְיִתְהַדָּר וְיִתְעַלֶּה וְיִתְהַלָּל
שְׁמֵהּ דְּקֻדְשָׁא בְּרִיךְ הוּא (קהל: בְּרִיךְ הוּא)
לְעֵלָּא מִן כָּל בִּרְכָתָא וְשִׁירָתָא, תֻּשְׁבְּחָתָא וְנֶחֱמָתָא
דַּאֲמִירָן בְּעָלְמָא, וְאִמְרוּ אָמֵן. (קהל: אָמֵן)

עַל יִשְׂרָאֵל וְעַל רַבָּנָן
וְעַל תַּלְמִידֵיהוֹן וְעַל כָּל תַּלְמִידֵי תַלְמִידֵיהוֹן
וְעַל כָּל מָאן דְּעָסְקִין בְּאוֹרַיְתָא
דִּי בְּאַתְרָא (בארץ ישראל: קַדִּישָׁא) הָדֵין, וְדִי בְּכָל אֲתַר וַאֲתַר
יְהֵא לְהוֹן וּלְכוֹן שְׁלָמָא רַבָּא
חִנָּא וְחִסְדָּא, וְרַחֲמֵי, וְחַיֵּי אֲרִיכֵי, וּמְזוֹנֵי רְוִיחֵי
וּפֻרְקָנָא מִן קֳדָם אֲבוּהוֹן דִּי בִשְׁמַיָּא, וְאִמְרוּ אָמֵן. (קהל: אָמֵן)

יְהֵא שְׁלָמָא רַבָּא מִן שְׁמַיָּא
וְחַיִּים (טוֹבִים) עָלֵינוּ וְעַל כָּל יִשְׂרָאֵל, וְאִמְרוּ אָמֵן. (קהל: אָמֵן)

Bow, take three steps back, as if taking leave of the Divine Presence,
then bow, first left, then right, then center, while saying:

עֹשֶׂה שָׁלוֹם בִּמְרוֹמָיו
הוּא יַעֲשֶׂה בְרַחֲמָיו שָׁלוֹם
עָלֵינוּ וְעַל כָּל יִשְׂרָאֵל, וְאִמְרוּ אָמֵן. (קהל: אָמֵן)

On חול המועד *weekdays (except for* הושענא רבה*), continue* שחרית *on page 599.*
On יום טוב, שבת חול המועד *and* הושענא רבה *continue on the next page.*

Shaḥarit for Shabbat and Yom Tov

A PSALM BEFORE VERSES OF PRAISE

מִזְמוֹר שִׁיר A psalm of David. *Ps. 30*
A song for the dedication of the House.
I will exalt You, LORD, for You have lifted me up,
and not let my enemies rejoice over me.
LORD, my God, I cried to You for help and You healed me.
LORD, You lifted my soul from the grave;
You spared me from going down to the pit.
Sing to the LORD, you His devoted ones,
and give thanks to His holy name.
For His anger is for a moment, but His favor for a lifetime.
At night there may be weeping, but in the morning there is joy.
When I felt secure, I said, "I shall never be shaken."
LORD, when You favored me,
You made me stand firm as a mountain,
but when You hid Your face, I was terrified.
To You, LORD, I called; I pleaded with my LORD:
"What gain would there be if I died and went down to the grave?
Can dust thank You? Can it declare Your truth?
Hear, LORD, and be gracious to me; LORD, be my help."
You have turned my sorrow into dancing.
▸ You have removed my sackcloth and clothed me with joy,
so that my soul may sing to You and not be silent.
LORD my God, for ever will I thank You.

---

to be sung on that occasion (Rashi). In it David relates how, when his life was in danger, God delivered him to safety. Set here, it beautifully connects the dawn blessings (waking from sleep as a miniature experience of being saved from death to life) with the Verses of Praise that are about to follow ("So that my soul may sing to You").

שחרית לשבת וליום טוב

מזמור לפני פסוקי דזמרה

מִזְמוֹר שִׁיר־חֲנֻכַּת הַבַּיִת לְדָוִד: תהלים ל
אֲרוֹמִמְךָ יהוה כִּי דִלִּיתָנִי, וְלֹא־שִׂמַּחְתָּ אֹיְבַי לִי:
יהוה אֱלֹהָי, שִׁוַּעְתִּי אֵלֶיךָ וַתִּרְפָּאֵנִי:
יהוה, הֶעֱלִיתָ מִן־שְׁאוֹל נַפְשִׁי, חִיִּיתַנִי מִיָּרְדִי־בוֹר:
זַמְּרוּ לַיהוה חֲסִידָיו, וְהוֹדוּ לְזֵכֶר קָדְשׁוֹ:
כִּי רֶגַע בְּאַפּוֹ, חַיִּים בִּרְצוֹנוֹ, בָּעֶרֶב יָלִין בֶּכִי וְלַבֹּקֶר רִנָּה:
וַאֲנִי אָמַרְתִּי בְשַׁלְוִי, בַּל־אֶמּוֹט לְעוֹלָם:
יהוה, בִּרְצוֹנְךָ הֶעֱמַדְתָּה לְהַרְרִי עֹז
הִסְתַּרְתָּ פָנֶיךָ הָיִיתִי נִבְהָל:
אֵלֶיךָ יהוה אֶקְרָא, וְאֶל־אֲדֹנָי אֶתְחַנָּן:
מַה־בֶּצַע בְּדָמִי, בְּרִדְתִּי אֶל שָׁחַת, הֲיוֹדְךָ עָפָר, הֲיַגִּיד אֲמִתֶּךָ:
שְׁמַע־יהוה וְחָנֵּנִי, יהוה הֱיֵה־עֹזֵר לִי:
◂ הָפַכְתָּ מִסְפְּדִי לְמָחוֹל לִי, פִּתַּחְתָּ שַׂקִּי, וַתְּאַזְּרֵנִי שִׂמְחָה:
לְמַעַן יְזַמֶּרְךָ כָבוֹד וְלֹא יִדֹּם, יהוה אֱלֹהַי, לְעוֹלָם אוֹדֶךָּ:

מִזְמוֹר שִׁיר *Psalm 30.* This psalm was a late addition to the morning prayers, appearing for the first time in the seventeenth century. Although entitled "A psalm of David. A song for the dedication of the House," we know that the Temple was not built in his lifetime. As a soldier and military leader he was deemed not to be privileged to build a Temple that symbolized peace (1 Chr. 22:8). Hence it was built by his son King Solomon, whose name means peace and whose reign was marked by peace. Nonetheless, since it was David who conceived the plan to build the Temple, he wrote this psalm

MOURNER'S KADDISH

The following prayer, said by mourners, requires the presence of a minyan. A transliteration can be found on page 1467.

Mourner: יִתְגַּדַּל Magnified and sanctified
may His great name be,
in the world He created by His will.
May He establish His kingdom
in your lifetime and in your days,
and in the lifetime
of all the house of Israel,
swiftly and soon –
and say: Amen.

All: May His great name be blessed
for ever and all time.

Mourner: Blessed and praised, glorified and exalted,
raised and honored,
uplifted and lauded
be the name of the Holy One,
blessed be He,
beyond any blessing,
song, praise and consolation
uttered in the world –
and say: Amen.

May there be great peace from heaven,
and life for us and all Israel –
and say: Amen.

Bow, take three steps back, as if taking leave of the Divine Presence, then bow, first left, then right, then center, while saying:

May He who makes peace in His high places,
make peace for us and all Israel –
and say: Amen.

קדיש יתום

The following prayer, said by mourners, requires the presence of a מנין.
A transliteration can be found on page 1467.

אבל: יִתְגַּדַּל וְיִתְקַדַּשׁ שְׁמֵהּ רַבָּא (קהל: אָמֵן)
בְּעָלְמָא דִּי בְרָא כִרְעוּתֵהּ
וְיַמְלִיךְ מַלְכוּתֵהּ
בְּחַיֵּיכוֹן וּבְיוֹמֵיכוֹן וּבְחַיֵּי דְכָל בֵּית יִשְׂרָאֵל
בַּעֲגָלָא וּבִזְמַן קָרִיב
וְאִמְרוּ אָמֵן. (קהל: אָמֵן)

קהל ואבל: יְהֵא שְׁמֵהּ רַבָּא מְבָרַךְ לְעָלַם וּלְעָלְמֵי עָלְמַיָּא.

אבל: יִתְבָּרַךְ וְיִשְׁתַּבַּח וְיִתְפָּאַר
וְיִתְרוֹמַם וְיִתְנַשֵּׂא וְיִתְהַדָּר וְיִתְעַלֶּה וְיִתְהַלָּל
שְׁמֵהּ דְּקֻדְשָׁא בְּרִיךְ הוּא (קהל: בְּרִיךְ הוּא)
לְעֵלָּא מִן כָּל בִּרְכָתָא וְשִׁירָתָא, תֻּשְׁבְּחָתָא וְנֶחֱמָתָא
דַּאֲמִירָן בְּעָלְמָא
וְאִמְרוּ אָמֵן. (קהל: אָמֵן)

יְהֵא שְׁלָמָא רַבָּא מִן שְׁמַיָּא
וְחַיִּים, עָלֵינוּ וְעַל כָּל יִשְׂרָאֵל
וְאִמְרוּ אָמֵן. (קהל: אָמֵן)

Bow, take three steps back, as if taking leave of the Divine Presence,
then bow, first left, then right, then center, while saying:

עֹשֶׂה שָׁלוֹם בִּמְרוֹמָיו
הוּא יַעֲשֶׂה שָׁלוֹם עָלֵינוּ
וְעַל כָּל יִשְׂרָאֵל
וְאִמְרוּ אָמֵן. (קהל: אָמֵן)

PESUKEI DEZIMRA

The following introductory blessing to the Pesukei DeZimra (Verses of Praise) is said standing, while holding the two front tzitziot of the tallit. They are kissed and released at the end of the blessing at "songs of praise" (on the next page). From the beginning of this prayer to the end of the Amida, conversation is forbidden.

Some say:
I hereby prepare my mouth to thank, praise and laud my Creator, for the sake of the unification of the Holy One, blessed be He, and His Divine Presence, through that which is hidden and concealed, in the name of all Israel.

BLESSED IS HE WHO SPOKE

and the world came into being, blessed is He.
Blessed is He who creates the universe.
Blessed is He who speaks and acts.
Blessed is He who decrees and fulfills.
Blessed is He who shows compassion to the earth.
Blessed is He who shows compassion to all creatures.
Blessed is He who gives a good reward
to those who fear Him.
Blessed is He who lives for ever and exists to eternity.
Blessed is He who redeems and saves.
Blessed is His name.

145–150, of the book of Psalms, which correspond to the six days of creation in Genesis 1.

בָּרוּךְ שֶׁאָמַר וְהָיָה הָעוֹלָם *Blessed is He who spoke and the world came into being.* In the sharpest possible contrast to the mythology of the pagan world, creation unfolds in Genesis 1 without clash or conflict between the elements. God said, "Let there be" and there was. There is an essential underlying harmony in the universe. All that exists is the result of a single creative will. The world is fundamentally good – the word "good" appears seven times in the opening chapter. The opening section of this two-part blessing is a ten-line litany of blessings, corresponding to the ten times in Genesis 1 in which the phrase, "And God said" appears: the "ten utterances" by which the world was made (*Avot* 5:1).

פסוקי דזמרה

The following introductory blessing to the פסוקי דזמרה *is said standing, while holding the two front* ציציות *of the* טלית*. They are kissed and released at the end of the blessing at* בַּתִּשְׁבָּחוֹת *(on the next page). From the beginning of this prayer to the end of the* עמידה*, conversation is forbidden.*

Some say:

הֲרֵינִי מְזַמֵּן אֶת פִּי לְהוֹדוֹת וּלְהַלֵּל וּלְשַׁבֵּחַ אֶת בּוֹרְאִי, לְשֵׁם יִחוּד קֻדְשָׁא בְּרִיךְ הוּא וּשְׁכִינְתֵּהּ עַל יְדֵי הַהוּא טָמִיר וְנֶעְלָם בְּשֵׁם כָּל יִשְׂרָאֵל.

בָּרוּךְ שֶׁאָמַר
וְהָיָה הָעוֹלָם, בָּרוּךְ הוּא.
בָּרוּךְ עוֹשֶׂה בְרֵאשִׁית
בָּרוּךְ אוֹמֵר וְעוֹשֶׂה
בָּרוּךְ גּוֹזֵר וּמְקַיֵּם
בָּרוּךְ מְרַחֵם עַל הָאָרֶץ
בָּרוּךְ מְרַחֵם עַל הַבְּרִיּוֹת
בָּרוּךְ מְשַׁלֵּם שָׂכָר טוֹב לִירֵאָיו
בָּרוּךְ חַי לָעַד וְקַיָּם לָנֶצַח
בָּרוּךְ פּוֹדֶה וּמַצִּיל
בָּרוּךְ שְׁמוֹ

בָּרוּךְ שֶׁאָמַר *Blessed is He who spoke.* An introductory blessing to the Verses of Praise that follow, mainly taken from the Psalms. Their essential theme is God as He exists in Creation, designing and sustaining the universe in wisdom, justice and compassion. At their core are the last six psalms,

Blessed are You, LORD our God, King of the Universe,
God, compassionate Father, extolled by the mouth of His people,
praised and glorified by the tongue of His devoted ones
and those who serve Him.
With the songs of Your servant David
we will praise You, O LORD our God.
With praises and psalms we will magnify and praise You, glorify You,
Speak Your name and proclaim Your kingship,
our King, our God, ▸ the only One, Giver of life to the worlds
the King whose great name is praised and glorified to all eternity.
Blessed are You, LORD,
the King extolled with songs of praise.

הודו Thank the LORD, call on His name, make His acts known among the peoples. Sing to Him, make music to Him, tell of all His wonders. Glory in His holy name; let the hearts of those who seek the LORD rejoice. Search out the LORD and His strength; seek His presence at all times. Remember the wonders He has done, His miracles, and the judgments He pronounced. Descendants of Yisrael His servant, sons of Jacob His chosen ones: He is the LORD our God. His judgments are throughout the earth. Remember His covenant for ever, the word He commanded for a thousand generations. He made it with Abraham, vowed it to Isaac, and confirmed it to Jacob as a statute and to Israel as an everlasting covenant, saying, *1 Chr. 16*

מְבַקְשֵׁי יהוה *Those who seek the LORD.* including those of other nations (Radak).

בַּקְּשׁוּ פָנָיו *Seek His presence.* in prayer (Radak), or contemplation (Malbim; see commentary on Psalms 105:4).

וּמִשְׁפְּטֵי־פִיהוּ *The judgments He pronounced.* the warnings God sends in advance through His prophets, as Moses warned Pharaoh of the impending plagues (Radak, Ps. 105:5).

לְאֶלֶף דּוֹר *For a thousand generations.* a poetic way of saying "forever."

אַבְרָהָם, יִצְחָק, יַעֲקֹב *Abraham, Isaac, Jacob.* God made a promise to each of the three patriarchs that their descendants would inherit the land.

בָּרוּךְ אַתָּה יהוה אֱלֹהֵינוּ מֶלֶךְ הָעוֹלָם
הָאֵל הָאָב הָרַחֲמָן הַמְהֻלָּל בְּפִי עַמּוֹ
מְשֻׁבָּח וּמְפֹאָר בִּלְשׁוֹן חֲסִידָיו וַעֲבָדָיו
וּבְשִׁירֵי דָוִד עַבְדֶּךָ, נְהַלֶּלְךָ יהוה אֱלֹהֵינוּ.
בִּשְׁבָחוֹת וּבִזְמִירוֹת
נְגַדֶּלְךָ וּנְשַׁבֵּחֲךָ וּנְפָאֶרְךָ, וְנַזְכִּיר שִׁמְךָ וְנַמְלִיכְךָ
מַלְכֵּנוּ אֱלֹהֵינוּ, ◂ יָחִיד חֵי הָעוֹלָמִים
מֶלֶךְ, מְשֻׁבָּח וּמְפֹאָר עֲדֵי עַד שְׁמוֹ הַגָּדוֹל
בָּרוּךְ אַתָּה יהוה, מֶלֶךְ מְהֻלָּל בַּתִּשְׁבָּחוֹת.

הוֹדוּ לַיהוה קִרְאוּ בִשְׁמוֹ, הוֹדִיעוּ בָעַמִּים עֲלִילֹתָיו: שִׁירוּ לוֹ, דברי הימים א׳ טז
זַמְּרוּ־לוֹ, שִׂיחוּ בְּכָל־נִפְלְאוֹתָיו: הִתְהַלְלוּ בְּשֵׁם קָדְשׁוֹ, יִשְׂמַח לֵב
מְבַקְשֵׁי יהוה: דִּרְשׁוּ יהוה וְעֻזּוֹ, בַּקְּשׁוּ פָנָיו תָּמִיד: זִכְרוּ נִפְלְאֹתָיו
אֲשֶׁר עָשָׂה, מֹפְתָיו וּמִשְׁפְּטֵי־פִיהוּ: זֶרַע יִשְׂרָאֵל עַבְדּוֹ, בְּנֵי יַעֲקֹב
בְּחִירָיו: הוּא יהוה אֱלֹהֵינוּ בְּכָל־הָאָרֶץ מִשְׁפָּטָיו: זִכְרוּ לְעוֹלָם
בְּרִיתוֹ, דָּבָר צִוָּה לְאֶלֶף דּוֹר: אֲשֶׁר כָּרַת אֶת־אַבְרָהָם, וּשְׁבוּעָתוֹ
לְיִצְחָק: וַיַּעֲמִידֶהָ לְיַעֲקֹב לְחֹק, לְיִשְׂרָאֵל בְּרִית עוֹלָם: לֵאמֹר, לְךָ

בָּרוּךְ אַתָּה *Blessed are You.* The second part of this two-part blessing is an introduction to the biblical passages that follow.

וּבְשִׁירֵי דָוִד עַבְדֶּךָ *With the songs of Your servant David.* A reference to the psalms that form the core of the Verses of Praise.

הוֹדוּ לַיהוה *Thank the Lord.* A joyous celebration of Jewish history, this is the song David composed for the day the Ark was brought, in joy and dance, to Jerusalem.

הוֹדִיעוּ בָעַמִּים עֲלִילֹתָיו *Make His acts known among the peoples.* According to Radak this is a reference to the miraculous afflictions that struck the Philistines when they captured the Ark (1 Sam. 5).

"To you I will give the land of Canaan as your allotted heritage." You were then small in number, few, strangers there, wandering from nation to nation, from one kingdom to another, but He let no man oppress them, and for their sake He rebuked kings: "Do not touch My anointed ones, and do My prophets no harm." Sing to the LORD, all the earth; proclaim His salvation daily. Declare His glory among the nations, His marvels among all the peoples. For great is the LORD and greatly to be praised; He is awesome beyond all heavenly powers. ▸ For all the gods of the peoples are mere idols; it was the LORD who made the heavens.

Before Him are majesty and splendor; there is strength and beauty in His holy place. Render to the LORD, families of the peoples, render to the LORD honor and might. Render to the LORD the glory due to His name; bring an offering and come before Him; bow down to the LORD in the splendor of holiness. Tremble before Him, all the earth; the world stands firm, it will not be shaken. Let the heavens rejoice and the earth be glad; let them declare among the nations, "The LORD is King." Let the sea roar, and all that is in it; let the fields be jubilant, and all they contain. Then the trees of the forest will sing for joy before the LORD, for He is coming to judge the earth. Thank the LORD for He is good; His loving-kindness is for ever. Say: "Save us, God of our salvation; gather us and rescue us from the nations, to acknowledge Your holy name and glory in Your praise. Blessed is the LORD, God of Israel, from this world to eternity." And let all the people say "Amen" and "Praise the LORD."

---

pagans worshiped the sun, moon and stars as gods, not realizing that none was an independent power. Each had been made by the One God.

יִשְׂמְחוּ הַשָּׁמַיִם *Let the heavens rejoice.* A sentiment typical of the radiant vision of the Psalms: the universe moves in accordance with both the natural and moral laws that ensure its order and stability. Nature is not something to fear, but to celebrate.

וַיֹּאמְרוּ כָל־הָעָם *And let all the people say.* This was their response to the song sung the day the Ark was brought to Jerusalem (Ralbag).

אֶתֵּן אֶרֶץ־כְּנָעַן, חֶבֶל נַחֲלַתְכֶם: בִּהְיוֹתְכֶם מְתֵי מִסְפָּר, כִּמְעַט וְגָרִים בָּהּ: וַיִּתְהַלְּכוּ מִגּוֹי אֶל־גּוֹי, וּמִמַּמְלָכָה אֶל־עַם אַחֵר: לֹא־הִנִּיחַ לְאִישׁ לְעָשְׁקָם, וַיּוֹכַח עֲלֵיהֶם מְלָכִים: אַל־תִּגְּעוּ בִּמְשִׁיחָי, וּבִנְבִיאַי אַל־תָּרֵעוּ: שִׁירוּ לַיהוה כָּל־הָאָרֶץ, בַּשְּׂרוּ מִיּוֹם־אֶל־יוֹם יְשׁוּעָתוֹ: סַפְּרוּ בַגּוֹיִם אֶת־כְּבוֹדוֹ, בְּכָל־הָעַמִּים נִפְלְאֹתָיו: כִּי גָדוֹל יהוה וּמְהֻלָּל מְאֹד, וְנוֹרָא הוּא עַל־כָּל־אֱלֹהִים: ◂ כִּי כָּל־אֱלֹהֵי הָעַמִּים אֱלִילִים, וַיהוה שָׁמַיִם עָשָׂה:

הוֹד וְהָדָר לְפָנָיו, עֹז וְחֶדְוָה בִּמְקֹמוֹ: הָבוּ לַיהוה מִשְׁפְּחוֹת עַמִּים, הָבוּ לַיהוה כָּבוֹד וָעֹז: הָבוּ לַיהוה כְּבוֹד שְׁמוֹ, שְׂאוּ מִנְחָה וּבֹאוּ לְפָנָיו, הִשְׁתַּחֲווּ לַיהוה בְּהַדְרַת־קֹדֶשׁ: חִילוּ מִלְּפָנָיו כָּל־הָאָרֶץ, אַף־תִּכּוֹן תֵּבֵל בַּל־תִּמּוֹט: יִשְׂמְחוּ הַשָּׁמַיִם וְתָגֵל הָאָרֶץ, וְיֹאמְרוּ בַגּוֹיִם יהוה מָלָךְ: יִרְעַם הַיָּם וּמְלוֹאוֹ, יַעֲלֹץ הַשָּׂדֶה וְכָל־אֲשֶׁר־בּוֹ: אָז יְרַנְּנוּ עֲצֵי הַיָּעַר, מִלִּפְנֵי יהוה, כִּי־בָא לִשְׁפּוֹט אֶת־הָאָרֶץ: הוֹדוּ לַיהוה כִּי טוֹב, כִּי לְעוֹלָם חַסְדּוֹ: וְאִמְרוּ, הוֹשִׁיעֵנוּ אֱלֹהֵי יִשְׁעֵנוּ, וְקַבְּצֵנוּ וְהַצִּילֵנוּ מִן־הַגּוֹיִם, לְהֹדוֹת לְשֵׁם קָדְשֶׁךָ, לְהִשְׁתַּבֵּחַ בִּתְהִלָּתֶךָ: בָּרוּךְ יהוה אֱלֹהֵי יִשְׂרָאֵל מִן־הָעוֹלָם וְעַד־הָעֹלָם, וַיֹּאמְרוּ כָל־הָעָם אָמֵן, וְהַלֵּל לַיהוה:

וַיִּתְהַלְּכוּ *Wandering.* Each of the patriarchs was forced to leave the land because of famine.

וַיּוֹכַח עֲלֵיהֶם מְלָכִים *For their sake He rebuked kings.* A reference to God's affliction of Pharaoh (Gen. 12:17) and Abimelech, King of Gerar (Gen. 20:18) for taking Sarah; and Laban when he was pursuing Jacob (Gen. 31:24, 29).

מְשִׁיחָי *My anointed ones.* Although only kings and high priests were anointed, here the phrase is used as a metaphor meaning "chosen ones."

אֱלִילִים, וַיהוה שָׁמַיִם עָשָׂה *Mere idols; it was the Lord who made the heavens.* The

▸ Exalt the LORD our God and bow before His footstool: He is *Ps. 99*
holy. Exalt the LORD our God and bow at His holy mountain; for
holy is the LORD our God.

He is compassionate. He forgives iniquity and does not destroy. *Ps. 78*
Repeatedly He suppresses His anger, not rousing His full wrath.
You, LORD: do not withhold Your compassion from me. May Your *Ps. 40*
loving-kindness and truth always guard me. Remember, LORD, *Ps. 25*
Your acts of compassion and love, for they have existed for ever.
Ascribe power to God, whose majesty is over Israel and whose *Ps. 68*
might is in the skies. You are awesome, God, in Your holy places.
It is the God of Israel who gives might and strength to the people,
may God be blessed. God of retribution, LORD, God of retribu- *Ps. 94*
tion, appear. Arise, Judge of the earth, to repay the arrogant their
just deserts. Salvation belongs to the LORD; may Your blessing *Ps. 3*
rest upon Your people, Selah! ▸ The LORD of hosts is with us, the *Ps. 46*
God of Jacob is our stronghold, Selah! LORD of hosts, happy is *Ps. 84*
the one who trusts in You. LORD, save! May the King answer us *Ps. 20*
on the day we call.

Save Your people and bless Your heritage; tend them and carry *Ps. 28*
them for ever. Our soul longs for the LORD; He is our Help and *Ps. 33*
Shield. For in Him our hearts rejoice, for in His holy name we
have trusted. May Your loving-kindness, LORD, be upon us, as we
have put our hope in You. Show us, LORD, Your loving-kindness *Ps. 85*
and grant us Your salvation. Arise, help us and redeem us for the *Ps. 44*
sake of Your love. I am the LORD your God who brought you *Ps. 81*
up from the land of Egypt: open your mouth wide and I will fill
it. Happy is the people for whom this is so; happy is the people *Ps. 144*
whose God the LORD. ▸ As for me, I trust in Your loving-kindness; *Ps. 13*
my heart rejoices in Your salvation. I will sing to the LORD for He
has been good to me.

---

divine justice and compassion, moving seamlessly from national to individual thanksgiving.

‹ רוֹמְמוּ יהוה אֱלֹהֵינוּ וְהִשְׁתַּחֲווּ לַהֲדֹם רַגְלָיו, קָדוֹשׁ הוּא: תהלים צט
רוֹמְמוּ יהוה אֱלֹהֵינוּ וְהִשְׁתַּחֲווּ לְהַר קָדְשׁוֹ, כִּי־קָדוֹשׁ יהוה
אֱלֹהֵינוּ:

וְהוּא רַחוּם, יְכַפֵּר עָוֹן וְלֹא־יַשְׁחִית, וְהִרְבָּה לְהָשִׁיב אַפּוֹ, תהלים עח
וְלֹא־יָעִיר כָּל־חֲמָתוֹ: אַתָּה יהוה לֹא־תִכְלָא רַחֲמֶיךָ מִמֶּנִּי, תהלים מ
חַסְדְּךָ וַאֲמִתְּךָ תָּמִיד יִצְּרוּנִי: זְכֹר־רַחֲמֶיךָ יהוה וַחֲסָדֶיךָ, כִּי תהלים כה
מֵעוֹלָם הֵמָּה: תְּנוּ עֹז לֵאלֹהִים, עַל־יִשְׂרָאֵל גַּאֲוָתוֹ, וְעֻזּוֹ תהלים סח
בַּשְּׁחָקִים: נוֹרָא אֱלֹהִים מִמִּקְדָּשֶׁיךָ, אֵל יִשְׂרָאֵל הוּא נֹתֵן עֹז
וְתַעֲצֻמוֹת לָעָם, בָּרוּךְ אֱלֹהִים: אֵל־נְקָמוֹת יהוה, אֵל נְקָמוֹת תהלים צד
הוֹפִיעַ: הִנָּשֵׂא שֹׁפֵט הָאָרֶץ, הָשֵׁב גְּמוּל עַל־גֵּאִים: לַיהוה תהלים ג
הַיְשׁוּעָה, עַל־עַמְּךָ בִרְכָתֶךָ סֶּלָה: ‹ יהוה צְבָאוֹת עִמָּנוּ, מִשְׂגָּב תהלים מו
לָנוּ אֱלֹהֵי יַעֲקֹב סֶלָה: יהוה צְבָאוֹת, אַשְׁרֵי אָדָם בֹּטֵחַ בָּךְ: תהלים פד
יהוה הוֹשִׁיעָה, הַמֶּלֶךְ יַעֲנֵנוּ בְיוֹם־קָרְאֵנוּ: תהלים כ

הוֹשִׁיעָה אֶת־עַמֶּךָ, וּבָרֵךְ אֶת־נַחֲלָתֶךָ, וּרְעֵם וְנַשְּׂאֵם תהלים כח
עַד־הָעוֹלָם: נַפְשֵׁנוּ חִכְּתָה לַיהוה, עֶזְרֵנוּ וּמָגִנֵּנוּ הוּא: כִּי־בוֹ תהלים לג
יִשְׂמַח לִבֵּנוּ, כִּי בְשֵׁם קָדְשׁוֹ בָטָחְנוּ: יְהִי־חַסְדְּךָ יהוה עָלֵינוּ,
כַּאֲשֶׁר יִחַלְנוּ לָךְ: הַרְאֵנוּ יהוה חַסְדֶּךָ, וְיֶשְׁעֲךָ תִּתֶּן־לָנוּ: קוּמָה תהלים פה תהלים מד
עֶזְרָתָה לָּנוּ, וּפְדֵנוּ לְמַעַן חַסְדֶּךָ: אָנֹכִי יהוה אֱלֹהֶיךָ הַמַּעַלְךָ תהלים פא
מֵאֶרֶץ מִצְרָיִם, הַרְחֶב־פִּיךָ וַאֲמַלְאֵהוּ: אַשְׁרֵי הָעָם שֶׁכָּכָה תהלים קמד
לּוֹ, אַשְׁרֵי הָעָם שֶׁיהוה אֱלֹהָיו: ‹ וַאֲנִי בְּחַסְדְּךָ בָטַחְתִּי, יָגֵל תהלים יג
לִבִּי בִּישׁוּעָתֶךָ, אָשִׁירָה לַיהוה, כִּי גָמַל עָלָי:

רוֹמְמוּ *Exalt.* A selection of verses from the book of Psalms, on the themes of

On Hoshana Raba the following psalm is said. The custom is to say it standing.

מִזְמוֹר A psalm of thanksgiving. Shout joyously to the LORD, all the earth. Serve the LORD with joy. Come before Him with jubilation. Know that the LORD is God. He made us and we are His. We are His people and the flock He tends. Enter His gates with thanksgiving, His courts with praise. Thank Him and bless His name. ▸ For the LORD is good, His loving-kindness is everlasting, and His faithfulness is for every generation. *Ps. 100*

לַמְנַצֵּחַ For the conductor of music. A psalm of David. *Ps. 19*
The heavens declare the glory of God;
the skies proclaim the work of His hands.
Day to day they pour forth speech;
night to night they communicate knowledge.
There is no speech, there are no words,
their voice is not heard.
Yet their music carries throughout the earth,
their words to the end of the world.
In them He has set a tent for the sun.
It emerges like a groom from his marriage chamber,
rejoicing like a champion about to run a race.
It rises at one end of the heaven
and makes its circuit to the other:
nothing is hidden from its heat.
The LORD's Torah is perfect, refreshing the soul.
The LORD's testimony is faithful, making the simple wise.
The LORD's precepts are just, gladdening the heart.
The LORD's commandment is radiant, giving light to the eyes.
The fear of the LORD is pure, enduring for ever.
The LORD's judgments are true, altogether righteous.

---

them is the idea of speech. First is the silent speech of the universe, the "music of the spheres," that the universe continually utters to its Creator. Then comes the audible speech of God to humankind, the revelation of His will in the form of the Torah. The Psalmist speaks ecstatically about the power of

On הושענא רבה *the following psalm is said. The custom is to say it standing.*

תהלים ק מִזְמוֹר לְתוֹדָה, הָרִֽיעוּ לַיהוה כׇּל־הָאָֽרֶץ: עִבְדוּ אֶת־יהוה בְּשִׂמְחָה,
בֹּֽאוּ לְפָנָיו בִּרְנָנָה: דְּעוּ כִּי־יהוה הוּא אֱלֹהִים, הוּא עָשָֽׂנוּ וְלוֹ אֲנַֽחְנוּ,
עַמּוֹ וְצֹאן מַרְעִיתוֹ: בֹּֽאוּ שְׁעָרָיו בְּתוֹדָה, חֲצֵרֹתָיו בִּתְהִלָּה, הֽוֹדוּ לוֹ,
בָּרְכוּ שְׁמוֹ: ‹ כִּי־טוֹב יהוה, לְעוֹלָם חַסְדּוֹ, וְעַד־דֹּר וָדֹר אֱמוּנָתוֹ:

תהלים יט לַמְנַצֵּֽחַ מִזְמוֹר לְדָוִד:
הַשָּׁמַֽיִם מְסַפְּרִים כְּבוֹד־אֵל, וּמַֽעֲשֵׂה יָדָיו מַגִּיד הָרָקִֽיעַ:
יוֹם לְיוֹם יַבִּֽיעַ אֹֽמֶר, וְלַֽיְלָה לְּלַֽיְלָה יְחַוֶּה־דָּֽעַת:
אֵין־אֹֽמֶר וְאֵין דְּבָרִים, בְּלִי נִשְׁמָע קוֹלָם:
בְּכׇל־הָאָֽרֶץ יָצָא קַוָּם, וּבִקְצֵה תֵבֵל מִלֵּיהֶם
לַשֶּֽׁמֶשׁ שָׂם־אֹֽהֶל בָּהֶם:
וְהוּא כְּחָתָן יֹצֵא מֵחֻפָּתוֹ, יָשִׂישׂ כְּגִבּוֹר לָרוּץ אֹֽרַח:
מִקְצֵה הַשָּׁמַֽיִם מוֹצָאוֹ, וּתְקוּפָתוֹ עַל־קְצוֹתָם
וְאֵין נִסְתָּר מֵחַמָּתוֹ:
תּוֹרַת יהוה תְּמִימָה, מְשִֽׁיבַת נָֽפֶשׁ
עֵדוּת יהוה נֶאֱמָנָה, מַחְכִּֽימַת פֶּֽתִי:
פִּקּוּדֵי יהוה יְשָׁרִים, מְשַׂמְּחֵי־לֵב
מִצְוַת יהוה בָּרָה, מְאִירַת עֵינָֽיִם:
יִרְאַת יהוה טְהוֹרָה, עוֹמֶֽדֶת לָעַד
מִשְׁפְּטֵי־יהוה אֱמֶת, צָדְקוּ יַחְדָּו:

לַמְנַצֵּֽחַ *Psalm 19.* A magnificent psalm in three parts, corresponding to the basic tripartite structure of Jewish belief: Creation, Revelation and Redemption. The first seven verses are a hymn about Creation as God's work. The second section (verses 8–11) is about Revelation – Torah – as God's word. The third is a prayer for forgiveness, ending with the word "Redeemer." What connects

More precious than gold, than much fine gold.
They are sweeter than honey, than honey from the comb.
Your servant, too, is careful of them,
for in observing them there is great reward.
Yet who can discern his errors?
Cleanse me of hidden faults.
Keep Your servant also from willful sins;
let them not have dominion over me.
Then shall I be blameless,
and innocent of grave sin.
▸ May the words of my mouth and the meditation of my heart
find favor before You, LORD, my Rock and my Redeemer.

לְדָוִד Of David. When he pretended to be insane before Abimelech, who drove him away, and he left. *Ps. 34*
I will bless the LORD at all times;
His praise will be always on my lips.
My soul will glory in the LORD;
let the lowly hear this and rejoice.
Magnify the LORD with me;
let us exalt His name together.
I sought the LORD, and He answered me;
He saved me from all my fears.
Those who look to Him are radiant;
Their faces are never downcast.
This poor man called, and the LORD heard;
He saved him from all his troubles.
The LORD's angel encamps around those who fear Him,
and He rescues them.

---

decided to pretend to be insane, "making marks on the doors of the gate and letting saliva run down his beard." The Philistine king, dismissing him as a madman, told his servants to remove him. Thus David was able to make good his escape (1 Sam. 21:11–16). He composed this psalm as a song of thanksgiving: "This poor man called, and the LORD heard… None who take refuge in Him shall be condemned." God is not on the side of those who embody

הַנֶּחֱמָדִים מִזָּהָב וּמִפַּז רָב, וּמְתוּקִים מִדְּבַשׁ וְנֹפֶת צוּפִים:
גַּם־עַבְדְּךָ נִזְהָר בָּהֶם, בְּשָׁמְרָם עֵקֶב רָב:
שְׁגִיאוֹת מִי־יָבִין, מִנִּסְתָּרוֹת נַקֵּנִי:
גַּם מִזֵּדִים חֲשֹׂךְ עַבְדֶּךָ, אַל־יִמְשְׁלוּ־בִי אָז אֵיתָם
וְנִקֵּיתִי מִפֶּשַׁע רָב:
◂ יִהְיוּ לְרָצוֹן אִמְרֵי־פִי וְהֶגְיוֹן לִבִּי לְפָנֶיךָ, יהוה, צוּרִי וְגֹאֲלִי:

תהלים לד

לְדָוִד, בְּשַׁנּוֹתוֹ אֶת־טַעְמוֹ לִפְנֵי אֲבִימֶלֶךְ, וַיְגָרְשֵׁהוּ וַיֵּלַךְ:
אֲבָרְכָה אֶת־יהוה בְּכָל־עֵת, תָּמִיד תְּהִלָּתוֹ בְּפִי:
בַּיהוה תִּתְהַלֵּל נַפְשִׁי, יִשְׁמְעוּ עֲנָוִים וְיִשְׂמָחוּ:
גַּדְּלוּ לַיהוה אִתִּי, וּנְרוֹמְמָה שְׁמוֹ יַחְדָּו:
דָּרַשְׁתִּי אֶת־יהוה וְעָנָנִי, וּמִכָּל־מְגוּרוֹתַי הִצִּילָנִי:
הִבִּיטוּ אֵלָיו וְנָהָרוּ, וּפְנֵיהֶם אַל־יֶחְפָּרוּ:
זֶה עָנִי קָרָא, וַיהוה שָׁמֵעַ, וּמִכָּל־צָרוֹתָיו הוֹשִׁיעוֹ:
חֹנֶה מַלְאַךְ־יהוה סָבִיב לִירֵאָיו, וַיְחַלְּצֵם:

Torah to transform those who open themselves to its radiance. In Creation we encounter the world that is, but in Revelation we catch a glimpse of the world that ought to be, and will come to be when we align our will with the will of God. Finally comes the speech of humanity to God ("the words of my mouth and the meditation of my heart") in the form of prayer.

שְׁגִיאוֹת מִי־יָבִין *Yet who can discern his errors?* The Psalmist notes the fundamental difference between humans and inanimate nature: the latter automatically conforms to the will of its Creator, but mankind does not. He therefore prays to be protected from sin, deliberate or unwitting.

יִהְיוּ לְרָצוֹן אִמְרֵי־פִי *May the words of my mouth.* A beautiful prayer we say at the end of every Amida.

לְדָוִד *Psalm 34.* David, fleeing from Saul, took refuge in the Philistine city of Gath. There he was recognized, and knew that his life was in danger. He

Taste and see that the LORD is good;
    happy is the man who takes refuge in Him.
Fear the LORD, you His holy ones,
    for those who fear Him lack nothing.
Young lions may grow weak and hungry,
    but those who seek the LORD lack no good thing.
Come, my children, listen to me;
    I will teach you the fear of the LORD.
Who desires life, loving each day to see good?
Then guard your tongue from evil
    and your lips from speaking deceit.
Turn from evil and do good;
    seek peace and pursue it.
The eyes of the LORD are on the righteous
    and His ears attentive to their cry;
The LORD's face is set against those who do evil,
    to erase their memory from the earth.
The righteous cry out, and the LORD hears them;
    delivering them from all their troubles.
The LORD is close to the brokenhearted,
    and saves those who are crushed in spirit.
Many troubles may befall the righteous,
    but the LORD delivers him from them all;
He protects all his bones,
    so that none of them will be broken.
Evil will slay the wicked;
    the enemies of the righteous will be condemned.
▸ The LORD redeems His servants;
    none who take refuge in Him shall be condemned.

תְּפִלָּה לְמֹשֶׁה A prayer of Moses, the man of God. LORD, You have *Ps. 90* been our shelter in every generation. Before the mountains were born, before You brought forth the earth and the world, from everlasting to everlasting You are God. You turn men back to dust, saying, "Return,

---

אִישׁ הָאֱלֹהִים *The man of God.* This description also occurs in Deuteronomy

טַעֲמוּ וּרְאוּ כִּי־טוֹב יהוה, אַשְׁרֵי הַגֶּבֶר יֶחֱסֶה־בּוֹ:
יְראוּ אֶת־יהוה קְדֹשָׁיו, כִּי־אֵין מַחְסוֹר לִירֵאָיו:
כְּפִירִים רָשׁוּ וְרָעֵבוּ, וְדֹרְשֵׁי יהוה לֹא־יַחְסְרוּ כָל־טוֹב:
לְכוּ־בָנִים שִׁמְעוּ־לִי, יִרְאַת יהוה אֲלַמֶּדְכֶם:
מִי־הָאִישׁ הֶחָפֵץ חַיִּים, אֹהֵב יָמִים לִרְאוֹת טוֹב:
נְצֹר לְשׁוֹנְךָ מֵרָע, וּשְׂפָתֶיךָ מִדַּבֵּר מִרְמָה:
סוּר מֵרָע וַעֲשֵׂה־טוֹב, בַּקֵּשׁ שָׁלוֹם וְרָדְפֵהוּ:
עֵינֵי יהוה אֶל־צַדִּיקִים, וְאָזְנָיו אֶל־שַׁוְעָתָם:
פְּנֵי יהוה בְּעֹשֵׂי רָע, לְהַכְרִית מֵאֶרֶץ זִכְרָם:
צָעֲקוּ וַיהוה שָׁמֵעַ, וּמִכָּל־צָרוֹתָם הִצִּילָם:
קָרוֹב יהוה לְנִשְׁבְּרֵי־לֵב, וְאֶת־דַּכְּאֵי־רוּחַ יוֹשִׁיעַ:
רַבּוֹת רָעוֹת צַדִּיק, וּמִכֻּלָּם יַצִּילֶנּוּ יהוה:
שֹׁמֵר כָּל־עַצְמוֹתָיו, אַחַת מֵהֵנָּה לֹא נִשְׁבָּרָה:
תְּמוֹתֵת רָשָׁע רָעָה, וְשֹׂנְאֵי צַדִּיק יֶאְשָׁמוּ:
◄ פּוֹדֶה יהוה נֶפֶשׁ עֲבָדָיו, וְלֹא יֶאְשְׁמוּ כָּל־הַחֹסִים בּוֹ:

תְּפִלָּה לְמֹשֶׁה אִישׁ־הָאֱלֹהִים, אֲדֹנָי, מָעוֹן אַתָּה הָיִיתָ לָּנוּ בְּדֹר תהלים צ
וָדֹר: בְּטֶרֶם הָרִים יֻלָּדוּ, וַתְּחוֹלֵל אֶרֶץ וְתֵבֵל, וּמֵעוֹלָם עַד־עוֹלָם
אַתָּה אֵל: תָּשֵׁב אֱנוֹשׁ עַד־דַּכָּא, וַתֹּאמֶר שׁוּבוּ בְנֵי־אָדָם: כִּי

---

the arrogance of power: "The Lord is close to the brokenhearted, and saves those who are crushed in spirit."

תְּפִלָּה לְמֹשֶׁה *Psalm 90.* A magnificent poem, the only psalm attributed to Moses, on God's eternity and our mortality. However long we live, our lives are a mere microsecond in the history of the cosmos. Wisdom consists in knowing how brief is our stay on earth, and in the determination to use every day in service of the right, the just and the holy. The good we do lives after us; the rest is oft interred with our bones.

you children of men." For a thousand years in Your sight are like yesterday when it has passed, like a watch in the night. You sweep men away; they sleep. In the morning they are like grass newly grown: in the morning it flourishes and is new, but by evening it withers and dries up. For we are consumed by Your anger, terrified by Your fury. You have set our iniquities before You, our secret sins in the light of Your presence. All our days pass away in Your wrath, we spend our years like a sigh. The span of our life is seventy years, or if we are strong, eighty years; but the best of them is trouble and sorrow, for they quickly pass, and we fly away. Who can know the force of Your anger? Your wrath matches the fear due to You. Teach us rightly to number our days, that we may gain a heart of wisdom. Relent, O LORD! How much longer? Be sorry for Your servants. Satisfy us in the morning with Your loving-kindness, that we may sing and rejoice all our days. Grant us joy for as many days as You have afflicted us, for as many years as we saw trouble. Let Your deeds be seen by Your servants, and Your glory by their children. ▸ May the pleasantness of the LORD our God be upon us. Establish for us the work of our hands, O establish the work of our hands.

יֹשֵׁב בְּסֵתֶר He who lives in the shelter of the Most High dwells in the shadow of the Almighty. I say of the LORD, my Refuge and Stronghold, my God in whom I trust, that He will save you from the fowler's snare and the deadly pestilence. With His pinions He will cover you, and beneath His wings you will find shelter; His faithfulness is an encircling shield. You need not fear terror by night, nor the arrow that flies by day; not the pestilence that stalks in darkness, nor the plague that ravages at noon. A thousand may fall at your side, ten thousand at your right hand, but it will not come near you. You will only look with your eyes and see the punishment of the wicked. Because you *Ps. 91*

---

achievements that last. According to the sages, this is the blessing Moses gave the Israelites when they completed the building of the Tabernacle.

יֹשֵׁב בְּסֵתֶר *Psalm 91.* A psalm for protection at a time of danger. There is no life without risk, and courage does not mean having no fear; it means feeling it yet overcoming it in the knowledge that we are not alone. "We have nothing to fear but fear itself," and faith is the antidote to fear. The psalm radiates a sense of confidence and trust even in a world full of hazards.

אֶלֶף שָׁנִים בְּעֵינֶיךָ, כְּיוֹם אֶתְמוֹל כִּי יַעֲבֹר, וְאַשְׁמוּרָה בַלָּיְלָה:
זְרַמְתָּם, שֵׁנָה יִהְיוּ, בַּבֹּקֶר כֶּחָצִיר יַחֲלֹף: בַּבֹּקֶר יָצִיץ וְחָלָף, לָעֶרֶב
יְמוֹלֵל וְיָבֵשׁ: כִּי־כָלִינוּ בְאַפֶּךָ, וּבַחֲמָתְךָ נִבְהָלְנוּ: שַׁתָּ עֲוֹנֹתֵינוּ
לְנֶגְדֶּךָ, עֲלֻמֵנוּ לִמְאוֹר פָּנֶיךָ: כִּי כָל־יָמֵינוּ פָּנוּ בְעֶבְרָתֶךָ, כִּלִּינוּ
שָׁנֵינוּ כְמוֹ־הֶגֶה: יְמֵי־שְׁנוֹתֵינוּ בָהֶם שִׁבְעִים שָׁנָה, וְאִם בִּגְבוּרֹת
שְׁמוֹנִים שָׁנָה, וְרָהְבָּם עָמָל וָאָוֶן, כִּי־גָז חִישׁ וַנָּעֻפָה: מִי־יוֹדֵעַ
עֹז אַפֶּךָ, וּכְיִרְאָתְךָ עֶבְרָתֶךָ, לִמְנוֹת יָמֵינוּ כֵּן הוֹדַע, וְנָבִא לְבַב
חָכְמָה: שׁוּבָה יהוה עַד־מָתָי, וְהִנָּחֵם עַל־עֲבָדֶיךָ: שַׂבְּעֵנוּ בַבֹּקֶר
חַסְדֶּךָ, וּנְרַנְּנָה וְנִשְׂמְחָה בְּכָל־יָמֵינוּ: שַׂמְּחֵנוּ כִּימוֹת עִנִּיתָנוּ, שְׁנוֹת
רָאִינוּ רָעָה: יֵרָאֶה אֶל־עֲבָדֶיךָ פָעֳלֶךָ, וַהֲדָרְךָ עַל־בְּנֵיהֶם: ◂ וִיהִי
נֹעַם אֲדֹנָי אֱלֹהֵינוּ עָלֵינוּ, וּמַעֲשֵׂה יָדֵינוּ כּוֹנְנָה עָלֵינוּ, וּמַעֲשֵׂה
יָדֵינוּ כּוֹנְנֵהוּ:

תהלים צא יֹשֵׁב בְּסֵתֶר עֶלְיוֹן, בְּצֵל שַׁדַּי יִתְלוֹנָן: אֹמַר לַיהוה מַחְסִי וּמְצוּדָתִי,
אֱלֹהַי אֶבְטַח־בּוֹ: כִּי הוּא יַצִּילְךָ מִפַּח יָקוּשׁ, מִדֶּבֶר הַוּוֹת:
בְּאֶבְרָתוֹ יָסֶךְ לָךְ, וְתַחַת־כְּנָפָיו תֶּחְסֶה, צִנָּה וְסֹחֵרָה אֲמִתּוֹ:
לֹא־תִירָא מִפַּחַד לָיְלָה, מֵחֵץ יָעוּף יוֹמָם: מִדֶּבֶר בָּאֹפֶל יַהֲלֹךְ,
מִקֶּטֶב יָשׁוּד צָהֳרָיִם: יִפֹּל מִצִּדְּךָ אֶלֶף, וּרְבָבָה מִימִינֶךָ, אֵלֶיךָ
לֹא יִגָּשׁ: רַק בְּעֵינֶיךָ תַבִּיט, וְשִׁלֻּמַת רְשָׁעִים תִּרְאֶה: כִּי־אַתָּה

33:1, prefacing Moses' final blessing to the people. In the Torah only Moses is given this description. Elsewhere in Tanakh it is used as a synonym for a prophet.

אֶלֶף שָׁנִים ... וְאַשְׁמוּרָה בַלָּיְלָה *A thousand years ... a watch in the night.* A dramatic contrast between God's time-scale and ours. Note the succession of poetic images conveying the brevity of human life: it flows as fast as a swollen river, as quickly as a sleep or a dream, it is like grass in a parched land that soon withers, it is like a sigh, a mere breath, like a bird that briefly lands then flies away.

וּמַעֲשֵׂה יָדֵינוּ כּוֹנְנָה עָלֵינוּ *Establish for us the work of our hands.* Help us create

said "The LORD is my Refuge," taking the Most High as your shelter, no harm will befall you, no plague will come near your tent, for He will command His angels about you, to guard you in all your ways. They will lift you in their hands, lest your foot stumble on a stone. You will tread on lions and vipers, you will trample on young lions and snakes. [God says] "Because he loves Me, I will rescue him; I will protect him, because he acknowledges My name. When he calls on Me, I will answer him, I will be with him in distress, I will deliver him and bring him honor. ▸ With long life I will satisfy him, and show him My salvation. With long life I will satisfy him, and show him My salvation."

הַלְלוּיָהּ Halleluya! Praise the name of the LORD. Praise Him, you servants of the LORD who stand in the LORD's House, in the courtyards of the House of our God. Praise the LORD, for the LORD is good; sing praises to His name, for it is lovely. For the LORD has chosen Jacob as His own, Israel as his treasure. For I know that the LORD is great, that our LORD is above all heavenly powers. Whatever pleases the LORD, He does, in heaven and on earth, in the seas and all the depths. He raises clouds from the ends of the earth; He sends lightning with the rain; He brings out the wind from His storehouses. He struck down the firstborn of Egypt, of both man and animals. He sent signs and wonders into your midst, Egypt – against Pharaoh and all his servants. He struck down many nations and slew mighty kings: Siḥon, King of the Amorites, Og, King of Bashan, and all the kingdoms of Canaan, giving their land as a heritage, a heritage for His people Israel. Your name, LORD, endures for ever; Your renown, LORD, for all generations. For the LORD will bring justice to His people, and have compassion on His servants. The idols of the nations are silver and gold, the work of human hands. They have mouths, but cannot speak; eyes, but cannot *Ps. 135*

פֶּה־לָהֶם וְלֹא יְדַבֵּרוּ *They have mouths, but cannot speak.* Those who put their faith in forces that are less than human, themselves become less than human. Many have been the idols of history: power, wealth, status, the nation, the race, the state, the ideology, the system. None has lasted, for each has crushed the human spirit. None has given rise to stable systems of liberty and dignity.

יהוה מַחְסִי, עֶלְיוֹן שַׂמְתָּ מְעוֹנֶךָ: לֹא־תְאֻנֶּה אֵלֶיךָ רָעָה, וְנֶגַע
לֹא־יִקְרַב בְּאָהֳלֶךָ: כִּי מַלְאָכָיו יְצַוֶּה־לָּךְ, לִשְׁמָרְךָ בְּכָל־דְּרָכֶיךָ:
עַל־כַּפַּיִם יִשָּׂאוּנְךָ, פֶּן־תִּגֹּף בָּאֶבֶן רַגְלֶךָ: עַל־שַׁחַל וָפֶתֶן תִּדְרֹךְ,
תִּרְמֹס כְּפִיר וְתַנִּין: כִּי בִי חָשַׁק וַאֲפַלְּטֵהוּ, אֲשַׂגְּבֵהוּ כִּי־יָדַע
שְׁמִי: יִקְרָאֵנִי וְאֶעֱנֵהוּ, עִמּוֹ אָנֹכִי בְצָרָה, אֲחַלְּצֵהוּ וַאֲכַבְּדֵהוּ:
◂ אֹרֶךְ יָמִים אַשְׂבִּיעֵהוּ, וְאַרְאֵהוּ בִּישׁוּעָתִי:
אֹרֶךְ יָמִים אַשְׂבִּיעֵהוּ, וְאַרְאֵהוּ בִּישׁוּעָתִי:

תהלים קלה הַלְלוּיָהּ, הַלְלוּ אֶת־שֵׁם יהוה, הַלְלוּ עַבְדֵי יהוה: שֶׁעֹמְדִים בְּבֵית
יהוה, בְּחַצְרוֹת בֵּית אֱלֹהֵינוּ: הַלְלוּיָהּ כִּי־טוֹב יהוה, זַמְּרוּ לִשְׁמוֹ
כִּי נָעִים: כִּי־יַעֲקֹב בָּחַר לוֹ יָהּ, יִשְׂרָאֵל לִסְגֻלָּתוֹ: כִּי אֲנִי יָדַעְתִּי
כִּי־גָדוֹל יהוה, וַאֲדֹנֵינוּ מִכָּל־אֱלֹהִים: כֹּל אֲשֶׁר־חָפֵץ יהוה עָשָׂה,
בַּשָּׁמַיִם וּבָאָרֶץ, בַּיַּמִּים וְכָל־תְּהֹמוֹת: מַעֲלֶה נְשִׂאִים מִקְצֵה
הָאָרֶץ, בְּרָקִים לַמָּטָר עָשָׂה, מוֹצֵא־רוּחַ מֵאוֹצְרוֹתָיו: שֶׁהִכָּה בְּכוֹרֵי
מִצְרָיִם, מֵאָדָם עַד־בְּהֵמָה: שָׁלַח אוֹתֹת וּמֹפְתִים בְּתוֹכֵכִי מִצְרָיִם,
בְּפַרְעֹה וּבְכָל־עֲבָדָיו: שֶׁהִכָּה גּוֹיִם רַבִּים, וְהָרַג מְלָכִים עֲצוּמִים:
לְסִיחוֹן מֶלֶךְ הָאֱמֹרִי, וּלְעוֹג מֶלֶךְ הַבָּשָׁן, וּלְכֹל מַמְלְכוֹת כְּנָעַן:
וְנָתַן אַרְצָם נַחֲלָה, נַחֲלָה לְיִשְׂרָאֵל עַמּוֹ: יהוה שִׁמְךָ לְעוֹלָם,
יהוה זִכְרְךָ לְדֹר־וָדֹר: כִּי־יָדִין יהוה עַמּוֹ, וְעַל־עֲבָדָיו יִתְנֶחָם:
עֲצַבֵּי הַגּוֹיִם כֶּסֶף וְזָהָב, מַעֲשֵׂה יְדֵי אָדָם: פֶּה־לָהֶם וְלֹא יְדַבֵּרוּ,

הַלְלוּיָהּ *Psalm 135*. Psalms 135 and 136 are a matched pair, describing the same events: the exodus from Egypt and the battles prior to the Israelites' entry into the Promised Land. What Psalm 135 says in prose, Psalm 136 says in poetry. Both are joyous celebrations of the redeeming power of God in history. Blaise Pascal thought that the history of the Jews was proof of the existence of God. Israel are the people who, in themselves, testify to something greater than themselves. Their miraculous survival is a signal of transcendence.

see; ears, but cannot hear; there is no breath in their mouths. Those who make them will become like them: so will all who trust in them. ▸ House of Israel, bless the LORD. House of Aaron, bless the LORD. House of Levi, bless the LORD. You who fear the LORD, bless the LORD. Blessed is the LORD from Zion, He who dwells in Jerusalem. Halleluya!

The custom is to stand for the following psalm.

הוֹדוּ Thank the LORD for He is good; His loving-kindness is for ever. *Ps. 136*
Thank the God of gods, His loving-kindness is for ever.
Thank the LORD of Lords, His loving-kindness is for ever.
To the One who alone works great wonders, His loving-kindness is for ever.
Who made the heavens with wisdom, His loving-kindness is for ever.
Who spread the earth upon the waters, His loving-kindness is for ever.
Who made the great lights, His loving-kindness is for ever.
The sun to rule by day, His loving-kindness is for ever.
The moon and the stars to rule by night; His loving-kindness is for ever.
Who struck Egypt through their firstborn, His loving-kindness is for ever.
And brought out Israel from their midst, His loving-kindness is for ever.
With a strong hand and outstretched arm, His loving-kindness is for ever.
Who split the Reed Sea into parts, His loving-kindness is for ever.
And made Israel pass through it, His loving-kindness is for ever.
Casting Pharaoh and his army into the Reed Sea; His loving-kindness is for ever.

כִּי־טוֹב *For He is good.* The phrase *ki tov* occurs repeatedly in Genesis 1: "And God said, Let there be … and there was … and God saw that it was good [*ki tov*]." Rabbi Yaakov Tzvi Mecklenburg suggested that the phrase be translated, as here, "and God saw, *because* He is good." The phrase does not mean merely that what God created was good. It means that He created because of His goodness. One who is good seeks to share good with others. It was God's desire to share the blessing of existence with others that led Him to create the universe.

עֵינַיִם לָהֶם וְלֹא יִרְאוּ: אָזְנַיִם לָהֶם וְלֹא יַאֲזִינוּ, אַף אֵין־יֶשׁ־רְוּחַ
בְּפִיהֶם: כְּמוֹהֶם יִהְיוּ עֹשֵׂיהֶם, כֹּל אֲשֶׁר־בֹּטֵחַ בָּהֶם: ‹ בֵּית יִשְׂרָאֵל
בָּרְכוּ אֶת־יהוה, בֵּית אַהֲרֹן בָּרְכוּ אֶת־יהוה: בֵּית הַלֵּוִי בָּרְכוּ
אֶת־יהוה, יִרְאֵי יהוה בָּרְכוּ אֶת־יהוה: בָּרוּךְ יהוה מִצִּיּוֹן, שֹׁכֵן
יְרוּשָׁלָםִ, הַלְלוּיָהּ:

The custom is to stand for the following psalm.

הוֹדוּ לַיהוה כִּי־טוֹב כִּי לְעוֹלָם חַסְדּוֹ: תהלים קלו
הוֹדוּ לֵאלֹהֵי הָאֱלֹהִים כִּי לְעוֹלָם חַסְדּוֹ:
הוֹדוּ לַאֲדֹנֵי הָאֲדֹנִים כִּי לְעוֹלָם חַסְדּוֹ:
לְעֹשֵׂה נִפְלָאוֹת גְּדֹלוֹת לְבַדּוֹ כִּי לְעוֹלָם חַסְדּוֹ:
לְעֹשֵׂה הַשָּׁמַיִם בִּתְבוּנָה כִּי לְעוֹלָם חַסְדּוֹ:
לְרֹקַע הָאָרֶץ עַל־הַמָּיִם כִּי לְעוֹלָם חַסְדּוֹ:
לְעֹשֵׂה אוֹרִים גְּדֹלִים כִּי לְעוֹלָם חַסְדּוֹ:
אֶת־הַשֶּׁמֶשׁ לְמֶמְשֶׁלֶת בַּיּוֹם כִּי לְעוֹלָם חַסְדּוֹ:
אֶת־הַיָּרֵחַ וְכוֹכָבִים לְמֶמְשְׁלוֹת בַּלָּיְלָה כִּי לְעוֹלָם חַסְדּוֹ:
לְמַכֵּה מִצְרַיִם בִּבְכוֹרֵיהֶם כִּי לְעוֹלָם חַסְדּוֹ:
וַיּוֹצֵא יִשְׂרָאֵל מִתּוֹכָם כִּי לְעוֹלָם חַסְדּוֹ:
בְּיָד חֲזָקָה וּבִזְרוֹעַ נְטוּיָה כִּי לְעוֹלָם חַסְדּוֹ:
לְגֹזֵר יַם־סוּף לִגְזָרִים כִּי לְעוֹלָם חַסְדּוֹ:
וְהֶעֱבִיר יִשְׂרָאֵל בְּתוֹכוֹ כִּי לְעוֹלָם חַסְדּוֹ:
וְנִעֵר פַּרְעֹה וְחֵילוֹ בְיַם־סוּף כִּי לְעוֹלָם חַסְדּוֹ:

הודו *Psalm 136.* This psalm, known as *Hallel HaGadol*, "the Great Hallel," is one of the earliest forms of a litany, a prayer in which the leader utters a series of praises to which the congregation responds with a set reply. Jewish prayer contains many litanies, most notably during *Seliḥot*, the penitential prayers prior to and during Yom Kippur, and the *Hoshanot* said on Sukkot and Hoshana Raba.

Who led His people
through the wilderness; His loving-kindness is for ever.
Who struck down great kings, His loving-kindness is for ever.
And slew mighty kings, His loving-kindness is for ever.
Siḥon, King of the Amorites, His loving-kindness is for ever.
And Og, King of Bashan, His loving-kindness is for ever.
And gave their land as a heritage, His loving-kindness is for ever.
A heritage for His servant Israel; His loving-kindness is for ever.
Who remembered us in our lowly state, His loving-kindness is for ever.
And rescued us from our tormentors, His loving-kindness is for ever.
▸ Who gives food to all flesh, His loving-kindness is for ever.
Give thanks to the God of heaven. His loving-kindness is for ever.

רַנְּנוּ Sing joyfully to the LORD, you righteous, for praise from the upright is seemly. Give thanks to the LORD with the harp; make music to Him on the ten-stringed lute. Sing Him a new song, play skillfully with shouts of joy. For the LORD's word is right, and all His deeds are done in faith. He loves righteousness and justice; the earth is full of the LORD's loving-kindness. By the LORD's word the heavens were made, and all their starry host by the breath of His mouth. He gathers the sea waters as a heap, and places the deep in storehouses. Let all the earth fear the LORD, and all the world's inhabitants stand in awe of Him. For He spoke, and it was; He commanded, and it stood firm. The LORD foils the plans of nations; He thwarts the intentions of peoples. The LORD's plans stand for ever, His heart's intents for all generations. Happy is the nation whose God is the LORD, the people He has chosen as His own. From heaven the LORD looks down and sees all mankind; from His dwelling place He oversees all who live on earth. He forms the hearts of all, and discerns Ps. 33

---

the universe has a moral as well as physical beauty: "The earth is full of the LORD's loving-kindness." Love and justice prevail in the end, not power and aggression. "No king is saved by the size of his army," and tyrannical regimes eventually fall.

לְמוֹלִיךְ עַמּוֹ בַּמִּדְבָּר כִּי לְעוֹלָם חַסְדּוֹ:
לְמַכֵּה מְלָכִים גְּדֹלִים כִּי לְעוֹלָם חַסְדּוֹ:
וַיַּהֲרֹג מְלָכִים אַדִּירִים כִּי לְעוֹלָם חַסְדּוֹ:
לְסִיחוֹן מֶלֶךְ הָאֱמֹרִי כִּי לְעוֹלָם חַסְדּוֹ:
וּלְעוֹג מֶלֶךְ הַבָּשָׁן כִּי לְעוֹלָם חַסְדּוֹ:
וְנָתַן אַרְצָם לְנַחֲלָה כִּי לְעוֹלָם חַסְדּוֹ:
נַחֲלָה לְיִשְׂרָאֵל עַבְדּוֹ כִּי לְעוֹלָם חַסְדּוֹ:
שֶׁבְּשִׁפְלֵנוּ זָכַר לָנוּ כִּי לְעוֹלָם חַסְדּוֹ:
וַיִּפְרְקֵנוּ מִצָּרֵינוּ כִּי לְעוֹלָם חַסְדּוֹ:
‣ נֹתֵן לֶחֶם לְכָל־בָּשָׂר כִּי לְעוֹלָם חַסְדּוֹ:
הוֹדוּ לְאֵל הַשָּׁמָיִם כִּי לְעוֹלָם חַסְדּוֹ:

תהלים לג
רַנְּנוּ צַדִּיקִים בַּיהוה, לַיְשָׁרִים נָאוָה תְהִלָּה: הוֹדוּ לַיהוה בְּכִנּוֹר,
בְּנֵבֶל עָשׂוֹר זַמְּרוּ־לוֹ: שִׁירוּ־לוֹ שִׁיר חָדָשׁ, הֵיטִיבוּ נַגֵּן בִּתְרוּעָה:
כִּי־יָשָׁר דְּבַר־יהוה, וְכָל־מַעֲשֵׂהוּ בֶּאֱמוּנָה: אֹהֵב צְדָקָה וּמִשְׁפָּט,
חֶסֶד יהוה מָלְאָה הָאָרֶץ: בִּדְבַר יהוה שָׁמַיִם נַעֲשׂוּ, וּבְרוּחַ פִּיו
כָּל־צְבָאָם: כֹּנֵס כַּנֵּד מֵי הַיָּם, נֹתֵן בְּאוֹצָרוֹת תְּהוֹמוֹת: יִירְאוּ
מֵיהוה כָּל־הָאָרֶץ, מִמֶּנּוּ יָגוּרוּ כָּל־יֹשְׁבֵי תֵבֵל: כִּי הוּא אָמַר וַיֶּהִי,
הוּא־צִוָּה וַיַּעֲמֹד: יהוה הֵפִיר עֲצַת־גּוֹיִם, הֵנִיא מַחְשְׁבוֹת עַמִּים:
עֲצַת יהוה לְעוֹלָם תַּעֲמֹד, מַחְשְׁבוֹת לִבּוֹ לְדֹר וָדֹר: אַשְׁרֵי הַגּוֹי
אֲשֶׁר־יהוה אֱלֹהָיו, הָעָם בָּחַר לְנַחֲלָה לוֹ: מִשָּׁמַיִם הִבִּיט יהוה,
רָאָה אֶת־כָּל־בְּנֵי הָאָדָם: מִמְּכוֹן־שִׁבְתּוֹ הִשְׁגִּיחַ, אֶל כָּל־יֹשְׁבֵי
הָאָרֶץ: הַיֹּצֵר יַחַד לִבָּם, הַמֵּבִין אֶל־כָּל־מַעֲשֵׂיהֶם: אֵין־הַמֶּלֶךְ

רַנְּנוּ *Psalm* 33. A joyous creation psalm inviting us to sing God's praises on the earth He created and in the midst of the history He guides. To the Psalmist

all their deeds. No king is saved by the size of his army; no warrior is delivered by great strength. A horse is a vain hope for deliverance; despite its great strength, it cannot save. The eye of the LORD is on those who fear Him, on those who place their hope in His unfailing love, to rescue their soul from death, and keep them alive in famine. Our soul waits for the LORD; He is our Help and Shield. ▸ In Him our hearts rejoice, for we trust in His holy name. Let Your unfailing love be upon us, LORD, as we have put our hope in You.

מִזְמוֹר שִׁיר A psalm. A song for the Sabbath day. It is good to thank *Ps. 92* the LORD and sing psalms to Your name, Most High – to tell of Your loving-kindness in the morning and Your faithfulness at night, to the music of the ten-stringed lyre and the melody of the harp. For You have made me rejoice by Your work, O LORD; I sing for joy at the deeds of Your hands. How great are Your deeds, LORD, and how very deep Your thoughts. A boor cannot know, nor can a fool understand, that though the wicked spring up like grass and all evildoers flourish, it is only that they may be destroyed for ever. But You, LORD, are eternally exalted. For behold Your enemies, LORD, behold Your enemies will perish; all evildoers will be scattered. You have raised my pride like that of a wild ox; I am anointed with fresh oil. My eyes shall look in triumph on my adversaries, my ears shall hear the downfall of the wicked who rise against me. ▸ The righteous will flourish like a palm tree and grow tall like a cedar in Lebanon. Planted in the LORD's House, blossoming in our God's courtyards, they will still bear fruit in old age, and stay vigorous and fresh, proclaiming that the LORD is upright: He is my Rock, in whom there is no wrong.

---

good if, all too often, evildoers seize power, injustice prevails, the innocent suffer and the guilty escape punishment? The psalm tells us that our time-horizon is too constricted. We look at the short term, not the long. Evil may win temporary victories but in the long run, right, justice and liberty prevail. Tyrants may seem impregnable in their day, but evil empires crumble, and are condemned by the full perspective of history. That is what "a fool cannot understand" but the wise know. The Sabbath of the psalm is thus not the Sabbath of past or present but of the future, the Messianic age, the "day that is entirely Shabbat," when there will be neither master nor slave, oppressor

נוֹשָׁע בְּרָב־חָיִל, גִּבּוֹר לֹא־יִנָּצֵל בְּרָב־כֹּחַ: שֶׁקֶר הַסּוּס לִתְשׁוּעָה, וּבְרֹב חֵילוֹ לֹא יְמַלֵּט: הִנֵּה עֵין יהוה אֶל־יְרֵאָיו, לַמְיַחֲלִים לְחַסְדּוֹ: לְהַצִּיל מִמָּוֶת נַפְשָׁם, וּלְחַיּוֹתָם בָּרָעָב: נַפְשֵׁנוּ חִכְּתָה לַיהוה, עֶזְרֵנוּ וּמָגִנֵּנוּ הוּא: ‹ כִּי־בוֹ יִשְׂמַח לִבֵּנוּ, כִּי בְשֵׁם קָדְשׁוֹ בָטָחְנוּ: יְהִי־חַסְדְּךָ יהוה עָלֵינוּ, כַּאֲשֶׁר יִחַלְנוּ לָךְ:

מִזְמוֹר שִׁיר לְיוֹם הַשַּׁבָּת: טוֹב לְהֹדוֹת לַיהוה, וּלְזַמֵּר לְשִׁמְךָ עֶלְיוֹן: לְהַגִּיד בַּבֹּקֶר חַסְדֶּךָ, וֶאֱמוּנָתְךָ בַּלֵּילוֹת: עֲלֵי־עָשׂוֹר וַעֲלֵי־נָבֶל, עֲלֵי הִגָּיוֹן בְּכִנּוֹר: כִּי שִׂמַּחְתַּנִי יהוה בְּפָעֳלֶךָ, בְּמַעֲשֵׂי יָדֶיךָ אֲרַנֵּן: מַה־גָּדְלוּ מַעֲשֶׂיךָ יהוה, מְאֹד עָמְקוּ מַחְשְׁבֹתֶיךָ: אִישׁ־בַּעַר לֹא יֵדָע, וּכְסִיל לֹא־יָבִין אֶת־זֹאת: בִּפְרֹחַ רְשָׁעִים כְּמוֹ עֵשֶׂב, וַיָּצִיצוּ כָּל־פֹּעֲלֵי אָוֶן, לְהִשָּׁמְדָם עֲדֵי־עַד: וְאַתָּה מָרוֹם לְעֹלָם יהוה: כִּי הִנֵּה אֹיְבֶיךָ יהוה, כִּי־הִנֵּה אֹיְבֶיךָ יֹאבֵדוּ, יִתְפָּרְדוּ כָּל־פֹּעֲלֵי אָוֶן: וַתָּרֶם כִּרְאֵים קַרְנִי, בַּלֹּתִי בְּשֶׁמֶן רַעֲנָן: וַתַּבֵּט עֵינִי בְּשׁוּרָי, בַּקָּמִים עָלַי מְרֵעִים תִּשְׁמַעְנָה אָזְנָי: ‹ צַדִּיק כַּתָּמָר יִפְרָח, כְּאֶרֶז בַּלְּבָנוֹן יִשְׂגֶּה: שְׁתוּלִים בְּבֵית יהוה, בְּחַצְרוֹת אֱלֹהֵינוּ יַפְרִיחוּ: עוֹד יְנוּבוּן בְּשֵׂיבָה, דְּשֵׁנִים וְרַעֲנַנִּים יִהְיוּ: לְהַגִּיד כִּי־יָשָׁר יהוה, צוּרִי, וְלֹא־עַוְלָתָה בּוֹ: תהלים צב

מִזְמוֹר שִׁיר *Psalm 92.* The sages interpreted the opening of this psalm as meaning not just "a song *for* the Sabbath day" but also "a song sung *by* the Sabbath day" (see page 544), as if the day itself gave testimony to the Creator, which in effect it does. By being the day on which we do no creative work, time itself makes us aware that we are not just creators; we are also creations. The more we understand about the nature of the universe, its vast complexity, and the way it is finely tuned for the emergence of life, the more we sense a vast intelligence at work, framing its "fearful symmetry."

Yet the psalm speaks not about creation but about justice. The universe is not simply matter and anti-matter governed by certain scientific laws. It is also – as Genesis 1 tells us seven times – "good." But how can we consider it

יהוה מָלָךְ The LORD reigns. He is robed in majesty. The LORD is robed, *Ps. 93*
girded with strength. The world is firmly established; it cannot be moved. Your throne stands firm as of old; You are eternal. Rivers lift up, LORD, rivers lift up their voice, rivers lift up their Crashing waves. ▸ Mightier than the noise of many waters, than the mighty waves of the sea is the LORD on high. Your testimonies are very sure; holiness adorns Your House, LORD, for evermore.

יְהִי כְבוֹד May the LORD's glory be for ever; may the LORD rejoice in *Ps. 104*
His works. May the LORD's name be blessed, now and for ever. From *Ps. 113*
the rising of the sun to its setting, may the LORD's name be praised.
The LORD is high above all nations; His glory is above the heavens.
LORD, Your name is for ever. Your renown, LORD, is for all generations. *Ps. 135*
The LORD has established His throne in heaven; His kingdom rules *Ps. 103*
all. Let the heavens rejoice and the earth be glad. Let them say among *1 Chr. 16*
the nations, "The LORD is King." The LORD is King, the LORD was
King, the LORD will be King for ever and all time. The LORD is King *Ps. 10*
for ever and all time; nations will perish from His land. The LORD foils *Ps. 33*
the plans of nations; He frustrates the intentions of peoples. Many are *Prov. 19*
the intentions in a person's mind, but the LORD's plan prevails. The *Ps. 33*
LORD's plan shall stand for ever, His mind's intent for all generations.
For He spoke and it was; He commanded and it stood firm. For the *Ps. 132*
LORD has chosen Zion; He desired it for His dwelling. For the LORD *Ps. 135*
has chosen Jacob, Israel as His special treasure. For the LORD will not *Ps. 94*
abandon His people; nor will He forsake His heritage. ▸ He is com- *Ps. 78*
passionate. He forgives iniquity and does not destroy. Repeatedly He
suppresses His anger, not rousing His full wrath. LORD, save! May the *Ps. 20*
King answer us on the day we call.

---

creative power, that the universe is fundamentally good, and that chaos is merely order of a complexity we can neither understand nor predict. This is beautifully expressed in this psalm which sees the roar of the oceans as part of creation paying homage to its Creator. God is beyond – not within – nature, time and space.

יְהִי כְבוֹד *May the LORD's glory.* An anthology of verses, mainly from the books of Psalms, Proverbs, and Chronicles. God created the universe; therefore He

יהוה מָלָךְ, גֵּאוּת לָבֵשׁ, לָבֵשׁ יהוה עֹז הִתְאַזָּר, אַף־תִּכּוֹן תֵּבֵל תהלים צג
בַּל־תִּמּוֹט: נָכוֹן כִּסְאֲךָ מֵאָז, מֵעוֹלָם אָתָּה: נָשְׂאוּ נְהָרוֹת יהוה,
נָשְׂאוּ נְהָרוֹת קוֹלָם, יִשְׂאוּ נְהָרוֹת דָּכְיָם: › מִקֹּלוֹת מַיִם רַבִּים,
אַדִּירִים מִשְׁבְּרֵי־יָם, אַדִּיר בַּמָּרוֹם יהוה: עֵדֹתֶיךָ נֶאֶמְנוּ מְאֹד
לְבֵיתְךָ נַאֲוָה־קֹּדֶשׁ, יהוה לְאֹרֶךְ יָמִים:

יְהִי כְבוֹד יהוה לְעוֹלָם, יִשְׂמַח יהוה בְּמַעֲשָׂיו: יְהִי שֵׁם יהוה מְבֹרָךְ, תהלים קד תהלים קיג
מֵעַתָּה וְעַד־עוֹלָם: מִמִּזְרַח־שֶׁמֶשׁ עַד־מְבוֹאוֹ, מְהֻלָּל שֵׁם יהוה:
רָם עַל־כָּל־גּוֹיִם יהוה, עַל הַשָּׁמַיִם כְּבוֹדוֹ: יהוה שִׁמְךָ לְעוֹלָם, תהלים קלה
יהוה זִכְרְךָ לְדֹר־וָדֹר: יהוה בַּשָּׁמַיִם הֵכִין כִּסְאוֹ, וּמַלְכוּתוֹ בַּכֹּל תהלים קג
מָשָׁלָה: יִשְׂמְחוּ הַשָּׁמַיִם וְתָגֵל הָאָרֶץ, וְיֹאמְרוּ בַגּוֹיִם יהוה מָלָךְ: דברי הימים א׳ טז
יהוה מֶלֶךְ, יהוה מָלָךְ, יהוה יִמְלֹךְ לְעוֹלָם וָעֶד. יהוה מֶלֶךְ עוֹלָם תהלים י
וָעֶד, אָבְדוּ גוֹיִם מֵאַרְצוֹ: יהוה הֵפִיר עֲצַת־גּוֹיִם, הֵנִיא מַחְשְׁבוֹת תהלים לג
עַמִּים: רַבּוֹת מַחֲשָׁבוֹת בְּלֶב־אִישׁ, וַעֲצַת יהוה הִיא תָקוּם: משלי יט
עֲצַת יהוה לְעוֹלָם תַּעֲמֹד, מַחְשְׁבוֹת לִבּוֹ לְדֹר וָדֹר: כִּי הוּא אָמַר תהלים לג
וַיֶּהִי, הוּא־צִוָּה וַיַּעֲמֹד: כִּי־בָחַר יהוה בְּצִיּוֹן, אִוָּהּ לְמוֹשָׁב לוֹ: תהלים קלב
כִּי־יַעֲקֹב בָּחַר לוֹ יָהּ, יִשְׂרָאֵל לִסְגֻלָּתוֹ: כִּי לֹא־יִטֹּשׁ יהוה עַמּוֹ, תהלים קלה תהלים צד
וְנַחֲלָתוֹ לֹא יַעֲזֹב: › וְהוּא רַחוּם, יְכַפֵּר עָוֹן וְלֹא־יַשְׁחִית, וְהִרְבָּה תהלים עח
לְהָשִׁיב אַפּוֹ, וְלֹא־יָעִיר כָּל־חֲמָתוֹ: יהוה הוֹשִׁיעָה, הַמֶּלֶךְ יַעֲנֵנוּ תהלים כ
בְיוֹם־קָרְאֵנוּ:

---

and oppressed, when hierarchies of power are abandoned and humanity finally recognizes the universe as God's work, and the human person as God's image. That is the ultimate Shabbat to which all our current Sabbaths are a prelude and preparation.

יהוה מָלָךְ *Psalm 93.* Almost all ancient polytheistic myths saw the sea as an independent force of chaos against which the gods were forced to do battle. The great revolution of monotheism was to insist that there is only one

The line beginning with "You open Your hand" should be said with special concentration, representing as it does the key idea of this psalm, and of Pesukei DeZimra as a whole, that God is the creator and sustainer of all.

אַשְׁרֵי Happy are those who dwell in Your House; Ps. 84
they shall continue to praise You, Selah!
Happy are the people for whom this is so; Ps. 144
happy are the people whose God is the LORD.
A song of praise by David. Ps. 145

I will exalt You, my God, the King, and bless Your name for ever and all time. Every day I will bless You, and praise Your name for ever and all time. Great is the LORD and greatly to be praised; His greatness is unfathomable. One generation will praise Your works to the next, and tell of Your mighty deeds. On the glorious splendor of Your majesty I will meditate, and on the acts of Your wonders. They shall talk of the power of Your awesome deeds, and I will tell of Your greatness. They shall recite the record of Your great goodness, and sing with joy of Your righteousness. The LORD is gracious and compassionate, slow to anger and great in loving-kindness. The LORD is good to all, and His compassion extends to all His works. All Your works shall thank You, LORD, and Your devoted ones shall bless You. They shall talk of the glory of Your kingship, and speak of Your might. To make known to mankind His mighty deeds and the glorious majesty of His kingship. Your kingdom is an everlasting kingdom, and Your reign is for all generations. The LORD supports all who fall, and raises all who are bowed down. All raise their eyes to

---

אַשְׁרֵי *Happy are those.* Psalm 145 was seen by the sages as the quintessential expression of the book of Psalms, especially the creation psalms that dominate the Verses of Praise, because (a) it is an alphabetic acrostic, praising God with each letter of the alphabet (with the exception of *nun,* a letter omitted lest it recall *nefila,* the fall of ancient Israel), and (b) because it contains the line, "You open Your hand, and satisfy every living thing with favor." It is also (c) the only poem to be explicitly called *tehilla,* "a psalm" (the book of Psalms is called, in Hebrew, *Sefer Tehillim*). To it have been added two verses at the beginning and one at the end, so that the psalm begins with the word *Ashrei,* the first word in the book of Psalms, and ends with *Halleluya,* the book's last word.

The line beginning with פּוֹתֵחַ אֶת יָדֶךָ *should be said with special concentration, representing as it does the key idea of this psalm, and of* פסוקי דזמרה *as a whole, that God is the creator and sustainer of all.*

אַשְׁרֵי יוֹשְׁבֵי בֵיתֶךָ, עוֹד יְהַלְלְוּךָ סֶּלָה: תהלים פד

אַשְׁרֵי הָעָם שֶׁכָּכָה לּוֹ, אַשְׁרֵי הָעָם שֶׁיהוה אֱלֹהָיו: תהלים קמד

תְּהִלָּה לְדָוִד תהלים קמה

אֲרוֹמִמְךָ אֱלוֹהַי הַמֶּלֶךְ, וַאֲבָרְכָה שִׁמְךָ לְעוֹלָם וָעֶד:

בְּכָל־יוֹם אֲבָרְכֶךָּ, וַאֲהַלְלָה שִׁמְךָ לְעוֹלָם וָעֶד:

גָּדוֹל יהוה וּמְהֻלָּל מְאֹד, וְלִגְדֻלָּתוֹ אֵין חֵקֶר:

דּוֹר לְדוֹר יְשַׁבַּח מַעֲשֶׂיךָ, וּגְבוּרֹתֶיךָ יַגִּידוּ:

הֲדַר כְּבוֹד הוֹדֶךָ, וְדִבְרֵי נִפְלְאֹתֶיךָ אָשִׂיחָה:

וֶעֱזוּז נוֹרְאֹתֶיךָ יֹאמֵרוּ, וּגְדוּלָּתְךָ אֲסַפְּרֶנָּה:

זֵכֶר רַב־טוּבְךָ יַבִּיעוּ, וְצִדְקָתְךָ יְרַנֵּנוּ:

חַנּוּן וְרַחוּם יהוה, אֶרֶךְ אַפַּיִם וּגְדָל־חָסֶד:

טוֹב־יהוה לַכֹּל, וְרַחֲמָיו עַל־כָּל־מַעֲשָׂיו:

יוֹדְוּךָ יהוה כָּל־מַעֲשֶׂיךָ, וַחֲסִידֶיךָ יְבָרְכוּכָה:

כְּבוֹד מַלְכוּתְךָ יֹאמֵרוּ, וּגְבוּרָתְךָ יְדַבֵּרוּ:

לְהוֹדִיעַ לִבְנֵי הָאָדָם גְּבוּרֹתָיו, וּכְבוֹד הֲדַר מַלְכוּתוֹ:

מַלְכוּתְךָ מַלְכוּת כָּל־עֹלָמִים, וּמֶמְשַׁלְתְּךָ בְּכָל־דּוֹר וָדֹר:

סוֹמֵךְ יהוה לְכָל־הַנֹּפְלִים, וְזוֹקֵף לְכָל־הַכְּפוּפִים:

---

is sole Sovereign of the universe, ruling nature through scientific law, and history through the moral law. Those who pit themselves against God are destined to fail: "Many are the intentions in a person's mind, but the Lord's plan prevails." Israel, as the people of the eternal God, is itself eternal, and though it often suffers persecution, it will never be destroyed, for divine compassion ultimately prevails over divine anger: "The Lord will not abandon His people."

You in hope, and You give them their food in due season. You open Your hand, and satisfy every living thing with favor. The LORD is righteous in all His ways, and kind in all He does. The LORD is close to all who call on Him, to all who call on Him in truth. He fulfills the will of those who revere Him; He hears their cry and saves them. The LORD guards all who love Him, but all the wicked He will destroy. ▸ My mouth shall speak the praise of the LORD, and all creatures shall bless His holy name for ever and all time.

We will bless the LORD now and for ever. Halleluya! *Ps. 115*

הַלְלוּיָהּ Halleluya! Praise the LORD, my soul. I will praise the LORD *Ps. 146* all my life; I will sing to my God as long as I live. Put not your trust in princes, or in mortal man who cannot save. His breath expires, he returns to the earth; on that day his plans come to an end. Happy is he whose help is the God of Jacob, whose hope is in the LORD his God who made heaven and earth, the sea and all they contain; He who keeps faith for ever. He secures justice for the oppressed. He gives food to the hungry. The LORD sets captives free. The LORD gives sight to the blind. The LORD raises those bowed down. The LORD loves the righteous. The LORD protects the stranger. He gives courage to the orphan and widow. He thwarts the way of the wicked. ▸ The LORD shall reign for ever. He is your God, Zion, for all generations. Halleluya!

הַלְלוּיָהּ Halleluya! How good it is to sing songs to our God; how pleas- *Ps. 147* ant and fitting to praise Him. The LORD rebuilds Jerusalem. He gathers the scattered exiles of Israel. He heals the brokenhearted and binds up their wounds. He counts the number of the stars, calling each by name. Great is our LORD and mighty in power; His understanding has no limit. The LORD gives courage to the humble, but casts the wicked

---

the victims of injustice, and those who have no one else to care for them. The supreme Power supremely cares for the powerless.

הַלְלוּיָהּ *Psalm 147.* God, the Shaper of history ("gathers the scattered exiles") and Architect of the cosmos ("counts the number of the stars"), is nonetheless

עֵינֵי־כֹל אֵלֶיךָ יְשַׂבֵּרוּ, וְאַתָּה נוֹתֵן־לָהֶם אֶת־אָכְלָם בְּעִתּוֹ:
פּוֹתֵחַ אֶת־יָדֶךָ, וּמַשְׂבִּיעַ לְכָל־חַי רָצוֹן:
צַדִּיק יהוה בְּכָל־דְּרָכָיו, וְחָסִיד בְּכָל־מַעֲשָׂיו:
קָרוֹב יהוה לְכָל־קֹרְאָיו, לְכֹל אֲשֶׁר יִקְרָאֻהוּ בֶאֱמֶת:
רְצוֹן־יְרֵאָיו יַעֲשֶׂה, וְאֶת־שַׁוְעָתָם יִשְׁמַע, וְיוֹשִׁיעֵם:
שׁוֹמֵר יהוה אֶת־כָּל־אֹהֲבָיו, וְאֵת כָּל־הָרְשָׁעִים יַשְׁמִיד:
‹ תְּהִלַּת יהוה יְדַבֶּר פִּי, וִיבָרֵךְ כָּל־בָּשָׂר שֵׁם קָדְשׁוֹ לְעוֹלָם וָעֶד:
וַאֲנַחְנוּ נְבָרֵךְ יָהּ מֵעַתָּה וְעַד־עוֹלָם, הַלְלוּיָהּ: תהלים קטו

הַלְלוּיָהּ, הַלְלִי נַפְשִׁי אֶת־יהוה: אֲהַלְלָה יהוה בְּחַיָּי, אֲזַמְּרָה תהלים קמו
לֵאלֹהַי בְּעוֹדִי: אַל־תִּבְטְחוּ בִנְדִיבִים, בְּבֶן־אָדָם שֶׁאֵין לוֹ
תְשׁוּעָה: תֵּצֵא רוּחוֹ, יָשֻׁב לְאַדְמָתוֹ, בַּיּוֹם הַהוּא אָבְדוּ עֶשְׁתֹּנֹתָיו:
אַשְׁרֵי שֶׁאֵל יַעֲקֹב בְּעֶזְרוֹ, שִׂבְרוֹ עַל־יהוה אֱלֹהָיו: עֹשֶׂה שָׁמַיִם
וָאָרֶץ, אֶת־הַיָּם וְאֶת־כָּל־אֲשֶׁר־בָּם, הַשֹּׁמֵר אֱמֶת לְעוֹלָם: עֹשֶׂה
מִשְׁפָּט לַעֲשׁוּקִים, נֹתֵן לֶחֶם לָרְעֵבִים, יהוה מַתִּיר אֲסוּרִים:
יהוה פֹּקֵחַ עִוְרִים, יהוה זֹקֵף כְּפוּפִים, יהוה אֹהֵב צַדִּיקִים: יהוה
שֹׁמֵר אֶת־גֵּרִים, יָתוֹם וְאַלְמָנָה יְעוֹדֵד, וְדֶרֶךְ רְשָׁעִים יְעַוֵּת:
‹ יִמְלֹךְ יהוה לְעוֹלָם, אֱלֹהַיִךְ צִיּוֹן לְדֹר וָדֹר, הַלְלוּיָהּ:

הַלְלוּיָהּ, כִּי־טוֹב זַמְּרָה אֱלֹהֵינוּ, כִּי־נָעִים נָאוָה תְהִלָּה: בּוֹנֵה תהלים קמז
יְרוּשָׁלַםִ יהוה, נִדְחֵי יִשְׂרָאֵל יְכַנֵּס: הָרוֹפֵא לִשְׁבוּרֵי לֵב, וּמְחַבֵּשׁ
לְעַצְּבוֹתָם: מוֹנֶה מִסְפָּר לַכּוֹכָבִים, לְכֻלָּם שֵׁמוֹת יִקְרָא: גָּדוֹל
אֲדוֹנֵינוּ וְרַב־כֹּחַ, לִתְבוּנָתוֹ אֵין מִסְפָּר: מְעוֹדֵד עֲנָוִים יהוה,

---

הַלְלוּיָהּ *Psalm 146.* A hymn of praise to God's justice and compassion. Put not your faith in mortals but in God, who cares for the oppressed, the hungry,

to the ground. Sing to the LORD in thanks; make music to our God on the harp. He covers the sky with clouds. He provides the earth with rain and makes grass grow on the hills. He gives food to the cattle and to the ravens when they cry. He does not take delight in the strength of horses nor pleasure in the fleetness of man. The LORD takes pleasure in those who fear Him, who put their hope in His loving care. Praise the LORD, Jerusalem; sing to your God, Zion, for He has strengthened the bars of your gates and blessed your children in your midst. He has brought peace to your borders, and satisfied you with the finest wheat. He sends His commandment to earth; swiftly runs His word. He spreads snow like fleece, sprinkles frost like ashes, scatters hail like crumbs. Who can stand His cold? He sends His word and melts them; He makes the wind blow and the waters flow. ▸ He has declared His words to Jacob, His statutes and laws to Israel. He has done this for no other nation; such laws they do not know. Halleluya!

הַלְלוּיָהּ Halleluya! Praise the LORD from the heavens, praise Him in the heights. Praise Him, all His angels; praise Him, all His hosts. Praise Him, sun and moon; praise Him, all shining stars. Praise Him, highest heavens and the waters above the heavens. Let them praise the name of the LORD, for He commanded and they were created. He established them for ever and all time, issuing a decree that will never change. Praise the LORD from the earth: sea monsters and all the deep seas; fire and hail, snow and mist, storm winds that obey His word; mountains and all hills, fruit trees and all cedars; wild animals and all cattle, creeping things and winged birds; kings of the earth and all nations, princes and all judges on earth; youths and maidens, old and young. ▸ Let them praise the name of the LORD, for His name alone *Ps. 148*

---

to Israel did He reveal an entire body of laws, the detailed architectonics of a society under the sovereignty of God, dedicated to justice, holiness and respect for human dignity.

הַלְלוּיָהּ *Psalm 148.* A cosmic psalm of praise, beginning with the heavens, sun, moon and stars; then moving to earth and all living things, culminating with humanity.

מַשְׁפִּיל רְשָׁעִים עֲדֵי־אָרֶץ: עֱנוּ לַיהוה בְּתוֹדָה, זַמְּרוּ לֵאלֹהֵינוּ בְכִנּוֹר: הַמְכַסֶּה שָׁמַיִם בְּעָבִים, הַמֵּכִין לָאָרֶץ מָטָר, הַמַּצְמִיחַ הָרִים חָצִיר: נוֹתֵן לִבְהֵמָה לַחְמָהּ, לִבְנֵי עֹרֵב אֲשֶׁר יִקְרָאוּ: לֹא בִגְבוּרַת הַסּוּס יֶחְפָּץ, לֹא־בְשׁוֹקֵי הָאִישׁ יִרְצֶה: רוֹצֶה יהוה אֶת־יְרֵאָיו, אֶת־הַמְיַחֲלִים לְחַסְדּוֹ: שַׁבְּחִי יְרוּשָׁלַםִ אֶת־יהוה, הַלְלִי אֱלֹהַיִךְ צִיּוֹן: כִּי־חִזַּק בְּרִיחֵי שְׁעָרָיִךְ, בֵּרַךְ בָּנַיִךְ בְּקִרְבֵּךְ: הַשָּׂם־גְּבוּלֵךְ שָׁלוֹם, חֵלֶב חִטִּים יַשְׂבִּיעֵךְ: הַשֹּׁלֵחַ אִמְרָתוֹ אָרֶץ, עַד־מְהֵרָה יָרוּץ דְּבָרוֹ: הַנֹּתֵן שֶׁלֶג כַּצָּמֶר, כְּפוֹר כָּאֵפֶר יְפַזֵּר: מַשְׁלִיךְ קַרְחוֹ כְפִתִּים, לִפְנֵי קָרָתוֹ מִי יַעֲמֹד: יִשְׁלַח דְּבָרוֹ וְיַמְסֵם, יַשֵּׁב רוּחוֹ יִזְּלוּ־מָיִם: ‹ מַגִּיד דְּבָרָו לְיַעֲקֹב, חֻקָּיו וּמִשְׁפָּטָיו לְיִשְׂרָאֵל: לֹא עָשָׂה כֵן לְכָל־גּוֹי, וּמִשְׁפָּטִים בַּל־יְדָעוּם, הַלְלוּיָהּ:

תהלים קמח הַלְלוּיָהּ, הַלְלוּ אֶת־יהוה מִן־הַשָּׁמַיִם, הַלְלוּהוּ בַּמְּרוֹמִים: הַלְלוּהוּ כָל־מַלְאָכָיו, הַלְלוּהוּ כָּל־צְבָאָו: הַלְלוּהוּ שֶׁמֶשׁ וְיָרֵחַ, הַלְלוּהוּ כָּל־כּוֹכְבֵי אוֹר: הַלְלוּהוּ שְׁמֵי הַשָּׁמָיִם, וְהַמַּיִם אֲשֶׁר מֵעַל הַשָּׁמָיִם: יְהַלְלוּ אֶת־שֵׁם יהוה, כִּי הוּא צִוָּה וְנִבְרָאוּ: וַיַּעֲמִידֵם לָעַד לְעוֹלָם, חָק־נָתַן וְלֹא יַעֲבוֹר: הַלְלוּ אֶת־יהוה מִן־הָאָרֶץ, תַּנִּינִים וְכָל־תְּהֹמוֹת: אֵשׁ וּבָרָד שֶׁלֶג וְקִיטוֹר, רוּחַ סְעָרָה עֹשָׂה דְבָרוֹ: הֶהָרִים וְכָל־גְּבָעוֹת, עֵץ פְּרִי וְכָל־אֲרָזִים: הַחַיָּה וְכָל־בְּהֵמָה, רֶמֶשׂ וְצִפּוֹר כָּנָף: מַלְכֵי־אֶרֶץ וְכָל־לְאֻמִּים, שָׂרִים וְכָל־שֹׁפְטֵי אָרֶץ: בַּחוּרִים וְגַם־בְּתוּלוֹת, זְקֵנִים עִם־נְעָרִים: ‹ יְהַלְלוּ אֶת־שֵׁם יהוה, כִּי־נִשְׂגָּב

---

close to us, healing the broken heart and ministering to our emotional wounds.

לֹא עָשָׂה כֵן לְכָל־גּוֹי *He has done this for no other nation.* Although there has been a covenant between God and all humanity since the days of Noah, only

is sublime; His majesty is above earth and heaven. He has raised the pride of His people, for the glory of all His devoted ones, the children of Israel, the people close to Him. Halleluya!

הַלְלוּיָהּ Halleluya! Sing to the LORD a new song, His praise in the assembly of the devoted. Let Israel rejoice in its Maker; let the children of Zion exult in their King. Let them praise His name with dancing; sing praises to Him with timbrel and harp. For the LORD delights in His people; He adorns the humble with salvation. Let the devoted revel in glory; let them sing for joy on their beds. Let high praises of God be in their throats, and a two-edged sword in their hand: to impose retribution on the nations, punishment on the peoples, ▸ binding their kings with chains, their nobles with iron fetters, carrying out the judgment written against them. This is the glory of all His devoted ones. Halleluya! *Ps. 149*

הַלְלוּיָהּ Halleluya! *Ps. 150*
Praise God in His holy place;
praise Him in the heavens of His power.
Praise Him for His mighty deeds;
praise Him for His surpassing greatness.
Praise Him with blasts of the shofar;
praise Him with the harp and lyre.
Praise Him with timbrel and dance;
praise Him with strings and flute.
▸ Praise Him with clashing cymbals;
praise Him with resounding cymbals.
Let all that breathes praise the LORD. Halleluya!
Let all that breathes praise the LORD. Halleluya!

כֹּל הַנְּשָׁמָה *Let all that breathes.* The psalm mentions nine musical and creative expressions of praise, culminating in the tenth, the breath of all that lives – echoing the tenfold blessing with which the Verses of Praise begin, itself an echo of the ten creative utterances with which God created the universe (the ten times the phrase "God said" appears in Genesis 1). Note the difference between a scientific and a religious way of describing the universe. "Not *how* the world is but *that* it is, is the mystical" (Wittgenstein).

שְׁמוֹ לְבַדּוֹ, הוֹדוֹ עַל־אֶרֶץ וְשָׁמָיִם: וַיָּרֶם קֶרֶן לְעַמּוֹ, תְּהִלָּה לְכָל־
חֲסִידָיו, לִבְנֵי יִשְׂרָאֵל עַם קְרֹבוֹ, הַלְלוּיָהּ:

תהלים קמט הַלְלוּיָהּ, שִׁירוּ לַיהוה שִׁיר חָדָשׁ, תְּהִלָּתוֹ בִּקְהַל חֲסִידִים: יִשְׂמַח
יִשְׂרָאֵל בְּעֹשָׂיו, בְּנֵי־צִיּוֹן יָגִילוּ בְמַלְכָּם: יְהַלְלוּ שְׁמוֹ בְמָחוֹל, בְּתֹף
וְכִנּוֹר יְזַמְּרוּ־לוֹ: כִּי־רוֹצֶה יהוה בְּעַמּוֹ, יְפָאֵר עֲנָוִים בִּישׁוּעָה:
יַעְלְזוּ חֲסִידִים בְּכָבוֹד, יְרַנְּנוּ עַל־מִשְׁכְּבוֹתָם: רוֹמְמוֹת אֵל בִּגְרוֹנָם,
וְחֶרֶב פִּיפִיּוֹת בְּיָדָם: לַעֲשׂוֹת נְקָמָה בַּגּוֹיִם, תּוֹכֵחוֹת בַּלְאֻמִּים:
› לֶאְסֹר מַלְכֵיהֶם בְּזִקִּים, וְנִכְבְּדֵיהֶם בְּכַבְלֵי בַרְזֶל: לַעֲשׂוֹת בָּהֶם
מִשְׁפָּט כָּתוּב, הָדָר הוּא לְכָל־חֲסִידָיו, הַלְלוּיָהּ:

תהלים קנ הַלְלוּיָהּ
הַלְלוּ־אֵל בְּקָדְשׁוֹ, הַלְלוּהוּ בִּרְקִיעַ עֻזּוֹ:
הַלְלוּהוּ בִגְבוּרֹתָיו, הַלְלוּהוּ כְּרֹב גֻּדְלוֹ:
הַלְלוּהוּ בְּתֵקַע שׁוֹפָר, הַלְלוּהוּ בְּנֵבֶל וְכִנּוֹר:
הַלְלוּהוּ בְתֹף וּמָחוֹל, הַלְלוּהוּ בְּמִנִּים וְעֻגָב:
› הַלְלוּהוּ בְצִלְצְלֵי־שָׁמַע, הַלְלוּהוּ בְּצִלְצְלֵי תְרוּעָה:
כֹּל הַנְּשָׁמָה תְּהַלֵּל יָהּ, הַלְלוּיָהּ:
כֹּל הַנְּשָׁמָה תְּהַלֵּל יָהּ, הַלְלוּיָהּ:

הַלְלוּיָהּ *Psalm 149.* A song of victory. Israel emerges triumphant over those who seek to destroy it, not because of its strength but because of its faith.

חֶרֶב פִּיפִיּוֹת *A two-edged sword.* Literally, "a sword of mouths." Israel does not live by the physical sword but by words: the power of prayer. Thus the "sword of mouths" echoes the previous phrase, "praises of God be in their throats" (*Or Penei Moshe*).

הַלְלוּיָהּ *Psalm 150.* The last psalm in the book of Psalms, gathering all previous praise into a majestic choral finale. More than a third of the words consist of various forms of the verb "to praise."

בָּרוּךְ Blessed be the LORD for ever. Amen and Amen. *Ps. 89*
Blessed from Zion be the LORD *Ps. 135*
who dwells in Jerusalem. Halleluya!
Blessed be the LORD, God of Israel, *Ps. 72*
who alone does wonders.
▸ Blessed be His glorious name for ever,
and may all the earth be filled with His glory.
Amen and Amen.

Stand until "The soul" on page 352.

וַיְבָרֶךְ David blessed the LORD in front of the entire assembly. David *1 Chr. 29*
said, "Blessed are You, LORD, God of our father Yisrael, for ever and ever. Yours, LORD, are the greatness and the power, the glory, majesty and splendor, for everything in heaven and earth is Yours. Yours, LORD, is the kingdom; You are exalted as Head over all. Both riches and honor are in Your gift and You reign over all things. In Your hand are strength and might. It is in Your power to make great and give strength to all. Therefore, our God, we thank You and
praise Your glorious name." You alone are the LORD. You *Neh. 9*
made the heavens, even the highest heavens, and all their hosts, the earth and all that is on it, the seas and all they contain. You give life to them all, and the hosts of heaven worship You. ▸ You are the LORD God who chose Abram and brought him out of Ur of the Chaldees, changing his name to Abraham. You found his heart faithful toward You, ◂ and You made a covenant with him to give to his descendants the land of the Canaanites, Hittites, Amorites, Perizzites, Jebusites and Girgashites. You fulfilled Your promise for

---

וַיְבָרֶךְ דָּוִיד *David blessed.* There now follow three biblical passages that strictly speaking do not belong to the Verses of Praise, either in source or subject matter. The Verses of Praise are "songs of Your servant David" – that is, passages from the book of Psalms – and they are about "He who spoke and the world came into being," about God as Creator and Sovereign of the universe. None of the following passages belongs to either category. They are (1) the national

בָּרוּךְ יהוה לְעוֹלָם, אָמֵן וְאָמֵן: תהלים פט
בָּרוּךְ יהוה מִצִּיּוֹן, שֹׁכֵן יְרוּשָׁלָיִם, הַלְלוּיָהּ: תהלים קלה
בָּרוּךְ יהוה אֱלֹהִים אֱלֹהֵי יִשְׂרָאֵל, עֹשֵׂה נִפְלָאוֹת לְבַדּוֹ: תהלים עב
◂ וּבָרוּךְ שֵׁם כְּבוֹדוֹ לְעוֹלָם
וְיִמָּלֵא כְבוֹדוֹ אֶת־כָּל־הָאָרֶץ
אָמֵן וְאָמֵן:

Stand until נִשְׁמַת *on page 353.*

וַיְבָרֶךְ דָּוִיד אֶת־יהוה לְעֵינֵי כָּל־הַקָּהָל, וַיֹּאמֶר דָּוִיד, בָּרוּךְ דברי הימים א׳ כט
אַתָּה יהוה, אֱלֹהֵי יִשְׂרָאֵל אָבִינוּ, מֵעוֹלָם וְעַד־עוֹלָם: לְךָ יהוה
הַגְּדֻלָּה וְהַגְּבוּרָה וְהַתִּפְאֶרֶת וְהַנֵּצַח וְהַהוֹד, כִּי־כֹל בַּשָּׁמַיִם
וּבָאָרֶץ, לְךָ יהוה הַמַּמְלָכָה וְהַמִּתְנַשֵּׂא לְכֹל לְרֹאשׁ: וְהָעֹשֶׁר
וְהַכָּבוֹד מִלְּפָנֶיךָ, וְאַתָּה מוֹשֵׁל בַּכֹּל, וּבְיָדְךָ כֹּחַ וּגְבוּרָה, וּבְיָדְךָ
לְגַדֵּל וּלְחַזֵּק לַכֹּל: וְעַתָּה אֱלֹהֵינוּ מוֹדִים אֲנַחְנוּ לָךְ, וּמְהַלְלִים
לְשֵׁם תִּפְאַרְתֶּךָ: אַתָּה־הוּא יהוה לְבַדֶּךָ, אַתָּ עָשִׂיתָ נחמיה ט
אֶת־הַשָּׁמַיִם, שְׁמֵי הַשָּׁמַיִם וְכָל־צְבָאָם, הָאָרֶץ וְכָל־אֲשֶׁר
עָלֶיהָ, הַיַּמִּים וְכָל־אֲשֶׁר בָּהֶם, וְאַתָּה מְחַיֶּה אֶת־כֻּלָּם, וּצְבָא
הַשָּׁמַיִם לְךָ מִשְׁתַּחֲוִים: ◂ אַתָּה הוּא יהוה הָאֱלֹהִים אֲשֶׁר בָּחַרְתָּ
בְּאַבְרָם, וְהוֹצֵאתוֹ מֵאוּר כַּשְׂדִּים, וְשַׂמְתָּ שְּׁמוֹ אַבְרָהָם: וּמָצָאתָ
אֶת־לְבָבוֹ נֶאֱמָן לְפָנֶיךָ, ◂ וְכָרוֹת עִמּוֹ הַבְּרִית לָתֵת אֶת־אֶרֶץ
הַכְּנַעֲנִי הַחִתִּי הָאֱמֹרִי וְהַפְּרִזִּי וְהַיְבוּסִי וְהַגִּרְגָּשִׁי, לָתֵת לְזַרְעוֹ,

---

בָּרוּךְ יהוה לְעוֹלָם *Blessed be the Lord for ever.* A passage marking the end of the Verses of Praise, consisting of four verses from Psalms, each opening with the word "Blessed," thus echoing the opening paragraph, "Blessed is He who spoke."

You are righteous. You saw the suffering of our ancestors in Egypt. You heard their cry at the Sea of Reeds. You sent signs and wonders against Pharaoh, all his servants and all the people of his land, because You knew how arrogantly the Egyptians treated them. You created for Yourself renown that remains to this day. ▸ You divided the sea before them, so that they passed through the sea on dry land, but You cast their pursuers into the depths, like a stone into mighty waters.

וַיּוֹשַׁע That day the LORD saved Israel from the hands of the Egyptians, and Israel saw the Egyptians lying dead on the seashore. ▸ When Israel saw the great power the LORD had displayed against the Egyptians, the people feared the LORD, and believed in the LORD and in His servant, Moses. *Ex. 14*

אָז יָשִׁיר־מֹשֶׁה Then Moses and the Israelites sang this song to the LORD, saying: *Ex. 15*

I will sing to the LORD, for He has triumphed gloriously;
horse and rider He has hurled into the sea.
The LORD is my strength and song; He has become my salvation.
This is my God, and I will beautify Him,
my father's God, and I will exalt Him.

---

phenomenon, a higher order of being. The *tzibbur* that prays is a microcosm of the Jewish people. At this moment of transition, therefore, we undergo a metamorphosis, and we do so by a historical reenactment, retracing the steps of our ancestors as they cast off their private concerns as individuals to become a community of faith dedicated to the collective worship of God.

THE SONG AT THE SEA

Rashi, explaining the Talmudic view (*Sota* 30b) that at the Sea of Reeds Moses and the Israelites spontaneously sang the song together, says that the holy spirit rested on them and miraculously the same words came into

וַתָּקֶם אֶת־דְּבָרֶיךָ, כִּי צַדִּיק אָתָּה: וַתֵּרֶא אֶת־עֳנִי אֲבֹתֵינוּ
בְּמִצְרָיִם, וְאֶת־זַעֲקָתָם שָׁמַעְתָּ עַל־יַם־סוּף: וַתִּתֵּן אֹתֹת וּמֹפְתִים
בְּפַרְעֹה וּבְכָל־עֲבָדָיו וּבְכָל־עַם אַרְצוֹ, כִּי יָדַעְתָּ כִּי הֵזִידוּ עֲלֵיהֶם,
וַתַּעַשׂ־לְךָ שֵׁם כְּהַיּוֹם הַזֶּה: ◂ וְהַיָּם בָּקַעְתָּ לִפְנֵיהֶם, וַיַּעַבְרוּ
בְתוֹךְ־הַיָּם בַּיַּבָּשָׁה, וְאֶת־רֹדְפֵיהֶם הִשְׁלַכְתָּ בִמְצוֹלֹת כְּמוֹ־
אֶבֶן, בְּמַיִם עַזִּים:

שמות יד וַיּוֹשַׁע יהוה בַּיּוֹם הַהוּא אֶת־יִשְׂרָאֵל מִיַּד מִצְרָיִם, וַיַּרְא יִשְׂרָאֵל
אֶת־מִצְרַיִם מֵת עַל־שְׂפַת הַיָּם: ◂ וַיַּרְא יִשְׂרָאֵל אֶת־הַיָּד הַגְּדֹלָה
אֲשֶׁר עָשָׂה יהוה בְּמִצְרַיִם, וַיִּירְאוּ הָעָם אֶת־יהוה, וַיַּאֲמִינוּ
בַּיהוה וּבְמֹשֶׁה עַבְדּוֹ:

שמות טו אָז יָשִׁיר־מֹשֶׁה וּבְנֵי יִשְׂרָאֵל אֶת־הַשִּׁירָה הַזֹּאת לַיהוה, וַיֹּאמְרוּ
לֵאמֹר, אָשִׁירָה לַיהוה כִּי־גָאֹה גָּאָה, סוּס
וְרֹכְבוֹ רָמָה בַיָּם: עָזִּי וְזִמְרָת יָהּ וַיְהִי־לִי
לִישׁוּעָה, זֶה אֵלִי וְאַנְוֵהוּ, אֱלֹהֵי

---

assembly convened by David shortly before his death to initiate the building of the Temple under the aegis of his son and successor Solomon; (2) the national assembly gathered by Ezra and Nehemiah to renew the covenant between Israel and God; and (3) the song sung by the Israelites after they had crossed the Sea of Reeds and become "the people You acquired." These were key historic moments when the Jewish people came together as a collective body to praise God and pledge their loyalty to Him. Their presence here marks the transition from private to public prayer, which is about to begin.

A *tzibbur*, a public, is more than a mere assemblage of individuals, just as the human body is more than a collection of cells. It is an emergent

The LORD is a Master of war; LORD is His name.
Pharaoh's chariots and army He cast into the sea;
    the best of his officers drowned in the Sea of Reeds.
The deep waters covered them;
    they went down to the depths like a stone.
Your right hand, LORD, is majestic in power.
    Your right hand, LORD, shatters the enemy.
In the greatness of Your majesty, You overthrew those who rose
    against You.
    You sent out Your fury; it consumed them like stubble.
By the blast of Your nostrils the waters piled up.
    The surging waters stood straight like a wall;
    the deeps congealed in the heart of the sea.
The enemy said, "I will pursue. I will overtake. I will divide the spoil.
    My desire shall have its fill of them.
    I will draw my sword. My hand will destroy them."
You blew with Your wind; the sea covered them.
    They sank in the mighty waters like lead.
Who is like You, LORD, among the mighty?
    Who is like You – majestic in holiness, awesome in glory,
    working wonders?
You stretched out Your right hand,
    the earth swallowed them.
In Your loving-kindness, You led the people You redeemed.
    In Your strength, You guided them to Your holy abode.
Nations heard and trembled;
    terror gripped Philistia's inhabitants.

Scruton calls music "an encounter with the pure subject, released from the world of objects, and moving in obedience to the laws of freedom alone." He quotes Rilke: "Words still go softly forth towards the unsayable. / And music, always new, from palpitating stones / Builds in useless space its godly home." The history of the Jewish spirit is written in its songs.

אָבִי וַאֲרֹמְמֶנְהוּ: יהוה אִישׁ מִלְחָמָה, יהוה
שְׁמוֹ: מַרְכְּבֹת פַּרְעֹה וְחֵילוֹ יָרָה בַיָּם, וּמִבְחַר
שָׁלִשָׁיו טֻבְּעוּ בְיַם־סוּף: תְּהֹמֹת יְכַסְיֻמוּ, יָרְדוּ בִמְצוֹלֹת כְּמוֹ־
אָבֶן: יְמִינְךָ יהוה נֶאְדָּרִי בַּכֹּחַ, יְמִינְךָ
יהוה תִּרְעַץ אוֹיֵב: וּבְרֹב גְּאוֹנְךָ תַּהֲרֹס
קָמֶיךָ, תְּשַׁלַּח חֲרֹנְךָ יֹאכְלֵמוֹ כַּקַּשׁ: וּבְרוּחַ
אַפֶּיךָ נֶעֶרְמוּ מַיִם, נִצְּבוּ כְמוֹ־נֵד
נֹזְלִים, קָפְאוּ תְהֹמֹת בְּלֶב־יָם: אָמַר
אוֹיֵב אֶרְדֹּף, אַשִּׂיג, אֲחַלֵּק שָׁלָל, תִּמְלָאֵמוֹ
נַפְשִׁי, אָרִיק חַרְבִּי תּוֹרִישֵׁמוֹ יָדִי: נָשַׁפְתָּ
בְרוּחֲךָ כִּסָּמוֹ יָם, צָלְלוּ כַּעוֹפֶרֶת בְּמַיִם
אַדִּירִים: מִי־כָמֹכָה בָּאֵלִם יהוה, מִי
כָּמֹכָה נֶאְדָּר בַּקֹּדֶשׁ, נוֹרָא תְהִלֹּת עֹשֵׂה
פֶלֶא: נָטִיתָ יְמִינְךָ תִּבְלָעֵמוֹ אָרֶץ: נָחִיתָ
בְחַסְדְּךָ עַם־זוּ גָּאָלְתָּ, נֵהַלְתָּ בְעָזְּךָ אֶל־נְוֵה
קָדְשֶׁךָ: שָׁמְעוּ עַמִּים יִרְגָּזוּן, חִיל
אָחַז יֹשְׁבֵי פְּלָשֶׁת: אָז נִבְהֲלוּ אַלּוּפֵי

their minds at the same time. It was a moment of collective epiphany, and it expressed itself as song.

When language aspires to the transcendent and the soul longs to break free of the gravitational pull of the earth, it modulates into song. Richter called music "the poetry of the air." Tolstoy called it "the shorthand of emotion." Goethe said, "Religious worship cannot do without music. It is one of the foremost means to work upon man with an effect of marvel." Words are the language of the mind. Music is the language of the soul.

Faith is the ability to hear the music beneath the noise. Philosopher Roger

The chiefs of Edom were dismayed,
Moab's leaders were seized with trembling,
the people of Canaan melted away.
Fear and dread fell upon them.
By the power of Your arm, they were still as stone –
until Your people crossed, LORD,
until the people You acquired crossed over.
You will bring them and plant them
on the mountain of Your heritage –
the place, LORD, You made for Your dwelling,
the Sanctuary, LORD, Your hands established.
The LORD will reign for ever and all time.

The LORD will reign for ever and all time.
The LORD's kingship is established for ever and to all eternity.

When Pharaoh's horses, chariots and riders went into the sea,
the LORD brought the waters of the sea back over them,
but the Israelites walked on dry land through the sea.

▸ For kingship is the LORD's *Ps. 22*
and He rules over the nations.
Saviors shall go up to Mount Zion *Ob. 1*
to judge Mount Esau,
and the LORD's shall be the kingdom.

Then the LORD shall be King over all the earth; *Zech. 14*
on that day the LORD shall be One and His name One,

(as it is written in Your Torah, saying:
Listen, Israel: the LORD is our God, the LORD is One.) *Deut. 6*

On Hoshana Raba continue with the Ḥol HaMo'ed weekday service,
from "May Your name be praised" on page 620.

On Simḥat Torah some say the piyut "The souls of those learned" on page 1443.

אֱדוֹם, אֵילֵי מוֹאָב יֹאחֲזֵמוֹ רָעַד, נָמֹגוּ
כֹּל יֹשְׁבֵי כְנָעַן: תִּפֹּל עֲלֵיהֶם אֵימָתָה
וָפַחַד, בִּגְדֹל זְרוֹעֲךָ יִדְּמוּ כָּאָבֶן, עַד־
יַעֲבֹר עַמְּךָ יהוה, עַד־יַעֲבֹר עַם־זוּ
קָנִיתָ: תְּבִאֵמוֹ וְתִטָּעֵמוֹ בְּהַר נַחֲלָתְךָ, מָכוֹן
לְשִׁבְתְּךָ פָּעַלְתָּ יהוה, מִקְּדָשׁ אֲדֹנָי כּוֹנְנוּ
יָדֶיךָ: יהוה יִמְלֹךְ לְעֹלָם וָעֶד:
יהוה יִמְלֹךְ לְעֹלָם וָעֶד.
יהוה מַלְכוּתֵהּ קָאֵם לְעָלַם וּלְעָלְמֵי עָלְמַיָּא.
כִּי
בָא סוּס פַּרְעֹה בְּרִכְבּוֹ וּבְפָרָשָׁיו בַּיָּם, וַיָּשֶׁב יהוה עֲלֵהֶם אֶת־מֵי
הַיָּם, וּבְנֵי יִשְׂרָאֵל הָלְכוּ בַיַּבָּשָׁה בְּתוֹךְ הַיָּם:

תהלים כב ‹ כִּי לַיהוה הַמְּלוּכָה וּמֹשֵׁל בַּגּוֹיִם:
עובדיה א וְעָלוּ מוֹשִׁעִים בְּהַר צִיּוֹן
לִשְׁפֹּט אֶת־הַר עֵשָׂו
וְהָיְתָה לַיהוה הַמְּלוּכָה:
זכריה יד וְהָיָה יהוה לְמֶלֶךְ עַל־כָּל־הָאָרֶץ
בַּיּוֹם הַהוּא יִהְיֶה יהוה אֶחָד וּשְׁמוֹ אֶחָד:

דברים ו (וּבְתוֹרָתְךָ כָּתוּב לֵאמֹר, שְׁמַע יִשְׂרָאֵל, יהוה אֱלֹהֵינוּ יהוה אֶחָד:)

On הושענא רבה *continue with the* חול המועד *service, from* יִשְׁתַּבַּח *on page 621.*

On שמחת תורה *some say the piyut* נִשְׁמַת מְלַמְּדֵי מוֹרָשָׁה *on page 1443.*

THE SOUL

of all that lives shall bless Your name, LORD our God,
and the spirit of all flesh shall always glorify
and exalt Your remembrance, our King.
From eternity to eternity You are God.
Without You, we have no King, Redeemer or Savior,
who liberates, rescues, sustains
and shows compassion in every time of trouble and distress.
We have no King but You, God of the first and last,
God of all creatures, Master of all ages,
extolled by a multitude of praises,
who guides His world with loving-kindness
and His creatures with compassion.
The LORD neither slumbers nor sleeps.
He rouses the sleepers and wakens the slumberers.
He makes the dumb speak, sets the bound free,
supports the fallen, and raises those bowed down.
To You alone we give thanks:
If our mouths were as full of song as the sea,
and our tongue with jubilation as its myriad waves,
if our lips were full of praise like the spacious heavens,
and our eyes shone like the sun and moon,
if our hands were outstretched like eagles of the sky,
and our feet as swift as hinds –

The second part, beginning "To You alone we give thanks," is mentioned in the Talmud (*Berakhot* 59b) as a thanksgiving prayer for rain.

The first section is an extended meditation on the last words of the book of Psalms: "Let all that breathes praise the LORD." Hebrew has many words for soul, all deriving from verbs related to breathing. *Neshama* – the word linking this passage to the end of Psalms, means to breathe deeply, as we are able to do in a state of rest. Hence the sages said that on Shabbat we have "an extra soul." In the still silence of the turning world, it is as if we hear all that lives sing a song of praise to God who brought the universe into being, sustains it, and guides the destinies of all things.

The second section is composed around a phrase from Psalms: "All my

נִשְׁמַת

כָּל חַי תְּבָרֵךְ אֶת שִׁמְךָ, יהוה אֱלֹהֵינוּ
וְרוּחַ כָּל בָּשָׂר תְּפָאֵר וּתְרוֹמֵם זִכְרְךָ מַלְכֵּנוּ תָּמִיד.
מִן הָעוֹלָם וְעַד הָעוֹלָם אַתָּה אֵל
וּמִבַּלְעָדֶיךָ אֵין לָנוּ מֶלֶךְ גּוֹאֵל וּמוֹשִׁיעַ
פּוֹדֶה וּמַצִּיל וּמְפַרְנֵס וּמְרַחֵם
בְּכָל עֵת צָרָה וְצוּקָה אֵין לָנוּ מֶלֶךְ אֶלָּא אָתָּה.
אֱלֹהֵי הָרִאשׁוֹנִים וְהָאַחֲרוֹנִים, אֱלוֹהַּ כָּל בְּרִיּוֹת
אֲדוֹן כָּל תּוֹלָדוֹת, הַמְהֻלָּל בְּרֹב הַתִּשְׁבָּחוֹת
הַמְנַהֵג עוֹלָמוֹ בְּחֶסֶד וּבְרִיּוֹתָיו בְּרַחֲמִים.
וַיהוה לֹא יָנוּם וְלֹא יִישָׁן
הַמְעוֹרֵר יְשֵׁנִים וְהַמֵּקִיץ נִרְדָּמִים
וְהַמֵּשִׂיחַ אִלְּמִים וְהַמַּתִּיר אֲסוּרִים
וְהַסּוֹמֵךְ נוֹפְלִים וְהַזּוֹקֵף כְּפוּפִים.
לְךָ לְבַדְּךָ אֲנַחְנוּ מוֹדִים.
אִלּוּ פִינוּ מָלֵא שִׁירָה כַּיָּם
וּלְשׁוֹנֵנוּ רִנָּה כַּהֲמוֹן גַּלָּיו
וְשִׂפְתוֹתֵינוּ שֶׁבַח כְּמֶרְחֲבֵי רָקִיעַ
וְעֵינֵינוּ מְאִירוֹת כַּשֶּׁמֶשׁ וְכַיָּרֵחַ
וְיָדֵינוּ פְרוּשׂוֹת כְּנִשְׁרֵי שָׁמָיִם
וְרַגְלֵינוּ קַלּוֹת כָּאַיָּלוֹת

נִשְׁמַת *The soul.* This magnificent poem is composed of two parts. The first, according to Rabbi Yoḥanan, is the "blessing of the song" mentioned in the Mishna as a conclusion to Hallel in the Pesaḥ Seder service (*Pesaḥim* 118a). Just as there, so here, it stands as a conclusion to the recitation of Psalms.

still we could not thank You enough,
LORD our God and God of our ancestors,
or bless Your name
for even one of the thousand thousands
and myriad myriads of favors
You did for our ancestors and for us.
You redeemed us from Egypt, LORD our God,
and freed us from the house of bondage.
In famine You nourished us; in times of plenty You sustained us.
You delivered us from the sword, saved us from the plague,
and spared us from serious and lasting illness.
Until now Your mercies have helped us.
Your love has not forsaken us.
May You, LORD our God, never abandon us.
Therefore the limbs You formed within us,
the spirit and soul You breathed into our nostrils,
and the tongue You placed in our mouth –
they will thank and bless, praise and glorify, exalt and esteem,
hallow and do homage to Your name, O our King.
For every mouth shall give thanks to You,
every tongue vow allegiance to You, every knee shall bend to You,
every upright body shall bow to You, all hearts shall fear You,
and our innermost being sing praises to Your name,
as is written:

"All my bones shall say: LORD, who is like You? *Ps. 35*
You save the poor from one stronger than him,
the poor and needy from one who would rob him."

Who is like You? Who is equal to You?
Who can be compared to You?
O great, mighty and awesome God, God Most High,
Maker of heaven and earth.
▸ We will laud, praise and glorify You and bless Your holy name,
as it is said:

"Of David. Bless the LORD, O my soul, *Ps. 103*
and all that is within me bless His holy name."

אֵין אֲנַחְנוּ מַסְפִּיקִים לְהוֹדוֹת לְךָ
יהוה אֱלֹהֵינוּ וֵאלֹהֵי אֲבוֹתֵינוּ
וּלְבָרֵךְ אֶת שְׁמֶךָ
עַל אַחַת מֵאֶלֶף אֶלֶף אַלְפֵי אֲלָפִים
וְרִבֵּי רְבָבוֹת פְּעָמִים הַטּוֹבוֹת שֶׁעָשִׂיתָ עִם אֲבוֹתֵינוּ וְעִמָּנוּ.
מִמִּצְרַיִם גְּאַלְתָּנוּ, יהוה אֱלֹהֵינוּ, וּמִבֵּית עֲבָדִים פְּדִיתָנוּ
בְּרָעָב זַנְתָּנוּ וּבְשָׂבָע כִּלְכַּלְתָּנוּ
מֵחֶרֶב הִצַּלְתָּנוּ וּמִדֶּבֶר מִלַּטְתָּנוּ
וּמֵחֳלָיִים רָעִים וְנֶאֱמָנִים דִּלִּיתָנוּ.
עַד הֵנָּה עֲזָרוּנוּ רַחֲמֶיךָ, וְלֹא עֲזָבוּנוּ חֲסָדֶיךָ
וְאַל תִּטְּשֵׁנוּ, יהוה אֱלֹהֵינוּ, לָנֶצַח.
עַל כֵּן אֵבָרִים שֶׁפִּלַּגְתָּ בָּנוּ
וְרוּחַ וּנְשָׁמָה שֶׁנָּפַחְתָּ בְּאַפֵּנוּ, וְלָשׁוֹן אֲשֶׁר שַׂמְתָּ בְּפִינוּ
הֵן הֵם יוֹדוּ וִיבָרְכוּ וִישַׁבְּחוּ וִיפָאֲרוּ
וִירוֹמְמוּ וְיַעֲרִיצוּ וְיַקְדִּישׁוּ וְיַמְלִיכוּ אֶת שִׁמְךָ מַלְכֵּנוּ
כִּי כָל פֶּה לְךָ יוֹדֶה וְכָל לָשׁוֹן לְךָ תִשָּׁבַע
וְכָל בֶּרֶךְ לְךָ תִכְרַע וְכָל קוֹמָה לְפָנֶיךָ תִשְׁתַּחֲוֶה
וְכָל לְבָבוֹת יִירָאוּךָ וְכָל קֶרֶב וּכְלָיוֹת יְזַמְּרוּ לִשְׁמֶךָ
כַּדָּבָר שֶׁכָּתוּב
כָּל עַצְמֹתַי תֹּאמַרְנָה יהוה מִי כָמוֹךָ | תהלים לה
מַצִּיל עָנִי מֵחָזָק מִמֶּנּוּ, וְעָנִי וְאֶבְיוֹן מִגֹּזְלוֹ:

מִי יִדְמֶה לָּךְ וּמִי יִשְׁוֶה לָּךְ וּמִי יַעֲרָךְ לָךְ
הָאֵל הַגָּדוֹל, הַגִּבּוֹר וְהַנּוֹרָא, אֵל עֶלְיוֹן, קוֹנֵה שָׁמַיִם וָאָרֶץ.
◂ נְהַלֶּלְךָ וּנְשַׁבֵּחֲךָ וּנְפָאֶרְךָ וּנְבָרֵךְ אֶת שֵׁם קָדְשֶׁךָ
כָּאָמוּר
לְדָוִד, בָּרְכִי נַפְשִׁי אֶת־יהוה, וְכָל־קְרָבַי אֶת־שֵׁם קָדְשׁוֹ: | תהלים קג

On Yom Tov the Leader begins here:

הָאֵל GOD –
in Your absolute power,
Great – in the glory of Your name,
Mighty – for ever,
Awesome – in Your awe-inspiring deeds,
The King – who sits on a throne.
High and lofty

On Shabbat of Ḥol HaMo'ed, the Leader begins here:

HE INHABITS ETERNITY;
exalted and holy is His name.
And it is written:

Sing joyfully to the LORD, you righteous, *Ps. 33*
for praise from the upright is seemly

▸ By the mouth of the upright You shall be praised.
By the words of the righteous You shall be blessed.
By the tongue of the devout You shall be extolled,
And in the midst of the holy You shall be sanctified.

On Shabbat and festivals it is often the custom to change prayer leaders between the Verses of Praise, essentially a preparation for public prayer, and public prayer itself, beginning with *Barekhu*. The dividing point varies according to the day and its central theme. On Shabbat the division occurs at "He inhabits eternity," emphasizing creation. On Rosh HaShana and Yom Kippur, it is at "The King," highlighting the ideas of justice and judgment. On festivals, it is at "God – in Your absolute power," evoking God as He acts in history, for the festivals are commemorations of the formative events of Jewish history.

יְשָׁרִים, צַדִּיקִים, חֲסִידִים, קְדוֹשִׁים *Upright, righteous, devout, holy.* A fourfold classification of the types of human excellence, from the most people-centered to the most God-centered. Upright means dealing honestly and with integrity. Righteous means one who practices equity and justice. Devout, says Maimonides, means going beyond the letter of the law, doing more than is

On יום טוב *the* שליח ציבור *begins here:*

הָאֵל

בְּתַעֲצוּמוֹת עֻזֶּךָ
הַגָּדוֹל בִּכְבוֹד שְׁמֶךָ
הַגִּבּוֹר לָנֶצַח וְהַנּוֹרָא בְּנוֹרְאוֹתֶיךָ
הַמֶּלֶךְ הַיּוֹשֵׁב עַל כִּסֵּא
רָם וְנִשָּׂא

On שבת חול המועד *the* שליח ציבור *begins here:*

שׁוֹכֵן עַד

מָרוֹם וְקָדוֹשׁ שְׁמוֹ
וְכָתוּב
רַנְּנוּ צַדִּיקִים בַּיהוה, לַיְשָׁרִים נָאוָה תְהִלָּה: תהלים לג

◂ בְּפִי	יְשָׁרִים	תִּתְהַלָּל
וּבְדִבְרֵי	צַדִּיקִים	תִּתְבָּרַךְ
וּבִלְשׁוֹן	חֲסִידִים	תִּתְרוֹמָם
וּבְקֶרֶב	קְדוֹשִׁים	תִּתְקַדָּשׁ

---

bones shall say, LORD, who is like You?" – thus ingeniously linking the Psalms of praise with the Song at the Sea, which contains the same phrase "Who is like You?" Through a fine series of images, the poet expresses the human inadequacy in thanking God, itemizing how the various limbs ("All my bones") may praise Him, yet "still we could not thank You enough."

הָאֵל בְּתַעֲצוּמוֹת עֻזֶּךָ *God – in Your absolute power.* A word-by-word explication of the four terms above: "O great, mighty and awesome God," a phrase used by Moses (Deut. 10:17).

וּבְמַקְהֲלוֹת And in the assemblies
of tens of thousands of Your people, the house of Israel,
with joyous song shall Your name, our King,
be glorified in every generation.
▸ For this is the duty of all creatures before You,
LORD our God and God of our ancestors:
to thank, praise, laud, glorify, exalt,
honor, bless, raise high and acclaim –
even beyond all the words of song and praise
of David, son of Jesse, Your servant, Your anointed.

Stand until after "Bless" on page 362.

יִשְׁתַּבַּח May Your name be praised forever, our King,
the great and holy God, King in heaven and on earth.
For to You, LORD our God and God of our ancestors,
it is right to offer song and praise,
hymn and psalm,
strength and dominion,
eternity, greatness and power,
song of praise and glory,
holiness and kingship,
▸ blessings and thanks, from now and for ever.

---

based on the prayers of the patriarchs or is it a reminder of the service in the Temple? Ultimately, of course, it is both, but as we approach the start of communal prayers, for which we require a *minyan*, we emphasize the public dimension, the thronged assemblies such as gathered in the Temple. "In the multitude of people is the glory of the King" (Prov. 14:28).

יִשְׁתַּבַּח שִׁמְךָ לָעַד *May Your name be praised for ever.* The concluding blessing over the Verses of Praise which, like the introductory blessing, is said standing. The fifteen terms of glorification equal the number of psalms in the Verses of Praise on Sabbaths and festivals, as well as the number of "Songs of Ascents."

וּבְמַקְהֲלוֹת רִבְבוֹת עַמְּךָ בֵּית יִשְׂרָאֵל
בְּרִנָּה יִתְפָּאַר שִׁמְךָ מַלְכֵּנוּ בְּכָל דּוֹר וָדוֹר
› שֶׁכֵּן חוֹבַת כָּל הַיְצוּרִים
לְפָנֶיךָ יהוה אֱלֹהֵינוּ וֵאלֹהֵי אֲבוֹתֵינוּ
לְהוֹדוֹת, לְהַלֵּל, לְשַׁבֵּחַ, לְפָאֵר, לְרוֹמֵם
לְהַדֵּר, לְבָרֵךְ, לְעַלֵּה וּלְקַלֵּס
עַל כָּל דִּבְרֵי שִׁירוֹת וְתִשְׁבְּחוֹת
דָּוִד בֶּן יִשַׁי, עַבְדְּךָ מְשִׁיחֶךָ.

Stand until after בָּרְכוּ *on page 363.*

יִשְׁתַּבַּח שִׁמְךָ לָעַד, מַלְכֵּנוּ
הָאֵל הַמֶּלֶךְ הַגָּדוֹל וְהַקָּדוֹשׁ בַּשָּׁמַיִם וּבָאָרֶץ
כִּי לְךָ נָאֶה, יהוה אֱלֹהֵינוּ וֵאלֹהֵי אֲבוֹתֵינוּ
שִׁיר וּשְׁבָחָה, הַלֵּל וְזִמְרָה
עֹז וּמֶמְשָׁלָה, נֶצַח, גְּדֻלָּה וּגְבוּרָה
תְּהִלָּה וְתִפְאֶרֶת, קְדֻשָּׁה וּמַלְכוּת
› בְּרָכוֹת וְהוֹדָאוֹת, מֵעַתָּה וְעַד עוֹלָם.

---

required (Laws of the Murderer and the Protection of Life 13:4). Holy means dedicated to God, unconcerned with worldly goods or values. The initial letters of the second word in each phrase spell the name Yitzḥak, probably the name of the composer of this prayer.

וּבְמַקְהֲלוֹת *And in the assemblies.* There is a difference of opinion between Maimonides and Nahmanides as to whether prayer in origin is private or public – the inner conversation between the soul and God, or the public celebration of His presence in the midst of nation and community (see Maimonides, Laws of Prayer 1:1, Laws of Kings 9:1; Nahmanides on Exodus 13:16). Is it

Blessed are You, LORD,
God and King, exalted in praises,
God of thanksgivings,
Master of wonders,
who delights in hymns of song,
King, God, Giver of life to the worlds.

HALF KADDISH

Leader: יִתְגַּדַּל Magnified and sanctified
may His great name be,
in the world He created by His will.
May He establish His kingdom
in your lifetime and in your days,
and in the lifetime of all the house of Israel,
swiftly and soon –
and say: Amen.

All: May His great name be blessed
for ever and all time.

Leader: Blessed and praised, glorified and exalted,
raised and honored, uplifted and lauded
be the name of the Holy One,
blessed be He,
beyond any blessing,
song, praise and consolation uttered in the world –
and say: Amen.

---

different movements of a symphony rather than the beginning of a new piece, the Half Kaddish denotes an internal break between two connected sections of prayer. Like all other versions of Kaddish it requires a quorum of ten men, the smallest number that constitutes a community as opposed to a group of individuals.

בָּרוּךְ אַתָּה יהוה
אֵל מֶלֶךְ גָּדוֹל בַּתִּשְׁבָּחוֹת
אֵל הַהוֹדָאוֹת
אֲדוֹן הַנִּפְלָאוֹת
הַבּוֹחֵר בְּשִׁירֵי זִמְרָה
מֶלֶךְ, אֵל, חֵי הָעוֹלָמִים.

חצי קדיש

ש״ץ: יִתְגַּדַּל וְיִתְקַדַּשׁ שְׁמֵהּ רַבָּא (קהל: אָמֵן)
בְּעָלְמָא דִּי בְרָא כִרְעוּתֵהּ
וְיַמְלִיךְ מַלְכוּתֵהּ
בְּחַיֵּיכוֹן וּבְיוֹמֵיכוֹן וּבְחַיֵּי דְכָל בֵּית יִשְׂרָאֵל
בַּעֲגָלָא וּבִזְמַן קָרִיב, וְאִמְרוּ אָמֵן. (קהל: אָמֵן)

קהל וש״ץ: יְהֵא שְׁמֵהּ רַבָּא מְבָרַךְ לְעָלַם וּלְעָלְמֵי עָלְמַיָּא.

ש״ץ: יִתְבָּרַךְ וְיִשְׁתַּבַּח וְיִתְפָּאַר וְיִתְרוֹמַם וְיִתְנַשֵּׂא
וְיִתְהַדָּר וְיִתְעַלֶּה וְיִתְהַלָּל
שְׁמֵהּ דְּקֻדְשָׁא בְּרִיךְ הוּא (קהל: בְּרִיךְ הוּא)
לְעֵלָּא מִן כָּל בִּרְכָתָא וְשִׁירָתָא
תֻּשְׁבְּחָתָא וְנֶחֱמָתָא
דַּאֲמִירָן בְּעָלְמָא, וְאִמְרוּ אָמֵן. (קהל: אָמֵן)

HALF KADDISH

This, the shortest of the five forms of Kaddish, marks the end of one section of the prayers. More like a semicolon than a period, or a pause between the

BLESSINGS OF THE SHEMA

The following blessing and response are said only in the presence of a minyan. They represent a formal summons to the congregation to engage in an act of collective prayer. The custom of bowing at this point is based on 1 Chronicles 29:20, "David said to the whole assembly, 'Now bless the LORD your God.' All the assembly blessed the LORD God of their fathers and bowed their heads low to the LORD and the King." The Leader says the following, bowing at "Bless," standing straight at "the LORD." The congregation, followed by the Leader, responds, bowing at "Bless," standing straight at "the LORD."

Leader: **BLESS**
the LORD, the blessed One.

Congregation: Bless the LORD, the blessed One,
for ever and all time.

Leader: Bless the LORD, the blessed One,
for ever and all time.

The custom is to sit from this point until the Amida, since the predominant emotion of this section of the prayers is love rather than awe. Conversation is forbidden until after the Amida.

Some congregations interweave piyutim (known as Yotzerot) within the blessings of the Shema. *For Yotzerot for the first day, turn to page 1400; for the second day, turn to page 1410; for Shabbat of Ḥol HaMo'ed, turn to page 1424; for Shemini Atzeret, turn to page 1428; and for Simḥat Torah, turn to page 1444.*

בָּרוּךְ Blessed are You, LORD our God, King of the Universe,
who forms light and creates darkness,
makes peace and creates all.

יוֹצֵר אוֹר וּבוֹרֵא חֹשֶׁךְ *Who forms light and creates darkness.* This affirmation, based on a verse in Isaiah (45:7), is an emphatic denial of dualism, the idea, whose origin lay in Greek Gnosticism, that there are two supreme and contending forces at work in the universe, one of good, the other of evil – known variously as the demiurge, the devil, Satan, Belial, Lucifer or the prince of darkness. Dualism arises as an attempt to explain the prevalence of evil in the world by attributing it to a malign power, the enemy of God and the good. Such a view is radically incompatible with monotheism. It is also

קריאת שמע וברכותיה

The following blessing and response are said only in the presence of a מנין.
They represent a formal summons to the קהל *to engage in an act of collective prayer.*
The custom of bowing at this point is based on דברי הימים א׳ כט, כ, *"David said to the whole assembly, 'Now bless the Lord your God.' All the assembly blessed the Lord God of their fathers and bowed their heads low to the Lord and the King."*
The שליח ציבור *says the following, bowing at* בָּרְכוּ*, standing straight at* ה׳.
The קהל*, followed by the* שליח ציבור*, responds, bowing at* בָּרוּךְ*, standing straight at* ה׳.

ש״ץ: בָּרְכוּ
אֶת יהוה הַמְבֹרָךְ.

קהל: בָּרוּךְ יהוה הַמְבֹרָךְ לְעוֹלָם וָעֶד.

ש״ץ: בָּרוּךְ יהוה הַמְבֹרָךְ לְעוֹלָם וָעֶד.

The custom is to sit from this point until the עמידה*, since the predominant emotion of this section of the prayers is love rather than awe.*
Conversation is forbidden until after the עמידה.

Some congregations interweave piyutim (known as יוצרות*) within the blessings of the* שמע.
For יוצרות *for the first day, turn to page 1400; for the second day, turn to page 1410; for* שבת חול המועד*, turn to page 1424; for* שמיני עצרת*, turn to page 1428; and for* שמחת תורה*, turn to page 1444.*

בָּרוּךְ אַתָּה יהוה אֱלֹהֵינוּ מֶלֶךְ הָעוֹלָם
יוֹצֵר אוֹר וּבוֹרֵא חֹשֶׁךְ
עֹשֶׂה שָׁלוֹם וּבוֹרֵא אֶת הַכֹּל.

בָּרְכוּ *Bless the Lord.* The formal start of communal prayer, to which the Verses of Praise have been a prelude and preparation. *Barekhu*, like the *zimmun* said before the Grace after Meals, is an invitation to others to join in an act of praise, based on the verse, "Magnify the Lord with me, let us exalt His name together" (Ps. 34:4).

On Shabbat continue with "All will thank You" on the next page.
On a weekday continue here:

הַמֵּאִיר In compassion He gives light to the earth and its inhabitants,
and in His goodness continually renews the work of creation,
day after day.
How numerous are Your works, LORD; Ps. 104
You made them all in wisdom;
the earth is full of Your creations.
He is the King exalted alone since the beginning of time –
praised, glorified and elevated since the world began.
Eternal God,
in Your great compassion, have compassion on us,
LORD of our strength, Rock of our refuge,
Shield of our salvation, Stronghold of our safety.
The blessed God, great in knowledge,
prepared and made the rays of the sun.
He who is good formed glory for His name,
surrounding His power with radiant stars.
The leaders of His hosts, the holy ones, exalt the Almighty,
constantly proclaiming God's glory and holiness.
▸ Be blessed, LORD our God, for the magnificence of Your handiwork
and for the radiant lights You have made.
May they glorify You, Selah!

Continue with "May You be blessed, our Rock" on page 370.

---

and then finding a smoother pebble or a prettier shell than ordinary, whilst the great ocean of truth lay all undiscovered before me." The more we discover about the universe, the greater its mystery and majesty inspire awe.

אֵל בָּרוּךְ *The blessed God.* An alphabetical acrostic of twenty-two words. Although this, the first blessing before the Shema, is about creation as a whole, the morning prayer emphasizes the element of which we are most conscious at the start of the day: the creation of light. Of this, there are two forms: the physical light of the sun, moon and stars, made on the fourth day of creation, and the spiritual light created on the first day ("Let there be light"). The prayer modulates from the first to the second, from the universe as we see it, to the mystical vision of God enthroned in glory, surrounded by angels.

On שבת *continue with* הַכֹּל יוֹדוּךָ *on the next page.*
On a weekday continue here:

הַמֵּאִיר לָאָרֶץ וְלַדָּרִים עָלֶיהָ בְּרַחֲמִים
וּבְטוּבוֹ מְחַדֵּשׁ בְּכָל יוֹם תָּמִיד מַעֲשֵׂה בְרֵאשִׁית.
מָה רַבּוּ מַעֲשֶׂיךָ יהוה, כֻּלָּם בְּחָכְמָה עָשִׂיתָ תהלים קד
מָלְאָה הָאָרֶץ קִנְיָנֶךָ:
הַמֶּלֶךְ הַמְרוֹמָם לְבַדּוֹ מֵאָז
הַמְשֻׁבָּח וְהַמְפֹאָר וְהַמִּתְנַשֵּׂא מִימוֹת עוֹלָם.
אֱלֹהֵי עוֹלָם
בְּרַחֲמֶיךָ הָרַבִּים רַחֵם עָלֵינוּ
אֲדוֹן עֻזֵּנוּ, צוּר מִשְׂגַּבֵּנוּ
מָגֵן יִשְׁעֵנוּ, מִשְׂגָּב בַּעֲדֵנוּ.
אֵל בָּרוּךְ גְּדוֹל דֵּעָה
הֵכִין וּפָעַל זָהֳרֵי חַמָּה
טוֹב יָצַר כָּבוֹד לִשְׁמוֹ
מְאוֹרוֹת נָתַן סְבִיבוֹת עֻזּוֹ
פִּנּוֹת צְבָאָיו קְדוֹשִׁים, רוֹמְמֵי שַׁדַּי
תָּמִיד מְסַפְּרִים כְּבוֹד אֵל וּקְדֻשָּׁתוֹ.
◂ תִּתְבָּרַךְ יהוה אֱלֹהֵינוּ, עַל שֶׁבַח מַעֲשֵׂה יָדֶיךָ
וְעַל מְאוֹרֵי אוֹר שֶׁעָשִׂיתָ, יְפָאֲרוּךָ סֶּלָה.

Continue with תִּתְבָּרַךְ, צוּרֵנוּ *on page 371.*

---

exceptionally dangerous: it has led some groups to see others as the personification of evil. Nonetheless, there is evidence that such views were held by some sectarian groups of Jews in the late Second Temple period; hence the need to discountenance it at the very start of communal prayer.

Isaac Newton, the greatest scientist of the seventeenth century, once said: "I do not know what I may appear to the world, but to myself I seem to have been only like a boy playing on the sea-shore, and diverting myself in now

On Shabbat continue here:

All will thank You. All will praise You.
All will declare: Nothing is as holy as the LORD.
All will exalt You, Selah, You who form all –
the God who daily opens the doors of the gates of the East
and cleaves the windows of the sky,
who brings out the sun from its place and the moon from its abode,
giving light to the whole world and its inhabitants
whom He created by the attribute of compassion.
In compassion He gives light to the earth and its inhabitants,
and in His goodness daily, continually, renews the work of creation.
He is the King who alone was exalted since time began,
praised, glorified and raised high from days of old.
Eternal God, in Your great compassion, have compassion on us,
LORD of our strength, Rock of our refuge,
Shield of our salvation, Stronghold of our safety.

אֵין כְּעֶרְכֶּךָ None can be compared to You, there is none besides You;
None without You. Who is like You?

▸ None can be compared to You, LORD our God –
in this world.
There is none besides You, our King –
in the life of the World to Come.
There is none but You, our Redeemer –
in the days of the Messiah.
There is none like You, our Savior –
at the resurrection of the dead.

---

joined the attribute of compassion (*Bereshit Raba* 8:5). One of the supreme ironies of literature is that Portia's speech in Shakespeare's *The Merchant of Venice*, framed in opposition to Jewish ethics, is in fact a precise statement of it:

> The quality of mercy is not strained. It droppeth as the gentle rain from heaven
> Upon the place beneath [...] / It is an attribute to God himself
> And earthly power doth then show likest God's
> Where mercy seasons justice. (IV, i)

On שבת *continue here:*

הַכֹּל יוֹדְוּךָ וְהַכֹּל יְשַׁבְּחְוּךָ
וְהַכֹּל יֹאמְרוּ אֵין קָדוֹשׁ כַּיהוה
הַכֹּל יְרוֹמְמְוּךָ סֶּלָה, יוֹצֵר הַכֹּל.
הָאֵל הַפּוֹתֵחַ בְּכָל יוֹם דַּלְתוֹת שַׁעֲרֵי מִזְרָח
וּבוֹקֵעַ חַלּוֹנֵי רָקִיעַ
מוֹצִיא חַמָּה מִמְּקוֹמָהּ וּלְבָנָה מִמְּכוֹן שִׁבְתָּהּ
וּמֵאִיר לָעוֹלָם כֻּלּוֹ וּלְיוֹשְׁבָיו, שֶׁבָּרָא בְּמִדַּת הָרַחֲמִים.
הַמֵּאִיר לָאָרֶץ וְלַדָּרִים עָלֶיהָ בְּרַחֲמִים
וּבְטוּבוֹ מְחַדֵּשׁ בְּכָל יוֹם תָּמִיד מַעֲשֵׂה בְרֵאשִׁית.
הַמֶּלֶךְ הַמְרוֹמָם לְבַדּוֹ מֵאָז
הַמְשֻׁבָּח וְהַמְפֹאָר וְהַמִּתְנַשֵּׂא מִימוֹת עוֹלָם.
אֱלֹהֵי עוֹלָם, בְּרַחֲמֶיךָ הָרַבִּים רַחֵם עָלֵינוּ
אֲדוֹן עֻזֵּנוּ, צוּר מִשְׂגַּבֵּנוּ, מָגֵן יִשְׁעֵנוּ, מִשְׂגָּב בַּעֲדֵנוּ.

אֵין כְּעֶרְכֶּךָ, וְאֵין זוּלָתֶךָ
אֶפֶס בִּלְתֶּךָ, וּמִי דּוֹמֶה לָּךְ.
◂ אֵין כְּעֶרְכְּךָ, יהוה אֱלֹהֵינוּ, בָּעוֹלָם הַזֶּה
וְאֵין זוּלָתְךָ, מַלְכֵּנוּ, לְחַיֵּי הָעוֹלָם הַבָּא
אֶפֶס בִּלְתְּךָ, גּוֹאֲלֵנוּ, לִימוֹת הַמָּשִׁיחַ
וְאֵין דּוֹמֶה לְּךָ, מוֹשִׁיעֵנוּ, לִתְחִיַּת הַמֵּתִים.

הַכֹּל יוֹדְוּךָ *All will thank You.* This passage, said on Shabbat, is longer than its weekday equivalent since Shabbat is a memorial of creation (*Roke'aḥ*).

שֶׁבָּרָא בְּמִדַּת הָרַחֲמִים *Whom He created by the attribute of compassion.* According to tradition, God initially sought to create the world under the attribute of strict justice, but saw that it could not survive. What did He do? To justice He

אֵל אָדוֹן God, Lord of all creation,
the Blessed, is blessed by every soul.
His greatness and goodness fill the world;
knowledge and wisdom surround Him.

Exalted above the holy Ḥayyot,
adorned in glory on the Chariot;
merit and right are before His throne,
kindness and compassion before His glory.

Good are the radiant stars our God created;
He formed them with knowledge,
understanding and deliberation.
He gave them strength and might
to rule throughout the world.

Full of splendor, radiating light,
beautiful is their splendor throughout the world.
Glad as they go forth, joyous as they return,
they fulfill with awe their Creator's will.

Glory and honor they give to His name,
jubilation and song at the mention of His majesty.
He called the sun into being and it shone with light.
He looked and fashioned the form of the moon.

All the hosts on high give Him praise;
the Seraphim, Ophanim and holy Ḥayyot
ascribe glory and greatness –

אֵל אָדוֹן עַל כָּל הַמַּעֲשִׂים *God, Lord of all creation.* An ancient prayer, influenced by *Merkava* mysticism, envisioning God surrounded by the angels and the myriad stars. *Merkava* or "Chariot" mysticism was based on the vision seen by Ezekiel and described by him in the first chapter of the book that bears his name.

כָּל צְבָא מָרוֹם *All the hosts on high.* Having mentioned the sun and moon, the Hebrew hints at the other planets of the Ptolemaic system: שֶׁבַח נוֹתְנִים לוֹ כָּל צְבָא מָרוֹם – the ש of *sheva*ḥ signaling Saturn (*Shabbetai*), and so on for Venus (נ for *Noga*), Mercury (כ for *Kokhav*), Jupiter (צ for *Tzedek*), and Mars (מ for *Maadim*).

אֵל אָדוֹן עַל כָּל הַמַּעֲשִׂים
בָּרוּךְ וּמְבֹרָךְ בְּפִי כָּל נְשָׁמָה
גָּדְלוֹ וְטוּבוֹ מָלֵא עוֹלָם
דַּעַת וּתְבוּנָה סוֹבְבִים אוֹתוֹ.

הַמִּתְגָּאֶה עַל חַיּוֹת הַקֹּדֶשׁ
וְנֶהְדָּר בְּכָבוֹד עַל הַמֶּרְכָּבָה
זְכוּת וּמִישׁוֹר לִפְנֵי כִסְאוֹ
חֶסֶד וְרַחֲמִים לִפְנֵי כְבוֹדוֹ.

טוֹבִים מְאוֹרוֹת שֶׁבָּרָא אֱלֹהֵינוּ
יְצָרָם בְּדַעַת בְּבִינָה וּבְהַשְׂכֵּל
כֹּחַ וּגְבוּרָה נָתַן בָּהֶם
לִהְיוֹת מוֹשְׁלִים בְּקֶרֶב תֵּבֵל.

מְלֵאִים זִיו וּמְפִיקִים נֹגַהּ
נָאֶה זִיוָם בְּכָל הָעוֹלָם
שְׂמֵחִים בְּצֵאתָם וְשָׂשִׂים בְּבוֹאָם
עוֹשִׂים בְּאֵימָה רְצוֹן קוֹנָם.

פְּאֵר וְכָבוֹד נוֹתְנִים לִשְׁמוֹ
צָהֳלָה וְרִנָּה לְזֵכֶר מַלְכוּתוֹ
קָרָא לַשֶּׁמֶשׁ וַיִּזְרַח אוֹר
רָאָה וְהִתְקִין צוּרַת הַלְּבָנָה.

שֶׁבַח נוֹתְנִים לוֹ כָּל צְבָא מָרוֹם
תִּפְאֶרֶת וּגְדֻלָּה, שְׂרָפִים וְאוֹפַנִּים וְחַיּוֹת הַקֹּדֶשׁ.

לָאֵל To God who rested from all works, and on the seventh day
ascended and sat on His throne of glory.
He robed the day of rest in glory and called the Sabbath day a delight.
This is the praise of the seventh day,
that on it God rested from all His work.
The seventh day itself gives praise, saying,
"A psalm, a song for the Sabbath day. *Ps. 92*
It is good to give thanks to the LORD."
Therefore let all He has formed glorify and bless God.
Let them give praise, honor and grandeur to God,
the King, who formed all things,
and in His holiness gave a heritage of rest
to His people Israel on the holy Sabbath day.
May Your name, O LORD our God, be sanctified,
and Your renown, O our King, be glorified
in the heavens above and on earth below.
May You be blessed, our Deliverer,
by the praises of Your handiwork,
and by the radiant lights You have made:
may they glorify You. Selah!

On all days continue here:

תִּתְבָּרַךְ May You be blessed,
our Rock, King and Redeemer,
Creator of holy beings.
May Your name be praised for ever,
our King, Creator of the ministering angels,
all of whom stand in the universe's heights,
proclaiming together, in awe, aloud,
the words of the living God, the eternal King.

---

understood not as a song *for* the Sabbath, but *by* the Sabbath. It is as if, in the silence of Shabbat, we hear the song creation sings to its Creator, the "music of the spheres."

תִּתְבָּרַךְ *May You be blessed.* Two prophets, Isaiah and Ezekiel, saw mystical visions of God enthroned among His heavenly host, the choir of angels.

לָאֵל אֲשֶׁר שָׁבַת מִכָּל הַמַּעֲשִׂים
בַּיּוֹם הַשְּׁבִיעִי נִתְעַלָּה וְיָשַׁב עַל כִּסֵּא כְבוֹדוֹ.
תִּפְאֶרֶת עָטָה לְיוֹם הַמְּנוּחָה
עֹנֶג קָרָא לְיוֹם הַשַּׁבָּת.
זֶה שֶׁבַח שֶׁלַּיּוֹם הַשְּׁבִיעִי
שֶׁבּוֹ שָׁבַת אֵל מִכָּל מְלַאכְתּוֹ
וְיוֹם הַשְּׁבִיעִי מְשַׁבֵּחַ וְאוֹמֵר
מִזְמוֹר שִׁיר לְיוֹם הַשַּׁבָּת, טוֹב לְהֹדוֹת לַיהוה: תהלים צב
לְפִיכָךְ יְפָאֲרוּ וִיבָרְכוּ לָאֵל כָּל יְצוּרָיו
שֶׁבַח יְקָר וּגְדֻלָּה יִתְּנוּ לָאֵל מֶלֶךְ יוֹצֵר כֹּל
הַמַּנְחִיל מְנוּחָה לְעַמּוֹ יִשְׂרָאֵל בִּקְדֻשָּׁתוֹ בְּיוֹם שַׁבַּת קֹדֶשׁ.
שִׁמְךָ יהוה אֱלֹהֵינוּ יִתְקַדַּשׁ, וְזִכְרְךָ מַלְכֵּנוּ יִתְפָּאַר
בַּשָּׁמַיִם מִמַּעַל וְעַל הָאָרֶץ מִתָּחַת.
תִּתְבָּרַךְ מוֹשִׁיעֵנוּ עַל שֶׁבַח מַעֲשֵׂה יָדֶיךָ
וְעַל מְאוֹרֵי אוֹר שֶׁעָשִׂיתָ, יְפָאֲרוּךָ סֶּלָה.

On all days continue here:

תִּתְבָּרַךְ
צוּרֵנוּ מַלְכֵּנוּ וְגוֹאֲלֵנוּ, בּוֹרֵא קְדוֹשִׁים
יִשְׁתַּבַּח שִׁמְךָ לָעַד
מַלְכֵּנוּ, יוֹצֵר מְשָׁרְתִים
וַאֲשֶׁר מְשָׁרְתָיו כֻּלָּם עוֹמְדִים בְּרוּם עוֹלָם
וּמַשְׁמִיעִים בְּיִרְאָה יַחַד בְּקוֹל
דִּבְרֵי אֱלֹהִים חַיִּים וּמֶלֶךְ עוֹלָם.

וְיוֹם הַשְּׁבִיעִי מְשַׁבֵּחַ *The seventh day itself gives praise.* A midrashic idea, based on the phrase that opens Psalm 92: "A psalm, a song of the Sabbath day," here

They are all beloved, all pure, all mighty,
and all perform in awe and reverence
the will of their Maker.
▸ All open their mouths
in holiness and purity,
with song and psalm,
and bless, praise, glorify,
revere, sanctify and declare the sovereignty of – ◂
the name of the great, mighty
and awesome God and King,
holy is He.
▸ All accept on themselves, one from another,
the yoke of the kingdom of heaven,
granting permission to one another
to sanctify the One who formed them,
in serene spirit,
pure speech and sweet melody.
All, as one, proclaim His holiness,
saying in awe:

All say aloud:

Holy, holy, holy is the LORD of hosts; *Is. 6*
the whole world is filled with His glory.

Some congregations say here a piyut (known as an Ophan).
For the Ophan for the first two days of Sukkot, turn to page 1401;
for Shabbat of Ḥol HaMo'ed, turn to page 1426;
for Shemini Atzeret, turn to page 1429; and for Simḥat Torah, turn to page 1446.

---

prayer, except on Shabbat and festivals, when the third is transferred to the afternoon.

This section of the prayers – the vision of the heavenly throne and the angels – is part of the mystical tradition in Judaism. Prayer is Jacob's ladder, stretching from earth to heaven, with "angels of the LORD" ascending and descending (*Zohar*). The three *kedushot* represent, respectively, the ascent, the summit, and the descent: the journey of the soul from earth to heaven and back again, transformed by our experience of the Divine.

כֻּלָּם אֲהוּבִים, כֻּלָּם בְּרוּרִים, כֻּלָּם גִּבּוֹרִים
וְכֻלָּם עוֹשִׂים בְּאֵימָה וּבְיִרְאָה רְצוֹן קוֹנָם
◂ וְכֻלָּם פּוֹתְחִים אֶת פִּיהֶם
בִּקְדֻשָּׁה וּבְטָהֳרָה
בְּשִׁירָה וּבְזִמְרָה
וּמְבָרְכִים וּמְשַׁבְּחִים וּמְפָאֲרִים
וּמַעֲרִיצִים וּמַקְדִּישִׁים וּמַמְלִיכִים ◂
אֶת שֵׁם הָאֵל הַמֶּלֶךְ הַגָּדוֹל, הַגִּבּוֹר וְהַנּוֹרָא
קָדוֹשׁ הוּא.
◂ וְכֻלָּם מְקַבְּלִים עֲלֵיהֶם עֹל מַלְכוּת שָׁמַיִם זֶה מִזֶּה
וְנוֹתְנִים רְשׁוּת זֶה לָזֶה
לְהַקְדִּישׁ לְיוֹצְרָם בְּנַחַת רוּחַ
בְּשָׂפָה בְרוּרָה וּבִנְעִימָה
קְדֻשָּׁה כֻּלָּם כְּאֶחָד
עוֹנִים וְאוֹמְרִים בְּיִרְאָה

All say aloud:

ישעיה ו
קָדוֹשׁ, קָדוֹשׁ, קָדוֹשׁ יהוה צְבָאוֹת
מְלֹא כָל־הָאָרֶץ כְּבוֹדוֹ:

Some congregations say here a piyut (known as an אופן*).*
For the אופן *for the first two days of* סוכות*, turn to page 1401;*
for שבת חול המועד*, turn to page 1426; for* שמיני עצרת*, turn to page 1429;*
and for שמחת תורה*, turn to page 1446.*

These visions, together with the words the prophets heard the angels sing ("Holy, holy, holy" in Isaiah's vision, "Blessed be the LORD's glory from His place" in Ezekiel's), form the heart of *Kedusha*, the "Holiness" prayer. This is recited three times in the morning prayers – (1) before the Shema, (2) during the Leader's Repetition of the Amida, and (3) toward the end of

▸ Then the Ophanim and the Holy Ḥayyot,
with a roar of noise,
raise themselves toward the Seraphim and,
facing them, give praise, saying:

All say aloud:
Blessed is the Lord's glory from His place. *Ezek. 3*

לְאֵל To the blessed God they offer melodies.
To the King, living and eternal God,
they say psalms and proclaim praises.
For it is He alone
who does mighty deeds and creates new things,
who is Master of battles and sows righteousness,
who makes salvation grow and creates cures,
who is is revered in praises, the Lord of wonders,
who in His goodness, continually renews the work of creation,
day after day,
as it is said:
"[Praise] Him who made the great lights, *Ps. 136*
for His love endures for ever."
▸ May You make a new light shine over Zion,
and may we all soon be worthy of its light.
Blessed are You, Lord,
who forms the radiant lights.

אַהֲבָה You have loved us with great love, Lord our God,
and with surpassing compassion
have You had compassion on us.
Our Father, our King,
for the sake of our ancestors who trusted in You,
and to whom You taught the laws of life,
be gracious also to us and teach us.

אַהֲבָה רַבָּה אֲהַבְתָּנוּ *You have loved us with great love.* Even before reciting the Shema with its command, "Love the Lord your God with all your heart,

▸ וְהָאוֹפַנִּים וְחַיּוֹת הַקֹּדֶשׁ
בְּרַעַשׁ גָּדוֹל מִתְנַשְּׂאִים לְעֻמַּת שְׂרָפִים
לְעֻמָּתָם מְשַׁבְּחִים וְאוֹמְרִים

All say aloud:

בָּרוּךְ כְּבוֹד־יהוה מִמְּקוֹמוֹ: יחזקאל ג

לָאֵל בָּרוּךְ נְעִימוֹת יִתֵּנוּ
לַמֶּלֶךְ אֵל חַי וְקַיָּם
זְמִירוֹת יֹאמֵרוּ וְתִשְׁבָּחוֹת יַשְׁמִיעוּ
כִּי הוּא לְבַדּוֹ
פּוֹעֵל גְּבוּרוֹת, עוֹשֶׂה חֲדָשׁוֹת
בַּעַל מִלְחָמוֹת, זוֹרֵעַ צְדָקוֹת
מַצְמִיחַ יְשׁוּעוֹת, בּוֹרֵא רְפוּאוֹת
נוֹרָא תְהִלּוֹת, אֲדוֹן הַנִּפְלָאוֹת
הַמְחַדֵּשׁ בְּטוּבוֹ בְּכָל יוֹם תָּמִיד מַעֲשֵׂה בְרֵאשִׁית
כָּאָמוּר
לְעֹשֵׂה אוֹרִים גְּדֹלִים, כִּי לְעוֹלָם חַסְדּוֹ: תהלים קלו
▸ אוֹר חָדָשׁ עַל צִיּוֹן תָּאִיר
וְנִזְכֶּה כֻלָּנוּ מְהֵרָה לְאוֹרוֹ.
בָּרוּךְ אַתָּה יהוה, יוֹצֵר הַמְּאוֹרוֹת.

אַהֲבָה רַבָּה אֲהַבְתָּנוּ, יהוה אֱלֹהֵינוּ
חֶמְלָה גְדוֹלָה וִיתֵרָה חָמַלְתָּ עָלֵינוּ.
אָבִינוּ מַלְכֵּנוּ
בַּעֲבוּר אֲבוֹתֵינוּ שֶׁבָּטְחוּ בְךָ, וַתְּלַמְּדֵם חֻקֵּי חַיִּים
כֵּן תְּחָנֵּנוּ וּתְלַמְּדֵנוּ.

Our Father, compassionate Father, ever compassionate,
have compassion on us.
Instill in our hearts the desire to understand and discern,
to listen, learn and teach, to observe, perform and fulfill
all the teachings of Your Torah in love.
Enlighten our eyes in Your Torah
and let our hearts cling to Your commandments.
Unite our hearts to love and revere Your name,
so that we may never be ashamed.
And because we have trusted
in Your holy, great and revered name,
may we be glad and rejoice in Your salvation.

At this point, gather the four tzitziot of the tallit, holding them in the left hand.

Bring us back in peace from the four quarters of the earth
and lead us upright to our land.
▸ For You are a God who performs acts of salvation,
and You chose us from all peoples and tongues,
bringing us close to Your great name for ever in truth,
that we may thank You
and proclaim Your Oneness in love.
Blessed are You, Lord,
who chooses His people Israel in love.

---

centrality of law in Judaism: "...the law of millennia, studied and lived, analyzed and rhapsodized, the law of everyday and of the day of death, petty and yet sublime, sober and yet woven in legend; a law which knows both the fire of the Sabbath candle and that of the martyr's stake" (Franz Rosenzweig, *On Jewish Learning*, 77). The law, through which Israel is charged with bringing the Divine Presence into the shared spaces of our common life, is itself based on a threefold love: for God, the neighbor, and the stranger. Through law – the choreography of grace in relationship – we redeem our finitude, turning the prose of daily life into religious poetry and making gentle the life of this world.

אָבִינוּ, הָאָב הָרַחֲמָן, הַמְרַחֵם
רַחֵם עָלֵינוּ
וְתֵן בְּלִבֵּנוּ לְהָבִין וּלְהַשְׂכִּיל
לִשְׁמֹעַ, לִלְמֹד וּלְלַמֵּד, לִשְׁמֹר וְלַעֲשׂוֹת, וּלְקַיֵּם
אֶת כָּל דִּבְרֵי תַלְמוּד תּוֹרָתֶךָ בְּאַהֲבָה.
וְהָאֵר עֵינֵינוּ בְּתוֹרָתֶךָ
וְדַבֵּק לִבֵּנוּ בְּמִצְוֹתֶיךָ
וְיַחֵד לְבָבֵנוּ לְאַהֲבָה וּלְיִרְאָה אֶת שְׁמֶךָ
וְלֹא נֵבוֹשׁ לְעוֹלָם וָעֶד.
כִּי בְשֵׁם קָדְשְׁךָ הַגָּדוֹל וְהַנּוֹרָא בָּטָחְנוּ
נָגִילָה וְנִשְׂמְחָה בִּישׁוּעָתֶךָ.

At this point, gather the four ציציות *of the* טלית*, holding them in the left hand.*

וַהֲבִיאֵנוּ לְשָׁלוֹם מֵאַרְבַּע כַּנְפוֹת הָאָרֶץ
וְתוֹלִיכֵנוּ קוֹמְמִיּוּת לְאַרְצֵנוּ.
◂ כִּי אֵל פּוֹעֵל יְשׁוּעוֹת אָתָּה
וּבָנוּ בָחַרְתָּ מִכָּל עַם וְלָשׁוֹן
וְקֵרַבְתָּנוּ לְשִׁמְךָ הַגָּדוֹל סֶלָה, בֶּאֱמֶת
לְהוֹדוֹת לְךָ וּלְיַחֶדְךָ בְּאַהֲבָה.
בָּרוּךְ אַתָּה יהוה, הַבּוֹחֵר בְּעַמּוֹ יִשְׂרָאֵל בְּאַהֲבָה.

---

with all your soul, and with all your might," we speak of God's love for us. Note how that love is expressed: in the fact that God taught us "the laws of life." Christianity at times contrasted law and love as if they were opposed. In Judaism law *is* love: the expression of God's love for us and ours for Him.

Franz Rosenzweig criticized Martin Buber for failing to understand the

The Shema must be said with intense concentration. In the first paragraph one should accept, with love, the sovereignty of God; in the second, the mitzvot as the will of God. The end of the third paragraph constitutes fulfillment of the mitzva to remember, morning and evening, the exodus from Egypt.

When not praying with a minyan, say:

God, faithful King!

The following verse should be said aloud, while covering the eyes with the right hand:

Listen, Israel: the Lord is our God, the Lord is One. Deut. 6

Quietly: Blessed be the name of His glorious kingdom for ever and all time.

וְאָהַבְתָּ Love the Lord your God with all your heart, with all your soul, and with all your might. These words which I command you today shall be on your heart. Teach them repeatedly to your children, speaking of them when you sit at home and when you travel on the way, when you lie down and when you rise. Bind them as a sign on your hand, and they shall be an emblem between your eyes. Write them on the doorposts of your house and gates. Deut. 6

וְהָיָה If you indeed heed My commandments with which I charge you today, to love the Lord your God and worship Him with all your heart and with all your soul, I will give rain in your land in its season, the early and late rain; and you shall gather in your grain, wine and oil. I will give grass in your field for your cattle, and you shall eat and be satisfied. Be careful lest your heart be tempted and Deut. 11

וְאָהַבְתָּ אֵת יהוה אֱלֹהֶיךָ *Love the Lord your God.* "What is the love of God that is befitting? It is to love God with a great and exceeding love, so strong that one's soul shall be knit up with the love of God, such that it is continually enraptured by it, like a lovesick individual whose mind is at no time free from passion for a particular woman and is enraptured by her at all times... Even more intense should be the love of God in the hearts of those who love Him; they should be enraptured by this love at all times" (Maimonides, Laws of Repentance, 10:3).

The שמע *must be said with intense concentration. In the first paragraph one should accept, with love, the sovereignty of God; in the second, the* מצוות *as the will of God. The end of the third paragraph constitutes fulfillment of the* מצווה *to remember, morning and evening, the exodus from Egypt.*

When not praying with a מנין*, say:*

אֵל מֶלֶךְ נֶאֱמָן

The following verse should be said aloud, while covering the eyes with the right hand:

שְׁמַע יִשְׂרָאֵל, יהוה אֱלֹהֵינוּ, יהוה ׀ אֶחָד׃ דברים ו

Quietly בָּרוּךְ שֵׁם כְּבוֹד מַלְכוּתוֹ לְעוֹלָם וָעֶד.

וְאָהַבְתָּ אֵת יהוה אֱלֹהֶיךָ, בְּכָל־לְבָבְךָ וּבְכָל־נַפְשְׁךָ וּבְכָל־מְאֹדֶךָ׃ דברים ו
וְהָיוּ הַדְּבָרִים הָאֵלֶּה, אֲשֶׁר אָנֹכִי מְצַוְּךָ הַיּוֹם, עַל־לְבָבֶךָ׃ וְשִׁנַּנְתָּם
לְבָנֶיךָ וְדִבַּרְתָּ בָּם, בְּשִׁבְתְּךָ בְּבֵיתֶךָ וּבְלֶכְתְּךָ בַדֶּרֶךְ, וּבְשָׁכְבְּךָ
וּבְקוּמֶךָ׃ וּקְשַׁרְתָּם לְאוֹת עַל־יָדֶךָ וְהָיוּ לְטֹטָפֹת בֵּין עֵינֶיךָ׃
וּכְתַבְתָּם עַל־מְזֻזוֹת בֵּיתֶךָ וּבִשְׁעָרֶיךָ׃

וְהָיָה אִם־שָׁמֹעַ תִּשְׁמְעוּ אֶל־מִצְוֺתַי אֲשֶׁר אָנֹכִי מְצַוֶּה אֶתְכֶם דברים יא
הַיּוֹם, לְאַהֲבָה אֶת־יהוה אֱלֹהֵיכֶם וּלְעָבְדוֹ, בְּכָל־לְבַבְכֶם וּבְכָל־
נַפְשְׁכֶם׃ וְנָתַתִּי מְטַר־אַרְצְכֶם בְּעִתּוֹ, יוֹרֶה וּמַלְקוֹשׁ, וְאָסַפְתָּ
דְגָנֶךָ וְתִירֹשְׁךָ וְיִצְהָרֶךָ׃ וְנָתַתִּי עֵשֶׂב בְּשָׂדְךָ לִבְהֶמְתֶּךָ, וְאָכַלְתָּ
וְשָׂבָעְתָּ׃ הִשָּׁמְרוּ לָכֶם פֶּן־יִפְתֶּה לְבַבְכֶם, וְסַרְתֶּם וַעֲבַדְתֶּם

שְׁמַע יִשְׂרָאֵל *Listen, Israel.* Most of the ancient civilizations, from Mesopotamia and Egypt to Greece and Rome, were predominantly visual, with monumental architecture and iconic use of art. Judaism with its faith in the invisible God emphasized hearing over seeing, and listening over looking. Hence the verb "Listen" in this key text, as well as our custom, when saying it, to cover our eyes, shutting out the visible world to concentrate on the commanding Voice.

you go astray and worship other gods, bowing down to them. Then the LORD's anger will flare against you and He will close the heavens so that there will be no rain. The land will not yield its crops, and you will perish swiftly from the good land that the LORD is giving you. Therefore, set these, My words, on your heart and soul. Bind them as a sign on your hand, and they shall be an emblem between your eyes. Teach them to your children, speaking of them when you sit at home and when you travel on the way, when you lie down and when you rise. Write them on the doorposts of your house and gates, so that you and your children may live long in the land that the LORD swore to your ancestors to give them, for as long as the heavens are above the earth.

Hold the tzitziot in the right hand also (some transfer to the right hand), kissing them at °.

וַיֹּאמֶר The LORD spoke to Moses, saying: Speak to the Israelites *Num. 15*
and tell them to make °tassels on the corners of their garments for all generations. They shall attach to the °tassel at each corner a thread of blue. This shall be your °tassel, and you shall see it and remember all of the LORD's commandments and keep them, not straying after your heart and after your eyes, following your own sinful desires. Thus you will be reminded to keep all My

---

cues to remind us of fundamental propositions: who we are and what we are called on to do. The Shema speaks of three such symbols: tefillin, mezuza and tzitzit. The first relates to who we are, the second to where we live, the third to how we dress and appear to the world and to ourselves.

וְלֹא תָתֻרוּ אַחֲרֵי לְבַבְכֶם וְאַחֲרֵי עֵינֵיכֶם *Not straying after your heart and after your eyes.* Note the unexpected order of the phrases. We would have thought that seeing gives rise to desiring rather than the other way around (see Rashi to Numbers 15:39). In fact, however, the story of the spies that precedes the command of tzitzit in the Torah (Num. 13–14) shows that the reverse is frequently the case. Our perception is framed and often distorted by our emotions. The spies were afraid: therefore they saw their enemies as giants and themselves as grasshoppers. They did not realize that the reverse was the case (see Joshua 2:9–11).

אֱלֹהִים אֲחֵרִים וְהִשְׁתַּחֲוִיתֶם לָהֶם: וְחָרָה אַף־יהוה בָּכֶם, וְעָצַר
אֶת־הַשָּׁמַיִם וְלֹא־יִהְיֶה מָטָר, וְהָאֲדָמָה לֹא תִתֵּן אֶת־יְבוּלָהּ,
וַאֲבַדְתֶּם מְהֵרָה מֵעַל הָאָרֶץ הַטֹּבָה אֲשֶׁר יהוה נֹתֵן לָכֶם:
וְשַׂמְתֶּם אֶת־דְּבָרַי אֵלֶּה עַל־לְבַבְכֶם וְעַל־נַפְשְׁכֶם, וּקְשַׁרְתֶּם
אֹתָם לְאוֹת עַל־יֶדְכֶם, וְהָיוּ לְטוֹטָפֹת בֵּין עֵינֵיכֶם: וְלִמַּדְתֶּם
אֹתָם אֶת־בְּנֵיכֶם לְדַבֵּר בָּם, בְּשִׁבְתְּךָ בְּבֵיתֶךָ וּבְלֶכְתְּךָ בַדֶּרֶךְ,
וּבְשָׁכְבְּךָ וּבְקוּמֶךָ: וּכְתַבְתָּם עַל־מְזוּזוֹת בֵּיתֶךָ וּבִשְׁעָרֶיךָ: לְמַעַן
יִרְבּוּ יְמֵיכֶם וִימֵי בְנֵיכֶם עַל הָאֲדָמָה אֲשֶׁר נִשְׁבַּע יהוה לַאֲבֹתֵיכֶם
לָתֵת לָהֶם, כִּימֵי הַשָּׁמַיִם עַל־הָאָרֶץ:

Hold the ציצית *in the right hand also (some transfer to the right hand), kissing them at °.*

וַיֹּאמֶר יהוה אֶל־מֹשֶׁה לֵּאמֹר: דַּבֵּר אֶל־בְּנֵי יִשְׂרָאֵל וְאָמַרְתָּ במדבר טו
אֲלֵהֶם, וְעָשׂוּ לָהֶם °צִיצִת עַל־כַּנְפֵי בִגְדֵיהֶם לְדֹרֹתָם, וְנָתְנוּ
°עַל־צִיצִת הַכָּנָף פְּתִיל תְּכֵלֶת: וְהָיָה לָכֶם °לְצִיצִת, וּרְאִיתֶם
אֹתוֹ וּזְכַרְתֶּם אֶת־כָּל־מִצְוֺת יהוה וַעֲשִׂיתֶם אֹתָם, וְלֹא תָתוּרוּ
אַחֲרֵי לְבַבְכֶם וְאַחֲרֵי עֵינֵיכֶם, אֲשֶׁר־אַתֶּם זֹנִים אַחֲרֵיהֶם: לְמַעַן

וְלִמַּדְתֶּם אֹתָם אֶת־בְּנֵיכֶם *Teach them to your children.* Jews are the only people to have predicated their very survival on education. The Mesopotamians built ziggurats, the Egyptians built pyramids, the Athenians the Parthenon and the Romans the Colosseum. Jews built schools and houses of study. Those other civilizations died and disappeared; Jews and Judaism survived.

לְמַעַן יִרְבּוּ יְמֵיכֶם וִימֵי בְנֵיכֶם *So that you and your children may live long.* Strong nations are impossible without strong families dedicated to passing on their heritage across the generations. Those who plan for one year plant crops. Those who plan for ten years plant trees. Those who plan for centuries educate children.

וּרְאִיתֶם אֹתוֹ, וּזְכַרְתֶּם *And you shall see it and remember.* Though Judaism is primarily a religion of hearing rather than seeing, we nonetheless need visual

commandments, and be holy to your God. I am the LORD your God, who brought you out of the land of Egypt to be your God. I am the LORD your God.

°True –

The Leader repeats:

‣ The LORD your God is true –

וְיַצִּיב And firm, established and enduring, right, faithful,
beloved, cherished, delightful, pleasant,
awesome, mighty, perfect, accepted,
good and beautiful
is this faith for us for ever.

True is the eternal God, our King, Rock of Jacob,
Shield of our salvation.
He exists and His name exists through all generations.
His throne is established,
His kingship and faithfulness endure for ever.

At °, kiss the tzitziot and release them.

His words live and persist, faithful and desirable
°for ever and all time.
‣ So they were for our ancestors, so they are for us,
and so they will be for our children
and all our generations and for all future generations
of the seed of Israel, Your servants.

---

your promises, being true to your word, doing what you said you would do. According to Rashi (to Exodus 6:3), the holiest name of God means "the One who is true to His word." This concept of truth serves as the bridge between the end of the Shema, with its reference to the exodus from Egypt, and the quintessential prayer, the Amida, that we are now approaching. The fact that God redeemed His people in the past is the basis of our prayer for redemption in the future. Just as God was true to His word then, so we pray He will be now. The sixfold repetition of *emet* acts as a reminder of the six steps we have

תִּזְכְּרוּ וַעֲשִׂיתֶם אֶת־כׇּל־מִצְוֺתָי, וִהְיִיתֶם קְדֹשִׁים לֵאלֹהֵיכֶם: אֲנִי יהוה אֱלֹהֵיכֶם, אֲשֶׁר הוֹצֵאתִי אֶתְכֶם מֵאֶרֶץ מִצְרַיִם, לִהְיוֹת לָכֶם לֵאלֹהִים, אֲנִי יהוה אֱלֹהֵיכֶם:

°אֱמֶת

The שליח ציבור *repeats:*

‹ יהוה אֱלֹהֵיכֶם אֱמֶת

וְיַצִּיב, וְנָכוֹן וְקַיָּם, וְיָשָׁר וְנֶאֱמָן
וְאָהוּב וְחָבִיב, וְנֶחְמָד וְנָעִים
וְנוֹרָא וְאַדִּיר, וּמְתֻקָּן וּמְקֻבָּל, וְטוֹב וְיָפֶה
הַדָּבָר הַזֶּה עָלֵינוּ לְעוֹלָם וָעֶד.

אֱמֶת אֱלֹהֵי עוֹלָם מַלְכֵּנוּ
צוּר יַעֲקֹב מָגֵן יִשְׁעֵנוּ
לְדוֹר וָדוֹר הוּא קַיָּם וּשְׁמוֹ קַיָּם
וְכִסְאוֹ נָכוֹן
וּמַלְכוּתוֹ וֶאֱמוּנָתוֹ לָעַד קַיֶּמֶת.

At °, kiss the ציציות *and release them.*

וּדְבָרָיו חָיִים וְקַיָּמִים
נֶאֱמָנִים וְנֶחֱמָדִים
°לָעַד וּלְעוֹלְמֵי עוֹלָמִים
‹ עַל אֲבוֹתֵינוּ וְעָלֵינוּ
עַל בָּנֵינוּ וְעַל דּוֹרוֹתֵינוּ
וְעַל כׇּל דּוֹרוֹת זֶרַע יִשְׂרָאֵל עֲבָדֶיךָ.

אֱמֶת *True.* The word *emet* does not just mean "true" in the narrow Western sense of something that corresponds to reality. In Hebrew it means honoring

For the early and the later generations
this faith has proved good and enduring for ever –
True and faithful, an irrevocable law.
True You are the LORD: our God and God of our ancestors,
▸ our King and King of our ancestors,
our Redeemer and Redeemer of our ancestors,
our Maker, Rock of our salvation,
our Deliverer and Rescuer: this has ever been Your name.
There is no God but You.

Some congregations say here a piyut (known as a Zulat).
For the Zulat for the first day, turn to page 1402; for the second day, turn to page 1412; for Shabbat of Ḥol HaMo'ed, turn to page 1426; for Shemini Atzeret, turn to page 1430; and for Simḥat Torah, turn to page 1448.

עֶזְרַת You have always been the help of our ancestors,
Shield and Savior of their children
after them in every generation.
Your dwelling is in the heights of the universe,
and Your judgments and righteousness
reach to the ends of the earth.
Happy is the one who obeys Your commandments
and takes to heart Your teaching and Your word.
True You are the Master of Your people
and a mighty King who pleads their cause.
True You are the first and You are the last.
Besides You, we have no king, redeemer or savior.
From Egypt You redeemed us, LORD our God,
and from the slave-house You delivered us.
All their firstborn You killed,
but Your firstborn You redeemed.
You split the Sea of Reeds and drowned the arrogant.
You brought Your beloved ones across.
The water covered their foes; not one of them was left. *Ps. 106*

---

taken – the three blessings surrounding the Shema and the three paragraphs of the Shema itself – toward the ultimate destination of prayer, the act of

עַל הָרִאשׁוֹנִים וְעַל הָאַחֲרוֹנִים
דָּבָר טוֹב וְקַיָּם לְעוֹלָם וָעֶד
אֱמֶת וֶאֱמוּנָה, חֹק וְלֹא יַעֲבֹר.
אֱמֶת שָׁאַתָּה הוּא יהוה אֱלֹהֵינוּ וֵאלֹהֵי אֲבוֹתֵינוּ
◂ מַלְכֵּנוּ מֶלֶךְ אֲבוֹתֵינוּ
גּוֹאֲלֵנוּ גּוֹאֵל אֲבוֹתֵינוּ, יוֹצְרֵנוּ צוּר יְשׁוּעָתֵנוּ
פּוֹדֵנוּ וּמַצִּילֵנוּ מֵעוֹלָם שְׁמֶךָ
אֵין אֱלֹהִים זוּלָתֶךָ.

Some congregations say here a piyut (known as a זולת*).*
For the זולת *for the first day, turn to page 1402; for the second day, turn to page 1412; for* שבת חול המועד*, turn to page 1426; for* שמיני עצרת*, turn to page 1430; and for* שמחת תורה*, turn to page 1448.*

עֶזְרַת אֲבוֹתֵינוּ אַתָּה הוּא מֵעוֹלָם
מָגֵן וּמוֹשִׁיעַ לִבְנֵיהֶם אַחֲרֵיהֶם בְּכָל דּוֹר וָדוֹר.
בְּרוּם עוֹלָם מוֹשָׁבֶךָ, וּמִשְׁפָּטֶיךָ וְצִדְקָתְךָ עַד אַפְסֵי אָרֶץ.
אַשְׁרֵי אִישׁ שֶׁיִּשְׁמַע לְמִצְוֹתֶיךָ
וְתוֹרָתְךָ וּדְבָרְךָ יָשִׂים עַל לִבּוֹ.
אֱמֶת אַתָּה הוּא אָדוֹן לְעַמֶּךָ
וּמֶלֶךְ גִּבּוֹר לָרִיב רִיבָם.
אֱמֶת אַתָּה הוּא רִאשׁוֹן וְאַתָּה הוּא אַחֲרוֹן
וּמִבַּלְעָדֶיךָ אֵין לָנוּ מֶלֶךְ גּוֹאֵל וּמוֹשִׁיעַ.
מִמִּצְרַיִם גְּאַלְתָּנוּ, יהוה אֱלֹהֵינוּ
וּמִבֵּית עֲבָדִים פְּדִיתָנוּ
כָּל בְּכוֹרֵיהֶם הָרַגְתָּ, וּבְכוֹרְךָ גָּאָלְתָּ
וְיַם סוּף בָּקַעְתָּ, וְזֵדִים טִבַּעְתָּ, וִידִידִים הֶעֱבַרְתָּ
וַיְכַסּוּ־מַיִם צָרֵיהֶם, אֶחָד מֵהֶם לֹא נוֹתָר: תהלים קו

For this, the beloved ones praised and exalted God,
the cherished ones sang psalms, songs and praises,
blessings and thanksgivings to the King,
the living and enduring God.
High and exalted, great and awesome,
He humbles the haughty and raises the lowly,
freeing captives and redeeming those in need, helping the poor
and answering His people when they cry out to Him.

Stand in preparation for the Amida. Take three steps back before beginning the Amida.

▸ Praises to God Most High,
the Blessed One who is blessed.
Moses and the children of Israel
recited to You a song with great joy,
and they all exclaimed:
"Who is like You, LORD, among the mighty? *Ex. 15*
Who is like You, majestic in holiness,
awesome in praises, doing wonders?"
▸ With a new song, the redeemed people praised
Your name at the seashore.
Together they all gave thanks,
proclaimed Your kingship, and declared:
"The LORD shall reign for ever and ever." *Ibid.*

Congregants should end the following blessing together with the Leader so as to be able to move directly from the words "redeemed Israel" to the Amida, without the interruption of saying Amen.

▸ צוּר יִשְׂרָאֵל Rock of Israel! Arise to the help of Israel.
Deliver, as You promised, Judah and Israel.
Our Redeemer, the LORD of hosts is His name, *Is. 47*
the Holy One of Israel.
Blessed are You, LORD, who redeemed Israel.

On Yom Tov, say the Amida on the next page.
On Shabbat of Ḥol HaMo'ed, say the Amida on page 788.

---

standing directly before God in the Amida. This is the seventh step, and in Judaism seven is the sign of the Holy.

עַל זֹאת שִׁבְּחוּ אֲהוּבִים, וְרוֹמְמוּ אֵל
וְנָתְנוּ יְדִידִים זְמִירוֹת, שִׁירוֹת וְתִשְׁבָּחוֹת
בְּרָכוֹת וְהוֹדָאוֹת לְמֶלֶךְ אֵל חַי וְקַיָּם
רָם וְנִשָּׂא, גָּדוֹל וְנוֹרָא
מַשְׁפִּיל גֵּאִים וּמַגְבִּיהַּ שְׁפָלִים
מוֹצִיא אֲסִירִים, וּפוֹדֶה עֲנָוִים וְעוֹזֵר דַּלִּים
וְעוֹנֶה לְעַמּוֹ בְּעֵת שַׁוְּעָם אֵלָיו.

Stand in preparation for the עמידה*. Take three steps back before beginning the* עמידה*.*

‹ תְּהִלּוֹת לְאֵל עֶלְיוֹן, בָּרוּךְ הוּא וּמְבֹרָךְ
מֹשֶׁה וּבְנֵי יִשְׂרָאֵל
לְךָ עָנוּ שִׁירָה בְּשִׂמְחָה רַבָּה
וְאָמְרוּ כֻלָּם
מִי־כָמֹכָה בָּאֵלִם, יהוה שמות טו
מִי כָּמֹכָה נֶאְדָּר בַּקֹּדֶשׁ, נוֹרָא תְהִלֹּת, עֹשֵׂה פֶלֶא:
‹ שִׁירָה חֲדָשָׁה שִׁבְּחוּ גְאוּלִים
לְשִׁמְךָ עַל שְׂפַת הַיָּם
יַחַד כֻּלָּם הוֹדוּ וְהִמְלִיכוּ
וְאָמְרוּ
יהוה יִמְלֹךְ לְעֹלָם וָעֶד: שם

The קהל *should end the following blessing together with the* שליח ציבור *so as to be able to move directly from the words* גָּאַל יִשְׂרָאֵל *to the* עמידה*, without the interruption of saying* אמן*.*

‹ צוּר יִשְׂרָאֵל, קוּמָה בְּעֶזְרַת יִשְׂרָאֵל
וּפְדֵה כִנְאֻמֶךָ יְהוּדָה וְיִשְׂרָאֵל.
גֹּאֲלֵנוּ יהוה צְבָאוֹת שְׁמוֹ, קְדוֹשׁ יִשְׂרָאֵל: ישעיה מז
בָּרוּךְ אַתָּה יהוה, גָּאַל יִשְׂרָאֵל.

On יום טוב*, say the* עמידה *on the next page.*
On שבת חול המועד*, say the* עמידה *on page 789.*

THE AMIDA

The following prayer, until "in former years" on page 402, is said silently, standing with feet together. If there is a minyan, the Amida is repeated aloud by the Leader. Take three steps forward and at the points indicated by ▾, bend the knees at the first word, bow at the second, and stand straight before saying God's name.

O Lord, open my lips, so that my mouth may declare Your praise. *Ps. 51*

PATRIARCHS

▾בָּרוּךְ▾ Blessed are You, Lord our God and God of our fathers,
God of Abraham, God of Isaac and God of Jacob;
the great, mighty and awesome God, God Most High,
who bestows acts of loving-kindness and creates all,
who remembers the loving-kindness of the fathers
and will bring a Redeemer to their children's children
for the sake of His name, in love.
King, Helper, Savior, Shield:
▾Blessed are You, Lord,
Shield of Abraham.

DIVINE MIGHT

אַתָּה גִּבּוֹר You are eternally mighty, Lord.
You give life to the dead
and have great power to save.

In Israel:
He causes the dew to fall.

On Simḥat Torah outside Israel:
He makes the wind blow and the rain fall.

He sustains the living with loving-kindness,
and with great compassion revives the dead.

---

when you were a bride; how you walked after Me in the desert, through a land not sown." The patriarchs and matriarchs were willing to undertake a physical and spiritual journey, fraught with risk, in response to the call of God. They listened to God. Therefore in their merit we ask God to listen to us. That is the historical basis on which we pray.

עמידה

The following prayer, until קַדְמֹנִיּוֹת *on page 403, is said silently, standing with feet together. If there is a* מנין*, the* עמידה *is repeated aloud by the* שליח ציבור*. Take three steps forward and at the points indicated by* ᵀ*, bend the knees at the first word, bow at the second, and stand straight before saying God's name.*

אֲדֹנָי, שְׂפָתַי תִּפְתָּח, וּפִי יַגִּיד תְּהִלָּתֶךָ: תהלים נא

אבות

ᵀבָּרוּךְ אַתָּה יהוה, אֱלֹהֵינוּ וֵאלֹהֵי אֲבוֹתֵינוּ
אֱלֹהֵי אַבְרָהָם, אֱלֹהֵי יִצְחָק, וֵאלֹהֵי יַעֲקֹב
הָאֵל הַגָּדוֹל הַגִּבּוֹר וְהַנּוֹרָא, אֵל עֶלְיוֹן
גּוֹמֵל חֲסָדִים טוֹבִים, וְקוֹנֵה הַכֹּל, וְזוֹכֵר חַסְדֵי אָבוֹת
וּמֵבִיא גוֹאֵל לִבְנֵי בְנֵיהֶם לְמַעַן שְׁמוֹ בְּאַהֲבָה.
מֶלֶךְ עוֹזֵר וּמוֹשִׁיעַ וּמָגֵן.
ᵀבָּרוּךְ אַתָּה יהוה, מָגֵן אַבְרָהָם.

גבורות

אַתָּה גִּבּוֹר לְעוֹלָם, אֲדֹנָי
מְחַיֵּה מֵתִים אַתָּה, רַב לְהוֹשִׁיעַ

In ארץ ישראל:

מוֹרִיד הַטָּל

On שמחת תורה *outside Israel:*

מַשִּׁיב הָרוּחַ וּמוֹרִיד הַגֶּשֶׁם

מְכַלְכֵּל חַיִּים בְּחֶסֶד, מְחַיֵּה מֵתִים בְּרַחֲמִים רַבִּים

וְזוֹכֵר חַסְדֵי אָבוֹת *Remembers the loving-kindness of the fathers.* The reference is not just to obvious acts of kindness like Abraham offering hospitality to passersby, or Rebecca bringing water for a stranger and his camels – though these acts were essential in establishing a template of Jewish character, in seeking to be a blessing to others. There is also, in this phrase, an echo of Jeremiah (2:2): "I remember of you the kindness of your youth, your love

He supports the fallen, heals the sick, sets captives free,
and keeps His faith with those who sleep in the dust.
Who is like You, Master of might,
and who can compare to You,
O King who brings death and gives life,
and makes salvation grow?
Faithful are You to revive the dead.
Blessed are You, LORD, who revives the dead.

When saying the Amida silently, continue with "You are holy" on the next page.

KEDUSHA

During the Leader's Repetition, the following is said standing with feet together, rising on the toes at the words indicated by ˄.

Cong. then Leader: נְקַדֵּשׁ We will sanctify Your name on earth, as they sanctify it in the highest heavens, as is written by Your prophet, "And they [the angels] call to one another saying: *Is. 6*

Cong. then Leader: ˄Holy, ˄holy, ˄holy is the LORD of hosts; the whole world is filled with His glory."

Then with a sound of mighty noise, majestic and strong, they make their voice heard, raising themselves toward the Seraphim, and facing them say: "Blessed –"

Cong. then Leader: "˄Blessed is the LORD's glory from His place." *Ezek. 3*

Reveal Yourself from Your place, O our King, and reign over us, for we are waiting for You. When will You reign in Zion? May it be soon in our days, and may You dwell there for ever and all time. May You be exalted and sanctified in the midst of Jerusalem, Your city, from generation to generation for evermore. May our eyes see Your kingdom, as is said in the songs of Your splendor, written by David Your righteous anointed one:

Cong. then Leader: "˄The LORD shall reign for ever. He is your God, Zion, from generation to generation, Halleluya!" *Ps. 146*

Leader: From generation to generation we will declare Your greatness, and we will proclaim Your holiness for evermore. Your praise, our God, shall not leave our mouth forever, for You, God, are a great and holy King. Blessed are You, LORD, the holy God.

The Leader continues with "You have chosen us" on the next page.

סוֹמֵךְ נוֹפְלִים, וְרוֹפֵא חוֹלִים, וּמַתִּיר אֲסוּרִים
וּמְקַיֵּם אֱמוּנָתוֹ לִישֵׁנֵי עָפָר.
מִי כָמְוֹךָ, בַּעַל גְּבוּרוֹת, וּמִי דּוֹמֶה לָּךְ
מֶלֶךְ, מֵמִית וּמְחַיֶּה וּמַצְמִיחַ יְשׁוּעָה.
וְנֶאֱמָן אַתָּה לְהַחֲיוֹת מֵתִים.
בָּרוּךְ אַתָּה יהוה, מְחַיֵּה הַמֵּתִים.

When saying the עמידה *silently, continue with* אַתָּה קָדוֹשׁ *on the next page.*

קדושה

During the חזרת הש״ץ*, the following is said standing with feet together, rising on the toes at the words indicated by* *.

קהל *then* ש״ץ: נְקַדֵּשׁ אֶת שִׁמְךָ בָּעוֹלָם, כְּשֵׁם שֶׁמַּקְדִּישִׁים אוֹתוֹ בִּשְׁמֵי מָרוֹם
כַּכָּתוּב עַל יַד נְבִיאֶךָ: וְקָרָא זֶה אֶל־זֶה וְאָמַר ישעיה ו

קהל *then* ש״ץ: *קָדוֹשׁ, *קָדוֹשׁ, *קָדוֹשׁ, יהוה צְבָאוֹת, מְלֹא כָל־הָאָרֶץ כְּבוֹדוֹ:
אָז בְּקוֹל רַעַשׁ גָּדוֹל אַדִּיר וְחָזָק, מַשְׁמִיעִים קוֹל
מִתְנַשְּׂאִים לְעֻמַּת שְׂרָפִים, לְעֻמָּתָם בָּרוּךְ יֹאמֵרוּ

קהל *then* ש״ץ: *בָּרוּךְ כְּבוֹד־יהוה מִמְּקוֹמוֹ: יחזקאל ג
מִמְּקוֹמְךָ מַלְכֵּנוּ תוֹפִיעַ וְתִמְלֹךְ עָלֵינוּ, כִּי מְחַכִּים אֲנַחְנוּ לָךְ
מָתַי תִּמְלֹךְ בְּצִיּוֹן, בְּקָרוֹב בְּיָמֵינוּ לְעוֹלָם וָעֶד תִּשְׁכֹּן
תִּתְגַּדַּל וְתִתְקַדַּשׁ בְּתוֹךְ יְרוּשָׁלַיִם עִירְךָ לְדוֹר וָדוֹר וּלְנֵצַח נְצָחִים.
וְעֵינֵינוּ תִרְאֶינָה מַלְכוּתֶךָ
כַּדָּבָר הָאָמוּר בְּשִׁירֵי עֻזֶּךָ עַל יְדֵי דָוִד מְשִׁיחַ צִדְקֶךָ

קהל *then* ש״ץ: *יִמְלֹךְ יהוה לְעוֹלָם, אֱלֹהַיִךְ צִיּוֹן לְדֹר וָדֹר, הַלְלוּיָהּ: תהלים קמו

ש״ץ: לְדוֹר וָדוֹר נַגִּיד גָּדְלֶךָ, וּלְנֵצַח נְצָחִים קְדֻשָּׁתְךָ נַקְדִּישׁ
וְשִׁבְחֲךָ אֱלֹהֵינוּ מִפִּינוּ לֹא יָמוּשׁ לְעוֹלָם וָעֶד
כִּי אֵל מֶלֶךְ גָּדוֹל וְקָדוֹשׁ אָתָּה.
בָּרוּךְ אַתָּה יהוה הָאֵל הַקָּדוֹשׁ.

The שליח ציבור *continues with* אַתָּה בְחַרְתָּנוּ *on the next page.*

When saying the Amida silently, continue here:

HOLINESS

אַתָּה קָדוֹשׁ You are holy and Your name is holy,
and holy ones praise You daily, Selah!
Blessed are You, Lord, the holy God.

HOLINESS OF THE DAY

אַתָּה בְחַרְתָּנוּ You have chosen us from among all peoples.
You have loved and favored us.
You have raised us above all tongues.
You have made us holy through Your commandments.
You have brought us near, our King, to Your service,
and have called us by Your great and holy name.

On Shabbat, add the words in parentheses:

וַתִּתֶּן לָנוּ And You, Lord our God, have given us in love
(Sabbaths for rest and) festivals for rejoicing,
holy days and seasons for joy, (this Sabbath day and) this day of:

On Sukkot: the festival of Sukkot, our time of rejoicing

On Shemini Atzeret & Simḥat Torah: the festival of the eighth day, Shemini Atzeret, our time of rejoicing

(with love), a holy assembly in memory of the exodus from Egypt.

אֱלֹהֵינוּ Our God and God of our ancestors,
may there rise, come, reach, appear, be favored, heard,
regarded and remembered before You,
our recollection and remembrance,
as well as the remembrance of our ancestors,
and of the Messiah son of David Your servant,
and of Jerusalem Your holy city,
and of all Your people the house of Israel –

---

story of the survival of the nation against all odds lies the most obvious outward sign of the Jewish mission, to be God's witnesses to the world.

זִכְרוֹנֵנוּ וּפִקְדּוֹנֵנוּ *Our recollection and remembrance.* According to Malbim (Gen. 21:1), the verb ז-כ-ר, "remember," means the opposite of "forget." It is cognitive.

When saying the עמידה silently, continue here:

קדושת השם

אַתָּה קָדוֹשׁ וְשִׁמְךָ קָדוֹשׁ, וּקְדוֹשִׁים בְּכָל יוֹם יְהַלְלְוּךָ סֶּלָה.
בָּרוּךְ אַתָּה יהוה, הָאֵל הַקָּדוֹשׁ.

קדושת היום

אַתָּה בְחַרְתָּנוּ מִכָּל הָעַמִּים
אָהַבְתָּ אוֹתָנוּ וְרָצִיתָ בָּנוּ, וְרוֹמַמְתָּנוּ מִכָּל הַלְּשׁוֹנוֹת
וְקִדַּשְׁתָּנוּ בְּמִצְוֹתֶיךָ, וְקֵרַבְתָּנוּ מַלְכֵּנוּ לַעֲבוֹדָתֶךָ
וְשִׁמְךָ הַגָּדוֹל וְהַקָּדוֹשׁ עָלֵינוּ קָרָאתָ.

On שבת, add the words in parentheses:

וַתִּתֶּן לָנוּ יהוה אֱלֹהֵינוּ בְּאַהֲבָה
(שַׁבָּתוֹת לִמְנוּחָה וּ)מוֹעֲדִים לְשִׂמְחָה, חַגִּים וּזְמַנִּים לְשָׂשׂוֹן
אֶת יוֹם (הַשַּׁבָּת הַזֶּה וְאֶת יוֹם)

בסוכות: חַג הַסֻּכּוֹת הַזֶּה, זְמַן שִׂמְחָתֵנוּ

בשמע״צ ובש״ת: הַשְּׁמִינִי חַג הָעֲצֶרֶת הַזֶּה, זְמַן שִׂמְחָתֵנוּ

(בְּאַהֲבָה) מִקְרָא קֹדֶשׁ, זֵכֶר לִיצִיאַת מִצְרָיִם.

אֱלֹהֵינוּ וֵאלֹהֵי אֲבוֹתֵינוּ
יַעֲלֶה וְיָבוֹא וְיַגִּיעַ וְיֵרָאֶה וְיֵרָצֶה וְיִשָּׁמַע
וְיִפָּקֵד וְיִזָּכֵר זִכְרוֹנֵנוּ וּפִקְדּוֹנֵנוּ וְזִכְרוֹן אֲבוֹתֵינוּ
וְזִכְרוֹן מָשִׁיחַ בֶּן דָּוִד עַבְדֶּךָ, וְזִכְרוֹן יְרוּשָׁלַיִם עִיר קָדְשֶׁךָ
וְזִכְרוֹן כָּל עַמְּךָ בֵּית יִשְׂרָאֵל, לְפָנֶיךָ

אַתָּה בְחַרְתָּנוּ *You have chosen us.* The three pilgrimage festivals, Pesaḥ, Shavuot and Sukkot are festivals of history. Therefore the Amida on these days emphasizes the uniqueness of Jewish history, for in and through the extraordinary

for deliverance and well-being,
grace, loving-kindness and compassion,
life and peace, on this day of:

On Sukkot: the festival of Sukkot.
On Shemini Atzeret & Simḥat Torah: the festival of Shemini Atzeret.

On it remember us, LORD our God, for good;
recollect us for blessing, and deliver us for life.
In accord with Your promise of salvation and compassion,
spare us and be gracious to us;
have compassion on us and deliver us,
for our eyes are turned to You
because You, God, are a gracious and compassionate King.

On Shabbat, add the words in parentheses:

וְהַשִּׂיאֵנוּ Bestow on us, LORD our God,
the blessings of Your festivals
for good life and peace, joy and gladness,
as You desired and promised to bless us.
(Our God and God of our fathers, find favor in our rest.)
Make us holy through Your commandments
and grant us a share in Your Torah.
Satisfy us with Your goodness, gladden us with Your salvation,
and purify our hearts to serve You in truth.
Grant us as our heritage, LORD our God (with love and favor,)
with joy and gladness, Your holy (Sabbath and) festivals,
and may Israel, who sanctify Your name, rejoice in You.
Blessed are You, LORD,
who sanctifies (the Sabbath and) Israel and the festive seasons.

---

(4) lifting, raising; and many others. The richness of resonances of the verb may reflect the multidimensional nature of the experience of the pilgrimage festivals: reliving history, celebrating the season and its harvest, together with the joy of journeying to Jerusalem, being in the Temple and being part of a thronged national celebration.

לִפְלֵיטָה, לְטוֹבָה, לְחֵן וּלְחֶסֶד וּלְרַחֲמִים
לְחַיִּים וּלְשָׁלוֹם בְּיוֹם

בסוכות: חַג הַסֻּכּוֹת הַזֶּה.

בשמע״צ ובש״ת: הַשְּׁמִינִי חַג הָעֲצֶרֶת הַזֶּה.

זָכְרֵנוּ יהוה אֱלֹהֵינוּ בּוֹ לְטוֹבָה
וּפָקְדֵנוּ בוֹ לִבְרָכָה, וְהוֹשִׁיעֵנוּ בוֹ לְחַיִּים.
וּבִדְבַר יְשׁוּעָה וְרַחֲמִים, חוּס וְחָנֵּנוּ, וְרַחֵם עָלֵינוּ וְהוֹשִׁיעֵנוּ
כִּי אֵלֶיךָ עֵינֵינוּ, כִּי אֵל מֶלֶךְ חַנּוּן וְרַחוּם אָתָּה.

On שבת, add the words in parentheses:

וְהַשִּׂיאֵנוּ יהוה אֱלֹהֵינוּ אֶת בִּרְכַּת מוֹעֲדֶיךָ
לְחַיִּים וּלְשָׁלוֹם, לְשִׂמְחָה וּלְשָׂשׂוֹן
כַּאֲשֶׁר רָצִיתָ וְאָמַרְתָּ לְבָרְכֵנוּ.
(אֱלֹהֵינוּ וֵאלֹהֵי אֲבוֹתֵינוּ, רְצֵה בִמְנוּחָתֵנוּ)
קַדְּשֵׁנוּ בְּמִצְוֹתֶיךָ, וְתֵן חֶלְקֵנוּ בְּתוֹרָתֶךָ
שַׂבְּעֵנוּ מִטּוּבֶךָ, וְשַׂמְּחֵנוּ בִּישׁוּעָתֶךָ
וְטַהֵר לִבֵּנוּ לְעָבְדְּךָ בֶּאֱמֶת.
וְהַנְחִילֵנוּ יהוה אֱלֹהֵינוּ (בְּאַהֲבָה וּבְרָצוֹן)
בְּשִׂמְחָה וּבְשָׂשׂוֹן (שַׁבָּת וּ)מוֹעֲדֵי קָדְשֶׁךָ
וְיִשְׂמְחוּ בְךָ יִשְׂרָאֵל מְקַדְּשֵׁי שְׁמֶךָ.
בָּרוּךְ אַתָּה יהוה, מְקַדֵּשׁ (הַשַּׁבָּת וְ)יִשְׂרָאֵל וְהַזְּמַנִּים.

The verb פ-ק-ד, "to recollect," refers to an act of focused attention and may also involve the emotions and the will.

וְהַשִּׂיאֵנוּ *Bestow on us.* A verb that has a multiplicity of meanings, among them: (1) giving a gift, (2) loading, (3) causing someone to receive a blessing,

TEMPLE SERVICE

רְצֵה Find favor, LORD our God,
in Your people Israel and their prayer.
Restore the service to Your most holy House,
and accept in love and favor
the fire-offerings of Israel and their prayer.
May the service of Your people Israel always find favor with You.
And may our eyes witness Your return to Zion in compassion.
Blessed are You, LORD, who restores His Presence to Zion.

THANKSGIVING

Bow at the first nine words.

מוֹדִים We give thanks to You,
for You are the LORD our God
and God of our ancestors
for ever and all time.
You are the Rock of our lives,
Shield of our salvation
from generation to generation.
We will thank You and
declare Your praise for our lives,
which are entrusted into Your hand;
for our souls,
which are placed in Your charge;
for Your miracles
which are with us every day;
and for Your wonders and favors
at all times, evening,
morning and midday.
You are good –
for Your compassion never fails.
You are compassionate –
for Your loving-kindnesses never cease.
We have always placed our hope in You.

During the Leader's Repetition, the congregation says quietly:

מוֹדִים We give thanks to You,
for You are the LORD our God
and God of our ancestors,
God of all flesh,
who formed us
and formed the universe.
Blessings and thanks
are due to Your great
and holy name for giving us
life and sustaining us.
May You continue
to give us life
and sustain us;
and may You gather our
exiles to Your holy courts,
to keep Your decrees,
do Your will and serve You
with a perfect heart,
for it is for us
to give You thanks.
Blessed be God to whom
thanksgiving is due.

עבודה

רְצֵה יהוה אֱלֹהֵינוּ בְּעַמְּךָ יִשְׂרָאֵל, וּבִתְפִלָּתָם
וְהָשֵׁב אֶת הָעֲבוֹדָה לִדְבִיר בֵּיתֶךָ
וְאִשֵּׁי יִשְׂרָאֵל וּתְפִלָּתָם בְּאַהֲבָה תְקַבֵּל בְּרָצוֹן
וּתְהִי לְרָצוֹן תָּמִיד עֲבוֹדַת יִשְׂרָאֵל עַמֶּךָ.
וְתֶחֱזֶינָה עֵינֵינוּ בְּשׁוּבְךָ לְצִיּוֹן בְּרַחֲמִים.
בָּרוּךְ אַתָּה יהוה, הַמַּחֲזִיר שְׁכִינָתוֹ לְצִיּוֹן.

הודאה

Bow at the first five words.

מוֹדִים אֲנַחְנוּ לָךְ
שָׁאַתָּה הוּא יהוה אֱלֹהֵינוּ
וֵאלֹהֵי אֲבוֹתֵינוּ לְעוֹלָם וָעֶד.
צוּר חַיֵּינוּ, מָגֵן יִשְׁעֵנוּ
אַתָּה הוּא לְדוֹר וָדוֹר.
נוֹדֶה לְּךָ וּנְסַפֵּר תְּהִלָּתֶךָ
עַל חַיֵּינוּ הַמְּסוּרִים בְּיָדֶךָ
וְעַל נִשְׁמוֹתֵינוּ הַפְּקוּדוֹת לָךְ
וְעַל נִסֶּיךָ שֶׁבְּכָל יוֹם עִמָּנוּ
וְעַל נִפְלְאוֹתֶיךָ וְטוֹבוֹתֶיךָ
שֶׁבְּכָל עֵת
עֶרֶב וָבֹקֶר וְצָהֳרָיִם.
הַטּוֹב, כִּי לֹא כָלוּ רַחֲמֶיךָ
וְהַמְרַחֵם, כִּי לֹא תַמּוּ חֲסָדֶיךָ
מֵעוֹלָם קִוִּינוּ לָךְ.

During the חזרת הש״ץ*, the* קהל *says quietly:*

מוֹדִים אֲנַחְנוּ לָךְ
שָׁאַתָּה הוּא יהוה אֱלֹהֵינוּ
וֵאלֹהֵי אֲבוֹתֵינוּ
אֱלֹהֵי כָל בָּשָׂר
יוֹצְרֵנוּ, יוֹצֵר בְּרֵאשִׁית.
בְּרָכוֹת וְהוֹדָאוֹת
לְשִׁמְךָ הַגָּדוֹל וְהַקָּדוֹשׁ
עַל שֶׁהֶחֱיִיתָנוּ וְקִיַּמְתָּנוּ.
כֵּן תְּחַיֵּנוּ וּתְקַיְּמֵנוּ
וְתֶאֱסֹף גָּלֻיּוֹתֵינוּ
לְחַצְרוֹת קָדְשֶׁךָ
לִשְׁמֹר חֻקֶּיךָ
וְלַעֲשׂוֹת רְצוֹנֶךָ וּלְעָבְדְּךָ
בְּלֵבָב שָׁלֵם
עַל שֶׁאֲנַחְנוּ מוֹדִים לָךְ.
בָּרוּךְ אֵל הַהוֹדָאוֹת.

וְעַל כֻּלָּם For all these things
may Your name be blessed and exalted, our King,
continually, for ever and all time.
Let all that lives thank You, Selah!
and praise Your name in truth, God, our Savior and Help, Selah!
▾Blessed are You, LORD,
whose name is "the Good" and to whom thanks are due.

When saying the Amida silently, continue with "Grant peace" on the next page.

On Simhat Torah, many congregations have the custom to say the Priestly Blessing in Shaharit. Some communities say an extended version of the Priestly Blessing on page 520.

BIRKAT KOHANIM

When the Priestly Blessing is not said, the Leader says the formula on the next page. The following supplication is recited quietly while the Leader says "Let all that lives" above.

In some communities, the congregation says:
יְהִי רָצוֹן May it be Your will, LORD our God and God of our ancestors, that this blessing with which You have commanded to bless Your people Israel should be a complete blessing, with neither hindrance nor sin, now and forever.

The Kohanim say:
יְהִי רָצוֹן May it be Your will, LORD our God and God of our ancestors, that this blessing with which You have commanded us to bless Your people Israel should be a complete blessing, with neither hindrance nor sin, now and forever.

The following is recited quietly by the Leader:
אֱלֹהֵינוּ Our God and God of our fathers, bless us with the threefold blessing in the Torah, written by the hand of Moses Your servant and pronounced by Aaron and his sons:

The Leader says aloud:
Kohanim!

In most places, the congregation responds:
Your holy people, as it said:

The Kohanim say the following blessing in unison:
בָּרוּךְ Blessed are You, LORD our God, King of the Universe, who has made us holy with the holiness of Aaron, and has commanded us to bless His people Israel with love.

The Leader calls word by word, followed by the Kohanim:
יְבָרֶכְךָ May the LORD bless you and protect you. (*Cong:* Amen.) *Num. 6*
May the LORD make His face shine on you and be gracious to you. (*Cong:* Amen.)
May the LORD turn His face towards you, and grant you peace. (*Cong:* Amen.)

The Leader continues with "Grant peace" on the next page.

וְעַל כֻּלָּם יִתְבָּרַךְ וְיִתְרוֹמַם שִׁמְךָ מַלְכֵּנוּ תָּמִיד לְעוֹלָם וָעֶד.
וְכֹל הַחַיִּים יוֹדְוּךָ סֶּלָה, וִיהַלְלוּ אֶת שִׁמְךָ בֶּאֱמֶת
הָאֵל יְשׁוּעָתֵנוּ וְעֶזְרָתֵנוּ סֶלָה.
ּבָּרוּךְ אַתָּה יהוה, הַטּוֹב שִׁמְךָ וּלְךָ נָאֶה לְהוֹדוֹת.

When saying the עמידה *silently, continue with* שִׂים שָׁלוֹם *on the next page.*

On שמחת תורה *many congregations have the custom to say* ברכת כוהנים *in* שחרית.
Some communities say an extended נוסח *of* ברכת כוהנים *on page 521.*

ברכת כוהנים

When ברכת כהנים *is not said, the* שליח ציבור *says the formula on the next page.*
The following supplication is recited quietly while the שליח ציבור *says* וְכֹל הַחַיִּים *above.*

In some communities, the קהל *says:*

יְהִי רָצוֹן מִלְּפָנֶיךָ, יהוה אֱלֹהֵינוּ וֵאלֹהֵי אֲבוֹתֵינוּ, שֶׁתְּהֵא הַבְּרָכָה הַזֹּאת שֶׁצִּוִּיתָ לְבָרֵךְ אֶת עַמְּךָ יִשְׂרָאֵל בְּרָכָה שְׁלֵמָה, וְלֹא יִהְיֶה בָּהּ שׁוּם מִכְשׁוֹל וְעָוֹן מֵעַתָּה וְעַד עוֹלָם.

The כהנים *say:*

יְהִי רָצוֹן מִלְּפָנֶיךָ, יהוה אֱלֹהֵינוּ וֵאלֹהֵי אֲבוֹתֵינוּ, שֶׁתְּהֵא הַבְּרָכָה הַזֹּאת שֶׁצִּוִּיתָנוּ לְבָרֵךְ אֶת עַמְּךָ יִשְׂרָאֵל בְּרָכָה שְׁלֵמָה, וְלֹא יִהְיֶה בָּהּ שׁוּם מִכְשׁוֹל וְעָוֹן מֵעַתָּה וְעַד עוֹלָם.

The following is recited quietly by the שליח ציבור:

אֱלֹהֵינוּ וֵאלֹהֵי אֲבוֹתֵינוּ, בָּרְכֵנוּ בַּבְּרָכָה הַמְשֻׁלֶּשֶׁת בַּתּוֹרָה
הַכְּתוּבָה עַל יְדֵי מֹשֶׁה עַבְדֶּךָ, הָאֲמוּרָה מִפִּי אַהֲרֹן וּבָנָיו

The שליח ציבור *says aloud:*

כֹּהֲנִים

In most places, the קהל *responds:*

עַם קְדוֹשֶׁךָ, כָּאָמוּר:

The כהנים *say the following blessing in unison:*

בָּרוּךְ אַתָּה יהוה אֱלֹהֵינוּ מֶלֶךְ הָעוֹלָם, אֲשֶׁר קִדְּשָׁנוּ בִּקְדֻשָּׁתוֹ שֶׁל אַהֲרֹן,
וְצִוָּנוּ לְבָרֵךְ אֶת עַמּוֹ יִשְׂרָאֵל בְּאַהֲבָה.

The שליח ציבור *calls word by word, followed by the* כהנים:

יְבָרֶכְךָ יהוה וְיִשְׁמְרֶךָ: קהל: אָמֵן במדבר ו
יָאֵר יהוה פָּנָיו אֵלֶיךָ וִיחֻנֶּךָּ: קהל: אָמֵן
יִשָּׂא יהוה פָּנָיו אֵלֶיךָ וְיָשֵׂם לְךָ שָׁלוֹם: קהל: אָמֵן

The שליח ציבור *continues with* שִׂים שָׁלוֹם *on the next page.*

The congregation says:

אַדִּיר Majestic One on high who dwells in power: You are peace and Your name is peace. May it be Your will to bestow on us and on Your people the house of Israel, life and blessing as a safeguard for peace.

The Kohanim say:

רִבּוֹנוֹ Master of the Universe: we have done what You have decreed for us. So too may You deal with us as You have promised us. Look down from Your holy dwelling place, from heaven, and bless Your people Israel and the land You have given us as You promised on oath to our ancestors, a land flowing with milk and honey. *Deut. 26*

If the Priestly Blessing is not said, the following is said by the Leader:

Our God and God of our fathers, bless us with the threefold blessing in the Torah, written by the hand of Moses Your servant and pronounced by Aaron and his sons the priests, Your holy people, as it is said:

May the LORD bless you and protect you. *Num. 6*
Cong: May it be Your will.
May the LORD make His face shine on you and be gracious to you.
Cong: May it be Your will.
May the LORD turn His face toward you, and grant you peace.
Cong: May it be Your will.

PEACE

שִׂים שָׁלוֹם Grant peace, goodness and blessing,
grace, loving-kindness and compassion
to us and all Israel Your people.
Bless us, our Father, all as one, with the light of Your face,
for by the light of Your face You have given us, LORD our God,
the Torah of life and love of kindness,
righteousness, blessing, compassion, life and peace.
May it be good in Your eyes to bless Your people Israel
at every time, in every hour, with Your peace.
Blessed are You, LORD,
who blesses His people Israel with peace.

The following verse concludes the Leader's Repetition of the Amida.
Some also say it here as part of the silent Amida.

May the words of my mouth and the meditation of my heart *Ps. 19*
find favor before You, LORD, my Rock and Redeemer.

The קהל *says:*

אַדִּיר בַּמָּרוֹם שׁוֹכֵן בִּגְבוּרָה, אַתָּה שָׁלוֹם וְשִׁמְךָ שָׁלוֹם. יְהִי רָצוֹן שֶׁתָּשִׂים עָלֵינוּ וְעַל כָּל עַמְּךָ בֵּית יִשְׂרָאֵל חַיִּים וּבְרָכָה לְמִשְׁמֶרֶת שָׁלוֹם.

The כהנים *say:*

רִבּוֹנוֹ שֶׁל עוֹלָם, עָשִׂינוּ מַה שֶּׁגָּזַרְתָּ עָלֵינוּ, אַף אַתָּה עֲשֵׂה עִמָּנוּ כְּמוֹ שֶׁהִבְטַחְתָּנוּ. הַשְׁקִיפָה מִמְּעוֹן קָדְשְׁךָ מִן־הַשָּׁמַיִם, וּבָרֵךְ אֶת־עַמְּךָ אֶת־יִשְׂרָאֵל, וְאֵת הָאֲדָמָה אֲשֶׁר נָתַתָּה לָנוּ, כַּאֲשֶׁר נִשְׁבַּעְתָּ לַאֲבֹתֵינוּ, אֶרֶץ זָבַת חָלָב וּדְבָשׁ: דברים כו

If ברכת כהנים *is not said, the following is said by the* שליח ציבור*:*

אֱלֹהֵינוּ וֵאלֹהֵי אֲבוֹתֵינוּ, בָּרְכֵנוּ בַבְּרָכָה הַמְשֻׁלֶּשֶׁת בַּתּוֹרָה, הַכְּתוּבָה עַל יְדֵי מֹשֶׁה עַבְדֶּךָ, הָאֲמוּרָה מִפִּי אַהֲרֹן וּבָנָיו כֹּהֲנִים עַם קְדוֹשֶׁיךָ, כָּאָמוּר

במדבר ו יְבָרֶכְךָ יהוה וְיִשְׁמְרֶךָ: קהל: כֵּן יְהִי רָצוֹן
יָאֵר יהוה פָּנָיו אֵלֶיךָ וִיחֻנֶּךָּ: קהל: כֵּן יְהִי רָצוֹן
יִשָּׂא יהוה פָּנָיו אֵלֶיךָ וְיָשֵׂם לְךָ שָׁלוֹם: קהל: כֵּן יְהִי רָצוֹן

ברכת שלום

שִׂים שָׁלוֹם טוֹבָה וּבְרָכָה
חֵן וָחֶסֶד וְרַחֲמִים עָלֵינוּ וְעַל כָּל יִשְׂרָאֵל עַמֶּךָ.
בָּרְכֵנוּ אָבִינוּ כֻּלָּנוּ כְּאֶחָד בְּאוֹר פָּנֶיךָ
כִּי בְאוֹר פָּנֶיךָ נָתַתָּ לָּנוּ יהוה אֱלֹהֵינוּ
תּוֹרַת חַיִּים וְאַהֲבַת חֶסֶד
וּצְדָקָה וּבְרָכָה וְרַחֲמִים וְחַיִּים וְשָׁלוֹם.
וְטוֹב בְּעֵינֶיךָ לְבָרֵךְ אֶת עַמְּךָ יִשְׂרָאֵל
בְּכָל עֵת וּבְכָל שָׁעָה בִּשְׁלוֹמֶךָ.
בָּרוּךְ אַתָּה יהוה, הַמְבָרֵךְ אֶת עַמּוֹ יִשְׂרָאֵל בַּשָּׁלוֹם.

The following verse concludes the חזרת הש״ץ.
Some also say it here as part of the silent עמידה.

תהלים יט יִהְיוּ לְרָצוֹן אִמְרֵי־פִי וְהֶגְיוֹן לִבִּי לְפָנֶיךָ, יהוה צוּרִי וְגֹאֲלִי:

אֱלֹהַי My God, Berakhot 17a
guard my tongue from evil and my lips from deceitful speech.
To those who curse me, let my soul be silent;
may my soul be to all like the dust.
Open my heart to Your Torah
and let my soul pursue Your commandments.
As for all who plan evil against me,
swiftly thwart their counsel and frustrate their plans.
Act for the sake of Your name;
act for the sake of Your right hand;
act for the sake of Your holiness;
act for the sake of Your Torah.
That Your beloved ones may be delivered, Ps. 60
save with Your right hand and answer me.
May the words of my mouth and the meditation of my heart Ps. 19
find favor before You, LORD, my Rock and Redeemer.

Bow, take three steps back, then bow, first left, then right, then center, while saying:

May He who makes peace in His high places,
make peace for us and all Israel – and say: Amen.

יְהִי רָצוֹן May it be Your will, LORD our God and God of our ancestors,
that the Temple be rebuilt speedily in our days,
and grant us a share in Your Torah.
And there we will serve You with reverence,
as in the days of old and as in former years.
Then the offering of Judah and Jerusalem Mal. 3
will be pleasing to the LORD as in the days of old and as in former years.

The Leader repeats the Amida (page 388).

*In congregations which recite piyutim on the first days of Sukkot,
the Repetition for the first day begins on page 1403; for the second day on page 1414.*

*On Sukkot continue with the Blessing on Taking the Lulav on the next page.
On Shabbat Hol HaMo'ed, Shemini Atzeret and Simhat
Torah continue with Hallel on page 408.*

אֱלֹהַי ברכות יז.
נְצֹר לְשׁוֹנִי מֵרָע וּשְׂפָתַי מִדַּבֵּר מִרְמָה
וְלִמְקַלְלַי נַפְשִׁי תִדֹּם, וְנַפְשִׁי כֶּעָפָר לַכֹּל תִּהְיֶה.
פְּתַח לִבִּי בְּתוֹרָתֶךָ, וּבְמִצְוֹתֶיךָ תִּרְדֹּף נַפְשִׁי.
וְכָל הַחוֹשְׁבִים עָלַי רָעָה
מְהֵרָה הָפֵר עֲצָתָם וְקַלְקֵל מַחֲשַׁבְתָּם.
עֲשֵׂה לְמַעַן שְׁמֶךָ, עֲשֵׂה לְמַעַן יְמִינֶךָ
עֲשֵׂה לְמַעַן קְדֻשָּׁתֶךָ, עֲשֵׂה לְמַעַן תּוֹרָתֶךָ.
תהלים ס לְמַעַן יֵחָלְצוּן יְדִידֶיךָ, הוֹשִׁיעָה יְמִינְךָ וַעֲנֵנִי:
תהלים יט יִהְיוּ לְרָצוֹן אִמְרֵי־פִי וְהֶגְיוֹן לִבִּי לְפָנֶיךָ, יהוה צוּרִי וְגֹאֲלִי:

Bow, take three steps back, then bow, first left, then right, then center, while saying:

עֹשֶׂה שָׁלוֹם בִּמְרוֹמָיו
הוּא יַעֲשֶׂה שָׁלוֹם עָלֵינוּ וְעַל כָּל יִשְׂרָאֵל, וְאִמְרוּ אָמֵן.

יְהִי רָצוֹן מִלְּפָנֶיךָ יהוה אֱלֹהֵינוּ וֵאלֹהֵי אֲבוֹתֵינוּ
שֶׁיִּבָּנֶה בֵּית הַמִּקְדָּשׁ בִּמְהֵרָה בְיָמֵינוּ
וְתֵן חֶלְקֵנוּ בְּתוֹרָתֶךָ
וְשָׁם נַעֲבָדְךָ בְּיִרְאָה כִּימֵי עוֹלָם וּכְשָׁנִים קַדְמֹנִיּוֹת.
מלאכי ג וְעָרְבָה לַיהוה מִנְחַת יְהוּדָה וִירוּשָׁלָיִם כִּימֵי עוֹלָם וּכְשָׁנִים קַדְמֹנִיּוֹת:

The שליח ציבור *repeats the* עמידה *(page 389).*

In congregations which recite piyutim on the first days of סוכות*,*
the חזרת הש״ץ *for the first day begins on page 1403;*
for the second day on page 1414.

On סוכות *continue with* סדר נטילת לולב *on the next page.*
On שבת חול המועד, שמיני עצרת *and* שמחת תורה *continue with* הלל *on page 409.*

Blessing on Taking the Lulav

On Sukkot, except on Shabbat, the lulav and etrog are taken before Hallel.

Some say the following:

יְהִי רָצוֹן May it be Your will, LORD my God and God of my fathers, that through the fruit of the citron tree, the palm frond, the myrtle branches and willows of the brook, the letters of Your unique name draw close to one another and become united in my hand. Make it known I am called by Your name, so that [evil] will fear to come close to me. When I wave them, may a rich flow of blessings flow from the supreme Source of wisdom to the place of the Tabernacle and the site of the House of our God. May the command of these four species be considered by You as if I had fulfilled it in all its details and roots, as well as the 613 commandments dependent on it, for it is my intention

---

resolved the seeming contradiction: In the Temple the four kinds were taken for seven days, elsewhere only on the first day. After the Temple was destroyed, Rabban Yoḥanan ben Zakkai ruled that they be taken everywhere for seven days, in memory of the Temple (Mishna, *Sukka* 3:12). They are not taken on Shabbat, as a preventive measure against carrying in a public domain (*Sukka* 42b-43a).

The lulav is waved in six directions: east, south, west and north, (i.e., straight ahead, right, rear, left) corresponding to the directions of the wind, then up and down. In each case it should be waved three times.

The four kinds represent four parts of the body. The lulav represents the spine, the myrtle the eyes, the willow the mouth, and the etrog the heart. King David said that when we hold the four kinds and praise God, it is as if "All my bones shall say, LORD, who is like You?" (Ps. 35:10, *Vayikra Raba* 30:14).

As the etrog has both aroma and fruit, so there are those in Israel who have knowledge of Torah and good deeds. As the palm tree has fruit but no aroma, so there are those in Israel who have knowledge of the Torah but not good deeds. As the myrtle has aroma but no fruit, so there are those in Israel who have good deeds but not knowledge of the Torah. And as the willow has neither aroma nor fruit, so there are those in Israel who have neither Torah nor good deeds. The Holy One, blessed be He, said: "To make it impossible for Israel to be destroyed, let all of them be bound together, and let each atone for the others" (*Pesikta deRav Kahana* 27:9).

The four kinds are a symbolic expression of our rejoicing that the Israelites left the wilderness, "A place with no grain or figs or vines or pomegranates; there

סדר נטילת לולב

On סוכות, *except on* שבת, *the* לולב *and* אתרוג *are taken before* הלל.

Some say the following:

יְהִי רָצוֹן מִלְּפָנֶיךָ יהוה אֱלֹהַי וֵאלֹהֵי אֲבוֹתַי, בִּפְרִי עֵץ הָדָר וְכַפֹּת תְּמָרִים וַעֲנַף עֵץ עָבֹת וְעַרְבֵי נַחַל, אוֹתִיּוֹת שִׁמְךָ הַמְיֻחָד תְּקָרֵב אֶחָד אֶל אֶחָד וְהָיוּ לַאֲחָדִים בְּיָדִי, וְלֵידַע אֵיךְ שִׁמְךָ נִקְרָא עָלַי וְיִירְאוּ מִגֶּשֶׁת אֵלַי. וּבְנַעֲנוּעִי אוֹתָם תַּשְׁפִּיעַ שֶׁפַע בְּרָכוֹת מִדֵּעַת עֶלְיוֹן לִנְוֵה אַפִּרְיוֹן לִמְכוֹן בֵּית אֱלֹהֵינוּ, וּתְהֵא חֲשׁוּבָה לְפָנֶיךָ מִצְוַת אַרְבָּעָה מִינִים אֵלּוּ כְּאִלּוּ קִיַּמְתִּיהָ בְּכָל פְּרָטוֹתֶיהָ וְשָׁרָשֶׁיהָ וְתַרְיַ״ג מִצְוֹת הַתְּלוּיוֹת בָּהּ, כִּי כַוָּנָתִי לְיַחֲדָא

TAKING THE LULAV

The "four kinds" is one of the essential commands of the festival. The Torah specifies: "On the first day, you shall take for yourselves a fruit of the citron tree, palm fronds, myrtle branches and willows of the brook, and be joyous in the presence of the Lord your God for seven days" (Lev. 23:40). It is noteworthy, however, that the Torah does not identify explicitly two of the four kinds; a strictly literal translation would read "the fruit of a goodly tree, palm fronds, boughs of a dense-leaved tree and willows…". It is the Oral Tradition which identifies "the fruit of a goodly tree" as the etrog (citron) and "a dense-leaved tree" as the myrtle.

What they have in common is that wherever you find them, there is water. They are the visible blessings of the rain that fell in the previous year. We take them now in thanks to God for the blessing of rain in the past year, and to pray for rain in the year to come.

The lulav, bound together with the myrtles and willow, is taken in the right hand. The etrog is taken, inverted, in the left. After the blessing is recited, the etrog is turned the right way up. This is because the blessing over a command must precede the fulfillment of the command. Since the command in this case is simply to "take" the four kinds, merely holding them in the correct manner fulfils it. In order *not* to perform the command before the blessing, we invert the etrog, only holding it the right way up immediately thereafter. The blessing refers only to the lulav, since it is the tallest and most conspicuous of the four kinds.

The verse in Leviticus about the four kinds begins with the phrase, "On the first day," and ends, "you shall be joyous… for seven days." The Oral Tradition

to unify the name of the Holy One, blessed be He, and His Divine Presence, in reverence and love, to unify the name *Yod-Heh* with *Vav-Heh*, in perfect unity in the name of all Israel, Amen. Blessed is the LORD forever, Amen and Amen. *Ps. 89*

The lulav is taken in the right hand, with the myrtle leaves on the right, willow leaves on the left. The etrog is taken in the left hand, with its pointed end toward the floor. If left-handed, take the etrog in the right hand and the lulav in the left. Then say the following blessing:

בָּרוּךְ Blessed are You, LORD our God, King of the Universe,
who has made us holy through His commandments,
and has commanded us about taking the lulav.

On the first day the lulav is taken, add:

בָּרוּךְ Blessed are You, LORD our God, King of the Universe,
who has given us life, sustained us and brought us to this time.

Invert the etrog, so that its pointed end is facing up. Face the front of the synagogue and wave the lulav and etrog in the following sequence, three times in each direction: ahead, right, back, left, up, down. Continue to hold the lulav and etrog during Hallel.

On his exit, the man came up to him, saying, "Revered Rabbi, please do not think me importunate, but since it concerns a matter of Torah, I seek to understand and learn. To visit the elderly is certainly a mitzva, but it can be done at any time, while obtaining an etrog for Sukkot occurs only once a year. I would have expected the rabbi to spend more time choosing it. As for visiting the old age home, he could surely do that during the festival, rather than before it."

Rabbi Levin took the man's hand and smiled: "My friend, there are two mitzvot in relation to which the Torah uses the word *hadar*, 'beauty.' One is the etrog, called by the Torah *pri etz hadar*, literally, 'fruit of the beautiful tree' (Lev. 23:40). The other is honoring the elderly, as it says, *vehadarta pnei zaken* (Lev. 19:32). However, the etrog is an object, and the aged individual a subject, a human being, not a fruit. I believe one should spend more time beautifying a command about a human being than beautifying a command relating to a fruit." (Adapted from Rabbi Shlomo Riskin, *Jerusalem Post*, 14 October 2001).

Each Sukkot morning, after taking the four kinds, the sixth Lubavitcher Rebbe, Rabbi Yosef Yitzhak Schneerson, would allow all who wished to do so to use his lulav and etrog. Many Hasidim did so even though they had a set of their own, believing it to be a privilege to perform the mitzva with the Rebbe's set.

שְׁמָא דְקֻדְשָׁא בְּרִיךְ הוּא וּשְׁכִינְתֵהּ בִּדְחִילוּ וּרְחִימוּ, לְיַחֵד שֵׁם י״ה בו״ה
בְּיִחוּדָא שְׁלִים בְּשֵׁם כָּל יִשְׂרָאֵל, אָמֵן. בָּרוּךְ יהוה לְעוֹלָם, אָמֵן וְאָמֵן: תהלים פט

The לולב *is taken in the right hand, with the* הדסים *on the right,* ערבות *on the left. The* אתרוג *is taken in the left hand, with its pointed end toward the floor. If left-handed, take the* אתרוג *in the right hand and the* לולב *in the left. Then say the following blessing:*

בָּרוּךְ אַתָּה יהוה אֱלֹהֵינוּ מֶלֶךְ הָעוֹלָם
אֲשֶׁר קִדְּשָׁנוּ בְּמִצְוֹתָיו וְצִוָּנוּ עַל נְטִילַת לוּלָב.

On the first day the לולב *is taken, add:*

בָּרוּךְ אַתָּה יהוה אֱלֹהֵינוּ מֶלֶךְ הָעוֹלָם
שֶׁהֶחֱיָנוּ וְקִיְּמָנוּ וְהִגִּיעָנוּ לַזְּמַן הַזֶּה.

Invert the אתרוג*, so that its pointed end is facing up. Face the front of the* בית כנסת *and wave the* לולב *and* אתרוג *in the following sequence, three times in each direction: ahead, right, back, left, up, down. Continue to hold the* לולב *and* אתרוג *during* הלל.

---

was not even water to drink" (Num. 20:5), and came to a country full of fruit trees and rivers. In order to remember this, we take the fruit which is the most pleasant of the land, branches that smell the best, the most beautiful leaves, and also the best of herbs, i.e., the willows of the brook. These four kinds have also these three purposes: First, they were plentiful in those days in the Land of Israel so that everyone could easily get them. Secondly, they have a good appearance, they are green; some of them, namely the citron and the myrtle, are also excellent as regards their smell, the branches of the palm tree and the willow having neither good nor bad smell. Thirdly, they keep fresh and green for seven days, which is not the case with peaches, pomegranates, asparagus, nuts and the like. (Maimonides, *Guide for the Perplexed*, 3:43)

The saintly Reb Aryeh Levin (1885–1969) was once seen buying his etrog in the Geula district of Jerusalem. To the surprise of onlookers, the rabbi quickly sorted through those on offer, bought one, paid, and left. One man witnessing the event was curious. To find a beautiful etrog for the four kinds is no small matter. People devote much time, energy, and expense to finding one. What then led the tzaddik this year to acquire one so rapidly? He decided to follow the rabbi. He saw him enter an old age home and stay there for an hour and a half.

Hallel

בָּרוּךְ Blessed are You, Lord our God, King of the Universe,
who has made us holy through His commandments
and has commanded us to recite the Hallel.

הַלְלוּיָהּ Halleluya! Servants of the Lord, give praise; praise the name of the Lord. Blessed be the name of the Lord now and for evermore. From the rising of the sun to its setting, may the Lord's name be praised. High is the Lord above all nations; His glory is above the *Ps. 113*

"Lord, please, save us," and other responses. It was colorful, atmospheric, joyous: a people coming to pay homage to God who had brought it to freedom, watched over its destinies and saved it from its enemies.

Hallel is the oldest extended sequence of prayer that has been preserved in its entirety. The sages sensed in it echoes of ancient songs of deliverance: Moses and the Israelites after they had crossed the Sea of Reeds; Joshua and the Israelites after their battles of conquest; Deborah and Barak after they had defeated Sisera; Hezekiah and the people who survived the siege of Sennacherib; Hananiah, Mishael and Azariah after surviving Nebuchadnezzar's fiery furnace; and Mordekhai and Esther after their deliverance from Haman (*Pesaḥim* 119a). The saying of Hallel was also ordained after the victory of the Maccabees against the Seleucid Greeks.

Hallel is said during Pesaḥ, Shavuot, Sukkot, Shemini Atzeret, Simḥat Torah and Ḥanukka – and in modern times, also on Yom HaAtzma'ut and Yom Yerushalayim. It is a feature of the Pesaḥ Seder service (some also say it in the synagogue at the end of Ma'ariv). On Rosh Ḥodesh and the last days of Pesaḥ, the custom arose to say an abridged form (known as "Half Hallel").

Hallel is supremely the poetry of the three pilgrimage festivals, as Jews remember the deliverances of the past, give thanks for the present, and pray for a safe future. It is constructed in three movements: (1) Psalms 113–115 are songs of collective gratitude and indebtedness to God, (2) Psalm 116 is a song sung over a thanksgiving-offering (*korban toda*), and (3) Psalms 117–118 reflect the joy of the pilgrims as they celebrate in the Temple.

הַלְלוּיָהּ *Psalm 113. Halleluya!* A prelude to the praises that follow. The verb ה-ל-ל,

סדר הלל

בָּרוּךְ אַתָּה יהוה אֱלֹהֵינוּ מֶלֶךְ הָעוֹלָם
אֲשֶׁר קִדְּשָׁנוּ בְּמִצְוֹתָיו וְצִוָּנוּ לִקְרֹא אֶת הַהַלֵּל.

הַלְלוּיָהּ, הַלְלוּ עַבְדֵי יהוה, הַלְלוּ אֶת־שֵׁם יהוה: יְהִי שֵׁם יהוה תהלים קיג
מְבֹרָךְ, מֵעַתָּה וְעַד־עוֹלָם: מִמִּזְרַח־שֶׁמֶשׁ עַד־מְבוֹאוֹ, מְהֻלָּל שֵׁם
יהוה: רָם עַל־כָּל־גּוֹיִם יהוה, עַל הַשָּׁמַיִם כְּבוֹדוֹ: מִי כַּיהוה אֱלֹהֵינוּ,

---

Once, after the Rebbe's etrog was returned to him bruised and stained from being handled by hundreds of hands, one of his Hasidim said to him: "Why do you allow so many people to use your etrog? It has lost its *hidur* (beauty)."

The Rebbe replied, "To the contrary, this is the most beautiful etrog of all. What greater *hidur* can there be for an etrog than the fact that hundreds of Jews have performed a mitzva with it?"

HALLEL

The six psalms, 113–118, known as Hallel, form a distinct unit that was sung on festivals in the Second Temple. It is sometimes known as the Egyptian Hallel (because of the reference to the exodus from Egypt in the second paragraph) to distinguish it from the daily Hallel (Psalms 145–150) and the "Great Hallel," Psalms 135 and 136, sung on Shabbat.

To get a sense of what Hallel in the Temple was like, we have to imagine the throng of pilgrims who have come to Jerusalem from all over Israel to "be seen by the Lord your God, three times each year" (Ex. 34:24). Eyewitness testimony tells us that on one Pesaḥ when the worshipers were counted, there were found to be 1.2 million people, "twice the number of those who came out of Egypt" (*Pesaḥim* 64b). Jerusalem was packed, the roads leading up to it often blocked by the sheer number of pilgrims, and the Temple courtyard so full that it was considered a miracle that "though people stood crowded together, there was room enough for them to prostrate themselves."

The Levites sang, musical instruments played (something not permitted on holy days outside the Temple), and as the leader sang the verses, the crowd responded with refrains: "Halleluya," "His loving-kindness is for ever,"

heavens. Who is like the LORD our God, who sits enthroned so high, yet turns so low to see the heavens and the earth? ▸ He raises the poor from the dust and the needy from the refuse heap, giving them a place alongside princes, the princes of His people. He makes the woman in a childless house a happy mother of children. Halleluya!

בְּצֵאת When Israel came out of Egypt, the house of Jacob from a people of foreign tongue, Judah became His sanctuary, Israel His dominion. The sea saw and fled; the Jordan turned back. The mountains skipped like rams, the hills like lambs. ▸ Why was it, sea, that you fled? Jordan, why did you turn back? Why, mountains, did you skip like rams, and you, hills, like lambs? It was at the presence of the LORD, Creator of the earth, at the presence of the God of Jacob, who turned the rock into a pool of water, flint into a flowing spring. *Ps. 114*

God's name until the penultimate verse. It builds to a tremendous climax, bringing together a series of miracles that happened to the Israelites in the days of Moses and Joshua. Inanimate nature – sea, river, mountains, hills, rock, flint – come alive, trembling and retreating at the approach of God.

הַיָּם רָאָה וַיָּנֹס *The sea saw and fled.* An elision of two separate events: the division of the Sea of Reeds in the days of Moses, and the parting of the Jordan in the days of Joshua.

הֶהָרִים רָקְדוּ *The mountains skipped.* A description, echoing Psalm 29, of how the earth moved when the Torah was given at Sinai.

מַה־לְּךָ *Why was it.* An unusual recasting of the previous two lines in the form of a series of rhetorical questions, heightening the tension before the triumphant declaration of the name of God.

הַהֹפְכִי הַצּוּר *Who turned the rock.* A reference to the occasions (Ex. 17; Num. 20) when God, through Moses, brought water from the rocks so that a parched and thirsty people could drink.

Rabbi Joseph Soloveitchik has an insightful comment on this passage. There are two types of personal and political change, one brought about by physical force (conquest), the other by spiritual transformation (sanctity). Conquest involves a change of masters, but slaves remain slaves. Sanctity involves a change in the person him- or herself. The slave, achieving inner freedom, is no longer existentially a slave. Thus in Jewish law a slave whose

הַמַּגְבִּיהִי לָשָׁבֶת: הַמַּשְׁפִּילִי לִרְאוֹת, בַּשָּׁמַיִם וּבָאָרֶץ: ◂ מְקִימִי
מֵעָפָר דָּל, מֵאַשְׁפֹּת יָרִים אֶבְיוֹן: לְהוֹשִׁיבִי עִם־נְדִיבִים, עִם נְדִיבֵי
עַמּוֹ: מוֹשִׁיבִי עֲקֶרֶת הַבַּיִת, אֵם־הַבָּנִים שְׂמֵחָה, הַלְלוּיָהּ:

בְּצֵאת יִשְׂרָאֵל מִמִּצְרָיִם, בֵּית יַעֲקֹב מֵעַם לֹעֵז: הָיְתָה יְהוּדָה תהלים קיד
לְקָדְשׁוֹ, יִשְׂרָאֵל מַמְשְׁלוֹתָיו: הַיָּם רָאָה וַיָּנֹס, הַיַּרְדֵּן יִסֹּב לְאָחוֹר:
הֶהָרִים רָקְדוּ כְאֵילִים, גְּבָעוֹת כִּבְנֵי־צֹאן: ◂ מַה־לְּךָ הַיָּם כִּי תָנוּס,
הַיַּרְדֵּן תִּסֹּב לְאָחוֹר: הֶהָרִים תִּרְקְדוּ כְאֵילִים, גְּבָעוֹת כִּבְנֵי־צֹאן:
מִלִּפְנֵי אָדוֹן חוּלִי אָרֶץ, מִלִּפְנֵי אֱלוֹהַּ יַעֲקֹב: הַהֹפְכִי הַצּוּר אֲגַם־
מָיִם, חַלָּמִישׁ לְמַעְיְנוֹ־מָיִם:

"to praise in joyous song" – from which come the words *Tehillim*, the generic name for the psalms, and *Halleluya*, "Praise God" – appears three times in the first verse, setting the mood of elation. It appears five times in the psalm, and ten times in Hallel as a whole.

מֵעַתָּה וְעַד־עוֹלָם: מִמִּזְרַח־שֶׁמֶשׁ *Now and for evermore. From the rising of the sun.* God's praises echo through all time and space.

הַמַּגְבִּיהִי לָשָׁבֶת: הַמַּשְׁפִּילִי לִרְאוֹת *Who sits enthroned so high, yet turns so low to see.* Though God is beyond the heavens, He sees all that happens on earth. God is close to all who seek to be close to Him, and He is never far from those who need His help.

מְקִימִי מֵעָפָר דָּל *He raises the poor from the dust.* This section is strikingly reminiscent of Hannah's song of thanksgiving after God answered her prayers for a child. She sang: "He lifts the poor out of the dust and rasises abject men from the dunghills, to seat them up there with princes, to bequeath them chairs of honor" (1 Sam. 2:6–7). God cares for great and small alike; in His eyes there are no distinctions of class or caste. God humbles the arrogant and lifts the humble. The deep underlying egalitarianism of the Hebrew Bible – that we are all equal in dignity under the sovereignty of God – was a revolutionary idea in the ancient world and remains so today.

בְּצֵאת יִשְׂרָאֵל מִמִּצְרָיִם *Psalm 114. When Israel came out of Egypt.* The psalm starts slowly, opening with a subordinate clause and delaying explicit mention of

לֹא לָנוּ Not to us, LORD, not to us, but to Your name give glory, for Your love, for Your faithfulness. Why should the nations say, "Where now is their God?" Our God is in heaven; whatever He wills He does. Their idols are silver and gold, made by human hands. They have mouths but cannot speak; eyes but cannot see. They have ears but cannot hear; noses but cannot smell. They have hands but cannot feel; feet but cannot walk. No sound comes from their throat. Those who make them become like them; so will all who trust in them. ▸ Israel, trust in the LORD – He is their Help and their Shield. House of Aaron, trust in the LORD – He is their Help and their Shield. You who fear the LORD, trust in the LORD – He is their Help and their Shield. Ps. 115

עֲצַבֵּיהֶם כֶּסֶף וְזָהָב *Their idols are silver and gold.* An extended polemic against idolatry. The contrast between God and the idols is brought out by the words *asa*, "Whatever He wills He does," and *ma'aseh*, "made by human hands." God *makes*; idols are *made*. God makes man in His image; man makes idols in his. Hence, "Those who make them become like them." We are shaped by what we worship. Those who worship lifeless icons become lifeless. Only by worshiping the God of life do we truly live.

יִשְׂרָאֵל בְּטַח בַּיהוה *Israel, trust in the LORD.* The Psalmist turns to three groups of people worshiping in the Temple: *Israel*, the Jewish worshipers, *House of Aaron*, the officiating priests and Levites, and *You who fear the* LORD, meaning converts (Rashi) or righteous gentiles of all nations (Ibn Ezra). In his song at the dedication of the Temple, Solomon foresaw that gentiles, not just Jews, would come to the Temple to pray (1 Kings 8:41–43). Isaiah envisions the day when "My House shall be called a house of prayer for all peoples" (Is. 56:7). The sharp opposition to idolatry in this psalm does not preclude a universalistic openness to humanity as a whole.

עֶזְרָם וּמָגִנָּם הוּא *He is their Help and their Shield.* This thrice-repeated phrase may originally have been a congregational response.

יהוה זְכָרָנוּ *The LORD remembers us.* Still part of Psalm 115, the Psalmist asks God to bless the same three groups as above: Israel, the House of Aaron and those who fear the LORD among the nations.

הַשָּׁמַיִם שָׁמַיִם לַיהוה, וְהָאָרֶץ נָתַן לִבְנֵי־אָדָם *The heavens are the LORD's, but the earth He has given over to mankind.* When God is God, humanity can be humane,

לֹא לָנוּ יהוה לֹא לָנוּ, כִּי־לְשִׁמְךָ תֵּן כָּבוֹד, עַל־חַסְדְּךָ עַל־אֲמִתֶּךָ: תהלים קטו
לָמָּה יֹאמְרוּ הַגּוֹיִם אַיֵּה־נָא אֱלֹהֵיהֶם: וֵאלֹהֵינוּ בַשָּׁמָיִם, כֹּל אֲשֶׁר־
חָפֵץ עָשָׂה: עֲצַבֵּיהֶם כֶּסֶף וְזָהָב, מַעֲשֵׂה יְדֵי אָדָם: פֶּה־לָהֶם וְלֹא
יְדַבֵּרוּ, עֵינַיִם לָהֶם וְלֹא יִרְאוּ: אָזְנַיִם לָהֶם וְלֹא יִשְׁמָעוּ, אַף לָהֶם
וְלֹא יְרִיחוּן: יְדֵיהֶם וְלֹא יְמִישׁוּן, רַגְלֵיהֶם וְלֹא יְהַלֵּכוּ, לֹא־יֶהְגּוּ
בִּגְרוֹנָם: כְּמוֹהֶם יִהְיוּ עֹשֵׂיהֶם, כֹּל אֲשֶׁר־בֹּטֵחַ בָּהֶם: ◂ יִשְׂרָאֵל
בְּטַח בַּיהוה, עֶזְרָם וּמָגִנָּם הוּא: בֵּית אַהֲרֹן בִּטְחוּ בַיהוה, עֶזְרָם
וּמָגִנָּם הוּא: יִרְאֵי יהוה בִּטְחוּ בַיהוה, עֶזְרָם וּמָגִנָּם הוּא:

---

master puts tefillin on him goes free (*Gittin* 40a), and a slave from outside Israel who escapes to Israel is not returned to his master (*Gittin* 45a). Sanctity liberates from within.

That is why the Israelites had to celebrate the first Passover while they were still in Egypt. "Had the Jews not first redeemed themselves by self-sanctification on that night-of-watching in Egypt, the redemption through conquest [the signs and wonders of the exodus] would not have been complete." Hence *When Israel came out of Egypt… Judah became His sanctuary, Israel His dominion.* Only after that, *the sea saw and fled.* The inner liberation had to precede the outer redemption (Rabbi J. Soloveitchik, *Festival of Freedom*).

לֹא לָנוּ *Psalm 115. Not to us.* According to some, this psalm is a continuation of the previous one. Recalling its past, Israel pledges itself to faith in God in the future (Radak). In the first three verses, the Psalmist pleads with God to protect His people, for His sake not ours.

לָמָּה יֹאמְרוּ הַגּוֹיִם אַיֵּה־נָא אֱלֹהֵיהֶם *Why should the nations say, "Where now is their God?"* The idea that Israel's sufferings constitute a desecration of God's name is first heard in Moses' plea after the sin of the golden calf: "Why should Egypt speak, and say, 'In an evil hour did He bring them out'" (Ex. 32:12). It is repeated in Moses' song at the end of his life, "I dreaded the taunt of the enemy, lest the adversary misunderstand and say, 'Our hand has triumphed; the Lord has not done all this'" (Deut. 32:27), and developed at length in Ezekiel 20. Israel are God's witnesses (Is. 43; 44). Therefore their fate affects how people think of God.

יהוה זְכָרָנוּ The LORD remembers us and will bless us. He will bless the house of Israel. He will bless the house of Aaron. He will bless those who fear the LORD, small and great alike. May the LORD give you increase: you and your children. May you be blessed by the LORD, Maker of heaven and earth. ▸ The heavens are the LORD's, but the earth He has given over to mankind. It is not the dead who praise the LORD, nor those who go down to the silent grave. But we will bless the LORD, now and for ever. Halleluya!

אָהַבְתִּי I love the LORD, for He hears my voice, my pleas. He turns His ear Ps. 116
to me whenever I call. The bonds of death encompassed me, the anguish of the grave came upon me, I was overcome by trouble and sorrow. Then I called on the name of the LORD: "LORD, I pray, save my life." Gracious is the LORD, and righteous; our God is full of compassion. The LORD protects the simple hearted. When I was brought low, He saved me. My soul, be at peace once more, for the LORD has been good to you. For You have rescued me from death, my eyes from weeping, my feet from stumbling. ▸ I shall walk in the presence of the LORD in the land of the living. I had faith, even when I said, "I am greatly afflicted," even when I said rashly, "All men are liars."

---

preceding it. It is deeply personal; it consistently uses the first person singular, "I" and "my." It tells of how the speaker turned to God in deep distress, close to death. God answered his prayer and saved him. Therefore he is bringing a thanksgiving-offering to fulfill the vow he made then. Several of the words have unusual, antiquated and poeticized endings which further slow the pace. At the end the poet turns to address Jerusalem in the second person ("in your midst, Jerusalem") as if it were an intimate friend.

שֹׁמֵר פְּתָאיִם יהוה... שׁוּבִי נַפְשִׁי לִמְנוּחָיְכִי *The LORD protects the simple hearted... My soul, be at peace once more.* It is simple trust that has brought God's healing; therefore the poet urges himself not to be anxious but to trust and stay calm.

כִּי חִלַּצְתָּ נַפְשִׁי *For You have rescued me.* Now, becalmed, the poet turns directly to God, thanking Him for His deliverance.

בְּאַרְצוֹת הַחַיִּים *In the land of the living.* As was said in the previous psalm, "It is not the dead who praise the LORD." The poet is thanking God for the

יהוה זְכָרָנוּ יְבָרֵךְ, יְבָרֵךְ אֶת־בֵּית יִשְׂרָאֵל, יְבָרֵךְ אֶת־בֵּית אַהֲרֹן: יְבָרֵךְ יִרְאֵי יהוה, הַקְּטַנִּים עִם־הַגְּדֹלִים: יֹסֵף יהוה עֲלֵיכֶם, עֲלֵיכֶם וְעַל־בְּנֵיכֶם: בְּרוּכִים אַתֶּם לַיהוה, עֹשֵׂה שָׁמַיִם וָאָרֶץ: ‹ הַשָּׁמַיִם שָׁמַיִם לַיהוה, וְהָאָרֶץ נָתַן לִבְנֵי־אָדָם: לֹא הַמֵּתִים יְהַלְלוּ־יָהּ, וְלֹא כָּל־יֹרְדֵי דוּמָה: וַאֲנַחְנוּ נְבָרֵךְ יָהּ, מֵעַתָּה וְעַד־עוֹלָם, הַלְלוּיָהּ:

תהלים קטז אָהַבְתִּי, כִּי־יִשְׁמַע יהוה, אֶת־קוֹלִי תַּחֲנוּנָי: כִּי־הִטָּה אָזְנוֹ לִי, וּבְיָמַי אֶקְרָא: אֲפָפוּנִי חֶבְלֵי־מָוֶת, וּמְצָרֵי שְׁאוֹל מְצָאוּנִי, צָרָה וְיָגוֹן אֶמְצָא: וּבְשֵׁם־יהוה אֶקְרָא, אָנָּה יהוה מַלְּטָה נַפְשִׁי: חַנּוּן יהוה וְצַדִּיק, וֵאלֹהֵינוּ מְרַחֵם: שֹׁמֵר פְּתָאִים יהוה, דַּלּוֹתִי וְלִי יְהוֹשִׁיעַ: שׁוּבִי נַפְשִׁי לִמְנוּחָיְכִי, כִּי־יהוה גָּמַל עָלָיְכִי: כִּי חִלַּצְתָּ נַפְשִׁי מִמָּוֶת, אֶת־עֵינִי מִן־דִּמְעָה, אֶת־רַגְלִי מִדֶּחִי: ‹ אֶתְהַלֵּךְ לִפְנֵי יהוה, בְּאַרְצוֹת הַחַיִּים: הֶאֱמַנְתִּי כִּי אֲדַבֵּר, אֲנִי עָנִיתִי מְאֹד: אֲנִי אָמַרְתִּי בְחָפְזִי, כָּל־הָאָדָם כֹּזֵב:

---

but when man tries to be like God he becomes inhumane. It was the attempt to build "a tower that reaches to the heavens" that was the sin of the builders of Babel (Gen. 11:4). God has given us the earth, but He reigns supreme; and we must have humility, knowing the proper limits of our striving. When humans have worshiped other humans as gods, the result has been hubris followed by nemesis, often involving tyranny and bloodshed on a massive scale.

לֹא הַמֵּתִים יְהַלְלוּ־יָהּ *It is not the dead who praise the Lord.* A theme sounded often in the book of Psalms. The God of life is to be found in life.

וַאֲנַחְנוּ נְבָרֵךְ יָהּ *But we will bless the Lord.* One of the best-known lines of Psalms, having been added as a conclusion to *Ashrei* and thus said three times daily.

אָהַבְתִּי *Psalm 116. I love the Lord.* The second section of Hallel is the slow movement in the symphony, significantly different in tone from those

מָה־אָשִׁיב How can I repay the LORD for all His goodness to me? I will lift the cup of salvation and call on the name of the LORD. I will fulfill my vows to the LORD in the presence of all His people. Grievous in the LORD's sight is the death of His devoted ones. Truly, LORD, I am Your servant; I am Your servant, the son of Your maidservant. You set me free from my chains. ▸ To You I shall bring a thanksgiving-offering and call on the LORD by name. I will fulfill my vows to the LORD in the presence of all His people, in the courts of the House of the LORD, in your midst, Jerusalem. Halleluya.

הַלְלוּ Praise the LORD, all nations; acclaim Him, all you peoples; *Ps. 117*
for His loving-kindness to us is strong,
and the LORD's faithfulness is everlasting. Halleluya.

הַלְלוּ *Psalm 117. Praise.* The briefest of psalms, the shortest chapter in Tanakh, this psalm fulfills three functions. First, it reestablishes the mood of public worship after the introspective and private nature of the previous psalm. Second, it serves as a prelude to the great psalm that follows. Third, it is a call, a summons to the crowd inviting them to take part in what is about to follow: an act of praise and thanks that will involve their active participation.

At one level the leader is inviting the entire crowd, both Jews and gentiles (the "God-fearers" of the previous psalms) to join in an act of praise. At a deeper level he is articulating a belief that runs through Jewish history, beginning with God's first call to Abraham: "Through you all the nations of the earth shall be blessed." Jewish history is of significance not just to Jews but to humanity. Jews are God's witnesses to the world. Those who try to destroy people's belief in God – the God who stands above all nations and powers – try to destroy the Jewish people. Those who respect God tend to respect the Jewish people. The Jews are God's question mark over all attempts to rule by power and persuade by force.

חַסְדּוֹ, וֶאֱמֶת *His loving-kindness…faithfulness. Ḥesed* and *emet*, the two words used here, often appear together in Tanakh. They are the central covenantal virtues. Often translated as "kindness" and "truth," they have a highly specific meaning in the context of Judaism. *Ḥesed* is love-as-loyalty and loyalty-as-love. It means love not as an emotion but as a moral commitment, as in marriage. *Emet* means being true to your word, keeping your promises, honoring your pledge. It is not a cognitive term but a moral one, so it is best translated

מָה־אָשִׁיב לַיהוה, כָּל־תַּגְמוּלוֹהִי עָלָי: כּוֹס־יְשׁוּעוֹת אֶשָּׂא, וּבְשֵׁם יהוה אֶקְרָא: נְדָרַי לַיהוה אֲשַׁלֵּם, נֶגְדָה־נָּא לְכָל־עַמּוֹ: יָקָר בְּעֵינֵי יהוה, הַמָּוְתָה לַחֲסִידָיו: אָנָּה יהוה כִּי־אֲנִי עַבְדֶּךָ, אֲנִי־עַבְדְּךָ בֶּן־אֲמָתֶךָ, פִּתַּחְתָּ לְמוֹסֵרָי: › לְךָ־אֶזְבַּח זֶבַח תּוֹדָה, וּבְשֵׁם יהוה אֶקְרָא: נְדָרַי לַיהוה אֲשַׁלֵּם, נֶגְדָה־נָּא לְכָל־עַמּוֹ: בְּחַצְרוֹת בֵּית יהוה, בְּתוֹכֵכִי יְרוּשָׁלָםִ, הַלְלוּיָהּ:

תהלים קיז

הַלְלוּ אֶת־יהוה כָּל־גּוֹיִם, שַׁבְּחוּהוּ כָּל־הָאֻמִּים:
כִּי גָבַר עָלֵינוּ חַסְדּוֹ, וֶאֱמֶת־יהוה לְעוֹלָם, הַלְלוּיָהּ:

---

physical gift of life and the spiritual gift of being able to "walk in the presence of the LORD."

הֶאֱמַנְתִּי ... אֲנִי אָמַרְתִּי בְחָפְזִי, כָּל־הָאָדָם כֹּזֵב *I had faith ... even when I said rashly, "All men are liars."* The commentators relate this to King David who, when forced to flee from Saul, felt betrayed by everyone. Alternatively, "Even when I was fleeing for my life, I knew that those [who preached despair] were false" (Radak).

מָה־אָשִׁיב לַיהוה *How can I repay the LORD.* A rhetorical question. We cannot repay God for what He has given us. Faith is, among other things, gratitude – the sense of life-as-a-gift that we often only have when we have come close to losing it.

כּוֹס־יְשׁוּעוֹת אֶשָּׂא *I will lift the cup of salvation.* A reference to the wine libation that accompanied a thanksgiving-offering (Rashi).

יָקָר בְּעֵינֵי יהוה, הַמָּוְתָה לַחֲסִידָיו *Grievous in the LORD's sight is the death of His devoted ones.* A reference back to the deliverance from death, to the memory of which this psalm is dedicated.

אָנָּה יהוה כִּי־אֲנִי עַבְדֶּךָ *Truly, LORD, I am Your servant.* The poet speaks of himself during his crisis, feeling as if he were a slave enchained by an angry master. Now, healed, he feels both forgiven and released.

נְדָרַי לַיהוה אֲשַׁלֵּם *I will fulfill my vows to the LORD.* This sentence appears twice in the psalm, which contains a number of other repetitions (such as "I am Your servant") for poetic effect.

The following verses are chanted by the Leader.
At the end of each verse, the congregation responds, "Thank the LORD for He is good; His loving-kindness is for ever."
On Sukkot the lulav and etrog are waved, three waves for each word of the verse (except God's name). On the first word, wave forward, then, on subsequent words, wave right, back, left, up and down respectively. The Leader waves only for the first two verses. The congregation waves each time the first verse is said in response.

הוֹדוּ Thank the LORD for He is good; His loving-kindness is for ever. *Ps. 118*
Let Israel say His loving-kindness is for ever.
Let the house of Aaron say His loving-kindness is for ever.
Let those who fear the LORD say His loving-kindness is for ever.

מִן־הַמֵּצַר In my distress I called on the LORD. The LORD answered me and set me free. The LORD is with me; I will not be afraid. What can man do to me? The LORD is with me. He is my Helper. I will see the downfall of my enemies. It is better to take refuge in the LORD than to trust in man. It is better to take refuge in the LORD than to trust in princes. The nations all surrounded me, but in the LORD's name I drove

---

speaking of the rescue of the nation from its foes. Note how, throughout this section of the psalm, phrases repeat themselves ("the LORD is with me," "It is better to take refuge," "they surrounded me," "right hand") two or three times. This may be because different lines were sung by different choirs, or alternately by leader, Levites and congregation. The effect in any case is choral.

מִן־הַמֵּצַר... בַּמֶּרְחָב *In my distress... set me free.* The Hebrew words carry the literal meanings of narrow straits and wide open spaces, conveying an almost physical sense of confinement and release.

טוֹב לַחֲסוֹת בַּיהוה *It is better to take refuge in the LORD.* A sentiment found repeatedly in Psalms. People disappoint, betray, fail to keep their promises, prove untrustworthy. Former allies become enemies. People in pursuit of wealth or power often let advantage override principle and loyalty. Hence the loneliness of public life. Trust in God is ultimately the only reliable source of strength.

כָּל־גּוֹיִם סְבָבוּנִי *The nations all surrounded me.* The geographical position of Israel meant that in both ancient and modern times it was peculiarly vulnerable to attack, bordering as it did on several states and within the reach of larger imperial powers.

The following verses are chanted by the שליח ציבור.
At the end of each verse, the קהל *responds:* .הודוּ לַיהוה כִּי־טוֹב, כִּי לְעוֹלָם חַסְדּוֹ
On סוכות *the* לולב *and* אתרוג *are waved, three waves for each word of the verse (except God's name). On the first word, wave forward, then, on subsequent words, wave right, back, left, up and down respectively. The* שליח ציבור *waves only for the first two verses. The* קהל *waves each time the first verse is said in response.*

תהלים קיח

הוֹדוּ לַיהוה כִּי־טוֹב כִּי לְעוֹלָם חַסְדּוֹ:
יֹאמַר־נָא יִשְׂרָאֵל כִּי לְעוֹלָם חַסְדּוֹ:
יֹאמְרוּ־נָא בֵית־אַהֲרֹן כִּי לְעוֹלָם חַסְדּוֹ:
יֹאמְרוּ־נָא יִרְאֵי יהוה כִּי לְעוֹלָם חַסְדּוֹ:

מִן־הַמֵּצַר קָרָאתִי יָּהּ, עָנָנִי בַמֶּרְחָב יָהּ: יהוה לִי לֹא אִירָא, מַה־יַּעֲשֶׂה לִי אָדָם: יהוה לִי בְּעֹזְרָי, וַאֲנִי אֶרְאֶה בְשֹׂנְאָי: טוֹב לַחֲסוֹת בַּיהוה, מִבְּטֹחַ בָּאָדָם: טוֹב לַחֲסוֹת בַּיהוה, מִבְּטֹחַ בִּנְדִיבִים: כָּל־גּוֹיִם סְבָבוּנִי, בְּשֵׁם יהוה כִּי אֲמִילַם: סַבּוּנִי גַם־סְבָבוּנִי, בְּשֵׁם

---

as "faithfulness." The Psalmist is calling on the world to witness and celebrate the special covenantal bond between God and His people.

הודו *Psalm 118. Thank.* This extended psalm, written in four or five movements, is written to be sung antiphonally, the leader singing a line or half-line, with the congregation then responding. We do not know exactly how the psalm was sung in Temple times, and there are differences of custom even today, but this was the moment of maximum participation by the pilgrims, many of whom had traveled long distances to be there. It was a high point in the Temple service: a nation celebrating its past and praying for the future.

הודו לַיהוה כִּי־טוֹב *Thank the Lord for He is good.* This verse was first recited by King David when he brought the ark to Jerusalem (1 Chron. 16:34).

יֹאמַר־נָא יִשְׂרָאֵל *Let Israel say.* The Psalmist turns to the same three groups – Israel, the House of Aaron, and God-fearers – as he has done in previous psalms.

מִן־הַמֵּצַר *In my distress.* Here, personal and national sentiments merge. At one level the Psalmist is speaking of an individual deliverance, at another he is

them off. They surrounded me on every side, but in the LORD's name I drove them off. They surrounded me like bees, they attacked me as fire attacks brushwood, but in the LORD's name I drove them off. They thrust so hard against me, I nearly fell, but the LORD came to my help. The LORD is my strength and my song; He has become my salvation. Sounds of song and salvation resound in the tents of the righteous: "The LORD's right hand has done mighty deeds. The LORD's right hand is lifted high. The LORD's right hand has done mighty deeds." I will not die but live, and tell what the LORD has done. The LORD has chastened me severely, but He has not given me over to death. ▸ Open for me the gates of righteousness that I may enter them and thank the LORD. This is the gateway to the LORD; through it, the righteous shall enter.

אוֹדְךָ I will thank You, for You answered me,
and became my salvation.
I will thank You, for You answered me, and became my salvation.

The stone the builders rejected
has become the main cornerstone.
The stone the builders rejected has become the main cornerstone.

This is the LORD's doing.
It is wondrous in our eyes.
This is the LORD's doing. It is wondrous in our eyes.

This is the day the LORD has made.
Let us rejoice and be glad in it.
This is the day the LORD has made. Let us rejoice and be glad in it.

זֶה־הַשַּׁעַר *This is the gateway.* A response to the pilgrims by the gatekeepers.

אוֹדְךָ *I will thank You.* From here to the end of the psalm the lines are repeated, in memory of the way they were sung responsively in the Temple.

אֶבֶן מָאֲסוּ הַבּוֹנִים *The stone the builders rejected.* This is a reference to the people of Israel. Two of the first references to Israel in non-Jewish sources – the Merneptah stele (Egypt, thirteenth century BCE) and the Mesha stele (Moab, ninth century BCE) – both declare that Israel has been destroyed. Israel is the people that outlives its obituaries.

יהוה כִּי אֲמִילַם: סַבּוּנִי כִדְבֹרִים, דֹּעֲכוּ כְּאֵשׁ קוֹצִים, בְּשֵׁם יהוה כִּי אֲמִילַם: דָּחֹה דְחִיתַנִי לִנְפֹּל, וַיהוה עֲזָרָנִי: עָזִּי וְזִמְרָת יָהּ, וַיְהִי־לִי לִישׁוּעָה: קוֹל רִנָּה וִישׁוּעָה בְּאָהֳלֵי צַדִּיקִים, יְמִין יהוה עֹשָׂה חָיִל: יְמִין יהוה רוֹמֵמָה, יְמִין יהוה עֹשָׂה חָיִל: לֹא־אָמוּת כִּי־אֶחְיֶה, וַאֲסַפֵּר מַעֲשֵׂי יָהּ: יַסֹּר יִסְּרַנִּי יָּהּ, וְלַמָּוֶת לֹא נְתָנָנִי: ‹ פִּתְחוּ־לִי שַׁעֲרֵי־צֶדֶק, אָבֹא־בָם אוֹדֶה יָהּ: זֶה־הַשַּׁעַר לַיהוה, צַדִּיקִים יָבֹאוּ בוֹ:

אוֹדְךָ כִּי עֲנִיתָנִי, וַתְּהִי־לִי לִישׁוּעָה:
אוֹדְךָ כִּי עֲנִיתָנִי, וַתְּהִי־לִי לִישׁוּעָה:

אֶבֶן מָאֲסוּ הַבּוֹנִים, הָיְתָה לְרֹאשׁ פִּנָּה:
אֶבֶן מָאֲסוּ הַבּוֹנִים, הָיְתָה לְרֹאשׁ פִּנָּה:

מֵאֵת יהוה הָיְתָה זֹּאת, הִיא נִפְלָאת בְּעֵינֵינוּ:
מֵאֵת יהוה הָיְתָה זֹּאת, הִיא נִפְלָאת בְּעֵינֵינוּ:

זֶה־הַיּוֹם עָשָׂה יהוה, נָגִילָה וְנִשְׂמְחָה בוֹ:
זֶה־הַיּוֹם עָשָׂה יהוה, נָגִילָה וְנִשְׂמְחָה בוֹ:

כְּאֵשׁ קוֹצִים *As fire attacks brushwood.* Flaring up dramatically but quickly burning itself out.

קוֹל רִנָּה *Sounds of song.* A prelude to the dramatic choral piece that follows, three phrases each beginning, "The Lord's right hand."

לֹא־אָמוּת כִּי־אֶחְיֶה, וַאֲסַפֵּר *I will not die but live, and tell.* A quintessential expression of the Jewish instinct for survival, itself intimately connected to the role of Jews as witnesses. A witness must survive if truth is not to be buried.

פִּתְחוּ־לִי שַׁעֲרֵי־צֶדֶק *Open for me the gates of righteousness.* In Temple times this referred literally to the gates of the city, and would have resonated with the pilgrims as they entered Jerusalem.

On Sukkot the lulav and etrog are waved while saying "Lord, please, save us," three waves in each direction (not for God's name). On the first word, wave forward and right; third word: back and left; fourth word: up and down.

Leader followed by congregation:

אָנָּא Lord, please, save us.
Lord, please, save us.
Lord, please, grant us success.
Lord, please, grant us success.

בָּרוּךְ Blessed is one who comes in the name of the Lord; we bless you from the House of the Lord.
Blessed is one who comes in the name of the Lord; we bless you from the House of the Lord.

The Lord is God; He has given us light. Bind the festival offering with thick cords [and bring it] to the horns of the altar.
The Lord is God; He has given us light. Bind the festival offering with thick cords [and bring it] to the horns of the altar.

You are my God and I will thank You; You are my God, I will exalt You.
You are my God and I will thank You; You are my God, I will exalt You.

Thank the Lord for He is good; His loving-kindness is for ever.
Thank the Lord for He is good; His loving-kindness is for ever.

יְהַלְלוּךָ All Your works will praise You, Lord our God, and Your devoted ones – the righteous who do Your will, together with all Your people the house of Israel – will joyously thank, bless, praise, glorify, exalt, revere, sanctify, and proclaim the sovereignty of Your name, our King. ▸ For it is good to thank You and fitting to sing

---

to bring to the altar a festival offering: *ḥag* in biblical Hebrew, *ḥagiga* in rabbinic Hebrew.

אֵלִי אַתָּה *You are my God.* Said by the offerer at the time of the offering.

הודו ליהוה כי־טוב *Thank the Lord for He is good.* The psalm ends with the same verse with which it began. Note the difference between praise (*hallel, shevaḥ*) and thanks (*hoda'a*). Worship, both in the Temple and the synagogue, in both Hallel and the Amida, begins with praise and ends with thanks. Praise is more external and formal, thanks more inward and deeply felt.

יְהַלְלוּךָ ... כָּל מַעֲשֶׂיךָ *All Your works will praise You.* Not part of Hallel itself, this

On סוכות *the* לולב *and* אתרוג *are waved while saying* אָנָּא יהוה הוֹשִׁיעָה נָּא, *three waves in each direction (not for God's name). On the first word, wave forward and right; third word: back and left; fourth word: up and down.*

קהל *followed by* שליח ציבור:

אָנָּא יהוה הוֹשִׁיעָה נָּא:

אָנָּא יהוה הוֹשִׁיעָה נָּא:

אָנָּא יהוה הַצְלִיחָה נָא:

אָנָּא יהוה הַצְלִיחָה נָא:

בָּרוּךְ הַבָּא בְּשֵׁם יהוה, בֵּרַכְנוּכֶם מִבֵּית יהוה:
בָּרוּךְ הַבָּא בְּשֵׁם יהוה, בֵּרַכְנוּכֶם מִבֵּית יהוה:

אֵל יהוה וַיָּאֶר לָנוּ, אִסְרוּ־חַג בַּעֲבֹתִים עַד־קַרְנוֹת הַמִּזְבֵּחַ:
אֵל יהוה וַיָּאֶר לָנוּ, אִסְרוּ־חַג בַּעֲבֹתִים עַד־קַרְנוֹת הַמִּזְבֵּחַ:

אֵלִי אַתָּה וְאוֹדֶךָּ, אֱלֹהַי אֲרוֹמְמֶךָּ:
אֵלִי אַתָּה וְאוֹדֶךָּ, אֱלֹהַי אֲרוֹמְמֶךָּ:

הוֹדוּ לַיהוה כִּי־טוֹב, כִּי לְעוֹלָם חַסְדּוֹ:
הוֹדוּ לַיהוה כִּי־טוֹב, כִּי לְעוֹלָם חַסְדּוֹ:

יְהַלְלְוּךָ יהוה אֱלֹהֵינוּ כָּל מַעֲשֶׂיךָ, וַחֲסִידֶיךָ צַדִּיקִים עוֹשֵׂי רְצוֹנֶךָ, וְכָל עַמְּךָ בֵּית יִשְׂרָאֵל בְּרִנָּה יוֹדוּ וִיבָרְכוּ וִישַׁבְּחוּ וִיפָאֲרוּ וִירוֹמְמוּ וְיַעֲרִיצוּ וְיַקְדִּישׁוּ וְיַמְלִיכוּ אֶת שִׁמְךָ מַלְכֵּנוּ, • כִּי לְךָ טוֹב

אָנָּא יהוה הוֹשִׁיעָה נָּא *Lord, please, save us.* A dramatic sequence in which leader and congregation turn directly in plea to God. It became the basis of the extended litanies said on Sukkot during *Hakafot*, the procession around the altar in the Temple and the *bima* in the synagogue, as well as the source of the English word "hosanna" (=*hosha na*).

בָּרוּךְ הַבָּא *Blessed is one who comes.* A greeting by the priests to the pilgrims (Rashi, Radak).

אֵל יהוה *The Lord is God.* A response by the pilgrims, declaring their intent

psalms to Your name, for from eternity to eternity You are God. Blessed are You, LORD, King who is extolled with praises.

Some say at this point Hoshanot on page 530, before Full Kaddish.

FULL KADDISH

Some have the custom to include additional responses in Full Kaddish. They can be found in the version on page 1464.

Leader: יִתְגַּדַּל Magnified and sanctified may His great name be,
in the world He created by His will.
May He establish His kingdom
in your lifetime and in your days,
and in the lifetime of all the house of Israel,
swiftly and soon – and say: Amen.

All: May His great name be blessed for ever and all time.

Leader: Blessed and praised, glorified and exalted,
raised and honored, uplifted and lauded be
the name of the Holy One, blessed be He,
beyond any blessing, song, praise and consolation
uttered in the world – and say: Amen.

May the prayers and pleas of all Israel
be accepted by their Father in heaven – and say: Amen.

May there be great peace from heaven,
and life for us and all Israel – and say: Amen.

Bow, take three steps back, as if taking leave of the Divine Presence, then bow, first left, then right, then center, while saying:
May He who makes peace in His high places,
make peace for us and all Israel – and say: Amen.

If the first day of Sukkot and Shemini Atzeret fall on Shabbat, Ecclesiastes is read on Shemini Atzeret at this point (page 812), followed by the Mourner's Kaddish. In Israel, it is read on the first day of Sukkot.

On Shemini Atzeret which falls on a weekday, continue with The Removal of the Torah on page 1080. On Simhat Torah, continue with Hakafot on page 1206. On other days of Yom Tov continue on the next page.

---

is a concluding blessing, similar to the one said after the Verses of Praise in the morning service.

לְהוֹדוֹת וּלְשִׁמְךָ נָאֶה לְזַמֵּר, כִּי מֵעוֹלָם וְעַד עוֹלָם אַתָּה אֵל. בָּרוּךְ אַתָּה יהוה, מֶלֶךְ מְהֻלָּל בַּתִּשְׁבָּחוֹת.

Some say at this point הושענות *on page 531, before* קדיש שלם.

קדיש שלם

Some have the custom to include additional responses in קדיש שלם. *They can be found in the version on page 1465.*

ש״ץ: יִתְגַּדַּל וְיִתְקַדַּשׁ שְׁמֵהּ רַבָּא (קהל: אָמֵן)
בְּעָלְמָא דִּי בְרָא כִרְעוּתֵהּ, וְיַמְלִיךְ מַלְכוּתֵהּ
בְּחַיֵּיכוֹן וּבְיוֹמֵיכוֹן וּבְחַיֵּי דְכָל בֵּית יִשְׂרָאֵל
בַּעֲגָלָא וּבִזְמַן קָרִיב, וְאִמְרוּ אָמֵן. (קהל: אָמֵן)

קהל וש״ץ: יְהֵא שְׁמֵהּ רַבָּא מְבָרַךְ לְעָלַם וּלְעָלְמֵי עָלְמַיָּא.

ש״ץ: יִתְבָּרַךְ וְיִשְׁתַּבַּח וְיִתְפָּאַר
וְיִתְרוֹמַם וְיִתְנַשֵּׂא וְיִתְהַדָּר וְיִתְעַלֶּה וְיִתְהַלָּל
שְׁמֵהּ דְּקֻדְשָׁא בְּרִיךְ הוּא (קהל: בְּרִיךְ הוּא)
לְעֵלָּא מִן כָּל בִּרְכָתָא וְשִׁירָתָא, תֻּשְׁבְּחָתָא וְנֶחֱמָתָא
דַּאֲמִירָן בְּעָלְמָא, וְאִמְרוּ אָמֵן. (קהל: אָמֵן)

תִּתְקַבַּל צְלוֹתְהוֹן וּבָעוּתְהוֹן דְּכָל יִשְׂרָאֵל
קֳדָם אֲבוּהוֹן דִּי בִשְׁמַיָּא, וְאִמְרוּ אָמֵן. (קהל: אָמֵן)

יְהֵא שְׁלָמָא רַבָּא מִן שְׁמַיָּא
וְחַיִּים, עָלֵינוּ וְעַל כָּל יִשְׂרָאֵל, וְאִמְרוּ אָמֵן. (קהל: אָמֵן)

Bow, take three steps back, as if taking leave of the Divine Presence, then bow, first left, then right, then center, while saying:

עֹשֶׂה שָׁלוֹם בִּמְרוֹמָיו
הוּא יַעֲשֶׂה שָׁלוֹם עָלֵינוּ וְעַל כָּל יִשְׂרָאֵל, וְאִמְרוּ אָמֵן. (קהל: אָמֵן)

If the first day of סוכות *and* שמיני עצרת *fall on* שבת, קהלת *is read on* שמיני עצרת *at this point (page 813), followed by* קדיש יתום. *In* ארץ ישראל, *it is read on the first day of* סוכות.

On שמיני עצרת *which falls on a weekday, continue with* הוצאת ספר תורה *on page 1081. On* שמחת תורה, *continue with* הקפות *on page 1207. On other days of* יום טוב *continue on the next page.*

REMOVING THE TORAH FROM THE ARK

אֵין־כָּמְוֹךָ There is none like You among the heavenly powers, *Ps. 86*
LORD, and there are no works like Yours.
Your kingdom is an eternal kingdom, *Ps. 145*
and Your dominion is for all generations.

The LORD is King, the LORD was King,
the LORD shall be King for ever and all time.
The LORD will give strength to His people; *Ps. 29*
the LORD will bless His people with peace.

Father of compassion,
favor Zion with Your goodness; rebuild the walls of Jerusalem. *Ps. 51*
For we trust in You alone, King, God, high and exalted, Master of worlds.

The Ark is opened and the congregation stands. All say:

וַיְהִי בִּנְסֹעַ Whenever the Ark set out, Moses would say, *Num. 10*
"Arise, LORD, and may Your enemies be scattered.
May those who hate You flee before You."
For the Torah shall come forth from Zion, *Is. 2*
and the word of the LORD from Jerusalem.
Blessed is He who in His Holiness gave the Torah to His people Israel.

On Shabbat, continue with "Blessed is the name" on page 430.

Thus from its earliest days the synagogue was a place of study as well as prayer. In Second Temple and later eras, the reading was accompanied by verse-by-verse translation into the vernacular, mainly Aramaic. In the course of time the act of taking the Torah from, and returning it to, the Ark became ceremonial moments in their own right.

אֵין־כָּמְוֹךָ בָאֱלֹהִים *There is none like You among the heavenly powers.* A collection of verses and phrases from the book of Psalms, focusing on God's sovereignty.

וַיְהִי בִּנְסֹעַ הָאָרֹן *Whenever the Ark set out.* A description of the Ark during the journeys of the Israelites in the wilderness. The parallel verse, "When the Ark came to rest," is recited when the Torah is returned to the Ark. Thus the taking of the *Sefer Torah* from the Ark and its return, recall the Ark of the Covenant which accompanied the Israelites in the days of Moses.

כִּי מִצִּיּוֹן תֵּצֵא תוֹרָה *For the Torah shall come forth from Zion.* Part of Isaiah's famous vision (2:2–4) of the end of days.

הוצאת ספר תורה

אֵין־כָּמְוֹךָ בָאֱלֹהִים, אֲדֹנָי, וְאֵין כְּמַעֲשֶׂיךָ: תהלים פו
מַלְכוּתְךָ מַלְכוּת כָּל־עֹלָמִים, וּמֶמְשַׁלְתְּךָ בְּכָל־דּוֹר וָדֹר: תהלים קמה
יהוה מֶלֶךְ, יהוה מָלָךְ, יהוה יִמְלֹךְ לְעֹלָם וָעֶד.
יהוה עֹז לְעַמּוֹ יִתֵּן, יהוה יְבָרֵךְ אֶת־עַמּוֹ בַשָּׁלוֹם: תהלים כט

אַב הָרַחֲמִים, הֵיטִיבָה בִרְצוֹנְךָ אֶת־צִיּוֹן תִּבְנֶה חוֹמוֹת יְרוּשָׁלָֽםִ: תהלים נא
כִּי בְךָ לְבַד בָּטָחְנוּ, מֶלֶךְ אֵל רָם וְנִשָּׂא, אֲדוֹן עוֹלָמִים.

The ארון קודש *is opened and the* קהל *stands. All say:*

וַיְהִי בִּנְסֹעַ הָאָרֹן וַיֹּאמֶר מֹשֶׁה במדבר י
קוּמָה יהוה וְיָפֻצוּ אֹיְבֶיךָ וְיָנֻסוּ מְשַׂנְאֶיךָ מִפָּנֶיךָ:
כִּי מִצִּיּוֹן תֵּצֵא תוֹרָה וּדְבַר־יהוה מִירוּשָׁלָֽםִ: ישעיה ב
בָּרוּךְ שֶׁנָּתַן תּוֹרָה לְעַמּוֹ יִשְׂרָאֵל בִּקְדֻשָּׁתוֹ.

On שבת*, continue with* בְּרִיךְ שְׁמֵהּ *on page 431.*

READING OF THE TORAH
Since the revelation at Mount Sinai, the Jewish people has been a nation defined by a book: the Torah. The Mosaic books are more than sacred literature. They are the written constitution of the house of Israel as a nation under the sovereignty of God, the basis of its collective memory, the record of its covenant with God, the template of its existence as "a kingdom of priests and a holy nation" (Ex. 19:6), and the detailed specification of the task it is called on to perform – to construct a society on the basis of justice and compassion and the inalienable dignity of the human person as the image of God. Just as the Torah is central to Jewish life, so the reading of the Torah is central to the synagogue service.

The penultimate command Moses gave to the Israelites was the institution of a national assembly once every seven years when the king would read the Torah to the people (Deut. 31:10–13). The Tanakh records several key moments in Jewish history when national rededication was accompanied by a public reading of the Torah, most famously in the days of king Josiah (II Kings 23) and Ezra (Neh. 8). According to tradition, Moses ordained that the Torah be read regularly and publicly; a long reading on Shabbat morning and shorter readings on Mondays and Thursdays. Ezra, reinstituting this practice, added the reading on Shabbat afternoon.

The following (The Thirteen Attributes of Mercy) is said three times:

יהוה The Lord, the Lord, compassionate and gracious God, *Ex. 34*
slow to anger, abounding in loving-kindness and truth,
extending loving-kindness to a thousand generations,
forgiving iniquity, rebellion and sin,
and absolving [the guilty who repent].

Each individual says silently, inserting appropriate phrase/s in parentheses:

רִבּוֹנוֹ Master of the Universe, fulfill my heart's requests for good. Satisfy my desire, grant my request, and enable me (*name*, son/daughter of *father's name*), (and my wife/ husband, and my sons/daughters) and all the members of my household to do Your will with a perfect heart. Deliver us from the evil impulse, grant us our share in Your Torah, and make us worthy that Your Presence may rest upon us. Confer on us a spirit of wisdom and understanding, and may there be fulfilled in us the verse: "The spirit of the Lord *Is. 11*
will rest upon him – a spirit of wisdom and understanding, a spirit of counsel and strength, a spirit of knowledge and reverence for the Lord." So too may it be Your will, Lord our God and God of our ancestors, that we be worthy to do deeds that are good in Your sight, and to walk before You in the ways of the upright. Make us holy through Your holiness, so that we may be worthy of a good and long life, and of the World to Come. Guard us from evil deeds and bad times that threaten to bring turmoil to the world. May *Ps. 32*
loving-kindness surround one who trusts in the Lord. Amen.

יִהְיוּ May the words of my mouth and the meditation of my *Ps. 19*
heart find favor before You, Lord, my Rock and Redeemer.

Say the following verse three times:

וַאֲנִי As for me, may my prayer come to You, Lord, *Ps. 69*
at a time of favor. O God, in Your great love,
answer me with Your faithful salvation.

רִבּוֹנוֹ שֶׁל עוֹלָם *Master of the Universe.* The festivals are heightened times of holiness, and the opening of the Ark is a moment when we most intensely feel the transformative energy of the Divine Presence. Thus, when these two sacred moments coincide, we say a personal prayer for God's blessing in our lives and the lives of our family, that we may have a material and spiritual environment that will allow us to serve God without distraction or hindrance.

The following (י״ג מידות הרחמים) *is said three times:*

יהוה, יהוה, אֵל רַחוּם וְחַנּוּן, אֶרֶךְ אַפַּיִם וְרַב־חֶסֶד וֶאֱמֶת: שמות לד
נֹצֵר חֶסֶד לָאֲלָפִים, נֹשֵׂא עָוֹן וָפֶשַׁע וְחַטָּאָה, וְנַקֵּה:

Each individual says silently, inserting appropriate phrase/s in parentheses:

רִבּוֹנוֹ שֶׁל עוֹלָם, מַלֵּא מִשְׁאֲלוֹת לִבִּי לְטוֹבָה, וְהָפֵק רְצוֹנִי וְתֵן שְׁאֵלָתִי, וְזַכֵּה
לִי (פלוני(ת) בֶּן/בַּת פלוני) (וְאִשְׁתִּי/בַּעְלִי וּבָנַי וּבְנוֹתַי) וְכָל בְּנֵי בֵיתִי, לַעֲשׂוֹת
רְצוֹנְךָ בְּלֵבָב שָׁלֵם, וּמַלְּטֵנוּ מִיֵּצֶר הָרָע, וְתֵן חֶלְקֵנוּ בְּתוֹרָתֶךָ, וְזַכֵּנוּ שֶׁתִּשְׁרֶה
שְׁכִינָתְךָ עָלֵינוּ, וְהוֹפַע עָלֵינוּ רוּחַ חָכְמָה וּבִינָה. וְיִתְקַיֵּם בָּנוּ מִקְרָא שֶׁכָּתוּב:
וְנָחָה עָלָיו רוּחַ יהוה, רוּחַ חָכְמָה וּבִינָה, רוּחַ עֵצָה וּגְבוּרָה, רוּחַ דַּעַת וְיִרְאַת ישעיה יא
יהוה: וּבְכֵן יְהִי רָצוֹן מִלְּפָנֶיךָ יהוה אֱלֹהֵינוּ וֵאלֹהֵי אֲבוֹתֵינוּ, שֶׁתְּזַכֵּנוּ לַעֲשׂוֹת
מַעֲשִׂים טוֹבִים בְּעֵינֶיךָ וְלָלֶכֶת בְּדַרְכֵי יְשָׁרִים לְפָנֶיךָ, וְקַדְּשֵׁנוּ בִּקְדֻשָּׁתֶךָ
כְּדֵי שֶׁנִּזְכֶּה לְחַיִּים טוֹבִים וַאֲרוּכִים וּלְחַיֵּי הָעוֹלָם הַבָּא, וְתִשְׁמְרֵנוּ מִמַּעֲשִׂים
רָעִים וּמִשָּׁעוֹת רָעוֹת הַמִּתְרַגְּשׁוֹת לָבוֹא לָעוֹלָם, וְהַבּוֹטֵחַ בַּיהוה חֶסֶד תהלים לב
יְסוֹבְבֶנּוּ: אָמֵן.

יִהְיוּ לְרָצוֹן אִמְרֵי־פִי וְהֶגְיוֹן לִבִּי לְפָנֶיךָ, יהוה צוּרִי וְגֹאֲלִי: תהלים יט

Say the following verse three times:

וַאֲנִי תְפִלָּתִי־לְךָ יהוה, עֵת רָצוֹן, אֱלֹהִים בְּרָב־חַסְדֶּךָ תהלים סט
עֲנֵנִי בֶּאֱמֶת יִשְׁעֶךָ:

THE THIRTEEN ATTRIBUTES OF MERCY

The "Thirteen attributes of compassion" is the name given by the sages to God's declaration to Moses when he prayed on the people's behalf after the golden calf. They constitute God's Self-definition as the source of compassion and pardon that frames the moral life. According to the Talmud (*Rosh HaShana* 17b), God made a covenant that no prayer for forgiveness accompanied by these words would go unanswered. This and the following prayer are not said on Shabbat since we do not make personal requests of God on that day.

On all days continue:

בְּרִיךְ Blessed is the name of the Master of the Universe. Blessed is Your crown and Your place. May Your favor always be with Your people Israel. Show Your people the salvation of Your right hand in Your Temple. Grant us the gift of Your good light, and accept our prayers in mercy. May it be Your will to prolong our life in goodness. May I be counted among the righteous, so that You will have compassion on me and protect me and all that is mine and all that is Your people Israel's. You feed all; You sustain all; You rule over all; You rule over kings, for sovereignty is Yours. I am a servant of the Holy One, blessed be He, before whom and before whose glorious Torah I bow at all times. Not in man do I trust, nor on any angel do I rely, but on the God of heaven who is the God of truth, whose Torah is truth, whose prophets speak truth, and who abounds in acts of love and truth. ▸ In Him I trust, and to His holy and glorious name I offer praises. May it be Your will to open my heart to the Torah, and to fulfill the wishes of my heart and of the hearts of all Your people Israel for good, for life, and for peace. *Zohar, Vayak-hel*

Two Torah scrolls are removed from the Ark. The Leader takes one in his right arm and, followed by the congregation, says:

Listen, Israel: the LORD is our God, the LORD is One. *Deut. 6*

Leader then congregation:

One is our God; great is our Master;
holy is His name.

The Leader turns to face the Ark, bows and says:

Magnify the LORD with me, and let us exalt His name together. *Ps. 34*

The Ark is closed. The Leader carries the Torah scroll to the bima and the congregation says:

לְךָ Yours, LORD, are the greatness and the power, the glory and the majesty and splendor, for everything in heaven and earth is Yours. Yours, LORD, is the kingdom; You are exalted as Head over all. *1 Chr. 29*

---

of reciting it has its origins in the circle of mystics in Safed associated with Rabbi Isaac Luria. It is a beautiful prayer in which we yearn to be open to the Torah and faithful to our vocation as a servant of the Holy One, for the highest privilege is to serve the Author of all. As the doors of the Ark open, so we open our hearts.

On all days continue:

זוהר ויקהל בְּרִיךְ שְׁמֵהּ דְּמָרֵא עָלְמָא, בְּרִיךְ כִּתְרָךְ וְאַתְרָךְ. יְהֵא רְעוּתָךְ עִם עַמָּךְ יִשְׂרָאֵל לְעָלַם, וּפֻרְקַן יְמִינָךְ אַחֲזֵי לְעַמָּךְ בְּבֵית מַקְדְּשָׁךְ, וּלְאַמְטוּיֵי לַנָא מִטּוּב נְהוֹרָךְ, וּלְקַבֵּל צְלוֹתַנָא בְּרַחֲמִין. יְהֵא רַעֲוָא קֳדָמָךְ דְּתוֹרִיךְ לַן חַיִּין בְּטִיבוּ, וְלֶהֱוֵי אֲנָא פְקִידָא בְּגוֹ צַדִּיקַיָּא, לְמִרְחַם עֲלַי וּלְמִנְטַר יָתִי וְיַת כָּל דִּי לִי וְדִי לְעַמָּךְ יִשְׂרָאֵל. אַנְתְּ הוּא זָן לְכֹלָּא וּמְפַרְנֵס לְכֹלָּא, אַנְתְּ הוּא שַׁלִּיט עַל כֹּלָּא, אַנְתְּ הוּא דְּשַׁלִּיט עַל מַלְכַיָּא, וּמַלְכוּתָא דִּילָךְ הִיא. אֲנָא עַבְדָּא דְקֻדְשָׁא בְּרִיךְ הוּא, דְּסָגֵדְנָא קַמֵּהּ וּמִקַּמֵּי דִּיקַר אוֹרַיְתֵהּ בְּכָל עִדָּן וְעִדָּן. לָא עַל אֱנָשׁ רָחִיצְנָא וְלָא עַל בַּר אֱלָהִין סָמִיכְנָא, אֶלָּא בֶּאֱלָהָא דִשְׁמַיָּא, דְּהוּא אֱלָהָא קְשׁוֹט, וְאוֹרַיְתֵהּ קְשׁוֹט, וּנְבִיאוֹהִי קְשׁוֹט, וּמַסְגֵּא לְמֶעְבַּד טַבְוָן וּקְשׁוֹט. ◂ בֵּהּ אֲנָא רָחִיץ, וְלִשְׁמֵהּ קַדִּישָׁא יַקִּירָא אֲנָא אֵמַר תֻּשְׁבְּחָן. יְהֵא רַעֲוָא קֳדָמָךְ דְּתִפְתַּח לִבַּאי בְּאוֹרַיְתָא, וְתַשְׁלִים מִשְׁאֲלִין דְּלִבַּאי וְלִבָּא דְכָל עַמָּךְ יִשְׂרָאֵל לְטָב וּלְחַיִּין וְלִשְׁלָם.

Two ספרי תורה *are removed from the* ארון קודש. *The* שליח צבור *takes one in his right arm, and, followed by the* קהל*, says:*

דברים ו שְׁמַע יִשְׂרָאֵל, יהוה אֱלֹהֵינוּ, יהוה אֶחָד׃

קהל *then* שליח ציבור:

אֶחָד אֱלֹהֵינוּ, גָּדוֹל אֲדוֹנֵינוּ, קָדוֹשׁ שְׁמוֹ.

The שליח ציבור *turns to face the* ארון קודש*, bows and says:*

תהלים לד גַּדְּלוּ לַיהוה אִתִּי וּנְרוֹמְמָה שְׁמוֹ יַחְדָּו׃

The ארון קודש *is closed. The* שליח ציבור *carries the* ספר תורה *to the* בימה *and the* קהל *says:*

דברי הימים א׳ כט לְךָ יהוה הַגְּדֻלָּה וְהַגְּבוּרָה וְהַתִּפְאֶרֶת וְהַנֵּצַח וְהַהוֹד, כִּי־כֹל בַּשָּׁמַיִם וּבָאָרֶץ, לְךָ יהוה הַמַּמְלָכָה וְהַמִּתְנַשֵּׂא לְכֹל לְרֹאשׁ׃

בְּרִיךְ שְׁמֵהּ *Blessed is the name.* This passage, from the mystical text, the *Zohar,* is prefaced in its original context with the words: "Rabbi Shimon said: When the scroll of the Torah is taken out to be read in public, the Gates of Compassion are opened, and love is aroused on high. Therefore one should say [at this time] ..." The words "Blessed is the name" then follow. The custom

רוֹמְמוּ Exalt the LORD our God and bow to His footstool; He is holy. Ps. 99
Exalt the LORD our God, and bow at His holy mountain, for holy is the LORD our God.

Over all may the name of the Supreme King of kings, the Holy One blessed be He, be magnified and sanctified, praised and glorified, exalted and extolled, in the worlds that He has created – this world and the World to Come – in accordance with His will, and the will of those who fear Him, and the will of the whole house of Israel. He is the Rock of worlds, LORD of all creatures, God of all souls, who dwells in the spacious heights and inhabits the high heavens of old. His holiness is over the Ḥayyot and over the throne of glory. Therefore may Your name, LORD our God, be sanctified among us in the sight of all that lives. Let us sing before Him a new song,
as it is written: "Sing to God, make music for His name, extol Him who rides the Ps. 68
clouds – the LORD is His name – and exult before Him." And may we see Him eye
to eye when He returns to His abode as it is written: "For they shall see eye to eye Is. 52
when the LORD returns to Zion." And it is said: "Then will the glory of the LORD be Is. 40
revealed, and all mankind together shall see that the mouth of the LORD has spoken."

Father of mercy, have compassion on the people borne by Him. May He remember the covenant with the mighty (patriarchs), and deliver us from evil times. May He reproach the evil instinct in the people by Him, and graciously grant that we be an eternal remnant. May He fulfill in good measure our requests for salvation and compassion.

The Torah scroll is placed on the bima and the Gabbai calls a Kohen to the Torah.

וְיַעֲזֹר May He help, shield and save all who seek refuge in Him, and let us say: Amen. Let us all render greatness to our God and give honor to the Torah. *Let the Kohen come forward. Arise (*name* son of *father's name*), the Kohen.

**If no Kohen is present, a Levi or Yisrael is called up as follows:*

/As there is no Kohen, arise (*name* son of *father's name*) in place of a Kohen./

Blessed is He who, in His holiness, gave the Torah to His people Israel.

The congregation followed by the Gabbai:

You who cling to the LORD your God are all alive today. Deut. 4

The Torah portions for the first two days of Sukkot can be found from page 440.

---

known as the *ba'al koreh*), "so as not to shame those who do not know how to read" their own portions (see *Beit Yosef, Oraḥ Ḥayyim* 141). Instead, the *oleh* says the blessings before and after the portion, and recites the text silently along with the reader.

תהלים צט רוֹמְמוּ יהוה אֱלֹהֵינוּ וְהִשְׁתַּחֲווּ לַהֲדֹם רַגְלָיו, קָדוֹשׁ הוּא: רוֹמְמוּ
יהוה אֱלֹהֵינוּ וְהִשְׁתַּחֲווּ לְהַר קָדְשׁוֹ, כִּי־קָדוֹשׁ יהוה אֱלֹהֵינוּ:

עַל הַכֹּל יִתְגַּדַּל וְיִתְקַדַּשׁ וְיִשְׁתַּבַּח וְיִתְפָּאַר וְיִתְרוֹמַם וְיִתְנַשֵּׂא שְׁמוֹ שֶׁל מֶלֶךְ
מַלְכֵי הַמְּלָכִים הַקָּדוֹשׁ בָּרוּךְ הוּא בָּעוֹלָמוֹת שֶׁבָּרָא, הָעוֹלָם הַזֶּה וְהָעוֹלָם הַבָּא,
כִּרְצוֹנוֹ וְכִרְצוֹן יְרֵאָיו וְכִרְצוֹן כָּל בֵּית יִשְׂרָאֵל. צוּר הָעוֹלָמִים, אֲדוֹן כָּל הַבְּרִיּוֹת,
אֱלוֹהַּ כָּל הַנְּפָשׁוֹת, הַיּוֹשֵׁב בְּמֶרְחֲבֵי מָרוֹם, הַשּׁוֹכֵן בִּשְׁמֵי שְׁמֵי קֶדֶם, קְדֻשָּׁתוֹ עַל
הַחַיּוֹת, וּקְדֻשָּׁתוֹ עַל כִּסֵּא הַכָּבוֹד. וּבְכֵן יִתְקַדַּשׁ שִׁמְךָ בָּנוּ יהוה אֱלֹהֵינוּ לְעֵינֵי
תהלים סח כָּל חָי, וְנֹאמַר לְפָנָיו שִׁיר חָדָשׁ, כַּכָּתוּב: שִׁירוּ לֵאלֹהִים זַמְּרוּ שְׁמוֹ, סֹלּוּ לָרֹכֵב
ישעיה נב בָּעֲרָבוֹת, בְּיָהּ שְׁמוֹ, וְעִלְזוּ לְפָנָיו: וְנִרְאֵהוּ עַיִן בְּעַיִן בְּשׁוּבוֹ אֶל נָוֵהוּ, כַּכָּתוּב: כִּי
ישעיה מ עַיִן בְּעַיִן יִרְאוּ בְּשׁוּב יהוה צִיּוֹן: וְנֶאֱמַר: וְנִגְלָה כְּבוֹד יהוה, וְרָאוּ כָל־בָּשָׂר יַחְדָּו
כִּי פִּי יהוה דִּבֵּר:

אַב הָרַחֲמִים הוּא יְרַחֵם עַם עֲמוּסִים, וְיִזְכֹּר בְּרִית אֵיתָנִים, וְיַצִּיל נַפְשׁוֹתֵינוּ מִן
הַשָּׁעוֹת הָרָעוֹת, וְיִגְעַר בְּיֵצֶר הָרָע מִן הַנְּשׂוּאִים, וְיָחֹן אוֹתָנוּ לִפְלֵיטַת עוֹלָמִים,
וִימַלֵּא מִשְׁאֲלוֹתֵינוּ בְּמִדָּה טוֹבָה יְשׁוּעָה וְרַחֲמִים.

The ספר תורה *is placed on the* שולחן *and the* גבאי *calls a* כהן *to the* תורה.

וְיַעֲזֹר וְיָגֵן וְיוֹשִׁיעַ לְכָל הַחוֹסִים בּוֹ, וְנֹאמַר אָמֵן. הַכֹּל הָבוּ גֹדֶל לֵאלֹהֵינוּ
וּתְנוּ כָבוֹד לַתּוֹרָה. *כֹּהֵן קְרַב, יַעֲמֹד (פלוני בֶּן פלוני) הַכֹּהֵן.

**If no* כהן *is present, a* לוי *or* ישראל *is called up as follows:*

/אֵין כָּאן כֹּהֵן, יַעֲמֹד (פלוני בֶּן פלוני) בִּמְקוֹם כֹּהֵן./

בָּרוּךְ שֶׁנָּתַן תּוֹרָה לְעַמּוֹ יִשְׂרָאֵל בִּקְדֻשָּׁתוֹ.

The קהל *followed by the* גבאי*:*

דברים ד וְאַתֶּם הַדְּבֵקִים בַּיהוה אֱלֹהֵיכֶם חַיִּים כֻּלְּכֶם הַיּוֹם:

The תורה *portions for the first two days of* סוכות
can be found from page 441.

ASCENT TO THE TORAH

The original custom was that each of those called to the Torah read his own portion. Not everyone was able to do this, so the practice developed of entrusting the reading to one with expertise (commonly, though ungrammatically,

The Reader shows the oleh the section to be read. The oleh touches the scroll at that place with the tzitzit of his tallit, which he then kisses. Holding the handles of the scroll, he says:

Oleh: Bless the LORD, the blessed One.

Cong: Bless the LORD, the blessed One, for ever and all time.

Oleh: Bless the LORD, the blessed One, for ever and all time.
Blessed are You, LORD our God, King of the Universe,
who has chosen us from all peoples
and has given us His Torah.
Blessed are You, LORD, Giver of the Torah.

After the reading, the oleh says:

Oleh: Blessed are You, LORD our God, King of the Universe,
who has given us the Torah of truth,
planting everlasting life in our midst.
Blessed are You, LORD, Giver of the Torah.

One who has survived a situation of danger, says:

Blessed are You, LORD our God, King of the Universe, who bestows good on the unworthy, who has bestowed on me much good.

The congregation responds:

Amen. May He who bestowed much good on you
continue to bestow on you much good, Selah.

After a Bar Mitzva boy has finished the Torah blessing, his father says aloud:

Blessed is He who has released me from the responsibility for this child.

אֲשֶׁר נָתַן לָנוּ תּוֹרַת אֱמֶת *Who has given us the Torah of truth.* An act of affirmation following the reading. There is truth that is thought and there is truth that is lived. Judaism is about the transformative truths that we enact when we align our will with that of God.

וְחַיֵּי עוֹלָם *Everlasting life.* Immortality lies not in how long we live but in how we live. Reaching out to the Eternal and finding Him reaching out to us, we touch eternity.

The קורא *shows the* עולה *the section to be read. The* עולה *touches the scroll at that place with the* ציצית *of his* טלית*, which he then kisses. Holding the handles of the scroll, he says:*

עולה: בָּרְכוּ אֶת יהוה הַמְבֹרָךְ.

קהל: בָּרוּךְ יהוה הַמְבֹרָךְ לְעוֹלָם וָעֶד.

עולה: בָּרוּךְ יהוה הַמְבֹרָךְ לְעוֹלָם וָעֶד.
בָּרוּךְ אַתָּה יהוה, אֱלֹהֵינוּ מֶלֶךְ הָעוֹלָם
אֲשֶׁר בָּחַר בָּנוּ מִכָּל הָעַמִּים וְנָתַן לָנוּ אֶת תּוֹרָתוֹ.
בָּרוּךְ אַתָּה יהוה, נוֹתֵן הַתּוֹרָה.

After the קריאת התורה*, the* עולה *says:*

עולה: בָּרוּךְ אַתָּה יהוה אֱלֹהֵינוּ מֶלֶךְ הָעוֹלָם
אֲשֶׁר נָתַן לָנוּ תּוֹרַת אֱמֶת וְחַיֵּי עוֹלָם נָטַע בְּתוֹכֵנוּ.
בָּרוּךְ אַתָּה יהוה, נוֹתֵן הַתּוֹרָה.

One who has survived a situation of danger, says:

בָּרוּךְ אַתָּה יהוה אֱלֹהֵינוּ מֶלֶךְ הָעוֹלָם
הַגּוֹמֵל לְחַיָּבִים טוֹבוֹת, שֶׁגְּמָלַנִי כָּל טוֹב.

The קהל *responds:*

אָמֵן. מִי שֶׁגְּמָלְךָ כָּל טוֹב הוּא יִגְמָלְךָ כָּל טוֹב, סֶלָה.

After a בר מצווה *has finished the* תורה *blessing, his father says aloud:*

בָּרוּךְ שֶׁפְּטָרַנִי מֵעָנְשׁוֹ שֶׁלָּזֶה.

בָּרוּךְ יהוה *Bless the Lord.* An invitation to the congregation to join in blessing God, similar to the one that precedes communal prayer in the morning and evening services.

אֲשֶׁר בָּחַר בָּנוּ מִכָּל הָעַמִּים *Who has chosen us from all peoples.* This ancient blessing, to be said before Torah study as well as before the public reading of the Torah, makes it clear that chosenness is not a right but a responsibility.

FOR AN OLEH

May He who blessed our fathers, Abraham, Isaac and Jacob, bless (*name, son of father's name*) who has been called up in honor of the All-Present, in honor of the Torah, and in honor of (*On Shabbat:* the Sabbath and in honor of) the festival. As a reward for this, may the Holy One, blessed be He, protect and deliver him from all trouble and distress, all infection and illness, and send blessing and success to all the work of his hands, and may he merit to go up to Jerusalem for the festivals, together with all Israel, his brethren, and let us say: Amen.

FOR A SICK MAN

May He who blessed our fathers, Abraham, Isaac and Jacob, Moses and Aaron, David and Solomon, bless and heal one who is ill, (*sick person's name*, son of *mother's name*), on whose behalf (*name of the one making the offering*) is making a contribution to charity. As a reward for this, may the Holy One, blessed be He, be filled with compassion for him, to restore his health, cure him, strengthen and revive him, sending him a swift and full recovery from heaven to all his 248 organs and 365 sinews, amongst the other sick ones in Israel, a healing of the spirit and a healing of the body – though on (*On Shabbat:* the Sabbath and) festivals it is forbidden to cry out, may healing be quick to come – now, swiftly and soon, and let us say: Amen.

FOR A SICK WOMAN

May He who blessed our fathers, Abraham, Isaac and Jacob, Moses and Aaron, David and Solomon, bless and heal one who is ill, (*sick person's name*, daughter of *mother's name*), on whose behalf (*name of the one making the offering*) is making a contribution to charity. As a reward for this, may the Holy One, blessed be He, be filled with compassion for her, to restore her health, cure her, strengthen and revive her, sending her a swift and full recovery from heaven to all her organs and sinews, amongst the other sick ones in Israel, a healing of the spirit and a healing of the body – though on (*On Shabbat:* the Sabbath and) festivals it is forbidden to cry out, may healing be quick to come – now, swiftly and soon, and let us say: Amen.

מי שברך לעולה לתורה

מִי שֶׁבֵּרַךְ אֲבוֹתֵינוּ אַבְרָהָם יִצְחָק וְיַעֲקֹב, הוּא יְבָרֵךְ אֶת (פלוני בֶּן פלוני), בַּעֲבוּר שֶׁעָלָה לִכְבוֹד הַמָּקוֹם וְלִכְבוֹד הַתּוֹרָה (בשבת: וְלִכְבוֹד הַשַּׁבָּת) וְלִכְבוֹד הָרֶגֶל. בִּשְׂכַר זֶה הַקָּדוֹשׁ בָּרוּךְ הוּא יִשְׁמְרֵהוּ וְיַצִּילֵהוּ מִכָּל צָרָה וְצוּקָה וּמִכָּל נֶגַע וּמַחֲלָה, וְיִשְׁלַח בְּרָכָה וְהַצְלָחָה בְּכָל מַעֲשֵׂה יָדָיו, וְיִזְכֶּה לַעֲלוֹת לָרֶגֶל עִם כָּל יִשְׂרָאֵל אֶחָיו, וְנֹאמַר אָמֵן.

מי שברך לחולֶה

מִי שֶׁבֵּרַךְ אֲבוֹתֵינוּ אַבְרָהָם יִצְחָק וְיַעֲקֹב, מֹשֶׁה וְאַהֲרֹן דָּוִד וּשְׁלֹמֹה הוּא יְבָרֵךְ וִירַפֵּא אֶת הַחוֹלֶה (פלוני בֶּן פלונית) בַּעֲבוּר שֶׁ(פלוני בֶּן פלוני) נוֹדֵר צְדָקָה בַּעֲבוּרוֹ. בִּשְׂכַר זֶה הַקָּדוֹשׁ בָּרוּךְ הוּא יִמָּלֵא רַחֲמִים עָלָיו לְהַחֲלִימוֹ וּלְרַפֹּאתוֹ וּלְהַחֲזִיקוֹ וּלְהַחֲיוֹתוֹ וְיִשְׁלַח לוֹ מְהֵרָה רְפוּאָה שְׁלֵמָה מִן הַשָּׁמַיִם לִרְמַ״ח אֵבָרָיו וּשְׁסָ״ה גִּידָיו בְּתוֹךְ שְׁאָר חוֹלֵי יִשְׂרָאֵל, רְפוּאַת הַנֶּפֶשׁ וּרְפוּאַת הַגּוּף. יוֹם טוֹב הוּא מִלִּזְעֹק (בשבת: שַׁבָּת וְיוֹם טוֹב הֵם) וּרְפוּאָה קְרוֹבָה לָבוֹא, הַשְׁתָּא בַּעֲגָלָא וּבִזְמַן קָרִיב, וְנֹאמַר אָמֵן.

מי שברך לחולָה

מִי שֶׁבֵּרַךְ אֲבוֹתֵינוּ אַבְרָהָם יִצְחָק וְיַעֲקֹב, מֹשֶׁה וְאַהֲרֹן דָּוִד וּשְׁלֹמֹה הוּא יְבָרֵךְ וִירַפֵּא אֶת הַחוֹלָה (פלונית בַּת פלונית) בַּעֲבוּר שֶׁ(פלוני בֶּן פלוני) נוֹדֵר צְדָקָה בַּעֲבוּרָהּ. בִּשְׂכַר זֶה הַקָּדוֹשׁ בָּרוּךְ הוּא יִמָּלֵא רַחֲמִים עָלֶיהָ לְהַחֲלִימָהּ וּלְרַפֹּאתָהּ וּלְהַחֲזִיקָהּ וּלְהַחֲיוֹתָהּ וְיִשְׁלַח לָהּ מְהֵרָה רְפוּאָה שְׁלֵמָה מִן הַשָּׁמַיִם לְכָל אֵבָרֶיהָ וּלְכָל גִּידֶיהָ בְּתוֹךְ שְׁאָר חוֹלֵי יִשְׂרָאֵל, רְפוּאַת הַנֶּפֶשׁ וּרְפוּאַת הַגּוּף. יוֹם טוֹב הוּא (בשבת: שַׁבָּת וְיוֹם טוֹב הֵם) מִלִּזְעֹק וּרְפוּאָה קְרוֹבָה לָבוֹא, הַשְׁתָּא בַּעֲגָלָא וּבִזְמַן קָרִיב, וְנֹאמַר אָמֵן.

ON THE BIRTH OF A SON

May He who blessed our fathers, Abraham, Isaac and Jacob, Moses and Aaron, David and Solomon, Sarah, Rebecca, Rachel and Leah, bless the woman (*name*, daughter of *father's name*) who has given birth, and her son who has been born to her as an auspicious sign. Her husband, the child's father, is making a contribution to charity. As a reward for this, may father and mother merit to bring the child into the covenant of Abraham and to a life of Torah, to the marriage canopy and to good deeds, and let us say: Amen.

ON THE BIRTH OF A DAUGHTER

May He who blessed our fathers, Abraham, Isaac and Jacob, Moses and Aaron, David and Solomon, Sarah, Rebecca, Rachel and Leah, bless the woman (*name*, daughter of *father's name*) who has given birth, and her daughter who has been born to her as an auspicious sign; and may her name be called in Israel (*baby's name*, daughter of *father's name*). Her husband, the child's father, is making a contribution to charity. As a reward for this, may father and mother merit to raise her to a life of Torah, to the marriage canopy, and to good deeds, and let us say: Amen.

FOR A BAR MITZVA

May He who blessed our fathers, Abraham, Isaac and Jacob, bless (*name*, son of *father's name*) who has completed thirteen years and attained the age of the commandments, who has been called to the Torah to give praise and thanks to God, may His name be blessed, for all the good He has bestowed on him. May the Holy One, blessed be He, protect and sustain him and direct his heart to be perfect with God, to walk in His ways and keep the commandments all the days of his life, and let us say: Amen.

FOR A BAT MITZVA

May He who blessed our fathers, Abraham, Isaac and Jacob, Sarah, Rebecca, Rachel and Leah, bless (*name*, daughter of *father's name*) who has completed twelve years and attained the age of the commandments, and gives praise and thanks to God, may His name be blessed, for all the good He has bestowed on her. May the Holy One, blessed be He, protect and sustain her and direct her heart to be perfect with God, to walk in His ways and keep the commandments all the days of her life, and let us say: Amen.

מי שברך ליולדת בן

מִי שֶׁבֵּרַךְ אֲבוֹתֵינוּ אַבְרָהָם יִצְחָק וְיַעֲקֹב, מֹשֶׁה וְאַהֲרֹן דָּוִד וּשְׁלֹמֹה, שָׂרָה רִבְקָה רָחֵל וְלֵאָה הוּא יְבָרֵךְ אֶת הָאִשָּׁה הַיּוֹלֶדֶת (פלונית בַּת פלוני) וְאֶת בְּנָהּ שֶׁנּוֹלַד לָהּ לְמַזָּל טוֹב בַּעֲבוּר שֶׁבַּעְלָהּ וְאָבִיו נוֹדֵר צְדָקָה בַּעֲדָם. בִּשְׂכַר זֶה יִזְכּוּ אָבִיו וְאִמּוֹ לְהַכְנִיסוֹ בִּבְרִיתוֹ שֶׁל אַבְרָהָם אָבִינוּ וּלְגַדְּלוֹ לְתוֹרָה וּלְחֻפָּה וּלְמַעֲשִׂים טוֹבִים, וְנֹאמַר אָמֵן.

מי שברך ליולדת בת

מִי שֶׁבֵּרַךְ אֲבוֹתֵינוּ אַבְרָהָם יִצְחָק וְיַעֲקֹב, מֹשֶׁה וְאַהֲרֹן דָּוִד וּשְׁלֹמֹה, שָׂרָה רִבְקָה רָחֵל וְלֵאָה הוּא יְבָרֵךְ אֶת הָאִשָּׁה הַיּוֹלֶדֶת (פלונית בַּת פלוני) וְאֶת בִּתָּהּ שֶׁנּוֹלְדָה לָהּ לְמַזָּל טוֹב וְיִקָּרֵא שְׁמָהּ בְּיִשְׂרָאֵל (פלונית בַּת פלוני), בַּעֲבוּר שֶׁבַּעְלָהּ וְאָבִיהָ נוֹדֵר צְדָקָה בַּעֲדָן. בִּשְׂכַר זֶה יִזְכּוּ אָבִיהָ וְאִמָּהּ לְגַדְּלָהּ לְתוֹרָה וּלְחֻפָּה וּלְמַעֲשִׂים טוֹבִים, וְנֹאמַר אָמֵן.

מי שברך לבר מצווה

מִי שֶׁבֵּרַךְ אֲבוֹתֵינוּ אַבְרָהָם יִצְחָק וְיַעֲקֹב הוּא יְבָרֵךְ אֶת (פלוני בֶּן פלוני) שֶׁמָּלְאוּ לוֹ שְׁלֹשׁ עֶשְׂרֵה שָׁנָה וְהִגִּיעַ לְמִצְוֹת, וְעָלָה לַתּוֹרָה, לָתֵת שֶׁבַח וְהוֹדָיָה לְהַשֵּׁם יִתְבָּרַךְ עַל כָּל הַטּוֹבָה שֶׁגָּמַל אִתּוֹ. יִשְׁמְרֵהוּ הַקָּדוֹשׁ בָּרוּךְ הוּא וִיחַיֵּהוּ, וִיכוֹנֵן אֶת לִבּוֹ לִהְיוֹת שָׁלֵם עִם יהוה וְלָלֶכֶת בִּדְרָכָיו וְלִשְׁמֹר מִצְוֹתָיו כָּל הַיָּמִים, וְנֹאמַר אָמֵן.

מי שברך לבת מצווה

מִי שֶׁבֵּרַךְ אֲבוֹתֵינוּ אַבְרָהָם יִצְחָק וְיַעֲקֹב, שָׂרָה רִבְקָה רָחֵל וְלֵאָה, הוּא יְבָרֵךְ אֶת (פלונית בַּת פלוני) שֶׁמָּלְאוּ לָהּ שְׁתֵּים עֶשְׂרֵה שָׁנָה וְהִגִּיעָה לְמִצְוֹת, וְנוֹתֶנֶת שֶׁבַח וְהוֹדָיָה לְהַשֵּׁם יִתְבָּרַךְ עַל כָּל הַטּוֹבָה שֶׁגָּמַל אִתָּהּ. יִשְׁמְרֶהָ הַקָּדוֹשׁ בָּרוּךְ הוּא וִיחַיֶּהָ, וִיכוֹנֵן אֶת לִבָּהּ לִהְיוֹת שָׁלֵם עִם יהוה וְלָלֶכֶת בִּדְרָכָיו וְלִשְׁמֹר מִצְוֹתָיו כָּל הַיָּמִים, וְנֹאמַר אָמֵן.

TORAH READING FOR THE FIRST AND SECOND DAY OF YOM TOV

On the first two days of Sukkot say (in Israel, the first day only):

The LORD spoke to Moses, saying: When a bullock or lamb or goat is born, it shall remain with its mother for seven days; from the eighth day onwards it will be accepted as a sacrifice, a fire-offering to the LORD. Whether a bullock or a sheep, you may not slaughter the animal and its offspring on the same day. If you bring an offering of thanksgiving to God, offer it so that it will be accepted from you. It must be eaten on that very day; let none of it remain until morning; I am the LORD. Safeguard My commandments and perform them; I am the LORD. Do not profane My holy name; I shall be sanctified among the children of Israel; I am the LORD who sanctifies you, who has taken you out of the land of Egypt to be your God: I am the LORD. *Lev. 22:26–23:44*

The LORD spoke to Moses, saying: Speak to the children of Israel, saying to them: The appointed times of the LORD which you shall proclaim to be days of sacred assembly: these are My appointed times: For six days shall work be done, but the seventh day is a Sabbath of utter rest, a sacred assembly; *(Shabbat* LEVI)

---

extinction of species. If either parent or child survives, they can have further offspring, but not if both are killed (see *Bereshit Raba* 75:13).

אֲשֶׁר־תִּקְרְאוּ אֹתָם *Which you shall proclaim.* The determination of the calendar – whether a month is twenty-nine or thirty days, and whether to make a year a leap year by adding a month – is handed to the authority of the human court. The fixing of the calendar was the first command given to the Israelites as a people (Ex. 12:2). Only in Israel does the court have this authority, so in the fourth century, when the center of Jewish life moved to Babylon, the court authorized a decision to determine the calendar on the basis of astronomical calculation, rather than monthly and yearly decisions of the court.

אֵלֶּה הֵם מוֹעֲדָי *These are My appointed times.* The word *mo'ed* has the connotation of "meeting" (see Exodus 33:7 and Rashi ad loc.). These were days on which God and Israel "met." They were times designated for a collective encounter with the Divine.

שַׁבָּת *Sabbath.* Here included among the festivals. Shabbat means to cease,

קריאה ליום הראשון והשני של יום טוב

On the first two days of סוכות *say* (*in* ארץ ישראל, *the first day only*):

וַיְדַבֵּר יהוה אֶל־מֹשֶׁה לֵּאמֹר: שׁוֹר אוֹ־כֶשֶׂב אוֹ־עֵז כִּי יִוָּלֵד וְהָיָה ויקרא כב: כו–כג:מד
שִׁבְעַת יָמִים תַּחַת אִמּוֹ וּמִיּוֹם הַשְּׁמִינִי וָהָלְאָה יֵרָצֶה לְקָרְבַּן
אִשֶּׁה לַיהוה: וְשׁוֹר אוֹ־שֶׂה אֹתוֹ וְאֶת־בְּנוֹ לֹא תִשְׁחֲטוּ בְּיוֹם
אֶחָד: וְכִי־תִזְבְּחוּ זֶבַח־תּוֹדָה לַיהוה לִרְצֹנְכֶם תִּזְבָּחוּ: בַּיּוֹם
הַהוּא יֵאָכֵל לֹא־תוֹתִירוּ מִמֶּנּוּ עַד־בֹּקֶר אֲנִי יהוה: וּשְׁמַרְתֶּם
מִצְוֺתַי וַעֲשִׂיתֶם אֹתָם אֲנִי יהוה: וְלֹא תְחַלְּלוּ אֶת־שֵׁם קָדְשִׁי
וְנִקְדַּשְׁתִּי בְּתוֹךְ בְּנֵי יִשְׂרָאֵל אֲנִי יהוה מְקַדִּשְׁכֶם: הַמּוֹצִיא אֶתְכֶם
מֵאֶרֶץ מִצְרַיִם לִהְיוֹת לָכֶם לֵאלֹהִים אֲנִי יהוה:

וַיְדַבֵּר יהוה אֶל־מֹשֶׁה לֵּאמֹר: דַּבֵּר אֶל־בְּנֵי יִשְׂרָאֵל וְאָמַרְתָּ (בשבת לוי)
אֲלֵהֶם מוֹעֲדֵי יהוה אֲשֶׁר־תִּקְרְאוּ אֹתָם מִקְרָאֵי קֹדֶשׁ אֵלֶּה
הֵם מוֹעֲדָי: שֵׁשֶׁת יָמִים תֵּעָשֶׂה מְלָאכָה וּבַיּוֹם הַשְּׁבִיעִי שַׁבַּת

TORAH READING FOR THE FIRST TWO DAYS

The core reading is Leviticus 23, the first of three extended accounts of the festivals in the Torah. This sets out the basic structure of the Jewish calendar as a rhythm of holiness in time. The second, in Numbers 28–29, is a detailed account of the sacrifices to be offered on these days. The third, in Deuteronomy 16, emphasizes the pilgrimage character of Pesaḥ, Shavuot and Sukkot, together with the principle of social inclusion – they were days on which the widow, orphan, Levite, and stranger were all to be included in the celebration. Note the significance of the number seven in the architectonics of holy time. The seventh day, Shabbat, is holy. There are seven other holy days: the first and last day of Pesaḥ, Shavuot, Rosh HaShana, Yom Kippur, Sukkot and Shemini Atzeret. The greatest concentration of festivals is in the seventh month.

אֹתוֹ וְאֶת־בְּנוֹ *The animal and its offspring.* Maimonides says that the reason is compassion. The maternal instinct is strong in animals as in humans, and it is cruel to kill young animals in the sight of the mother. The same logic applies to the rule of sending the mother bird away (*Guide for the Perplexed* 3:48). Others give an ecological explanation. To kill both parent and child is to risk the

you may not do any work. It is a Sabbath for the LORD in all of your dwellings.

These are the appointed times of the LORD, sacred assemblies, which you shall announce in their due seasons: In the first month, on the fourteenth of that month, in the afternoon, the Pesaḥ [offering shall be brought] to the LORD. And the fifteenth day of that month will be the festival of Matzot to the LORD; for seven days you shall eat matzot. On the first day there will be a sacred assembly; you shall do no laborious work. And you shall bring an offering consumed by fire to the LORD on each of the seven days; on the seventh day there shall be a sacred assembly: you shall do no laborious work.

LEVI (*Shabbat* SHELISHI)

The LORD spoke to Moses, saying: Speak to the children of Israel and tell them: When you enter the land which I am giving you, and you harvest its grains, you shall bring the first omer measure of your harvest to the priest. He shall wave the omer in the presence of the LORD so that it may be accepted from you; the priest shall wave it on the day following the [Pesaḥ] rest day. And on the day of waving the omer, you shall offer an unblemished yearling

(*Shabbat* REVI'I)

---

less, since the festival was preceded by the offering of the Pesaḥ, the Paschal Lamb, it eventually gave its name to the whole. The word *ḥag*, "festival," has the specific meaning of a pilgrimage, i.e., a journey to the central place of worship, the Temple.

מְלֶאכֶת עֲבֹדָה *Laborious work.* There is a fundamental difference between *melakha*, "work," forbidden on Shabbat, and *melekhet avoda*, "burdensome work," forbidden on festivals. The Torah itself (Ex. 12:16) clarifies this distinction: work involved in the preparation of food is work but not burdensome; therefore it is forbidden on the Sabbath but permitted on festivals.

מִמָּחֳרַת הַשַּׁבָּת *The day following the [Pesaḥ] rest day.* The meaning of this phrase became the cause of one of the great controversies in Judaism between the Pharisees and those groups that did not accept the authority of the Oral Law, and thus read "the Sabbath" as meaning the seventh day of the week.

שַׁבָּתוֹן מִקְרָא־קֹדֶשׁ כָּל־מְלָאכָה לֹא תַעֲשׂוּ שַׁבָּת הִוא לַיהוָה
בְּכֹל מוֹשְׁבֹתֵיכֶם׃

לוי (בשבת שלישי) אֵלֶּה מוֹעֲדֵי יְהוָה מִקְרָאֵי קֹדֶשׁ אֲשֶׁר־תִּקְרְאוּ אֹתָם בְּמוֹעֲדָם׃
בַּחֹדֶשׁ הָרִאשׁוֹן בְּאַרְבָּעָה עָשָׂר לַחֹדֶשׁ בֵּין הָעַרְבָּיִם פֶּסַח
לַיהוָה׃ וּבַחֲמִשָּׁה עָשָׂר יוֹם לַחֹדֶשׁ הַזֶּה חַג הַמַּצּוֹת לַיהוָה
שִׁבְעַת יָמִים מַצּוֹת תֹּאכֵלוּ׃ בַּיּוֹם הָרִאשׁוֹן מִקְרָא־קֹדֶשׁ יִהְיֶה
לָכֶם כָּל־מְלֶאכֶת עֲבֹדָה לֹא תַעֲשׂוּ׃ וְהִקְרַבְתֶּם אִשֶּׁה לַיהוָה
שִׁבְעַת יָמִים בַּיּוֹם הַשְּׁבִיעִי מִקְרָא־קֹדֶשׁ כָּל־מְלֶאכֶת עֲבֹדָה
לֹא תַעֲשׂוּ׃

(בשבת רביעי) וַיְדַבֵּר יְהוָה אֶל־מֹשֶׁה לֵּאמֹר׃ דַּבֵּר אֶל־בְּנֵי יִשְׂרָאֵל וְאָמַרְתָּ
אֲלֵהֶם כִּי־תָבֹאוּ אֶל־הָאָרֶץ אֲשֶׁר אֲנִי נֹתֵן לָכֶם וּקְצַרְתֶּם אֶת־
קְצִירָהּ וַהֲבֵאתֶם אֶת־עֹמֶר רֵאשִׁית קְצִירְכֶם אֶל־הַכֹּהֵן׃ וְהֵנִיף
אֶת־הָעֹמֶר לִפְנֵי יְהוָה לִרְצֹנְכֶם מִמָּחֳרַת הַשַּׁבָּת יְנִיפֶנּוּ הַכֹּהֵן׃
וַעֲשִׂיתֶם בְּיוֹם הֲנִיפְכֶם אֶת־הָעֹמֶר כֶּבֶשׂ תָּמִים בֶּן־שְׁנָתוֹ לְעֹלָה

---

desist. Bodies persist in motion. Nature never rests. What makes humans different, and in the image of God, is that they can stop. "Why is God called *Shadai*? Because He said to the universe, *Dai*, Enough" (Rashi on Gen. 43:14). The ability to stop, cease, pause and rest, marks the primacy of choice over necessity, will over nature.

מִקְרָא־קֹדֶשׁ *A sacred assembly.* From the word *k-r-a*, which means "to call, summon." These were times when the nation assembled, locally or centrally in Jerusalem (Nahmanides). There may also be a hint that these were times when the Torah was read or proclaimed (*mikra* became a Hebrew synonym for Torah).

חַג הַמַּצּוֹת *The festival of Matzot.* Traditionally the festival of unleavened bread is known as Pesaḥ, but in fact these are different days. Pesaḥ was the offering of the Paschal Lamb on 14 Nisan. It was a preparation for the festival, not a festival itself in the sense of a day on which it is forbidden to work. Nonethe-

lamb as a burnt-offering to the Lord. And its meal-offering shall be two tenths of an ephah of fine flour mixed with oil, an offering consumed by fire, a pleasing scent for the Lord; its libation shall be a fourth of a hin of wine. You may not eat any bread, roasted grains or fresh kernels (of the new harvest) until this day, until you bring the offering of your God – this is an eternal ordinance for all your generations in all of your dwellings.

SHELISHI (*Shabbat* HAMISHI)

And you shall count seven complete weeks from the day following the [Pesaḥ] rest day, when you brought the omer as a wave-offering. To the day after the seventh week you shall count fifty days. Then you shall present a meal-offering of new grain to the Lord. You shall bring two loaves from your settlements as a wave-offering: they shall be made from two tenths of an ephah of fine flour; they shall be baked as leavened bread; first harvest for the Lord. And with this bread you shall offer seven unblemished yearling lambs, one young bullock and two rams: all as a burnt-offering to the Lord along with their meal-offerings and wine-libations, an offering consumed by fire, a pleasant scent for the Lord. And you shall bring one male goat for atonement and two yearling lambs as a peace-offering. And the priest shall wave them over the loaves made from the first harvest as a wave-offering in the presence of the Lord, and upon the two lambs – they shall be sanctified to the Lord, for the priest. And you shall proclaim on that day – it shall be a sacred assembly for you: you may not perform any laborious work – this is an eternal ordinance for all your generations in all of your dwellings. And when you reap the grain of your land, do not

---

led Nahmanides to conclude that the seven weeks between Pesaḥ and Shavuot are like the seven days between Sukkot and Shemini Atzeret. According to this view Pesaḥ and Shavuot are the beginning and end of a single extended festival, agriculturally the start and finish of the grain harvest, historically the journey from Egypt to Mount Sinai, from exodus to revelation.

וּבְקֻצְרְכֶם אֶת־קְצִיר אַרְצְכֶם *And when you reap the grain of your land.* The laws of provisions for the poor are spelled out in greater detail elsewhere. They are

לַיהוָה: וּמִנְחָתוֹ שְׁנֵי עֶשְׂרֹנִים סֹלֶת בְּלוּלָה בַשֶּׁמֶן אִשֶּׁה לַיהוָה
רֵיחַ נִיחֹחַ וְנִסְכֹּה יַיִן רְבִיעִת הַהִין: וְלֶחֶם וְקָלִי וְכַרְמֶל לֹא
תֹאכְלוּ עַד־עֶצֶם הַיּוֹם הַזֶּה עַד הֲבִיאֲכֶם אֶת־קָרְבַּן אֱלֹהֵיכֶם
חֻקַּת עוֹלָם לְדֹרֹתֵיכֶם בְּכֹל מֹשְׁבֹתֵיכֶם: *וּסְפַרְתֶּם שלישי (בשבת חמישי)
לָכֶם מִמָּחֳרַת הַשַּׁבָּת מִיּוֹם הֲבִיאֲכֶם אֶת־עֹמֶר הַתְּנוּפָה שֶׁבַע
שַׁבָּתוֹת תְּמִימֹת תִּהְיֶינָה: עַד מִמָּחֳרַת הַשַּׁבָּת הַשְּׁבִיעִת תִּסְפְּרוּ
חֲמִשִּׁים יוֹם וְהִקְרַבְתֶּם מִנְחָה חֲדָשָׁה לַיהוָה: מִמּוֹשְׁבֹתֵיכֶם
תָּבִיאוּ ׀ לֶחֶם תְּנוּפָה שְׁתַּיִם שְׁנֵי עֶשְׂרֹנִים סֹלֶת תִּהְיֶינָה חָמֵץ
תֵּאָפֶינָה בִּכּוּרִים לַיהוָה: וְהִקְרַבְתֶּם עַל־הַלֶּחֶם שִׁבְעַת כְּבָשִׂים
תְּמִימִם בְּנֵי שָׁנָה וּפַר בֶּן־בָּקָר אֶחָד וְאֵילִם שְׁנָיִם יִהְיוּ עֹלָה
לַיהוָה וּמִנְחָתָם וְנִסְכֵּיהֶם אִשֵּׁה רֵיחַ־נִיחֹחַ לַיהוָה: וַעֲשִׂיתֶם
שְׂעִיר־עִזִּים אֶחָד לְחַטָּאת וּשְׁנֵי כְבָשִׂים בְּנֵי שָׁנָה לְזֶבַח שְׁלָמִים:
וְהֵנִיף הַכֹּהֵן ׀ אֹתָם עַל לֶחֶם הַבִּכֻּרִים תְּנוּפָה לִפְנֵי יְהוָה עַל־שְׁנֵי
כְּבָשִׂים קֹדֶשׁ יִהְיוּ לַיהוָה לַכֹּהֵן: וּקְרָאתֶם בְּעֶצֶם ׀ הַיּוֹם הַזֶּה
מִקְרָא־קֹדֶשׁ יִהְיֶה לָכֶם כָּל־מְלֶאכֶת עֲבֹדָה לֹא תַעֲשׂוּ חֻקַּת
עוֹלָם בְּכָל־מוֹשְׁבֹתֵיכֶם לְדֹרֹתֵיכֶם: וּבְקֻצְרְכֶם אֶת־קְצִיר אַרְצְכֶם

The Boethusians, Sadducees and Karaites understood it as the day after the Sabbath during the festival week. The Qumran sect understood it as the Sunday after the end of the festival week. The Oral Tradition understood it to mean the day after the first day of the festival: "the Sabbath" thus means "the day of rest."

וְלֶחֶם... לֹא תֹאכְלוּ *You may not eat any bread.* The offering of the Omer permitted new produce to be eaten. Before satisfying our own hunger we must acknowledge God, thanking Him for the produce of the land.

וּסְפַרְתֶּם לָכֶם *And you shall count.* Shavuot is the one festival given no fixed calendrical date in the Torah. Depending on whether Nisan and Iyar were long or short months, it could fall on the fifth, sixth or seventh of Sivan. This

finish reaping the corner of your field, and do not collect the fallen remnants of your harvest: you must leave them for the poor and for the stranger – I am the LORD your God.

The LORD spoke to Moses, saying: Speak to the children of Israel, saying: In the seventh month, on the first day of the month, you shall hold a rest day of remembrance by the shofar, a sacred assembly. You may not perform any laborious work, and you shall bring a fire-offering to the LORD. REVI'I (Shabbat SHISHI)

The LORD spoke to Moses, saying: Speak to the children of Israel, saying: On the tenth day of that seventh month, there shall be a Day of Atonement; it is a sacred assembly for you; you shall afflict your souls, and bring a fire-offering to the LORD. You may not perform any work on this day, for it is a Day of Atonements, to atone for you before the LORD your God. For any soul that is not afflicted on this very day will be cut off from its people. And any soul that performs any work on this very day – I shall cause that soul to be lost from among its people. You shall perform no work – this is an eternal ordinance for all your generations in all of your dwellings. It is a Sabbath of Sabbaths for you; you shall afflict your souls from the ninth of the month in the evening; you shall rest on your Sabbath until the following evening.

The LORD spoke to Moses, saying: Speak to the children of Israel, HAMISHI (Shabbat SHEVI'I)

---

through the ages to make sacrifices for the sake of their faith (*Rosh HaShana* 16a), or God's call to us to return to Him (Maimonides, *Laws of Repentance* 3:4). Traditionally this is the beginning of a ten-day process of repentance culminating in Yom Kippur.

יוֹם הַכִּפֻּרִים *Day of Atonements.* In the plural, meaning both individual and collective. This is the supreme day of repentance and forgiveness.

וְעִנִּיתֶם אֶת־נַפְשֹׁתֵיכֶם *You shall afflict your souls.* This phrase is mentioned five times in the Torah, and is thus understood as five forms of abstinence, from (1) eating and drinking, (2) bathing, (3) anointing, (4) sexual relations and (5) the wearing of (leather) shoes.

לֹא־תְכַלֶּה פְּאַת שָׂדְךָ בְּקֻצְרֶךָ וְלֶקֶט קְצִירְךָ לֹא תְלַקֵּט לֶעָנִי
וְלַגֵּר תַּעֲזֹב אֹתָם אֲנִי יהוה אֱלֹהֵיכֶם׃
רביעי (בשבת שישי) וַיְדַבֵּר יהוה אֶל־מֹשֶׁה לֵּאמֹר׃ דַּבֵּר אֶל־בְּנֵי יִשְׂרָאֵל לֵאמֹר
בַּחֹדֶשׁ הַשְּׁבִיעִי בְּאֶחָד לַחֹדֶשׁ יִהְיֶה לָכֶם שַׁבָּתוֹן זִכְרוֹן תְּרוּעָה
מִקְרָא־קֹדֶשׁ׃ כָּל־מְלֶאכֶת עֲבֹדָה לֹא תַעֲשׂוּ וְהִקְרַבְתֶּם אִשֶּׁה
לַיהוה׃ וַיְדַבֵּר יהוה אֶל־מֹשֶׁה לֵּאמֹר׃ אַךְ בֶּעָשׂוֹר
לַחֹדֶשׁ הַשְּׁבִיעִי הַזֶּה יוֹם הַכִּפֻּרִים הוּא מִקְרָא־קֹדֶשׁ יִהְיֶה לָכֶם
וְעִנִּיתֶם אֶת־נַפְשֹׁתֵיכֶם וְהִקְרַבְתֶּם אִשֶּׁה לַיהוה׃ וְכָל־מְלָאכָה
לֹא תַעֲשׂוּ בְּעֶצֶם הַיּוֹם הַזֶּה כִּי יוֹם כִּפֻּרִים הוּא לְכַפֵּר עֲלֵיכֶם לִפְנֵי
יהוה אֱלֹהֵיכֶם׃ כִּי כָל־הַנֶּפֶשׁ אֲשֶׁר לֹא־תְעֻנֶּה בְּעֶצֶם הַיּוֹם הַזֶּה
וְנִכְרְתָה מֵעַמֶּיהָ׃ וְכָל־הַנֶּפֶשׁ אֲשֶׁר תַּעֲשֶׂה כָּל־מְלָאכָה בְּעֶצֶם
הַיּוֹם הַזֶּה וְהַאֲבַדְתִּי אֶת־הַנֶּפֶשׁ הַהִוא מִקֶּרֶב עַמָּהּ׃ כָּל־מְלָאכָה
לֹא תַעֲשׂוּ חֻקַּת עוֹלָם לְדֹרֹתֵיכֶם בְּכֹל מֹשְׁבֹתֵיכֶם׃ שַׁבַּת שַׁבָּתוֹן
הוּא לָכֶם וְעִנִּיתֶם אֶת־נַפְשֹׁתֵיכֶם בְּתִשְׁעָה לַחֹדֶשׁ בָּעֶרֶב מֵעֶרֶב
עַד־עֶרֶב תִּשְׁבְּתוּ שַׁבַּתְּכֶם׃
חמישי (בשבת שביעי) וַיְדַבֵּר יהוה אֶל־מֹשֶׁה לֵּאמֹר׃ דַּבֵּר אֶל־בְּנֵי יִשְׂרָאֵל לֵאמֹר

---

mentioned here because of the association of Shavuot with the grain harvest. The book of Ruth gives us a picture of what this was like in practice. The festivals were to be times of national, collective celebration, from which no one was to be excluded. The solidarity and fraternity the people experienced through their sufferings in Egypt, and their long stay in the desert, were not to be forgotten when they entered the land. The welfare of the poor, and inclusion of the lonely, were fundamental to the ethos of the nation under God.

זִכְרוֹן תְּרוּעָה *Remembrance by the shofar.* This day later became known as Rosh HaShana, though it is not described as such in Tanakh. The blasts were to be sounded using a ram's horn (see Joshua 6:5) rather than the silver trumpets mentioned in Numbers 10. Later tradition understood the blasts as either our call to God to remember the binding of Isaac and the willingness of Jews

and tell them: On the fifteenth day of this seventh month, there shall be a Festival of Booths for the LORD, for seven days. On the first day there shall be a sacred assembly; you shall do no laborious work. For seven days, you shall bring fire-offerings to the LORD; on the eighth day there will be a sacred assembly, and you shall bring another fire-offering to the LORD – it is a day of gathering; you shall do no laborious work. These are the appointed times of the LORD which you shall proclaim to be days of sacred assembly, bringing fire-offerings to the LORD: burnt-offerings, meal-offerings, peace-offerings and wine-libations, as ordained for each day, in addition to the LORD's Sabbath offerings, and your donated offerings, and all the vows and voluntary offerings which you may offer to the LORD. But on the fifteenth day of the seventh month, when you gather the harvest of the land, you shall celebrate the LORD's holiday for seven days; the first day shall be a day of rest, and the eighth day shall be a day of rest. And on the first day, you shall take for yourselves a fruit of the citron tree, palm fronds, myrtle branches and willows of the brook, and be joyous in the presence of the LORD your God for seven days. You shall celebrate it, a holiday for the LORD, seven days a year – this is an eternal ordinance for all your generations – you shall celebrate it in the seventh month. You shall dwell in booths for seven days; all those born among Israel shall dwell in booths, so that your descendants will know that I settled the children of Israel in booths when I brought them out of the land of Egypt; I am the LORD your God. And Moses related all of the LORD's festivals to the children of Israel.

---

understands it to mean "holding back," a request by God not to leave after the seventh day of Sukkot, but to stay an extra day. Ḥizkuni explains that this is because of the long gap of time – almost six months – before the people would gather again at the Temple.

בַּסֻּכֹּת *In booths.* According to Rashbam the point of the command is that, when the Israelites celebrate the ingathering of the harvest, they should remember the forty years when they wandered in the desert with a land or permanent home, and thus avoid the hubris of thinking "My power and the

בַּחֲמִשָּׁה עָשָׂר יוֹם לַחֹדֶשׁ הַשְּׁבִיעִי הַזֶּה חַג הַסֻּכּוֹת שִׁבְעַת
יָמִים לַיהוָה׃ בַּיּוֹם הָרִאשׁוֹן מִקְרָא־קֹדֶשׁ כָּל־מְלֶאכֶת עֲבֹדָה
לֹא תַעֲשׂוּ׃ שִׁבְעַת יָמִים תַּקְרִיבוּ אִשֶּׁה לַיהוָה בַּיּוֹם הַשְּׁמִינִי
מִקְרָא־קֹדֶשׁ יִהְיֶה לָכֶם וְהִקְרַבְתֶּם אִשֶּׁה לַיהוָה עֲצֶרֶת הִוא
כָּל־מְלֶאכֶת עֲבֹדָה לֹא תַעֲשׂוּ׃ אֵלֶּה מוֹעֲדֵי יְהוָה אֲשֶׁר־תִּקְרְאוּ
אֹתָם מִקְרָאֵי קֹדֶשׁ לְהַקְרִיב אִשֶּׁה לַיהוָה עֹלָה וּמִנְחָה זֶבַח
וּנְסָכִים דְּבַר־יוֹם בְּיוֹמוֹ׃ מִלְּבַד שַׁבְּתֹת יְהוָה וּמִלְּבַד מַתְּנוֹתֵיכֶם
וּמִלְּבַד כָּל־נִדְרֵיכֶם וּמִלְּבַד כָּל־נִדְבֹתֵיכֶם אֲשֶׁר תִּתְּנוּ לַיהוָה׃
אַךְ בַּחֲמִשָּׁה עָשָׂר יוֹם לַחֹדֶשׁ הַשְּׁבִיעִי בְּאָסְפְּכֶם אֶת־תְּבוּאַת
הָאָרֶץ תָּחֹגּוּ אֶת־חַג־יְהוָה שִׁבְעַת יָמִים בַּיּוֹם הָרִאשׁוֹן שַׁבָּתוֹן
וּבַיּוֹם הַשְּׁמִינִי שַׁבָּתוֹן׃ וּלְקַחְתֶּם לָכֶם בַּיּוֹם הָרִאשׁוֹן פְּרִי עֵץ
הָדָר כַּפֹּת תְּמָרִים וַעֲנַף עֵץ־עָבֹת וְעַרְבֵי־נָחַל וּשְׂמַחְתֶּם לִפְנֵי
יְהוָה אֱלֹהֵיכֶם שִׁבְעַת יָמִים׃ וְחַגֹּתֶם אֹתוֹ חַג לַיהוָה שִׁבְעַת יָמִים
בַּשָּׁנָה חֻקַּת עוֹלָם לְדֹרֹתֵיכֶם בַּחֹדֶשׁ הַשְּׁבִיעִי תָּחֹגּוּ אֹתוֹ׃ בַּסֻּכֹּת
תֵּשְׁבוּ שִׁבְעַת יָמִים כָּל־הָאֶזְרָח בְּיִשְׂרָאֵל יֵשְׁבוּ בַּסֻּכֹּת׃ לְמַעַן
יֵדְעוּ דֹרֹתֵיכֶם כִּי בַסֻּכּוֹת הוֹשַׁבְתִּי אֶת־בְּנֵי יִשְׂרָאֵל בְּהוֹצִיאִי
אוֹתָם מֵאֶרֶץ מִצְרָיִם אֲנִי יְהוָה אֱלֹהֵיכֶם׃ וַיְדַבֵּר מֹשֶׁה אֶת־מֹעֲדֵי
יְהוָה אֶל־בְּנֵי יִשְׂרָאֵל׃

בַּחֲמִשָּׁה עָשָׂר יוֹם *On the fifteenth day.* The festival of Sukkot, beginning on the night of the full moon of the seventh month, stands at the opposite end of the calendar from the festival of unleavened bread, which begins on the night of the full moon of the first month. Whereas the latter recalls the affliction and bitterness of slavery, Sukkot, the festival of ingathering of the produce of the land, is supremely a time of joy.

עֲצֶרֶת *A day of gathering.* The day we now call Shemini Atzeret. The word may mean "restraint" from doing work (Ibn Ezra, Rashbam), or "binding," meaning the day that brings closure to the festival cycle (Ramban). Rashi

HALF KADDISH

Before Maftir is read, the second Sefer Torah is placed on the bima and the Reader says Half Kaddish:

Reader: יִתְגַּדַּל Magnified and sanctified may His great name be,
in the world He created by His will.
May He establish His kingdom
in your lifetime and in your days,
and in the lifetime of all the house of Israel,
swiftly and soon – and say: Amen.

All: May His great name be blessed for ever and all time.

Reader: Blessed and praised, glorified and exalted,
raised and honored, uplifted and lauded
be the name of the Holy One, blessed be He,
beyond any blessing,
song, praise and consolation
uttered in the world – and say: Amen.

HAGBAHA AND GELILA

The first Torah scroll is lifted and the congregation says:

וְזֹאת הַתּוֹרָה This is the Torah *Deut. 4*
that Moses placed before the children of Israel,
at the LORD's commandment, by the hand of Moses. *Num. 9*

Some add: It is a tree of life to those who grasp it, *Prov. 3*
and those who uphold it are happy.
Its ways are ways of pleasantness, and all its paths are peace.
Long life is in its right hand; in its left, riches and honor.
It pleased the LORD for the sake of [Israel's] righteousness, *Is. 42*
to make the Torah great and glorious.

The first Torah scroll is bound and covered and the oleh for Maftir is called to the second Torah scroll.

---

strength of my hands have produced this wealth for me" (Deut. 8:17). According to Rashi, the reference is to the Clouds of Glory that surrounded the Israelites during their years in the wilderness.

חצי קדיש

Before מפטיר *is read, the second* ספר תורה *is placed on the* שולחן *and the* קורא *says* חצי קדיש:

קורא: יִתְגַּדַּל וְיִתְקַדַּשׁ שְׁמֵהּ רַבָּא (קהל: אָמֵן)
בְּעָלְמָא דִּי בְרָא כִרְעוּתֵהּ
וְיַמְלִיךְ מַלְכוּתֵהּ
בְּחַיֵּיכוֹן וּבְיוֹמֵיכוֹן וּבְחַיֵּי דְכָל בֵּית יִשְׂרָאֵל
בַּעֲגָלָא וּבִזְמַן קָרִיב
וְאִמְרוּ אָמֵן. (קהל: אָמֵן)

קהל וקורא: יְהֵא שְׁמֵהּ רַבָּא מְבָרַךְ לְעָלַם וּלְעָלְמֵי עָלְמַיָּא.

קורא: יִתְבָּרַךְ וְיִשְׁתַּבַּח וְיִתְפָּאַר וְיִתְרוֹמַם וְיִתְנַשֵּׂא
וְיִתְהַדָּר וְיִתְעַלֶּה וְיִתְהַלָּל
שְׁמֵהּ דְּקֻדְשָׁא בְּרִיךְ הוּא (קהל: בְּרִיךְ הוּא)
לְעֵלָּא מִן כָּל בִּרְכָתָא וְשִׁירָתָא
תֻּשְׁבְּחָתָא וְנֶחֱמָתָא
דַּאֲמִירָן בְּעָלְמָא
וְאִמְרוּ אָמֵן. (קהל: אָמֵן)

הגבהה וגלילה

The first ספר תורה *is lifted and the* קהל *says:*

וְזֹאת הַתּוֹרָה אֲשֶׁר־שָׂם מֹשֶׁה לִפְנֵי בְּנֵי יִשְׂרָאֵל: דברים ד
עַל־פִּי יהוה בְּיַד מֹשֶׁה: במדבר ט

Some add עֵץ־חַיִּים הִיא לַמַּחֲזִיקִים בָּהּ וְתֹמְכֶיהָ מְאֻשָּׁר: משלי ג
דְּרָכֶיהָ דַרְכֵי־נֹעַם וְכָל־נְתִיבֹתֶיהָ שָׁלוֹם:
אֹרֶךְ יָמִים בִּימִינָהּ, בִּשְׂמֹאולָהּ עֹשֶׁר וְכָבוֹד:
יהוה חָפֵץ לְמַעַן צִדְקוֹ יַגְדִּיל תּוֹרָה וְיַאְדִּיר: ישעיה מב

The first ספר תורה *is bound and covered and the* עולה *for* מפטיר *is called to the second* ספר תורה.

MAFTIR

On the first two days of Sukkot say (in Israel, the first day only):

וּבַחֲמִשָּׁה עָשָׂר On the fifteenth day of the seventh month you shall hold a sacred assembly. You shall do no laborious work, and you shall celebrate a festival to the LORD for seven days. You shall offer a burnt-offering, a fire-offering of pleasing aroma to the LORD: thirteen young bullocks, two rams, and fourteen yearling male lambs; they shall be without blemish. And also their meal-offerings, fine flour mixed with oil, three-tenths of an ephah for each of the thirteen bulls, two-tenths of an ephah for each of the two rams, and an ephah each for every one of the fourteen lambs. And one male goat as a sin-offering, as well as the regular daily sacrifice, its meal-offering and its libation. *Num. 29: 12–16*

HAGBAHA AND GELILA

The second Torah scroll is lifted and the congregation says:

וְזֹאת הַתּוֹרָה This is the Torah *Deut. 4*
that Moses placed before the children of Israel,
at the LORD's commandment, by the hand of Moses. *Num. 9*

Some add: It is a tree of life to those who grasp it, *Prov. 3*
and those who uphold it are happy.
Its ways are ways of pleasantness, and all its paths are peace.
Long life is in its right hand; in its left, riches and honor.
It pleased the LORD for the sake of [Israel's] righteousness, *Is. 42*
to make the Torah great and glorious.

The second Torah scroll is bound and covered and the oleh for Maftir reads the Haftara.

BLESSING BEFORE READING THE HAFTARA

Before reading the Haftara, the person called up for Maftir says:

בָּרוּךְ Blessed are You, LORD our God, King of the Universe, who chose good prophets and was pleased with their words, spoken in truth. Blessed are You, LORD, who chose the Torah, His servant Moses, His people Israel, and the prophets of truth and righteousness.

מפטיר

On the first two days of סוכות *say (in* ארץ ישראל*, the first day only):*

וּבַחֲמִשָּׁה עָשָׂר יוֹם לַחֹדֶשׁ הַשְּׁבִיעִי מִקְרָא־קֹדֶשׁ יִהְיֶה לָכֶם במדבר כט:יב–טז
כָּל־מְלֶאכֶת עֲבֹדָה לֹא תַעֲשׂוּ וְחַגֹּתֶם חַג לַיהוה שִׁבְעַת יָמִים׃
וְהִקְרַבְתֶּם עֹלָה אִשֵּׁה רֵיחַ נִיחֹחַ לַיהוה פָּרִים בְּנֵי־בָקָר שְׁלֹשָׁה
עָשָׂר אֵילִם שְׁנָיִם כְּבָשִׂים בְּנֵי־שָׁנָה אַרְבָּעָה עָשָׂר תְּמִימִם יִהְיוּ׃
וּמִנְחָתָם סֹלֶת בְּלוּלָה בַשָּׁמֶן שְׁלֹשָׁה עֶשְׂרֹנִים לַפָּר הָאֶחָד
לִשְׁלֹשָׁה עָשָׂר פָּרִים שְׁנֵי עֶשְׂרֹנִים לָאַיִל הָאֶחָד לִשְׁנֵי הָאֵילִם׃
וְעִשָּׂרוֹן עִשָּׂרוֹן לַכֶּבֶשׂ הָאֶחָד לְאַרְבָּעָה עָשָׂר כְּבָשִׂים׃ וּשְׂעִיר־
עִזִּים אֶחָד חַטָּאת מִלְּבַד עֹלַת הַתָּמִיד מִנְחָתָהּ וְנִסְכָּהּ׃

הגבהה וגלילה

The second ספר תורה *is lifted and the* קהל *says:*

וְזֹאת הַתּוֹרָה אֲשֶׁר־שָׂם מֹשֶׁה לִפְנֵי בְּנֵי יִשְׂרָאֵל׃ דברים ד
עַל־פִּי יהוה בְּיַד מֹשֶׁה׃ במדבר ט

Some add עֵץ־חַיִּים הִיא לַמַּחֲזִיקִים בָּהּ וְתֹמְכֶיהָ מְאֻשָּׁר׃ משלי ג
דְּרָכֶיהָ דַרְכֵי־נֹעַם וְכָל־נְתִיבוֹתֶיהָ שָׁלוֹם׃
אֹרֶךְ יָמִים בִּימִינָהּ, בִּשְׂמֹאולָהּ עֹשֶׁר וְכָבוֹד׃
יהוה חָפֵץ לְמַעַן צִדְקוֹ יַגְדִּיל תּוֹרָה וְיַאְדִּיר׃ ישעיה מב

The second ספר תורה *is bound and covered and the* עולה *for* מפטיר *reads the* הפטרה.

ברכה קודם ההפטרה

Before reading the הפטרה*, the person called up for* מפטיר *says:*

בָּרוּךְ אַתָּה יהוה אֱלֹהֵינוּ מֶלֶךְ הָעוֹלָם אֲשֶׁר בָּחַר בִּנְבִיאִים טוֹבִים, וְרָצָה בְדִבְרֵיהֶם הַנֶּאֱמָרִים בֶּאֱמֶת. בָּרוּךְ אַתָּה יהוה, הַבּוֹחֵר בַּתּוֹרָה וּבְמֹשֶׁה עַבְדּוֹ וּבְיִשְׂרָאֵל עַמּוֹ וּבִנְבִיאֵי הָאֱמֶת וָצֶדֶק.

The Haftara for the second day (outside Israel) of Sukkot is on page 460.

HAFTARA FOR THE FIRST DAY OF SUKKOT

Behold, a day of the LORD is coming; your spoil will be divided up in your midst. I will gather all the nations to Jerusalem for war: the city will be taken, the houses will be plundered, and the women will be raped; half of the city will go out into exile, but the remainder of the people will not be cut off from the city. And the LORD will go out and He will fight against these nations, as He has fought on days of battle: on that day, His feet will stand upon the Mount of Olives which faces Jerusalem on the east, and the Mount of Olives will split through its middle – in to a very great valley – from east to west; and half the mountain will shift northward and half *Zecharia. 14:1–21*

---

the people of the covenant, at a low ebb economically, politically and spiritually, are caught in a vortex of alien forces.

The late prophets lost none of their faith in the eventual restoration of Israel and the rebuilding of the Temple. But there is a mounting sense that this will not happen within the normal terms of history. There will be a major confrontation in which the universe will be shaken to its foundations, after which Israel will emerge triumphant and at peace, and Jerusalem, especially on Sukkot, will be acknowledged as the spiritual center of the world.

יוֹם־בָּא לַה׳ *A day of the LORD.* The time before the end of time, the war that will put an end to war, the storm before the peace. The nations of the world will wage a battle against Jerusalem. Initially the war will go badly – the city will be conquered, and half its inhabitants taken captive. Then, though, God will intervene in a miraculous manner as He did in an earlier age at the Red Sea.

וְנִבְקַע הַר הַזֵּיתִים מֵחֶצְיוֹ *Mount of Olives will split through its middle.* There will be an earthquake that will split the Mount of Olives, similar to the one that occurred in the days of Uzzia, some 165 years before the destruction of the First Temple (see Amos 1:1). Regarding this earlier event, Josephus writes that "a great earthquake shook the ground, and a rent was made in

The הפטרה *for the second day (outside* ארץ ישראל*) of* סוכות *is on page 461.*

הפטרה ליום הראשון של סוכות

הִנֵּה יוֹם־בָּא לַיהוָה וְחֻלַּק שְׁלָלֵךְ בְּקִרְבֵּךְ׃ וְאָסַפְתִּי אֶת־כָּל־ זכריה יד:א–כא
הַגּוֹיִם ׀ אֶל־יְרוּשָׁלִַם לַמִּלְחָמָה וְנִלְכְּדָה הָעִיר וְנָשַׁסּוּ הַבָּתִּים
וְהַנָּשִׁים תשגלנה וְיָצָא חֲצִי הָעִיר בַּגּוֹלָה וְיֶתֶר הָעָם לֹא יִכָּרֵת תִּשָּׁכַבְנָה
מִן־הָעִיר׃ וְיָצָא יְהוָה וְנִלְחַם בַּגּוֹיִם הָהֵם כְּיוֹם הִלָּחֲמוֹ בְּיוֹם
קְרָב׃ וְעָמְדוּ רַגְלָיו בַּיּוֹם־הַהוּא עַל־הַר הַזֵּיתִים אֲשֶׁר עַל־
פְּנֵי יְרוּשָׁלִַם מִקֶּדֶם וְנִבְקַע הַר הַזֵּיתִים מֵחֶצְיוֹ מִזְרָחָה וָיָמָּה
גֵּיא גְּדוֹלָה מְאֹד וּמָשׁ חֲצִי הָהָר צָפוֹנָה וְחֶצְיוֹ נֶגְבָּה׃ וְנַסְתֶּם

HAFTARA FOR THE FIRST DAY

Zechariah was one of the last of the prophets. He began his prophetic career around the year 520 BCE, as the first of the exiles were returning from Babylon. Along with the prophet Haggai he encouraged the rebuilding of the Temple and the revitalizing of Jewish life under Joshua the High Priest and the governor Zerubavel. The connection between the haftara, the last chapter of his book, and Sukkot, is direct. In a verse that became one of the best known in the prayer book, Zechariah foresees a day when all the nations of the world will acknowledge the sovereignty of God ("On that day the LORD shall be One and His name One"). They will come to worship in Jerusalem to celebrate Sukkot, which will become the universal festival of rain.

Before that happens, however, there will be a major confrontation between Israel and its enemies. Initially Jews will suffer setbacks, but God will then fight for His people and defeat its enemies for all time. Jerusalem will re-emerge as the diadem of the earth, the world center of faith in a new order of peace.

A new tone entered prophecy during and especially after the Babylonian exile. Beginning in Babylon with Ezekiel, we gain a sense of the prophets "wandering between two worlds," a past that has gone, and a future seemingly powerless to be born. The times are out of joint, there is global disorder, new empires are battling for supremacy, barbarians are invading the region, and

southward. And you will flee from this Valley of the Mountains – the Valley of the Mountains will reach as far as Atzal – you will flee as you fled from the earthquake in the days of Uziah the King of Judah; and the LORD will come, my God, all the holy ones with You. And it will be: on that day there will be neither bright light nor thick darkness. And it will be: this one day will be known as the LORD's, it will be neither day nor night but at evening time there will be light. And it will be: on that day living waters will flow out from Jerusalem, half to the eastern sea and half to the western sea; in summer and winter it will be so. Then the LORD shall be King over all the earth; on that day the LORD shall be One and His name One. The whole country will be smoothed out like the Arava, from Geva to Rimon south of Jerusalem – and [Jerusalem] will be lifted up, in her place; and from the gate of Binyamin to the site of the first gate and to the corner gate, and from the tower of Ḥananel to the king's winery, they will inhabit her. There will be no more devastation – and Jerusalem will live in safety.

And this will be the plague that the LORD will bring upon all the peoples who fought against Jerusalem: their flesh will rot away as they stand on their feet, their eyes will rot in their sockets and their tongues will rot in their mouths. And it will be: on that day, the turmoil the LORD brings on them will be great and each man will seize his neighbor by the arm to raise his hand against his neighbor's hand. And Judah too will fight in Jerusalem and the wealth

---

in Zephaniah (3:9), "Then I will restore to the peoples a pure speech, so that all of them will call on the name of the LORD and will serve Him with one accord."

וְרָאֲמָה *Will be lifted up.* The landscape will be transformed. The surrounding countryside will become a level plain, with Jerusalem the highpoint of the landscape: it will be exalted physically as well as spiritually.

הַמַּגֵּפָה *The plague.* The attacking armies will be struck by a plague, as hap-

גֵיא־הָרַי כִּי־יַגִּיעַ גֵּי־הָרִים אֶל־אָצַל וְנַסְתֶּם כַּאֲשֶׁר נַסְתֶּם מִפְּנֵי
הָרַעַשׁ בִּימֵי עֻזִּיָּה מֶלֶךְ־יְהוּדָה וּבָא יהוה אֱלֹהַי כָּל־קְדֹשִׁים
עִמָּךְ׃ וְהָיָה בַּיּוֹם הַהוּא לֹא־יִהְיֶה אוֹר יְקָרוֹת יקפאון׃ וְהָיָה וְקִפָּאוֹן
יוֹם־אֶחָד הוּא יִוָּדַע לַיהוה לֹא־יוֹם וְלֹא־לָיְלָה וְהָיָה לְעֵת־
עֶרֶב יִהְיֶה־אוֹר׃ וְהָיָה ׀ בַּיּוֹם הַהוּא יֵצְאוּ מַיִם־חַיִּים מִירוּשָׁלִַם
חֶצְיָם אֶל־הַיָּם הַקַּדְמוֹנִי וְחֶצְיָם אֶל־הַיָּם הָאַחֲרוֹן בַּקַּיִץ
וּבָחֹרֶף יִהְיֶה׃ וְהָיָה יהוה לְמֶלֶךְ עַל־כָּל־הָאָרֶץ בַּיּוֹם הַהוּא
יִהְיֶה יהוה אֶחָד וּשְׁמוֹ אֶחָד׃ יִסּוֹב כָּל־הָאָרֶץ כָּעֲרָבָה מִגֶּבַע
לְרִמּוֹן נֶגֶב יְרוּשָׁלִָם וְרָאֲמָה וְיָשְׁבָה תַחְתֶּיהָ לְמִשַּׁעַר בִּנְיָמִן
עַד־מְקוֹם שַׁעַר הָרִאשׁוֹן עַד־שַׁעַר הַפִּנִּים וּמִגְדַּל חֲנַנְאֵל עַד
יִקְבֵי הַמֶּלֶךְ׃ וְיָשְׁבוּ בָהּ וְחֵרֶם לֹא יִהְיֶה־עוֹד וְיָשְׁבָה יְרוּשָׁלִַם
לָבֶטַח׃ וְזֹאת ׀ תִּהְיֶה הַמַּגֵּפָה אֲשֶׁר יִגֹּף יהוה אֶת־
כָּל־הָעַמִּים אֲשֶׁר צָבְאוּ עַל־יְרוּשָׁלִָם הָמֵק ׀ בְּשָׂרוֹ וְהוּא עֹמֵד
עַל־רַגְלָיו וְעֵינָיו תִּמַּקְנָה בְחֹרֵיהֶן וּלְשׁוֹנוֹ תִּמַּק בְּפִיהֶם׃ וְהָיָה
בַּיּוֹם הַהוּא תִּהְיֶה מְהוּמַת־יהוה רַבָּה בָּהֶם וְהֶחֱזִיקוּ אִישׁ יַד
רֵעֵהוּ וְעָלְתָה יָדוֹ עַל־יַד רֵעֵהוּ׃ וְגַם־יְהוּדָה תִּלָּחֵם בִּירוּשָׁלִָם

---

the Temple.... And before the city at a place called Eroge, half the mountain broke off from the rest on the west and rolled itself four furlongs." (*Antiquities*, 9:10:4).

מַיִם־חַיִּים *Living waters.* A vision shared by Joel (4:18) and Ezekiel (47:1–12). Water will flow from Jerusalem, irrigating the whole land, half flowing toward the Dead Sea, half toward the Mediterranean.

יִהְיֶה ה׳ אֶחָד וּשְׁמוֹ אֶחָד *The Lord shall be One and His name One.* The nations will acknowledge that there is only one God, and will invoke His name alone. Monotheism will become the universal faith. There is a similar prophecy

of all the surrounding nations, great quantities of gold, silver and clothing, will be gathered in. And there will be a plague just like this plague, on the horse, the mule, the camel and the donkey and on every animal in those camps.

And it will be: those remaining from all the nations who came up against Jerusalem will go up year upon year to bow down to the King, LORD of Hosts, and to celebrate the Festival of Sukkot. And it will be: those from the earth's families who do not go up to Jerusalem and bow down to the King, LORD of Hosts – rain shall not fall for them; and if the family of Egypt does not go up, does not come – they will have no [overflow]. This will be the plague that the LORD will bring upon the nations who do not go up to celebrate the Festival of Sukkot; such will be the punishment of Egypt and the punishment of all the nations who do not come up to celebrate the Festival of Sukkot.

On that day even the bells of the horses will be inscribed "sacred to the LORD"; and the pots in the House of the LORD will be like basins before the Altar. And it will be: every pot in Jerusalem and in Judah will be sacred to the LORD of Hosts, and all those who come to sacrifice will take them and will cook in them; and on that day, there will be no more need for traders in the House of the LORD of Hosts.

Continue with the blessings after the Haftara on page 464.

---

give thanks for the harvest of the past year, and to pray for rain in the year to come. Nations that do not participate will be deprived of rain. Egypt, which depended not on rain but on the waters of the Nile, would nevertheless suffer drought.

עַל־מְצִלּוֹת הַסּוּס *Even the bells of the horses.* A sign that they are carrying pilgrims to celebrate the festival (Abarbanel). There will be so many sacrifices brought for the festival that there will be no more need for animals or pots to be purchased from traders.

וְאֻסַּף חֵיל כָּל־הַגּוֹיִם סָבִיב זָהָב וָכֶסֶף וּבְגָדִים לָרֹב מְאֹד׃ וְכֵן
תִּהְיֶה מַגֵּפַת הַסּוּס הַפֶּרֶד הַגָּמָל וְהַחֲמוֹר וְכָל־הַבְּהֵמָה אֲשֶׁר
יִהְיֶה בַּמַּחֲנוֹת הָהֵמָּה כַּמַּגֵּפָה הַזֹּאת׃ וְהָיָה כָּל־הַנּוֹתָר מִכָּל־
הַגּוֹיִם הַבָּאִים עַל־יְרוּשָׁלָםִ וְעָלוּ מִדֵּי שָׁנָה בְשָׁנָה לְהִשְׁתַּחֲוֹת
לְמֶלֶךְ יהוה צְבָאוֹת וְלָחֹג אֶת־חַג הַסֻּכּוֹת׃ וְהָיָה אֲשֶׁר לֹא־
יַעֲלֶה מֵאֵת מִשְׁפְּחוֹת הָאָרֶץ אֶל־יְרוּשָׁלַםִ לְהִשְׁתַּחֲוֹת לְמֶלֶךְ
יהוה צְבָאוֹת וְלֹא עֲלֵיהֶם יִהְיֶה הַגָּשֶׁם׃ וְאִם־מִשְׁפַּחַת מִצְרַיִם
לֹא־תַעֲלֶה וְלֹא בָאָה וְלֹא עֲלֵיהֶם תִּהְיֶה הַמַּגֵּפָה אֲשֶׁר יִגֹּף יהוה
אֶת־הַגּוֹיִם אֲשֶׁר לֹא יַעֲלוּ לָחֹג אֶת־חַג הַסֻּכּוֹת׃ זֹאת תִּהְיֶה
חַטַּאת מִצְרָיִם וְחַטַּאת כָּל־הַגּוֹיִם אֲשֶׁר לֹא יַעֲלוּ לָחֹג אֶת־חַג
הַסֻּכּוֹת׃ בַּיּוֹם הַהוּא יִהְיֶה עַל־מְצִלּוֹת הַסּוּס קֹדֶשׁ לַיהוה וְהָיָה
הַסִּירוֹת בְּבֵית יהוה כַּמִּזְרָקִים לִפְנֵי הַמִּזְבֵּחַ׃ וְהָיָה כָּל־סִיר
בִּירוּשָׁלַםִ וּבִיהוּדָה קֹדֶשׁ לַיהוה צְבָאוֹת וּבָאוּ כָּל־הַזֹּבְחִים
וְלָקְחוּ מֵהֶם וּבִשְּׁלוּ בָהֶם וְלֹא־יִהְיֶה כְנַעֲנִי עוֹד בְּבֵית־יהוה
צְבָאוֹת בַּיּוֹם הַהוּא׃

Continue with the blessings after the הפטרה *on page 465.*

---

pened to the Assyrian army under Sennacherib (II Kings 19:35, Is. 37:36). In the fog of war, confusion will reign.

לָחֹג אֶת־חַג הַסֻּכּוֹת *To celebrate the Festival of Sukkot.* According to the sages, this was the time at which rainfall was determined for the coming year (Mishna *Rosh HaShana* 1:2). Sukkot was the most universal of the festivals. Tradition identified the seventy bullocks offered during its seven days with the seventy nations of the world (see Num. 29:12–34, Gen. 10, *Tanḥuma, Pinḥas* 16). The defeat of Israel's enemies will take place on Sukkot, after which the festival will be celebrated by all the nations. They will come to Jerusalem to

HAFTARA FOR THE SECOND DAY OF SUKKOT

It was in the month of Eitanim, at the Festival (in the seventh month, that is), that all the people of Israel gathered together to King Solomon. All the elders of Israel came; and the Priests were bearing the Ark with them. The Priests and the Levites brought the Ark of the LORD, and the Tent of Meeting and all the holy vessels that used to be in it, up [to the top of Mount Zion]. And King Solomon, and all the people of Israel who had come with him before the Ark, brought offerings from the flock and the herd; offerings that could not be counted or listed, so numerous were they. The priests brought the Ark of the LORD's Covenant to its place: to the Sanctuary of the House – to the Holy of Holies – to the shade of the Cherubim's wings. For the Cherubim stretched their wings out over the place of the Ark; and they covered the Ark and its poles above. The poles themselves extended outwards, and their ends were discernible from the Holy Place, the Sanctuary, but they could not be seen from outside; and this is where they remain to this day. The Ark held nothing else but the two stone tablets that Moses had placed there at Horev, that the LORD had hewed out with the children of Israel as they left Egypt. *I Kings 8:2–21*

---

cration took place, the celebrations lasting for two weeks. The second week coincided with Sukkot, which thereafter became associated with the Temple and its consecration. The Second Temple was also inaugurated on Sukkot (Ezra 3:1–6), and even the re-consecration by the Maccabees after the defilement of the Greeks, though it took place later in the year, on Hanukka, was also modeled on Sukkot (see II Maccabees 10:6–8).

בֶּחָג *Gathered together.* The entire ceremony took fourteen days, the last seven of which were Sukkot. Eitanim was the original name for the seventh month. After the Babylonian exile, it became known as Tishrei.

אֹהֶל מוֹעֵד *The Tent of Meeting.* Made by Moses, it had been in Gibeon. The Ark of the Covenant and other items had been kept in a tent within David's city.

רָאשֵׁי הַבַּדִּים *Their ends.* They (the poles of the Ark) extended outward, press-

הפטרה ליום שני בחו״ל של סוכות

מלכים א׳ ח:ב–כא

וַיִּקָּהֲלוּ אֶל־הַמֶּלֶךְ שְׁלֹמֹה כָּל־אִישׁ יִשְׂרָאֵל בְּיֶרַח הָאֵתָנִים בֶּחָג
הוּא הַחֹדֶשׁ הַשְּׁבִיעִי: וַיָּבֹאוּ כֹּל זִקְנֵי יִשְׂרָאֵל וַיִּשְׂאוּ הַכֹּהֲנִים
אֶת־הָאָרוֹן: וַיַּעֲלוּ אֶת־אֲרוֹן יהוה וְאֶת־אֹהֶל מוֹעֵד וְאֶת־כָּל־
כְּלֵי הַקֹּדֶשׁ אֲשֶׁר בָּאֹהֶל וַיַּעֲלוּ אֹתָם הַכֹּהֲנִים וְהַלְוִיִּם: וְהַמֶּלֶךְ
שְׁלֹמֹה וְכָל־עֲדַת יִשְׂרָאֵל הַנּוֹעָדִים עָלָיו אִתּוֹ לִפְנֵי הָאָרוֹן
מְזַבְּחִים צֹאן וּבָקָר אֲשֶׁר לֹא־יִסָּפְרוּ וְלֹא יִמָּנוּ מֵרֹב: וַיָּבִאוּ
הַכֹּהֲנִים אֶת־אֲרוֹן בְּרִית־יהוה אֶל־מְקוֹמוֹ אֶל־דְּבִיר הַבַּיִת
אֶל־קֹדֶשׁ הַקֳּדָשִׁים אֶל־תַּחַת כַּנְפֵי הַכְּרוּבִים: כִּי הַכְּרוּבִים
פֹּרְשִׂים כְּנָפַיִם אֶל־מְקוֹם הָאָרוֹן וַיָּסֹכּוּ הַכְּרֻבִים עַל־הָאָרוֹן
וְעַל־בַּדָּיו מִלְמָעְלָה: וַיַּאֲרִכוּ הַבַּדִּים וַיֵּרָאוּ רָאשֵׁי הַבַּדִּים מִן־
הַקֹּדֶשׁ עַל־פְּנֵי הַדְּבִיר וְלֹא יֵרָאוּ הַחוּצָה וַיִּהְיוּ שָׁם עַד הַיּוֹם
הַזֶּה: אֵין בָּאָרוֹן רַק שְׁנֵי לֻחוֹת הָאֲבָנִים אֲשֶׁר הִנִּחַ שָׁם מֹשֶׁה
בְּחֹרֵב אֲשֶׁר כָּרַת יהוה עִם־בְּנֵי יִשְׂרָאֵל בְּצֵאתָם מֵאֶרֶץ מִצְרָיִם:

HAFTARA FOR THE SECOND DAY

Four hundred and eighty years after the exodus, King Solomon set in motion the building of the Temple, bringing the entire journey of slavery-to-freedom to its culmination. The nation now had a land, a king, and a capital city, Jerusalem. But there was as yet no permanent home for God at the spiritual center-point of the nation. The plan to build a Temple had been conceived by King David, but he was told by God, through the prophet Nathan, that it would be his son who would build it (II Sam. 7). The idea of such a sanctuary had been anticipated long before, in the Song at the Sea, at a critical moment in the exodus itself: "You will bring them in and plant them on the mountain of Your inheritance – the place, Lord, You made for Your dwelling, the sanctuary, Lord, Your hands established" (Ex. 15:17).

The construction took seven years. Eleven months later the formal conse-

And when the Priests left the Holy Place, the cloud filled the House of the LORD. And the Priests could not stand up to serve because of the cloud – for the glory of the LORD filled the LORD's House.

It was then that Solomon said:
"The LORD said His Presence
would rest in the darkness.
I have built, I have built You a House of Worship;
a place for Your dwelling forever."

Then the king turned his face and blessed all the congregation of Israel: "Blessed be the LORD God of Israel, whose mouth spoke to David my father, and whose hand fulfilled; for He said: 'From the day I brought My people Israel from Egypt I never chose a town in all the tribes of Israel to build My House, to rest My name there; but now I choose David to rule My people Israel.' And He was with the heart of my father, David, who longed to build a House for the name of the LORD God of Israel, and He said to my father, David: 'Because it was in your heart to build a House for My name, you pleased Me by having this in your heart. You shall not build the House – but your son, your seed, will build a House for My name.' And the LORD has fulfilled the word He spoke, and I have followed my father David, to sit upon the throne of Israel, as the LORD promised. And I have built a House for the name of the LORD God of Israel. And there I made a place for the Ark with the LORD's Covenant in it; the one that He hewed out with our fathers, when He brought them out of the Land of Egypt."

---

done after the construction of the Tabernacle (Ex. 39:43. See also Lev. 9:23). Solomon now reviews the history of the project, David's initial plan, and God's instruction that it should not be done in his reign but in his son's.

בְּרִית ה׳ *The LORD's Covenant.* The tablets of stone given to Moses at Mount Sinai, and kept in the Ark.

וַיְהִי בְּצֵאת הַכֹּהֲנִים מִן־הַקֹּדֶשׁ וְהֶעָנָן מָלֵא אֶת־בֵּית יהוה׃
וְלֹא־יָכְלוּ הַכֹּהֲנִים לַעֲמֹד לְשָׁרֵת מִפְּנֵי הֶעָנָן כִּי־מָלֵא כְבוֹד־
יהוה אֶת־בֵּית יהוה׃ אָז אָמַר שְׁלֹמֹה יהוה אָמַר
לִשְׁכֹּן בָּעֲרָפֶל׃ בָּנֹה בָנִיתִי בֵּית זְבֻל לָךְ מָכוֹן לְשִׁבְתְּךָ עוֹלָמִים׃
וַיַּסֵּב הַמֶּלֶךְ אֶת־פָּנָיו וַיְבָרֶךְ אֵת כָּל־קְהַל יִשְׂרָאֵל וְכָל־קְהַל
יִשְׂרָאֵל עֹמֵד׃ וַיֹּאמֶר בָּרוּךְ יהוה אֱלֹהֵי יִשְׂרָאֵל אֲשֶׁר דִּבֶּר
בְּפִיו אֵת דָּוִד אָבִי וּבְיָדוֹ מִלֵּא לֵאמֹר׃ מִן־הַיּוֹם אֲשֶׁר הוֹצֵאתִי
אֶת־עַמִּי אֶת־יִשְׂרָאֵל מִמִּצְרַיִם לֹא־בָחַרְתִּי בְעִיר מִכֹּל שִׁבְטֵי
יִשְׂרָאֵל לִבְנוֹת בַּיִת לִהְיוֹת שְׁמִי שָׁם וָאֶבְחַר בְּדָוִד לִהְיוֹת
עַל־עַמִּי יִשְׂרָאֵל׃ וַיְהִי עִם־לְבַב דָּוִד אָבִי לִבְנוֹת בַּיִת לְשֵׁם
יהוה אֱלֹהֵי יִשְׂרָאֵל׃ וַיֹּאמֶר יהוה אֶל־דָּוִד אָבִי יַעַן אֲשֶׁר הָיָה
עִם־לְבָבְךָ לִבְנוֹת בַּיִת לִשְׁמִי הֱטִיבֹתָ כִּי הָיָה עִם־לְבָבֶךָ׃ רַק
אַתָּה לֹא תִבְנֶה הַבָּיִת כִּי אִם־בִּנְךָ הַיֹּצֵא מֵחֲלָצֶיךָ הוּא־יִבְנֶה
הַבַּיִת לִשְׁמִי׃ וַיָּקֶם יהוה אֶת־דְּבָרוֹ אֲשֶׁר דִּבֵּר וָאָקֻם תַּחַת
דָּוִד אָבִי וָאֵשֵׁב ׀ עַל־כִּסֵּא יִשְׂרָאֵל כַּאֲשֶׁר דִּבֶּר יהוה וָאֶבְנֶה
הַבַּיִת לְשֵׁם יהוה אֱלֹהֵי יִשְׂרָאֵל׃ וָאָשִׂם שָׁם מָקוֹם לָאָרוֹן
אֲשֶׁר־שָׁם בְּרִית יהוה אֲשֶׁר כָּרַת עִם־אֲבֹתֵינוּ בְּהוֹצִיאוֹ אֹתָם
מֵאֶרֶץ מִצְרָיִם׃

---

ing against the veil that separated the Holy (*heikhal*) from the Holy of Holies (*dvir*), but not visible beyond it.

וְהֶעָנָן מָלֵא *The cloud filled.* as it had done in the sanctuary established by Moses in the wilderness (see Ex. 40:34–35). The cloud was the visible sign of the Divine Presence, "the Glory of God."

וַיְבָרֶךְ אֵת כָּל־קְהַל יִשְׂרָאֵל *Blessed all the congregation of Israel.* As Moses had

BLESSINGS AFTER THE HAFTARA

After the Haftara, the person called up for Maftir says the following blessings:

בָּרוּךְ Blessed are You, Lord our God, King of the Universe, Rock of all worlds, righteous for all generations, the faithful God who says and does, speaks and fulfills, all of whose words are truth and righteousness. You are faithful, Lord our God, and faithful are Your words, not one of which returns unfulfilled, for You, God, are a faithful (and compassionate) King. Blessed are You, Lord, faithful in all His words.

רַחֵם Have compassion on Zion for it is the source of our life, and save the one grieved in spirit swiftly in our days. Blessed are You, Lord, who makes Zion rejoice in her children.

שַׂמְּחֵנוּ Grant us joy, Lord our God, through Elijah the prophet Your servant, and through the kingdom of the house of David Your anointed – may he soon come and make our hearts glad. May no stranger sit on his throne, and may others not continue to inherit his glory, for You promised him by Your holy name that his light would never be extinguished. Blessed are You, Lord, Shield of David.

רַחֵם עַל צִיּוֹן *Have compassion on Zion.* Zion is a synonym for Jerusalem. There is, in this brief blessing, a piercing note of love for the holy city ("the source of our life") as well as sadness for its ruined state ("grieved in spirit"). Jerusalem is the home of the Jewish heart, the place from which the Divine Presence was never exiled (Maimonides, Laws of the Chosen House 6:16).

עַל כִּסְאוֹ לֹא יֵשֵׁב זָר *May no stranger sit on his throne.* A prayer for the return of the Davidic monarchy and the restoration of Jewish sovereignty over the land of Israel. There may be the hint here of a polemic against rival claims to sovereignty such as that of the Hasmonean kings of the Second Temple period who were not from the house of David.

ברכות לאחר ההפטרה

After the הפטרה*, the person called up for* מפטיר *says the following blessings:*

בָּרוּךְ אַתָּה יהוה אֱלֹהֵינוּ מֶלֶךְ הָעוֹלָם, צוּר כָּל הָעוֹלָמִים, צַדִּיק בְּכָל הַדּוֹרוֹת, הָאֵל הַנֶּאֱמָן, הָאוֹמֵר וְעוֹשֶׂה, הַמְדַבֵּר וּמְקַיֵּם, שֶׁכָּל דְּבָרָיו אֱמֶת וָצֶדֶק. נֶאֱמָן אַתָּה הוּא יהוה אֱלֹהֵינוּ וְנֶאֱמָנִים דְּבָרֶיךָ, וְדָבָר אֶחָד מִדְּבָרֶיךָ אָחוֹר לֹא יָשׁוּב רֵיקָם, כִּי אֵל מֶלֶךְ נֶאֱמָן (וְרַחֲמָן) אָתָּה. בָּרוּךְ אַתָּה יהוה, הָאֵל הַנֶּאֱמָן בְּכָל דְּבָרָיו.

רַחֵם עַל צִיּוֹן כִּי הִיא בֵּית חַיֵּינוּ, וְלַעֲלוּבַת נֶפֶשׁ תּוֹשִׁיעַ בִּמְהֵרָה בְיָמֵינוּ. בָּרוּךְ אַתָּה יהוה, מְשַׂמֵּחַ צִיּוֹן בְּבָנֶיהָ.

שַׂמְּחֵנוּ יהוה אֱלֹהֵינוּ בְּאֵלִיָּהוּ הַנָּבִיא עַבְדֶּךָ, וּבְמַלְכוּת בֵּית דָּוִד מְשִׁיחֶךָ, בִּמְהֵרָה יָבוֹא וְיָגֵל לִבֵּנוּ. עַל כִּסְאוֹ לֹא יֵשֶׁב זָר, וְלֹא יִנְחֲלוּ עוֹד אֲחֵרִים אֶת כְּבוֹדוֹ, כִּי בְשֵׁם קָדְשְׁךָ נִשְׁבַּעְתָּ לּוֹ שֶׁלֹּא יִכְבֶּה נֵרוֹ לְעוֹלָם וָעֶד. בָּרוּךְ אַתָּה יהוה, מָגֵן דָּוִד.

BLESSINGS AFTER THE HAFTARA

There are three blessings after each Haftara; a fourth is added on Shabbat and festivals.

בָּרוּךְ אַתָּה *Blessed are You.* The first of a sequence of blessings begins with this formula, but not the subsequent ones. The key word of this first paragraph is *ne'eman*, "faithful," meaning: God keeps His word. Many of the haftarot are prophetic visions of the future, communicated to the prophet by God Himself. Historically these have formed the basis of Jewish hope. Hence we affirm our faith that the visions will come true. What God has promised, He will fulfill.

On Shabbat, add the words in parentheses:

עַל הַתּוֹרָה For the Torah, for Divine worship, for the prophets (and for this Sabbath day), and for this day of the festival of Sukkot which You, LORD our God, have given us (for holiness and rest) for gladness and joy, for honor and glory – for all these we thank and bless You, LORD our God, and may Your name be blessed by the mouth of all that lives, continually, for ever and all time. Blessed are You, LORD, who sanctifies (the Sabbath and) Israel and the festive seasons.

On a weekday, the service continues with the various prayers for government on page 470.

On Shabbat continue:

יְקוּם פֻּרְקָן May deliverance arise from heaven, bringing grace, love and compassion, long life, ample sustenance and heavenly help, physical health and enlightenment of mind, living and thriving children who will neither interrupt nor cease from the words of the Torah – to our masters and teachers of the holy communities in the land of Israel and Babylon; to the leaders of assemblies and the leaders of communities in exile; to the heads of academies and to the judges in the gates; to all their disciples and their disciples' disciples, and to all who occupy themselves in study of the Torah. May the King of the Universe bless them, prolonging their lives, increasing their days, and adding to their years. May they be redeemed and delivered from all distress and illness. May our Master in heaven be their help at all times and seasons; and let us say: Amen.

יְקוּם פֻּרְקָן *May deliverance arise.* Two Aramaic prayers originating in Babylon in the age of the Geonim (late sixth to early eleventh century) for the welfare of the leaders of the Jewish community. The "leaders of as-

On שבת, add the words in parentheses:

עַל הַתּוֹרָה וְעַל הָעֲבוֹדָה וְעַל הַנְּבִיאִים (וְעַל יוֹם הַשַּׁבָּת הַזֶּה), וְעַל יוֹם חַג הַסֻּכּוֹת הַזֶּה שֶׁנָּתַתָּ לָּנוּ יהוה אֱלֹהֵינוּ (לִקְדֻשָּׁה וְלִמְנוּחָה) לְשָׂשׂוֹן וּלְשִׂמְחָה, לְכָבוֹד וּלְתִפְאָרֶת. עַל הַכֹּל יהוה אֱלֹהֵינוּ אֲנַחְנוּ מוֹדִים לָךְ וּמְבָרְכִים אוֹתָךְ, יִתְבָּרַךְ שִׁמְךָ בְּפִי כָּל חַי תָּמִיד לְעוֹלָם וָעֶד. בָּרוּךְ אַתָּה יהוה, מְקַדֵּשׁ (הַשַּׁבָּת וְ)יִשְׂרָאֵל וְהַזְּמַנִּים.

On a weekday, the service continues with the various prayers for government on page 471.

On שבת continue:

יְקוּם פֻּרְקָן מִן שְׁמַיָּא, חִנָּא וְחִסְדָּא וְרַחֲמֵי וְחַיֵּי אֲרִיכֵי וּמְזוֹנֵי רְוִיחֵי, וְסִיַּעְתָּא דִשְׁמַיָּא, וּבַרְיוּת גּוּפָא וּנְהוֹרָא מְעַלְיָא, זַרְעָא חַיָּא וְקַיָּמָא, זַרְעָא דִּי לָא יִפְסֻק וְדִי לָא יִבְטֻל מִפִּתְגָּמֵי אוֹרַיְתָא, לְמָרָנָן וְרַבָּנָן חֲבוּרָתָא קַדִּישָׁתָא דִּי בְאַרְעָא דְיִשְׂרָאֵל וְדִי בְבָבֶל, לְרֵישֵׁי כַלָּה, וּלְרֵישֵׁי גַלְוָתָא, וּלְרֵישֵׁי מְתִיבָתָא, וּלְדַיָּנֵי דְבָבָא, לְכָל תַּלְמִידֵיהוֹן, וּלְכָל תַּלְמִידֵי תַלְמִידֵיהוֹן, וּלְכָל מָאן דְּעָסְקִין בְּאוֹרַיְתָא. מַלְכָּא דְעָלְמָא יְבָרֵךְ יָתְהוֹן, יַפֵּשׁ חַיֵּיהוֹן וְיַסְגֵּא יוֹמֵיהוֹן, וְיִתֵּן אַרְכָא לִשְׁנֵיהוֹן, וְיִתְפָּרְקוּן וְיִשְׁתֵּיזְבוּן מִן כָּל עָקָא וּמִן כָּל מַרְעִין בִּישִׁין. מָרַן דִּי בִשְׁמַיָּא יְהֵא בְסַעְדְּהוֹן כָּל זְמַן וְעִדָּן, וְנֹאמַר אָמֵן.

עַל הַתּוֹרָה *For the Torah.* A prayer specific to the day, be it Shabbat, festival or both.

יְקוּם פֻּרְקָן May deliverance arise from heaven, bringing grace, love and compassion, long life, ample sustenance and heavenly help, physical health and enlightenment of mind, living and thriving children who will neither interrupt nor cease from the words of the Torah – to all this holy congregation, great and small, women and children. May the King of the Universe bless you, prolonging your lives, increasing your days, and adding to your years. May you be redeemed and delivered from all distress and illness. May our Master in heaven be your help at all times and seasons; and let us say: Amen.

מִי שֶׁבֵּרַךְ May He who blessed our fathers, Abraham, Isaac and Jacob, bless all this holy congregation, together with all other holy congregations: them, their wives, their sons and daughters, and all that is theirs. May He bless those who unite to form synagogues for prayer and those who come there to pray; those who provide lamps for light and wine for Kiddush and Havdala, food for visitors and charity for the poor, and all who faithfully occupy themselves with the needs of the community. May the Holy One, blessed be He, give them their reward; may He remove from them all illness, grant them complete healing, and forgive all their sins. May He send blessing and success to all the work of their hands, together with all Israel their brethren; and let us say: Amen.

---

especially those who contribute by time or money to its upkeep. Just as the Tabernacle – the first collective house of worship of the Jewish people – was made from voluntary contributions, so Jewish communities and their religious, educational and welfare institutions have been sustained ever since by offerings "from everyone whose heart prompts them to give" (Ex. 25:2). These three prayers were instituted to be said on the Sabbath and are usually not said at other times.

יְקוּם פֻּרְקָן מִן שְׁמַיָּא, חִנָּא וְחִסְדָּא וְרַחֲמֵי וְחַיֵּי אֲרִיכֵי וּמְזוֹנֵי רְוִיחֵי, וְסִיַּעְתָּא דִשְׁמַיָּא, וּבַרְיוּת גּוּפָא וּנְהוֹרָא מְעַלְיָא, זַרְעָא חַיָּא וְקַיָּמָא, זַרְעָא דִּי לָא יִפְסֻק וְדִי לָא יִבְטֻל מִפִּתְגָּמֵי אוֹרַיְתָא, לְכָל קְהָלָא קַדִּישָׁא הָדֵין, רַבְרְבַיָּא עִם זְעֵרַיָּא, טַפְלָא וּנְשַׁיָּא. מַלְכָּא דְעָלְמָא יְבָרֵךְ יָתְכוֹן, יַפֵּשׁ חַיֵּיכוֹן וְיַסְגֵּא יוֹמֵיכוֹן, וְיִתֵּן אַרְכָא לִשְׁנֵיכוֹן, וְתִתְפָּרְקוּן וְתִשְׁתֵּיזְבוּן מִן כָּל עָקָא וּמִן כָּל מַרְעִין בִּישִׁין. מָרַן דִּי בִשְׁמַיָּא יְהֵא בְסַעְדְּכוֹן כָּל זְמַן וְעִדָּן, וְנֹאמַר אָמֵן.

מִי שֶׁבֵּרַךְ אֲבוֹתֵינוּ אַבְרָהָם יִצְחָק וְיַעֲקֹב, הוּא יְבָרֵךְ אֶת כָּל הַקָּהָל הַקָּדוֹשׁ הַזֶּה עִם כָּל קְהִלּוֹת הַקֹּדֶשׁ, הֵם וּנְשֵׁיהֶם וּבְנֵיהֶם וּבְנוֹתֵיהֶם וְכֹל אֲשֶׁר לָהֶם, וּמִי שֶׁמְּיַחֲדִים בָּתֵּי כְנֵסִיּוֹת לִתְפִלָּה, וּמִי שֶׁבָּאִים בְּתוֹכָם לְהִתְפַּלֵּל, וּמִי שֶׁנּוֹתְנִים נֵר לַמָּאוֹר וְיַיִן לְקִדּוּשׁ וּלְהַבְדָּלָה וּפַת לָאוֹרְחִים וּצְדָקָה לָעֲנִיִּים, וְכָל מִי שֶׁעוֹסְקִים בְּצָרְכֵי צִבּוּר בֶּאֱמוּנָה. הַקָּדוֹשׁ בָּרוּךְ הוּא יְשַׁלֵּם שְׂכָרָם, וְיָסִיר מֵהֶם כָּל מַחֲלָה, וְיִרְפָּא לְכָל גּוּפָם, וְיִסְלַח לְכָל עֲוֹנָם, וְיִשְׁלַח בְּרָכָה וְהַצְלָחָה בְּכָל מַעֲשֵׂי יְדֵיהֶם עִם כָּל יִשְׂרָאֵל אֲחֵיהֶם, וְנֹאמַר אָמֵן.

---

semblies" were scholars who taught the public on Sabbaths and festivals. "Leaders of communities in exile" were the lay-leaders, headed in Babylon by the Exilarch. The second prayer is for the welfare of the members of the congregation.

מִי שֶׁבֵּרַךְ *May He who blessed.* This third prayer, a Hebrew equivalent and expansion of the previous one, is for the members of the congregation,

The Prayer for the Welfare of the Canadian Government is on the next page.

PRAYER FOR THE WELFARE OF THE AMERICAN GOVERNMENT

The Leader says the following:

הַנּוֹתֵן תְּשׁוּעָה May He who gives salvation to kings and dominion to princes, whose kingdom is an everlasting kingdom, who delivers His servant David from the evil sword, who makes a way in the sea and a path through the mighty waters, bless and protect, guard and help, exalt, magnify and uplift the President, Vice President and all officials of this land. May the Supreme King of kings in His mercy put into their hearts and the hearts of all their counselors and officials, to deal kindly with us and all Israel. In their days and in ours, may Judah be saved and Israel dwell in safety, and may the Redeemer come to Zion. May this be His will, and let us say: Amen.

PRAYER FOR THE SAFETY OF THE AMERICAN MILITARY FORCES

The Leader says the following:

אַדִּיר בַּמָּרוֹם God on high who dwells in might, the King to whom peace belongs, look down from Your holy habitation and bless the soldiers of the American military forces who risk their lives for the sake of peace on earth. Be their shelter and stronghold, and let them not falter. Give them the strength and courage to thwart the plans of the enemy and end the rule of evil. May their enemies be scattered and their foes flee before them, and may they rejoice in Your salvation. Bring them back safely to their homes, as is written: "The LORD *Ps. 121*
will guard you from all harm, He will guard your life. The LORD will guard your going and coming, now and for evermore." And may there be fulfilled for us the verse: "Nation shall not lift up sword against *Is. 2*
nation, nor shall they learn war any more." Let all the inhabitants on earth know that sovereignty is Yours and Your name inspires awe over all You have created – and let us say: Amen.

---

its peace, you shall find peace." This is the first statement in history of what it is to be a creative minority, integrating without assimilating, maintaining one's identity while contributing to society as a whole. Similar guidance

The Prayer for the Welfare of the Canadian Government is on the next page.

תפילה לשלום המלכות (ארה״ב)

The שליח ציבור *says the following:*

הַנּוֹתֵן תְּשׁוּעָה לַמְּלָכִים וּמֶמְשָׁלָה לַנְּסִיכִים, מַלְכוּתוֹ מַלְכוּת כָּל עוֹלָמִים, הַפּוֹצֶה אֶת דָּוִד עַבְדּוֹ מֵחֶרֶב רָעָה, הַנּוֹתֵן בַּיָּם דֶּרֶךְ וּבְמַיִם עַזִּים נְתִיבָה, הוּא יְבָרֵךְ וְיִשְׁמֹר וְיִנְצֹר וְיַעֲזֹר וִירוֹמֵם וִיגַדֵּל וִינַשֵּׂא לְמַעְלָה אֶת הַנָּשִׂיא וְאֵת מִשְׁנֵהוּ וְאֶת כָּל שָׂרֵי הָאָרֶץ הַזֹּאת. מֶלֶךְ מַלְכֵי הַמְּלָכִים, בְּרַחֲמָיו יִתֵּן בְּלִבָּם וּבְלֵב כָּל יוֹעֲצֵיהֶם וְשָׂרֵיהֶם לַעֲשׂוֹת טוֹבָה עִמָּנוּ וְעִם כָּל יִשְׂרָאֵל. בִּימֵיהֶם וּבְיָמֵינוּ תִּוָּשַׁע יְהוּדָה, וְיִשְׂרָאֵל יִשְׁכֹּן לָבֶטַח, וּבָא לְצִיּוֹן גּוֹאֵל. וְכֵן יְהִי רָצוֹן, וְנֹאמַר אָמֵן.

תפילה לשלום חיילי צבא ארצות הברית

The שליח ציבור *says the following:*

אַדִּיר בַּמָּרוֹם שׁוֹכֵן בִּגְבוּרָה, מֶלֶךְ שֶׁהַשָּׁלוֹם שֶׁלּוֹ, הַשְׁקִיפָה מִמְּעוֹן
קָדְשֶׁךָ, וּבָרֵךְ אֶת חַיָּלֵי צְבָא אַרְצוֹת הַבְּרִית, הַמְחָרְפִים נַפְשָׁם
בְּלֶכְתָּם לָשִׂים שָׁלוֹם בָּאָרֶץ. הֱיֵה נָא לָהֶם מַחֲסֶה וּמָעוֹז, וְאַל תִּתֵּן
לַמּוֹט רַגְלָם, חַזֵּק יְדֵיהֶם וְאַמֵּץ רוּחָם לְהָפֵר עֲצַת אוֹיֵב וּלְהַעֲבִיר
מֶמְשֶׁלֶת זָדוֹן, יָפֽוּצוּ אוֹיְבֵיהֶם וְיָנֽוּסוּ מְשַׂנְאֵיהֶם מִפְּנֵיהֶם, וְיִשְׂמְחוּ
בִּישׁוּעָתֶךָ. הֲשִׁיבֵם בְּשָׁלוֹם אֶל בֵּיתָם, כַּכָּתוּב בְּדִבְרֵי קָדְשֶׁךָ: יהוה תהלים קכא
יִשְׁמָרְךָ מִכָּל־רָע, יִשְׁמֹר אֶת־נַפְשֶׁךָ: יהוה יִשְׁמָר־צֵאתְךָ וּבוֹאֶךָ,
מֵעַתָּה וְעַד־עוֹלָם: וְקַיֵּם בָּֽנוּ מִקְרָא שֶׁכָּתוּב: לֹא־יִשָּׂא גוֹי אֶל־גּוֹי ישעיה ב
חֶרֶב, וְלֹא־יִלְמְדוּ עוֹד מִלְחָמָה: וְיֵדְעוּ כָּל יוֹשְׁבֵי תֵבֵל כִּי לְךָ מְלוּכָה
יָאֲתָה, וְשִׁמְךָ נוֹרָא עַל כָּל מַה שֶּׁבָּרָֽאתָ. וְנֹאמַר אָמֵן.

PRAYER FOR THE WELFARE OF THE GOVERNMENT

This prayer echoes the instruction of Jeremiah (29:7) to those dispersed at the time of the Babylonian exile (sixth century BCE): "Seek the peace of the city to which I have carried you in exile. Pray to the LORD for it, because in

PRAYER FOR THE WELFARE OF THE CANADIAN GOVERNMENT

The Leader says the following:

הַנּוֹתֵן תְּשׁוּעָה May He who gives salvation to kings and dominion to princes, whose kingdom is an everlasting kingdom, who delivers His servant David from the evil sword, who makes a way in the sea and a path through the mighty waters, bless and protect, guard and help, exalt, magnify and uplift the Prime Minister and all the elected and appointed officials of Canada. May the Supreme King of kings in His mercy put into their hearts and the hearts of all their counselors and officials, to deal kindly with us and all Israel. In their days and in ours, may Judah be saved and Israel dwell in safety, and may the Redeemer come to Zion. May this be His will, and let us say: Amen.

PRAYER FOR THE SAFETY OF THE CANADIAN FORCES

The Leader says the following:

אַדִּיר בַּמָּרוֹם God on high who dwells in might, the King to whom peace belongs, look down from Your holy habitation and bless the soldiers of the Canadian Forces who risk their lives for the sake of peace on earth. Be their shelter and stronghold, and let them not falter. Give them the strength and courage to thwart the plans of the enemy and end the rule of evil. May their enemies be scattered and their foes flee before them, and may they rejoice in Your salvation. Bring them back safely to their homes, as is written: "The LORD will *Ps. 121*
guard you from all harm, He will guard your life. The LORD will guard your going and coming, now and for evermore." And may there be fulfilled for us the verse: "Nation shall not lift up sword *Is. 2*
against nation, nor shall they learn war any more." Let all the inhabitants on earth know that sovereignty is Yours and Your name inspires awe over all You have created – and let us say: Amen.

---

we live, to work for the common good and for the good of all humankind, to care for the welfare of others, and to work for good relations between different groups.

תפילה לשלום המלכות (קנדה)

The שליח ציבור *says the following:*

הַנּוֹתֵן תְּשׁוּעָה לַמְּלָכִים וּמֶמְשָׁלָה לַנְּסִיכִים, מַלְכוּתוֹ מַלְכוּת כָּל עוֹלָמִים, הַפּוֹצֶה אֶת דָּוִד עַבְדּוֹ מֵחֶרֶב רָעָה, הַנּוֹתֵן בַּיָּם דֶּרֶךְ וּבְמַיִם עַזִּים נְתִיבָה, הוּא יְבָרֵךְ וְיִשְׁמֹר וְיִנְצֹר וְיַעֲזֹר וִירוֹמֵם וִיגַדֵּל וִינַשֵּׂא לְמַעְלָה אֶת רֹאשׁ הַמֶּמְשָׁלָה וְאֶת כָּל שָׂרֵי הָאָרֶץ הַזֹּאת. מֶלֶךְ מַלְכֵי הַמְּלָכִים, בְּרַחֲמָיו יִתֵּן בְּלִבָּם וּבְלֵב כָּל יוֹעֲצֵיהֶם וְשָׂרֵיהֶם לַעֲשׂוֹת טוֹבָה עִמָּנוּ וְעִם כָּל יִשְׂרָאֵל. בִּימֵיהֶם וּבְיָמֵינוּ תִּוָּשַׁע יְהוּדָה, וְיִשְׂרָאֵל יִשְׁכֹּן לָבֶטַח, וּבָא לְצִיּוֹן גּוֹאֵל. וְכֵן יְהִי רָצוֹן, וְנֹאמַר אָמֵן.

תפילה לשלום חיילי צבא קנדה

The שליח ציבור *says the following:*

אַדִּיר בַּמָּרוֹם שׁוֹכֵן בִּגְבוּרָה, מֶלֶךְ שֶׁהַשָּׁלוֹם שֶׁלּוֹ, הַשְׁקִיפָה מִמְּעוֹן
קָדְשְׁךָ, וּבָרֵךְ אֶת חַיָּלֵי צְבָא קָנָדָה, הַמְחָרְפִים נַפְשָׁם בְּלֶכְתָּם לָשִׂים
שָׁלוֹם בָּאָרֶץ. הֱיֵה נָא לָהֶם מַחֲסֶה וּמָעוֹז, וְאַל תִּתֵּן לַמּוֹט רַגְלָם, חַזֵּק
יְדֵיהֶם וְאַמֵּץ רוּחָם לְהָפֵר עֲצַת אוֹיֵב וּלְהַעֲבִיר מֶמְשֶׁלֶת זָדוֹן, יָפוּצוּ
אוֹיְבֵיהֶם וְיָנוּסוּ מְשַׂנְאֵיהֶם מִפְּנֵיהֶם, וְיִשְׂמְחוּ בִּישׁוּעָתֶךָ. הֲשִׁיבֵם
בְּשָׁלוֹם אֶל בֵּיתָם, כַּכָּתוּב בְּדִבְרֵי קָדְשֶׁךָ: יהוה יִשְׁמָרְךָ מִכָּל־רָע, תהלים קכא
יִשְׁמֹר אֶת־נַפְשֶׁךָ: יהוה יִשְׁמָר־צֵאתְךָ וּבוֹאֶךָ, מֵעַתָּה וְעַד־עוֹלָם:
וְקַיֵּם בָּנוּ מִקְרָא שֶׁכָּתוּב: לֹא־יִשָּׂא גוֹי אֶל־גּוֹי חֶרֶב, וְלֹא־יִלְמְדוּ עוֹד ישעיה ב
מִלְחָמָה: וְיֵדְעוּ כָּל יוֹשְׁבֵי תֵבֵל כִּי לְךָ מְלוּכָה יָאֲתָה, וְשִׁמְךָ נוֹרָא
עַל כָּל מַה שֶּׁבָּרָאתָ. וְנֹאמַר אָמֵן.

---

was given at a later period (first century CE) after the Roman conquest of Jerusalem: "Rabbi Ḥanina, the deputy High Priest, said: Pray for the welfare of the government, for were it not for fear of it, people would swallow one another alive" (*Avot* 3:2). To be a Jew is to be loyal to the country in which

PRAYER FOR THE STATE OF ISRAEL

The Leader says the following prayer:

אָבִינוּ שֶׁבַּשָּׁמַיִם Heavenly Father, Israel's Rock and Redeemer, bless the State of Israel, the first flowering of our redemption. Shield it under the wings of Your loving-kindness and spread over it the Tabernacle of Your peace. Send Your light and truth to its leaders, ministers and counselors, and direct them with good counsel before You.

Strengthen the hands of the defenders of our Holy Land; grant them deliverance, our God, and crown them with the crown of victory. Grant peace in the land and everlasting joy to its inhabitants.

As for our brothers, the whole house of Israel, remember them in all the lands of our (*In Israel say:* their) dispersion, and swiftly lead us (*In Israel say:* them) upright to Zion Your city, and Jerusalem Your dwelling place, as is written in the Torah of Moses Your servant: "Even if *Deut. 30* you are scattered to the furthermost lands under the heavens, from there the LORD your God will gather you and take you back. The LORD your God will bring you to the land your ancestors possessed and you will possess it; and He will make you more prosperous and numerous than your ancestors. Then the LORD your God will open up your heart and the heart of your descendants, to love the LORD your God with all your heart and with all your soul, that you may live."

Unite our hearts to love and revere Your name and observe all the words of Your Torah, and swiftly send us Your righteous anointed one of the house of David, to redeem those who long for Your salvation.

Appear in Your glorious majesty over all the dwellers on earth, and let all who breathe declare: The LORD God of Israel is King and His kingship has dominion over all. Amen, Selah.

---

powerlessness. It is hard not to see in this event the fulfillment of the vision of Moses at the end of his life: "Even if you are scattered to the furthermost lands under the heavens, from there the LORD your God will gather you and take you back" (Deut. 30:4).

תפילה לשלום מדינת ישראל

The שליח ציבור *says the following prayer:*

אָבִינוּ שֶׁבַּשָּׁמַיִם, צוּר יִשְׂרָאֵל וְגוֹאֲלוֹ, בָּרֵךְ אֶת מְדִינַת יִשְׂרָאֵל, רֵאשִׁית צְמִיחַת גְּאֻלָּתֵנוּ. הָגֵן עָלֶיהָ בְּאֶבְרַת חַסְדֶּךָ וּפְרֹשׂ עָלֶיהָ סֻכַּת שְׁלוֹמֶךָ, וּשְׁלַח אוֹרְךָ וַאֲמִתְּךָ לְרָאשֶׁיהָ, שָׂרֶיהָ וְיוֹעֲצֶיהָ, וְתַקְּנֵם בְּעֵצָה טוֹבָה מִלְּפָנֶיךָ.

חַזֵּק אֶת יְדֵי מְגִנֵּי אֶרֶץ קָדְשֵׁנוּ, וְהַנְחִילֵם אֱלֹהֵינוּ יְשׁוּעָה וַעֲטֶרֶת נִצָּחוֹן תְּעַטְּרֵם, וְנָתַתָּ שָׁלוֹם בָּאָרֶץ וְשִׂמְחַת עוֹלָם לְיוֹשְׁבֶיהָ.

וְאֶת אַחֵינוּ כָּל בֵּית יִשְׂרָאֵל, פְּקָד נָא בְּכָל אַרְצוֹת פְּזוּרֵינוּ, וְתוֹלִיכֵנוּ /בארץ ישראל: פְּזוּרֵיהֶם, וְתוֹלִיכֵם/ מְהֵרָה קוֹמְמִיּוּת לְצִיּוֹן עִירֶךָ וְלִירוּשָׁלַיִם מִשְׁכַּן שְׁמֶךָ, כַּכָּתוּב בְּתוֹרַת מֹשֶׁה עַבְדֶּךָ: אִם־יִהְיֶה נִדַּחֲךָ בִּקְצֵה דברים ל הַשָּׁמָיִם, מִשָּׁם יְקַבֶּצְךָ יהוה אֱלֹהֶיךָ וּמִשָּׁם יִקָּחֶךָ: וֶהֱבִיאֲךָ יהוה אֱלֹהֶיךָ אֶל־הָאָרֶץ אֲשֶׁר־יָרְשׁוּ אֲבֹתֶיךָ וִירִשְׁתָּהּ, וְהֵיטִבְךָ וְהִרְבְּךָ מֵאֲבֹתֶיךָ: וּמָל יהוה אֱלֹהֶיךָ אֶת־לְבָבְךָ וְאֶת־לְבַב זַרְעֶךָ, לְאַהֲבָה אֶת־יהוה אֱלֹהֶיךָ בְּכָל־לְבָבְךָ וּבְכָל־נַפְשְׁךָ, לְמַעַן חַיֶּיךָ:

וְיַחֵד לְבָבֵנוּ לְאַהֲבָה וּלְיִרְאָה אֶת שְׁמֶךָ, וְלִשְׁמֹר אֶת כָּל דִּבְרֵי תוֹרָתֶךָ, וּשְׁלַח לָנוּ מְהֵרָה בֶּן דָּוִד מְשִׁיחַ צִדְקֶךָ, לִפְדּוֹת מְחַכֵּי קֵץ יְשׁוּעָתֶךָ.

וְהוֹפַע בַּהֲדַר גְּאוֹן עֻזֶּךָ עַל כָּל יוֹשְׁבֵי תֵבֵל אַרְצֶךָ וְיֹאמַר כֹּל אֲשֶׁר נְשָׁמָה בְאַפּוֹ, יהוה אֱלֹהֵי יִשְׂרָאֵל מֶלֶךְ וּמַלְכוּתוֹ בַּכֹּל מָשָׁלָה, אָמֵן סֶלָה.

PRAYER FOR THE STATE OF ISRAEL

Introduced after the birth of the modern State of Israel in 1948 and the restoration of Jewish sovereignty after almost two millennia of homelessness and

PRAYER FOR ISRAEL'S DEFENSE FORCES

The Leader says the following prayer:

מִי שֶׁבֵּרַךְ May He who blessed our ancestors, Abraham, Isaac and Jacob, bless the members of Israel's Defense Forces and its security services who stand guard over our land and the cities of our God from the Lebanese border to the Egyptian desert, from the Mediterranean sea to the approach of the Aravah, and wherever else they are, on land, in air and at sea. May the LORD make the enemies who rise against us be struck down before them. May the Holy One, blessed be He, protect and deliver them from all trouble and distress, affliction and illness, and send blessing and success to all the work of their hands. May He subdue our enemies under them and crown them with deliverance and victory. And may there be
fulfilled in them the verse, "It is the LORD your God who goes with you to *Deut. 20*
fight for you against your enemies, to deliver you." And let us say: Amen.

PRAYER FOR THOSE BEING HELD IN CAPTIVITY

If Israeli soldiers or civilians are being held in captivity, the Leader says the following:

מִי שֶׁבֵּרַךְ May He who blessed our ancestors, Abraham, Isaac and Jacob, Joseph, Moses and Aaron, David and Solomon, bless, protect and guard the members of Israel's Defense Forces missing in action or held captive, and other captives among our brethren, the whole house of Israel, who are in distress or captivity, as we, the members of this holy congregation, pray on their behalf. May the Holy One, blessed be He, have compassion on them and bring them out from darkness and the shadow of death; may He break their bonds, deliver them from their distress, and bring them
swiftly back to their families' embrace. Give thanks to the LORD for His *Ps. 107*
loving-kindness and for the wonders He does for the children of men;
and may there be fulfilled in them the verse: "Those redeemed by the *Is. 35*
LORD will return; they will enter Zion with singing, and everlasting joy will crown their heads. Gladness and joy will overtake them, and sorrow and sighing will flee away." And let us say: Amen.

On weekdays continue with "LORD my God" on the next page; on Shabbat, some congregations omit "LORD my God" and continue with "Happy are those" on page 480.

---

neighbors, places its faith in God and the justice of its cause, not on military might alone.

מי שברך לחיילי צה״ל

The שליח ציבור *says the following prayer:*

מִי שֶׁבֵּרַךְ אֲבוֹתֵינוּ אַבְרָהָם יִצְחָק וְיַעֲקֹב הוּא יְבָרֵךְ אֶת חַיָּלֵי צְבָא
הַהֲגָנָה לְיִשְׂרָאֵל וְאַנְשֵׁי כֹּחוֹת הַבִּטָּחוֹן, הָעוֹמְדִים עַל מִשְׁמַר אַרְצֵנוּ
וְעָרֵי אֱלֹהֵינוּ, מִגְּבוּל הַלְּבָנוֹן וְעַד מִדְבַּר מִצְרַיִם וּמִן הַיָּם הַגָּדוֹל עַד
לְבוֹא הָעֲרָבָה וּבְכָל מָקוֹם שֶׁהֵם, בַּיַּבָּשָׁה, בָּאֲוִיר וּבַיָּם. יִתֵּן יהוה אֶת
אוֹיְבֵינוּ הַקָּמִים עָלֵינוּ נִגָּפִים לִפְנֵיהֶם. הַקָּדוֹשׁ בָּרוּךְ הוּא יִשְׁמֹר וְיַצִּיל
אֶת חַיָּלֵינוּ מִכָּל צָרָה וְצוּקָה וּמִכָּל נֶגַע וּמַחֲלָה, וְיִשְׁלַח בְּרָכָה וְהַצְלָחָה
בְּכָל מַעֲשֵׂי יְדֵיהֶם. יַדְבֵּר שׂוֹנְאֵינוּ תַּחְתֵּיהֶם וִיעַטְּרֵם בְּכֶתֶר יְשׁוּעָה
דברים כ וּבַעֲטֶרֶת נִצָּחוֹן. וִיקֻיַּם בָּהֶם הַכָּתוּב: כִּי יהוה אֱלֹהֵיכֶם הַהֹלֵךְ עִמָּכֶם
לְהִלָּחֵם לָכֶם עִם־אֹיְבֵיכֶם לְהוֹשִׁיעַ אֶתְכֶם: וְנֹאמַר אָמֵן.

מי שברך לשבויים

If Israeli soldiers or civilians are being held in captivity, the שליח ציבור *says the following:*

מִי שֶׁבֵּרַךְ אֲבוֹתֵינוּ אַבְרָהָם יִצְחָק וְיַעֲקֹב, יוֹסֵף מֹשֶׁה וְאַהֲרֹן, דָּוִד
וּשְׁלֹמֹה, הוּא יְבָרֵךְ וְיִשְׁמֹר וְיִנְצֹר אֶת נֶעְדְּרֵי צְבָא הַהֲגָנָה לְיִשְׂרָאֵל
וּשְׁבוּיָו, וְאֶת כָּל אַחֵינוּ הַנְּתוּנִים בְּצָרָה וּבְשִׁבְיָה, בַּעֲבוּר שֶׁכָּל הַקָּהָל
הַקָּדוֹשׁ הַזֶּה מִתְפַּלֵּל בַּעֲבוּרָם. הַקָּדוֹשׁ בָּרוּךְ הוּא יִמָּלֵא רַחֲמִים
עֲלֵיהֶם, וְיוֹצִיאֵם מֵחֹשֶׁךְ וְצַלְמָוֶת, וּמוֹסְרוֹתֵיהֶם יְנַתֵּק, וּמִמְּצוּקוֹתֵיהֶם
תהלים קז יוֹשִׁיעֵם, וִישִׁיבֵם מְהֵרָה לְחֵיק מִשְׁפְּחוֹתֵיהֶם. יוֹדוּ לַיהוה חַסְדּוֹ
ישעיה לה וְנִפְלְאוֹתָיו לִבְנֵי אָדָם: וִיקֻיַּם בָּהֶם מִקְרָא שֶׁכָּתוּב: וּפְדוּיֵי יהוה יְשֻׁבוּן,
וּבָאוּ צִיּוֹן בְּרִנָּה, וְשִׂמְחַת עוֹלָם עַל־רֹאשָׁם, שָׂשׂוֹן וְשִׂמְחָה יַשִּׂיגוּ, וְנָסוּ
יָגוֹן וַאֲנָחָה: וְנֹאמַר אָמֵן.

*On weekdays continue with "*יָהּ אֵלִי*" on the next page; on* שבת*, some congregations omit "*יָהּ אֵלִי*" and continue with "*אַשְׁרֵי*" on page 481.*

PRAYER FOR ISRAEL'S DEFENSE FORCES

The verse with which the prayer ends is taken from the speech that the "priest anointed for war" spoke to the Israelites before they went into battle in biblical times (Deut. 20:4). Israel, always small and outnumbered by its

Some congregations omit the following on Shabbat.

יָהּ אֵלִי LORD my God and Redeemer, I will stand to greet You;
[God] who was and will be, was and is,
the land of every nation is Yours.

The thanksgiving-offering, burnt-offering, meal-offering, sin-offering, guilt-offering, peace-offering and inauguration-offering are all offerings to You. Remember the weary nation that has borne much, and bring it back to Your land. I will always praise You with "Happy are those who dwell in Your House."

Fine beyond fine, undecipherable, His understanding is unfathomable,
Awesome God who distinguishes between
good and evil with a single glance.

The thanksgiving-offering, burnt-offering, meal-offering, sin-offering, guilt-offering, peace-offering and inauguration-offering are all offerings to You. Remember the weary nation that has borne much, and bring it back to Your land. I will always praise You with "Happy are those who dwell in Your House."

LORD of hosts, with many wonders, He joined all His tent,
making all blossom in the ways of the heart:
the Rock, perfect is His work.

The thanksgiving-offering, burnt-offering, meal-offering, sin-offering, guilt-offering, peace-offering and inauguration-offering are all offerings to You. Remember the weary nation that has borne much, and bring it back to Your land. I will always praise You with "Happy are those who dwell in Your House."

---

the holiest name of God is that He is past, present and future, both in and beyond time.

דַּק עַל דַּק *Fine beyond fine.* The universe is finely tuned for the emergence of life, its delicately balanced mechanisms beyond the reach of human senses and understanding.

בְּאַחַת סְקִירָה *With a single glance.* There is no time-lag between an event and God's knowledge and judgment of it.

כָּל אָהֳלוֹ *All His tent.* A metaphor for the universe as a whole.

בִּנְתִיבוֹת לֵב *In the ways of the heart.* A mystical reference to thirty-two (the numerical value of *lev*, "heart") paths of wisdom with which the universe was created (*Sefer Yetzira*). God's name "*Elohim*" appears thirty-two times in Genesis 1.

Some congregations omit the following on שבת.

יָהּ אֵלִי וְגוֹאֲלִי, אֶתְיַצְּבָה לִקְרָאתֶךָ
הָיָה וְיִהְיֶה, הָיָה וְהֹוֶה, כָּל גּוֹי אַדְמָתֶךָ.
וְתוֹדָה וְלָעוֹלָה וְלַמִּנְחָה וְלַחַטָּאת וְלָאָשָׁם
וְלַשְּׁלָמִים וְלַמִּלּוּאִים כָּל קָרְבָּנֶךָ.
זְכֹר נִלְאָה אֲשֶׁר נָשְׂאָה וְהָשִׁיבָה לְאַדְמָתֶךָ
סֶלָה אֲהַלְלָךְ בְּאַשְׁרֵי יוֹשְׁבֵי בֵיתֶךָ.

דַּק עַל דַּק, עַד אֵין נִבְדַּק, וְלִתְבוּנָתוֹ אֵין חֵקֶר
הָאֵל נוֹרָא, בְּאַחַת סְקִירָה, בֵּין טוֹב לָרַע יְבַקֵּר.
וְתוֹדָה וְלָעוֹלָה וְלַמִּנְחָה וְלַחַטָּאת וְלָאָשָׁם
וְלַשְּׁלָמִים וְלַמִּלּוּאִים כָּל קָרְבָּנֶךָ.
זְכֹר נִלְאָה אֲשֶׁר נָשְׂאָה וְהָשִׁיבָה לְאַדְמָתֶךָ
סֶלָה אֲהַלְלָךְ בְּאַשְׁרֵי יוֹשְׁבֵי בֵיתֶךָ.

אֲדוֹן צְבָאוֹת, בְּרֹב פְּלָאוֹת, חִבֵּר כָּל אָהֳלוֹ
בִּנְתִיבוֹת לֵב לִבְלֵב, הַצּוּר תָּמִים פָּעֳלוֹ.
וְתוֹדָה וְלָעוֹלָה וְלַמִּנְחָה וְלַחַטָּאת וְלָאָשָׁם
וְלַשְּׁלָמִים וְלַמִּלּוּאִים כָּל קָרְבָּנֶךָ.
זְכֹר נִלְאָה אֲשֶׁר נָשְׂאָה וְהָשִׁיבָה לְאַדְמָתֶךָ
סֶלָה אֲהַלְלָךְ בְּאַשְׁרֵי יוֹשְׁבֵי בֵיתֶךָ.

יָהּ אֵלִי *Lord my God.* A poem that originated in mystical circles, appearing for the first time in the Siddur of Rabbi Isaiah Horowitz (c. 1565–1630; known as *Shela*). It is a prelude, specific to the three pilgrimage festivals, to *Ashrei*, the first three words of which form its refrain. It expresses the sadness that we can no longer be present at the Temple bringing our offerings and rejoicing as our ancestors once did on these days when the nation came together in celebration. Some do not say it on Shabbat; some omit it on days when *Yizkor* is said, when our grief is specifically focused remembering the deceased.

הָיָה וְיִהְיֶה, הָיָה וְהֹוֶה *Who was and will be, was and is.* One of the senses of

אַשְׁרֵי Happy are those who dwell in Your House; Ps. 84
they shall continue to praise You, Selah!
Happy are the people for whom this is so; Ps. 144
happy are the people whose God is the Lord.
A song of praise by David. Ps. 145

I will exalt You, my God, the King, and bless Your name for ever and all time. Every day I will bless You, and praise Your name for ever and all time. Great is the Lord and greatly to be praised; His greatness is unfathomable. One generation will praise Your works to the next, and tell of Your mighty deeds. On the glorious splendor of Your majesty I will meditate, and on the acts of Your wonders. They shall talk of the power of Your awesome deeds, and I will tell of Your greatness. They shall recite the record of Your great goodness, and sing with joy of Your righteousness. The Lord is gracious and compassionate, slow to anger and great in loving-kindness. The Lord is good to all, and His compassion extends to all His works. All Your works shall thank You, Lord, and Your devoted ones shall bless You. They shall talk of the glory of Your kingship, and speak of Your might. To make known to mankind His mighty deeds and the glorious majesty of His kingship. Your kingdom is an everlasting kingdom, and Your reign is for all generations. The Lord supports all who fall, and raises all who are bowed down. All raise their eyes to You in hope, and You give them their food in due season. You open Your hand, and satisfy every living thing with favor. The Lord is righteous in all His ways, and kind in all He does. The Lord is close to all who call on Him, to all who call on Him in truth. He fulfills the will of those who revere Him; He hears their cry and saves them. The Lord guards all who love Him, but all the wicked He will destroy. ▸ My mouth shall speak the praise of the Lord, and all creatures shall bless His holy name for ever and all time.

We will bless the Lord now and for ever. Halleluya! Ps. 115

תהלים פד
אַשְׁרֵי יוֹשְׁבֵי בֵיתֶךָ, עוֹד יְהַלְלְוּךָ סֶּלָה:

תהלים קמד
אַשְׁרֵי הָעָם שֶׁכָּכָה לּוֹ, אַשְׁרֵי הָעָם שֶׁיהוה אֱלֹהָיו:

תהלים קמה
תְּהִלָּה לְדָוִד

אֲרוֹמִמְךָ אֱלוֹהַי הַמֶּלֶךְ, וַאֲבָרְכָה שִׁמְךָ לְעוֹלָם וָעֶד:
בְּכָל־יוֹם אֲבָרְכֶךָּ, וַאֲהַלְלָה שִׁמְךָ לְעוֹלָם וָעֶד:
גָּדוֹל יהוה וּמְהֻלָּל מְאֹד, וְלִגְדֻלָּתוֹ אֵין חֵקֶר:
דּוֹר לְדוֹר יְשַׁבַּח מַעֲשֶׂיךָ, וּגְבוּרֹתֶיךָ יַגִּידוּ:
הֲדַר כְּבוֹד הוֹדֶךָ, וְדִבְרֵי נִפְלְאֹתֶיךָ אָשִׂיחָה:
וֶעֱזוּז נוֹרְאוֹתֶיךָ יֹאמֵרוּ, וּגְדוּלָּתְךָ אֲסַפְּרֶנָּה:
זֵכֶר רַב־טוּבְךָ יַבִּיעוּ, וְצִדְקָתְךָ יְרַנֵּנוּ:
חַנּוּן וְרַחוּם יהוה, אֶרֶךְ אַפַּיִם וּגְדָל־חָסֶד:
טוֹב־יהוה לַכֹּל, וְרַחֲמָיו עַל־כָּל־מַעֲשָׂיו:
יוֹדְוּךָ יהוה כָּל־מַעֲשֶׂיךָ, וַחֲסִידֶיךָ יְבָרְכוּכָה:
כְּבוֹד מַלְכוּתְךָ יֹאמֵרוּ, וּגְבוּרָתְךָ יְדַבֵּרוּ:
לְהוֹדִיעַ לִבְנֵי הָאָדָם גְּבוּרֹתָיו, וּכְבוֹד הֲדַר מַלְכוּתוֹ:
מַלְכוּתְךָ מַלְכוּת כָּל־עֹלָמִים, וּמֶמְשַׁלְתְּךָ בְּכָל־דּוֹר וָדֹר:
סוֹמֵךְ יהוה לְכָל־הַנֹּפְלִים, וְזוֹקֵף לְכָל־הַכְּפוּפִים:
עֵינֵי־כֹל אֵלֶיךָ יְשַׂבֵּרוּ, וְאַתָּה נוֹתֵן־לָהֶם אֶת־אָכְלָם בְּעִתּוֹ:
פּוֹתֵחַ אֶת־יָדֶךָ, וּמַשְׂבִּיעַ לְכָל־חַי רָצוֹן:
צַדִּיק יהוה בְּכָל־דְּרָכָיו, וְחָסִיד בְּכָל־מַעֲשָׂיו:
קָרוֹב יהוה לְכָל־קֹרְאָיו, לְכֹל אֲשֶׁר יִקְרָאֻהוּ בֶאֱמֶת:
רְצוֹן־יְרֵאָיו יַעֲשֶׂה, וְאֶת־שַׁוְעָתָם יִשְׁמַע, וְיוֹשִׁיעֵם:
שׁוֹמֵר יהוה אֶת־כָּל־אֹהֲבָיו, וְאֵת כָּל־הָרְשָׁעִים יַשְׁמִיד:
◂ תְּהִלַּת יהוה יְדַבֶּר פִּי, וִיבָרֵךְ כָּל־בָּשָׂר שֵׁם קָדְשׁוֹ לְעוֹלָם וָעֶד:

תהלים קטו
וַאֲנַחְנוּ נְבָרֵךְ יָהּ מֵעַתָּה וְעַד־עוֹלָם, הַלְלוּיָהּ:

RETURNING THE TORAH TO THE ARK

The Ark is opened. All stand.
The Leader takes one of the Torah scrolls and says:

יְהַלְלוּ Let them praise the name of the Lord, Ps. 148
for His name alone is sublime.

The congregation responds:

הוֹדוֹ His majesty is above earth and heaven.
He has raised the horn of His people,
for the glory of all His devoted ones,
the children of Israel, the people close to Him.
Halleluya!

While the Torah scrolls are being returned to the Ark, on a weekday the following is said. On Shabbat, Psalm 29, on the next page, is said.

לְדָוִד מִזְמוֹר A psalm of David. The earth is the Lord's and all it Ps. 24
contains, the world and all who live in it. For He founded it on the seas and established it on the streams. Who may climb the mountain of the Lord? Who may stand in His holy place? He who has clean hands and a pure heart, who has not taken My name in vain, or sworn deceitfully. He shall receive blessing from the Lord, and just reward from God, his salvation. This is a generation of those who seek Him, the descendants of Jacob who seek Your presence, Selah! Lift up your heads, O gates; be uplifted, eternal doors, so that the King of glory may enter. Who is the King of glory? It is the Lord, strong and mighty, the Lord mighty in battle. Lift up your heads, O gates; be uplifted, eternal doors, so that the King of glory may enter. ▸ Who is He, the King of glory? The Lord of hosts, He is the King of glory, Selah!

"Lift up your heads, O gates" – makes this an appropriate psalm to say as we open the doors of the Ark to receive the Torah scrolls.

הכנסת ספר תורה

The ארון קודש *is opened. All stand.*
The שליח ציבור *takes one of the* ספרי תורה *and says:*

יְהַלְלוּ אֶת־שֵׁם יהוה, כִּי־נִשְׂגָּב שְׁמוֹ, לְבַדּוֹ תהלים קמח

The קהל *responds:*

הוֹדוֹ עַל־אֶרֶץ וְשָׁמָיִם:
וַיָּרֶם קֶרֶן לְעַמּוֹ
תְּהִלָּה לְכָל־חֲסִידָיו
לִבְנֵי יִשְׂרָאֵל עַם קְרֹבוֹ
הַלְלוּיָהּ:

While the ספרי תורה *are being returned to the* ארון קודש*, on a weekday the following is said. On* שבת*, Psalm 29, on the next page, is said.*

לְדָוִד מִזְמוֹר, לַיהוה הָאָרֶץ וּמְלוֹאָהּ, תֵּבֵל וְיֹשְׁבֵי בָהּ: כִּי־הוּא עַל־יַמִּים יְסָדָהּ, וְעַל־נְהָרוֹת יְכוֹנְנֶהָ: מִי־יַעֲלֶה בְהַר־יהוה, וּמִי־יָקוּם בִּמְקוֹם קָדְשׁוֹ: נְקִי כַפַּיִם וּבַר־לֵבָב, אֲשֶׁר לֹא־נָשָׂא לַשָּׁוְא נַפְשִׁי וְלֹא נִשְׁבַּע לְמִרְמָה: יִשָּׂא בְרָכָה מֵאֵת יהוה, וּצְדָקָה מֵאֱלֹהֵי יִשְׁעוֹ: זֶה דּוֹר דֹּרְשָׁו, מְבַקְשֵׁי פָנֶיךָ, יַעֲקֹב, סֶלָה: שְׂאוּ שְׁעָרִים רָאשֵׁיכֶם, וְהִנָּשְׂאוּ פִּתְחֵי עוֹלָם, וְיָבוֹא מֶלֶךְ הַכָּבוֹד: מִי זֶה מֶלֶךְ הַכָּבוֹד, יהוה עִזּוּז וְגִבּוֹר, יהוה גִּבּוֹר מִלְחָמָה: שְׂאוּ שְׁעָרִים רָאשֵׁיכֶם, וּשְׂאוּ פִּתְחֵי עוֹלָם, וְיָבֹא מֶלֶךְ הַכָּבוֹד: ‹ מִי הוּא זֶה מֶלֶךְ הַכָּבוֹד, יהוה צְבָאוֹת הוּא מֶלֶךְ הַכָּבוֹד, סֶלָה: תהלים כד

לְדָוִד מִזְמוֹר *Psalm 24.* Associated with the occasion on which Solomon brought the Ark into the Temple. The reference to the opening of the gates –

On Shabbat the following is said:

מִזְמוֹר לְדָוִד A psalm of David. Render to the LORD, you angelic Ps. 29
powers, render to the LORD glory and might. Render to the LORD the glory due to His name. Bow to the LORD in the beauty of holiness. The LORD's voice echoes over the waters; the God of glory thunders; the LORD is over the mighty waters. The LORD's voice in power, the LORD's voice in beauty, the LORD's voice breaks cedars, the LORD shatters the cedars of Lebanon. He makes Lebanon skip like a calf, Sirion like a young wild ox. The LORD's voice cleaves flames of fire. The LORD's voice makes the desert quake, the LORD shakes the desert of Kadesh. The LORD's voice makes hinds calve and strips the forests bare, and in His temple all say: "Glory!" ▸ The LORD sat enthroned at the Flood, the LORD sits enthroned as King for ever. The LORD will give strength to His people; the LORD will bless His people with peace.

As the Torah scrolls are placed into the Ark, all say:

וּבְנֻחֹה יֹאמַר When the Ark came to rest, Moses would say:
"Return, O LORD, to the myriad thousands of Israel." Num. 10
Advance, LORD, to Your resting place, Ps. 132
You and Your mighty Ark.
Your priests are clothed in righteousness,
and Your devoted ones sing in joy.
For the sake of Your servant David,
do not reject Your anointed one.
For I give you good instruction; Prov. 4
do not forsake My Torah.
It is a tree of life to those who grasp it, Prov. 3
and those who uphold it are happy.

---

past, when the Israelites carried the Ark, containing the Tablets, with them on all their journeys.

עֵץ־חַיִּים הִיא לַמַּחֲזִיקִים בָּהּ *It is a tree of life to those who grasp it.* The first humans

On שבת *the following is said:*

תהלים כט מִזְמוֹר לְדָוִד, הָבוּ לַיהוה בְּנֵי אֵלִים, הָבוּ לַיהוה כָּבוֹד וָעֹז: הָבוּ
לַיהוה כְּבוֹד שְׁמוֹ, הִשְׁתַּחֲווּ לַיהוה בְּהַדְרַת־קֹדֶשׁ: קוֹל יהוה
עַל־הַמָּיִם, אֵל־הַכָּבוֹד הִרְעִים, יהוה עַל־מַיִם רַבִּים: קוֹל־יהוה
בַּכֹּחַ, קוֹל יהוה בֶּהָדָר: קוֹל יהוה שֹׁבֵר אֲרָזִים, וַיְשַׁבֵּר יהוה אֶת־
אַרְזֵי הַלְּבָנוֹן: וַיַּרְקִידֵם כְּמוֹ־עֵגֶל, לְבָנוֹן וְשִׂרְיוֹן כְּמוֹ בֶן־רְאֵמִים:
קוֹל־יהוה חֹצֵב לַהֲבוֹת אֵשׁ: קוֹל יהוה יָחִיל מִדְבָּר, יָחִיל יהוה
מִדְבַּר קָדֵשׁ: קוֹל יהוה יְחוֹלֵל אַיָּלוֹת וַיֶּחֱשֹׂף יְעָרוֹת, וּבְהֵיכָלוֹ,
כֻּלּוֹ אֹמֵר כָּבוֹד: ‹ יהוה לַמַּבּוּל יָשָׁב, וַיֵּשֶׁב יהוה מֶלֶךְ לְעוֹלָם:
יהוה עֹז לְעַמּוֹ יִתֵּן, יהוה יְבָרֵךְ אֶת־עַמּוֹ בַשָּׁלוֹם:

As the ספרי תורה *are placed into the* ארון קודש*, all say:*

במדבר י וּבְנֻחֹה יֹאמַר, שׁוּבָה יהוה רִבְבוֹת אַלְפֵי יִשְׂרָאֵל:
תהלים קלב קוּמָה יהוה לִמְנוּחָתֶךָ, אַתָּה וַאֲרוֹן עֻזֶּךָ:
כֹּהֲנֶיךָ יִלְבְּשׁוּ־צֶדֶק, וַחֲסִידֶיךָ יְרַנֵּנוּ:
בַּעֲבוּר דָּוִד עַבְדֶּךָ אַל־תָּשֵׁב פְּנֵי מְשִׁיחֶךָ:
משלי ד כִּי לֶקַח טוֹב נָתַתִּי לָכֶם, תּוֹרָתִי אַל־תַּעֲזֹבוּ:
משלי ג עֵץ־חַיִּים הִיא לַמַּחֲזִיקִים בָּהּ, וְתֹמְכֶיהָ מְאֻשָּׁר:

מִזְמוֹר לְדָוִד *Psalm 29.* A psalm whose sevenfold reference to the "voice" of God shaking the earth and making the wilderness tremble is taken as an allusion to the giving of the Torah at Mount Sinai accompanied by thunder and lighting, when the mountain "trembled violently" (Exodus 19:18).

וּבְנֻחֹה יֹאמַר *When the Ark came to rest.* This is the verse (Num. 10:36) that describes the occasions in the wilderness years when the Israelites encamped. As at the opening of the Ark, a ceremony in the present recalls the ancient

Its ways are ways of pleasantness, and all its paths are peace.
▸ Turn us back, O Lord, to You, and we will return. *Lam. 5*
Renew our days as of old.

The Ark is closed.

HALF KADDISH

Leader: יִתְגַּדַּל Magnified and sanctified
may His great name be,
in the world He created by His will.
May He establish His kingdom
in your lifetime and in your days,
and in the lifetime of all the house of Israel,
swiftly and soon –
and say: Amen.

All: May His great name be blessed
for ever and all time.

Leader: Blessed and praised,
glorified and exalted,
raised and honored,
uplifted and lauded
be the name of the Holy One,
blessed be He,
beyond any blessing,
song, praise and consolation
uttered in the world –
and say: Amen.

חַדֵּשׁ יָמֵינוּ כְּקֶדֶם *Renew our days as of old.* A poignant verse taken from the book of Lamentations. In Judaism – the world's oldest monotheistic faith – the new is old, and the old remains new. The symbol of this constant renewal is the Torah, the word of the One beyond time.

דְּרָכֶיהָ דַרְכֵי־נֹעַם וְכָל־נְתִיבוֹתֶיהָ שָׁלוֹם:

▸ הֲשִׁיבֵנוּ יהוה אֵלֶיךָ וְנָשׁוּבָה, חַדֵּשׁ יָמֵינוּ כְּקֶדֶם: איכה ה

The ארון קודש *is closed.*

חצי קדיש

ש״ץ: יִתְגַּדַּל וְיִתְקַדַּשׁ שְׁמֵהּ רַבָּא (קהל: אָמֵן)
בְּעָלְמָא דִּי בְרָא כִרְעוּתֵהּ
וְיַמְלִיךְ מַלְכוּתֵהּ
בְּחַיֵּיכוֹן וּבְיוֹמֵיכוֹן וּבְחַיֵּי דְכָל בֵּית יִשְׂרָאֵל
בַּעֲגָלָא וּבִזְמַן קָרִיב
וְאִמְרוּ אָמֵן. (קהל: אָמֵן)

קהל וש״ץ: יְהֵא שְׁמֵהּ רַבָּא מְבָרַךְ לְעָלַם וּלְעָלְמֵי עָלְמַיָּא.

ש״ץ: יִתְבָּרַךְ וְיִשְׁתַּבַּח וְיִתְפָּאַר וְיִתְרוֹמַם וְיִתְנַשֵּׂא
וְיִתְהַדָּר וְיִתְעַלֶּה וְיִתְהַלָּל
שְׁמֵהּ דְּקֻדְשָׁא בְּרִיךְ הוּא (קהל: בְּרִיךְ הוּא)
לְעֵלָּא מִן כָּל בִּרְכָתָא וְשִׁירָתָא
תֻּשְׁבְּחָתָא וְנֶחֱמָתָא
דַּאֲמִירָן בְּעָלְמָא
וְאִמְרוּ אָמֵן. (קהל: אָמֵן)

---

were forbidden to eat from the Tree of Life "lest they live forever" (Gen. 3:22). In this fine instance of intertextuality the book of Proverbs tells us that immortality is to be found in how we live, not how long. In the union of divine word and human mind we become part of something beyond time, chance and change. The first humans may have lost paradise, but by giving us the Torah, God has given us access to it again.

Musaf for Sukkot

The following prayer, until "in former years" on page 504, is said silently, standing with feet together. Take three steps forward and at the points indicated by ▾, *bend the knees at the first word, bow at the second, and stand straight before saying God's name.*

When I proclaim the LORD's name, give glory to our God. *Deut. 32*
O LORD, open my lips, so that my mouth may declare Your praise. *Ps. 51*

PATRIARCHS

▾בָּרוּךְ▾ Blessed are You, LORD our God and God of our fathers,
God of Abraham, God of Isaac and God of Jacob;
the great, mighty and awesome God, God Most High,
who bestows acts of loving-kindness and creates all,
who remembers the loving-kindness of the fathers
and will bring a Redeemer to their children's children
for the sake of His name, in love.
King, Helper, Savior, Shield:
▾Blessed are You, LORD, Shield of Abraham.

DIVINE MIGHT

אַתָּה גִּבּוֹר You are eternally mighty, LORD.
You give life to the dead and have great power to save.

In Israel:
He causes the dew to fall.

---

for a sacrifice. As our ancestors brought offerings in the Temple so we bring an offering of words.

אֱלֹהֵינוּ וֵאלֹהֵי אֲבוֹתֵינוּ *Our God and God of our fathers.* This is the same sequence as in the Song at the Sea: "This is my God, and I will beautify Him, my father's God, and I will exalt Him" (Ex. 15:2). There are two kinds of inheritance. If I inherit gold, I need do nothing to maintain its value: it will happen inevitably. But if I inherit a business and do not work to maintain it, it will eventually be valueless. Faith is less like gold than like a business. I have to work to sustain its value if I am truly to inherit it. We have to make God *our* God if we are truly to honor the God of our ancestors.

אַתָּה גִּבּוֹר *You are eternally mighty.* This paragraph, with its fivefold reference to the resurrection of the dead, reflects one of the major areas of contention

מוסף לסוכות

The following prayer, until קַדְמֹנִיּוֹת *on page 505, is said silently, standing with feet together. Take three steps forward and at the points indicated by* ˚, *bend the knees at the first word, bow at the second, and stand straight before saying God's name.*

כִּי שֵׁם יהוה אֶקְרָא, הָבוּ גֹדֶל לֵאלֹהֵינוּ: דברים לב
אֲדֹנָי, שְׂפָתַי תִּפְתָּח, וּפִי יַגִּיד תְּהִלָּתֶךָ: תהלים נא

אבות

˚בָּרוּךְ אַתָּה יהוה, אֱלֹהֵינוּ וֵאלֹהֵי אֲבוֹתֵינוּ
אֱלֹהֵי אַבְרָהָם, אֱלֹהֵי יִצְחָק, וֵאלֹהֵי יַעֲקֹב
הָאֵל הַגָּדוֹל הַגִּבּוֹר וְהַנּוֹרָא, אֵל עֶלְיוֹן
גּוֹמֵל חֲסָדִים טוֹבִים, וְקוֹנֵה הַכֹּל, וְזוֹכֵר חַסְדֵי אָבוֹת
וּמֵבִיא גוֹאֵל לִבְנֵי בְנֵיהֶם לְמַעַן שְׁמוֹ בְּאַהֲבָה.
מֶלֶךְ עוֹזֵר וּמוֹשִׁיעַ וּמָגֵן.
˚בָּרוּךְ אַתָּה יהוה, מָגֵן אַבְרָהָם.

גבורות

אַתָּה גִּבּוֹר לְעוֹלָם, אֲדֹנָי
מְחַיֵּה מֵתִים אַתָּה, רַב לְהוֹשִׁיעַ

In ארץ ישראל:

מוֹרִיד הַטָּל

MUSAF

The Musaf service corresponds to the additional sacrifice that was offered in Temple times on Shabbat and festivals. The sacrificial element is more pronounced in Musaf than in other services, since the other services have a double aspect. On the one hand, they too represent sacrifice (except Ma'ariv, the evening service, because no sacrifices were offered at night). But they also represent the prayers of the patriarchs: the morning service is associated with Abraham, the afternoon service with Isaac, and the evening service with Jacob. Musaf has no such additional dimension. It is, simply, the substitute

He sustains the living with loving-kindness,
and with great compassion revives the dead.
He supports the fallen, heals the sick, sets captives free,
and keeps His faith with those who sleep in the dust.
Who is like You, Master of might,
and who can compare to You,
O King who brings death and gives life,
and makes salvation grow?
Faithful are You to revive the dead.
Blessed are You, LORD, who revives the dead.

HOLINESS

אַתָּה קָדוֹשׁ You are holy and Your name is holy,
and holy ones praise You daily, Selah!
Blessed are You, LORD, the holy God.

HOLINESS OF THE DAY

אַתָּה בְחַרְתָּנוּ You have chosen us from among all peoples.
You have loved and favored us.
You have raised us above all tongues.
You have made us holy through Your commandments.
You have brought us near, our King, to Your service,
and have called us by Your great and holy name.

אַתָּה קָדוֹשׁ *You are holy.* The infinite light of God is hidden in the finite spaces of the physical universe. Indeed the word *olam*, universe, is semantically linked to the word *ne'elam*, hidden. "Holy" is the name we give to those special times, places, people and deeds that are signals of transcendence, points at which the infinity of God becomes manifest within the finite world. The holiness of God therefore refers to divine transcendence: God beyond, not within, the world. The holiness of Israel ("Be holy, for I the LORD your God am holy" [Lev. 19:2]) refers to the points within our life where we efface ourselves in order to become a vehicle through which God's light flows into the world.

אַתָּה בְחַרְתָּנוּ *You have chosen us.* The form of sacrifice in Judaism is differ-

מְכַלְכֵּל חַיִּים בְּחֶסֶד, מְחַיֵּה מֵתִים בְּרַחֲמִים רַבִּים
סוֹמֵךְ נוֹפְלִים, וְרוֹפֵא חוֹלִים, וּמַתִּיר אֲסוּרִים
וּמְקַיֵּם אֱמוּנָתוֹ לִישֵׁנֵי עָפָר.
מִי כָמְוֹךָ, בַּעַל גְּבוּרוֹת, וּמִי דּוֹמֶה לָּךְ
מֶלֶךְ, מֵמִית וּמְחַיֶּה וּמַצְמִיחַ יְשׁוּעָה.
וְנֶאֱמָן אַתָּה לְהַחֲיוֹת מֵתִים.
בָּרוּךְ אַתָּה יהוה, מְחַיֵּה הַמֵּתִים.

קדושת השם

אַתָּה קָדוֹשׁ וְשִׁמְךָ קָדוֹשׁ
וּקְדוֹשִׁים בְּכָל יוֹם יְהַלְלְוּךָ סֶּלָה.
בָּרוּךְ אַתָּה יהוה, הָאֵל הַקָּדוֹשׁ.

קדושת היום

אַתָּה בְחַרְתָּנוּ מִכָּל הָעַמִּים, אָהַבְתָּ אוֹתָנוּ וְרָצִיתָ בָּנוּ
וְרוֹמַמְתָּנוּ מִכָּל הַלְּשׁוֹנוֹת, וְקִדַּשְׁתָּנוּ בְּמִצְוֹתֶיךָ
וְקֵרַבְתָּנוּ מַלְכֵּנוּ לַעֲבוֹדָתֶךָ
וְשִׁמְךָ הַגָּדוֹל וְהַקָּדוֹשׁ עָלֵינוּ קָרָאתָ.

---

between the Pharisees and Sadducees in Second Temple times. The Sadducees, influenced by the Greeks, believed that the true home of the soul is in heaven, not on earth. Therefore the highest state is *Olam HaBa*, the World to Come, life after death. That anyone, having experienced such serenity and closeness to God, might wish to return to bodily life on earth was as unintelligible to them as it would have been to Plato. The Pharisees believed otherwise, that justice belongs on earth not only in heaven, and that those who died – including those who died unjustly or before their time – will one day live again, not just immortally in heaven but physically on earth. There is a World to Come, life after death, but there will also be in the future a resurrection of those who died. This is a deep and fundamental statement of Jewish faith.

On Shabbat, add the words in parentheses:

וַתִּתֶּן לָנוּ And You, Lord our God, have given us in love
(Sabbaths for rest and) festivals for rejoicing,
holy days and seasons for joy,
(this Sabbath day and) this day of
the festival of Sukkot, our time of rejoicing
(with love), a holy assembly
in memory of the exodus from Egypt.

וּמִפְּנֵי חֲטָאֵינוּ But because of our sins we were exiled from our land
and driven far from our country.
We cannot go up to appear and bow before You,
and to perform our duties in Your chosen House,
the great and holy Temple that was called by Your name,
because of the hand that was stretched out against Your Sanctuary.
May it be Your will, Lord our God and God of our ancestors,
merciful King,

God we are a mere concatenation of chemicals that will one day turn to dust. Only by the gift of self to the eternal God do we touch – and are touched by – eternity.

וּמִפְּנֵי חֲטָאֵינוּ גָּלִינוּ מֵאַרְצֵנוּ *But because of our sins we were exiled from our land.* An explanation of why we are no longer able to offer sacrifices in the Temple. The word *ḥet*, "sin," also means to miss a target. *Avera*, like the English word "transgression," means to cross a boundary into forbidden territory. Thus a sin is an act in the wrong place, one that disturbs the moral order of the universe. Its punishment, measure for measure, is that the sinner is sent to the wrong place, that is, into exile. For their sin, Adam and Eve were exiled from Eden. For our ancestors' sins they were exiled from their land. The Hebrew word *teshuva*, the proper response to sin, thus has the double sense of spiritual *repentance* for wrongdoing and physical *return* to the land.

וַתִּתֶּן לָנוּ ... וּמִפְּנֵי חֲטָאֵינוּ ... אֱלֹהֵינוּ וֵאלֹהֵי אֲבוֹתֵינוּ *And You [Lord our God] have given us ... But because of our sins ... Our God and God of our ancestors.* Rabbi Joseph

On שבת*, add the words in parentheses:*

וַתִּתֶּן לָנוּ יהוה אֱלֹהֵינוּ בְּאַהֲבָה
(שַׁבָּתוֹת לִמְנוּחָה וּ)מוֹעֲדִים לְשִׂמְחָה, חַגִּים וּזְמַנִּים לְשָׂשׂוֹן
אֶת יוֹם (הַשַּׁבָּת הַזֶּה וְאֶת יוֹם)
חַג הַסֻּכּוֹת הַזֶּה, זְמַן שִׂמְחָתֵנוּ
(בְּאַהֲבָה) מִקְרָא קֹדֶשׁ, זֵכֶר לִיצִיאַת מִצְרָיִם.

וּמִפְּנֵי חֲטָאֵינוּ גָּלִינוּ מֵאַרְצֵנוּ, וְנִתְרַחַקְנוּ מֵעַל אַדְמָתֵנוּ
וְאֵין אֲנַחְנוּ יְכוֹלִים לַעֲלוֹת וְלֵרָאוֹת וּלְהִשְׁתַּחֲווֹת לְפָנֶיךָ
וְלַעֲשׂוֹת חוֹבוֹתֵינוּ בְּבֵית בְּחִירָתֶךָ
בַּבַּיִת הַגָּדוֹל וְהַקָּדוֹשׁ שֶׁנִּקְרָא שִׁמְךָ עָלָיו
מִפְּנֵי הַיָּד שֶׁנִּשְׁתַּלְּחָה בְּמִקְדָּשֶׁךָ.
יְהִי רָצוֹן מִלְּפָנֶיךָ יהוה אֱלֹהֵינוּ וֵאלֹהֵי אֲבוֹתֵינוּ
מֶלֶךְ רַחֲמָן

---

ent with and without a Temple, but its centrality remains. Where once our ancestors offered animals, now, lacking a Temple, we offer words. Yet the essential act is the same in both cases: a giving of self to God. In Judaism, to love is to give. Jewish marriage is consecrated by the gift of a ring. It is not that the recipient needs to receive. It is that love is emotion turned outward. Love is the sacrifice of self to other, and the result is ק-ר-ב, the "coming close" that is the root of the word *korban*, "sacrifice." At the beginning of Leviticus, the book containing many of the details of the sacrifices, the Torah states, "When a person offers *of you* an offering to the Lord" (Lev. 1:2). The order of the words is unexpected: it would be more natural to say, "When one of you brings an offering." From this, the Jewish mystics concluded that the real offering is "of you," that is, of self. The animals were the outer form of the command, but its essential core is the inward act of self-sacrificing love. That is why, after the destruction of the Temple, prayer could substitute for sacrifice, for true prayer *is* the giving of self, the acknowledgment that without

that You in Your abounding compassion may once more
have mercy on us and on Your Sanctuary,
rebuilding it swiftly and adding to its glory.
Our Father, our King,
reveal the glory of Your kingdom to us swiftly.
Appear and be exalted over us in the sight of all that lives.
Bring back our scattered ones from among the nations,
and gather our dispersed people from the ends of the earth.
Lead us to Zion, Your city, in jubilation,
and to Jerusalem, home of Your Temple, with everlasting joy.
There we will prepare for You our obligatory offerings:
the regular daily offerings in their order
and the additional offerings according to their law.
And the additional offering(s of this Sabbath day and)
of this day of the festival of Sukkot.
we will prepare and offer before You in love,
in accord with Your will's commandment,
as You wrote for us in Your Torah
through Your servant Moses,
by Your own word, as it is said:

On Shabbat:
וּבְיוֹם הַשַּׁבָּת On the Sabbath day, make an offering *Num. 28*
of two lambs a year old, without blemish,
together with two-tenths of an ephah of fine flour
mixed with oil as a meal-offering,
and its appropriate libation.
This is the burnt-offering for every Sabbath,
in addition to the regular daily burnt-offering and its libation.

---

the festivals. The second corresponds to Numbers 28–29, which specifies the sacrifices offered on each holy day. The third, with its reference to a reinstatement of pilgrimage to a rebuilt Temple, echoes a key theme of Deuteronomy 16.

שֶׁתָּשׁוּב וּתְרַחֵם עָלֵינוּ וְעַל מִקְדָּשְׁךָ בְּרַחֲמֶיךָ הָרַבִּים
וְתִבְנֵהוּ מְהֵרָה וּתְגַדֵּל כְּבוֹדוֹ.
אָבִינוּ מַלְכֵּנוּ, גַּלֵּה כְּבוֹד מַלְכוּתְךָ עָלֵינוּ מְהֵרָה
וְהוֹפַע וְהִנָּשֵׂא עָלֵינוּ לְעֵינֵי כָּל חָי
וְקָרֵב פְּזוּרֵינוּ מִבֵּין הַגּוֹיִם
וּנְפוּצוֹתֵינוּ כַּנֵּס מִיַּרְכְּתֵי אָרֶץ.
וַהֲבִיאֵנוּ לְצִיּוֹן עִירְךָ בְּרִנָּה
וְלִירוּשָׁלַיִם בֵּית מִקְדָּשְׁךָ בְּשִׂמְחַת עוֹלָם
וְשָׁם נַעֲשֶׂה לְפָנֶיךָ אֶת קָרְבְּנוֹת חוֹבוֹתֵינוּ
תְּמִידִים כְּסִדְרָם וּמוּסָפִים כְּהִלְכָתָם
וְאֶת מוּסַף יוֹם / שבת: וְאֶת מוּסְפֵי יוֹם הַשַּׁבָּת הַזֶּה וְיוֹם/
חַג הַסֻּכּוֹת הַזֶּה.
נַעֲשֶׂה וְנַקְרִיב לְפָנֶיךָ בְּאַהֲבָה כְּמִצְוַת רְצוֹנֶךָ
כְּמוֹ שֶׁכָּתַבְתָּ עָלֵינוּ בְּתוֹרָתֶךָ
עַל יְדֵי מֹשֶׁה עַבְדֶּךָ
מִפִּי כְבוֹדֶךָ, כָּאָמוּר

On שבת:

במדבר כח
וּבְיוֹם הַשַּׁבָּת, שְׁנֵי־כְבָשִׂים בְּנֵי־שָׁנָה תְּמִימִם
וּשְׁנֵי עֶשְׂרֹנִים סֹלֶת מִנְחָה בְּלוּלָה בַשֶּׁמֶן וְנִסְכּוֹ:
עֹלַת שַׁבַּת בְּשַׁבַּתּוֹ, עַל־עֹלַת הַתָּמִיד וְנִסְכָּהּ:

Soloveitchik suggests that this three-paragraph structure of the middle section of Musaf corresponds to the three passages in the Torah dealing with the festivals. The first paragraph, which identifies the theme of the festival, corresponds to Leviticus 23, which sets out the character and dates of

וּבַחֲמִשָּׁה עָשָׂר On the fifteenth day of the seventh month *Num. 29*
you shall hold a sacred assembly.
You shall do no laborious work,
and you shall celebrate a festival to the LORD for seven days.
You shall offer a burnt-offering,
a fire-offering of pleasing aroma to the LORD:
thirteen young bullocks, two rams,
and fourteen yearling male lambs; they shall be without blemish.

And their meal-offerings and wine-libations as ordained:
three-tenths of an ephah for each bull,
two-tenths of an ephah for each ram,
one-tenth of an ephah for each lamb,
wine for the libations, a male goat for atonement,
and two regular daily offerings according to their law.

On Shabbat:
יִשְׂמְחוּ Those who keep the Sabbath and call it a delight
shall rejoice in Your kingship.
The people who sanctify the seventh day shall all be satisfied
and take delight in Your goodness,
for You favored the seventh day and declared it holy.
You called it "most desirable of days" in remembrance of Creation.

אֱלֹהֵינוּ Our God and God of our ancestors,
merciful King, have compassion upon us.
You who are good and do good, respond to our call.
Return to us in Your abounding mercy
for the sake of our fathers who did Your will.
Rebuild Your Temple as at the beginning,
and establish Your Sanctuary on its site.
Let us witness its rebuilding and gladden us by its restoration.
Bring the priests back to their service,
the Levites to their song and music,
and the Israelites to their homes.

וּבַחֲמִשָּׁה עָשָׂר יוֹם לַחֹדֶשׁ הַשְּׁבִיעִי במדבר כט
מִקְרָא־קֹדֶשׁ יִהְיֶה לָכֶם
כָּל־מְלֶאכֶת עֲבֹדָה לֹא תַעֲשׂוּ
וְחַגֹּתֶם חַג לַיהוה שִׁבְעַת יָמִים:
וְהִקְרַבְתֶּם עֹלָה אִשֵּׁה רֵיחַ נִיחֹחַ לַיהוה
פָּרִים בְּנֵי־בָקָר שְׁלֹשָׁה עָשָׂר, אֵילִם שְׁנָיִם
כְּבָשִׂים בְּנֵי־שָׁנָה אַרְבָּעָה עָשָׂר, תְּמִימִם יִהְיוּ:

וּמִנְחָתָם וְנִסְכֵּיהֶם כִּמְדֻבָּר
שְׁלֹשָׁה עֶשְׂרֹנִים לַפָּר וּשְׁנֵי עֶשְׂרֹנִים לָאָיִל, וְעִשָּׂרוֹן לַכֶּבֶשׂ
וְיַיִן כְּנִסְכּוֹ, וְשָׂעִיר לְכַפֵּר, וּשְׁנֵי תְמִידִים כְּהִלְכָתָם.

On שבת:

יִשְׂמְחוּ בְמַלְכוּתְךָ שׁוֹמְרֵי שַׁבָּת וְקוֹרְאֵי עֹנֶג.
עַם מְקַדְּשֵׁי שְׁבִיעִי כֻּלָּם יִשְׂבְּעוּ וְיִתְעַנְּגוּ מִטּוּבֶךָ
וּבַשְּׁבִיעִי רָצִיתָ בּוֹ וְקִדַּשְׁתּוֹ
חֶמְדַּת יָמִים אוֹתוֹ קָרָאתָ, זֵכֶר לְמַעֲשֵׂה בְרֵאשִׁית.

אֱלֹהֵינוּ וֵאלֹהֵי אֲבוֹתֵינוּ
מֶלֶךְ רַחֲמָן רַחֵם עָלֵינוּ, טוֹב וּמֵטִיב הִדָּרֶשׁ לָנוּ
שׁוּבָה אֵלֵינוּ בַּהֲמוֹן רַחֲמֶיךָ
בִּגְלַל אָבוֹת שֶׁעָשׂוּ רְצוֹנֶךָ.
בְּנֵה בֵיתְךָ כְּבַתְּחִלָּה, וְכוֹנֵן מִקְדָּשְׁךָ עַל מְכוֹנוֹ
וְהַרְאֵנוּ בְּבִנְיָנוֹ, וְשַׂמְּחֵנוּ בְּתִקּוּנוֹ
וְהָשֵׁב כֹּהֲנִים לַעֲבוֹדָתָם, וּלְוִיִּם לְשִׁירָם וּלְזִמְרָם
וְהָשֵׁב יִשְׂרָאֵל לִנְוֵיהֶם.

וְשָׁם נַעֲלֶה There we will go up and appear and bow before You
on the three pilgrimage festivals,
as is written in Your Torah:

> "Three times in the year all your males shall appear *Deut. 16*
> before the LORD your God
> at the place He will choose:
> on Pesaḥ, Shavuot and Sukkot.
> They shall not appear before the LORD empty-handed.
> Each shall bring such a gift as he can,
> in proportion to the blessing
> that the LORD your God grants you."

On Shabbat add the words in parentheses:

וְהַשִּׂיאֵנוּ Bestow on us, LORD our God,
the blessing of Your festivals
for life and peace, joy and gladness,
as You desired and promised to bless us.
(Our God and God of our fathers, find favor in our rest.)
Make us holy through Your commandments
and grant us a share in Your Torah;
satisfy us with Your goodness,
gladden us with Your salvation,
and purify our hearts to serve You in truth.
And grant us a heritage, LORD our God,
(with love and favor,) with joy and gladness,
Your holy (Sabbath and) festivals.
May Israel, who sanctify Your name, rejoice in You.
Blessed are You, LORD,
who sanctifies (the Sabbath and) Israel and the festive seasons.

---

the other. A person can be inwardly joyful without showing it, or be dressed in festive clothes while feeling inwardly sad. Festivals are a time for both. They are or should be times of inward joy: that is why in Jewish law a festival

וְשָׁם נַעֲלֶה וְנֵרָאֶה וְנִשְׁתַּחֲוֶה לְפָנֶיךָ בְּשָׁלֹשׁ פַּעֲמֵי רְגָלֵינוּ
כַּכָּתוּב בְּתוֹרָתֶךָ
שָׁלוֹשׁ פְּעָמִים בַּשָּׁנָה יֵרָאֶה כָל־זְכוּרְךָ דברים טז
אֶת־פְּנֵי יהוה אֱלֹהֶיךָ
בַּמָּקוֹם אֲשֶׁר יִבְחָר
בְּחַג הַמַּצּוֹת, וּבְחַג הַשָּׁבֻעוֹת, וּבְחַג הַסֻּכּוֹת
וְלֹא יֵרָאֶה אֶת־פְּנֵי יהוה רֵיקָם:
אִישׁ כְּמַתְּנַת יָדוֹ, כְּבִרְכַּת יהוה אֱלֹהֶיךָ אֲשֶׁר נָתַן־לָךְ:

On שבת *add the words in parentheses:*

וְהַשִּׂיאֵנוּ יהוה אֱלֹהֵינוּ אֶת בִּרְכַּת מוֹעֲדֶיךָ
לְחַיִּים וּלְשָׁלוֹם, לְשִׂמְחָה וּלְשָׂשׂוֹן
כַּאֲשֶׁר רָצִיתָ וְאָמַרְתָּ לְבָרְכֵנוּ.
(אֱלֹהֵינוּ וֵאלֹהֵי אֲבוֹתֵינוּ, רְצֵה בִמְנוּחָתֵנוּ)
קַדְּשֵׁנוּ בְּמִצְוֹתֶיךָ, וְתֵן חֶלְקֵנוּ בְּתוֹרָתֶךָ
שַׂבְּעֵנוּ מִטּוּבֶךָ, וְשַׂמְּחֵנוּ בִּישׁוּעָתֶךָ
וְטַהֵר לִבֵּנוּ לְעָבְדְּךָ בֶּאֱמֶת
וְהַנְחִילֵנוּ יהוה אֱלֹהֵינוּ (בְּאַהֲבָה וּבְרָצוֹן)
בְּשִׂמְחָה וּבְשָׂשׂוֹן (שַׁבָּת וּ) מוֹעֲדֵי קָדְשֶׁךָ
וְיִשְׂמְחוּ בְךָ יִשְׂרָאֵל מְקַדְּשֵׁי שְׁמֶךָ.
בָּרוּךְ אַתָּה יהוה, מְקַדֵּשׁ (הַשַּׁבָּת וְ) יִשְׂרָאֵל וְהַזְּמַנִּים.

לְשִׂמְחָה וּלְשָׂשׂוֹן *Joy and gladness.* The difference between these two terms, according to Malbim, is that *simḥa*, joy, refers to inward emotion. *Sasson*, gladness, refers to the outward signs of celebration. One can exist without

TEMPLE SERVICE

רְצֵה Find favor, Lord our God,
in Your people Israel and their prayer.
Restore the service to Your most holy House,
and accept in love and favor
the fire-offerings of Israel and their prayer.
May the service of Your people Israel
always find favor with You.
And may our eyes witness Your return to Zion in compassion.
Blessed are You, Lord,
who restores His Presence to Zion.

THANKSGIVING

Bow at the first nine words.

מוֹדִים We give thanks to You,
for You are the Lord our God and God of our ancestors
for ever and all time.
You are the Rock of our lives,
Shield of our salvation from generation to generation.
We will thank You and declare Your praise for our lives,
which are entrusted into Your hand;
for our souls, which are placed in Your charge;
for Your miracles which are with us every day;
and for Your wonders and favors
at all times, evening, morning and midday.
You are good – for Your compassion never fails.
You are compassionate –
for Your loving-kindnesses never cease.
We have always placed our hope in You.

מוֹדִים אֲנַחְנוּ לָךְ *We give thanks to You.* This, the middle of the closing three blessings, mirrors the middle of the first three blessings, with this difference – that where that paragraph spoke of God who restores life to the dead, here

עבודה

רְצֵה יהוה אֱלֹהֵינוּ בְּעַמְּךָ יִשְׂרָאֵל, וּבִתְפִלָּתָם
וְהָשֵׁב אֶת הָעֲבוֹדָה לִדְבִיר בֵּיתֶךָ
וְאִשֵּׁי יִשְׂרָאֵל וּתְפִלָּתָם בְּאַהֲבָה תְקַבֵּל בְּרָצוֹן
וּתְהִי לְרָצוֹן תָּמִיד עֲבוֹדַת יִשְׂרָאֵל עַמֶּךָ.
וְתֶחֱזֶינָה עֵינֵינוּ בְּשׁוּבְךָ לְצִיּוֹן בְּרַחֲמִים.
בָּרוּךְ אַתָּה יהוה, הַמַּחֲזִיר שְׁכִינָתוֹ לְצִיּוֹן.

הודאה

Bow at the first five words.

מוֹדִים אֲנַחְנוּ לָךְ
שָׁאַתָּה הוּא יהוה אֱלֹהֵינוּ וֵאלֹהֵי אֲבוֹתֵינוּ לְעוֹלָם וָעֶד.
צוּר חַיֵּינוּ, מָגֵן יִשְׁעֵנוּ, אַתָּה הוּא לְדוֹר וָדוֹר.
נוֹדֶה לְּךָ וּנְסַפֵּר תְּהִלָּתֶךָ
עַל חַיֵּינוּ הַמְּסוּרִים בְּיָדֶךָ
וְעַל נִשְׁמוֹתֵינוּ הַפְּקוּדוֹת לָךְ
וְעַל נִסֶּיךָ שֶׁבְּכָל יוֹם עִמָּנוּ
וְעַל נִפְלְאוֹתֶיךָ וְטוֹבוֹתֶיךָ
שֶׁבְּכָל עֵת, עֶרֶב וָבֹקֶר וְצָהֳרָיִם.
הַטּוֹב, כִּי לֹא כָלוּ רַחֲמֶיךָ
וְהַמְרַחֵם, כִּי לֹא תַמּוּ חֲסָדֶיךָ
מֵעוֹלָם קִוִּינוּ לָךְ.

---

brings to an end a time of mourning. They are also times of public gladness where we celebrate together by the way we dress, eat and sing.

For all these things may Your name be blessed and exalted,
our King, continually, for ever and all time.
Let all that lives thank You, Selah!
and praise Your name in truth,
God, our Savior and Help, Selah!
▾Blessed are You, LORD,
whose name is "the Good"
and to whom thanks are due.

PEACE

שִׂים שָׁלוֹם Grant peace, goodness and blessing,
grace, loving-kindness and compassion to us
and all Israel Your people.
Bless us, our Father, all as one,
with the light of Your face,
for by the light of Your face You have given us,
LORD our God,
the Torah of life and love of kindness,
righteousness, blessing, compassion, life and peace.
May it be good in Your eyes to bless Your people Israel
at every time, in every hour, with Your peace.
Blessed are You, LORD,
who blesses His people Israel with peace.

Some say the following verse:
May the words of my mouth and the meditation of my heart *Ps. 19*
find favor before You, LORD, my Rock and Redeemer.

---

the more we recognize all the "wonders" that are with us at every moment. If we would only open our eyes to the sheer improbability of existence we would realize that we are surrounded by the astonishing, intricate beauty of God's constant creativity: "Lift up your eyes on high, and see who has created these things" (Is. 40:26).

וְעַל כֻּלָּם יִתְבָּרַךְ וְיִתְרוֹמַם שִׁמְךָ מַלְכֵּנוּ תָּמִיד לְעוֹלָם וָעֶד.
וְכֹל הַחַיִּים יוֹדְוּךָ סֶּלָה, וִיהַלְלוּ אֶת שִׁמְךָ בֶּאֱמֶת
הָאֵל יְשׁוּעָתֵנוּ וְעֶזְרָתֵנוּ סֶלָה.
בָּרוּךְ אַתָּה יהוה, הַטּוֹב שִׁמְךָ וּלְךָ נָאֶה לְהוֹדוֹת.

שלום

שִׂים שָׁלוֹם טוֹבָה וּבְרָכָה חֵן וָחֶסֶד וְרַחֲמִים
עָלֵינוּ וְעַל כָּל יִשְׂרָאֵל עַמֶּךָ.
בָּרְכֵנוּ אָבִינוּ כֻּלָּנוּ כְּאֶחָד בְּאוֹר פָּנֶיךָ
כִּי בְאוֹר פָּנֶיךָ נָתַתָּ לָּנוּ, יהוה אֱלֹהֵינוּ
תּוֹרַת חַיִּים וְאַהֲבַת חֶסֶד
וּצְדָקָה וּבְרָכָה וְרַחֲמִים וְחַיִּים וְשָׁלוֹם.
וְטוֹב בְּעֵינֶיךָ לְבָרֵךְ אֶת עַמְּךָ יִשְׂרָאֵל
בְּכָל עֵת וּבְכָל שָׁעָה בִּשְׁלוֹמֶךָ.
בָּרוּךְ אַתָּה יהוה, הַמְבָרֵךְ אֶת עַמּוֹ יִשְׂרָאֵל בַּשָּׁלוֹם.

Some say the following verse:

יִהְיוּ לְרָצוֹן אִמְרֵי־פִי וְהֶגְיוֹן לִבִּי לְפָנֶיךָ, יהוה צוּרִי וְגֹאֲלִי: תהלים יט

---

we speak of the no less miraculous fact that God gives life to the living. The fact that increasingly we can give scientific explanations for the *how* of life, does not diminish – indeed should intensify – our sense of wonder and gratitude at the *gift* of life. There is nothing "mere" about the fact that we are here. The more we learn about cosmology (the birth of the physical universe), life (the emergence of forms of self-organizing complexity), sentience (the fact that we can feel) and self-consciousness (the fact that we can stand outside our feelings, exercising freedom and asking the question, Why?) –

אֱלֹהַי My God, Berakhot 17a
guard my tongue from evil and my lips from deceitful speech.
To those who curse me, let my soul be silent;
may my soul be to all like the dust.
Open my heart to Your Torah
and let my soul pursue Your commandments.
As for all who plan evil against me,
swiftly thwart their counsel and frustrate their plans.
Act for the sake of Your name;
act for the sake of Your right hand;
act for the sake of Your holiness;
act for the sake of Your Torah.
That Your beloved ones may be delivered, Ps. 60
save with Your right hand and answer me.
May the words of my mouth Ps. 19
and the meditation of my heart find favor before You,
Lord, my Rock and Redeemer.

Bow, take three steps back, then bow, first left, then right, then center, while saying:
May He who makes peace in His high places,
make peace for us and all Israel –
and say: Amen.

יְהִי רָצוֹן May it be Your will, Lord our God and God of our ancestors,
that the Temple be rebuilt speedily in our days,
and grant us a share in Your Torah.
And there we will serve You with reverence,
as in the days of old and as in former years.
Then the offering of Judah and Jerusalem Mal. 3
will be pleasing to the Lord as in the days of old and as in former years.

נַפְשִׁי תִדֹּם *Let my soul be silent.* "The way of the just is to be insulted but not to insult; to hear yourself reviled but not to reply; to act out of love and to rejoice even in affliction" (Maimonides, Laws of Ethical Character 2:3, based on *Yoma* 23a).

אֱלֹהַי ברכות יז.

נְצֹר לְשׁוֹנִי מֵרָע וּשְׂפָתַי מִדַּבֵּר מִרְמָה

וְלִמְקַלְלַי נַפְשִׁי תִדֹּם, וְנַפְשִׁי כֶּעָפָר לַכֹּל תִּהְיֶה.

פְּתַח לִבִּי בְּתוֹרָתֶךָ, וּבְמִצְוֹתֶיךָ תִּרְדֹּף נַפְשִׁי.

וְכָל הַחוֹשְׁבִים עָלַי רָעָה

מְהֵרָה הָפֵר עֲצָתָם וְקַלְקֵל מַחֲשַׁבְתָּם.

עֲשֵׂה לְמַעַן שְׁמֶךָ

עֲשֵׂה לְמַעַן יְמִינֶךָ

עֲשֵׂה לְמַעַן קְדֻשָּׁתֶךָ

עֲשֵׂה לְמַעַן תּוֹרָתֶךָ.

לְמַעַן יֵחָלְצוּן יְדִידֶיךָ, הוֹשִׁיעָה יְמִינְךָ וַעֲנֵנִי: תהלים ס

יִהְיוּ לְרָצוֹן אִמְרֵי־פִי וְהֶגְיוֹן לִבִּי לְפָנֶיךָ, יהוה צוּרִי וְגוֹאֲלִי: תהלים יט

Bow, take three steps back, then bow, first left, then right, then center, while saying:

עֹשֶׂה שָׁלוֹם בִּמְרוֹמָיו

הוּא יַעֲשֶׂה שָׁלוֹם עָלֵינוּ וְעַל כָּל יִשְׂרָאֵל, וְאִמְרוּ אָמֵן.

יְהִי רָצוֹן מִלְּפָנֶיךָ יהוה אֱלֹהֵינוּ וֵאלֹהֵי אֲבוֹתֵינוּ

שֶׁיִּבָּנֶה בֵּית הַמִּקְדָּשׁ בִּמְהֵרָה בְיָמֵינוּ, וְתֵן חֶלְקֵנוּ בְּתוֹרָתֶךָ

וְשָׁם נַעֲבָדְךָ בְּיִרְאָה כִּימֵי עוֹלָם וּכְשָׁנִים קַדְמֹנִיּוֹת.

וְעָרְבָה לַיהוה מִנְחַת יְהוּדָה וִירוּשָׁלָםִ כִּימֵי עוֹלָם וּכְשָׁנִים קַדְמֹנִיּוֹת: מלאכי ג

אֱלֹהַי, נְצֹר לְשׁוֹנִי *My God, guard my tongue.* Having asked God at the beginning of the Amida to "Open my lips, so that my mouth may declare Your praise," we now, at the end, ask God to help us close our lips from speaking harshly or deceitfully to others. Evil speech is one of the worst of all sins. It is especially wrong to pass from speaking well to God to speaking badly to our fellow humans, as if the one compensated for the other.

Leader's Repetition for Musaf

The Leader takes three steps forward and at the points indicated by ▾, bends the knees at the first word, bows at the second, and stands straight before saying God's name.

When I proclaim the LORD's name, give glory to our God. *Deut. 32*
O LORD, open my lips, so that my mouth may declare Your praise. *Ps. 51*

PATRIARCHS

▾בָּרוּךְ▾ Blessed are You, LORD our God and God of our fathers,
God of Abraham, God of Isaac and God of Jacob;
the great, mighty and awesome God, God Most High,
who bestows acts of loving-kindness and creates all,
who remembers the loving-kindness of the fathers
and will bring a Redeemer
to their children's children
for the sake of His name, in love.
King, Helper, Savior, Shield:
▾Blessed are You, LORD, Shield of Abraham.

DIVINE MIGHT

אַתָּה גִּבּוֹר You are eternally mighty, LORD.
You give life to the dead and have great power to save.

In Israel:
He causes the dew to fall.

He sustains the living with loving-kindness,
and with great compassion revives the dead.
He supports the fallen, heals the sick, sets captives free,
and keeps His faith with those who sleep in the dust.
Who is like You, Master of might,
and who can compare to You,
O King who brings death and gives life,
and makes salvation grow?
Faithful are You to revive the dead.
Blessed are You, LORD, who revives the dead.

חזרת הש״ץ למוסף

The שליח ציבור *takes three steps forward and at the points indicated by* ׳, *bends the knees at the first word, bows at the second, and stands straight before saying God's name.*

דברים לב כִּי שֵׁם יהוה אֶקְרָא, הָבוּ גֹדֶל לֵאלֹהֵינוּ:
תהלים נא אֲדֹנָי, שְׂפָתַי תִּפְתָּח, וּפִי יַגִּיד תְּהִלָּתֶךָ:

אבות

׳בָּרוּךְ אַתָּה יהוה, אֱלֹהֵינוּ וֵאלֹהֵי אֲבוֹתֵינוּ
אֱלֹהֵי אַבְרָהָם, אֱלֹהֵי יִצְחָק, וֵאלֹהֵי יַעֲקֹב
הָאֵל הַגָּדוֹל הַגִּבּוֹר וְהַנּוֹרָא, אֵל עֶלְיוֹן
גּוֹמֵל חֲסָדִים טוֹבִים, וְקוֹנֵה הַכֹּל, וְזוֹכֵר חַסְדֵי אָבוֹת
וּמֵבִיא גוֹאֵל לִבְנֵי בְנֵיהֶם לְמַעַן שְׁמוֹ בְּאַהֲבָה.
מֶלֶךְ עוֹזֵר וּמוֹשִׁיעַ וּמָגֵן.
׳בָּרוּךְ אַתָּה יהוה, מָגֵן אַבְרָהָם.

גבורות

אַתָּה גִּבּוֹר לְעוֹלָם אֲדֹנָי
מְחַיֵּה מֵתִים אַתָּה, רַב לְהוֹשִׁיעַ

In ארץ ישראל:

מוֹרִיד הַטָּל

מְכַלְכֵּל חַיִּים בְּחֶסֶד, מְחַיֵּה מֵתִים בְּרַחֲמִים רַבִּים
סוֹמֵךְ נוֹפְלִים, וְרוֹפֵא חוֹלִים, וּמַתִּיר אֲסוּרִים
וּמְקַיֵּם אֱמוּנָתוֹ לִישֵׁנֵי עָפָר.
מִי כָמְוֹךָ, בַּעַל גְּבוּרוֹת, וּמִי דּוֹמֶה לָּךְ
מֶלֶךְ, מֵמִית וּמְחַיֶּה וּמַצְמִיחַ יְשׁוּעָה.
וְנֶאֱמָן אַתָּה לְהַחֲיוֹת מֵתִים.
בָּרוּךְ אַתָּה יהוה, מְחַיֵּה הַמֵּתִים.

KEDUSHA

The following is said standing with feet together, rising on the toes at the words indicated by ˄.

Cong. then Leader: נַעֲרִיצְךָ We will revere and sanctify You with the words uttered by the holy Seraphim who sanctify Your name in the Sanctuary; as is written by Your prophet: "They call out to one another, saying: *Is. 6*

Cong. then Leader: ˄Holy, ˄holy, ˄holy is the LORD of hosts; the whole world is filled with His glory." His glory fills the universe. His ministering angels ask each other, "Where is the place of His glory?" Those facing them say "Blessed –"

Cong. then Leader: "˄Blessed is the LORD's glory from His place." *Ezek. 3*
From His place may He turn with compassion and be gracious to the people who proclaim the unity of His name, morning and evening, every day, continually, twice each day reciting in love the Shema:

Cong. then Leader: "Listen, Israel, the LORD is our God, the LORD is One." *Deut. 6*
He is our God, He is our Father, He is our King, He is our Savior – and He, in His compassion, will let us hear a second time in the presence of all that lives, His promise "to be your God. I am the LORD your God." *Num. 15*

---

seeks is *our* praise – the praise of free, fallible, finite agents for whom God is often hidden, who sometimes sin and despair and lose their faith, but who still turn their thoughts and hearts to the creative Source of the universe and the redeeming Presence of history, the Infinite before whom we stand, to whom we offer praise.

שְׁמַע יִשְׂרָאֵל *Listen, Israel.* With the exception of Yom Kippur, the Musaf *Kedusha* is the only one to contain the first verse of the Shema. According to a Geonic tradition (cited in *Or Zarua* 2:50), the custom to so include it originated at a time of persecution when Jews were forbidden publicly to declare their faith by saying the Shema in the synagogue. To circumvent this they incorporated its first line into the Musaf *Kedusha*, where it remains to this day.

קדושה

The following is said standing with feet together, rising on the toes at the words indicated by ▲.

then קהל ש״ץ: נַעֲרִיצְךָ וְנַקְדִּישְׁךָ כְּסוֹד שִׂיחַ שַׂרְפֵי קֹדֶשׁ, הַמַּקְדִּישִׁים שִׁמְךָ בַּקֹּדֶשׁ, כַּכָּתוּב עַל יַד נְבִיאֶךָ: וְקָרָא זֶה אֶל־זֶה וְאָמַר ישעיה ו

then קהל ש״ץ: ▲קָדוֹשׁ, ▲קָדוֹשׁ, ▲קָדוֹשׁ, יהוה צְבָאוֹת, מְלֹא כָל־הָאָרֶץ כְּבוֹדוֹ: כְּבוֹדוֹ מָלֵא עוֹלָם, מְשָׁרְתָיו שׁוֹאֲלִים זֶה לָזֶה, אַיֵּה מְקוֹם כְּבוֹדוֹ לְעֻמָּתָם בָּרוּךְ יֹאמֵרוּ

then קהל ש״ץ: ▲בָּרוּךְ כְּבוֹד־יהוה מִמְּקוֹמוֹ: יחזקאל ג
מִמְּקוֹמוֹ הוּא יִפֶן בְּרַחֲמִים, וְיָחֹן עַם הַמְיַחֲדִים שְׁמוֹ, עֶרֶב וָבֹקֶר בְּכָל יוֹם תָּמִיד, פַּעֲמַיִם בְּאַהֲבָה שְׁמַע אוֹמְרִים

then קהל ש״ץ: שְׁמַע יִשְׂרָאֵל, יהוה אֱלֹהֵינוּ, יהוה אֶחָד: דברים ו
הוּא אֱלֹהֵינוּ, הוּא אָבִינוּ, הוּא מַלְכֵּנוּ, הוּא מוֹשִׁיעֵנוּ, וְהוּא יַשְׁמִיעֵנוּ בְּרַחֲמָיו שֵׁנִית לְעֵינֵי כָּל חָי, לִהְיוֹת לָכֶם לֵאלֹהִים, אֲנִי יהוה אֱלֹהֵיכֶם: במדבר טו

KEDUSHA

Kedusha is the Everest of prayer, the summit of the spiritual life. It is based on the two mystical visions in which Isaiah and Ezekiel saw God in heaven, enthroned in glory and surrounded by a chorus of angels singing His praises. Isaiah heard them say "Holy, holy, holy… the whole world is filled with His glory" (Is. 6:3). Ezekiel heard them say, "Blessed is the LORD's glory from His place" (Ezek. 3:12). By saying *Kedusha* we join the angelic chorus, singing God's praises on earth as they do in heaven. What empowers us to do so is the declaration of Psalm 8:5–6, "What is man, that You are mindful of him, the son of man, that You think of him? Yet You have made him but little lower than the angels, and crowned him with glory and honor." The paradox is that though God is surrounded by angels singing His praises, what He

Cong. then Leader: Glorious is our Glorious One, LORD our Master, and glorious is Your name throughout the earth. Then the LORD shall be King over all the earth; on that day the LORD shall be One and His name One. *Ps. 8* *Zech. 14*

Leader: And in Your holy Writings it is written:

Cong. then Leader: "▲The LORD shall reign for ever. He is your God, Zion, from generation to generation, Halleluya!" *Ps. 146*

Leader: לְדוֹר וָדוֹר From generation to generation we will declare Your greatness, and we will proclaim Your holiness for evermore. Your praise, our God, shall not leave our mouth forever, for You, God, are a great and holy King. Blessed are You, LORD, the holy God.

HOLINESS OF THE DAY

אַתָּה בְחַרְתָּנוּ You have chosen us from among all peoples.
You have loved and favored us.
You have raised us above all tongues.
You have made us holy through Your commandments.
You have brought us near, our King, to Your service,
and have called us by Your great and holy name.

On Shabbat, add the words in parentheses:

וַתִּתֶּן לָנוּ And You, LORD our God, have given us in love
(Sabbaths for rest and) festivals for rejoicing,
holy days and seasons for joy, (this Sabbath day and) this day of
the festival of Sukkot, our time of rejoicing
(with love), a holy assembly in memory of the exodus from Egypt.

וּמִפְּנֵי חֲטָאֵינוּ But because of our sins we were exiled from our land
and driven far from our country.
We cannot go up to appear and bow before You,
and to perform our duties in Your chosen House,
the great and holy Temple that was called by Your name,
because of the hand that was stretched out
against Your Sanctuary.

then קהל ש״ץ: אַדִּיר אַדִּירֵנוּ, יהוה אֲדֹנֵינוּ, מָה־אַדִּיר שִׁמְךָ בְּכָל־הָאָרֶץ: תהלים ח
וְהָיָה יהוה לְמֶלֶךְ עַל־כָּל־הָאָרֶץ, בַּיּוֹם הַהוּא יִהְיֶה יהוה זכריה יד
אֶחָד וּשְׁמוֹ אֶחָד:

ש״ץ: וּבְדִבְרֵי קָדְשְׁךָ כָּתוּב לֵאמֹר

then קהל ש״ץ: יִמְלֹךְ יהוה לְעוֹלָם, אֱלֹהַיִךְ צִיּוֹן לְדֹר וָדֹר, הַלְלוּיָהּ: תהלים קמו

ש״ץ: לְדוֹר וָדוֹר נַגִּיד גָּדְלֶךָ, וּלְנֵצַח נְצָחִים קְדֻשָּׁתְךָ נַקְדִּישׁ,
וְשִׁבְחֲךָ אֱלֹהֵינוּ מִפִּינוּ לֹא יָמוּשׁ לְעוֹלָם וָעֶד, כִּי אֵל מֶלֶךְ
גָּדוֹל וְקָדוֹשׁ אָתָּה. בָּרוּךְ אַתָּה יהוה, הָאֵל הַקָּדוֹשׁ.

קדושת היום

אַתָּה בְחַרְתָּנוּ מִכָּל הָעַמִּים
אָהַבְתָּ אוֹתָנוּ וְרָצִיתָ בָּנוּ, וְרוֹמַמְתָּנוּ מִכָּל הַלְּשׁוֹנוֹת
וְקִדַּשְׁתָּנוּ בְּמִצְוֹתֶיךָ, וְקֵרַבְתָּנוּ מַלְכֵּנוּ לַעֲבוֹדָתֶךָ
וְשִׁמְךָ הַגָּדוֹל וְהַקָּדוֹשׁ עָלֵינוּ קָרָאתָ.

On שבת, add the words in parentheses:

וַתִּתֶּן לָנוּ יהוה אֱלֹהֵינוּ בְּאַהֲבָה
(שַׁבָּתוֹת לִמְנוּחָה וּ)מוֹעֲדִים לְשִׂמְחָה, חַגִּים וּזְמַנִּים לְשָׂשׂוֹן
אֶת יוֹם (הַשַּׁבָּת הַזֶּה וְאֶת יוֹם) חַג הַסֻּכּוֹת הַזֶּה, זְמַן שִׂמְחָתֵנוּ
(בְּאַהֲבָה) מִקְרָא קֹדֶשׁ, זֵכֶר לִיצִיאַת מִצְרָיִם.

וּמִפְּנֵי חֲטָאֵינוּ גָּלִינוּ מֵאַרְצֵנוּ, וְנִתְרַחַקְנוּ מֵעַל אַדְמָתֵנוּ
וְאֵין אֲנַחְנוּ יְכוֹלִים לַעֲלוֹת וְלֵרָאוֹת וּלְהִשְׁתַּחֲווֹת לְפָנֶיךָ
וְלַעֲשׂוֹת חוֹבוֹתֵינוּ בְּבֵית בְּחִירָתֶךָ
בַּבַּיִת הַגָּדוֹל וְהַקָּדוֹשׁ שֶׁנִּקְרָא שִׁמְךָ עָלָיו
מִפְּנֵי הַיָּד שֶׁנִּשְׁתַּלְּחָה בְּמִקְדָּשֶׁךָ.

May it be Your will, LORD our God and God of our ancestors,
merciful King,
that You in Your abounding compassion may once more
have mercy on us and on Your Sanctuary,
rebuilding it swiftly and adding to its glory.
Our Father, our King, reveal the glory of Your kingdom to us swiftly.
Appear and be exalted over us in the sight of all that lives.
Bring back our scattered ones from among the nations,
and gather our dispersed people from the ends of the earth.

Lead us to Zion, Your city, in jubilation,
and to Jerusalem, home of Your Temple, with everlasting joy.
There we will prepare for You our obligatory offerings:
the regular daily offerings in their order
and the additional offerings according to their law.
And the additional offering(s of this Sabbath day and)
of this day of the festival of Sukkot.
we will prepare and offer before You in love,
in accord with Your will's commandment,
as You wrote for us in Your Torah
through Your servant Moses, by Your own word, as it is said:

On Shabbat:

וּבְיוֹם הַשַּׁבָּת On the Sabbath day, make an offering of two lambs a year old, without blemish, together with two-tenths of an ephah of fine flour mixed with oil as a meal-offering, and its appropriate libation. This is the burnt-offering for every Sabbath, in addition to the regular daily burnt-offering and its libation. *Num. 28*

וּבַחֲמִשָּׁה עָשָׂר On the fifteenth day of the seventh month *Num. 29*
you shall hold a sacred assembly.
You shall do no laborious work,
and you shall celebrate a festival to the LORD for seven days.
You shall offer a burnt-offering,
a fire-offering of pleasing aroma to the LORD:
thirteen young bullocks, two rams,
and fourteen yearling male lambs; they shall be without blemish.

יְהִי רָצוֹן מִלְּפָנֶיךָ יהוה אֱלֹהֵינוּ וֵאלֹהֵי אֲבוֹתֵינוּ, מֶלֶךְ רַחֲמָן
שֶׁתָּשׁוּב וּתְרַחֵם עָלֵינוּ וְעַל מִקְדָּשְׁךָ בְּרַחֲמֶיךָ הָרַבִּים
וְתִבְנֵהוּ מְהֵרָה וּתְגַדֵּל כְּבוֹדוֹ.
אָבִינוּ מַלְכֵּנוּ, גַּלֵּה כְּבוֹד מַלְכוּתְךָ עָלֵינוּ מְהֵרָה
וְהוֹפַע וְהִנָּשֵׂא עָלֵינוּ לְעֵינֵי כָּל חָי
וְקָרֵב פְּזוּרֵינוּ מִבֵּין הַגּוֹיִם, וּנְפוּצוֹתֵינוּ כַּנֵּס מִיַּרְכְּתֵי אָרֶץ.

וַהֲבִיאֵנוּ לְצִיּוֹן עִירְךָ בְּרִנָּה
וְלִירוּשָׁלַיִם בֵּית מִקְדָּשְׁךָ בְּשִׂמְחַת עוֹלָם
וְשָׁם נַעֲשֶׂה לְפָנֶיךָ אֶת קָרְבְּנוֹת חוֹבוֹתֵינוּ
תְּמִידִים כְּסִדְרָם וּמוּסָפִים כְּהִלְכָתָם
וְאֶת מוּסַף יוֹם / שבת: וְאֶת מוּסְפֵי יוֹם הַשַּׁבָּת הַזֶּה וְיוֹם/
חַג הַסֻּכּוֹת הַזֶּה
נַעֲשֶׂה וְנַקְרִיב לְפָנֶיךָ בְּאַהֲבָה כְּמִצְוַת רְצוֹנֶךָ
כְּמוֹ שֶׁכָּתַבְתָּ עָלֵינוּ בְּתוֹרָתֶךָ
עַל יְדֵי מֹשֶׁה עַבְדֶּךָ מִפִּי כְבוֹדֶךָ, כָּאָמוּר

On שבת:

וּבְיוֹם הַשַּׁבָּת, שְׁנֵי־כְבָשִׂים בְּנֵי־שָׁנָה תְּמִימִם וּשְׁנֵי עֶשְׂרֹנִים סֹלֶת מִנְחָה בְּלוּלָה בַשֶּׁמֶן וְנִסְכּוֹ: עֹלַת שַׁבַּת בְּשַׁבַּתּוֹ, עַל־עֹלַת הַתָּמִיד וְנִסְכָּהּ: במדבר כח

וּבַחֲמִשָּׁה עָשָׂר יוֹם לַחֹדֶשׁ הַשְּׁבִיעִי, מִקְרָא־קֹדֶשׁ יִהְיֶה לָכֶם במדבר כט
כָּל־מְלֶאכֶת עֲבֹדָה לֹא תַעֲשׂוּ
וְחַגֹּתֶם חַג לַיהוה שִׁבְעַת יָמִים:
וְהִקְרַבְתֶּם עֹלָה אִשֵּׁה רֵיחַ נִיחֹחַ לַיהוה
פָּרִים בְּנֵי־בָקָר שְׁלֹשָׁה עָשָׂר, אֵילִם שְׁנָיִם
כְּבָשִׂים בְּנֵי־שָׁנָה אַרְבָּעָה עָשָׂר, תְּמִימִם יִהְיוּ:

And their meal-offerings and wine-libations as ordained:
three-tenths of an ephah for each bull,
two-tenths of an ephah for the ram,
one-tenth of an ephah for each lamb,
wine for the libations, a male goat for atonement,
and two regular daily offerings according to their law.

On Shabbat:

יִשְׂמְחוּ Those who keep the Sabbath and call it a delight shall rejoice in Your kingship. The people who sanctify the seventh day shall all be satisfied and take delight in Your goodness, for You favored the seventh day and declared it holy. You called it "most desirable of days" in remembrance of Creation.

אֱלֹהֵינוּ Our God and God of our ancestors,
merciful King, have compassion upon us.
You who are good and do good, respond to our call.
Return to us in Your abounding mercy
for the sake of our fathers who did Your will.
Rebuild Your Temple as at the beginning,
and establish Your Sanctuary on its site.
Let us witness its rebuilding
and gladden us by its restoration.
Bring the priests back to their service,
the Levites to their song and music,
and the Israelites to their homes.

וְשָׁם נַעֲלֶה There we will go up and appear and bow before You
on the three pilgrimage festivals, as is written in Your Torah:

"Three times in the year all your males shall appear *Deut. 16*
before the Lord your God at the place He will choose:
on Pesaḥ, Shavuot and Sukkot.
They shall not appear before the Lord empty-handed.
Each shall bring such a gift as he can, in proportion
to the blessing that the Lord your God grants you."

וּמִנְחָתָם וְנִסְכֵּיהֶם כִּמְדֻבָּר
שְׁלֹשָׁה עֶשְׂרֹנִים לַפָּר וּשְׁנֵי עֶשְׂרֹנִים לָאָיִל, וְעִשָּׂרוֹן לַכֶּבֶשׂ
וְיַיִן כְּנִסְכּוֹ, וְשָׂעִיר לְכַפֵּר, וּשְׁנֵי תְמִידִים כְּהִלְכָתָם.

On שבת:

יִשְׂמְחוּ בְמַלְכוּתְךָ שׁוֹמְרֵי שַׁבָּת וְקוֹרְאֵי עֹנֶג. עַם מְקַדְּשֵׁי שְׁבִיעִי כֻּלָּם יִשְׂבְּעוּ וְיִתְעַנְּגוּ מִטּוּבֶךָ, וּבַשְּׁבִיעִי רָצִיתָ בּוֹ וְקִדַּשְׁתּוֹ, חֶמְדַּת יָמִים אוֹתוֹ קָרָאתָ, זֵכֶר לְמַעֲשֵׂה בְרֵאשִׁית.

אֱלֹהֵינוּ וֵאלֹהֵי אֲבוֹתֵינוּ, מֶלֶךְ רַחֲמָן רַחֵם עָלֵינוּ
טוֹב וּמֵטִיב הִדָּרֶשׁ לָנוּ
שׁוּבָה אֵלֵינוּ בַּהֲמוֹן רַחֲמֶיךָ
בִּגְלַל אָבוֹת שֶׁעָשׂוּ רְצוֹנֶךָ.
בְּנֵה בֵיתְךָ כְּבַתְּחִלָּה וְכוֹנֵן מִקְדָּשְׁךָ עַל מְכוֹנוֹ
וְהַרְאֵנוּ בְּבִנְיָנוֹ, וְשַׂמְּחֵנוּ בְּתִקּוּנוֹ
וְהָשֵׁב כֹּהֲנִים לַעֲבוֹדָתָם, וּלְוִיִּם לְשִׁירָם וּלְזִמְרָם
וְהָשֵׁב יִשְׂרָאֵל לִנְוֵיהֶם.

וְשָׁם נַעֲלֶה וְנֵרָאֶה וְנִשְׁתַּחֲוֶה לְפָנֶיךָ בְּשָׁלֹשׁ פַּעֲמֵי רְגָלֵינוּ
כַּכָּתוּב בְּתוֹרָתֶךָ

שָׁלוֹשׁ פְּעָמִים בַּשָּׁנָה יֵרָאֶה כָל־זְכוּרְךָ אֶת־פְּנֵי יהוה אֱלֹהֶיךָ דברים טז
בַּמָּקוֹם אֲשֶׁר יִבְחָר
בְּחַג הַמַּצּוֹת, וּבְחַג הַשָּׁבֻעוֹת, וּבְחַג הַסֻּכּוֹת
וְלֹא יֵרָאֶה אֶת־פְּנֵי יהוה רֵיקָם:
אִישׁ כְּמַתְּנַת יָדוֹ, כְּבִרְכַּת יהוה אֱלֹהֶיךָ אֲשֶׁר נָתַן־לָךְ:

On Shabbat add the words in parentheses:

וְהַשִּׂיאֵנוּ Bestow on us, LORD our God,
the blessing of Your festivals
for life and peace, joy and gladness,
as You desired and promised to bless us.
(Our God and God of our fathers, find favor in our rest.)
Make us holy through Your commandments
and grant us a share in Your Torah;
satisfy us with Your goodness, gladden us with Your salvation,
and purify our hearts to serve You in truth.
And grant us a heritage, LORD our God, (with love and favor,)
with joy and gladness, Your holy (Sabbath and) festivals.
May Israel, who sanctify Your name, rejoice in You.
Blessed are You, LORD,
who sanctifies (the Sabbath and) Israel and the festive seasons.

TEMPLE SERVICE

רְצֵה Find favor, LORD our God, in Your people Israel
and their prayer.
Restore the service to Your most holy House,
and accept in love and favor the fire-offerings of Israel
and their prayer.
May the service of Your people Israel always find favor with You.

If Kohanim say the Priestly Blessing during the Leader's Repetition, the following is said (In Israel the formula on the next page is said); otherwise the Leader continues with "And may our eyes" on the next page.

All: וְתֶעֱרַב May our entreaty be as pleasing to You as a burnt-offering and sacrifice. Please, Compassionate One, in Your abounding mercy restore Your Presence to Zion, Your city, and the order of the Temple service to Jerusalem. And may our eyes witness Your return to Zion in compassion, there we may serve You with reverence as in the days of old and as in former years.

Leader: Blessed are You, LORD, for You alone do we serve with reverence.

The service continues with "We give thanks" on the next page.

On שבת *add the words in parentheses:*

וְהַשִּׂיאֵנוּ יהוה אֱלֹהֵינוּ אֶת בִּרְכַּת מוֹעֲדֶיךָ
לְחַיִּים וּלְשָׁלוֹם, לְשִׂמְחָה וּלְשָׂשׂוֹן
כַּאֲשֶׁר רָצִיתָ וְאָמַרְתָּ לְבָרְכֵנוּ.
(אֱלֹהֵינוּ וֵאלֹהֵי אֲבוֹתֵינוּ, רְצֵה בִמְנוּחָתֵנוּ)
קַדְּשֵׁנוּ בְּמִצְוֹתֶיךָ, וְתֵן חֶלְקֵנוּ בְּתוֹרָתֶךָ
שַׂבְּעֵנוּ מִטּוּבֶךָ, וְשַׂמְּחֵנוּ בִּישׁוּעָתֶךָ
וְטַהֵר לִבֵּנוּ לְעָבְדְּךָ בֶּאֱמֶת
וְהַנְחִילֵנוּ יהוה אֱלֹהֵינוּ (בְּאַהֲבָה וּבְרָצוֹן) בְּשִׂמְחָה וּבְשָׂשׂוֹן
(שַׁבָּת וּ)מוֹעֲדֵי קָדְשֶׁךָ וְיִשְׂמְחוּ בְךָ יִשְׂרָאֵל מְקַדְּשֵׁי שְׁמֶךָ.
בָּרוּךְ אַתָּה יהוה, מְקַדֵּשׁ (הַשַּׁבָּת וְ)יִשְׂרָאֵל וְהַזְּמַנִּים.

עבודה

רְצֵה יהוה אֱלֹהֵינוּ בְּעַמְּךָ יִשְׂרָאֵל, וּבִתְפִלָּתָם
וְהָשֵׁב אֶת הָעֲבוֹדָה לִדְבִיר בֵּיתֶךָ
וְאִשֵּׁי יִשְׂרָאֵל וּתְפִלָּתָם בְּאַהֲבָה תְקַבֵּל בְּרָצוֹן
וּתְהִי לְרָצוֹן תָּמִיד עֲבוֹדַת יִשְׂרָאֵל עַמֶּךָ.

If כהנים *say* ברכת כהנים *during* חזרת הש״ץ,
the following is said (*In* ארץ ישראל *the formula on the next page is said*);
otherwise the שליח ציבור *continues with* וְתֶחֱזֶינָה *on the next page.*

קהל וש״ץ: וְתֶעֱרַב עָלֶיךָ עֲתִירָתֵנוּ כְּעוֹלָה וּכְקָרְבָּן. אָנָּא רַחוּם, בְּרַחֲמֶיךָ הָרַבִּים הָשֵׁב שְׁכִינָתְךָ לְצִיּוֹן עִירֶךָ, וְסֵדֶר הָעֲבוֹדָה לִירוּשָׁלָיִם. וְתֶחֱזֶינָה עֵינֵינוּ בְּשׁוּבְךָ לְצִיּוֹן בְּרַחֲמִים. וְשָׁם נַעֲבָדְךָ בְּיִרְאָה כִּימֵי עוֹלָם וּכְשָׁנִים קַדְמוֹנִיּוֹת.

ש״ץ: בָּרוּךְ אַתָּה יהוה שֶׁאוֹתְךָ לְבַדְּךָ בְּיִרְאָה נַעֲבֹד.

The service continues with מוֹדִים *on the next page.*

In Israel the following formula is used instead:

All: וְתֶעֱרַב May our entreaty be as pleasing to You as a burnt-offering and sacrifice. Please, Compassionate One, in Your abounding mercy restore Your Presence to Zion, Your city, and the order of the Temple service to Jerusalem. That there we may serve You with reverence as in the days of old and as in former years.

When the Priestly Blessing is not said, and also in Israel, the Leader continues:

And may our eyes witness Your return to Zion in compassion.
Blessed are You, LORD, who restores His Presence to Zion.

THANKSGIVING

Bow at the first nine words.

מוֹדִים We give thanks to You,
for You are the LORD our God
and God of our ancestors
for ever and all time.
You are the Rock of our lives,
Shield of our salvation
from generation to generation.
We will thank You and
declare Your praise for our lives,
which are entrusted into Your hand;
for our souls,
which are placed in Your charge;
for Your miracles
which are with us every day;
and for Your wonders and favors
at all times, evening,
morning and midday.
You are good –
for Your compassion never fails.
You are compassionate –
for Your loving-kindnesses never cease.
We have always placed our hope in You.

As the Leader recites Modim, the congregation says quietly:

מוֹדִים We give thanks to You,
for You are the LORD our God
and God of our ancestors,
God of all flesh,
who formed us
and formed the universe.
Blessings and thanks
are due to Your great
and holy name for giving us
life and sustaining us.
May You continue
to give us life
and sustain us;
and may You gather our
exiles to Your holy courts,
to keep Your decrees,
do Your will and serve You
with a perfect heart,
for it is for us
to give You thanks.
Blessed be God to whom
thanksgiving is due.

In ארץ ישראל *the following formula is used instead:*

קהל וש״ץ: וְתֶעֱרַב עָלֶיךָ עֲתִירָתֵנוּ כְּעוֹלָה וּכְקָרְבָּן. אָנָּא רַחוּם, בְּרַחֲמֶיךָ הָרַבִּים הָשֵׁב שְׁכִינָתְךָ לְצִיּוֹן עִירְךָ, וְסֵדֶר הָעֲבוֹדָה לִירוּשָׁלָיִם. וְשָׁם נַעֲבָדְךָ בְּיִרְאָה כִּימֵי עוֹלָם וּכְשָׁנִים קַדְמוֹנִיּוֹת.

When ברכת כהנים *is not said, and also in* ארץ ישראל*, the* שליח ציבור *continues:*

וְתֶחֱזֶינָה עֵינֵינוּ בְּשׁוּבְךָ לְצִיּוֹן בְּרַחֲמִים.
בָּרוּךְ אַתָּה יהוה, הַמַּחֲזִיר שְׁכִינָתוֹ לְצִיּוֹן.

הודאה

Bow at the first five words.

מוֹדִים אֲנַחְנוּ לָךְ
שָׁאַתָּה הוּא יהוה אֱלֹהֵינוּ
וֵאלֹהֵי אֲבוֹתֵינוּ לְעוֹלָם וָעֶד.
צוּר חַיֵּינוּ, מָגֵן יִשְׁעֵנוּ
אַתָּה הוּא לְדוֹר וָדוֹר.
נוֹדֶה לְּךָ וּנְסַפֵּר תְּהִלָּתֶךָ
עַל חַיֵּינוּ הַמְּסוּרִים בְּיָדֶךָ
וְעַל נִשְׁמוֹתֵינוּ הַפְּקוּדוֹת לָךְ
וְעַל נִסֶּיךָ שֶׁבְּכָל יוֹם עִמָּנוּ
וְעַל נִפְלְאוֹתֶיךָ וְטוֹבוֹתֶיךָ
שֶׁבְּכָל עֵת
עֶרֶב וָבֹקֶר וְצָהֳרָיִם.
הַטּוֹב, כִּי לֹא כָלוּ רַחֲמֶיךָ
וְהַמְרַחֵם, כִּי לֹא תַמּוּ חֲסָדֶיךָ
מֵעוֹלָם קִוִּינוּ לָךְ.

As the שליח ציבור *recites* מודים*, the* קהל *says quietly:*

מוֹדִים אֲנַחְנוּ לָךְ
שָׁאַתָּה הוּא יהוה אֱלֹהֵינוּ
וֵאלֹהֵי אֲבוֹתֵינוּ
אֱלֹהֵי כָל בָּשָׂר
יוֹצְרֵנוּ, יוֹצֵר בְּרֵאשִׁית.
בְּרָכוֹת וְהוֹדָאוֹת
לְשִׁמְךָ הַגָּדוֹל וְהַקָּדוֹשׁ
עַל שֶׁהֶחֱיִיתָנוּ וְקִיַּמְתָּנוּ.
כֵּן תְּחַיֵּנוּ וּתְקַיְּמֵנוּ
וְתֶאֱסֹף גָּלֻיּוֹתֵינוּ
לְחַצְרוֹת קָדְשֶׁךָ
לִשְׁמֹר חֻקֶּיךָ
וְלַעֲשׂוֹת רְצוֹנֶךָ וּלְעָבְדְּךָ
בְּלֵבָב שָׁלֵם
עַל שֶׁאֲנַחְנוּ מוֹדִים לָךְ.
בָּרוּךְ אֵל הַהוֹדָאוֹת.

וְעַל כֻּלָּם For all these things may Your name be
blessed and exalted, our King, continually, for ever and all time.
Let all that lives thank You, Selah! and praise Your name in truth,
God, our Savior and Help, Selah!
▾Blessed are You, LORD, whose name is "the Good"
and to whom thanks are due.

BIRKAT KOHANIM

When the Priestly Blessing is not said, the Leader says the formula on page 528.
The following supplication is recited quietly while the Leader says "Let all that lives" above.

In some communities, the congregation says:
יְהִי רָצוֹן May it be Your will, LORD our God and God of our ancestors, that this blessing with which You have commanded to bless Your people Israel should be a complete blessing, with neither hindrance nor sin, now and forever.

The Kohanim say:
יְהִי רָצוֹן May it be Your will, LORD our God and God of our ancestors, that this blessing with which You have commanded us to bless Your people Israel should be a complete blessing, with neither hindrance nor sin, now and forever.

In Israel the Priestly Blessing on page 1396 is said.
The following is recited quietly by the Leader:
אֱלֹהֵינוּ Our God and God of our fathers,
bless us with the threefold blessing in the Torah,
written by the hand of Moses Your servant
and pronounced by Aaron and his sons:

---

in Israel. Outside Israel, our custom is that the priestly blessings are said only on festivals, for only then do we experience the joy that those who live in God's land feel every day.

During the Leader's Repetition of the Amida, and prior to the Priestly Blessings, the Kohanim remove their shoes and wash their hands in water poured from a special vessel by the Levites. When the Leader reaches "Find favor," they ascend to stand in front of the Ark. They cover the head and upper body with the tallit.

When blessing the people, the Kohanim raise their arms and hands as Aaron did when he first blessed the people (Lev. 9:22). Their fingers are spread apart, as a symbol of generosity of spirit (the closed hand symbolizes possessiveness [Deut. 15:7]) and of the Divine Presence that shines through the spaces like the beloved in the Song of Songs who "peers through the

וְעַל כֻּלָּם יִתְבָּרַךְ וְיִתְרוֹמַם שִׁמְךָ מַלְכֵּנוּ תָּמִיד לְעוֹלָם וָעֶד.
וְכֹל הַחַיִּים יוֹדְוּךָ סֶּלָה, וִיהַלְלוּ אֶת שִׁמְךָ בֶּאֱמֶת
הָאֵל יְשׁוּעָתֵנוּ וְעֶזְרָתֵנוּ סֶלָה.
בָּרוּךְ אַתָּה יהוה, הַטּוֹב שִׁמְךָ וּלְךָ נָאֶה לְהוֹדוֹת.

ברכת כוהנים

When ברכת כהנים *is not said, the* שליח ציבור *says the formula on page 529.*
The following supplication is recited quietly while the שליח ציבור *says* וְכֹל הַחַיִּים *above.*

In some communities, the קהל *says:*

יְהִי רָצוֹן מִלְּפָנֶיךָ, יהוה אֱלֹהֵינוּ וֵאלֹהֵי אֲבוֹתֵינוּ, שֶׁתְּהֵא הַבְּרָכָה הַזֹּאת שֶׁצִּוִּיתָ לְבָרֵךְ אֶת עַמְּךָ יִשְׂרָאֵל בְּרָכָה שְׁלֵמָה, וְלֹא יִהְיֶה בָּהּ שׁוּם מִכְשׁוֹל וְעָוֹן מֵעַתָּה וְעַד עוֹלָם.

The כהנים *say:*

יְהִי רָצוֹן מִלְּפָנֶיךָ, יהוה אֱלֹהֵינוּ וֵאלֹהֵי אֲבוֹתֵינוּ, שֶׁתְּהֵא הַבְּרָכָה הַזֹּאת שֶׁצִּוִּיתָנוּ לְבָרֵךְ אֶת עַמְּךָ יִשְׂרָאֵל בְּרָכָה שְׁלֵמָה, וְלֹא יִהְיֶה בָּהּ שׁוּם מִכְשׁוֹל וְעָוֹן מֵעַתָּה וְעַד עוֹלָם.

In ארץ ישראל *the* ברכת כהנים *on page 1397 is said.*
The following is recited quietly by the שליח ציבור:

אֱלֹהֵינוּ וֵאלֹהֵי אֲבוֹתֵינוּ, בָּרְכֵנוּ בַּבְּרָכָה הַמְשֻׁלֶּשֶׁת בַּתּוֹרָה
הַכְּתוּבָה עַל יְדֵי מֹשֶׁה עַבְדֶּךָ, הָאֲמוּרָה מִפִּי אַהֲרֹן וּבָנָיו

BIRKAT KOHANIM

The Priestly Blessings are unique among our prayers: not only are they ordained by the Torah itself, but so is their precise wording (Num. 6:24–26). They are therefore our most ancient prayer. Beautifully constructed, the blessings grow in length – the first line has three words; the second, five; the third, seven – and in each, God's holiest name is the second word of the blessing. They ascend thematically: the first is for material blessing, the second for spiritual blessing, and the third for peace, without which no blessings can be enjoyed.

The Torah is careful to state: "So they (the priests) shall place My name on the Israelites and I will bless them" (Num. 6:27). Thus it is not the priests who bless the people, but God. The priests – whose entire lives were dedicated to divine service – were holy vehicles through which divine blessing flowed. In Temple times, the priests blessed the people daily. That remains the custom

The Leader says aloud:

Kohanim!

In most places, the congregation responds:

Your holy people, as it said:

The Kohanim say the following blessing in unison:

בָּרוּךְ Blessed are You, LORD our God, King of the Universe, who has made us holy with the holiness of Aaron, and has commanded us to bless His people Israel with love.

The first word in each sentence is said by the Leader, followed by the Kohanim. Some read silently the accompanying verses. One should remain silent and not look at the Kohanim while the blessings are being said.

May [He] bless you	May the LORD, Maker of heaven and earth, bless you from Zion.	*Ps. 134*
The LORD	LORD our Master, how majestic is Your name throughout the earth.	*Ps. 8*
And protect you.	Protect me, God, for in You I take refuge.	*Ps. 16*

Read the following silently while the Kohanim chant. Omit on Shabbat.

Master of the Universe, I am Yours and my dreams are Yours. I have dreamt a dream and I do not know what it means. May it be Your will, LORD my God and God of my fathers, that all my dreams be, for me and all Israel, for good, whether I have

---

וְצִוָּנוּ לְבָרֵךְ אֶת עַמּוֹ יִשְׂרָאֵל בְּאַהֲבָה *And has commended us to bless His people Israel with love.* A unique stipulation ("with love") which we do not find in connection with any other command. According to Rashi (to Numbers 6:23), God told Moses to instruct the priests that they should make the blessing "with concentration and a full heart." Hillel suggested that it was Aaron's gift for love and peace that made him and his children the conduit for divine blessings: "Be among the disciples of Aaron, loving peace and pursuing peace, loving people and drawing them close to Torah" (*Avot* 1:12). Love is the conduit through which divine energy flows into the world.

יְבָרֶכְךָ *May the LORD bless you* with your material needs and good health and protect you from harm. *May the LORD make His face shine on you,* granting you spiritual growth, especially through Torah study (*Targum Yonatan*), *and be gracious to you,* so that you find favor in the eyes of God and your

The שליח ציבור *says aloud:*

כֹּהֲנִים

In most places, the קהל *responds:*

עַם קְדוֹשֶׁךָ, כָּאָמוּר:

The כהנים *say the following blessing in unison:*

בָּרוּךְ אַתָּה יהוה אֱלֹהֵינוּ מֶלֶךְ הָעוֹלָם, אֲשֶׁר קִדְּשָׁנוּ בִּקְדֻשָּׁתוֹ שֶׁל אַהֲרֹן, וְצִוָּנוּ לְבָרֵךְ אֶת עַמּוֹ יִשְׂרָאֵל בְּאַהֲבָה.

The first word in each sentence is said by the שליח ציבור*, followed by the* כהנים*. Some read silently the accompanying verses. One should remain silent and not look at the* כהנים *while the blessings are being said.*

תהלים קלד **יְבָרֶכְךָ** יְבָרֶכְךָ יהוה מִצִּיּוֹן, עֹשֵׂה שָׁמַיִם וָאָרֶץ:

תהלים ח **יהוה** יהוה אֲדֹנֵינוּ, מָה־אַדִּיר שִׁמְךָ בְּכָל־הָאָרֶץ:

תהלים טז **וְיִשְׁמְרֶךָ:** שָׁמְרֵנִי אֵל, כִּי־חָסִיתִי בָךְ:

Read the following silently while the כהנים *chant. Omit on* שבת.

רִבּוֹנוֹ שֶׁל עוֹלָם, אֲנִי שֶׁלָּךְ וַחֲלוֹמוֹתַי שֶׁלָּךְ. חֲלוֹם חָלַמְתִּי וְאֵינִי יוֹדֵעַ מַה הוּא. יְהִי רָצוֹן מִלְּפָנֶיךָ, יהוה אֱלֹהַי וֵאלֹהֵי אֲבוֹתַי, שֶׁיִּהְיוּ כָּל חֲלוֹמוֹתַי עָלַי וְעַל כָּל יִשְׂרָאֵל

---

lattices" (Song. 2:9; *Bemidbar Raba* 11:2). The priests cover their hands and faces with the tallit in memory of the Holy of Holies that was screened from public gaze by a curtain (*Beit Yosef*, *OḤ* 128).

The biblical command is preceded by the words, "The LORD said to Moses, 'Tell Aaron and his sons: This is how you are to bless the Israelites. *Say to them…*" (Num. 6:22–23). In memory of Moses instructing the priests, the custom is that the Leader recites each word, followed by the Kohanim (Maimonides, Laws of Prayer 14:3; others argue that the custom is merely to avoid error on the part of the priests).

During the blessings, the members of the congregation should be in front of the Kohanim. Those sitting behind should move forward at this time. Their faces should be turned toward the Kohanim, but they should not look directly at them while the blessings are being said (Rema, *OḤ* 128:23, following the Yerushalmi).

dreamt about myself, or about others, or others have dreamt about me. If they are good, strengthen and reinforce them, and may they be fulfilled in me and them like the dreams of the righteous Joseph. If, though, they need healing, heal them as You healed Hezekiah King of Judah from his illness, like Miriam the prophetess from her leprosy, like Na'aman from his leprosy, like the waters of Mara by Moses our teacher, and like the waters of Jericho by Elisha. And just as You turned the curses of Balaam the wicked from curse to blessing, so turn all my dreams about me and all Israel to good; protect me, be gracious to me and accept me. Amen.

May [He] make shine	May God be gracious to us and bless us; may He make His face shine upon us, Selah.	*Ps. 67*
The Lord	The Lord, the Lord, compassionate and gracious God, slow to anger, abounding in kindness and truth.	*Ex. 34*
His face	Turn to me and be gracious to me, for I am alone and afflicted.	*Ps. 25*
On you	To You, Lord, I lift up my soul.	*Ps. 25*
And be gracious to you.	As the eyes of slaves turn to their master's hand, or the eyes of a slave-girl to the hand of her mistress, so our eyes are turned to the Lord our God, awaiting His favor.	*Ps. 123*

Read the following silently while the Kohanim chant. Omit on Shabbat.

Master of the Universe, I am Yours and my dreams are Yours. I have dreamt a dream and I do not know what it means. May it be Your will, Lord my God and God of my fathers, that all my dreams be, for me and all Israel, for good, whether I have dreamt about myself, or about others, or others have dreamt about me. If they are good, strengthen and reinforce them, and may they be fulfilled in me and them like the dreams of the righteous Joseph. If, though, they need healing, heal them as You healed Hezekiah King of Judah from his illness, like Miriam the prophetess from her leprosy, like Na'aman from his leprosy, like the waters of Mara by Moses our teacher, and like the waters of Jericho by Elisha. And just as You turned the curses of Balaam the wicked from curse to blessing, so turn all my dreams about me and all Israel to good; protect me, be gracious to me and accept me. Amen.

(Sforno), *and grant you peace,* external and internal, harmony with the world and with yourself.

לְטוֹבָה, בֵּין שֶׁחָלַמְתִּי עַל עַצְמִי, וּבֵין שֶׁחָלַמְתִּי עַל אֲחֵרִים, וּבֵין שֶׁחָלְמוּ אֲחֵרִים עָלָי. אִם טוֹבִים הֵם, חַזְּקֵם וְאַמְּצֵם, וְיִתְקַיְּמוּ בִי וּבָהֶם, כַּחֲלוֹמוֹתָיו שֶׁל יוֹסֵף הַצַּדִּיק. וְאִם צְרִיכִים רְפוּאָה, רְפָאֵם כְּחִזְקִיָּהוּ מֶלֶךְ יְהוּדָה מֵחָלְיוֹ, וּכְמִרְיָם הַנְּבִיאָה מִצָּרַעְתָּהּ, וּכְנַעֲמָן מִצָּרַעְתּוֹ, וּכְמֵי מָרָה עַל יְדֵי מֹשֶׁה רַבֵּנוּ, וּכְמֵי יְרִיחוֹ עַל יְדֵי אֱלִישָׁע. וּכְשֵׁם שֶׁהָפַכְתָּ אֶת קִלְלַת בִּלְעָם הָרָשָׁע מִקְּלָלָה לִבְרָכָה, כֵּן תַּהֲפֹךְ כָּל חֲלוֹמוֹתַי עָלַי וְעַל כָּל יִשְׂרָאֵל לְטוֹבָה, וְתִשְׁמְרֵנִי וּתְחָנֵּנִי וְתִרְצֵנִי. אָמֵן.

יָאֵר אֱלֹהִים יְחָנֵּנוּ וִיבָרְכֵנוּ, יָאֵר פָּנָיו אִתָּנוּ סֶלָה: תהלים סז

יהוה יהוה, יהוה, אֵל רַחוּם וְחַנּוּן שמות לד
אֶרֶךְ אַפַּיִם וְרַב־חֶסֶד וֶאֱמֶת:

פָּנָיו פְּנֵה־אֵלַי וְחָנֵּנִי, כִּי־יָחִיד וְעָנִי אָנִי: תהלים כה

אֵלֶיךָ אֵלֶיךָ יהוה נַפְשִׁי אֶשָּׂא: תהלים כה

וִיחֻנֶּךָּ: הִנֵּה כְעֵינֵי עֲבָדִים אֶל־יַד אֲדוֹנֵיהֶם תהלים קכג
כְּעֵינֵי שִׁפְחָה אֶל־יַד גְּבִרְתָּהּ, כֵּן עֵינֵינוּ אֶל־יהוה אֱלֹהֵינוּ
עַד שֶׁיְּחָנֵּנוּ:

Read the following silently while the כהנים *chant. Omit on* שבת.

רִבּוֹנוֹ שֶׁל עוֹלָם, אֲנִי שֶׁלָּךְ וַחֲלוֹמוֹתַי שֶׁלָּךְ. חֲלוֹם חָלַמְתִּי וְאֵינִי יוֹדֵעַ מַה הוּא. יְהִי רָצוֹן מִלְּפָנֶיךָ, יהוה אֱלֹהַי וֵאלֹהֵי אֲבוֹתַי, שֶׁיִּהְיוּ כָּל חֲלוֹמוֹתַי עָלַי וְעַל כָּל יִשְׂרָאֵל לְטוֹבָה, בֵּין שֶׁחָלַמְתִּי עַל עַצְמִי, וּבֵין שֶׁחָלַמְתִּי עַל אֲחֵרִים, וּבֵין שֶׁחָלְמוּ אֲחֵרִים עָלָי. אִם טוֹבִים הֵם, חַזְּקֵם וְאַמְּצֵם, וְיִתְקַיְּמוּ בִי וּבָהֶם, כַּחֲלוֹמוֹתָיו שֶׁל יוֹסֵף הַצַּדִּיק. וְאִם צְרִיכִים רְפוּאָה, רְפָאֵם כְּחִזְקִיָּהוּ מֶלֶךְ יְהוּדָה מֵחָלְיוֹ, וּכְמִרְיָם הַנְּבִיאָה מִצָּרַעְתָּהּ, וּכְנַעֲמָן מִצָּרַעְתּוֹ, וּכְמֵי מָרָה עַל יְדֵי מֹשֶׁה רַבֵּנוּ, וּכְמֵי יְרִיחוֹ עַל יְדֵי אֱלִישָׁע. וּכְשֵׁם שֶׁהָפַכְתָּ אֶת קִלְלַת בִּלְעָם הָרָשָׁע מִקְּלָלָה לִבְרָכָה, כֵּן תַּהֲפֹךְ כָּל חֲלוֹמוֹתַי עָלַי וְעַל כָּל יִשְׂרָאֵל לְטוֹבָה, וְתִשְׁמְרֵנִי וּתְחָנֵּנִי וְתִרְצֵנִי. אָמֵן.

---

fellow humans. *May the* Lord *turn His face toward you,* bestowing on you His providential care (Rashbam, Ibn Ezra), or, may He grant you eternal life

May [He] turn	May he receive a blessing from the LORD and a just reward from the God of his salvation. And he will win grace and good favor in the eyes of God and man.	Ps. 24 Prov. 3
The LORD	LORD, be gracious to us; we yearn for You. Be their strength every morning, our salvation in time of distress.	Is. 33
His face	Do not hide Your face from me in the day of my distress. Turn Your ear to me; on the day I call, swiftly answer me.	Ps. 102
Toward you	To You, enthroned in heaven, I lift my eyes.	Ps. 123
And give	They shall place My name on the children of Israel, and I will bless them.	Num. 6
You	Yours, LORD, are the greatness and the power, the glory, majesty and splendor, for everything in heaven and earth is Yours. Yours, LORD, is the kingdom; You are exalted as Head over all.	1 Chr. 29
Peace.	"Peace, peace, to those far and near," says the LORD, "and I will heal him."	Is. 57

Read the following silently while the Kohanim chant. Omit on Shabbat.

May it be Your will, LORD my God and God of my fathers, that You act for the sake of Your simple, sacred kindness and great compassion, and for the purity of Your great, mighty and awesome name of twenty-two letters derived from the verses of the priestly blessing spoken by Aaron and his sons, Your holy people. May You be close to me when I call to You. May You hear my prayer, plea and cry as You did the cry of Jacob Your perfect one who was called "a plain man." May You grant me and all the members of my household our food and sustenance, generously not meagerly, honestly not otherwise, with satisfaction not pain, from Your generous hand, just as You gave a portion of bread to eat and clothes to wear to Jacob our father who was called "a plain man." May we find love, grace, kindness and compassion in Your sight and in the eyes of all who see us. May my words in service to You be heard, as You granted Joseph Your righteous one, at the time when he was robed by his father in a cloak of fine wool, that he find grace, kindness and compassion in Your sight and in the eyes of all who saw him. May You do wonders and miracles with me, and a sign for good. Grant me success in my paths, and set in my heart understanding that I may understand, discern and fulfill all the words of Your Torah's teachings and mysteries. Save me from errors and purify my thoughts and my heart to serve You and be in awe of You. Prolong my days (*add, where appropriate:* and those of my father, mother, wife, husband, son/s, and daughter/s) in joy and happiness, with much strength and peace. Amen, Selah.

The Leader continues with "Grant peace" on the next page.

יִשָּׂא יִשָּׂא בְרָכָה מֵאֵת יהוה, וּצְדָקָה מֵאֱלֹהֵי יִשְׁעוֹ: תהלים כד
וּמְצָא־חֵן וְשֵׂכֶל־טוֹב בְּעֵינֵי אֱלֹהִים וְאָדָם: משלי ג

יהוה יהוה חָנֵּנוּ, לְךָ קִוִּינוּ, הֱיֵה זְרֹעָם לַבְּקָרִים ישעיה לג
אַף־יְשׁוּעָתֵנוּ בְּעֵת צָרָה:

פָּנָיו אַל־תַּסְתֵּר פָּנֶיךָ מִמֶּנִּי בְּיוֹם צַר לִי, הַטֵּה־אֵלַי אָזְנֶךָ תהלים קב
בְּיוֹם אֶקְרָא מַהֵר עֲנֵנִי:

אֵלֶיךָ אֵלֶיךָ נָשָׂאתִי אֶת־עֵינַי, הַיֹּשְׁבִי בַּשָּׁמָיִם: תהלים קכג

וְיָשֵׂם וְשָׂמוּ אֶת־שְׁמִי עַל־בְּנֵי יִשְׂרָאֵל, וַאֲנִי אֲבָרְכֵם: במדבר ו

לְךָ לְךָ יהוה הַגְּדֻלָּה וְהַגְּבוּרָה וְהַתִּפְאֶרֶת וְהַנֵּצַח וְהַהוֹד דברי הימים א׳ כט
כִּי־כֹל בַּשָּׁמַיִם וּבָאָרֶץ, לְךָ יהוה הַמַּמְלָכָה
וְהַמִּתְנַשֵּׂא לְכֹל לְרֹאשׁ:

שָׁלוֹם: שָׁלוֹם שָׁלוֹם לָרָחוֹק וְלַקָּרוֹב, אָמַר יהוה, וּרְפָאתִיו: ישעיה נז

Read the following silently while the כהנים *chant. Omit on* שבת*.*

יְהִי רָצוֹן מִלְּפָנֶיךָ, יהוה אֱלֹהַי וֵאלֹהֵי אֲבוֹתַי, שֶׁתַּעֲשֶׂה לְמַעַן קְדֻשַּׁת חֲסָדֶיךָ וְגֹדֶל רַחֲמֶיךָ הַפְּשׁוּטִים, וּלְמַעַן טָהֳרַת שִׁמְךָ הַגָּדוֹל הַגִּבּוֹר וְהַנּוֹרָא, בֶּן עֶשְׂרִים וּשְׁתַּיִם אוֹתִיּוֹת הַיּוֹצֵא מִפְּסוּקִים שֶׁל בִּרְכַּת כֹּהֲנִים הָאֲמוּרָה מִפִּי אַהֲרֹן וּבָנָיו עַם קְדוֹשֶׁךָ, שֶׁתִּהְיֶה קָרוֹב לִי בְּקָרְאִי לָךְ, וְתִשְׁמַע תְּפִלָּתִי נַאֲקָתִי וְאֶנְקָתִי תָּמִיד, כְּשֵׁם שֶׁשָּׁמַעְתָּ אֶנְקַת יַעֲקֹב תְּמִימֶךָ הַנִּקְרָא אִישׁ תָּם. וְתִתֶּן לִי וּלְכָל נַפְשׁוֹת בֵּיתִי מְזוֹנוֹתֵינוּ וּפַרְנָסָתֵנוּ בְּרֶוַח וְלֹא בְצִמְצוּם, בְּהֶתֵּר וְלֹא בְאִסּוּר, בְּנַחַת וְלֹא בְצַעַר, מִתַּחַת יָדְךָ הָרְחָבָה, כְּשֵׁם שֶׁנָּתַתָּ פִּסַּת לֶחֶם לֶאֱכֹל וּבֶגֶד לִלְבֹּשׁ לְיַעֲקֹב אָבִינוּ הַנִּקְרָא אִישׁ תָּם. וְתִתְּנֵנוּ לְאַהֲבָה, לְחֵן וּלְחֶסֶד וּלְרַחֲמִים בְּעֵינֶיךָ וּבְעֵינֵי כָל רוֹאֵינוּ, וְיִהְיוּ דְבָרַי נִשְׁמָעִים לַעֲבוֹדָתֶךָ, כְּשֵׁם שֶׁנָּתַתָּ אֶת יוֹסֵף צַדִּיקֶךָ בְּשָׁעָה שֶׁהִלְבִּישׁוֹ אָבִיו כְּתֹנֶת פַּסִּים לְחֵן וּלְחֶסֶד וּלְרַחֲמִים בְּעֵינֶיךָ וּבְעֵינֵי כָל רוֹאָיו. וְתַעֲשֶׂה עִמִּי נִפְלָאוֹת וְנִסִּים, וּלְטוֹבָה אוֹת, וְתַצְלִיחֵנִי בִּדְרָכַי, וְתֵן בְּלִבִּי בִּינָה לְהָבִין וּלְהַשְׂכִּיל וּלְקַיֵּם אֶת כָּל דִּבְרֵי תַלְמוּד תּוֹרָתֶךָ וְסוֹדוֹתֶיהָ, וְתַצִּילֵנִי מִשְּׁגִיאוֹת, וּתְטַהֵר רַעְיוֹנַי וְלִבִּי לַעֲבוֹדָתֶךָ, וְתַאֲרִיךְ יָמַי (וִימֵי אָבִי וְאִמִּי / וְאִשְׁתִּי / וּבַעְלִי / וּבָנַי וּבְנוֹתַי) בְּטוֹב וּבִנְעִימוֹת, בְּרֹב עֹז וְשָׁלוֹם, אָמֵן סֶלָה.

The שליח ציבור *continues with* שִׂים שָׁלוֹם *on the next page.*

The congregation says:

אַדִּיר Majestic One on high who dwells in power: You are peace and Your name is peace. May it be Your will to bestow on us and on Your people the house of Israel, life and blessing as a safeguard for peace.

The Kohanim say:

רִבּוֹנוֹ Master of the Universe: we have done what You have decreed for us. So too may You deal with us as You have promised us. Look down *Deut. 26* from Your holy dwelling place, from heaven, and bless Your people Israel and the land You have given us as You promised on oath to our ancestors, a land flowing with milk and honey.

If the Priestly Blessing is not said, the following is said by the Leader:

Our God and God of our fathers, bless us with the threefold blessing in the Torah, written by the hand of Moses Your servant and pronounced by Aaron and his sons the priests, Your holy people, as it is said:

May the LORD bless you and protect you. *Num. 6*
Cong: May it be Your will.
May the LORD make His face shine on you and be gracious to you.
Cong: May it be Your will.
May the LORD turn His face toward you, and grant you peace.
Cong: May it be Your will.

PEACE

שִׂים שָׁלוֹם Grant peace, goodness and blessing,
grace, loving-kindness and compassion to us
and all Israel Your people.
Bless us, our Father, all as one,
with the light of Your face,
for by the light of Your face You have given us, LORD our God,
the Torah of life and love of kindness,
righteousness, blessing, compassion, life and peace.
May it be good in Your eyes to bless Your people Israel
at every time, in every hour, with Your peace.
Blessed are You, LORD,
who blesses His people Israel with peace.

Some also say it here as part of the silent Amida.

May the words of my mouth and the meditation of my heart *Ps. 19*
find favor before You, LORD, my Rock and Redeemer.

The קהל *says:*

אַדִּיר בַּמָּרוֹם שׁוֹכֵן בִּגְבוּרָה, אַתָּה שָׁלוֹם וְשִׁמְךָ שָׁלוֹם. יְהִי רָצוֹן שֶׁתָּשִׂים עָלֵינוּ וְעַל כָּל עַמְּךָ בֵּית יִשְׂרָאֵל חַיִּים וּבְרָכָה לְמִשְׁמֶרֶת שָׁלוֹם.

The כהנים *say:*

רִבּוֹנוֹ שֶׁל עוֹלָם, עָשִׂינוּ מַה שֶּׁגָּזַרְתָּ עָלֵינוּ, אַף אַתָּה עֲשֵׂה עִמָּנוּ כְּמוֹ שֶׁהִבְטַחְתָּנוּ. הַשְׁקִיפָה מִמְּעוֹן קָדְשְׁךָ מִן־הַשָּׁמַיִם, וּבָרֵךְ אֶת־עַמְּךָ אֶת־יִשְׂרָאֵל, וְאֵת הָאֲדָמָה אֲשֶׁר נָתַתָּה לָנוּ, כַּאֲשֶׁר נִשְׁבַּעְתָּ לַאֲבֹתֵינוּ, אֶרֶץ זָבַת חָלָב וּדְבָשׁ: דברים כו

If ברכת כהנים *is not said, the following is said by the* שליח ציבור*:*

אֱלֹהֵינוּ וֵאלֹהֵי אֲבוֹתֵינוּ, בָּרְכֵנוּ בַּבְּרָכָה הַמְשֻׁלֶּשֶׁת בַּתּוֹרָה, הַכְּתוּבָה עַל יְדֵי מֹשֶׁה עַבְדֶּךָ, הָאֲמוּרָה מִפִּי אַהֲרֹן וּבָנָיו כֹּהֲנִים עַם קְדוֹשֶׁיךָ, כָּאָמוּר

במדבר ו יְבָרֶכְךָ יהוה וְיִשְׁמְרֶךָ: קהל: כֵּן יְהִי רָצוֹן
יָאֵר יהוה פָּנָיו אֵלֶיךָ וִיחֻנֶּךָּ: קהל: כֵּן יְהִי רָצוֹן
יִשָּׂא יהוה פָּנָיו אֵלֶיךָ וְיָשֵׂם לְךָ שָׁלוֹם: קהל: כֵּן יְהִי רָצוֹן

שלום

שִׂים שָׁלוֹם טוֹבָה וּבְרָכָה, חֵן וָחֶסֶד וְרַחֲמִים
עָלֵינוּ וְעַל כָּל יִשְׂרָאֵל עַמֶּךָ.
בָּרְכֵנוּ אָבִינוּ כֻּלָּנוּ כְּאֶחָד בְּאוֹר פָּנֶיךָ
כִּי בְאוֹר פָּנֶיךָ נָתַתָּ לָּנוּ, יהוה אֱלֹהֵינוּ
תּוֹרַת חַיִּים וְאַהֲבַת חֶסֶד
וּצְדָקָה וּבְרָכָה וְרַחֲמִים וְחַיִּים וְשָׁלוֹם.
וְטוֹב בְּעֵינֶיךָ לְבָרֵךְ אֶת עַמְּךָ יִשְׂרָאֵל
בְּכָל עֵת וּבְכָל שָׁעָה בִּשְׁלוֹמֶךָ.
בָּרוּךְ אַתָּה יהוה, הַמְבָרֵךְ אֶת עַמּוֹ יִשְׂרָאֵל בַּשָּׁלוֹם.

The following verse concludes the חזרת הש״ץ

תהלים יט יִהְיוּ לְרָצוֹן אִמְרֵי־פִי וְהֶגְיוֹן לִבִּי לְפָנֶיךָ, יהוה צוּרִי וְגֹאֲלִי:

אַדִּיר בַּמָּרוֹם *Majestic One on high.* A prayer by the congregation, echoing three times the last word of the priestly blessing: peace.

Hoshanot

Hoshanot are said after the Leader's Repetition of the Amida of Musaf (and in some congregations after Hallel) on every day of Sukkot.

On weekdays, the Ark is opened, and a Torah scroll is taken to the Bima. Members of the congregation who have a Lulav and Etrog make a circuit around the Bima and say Hoshanot. Mourners do not participate in the circuit.

At the conclusion of the Hoshanot, the Torah scroll is returned to the Ark, which is then closed.

On Shabbat, turn to page 916.

Leader then congregation:

הוֹשַׁע נָא Save us, please for Your sake, our God, save us please.

Leader then congregation:

Save us, please for Your sake, our Creator, save us, please.

Leader then congregation:

Save us, please for Your sake, our Redeemer, save us, please.

Leader then congregation:

Save us, please for Your sake, You who seek us, save us, please.

For the first day of Yom Tov continue on the next page and for the second day turn to page 534.

---

members of the congregation stands holding a Sefer Torah, represents the altar.

The processions themselves follow the ritual described in the book of Joshua during the Israelites' campaign against Jericho. The people were commanded by God to walk around the city for seven days – once on each of the first six days, seven times on the seventh – at the end of which the walls collapsed (Joshua 6:1–20; see Yerushalmi, *Sukka* 4:3). This was the first great victory in the conquest of the land. Abudarham also finds a hint of the custom in a verse in Psalms (26:6), "I wash my hands in innocence and *walk around Your altar,* O Lord."

A circular procession is a way of focusing spiritual energy. There is a mystical custom for a bride to circle her husband seven times before the marriage ceremony. The Talmud (*Taanit* 31a) says that in the world to come the righ-

הושענות

הושענות are said after the חזרת הש״ץ of the מוסף עמידה
(and in some congregations after הלל) on every day of סוכות.
On weekdays, the ארון קודש is opened, and a ספר תורה is taken to the בימה.
Members of the קהל who have a לולב and אתרוג make a circuit around the בימה and say הושענות. Mourners do not participate in the circuit.
At the conclusion of the הושענות, the ספר תורה is returned to the ארון קודש, which is then closed.

On שבת, turn to page 917.

קהל then שליח ציבור:

הוֹשַׁע נָא לְמַעַנְךָ אֱלֹהֵינוּ הוֹשַׁע נָא.

קהל then שליח ציבור:

הוֹשַׁע נָא לְמַעַנְךָ בּוֹרְאֵנוּ הוֹשַׁע נָא.

קהל then שליח ציבור:

הוֹשַׁע נָא לְמַעַנְךָ גּוֹאֲלֵנוּ הוֹשַׁע נָא.

קהל then שליח ציבור:

הוֹשַׁע נָא לְמַעַנְךָ דּוֹרְשֵׁנוּ הוֹשַׁע נָא.

For the first day of יום טוב continue on the next page and for the second day turn to page 535.

HOSHANOT

The *Hakafot*, processions, and *Hoshanot*, the prayers that accompany them, go back to Temple times. According to the Mishna (*Sukka* 4:5) priests would take willow branches and circle the altar, once on each of the first six days of Sukkot, and seven times on the seventh day. Nowadays we observe the custom of taking willow branches on their own only on Hoshana Raba. Other texts speak of a procession in which people held the lulav, myrtle, willow and etrog (*Midrash Tehillim* 26:5). The Book of Jubilees (16:31) dates the custom back to Abraham. Our procession around the *bima* is a conscious evocation of this aspect of the Temple service. The *bima*, on which one of the

On the first day (second day if the first day falls on Shabbat) of Yom Tov say:

Save us, please –

לְמַעַן אֲמִתָּךְ For the sake of Your truth – for the sake of Your covenant – for the sake of Your greatness and glory – for the sake of Your Law – for the sake of Your majesty – for the sake of Your promise – for the sake of Your remembrance – for the sake of Your love – for the sake of Your goodness – for the sake of Your Oneness – for the sake of Your honor – for the sake of Your wisdom – for the sake of Your kingship – for the sake of Your eternity – for the sake of Your mystery – for the sake of Your might – for the sake of Your splendor – for the sake of Your righteousness – for the sake of Your holiness – for the sake of Your great compassion – for the sake of Your Presence – for the sake of Your praise – Save us, please.

Continue with "I and HE: save us, please." on page 536.

---

fasts, usually held to pray for rain during a drought: hence the connection with Sukkot, the festival of rain.

Many of the *Hoshanot* as we have them today were composed by the great sixth-century liturgical poet R. Elazar HaKalir, though some are later and by other hands. Note how HaKalir, a virtuoso who generally used complex structures, rarefied words and elaborate allusions, here keeps to the simple form of the litany, so central was it to the mood of Sukkot in Temple times. Each of the *Hoshanot* has a single overarching theme.

הוֹשַׁע נָא *Save us, please.* Note the *Hoshanot* are built on the single phrase, "Save us please," and not the line following it in Hallel, "Please grant us success." Our faith in God does not depend on success. As the prophet Habakkuk said in a beautiful prayer: "Though the fig tree does not bud and there are no grapes on the vines, though the olive crop fails and the fields produce no food, though there are no sheep in the pen and no cattle in the stalls, yet I will rejoice in the LORD, I will be joyful in God my Savior" (Hab. 3:17–18).

DAY 1

לְמַעַן אֲמִתָּךְ *For the sake of Your truth.*
The theme of this *Hoshana* is redemption from exile. The *Hakafot* and *Hosha-*

On the first day (second day if the first day falls on שבת*) of* יום טוב *say:*

הוֹשַׁע נָא

לְמַעַן אֲמִתָּךְ. לְמַעַן בְּרִיתָךְ. לְמַעַן גָּדְלָךְ וְתִפְאַרְתָּךְ. לְמַעַן דָּתָךְ. לְמַעַן הוֹדָךְ. לְמַעַן וִעוּדָךְ. לְמַעַן זִכְרָךְ. לְמַעַן חַסְדָּךְ. לְמַעַן טוּבָךְ. לְמַעַן יִחוּדָךְ. לְמַעַן כְּבוֹדָךְ. לְמַעַן לִמּוּדָךְ. לְמַעַן מַלְכוּתָךְ. לְמַעַן נִצְחָךְ. לְמַעַן סוֹדָךְ. לְמַעַן עֻזָּךְ. לְמַעַן פְּאֵרָךְ. לְמַעַן צִדְקָתָךְ. לְמַעַן קְדֻשָּׁתָךְ. לְמַעַן רַחֲמֶיךָ הָרַבִּים. לְמַעַן שְׁכִינָתָךְ. לְמַעַן תְּהִלָּתָךְ. הוֹשַׁע נָא.

Continue with אֲנִי וָהוּ הוֹשִׁיעָה נָּא *on page 537.*

---

teous will dance in a circle with God Himself in the center. The circle is a way in which people define themselves in relation to a center from which each is equidistant. The Jewish people is the circumference of a circle at whose center is God.

According to the Mishna (*Sukka* 4:5), while the priests circled the Altar they recited the phrase from Hallel, "Lord please save us." *Hoshana* is an elision of the words *Hoshia na*, "Please save," and entered the English language via the Greek translation of the Bible as *hosanna*, meaning "an expression of adoration, praise or joy." On Sukkot, the Temple precincts were thronged with pilgrims. The sight of the crowds with their lulavim, and the sound of their jubilant cries of *Hoshana*, formed an unforgettable climax of national joy: God's people celebrating the harvest He had blessed, in the land to which He had brought them, in the House that was His earthly home.

The prayers themselves, known as *Hoshanot*, are litanies. Each consists of a series of short phrases said by the leader, structured as a simple alphabetical acrostic, followed by a standard response from the congregation. The crowds of pilgrims in the Temple Courtyard needed prayers that could easily involve them. The form of a litany was perfect for such a vast processional. It allowed everyone to join in with the response, "Save us, please," while only the leader of prayer needed to know the changing words.

Other prayers structured as litanies include *Dayenu* ("It would have been sufficient") in the Seder on Pesaḥ, and several of the Seliḥot prayers, with the refrain "Answer us" in place of "Save us." Seliḥot were originally said on public

On the second day of Yom Tov say:

Save us, please –

אֶבֶן שְׁתִיָּה The Foundation Stone – the House You chose – the threshing-floor of Ornan – the hidden Shrine – Mount Moriah – where He shall be seen – Your glorious Sanctuary – where David camped – the best of Lebanon – the Beauty of Heights, Joy of all the earth – the Place of Perfect Beauty – the Lodge of Goodness – the Place of Your dwelling – the Shelter of Shalem – the tribes' Pilgrimage – the precious Cornerstone – shining Zion – the Holy of Holies – [the walls] lined with love – Residence of Your glory – the Hill toward which all mouths pray – Save us, please.

גֹּרֶן אָרְנָן *The threshing-floor of Ornan.* Purchased by King David as the site on which the Temple would be built (II Sam. 24).

דְּבִיר הַמֻּצְנָע *The hidden Shrine.* The Holy of Holies, hidden behind a curtain.

וְהַר יֵרָאֶה *Where the LORD shall be seen.* The name given to the place after the binding of Isaac (Gen. 22:14).

טוֹב הַלְּבָנוֹן *The best of Lebanon.* From where the cedar wood was brought by Solomon for the Temple (I Kings 5:16–25).

מְשׂוֹשׂ כָּל הָאָרֶץ. כְּלִילַת יֹפִי. לִינַת הַצֶּדֶק *Joy of all the earth… place of perfect beauty… Lodge of goodness.* Descriptions of Jerusalem in Psalms 48:3, Lamentations 2:15, and Isaiah 1:21.

סֻכַּת שָׁלֵם *Shelter of Shalem.* Shalem was the original name of the city in the days of Abraham (Gen. 14:18). In Psalms (76:3), the Temple is described as a Tabernacle in Shalem.

פִּנַּת יִקְרַת *Precious cornerstone.* A phrase from Isaiah 28:16. Tradition identified it as the seat of the Sanhedrin, Israel's Supreme Court.

תֵּל תַּלְפִּיּוֹת *Hill toward which all mouths pray. Talpiyot* comes from Song of Songs 4:4. It was interpreted by the sages as "the place to which all mouths turn" when they pray (*Berakhot* 30a).

On the second day of יום טוב *say:*

הוֹשַׁע נָא

אֶבֶן שְׁתִיָּה. בֵּית הַבְּחִירָה. גֹּרֶן אָרְנָן. דְּבִיר הַמֻּצְנָע. הַר הַמּוֹרִיָּה. וְהַר יֵרָאֶה. זְבוּל תִּפְאַרְתֶּךָ. חָנָה דָוִד. טוֹב הַלְּבָנוֹן. יְפֵה נוֹף מְשׂוֹשׂ כָּל הָאָרֶץ. כְּלִילַת יֹפִי. לִינַת הַצֶּדֶק. מָכוֹן לְשִׁבְתֶּךָ. נָוֶה שַׁאֲנָן. סֻכַּת שָׁלֵם. עֲלִיַּת שְׁבָטִים. פִּנַּת יִקְרַת. צִיּוֹן הַמְצֻיֶּנֶת. קֹדֶשׁ הַקֳּדָשִׁים. רָצוּף אַהֲבָה. שְׁכִינַת כְּבוֹדֶךָ. תֵּל תַּלְפִּיּוֹת. הוֹשַׁע נָא.

---

not are peculiarly intense reminders of the ceremony in the Temple. Hence the poignancy and urgency of this *Hoshana*, calling on God to redeem His people for His sake, not for ours. Behind it is the idea that when Israel are in exile, banished from their land, it is not only a tragedy for them. It is, as it were, a *Ḥillul Hashem*, a desecration of God's name, since it must seem to the world as if He were unable to redeem His people. Therefore, says the *Hoshana*, redeem them for the sake of Your truth, that is, Your promise to the people that they would inherit the land. The words in the Hoshana all relate to the attributes of God as He is perceived by humans, especially in relation to the fate of Israel, the people of the covenant. The custom with each of the *Hoshanot* is to add the word *Hoshana* to each of the phrases, at the beginning or end, or both.

DAY 2

אֶבֶן שְׁתִיָּה *The Foundation Stone.*
The theme of this *Hoshana* is Jerusalem and the Temple where the procession originally took place.

אֶבֶן שְׁתִיָּה *The foundation stone.* "The land of Israel is at the center of the world. At the center of Israel is Jerusalem, at the center of Jerusalem is the Temple, at the center of the Temple is the Hall, at the center of the Hall is the Ark, and at the front of the Hall is the Foundation Stone on which the world rests" (*Tanḥuma, Buber, Kedoshim* 10).

I and *HE*: save us, please.

כְּהוֹשַׁעְתָּ As You saved the mighty ones in Lud with You,
coming down for Your people's deliverance – save us, please.

As You saved nation and God together,
[the people] called for God's salvation – save us, please.

As You saved the crowding hosts,
and angelic hosts along with them – save us, please.

As You saved pure ones from the grip of slavery,
Gracious One; enslaved in cruel hands – save us, please.

As You saved those submerged between slices of the deep,
and brought Your own glory through it with them –
save us, please.

---

is with Israel in exile: "*And I* was in the midst of the exile" (Ezekiel 1:1) and "*And He* was bound in chains with all the exiles..." (Jer. 40:1), interpreted by the Midrash as if they were speaking of God Himself. From these two verses come the words "*I and He.*"

כְּהוֹשַׁעְתָּ אֵלִים *As You saved the mighty ones*
This *Hoshana*, a litany of the saving acts of God in the past, is an extended commentary on the phrase "I and He," understood to mean that the Divine Presence is always with God's people, suffering when they suffer. When Israel is in exile, so is the Divine Presence. When Jerusalem is in ruins, God too weeps (see *Berakhot* 3a). Hence the power and passion of this daring prayer: Save us, for in saving us it is as if You were saving Yourself, that is, rescuing the Divine Presence from its exile.

אֵלִים *The mighty ones.* A reference to the descendants of the patriarchs (see Rashi to Ps. 29:1). Alternatively it may mean "the terebinths" (see Rashi, Ibn Ezra and Radak to Is. 61:3).

בְּלוּד *In Lud.* An alternative name for Egypt.

עִמָּךְ *With You.* "I will be with him in distress," says God (Ps. 91:15).

מַלְאֲכֵי צְבָאוֹת *Angelic hosts.* On the phrase, "All the LORD's hosts left Egypt," the Midrash says, "This refers to the ministering angels" (Ex. 12:41 and *Mekhilta* ad loc.).

אֲנִי וָהוֹ הוֹשִׁיעָה נָּא.

כְּהוֹשַׁעְתָּ אֵלִים בְּלוּד עִמָּךְ.
בְּצֵאתְךָ לְיֵשַׁע עַמָּךְ. כֵּן הוֹשַׁע נָא.
כְּהוֹשַׁעְתָּ גּוֹי וֵאלֹהִים.
דְּרוּשִׁים לְיֵשַׁע אֱלֹהִים. כֵּן הוֹשַׁע נָא.
כְּהוֹשַׁעְתָּ הֲמוֹן צְבָאוֹת.
וְעִמָּם מַלְאֲכֵי צְבָאוֹת. כֵּן הוֹשַׁע נָא.
כְּהוֹשַׁעְתָּ זַכִּים מִבֵּית עֲבָדִים.
חַנּוּן בְּיָדָם מַעֲבִידִים. כֵּן הוֹשַׁע נָא.
כְּהוֹשַׁעְתָּ טְבוּעִים בְּצוּל גְּזָרִים.
יְקָרְךָ עִמָּם מַעֲבִירִים. כֵּן הוֹשַׁע נָא.

אֲנִי וָהוֹ *I and HE*

"Every day [in the Temple, the pilgrims] would circle the Altar once, saying 'LORD, please, save us. LORD, please, grant us success' (Ps. 118). Rabbi Yehuda says: '*Ani Vahu*, please, save us'" (Mishna *Sukka* 4:5). Rashi's understanding of this enigmatic phrase is that the phrase *Ani Vahu* replaces "LORD, please," in Psalm 118:25 on which the prayer is based. Rabbi Yehuda is telling us that rather than voicing the full name of God as they sang, the people used a known modification to the letters, respectfully substituting for it.

Rabbi Yehuda's phrase is understood differently in the Jerusalem Talmud. There the spelling is not אני והו, but אני והוא – "I and He, please, save us." Maimonides in his commentary to the Mishna suggests that this is in reference to the passage in Deuteronomy (32:39) – "See now that I, *I am He*, there is no god beside Me" – in which God promises to vindicate His people: appropriate in a prayer for salvation. However he also reports (in the name of the Geonim) that some related the phrase to the tradition that when Israel suffer, God suffers with them. When Israel are in exile, God follows them into the darkness of exile to comfort them (see *Eikha Raba, Petiḥta* 34). "I and He" would thus mean, "He who is with me in distress." Alternatively, the reference may be to the verses cited by the Midrash to prove that God

As You saved the stem as they sang "And God saved" –
but the Deliverer reads it, "God was saved" – save us, please.

As You saved, and You said, "I took you out,"
but let it be pointed, "I was taken out with you" – save us, please.

As You saved those who encompassed the Altar,
bearing their willows to encircle the Altar – save us, please.

As You saved the Ark of wonders that was wronged,
tormenting Philistia with fury, and saving it – save us, please.

As You saved the communities You sent away to Babylon,
being sent too, for them, Your compassionate Self –
save us, please.

As You saved the returning exiles of the tribes of Jacob,
so come back and return the exiles of the tents of Jacob –
and save us, please.

As You saved those who kept Your commandments and waited for
salvation, / God of all salvation – and save us, please.

I and *HE*: save us, please.

The Torah scroll is returned to the Ark.

הוֹשִׁיעָה Save Your people; bless Your legacy; tend them and carry *Ps. 28*
them forever. Let these words with which I have pleaded with the LORD *1 Kings 8*
be close to the LORD our God day and night, that He may do justice for His servant, and justice for His people Israel, day after day; so that all the peoples of the earth will know that the LORD is God. There is no other.

The Ark is closed.

---

only rescuing the Israelites; it is as if He were liberating His own Divine Presence, that was suffering alongside His people.

הוֹשִׁיעָה אֶת־עַמֶּךָ *Save Your people.* Two passages with a specific connection with Sukkot. The first, from psalm 28, uses the verb *hoshia*, "save," that is the leitmotif of the *Hoshanot*. The second is the culmination of King Solomon's prayer at the dedication of the Temple, which took place on Sukkot and forms the subject of the Haftara on the second day.

כְּהוֹשַׁעְתָּ כַּנָּה מְשׁוֹרֶרֶת וַיּוֹשַׁע.
לְגוֹחָה מְצַיֶּנֶת וַיִּוָּשַׁע. כֵּן הוֹשַׁע נָא.

כְּהוֹשַׁעְתָּ מַאֲמַר וְהוֹצֵאתִי אֶתְכֶם.
נָקוּב וְהוּצֵאתִי אִתְּכֶם. כֵּן הוֹשַׁע נָא.

כְּהוֹשַׁעְתָּ סוֹבְבֵי מִזְבֵּחַ.
עוֹמְסֵי עֲרָבָה לְהַקִּיף מִזְבֵּחַ. כֵּן הוֹשַׁע נָא.

כְּהוֹשַׁעְתָּ פִּלְאֵי אָרוֹן כְּהֻפְשַׁע.
צִעֵר פְּלֶשֶׁת בַּחֲרוֹן אַף, וְנוֹשַׁע. כֵּן הוֹשַׁע נָא.

כְּהוֹשַׁעְתָּ קְהִלּוֹת בָּבֶלָה שִׁלַּחְתָּ.
רַחוּם לְמַעֲנָם שֻׁלַּחְתָּ. כֵּן הוֹשַׁע נָא.

כְּהוֹשַׁעְתָּ שְׁבוּת שִׁבְטֵי יַעֲקֹב.
תָּשׁוּב וְתָשִׁיב שְׁבוּת אָהֳלֵי יַעֲקֹב. וְהוֹשִׁיעָה נָּא.

כְּהוֹשַׁעְתָּ שׁוֹמְרֵי מִצְוֹת וְחוֹכֵי יְשׁוּעוֹת.
אֵל לְמוֹשָׁעוֹת. וְהוֹשִׁיעָה נָּא.

אֲנִי וָהוֹ הוֹשִׁיעָה נָּא.

The ספר תורה *is returned to the* ארון קודש.

תהלים כח **הוֹשִׁיעָה אֶת־עַמֶּךָ, וּבָרֵךְ אֶת־נַחֲלָתֶךָ, וּרְעֵם וְנַשְּׂאֵם עַד־הָעוֹלָם: וְיִהְיוּ**
מלכים א׳ ח **דְבָרַי אֵלֶּה, אֲשֶׁר הִתְחַנַּנְתִּי לִפְנֵי יהוה, קְרֹבִים אֶל־יהוה אֱלֹהֵינוּ יוֹמָם**
וָלָיְלָה, לַעֲשׂוֹת מִשְׁפַּט עַבְדּוֹ וּמִשְׁפַּט עַמּוֹ יִשְׂרָאֵל, דְּבַר־יוֹם בְּיוֹמוֹ:
לְמַעַן דַּעַת כָּל־עַמֵּי הָאָרֶץ כִּי יהוה הוּא הָאֱלֹהִים, אֵין עוֹד:

The ארון קודש *is closed.*

וַיִּוָּשַׁע ... וְהוּצֵאתִי *God was saved ... I was taken out.* Hebrew was originally written without vowels. Thus active verbs – "God saved," He "took out" – could be read with a change of vowels as passive, to mean that God was not

FULL KADDISH

Some have the custom to include additional responses in Full Kaddish. They can be found in the version on page 1464.

Leader: יִתְגַּדַּל Magnified and sanctified
may His great name be,
in the world He created by His will.
May He establish His kingdom
in your lifetime and in your days,
and in the lifetime of all the house of Israel,
swiftly and soon –
and say: Amen.

All: May His great name be blessed
for ever and all time.

Leader: Blessed and praised,
glorified and exalted,
raised and honored,
uplifted and lauded be the name of the Holy One,
blessed be He,
beyond any blessing,
song, praise and consolation
uttered in the world –
and say: Amen.

May the prayers and pleas of all Israel
be accepted by their Father in heaven –
and say: Amen.

May there be great peace from heaven,
and life for us and all Israel –
and say: Amen.

Bow, take three steps back, as if taking leave of the Divine Presence, then bow, first left, then right, then center, while saying:

May He who makes peace in His high places,
make peace for us and all Israel –
and say: Amen.

קדיש שלם

Some have the custom to include additional responses in קדיש שלם*.*
They can be found in the version on page 1465.

ש״ץ: יִתְגַּדַּל וְיִתְקַדַּשׁ שְׁמֵהּ רַבָּא (קהל: אָמֵן)
בְּעָלְמָא דִּי בְרָא כִרְעוּתֵהּ
וְיַמְלִיךְ מַלְכוּתֵהּ
בְּחַיֵּיכוֹן וּבְיוֹמֵיכוֹן וּבְחַיֵּי דְכָל בֵּית יִשְׂרָאֵל
בַּעֲגָלָא וּבִזְמַן קָרִיב
וְאִמְרוּ אָמֵן. (קהל: אָמֵן)

קהל וש״ץ: יְהֵא שְׁמֵהּ רַבָּא מְבָרַךְ לְעָלַם וּלְעָלְמֵי עָלְמַיָּא.

ש״ץ: יִתְבָּרַךְ וְיִשְׁתַּבַּח וְיִתְפָּאַר
וְיִתְרוֹמַם וְיִתְנַשֵּׂא וְיִתְהַדָּר וְיִתְעַלֶּה וְיִתְהַלָּל
שְׁמֵהּ דְּקֻדְשָׁא בְּרִיךְ הוּא (קהל: בְּרִיךְ הוּא)
לְעֵלָּא מִן כָּל בִּרְכָתָא וְשִׁירָתָא, תֻּשְׁבְּחָתָא וְנֶחֱמָתָא
דַּאֲמִירָן בְּעָלְמָא
וְאִמְרוּ אָמֵן. (קהל: אָמֵן)

תִּתְקַבַּל צְלוֹתְהוֹן וּבָעוּתְהוֹן דְּכָל יִשְׂרָאֵל
קֳדָם אֲבוּהוֹן דִּי בִשְׁמַיָּא
וְאִמְרוּ אָמֵן. (קהל: אָמֵן)

יְהֵא שְׁלָמָא רַבָּא מִן שְׁמַיָּא
וְחַיִּים, עָלֵינוּ וְעַל כָּל יִשְׂרָאֵל
וְאִמְרוּ אָמֵן. (קהל: אָמֵן)

Bow, take three steps back, as if taking leave of the Divine Presence,
then bow, first left, then right, then center, while saying:

עֹשֶׂה שָׁלוֹם בִּמְרוֹמָיו
הוּא יַעֲשֶׂה שָׁלוֹם עָלֵינוּ וְעַל כָּל יִשְׂרָאֵל
וְאִמְרוּ אָמֵן. (קהל: אָמֵן)

אֵין כֵּאלֹהֵינוּ There is none like our God, none like our LORD,
none like our King, none like our Savior.
Who is like our God? Who is like our LORD?
Who is like our King? Who is like our Savior?
We will thank our God, we will thank our LORD,
we will thank our King, we will thank our Savior.
Blessed is our God, blessed is our LORD,
blessed is our King, blessed is our Savior.
You are our God, You are our LORD,
You are our King, You are our Savior.
You are He to whom our ancestors offered the fragrant incense.

פִּטּוּם הַקְּטֹרֶת The incense mixture consisted of balsam, onycha, galbanum and frankincense, each weighing seventy manehs; myrrh, cassia, spikenard and saffron, each weighing sixteen manehs; twelve manehs of costus, three of aromatic bark; nine of cinnamon; nine kabs of Carsina lye; three seahs and three kabs of Cyprus wine. If Cyprus wine was not available, old white wine might be used. A quarter of a kab of Sodom salt, and a minute amount of a smoke-raising herb. Rabbi Nathan says: Also a minute amount of Jordan amber. If one added honey to the mixture, he rendered it unfit for sacred use. If he omitted any one of its ingredients, he is guilty of a capital offense. *Keritot 6a*

Rabban Shimon ben Gamliel says: "Balsam" refers to the sap that drips from the balsam tree. The Carsina lye was used for bleaching the onycha to improve it. The Cyprus wine was used to soak the onycha in it to make it pungent. Though urine is suitable for this purpose, it is not brought into the Temple out of respect.

These were the psalms which the Levites used to recite in the Temple: *Mishna, Tamid 7*
On the first day of the week they used to say:
"The earth is the LORD's and all it contains, *Ps. 24*
the world and all who live in it."

פִּטּוּם הַקְּטֹרֶת *The incense mixture.* A Talmudic passage (*Keritot* 6a) describing the composition of the incense, burned in the Temple every morning and evening (Ex. 30:7–9).

הַשִּׁיר שֶׁהַלְוִיִּם הָיוּ אוֹמְרִים *These were the psalms which the Levites used to recite.* Each day of the week, after the regular offerings in the Temple, the Levites

אֵין כֵּאלֹהֵינוּ, אֵין כַּאדוֹנֵינוּ, אֵין כְּמַלְכֵּנוּ, אֵין כְּמוֹשִׁיעֵנוּ.
מִי כֵאלֹהֵינוּ, מִי כַאדוֹנֵינוּ, מִי כְמַלְכֵּנוּ, מִי כְמוֹשִׁיעֵנוּ.
נוֹדֶה לֵאלֹהֵינוּ, נוֹדֶה לַאדוֹנֵינוּ, נוֹדֶה לְמַלְכֵּנוּ, נוֹדֶה לְמוֹשִׁיעֵנוּ.
בָּרוּךְ אֱלֹהֵינוּ, בָּרוּךְ אֲדוֹנֵינוּ, בָּרוּךְ מַלְכֵּנוּ, בָּרוּךְ מוֹשִׁיעֵנוּ.
אַתָּה הוּא אֱלֹהֵינוּ, אַתָּה הוּא אֲדוֹנֵינוּ,
אַתָּה הוּא מַלְכֵּנוּ, אַתָּה הוּא מוֹשִׁיעֵנוּ.
אַתָּה הוּא שֶׁהִקְטִירוּ אֲבוֹתֵינוּ לְפָנֶיךָ אֶת קְטֹרֶת הַסַּמִּים.

פִּטּוּם הַקְּטֹרֶת. הַצֳּרִי, וְהַצִּפֹּרֶן, וְהַחֶלְבְּנָה, וְהַלְּבוֹנָה מִשְׁקַל שִׁבְעִים שִׁבְעִים מָנֶה, מֹר, וּקְצִיעָה, שִׁבֹּלֶת נֵרְדְּ, וְכַרְכֹּם מִשְׁקַל שִׁשָּׁה עָשָׂר שִׁשָּׁה עָשָׂר מָנֶה, הַקֹּשְׁטְ שְׁנֵים עָשָׂר, קִלּוּפָה שְׁלֹשָׁה, וְקִנָּמוֹן תִּשְׁעָה, בֹּרִית כַּרְשִׁינָה תִּשְׁעָה קַבִּין, יֵין קַפְרִיסִין סְאִין תְּלָת וְקַבִּין תְּלָתָא, וְאִם אֵין לוֹ יֵין קַפְרִיסִין, מֵבִיא חֲמַר חִוַּרְיָן עַתִּיק. מֶלַח סְדוֹמִית רֹבַע, מַעֲלֶה עָשָׁן כָּל שֶׁהוּא. רַבִּי נָתָן הַבַּבְלִי אוֹמֵר: אַף כִּפַּת הַיַּרְדֵּן כָּל שֶׁהוּא, וְאִם נָתַן בָּהּ דְּבַשׁ פְּסָלָהּ, וְאִם חִסַּר אֶחָד מִכָּל סַמָּנֶיהָ, חַיָּב מִיתָה. כריתות ו.

רַבָּן שִׁמְעוֹן בֶּן גַּמְלִיאֵל אוֹמֵר: הַצֳּרִי אֵינוֹ אֶלָּא שְׂרָף הַנּוֹטֵף מֵעֲצֵי הַקְּטָף. בֹּרִית כַּרְשִׁינָה שֶׁשָּׁפִין בָּהּ אֶת הַצִּפֹּרֶן כְּדֵי שֶׁתְּהֵא נָאָה, יֵין קַפְרִיסִין שֶׁשּׁוֹרִין בּוֹ אֶת הַצִּפֹּרֶן כְּדֵי שֶׁתְּהֵא עַזָּה, וַהֲלֹא מֵי רַגְלַיִם יָפִין לָהּ, אֶלָּא שֶׁאֵין מַכְנִיסִין מֵי רַגְלַיִם בַּמִּקְדָּשׁ מִפְּנֵי הַכָּבוֹד.

הַשִּׁיר שֶׁהַלְוִיִּם הָיוּ אוֹמְרִים בְּבֵית הַמִּקְדָּשׁ: משנה תמיד ז
בַּיּוֹם הָרִאשׁוֹן הָיוּ אוֹמְרִים
לַיהוה הָאָרֶץ וּמְלוֹאָהּ, תֵּבֵל וְיֹשְׁבֵי בָהּ: תהלים כד

אֵין כֵּאלֹהֵינוּ *There is none like our God.* A poetic introduction to the reading of the passage about the incense offering in the Temple. The initial letters of the first three lines spell Amen, followed by several phrases beginning with "Blessed." Thus the poem is also a way of reaffirming the preceding prayers, a coded coda to the service as a whole.

On the second day they used to say:
"Great is the LORD and greatly to be praised Ps. 48
in the city of God, on His holy mountain."
On the third day they used to say:
"God stands in the divine assembly. Ps. 82
Among the judges He delivers judgment."
On the fourth day they used to say:
"God of retribution, LORD, God of retribution, appear." Ps. 94
On the fifth day they used to say:
"Sing for joy to God, our strength. Ps. 81
Shout aloud to the God of Jacob."
On the sixth day they used to say:
"The LORD reigns: He is robed in majesty; Ps. 93
the LORD is robed, girded with strength;
the world is firmly established; it cannot be moved."
On the Sabbath they used to say:
"A psalm, a song for the Sabbath day" – Ps. 92
[meaning] a psalm and song for the time to come,
for the day which will be entirely Sabbath and rest for life everlasting.

It was taught in the Academy of Elijah: Whoever studies [Torah] laws every day *Megilla 28b* is assured that he will be destined for the World to Come, as it is said, "The ways *Hab. 3* of the world are His" – read not, "ways" [*halikhot*] but "laws" [*halakhot*].

Rabbi Elazar said in the name of Rabbi Ḥanina: The disciples of the sages *Berakhot 64a* increase peace in the world, as it is said, "And all your children shall be taught *Is. 54* of the LORD, and great shall be the peace of your children [*banayikh*]." Read not *banayikh*, "your children," but *bonayikh*, "your builders." Those who love *Ps. 119* Your Torah have great peace; there is no stumbling block for them. May there *Ps. 122* be peace within your ramparts, prosperity in your palaces. For the sake of my brothers and friends, I shall say, "Peace be within you." For the sake of the House of the LORD our God, I will seek your good. ▸ May the LORD grant *Ps. 29* strength to His people; may the LORD bless His people with peace.

---

banayikh, 'your children' but *bonayikh* 'your builders.'" When scholars are also builders, they create peace. At many stages during their wanderings in the desert, there was dissension among the Israelites, but when they were building the Tabernacle there was harmony. The best way to bring peace to any fractured group is to build something together.

בַּשֵּׁנִי הָיוּ אוֹמְרִים
גָּדוֹל יהוה וּמְהֻלָּל מְאֹד, בְּעִיר אֱלֹהֵינוּ הַר־קָדְשׁוֹ: תהלים מח
בַּשְּׁלִישִׁי הָיוּ אוֹמְרִים
אֱלֹהִים נִצָּב בַּעֲדַת־אֵל, בְּקֶרֶב אֱלֹהִים יִשְׁפֹּט: תהלים פב
בָּרְבִיעִי הָיוּ אוֹמְרִים
אֵל־נְקָמוֹת יהוה, אֵל נְקָמוֹת הוֹפִיעַ: תהלים צד
בַּחֲמִישִׁי הָיוּ אוֹמְרִים
הַרְנִינוּ לֵאלֹהִים עוּזֵּנוּ, הָרִיעוּ לֵאלֹהֵי יַעֲקֹב: תהלים פא
בַּשִּׁשִּׁי הָיוּ אוֹמְרִים
יהוה מָלָךְ גֵּאוּת לָבֵשׁ לָבֵשׁ יהוה עֹז הִתְאַזָּר תהלים צג
אַף־תִּכּוֹן תֵּבֵל בַּל־תִּמּוֹט:
בַּשַּׁבָּת הָיוּ אוֹמְרִים
מִזְמוֹר שִׁיר לְיוֹם הַשַּׁבָּת: תהלים צב
מִזְמוֹר שִׁיר לֶעָתִיד לָבוֹא
לְיוֹם שֶׁכֻּלּוֹ שַׁבָּת וּמְנוּחָה לְחַיֵּי הָעוֹלָמִים.

תָּנָא דְבֵי אֵלִיָּהוּ: כָּל הַשּׁוֹנֶה הֲלָכוֹת בְּכָל יוֹם, מֻבְטָח לוֹ שֶׁהוּא בֶּן עוֹלָם מגילה כח:
הַבָּא, שֶׁנֶּאֱמַר, הֲלִיכוֹת עוֹלָם לוֹ: אַל תִּקְרֵי הֲלִיכוֹת אֶלָּא הֲלָכוֹת. חבקוק ג

אָמַר רַבִּי אֶלְעָזָר, אָמַר רַבִּי חֲנִינָא: תַּלְמִידֵי חֲכָמִים מַרְבִּים שָׁלוֹם בָּעוֹלָם, ברכות סד.
שֶׁנֶּאֱמַר, וְכָל־בָּנַיִךְ לִמּוּדֵי יהוה, וְרַב שְׁלוֹם בָּנָיִךְ: אַל תִּקְרֵי בָּנָיִךְ, אֶלָּא ישעיה נד
בּוֹנָיִךְ. שָׁלוֹם רָב לְאֹהֲבֵי תוֹרָתֶךָ, וְאֵין־לָמוֹ מִכְשׁוֹל: יְהִי־שָׁלוֹם בְּחֵילֵךְ, תהלים קיט תהלים קכב
שַׁלְוָה בְּאַרְמְנוֹתָיִךְ: לְמַעַן אַחַי וְרֵעָי אֲדַבְּרָה־נָּא שָׁלוֹם בָּךְ: לְמַעַן בֵּית־יהוה
אֱלֹהֵינוּ אֲבַקְשָׁה טוֹב לָךְ: ◂ יהוה עֹז לְעַמּוֹ יִתֵּן, יהוה יְבָרֵךְ אֶת־עַמּוֹ בַשָּׁלוֹם: תהלים כט

---

would sing a particular psalm. We still say these psalms, usually at the end of the service. In this way, a further connection is made between our prayers and the Temple service.

תַּלְמִידֵי חֲכָמִים מַרְבִּים שָׁלוֹם בָּעוֹלָם *The disciples of the sages increase peace in the world.* The full meaning of this statement is clear only at the end: "Read not

THE RABBIS' KADDISH

The following prayer, said by mourners, requires the presence of a minyan.
A transliteration can be found on page 1466.

Mourner: יִתְגַּדַּל Magnified and sanctified
may His great name be,
in the world He created by His will.
May He establish His kingdom in your lifetime
and in your days,
and in the lifetime of all the house of Israel,
swiftly and soon –
and say: Amen.

All: May His great name be blessed for ever and all time.

Mourner: Blessed and praised, glorified and exalted,
raised and honored, uplifted and lauded
be the name of the Holy One, blessed be He,
beyond any blessing,
song, praise and consolation uttered in the world –
and say: Amen.

To Israel, to the teachers,
their disciples and their disciples' disciples,
and to all who engage in the study of Torah,
in this (*in Israel add:* holy) place or elsewhere,
may there come to them and you great peace,
grace, kindness and compassion, long life, ample sustenance
and deliverance, from their Father in Heaven –
and say: Amen.

May there be great peace from heaven,
and (good) life for us and all Israel –
and say: Amen.

Bow, take three steps back, as if taking leave of the Divine Presence,
then bow, first left, then right, then center, while saying:
May He who makes peace in His high places,
in His compassion make peace for us and all Israel –
and say: Amen.

קדיש דרבנן

The following prayer, said by mourners, requires the presence of a מנין.
A transliteration can be found on page 1466.

אבל: יִתְגַּדַּל וְיִתְקַדַּשׁ שְׁמֵהּ רַבָּא (קהל: אָמֵן)
בְּעָלְמָא דִּי בְרָא כִרְעוּתֵהּ
וְיַמְלִיךְ מַלְכוּתֵהּ
בְּחַיֵּיכוֹן וּבְיוֹמֵיכוֹן וּבְחַיֵּי דְכָל בֵּית יִשְׂרָאֵל
בַּעֲגָלָא וּבִזְמַן קָרִיב, וְאִמְרוּ אָמֵן. (קהל: אָמֵן)

קהל ואבל: יְהֵא שְׁמֵהּ רַבָּא מְבָרַךְ לְעָלַם וּלְעָלְמֵי עָלְמַיָּא.

אבל: יִתְבָּרַךְ וְיִשְׁתַּבַּח וְיִתְפָּאַר וְיִתְרוֹמַם וְיִתְנַשֵּׂא
וְיִתְהַדָּר וְיִתְעַלֶּה וְיִתְהַלָּל
שְׁמֵהּ דְּקֻדְשָׁא בְּרִיךְ הוּא (קהל: בְּרִיךְ הוּא)
לְעֵלָּא מִן כָּל בִּרְכָתָא וְשִׁירָתָא, תֻּשְׁבְּחָתָא וְנֶחֱמָתָא
דַּאֲמִירָן בְּעָלְמָא, וְאִמְרוּ אָמֵן. (קהל: אָמֵן)

עַל יִשְׂרָאֵל וְעַל רַבָּנָן
וְעַל תַּלְמִידֵיהוֹן וְעַל כָּל תַּלְמִידֵי תַלְמִידֵיהוֹן
וְעַל כָּל מָאן דְּעָסְקִין בְּאוֹרַיְתָא
דִּי בְאַתְרָא (בארץ ישראל: קַדִּישָׁא) הָדֵין, וְדִי בְכָל אֲתַר וַאֲתַר
יְהֵא לְהוֹן וּלְכוֹן שְׁלָמָא רַבָּא
חִנָּא וְחִסְדָּא, וְרַחֲמֵי, וְחַיֵּי אֲרִיכֵי, וּמְזוֹנֵי רְוִיחֵי
וּפֻרְקָנָא מִן קֳדָם אֲבוּהוֹן דִּי בִשְׁמַיָּא, וְאִמְרוּ אָמֵן. (קהל: אָמֵן)

יְהֵא שְׁלָמָא רַבָּא מִן שְׁמַיָּא
וְחַיִּים (טוֹבִים) עָלֵינוּ וְעַל כָּל יִשְׂרָאֵל, וְאִמְרוּ אָמֵן. (קהל: אָמֵן)

Bow, take three steps back, as if taking leave of the Divine Presence, then bow, first left, then right, then center, while saying:

עֹשֶׂה שָׁלוֹם בִּמְרוֹמָיו
הוּא יַעֲשֶׂה בְרַחֲמָיו שָׁלוֹם
עָלֵינוּ וְעַל כָּל יִשְׂרָאֵל, וְאִמְרוּ אָמֵן. (קהל: אָמֵן)

Stand while saying Aleinu. Bow at ▾.

עָלֵינוּ It is our duty to praise the Master of all,
and ascribe greatness to the Author of creation,
who has not made us like the nations of the lands
nor placed us like the families of the earth;
who has not made our portion like theirs,
nor our destiny like all their multitudes.
(For they worship vanity and emptiness,
and pray to a god who cannot save.)
▾But we bow in worship
and thank the Supreme King of kings, the Holy One, blessed be He,
who extends the heavens and establishes the earth,
whose throne of glory is in the heavens above,
and whose power's Presence is in the highest of heights.
He is our God; there is no other.
Truly He is our King, there is none else,
as it is written in His Torah:
"You shall know and take to heart this day that the LORD is God, *Deut. 4*
in heaven above and on earth below.
There is no other."

Therefore, we place our hope in You, LORD our God,
that we may soon see the glory of Your power,
when You will remove abominations from the earth,
and idols will be utterly destroyed,
when the world will be perfected
under the sovereignty of the Almighty,
when all humanity will call on Your name,
to turn all the earth's wicked toward You.
All the world's inhabitants will realize and know
that to You every knee must bow and every tongue swear loyalty.
Before You, LORD our God, they will kneel and bow down
and give honor to Your glorious name.
They will all accept the yoke of Your kingdom,
and You will reign over them soon and for ever.
For the kingdom is Yours, and to all eternity You will reign in glory,
as it is written in Your Torah: "The LORD will reign for ever and ever." *Ex. 15*

Stand while saying עָלֵינוּ. *Bow at* ˚.

עָלֵינוּ לְשַׁבֵּחַ לַאֲדוֹן הַכֹּל, לָתֵת גְּדֻלָּה לְיוֹצֵר בְּרֵאשִׁית
שֶׁלֹּא עָשָׂנוּ כְּגוֹיֵי הָאֲרָצוֹת, וְלֹא שָׂמָנוּ כְּמִשְׁפְּחוֹת הָאֲדָמָה
שֶׁלֹּא שָׂם חֶלְקֵנוּ כָּהֶם וְגוֹרָלֵנוּ כְּכָל הֲמוֹנָם.
(שֶׁהֵם מִשְׁתַּחֲוִים לְהֶבֶל וָרִיק וּמִתְפַּלְלִים אֶל אֵל לֹא יוֹשִׁיעַ.)
˚וַאֲנַחְנוּ כּוֹרְעִים וּמִשְׁתַּחֲוִים וּמוֹדִים
לִפְנֵי מֶלֶךְ מַלְכֵי הַמְּלָכִים, הַקָּדוֹשׁ בָּרוּךְ הוּא
שֶׁהוּא נוֹטֶה שָׁמַיִם וְיוֹסֵד אָרֶץ
וּמוֹשַׁב יְקָרוֹ בַּשָּׁמַיִם מִמַּעַל
וּשְׁכִינַת עֻזּוֹ בְּגָבְהֵי מְרוֹמִים.
הוּא אֱלֹהֵינוּ, אֵין עוֹד.
אֱמֶת מַלְכֵּנוּ, אֶפֶס זוּלָתוֹ, כַּכָּתוּב בְּתוֹרָתוֹ
וְיָדַעְתָּ הַיּוֹם וַהֲשֵׁבֹתָ אֶל־לְבָבֶךָ דברים ד
כִּי יהוה הוּא הָאֱלֹהִים בַּשָּׁמַיִם מִמַּעַל וְעַל־הָאָרֶץ מִתָּחַת
אֵין עוֹד:

עַל כֵּן נְקַוֶּה לְּךָ יהוה אֱלֹהֵינוּ, לִרְאוֹת מְהֵרָה בְּתִפְאֶרֶת עֻזֶּךָ
לְהַעֲבִיר גִּלּוּלִים מִן הָאָרֶץ, וְהָאֱלִילִים כָּרוֹת יִכָּרֵתוּן
לְתַקֵּן עוֹלָם בְּמַלְכוּת שַׁדַּי.
וְכָל בְּנֵי בָשָׂר יִקְרְאוּ בִשְׁמֶךָ לְהַפְנוֹת אֵלֶיךָ כָּל רִשְׁעֵי אָרֶץ.
יַכִּירוּ וְיֵדְעוּ כָּל יוֹשְׁבֵי תֵבֵל
כִּי לְךָ תִּכְרַע כָּל בֶּרֶךְ, תִּשָּׁבַע כָּל לָשׁוֹן.
לְפָנֶיךָ יהוה אֱלֹהֵינוּ יִכְרְעוּ וְיִפֹּלוּ, וְלִכְבוֹד שִׁמְךָ יְקָר יִתֵּנוּ
וִיקַבְּלוּ כֻלָּם אֶת עֹל מַלְכוּתֶךָ
וְתִמְלֹךְ עֲלֵיהֶם מְהֵרָה לְעוֹלָם וָעֶד.
כִּי הַמַּלְכוּת שֶׁלְּךָ הִיא וּלְעוֹלְמֵי עַד תִּמְלֹךְ בְּכָבוֹד
כַּכָּתוּב בְּתוֹרָתֶךָ, יהוה יִמְלֹךְ לְעֹלָם וָעֶד: שמות טו

▸ And it is said: "Then the LORD shall be King over all the earth; on that day the LORD shall be One and His name One." *Zech. 14*

Some add:

Have no fear of sudden terror or of the ruin when it overtakes the wicked. *Prov. 3*
Devise your strategy, but it will be thwarted; propose your plan, *Is. 8*
but it will not stand, for God is with us.
When you grow old, I will still be the same. *Is. 46*
When your hair turns gray, I will still carry you.
I made you, I will bear you, I will carry you, and I will rescue you.

MOURNER'S KADDISH

The following prayer, said by mourners, requires the presence of a minyan.
A transliteration can be found on page 1467.

Mourner: יִתְגַּדַּל Magnified and sanctified
may His great name be,
in the world He created by His will.
May He establish His kingdom
in your lifetime and in your days,
and in the lifetime of all the house of Israel,
swiftly and soon –
and say: Amen.

All: May His great name be blessed for ever and all time.

Mourner: Blessed and praised, glorified and exalted,
raised and honored, uplifted and lauded
be the name of the Holy One, blessed be He,
beyond any blessing, song, praise and consolation
uttered in the world –
and say: Amen.

May there be great peace from heaven,
and life for us and all Israel –
and say: Amen.

Bow, take three steps back, as if taking leave of the Divine Presence,
then bow, first left, then right, then center, while saying:

May He who makes peace in His high places,
make peace for us and all Israel –
and say: Amen.

◂ וְנֶאֱמַר, וְהָיָה יהוה לְמֶלֶךְ עַל־כָּל־הָאָרֶץ בַּיּוֹם הַהוּא יִהְיֶה יהוה אֶחָד וּשְׁמוֹ אֶחָד: זכריה יד

Some add:

אַל־תִּירָא מִפַּחַד פִּתְאֹם וּמִשֹּׁאַת רְשָׁעִים כִּי תָבֹא: משלי ג

עֻצוּ עֵצָה וְתֻפָר, דַּבְּרוּ דָבָר וְלֹא יָקוּם, כִּי עִמָּנוּ אֵל: ישעיה ח

וְעַד־זִקְנָה אֲנִי הוּא, וְעַד־שֵׂיבָה אֲנִי אֶסְבֹּל, אֲנִי עָשִׂיתִי וַאֲנִי אֶשָּׂא וַאֲנִי אֶסְבֹּל וַאֲמַלֵּט: ישעיה מו

קדיש יתום

The following prayer, said by mourners, requires the presence of a מנין.
A transliteration can be found on page 1467.

אבל: יִתְגַּדַּל וְיִתְקַדַּשׁ שְׁמֵהּ רַבָּא (קהל: אָמֵן)
בְּעָלְמָא דִּי בְרָא כִרְעוּתֵהּ
וְיַמְלִיךְ מַלְכוּתֵהּ
בְּחַיֵּיכוֹן וּבְיוֹמֵיכוֹן וּבְחַיֵּי דְכָל בֵּית יִשְׂרָאֵל
בַּעֲגָלָא וּבִזְמַן קָרִיב, וְאִמְרוּ אָמֵן. (קהל: אָמֵן)

קהל ואבל: יְהֵא שְׁמֵהּ רַבָּא מְבָרַךְ לְעָלַם וּלְעָלְמֵי עָלְמַיָּא.

אבל: יִתְבָּרַךְ וְיִשְׁתַּבַּח וְיִתְפָּאַר
וְיִתְרוֹמַם וְיִתְנַשֵּׂא וְיִתְהַדָּר וְיִתְעַלֶּה וְיִתְהַלָּל
שְׁמֵהּ דְּקֻדְשָׁא בְּרִיךְ הוּא (קהל: בְּרִיךְ הוּא)
לְעֵלָּא מִן כָּל בִּרְכָתָא וְשִׁירָתָא, תֻּשְׁבְּחָתָא וְנֶחֱמָתָא
דַּאֲמִירָן בְּעָלְמָא, וְאִמְרוּ אָמֵן. (קהל: אָמֵן)

יְהֵא שְׁלָמָא רַבָּא מִן שְׁמַיָּא
וְחַיִּים, עָלֵינוּ וְעַל כָּל יִשְׂרָאֵל, וְאִמְרוּ אָמֵן. (קהל: אָמֵן)

Bow, take three steps back, as if taking leave of the Divine Presence, then bow, first left, then right, then center, while saying:

עֹשֶׂה שָׁלוֹם בִּמְרוֹמָיו
הוּא יַעֲשֶׂה שָׁלוֹם עָלֵינוּ וְעַל כָּל יִשְׂרָאֵל
וְאִמְרוּ אָמֵן. (קהל: אָמֵן)

THE DAILY PSALM

One of the following psalms is said on the appropriate day of the week as indicated.
After the psalm, the Mourner's Kaddish is said.
Many congregations say the Daily Psalm after the Song of Glory, page 564.

Sunday: הַיּוֹם Today is the first day of the week,
on which the Levites used to say this psalm in the Temple:

לְדָוִד מִזְמוֹר A psalm of David. The earth is the LORD's and all it contains, the world and all who live in it. For He founded it on the seas and established it on the streams. Who may climb the mountain of the LORD? Who may stand in His holy place? He who has clean hands and a pure heart, who has not taken My name in vain or sworn deceitfully. He shall receive a blessing from the LORD, and just reward from the God of his salvation. This is a generation of those who seek Him, the descendants of Jacob who seek Your presence, Selah! Lift up your heads, O gates; be uplifted, eternal doors, so that the King of glory may enter. Who is the King of glory? It is the LORD, strong and mighty, the LORD mighty in battle. Lift up your heads, O gates; be uplifted, eternal doors, that the King of glory may enter. ▸ Who is He, the King of glory? The LORD of hosts, He is the King of glory, Selah! *Ps. 24*

Mourner's Kaddish (page 560)

Monday: הַיּוֹם Today is the second day of the week,
on which the Levites used to say this psalm in the Temple:

שִׁיר מִזְמוֹר A song. A psalm of the sons of Koraḥ. Great is the LORD and greatly to be praised in the city of God, on His holy mountain – beautiful in its heights, joy of all the earth, Mount Zion on its northern side, city of the great King. In its citadels God is known as a stronghold. See how the kings joined forces, advancing together. They saw, they were astounded, they panicked, they fled. There fear seized them, like the pains of a woman giving *Ps. 48*

שִׁיר מִזְמוֹר לִבְנֵי־קֹרַח *Monday: Psalm 48.* A hymn of praise to the beauty and endurance of Jerusalem, the city that outlived all those who sought to conquer it.

A score of conquerors have held it as their choicest prize; and more than a dozen times has it been utterly destroyed. The Babylonians burnt it, and deported its population; the Romans slew a million of its inhabitants, razed it to the ground, passed the ploughshare over it, and strewed its furrows with salt; Hadrian banished its very name from the lips of men, changed it to *Aelia*

שיר של יום

One of the following psalms is said on the appropriate day of the week as indicated.
After the psalm, קדיש יתום *is said.*
Many congregations say the שיר של יום *after the* שיר הכבוד*, page 565.*

Sunday הַיּוֹם יוֹם רִאשׁוֹן בְּשַׁבָּת, שֶׁבּוֹ הָיוּ הַלְוִיִּם אוֹמְרִים בְּבֵית הַמִּקְדָּשׁ:

תהלים כד לְדָוִד מִזְמוֹר, לַיהוה הָאָרֶץ וּמְלוֹאָהּ, תֵּבֵל וְיֹשְׁבֵי בָהּ: כִּי־הוּא עַל־
יַמִּים יְסָדָהּ, וְעַל־נְהָרוֹת יְכוֹנְנֶהָ: מִי־יַעֲלֶה בְהַר־יהוה, וּמִי־יָקוּם
בִּמְקוֹם קָדְשׁוֹ: נְקִי כַפַּיִם וּבַר־לֵבָב, אֲשֶׁר לֹא־נָשָׂא לַשָּׁוְא נַפְשִׁי,
וְלֹא נִשְׁבַּע לְמִרְמָה: יִשָּׂא בְרָכָה מֵאֵת יהוה, וּצְדָקָה מֵאֱלֹהֵי יִשְׁעוֹ:
זֶה דּוֹר דֹּרְשָׁו, מְבַקְשֵׁי פָנֶיךָ יַעֲקֹב סֶלָה: שְׂאוּ שְׁעָרִים רָאשֵׁיכֶם,
וְהִנָּשְׂאוּ פִּתְחֵי עוֹלָם, וְיָבוֹא מֶלֶךְ הַכָּבוֹד: מִי זֶה מֶלֶךְ הַכָּבוֹד, יהוה
עִזּוּז וְגִבּוֹר, יהוה גִּבּוֹר מִלְחָמָה: שְׂאוּ שְׁעָרִים רָאשֵׁיכֶם, וּשְׂאוּ פִּתְחֵי
עוֹלָם, וְיָבֹא מֶלֶךְ הַכָּבוֹד: ◂ מִי הוּא זֶה מֶלֶךְ הַכָּבוֹד, יהוה צְבָאוֹת
הוּא מֶלֶךְ הַכָּבוֹד סֶלָה:

קדיש יתום (*page 561*)

Monday הַיּוֹם יוֹם שֵׁנִי בְּשַׁבָּת, שֶׁבּוֹ הָיוּ הַלְוִיִּם אוֹמְרִים בְּבֵית הַמִּקְדָּשׁ:

תהלים מח שִׁיר מִזְמוֹר לִבְנֵי־קֹרַח: גָּדוֹל יהוה וּמְהֻלָּל מְאֹד, בְּעִיר אֱלֹהֵינוּ, הַר־
קָדְשׁוֹ: יְפֵה נוֹף מְשׂוֹשׂ כָּל־הָאָרֶץ, הַר־צִיּוֹן יַרְכְּתֵי צָפוֹן, קִרְיַת מֶלֶךְ
רָב: אֱלֹהִים בְּאַרְמְנוֹתֶיהָ נוֹדַע לְמִשְׂגָּב: כִּי־הִנֵּה הַמְּלָכִים נוֹעֲדוּ,
עָבְרוּ יַחְדָּו: הֵמָּה רָאוּ כֵּן תָּמָהוּ, נִבְהֲלוּ נֶחְפָּזוּ: רְעָדָה אֲחָזָתַם שָׁם,

---

THE DAILY PSALM

A special psalm was said in the Temple on each of the seven days of the week. We say them still, in memory of those days and in hope of future restoration.

לְדָוִד מִזְמוֹר *Sunday: Psalm 24.* The opening verses mirror the act of creation, reminding us that each week mirrors the seven days of creation itself. The psalm also alludes to the Temple, built on "the mountain of the Lord." The connection between the two is based on the idea that the Temple was a microcosm of the universe, and its construction a human counterpart to the divine creation of the cosmos.

birth, like ships of Tarshish wrecked by an eastern wind. What we had heard, now we have seen, in the city of the Lord of hosts, in the city of our God. May God preserve it for ever, Selah! In the midst of Your Temple, God, we meditate on Your love. As is Your name, God, so is Your praise: it reaches to the ends of the earth. Your right hand is filled with righteousness. Let Mount Zion rejoice, let the towns of Judah be glad, because of Your judgments. Walk around Zion and encircle it. Count its towers, note its strong walls, view its citadels, so that you may tell a future generation ▸ that this is God, our God, for ever and ever. He will guide us for evermore.

Mourner's Kaddish (page 560)

Tuesday: הַיּוֹם Today is the third day of the week,
on which the Levites used to say this psalm in the Temple:

מִזְמוֹר לְאָסָף A psalm of Asaph. God stands in the Divine assembly. Among *Ps. 82*
the judges He delivers judgment. How long will you judge unjustly, showing favor to the wicked? Selah. Do justice to the weak and the orphaned. Vindicate the poor and destitute. Rescue the weak and needy. Save them from the hand of the wicked. They do not know nor do they understand. They walk about in darkness while all the earth's foundations shake. I once said, "You are like gods, all of you are sons of the Most High." But you shall die like mere men, you will fall like any prince. ▸ Arise, O Lord, judge the earth, for all the nations are Your possession.

Mourner's Kaddish (page 560)

Wednesday: הַיּוֹם Today is the fourth day of the week,
on which the Levites used to say this psalm in the Temple:

אֵל־נְקָמוֹת God of retribution, Lord, God of retribution, appear! Rise up, *Ps. 94*
Judge of the earth. Repay to the arrogant what they deserve. How long shall the wicked, Lord, how long shall the wicked triumph? They pour out

---

application of law, brings order to society as scientific law brings order to the cosmos. Justice ultimately belongs to God. A judge must therefore act with humility and integrity, bringing divine order to human chaos. "A judge who delivers a true judgment becomes a partner of the Holy One, blessed be He, in the work of creation" (*Shabbat* 10a).

אֵל־נְקָמוֹת יהוה *Wednesday: Psalm 94.* A psalm of intense power about the connection between religious faith and ethical conduct and their opposite: lack

חִיל כַּיּוֹלֵדָה: בְּרוּחַ קָדִים תְּשַׁבֵּר אֳנִיּוֹת תַּרְשִׁישׁ: כַּאֲשֶׁר שָׁמַעְנוּ כֵּן
רָאִינוּ, בְּעִיר־יהוה צְבָאוֹת, בְּעִיר אֱלֹהֵינוּ, אֱלֹהִים יְכוֹנְנֶהָ עַד־עוֹלָם
סֶלָה: דִּמִּינוּ אֱלֹהִים חַסְדֶּךָ, בְּקֶרֶב הֵיכָלֶךָ: כְּשִׁמְךָ אֱלֹהִים כֵּן תְּהִלָּתְךָ
עַל־קַצְוֵי־אֶרֶץ, צֶדֶק מָלְאָה יְמִינֶךָ: יִשְׂמַח הַר־צִיּוֹן, תָּגֵלְנָה בְּנוֹת
יְהוּדָה, לְמַעַן מִשְׁפָּטֶיךָ: סֹבּוּ צִיּוֹן וְהַקִּיפוּהָ, סִפְרוּ מִגְדָּלֶיהָ: שִׁיתוּ לִבְּכֶם
לְחֵילָה, פַּסְּגוּ אַרְמְנוֹתֶיהָ, לְמַעַן תְּסַפְּרוּ לְדוֹר אַחֲרוֹן: ‹ כִּי זֶה אֱלֹהִים
אֱלֹהֵינוּ עוֹלָם וָעֶד, הוּא יְנַהֲגֵנוּ עַל־מוּת: קדיש יתום (*page 561*)

Tuesday הַיּוֹם יוֹם שְׁלִישִׁי בְּשַׁבָּת, שֶׁבּוֹ הָיוּ הַלְוִיִּם אוֹמְרִים בְּבֵית הַמִּקְדָּשׁ:

תהלים פב מִזְמוֹר לְאָסָף, אֱלֹהִים נִצָּב בַּעֲדַת־אֵל, בְּקֶרֶב אֱלֹהִים יִשְׁפֹּט: עַד־מָתַי
תִּשְׁפְּטוּ־עָוֶל, וּפְנֵי רְשָׁעִים תִּשְׂאוּ־סֶלָה: שִׁפְטוּ־דַל וְיָתוֹם, עָנִי וָרָשׁ
הַצְדִּיקוּ: פַּלְּטוּ־דַל וְאֶבְיוֹן, מִיַּד רְשָׁעִים הַצִּילוּ: לֹא יָדְעוּ וְלֹא יָבִינוּ,
בַּחֲשֵׁכָה יִתְהַלָּכוּ, יִמּוֹטוּ כָּל־מוֹסְדֵי אָרֶץ: אֲנִי־אָמַרְתִּי אֱלֹהִים אַתֶּם,
וּבְנֵי עֶלְיוֹן כֻּלְּכֶם: אָכֵן כְּאָדָם תְּמוּתוּן, וּכְאַחַד הַשָּׂרִים תִּפֹּלוּ: ‹ קוּמָה
אֱלֹהִים שָׁפְטָה הָאָרֶץ, כִּי־אַתָּה תִנְחַל בְּכָל־הַגּוֹיִם:
קדיש יתום (*page 561*)

Wednesday הַיּוֹם יוֹם רְבִיעִי בְּשַׁבָּת, שֶׁבּוֹ הָיוּ הַלְוִיִּם אוֹמְרִים בְּבֵית הַמִּקְדָּשׁ:

תהלים צד אֵל־נְקָמוֹת יהוה, אֵל נְקָמוֹת הוֹפִיעַ: הִנָּשֵׂא שֹׁפֵט הָאָרֶץ, הָשֵׁב גְּמוּל
עַל־גֵּאִים: עַד־מָתַי רְשָׁעִים, יהוה, עַד־מָתַי רְשָׁעִים יַעֲלֹזוּ: יַבִּיעוּ
יְדַבְּרוּ עָתָק, יִתְאַמְּרוּ כָּל־פֹּעֲלֵי אָוֶן: עַמְּךָ יהוה יְדַכְּאוּ, וְנַחֲלָתְךָ יְעַנּוּ:

Capitolina, and prohibited any Jew from entering its precincts on pain of death. Persians and Arabs, Barbarians and Crusaders and Turks took it and retook it, ravaged it and burnt it; and yet, marvellous to relate, it ever rises from its ashes to renewed life and glory. It is the Eternal City of the Eternal People. (Rabbi J.H. Hertz)

מִזְמוֹר לְאָסָף *Tuesday: Psalm 82.* A psalm about judges and justice. Justice, the

insolent words. All the evildoers are full of boasting. They crush Your people, LORD, and oppress Your inheritance. They kill the widow and the stranger. They murder the orphaned. They say, "The LORD does not see. The God of Jacob pays no heed." Take heed, you most brutish people. You fools, when will you grow wise? Will He who implants the ear not hear? Will He who formed the eye not see? Will He who disciplines nations – He who teaches man knowledge – not punish? The LORD knows that the thoughts of man are a mere fleeting breath. Happy is the man whom You discipline, LORD, the one You instruct in Your Torah, giving him tranquility in days of trouble, until a pit is dug for the wicked. For the LORD will not forsake His people, nor abandon His heritage. Judgment shall again accord with justice, and all the upright in heart will follow it. Who will rise up for me against the wicked? Who will stand up for me against wrongdoers? Had the LORD not been my help, I would soon have dwelt in death's silence. When I thought my foot was slipping, Your loving-kindness, LORD, gave me support. When I was filled with anxiety, Your consolations soothed my soul. Can a corrupt throne be allied with You? Can injustice be framed into law? They join forces against the life of the righteous, and condemn the innocent to death. But the LORD is my stronghold, my God is the Rock of my refuge. He will bring back on them their wickedness, and destroy them for their evil deeds. The LORD our God will destroy them.

▸ Come, let us sing for joy to the LORD; let us shout aloud to the Rock of our salvation. Let us greet Him with thanksgiving, shout aloud to Him with songs of praise. For the LORD is the great God, the King great above all powers. *Ps. 95*

Mourner's Kaddish (page 560)

Thursday: הַיּוֹם Today is the fifth day of the week,
on which the Levites used to say this psalm in the Temple:

לַמְנַצֵּחַ For the conductor of music. On the Gittit. By Asaph. Sing for joy to God, our strength. Shout aloud to the God of Jacob. Raise a song, beat the drum, play the sweet harp and lyre. Sound the shofar on the new moon, on our feast day when the moon is hidden. For it is a statute for Israel, an ordinance of the God of Jacob. He established it as a testimony for Joseph *Ps. 81*

לַמְנַצֵּחַ *Thursday: Psalm 81.* God pleads with His people: a classic expression of one of the great themes of the prophetic literature, the divine pathos – God's

אַלְמָנָה וְגֵר יַהֲרֹגוּ, וִיתוֹמִים יְרַצֵּחוּ: וַיֹּאמְרוּ לֹא יִרְאֶה־יָּהּ, וְלֹא־יָבִין
אֱלֹהֵי יַעֲקֹב: בִּינוּ בֹּעֲרִים בָּעָם, וּכְסִילִים מָתַי תַּשְׂכִּילוּ: הֲנֹטַע אֹזֶן
הֲלֹא יִשְׁמָע, אִם־יֹצֵר עַיִן הֲלֹא יַבִּיט: הֲיֹסֵר גּוֹיִם הֲלֹא יוֹכִיחַ, הַמְלַמֵּד
אָדָם דָּעַת: יהוה יֹדֵעַ מַחְשְׁבוֹת אָדָם, כִּי־הֵמָּה הָבֶל: אַשְׁרֵי הַגֶּבֶר
אֲשֶׁר־תְּיַסְּרֶנּוּ יָּהּ, וּמִתּוֹרָתְךָ תְלַמְּדֶנּוּ: לְהַשְׁקִיט לוֹ מִימֵי רָע, עַד
יִכָּרֶה לָרָשָׁע שָׁחַת: כִּי לֹא־יִטֹּשׁ יהוה עַמּוֹ, וְנַחֲלָתוֹ לֹא יַעֲזֹב: כִּי־עַד־
צֶדֶק יָשׁוּב מִשְׁפָּט, וְאַחֲרָיו כָּל־יִשְׁרֵי־לֵב: מִי־יָקוּם לִי עִם־מְרֵעִים,
מִי־יִתְיַצֵּב לִי עִם־פֹּעֲלֵי אָוֶן: לוּלֵי יהוה עֶזְרָתָה לִּי, כִּמְעַט שָׁכְנָה
דוּמָה נַפְשִׁי: אִם־אָמַרְתִּי מָטָה רַגְלִי, חַסְדְּךָ יהוה יִסְעָדֵנִי: בְּרֹב
שַׂרְעַפַּי בְּקִרְבִּי, תַּנְחוּמֶיךָ יְשַׁעַשְׁעוּ נַפְשִׁי: הַיְחָבְרְךָ כִּסֵּא הַוּוֹת, יֹצֵר
עָמָל עֲלֵי־חֹק: יָגוֹדּוּ עַל־נֶפֶשׁ צַדִּיק, וְדָם נָקִי יַרְשִׁיעוּ: וַיְהִי יהוה
לִי לְמִשְׂגָּב, וֵאלֹהַי לְצוּר מַחְסִי: וַיָּשֶׁב עֲלֵיהֶם אֶת־אוֹנָם, וּבְרָעָתָם
יַצְמִיתֵם, יַצְמִיתֵם יהוה אֱלֹהֵינוּ:

‹ לְכוּ נְרַנְּנָה לַיהוה, נָרִיעָה לְצוּר יִשְׁעֵנוּ: נְקַדְּמָה פָנָיו בְּתוֹדָה, בִּזְמִרוֹת תהלים צה
נָרִיעַ לוֹ: כִּי אֵל גָּדוֹל יהוה, וּמֶלֶךְ גָּדוֹל עַל־כָּל־אֱלֹהִים:

קדיש יתום (*page 561*)

Thursday הַיּוֹם יוֹם חֲמִישִׁי בְּשַׁבָּת, שֶׁבּוֹ הָיוּ הַלְוִיִּם אוֹמְרִים בְּבֵית הַמִּקְדָּשׁ:

לַמְנַצֵּחַ עַל־הַגִּתִּית לְאָסָף: הַרְנִינוּ לֵאלֹהִים עוּזֵּנוּ, הָרִיעוּ לֵאלֹהֵי תהלים פא
יַעֲקֹב: שְׂאוּ־זִמְרָה וּתְנוּ־תֹף, כִּנּוֹר נָעִים עִם־נָבֶל: תִּקְעוּ בַחֹדֶשׁ שׁוֹפָר,
בַּכֵּסֶה לְיוֹם חַגֵּנוּ: כִּי חֹק לְיִשְׂרָאֵל הוּא, מִשְׁפָּט לֵאלֹהֵי יַעֲקֹב: עֵדוּת
בִּיהוֹסֵף שָׂמוֹ, בְּצֵאתוֹ עַל־אֶרֶץ מִצְרָיִם, שְׂפַת לֹא־יָדַעְתִּי אֶשְׁמָע:

---

of faith and a failure of humanity. When man begins to worship himself, he dreams of becoming a god but ends by becoming lower than the beasts. Appropriately, some communities recite this psalm on *Yom HaSho'a*, Holocaust Memorial Day (27 Nisan).

when He went forth against the land of Egypt, where I heard a language that I did not know. I relieved his shoulder of the burden. His hands were freed from the builder's basket. In distress you called and I rescued you. I answered you from the secret place of thunder; I tested you at the waters of Meribah, Selah! Hear, My people, and I will warn you. Israel, if you would only listen to Me! Let there be no strange god among you. Do not bow down to an alien god. I am the LORD your God who brought you out of the land of Egypt. Open your mouth wide and I will fill it. But My people would not listen to Me. Israel would have none of Me. So I left them to their stubborn hearts, letting them follow their own devices. If only My people would listen to Me, if Israel would walk in My ways, I would soon subdue their enemies, and turn My hand against their foes. Those who hate the LORD would cower before Him and their doom would last for ever. ▸ He would feed Israel with the finest wheat – with honey from the rock I would satisfy you.

Mourner's Kaddish (on the next page)

Friday: הַיּוֹם Today is the sixth day of the week,
on which the Levites used to say this psalm in the Temple:

יהוה מָלָךְ The LORD reigns. He is robed in majesty. The LORD is robed, girded with strength. The world is firmly established; it cannot be moved. Your throne stands firm as of old; You are eternal. Rivers lift up, LORD, rivers lift up their voice, rivers lift up their crashing waves. Mightier than the noise of many waters, than the mighty waves of the sea is the LORD on high. ▸ Your testimonies are very sure; holiness adorns Your House, LORD, for evermore. *Ps. 93*

Mourner's Kaddish (on the next page)

Shabbat: הַיּוֹם Today is the holy Sabbath,
on which the Levites used to say this psalm in the Temple:

מִזְמוֹר A psalm. A song for the Sabbath day. It is good to thank the LORD and sing psalms to Your name, Most High – to tell of Your loving-kindness in the morning and Your faithfulness at night, to the music of the ten-stringed lyre and the melody of the harp. For You have made me rejoice by Your work, O *Ps. 92*

---

day, when "the heavens and the earth were completed, and all their array" (Gen. 2:1).

מִזְמוֹר *The Sabbath: Psalm 92.* A psalm about the Sabbath of the end of days when the world will be restored to its primal harmony, violence will cease,

הֲסִירוֹתִי מִסֵּבֶל שִׁכְמוֹ, כַּפָּיו מִדּוּד תַּעֲבֹרְנָה: בַּצָּרָה קָרָאתָ וָאֲחַלְּצֶךָּ,
אֶעֶנְךָ בְּסֵתֶר רַעַם, אֶבְחָנְךָ עַל־מֵי מְרִיבָה סֶלָה: שְׁמַע עַמִּי וְאָעִידָה
בָּךְ, יִשְׂרָאֵל אִם־תִּשְׁמַע־לִי: לֹא־יִהְיֶה בְךָ אֵל זָר, וְלֹא תִשְׁתַּחֲוֶה
לְאֵל נֵכָר: אָנֹכִי יהוה אֱלֹהֶיךָ, הַמַּעַלְךָ מֵאֶרֶץ מִצְרָיִם, הַרְחֶב־פִּיךָ
וַאֲמַלְאֵהוּ: וְלֹא־שָׁמַע עַמִּי לְקוֹלִי, וְיִשְׂרָאֵל לֹא־אָבָה לִי: וָאֲשַׁלְּחֵהוּ
בִּשְׁרִירוּת לִבָּם, יֵלְכוּ בְּמוֹעֲצוֹתֵיהֶם: לוּ עַמִּי שֹׁמֵעַ לִי, יִשְׂרָאֵל בִּדְרָכַי
יְהַלֵּכוּ: כִּמְעַט אוֹיְבֵיהֶם אַכְנִיעַ, וְעַל־צָרֵיהֶם אָשִׁיב יָדִי: מְשַׂנְאֵי יהוה
יְכַחֲשׁוּ־לוֹ, וִיהִי עִתָּם לְעוֹלָם: ‹ וַיַּאֲכִילֵהוּ מֵחֵלֶב חִטָּה, וּמִצּוּר, דְּבַשׁ
אַשְׂבִּיעֶךָ:

קדיש יתום (*on the next page*)

Friday הַיּוֹם יוֹם שִׁשִּׁי בְּשַׁבָּת, שֶׁבּוֹ הָיוּ הַלְוִיִּם אוֹמְרִים בְּבֵית הַמִּקְדָּשׁ:

תהלים צג
יהוה מָלָךְ, גֵּאוּת לָבֵשׁ, לָבֵשׁ יהוה עֹז הִתְאַזָּר, אַף־תִּכּוֹן תֵּבֵל בַּל־
תִּמּוֹט: נָכוֹן כִּסְאֲךָ מֵאָז, מֵעוֹלָם אָתָּה: נָשְׂאוּ נְהָרוֹת יהוה, נָשְׂאוּ
נְהָרוֹת קוֹלָם, יִשְׂאוּ נְהָרוֹת דָּכְיָם: מִקֹּלוֹת מַיִם רַבִּים, אַדִּירִים מִשְׁבְּרֵי־
יָם, אַדִּיר בַּמָּרוֹם יהוה: ‹ עֵדֹתֶיךָ נֶאֶמְנוּ מְאֹד, לְבֵיתְךָ נַאֲוָה־קֹּדֶשׁ,
יהוה לְאֹרֶךְ יָמִים:

קדיש יתום (*on the next page*)

שבת הַיּוֹם יוֹם שַׁבַּת קֹדֶשׁ, שֶׁבּוֹ הָיוּ הַלְוִיִּם אוֹמְרִים בְּבֵית הַמִּקְדָּשׁ:

תהלים צב
מִזְמוֹר שִׁיר לְיוֹם הַשַּׁבָּת: טוֹב לְהֹדוֹת לַיהוה, וּלְזַמֵּר לְשִׁמְךָ עֶלְיוֹן:
לְהַגִּיד בַּבֹּקֶר חַסְדֶּךָ, וֶאֱמוּנָתְךָ בַּלֵּילוֹת: עֲלֵי־עָשׂוֹר וַעֲלֵי־נָבֶל, עֲלֵי
הִגָּיוֹן בְּכִנּוֹר: כִּי שִׂמַּחְתַּנִי יהוה בְּפָעֳלֶךָ, בְּמַעֲשֵׂי יָדֶיךָ אֲרַנֵּן: מַה־גָּדְלוּ

---

love for, but exasperation with, His children. "If only My people would listen to Me."

יהוה מָלָךְ *Friday: Psalm 93.* Speaking as it does of the completion of creation ("the world is firmly established"), this psalm is appropriate for the sixth

Lord; I sing for joy at the deeds of Your hands. How great are Your deeds, Lord, and how very deep Your thoughts. A boor cannot know, nor can a fool understand, that though the wicked spring up like grass and all evildoers flourish, it is only that they may be destroyed for ever. But You, Lord, are eternally exalted. For behold Your enemies, Lord, behold Your enemies will perish; all evildoers will be scattered. You have raised my pride like that of a wild ox; I am anointed with fresh oil. My eyes shall look in triumph on my adversaries; my ears shall hear the downfall of the wicked who rise against me. The righteous will flourish like a palm tree and grow tall like a cedar in Lebanon. Planted in the Lord's House, blossoming in our God's courtyards, ▸ they will still bear fruit in old age, and stay vigorous and fresh, proclaiming that the Lord is upright: He is my Rock, in whom there is no wrong.

MOURNER'S KADDISH

The following prayer, said by mourners, requires the presence of a minyan.
A transliteration can be found on page 1467.

Mourner: יִתְגַּדַּל Magnified and sanctified
may His great name be,
in the world He created by His will.
May He establish His kingdom
in your lifetime and in your days,
and in the lifetime of all the house of Israel,
swiftly and soon –
and say: Amen.

All: May His great name be blessed for ever and all time.

Mourner: Blessed and praised, glorified and exalted,
raised and honored,
uplifted and lauded
be the name of the Holy One,
blessed be He,

---

come, for the day which will be entirely Sabbath and rest for life everlasting" (Mishna, *Tamid* 7:4).

מַעֲשֶׂיךָ יהוה, מְאֹד עָמְקוּ מַחְשְׁבֹתֶיךָ: אִישׁ־בַּעַר לֹא יֵדָע, וּכְסִיל לֹא־יָבִין אֶת־זֹאת: בִּפְרֹחַ רְשָׁעִים כְּמוֹ־עֵשֶׂב, וַיָּצִיצוּ כָּל־פֹּעֲלֵי אָוֶן, לְהִשָּׁמְדָם עֲדֵי־עַד: וְאַתָּה מָרוֹם לְעֹלָם יהוה: כִּי הִנֵּה אֹיְבֶיךָ יהוה, כִּי־הִנֵּה אֹיְבֶיךָ יֹאבֵדוּ, יִתְפָּרְדוּ כָּל־פֹּעֲלֵי אָוֶן: וַתָּרֶם כִּרְאֵים קַרְנִי, בַּלֹּתִי בְּשֶׁמֶן רַעֲנָן: וַתַּבֵּט עֵינִי בְּשׁוּרָי, בַּקָּמִים עָלַי מְרֵעִים תִּשְׁמַעְנָה אָזְנָי: צַדִּיק כַּתָּמָר יִפְרָח, כְּאֶרֶז בַּלְּבָנוֹן יִשְׂגֶּה: שְׁתוּלִים בְּבֵית יהוה, בְּחַצְרוֹת אֱלֹהֵינוּ יַפְרִיחוּ: › עוֹד יְנוּבוּן בְּשֵׂיבָה, דְּשֵׁנִים וְרַעֲנַנִּים יִהְיוּ: לְהַגִּיד כִּי־יָשָׁר יהוה, צוּרִי, וְלֹא־עַוְלָתָה בּוֹ:

קדיש יתום

The following prayer, said by mourners, requires the presence of a מנין.
A transliteration can be found on page 1467.

אבל: יִתְגַּדַּל וְיִתְקַדַּשׁ שְׁמֵהּ רַבָּא (קהל: אָמֵן)
בְּעָלְמָא דִּי בְרָא כִרְעוּתֵהּ
וְיַמְלִיךְ מַלְכוּתֵהּ
בְּחַיֵּיכוֹן וּבְיוֹמֵיכוֹן וּבְחַיֵּי דְכָל בֵּית יִשְׂרָאֵל
בַּעֲגָלָא וּבִזְמַן קָרִיב
וְאִמְרוּ אָמֵן. (קהל: אָמֵן)

קהל ואבל: יְהֵא שְׁמֵהּ רַבָּא מְבָרַךְ לְעָלַם וּלְעָלְמֵי עָלְמַיָּא.

אבל: יִתְבָּרַךְ וְיִשְׁתַּבַּח וְיִתְפָּאַר
וְיִתְרוֹמַם וְיִתְנַשֵּׂא וְיִתְהַדָּר וְיִתְעַלֶּה וְיִתְהַלָּל
שְׁמֵהּ דְּקֻדְשָׁא בְּרִיךְ הוּא (קהל: בְּרִיךְ הוּא)

---

lives will not be cut short by war or terror, and each being will recognize its integrity in the scheme of creation. It is, said the sages, a "song for the time to

beyond any blessing,
song, praise and consolation
uttered in the world –
and say: Amen.

May there be great peace from heaven,
and life for us and all Israel –
and say: Amen.

Bow, take three steps back, as if taking leave of the Divine Presence, then bow, first left, then right, then center, while saying:

May He who makes peace in His high places,
make peace for us and all Israel –
and say: Amen.

לְדָוִד A psalm of David. The LORD is my light and my salvation – whom *Ps. 27* then shall I fear? The LORD is the stronghold of my life – of whom shall I be afraid? When evil men close in on me to devour my flesh, it is they, my enemies and foes, who stumble and fall. Should an army besiege me, my heart would not fear. Should war break out against me, still I would be confident. One thing I ask of the LORD, only this do I seek: to live in the House of the LORD all the days of my life, to gaze on the beauty of the LORD and worship in His Temple. For He will keep me safe in His pavilion on the day of trouble. He will hide me under the cover of His tent. He will set me high upon a rock. Now my head is high above my enemies who surround me. I will sacrifice in His tent with shouts of joy. I will sing and chant praises to the LORD. LORD, hear my voice when I call. Be gracious to me and answer me. On Your behalf my heart says, "Seek My face." Your face, LORD, will I seek. Do not hide Your face from me. Do not turn Your servant away in anger. You have been my help. Do not reject or forsake me, God, my Savior. Were my father and my mother to forsake me, the LORD would take me in. Teach me Your way, LORD, and lead me on a level path, because of my oppressors. Do not abandon me to the will of my foes, for false witnesses have risen against me, breathing violence. ▸ Were it not for my faith that I shall see the LORD's goodness in the land of the living. Hope in the LORD. Be strong and of good courage, and hope in the LORD!

Mourner's Kaddish (previous page)

לְעֵֽלָּא מִן כָּל בִּרְכָתָא וְשִׁירָתָא, תֻּשְׁבְּחָתָא וְנֶחֱמָתָא
דַּאֲמִירָן בְּעָלְמָא
וְאִמְרוּ אָמֵן. (קהל: אָמֵן)

יְהֵא שְׁלָמָא רַבָּא מִן שְׁמַיָּא
וְחַיִּים, עָלֵֽינוּ וְעַל כָּל יִשְׂרָאֵל
וְאִמְרוּ אָמֵן. (קהל: אָמֵן)

Bow, take three steps back, as if taking leave of the Divine Presence, then bow, first left, then right, then center, while saying:

עֹשֶׂה שָׁלוֹם בִּמְרוֹמָיו
הוּא יַעֲשֶׂה שָׁלוֹם עָלֵֽינוּ וְעַל כָּל יִשְׂרָאֵל
וְאִמְרוּ אָמֵן. (קהל: אָמֵן)

לְדָוִד, יהוה אוֹרִי וְיִשְׁעִי, מִמִּי אִירָא, יהוה מָעוֹז־חַיַּי, מִמִּי אֶפְחָד: בִּקְרֹב עָלַי מְרֵעִים לֶאֱכֹל אֶת־בְּשָׂרִי, צָרַי וְאֹיְבַי לִי, הֵמָּה כָשְׁלוּ וְנָפָֽלוּ: אִם־תַּחֲנֶה עָלַי מַחֲנֶה, לֹא־יִירָא לִבִּי, אִם־תָּקוּם עָלַי מִלְחָמָה, בְּזֹאת אֲנִי בוֹטֵֽחַ: אַחַת שָׁאַלְתִּי מֵאֵת־יהוה, אוֹתָהּ אֲבַקֵּשׁ, שִׁבְתִּי בְּבֵית־יהוה כָּל־יְמֵי חַיַּי, לַחֲזוֹת בְּנֹֽעַם־יהוה, וּלְבַקֵּר בְּהֵיכָלוֹ: כִּי יִצְפְּנֵֽנִי בְּסֻכֹּה בְּיוֹם רָעָה, יַסְתִּרֵֽנִי בְּסֵֽתֶר אָהֳלוֹ, בְּצוּר יְרוֹמְמֵֽנִי: וְעַתָּה יָרוּם רֹאשִׁי עַל אֹיְבַי סְבִיבוֹתַי, וְאֶזְבְּחָה בְאָהֳלוֹ זִבְחֵי תְרוּעָה, אָשִֽׁירָה וַאֲזַמְּרָה לַיהוה: שְׁמַע־יהוה קוֹלִי אֶקְרָא, וְחָנֵּֽנִי וַעֲנֵֽנִי: לְךָ אָמַר לִבִּי בַּקְּשׁוּ פָנָי, אֶת־פָּנֶֽיךָ יהוה אֲבַקֵּשׁ: אַל־תַּסְתֵּר פָּנֶֽיךָ מִמֶּֽנִּי, אַל תַּט־בְּאַף עַבְדֶּֽךָ, עֶזְרָתִי הָיִֽיתָ, אַל־תִּטְּשֵֽׁנִי וְאַל־תַּעַזְבֵֽנִי, אֱלֹהֵי יִשְׁעִי: כִּי־אָבִי וְאִמִּי עֲזָבֽוּנִי, וַיהוה יַאַסְפֵֽנִי: הוֹרֵֽנִי יהוה דַּרְכֶּֽךָ, וּנְחֵֽנִי בְּאֹֽרַח מִישׁוֹר, לְמַֽעַן שׁוֹרְרָי: אַל־תִּתְּנֵֽנִי בְּנֶֽפֶשׁ צָרָי, כִּי קָֽמוּ־בִי עֵדֵי־שֶֽׁקֶר, וִיפֵֽחַ חָמָס: › לוּלֵא הֶאֱמַֽנְתִּי לִרְאוֹת בְּטוּב־יהוה בְּאֶֽרֶץ חַיִּים: קַוֵּה אֶל־יהוה, חֲזַק וְיַאֲמֵץ לִבֶּֽךָ, וְקַוֵּה אֶל־יהוה: תהלים כז

קדיש יתום (*previous page*)

SONG OF GLORY

The Ark is opened and all stand.

Leader: I will sing sweet psalms and I will weave songs,
to You for whom my soul longs.

Cong: My soul yearns for the shelter of Your hand,
that all Your mystic secrets I might understand.

Leader: Whenever I speak of Your glory above,
my heart is yearning for Your love.

Cong: So Your glories I will proclaim,
and in songs of love give honor to Your name.

Leader: I will tell of Your glory though I have not seen You,
imagine and describe You, though I have not known You.

Cong: By the hand of Your prophets, through Your servants' mystery,
You gave a glimpse of Your wondrous majesty.

Leader: Recounting Your grandeur and Your glory,
of Your great deeds they told the story.

Cong: They depicted You, though not as You are,
but as You do: Your acts, Your power.

Leader: They represented You in many visions;
through them all You are One without divisions.

Cong: They saw You, now old, then young,
Your head with gray, with black hair hung.

Leader: Aged on the day of judgment, yet on the day of war,
a young warrior with mighty hands they saw.

Cong: Triumph like a helmet He wore on his head;
His right hand and holy arm to victory have led.

הִנְּךָ אֶחָד בְּכָל דִּמְיוֹנוֹת *Through them all, You are One without divisions.* Literally, "You are One through all the images," a preface to the following verses which give examples of this theme.

זִקְנָה בְּיוֹם דִּין *Aged on the day of judgment.* A reference to the mystical vision in Daniel (7:9) of God sitting on the throne of judgment: "The hair of His head was white as wool."

בְּיוֹם קְרָב *Yet on the day of war.* From the vision of Zechariah (14:3).

שיר הכבוד

The ארון קודש *is opened and all stand.*

ש״ץ: אַנְעִים זְמִירוֹת וְשִׁירִים אֶאֱרֹג, כִּי אֵלֶיךָ נַפְשִׁי תַעֲרֹג.
קהל: נַפְשִׁי חָמְדָה בְּצֵל יָדֶךָ, לָדַעַת כָּל רָז סוֹדֶךָ.

ש״ץ: מִדֵּי דַבְּרִי בִּכְבוֹדֶךָ, הוֹמֶה לִבִּי אֶל דּוֹדֶיךָ.
קהל: עַל כֵּן אֲדַבֵּר בְּךָ נִכְבָּדוֹת, וְשִׁמְךָ אֲכַבֵּד בְּשִׁירֵי יְדִידוֹת.

ש״ץ: אֲסַפְּרָה כְבוֹדְךָ וְלֹא רְאִיתִיךָ, אֲדַמְּךָ אֲכַנְּךָ וְלֹא יְדַעְתִּיךָ.
קהל: בְּיַד נְבִיאֶיךָ בְּסוֹד עֲבָדֶיךָ, דִּמִּיתָ הֲדַר כְּבוֹד הוֹדֶךָ.

ש״ץ: גְּדֻלָּתְךָ וּגְבוּרָתֶךָ, כִּנּוּ לְתֹקֶף פְּעֻלָּתֶךָ.
קהל: דִּמּוּ אוֹתְךָ וְלֹא כְּפִי יֶשְׁךָ, וַיְשַׁוּוּךָ לְפִי מַעֲשֶׂיךָ.

ש״ץ: הִמְשִׁילוּךָ בְּרֹב חֶזְיוֹנוֹת, הִנְּךָ אֶחָד בְּכָל דִּמְיוֹנוֹת.
קהל: וַיֶּחֱזוּ בְךָ זִקְנָה וּבַחֲרוּת, וּשְׂעַר רֹאשְׁךָ בְּשֵׂיבָה וְשַׁחֲרוּת.

ש״ץ: זִקְנָה בְּיוֹם דִּין וּבַחֲרוּת בְּיוֹם קְרָב, כְּאִישׁ מִלְחָמוֹת יָדָיו לוֹ רָב.
קהל: חָבַשׁ כּוֹבַע יְשׁוּעָה בְּרֹאשׁוֹ, הוֹשִׁיעָה לּוֹ יְמִינוֹ וּזְרוֹעַ קָדְשׁוֹ.

ANIM ZEMIROT – SONG OF GLORY

Attributed to either Rabbi Yehuda HeḤasid (d. 1217) or his father Rabbi Shmuel, a hymn structured as an alphabetical acrostic, with a (non-acrostic) four-line introduction and a three-line conclusion, followed by biblical verses. The poem, with great grace and depth, speaks about the limits of language in describing the experience of God. On the one hand, God – infinite, eternal, invisible – is beyond the reach of language. On the other, we can only address Him in and through language. Hence the various literary forms – metaphor, image, mystic vision – used by the prophets and poets and their successors to indicate, through words, that which lies beyond words. The images are many, but God is One.

בְּצֵל יָדֶךָ *The shelter of Your hand.* An image of intimacy and protection (see Isaiah 49:2, 51:16; Song of Songs 2:3).

אֲדַמְּךָ אֲכַנְּךָ וְלֹא יְדַעְתִּיךָ *Imagine and describe You, though I have not known You.* The finite cannot truly know the Infinite; physical beings cannot fully understand the One who is non-physical.

Leader: His curls are filled with dew drops of light,
His locks with fragments of the night.

Cong: He will glory in me, for He delights in me;
My diadem of beauty He shall be.

Leader: His head is like pure beaten gold;
Engraved on His brow, His sacred name behold.

Cong: For grace and glory, beauty and renown,
His people have adorned Him with a crown.

Leader: Like a youth's, His hair in locks unfurls;
Its black tresses flowing in curls.

Cong: Jerusalem, His splendor, is the dwelling place of right;
may He prize it as His highest delight.

Leader: Like a crown in His hand may His treasured people be,
a turban of beauty and of majesty.

Cong: He bore them, carried them, with a crown He adorned them.
They were precious in His sight, and He honored them.

Leader: His glory is on me; my glory is on Him.
He is near to me when I call to Him.

Cong: He is bright and rosy; red will be His dress,
when He comes from Edom, treading the winepress.

Leader: He showed the tefillin-knot to Moses, humble, wise,
when the Lord's likeness was before his eyes.

Cong: He delights in His people; the humble He does raise –
He glories in them; He sits enthroned upon their praise.

Leader: Your first word, Your call to every age, is true:
O seek the people who seek You.

Cong: My many songs please take and hear
and may my hymn of joy to You come near.

Leader: May my praise be a crown for Your head,
and like incense before You, the prayers I have said.

Cong: May a poor man's song be precious in Your eyes,
like a song sung over sacrifice.

---

days, taken from Isaiah 63:1–3. By invoking some of the most dramatic images of God in the Bible and rabbinic literature, the poet tells us that they are not to be understood literally: poetry, metaphor and imagery are ways in which prophets and mystics intimate what lies beyond the sayable.

ש״ץ: טַלְלֵי אוֹרוֹת רֹאשׁוֹ נִמְלָא, קְוֻצּוֹתָיו רְסִיסֵי לָיְלָה.
קהל: יִתְפָּאֵר בִּי כִּי חָפֵץ בִּי, וְהוּא יִהְיֶה לִּי לַעֲטֶרֶת צְבִי.

ש״ץ: כֶּתֶם טָהוֹר פָּז דְּמוּת רֹאשׁוֹ, וְחַק עַל מֵצַח כְּבוֹד שֵׁם קָדְשׁוֹ.
קהל: לְחֵן וּלְכָבוֹד צְבִי תִפְאָרָה, אֻמָּתוֹ לוֹ עִטְּרָה עֲטָרָה.

ש״ץ: מַחְלְפוֹת רֹאשׁוֹ כְּבִימֵי בְחוּרוֹת, קְוֻצּוֹתָיו תַּלְתַּלִּים שְׁחוֹרוֹת.
קהל: נְוֵה הַצֶּדֶק צְבִי תִפְאַרְתּוֹ, יַעֲלֶה נָּא עַל רֹאשׁ שִׂמְחָתוֹ.

ש״ץ: סְגֻלָּתוֹ תְּהִי בְיָדוֹ עֲטֶרֶת, וּצְנִיף מְלוּכָה צְבִי תִפְאֶרֶת.
קהל: עֲמוּסִים נְשָׂאָם, עֲטֶרֶת עִנְּדָם, מֵאֲשֶׁר יָקְרוּ בְעֵינָיו כִּבְּדָם.

ש״ץ: פְּאֵרוֹ עָלַי וּפְאֵרִי עָלָיו, וְקָרוֹב אֵלַי בְּקָרְאִי אֵלָיו.
קהל: צַח וְאָדֹם לִלְבוּשׁוֹ אָדֹם, פּוּרָה בְדָרְכוֹ בְּבוֹאוֹ מֵאֱדוֹם.

ש״ץ: קֶשֶׁר תְּפִלִּין הֶרְאָה לֶעָנָו, תְּמוּנַת יהוה לְנֶגֶד עֵינָיו.
קהל: רוֹצֶה בְעַמּוֹ עֲנָוִים יְפָאֵר, יוֹשֵׁב תְּהִלּוֹת בָּם לְהִתְפָּאֵר.

ש״ץ: רֹאשׁ דְּבָרְךָ אֱמֶת קוֹרֵא מֵרֹאשׁ דּוֹר וָדוֹר, עַם דּוֹרֶשְׁךָ דְּרֹשׁ.
קהל: שִׁית הֲמוֹן שִׁירַי נָא עָלֶיךָ, וְרִנָּתִי תִּקְרַב אֵלֶיךָ.

ש״ץ: תְּהִלָּתִי תְּהִי לְרֹאשְׁךָ עֲטֶרֶת, וּתְפִלָּתִי תִּכּוֹן קְטֹרֶת.
קהל: תִּיקַר שִׁירַת רָשׁ בְּעֵינֶיךָ, כַּשִּׁיר יוּשַׁר עַל קָרְבָּנֶיךָ.

טַלְלֵי אוֹרוֹת *Dew drops of light.* These and the following images are drawn from Isaiah and the Song of Songs.

פְּאֵרוֹ עָלַי וּפְאֵרִי עָלָיו *His glory is on me; my glory is on Him.* A reference to the daring metaphor of the sages (*Berakhot* 6a), that just as the children of Israel wear tefillin (an emblem of glory) containing the verse *Shema Yisrael*, proclaiming the Oneness of God, so God, as it were, wears tefillin containing the verse, "Who is like Your people Israel, a nation unique on earth?" – proclaiming the uniqueness of Israel. This is reiterated in the phrase of the next stanza, "He showed the tefillin-knot to Moses," a reference to Exodus 33:23, "You will see My back." Tefillin symbolize the bond of love between God and His people.

בְּבוֹאוֹ מֵאֱדוֹם *When He comes from Edom.* An image of judgment at the end of

Leader: To the One who sustains all, may my blessing take flight:
Creator, Life-Giver, God of right and might.

Cong: And when I offer blessing, to me Your head incline:
accepting it as spice, fragrant and fine.

Leader: May my prayer be to You sweet song.
For You my soul will always long.

The Ark is closed.

Yours, LORD, are the greatness and the power, the glory, the majesty and splendor, *1 Chr. 29*
for everything in heaven and earth is Yours. Yours, LORD, is the kingdom; You
are exalted as Head over all. ▸ Who can tell of the mighty acts of the LORD and *Ps. 106*
make all His praise be heard?

Mourner's Kaddish (page 560)

Many congregations sing Adon Olam at this point.

LORD OF THE UNIVERSE,
who reigned before the birth of any thing –

When by His will all things were made
then was His name proclaimed King.

And when all things shall cease to be
He alone will reign in awe.

He was, He is, and He shall be
glorious for evermore.

He is One, there is none else,
alone, unique, beyond compare;

Without beginning, without end,
His might, His rule are everywhere.

He is my God; my Redeemer lives.
He is the Rock on whom I rely –

My banner and my safe retreat,
my cup, my portion when I cry.

Into His hand my soul I place,
when I awake and when I sleep.

The LORD is with me, I shall not fear;
body and soul from harm will He keep.

ש״ץ: בִּרְכָתִי תַעֲלֶה לְרֹאשׁ מַשְׁבִּיר, מְחוֹלֵל וּמוֹלִיד, צַדִּיק כַּבִּיר.

קהל: וּבְבִרְכָתִי תְנַעֲנַע לִי רֹאשׁ, וְאוֹתָהּ קַח לְךָ כִּבְשָׂמִים רֹאשׁ.

ש״ץ: יֶעֱרַב נָא שִׂיחִי עָלֶיךָ, כִּי נַפְשִׁי תַעֲרֹג אֵלֶיךָ.

The ארון קודש *is closed.*

לְךָ יהוה הַגְּדֻלָּה וְהַגְּבוּרָה וְהַתִּפְאֶרֶת וְהַנֵּצַח וְהַהוֹד כִּי־כֹל בַּשָּׁמַיִם וּבָאָרֶץ, לְךָ יהוה הַמַּמְלָכָה וְהַמִּתְנַשֵּׂא לְכֹל לְרֹאשׁ: דברי הימים א׳ כט

› מִי יְמַלֵּל גְּבוּרוֹת יהוה, יַשְׁמִיעַ כָּל־תְּהִלָּתוֹ: תהלים קו

קדיש יתום (*page 561*)

Many congregations sing אֲדוֹן עוֹלָם *at this point.*

אֲדוֹן עוֹלָם

אֲשֶׁר מָלַךְ בְּטֶרֶם כָּל־יְצִיר נִבְרָא.
לְעֵת נַעֲשָׂה בְחֶפְצוֹ כֹּל אֲזַי מֶלֶךְ שְׁמוֹ נִקְרָא.
וְאַחֲרֵי כִּכְלוֹת הַכֹּל לְבַדּוֹ יִמְלֹךְ נוֹרָא.
וְהוּא הָיָה וְהוּא הֹוֶה וְהוּא יִהְיֶה בְּתִפְאָרָה.
וְהוּא אֶחָד וְאֵין שֵׁנִי לְהַמְשִׁיל לוֹ לְהַחְבִּירָה.
בְּלִי רֵאשִׁית בְּלִי תַכְלִית וְלוֹ הָעֹז וְהַמִּשְׂרָה.
וְהוּא אֵלִי וְחַי גּוֹאֲלִי וְצוּר חֶבְלִי בְּעֵת צָרָה.
וְהוּא נִסִּי וּמָנוֹס לִי מְנָת כּוֹסִי בְּיוֹם אֶקְרָא.
בְּיָדוֹ אַפְקִיד רוּחִי בְּעֵת אִישַׁן וְאָעִירָה.
וְעִם רוּחִי גְּוִיָּתִי יהוה לִי וְלֹא אִירָא.

כִּי נַפְשִׁי תַעֲרֹג אֵלֶיךָ *For You my soul will always long.* The poet brings the song to an end by referring back to the line with which it began.

Kiddush for Yom Tov Morning

On a Yom Tov that falls on Shabbat, start Kiddush here
(some begin at "Therefore the LORD blessed" below):

וְשָׁמְרוּ The children of Israel must keep the Sabbath, observing the Sabbath in every generation as an everlasting covenant. It is a sign between Me and the children of Israel for ever, for in six days the LORD made the heavens and the earth, but on the seventh day He ceased work and refreshed Himself. *Ex. 31*

זָכוֹר Remember the Sabbath day to keep it holy. Six days you shall labor and do all your work, but the seventh day is a Sabbath of the LORD your God; on it you shall not do any work – you, your son or daughter, your male or female slave, or your cattle, or the stranger within your gates. For in six days the LORD made heaven and earth and sea and all that is in them, and rested on the seventh day; *Ex. 20*

On a Yom Tov that falls on Shabbat, some start Kiddush here instead:

Therefore the LORD blessed the Sabbath day and declared it holy.

On a Yom Tov that falls on a weekday, start here:

אֵלֶּה These are the appointed times of the LORD, *Lev. 23*
sacred assemblies, which you shall announce in their due season.
Thus Moses announced the LORD's appointed seasons
to the children of Israel.

When saying Kiddush for others, add: Please pay attention, my masters.

בָּרוּךְ Blessed are You, LORD our God, King of the Universe,
who creates the fruit of the vine.

If one is unable to sit in a sukka the following is not said.

בָּרוּךְ Blessed are You, LORD our God, King of the Universe,
who has made us holy through His commandments
and has commanded us to dwell in the sukka.

---

preceded by scriptural verses which speak of the honor or joy of the day. It is called "the great Kiddush" as if not to put it to shame when compared with its biblically mandated counterpart. There is a moral lesson here. If we institute customs (like covering the ḥalla or matza when making a declaration over wine) so as not to shame inanimate objects or abstract entities, how much more so should be careful never to shame a human being.

קידושא רבה

On יום טוב *that falls on* שבת, *start* קידוש *here (some begin at* עַל־כֵּן בֵּרַךְ *below):*

שמות לא וְשָׁמְרוּ בְנֵי־יִשְׂרָאֵל אֶת־הַשַּׁבָּת, לַעֲשׂוֹת אֶת־הַשַּׁבָּת לְדֹרֹתָם בְּרִית עוֹלָם: בֵּינִי וּבֵין בְּנֵי יִשְׂרָאֵל אוֹת הִוא לְעֹלָם, כִּי־שֵׁשֶׁת יָמִים עָשָׂה יהוה אֶת־הַשָּׁמַיִם וְאֶת־הָאָרֶץ וּבַיּוֹם הַשְּׁבִיעִי שָׁבַת וַיִּנָּפַשׁ:

שמות כ זָכוֹר אֶת־יוֹם הַשַּׁבָּת לְקַדְּשׁוֹ: שֵׁשֶׁת יָמִים תַּעֲבֹד, וְעָשִׂיתָ כָּל־מְלַאכְתֶּךָ: וְיוֹם הַשְּׁבִיעִי שַׁבָּת לַיהוה אֱלֹהֶיךָ, לֹא־תַעֲשֶׂה כָל־מְלָאכָה אַתָּה וּבִנְךָ וּבִתֶּךָ, עַבְדְּךָ וַאֲמָתְךָ וּבְהֶמְתֶּךָ, וְגֵרְךָ אֲשֶׁר בִּשְׁעָרֶיךָ: כִּי שֵׁשֶׁת־יָמִים עָשָׂה יהוה אֶת־הַשָּׁמַיִם וְאֶת־הָאָרֶץ אֶת־הַיָּם וְאֶת־כָּל־אֲשֶׁר־בָּם, וַיָּנַח בַּיּוֹם הַשְּׁבִיעִי

On יום טוב *that falls on* שבת, *some start* קידוש *here instead:*

עַל־כֵּן בֵּרַךְ יהוה אֶת־יוֹם הַשַּׁבָּת וַיְקַדְּשֵׁהוּ:

On יום טוב *that falls on a weekday, start here:*

ויקרא כג אֵלֶּה מוֹעֲדֵי יהוה מִקְרָאֵי קֹדֶשׁ אֲשֶׁר־תִּקְרְאוּ אֹתָם בְּמוֹעֲדָם:
וַיְדַבֵּר מֹשֶׁה אֶת־מֹעֲדֵי יהוה אֶל־בְּנֵי יִשְׂרָאֵל:

When saying קידוש *for others, add* סַבְרִי מָרָנָן

בָּרוּךְ אַתָּה יהוה אֱלֹהֵינוּ מֶלֶךְ הָעוֹלָם, בּוֹרֵא פְּרִי הַגָּפֶן.

If one is unable to sit in a סוכה *the following is not said.*

בָּרוּךְ אַתָּה יהוה אֱלֹהֵינוּ מֶלֶךְ הָעוֹלָם
אֲשֶׁר קִדְּשָׁנוּ בְּמִצְוֹתָיו וְצִוָּנוּ לֵישֵׁב בַּסֻּכָּה.

KIDDUSH

Kiddush on Sabbath and festival mornings is halakhically different from its evening counterpart. In the evening, Kiddush is a biblically ordained performative utterance, declaring the day holy in fulfillment of the command "Remember the Sabbath day to keep it holy," meaning, declare it holy by a blessing made, if possible, over wine (Ex. 20:8; *Pesaḥim* 106a). In the morning, the blessing over wine is a rabbinic command, part of a different mitzva, *kevod Shabbat*, "honoring Shabbat" or *simḥat haregel*, rejoicing on the festival (*Mishna Berura* 271:2). Hence it consists only of a blessing over wine,

Minḥa for Yom Tov

אַשְׁרֵי Happy are those who dwell in Your House; Ps. 84
they shall continue to praise You, Selah!
Happy are the people for whom this is so; Ps. 144
happy are the people whose God is the LORD.
A song of praise by David. Ps. 145

I will exalt You, my God, the King, and bless Your name for ever and all time. Every day I will bless You, and praise Your name for ever and all time. Great is the LORD and greatly to be praised; His greatness is unfathomable. One generation will praise Your works to the next, and tell of Your mighty deeds. On the glorious splendor of Your majesty I will meditate, and on the acts of Your wonders. They shall talk of the power of Your awesome deeds, and I will tell of Your greatness. They shall recite the record of Your great goodness, and sing with joy of Your righteousness. The LORD is gracious and compassionate, slow to anger and great in loving-kindness. The LORD is good to all, and His compassion extends to all His works. All Your works shall thank You, LORD, and Your devoted ones shall bless You. They shall talk of the glory of Your kingship, and speak of Your might. To make known to mankind His mighty deeds and the glorious majesty of His kingship. Your kingdom is an everlasting kingdom, and Your reign is for all generations. The LORD supports all who fall, and raises all who are bowed down. All raise their eyes to You in hope, and You give them their food in due season. You open Your hand, and satisfy every living thing with favor. The LORD is righteous in all His ways, and kind in all He does. The LORD is close to all who call on Him, to all who call on Him in truth. He fulfills the will of those who revere Him; He hears their cry and saves them. The LORD guards all who love Him, but all the wicked He will destroy. ▸ My mouth shall speak the praise of the LORD, and all creatures shall bless His holy name for ever and all time.

We will bless the LORD now and for ever. Halleluya! Ps. 115

מנחה ליום טוב

אַשְׁרֵי יוֹשְׁבֵי בֵיתֶךָ, עוֹד יְהַלְלוּךָ סֶּלָה: תהלים פד

אַשְׁרֵי הָעָם שֶׁכָּכָה לּוֹ, אַשְׁרֵי הָעָם שֶׁיהוה אֱלֹהָיו: תהלים קמד

תְּהִלָּה לְדָוִד תהלים קמה

אֲרוֹמִמְךָ אֱלוֹהַי הַמֶּלֶךְ, וַאֲבָרְכָה שִׁמְךָ לְעוֹלָם וָעֶד:

בְּכָל־יוֹם אֲבָרְכֶךָּ, וַאֲהַלְלָה שִׁמְךָ לְעוֹלָם וָעֶד:

גָּדוֹל יהוה וּמְהֻלָּל מְאֹד, וְלִגְדֻלָּתוֹ אֵין חֵקֶר:

דּוֹר לְדוֹר יְשַׁבַּח מַעֲשֶׂיךָ, וּגְבוּרֹתֶיךָ יַגִּידוּ:

הֲדַר כְּבוֹד הוֹדֶךָ, וְדִבְרֵי נִפְלְאֹתֶיךָ אָשִׂיחָה:

וֶעֱזוּז נוֹרְאֹתֶיךָ יֹאמֵרוּ, וּגְדוּלָּתְךָ אֲסַפְּרֶנָּה:

זֵכֶר רַב־טוּבְךָ יַבִּיעוּ, וְצִדְקָתְךָ יְרַנֵּנוּ:

חַנּוּן וְרַחוּם יהוה, אֶרֶךְ אַפַּיִם וּגְדָל־חָסֶד:

טוֹב־יהוה לַכֹּל, וְרַחֲמָיו עַל־כָּל־מַעֲשָׂיו:

יוֹדוּךָ יהוה כָּל־מַעֲשֶׂיךָ, וַחֲסִידֶיךָ יְבָרְכוּכָה:

כְּבוֹד מַלְכוּתְךָ יֹאמֵרוּ, וּגְבוּרָתְךָ יְדַבֵּרוּ:

לְהוֹדִיעַ לִבְנֵי הָאָדָם גְּבוּרֹתָיו, וּכְבוֹד הֲדַר מַלְכוּתוֹ:

מַלְכוּתְךָ מַלְכוּת כָּל־עֹלָמִים, וּמֶמְשַׁלְתְּךָ בְּכָל־דּוֹר וָדֹר:

סוֹמֵךְ יהוה לְכָל־הַנֹּפְלִים, וְזוֹקֵף לְכָל־הַכְּפוּפִים:

עֵינֵי־כֹל אֵלֶיךָ יְשַׂבֵּרוּ, וְאַתָּה נוֹתֵן־לָהֶם אֶת־אָכְלָם בְּעִתּוֹ:

פּוֹתֵחַ אֶת־יָדֶךָ, וּמַשְׂבִּיעַ לְכָל־חַי רָצוֹן:

צַדִּיק יהוה בְּכָל־דְּרָכָיו, וְחָסִיד בְּכָל־מַעֲשָׂיו:

קָרוֹב יהוה לְכָל־קֹרְאָיו, לְכֹל אֲשֶׁר יִקְרָאֻהוּ בֶאֱמֶת:

רְצוֹן־יְרֵאָיו יַעֲשֶׂה, וְאֶת־שַׁוְעָתָם יִשְׁמַע, וְיוֹשִׁיעֵם:

שׁוֹמֵר יהוה אֶת־כָּל־אֹהֲבָיו, וְאֵת כָּל־הָרְשָׁעִים יַשְׁמִיד:

◂ תְּהִלַּת יהוה יְדַבֶּר פִּי, וִיבָרֵךְ כָּל־בָּשָׂר שֵׁם קָדְשׁוֹ לְעוֹלָם וָעֶד:

וַאֲנַחְנוּ נְבָרֵךְ יָהּ מֵעַתָּה וְעַד־עוֹלָם, הַלְלוּיָהּ: תהלים קטו

וּבָא לְצִיּוֹן גּוֹאֵל "A redeemer will come to Zion, *Is. 59*
to those of Jacob who repent of their sins," declares the LORD.
"As for Me, this is My covenant with them," says the LORD.
"My spirit, that is on you, and My words I have placed in your mouth will not depart from your mouth, or from the mouth of your children, or from the mouth of their descendants from this time on and for ever," says the LORD.

▸ You are the Holy One, enthroned on the praises of Israel. *Ps. 22*
And [the angels] call to one another, saying, ◂ "Holy, holy, holy *Is. 6*
is the LORD of hosts; the whole world is filled with His glory."

And they receive permission from one another, saying: *Targum Yonatan Is. 6*
"Holy in the highest heavens, home of His Presence; holy on earth,
the work of His strength; holy for ever and all time is the LORD of hosts;
the whole earth is full of His radiant glory."

▸ Then a wind lifted me up and I heard behind me the sound of a great *Ezek. 3*
noise, saying, ◂ "Blessed is the LORD's glory from His place."

Then a wind lifted me up and I heard behind me *Targum Yonatan Ezek. 3*
the sound of a great tempest of those who uttered praise, saying,
"Blessed is the LORD's glory from the place of the home of His Presence."

The LORD shall reign for ever and all time. *Ex. 15*
The LORD's kingdom is established for ever and all time. *Targum Onkelos Ex. 15*

יהוה LORD, God of Abraham, Isaac and Yisrael, our ancestors, may *1 Chr. 29*
You keep this for ever so that it forms the thoughts in Your people's
heart, and directs their heart toward You. He is compassionate. He *Ps. 78*
forgives iniquity and does not destroy. Repeatedly He suppresses His
anger, not rousing His full wrath. For You, my LORD, are good and *Ps. 86*
forgiving, abundantly kind to all who call on You. Your righteousness *Ps. 119*
is eternally righteous, and Your Torah is truth. Grant truth to Jacob, *Mic. 7*
loving-kindness to Abraham, as You promised our ancestors in ancient
times. Blessed is my LORD for day after day He burdens us [with His *Ps. 68*
blessings]; is our salvation, Selah! The LORD of hosts is with us; the *Ps. 46*
God of Jacob is our refuge, Selah! LORD of hosts, happy is the one who *Ps. 84*
trusts in You. LORD, save. May the King answer us on the day we call. *Ps. 20*

וּבָא לְצִיּוֹן גּוֹאֵל, וּלְשָׁבֵי פֶשַׁע בְּיַעֲקֹב, נְאֻם יהוה: ישעיה נט
וַאֲנִי זֹאת בְּרִיתִי אוֹתָם, אָמַר יהוה
רוּחִי אֲשֶׁר עָלֶיךָ וּדְבָרַי אֲשֶׁר־שַׂמְתִּי בְּפִיךָ
לֹא־יָמוּשׁוּ מִפִּיךָ וּמִפִּי זַרְעֲךָ וּמִפִּי זֶרַע זַרְעֲךָ
אָמַר יהוה, מֵעַתָּה וְעַד־עוֹלָם:

◂ וְאַתָּה קָדוֹשׁ יוֹשֵׁב תְּהִלּוֹת יִשְׂרָאֵל: וְקָרָא זֶה אֶל־זֶה וְאָמַר ◂ תהלים כב ישעיה ו
קָדוֹשׁ, קָדוֹשׁ, קָדוֹשׁ, יהוה צְבָאוֹת, מְלֹא כָל־הָאָרֶץ כְּבוֹדוֹ:
וּמְקַבְּלִין דֵּין מִן דֵּין וְאָמְרִין, קַדִּישׁ בִּשְׁמֵי מְרוֹמָא עִלָּאָה בֵּית שְׁכִינְתֵּהּ תרגום יונתן ישעיה ו
קַדִּישׁ עַל אַרְעָא עוֹבַד גְּבוּרְתֵּהּ, קַדִּישׁ לְעָלַם וּלְעָלְמֵי עָלְמַיָּא
יהוה צְבָאוֹת, מַלְיָא כָל אַרְעָא זִיו יְקָרֵהּ.

◂ וַתִּשָּׂאֵנִי רוּחַ, וָאֶשְׁמַע אַחֲרַי קוֹל רַעַשׁ גָּדוֹל ◂ יחזקאל ג
בָּרוּךְ כְּבוֹד־יהוה מִמְּקוֹמוֹ:
וּנְטָלַתְנִי רוּחָא, וּשְׁמָעִית בַּתְרַי קָל זִיעַ סַגִּיא, דִּמְשַׁבְּחִין וְאָמְרִין תרגום יונתן יחזקאל ג
בְּרִיךְ יְקָרָא דַיהוה מֵאֲתַר בֵּית שְׁכִינְתֵּהּ.

יהוה יִמְלֹךְ לְעֹלָם וָעֶד: שמות טו
יהוה מַלְכוּתֵהּ קָאֵם לְעָלַם וּלְעָלְמֵי עָלְמַיָּא. תרגום אונקלוס שמות טו

יהוה אֱלֹהֵי אַבְרָהָם יִצְחָק וְיִשְׂרָאֵל אֲבֹתֵינוּ, שָׁמְרָה־זֹּאת לְעוֹלָם דברי הימים א׳, כט
לְיֵצֶר מַחְשְׁבוֹת לְבַב עַמֶּךָ, וְהָכֵן לְבָבָם אֵלֶיךָ: וְהוּא רַחוּם יְכַפֵּר עָוֹן תהלים עח
וְלֹא־יַשְׁחִית, וְהִרְבָּה לְהָשִׁיב אַפּוֹ, וְלֹא־יָעִיר כָּל־חֲמָתוֹ: כִּי־אַתָּה אֲדֹנָי תהלים פו
טוֹב וְסַלָּח, וְרַב־חֶסֶד לְכָל־קֹרְאֶיךָ: צִדְקָתְךָ צֶדֶק לְעוֹלָם וְתוֹרָתְךָ תהלים קיט
אֱמֶת: תִּתֵּן אֱמֶת לְיַעֲקֹב, חֶסֶד לְאַבְרָהָם, אֲשֶׁר־נִשְׁבַּעְתָּ לַאֲבֹתֵינוּ מיכה ז
מִימֵי קֶדֶם: בָּרוּךְ אֲדֹנָי יוֹם יוֹם יַעֲמָס־לָנוּ, הָאֵל יְשׁוּעָתֵנוּ סֶלָה: יהוה תהלים סח תהלים מו
צְבָאוֹת עִמָּנוּ, מִשְׂגָּב לָנוּ אֱלֹהֵי יַעֲקֹב סֶלָה: יהוה צְבָאוֹת, אַשְׁרֵי תהלים כ
אָדָם בֹּטֵחַ בָּךְ: יהוה הוֹשִׁיעָה, הַמֶּלֶךְ יַעֲנֵנוּ בְיוֹם־קָרְאֵנוּ: תהלים פד

בָּרוּךְ Blessed is He, our God, who created us for His glory, separating us from those who go astray; who gave us the Torah of truth, planting within us eternal life. May He open our heart to His Torah, imbuing our heart with the love and awe of Him, that we may do His will and serve Him with a perfect heart, so that we neither toil in vain nor give birth to confusion.

יְהִי רָצוֹן May it be Your will, O Lord our God and God of our ancestors, that we keep Your laws in this world, and thus be worthy to live, see and inherit goodness and blessing in the Messianic Age and in
the life of the World to Come. So that my soul may sing to You and *Ps. 30*
not be silent. Lord, my God, for ever I will thank You. Blessed is the *Jer. 17*
man who trusts in the Lord, whose trust is in the Lord alone. Trust *Is. 26*
in the Lord for evermore, for God, the Lord, is an everlasting Rock. *Ps. 9*
▸ Those who know Your name trust in You, for You, Lord, do not for-
sake those who seek You. The Lord desired, for the sake of Israel's *Is. 42*
merit, to make the Torah great and glorious.

HALF KADDISH

Leader: יִתְגַּדַּל Magnified and sanctified may His great name be,
in the world He created by His will.
May He establish His kingdom
in your lifetime and in your days,
and in the lifetime of all the house of Israel,
swiftly and soon – and say: Amen.

All: May His great name be blessed for ever and all time.

Leader: Blessed and praised, glorified and exalted,
raised and honored,
uplifted and lauded
be the name of the Holy One, blessed be He,
beyond any blessing,
song, praise and consolation
uttered in the world – and say: Amen.

On Yom Tov falling on Shabbat, the Torah is read; continue with "As for me" on page 954.
On a weekday continue with the Amida on the next page.

בָּרוּךְ הוּא אֱלֹהֵינוּ שֶׁבְּרָאָנוּ לִכְבוֹדוֹ, וְהִבְדִּילָנוּ מִן הַתּוֹעִים, וְנָתַן לָנוּ תּוֹרַת אֱמֶת, וְחַיֵּי עוֹלָם נָטַע בְּתוֹכֵנוּ. הוּא יִפְתַּח לִבֵּנוּ בְּתוֹרָתוֹ, וְיָשֵׂם בְּלִבֵּנוּ אַהֲבָתוֹ וְיִרְאָתוֹ וְלַעֲשׂוֹת רְצוֹנוֹ וּלְעָבְדוֹ בְּלֵבָב שָׁלֵם, לְמַעַן לֹא נִיגַע לָרִיק וְלֹא נֵלֵד לַבֶּהָלָה.

יְהִי רָצוֹן מִלְּפָנֶיךָ יהוה אֱלֹהֵינוּ וֵאלֹהֵי אֲבוֹתֵינוּ, שֶׁנִּשְׁמֹר חֻקֶּיךָ
בָּעוֹלָם הַזֶּה, וְנִזְכֶּה וְנִחְיֶה וְנִרְאֶה וְנִירַשׁ טוֹבָה וּבְרָכָה, לִשְׁנֵי יְמוֹת
הַמָּשִׁיחַ וּלְחַיֵּי הָעוֹלָם הַבָּא. לְמַעַן יְזַמֶּרְךָ כָבוֹד וְלֹא יִדֹּם, יהוה תהלים ל
אֱלֹהַי, לְעוֹלָם אוֹדֶךָּ: בָּרוּךְ הַגֶּבֶר אֲשֶׁר יִבְטַח בַּיהוה, וְהָיָה יהוה ירמיה יז
מִבְטַחוֹ: בִּטְחוּ בַיהוה עֲדֵי־עַד, כִּי בְּיָהּ יהוה צוּר עוֹלָמִים: ◂ וְיִבְטְחוּ ישעיה כו תהלים ט
בְךָ יוֹדְעֵי שְׁמֶךָ, כִּי לֹא־עָזַבְתָּ דֹרְשֶׁיךָ, יהוה: יהוה חָפֵץ לְמַעַן צִדְקוֹ, ישעיה מב
יַגְדִּיל תּוֹרָה וְיַאְדִּיר:

חצי קדיש

ש״ץ: יִתְגַּדַּל וְיִתְקַדַּשׁ שְׁמֵהּ רַבָּא (קהל: אָמֵן)
בְּעָלְמָא דִּי בְרָא כִרְעוּתֵהּ
וְיַמְלִיךְ מַלְכוּתֵהּ
בְּחַיֵּיכוֹן וּבְיוֹמֵיכוֹן וּבְחַיֵּי דְכָל בֵּית יִשְׂרָאֵל
בַּעֲגָלָא וּבִזְמַן קָרִיב, וְאִמְרוּ אָמֵן. (קהל: אָמֵן)

קהל וש״ץ: יְהֵא שְׁמֵהּ רַבָּא מְבָרַךְ לְעָלַם וּלְעָלְמֵי עָלְמַיָּא.

ש״ץ: יִתְבָּרַךְ וְיִשְׁתַּבַּח וְיִתְפָּאַר וְיִתְרוֹמַם
וְיִתְנַשֵּׂא וְיִתְהַדָּר וְיִתְעַלֶּה וְיִתְהַלָּל
שְׁמֵהּ דְּקֻדְשָׁא בְּרִיךְ הוּא (קהל: בְּרִיךְ הוּא)
לְעֵלָּא מִן כָּל בִּרְכָתָא וְשִׁירָתָא, תֻּשְׁבְּחָתָא וְנֶחֱמָתָא
דַּאֲמִירָן בְּעָלְמָא, וְאִמְרוּ אָמֵן. (קהל: אָמֵן)

On יום טוב *falling on* שבת*, the Torah is read; continue with* וַאֲנִי תְפִלָּתִי־לְךָ *on page 955.*
On a weekday continue with the עמידה *on the next page.*

THE AMIDA

The following prayer, until "in former years" on page 590, is said silently, standing with feet together. If there is a minyan, the Amida is then repeated aloud by the Leader. Take three steps forward and at the points indicated by ▾, bend the knees at the first word, bow at the second, and stand straight before saying God's name.

When I proclaim the LORD's name, give glory to our God. *Deut. 32*
O LORD, open my lips, so that my mouth may declare Your praise. *Ps. 51*

PATRIARCHS

▾בָּרוּךְ▾ Blessed are You, LORD our God and God of our fathers,
God of Abraham, God of Isaac and God of Jacob;
the great, mighty and awesome God, God Most High,
who bestows acts of loving-kindness and creates all,
who remembers the loving-kindness of the fathers
and will bring a Redeemer
to their children's children
for the sake of His name, in love.
King, Helper, Savior, Shield:
▾Blessed are You,
LORD, Shield of Abraham.

DIVINE MIGHT

אַתָּה גִּבּוֹר You are eternally mighty, LORD.
You give life to the dead
and have great power to save.

In Israel on Sukkot:
He causes the dew to fall.

On Shemini Atzeret & Simhat Torah:
He makes the wind blow and the rain fall.

He sustains the living with loving-kindness,
and with great compassion revives the dead.
He supports the fallen, heals the sick, sets captives free,
and keeps His faith with those who sleep in the dust.

עמידה

The following prayer, until קְדמֹנִיּוֹת *on page 591, is said silently, standing with feet together. If there is a* מנין*, the* עמידה *is then repeated aloud by the* שליח ציבור*. Take three steps forward and at the points indicated by* °*, bend the knees at the first word, bow at the second, and stand straight before saying God's name.*

דברים לב כִּי שֵׁם יהוה אֶקְרָא, הָבוּ גֹדֶל לֵאלֹהֵינוּ:

תהלים נא אֲדֹנָי, שְׂפָתַי תִּפְתָּח, וּפִי יַגִּיד תְּהִלָּתֶךָ:

אבות

°בָּרוּךְ אַתָּה יהוה, אֱלֹהֵינוּ וֵאלֹהֵי אֲבוֹתֵינוּ
אֱלֹהֵי אַבְרָהָם, אֱלֹהֵי יִצְחָק, וֵאלֹהֵי יַעֲקֹב
הָאֵל הַגָּדוֹל הַגִּבּוֹר וְהַנּוֹרָא, אֵל עֶלְיוֹן
גּוֹמֵל חֲסָדִים טוֹבִים, וְקוֹנֵה הַכֹּל
וְזוֹכֵר חַסְדֵי אָבוֹת
וּמֵבִיא גוֹאֵל לִבְנֵי בְנֵיהֶם לְמַעַן שְׁמוֹ בְּאַהֲבָה.
מֶלֶךְ עוֹזֵר וּמוֹשִׁיעַ וּמָגֵן.
°בָּרוּךְ אַתָּה יהוה, מָגֵן אַבְרָהָם.

גבורות

אַתָּה גִּבּוֹר לְעוֹלָם, אֲדֹנָי
מְחַיֵּה מֵתִים אַתָּה, רַב לְהוֹשִׁיעַ

In ארץ ישראל *on Sukkot:*

מוֹרִיד הַטָּל

On שמיני עצרת *and* שמחת תורה*:*

מַשִּׁיב הָרְוּחַ וּמוֹרִיד הַגֶּשֶׁם

מְכַלְכֵּל חַיִּים בְּחֶסֶד, מְחַיֵּה מֵתִים בְּרַחֲמִים רַבִּים
סוֹמֵךְ נוֹפְלִים, וְרוֹפֵא חוֹלִים, וּמַתִּיר אֲסוּרִים
וּמְקַיֵּם אֱמוּנָתוֹ לִישֵׁנֵי עָפָר.

Who is like You, Master of might, and who can compare to You,
O King who brings death and gives life,
and makes salvation grow?
Faithful are You to revive the dead.
Blessed are You,
LORD, who revives the dead.

When saying the Amida silently, continue with "You are holy" below.

KEDUSHA

During the Leader's Repetition, the following is said standing with feet together, rising on the toes at the words indicated by ▴.

Cong. then Leader: נְקַדֵּשׁ We will sanctify Your name on earth,
as they sanctify it in the highest heavens,
as is written by Your prophet,
"And they [the angels] call to one another saying: *Is. 6*

Cong. then Leader: ▴Holy, ▴holy, ▴holy is the LORD of hosts;
the whole world is filled with His glory."
Those facing them say "Blessed –"

Cong. then Leader: ▴"Blessed is the LORD's glory from His place." *Ezek. 3*
And in Your holy Writings it is written thus:

Cong. then Leader: ▴"The LORD shall reign for ever. He is your God, Zion, *Ps. 146*
from generation to generation, Halleluya!"

Leader: From generation to generation we will declare Your greatness,
and we will proclaim Your holiness for evermore.
Your praise, our God, shall not leave our mouth forever,
for You, God, are a great and holy King.
Blessed are You, LORD, the holy God.

The Leader continues with "You have chosen us" on the next page.

When saying the Amida silently, continue here:

HOLINESS

אַתָּה קָדוֹשׁ You are holy and Your name is holy,
and holy ones praise You daily, Selah!
Blessed are You, LORD,
the holy God.

מִי כָמְוֹךָ, בַּעַל גְּבוּרוֹת, וּמִי דְּוֹמֶה לָּךְ
מֶלֶךְ, מֵמִית וּמְחַיֶּה וּמַצְמִיחַ יְשׁוּעָה.
וְנֶאֱמָן אַתָּה לְהַחֲיוֹת מֵתִים.
בָּרוּךְ אַתָּה יהוה, מְחַיֵּה הַמֵּתִים.

When saying the עמידה *silently, continue with* אַתָּה קָדוֹשׁ *below*

קדושה

During the חזרת הש״ץ, *the following is said standing with feet together, rising on the toes at the words indicated by* ^.

קהל *then* ש״ץ: נְקַדֵּשׁ אֶת שִׁמְךָ בָּעוֹלָם, כְּשֵׁם שֶׁמַּקְדִּישִׁים אוֹתוֹ בִּשְׁמֵי מָרוֹם
כַּכָּתוּב עַל יַד נְבִיאֶךָ: וְקָרָא זֶה אֶל־זֶה וְאָמַר ישעיה ו

קהל *then* ש״ץ: ^קָדוֹשׁ, ^קָדוֹשׁ, ^קָדוֹשׁ, יהוה צְבָאוֹת, מְלֹא כָל־הָאָרֶץ כְּבוֹדוֹ:
לְעֻמָּתָם בָּרוּךְ יֹאמֵרוּ

קהל *then* ש״ץ: ^בָּרוּךְ כְּבוֹד־יהוה מִמְּקוֹמוֹ: יחזקאל ג
וּבְדִבְרֵי קָדְשְׁךָ כָּתוּב לֵאמֹר

קהל *then* ש״ץ: ^יִמְלֹךְ יהוה לְעוֹלָם, אֱלֹהַיִךְ צִיּוֹן לְדֹר וָדֹר, הַלְלוּיָהּ: תהלים קמו

ש״ץ: לְדוֹר וָדוֹר נַגִּיד גָּדְלֶךָ, וּלְנֵצַח נְצָחִים קְדֻשָּׁתְךָ נַקְדִּישׁ
וְשִׁבְחֲךָ אֱלֹהֵינוּ מִפִּינוּ לֹא יָמוּשׁ לְעוֹלָם וָעֶד
כִּי אֵל מֶלֶךְ גָּדוֹל וְקָדוֹשׁ אָתָּה.
בָּרוּךְ אַתָּה יהוה הָאֵל הַקָּדוֹשׁ.

The שליח ציבור *continues with* אַתָּה בְחַרְתָּנוּ *on the next page.*

When saying the עמידה *silently, continue here:*

קדושת השם

אַתָּה קָדוֹשׁ וְשִׁמְךָ קָדוֹשׁ
וּקְדוֹשִׁים בְּכָל יוֹם יְהַלְלְוּךָ סֶּלָה.
בָּרוּךְ אַתָּה יהוה, הָאֵל הַקָּדוֹשׁ.

HOLINESS OF THE DAY

אַתָּה בְחַרְתָּנוּ You have chosen us from among all peoples.
You have loved and favored us.
You have raised us above all tongues.
You have made us holy through Your commandments.
You have brought us near, our King, to Your service,
and have called us by Your great and holy name.

On Shabbat, add the words in parentheses:

וַתִּתֶּן לָנוּ And You, Lord our God, have given us in love
(Sabbaths for rest and) festivals for rejoicing,
holy days and seasons for joy, (this Sabbath day and)
this day of:

On Sukkot: the festival of Sukkot,
our time of rejoicing

On Shemini Atzeret & Simḥat Torah: the festival of the eighth day, Shemini Atzeret,
our time of rejoicing

(with love), a holy assembly
in memory of the exodus from Egypt.

אֱלֹהֵינוּ Our God and God of our ancestors,
may there rise, come, reach, appear,
be favored, heard, regarded and remembered before You,
our recollection and remembrance,
as well as the remembrance of our ancestors,
and of the Messiah son of David Your servant,
and of Jerusalem Your holy city,
and of all Your people the house of Israel – for deliverance
and well-being, grace, loving-kindness and compassion,
life and peace, on this day of:

On Sukkot: the festival of Sukkot.

On Shemini Atzeret & Simḥat Torah: the festival of Shemini Atzeret.

קדושת היום

אַתָּה בְחַרְתָּנוּ מִכָּל הָעַמִּים
אָהַבְתָּ אוֹתָנוּ וְרָצִיתָ בָּנוּ
וְרוֹמַמְתָּנוּ מִכָּל הַלְּשׁוֹנוֹת
וְקִדַּשְׁתָּנוּ בְּמִצְוֹתֶיךָ
וְקֵרַבְתָּנוּ מַלְכֵּנוּ לַעֲבוֹדָתֶךָ
וְשִׁמְךָ הַגָּדוֹל וְהַקָּדוֹשׁ עָלֵינוּ קָרָאתָ.

On שבת, add the words in parentheses:

וַתִּתֶּן לָנוּ יהוה אֱלֹהֵינוּ בְּאַהֲבָה
(שַׁבָּתוֹת לִמְנוּחָה וּ)מוֹעֲדִים לְשִׂמְחָה, חַגִּים וּזְמַנִּים לְשָׂשׂוֹן
אֶת יוֹם (הַשַּׁבָּת הַזֶּה וְאֶת יוֹם)

בסוכות: חַג הַסֻּכּוֹת הַזֶּה, זְמַן שִׂמְחָתֵנוּ
בשמע״צ ובש״ת: הַשְּׁמִינִי חַג הָעֲצֶרֶת הַזֶּה, זְמַן שִׂמְחָתֵנוּ

(בְּאַהֲבָה) מִקְרָא קֹדֶשׁ, זֵכֶר לִיצִיאַת מִצְרָיִם.

אֱלֹהֵינוּ וֵאלֹהֵי אֲבוֹתֵינוּ
יַעֲלֶה וְיָבוֹא וְיַגִּיעַ, וְיֵרָאֶה וְיֵרָצֶה וְיִשָּׁמַע
וְיִפָּקֵד וְיִזָּכֵר זִכְרוֹנֵנוּ וּפִקְדּוֹנֵנוּ וְזִכְרוֹן אֲבוֹתֵינוּ
וְזִכְרוֹן מָשִׁיחַ בֶּן דָּוִד עַבְדֶּךָ, וְזִכְרוֹן יְרוּשָׁלַיִם עִיר קָדְשֶׁךָ
וְזִכְרוֹן כָּל עַמְּךָ בֵּית יִשְׂרָאֵל, לְפָנֶיךָ
לִפְלֵיטָה, לְטוֹבָה, לְחֵן וּלְחֶסֶד וּלְרַחֲמִים
לְחַיִּים וּלְשָׁלוֹם בְּיוֹם

בסוכות: חַג הַסֻּכּוֹת הַזֶּה.
בשמע״צ ובש״ת: הַשְּׁמִינִי חַג הָעֲצֶרֶת הַזֶּה.

On it remember us, Lord our God, for good;
recollect us for blessing, and deliver us for life.
In accord with Your promise of salvation and compassion,
spare us and be gracious to us;
have compassion on us and deliver us,
for our eyes are turned to You
because You, God, are a gracious and compassionate King.

On Shabbat, add the words in parentheses:

וְהַשִּׂיאֵנוּ Bestow on us, Lord our God,
the blessings of Your festivals
for good life and peace, joy and gladness,
as You desired and promised to bless us.
(Our God and God of our fathers, find favor in our rest.)
Make us holy through Your commandments
and grant us a share in Your Torah.
Satisfy us with Your goodness, gladden us with Your salvation,
and purify our hearts to serve You in truth.
Grant us as our heritage, Lord our God (with love and favor,)
with joy and gladness, Your holy (Sabbath and) festivals,
and may Israel, who sanctify Your name, rejoice in You.
Blessed are You, Lord,
who sanctifies (the Sabbath and) Israel and the festive seasons.

TEMPLE SERVICE

רְצֵה Find favor, Lord our God,
in Your people Israel and their prayer.
Restore the service to Your most holy House,
and accept in love and favor
the fire-offerings of Israel and their prayer.
May the service of Your people Israel always find favor with You.
And may our eyes witness Your return to Zion in compassion.
Blessed are You, Lord,
who restores His Presence to Zion.

זָכְרֵנוּ יהוה אֱלֹהֵינוּ בּוֹ לְטוֹבָה
וּפָקְדֵנוּ בוֹ לִבְרָכָה, וְהוֹשִׁיעֵנוּ בוֹ לְחַיִּים.
וּבִדְבַר יְשׁוּעָה וְרַחֲמִים, חוּס וְחָנֵּנוּ, וְרַחֵם עָלֵינוּ וְהוֹשִׁיעֵנוּ
כִּי אֵלֶיךָ עֵינֵינוּ כִּי אֵל מֶלֶךְ חַנּוּן וְרַחוּם אָתָּה.

On שבת*, add the words in parentheses:*

וְהַשִּׂיאֵנוּ יהוה אֱלֹהֵינוּ אֶת בִּרְכַּת מוֹעֲדֶיךָ
לְחַיִּים וּלְשָׁלוֹם, לְשִׂמְחָה וּלְשָׂשׂוֹן
כַּאֲשֶׁר רָצִיתָ וְאָמַרְתָּ לְבָרְכֵנוּ.
(אֱלֹהֵינוּ וֵאלֹהֵי אֲבוֹתֵינוּ, רְצֵה בִמְנוּחָתֵנוּ)
קַדְּשֵׁנוּ בְּמִצְוֹתֶיךָ וְתֵן חֶלְקֵנוּ בְּתוֹרָתֶךָ
שַׂבְּעֵנוּ מִטּוּבֶךָ, וְשַׂמְּחֵנוּ בִּישׁוּעָתֶךָ
וְטַהֵר לִבֵּנוּ לְעָבְדְּךָ בֶּאֱמֶת.
וְהַנְחִילֵנוּ יהוה אֱלֹהֵינוּ (בְּאַהֲבָה וּבְרָצוֹן)
בְּשִׂמְחָה וּבְשָׂשׂוֹן (שַׁבָּת וּ)מוֹעֲדֵי קָדְשֶׁךָ
וְיִשְׂמְחוּ בְךָ יִשְׂרָאֵל מְקַדְּשֵׁי שְׁמֶךָ.
בָּרוּךְ אַתָּה יהוה, מְקַדֵּשׁ (הַשַּׁבָּת וְ)יִשְׂרָאֵל וְהַזְּמַנִּים.

עבודה

רְצֵה יהוה אֱלֹהֵינוּ בְּעַמְּךָ יִשְׂרָאֵל, וּבִתְפִלָּתָם
וְהָשֵׁב אֶת הָעֲבוֹדָה לִדְבִיר בֵּיתֶךָ
וְאִשֵּׁי יִשְׂרָאֵל וּתְפִלָּתָם בְּאַהֲבָה תְקַבֵּל בְּרָצוֹן
וּתְהִי לְרָצוֹן תָּמִיד עֲבוֹדַת יִשְׂרָאֵל עַמֶּךָ.
וְתֶחֱזֶינָה עֵינֵינוּ בְּשׁוּבְךָ לְצִיּוֹן בְּרַחֲמִים.
בָּרוּךְ אַתָּה יהוה, הַמַּחֲזִיר שְׁכִינָתוֹ לְצִיּוֹן.

THANKSGIVING

Bow at the first nine words.

מוֹדִים We give thanks to You,
for You are the LORD our God
and God of our ancestors
for ever and all time.
You are the Rock of our lives,
Shield of our salvation
from generation to generation.
We will thank You and
declare Your praise for our lives,
which are entrusted into Your hand;
for our souls,
which are placed in Your charge;
for Your miracles
which are with us every day;
and for Your wonders and favors
at all times, evening,
morning and midday.
You are good –
for Your compassion never fails.
You are compassionate –
for Your loving-kindnesses never cease.
We have always placed our hope in You.

During the Leader's Repetition, the congregation says quietly:
מוֹדִים We give thanks to You,
for You are the LORD our God
and God of our ancestors,
God of all flesh,
who formed us
and formed the universe.
Blessings and thanks
are due to Your great
and holy name for giving us
life and sustaining us.
May You continue
to give us life
and sustain us;
and may You gather our
exiles to Your holy courts,
to keep Your decrees,
do Your will and serve You
with a perfect heart,
for it is for us
to give You thanks.
Blessed be God to whom
thanksgiving is due.

וְעַל כֻּלָּם For all these things
may Your name be blessed and exalted, our King,
continually, for ever and all time.
Let all that lives thank You, Selah!
and praise Your name in truth, God, our Savior and Help, Selah!
Blessed are You, LORD,
whose name is "the Good" and to whom thanks are due.

הודאה

Bow at the first five words.

'מוֹדִים אֲנַחְנוּ לָךְ
שָׁאַתָּה הוּא יהוה אֱלֹהֵינוּ
וֵאלֹהֵי אֲבוֹתֵינוּ לְעוֹלָם וָעֶד.
צוּר חַיֵּינוּ, מָגֵן יִשְׁעֵנוּ
אַתָּה הוּא לְדוֹר וָדוֹר.
נוֹדֶה לְּךָ וּנְסַפֵּר תְּהִלָּתֶךָ
עַל חַיֵּינוּ הַמְּסוּרִים בְּיָדֶךָ
וְעַל נִשְׁמוֹתֵינוּ הַפְּקוּדוֹת לָךְ
וְעַל נִסֶּיךָ שֶׁבְּכָל יוֹם עִמָּנוּ
וְעַל נִפְלְאוֹתֶיךָ וְטוֹבוֹתֶיךָ
שֶׁבְּכָל עֵת
עֶרֶב וָבֹקֶר וְצָהֳרָיִם.
הַטּוֹב, כִּי לֹא כָלוּ רַחֲמֶיךָ
וְהַמְרַחֵם, כִּי לֹא תַמּוּ חֲסָדֶיךָ
מֵעוֹלָם קִוִּינוּ לָךְ.

During the חזרת הש״ץ, *the* קהל *says quietly:*

'מוֹדִים אֲנַחְנוּ לָךְ
שָׁאַתָּה הוּא יהוה אֱלֹהֵינוּ
וֵאלֹהֵי אֲבוֹתֵינוּ
אֱלֹהֵי כָל בָּשָׂר
יוֹצְרֵנוּ, יוֹצֵר בְּרֵאשִׁית.
בְּרָכוֹת וְהוֹדָאוֹת
לְשִׁמְךָ הַגָּדוֹל וְהַקָּדוֹשׁ
עַל שֶׁהֶחֱיִיתָנוּ וְקִיַּמְתָּנוּ.
כֵּן תְּחַיֵּנוּ וּתְקַיְּמֵנוּ
וְתֶאֱסֹף גָּלֻיּוֹתֵינוּ
לְחַצְרוֹת קָדְשֶׁךָ
לִשְׁמֹר חֻקֶּיךָ
וְלַעֲשׂוֹת רְצוֹנֶךָ
וּלְעָבְדְּךָ בְּלֵבָב שָׁלֵם
עַל שֶׁאֲנַחְנוּ מוֹדִים לָךְ.
בָּרוּךְ אֵל הַהוֹדָאוֹת.

וְעַל כֻּלָּם יִתְבָּרַךְ וְיִתְרוֹמַם שִׁמְךָ מַלְכֵּנוּ תָּמִיד לְעוֹלָם וָעֶד.
וְכֹל הַחַיִּים יוֹדוּךָ סֶּלָה
וִיהַלְלוּ אֶת שִׁמְךָ בֶּאֱמֶת, הָאֵל יְשׁוּעָתֵנוּ וְעֶזְרָתֵנוּ סֶלָה.
'בָּרוּךְ אַתָּה יהוה
הַטּוֹב שִׁמְךָ וּלְךָ נָאֶה לְהוֹדוֹת.

PEACE

	In Israel on Shabbat:
שָׁלוֹם רָב Grant great peace to Your people Israel for ever, for You are the sovereign LORD of all peace; and may it be good in Your eyes to bless Your people Israel at every time, at every hour, with Your peace.	שִׂים שָׁלוֹם Grant peace, goodness and blessing, grace, loving-kindness and compassion to us and all Israel Your people. Bless us, our Father, all as one, with the light of Your face, for by the light of Your face You have given us, LORD our God, the Torah of life and love of kindness, righteousness, blessing, compassion, life and peace. May it be good in Your eyes to bless Your people Israel at every time, in every hour, with Your peace.

Blessed are You, LORD,
who blesses His people Israel with peace.

The following verse concludes the Leader's Repetition of the Amida. Some also say it here as part of the silent Amida.

May the words of my mouth and the meditation of my heart *Ps. 19*
find favor before You, LORD, my Rock and Redeemer.

אֱלֹהַי My God, *Berakhot 17a*
guard my tongue from evil and my lips from deceitful speech.
To those who curse me, let my soul be silent;
may my soul be to all like the dust.
Open my heart to Your Torah
and let my soul pursue Your commandments.
As for all who plan evil against me,
swiftly thwart their counsel and frustrate their plans.
Act for the sake of Your name;
act for the sake of Your right hand;
act for the sake of Your holiness;
act for the sake of Your Torah.

ברכת שלום

שָׁלוֹם רָב
עַל יִשְׂרָאֵל עַמְּךָ
תָּשִׂים לְעוֹלָם
כִּי אַתָּה הוּא מֶלֶךְ אָדוֹן
לְכָל הַשָּׁלוֹם.
וְטוֹב בְּעֵינֶיךָ לְבָרֵךְ
אֶת עַמְּךָ יִשְׂרָאֵל
בְּכָל עֵת וּבְכָל שָׁעָה
בִּשְׁלוֹמֶךָ.

In ארץ ישראל *on* שבת:
שִׂים שָׁלוֹם טוֹבָה וּבְרָכָה
חֵן וָחֶסֶד וְרַחֲמִים
עָלֵינוּ וְעַל כָּל יִשְׂרָאֵל עַמֶּךָ.
בָּרְכֵנוּ אָבִינוּ כֻּלָּנוּ כְּאֶחָד בְּאוֹר פָּנֶיךָ
כִּי בְאוֹר פָּנֶיךָ נָתַתָּ לָּנוּ יהוה אֱלֹהֵינוּ
תּוֹרַת חַיִּים וְאַהֲבַת חֶסֶד
וּצְדָקָה וּבְרָכָה, וְרַחֲמִים וְחַיִּים וְשָׁלוֹם.
וְטוֹב בְּעֵינֶיךָ לְבָרֵךְ אֶת עַמְּךָ יִשְׂרָאֵל
בְּכָל עֵת וּבְכָל שָׁעָה בִּשְׁלוֹמֶךָ.

בָּרוּךְ אַתָּה יהוה, הַמְבָרֵךְ אֶת עַמּוֹ יִשְׂרָאֵל בַּשָּׁלוֹם.

The following verse concludes the חזרת הש״ץ.
Some also say it here as part of the silent עמידה.

יִהְיוּ לְרָצוֹן אִמְרֵי־פִי וְהֶגְיוֹן לִבִּי לְפָנֶיךָ, יהוה צוּרִי וְגֹאֲלִי: תהלים יט

אֱלֹהַי ברכות יז.
נְצֹר לְשׁוֹנִי מֵרָע וּשְׂפָתַי מִדַּבֵּר מִרְמָה
וְלִמְקַלְלַי נַפְשִׁי תִדֹּם, וְנַפְשִׁי כֶּעָפָר לַכֹּל תִּהְיֶה.
פְּתַח לִבִּי בְּתוֹרָתֶךָ, וּבְמִצְוֹתֶיךָ תִּרְדֹּף נַפְשִׁי.
וְכָל הַחוֹשְׁבִים עָלַי רָעָה
מְהֵרָה הָפֵר עֲצָתָם וְקַלְקֵל מַחֲשַׁבְתָּם.
עֲשֵׂה לְמַעַן שְׁמֶךָ
עֲשֵׂה לְמַעַן יְמִינֶךָ
עֲשֵׂה לְמַעַן קְדֻשָּׁתֶךָ
עֲשֵׂה לְמַעַן תּוֹרָתֶךָ.

That Your beloved ones may be delivered, Ps. 60
save with Your right hand and answer me.
May the words of my mouth and the meditation of my heart Ps. 19
find favor before You, LORD, my Rock and Redeemer.

Bow, take three steps back, then bow, first left, then right, then center, while saying:

May He who makes peace in His high places,
make peace for us and all Israel –
and say: Amen.

יְהִי רָצוֹן May it be Your will, LORD our God and God of our ancestors,
that the Temple be rebuilt speedily in our days,
and grant us a share in Your Torah.
And there we will serve You with reverence,
as in the days of old and as in former years.
Then the offering of Judah and Jerusalem Mal. 3
will be pleasing to the LORD as in the days of old and as in former years.

FULL KADDISH

Some have the custom to include additional responses in Full Kaddish. They can be found in the version on page 1464.

Leader: יִתְגַּדַּל Magnified and sanctified
may His great name be,
in the world He created by His will.
May He establish His kingdom
in your lifetime and in your days,
and in the lifetime of all the house of Israel,
swiftly and soon –
and say: Amen.

All: May His great name be blessed for ever and all time.

Leader: Blessed and praised,
glorified and exalted,
raised and honored, uplifted and lauded be
the name of the Holy One,
blessed be He,

לְמַעַן יֵחָלְצוּן יְדִידֶיךָ, הוֹשִׁיעָה יְמִינְךָ וַעֲנֵנִי: תהלים ס
יִהְיוּ לְרָצוֹן אִמְרֵי־פִי וְהֶגְיוֹן לִבִּי לְפָנֶיךָ, יהוה צוּרִי וְגֹאֲלִי: תהלים יט

Bow, take three steps back, then bow, first left, then right, then center, while saying:

עֹשֶׂה שָׁלוֹם בִּמְרוֹמָיו
הוּא יַעֲשֶׂה שָׁלוֹם עָלֵינוּ וְעַל כָּל יִשְׂרָאֵל
וְאִמְרוּ אָמֵן.

יְהִי רָצוֹן מִלְּפָנֶיךָ יהוה אֱלֹהֵינוּ וֵאלֹהֵי אֲבוֹתֵינוּ
שֶׁיִּבָּנֶה בֵּית הַמִּקְדָּשׁ בִּמְהֵרָה בְיָמֵינוּ
וְתֵן חֶלְקֵנוּ בְּתוֹרָתֶךָ
וְשָׁם נַעֲבָדְךָ בְּיִרְאָה כִּימֵי עוֹלָם וּכְשָׁנִים קַדְמֹנִיּוֹת.
וְעָרְבָה לַיהוה מִנְחַת יְהוּדָה וִירוּשָׁלָיִם כִּימֵי עוֹלָם וּכְשָׁנִים קַדְמֹנִיּוֹת: מלאכי ג

קדיש שלם

Some have the custom to include additional responses in קדיש שלם.
They can be found in the version on page 1465.

ש״ץ: יִתְגַּדַּל וְיִתְקַדַּשׁ שְׁמֵהּ רַבָּא (קהל: אָמֵן)
בְּעָלְמָא דִּי בְרָא כִרְעוּתֵהּ
וְיַמְלִיךְ מַלְכוּתֵהּ
בְּחַיֵּיכוֹן וּבְיוֹמֵיכוֹן וּבְחַיֵּי דְכָל בֵּית יִשְׂרָאֵל
בַּעֲגָלָא וּבִזְמַן קָרִיב
וְאִמְרוּ אָמֵן. (קהל: אָמֵן)

קהל וש״ץ: יְהֵא שְׁמֵהּ רַבָּא מְבָרַךְ לְעָלַם וּלְעָלְמֵי עָלְמַיָּא.

ש״ץ: יִתְבָּרַךְ וְיִשְׁתַּבַּח וְיִתְפָּאַר
וְיִתְרוֹמַם וְיִתְנַשֵּׂא וְיִתְהַדָּר וְיִתְעַלֶּה וְיִתְהַלָּל
שְׁמֵהּ דְּקֻדְשָׁא בְּרִיךְ הוּא (קהל: בְּרִיךְ הוּא)

beyond any blessing,
song, praise and consolation
uttered in the world –
and say: Amen.

May the prayers and pleas of all Israel
be accepted by their Father in heaven –
and say: Amen.

May there be great peace from heaven,
and life for us
and all Israel –
and say: Amen.

Bow, take three steps back, as if taking leave of the Divine Presence, then bow, first left, then right, then center, while saying:
May He who makes peace in His high places,
make peace for us
and all Israel –
and say: Amen.

Stand while saying Aleinu. Bow at ▾.

עָלֵינוּ It is our duty to praise the Master of all,
and ascribe greatness to the Author of creation,
who has not made us like the nations of the lands
nor placed us like the families of the earth;
who has not made our portion like theirs,
nor our destiny like all their multitudes.
(For they worship vanity and emptiness,
and pray to a god who cannot save.)
▾But we bow in worship
and thank the Supreme King of kings,
the Holy One, blessed be He,
who extends the heavens and establishes the earth,
whose throne of glory is in the heavens above,
and whose power's Presence is in the highest of heights.

לְעֵלָּא מִן כָּל בִּרְכָתָא
וְשִׁירָתָא, תֻּשְׁבְּחָתָא וְנֶחֱמָתָא
דַּאֲמִירָן בְּעָלְמָא, וְאִמְרוּ אָמֵן. (קהל: אָמֵן)

תִּתְקַבַּל צְלוֹתְהוֹן וּבָעוּתְהוֹן דְּכָל יִשְׂרָאֵל
קֳדָם אֲבוּהוֹן דִּי בִשְׁמַיָּא
וְאִמְרוּ אָמֵן. (קהל: אָמֵן)

יְהֵא שְׁלָמָא רַבָּא מִן שְׁמַיָּא
וְחַיִּים, עָלֵינוּ וְעַל כָּל יִשְׂרָאֵל
וְאִמְרוּ אָמֵן. (קהל: אָמֵן)

Bow, take three steps back, as if taking leave of the Divine Presence, then bow, first left, then right, then center, while saying:

עֹשֶׂה שָׁלוֹם בִּמְרוֹמָיו
הוּא יַעֲשֶׂה שָׁלוֹם עָלֵינוּ וְעַל כָּל יִשְׂרָאֵל
וְאִמְרוּ אָמֵן. (קהל: אָמֵן)

Stand while saying עָלֵינוּ*. Bow at* ▾*.*

עָלֵינוּ לְשַׁבֵּחַ לַאֲדוֹן הַכֹּל, לָתֵת גְּדֻלָּה לְיוֹצֵר בְּרֵאשִׁית
שֶׁלֹּא עָשָׂנוּ כְּגוֹיֵי הָאֲרָצוֹת, וְלֹא שָׂמָנוּ כְּמִשְׁפְּחוֹת הָאֲדָמָה
שֶׁלֹּא שָׂם חֶלְקֵנוּ כָּהֶם וְגוֹרָלֵנוּ כְּכָל הֲמוֹנָם.
(שֶׁהֵם מִשְׁתַּחֲוִים לְהֶבֶל וָרִיק וּמִתְפַּלְלִים אֶל אֵל לֹא יוֹשִׁיעַ.)
▾וַאֲנַחְנוּ כּוֹרְעִים וּמִשְׁתַּחֲוִים וּמוֹדִים
לִפְנֵי מֶלֶךְ מַלְכֵי הַמְּלָכִים, הַקָּדוֹשׁ בָּרוּךְ הוּא
שֶׁהוּא נוֹטֶה שָׁמַיִם וְיוֹסֵד אָרֶץ
וּמוֹשַׁב יְקָרוֹ בַּשָּׁמַיִם מִמַּעַל
וּשְׁכִינַת עֻזּוֹ בְּגָבְהֵי מְרוֹמִים.

He is our God; there is no other.
Truly He is our King, there is none else,
as it is written in His Torah:
"You shall know and take to heart this day *Deut. 4*
that the LORD is God, in heaven above and on earth below.
There is no other."

Therefore, we place our hope in You, LORD our God,
that we may soon see the glory of Your power,
when You will remove abominations from the earth,
and idols will be utterly destroyed,
when the world will be perfected
under the sovereignty of the Almighty,
when all humanity will call on Your name,
to turn all the earth's wicked toward You.
All the world's inhabitants will realize and know
that to You every knee must bow and every tongue swear loyalty.
Before You, LORD our God, they will kneel and bow down
and give honor to Your glorious name.
They will all accept the yoke of Your kingdom,
and You will reign over them soon and for ever.
For the kingdom is Yours,
and to all eternity You will reign in glory,
as it is written in Your Torah:
"The LORD will reign for ever and ever." *Ex. 15*
▸ And it is said:
"Then the LORD shall be King over all the earth; *Zech. 14*
on that day the LORD shall be One and His name One."

Some add:
Have no fear of sudden terror or of the ruin when it overtakes the wicked. *Prov. 3*
Devise your strategy, but it will be thwarted; *Is. 8*
propose your plan, but it will not stand, for God is with us.
When you grow old, I will still be the same. *Is. 46*
When your hair turns gray, I will still carry you.
I made you, I will bear you,
I will carry you, and I will rescue you.

הוּא אֱלֹהֵינוּ, אֵין עוֹד.
אֱמֶת מַלְכֵּנוּ, אֶפֶס זוּלָתוֹ, כַּכָּתוּב בְּתוֹרָתוֹ
וְיָדַעְתָּ הַיּוֹם וַהֲשֵׁבֹתָ אֶל־לְבָבֶךָ דברים ד
כִּי יהוה הוּא הָאֱלֹהִים בַּשָּׁמַיִם מִמַּעַל וְעַל־הָאָרֶץ מִתָּחַת
אֵין עוֹד:

עַל כֵּן נְקַוֶּה לְּךָ יהוה אֱלֹהֵינוּ, לִרְאוֹת מְהֵרָה בְּתִפְאֶרֶת עֻזֶּךָ
לְהַעֲבִיר גִּלּוּלִים מִן הָאָרֶץ
וְהָאֱלִילִים כָּרוֹת יִכָּרֵתוּן
לְתַקֵּן עוֹלָם בְּמַלְכוּת שַׁדַּי.
וְכָל בְּנֵי בָשָׂר יִקְרְאוּ בִשְׁמֶךָ לְהַפְנוֹת אֵלֶיךָ כָּל רִשְׁעֵי אָרֶץ.
יַכִּירוּ וְיֵדְעוּ כָּל יוֹשְׁבֵי תֵבֵל
כִּי לְךָ תִּכְרַע כָּל בֶּרֶךְ, תִּשָּׁבַע כָּל לָשׁוֹן.
לְפָנֶיךָ יהוה אֱלֹהֵינוּ יִכְרְעוּ וְיִפֹּלוּ
וְלִכְבוֹד שִׁמְךָ יְקָר יִתֵּנוּ
וִיקַבְּלוּ כֻלָּם אֶת עֹל מַלְכוּתֶךָ
וְתִמְלֹךְ עֲלֵיהֶם מְהֵרָה לְעוֹלָם וָעֶד.
כִּי הַמַּלְכוּת שֶׁלְּךָ הִיא וּלְעוֹלְמֵי עַד תִּמְלֹךְ בְּכָבוֹד
כַּכָּתוּב בְּתוֹרָתֶךָ, יהוה יִמְלֹךְ לְעֹלָם וָעֶד: שמות טו
◂ וְנֶאֱמַר, וְהָיָה יהוה לְמֶלֶךְ עַל־כָּל־הָאָרֶץ זכריה יד
בַּיּוֹם הַהוּא יִהְיֶה יהוה אֶחָד וּשְׁמוֹ אֶחָד:

Some add:

אַל־תִּירָא מִפַּחַד פִּתְאֹם וּמִשֹּׁאַת רְשָׁעִים כִּי תָבֹא: משלי ג
עֻצוּ עֵצָה וְתֻפָר, דַּבְּרוּ דָבָר וְלֹא יָקוּם, כִּי עִמָּנוּ אֵל: ישעיה ח
וְעַד־זִקְנָה אֲנִי הוּא, וְעַד־שֵׂיבָה אֲנִי אֶסְבֹּל ישעיה מו
אֲנִי עָשִׂיתִי וַאֲנִי אֶשָּׂא וַאֲנִי אֶסְבֹּל וַאֲמַלֵּט:

MOURNER'S KADDISH

The following prayer, said by mourners, requires the presence of a minyan. A transliteration can be found on page 1467.

Mourner: יִתְגַּדַּל Magnified and sanctified
may His great name be,
in the world He created by His will.
May He establish His kingdom in your lifetime
and in your days,
and in the lifetime of all the house of Israel,
swiftly and soon –
and say: Amen.

All: May His great name be blessed for ever and all time.

Mourner: Blessed and praised,
glorified and exalted,
raised and honored,
uplifted and lauded
be the name of the Holy One,
blessed be He,
beyond any blessing,
song, praise and consolation
uttered in the world –
and say: Amen.

May there be great peace from heaven,
and life for us and all Israel –
and say: Amen.

Bow, take three steps back, as if taking leave of the Divine Presence, then bow, first left, then right, then center, while saying:

May He who makes peace in His high places,
make peace for us and all Israel –
and say: Amen.

For Ma'ariv of Yom Tov, turn to page 44. For Ma'ariv of Shabbat Ḥol HaMo'ed, turn to page 740. For Ma'ariv of Ḥol HaMo'ed and Motza'ei Yom Tov, turn to page 1336.

קדיש יתום

The following prayer, said by mourners, requires the presence of a מנין.
A transliteration can be found on page 1467.

אבל: יִתְגַּדַּל וְיִתְקַדַּשׁ שְׁמֵהּ רַבָּא (קהל: אָמֵן)
בְּעָלְמָא דִּי בְרָא כִרְעוּתֵהּ
וְיַמְלִיךְ מַלְכוּתֵהּ
בְּחַיֵּיכוֹן וּבְיוֹמֵיכוֹן וּבְחַיֵּי דְכָל בֵּית יִשְׂרָאֵל
בַּעֲגָלָא וּבִזְמַן קָרִיב
וְאִמְרוּ אָמֵן. (קהל: אָמֵן)

קהל ואבל: יְהֵא שְׁמֵהּ רַבָּא מְבָרַךְ לְעָלַם וּלְעָלְמֵי עָלְמַיָּא.

אבל: יִתְבָּרַךְ וְיִשְׁתַּבַּח וְיִתְפָּאַר
וְיִתְרוֹמַם וְיִתְנַשֵּׂא וְיִתְהַדָּר וְיִתְעַלֶּה וְיִתְהַלָּל
שְׁמֵהּ דְּקֻדְשָׁא בְּרִיךְ הוּא (קהל: בְּרִיךְ הוּא)
לְעֵלָּא מִן כָּל בִּרְכָתָא וְשִׁירָתָא, תֻּשְׁבְּחָתָא וְנֶחֱמָתָא
דַּאֲמִירָן בְּעָלְמָא
וְאִמְרוּ אָמֵן. (קהל: אָמֵן)

יְהֵא שְׁלָמָא רַבָּא מִן שְׁמַיָּא
וְחַיִּים, עָלֵינוּ וְעַל כָּל יִשְׂרָאֵל
וְאִמְרוּ אָמֵן. (קהל: אָמֵן)

Bow, take three steps back, as if taking leave of the Divine Presence, then bow, first left, then right, then center, while saying:

עֹשֶׂה שָׁלוֹם בִּמְרוֹמָיו
הוּא יַעֲשֶׂה שָׁלוֹם עָלֵינוּ וְעַל כָּל יִשְׂרָאֵל
וְאִמְרוּ אָמֵן. (קהל: אָמֵן)

For מעריב *of* יום טוב, *turn to page 45. For* מעריב *of* שבת חול המועד, *turn to page 741.*
For מעריב *of* חול המועד *and* מוצאי יום טוב, *turn to page 1337.*

Shaḥarit for Ḥol HaMo'ed

Begin as on Yom Tov, pages 258–304.

A PSALM BEFORE VERSES OF PRAISE

מִזְמוֹר שִׁיר A psalm of David. A song for the dedication of the House. *Ps. 30*
I will exalt You, LORD, for You have lifted me up,
and not let my enemies rejoice over me.
LORD, my God, I cried to You for help and You healed me.
LORD, You lifted my soul from the grave;
You spared me from going down to the pit.
Sing to the LORD, you His devoted ones,
and give thanks to His holy name.
For His anger is for a moment, but His favor for a lifetime.
At night there may be weeping, but in the morning there is joy.
When I felt secure, I said, "I shall never be shaken."
LORD, when You favored me,
You made me stand firm as a mountain,
but when You hid Your face, I was terrified.
To You, LORD, I called; I pleaded with my LORD:
"What gain would there be if I died and went down to the grave?
Can dust thank You? Can it declare Your truth?
Hear, LORD, and be gracious to me; LORD, be my help."
You have turned my sorrow into dancing.
▸ You have removed my sackcloth and clothed me with joy,
so that my soul may sing to You and not be silent.
LORD my God, for ever will I thank You.

---

from rabbinic law. If the *ot* derives from the extra mitzvot of this period then these pertain to Ḥol HaMo'ed as well.

The Sephardi tradition forbids *tefillin* on Ḥol HaMo'ed. The Ashkenazi tradition requires *tefillin* on Ḥol HaMo'ed. A compromise position is to wear *tefillin* without a blessing, which is the practice recommended by the *Mishna Berura* (31:8). Both Ashkenazi and Sephardi communities in Israel do not wear *tefillin*.

שחרית לחול המועד

Begin as on יום טוב*, pages 259–305.*

מזמור לפני פסוקי דזמרה

מִזְמוֹר שִׁיר־חֲנֻכַּת הַבַּיִת לְדָוִד: תהלים ל
אֲרוֹמִמְךָ יהוה כִּי דִלִּיתָנִי, וְלֹא־שִׂמַּחְתָּ אֹיְבַי לִי:
יהוה אֱלֹהָי, שִׁוַּעְתִּי אֵלֶיךָ וַתִּרְפָּאֵנִי:
יהוה, הֶעֱלִיתָ מִן־שְׁאוֹל נַפְשִׁי, חִיִּיתַנִי מִיָּרְדִי־בוֹר:
זַמְּרוּ לַיהוה חֲסִידָיו, וְהוֹדוּ לְזֵכֶר קָדְשׁוֹ:
כִּי רֶגַע בְּאַפּוֹ, חַיִּים בִּרְצוֹנוֹ
בָּעֶרֶב יָלִין בֶּכִי וְלַבֹּקֶר רִנָּה:
וַאֲנִי אָמַרְתִּי בְשַׁלְוִי, בַּל־אֶמּוֹט לְעוֹלָם:
יהוה, בִּרְצוֹנְךָ הֶעֱמַדְתָּה לְהַרְרִי עֹז
הִסְתַּרְתָּ פָנֶיךָ הָיִיתִי נִבְהָל:
אֵלֶיךָ יהוה אֶקְרָא, וְאֶל־אֲדֹנָי אֶתְחַנָּן:
מַה־בֶּצַע בְּדָמִי, בְּרִדְתִּי אֶל שָׁחַת, הֲיוֹדְךָ עָפָר, הֲיַגִּיד אֲמִתֶּךָ:
שְׁמַע־יהוה וְחָנֵּנִי, יהוה הֱיֵה־עֹזֵר לִי:
◂ הָפַכְתָּ מִסְפְּדִי לְמָחוֹל לִי, פִּתַּחְתָּ שַׂקִּי, וַתְּאַזְּרֵנִי שִׂמְחָה:
לְמַעַן יְזַמֶּרְךָ כָבוֹד וְלֹא יִדֹּם, יהוה אֱלֹהַי, לְעוֹלָם אוֹדֶךָּ:

TEFILLIN ON ḤOL HAMO'ED

The wearing of *tefillin* on Ḥol HaMo'ed is the subject of rich debate. Essentially, the question goes to the heart of the nature of Shabbat and Yom Tov. What is their "*ot*" or distinguishing sign? Are they defined more by what is forbidden (*isur melakha*) or by what is required in the performance of extra mitzvot? If it is the former then *tefillin* would be required since *melakha* is only prohibited on Shabbat and Yom Tov. The Ḥol HaMo'ed restrictions on *melakha* stem

MOURNER'S KADDISH

The following prayer, said by mourners, requires the presence of a minyan. A transliteration can be found on page 1467.

Mourner: יִתְגַּדַּל Magnified and sanctified
may His great name be,
in the world He created by His will.
May He establish His kingdom
in your lifetime
and in your days,
and in the lifetime of all the house of Israel,
swiftly and soon –
and say: Amen.

All: May His great name be blessed
for ever and all time.

Mourner: Blessed and praised,
glorified and exalted,
raised and honored,
uplifted and lauded
be the name of the Holy One,
blessed be He,
beyond any blessing,
song, praise and consolation
uttered in the world –
and say: Amen.

May there be great peace from heaven,
and life for us and all Israel – and say: Amen.

Bow, take three steps back, as if taking leave of the Divine Presence, then bow, first left, then right, then center, while saying:

May He who makes peace in His high places,
make peace for us and all Israel –
and say: Amen.

קדיש יתום

The following prayer, said by mourners, requires the presence of a מנין*.*
A transliteration can be found on page 1467.

אבל: יִתְגַּדַּל וְיִתְקַדַּשׁ שְׁמֵהּ רַבָּא (קהל: אָמֵן)
בְּעָלְמָא דִּי בְרָא כִרְעוּתֵהּ
וְיַמְלִיךְ מַלְכוּתֵהּ
בְּחַיֵּיכוֹן וּבְיוֹמֵיכוֹן וּבְחַיֵּי דְכָל בֵּית יִשְׂרָאֵל
בַּעֲגָלָא וּבִזְמַן קָרִיב
וְאִמְרוּ אָמֵן. (קהל: אָמֵן)

קהל ואבל: יְהֵא שְׁמֵהּ רַבָּא מְבָרַךְ לְעָלַם וּלְעָלְמֵי עָלְמַיָּא.

אבל: יִתְבָּרַךְ וְיִשְׁתַּבַּח וְיִתְפָּאַר
וְיִתְרוֹמַם וְיִתְנַשֵּׂא וְיִתְהַדָּר וְיִתְעַלֶּה וְיִתְהַלָּל
שְׁמֵהּ דְּקֻדְשָׁא בְּרִיךְ הוּא (קהל: בְּרִיךְ הוּא)
לְעֵלָּא מִן כָּל בִּרְכָתָא וְשִׁירָתָא
תֻּשְׁבְּחָתָא וְנֶחֱמָתָא
דַּאֲמִירָן בְּעָלְמָא
וְאִמְרוּ אָמֵן. (קהל: אָמֵן)

יְהֵא שְׁלָמָא רַבָּא מִן שְׁמַיָּא
וְחַיִּים, עָלֵינוּ וְעַל כָּל יִשְׂרָאֵל
וְאִמְרוּ אָמֵן. (קהל: אָמֵן)

Bow, take three steps back, as if taking leave of the Divine Presence,
then bow, first left, then right, then center, while saying:

עֹשֶׂה שָׁלוֹם בִּמְרוֹמָיו
הוּא יַעֲשֶׂה שָׁלוֹם עָלֵינוּ וְעַל כָּל יִשְׂרָאֵל
וְאִמְרוּ אָמֵן. (קהל: אָמֵן)

PESUKEI DEZIMRA

The introductory blessing to the Pesukei DeZimra (Verses of Praise) is said standing, while holding the two front tzitziot of the tallit. They are kissed and released at the end of the blessing at "songs of praise" (on the next page). From the beginning of this prayer to the end of the Amida, conversation is forbidden.

Some say:

I hereby prepare my mouth to thank, praise and laud my Creator, for the sake of the unification of the Holy One, blessed be He, and His Divine Presence, through that which is hidden and concealed, in the name of all Israel.

BLESSED IS HE WHO SPOKE

and the world came into being, blessed is He.
Blessed is He who creates the universe.
Blessed is He who speaks and acts.
Blessed is He who decrees and fulfills.
Blessed is He who shows compassion to the earth.
Blessed is He who shows compassion to all creatures.
Blessed is He who gives a good reward
to those who fear Him.
Blessed is He who lives for ever and exists to eternity.
Blessed is He who redeems and saves.
Blessed is His name.

---

the "Verses of Praise." The morning service from this point until the end is constructed in three movements, whose themes are: (1) *Creation:* God as He is in nature; (2) *Revelation:* God as He is in Torah and prayer; and (3) *Redemption:* God as He is in history and our lives. The theme of the Verses of Praise is Creation – God as Architect and Maker of a universe of splendor and diversity, whose orderliness testifies to the single creative will that underlies all that exists. The psalms tell this story not in scientific prose but majestic poetry, not *proving* but *proclaiming* the One at the heart of all.

פסוקי דזמרה

The introductory blessing to the פסוקי דזמרה *is said standing, while holding the two front* ציציות *of the* טלית*. They are kissed and released at the end of the blessing at* בַּתִּשְׁבָּחוֹת *(on the next page). From the beginning of this prayer to the end of the* עמידה*, conversation is forbidden.*

Some say:

הֲרֵינִי מְזַמֵּן אֶת פִּי לְהוֹדוֹת וּלְהַלֵּל וּלְשַׁבֵּחַ אֶת בּוֹרְאִי, לְשֵׁם יִחוּד קֻדְשָׁא בְּרִיךְ הוּא וּשְׁכִינְתֵּהּ עַל יְדֵי הַהוּא טָמִיר וְנֶעְלָם בְּשֵׁם כָּל יִשְׂרָאֵל.

בָּרוּךְ שֶׁאָמַר
וְהָיָה הָעוֹלָם, בָּרוּךְ הוּא.
בָּרוּךְ עוֹשֶׂה בְרֵאשִׁית
בָּרוּךְ אוֹמֵר וְעוֹשֶׂה
בָּרוּךְ גּוֹזֵר וּמְקַיֵּם
בָּרוּךְ מְרַחֵם עַל הָאָרֶץ
בָּרוּךְ מְרַחֵם עַל הַבְּרִיּוֹת
בָּרוּךְ מְשַׁלֵּם שָׂכָר טוֹב לִירֵאָיו
בָּרוּךְ חַי לָעַד וְקַיָּם לָנֶצַח
בָּרוּךְ פּוֹדֶה וּמַצִּיל
בָּרוּךְ שְׁמוֹ.

PESUKEI DEZIMRA / VERSES OF PRAISE

"A person should first recount the praise of the Holy One, blessed be He, and then pray" (*Berakhot* 32b), hence the passages that follow, known as

Blessed are You, LORD our God, King of the Universe,
God, compassionate Father,
extolled by the mouth of His people,
praised and glorified
by the tongue of His devoted ones and those who serve Him.
With the songs of Your servant David
we will praise You, O LORD our God.
With praises and psalms
we will magnify and praise You, glorify You,
Speak Your name and proclaim Your kingship,
our King, our God, ‣ the only One, Giver of life to the worlds,
the King whose great name is praised and glorified to all eternity.
Blessed are You, LORD, the King extolled with songs of praise.

הודו לַיהוה Thank the LORD, call on His name, make His acts known *1 Chr. 16*
among the peoples. Sing to Him, make music to Him, tell of all His wonders. Glory in His holy name; let the hearts of those who seek the LORD rejoice. Search out the LORD and His strength; seek His presence at all times. Remember the wonders He has done, His miracles, and the judgments He pronounced. Descendants of Yisrael His servant, sons of Jacob His chosen ones: He is the LORD our God. His judgments are throughout the earth. Remember His covenant for ever, the word He commanded for a thousand generations. He made it with Abraham, vowed it to Isaac, and confirmed it to Jacob as a statute and to Israel as an everlasting covenant, saying, "To you I will give the land of Canaan as your allotted heritage." You were then small in number, few, strangers there, wandering from nation to nation, from one kingdom to another, but He let no man oppress them, and for their sake He rebuked kings: "Do not touch My anointed ones, and do My prophets no harm." Sing to the LORD, all the earth; proclaim His salvation daily. Declare His glory among the nations, His marvels among all the peoples. For great is the LORD and greatly to be praised; He is awesome beyond all heavenly powers. ‣ For all the gods of the peoples are mere idols; it was the LORD who made the heavens.

בָּרוּךְ אַתָּה יהוה אֱלֹהֵינוּ מֶלֶךְ הָעוֹלָם
הָאֵל הָאָב הָרַחֲמָן הַמְהֻלָּל בְּפִי עַמּוֹ
מְשֻׁבָּח וּמְפֹאָר בִּלְשׁוֹן חֲסִידָיו וַעֲבָדָיו
וּבְשִׁירֵי דָוִד עַבְדֶּךָ, נְהַלֶּלְךָ יהוה אֱלֹהֵינוּ.
בִּשְׁבָחוֹת וּבִזְמִירוֹת, נְגַדֶּלְךָ וּנְשַׁבֵּחֲךָ וּנְפָאֶרְךָ
וְנַזְכִּיר שִׁמְךָ וְנַמְלִיכְךָ
מַלְכֵּנוּ אֱלֹהֵינוּ, ◂ יָחִיד חֵי הָעוֹלָמִים
מֶלֶךְ, מְשֻׁבָּח וּמְפֹאָר עֲדֵי עַד שְׁמוֹ הַגָּדוֹל
בָּרוּךְ אַתָּה יהוה, מֶלֶךְ מְהֻלָּל בַּתִּשְׁבָּחוֹת.

הוֹדוּ לַיהוה קִרְאוּ בִשְׁמוֹ, הוֹדִיעוּ בָעַמִּים עֲלִילֹתָיו: שִׁירוּ לוֹ, דברי הימים א׳, טז
זַמְּרוּ־לוֹ, שִׂיחוּ בְּכָל־נִפְלְאוֹתָיו: הִתְהַלְלוּ בְּשֵׁם קָדְשׁוֹ, יִשְׂמַח
לֵב מְבַקְשֵׁי יהוה: דִּרְשׁוּ יהוה וְעֻזּוֹ, בַּקְּשׁוּ פָנָיו תָּמִיד: זִכְרוּ
נִפְלְאֹתָיו אֲשֶׁר עָשָׂה, מֹפְתָיו וּמִשְׁפְּטֵי־פִיהוּ: זֶרַע יִשְׂרָאֵל עַבְדּוֹ,
בְּנֵי יַעֲקֹב בְּחִירָיו: הוּא יהוה אֱלֹהֵינוּ בְּכָל־הָאָרֶץ מִשְׁפָּטָיו:
זִכְרוּ לְעוֹלָם בְּרִיתוֹ, דָּבָר צִוָּה לְאֶלֶף דּוֹר: אֲשֶׁר כָּרַת אֶת־
אַבְרָהָם, וּשְׁבוּעָתוֹ לְיִצְחָק: וַיַּעֲמִידֶהָ לְיַעֲקֹב לְחֹק, לְיִשְׂרָאֵל
בְּרִית עוֹלָם: לֵאמֹר, לְךָ אֶתֵּן אֶרֶץ־כְּנָעַן, חֶבֶל נַחֲלַתְכֶם:
בִּהְיוֹתְכֶם מְתֵי מִסְפָּר, כִּמְעַט וְגָרִים בָּהּ: וַיִּתְהַלְּכוּ מִגּוֹי אֶל־
גּוֹי, וּמִמַּמְלָכָה אֶל־עַם אַחֵר: לֹא־הִנִּיחַ לְאִישׁ לְעָשְׁקָם, וַיּוֹכַח
עֲלֵיהֶם מְלָכִים: אַל־תִּגְּעוּ בִּמְשִׁיחָי, וּבִנְבִיאַי אַל־תָּרֵעוּ: שִׁירוּ
לַיהוה כָּל־הָאָרֶץ, בַּשְּׂרוּ מִיּוֹם־אֶל־יוֹם יְשׁוּעָתוֹ: סַפְּרוּ בַגּוֹיִם
אֶת־כְּבוֹדוֹ, בְּכָל־הָעַמִּים נִפְלְאֹתָיו: כִּי גָדוֹל יהוה וּמְהֻלָּל מְאֹד,
וְנוֹרָא הוּא עַל־כָּל־אֱלֹהִים: ◂ כִּי כָּל־אֱלֹהֵי הָעַמִּים אֱלִילִים, וַיהוה
שָׁמַיִם עָשָׂה:

Before Him are majesty and splendor; there is strength and beauty in His holy place. Render to the LORD, families of the peoples, render to the LORD honor and might. Render to the LORD the glory due to His name; bring an offering and come before Him; bow down to the LORD in the splendor of holiness. Tremble before Him, all the earth; the world stands firm, it will not be shaken. Let the heavens rejoice and the earth be glad; let them declare among the nations, "The LORD is King." Let the sea roar, and all that is in it; let the fields be jubilant, and all they contain. Then the trees of the forest will sing for joy before the LORD, for He is coming to judge the earth. Thank the LORD for He is good; His loving-kindness is for ever. Say: "Save us, God of our salvation; gather us and rescue us from the nations, to acknowledge Your holy name and glory in Your praise. Blessed is the LORD, God of Israel, from this world to eternity." And let all the people say "Amen" and "Praise the LORD."

▸ Exalt the LORD our God and bow before His footstool: He is holy. Ps. 99
Exalt the LORD our God and bow at His holy mountain; for holy is the LORD our God.

He is compassionate. He forgives iniquity and does not destroy. Ps. 78
Repeatedly He suppresses His anger, not rousing His full wrath. You, Ps. 40
LORD: do not withhold Your compassion from me. May Your loving-
kindness and truth always guard me. Remember, LORD, Your acts of Ps. 25
compassion and love, for they have existed for ever. Ascribe power Ps. 68
to God, whose majesty is over Israel and whose might is in the skies.
You are awesome, God, in Your holy places. It is the God of Israel who
gives might and strength to the people, may God be blessed. God of Ps. 94
retribution, LORD, God of retribution, appear. Arise, Judge of the earth,
to repay the arrogant their just deserts. Salvation belongs to the LORD; Ps. 3
may Your blessing rest upon Your people, Selah! ▸ The LORD of hosts Ps. 46
is with us, the God of Jacob is our stronghold, Selah! LORD of hosts, Ps. 84
happy is the one who trusts in You. LORD, save! May the King answer Ps. 20
us on the day we call.

Save Your people and bless Your heritage; tend them and carry them Ps. 28
for ever. Our soul longs for the LORD; He is our Help and Shield. For Ps. 33
in Him our hearts rejoice, for in His holy name we have trusted. May
Your loving-kindness, LORD, be upon us, as we have put our hope in You.
Show us, LORD, Your loving-kindness and grant us Your salvation. Arise, Ps. 85 Ps. 44

הוֹד וְהָדָר לְפָנָיו, עֹז וְחֶדְוָה בִּמְקֹמוֹ: הָבוּ לַיהוה מִשְׁפְּחוֹת
עַמִּים, הָבוּ לַיהוה כָּבוֹד וָעֹז: הָבוּ לַיהוה כְּבוֹד שְׁמוֹ, שְׂאוּ מִנְחָה
וּבֹאוּ לְפָנָיו, הִשְׁתַּחֲווּ לַיהוה בְּהַדְרַת־קֹדֶשׁ: חִילוּ מִלְּפָנָיו כָּל־
הָאָרֶץ, אַף־תִּכּוֹן תֵּבֵל בַּל־תִּמּוֹט: יִשְׂמְחוּ הַשָּׁמַיִם וְתָגֵל הָאָרֶץ,
וְיֹאמְרוּ בַגּוֹיִם יהוה מָלָךְ: יִרְעַם הַיָּם וּמְלוֹאוֹ, יַעֲלֹץ הַשָּׂדֶה וְכָל־
אֲשֶׁר־בּוֹ: אָז יְרַנְּנוּ עֲצֵי הַיָּעַר, מִלִּפְנֵי יהוה, כִּי־בָא לִשְׁפּוֹט אֶת־
הָאָרֶץ: הוֹדוּ לַיהוה כִּי טוֹב, כִּי לְעוֹלָם חַסְדּוֹ: וְאִמְרוּ, הוֹשִׁיעֵנוּ
אֱלֹהֵי יִשְׁעֵנוּ, וְקַבְּצֵנוּ וְהַצִּילֵנוּ מִן־הַגּוֹיִם, לְהֹדוֹת לְשֵׁם קָדְשֶׁךָ,
לְהִשְׁתַּבֵּחַ בִּתְהִלָּתֶךָ: בָּרוּךְ יהוה אֱלֹהֵי יִשְׂרָאֵל מִן־הָעוֹלָם וְעַד־
הָעֹלָם, וַיֹּאמְרוּ כָל־הָעָם אָמֵן, וְהַלֵּל לַיהוה:

◂ רוֹמְמוּ יהוה אֱלֹהֵינוּ וְהִשְׁתַּחֲווּ לַהֲדֹם רַגְלָיו, קָדוֹשׁ הוּא: תהלים צט
רוֹמְמוּ יהוה אֱלֹהֵינוּ וְהִשְׁתַּחֲווּ לְהַר קָדְשׁוֹ, כִּי־קָדוֹשׁ יהוה אֱלֹהֵינוּ:

וְהוּא רַחוּם, יְכַפֵּר עָוֹן וְלֹא־יַשְׁחִית, וְהִרְבָּה לְהָשִׁיב אַפּוֹ, תהלים עח
וְלֹא־יָעִיר כָּל־חֲמָתוֹ: אַתָּה יהוה לֹא־תִכְלָא רַחֲמֶיךָ מִמֶּנִּי, חַסְדְּךָ תהלים מ
וַאֲמִתְּךָ תָּמִיד יִצְּרוּנִי: זְכֹר־רַחֲמֶיךָ יהוה וַחֲסָדֶיךָ, כִּי מֵעוֹלָם הֵמָּה: תהלים כה
תְּנוּ עֹז לֵאלֹהִים, עַל־יִשְׂרָאֵל גַּאֲוָתוֹ, וְעֻזּוֹ בַּשְּׁחָקִים: נוֹרָא אֱלֹהִים תהלים סח
מִמִּקְדָּשֶׁיךָ, אֵל יִשְׂרָאֵל הוּא נֹתֵן עֹז וְתַעֲצֻמוֹת לָעָם, בָּרוּךְ אֱלֹהִים:
אֵל־נְקָמוֹת יהוה, אֵל נְקָמוֹת הוֹפִיעַ: הִנָּשֵׂא שֹׁפֵט הָאָרֶץ, הָשֵׁב תהלים צד
גְּמוּל עַל־גֵּאִים: לַיהוה הַיְשׁוּעָה, עַל־עַמְּךָ בִרְכָתֶךָ סֶּלָה: ◂ יהוה תהלים ג תהלים מו
צְבָאוֹת עִמָּנוּ, מִשְׂגָּב לָנוּ אֱלֹהֵי יַעֲקֹב סֶלָה: יהוה צְבָאוֹת, אַשְׁרֵי תהלים פד
אָדָם בֹּטֵחַ בָּךְ: יהוה הוֹשִׁיעָה, הַמֶּלֶךְ יַעֲנֵנוּ בְיוֹם־קָרְאֵנוּ: תהלים כ

הוֹשִׁיעָה אֶת־עַמֶּךָ, וּבָרֵךְ אֶת־נַחֲלָתֶךָ, וּרְעֵם וְנַשְּׂאֵם עַד־ תהלים כח
הָעוֹלָם: נַפְשֵׁנוּ חִכְּתָה לַיהוה, עֶזְרֵנוּ וּמָגִנֵּנוּ הוּא: כִּי־בוֹ יִשְׂמַח תהלים לג
לִבֵּנוּ, כִּי בְשֵׁם קָדְשׁוֹ בָטָחְנוּ: יְהִי־חַסְדְּךָ יהוה עָלֵינוּ, כַּאֲשֶׁר
יִחַלְנוּ לָךְ: הַרְאֵנוּ יהוה חַסְדֶּךָ, וְיֶשְׁעֲךָ תִּתֶּן־לָנוּ: קוּמָה עֶזְרָתָה תהלים פה תהלים מד

help us and redeem us for the sake of Your love. I am the LORD your Ps. 81
God who brought you up from the land of Egypt: open your mouth
wide and I will fill it. Happy is the people for whom this is so; happy is Ps. 144
the people whose God is the LORD. ▸ As for me, I trust in Your loving- Ps. 13
kindness; my heart rejoices in Your salvation. I will sing to the LORD
for He has been good to me.

The custom is to say this psalm standing.

מִזְמוֹר A psalm of thanksgiving. Shout joyously to the LORD, all Ps. 100
the earth. Serve the LORD with joy. Come before Him with jubilation. Know that the LORD is God. He made us and we are His. We are His people and the flock He tends. Enter His gates with thanksgiving, His courts with praise. Thank Him and bless His name. ▸ For the LORD is good, His loving-kindness is everlasting, and His faithfulness is for every generation.

יְהִי כְבוֹד May the LORD's glory be for ever; may the LORD rejoice in His Ps. 104
works. May the LORD's name be blessed, now and for ever. From the Ps. 113
rising of the sun to its setting, may the LORD's name be praised. The
LORD is high above all nations; His glory is above the heavens. LORD, Ps. 135
Your name is for ever. Your renown, LORD, is for all generations. The Ps. 103
LORD has established His throne in heaven; His kingdom rules all. Let 1 Chr. 16
the heavens rejoice and the earth be glad. Let them say among the
nations, "The LORD is King." The LORD is King, the LORD was King,
the LORD will be King for ever and all time. The LORD is King for ever Ps. 10
and all time; nations will perish from His land. The LORD foils the plans Ps. 33
of nations; He frustrates the intentions of peoples. Many are the inten- Prov. 19
tions in a person's mind, but the LORD's plan prevails. The LORD's plan Ps. 33
shall stand for ever, His mind's intent for all generations. For He spoke
and it was; He commanded and it stood firm. For the LORD has chosen Ps. 132
Zion; He desired it for His dwelling. For the LORD has chosen Jacob as Ps. 135
His own, Israel as His special treasure. For the LORD will not abandon Ps. 94
His people; nor will He forsake His heritage. ▸ He is compassionate. He Ps. 78
forgives iniquity and does not destroy. Repeatedly He suppresses His
anger, not rousing His full wrath. LORD, save! May the King answer us Ps. 20
on the day we call.

לָנוּ, וּפְדֵנוּ לְמַעַן חַסְדֶּךָ: אָנֹכִי יהוה אֱלֹהֶיךָ הַמַּעַלְךָ מֵאֶרֶץ תהלים פא
מִצְרָיִם, הַרְחֶב־פִּיךָ וַאֲמַלְאֵהוּ: אַשְׁרֵי הָעָם שֶׁכָּכָה לּוֹ, אַשְׁרֵי תהלים קמד
הָעָם שֶׁיהוה אֱלֹהָיו: › וַאֲנִי בְּחַסְדְּךָ בָטַחְתִּי, יָגֵל לִבִּי בִּישׁוּעָתֶךָ, תהלים יג
אָשִׁירָה לַיהוה, כִּי גָמַל עָלָי:

The custom is to say this psalm standing.

מִזְמוֹר לְתוֹדָה, הָרִיעוּ לַיהוה כָּל־הָאָרֶץ: עִבְדוּ אֶת־יהוה תהלים ק
בְּשִׂמְחָה, בֹּאוּ לְפָנָיו בִּרְנָנָה: דְּעוּ כִּי־יהוה הוּא אֱלֹהִים,
הוּא עָשָׂנוּ וְלוֹ אֲנַחְנוּ, עַמּוֹ וְצֹאן מַרְעִיתוֹ: בֹּאוּ שְׁעָרָיו
בְּתוֹדָה, חֲצֵרֹתָיו בִּתְהִלָּה, הוֹדוּ לוֹ, בָּרְכוּ שְׁמוֹ: › כִּי־טוֹב
יהוה, לְעוֹלָם חַסְדּוֹ, וְעַד־דֹּר וָדֹר אֱמוּנָתוֹ:

יְהִי כְבוֹד יהוה לְעוֹלָם, יִשְׂמַח יהוה בְּמַעֲשָׂיו: יְהִי שֵׁם יהוה תהלים קד תהלים קיג
מְבֹרָךְ, מֵעַתָּה וְעַד־עוֹלָם: מִמִּזְרַח־שֶׁמֶשׁ עַד־מְבוֹאוֹ, מְהֻלָּל
שֵׁם יהוה: רָם עַל־כָּל־גּוֹיִם יהוה, עַל הַשָּׁמַיִם כְּבוֹדוֹ: יהוה שִׁמְךָ תהלים קלה
לְעוֹלָם, יהוה זִכְרְךָ לְדֹר־וָדֹר: יהוה בַּשָּׁמַיִם הֵכִין כִּסְאוֹ, וּמַלְכוּתוֹ תהלים קג
בַּכֹּל מָשָׁלָה: יִשְׂמְחוּ הַשָּׁמַיִם וְתָגֵל הָאָרֶץ, וְיֹאמְרוּ בַגּוֹיִם יהוה דברי הימים א׳ טז
מָלָךְ: יהוה מֶלֶךְ, יהוה מָלָךְ, יהוה יִמְלֹךְ לְעוֹלָם וָעֶד. יהוה מֶלֶךְ תהלים י
עוֹלָם וָעֶד, אָבְדוּ גוֹיִם מֵאַרְצוֹ: יהוה הֵפִיר עֲצַת־גּוֹיִם, הֵנִיא תהלים לג
מַחְשְׁבוֹת עַמִּים: רַבּוֹת מַחֲשָׁבוֹת בְּלֶב־אִישׁ, וַעֲצַת יהוה הִיא משלי יט
תָקוּם: עֲצַת יהוה לְעוֹלָם תַּעֲמֹד, מַחְשְׁבוֹת לִבּוֹ לְדֹר וָדֹר: כִּי הוּא תהלים לג
אָמַר וַיֶּהִי, הוּא־צִוָּה וַיַּעֲמֹד: כִּי־בָחַר יהוה בְּצִיּוֹן, אִוָּהּ לְמוֹשָׁב תהלים קלב
לוֹ: כִּי־יַעֲקֹב בָּחַר לוֹ יָהּ, יִשְׂרָאֵל לִסְגֻלָּתוֹ: כִּי לֹא־יִטֹּשׁ יהוה עַמּוֹ, תהלים קלה תהלים צד
וְנַחֲלָתוֹ לֹא יַעֲזֹב: › וְהוּא רַחוּם, יְכַפֵּר עָוֹן וְלֹא־יַשְׁחִית, וְהִרְבָּה תהלים עח
לְהָשִׁיב אַפּוֹ, וְלֹא־יָעִיר כָּל־חֲמָתוֹ: יהוה הוֹשִׁיעָה, הַמֶּלֶךְ יַעֲנֵנוּ תהלים כ
בְיוֹם־קָרְאֵנוּ:

The line beginning with "You open Your hand" should be said with special concentration, representing as it does the key idea of this Psalm, and of Pesukei DeZimra as a whole, that God is the creator and sustainer of all. Some have the custom to touch the hand-tefillin at °, and the head-tefillin at °°.

אַשְׁרֵי Happy are those who dwell in Your House; *Ps. 84*
they shall continue to praise You, Selah!
Happy are the people for whom this is so; *Ps. 144*
happy are the people whose God is the LORD.

A song of praise by David. *Ps. 145*

I will exalt You, my God, the King, and bless Your name for ever and all time. Every day I will bless You, and praise Your name for ever and all time. Great is the LORD and greatly to be praised; His greatness is unfathomable. One generation will praise Your works to the next, and tell of Your mighty deeds. On the glorious splendor of Your majesty I will meditate, and on the acts of Your wonders. They shall talk of the power of Your awesome deeds, and I will tell of Your greatness. They shall recite the record of Your great goodness, and sing with joy of Your righteousness. The LORD is gracious and compassionate, slow to anger and great in loving-kindness. The LORD is good to all, and His compassion extends to all His works. All Your works shall thank You, LORD, and Your devoted ones shall bless You. They shall talk of the glory of Your kingship, and speak of Your might. To make known to mankind His mighty deeds and the glorious majesty of His kingship. Your kingdom is an everlasting kingdom, and Your reign is for all generations. The LORD supports all who fall, and raises all who are bowed down. All raise their eyes to You in hope, and You give them their food in due season. °You open Your hand, °°and satisfy every living thing with favor. The LORD is righteous in all His ways, and kind in all He does. The LORD is close to all who call on Him, to all who call on Him in truth. He fulfills the will of those who revere Him; He hears their cry and saves them. The LORD guards all who love Him, but all the wicked He will destroy. ▸ My mouth shall speak the praise of the LORD, and all creatures shall bless His holy name for ever and all time.

We will bless the LORD now and for ever. Halleluya! *Ps. 115*

The line beginning with פּוֹתֵחַ אֶת יָדֶךָ *should be said with special concentration, representing as it does the key idea of this psalm, and of* פסוקי דזמרה *as a whole, that God is the creator and sustainer of all. Some have the custom to touch the* תפילין של יד *at °, and the* תפילין של ראש *at °°.*

אַשְׁרֵי יוֹשְׁבֵי בֵיתֶךָ, עוֹד יְהַלְלְוּךָ סֶּלָה: תהלים פד

אַשְׁרֵי הָעָם שֶׁכָּכָה לּוֹ, אַשְׁרֵי הָעָם שֶׁיהוה אֱלֹהָיו: תהלים קמד

תְּהִלָּה לְדָוִד תהלים קמה

אֲרוֹמִמְךָ אֱלוֹהַי הַמֶּלֶךְ, וַאֲבָרְכָה שִׁמְךָ לְעוֹלָם וָעֶד:
בְּכָל־יוֹם אֲבָרְכֶךָּ, וַאֲהַלְלָה שִׁמְךָ לְעוֹלָם וָעֶד:
גָּדוֹל יהוה וּמְהֻלָּל מְאֹד, וְלִגְדֻלָּתוֹ אֵין חֵקֶר:
דּוֹר לְדוֹר יְשַׁבַּח מַעֲשֶׂיךָ, וּגְבוּרֹתֶיךָ יַגִּידוּ:
הֲדַר כְּבוֹד הוֹדֶךָ, וְדִבְרֵי נִפְלְאֹתֶיךָ אָשִׂיחָה:
וֶעֱזוּז נוֹרְאֹתֶיךָ יֹאמֵרוּ, וּגְדוּלָּתְךָ אֲסַפְּרֶנָּה:
זֵכֶר רַב־טוּבְךָ יַבִּיעוּ, וְצִדְקָתְךָ יְרַנֵּנוּ:
חַנּוּן וְרַחוּם יהוה, אֶרֶךְ אַפַּיִם וּגְדָל־חָסֶד:
טוֹב־יהוה לַכֹּל, וְרַחֲמָיו עַל־כָּל־מַעֲשָׂיו:
יוֹדוּךָ יהוה כָּל־מַעֲשֶׂיךָ, וַחֲסִידֶיךָ יְבָרְכוּכָה:
כְּבוֹד מַלְכוּתְךָ יֹאמֵרוּ, וּגְבוּרָתְךָ יְדַבֵּרוּ:
לְהוֹדִיעַ לִבְנֵי הָאָדָם גְּבוּרֹתָיו, וּכְבוֹד הֲדַר מַלְכוּתוֹ:
מַלְכוּתְךָ מַלְכוּת כָּל־עֹלָמִים, וּמֶמְשַׁלְתְּךָ בְּכָל־דּוֹר וָדֹר:
סוֹמֵךְ יהוה לְכָל־הַנֹּפְלִים, וְזוֹקֵף לְכָל־הַכְּפוּפִים:
עֵינֵי־כֹל אֵלֶיךָ יְשַׂבֵּרוּ, וְאַתָּה נוֹתֵן־לָהֶם אֶת־אָכְלָם בְּעִתּוֹ:
°פּוֹתֵחַ אֶת־יָדֶךָ, °°וּמַשְׂבִּיעַ לְכָל־חַי רָצוֹן:
צַדִּיק יהוה בְּכָל־דְּרָכָיו, וְחָסִיד בְּכָל־מַעֲשָׂיו:
קָרוֹב יהוה לְכָל־קֹרְאָיו, לְכֹל אֲשֶׁר יִקְרָאֻהוּ בֶאֱמֶת:
רְצוֹן־יְרֵאָיו יַעֲשֶׂה, וְאֶת־שַׁוְעָתָם יִשְׁמַע, וְיוֹשִׁיעֵם:
שׁוֹמֵר יהוה אֶת־כָּל־אֹהֲבָיו, וְאֵת כָּל־הָרְשָׁעִים יַשְׁמִיד:
› תְּהִלַּת יהוה יְדַבֶּר פִּי, וִיבָרֵךְ כָּל־בָּשָׂר שֵׁם קָדְשׁוֹ לְעוֹלָם וָעֶד:

וַאֲנַחְנוּ נְבָרֵךְ יָהּ מֵעַתָּה וְעַד־עוֹלָם, הַלְלוּיָהּ: תהלים קטו

הַלְלוּיָהּ Halleluya! Praise the LORD, my soul. I will praise the LORD *Ps. 146* all my life; I will sing to my God as long as I live. Put not your trust in princes, or in mortal man who cannot save. His breath expires, he returns to the earth; on that day his plans come to an end. Happy is he whose help is the God of Jacob, whose hope is in the LORD his God who made heaven and earth, the sea and all they contain; He who keeps faith for ever. He secures justice for the oppressed. He gives food to the hungry. The LORD sets captives free. The LORD gives sight to the blind. The LORD raises those bowed down. The LORD loves the righteous. The LORD protects the stranger. He gives courage to the orphan and widow. He thwarts the way of the wicked. ▸ The LORD shall reign for ever. He is your God, Zion, for all generations. Halleluya!

הַלְלוּיָהּ Halleluya! How good it is to sing songs to our God; how pleas- *Ps. 147* ant and fitting to praise Him. The LORD rebuilds Jerusalem. He gathers the scattered exiles of Israel. He heals the brokenhearted and binds up their wounds. He counts the number of the stars, calling each by name. Great is our LORD and mighty in power; His understanding has no limit. The LORD gives courage to the humble, but casts the wicked to the ground. Sing to the LORD in thanks; make music to our God on the harp. He covers the sky with clouds. He provides the earth with rain and makes grass grow on the hills. He gives food to the cattle and to the ravens when they cry. He does not take delight in the strength of horses nor pleasure in the fleetness of man. The LORD takes pleasure in those who fear Him, who put their hope in His loving care. Praise the LORD, Jerusalem; sing to your God, Zion, for He has strengthened the bars of your gates and blessed your children in your midst. He has brought peace to your borders, and satisfied you with the finest wheat. He sends His commandment to earth; swiftly runs His word. He spreads snow like fleece, sprinkles frost like ashes, scatters hail like crumbs. Who can stand His cold? He sends His word and melts them; He makes the wind blow and the waters flow. ▸ He has declared His words to Jacob, His statutes and laws to Israel. He has done this for no other nation; such laws they do not know. Halleluya!

הַלְלוּיָהּ, הַלְלִי נַפְשִׁי אֶת־יהוה: אֲהַלְלָה יהוה בְּחַיָּי, אֲזַמְּרָה תהלים קמו
לֵאלֹהַי בְּעוֹדִי: אַל־תִּבְטְחוּ בִנְדִיבִים, בְּבֶן־אָדָם שֶׁאֵין לוֹ תְשׁוּעָה:
תֵּצֵא רוּחוֹ, יָשֻׁב לְאַדְמָתוֹ, בַּיּוֹם הַהוּא אָבְדוּ עֶשְׁתֹּנֹתָיו: אַשְׁרֵי
שֶׁאֵל יַעֲקֹב בְּעֶזְרוֹ, שִׂבְרוֹ עַל־יהוה אֱלֹהָיו: עֹשֶׂה שָׁמַיִם וָאָרֶץ,
אֶת־הַיָּם וְאֶת־כָּל־אֲשֶׁר־בָּם, הַשֹּׁמֵר אֱמֶת לְעוֹלָם: עֹשֶׂה מִשְׁפָּט
לַעֲשׁוּקִים, נֹתֵן לֶחֶם לָרְעֵבִים, יהוה מַתִּיר אֲסוּרִים: יהוה פֹּקֵחַ
עִוְרִים, יהוה זֹקֵף כְּפוּפִים, יהוה אֹהֵב צַדִּיקִים: יהוה שֹׁמֵר אֶת־
גֵּרִים, יָתוֹם וְאַלְמָנָה יְעוֹדֵד, וְדֶרֶךְ רְשָׁעִים יְעַוֵּת: › יִמְלֹךְ יהוה
לְעוֹלָם, אֱלֹהַיִךְ צִיּוֹן לְדֹר וָדֹר, הַלְלוּיָהּ:

הַלְלוּיָהּ, כִּי־טוֹב זַמְּרָה אֱלֹהֵינוּ, כִּי־נָעִים נָאוָה תְהִלָּה: בּוֹנֵה תהלים קמז
יְרוּשָׁלַםִ יהוה, נִדְחֵי יִשְׂרָאֵל יְכַנֵּס: הָרוֹפֵא לִשְׁבוּרֵי לֵב, וּמְחַבֵּשׁ
לְעַצְּבוֹתָם: מוֹנֶה מִסְפָּר לַכּוֹכָבִים, לְכֻלָּם שֵׁמוֹת יִקְרָא: גָּדוֹל
אֲדוֹנֵינוּ וְרַב־כֹּחַ, לִתְבוּנָתוֹ אֵין מִסְפָּר: מְעוֹדֵד עֲנָוִים יהוה, מַשְׁפִּיל
רְשָׁעִים עֲדֵי־אָרֶץ: עֱנוּ לַיהוה בְּתוֹדָה, זַמְּרוּ לֵאלֹהֵינוּ בְכִנּוֹר:
הַמְכַסֶּה שָׁמַיִם בְּעָבִים, הַמֵּכִין לָאָרֶץ מָטָר, הַמַּצְמִיחַ הָרִים חָצִיר:
נוֹתֵן לִבְהֵמָה לַחְמָהּ, לִבְנֵי עֹרֵב אֲשֶׁר יִקְרָאוּ: לֹא בִגְבוּרַת הַסּוּס
יֶחְפָּץ, לֹא־בְשׁוֹקֵי הָאִישׁ יִרְצֶה: רוֹצֶה יהוה אֶת־יְרֵאָיו, אֶת־
הַמְיַחֲלִים לְחַסְדּוֹ: שַׁבְּחִי יְרוּשָׁלַםִ אֶת־יהוה, הַלְלִי אֱלֹהַיִךְ צִיּוֹן:
כִּי־חִזַּק בְּרִיחֵי שְׁעָרָיִךְ, בֵּרַךְ בָּנַיִךְ בְּקִרְבֵּךְ: הַשָּׂם־גְּבוּלֵךְ שָׁלוֹם,
חֵלֶב חִטִּים יַשְׂבִּיעֵךְ: הַשֹּׁלֵחַ אִמְרָתוֹ אָרֶץ, עַד־מְהֵרָה יָרוּץ דְּבָרוֹ:
הַנֹּתֵן שֶׁלֶג כַּצָּמֶר, כְּפוֹר כָּאֵפֶר יְפַזֵּר: מַשְׁלִיךְ קַרְחוֹ כְפִתִּים, לִפְנֵי
קָרָתוֹ מִי יַעֲמֹד: יִשְׁלַח דְּבָרוֹ וְיַמְסֵם, יַשֵּׁב רוּחוֹ יִזְּלוּ־מָיִם: › מַגִּיד
דְּבָרָו לְיַעֲקֹב, חֻקָּיו וּמִשְׁפָּטָיו לְיִשְׂרָאֵל: לֹא עָשָׂה כֵן לְכָל־גּוֹי,
וּמִשְׁפָּטִים בַּל־יְדָעוּם, הַלְלוּיָהּ:

הַלְלוּיָהּ Halleluya! Praise the LORD from the heavens, praise Him Ps. 148
in the heights. Praise Him, all His angels; praise Him, all His hosts. Praise Him, sun and moon; praise Him, all shining stars. Praise Him, highest heavens and the waters above the heavens. Let them praise the name of the LORD, for He commanded and they were created. He established them for ever and all time, issuing a decree that will never change. Praise the LORD from the earth: sea monsters and all the deep seas; fire and hail, snow and mist, storm winds that obey His word; mountains and all hills, fruit trees and all cedars; wild animals and all cattle, creeping things and winged birds; kings of the earth and all nations, princes and all judges on earth; youths and maidens, old and young. ▸ Let them praise the name of the LORD, for His name alone is sublime; His majesty is above earth and heaven. He has raised the pride of His people, for the glory of all His devoted ones, the children of Israel, the people close to Him. Halleluya!

הַלְלוּיָהּ Halleluya! Sing to the LORD a new song, His praise in the Ps. 149
assembly of the devoted. Let Israel rejoice in its Maker; let the children of Zion exult in their King. Let them praise His name with dancing; sing praises to Him with timbrel and harp. For the LORD delights in His people; He adorns the humble with salvation. Let the devoted revel in glory; let them sing for joy on their beds. Let high praises of God be in their throats, and a two-edged sword in their hand: to impose retribution on the nations, punishment on the peoples, ▸ binding their kings with chains, their nobles with iron fetters, carrying out the judgment written against them. This is the glory of all His devoted ones. Halleluya!

הַלְלוּיָהּ Halleluya! Praise God in His holy place; praise Him in the Ps. 150
heavens of His power. Praise Him for His mighty deeds; praise Him for His surpassing greatness. Praise Him with blasts of the shofar; praise Him with the harp and lyre. Praise Him with timbrel and dance; praise Him with strings and flute. Praise Him with clashing cymbals; praise Him with resounding cymbals. ▸ Let all that breathes praise the LORD. Halleluya! Let all that breathes praise the LORD. Halleluya!

תהלים קמח
הַלְלוּיָהּ, הַלְלוּ אֶת־יהוה מִן־הַשָּׁמַיִם, הַלְלוּהוּ בַּמְּרוֹמִים: הַלְלוּהוּ כָל־מַלְאָכָיו, הַלְלוּהוּ כָּל־צְבָאָו: הַלְלוּהוּ שֶׁמֶשׁ וְיָרֵחַ, הַלְלוּהוּ כָּל־כּוֹכְבֵי אוֹר: הַלְלוּהוּ שְׁמֵי הַשָּׁמָיִם, וְהַמַּיִם אֲשֶׁר מֵעַל הַשָּׁמָיִם: יְהַלְלוּ אֶת־שֵׁם יהוה, כִּי הוּא צִוָּה וְנִבְרָאוּ: וַיַּעֲמִידֵם לָעַד לְעוֹלָם, חָק־נָתַן וְלֹא יַעֲבוֹר: הַלְלוּ אֶת־יהוה מִן־הָאָרֶץ, תַּנִּינִים וְכָל־תְּהֹמוֹת: אֵשׁ וּבָרָד שֶׁלֶג וְקִיטוֹר, רוּחַ סְעָרָה עֹשָׂה דְבָרוֹ: הֶהָרִים וְכָל־גְּבָעוֹת, עֵץ פְּרִי וְכָל־אֲרָזִים: הַחַיָּה וְכָל־בְּהֵמָה, רֶמֶשׂ וְצִפּוֹר כָּנָף: מַלְכֵי־אֶרֶץ וְכָל־לְאֻמִּים, שָׂרִים וְכָל־שֹׁפְטֵי אָרֶץ: בַּחוּרִים וְגַם־בְּתוּלוֹת, זְקֵנִים עִם־נְעָרִים: ‹ יְהַלְלוּ אֶת־שֵׁם יהוה, כִּי־נִשְׂגָּב שְׁמוֹ לְבַדּוֹ, הוֹדוֹ עַל־אֶרֶץ וְשָׁמָיִם: וַיָּרֶם קֶרֶן לְעַמּוֹ, תְּהִלָּה לְכָל־חֲסִידָיו, לִבְנֵי יִשְׂרָאֵל עַם קְרֹבוֹ, הַלְלוּיָהּ:

תהלים קמט
הַלְלוּיָהּ, שִׁירוּ לַיהוה שִׁיר חָדָשׁ, תְּהִלָּתוֹ בִּקְהַל חֲסִידִים: יִשְׂמַח יִשְׂרָאֵל בְּעֹשָׂיו, בְּנֵי־צִיּוֹן יָגִילוּ בְמַלְכָּם: יְהַלְלוּ שְׁמוֹ בְמָחוֹל, בְּתֹף וְכִנּוֹר יְזַמְּרוּ־לוֹ: כִּי־רוֹצֶה יהוה בְּעַמּוֹ, יְפָאֵר עֲנָוִים בִּישׁוּעָה: יַעְלְזוּ חֲסִידִים בְּכָבוֹד, יְרַנְּנוּ עַל־מִשְׁכְּבוֹתָם: רוֹמְמוֹת אֵל בִּגְרוֹנָם, וְחֶרֶב פִּיפִיּוֹת בְּיָדָם: לַעֲשׂוֹת נְקָמָה בַּגּוֹיִם, תּוֹכֵחוֹת בַּלְאֻמִּים: ‹ לֶאְסֹר מַלְכֵיהֶם בְּזִקִּים, וְנִכְבְּדֵיהֶם בְּכַבְלֵי בַרְזֶל: לַעֲשׂוֹת בָּהֶם מִשְׁפָּט כָּתוּב, הָדָר הוּא לְכָל־חֲסִידָיו, הַלְלוּיָהּ:

תהלים קנ
הַלְלוּיָהּ, הַלְלוּ־אֵל בְּקָדְשׁוֹ, הַלְלוּהוּ בִּרְקִיעַ עֻזּוֹ: הַלְלוּהוּ בִגְבוּרֹתָיו, הַלְלוּהוּ כְּרֹב גֻּדְלוֹ: הַלְלוּהוּ בְּתֵקַע שׁוֹפָר, הַלְלוּהוּ בְּנֵבֶל וְכִנּוֹר: הַלְלוּהוּ בְתֹף וּמָחוֹל, הַלְלוּהוּ בְּמִנִּים וְעֻגָב: הַלְלוּהוּ בְצִלְצְלֵי־שָׁמַע, הַלְלוּהוּ בְּצִלְצְלֵי תְרוּעָה: ‹ כֹּל הַנְּשָׁמָה תְּהַלֵּל יָהּ, הַלְלוּיָהּ: כֹּל הַנְּשָׁמָה תְּהַלֵּל יָהּ, הַלְלוּיָהּ:

בָּרוּךְ Blessed be the LORD for ever. Amen and Amen. Ps. 89
Blessed from Zion be the LORD Ps. 135
who dwells in Jerusalem. Halleluya!
Blessed be the LORD, God of Israel, Ps. 72
who alone does wonders.
▸ Blessed be His glorious name for ever,
and may all the earth be filled with His glory.
Amen and Amen.

Stand until after "Bless the LORD" on page 624.

וַיְבָרֶךְ David blessed the LORD in front of the entire assembly. David *1 Chr. 29*
said, "Blessed are You, LORD, God of our father Yisrael, for ever and ever. Yours, LORD, are the greatness and the power, the glory, majesty and splendor, for everything in heaven and earth is Yours. Yours, LORD, is the kingdom; You are exalted as Head over all. Both riches and honor are in Your gift and You reign over all things. In Your hand are strength and might. It is in Your power to make great and give strength to all. Therefore, our God, we thank You and
praise Your glorious name." You alone are the LORD. You *Neh. 9*
made the heavens, even the highest heavens, and all their hosts, the earth and all that is on it, the seas and all they contain. You give life to them all, and the hosts of heaven worship You. ▸ You are the LORD God who chose Abram and brought him out of Ur of the Chaldees, changing his name to Abraham. You found his heart faithful toward You, ◂ and You made a covenant with him to give to his descendants the land of the Canaanites, Hittites, Amorites, Perizzites, Jebusites and Girgashites. You fulfilled Your promise for You are righteous. You saw the suffering of our ancestors in Egypt. You heard their cry at the Sea of Reeds. You sent signs and wonders against Pharaoh, all his servants and all the people of his land, because You knew how arrogantly the Egyptians treated them. You created for Yourself renown that remains to this day. ▸ You divided the sea before them, so that they passed through the sea on dry land, but You cast their pursuers into the depths, like a stone into mighty waters.

בָּרוּךְ יהוה לְעוֹלָם, אָמֵן וְאָמֵן: תהלים פט
בָּרוּךְ יהוה מִצִּיּוֹן, שֹׁכֵן יְרוּשָׁלָםִ, הַלְלוּיָהּ: תהלים קלה
בָּרוּךְ יהוה אֱלֹהִים אֱלֹהֵי יִשְׂרָאֵל, עֹשֵׂה נִפְלָאוֹת לְבַדּוֹ: תהלים עב
◂ וּבָרוּךְ שֵׁם כְּבוֹדוֹ לְעוֹלָם
וְיִמָּלֵא כְבוֹדוֹ אֶת־כָּל־הָאָרֶץ
אָמֵן וְאָמֵן:

Stand until after בָּרְכוּ *on page 625.*

וַיְבָרֶךְ דָּוִיד אֶת־יהוה לְעֵינֵי כָּל־הַקָּהָל, וַיֹּאמֶר דָּוִיד, בָּרוּךְ דברי הימים א׳, כט
אַתָּה יהוה, אֱלֹהֵי יִשְׂרָאֵל אָבִינוּ, מֵעוֹלָם וְעַד־עוֹלָם: לְךָ יהוה
הַגְּדֻלָּה וְהַגְּבוּרָה וְהַתִּפְאֶרֶת וְהַנֵּצַח וְהַהוֹד, כִּי־כֹל בַּשָּׁמַיִם
וּבָאָרֶץ, לְךָ יהוה הַמַּמְלָכָה וְהַמִּתְנַשֵּׂא לְכֹל לְרֹאשׁ: וְהָעֹשֶׁר
וְהַכָּבוֹד מִלְּפָנֶיךָ, וְאַתָּה מוֹשֵׁל בַּכֹּל, וּבְיָדְךָ כֹּחַ וּגְבוּרָה, וּבְיָדְךָ
לְגַדֵּל וּלְחַזֵּק לַכֹּל: וְעַתָּה אֱלֹהֵינוּ מוֹדִים אֲנַחְנוּ לָךְ, וּמְהַלְלִים
לְשֵׁם תִּפְאַרְתֶּךָ: אַתָּה־הוּא יהוה לְבַדֶּךָ, אַתָּ עָשִׂיתָ נחמיה ט
אֶת־הַשָּׁמַיִם, שְׁמֵי הַשָּׁמַיִם וְכָל־צְבָאָם, הָאָרֶץ וְכָל־אֲשֶׁר עָלֶיהָ,
הַיַּמִּים וְכָל־אֲשֶׁר בָּהֶם, וְאַתָּה מְחַיֶּה אֶת־כֻּלָּם, וּצְבָא הַשָּׁמַיִם לְךָ
מִשְׁתַּחֲוִים: ◂ אַתָּה הוּא יהוה הָאֱלֹהִים אֲשֶׁר בָּחַרְתָּ בְּאַבְרָם,
וְהוֹצֵאתוֹ מֵאוּר כַּשְׂדִּים, וְשַׂמְתָּ שְּׁמוֹ אַבְרָהָם: וּמָצָאתָ אֶת־לְבָבוֹ
נֶאֱמָן לְפָנֶיךָ, ◂ וְכָרוֹת עִמּוֹ הַבְּרִית לָתֵת אֶת־אֶרֶץ הַכְּנַעֲנִי הַחִתִּי
הָאֱמֹרִי וְהַפְּרִזִּי וְהַיְבוּסִי וְהַגִּרְגָּשִׁי, לָתֵת לְזַרְעוֹ, וַתָּקֶם אֶת־דְּבָרֶיךָ,
כִּי צַדִּיק אָתָּה: וַתֵּרֶא אֶת־עֳנִי אֲבֹתֵינוּ בְּמִצְרָיִם, וְאֶת־זַעֲקָתָם
שָׁמַעְתָּ עַל־יַם־סוּף: וַתִּתֵּן אֹתֹת וּמֹפְתִים בְּפַרְעֹה וּבְכָל־עֲבָדָיו
וּבְכָל־עַם אַרְצוֹ, כִּי יָדַעְתָּ כִּי הֵזִידוּ עֲלֵיהֶם, וַתַּעַשׂ־לְךָ שֵׁם כְּהַיּוֹם
הַזֶּה: ◂ וְהַיָּם בָּקַעְתָּ לִפְנֵיהֶם, וַיַּעַבְרוּ בְתוֹךְ־הַיָּם בַּיַּבָּשָׁה, וְאֶת־
רֹדְפֵיהֶם הִשְׁלַכְתָּ בִמְצוֹלֹת כְּמוֹ־אֶבֶן, בְּמַיִם עַזִּים:

וַיּוֹשַׁע That day the LORD saved Israel from the hands of the Egyptians, *Ex. 14*
and Israel saw the Egyptians lying dead on the seashore. ▸ When Israel saw the great power the LORD had displayed against the Egyptians, the people feared the LORD, and believed in the LORD and in His servant, Moses.

אָז יָשִׁיר־מֹשֶׁה Then Moses and the Israelites sang this song *Ex. 15*
to the LORD, saying:
I will sing to the LORD, for He has triumphed gloriously;
horse and rider He has hurled into the sea.
The LORD is my strength and song; He has become my salvation.
This is my God, and I will beautify Him,
my father's God, and I will exalt Him.
The LORD is a Master of war; LORD is His name.
Pharaoh's chariots and army He cast into the sea;
the best of his officers drowned in the Sea of Reeds.
The deep waters covered them;
they went down to the depths like a stone.
Your right hand, LORD, is majestic in power.
Your right hand, LORD, shatters the enemy.
In the greatness of Your majesty,
You overthrew those who rose against You.
You sent out Your fury; it consumed them like stubble.
By the blast of Your nostrils the waters piled up.
The surging waters stood straight like a wall;
the deeps congealed in the heart of the sea.
The enemy said, "I will pursue. I will overtake. I will divide the spoil.
My desire shall have its fill of them.
I will draw my sword. My hand will destroy them."
You blew with Your wind; the sea covered them.
They sank in the mighty waters like lead.
Who is like You, LORD, among the mighty?
Who is like You – majestic in holiness, awesome in glory, working wonders?
You stretched out Your right hand, the earth swallowed them.
In Your loving-kindness, You led the people You redeemed.
In Your strength, You guided them to Your holy abode.
Nations heard and trembled;
terror gripped Philistia's inhabitants.

וַיּֽוֹשַׁע יהוה בַּיּוֹם הַהוּא אֶת־יִשְׂרָאֵל מִיַּד מִצְרָיִם, וַיַּרְא יִשְׂרָאֵל שמות יד
אֶת־מִצְרַיִם מֵת עַל־שְׂפַת הַיָּם: • וַיַּרְא יִשְׂרָאֵל אֶת־הַיָּד הַגְּדֹלָה
אֲשֶׁר עָשָׂה יהוה בְּמִצְרַיִם, וַיִּירְאוּ הָעָם אֶת־יהוה, וַיַּאֲמִינוּ בַּיהוה
וּבְמֹשֶׁה עַבְדּוֹ:

אָז יָשִׁיר־מֹשֶׁה וּבְנֵי יִשְׂרָאֵל אֶת־הַשִּׁירָה הַזֹּאת לַיהוה, וַיֹּאמְרוּ שמות טו
לֵאמֹר, אָשִֽׁירָה לַיהוה כִּי־גָאֹה גָּאָה, סוּס
וְרֹכְבוֹ רָמָה בַיָּם: עָזִּי וְזִמְרָת יָהּ וַיְהִי־לִי
לִישׁוּעָה, זֶה אֵלִי וְאַנְוֵהוּ, אֱלֹהֵי
אָבִי וַאֲרֹמְמֶנְהוּ: יהוה אִישׁ מִלְחָמָה, יהוה
שְׁמוֹ: מַרְכְּבֹת פַּרְעֹה וְחֵילוֹ יָרָה בַיָּם, וּמִבְחַר
שָׁלִשָׁיו טֻבְּעוּ בְיַם־סוּף: תְּהֹמֹת יְכַסְיֻמוּ, יָרְדוּ בִמְצוֹלֹת כְּמוֹ־
אָבֶן: יְמִינְךָ יהוה נֶאְדָּרִי בַּכֹּחַ, יְמִינְךָ
יהוה תִּרְעַץ אוֹיֵב: וּבְרֹב גְּאוֹנְךָ תַּהֲרֹס
קָמֶיךָ, תְּשַׁלַּח חֲרֹנְךָ יֹאכְלֵמוֹ כַּקַּשׁ: וּבְרוּחַ
אַפֶּיךָ נֶעֶרְמוּ מַיִם, נִצְּבוּ כְמוֹ־נֵד
נֹזְלִים, קָפְאוּ תְהֹמֹת בְּלֶב־יָם: אָמַר
אוֹיֵב אֶרְדֹּף, אַשִּׂיג, אֲחַלֵּק שָׁלָל, תִּמְלָאֵמוֹ
נַפְשִׁי, אָרִיק חַרְבִּי תּוֹרִישֵׁמוֹ יָדִי: נָשַׁפְתָּ
בְרוּחֲךָ כִּסָּמוֹ יָם, צָלְלוּ כַּעוֹפֶרֶת בְּמַיִם
אַדִּירִים: מִי־כָמֹכָה בָּאֵלִם יהוה, מִי
כָּמֹכָה נֶאְדָּר בַּקֹּדֶשׁ, נוֹרָא תְהִלֹּת עֹשֵׂה
פֶלֶא: נָטִיתָ יְמִינְךָ תִּבְלָעֵמוֹ אָרֶץ: נָחִיתָ
בְחַסְדְּךָ עַם־זוּ גָּאָלְתָּ, נֵהַלְתָּ בְעָזְּךָ אֶל־נְוֵה
קָדְשֶׁךָ: שָׁמְעוּ עַמִּים יִרְגָּזוּן, חִיל
אָחַז יֹשְׁבֵי פְּלָשֶׁת: אָז נִבְהֲלוּ אַלּוּפֵי

The chiefs of Edom were dismayed,
Moab's leaders were seized with trembling,
the people of Canaan melted away.
Fear and dread fell upon them.
By the power of Your arm, they were still as stone –
until Your people crossed, LORD,
until the people You acquired crossed over.
You will bring them and plant them
on the mountain of Your heritage –
the place, LORD, You made for Your dwelling,
the Sanctuary, LORD, Your hands established.
The LORD will reign for ever and all time.

The LORD will reign for ever and all time.
The LORD's kingship is established for ever and to all eternity.

When Pharaoh's horses, chariots and riders went into the sea,
the LORD brought the waters of the sea back over them, but
the Israelites walked on dry land through the sea.

▸ For kingship is the LORD's *Ps. 22*
and He rules over the nations.
Saviors shall go up to Mount Zion to judge Mount Esau, *Ob. 1*
and the LORD's shall be the kingdom.
Then the LORD shall be King over all the earth; *Zech. 14*
on that day the LORD shall be One and His name One,

(as it is written in Your Torah, saying:
Listen, Israel: the LORD is our God, the LORD is One.) *Deut. 6*

יִשְׁתַּבַּח May Your name be praised for ever, our King,
the great and holy God, King in heaven and on earth.
For to You, LORD our God and God of our ancestors,
it is right to offer song and praise,
hymn and psalm,
strength and dominion,
eternity, greatness and power,

אֱדוֹם, אֵילֵי מוֹאָב יֹאחֲזֵמוֹ רָעַד, נָמֹגוּ
כֹּל יֹשְׁבֵי כְנָעַן: תִּפֹּל עֲלֵיהֶם אֵימָתָה
וָפַחַד, בִּגְדֹל זְרוֹעֲךָ יִדְּמוּ כָּאָבֶן, עַד־
יַעֲבֹר עַמְּךָ יהוה, עַד־יַעֲבֹר עַם־זוּ
קָנִיתָ: תְּבִאֵמוֹ וְתִטָּעֵמוֹ בְּהַר נַחֲלָתְךָ, מָכוֹן
לְשִׁבְתְּךָ פָּעַלְתָּ יהוה, מִקְּדָשׁ אֲדֹנָי כּוֹנְנוּ
יָדֶיךָ: יהוה יִמְלֹךְ לְעֹלָם וָעֶד:

יהוה יִמְלֹךְ לְעֹלָם וָעֶד.
יהוה מַלְכוּתֵהּ קָאֵם לְעָלַם וּלְעָלְמֵי עָלְמַיָּא.

כִּי
בָא סוּס פַּרְעֹה בְּרִכְבּוֹ וּבְפָרָשָׁיו בַּיָּם, וַיָּשֶׁב יהוה עֲלֵהֶם אֶת־מֵי
הַיָּם, וּבְנֵי יִשְׂרָאֵל הָלְכוּ בַיַּבָּשָׁה בְּתוֹךְ הַיָּם:

◂ כִּי לַיהוה הַמְּלוּכָה וּמֹשֵׁל בַּגּוֹיִם: תהלים כב
וְעָלוּ מוֹשִׁעִים בְּהַר צִיּוֹן, לִשְׁפֹּט אֶת־הַר עֵשָׂו עובדיה א
וְהָיְתָה לַיהוה הַמְּלוּכָה:
וְהָיָה יהוה לְמֶלֶךְ עַל־כָּל־הָאָרֶץ זכריה יד
בַּיּוֹם הַהוּא יִהְיֶה יהוה אֶחָד וּשְׁמוֹ אֶחָד:

(וּבְתוֹרָתְךָ כָּתוּב לֵאמֹר, שְׁמַע יִשְׂרָאֵל, יהוה אֱלֹהֵינוּ יהוה אֶחָד:) דברים ו

יִשְׁתַּבַּח שִׁמְךָ לָעַד, מַלְכֵּנוּ
הָאֵל הַמֶּלֶךְ הַגָּדוֹל וְהַקָּדוֹשׁ בַּשָּׁמַיִם וּבָאָרֶץ
כִּי לְךָ נָאֶה, יהוה אֱלֹהֵינוּ וֵאלֹהֵי אֲבוֹתֵינוּ
שִׁיר וּשְׁבָחָה, הַלֵּל וְזִמְרָה
עֹז וּמֶמְשָׁלָה, נֶצַח, גְּדֻלָּה וּגְבוּרָה

song of praise and glory, holiness and kingship,
▸ blessings and thanks, from now and for ever.
Blessed are You, LORD,
God and King, exalted in praises,
God of thanksgivings, Master of wonders,
who delights in hymns of song,
King, God, Giver of life to the worlds.

On Hoshana Raba, many congregations open the Ark and say this psalm responsively, verse by verse.

שִׁיר הַמַּעֲלוֹת A song of ascents. From the depths I have called to You, LORD. LORD, hear my voice; let Your ears be attentive to my plea. If You, LORD, should keep account of sins, O LORD, who could stand? But with You there is forgiveness, that You may be held in awe. I wait for the LORD, my soul waits, and in His word I put my hope. My soul waits for the LORD more than watchmen wait for the morning, more than watchmen wait for the morning. Israel, put your hope in the LORD, for with the LORD there is loving-kindness, and great is His power to redeem. It is He who will redeem Israel from all their sins. *Ps. 130*

HALF KADDISH

Leader: יִתְגַּדַּל Magnified and sanctified
may His great name be,
in the world He created by His will.
May He establish His kingdom
in your lifetime and in your days,
and in the lifetime of all the house of Israel,
swiftly and soon – and say: Amen.

All: May His great name be blessed for ever and all time.

Leader: Blessed and praised, glorified and exalted,
raised and honored, uplifted and lauded
be the name of the Holy One,
blessed be He,
beyond any blessing,
song, praise and consolation
uttered in the world – and say: Amen.

תְּהִלָּה וְתִפְאֶרֶת, קְדֻשָּׁה וּמַלְכוּת
◄ בְּרָכוֹת וְהוֹדָאוֹת, מֵעַתָּה וְעַד עוֹלָם.
בָּרוּךְ אַתָּה יהוה
אֵל מֶלֶךְ גָּדוֹל בַּתִּשְׁבָּחוֹת
אֵל הַהוֹדָאוֹת, אֲדוֹן הַנִּפְלָאוֹת
הַבּוֹחֵר בְּשִׁירֵי זִמְרָה, מֶלֶךְ, אֵל, חֵי הָעוֹלָמִים.

On הושענא רבה*, many congregations open the* ארון קודש *and say this psalm responsively, verse by verse.*

שִׁיר הַמַּעֲלוֹת, מִמַּעֲמַקִּים קְרָאתִיךָ יהוה: אֲדֹנָי שִׁמְעָה בְקוֹלִי, תהלים קל
תִּהְיֶינָה אָזְנֶיךָ קַשֻּׁבוֹת לְקוֹל תַּחֲנוּנָי: אִם־עֲוֹנוֹת תִּשְׁמָר־יָהּ,
אֲדֹנָי מִי יַעֲמֹד: כִּי־עִמְּךָ הַסְּלִיחָה, לְמַעַן תִּוָּרֵא: קִוִּיתִי יהוה
קִוְּתָה נַפְשִׁי, וְלִדְבָרוֹ הוֹחָלְתִּי: נַפְשִׁי לַאדֹנָי, מִשֹּׁמְרִים לַבֹּקֶר,
שֹׁמְרִים לַבֹּקֶר: יַחֵל יִשְׂרָאֵל אֶל יהוה, כִּי־עִם־יהוה הַחֶסֶד,
וְהַרְבֵּה עִמּוֹ פְדוּת: וְהוּא יִפְדֶּה אֶת־יִשְׂרָאֵל, מִכֹּל עֲוֹנוֹתָיו:

חצי קדיש

ש״ץ: יִתְגַּדַּל וְיִתְקַדַּשׁ שְׁמֵהּ רַבָּא (קהל: אָמֵן)
בְּעָלְמָא דִּי בְרָא כִרְעוּתֵהּ
וְיַמְלִיךְ מַלְכוּתֵהּ
בְּחַיֵּיכוֹן וּבְיוֹמֵיכוֹן וּבְחַיֵּי דְכָל בֵּית יִשְׂרָאֵל
בַּעֲגָלָא וּבִזְמַן קָרִיב, וְאִמְרוּ אָמֵן. (קהל: אָמֵן)

קהל וש״ץ: יְהֵא שְׁמֵהּ רַבָּא מְבָרַךְ לְעָלַם וּלְעָלְמֵי עָלְמַיָּא.

ש״ץ: יִתְבָּרַךְ וְיִשְׁתַּבַּח וְיִתְפָּאַר וְיִתְרוֹמַם וְיִתְנַשֵּׂא
וְיִתְהַדָּר וְיִתְעַלֶּה וְיִתְהַלָּל
שְׁמֵהּ דְּקֻדְשָׁא בְּרִיךְ הוּא (קהל: בְּרִיךְ הוּא)
לְעֵלָּא מִן כָּל בִּרְכָתָא וְשִׁירָתָא, תֻּשְׁבְּחָתָא וְנֶחֱמָתָא
דַּאֲמִירָן בְּעָלְמָא, וְאִמְרוּ אָמֵן. (קהל: אָמֵן)

BLESSINGS OF THE SHEMA

The following blessing and response are said only in the presence of a minyan. They represent a formal summons to the congregation to engage in an act of collective prayer. The custom of bowing at this point is based on 1 Chronicles 29:20, "David said to the whole assembly, 'Now bless the LORD your God.' All the assembly blessed the LORD God of their fathers and bowed their heads low to the LORD and the King." The Leader says the following, bowing at "Bless," standing straight at "the LORD." The congregation, followed by the Leader, responds, bowing at "Bless," standing straight at "the LORD."

Leader: **BLESS**
the LORD, the blessed One.

Congregation: Bless the LORD, the blessed One,
for ever and all time.

Leader: Bless the LORD, the blessed One,
for ever and all time.

The custom is to sit from this point until the Amida, since the predominant emotion of this section of the prayers is love rather than awe. Conversation is forbidden until after the Amida.

בָּרוּךְ Blessed are You, LORD our God,
King of the Universe,
who forms light and creates darkness, Is. 45
makes peace and creates all.

הַמֵּאִיר In compassion He gives light to the earth
and its inhabitants,
and in His goodness continually renews the work of creation,
day after day.
How numerous are Your works, LORD; Ps. 104
You made them all in wisdom;
the earth is full of Your creations.
He is the King exalted alone since the beginning of time –
praised, glorified and elevated since the world began.

קריאת שמע וברכותיה

The following blessing and response are said only in the presence of a מנין*. They represent a formal summons to the* קהל *to engage in an act of collective prayer. The custom of bowing at this point is based on* דברי הימים א׳ כט כ*, "David said to the whole assembly, 'Now bless the* Lord *your God.' All the assembly blessed the* Lord *God of their fathers and bowed their heads low to the* Lord *and the King." The* שליח ציבור *says the following, bowing at* בָּרְכוּ*, standing straight at* ה׳*. The* קהל*, followed by the* שליח ציבור*, responds, bowing at* בָּרוּךְ*, standing straight at* ה׳*.*

ש״ץ: בָּרְכוּ
אֶת יהוה הַמְבֹרָךְ.

קהל: בָּרוּךְ יהוה הַמְבֹרָךְ לְעוֹלָם וָעֶד.

ש״ץ: בָּרוּךְ יהוה הַמְבֹרָךְ לְעוֹלָם וָעֶד.

The custom is to sit from this point until the עמידה*, since the predominant emotion of this section of the prayers is love rather than awe. Conversation is forbidden until after the* עמידה*.*

בָּרוּךְ אַתָּה יהוה אֱלֹהֵינוּ מֶלֶךְ הָעוֹלָם
יוֹצֵר אוֹר וּבוֹרֵא חֹשֶׁךְ ישעיה מה
עֹשֶׂה שָׁלוֹם וּבוֹרֵא אֶת הַכֹּל.

הַמֵּאִיר לָאָרֶץ וְלַדָּרִים עָלֶיהָ בְּרַחֲמִים
וּבְטוּבוֹ מְחַדֵּשׁ בְּכָל יוֹם תָּמִיד מַעֲשֵׂה בְרֵאשִׁית.
מָה־רַבּוּ מַעֲשֶׂיךָ יהוה, כֻּלָּם בְּחָכְמָה עָשִׂיתָ תהלים קד
מָלְאָה הָאָרֶץ קִנְיָנֶךָ:
הַמֶּלֶךְ הַמְרוֹמָם לְבַדּוֹ מֵאָז
הַמְשֻׁבָּח וְהַמְפֹאָר וְהַמִּתְנַשֵּׂא מִימוֹת עוֹלָם.

Eternal God,
in Your great compassion, have compassion on us,
Lord of our strength, Rock of our refuge,
Shield of our salvation, You are our stronghold.
The blessed God,
great in knowledge,
prepared and made the rays of the sun.
He who is good formed glory for His name,
surrounding His power with radiant stars.
The leaders of His hosts,
the holy ones,
exalt the Almighty,
constantly proclaiming God's glory and holiness.
Be blessed, Lord our God,
for the magnificence of Your handiwork
and for the radiant lights You have made.
May they glorify You, Selah!

תִּתְבָּרַךְ May You be blessed,
our Rock, King and Redeemer,
Creator of holy beings.
May Your name be praised for ever,
our King, Creator of the ministering angels,
all of whom stand in the universe's heights,
proclaiming together,
in awe, aloud,
the words of the living God, the eternal King.
They are all beloved, all pure, all mighty,
and all perform in awe and reverence the will of their Maker.
▸ All open their mouths in holiness and purity,
with song and psalm,
and bless, praise, glorify,
revere, sanctify and declare the sovereignty of – ◂
The name of the great, mighty and awesome God and King,
holy is He.

אֱלֹהֵי עוֹלָם
בְּרַחֲמֶיךָ הָרַבִּים רַחֵם עָלֵינוּ
אֲדוֹן עֻזֵּנוּ, צוּר מִשְׂגַּבֵּנוּ
מָגֵן יִשְׁעֵנוּ, מִשְׂגָּב בַּעֲדֵנוּ.
אֵל בָּרוּךְ גְּדוֹל דֵּעָה, הֵכִין וּפָעַל זָהֳרֵי חַמָּה
טוֹב יָצַר כָּבוֹד לִשְׁמוֹ, מְאוֹרוֹת נָתַן סְבִיבוֹת עֻזּוֹ
פִּנּוֹת צְבָאָיו קְדוֹשִׁים, רוֹמְמֵי שַׁדַּי
תָּמִיד מְסַפְּרִים כְּבוֹד אֵל וּקְדֻשָּׁתוֹ.
תִּתְבָּרַךְ יהוה אֱלֹהֵינוּ, עַל שֶׁבַח מַעֲשֵׂה יָדֶיךָ.
וְעַל מְאוֹרֵי אוֹר שֶׁעָשִׂיתָ, יְפָאֲרוּךָ סֶּלָה.

תִּתְבָּרַךְ
צוּרֵנוּ מַלְכֵּנוּ וְגוֹאֲלֵנוּ, בּוֹרֵא קְדוֹשִׁים
יִשְׁתַּבַּח שִׁמְךָ לָעַד
מַלְכֵּנוּ, יוֹצֵר מְשָׁרְתִים
וַאֲשֶׁר מְשָׁרְתָיו כֻּלָּם עוֹמְדִים בְּרוּם עוֹלָם
וּמַשְׁמִיעִים בְּיִרְאָה יַחַד בְּקוֹל
דִּבְרֵי אֱלֹהִים חַיִּים וּמֶלֶךְ עוֹלָם.
כֻּלָּם אֲהוּבִים, כֻּלָּם בְּרוּרִים, כֻּלָּם גִּבּוֹרִים
וְכֻלָּם עוֹשִׂים בְּאֵימָה וּבְיִרְאָה רְצוֹן קוֹנָם
◂ וְכֻלָּם פּוֹתְחִים אֶת פִּיהֶם בִּקְדֻשָּׁה וּבְטָהֳרָה
בְּשִׁירָה וּבְזִמְרָה
וּמְבָרְכִים וּמְשַׁבְּחִים וּמְפָאֲרִים
◂ וּמַעֲרִיצִים וּמַקְדִּישִׁים וּמַמְלִיכִים
אֶת שֵׁם הָאֵל הַמֶּלֶךְ הַגָּדוֹל, הַגִּבּוֹר וְהַנּוֹרָא
קָדוֹשׁ הוּא.

▸ All accept on themselves,
one from another,
the yoke of the kingdom of heaven,
granting permission to one another
to sanctify the One who formed them,
in serene spirit,
pure speech and sweet melody.
All, as one,
proclaim His holiness,
saying in awe:

All say aloud: Holy, holy, holy is the LORD of hosts; *Is. 6*
the whole world is filled with His glory.

▸ Then the Ophanim and the Holy Ḥayyot,
with a roar of noise,
raise themselves toward the Seraphim and,
facing them, give praise, saying:

All say aloud: Blessed is the LORD's glory from His place. *Ezek. 3*

לְאֵל To the blessed God they offer melodies.
To the King, living and eternal God,
they say psalms and proclaim praises.
For it is He alone
who does mighty deeds and creates new things,
who is Master of battles, and sows righteousness,
who makes salvation grow and creates cures,
who is revered in praises, LORD of wonders,
who in His goodness,
continually renews the work of creation, day after day,
as it is said:
"[Praise] Him who made the great lights, *Ps. 136*
for His love endures for ever."

▸ May You make a new light shine over Zion,
and may we all soon be worthy of its light.
Blessed are You, LORD, who forms the radiant lights.

› וְכֻלָּם מְקַבְּלִים עֲלֵיהֶם עֹל מַלְכוּת שָׁמַיִם זֶה מִזֶּה
וְנוֹתְנִים רְשׁוּת זֶה לָזֶה
לְהַקְדִּישׁ לְיוֹצְרָם בְּנַחַת רוּחַ
בְּשָׂפָה בְרוּרָה וּבִנְעִימָה
קְדֻשָּׁה כֻּלָּם כְּאֶחָד
עוֹנִים וְאוֹמְרִים בְּיִרְאָה

All say aloud קָדוֹשׁ, קָדוֹשׁ, קָדוֹשׁ יהוה צְבָאוֹת ישעיה ו
מְלֹא כָל־הָאָרֶץ כְּבוֹדוֹ:

› וְהָאוֹפַנִּים וְחַיּוֹת הַקֹּדֶשׁ
בְּרַעַשׁ גָּדוֹל מִתְנַשְּׂאִים לְעֻמַּת שְׂרָפִים
לְעֻמָּתָם מְשַׁבְּחִים וְאוֹמְרִים

All say aloud בָּרוּךְ כְּבוֹד־יהוה מִמְּקוֹמוֹ: יחזקאל ג

לָאֵל בָּרוּךְ נְעִימוֹת יִתֵּנוּ, לַמֶּלֶךְ אֵל חַי וְקַיָּם
זְמִירוֹת יֹאמֵרוּ וְתִשְׁבָּחוֹת יַשְׁמִיעוּ
כִּי הוּא לְבַדּוֹ
פּוֹעֵל גְּבוּרוֹת, עוֹשֶׂה חֲדָשׁוֹת
בַּעַל מִלְחָמוֹת, זוֹרֵעַ צְדָקוֹת
מַצְמִיחַ יְשׁוּעוֹת, בּוֹרֵא רְפוּאוֹת
נוֹרָא תְהִלּוֹת, אֲדוֹן הַנִּפְלָאוֹת
הַמְחַדֵּשׁ בְּטוּבוֹ בְּכָל יוֹם תָּמִיד מַעֲשֵׂה בְרֵאשִׁית
כָּאָמוּר
לְעֹשֵׂה אוֹרִים גְּדֹלִים, כִּי לְעוֹלָם חַסְדּוֹ: תהלים קלו
› אוֹר חָדָשׁ עַל צִיּוֹן תָּאִיר וְנִזְכֶּה כֻלָּנוּ מְהֵרָה לְאוֹרוֹ.
בָּרוּךְ אַתָּה יהוה, יוֹצֵר הַמְּאוֹרוֹת.

אַהֲבָה You have loved us with great love, LORD our God,
and with surpassing compassion
have You had compassion on us.
Our Father, our King,
for the sake of our ancestors who trusted in You,
and to whom You taught the laws of life,
be gracious also to us and teach us.
Our Father, compassionate Father,
ever compassionate,
have compassion on us.
Instill in our hearts
the desire to understand and discern,
to listen, learn and teach,
to observe, perform and fulfill
all the teachings of Your Torah in love.
Enlighten our eyes in Your Torah
and let our hearts cling to Your commandments.
Unite our hearts to love and revere Your name,
so that we may never be ashamed.
And because we have trusted
in Your holy, great and revered name,
may we be glad and rejoice in Your salvation.

At this point, gather the four tzitziot of the tallit, holding them in the left hand.

Bring us back in peace
from the four quarters of the earth
and lead us upright to our land.
▸ For You are a God who performs acts of salvation,
and You chose us from all peoples and tongues,
bringing us close to Your great name for ever in truth,
that we may thank You
and proclaim Your Oneness in love.
Blessed are You, LORD,
who chooses His people Israel in love.

אַהֲבָה רַבָּה אֲהַבְתָּנוּ, יהוה אֱלֹהֵינוּ
חֶמְלָה גְדוֹלָה וִיתֵרָה חָמַלְתָּ עָלֵינוּ.
אָבִינוּ מַלְכֵּנוּ
בַּעֲבוּר אֲבוֹתֵינוּ שֶׁבָּטְחוּ בְךָ
וַתְּלַמְּדֵם חֻקֵּי חַיִּים
כֵּן תְּחָנֵּנוּ וּתְלַמְּדֵנוּ.
אָבִינוּ, הָאָב הָרַחֲמָן, הַמְרַחֵם
רַחֵם עָלֵינוּ
וְתֵן בְּלִבֵּנוּ לְהָבִין וּלְהַשְׂכִּיל
לִשְׁמֹעַ, לִלְמֹד וּלְלַמֵּד, לִשְׁמֹר וְלַעֲשׂוֹת, וּלְקַיֵּם
אֶת כָּל דִּבְרֵי תַלְמוּד תּוֹרָתֶךָ בְּאַהֲבָה.
וְהָאֵר עֵינֵינוּ בְּתוֹרָתֶךָ, וְדַבֵּק לִבֵּנוּ בְּמִצְוֹתֶיךָ
וְיַחֵד לְבָבֵנוּ לְאַהֲבָה וּלְיִרְאָה אֶת שְׁמֶךָ
וְלֹא נֵבוֹשׁ לְעוֹלָם וָעֶד.
כִּי בְשֵׁם קָדְשְׁךָ הַגָּדוֹל וְהַנּוֹרָא בָּטָחְנוּ
נָגִילָה וְנִשְׂמְחָה בִּישׁוּעָתֶךָ.

At this point, gather the four ציצית *of the* טלית*, holding them in the left hand.*

וַהֲבִיאֵנוּ לְשָׁלוֹם מֵאַרְבַּע כַּנְפוֹת הָאָרֶץ
וְתוֹלִיכֵנוּ קוֹמְמִיּוּת לְאַרְצֵנוּ.
◂ כִּי אֵל פּוֹעֵל יְשׁוּעוֹת אָתָּה
וּבָנוּ בָחַרְתָּ מִכָּל עַם וְלָשׁוֹן
וְקֵרַבְתָּנוּ לְשִׁמְךָ הַגָּדוֹל סֶלָה, בֶּאֱמֶת
לְהוֹדוֹת לְךָ וּלְיַחֶדְךָ בְּאַהֲבָה.
בָּרוּךְ אַתָּה יהוה, הַבּוֹחֵר בְּעַמּוֹ יִשְׂרָאֵל בְּאַהֲבָה.

The Shema must be said with intense concentration. In the first paragraph one should accept, with love, the sovereignty of God; in the second, the mitzvot as the will of God. The end of the third paragraph constitutes fulfillment of the mitzva to remember, morning and evening, the exodus from Egypt.
When not praying with a minyan, say:

God, faithful King!

The following verse should be said aloud, while covering the eyes with the right hand:

Listen, Israel: the LORD is our God, the LORD is One. *Deut. 6*

Quietly: Blessed be the name of His glorious kingdom for ever and all time.

Touch the hand-tefillin at ° and the head-tefillin at °°.

וְאָהַבְתָּ Love the LORD your God with all your heart, with all your soul, and with all your might. These words which I command you today shall be on your heart. Teach them repeatedly to your children, speaking of them when you sit at home and when you travel on the way, when you lie down and when you rise. °Bind them as a sign on your hand, and °°they shall be an emblem between your eyes. Write them on the doorposts of your house and gates. *Deut. 6*

Touch the hand-tefillin at ° and the head-tefillin at °°.

וְהָיָה If you indeed heed My commandments with which I charge you today, to love the LORD your God and worship Him with all your heart and with all your soul, I will give rain in your land in its season, the early and late rain; and you shall gather in your grain, wine and oil. I will give grass in your field for your cattle, and you shall eat and be satisfied. Be careful lest your heart be tempted and you go astray and worship other gods, bowing down to them. Then the LORD's anger will flare against you and He will close the heavens so that there will be no rain. The land will not yield its crops, and you will perish swiftly from the good land that the LORD is giving you. Therefore, set these, My words, on your heart and soul. °Bind them as a sign on your hand, °°and they shall be an emblem between your eyes. Teach them to your children, speaking of them *Deut. 11*

The שמע *must be said with intense concentration. In the first paragraph one should accept, with love, the sovereignty of God; in the second, the* מצוות *as the will of God. The end of the third paragraph constitutes fulfillment of the* מצווה *to remember, morning and evening, the exodus from Egypt.*
When not praying with a מנין*, say:*

אֵל מֶלֶךְ נֶאֱמָן

The following verse should be said aloud, while covering the eyes with the right hand:

שְׁמַע יִשְׂרָאֵל, יהוה אֱלֹהֵינוּ, יהוה | אֶחָד: דברים ו

Quietly בָּרוּךְ שֵׁם כְּבוֹד מַלְכוּתוֹ לְעוֹלָם וָעֶד.

Touch the תפילין של יד *at* ° *and the* תפילין של ראש *at* °°.

וְאָהַבְתָּ אֵת יהוה אֱלֹהֶיךָ, בְּכָל־לְבָבְךָ וּבְכָל־נַפְשְׁךָ וּבְכָל־מְאֹדֶךָ: וְהָיוּ הַדְּבָרִים הָאֵלֶּה, אֲשֶׁר אָנֹכִי מְצַוְּךָ הַיּוֹם, עַל־לְבָבֶךָ: וְשִׁנַּנְתָּם לְבָנֶיךָ וְדִבַּרְתָּ בָּם, בְּשִׁבְתְּךָ בְּבֵיתֶךָ וּבְלֶכְתְּךָ בַדֶּרֶךְ, וּבְשָׁכְבְּךָ וּבְקוּמֶךָ: °וּקְשַׁרְתָּם לְאוֹת עַל־יָדֶךָ °°וְהָיוּ לְטֹטָפֹת בֵּין עֵינֶיךָ: וּכְתַבְתָּם עַל־מְזֻזוֹת בֵּיתֶךָ וּבִשְׁעָרֶיךָ: דברים ו

Touch the תפילין של יד *at* ° *and the* תפילין של ראש *at* °°.

וְהָיָה אִם־שָׁמֹעַ תִּשְׁמְעוּ אֶל־מִצְוֺתַי אֲשֶׁר אָנֹכִי מְצַוֶּה אֶתְכֶם הַיּוֹם, לְאַהֲבָה אֶת־יהוה אֱלֹהֵיכֶם וּלְעָבְדוֹ, בְּכָל־לְבַבְכֶם וּבְכָל־נַפְשְׁכֶם: וְנָתַתִּי מְטַר־אַרְצְכֶם בְּעִתּוֹ, יוֹרֶה וּמַלְקוֹשׁ, וְאָסַפְתָּ דְגָנֶךָ וְתִירֹשְׁךָ וְיִצְהָרֶךָ: וְנָתַתִּי עֵשֶׂב בְּשָׂדְךָ לִבְהֶמְתֶּךָ, וְאָכַלְתָּ וְשָׂבָעְתָּ: הִשָּׁמְרוּ לָכֶם פֶּן־יִפְתֶּה לְבַבְכֶם, וְסַרְתֶּם וַעֲבַדְתֶּם אֱלֹהִים אֲחֵרִים וְהִשְׁתַּחֲוִיתֶם לָהֶם: וְחָרָה אַף־יהוה בָּכֶם, וְעָצַר אֶת־הַשָּׁמַיִם וְלֹא־יִהְיֶה מָטָר, וְהָאֲדָמָה לֹא תִתֵּן אֶת־יְבוּלָהּ, וַאֲבַדְתֶּם מְהֵרָה מֵעַל הָאָרֶץ הַטֹּבָה אֲשֶׁר יהוה נֹתֵן לָכֶם: וְשַׂמְתֶּם אֶת־דְּבָרַי אֵלֶּה עַל־לְבַבְכֶם וְעַל־נַפְשְׁכֶם, °וּקְשַׁרְתֶּם אֹתָם לְאוֹת עַל־יֶדְכֶם, °°וְהָיוּ לְטוֹטָפֹת בֵּין עֵינֵיכֶם: וְלִמַּדְתֶּם דברים יא

when you sit at home and when you travel on the way, when you lie down and when you rise. Write them on the doorposts of your house and gates, so that you and your children may live long in the land that the LORD swore to your ancestors to give them, for as long as the heavens are above the earth.

Hold the tzitziot in the right hand also (some transfer to the right hand), kissing them at °.

וַיֹּאמֶר The LORD spoke to Moses, saying: Speak to the Israelites *Num. 15*
and tell them to make °tassels on the corners of their garments for all generations. They shall attach to the °tassel at each corner a thread of blue. This shall be your °tassel, and you shall see it and remember all of the LORD's commandments and keep them, not straying after your heart and after your eyes, following your own sinful desires. Thus you will be reminded to keep all My commandments, and be holy to your God. I am the LORD your God, who brought you out of the land of Egypt to be your God. I am the LORD your God.

°True –

The Leader repeats:

▸ The LORD your God is true –

וְיַצִּיב And firm, established and enduring,
right, faithful,
beloved, cherished, delightful, pleasant,
awesome, mighty, perfect, accepted,
good and beautiful
is this faith for us for ever.

True is the eternal God, our King,
Rock of Jacob,
Shield of our salvation.
He exists and His name exists
through all generations.
His throne is established,
His kingship and faithfulness endure for ever.

אֹתָם אֶת־בְּנֵיכֶם לְדַבֵּר בָּם, בְּשִׁבְתְּךָ בְּבֵיתֶךָ וּבְלֶכְתְּךָ בַדֶּרֶךְ,
וּבְשָׁכְבְּךָ וּבְקוּמֶךָ: וּכְתַבְתָּם עַל־מְזוּזוֹת בֵּיתֶךָ וּבִשְׁעָרֶיךָ: לְמַעַן
יִרְבּוּ יְמֵיכֶם וִימֵי בְנֵיכֶם עַל הָאֲדָמָה אֲשֶׁר נִשְׁבַּע יהוה לַאֲבֹתֵיכֶם
לָתֵת לָהֶם, כִּימֵי הַשָּׁמַיִם עַל־הָאָרֶץ:

Hold the ציציות *in the right hand also (some transfer to the right hand), kissing them at °.*

וַיֹּאמֶר יהוה אֶל־מֹשֶׁה לֵּאמֹר: דַּבֵּר אֶל־בְּנֵי יִשְׂרָאֵל וְאָמַרְתָּ במדבר טו
אֲלֵהֶם, וְעָשׂוּ לָהֶם °צִיצִת עַל־כַּנְפֵי בִגְדֵיהֶם לְדֹרֹתָם, וְנָתְנוּ
°עַל־צִיצִת הַכָּנָף פְּתִיל תְּכֵלֶת: וְהָיָה לָכֶם °לְצִיצִת, וּרְאִיתֶם
אֹתוֹ וּזְכַרְתֶּם אֶת־כָּל־מִצְוֺת יהוה וַעֲשִׂיתֶם אֹתָם, וְלֹא תָתוּרוּ
אַחֲרֵי לְבַבְכֶם וְאַחֲרֵי עֵינֵיכֶם, אֲשֶׁר־אַתֶּם זֹנִים אַחֲרֵיהֶם: לְמַעַן
תִּזְכְּרוּ וַעֲשִׂיתֶם אֶת־כָּל־מִצְוֺתָי, וִהְיִיתֶם קְדֹשִׁים לֵאלֹהֵיכֶם: אֲנִי
יהוה אֱלֹהֵיכֶם, אֲשֶׁר הוֹצֵאתִי אֶתְכֶם מֵאֶרֶץ מִצְרַיִם, לִהְיוֹת לָכֶם
לֵאלֹהִים, אֲנִי יהוה אֱלֹהֵיכֶם:

°אֱמֶת

The שליח ציבור *repeats:*

› יהוה אֱלֹהֵיכֶם אֱמֶת

וְיַצִּיב, וְנָכוֹן וְקַיָּם, וְיָשָׁר וְנֶאֱמָן
וְאָהוּב וְחָבִיב, וְנֶחְמָד וְנָעִים
וְנוֹרָא וְאַדִּיר, וּמְתֻקָּן וּמְקֻבָּל, וְטוֹב וְיָפֶה
הַדָּבָר הַזֶּה עָלֵינוּ לְעוֹלָם וָעֶד.

אֱמֶת אֱלֹהֵי עוֹלָם מַלְכֵּנוּ
צוּר יַעֲקֹב מָגֵן יִשְׁעֵנוּ
לְדוֹר וָדוֹר הוּא קַיָּם וּשְׁמוֹ קַיָּם
וְכִסְאוֹ נָכוֹן, וּמַלְכוּתוֹ וֶאֱמוּנָתוֹ לָעַד קַיֶּמֶת.

At °, kiss the tzitziot and release them.

His words live and persist,
faithful and desirable
°for ever and all time.
▸ So they were for our ancestors,
so they are for us,
and so they will be for our children
and all our generations
and for all future generations
of the seed of Israel, Your servants. ◂
For the early and the later generations
this faith has proved good
and enduring for ever –
True and faithful, an irrevocable law.

True You are the LORD: our God and God of our ancestors,
▸ our King and King of our ancestors,
our Redeemer and Redeemer of our ancestors,
our Maker,
Rock of our salvation,
our Deliverer and Rescuer:
this has ever been Your name.
There is no God but You.

עֶזְרַת You have always been the help of our ancestors,
Shield and Savior of their children after them
in every generation.
Your dwelling is in the heights of the universe,
and Your judgments and righteousness
reach to the ends of the earth.

Happy is the one who obeys Your commandments
and takes to heart Your teaching and Your word.

True You are the Master of Your people
and a mighty King who pleads their cause.

At °, kiss the ציציות and release them.

וּדְבָרָיו חָיִים וְקַיָּמִים
נֶאֱמָנִים וְנֶחֱמָדִים
°לָעַד וּלְעוֹלְמֵי עוֹלָמִים
◂ עַל אֲבוֹתֵינוּ וְעָלֵינוּ
עַל בָּנֵינוּ וְעַל דּוֹרוֹתֵינוּ
וְעַל כָּל דּוֹרוֹת זֶרַע יִשְׂרָאֵל עֲבָדֶיךָ. ◂
עַל הָרִאשׁוֹנִים וְעַל הָאַחֲרוֹנִים
דָּבָר טוֹב וְקַיָּם לְעוֹלָם וָעֶד
אֱמֶת וֶאֱמוּנָה, חֹק וְלֹא יַעֲבֹר.

אֱמֶת שָׁאַתָּה הוּא יהוה אֱלֹהֵינוּ וֵאלֹהֵי אֲבוֹתֵינוּ
◂ מַלְכֵּנוּ מֶלֶךְ אֲבוֹתֵינוּ
גּוֹאֲלֵנוּ גּוֹאֵל אֲבוֹתֵינוּ
יוֹצְרֵנוּ צוּר יְשׁוּעָתֵנוּ
פּוֹדֵנוּ וּמַצִּילֵנוּ מֵעוֹלָם שְׁמֶךָ
אֵין אֱלֹהִים זוּלָתֶךָ.

עֶזְרַת אֲבוֹתֵינוּ אַתָּה הוּא מֵעוֹלָם
מָגֵן וּמוֹשִׁיעַ לִבְנֵיהֶם אַחֲרֵיהֶם בְּכָל דּוֹר וָדוֹר.
בְּרוּם עוֹלָם מוֹשָׁבֶךָ
וּמִשְׁפָּטֶיךָ וְצִדְקָתְךָ עַד אַפְסֵי אָרֶץ.
אַשְׁרֵי אִישׁ שֶׁיִּשְׁמַע לְמִצְוֹתֶיךָ
וְתוֹרָתְךָ וּדְבָרְךָ יָשִׂים עַל לִבּוֹ.
אֱמֶת אַתָּה הוּא אָדוֹן לְעַמֶּךָ
וּמֶלֶךְ גִּבּוֹר לָרִיב רִיבָם.

True You are the first and You are the last.
Beside You, we have no king, redeemer or savior.

From Egypt You redeemed us,
Lord our God,
and from the slave-house You delivered us.
All their firstborn You killed,
but Your firstborn You redeemed.
You split the Sea of Reeds
and drowned the arrogant.
You brought Your beloved ones across.
The water covered their foes; *Ps. 106*
not one of them was left.

For this, the beloved ones praised
and exalted God,
the cherished ones sang psalms, songs and praises,
blessings and thanksgivings to the King,
the living and enduring God.
High and exalted, great and awesome,
He humbles the haughty and raises the lowly,
freeing captives and redeeming those in need,
helping the poor
and answering His people when they cry out to Him.

Stand in preparation for the Amida.
Take three steps back before beginning the Amida.

▸ Praises to God Most High,
the Blessed One who is blessed.
Moses and the children of Israel
recited to You a song with great joy,
and they all exclaimed:

"Who is like You, Lord, among the mighty? *Ex. 15*
Who is like You, majestic in holiness,
awesome in praises, doing wonders?"

אֱמֶת אַתָּה הוּא רִאשׁוֹן וְאַתָּה הוּא אַחֲרוֹן
וּמִבַּלְעָדֶיךָ אֵין לָנוּ מֶלֶךְ גּוֹאֵל וּמוֹשִׁיעַ.
מִמִּצְרַיִם גְּאַלְתָּנוּ, יהוה אֱלֹהֵינוּ
וּמִבֵּית עֲבָדִים פְּדִיתָנוּ
כָּל בְּכוֹרֵיהֶם הָרָגְתָּ, וּבְכוֹרְךָ גָּאָלְתָּ
וְיַם סוּף בָּקַעְתָּ
וְזֵדִים טִבַּעְתָּ
וִידִידִים הֶעֱבַרְתָּ
וַיְכַסּוּ־מַיִם צָרֵיהֶם, אֶחָד מֵהֶם לֹא נוֹתָר: תהלים קו

עַל זֹאת שִׁבְּחוּ אֲהוּבִים, וְרוֹמְמוּ אֵל
וְנָתְנוּ יְדִידִים זְמִירוֹת, שִׁירוֹת וְתִשְׁבָּחוֹת
בְּרָכוֹת וְהוֹדָאוֹת לְמֶלֶךְ אֵל חַי וְקַיָּם
רָם וְנִשָּׂא, גָּדוֹל וְנוֹרָא
מַשְׁפִּיל גֵּאִים וּמַגְבִּיהַ שְׁפָלִים
מוֹצִיא אֲסִירִים, וּפוֹדֶה עֲנָוִים וְעוֹזֵר דַּלִּים
וְעוֹנֶה לְעַמּוֹ בְּעֵת שַׁוְּעָם אֵלָיו.

Stand in preparation for the עמידה. Take three steps back before beginning the עמידה.

◂ תְּהִלּוֹת לְאֵל עֶלְיוֹן, בָּרוּךְ הוּא וּמְבֹרָךְ
מֹשֶׁה וּבְנֵי יִשְׂרָאֵל
לְךָ עָנוּ שִׁירָה בְּשִׂמְחָה רַבָּה
וְאָמְרוּ כֻלָּם
מִי־כָמֹכָה בָּאֵלִם, יהוה שמות טו
מִי כָּמֹכָה נֶאְדָּר בַּקֹּדֶשׁ
נוֹרָא תְהִלֹּת, עֹשֵׂה פֶלֶא:

▸ With a new song, the redeemed people praised
Your name at the seashore.
Together they all gave thanks,
proclaimed Your kingship,
and declared:
"The LORD shall reign for ever and ever." *Ex. 15*

Congregants should end the following blessing together with the Leader so as to be able to move directly from the words "redeemed Israel" to the Amida, without the interruption of saying Amen.

▸ צוּר יִשְׂרָאֵל ▸ Rock of Israel! Arise to the help of Israel.
Deliver, as You promised, Judah and Israel.
Our Redeemer, the LORD of hosts is His name, *Is. 47*
the Holy One of Israel.
Blessed are You, LORD, who redeemed Israel.

THE AMIDA

The following prayer, until "in former years" on page 656, is said standing with feet together in imitation of the angels in Ezekiel's vision (Ezek. 1:7). The Amida is said silently, following the precedent of Hannah when she prayed for a child (1 Sam. 1:13). If there is a minyan, it is repeated aloud by the Leader. Take three steps forward, as if formally entering the place of the Divine Presence. At the points indicated by ▾, bend the knees at the first word, bow at the second, and stand straight before saying God's name.

O LORD, open my lips, *Ps. 51*
so that my mouth may declare Your praise.

PATRIARCHS

▾בָּרוּךְ Blessed are You, LORD our God and God of our fathers,
God of Abraham, God of Isaac and God of Jacob;
the great, mighty and awesome God, God Most High,
who bestows acts of loving-kindness and creates all,
who remembers the loving-kindness of the fathers and will bring
a Redeemer to their children's children
for the sake of His name, in love.
King, Helper, Savior, Shield:
▾Blessed are You,
LORD, Shield of Abraham.

◂ שִׁירָה חֲדָשָׁה שִׁבְּחוּ גְאוּלִים
לְשִׁמְךָ עַל שְׂפַת הַיָּם
יַחַד כֻּלָּם הוֹדוּ וְהִמְלִיכוּ
וְאָמְרוּ
יהוה יִמְלֹךְ לְעֹלָם וָעֶד: שמות טו

The קהל *should end the following blessing together with the* שליח ציבור *so as to be able to move directly from the words* גָּאַל יִשְׂרָאֵל *to the* עמידה*, without the interruption of saying* אמן*.*

◂ צוּר יִשְׂרָאֵל, קוּמָה בְּעֶזְרַת יִשְׂרָאֵל
וּפְדֵה כִנְאֻמֶךָ יְהוּדָה וְיִשְׂרָאֵל.
גֹּאֲלֵנוּ יהוה צְבָאוֹת שְׁמוֹ, קְדוֹשׁ יִשְׂרָאֵל: ישעיה מז
בָּרוּךְ אַתָּה יהוה, גָּאַל יִשְׂרָאֵל.

עמידה

The following prayer, until קַדְמֹנִיּוֹת *on page 657, is said standing with feet together in imitation of the angels in Ezekiel's vision (*יחזקאל א, ז*). The* עמידה *is said silently, following the precedent of Hannah when she prayed for a child (*שמואל א׳ א, יג*). If there is a* מנין*, it is repeated aloud by the* שליח ציבור*. Take three steps forward, as if formally entering the place of the Divine Presence. At the points indicated by* ᵀ*, bend the knees at the first word, bow at the second, and stand straight before saying God's name.*

אֲדֹנָי, שְׂפָתַי תִּפְתָּח, וּפִי יַגִּיד תְּהִלָּתֶךָ: תהלים נא

אבות

ᵀבָּרוּךְ אַתָּה יהוה, אֱלֹהֵינוּ וֵאלֹהֵי אֲבוֹתֵינוּ
אֱלֹהֵי אַבְרָהָם, אֱלֹהֵי יִצְחָק, וֵאלֹהֵי יַעֲקֹב
הָאֵל הַגָּדוֹל הַגִּבּוֹר וְהַנּוֹרָא, אֵל עֶלְיוֹן
גּוֹמֵל חֲסָדִים טוֹבִים, וְקֹנֵה הַכֹּל
וְזוֹכֵר חַסְדֵי אָבוֹת
וּמֵבִיא גוֹאֵל לִבְנֵי בְנֵיהֶם לְמַעַן שְׁמוֹ בְּאַהֲבָה.
מֶלֶךְ עוֹזֵר וּמוֹשִׁיעַ וּמָגֵן.
ᵀבָּרוּךְ אַתָּה יהוה, מָגֵן אַבְרָהָם.

DIVINE MIGHT

אַתָּה גִּבּוֹר You are eternally mighty, LORD.
You give life to the dead and have great power to save.

In Israel: He causes the dew to fall.

He sustains the living with loving-kindness,
and with great compassion revives the dead.
He supports the fallen, heals the sick, sets captives free,
and keeps His faith with those who sleep in the dust.
Who is like You, Master of might, and who can compare to You,
O King who brings death and gives life,
and makes salvation grow?
Faithful are You to revive the dead.
Blessed are You, LORD, who revives the dead.

When saying the Amida silently, continue with "You are holy" on the next page.

KEDUSHA

During the Leader's Repetition, the following is said standing with feet together, rising on the toes at the words indicated by ▲.

Cong. then Leader: נְקַדֵּשׁ We will sanctify Your name on earth,
as they sanctify it in the highest heavens,
as is written by Your prophet,
"And they [the angels] call to one another saying: *Is. 6*

Cong. then Leader: ▲Holy, ▲holy, ▲holy is the LORD of hosts;
the whole world is filled with His glory."
Those facing them say "Blessed –"

Cong. then Leader: "▲Blessed is the LORD's glory from His place." *Ezek. 3*
And in Your holy Writings it is written thus:

Cong. then Leader: "▲The LORD shall reign for ever. He is your God, Zion, *Ps. 146*
from generation to generation, Halleluya!"

Leader: From generation to generation we will declare Your greatness,
and we will proclaim Your holiness for evermore.
Your praise, our God, shall not leave our mouth forever,
for You, God, are a great and holy King.
Blessed are You, LORD, the holy God.

The Leader continues with "You grace humanity" on the next page.

גבורות

אַתָּה גִּבּוֹר לְעוֹלָם, אֲדֹנָי, מְחַיֵּה מֵתִים אַתָּה, רַב לְהוֹשִׁיעַ

In ארץ ישראל מוֹרִיד הַטָּל

מְכַלְכֵּל חַיִּים בְּחֶסֶד, מְחַיֵּה מֵתִים בְּרַחֲמִים רַבִּים
סוֹמֵךְ נוֹפְלִים, וְרוֹפֵא חוֹלִים, וּמַתִּיר אֲסוּרִים
וּמְקַיֵּם אֱמוּנָתוֹ לִישֵׁנֵי עָפָר.
מִי כָמְוֹךָ, בַּעַל גְּבוּרוֹת, וּמִי דּוֹמֶה לָּךְ
מֶלֶךְ, מֵמִית וּמְחַיֶּה וּמַצְמִיחַ יְשׁוּעָה.
וְנֶאֱמָן אַתָּה לְהַחֲיוֹת מֵתִים.
בָּרוּךְ אַתָּה יהוה, מְחַיֵּה הַמֵּתִים.

When saying the עמידה *silently, continue with* אַתָּה קָדוֹשׁ *on the next page.*

קדושה

During חזרת הש״ץ*, the following is said standing with feet together, rising on the toes at the words indicated by* ^.

then קהל ש״ץ: נְקַדֵּשׁ אֶת שִׁמְךָ בָּעוֹלָם, כְּשֵׁם שֶׁמַּקְדִּישִׁים אוֹתוֹ בִּשְׁמֵי מָרוֹם
כַּכָּתוּב עַל יַד נְבִיאֶךָ, וְקָרָא זֶה אֶל־זֶה וְאָמַר ישעיה ו

then קהל ש״ץ: ^קָדוֹשׁ, ^קָדוֹשׁ, ^קָדוֹשׁ, יהוה צְבָאוֹת, מְלֹא כָל־הָאָרֶץ כְּבוֹדוֹ:
לְעֻמָּתָם בָּרוּךְ יֹאמֵרוּ

then קהל ש״ץ: ^בָּרוּךְ כְּבוֹד־יהוה מִמְּקוֹמוֹ: יחזקאל ג
וּבְדִבְרֵי קָדְשְׁךָ כָּתוּב לֵאמֹר

then קהל ש״ץ: ^יִמְלֹךְ יהוה לְעוֹלָם, אֱלֹהַיִךְ צִיּוֹן לְדֹר וָדֹר, הַלְלוּיָהּ: תהלים קמו

ש״ץ: לְדוֹר וָדוֹר נַגִּיד גָּדְלֶךָ, וּלְנֵצַח נְצָחִים קְדֻשָּׁתְךָ נַקְדִּישׁ
וְשִׁבְחֲךָ אֱלֹהֵינוּ מִפִּינוּ לֹא יָמוּשׁ לְעוֹלָם וָעֶד
כִּי אֵל מֶלֶךְ גָּדוֹל וְקָדוֹשׁ אָתָּה.
בָּרוּךְ אַתָּה יהוה, הָאֵל הַקָּדוֹשׁ.

The שליח ציבור *continues with* אַתָּה חוֹנֵן *on the next page.*

HOLINESS

אַתָּה קָדוֹשׁ You are holy and Your name is holy,
and holy ones praise You daily, Selah!
Blessed are You, LORD,
the holy God.

KNOWLEDGE

אַתָּה חוֹנֵן You grace humanity with knowledge
and teach mortals understanding.
Grace us with the knowledge, understanding
and discernment that come from You.
Blessed are You, LORD,
who graciously grants knowledge.

REPENTANCE

הֲשִׁיבֵנוּ Bring us back, our Father, to Your Torah.
Draw us near, our King, to Your service.
Lead us back to You in perfect repentance.
Blessed are You,
LORD, who desires repentance.

FORGIVENESS

Strike the left side of the chest at °.

סְלַח לָנוּ Forgive us, our Father, for we have °sinned.
Pardon us, our King, for we have °transgressed;
for You pardon and forgive.
Blessed are You, LORD,
the gracious One who repeatedly forgives.

REDEMPTION

רְאֵה Look on our affliction, plead our cause,
and redeem us soon for Your name's sake,
for You are a powerful Redeemer.
Blessed are You, LORD,
the Redeemer of Israel.

קדושת השם

אַתָּה קָדוֹשׁ וְשִׁמְךָ קָדוֹשׁ
וּקְדוֹשִׁים בְּכָל יוֹם יְהַלְלְוּךָ סֶּלָה.
בָּרוּךְ אַתָּה יהוה, הָאֵל הַקָּדוֹשׁ.

דעת

אַתָּה חוֹנֵן לְאָדָם דַּעַת
וּמְלַמֵּד לֶאֱנוֹשׁ בִּינָה.
חָנֵּנוּ מֵאִתְּךָ דֵּעָה בִּינָה וְהַשְׂכֵּל.
בָּרוּךְ אַתָּה יהוה, חוֹנֵן הַדָּעַת.

תשובה

הֲשִׁיבֵנוּ אָבִינוּ לְתוֹרָתֶךָ
וְקָרְבֵנוּ מַלְכֵּנוּ לַעֲבוֹדָתֶךָ
וְהַחֲזִירֵנוּ בִּתְשׁוּבָה שְׁלֵמָה לְפָנֶיךָ.
בָּרוּךְ אַתָּה יהוה, הָרוֹצֶה בִּתְשׁוּבָה.

סליחה

Strike the left side of the chest at °.

סְלַח לָנוּ אָבִינוּ כִּי °חָטָאנוּ
מְחַל לָנוּ מַלְכֵּנוּ כִּי °פָשָׁעְנוּ
כִּי מוֹחֵל וְסוֹלֵחַ אָתָּה.
בָּרוּךְ אַתָּה יהוה, חַנּוּן הַמַּרְבֶּה לִסְלֹחַ.

גאולה

רְאֵה בְעָנְיֵנוּ, וְרִיבָה רִיבֵנוּ
וּגְאָלֵנוּ מְהֵרָה לְמַעַן שְׁמֶךָ
כִּי גּוֹאֵל חָזָק אָתָּה.
בָּרוּךְ אַתָּה יהוה, גּוֹאֵל יִשְׂרָאֵל.

HEALING

רְפָאֵנוּ Heal us, LORD, and we shall be healed.
Save us and we shall be saved,
for You are our praise.
Bring complete recovery for all our ailments,

The following prayer for a sick person may be said here:
May it be Your will, O LORD my God and God of my ancestors, that You speedily send a complete recovery from heaven, a healing of both soul and body, to the patient (*name*), son/daughter of (*mother's name*) among the other afflicted of Israel.

---

for You, God, King, are a faithful and compassionate Healer.
Blessed are You, LORD,
Healer of the sick of His people Israel.

PROSPERITY

בָּרֵךְ Bless this year for us, LORD our God,
and all its types of produce for good.
Grant blessing on the face of the earth,
and from its goodness satisfy us,
blessing our year as the best of years.
Blessed are You, LORD,
who blesses the years.

INGATHERING OF EXILES

תְּקַע Sound the great shofar for our freedom,
raise high the banner to gather our exiles,
and gather us together from the four quarters of the earth.
Blessed are You, LORD,
who gathers the dispersed of His people Israel.

JUSTICE

הָשִׁיבָה Restore our judges as at first,
and our counselors as at the beginning,
and remove from us sorrow and sighing.

רפואה

רְפָאֵנוּ יהוה וְנֵרָפֵא
הוֹשִׁיעֵנוּ וְנִוָּשֵׁעָה, כִּי תְהִלָּתֵנוּ אָתָּה
וְהַעֲלֵה רְפוּאָה שְׁלֵמָה לְכָל מַכּוֹתֵינוּ

The following prayer for a sick person may be said here:

יְהִי רָצוֹן מִלְּפָנֶיךָ יהוה אֱלֹהַי וֵאלֹהֵי אֲבוֹתַי, שֶׁתִּשְׁלַח מְהֵרָה רְפוּאָה שְׁלֵמָה
מִן הַשָּׁמַיִם רְפוּאַת הַנֶּפֶשׁ וּרְפוּאַת הַגּוּף לַחוֹלֶה/לַחוֹלָה *name of patient*
בֶּן/בַּת *mother's name* בְּתוֹךְ שְׁאָר חוֹלֵי יִשְׂרָאֵל.

כִּי אֵל מֶלֶךְ רוֹפֵא נֶאֱמָן וְרַחֲמָן אָתָּה.
בָּרוּךְ אַתָּה יהוה, רוֹפֵא חוֹלֵי עַמּוֹ יִשְׂרָאֵל.

ברכת השנים

בָּרֵךְ עָלֵינוּ יהוה אֱלֹהֵינוּ אֶת הַשָּׁנָה הַזֹּאת
וְאֶת כָּל מִינֵי תְבוּאָתָהּ, לְטוֹבָה
וְתֵן בְּרָכָה עַל פְּנֵי הָאֲדָמָה, וְשַׂבְּעֵנוּ מִטּוּבָהּ
וּבָרֵךְ שְׁנָתֵנוּ כַּשָּׁנִים הַטּוֹבוֹת.
בָּרוּךְ אַתָּה יהוה, מְבָרֵךְ הַשָּׁנִים.

קבוץ גלויות

תְּקַע בְּשׁוֹפָר גָּדוֹל לְחֵרוּתֵנוּ, וְשָׂא נֵס לְקַבֵּץ גָּלֻיּוֹתֵינוּ
וְקַבְּצֵנוּ יַחַד מֵאַרְבַּע כַּנְפוֹת הָאָרֶץ.
בָּרוּךְ אַתָּה יהוה, מְקַבֵּץ נִדְחֵי עַמּוֹ יִשְׂרָאֵל.

השבת המשפט

הָשִׁיבָה שׁוֹפְטֵינוּ כְּבָרִאשׁוֹנָה
וְיוֹעֲצֵינוּ כְּבַתְּחִלָּה
וְהָסֵר מִמֶּנּוּ יָגוֹן וַאֲנָחָה

May You alone, LORD,
reign over us with loving-kindness and compassion,
and vindicate us in justice.
Blessed are You, LORD,
the King who loves righteousness and justice.

AGAINST INFORMERS

וְלַמַּלְשִׁינִים For the slanderers let there be no hope,
and may all wickedness perish in an instant.
May all Your people's enemies swiftly be cut down.
May You swiftly uproot, crush, cast down
and humble the arrogant swiftly in our days.
Blessed are You, LORD,
who destroys enemies and humbles the arrogant.

THE RIGHTEOUS

עַל הַצַּדִּיקִים To the righteous, the pious,
the elders of Your people the house of Israel,
the remnant of their scholars, the righteous converts, and to us,
may Your compassion be aroused, LORD our God.
Grant a good reward to all who sincerely trust in Your name.
Set our lot with them,
so that we may never be ashamed, for in You we trust.
Blessed are You, LORD,
who is the support and trust of the righteous.

REBUILDING JERUSALEM

וְלִירוּשָׁלַיִם To Jerusalem, Your city, may You return in compassion,
and may You dwell in it as You promised.
May You rebuild it rapidly in our days as an everlasting structure,
and install within it soon the throne of David.
Blessed are You, LORD,
who builds Jerusalem.

וּמְלֹךְ עָלֵינוּ אַתָּה יהוה לְבַדְּךָ בְּחֶסֶד וּבְרַחֲמִים
וְצַדְּקֵנוּ בַּמִּשְׁפָּט.
בָּרוּךְ אַתָּה יהוה, מֶלֶךְ אוֹהֵב צְדָקָה וּמִשְׁפָּט.

ברכת המינים

וְלַמַּלְשִׁינִים אַל תְּהִי תִקְוָה, וְכָל הָרִשְׁעָה כְּרֶגַע תֹּאבֵד
וְכָל אוֹיְבֵי עַמְּךָ מְהֵרָה יִכָּרֵתוּ
וְהַזֵּדִים מְהֵרָה תְעַקֵּר וּתְשַׁבֵּר וּתְמַגֵּר וְתַכְנִיעַ
בִּמְהֵרָה בְיָמֵינוּ.
בָּרוּךְ אַתָּה יהוה, שׁוֹבֵר אוֹיְבִים וּמַכְנִיעַ זֵדִים.

על הצדיקים

עַל הַצַּדִּיקִים וְעַל הַחֲסִידִים
וְעַל זִקְנֵי עַמְּךָ בֵּית יִשְׂרָאֵל
וְעַל פְּלֵיטַת סוֹפְרֵיהֶם, וְעַל גֵּרֵי הַצֶּדֶק, וְעָלֵינוּ
יֶהֱמוּ רַחֲמֶיךָ יהוה אֱלֹהֵינוּ
וְתֵן שָׂכָר טוֹב לְכָל הַבּוֹטְחִים בְּשִׁמְךָ בֶּאֱמֶת
וְשִׂים חֶלְקֵנוּ עִמָּהֶם, וּלְעוֹלָם לֹא נֵבוֹשׁ כִּי בְךָ בָטָחְנוּ.
בָּרוּךְ אַתָּה יהוה, מִשְׁעָן וּמִבְטָח לַצַּדִּיקִים.

בניין ירושלים

וְלִירוּשָׁלַיִם עִירְךָ בְּרַחֲמִים תָּשׁוּב
וְתִשְׁכֹּן בְּתוֹכָהּ כַּאֲשֶׁר דִּבַּרְתָּ
וּבְנֵה אוֹתָהּ בְּקָרוֹב בְּיָמֵינוּ בִּנְיַן עוֹלָם
וְכִסֵּא דָוִד מְהֵרָה לְתוֹכָהּ תָּכִין.
בָּרוּךְ אַתָּה יהוה, בּוֹנֵה יְרוּשָׁלָיִם.

KINGDOM OF DAVID

אֶת צֶמַח May the offshoot of Your servant David soon flower,
and may his pride be raised high by Your salvation,
for we wait for Your salvation all day.
Blessed are You, LORD,
who makes the glory of salvation flourish.

RESPONSE TO PRAYER

שְׁמַע קוֹלֵנוּ Listen to our voice, LORD our God.
Spare us and have compassion on us,
and in compassion and favor accept our prayer,
for You, God, listen to prayers and pleas.
Do not turn us away, O our King,
empty-handed from Your presence,
for You listen with compassion to the prayer of Your people Israel.
Blessed are You, LORD, who listens to prayer.

TEMPLE SERVICE

רְצֵה Find favor, LORD our God,
in Your people Israel and their prayer.
Restore the service to Your most holy House,
and accept in love and favor
the fire-offerings of Israel and their prayer.
May the service of Your people Israel always find favor with You.

אֱלֹהֵינוּ Our God and God of our ancestors,
may there rise, come, reach, appear, be favored, heard,
regarded and remembered before You,
our recollection and remembrance,
as well as the remembrance of our ancestors,
and of the Messiah son of David Your servant,
and of Jerusalem Your holy city,
and of all Your people the house of Israel –
for deliverance and well-being,
grace, loving-kindness and compassion, life and peace,
on this day of the Festival of Sukkot.

מלכות בית דוד

אֶת צֶמַח דָּוִד עַבְדְּךָ מְהֵרָה תַצְמִיחַ
וְקַרְנוֹ תָּרוּם בִּישׁוּעָתֶךָ
כִּי לִישׁוּעָתְךָ קִוִּינוּ כָּל הַיּוֹם.
בָּרוּךְ אַתָּה יהוה, מַצְמִיחַ קֶרֶן יְשׁוּעָה.

שומע תפלה

שְׁמַע קוֹלֵנוּ יהוה אֱלֹהֵינוּ
חוּס וְרַחֵם עָלֵינוּ, וְקַבֵּל בְּרַחֲמִים וּבְרָצוֹן אֶת תְּפִלָּתֵנוּ
כִּי אֵל שׁוֹמֵעַ תְּפִלּוֹת וְתַחֲנוּנִים אָתָּה
וּמִלְּפָנֶיךָ מַלְכֵּנוּ רֵיקָם אַל תְּשִׁיבֵנוּ
כִּי אַתָּה שׁוֹמֵעַ תְּפִלַּת עַמְּךָ יִשְׂרָאֵל בְּרַחֲמִים.
בָּרוּךְ אַתָּה יהוה, שׁוֹמֵעַ תְּפִלָּה.

עבודה

רְצֵה יהוה אֱלֹהֵינוּ בְּעַמְּךָ יִשְׂרָאֵל, וּבִתְפִלָּתָם
וְהָשֵׁב אֶת הָעֲבוֹדָה לִדְבִיר בֵּיתֶךָ
וְאִשֵּׁי יִשְׂרָאֵל וּתְפִלָּתָם בְּאַהֲבָה תְקַבֵּל בְּרָצוֹן
וּתְהִי לְרָצוֹן תָּמִיד עֲבוֹדַת יִשְׂרָאֵל עַמֶּךָ.

אֱלֹהֵינוּ וֵאלֹהֵי אֲבוֹתֵינוּ
יַעֲלֶה וְיָבוֹא וְיַגִּיעַ, וְיֵרָאֶה וְיֵרָצֶה וְיִשָּׁמַע
וְיִפָּקֵד וְיִזָּכֵר זִכְרוֹנֵנוּ וּפִקְדוֹנֵנוּ וְזִכְרוֹן אֲבוֹתֵינוּ
וְזִכְרוֹן מָשִׁיחַ בֶּן דָּוִד עַבְדֶּךָ
וְזִכְרוֹן יְרוּשָׁלַיִם עִיר קָדְשֶׁךָ
וְזִכְרוֹן כָּל עַמְּךָ בֵּית יִשְׂרָאֵל, לְפָנֶיךָ
לִפְלֵיטָה לְטוֹבָה, לְחֵן וּלְחֶסֶד וּלְרַחֲמִים, לְחַיִּים וּלְשָׁלוֹם
בְּיוֹם חַג הַסֻּכּוֹת הַזֶּה.

On it remember us, LORD our God, for good;
recollect us for blessing, and deliver us for life.
In accord with Your promise of salvation and compassion,
spare us and be gracious to us;
have compassion on us and deliver us,
for our eyes are turned to You
because You, God, are a gracious and compassionate King.
And may our eyes witness Your return to Zion in compassion.
Blessed are You, LORD, who restores His Presence to Zion.

THANKSGIVING

Bow at the first nine words.

מוֹדִים We give thanks to You,
for You are the LORD our God
and God of our ancestors
for ever and all time.
You are the Rock of our lives,
Shield of our salvation
from generation to generation.
We will thank You and
declare Your praise for our lives,
which are entrusted into Your hand;
for our souls,
which are placed in Your charge;
for Your miracles
which are with us every day;
and for Your wonders and favors
at all times, evening,
morning and midday.
You are good –
for Your compassion never fails.
You are compassionate –
for Your loving-kindnesses never cease.
We have always placed our hope in You.

During the Leader's Repetition, the congregation says quietly:

מוֹדִים We give thanks to You,
for You are the LORD our God
and God of our ancestors,
God of all flesh,
who formed us
and formed the universe.
Blessings and thanks are due
to Your great and holy name
for giving us life
and sustaining us.
May You continue
to give us life and sustain us;
and may You gather our exiles
to Your holy courts,
to keep Your decrees,
do Your will and serve You
with a perfect heart,
for it is for us to give You thanks.
Blessed be God to whom
thanksgiving is due.

זָכְרֵנוּ יהוה אֱלֹהֵינוּ בּוֹ לְטוֹבָה
וּפָקְדֵנוּ בוֹ לִבְרָכָה, וְהוֹשִׁיעֵנוּ בוֹ לְחַיִּים.
וּבִדְבַר יְשׁוּעָה וְרַחֲמִים
חוּס וְחָנֵּנוּ, וְרַחֵם עָלֵינוּ וְהוֹשִׁיעֵנוּ
כִּי אֵלֶיךָ עֵינֵינוּ, כִּי אֵל מֶלֶךְ חַנּוּן וְרַחוּם אָתָּה.
וְתֶחֱזֶינָה עֵינֵינוּ בְּשׁוּבְךָ לְצִיּוֹן בְּרַחֲמִים.
בָּרוּךְ אַתָּה יהוה, הַמַּחֲזִיר שְׁכִינָתוֹ לְצִיּוֹן.

הודאה

Bow at the first five words.

ˈמוֹדִים אֲנַחְנוּ לָךְ
שָׁאַתָּה הוּא יהוה אֱלֹהֵינוּ
וֵאלֹהֵי אֲבוֹתֵינוּ לְעוֹלָם וָעֶד.
צוּר חַיֵּינוּ, מָגֵן יִשְׁעֵנוּ
אַתָּה הוּא לְדוֹר וָדוֹר.
נוֹדֶה לְּךָ וּנְסַפֵּר תְּהִלָּתֶךָ
עַל חַיֵּינוּ הַמְּסוּרִים בְּיָדֶךָ
וְעַל נִשְׁמוֹתֵינוּ הַפְּקוּדוֹת לָךְ
וְעַל נִסֶּיךָ שֶׁבְּכָל יוֹם עִמָּנוּ
וְעַל נִפְלְאוֹתֶיךָ וְטוֹבוֹתֶיךָ
שֶׁבְּכָל עֵת
עֶרֶב וָבֹקֶר וְצָהֳרָיִם.
הַטּוֹב, כִּי לֹא כָלוּ רַחֲמֶיךָ
וְהַמְרַחֵם, כִּי לֹא תַמּוּ חֲסָדֶיךָ
מֵעוֹלָם קִוִּינוּ לָךְ.

During חזרת הש״ץ, the קהל says quietly:

ˈמוֹדִים אֲנַחְנוּ לָךְ
שָׁאַתָּה הוּא יהוה אֱלֹהֵינוּ
וֵאלֹהֵי אֲבוֹתֵינוּ
אֱלֹהֵי כָל בָּשָׂר
יוֹצְרֵנוּ, יוֹצֵר בְּרֵאשִׁית.
בְּרָכוֹת וְהוֹדָאוֹת
לְשִׁמְךָ הַגָּדוֹל וְהַקָּדוֹשׁ
עַל שֶׁהֶחֱיִיתָנוּ וְקִיַּמְתָּנוּ.
כֵּן תְּחַיֵּנוּ וּתְקַיְּמֵנוּ
וְתֶאֱסֹף גָּלֻיּוֹתֵינוּ
לְחַצְרוֹת קָדְשֶׁךָ
לִשְׁמֹר חֻקֶּיךָ וְלַעֲשׂוֹת רְצוֹנֶךָ
וּלְעָבְדְּךָ בְּלֵבָב שָׁלֵם
עַל שֶׁאֲנַחְנוּ מוֹדִים לָךְ.
בָּרוּךְ אֵל הַהוֹדָאוֹת.

וְעַל כֻּלָּם For all these things may Your name be blessed
and exalted, our King, continually, for ever and all time.
Let all that lives thank You, Selah!
and praise Your name in truth,
God, our Savior and Help, Selah!
▾Blessed are You, LORD, whose name is "the Good"
and to whom thanks are due.

The following is said by the Leader during the Repetition of the Amida.
In Israel, if Kohanim bless the congregation, *turn to page 1396.*

Our God and God of our fathers, bless us with the threefold blessing in the Torah, written by the hand of Moses Your servant and pronounced by Aaron and his sons the priests, Your holy people, as it is said:

May the LORD bless you and protect you. *Num. 6*
Cong: May it be Your will.
May the LORD make His face shine on you and be gracious to you.
Cong: May it be Your will.
May the LORD turn His face toward you, and grant you peace.
Cong: May it be Your will.

PEACE

שִׂים שָׁלוֹם Grant peace, goodness and blessing,
grace, loving-kindness and compassion
to us and all Israel Your people.
Bless us, our Father, all as one, with the light of Your face,
for by the light of Your face You have given us, LORD our God,
the Torah of life and love of kindness,
righteousness, blessing, compassion, life and peace.
May it be good in Your eyes to bless Your people Israel
at every time, in every hour, with Your peace.
Blessed are You, LORD, who blesses His people Israel with peace.

The following verse concludes the Leader's Repetition of the Amida.
Some also say it here as part of the silent Amida.

May the words of my mouth and the meditation of my heart *Ps. 19*
find favor before You, LORD, my Rock and Redeemer.

וְעַל כֻּלָּם יִתְבָּרַךְ וְיִתְרוֹמַם שִׁמְךָ מַלְכֵּנוּ תָּמִיד לְעוֹלָם וָעֶד.
וְכֹל הַחַיִּים יוֹדְוּךָ סֶּלָה, וִיהַלְלוּ אֶת שִׁמְךָ בֶּאֱמֶת
הָאֵל יְשׁוּעָתֵנוּ וְעֶזְרָתֵנוּ סֶלָה.
בָּרוּךְ אַתָּה יהוה, הַטּוֹב שִׁמְךָ וּלְךָ נָאֶה לְהוֹדוֹת.

The following is said by the שליח ציבור *during* חורת הש״ץ.
In ארץ ישראל *if* כהנים *say* ברכת כהנים *turn to page 1397.*

אֱלֹהֵינוּ וֵאלֹהֵי אֲבוֹתֵינוּ, בָּרְכֵנוּ בַבְּרָכָה הַמְשֻׁלֶּשֶׁת בַּתּוֹרָה, הַכְּתוּבָה עַל יְדֵי מֹשֶׁה עַבְדֶּךָ, הָאֲמוּרָה מִפִּי אַהֲרֹן וּבָנָיו כֹּהֲנִים עַם קְדוֹשֶׁךָ, כָּאָמוּר

במדבר ו
יְבָרֶכְךָ יהוה וְיִשְׁמְרֶךָ: קהל: כֵּן יְהִי רָצוֹן
יָאֵר יהוה פָּנָיו אֵלֶיךָ וִיחֻנֶּךָּ: קהל: כֵּן יְהִי רָצוֹן
יִשָּׂא יהוה פָּנָיו אֵלֶיךָ וְיָשֵׂם לְךָ שָׁלוֹם: קהל: כֵּן יְהִי רָצוֹן

שלום

שִׂים שָׁלוֹם טוֹבָה וּבְרָכָה
חֵן וָחֶסֶד וְרַחֲמִים עָלֵינוּ וְעַל כָּל יִשְׂרָאֵל עַמֶּךָ.
בָּרְכֵנוּ אָבִינוּ כֻּלָּנוּ כְּאֶחָד בְּאוֹר פָּנֶיךָ
כִּי בְאוֹר פָּנֶיךָ נָתַתָּ לָּנוּ יהוה אֱלֹהֵינוּ
תּוֹרַת חַיִּים וְאַהֲבַת חֶסֶד
וּצְדָקָה וּבְרָכָה וְרַחֲמִים וְחַיִּים וְשָׁלוֹם.
וְטוֹב בְּעֵינֶיךָ לְבָרֵךְ אֶת עַמְּךָ יִשְׂרָאֵל
בְּכָל עֵת וּבְכָל שָׁעָה בִּשְׁלוֹמֶךָ.
בָּרוּךְ אַתָּה יהוה, הַמְבָרֵךְ אֶת עַמּוֹ יִשְׂרָאֵל בַּשָּׁלוֹם.

The following verse concludes the חורת הש״ץ.
Some also say it here as part of the silent עמידה.

תהלים יט
יִהְיוּ לְרָצוֹן אִמְרֵי־פִי וְהֶגְיוֹן לִבִּי לְפָנֶיךָ, יהוה צוּרִי וְגֹאֲלִי:

אֱלֹהַי My God, *Berakhot 17a*
guard my tongue from evil and my lips from deceitful speech.
To those who curse me, let my soul be silent;
may my soul be to all like the dust.
Open my heart to Your Torah and let my soul
pursue Your commandments.
As for all who plan evil against me,
swiftly thwart their counsel and frustrate their plans.
Act for the sake of Your name;
act for the sake of Your right hand;
act for the sake of Your holiness;
act for the sake of Your Torah.
That Your beloved ones may be delivered, *Ps. 60*
save with Your right hand and answer me.
May the words of my mouth and the meditation of my heart *Ps. 19*
find favor before You, LORD, my Rock and Redeemer.

Bow, take three steps back, then bow, first left, then right, then center, while saying:

May He who makes peace in His high places,
make peace for us and all Israel –
and say: Amen.

יְהִי רָצוֹן May it be Your will, LORD our God and God of our ancestors,
that the Temple be rebuilt speedily in our days,
and grant us a share in Your Torah.
And there we will serve You with reverence,
as in the days of old and as in former years.
Then the offering of Judah and Jerusalem will be pleasing to the LORD *Mal. 3*
as in the days of old and as in former years.

*When praying with a minyan, the Amida is repeated aloud by the Leader.
After the Repetition, the congregants remove their tefillin; some hold
that the Leader keeps them on until the Full Kaddish.*

אֱלֹהַי ברכות יז.
נְצֹר לְשׁוֹנִי מֵרָע וּשְׂפָתַי מִדַּבֵּר מִרְמָה
וְלִמְקַלְלַי נַפְשִׁי תִדֹּם, וְנַפְשִׁי כֶּעָפָר לַכֹּל תִּהְיֶה.
פְּתַח לִבִּי בְּתוֹרָתֶךָ, וּבְמִצְוֹתֶיךָ תִּרְדֹּף נַפְשִׁי.
וְכָל הַחוֹשְׁבִים עָלַי רָעָה
מְהֵרָה הָפֵר עֲצָתָם וְקַלְקֵל מַחֲשַׁבְתָּם.
עֲשֵׂה לְמַעַן שְׁמֶךָ
עֲשֵׂה לְמַעַן יְמִינֶךָ
עֲשֵׂה לְמַעַן קְדֻשָּׁתֶךָ
עֲשֵׂה לְמַעַן תּוֹרָתֶךָ.
לְמַעַן יֵחָלְצוּן יְדִידֶיךָ, הוֹשִׁיעָה יְמִינְךָ וַעֲנֵנִי: תהלים ס
יִהְיוּ לְרָצוֹן אִמְרֵי־פִי וְהֶגְיוֹן לִבִּי לְפָנֶיךָ, יהוה צוּרִי וְגֹאֲלִי: תהלים יט

Bow, take three steps back, then bow, first left, then right, then center, while saying:

עֹשֶׂה שָׁלוֹם בִּמְרוֹמָיו
הוּא יַעֲשֶׂה שָׁלוֹם עָלֵינוּ וְעַל כָּל יִשְׂרָאֵל
וְאִמְרוּ אָמֵן.

יְהִי רָצוֹן מִלְּפָנֶיךָ יהוה אֱלֹהֵינוּ וֵאלֹהֵי אֲבוֹתֵינוּ
שֶׁיִּבָּנֶה בֵּית הַמִּקְדָּשׁ בִּמְהֵרָה בְיָמֵינוּ, וְתֵן חֶלְקֵנוּ בְּתוֹרָתֶךָ
וְשָׁם נַעֲבָדְךָ בְּיִרְאָה כִּימֵי עוֹלָם וּכְשָׁנִים קַדְמֹנִיּוֹת.
וְעָרְבָה לַיהוה מִנְחַת יְהוּדָה וִירוּשָׁלָםִ כִּימֵי עוֹלָם וּכְשָׁנִים קַדְמֹנִיּוֹת: מלאכי ג

When praying with a מנין*, the* עמידה *is repeated aloud by the* שליח ציבור*.*
After חזרת הש״ץ*, the congregants remove their* תפילין*; some hold that the* שליח ציבור *keeps them on until the* קדיש שלם*.*

Blessing on Taking the Lulav

The lulav and etrog are taken before Hallel.

Some say the following:

יְהִי רָצוֹן May it be Your will, LORD my God and God of my fathers, that through the fruit of the citron tree, the palm frond, the myrtle branches and willows of the brook, the letters of Your unique name draw close to one another and become united in my hand. Make it known I am called by Your name, so that [evil] will fear to come close to me. When I wave them, may a rich flow of blessings flow from the supreme Source of wisdom to the place of the Tabernacle and the site of the House of our God. May the command of these four species be considered by You as if I had fulfilled it in all its details and roots, as well as the 613 commandments dependent on it, for it is my intention to unify the name of the Holy One, blessed be He, and His Divine Presence, in reverence and love, to unify the name *Yod-Heh* with *Vav-Heh*, in perfect unity in the name of all Israel, Amen. Blessed is the LORD forever, Amen and Amen. *Ps. 89*

The lulav is taken in the right hand, with the myrtle leaves on the right, willow leaves on the left. The etrog is taken in the left hand, with its pointed end toward the floor. If left-handed, take the etrog in the right hand and the lulav in the left. Then say the following blessing:

בָּרוּךְ Blessed are You, LORD our God, King of the Universe,
who has made us holy through His commandments,
and has commanded us about taking the lulav.

If the first day of Sukkot falls on a Shabbat, in Israel on the first day of Hol HaMo'ed the lulav is taken, then add:

בָּרוּךְ Blessed are You, LORD our God, King of the Universe,
who has given us life, sustained us and brought us to this time.

Invert the etrog, so that its pointed end is facing up. Face the front of the synagogue and wave the lulav and etrog in the following sequence, three times in each direction: ahead, right, back, left, up, down. Continue to hold the lulav and etrog during Hallel.

סדר נטילת לולב

The לולב *and* אתרוג *are taken before* הלל.

Some say the following:

יְהִי רָצוֹן מִלְּפָנֶיךָ יהוה אֱלֹהַי וֵאלֹהֵי אֲבוֹתַי, בִּפְרִי עֵץ הָדָר וְכַפֹּת תְּמָרִים וַעֲנַף עֵץ עָבוֹת וְעַרְבֵי נַחַל, אוֹתִיּוֹת שִׁמְךָ הַמְיֻחָד תְּקָרֵב אֶחָד אֶל אֶחָד וְהָיוּ לַאֲחָדִים בְּיָדִי, וְלֵידַע אֵיךְ שִׁמְךָ נִקְרָא עָלַי וְיִירְאוּ מִגֶּשֶׁת אֵלַי. וּבְנַעֲנוּעִי אוֹתָם תַּשְׁפִּיעַ שֶׁפַע בְּרָכוֹת מִדַּעַת עֶלְיוֹן לִנְוֵה אַפִּרְיוֹן לִמְכוֹן בֵּית אֱלֹהֵינוּ, וּתְהֵא חֲשׁוּבָה לְפָנֶיךָ מִצְוַת אַרְבָּעָה מִינִים אֵלּוּ כְּאִלּוּ קִיַּמְתִּיהָ בְּכָל פְּרָטוֹתֶיהָ וְשָׁרָשֶׁיהָ וְתַרְיַ״ג מִצְוֹת הַתְּלוּיוֹת בָּהּ, כִּי כַוָּנָתִי לְיַחֲדָא שְׁמָא דְקֻדְשָׁא בְּרִיךְ הוּא וּשְׁכִינְתֵּהּ בִּדְחִילוּ וּרְחִימוּ, לְיַחֵד שֵׁם י״ה בו״ה בְּיִחוּדָא שְׁלִים בְּשֵׁם כָּל יִשְׂרָאֵל, אָמֵן. בָּרוּךְ יהוה לְעוֹלָם, אָמֵן וְאָמֵן: תהלים פט

The לולב *is taken in the right hand, with the* הדסים *on the right,* ערבות *on the left. The* אתרוג *is taken in the left hand, with its pointed end toward the floor. If left-handed, take the* אתרוג *in the right hand and the* לולב *in the left. Then say the following blessing:*

בָּרוּךְ אַתָּה יהוה אֱלֹהֵינוּ מֶלֶךְ הָעוֹלָם
אֲשֶׁר קִדְּשָׁנוּ בְּמִצְוֹתָיו וְצִוָּנוּ עַל נְטִילַת לוּלָב.

If the first day of סוכות *falls on a* שבת*, in* ארץ ישראל *on the first day of* חול המועד *the* לולב *is taken for the first time, then add:*

בָּרוּךְ אַתָּה יהוה אֱלֹהֵינוּ מֶלֶךְ הָעוֹלָם
שֶׁהֶחֱיָנוּ וְקִיְּמָנוּ וְהִגִּיעָנוּ לַזְּמַן הַזֶּה.

Invert the אתרוג*, so that its pointed end is facing up. Face the front of the* בית כנסת *and wave the* לולב *and* אתרוג *in the following sequence, three times in each direction: ahead, right, back, left, up, down. Continue to hold the* לולב *and* אתרוג *during* הלל.

HALLEL

בָּרוּךְ Blessed are You, LORD our God, King of the Universe, who has made us holy through His commandments and has commanded us to recite the Hallel.

הַלְלוּיָהּ Halleluya! Servants of the LORD, give praise; praise the name of the LORD. Blessed be the name of the LORD now and for evermore. From the rising of the sun to its setting, may the LORD's name be praised. High is the LORD above all nations; His glory is above the heavens. Who is like the LORD our God, who sits enthroned so high, yet turns so low to see the heavens and the earth? ▸ He raises the poor from the dust and the needy from the refuse heap, giving them a place alongside princes, the princes of His people. He makes the woman in a childless house a happy mother of children. Halleluya! *Ps. 113*

בְּצֵאת When Israel came out of Egypt, the house of Jacob from a people of foreign tongue, Judah became His sanctuary, Israel His dominion. The sea saw and fled; the Jordan turned back. The mountains skipped like rams, the hills like lambs. ▸ Why was it, sea, that you fled? Jordan, why did you turn back? Why, mountains, did you skip like rams, and you, hills, like lambs? It was at the presence of the LORD, Creator of the earth, at the presence of the God of Jacob, who turned the rock into a pool of water, flint into a flowing spring. *Ps. 114*

לֹא לָנוּ Not to us, LORD, not to us, but to Your name give glory, for Your love, for Your faithfulness. Why should the nations say, "Where now is their God?" Our God is in heaven; whatever He wills He does. Their idols are silver and gold, made by human hands. They have mouths but cannot speak; eyes but cannot see. They have ears but cannot hear; noses but cannot smell. They have hands but cannot feel; feet but cannot walk. No sound comes from their throat. Those who make them become like them; so will all who trust in them. ▸ Israel, trust in the LORD – He is their Help and their Shield. House of Aaron, trust in the LORD – He is their Help and their Shield. You who fear the LORD, trust in the LORD – He is their Help and their Shield. *Ps. 115*

הלל

בָּרוּךְ אַתָּה יהוה אֱלֹהֵינוּ מֶלֶךְ הָעוֹלָם
אֲשֶׁר קִדְּשָׁנוּ בְּמִצְוֹתָיו וְצִוָּנוּ לִקְרֹא אֶת הַהַלֵּל.

תהלים קיג
הַלְלוּיָהּ, הַלְלוּ עַבְדֵי יהוה, הַלְלוּ אֶת־שֵׁם יהוה: יְהִי שֵׁם יהוה מְבֹרָךְ, מֵעַתָּה וְעַד־עוֹלָם: מִמִּזְרַח־שֶׁמֶשׁ עַד־מְבוֹאוֹ, מְהֻלָּל שֵׁם יהוה: רָם עַל־כָּל־גּוֹיִם יהוה, עַל הַשָּׁמַיִם כְּבוֹדוֹ: מִי כַּיהוה אֱלֹהֵינוּ, הַמַּגְבִּיהִי לָשָׁבֶת: הַמַּשְׁפִּילִי לִרְאוֹת, בַּשָּׁמַיִם וּבָאָרֶץ: ◂ מְקִימִי מֵעָפָר דָּל, מֵאַשְׁפֹּת יָרִים אֶבְיוֹן: לְהוֹשִׁיבִי עִם־נְדִיבִים, עִם נְדִיבֵי עַמּוֹ: מוֹשִׁיבִי עֲקֶרֶת הַבַּיִת, אֵם־הַבָּנִים שְׂמֵחָה, הַלְלוּיָהּ:

תהלים קיד
בְּצֵאת יִשְׂרָאֵל מִמִּצְרָיִם, בֵּית יַעֲקֹב מֵעַם לֹעֵז: הָיְתָה יְהוּדָה לְקָדְשׁוֹ, יִשְׂרָאֵל מַמְשְׁלוֹתָיו: הַיָּם רָאָה וַיָּנֹס, הַיַּרְדֵּן יִסֹּב לְאָחוֹר: הֶהָרִים רָקְדוּ כְאֵילִים, גְּבָעוֹת כִּבְנֵי־צֹאן: ◂ מַה־לְּךָ הַיָּם כִּי תָנוּס, הַיַּרְדֵּן תִּסֹּב לְאָחוֹר: הֶהָרִים תִּרְקְדוּ כְאֵילִים, גְּבָעוֹת כִּבְנֵי־צֹאן: מִלִּפְנֵי אָדוֹן חוּלִי אָרֶץ, מִלִּפְנֵי אֱלוֹהַּ יַעֲקֹב: הַהֹפְכִי הַצּוּר אֲגַם־מָיִם, חַלָּמִישׁ לְמַעְיְנוֹ־מָיִם:

תהלים קטו
לֹא לָנוּ יהוה לֹא לָנוּ, כִּי־לְשִׁמְךָ תֵּן כָּבוֹד, עַל־חַסְדְּךָ עַל־אֲמִתֶּךָ: לָמָּה יֹאמְרוּ הַגּוֹיִם אַיֵּה־נָא אֱלֹהֵיהֶם: וֵאלֹהֵינוּ בַשָּׁמָיִם, כֹּל אֲשֶׁר־חָפֵץ עָשָׂה: עֲצַבֵּיהֶם כֶּסֶף וְזָהָב, מַעֲשֵׂה יְדֵי אָדָם: פֶּה־לָהֶם וְלֹא יְדַבֵּרוּ, עֵינַיִם לָהֶם וְלֹא יִרְאוּ: אָזְנַיִם לָהֶם וְלֹא יִשְׁמָעוּ, אַף לָהֶם וְלֹא יְרִיחוּן: יְדֵיהֶם וְלֹא יְמִישׁוּן, רַגְלֵיהֶם וְלֹא יְהַלֵּכוּ, לֹא־יֶהְגּוּ בִּגְרוֹנָם: כְּמוֹהֶם יִהְיוּ עֹשֵׂיהֶם, כֹּל אֲשֶׁר־בֹּטֵחַ בָּהֶם: ◂ יִשְׂרָאֵל בְּטַח בַּיהוה, עֶזְרָם וּמָגִנָּם הוּא: בֵּית אַהֲרֹן בִּטְחוּ בַיהוה, עֶזְרָם וּמָגִנָּם הוּא: יִרְאֵי יהוה בִּטְחוּ בַיהוה, עֶזְרָם וּמָגִנָּם הוּא:

יהוה זְכָרָנוּ The LORD remembers us and will bless us. He will bless the house of Israel. He will bless the house of Aaron. He will bless those who fear the LORD, small and great alike. May the LORD give you increase: you and your children. May you be blessed by the LORD, Maker of heaven and earth. ▸ The heavens are the LORD's, but the earth He has given over to mankind. It is not the dead who praise the LORD, nor those who go down to the silent grave. But we will bless the LORD, now and for ever. Halleluya! *Ps. 115*

אָהַבְתִּי I love the LORD, for He hears my voice, my pleas. He turns His ear to me whenever I call. The bonds of death encompassed me, the anguish of the grave came upon me, I was overcome by trouble and sorrow. Then I called on the name of the LORD: "LORD, I pray, save my life." Gracious is the LORD, and righteous; our God is full of compassion. The LORD protects the simple hearted. When I was brought low, He saved me. My soul, be at peace once more, for the LORD has been good to you. For You have rescued me from death, my eyes from weeping, my feet from stumbling. ▸ I shall walk in the presence of the LORD in the land of the living. I had faith, even when I said, "I am greatly afflicted," even when I said rashly, "All men are liars." *Ps. 116*

מָה־אָשִׁיב How can I repay the LORD for all His goodness to me? I will lift the cup of salvation and call on the name of the LORD. I will fulfill my vows to the LORD in the presence of all His people. Grievous in the LORD's sight is the death of His devoted ones. Truly, LORD, I am Your servant; I am Your servant, the son of Your maidservant. You set me free from my chains. ▸ To You I shall bring a thanksgiving-offering and call on the LORD by name. I will fulfill my vows to the LORD in the presence of all His people, in the courts of the House of the LORD, in your midst, Jerusalem. Halleluya. *Ps. 116*

הַלְלוּ Praise the LORD, all nations; acclaim Him, all you peoples; *Ps. 117*
for His loving-kindness to us is strong,
and the LORD's faithfulness is everlasting.
Halleluya.

יְהוה זְכָרָנוּ יְבָרֵךְ, יְבָרֵךְ אֶת־בֵּית יִשְׂרָאֵל, יְבָרֵךְ אֶת־בֵּית אַהֲרֹן: תהלים קטו
יְבָרֵךְ יִרְאֵי יהוה, הַקְּטַנִּים עִם־הַגְּדֹלִים: יֹסֵף יהוה עֲלֵיכֶם, עֲלֵיכֶם
וְעַל־בְּנֵיכֶם: בְּרוּכִים אַתֶּם לַיהוה, עֹשֵׂה שָׁמַיִם וָאָרֶץ: ◂ הַשָּׁמַיִם
שָׁמַיִם לַיהוה, וְהָאָרֶץ נָתַן לִבְנֵי־אָדָם: לֹא הַמֵּתִים יְהַלְלוּ־יָהּ, וְלֹא
כָּל־יֹרְדֵי דוּמָה: וַאֲנַחְנוּ נְבָרֵךְ יָהּ, מֵעַתָּה וְעַד־עוֹלָם, הַלְלוּיָהּ:

אָהַבְתִּי, כִּי־יִשְׁמַע יהוה, אֶת־קוֹלִי תַּחֲנוּנָי: כִּי־הִטָּה אָזְנוֹ לִי, תהלים קטז
וּבְיָמַי אֶקְרָא: אֲפָפוּנִי חֶבְלֵי־מָוֶת, וּמְצָרֵי שְׁאוֹל מְצָאוּנִי, צָרָה
וְיָגוֹן אֶמְצָא: וּבְשֵׁם־יהוה אֶקְרָא, אָנָּה יהוה מַלְּטָה נַפְשִׁי: חַנּוּן
יהוה וְצַדִּיק, וֵאלֹהֵינוּ מְרַחֵם: שֹׁמֵר פְּתָאיִם יהוה, דַּלּוֹתִי וְלִי
יְהוֹשִׁיעַ: שׁוּבִי נַפְשִׁי לִמְנוּחָיְכִי, כִּי־יהוה גָּמַל עָלָיְכִי: כִּי חִלַּצְתָּ
נַפְשִׁי מִמָּוֶת, אֶת־עֵינִי מִן־דִּמְעָה, אֶת־רַגְלִי מִדֶּחִי: ◂ אֶתְהַלֵּךְ לִפְנֵי
יהוה, בְּאַרְצוֹת הַחַיִּים: הֶאֱמַנְתִּי כִּי אֲדַבֵּר, אֲנִי עָנִיתִי מְאֹד: אֲנִי
אָמַרְתִּי בְחָפְזִי, כָּל־הָאָדָם כֹּזֵב:

מָה־אָשִׁיב לַיהוה, כָּל־תַּגְמוּלוֹהִי עָלָי: כּוֹס־יְשׁוּעוֹת אֶשָּׂא, וּבְשֵׁם תהלים קטז
יהוה אֶקְרָא: נְדָרַי לַיהוה אֲשַׁלֵּם, נֶגְדָה־נָּא לְכָל־עַמּוֹ: יָקָר בְּעֵינֵי
יהוה, הַמָּוְתָה לַחֲסִידָיו: אָנָּה יהוה כִּי־אֲנִי עַבְדֶּךָ, אֲנִי־עַבְדְּךָ
בֶּן־אֲמָתֶךָ, פִּתַּחְתָּ לְמוֹסֵרָי: ◂ לְךָ־אֶזְבַּח זֶבַח תּוֹדָה, וּבְשֵׁם יהוה
אֶקְרָא: נְדָרַי לַיהוה אֲשַׁלֵּם, נֶגְדָה־נָּא לְכָל־עַמּוֹ: בְּחַצְרוֹת בֵּית
יהוה, בְּתוֹכֵכִי יְרוּשָׁלָםִ, הַלְלוּיָהּ:

הַלְלוּ אֶת־יהוה כָּל־גּוֹיִם, שַׁבְּחוּהוּ כָּל־הָאֻמִּים: תהלים קיז
כִּי גָבַר עָלֵינוּ חַסְדּוֹ, וֶאֱמֶת־יהוה לְעוֹלָם
הַלְלוּיָהּ:

The following verses are chanted by the Leader. At the end of each verse, the congregation responds, "Thank the LORD for He is good; His loving-kindness is for ever."
The lulav and etrog are waved, three waves for each word of the verse (except God's name). On the first word, wave forward, then, on subsequent words, wave right, back, left, up and down respectively. The Leader waves only for the first two verses. The congregation waves each time the first verse is said in response.

הודו Thank the LORD for He is good; His loving-kindness is for ever. *Ps. 118*
Let Israel say His loving-kindness is for ever.
Let the house of Aaron say His loving-kindness is for ever.
Let those who fear the LORD say His loving-kindness is for ever.

מִן־הַמֵּצַר In my distress I called on the LORD. The LORD answered me and set me free. The LORD is with me; I will not be afraid. What can man do to me? The LORD is with me. He is my Helper. I will see the downfall of my enemies. It is better to take refuge in the LORD than to trust in man. It is better to take refuge in the LORD than to trust in princes. The nations all surrounded me, but in the LORD's name I drove them off. They surrounded me on every side, but in the LORD's name I drove them off. They surrounded me like bees, they attacked me as fire attacks brushwood, but in the LORD's name I drove them off. They thrust so hard against me, I nearly fell, but the LORD came to my help. The LORD is my strength and my song; He has become my salvation. Sounds of song and salvation resound in the tents of the righteous: "The LORD's right hand has done mighty deeds. The LORD's right hand is lifted high. The LORD's right hand has done mighty deeds." I will not die but live, and tell what the LORD has done. The LORD has chastened me severely, but He has not given me over to death. ▸ Open for me the gates of righteousness that I may enter them and thank the LORD. This is the gateway to the LORD; through it, the righteous shall enter.

אוֹדְךָ I will thank You, for You answered me, and became my salvation.
I will thank You, for You answered me, and became my salvation.

The stone the builders rejected has become the main cornerstone.
The stone the builders rejected has become the main cornerstone.

This is the LORD's doing. It is wondrous in our eyes.
This is the LORD's doing. It is wondrous in our eyes.

This is the day the LORD has made. Let us rejoice and be glad in it.
This is the day the LORD has made. Let us rejoice and be glad in it.

The following verses are chanted by the שליח ציבור*.*
At the end of each verse, the קהל *responds:* הוֹדוּ לַיהוה כִּי־טוֹב, כִּי לְעוֹלָם חַסְדּוֹ.

The לולב *and* אתרוג *are waved, three waves for each word of the verse (except God's name). On the first word, wave forward, then, on subsequent words, wave right, back, left, up and down respectively. The* שליח ציבור *waves only for the first two verses. The* קהל *waves each time the first verse is said in response.*

הוֹדוּ לַיהוה כִּי־טוֹב כִּי לְעוֹלָם חַסְדּוֹ: תהלים קיח
יֹאמַר־נָא יִשְׂרָאֵל כִּי לְעוֹלָם חַסְדּוֹ:
יֹאמְרוּ־נָא בֵית־אַהֲרֹן כִּי לְעוֹלָם חַסְדּוֹ:
יֹאמְרוּ־נָא יִרְאֵי יהוה כִּי לְעוֹלָם חַסְדּוֹ:

מִן־הַמֵּצַר קָרָאתִי יָּהּ, עָנָנִי בַמֶּרְחָב יָהּ: יהוה לִי לֹא אִירָא, מַה־יַּעֲשֶׂה לִי אָדָם: יהוה לִי בְּעֹזְרָי, וַאֲנִי אֶרְאֶה בְשֹׂנְאָי: טוֹב לַחֲסוֹת בַּיהוה, מִבְּטֹחַ בָּאָדָם: טוֹב לַחֲסוֹת בַּיהוה, מִבְּטֹחַ בִּנְדִיבִים: כָּל־גּוֹיִם סְבָבוּנִי, בְּשֵׁם יהוה כִּי אֲמִילַם: סַבּוּנִי גַם־סְבָבוּנִי, בְּשֵׁם יהוה כִּי אֲמִילַם: סַבּוּנִי כִדְבֹרִים, דֹּעֲכוּ כְּאֵשׁ קוֹצִים, בְּשֵׁם יהוה כִּי אֲמִילַם: דַּחֹה דְחִיתַנִי לִנְפֹּל, וַיהוה עֲזָרָנִי: עָזִּי וְזִמְרָת יָהּ, וַיְהִי־לִי לִישׁוּעָה: קוֹל רִנָּה וִישׁוּעָה בְּאָהֳלֵי צַדִּיקִים, יְמִין יהוה עֹשָׂה חָיִל: יְמִין יהוה רוֹמֵמָה, יְמִין יהוה עֹשָׂה חָיִל: לֹא־אָמוּת כִּי־אֶחְיֶה, וַאֲסַפֵּר מַעֲשֵׂי יָהּ: יַסֹּר יִסְּרַנִּי יָּהּ, וְלַמָּוֶת לֹא נְתָנָנִי: › פִּתְחוּ־לִי שַׁעֲרֵי־צֶדֶק, אָבֹא־בָם אוֹדֶה יָהּ: זֶה־הַשַּׁעַר לַיהוה, צַדִּיקִים יָבֹאוּ בוֹ:

אוֹדְךָ כִּי עֲנִיתָנִי, וַתְּהִי־לִי לִישׁוּעָה:
אוֹדְךָ כִּי עֲנִיתָנִי, וַתְּהִי־לִי לִישׁוּעָה:

אֶבֶן מָאֲסוּ הַבּוֹנִים, הָיְתָה לְרֹאשׁ פִּנָּה:
אֶבֶן מָאֲסוּ הַבּוֹנִים, הָיְתָה לְרֹאשׁ פִּנָּה:

מֵאֵת יהוה הָיְתָה זֹּאת, הִיא נִפְלָאת בְּעֵינֵינוּ:
מֵאֵת יהוה הָיְתָה זֹּאת, הִיא נִפְלָאת בְּעֵינֵינוּ:

זֶה־הַיּוֹם עָשָׂה יהוה, נָגִילָה וְנִשְׂמְחָה בוֹ:
זֶה־הַיּוֹם עָשָׂה יהוה, נָגִילָה וְנִשְׂמְחָה בוֹ:

The lulav and etrog are waved while saying "Lord, please, save us," three waves in each direction (not for God's name). On the first word, wave forward and right; third word: back and left; fourth word: up and down.

Leader followed by congregation:

אָנָּא Lord, please, save us.
Lord, please, save us.
Lord, please, grant us success.
Lord, please, grant us success.

בָּרוּךְ Blessed is one who comes in the name of the Lord;
we bless you from the House of the Lord.
Blessed is one who comes in the name of the Lord;
we bless you from the House of the Lord.

The Lord is God; He has given us light. Bind the festival offering with thick cords [and bring it] to the horns of the altar.
The Lord is God; He has given us light. Bind the festival offering with thick cords [and bring it] to the horns of the altar.

You are my God and I will thank You;
You are my God, I will exalt You.
You are my God and I will thank You;
You are my God, I will exalt You.

Thank the Lord for He is good;
His loving-kindness is for ever.
Thank the Lord for He is good;
His loving-kindness is for ever.

יְהַלְלוּךָ All Your works will praise You, Lord our God,
and Your devoted ones – the righteous who do Your will,
together with all Your people the house of Israel –
will joyously thank, bless, praise, glorify, exalt, revere, sanctify,
and proclaim the sovereignty of Your name, our King.
▸ For it is good to thank You and fitting to sing psalms to Your name,
for from eternity to eternity You are God.
Blessed are You, Lord, King who is extolled with praises.

Some say at this point Hoshanot on page 710, then Full Kaddish.

The לולב *and* אתרוג *are waved while saying* אָנָּא יהוה הוֹשִׁיעָה נָּא, *three waves in each direction (not for God's name). On the first word, wave forward and right; third word: back and left; fourth word: up and down.*

שליח ציבור *followed by* קהל:

אָנָּא יהוה הוֹשִׁיעָה נָּא:
אָנָּא יהוה הוֹשִׁיעָה נָּא:
אָנָּא יהוה הַצְלִיחָה נָא:
אָנָּא יהוה הַצְלִיחָה נָא:

בָּרוּךְ הַבָּא בְּשֵׁם יהוה, בֵּרַכְנוּכֶם מִבֵּית יהוה:
בָּרוּךְ הַבָּא בְּשֵׁם יהוה, בֵּרַכְנוּכֶם מִבֵּית יהוה:
אֵל יהוה וַיָּאֶר לָנוּ, אִסְרוּ־חַג בַּעֲבֹתִים עַד־קַרְנוֹת הַמִּזְבֵּחַ:
אֵל יהוה וַיָּאֶר לָנוּ, אִסְרוּ־חַג בַּעֲבֹתִים עַד־קַרְנוֹת הַמִּזְבֵּחַ:
אֵלִי אַתָּה וְאוֹדֶךָּ, אֱלֹהַי אֲרוֹמְמֶךָּ:
אֵלִי אַתָּה וְאוֹדֶךָּ, אֱלֹהַי אֲרוֹמְמֶךָּ:
הוֹדוּ לַיהוה כִּי־טוֹב, כִּי לְעוֹלָם חַסְדּוֹ:
הוֹדוּ לַיהוה כִּי־טוֹב, כִּי לְעוֹלָם חַסְדּוֹ:

יְהַלְלְוּךָ יהוה אֱלֹהֵינוּ כָּל מַעֲשֶׂיךָ
וַחֲסִידֶיךָ צַדִּיקִים עוֹשֵׂי רְצוֹנֶךָ
וְכָל עַמְּךָ בֵּית יִשְׂרָאֵל בְּרִנָּה יוֹדוּ
וִיבָרְכוּ וִישַׁבְּחוּ וִיפָאֲרוּ וִירוֹמְמוּ וְיַעֲרִיצוּ וְיַקְדִּישׁוּ
וְיַמְלִיכוּ אֶת שִׁמְךָ מַלְכֵּנוּ
◂ כִּי לְךָ טוֹב לְהוֹדוֹת וּלְשִׁמְךָ נָאֶה לְזַמֵּר
כִּי מֵעוֹלָם וְעַד עוֹלָם אַתָּה אֵל.
בָּרוּךְ אַתָּה יהוה, מֶלֶךְ מְהֻלָּל בַּתִּשְׁבָּחוֹת.

Some say at this point הושענות *on page 711**, then* קדיש שלם.

FULL KADDISH

Some have the custom to include additional responses in Full Kaddish. They can be found in the version on page 1464.

Leader: יִתְגַּדַּל Magnified and sanctified
may His great name be,
in the world He created by His will.
May He establish His kingdom
in your lifetime and in your days,
and in the lifetime of all the house of Israel,
swiftly and soon –
and say: Amen.

All: May His great name be blessed
for ever and all time.

Leader: Blessed and praised, glorified and exalted,
raised and honored, uplifted and lauded be
the name of the Holy One,
blessed be He,
beyond any blessing,
song, praise and consolation
uttered in the world –
and say: Amen.

May the prayers and pleas of all Israel
be accepted by their Father in heaven –
and say: Amen.

May there be great peace from heaven,
and life for us and all Israel –
and say: Amen.

Bow, take three steps back, as if taking leave of the Divine Presence, then bow, first left, then right, then center, while saying:

May He who makes peace in His high places,
make peace for us and all Israel –
and say: Amen.

On Hoshana Raba, continue with The Removing of the Torah on page 984.

קדיש שלם

Some have the custom to include additional responses in קדיש שלם*.*
They can be found in the version on page 1465.

ש״ץ: יִתְגַּדַּל וְיִתְקַדַּשׁ שְׁמֵהּ רַבָּא (קהל: אָמֵן)
בְּעָלְמָא דִּי בְרָא כִרְעוּתֵהּ
וְיַמְלִיךְ מַלְכוּתֵהּ
בְּחַיֵּיכוֹן וּבְיוֹמֵיכוֹן וּבְחַיֵּי דְכָל בֵּית יִשְׂרָאֵל
בַּעֲגָלָא וּבִזְמַן קָרִיב
וְאִמְרוּ אָמֵן. (קהל: אָמֵן)

קהל וש״ץ: יְהֵא שְׁמֵהּ רַבָּא מְבָרַךְ לְעָלַם וּלְעָלְמֵי עָלְמַיָּא.

ש״ץ: יִתְבָּרַךְ וְיִשְׁתַּבַּח וְיִתְפָּאַר
וְיִתְרוֹמַם וְיִתְנַשֵּׂא וְיִתְהַדָּר וְיִתְעַלֶּה וְיִתְהַלָּל
שְׁמֵהּ דְּקֻדְשָׁא בְּרִיךְ הוּא (קהל: בְּרִיךְ הוּא)
לְעֵלָּא מִן כָּל בִּרְכָתָא וְשִׁירָתָא, תֻּשְׁבְּחָתָא וְנֶחֱמָתָא
דַּאֲמִירָן בְּעָלְמָא
וְאִמְרוּ אָמֵן. (קהל: אָמֵן)

תִּתְקַבַּל צְלוֹתְהוֹן וּבָעוּתְהוֹן דְּכָל יִשְׂרָאֵל
קֳדָם אֲבוּהוֹן דִּי בִשְׁמַיָּא
וְאִמְרוּ אָמֵן. (קהל: אָמֵן)

יְהֵא שְׁלָמָא רַבָּא מִן שְׁמַיָּא וְחַיִּים
עָלֵינוּ וְעַל כָּל יִשְׂרָאֵל
וְאִמְרוּ אָמֵן. (קהל: אָמֵן)

Bow, take three steps back, as if taking leave of the Divine Presence,
then bow, first left, then right, then center, while saying:

עֹשֶׂה שָׁלוֹם בִּמְרוֹמָיו
הוּא יַעֲשֶׂה שָׁלוֹם עָלֵינוּ וְעַל כָּל יִשְׂרָאֵל
וְאִמְרוּ אָמֵן. (קהל: אָמֵן)

On הושענא רבה*, continue with The Removing of the Torah on page 985.*

REMOVING THE TORAH FROM THE ARK

The Ark is opened and the congregation stands. All say:

וַיְהִי בִּנְסֹעַ Whenever the Ark set out, Moses would say, *Num. 10*
"Arise, LORD, and may Your enemies be scattered.
May those who hate You flee before You."
For the Torah shall come forth from Zion, *Is. 2*
and the word of the LORD from Jerusalem.
Blessed is He who in His holiness
gave the Torah to His people Israel.

Blessed is the name of the Master of the Universe. Blessed is Your crown and Your place. May Your favor always be with Your people Israel. Show Your people the salvation of Your right hand in Your Temple. Grant us the gift of Your good light, and accept our prayers in mercy. May it be Your will to prolong our life in goodness. May I be counted among the righteous, so that You will have compassion on me and protect me and all that is mine and all that is Your people Israel's. You feed all; You sustain all; You rule over all; You rule over kings, for sovereignty is Yours. I am a servant of the Holy One, blessed be He, before whom and before whose glorious Torah I bow at all times. Not in man do I trust, nor on any angel do I rely, but on the God of heaven who is the God of truth, whose Torah is truth, whose prophets speak truth, and who abounds in acts of love and truth. ▸ In Him I trust, and to His holy and glorious name I offer praises. May it be Your will to open my heart to the Torah, and to fulfill the wishes of my heart and of the hearts of all Your people Israel for good, for life, and for peace. *Zohar, Vayak-hel*

The Torah scroll is removed from the Ark. The Leader takes it in his right arm and, followed by the congregation, says:

Magnify the LORD with me,
and let us exalt His name together. *Ps. 34*

The Ark is closed. The Leader carries the Torah scroll to the bima and the congregation says:

לְךָ Yours, LORD, are the greatness and the power, the glory and the majesty and splendor, for everything in heaven and earth is Yours. Yours, LORD, is the kingdom; You are exalted as Head over all. *1 Chr. 29*

רוֹמְמוּ Exalt the LORD our God and bow to His footstool; He is holy. Exalt the LORD our God, and bow at His holy mountain, for holy is the LORD our God. *Ps. 99*

הוצאת ספר תורה

The ארון קודש *is opened and the* קהל *stands. All say:*

וַיְהִי בִּנְסֹעַ הָאָרֹן וַיֹּאמֶר מֹשֶׁה במדבר י
קוּמָה יהוה וְיָפֻצוּ אֹיְבֶיךָ וְיָנֻסוּ מְשַׂנְאֶיךָ מִפָּנֶיךָ:
כִּי מִצִּיּוֹן תֵּצֵא תוֹרָה וּדְבַר־יהוה מִירוּשָׁלָםִ: ישעיה ב
בָּרוּךְ שֶׁנָּתַן תּוֹרָה לְעַמּוֹ יִשְׂרָאֵל בִּקְדֻשָּׁתוֹ.

בְּרִיךְ שְׁמֵהּ דְּמָרֵא עָלְמָא, בְּרִיךְ כִּתְרָךְ וְאַתְרָךְ. יְהֵא רְעוּתָךְ עִם עַמָּךְ יִשְׂרָאֵל לְעָלַם, וּפֻרְקַן יְמִינָךְ אַחֲזֵי לְעַמָּךְ בְּבֵית מַקְדְּשָׁךְ, וּלְאַמְטוּיֵי לַנָא מִטּוּב נְהוֹרָךְ, וּלְקַבֵּל צְלוֹתַנָא בְּרַחֲמִין. יְהֵא רַעֲוָא קֳדָמָךְ דְּתוֹרִיךְ לַן חַיִּין בְּטִיבוּ, וְלֶהֱוֵי אֲנָא פְּקִידָא בְּגוֹ צַדִּיקַיָּא, לְמִרְחַם עֲלַי וּלְמִנְטַר יָתִי וְיַת כָּל דִּי לִי וְדִי לְעַמָּךְ יִשְׂרָאֵל. אַנְתְּ הוּא זָן לְכֹלָּא וּמְפַרְנֵס לְכֹלָּא, אַנְתְּ הוּא שַׁלִּיט עַל כֹּלָּא, אַנְתְּ הוּא דְשַׁלִּיט עַל מַלְכַיָּא, וּמַלְכוּתָא דִּילָךְ הִיא. אֲנָא עַבְדָּא דְקֻדְשָׁא בְּרִיךְ הוּא, דְּסָגֵדְנָא קַמֵּהּ וּמִקַּמֵּי דִּיקַר אוֹרַיְתֵהּ בְּכָל עִדָּן וְעִדָּן. לָא עַל אֱנָשׁ רָחִיצְנָא וְלָא עַל בַּר אֱלָהִין סָמִיכְנָא, אֶלָּא בֶּאֱלָהָא דִשְׁמַיָּא, דְּהוּא אֱלָהָא קְשׁוֹט, וְאוֹרַיְתֵהּ קְשׁוֹט, וּנְבִיאוֹהִי קְשׁוֹט, וּמַסְגֵּא לְמֶעְבַּד טַבְוָן וּקְשׁוֹט. • בֵּהּ אֲנָא רָחִיץ, וְלִשְׁמֵהּ קַדִּישָׁא יַקִּירָא אֲנָא אֵמַר תֻּשְׁבְּחָן. יְהֵא רַעֲוָא קֳדָמָךְ דְּתִפְתַּח לִבַּאי בְּאוֹרַיְתָא, וְתַשְׁלִים מִשְׁאֲלִין דְּלִבַּאי וְלִבָּא דְכָל עַמָּךְ יִשְׂרָאֵל לְטָב וּלְחַיִּין וְלִשְׁלָם. זוהר ויקהל

The ספר תורה *is removed from the* ארון קודש*. The* שליח ציבור *takes it in his right arm and, followed by the* קהל*, says:*

גַּדְּלוּ לַיהוה אִתִּי וּנְרוֹמְמָה שְׁמוֹ יַחְדָּו: תהלים לד

The ארון קודש *is closed. The* שליח ציבור *carries the* ספר תורה *to the* בימה *and the* קהל *says:*

לְךָ יהוה הַגְּדֻלָּה וְהַגְּבוּרָה וְהַתִּפְאֶרֶת וְהַנֵּצַח וְהַהוֹד, כִּי־כֹל בַּשָּׁמַיִם וּבָאָרֶץ, לְךָ יהוה הַמַּמְלָכָה וְהַמִּתְנַשֵּׂא לְכֹל לְרֹאשׁ: דברי הימים א, כט

רוֹמְמוּ יהוה אֱלֹהֵינוּ וְהִשְׁתַּחֲווּ לַהֲדֹם רַגְלָיו, קָדוֹשׁ הוּא: רוֹמְמוּ יהוה אֱלֹהֵינוּ וְהִשְׁתַּחֲווּ לְהַר קָדְשׁוֹ, כִּי־קָדוֹשׁ יהוה אֱלֹהֵינוּ: תהלים צט

אַב הָרַחֲמִים May the Father of compassion have compassion on the people borne by Him. May He remember the covenant with the mighty [patriarchs], and deliver us from evil times. May He reproach the evil instinct in the people carried by Him, and graciously grant that we be an everlasting remnant. May He fulfill in good measure our requests for salvation and compassion.

The Torah scroll is placed on the bima and the Gabbai calls a Kohen to the Torah.

May His kingship over us be soon revealed and made manifest. May He be gracious to our surviving remnant, the remnant of His people the house of Israel in grace, loving-kindness, compassion and favor, and let us say: Amen. Let us all render greatness to our God and give honor to the Torah. *Let the Kohen come forward. Arise (*name* son of *father's name*), the Kohen.

**If no Kohen is present, a Levi or Yisrael is called up as follows:*

/As there is no Kohen, arise (*name* son of *father's name*) in place of a Kohen./

Blessed is He who, in His holiness, gave the Torah to His people Israel.

Congregation followed by the Gabbai:

You who cling to the LORD your God are all alive today. *Deut. 4*

The Reader shows the oleh the section to be read. The oleh touches the scroll at that place with the tzitzit of his tallit, which he then kisses. Holding the handles of the scroll, he says:

Oleh: Bless the LORD, the blessed One.

Cong: Bless the LORD, the blessed One, for ever and all time.

Oleh: Bless the LORD, the blessed One,
for ever and all time.

Blessed are You, LORD our God, King of the Universe,
who has chosen us from all peoples
and has given us His Torah.
Blessed are You, LORD, Giver of the Torah.

After the reading, the oleh says:

Oleh: Blessed are You, LORD our God, King of the Universe,
who has given us the Torah of truth,
planting everlasting life in our midst.
Blessed are You, LORD, Giver of the Torah.

אַב הָרַחֲמִים הוּא יְרַחֵם עַם עֲמוּסִים, וְיִזְכֹּר בְּרִית אֵיתָנִים, וְיַצִּיל נַפְשׁוֹתֵינוּ מִן הַשָּׁעוֹת הָרָעוֹת, וְיִגְעַר בְּיֵצֶר הָרָע מִן הַנְּשׂוּאִים, וְיָחֹן אוֹתָנוּ לִפְלֵיטַת עוֹלָמִים, וִימַלֵּא מִשְׁאֲלוֹתֵינוּ בְּמִדָּה טוֹבָה יְשׁוּעָה וְרַחֲמִים.

The ספר תורה is placed on the שולחן and the גבאי calls a כהן to the תורה.

וְתִגָּלֶה וְתֵרָאֶה מַלְכוּתוֹ עָלֵינוּ בִּזְמַן קָרוֹב, וְיָחֹן פְּלֵיטָתֵנוּ וּפְלֵיטַת עַמּוֹ בֵּית יִשְׂרָאֵל לְחֵן וּלְחֶסֶד וּלְרַחֲמִים וּלְרָצוֹן וְנֹאמַר אָמֵן. הַכֹּל הָבוּ גֹדֶל לֵאלֹהֵינוּ וּתְנוּ כָבוֹד לַתּוֹרָה. *כֹּהֵן קְרָב, יַעֲמֹד (פלוני בֶּן פלוני) הַכֹּהֵן.

**If no כהן is present, a לוי or ישראל is called up as follows:*

/אֵין כָּאן כֹּהֵן, יַעֲמֹד (פלוני בֶּן פלוני) בִּמְקוֹם כֹּהֵן./

בָּרוּךְ שֶׁנָּתַן תּוֹרָה לְעַמּוֹ יִשְׂרָאֵל בִּקְדֻשָּׁתוֹ.

The קהל followed by the גבאי:

וְאַתֶּם הַדְּבֵקִים בַּיהוה אֱלֹהֵיכֶם חַיִּים כֻּלְּכֶם הַיּוֹם: דברים ד

The קורא shows the עולה the section to be read. The עולה touches the scroll at that place with the ציצית of his טלית, which he then kisses. Holding the handles of the scroll, he says:

עולה: בָּרְכוּ אֶת יהוה הַמְבֹרָךְ.

קהל: בָּרוּךְ יהוה הַמְבֹרָךְ לְעוֹלָם וָעֶד.

עולה: בָּרוּךְ יהוה הַמְבֹרָךְ לְעוֹלָם וָעֶד.
בָּרוּךְ אַתָּה יהוה, אֱלֹהֵינוּ מֶלֶךְ הָעוֹלָם
אֲשֶׁר בָּחַר בָּנוּ מִכָּל הָעַמִּים וְנָתַן לָנוּ אֶת תּוֹרָתוֹ.
בָּרוּךְ אַתָּה יהוה, נוֹתֵן הַתּוֹרָה.

After the קריאת התורה, the עולה says:

עולה: בָּרוּךְ אַתָּה יהוה אֱלֹהֵינוּ מֶלֶךְ הָעוֹלָם
אֲשֶׁר נָתַן לָנוּ תּוֹרַת אֱמֶת וְחַיֵּי עוֹלָם נָטַע בְּתוֹכֵנוּ.
בָּרוּךְ אַתָּה יהוה, נוֹתֵן הַתּוֹרָה.

One who has survived a situation of danger says:

Blessed are You, LORD our God, King of the Universe, who bestows good on the unworthy, who has bestowed on me much good.

The congregation responds:

Amen. May He who bestowed much good on you continue to bestow on you much good, Selah.

TORAH READING FOR THE FIRST DAY OF HOL HAMO'ED

In Israel, the first three verses, "On the second day" through "its meal offering and their libations," are read for each of the four aliyot.

On the second day, twelve young bullocks, two rams, and fourteen unblemished yearling male lambs. And you shall perform their meal-offerings and their libations, for each of the bullocks, the rams and the lambs, in the proper quantities, according to the law. And likewise a male goat for atonement, as well as the regular daily offering and its meal offering and their libations. *Num. 29:17–25*

LEVI On the third day, eleven young bullocks, two rams, and fourteen unblemished yearling male lambs. And you shall perform their meal-offerings and their libations, for each of the bullocks, the rams and the lambs, in the proper quantities, according to the law. And likewise a male goat for atonement, as well as the regular daily offering and its meal offering and its libation.

SHELISHI On the fourth day, ten young bullocks, two rams, and fourteen unblemished yearling male lambs. And you shall perform their meal-offerings and their libations, for each of the bullocks, the rams and the lambs, in the proper quantities, according to the law. And likewise a male goat for atonement, as well as the regular daily offering and its meal offering and its libation.

REVI'I On the second day, twelve young bullocks, two rams, and fourteen unblemished yearling male lambs. And you shall perform their meal-offerings and their libations, for each of the bullocks, the rams and the lambs, in the proper quantities, according to the law. And likewise a male goat for atonement, as well as the regular daily offering and its meal offering and their libations.

On the third day, eleven young bullocks, two rams, and fourteen unblemished yearling male lambs. And you shall perform their meal-offerings and their libations, for each of the bullocks, the rams and the lambs, in

One who has survived a situation of danger says:

בָּרוּךְ אַתָּה יהוה אֱלֹהֵינוּ מֶלֶךְ הָעוֹלָם הַגּוֹמֵל לְחַיָּבִים טוֹבוֹת שֶׁגְּמָלַנִי כָּל טוֹב.

The קהל *responds:*

אָמֵן. מִי שֶׁגְּמָלְךָ כָּל טוֹב הוּא יִגְמָלְךָ כָּל טוֹב, סֶלָה.

קריאה ליום הראשון דחול המועד

In ארץ ישראל*, the first three verses,* וּבַיּוֹם הַשֵּׁנִי *through* וּמִנְחָתָהּ וְנִסְכֵּיהֶם*, are read for each of the four* עליות*.*

במדבר כט:יז–כה וּבַיּוֹם הַשֵּׁנִי פָּרִים בְּנֵי־בָקָר שְׁנֵים עָשָׂר אֵילִם שְׁנָיִם כְּבָשִׂים בְּנֵי־
שָׁנָה אַרְבָּעָה עָשָׂר תְּמִימִם: וּמִנְחָתָם וְנִסְכֵּיהֶם לַפָּרִים לָאֵילִם
וְלַכְּבָשִׂים בְּמִסְפָּרָם כַּמִּשְׁפָּט: וּשְׂעִיר־עִזִּים אֶחָד חַטָּאת מִלְּבַד
לוי עֹלַת הַתָּמִיד וּמִנְחָתָהּ וְנִסְכֵּיהֶם: *וּבַיּוֹם הַשְּׁלִישִׁי
פָּרִים עַשְׁתֵּי־עָשָׂר אֵילִם שְׁנָיִם כְּבָשִׂים בְּנֵי־שָׁנָה אַרְבָּעָה עָשָׂר
תְּמִימִם: וּמִנְחָתָם וְנִסְכֵּיהֶם לַפָּרִים לָאֵילִם וְלַכְּבָשִׂים בְּמִסְפָּרָם
כַּמִּשְׁפָּט: וּשְׂעִיר חַטָּאת אֶחָד מִלְּבַד עֹלַת הַתָּמִיד וּמִנְחָתָהּ
שלישי וְנִסְכָּהּ: *וּבַיּוֹם הָרְבִיעִי פָּרִים עֲשָׂרָה אֵילִם שְׁנָיִם
כְּבָשִׂים בְּנֵי־שָׁנָה אַרְבָּעָה עָשָׂר תְּמִימִם: מִנְחָתָם וְנִסְכֵּיהֶם
לַפָּרִים לָאֵילִם וְלַכְּבָשִׂים בְּמִסְפָּרָם כַּמִּשְׁפָּט: וּשְׂעִיר־עִזִּים אֶחָד
חַטָּאת מִלְּבַד עֹלַת הַתָּמִיד מִנְחָתָהּ וְנִסְכָּהּ:

רביעי וּבַיּוֹם הַשֵּׁנִי פָּרִים בְּנֵי־בָקָר שְׁנֵים עָשָׂר אֵילִם שְׁנָיִם כְּבָשִׂים
בְּנֵי־שָׁנָה אַרְבָּעָה עָשָׂר תְּמִימִם: וּמִנְחָתָם וְנִסְכֵּיהֶם לַפָּרִים
לָאֵילִם וְלַכְּבָשִׂים בְּמִסְפָּרָם כַּמִּשְׁפָּט: וּשְׂעִיר־עִזִּים אֶחָד חַטָּאת
מִלְּבַד עֹלַת הַתָּמִיד וּמִנְחָתָהּ וְנִסְכֵּיהֶם: וּבַיּוֹם
הַשְּׁלִישִׁי פָּרִים עַשְׁתֵּי־עָשָׂר אֵילִם שְׁנָיִם כְּבָשִׂים בְּנֵי־שָׁנָה
אַרְבָּעָה עָשָׂר תְּמִימִם: וּמִנְחָתָם וְנִסְכֵּיהֶם לַפָּרִים לָאֵילִם

the proper quantities, according to the law. And likewise a male goat for atonement, as well as the regular daily offering and its meal offering and its libation.

Continue with Half Kaddish on page 682.

TORAH READING FOR THE SECOND DAY OF ḤOL HAMO'ED

In Israel, the first three verses, "On the third day" through "its meal offering and its libation," are read for each of the four aliyot.

On the third day, eleven young bullocks, two rams, and fourteen unblemished yearling male lambs. And you shall perform their meal-offerings and their libations, for each of the bullocks, the rams and the lambs, in the proper quantities, according to the law. And likewise a male goat for atonement, as well as the regular daily offering and its meal offering and its libation. *Num. 29:20–28*

LEVI On the fourth day, ten young bullocks, two rams, and fourteen unblemished yearling male lambs. And you shall perform their meal-offerings and their libations, for each of the bullocks, the rams and the lambs, in the proper quantities, according to the law. And likewise a male goat for atonement, as well as the regular daily offering and its meal offering and its libation.

SHELISHI On the fifth day, nine young bullocks, two rams, and fourteen unblemished yearling male lambs. And you shall perform their meal-offerings and their libations, for each of the bullocks, the rams and the lambs, in the proper quantities, according to the law. And likewise a male goat for atonement, as well as the regular daily offering and its meal offering and its libation.

REVI'I On the third day, eleven young bullocks, two rams, and fourteen unblemished yearling male lambs. And you shall perform their meal-offerings and their libations, for each of the bullocks, the rams and the lambs, in the proper quantities, according to the law. And likewise a male goat for atonement, as well as the regular daily offering and its meal offering and its libation.

On the fourth day, ten young bullocks, two rams, and fourteen unblemished yearling male lambs. And you shall perform their meal-offerings and their libations, for each of the bullocks, the rams and the lambs, in the proper quantities, according to the law. And likewise a male goat for atonement, as well as the regular daily offering and its meal offering and its libation.

Continue with Half Kaddish on page 682.

וְלַכְּבָשִׂ֛ים בְּמִסְפָּרָ֖ם כַּמִּשְׁפָּֽט׃ וּשְׂעִ֥יר חַטָּ֖את אֶחָ֑ד מִלְּבַד֙ עֹלַ֣ת
הַתָּמִ֔יד וּמִנְחָתָ֖הּ וְנִסְכָּֽהּ׃

Continue with חצי קדיש *on page 683.*

קריאה ליום השני דחול המועד

In ארץ ישראל*, the first three verses,* וּבַיּוֹם הַשְּׁלִישִׁי *through* וּמִנְחָתָהּ וְנִסְכָּהּ*, are read for each of the four* עליות*.*

וּבַיּ֧וֹם הַשְּׁלִישִׁ֛י פָּרִ֥ים עַשְׁתֵּי־עָשָׂ֖ר אֵילִ֣ם שְׁנָ֑יִם כְּבָשִׂ֧ים בְּנֵי־ במדבר כט:כ–כח
שָׁנָ֛ה אַרְבָּעָ֥ה עָשָׂ֖ר תְּמִימִֽם׃ וּמִנְחָתָ֣ם וְנִסְכֵּיהֶ֡ם לַ֠פָּרִים לָֽאֵילִ֧ם
וְלַכְּבָשִׂ֛ים בְּמִסְפָּרָ֖ם כַּמִּשְׁפָּֽט׃ וּשְׂעִ֥יר חַטָּ֖את אֶחָ֑ד מִלְּבַד֙ עֹלַ֣ת
הַתָּמִ֔יד וּמִנְחָתָ֖הּ וְנִסְכָּֽהּ׃ ★וּבַיּ֧וֹם הָרְבִיעִ֛י פָּרִ֥ים לוי
עֲשָׂרָ֖ה אֵילִ֣ם שְׁנָ֑יִם כְּבָשִׂ֧ים בְּנֵי־שָׁנָ֛ה אַרְבָּעָ֥ה עָשָׂ֖ר תְּמִימִֽם׃
מִנְחָתָ֣ם וְנִסְכֵּיהֶ֡ם לַ֠פָּרִים לָאֵילִ֧ם וְלַכְּבָשִׂ֛ים בְּמִסְפָּרָ֖ם כַּמִּשְׁפָּֽט׃
וּשְׂעִיר־עִזִּ֥ים אֶחָ֖ד חַטָּ֑את מִלְּבַד֙ עֹלַ֣ת הַתָּמִ֔יד מִנְחָתָ֖הּ
וְנִסְכָּֽהּ׃ ★וּבַיּ֧וֹם הַחֲמִישִׁ֛י פָּרִ֥ים תִּשְׁעָ֖ה אֵילִ֣ם שְׁנָ֑יִם שלישי
כְּבָשִׂ֧ים בְּנֵי־שָׁנָ֛ה אַרְבָּעָ֥ה עָשָׂ֖ר תְּמִימִֽם׃ וּמִנְחָתָ֣ם וְנִסְכֵּיהֶ֡ם
לַ֠פָּרִים לָאֵילִ֧ם וְלַכְּבָשִׂ֛ים בְּמִסְפָּרָ֖ם כַּמִּשְׁפָּֽט׃ וּשְׂעִ֥יר חַטָּ֖את
אֶחָ֑ד מִלְּבַד֙ עֹלַ֣ת הַתָּמִ֔יד וּמִנְחָתָ֖הּ וְנִסְכָּֽהּ׃
וּבַיּ֧וֹם הַשְּׁלִישִׁ֛י פָּרִ֥ים עַשְׁתֵּי־עָשָׂ֖ר אֵילִ֣ם שְׁנָ֑יִם כְּבָשִׂ֧ים בְּנֵי־ רביעי
שָׁנָ֛ה אַרְבָּעָ֥ה עָשָׂ֖ר תְּמִימִֽם׃ וּמִנְחָתָ֣ם וְנִסְכֵּיהֶ֡ם לַ֠פָּרִים לָֽאֵילִ֧ם
וְלַכְּבָשִׂ֛ים בְּמִסְפָּרָ֖ם כַּמִּשְׁפָּֽט׃ וּשְׂעִ֥יר חַטָּ֖את אֶחָ֑ד מִלְּבַד֙
עֹלַ֣ת הַתָּמִ֔יד וּמִנְחָתָ֖הּ וְנִסְכָּֽהּ׃ וּבַיּ֧וֹם הָרְבִיעִ֛י
פָּרִ֥ים עֲשָׂרָ֖ה אֵילִ֣ם שְׁנָ֑יִם כְּבָשִׂ֧ים בְּנֵי־שָׁנָ֛ה אַרְבָּעָ֥ה עָשָׂ֖ר
תְּמִימִֽם׃ מִנְחָתָ֣ם וְנִסְכֵּיהֶ֡ם לַ֠פָּרִים לָאֵילִ֧ם וְלַכְּבָשִׂ֛ים בְּמִסְפָּרָ֖ם
כַּמִּשְׁפָּֽט׃ וּשְׂעִיר־עִזִּ֥ים אֶחָ֖ד חַטָּ֑את מִלְּבַד֙ עֹלַ֣ת הַתָּמִ֔יד
מִנְחָתָ֖הּ וְנִסְכָּֽהּ׃

Continue with חצי קדיש *on page 683.*

TORAH READING FOR THE THIRD DAY OF ḤOL HAMO'ED

In Israel, the first three verses, "On the fourth day" through "its meal offering and its libation," are read for each of the four aliyot.

On the fourth day, ten young bullocks, two rams, and fourteen unblemished yearling male lambs. And you shall perform their meal-offerings and their libations, for each of the bullocks, the rams and the lambs, in the proper quantities, according to the law. And likewise a male goat for atonement, as well as the regular daily offering and its meal offering and its libation. *Num. 29:23–31*

LEVI On the fifth day, nine young bullocks, two rams, and fourteen unblemished yearling male lambs. And you shall perform their meal-offerings and their libations, for each of the bullocks, the rams and the lambs, in the proper quantities, according to the law. And likewise a male goat for atonement, as well as the regular daily offering and its meal offering and its libation.

SHELISHI On the sixth day, eighth young bullocks, two rams, and fourteen unblemished yearling male lambs. And you shall perform their meal-offerings and their libations, for each of the bullocks, the rams and the lambs, in the proper quantities, according to the law. And likewise a male goat for atonement, as well as the regular daily offering and its meal offering and its libations.

REVI'I On the fourth day, ten young bullocks, two rams, and fourteen unblemished yearling male lambs. And you shall perform their meal-offerings and their libations, for each of the bullocks, the rams and the lambs, in the proper quantities, according to the law. And likewise a male goat for atonement, as well as the regular daily offering and its meal offering and its libation.

On the fifth day, nine young bullocks, two rams, and fourteen unblemished yearling male lambs. And you shall perform their meal-offerings and their libations, for each of the bullocks, the rams and the lambs, in the proper quantities, according to the law. And likewise a male goat for atonement, as well as the regular daily offering and its meal offering and its libation.

Continue with Half Kaddish on page 682.

TORAH READING FOR THE FOURTH DAY OF ḤOL HAMO'ED

In Israel, the first three verses, "On the fifth day" through "its meal offering and its libation," are read for each of the four aliyot.

On the fifth day, nine young bullocks, two rams, and fourteen unblemished *Num. 29:26–34*

קריאה ליום השלישי דחול המועד

In ארץ ישראל*, the first three verses,* וּבַיּוֹם הָרְבִיעִי *through* מִנְחָתָהּ וְנִסְכָּהּ*, are read for each of the four* עליות*.*

במדבר כט:כג–לא וּבַיּוֹם הָרְבִיעִי פָּרִים עֲשָׂרָה אֵילִם שְׁנָיִם כְּבָשִׂים בְּנֵי־שָׁנָה
אַרְבָּעָה עָשָׂר תְּמִימִם: מִנְחָתָם וְנִסְכֵּיהֶם לַפָּרִים לָאֵילִם
וְלַכְּבָשִׂים בְּמִסְפָּרָם כַּמִּשְׁפָּט: וּשְׂעִיר־עִזִּים אֶחָד חַטָּאת מִלְּבַד
לוי עֹלַת הַתָּמִיד מִנְחָתָהּ וְנִסְכָּהּ: *וּבַיּוֹם הַחֲמִישִׁי
פָּרִים תִּשְׁעָה אֵילִם שְׁנָיִם כְּבָשִׂים בְּנֵי־שָׁנָה אַרְבָּעָה עָשָׂר
תְּמִימִם: וּמִנְחָתָם וְנִסְכֵּיהֶם לַפָּרִים לָאֵילִם וְלַכְּבָשִׂים בְּמִסְפָּרָם
כַּמִּשְׁפָּט: וּשְׂעִיר חַטָּאת אֶחָד מִלְּבַד עֹלַת הַתָּמִיד וּמִנְחָתָהּ
שלישי וְנִסְכָּהּ: *וּבַיּוֹם הַשִּׁשִּׁי פָּרִים שְׁמֹנָה אֵילִם שְׁנָיִם
כְּבָשִׂים בְּנֵי־שָׁנָה אַרְבָּעָה עָשָׂר תְּמִימִם: וּמִנְחָתָם וְנִסְכֵּיהֶם
לַפָּרִים לָאֵילִם וְלַכְּבָשִׂים בְּמִסְפָּרָם כַּמִּשְׁפָּט: וּשְׂעִיר חַטָּאת
אֶחָד מִלְּבַד עֹלַת הַתָּמִיד מִנְחָתָהּ וּנְסָכֶיהָ:

רביעי וּבַיּוֹם הָרְבִיעִי פָּרִים עֲשָׂרָה אֵילִם שְׁנָיִם כְּבָשִׂים בְּנֵי־שָׁנָה אַרְבָּעָה
עָשָׂר תְּמִימִם: מִנְחָתָם וְנִסְכֵּיהֶם לַפָּרִים לָאֵילִם וְלַכְּבָשִׂים
בְּמִסְפָּרָם כַּמִּשְׁפָּט: וּשְׂעִיר־עִזִּים אֶחָד חַטָּאת מִלְּבַד עֹלַת
הַתָּמִיד מִנְחָתָהּ וְנִסְכָּהּ: וּבַיּוֹם הַחֲמִישִׁי פָּרִים
תִּשְׁעָה אֵילִם שְׁנָיִם כְּבָשִׂים בְּנֵי־שָׁנָה אַרְבָּעָה עָשָׂר תְּמִימִם:
וּמִנְחָתָם וְנִסְכֵּיהֶם לַפָּרִים לָאֵילִם וְלַכְּבָשִׂים בְּמִסְפָּרָם כַּמִּשְׁפָּט:
וּשְׂעִיר חַטָּאת אֶחָד מִלְּבַד עֹלַת הַתָּמִיד וּמִנְחָתָהּ וְנִסְכָּהּ:

Continue with חצי קדיש *on page 683.*

קריאה ליום הרביעי דחול המועד

In ארץ ישראל*, the first three verses,* וּבַיּוֹם הַחֲמִישִׁי *through* וּמִנְחָתָהּ וְנִסְכָּהּ*, are read for each of the four* עליות*.*

במדבר כט:כו–לד וּבַיּוֹם הַחֲמִישִׁי פָּרִים תִּשְׁעָה אֵילִם שְׁנָיִם כְּבָשִׂים בְּנֵי־שָׁנָה

yearling male lambs. And you shall perform their meal-offerings and their libations, for each of the bullocks, the rams and the lambs, in the proper quantities, according to the law. And likewise a male goat for atonement, as well as the regular daily offering and its meal offering and its libation.

On the sixth day, eight young bullocks, two rams, and fourteen unblemished yearling male lambs. And you shall perform their meal-offerings and their libations, for each of the bullocks, the rams and the lambs, in the proper quantities, according to the law. And likewise a male goat for atonement, as well as the regular daily offering and its meal offering and its libations. LEVI

On the seventh day, seven young bullocks, two rams, and fourteen unblemished yearling male lambs. And you shall perform their meal-offerings and their libations, for each of the bullocks, the rams and the lambs, in the proper quantities, according to the law. And likewise a male goat for atonement, as well as the regular daily offering and its meal offering and its libation. SHELISHI

On the fifth day, nine young bullocks, two rams, and fourteen unblemished yearling male lambs. And you shall perform their meal-offerings and their libations, for each of the bullocks, the rams and the lambs, in the proper quantities, according to the law. And likewise a male goat for atonement, as well as the regular daily offering and its meal offering and its libation. REVI'I

On the sixth day, eight young bullocks, two rams, and fourteen unblemished yearling male lambs. And you shall perform their meal-offerings and their libations, for each of the bullocks, the rams and the lambs, in the proper quantities, according to the law. And likewise a male goat for atonement, as well as the regular daily offering and its meal offering and its libations.

Continue with Half Kaddish on the next page.

TORAH READING FOR THE FIFTH DAY OF ḤOL HAMO'ED IN ISRAEL

In Israel, the following is read for each of the four aliyot.

On the sixth day, eight young bullocks, two rams, and fourteen unblemished yearling male lambs. And you shall perform their meal-offerings and their libations, for each of the bullocks, the rams and the lambs, in the proper quantities, according to the law. And likewise a male goat for atonement, as well as the regular daily offering and its meal offering and its libations. *Num. 29:29–31*

ארבעה עשר תמימם: ומנחתם ונסכיהם לפרים לאילם ולכבשים במספרם כמשפט: ושעיר חטאת אחד מלבד עלת התמיד ומנחתה ונסכה: *וביום הששי לוי
פרים שמנה אילם שנים כבשים בני־שנה ארבעה עשר תמימם: ומנחתם ונסכיהם לפרים לאילם ולכבשים במספרם כמשפט: ושעיר חטאת אחד מלבד עלת התמיד מנחתה ונסכיה: *וביום השביעי פרים שבעה אילם שנים שלישי
כבשים בני־שנה ארבעה עשר תמימם: ומנחתם ונסכהם לפרים לאילם ולכבשים במספרם כמשפטם: ושעיר חטאת אחד מלבד עלת התמיד מנחתה ונסכה:

וביום החמישי פרים תשעה אילם שנים כבשים בני־שנה רביעי
ארבעה עשר תמימם: ומנחתם ונסכיהם לפרים לאילם ולכבשים במספרם כמשפט: ושעיר חטאת אחד מלבד עלת התמיד ומנחתה ונסכה: וביום הששי פרים שמנה אילם שנים כבשים בני־שנה ארבעה עשר תמימם: ומנחתם ונסכיהם לפרים לאילם ולכבשים במספרם כמשפט: ושעיר חטאת אחד מלבד עלת התמיד מנחתה ונסכיה:

Continue with חצי קדיש *on the next page.*

קריאה ליום החמישי דחול המועד סוכות בארץ ישראל

In ארץ ישראל*, the following is read for each of the four* עליות*.*

וביום הששי פרים שמנה אילם שנים כבשים בני־שנה ארבעה במדבר כט:כט–לא
עשר תמימם: ומנחתם ונסכיהם לפרים לאילם ולכבשים במספרם כמשפט: ושעיר חטאת אחד מלבד עלת התמיד מנחתה ונסכיה:

HALF KADDISH

After the Reading of the Torah, the Reader says Half Kaddish:

Reader: יִתְגַּדַּל Magnified and sanctified
may His great name be,
in the world He created by His will.
May He establish His kingdom
in your lifetime and in your days,
and in the lifetime of all the house of Israel,
swiftly and soon –
and say: Amen.

All: May His great name be blessed for ever and all time.

Reader: Blessed and praised,
glorified and exalted,
raised and honored,
uplifted and lauded
be the name of the Holy One,
blessed be He,
beyond any blessing, song,
praise and consolation
uttered in the world –
and say: Amen.

HAGBAHA AND GELILA

The Torah scroll is lifted and the congregation says:

וְזֹאת הַתּוֹרָה This is the Torah *Deut. 4*
that Moses placed before the children of Israel,
at the LORD's commandment, by the hand of Moses. *Num. 9*

Some add:
It is a tree of life to those who grasp it, and those who uphold it are happy. *Prov. 3*
Its ways are ways of pleasantness, and all its paths are peace.
Long life is at its right hand; at its left, riches and honor.
It pleased the LORD for the sake of [Israel's] righteousness, *Is. 42*
to make the Torah great and glorious.

חצי קדיש

After קריאת התורה, *the* קורא *says* חצי קדיש:

קורא: יִתְגַּדַּל וְיִתְקַדַּשׁ שְׁמֵהּ רַבָּא (קהל: אָמֵן)
בְּעָלְמָא דִּי בְרָא כִרְעוּתֵהּ
וְיַמְלִיךְ מַלְכוּתֵהּ
בְּחַיֵּיכוֹן וּבְיוֹמֵיכוֹן וּבְחַיֵּי דְכָל בֵּית יִשְׂרָאֵל
בַּעֲגָלָא וּבִזְמַן קָרִיב
וְאִמְרוּ אָמֵן. (קהל: אָמֵן)

קהל וקורא: יְהֵא שְׁמֵהּ רַבָּא מְבָרַךְ לְעָלַם וּלְעָלְמֵי עָלְמַיָּא.

קורא: יִתְבָּרַךְ וְיִשְׁתַּבַּח וְיִתְפָּאַר וְיִתְרוֹמַם וְיִתְנַשֵּׂא
וְיִתְהַדָּר וְיִתְעַלֶּה וְיִתְהַלָּל
שְׁמֵהּ דְּקֻדְשָׁא בְּרִיךְ הוּא (קהל: בְּרִיךְ הוּא)
לְעֵלָּא מִן כָּל בִּרְכָתָא וְשִׁירָתָא
תֻּשְׁבְּחָתָא וְנֶחֱמָתָא
דַּאֲמִירָן בְּעָלְמָא
וְאִמְרוּ אָמֵן. (קהל: אָמֵן)

הגבהה וגלילה

The ספר תורה *is lifted and the* קהל *says:*

דברים ד וְזֹאת הַתּוֹרָה אֲשֶׁר־שָׂם מֹשֶׁה לִפְנֵי בְּנֵי יִשְׂרָאֵל:
במדבר ט עַל־פִּי יהוה בְּיַד מֹשֶׁה:

Some add

משלי ג עֵץ־חַיִּים הִיא לַמַּחֲזִיקִים בָּהּ וְתֹמְכֶיהָ מְאֻשָּׁר:
דְּרָכֶיהָ דַרְכֵי־נֹעַם וְכָל־נְתִיבֹתֶיהָ שָׁלוֹם:
אֹרֶךְ יָמִים בִּימִינָהּ, בִּשְׂמֹאולָהּ עֹשֶׁר וְכָבוֹד:
ישעיה מב יהוה חָפֵץ לְמַעַן צִדְקוֹ יַגְדִּיל תּוֹרָה וְיַאְדִּיר:

RETURNING THE TORAH TO THE ARK

The Ark is opened. The Leader takes the Torah scroll and says:

יְהַלְלוּ Let them praise the name of the LORD, Ps. 148
for His name alone is sublime.

The congregation responds:

הוֹדוֹ His majesty is above earth and heaven.
He has raised the horn of His people,
for the glory of all His devoted ones,
the children of Israel, the people close to Him.
Halleluya!

As the Torah scroll is returned to the Ark, say:

לְדָוִד מִזְמוֹר A psalm of David. The earth is the LORD's and all it contains, Ps. 24
the world and all who live in it. For He founded it on the seas and established it on the streams. Who may climb the mountain of the LORD? Who may stand in His holy place? He who has clean hands and a pure heart, who has not taken My name in vain, or sworn deceitfully. He shall receive blessing from the LORD, and just reward from God, his salvation. This is a generation of those who seek Him, the descendants of Jacob who seek Your presence, Selah! Lift up your heads, O gates; be uplifted, eternal doors, so that the King of glory may enter. Who is the King of glory? It is the LORD, strong and mighty, the LORD mighty in battle. ▸ Lift up your heads, O gates; be uplifted, eternal doors, so that the King of glory may enter. Who is He, the King of glory? The LORD of hosts, He is the King of glory, Selah!

As the Torah scroll is placed into the Ark, say:

וּבְנֻחֹה יֹאמַר When the Ark came to rest, Moses would say: "Return, Num. 10
O LORD, to the myriad thousands of Israel." Advance, LORD, to Your Ps. 132
resting place, You and Your mighty Ark. Your priests are clothed in righteousness, and Your devoted ones sing in joy. For the sake of Your
servant David, do not reject Your anointed one. For I give you good Prov. 4
instruction; do not forsake My Torah. It is a tree of life to those who Prov. 3
grasp it, and those who uphold it are happy. Its ways are ways of pleasantness, and all its paths are peace. ▸ Turn us back, O LORD, to You, and Lam. 5
we will return. Renew our days as of old.

The Ark is closed.

הכנסת ספר תורה

The ארון קודש is opened. The שליח ציבור takes the ספר תורה and says:

יְהַלְלוּ אֶת־שֵׁם יהוה, כִּי נִשְׂגָּב־שְׁמוֹ, לְבַדּוֹ תהלים קמח

The קהל responds:

הוֹדוֹ עַל־אֶרֶץ וְשָׁמָיִם:
וַיָּרֶם קֶרֶן לְעַמּוֹ
תְּהִלָּה לְכָל־חֲסִידָיו
לִבְנֵי יִשְׂרָאֵל עַם קְרֹבוֹ, הַלְלוּיָהּ:

As the ספר תורה is returned to the ארון קודש, say:

לְדָוִד מִזְמוֹר, לַיהוה הָאָרֶץ וּמְלוֹאָהּ, תֵּבֵל וְיֽשְׁבֵי בָהּ: כִּי־הוּא עַל־ תהלים כד
יַמִּים יְסָדָהּ, וְעַל־נְהָרוֹת יְכוֹנְנֶהָ: מִי־יַעֲלֶה בְהַר־יהוה, וּמִי־יָקוּם
בִּמְקוֹם קָדְשׁוֹ: נְקִי כַפַּיִם וּבַר־לֵבָב, אֲשֶׁר לֹא־נָשָׂא לַשָּׁוְא נַפְשִׁי
וְלֹא נִשְׁבַּע לְמִרְמָה: יִשָּׂא בְרָכָה מֵאֵת יהוה, וּצְדָקָה מֵאֱלֹהֵי יִשְׁעוֹ:
זֶה דּוֹר דֹּרְשָׁו, מְבַקְשֵׁי פָנֶיךָ, יַעֲקֹב, סֶלָה: שְׂאוּ שְׁעָרִים רָאשֵׁיכֶם,
וְהִנָּשְׂאוּ פִּתְחֵי עוֹלָם, וְיָבוֹא מֶלֶךְ הַכָּבוֹד: מִי זֶה מֶלֶךְ הַכָּבוֹד, יהוה
עִזּוּז וְגִבּוֹר, יהוה גִּבּוֹר מִלְחָמָה: ‹ שְׂאוּ שְׁעָרִים רָאשֵׁיכֶם, וּשְׂאוּ
פִּתְחֵי עוֹלָם, וְיָבֹא מֶלֶךְ הַכָּבוֹד: מִי הוּא זֶה מֶלֶךְ הַכָּבוֹד, יהוה
צְבָאוֹת הוּא מֶלֶךְ הַכָּבוֹד, סֶלָה:

As the ספר תורה is placed into the ארון קודש, say:

וּבְנֻחֹה יֹאמַר, שׁוּבָה יהוה רִבְבוֹת אַלְפֵי יִשְׂרָאֵל: קוּמָה יהוה במדבר י
לִמְנוּחָתֶךָ, אַתָּה וַאֲרוֹן עֻזֶּךָ: כֹּהֲנֶיךָ יִלְבְּשׁוּ־צֶדֶק, וַחֲסִידֶיךָ יְרַנֵּנוּ: תהלים קלב
בַּעֲבוּר דָּוִד עַבְדֶּךָ אַל־תָּשֵׁב פְּנֵי מְשִׁיחֶךָ: כִּי לֶקַח טוֹב נָתַתִּי משלי ד
לָכֶם, תּוֹרָתִי אַל־תַּעֲזֹבוּ: עֵץ־חַיִּים הִיא לַמַּחֲזִיקִים בָּהּ, וְתֹמְכֶיהָ משלי ג
מְאֻשָּׁר: דְּרָכֶיהָ דַרְכֵי־נֹעַם וְכָל־נְתִיבֹתֶיהָ שָׁלוֹם: ‹ הֲשִׁיבֵנוּ יהוה איכה ה
אֵלֶיךָ וְנָשׁוּבָ, חַדֵּשׁ יָמֵינוּ כְּקֶדֶם:

The ארון קודש is closed.

אַשְׁרֵי Happy are those who dwell in Your House; Ps. 84
they shall continue to praise You, Selah!
Happy are the people for whom this is so; Ps. 144
happy are the people whose God is the LORD.
A song of praise by David. Ps. 145

I will exalt You, my God, the King, and bless Your name for ever and all time. Every day I will bless You, and praise Your name for ever and all time. Great is the LORD and greatly to be praised; His greatness is unfathomable. One generation will praise Your works to the next, and tell of Your mighty deeds. On the glorious splendor of Your majesty I will meditate, and on the acts of Your wonders. They shall talk of the power of Your awesome deeds, and I will tell of Your greatness. They shall recite the record of Your great goodness, and sing with joy of Your righteousness. The LORD is gracious and compassionate, slow to anger and great in loving-kindness. The LORD is good to all, and His compassion extends to all His works. All Your works shall thank You, LORD, and Your devoted ones shall bless You. They shall talk of the glory of Your kingship, and speak of Your might. To make known to mankind His mighty deeds and the glorious majesty of His kingship. Your kingdom is an everlasting kingdom, and Your reign is for all generations. The LORD supports all who fall, and raises all who are bowed down. All raise their eyes to You in hope, and You give them their food in due season. You open Your hand, and satisfy every living thing with favor. The LORD is righteous in all His ways, and kind in all He does. The LORD is close to all who call on Him, to all who call on Him in truth. He fulfills the will of those who revere Him; He hears their cry and saves them. The LORD guards all who love Him, but all the wicked He will destroy. ▸ My mouth shall speak the praise of the LORD, and all creatures shall bless His holy name for ever and all time.

We will bless the LORD now and for ever. Halleluya! Ps. 115

אַשְׁרֵי יוֹשְׁבֵי בֵיתֶךָ, עוֹד יְהַלְלוּךָ סֶּלָה: תהלים פד

אַשְׁרֵי הָעָם שֶׁכָּכָה לּוֹ, אַשְׁרֵי הָעָם שֶׁיהוה אֱלֹהָיו: תהלים קמד

תְּהִלָּה לְדָוִד תהלים קמה

אֲרוֹמִמְךָ אֱלוֹהַי הַמֶּלֶךְ, וַאֲבָרְכָה שִׁמְךָ לְעוֹלָם וָעֶד:

בְּכָל־יוֹם אֲבָרְכֶךָּ, וַאֲהַלְלָה שִׁמְךָ לְעוֹלָם וָעֶד:

גָּדוֹל יהוה וּמְהֻלָּל מְאֹד, וְלִגְדֻלָּתוֹ אֵין חֵקֶר:

דּוֹר לְדוֹר יְשַׁבַּח מַעֲשֶׂיךָ, וּגְבוּרֹתֶיךָ יַגִּידוּ:

הֲדַר כְּבוֹד הוֹדֶךָ, וְדִבְרֵי נִפְלְאֹתֶיךָ אָשִׂיחָה:

וֶעֱזוּז נוֹרְאֹתֶיךָ יֹאמֵרוּ, וּגְדוּלָּתְךָ אֲסַפְּרֶנָּה:

זֵכֶר רַב־טוּבְךָ יַבִּיעוּ, וְצִדְקָתְךָ יְרַנֵּנוּ:

חַנּוּן וְרַחוּם יהוה, אֶרֶךְ אַפַּיִם וּגְדָל־חָסֶד:

טוֹב־יהוה לַכֹּל, וְרַחֲמָיו עַל־כָּל־מַעֲשָׂיו:

יוֹדוּךָ יהוה כָּל־מַעֲשֶׂיךָ, וַחֲסִידֶיךָ יְבָרְכוּכָה:

כְּבוֹד מַלְכוּתְךָ יֹאמֵרוּ, וּגְבוּרָתְךָ יְדַבֵּרוּ:

לְהוֹדִיעַ לִבְנֵי הָאָדָם גְּבוּרֹתָיו, וּכְבוֹד הֲדַר מַלְכוּתוֹ:

מַלְכוּתְךָ מַלְכוּת כָּל־עֹלָמִים, וּמֶמְשַׁלְתְּךָ בְּכָל־דּוֹר וָדֹר:

סוֹמֵךְ יהוה לְכָל־הַנֹּפְלִים, וְזוֹקֵף לְכָל־הַכְּפוּפִים:

עֵינֵי־כֹל אֵלֶיךָ יְשַׂבֵּרוּ, וְאַתָּה נוֹתֵן־לָהֶם אֶת־אָכְלָם בְּעִתּוֹ:

פּוֹתֵחַ אֶת־יָדֶךָ, וּמַשְׂבִּיעַ לְכָל־חַי רָצוֹן:

צַדִּיק יהוה בְּכָל־דְּרָכָיו, וְחָסִיד בְּכָל־מַעֲשָׂיו:

קָרוֹב יהוה לְכָל־קֹרְאָיו, לְכֹל אֲשֶׁר יִקְרָאֻהוּ בֶאֱמֶת:

רְצוֹן־יְרֵאָיו יַעֲשֶׂה, וְאֶת־שַׁוְעָתָם יִשְׁמַע, וְיוֹשִׁיעֵם:

שׁוֹמֵר יהוה אֶת־כָּל־אֹהֲבָיו, וְאֵת כָּל־הָרְשָׁעִים יַשְׁמִיד:

◂ תְּהִלַּת יהוה יְדַבֶּר פִּי, וִיבָרֵךְ כָּל־בָּשָׂר שֵׁם קָדְשׁוֹ לְעוֹלָם וָעֶד:

וַאֲנַחְנוּ נְבָרֵךְ יָהּ מֵעַתָּה וְעַד־עוֹלָם, הַלְלוּיָהּ: תהלים קטו

וּבָא לְצִיּוֹן גּוֹאֵל "A redeemer will come to Zion, *Is. 59*
to those of Jacob who repent of their sins," declares the LORD.
"As for Me, this is My covenant with them," says the LORD.
"My spirit, that is on you, and My words I have placed in your mouth will not depart from your mouth, or from the mouth of your children, or from the mouth of their descendants from this time on and for ever," says the LORD.

▸ You are the Holy One, enthroned on the praises of Israel. *Ps. 22*
And [the angels] call to one another, saying, ◂ "Holy, holy, holy *Is. 6*
is the LORD of hosts; the whole world is filled with His glory."
And they receive permission from one another, saying: *Targum Yonatan Is. 6*
"Holy in the highest heavens, home of His Presence; holy on earth,
the work of His strength; holy for ever and all time is the LORD of hosts;
the whole earth is full of His radiant glory."

▸ Then a wind lifted me up and I heard behind me the sound of a great *Ezek. 3*
noise, saying, ◂ "Blessed is the LORD's glory from His place."
Then a wind lifted me up and I heard behind me *Targum Yonatan Ezek. 3*
the sound of a great tempest of those who uttered praise, saying,
"Blessed is the LORD's glory from the place of the home of His Presence."

The LORD shall reign for ever and all time. *Ex. 15*
The LORD's kingdom is established for ever and all time. *Targum Onkelos Ex. 15*

יהוה LORD, God of Abraham, Isaac and Yisrael, our ancestors, may *1 Chr. 29*
You keep this for ever so that it forms the thoughts in Your people's
heart, and directs their heart toward You. He is compassionate. He *Ps. 78*
forgives iniquity and does not destroy. Repeatedly He suppresses His
anger, not rousing His full wrath. For You, my LORD, are good and *Ps. 86*
forgiving, abundantly kind to all who call on You. Your righteousness *Ps. 119*
is eternally righteous, and Your Torah is truth. Grant truth to Jacob, *Mic. 7*
loving-kindness to Abraham, as You promised our ancestors in ancient
times. Blessed is my LORD for day after day He burdens us [with His *Ps. 68*
blessings]; is our salvation, Selah! The LORD of hosts is with us; the *Ps. 46*
God of Jacob is our refuge, Selah! LORD of hosts, happy is the one who *Ps. 84*
trusts in You. LORD, save. May the King answer us on the day we call. *Ps. 20*

וּבָא לְצִיּוֹן גּוֹאֵל, וּלְשָׁבֵי פֶשַׁע בְּיַעֲקֹב, נְאֻם יהוה: ישעיה נט
וַאֲנִי זֹאת בְּרִיתִי אוֹתָם, אָמַר יהוה
רוּחִי אֲשֶׁר עָלֶיךָ וּדְבָרַי אֲשֶׁר־שַׂמְתִּי בְּפִיךָ
לֹא־יָמוּשׁוּ מִפִּיךָ וּמִפִּי זַרְעֲךָ וּמִפִּי זֶרַע זַרְעֲךָ
אָמַר יהוה, מֵעַתָּה וְעַד־עוֹלָם:

◂ וְאַתָּה קָדוֹשׁ יוֹשֵׁב תְּהִלּוֹת יִשְׂרָאֵל: וְקָרָא זֶה אֶל־זֶה וְאָמַר ◂ תהלים כב
קָדוֹשׁ, קָדוֹשׁ, קָדוֹשׁ, יהוה צְבָאוֹת, מְלֹא כָל־הָאָרֶץ כְּבוֹדוֹ: ישעיה ו
וּמְקַבְּלִין דֵּין מִן דֵּין וְאָמְרִין, קַדִּישׁ בִּשְׁמֵי מְרוֹמָא עִלָּאָה בֵּית שְׁכִינְתֵּהּ תרגום יונתן
קַדִּישׁ עַל אַרְעָא עוֹבַד גְּבוּרְתֵּהּ, קַדִּישׁ לְעָלַם וּלְעָלְמֵי עָלְמַיָּא ישעיה ו
יהוה צְבָאוֹת, מַלְיָא כָל אַרְעָא זִיו יְקָרֵהּ.

◂ וַתִּשָּׂאֵנִי רוּחַ, וָאֶשְׁמַע אַחֲרַי קוֹל רַעַשׁ גָּדוֹל ◂ יחזקאל ג
בָּרוּךְ כְּבוֹד־יהוה מִמְּקוֹמוֹ:
וּנְטָלַתְנִי רוּחָא, וּשְׁמָעִית בַּתְרַי קָל זִיעַ סַגִּיא, דִּמְשַׁבְּחִין וְאָמְרִין תרגום יונתן
בְּרִיךְ יְקָרָא דַיהוה מֵאֲתַר בֵּית שְׁכִינְתֵּהּ. יחזקאל ג

יהוה יִמְלֹךְ לְעֹלָם וָעֶד: שמות טו
יהוה מַלְכוּתֵהּ קָאֵם לְעָלַם וּלְעָלְמֵי עָלְמַיָּא. תרגום אונקלוס שמות טו

יהוה אֱלֹהֵי אַבְרָהָם יִצְחָק וְיִשְׂרָאֵל אֲבֹתֵינוּ, שָׁמְרָה־זֹּאת לְעוֹלָם דברי הימים א, כט
לְיֵצֶר מַחְשְׁבוֹת לְבַב עַמֶּךָ, וְהָכֵן לְבָבָם אֵלֶיךָ: וְהוּא רַחוּם יְכַפֵּר עָוֹן תהלים עח
וְלֹא־יַשְׁחִית, וְהִרְבָּה לְהָשִׁיב אַפּוֹ, וְלֹא־יָעִיר כָּל־חֲמָתוֹ: כִּי־אַתָּה תהלים פו
אֲדֹנָי טוֹב וְסַלָּח, וְרַב־חֶסֶד לְכָל־קֹרְאֶיךָ: צִדְקָתְךָ צֶדֶק לְעוֹלָם תהלים קיט
וְתוֹרָתְךָ אֱמֶת: תִּתֵּן אֱמֶת לְיַעֲקֹב, חֶסֶד לְאַבְרָהָם, אֲשֶׁר־נִשְׁבַּעְתָּ מיכה ז
לַאֲבֹתֵינוּ מִימֵי קֶדֶם: בָּרוּךְ אֲדֹנָי יוֹם יוֹם יַעֲמָס־לָנוּ, הָאֵל יְשׁוּעָתֵנוּ תהלים סח
סֶלָה: יהוה צְבָאוֹת עִמָּנוּ, מִשְׂגָּב לָנוּ אֱלֹהֵי יַעֲקֹב סֶלָה: יהוה צְבָאוֹת, תהלים מו תהלים פד
אַשְׁרֵי אָדָם בֹּטֵחַ בָּךְ: יהוה הוֹשִׁיעָה, הַמֶּלֶךְ יַעֲנֵנוּ בְיוֹם־קָרְאֵנוּ: תהלים כ

בָּרוּךְ Blessed is He, our God, who created us for His glory, separating us from those who go astray; who gave us the Torah of truth, planting within us eternal life. May He open our heart to His Torah, imbuing our heart with the love and awe of Him, that we may do His will and serve Him with a perfect heart, so that we neither toil in vain nor give birth to confusion.

יְהִי רָצוֹן May it be Your will, O LORD our God and God of our ancestors, that we keep Your laws in this world, and thus be worthy to live, see and inherit goodness and blessing in the Messianic Age and in the
life of the World to Come. So that my soul may sing to You and not *Ps. 30*
be silent. LORD, my God, for ever I will thank You. Blessed is the man *Jer. 17*
who trusts in the LORD, whose trust is in the LORD alone. Trust in the *Is. 26*
LORD for evermore, for God, the LORD, is an everlasting Rock. ▸ Those *Ps. 9*
who know Your name trust in You, for You, LORD, do not forsake those
who seek You. The LORD desired, for the sake of Israel's merit, to make *Is. 42*
the Torah great and glorious.

HALF KADDISH

Leader: יִתְגַּדַּל Magnified and sanctified
may His great name be,
in the world He created by His will.
May He establish His kingdom
in your lifetime and in your days,
and in the lifetime of all the house of Israel,
swiftly and soon –
and say: Amen.

All: May His great name be blessed for ever and all time.

Leader: Blessed and praised, glorified and exalted,
raised and honored, uplifted and lauded
be the name of the Holy One, blessed be He,
beyond any blessing,
song, praise and consolation
uttered in the world –
and say: Amen.

בָּרוּךְ הוּא אֱלֹהֵינוּ שֶׁבְּרָאָנוּ לִכְבוֹדוֹ, וְהִבְדִּילָנוּ מִן הַתּוֹעִים, וְנָתַן לָנוּ תּוֹרַת אֱמֶת, וְחַיֵּי עוֹלָם נָטַע בְּתוֹכֵנוּ. הוּא יִפְתַּח לִבֵּנוּ בְּתוֹרָתוֹ, וְיָשֵׂם בְּלִבֵּנוּ אַהֲבָתוֹ וְיִרְאָתוֹ וְלַעֲשׂוֹת רְצוֹנוֹ וּלְעָבְדוֹ בְּלֵבָב שָׁלֵם, לְמַעַן לֹא נִיגַע לָרִיק וְלֹא נֵלֵד לַבֶּהָלָה.

יְהִי רָצוֹן מִלְּפָנֶיךָ יהוה אֱלֹהֵינוּ וֵאלֹהֵי אֲבוֹתֵינוּ, שֶׁנִּשְׁמֹר חֻקֶּיךָ
בָּעוֹלָם הַזֶּה, וְנִזְכֶּה וְנִחְיֶה וְנִרְאֶה וְנִירַשׁ טוֹבָה וּבְרָכָה, לִשְׁנֵי יְמוֹת
הַמָּשִׁיחַ וּלְחַיֵּי הָעוֹלָם הַבָּא. לְמַעַן יְזַמֶּרְךָ כָבוֹד וְלֹא יִדֹּם, יהוה תהלים ל
אֱלֹהַי, לְעוֹלָם אוֹדֶךָּ: בָּרוּךְ הַגֶּבֶר אֲשֶׁר יִבְטַח בַּיהוה, וְהָיָה יהוה ירמיה יז
מִבְטַחוֹ: בִּטְחוּ בַיהוה עֲדֵי־עַד, כִּי בְּיָהּ יהוה צוּר עוֹלָמִים: ◂ וְיִבְטְחוּ ישעיה כו תהלים ט
בְךָ יוֹדְעֵי שְׁמֶךָ, כִּי לֹא־עָזַבְתָּ דֹרְשֶׁיךָ, יהוה: יהוה חָפֵץ לְמַעַן צִדְקוֹ, ישעיה מב
יַגְדִּיל תּוֹרָה וְיַאְדִּיר:

חצי קדיש

ש״ץ: יִתְגַּדַּל וְיִתְקַדַּשׁ שְׁמֵהּ רַבָּא (קהל: אָמֵן)
בְּעָלְמָא דִּי בְרָא כִרְעוּתֵהּ
וְיַמְלִיךְ מַלְכוּתֵהּ
בְּחַיֵּיכוֹן וּבְיוֹמֵיכוֹן וּבְחַיֵּי דְכָל בֵּית יִשְׂרָאֵל
בַּעֲגָלָא וּבִזְמַן קָרִיב, וְאִמְרוּ אָמֵן. (קהל: אָמֵן)

קהל וש״ץ: יְהֵא שְׁמֵהּ רַבָּא מְבָרַךְ לְעָלַם וּלְעָלְמֵי עָלְמַיָּא.

ש״ץ: יִתְבָּרַךְ וְיִשְׁתַּבַּח וְיִתְפָּאַר וְיִתְרוֹמַם וְיִתְנַשֵּׂא
וְיִתְהַדָּר וְיִתְעַלֶּה וְיִתְהַלָּל
שְׁמֵהּ דְּקֻדְשָׁא בְּרִיךְ הוּא (קהל: בְּרִיךְ הוּא)
לְעֵלָּא מִן כָּל בִּרְכָתָא וְשִׁירָתָא
תֻּשְׁבְּחָתָא וְנֶחֱמָתָא
דַּאֲמִירָן בְּעָלְמָא, וְאִמְרוּ אָמֵן. (קהל: אָמֵן)

Musaf for Ḥol HaMo'ed

The following prayer, until "in former years" on page 708, is said silently, standing with feet together. If there is a minyan, the Amida is repeated aloud by the Leader. Take three steps forward and at the points indicated by ▾, bend the knees at the first word, bow at the second, and stand straight before saying God's name.

When I proclaim the LORD's name, give glory to our God. *Deut. 32*
O LORD, open my lips, so that my mouth may declare Your praise. *Ps. 51*

PATRIARCHS

▾בָּרוּךְ Blessed are You, LORD our God and God of our fathers,
God of Abraham, God of Isaac and God of Jacob;
the great, mighty and awesome God, God Most High,
who bestows acts of loving-kindness and creates all,
who remembers the loving-kindness of the fathers
and will bring a Redeemer to their children's children
for the sake of His name, in love.
King, Helper, Savior, Shield:
▾Blessed are You, LORD, Shield of Abraham.

DIVINE MIGHT

אַתָּה גִּבּוֹר You are eternally mighty, LORD.
You give life to the dead
and have great power to save.

In Israel: He causes the dew to fall.

He sustains the living with loving-kindness,
and with great compassion revives the dead.
He supports the fallen, heals the sick, sets captives free,
and keeps His faith with those who sleep in the dust.
Who is like You, Master of might,
and who can compare to You,
O King who brings death and gives life,
and makes salvation grow?
Faithful are You to revive the dead.
Blessed are You, LORD, who revives the dead.

תפילת מוסף לחול המועד

The following prayer, until קַדְמֹנִיּוֹת *on page 709, is said silently, standing with feet together. If there is a* מנין*, the* עמידה *is repeated aloud by the* שליח ציבור*. Take three steps forward and at the points indicated by* ᵎ*, bend the knees at the first word, bow at the second, and stand straight before saying God's name.*

כִּי שֵׁם יהוה אֶקְרָא, הָבוּ גֹדֶל לֵאלֹהֵינוּ: דברים לב

אֲדֹנָי, שְׂפָתַי תִּפְתָּח, וּפִי יַגִּיד תְּהִלָּתֶךָ: תהלים נא

אבות

ᵎבָּרוּךְ אַתָּה יהוה, אֱלֹהֵינוּ וֵאלֹהֵי אֲבוֹתֵינוּ
אֱלֹהֵי אַבְרָהָם, אֱלֹהֵי יִצְחָק, וֵאלֹהֵי יַעֲקֹב
הָאֵל הַגָּדוֹל הַגִּבּוֹר וְהַנּוֹרָא, אֵל עֶלְיוֹן
גּוֹמֵל חֲסָדִים טוֹבִים, וְקוֹנֵה הַכֹּל, וְזוֹכֵר חַסְדֵי אָבוֹת
וּמֵבִיא גוֹאֵל לִבְנֵי בְנֵיהֶם לְמַעַן שְׁמוֹ בְּאַהֲבָה.
מֶלֶךְ עוֹזֵר וּמוֹשִׁיעַ וּמָגֵן.
ᵎבָּרוּךְ אַתָּה יהוה, מָגֵן אַבְרָהָם.

גבורות

אַתָּה גִּבּוֹר לְעוֹלָם, אֲדֹנָי
מְחַיֵּה מֵתִים אַתָּה, רַב לְהוֹשִׁיעַ

In ארץ ישראל מוֹרִיד הַטָּל

מְכַלְכֵּל חַיִּים בְּחֶסֶד, מְחַיֵּה מֵתִים בְּרַחֲמִים רַבִּים
סוֹמֵךְ נוֹפְלִים, וְרוֹפֵא חוֹלִים, וּמַתִּיר אֲסוּרִים
וּמְקַיֵּם אֱמוּנָתוֹ לִישֵׁנֵי עָפָר.
מִי כָמוֹךָ, בַּעַל גְּבוּרוֹת, וּמִי דּוֹמֶה לָּךְ
מֶלֶךְ, מֵמִית וּמְחַיֶּה וּמַצְמִיחַ יְשׁוּעָה.
וְנֶאֱמָן אַתָּה לְהַחֲיוֹת מֵתִים.
בָּרוּךְ אַתָּה יהוה, מְחַיֵּה הַמֵּתִים.

When saying the Amida silently, continue with "You are holy" below.

KEDUSHA

During the Leader's Repetition, the following is said standing with feet together, rising on the toes at the words indicated by ▴.

Cong. then Leader: נְקַדֵּשׁ We will sanctify Your name on earth,
as they sanctify it in the highest heavens,
as is written by Your prophet,
"And they [the angels] call to one another saying: *Is. 6*

Cong. then Leader: ▴Holy, ▴holy, ▴holy is the LORD of hosts;
the whole world is filled with His glory."
Those facing them say "Blessed –"

Cong. then Leader: ▴"Blessed is the LORD's glory from His place." *Ezek. 3*
And in Your holy Writings it is written thus:

Cong. then Leader: ▴"The LORD shall reign for ever. He is your God, Zion, *Ps. 146*
from generation to generation, Halleluya!"

Leader: From generation to generation we will declare Your greatness,
and we will proclaim Your holiness for evermore.
Your praise, our God, shall not leave our mouth forever,
for You, God, are a great and holy King.
Blessed are You, LORD, the holy God.

The Leader continues with "You have chosen us" below.

HOLINESS

אַתָּה קָדוֹשׁ You are holy and Your name is holy,
and holy ones praise You daily, Selah!
Blessed are You, LORD, the holy God.

HOLINESS OF THE DAY

אַתָּה בְחַרְתָּנוּ You have chosen us
from among all peoples.
You have loved and favored us.
You have raised us above all tongues.
You have made us holy through Your commandments.
You have brought us near, our King, to Your service,
and have called us by Your great and holy name.

When saying the עמידה *silently, continue with* אַתָּה קָדוֹשׁ *below.*

קדושה

During the חזרת הש״ץ*, the following is said standing with feet together, rising on the toes at the words indicated by* ^.

קהל *then* ש״ץ: נְקַדֵּשׁ אֶת שִׁמְךָ בָּעוֹלָם, כְּשֵׁם שֶׁמַּקְדִּישִׁים אוֹתוֹ בִּשְׁמֵי מָרוֹם
כַּכָּתוּב עַל יַד נְבִיאֶךָ: וְקָרָא זֶה אֶל־זֶה וְאָמַר ישעיה ו

קהל *then* ש״ץ: ^קָדוֹשׁ, ^קָדוֹשׁ, ^קָדוֹשׁ, יהוה צְבָאוֹת, מְלֹא כָל־הָאָרֶץ כְּבוֹדוֹ:
לְעֻמָּתָם בָּרוּךְ יֹאמֵרוּ

קהל *then* ש״ץ: ^בָּרוּךְ כְּבוֹד־יהוה מִמְּקוֹמוֹ: יחזקאל ג
וּבְדִבְרֵי קָדְשְׁךָ כָּתוּב לֵאמֹר

קהל *then* ש״ץ: ^יִמְלֹךְ יהוה לְעוֹלָם, אֱלֹהַיִךְ צִיּוֹן לְדֹר וָדֹר, הַלְלוּיָהּ: תהלים קמו

ש״ץ: לְדוֹר וָדוֹר נַגִּיד גָּדְלֶךָ, וּלְנֵצַח נְצָחִים קְדֻשָּׁתְךָ נַקְדִּישׁ
וְשִׁבְחֲךָ אֱלֹהֵינוּ מִפִּינוּ לֹא יָמוּשׁ לְעוֹלָם וָעֶד
כִּי אֵל מֶלֶךְ גָּדוֹל וְקָדוֹשׁ אָתָּה.
בָּרוּךְ אַתָּה יהוה, הָאֵל הַקָּדוֹשׁ.

The שליח ציבור *continues with* אַתָּה בְחַרְתָּנוּ *below.*

קדושת השם

אַתָּה קָדוֹשׁ וְשִׁמְךָ קָדוֹשׁ
וּקְדוֹשִׁים בְּכָל יוֹם יְהַלְלוּךָ סֶּלָה.
בָּרוּךְ אַתָּה יהוה, הָאֵל הַקָּדוֹשׁ.

קדושת היום

אַתָּה בְחַרְתָּנוּ מִכָּל הָעַמִּים
אָהַבְתָּ אוֹתָנוּ וְרָצִיתָ בָּנוּ, וְרוֹמַמְתָּנוּ מִכָּל הַלְּשׁוֹנוֹת
וְקִדַּשְׁתָּנוּ בְּמִצְוֹתֶיךָ, וְקֵרַבְתָּנוּ מַלְכֵּנוּ לַעֲבוֹדָתֶךָ
וְשִׁמְךָ הַגָּדוֹל וְהַקָּדוֹשׁ עָלֵינוּ קָרָאתָ.

וַתִּתֶּן לָנוּ And You, Lord our God, have given us in love
festivals for rejoicing, holy days and seasons for joy,
this day of the festival of Sukkot, our time of rejoicing,
a holy assembly in memory of the exodus from Egypt.

וּמִפְּנֵי חֲטָאֵינוּ But because of our sins we were exiled from our land
and driven far from our country.
We cannot go up to appear and bow before You,
and to perform our duties in Your chosen House,
the great and holy Temple that was called by Your name,
because of the hand that was stretched out against Your Sanctuary.
May it be Your will, Lord our God and God of our ancestors,
merciful King,
that You in Your abounding compassion may once more
have mercy on us and on Your Sanctuary,
rebuilding it swiftly and adding to its glory.
Our Father, our King,
reveal the glory of Your kingdom to us swiftly.
Appear and be exalted over us in the sight of all that lives.
Bring back our scattered ones from among the nations,
and gather our dispersed people from the ends of the earth.
Lead us to Zion, Your city, in jubilation,
and to Jerusalem, home of Your Temple,
with everlasting joy.
There we will prepare for You our obligatory offerings:
the regular daily offerings in their order
and the additional offerings according to their law.
And the additional offering of this day of the festival of Sukkot
we will prepare and offer before You in love,
in accord with Your will's commandment,
as You wrote for us in Your Torah
through Your servant Moses,
by Your own word, as it is said:

וַתִּתֶּן לָנוּ יהוה אֱלֹהֵינוּ בְּאַהֲבָה
מוֹעֲדִים לְשִׂמְחָה, חַגִּים וּזְמַנִּים לְשָׂשׂוֹן
אֶת יוֹם חַג הַסֻּכּוֹת הַזֶּה, זְמַן שִׂמְחָתֵנוּ
מִקְרָא קֹדֶשׁ, זֵכֶר לִיצִיאַת מִצְרָיִם.

וּמִפְּנֵי חֲטָאֵינוּ גָּלִינוּ מֵאַרְצֵנוּ, וְנִתְרַחַקְנוּ מֵעַל אַדְמָתֵנוּ
וְאֵין אֲנַחְנוּ יְכוֹלִים לַעֲלוֹת וְלֵרָאוֹת וּלְהִשְׁתַּחֲווֹת לְפָנֶיךָ
וְלַעֲשׂוֹת חוֹבוֹתֵינוּ בְּבֵית בְּחִירָתֶךָ
בַּבַּיִת הַגָּדוֹל וְהַקָּדוֹשׁ שֶׁנִּקְרָא שִׁמְךָ עָלָיו
מִפְּנֵי הַיָּד שֶׁנִּשְׁתַּלְּחָה בְּמִקְדָּשֶׁךָ.
יְהִי רָצוֹן מִלְּפָנֶיךָ יהוה אֱלֹהֵינוּ וֵאלֹהֵי אֲבוֹתֵינוּ, מֶלֶךְ רַחֲמָן
שֶׁתָּשׁוּב וּתְרַחֵם עָלֵינוּ וְעַל מִקְדָּשְׁךָ בְּרַחֲמֶיךָ הָרַבִּים
וְתִבְנֵהוּ מְהֵרָה וּתְגַדֵּל כְּבוֹדוֹ.
אָבִינוּ מַלְכֵּנוּ, גַּלֵּה כְּבוֹד מַלְכוּתְךָ עָלֵינוּ מְהֵרָה
וְהוֹפַע וְהִנָּשֵׂא עָלֵינוּ לְעֵינֵי כָּל חָי
וְקָרֵב פְּזוּרֵינוּ מִבֵּין הַגּוֹיִם, וּנְפוּצוֹתֵינוּ כַּנֵּס מִיַּרְכְּתֵי אָרֶץ.
וַהֲבִיאֵנוּ לְצִיּוֹן עִירְךָ בְּרִנָּה
וְלִירוּשָׁלַיִם בֵּית מִקְדָּשְׁךָ בְּשִׂמְחַת עוֹלָם
וְשָׁם נַעֲשֶׂה לְפָנֶיךָ אֶת קָרְבְּנוֹת חוֹבוֹתֵינוּ
תְּמִידִים כְּסִדְרָם וּמוּסָפִים כְּהִלְכָתָם
וְאֶת מוּסַף יוֹם חַג הַסֻּכּוֹת הַזֶּה
נַעֲשֶׂה וְנַקְרִיב לְפָנֶיךָ בְּאַהֲבָה כְּמִצְוַת רְצוֹנֶךָ
כְּמוֹ שֶׁכָּתַבְתָּ עָלֵינוּ בְּתוֹרָתֶךָ
עַל יְדֵי מֹשֶׁה עַבְדֶּךָ מִפִּי כְבוֹדֶךָ, כָּאָמוּר

On the first day of Ḥol HaMo'ed Sukkot,
say the following two paragraphs (in Israel say only the first):

וּבַיּוֹם הַשֵּׁנִי On the second day you shall offer twelve young bullocks, two rams, fourteen yearling male lambs without blemish. And their meal-offerings and wine-libations as ordained: three-tenths of an ephah for each bull, two-tenths of an ephah for each ram, one-tenth of an ephah for each lamb, wine for the libations, a male goat for atonement, and two regular daily offerings according to their law. *Num. 29*

וּבַיּוֹם הַשְּׁלִישִׁי On the third day you shall offer eleven bullocks, two rams, fourteen yearling male lambs without blemish. And their meal-offerings and wine-libations as ordained: three-tenths of an ephah for each bull, two-tenths of an ephah for the ram, one-tenth of an ephah for each lamb, wine for the libations, a male goat for atonement, and two regular daily offerings according to their law. *Num. 29*

On weekdays, continue with "Our God and God of our ancestors" on page 702.

On the second day of Ḥol HaMo'ed Sukkot,
say the following two paragraphs (in Israel say only the first):

וּבַיּוֹם הַשְּׁלִישִׁי On the third day you shall offer eleven bullocks, two rams, fourteen yearling male lambs without blemish. And their meal-offerings and wine-libations as ordained: three-tenths of an ephah for each bull, two-tenths of an ephah for each ram, one-tenth of an ephah for each lamb, wine for the libations, a male goat for atonement, and two regular daily offerings according to their law. *Num. 29*

וּבַיּוֹם הָרְבִיעִי On the fourth day you shall offer ten bullocks, two rams, fourteen yearling male lambs without blemish. And their meal-offerings and wine-libations as ordained: three-tenths of an ephah for each bull, two-tenths of an ephah for each ram, one-tenth of an ephah for each lamb, wine for the libations, a male goat for atonement, and two regular daily offerings according to their law. *Num. 29*

On weekdays, continue with "Our God and God of our ancestors" on page 702.

On the third day of Ḥol HaMo'ed Sukkot,
say the following two paragraphs (in Israel say only the first):

וּבַיּוֹם הָרְבִיעִי On the fourth day you shall offer ten bullocks, two rams, fourteen yearling male lambs without blemish. And their *Num. 29*

On the first day of חול המועד סוכות,
say the following two paragraphs (in ארץ ישראל *say only the first):*

וּבַיּוֹם הַשֵּׁנִי, פָּרִים בְּנֵי־בָקָר שְׁנֵים עָשָׂר, אֵילִם שְׁנָיִם, כְּבָשִׂים בְּנֵי־שָׁנָה אַרְבָּעָה עָשָׂר, תְּמִימִם: וּמִנְחָתָם וְנִסְכֵּיהֶם כִּמְדֻבָּר, שְׁלֹשָׁה עֶשְׂרֹנִים לַפָּר, וּשְׁנֵי עֶשְׂרֹנִים לָאָיִל, וְעִשָּׂרוֹן לַכֶּבֶשׂ, וְיַיִן כְּנִסְכּוֹ, וְשָׂעִיר לְכַפֵּר, וּשְׁנֵי תְמִידִים כְּהִלְכָתָם. במדבר כט

וּבַיּוֹם הַשְּׁלִישִׁי, פָּרִים עַשְׁתֵּי־עָשָׂר, אֵילִם שְׁנָיִם, כְּבָשִׂים בְּנֵי־שָׁנָה אַרְבָּעָה עָשָׂר, תְּמִימִם: וּמִנְחָתָם וְנִסְכֵּיהֶם כִּמְדֻבָּר, שְׁלֹשָׁה עֶשְׂרֹנִים לַפָּר, וּשְׁנֵי עֶשְׂרֹנִים לָאָיִל, וְעִשָּׂרוֹן לַכֶּבֶשׂ, וְיַיִן כְּנִסְכּוֹ, וְשָׂעִיר לְכַפֵּר, וּשְׁנֵי תְמִידִים כְּהִלְכָתָם. במדבר כט

Continue with אֱלֹהֵינוּ וֵאלֹהֵי אֲבוֹתֵינוּ *on page 703.*

On the second day of חול המועד סוכות,
say the following two paragraphs (in ארץ ישראל *say only the first):*

וּבַיּוֹם הַשְּׁלִישִׁי, פָּרִים עַשְׁתֵּי־עָשָׂר, אֵילִם שְׁנָיִם, כְּבָשִׂים בְּנֵי־שָׁנָה אַרְבָּעָה עָשָׂר, תְּמִימִם: וּמִנְחָתָם וְנִסְכֵּיהֶם כִּמְדֻבָּר, שְׁלֹשָׁה עֶשְׂרֹנִים לַפָּר, וּשְׁנֵי עֶשְׂרֹנִים לָאָיִל, וְעִשָּׂרוֹן לַכֶּבֶשׂ, וְיַיִן כְּנִסְכּוֹ, וְשָׂעִיר לְכַפֵּר, וּשְׁנֵי תְמִידִים כְּהִלְכָתָם. במדבר כט

וּבַיּוֹם הָרְבִיעִי, פָּרִים עֲשָׂרָה, אֵילִם שְׁנָיִם, כְּבָשִׂים בְּנֵי־שָׁנָה אַרְבָּעָה עָשָׂר, תְּמִימִם: וּמִנְחָתָם וְנִסְכֵּיהֶם כִּמְדֻבָּר, שְׁלֹשָׁה עֶשְׂרֹנִים לַפָּר, וּשְׁנֵי עֶשְׂרֹנִים לָאָיִל, וְעִשָּׂרוֹן לַכֶּבֶשׂ, וְיַיִן כְּנִסְכּוֹ, וְשָׂעִיר לְכַפֵּר, וּשְׁנֵי תְמִידִים כְּהִלְכָתָם. במדבר כט

Continue with אֱלֹהֵינוּ וֵאלֹהֵי אֲבוֹתֵינוּ *on page 703.*

On the third day of חול המועד סוכות,
say the following two paragraphs (in ארץ ישראל *say only the first):*

וּבַיּוֹם הָרְבִיעִי, פָּרִים עֲשָׂרָה, אֵילִם שְׁנָיִם, כְּבָשִׂים בְּנֵי־שָׁנָה במדבר כט

meal-offerings and wine-libations as ordained: three-tenths of an ephah for each bull, two-tenths of an ephah for each ram, one-tenth of an ephah for each lamb, wine for the libations, a male goat for atonement, and two regular daily offerings according to their law.

וּבַיּוֹם הַחֲמִישִׁי On the fifth day you shall offer nine bullocks, two rams, fourteen yearling male lambs without blemish. And their meal-offerings and wine-libations as ordained: three-tenths of an ephah for each bull, two-tenths of an ephah for each ram, one-tenth of an ephah for each lamb, wine for the libations, a male goat for atonement, and two regular daily offerings according to their law. *Num. 29*

Continue with "Our God and God of our ancestors" on the next page.

On the fourth day of Ḥol HaMo'ed Sukkot,
say the following two paragraphs (in Israel say only the first):

וּבַיּוֹם הַחֲמִישִׁי On the fifth day you shall offer nine bullocks, two rams, fourteen yearling male lambs without blemish. And their meal-offerings and wine-libations as ordained: three-tenths of an ephah for each bull, two-tenths of an ephah for each ram, one-tenth of an ephah for each lamb, wine for the libations, a male goat for atonement, and two regular daily offerings according to their law. *Num. 29*

וּבַיּוֹם הַשִּׁשִּׁי On the sixth day you shall offer eight bullocks, two rams, fourteen yearling male lambs without blemish. And their meal-offerings and wine-libations as ordained: three-tenths of an ephah for each bull, two-tenths of an ephah for each ram, one-tenth of an ephah for each lamb, wine for the libations, a male goat for atonement, and two regular daily offerings according to their law. *Num. 29*

Continue with "Our God and God of our ancestors" on the next page.

On the fifth day of Ḥol HaMo'ed, in Israel, say this paragraph.

וּבַיּוֹם הַשִּׁשִּׁי On the sixth day you shall offer eight bullocks, two rams, fourteen yearling male lambs without blemish. And their meal-offerings and wine-libations as ordained: three-tenths of an ephah for each bull, two-tenths of an ephah for each ram, one-tenth of an ephah for each lamb, wine for the libations, a male goat for atonement, and two regular daily offerings according to their law. *Num. 29*

אַרְבָּעָה עָשָׂר, תְּמִימִם: וּמִנְחָתָם וְנִסְכֵּיהֶם כִּמְדֻבָּר,
שְׁלֹשָׁה עֶשְׂרֹנִים לַפָּר, וּשְׁנֵי עֶשְׂרֹנִים לָאָיִל, וְעִשָּׂרוֹן לַכֶּבֶשׂ,
וְיַיִן כְּנִסְכּוֹ, וְשָׂעִיר לְכַפֵּר, וּשְׁנֵי תְמִידִים כְּהִלְכָתָם.

וּבַיּוֹם הַחֲמִישִׁי, פָּרִים תִּשְׁעָה, אֵילִם שְׁנָיִם, כְּבָשִׂים בְּנֵי־שָׁנָה במדבר כט
אַרְבָּעָה עָשָׂר, תְּמִימִם: וּמִנְחָתָם וְנִסְכֵּיהֶם כִּמְדֻבָּר,
שְׁלֹשָׁה עֶשְׂרֹנִים לַפָּר, וּשְׁנֵי עֶשְׂרֹנִים לָאָיִל, וְעִשָּׂרוֹן לַכֶּבֶשׂ,
וְיַיִן כְּנִסְכּוֹ, וְשָׂעִיר לְכַפֵּר, וּשְׁנֵי תְמִידִים כְּהִלְכָתָם.

Continue with אֱלֹהֵינוּ וֵאלֹהֵי אֲבוֹתֵינוּ *on the next page.*

On the fourth day of חול המועד סוכות*, say the following two paragraphs (in* ארץ ישראל *say only the first):*

וּבַיּוֹם הַחֲמִישִׁי, פָּרִים תִּשְׁעָה, אֵילִם שְׁנָיִם, כְּבָשִׂים בְּנֵי־שָׁנָה במדבר כט
אַרְבָּעָה עָשָׂר, תְּמִימִם: וּמִנְחָתָם וְנִסְכֵּיהֶם כִּמְדֻבָּר, שְׁלֹשָׁה
עֶשְׂרֹנִים לַפָּר, וּשְׁנֵי עֶשְׂרֹנִים לָאָיִל, וְעִשָּׂרוֹן לַכֶּבֶשׂ, וְיַיִן
כְּנִסְכּוֹ, וְשָׂעִיר לְכַפֵּר, וּשְׁנֵי תְמִידִים כְּהִלְכָתָם.

וּבַיּוֹם הַשִּׁשִּׁי, פָּרִים שְׁמֹנָה, אֵילִם שְׁנָיִם, כְּבָשִׂים בְּנֵי־שָׁנָה במדבר כט
אַרְבָּעָה עָשָׂר, תְּמִימִם: וּמִנְחָתָם וְנִסְכֵּיהֶם כִּמְדֻבָּר, שְׁלֹשָׁה
עֶשְׂרֹנִים לַפָּר, וּשְׁנֵי עֶשְׂרֹנִים לָאָיִל, וְעִשָּׂרוֹן לַכֶּבֶשׂ, וְיַיִן
כְּנִסְכּוֹ, וְשָׂעִיר לְכַפֵּר, וּשְׁנֵי תְמִידִים כְּהִלְכָתָם.

Continue with אֱלֹהֵינוּ וֵאלֹהֵי אֲבוֹתֵינוּ *on the next page.*

On the fifth day of חול המועד*, in* ארץ ישראל*, say this paragraph:*

וּבַיּוֹם הַשִּׁשִּׁי, פָּרִים שְׁמֹנָה, אֵילִם שְׁנָיִם, כְּבָשִׂים בְּנֵי־שָׁנָה במדבר כט
אַרְבָּעָה עָשָׂר, תְּמִימִם: וּמִנְחָתָם וְנִסְכֵּיהֶם כִּמְדֻבָּר, שְׁלֹשָׁה
עֶשְׂרֹנִים לַפָּר, וּשְׁנֵי עֶשְׂרֹנִים לָאָיִל, וְעִשָּׂרוֹן לַכֶּבֶשׂ, וְיַיִן
כְּנִסְכּוֹ, וְשָׂעִיר לְכַפֵּר, וּשְׁנֵי תְמִידִים כְּהִלְכָתָם.

אֱלֹהֵינוּ Our God and God of our ancestors,
merciful King, have compassion upon us.
You who are good and do good, respond to our call.
Return to us in Your abounding mercy
for the sake of our fathers who did Your will.
Rebuild Your Temple as at the beginning,
and establish Your Sanctuary on its site.
Let us witness its rebuilding and gladden us by its restoration.
Bring the priests back to their service,
the Levites to their song and music,
and the Israelites to their homes.

וְשָׁם נַעֲלֶה There we will go up and appear and bow before You
on the three pilgrimage festivals, as is written in Your Torah:
"Three times in the year all your males shall appear *Deut. 16*
before the LORD your God at the place He will choose:
on Pesaḥ, Shavuot and Sukkot.
They shall not appear before the LORD empty-handed.
Each shall bring such a gift as he can,
in proportion to the blessing
that the LORD your God grants you."

וְהַשִּׂיאֵנוּ Bestow on us, LORD our God,
the blessings of Your festivals
for good life and peace, joy and gladness,
as You desired and promised to bless us.
Make us holy through Your commandments
and grant us a share in Your Torah.
Satisfy us with Your goodness, gladden us with Your salvation,
and purify our hearts to serve You in truth.
Grant us as our heritage,
LORD our God with joy and gladness, Your holy festivals,
and may Israel, who sanctify Your name, rejoice in You.
Blessed are You, LORD, who sanctifies Israel and the festive seasons.

אֱלֹהֵינוּ וֵאלֹהֵי אֲבוֹתֵינוּ
מֶלֶךְ רַחֲמָן רַחֵם עָלֵינוּ, טוֹב וּמֵטִיב הִדָּרֶשׁ לָנוּ
שׁוּבָה אֵלֵינוּ בַּהֲמוֹן רַחֲמֶיךָ בִּגְלַל אָבוֹת שֶׁעָשׂוּ רְצוֹנֶךָ.
בְּנֵה בֵיתְךָ כְּבַתְּחִלָּה, וְכוֹנֵן מִקְדָּשְׁךָ עַל מְכוֹנוֹ
וְהַרְאֵנוּ בְּבִנְיָנוֹ, וְשַׂמְּחֵנוּ בְּתִקּוּנוֹ
וְהָשֵׁב כֹּהֲנִים לַעֲבוֹדָתָם, וּלְוִיִּם לְשִׁירָם וּלְזִמְרָם
וְהָשֵׁב יִשְׂרָאֵל לִנְוֵיהֶם.

וְשָׁם נַעֲלֶה וְנֵרָאֶה וְנִשְׁתַּחֲוֶה לְפָנֶיךָ בְּשָׁלֹשׁ פַּעֲמֵי רְגָלֵינוּ
כַּכָּתוּב בְּתוֹרָתֶךָ
שָׁלוֹשׁ פְּעָמִים בַּשָּׁנָה יֵרָאֶה כָל־זְכוּרְךָ אֶת־פְּנֵי יהוה אֱלֹהֶיךָ דברים טז
בַּמָּקוֹם אֲשֶׁר יִבְחָר
בְּחַג הַמַּצּוֹת, וּבְחַג הַשָּׁבֻעוֹת, וּבְחַג הַסֻּכּוֹת
וְלֹא יֵרָאֶה אֶת־פְּנֵי יהוה רֵיקָם:
אִישׁ כְּמַתְּנַת יָדוֹ, כְּבִרְכַּת יהוה אֱלֹהֶיךָ אֲשֶׁר נָתַן־לָךְ:

וְהַשִּׂיאֵנוּ יהוה אֱלֹהֵינוּ אֶת בִּרְכַּת מוֹעֲדֶיךָ
לְחַיִּים וּלְשָׁלוֹם, לְשִׂמְחָה וּלְשָׂשׂוֹן
כַּאֲשֶׁר רָצִיתָ וְאָמַרְתָּ לְבָרְכֵנוּ.
קַדְּשֵׁנוּ בְּמִצְוֹתֶיךָ, וְתֵן חֶלְקֵנוּ בְּתוֹרָתֶךָ
שַׂבְּעֵנוּ מִטּוּבֶךָ, וְשַׂמְּחֵנוּ בִּישׁוּעָתֶךָ
וְטַהֵר לִבֵּנוּ לְעָבְדְּךָ בֶּאֱמֶת.
וְהַנְחִילֵנוּ יהוה אֱלֹהֵינוּ בְּשִׂמְחָה וּבְשָׂשׂוֹן מוֹעֲדֵי קָדְשֶׁךָ
וְיִשְׂמְחוּ בְךָ יִשְׂרָאֵל מְקַדְּשֵׁי שְׁמֶךָ.
בָּרוּךְ אַתָּה יהוה, מְקַדֵּשׁ יִשְׂרָאֵל וְהַזְּמַנִּים.

TEMPLE SERVICE

רְצֵה Find favor, LORD our God, in Your people Israel
and their prayer.
Restore the service to Your most holy House,
and accept in love and favor
the fire-offerings of Israel and their prayer.
May the service of Your people Israel always find favor with You.
And may our eyes witness Your return to Zion in compassion.
Blessed are You, LORD, who restores His Presence to Zion.

THANKSGIVING

Bow at the first nine words.

מוֹדִים We give thanks to You,
for You are the LORD our God
and God of our ancestors
for ever and all time.
You are the Rock of our lives,
Shield of our salvation
from generation to generation.
We will thank You and
declare Your praise for our lives,
which are entrusted into Your hand;
for our souls,
which are placed in Your charge;
for Your miracles
which are with us every day;
and for Your wonders and favors
at all times, evening,
morning and midday.
You are good –
for Your compassion never fails.
You are compassionate –
for Your loving-kindnesses never cease.
We have always placed our hope in You.

During the Leader's Repetition, the congregation says quietly:

מוֹדִים We give thanks to You,
for You are the LORD our God
and God of our ancestors,
God of all flesh,
who formed us
and formed the universe.
Blessings and thanks
are due to Your great
and holy name for giving us
life and sustaining us.
May You continue
to give us life
and sustain us;
and may You gather our
exiles to Your holy courts,
to keep Your decrees,
do Your will and serve You
with a perfect heart,
for it is for us
to give You thanks.
Blessed be God to whom
thanksgiving is due.

עבודה

רְצֵה יהוה אֱלֹהֵינוּ בְּעַמְּךָ יִשְׂרָאֵל, וּבִתְפִלָּתָם
וְהָשֵׁב אֶת הָעֲבוֹדָה לִדְבִיר בֵּיתֶךָ
וְאִשֵּׁי יִשְׂרָאֵל וּתְפִלָּתָם בְּאַהֲבָה תְקַבֵּל בְּרָצוֹן
וּתְהִי לְרָצוֹן תָּמִיד עֲבוֹדַת יִשְׂרָאֵל עַמֶּךָ.
וְתֶחֱזֶינָה עֵינֵינוּ בְּשׁוּבְךָ לְצִיּוֹן בְּרַחֲמִים.
בָּרוּךְ אַתָּה יהוה, הַמַּחֲזִיר שְׁכִינָתוֹ לְצִיּוֹן.

הודאה

Bow at the first five words.

מוֹדִים אֲנַחְנוּ לָךְ
שָׁאַתָּה הוּא יהוה אֱלֹהֵינוּ
וֵאלֹהֵי אֲבוֹתֵינוּ לְעוֹלָם וָעֶד.
צוּר חַיֵּינוּ, מָגֵן יִשְׁעֵנוּ
אַתָּה הוּא לְדוֹר וָדוֹר.
נוֹדֶה לְּךָ וּנְסַפֵּר תְּהִלָּתֶךָ
עַל חַיֵּינוּ הַמְּסוּרִים בְּיָדֶךָ
וְעַל נִשְׁמוֹתֵינוּ הַפְּקוּדוֹת לָךְ
וְעַל נִסֶּיךָ שֶׁבְּכָל יוֹם עִמָּנוּ
וְעַל נִפְלְאוֹתֶיךָ וְטוֹבוֹתֶיךָ
שֶׁבְּכָל עֵת
עֶרֶב וָבֹקֶר וְצָהֳרָיִם.
הַטּוֹב, כִּי לֹא כָלוּ רַחֲמֶיךָ
וְהַמְרַחֵם, כִּי לֹא תַמּוּ חֲסָדֶיךָ
מֵעוֹלָם קִוִּינוּ לָךְ.

During the חזרת הש״ץ, *the* קהל *says quietly:*

מוֹדִים אֲנַחְנוּ לָךְ
שָׁאַתָּה הוּא יהוה אֱלֹהֵינוּ
וֵאלֹהֵי אֲבוֹתֵינוּ
אֱלֹהֵי כָל בָּשָׂר
יוֹצְרֵנוּ, יוֹצֵר בְּרֵאשִׁית.
בְּרָכוֹת וְהוֹדָאוֹת
לְשִׁמְךָ הַגָּדוֹל וְהַקָּדוֹשׁ
עַל שֶׁהֶחֱיִיתָנוּ וְקִיַּמְתָּנוּ.
כֵּן תְּחַיֵּנוּ וּתְקַיְּמֵנוּ
וְתֶאֱסֹף גָּלֻיּוֹתֵינוּ
לְחַצְרוֹת קָדְשֶׁךָ
לִשְׁמֹר חֻקֶּיךָ וְלַעֲשׂוֹת רְצוֹנֶךָ
וּלְעָבְדְּךָ בְּלֵבָב שָׁלֵם
עַל שֶׁאֲנַחְנוּ מוֹדִים לָךְ.
בָּרוּךְ אֵל הַהוֹדָאוֹת.

וְעַל כֻּלָּם For all these things
may Your name be blessed and exalted, our King,
continually, for ever and all time. Let all that lives thank You, Selah!
and praise Your name in truth, God, our Savior and Help, Selah!
▾Blessed are You, LORD, whose name is "the Good"
and to whom thanks are due.

For the blessing of the Kohanim in Israel, see page 1396.
The Leader says the following during the Repetition of the Musaf Amida.
It is also said in Israel when no Kohanim bless the congregation.

Our God and God of our fathers, bless us with the threefold blessing in the Torah, written by the hand of Moses Your servant and pronounced by Aaron and his sons the priests, Your holy people, as it is said:

May the LORD bless you and protect you. *Num. 6*
Cong: May it be Your will.
May the LORD make His face shine on you and be gracious to you.
Cong: May it be Your will.
May the LORD turn His face toward you, and grant you peace.
Cong: May it be Your will.

PEACE

שִׂים שָׁלוֹם Grant peace, goodness and blessing,
grace, loving-kindness and compassion
to us and all Israel Your people.
Bless us, our Father, all as one,
with the light of Your face,
for by the light of Your face You have given us, LORD our God,
the Torah of life and love of kindness,
righteousness, blessing, compassion, life and peace.
May it be good in Your eyes to bless Your people Israel
at every time, in every hour, with Your peace.
Blessed are You, LORD, who blesses His people Israel with peace.

The following verse concludes the Leader's Repetition of the Amida.
Some also say it here as part of the silent Amida.

May the words of my mouth and the meditation of my heart *Ps. 19*
find favor before You, LORD, my Rock and Redeemer.

וְעַל כֻּלָּם יִתְבָּרַךְ וְיִתְרוֹמַם שִׁמְךָ מַלְכֵּנוּ תָּמִיד לְעוֹלָם וָעֶד.
וְכֹל הַחַיִּים יוֹדְוּךָ סֶּלָה, וִיהַלְלוּ אֶת שִׁמְךָ בֶּאֱמֶת
הָאֵל יְשׁוּעָתֵנוּ וְעֶזְרָתֵנוּ סֶלָה.
בָּרוּךְ אַתָּה יהוה, הַטּוֹב שִׁמְךָ וּלְךָ נָאֶה לְהוֹדוֹת.

For the blessing of the כהנים *in* ארץ ישראל *see page 1397.*
The שליח ציבור *says the following during the* חזרת הש״ץ *of* מוסף.
It is also said in ארץ ישראל *when no* כהנים *bless the* קהל.

אֱלֹהֵינוּ וֵאלֹהֵי אֲבוֹתֵינוּ, בָּרְכֵנוּ בַּבְּרָכָה הַמְשֻׁלֶּשֶׁת בַּתּוֹרָה, הַכְּתוּבָה עַל יְדֵי מֹשֶׁה עַבְדֶּךָ, הָאֲמוּרָה מִפִּי אַהֲרֹן וּבָנָיו כֹּהֲנִים עַם קְדוֹשֶׁיךָ, כָּאָמוּר

במדבר ו
יְבָרֶכְךָ יהוה וְיִשְׁמְרֶךָ: קהל: כֵּן יְהִי רָצוֹן
יָאֵר יהוה פָּנָיו אֵלֶיךָ וִיחֻנֶּךָּ: קהל: כֵּן יְהִי רָצוֹן
יִשָּׂא יהוה פָּנָיו אֵלֶיךָ וְיָשֵׂם לְךָ שָׁלוֹם: קהל: כֵּן יְהִי רָצוֹן

שלום

שִׂים שָׁלוֹם טוֹבָה וּבְרָכָה
חֵן וָחֶסֶד וְרַחֲמִים עָלֵינוּ וְעַל כָּל יִשְׂרָאֵל עַמֶּךָ.
בָּרְכֵנוּ אָבִינוּ כֻּלָּנוּ כְּאֶחָד בְּאוֹר פָּנֶיךָ
כִּי בְאוֹר פָּנֶיךָ נָתַתָּ לָּנוּ יהוה אֱלֹהֵינוּ
תּוֹרַת חַיִּים וְאַהֲבַת חֶסֶד
וּצְדָקָה וּבְרָכָה וְרַחֲמִים וְחַיִּים וְשָׁלוֹם.
וְטוֹב בְּעֵינֶיךָ לְבָרֵךְ אֶת עַמְּךָ יִשְׂרָאֵל
בְּכָל עֵת וּבְכָל שָׁעָה בִּשְׁלוֹמֶךָ.
בָּרוּךְ אַתָּה יהוה, הַמְבָרֵךְ אֶת עַמּוֹ יִשְׂרָאֵל בַּשָּׁלוֹם.

The following verse concludes the חזרת הש״ץ.
Some also say it here as part of the silent עמידה.

תהלים יט
יִהְיוּ לְרָצוֹן אִמְרֵי־פִי וְהֶגְיוֹן לִבִּי לְפָנֶיךָ, יהוה צוּרִי וְגֹאֲלִי:

אֱלֹהַי My God, *Berakhot 17a*
guard my tongue from evil and my lips from deceitful speech.
To those who curse me, let my soul be silent;
may my soul be to all like the dust.
Open my heart to Your Torah
and let my soul pursue Your commandments.
As for all who plan evil against me,
swiftly thwart their counsel and frustrate their plans.
Act for the sake of Your name;
act for the sake of Your right hand;
act for the sake of Your holiness;
act for the sake of Your Torah.
That Your beloved ones may be delivered, *Ps. 60*
save with Your right hand and answer me.
May the words of my mouth and the meditation of my heart *Ps. 19*
find favor before You, LORD, my Rock and Redeemer.

Bow, take three steps back, then bow, first left, then right, then center, while saying:
May He who makes peace in His high places,
make peace for us and all Israel –
and say: Amen.

יְהִי רָצוֹן May it be Your will, LORD our God and God of our ancestors,
that the Temple be rebuilt speedily in our days,
and grant us a share in Your Torah.
And there we will serve You with reverence,
as in the days of old and as in former years.
Then the offering of Judah and Jerusalem *Mal. 3*
will be pleasing to the LORD
as in the days of old and as in former years.

The Leader repeats the Amida (page 692).

ברכות יז.

אֱלֹהַי
נְצֹר לְשׁוֹנִי מֵרָע וּשְׂפָתַי מִדַּבֵּר מִרְמָה
וְלִמְקַלְלַי נַפְשִׁי תִדֹּם, וְנַפְשִׁי כֶּעָפָר לַכֹּל תִּהְיֶה.
פְּתַח לִבִּי בְּתוֹרָתֶךָ, וּבְמִצְוֹתֶיךָ תִּרְדֹּף נַפְשִׁי.
וְכָל הַחוֹשְׁבִים עָלַי רָעָה
מְהֵרָה הָפֵר עֲצָתָם וְקַלְקֵל מַחֲשַׁבְתָּם.
עֲשֵׂה לְמַעַן שְׁמֶךָ
עֲשֵׂה לְמַעַן יְמִינֶךָ
עֲשֵׂה לְמַעַן קְדֻשָּׁתֶךָ
עֲשֵׂה לְמַעַן תּוֹרָתֶךָ.
תהלים ס לְמַעַן יֵחָלְצוּן יְדִידֶיךָ, הוֹשִׁיעָה יְמִינְךָ וַעֲנֵנִי:
תהלים יט יִהְיוּ לְרָצוֹן אִמְרֵי־פִי וְהֶגְיוֹן לִבִּי לְפָנֶיךָ, יהוה צוּרִי וְגוֹאֲלִי:

Bow, take three steps back, then bow, first left, then right, then center, while saying:

עֹשֶׂה שָׁלוֹם בִּמְרוֹמָיו
הוּא יַעֲשֶׂה שָׁלוֹם עָלֵינוּ וְעַל כָּל יִשְׂרָאֵל
וְאִמְרוּ אָמֵן.

יְהִי רָצוֹן מִלְּפָנֶיךָ יהוה אֱלֹהֵינוּ וֵאלֹהֵי אֲבוֹתֵינוּ
שֶׁיִּבָּנֶה בֵּית הַמִּקְדָּשׁ בִּמְהֵרָה בְיָמֵינוּ
וְתֵן חֶלְקֵנוּ בְּתוֹרָתֶךָ
וְשָׁם נַעֲבָדְךָ בְּיִרְאָה כִּימֵי עוֹלָם וּכְשָׁנִים קַדְמוֹנִיּוֹת.
מלאכי ג וְעָרְבָה לַיהוה מִנְחַת יְהוּדָה וִירוּשָׁלָיִם כִּימֵי עוֹלָם וּכְשָׁנִים קַדְמֹנִיּוֹת:

The Leader repeats the עמידה *(page 693)*.

Hoshanot

Hoshanot are said after the Leader's Repetition of the Amida of Musaf (and in some congregations after Hallel) on every day of Sukkot.
On weekdays, the Ark is opened, and a Torah scroll is taken to the Bima. Members of the congregation who have a Lulav and Etrog make a circuit around the Bima and say Hoshanot. Mourners do not participate in the circuit.
At the conclusion of the Hoshanot, the Torah scroll is returned to the Ark, which is then closed.

In Israel, on the first day of Ḥol HaMo'ed, "The Foundation Stone" on the next page is said; and if it is Sunday, "For the sake of Your truth" on page 532. On subsequent days, the same Hashanot are said as outside Israel.

If first day of Sukkot falls on	*On the first day of Ḥol HaMo'ed*	*On second day of Ḥol HaMo'ed*	*On third day of Ḥol HaMo'ed*	*On fourth day of Ḥol HaMo'ed*
Monday	I shall lay out my prayer	"I am a wall," said the people	God of all salvation	A people guarded
Tuesday	I shall lay out my prayer	God of all salvation	A people guarded	Master who saves
Thursday	A people guarded	I shall lay out my prayer	God of all salvation	Master who saves
Shabbat	I shall lay out my prayer	The Foundation Stone	God of all salvation	Master who saves

Leader then congregation:

הוֹשַׁע נָא Save us, please for Your sake, our God, save us please.

Leader then congregation:

Save us, please for Your sake, our Creator, save us, please.

Leader then congregation:

Save us, please for Your sake, our Redeemer, save us, please.

Leader then congregation:

Save us, please for Your sake, You who seek us, save us, please.

Save us, please –

אֶעֱרֹךְ שׁוּעִי I shall lay out my prayer – in the house of my prayer – I found my sin, fasting – I seek You from there, to save me – heed the sound of my prayer – and rise up to my aid – remember with compassion, my Savior – making life my

---

אֶעֱרֹךְ שׁוּעִי *I shall lay out my prayer.* A *Hoshana* on the theme of repentance, referring back to Yom Kippur, and the fasting and confessions of that day.

הושענות

הושענות are said after the חזרת הש״ץ of the מוסף עמידה (and in some congregations after הלל) on every day of סוכות.
The ארון קודש is opened, and a ספר תורה is taken to the בימה. Members of the קהל who have a לולב and אתרוג make a circuit around the בימה and say הושענות. Mourners do not participate in the circuit.
At the conclusion of the הושענות, the ספר תורה is returned to the ארון קודש, which is then closed.

In ארץ ישראל, on the first day of חול המועד, אֶבֶן שְׁתִיָּה on the next page is said; and if it is Sunday, לְמַעַן אֲמִתָּךְ on page 533.
On subsequent days, the same הושענות are said as outside ארץ ישראל.

On fourth day of חול המועד	On third day of חול המועד	On second day of חול המועד	On first day of חול המועד	If first day of סוכות falls on
אֹם נְצוּרָה	אֵל לְמוֹשָׁעוֹת	אֹם אֲנִי חוֹמָה	אֶעֱרֹךְ שׁוּעִי	Monday
אָדוֹן הַמּוֹשִׁיעַ	אֹם נְצוּרָה	אֵל לְמוֹשָׁעוֹת	אֶעֱרֹךְ שׁוּעִי	Tuesday
אָדוֹן הַמּוֹשִׁיעַ	אֵל לְמוֹשָׁעוֹת	אֶעֱרֹךְ שׁוּעִי	אֹם נְצוּרָה	Thursday
אָדוֹן הַמּוֹשִׁיעַ	אֵל לְמוֹשָׁעוֹת	אֶבֶן שְׁתִיָּה	אֶעֱרֹךְ שׁוּעִי	שבת

שליח ציבור then קהל:

הוֹשַׁע נָא לְמַעַנְךָ אֱלֹהֵינוּ הוֹשַׁע נָא.

שליח ציבור then קהל:

הוֹשַׁע נָא לְמַעַנְךָ בּוֹרְאֵנוּ הוֹשַׁע נָא.

שליח ציבור then קהל:

הוֹשַׁע נָא לְמַעַנְךָ גּוֹאֲלֵנוּ הוֹשַׁע נָא.

שליח ציבור then קהל:

הוֹשַׁע נָא לְמַעַנְךָ דּוֹרְשֵׁנוּ הוֹשַׁע נָא.

הוֹשַׁע נָא

אֶעֱרֹךְ שׁוּעִי. בְּבֵית שַׁוְעִי. גִּלִּיתִי בַצּוֹם פִּשְׁעִי. דְּרַשְׁתִּיךָ בּוֹ לְהוֹשִׁיעִי. הַקְשִׁיבָה לְקוֹל שַׁוְעִי. וְקוּמָה וְהוֹשִׁיעִי. זְכֹר וְרַחֵם מוֹשִׁיעִי. חַי כֵּן

delight – Beneficent One, hear my groaning – quickly, bring my savior – put an end to my accuser – that he condemn me no more – quickly, God of my salvation – make eternal my salvation – bear the iniquity of my wickedness – pass over my sin – turn to me and save me – righteous Rock, my Savior – receive, please, my prayer – raise the horn of my salvation – Almighty One, my Savior – come, show Yourself and save me – Save us, please.

Continue with "I and HE: save us, please" on page 716.

Save us, please –

אֶבֶן שְׁתִיָּה The Foundation Stone – the House You chose – the threshing-floor of Arnan – the hidden Shrine – Mount Moriah – where He shall be seen – Your glorious Sanctuary – where David camped – the best of Lebanon – the Beauty of Heights, Joy of all the earth – the Place of Perfect Beauty – the Lodge of Goodness – the Place of Your dwelling – the Shelter of Shalem – the tribes' Pilgrimage – the precious Cornerstone – shining Zion – the Holy of Holies – [the walls] lined with love – Residence of Your glory – the Hill toward which all mouths pray – Save us, please.

Continue with "I and HE: save us, please" on page 716.

Save us, please –

אֹם אֲנִי חוֹמָה "I am a wall," said the people – bright as the sun – exiled and reviled – fair like a date palm – killed on account of You – like sheep to the slaughter – dispersed among tormentors – wrapped in Your embrace,

---

אֹם אֲנִי חוֹמָה I AM A WALL

An anguished *Hoshana* from a people in exile. Suffering persecution, clinging fast to God, yet reviled by their fellow humans.

אֹם אֲנִי חוֹמָה *I am a wall.* A phrase from Song of Songs (8:10), meaning here, "holding fast to Your law, refusing to be moved," despite all the blandishments and threats.

כְּצֹאן טִבְחָה *Like sheep to the slaughter.* "Yet for Your sake we are killed all the day long; we are regarded as sheep to be slaughtered" (Ps. 44:23).

חֲבוּקָה ... בָּךְ *Wrapped in Your embrace.* Refusing to let our sufferings distance us from You.

תְּשַׁעְשְׁעִי. טוֹב בְּאֶנֶק שְׁעִי. יוֹחַשׁ מוֹשִׁיעִי. כַּלֵּה מַרְשִׁיעִי. לְבַל עוֹד יַרְשִׁיעִי. מַהֵר אֱלֹהֵי יִשְׁעִי. נֶצַח לְהוֹשִׁיעִי. שָׂא נָא עֲוֹן רִשְׁעִי. עֲבֹר עַל פִּשְׁעִי. פְּנֵה נָא לְהוֹשִׁיעִי. צוּר צַדִּיק מוֹשִׁיעִי. קַבֵּל נָא שַׁוְעִי. רוֹמֵם קֶרֶן יִשְׁעִי. שַׁדַּי מוֹשִׁיעִי. תּוֹפִיעַ וְתוֹשִׁיעִי. הוֹשַׁע נָא.

Continue with אֲנִי וָהוּ הוֹשִׁיעָה נָּא *on page 717.*

הוֹשַׁע נָא

אֶבֶן שְׁתִיָּה. בֵּית הַבְּחִירָה. גֹּרֶן אָרְנָן. דְּבִיר הַמֻּצְנָע. הַר הַמּוֹרִיָּה. וְהַר יֵרָאֶה. זְבוּל תִּפְאַרְתֶּךָ. חָנָה דָוִד. טוֹב הַלְּבָנוֹן. יְפֵה נוֹף מְשׂוֹשׂ כָּל הָאָרֶץ. כְּלִילַת יֹפִי. לִינַת הַצֶּדֶק. מָכוֹן לְשִׁבְתֶּךָ. נָוֶה שַׁאֲנָן. סֻכַּת שָׁלֵם. עֲלִיַּת שְׁבָטִים. פִּנַּת יִקְרַת. צִיּוֹן הַמְצֻיֶּנֶת. קֹדֶשׁ הַקֳּדָשִׁים. רָצוּף אַהֲבָה. שְׁכִינַת כְּבוֹדֶךָ. תֵּל תַּלְפִּיּוֹת. הוֹשַׁע נָא.

Continue with אֲנִי וָהוּ הוֹשִׁיעָה נָּא *on page 717.*

הוֹשַׁע נָא

אֹם אֲנִי חוֹמָה. בָּרָה כַּחַמָּה. גּוֹלָה וְסוּרָה. דָּמְתָה לְתָמָר. הַהֲרוּגָה עָלֶיךָ. וְנֶחְשֶׁבֶת כְּצֹאן טִבְחָה. זְרוּיָה בֵּין מַכְעִיסֶיהָ. חֲבוּקָה וּדְבוּקָה בָּךְ. טוֹעֶנֶת

אֶעֱרֹךְ שׁוּעִי *I shall lay out my prayer (previous page).* Based on a phrase in Job. 36:19.

כַּלֵּה מַרְשִׁיעִי *Put an end to my accuser.* Traditionally the role ascribed to Satan, understood in Judaism as the prosecuting attorney in the Heavenly court.

פְּנֵה נָא *Turn to me.* Based on Isaiah 45:22, where God says, "Turn to Me and be saved."

צוּר צַדִּיק *Righteous Rock.* Based on Deut. 32:4, "He is the Rock, His works are perfect, and all His ways are just: a faithful God who does no wrong, righteous and just is He."

אֶבֶן שְׁתִיָּה *The foundation Stone.* For commentary, see page 535.

clinging to You – bearing Your yoke – the one to know Your Oneness – beaten down in exile – learning the awe of You – our faces scratched – given over to the violent – weighed down beneath Your burden – oppressed and in turmoil – redeemed by [Moses] Toviya – holy flock – the communities of Jacob – marked out with Your name – roaring, "Save us, please!" – leaning on You – Save us, please.

Continue with "I and HE: save us, please" on the next page.

Save us, please –

אֵל לְמוֹשָׁעוֹת God of all salvation – for keeping our four vows – we who draw close in prayer – who come knocking to lay out our prayer – who speak Your words of delight – who revel in their questions – crying out to be heard – we who watch for the Redemption – hear those who hold on to You – who understand Your calendar – who bow to You and pray – to comprehend Your message – as it comes from Your mouth – (You who give salvation) – telling their stories – making known Your testament – You who work salvation – bring a righteous [leader] for the saved – bring close our salvations – with noise, amid thundering – in three brief hours – speed us our salvation – Save us, please.

Continue with "I and HE: save us, please" on the next page.

---

read the phrase as "four weeks", referring to the four weeks of Tishrei during which the world is judged (R. Isaac Landau).

וְחִידוֹת מִשְׁתַּעַשְׁעוֹת *Revel in their questions.* A reference to Prov. 1:6, "the sayings and riddles of the wise," that is, who take pleasure in unraveling the cryptic utterances of the sages.

יוֹדְעֵי בֵּין שָׁעוֹת *Who understand Your calendar.* That is, the Great Sanhedrin who were charged with the determining the calendar. This, according to tradition, was the first command given to the Israelites as a nation (Ex. 12:2).

רְגֶשׁ תְּשׁוּאוֹת *With noise, amid thundering.* A reference to the battle described by Zechariah and Ezekiel that will precede and usher in the messianic age.

שָׁלֹשׁ שָׁעוֹת *In three brief hours.* A reference to the threefold "now" in Isaiah 33:10, a verse referring to future redemption: "'Now will I arise,' says the LORD. 'Now will I be exalted; now will I be lifted up,'" emphasizing the speed of the defeat of Israel's enemies (*Shir HaShirim Raba* 4:8).

עַלֶּךָ. יְחִידָה לְיַחֲדָךְ. כְּבוּשָׁה בַגּוֹלָה. לוֹמֶדֶת יִרְאָתָךְ. מְרוּטַת לֶחִי. נְתוּנָה לְמַכִּים. סוֹבֶלֶת סִבְלָךְ. עֲנִיָּה סוֹעֲרָה. פְּדוּיַת טוֹבִיָּה. צֹאן קָדָשִׁים. קְהִלּוֹת יַעֲקֹב. רְשׁוּמִים בִּשְׁמֶךָ. שׁוֹאֲגִים הוֹשַׁע נָא. תְּמוּכִים עָלֶיךָ. הוֹשַׁע נָא.

Continue with אֲנִי וָהוּ הוֹשִׁיעָה נָּא *on the next page.*

הוֹשַׁע נָא

אֵל לְמוֹשָׁעוֹת. בְּאַרְבַּע שְׁבוּעוֹת. גָּשִׁים בְּשַׁוְעוֹת. דּוֹפְקֵי עֶרֶךְ שׁוּעוֹת. הוֹגֵי שַׁעֲשׁוּעוֹת. וְחִידוֹת מִשְׁתַּעְשְׁעוֹת. זוֹעֲקִים לְהַשְׁעוֹת. חוֹכֵי יְשׁוּעוֹת. טְפוּלִים בְּךָ שְׁעוֹת. יוֹדְעֵי בֵּין שָׁעוֹת. כּוֹרְעֶיךָ בְּשַׁוְעוֹת. לְהָבִין שְׁמוּעוֹת. מִפִּיךָ נִשְׁמָעוֹת. נוֹתֵן תְּשׁוּעוֹת. סְפּוּרוֹת מַשְׁמָעוֹת. עֵדוּת מַשְׁמִיעוֹת. פּוֹעֵל יְשׁוּעוֹת. צַדִּיק נוֹשָׁעוֹת. קִרְיַת תְּשׁוּעוֹת. רֶגֶשׁ תְּשׁוּאוֹת. שָׁלֹשׁ שָׁעוֹת. תָּחִישׁ לִתְשׁוּעוֹת. הוֹשַׁע נָא.

Continue with אֲנִי וָהוּ הוֹשִׁיעָה נָּא *on the next page.*

מְרוּטַת לֶחִי *Our faces scratched.* "I offered my back to those who beat me, my cheeks to those who pulled out my beard; I did not hide my face from mocking and spitting" (Is. 50:6), a terrible commentary on how Jews have been treated through the ages.

טוֹבִיָּה *Tovia.* According to R. Judah, the name given to Moses by his mother Yokheved, based on the phrase, "She saw that he was good [*tov*]" (Ex. 2:2, *Sota* 12a).

אֵל לְמוֹשָׁעוֹת *God of all salvation.* A *Hoshana* on the theme of redemption from exile, involving complex literary play on the root י-ש-ע and similar-sounding words.

בְּאַרְבַּע שְׁבוּעוֹת *Four vows.* The four oaths God took in promising salvation: "The Lord Almighty has sworn by Himself" (Jer. 51:14); "The Lord has sworn by His right hand and by His mighty arm" (Is. 62:8); "To Me this is like the days of Noah, when I swore that the waters of Noah would never again cover the earth. So now I have sworn not to be angry with you, never to rebuke you again" (Is. 54:9); and "By Myself I have sworn, My mouth has uttered in all integrity a word that will not be revoked" (Is. 45:23). Others

Save us, please –

אָדוֹן הַמּוֹשִׁיעַ Master who saves – there is no one else – mighty, with great power to save – when I was brought low, He saved me – God who saves – who delivers and saves – save those who cry out to You – those who yet watch for You – nourish Your young lambs – make the harvest lavish – sprout every growing thing and save us – do not condemn this valley – make the good fruits sweet and save us – carry the clouds to us – shake down the raindrops – do not hold back the clouds – You who open Your hand and satisfy – relieve those who thirst for You – save those who call to You – save those You have loved – rescue those who rise to seek You – save Your innocent ones – Save us, please.

I and *HE*: save us, please.

כְּהוֹשַׁעְתָּ As You saved the mighty ones in Lud with You,
coming down for Your people's deliverance – save us, please.

As You saved nation and God together,
[the people] called for God's salvation – save us, please.

As You saved the crowding hosts,
and angelic hosts along with them – save us, please.

As You saved pure ones from the grip of slavery,
Gracious One; enslaved in cruel hands – save us, please.

As You saved those submerged between slices of the deep,
and brought Your own glory through it with them – save us, please.

As You saved the stem as they sang "And God saved" –
but the Deliverer reads it, "God was saved" – save us, please.

As You saved, and You said, "I took you out,"
but let it be pointed, "I was taken out with you" – save us, please.

As You saved those who encompassed the Altar,
bearing their willows to encircle the Altar – save us, please.

אָדוֹן הַמּוֹשִׁיעַ *Master who saves.* For commentary see page 1025.

כְּהוֹשַׁעְתָּ *As you saved.* For commentary see page 537.

הוֹשַׁע נָא

אָדוֹן הַמּוֹשִׁיעַ. בִּלְתְּךָ אֵין לְהוֹשִׁיעַ. גִּבּוֹר וְרַב לְהוֹשִׁיעַ. דַּלּוֹתִי וְלִי יְהוֹשִׁיעַ. הָאֵל הַמּוֹשִׁיעַ. וּמַצִּיל וּמוֹשִׁיעַ. זוֹעֲקֶיךָ תּוֹשִׁיעַ. חוֹכֶיךָ הוֹשִׁיעַ. טְלָאֶיךָ תַּשְׂבִּיעַ. יְבוּל לְהַשְׁפִּיעַ. כָּל שִׂיחַ תַּדְשֵׁא וְתוֹשִׁיעַ. לְגֵיא בַּל תַּרְשִׁיעַ. מְגָדִים תַּמְתִּיק וְתוֹשִׁיעַ. נְשִׂיאִים לְהַסִּיעַ. שְׂעִירִים לְהָנִיעַ. עֲנָנִים מִלְּהַמְנִיעַ. פּוֹתֵחַ יָד וּמַשְׂבִּיעַ. צְמֵאֶיךָ תַּשְׂבִּיעַ. קוֹרְאֶיךָ תּוֹשִׁיעַ. רְחוּמֶיךָ תּוֹשִׁיעַ. שׁוֹחֲרֶיךָ הוֹשִׁיעַ. תְּמִימֶיךָ תּוֹשִׁיעַ. הוֹשַׁע נָא.

אֲנִי וָהוֹ הוֹשִׁיעָה נָּא.

כְּהוֹשַׁעְתָּ אֵלִים בְּלוּד עִמָּךְ.
בְּצֵאתְךָ לְיֵשַׁע עַמָּךְ. כֵּן הוֹשַׁע נָא.

כְּהוֹשַׁעְתָּ גּוֹי וֵאלֹהִים.
דְּרוּשִׁים לְיֵשַׁע אֱלֹהִים. כֵּן הוֹשַׁע נָא.

כְּהוֹשַׁעְתָּ הֲמוֹן צְבָאוֹת.
וְעִמָּם מַלְאֲכֵי צְבָאוֹת. כֵּן הוֹשַׁע נָא.

כְּהוֹשַׁעְתָּ זַכִּים מִבֵּית עֲבָדִים.
חַנּוּן בְּיָדָם מַעֲבִידִים. כֵּן הוֹשַׁע נָא.

כְּהוֹשַׁעְתָּ טְבוּעִים בְּצוּל גְּזָרִים.
יְקָרְךָ עִמָּם מַעֲבִירִים. כֵּן הוֹשַׁע נָא.

כְּהוֹשַׁעְתָּ כַּנָּה מְשׁוֹרֶרֶת וַיּוֹשַׁע.
לְגוֹחָה מְצֻיֶּנֶת וַיִּוָּשַׁע. כֵּן הוֹשַׁע נָא.

כְּהוֹשַׁעְתָּ מַאֲמַר וְהוֹצֵאתִי אֶתְכֶם.
נָקוּב וְהוּצֵאתִי אִתְּכֶם. כֵּן הוֹשַׁע נָא.

כְּהוֹשַׁעְתָּ סוֹבְבֵי מִזְבֵּחַ.
עוֹמְסֵי עֲרָבָה לְהַקִּיף מִזְבֵּחַ. כֵּן הוֹשַׁע נָא.

As You saved the Ark of wonders that was wronged,
tormenting Philistia with fury, and saving it – save us, please.

As You saved the communities You sent away to Babylon,
being sent too, for them, Your compassionate Self – save us, please.

As You saved the returning exiles of the tribes of Jacob,
so come back and return the exiles of the tents of Jacob –
and save us, please.

As You saved those who kept Your commandments and waited for
salvation, / God of all salvation – and save us, please.

I and *HE*: save us, please.

The Torah scroll is returned to the Ark.

הוֹשִׁיעָה Save Your people; bless Your legacy; tend them and carry *Ps. 28*
them forever. Let these words with which I have pleaded with the *1 Kings 8*
LORD be close to the LORD our God day and night, that He may do justice for His servant, and justice for His people Israel, day after day; so that all the peoples of the earth will know that the LORD is God. There is no other.

The Ark is closed.

FULL KADDISH

Some have the custom to include additional responses in Full Kaddish. They can be found in the version on *page 1464.*

Leader: יִתְגַּדַּל Magnified and sanctified may His great name be,
in the world He created by His will.
May He establish His kingdom
in your lifetime and in your days,
and in the lifetime of all the house of Israel,
swiftly and soon –
and say: Amen.

All: May His great name be blessed
for ever and all time.

כְּהוֹשַׁעְתָּ פְּלָאֵי אָרוֹן כְּהֻפְשַׁע.
צַעַר פְּלֶשֶׁת בַּחֲרוֹן אַף, וְנוֹשַׁע. כֵּן הוֹשַׁע נָא.

כְּהוֹשַׁעְתָּ קְהִלּוֹת בָּבֶלָה שִׁלַּחְתָּ.
רַחוּם לְמַעֲנָם שֻׁלַּחְתָּ. כֵּן הוֹשַׁע נָא.

כְּהוֹשַׁעְתָּ שְׁבוּת שִׁבְטֵי יַעֲקֹב.
תָּשׁוּב וְתָשִׁיב שְׁבוּת אָהֳלֵי יַעֲקֹב. וְהוֹשִׁיעָה נָּא.

כְּהוֹשַׁעְתָּ שׁוֹמְרֵי מִצְוֹת וְחוֹכֵי יְשׁוּעוֹת.
אֵל לְמוֹשָׁעוֹת. וְהוֹשִׁיעָה נָּא.

אֲנִי וָהוּ הוֹשִׁיעָה נָּא.

The ספר תורה *is returned to the* ארון קודש.

תהלים כח
מלכים א׳ ח

הוֹשִׁיעָה אֶת־עַמֶּךָ, וּבָרֵךְ אֶת־נַחֲלָתֶךָ, וּרְעֵם וְנַשְּׂאֵם עַד־הָעוֹלָם: וְיִהְיוּ דְבָרַי אֵלֶּה, אֲשֶׁר הִתְחַנַּנְתִּי לִפְנֵי יהוה, קְרֹבִים אֶל־יהוה אֱלֹהֵינוּ יוֹמָם וָלָיְלָה, לַעֲשׂוֹת מִשְׁפַּט עַבְדּוֹ וּמִשְׁפַּט עַמּוֹ יִשְׂרָאֵל, דְּבַר־יוֹם בְּיוֹמוֹ: לְמַעַן דַּעַת כָּל־עַמֵּי הָאָרֶץ כִּי יהוה הוּא הָאֱלֹהִים, אֵין עוֹד:

The ארון קודש *is closed.*

קדיש שלם

Some have the custom to include additional responses in קדיש שלם.
They can be found in the version on page 1465.

ש״ץ: **יִתְגַּדַּל וְיִתְקַדַּשׁ שְׁמֵהּ רַבָּא** (קהל: אָמֵן)
בְּעָלְמָא דִּי בְרָא כִרְעוּתֵהּ
וְיַמְלִיךְ מַלְכוּתֵהּ
בְּחַיֵּיכוֹן וּבְיוֹמֵיכוֹן וּבְחַיֵּי דְכָל בֵּית יִשְׂרָאֵל
בַּעֲגָלָא וּבִזְמַן קָרִיב
וְאִמְרוּ אָמֵן. (קהל: אָמֵן)

קהל וש״ץ: **יְהֵא שְׁמֵהּ רַבָּא מְבָרַךְ לְעָלַם וּלְעָלְמֵי עָלְמַיָּא.**

Leader: Blessed and praised, glorified and exalted,
raised and honored, uplifted and lauded
be the name of the Holy One,
blessed be He,
beyond any blessing,
song, praise and consolation
uttered in the world – and say: Amen.

May the prayers and pleas of all Israel
be accepted by their Father in heaven – and say: Amen.

May there be great peace from heaven,
and life for us and all Israel – and say: Amen.

Bow, take three steps back, as if taking leave of the Divine Presence, then bow, first left, then right, then center, while saying:

May He who makes peace in His high places,
make peace for us and all Israel – and say: Amen.

Stand while saying Aleinu. Bow at ▾.

עָלֵינוּ It is our duty to praise the Master of all,
and ascribe greatness to the Author of creation,
who has not made us like the nations of the lands
nor placed us like the families of the earth;
who has not made our portion like theirs,
nor our destiny like all their multitudes.
(For they worship vanity and emptiness,
and pray to a god who cannot save.)
▾But we bow in worship
and thank the Supreme King of kings, the Holy One,
blessed be He,
who extends the heavens and establishes the earth,
whose throne of glory is in the heavens above,
and whose power's Presence is in the highest of heights.
He is our God; there is no other.

ש״ץ: יִתְבָּרַךְ וְיִשְׁתַּבַּח וְיִתְפָּאַר
וְיִתְרוֹמַם וְיִתְנַשֵּׂא וְיִתְהַדָּר וְיִתְעַלֶּה וְיִתְהַלָּל
שְׁמֵהּ דְּקֻדְשָׁא בְּרִיךְ הוּא (קהל: בְּרִיךְ הוּא)
לְעֵלָּא מִן כָּל בִּרְכָתָא וְשִׁירָתָא, תֻּשְׁבְּחָתָא וְנֶחֱמָתָא
דַּאֲמִירָן בְּעָלְמָא, וְאִמְרוּ אָמֵן. (קהל: אָמֵן)

תִּתְקַבַּל צְלוֹתְהוֹן וּבָעוּתְהוֹן דְּכָל יִשְׂרָאֵל
קֳדָם אֲבוּהוֹן דִּי בִשְׁמַיָּא, וְאִמְרוּ אָמֵן. (קהל: אָמֵן)

יְהֵא שְׁלָמָא רַבָּא מִן שְׁמַיָּא
וְחַיִּים, עָלֵינוּ וְעַל כָּל יִשְׂרָאֵל, וְאִמְרוּ אָמֵן. (קהל: אָמֵן)

Bow, take three steps back, as if taking leave of the Divine Presence, then bow, first left, then right, then center, while saying:

עֹשֶׂה שָׁלוֹם בִּמְרוֹמָיו
הוּא יַעֲשֶׂה שָׁלוֹם
עָלֵינוּ וְעַל כָּל יִשְׂרָאֵל, וְאִמְרוּ אָמֵן. (קהל: אָמֵן)

Stand while saying עָלֵינוּ. *Bow at* ▾.

עָלֵינוּ לְשַׁבֵּחַ לַאֲדוֹן הַכֹּל, לָתֵת גְּדֻלָּה לְיוֹצֵר בְּרֵאשִׁית
שֶׁלֹּא עָשָׂנוּ כְּגוֹיֵי הָאֲרָצוֹת, וְלֹא שָׂמָנוּ כְּמִשְׁפְּחוֹת הָאֲדָמָה
שֶׁלֹּא שָׂם חֶלְקֵנוּ כָּהֶם וְגוֹרָלֵנוּ כְּכָל הֲמוֹנָם.
(שֶׁהֵם מִשְׁתַּחֲוִים לְהֶבֶל וָרִיק וּמִתְפַּלְלִים אֶל אֵל לֹא יוֹשִׁיעַ.)
▾וַאֲנַחְנוּ כּוֹרְעִים וּמִשְׁתַּחֲוִים וּמוֹדִים
לִפְנֵי מֶלֶךְ מַלְכֵי הַמְּלָכִים, הַקָּדוֹשׁ בָּרוּךְ הוּא
שֶׁהוּא נוֹטֶה שָׁמַיִם וְיוֹסֵד אָרֶץ
וּמוֹשַׁב יְקָרוֹ בַּשָּׁמַיִם מִמַּעַל
וּשְׁכִינַת עֻזּוֹ בְּגָבְהֵי מְרוֹמִים.
הוּא אֱלֹהֵינוּ, אֵין עוֹד.

Truly He is our King, there is none else,
as it is written in His Torah:
"You shall know and take to heart this day that the LORD is God, *Deut. 4*
in heaven above and on earth below.
There is no other."

Therefore, we place our hope in You, LORD our God,
that we may soon see the glory of Your power,
when You will remove abominations from the earth,
and idols will be utterly destroyed,
when the world will be perfected
under the sovereignty of the Almighty,
when all humanity will call on Your name,
to turn all the earth's wicked toward You.
All the world's inhabitants will realize and know
that to You every knee must bow and every tongue swear loyalty.
Before You, LORD our God, they will kneel and bow down
and give honor to Your glorious name.
They will all accept the yoke of Your kingdom,
and You will reign over them soon and for ever.
For the kingdom is Yours,
and to all eternity You will reign in glory,
as it is written in Your Torah:
"The LORD will reign for ever and ever." *Ex. 15*
▸ And it is said:
"Then the LORD shall be King over all the earth; *Zech. 14*
on that day the LORD shall be One and His name One."

Some add:

Have no fear of sudden terror or of the ruin when it overtakes the wicked. *Prov. 3*
Devise your strategy, but it will be thwarted; propose your plan, *Is. 8*
but it will not stand, for God is with us.
When you grow old, I will still be the same. *Is. 46*
When your hair turns gray, I will still carry you.
I made you, I will bear you, I will carry you, and I will rescue you.

אֱמֶת מַלְכֵּנוּ, אֶפֶס זוּלָתוֹ, כַּכָּתוּב בְּתוֹרָתוֹ

וְיָדַעְתָּ הַיּוֹם וַהֲשֵׁבֹתָ אֶל־לְבָבֶךָ דברים ד

כִּי יהוה הוּא הָאֱלֹהִים בַּשָּׁמַיִם מִמַּעַל וְעַל־הָאָרֶץ מִתָּחַת

אֵין עוֹד:

עַל כֵּן נְקַוֶּה לְּךָ יהוה אֱלֹהֵינוּ, לִרְאוֹת מְהֵרָה בְּתִפְאֶרֶת עֻזֶּךָ

לְהַעֲבִיר גִּלּוּלִים מִן הָאָרֶץ

וְהָאֱלִילִים כָּרוֹת יִכָּרֵתוּן

לְתַקֵּן עוֹלָם בְּמַלְכוּת שַׁדַּי.

וְכָל בְּנֵי בָשָׂר יִקְרְאוּ בִשְׁמֶךָ לְהַפְנוֹת אֵלֶיךָ כָּל רִשְׁעֵי אָרֶץ.

יַכִּירוּ וְיֵדְעוּ כָּל יוֹשְׁבֵי תֵבֵל

כִּי לְךָ תִּכְרַע כָּל בֶּרֶךְ, תִּשָּׁבַע כָּל לָשׁוֹן.

לְפָנֶיךָ יהוה אֱלֹהֵינוּ יִכְרְעוּ וְיִפֹּלוּ

וְלִכְבוֹד שִׁמְךָ יְקָר יִתֵּנוּ

וִיקַבְּלוּ כֻלָּם אֶת עֹל מַלְכוּתֶךָ

וְתִמְלֹךְ עֲלֵיהֶם מְהֵרָה לְעוֹלָם וָעֶד.

כִּי הַמַּלְכוּת שֶׁלְּךָ הִיא וּלְעוֹלְמֵי עַד תִּמְלֹךְ בְּכָבוֹד

כַּכָּתוּב בְּתוֹרָתֶךָ

יהוה יִמְלֹךְ לְעֹלָם וָעֶד: שמות טו

◂ וְנֶאֱמַר, וְהָיָה יהוה לְמֶלֶךְ עַל־כָּל־הָאָרֶץ זכריה יד

בַּיּוֹם הַהוּא יִהְיֶה יהוה אֶחָד וּשְׁמוֹ אֶחָד:

Some add:

אַל־תִּירָא מִפַּחַד פִּתְאֹם וּמִשֹּׁאַת רְשָׁעִים כִּי תָבֹא: משלי ג

עֻצוּ עֵצָה וְתֻפָר, דַּבְּרוּ דָבָר וְלֹא יָקוּם, כִּי עִמָּנוּ אֵל: ישעיה ח

וְעַד־זִקְנָה אֲנִי הוּא, וְעַד־שֵׂיבָה אֲנִי אֶסְבֹּל ישעיה מו

אֲנִי עָשִׂיתִי וַאֲנִי אֶשָּׂא וַאֲנִי אֶסְבֹּל וַאֲמַלֵּט:

MOURNER'S KADDISH

The following prayer, said by mourners, requires the presence of a minyan. A transliteration can be found on page 1467.

Mourner: יִתְגַּדַּל Magnified and sanctified
may His great name be,
in the world He created by His will.
May He establish His kingdom
in your lifetime and in your days,
and in the lifetime of all the house of Israel,
swiftly and soon –
and say: Amen.

All: May His great name
be blessed for ever and all time.

Mourner: Blessed and praised,
glorified and exalted,
raised and honored, uplifted and lauded
be the name of the Holy One,
blessed be He,
beyond any blessing,
song, praise and consolation
uttered in the world –
and say: Amen.

May there be great peace from heaven,
and life for us and all Israel –
and say: Amen.

Bow, take three steps back, as if taking leave of the Divine Presence, then bow, first left, then right, then center, while saying:

May He who makes peace in His high places,
make peace for us and all Israel –
and say: Amen.

קדיש יתום

The following prayer, said by mourners, requires the presence of a מנין.
A transliteration can be found on page 1467.

אבל: יִתְגַּדַּל וְיִתְקַדַּשׁ שְׁמֵהּ רַבָּא (קהל: אָמֵן)
בְּעָלְמָא דִּי בְרָא כִרְעוּתֵהּ
וְיַמְלִיךְ מַלְכוּתֵהּ
בְּחַיֵּיכוֹן וּבְיוֹמֵיכוֹן וּבְחַיֵּי דְכָל בֵּית יִשְׂרָאֵל
בַּעֲגָלָא וּבִזְמַן קָרִיב
וְאִמְרוּ אָמֵן. (קהל: אָמֵן)

קהל ואבל: יְהֵא שְׁמֵהּ רַבָּא מְבָרַךְ לְעָלַם וּלְעָלְמֵי עָלְמַיָּא.

אבל: יִתְבָּרַךְ וְיִשְׁתַּבַּח וְיִתְפָּאַר
וְיִתְרוֹמַם וְיִתְנַשֵּׂא וְיִתְהַדָּר וְיִתְעַלֶּה וְיִתְהַלָּל
שְׁמֵהּ דְּקֻדְשָׁא בְּרִיךְ הוּא (קהל: בְּרִיךְ הוּא)
לְעֵלָּא מִן כָּל בִּרְכָתָא וְשִׁירָתָא, תֻּשְׁבְּחָתָא וְנֶחֱמָתָא
דַּאֲמִירָן בְּעָלְמָא
וְאִמְרוּ אָמֵן. (קהל: אָמֵן)

יְהֵא שְׁלָמָא רַבָּא מִן שְׁמַיָּא
וְחַיִּים, עָלֵינוּ וְעַל כָּל יִשְׂרָאֵל
וְאִמְרוּ אָמֵן. (קהל: אָמֵן)

Bow, take three steps back, as if taking leave of the Divine Presence, then bow, first left, then right, then center, while saying:

עֹשֶׂה שָׁלוֹם בִּמְרוֹמָיו
הוּא יַעֲשֶׂה שָׁלוֹם עָלֵינוּ וְעַל כָּל יִשְׂרָאֵל
וְאִמְרוּ אָמֵן. (קהל: אָמֵן)

THE DAILY PSALM

One of the following psalms is said on the appropriate day of the week as indicated.

Sunday: Today is the first day of the week,
on which the Levites used to say this psalm in the Temple:

לְדָוִד מִזְמוֹר A psalm of David. The earth is the LORD's and all it contains, *Ps. 24*
the world and all who live in it. For He founded it on the seas and established it on the streams. Who may climb the mountain of the LORD? Who may stand in His holy place? He who has clean hands and a pure heart, who has not taken My name in vain or sworn deceitfully. He shall receive a blessing from the LORD, and just reward from the God of his salvation. This is a generation of those who seek Him, the descendants of Jacob who seek Your presence, Selah! Lift up your heads, O gates; be uplifted, eternal doors, so that the King of glory may enter. Who is the King of glory? It is the LORD, strong and mighty, the LORD mighty in battle. Lift up your heads, O gates; be uplifted, eternal doors, that the King of glory may enter. ▸ Who is He, the King of glory? The LORD of hosts, He is the King of glory, Selah!

Mourner's Kaddish (page 732)

Monday: Today is the second day of the week,
on which the Levites used to say this psalm in the Temple:

שִׁיר מִזְמוֹר A song. A psalm of the sons of Koraḥ. Great is the LORD and *Ps. 48*
greatly to be praised in the city of God, on His holy mountain – beautiful in its heights, joy of all the earth, Mount Zion on its northern side, city of the great King. In its citadels God is known as a stronghold. See how the kings joined forces, advancing together. They saw, they were astounded, they panicked, they fled. There fear seized them, like the pains of a woman giving birth, like ships of Tarshish wrecked by an eastern wind. What we had heard, now we have seen, in the city of the LORD of hosts, in the city of our God. May God preserve it for ever, Selah! In the midst of Your Temple, God, we meditate on Your love. As is Your name, God, so is Your praise: it reaches to the ends of the earth. Your right hand is filled with righteousness. Let Mount Zion rejoice, let the towns of Judah be glad, because of Your judgments. Walk around Zion and encircle it. Count its towers, note its strong walls, view its citadels,

שיר של יום

One of the following psalms is said on the appropriate day of the week as indicated.

Sunday הַיּוֹם יוֹם רִאשׁוֹן בְּשַׁבָּת, שֶׁבּוֹ הָיוּ הַלְוִיִּם אוֹמְרִים בְּבֵית הַמִּקְדָּשׁ:

לְדָוִד מִזְמוֹר, לַיהוה הָאָרֶץ וּמְלוֹאָהּ, תֵּבֵל וְיְשְׁבֵי בָהּ: כִּי־הוּא עַל־ תהלים כד
יַמִּים יְסָדָהּ, וְעַל־נְהָרוֹת יְכוֹנְנֶהָ: מִי־יַעֲלֶה בְהַר־יהוה, וּמִי־יָקוּם
בִּמְקוֹם קָדְשׁוֹ: נְקִי כַפַּיִם וּבַר־לֵבָב, אֲשֶׁר לֹא־נָשָׂא לַשָּׁוְא נַפְשִׁי,
וְלֹא נִשְׁבַּע לְמִרְמָה: יִשָּׂא בְרָכָה מֵאֵת יהוה, וּצְדָקָה מֵאֱלֹהֵי יִשְׁעוֹ:
זֶה דּוֹר דֹּרְשָׁו, מְבַקְשֵׁי פָנֶיךָ יַעֲקֹב סֶלָה: שְׂאוּ שְׁעָרִים רָאשֵׁיכֶם,
וְהִנָּשְׂאוּ פִּתְחֵי עוֹלָם, וְיָבוֹא מֶלֶךְ הַכָּבוֹד: מִי זֶה מֶלֶךְ הַכָּבוֹד,
יהוה עִזּוּז וְגִבּוֹר, יהוה גִּבּוֹר מִלְחָמָה: שְׂאוּ שְׁעָרִים רָאשֵׁיכֶם,
וּשְׂאוּ פִּתְחֵי עוֹלָם, וְיָבֹא מֶלֶךְ הַכָּבוֹד: ‹ מִי הוּא זֶה מֶלֶךְ הַכָּבוֹד,
יהוה צְבָאוֹת הוּא מֶלֶךְ הַכָּבוֹד סֶלָה:

קדיש יתום (*page 733*)

Monday הַיּוֹם יוֹם שֵׁנִי בְּשַׁבָּת, שֶׁבּוֹ הָיוּ הַלְוִיִּם אוֹמְרִים בְּבֵית הַמִּקְדָּשׁ:

שִׁיר מִזְמוֹר לִבְנֵי־קֹרַח: גָּדוֹל יהוה וּמְהֻלָּל מְאֹד, בְּעִיר אֱלֹהֵינוּ, תהלים מח
הַר־קָדְשׁוֹ: יְפֵה נוֹף מְשׂוֹשׂ כָּל־הָאָרֶץ, הַר־צִיּוֹן יַרְכְּתֵי צָפוֹן, קִרְיַת
מֶלֶךְ רָב: אֱלֹהִים בְּאַרְמְנוֹתֶיהָ נוֹדַע לְמִשְׂגָּב: כִּי־הִנֵּה הַמְּלָכִים
נוֹעֲדוּ, עָבְרוּ יַחְדָּו: הֵמָּה רָאוּ כֵּן תָּמָהוּ, נִבְהֲלוּ נֶחְפָּזוּ: רְעָדָה
אֲחָזָתַם שָׁם, חִיל כַּיּוֹלֵדָה: בְּרוּחַ קָדִים תְּשַׁבֵּר אֳנִיּוֹת תַּרְשִׁישׁ:
כַּאֲשֶׁר שָׁמַעְנוּ כֵּן רָאִינוּ, בְּעִיר־יהוה צְבָאוֹת, בְּעִיר אֱלֹהֵינוּ,
אֱלֹהִים יְכוֹנְנֶהָ עַד־עוֹלָם סֶלָה: דִּמִּינוּ אֱלֹהִים חַסְדֶּךָ, בְּקֶרֶב
הֵיכָלֶךָ: כְּשִׁמְךָ אֱלֹהִים כֵּן תְּהִלָּתְךָ עַל־קַצְוֵי־אֶרֶץ, צֶדֶק מָלְאָה
יְמִינֶךָ: יִשְׂמַח הַר־צִיּוֹן, תָּגֵלְנָה בְּנוֹת יְהוּדָה, לְמַעַן מִשְׁפָּטֶיךָ:
סֹבּוּ צִיּוֹן וְהַקִּיפוּהָ, סִפְרוּ מִגְדָּלֶיהָ: שִׁיתוּ לִבְּכֶם לְחֵילָה, פַּסְּגוּ

so that you may tell a future generation ▸ that this is God, our God, for ever and ever. He will guide us for evermore.

Mourner's Kaddish (*page* 732)

Tuesday: Today is the third day of the week,
on which the Levites used to say this psalm in the Temple:

מִזְמוֹר לְאָסָף A psalm of Asaph. God stands in the Divine assembly. Among *Ps. 82*
the judges He delivers judgment. How long will you judge unjustly, showing favor to the wicked? Selah. Do justice to the weak and the orphaned. Vindicate the poor and destitute. Rescue the weak and needy. Save them from the hand of the wicked. They do not know nor do they understand. They walk about in darkness while all the earth's foundations shake. I once said, "You are like gods, all of you are sons of the Most High." But you shall die like mere men, you will fall like any prince. ▸ Arise, O Lord, judge the earth, for all the nations are Your possession.

Mourner's Kaddish (*page* 732)

Wednesday: Today is the fourth day of the week,
on which the Levites used to say this psalm in the Temple:

אֵל־נְקָמוֹת God of retribution, Lord, God of retribution, appear! Rise up, *Ps. 94*
Judge of the earth. Repay to the arrogant what they deserve. How long shall the wicked, Lord, how long shall the wicked triumph? They pour out insolent words. All the evildoers are full of boasting. They crush Your people, Lord, and oppress Your inheritance. They kill the widow and the stranger. They murder the orphaned. They say, "The Lord does not see. The God of Jacob pays no heed." Take heed, you most brutish people. You fools, when will you grow wise? Will He who implants the ear not hear? Will He who formed the eye not see? Will He who disciplines nations – He who teaches man knowledge – not punish? The Lord knows that the thoughts of man are a mere fleeting breath. Happy is the man whom You discipline, Lord, the one You instruct in Your Torah, giving him tranquility in days of trouble, until a pit is dug for the wicked. For the Lord will not forsake His people, nor abandon His heritage. Judgment shall again accord with justice, and all the upright in heart will follow it. Who will rise up for me against the wicked? Who will stand up for me against wrongdoers? Had the Lord not been my help, I would soon

אַרְמְנוֹתֶיהָ, לְמַעַן תְּסַפְּרוּ לְדוֹר אַחֲרוֹן: ‹ כִּי זֶה אֱלֹהִים אֱלֹהֵינוּ
עוֹלָם וָעֶד, הוּא יְנַהֲגֵנוּ עַל־מוּת: קדיש יתום (*page 733*)

Tuesday הַיּוֹם יוֹם שְׁלִישִׁי בְּשַׁבָּת, שֶׁבּוֹ הָיוּ הַלְוִיִּם אוֹמְרִים בְּבֵית הַמִּקְדָּשׁ:

מִזְמוֹר לְאָסָף, אֱלֹהִים נִצָּב בַּעֲדַת־אֵל, בְּקֶרֶב אֱלֹהִים יִשְׁפֹּט: עַד־ תהלים פב
מָתַי תִּשְׁפְּטוּ־עָוֶל, וּפְנֵי רְשָׁעִים תִּשְׂאוּ־סֶלָה: שִׁפְטוּ־דַל וְיָתוֹם,
עָנִי וָרָשׁ הַצְדִּיקוּ: פַּלְּטוּ־דַל וְאֶבְיוֹן, מִיַּד רְשָׁעִים הַצִּילוּ: לֹא יָדְעוּ
וְלֹא יָבִינוּ, בַּחֲשֵׁכָה יִתְהַלָּכוּ, יִמּוֹטוּ כָּל־מוֹסְדֵי אָרֶץ: אֲנִי־אָמַרְתִּי
אֱלֹהִים אַתֶּם, וּבְנֵי עֶלְיוֹן כֻּלְּכֶם: אָכֵן כְּאָדָם תְּמוּתוּן, וּכְאַחַד
הַשָּׂרִים תִּפֹּלוּ: ‹ קוּמָה אֱלֹהִים שָׁפְטָה הָאָרֶץ, כִּי־אַתָּה תִנְחַל
בְּכָל־הַגּוֹיִם: קדיש יתום (*page 733*)

Wednesday הַיּוֹם יוֹם רְבִיעִי בְּשַׁבָּת, שֶׁבּוֹ הָיוּ הַלְוִיִּם אוֹמְרִים בְּבֵית הַמִּקְדָּשׁ:

אֵל־נְקָמוֹת יהוה, אֵל נְקָמוֹת הוֹפִיעַ: הִנָּשֵׂא שֹׁפֵט הָאָרֶץ, הָשֵׁב תהלים צד
גְּמוּל עַל־גֵּאִים: עַד־מָתַי רְשָׁעִים, יהוה, עַד־מָתַי רְשָׁעִים יַעֲלֹזוּ:
יַבִּיעוּ יְדַבְּרוּ עָתָק, יִתְאַמְּרוּ כָּל־פֹּעֲלֵי אָוֶן: עַמְּךָ יהוה יְדַכְּאוּ,
וְנַחֲלָתְךָ יְעַנּוּ: אַלְמָנָה וְגֵר יַהֲרֹגוּ, וִיתוֹמִים יְרַצֵּחוּ: וַיֹּאמְרוּ לֹא
יִרְאֶה־יָּהּ, וְלֹא־יָבִין אֱלֹהֵי יַעֲקֹב: בִּינוּ בֹּעֲרִים בָּעָם, וּכְסִילִים מָתַי
תַּשְׂכִּילוּ: הֲנֹטַע אֹזֶן הֲלֹא יִשְׁמָע, אִם־יֹצֵר עַיִן הֲלֹא יַבִּיט: הֲיֹסֵר
גּוֹיִם הֲלֹא יוֹכִיחַ, הַמְלַמֵּד אָדָם דָּעַת: יהוה יֹדֵעַ מַחְשְׁבוֹת אָדָם,
כִּי־הֵמָּה הָבֶל: אַשְׁרֵי הַגֶּבֶר אֲשֶׁר־תְּיַסְּרֶנּוּ יָּהּ, וּמִתּוֹרָתְךָ תְלַמְּדֶנּוּ:
לְהַשְׁקִיט לוֹ מִימֵי רָע, עַד יִכָּרֶה לָרָשָׁע שָׁחַת: כִּי לֹא־יִטֹּשׁ יהוה
עַמּוֹ, וְנַחֲלָתוֹ לֹא יַעֲזֹב: כִּי־עַד־צֶדֶק יָשׁוּב מִשְׁפָּט, וְאַחֲרָיו כָּל־
יִשְׁרֵי־לֵב: מִי־יָקוּם לִי עִם־מְרֵעִים, מִי־יִתְיַצֵּב לִי עִם־פֹּעֲלֵי אָוֶן:

have dwelt in death's silence. When I thought my foot was slipping, Your loving-kindness, LORD, gave me support. When I was filled with anxiety, Your consolations soothed my soul. Can a corrupt throne be allied with You? Can injustice be framed into law? They join forces against the life of the righteous, and condemn the innocent to death. But the LORD is my stronghold, my God is the Rock of my refuge. He will bring back on them their wickedness, and destroy them for their evil deeds. The LORD our God will destroy them.

▸ Come, let us sing for joy to the LORD; let us shout aloud to the Rock of Ps. 95
our salvation. Let us greet Him with thanksgiving, shout aloud to Him with songs of praise. For the LORD is the great God, the King great above all powers.

Mourner's Kaddish on the next page.

Thursday: Today is the fifth day of the week,
on which the Levites used to say this psalm in the Temple:

לַמְנַצֵּחַ For the conductor of music. On the Gittit. By Asaph. Sing for joy Ps. 81
to God, our strength. Shout aloud to the God of Jacob. Raise a song, beat the drum, play the sweet harp and lyre. Sound the shofar on the new moon, on our feast day when the moon is hidden. For it is a statute for Israel, an ordinance of the God of Jacob. He established it as a testimony for Joseph when He went forth against the land of Egypt, where I heard a language that I did not know. I relieved his shoulder of the burden. His hands were freed from the builder's basket. In distress you called and I rescued you. I answered you from the secret place of thunder; I tested you at the waters of Meribah, Selah! Hear, My people, and I will warn you. Israel, if you would only listen to Me! Let there be no strange god among you. Do not bow down to an alien god. I am the LORD your God who brought you out of the land of Egypt. Open your mouth wide and I will fill it. But My people would not listen to Me. Israel would have none of Me. So I left them to their stubborn hearts, letting them follow their own devices. If only My people would listen to Me, if Israel would walk in My ways, I would soon subdue their enemies, and turn My hand against their foes. Those who hate the LORD would cower before Him and their doom would last for ever.
▸ He would feed Israel with the finest wheat – with honey from the rock I would satisfy you.

Mourner's Kaddish on the next page.

לוּלֵי יהוה עֶזְרָתָה לִּי, כִּמְעַט שָׁכְנָה דוּמָה נַפְשִׁי: אִם־אָמַרְתִּי
מָטָה רַגְלִי, חַסְדְּךָ יהוה יִסְעָדֵנִי: בְּרֹב שַׂרְעַפַּי בְּקִרְבִּי, תַּנְחוּמֶיךָ
יְשַׁעַשְׁעוּ נַפְשִׁי: הַיְחָבְרְךָ כִּסֵּא הַוּוֹת, יֹצֵר עָמָל עֲלֵי־חֹק: יָגוֹדּוּ
עַל־נֶפֶשׁ צַדִּיק, וְדָם נָקִי יַרְשִׁיעוּ: וַיְהִי יהוה לִי לְמִשְׂגָּב, וֵאלֹהַי
לְצוּר מַחְסִי: וַיָּשֶׁב עֲלֵיהֶם אֶת־אוֹנָם, וּבְרָעָתָם יַצְמִיתֵם, יַצְמִיתֵם
יהוה אֱלֹהֵינוּ:

תהלים צה ‹ לְכוּ נְרַנְּנָה לַיהוה, נָרִיעָה לְצוּר יִשְׁעֵנוּ: נְקַדְּמָה פָנָיו בְּתוֹדָה,
בִּזְמִרוֹת נָרִיעַ לוֹ: כִּי אֵל גָּדוֹל יהוה, וּמֶלֶךְ גָּדוֹל עַל־כָּל־אֱלֹהִים:

קדיש יתום *on the next page.*

Thursday הַיּוֹם יוֹם חֲמִישִׁי בְּשַׁבָּת, שֶׁבּוֹ הָיוּ הַלְוִיִּם אוֹמְרִים בְּבֵית הַמִּקְדָּשׁ:

תהלים פא לַמְנַצֵּחַ עַל־הַגִּתִּית לְאָסָף: הַרְנִינוּ לֵאלֹהִים עוּזֵּנוּ, הָרִיעוּ לֵאלֹהֵי
יַעֲקֹב: שְׂאוּ־זִמְרָה וּתְנוּ־תֹף, כִּנּוֹר נָעִים עִם־נָבֶל: תִּקְעוּ בַחֹדֶשׁ
שׁוֹפָר, בַּכֵּסֶה לְיוֹם חַגֵּנוּ: כִּי חֹק לְיִשְׂרָאֵל הוּא, מִשְׁפָּט לֵאלֹהֵי
יַעֲקֹב: עֵדוּת בִּיהוֹסֵף שָׂמוֹ, בְּצֵאתוֹ עַל־אֶרֶץ מִצְרָיִם, שְׂפַת לֹא־
יָדַעְתִּי אֶשְׁמָע: הֲסִירוֹתִי מִסֵּבֶל שִׁכְמוֹ, כַּפָּיו מִדּוּד תַּעֲבֹרְנָה:
בַּצָּרָה קָרָאתָ וָאֲחַלְּצֶךָּ, אֶעֶנְךָ בְּסֵתֶר רַעַם, אֶבְחָנְךָ עַל־מֵי
מְרִיבָה סֶלָה: שְׁמַע עַמִּי וְאָעִידָה בָּךְ, יִשְׂרָאֵל אִם־תִּשְׁמַע־לִי:
לֹא־יִהְיֶה בְךָ אֵל זָר, וְלֹא תִשְׁתַּחֲוֶה לְאֵל נֵכָר: אָנֹכִי יהוה אֱלֹהֶיךָ,
הַמַּעַלְךָ מֵאֶרֶץ מִצְרָיִם, הַרְחֶב־פִּיךָ וַאֲמַלְאֵהוּ: וְלֹא־שָׁמַע
עַמִּי לְקוֹלִי, וְיִשְׂרָאֵל לֹא־אָבָה לִי: וָאֲשַׁלְּחֵהוּ בִּשְׁרִירוּת לִבָּם,
יֵלְכוּ בְּמוֹעֲצוֹתֵיהֶם: לוּ עַמִּי שֹׁמֵעַ לִי, יִשְׂרָאֵל בִּדְרָכַי יְהַלֵּכוּ:
כִּמְעַט אוֹיְבֵיהֶם אַכְנִיעַ, וְעַל־צָרֵיהֶם אָשִׁיב יָדִי: מְשַׂנְאֵי יהוה
יְכַחֲשׁוּ־לוֹ, וִיהִי עִתָּם לְעוֹלָם: ‹ וַיַּאֲכִילֵהוּ מֵחֵלֶב חִטָּה, וּמִצּוּר,
דְּבַשׁ אַשְׂבִּיעֶךָ:

קדיש יתום *on the next page.*

Friday: Today is the sixth day of the week,
on which the Levites used to say this psalm in the Temple:

יְהוָה מָלָךְ The LORD reigns. He is robed in majesty. The LORD is robed, *Ps. 93*
girded with strength. The world is firmly established; it cannot be moved. Your throne stands firm as of old; You are eternal. Rivers lift up, LORD, rivers lift up their voice, rivers lift up their crashing waves. Mightier than the noise of many waters, than the mighty waves of the sea is the LORD on high. ▸ Your testimonies are very sure; holiness adorns Your House, LORD, for evermore.

MOURNER'S KADDISH

The following prayer, said by mourners, requires the presence of a minyan.
A transliteration can be found on page 1467.

Mourner: יִתְגַּדַּל Magnified and sanctified
may His great name be,
in the world He created by His will.
May He establish His kingdom
in your lifetime and in your days,
and in the lifetime of all the house of Israel,
swiftly and soon –
and say: Amen.

All: May His great name
be blessed for ever and all time.

Mourner: Blessed and praised, glorified and exalted,
raised and honored,
uplifted and lauded
be the name of the Holy One,
blessed be He,
beyond any blessing,
song, praise and consolation
uttered in the world –
and say: Amen.

Friday הַיּוֹם יוֹם שִׁשִּׁי בְּשַׁבָּת, שֶׁבּוֹ הָיוּ הַלְוִיִּם אוֹמְרִים בְּבֵית הַמִּקְדָּשׁ:

יהוה מָלָךְ, גֵּאוּת לָבֵשׁ, לָבֵשׁ יהוה עֹז הִתְאַזָּר, אַף־תִּכּוֹן תֵּבֵל בַּל־ תהלים צג
תִּמּוֹט: נָכוֹן כִּסְאֲךָ מֵאָז, מֵעוֹלָם אָתָּה: נָשְׂאוּ נְהָרוֹת יהוה, נָשְׂאוּ
נְהָרוֹת קוֹלָם, יִשְׂאוּ נְהָרוֹת דָּכְיָם: מִקֹּלוֹת מַיִם רַבִּים, אַדִּירִים
מִשְׁבְּרֵי־יָם, אַדִּיר בַּמָּרוֹם יהוה: ‹ עֵדֹתֶיךָ נֶאֶמְנוּ מְאֹד, לְבֵיתְךָ
נַאֲוָה־קֹּדֶשׁ, יהוה לְאֹרֶךְ יָמִים:

קדיש יתום

The following prayer, said by mourners, requires the presence of a מנין.
A transliteration can be found on page 1467.

אבל: יִתְגַּדַּל וְיִתְקַדַּשׁ שְׁמֵהּ רַבָּא (קהל: אָמֵן)
בְּעָלְמָא דִּי בְרָא כִרְעוּתֵהּ
וְיַמְלִיךְ מַלְכוּתֵהּ
בְּחַיֵּיכוֹן וּבְיוֹמֵיכוֹן וּבְחַיֵּי דְכָל בֵּית יִשְׂרָאֵל
בַּעֲגָלָא וּבִזְמַן קָרִיב
וְאִמְרוּ אָמֵן. (קהל: אָמֵן)

קהל ואבל: יְהֵא שְׁמֵהּ רַבָּא מְבָרַךְ לְעָלַם וּלְעָלְמֵי עָלְמַיָּא.

אבל: יִתְבָּרַךְ וְיִשְׁתַּבַּח וְיִתְפָּאַר
וְיִתְרוֹמַם וְיִתְנַשֵּׂא וְיִתְהַדָּר וְיִתְעַלֶּה וְיִתְהַלָּל
שְׁמֵהּ דְּקֻדְשָׁא בְּרִיךְ הוּא (קהל: בְּרִיךְ הוּא)
לְעֵלָּא מִן כָּל בִּרְכָתָא וְשִׁירָתָא
תֻּשְׁבְּחָתָא וְנֶחֱמָתָא
דַּאֲמִירָן בְּעָלְמָא
וְאִמְרוּ אָמֵן. (קהל: אָמֵן)

May there be great peace from heaven,
and life for us and all Israel –
and say: Amen.

Bow, take three steps back, as if taking leave of the Divine Presence, then bow, first left, then right, then center, while saying:

May He who makes peace in His high places,
make peace for us and all Israel –
and say: Amen.

לְדָוִד A psalm of David. The LORD is my light and my salvation – whom *Ps. 27*
then shall I fear? The LORD is the stronghold of my life – of whom shall I be afraid? When evil men close in on me to devour my flesh, it is they, my enemies and foes, who stumble and fall. Should an army besiege me, my heart would not fear. Should war break out against me, still I would be confident. One thing I ask of the LORD, only this do I seek: to live in the House of the LORD all the days of my life, to gaze on the beauty of the LORD and worship in His Temple. For He will keep me safe in His pavilion on the day of trouble. He will hide me under the cover of His tent. He will set me high upon a rock. Now my head is high above my enemies who surround me. I will sacrifice in His tent with shouts of joy. I will sing and chant praises to the LORD. LORD, hear my voice when I call. Be gracious to me and answer me. On Your behalf my heart says, "Seek My face." Your face, LORD, will I seek. Do not hide Your face from me. Do not turn Your servant away in anger. You have been my help. Do not reject or forsake me, God, my Savior. Were my father and my mother to forsake me, the LORD would take me in. Teach me Your way, LORD, and lead me on a level path, because of my oppressors. Do not abandon me to the will of my foes, for false witnesses have risen against me, breathing violence. ▸ Were it not for my faith that I shall see the LORD's goodness in the land of the living. Hope in the LORD. Be strong and of good courage, and hope in the LORD!

Mourner's Kaddish (*on the previous page*)

In Israel, continue on the next page.

יְהֵא שְׁלָמָא רַבָּא מִן שְׁמַיָּא
וְחַיִּים, עָלֵינוּ וְעַל כָּל יִשְׂרָאֵל
וְאִמְרוּ אָמֵן. (קהל: אָמֵן)

Bow, take three steps back, as if taking leave of the Divine Presence, then bow, first left, then right, then center, while saying:

עֹשֶׂה שָׁלוֹם בִּמְרוֹמָיו
הוּא יַעֲשֶׂה שָׁלוֹם עָלֵינוּ וְעַל כָּל יִשְׂרָאֵל
וְאִמְרוּ אָמֵן. (קהל: אָמֵן)

תהלים כז לְדָוִד, יהוה אוֹרִי וְיִשְׁעִי, מִמִּי אִירָא, יהוה מָעוֹז־חַיַּי, מִמִּי אֶפְחָד: בִּקְרֹב עָלַי מְרֵעִים לֶאֱכֹל אֶת־בְּשָׂרִי, צָרַי וְאֹיְבַי לִי, הֵמָּה כָשְׁלוּ וְנָפָלוּ: אִם־תַּחֲנֶה עָלַי מַחֲנֶה, לֹא־יִירָא לִבִּי, אִם־תָּקוּם עָלַי מִלְחָמָה, בְּזֹאת אֲנִי בוֹטֵחַ: אַחַת שָׁאַלְתִּי מֵאֵת־יהוה, אוֹתָהּ אֲבַקֵּשׁ, שִׁבְתִּי בְּבֵית־יהוה כָּל־יְמֵי חַיַּי, לַחֲזוֹת בְּנֹעַם־יהוה, וּלְבַקֵּר בְּהֵיכָלוֹ: כִּי יִצְפְּנֵנִי בְּסֻכֹּה בְּיוֹם רָעָה, יַסְתִּרֵנִי בְּסֵתֶר אָהֳלוֹ, בְּצוּר יְרוֹמְמֵנִי: וְעַתָּה יָרוּם רֹאשִׁי עַל אֹיְבַי סְבִיבוֹתַי, וְאֶזְבְּחָה בְאָהֳלוֹ זִבְחֵי תְרוּעָה, אָשִׁירָה וַאֲזַמְּרָה לַיהוה: שְׁמַע־יהוה קוֹלִי אֶקְרָא, וְחָנֵּנִי וַעֲנֵנִי: לְךָ אָמַר לִבִּי בַּקְּשׁוּ פָנָי, אֶת־פָּנֶיךָ יהוה אֲבַקֵּשׁ: אַל־תַּסְתֵּר פָּנֶיךָ מִמֶּנִּי, אַל תַּט־בְּאַף עַבְדֶּךָ, עֶזְרָתִי הָיִיתָ, אַל־תִּטְּשֵׁנִי וְאַל־תַּעַזְבֵנִי, אֱלֹהֵי יִשְׁעִי: כִּי־אָבִי וְאִמִּי עֲזָבוּנִי, וַיהוה יַאַסְפֵנִי: הוֹרֵנִי יהוה דַּרְכֶּךָ, וּנְחֵנִי בְּאֹרַח מִישׁוֹר, לְמַעַן שׁוֹרְרָי: אַל־תִּתְּנֵנִי בְּנֶפֶשׁ צָרָי, כִּי קָמוּ־בִי עֵדֵי־שֶׁקֶר, וִיפֵחַ חָמָס: ◂ לוּלֵא הֶאֱמַנְתִּי לִרְאוֹת בְּטוּב־יהוה בְּאֶרֶץ חַיִּים: קַוֵּה אֶל־יהוה, חֲזַק וְיַאֲמֵץ לִבֶּךָ, וְקַוֵּה אֶל־יהוה:

קדיש יתום (*on the previous page*)

In ארץ ישראל*, continue on the next page.*

אֵין כֵּאלֹהֵינוּ There is none like our God, none like our LORD,
none like our King, none like our Savior.
Who is like our God? Who is like our LORD?
Who is like our King? Who is like our Savior?
We will thank our God, we will thank our LORD,
we will thank our King, we will thank our Savior.
Blessed is our God, blessed is our LORD,
blessed is our King, blessed is our Savior.
You are our God, You are our LORD,
You are our King, You are our Savior.
You are He to whom our ancestors offered the fragrant incense.

פִּטּוּם הַקְּטֹרֶת The incense mixture consisted of balsam, onycha, galbanum and frankincense, each weighing seventy manehs; myrrh, cassia, spikenard and saffron, each weighing sixteen manehs; twelve manehs of costus, three of aromatic bark; nine of cinnamon; nine kabs of Carsina lye; three seahs and three kabs of Cyprus wine. If Cyprus wine was not available, old white wine might be used. A quarter of a kab of Sodom salt, and a minute amount of a smoke-raising herb. Rabbi Nathan says: Also a minute amount of Jordan amber. If one added honey to the mixture, he rendered it unfit for sacred use. If he omitted any one of its ingredients, he is guilty of a capital offense. *Keritot 6a*

Rabban Shimon ben Gamliel says: "Balsam" refers to the sap that drips from the balsam tree. The Carsina lye was used for bleaching the onycha to improve it. The Cyprus wine was used to soak the onycha in it to make it pungent. Though urine is suitable for this purpose, it is not brought into the Temple out of respect.

It was taught in the Academy of Elijah: Whoever studies [Torah] laws every day is assured that he will be destined for the World to Come, as it is said, "The ways of the world are His" – read not, "ways" [*halikhot*] but "laws" [*halakhot*]. *Megilla 28b* *Hab. 3*

Rabbi Elazar said in the name of Rabbi Ḥanina: The disciples of the sages increase peace in the world, as it is said, "And all your children shall be taught of the LORD, and great shall be the peace of your children [*banayikh*]." Read not *banayikh*, "your children," but *bonayikh*, "your builders." Those who love Your Torah have great peace; there is no stumbling block for them. May there be peace within your ramparts, prosperity in your palaces. For the sake of my brothers and friends, I shall say, "Peace be within you." For the sake of the House of the LORD our God, I will seek your good. ▸ May the LORD grant strength to His people; may the LORD bless His people with peace. *Berakhot 64a* *Is. 54* *Ps. 119* *Ps. 122* *Ps. 29*

אֵין כֵּאלֹהֵינוּ, אֵין כַּאדוֹנֵינוּ, אֵין כְּמַלְכֵּנוּ, אֵין כְּמוֹשִׁיעֵנוּ.
מִי כֵאלֹהֵינוּ, מִי כַאדוֹנֵינוּ, מִי כְמַלְכֵּנוּ, מִי כְמוֹשִׁיעֵנוּ.
נוֹדֶה לֵאלֹהֵינוּ, נוֹדֶה לַאדוֹנֵינוּ, נוֹדֶה לְמַלְכֵּנוּ, נוֹדֶה לְמוֹשִׁיעֵנוּ.
בָּרוּךְ אֱלֹהֵינוּ, בָּרוּךְ אֲדוֹנֵינוּ, בָּרוּךְ מַלְכֵּנוּ, בָּרוּךְ מוֹשִׁיעֵנוּ.
אַתָּה הוּא אֱלֹהֵינוּ, אַתָּה הוּא אֲדוֹנֵינוּ,
אַתָּה הוּא מַלְכֵּנוּ, אַתָּה הוּא מוֹשִׁיעֵנוּ.
אַתָּה הוּא שֶׁהִקְטִירוּ אֲבוֹתֵינוּ לְפָנֶיךָ אֶת קְטֹרֶת הַסַּמִּים.

פִּטּוּם הַקְּטֹרֶת. הַצֳּרִי, וְהַצִּפֹּרֶן, וְהַחֶלְבְּנָה, וְהַלְּבוֹנָה מִשְׁקַל שִׁבְעִים שִׁבְעִים מָנֶה, מֹר, וּקְצִיעָה, שִׁבֹּלֶת נֵרְדְּ, וְכַרְכֹּם מִשְׁקַל שִׁשָּׁה עָשָׂר שִׁשָּׁה עָשָׂר מָנֶה, הַקֹּשְׁטְ שְׁנֵים עָשָׂר, קִלּוּפָה שְׁלֹשָׁה, וְקִנָּמוֹן תִּשְׁעָה, בֹּרִית כַּרְשִׁינָה תִּשְׁעָה קַבִּין, יֵין קַפְרִיסִין סְאִין תְּלָת וְקַבִּין תְּלָתָא, וְאִם אֵין לוֹ יֵין קַפְרִיסִין, מֵבִיא חֲמַר חִוַּרְיָן עַתִּיק. מֶלַח סְדוֹמִית רֹבַע, מַעֲלֶה עָשָׁן כָּל שֶׁהוּא. רַבִּי נָתָן הַבַּבְלִי אוֹמֵר: אַף כִּפַּת הַיַּרְדֵּן כָּל שֶׁהוּא, וְאִם נָתַן בָּהּ דְּבַשׁ פְּסָלָהּ, וְאִם חִסַּר אֶחָד מִכָּל סַמָּנֶיהָ, חַיָּב מִיתָה. כריתות ו.

רַבָּן שִׁמְעוֹן בֶּן גַּמְלִיאֵל אוֹמֵר: הַצֳּרִי אֵינוֹ אֶלָּא שְׂרָף הַנּוֹטֵף מֵעֲצֵי הַקְּטָף. בֹּרִית כַּרְשִׁינָה שֶׁשָּׁפִין בָּהּ אֶת הַצִּפֹּרֶן כְּדֵי שֶׁתְּהֵא נָאָה, יֵין קַפְרִיסִין שֶׁשּׁוֹרִין בּוֹ אֶת הַצִּפֹּרֶן כְּדֵי שֶׁתְּהֵא עַזָּה, וַהֲלֹא מֵי רַגְלַיִם יָפִין לָהּ, אֶלָּא שֶׁאֵין מַכְנִיסִין מֵי רַגְלַיִם בַּמִּקְדָּשׁ מִפְּנֵי הַכָּבוֹד.

תָּנָא דְבֵי אֵלִיָּהוּ: כָּל הַשּׁוֹנֶה הֲלָכוֹת בְּכָל יוֹם, מֻבְטָח לוֹ שֶׁהוּא בֶּן עוֹלָם מגילה כח:
הַבָּא, שֶׁנֶּאֱמַר: הֲלִיכוֹת עוֹלָם לוֹ: אַל תִּקְרֵי הֲלִיכוֹת אֶלָּא הֲלָכוֹת. חבקוק ג

אָמַר רַבִּי אֶלְעָזָר, אָמַר רַבִּי חֲנִינָא: תַּלְמִידֵי חֲכָמִים מַרְבִּים שָׁלוֹם בָּעוֹלָם, ברכות סד.
שֶׁנֶּאֱמַר, וְכָל־בָּנַיִךְ לִמּוּדֵי יהוה, וְרַב שְׁלוֹם בָּנָיִךְ: אַל תִּקְרֵי בָּנָיִךְ, אֶלָּא ישעיה נד
בּוֹנָיִךְ. שָׁלוֹם רָב לְאֹהֲבֵי תוֹרָתֶךָ, וְאֵין־לָמוֹ מִכְשׁוֹל: יְהִי־שָׁלוֹם בְּחֵילֵךְ, תהלים קיט תהלים קכב
שַׁלְוָה בְּאַרְמְנוֹתָיִךְ: לְמַעַן אַחַי וְרֵעָי אֲדַבְּרָה־נָּא שָׁלוֹם בָּךְ: לְמַעַן
בֵּית־יהוה אֱלֹהֵינוּ אֲבַקְשָׁה טוֹב לָךְ: ◂ יהוה עֹז לְעַמּוֹ יִתֵּן, יהוה יְבָרֵךְ אֶת־ תהלים כט
עַמּוֹ בַשָּׁלוֹם:

THE RABBIS' KADDISH

The following prayer, said by mourners, requires the presence of a minyan.
A transliteration can be found on page 1466.

Mourner: יִתְגַּדַּל Magnified and sanctified
may His great name be, in the world He created by His will.
May He establish His kingdom in your lifetime
and in your days, and in the lifetime of all the house of Israel,
swiftly and soon –
and say: Amen.

All: May His great name be blessed for ever and all time.

Mourner: Blessed and praised, glorified and exalted,
raised and honored, uplifted and lauded be
the name of the Holy One,
blessed be He,
beyond any blessing,
song, praise and consolation
uttered in the world –
and say: Amen.

To Israel, to the teachers,
their disciples and their disciples' disciples,
and to all who engage in the study of Torah,
in this (*in Israel add:* holy) place or elsewhere,
may there come to them and you great peace,
grace, kindness and compassion,
long life, ample sustenance
and deliverance, from their Father in Heaven –
and say: Amen.

May there be great peace from heaven,
and (good) life for us and all Israel –
and say: Amen.

Bow, take three steps back, as if taking leave of the Divine Presence, then bow, first left, then right, then center, while saying:

May He who makes peace in His high places,
in His compassion make peace for us and all Israel –
and say: Amen.

קדיש דרבנן

The following prayer, said by mourners, requires the presence of a מנין*.*
A transliteration can be found on page 1466.

אבל: יִתְגַּדַּל וְיִתְקַדַּשׁ שְׁמֵהּ רַבָּא (קהל: אָמֵן)
בְּעָלְמָא דִּי בְרָא כִרְעוּתֵהּ
וְיַמְלִיךְ מַלְכוּתֵהּ
בְּחַיֵּיכוֹן וּבְיוֹמֵיכוֹן וּבְחַיֵּי דְכָל בֵּית יִשְׂרָאֵל
בַּעֲגָלָא וּבִזְמַן קָרִיב, וְאִמְרוּ אָמֵן. (קהל: אָמֵן)

קהל ואבל: יְהֵא שְׁמֵהּ רַבָּא מְבָרַךְ לְעָלַם וּלְעָלְמֵי עָלְמַיָּא.

אבל: יִתְבָּרַךְ וְיִשְׁתַּבַּח וְיִתְפָּאַר וְיִתְרוֹמַם וְיִתְנַשֵּׂא
וְיִתְהַדָּר וְיִתְעַלֶּה וְיִתְהַלָּל
שְׁמֵהּ דְּקֻדְשָׁא בְּרִיךְ הוּא (קהל: בְּרִיךְ הוּא)
לְעֵלָּא מִן כָּל בִּרְכָתָא וְשִׁירָתָא, תֻּשְׁבְּחָתָא וְנֶחֱמָתָא
דַּאֲמִירָן בְּעָלְמָא, וְאִמְרוּ אָמֵן. (קהל: אָמֵן)

עַל יִשְׂרָאֵל וְעַל רַבָּנָן
וְעַל תַּלְמִידֵיהוֹן וְעַל כָּל תַּלְמִידֵי תַלְמִידֵיהוֹן
וְעַל כָּל מָאן דְּעָסְקִין בְּאוֹרַיְתָא
דִּי בְּאַתְרָא (בארץ ישראל: קַדִּישָׁא) הָדֵין, וְדִי בְּכָל אֲתַר וַאֲתַר
יְהֵא לְהוֹן וּלְכוֹן שְׁלָמָא רַבָּא
חִנָּא וְחִסְדָּא, וְרַחֲמֵי, וְחַיֵּי אֲרִיכֵי, וּמְזוֹנֵי רְוִיחֵי
וּפֻרְקָנָא מִן קֳדָם אֲבוּהוֹן דִּי בִשְׁמַיָּא, וְאִמְרוּ אָמֵן. (קהל: אָמֵן)

יְהֵא שְׁלָמָא רַבָּא מִן שְׁמַיָּא
וְחַיִּים (טוֹבִים) עָלֵינוּ וְעַל כָּל יִשְׂרָאֵל, וְאִמְרוּ אָמֵן. (קהל: אָמֵן)

Bow, take three steps back, as if taking leave of the Divine Presence, then bow, first left, then right, then center, while saying:

עֹשֶׂה שָׁלוֹם בִּמְרוֹמָיו
הוּא יַעֲשֶׂה בְרַחֲמָיו שָׁלוֹם
עָלֵינוּ וְעַל כָּל יִשְׂרָאֵל, וְאִמְרוּ אָמֵן. (קהל: אָמֵן)

Ma'ariv for Shabbat Ḥol HaMo'ed

KABBALAT SHABBAT

מִזְמוֹר A psalm. A song for the Sabbath day. Ps. 92
It is good to thank the LORD
and sing psalms to Your name, Most High –
to tell of Your loving-kindness in the morning
and Your faithfulness at night,
to the music of the ten-stringed lyre and the melody of the harp.
For You have made me rejoice by Your work, O LORD;
I sing for joy at the deeds of Your hands.
How great are Your deeds, LORD,
and how very deep Your thoughts.
A boor cannot know, nor can a fool understand,
that though the wicked spring up like grass
and all evildoers flourish,
it is only that they may be destroyed for ever.
But You, LORD, are eternally exalted.

---

for evening, morning, and afternoon are different, a phenomenon unique to Shabbat). There is the Shabbat of the past – Shabbat as a memorial of creation. There is the Shabbat of the present – the Shabbat of revelation when, resting from work, we encounter the divine presence more acutely than at other times, and we read the Torah, itself the record of revelation. And there is the Shabbat of the future, the Messianic Age, when all of humanity will acknowledge the One God, and peace will reign. It is this Shabbat of the future to which the psalm is dedicated. People will then look back on the history of suffering that humans have caused one another, and see clearly how, though the wicked flourished briefly "like grass," in the long run justice prevailed. "A fool cannot understand" that evil, however invulnerable it seems at the time, has a short life-span. It never wins the final victory. The psalm ends with a vindication of God's justice.

מעריב לשבת חול המועד

קבלת שבת

מִזְמוֹר שִׁיר לְיוֹם הַשַּׁבָּת: תהלים צב
טוֹב לְהֹדוֹת לַיהוה, וּלְזַמֵּר לְשִׁמְךָ עֶלְיוֹן:
לְהַגִּיד בַּבֹּקֶר חַסְדֶּךָ, וֶאֱמוּנָתְךָ בַּלֵּילוֹת:
עֲלֵי־עָשׂוֹר וַעֲלֵי־נָבֶל, עֲלֵי הִגָּיוֹן בְּכִנּוֹר:
כִּי שִׂמַּחְתַּנִי יהוה בְּפָעֳלֶךָ, בְּמַעֲשֵׂי יָדֶיךָ אֲרַנֵּן:
מַה־גָּדְלוּ מַעֲשֶׂיךָ יהוה, מְאֹד עָמְקוּ מַחְשְׁבֹתֶיךָ:
אִישׁ־בַּעַר לֹא יֵדָע, וּכְסִיל לֹא־יָבִין אֶת־זֹאת:
בִּפְרֹחַ רְשָׁעִים כְּמוֹ עֵשֶׂב, וַיָּצִיצוּ כָּל־פֹּעֲלֵי אָוֶן
לְהִשָּׁמְדָם עֲדֵי־עַד:
וְאַתָּה מָרוֹם לְעֹלָם יהוה:

KABBALAT SHABBAT / WELCOMING SHABBAT
Our normal service for Kabbalat Shabbat dates back to the sixteenth century and the circle of Jewish mystics in Safed. However, the custom of saying psalms 92 and 93, respectively the psalms for Shabbat and for Friday – the day the first humans were created – goes back many centuries before this. Therefore, when Yom Tov or Ḥol HaMo'ed falls on Shabbat, we say only these psalms, regarded as more obligatory than the other psalms and the song "Come my beloved" (*Pri Megadim* 488:1).

מִזְמוֹר שִׁיר *Psalm 92.* The superscription, "A psalm. A song for the Sabbath day" is part of the psalm itself, testifying to the antiquity of the custom of saying it on Shabbat as part of the Temple service. The connection between it and Shabbat is not immediately clear. The explanation is that there are three dimensions of Shabbat (that is why on a regular Shabbat the Amida prayers

For behold Your enemies, LORD, behold Your enemies will perish;
all evildoers will be scattered.
You have raised my pride like that of a wild ox;
I am anointed with fresh oil.
My eyes shall look in triumph on my adversaries,
my ears shall hear the downfall of the wicked who rise against me.
▸ The righteous will flourish like a palm tree
and grow tall like a cedar in Lebanon.
Planted in the LORD's House,
blossoming in our God's courtyards,
they will still bear fruit in old age,
and stay vigorous and fresh,
proclaiming that the LORD is upright:
He is my Rock, in whom there is no wrong.

יהוה מָלָךְ The LORD reigns. He is robed in majesty. *Ps. 93*
The LORD is robed, girded with strength.
The world is firmly established; it cannot be moved.
Your throne stands firm as of old; You are eternal.
Rivers lift up, LORD, rivers lift up their voice,
rivers lift up their crashing waves.
▸ Mightier than the noise of many waters,
than the mighty waves of the sea is the LORD on high.
Your testimonies are very sure;
holiness adorns Your House, LORD, for evermore.

Intelligence; therefore struggle and combat are not written into its script. Faith is the ability to hear the music beneath the noise, the order beneath the seeming chaos.

נָשְׂאוּ נְהָרוֹת *Rivers lift up.* The repetitions in this verse, and the rhythms of the next, capture in sound the rolling of mighty waves, culminating in the magnificent, "LORD on high," the great affirmation ringing out above the sound of the sea.

כִּי הִנֵּה אֹיְבֶיךָ יהוה, כִּי־הִנֵּה אֹיְבֶיךָ יֹאבֵדוּ

יִתְפָּרְדוּ כָּל־פֹּעֲלֵי אָוֶן:

וַתָּרֶם כִּרְאֵים קַרְנִי, בַּלֹּתִי בְּשֶׁמֶן רַעֲנָן:

וַתַּבֵּט עֵינִי בְּשׁוּרָי, בַּקָּמִים עָלַי מְרֵעִים תִּשְׁמַעְנָה אָזְנָי:

◂ צַדִּיק כַּתָּמָר יִפְרָח, כְּאֶרֶז בַּלְּבָנוֹן יִשְׂגֶּה:

שְׁתוּלִים בְּבֵית יהוה, בְּחַצְרוֹת אֱלֹהֵינוּ יַפְרִיחוּ:

עוֹד יְנוּבוּן בְּשֵׂיבָה, דְּשֵׁנִים וְרַעֲנַנִּים יִהְיוּ:

לְהַגִּיד כִּי־יָשָׁר יהוה, צוּרִי, וְלֹא־עַוְלָתָה בּוֹ:

תהלים צג יהוה מָלָךְ, גֵּאוּת לָבֵשׁ

לָבֵשׁ יהוה עֹז הִתְאַזָּר, אַף־תִּכּוֹן תֵּבֵל בַּל־תִּמּוֹט:

נָכוֹן כִּסְאֲךָ מֵאָז, מֵעוֹלָם אָתָּה:

נָשְׂאוּ נְהָרוֹת יהוה, נָשְׂאוּ נְהָרוֹת קוֹלָם, יִשְׂאוּ נְהָרוֹת דָּכְיָם:

◂ מִקֹּלוֹת מַיִם רַבִּים, אַדִּירִים מִשְׁבְּרֵי־יָם, אַדִּיר בַּמָּרוֹם יהוה:

עֵדֹתֶיךָ נֶאֶמְנוּ מְאֹד, לְבֵיתְךָ נַאֲוָה־קֹדֶשׁ, יהוה לְאֹרֶךְ יָמִים:

כַּתָּמָר ... כְּאֶרֶז *Like a palm tree… a cedar.* The difference between a date palm and a cedar is that we benefit from the palm tree while it is alive: we eat its fruit, we sit in its shade. A cedar is used for its wood. Only when a cedar is cut down do we realize how tall it was. With the righteous, both of these are true. While they live, we enjoy their presence: we eat the fruit of their wisdom, we sit in the shade of their presence. When they are cut down and are no longer with us, only then do we realize their true stature.

יהוה מָלָךְ *Psalm 93. The Lord reigns.* This psalm is, among other things, a polemic against the world of myth. In many ancient myths there was a struggle between the god of order and the forces of chaos, represented by the god or goddess of the primordial sea. Not so, says the psalm. The waters may roar but God is supreme over all. The universe is the result of a single creative

MOURNER'S KADDISH

The following prayer, said by mourners, requires the presence of a minyan. A transliteration can be found on page 1467.

Mourner: יִתְגַּדַּל Magnified and sanctified
may His great name be,
in the world He created by His will.
May He establish His kingdom
in your lifetime and in your days,
and in the lifetime of all the house of Israel,
swiftly and soon –
and say: Amen.

All: May His great name
be blessed for ever and all time.

Mourner: Blessed and praised,
glorified and exalted,
raised and honored,
uplifted and lauded
be the name of the Holy One,
blessed be He,
beyond any blessing,
song, praise and consolation
uttered in the world –
and say: Amen.

May there be great peace from heaven,
and life for us and all Israel –
and say: Amen.

Bow, take three steps back, as if taking leave of the Divine Presence, then bow, first left, then right, then center, while saying:

May He who makes peace in His high places,
make peace for us and all Israel –
and say: Amen.

קדיש יתום

The following prayer, said by mourners, requires the presence of a מנין.
A transliteration can be found on page 1467.

אבל: יִתְגַּדַּל וְיִתְקַדַּשׁ שְׁמֵהּ רַבָּא (קהל: אָמֵן)
בְּעָלְמָא דִּי בְרָא כִרְעוּתֵהּ
וְיַמְלִיךְ מַלְכוּתֵהּ
בְּחַיֵּיכוֹן וּבְיוֹמֵיכוֹן וּבְחַיֵּי דְכָל בֵּית יִשְׂרָאֵל
בַּעֲגָלָא וּבִזְמַן קָרִיב
וְאִמְרוּ אָמֵן. (קהל: אָמֵן)

קהל ואבל: יְהֵא שְׁמֵהּ רַבָּא מְבָרַךְ לְעָלַם וּלְעָלְמֵי עָלְמַיָּא.

אבל: יִתְבָּרַךְ וְיִשְׁתַּבַּח וְיִתְפָּאַר
וְיִתְרוֹמַם וְיִתְנַשֵּׂא וְיִתְהַדָּר וְיִתְעַלֶּה וְיִתְהַלָּל
שְׁמֵהּ דְּקֻדְשָׁא בְּרִיךְ הוּא (קהל: בְּרִיךְ הוּא)
לְעֵֽלָּא מִן כָּל בִּרְכָתָא וְשִׁירָתָא
תֻּשְׁבְּחָתָא וְנֶחֱמָתָא
דַּאֲמִירָן בְּעָלְמָא
וְאִמְרוּ אָמֵן. (קהל: אָמֵן)

יְהֵא שְׁלָמָא רַבָּא מִן שְׁמַיָּא
וְחַיִּים, עָלֵינוּ וְעַל כָּל יִשְׂרָאֵל
וְאִמְרוּ אָמֵן. (קהל: אָמֵן)

Bow, take three steps back, as if taking leave of the Divine Presence, then bow, first left, then right, then center, while saying:

עֹשֶׂה שָׁלוֹם בִּמְרוֹמָיו
הוּא יַעֲשֶׂה שָׁלוֹם עָלֵינוּ וְעַל כָּל יִשְׂרָאֵל
וְאִמְרוּ אָמֵן. (קהל: אָמֵן)

BLESSINGS OF THE SHEMA

The Leader says the following, bowing at "Bless," standing straight at "the Lord." The congregation, followed by the Leader, responds, bowing at "Bless," standing straight at "the Lord."

Leader: **BLESS**
the Lord, the blessed One.

Congregation: Bless the Lord, the blessed One,
for ever and all time.

Leader: Bless the Lord, the blessed One,
for ever and all time.

בָּרוּךְ Blessed are You,
Lord our God, King of the Universe,
who by His word brings on evenings,
by His wisdom opens the gates of heaven,
with understanding makes time change
and the seasons rotate,
and by His will
orders the stars in their constellations in the sky.
He creates day and night,
rolling away the light before the darkness,
and darkness before the light.
▸ He makes the day pass and brings on night,
distinguishing day from night:
the Lord of hosts is His name.
May the living and forever enduring God
rule over us for all time.
Blessed are You, Lord, who brings on evenings.

קריאת שמע וברכותיה

The שליח ציבור *says the following, bowing at* בָּרְכוּ*, standing straight at* ה׳*. The* קהל*, followed by the* שליח ציבור*, responds, bowing at* בָּרוּךְ*, standing straight at* ה׳*.*

ש״ץ: בָּרְכוּ
אֶת יהוה הַמְבֹרָךְ.

קהל: בָּרוּךְ יהוה הַמְבֹרָךְ לְעוֹלָם וָעֶד.

ש״ץ: בָּרוּךְ יהוה הַמְבֹרָךְ לְעוֹלָם וָעֶד.

בָּרוּךְ אַתָּה יהוה אֱלֹהֵינוּ מֶלֶךְ הָעוֹלָם
אֲשֶׁר בִּדְבָרוֹ מַעֲרִיב עֲרָבִים
בְּחָכְמָה פּוֹתֵחַ שְׁעָרִים
וּבִתְבוּנָה מְשַׁנֶּה עִתִּים וּמַחֲלִיף אֶת הַזְּמַנִּים
וּמְסַדֵּר אֶת הַכּוֹכָבִים בְּמִשְׁמְרוֹתֵיהֶם בָּרָקִיעַ כִּרְצוֹנוֹ.
בּוֹרֵא יוֹם וָלָיְלָה
גּוֹלֵל אוֹר מִפְּנֵי חֹשֶׁךְ וְחֹשֶׁךְ מִפְּנֵי אוֹר
◂ וּמַעֲבִיר יוֹם וּמֵבִיא לָיְלָה
וּמַבְדִּיל בֵּין יוֹם וּבֵין לָיְלָה
יהוה צְבָאוֹת שְׁמוֹ.
אֵל חַי וְקַיָּם תָּמִיד, יִמְלֹךְ עָלֵינוּ לְעוֹלָם וָעֶד.
בָּרוּךְ אַתָּה יהוה, הַמַּעֲרִיב עֲרָבִים.

אַהֲבַת עוֹלָם With everlasting love
have You loved Your people, the house of Israel.
You have taught us Torah and commandments,
decrees and laws of justice.
Therefore, LORD our God, when we lie down and when we rise up
we will speak of Your decrees, rejoicing in the words of Your Torah
and Your commandments for ever.
▸ For they are our life and the length of our days;
on them will we meditate day and night.
May You never take away Your love from us.
Blessed are You, LORD, who loves His people Israel.

The Shema must be said with intense concentration.
When not with a minyan, say:
God, faithful King!

The following verse should be said aloud, while covering the eyes with the right hand:

Listen, Israel: the LORD is our God, the LORD is One.

Deut. 6

Quietly: Blessed be the name of His glorious kingdom for ever and all time.

וְאָהַבְתָּ Love the LORD your God with all your heart, with all your soul, and with all your might. These words which I command you today shall be on yourheart. Teach them repeatedly to your children, speaking of them when you sit at home and when you travel on the way, when you lie down and when you rise. Bind them as a sign on your hand, and they shall be an emblem between your eyes. Write them on the doorposts of your house and gates. *Deut. 6*

וְהָיָה If you indeed heed My commandments with which I charge you today, to love the LORD your God and worship Him with all your heart and with all your soul, I will give rain in your land in its season, the early and late rain; and you shall gather in your grain, wine and oil. I will give grass in your field for your cattle, and you shall eat and be satisfied. Be careful lest your heart be *Deut. 11*

אַהֲבַת עוֹלָם בֵּית יִשְׂרָאֵל עַמְּךָ אָהָבְתָּ
תּוֹרָה וּמִצְוֹת, חֻקִּים וּמִשְׁפָּטִים, אוֹתָנוּ לִמַּדְתָּ
עַל כֵּן יהוה אֱלֹהֵינוּ בְּשָׁכְבֵנוּ וּבְקוּמֵנוּ נָשִׂיחַ בְּחֻקֶּיךָ
וְנִשְׂמַח בְּדִבְרֵי תוֹרָתֶךָ וּבְמִצְוֹתֶיךָ לְעוֹלָם וָעֶד
◂ כִּי הֵם חַיֵּינוּ וְאֹרֶךְ יָמֵינוּ, וּבָהֶם נֶהְגֶּה יוֹמָם וָלָיְלָה.
וְאַהֲבָתְךָ אַל תָּסִיר מִמֶּנּוּ לְעוֹלָמִים.
בָּרוּךְ אַתָּה יהוה, אוֹהֵב עַמּוֹ יִשְׂרָאֵל.

The שמע *must be said with intense concentration.*
When not with a מנין*, say:*

אֵל מֶלֶךְ נֶאֱמָן

The following verse should be said aloud, while covering the eyes with the right hand:

שְׁמַע יִשְׂרָאֵל, יהוה אֱלֹהֵינוּ, יהוה | אֶחָד׃ דברים ו

Quietly בָּרוּךְ שֵׁם כְּבוֹד מַלְכוּתוֹ לְעוֹלָם וָעֶד.

וְאָהַבְתָּ אֵת יהוה אֱלֹהֶיךָ, בְּכָל־לְבָבְךָ וּבְכָל־נַפְשְׁךָ וּבְכָל־ דברים ו
מְאֹדֶךָ׃ וְהָיוּ הַדְּבָרִים הָאֵלֶּה, אֲשֶׁר אָנֹכִי מְצַוְּךָ הַיּוֹם, עַל־לְבָבֶךָ׃
וְשִׁנַּנְתָּם לְבָנֶיךָ וְדִבַּרְתָּ בָּם, בְּשִׁבְתְּךָ בְּבֵיתֶךָ וּבְלֶכְתְּךָ בַדֶּרֶךְ,
וּבְשָׁכְבְּךָ וּבְקוּמֶךָ׃ וּקְשַׁרְתָּם לְאוֹת עַל־יָדֶךָ וְהָיוּ לְטֹטָפֹת בֵּין
עֵינֶיךָ׃ וּכְתַבְתָּם עַל־מְזֻזוֹת בֵּיתֶךָ וּבִשְׁעָרֶיךָ׃

וְהָיָה אִם־שָׁמֹעַ תִּשְׁמְעוּ אֶל־מִצְוֹתַי אֲשֶׁר אָנֹכִי מְצַוֶּה אֶתְכֶם דברים יא
הַיּוֹם, לְאַהֲבָה אֶת־יהוה אֱלֹהֵיכֶם וּלְעָבְדוֹ, בְּכָל־לְבַבְכֶם וּבְכָל־
נַפְשְׁכֶם׃ וְנָתַתִּי מְטַר־אַרְצְכֶם בְּעִתּוֹ, יוֹרֶה וּמַלְקוֹשׁ, וְאָסַפְתָּ
דְגָנֶךָ וְתִירֹשְׁךָ וְיִצְהָרֶךָ׃ וְנָתַתִּי עֵשֶׂב בְּשָׂדְךָ לִבְהֶמְתֶּךָ, וְאָכַלְתָּ
וְשָׂבָעְתָּ׃ הִשָּׁמְרוּ לָכֶם פֶּן־יִפְתֶּה לְבַבְכֶם, וְסַרְתֶּם וַעֲבַדְתֶּם

tempted and you go astray and worship other gods, bowing down to them. Then the LORD's anger will flare against you and He will close the heavens so that there will be no rain. The land will not yield its crops, and you will perish swiftly from the good land that the LORD is giving you. Therefore, set these, My words, on your heart and soul. Bind them as a sign on your hand, and they shall be an emblem between your eyes. Teach them to your children, speaking of them when you sit at home and when you travel on the way, when you lie down and when you rise. Write them on the doorposts of your house and gates, so that you and your children may live long in the land that the LORD swore to your ancestors to give them, for as long as the heavens are above the earth.

וַיֹּאמֶר The LORD spoke to Moses, saying: Speak to the Israelites *Num. 15*
and tell them to make tassels on the corners of their garments for all generations. They shall attach to the tassel at each corner a thread of blue. This shall be your tassel, and you shall see it and remember all of the LORD's commandments and keep them, not straying after your heart and after your eyes, following your own sinful desires. Thus you will be reminded to keep all My commandments, and be holy to your God. I am the LORD your God, who brought you out of the land of Egypt to be your God. I am the LORD your God.

True –

The Leader repeats:

▸ The LORD your God is true –

וֶאֱמוּנָה – and faithful is all this,
and firmly established for us
that He is the LORD our God,
and there is none beside Him,
and that we, Israel, are His people.

אֱלֹהִים אֲחֵרִים וְהִשְׁתַּחֲוִיתֶם לָהֶם: וְחָרָה אַף־יהוה בָּכֶם, וְעָצַר אֶת־הַשָּׁמַיִם וְלֹא־יִהְיֶה מָטָר, וְהָאֲדָמָה לֹא תִתֵּן אֶת־יְבוּלָהּ, וַאֲבַדְתֶּם מְהֵרָה מֵעַל הָאָרֶץ הַטֹּבָה אֲשֶׁר יהוה נֹתֵן לָכֶם: וְשַׂמְתֶּם אֶת־דְּבָרַי אֵלֶּה עַל־לְבַבְכֶם וְעַל־נַפְשְׁכֶם, וּקְשַׁרְתֶּם אֹתָם לְאוֹת עַל־יֶדְכֶם, וְהָיוּ לְטוֹטָפֹת בֵּין עֵינֵיכֶם: וְלִמַּדְתֶּם אֹתָם אֶת־בְּנֵיכֶם לְדַבֵּר בָּם, בְּשִׁבְתְּךָ בְּבֵיתֶךָ וּבְלֶכְתְּךָ בַדֶּרֶךְ, וּבְשָׁכְבְּךָ וּבְקוּמֶךָ: וּכְתַבְתָּם עַל־מְזוּזוֹת בֵּיתֶךָ וּבִשְׁעָרֶיךָ: לְמַעַן יִרְבּוּ יְמֵיכֶם וִימֵי בְנֵיכֶם עַל הָאֲדָמָה אֲשֶׁר נִשְׁבַּע יהוה לַאֲבֹתֵיכֶם לָתֵת לָהֶם, כִּימֵי הַשָּׁמַיִם עַל־הָאָרֶץ:

וַיֹּאמֶר יהוה אֶל־מֹשֶׁה לֵּאמֹר: דַּבֵּר אֶל־בְּנֵי יִשְׂרָאֵל וְאָמַרְתָּ במדבר טו
אֲלֵהֶם, וְעָשׂוּ לָהֶם צִיצִת עַל־כַּנְפֵי בִגְדֵיהֶם לְדֹרֹתָם, וְנָתְנוּ עַל־צִיצִת הַכָּנָף פְּתִיל תְּכֵלֶת: וְהָיָה לָכֶם לְצִיצִת, וּרְאִיתֶם אֹתוֹ וּזְכַרְתֶּם אֶת־כָּל־מִצְוֹת יהוה וַעֲשִׂיתֶם אֹתָם, וְלֹא תָתוּרוּ אַחֲרֵי לְבַבְכֶם וְאַחֲרֵי עֵינֵיכֶם, אֲשֶׁר־אַתֶּם זֹנִים אַחֲרֵיהֶם: לְמַעַן תִּזְכְּרוּ וַעֲשִׂיתֶם אֶת־כָּל־מִצְוֹתָי, וִהְיִיתֶם קְדֹשִׁים לֵאלֹהֵיכֶם: אֲנִי יהוה אֱלֹהֵיכֶם, אֲשֶׁר הוֹצֵאתִי אֶתְכֶם מֵאֶרֶץ מִצְרַיִם, לִהְיוֹת לָכֶם לֵאלֹהִים, אֲנִי יהוה אֱלֹהֵיכֶם:

אֱמֶת

The שליח ציבור *repeats.*

◂ יהוה אֱלֹהֵיכֶם אֱמֶת

וֶאֱמוּנָה כָּל זֹאת וְקַיָּם עָלֵינוּ
כִּי הוּא יהוה אֱלֹהֵינוּ וְאֵין זוּלָתוֹ
וַאֲנַחְנוּ יִשְׂרָאֵל עַמּוֹ.

He is our King, who redeems us from the hand of kings
and delivers us from the grasp of all tyrants.
He is our God, who on our behalf repays our foes
and brings just retribution on our mortal enemies;
who performs great deeds beyond understanding
and wonders beyond number;
who kept us alive, not letting our foot slip; *Ps. 66*
who led us on the high places of our enemies,
raising our pride above all our foes;
who did miracles for us
and brought vengeance against Pharaoh;
who performed signs and wonders
in the land of Ham's children;
who smote in His wrath all the firstborn of Egypt,
and brought out His people Israel from their midst
into everlasting freedom;
who led His children
through the divided Reed Sea,
plunging their pursuers and enemies into the depths.
When His children saw His might,
they gave praise and thanks to His name,
▸ and willingly accepted His Sovereignty.
Moses and the children of Israel
then sang a song to You with great joy,
and they all exclaimed:

> "Who is like You, LORD, among the mighty? *Ex. 15*
> Who is like You, majestic in holiness,
> awesome in praises, doing wonders?"

▸ Your children beheld Your majesty
as You parted the sea before Moses.
"This is my God!" they responded, and then said:

> "The LORD shall reign for ever and ever." *Ex. 15*

הַפּוֹדֵנוּ מִיַּד מְלָכִים
מַלְכֵּנוּ הַגּוֹאֲלֵנוּ מִכַּף כָּל הֶעָרִיצִים.
הָאֵל הַנִּפְרָע לָנוּ מִצָּרֵינוּ
וְהַמְשַׁלֵּם גְּמוּל לְכָל אוֹיְבֵי נַפְשֵׁנוּ.
הָעוֹשֶׂה גְדוֹלוֹת עַד אֵין חֵקֶר, וְנִפְלָאוֹת עַד אֵין מִסְפָּר
הַשָּׂם נַפְשֵׁנוּ בַּחַיִּים, וְלֹא־נָתַן לַמּוֹט רַגְלֵנוּ: תהלים סו
הַמַּדְרִיכֵנוּ עַל בָּמוֹת אוֹיְבֵינוּ
וַיָּרֶם קַרְנֵנוּ עַל כָּל שׂוֹנְאֵינוּ.
הָעוֹשֶׂה לָּנוּ נִסִּים וּנְקָמָה בְּפַרְעֹה
אוֹתוֹת וּמוֹפְתִים בְּאַדְמַת בְּנֵי חָם.
הַמַּכֶּה בְעֶבְרָתוֹ כָּל בְּכוֹרֵי מִצְרָיִם
וַיּוֹצֵא אֶת עַמּוֹ יִשְׂרָאֵל מִתּוֹכָם לְחֵרוּת עוֹלָם.
הַמַּעֲבִיר בָּנָיו בֵּין גִּזְרֵי יַם סוּף
אֶת רוֹדְפֵיהֶם וְאֶת שׂוֹנְאֵיהֶם בִּתְהוֹמוֹת טִבַּע
וְרָאוּ בָנָיו גְּבוּרָתוֹ, שִׁבְּחוּ וְהוֹדוּ לִשְׁמוֹ
◂ וּמַלְכוּתוֹ בְּרָצוֹן קִבְּלוּ עֲלֵיהֶם.
מֹשֶׁה וּבְנֵי יִשְׂרָאֵל, לְךָ עָנוּ שִׁירָה בְּשִׂמְחָה רַבָּה
וְאָמְרוּ כֻלָּם

מִי־כָמֹכָה בָּאֵלִם יהוה שמות טו
מִי כָּמֹכָה נֶאְדָּר בַּקֹּדֶשׁ
נוֹרָא תְהִלֹּת עֹשֵׂה פֶלֶא:

◂ מַלְכוּתְךָ רָאוּ בָנֶיךָ, בּוֹקֵעַ יָם לִפְנֵי מֹשֶׁה
זֶה אֵלִי עָנוּ, וְאָמְרוּ
יהוה יִמְלֹךְ לְעֹלָם וָעֶד: שמות טו

▸ And it is said,
"For the LORD has redeemed Jacob Jer. 31
and rescued him from a power
stronger than his own."
Blessed are You, LORD,
who redeemed Israel.

הַשְׁכִּיבֵנוּ Help us lie down,
O LORD our God, in peace,
and rise up, O our King, to life.
Spread over us Your canopy of peace.
Direct us with Your good counsel,
and save us for the sake of Your name.
Shield us and remove from us every enemy,
plague, sword, famine and sorrow.
Remove the adversary from before and behind us.
Shelter us in the shadow of Your wings,
for You, God, are our Guardian and Deliverer;
You, God, are a gracious and compassionate King.
▸ Guard our going out and our coming in,
for life and peace, from now and for ever.
Spread over us Your canopy of peace.
Blessed are You, LORD,
who spreads a canopy of peace over us,
over all His people Israel, and over Jerusalem.

All stand and say:

וְשָׁמְרוּ The children of Israel must keep the Sabbath, Ex. 31
observing the Sabbath in every generation
as an everlasting covenant.
It is a sign between Me and the children of Israel for ever,
for in six days God made the heavens and the earth,
but on the seventh day He ceased work
and refreshed Himself.

◂ וְנֶאֱמַר
כִּי־פָדָה יהוה אֶת־יַעֲקֹב, וּגְאָלוֹ מִיַּד חָזָק מִמֶּנּוּ: ירמיה לא
בָּרוּךְ אַתָּה יהוה, גָּאַל יִשְׂרָאֵל.

הַשְׁכִּיבֵנוּ יהוה אֱלֹהֵינוּ לְשָׁלוֹם
וְהַעֲמִידֵנוּ מַלְכֵּנוּ לְחַיִּים
וּפְרֹשׂ עָלֵינוּ סֻכַּת שְׁלוֹמֶךָ
וְתַקְּנֵנוּ בְּעֵצָה טוֹבָה מִלְּפָנֶיךָ
וְהוֹשִׁיעֵנוּ לְמַעַן שְׁמֶךָ.
וְהָגֵן בַּעֲדֵנוּ
וְהָסֵר מֵעָלֵינוּ אוֹיֵב, דֶּבֶר וְחֶרֶב וְרָעָב וְיָגוֹן
וְהָסֵר שָׂטָן מִלְּפָנֵינוּ וּמֵאַחֲרֵינוּ, וּבְצֵל כְּנָפֶיךָ תַּסְתִּירֵנוּ
כִּי אֵל שׁוֹמְרֵנוּ וּמַצִּילֵנוּ אָתָּה
כִּי אֵל מֶלֶךְ חַנּוּן וְרַחוּם אָתָּה.
◂ וּשְׁמֹר צֵאתֵנוּ וּבוֹאֵנוּ לְחַיִּים וּלְשָׁלוֹם מֵעַתָּה וְעַד עוֹלָם.
וּפְרֹשׂ עָלֵינוּ סֻכַּת שְׁלוֹמֶךָ.
בָּרוּךְ אַתָּה יהוה
הַפּוֹרֵשׂ סֻכַּת שָׁלוֹם עָלֵינוּ
וְעַל כָּל עַמּוֹ יִשְׂרָאֵל וְעַל יְרוּשָׁלָיִם.

All stand and say:

וְשָׁמְרוּ בְנֵי־יִשְׂרָאֵל אֶת־הַשַּׁבָּת שמות לא
לַעֲשׂוֹת אֶת־הַשַּׁבָּת לְדֹרֹתָם בְּרִית עוֹלָם:
בֵּינִי וּבֵין בְּנֵי יִשְׂרָאֵל, אוֹת הִוא לְעֹלָם
כִּי־שֵׁשֶׁת יָמִים עָשָׂה יהוה אֶת־הַשָּׁמַיִם וְאֶת־הָאָרֶץ
וּבַיּוֹם הַשְּׁבִיעִי שָׁבַת וַיִּנָּפַשׁ:

HALF KADDISH

Leader: יִתְגַּדַּל Magnified and sanctified may His great name be,
in the world He created by His will.
May He establish His kingdom
in your lifetime and in your days,
and in the lifetime of all the house of Israel,
swiftly and soon – and say: Amen.

All: May His great name be blessed for ever and all time.

Leader: Blessed and praised, glorified and exalted,
raised and honored, uplifted and lauded
be the name of the Holy One,
blessed be He, beyond any blessing,
song, praise and consolation
uttered in the world – and say: Amen.

THE AMIDA

The following prayer, until "in former years" on page 764, is said silently, standing with feet together. Take three steps forward and at the points indicated by ▾, bend the knees at the first word, bow at the second, and stand straight before saying God's name.

O Lord, open my lips, *Ps. 51*
so that my mouth may declare Your praise.

PATRIARCHS

▾בָּרוּךְ Blessed are You, Lord our God and God of our fathers,
God of Abraham, God of Isaac and God of Jacob;
the great, mighty and awesome God, God Most High,
who bestows acts of loving-kindness and creates all,
who remembers the loving-kindness of the fathers
and will bring a Redeemer
to their children's children
for the sake of His name, in love.
King, Helper, Savior, Shield:
▾Blessed are You, Lord, Shield of Abraham.

חצי קדיש

ש״ץ: יִתְגַּדַּל וְיִתְקַדַּשׁ שְׁמֵהּ רַבָּא (קהל: אָמֵן)
בְּעָלְמָא דִּי בְרָא כִרְעוּתֵהּ
וְיַמְלִיךְ מַלְכוּתֵהּ
בְּחַיֵּיכוֹן וּבְיוֹמֵיכוֹן וּבְחַיֵּי דְכָל בֵּית יִשְׂרָאֵל
בַּעֲגָלָא וּבִזְמַן קָרִיב, וְאִמְרוּ אָמֵן. (קהל: אָמֵן)

קהל וש״ץ: יְהֵא שְׁמֵהּ רַבָּא מְבָרַךְ לְעָלַם וּלְעָלְמֵי עָלְמַיָּא.

ש״ץ: יִתְבָּרַךְ וְיִשְׁתַּבַּח וְיִתְפָּאַר וְיִתְרוֹמַם וְיִתְנַשֵּׂא
וְיִתְהַדָּר וְיִתְעַלֶּה וְיִתְהַלָּל
שְׁמֵהּ דְּקֻדְשָׁא בְּרִיךְ הוּא (קהל: בְּרִיךְ הוּא)
לְעֵלָּא מִן כָּל בִּרְכָתָא וְשִׁירָתָא, תֻּשְׁבְּחָתָא וְנֶחֱמָתָא
דַּאֲמִירָן בְּעָלְמָא, וְאִמְרוּ אָמֵן. (קהל: אָמֵן)

עמידה

The following prayer, until קַדְמֹנִיּוֹת *on page 765, is said silently, standing with feet together. Take three steps forward and at the points indicated by* ˺*, bend the knees at the first word, bow at the second, and stand straight before saying God's name.*

אֲדֹנָי, שְׂפָתַי תִּפְתָּח, וּפִי יַגִּיד תְּהִלָּתֶךָ: תהלים נא

אבות

˺בָּרוּךְ אַתָּה יהוה, אֱלֹהֵינוּ וֵאלֹהֵי אֲבוֹתֵינוּ
אֱלֹהֵי אַבְרָהָם, אֱלֹהֵי יִצְחָק, וֵאלֹהֵי יַעֲקֹב
הָאֵל הַגָּדוֹל הַגִּבּוֹר וְהַנּוֹרָא, אֵל עֶלְיוֹן
גּוֹמֵל חֲסָדִים טוֹבִים, וְקוֹנֵה הַכֹּל
וְזוֹכֵר חַסְדֵי אָבוֹת
וּמֵבִיא גוֹאֵל לִבְנֵי בְנֵיהֶם לְמַעַן שְׁמוֹ בְּאַהֲבָה.
מֶלֶךְ עוֹזֵר וּמוֹשִׁיעַ וּמָגֵן.
˺בָּרוּךְ אַתָּה יהוה, מָגֵן אַבְרָהָם.

DIVINE MIGHT

אַתָּה גִּבּוֹר You are eternally mighty, LORD.
You give life to the dead
and have great power to save.

In Israel: He causes the dew to fall.

He sustains the living with loving-kindness,
and with great compassion revives the dead.
He supports the fallen, heals the sick, sets captives free,
and keeps His faith with those who sleep in the dust.
Who is like You, Master of might,
and who can compare to You,
O King who brings death and gives life,
and makes salvation grow?
Faithful are You to revive the dead.
Blessed are You, LORD, who revives the dead.

HOLINESS

אַתָּה קָדוֹשׁ You are holy and Your name is holy,
and holy ones praise You daily, Selah!
Blessed are You, LORD, the holy God.

HOLINESS OF THE DAY

אַתָּה קִדַּשְׁתָּ You sanctified the seventh day
for Your name's sake,
as the culmination of the creation of heaven and earth.
Of all days, You blessed it; of all seasons You sanctified it –
and so it is written in Your Torah:

וַיְכֻלּוּ Then the heavens and the earth were completed, *Gen. 2*
and all their array.
With the seventh day, God completed the work He had done.
He ceased on the seventh day from all the work He had done.
God blessed the seventh day and declared it holy,
because on it He ceased from all His work
He had created to do.

גבורות

אַתָּה גִּבּוֹר לְעוֹלָם, אֲדֹנָי
מְחַיֵּה מֵתִים אַתָּה, רַב לְהוֹשִׁיעַ

In ארץ ישראל מוֹרִיד הַטָּל

מְכַלְכֵּל חַיִּים בְּחֶסֶד, מְחַיֵּה מֵתִים בְּרַחֲמִים רַבִּים
סוֹמֵךְ נוֹפְלִים, וְרוֹפֵא חוֹלִים, וּמַתִּיר אֲסוּרִים
וּמְקַיֵּם אֱמוּנָתוֹ לִישֵׁנֵי עָפָר.
מִי כָמְוֹךָ, בַּעַל גְּבוּרוֹת, וּמִי דּוֹמֶה לָּךְ
מֶלֶךְ, מֵמִית וּמְחַיֶּה וּמַצְמִיחַ יְשׁוּעָה.
וְנֶאֱמָן אַתָּה לְהַחֲיוֹת מֵתִים.
בָּרוּךְ אַתָּה יהוה, מְחַיֵּה הַמֵּתִים.

קדושת השם

אַתָּה קָדוֹשׁ וְשִׁמְךָ קָדוֹשׁ, וּקְדוֹשִׁים בְּכָל יוֹם יְהַלְלוּךָ סֶּלָה.
בָּרוּךְ אַתָּה יהוה, הָאֵל הַקָּדוֹשׁ.

קדושת היום

אַתָּה קִדַּשְׁתָּ אֶת יוֹם הַשְּׁבִיעִי לִשְׁמֶךָ
תַּכְלִית מַעֲשֵׂה שָׁמַיִם וָאָרֶץ
וּבֵרַכְתּוֹ מִכָּל הַיָּמִים, וְקִדַּשְׁתּוֹ מִכָּל הַזְּמַנִּים
וְכֵן כָּתוּב בְּתוֹרָתֶךָ

וַיְכֻלּוּ הַשָּׁמַיִם וְהָאָרֶץ וְכָל־צְבָאָם: בראשית ב
וַיְכַל אֱלֹהִים בַּיּוֹם הַשְּׁבִיעִי מְלַאכְתּוֹ אֲשֶׁר עָשָׂה
וַיִּשְׁבֹּת בַּיּוֹם הַשְּׁבִיעִי מִכָּל־מְלַאכְתּוֹ אֲשֶׁר עָשָׂה:
וַיְבָרֶךְ אֱלֹהִים אֶת־יוֹם הַשְּׁבִיעִי, וַיְקַדֵּשׁ אֹתוֹ
כִּי בוֹ שָׁבַת מִכָּל־מְלַאכְתּוֹ, אֲשֶׁר־בָּרָא אֱלֹהִים לַעֲשׂוֹת:

אֱלֹהֵינוּ Our God and God of our ancestors,
may You find favor in our rest.
Make us holy through Your commandments
and grant us our share in Your Torah.
Satisfy us with Your goodness,
grant us joy in Your salvation,
and purify our hearts to serve You in truth.
In love and favor, O LORD our God,
grant us as our heritage Your holy Shabbat,
so that Israel, who sanctify Your name, may find rest on it.
Blessed are You, LORD, who sanctifies the Sabbath.

TEMPLE SERVICE
רְצֵה Find favor, LORD our God,
in Your people Israel and their prayer.
Restore the service to Your most holy House,
and accept in love and favor
the fire-offerings of Israel and their prayer.
May the service of Your people Israel
always find favor with You.

אֱלֹהֵינוּ Our God and God of our ancestors,
may there rise, come, reach, appear, be favored, heard,
regarded and remembered before You,
our recollection and remembrance,
as well as the remembrance of our ancestors,
and of the Messiah son of David Your servant,
and of Jerusalem Your holy city,
and of all Your people the house of Israel –
for deliverance and well-being,
grace, loving-kindness and compassion,
life and peace,
on this day of the festival of Sukkot.

אֱלֹהֵינוּ וֵאלֹהֵי אֲבוֹתֵינוּ, רְצֵה בִמְנוּחָתֵנוּ.
קַדְּשֵׁנוּ בְּמִצְוֹתֶיךָ, וְתֵן חֶלְקֵנוּ בְּתוֹרָתֶךָ
שַׂבְּעֵנוּ מִטּוּבֶךָ, וְשַׂמְּחֵנוּ בִּישׁוּעָתֶךָ
וְטַהֵר לִבֵּנוּ לְעָבְדְּךָ בֶּאֱמֶת.
וְהַנְחִילֵנוּ, יהוה אֱלֹהֵינוּ
בְּאַהֲבָה וּבְרָצוֹן שַׁבַּת קָדְשֶׁךָ
וְיָנוּחוּ בָהּ יִשְׂרָאֵל מְקַדְּשֵׁי שְׁמֶךָ.
בָּרוּךְ אַתָּה יהוה, מְקַדֵּשׁ הַשַּׁבָּת.

עבודה

רְצֵה יהוה אֱלֹהֵינוּ בְּעַמְּךָ יִשְׂרָאֵל, וּבִתְפִלָּתָם
וְהָשֵׁב אֶת הָעֲבוֹדָה לִדְבִיר בֵּיתֶךָ
וְאִשֵּׁי יִשְׂרָאֵל וּתְפִלָּתָם בְּאַהֲבָה תְקַבֵּל בְּרָצוֹן
וּתְהִי לְרָצוֹן תָּמִיד עֲבוֹדַת יִשְׂרָאֵל עַמֶּךָ.

אֱלֹהֵינוּ וֵאלֹהֵי אֲבוֹתֵינוּ
יַעֲלֶה וְיָבוֹא וְיַגִּיעַ, וְיֵרָאֶה וְיֵרָצֶה וְיִשָּׁמַע
וְיִפָּקֵד וְיִזָּכֵר זִכְרוֹנֵנוּ וּפִקְדוֹנֵנוּ
וְזִכְרוֹן אֲבוֹתֵינוּ
וְזִכְרוֹן מָשִׁיחַ בֶּן דָּוִד עַבְדֶּךָ
וְזִכְרוֹן יְרוּשָׁלַיִם עִיר קָדְשֶׁךָ
וְזִכְרוֹן כָּל עַמְּךָ בֵּית יִשְׂרָאֵל, לְפָנֶיךָ
לִפְלֵיטָה, לְטוֹבָה, לְחֵן וּלְחֶסֶד וּלְרַחֲמִים
לְחַיִּים וּלְשָׁלוֹם
בְּיוֹם חַג הַסֻּכּוֹת הַזֶּה.

On it remember us, LORD our God, for good;
recollect us for blessing, and deliver us for life.
In accord with Your promise of salvation and compassion,
spare us and be gracious to us;
have compassion on us and deliver us,
for our eyes are turned to You
because You, God, are a gracious and compassionate King.

וְתֶחֱזֶינָה And may our eyes witness
Your return to Zion in compassion.
Blessed are You, LORD, who restores His Presence to Zion.

THANKSGIVING

Bow at the first nine words.

מוֹדִים We give thanks to You,
for You are the LORD our God and God of our ancestors
for ever and all time.
You are the Rock of our lives, Shield of our salvation
from generation to generation.
We will thank You and declare Your praise for our lives,
which are entrusted into Your hand;
for our souls, which are placed in Your charge;
for Your miracles which are with us every day;
and for Your wonders and favors
at all times, evening, morning and midday.
You are good – for Your compassion never fails.
You are compassionate – for Your loving-kindnesses never cease.
We have always placed our hope in You.
For all these things
may Your name be blessed and exalted, our King,
continually, for ever and all time.
Let all that lives thank You, Selah! and praise Your name in truth,
God, our Savior and Help, Selah!
▾Blessed are You, LORD,
whose name is "the Good" and to whom thanks are due.

זָכְרֵנוּ יהוה אֱלֹהֵינוּ בּוֹ לְטוֹבָה, וּפָקְדֵנוּ בוֹ לִבְרָכָה
וְהוֹשִׁיעֵנוּ בוֹ לְחַיִּים.
וּבִדְבַר יְשׁוּעָה וְרַחֲמִים, חוּס וְחָנֵּנוּ, וְרַחֵם עָלֵינוּ וְהוֹשִׁיעֵנוּ
כִּי אֵלֶיךָ עֵינֵינוּ, כִּי אֵל מֶלֶךְ חַנּוּן וְרַחוּם אָתָּה.

וְתֶחֱזֶינָה עֵינֵינוּ בְּשׁוּבְךָ לְצִיּוֹן בְּרַחֲמִים.
בָּרוּךְ אַתָּה יהוה, הַמַּחֲזִיר שְׁכִינָתוֹ לְצִיּוֹן.

הודאה

Bow at the first five words.

מוֹדִים אֲנַחְנוּ לָךְ
שָׁאַתָּה הוּא יהוה אֱלֹהֵינוּ וֵאלֹהֵי אֲבוֹתֵינוּ לְעוֹלָם וָעֶד.
צוּר חַיֵּינוּ, מָגֵן יִשְׁעֵנוּ, אַתָּה הוּא לְדוֹר וָדוֹר.
נוֹדֶה לְּךָ וּנְסַפֵּר תְּהִלָּתֶךָ
עַל חַיֵּינוּ הַמְּסוּרִים בְּיָדֶךָ
וְעַל נִשְׁמוֹתֵינוּ הַפְּקוּדוֹת לָךְ
וְעַל נִסֶּיךָ שֶׁבְּכָל יוֹם עִמָּנוּ
וְעַל נִפְלְאוֹתֶיךָ וְטוֹבוֹתֶיךָ
שֶׁבְּכָל עֵת, עֶרֶב וָבֹקֶר וְצָהֳרָיִם.
הַטּוֹב, כִּי לֹא כָלוּ רַחֲמֶיךָ
וְהַמְרַחֵם, כִּי לֹא תַמּוּ חֲסָדֶיךָ
מֵעוֹלָם קִוִּינוּ לָךְ.
וְעַל כֻּלָּם יִתְבָּרַךְ וְיִתְרוֹמַם שִׁמְךָ מַלְכֵּנוּ תָּמִיד לְעוֹלָם וָעֶד.
וְכֹל הַחַיִּים יוֹדוּךָ סֶּלָה, וִיהַלְלוּ אֶת שִׁמְךָ בֶּאֱמֶת
הָאֵל יְשׁוּעָתֵנוּ וְעֶזְרָתֵנוּ סֶלָה.
בָּרוּךְ אַתָּה יהוה, הַטּוֹב שִׁמְךָ וּלְךָ נָאֶה לְהוֹדוֹת.

PEACE

שָׁלוֹם רָב Grant great peace to Your people Israel for ever,
for You are the sovereign LORD of all peace;
and may it be good in Your eyes to bless Your people Israel
at every time, at every hour, with Your peace.
Blessed are You, LORD, who blesses His people Israel with peace.

Some say the following verse.
May the words of my mouth and the meditation of my heart *Ps. 19*
find favor before You, LORD, my Rock and Redeemer.

אֱלֹהַי My God, *Berakhot 17a*
guard my tongue from evil and my lips from deceitful speech.
To those who curse me, let my soul be silent;
may my soul be to all like the dust.
Open my heart to Your Torah
and let my soul pursue Your commandments.
As for all who plan evil against me,
swiftly thwart their counsel and frustrate their plans.
Act for the sake of Your name; act for the sake of Your right hand;
act for the sake of Your holiness; act for the sake of Your Torah.
That Your beloved ones may be delivered, *Ps. 60*
save with Your right hand and answer me.
May the words of my mouth and the meditation of my heart *Ps. 19*
find favor before You, LORD, my Rock and Redeemer.

Bow, take three steps back, then bow, first left, then right, then center, while saying:
May He who makes peace in His high places,
make peace for us and all Israel – and say: Amen.

יְהִי רָצוֹן May it be Your will, LORD our God and God of our ancestors,
that the Temple be rebuilt speedily in our days,
and grant us a share in Your Torah.
And there we will serve You with reverence,
as in the days of old and as in former years.
Then the offering of Judah and Jerusalem *Mal. 3*
will be pleasing to the LORD as in the days of old and as in former years.

ברכת שלום

שָׁלוֹם רָב עַל יִשְׂרָאֵל עַמְּךָ תָּשִׂים לְעוֹלָם
כִּי אַתָּה הוּא מֶלֶךְ אָדוֹן לְכָל הַשָּׁלוֹם.
וְטוֹב בְּעֵינֶיךָ לְבָרֵךְ אֶת עַמְּךָ יִשְׂרָאֵל
בְּכָל עֵת וּבְכָל שָׁעָה בִּשְׁלוֹמֶךָ.
בָּרוּךְ אַתָּה יהוה, הַמְבָרֵךְ אֶת עַמּוֹ יִשְׂרָאֵל בַּשָּׁלוֹם.

Some say the following verse.

יִהְיוּ לְרָצוֹן אִמְרֵי־פִי וְהֶגְיוֹן לִבִּי לְפָנֶיךָ, יהוה צוּרִי וְגֹאֲלִי: תהלים יט

אֱלֹהַי ברכות יז.
נְצֹר לְשׁוֹנִי מֵרָע וּשְׂפָתַי מִדַּבֵּר מִרְמָה
וְלִמְקַלְלַי נַפְשִׁי תִדֹּם, וְנַפְשִׁי כֶּעָפָר לַכֹּל תִּהְיֶה.
פְּתַח לִבִּי בְּתוֹרָתֶךָ, וּבְמִצְוֹתֶיךָ תִּרְדֹּף נַפְשִׁי.
וְכָל הַחוֹשְׁבִים עָלַי רָעָה
מְהֵרָה הָפֵר עֲצָתָם וְקַלְקֵל מַחֲשַׁבְתָּם.
עֲשֵׂה לְמַעַן שְׁמֶךָ, עֲשֵׂה לְמַעַן יְמִינֶךָ
עֲשֵׂה לְמַעַן קְדֻשָּׁתֶךָ, עֲשֵׂה לְמַעַן תּוֹרָתֶךָ.
לְמַעַן יֵחָלְצוּן יְדִידֶיךָ, הוֹשִׁיעָה יְמִינְךָ וַעֲנֵנִי: תהלים ס
יִהְיוּ לְרָצוֹן אִמְרֵי־פִי וְהֶגְיוֹן לִבִּי לְפָנֶיךָ, יהוה צוּרִי וְגֹאֲלִי: תהלים יט

Bow, take three steps back, then bow, first left, then right, then center, while saying:

עֹשֶׂה שָׁלוֹם בִּמְרוֹמָיו
הוּא יַעֲשֶׂה שָׁלוֹם עָלֵינוּ וְעַל כָּל יִשְׂרָאֵל, וְאִמְרוּ אָמֵן.

יְהִי רָצוֹן מִלְּפָנֶיךָ יהוה אֱלֹהֵינוּ וֵאלֹהֵי אֲבוֹתֵינוּ
שֶׁיִּבָּנֶה בֵּית הַמִּקְדָּשׁ בִּמְהֵרָה בְיָמֵינוּ, וְתֵן חֶלְקֵנוּ בְּתוֹרָתֶךָ
וְשָׁם נַעֲבָדְךָ בְּיִרְאָה כִּימֵי עוֹלָם וּכְשָׁנִים קַדְמוֹנִיּוֹת.
וְעָרְבָה לַיהוה מִנְחַת יְהוּדָה וִירוּשָׁלָיִם כִּימֵי עוֹלָם וּכְשָׁנִים קַדְמוֹנִיּוֹת: מלאכי ג

All stand and say:

וַיְכֻלּוּ Then the heavens and the earth were completed, *Gen. 2*
and all their array.
With the seventh day, God completed the work He had done.
He ceased on the seventh day from all the work He had done.
God blessed the seventh day and declared it holy,
because on it He ceased from all His work He had created to do.

The Leader continues:

בָּרוּךְ Blessed are You, LORD our God and God of our fathers,
God of Abraham, God of Isaac and God of Jacob,
the great, mighty and awesome God,
God Most High, Creator of heaven and earth.

The congregation then the Leader:

מָגֵן אָבוֹת By His word, He was the Shield of our ancestors.
By His promise, He will revive the dead.
There is none like the holy God
who gives rest to His people on His holy Sabbath day,
for He found them worthy of His favor to give them rest.
Before Him we will come in worship with reverence and awe,
giving thanks to His name daily, continually, with due blessings.
He is God to whom thanks are due, the LORD of peace
who sanctifies the Sabbath and blesses the seventh day,
and in holiness gives rest to a people filled with delight,
in remembrance of the work of creation.

The Leader continues:

אֱלֹהֵינוּ Our God and God of our ancestors,
may You find favor in our rest.
Make us holy through Your commandments
and grant us our share in Your Torah.
Satisfy us with Your goodness, grant us joy in Your salvation,
and purify our hearts to serve You in truth.

---

ascribes it to the fact that in Babylon – where synagogues were, for the most part, outside town – going home at night was fraught with danger. This prayer was added for the benefit of latecomers, so that the congregation could leave together.

All stand and say:

וַיְכֻלּוּ הַשָּׁמַיִם וְהָאָרֶץ וְכָל־צְבָאָם: בראשית ב
וַיְכַל אֱלֹהִים בַּיּוֹם הַשְּׁבִיעִי מְלַאכְתּוֹ אֲשֶׁר עָשָׂה
וַיִּשְׁבֹּת בַּיּוֹם הַשְּׁבִיעִי מִכָּל־מְלַאכְתּוֹ אֲשֶׁר עָשָׂה:
וַיְבָרֶךְ אֱלֹהִים אֶת־יוֹם הַשְּׁבִיעִי, וַיְקַדֵּשׁ אֹתוֹ
כִּי בוֹ שָׁבַת מִכָּל־מְלַאכְתּוֹ, אֲשֶׁר־בָּרָא אֱלֹהִים, לַעֲשׂוֹת:

The שליח ציבור *continues:*

בָּרוּךְ אַתָּה יהוה, אֱלֹהֵינוּ וֵאלֹהֵי אֲבוֹתֵינוּ
אֱלֹהֵי אַבְרָהָם, אֱלֹהֵי יִצְחָק, וֵאלֹהֵי יַעֲקֹב
הָאֵל הַגָּדוֹל הַגִּבּוֹר וְהַנּוֹרָא, אֵל עֶלְיוֹן, קֹנֵה שָׁמַיִם וָאָרֶץ.

The קהל *then the* שליח ציבור*:*

מָגֵן אָבוֹת בִּדְבָרוֹ, מְחַיֵּה מֵתִים בְּמַאֲמָרוֹ
הָאֵל הַקָּדוֹשׁ שֶׁאֵין כָּמְוֹהוּ
הַמֵּנִיחַ לְעַמּוֹ בְּיוֹם שַׁבַּת קָדְשׁוֹ, כִּי בָם רָצָה לְהָנִיחַ לָהֶם
לְפָנָיו נַעֲבֹד בְּיִרְאָה וָפַחַד
וְנוֹדֶה לִשְׁמוֹ בְּכָל יוֹם תָּמִיד, מֵעֵין הַבְּרָכוֹת
אֵל הַהוֹדָאוֹת, אֲדוֹן הַשָּׁלוֹם
מְקַדֵּשׁ הַשַּׁבָּת וּמְבָרֵךְ שְׁבִיעִי
וּמֵנִיחַ בִּקְדֻשָּׁה לְעַם מְדֻשְּׁנֵי עֹנֶג, זֵכֶר לְמַעֲשֵׂה בְרֵאשִׁית.

The שליח ציבור *continues:*

אֱלֹהֵינוּ וֵאלֹהֵי אֲבוֹתֵינוּ, רְצֵה בִמְנוּחָתֵנוּ.
קַדְּשֵׁנוּ בְּמִצְוֹתֶיךָ וְתֵן חֶלְקֵנוּ בְּתוֹרָתֶךָ
שַׂבְּעֵנוּ מִטּוּבֶךָ וְשַׂמְּחֵנוּ בִּישׁוּעָתֶךָ
וְטַהֵר לִבֵּנוּ לְעָבְדְּךָ בֶּאֱמֶת.

מָגֵן אָבוֹת בִּדְבָרוֹ *By His word, He was the Shield of our ancestors:* A summary of the seven blessings of the Amida, which is unique to Friday evening. Tradition

In love and favor, LORD our God,
grant us as our heritage Your holy Sabbath,
so that Israel who sanctify Your name may find rest on it.
Blessed are You, LORD, who sanctifies the Sabbath.

FULL KADDISH

Some have the custom to include additional responses in Full Kaddish. They can be found in the version on page 1464.

Leader: יִתְגַּדַּל Magnified and sanctified may His great name be,
in the world He created by His will.
May He establish His kingdom
in your lifetime and in your days,
and in the lifetime of all the house of Israel,
swiftly and soon –
and say: Amen.

All: May His great name be blessed for ever and all time.

Leader: Blessed and praised, glorified and exalted,
raised and honored, uplifted and lauded be
the name of the Holy One,
blessed be He, beyond any blessing,
song, praise and consolation
uttered in the world –
and say: Amen.

May the prayers and pleas of all Israel
be accepted by their Father in heaven –
and say: Amen.

May there be great peace from heaven,
and life for us and all Israel –
and say: Amen.

Bow, take three steps back, as if taking leave of the Divine Presence, then bow, first left, then right, then center, while saying:

May He who makes peace in His high places,
make peace for us and all Israel –
and say: Amen.

וְהַנְחִילֵנוּ יהוה אֱלֹהֵינוּ בְּאַהֲבָה וּבְרָצוֹן שַׁבַּת קָדְשֶׁךָ
וְיָנוּחוּ בָהּ יִשְׂרָאֵל מְקַדְּשֵׁי שְׁמֶךָ.
בָּרוּךְ אַתָּה יהוה, מְקַדֵּשׁ הַשַּׁבָּת.

קדיש שלם

Some have the custom to include additional responses in קדיש שלם*.*
They can be found in the version on page 1465.

ש״ץ: יִתְגַּדַּל וְיִתְקַדַּשׁ שְׁמֵהּ רַבָּא (קהל: אָמֵן)
בְּעָלְמָא דִּי בְרָא כִרְעוּתֵהּ
וְיַמְלִיךְ מַלְכוּתֵהּ
בְּחַיֵּיכוֹן וּבְיוֹמֵיכוֹן וּבְחַיֵּי דְכָל בֵּית יִשְׂרָאֵל
בַּעֲגָלָא וּבִזְמַן קָרִיב, וְאִמְרוּ אָמֵן. (קהל: אָמֵן)

קהל וש״ץ: יְהֵא שְׁמֵהּ רַבָּא מְבָרַךְ לְעָלַם וּלְעָלְמֵי עָלְמַיָּא.

ש״ץ: יִתְבָּרַךְ וְיִשְׁתַּבַּח וְיִתְפָּאַר
וְיִתְרוֹמַם וְיִתְנַשֵּׂא וְיִתְהַדָּר וְיִתְעַלֶּה וְיִתְהַלָּל
שְׁמֵהּ דְּקֻדְשָׁא בְּרִיךְ הוּא (קהל: בְּרִיךְ הוּא)
לְעֵלָּא מִן כָּל בִּרְכָתָא וְשִׁירָתָא, תֻּשְׁבְּחָתָא וְנֶחֱמָתָא
דַּאֲמִירָן בְּעָלְמָא, וְאִמְרוּ אָמֵן. (קהל: אָמֵן)

תִּתְקַבַּל צְלוֹתְהוֹן וּבָעוּתְהוֹן דְּכָל יִשְׂרָאֵל
קֳדָם אֲבוּהוֹן דִּי בִשְׁמַיָּא, וְאִמְרוּ אָמֵן. (קהל: אָמֵן)

יְהֵא שְׁלָמָא רַבָּא מִן שְׁמַיָּא
וְחַיִּים, עָלֵינוּ וְעַל כָּל יִשְׂרָאֵל, וְאִמְרוּ אָמֵן. (קהל: אָמֵן)

Bow, take three steps back, as if taking leave of the Divine Presence, then bow, first left, then right, then center, while saying:

עֹשֶׂה שָׁלוֹם בִּמְרוֹמָיו
הוּא יַעֲשֶׂה שָׁלוֹם
עָלֵינוּ וְעַל כָּל יִשְׂרָאֵל, וְאִמְרוּ אָמֵן. (קהל: אָמֵן)

KIDDUSH IN THE SYNAGOGUE

Kiddush is recited in the Sukka. The Leader raises a cup of wine and says:

Please pay attention, my masters.

בָּרוּךְ Blessed are You, LORD our God, King of the Universe,
who creates the fruit of the vine.

בָּרוּךְ Blessed are You, LORD our God, King of the Universe, who has made us holy with His commandments, has favored us, and in love and favor given us His holy Sabbath as a heritage, a remembrance of the work of creation. It is the first among the holy days of assembly, a remembrance of the exodus from Egypt. For You chose us and sanctified us from all the peoples, and in love and favor gave us Your holy Sabbath as a heritage. Blessed are You, LORD, who sanctifies the Sabbath.

בָּרוּךְ Blessed are You, LORD our God, King of the Universe,
who has made us holy through His commandments
and has commanded us to dwell in the sukka.

The wine should be drunk by children under the age of Bar/Bat Mitzva or, if there are none, by the Leader.

Stand while saying Aleinu. Bow at ▾.

עָלֵינוּ It is our duty to praise the Master of all,
and ascribe greatness to the Author of creation,
who has not made us like the nations of the lands
nor placed us like the families of the earth;
who has not made our portion like theirs,
nor our destiny like all their multitudes.
(For they worship vanity and emptiness,
and pray to a god who cannot save.)
▾But we bow in worship
and thank the Supreme King of kings, the Holy One, blessed be He,
who extends the heavens and establishes the earth,
whose throne of glory is in the heavens above,
and whose power's Presence is in the highest of heights.
He is our God; there is no other.
Truly He is our King, there is none else,
as it is written in His Torah: "You shall know and take to heart this day *Deut. 4*
that the LORD is God, in heaven above and on earth below.
There is no other."

קידוש בבית הכנסת

קידוש is recited in the סוכה. The שליח ציבור raises a cup of wine and says:

סַבְרִי מָרָנָן

בָּרוּךְ אַתָּה יהוה אֱלֹהֵינוּ מֶלֶךְ הָעוֹלָם בּוֹרֵא פְּרִי הַגָּפֶן.

בָּרוּךְ אַתָּה יהוה אֱלֹהֵינוּ מֶלֶךְ הָעוֹלָם, אֲשֶׁר קִדְּשָׁנוּ בְּמִצְוֹתָיו, וְרָצָה בָנוּ, וְשַׁבַּת קָדְשׁוֹ בְּאַהֲבָה וּבְרָצוֹן הִנְחִילָנוּ, זִכָּרוֹן לְמַעֲשֵׂה בְרֵאשִׁית, כִּי הוּא יוֹם תְּחִלָּה לְמִקְרָאֵי קֹדֶשׁ, זֵכֶר לִיצִיאַת מִצְרָיִם, כִּי בָנוּ בָחַרְתָּ וְאוֹתָנוּ קִדַּשְׁתָּ מִכָּל הָעַמִּים, וְשַׁבַּת קָדְשְׁךָ בְּאַהֲבָה וּבְרָצוֹן הִנְחַלְתָּנוּ. בָּרוּךְ אַתָּה יהוה, מְקַדֵּשׁ הַשַּׁבָּת.

בָּרוּךְ אַתָּה יהוה אֱלֹהֵינוּ מֶלֶךְ הָעוֹלָם
אֲשֶׁר קִדְּשָׁנוּ בְּמִצְוֹתָיו וְצִוָּנוּ לֵישֵׁב בַּסֻּכָּה.

The wine should be drunk by children under the age of בר מצווה or בת מצווה or, if there are none, by the שליח ציבור.

*Stand while saying עָלֵינוּ. Bow at *.*

עָלֵינוּ לְשַׁבֵּחַ לַאֲדוֹן הַכֹּל, לָתֵת גְּדֻלָּה לְיוֹצֵר בְּרֵאשִׁית
שֶׁלֹּא עָשָׂנוּ כְּגוֹיֵי הָאֲרָצוֹת, וְלֹא שָׂמָנוּ כְּמִשְׁפְּחוֹת הָאֲדָמָה
שֶׁלֹּא שָׂם חֶלְקֵנוּ כָּהֶם וְגוֹרָלֵנוּ כְּכָל הֲמוֹנָם.
(שֶׁהֵם מִשְׁתַּחֲוִים לְהֶבֶל וָרִיק וּמִתְפַּלְלִים אֶל אֵל לֹא יוֹשִׁיעַ.)
*וַאֲנַחְנוּ כּוֹרְעִים וּמִשְׁתַּחֲוִים וּמוֹדִים
לִפְנֵי מֶלֶךְ מַלְכֵי הַמְּלָכִים, הַקָּדוֹשׁ בָּרוּךְ הוּא
שֶׁהוּא נוֹטֶה שָׁמַיִם וְיוֹסֵד אָרֶץ, וּמוֹשַׁב יְקָרוֹ בַּשָּׁמַיִם מִמַּעַל
וּשְׁכִינַת עֻזּוֹ בְּגָבְהֵי מְרוֹמִים.
הוּא אֱלֹהֵינוּ, אֵין עוֹד.
אֱמֶת מַלְכֵּנוּ, אֶפֶס זוּלָתוֹ
כַּכָּתוּב בְּתוֹרָתוֹ, וְיָדַעְתָּ הַיּוֹם וַהֲשֵׁבֹתָ אֶל־לְבָבֶךָ דברים ד
כִּי יהוה הוּא הָאֱלֹהִים בַּשָּׁמַיִם מִמַּעַל וְעַל־הָאָרֶץ מִתָּחַת, אֵין עוֹד:

Therefore, we place our hope in You, LORD our God,
that we may soon see the glory of Your power,
when You will remove abominations from the earth,
and idols will be utterly destroyed,
when the world will be perfected under the sovereignty of the Almighty,
when all humanity will call on Your name,
to turn all the earth's wicked toward You.
All the world's inhabitants will realize and know
that to You every knee must bow and every tongue swear loyalty.
Before You, LORD our God, they will kneel and bow down
and give honor to Your glorious name.
They will all accept the yoke of Your kingdom,
and You will reign over them soon and for ever.
For the kingdom is Yours,
and to all eternity You will reign in glory,
as it is written in Your Torah:
"The LORD will reign for ever and ever." *Ex. 15*
▸ And it is said: "Then the LORD shall be King over all the earth; *Zech. 14*
on that day the LORD shall be One and His name One."

Some add:

Have no fear of sudden terror or of the ruin when it overtakes the wicked. *Prov. 3*
Devise your strategy, but it will be thwarted; *Is. 8*
propose your plan, but it will not stand, for God is with us.
When you grow old, I will still be the same. *Is. 46*
When your hair turns gray, I will still carry you.
I made you, I will bear you, I will carry you, and I will rescue you.

MOURNER'S KADDISH

The following prayer, said by mourners, requires the presence of a minyan.
A transliteration can be found on page 1467.

Mourner: יִתְגַּדַּל Magnified and sanctified may His great name be,
in the world He created by His will.
May He establish His kingdom
in your lifetime and in your days,
and in the lifetime of all the house of Israel,
swiftly and soon –
and say: Amen.

עַל כֵּן נְקַוֶּה לְּךָ יהוה אֱלֹהֵינוּ, לִרְאוֹת מְהֵרָה בְּתִפְאֶרֶת עֻזֶּךָ
לְהַעֲבִיר גִּלּוּלִים מִן הָאָרֶץ, וְהָאֱלִילִים כָּרוֹת יִכָּרֵתוּן
לְתַקֵּן עוֹלָם בְּמַלְכוּת שַׁדַּי.
וְכָל בְּנֵי בָשָׂר יִקְרְאוּ בִשְׁמֶךָ לְהַפְנוֹת אֵלֶיךָ כָּל רִשְׁעֵי אָרֶץ.
יַכִּירוּ וְיֵדְעוּ כָּל יוֹשְׁבֵי תֵבֵל
כִּי לְךָ תִּכְרַע כָּל בֶּרֶךְ, תִּשָּׁבַע כָּל לָשׁוֹן.
לְפָנֶיךָ יהוה אֱלֹהֵינוּ יִכְרְעוּ וְיִפֹּלוּ, וְלִכְבוֹד שִׁמְךָ יְקָר יִתֵּנוּ
וִיקַבְּלוּ כֻלָּם אֶת עֹל מַלְכוּתֶךָ
וְתִמְלֹךְ עֲלֵיהֶם מְהֵרָה לְעוֹלָם וָעֶד.
כִּי הַמַּלְכוּת שֶׁלְּךָ הִיא וּלְעוֹלְמֵי עַד תִּמְלֹךְ בְּכָבוֹד
כַּכָּתוּב בְּתוֹרָתֶךָ, יהוה יִמְלֹךְ לְעֹלָם וָעֶד: שמות טו
► וְנֶאֱמַר, וְהָיָה יהוה לְמֶלֶךְ עַל־כָּל־הָאָרֶץ זכריה יד
בַּיּוֹם הַהוּא יִהְיֶה יהוה אֶחָד וּשְׁמוֹ אֶחָד:

Some add:

אַל־תִּירָא מִפַּחַד פִּתְאֹם וּמִשֹּׁאַת רְשָׁעִים כִּי תָבֹא: משלי ג
עֻצוּ עֵצָה וְתֻפָר, דַּבְּרוּ דָבָר וְלֹא יָקוּם, כִּי עִמָּנוּ אֵל: ישעיה ח
וְעַד־זִקְנָה אֲנִי הוּא, וְעַד־שֵׂיבָה אֲנִי אֶסְבֹּל ישעיה מו
אֲנִי עָשִׂיתִי וַאֲנִי אֶשָּׂא וַאֲנִי אֶסְבֹּל וַאֲמַלֵּט:

קדיש יתום

The following prayer, said by mourners, requires the presence of a מנין*.*
A transliteration can be found on page 1467.

אבל: יִתְגַּדַּל וְיִתְקַדַּשׁ שְׁמֵהּ רַבָּא (קהל: אָמֵן)
בְּעָלְמָא דִּי בְרָא כִרְעוּתֵהּ
וְיַמְלִיךְ מַלְכוּתֵהּ
בְּחַיֵּיכוֹן וּבְיוֹמֵיכוֹן וּבְחַיֵּי דְכָל בֵּית יִשְׂרָאֵל
בַּעֲגָלָא וּבִזְמַן קָרִיב
וְאִמְרוּ אָמֵן. (קהל: אָמֵן)

All: May His great name be blessed for ever and all time.

Mourner: Blessed and praised, glorified and exalted,
raised and honored, uplifted and lauded
be the name of the Holy One,
blessed be He,
beyond any blessing,
song, praise and consolation
uttered in the world –
and say: Amen.

May there be great peace from heaven,
and life for us and all Israel –
and say: Amen.

Bow, take three steps back, as if taking leave of the Divine Presence, then bow, first left, then right, then center, while saying:

May He who makes peace in His high places,
make peace for us and all Israel –
and say: Amen.

לְדָוִד A psalm of David. The LORD is my light and my salvation – whom *Ps. 27*
then shall I fear? The LORD is the stronghold of my life – of whom shall I be afraid? When evil men close in on me to devour my flesh, it is they, my enemies and foes, who stumble and fall. Should an army besiege me, my heart would not fear. Should war break out against me, still I would be confident. One thing I ask of the LORD, only this do I seek: to live in the House of the LORD all the days of my life, to gaze on the beauty of the LORD and worship in His Temple. For He will keep me safe in His pavilion on the day of trouble. He will hide me under the cover of His tent. He will set me high upon a rock. Now my head is high above my enemies who surround me. I will sacrifice in His tent with shouts of joy. I will sing and chant praises to the LORD. LORD, hear my voice when I call. Be gracious to me and answer me. On Your behalf my heart says, "Seek My face." Your face, LORD, will I seek. Do not hide Your face from me. Do not turn Your servant away in anger. You have been my help. Do not reject or forsake me, God, my Savior. Were my father and my mother to forsake me, the LORD would take me in. Teach me Your way, LORD, and

קהל ואבל: יְהֵא שְׁמֵהּ רַבָּא מְבָרַךְ לְעָלַם וּלְעָלְמֵי עָלְמַיָּא.

אבל: יִתְבָּרַךְ וְיִשְׁתַּבַּח וְיִתְפָּאַר
וְיִתְרוֹמַם וְיִתְנַשֵּׂא וְיִתְהַדָּר וְיִתְעַלֶּה וְיִתְהַלָּל
שְׁמֵהּ דְּקֻדְשָׁא בְּרִיךְ הוּא (קהל: בְּרִיךְ הוּא)
לְעֵלָּא מִן כָּל בִּרְכָתָא וְשִׁירָתָא, תֻּשְׁבְּחָתָא וְנֶחֱמָתָא
דַּאֲמִירָן בְּעָלְמָא
וְאִמְרוּ אָמֵן. (קהל: אָמֵן)

יְהֵא שְׁלָמָא רַבָּא מִן שְׁמַיָּא
וְחַיִּים, עָלֵינוּ וְעַל כָּל יִשְׂרָאֵל
וְאִמְרוּ אָמֵן. (קהל: אָמֵן)

Bow, take three steps back, as if taking leave of the Divine Presence, then bow, first left, then right, then center, while saying:

עֹשֶׂה שָׁלוֹם בִּמְרוֹמָיו
הוּא יַעֲשֶׂה שָׁלוֹם עָלֵינוּ וְעַל כָּל יִשְׂרָאֵל
וְאִמְרוּ אָמֵן. (קהל: אָמֵן)

תהלים כז לְדָוִד, יהוה אוֹרִי וְיִשְׁעִי, מִמִּי אִירָא, יהוה מָעוֹז־חַיַּי, מִמִּי אֶפְחָד:
בִּקְרֹב עָלַי מְרֵעִים לֶאֱכֹל אֶת־בְּשָׂרִי, צָרַי וְאֹיְבַי לִי, הֵמָּה כָשְׁלוּ
וְנָפָלוּ: אִם־תַּחֲנֶה עָלַי מַחֲנֶה, לֹא־יִירָא לִבִּי, אִם־תָּקוּם עָלַי מִלְחָמָה,
בְּזֹאת אֲנִי בוֹטֵחַ: אַחַת שָׁאַלְתִּי מֵאֵת־יהוה, אוֹתָהּ אֲבַקֵּשׁ, שִׁבְתִּי
בְּבֵית־יהוה כָּל־יְמֵי חַיַּי, לַחֲזוֹת בְּנֹעַם־יהוה, וּלְבַקֵּר בְּהֵיכָלוֹ: כִּי
יִצְפְּנֵנִי בְּסֻכֹּה בְּיוֹם רָעָה, יַסְתִּרֵנִי בְּסֵתֶר אָהֳלוֹ, בְּצוּר יְרוֹמְמֵנִי:
וְעַתָּה יָרוּם רֹאשִׁי עַל אֹיְבַי סְבִיבוֹתַי, וְאֶזְבְּחָה בְאָהֳלוֹ זִבְחֵי תְרוּעָה,
אָשִׁירָה וַאֲזַמְּרָה לַיהוה: שְׁמַע־יהוה קוֹלִי אֶקְרָא, וְחָנֵּנִי וַעֲנֵנִי: לְךָ
אָמַר לִבִּי בַּקְּשׁוּ פָנָי, אֶת־פָּנֶיךָ יהוה אֲבַקֵּשׁ: אַל־תַּסְתֵּר פָּנֶיךָ מִמֶּנִּי,

lead me on a level path, because of my oppressors. Do not abandon me to the will of my foes, for false witnesses have risen against me, breathing violence. ▸ Were it not for my faith that I shall see the LORD's goodness in the land of the living. Hope in the LORD. Be strong and of good courage, and hope in the LORD!

Mourner's Kaddish (on page 772)

Most congregations sing Yigdal at this point. Some add Adon Olam (page 270).

GREAT

is the living God and praised.
He exists, and His existence is beyond time.

He is One, and there is no unity like His.
Unfathomable, His Oneness is infinite.

He has neither bodily form nor substance;
His holiness is beyond compare.

He preceded all that was created.
He was first: there was no beginning to His beginning.

Behold He is Master of the Universe; every creature
shows His greatness and majesty.

The rich flow of His prophecy He gave
to His treasured people in whom He gloried.

Never in Israel has there arisen another like Moses,
a prophet who beheld God's image.

God gave His people a Torah of truth
by the hand of His prophet, most faithful of His House.

God will not alter or change His law
for any other, for eternity.

He sees and knows our secret thoughts;
as soon as something is begun, He foresees its end.

He rewards people with loving-kindness according to their deeds;
He punishes the wicked according to his wickedness.

At the end of days He will send our Messiah,
to redeem those who await His final salvation.

God will revive the dead in His great loving-kindness.
Blessed for evermore is His glorious name!

אַל תַּט־בְּאַף עַבְדֶּךָ, עֶזְרָתִי הָיִיתָ, אַל־תִּטְּשֵׁנִי וְאַל־תַּעַזְבֵנִי, אֱלֹהֵי יִשְׁעִי: כִּי־אָבִי וְאִמִּי עֲזָבוּנִי, וַיהוה יַאַסְפֵנִי: הוֹרֵנִי יהוה דַּרְכֶּךָ, וּנְחֵנִי בְּאֹרַח מִישׁוֹר, לְמַעַן שׁוֹרְרָי: אַל־תִּתְּנֵנִי בְּנֶפֶשׁ צָרָי, כִּי קָמוּ־בִי עֵדֵי־שֶׁקֶר, וִיפֵחַ חָמָס: ◂ לוּלֵא הֶאֱמַנְתִּי לִרְאוֹת בְּטוּב־יהוה בְּאֶרֶץ חַיִּים: קַוֵּה אֶל־יהוה, חֲזַק וְיַאֲמֵץ לִבֶּךָ, וְקַוֵּה אֶל־יהוה:

קדיש יתום (*on page 773*)

Most congregations sing יִגְדַּל *at this point. Some add* אֲדוֹן עוֹלָם (*page 271*).

יִגְדַּל

אֱלֹהִים חַי וְיִשְׁתַּבַּח, נִמְצָא וְאֵין עֵת אֶל מְצִיאוּתוֹ.
אֶחָד וְאֵין יָחִיד כְּיִחוּדוֹ, נֶעְלָם וְגַם אֵין סוֹף לְאַחְדּוּתוֹ.
אֵין לוֹ דְּמוּת הַגּוּף וְאֵינוֹ גוּף, לֹא נַעֲרֹךְ אֵלָיו קְדֻשָּׁתוֹ.
קַדְמוֹן לְכָל דָּבָר אֲשֶׁר נִבְרָא, רִאשׁוֹן וְאֵין רֵאשִׁית לְרֵאשִׁיתוֹ.
הִנּוֹ אֲדוֹן עוֹלָם, וְכָל נוֹצָר יוֹרֶה גְדֻלָּתוֹ וּמַלְכוּתוֹ.
שֶׁפַע נְבוּאָתוֹ נְתָנוֹ אֶל־אַנְשֵׁי סְגֻלָּתוֹ וְתִפְאַרְתּוֹ.
לֹא קָם בְּיִשְׂרָאֵל כְּמֹשֶׁה עוֹד נָבִיא וּמַבִּיט אֶת תְּמוּנָתוֹ.
תּוֹרַת אֱמֶת נָתַן לְעַמּוֹ אֵל עַל יַד נְבִיאוֹ נֶאֱמַן בֵּיתוֹ.
לֹא יַחֲלִיף הָאֵל וְלֹא יָמִיר דָּתוֹ לְעוֹלָמִים לְזוּלָתוֹ.
צוֹפֶה וְיוֹדֵעַ סְתָרֵינוּ, מַבִּיט לְסוֹף דָּבָר בְּקַדְמָתוֹ.
גּוֹמֵל לְאִישׁ חֶסֶד כְּמִפְעָלוֹ, נוֹתֵן לְרָשָׁע רָע כְּרִשְׁעָתוֹ.
יִשְׁלַח לְקֵץ יָמִין מְשִׁיחֵנוּ לִפְדּוֹת מְחַכֵּי קֵץ יְשׁוּעָתוֹ.
מֵתִים יְחַיֶּה אֵל בְּרֹב חַסְדּוֹ, בָּרוּךְ עֲדֵי עַד שֵׁם תְּהִלָּתוֹ.

Kiddush for Shabbat Evening

BLESSING THE CHILDREN

On the evening of Shabbat, many have the custom to bless their children.

To sons, say:

יְשִׂמְךָ May God
make you like Ephraim
and Manasseh.

To daughters, say: *Gen. 48*

יְשִׂימֵךְ May God
make you like Sarah, Rebecca,
Rachel and Leah.

יְבָרֶכְךָ May the LORD bless you and protect you. *Num. 6*
May the LORD make His face shine on you and be gracious to you.
May the LORD turn His face toward you and grant you peace.

Many people sing each of the four verses of the following song three times:

שָׁלוֹם עֲלֵיכֶם Welcome,
ministering angels, angels of the Most High,
from the Supreme King of kings,
the Holy One, blessed be He.

Enter in peace,
angels of peace, angels of the Most High,
from the Supreme King of kings,
the Holy One, blessed be He.

Bless me with peace,
angels of peace, angels of the Most High,
from the Supreme King of kings,
the Holy One, blessed be He.

Go in peace,
angels of peace, angels of the Most High,
from the Supreme King of kings,
the Holy One, blessed be He.

כִּי מַלְאָכָיו He will command His angels about you, *Ps. 91*
to guard you in all your ways.
May the LORD guard your going out and your return, *Ps. 121*
from now and for all time.

קידוש לליל שבת

ברכת הבנים

On ליל שבת, many have the custom to bless their children.

To sons, say:

יְשִׂמְךָ אֱלֹהִים
כְּאֶפְרַיִם וְכִמְנַשֶּׁה: בראשית מח

To daughters, say:

יְשִׂימֵךְ אֱלֹהִים
כְּשָׂרָה רִבְקָה רָחֵל וְלֵאָה.

במדבר ו יְבָרֶכְךָ יהוה וְיִשְׁמְרֶךָ:
יָאֵר יהוה פָּנָיו אֵלֶיךָ וִיחֻנֶּךָּ:
יִשָּׂא יהוה פָּנָיו אֵלֶיךָ וְיָשֵׂם לְךָ שָׁלוֹם:

Many people sing each of the four verses of the following song three times:

שָׁלוֹם עֲלֵיכֶם
מַלְאֲכֵי הַשָּׁרֵת, מַלְאֲכֵי עֶלְיוֹן
מִמֶּלֶךְ מַלְכֵי הַמְּלָכִים, הַקָּדוֹשׁ בָּרוּךְ הוּא.

בּוֹאֲכֶם לְשָׁלוֹם
מַלְאֲכֵי הַשָּׁלוֹם, מַלְאֲכֵי עֶלְיוֹן
מִמֶּלֶךְ מַלְכֵי הַמְּלָכִים, הַקָּדוֹשׁ בָּרוּךְ הוּא.

בָּרְכוּנִי לְשָׁלוֹם
מַלְאֲכֵי הַשָּׁלוֹם, מַלְאֲכֵי עֶלְיוֹן
מִמֶּלֶךְ מַלְכֵי הַמְּלָכִים, הַקָּדוֹשׁ בָּרוּךְ הוּא.

צֵאתְכֶם לְשָׁלוֹם
מַלְאֲכֵי הַשָּׁלוֹם, מַלְאֲכֵי עֶלְיוֹן
מִמֶּלֶךְ מַלְכֵי הַמְּלָכִים, הַקָּדוֹשׁ בָּרוּךְ הוּא.

תהלים צא כִּי מַלְאָכָיו יְצַוֶּה־לָּךְ, לִשְׁמָרְךָ בְּכָל־דְּרָכֶיךָ:
תהלים קכא יהוה יִשְׁמָר־צֵאתְךָ וּבוֹאֶךָ, מֵעַתָּה וְעַד־עוֹלָם:

Some say:

רִבּוֹן כָּל הָעוֹלָמִים Master of all worlds, Lord of all souls, Lord of peace, mighty, blessed and great King, King who speaks peace, King who is glorious, enduring and pure, King who gives life to worlds, King who is good and does good, King alone and unique, great King who robes Himself in compassion, King who reigns over all kings, who is exalted and supports those who fall, King who is Author of creation, who redeems and rescues, who is radiant and ruddy, King who is holy, high and exalted, King who hears prayer, King whose way is just: I thank You, Lord my God and God of my ancestors, for all the loving-kindness You have done and will do for me, and all the members of my household and all my fellow creatures. Blessed are Your angels, holy and pure, who do Your will. Lord of peace, King to whom peace belongs, bless me with peace, and grant me and the members of my household, and all Your people the house of Israel, a good and peaceful life. King exalted over all the heavenly array, who formed me and who formed creation, I entreat Your radiant presence, that You find me and all the members of my household worthy of grace and good favor in Your eyes and the eyes of all people and all who see us, that we may serve You. May we be worthy to receive Sabbaths amidst great joy, wealth and honor, and few sins. May You remove from me and all the members of my household and all Your people the house of Israel all sickness and disease, all poverty, hardship and destitution. Grant us a virtuous desire to serve You in truth, awe and love. May we find honor in Your eyes and the eyes of all who see us, for You are the King of honor: to You it belongs, to You it accords. Please, King who reigns over all kings, command Your angels, ministering angels who minister to the Most High, to act compassionately toward me when they enter my house on our holy day, for I have lit my lights, spread my couch and changed my clothes in honor of the Sabbath; I have come to Your House to lay my pleas before You that You remove my sighs; I have testified that in six days You created all things, and said it a second time, and will testify to it a third time over my cup, in joy, as You commanded me to remember it, delighting in the extra soul You have given me. On it [the Sabbath] I shall rest as You have commanded me, thereby to serve You. So too I will declare Your greatness in joyful song, for I have set the Lord before me, that You may have compassion upon me in my exile, redeeming me and awakening my heart to Your love. Then I will keep Your commands and statutes without sadness, praying correctly as is right and fitting. Angels of peace, come in peace and bless me with peace; declare blessed the table I have prepared, and go in peace, now and forever. Amen, Selah.

Some say:

רִבּוֹן כָּל הָעוֹלָמִים, אֲדוֹן כָּל הַנְּשָׁמוֹת, אֲדוֹן הַשָּׁלוֹם. מֶלֶךְ אַבִּיר, מֶלֶךְ בָּרוּךְ, מֶלֶךְ גָּדוֹל, מֶלֶךְ דּוֹבֵר שָׁלוֹם, מֶלֶךְ הָדוּר, מֶלֶךְ וָתִיק, מֶלֶךְ זַךְ, מֶלֶךְ חֵי הָעוֹלָמִים, מֶלֶךְ טוֹב וּמֵטִיב, מֶלֶךְ יָחִיד וּמְיֻחָד, מֶלֶךְ כַּבִּיר, מֶלֶךְ לוֹבֵשׁ רַחֲמִים, מֶלֶךְ מַלְכֵי הַמְּלָכִים, מֶלֶךְ נִשְׂגָּב, מֶלֶךְ סוֹמֵךְ נוֹפְלִים, מֶלֶךְ עֹשֶׂה מַעֲשֵׂה בְרֵאשִׁית, מֶלֶךְ פּוֹדֶה וּמַצִּיל, מֶלֶךְ צַח וְאָדֹם, מֶלֶךְ קָדוֹשׁ, מֶלֶךְ רָם וְנִשָּׂא, מֶלֶךְ שׁוֹמֵעַ תְּפִלָּה, מֶלֶךְ תָּמִים דַּרְכּוֹ. מוֹדֶה אֲנִי לְפָנֶיךָ, יהוה אֱלֹהַי וֵאלֹהֵי אֲבוֹתַי, עַל כָּל הַחֶסֶד אֲשֶׁר עָשִׂיתָ עִמָּדִי וַאֲשֶׁר אַתָּה עָתִיד לַעֲשׂוֹת עִמִּי וְעִם כָּל בְּנֵי בֵיתִי וְעִם כָּל בְּרִיּוֹתֶיךָ, בְּנֵי בְרִיתִי. וּבְרוּכִים הֵם מַלְאָכֶיךָ הַקְּדוֹשִׁים וְהַטְּהוֹרִים שֶׁעוֹשִׂים רְצוֹנֶךָ. אֲדוֹן הַשָּׁלוֹם, מֶלֶךְ שֶׁהַשָּׁלוֹם שֶׁלּוֹ, בָּרְכֵנִי בַשָּׁלוֹם, וְתִפְקֹד אוֹתִי וְאֶת כָּל בְּנֵי בֵיתִי וְכָל עַמְּךָ בֵּית יִשְׂרָאֵל לְחַיִּים טוֹבִים וּלְשָׁלוֹם. מֶלֶךְ עֶלְיוֹן עַל כָּל צְבָא מָרוֹם, יוֹצְרֵנוּ, יוֹצֵר בְּרֵאשִׁית, אֲחַלֶּה פָנֶיךָ הַמְּאִירִים, שֶׁתְּזַכֶּה אוֹתִי וְאֶת כָּל בְּנֵי בֵיתִי לִמְצֹא חֵן וְשֵׂכֶל טוֹב בְּעֵינֶיךָ וּבְעֵינֵי כָּל בְּנֵי אָדָם וּבְעֵינֵי כָל רוֹאֵינוּ לַעֲבוֹדָתֶךָ. וְזַכֵּנוּ לְקַבֵּל שַׁבָּתוֹת מִתּוֹךְ רֹב שִׂמְחָה וּמִתּוֹךְ עֹשֶׁר וְכָבוֹד וּמִתּוֹךְ מִעוּט עֲוֹנוֹת. וְהָסֵר מִמֶּנִּי וּמִכָּל בְּנֵי בֵיתִי וּמִכָּל עַמְּךָ בֵּית יִשְׂרָאֵל כָּל מִינֵי חֹלִי וְכָל מִינֵי מַדְוֶה וְכָל מִינֵי דַלּוּת וַעֲנִיּוּת וְאֶבְיוֹנוּת. וְתֵן בָּנוּ יֵצֶר טוֹב לְעָבְדְּךָ בֶּאֱמֶת וּבְיִרְאָה וּבְאַהֲבָה. וְנִהְיֶה מְכֻבָּדִים בְּעֵינֶיךָ וּבְעֵינֵי כָל רוֹאֵינוּ, כִּי אַתָּה הוּא מֶלֶךְ הַכָּבוֹד, כִּי לְךָ נָאֶה, כִּי לְךָ יָאֶה. אָנָּא, מֶלֶךְ מַלְכֵי הַמְּלָכִים, צַוֵּה לְמַלְאָכֶיךָ, מַלְאֲכֵי הַשָּׁרֵת, מְשָׁרְתֵי עֶלְיוֹן, שֶׁיִּפְקְדוּנִי בְּרַחֲמִים וִיבָרְכוּנִי בְּבוֹאָם לְבֵיתִי בְּיוֹם קָדְשֵׁנוּ, כִּי הִדְלַקְתִּי נֵרוֹתַי וְהִצַּעְתִּי מִטָּתִי וְהֶחֱלַפְתִּי שִׂמְלוֹתַי לִכְבוֹד יוֹם הַשַּׁבָּת וּבָאתִי לְבֵיתְךָ לְהַפִּיל תְּחִנָּתִי לְפָנֶיךָ, שֶׁתַּעֲבִיר אַנְחָתִי, וָאָעִיד אֲשֶׁר בָּרָאתָ בְשִׁשָּׁה יָמִים כָּל הַיְצוּר, וָאֶשְׁנֶה וַאֲשַׁלֵּשׁ עוֹד לְהָעִיד עַל כּוֹסִי בְּתוֹךְ שִׂמְחָתִי, כַּאֲשֶׁר צִוִּיתַנִי לְזָכְרוֹ וּלְהִתְעַנֵּג בְּיֶתֶר נִשְׁמָתִי אֲשֶׁר נָתַתָּ בִּי. בּוֹ אֶשְׁבֹּת כַּאֲשֶׁר צִוִּיתַנִי לְשָׁרְתֶךָ, וְכֵן אַגִּיד גְּדֻלָּתְךָ בְּרִנָּה, וְשִׁוִּיתִי יהוה לִקְרָאתִי שֶׁתְּרַחֲמֵנִי עוֹד בְּגָלוּתִי לְגָאֳלֵנִי לְעוֹרֵר לִבִּי לְאַהֲבָתֶךָ. וְאָז אֶשְׁמֹר פִּקּוּדֶיךָ וְחֻקֶּיךָ בְּלִי עֶצֶב, וְאֶתְפַּלֵּל כַּדָּת כָּרָאוּי וְכַנָּכוֹן. מַלְאֲכֵי הַשָּׁלוֹם, בּוֹאֲכֶם לְשָׁלוֹם, בָּרְכוּנִי לְשָׁלוֹם, וְאִמְרוּ בָּרוּךְ לְשֻׁלְחָנִי הֶעָרוּךְ, וְצֵאתְכֶם לְשָׁלוֹם מֵעַתָּה וְעַד עוֹלָם, אָמֵן סֶלָה.

אֵשֶׁת־חַיִל A woman of strength, who can find? *Prov. 31*
Her worth is far beyond pearls.
Her husband's heart trusts in her, and he has no lack of gain.
She brings him good, not harm, all the days of her life.
She seeks wool and linen, and works with willing hands.
She is like a ship laden with merchandise, bringing her food from afar.
She rises while it is still night, providing food for her household,
portions for her maids.
She considers a field and buys it;
from her earnings she plants a vineyard.
She girds herself with strength, and braces her arms for her tasks.
She sees that her business goes well; her lamp does not go out at night.
She holds the distaff in her hand,
and grasps the spindle with her palms.
She reaches out her palm to the poor,
and extends her hand to the needy.
She has no fear for her family when it snows,
for all her household is clothed in crimson wool.
She makes elegant coverings;
her clothing is fine linen and purple wool.
Her husband is well known in the gates,
where he sits with the elders of the land.
She makes linen garments and sells them,
and supplies merchants with sashes.
She is clothed with strength and dignity;
she can laugh at the days to come.
She opens her mouth with wisdom,
and the law of kindness is on her tongue.
She watches over the ways of her household,
and never eats the bread of idleness.
Her children rise and call her happy; her husband also praises her:
"Many women have excelled, but you surpass them all."
Charm is deceptive and beauty vain:
it is the God-fearing woman who deserves praise.
Give her the reward she has earned;
let her deeds bring her praise in the gates.

משלי לא

אֵשֶׁת־חַיִל מִי יִמְצָא, וְרָחֹק מִפְּנִינִים מִכְרָהּ:
בָּטַח בָּהּ לֵב בַּעְלָהּ, וְשָׁלָל לֹא יֶחְסָר:
גְּמָלַתְהוּ טוֹב וְלֹא־רָע, כֹּל יְמֵי חַיֶּיהָ:
דָּרְשָׁה צֶמֶר וּפִשְׁתִּים, וַתַּעַשׂ בְּחֵפֶץ כַּפֶּיהָ:
הָיְתָה כָּאֳנִיּוֹת סוֹחֵר, מִמֶּרְחָק תָּבִיא לַחְמָהּ:
וַתָּקָם בְּעוֹד לַיְלָה, וַתִּתֵּן טֶרֶף לְבֵיתָהּ, וְחֹק לְנַעֲרֹתֶיהָ:
זָמְמָה שָׂדֶה וַתִּקָּחֵהוּ, מִפְּרִי כַפֶּיהָ נָטְעָה כָּרֶם:
חָגְרָה בְעוֹז מָתְנֶיהָ, וַתְּאַמֵּץ זְרוֹעֹתֶיהָ:
טָעֲמָה כִּי־טוֹב סַחְרָהּ, לֹא־יִכְבֶּה בַלַּיְלָה נֵרָהּ:
יָדֶיהָ שִׁלְּחָה בַכִּישׁוֹר, וְכַפֶּיהָ תָּמְכוּ פָלֶךְ:
כַּפָּהּ פָּרְשָׂה לֶעָנִי, וְיָדֶיהָ שִׁלְּחָה לָאֶבְיוֹן:
לֹא־תִירָא לְבֵיתָהּ מִשָּׁלֶג, כִּי כָל־בֵּיתָהּ לָבֻשׁ שָׁנִים:
מַרְבַדִּים עָשְׂתָה־לָּהּ, שֵׁשׁ וְאַרְגָּמָן לְבוּשָׁהּ:
נוֹדָע בַּשְּׁעָרִים בַּעְלָהּ, בְּשִׁבְתּוֹ עִם־זִקְנֵי־אָרֶץ:
סָדִין עָשְׂתָה וַתִּמְכֹּר, וַחֲגוֹר נָתְנָה לַכְּנַעֲנִי:
עוֹז־וְהָדָר לְבוּשָׁהּ, וַתִּשְׂחַק לְיוֹם אַחֲרוֹן:
פִּיהָ פָּתְחָה בְחָכְמָה, וְתוֹרַת־חֶסֶד עַל־לְשׁוֹנָהּ:
צוֹפִיָּה הֲלִיכוֹת בֵּיתָהּ, וְלֶחֶם עַצְלוּת לֹא תֹאכֵל:
קָמוּ בָנֶיהָ וַיְאַשְּׁרוּהָ, בַּעְלָהּ וַיְהַלְלָהּ:
רַבּוֹת בָּנוֹת עָשׂוּ חָיִל, וְאַתְּ עָלִית עַל־כֻּלָּנָה:
שֶׁקֶר הַחֵן וְהֶבֶל הַיֹּפִי, אִשָּׁה יִרְאַת־יהוה הִיא תִתְהַלָּל:
תְּנוּ־לָהּ מִפְּרִי יָדֶיהָ, וִיהַלְלוּהָ בַשְּׁעָרִים מַעֲשֶׂיהָ:

Some say:

Prepare the feast of perfect faith, joy of the holy King.
Prepare the royal feast.

This is the feast [mystically known as] 'the Field of Holy Apples' –
and 'the Small Face' and 'the Holy Ancient One'
[mystical terms for aspects of the Divine] come to partake in the feast with it.

With songs of praise I will cut away [evil forces],
to enter the holy gates of 'the Field of Apples.'
We now invite Her [the Divine Presence] with a newly prepared table
and a fine candelabrum spreading light upon our heads.
Between right and left is the bride, decked with jewelry, adorned and robed.
Her husband embraces her, and in the joy of their togetherness
[evil forces] are crushed.
Cries and suffering stop and cease; a new face comes upon spirits and souls.
She will have great and doubled joy; light will come, and bounteous blessing.
Come near, dear friends, and prepare delicacies of many kinds, and fish and fowl.
Renewing souls and spirits through the thirty-two [paths of wisdom]
and the three branches [of Scripture].
She [the Divine Presence] has seventy crowns, and above,
the King is crowned with all in the Holy of Holies.
Engraved and hidden with her are all worlds,
but the pestle of the Ancient of Days releases all that is hidden.
May it be His will that the Divine Presence rest on His people who,
for His name's sake, delight in sweet foods and honey.
To the south, I will arrange the candelabrum of hidden [wisdom],
to the north I will set the table with bread.
With wine in the cup, and myrtle clusters for bridegroom and bride,
the weak will be given strength.
Let us make them crowns of precious words, seventy crowns beyond the fifty.
May the Divine Presence be crowned with six loaves on each side, like
the two sets of six loaves [of showbread] and other articles [in the Temple].
[On the Sabbath] impure powers and afflicting angels cease and desist; and
those who are confined have respite.
To break bread the size of an olive or an egg, for there are two ways of
interpreting the *Yod* [of the Divine name], restrictively or expansively.
It is like pure olive oil, pressed in a mill, flowing like rivers, whispering secrets.
Let us speak of mysteries, secrets unrevealed, hidden and concealed.
To crown the bride with mysteries above, at this,
the holy angels' wedding celebration.

Some say:

אַתְקֵינוּ סְעוּדָתָא דִמְהֵימְנוּתָא שְׁלִימְתָא
חֶדְוְתָא דְמַלְכָּא קַדִּישָׁא.
אַתְקֵינוּ סְעוּדָתָא דְמַלְכָּא.

דָּא הִיא סְעוּדָתָא דַּחֲקַל תַּפּוּחִין קַדִּישִׁין
וּזְעֵיר אַנְפִּין וְעַתִּיקָא קַדִּישָׁא אָתְיָן לְסַעֲדָה בַּהֲדַהּ.

אֲזַמֵּר בִּשְׁבָחִין / לְמֵעַל גּוֹ פִתְחִין / דְּבַחֲקַל תַּפּוּחִין / דְּאִנּוּן קַדִּישִׁין.
נְזַמֵּן לַהּ הַשְׁתָּא / בְּפָתוֹרָא חַדְתָּא / וּבִמְנָרְתָא טָבְתָא / דְּנָהֲרָה עַל רֵישִׁין.
יְמִינָא וּשְׂמָאלָא / וּבֵינַיְהוּ כַלָּה / בְּקִשּׁוּטִין אָזְלָא / וּמָנִין וּלְבוּשִׁין.
יְחַבֵּק לַהּ בַּעְלָהּ / וּבִיסוֹדָא דִי לַהּ / דְּעָבֵד נַיְחָא לַהּ / יְהֵא כָתֵשׁ כְּתִישִׁין.
צְוָחִין אוּף עָקְתִין / בְּטִילִין וּשְׁבִיתִין / בְּרַם אַנְפִּין חַדְתִּין / וְרוּחִין עִם נַפְשִׁין.
חֲדוּ סַגִּי יֵיתֵי / וְעַל חֲדָה תַרְתֵּי / נְהוֹרָא לַהּ יַמְטֵי / וּבִרְכָן דִּנְפִישִׁין.
קְרִיבוּ שׁוֹשְׁבִינִין / עֲבִידוּ תִקּוּנִין / לְאַפָּשָׁה זֵינִין / וְנוּנִין עִם רַחְשִׁין.
לְמֶעְבַּד נִשְׁמָתִין / וְרוּחִין חַדְתִּין / בְּתַרְתֵּי וּתְלָתִין / וּבִתְלָתָא שִׁבְשִׁין.
וְעִטְרִין שַׁבְעִין לַהּ / וּמַלְכָּא דִלְעֵלָּא / דְּיִתְעַטַּר כֹּלָּא / בְּקַדִּישׁ קַדִּישִׁין.
רְשִׁימִין וּסְתִימִין / בְּגַוַּהּ כָּל עָלְמִין / בְּרַם עַתִּיק יוֹמִין / הֲלָא בָטֵשׁ בְּטִישִׁין.
יְהֵא רַעֲוָה קַמֵּהּ / דְּתִשְׁרֵי עַל עַמֵּהּ / דְּיִתְעַנַּג לִשְׁמֵהּ / בְּמִתְקִין וְדֻבְשִׁין.
אֲסַדֵּר לִדְרוֹמָא / מְנָרְתָא דִסְתִימָא / וְשֻׁלְחָן עִם נַהֲמָא / בִּצְפוֹנָא אַדְשִׁין.
בְּחַמְרָא גוֹ כָסָא / וּמַדַּנֵּי אָסָא / לְאָרוּס וַאֲרוּסָה / לְאַתְקָפָא חַלְשִׁין.
נְעַבֵּד לוֹן כִּתְרִין / בְּמִלִּין יַקִּירִין / בְּשַׁבְעִין עִטּוּרִין / דְּעַל גַּבֵּי חַמְשִׁין.
שְׁכִינְתָּא תִתְעַטַּר / בְּשִׁית נַהֲמֵי לִסְטַר / בְּוָוִין תִּתְקַטַּר / וְזֵינִין דִּכְנִישִׁין.
(שְׁבִיתִין וּשְׁבִיקִין / מְסָאֲבִין דְּדָחֲקִין / חֲבִילִין דִּמְעִיקִין / וְכָל זֵינֵי חַרְשִׁין.)
לְמִבְצַע עַל רִיפְתָּא / כְּזֵיתָא וּכְבֵיעְתָא / תְּרֵין יוּדִין נָקְטָא / סְתִימִין וּפְרִישִׁין.
מְשַׁח זֵיתָא דָּכְיָא / דְּטָחֲנִין רֵחַיָּא / וְנָגְדִין נַחְלַיָּא / בְּגַוַּהּ בִּלְחִישִׁין.
הֲלָא נֵימָא רָזִין / וּמִלִּין דִּגְנִיזִין / דְּלֵיתֵיהוֹן מִתְחֲזִין / טְמִירִין וּכְבִישִׁין.
לְאַעְטָרָה כַלָּה / בְּרָזִין דִּלְעֵלָּא / בְּגוֹ הַאי הִלּוּלָה / דְּעִירִין קַדִּישִׁין.

KIDDUSH FOR SHABBAT EVENING

For Kiddush on Yom Tov see page 188.

Quietly: And it was evening, and it was morning – Gen. 1

יוֹם הַשִּׁשִּׁי the sixth day.

Then the heavens and the earth were completed, Gen. 2
and all their array.
With the seventh day, God completed the work He had done.
He ceased on the seventh day from all the work He had done.
God blessed the seventh day and declared it holy,
because on it He ceased from all His work He had created to do.

When saying Kiddush for others, add:
Please pay attention, my masters.

Blessed are You, Lord our God, King of the Universe,
who creates the fruit of the vine.

Blessed are You, Lord our God, King of the Universe,
who has made us holy through His commandments,
who has favored us,
and in love and favor gave us His holy Sabbath as a heritage,
a remembrance of the work of creation.
It is the first among the holy days of assembly,
a remembrance of the exodus from Egypt.
For You chose us and sanctified us from all the peoples,
and in love and favor gave us Your holy Sabbath as a heritage.
Blessed are You, Lord,
who sanctifies the Sabbath.

If one is unable to sit in a sukka this blessing is not said.

בָּרוּךְ Blessed are You, Lord our God, King of the Universe,
who has made us holy though His commandments,
and has commanded us to dwell in the sukka.

קידוש לליל שבת

For קידוש *on* יום טוב *see page 189.*

Quietly וַיְהִי־עֶרֶב וַיְהִי־בֹקֶר בראשית א

יוֹם הַשִּׁשִּׁי:

וַיְכֻלּוּ הַשָּׁמַיִם וְהָאָרֶץ וְכָל־צְבָאָם: בראשית ב
וַיְכַל אֱלֹהִים בַּיּוֹם הַשְּׁבִיעִי מְלַאכְתּוֹ אֲשֶׁר עָשָׂה
וַיִּשְׁבֹּת בַּיּוֹם הַשְּׁבִיעִי מִכָּל־מְלַאכְתּוֹ אֲשֶׁר עָשָׂה:
וַיְבָרֶךְ אֱלֹהִים אֶת־יוֹם הַשְּׁבִיעִי, וַיְקַדֵּשׁ אֹתוֹ
כִּי בוֹ שָׁבַת מִכָּל־מְלַאכְתּוֹ, אֲשֶׁר־בָּרָא אֱלֹהִים, לַעֲשׂוֹת:

When saying קידוש *for others, add:*

סַבְרִי מָרָנָן

בָּרוּךְ אַתָּה יהוה אֱלֹהֵינוּ מֶלֶךְ הָעוֹלָם בּוֹרֵא פְּרִי הַגָּפֶן.

בָּרוּךְ אַתָּה יהוה אֱלֹהֵינוּ מֶלֶךְ הָעוֹלָם
אֲשֶׁר קִדְּשָׁנוּ בְּמִצְוֹתָיו, וְרָצָה בָנוּ
וְשַׁבַּת קָדְשׁוֹ בְּאַהֲבָה וּבְרָצוֹן הִנְחִילָנוּ
זִכָּרוֹן לְמַעֲשֵׂה בְרֵאשִׁית
כִּי הוּא יוֹם תְּחִלָּה לְמִקְרָאֵי קֹדֶשׁ, זֵכֶר לִיצִיאַת מִצְרָיִם
כִּי בָנוּ בָחַרְתָּ וְאוֹתָנוּ קִדַּשְׁתָּ מִכָּל הָעַמִּים
וְשַׁבַּת קָדְשְׁךָ בְּאַהֲבָה וּבְרָצוֹן הִנְחַלְתָּנוּ.
בָּרוּךְ אַתָּה יהוה, מְקַדֵּשׁ הַשַּׁבָּת.

If one is unable to sit in a סוכה *this blessing is not said.*

בָּרוּךְ אַתָּה יהוה אֱלֹהֵינוּ מֶלֶךְ הָעוֹלָם
אֲשֶׁר קִדְּשָׁנוּ בְּמִצְוֹתָיו וְצִוָּנוּ לֵישֵׁב בַּסֻּכָּה.

Shaḥarit for Shabbat Ḥol HaMo'ed

Shaḥarit begins as on Yom Tov, from pages 258–386.

THE AMIDA

The following prayer, until "in former years" on page 800, is said silently, standing with feet together. If there is a minyan, the Amida is repeated aloud by the Leader. Take three steps forward and at the points indicated by ˅, bend the knees at the first word, bow at the second, and stand straight before saying God's name.

O LORD, open my lips, so that my mouth may declare Your praise. *Ps. 51*

PATRIARCHS

˅בָּרוּךְ˅ Blessed are You, LORD our God and God of our fathers,
God of Abraham, God of Isaac and God of Jacob;
the great, mighty and awesome God, God Most High,
who bestows acts of loving-kindness and creates all,
who remembers the loving-kindness of the fathers
and will bring a Redeemer
to their children's children
for the sake of His name, in love.
King, Helper, Savior, Shield:
˅Blessed are You, LORD, Shield of Abraham.

DIVINE MIGHT

אַתָּה גִּבּוֹר You are eternally mighty, LORD.
You give life to the dead
and have great power to save.

In Israel:
He causes the dew to fall.

He sustains the living with loving-kindness,
and with great compassion revives the dead.
He supports the fallen, heals the sick, sets captives free,
and keeps His faith with those who sleep in the dust.

שחרית לשבת חול המועד

שחרית begins as on יום טוב, from pages 259–387.

עמידה

The following prayer, until קַדְמֹנִיּוֹת on page 801, is said silently, standing with feet together. If there is a מנין, the עמידה is repeated aloud by the שליח ציבור. Take three steps forward and at the points indicated by ˚, bend the knees at the first word, bow at the second, and stand straight before saying God's name.

אֲדֹנָי, שְׂפָתַי תִּפְתָּח, וּפִי יַגִּיד תְּהִלָּתֶךָ: תהלים נא

אבות

˚בָּרוּךְ אַתָּה יהוה, אֱלֹהֵינוּ וֵאלֹהֵי אֲבוֹתֵינוּ
אֱלֹהֵי אַבְרָהָם, אֱלֹהֵי יִצְחָק, וֵאלֹהֵי יַעֲקֹב
הָאֵל הַגָּדוֹל הַגִּבּוֹר וְהַנּוֹרָא, אֵל עֶלְיוֹן
גּוֹמֵל חֲסָדִים טוֹבִים, וְקוֹנֵה הַכֹּל
וְזוֹכֵר חַסְדֵי אָבוֹת
וּמֵבִיא גוֹאֵל לִבְנֵי בְנֵיהֶם לְמַעַן שְׁמוֹ בְּאַהֲבָה.
מֶלֶךְ עוֹזֵר וּמוֹשִׁיעַ וּמָגֵן.
˚בָּרוּךְ אַתָּה יהוה, מָגֵן אַבְרָהָם.

גבורות

אַתָּה גִּבּוֹר לְעוֹלָם, אֲדֹנָי
מְחַיֵּה מֵתִים אַתָּה, רַב לְהוֹשִׁיעַ

In ארץ ישראל:
מוֹרִיד הַטָּל

מְכַלְכֵּל חַיִּים בְּחֶסֶד, מְחַיֵּה מֵתִים בְּרַחֲמִים רַבִּים
סוֹמֵךְ נוֹפְלִים, וְרוֹפֵא חוֹלִים, וּמַתִּיר אֲסוּרִים
וּמְקַיֵּם אֱמוּנָתוֹ לִישֵׁנֵי עָפָר.

Who is like You, Master of might,
and who can compare to You,
O King who brings death and gives life,
and makes salvation grow?
Faithful are You to revive the dead.
Blessed are You, Lord, who revives the dead.

When saying the Amida silently, continue with "You are holy" on the next page.

KEDUSHA

During the Leader's Repetition, the following is said standing with feet together, rising on the toes at the words indicated by ▴.

Cong. then Leader: נְקַדֵּשׁ We will sanctify Your name on earth, as they sanctify it in the highest heavens, as is written by Your prophet,
"And they [the angels] call to one another saying: *Is. 6*

Cong. then Leader: ▴Holy, ▴holy, ▴holy is the Lord of hosts the whole world is filled with His glory."
Then with a sound of mighty noise, majestic and strong, they make their voice heard, raising themselves toward the Seraphim, and facing them say: "Blessed –"

Cong. then Leader: "▴Blessed is the Lord's glory from His place." *Ezek. 3*
Reveal Yourself from Your place, O our King, and reign over us, for we are waiting for You. When will You reign in Zion? May it be soon in our days, and may You dwell there for ever and all time. May You be exalted and sanctified in the midst of Jerusalem, Your city, from generation to generation for evermore. May our eyes see Your kingdom, as is said in the songs of Your splendor, written by David Your righteous anointed one:

Cong. then Leader: "▴The Lord shall reign for ever. He is your God, Zion, from generation to generation, Halleluya!" *Ps. 146*

Leader: From generation to generation we will declare Your greatness, and we will proclaim Your holiness for evermore.
Your praise, our God, shall not leave our mouth forever,
for You, God, are a great and holy King.
Blessed are You, Lord, the holy God.

The Leader continues with "Moses rejoiced" on the next page.

מִי כָמְוֹךָ, בַּעַל גְּבוּרוֹת
וּמִי דְּוֹמֶה לָּךְ
מֶלֶךְ, מֵמִית וּמְחַיֶּה וּמַצְמִיחַ יְשׁוּעָה.
וְנֶאֱמָן אַתָּה לְהַחֲיוֹת מֵתִים.
בָּרוּךְ אַתָּה יהוה, מְחַיֵּה הַמֵּתִים.

When saying the עמידה silently, continue with אַתָּה קָדוֹשׁ on the next page.

קדושה

During the חזרת הש״ץ, the following is said standing with feet together, rising on the toes at the words indicated by ˄.

then קהל ש״ץ: נְקַדֵּשׁ אֶת שִׁמְךָ בָּעוֹלָם, כְּשֵׁם שֶׁמַּקְדִּישִׁים אוֹתוֹ בִּשְׁמֵי מָרוֹם
ישעיה ו כַּכָּתוּב עַל יַד נְבִיאֶךָ: וְקָרָא זֶה אֶל־זֶה וְאָמַר

then קהל ש״ץ: ˄קָדוֹשׁ, ˄קָדוֹשׁ, ˄קָדוֹשׁ, יהוה צְבָאוֹת, מְלֹא כָל־הָאָרֶץ כְּבוֹדוֹ:
אָז בְּקוֹל רַעַשׁ גָּדוֹל אַדִּיר וְחָזָק, מַשְׁמִיעִים קוֹל
מִתְנַשְּׂאִים לְעֻמַּת שְׂרָפִים, לְעֻמָּתָם בָּרוּךְ יֹאמֵרוּ

יחזקאל ג then קהל ש״ץ: ˄בָּרוּךְ כְּבוֹד־יהוה מִמְּקוֹמוֹ:
מִמְּקוֹמְךָ מַלְכֵּנוּ תוֹפִיעַ וְתִמְלֹךְ עָלֵינוּ, כִּי מְחַכִּים אֲנַחְנוּ לָךְ
מָתַי תִּמְלֹךְ בְּצִיּוֹן, בְּקָרוֹב בְּיָמֵינוּ לְעוֹלָם וָעֶד תִּשְׁכֹּן
תִּתְגַּדַּל וְתִתְקַדַּשׁ בְּתוֹךְ יְרוּשָׁלַיִם עִירְךָ לְדוֹר וָדוֹר וּלְנֵצַח נְצָחִים.
וְעֵינֵינוּ תִרְאֶינָה מַלְכוּתֶךָ
כַּדָּבָר הָאָמוּר בְּשִׁירֵי עֻזֶּךָ עַל יְדֵי דָוִד מְשִׁיחַ צִדְקֶךָ

תהלים קמו then קהל ש״ץ: ˄יִמְלֹךְ יהוה לְעוֹלָם, אֱלֹהַיִךְ צִיּוֹן לְדֹר וָדֹר, הַלְלוּיָהּ:

ש״ץ: לְדוֹר וָדוֹר נַגִּיד גָּדְלֶךָ, וּלְנֵצַח נְצָחִים קְדֻשָּׁתְךָ נַקְדִּישׁ
וְשִׁבְחֲךָ אֱלֹהֵינוּ מִפִּינוּ לֹא יָמוּשׁ לְעוֹלָם וָעֶד
כִּי אֵל מֶלֶךְ גָּדוֹל וְקָדוֹשׁ אָתָּה.
בָּרוּךְ אַתָּה יהוה, הָאֵל הַקָּדוֹשׁ.

The שליח ציבור continues with יִשְׂמַח מֹשֶׁה on the next page.

HOLINESS

אַתָּה קָדוֹשׁ You are holy and Your name is holy,
and holy ones praise You daily, Selah!
Blessed are You, LORD, the holy God.

HOLINESS OF THE DAY

יִשְׂמַח Moses rejoiced at the gift of his portion
when You called him "faithful servant."
A crown of glory
You placed on his head
when he stood before You on Mount Sinai.
He brought down in his hands two tablets of stone
on which was engraved the observance of the Sabbath.
So it is written in Your Torah:

וְשָׁמְרוּ The children of Israel must keep the Sabbath, *Ex. 31*
observing the Sabbath in every generation
as an everlasting covenant.
It is a sign between Me and the children of Israel for ever,
for in six days God made the heavens and the earth,
but on the seventh day
He ceased work and refreshed Himself.

וְלֹא You, O LORD our God, did not give it
to the other nations of the world,
nor did You, our King,
give it as a heritage to those who worship idols.
In its rest the uncircumcised do not dwell,
for You gave it in love to Israel Your people,
to the descendants of Jacob whom You chose.
May the people who sanctify the seventh day
all find satisfaction and delight in Your goodness,
for You favored the seventh day and made it holy,
calling it the most cherished of days,
a remembrance of the act of creation.

קדושת השם

אַתָּה קָדוֹשׁ וְשִׁמְךָ קָדוֹשׁ, וּקְדוֹשִׁים בְּכָל יוֹם יְהַלְלְוּךָ סֶּלָה.
בָּרוּךְ אַתָּה יהוה, הָאֵל הַקָּדוֹשׁ.

קדושת היום

יִשְׂמַח מֹשֶׁה בְּמַתְּנַת חֶלְקוֹ
כִּי עֶבֶד נֶאֱמָן קָרָאתָ לּוֹ
כְּלִיל תִּפְאֶרֶת בְּרֹאשׁוֹ נָתַתָּ לּוֹ
בְּעָמְדוֹ לְפָנֶיךָ עַל הַר סִינַי
וּשְׁנֵי לוּחוֹת אֲבָנִים הוֹרִיד בְּיָדוֹ
וְכָתוּב בָּהֶם שְׁמִירַת שַׁבָּת
וְכֵן כָּתוּב בְּתוֹרָתֶךָ

וְשָׁמְרוּ בְנֵי־יִשְׂרָאֵל אֶת־הַשַּׁבָּת שמות לא
לַעֲשׂוֹת אֶת־הַשַּׁבָּת לְדֹרֹתָם בְּרִית עוֹלָם:
בֵּינִי וּבֵין בְּנֵי יִשְׂרָאֵל אוֹת הִוא לְעֹלָם
כִּי־שֵׁשֶׁת יָמִים עָשָׂה יהוה אֶת־הַשָּׁמַיִם וְאֶת־הָאָרֶץ
וּבַיּוֹם הַשְּׁבִיעִי שָׁבַת וַיִּנָּפַשׁ:

וְלֹא נְתַתּוֹ, יהוה אֱלֹהֵינוּ, לְגוֹיֵי הָאֲרָצוֹת
וְלֹא הִנְחַלְתּוֹ, מַלְכֵּנוּ, לְעוֹבְדֵי פְסִילִים
וְגַם בִּמְנוּחָתוֹ לֹא יִשְׁכְּנוּ עֲרֵלִים
כִּי לְיִשְׂרָאֵל עַמְּךָ נְתַתּוֹ בְּאַהֲבָה
לְזֶרַע יַעֲקֹב אֲשֶׁר בָּם בָּחָרְתָּ.
עַם מְקַדְּשֵׁי שְׁבִיעִי, כֻּלָּם יִשְׂבְּעוּ וְיִתְעַנְּגוּ מִטּוּבֶךָ
וּבַשְּׁבִיעִי רָצִיתָ בּוֹ וְקִדַּשְׁתּוֹ
חֶמְדַּת יָמִים אוֹתוֹ קָרָאתָ, זֵכֶר לְמַעֲשֵׂה בְרֵאשִׁית.

אֱלֹהֵינוּ Our God and God of our ancestors,
find favor in our rest.
Make us holy through Your commandments
and grant us our share in Your Torah.
Satisfy us with Your goodness,
grant us joy in Your salvation,
and purify our hearts to serve You in truth.
In love and favor, LORD our God,
grant us as our heritage Your holy Sabbath,
so that Israel who sanctify Your name may find rest on it.
Blessed are You, LORD,
who sanctifies the Sabbath.

TEMPLE SERVICE

רְצֵה Find favor, LORD our God,
in Your people Israel and their prayer.
Restore the service to Your most holy House,
and accept in love and favor
the fire-offerings of Israel and their prayer.
May the service of Your people Israel
always find favor with You.

אֱלֹהֵינוּ Our God and God of our ancestors,
may there rise, come, reach, appear,
be favored, heard, regarded and remembered before You,
our recollection and remembrance,
as well as the remembrance of our ancestors,
and of the Messiah son of David Your servant,
and of Jerusalem Your holy city,
and of all Your people the house of Israel –
for deliverance and well-being,
grace, loving-kindness and compassion,
life and peace,
on this day of the Festival of Sukkot.

אֱלֹהֵינוּ וֵאלֹהֵי אֲבוֹתֵינוּ, רְצֵה בִמְנוּחָתֵנוּ
קַדְּשֵׁנוּ בְּמִצְוֹתֶיךָ וְתֵן חֶלְקֵנוּ בְּתוֹרָתֶךָ
שַׂבְּעֵנוּ מִטּוּבֶךָ וְשַׂמְּחֵנוּ בִּישׁוּעָתֶךָ
וְטַהֵר לִבֵּנוּ לְעָבְדְּךָ בֶּאֱמֶת
וְהַנְחִילֵנוּ, יהוה אֱלֹהֵינוּ
בְּאַהֲבָה וּבְרָצוֹן שַׁבַּת קָדְשֶׁךָ
וְיָנוּחוּ בוֹ יִשְׂרָאֵל מְקַדְּשֵׁי שְׁמֶךָ.
בָּרוּךְ אַתָּה יהוה, מְקַדֵּשׁ הַשַּׁבָּת.

עבודה

רְצֵה יהוה אֱלֹהֵינוּ בְּעַמְּךָ יִשְׂרָאֵל, וּבִתְפִלָּתָם
וְהָשֵׁב אֶת הָעֲבוֹדָה לִדְבִיר בֵּיתֶךָ
וְאִשֵּׁי יִשְׂרָאֵל וּתְפִלָּתָם בְּאַהֲבָה תְקַבֵּל בְּרָצוֹן
וּתְהִי לְרָצוֹן תָּמִיד עֲבוֹדַת יִשְׂרָאֵל עַמֶּךָ.

אֱלֹהֵינוּ וֵאלֹהֵי אֲבוֹתֵינוּ
יַעֲלֶה וְיָבוֹא וְיַגִּיעַ, וְיֵרָאֶה וְיֵרָצֶה וְיִשָּׁמַע
וְיִפָּקֵד וְיִזָּכֵר זִכְרוֹנֵנוּ וּפִקְדוֹנֵנוּ
וְזִכְרוֹן אֲבוֹתֵינוּ
וְזִכְרוֹן מָשִׁיחַ בֶּן דָּוִד עַבְדֶּךָ
וְזִכְרוֹן יְרוּשָׁלַיִם עִיר קָדְשֶׁךָ
וְזִכְרוֹן כָּל עַמְּךָ בֵּית יִשְׂרָאֵל, לְפָנֶיךָ
לִפְלֵיטָה לְטוֹבָה, לְחֵן וּלְחֶסֶד וּלְרַחֲמִים
לְחַיִּים וּלְשָׁלוֹם
בְּיוֹם חַג הַסֻּכּוֹת הַזֶּה.

On it remember us, LORD our God, for good;
recollect us for blessing, and deliver us for life.
In accord with Your promise of salvation and compassion,
spare us and be gracious to us;
have compassion on us and deliver us,
for our eyes are turned to You
because You, God, are a gracious and compassionate King.

And may our eyes witness Your return to Zion in compassion.
Blessed are You, LORD, who restores His Presence to Zion

THANKSGIVING

Bow at the first nine words.

מוֹדִים We give thanks to You,
for You are the LORD our God
and God of our ancestors
for ever and all time.
You are the Rock of our lives,
Shield of our salvation
from generation to generation.
We will thank You and
declare Your praise for our lives,
which are entrusted into Your hand;
for our souls,
which are placed in Your charge;
for Your miracles
which are with us every day;
and for Your wonders and favors
at all times, evening,
morning and midday.
You are good –
for Your compassion never fails.
You are compassionate –
for Your loving-kindnesses never cease.
We have always placed our hope in You.

During the Leader's Repetition, the congregation says quietly:
מוֹדִים We give thanks to You,
for You are the LORD our God
and God of our ancestors,
God of all flesh,
who formed us
and formed the universe.
Blessings and thanks
are due to Your great
and holy name for giving us
life and sustaining us.
May You continue
to give us life
and sustain us;
and may You gather our
exiles to Your holy courts,
to keep Your decrees,
do Your will and serve You
with a perfect heart,
for it is for us
to give You thanks.
Blessed be God to whom
thanksgiving is due.

זָכְרֵנוּ יהוה אֱלֹהֵינוּ בּוֹ לְטוֹבָה
וּפָקְדֵנוּ בוֹ לִבְרָכָה
וְהוֹשִׁיעֵנוּ בוֹ לְחַיִּים.
וּבִדְבַר יְשׁוּעָה וְרַחֲמִים
חוּס וְחָנֵּנוּ, וְרַחֵם עָלֵינוּ וְהוֹשִׁיעֵנוּ
כִּי אֵלֶיךָ עֵינֵינוּ, כִּי אֵל מֶלֶךְ חַנּוּן וְרַחוּם אָתָּה.

וְתֶחֱזֶינָה עֵינֵינוּ בְּשׁוּבְךָ לְצִיּוֹן בְּרַחֲמִים.
בָּרוּךְ אַתָּה יהוה, הַמַּחֲזִיר שְׁכִינָתוֹ לְצִיּוֹן.

הודאה

Bow at the first five words.

מוֹדִים אֲנַחְנוּ לָךְ
שָׁאַתָּה הוּא יהוה אֱלֹהֵינוּ
וֵאלֹהֵי אֲבוֹתֵינוּ לְעוֹלָם וָעֶד.
צוּר חַיֵּינוּ, מָגֵן יִשְׁעֵנוּ
אַתָּה הוּא לְדוֹר וָדוֹר.
נוֹדֶה לְּךָ וּנְסַפֵּר תְּהִלָּתֶךָ
עַל חַיֵּינוּ הַמְּסוּרִים בְּיָדֶךָ
וְעַל נִשְׁמוֹתֵינוּ הַפְּקוּדוֹת לָךְ
וְעַל נִסֶּיךָ שֶׁבְּכָל יוֹם עִמָּנוּ
וְעַל נִפְלְאוֹתֶיךָ וְטוֹבוֹתֶיךָ
שֶׁבְּכָל עֵת, עֶרֶב וָבֹקֶר וְצָהֳרָיִם.
הַטּוֹב, כִּי לֹא כָלוּ רַחֲמֶיךָ
וְהַמְרַחֵם, כִּי לֹא תַמּוּ חֲסָדֶיךָ
מֵעוֹלָם קִוִּינוּ לָךְ.

During the חזרת הש״ץ, *the* קהל *says quietly:*

מוֹדִים אֲנַחְנוּ לָךְ
שָׁאַתָּה הוּא יהוה אֱלֹהֵינוּ
וֵאלֹהֵי אֲבוֹתֵינוּ
אֱלֹהֵי כָל בָּשָׂר
יוֹצְרֵנוּ, יוֹצֵר בְּרֵאשִׁית.
בְּרָכוֹת וְהוֹדָאוֹת
לְשִׁמְךָ הַגָּדוֹל וְהַקָּדוֹשׁ
עַל שֶׁהֶחֱיִיתָנוּ וְקִיַּמְתָּנוּ.
כֵּן תְּחַיֵּנוּ וּתְקַיְּמֵנוּ
וְתֶאֱסֹף גָּלֻיּוֹתֵינוּ
לְחַצְרוֹת קָדְשֶׁךָ
לִשְׁמֹר חֻקֶּיךָ וְלַעֲשׂוֹת רְצוֹנֶךָ
וּלְעָבְדְּךָ בְּלֵבָב שָׁלֵם
עַל שֶׁאֲנַחְנוּ מוֹדִים לָךְ.
בָּרוּךְ אֵל הַהוֹדָאוֹת.

וְעַל כֻּלָּם For all these things may Your name be blessed and exalted,
our King, continually, for ever and all time.
Let all that lives thank You, Selah!
and praise Your name in truth,
God, our Savior and Help, Selah!
▾Blessed are You, LORD, whose name is "the Good"
and to whom thanks are due.

The following is said by the Leader during the Repetition of the Amida.
In Israel, if Kohanim bless the congregation, *turn to page 1396.*

Our God and God of our fathers, bless us with the threefold blessing in the Torah, written by the hand of Moses Your servant and pronounced by Aaron and his sons the priests, Your holy people, as it is said:

May the LORD bless you and protect you. *Num. 6*
Cong: May it be Your will.
May the LORD make His face shine on you and be gracious to you.
Cong: May it be Your will.
May the LORD turn His face toward you, and grant you peace.
Cong: May it be Your will.

PEACE

שִׂים שָׁלוֹם Grant peace, goodness and blessing,
grace, loving-kindness and compassion
to us and all Israel Your people.
Bless us, our Father, all as one, with the light of Your face,
for by the light of Your face You have given us, LORD our God,
the Torah of life and love of kindness,
righteousness, blessing, compassion, life and peace.
May it be good in Your eyes to bless Your people Israel
at every time, in every hour, with Your peace.
Blessed are You, LORD,
who blesses His people Israel with peace.

The following verse concludes the Leader's Repetition of the Amida.
Some also say it here as part of the silent Amida.

May the words of my mouth and the meditation of my heart *Ps. 19*
find favor before You, LORD, my Rock and Redeemer.

וְעַל כֻּלָּם יִתְבָּרַךְ וְיִתְרוֹמַם שִׁמְךָ מַלְכֵּנוּ תָּמִיד לְעוֹלָם וָעֶד.
וְכֹל הַחַיִּים יוֹדְוּךָ סֶּלָה, וִיהַלְלוּ אֶת שִׁמְךָ בֶּאֱמֶת
הָאֵל יְשׁוּעָתֵנוּ וְעֶזְרָתֵנוּ סֶלָה.
בָּרוּךְ אַתָּה יהוה, הַטּוֹב שִׁמְךָ וּלְךָ נָאֶה לְהוֹדוֹת.

The following is said by the שליח ציבור *during* חורת הש״ץ.
In ארץ ישראל *if* כהנים *say* ברכת כהנים *turn to page 1397.*

אֱלֹהֵינוּ וֵאלֹהֵי אֲבוֹתֵינוּ, בָּרְכֵנוּ בַבְּרָכָה הַמְשֻׁלֶּשֶׁת בַּתּוֹרָה, הַכְּתוּבָה עַל יְדֵי מֹשֶׁה עַבְדֶּךָ, הָאֲמוּרָה מִפִּי אַהֲרֹן וּבָנָיו כֹּהֲנִים עַם קְדוֹשֶׁיךָ, כָּאָמוּר

יְבָרֶכְךָ יהוה וְיִשְׁמְרֶךָ: קהל: כֵּן יְהִי רָצוֹן במדבר ו
יָאֵר יהוה פָּנָיו אֵלֶיךָ וִיחֻנֶּךָּ: קהל: כֵּן יְהִי רָצוֹן
יִשָּׂא יהוה פָּנָיו אֵלֶיךָ וְיָשֵׂם לְךָ שָׁלוֹם: קהל: כֵּן יְהִי רָצוֹן

שלום

שִׂים שָׁלוֹם טוֹבָה וּבְרָכָה
חֵן וָחֶסֶד וְרַחֲמִים
עָלֵינוּ וְעַל כָּל יִשְׂרָאֵל עַמֶּךָ.
בָּרְכֵנוּ אָבִינוּ כֻּלָּנוּ כְּאֶחָד בְּאוֹר פָּנֶיךָ
כִּי בְאוֹר פָּנֶיךָ נָתַתָּ לָּנוּ יהוה אֱלֹהֵינוּ
תּוֹרַת חַיִּים וְאַהֲבַת חֶסֶד
וּצְדָקָה וּבְרָכָה וְרַחֲמִים וְחַיִּים וְשָׁלוֹם.
וְטוֹב בְּעֵינֶיךָ לְבָרֵךְ אֶת עַמְּךָ יִשְׂרָאֵל
בְּכָל עֵת וּבְכָל שָׁעָה בִּשְׁלוֹמֶךָ.
בָּרוּךְ אַתָּה יהוה, הַמְבָרֵךְ אֶת עַמּוֹ יִשְׂרָאֵל בַּשָּׁלוֹם.

The following verse concludes the חורת הש״ץ.
Some also say it here as part of the silent עמידה.

יִהְיוּ לְרָצוֹן אִמְרֵי־פִי וְהֶגְיוֹן לִבִּי לְפָנֶיךָ, יהוה צוּרִי וְגֹאֲלִי: תהלים יט

אֱלֹהַי My God, *Berakhot 17a*
guard my tongue from evil and my lips from deceitful speech.
To those who curse me, let my soul be silent;
may my soul be to all like the dust.
Open my heart to Your Torah and let my soul
pursue Your commandments.
As for all who plan evil against me,
swiftly thwart their counsel and frustrate their plans.
Act for the sake of Your name;
act for the sake of Your right hand;
act for the sake of Your holiness;
act for the sake of Your Torah.
That Your beloved ones may be delivered, *Ps. 60*
save with Your right hand and answer me.
May the words of my mouth and the meditation of my heart *Ps. 19*
find favor before You, LORD, my Rock and Redeemer.

Bow, take three steps back, then bow, first left, then right, then center, while saying:

May He who makes peace in His high places,
make peace for us and all Israel –
and say: Amen.

יְהִי רָצוֹן May it be Your will, LORD our God and God of our ancestors,
that the Temple be rebuilt speedily in our days,
and grant us a share in Your Torah.
And there we will serve You with reverence,
as in the days of old and as in former years.
Then the offering of Judah and Jerusalem will be pleasing to the LORD *Mal. 3*
as in the days of old and as in former years.

When praying with a minyan, the Amida is repeated aloud by the Leader.

ברכות יז.

אֱלֹהַי
נְצֹר לְשׁוֹנִי מֵרָע וּשְׂפָתַי מִדַּבֵּר מִרְמָה
וְלִמְקַלְלַי נַפְשִׁי תִדֹּם, וְנַפְשִׁי כֶּעָפָר לַכֹּל תִּהְיֶה.
פְּתַח לִבִּי בְּתוֹרָתֶךָ, וּבְמִצְוֹתֶיךָ תִּרְדֹּף נַפְשִׁי.
וְכָל הַחוֹשְׁבִים עָלַי רָעָה
מְהֵרָה הָפֵר עֲצָתָם וְקַלְקֵל מַחֲשַׁבְתָּם.
עֲשֵׂה לְמַעַן שְׁמֶךָ
עֲשֵׂה לְמַעַן יְמִינֶךָ
עֲשֵׂה לְמַעַן קְדֻשָּׁתֶךָ
עֲשֵׂה לְמַעַן תּוֹרָתֶךָ.

תהלים ס לְמַעַן יֵחָלְצוּן יְדִידֶיךָ, הוֹשִׁיעָה יְמִינְךָ וַעֲנֵנִי:

תהלים יט יִהְיוּ לְרָצוֹן אִמְרֵי־פִי וְהֶגְיוֹן לִבִּי לְפָנֶיךָ, יהוה צוּרִי וְגֹאֲלִי:

Bow, take three steps back, then bow, first left, then right, then center, while saying:

עֹשֶׂה שָׁלוֹם בִּמְרוֹמָיו
הוּא יַעֲשֶׂה שָׁלוֹם עָלֵינוּ וְעַל כָּל יִשְׂרָאֵל
וְאִמְרוּ אָמֵן.

יְהִי רָצוֹן מִלְּפָנֶיךָ יהוה אֱלֹהֵינוּ וֵאלֹהֵי אֲבוֹתֵינוּ
שֶׁיִּבָּנֶה בֵּית הַמִּקְדָּשׁ בִּמְהֵרָה בְיָמֵינוּ
וְתֵן חֶלְקֵנוּ בְּתוֹרָתֶךָ
וְשָׁם נַעֲבָדְךָ בְּיִרְאָה כִּימֵי עוֹלָם וּכְשָׁנִים קַדְמֹנִיּוֹת.

מלאכי ג וְעָרְבָה לַיהוה מִנְחַת יְהוּדָה וִירוּשָׁלָיִם כִּימֵי עוֹלָם וּכְשָׁנִים קַדְמֹנִיּוֹת:

When praying with a מנין, *the* עמידה *is repeated aloud by the* שליח ציבור.

Hallel

בָּרוּךְ Blessed are You, LORD our God, King of the Universe,
who has made us holy through His commandments
and has commanded us to recite the Hallel.

הַלְלוּיָהּ Halleluya! Servants of the LORD, give praise; praise the name of the LORD. Blessed be the name of the LORD now and for evermore. From the rising of the sun to its setting, may the LORD's name be praised. High is the LORD above all nations; His glory is above the heavens. Who is like the LORD our God, who sits enthroned so high, yet turns so low to see the heavens and the earth? ▸ He raises the poor from the dust and the needy from the refuse heap, giving them a place alongside princes, the princes of His people. He makes the woman in a childless house a happy mother of children. Halleluya! *Ps. 113*

בְּצֵאת When Israel came out of Egypt, the house of Jacob from a people of foreign tongue, Judah became His sanctuary, Israel His dominion. The sea saw and fled; the Jordan turned back. The mountains skipped like rams, the hills like lambs. ▸ Why was it, sea, that you fled? Jordan, why did you turn back? Why, mountains, did you skip like rams, and you, hills, like lambs? It was at the presence of the LORD, Creator of the earth, at the presence of the God of Jacob, who turned the rock into a pool of water, flint into a flowing spring. *Ps. 114*

לֹא לָנוּ Not to us, LORD, not to us, but to Your name give glory, for Your love, for Your faithfulness. Why should the nations say, "Where now is their God?" Our God is in heaven; whatever He wills He does. Their idols are silver and gold, made by human hands. They have mouths but cannot speak; eyes but cannot see. They have ears but cannot hear; noses but cannot smell. They have hands but cannot feel; feet but cannot walk. No sound comes from their throat. Those who make them become like them; so will all who trust in them. ▸ Israel, trust in the LORD – He is their Help and their Shield. House of Aaron, trust in the LORD – He is their Help and their Shield. You who fear the LORD, trust in the LORD – He is their Help and their Shield. *Ps. 115*

סדר הלל

בָּרוּךְ אַתָּה יהוה אֱלֹהֵינוּ מֶלֶךְ הָעוֹלָם
אֲשֶׁר קִדְּשָׁנוּ בְּמִצְוֹתָיו וְצִוָּנוּ לִקְרֹא אֶת הַהַלֵּל.

הַלְלוּיָהּ, הַלְלוּ עַבְדֵי יהוה, הַלְלוּ אֶת־שֵׁם יהוה: יְהִי שֵׁם יהוה תהלים קיג
מְבֹרָךְ, מֵעַתָּה וְעַד־עוֹלָם: מִמִּזְרַח־שֶׁמֶשׁ עַד־מְבוֹאוֹ, מְהֻלָּל שֵׁם
יהוה: רָם עַל־כָּל־גּוֹיִם יהוה, עַל הַשָּׁמַיִם כְּבוֹדוֹ: מִי כַּיהוה אֱלֹהֵינוּ,
הַמַּגְבִּיהִי לָשָׁבֶת: הַמַּשְׁפִּילִי לִרְאוֹת, בַּשָּׁמַיִם וּבָאָרֶץ: ◂ מְקִימִי
מֵעָפָר דָּל, מֵאַשְׁפֹּת יָרִים אֶבְיוֹן: לְהוֹשִׁיבִי עִם־נְדִיבִים, עִם נְדִיבֵי
עַמּוֹ: מוֹשִׁיבִי עֲקֶרֶת הַבַּיִת, אֵם־הַבָּנִים שְׂמֵחָה, הַלְלוּיָהּ:

בְּצֵאת יִשְׂרָאֵל מִמִּצְרָיִם, בֵּית יַעֲקֹב מֵעַם לֹעֵז: הָיְתָה יְהוּדָה תהלים קיד
לְקָדְשׁוֹ, יִשְׂרָאֵל מַמְשְׁלוֹתָיו: הַיָּם רָאָה וַיָּנֹס, הַיַּרְדֵּן יִסֹּב לְאָחוֹר:
הֶהָרִים רָקְדוּ כְאֵילִים, גְּבָעוֹת כִּבְנֵי־צֹאן: ◂ מַה־לְּךָ הַיָּם כִּי תָנוּס,
הַיַּרְדֵּן תִּסֹּב לְאָחוֹר: הֶהָרִים תִּרְקְדוּ כְאֵילִים, גְּבָעוֹת כִּבְנֵי־צֹאן:
מִלִּפְנֵי אָדוֹן חְוּלִי אָרֶץ, מִלִּפְנֵי אֱלוֹהַּ יַעֲקֹב: הַהֹפְכִי הַצּוּר אֲגַם־
מָיִם, חַלָּמִישׁ לְמַעְיְנוֹ־מָיִם:

לֹא לָנוּ יהוה לֹא לָנוּ, כִּי־לְשִׁמְךָ תֵּן כָּבוֹד, עַל־חַסְדְּךָ עַל־אֲמִתֶּךָ: תהלים קטו
לָמָּה יֹאמְרוּ הַגּוֹיִם אַיֵּה־נָא אֱלֹהֵיהֶם: וֵאלֹהֵינוּ בַשָּׁמָיִם, כֹּל אֲשֶׁר־
חָפֵץ עָשָׂה: עֲצַבֵּיהֶם כֶּסֶף וְזָהָב, מַעֲשֵׂה יְדֵי אָדָם: פֶּה־לָהֶם וְלֹא
יְדַבֵּרוּ, עֵינַיִם לָהֶם וְלֹא יִרְאוּ: אָזְנַיִם לָהֶם וְלֹא יִשְׁמָעוּ, אַף לָהֶם
וְלֹא יְרִיחוּן: יְדֵיהֶם וְלֹא יְמִישׁוּן, רַגְלֵיהֶם וְלֹא יְהַלֵּכוּ, לֹא־יֶהְגּוּ
בִּגְרוֹנָם: כְּמוֹהֶם יִהְיוּ עֹשֵׂיהֶם, כֹּל אֲשֶׁר־בֹּטֵחַ בָּהֶם: ◂ יִשְׂרָאֵל
בְּטַח בַּיהוה, עֶזְרָם וּמָגִנָּם הוּא: בֵּית אַהֲרֹן בִּטְחוּ בַיהוה, עֶזְרָם
וּמָגִנָּם הוּא: יִרְאֵי יהוה בִּטְחוּ בַיהוה, עֶזְרָם וּמָגִנָּם הוּא:

יהוה זְכָרָנוּ The Lord remembers us and will bless us. He will bless the house of Israel. He will bless the house of Aaron. He will bless those who fear the Lord, small and great alike. May the Lord give you increase: you and your children. May you be blessed by the Lord, Maker of heaven and earth. ▸ The heavens are the Lord's, but the earth He has given over to mankind. It is not the dead who praise the Lord, nor those who go down to the silent grave. But we will bless the Lord, now and for ever. Halleluya!

אָהַבְתִּי I love the Lord, for He hears my voice, my pleas. He turns His ear to me whenever I call. The bonds of death encompassed me, the anguish of the grave came upon me, I was overcome by trouble and sorrow. Then I called on the name of the Lord: "Lord, I pray, save my life." Gracious is the Lord, and righteous; our God is full of compassion. The Lord protects the simple hearted. When I was brought low, He saved me. My soul, be at peace once more, for the Lord has been good to you. For You have rescued me from death, my eyes from weeping, my feet from stumbling. ▸ I shall walk in the presence of the Lord in the land of the living. I had faith, even when I said, "I am greatly afflicted," even when I said rashly, "All men are liars." *Ps. 116*

מָה־אָשִׁיב How can I repay the Lord for all His goodness to me? I will lift the cup of salvation and call on the name of the Lord. I will fulfill my vows to the Lord in the presence of all His people. Grievous in the Lord's sight is the death of His devoted ones. Truly, Lord, I am Your servant; I am Your servant, the son of Your maidservant. You set me free from my chains. ▸ To You I shall bring a thanksgiving-offering and call on the Lord by name. I will fulfill my vows to the Lord in the presence of all His people, in the courts of the House of the Lord, in your midst, Jerusalem. Halleluya.

הַלְלוּ Praise the Lord, all nations; acclaim Him, all you peoples; *Ps. 117*
for His loving-kindness to us is strong,
and the Lord's faithfulness is everlasting.
Halleluya.

יהוה זְכָרָנוּ יְבָרֵךְ, יְבָרֵךְ אֶת־בֵּית יִשְׂרָאֵל, יְבָרֵךְ אֶת־בֵּית אַהֲרֹן: יְבָרֵךְ יִרְאֵי יהוה, הַקְּטַנִּים עִם־הַגְּדֹלִים: יֹסֵף יהוה עֲלֵיכֶם, עֲלֵיכֶם וְעַל־בְּנֵיכֶם: בְּרוּכִים אַתֶּם לַיהוה, עֹשֵׂה שָׁמַיִם וָאָרֶץ: ‹ הַשָּׁמַיִם שָׁמַיִם לַיהוה, וְהָאָרֶץ נָתַן לִבְנֵי־אָדָם: לֹא הַמֵּתִים יְהַלְלוּ־יָהּ, וְלֹא כָּל־יֹרְדֵי דוּמָה: וַאֲנַחְנוּ נְבָרֵךְ יָהּ, מֵעַתָּה וְעַד־עוֹלָם, הַלְלוּיָהּ:

תהלים קטז

אָהַבְתִּי, כִּי־יִשְׁמַע יהוה, אֶת־קוֹלִי תַּחֲנוּנָי: כִּי־הִטָּה אָזְנוֹ לִי, וּבְיָמַי אֶקְרָא: אֲפָפוּנִי חֶבְלֵי־מָוֶת, וּמְצָרֵי שְׁאוֹל מְצָאוּנִי, צָרָה וְיָגוֹן אֶמְצָא: וּבְשֵׁם־יהוה אֶקְרָא, אָנָּה יהוה מַלְּטָה נַפְשִׁי: חַנּוּן יהוה וְצַדִּיק, וֵאלֹהֵינוּ מְרַחֵם: שֹׁמֵר פְּתָאִים יהוה, דַּלּוֹתִי וְלִי יְהוֹשִׁיעַ: שׁוּבִי נַפְשִׁי לִמְנוּחָיְכִי, כִּי־יהוה גָּמַל עָלָיְכִי: כִּי חִלַּצְתָּ נַפְשִׁי מִמָּוֶת, אֶת־עֵינִי מִן־דִּמְעָה, אֶת־רַגְלִי מִדֶּחִי: ‹ אֶתְהַלֵּךְ לִפְנֵי יהוה, בְּאַרְצוֹת הַחַיִּים: הֶאֱמַנְתִּי כִּי אֲדַבֵּר, אֲנִי עָנִיתִי מְאֹד: אֲנִי אָמַרְתִּי בְחָפְזִי, כָּל־הָאָדָם כֹּזֵב:

מָה־אָשִׁיב לַיהוה, כָּל־תַּגְמוּלוֹהִי עָלָי: כּוֹס־יְשׁוּעוֹת אֶשָּׂא, וּבְשֵׁם יהוה אֶקְרָא: נְדָרַי לַיהוה אֲשַׁלֵּם, נֶגְדָה־נָּא לְכָל־עַמּוֹ: יָקָר בְּעֵינֵי יהוה, הַמָּוְתָה לַחֲסִידָיו: אָנָּה יהוה כִּי־אֲנִי עַבְדֶּךָ, אֲנִי־עַבְדְּךָ בֶּן־אֲמָתֶךָ, פִּתַּחְתָּ לְמוֹסֵרָי: ‹ לְךָ־אֶזְבַּח זֶבַח תּוֹדָה, וּבְשֵׁם יהוה אֶקְרָא: נְדָרַי לַיהוה אֲשַׁלֵּם, נֶגְדָה־נָּא לְכָל־עַמּוֹ: בְּחַצְרוֹת בֵּית יהוה, בְּתוֹכֵכִי יְרוּשָׁלָםִ, הַלְלוּיָהּ:

תהלים קיז

הַלְלוּ אֶת־יהוה כָּל־גּוֹיִם, שַׁבְּחוּהוּ כָּל־הָאֻמִּים:
כִּי גָבַר עָלֵינוּ חַסְדּוֹ, וֶאֱמֶת־יהוה לְעוֹלָם
הַלְלוּיָהּ:

The following verses are chanted by the Leader. At the end of each verse, the congregation responds, "Thank the LORD for He is good; His loving-kindness is for ever."

הודו Thank the LORD for He is good; His loving-kindness is for ever. *Ps. 118*
Let Israel say His loving-kindness is for ever.
Let the house of Aaron say His loving-kindness is for ever.
Let those who fear the LORD say His loving-kindness is for ever.

מִן־הַמֵּצַר In my distress I called on the LORD. The LORD answered me and set me free. The LORD is with me; I will not be afraid. What can man do to me? The LORD is with me. He is my Helper. I will see the downfall of my enemies. It is better to take refuge in the LORD than to trust in man. It is better to take refuge in the LORD than to trust in princes. The nations all surrounded me, but in the LORD's name I drove them off. They surrounded me on every side, but in the LORD's name I drove them off. They surrounded me like bees, they attacked me as fire attacks brushwood, but in the LORD's name I drove them off. They thrust so hard against me, I nearly fell, but the LORD came to my help. The LORD is my strength and my song; He has become my salvation. Sounds of song and salvation resound in the tents of the righteous: "The LORD's right hand has done mighty deeds. The LORD's right hand is lifted high. The LORD's right hand has done mighty deeds." I will not die but live, and tell what the LORD has done. The LORD has chastened me severely, but He has not given me over to death. ▸ Open for me the gates of righteousness that I may enter them and thank the LORD. This is the gateway to the LORD; through it, the righteous shall enter.

אוֹדְךָ I will thank You, for You answered me, and became my salvation.
I will thank You, for You answered me, and became my salvation.

The stone the builders rejected has become the main cornerstone.
The stone the builders rejected has become the main cornerstone.

This is the LORD's doing. It is wondrous in our eyes.
This is the LORD's doing. It is wondrous in our eyes.

This is the day the LORD has made. Let us rejoice and be glad in it.
This is the day the LORD has made. Let us rejoice and be glad in it.

The following verses are chanted by the שליח ציבור.
At the end of each verse, the קהל *responds:* הודו לַיהוה כִּי־טוֹב, כִּי לְעוֹלָם חַסְדּוֹ.

הוֹדוּ לַיהוה כִּי־טוֹב כִּי לְעוֹלָם חַסְדּוֹ: תהלים קיח
יֹאמַר־נָא יִשְׂרָאֵל כִּי לְעוֹלָם חַסְדּוֹ:
יֹאמְרוּ־נָא בֵית־אַהֲרֹן כִּי לְעוֹלָם חַסְדּוֹ:
יֹאמְרוּ־נָא יִרְאֵי יהוה כִּי לְעוֹלָם חַסְדּוֹ:

מִן־הַמֵּצַר קָרָאתִי יָּהּ, עָנָנִי בַמֶּרְחָב יָהּ: יהוה לִי לֹא אִירָא, מַה־יַּעֲשֶׂה לִי אָדָם: יהוה לִי בְּעֹזְרָי, וַאֲנִי אֶרְאֶה בְשֹׂנְאָי: טוֹב לַחֲסוֹת בַּיהוה, מִבְּטֹחַ בָּאָדָם: טוֹב לַחֲסוֹת בַּיהוה, מִבְּטֹחַ בִּנְדִיבִים: כָּל־גּוֹיִם סְבָבוּנִי, בְּשֵׁם יהוה כִּי אֲמִילַם: סַבּוּנִי גַם־סְבָבוּנִי, בְּשֵׁם יהוה כִּי אֲמִילַם: סַבּוּנִי כִדְבֹרִים, דֹּעֲכוּ כְּאֵשׁ קוֹצִים, בְּשֵׁם יהוה כִּי אֲמִילַם: דָּחֹה דְחִיתַנִי לִנְפֹּל, וַיהוה עֲזָרָנִי: עָזִּי וְזִמְרָת יָהּ, וַיְהִי־לִי לִישׁוּעָה: קוֹל רִנָּה וִישׁוּעָה בְּאָהֳלֵי צַדִּיקִים, יְמִין יהוה עֹשָׂה חָיִל: יְמִין יהוה רוֹמֵמָה, יְמִין יהוה עֹשָׂה חָיִל: לֹא־אָמוּת כִּי־אֶחְיֶה, וַאֲסַפֵּר מַעֲשֵׂי יָהּ: יַסֹּר יִסְּרַנִּי יָּהּ, וְלַמָּוֶת לֹא נְתָנָנִי: ‹ פִּתְחוּ־לִי שַׁעֲרֵי־צֶדֶק, אָבֹא־בָם אוֹדֶה יָהּ: זֶה־הַשַּׁעַר לַיהוה, צַדִּיקִים יָבֹאוּ בוֹ:

אוֹדְךָ כִּי עֲנִיתָנִי, וַתְּהִי־לִי לִישׁוּעָה:
אוֹדְךָ כִּי עֲנִיתָנִי, וַתְּהִי־לִי לִישׁוּעָה:

אֶבֶן מָאֲסוּ הַבּוֹנִים, הָיְתָה לְרֹאשׁ פִּנָּה:
אֶבֶן מָאֲסוּ הַבּוֹנִים, הָיְתָה לְרֹאשׁ פִּנָּה:

מֵאֵת יהוה הָיְתָה זֹּאת, הִיא נִפְלָאת בְּעֵינֵינוּ:
מֵאֵת יהוה הָיְתָה זֹּאת, הִיא נִפְלָאת בְּעֵינֵינוּ:

זֶה־הַיּוֹם עָשָׂה יהוה, נָגִילָה וְנִשְׂמְחָה בוֹ:
זֶה־הַיּוֹם עָשָׂה יהוה, נָגִילָה וְנִשְׂמְחָה בוֹ:

Leader followed by congregation:

אָנָּא LORD, please, save us.
LORD, please, save us.
LORD, please, grant us success.
LORD, please, grant us success.

בָּרוּךְ Blessed is one who comes in the name of the LORD;
we bless you from the House of the LORD.
Blessed is one who comes in the name of the LORD;
we bless you from the House of the LORD.

The LORD is God; He has given us light. Bind the festival offering with thick cords [and bring it] to the horns of the altar.
The LORD is God; He has given us light. Bind the festival offering with thick cords [and bring it] to the horns of the altar.

You are my God and I will thank You; You are my God, I will exalt You.
You are my God and I will thank You; You are my God, I will exalt You.

Thank the LORD for He is good; His loving-kindness is for ever.
Thank the LORD for He is good; His loving-kindness is for ever.

יְהַלְלוּךָ All Your works will praise You, LORD our God,
and Your devoted ones – the righteous who do Your will,
together with all Your people the house of Israel –
will joyously thank, bless, praise, glorify, exalt, revere, sanctify,
and proclaim the sovereignty of Your name, our King.
▸ For it is good to thank You
and fitting to sing psalms to Your name,
for from eternity to eternity You are God.
Blessed are You, LORD,
King who is extolled with praises.

Some say at this point Hoshanot on page 916, then Full Kaddish.

followed by שליח ציבור קהל:

אָנָּא יהוה הוֹשִׁיעָה נָּא:
אָנָּא יהוה הוֹשִׁיעָה נָּא:
אָנָּא יהוה הַצְלִיחָה נָא:
אָנָּא יהוה הַצְלִיחָה נָא:

בָּרוּךְ הַבָּא בְּשֵׁם יהוה, בֵּרַכְנוּכֶם מִבֵּית יהוה:
בָּרוּךְ הַבָּא בְּשֵׁם יהוה, בֵּרַכְנוּכֶם מִבֵּית יהוה:

אֵל יהוה וַיָּאֶר לָנוּ, אִסְרוּ־חַג בַּעֲבֹתִים עַד־קַרְנוֹת הַמִּזְבֵּחַ:
אֵל יהוה וַיָּאֶר לָנוּ, אִסְרוּ־חַג בַּעֲבֹתִים עַד־קַרְנוֹת הַמִּזְבֵּחַ:

אֵלִי אַתָּה וְאוֹדֶךָּ, אֱלֹהַי אֲרוֹמְמֶךָּ:
אֵלִי אַתָּה וְאוֹדֶךָּ, אֱלֹהַי אֲרוֹמְמֶךָּ:

הוֹדוּ לַיהוה כִּי־טוֹב, כִּי לְעוֹלָם חַסְדּוֹ:
הוֹדוּ לַיהוה כִּי־טוֹב, כִּי לְעוֹלָם חַסְדּוֹ:

יְהַלְלְוּךָ יהוה אֱלֹהֵינוּ כָּל מַעֲשֶׂיךָ
וַחֲסִידֶיךָ צַדִּיקִים עוֹשֵׂי רְצוֹנֶךָ
וְכָל עַמְּךָ בֵּית יִשְׂרָאֵל בְּרִנָּה יוֹדוּ וִיבָרְכוּ וִישַׁבְּחוּ וִיפָאֲרוּ
וִירוֹמְמוּ וְיַעֲרִיצוּ וְיַקְדִּישׁוּ וְיַמְלִיכוּ אֶת שִׁמְךָ מַלְכֵּנוּ
◂ כִּי לְךָ טוֹב לְהוֹדוֹת וּלְשִׁמְךָ נָאֶה לְזַמֵּר
כִּי מֵעוֹלָם וְעַד עוֹלָם אַתָּה אֵל.
בָּרוּךְ אַתָּה יהוה, מֶלֶךְ מְהֻלָּל בַּתִּשְׁבָּחוֹת.

Some say at this point הושענות *on page 917, then* קדיש שלם.

FULL KADDISH

Some have the custom to include additional responses in Full Kaddish. They can be found in the version on page 1464.

Leader: יִתְגַּדַּל Magnified and sanctified may His great name be,
in the world He created by His will.
May He establish His kingdom
in your lifetime and in your days,
and in the lifetime of all the house of Israel,
swiftly and soon –
and say: Amen.

All: May His great name be blessed
for ever and all time.

Leader: Blessed and praised,
glorified and exalted,
raised and honored,
uplifted and lauded be
the name of the Holy One,
blessed be He,
beyond any blessing,
song, praise and consolation
uttered in the world –
and say: Amen.

May the prayers and pleas of all Israel
be accepted by their Father in heaven –
and say: Amen.

May there be great peace from heaven,
and life for us and all Israel –
and say: Amen.

Bow, take three steps back, as if taking leave of the Divine Presence, then bow, first left, then right, then center, while saying:

May He who makes peace in His high places,
make peace for us and all Israel –
and say: Amen.

קדיש שלם

Some have the custom to include additional responses in קדיש שלם*. They can be found in the version on page 1465.*

ש״ץ: יִתְגַּדַּל וְיִתְקַדַּשׁ שְׁמֵהּ רַבָּא (קהל: אָמֵן)
בְּעָלְמָא דִּי בְרָא כִרְעוּתֵהּ
וְיַמְלִיךְ מַלְכוּתֵהּ
בְּחַיֵּיכוֹן וּבְיוֹמֵיכוֹן וּבְחַיֵּי דְכָל בֵּית יִשְׂרָאֵל
בַּעֲגָלָא וּבִזְמַן קָרִיב
וְאִמְרוּ אָמֵן. (קהל: אָמֵן)

קהל וש״ץ: יְהֵא שְׁמֵהּ רַבָּא מְבָרַךְ לְעָלַם וּלְעָלְמֵי עָלְמַיָּא.

ש״ץ: יִתְבָּרַךְ וְיִשְׁתַּבַּח וְיִתְפָּאַר
וְיִתְרוֹמַם וְיִתְנַשֵּׂא וְיִתְהַדָּר וְיִתְעַלֶּה וְיִתְהַלָּל
שְׁמֵהּ דְּקֻדְשָׁא בְּרִיךְ הוּא (קהל: בְּרִיךְ הוּא)
לְעֵלָּא מִן כָּל בִּרְכָתָא וְשִׁירָתָא, תֻּשְׁבְּחָתָא וְנֶחֱמָתָא
דַּאֲמִירָן בְּעָלְמָא
וְאִמְרוּ אָמֵן. (קהל: אָמֵן)

תִּתְקַבַּל צְלוֹתְהוֹן וּבָעוּתְהוֹן דְּכָל יִשְׂרָאֵל
קֳדָם אֲבוּהוֹן דִּי בִשְׁמַיָּא
וְאִמְרוּ אָמֵן. (קהל: אָמֵן)

יְהֵא שְׁלָמָא רַבָּא מִן שְׁמַיָּא
וְחַיִּים, עָלֵינוּ וְעַל כָּל יִשְׂרָאֵל
וְאִמְרוּ אָמֵן. (קהל: אָמֵן)

Bow, take three steps back, as if taking leave of the Divine Presence, then bow, first left, then right, then center, while saying:

עֹשֶׂה שָׁלוֹם בִּמְרוֹמָיו
הוּא יַעֲשֶׂה שָׁלוֹם עָלֵינוּ וְעַל כָּל יִשְׂרָאֵל
וְאִמְרוּ אָמֵן. (קהל: אָמֵן)

Kohelet / Ecclesiastes

On Shabbat, Ecclesiastes is read at this point. If the first day of Sukkot and Shemini Atzeret fall on Shabbat, Ecclesiastes is read on Shemini Atzeret (In Israel on the first day of Sukkot).

1 The sayings of Kohelet son of David, King of Israel in Jerusalem:
Shallowest breath, said Kohelet; the shallowest breath, it is all but

---

It is the delight in knowing that we are here by God's grace, living, breathing, experiencing, celebrating. To feel joy you need neither wealth nor power. Joy is born in love, work, and thanksgiving. Life may be a mere breath, but it is the breath of God. Kohelet, like Sukkot, is about joy in the midst of temporariness and vulnerability.

Third, just as Sukkot is the most universalist of the three pilgrim festivals, so Kohelet is the most universalist of books. The word God appears no less than 42 times, but always as *Elokim*, God in His universality as Creator and Source of wisdom, never as *Hashem*, the God of revelation and particularity. The word *adam*, "man," appears 49 times, "Israel" only once ("I, Kohelet, was king of Israel in Jerusalem"). The specificity of Judaism and the Jewish people plays no part in the text.

Kohelet is supremely a book of wisdom – *ḥ-kh-m*, "wise," in one or other form, appears 53 times – and wisdom is universal ("If they tell you there is wisdom among the nations, believe it," *Eikha Raba* 2:13). There is nothing here about the Torah of the priest or the divine word of the prophet, Judaism's particularities. But Kohelet is also about the limits of wisdom. It is better to be wise than to be a fool. But the more wisdom the more pain, and the more aware we become of our limitations.

Kohelet is an exploration of how much it is possible to discover by wisdom alone, without revelation. His answer is much about how the world *is* "under the sun," but little about how it ought to be. The conclusion "Fear God, and keep His commandments: for this is the whole of man" is not a pious afterthought, but rather the conclusion to which Kohelet has been tending all along. Reason without revelation ends in a tragic sense of life: stoicism, Epicureanism, cynicism, skepticism, even nihilism. Kohelet is a deeply religious book, driven by the author's sense of sadness that he has spent much of his life in pursuit of the wrong things. His saving grace is candor. The conclusion is poignant: Kohelet sought to find *divrei ḥefetz*, "pleasing words" (translated here as "choicest words"), but in the end felt forced to write "words of truth honestly" (12:10).

God has placed "eternity in our minds" (3:11). The universe is almost

קהלת

On שבת, קהלת *is read at this point. If the first day of* סוכות *and* שמיני עצרת *fall on* שבת, קהלת *is read on* שמיני עצרת (*in* ארץ ישראל *on the first day of* סוכות).

א דִּבְרֵי֙ קֹהֶ֣לֶת בֶּן־דָּוִ֔ד מֶ֖לֶךְ בִּירוּשָׁלָֽ͏ִם׃ הֲבֵ֤ל הֲבָלִים֙ אָמַ֣ר קֹהֶ֔לֶת

KOHELET

For an essay on Kohelet, see Introduction, page xxxi.

Kohelet is a difficult, disturbing book, until one places it in the context of Sukkot, at which point the interpretive difficulties fade away. It is about three themes, each of which is also a theme of the festival.

First, it is about vulnerability and temporariness. Living in a Sukka means exposure to the elements, the wind, the rain and the night-time cold. The definition of a Sukka is that it is a *dirat arai*, a temporary dwelling (*Sukka* 2a). For Kohelet, that is precisely the shape of a human life.

The key word Kohelet uses to drive the point home is *hevel*, which appears thirty-seven times in the book, five in the second verse alone. It has been translated as "meaningless," "futile," "empty," "pointless," and "vanity," but it literally means "a shallow breath." That, says Kohelet, is all a human life is: a fleeting breath, a microsecond, set against the long history of the universe. Breath is all that separates us from death. The human body is no more than a Sukka, a temporary dwelling. Kohelet is obsessed by this. For him it threatened to rob life of all meaning.

He sought to make himself invulnerable by the pursuit of wealth, possessions, power, pleasure and wisdom. He discovered, though, that none of these brings immunity to the ravages of time. *Et in Arcadia ego*: even in a this-worldly paradise, death is there. We are temporary dwellers here on earth.

Second, and surprisingly, Kohelet is about the key word of Sukkot, namely *simha*, "joy." The word, in one or other of its forms, appears seventeen times in the book – more than in all five Mosaic books combined. After every gloomy meditation, Kohelet ends with an injunction to rejoice. This happens seven times in the book, followed by an extended eighth that forms the closing crescendo beginning, "Young man, rejoice now in your youth" (11:9). The structure of the text, in other words, mirrors that of Sukkot itself: seven days of joy followed by the eighth of Shemini Atzeret.

Kohelet is not about happiness. The word appears only once and in an impersonal context (10:17, "Happy is the land"). Happiness has to do with life as a whole. Joy means celebrating the moment, knowing it will not last.

breath. What profit remains of all the labor one toils over beneath the sun? One age departs, another comes; the earth stands still forever. The sun rises, the sun sets. It heaves towards its place, and there it rises. Blowing south, turning north, turning then turning blows the wind, and back upon its turnings, the wind returns. All streams flow into the sea. The sea is still not full. Into the place where the streams flow, they turn to flow again. Everything is tiresome. One can say nothing, the eye can never see enough, the ear is never filled with hearing. What is to be – is what has been already, what is to be done is what is done, and there is nothing new at all beneath the sun. Something may make a person say, "Look at this: new!" – It has been here already, in all the eternities that came before us. The earliest left no memory behind; and those who are to come will still leave no memorial with the last ones who will be.

I, Kohelet, was king of Israel in Jerusalem. And I gave my mind over to searching and exploring with Wisdom, all that is done beneath the

---

dedication took place on Sukkot (Netziv suggests that the teachings of Kohelet were delivered that day).

Third, Solomon's Temple itself was a replacement for the *Mishkan*, the portable Tabernacle that accompanied the Israelites during their journeys through the desert. The passage in which Moses instructed the people about the sanctuary begins with the word *Vayak-hel*, "and Moses assembled," again from the same root as Kohelet. Moses issued this command on the day after Yom Kippur (see Rashi on Ex. 35:1), the day when, according to custom, we begin building the Sukka. "Kohelet" therefore has multiple associations with Sukkot, Solomon, Tabernacle, Temple, and the idea of a king teaching wisdom to the people.

הֲבֵל הֲבָלִים *Shallowest breath (Previous page).* A sustained contrast between the seeming eternity of the universe and the brevity of a human life. What difference do we, can we, make when we are here so briefly? The repetition of the word *hevel*, shallow breath, mirrors Kohelet's description of the repetitiveness of time itself.

אֲנִי קֹהֶלֶת הָיִיתִי מֶלֶךְ עַל־יִשְׂרָאֵל *I, Kohelet, was king of Israel.* This is the beginning of Kohelet's autobiographical account of how he sought meaning, first

הֲבֵל הֲבָלִים הַכֹּל הָבֶל׃ מַה־יִּתְרוֹן לָאָדָם בְּכָל־עֲמָלוֹ שֶׁיַּעֲמֹל
תַּחַת הַשָּׁמֶשׁ׃ דּוֹר הֹלֵךְ וְדוֹר בָּא וְהָאָרֶץ לְעוֹלָם עֹמָדֶת׃
וְזָרַח הַשֶּׁמֶשׁ וּבָא הַשָּׁמֶשׁ וְאֶל־מְקוֹמוֹ שׁוֹאֵף זוֹרֵחַ הוּא שָׁם׃
הוֹלֵךְ אֶל־דָּרוֹם וְסוֹבֵב אֶל־צָפוֹן סוֹבֵב ׀ סֹבֵב הוֹלֵךְ הָרוּחַ
וְעַל־סְבִיבֹתָיו שָׁב הָרוּחַ׃ כָּל־הַנְּחָלִים הֹלְכִים אֶל־הַיָּם וְהַיָּם
אֵינֶנּוּ מָלֵא אֶל־מְקוֹם שֶׁהַנְּחָלִים הֹלְכִים שָׁם הֵם שָׁבִים לָלָכֶת׃
כָּל־הַדְּבָרִים יְגֵעִים לֹא־יוּכַל אִישׁ לְדַבֵּר לֹא־תִשְׂבַּע עַיִן לִרְאוֹת
וְלֹא־תִמָּלֵא אֹזֶן מִשְּׁמֹעַ׃ מַה־שֶּׁהָיָה הוּא שֶׁיִּהְיֶה וּמַה־שֶּׁנַּעֲשָׂה
הוּא שֶׁיֵּעָשֶׂה וְאֵין כָּל־חָדָשׁ תַּחַת הַשָּׁמֶשׁ׃ יֵשׁ דָּבָר שֶׁיֹּאמַר
רְאֵה־זֶה חָדָשׁ הוּא כְּבָר הָיָה לְעֹלָמִים אֲשֶׁר הָיָה מִלְּפָנֵנוּ׃ אֵין
זִכְרוֹן לָרִאשֹׁנִים וְגַם לָאַחֲרֹנִים שֶׁיִּהְיוּ לֹא־יִהְיֶה לָהֶם זִכָּרוֹן עִם
שֶׁיִּהְיוּ לָאַחֲרֹנָה׃
אֲנִי קֹהֶלֶת הָיִיתִי מֶלֶךְ עַל־יִשְׂרָאֵל בִּירוּשָׁלָםִ׃ וְנָתַתִּי אֶת־לִבִּי
לִדְרוֹשׁ וְלָתוּר בַּחָכְמָה עַל כָּל־אֲשֶׁר נַעֲשָׂה תַּחַת הַשָּׁמָיִם

---

infinitely vast, while we are almost infinitesimally small. Yet we can experience eternity, not by living forever, but by living in the moment, encountering God in the here-and-nowness of time, loving for the sake of love, working for the sake of honest toil, seeking wisdom for the sake of wisdom, and knowing that though we are physically the quintessence of dust, there is within us the breath of God.

דִּבְרֵי קֹהֶלֶת *Kohelet (Previous page).* From the root ק-ה-ל, meaning "gather, convene, assemble." The word is not found elsewhere in Tanakh, but it has three resonances with Sukkot. First, it recalls the commandment that on Sukkot at the end of a sabbatical year the king was to convene a national assembly and read to the people from the Torah (Abudarham, based on Deut. 31:10–13). The command is known as *Hak-hel,* from the same Hebrew root as Kohelet.

Second, it recalls the dedication by King Solomon of the Temple, in the narrative of which (1 Kings 8) the root ק-ה-ל appears seven times. The

sky. A wretched occupation, this, given by God to mortal man, with
which to be oppressed. I saw everything that is done beneath the
sun. It is nothing but fleeting breath, but courting the wind. What is
crooked can never be straightened; what is lost can never be counted.
I said to my mind, I have built up and gathered more wisdom than
anyone who has ruled over Jerusalem before, and my mind has seen
much wisdom and insight. And I gave my mind over to understand
wisdom; and to understand delirium and folly. I know that too is but
courting the wind. For in great wisdom lies great bitterness; and one
who gathers insight gathers pain.

2 I said to my mind, Come, let me try you with joy, come and see
good living. I found that too to be but shallow breath. Delirium, I
called laughter; told joy, What comes of this? And so I explored on,
through my mind, steeping my body in wine, and my mind at the
helm remained wise – that I might catch hold of folly, and finally
see what is good for mortal man to do beneath the sky, for as long
as he should live. I amassed a great estate. I built myself houses,
planted for myself vineyards, acquired for myself gardens and
orchards and planted them with every kind of fruit tree. I ordered
for myself pools of water, to irrigate a forest burgeoning forth with
trees. I bought slaves and maidservants, and others were born in
my house; I had livestock also, cattle and flock, more than anyone
else who came before me in Jerusalem. I collected silver and gold,

---

of the universe lies outside the universe. By worshipping a transcendental God, Judaism invests life with meaning. But this cannot be achieved by "wisdom" alone, focusing exclusively on what is "beneath the sun" or "beneath the sky." Purely philosophical speculation always ends with a "tragic sense of life."

הִגְדַּלְתִּי מַעֲשָׂי *I amassed a great estate.* The Hebrew text uses the first person singular in this passage more than anywhere else in Tanakh, and with a double emphasis: "I built, planted, acquired *for myself*." Kohelet is here hinting why the pursuit of pleasure ultimately fails. It is self-centered rather than other-centered. Therefore it merely locks us more tightly in the narrow world of the ego, the smallest, yet strongest, of prisons.

הוּא ׀ עִנְיַן רָע נָתַן אֱלֹהִים לִבְנֵי הָאָדָם לַעֲנוֹת בּוֹ׃ רָאִיתִי אֶת־
כָּל־הַמַּעֲשִׂים שֶׁנַּעֲשׂוּ תַּחַת הַשָּׁמֶשׁ וְהִנֵּה הַכֹּל הֶבֶל וּרְעוּת
רוּחַ׃ מְעֻוָּת לֹא־יוּכַל לִתְקֹן וְחֶסְרוֹן לֹא־יוּכַל לְהִמָּנוֹת׃ דִּבַּרְתִּי
אֲנִי עִם־לִבִּי לֵאמֹר אֲנִי הִנֵּה הִגְדַּלְתִּי וְהוֹסַפְתִּי חָכְמָה עַל כָּל־
אֲשֶׁר־הָיָה לְפָנַי עַל־יְרוּשָׁלִָם וְלִבִּי רָאָה הַרְבֵּה חָכְמָה וָדָעַת׃
וָאֶתְּנָה לִבִּי לָדַעַת חָכְמָה וְדַעַת הֹלֵלוֹת וְשִׂכְלוּת יָדַעְתִּי שֶׁגַּם־
זֶה הוּא רַעְיוֹן רוּחַ׃ כִּי בְּרֹב חָכְמָה רָב־כָּעַס וְיוֹסִיף דַּעַת יוֹסִיף
ב מַכְאוֹב׃ אָמַרְתִּי אֲנִי בְּלִבִּי לְכָה־נָּא אֲנַסְּכָה בְשִׂמְחָה וּרְאֵה בְטוֹב
וְהִנֵּה גַם־הוּא הָבֶל׃ לִשְׂחוֹק אָמַרְתִּי מְהוֹלָל וּלְשִׂמְחָה מַה־זֹּה
עֹשָׂה׃ תַּרְתִּי בְלִבִּי לִמְשׁוֹךְ בַּיַּיִן אֶת־בְּשָׂרִי וְלִבִּי נֹהֵג בַּחָכְמָה
וְלֶאֱחֹז בְּסִכְלוּת עַד אֲשֶׁר־אֶרְאֶה אֵי־זֶה טוֹב לִבְנֵי הָאָדָם אֲשֶׁר
יַעֲשׂוּ תַּחַת הַשָּׁמַיִם מִסְפַּר יְמֵי חַיֵּיהֶם׃ הִגְדַּלְתִּי מַעֲשָׂי בָּנִיתִי
לִי בָּתִּים נָטַעְתִּי לִי כְּרָמִים׃ עָשִׂיתִי לִי גַּנּוֹת וּפַרְדֵּסִים וְנָטַעְתִּי
בָהֶם עֵץ כָּל־פֶּרִי׃ עָשִׂיתִי לִי בְּרֵכוֹת מָיִם לְהַשְׁקוֹת מֵהֶם יַעַר
צוֹמֵחַ עֵצִים׃ קָנִיתִי עֲבָדִים וּשְׁפָחוֹת וּבְנֵי־בַיִת הָיָה לִי גַּם מִקְנֶה
בָקָר וָצֹאן הַרְבֵּה הָיָה לִי מִכֹּל שֶׁהָיוּ לְפָנַי בִּירוּשָׁלִָם׃ כָּנַסְתִּי

---

in wisdom, then pleasure, then wealth and possessions, but failed to find it. The more we understand, the more we know how little we understand. The more we pursue pleasure, the duller it becomes. "The more posessions, the more worries" (*Avot* 2:8). Hence the surprising fact that Kohelet, a book of wisdom, is at the same time a critique of wisdom.

רַעְיוֹן רוּחַ *Courting the wind.* Wisdom, *ḥokhma,* refers to the truths we discover by observation and reflection, as opposed to those we receive through revelation and tradition. Kohelet now realizes that wisdom constantly strives for something that always eludes it. It seeks truth that is demonstrable, provable, and at the same time capable of investing life with meaning. There is no such thing. The meaning of a system lies outside the system. The meaning

and the treasures of kings and provinces; I called for singers, male and female, and all the delights of mankind, took women, many women.

I grew great and gathered more than anyone who had come before me in Jerusalem, and my wisdom too stood by me. I withheld from my eyes nothing that they sought after. I did not withhold any joy from myself. For my mind rejoiced in the fruits of my labor; and that was my share for all my toil. And then I turned to look at all my works, at the work of my hands, at all that I had labored to achieve – and this is what I saw: it is nothing but fleeting breath, but courting the wind, and there is no true profit beneath the sun. And I turned to look at wisdom and delirium and folly; for who is the man who will come after the king, when he has done what he has done? And I saw that there is some advantage to wisdom over foolishness, like the advantage of light over darkness. For the wise man has eyes in his head, while the fool walks in darkness; and still I know: the same fate awaits them both.

I said to myself, the fate of the fool awaits me also; why then should I be wiser? And I told myself that this too is empty breath. For the wise man, like the fool, leaves no memory forever. As soon as the coming days arrive, all are forgotten. How can it be that the wise man dies like the fool? I hated life; this work that is done beneath the sun is evil to me. Nothing but fleeting breath, but courting the wind.

And I hated all the toil of my labor beneath the sun; all to be left to one who will come after me. Who knows whether he will be wise or a fool; but he will lord over all that labor, over all that I toiled for wisely beneath the sun; making that too as empty as breath. And I turned to despair over all the labor I had toiled over beneath the sun. For so often one

---

that the opposite of a superficial truth is a falsehood, while the opposite of a profound truth may be another profound truth (Niels Bohr). In this case the conflict is resolved by asking of any labor, not what do I achieve by it, but what do I become through it. "It is good to combine Torah study with a worldly occupation, for the effort involved in both makes one forget sin. Torah study without an occupation will in the end fail and lead to sin" (*Avot* 2:2).

לִי גַּם־כֶּסֶף וְזָהָב וּסְגֻלַּת מְלָכִים וְהַמְּדִינוֹת עָשִׂיתִי לִי שָׁרִים
וְשָׁרוֹת וְתַעֲנוּגֹת בְּנֵי הָאָדָם שִׁדָּה וְשִׁדּוֹת׃ וְגָדַלְתִּי וְהוֹסַפְתִּי
מִכֹּל שֶׁהָיָה לְפָנַי בִּירוּשָׁלִָם אַף חָכְמָתִי עָמְדָה לִּי׃ וְכֹל אֲשֶׁר
שָׁאֲלוּ עֵינַי לֹא אָצַלְתִּי מֵהֶם לֹא־מָנַעְתִּי אֶת־לִבִּי מִכָּל־שִׂמְחָה
כִּי־לִבִּי שָׂמֵחַ מִכָּל־עֲמָלִי וְזֶה־הָיָה חֶלְקִי מִכָּל־עֲמָלִי׃ וּפָנִיתִי
אֲנִי בְּכָל־מַעֲשַׂי שֶׁעָשׂוּ יָדַי וּבֶעָמָל שֶׁעָמַלְתִּי לַעֲשׂוֹת וְהִנֵּה
הַכֹּל הֶבֶל וּרְעוּת רוּחַ וְאֵין יִתְרוֹן תַּחַת הַשָּׁמֶשׁ׃ וּפָנִיתִי אֲנִי
לִרְאוֹת חָכְמָה וְהוֹלֵלוֹת וְסִכְלוּת כִּי ׀ מֶה הָאָדָם שֶׁיָּבוֹא אַחֲרֵי
הַמֶּלֶךְ אֵת אֲשֶׁר־כְּבָר עָשׂוּהוּ׃ וְרָאִיתִי אָנִי שֶׁיֵּשׁ יִתְרוֹן לַחָכְמָה
מִן־הַסִּכְלוּת כִּיתְרוֹן הָאוֹר מִן־הַחֹשֶׁךְ׃ הֶחָכָם עֵינָיו בְּרֹאשׁוֹ
וְהַכְּסִיל בַּחֹשֶׁךְ הוֹלֵךְ וְיָדַעְתִּי גַם־אָנִי שֶׁמִּקְרֶה אֶחָד יִקְרֶה אֶת־
כֻּלָּם׃ וְאָמַרְתִּי אֲנִי בְּלִבִּי כְּמִקְרֵה הַכְּסִיל גַּם־אֲנִי יִקְרֵנִי וְלָמָּה
חָכַמְתִּי אֲנִי אָז יוֹתֵר וְדִבַּרְתִּי בְלִבִּי שֶׁגַּם־זֶה הָבֶל׃ כִּי אֵין זִכְרוֹן
לֶחָכָם עִם־הַכְּסִיל לְעוֹלָם בְּשֶׁכְּבָר הַיָּמִים הַבָּאִים הַכֹּל נִשְׁכָּח
וְאֵיךְ יָמוּת הֶחָכָם עִם־הַכְּסִיל׃ וְשָׂנֵאתִי אֶת־הַחַיִּים כִּי רַע עָלַי
הַמַּעֲשֶׂה שֶׁנַּעֲשָׂה תַּחַת הַשָּׁמֶשׁ כִּי־הַכֹּל הֶבֶל וּרְעוּת רוּחַ׃
וְשָׂנֵאתִי אֲנִי אֶת־כָּל־עֲמָלִי שֶׁאֲנִי עָמֵל תַּחַת הַשָּׁמֶשׁ שֶׁאַנִּיחֶנּוּ
לָאָדָם שֶׁיִּהְיֶה אַחֲרָי׃ וּמִי יוֹדֵעַ הֶחָכָם יִהְיֶה אוֹ סָכָל וְיִשְׁלַט בְּכָל־
עֲמָלִי שֶׁעָמַלְתִּי וְשֶׁחָכַמְתִּי תַּחַת הַשָּׁמֶשׁ גַּם־זֶה הָבֶל׃ וְסַבּוֹתִי
אֲנִי לְיַאֵשׁ אֶת־לִבִּי עַל כָּל־הֶעָמָל שֶׁעָמַלְתִּי תַּחַת הַשָּׁמֶשׁ׃

וְשָׂנֵאתִי אֲנִי אֶת־כָּל־עֲמָלִי *And I hated all the toil of my labor.* This is the first part of one of the many seeming contradictions in the book. Later, Kohelet seems to say the opposite: "The sleep of a worker is sweet" (5:11). The use of contradiction and paradox is one of Kohelet's literary devices. He knows

labors with wisdom and insight and skill – and then gives all his share to one who has not labored; this too is empty as breath, and a great evil. For what remains to one of all the labor and of all one's mind's pursuits, for which one has toiled beneath the sky? All your days are pain, your occupation bitterness, and even at night your mind does not rest, and this too is empty breath.

There is no good for man to find, but that he eat and drink and show himself some good of all his labor; this I saw to be a gift from God. For who will eat, who will hasten after my craving if not I? He gave wisdom and insight and joy to those who are satisfied with what they have; and to sinners He gave a preoccupation with gathering and collecting, only to give it all to the one who pleases God. This too is shallow breath; but courting the wind.

3 Everything has its moment; a time for every deed beneath the sky.
A time for birth, a time for death;
a time to plant and a time to uproot what is planted.
A time to kill, a time to heal;
a time to tear down and a time to build up.
A time to weep, a time to laugh;
a time for eulogy and a time for dance.
A time to cast away stones, a time to gather up stones;
a time to embrace and a time to hold back from embracing.

---

sages in literature. Though time is endless and cyclical, it is not all the same. Different times call for different responses. Wisdom consists in knowing the appropriate response to a specific moment.

עֵת לָלֶדֶת *A time for birth.* Usually translated, "to be born," but the *kal* form of the verb always means "to give birth" rather than the passive, to be born.

עֵת לִבְכּוֹת *A time to weep.* Rashi relates this to Tisha B'Av, when we remember the destruction of the two Temples as well as many other tragedies in Jewish history.

וְעֵת לִשְׂחוֹק *A time to laugh.* refers, for Rashi, to "the time to come" when humanly inflicted tragedy will be at an end and we learn to live in peace.

כִּי־יֵשׁ אָדָם שֶׁעֲמָלוֹ בְּחָכְמָה וּבְדַעַת וּבְכִשְׁרוֹן וּלְאָדָם שֶׁלֹּא
עָמַל־בּוֹ יִתְּנֶנּוּ חֶלְקוֹ גַּם־זֶה הֶבֶל וְרָעָה רַבָּה: כִּי מֶה־הֹוֶה לָאָדָם
בְּכָל־עֲמָלוֹ וּבְרַעְיוֹן לִבּוֹ שֶׁהוּא עָמֵל תַּחַת הַשָּׁמֶשׁ: כִּי כָל־יָמָיו
מַכְאֹבִים וָכַעַס עִנְיָנוֹ גַּם־בַּלַּיְלָה לֹא־שָׁכַב לִבּוֹ גַּם־זֶה הֶבֶל הוּא:
אֵין־טוֹב בָּאָדָם שֶׁיֹּאכַל וְשָׁתָה וְהֶרְאָה אֶת־נַפְשׁוֹ טוֹב בַּעֲמָלוֹ
גַּם־זֹה רָאִיתִי אָנִי כִּי מִיַּד הָאֱלֹהִים הִיא: כִּי מִי יֹאכַל וּמִי יָחוּשׁ
חוּץ מִמֶּנִּי: כִּי לְאָדָם שֶׁטּוֹב לְפָנָיו נָתַן חָכְמָה וְדַעַת וְשִׂמְחָה
וְלַחוֹטֶא נָתַן עִנְיָן לֶאֱסוֹף וְלִכְנוֹס לָתֵת לְטוֹב לִפְנֵי הָאֱלֹהִים גַּם־
ג זֶה הֶבֶל וּרְעוּת רוּחַ: לַכֹּל זְמָן וְעֵת לְכָל־חֵפֶץ תַּחַת הַשָּׁמָיִם:

עֵת לָלֶדֶת וְעֵת לָמוּת
עֵת לָטַעַת וְעֵת לַעֲקוֹר נָטוּעַ:
עֵת לַהֲרוֹג וְעֵת לִרְפּוֹא
עֵת לִפְרוֹץ וְעֵת לִבְנוֹת:
עֵת לִבְכּוֹת וְעֵת לִשְׂחוֹק
עֵת סְפוֹד וְעֵת רְקוֹד:
עֵת לְהַשְׁלִיךְ אֲבָנִים וְעֵת כְּנוֹס אֲבָנִים
עֵת לַחֲבוֹק וְעֵת לִרְחֹק מֵחַבֵּק:

כִּי מֶה־הֹוֶה לָאָדָם בְּכָל־עֲמָלוֹ *For what remains to one of all the labor.* This is the first of eight passages in which Kohelet suddenly changes mood and insists, despite the seeming disillusion and despair, that the right response to human mortality is joy. Joy comes from the consciousness of being alive and knowing that this is the ultimate gift of God. To live in the moment, unburdened by the past, unworried about the future, is to follow the way of Hillel the Elder, who used to say, "Blessed be God day by day" (*Beitza* 16a). Joy is not elsewhere but here, celebrating what we have.

לַכֹּל זְמָן וְעֵת לְכָל־חֵפֶץ *Everything has its moments.* One of the most famous pas-

A time to seek, a time to lose;
a time to keep and a time to cast aside.
A time to sever, a time to sew;
a time to be silent and a time to speak.
A time to love, a time to hate;
a time of war and a time for peace.

What profit has the one who works, from all his labor? I have seen the occupation that God gave mortal man to torment himself with. He made everything right in its proper time, He placed eternity in their minds; and no man ever fathoms what it is that God is working from beginning to end. And so I know that there is no good for them but to be joyful and to do what is good in their lifetime. And if any man eats and drinks and sees some good of all his labor – that is a gift from God. And I know that whatever God does will be forever. There is no adding to it, there is no taking away; and God has made quite sure that He be feared. That which has been is already here, and that which is to be has already been. And God is seeking after the pursued. Another thing that I saw beneath the sun: In a place of judgment – there are the evils. In a place of justice – evil is there. I said to my mind: God will judge both the righteous and the wicked, for the time comes for every

---

גַּם אֶת־הָעֹלָם נָתַן בְּלִבָּם *He placed eternity in their minds.* Rashi reads this as "hiddenness" – we cannot comprehend the infinite or the eternal, yet we have immortal longings. If we are fortunate, we understand the time we are in, and what it calls for: whether speech or silence, war or peace. Only God can fathom eternity.

יָדַעְתִּי *And so I know.* Another of Kohelet's rejections of despair. There is much we do not understand, much that we will never know, but this is not a reason to mourn: it is a reason to celebrate the breath of life itself.

מַה־שֶּׁהָיָה כְּבָר הוּא *That which has been is already here.* We are part of a larger narrative, scripted by God, whose full meaning will always elude us, for we are finite and live within time, while God is infinite, and lives beyond time.

עֵת לְבַקֵּשׁ וְעֵת לְאַבֵּד
עֵת לִשְׁמוֹר וְעֵת לְהַשְׁלִיךְ׃
עֵת לִקְרוֹעַ וְעֵת לִתְפּוֹר
עֵת לַחֲשׁוֹת וְעֵת לְדַבֵּר׃
עֵת לֶאֱהֹב וְעֵת לִשְׂנֹא
עֵת מִלְחָמָה וְעֵת שָׁלוֹם׃

מַה־יִּתְרוֹן הָעוֹשֶׂה בַּאֲשֶׁר הוּא עָמֵל׃ רָאִיתִי אֶת־הָעִנְיָן אֲשֶׁר
נָתַן אֱלֹהִים לִבְנֵי הָאָדָם לַעֲנוֹת בּוֹ׃ אֶת־הַכֹּל עָשָׂה יָפֶה בְעִתּוֹ
גַּם אֶת־הָעֹלָם נָתַן בְּלִבָּם מִבְּלִי אֲשֶׁר לֹא־יִמְצָא הָאָדָם אֶת־
הַמַּעֲשֶׂה אֲשֶׁר־עָשָׂה הָאֱלֹהִים מֵרֹאשׁ וְעַד־סוֹף׃ יָדַעְתִּי כִּי אֵין
טוֹב בָּם כִּי אִם־לִשְׂמוֹחַ וְלַעֲשׂוֹת טוֹב בְּחַיָּיו׃ וְגַם כָּל־הָאָדָם
שֶׁיֹּאכַל וְשָׁתָה וְרָאָה טוֹב בְּכָל־עֲמָלוֹ מַתַּת אֱלֹהִים הִיא׃ יָדַעְתִּי
כִּי כָּל־אֲשֶׁר יַעֲשֶׂה הָאֱלֹהִים הוּא יִהְיֶה לְעוֹלָם עָלָיו אֵין לְהוֹסִיף
וּמִמֶּנּוּ אֵין לִגְרֹעַ וְהָאֱלֹהִים עָשָׂה שֶׁיִּרְאוּ מִלְּפָנָיו׃ מַה־שֶּׁהָיָה
כְּבָר הוּא וַאֲשֶׁר לִהְיוֹת כְּבָר הָיָה וְהָאֱלֹהִים יְבַקֵּשׁ אֶת־נִרְדָּף׃
וְעוֹד רָאִיתִי תַּחַת הַשָּׁמֶשׁ מְקוֹם הַמִּשְׁפָּט שָׁמָּה הָרֶשַׁע וּמְקוֹם
הַצֶּדֶק שָׁמָּה הָרָשַׁע׃ אָמַרְתִּי אֲנִי בְּלִבִּי אֶת־הַצַּדִּיק וְאֶת־הָרָשָׁע

וְעֵת שָׁלוֹם *A time for peace.* Note that Kohelet ends his prose-poem with the word "peace." Peace is the last word of many Jewish prayers. To be a Jew is to long for peace.

אֶת־הַכֹּל עָשָׂה יָפֶה בְעִתּוֹ *He made everything right in its proper time.* All achievement is dependent on time, circumstance and fortune. Only God can foresee the future; we cannot. Therefore, do not weep if your efforts fail. God has His reasons, which we cannot fathom. We are part of a larger story, whose script we cannot read. Failure does not negate the effort, which is its own reward.

deed, for all that is done, there. And I said to my mind of the sons of man: God set them apart, to find that they are nothing but cattle. For the fate of man is the fate of cattle; the same fate awaits them both, the death of one is like the death of the other, and their spirits are the same, and the pre-eminence of man over beast is nothing, for it is all but shallow breath. All end in the same place; all emerge from dust and all go back to dust. Who can say that the spirit of a man rises up while the spirit of a beast sinks into the ground? I saw that there is no good at all but for man to take pleasure in his works; for that is his share. For who will bring him to see what will become of it all when he is gone?

4 But I turned again and saw all those made victims beneath the sun. There they were: the victims' tears and none to console them; power at the hands of their oppressors, and none to console them. And I thought the dead more fortunate, who have died already, than the living who yet live. But better than either, are those who are yet to be, for they have seen none of the evil that is wrought beneath the sun.

And I saw all the labor that is performed, all the skill – saw that it is all but one man's jealousy for another; this too is shallow breath and courting the wind. The fool crosses his hands and eats his own flesh. Better a handful of peace than two hands full of labor and courting the wind.

I turned again and saw shallow breath beneath the sun. It happens that a man may be alone, with no fellow, no child even, or brother, and there

---

Halakhic Man). The sage sees the dissonance between the world that is and the world that ought to be, and hears in it the call of God to relieve human suffering.

וְשַׁבֵּחַ אֲנִי אֶת־הַמֵּתִים שֶׁכְּבָר מֵתוּ *I thought the dead more fortunate, who have died already.* "For two and a half years the schools of Shammai and Hillel debated whether it would have been better for man be created or not. Eventually they voted and concluded: It would have been better for man not to have been created, but now that he has been, let him examine his deeds" (*Eiruvin* 13b).

יֵשׁ אֶחָד וְאֵין שֵׁנִי *A man may be alone.* The first time the words "not good" ap-

יִשְׁפֹּט הָאֱלֹהִים כִּי־עֵת לְכָל־חֵפֶץ וְעַל כָּל־הַמַּעֲשֶׂה שָׁם: אָמַרְתִּי
אֲנִי בְּלִבִּי עַל־דִּבְרַת בְּנֵי הָאָדָם לְבָרָם הָאֱלֹהִים וְלִרְאוֹת שְׁהֶם־
בְּהֵמָה הֵמָּה לָהֶם: כִּי מִקְרֶה בְנֵי־הָאָדָם וּמִקְרֶה הַבְּהֵמָה וּמִקְרֶה
אֶחָד לָהֶם כְּמוֹת זֶה כֵּן מוֹת זֶה וְרוּחַ אֶחָד לַכֹּל וּמוֹתַר הָאָדָם
מִן־הַבְּהֵמָה אָיִן כִּי הַכֹּל הָבֶל: הַכֹּל הוֹלֵךְ אֶל־מָקוֹם אֶחָד הַכֹּל
הָיָה מִן־הֶעָפָר וְהַכֹּל שָׁב אֶל־הֶעָפָר: מִי יוֹדֵעַ רוּחַ בְּנֵי הָאָדָם
הָעֹלָה הִיא לְמָעְלָה וְרוּחַ הַבְּהֵמָה הַיֹּרֶדֶת הִיא לְמַטָּה לָאָרֶץ:
וְרָאִיתִי כִּי אֵין טוֹב מֵאֲשֶׁר יִשְׂמַח הָאָדָם בְּמַעֲשָׂיו כִּי־הוּא חֶלְקוֹ
ד כִּי מִי יְבִיאֶנּוּ לִרְאוֹת בְּמֶה שֶׁיִּהְיֶה אַחֲרָיו: וְשַׁבְתִּי אֲנִי וָאֶרְאֶה
אֶת־כָּל־הָעֲשֻׁקִים אֲשֶׁר נַעֲשִׂים תַּחַת הַשָּׁמֶשׁ וְהִנֵּה ׀ דִּמְעַת
הָעֲשֻׁקִים וְאֵין לָהֶם מְנַחֵם וּמִיַּד עֹשְׁקֵיהֶם כֹּחַ וְאֵין לָהֶם מְנַחֵם:
וְשַׁבֵּחַ אֲנִי אֶת־הַמֵּתִים שֶׁכְּבָר מֵתוּ מִן־הַחַיִּים אֲשֶׁר הֵמָּה חַיִּים
עֲדֶנָה: וְטוֹב מִשְּׁנֵיהֶם אֵת אֲשֶׁר־עֲדֶן לֹא הָיָה אֲשֶׁר לֹא־רָאָה
אֶת־הַמַּעֲשֶׂה הָרָע אֲשֶׁר נַעֲשָׂה תַּחַת הַשָּׁמֶשׁ: וְרָאִיתִי אֲנִי
אֶת־כָּל־עָמָל וְאֵת כָּל־כִּשְׁרוֹן הַמַּעֲשֶׂה כִּי הִיא קִנְאַת־אִישׁ
מֵרֵעֵהוּ גַּם־זֶה הֶבֶל וּרְעוּת רוּחַ: הַכְּסִיל חֹבֵק אֶת־יָדָיו וְאֹכֵל
אֶת־בְּשָׂרוֹ: טוֹב מְלֹא כַף נָחַת מִמְּלֹא חָפְנַיִם עָמָל וּרְעוּת רוּחַ:
וְשַׁבְתִּי אֲנִי וָאֶרְאֶה הֶבֶל תַּחַת הַשָּׁמֶשׁ: יֵשׁ אֶחָד וְאֵין שֵׁנִי גַּם

וּמוֹתַר הָאָדָם מִן־הַבְּהֵמָה אָיִן *The pre-eminence of man over beast is nothing.* The basis of one of the first prayers we say each morning, and a standing rebuke to hubris, the idea that men can become like God. A sharp sense of our mortality is the best tutorial in humility.

דִּמְעַת הָעֲשׁוּקִים *The victims' tears.* Rabbi Chaim of Brisk, when asked what is the role of the rabbi, replied, "To redress the grievances of those who are abandoned and alone, to protect the dignity of the poor, and to rescue the oppressed from the hand of his oppressor" (Rabbi Joseph Soloveitchik,

may be no end to all his labor. His eye, too, will never see enough of riches; and who, after all, am I laboring for, and starving my spirit of good? This too is shallow breath and a wretched business. Two are better than one, for they have some good return for all their labor. For if they fall down, they will help each other rise. But pity the one who falls alone, for who will ever raise him? Two people lying down together are warm; but how can one ever be warm alone? If one man should assault another, then two can stand against him; and a three-stranded thread is not readily broken.

Better a poor and clever child, than an old and foolish king, who does not know how to take heed any more. For he may come straight out of prison to rule; and in his reign too, a poor child will be born. Yes, I saw all of life moving about beneath the sun, with the next child born to rise up after the last. There is no end to this people, to all that came before them; and those who come after them also, will not rejoice in him. This too: shallow breath; courting the wind. Watch your steps when you walk to the House of God. Better to take heed than to bring a fool's offering; for they know not what doing wrong means.

5 Do not hasten your lips, do not hurry your heart, to bring forth words in the presence of God; for God is in heaven, and you are here on earth; and so let your words be few. For as dreams come of too much preoccupation, so is a fool's voice known by too many words.

If you make a vow to God, do not delay to fulfill it; for there is no use being a fool – whatever you vow, fulfill. Better not to vow, than to vow and not fulfill. Do not let your mouth bring your flesh to punishment; and do not tell the messenger that it was a mistake; why should you have God rage at your words, and destroy the work of your hands? For

---

tween humans to those between us and God. The same rule applies to both: Say little, do much, and always do what you said you would. Never take vows or make promises you cannot fulfill. Vows can be annulled, but better not to vow than to vow and then annul, for the latter causes an erosion of trust that devalues the sanctity of the commitment implicit in a vow.

בֵּ֣ן וָאָח֮ אֵֽין־לוֹ֒ וְאֵ֥ין קֵץ֙ לְכָל־עֲמָל֔וֹ גַּם־עֵינָ֖יו לֹא־תִשְׂבַּ֣ע עֹ֑שֶׁר עֵינ֖וֹ
וּלְמִ֣י ׀ אֲנִ֣י עָמֵ֗ל וּמְחַסֵּ֤ר אֶת־נַפְשִׁי֙ מִטּוֹבָ֔ה גַּם־זֶ֥ה הֶ֛בֶל וְעִנְיַ֥ן
רָ֖ע הֽוּא׃ טוֹבִ֥ים הַשְּׁנַ֖יִם מִן־הָאֶחָ֑ד אֲשֶׁ֧ר יֵשׁ־לָהֶ֛ם שָׂכָ֥ר ט֖וֹב
בַּעֲמָלָֽם׃ כִּ֤י אִם־יִפֹּ֔לוּ הָאֶחָ֖ד יָקִ֣ים אֶת־חֲבֵר֑וֹ וְאִ֣ילוֹ הָאֶחָד֙ שֶׁיִּפֹּ֔ל
וְאֵ֥ין שֵׁנִ֖י לַהֲקִימֽוֹ׃ גַּ֛ם אִם־יִשְׁכְּב֥וּ שְׁנַ֖יִם וְחַ֣ם לָהֶ֑ם וּלְאֶחָ֖ד אֵ֥יךְ
יֵחָֽם׃ וְאִֽם־יִתְקְפוֹ֙ הָאֶחָ֔ד הַשְּׁנַ֖יִם יַעַמְד֣וּ נֶגְדּ֑וֹ וְהַחוּט֙ הַֽמְשֻׁלָּ֔שׁ
לֹ֥א בִמְהֵרָ֖ה יִנָּתֵֽק׃ ט֛וֹב יֶ֥לֶד מִסְכֵּ֖ן וְחָכָ֑ם מִמֶּ֤לֶךְ זָקֵן֙ וּכְסִ֔יל אֲשֶׁ֛ר
לֹא־יָדַ֥ע לְהִזָּהֵ֖ר עֽוֹד׃ כִּֽי־מִבֵּ֥ית הָסוּרִ֖ים יָצָ֣א לִמְלֹ֑ךְ כִּ֛י גַּ֥ם
בְּמַלְכוּת֖וֹ נוֹלַ֥ד רָֽשׁ׃ רָאִ֙יתִי֙ אֶת־כָּל־הַ֣חַיִּ֔ים הַֽמְהַלְּכִ֖ים תַּ֣חַת
הַשָּׁ֑מֶשׁ עִ֚ם הַיֶּ֣לֶד הַשֵּׁנִ֔י אֲשֶׁ֥ר יַעֲמֹ֖ד תַּחְתָּֽיו׃ אֵֽין־קֵ֣ץ לְכָל־הָעָ֗ם
לְכֹ֤ל אֲשֶׁר־הָיָה֙ לִפְנֵיהֶ֔ם גַּ֥ם הָאַחֲרוֹנִ֖ים לֹ֣א יִשְׂמְחוּ־ב֑וֹ כִּֽי־גַם־זֶ֥ה
הֶ֖בֶל וְרַעְי֥וֹן רֽוּחַ׃ שְׁמֹ֣ר רגליך כַּאֲשֶׁ֤ר תֵּלֵךְ֙ אֶל־בֵּ֣ית הָאֱלֹהִ֔ים רַגְלְךָ֗
וְקָר֣וֹב לִשְׁמֹ֔עַ מִתֵּ֥ת הַכְּסִילִ֖ים זָ֑בַח כִּֽי־אֵינָ֥ם יוֹדְעִ֖ים לַעֲשׂ֥וֹת
ה רָֽע׃ אַל־תְּבַהֵ֨ל עַל־פִּ֜יךָ וְלִבְּךָ֛ אַל־יְמַהֵ֥ר לְהוֹצִ֥יא דָבָ֖ר לִפְנֵ֣י
הָאֱלֹהִ֑ים כִּ֨י הָאֱלֹהִ֤ים בַּשָּׁמַ֙יִם֙ וְאַתָּ֣ה עַל־הָאָ֔רֶץ עַל־כֵּ֛ן יִהְי֥וּ
דְבָרֶ֖יךָ מְעַטִּֽים׃ כִּ֛י בָּ֥א הַחֲל֖וֹם בְּרֹ֣ב עִנְיָ֑ן וְק֥וֹל כְּסִ֖יל בְּרֹ֥ב דְּבָרִֽים׃
כַּאֲשֶׁ֨ר תִּדֹּ֜ר נֶ֣דֶר לֵאלֹהִ֗ים אַל־תְּאַחֵר֙ לְשַׁלְּמ֔וֹ כִּ֛י אֵ֥ין חֵ֖פֶץ
בַּכְּסִילִ֑ים אֵ֥ת אֲשֶׁר־תִּדֹּ֖ר שַׁלֵּֽם׃ ט֖וֹב אֲשֶׁ֣ר לֹֽא־תִדֹּ֑ר מִשֶּׁתִּדּ֖וֹר
וְלֹ֥א תְשַׁלֵּֽם׃ אַל־תִּתֵּ֤ן אֶת־פִּ֙יךָ֙ לַחֲטִ֣יא אֶת־בְּשָׂרֶ֔ךָ וְאַל־תֹּאמַר֙
לִפְנֵ֣י הַמַּלְאָ֔ךְ כִּ֥י שְׁגָגָ֖ה הִ֑יא לָ֣מָּה יִקְצֹ֤ף הָאֱלֹהִים֙ עַל־קוֹלֶ֔ךָ וְחִבֵּ֖ל

---

pear in the Torah is in Genesis 2:18: "It is not good for man to be alone." The source of happiness is not the "I" but the "You," not our self, but our relationships with others.

אַל־תְּבַהֵל עַל־פִּיךָ *Do not hasten your lips.* Kohelet moves from relationships be-

so many dreams and so much shallow breath, so many words – better only to fear God.

If you see oppression of a poor person, or any perversion of law and justice in the province – do not wonder at the fact; for every watchman has a watchman over him, and there are higher ones yet above. Yet the earth below has the advantage over all; even a king is enslaved to the field.

One who loves money will never be satisfied with money; nor one who loves abundance, with produce. That too is fleeting breath. As goodness multiplies, so do those who would consume it; and what gain does it bring its master but longing eyes? The sleep of a worker is sweet, whether he eats much or little, but the rich man's fullness will not let him sleep in peace.

There is a sickly evil I have seen beneath the sun: wealth hoarded up for its owner, only to harm him. That wealth may be destroyed by some evil event, and a child is born to him with not the smallest thing to his name. Naked as he emerged from his own mother's womb, just so will he return. And not the slightest thing will he hold from all his labor to bring with him.

This too is a sickly evil; just as one comes, so shall one leave again. And what profit does one gain for toiling after the wind? All his days he eats in darkness, and with great bitterness, and sickness, and fury.

This is what I have seen that is good: the beauty of eating and drinking and seeing some good of all the labor one toils over beneath the sun, all the days of the life God has given one – for this is one's share. For if God gives any man wealth and belongings, and grants him the power to eat of them, to take hold of what is his, to take pleasure in his

---

וְאָבַד הָעֹשֶׁר הַהוּא בְּעִנְיַן רָע *That wealth may be destroyed by some evil event.* Maimonides, in his *Guide for the Perplexed* (3:54), explains that possessions are externalities. They are what we *have*, not what we *are*. Therefore we can lose them overnight. Even if we keep them for a lifetime, possessions themselves are no testimony to the worth of their possessor.

אֶת־מַעֲשֵׂה יָדֶיךָ׃ כִּי בְרֹב חֲלֹמוֹת וַהֲבָלִים וּדְבָרִים הַרְבֵּה כִּי
אֶת־הָאֱלֹהִים יְרָא׃ אִם־עֹשֶׁק רָשׁ וְגֵזֶל מִשְׁפָּט וָצֶדֶק תִּרְאֶה
בַמְּדִינָה אַל־תִּתְמַהּ עַל־הַחֵפֶץ כִּי גָבֹהַּ מֵעַל גָּבֹהַּ שֹׁמֵר וּגְבֹהִים
עֲלֵיהֶם׃ וְיִתְרוֹן אֶרֶץ בַּכֹּל הִיא מֶלֶךְ לְשָׂדֶה נֶעֱבָד׃ אֹהֵב כֶּסֶף הוּא
לֹא־יִשְׂבַּע כֶּסֶף וּמִי־אֹהֵב בֶּהָמוֹן לֹא תְבוּאָה גַּם־זֶה הָבֶל׃
בִּרְבוֹת הַטּוֹבָה רַבּוּ אוֹכְלֶיהָ וּמַה־כִּשְׁרוֹן לִבְעָלֶיהָ כִּי אִם־ראית רְאוּת
עֵינָיו׃ מְתוּקָה שְׁנַת הָעֹבֵד אִם־מְעַט וְאִם־הַרְבֵּה יֹאכֵל וְהַשָּׂבָע
לֶעָשִׁיר אֵינֶנּוּ מַנִּיחַ לוֹ לִישׁוֹן׃ יֵשׁ רָעָה חוֹלָה רָאִיתִי תַּחַת
הַשָּׁמֶשׁ עֹשֶׁר שָׁמוּר לִבְעָלָיו לְרָעָתוֹ׃ וְאָבַד הָעֹשֶׁר הַהוּא בְּעִנְיַן
רָע וְהוֹלִיד בֵּן וְאֵין בְּיָדוֹ מְאוּמָה׃ כַּאֲשֶׁר יָצָא מִבֶּטֶן אִמּוֹ עָרוֹם
יָשׁוּב לָלֶכֶת כְּשֶׁבָּא וּמְאוּמָה לֹא־יִשָּׂא בַעֲמָלוֹ שֶׁיֹּלֵךְ בְּיָדוֹ׃
וְגַם־זֹה רָעָה חוֹלָה כָּל־עֻמַּת שֶׁבָּא כֵּן יֵלֵךְ וּמַה־יִּתְרוֹן לוֹ שֶׁיַּעֲמֹל
לָרוּחַ׃ גַּם כָּל־יָמָיו בַּחֹשֶׁךְ יֹאכֵל וְכָעַס הַרְבֵּה וְחָלְיוֹ וָקָצֶף׃ הִנֵּה
אֲשֶׁר־רָאִיתִי אָנִי טוֹב אֲשֶׁר־יָפֶה לֶאֱכוֹל וְלִשְׁתּוֹת וְלִרְאוֹת טוֹבָה
בְּכָל־עֲמָלוֹ ׀ שֶׁיַּעֲמֹל תַּחַת־הַשֶּׁמֶשׁ מִסְפַּר יְמֵי־חַיָּו אֲשֶׁר־נָתַן־
לוֹ הָאֱלֹהִים כִּי־הוּא חֶלְקוֹ׃ גַּם כָּל־הָאָדָם אֲשֶׁר נָתַן־לוֹ הָאֱלֹהִים
עֹשֶׁר וּנְכָסִים וְהִשְׁלִיטוֹ לֶאֱכֹל מִמֶּנּוּ וְלָשֵׂאת אֶת־חֶלְקוֹ וְלִשְׂמֹחַ

אִם־עֹשֶׁק רָשׁ וְגֵזֶל *If you see oppression of a poor person.* Kohelet here seems to suggest that bureaucracy – watchmen over watchmen – begets corruption: manifestly the case during the Holocaust, whose perpetrators later claimed they were merely obeying orders.

אֹהֵב כֶּסֶף *One who loves money.* For some, money becomes an end in itself. The more they have, the more they want. Money, in and of itself, does not satisfy, because it is a means, not an end. Better, therefore, a simple, modest life with peace of mind, than a life obsessed with material gain. "Who is rich? One who rejoices in what he has" (*Avot* 4:1).

labors – that is a gift from God. For he will not think too much about the days of his life; for God has given him the joy of his heart to be occupied with.

6 There is an evil I have seen beneath the sun, and it is rife among men. There will be a man to whom God gives wealth and possessions and honor, so that he lacks nothing his heart desires. And then God will not grant him the power to partake of it, and a stranger will consume it all; this is shallow breath and an evil sickness.

And a man may have a hundred children and live for many years, and as many as his years may be, his soul will never be satisfied with all that goodness; though he may not receive even a burial, I say a stillborn child is better off than he. For he came at a breath and leaves in darkness, and in darkness is his name covered over. That child will never see sunlight and never know; and yet he has more peace than such a man. If one lives a thousand years twice over, and sees no goodness – well, do we not all go to the same place in the end?

All of man's labor is only for his mouth; his soul will never be filled. What advantage does a wise man hold over a fool? And what does an oppressed man profit from knowing how to walk with life? Better what the eyes can see than what the soul goes walking after. Both are empty breath and courting the wind.

Whatever has been was called forth by name – and it is known by now that this is but a man, who cannot contend with one more powerful than he. There are so many things, such proliferation of empty breath, and what profit do they bring to man? For who knows what is good for a man in his lifetime; during the numbered days of his breath, that he lives as a shadow; for who can tell what his fate will be beneath the sun?

---

yet people still wrong one another, and we cannot know when and how God will reward virtue and punish evil. The two life-shaping truths are that we will one day die, and that the future is unknowable. It follows that God gives "wisdom and insight and joy to those who are satisfied with what they have" (2:26).

בְּעַמְלוֹ זֹה מַתַּת אֱלֹהִים הִיא: כִּי לֹא הַרְבֵּה יִזְכֹּר אֶת־יְמֵי חַיָּיו
ו כִּי הָאֱלֹהִים מַעֲנֶה בְּשִׂמְחַת לִבּוֹ: יֵשׁ רָעָה אֲשֶׁר רָאִיתִי תַּחַת
הַשָּׁמֶשׁ וְרַבָּה הִיא עַל־הָאָדָם: אִישׁ אֲשֶׁר יִתֶּן־לוֹ הָאֱלֹהִים עֹשֶׁר
וּנְכָסִים וְכָבוֹד וְאֵינֶנּוּ חָסֵר לְנַפְשׁוֹ ׀ מִכֹּל אֲשֶׁר־יִתְאַוֶּה וְלֹא־
יַשְׁלִיטֶנּוּ הָאֱלֹהִים לֶאֱכֹל מִמֶּנּוּ כִּי אִישׁ נׇכְרִי יֹאכְלֶנּוּ זֶה הֶבֶל
וׇחֳלִי רָע הוּא: אִם־יוֹלִיד אִישׁ מֵאָה וְשָׁנִים רַבּוֹת יִחְיֶה וְרַב ׀
שֶׁיִּהְיוּ יְמֵי־שָׁנָיו וְנַפְשׁוֹ לֹא־תִשְׂבַּע מִן־הַטּוֹבָה וְגַם־קְבוּרָה לֹא־
הָיְתָה לּוֹ אָמַרְתִּי טוֹב מִמֶּנּוּ הַנָּפֶל: כִּי־בַהֶבֶל בָּא וּבַחֹשֶׁךְ יֵלֵךְ
וּבַחֹשֶׁךְ שְׁמוֹ יְכֻסֶּה: גַּם־שֶׁמֶשׁ לֹא־רָאָה וְלֹא יָדָע נַחַת לָזֶה מִזֶּה:
וְאִלּוּ חָיָה אֶלֶף שָׁנִים פַּעֲמַיִם וְטוֹבָה לֹא רָאָה הֲלֹא אֶל־מָקוֹם
אֶחָד הַכֹּל הוֹלֵךְ: כׇּל־עֲמַל הָאָדָם לְפִיהוּ וְגַם־הַנֶּפֶשׁ לֹא תִמָּלֵא:
כִּי מַה־יּוֹתֵר לֶחָכָם מִן־הַכְּסִיל מַה־לֶּעָנִי יוֹדֵעַ לַהֲלֹךְ נֶגֶד הַחַיִּים:
טוֹב מַרְאֵה עֵינַיִם מֵהֲלׇךְ־נָפֶשׁ גַּם־זֶה הֶבֶל וּרְעוּת רוּחַ: מַה־
שֶּׁהָיָה כְּבָר נִקְרָא שְׁמוֹ וְנוֹדָע אֲשֶׁר־הוּא אָדָם וְלֹא־יוּכַל לָדִין
שֶׁתַּקִּיף עִם שהתקיף מִמֶּנּוּ: כִּי יֵשׁ־דְּבָרִים הַרְבֵּה מַרְבִּים הָבֶל מַה־יֹּתֵר
לָאָדָם: כִּי מִי־יוֹדֵעַ מַה־טּוֹב לָאָדָם בַּחַיִּים מִסְפַּר יְמֵי־חַיֵּי
הֶבְלוֹ וְיַעֲשֵׂם כַּצֵּל אֲשֶׁר מִי־יַגִּיד לָאָדָם מַה־יִּהְיֶה אַחֲרָיו תַּחַת

וְגַם־הַנֶּפֶשׁ לֹא תִמָּלֵא *His soul will never be filled.* The consumer society, by making us focus on what we do not yet have, rather than on enjoying what we have, is a system for the production and distribution of unhappiness.

כִּי מִי־יוֹדֵעַ מַה־טּוֹב לָאָדָם *For who knows what is good for a man?* This brings to an end the first part of Kohelet, his personal journey in search of wisdom. He has seen a world in which people spend their lives in pursuit of aims they think will bring happiness, but do not. He knows this from his own experience. He has witnessed much injustice and many cruel blows of fate. He does not doubt the existence of God, nor that God will bring all to justice,

7 Better a good name than fine oil. Better the day of death than of birth. Better to frequent a house of mourning than a feast; for that is the end of all men, and the living had better keep that in mind. Better bitterness than laughter, for while the face is troubled, the mind is bettering itself. A wise man's heart is in the house of mourning, and a fool's is in the house of celebration. Better to heed the rebuke of the wise than to hear the song of fools. For those fools' cackling is like the crackling of thorns under the pot. And that too is empty breath. For oppression turns a wise man delirious, and bribery comes at the cost of one's mind.

The end of a thing is better than its beginning. Patience is better than pride. Do not be so quick to anger, for anger lies in the lap of the fool. Do not say, "What went wrong, that times gone by were better than these?" It is not wisdom that brings you to ask.

Wisdom is better with an estate, though it profits all who see the sun. For a man in the shade of wisdom is in the shade of money too; and the profit of understanding is greater, for wisdom brings life to those who master it. Look at the word of God; for nobody can straighten what He has made crooked. On a good day, live goodness, and on a bad day look and see: God has made both things, one alongside the other; and no man can find fault with Him after.

---

abusive, to become so, and for the abused to accept their abuse. Without exceptional moral strength, we can become prisoners of our situation.

וִיאַבֵּד אֶת־לֵב מַתָּנָה *Bribery comes at the cost.* "Bribes blind those who see and prevert the words of the righteous" (Ex. 23:8).

טוֹב אַחֲרִית דָּבָר *The end of a thing is better.* After the one-per-cent of inspiration must come the ninety-per-cent of perspiration.

שֶׁהַיָּמִים הָרִאשֹׁנִים הָיוּ *The times gone by.* Avoid false nostalgia. Memory misleads. Things in the past were rarely as good or as bad as we think they were.

בְּיוֹם טוֹבָה הֱיֵה בְטוֹב *On a good day, live goodness.* The Targum reads: "On a day when God is good to you, you also be in goodness, and do good for all the world."

ז הַשָּׁמֶשׁ: טוֹב שֵׁם מִשֶּׁמֶן טוֹב וְיוֹם הַמָּוֶת מִיּוֹם הִוָּלְדוֹ:
טוֹב לָלֶכֶת אֶל־בֵּית־אֵבֶל מִלֶּכֶת אֶל־בֵּית מִשְׁתֶּה בַּאֲשֶׁר הוּא
סוֹף כָּל־הָאָדָם וְהַחַי יִתֵּן אֶל־לִבּוֹ: טוֹב כַּעַס מִשְּׂחוֹק כִּי־בְרֹעַ
פָּנִים יִיטַב לֵב: לֵב חֲכָמִים בְּבֵית אֵבֶל וְלֵב כְּסִילִים בְּבֵית
שִׂמְחָה: טוֹב לִשְׁמוֹעַ גַּעֲרַת חָכָם מֵאִישׁ שֹׁמֵעַ שִׁיר כְּסִילִים: כִּי
כְקוֹל הַסִּירִים תַּחַת הַסִּיר כֵּן שְׂחֹק הַכְּסִיל וְגַם־זֶה הָבֶל: כִּי
הָעֹשֶׁק יְהוֹלֵל חָכָם וִיאַבֵּד אֶת־לֵב מַתָּנָה: טוֹב אַחֲרִית דָּבָר
מֵרֵאשִׁיתוֹ טוֹב אֶרֶךְ־רוּחַ מִגְּבַהּ רוּחַ: אַל־תְּבַהֵל בְּרוּחֲךָ לִכְעוֹס
כִּי כַעַס בְּחֵיק כְּסִילִים יָנוּחַ: אַל־תֹּאמַר מֶה הָיָה שֶׁהַיָּמִים
הָרִאשֹׁנִים הָיוּ טוֹבִים מֵאֵלֶּה כִּי לֹא מֵחָכְמָה שָׁאַלְתָּ עַל־זֶה:
טוֹבָה חָכְמָה עִם־נַחֲלָה וְיֹתֵר לְרֹאֵי הַשָּׁמֶשׁ: כִּי בְּצֵל הַחָכְמָה
בְּצֵל הַכָּסֶף וְיִתְרוֹן דַּעַת הַחָכְמָה תְּחַיֶּה בְעָלֶיהָ: רְאֵה אֶת־
מַעֲשֵׂה הָאֱלֹהִים כִּי מִי יוּכַל לְתַקֵּן אֵת אֲשֶׁר עִוְּתוֹ: בְּיוֹם טוֹבָה
הֱיֵה בְטוֹב וּבְיוֹם רָעָה רְאֵה גַּם אֶת־זֶה לְעֻמַּת־זֶה עָשָׂה הָאֱלֹהִים
עַל־דִּבְרַת שֶׁלֹּא יִמְצָא הָאָדָם אַחֲרָיו מְאוּמָה: אֶת־הַכֹּל רָאִיתִי

טוֹב שֵׁם *Better a good name.* A series of wisdom aphorisms, many of them built on the construction, "Better X than Y."

טוֹב לָלֶכֶת אֶל־בֵּית־אֵבֶל *Better to frequent a house of mourning.* Visiting a house of mourning reminds us of the brevity of life, and the importance of "eulogy virtues" as opposed to "résumé virtues," qualities of character, as opposed to external achievements. The presence of death reminds us of the Psalmist's prayer: "Teach us rightly to number our days, that we may gain a heart of wisdom" (Ps. 90:12).

כִּי הָעֹשֶׁק יְהוֹלֵל חָכָם *For oppression turns a wise man delirious.* The Stanford Experiment (1971) showed how easy it is for those given the chance to be

I have seen it all in the days of my shallow breath; righteous men who die in their righteousness, and wicked ones who live long in their wickedness. So do not be too righteous, do not be so much wiser; for why should you become desolate? Do not be too wicked, and never be a fool, for why should you die before your time? Better to hold the one part, never loosening your hand upon the other; for a God-fearing man will escape both dangers. Wisdom gives the wise man more power than ten rulers in a city.

Yes, there is no one in this world so righteous that he does good and never sins. Do not take to heart all the words you hear said; do not overhear it when your slave insults you. For many times, as your heart well knows, you yourself have insulted others.

I tried all this with my wisdom. I said, "I shall be wiser"; but it was far away from me. All that has been is far away, deep, deep beyond fathoming. I turned, I and my mind, to understand and to explore and seek wisdom and reason; and to know the wickedness of foolishness, to know folly and delirium. And this is what I found: woman is more bitter than death, for she is all traps, with nets laid in her heart; her arms

---

Others have seen humans as invariably tainted by original sin, incapable of doing good except by divine grace. Judaism rejects both of these alternatives. No one is perfect: the Hebrew Bible unsparingly chronicles the faults of even the greatest. Yet there is repentance, atonement and forgiveness. We should refrain equally from too high and too low an opinion of ourselves and others.

מַר מִמָּוֶת אֶת־הָאִשָּׁה *Woman is more bitter.* To understand this statement we must set it in context of Solomon's life. 1 Kings 11:3 tells us that he had "seven hundred wives of royal birth and three hundred concubines," and that "they led him astray." This was in direct contravention of the biblical command about a king that "He must not take many wives, or his heart will be led astray." (Deut. 17:17). According to the sages (*Sanhedrin* 21a), Solomon, wisest of men, believed that he could take many wives without his heart being led astray, and he was wrong. The result was catastrophic: "As Solomon grew old, his wives turned his heart after other gods, and his heart was not

בִּימֵי הֶבְלִי יֵשׁ צַדִּיק אֹבֵד בְּצִדְקוֹ וְיֵשׁ רָשָׁע מַאֲרִיךְ בְּרָעָתוֹ:
אַל־תְּהִי צַדִּיק הַרְבֵּה וְאַל־תִּתְחַכַּם יוֹתֵר לָמָּה תִּשּׁוֹמֵם: אַל־
תִּרְשַׁע הַרְבֵּה וְאַל־תְּהִי סָכָל לָמָּה תָמוּת בְּלֹא עִתֶּךָ: טוֹב אֲשֶׁר
תֶּאֱחֹז בָּזֶה וְגַם־מִזֶּה אַל־תַּנַּח אֶת־יָדֶךָ כִּי־יְרֵא אֱלֹהִים יֵצֵא
אֶת־כֻּלָּם: הַחָכְמָה תָּעֹז לֶחָכָם מֵעֲשָׂרָה שַׁלִּיטִים אֲשֶׁר הָיוּ
בָּעִיר: כִּי אָדָם אֵין צַדִּיק בָּאָרֶץ אֲשֶׁר יַעֲשֶׂה־טּוֹב וְלֹא יֶחֱטָא:
גַּם לְכָל־הַדְּבָרִים אֲשֶׁר יְדַבֵּרוּ אַל־תִּתֵּן לִבֶּךָ אֲשֶׁר לֹא־תִשְׁמַע
אֶת־עַבְדְּךָ מְקַלְלֶךָ: כִּי גַּם־פְּעָמִים רַבּוֹת יָדַע לִבֶּךָ אֲשֶׁר גַּם־אַתָּ
קִלַּלְתָּ אֲחֵרִים: כָּל־זֹה נִסִּיתִי בַחָכְמָה אָמַרְתִּי אֶחְכָּמָה וְהִיא
רְחוֹקָה מִמֶּנִּי: רָחוֹק מַה־שֶּׁהָיָה וְעָמֹק ׀ עָמֹק מִי יִמְצָאֶנּוּ: סַבּוֹתִי
אֲנִי וְלִבִּי לָדַעַת וְלָתוּר וּבַקֵּשׁ חָכְמָה וְחֶשְׁבּוֹן וְלָדַעַת רֶשַׁע כֶּסֶל
וְהַסִּכְלוּת הוֹלֵלוֹת: וּמוֹצֶא אֲנִי מַר מִמָּוֶת אֶת־הָאִשָּׁה אֲשֶׁר־הִיא
מְצוֹדִים וַחֲרָמִים לִבָּהּ אֲסוּרִים יָדֶיהָ טוֹב לִפְנֵי הָאֱלֹהִים יִמָּלֵט

אַל־תְּהִי צַדִּיק הַרְבֵּה *So do not be too righteous.* "A person might say, 'Since envy, desire, the pursuit of honor and the like, are a wrong path, and drive a person from the world, I shall separate from them to a great degree…' with the result that he decides not to eat meat or drink wine or live in a pleasant home or wear good clothes…. This, too, is a bad path, and it is forbidden to walk along it. Whoever follows this path is called a sinner…. Therefore, our sages directed us to abstain only from those things which the Torah forbids…. Our sages stated: 'Is it not sufficient for you what the Torah has prohibited, that you must forbid additional things to yourself?' … On this and similar matters, Solomon instructed and said: 'Do not be too righteous, do not be so much wiser; for why should you become desolate?'" (Maimonides, Laws of Ethical Behavior 3:1).

כִּי אָדָם אֵין צַדִּיק בָּאָרֶץ *Yes, there is no one in this world so righteous.* This is one of Judaism's most humanizing beliefs. Civilizations have differed in their view of the human condition. Some have deified human beings as almost godlike.

are a prison; one favored by God escapes her, while a sinner becomes entrapped. See what I found, said Kohelet, searching one by one to find by reason. This too my soul sought and did not find: one man in a thousand I found; but even one such woman I did not. Yes, all that I found is this; that God created man straightforward; but they go seeking endless inventions.

8 Who is like a wise man, able to see meaning? The wisdom a person has lights up his face, and the pride in his face is changed. Obey the king's word, I say; and the word of your oath to God. Do not take flight; walk clear away; do not be present when evil is brewing, for a king will do what it pleases him to do. For a king's word is rule, and who can say to him, "What is it you do?" One who heeds the command will know no harm; and a wise mind will know justice in its time. For every deed has its time and its judgment – for great is the evil man must suffer – for man cannot know what will be; for who would tell him what may be? Man has no power over the wind, he cannot cage up the wind; no one rules on the day of death, and no one will take your place in battle, and evil will not save those who perform it.

All this have I seen, and I took it to heart; all that is done here beneath the sun, wherever man wields power over man to harm him. As I observed, I saw wicked men buried honorably, processed away from a holy place; while those who acted with decency are forgotten from the town – here again: shallow breath. For it is not soon that judgment is passed after evil, and so a person's mind is filled with thoughts of doing

---

bitter self-reproach of a man who ignored God's command believing that he was cleverer and stronger than other men.

אֶת־כָּל־זֶה רָאִיתִי *All this I have seen.* A savage judgment about the nature of politics. "All power tends to corrupt," and in the world of power, evil men are sometimes feted while they live and given elaborate funerals and memorials when they die, while the good are often outmaneuvered, sidelined and forgotten.

מִמֶּנָּה וְחוֹטֵא יִלָּכֶד בָּהּ׃ רְאֵה זֶה מָצָאתִי אָמְרָה קֹהֶלֶת אַחַת
לְאַחַת לִמְצֹא חֶשְׁבּוֹן׃ אֲשֶׁר עוֹד־בִּקְשָׁה נַפְשִׁי וְלֹא מָצָאתִי
אָדָם אֶחָד מֵאֶלֶף מָצָאתִי וְאִשָּׁה בְכָל־אֵלֶּה לֹא מָצָאתִי׃ לְבַד
רְאֵה־זֶה מָצָאתִי אֲשֶׁר עָשָׂה הָאֱלֹהִים אֶת־הָאָדָם יָשָׁר וְהֵמָּה
ח בִקְשׁוּ חִשְּׁבֹנוֹת רַבִּים׃ מִי כְּהֶחָכָם וּמִי יוֹדֵעַ פֵּשֶׁר דָּבָר חָכְמַת
אָדָם תָּאִיר פָּנָיו וְעֹז פָּנָיו יְשֻׁנֶּא׃ אֲנִי פִּי־מֶלֶךְ שְׁמֹר וְעַל דִּבְרַת
שְׁבוּעַת אֱלֹהִים׃ אַל־תִּבָּהֵל מִפָּנָיו תֵּלֵךְ אַל־תַּעֲמֹד בְּדָבָר רָע
כִּי כָּל־אֲשֶׁר יַחְפֹּץ יַעֲשֶׂה׃ בַּאֲשֶׁר דְּבַר־מֶלֶךְ שִׁלְטוֹן וּמִי יֹאמַר־
לוֹ מַה־תַּעֲשֶׂה׃ שׁוֹמֵר מִצְוָה לֹא יֵדַע דָּבָר רָע וְעֵת וּמִשְׁפָּט
יֵדַע לֵב חָכָם׃ כִּי לְכָל־חֵפֶץ יֵשׁ עֵת וּמִשְׁפָּט כִּי־רָעַת הָאָדָם
רַבָּה עָלָיו׃ כִּי־אֵינֶנּוּ יֹדֵעַ מַה־שֶּׁיִּהְיֶה כִּי כַּאֲשֶׁר יִהְיֶה מִי יַגִּיד
לוֹ׃ אֵין אָדָם שַׁלִּיט בָּרוּחַ לִכְלוֹא אֶת־הָרוּחַ וְאֵין שִׁלְטוֹן בְּיוֹם
הַמָּוֶת וְאֵין מִשְׁלַחַת בַּמִּלְחָמָה וְלֹא־יְמַלֵּט רֶשַׁע אֶת־בְּעָלָיו׃
אֶת־כָּל־זֶה רָאִיתִי וְנָתוֹן אֶת־לִבִּי לְכָל־מַעֲשֶׂה אֲשֶׁר נַעֲשָׂה
תַּחַת הַשָּׁמֶשׁ עֵת אֲשֶׁר שָׁלַט הָאָדָם בְּאָדָם לְרַע לוֹ׃ וּבְכֵן רָאִיתִי
רְשָׁעִים קְבֻרִים וָבָאוּ וּמִמְּקוֹם קָדוֹשׁ יְהַלֵּכוּ וְיִשְׁתַּכְּחוּ בָעִיר
אֲשֶׁר כֵּן־עָשׂוּ גַּם־זֶה הָבֶל׃ אֲשֶׁר אֵין־נַעֲשָׂה פִתְגָם מַעֲשֵׂה

---

fully devoted to the Lord his God, as the heart of David his father had been" (1 Kings 11:4). The man who built the Temple became the man who introduced idolatry into Israel at the highest level. Not only was Israel's spiritual life damaged; so was its political life. After Solomon's death, the kingdom split in two, and never recovered its former glory. Solomon's bitterness toward women here is less about women than about himself. He was the "sinner" who became "entrapped." Hence the last sentence of the passage: "God created man straightforward, but they go seeking endless inventions" – the

evil. A sinner does a hundred evils and is granted long years for it. Yes, I know that good will come to those who fear God, for fearing Him. And good will not come to an evil man, and he will not live long – he passes like a shadow, for he does not fear God.

Yet see this thing of breath that happens on this earth: the righteous to whom the same arrives as to the wicked; and the wicked to whom the same as the righteous comes – and I say: Here again is empty breath. And so I praise joy – for there is no good for man beneath the sun, but to eat and drink and be joyful. This is what he has to accompany him in his labors, through that life that God has given him beneath the sun. When I set my mind to knowing wisdom; to seeing what it is that is done upon this earth – and all day, all night, no sleep do one's eyes see – I saw all the work of God; saw that no man can fathom out the work that is done beneath the sun. One labors to seek it out and will never find it; if a wise man says he knows – no; and never will he be able to find out.

9 All this I took into my mind, trying to understand, all this: that the righteous and the wise and all their actions – all are in the hand of God. Their love, their hate, none of it is known; it is all just placed before them. All is as it is for all. The same fate awaits the righteous

---

we have. We should not let the fractures of the human world rob us of our ability to rejoice in the miracle of life itself.

אֶת־כָּל־זֶה נָתַתִּי אֶל־לִבִּי *All this I took into my mind.* Kohelet here brings his argument to a paradoxical climax. Having said that the dead are more fortunate than the living (4:2), he now says "Better to be a living dog than a dead lion" (9:4), exemplifying the dictum that "The test of a first-rate intelligence is the ability to hold two opposed ideas in mind at the same time and still retain the ability to function." In one sense the dead are better off than the living: they feel no pain. In another, even the most painful life is better than no life at all. That all books end does not mean that books are useless or are all the same. The same is true of life. The very brevity of life means that we should cherish each day. Wisdom and virtue may not make us live forever, but they make us live better, and that is what matters.

הָרָעָה מְהֵרָה עַל־כֵּן מָלֵא לֵב בְּנֵי־הָאָדָם בָּהֶם לַעֲשׂוֹת רָע׃
אֲשֶׁר חֹטֶא עֹשֶׂה רָע מְאַת וּמַאֲרִיךְ לוֹ כִּי גַּם־יוֹדֵעַ אָנִי אֲשֶׁר
יִהְיֶה־טּוֹב לְיִרְאֵי הָאֱלֹהִים אֲשֶׁר יִירְאוּ מִלְּפָנָיו׃ וְטוֹב לֹא־יִהְיֶה
לָרָשָׁע וְלֹא־יַאֲרִיךְ יָמִים כַּצֵּל אֲשֶׁר אֵינֶנּוּ יָרֵא מִלִּפְנֵי אֱלֹהִים׃
יֶשׁ־הֶבֶל אֲשֶׁר נַעֲשָׂה עַל־הָאָרֶץ אֲשֶׁר ׀ יֵשׁ צַדִּיקִים אֲשֶׁר מַגִּיעַ
אֲלֵהֶם כְּמַעֲשֵׂה הָרְשָׁעִים וְיֵשׁ רְשָׁעִים שֶׁמַּגִּיעַ אֲלֵהֶם כְּמַעֲשֵׂה
הַצַּדִּיקִים אָמַרְתִּי שֶׁגַּם־זֶה הָבֶל׃ וְשִׁבַּחְתִּי אֲנִי אֶת־הַשִּׂמְחָה
אֲשֶׁר אֵין־טוֹב לָאָדָם תַּחַת הַשֶּׁמֶשׁ כִּי אִם־לֶאֱכֹל וְלִשְׁתּוֹת
וְלִשְׂמוֹחַ וְהוּא יִלְוֶנּוּ בַעֲמָלוֹ יְמֵי חַיָּיו אֲשֶׁר־נָתַן־לוֹ הָאֱלֹהִים
תַּחַת הַשָּׁמֶשׁ׃ כַּאֲשֶׁר נָתַתִּי אֶת־לִבִּי לָדַעַת חָכְמָה וְלִרְאוֹת
אֶת־הָעִנְיָן אֲשֶׁר נַעֲשָׂה עַל־הָאָרֶץ כִּי גַם בַּיּוֹם וּבַלַּיְלָה שֵׁנָה
בְּעֵינָיו אֵינֶנּוּ רֹאֶה׃ וְרָאִיתִי אֶת־כָּל־מַעֲשֵׂה הָאֱלֹהִים כִּי לֹא יוּכַל
הָאָדָם לִמְצוֹא אֶת־הַמַּעֲשֶׂה אֲשֶׁר נַעֲשָׂה תַחַת־הַשֶּׁמֶשׁ בְּשֶׁל
אֲשֶׁר יַעֲמֹל הָאָדָם לְבַקֵּשׁ וְלֹא יִמְצָא וְגַם אִם־יֹאמַר הֶחָכָם
ט לָדַעַת לֹא יוּכַל לִמְצֹא׃ כִּי אֶת־כָּל־זֶה נָתַתִּי אֶל־לִבִּי וְלָבוּר
אֶת־כָּל־זֶה אֲשֶׁר הַצַּדִּיקִים וְהַחֲכָמִים וַעֲבָדֵיהֶם בְּיַד הָאֱלֹהִים
גַּם־אַהֲבָה גַם־שִׂנְאָה אֵין יוֹדֵעַ הָאָדָם הַכֹּל לִפְנֵיהֶם׃ הַכֹּל כַּאֲשֶׁר

כִּי גַּם־יוֹדֵעַ אָנִי אֲשֶׁר יִהְיֶה־טּוֹב *Yes, I know that good will come.* "The arc of the moral universe is long, but it bends towards justice" (M. L. King).

יֶשׁ־הֶבֶל אֲשֶׁר נַעֲשָׂה *Yet see this thing of breath.* Given the crooked timber of humanity, the world "beneath the sun" only roughly approximates to justice. There are good people who suffer, and bad people who flourish. Why this is so is the deepest question in Judaism, asked, among others, by Moses, Jeremiah and Job, but it is not Kohelet's primary interest. His question is: given that this is so, how shall we live? His answer is: by focusing on joy. This life is all

and the wicked, the good and the pure and the impure, the one who brings offerings and the one who does not. For a good man just as for a sinner; the one who swears falsely with the one who fears his oath. This is the evil in all that is done beneath the sun: the same fate attends everyone. And the hearts of man are weighed down with evil; delirium clouds their minds all their lives – and then they go to the dead.

For one who is still bound to life has something to rely upon: Better to be a living dog than a dead lion. For the living know at least that they must die; while the dead know nothing. No more reward for their actions; their names are forgotten. Their love, their hate, their passions – all are already lost. And they have no more share, no longer; no part in what is done beneath the sun. Go, eat your bread in joy, and drink your wine with a joyful heart, for God has accepted your deeds. Let your clothes at all times be white; let your head never lack anointing oil. Live well, with the woman you love, all the days of the shallow breath He has given you here beneath the sun, for this is your share in life, and in all the toil over which you labor beneath the sun. Whatever you find it in your hands to do – do that with all your strength. For there is no work or reason, no understanding or wisdom, in the grave to which you are going.

Then I turned again and saw beneath the sun – that the race is not given to the swift, nor the war to the mighty; bread is not promised to the wise, nor to the understanding, wealth; no more to the knowing, favor; for time, for misfortune, comes to them all. And man never knows when his time will come: as fish are entrapped in the deadly net, as birds are trapped in the snare, so too are people caught, at just that time of harm that will fall upon them without warning.

This too I saw of wisdom beneath the sun, great beyond my understanding. A small town. Few people in it. A great king came and

---

celebration. The rest – wealth, possessions, position, power – are the gift wrappings of a life, not life itself.

גַּם־זֹה רָאִיתִי חָכְמָה *This too I saw of wisdom.* A powerful story to show that

לַכֹּל מִקְרֶה אֶחָד לַצַּדִּיק וְלָרָשָׁע לַטּוֹב וְלַטָּהוֹר וְלַטָּמֵא וְלַזֹּבֵחַ
וְלַאֲשֶׁר אֵינֶנּוּ זֹבֵחַ כַּטּוֹב כַּחֹטֶא הַנִּשְׁבָּע כַּאֲשֶׁר שְׁבוּעָה יָרֵא׃
זֶה ׀ רָע בְּכֹל אֲשֶׁר־נַעֲשָׂה תַּחַת הַשֶּׁמֶשׁ כִּי־מִקְרֶה אֶחָד לַכֹּל
וְגַם לֵב בְּנֵי־הָאָדָם מָלֵא־רָע וְהוֹלֵלוֹת בִּלְבָבָם בְּחַיֵּיהֶם וְאַחֲרָיו
אֶל־הַמֵּתִים׃ כִּי־מִי אֲשֶׁר יבחר אֶל כָּל־הַחַיִּים יֵשׁ בִּטָּחוֹן כִּי־ יְחֻבַּר
לְכֶלֶב חַי הוּא טוֹב מִן־הָאַרְיֵה הַמֵּת׃ כִּי הַחַיִּים יוֹדְעִים שֶׁיָּמֻתוּ
וְהַמֵּתִים אֵינָם יוֹדְעִים מְאוּמָה וְאֵין־עוֹד לָהֶם שָׂכָר כִּי נִשְׁכַּח
זִכְרָם׃ גַּם אַהֲבָתָם גַּם־שִׂנְאָתָם גַּם־קִנְאָתָם כְּבָר אָבָדָה וְחֵלֶק
אֵין־לָהֶם עוֹד לְעוֹלָם בְּכֹל אֲשֶׁר־נַעֲשָׂה תַּחַת הַשָּׁמֶשׁ׃ לֵךְ אֱכֹל
בְּשִׂמְחָה לַחְמֶךָ וּשְׁתֵה בְלֶב־טוֹב יֵינֶךָ כִּי כְבָר רָצָה הָאֱלֹהִים
אֶת־מַעֲשֶׂיךָ׃ בְּכָל־עֵת יִהְיוּ בְגָדֶיךָ לְבָנִים וְשֶׁמֶן עַל־רֹאשְׁךָ
אַל־יֶחְסָר׃ רְאֵה חַיִּים עִם־אִשָּׁה אֲשֶׁר־אָהַבְתָּ כָּל־יְמֵי חַיֵּי הֶבְלֶךָ
אֲשֶׁר נָתַן־לְךָ תַּחַת הַשֶּׁמֶשׁ כֹּל יְמֵי הֶבְלֶךָ כִּי הוּא חֶלְקְךָ בַּחַיִּים
וּבַעֲמָלְךָ אֲשֶׁר־אַתָּה עָמֵל תַּחַת הַשָּׁמֶשׁ׃ כֹּל אֲשֶׁר תִּמְצָא יָדְךָ
לַעֲשׂוֹת בְּכֹחֲךָ עֲשֵׂה כִּי אֵין מַעֲשֶׂה וְחֶשְׁבּוֹן וְדַעַת וְחָכְמָה
בִּשְׁאוֹל אֲשֶׁר אַתָּה הֹלֵךְ שָׁמָּה׃ שַׁבְתִּי וְרָאֹה תַחַת־הַשֶּׁמֶשׁ כִּי
לֹא לַקַּלִּים הַמֵּרוֹץ וְלֹא לַגִּבּוֹרִים הַמִּלְחָמָה וְגַם לֹא לַחֲכָמִים
לֶחֶם וְגַם לֹא לַנְּבֹנִים עֹשֶׁר וְגַם לֹא לַיֹּדְעִים חֵן כִּי־עֵת וָפֶגַע יִקְרֶה
אֶת־כֻּלָּם׃ כִּי גַּם לֹא־יֵדַע הָאָדָם אֶת־עִתּוֹ כַּדָּגִים שֶׁנֶּאֱחָזִים
בִּמְצוֹדָה רָעָה וְכַצִּפֳּרִים הָאֲחֻזוֹת בַּפָּח כָּהֵם יוּקָשִׁים בְּנֵי הָאָדָם
לְעֵת רָעָה כְּשֶׁתִּפּוֹל עֲלֵיהֶם פִּתְאֹם׃ גַּם־זֹה רָאִיתִי חָכְמָה תַחַת

לֵךְ אֱכֹל בְּשִׂמְחָה לַחְמֶךָ *Go, eat your bread in joy.* Kohelet's ultimate judgment about what makes a life worth living: love, work, wholeheartedness, and

surrounded it and built great siege-walls all around. And one poor wise man was there to be found, able to save the whole town by his wisdom; and not a soul remembered that poor man. And I said: Wisdom is better than might; but the wisdom of a poor man is scorned, his words unheeded. The quiet words of the wise are heeded more than the shout of a ruler among fools. Better wisdom than weaponry – yet one lone sinner can destroy much good.

10 Dead flies ferment and putrefy perfumer's oils. More costly than wisdom, than honor – is one small dose of foolishness. A wise man's mind is to his right hand; and the mind of a fool to his left. Even as he walks along the way, a fool's mind is missing, telling every passerby that he is a fool.

If a ruler's spirit turns against you, do not leave your place, for appeasement can lay great sins to rest. Here is an evil I have seen beneath the sun, like an error coming forth from the ruler's mouth: fools are raised to the greatest heights, while rich men sit in the gutter. I have seen slaves riding on horseback, and princes walking like slaves on the ground.

He who digs the pit may fall into it, and he who tears down walls – a snake may bite him. He who quarries the stone will come to grief by it; and he who chops the tree may by that tree be harmed. If the axe grows blunt and is not polished, then the one who wields it must add force; for skill yields profit only through wisdom. If the snake that cannot be charmed bites, there is no profit to the charmer then. The words of the wise bring favor, while the lips of a fool will swallow him up. His speech begins with foolishness, and ends with evil delirium. Yet the fool speaks on and on. Man does not know what will be; yes, who may tell him what will come after? The labor of fools exhausts them; they know not even the way to the city.

Right connotes strength, focus and skill. Seforno says the distinction between right and left is between direction and desire.

הַכְּסִילִים ... לֹא־יָדַע לָלֶכֶת אֶל־עִיר *Fools… know not even the way to the city.* An idiomatic expression for lacking an elementary sense of direction in life.

הַשֶּׁמֶשׁ וּגְדוֹלָה הִיא אֵלָי׃ עִיר קְטַנָּה וַאֲנָשִׁים בָּהּ מְעָט וּבָא־
אֵלֶיהָ מֶלֶךְ גָּדוֹל וְסָבַב אֹתָהּ וּבָנָה עָלֶיהָ מְצוֹדִים גְּדֹלִים׃ וּמָצָא
בָהּ אִישׁ מִסְכֵּן חָכָם וּמִלַּט־הוּא אֶת־הָעִיר בְּחָכְמָתוֹ וְאָדָם לֹא
זָכַר אֶת־הָאִישׁ הַמִּסְכֵּן הַהוּא׃ וְאָמַרְתִּי אָנִי טוֹבָה חָכְמָה
מִגְּבוּרָה וְחָכְמַת הַמִּסְכֵּן בְּזוּיָה וּדְבָרָיו אֵינָם נִשְׁמָעִים׃ דִּבְרֵי
חֲכָמִים בְּנַחַת נִשְׁמָעִים מִזַּעֲקַת מוֹשֵׁל בַּכְּסִילִים׃ טוֹבָה חָכְמָה
מִכְּלֵי קְרָב וְחוֹטֶא אֶחָד יְאַבֵּד טוֹבָה הַרְבֵּה׃ זְבוּבֵי מָוֶת יַבְאִישׁ י
יַבִּיעַ שֶׁמֶן רוֹקֵחַ יָקָר מֵחָכְמָה מִכָּבוֹד סִכְלוּת מְעָט׃ לֵב חָכָם
לִימִינוֹ וְלֵב כְּסִיל לִשְׂמֹאלוֹ׃ וְגַם־בַּדֶּרֶךְ כשהסכל הֹלֵךְ לִבּוֹ חָסֵר כְּשֶׁסָּכָל
וְאָמַר לַכֹּל סָכָל הוּא׃ אִם־רוּחַ הַמּוֹשֵׁל תַּעֲלֶה עָלֶיךָ מְקוֹמְךָ
אַל־תַּנַּח כִּי מַרְפֵּא יַנִּיחַ חֲטָאִים גְּדוֹלִים׃ יֵשׁ רָעָה רָאִיתִי תַּחַת
הַשָּׁמֶשׁ כִּשְׁגָגָה שֶׁיֹּצָא מִלִּפְנֵי הַשַּׁלִּיט׃ נִתַּן הַסֶּכֶל בַּמְּרוֹמִים
רַבִּים וַעֲשִׁירִים בַּשֵּׁפֶל יֵשֵׁבוּ׃ רָאִיתִי עֲבָדִים עַל־סוּסִים וְשָׂרִים
הֹלְכִים כַּעֲבָדִים עַל־הָאָרֶץ׃ חֹפֵר גּוּמָּץ בּוֹ יִפּוֹל וּפֹרֵץ גָּדֵר יִשְּׁכֶנּוּ
נָחָשׁ׃ מַסִּיעַ אֲבָנִים יֵעָצֵב בָּהֶם בּוֹקֵעַ עֵצִים יִסָּכֶן בָּם׃ אִם־קֵהָה
הַבַּרְזֶל וְהוּא לֹא־פָנִים קִלְקַל וַחֲיָלִים יְגַבֵּר וְיִתְרוֹן הַכְשֵׁיר
חָכְמָה׃ אִם־יִשֹּׁךְ הַנָּחָשׁ בְּלוֹא־לָחַשׁ וְאֵין יִתְרוֹן לְבַעַל הַלָּשׁוֹן׃
דִּבְרֵי פִי־חָכָם חֵן וְשִׂפְתוֹת כְּסִיל תְּבַלְּעֶנּוּ׃ תְּחִלַּת דִּבְרֵי־פִיהוּ
סִכְלוּת וְאַחֲרִית פִּיהוּ הוֹלֵלוּת רָעָה׃ וְהַסָּכָל יַרְבֶּה דְבָרִים לֹא־
יֵדַע הָאָדָם מַה־שֶּׁיִּהְיֶה וַאֲשֶׁר יִהְיֶה מֵאַחֲרָיו מִי יַגִּיד לוֹ׃ עֲמַל
הַכְּסִילִים תְּיַגְּעֶנּוּ אֲשֶׁר לֹא־יָדַע לָלֶכֶת אֶל־עִיר׃ אִי־לָךְ אֶרֶץ

---

though wisdom is the greatest human gift, it does not necessarily bring recognition or reward. It is, and will always be, its own reward.

לֵב חָכָם לִימִינוֹ *A wise man's mind is to his right hand.* Not, of course, literally.

I pity you, the land whose king is a boy, whose princes feast in the morning. Happy the land whose king is a nobleman, and whose princes eat at the right time, strong, without drunkenness. The roof caves in for much laziness; and hands laid down spring leaks in the house. Feasts are made for laughter, and wine fills life with joy – and money will answer for everything.

Never curse a king, not even in your mind, nor a rich man, even in your innermost room. For a bird of the sky will carry that voice; a winged creature will repeat the word.

1 Cast your bread out onto the waters, for in the long passage of days you will find it again. Give of what is yours to seven, to eight, for on this earth you cannot know what evil may yet come. If the clouds fill with rain, they must empty it onto the earth. If a tree falls to the south, to the north – wherever that tree falls, there it will lie. One who watches for the wind will never sow; one who gazes at the clouds will never reap. And just as you know not the way of the wind, nor what frame fills a pregnant woman's womb, so you cannot know the work of God; and everything is His work. Sow your seeds in the morning, and by evening do not lay your hands down – for you do not know which will prove fit, these seeds or those, or whether the two are as good as one another. There is a sweetness in the light; it is good for the eyes to see the sun. And should a man live many years he should rejoice in all of them, remembering, too, the days of darkness, for there will be many. All that comes is but a breath.

Young man, rejoice now in your youth; let your heart ease you while

---

אִם־יִמָּלְאוּ הֶעָבִים גֶּשֶׁם *If the clouds fill with rain.* If you prosper, share some of your blessings with others.

שֹׁמֵר רוּחַ *One who watches for the wind.* All creative endeavor involves risk. Do not wait for certainty. It will never come.

וּמָתוֹק הָאוֹר *There is a sweetness in the light.* A change of tone as Kohelet prepares for the culmination of his argument. Having shown how much suffering, injustice, and uncertainty there is in life, he now turns to its moments of beauty.

בָּחוּר *Young man.* The point to which Kohelet has been tending since the

שֶׁמַּלְכֵּךְ נָעַר וְשָׂרַיִךְ בַּבֹּקֶר יֹאכֵלוּ: אַשְׁרֵיךְ אֶרֶץ שֶׁמַּלְכֵּךְ בֶּן־
חוֹרִים וְשָׂרַיִךְ בָּעֵת יֹאכֵלוּ בִּגְבוּרָה וְלֹא בַשְּׁתִי: בַּעֲצַלְתַּיִם יִמַּךְ
הַמְּקָרֶה וּבְשִׁפְלוּת יָדַיִם יִדְלֹף הַבָּיִת: לִשְׂחוֹק עֹשִׂים לֶחֶם וְיַיִן
יְשַׂמַּח חַיִּים וְהַכֶּסֶף יַעֲנֶה אֶת־הַכֹּל: גַּם בְּמַדָּעֲךָ מֶלֶךְ אַל־תְּקַלֵּל
וּבְחַדְרֵי מִשְׁכָּבְךָ אַל־תְּקַלֵּל עָשִׁיר כִּי עוֹף הַשָּׁמַיִם יוֹלִיךְ אֶת־
כְּנָפַיִם הַקּוֹל וּבַעַל הכנפים יַגֵּיד דָּבָר: שַׁלַּח לַחְמְךָ עַל־פְּנֵי הַמָּיִם א
כִּי־בְרֹב הַיָּמִים תִּמְצָאֶנּוּ: תֶּן־חֵלֶק לְשִׁבְעָה וְגַם לִשְׁמוֹנָה כִּי לֹא
תֵדַע מַה־יִּהְיֶה רָעָה עַל־הָאָרֶץ: אִם־יִמָּלְאוּ הֶעָבִים גֶּשֶׁם עַל־
הָאָרֶץ יָרִיקוּ וְאִם־יִפּוֹל עֵץ בַּדָּרוֹם וְאִם בַּצָּפוֹן מְקוֹם שֶׁיִּפּוֹל
הָעֵץ שָׁם יְהוּא: שֹׁמֵר רוּחַ לֹא יִזְרָע וְרֹאֶה בֶעָבִים לֹא יִקְצוֹר:
כַּאֲשֶׁר אֵינְךָ יוֹדֵעַ מַה־דֶּרֶךְ הָרוּחַ כַּעֲצָמִים בְּבֶטֶן הַמְּלֵאָה כָּכָה
לֹא תֵדַע אֶת־מַעֲשֵׂה הָאֱלֹהִים אֲשֶׁר יַעֲשֶׂה אֶת־הַכֹּל: בַּבֹּקֶר
זְרַע אֶת־זַרְעֶךָ וְלָעֶרֶב אַל־תַּנַּח יָדֶךָ כִּי אֵינְךָ יוֹדֵעַ אֵי זֶה יִכְשַׁר
הֲזֶה אוֹ־זֶה וְאִם־שְׁנֵיהֶם כְּאֶחָד טוֹבִים: וּמָתוֹק הָאוֹר וְטוֹב
לַעֵינַיִם לִרְאוֹת אֶת־הַשָּׁמֶשׁ: כִּי אִם־שָׁנִים הַרְבֵּה יִחְיֶה הָאָדָם
בְּכֻלָּם יִשְׂמָח וְיִזְכֹּר אֶת־יְמֵי הַחֹשֶׁךְ כִּי־הַרְבֵּה יִהְיוּ כָּל־שֶׁבָּא
הָבֶל: שְׂמַח בָּחוּר בְּיַלְדוּתֶךָ וִיטִיבְךָ לִבְּךָ בִּימֵי בְחוּרוֹתֶיךָ וְהַלֵּךְ

גַּם בְּמַדָּעֲךָ *Not even in your mind.* Negative thoughts eventually find expression in speech, similar to the English expression, "Don't even think of it."

שַׁלַּח לַחְמְךָ *Cast your bread.* A series of ideas, part moral, part pragmatic, about how to act, knowing the unpredictability of the future. Be generous to others because, for the most part, they will be generous to you: the principle of reciprocal altruism.

תֶּן־חֵלֶק לְשִׁבְעָה וְגַם לִשְׁמוֹנָה *Give of what is yours to seven, to eight.* Rashi relates this to the recipients of charity. Ibn Ezra relates it to days: give all week and then begin again.

you are young. Follow your heart where it leads you, your eyes where they allure you – and know that God will bring you into judgment for all this. So clear your heart of bitterness and free your flesh of pain, for youth and dark-haired days pass by like breath.

2 And remember your Creator in these days of your youth; before the
days of despair, before years come when you shall say: There is nothing here that I desire. Before the sun is darkened and the light, the moon and stars, and clouds return again after the rain. The day when the guards of the house will shake, and the soldiers buckle; when the grinders sit idle, grown few, and the women at the windows sit in darkness. When all the doors in the street are closed, as the mill-stone falls silent, and a man starts up at the sound of a bird, but the singing girls'

---

desire. On Shavuot, at the beginning of summer, we read in Ruth about love as companionship, faithfulness, marriage, and family. On Sukkot, we read of the love Kohelet has found in old age (*"Live well, with the woman you love"* – 9:9). The book ends with the elderly author addressing the youth of the next generation, and so the cycle begins again.

וּזְכֹר אֶת־בּוֹרְאֶיךָ בִּימֵי בְּחוּרֹתֶיךָ *And remember your Creator in these days of your youth.* One of the great passages in literature, a moving meditation on old age. The prose slows to an adagio. Kohelet uses a montage of images, each one fading into the next, each suggesting darkness and decay. First of light fading and clouds covering the sky, then of a house, once grand and full of laughter, now dilapidated and falling into ruin, then of a lamp that has fallen to the ground, then of vessels once used to draw water from a well, but which now lie broken and abandoned.

עַד אֲשֶׁר ... הַשֶּׁמֶשׁ וְהָאוֹר *Before the sun ... and the light*: Before you begin to lose the sharpness of your senses.

שֹׁמְרֵי הַבַּיִת *The guards of the house.* The sinews.

אַנְשֵׁי הֶחָיִל *The grinders.* Teeth.

הָרֹאוֹת *Windows.* The eyes.

דְלָתַיִם *Doors.* Lips.

וְיָקוּם לְקוֹל הַצִּפּוֹר *Starts up at the sound of a bird.* The old sleep lightly and are easily woken.

בְּדַרְכֵי לִבְּךָ ובמראי עֵינֶיךָ וְדָע כִּי עַל־כׇּל־אֵלֶּה יְבִיאֲךָ הָאֱלֹהִים וּבְמַרְאֵה
בַּמִּשְׁפָּט׃ וְהָסֵר כַּעַס מִלִּבֶּךָ וְהַעֲבֵר רָעָה מִבְּשָׂרֶךָ כִּי־הַיַּלְדוּת
וְהַשַּׁחֲרוּת הָבֶל׃ וּזְכֹר אֶת־בּוֹרְאֶיךָ בִּימֵי בְּחוּרֹתֶיךָ עַד אֲשֶׁר ב
לֹא־יָבֹאוּ יְמֵי הָרָעָה וְהִגִּיעוּ שָׁנִים אֲשֶׁר תֹּאמַר אֵין־לִי בָהֶם
חֵפֶץ׃ עַד אֲשֶׁר לֹא־תֶחְשַׁךְ הַשֶּׁמֶשׁ וְהָאוֹר וְהַיָּרֵחַ וְהַכּוֹכָבִים
וְשָׁבוּ הֶעָבִים אַחַר הַגָּשֶׁם׃ בַּיּוֹם שֶׁיָּזֻעוּ שֹׁמְרֵי הַבַּיִת וְהִתְעַוְּתוּ
אַנְשֵׁי הֶחָיִל וּבָטְלוּ הַטֹּחֲנוֹת כִּי מִעֵטוּ וְחָשְׁכוּ הָרֹאוֹת בָּאֲרֻבּוֹת׃
וְסֻגְּרוּ דְלָתַיִם בַּשּׁוּק בִּשְׁפַל קוֹל הַטַּחֲנָה וְיָקוּם לְקוֹל הַצִּפּוֹר

---

beginning. He is now an old man, and despite his wealth, power and supposed wisdom, he now knows that for much of his life he was traveling in the wrong direction. He wants to pass on this knowledge to the next generation. His fundamental mistake, made by so many, was to seek happiness in externalities, pursuing the worldly markers of success. But even by worldly standards, these do not deliver what they promise. Wealth may be lost. Justice does not always win in the affairs of humankind. Wisdom often goes unrecognized and unrewarded. We will never know what became of our legacy to the future, for by then we will not be here.

Our fundamental error, Kohelet discovers in old age, is to pursue happiness tomorrow by sacrificing today. We can be so busy making a living that we forget how to live. So intent are we on our destination that we travel forgetting to enjoy the view. Hence Kohelet's conclusion: the importance of intrinsic motivation, of acting *lishma,* for the sake of the act itself. Seek wisdom for the sake of wisdom, give love for the sake of love, and labor for the sake of honest toil. What matters is not what these bring you but what they make you. Work for tomorrow but celebrate today. Focus less on happiness than on joy. Above all, seek joy when you are young, because the future is unknowable, and life is hazardous and short. Do not miss out on inhaling life to the full while you still have the strength and passion to do so.

Thus Kohelet, which begins with the greatest statement in Tanakh of cyclical time, ends by closing the circle of the year. The three *megillot* we read on the pilgrimage festivals track the seasons of the year, and of life. On Pesaḥ, we read Song of Songs, about love in the springtime of youth, as passionate

voices drop low. And one lives in terror of heights, and all the pitfalls on the road. The almond blossoms, the grasshopper bears its burden, the caper fruit breaks asunder, but man is departing for his eternal home, and the mourners turn about around the streets. Remember – before the silver cord snaps, and the gold bowl is shattered, and the jug is broken beside the spring, and the basin is smashed against the well, the dust returns to the earth where it began, and the spirit returns to God who gave it. Shallowest breath, says Kohelet. It is all but shallow breath.

Kohelet's wisdom went further than this; he taught the people understanding always, and weighed and explored and assembled many wise sayings. Kohelet sought out choicest words, and wrote words of truth honestly. The words of the wise are like goads; like pointed nails are the scholars' sayings. One Shepherd gave them all. And further than this, my child, take heed; there is no end to the making of many books, and much study wearies the flesh.

The final word: it has all been said. Hold God in awe, and heed His commands, for that is all man has. And all that is done – God shall bring it to judgment; all that is hidden, the good and the bad.

The final word: it has all been said.
Hold God in awe, and heed His commands, for that is all man has.

[if it is open to so many conflicting interpretations]?' Therefore it is written, *One Shepherd gave them all* – one God gave them, and one leader [Moses] declared them from the mouth of the Lord of all, blessed be He" (*Ḥagiga* 3b).

אֶת־הָאֱלֹהִים יְרָא *Hold God in awe.* This is not a contrived ending, added to mitigate the seeming disillusionment of the rest of the text, but rather one that has been implicit throughout. Though wisdom is the highest of human accomplishments, it is profoundly limited. What was said of another sage is eminently true of Kohelet: He was the wisest of men because he knew how little he knew. There is much we cannot, and will never, understand. Our lives are short, our intellect limited, and our capacity for self-deception immense. That is why revelation is necessary. Wisdom can never supplant the word of the One who spoke and brought the universe into being. For all its skepticism, Kohelet is a deeply pious work of one who has seen how small we are in the scheme of things, made wise only by humility and awe in the conscious presence of God's eternity.

וְיִשַּׁחוּ כׇּל־בְּנוֹת הַשִּׁיר׃ גַּם מִגָּבֹהַּ יִרָאוּ וְחַתְחַתִּים בַּדֶּרֶךְ וְיָנֵאץ
הַשָּׁקֵד וְיִסְתַּבֵּל הֶחָגָב וְתָפֵר הָאֲבִיּוֹנָה כִּי־הֹלֵךְ הָאָדָם אֶל־בֵּית
עוֹלָמוֹ וְסָבְבוּ בַשּׁוּק הַסּוֹפְדִים׃ עַד אֲשֶׁר לֹא־ירחק חֶבֶל הַכֶּסֶף יֵרָתֵק
וְתָרֻץ גֻּלַּת הַזָּהָב וְתִשָּׁבֶר כַּד עַל־הַמַּבּוּעַ וְנָרֹץ הַגַּלְגַּל אֶל־הַבּוֹר׃
וְיָשֹׁב הֶעָפָר עַל־הָאָרֶץ כְּשֶׁהָיָה וְהָרוּחַ תָּשׁוּב אֶל־הָאֱלֹהִים
אֲשֶׁר נְתָנָהּ׃ הֲבֵל הֲבָלִים אָמַר הַקּוֹהֶלֶת הַכֹּל הָבֶל׃ וְיֹתֵר שֶׁהָיָה
קֹהֶלֶת חָכָם עוֹד לִמַּד־דַּעַת אֶת־הָעָם וְאִזֵּן וְחִקֵּר תִּקֵּן מְשָׁלִים
הַרְבֵּה׃ בִּקֵּשׁ קֹהֶלֶת לִמְצֹא דִּבְרֵי־חֵפֶץ וְכָתוּב יֹשֶׁר דִּבְרֵי אֱמֶת׃
דִּבְרֵי חֲכָמִים כַּדׇּרְבֹנוֹת וּכְמַשְׂמְרוֹת נְטוּעִים בַּעֲלֵי אֲסֻפּוֹת נִתְּנוּ
מֵרֹעֶה אֶחָד׃ וְיֹתֵר מֵהֵמָּה בְּנִי הִזָּהֵר עֲשׂוֹת סְפָרִים הַרְבֵּה אֵין
קֵץ וְלַהַג הַרְבֵּה יְגִעַת בָּשָׂר׃ סוֹף דָּבָר הַכֹּל נִשְׁמָע אֶת־הָאֱלֹהִים
יְרָא וְאֶת־מִצְוֺתָיו שְׁמוֹר כִּי־זֶה כׇּל־הָאָדָם׃ כִּי אֶת־כׇּל־מַעֲשֶׂה
הָאֱלֹהִים יָבִא בְמִשְׁפָּט עַל כׇּל־נֶעְלָם אִם־טוֹב וְאִם־רָע׃

סוף דבר הכל נשמע
את האלהים ירא ואת מצותיו שמור כי זה כל האדם

מִגָּבֹהַּ יִרָאוּ *Terror of heights.* The elderly fear falling.

וְיָנֵאץ הַשָּׁקֵד *The almond blossoms.* Hair turns white.

הֶחָגָב *The grasshopper.* Once light and sprightly, now overburdened and slow.

הֲבֵל הֲבָלִים *Shallowest breath.* With fine artistry, Kohelet ends where he began. For as he wrote at the beginning, a generation goes and another generation comes. He is about to leave this life, and wishes to leave his greatest legacy – the wisdom whose price was pain – to the young. On this harvest festival, this is Kohelet's harvest: the gleanings of a life.

דִּבְרֵי חֲכָמִים כַּדׇּרְבֹנוֹת *The words of the wise are like goads.* They are not comfortable or comforting, but they give direction and help us avoid losing our way.

בַּעֲלֵי אֲסֻפּוֹת *The scholars' sayings.* "This refers to the scholars who sit in assembly studying the Torah, some declaring 'Clean,' others 'Unclean,' some forbidding, others permitting. One might then say, 'How can I learn the Torah

MOURNER'S KADDISH

The following prayer, said by mourners, requires the presence of a minyan.
A transliteration can be found on page 1467.

Mourner: יִתְגַּדַּל Magnified and sanctified
may His great name be,
in the world He created by His will.
May He establish His kingdom
in your lifetime and in your days,
and in the lifetime of all the house of Israel,
swiftly and soon –
and say: Amen.

All: May His great name be blessed for ever and all time.

Mourner: Blessed and praised,
glorified and exalted,
raised and honored,
uplifted and lauded
be the name of the Holy One,
blessed be He,
beyond any blessing,
song, praise and consolation
uttered in the world –
and say: Amen.

May there be great peace from heaven,
and life for us and all Israel –
and say: Amen.

Bow, take three steps back, as if taking leave of the Divine Presence,
then bow, first left, then right, then center, while saying:
May He who makes peace in His high places,
make peace for us and all Israel –
and say: Amen.

On Shemini Atzeret, continue on page 1080.
In Israel, on the first day of Sukkot, continue on page 426.

קדיש יתום

The following prayer, said by mourners, requires the presence of a מנין.
A transliteration can be found on page 1467.

אבל: יִתְגַּדַּל וְיִתְקַדַּשׁ שְׁמֵהּ רַבָּא (קהל: אָמֵן)
בְּעָלְמָא דִּי בְרָא כִרְעוּתֵהּ
וְיַמְלִיךְ מַלְכוּתֵהּ
בְּחַיֵּיכוֹן וּבְיוֹמֵיכוֹן וּבְחַיֵּי דְכָל בֵּית יִשְׂרָאֵל
בַּעֲגָלָא וּבִזְמַן קָרִיב
וְאִמְרוּ אָמֵן. (קהל: אָמֵן)

קהל ואבל: יְהֵא שְׁמֵהּ רַבָּא מְבָרַךְ לְעָלַם וּלְעָלְמֵי עָלְמַיָּא.

אבל: יִתְבָּרַךְ וְיִשְׁתַּבַּח וְיִתְפָּאַר
וְיִתְרוֹמַם וְיִתְנַשֵּׂא וְיִתְהַדָּר וְיִתְעַלֶּה וְיִתְהַלָּל
שְׁמֵהּ דְּקֻדְשָׁא בְּרִיךְ הוּא (קהל: בְּרִיךְ הוּא)
לְעֵלָּא מִן כָּל בִּרְכָתָא וְשִׁירָתָא, תֻּשְׁבְּחָתָא וְנֶחֱמָתָא
דַּאֲמִירָן בְּעָלְמָא
וְאִמְרוּ אָמֵן. (קהל: אָמֵן)

יְהֵא שְׁלָמָא רַבָּא מִן שְׁמַיָּא
וְחַיִּים, עָלֵינוּ וְעַל כָּל יִשְׂרָאֵל
וְאִמְרוּ אָמֵן. (קהל: אָמֵן)

Bow, take three steps back, as if taking leave of the Divine Presence, then bow, first left, then right, then center, while saying:

עֹשֶׂה שָׁלוֹם בִּמְרוֹמָיו
הוּא יַעֲשֶׂה שָׁלוֹם עָלֵינוּ וְעַל כָּל יִשְׂרָאֵל
וְאִמְרוּ אָמֵן. (קהל: אָמֵן)

On שמיני עצרת*, continue on page 1081.*
In ארץ ישראל*, on the first day of* סוכות*, continue on page 427.*

REMOVING THE TORAH FROM THE ARK

אֵין־כָּמְוֹךָ There is none like You among the heavenly powers, *Ps. 86*
LORD, and there are no works like Yours.
Your kingdom is an eternal kingdom, *Ps. 145*
and Your dominion is for all generations.

The LORD is King, the LORD was King,
the LORD shall be King for ever and all time.
The LORD will give strength to His people; *Ps. 29*
the LORD will bless His people with peace.

Father of compassion,
favor Zion with Your goodness; rebuild the walls of Jerusalem. *Ps. 51*
For we trust in You alone, King, God,
high and exalted, Master of worlds.

The Ark is opened and the congregation stands. All say:

וַיְהִי בִּנְסֹעַ Whenever the Ark set out, Moses would say, *Num. 10*
"Arise, LORD, and may Your enemies be scattered.
May those who hate You flee before You."
For the Torah shall come forth from Zion, *Is. 2*
and the word of the LORD from Jerusalem.
Blessed is He who in His holiness
gave the Torah to His people Israel.

Zohar, Vayak-hel

Blessed is the name of the Master of the Universe. Blessed is Your crown and Your place. May Your favor always be with Your people Israel. Show Your people the salvation of Your right hand in Your Temple. Grant us the gift of Your good light, and accept our prayers in mercy. May it be Your will to prolong our life in goodness. May I be counted among the righteous, so that You will have compassion on me and protect me and all that is mine and all that is Your people Israel's. You feed all; You sustain all; You rule over all; You rule over kings, for sovereignty is Yours. I am a servant of the Holy One, blessed be He, before whom and before whose glorious Torah I bow at all times. Not in man do I trust, nor on any angel do I rely, but on the God of heaven who is the God of truth, whose Torah is truth, whose prophets speak truth, and who abounds in acts of love and truth. ▸ In Him I trust, and to His holy and glorious name I offer praises. May it be Your will to open my heart to the Torah, and to fulfill the wishes of my heart and of the hearts of all Your people Israel for good, for life, and for peace.

הוצאת ספר תורה

אֵין־כָּמְוֹךָ בָאֱלֹהִים, אֲדֹנָי, וְאֵין כְּמַעֲשֶׂיךָ: תהלים פו
מַלְכוּתְךָ מַלְכוּת כָּל־עֹלָמִים, וּמֶמְשַׁלְתְּךָ בְּכָל־דּוֹר וָדֹר: תהלים קמה

יהוה מֶלֶךְ, יהוה מָלָךְ, יהוה יִמְלֹךְ לְעֹלָם וָעֶד.
יהוה עֹז לְעַמּוֹ יִתֵּן, יהוה יְבָרֵךְ אֶת־עַמּוֹ בַשָּׁלוֹם: תהלים כט

אַב הָרַחֲמִים, הֵיטִיבָה בִרְצוֹנְךָ אֶת־צִיּוֹן תִּבְנֶה חוֹמוֹת יְרוּשָׁלָםִ: תהלים נא
כִּי בְךָ לְבַד בָּטָחְנוּ, מֶלֶךְ אֵל רָם וְנִשָּׂא, אֲדוֹן עוֹלָמִים.

The ארון קודש is opened and the קהל stands. All say:

וַיְהִי בִּנְסֹעַ הָאָרֹן וַיֹּאמֶר מֹשֶׁה במדבר י
קוּמָה יהוה וְיָפֻצוּ אֹיְבֶיךָ וְיָנֻסוּ מְשַׂנְאֶיךָ מִפָּנֶיךָ:
כִּי מִצִּיּוֹן תֵּצֵא תוֹרָה וּדְבַר־יהוה מִירוּשָׁלָםִ: ישעיה ב
בָּרוּךְ שֶׁנָּתַן תּוֹרָה לְעַמּוֹ יִשְׂרָאֵל בִּקְדֻשָּׁתוֹ.

בְּרִיךְ שְׁמֵהּ דְּמָרֵא עָלְמָא, בְּרִיךְ כִּתְרָךְ וְאַתְרָךְ. יְהֵא רְעוּתָךְ עִם עַמָּךְ יִשְׂרָאֵל זוהר ויקהל
לְעָלַם, וּפֻרְקַן יְמִינָךְ אַחֲזֵי לְעַמָּךְ בְּבֵית מַקְדְּשָׁךְ, וּלְאַמְטוּיֵי לָנָא מִטּוּב נְהוֹרָךְ, וּלְקַבֵּל צְלוֹתָנָא בְּרַחֲמִין. יְהֵא רַעֲוָא קֳדָמָךְ דְּתוֹרִיךְ לָן חַיִּין בְּטִיבוּ, וְלֶהֱוֵי אֲנָא פְקִידָא בְּגוֹ צַדִּיקַיָּא, לְמִרְחַם עָלַי וּלְמִנְטַר יָתִי וְיַת כָּל דִּי לִי וְדִי לְעַמָּךְ יִשְׂרָאֵל. אַנְתְּ הוּא זָן לְכֹלָּא וּמְפַרְנֵס לְכֹלָּא, אַנְתְּ הוּא שַׁלִּיט עַל כֹּלָּא, אַנְתְּ הוּא דְּשַׁלִּיט עַל מַלְכַיָּא, וּמַלְכוּתָא דִּילָךְ הִיא. אֲנָא עַבְדָּא דְקֻדְשָׁא בְּרִיךְ הוּא, דְּסָגִידְנָא קַמֵּהּ וּמִקַּמֵּי דִּיקַר אוֹרַיְתֵהּ בְּכָל עִדָּן וְעִדָּן. לָא עַל אֱנָשׁ רְחִיצְנָא וְלָא עַל בַּר אֱלָהִין סָמִיכְנָא, אֶלָּא בֶּאֱלָהָא דִשְׁמַיָּא, דְּהוּא אֱלָהָא קְשׁוֹט, וְאוֹרַיְתֵהּ קְשׁוֹט, וּנְבִיאוֹהִי קְשׁוֹט, וּמַסְגֵּא לְמֶעְבַּד טַבְוָן וּקְשׁוֹט. ◄ בֵּהּ אֲנָא רָחִיץ, וְלִשְׁמֵהּ קַדִּישָׁא יַקִּירָא אֲנָא אֵמַר תֻּשְׁבְּחָן. יְהֵא רַעֲוָא קֳדָמָךְ דְּתִפְתַּח לִבָּאִי בְּאוֹרַיְתָא, וְתַשְׁלִים מִשְׁאֲלִין דְּלִבָּאִי וְלִבָּא דְכָל עַמָּךְ יִשְׂרָאֵל לְטָב וּלְחַיִּין וְלִשְׁלָם.

Two Torah scrolls are removed from the Ark. The Leader takes one in his right arm and, followed by the congregation, says:

Listen, Israel: the LORD is our God, the LORD is One. *Deut. 6*

Leader then congregation:

One is our God; great is our Master; holy is His name.

The Leader takes the Torah scroll in his right arm, bows toward the Ark and says:

Magnify the LORD with me, and let us exalt His name together. *Ps. 34*

The Ark is closed. The Leader carries the Torah scroll to the bima and the congregation says:

לְךָ Yours, LORD, are the greatness and the power, the glory and the *1 Chr. 29*
majesty and splendor, for everything in heaven and earth is Yours. Yours, LORD, is the kingdom; You are exalted as Head over all.

רוֹמְמוּ Exalt the LORD our God and bow to His footstool; He is holy. *Ps. 99*
Exalt the LORD our God, and bow at His holy mountain, for holy is the LORD our God.

Over all may the name of the Supreme King of kings, the Holy One blessed be He, be magnified and sanctified, praised and glorified, exalted and extolled, in the worlds that He has created – this world and the World to Come – in accordance with His will, and the will of those who fear Him, and the will of the whole house of Israel. He is the Rock of worlds, LORD of all creatures, God of all souls, who dwells in the spacious heights and inhabits the high heavens of old. His holiness is over the Ḥayyot and over the throne of glory. Therefore may Your name, LORD our God, be sanctified among us in the sight of all that lives.
Let us sing before Him a new song, as it is written: "Sing to God, make music for *Ps. 68*
His name, extol Him who rides the clouds – the LORD is His name – and exult before Him." And may we see Him eye to eye when He returns to His abode
as it is written: "For they shall see eye to eye when the LORD returns to Zion." *Is. 52*
And it is said: "Then will the glory of the LORD be revealed, and all mankind *Is. 40*
together shall see that the mouth of the LORD has spoken."

Father of mercy, have compassion on the people borne by Him. May He remember the covenant with the mighty (patriarchs), and deliver us from evil times. May He reproach the evil instinct in the people by Him, and graciously grant that we be an eternal remnant. May He fulfill in good measure our requests for salvation and compassion.

Two ספרי תורה *are removed from the* ארון קודש. *The* שליח ציבור *takes one in his right arm and, followed by the* קהל, *says:*

דברים ו **שְׁמַע יִשְׂרָאֵל, יהוה אֱלֹהֵינוּ, יהוה אֶחָד:**

קהל *then* שליח ציבור:

אֶחָד אֱלֹהֵינוּ, גָּדוֹל אֲדוֹנֵינוּ, קָדוֹשׁ שְׁמוֹ.

The שליח ציבור *takes the* ספר תורה *in his right arm, bows toward the* ארון קודש *and says:*

תהלים לד **גַּדְּלוּ לַיהוה אִתִּי וּנְרוֹמְמָה שְׁמוֹ יַחְדָּו:**

The ארון קודש *is closed. The* שליח ציבור *carries the* ספר תורה *to the* בימה *and the* קהל *says:*

דברי הימים א׳ כט **לְךָ יהוה הַגְּדֻלָּה וְהַגְּבוּרָה וְהַתִּפְאֶרֶת וְהַנֵּצַח וְהַהוֹד, כִּי־כֹל בַּשָּׁמַיִם וּבָאָרֶץ, לְךָ יהוה הַמַּמְלָכָה וְהַמִּתְנַשֵּׂא לְכֹל לְרֹאשׁ:**

תהלים צט **רוֹמְמוּ יהוה אֱלֹהֵינוּ וְהִשְׁתַּחֲווּ לַהֲדֹם רַגְלָיו, קָדוֹשׁ הוּא: רוֹמְמוּ יהוה אֱלֹהֵינוּ וְהִשְׁתַּחֲווּ לְהַר קָדְשׁוֹ, כִּי־קָדוֹשׁ יהוה אֱלֹהֵינוּ:**

עַל הַכֹּל יִתְגַּדַּל וְיִתְקַדַּשׁ וְיִשְׁתַּבַּח וְיִתְפָּאַר וְיִתְרוֹמַם וְיִתְנַשֵּׂא שְׁמוֹ שֶׁל מֶלֶךְ מַלְכֵי הַמְּלָכִים הַקָּדוֹשׁ בָּרוּךְ הוּא בָּעוֹלָמוֹת שֶׁבָּרָא, הָעוֹלָם הַזֶּה וְהָעוֹלָם הַבָּא, כִּרְצוֹנוֹ וְכִרְצוֹן יְרֵאָיו וְכִרְצוֹן כָּל בֵּית יִשְׂרָאֵל. צוּר הָעוֹלָמִים, אֲדוֹן כָּל הַבְּרִיּוֹת, אֱלוֹהַּ כָּל הַנְּפָשׁוֹת, הַיּוֹשֵׁב בְּמֶרְחֲבֵי מָרוֹם, הַשּׁוֹכֵן בִּשְׁמֵי שְׁמֵי קֶדֶם, קְדֻשָּׁתוֹ עַל הַחַיּוֹת, וּקְדֻשָּׁתוֹ עַל כִּסֵּא הַכָּבוֹד. וּבְכֵן יִתְקַדַּשׁ שִׁמְךָ בָּנוּ יהוה
תהלים סח אֱלֹהֵינוּ לְעֵינֵי כָּל חָי, וְנֹאמַר לְפָנָיו שִׁיר חָדָשׁ, כַּכָּתוּב: שִׁירוּ לֵאלֹהִים זַמְּרוּ
שְׁמוֹ, סֹלּוּ לָרֹכֵב בָּעֲרָבוֹת, בְּיָהּ שְׁמוֹ, וְעִלְזוּ לְפָנָיו: וְנִרְאֵהוּ עַיִן בְּעַיִן בְּשׁוּבוֹ
ישעיה נב אֶל נָוֵהוּ, כַּכָּתוּב: כִּי עַיִן בְּעַיִן יִרְאוּ בְּשׁוּב יהוה צִיּוֹן: וְנֶאֱמַר: וְנִגְלָה כְּבוֹד
ישעיה מ יהוה, וְרָאוּ כָל־בָּשָׂר יַחְדָּו כִּי פִּי יהוה דִּבֵּר:

אַב הָרַחֲמִים הוּא יְרַחֵם עַם עֲמוּסִים, וְיִזְכֹּר בְּרִית אֵיתָנִים, וְיַצִּיל נַפְשׁוֹתֵינוּ מִן הַשָּׁעוֹת הָרָעוֹת, וְיִגְעַר בְּיֵצֶר הָרָע מִן הַנְּשׂוּאִים, וְיָחֹן אוֹתָנוּ לִפְלֵיטַת עוֹלָמִים, וִימַלֵּא מִשְׁאֲלוֹתֵינוּ בְּמִדָּה טוֹבָה יְשׁוּעָה וְרַחֲמִים.

The Torah scroll is placed on the bima and the Gabbai calls a Kohen to the Torah.

וְיַעֲזֹר May He help, shield and save all who seek refuge in Him,
and let us say: Amen. Let us all render greatness to our God
and give honor to the Torah. *Let the Kohen come forward.
Arise (*name* son of *father's name*), the Kohen.

**If no Kohen is present, a Levi or Yisrael is called up as follows:*
/As there is no Kohen, arise (*name* son of *father's name*) in place of a Kohen./

Blessed is He who, in His holiness, gave the Torah to His people Israel.

The congregation followed by the Gabbai:

You who cling to the LORD your God are all alive today. *Deut. 4*

*The Reader shows the oleh the section to be read.
The oleh touches the scroll at that place with the tzitzit of his tallit,
which he then kisses. Holding the handles of the scroll, he says:*

Oleh: Bless the LORD, the blessed One.

Cong: Bless the LORD, the blessed One, for ever and all time.

Oleh: Bless the LORD, the blessed One, for ever and all time.

Blessed are You, LORD our God, King of the Universe,
who has chosen us from all peoples
and has given us His Torah.
Blessed are You, LORD, Giver of the Torah.

After the reading, the oleh says:

Oleh: Blessed are You, LORD our God, King of the Universe,
who has given us the Torah of truth,
planting everlasting life in our midst.
Blessed are You, LORD, Giver of the Torah.

*After a Bar Mitzva boy has finished the Torah blessing,
his father says aloud:*

Blessed is He who has released me
from the responsibility for this child.

The ספר תורה *is placed on the* שולחן *and the* גבאי *calls a* כהן *to the* תורה.

וְיַעֲזֹר וְיָגֵן וְיוֹשִׁיעַ לְכָל הַחוֹסִים בּוֹ, וְנֹאמַר אָמֵן. הַכֹּל הָבוּ גֹדֶל לֵאלֹהֵינוּ וּתְנוּ כָבוֹד לַתּוֹרָה. *כֹּהֵן קְרַב, יַעֲמֹד (פלוני בֶּן פלוני) הַכֹּהֵן.

**If no* כהן *is present, a* לוי *or* ישראל *is called up as follows:*

/אֵין כָּאן כֹּהֵן, יַעֲמֹד (פלוני בֶּן פלוני) בִּמְקוֹם כֹּהֵן./

בָּרוּךְ שֶׁנָּתַן תּוֹרָה לְעַמּוֹ יִשְׂרָאֵל בִּקְדֻשָּׁתוֹ.

The קהל *followed by the* גבאי:

וְאַתֶּם הַדְּבֵקִים בַּיהוה אֱלֹהֵיכֶם חַיִּים כֻּלְּכֶם הַיּוֹם: דברים ד

The קורא *shows the* עולה *the section to be read.*
The עולה *touches the scroll at that place with the* ציצית *of his* טלית,
which he then kisses. Holding the handles of the scroll, he says:

עולה: בָּרְכוּ אֶת יהוה הַמְבֹרָךְ.

קהל: בָּרוּךְ יהוה הַמְבֹרָךְ לְעוֹלָם וָעֶד.

עולה: בָּרוּךְ יהוה הַמְבֹרָךְ לְעוֹלָם וָעֶד.
בָּרוּךְ אַתָּה יהוה, אֱלֹהֵינוּ מֶלֶךְ הָעוֹלָם
אֲשֶׁר בָּחַר בָּנוּ מִכָּל הָעַמִּים
וְנָתַן לָנוּ אֶת תּוֹרָתוֹ.
בָּרוּךְ אַתָּה יהוה, נוֹתֵן הַתּוֹרָה.

After the קריאת התורה, *the* עולה *says:*

עולה: בָּרוּךְ אַתָּה יהוה אֱלֹהֵינוּ מֶלֶךְ הָעוֹלָם
אֲשֶׁר נָתַן לָנוּ תּוֹרַת אֱמֶת
וְחַיֵּי עוֹלָם נָטַע בְּתוֹכֵנוּ.
בָּרוּךְ אַתָּה יהוה, נוֹתֵן הַתּוֹרָה.

After a בר מצווה *has finished the* תורה *blessing, his father says aloud:*

בָּרוּךְ שֶׁפְּטָרַנִי מֵעָנְשׁוֹ שֶׁלָּזֶה.

FOR AN OLEH

May He who blessed our fathers, Abraham, Isaac and Jacob, bless (*name*, son of *father's name*) who has been called up in honor of the All-Present, in honor of the Torah, and in honor of Shabbat. As a reward for this, may the Holy One, blessed be He, protect and deliver him from all trouble and distress, all infection and illness, and send blessing and success to all the work of his hands, together with all Israel, his brethren, and let us say: Amen.

FOR A SICK MAN

May He who blessed our fathers, Abraham, Isaac and Jacob, Moses and Aaron, David and Solomon, bless and heal one who is ill, (*sick person's name*, son of *mother's name*), on whose behalf (*name of the one making the offering*) is making a contribution to charity. As a reward for this, may the Holy One, blessed be He, be filled with compassion for him, to restore his health, cure him, strengthen and revive him, sending him a swift and full recovery from heaven to all his 248 organs and 365 sinews, amongst the other sick ones in Israel, a healing of the spirit and a healing of the body – though on Shabbat it is forbidden to cry out, may healing be quick to come – now, swiftly and soon, and let us say: Amen.

FOR A SICK WOMAN

May He who blessed our fathers, Abraham, Isaac and Jacob, Moses and Aaron, David and Solomon, bless and heal one who is ill, (*sick person's name*, daughter of *mother's name*), on whose behalf (*name of the one making the offering*) is making a contribution to charity. As a reward for this, may the Holy One, blessed be He, be filled with compassion for her, to restore her health, cure her, strengthen and revive her, sending her a swift and full recovery from heaven to all her organs and sinews, amongst the other sick ones in Israel, a healing of the spirit and a healing of the body – though on Shabbat it is forbidden to cry out, may healing be quick to come – now, swiftly and soon, and let us say: Amen.

ON THE BIRTH OF A SON

May He who blessed our fathers, Abraham, Isaac and Jacob, Moses and Aaron, David and Solomon, Sarah, Rebecca, Rachel and Leah, bless

מי שברך לעולה לתורה

מִי שֶׁבֵּרַךְ אֲבוֹתֵינוּ אַבְרָהָם יִצְחָק וְיַעֲקֹב, הוּא יְבָרֵךְ אֶת (פלוני בֶּן פלוני), בַּעֲבוּר שֶׁעָלָה לִכְבוֹד הַמָּקוֹם וְלִכְבוֹד הַתּוֹרָה וְלִכְבוֹד הַשַּׁבָּת. בִּשְׂכַר זֶה הַקָּדוֹשׁ בָּרוּךְ הוּא יִשְׁמְרֵהוּ וְיַצִּילֵהוּ מִכָּל צָרָה וְצוּקָה וּמִכָּל נֶגַע וּמַחֲלָה, וְיִשְׁלַח בְּרָכָה וְהַצְלָחָה בְּכָל מַעֲשֵׂה יָדָיו עִם כָּל יִשְׂרָאֵל אֶחָיו, וְנֹאמַר אָמֵן.

מי שברך לחולֶה

מִי שֶׁבֵּרַךְ אֲבוֹתֵינוּ אַבְרָהָם יִצְחָק וְיַעֲקֹב, מֹשֶׁה וְאַהֲרֹן דָּוִד וּשְׁלֹמֹה הוּא יְבָרֵךְ וִירַפֵּא אֶת הַחוֹלֶה (פלוני בֶּן פלונית) בַּעֲבוּר שֶׁ(פלוני בֶּן פלוני) נוֹדֵר צְדָקָה בַּעֲבוּרוֹ. בִּשְׂכַר זֶה הַקָּדוֹשׁ בָּרוּךְ הוּא יִמָּלֵא רַחֲמִים עָלָיו לְהַחֲלִימוֹ וּלְרַפְּאֹתוֹ וּלְהַחֲזִיקוֹ וּלְהַחֲיוֹתוֹ וְיִשְׁלַח לוֹ מְהֵרָה רְפוּאָה שְׁלֵמָה מִן הַשָּׁמַיִם לִרְמַ״ח אֵבָרָיו וּשְׁסָ״ה גִּידָיו בְּתוֹךְ שְׁאָר חוֹלֵי יִשְׂרָאֵל, רְפוּאַת הַנֶּפֶשׁ וּרְפוּאַת הַגּוּף. שַׁבָּת הִיא מִלִּזְעֹק וּרְפוּאָה קְרוֹבָה לָבוֹא, הַשְׁתָּא בַּעֲגָלָא וּבִזְמַן קָרִיב, וְנֹאמַר אָמֵן.

מי שברך לחולָה

מִי שֶׁבֵּרַךְ אֲבוֹתֵינוּ אַבְרָהָם יִצְחָק וְיַעֲקֹב, מֹשֶׁה וְאַהֲרֹן דָּוִד וּשְׁלֹמֹה הוּא יְבָרֵךְ וִירַפֵּא אֶת הַחוֹלָה (פלונית בַּת פלונית) בַּעֲבוּר שֶׁ(פלוני בֶּן פלוני) נוֹדֵר צְדָקָה בַּעֲבוּרָהּ. בִּשְׂכַר זֶה הַקָּדוֹשׁ בָּרוּךְ הוּא יִמָּלֵא רַחֲמִים עָלֶיהָ לְהַחֲלִימָהּ וּלְרַפְּאֹתָהּ וּלְהַחֲזִיקָהּ וּלְהַחֲיוֹתָהּ וְיִשְׁלַח לָהּ מְהֵרָה רְפוּאָה שְׁלֵמָה מִן הַשָּׁמַיִם לְכָל אֵבָרֶיהָ וּלְכָל גִּידֶיהָ בְּתוֹךְ שְׁאָר חוֹלֵי יִשְׂרָאֵל, רְפוּאַת הַנֶּפֶשׁ וּרְפוּאַת הַגּוּף. שַׁבָּת הִיא מִלִּזְעֹק וּרְפוּאָה קְרוֹבָה לָבוֹא, הַשְׁתָּא בַּעֲגָלָא וּבִזְמַן קָרִיב, וְנֹאמַר אָמֵן.

מי שברך ליולדת בן

מִי שֶׁבֵּרַךְ אֲבוֹתֵינוּ אַבְרָהָם יִצְחָק וְיַעֲקֹב, מֹשֶׁה וְאַהֲרֹן דָּוִד וּשְׁלֹמֹה, שָׂרָה רִבְקָה רָחֵל וְלֵאָה הוּא יְבָרֵךְ אֶת הָאִשָּׁה הַיּוֹלֶדֶת (פלונית

the woman (*name*, daughter of *father's name*) who has given birth, and her son who has been born to her as an auspicious sign. Her husband, the child's father, is making a contribution to charity. As a reward for this, may father and mother merit to bring the child into the covenant of Abraham and to a life of Torah, to the marriage canopy and to good deeds, and let us say: Amen.

ON THE BIRTH OF A DAUGHTER

May He who blessed our fathers, Abraham, Isaac and Jacob, Moses and Aaron, David and Solomon, Sarah, Rebecca, Rachel and Leah, bless the woman (*name*, daughter of *father's name*) who has given birth, and her daughter who has been born to her as an auspicious sign; and may her name be called in Israel (*baby's name*, daughter of *father's name*). Her husband, the child's father, is making a contribution to charity. As a reward for this, may father and mother merit to raise her to a life of Torah, to the marriage canopy, and to good deeds, and let us say: Amen.

FOR A BAR MITZVA

May He who blessed our fathers, Abraham, Isaac and Jacob, bless (*name*, son of *father's name*) who has completed thirteen years and attained the age of the commandments, who has been called to the Torah to give praise and thanks to God, may His name be blessed, for all the good He has bestowed on him. May the Holy One, blessed be He, protect and sustain him and direct his heart to be perfect with God, to walk in His ways and keep the commandments all the days of his life, and let us say: Amen.

FOR A BAT MITZVA

May He who blessed our fathers, Abraham, Isaac and Jacob, Sarah, Rebecca, Rachel and Leah, bless (*name*, daughter of *father's name*) who has completed twelve years and attained the age of the commandments, and gives praise and thanks to God, may His name be blessed, for all the good He has bestowed on her. May the Holy One, blessed be He, protect and sustain her and direct her heart to be perfect with God, to walk in His ways and keep the commandments all the days of her life, and let us say: Amen.

(פלונית בַּת פלוני) וְאֶת בְּנָהּ שֶׁנּוֹלַד לָהּ לְמַזָּל טוֹב בַּעֲבוּר שֶׁבַּעְלָהּ וְאָבִיו נוֹדֵר צְדָקָה בַּעֲדָם. בִּשְׂכַר זֶה יִזְכּוּ אָבִיו וְאִמּוֹ לְהַכְנִיסוֹ בִּבְרִיתוֹ שֶׁל אַבְרָהָם אָבִינוּ וּלְגַדְּלוֹ לְתוֹרָה וּלְחֻפָּה וּלְמַעֲשִׂים טוֹבִים, וְנֹאמַר אָמֵן.

מי שברך ליולדת בת

מִי שֶׁבֵּרַךְ אֲבוֹתֵינוּ אַבְרָהָם יִצְחָק וְיַעֲקֹב, מֹשֶׁה וְאַהֲרֹן דָּוִד וּשְׁלֹמֹה, שָׂרָה רִבְקָה רָחֵל וְלֵאָה הוּא יְבָרֵךְ אֶת הָאִשָּׁה הַיּוֹלֶדֶת (פלונית בַּת פלוני) וְאֶת בִּתָּהּ שֶׁנּוֹלְדָה לָהּ לְמַזָּל טוֹב וְיִקָּרֵא שְׁמָהּ בְּיִשְׂרָאֵל (פלונית בַּת פלוני), בַּעֲבוּר שֶׁבַּעְלָהּ וְאָבִיהָ נוֹדֵר צְדָקָה בַּעֲדָן. בִּשְׂכַר זֶה יִזְכּוּ אָבִיהָ וְאִמָּהּ לְגַדְּלָהּ לְתוֹרָה וּלְחֻפָּה וּלְמַעֲשִׂים טוֹבִים, וְנֹאמַר אָמֵן.

מי שברך לבר מצווה

מִי שֶׁבֵּרַךְ אֲבוֹתֵינוּ אַבְרָהָם יִצְחָק וְיַעֲקֹב הוּא יְבָרֵךְ אֶת (פלוני בֶּן פלוני) שֶׁמָּלְאוּ לוֹ שְׁלֹשׁ עֶשְׂרֵה שָׁנָה וְהִגִּיעַ לְמִצְוֹת, וְעָלָה לַתּוֹרָה, לָתֵת שֶׁבַח וְהוֹדָיָה לְהַשֵּׁם יִתְבָּרַךְ עַל כָּל הַטּוֹבָה שֶׁגָּמַל אִתּוֹ. יִשְׁמְרֵהוּ הַקָּדוֹשׁ בָּרוּךְ הוּא וִיחַיֵּהוּ, וִיכוֹנֵן אֶת לִבּוֹ לִהְיוֹת שָׁלֵם עִם יהוה וְלָלֶכֶת בִּדְרָכָיו וְלִשְׁמֹר מִצְוֹתָיו כָּל הַיָּמִים, וְנֹאמַר אָמֵן.

מי שברך לבת מצווה

מִי שֶׁבֵּרַךְ אֲבוֹתֵינוּ אַבְרָהָם יִצְחָק וְיַעֲקֹב, שָׂרָה רִבְקָה רָחֵל וְלֵאָה, הוּא יְבָרֵךְ אֶת (פלונית בַּת פלוני) שֶׁמָּלְאוּ לָהּ שְׁתֵּים עֶשְׂרֵה שָׁנָה וְהִגִּיעָה לְמִצְוֹת, וְנוֹתֶנֶת שֶׁבַח וְהוֹדָיָה לְהַשֵּׁם יִתְבָּרַךְ עַל כָּל הַטּוֹבָה שֶׁגָּמַל אִתָּהּ. יִשְׁמְרֶהָ הַקָּדוֹשׁ בָּרוּךְ הוּא וִיחַיֶּהָ, וִיכוֹנֵן אֶת לִבָּהּ לִהְיוֹת שָׁלֵם עִם יהוה וְלָלֶכֶת בִּדְרָכָיו וְלִשְׁמֹר מִצְוֹתָיו כָּל הַיָּמִים, וְנֹאמַר אָמֵן.

TORAH READING FOR SHABBAT HOL HAMO'ED

Moses said to the LORD: Behold, You have told me to bring this people
up [to the Land], but You have yet to inform me whom You shall send 34:26
along with me; You have told me that You have singled me out and that I have found favor in Your eyes. Now, if I indeed find favor in Your eyes, let me know Your ways, so that I might become acquainted with You, so that I find favor in Your eyes: behold, this people is Your nation! He replied: My presence shall go forth and guide You. He said to Him: If Your countenance does not go with us, do not remove us from this place. How am I to know that I have found favor in Your eyes – I and Your people – if not through Your presence among us? Let me and Your people be chosen from all other nations in the land.

The LORD said to Moses: I shall do this thing that you said, for you LEVI
have found favor in My eyes, and I recognize you by name. He said: Please, show me Your glory! He said: I shall pass all My beneficence before you, calling out the name of the LORD in your presence, and I shall be gracious to whom I shall be gracious; I shall be merciful to
whom I shall be merciful. He said: You cannot see My face, for no man SHELISHI
can see Me and live. The LORD said: Behold, there is a place near Me,

---

meant that God was both inconceivably vast and terrifyingly remote, further than the most distant star. Yet it is hard for people to bear a distant God. We need to feel Him close, which indeed He always is. Hence Moses' redoubled plea that God be tangibly, palpably close (this was one of the reasons why God commanded the Israelites to build the Tabernacle so that they could sense the Divine Presence in their midst). Moses' prayer was answered, as he reminds the next generation at the end of his life: "What nation is so great that they have God close to it, the way the LORD our God is close to us whenever we pray to Him?" (Deut. 4:7).

וְחַנֹּתִי אֶת־אֲשֶׁר אָחֹן וְרִחַמְתִּי אֶת־אֲשֶׁר אֲרַחֵם *I shall be gracious to whom I shall be gracious; I shall be merciful to whom I shall be merciful.* A statement similar in import to God's reply to Moses at the burning bush when he asked for God's name: "I will be who I will be" (Ex. 3:14). The God who exists beyond the universe cannot be fully understood by those who exist within

קריאה לשבת חול המועד

שמות לג, יב–לד, כו וַיֹּאמֶר מֹשֶׁה אֶל־יהוה רְאֵה אַתָּה אֹמֵר אֵלַי הַעַל אֶת־הָעָם
הַזֶּה וְאַתָּה לֹא הוֹדַעְתַּנִי אֵת אֲשֶׁר־תִּשְׁלַח עִמִּי וְאַתָּה אָמַרְתָּ
יְדַעְתִּיךָ בְשֵׁם וְגַם־מָצָאתָ חֵן בְּעֵינָי: וְעַתָּה אִם־נָא מָצָאתִי חֵן
בְּעֵינֶיךָ הוֹדִעֵנִי נָא אֶת־דְּרָכֶךָ וְאֵדָעֲךָ לְמַעַן אֶמְצָא־חֵן בְּעֵינֶיךָ
וּרְאֵה כִּי עַמְּךָ הַגּוֹי הַזֶּה: וַיֹּאמַר פָּנַי יֵלֵכוּ וַהֲנִחֹתִי לָךְ: וַיֹּאמֶר
אֵלָיו אִם־אֵין פָּנֶיךָ הֹלְכִים אַל־תַּעֲלֵנוּ מִזֶּה: וּבַמֶּה ׀ יִוָּדַע אֵפוֹא
כִּי־מָצָאתִי חֵן בְּעֵינֶיךָ אֲנִי וְעַמֶּךָ הֲלוֹא בְּלֶכְתְּךָ עִמָּנוּ וְנִפְלֵינוּ
אֲנִי וְעַמְּךָ מִכָּל־הָעָם אֲשֶׁר עַל־פְּנֵי הָאֲדָמָה:
לוי וַיֹּאמֶר יהוה אֶל־מֹשֶׁה גַּם אֶת־הַדָּבָר הַזֶּה אֲשֶׁר דִּבַּרְתָּ אֶעֱשֶׂה
כִּי־מָצָאתָ חֵן בְּעֵינַי וָאֵדָעֲךָ בְּשֵׁם: וַיֹּאמַר הַרְאֵנִי נָא אֶת־כְּבֹדֶךָ:
וַיֹּאמֶר אֲנִי אַעֲבִיר כָּל־טוּבִי עַל־פָּנֶיךָ וְקָרָאתִי בְשֵׁם יהוה לְפָנֶיךָ
שלישי וְחַנֹּתִי אֶת־אֲשֶׁר אָחֹן וְרִחַמְתִּי אֶת־אֲשֶׁר אֲרַחֵם: וַיֹּאמֶר לֹא
תוּכַל לִרְאֹת אֶת־פָּנָי כִּי לֹא־יִרְאַנִי הָאָדָם וָחָי: וַיֹּאמֶר יהוה

TORAH READING FOR SHABBAT OF ḤOL HAMO'ED

וַיֹּאמֶר מֹשֶׁה *Moses said.* The Israelites had made a golden calf, one of their most grievous sins in the wilderness. Moses had interceded with God on their behalf, descended, smashed the tablets, reprimanded the people, and punished the wrongdoers. Now Moses ascends the mountain to plead on their behalf again. He asks three things of God, first that His presence, not just an angel, should go with the people; second, that God "let him know His ways" so that he can understand the nature of divine justice; and third that God should reaffirm that Israel is indeed His people – that He has not distanced Himself from them.

פָּנַי *My presence.* Literally "My face," a strong statement of Divine immanence. Moses then reiterates how essential this is to the people. The idea of a transcendent God – the fundamental revolution of Abrahamic monotheism –

where you can stand upon the rock. When My glory passes, I shall put you in the rock's cave, and cover you with My palm until I pass. Then I shall remove My palm and you shall see My back, but My face may not be seen.

The LORD said to Moses: Carve out two stone tablets for yourself, like the first ones, and I will inscribe on them the same words that were on the first tablets, which you broke. Prepare yourself by morning, for in the morning you shall go up to Mount Sinai and stand before Me there, at the summit. No one shall go up with you, nor shall anyone be seen anywhere on the mountain; even the sheep and cattle may not graze in front of that mountain. So he carved out two stone tablets like the first ones; Moses arose early in the morning and walked up Mount Sinai as the LORD had commanded him, taking in his hand the two stone tablets. The LORD descended in a cloud, and stood with him there; and proclaimed in the name of the LORD. And the LORD passed by before him and proclaimed: "The LORD, the LORD, compassionate

REVI'I

HAMISHI

---

metaphorical way of saying that only in retrospect do we see the presence of God in events. We live life forward but understand it only backward.

פְּסָל־לְךָ שְׁנֵי־לֻחֹת אֲבָנִים *Carve out two stone tablets.* The first tablets, entirely the work of God, were broken. The second, the work of God but with the participation of man, endured. So it is in the life of the spirit. The Divine Presence rests securely in this world only when we do something to create space for it.

ה׳ ה׳ *The LORD, the LORD.* The "Thirteen Attributes of Divine compassion," the greatest statement of God's relationship with humanity, His Self-definition as the source of compassion and pardon that frames the moral life. It subsequently became the basis of penitential prayer, *Seliḥot*, in Judaism. It tells us that God does not "desire the death of the wicked, but that the wicked should come back from his way and live" (Ezekiel 33:11). When we repent and make good the harm we have done, God forgives. The Thirteen Attributes are: (1) *The LORD*: The name that signifies God's attribute of compassion as opposed to strict justice. (2) *The LORD*: God retains the same compassion even after we have sinned, thus making repentance possible. (3) *God*: The power and force through which God sustains the universe and all that lives. (4) *Compassionate*: The root ר-ח-מ is the same as "womb." Hence it means

הִנֵּה מָקוֹם אִתִּי וְנִצַּבְתָּ עַל־הַצּוּר: וְהָיָה בַּעֲבֹר כְּבֹדִי וְשַׂמְתִּיךָ
בְּנִקְרַת הַצּוּר וְשַׂכֹּתִי כַפִּי עָלֶיךָ עַד־עָבְרִי: וַהֲסִרֹתִי אֶת־כַּפִּי
וְרָאִיתָ אֶת־אֲחֹרָי וּפָנַי לֹא יֵרָאוּ:
וַיֹּאמֶר יהוה אֶל־מֹשֶׁה פְּסׇל־לְךָ שְׁנֵי־לֻחֹת אֲבָנִים כָּרִאשֹׁנִים רביעי
וְכָתַבְתִּי עַל־הַלֻּחֹת אֶת־הַדְּבָרִים אֲשֶׁר הָיוּ עַל־הַלֻּחֹת
הָרִאשֹׁנִים אֲשֶׁר שִׁבַּרְתָּ: וֶהְיֵה נָכוֹן לַבֹּקֶר וְעָלִיתָ בַבֹּקֶר אֶל־הַר
סִינַי וְנִצַּבְתָּ לִי שָׁם עַל־רֹאשׁ הָהָר: וְאִישׁ לֹא־יַעֲלֶה עִמָּךְ וְגַם־
אִישׁ אַל־יֵרָא בְּכׇל־הָהָר גַּם־הַצֹּאן וְהַבָּקָר אַל־יִרְעוּ אֶל־מוּל
הָהָר הַהוּא: וַיִּפְסֹל שְׁנֵי־לֻחֹת אֲבָנִים כָּרִאשֹׁנִים וַיַּשְׁכֵּם מֹשֶׁה חמישי
בַבֹּקֶר וַיַּעַל אֶל־הַר סִינַי כַּאֲשֶׁר צִוָּה יהוה אֹתוֹ וַיִּקַּח בְּיָדוֹ שְׁנֵי
לֻחֹת אֲבָנִים: וַיֵּרֶד יהוה בֶּעָנָן וַיִּתְיַצֵּב עִמּוֹ שָׁם וַיִּקְרָא בְשֵׁם
יהוה: וַיַּעֲבֹר יהוה ׀ עַל־פָּנָיו וַיִּקְרָא יהוה ׀ יהוה אֵל רַחוּם

---

the universe any more than a fetus within the womb can understand the world outside. Nor can the God of freedom and choice fall within the predictabilities of science. The attempt to understand God, whether in ancient or modern times, is ultimately the desire to control God, which is the root of idolatry. In this case, God is explaining to Moses a simple principle. God is the God of righteousness (*tzedaka*) and justice (*mishpat*; see Gen. 18:19). But He is also, as He explains here, the God of mercy (*ḥen*) and compassion (*raḥamim*). These two sets of values conflict. Righteousness and justice have to do with the impartial process of law. Mercy and compassion have to do with relationship, and going beyond the letter of the law. There is no way of knowing in advance which will prevail. It depends on the total knowledge of circumstance and consequence that exists only for God, not us. Thus even Moses, the greatest of the prophets, could not in principle fully understand the ways of Providence (see *Berakhot* 7a). Yet this we know: that they are a combination of righteousness, justice, mercy and compassion, and these are the values we are commanded to pursue.

וְרָאִיתָ אֶת־אֲחֹרָי וּפָנַי לֹא יֵרָאוּ *You will see My back but My face may not be seen.* A

and gracious God, slow to anger, abounding in loving-kindness and truth, extending loving-kindness to a thousand generations, forgiving iniquity, rebellion and sin, and absolving [the guilty who repent]; He shall not absolve [those who do not repent], but shall visit the punishment of fathers' sins upon their children and grandchildren to the third and fourth generation." And Moses hastened to bow to the ground, prostrating himself. He said: "O LORD, if I find favor in Your eyes, please, let the LORD go forth in our midst, for this is a stiff-necked people; forgive us our iniquity and our sin, and take us as Your inheritance." He said: "Behold, I will forge a covenant: in the presence of your entire people I will work wonders like none ever formed in all the world or for any nation; this people among whom you dwell shall witness the works of the LORD, for what I will do for you is awesome indeed. Keep what I command you today; I shall SHISHI expel the Amorites, the Canaanites, the Hittites, the Perizzites, the Hivites and the Jebusites for you. Guard yourselves against forging any covenant with the inhabitants of the land that you are about to enter, so that they do not become a snare in your path. Instead,

---

וַיֹּאמֶר הִנֵּה אָנֹכִי כֹּרֵת בְּרִית *He said: Behold, I will forge a covenant.* God renews the covenant in response to Moses' prayer.

נִפְלָאֹת *Wonders.* The word here does not necessarily mean "miracles" but rather "confer distinction" (see above, "Let me and Your people be chosen from all other nations in the land"). Jewish history will bear God's handwriting. In itself it will point to something beyond itself. "I remember how the materialist interpretation of history, when I attempted in my youth to verify it by applying it to the destinies of peoples, broke down in the case of the Jews, where destiny seemed absolutely inexplicable from the materialistic standpoint.... The survival of the Jews, their resistance to destruction, their endurance under absolutely peculiar conditions, and the fateful role played by them in history: all these point to the particular and mysterious foundations of their destiny" (Nikolai Berdyaev, *The Meaning of History*).

שְׁמָר־לְךָ ... בַּחֲלֵב אִמּוֹ *34:11–26:* The prohibition of idolatry and anything that might lead to it, followed by an account of the three pilgrimage festivals. These are essential terms of the covenant. The prohibition of idolatry

וְחַנּוּן אֶרֶךְ אַפַּיִם וְרַב־חֶסֶד וֶאֱמֶת׃ נֹצֵר חֶסֶד לָאֲלָפִים נֹשֵׂא
עָוֺן וָפֶשַׁע וְחַטָּאָה וְנַקֵּה לֹא יְנַקֶּה פֹּקֵד ׀ עֲוֺן אָבוֹת עַל־בָּנִים
וְעַל־בְּנֵי בָנִים עַל־שִׁלֵּשִׁים וְעַל־רִבֵּעִים׃ וַיְמַהֵר מֹשֶׁה וַיִּקֹּד
אַרְצָה וַיִּשְׁתָּחוּ׃ וַיֹּאמֶר אִם־נָא מָצָאתִי חֵן בְּעֵינֶיךָ אֲדֹנָי יֵלֶךְ־נָא
אֲדֹנָי בְּקִרְבֵּנוּ כִּי עַם־קְשֵׁה־עֹרֶף הוּא וְסָלַחְתָּ לַעֲוֺנֵנוּ וּלְחַטָּאתֵנוּ
וּנְחַלְתָּנוּ׃ וַיֹּאמֶר הִנֵּה אָנֹכִי כֹּרֵת בְּרִית נֶגֶד כָּל־עַמְּךָ אֶעֱשֶׂה
נִפְלָאֹת אֲשֶׁר לֹא־נִבְרְאוּ בְכָל־הָאָרֶץ וּבְכָל־הַגּוֹיִם וְרָאָה כָל־
הָעָם אֲשֶׁר־אַתָּה בְקִרְבּוֹ אֶת־מַעֲשֵׂה יהוה כִּי־נוֹרָא הוּא אֲשֶׁר
אֲנִי עֹשֶׂה עִמָּךְ׃ שְׁמָר־לְךָ אֵת אֲשֶׁר אָנֹכִי מְצַוְּךָ הַיּוֹם הִנְנִי גֹרֵשׁ ששי
מִפָּנֶיךָ אֶת־הָאֱמֹרִי וְהַכְּנַעֲנִי וְהַחִתִּי וְהַפְּרִזִּי וְהַחִוִּי וְהַיְבוּסִי׃
הִשָּׁמֶר לְךָ פֶּן־תִּכְרֹת בְּרִית לְיוֹשֵׁב הָאָרֶץ אֲשֶׁר אַתָּה בָּא
עָלֶיהָ פֶּן־יִהְיֶה לְמוֹקֵשׁ בְּקִרְבֶּךָ׃ כִּי אֶת־מִזְבְּחֹתָם תִּתֹּצוּן וְאֶת־

---

the kind of compassion a mother has for a child. (5) *Gracious*: The root ח-נ-נ refers to behavior that comes from the generosity of the one who does it, not the merits of the one to or for whom it is done. (6) *Slow to anger*: Thus giving time for wrongdoers to repent. (7) *Abounding in loving-kindness*: According to a person's needs, not their deserts. (8) *And truth*: Giving a just reward to those who do His will. (9) *Extending loving-kindness to thousands of generations*: God remembers through the ages the kindness of the patriarchs and the merits of our ancestors. (10) *Forgiving iniquity*: Sins committed knowingly. (11) *Rebellion*: Sins committed in a spirit of defiance. (12) *And sin*: Sins committed unwittingly, either because we did not know what we were doing or did not know that it was forbidden. (13) *And absolving*: Literally "cleansing" those who repent.

עֲוֺן אָבוֹת עַל־בָּנִים *Visit the punishment of fathers' sins upon their children.* According to the Talmud (*Berakhot* 7a), only when the children repeat the sins of the fathers.

וַיְמַהֵר מֹשֶׁה *Moses hastened.* God's Self-revelation becomes the basis of Moses' prayer, here and later, after the sin of the spies (Num. 14:18–19).

shatter their altars, break apart their sacred pillars, and cut down their worshiped trees. For you may not bow to any other god, for the LORD's name is Jealous; He is a jealous God. [And so do this,] lest you make a covenant with an inhabitant of the land and, when they stray after their gods and offer sacrifices to them, he invite you to partake of his sacrifice, and you do. And lest you take of his daughters to marry your sons; and these daughters stray after their gods and cause your sons to worship them too. Do not make molten gods for
yourselves. Observe the Festival of Matzot: you shall eat matzot for SHEVI'I
seven days as I have commanded you, at the season of the month of Aviv, for in the month of Aviv you went out of Egypt. Every firstborn that opens the womb is Mine, as well as every firstborn male of your herd, whether bullock or lamb. A firstborn donkey must be redeemed with a lamb, and if you do not redeem it, you must behead it; each of your own firstborn sons must be redeemed: do not approach Me empty-handed. Six days you shall do your work but on the seventh day you shall rest: in plowing and in sowing seasons too, you must rest. You shall celebrate a Festival of Weeks [Shavuot] at the time of the first wheat harvest, and a festival of ingathering [Sukkot] at the completion of the year. Three times a year all males shall present themselves before their Master, the LORD God of Israel. When I conquer nations for you and extend your borders, no one will covet your land when you go up to be seen by the LORD your God, three times each year. Do not slaughter My [Pesaḥ] offering along with leaven; the offering of the Pesaḥ festival must not be allowed to remain until morning. You shall bring the first fruits of your land to the house of the LORD your God. Do not cook a kid in its mother's milk.

לֹא־תְבַשֵּׁל גְּדִי בַּחֲלֵב אִמּוֹ *Do not cook a kid in its mother's milk.* The origin of the prohibition against mixing meat and milk. Maimonides infers from its association with the festivals that this was an idolatrous practice associated with pagan festivities (*Guide for the Perplexed* 3:48). The biblical imagination is predicated on clear boundaries. The pagan imagination often celebrated the blurring of boundaries: man-god, man-beast, androgyny, and other hybrids.

מַצֵּבֹתָם תְּשַׁבֵּרוּן וְאֶת־אֲשֵׁרָיו תִּכְרֹתוּן: כִּי לֹא תִשְׁתַּחֲוֶה לְאֵל
אַחֵר כִּי יהוה קַנָּא שְׁמוֹ אֵל קַנָּא הוּא: פֶּן־תִּכְרֹת בְּרִית לְיוֹשֵׁב
הָאָרֶץ וְזָנוּ ׀ אַחֲרֵי אֱלֹהֵיהֶם וְזָבְחוּ לֵאלֹהֵיהֶם וְקָרָא לְךָ וְאָכַלְתָּ
מִזִּבְחוֹ: וְלָקַחְתָּ מִבְּנֹתָיו לְבָנֶיךָ וְזָנוּ בְנֹתָיו אַחֲרֵי אֱלֹהֵיהֶן וְהִזְנוּ
אֶת־בָּנֶיךָ אַחֲרֵי אֱלֹהֵיהֶן: אֱלֹהֵי מַסֵּכָה לֹא תַעֲשֶׂה־לָּךְ: אֶת־ שביעי
חַג הַמַּצּוֹת תִּשְׁמֹר שִׁבְעַת יָמִים תֹּאכַל מַצּוֹת אֲשֶׁר צִוִּיתִךָ
לְמוֹעֵד חֹדֶשׁ הָאָבִיב כִּי בְּחֹדֶשׁ הָאָבִיב יָצָאתָ מִמִּצְרָיִם: כָּל־
פֶּטֶר רֶחֶם לִי וְכָל־מִקְנְךָ תִּזָּכָר פֶּטֶר שׁוֹר וָשֶׂה: וּפֶטֶר חֲמוֹר
תִּפְדֶּה בְשֶׂה וְאִם־לֹא תִפְדֶּה וַעֲרַפְתּוֹ כֹּל בְּכוֹר בָּנֶיךָ תִּפְדֶּה
וְלֹא־יֵרָאוּ פָנַי רֵיקָם: שֵׁשֶׁת יָמִים תַּעֲבֹד וּבַיּוֹם הַשְּׁבִיעִי תִּשְׁבֹּת
בֶּחָרִישׁ וּבַקָּצִיר תִּשְׁבֹּת: וְחַג שָׁבֻעֹת תַּעֲשֶׂה לְךָ בִּכּוּרֵי קְצִיר
חִטִּים וְחַג הָאָסִיף תְּקוּפַת הַשָּׁנָה: שָׁלֹשׁ פְּעָמִים בַּשָּׁנָה יֵרָאֶה
כָּל־זְכוּרְךָ אֶת־פְּנֵי הָאָדֹן ׀ יהוה אֱלֹהֵי יִשְׂרָאֵל: כִּי־אוֹרִישׁ
גּוֹיִם מִפָּנֶיךָ וְהִרְחַבְתִּי אֶת־גְּבֻלֶךָ וְלֹא־יַחְמֹד אִישׁ אֶת־אַרְצְךָ
בַּעֲלֹתְךָ לֵרָאוֹת אֶת־פְּנֵי יהוה אֱלֹהֶיךָ שָׁלֹשׁ פְּעָמִים בַּשָּׁנָה:
לֹא־תִשְׁחַט עַל־חָמֵץ דַּם־זִבְחִי וְלֹא־יָלִין לַבֹּקֶר זֶבַח חַג הַפָּסַח:
רֵאשִׁית בִּכּוּרֵי אַדְמָתְךָ תָּבִיא בֵּית יהוה אֱלֹהֶיךָ לֹא־תְבַשֵּׁל גְּדִי
בַּחֲלֵב אִמּוֹ:

---

follows from Israel's exclusive covenant of loyalty with God. The festivals testify to God's presence in Israel's history.

חֹדֶשׁ הָאָבִיב *The month of Aviv.* i.e., spring. This requirement that "the festival of unleavened bread" be in the spring determined the dual character of the Jewish calendar, lunar in relation to months, solar in relation to the year. Hence the need from time to time to add an extra month to the year to bring the two cycles into alignment.

HALF KADDISH

Before Maftir is read, the second Sefer Torah is placed on the bima and the Reader says Half Kaddish:

Reader: יִתְגַּדַּל Magnified and sanctified
may His great name be,
in the world He created by His will.
May He establish His kingdom
in your lifetime and in your days,
and in the lifetime of all the house of Israel,
swiftly and soon –
and say: Amen.

All: May His great name be blessed
for ever and all time.

Reader: Blessed and praised,
glorified and exalted,
raised and honored,
uplifted and lauded
be the name of the Holy One, blessed be He,
beyond any blessing,
song, praise and consolation
uttered in the world –
and say: Amen.

HAGBAHA AND GELILA

The Torah scroll is lifted and the congregation says:

וְזֹאת הַתּוֹרָה This is the Torah *Deut. 4*
that Moses placed before the children of Israel,
at the LORD's commandment, by the hand of Moses. *Num. 9*

Some add: It is a tree of life to those who grasp it, and those who uphold it are happy. *Prov. 3*
Its ways are ways of pleasantness, and all its paths are peace.
Long life is in its right hand; in its left, riches and honor.
It pleased the LORD for the sake of [Israel's] righteousness, *Is. 42*
to make the Torah great and glorious.

The first Torah scroll is bound and covered and the oleh for Maftir is called to the second Torah scroll.

חצי קדיש

Before מפטיר *is read, the second* ספר תורה *is placed on the* בימה*, and the* קורא *says* חצי קדיש:

קורא: יִתְגַּדַּל וְיִתְקַדַּשׁ שְׁמֵהּ רַבָּא (קהל: אָמֵן)
בְּעָלְמָא דִּי בְרָא כִרְעוּתֵהּ
וְיַמְלִיךְ מַלְכוּתֵהּ
בְּחַיֵּיכוֹן וּבְיוֹמֵיכוֹן וּבְחַיֵּי דְכָל בֵּית יִשְׂרָאֵל
בַּעֲגָלָא וּבִזְמַן קָרִיב
וְאִמְרוּ אָמֵן. (קהל: אָמֵן)

קהל וקורא: יְהֵא שְׁמֵהּ רַבָּא מְבָרַךְ לְעָלַם וּלְעָלְמֵי עָלְמַיָּא.

קורא: יִתְבָּרַךְ וְיִשְׁתַּבַּח וְיִתְפָּאַר וְיִתְרוֹמַם וְיִתְנַשֵּׂא
וְיִתְהַדָּר וְיִתְעַלֶּה וְיִתְהַלָּל
שְׁמֵהּ דְּקֻדְשָׁא בְּרִיךְ הוּא (קהל: בְּרִיךְ הוּא)
לְעֵלָּא מִן כָּל בִּרְכָתָא וְשִׁירָתָא
תֻּשְׁבְּחָתָא וְנֶחֱמָתָא
דַּאֲמִירָן בְּעָלְמָא
וְאִמְרוּ אָמֵן. (קהל: אָמֵן)

הגבהה וגלילה

The ספר תורה *is lifted and the* קהל *says:*

דברים ד וְזֹאת הַתּוֹרָה אֲשֶׁר־שָׂם מֹשֶׁה לִפְנֵי בְּנֵי יִשְׂרָאֵל:
במדבר ט עַל־פִּי יהוה בְּיַד מֹשֶׁה:

משלי ג *Some add* עֵץ־חַיִּים הִיא לַמַּחֲזִיקִים בָּהּ וְתֹמְכֶיהָ מְאֻשָּׁר:
דְּרָכֶיהָ דַרְכֵי־נֹעַם וְכָל־נְתִיבֹתֶיהָ שָׁלוֹם:
אֹרֶךְ יָמִים בִּימִינָהּ, בִּשְׂמֹאולָהּ עֹשֶׁר וְכָבוֹד:
ישעיה מב יהוה חָפֵץ לְמַעַן צִדְקוֹ יַגְדִּיל תּוֹרָה וְיַאְדִּיר:

The first ספר תורה *is bound and covered and the* עולה *for* מפטיר *is called to the second* ספר תורה.

MAFTIR FOR THE FIRST DAY (SECOND IN ISRAEL) OF ḤOL HAMO'ED

In Israel, the last three verses from "On the third day" through "its meal offering and its libation," are read.

On the second day, twelve young bullocks, two rams, and fourteen unblemished yearling male lambs. And you shall perform their meal-offerings and their libations, for each of the bullocks, the rams and the lambs, in the proper quantities, according to the law. And likewise a male goat for atonement, as well as the regular daily offering and its meal offering and their libations. *Num. 29:17–22*

On the third day, eleven young bullocks, two rams, and fourteen unblemished yearling male lambs. And you shall perform their meal-offerings and their libations, for each of the bullocks, the rams and the lambs, in the proper quantities, according to the law. And likewise a male goat for atonement, as well as the regular daily offering and its meal offering and its libation.

MAFTIR FOR THE THIRD DAY (FOURTH IN ISRAEL) OF ḤOL HAMO'ED

In Israel, the last three verses from "On the fifth day" through "its meal offering and its libation," are read.

On the fourth day, ten young bullocks, two rams, and fourteen unblemished yearling male lambs. And you shall perform their meal-offerings and their libations, for each of the bullocks, the rams and the lambs, in the proper quantities, according to the law. And likewise a male goat for atonement, as well as the regular daily offering and its meal offering and its libation. *Num. 29:23–28*

On the fifth day, nine young bullocks, two rams, and fourteen unblemished yearling male lambs. And you shall perform their meal-offerings and their libations, for each of the bullocks, the rams and the lambs, in the proper quantities, according to the law. And likewise a male goat for atonement, as well as the regular daily offering and its meal offering and its libation.

MAFTIR FOR THE FOURTH DAY (FIFTH IN ISRAEL) OF ḤOL HAMO'ED

In Israel, the last three verses from "On the sixth day" through "its meal offering and its libations," are read.

On the fifth day, nine young bullocks, two rams, and fourteen unblemished yearling male lambs. And you shall perform their meal-offerings and their libations, for each of the bullocks, the rams and the lambs, in the proper quantities, according to the law. And likewise a male goat for *Num. 29:26–31*

מפטיר ליום הראשון (השני בארץ ישראל) דחול המועד

In ארץ ישראל*, the last three verses from* וּבַיּוֹם הַשְּׁלִישִׁי *through* וּמִנְחָתָהּ וְנִסְכָּהּ*, are read.*

במדבר כט:יז–כב
וּבַיּוֹם הַשֵּׁנִי פָּרִים בְּנֵי־בָקָר שְׁנֵים עָשָׂר אֵילִם שְׁנָיִם כְּבָשִׂים בְּנֵי־
שָׁנָה אַרְבָּעָה עָשָׂר תְּמִימִם: וּמִנְחָתָם וְנִסְכֵּיהֶם לַפָּרִים לָאֵילִם
וְלַכְּבָשִׂים בְּמִסְפָּרָם כַּמִּשְׁפָּט: וּשְׂעִיר־עִזִּים אֶחָד חַטָּאת מִלְּבַד
עֹלַת הַתָּמִיד וּמִנְחָתָהּ וְנִסְכֵּיהֶם: וּבַיּוֹם הַשְּׁלִישִׁי
פָּרִים עַשְׁתֵּי־עָשָׂר אֵילִם שְׁנָיִם כְּבָשִׂים בְּנֵי־שָׁנָה אַרְבָּעָה עָשָׂר
תְּמִימִם: וּמִנְחָתָם וְנִסְכֵּיהֶם לַפָּרִים לָאֵילִם וְלַכְּבָשִׂים בְּמִסְפָּרָם
כַּמִּשְׁפָּט: וּשְׂעִיר חַטָּאת אֶחָד מִלְּבַד עֹלַת הַתָּמִיד וּמִנְחָתָהּ
וְנִסְכָּהּ:

מפטיר ליום השלישי (הרביעי בארץ ישראל) דחול המועד

In ארץ ישראל*, the last three verses from* וּבַיּוֹם הַחֲמִישִׁי *through* וּמִנְחָתָהּ וְנִסְכָּהּ*, are read.*

במדבר כט:כג–כח
וּבַיּוֹם הָרְבִיעִי פָּרִים עֲשָׂרָה אֵילִם שְׁנָיִם כְּבָשִׂים בְּנֵי־שָׁנָה
אַרְבָּעָה עָשָׂר תְּמִימִם: מִנְחָתָם וְנִסְכֵּיהֶם לַפָּרִים לָאֵילִם
וְלַכְּבָשִׂים בְּמִסְפָּרָם כַּמִּשְׁפָּט: וּשְׂעִיר־עִזִּים אֶחָד חַטָּאת מִלְּבַד
עֹלַת הַתָּמִיד מִנְחָתָהּ וְנִסְכָּהּ: וּבַיּוֹם הַחֲמִישִׁי פָּרִים
תִּשְׁעָה אֵילִם שְׁנָיִם כְּבָשִׂים בְּנֵי־שָׁנָה אַרְבָּעָה עָשָׂר תְּמִימִם:
וּמִנְחָתָם וְנִסְכֵּיהֶם לַפָּרִים לָאֵילִם וְלַכְּבָשִׂים בְּמִסְפָּרָם כַּמִּשְׁפָּט:
וּשְׂעִיר חַטָּאת אֶחָד מִלְּבַד עֹלַת הַתָּמִיד וּמִנְחָתָהּ וְנִסְכָּהּ:

מפטיר ליום הרביעי (החמישי בארץ ישראל) דחול המועד

In ארץ ישראל*, the last three verses from* וּבַיּוֹם הַשִּׁשִּׁי *through* מִנְחָתָהּ וּנְסָכֶיהָ*, are read.*

במדבר כט:כו–לא
וּבַיּוֹם הַחֲמִישִׁי פָּרִים תִּשְׁעָה אֵילִם שְׁנָיִם כְּבָשִׂים בְּנֵי־שָׁנָה
אַרְבָּעָה עָשָׂר תְּמִימִם: וּמִנְחָתָם וְנִסְכֵּיהֶם לַפָּרִים לָאֵילִם
וְלַכְּבָשִׂים בְּמִסְפָּרָם כַּמִּשְׁפָּט: וּשְׂעִיר חַטָּאת אֶחָד מִלְּבַד עֹלַת

atonement, as well as the regular daily offering and its meal offering and its libation.

On the sixth day, eight young bullocks, two rams, and fourteen unblemished yearling male lambs. And you shall perform their meal-offerings and their libations, for each of the bullocks, the rams and the lambs, in the proper quantities, according to the law. And likewise a male goat for atonement, as well as the regular daily offering and its meal offering and its libations.

HAGBAHA AND GELILA

The second Torah scroll is lifted and the congregation says:

וְזֹאת הַתּוֹרָה This is the Torah Deut. 4
that Moses placed before the children of Israel,
at the LORD's commandment, by the hand of Moses. Num. 9

Some add: It is a tree of life to those who grasp it, Prov. 3
and those who uphold it are happy.
Its ways are ways of pleasantness, and all its paths are peace.
Long life is in its right hand; in its left, riches and honor.
It pleased the LORD for the sake of [Israel's] righteousness, Is. 42
to make the Torah great and glorious.

The second Torah scroll is bound and covered and the oleh for Maftir reads the Haftara.

BLESSING BEFORE READING THE HAFTARA

Before reading the Haftara, the person called up for Maftir says:

בָּרוּךְ Blessed are You, LORD our God, King of the Universe, who chose good prophets and was pleased with their words, spoken in truth. Blessed are You, LORD, who chose the Torah, His servant Moses, His people Israel, and the prophets of truth and righteousness.

HAFTARA

And it shall be, on the day that Gog comes onto the soil of Israel, Ezek. 38:18–39:16
says the LORD God: My anger will rise up in My nostrils; in My

---

Ezekiel was supremely a prophet of exile. He was among the first group of exiles taken by Nebuchadnezzar to Babylon in 597 BCE. The Jews who remained believed that their initial defeat was only a temporary setback. Ezekiel,

הַתָּמִיד וּמִנְחָתָהּ וְנִסְכָּהּ׃ וּבַיּוֹם הַשִּׁשִּׁי פָּרִים שְׁמֹנָה
אֵילִם שְׁנָיִם כְּבָשִׂים בְּנֵי־שָׁנָה אַרְבָּעָה עָשָׂר תְּמִימִם׃ וּמִנְחָתָם
וְנִסְכֵּיהֶם לַפָּרִים לָאֵילִם וְלַכְּבָשִׂים בְּמִסְפָּרָם כַּמִּשְׁפָּט׃ וּשְׂעִיר
חַטָּאת אֶחָד מִלְּבַד עֹלַת הַתָּמִיד מִנְחָתָהּ וּנְסָכֶיהָ׃

הגבהה וגלילה

The second ספר תורה *is lifted and the* קהל *says:*

וְזֹאת הַתּוֹרָה אֲשֶׁר־שָׂם מֹשֶׁה לִפְנֵי בְּנֵי יִשְׂרָאֵל׃ דברים ד
עַל־פִּי יהוה בְּיַד מֹשֶׁה׃ במדבר ט

Some add עֵץ־חַיִּים הִיא לַמַּחֲזִיקִים בָּהּ וְתֹמְכֶיהָ מְאֻשָּׁר׃ משלי ג
דְּרָכֶיהָ דַרְכֵי־נֹעַם וְכָל־נְתִיבֹתֶיהָ שָׁלוֹם׃
אֹרֶךְ יָמִים בִּימִינָהּ, בִּשְׂמֹאולָהּ עֹשֶׁר וְכָבוֹד׃
יהוה חָפֵץ לְמַעַן צִדְקוֹ יַגְדִּיל תּוֹרָה וְיַאְדִּיר׃ ישעיה מב

The second ספר תורה *is bound and covered and the* עולה *for* מפטיר *reads the* הפטרה.

ברכה קודם ההפטרה

Before reading the הפטרה*, the person called up for* מפטיר *says:*

בָּרוּךְ אַתָּה יהוה אֱלֹהֵינוּ מֶלֶךְ הָעוֹלָם אֲשֶׁר בָּחַר בִּנְבִיאִים טוֹבִים,
וְרָצָה בְדִבְרֵיהֶם הַנֶּאֱמָרִים בֶּאֱמֶת. בָּרוּךְ אַתָּה יהוה, הַבּוֹחֵר
בַּתּוֹרָה וּבְמֹשֶׁה עַבְדּוֹ וּבְיִשְׂרָאֵל עַמּוֹ וּבִנְבִיאֵי הָאֱמֶת וָצֶדֶק.

הפטרה

וְהָיָה ׀ בַּיּוֹם הַהוּא בְּיוֹם בּוֹא גוֹג עַל־אַדְמַת יִשְׂרָאֵל נְאֻם אֲדֹנָי יחזקאל לח:יח–לט:ט
יֱהֹוִה תַּעֲלֶה חֲמָתִי בְּאַפִּי׃ וּבְקִנְאָתִי בְאֵשׁ־עֶבְרָתִי דִּבַּרְתִּי

HAFTARA FOR SHABBAT HOL HAMO'ED

A graphic vision of a battle that will take place at the end of days, in which Israel's enemies will be defeated, and God's name will be made great among the nations.

fury, in the fire of My rage, I have spoken: Surely, on that day there will be a great quaking upon the ground of Israel; the fish of the seas and the birds of the sky, the animals of the land, every creeping thing that crawls upon the earth and every man on the face of the earth will quake before Me; the mountains will be demolished, the terraces will collapse, and every wall shall fall to the ground. I will call the sword down on him from all My mountains, says the LORD, God: each man's sword will be turned against his brother. I will call judgment on him with pestilence and blood; I will pour down torrential rain and crystal hailstone, fire and sulphur over him and his troops, and over the many peoples who are with him. And

---

testify, in its strange and singular history, to the existence and sovereignty of the One God, Creator of heaven and earth.

The identity of Gog is unclear. His country, Magog, is mentioned in Genesis 10:2 as belonging to the descendants of Japheth (identified later with Asia Minor and Greece). Some have surmised that this is Gyges, also known as Goga, king of Lydia in Asia Minor (today, northwest Turkey) in the seventh century BCE. In later apocalyptic literature, Gog and Magog – now identified as a person, not a land – figured largely as initiators of a cosmic battle that would inaugurate the end of days.

The connection with Sukkot lies in the similarity between this vision and that of Zechariah 14 (the *haftara* for the first day), with its explicit reference to Sukkot. Since this was the time when both the first and second Temples were dedicated, it was natural to associate it with the restoration of cosmic order, in which Israel will be at peace, Jerusalem the spiritual center of the world, and God's presence manifest to all.

חֲמָתִי *My anger (previous page).* God's anger is directed at the fact that Gog is attacking a people "restored from the sword, gathered from the midst of many peoples," who are seeking to live quietly at peace (Ezekiel 38:8).

רַעַשׁ גָּדוֹל *A great quaking.* As if nature itself were rising in protest against this violation of peaceful coexistence.

דְּגֵי הַיָּם *The fish of the seas.* An evocation of the orderly creation described in the opening chapter of Genesis.

אֵשׁ וְגָפְרִית *Fire and sulphur.* An echo of the destruction of Sodom (Gen. 19:24).

אִם־לֹא ׀ בַּיּוֹם הַהוּא יִהְיֶה רַעַשׁ גָּדוֹל עַל אַדְמַת יִשְׂרָאֵל׃
וְרָעֲשׁוּ מִפָּנַי דְּגֵי הַיָּם וְעוֹף הַשָּׁמַיִם וְחַיַּת הַשָּׂדֶה וְכָל־הָרֶמֶשׂ
הָרֹמֵשׂ עַל־הָאֲדָמָה וְכֹל הָאָדָם אֲשֶׁר עַל־פְּנֵי הָאֲדָמָה וְנֶהֶרְסוּ
הֶהָרִים וְנָפְלוּ הַמַּדְרֵגוֹת וְכָל־חוֹמָה לָאָרֶץ תִּפּוֹל׃ וְקָרָאתִי
עָלָיו לְכָל־הָרַי חֶרֶב נְאֻם אֲדֹנָי יֱהוִה חֶרֶב אִישׁ בְּאָחִיו תִּהְיֶה׃
וְנִשְׁפַּטְתִּי אִתּוֹ בְּדֶבֶר וּבְדָם וְגֶשֶׁם שׁוֹטֵף וְאַבְנֵי אֶלְגָּבִישׁ אֵשׁ
וְגָפְרִית אַמְטִיר עָלָיו וְעַל־אֲגַפָּיו וְעַל־עַמִּים רַבִּים אֲשֶׁר אִתּוֹ׃

---

together with his older contemporary Jeremiah, prophesied otherwise: that the kingdom would be defeated again if it rose against Babylon, and the result would be an even greater catastrophe.

It was. In 586 BCE Jerusalem was conquered, the Temple destroyed, and much of the nation taken into captivity. In Babylon, Ezekiel became the voice of hope. The people, having forsaken the covenant, had been punished, God using Nebuchadnezzar as the instrument of His anger. But God would not allow His name to be desecrated by His people remaining captive, and would bring them back to their land. Ezekiel foresaw this in one of the most haunting of all biblical visions, in which he saw the nation as a valley of dry bones coming to life again through God's spirit, and heard God's promise to bring them back to their land.

In this, his next vision, Ezekiel envisioned a king, Gog, from the land of Magog, assembling a force to attack Israel even after their return. God Himself would intervene. There would be an earthquake, torrential rain, and burning sulphur. Israel's enemies would suffer a defeat so great that their weapons would be burned as fuel for seven years. God's sovereignty would be manifest to the world, the Temple would be rebuilt and Jews would live peaceably in their land.

Ezekiel lived at a time of immense turbulence. New empires were emerging. Old empires were being overturned. Bands of barbarian warriors were travelling southward. Their incursions reached, according to Herodotus, as far as Ashkelon. These hat-wearing invaders did not lay siege to cities, but rather targeted undefended small towns and villages, terrorizing populations with the aim of looting. Ezekiel's vision, then, is rooted in the turmoil of his times, when it seemed as if the very foundations of the world were being shaken. Yet his faith did not falter. Israel would outlive all its enemies, and

so I will be magnified and sanctified, I will make Myself known in the eyes of many nations – and they will know that I am the LORD.

And you, Man, prophesy against Gog and say: so says the LORD God: behold I am against you, Gog, prince, leader of Meshech and Tuval. I will turn you around, I will incite you on, and I will take you from the far-edge of the north and bring you to the mountains of Israel. I will strike your bow from your left hand, I will make the arrows fall from your right; upon the mountains of Israel, you will fall – you and your troops and all the peoples who are with you; I will give you up to the birds of prey, to every winged creature, to the animals of the land, to feed from; upon the open field, you will fall; so have I spoken, says the LORD God. And I will send fire on Magog and on those who live securely in their isles; they will know that I am the LORD.

I will make My holy name known among My people, Israel; I will no longer have My holy name profaned; and the nations will know that I am the LORD, holy among Israel. Behold: it is coming, it will be, says the LORD God: This is the day of which I have spoken.

And the inhabitants of the cities of Israel will come out, and they will kindle and burn the weapons, the shields and guards, the bows and arrows, the truncheons and spears; they will burn them for seven years, for fire: they will not take wood from the land, nor will they chop down any from the forests, for they will make their fires of weapons; they will despoil those who despoiled them, and plunder those who plundered them, says the LORD God.

And it will happen, on that day: I will grant Gog a burial-place there, in Israel, the Valley of the Travelers, east of the sea, and it will block the travelers; here they will bury Gog and his horde, they will call

---

it were, for God Himself, since it seemed to the nations as if He were unable to protect His people. This, for Ezekiel, was a *ḥillul Hashem*, a "desecration of God's name."

וְהִתְגַּדִּלְתִּי וְהִתְקַדִּשְׁתִּי וְנוֹדַעְתִּי לְעֵינֵי גּוֹיִם רַבִּים וְיָדְעוּ כִּי־
אֲנִי יְהוָה: וְאַתָּה בֶן־אָדָם הִנָּבֵא עַל־גּוֹג וְאָמַרְתָּ
כֹּה אָמַר אֲדֹנָי יֱהוִה הִנְנִי אֵלֶיךָ גּוֹג נְשִׂיא רֹאשׁ מֶשֶׁךְ וְתֻבָל:
וְשֹׁבַבְתִּיךָ וְשִׁשֵּׁאתִיךָ וְהַעֲלִיתִיךָ מִיַּרְכְּתֵי צָפוֹן וַהֲבֵאוֹתִיךָ עַל־
הָרֵי יִשְׂרָאֵל: וְהִכֵּיתִי קַשְׁתְּךָ מִיַּד שְׂמֹאולֶךָ וְחִצֶּיךָ מִיַּד יְמִינְךָ
אַפִּיל: עַל־הָרֵי יִשְׂרָאֵל תִּפּוֹל אַתָּה וְכָל־אֲגַפֶּיךָ וְעַמִּים אֲשֶׁר
אִתָּךְ לְעֵיט צִפּוֹר כָּל־כָּנָף וְחַיַּת הַשָּׂדֶה נְתַתִּיךָ לְאָכְלָה: עַל־
פְּנֵי הַשָּׂדֶה תִּפּוֹל כִּי אֲנִי דִבַּרְתִּי נְאֻם אֲדֹנָי יֱהוִה: וְשִׁלַּחְתִּי־
אֵשׁ בְּמָגוֹג וּבְיֹשְׁבֵי הָאִיִּים לָבֶטַח וְיָדְעוּ כִּי־אֲנִי יְהוָה: וְאֶת־
שֵׁם קָדְשִׁי אוֹדִיעַ בְּתוֹךְ עַמִּי יִשְׂרָאֵל וְלֹא־אַחֵל אֶת־שֵׁם־
קָדְשִׁי עוֹד וְיָדְעוּ הַגּוֹיִם כִּי־אֲנִי יְהוָה קָדוֹשׁ בְּיִשְׂרָאֵל: הִנֵּה
בָאָה וְנִהְיָתָה נְאֻם אֲדֹנָי יֱהוִה הוּא הַיּוֹם אֲשֶׁר דִּבַּרְתִּי: וְיָצְאוּ
יֹשְׁבֵי ׀ עָרֵי יִשְׂרָאֵל וּבִעֲרוּ וְהִשִּׂיקוּ בְּנֶשֶׁק וּמָגֵן וְצִנָּה בְּקֶשֶׁת
וּבְחִצִּים וּבְמַקֵּל יָד וּבְרֹמַח וּבִעֲרוּ בָהֶם אֵשׁ שֶׁבַע שָׁנִים: וְלֹא־
יִשְׂאוּ עֵצִים מִן־הַשָּׂדֶה וְלֹא יַחְטְבוּ מִן־הַיְּעָרִים כִּי בַנֶּשֶׁק
יְבַעֲרוּ־אֵשׁ וְשָׁלְלוּ אֶת־שֹׁלְלֵיהֶם וּבָזְזוּ אֶת־בֹּזְזֵיהֶם נְאֻם אֲדֹנָי
יֱהוִה: וְהָיָה בַיּוֹם הַהוּא אֶתֵּן לְגוֹג ׀ מְקוֹם־שָׁם קֶבֶר
בְּיִשְׂרָאֵל גֵּי הָעֹבְרִים קִדְמַת הַיָּם וְחֹסֶמֶת הִיא אֶת־הָעֹבְרִים
וְקָבְרוּ שָׁם אֶת־גּוֹג וְאֶת־כָּל־הֲמוֹנֹה וְקָרְאוּ גֵּיא הֲמוֹן גּוֹג: וּקְבָרוּם

וְהִתְגַּדִּלְתִּי וְהִתְקַדִּשְׁתִּי *I will be magnified and sanctified.* These words were adapted to become the opening words of the Kaddish, itself a prayer for the recognition of God's sovereignty throughout the world.

וְשֹׁבַבְתִּיךָ וְשִׁשֵּׁאתִיךָ *I will turn you around, I will incite you.* Those who seek the destruction of Israel will bring about their own destruction.

וְלֹא־אַחֵל אֶת־שֵׁם־קָדְשִׁי עוֹד *I will no longer have My holy name profaned.* To a unique degree, Ezekiel saw Israel's exile as a tragedy not only for Israel, but, as

it the Valley of the Hordes of Gog. For seven months, the house of Israel will bury them, to purify the land; all the people in the land will bury them, and it will make their name; it will be the day of My glory, says the LORD God. And they will select men to cross the land perpetually, burying those remains that lie upon the ground – with the travelers – to purify it; they will search from the end of seven months, and travelers passing through the land, whenever they see a human bone, will place a sign next to it, until the buriers have buried it in the Valley of the Hordes of Gog. A city will be named Hamona, [for his Hordes]. And so will they purify the land.

BLESSINGS AFTER READING THE HAFTARA

After the Haftara, the person called up for Maftir says the following blessings:

בָּרוּךְ Blessed are You, LORD our God, King of the Universe, Rock of all worlds, righteous for all generations, the faithful God who says and does, speaks and fulfills, all of whose words are truth and righteousness. You are faithful, LORD our God, and faithful are Your words, not one of which returns unfulfilled, for You, God, are a faithful (and compassionate) King. Blessed are You, LORD, faithful in all His words.

רַחֵם Have compassion on Zion for it is the source of our life, and save the one grieved in spirit swiftly in our days. Blessed are You, LORD, who makes Zion rejoice in her children.

שַׂמְּחֵנוּ Grant us joy, LORD our God, through Elijah the prophet Your servant, and through the kingdom of the house of David Your anointed – may he soon come and make our hearts glad. May no stranger sit on his throne, and may others not continue to inherit his glory, for You promised him by Your holy name that his light would never be extinguished. Blessed are You, LORD, Shield of David.

עַל הַתּוֹרָה For the Torah, for Divine worship, for the prophets, and for this Sabbath day and for this day of the Festival of Sukkot which You, LORD our God, have given us for holiness and rest, for joy and gladness, honor and glory – for all these we thank and bless You, LORD our God, and may Your name be blessed by the mouth of all that lives, continually, for ever and all time. Blessed are You, LORD, who sanctifies the Sabbath, Israel and the festivals.

בֵּית יִשְׂרָאֵל לְמַעַן טַהֵר אֶת־הָאָרֶץ שִׁבְעָה חֳדָשִׁים: וְקָבְרוּ כָּל־עַם הָאָרֶץ וְהָיָה לָהֶם לְשֵׁם יוֹם הִכָּבְדִי נְאֻם אֲדֹנָי יֱהֹוִה: וְאַנְשֵׁי תָמִיד יַבְדִּילוּ עֹבְרִים בָּאָרֶץ מְקַבְּרִים אֶת־הָעֹבְרִים אֶת־הַנּוֹתָרִים עַל־פְּנֵי הָאָרֶץ לְטַהֲרָהּ מִקְצֵה שִׁבְעָה־חֳדָשִׁים יַחְקֹרוּ: וְעָבְרוּ הָעֹבְרִים בָּאָרֶץ וְרָאָה עֶצֶם אָדָם וּבָנָה אֶצְלוֹ צִיּוּן עַד קָבְרוּ אֹתוֹ הַמְקַבְּרִים אֶל־גֵּיא הֲמוֹן גּוֹג: וְגַם שֶׁם־עִיר הֲמוֹנָה וְטִהֲרוּ הָאָרֶץ:

ברכות לאחר ההפטרה

After the הפטרה, the person called up for מפטיר says the following blessings:

בָּרוּךְ אַתָּה יהוה אֱלֹהֵינוּ מֶלֶךְ הָעוֹלָם, צוּר כָּל הָעוֹלָמִים, צַדִּיק בְּכָל הַדּוֹרוֹת, הָאֵל הַנֶּאֱמָן, הָאוֹמֵר וְעוֹשֶׂה, הַמְדַבֵּר וּמְקַיֵּם, שֶׁכָּל דְּבָרָיו אֱמֶת וָצֶדֶק. נֶאֱמָן אַתָּה הוּא יהוה אֱלֹהֵינוּ וְנֶאֱמָנִים דְּבָרֶיךָ, וְדָבָר אֶחָד מִדְּבָרֶיךָ אָחוֹר לֹא יָשׁוּב רֵיקָם, כִּי אֵל מֶלֶךְ נֶאֱמָן (וְרַחֲמָן) אָתָּה. בָּרוּךְ אַתָּה יהוה, הָאֵל הַנֶּאֱמָן בְּכָל דְּבָרָיו.

רַחֵם עַל צִיּוֹן כִּי הִיא בֵּית חַיֵּינוּ, וְלַעֲלוּבַת נֶפֶשׁ תּוֹשִׁיעַ בִּמְהֵרָה בְיָמֵינוּ. בָּרוּךְ אַתָּה יהוה, מְשַׂמֵּחַ צִיּוֹן בְּבָנֶיהָ.

שַׂמְּחֵנוּ יהוה אֱלֹהֵינוּ בְּאֵלִיָּהוּ הַנָּבִיא עַבְדֶּךָ, וּבְמַלְכוּת בֵּית דָּוִד מְשִׁיחֶךָ, בִּמְהֵרָה יָבוֹא וְיָגֵל לִבֵּנוּ. עַל כִּסְאוֹ לֹא יֵשֶׁב זָר, וְלֹא יִנְחֲלוּ עוֹד אֲחֵרִים אֶת כְּבוֹדוֹ, כִּי בְשֵׁם קָדְשְׁךָ נִשְׁבַּעְתָּ לּוֹ שֶׁלֹּא יִכְבֶּה נֵרוֹ לְעוֹלָם וָעֶד. בָּרוּךְ אַתָּה יהוה, מָגֵן דָּוִד.

עַל הַתּוֹרָה וְעַל הָעֲבוֹדָה וְעַל הַנְּבִיאִים וְעַל יוֹם הַשַּׁבָּת הַזֶּה, וְעַל יוֹם חַג הַסֻּכּוֹת הַזֶּה, שֶׁנָּתַתָּ לָּנוּ יהוה אֱלֹהֵינוּ לִקְדֻשָּׁה וְלִמְנוּחָה, לְשָׂשׂוֹן וּלְשִׂמְחָה, לְכָבוֹד וּלְתִפְאָרֶת. עַל הַכֹּל יהוה אֱלֹהֵינוּ אֲנַחְנוּ מוֹדִים לָךְ וּמְבָרְכִים אוֹתָךְ, יִתְבָּרַךְ שִׁמְךָ בְּפִי כָּל חַי תָּמִיד לְעוֹלָם וָעֶד. בָּרוּךְ אַתָּה יהוה, מְקַדֵּשׁ הַשַּׁבָּת וְיִשְׂרָאֵל וְהַזְּמַנִּים.

The following three paragraphs are only said when praying with a minyan (some say the first paragraph without a minyan).

יְקוּם פֻּרְקָן May deliverance arise from heaven, bringing grace, love and compassion, long life, ample sustenance and heavenly help, physical health and enlightenment of mind, living and thriving children who will neither interrupt nor cease from the words of the Torah – to our masters and teachers of the holy communities in the land of Israel and Babylon; to the leaders of assemblies and the leaders of communities in exile; to the heads of academies and to the judges in the gates; to all their disciples and their disciples' disciples, and to all who occupy themselves in study of the Torah. May the King of the Universe bless them, prolonging their lives, increasing their days, and adding to their years. May they be redeemed and delivered from all distress and illness. May our Master in heaven be their help at all times and seasons; and let us say: Amen.

יְקוּם פֻּרְקָן May deliverance arise from heaven, bringing grace, love and compassion, long life, ample sustenance and heavenly help, physical health and enlightenment of mind, living and thriving children who will neither interrupt nor cease from the words of the Torah – to all this holy congregation, great and small, women and children. May the King of the Universe bless you, prolonging your lives, increasing your days, and adding to your years. May you be redeemed and delivered from all distress and illness. May our Master in heaven be your help at all times and seasons; and let us say: Amen.

מִי שֶׁבֵּרַךְ May He who blessed our fathers, Abraham, Isaac and Jacob, bless all this holy congregation, together with all other holy congregations: them, their wives, their sons and daughters, and all that is theirs. May He bless those who unite to form synagogues for prayer and those who come there to pray; those who provide lamps for light and wine for Kiddush and Havdala, food for visitors and charity for the poor, and all who faithfully occupy themselves with the needs of the community. May the Holy One, blessed be He, give them their reward; may He remove from them all illness, grant them complete healing, and forgive all their sins. May He send blessing and success to all the work of their hands, together with all Israel their brethren; and let us say: Amen.

The following three paragraphs are only said when praying with a מנין (some say the first paragraph without a מנין).

יְקוּם פֻּרְקָן מִן שְׁמַיָּא, חִנָּא וְחִסְדָּא וְרַחֲמֵי וְחַיֵּי אֲרִיכֵי וּמְזוֹנֵי רְוִיחֵי, וְסִיַּעְתָּא דִשְׁמַיָּא, וּבַרְיוּת גּוּפָא וּנְהוֹרָא מְעַלְּיָא, זַרְעָא חַיָּא וְקַיָּמָא, זַרְעָא דִּי לָא יִפְסֻק וְדִי לָא יִבְטֻל מִפִּתְגָּמֵי אוֹרַיְתָא, לְמָרָנָן וְרַבָּנָן חֲבוּרָתָא קַדִּישָׁתָא דִּי בְאַרְעָא דְיִשְׂרָאֵל וְדִי בְּבָבֶל, לְרֵישֵׁי כַלָּה, וּלְרֵישֵׁי גַלְוָתָא, וּלְרֵישֵׁי מְתִיבָתָא, וּלְדַיָּנֵי דְבָבָא, לְכָל תַּלְמִידֵיהוֹן, וּלְכָל תַּלְמִידֵי תַלְמִידֵיהוֹן, וּלְכָל מָאן דְּעָסְקִין בְּאוֹרַיְתָא. מַלְכָּא דְעָלְמָא יְבָרֵךְ יָתְהוֹן, יַפֵּשׁ חַיֵּיהוֹן וְיַסְגֵּא יוֹמֵיהוֹן, וְיִתֵּן אַרְכָא לִשְׁנֵיהוֹן, וְיִתְפָּרְקוּן וְיִשְׁתֵּיזְבוּן מִן כָּל עָקָא וּמִן כָּל מַרְעִין בִּישִׁין. מָרַן דִּי בִשְׁמַיָּא יְהֵא בְסַעְדְּהוֹן כָּל זְמַן וְעִדָּן, וְנֹאמַר אָמֵן.

יְקוּם פֻּרְקָן מִן שְׁמַיָּא, חִנָּא וְחִסְדָּא וְרַחֲמֵי וְחַיֵּי אֲרִיכֵי וּמְזוֹנֵי רְוִיחֵי, וְסִיַּעְתָּא דִשְׁמַיָּא, וּבַרְיוּת גּוּפָא וּנְהוֹרָא מְעַלְּיָא, זַרְעָא חַיָּא וְקַיָּמָא, זַרְעָא דִּי לָא יִפְסֻק וְדִי לָא יִבְטֻל מִפִּתְגָּמֵי אוֹרַיְתָא, לְכָל קְהָלָא קַדִּישָׁא הָדֵין, רַבְרְבַיָּא עִם זְעֵרַיָּא, טַפְלָא וּנְשַׁיָּא. מַלְכָּא דְעָלְמָא יְבָרֵךְ יָתְכוֹן, יַפֵּשׁ חַיֵּיכוֹן וְיַסְגֵּא יוֹמֵיכוֹן, וְיִתֵּן אַרְכָא לִשְׁנֵיכוֹן, וְתִתְפָּרְקוּן וְתִשְׁתֵּיזְבוּן מִן כָּל עָקָא וּמִן כָּל מַרְעִין בִּישִׁין. מָרַן דִּי בִשְׁמַיָּא יְהֵא בְסַעְדְּכוֹן כָּל זְמַן וְעִדָּן, וְנֹאמַר אָמֵן.

מִי שֶׁבֵּרַךְ אֲבוֹתֵינוּ אַבְרָהָם יִצְחָק וְיַעֲקֹב, הוּא יְבָרֵךְ אֶת כָּל הַקָּהָל הַקָּדוֹשׁ הַזֶּה עִם כָּל קְהִלּוֹת הַקֹּדֶשׁ, הֵם וּנְשֵׁיהֶם וּבְנֵיהֶם וּבְנוֹתֵיהֶם וְכָל אֲשֶׁר לָהֶם, וּמִי שֶׁמְּיַחֲדִים בָּתֵּי כְנֵסִיּוֹת לִתְפִלָּה, וּמִי שֶׁבָּאִים בְּתוֹכָם לְהִתְפַּלֵּל, וּמִי שֶׁנּוֹתְנִים נֵר לַמָּאוֹר וְיַיִן לְקִדּוּשׁ וּלְהַבְדָּלָה, וּפַת לָאוֹרְחִים וּצְדָקָה לָעֲנִיִּים, וְכָל מִי שֶׁעוֹסְקִים בְּצָרְכֵי צִבּוּר בֶּאֱמוּנָה. הַקָּדוֹשׁ בָּרוּךְ הוּא יְשַׁלֵּם שְׂכָרָם, וְיָסִיר מֵהֶם כָּל מַחֲלָה, וְיִרְפָּא לְכָל גּוּפָם, וְיִסְלַח לְכָל עֲוֹנָם, וְיִשְׁלַח בְּרָכָה וְהַצְלָחָה בְּכָל מַעֲשֵׂי יְדֵיהֶם, עִם כָּל יִשְׂרָאֵל אֲחֵיהֶם, וְנֹאמַר אָמֵן.

The Prayer for the Welfare of the Canadian Government is on the next page.

PRAYER FOR THE WELFARE OF THE AMERICAN GOVERNMENT

The Leader says the following:

הַנּוֹתֵן תְּשׁוּעָה May He who gives salvation to kings and dominion to princes, whose kingdom is an everlasting kingdom, who delivers His servant David from the evil sword, who makes a way in the sea and a path through the mighty waters, bless and protect, guard and help, exalt, magnify and uplift the President, Vice President and all officials of this land. May the Supreme King of kings in His mercy put into their hearts and the hearts of all their counselors and officials, to deal kindly with us and all Israel. In their days and in ours, may Judah be saved and Israel dwell in safety, and may the Redeemer come to Zion. May this be His will, and let us say: Amen.

PRAYER FOR THE SAFETY OF THE AMERICAN MILITARY FORCES

The Leader says the following:

אַדִּיר בַּמָּרוֹם God on high who dwells in might, the King to whom peace belongs, look down from Your holy habitation and bless the soldiers of the American military forces who risk their lives for the sake of peace on earth. Be their shelter and stronghold, and let them not falter. Give them the strength and courage to thwart the plans of the enemy and end the rule of evil. May their enemies be scattered and their foes flee before them, and may they rejoice in Your salvation. Bring them back safely to their homes, as is written: "The LORD will guard you from all harm, He will guard *Ps. 121* your life. The LORD will guard your going and coming, now and for evermore." And may there be fulfilled for us the verse: "Nation *Is. 2* shall not lift up sword against nation, nor shall they learn war any more." Let all the inhabitants on earth know that sovereignty is Yours and Your name inspires awe over all You have created – and let us say: Amen.

The Prayer for the Welfare of the Canadian Government is on the next page.

תפילה לשלום המלכות (ארה״ב)

The שליח ציבור *says the following:*

הַנּוֹתֵן תְּשׁוּעָה לַמְּלָכִים וּמֶמְשָׁלָה לַנְּסִיכִים, מַלְכוּתוֹ מַלְכוּת כָּל עוֹלָמִים, הַפּוֹצֶה אֶת דָּוִד עַבְדּוֹ מֵחֶרֶב רָעָה, הַנּוֹתֵן בַּיָּם דֶּרֶךְ וּבְמַיִם עַזִּים נְתִיבָה, הוּא יְבָרֵךְ וְיִשְׁמֹר וְיִנְצֹר וְיַעֲזֹר וִירוֹמֵם וִיגַדֵּל וִינַשֵּׂא לְמַעְלָה אֶת הַנָּשִׂיא וְאֵת מִשְׁנֵהוּ וְאֶת כָּל שָׂרֵי הָאָרֶץ הַזֹּאת. מֶלֶךְ מַלְכֵי הַמְּלָכִים, בְּרַחֲמָיו יִתֵּן בְּלִבָּם וּבְלֵב כָּל יוֹעֲצֵיהֶם וְשָׂרֵיהֶם לַעֲשׂוֹת טוֹבָה עִמָּנוּ וְעִם כָּל יִשְׂרָאֵל. בִּימֵיהֶם וּבְיָמֵינוּ תִּוָּשַׁע יְהוּדָה, וְיִשְׂרָאֵל יִשְׁכֹּן לָבֶטַח, וּבָא לְצִיּוֹן גּוֹאֵל. וְכֵן יְהִי רָצוֹן, וְנֹאמַר אָמֵן.

תפילה לשלום חיילי צבא ארצות הברית

The שליח ציבור *says the following:*

אַדִּיר בַּמָּרוֹם שׁוֹכֵן בִּגְבוּרָה, מֶלֶךְ שֶׁהַשָּׁלוֹם שֶׁלּוֹ, הַשְׁקִיפָה מִמְּעוֹן
קָדְשְׁךָ, וּבָרֵךְ אֶת חַיָּלֵי צְבָא אַרְצוֹת הַבְּרִית, הַמְחָרְפִים נַפְשָׁם
בְּלֶכְתָּם לָשִׂים שָׁלוֹם בָּאָרֶץ. הֱיֵה נָא לָהֶם מַחֲסֶה וּמָעוֹז, וְאַל תִּתֵּן
לַמּוֹט רַגְלָם, חַזֵּק יְדֵיהֶם וְאַמֵּץ רוּחָם לְהָפֵר עֲצַת אוֹיֵב וּלְהַעֲבִיר
מֶמְשֶׁלֶת זָדוֹן, יָפוּצוּ אוֹיְבֵיהֶם וְיָנוּסוּ מְשַׂנְאֵיהֶם מִפְּנֵיהֶם, וְיִשְׂמְחוּ
בִּישׁוּעָתֶךָ. הֲשִׁיבֵם בְּשָׁלוֹם אֶל בֵּיתָם, כַּכָּתוּב בְּדִבְרֵי קָדְשֶׁךָ:
יהוה יִשְׁמָרְךָ מִכָּל־רָע, יִשְׁמֹר אֶת־נַפְשֶׁךָ: יהוה יִשְׁמָר־צֵאתְךָ תהלים קכא
וּבוֹאֶךָ, מֵעַתָּה וְעַד־עוֹלָם: וְקַיֵּם בָּנוּ מִקְרָא שֶׁכָּתוּב: לֹא־ ישעיה ב
יִשָּׂא גוֹי אֶל־גּוֹי חֶרֶב, וְלֹא־יִלְמְדוּ עוֹד מִלְחָמָה: וְיֵדְעוּ כָּל יוֹשְׁבֵי
תֵבֵל כִּי לְךָ מְלוּכָה יָאֲתָה, וְשִׁמְךָ נוֹרָא עַל כָּל מַה שֶּׁבָּרָאתָ.
וְנֹאמַר אָמֵן.

PRAYER FOR THE WELFARE OF THE CANADIAN GOVERNMENT

The Leader says the following:

הַנּוֹתֵן תְּשׁוּעָה May He who gives salvation to kings and dominion to princes, whose kingdom is an everlasting kingdom, who delivers His servant David from the evil sword, who makes a way in the sea and a path through the mighty waters, bless and protect, guard and help, exalt, magnify and uplift the Prime Minister and all the elected and appointed officials of Canada. May the Supreme King of kings in His mercy put into their hearts and the hearts of all their counselors and officials, to deal kindly with us and all Israel. In their days and in ours, may Judah be saved and Israel dwell in safety, and may the Redeemer come to Zion. May this be His will, and let us say: Amen.

PRAYER FOR THE SAFETY OF THE CANADIAN FORCES

The Leader says the following:

אַדִּיר בַּמָּרוֹם God on high who dwells in might, the King to whom peace belongs, look down from Your holy habitation and bless the soldiers of the Canadian Forces who risk their lives for the sake of peace on earth. Be their shelter and stronghold, and let them not falter. Give them the strength and courage to thwart the plans of the enemy and end the rule of evil. May their enemies be scattered and their foes flee before them, and may they rejoice in Your salvation. Bring them back safely to their homes, as is written: "The LORD will guard you from all harm, He will guard *Ps. 121*
your life. The LORD will guard your going and coming, now and for evermore." And may there be fulfilled for us the verse: "Nation *Is. 2*
shall not lift up sword against nation, nor shall they learn war any more." Let all the inhabitants on earth know that sovereignty is Yours and Your name inspires awe over all You have created – and let us say: Amen.

תפילה לשלום המלכות (קנדה)

The שליח ציבור *says the following:*

הַנּוֹתֵן תְּשׁוּעָה לַמְּלָכִים וּמֶמְשָׁלָה לַנְּסִיכִים, מַלְכוּתוֹ מַלְכוּת כָּל עוֹלָמִים, הַפּוֹצֶה אֶת דָּוִד עַבְדּוֹ מֵחֶרֶב רָעָה, הַנּוֹתֵן בַּיָּם דֶּרֶךְ וּבְמַיִם עַזִּים נְתִיבָה, הוּא יְבָרֵךְ וְיִשְׁמֹר וְיִנְצֹר וְיַעֲזֹר וִירוֹמֵם וִיגַדֵּל וִינַשֵּׂא לְמַעְלָה אֶת רֹאשׁ הַמֶּמְשָׁלָה וְאֶת כָּל שָׂרֵי הָאָרֶץ הַזֹּאת. מֶלֶךְ מַלְכֵי הַמְּלָכִים, בְּרַחֲמָיו יִתֵּן בְּלִבָּם וּבְלֵב כָּל יוֹעֲצֵיהֶם וְשָׂרֵיהֶם לַעֲשׂוֹת טוֹבָה עִמָּנוּ וְעִם כָּל יִשְׂרָאֵל. בִּימֵיהֶם וּבְיָמֵינוּ תִּוָּשַׁע יְהוּדָה, וְיִשְׂרָאֵל יִשְׁכֹּן לָבֶטַח, וּבָא לְצִיּוֹן גּוֹאֵל. וְכֵן יְהִי רָצוֹן, וְנֹאמַר אָמֵן.

תפילה לשלום חיילי צבא קנדה

The שליח ציבור *says the following:*

אַדִּיר בַּמָּרוֹם שׁוֹכֵן בִּגְבוּרָה, מֶלֶךְ שֶׁהַשָּׁלוֹם שֶׁלּוֹ, הַשְׁקִיפָה
מִמְּעוֹן קָדְשְׁךָ, וּבָרֵךְ אֶת חַיָּלֵי צְבָא קָנָדָה, הַמְחָרְפִים נַפְשָׁם
בְּלֶכְתָּם לָשִׂים שָׁלוֹם בָּאָרֶץ. הֱיֵה נָא לָהֶם מַחֲסֶה וּמָעוֹז, וְאַל
תִּתֵּן לַמּוֹט רַגְלָם, חַזֵּק יְדֵיהֶם וְאַמֵּץ רוּחָם לְהָפֵר עֲצַת אוֹיֵב
וּלְהַעֲבִיר מֶמְשֶׁלֶת זָדוֹן, יָפוּצוּ אוֹיְבֵיהֶם וְיָנוּסוּ מְשַׂנְאֵיהֶם
מִפְּנֵיהֶם, וְיִשְׂמְחוּ בִּישׁוּעָתֶךָ. הֲשִׁיבֵם בְּשָׁלוֹם אֶל בֵּיתָם, כַּכָּתוּב
בְּדִבְרֵי קָדְשֶׁךָ: יהוה יִשְׁמָרְךָ מִכָּל־רָע, יִשְׁמֹר אֶת־נַפְשֶׁךָ: יהוה תהלים קכא
יִשְׁמָר־צֵאתְךָ וּבוֹאֶךָ, מֵעַתָּה וְעַד־עוֹלָם: וְקַיֵּם בָּנוּ מִקְרָא שֶׁכָּתוּב:
לֹא־יִשָּׂא גוֹי אֶל־גּוֹי חֶרֶב, וְלֹא־יִלְמְדוּ עוֹד מִלְחָמָה: וְיֵדְעוּ כָּל ישעיה ב
יוֹשְׁבֵי תֵבֵל כִּי לְךָ מְלוּכָה יָאֲתָה, וְשִׁמְךָ נוֹרָא עַל כָּל מַה שֶּׁבָּרָאתָ.
וְנֹאמַר אָמֵן.

PRAYER FOR THE STATE OF ISRAEL

The Leader says the following prayer:

אָבִינוּ שֶׁבַּשָּׁמַיִם Heavenly Father, Israel's Rock and Redeemer, bless the State of Israel, the first flowering of our redemption. Shield it under the wings of Your loving-kindness and spread over it the Tabernacle of Your peace. Send Your light and truth to its leaders, ministers and counselors, and direct them with good counsel before You.

Strengthen the hands of the defenders of our Holy Land; grant them deliverance, our God, and crown them with the crown of victory. Grant peace in the land and everlasting joy to its inhabitants.

As for our brothers, the whole house of Israel, remember them in all the lands of our (*In Israel say:* their) dispersion, and swiftly lead us (*In Israel say:* them) upright to Zion Your city, and Jerusalem Your dwelling place, as is written in the Torah of Moses Your servant: "Even if you are scattered to the furthermost lands under the heavens, from there the LORD your God will gather you and take you back. The LORD your God will bring you to the land your ancestors possessed and you will possess it; and He will make you more prosperous and numerous than your ancestors. Then the LORD your God will open up your heart and the heart of your descendants, to love the LORD your God with all your heart and with all your soul, that you may live." *Deut. 30*

Unite our hearts to love and revere Your name and observe all the words of Your Torah, and swiftly send us Your righteous anointed one of the house of David, to redeem those who long for Your salvation.

Appear in Your glorious majesty over all the dwellers on earth, and let all who breathe declare: The LORD God of Israel is King and His kingship has dominion over all. Amen, Selah.

תפילה לשלום מדינת ישראל

The שליח ציבור *says the following prayer:*

אָבִינוּ שֶׁבַּשָּׁמַיִם, צוּר יִשְׂרָאֵל וְגוֹאֲלוֹ, בָּרֵךְ אֶת מְדִינַת יִשְׂרָאֵל, רֵאשִׁית צְמִיחַת גְּאֻלָּתֵנוּ. הָגֵן עָלֶיהָ בְּאֶבְרַת חַסְדֶּךָ וּפְרֹשׂ עָלֶיהָ סֻכַּת שְׁלוֹמֶךָ, וּשְׁלַח אוֹרְךָ וַאֲמִתְּךָ לְרָאשֶׁיהָ, שָׂרֶיהָ וְיוֹעֲצֶיהָ, וְתַקְּנֵם בְּעֵצָה טוֹבָה מִלְּפָנֶיךָ.

חַזֵּק אֶת יְדֵי מְגִנֵּי אֶרֶץ קָדְשֵׁנוּ, וְהַנְחִילֵם אֱלֹהֵינוּ יְשׁוּעָה וַעֲטֶרֶת נִצָּחוֹן תְּעַטְּרֵם, וְנָתַתָּ שָׁלוֹם בָּאָרֶץ וְשִׂמְחַת עוֹלָם לְיוֹשְׁבֶיהָ.

וְאֶת אַחֵינוּ כָּל בֵּית יִשְׂרָאֵל, פְּקָד נָא בְּכָל אַרְצוֹת פְּזוּרֵינוּ,
וְתוֹלִיכֵנוּ /בארץ ישראל: פְּזוּרֵיהֶם, וְתוֹלִיכֵם/ מְהֵרָה קוֹמְמִיּוּת לְצִיּוֹן
עִירֶךָ וְלִירוּשָׁלַיִם מִשְׁכַּן שְׁמֶךָ, כַּכָּתוּב בְּתוֹרַת מֹשֶׁה עַבְדֶּךָ:
אִם־יִהְיֶה נִדַּחֲךָ בִּקְצֵה הַשָּׁמָיִם, מִשָּׁם יְקַבֶּצְךָ יהוה אֱלֹהֶיךָ דברים ל
וּמִשָּׁם יִקָּחֶךָ: וֶהֱבִיאֲךָ יהוה אֱלֹהֶיךָ אֶל־הָאָרֶץ אֲשֶׁר־יָרְשׁוּ
אֲבֹתֶיךָ וִירִשְׁתָּהּ, וְהֵיטִבְךָ וְהִרְבְּךָ מֵאֲבֹתֶיךָ: וּמָל יהוה אֱלֹהֶיךָ
אֶת־לְבָבְךָ וְאֶת־לְבַב זַרְעֶךָ, לְאַהֲבָה אֶת־יהוה אֱלֹהֶיךָ בְּכָל־
לְבָבְךָ וּבְכָל־נַפְשְׁךָ, לְמַעַן חַיֶּיךָ:

וְיַחֵד לְבָבֵנוּ לְאַהֲבָה וּלְיִרְאָה אֶת שְׁמֶךָ, וְלִשְׁמֹר אֶת כָּל דִּבְרֵי תוֹרָתֶךָ, וּשְׁלַח לָנוּ מְהֵרָה בֶּן דָּוִד מְשִׁיחַ צִדְקֶךָ, לִפְדּוֹת מְחַכֵּי קֵץ יְשׁוּעָתֶךָ.

וְהוֹפַע בַּהֲדַר גְּאוֹן עֻזֶּךָ עַל כָּל יוֹשְׁבֵי תֵבֵל אַרְצֶךָ וְיֹאמַר כֹּל אֲשֶׁר נְשָׁמָה בְאַפּוֹ, יהוה אֱלֹהֵי יִשְׂרָאֵל מֶלֶךְ וּמַלְכוּתוֹ בַּכֹּל מָשָׁלָה, אָמֵן סֶלָה.

PRAYER FOR ISRAEL'S DEFENSE FORCES

The Leader says the following prayer:

מִי שֶׁבֵּרַךְ May He who blessed our ancestors, Abraham, Isaac and Jacob, bless the members of Israel's Defense Forces and its security services who stand guard over our land and the cities of our God from the Lebanese border to the Egyptian desert, from the Mediterranean sea to the approach of the Aravah, and wherever else they are, on land, in air and at sea. May the LORD make the enemies who rise against us be struck down before them. May the Holy One, blessed be He, protect and deliver them from all trouble and distress, affliction and illness, and send blessing and success to all the work of their hands. May He subdue our enemies under them and crown them with deliverance and victory. And may there be fulfilled in them the verse, "It is the LORD your God who goes with you to fight *Deut. 20*
for you against your enemies, to deliver you." And let us say: Amen.

PRAYER FOR THOSE BEING HELD IN CAPTIVITY

If Israeli soldiers or civilians are being held in captivity, the Leader says the following:

מִי שֶׁבֵּרַךְ May He who blessed our ancestors, Abraham, Isaac and Jacob, Joseph, Moses and Aaron, David and Solomon, bless, protect and guard the members of Israel's Defense Forces missing in action or held captive, and other captives among our brethren, the whole house of Israel, who are in distress or captivity, as we, the members of this holy congregation, pray on their behalf. May the Holy One, blessed be He, have compassion on them and bring them out from darkness and the shadow of death; may He break their bonds, deliver them from their distress, and bring them swiftly back to their families' embrace. Give thanks to the LORD for His loving-kindness *Ps. 107*
and for the wonders He does for the children of men; and may there be fulfilled in them the verse: "Those redeemed by the LORD will *Is. 35*
return; they will enter Zion with singing, and everlasting joy will crown their heads. Gladness and joy will overtake them, and sorrow and sighing will flee away." And let us say: Amen.

מי שברך לחיילי צה״ל

The שליח ציבור *says the following prayer:*

מִי שֶׁבֵּרַךְ אֲבוֹתֵינוּ אַבְרָהָם יִצְחָק וְיַעֲקֹב הוּא יְבָרֵךְ אֶת חַיָּלֵי
צְבָא הַהֲגָנָה לְיִשְׂרָאֵל וְאַנְשֵׁי כֹּחוֹת הַבִּטָּחוֹן, הָעוֹמְדִים עַל
מִשְׁמַר אַרְצֵנוּ וְעָרֵי אֱלֹהֵינוּ, מִגְּבוּל הַלְּבָנוֹן וְעַד מִדְבַּר מִצְרַיִם
וּמִן הַיָּם הַגָּדוֹל עַד לְבוֹא הָעֲרָבָה וּבְכָל מָקוֹם שֶׁהֵם, בַּיַּבָּשָׁה,
בָּאֲוִיר וּבַיָּם. יִתֵּן יהוה אֶת אוֹיְבֵינוּ הַקָּמִים עָלֵינוּ נִגָּפִים לִפְנֵיהֶם.
הַקָּדוֹשׁ בָּרוּךְ הוּא יִשְׁמֹר וְיַצִּיל אֶת חַיָּלֵינוּ מִכָּל צָרָה וְצוּקָה
וּמִכָּל נֶגַע וּמַחֲלָה, וְיִשְׁלַח בְּרָכָה וְהַצְלָחָה בְּכָל מַעֲשֵׂי יְדֵיהֶם.
יַדְבֵּר שׂוֹנְאֵינוּ תַּחְתֵּיהֶם וִיעַטְּרֵם בְּכֶתֶר יְשׁוּעָה וּבַעֲטֶרֶת נִצָּחוֹן.
וִיקֻיַּם בָּהֶם הַכָּתוּב: כִּי יהוה אֱלֹהֵיכֶם הַהֹלֵךְ עִמָּכֶם לְהִלָּחֵם דברים כ
לָכֶם עִם־אֹיְבֵיכֶם לְהוֹשִׁיעַ אֶתְכֶם: וְנֹאמַר אָמֵן.

מי שברך לשבויים

If Israeli soldiers or civilians are being held in captivity, the שליח ציבור *says the following:*

מִי שֶׁבֵּרַךְ אֲבוֹתֵינוּ אַבְרָהָם יִצְחָק וְיַעֲקֹב, יוֹסֵף מֹשֶׁה וְאַהֲרֹן,
דָּוִד וּשְׁלֹמֹה, הוּא יְבָרֵךְ וְיִשְׁמֹר וְיִנְצֹר אֶת נֶעְדְּרֵי צְבָא הַהֲגָנָה
לְיִשְׂרָאֵל וּשְׁבוּיָו, וְאֶת כָּל אַחֵינוּ הַנְּתוּנִים בְּצָרָה וּבְשִׁבְיָה,
בַּעֲבוּר שֶׁכָּל הַקָּהָל הַקָּדוֹשׁ הַזֶּה מִתְפַּלֵּל בַּעֲבוּרָם. הַקָּדוֹשׁ
בָּרוּךְ הוּא יִמָּלֵא רַחֲמִים עֲלֵיהֶם, וְיוֹצִיאֵם מֵחֹשֶׁךְ וְצַלְמָוֶת,
וּמוֹסְרוֹתֵיהֶם יְנַתֵּק, וּמִמְּצוּקוֹתֵיהֶם יוֹשִׁיעֵם, וִישִׁיבֵם מְהֵרָה
לְחֵיק מִשְׁפְּחוֹתֵיהֶם. יוֹדוּ לַיהוה חַסְדּוֹ וְנִפְלְאוֹתָיו לִבְנֵי אָדָם: תהלים קז
וִיקֻיַּם בָּהֶם מִקְרָא שֶׁכָּתוּב: וּפְדוּיֵי יהוה יְשֻׁבוּן, וּבָאוּ צִיּוֹן ישעיה לה
בְּרִנָּה, וְשִׂמְחַת עוֹלָם עַל־רֹאשָׁם, שָׂשׂוֹן וְשִׂמְחָה יַשִּׂיגוּ, וְנָסוּ
יָגוֹן וַאֲנָחָה: וְנֹאמַר אָמֵן.

The Leader says the first verse of Ashrei aloud and all continue:

אַשְׁרֵי Happy are those who dwell in Your House; Ps. 84
they shall continue to praise You, Selah!
Happy are the people for whom this is so; Ps. 144
happy are the people whose God is the LORD.
A song of praise by David. Ps. 145

I will exalt You, my God, the King, and bless Your name for ever and all time. Every day I will bless You, and praise Your name for ever and all time. Great is the LORD and greatly to be praised; His greatness is unfathomable. One generation will praise Your works to the next, and tell of Your mighty deeds. On the glorious splendor of Your majesty I will meditate, and on the acts of Your wonders. They shall talk of the power of Your awesome deeds, and I will tell of Your greatness. They shall recite the record of Your great goodness, and sing with joy of Your righteousness. The LORD is gracious and compassionate, slow to anger and great in loving-kindness. The LORD is good to all, and His compassion extends to all His works. All Your works shall thank You, LORD, and Your devoted ones shall bless You. They shall talk of the glory of Your kingship, and speak of Your might. To make known to mankind His mighty deeds and the glorious majesty of His kingship. Your kingdom is an everlasting kingdom, and Your reign is for all generations. The LORD supports all who fall, and raises all who are bowed down. All raise their eyes to You in hope, and You give them their food in due season. You open Your hand, and satisfy every living thing with favor. The LORD is righteous in all His ways, and kind in all He does. The LORD is close to all who call on Him, to all who call on Him in truth. He fulfills the will of those who revere Him; He hears their cry and saves them. The LORD guards all who love Him, but all the wicked He will destroy. ▸ My mouth shall speak the praise of the LORD, and all creatures shall bless His holy name for ever and all time.

We will bless the LORD now and for ever. Halleluya! Ps. 115

The שליח ציבור *says the first verse of* אשרי *aloud and all continue:*

תהלים פד אַשְׁרֵי יוֹשְׁבֵי בֵיתֶךָ, עוֹד יְהַלְלוּךָ סֶּלָה:
תהלים קמד אַשְׁרֵי הָעָם שֶׁכָּכָה לּוֹ, אַשְׁרֵי הָעָם שֶׁיהוה אֱלֹהָיו:
תהלים קמה תְּהִלָּה לְדָוִד

אֲרוֹמִמְךָ אֱלוֹהַי הַמֶּלֶךְ, וַאֲבָרְכָה שִׁמְךָ לְעוֹלָם וָעֶד:
בְּכָל־יוֹם אֲבָרְכֶךָּ, וַאֲהַלְלָה שִׁמְךָ לְעוֹלָם וָעֶד:
גָּדוֹל יהוה וּמְהֻלָּל מְאֹד, וְלִגְדֻלָּתוֹ אֵין חֵקֶר:
דּוֹר לְדוֹר יְשַׁבַּח מַעֲשֶׂיךָ, וּגְבוּרֹתֶיךָ יַגִּידוּ:
הֲדַר כְּבוֹד הוֹדֶךָ, וְדִבְרֵי נִפְלְאֹתֶיךָ אָשִׂיחָה:
וֶעֱזוּז נוֹרְאֹתֶיךָ יֹאמֵרוּ, וּגְדוּלָּתְךָ אֲסַפְּרֶנָּה:
זֵכֶר רַב־טוּבְךָ יַבִּיעוּ, וְצִדְקָתְךָ יְרַנֵּנוּ:
חַנּוּן וְרַחוּם יהוה, אֶרֶךְ אַפַּיִם וּגְדָל־חָסֶד:
טוֹב־יהוה לַכֹּל, וְרַחֲמָיו עַל־כָּל־מַעֲשָׂיו:
יוֹדוּךָ יהוה כָּל־מַעֲשֶׂיךָ, וַחֲסִידֶיךָ יְבָרְכוּכָה:
כְּבוֹד מַלְכוּתְךָ יֹאמֵרוּ, וּגְבוּרָתְךָ יְדַבֵּרוּ:
לְהוֹדִיעַ לִבְנֵי הָאָדָם גְּבוּרֹתָיו, וּכְבוֹד הֲדַר מַלְכוּתוֹ:
מַלְכוּתְךָ מַלְכוּת כָּל־עֹלָמִים, וּמֶמְשַׁלְתְּךָ בְּכָל־דּוֹר וָדֹר:
סוֹמֵךְ יהוה לְכָל־הַנֹּפְלִים, וְזוֹקֵף לְכָל־הַכְּפוּפִים:
עֵינֵי־כֹל אֵלֶיךָ יְשַׂבֵּרוּ, וְאַתָּה נוֹתֵן־לָהֶם אֶת־אָכְלָם בְּעִתּוֹ:
פּוֹתֵחַ אֶת־יָדֶךָ, וּמַשְׂבִּיעַ לְכָל־חַי רָצוֹן:
צַדִּיק יהוה בְּכָל־דְּרָכָיו, וְחָסִיד בְּכָל־מַעֲשָׂיו:
קָרוֹב יהוה לְכָל־קֹרְאָיו, לְכֹל אֲשֶׁר יִקְרָאֻהוּ בֶאֱמֶת:
רְצוֹן־יְרֵאָיו יַעֲשֶׂה, וְאֶת־שַׁוְעָתָם יִשְׁמַע, וְיוֹשִׁיעֵם:
שׁוֹמֵר יהוה אֶת־כָּל־אֹהֲבָיו, וְאֵת כָּל־הָרְשָׁעִים יַשְׁמִיד:
‹ תְּהִלַּת יהוה יְדַבֶּר פִּי, וִיבָרֵךְ כָּל־בָּשָׂר שֵׁם קָדְשׁוֹ לְעוֹלָם וָעֶד:
תהלים קטו וַאֲנַחְנוּ נְבָרֵךְ יָהּ מֵעַתָּה וְעַד־עוֹלָם, הַלְלוּיָהּ:

RETURNING THE TORAH TO THE ARK

The Ark is opened. All stand. The Leader takes one of the Torah scrolls and says:

יְהַלְלוּ Let them praise the name of the LORD, *Ps. 148*
for His name alone is sublime.

The congregation responds:

הוֹדוֹ His majesty is above earth and heaven.
He has raised the horn of His people,
for the glory of all His devoted ones,
the children of Israel, the people close to Him.
Halleluya!

While the Torah scrolls are being returned to the Ark, the following is said.

מִזְמוֹר לְדָוִד A psalm of David. *Ps. 29*
Render to the LORD, you angelic powers,
render to the LORD glory and might.
Render to the LORD the glory due to His name.
Bow down to the LORD in the splendor of holiness.
The LORD's voice echoes over the waters; the God of glory thunders;
the LORD is over the mighty waters.
The LORD's voice in power, the LORD's voice in beauty,
the LORD's voice breaks cedars,
the LORD shatters the cedars of Lebanon.
He makes Lebanon skip like a calf, Sirion like a young wild ox.
The LORD's voice cleaves flames of fire.
▸ The LORD's voice makes the desert quake,
the LORD shakes the desert of Kadesh.
The LORD's voice makes hinds calve and strips the forests bare,
and in His temple all say:
"Glory!" The LORD sat enthroned at the Flood,
the LORD sits enthroned as King for ever.
The LORD will give strength to His people;
the LORD will bless His people with peace.

הכנסת ספר תורה

The ארון קודש *is opened. All stand. The* שליח ציבור *takes one of the* ספרי תורה *and says:*

תהלים קמח

יְהַלְלוּ אֶת־שֵׁם יהוה, כִּי־נִשְׂגָּב שְׁמוֹ, לְבַדּוֹ

The קהל *responds:*

הוֹדוֹ עַל־אֶרֶץ וְשָׁמָיִם:
וַיָּרֶם קֶרֶן לְעַמּוֹ
תְּהִלָּה לְכָל־חֲסִידָיו
לִבְנֵי יִשְׂרָאֵל עַם קְרֹבוֹ
הַלְלוּיָהּ:

While the ספרי תורה *are being returned to the* ארון קודש*, the following is said.*

תהלים כט

מִזְמוֹר לְדָוִד, הָבוּ לַיהוה בְּנֵי אֵלִים, הָבוּ לַיהוה כָּבוֹד וָעֹז:
הָבוּ לַיהוה כְּבוֹד שְׁמוֹ, הִשְׁתַּחֲווּ לַיהוה בְּהַדְרַת־קֹדֶשׁ:
קוֹל יהוה עַל־הַמָּיִם, אֵל־הַכָּבוֹד הִרְעִים, יהוה עַל־מַיִם רַבִּים:
קוֹל־יהוה בַּכֹּחַ, קוֹל יהוה בֶּהָדָר:
קוֹל יהוה שֹׁבֵר אֲרָזִים, וַיְשַׁבֵּר יהוה אֶת־אַרְזֵי הַלְּבָנוֹן:
וַיַּרְקִידֵם כְּמוֹ־עֵגֶל, לְבָנוֹן וְשִׂרְיוֹן כְּמוֹ בֶן־רְאֵמִים:
קוֹל־יהוה חֹצֵב לַהֲבוֹת אֵשׁ:
קוֹל יהוה יָחִיל מִדְבָּר, יָחִיל יהוה מִדְבַּר קָדֵשׁ:
קוֹל יהוה יְחוֹלֵל אַיָּלוֹת וַיֶּחֱשֹׂף יְעָרוֹת
וּבְהֵיכָלוֹ, כֻּלּוֹ אֹמֵר כָּבוֹד:
יהוה לַמַּבּוּל יָשָׁב, וַיֵּשֶׁב יהוה מֶלֶךְ לְעוֹלָם:
יהוה עֹז לְעַמּוֹ יִתֵּן
יהוה יְבָרֵךְ אֶת־עַמּוֹ בַשָּׁלוֹם:

As the Torah scrolls are placed into the Ark, all say:

וּבְנֻחֹה יֹאמַר When the Ark came to rest, Moses would say: "Return, *Num. 10*
O LORD, to the myriad thousands of Israel." Advance, LORD, to Your *Ps. 132*
resting place, You and Your mighty Ark. Your priests are clothed in
righteousness, and Your devoted ones sing in joy. For the sake of
Your servant David, do not reject Your anointed one. For I give you *Prov. 4*
good instruction; do not forsake My Torah. It is a tree of life to those *Prov. 3*
who grasp it, and those who uphold it are happy. Its ways are ways of
pleasantness, and all its paths are peace. ▸ Turn us back, O LORD, to *Lam. 5*
You, and we will return. Renew our days as of old.

The Ark is closed.

HALF KADDISH

Reader: יִתְגַּדַּל Magnified and sanctified
may His great name be,
in the world He created by His will.
May He establish His kingdom
in your lifetime and in your days,
and in the lifetime of all the house of Israel,
swiftly and soon –
and say: Amen.

All: May His great name be blessed for ever and all time.

Reader: Blessed and praised,
glorified and exalted,
raised and honored,
uplifted and lauded
be the name of the Holy One, blessed be He,
beyond any blessing, song,
praise and consolation
uttered in the world –
and say: Amen.

As the ספרי תורה *are placed into the* ארון קודש, *all say:*

וּבְנֻחֹה יֹאמַר, שׁוּבָה יהוה רִבְבוֹת אַלְפֵי יִשְׂרָאֵל: קוּמָה יהוה במדבר י
לִמְנוּחָתֶךָ, אַתָּה וַאֲרוֹן עֻזֶּךָ: כֹּהֲנֶיךָ יִלְבְּשׁוּ־צֶדֶק, וַחֲסִידֶיךָ תהלים קלב
יְרַנֵּנוּ: בַּעֲבוּר דָּוִד עַבְדֶּךָ אַל־תָּשֵׁב פְּנֵי מְשִׁיחֶךָ: כִּי לֶקַח משלי ד
טוֹב נָתַתִּי לָכֶם, תּוֹרָתִי אַל־תַּעֲזֹבוּ: עֵץ־חַיִּים הִיא לַמַּחֲזִיקִים משלי ג
בָּהּ, וְתֹמְכֶיהָ מְאֻשָּׁר: דְּרָכֶיהָ דַרְכֵי־נֹעַם וְכָל־נְתִיבוֹתֶיהָ שָׁלוֹם:
‹ הֲשִׁיבֵנוּ יהוה אֵלֶיךָ וְנָשׁוּבָה, חַדֵּשׁ יָמֵינוּ כְּקֶדֶם: איכה ה

The ארון קודש *is closed.*

חצי קדיש

קורא: יִתְגַּדַּל וְיִתְקַדַּשׁ שְׁמֵהּ רַבָּא (קהל: אָמֵן)
בְּעָלְמָא דִּי בְרָא כִרְעוּתֵהּ
וְיַמְלִיךְ מַלְכוּתֵהּ
בְּחַיֵּיכוֹן וּבְיוֹמֵיכוֹן וּבְחַיֵּי דְכָל בֵּית יִשְׂרָאֵל
בַּעֲגָלָא וּבִזְמַן קָרִיב
וְאִמְרוּ אָמֵן. (קהל: אָמֵן)

קהל וקורא: יְהֵא שְׁמֵהּ רַבָּא מְבָרַךְ לְעָלַם וּלְעָלְמֵי עָלְמַיָּא.

קורא: יִתְבָּרַךְ וְיִשְׁתַּבַּח וְיִתְפָּאַר וְיִתְרוֹמַם וְיִתְנַשֵּׂא
וְיִתְהַדָּר וְיִתְעַלֶּה וְיִתְהַלָּל
שְׁמֵהּ דְּקֻדְשָׁא בְּרִיךְ הוּא (קהל: בְּרִיךְ הוּא)
לְעֵלָּא מִן כָּל בִּרְכָתָא וְשִׁירָתָא
תֻּשְׁבְּחָתָא וְנֶחֱמָתָא
דַּאֲמִירָן בְּעָלְמָא
וְאִמְרוּ אָמֵן. (קהל: אָמֵן)

Musaf for Shabbat Ḥol HaMo'ed

The following prayer, until "in former years" on page 914, is said silently, standing with feet together. If there is a minyan, the Amida is repeated aloud by the Leader. Take three steps forward and at the points indicated by ˅, bend the knees at the first word, bow at the second, and stand straight before saying God's name.

When I proclaim the LORD's name, give glory to our God. *Deut. 32*
O LORD, open my lips, so that my mouth may declare Your praise. *Ps. 51*

PATRIARCHS

˅בָּרוּךְ Blessed are You, LORD our God and God of our fathers,
God of Abraham, God of Isaac and God of Jacob;
the great, mighty and awesome God, God Most High,
who bestows acts of loving-kindness and creates all,
who remembers the loving-kindness of the fathers
and will bring a Redeemer to their children's children
for the sake of His name, in love.
King, Helper, Savior, Shield:
˅Blessed are You,
LORD, Shield of Abraham.

DIVINE MIGHT

אַתָּה גִּבּוֹר You are eternally mighty, LORD.
You give life to the dead and have great power to save.

In Israel:
He causes the dew to fall.

He sustains the living with loving-kindness,
and with great compassion revives the dead.
He supports the fallen, heals the sick, sets captives free,
and keeps His faith with those who sleep in the dust.
Who is like You, Master of might,
and who can compare to You,
O King who brings death and gives life,
and makes salvation grow?

מוסף לשבת חול המועד

The following prayer, until קַדְמֹנִיּוֹת *on page 915, is said silently, standing with feet together. If there is a* מנין*, the* עמידה *is repeated aloud by the* שליח ציבור*.*
Take three steps forward and at the points indicated by °*, bend the knees at the first word, bow at the second, and stand straight before saying God's name.*

דברים לב כִּי שֵׁם יהוה אֶקְרָא, הָבוּ גֹדֶל לֵאלֹהֵינוּ:
תהלים נא אֲדֹנָי, שְׂפָתַי תִּפְתָּח, וּפִי יַגִּיד תְּהִלָּתֶךָ:

אבות

°בָּרוּךְ אַתָּה יהוה, אֱלֹהֵינוּ וֵאלֹהֵי אֲבוֹתֵינוּ
אֱלֹהֵי אַבְרָהָם, אֱלֹהֵי יִצְחָק, וֵאלֹהֵי יַעֲקֹב
הָאֵל הַגָּדוֹל הַגִּבּוֹר וְהַנּוֹרָא, אֵל עֶלְיוֹן
גּוֹמֵל חֲסָדִים טוֹבִים, וְקוֹנֵה הַכֹּל
וְזוֹכֵר חַסְדֵי אָבוֹת
וּמֵבִיא גוֹאֵל לִבְנֵי בְנֵיהֶם לְמַעַן שְׁמוֹ בְּאַהֲבָה.
מֶלֶךְ עוֹזֵר וּמוֹשִׁיעַ וּמָגֵן.
°בָּרוּךְ אַתָּה יהוה, מָגֵן אַבְרָהָם.

גבורות

אַתָּה גִּבּוֹר לְעוֹלָם, אֲדֹנָי
מְחַיֵּה מֵתִים אַתָּה, רַב לְהוֹשִׁיעַ

In ארץ ישראל:
מוֹרִיד הַטָּל

מְכַלְכֵּל חַיִּים בְּחֶסֶד, מְחַיֵּה מֵתִים בְּרַחֲמִים רַבִּים
סוֹמֵךְ נוֹפְלִים, וְרוֹפֵא חוֹלִים, וּמַתִּיר אֲסוּרִים
וּמְקַיֵּם אֱמוּנָתוֹ לִישֵׁנֵי עָפָר.
מִי כָמוֹךָ, בַּעַל גְּבוּרוֹת, וּמִי דּוֹמֶה לָּךְ
מֶלֶךְ, מֵמִית וּמְחַיֶּה וּמַצְמִיחַ יְשׁוּעָה.

Faithful are You to revive the dead.
Blessed are You, LORD, who revives the dead.

When saying the Amida silently, continue with "You are holy" on the next page.

KEDUSHA

The following is said standing with feet together, rising on the toes at the words indicated by ▴.

Cong. then Leader: נַעֲרִיצְךָ We will revere and sanctify You with the words uttered by the holy Seraphim who sanctify Your name in the Sanctuary; as is written by Your prophet:
"They call out to one another, saying: *Is. 6*

Cong. then Leader: ▴Holy, ▴holy, ▴holy is the LORD of hosts;
the whole world is filled with His glory."
His glory fills the universe. His ministering angels ask each other,
"Where is the place of His glory?"
Those facing them say "Blessed –"

Cong. then Leader: "▴Blessed is the LORD's glory from His place." *Ezek. 3*
From His place may He turn with compassion
and be gracious to the people who proclaim the unity
of His name, morning and evening, every day, continually,
twice each day reciting in love the Shema:

Cong. then Leader: "Listen, Israel, the LORD is our God, the LORD is One." *Deut. 6*
He is our God, He is our Father, He is our King,
He is our Savior – and He, in His compassion,
will let us hear a second time in the presence of all that lives,
His promise to be "Your God." *Num. 15*
"I am the LORD your God."

Leader: And in Your holy Writings it is written:

Cong. then Leader: ▴"The LORD shall reign for ever. He is your God, Zion, *Ps. 146*
from generation to generation, Halleluya!"

Leader: From generation to generation we will declare Your greatness,
and we will proclaim Your holiness for evermore.
Your praise, our God, shall not leave our mouth forever,
for You, God, are a great and holy King.
Blessed are You, LORD, the holy God.

The Leader continues with "You have chosen us" on the next page.

וְנֶאֱמָן אַתָּה לְהַחֲיוֹת מֵתִים.
בָּרוּךְ אַתָּה יהוה, מְחַיֵּה הַמֵּתִים.

When saying the עמידה *silently, continue with* אַתָּה קָדוֹשׁ *on the next page.*

קדושה

The following is said standing with feet together, rising on the toes at the words indicated by ˄.

then קהל ש״ץ: נַעֲרִיצְךָ וְנַקְדִּישְׁךָ כְּסוֹד שִׂיחַ שַׂרְפֵי קֹדֶשׁ, הַמַּקְדִּישִׁים שִׁמְךָ
בַּקֹּדֶשׁ, כַּכָּתוּב עַל יַד נְבִיאֶךָ: וְקָרָא זֶה אֶל־זֶה וְאָמַר ישעיה ו

then קהל ש״ץ: ˄קָדוֹשׁ, ˄קָדוֹשׁ, ˄קָדוֹשׁ, יהוה צְבָאוֹת, מְלֹא כָל הָאָרֶץ כְּבוֹדוֹ:
כְּבוֹדוֹ מָלֵא עוֹלָם, מְשָׁרְתָיו שׁוֹאֲלִים זֶה לָזֶה, אַיֵּה מְקוֹם
כְּבוֹדוֹ, לְעֻמָּתָם בָּרוּךְ יֹאמֵרוּ

then קהל ש״ץ: ˄בָּרוּךְ כְּבוֹד־יהוה מִמְּקוֹמוֹ: יחזקאל ג
מִמְּקוֹמוֹ הוּא יִפֶן בְּרַחֲמִים, וְיָחֹן עַם הַמְיַחֲדִים שְׁמוֹ
עֶרֶב וָבֹקֶר בְּכָל יוֹם תָּמִיד, פַּעֲמַיִם בְּאַהֲבָה שְׁמַע אוֹמְרִים

then קהל ש״ץ: שְׁמַע יִשְׂרָאֵל, יהוה אֱלֹהֵינוּ, יהוה אֶחָד: דברים ו
הוּא אֱלֹהֵינוּ, הוּא אָבִינוּ, הוּא מַלְכֵּנוּ, הוּא מוֹשִׁיעֵנוּ
וְהוּא יַשְׁמִיעֵנוּ בְּרַחֲמָיו שֵׁנִית לְעֵינֵי כָּל חָי
לִהְיוֹת לָכֶם לֵאלֹהִים במדבר טו
אֲנִי יהוה אֱלֹהֵיכֶם:

ש״ץ: וּבְדִבְרֵי קָדְשְׁךָ כָּתוּב לֵאמֹר

then קהל ש״ץ: ˄יִמְלֹךְ יהוה לְעוֹלָם, אֱלֹהַיִךְ צִיּוֹן לְדֹר וָדֹר, הַלְלוּיָהּ: תהלים קמו

ש״ץ: לְדוֹר וָדוֹר נַגִּיד גָּדְלֶךָ, וּלְנֵצַח נְצָחִים קְדֻשָּׁתְךָ נַקְדִּישׁ
וְשִׁבְחֲךָ אֱלֹהֵינוּ מִפִּינוּ לֹא יָמוּשׁ לְעוֹלָם וָעֶד
כִּי אֵל מֶלֶךְ גָּדוֹל וְקָדוֹשׁ אָתָּה.
בָּרוּךְ אַתָּה יהוה, הָאֵל הַקָּדוֹשׁ.

The שליח ציבור *continues with* אַתָּה בְחַרְתָּנוּ *on the next page.*

HOLINESS

אַתָּה קָדוֹשׁ You are holy and Your name is holy,
and holy ones praise You daily, Selah!
Blessed are You, Lord, the holy God.

HOLINESS OF THE DAY

אַתָּה בְחַרְתָּנוּ You have chosen us from among all peoples.
You have loved and favored us.
You have raised us above all tongues.
You have made us holy through Your commandments.
You have brought us near, our King, to Your service,
and have called us by Your great and holy name.

וַתִּתֶּן לָנוּ And You, Lord our God, have given us in love
Sabbaths for rest and festivals for rejoicing,
holy days and seasons for joy,
this Sabbath day
and this day of the festival of Sukkot, our time of rejoicing
with love, a holy assembly
in memory of the exodus from Egypt.

וּמִפְּנֵי חֲטָאֵינוּ But because of our sins
we were exiled from our land
and driven far from our country.
We cannot go up to appear and bow before You,
and to perform our duties in Your chosen House,
the great and holy Temple that was called by Your name,
because of the hand that was stretched out
against Your Sanctuary.
May it be Your will, Lord our God and God of our ancestors,
merciful King,
that You in Your abounding compassion may once more
have mercy on us and on Your Sanctuary,
rebuilding it swiftly and adding to its glory.

קדושת השם

אַתָּה קָדוֹשׁ וְשִׁמְךָ קָדוֹשׁ וּקְדוֹשִׁים בְּכָל יוֹם יְהַלְלוּךָ סֶּלָה.
בָּרוּךְ אַתָּה יהוה, הָאֵל הַקָּדוֹשׁ.

קדושת היום

אַתָּה בְחַרְתָּנוּ מִכָּל הָעַמִּים
אָהַבְתָּ אוֹתָנוּ וְרָצִיתָ בָּנוּ
וְרוֹמַמְתָּנוּ מִכָּל הַלְּשׁוֹנוֹת
וְקִדַּשְׁתָּנוּ בְּמִצְוֹתֶיךָ
וְקֵרַבְתָּנוּ מַלְכֵּנוּ לַעֲבוֹדָתֶךָ
וְשִׁמְךָ הַגָּדוֹל וְהַקָּדוֹשׁ עָלֵינוּ קָרָאתָ.

וַתִּתֶּן לָנוּ יהוה אֱלֹהֵינוּ בְּאַהֲבָה
שַׁבָּתוֹת לִמְנוּחָה וּמוֹעֲדִים לְשִׂמְחָה
חַגִּים וּזְמַנִּים לְשָׂשׂוֹן
אֶת יוֹם הַשַּׁבָּת הַזֶּה וְאֶת יוֹם חַג הַסֻּכּוֹת הַזֶּה, זְמַן שִׂמְחָתֵנוּ
בְּאַהֲבָה מִקְרָא קֹדֶשׁ, זֵכֶר לִיצִיאַת מִצְרָיִם.

וּמִפְּנֵי חֲטָאֵינוּ גָּלִינוּ מֵאַרְצֵנוּ, וְנִתְרַחַקְנוּ מֵעַל אַדְמָתֵנוּ
וְאֵין אֲנַחְנוּ יְכוֹלִים לַעֲלוֹת וְלֵרָאוֹת וּלְהִשְׁתַּחֲווֹת לְפָנֶיךָ
וְלַעֲשׂוֹת חוֹבוֹתֵינוּ בְּבֵית בְּחִירָתֶךָ
בַּבַּיִת הַגָּדוֹל וְהַקָּדוֹשׁ שֶׁנִּקְרָא שִׁמְךָ עָלָיו
מִפְּנֵי הַיָּד שֶׁנִּשְׁתַּלְּחָה בְּמִקְדָּשֶׁךָ.
יְהִי רָצוֹן מִלְּפָנֶיךָ יהוה אֱלֹהֵינוּ וֵאלֹהֵי אֲבוֹתֵינוּ, מֶלֶךְ רַחֲמָן
שֶׁתָּשׁוּב וּתְרַחֵם עָלֵינוּ וְעַל מִקְדָּשְׁךָ בְּרַחֲמֶיךָ הָרַבִּים
וְתִבְנֵהוּ מְהֵרָה וּתְגַדֵּל כְּבוֹדוֹ.

Our Father, our King, reveal the glory of Your kingdom to us swiftly.
Appear and be exalted over us in the sight of all that lives.
Bring back our scattered ones from among the nations,
and gather our dispersed people from the ends of the earth.
Lead us to Zion, Your city, in jubilation,
and to Jerusalem, home of Your Temple, with everlasting joy.
There we will prepare for You our obligatory offerings:
the regular daily offerings in their order
and the additional offerings according to their law.
And the additional offerings of this Sabbath day
and of this day of the festival of Sukkot.
We will prepare and offer before You in love, in accord with
Your will's commandment, as You wrote for us in Your Torah
through Your servant Moses, by Your own word, as it is said:

וּבְיוֹם הַשַּׁבָּת On the Sabbath day, *Num. 28*
make an offering of two lambs a year old, without blemish,
together with two-tenths of an ephah of fine flour
mixed with oil as a meal-offering, and its appropriate libation.
This is the burnt-offering for every Sabbath,
in addition to the regular daily burnt-offering and its libation.

On the first day of Ḥol HaMo'ed Sukkot,
say the following two paragraphs (in Israel say only the second):

וּבַיּוֹם הַשֵּׁנִי On the second day you shall offer twelve young bullocks, two rams, fourteen yearling male lambs without blemish. And their meal-offerings and wine-libations as ordained: three-tenths of an ephah for each bull, two-tenths of an ephah for each ram, one-tenth of an ephah for each lamb, wine for the libations, a male goat for atonement, and two regular daily offerings according to their law. *Num. 29*

וּבַיּוֹם הַשְּׁלִישִׁי On the third day you shall offer eleven bullocks, two rams, fourteen yearling male lambs without blemish. And their meal-offerings and wine-libations as ordained: three-tenths of an ephah for each bull, two-tenths of an ephah for the ram, one-tenth of an ephah for each lamb, wine for the libations, a male goat for atonement, and two regular daily offerings according to their law. *Ibid.*

Continue with "Those who keep the Sabbath" on the next page.

אָבִינוּ מַלְכֵּנוּ, גַּלֵּה כְּבוֹד מַלְכוּתְךָ עָלֵינוּ מְהֵרָה
וְהוֹפַע וְהִנָּשֵׂא עָלֵינוּ לְעֵינֵי כָּל חָי
וְקָרֵב פְּזוּרֵינוּ מִבֵּין הַגּוֹיִם, וּנְפוּצוֹתֵינוּ כַּנֵּס מִיַּרְכְּתֵי אָרֶץ.
וַהֲבִיאֵנוּ לְצִיּוֹן עִירְךָ בְּרִנָּה
וְלִירוּשָׁלַיִם בֵּית מִקְדָּשְׁךָ בְּשִׂמְחַת עוֹלָם
וְשָׁם נַעֲשֶׂה לְפָנֶיךָ אֶת קָרְבְּנוֹת חוֹבוֹתֵינוּ
תְּמִידִים כְּסִדְרָם וּמוּסָפִים כְּהִלְכָתָם
וְאֶת מוּסְפֵי יוֹם הַשַּׁבָּת הַזֶּה וְיוֹם חַג הַסֻּכּוֹת הַזֶּה
נַעֲשֶׂה וְנַקְרִיב לְפָנֶיךָ בְּאַהֲבָה כְּמִצְוַת רְצוֹנֶךָ
כְּמוֹ שֶׁכָּתַבְתָּ עָלֵינוּ בְּתוֹרָתֶךָ
עַל יְדֵי מֹשֶׁה עַבְדֶּךָ מִפִּי כְבוֹדֶךָ, כָּאָמוּר

וּבְיוֹם הַשַּׁבָּת, שְׁנֵי־כְבָשִׂים בְּנֵי־שָׁנָה תְּמִימִם במדבר כח
וּשְׁנֵי עֶשְׂרֹנִים סֹלֶת מִנְחָה בְּלוּלָה בַשֶּׁמֶן וְנִסְכּוֹ:
עֹלַת שַׁבַּת בְּשַׁבַּתּוֹ, עַל־עֹלַת הַתָּמִיד וְנִסְכָּהּ:

On the first day of חול המועד*, say the following two paragraphs (in* ארץ ישראל *say only the second):*

וּבַיּוֹם הַשֵּׁנִי, פָּרִים בְּנֵי־בָקָר שְׁנֵים עָשָׂר, אֵילִם שְׁנָיִם, כְּבָשִׂים במדבר כט
בְּנֵי־שָׁנָה אַרְבָּעָה עָשָׂר, תְּמִימִם: וּמִנְחָתָם וְנִסְכֵּיהֶם
כִּמְדֻבָּר, שְׁלֹשָׁה עֶשְׂרֹנִים לַפָּר, וּשְׁנֵי עֶשְׂרֹנִים לָאָיִל, וְעִשָּׂרוֹן
לַכֶּבֶשׂ, וְיַיִן כְּנִסְכּוֹ, וְשָׂעִיר לְכַפֵּר, וּשְׁנֵי תְמִידִים כְּהִלְכָתָם.

וּבַיּוֹם הַשְּׁלִישִׁי, פָּרִים עַשְׁתֵּי־עָשָׂר, אֵילִם שְׁנָיִם, כְּבָשִׂים בְּנֵי־ שם
שָׁנָה אַרְבָּעָה עָשָׂר, תְּמִימִם: וּמִנְחָתָם וְנִסְכֵּיהֶם כִּמְדֻבָּר,
שְׁלֹשָׁה עֶשְׂרֹנִים לַפָּר, וּשְׁנֵי עֶשְׂרֹנִים לָאָיִל, וְעִשָּׂרוֹן לַכֶּבֶשׂ,
וְיַיִן כְּנִסְכּוֹ, וְשָׂעִיר לְכַפֵּר, וּשְׁנֵי תְמִידִים כְּהִלְכָתָם.

Continue with יִשְׂמְחוּ בְמַלְכוּתְךָ *on the next page.*

On the third day of Ḥol HaMo'ed Sukkot,
say the following two paragraphs (in Israel say only the second):

וּבַיּוֹם הָרְבִיעִי On the fourth day you shall offer ten bullocks, two rams, *Num. 29*
fourteen yearling male lambs without blemish. And their meal-offerings and wine-libations as ordained: three-tenths of an ephah for each bull, two-tenths of an ephah for each ram, one-tenth of an ephah for each lamb, wine for the libations, a male goat for atonement, and two regular daily offerings according to their law.

וּבַיּוֹם הַחֲמִישִׁי On the fifth day you shall offer nine bullocks, two rams, *Ibid.*
fourteen yearling male lambs without blemish. And their meal-offerings and wine-libations as ordained: three-tenths of an ephah for each bull, two-tenths of an ephah for each ram, one-tenth of an ephah for each lamb, wine for the libations, a male goat for atonement, and two regular daily offerings according to their law.

Continue with "Those who keep the Sabbath" below.

On the fourth day of Ḥol HaMo'ed Sukkot,
say the following two paragraphs (in Israel say only the second):

וּבַיּוֹם הַחֲמִישִׁי On the fifth day you shall offer nine bullocks, two rams, *Num. 29*
fourteen yearling male lambs without blemish. And their meal-offerings and wine-libations as ordained: three-tenths of an ephah for each bull, two-tenths of an ephah for each ram, one-tenth of an ephah for each lamb, wine for the libations, a male goat for atonement, and two regular daily offerings according to their law.

וּבַיּוֹם הַשִּׁשִּׁי On the sixth day you shall offer eight bullocks, two rams, *Ibid.*
fourteen yearling male lambs without blemish. And their meal-offerings and wine-libations as ordained: three-tenths of an ephah for each bull, two-tenths of an ephah for each ram, one-tenth of an ephah for each lamb, wine for the libations, a male goat for atonement, and two regular daily offerings according to their law.

יִשְׂמְחוּ Those who keep the Sabbath and call it a delight
shall rejoice in Your kingship.
The people who sanctify the seventh day
shall all be satisfied and take delight in Your goodness,
for You favored the seventh day and declared it holy.
You called it "most desirable of days" in remembrance of Creation.

On the third day of חול המועד סוכות*,*
say the following two paragraphs (in ארץ ישראל *say only the second):*

במדבר כט
וּבַיּוֹם הָרְבִיעִי, פָּרִים עֲשָׂרָה, אֵילִם שְׁנָיִם, כְּבָשִׂים בְּנֵי־שָׁנָה אַרְבָּעָה עָשָׂר, תְּמִימִם: וּמִנְחָתָם וְנִסְכֵּיהֶם כִּמְדֻבָּר, שְׁלֹשָׁה עֶשְׂרֹנִים לַפָּר, וּשְׁנֵי עֶשְׂרֹנִים לָאָיִל, וְעִשָּׂרוֹן לַכֶּבֶשׂ, וְיַיִן כְּנִסְכּוֹ, וְשָׂעִיר לְכַפֵּר, וּשְׁנֵי תְמִידִים כְּהִלְכָתָם.

שם
וּבַיּוֹם הַחֲמִישִׁי, פָּרִים תִּשְׁעָה, אֵילִם שְׁנָיִם, כְּבָשִׂים בְּנֵי־שָׁנָה אַרְבָּעָה עָשָׂר, תְּמִימִם: וּמִנְחָתָם וְנִסְכֵּיהֶם כִּמְדֻבָּר, שְׁלֹשָׁה עֶשְׂרֹנִים לַפָּר, וּשְׁנֵי עֶשְׂרֹנִים לָאָיִל, וְעִשָּׂרוֹן לַכֶּבֶשׂ, וְיַיִן כְּנִסְכּוֹ, וְשָׂעִיר לְכַפֵּר, וּשְׁנֵי תְמִידִים כְּהִלְכָתָם.

Continue with יִשְׂמְחוּ בְמַלְכוּתְךָ *below.*

On the fourth day of חול המועד סוכות*, say the following two paragraphs (in* ארץ ישראל *say only the second):*

במדבר כט
וּבַיּוֹם הַחֲמִישִׁי, פָּרִים תִּשְׁעָה, אֵילִם שְׁנָיִם, כְּבָשִׂים בְּנֵי־שָׁנָה אַרְבָּעָה עָשָׂר, תְּמִימִם: וּמִנְחָתָם וְנִסְכֵּיהֶם כִּמְדֻבָּר, שְׁלֹשָׁה עֶשְׂרֹנִים לַפָּר, וּשְׁנֵי עֶשְׂרֹנִים לָאָיִל, וְעִשָּׂרוֹן לַכֶּבֶשׂ, וְיַיִן כְּנִסְכּוֹ, וְשָׂעִיר לְכַפֵּר, וּשְׁנֵי תְמִידִים כְּהִלְכָתָם.

שם
וּבַיּוֹם הַשִּׁשִּׁי, פָּרִים שְׁמֹנָה, אֵילִם שְׁנָיִם, כְּבָשִׂים בְּנֵי־שָׁנָה אַרְבָּעָה עָשָׂר, תְּמִימִם: וּמִנְחָתָם וְנִסְכֵּיהֶם כִּמְדֻבָּר, שְׁלֹשָׁה עֶשְׂרֹנִים לַפָּר, וּשְׁנֵי עֶשְׂרֹנִים לָאָיִל, וְעִשָּׂרוֹן לַכֶּבֶשׂ, וְיַיִן כְּנִסְכּוֹ, וְשָׂעִיר לְכַפֵּר, וּשְׁנֵי תְמִידִים כְּהִלְכָתָם.

יִשְׂמְחוּ בְמַלְכוּתְךָ שׁוֹמְרֵי שַׁבָּת וְקוֹרְאֵי עֹנֶג.
עַם מְקַדְּשֵׁי שְׁבִיעִי כֻּלָּם יִשְׂבְּעוּ וְיִתְעַנְּגוּ מִטּוּבֶךָ
וּבַשְּׁבִיעִי רָצִיתָ בּוֹ וְקִדַּשְׁתּוֹ
חֶמְדַּת יָמִים אוֹתוֹ קָרָאתָ, זֵכֶר לְמַעֲשֵׂה בְרֵאשִׁית.

אֱלֹהֵינוּ Our God and God of our ancestors,
merciful King, have compassion upon us.
You who are good and do good, respond to our call.
Return to us in Your abounding mercy
for the sake of our fathers who did Your will.
Rebuild Your Temple as at the beginning,
and establish Your Sanctuary on its site.
Let us witness its rebuilding and gladden us by its restoration.
Bring the priests back to their service,
the Levites to their song and music,
and the Israelites to their homes.

וְשָׁם נַעֲלֶה There we will go up and appear and bow before You
on the three pilgrimage festivals, as is written in Your Torah:

"Three times in the year all your males shall appear *Deut. 16*
before the LORD your God
at the place He will choose:
on Pesaḥ, Shavuot and Sukkot.
They shall not appear before the LORD empty-handed.
Each shall bring such a gift as he can,
in proportion to the blessing
that the LORD your God grants you."

וְהַשִּׂיאֵנוּ Bestow on us, LORD our God, the blessing of Your festivals
for life and peace, joy and gladness,
as You desired and promised to bless us.
Our God and God of our fathers, find favor in our rest.
Make us holy through Your commandments
and grant us our share in Your Torah.
Satisfy us with Your goodness, grant us joy in Your salvation,
and purify our hearts to serve You in truth.
Grant us as our heritage, LORD our God, with love and favor,
with joy and gladness, Your holy Sabbath and festivals,
and may Israel, who sanctify Your name, rejoice in You.
Blessed are You, LORD,
who sanctifies the Sabbath and Israel and the festive seasons.

אֱלֹהֵינוּ וֵאלֹהֵי אֲבוֹתֵינוּ
מֶלֶךְ רַחֲמָן רַחֵם עָלֵינוּ, טוֹב וּמֵטִיב הִדָּרֶשׁ לָנוּ
שׁוּבָה אֵלֵינוּ בַּהֲמוֹן רַחֲמֶיךָ, בִּגְלַל אָבוֹת שֶׁעָשׂוּ רְצוֹנֶךָ.
בְּנֵה בֵיתְךָ כְּבַתְּחִלָּה, וְכוֹנֵן מִקְדָּשְׁךָ עַל מְכוֹנוֹ
וְהַרְאֵנוּ בְּבִנְיָנוֹ, וְשַׂמְּחֵנוּ בְּתִקּוּנוֹ
וְהָשֵׁב כֹּהֲנִים לַעֲבוֹדָתָם וּלְוִיִּם לְשִׁירָם וּלְזִמְרָם
וְהָשֵׁב יִשְׂרָאֵל לִנְוֵיהֶם.

וְשָׁם נַעֲלֶה וְנֵרָאֶה וְנִשְׁתַּחֲוֶה לְפָנֶיךָ בְּשָׁלֹשׁ פַּעֲמֵי רְגָלֵינוּ
כַּכָּתוּב בְּתוֹרָתֶךָ
שָׁלוֹשׁ פְּעָמִים בַּשָּׁנָה יֵרָאֶה כָל־זְכוּרְךָ אֶת־פְּנֵי יהוה אֱלֹהֶיךָ דברים טז
בַּמָּקוֹם אֲשֶׁר יִבְחָר
בְּחַג הַמַּצּוֹת, וּבְחַג הַשָּׁבֻעוֹת, וּבְחַג הַסֻּכּוֹת
וְלֹא יֵרָאֶה אֶת־פְּנֵי יהוה רֵיקָם:
אִישׁ כְּמַתְּנַת יָדוֹ, כְּבִרְכַּת יהוה אֱלֹהֶיךָ אֲשֶׁר נָתַן־לָךְ:

וְהַשִּׂיאֵנוּ יהוה אֱלֹהֵינוּ אֶת בִּרְכַּת מוֹעֲדֶיךָ
לְחַיִּים וּלְשָׁלוֹם, לְשִׂמְחָה וּלְשָׂשׂוֹן
כַּאֲשֶׁר רָצִיתָ וְאָמַרְתָּ לְבָרְכֵנוּ.
אֱלֹהֵינוּ וֵאלֹהֵי אֲבוֹתֵינוּ, רְצֵה בִמְנוּחָתֵנוּ
קַדְּשֵׁנוּ בְּמִצְוֹתֶיךָ וְתֵן חֶלְקֵנוּ בְּתוֹרָתֶךָ
שַׂבְּעֵנוּ מִטּוּבֶךָ וְשַׂמְּחֵנוּ בִּישׁוּעָתֶךָ
וְטַהֵר לִבֵּנוּ לְעָבְדְּךָ בֶּאֱמֶת
וְהַנְחִילֵנוּ, יהוה אֱלֹהֵינוּ, בְּאַהֲבָה וּבְרָצוֹן, בְּשִׂמְחָה וּבְשָׂשׂוֹן
שַׁבַּת וּמוֹעֲדֵי קָדְשֶׁךָ, וְיִשְׂמְחוּ בְךָ יִשְׂרָאֵל מְקַדְּשֵׁי שְׁמֶךָ.
בָּרוּךְ אַתָּה יהוה, מְקַדֵּשׁ הַשַּׁבָּת וְיִשְׂרָאֵל וְהַזְּמַנִּים.

TEMPLE SERVICE

רְצֵה Find favor, LORD our God, in Your people Israel
and their prayer.
Restore the service to Your most holy House,
and accept in love and favor the fire-offerings of Israel
and their prayer.
May the service of Your people Israel always find favor with You.
And may our eyes witness Your return to Zion in compassion.
Blessed are You, LORD, who restores His Presence to Zion.

THANKSGIVING

Bow at the first nine words.

מוֹדִים We give thanks to You,
for You are the LORD our God
and God of our ancestors
for ever and all time.
You are the Rock of our lives,
Shield of our salvation
from generation to generation.
We will thank You and
declare Your praise for our lives,
which are entrusted into Your hand;
for our souls,
which are placed in Your charge;
for Your miracles
which are with us every day;
and for Your wonders and favors
at all times, evening,
morning and midday.
You are good –
for Your compassion never fails.
You are compassionate –
for Your loving-kindnesses never cease.
We have always placed our hope in You.

During the Leader's Repetition, the congregation says quietly:

מוֹדִים We give thanks to You,
for You are the LORD our God
and God of our ancestors,
God of all flesh,
who formed us
and formed the universe.
Blessings and thanks
are due to Your great
and holy name for giving us
life and sustaining us.
May You continue
to give us life
and sustain us;
and may You gather our
exiles to Your holy courts,
to keep Your decrees,
do Your will and serve You
with a perfect heart,
for it is for us
to give You thanks.
Blessed be God to whom
thanksgiving is due.

עבודה

רְצֵה יהוה אֱלֹהֵינוּ בְּעַמְּךָ יִשְׂרָאֵל, וּבִתְפִלָּתָם
וְהָשֵׁב אֶת הָעֲבוֹדָה לִדְבִיר בֵּיתֶךָ
וְאִשֵּׁי יִשְׂרָאֵל וּתְפִלָּתָם בְּאַהֲבָה תְקַבֵּל בְּרָצוֹן
וּתְהִי לְרָצוֹן תָּמִיד עֲבוֹדַת יִשְׂרָאֵל עַמֶּךָ.
וְתֶחֱזֶינָה עֵינֵינוּ בְּשׁוּבְךָ לְצִיּוֹן בְּרַחֲמִים.
בָּרוּךְ אַתָּה יהוה, הַמַּחֲזִיר שְׁכִינָתוֹ לְצִיּוֹן.

הודאה

Bow at the first five words.

מוֹדִים אֲנַחְנוּ לָךְ
שָׁאַתָּה הוּא יהוה אֱלֹהֵינוּ
וֵאלֹהֵי אֲבוֹתֵינוּ לְעוֹלָם וָעֶד.
צוּר חַיֵּינוּ, מָגֵן יִשְׁעֵנוּ
אַתָּה הוּא לְדוֹר וָדוֹר.
נוֹדֶה לְּךָ וּנְסַפֵּר תְּהִלָּתֶךָ
עַל חַיֵּינוּ הַמְּסוּרִים בְּיָדֶךָ
וְעַל נִשְׁמוֹתֵינוּ הַפְּקוּדוֹת לָךְ
וְעַל נִסֶּיךָ שֶׁבְּכָל יוֹם עִמָּנוּ
וְעַל נִפְלְאוֹתֶיךָ וְטוֹבוֹתֶיךָ
שֶׁבְּכָל עֵת
עֶרֶב וָבֹקֶר וְצָהֳרָיִם.
הַטּוֹב, כִּי לֹא כָלוּ רַחֲמֶיךָ
וְהַמְרַחֵם, כִּי לֹא תַמּוּ חֲסָדֶיךָ
מֵעוֹלָם קִוִּינוּ לָךְ.

During the חזרת הש״ץ, *the* קהל *says quietly:*

מוֹדִים אֲנַחְנוּ לָךְ
שָׁאַתָּה הוּא יהוה אֱלֹהֵינוּ
וֵאלֹהֵי אֲבוֹתֵינוּ
אֱלֹהֵי כָל בָּשָׂר
יוֹצְרֵנוּ, יוֹצֵר בְּרֵאשִׁית.
בְּרָכוֹת וְהוֹדָאוֹת
לְשִׁמְךָ הַגָּדוֹל וְהַקָּדוֹשׁ
עַל שֶׁהֶחֱיִיתָנוּ וְקִיַּמְתָּנוּ.
כֵּן תְּחַיֵּנוּ וּתְקַיְּמֵנוּ
וְתֶאֱסֹף גָּלֻיּוֹתֵינוּ
לְחַצְרוֹת קָדְשֶׁךָ
לִשְׁמֹר חֻקֶּיךָ וְלַעֲשׂוֹת רְצוֹנֶךָ
וּלְעָבְדְּךָ בְּלֵבָב שָׁלֵם
עַל שֶׁאֲנַחְנוּ מוֹדִים לָךְ.
בָּרוּךְ אֵל הַהוֹדָאוֹת.

וְעַל כֻּלָּם For all these things may Your name be blessed and exalted,
our King, continually, for ever and all time.
Let all that lives thank You, Selah! and praise Your name in truth,
God, our Savior and Help, Selah!
▾Blessed are You, LORD, whose name is "the Good"
and to whom thanks are due.

The following is said by the Leader during the Repetition of the Amida. In Israel, if Kohanim bless the congregation, *turn to page 1396.*

Our God and God of our fathers, bless us with the threefold blessing in the Torah, written by the hand of Moses Your servant and pronounced by Aaron and his sons the priests, Your holy people, as it is said:

May the LORD bless you and protect you. Num. 6
Cong: May it be Your will.
May the LORD make His face shine on you and be gracious to you.
Cong: May it be Your will.
May the LORD turn His face toward you, and grant you peace.
Cong: May it be Your will.

PEACE

שִׂים שָׁלוֹם Grant peace, goodness and blessing,
grace, loving-kindness and compassion
to us and all Israel Your people.
Bless us, our Father, all as one,
with the light of Your face,
for by the light of Your face You have given us, LORD our God,
the Torah of life and love of kindness,
righteousness, blessing, compassion, life and peace.
May it be good in Your eyes to bless Your people Israel
at every time, in every hour, with Your peace.
Blessed are You, LORD, who blesses His people Israel with peace.

The following verse concludes the Leader's Repetition of the Amida. Some also say it here as part of the silent Amida.

יִהְיוּ לְרָצוֹן May the words of my mouth and the meditation of my heart Ps. 19
find favor before You, LORD, my Rock and Redeemer.

וְעַל כֻּלָּם יִתְבָּרַךְ וְיִתְרוֹמַם שִׁמְךָ מַלְכֵּנוּ תָּמִיד לְעוֹלָם וָעֶד.
וְכֹל הַחַיִּים יוֹדְוּךָ סֶּלָה, וִיהַלְלוּ אֶת שִׁמְךָ בֶּאֱמֶת
הָאֵל יְשׁוּעָתֵנוּ וְעֶזְרָתֵנוּ סֶלָה.
בָּרוּךְ אַתָּה יהוה, הַטּוֹב שִׁמְךָ וּלְךָ נָאֶה לְהוֹדוֹת.

The following is said by the שליח ציבור *during* חזרת הש״ץ.
In ארץ ישראל *if* כהנים *say* ברכת כהנים *turn to page 1397.*

אֱלֹהֵינוּ וֵאלֹהֵי אֲבוֹתֵינוּ, בָּרְכֵנוּ בַּבְּרָכָה הַמְשֻׁלֶּשֶׁת בַּתּוֹרָה, הַכְּתוּבָה עַל יְדֵי מֹשֶׁה עַבְדֶּךָ, הָאֲמוּרָה מִפִּי אַהֲרֹן וּבָנָיו כֹּהֲנִים עַם קְדוֹשֶׁיךָ, כָּאָמוּר

במדבר ו
יְבָרֶכְךָ יהוה וְיִשְׁמְרֶךָ: קהל: כֵּן יְהִי רָצוֹן
יָאֵר יהוה פָּנָיו אֵלֶיךָ וִיחֻנֶּךָּ: קהל: כֵּן יְהִי רָצוֹן
יִשָּׂא יהוה פָּנָיו אֵלֶיךָ וְיָשֵׂם לְךָ שָׁלוֹם: קהל: כֵּן יְהִי רָצוֹן

שלום

שִׂים שָׁלוֹם טוֹבָה וּבְרָכָה
חֵן וָחֶסֶד וְרַחֲמִים עָלֵינוּ וְעַל כָּל יִשְׂרָאֵל עַמֶּךָ.
בָּרְכֵנוּ אָבִינוּ כֻּלָּנוּ כְּאֶחָד בְּאוֹר פָּנֶיךָ
כִּי בְאוֹר פָּנֶיךָ נָתַתָּ לָּנוּ יהוה אֱלֹהֵינוּ
תּוֹרַת חַיִּים וְאַהֲבַת חֶסֶד
וּצְדָקָה וּבְרָכָה וְרַחֲמִים וְחַיִּים וְשָׁלוֹם.
וְטוֹב בְּעֵינֶיךָ לְבָרֵךְ אֶת עַמְּךָ יִשְׂרָאֵל
בְּכָל עֵת וּבְכָל שָׁעָה בִּשְׁלוֹמֶךָ.
בָּרוּךְ אַתָּה יהוה, הַמְבָרֵךְ אֶת עַמּוֹ יִשְׂרָאֵל בַּשָּׁלוֹם.

The following verse concludes the חזרת הש״ץ.
Some also say it here as part of the silent עמידה.

תהלים יט
יִהְיוּ לְרָצוֹן אִמְרֵי־פִי וְהֶגְיוֹן לִבִּי לְפָנֶיךָ, יהוה צוּרִי וְגֹאֲלִי:

אֱלֹהַי My God, *Berakhot 17a*
guard my tongue from evil and my lips from deceitful speech.
To those who curse me, let my soul be silent;
may my soul be to all like the dust.
Open my heart to Your Torah and let my soul
pursue Your commandments.
As for all who plan evil against me,
swiftly thwart their counsel and frustrate their plans.

Act for the sake of Your name;
act for the sake of Your right hand;
act for the sake of Your holiness;
act for the sake of Your Torah.

That Your beloved ones may be delivered, *Ps. 60*
save with Your right hand and answer me.
May the words of my mouth and the meditation of my heart *Ps. 19*
find favor before You, LORD, my Rock and Redeemer.

Bow, take three steps back, then bow, first left, then right, then center, while saying:

May He who makes peace in His high places,
make peace for us and all Israel –
and say: Amen.

יְהִי רָצוֹן May it be Your will, LORD our God and God of our ancestors,
that the Temple be rebuilt speedily in our days,
and grant us a share in Your Torah.
And there we will serve You with reverence,
as in the days of old and as in former years.
Then the offering of Judah and Jerusalem *Mal. 3*
will be pleasing to the LORD
as in the days of old and as in former years.

When praying with a minyan, the Amida is repeated aloud by the Leader.

אֱלֹהַי ברכות יז.
נְצֹר לְשׁוֹנִי מֵרָע וּשְׂפָתַי מִדַּבֵּר מִרְמָה
וְלִמְקַלְלַי נַפְשִׁי תִדֹּם, וְנַפְשִׁי כֶּעָפָר לַכֹּל תִּהְיֶה.
פְּתַח לִבִּי בְּתוֹרָתֶךָ, וּבְמִצְוֹתֶיךָ תִּרְדֹּף נַפְשִׁי.
וְכָל הַחוֹשְׁבִים עָלַי רָעָה
מְהֵרָה הָפֵר עֲצָתָם וְקַלְקֵל מַחֲשַׁבְתָּם.
עֲשֵׂה לְמַעַן שְׁמֶךָ
עֲשֵׂה לְמַעַן יְמִינֶךָ
עֲשֵׂה לְמַעַן קְדֻשָּׁתֶךָ
עֲשֵׂה לְמַעַן תּוֹרָתֶךָ.
לְמַעַן יֵחָלְצוּן יְדִידֶיךָ, הוֹשִׁיעָה יְמִינְךָ וַעֲנֵנִי: תהלים ס
יִהְיוּ לְרָצוֹן אִמְרֵי־פִי וְהֶגְיוֹן לִבִּי לְפָנֶיךָ, יהוה צוּרִי וְגֹאֲלִי: תהלים יט

Bow, take three steps back, then bow, first left, then right, then center, while saying:

עֹשֶׂה שָׁלוֹם בִּמְרוֹמָיו
הוּא יַעֲשֶׂה שָׁלוֹם עָלֵינוּ וְעַל כָּל יִשְׂרָאֵל
וְאִמְרוּ אָמֵן.

יְהִי רָצוֹן מִלְּפָנֶיךָ יהוה אֱלֹהֵינוּ וֵאלֹהֵי אֲבוֹתֵינוּ
שֶׁיִּבָּנֶה בֵּית הַמִּקְדָּשׁ בִּמְהֵרָה בְיָמֵינוּ
וְתֵן חֶלְקֵנוּ בְּתוֹרָתֶךָ
וְשָׁם נַעֲבָדְךָ בְּיִרְאָה כִּימֵי עוֹלָם וּכְשָׁנִים קַדְמֹנִיּוֹת.
וְעָרְבָה לַיהוה מִנְחַת יְהוּדָה וִירוּשָׁלָםִ כִּימֵי עוֹלָם וּכְשָׁנִים קַדְמֹנִיּוֹת: מלאכי ג

When praying with a מנין*, the* עמידה *is repeated aloud by the* שליח ציבור.

HOSHANOT FOR SHABBAT

The Ark is opened but no Torah scrolls are taken out.
The congregation does not walk around the Bima.

Leader then congregation:

הוֹשַׁע נָא Save us, please for Your sake, our God, save us please.

Leader then congregation:

Save us, please for Your sake, our Creator, save us, please.

Leader then congregation:

Save us, please for Your sake, our Redeemer, save us, please.

Leader then congregation:

Save us, please for Your sake, You who seek us, save us, please.

Save us, please –

אֹם נְצוּרָה כְּבָבַת A people guarded like the pupil of Your eye – who understand the Law that refreshes the spirit – who learn through all the laws of the Sabbath – who unfold the rules of carrying on the Sabbath – who fix two thousand cubits as our boundary for the Sabbath – and keep our feet from breaking the Sabbath – who remember early and keep hold of the Sabbath – and speed to hasten in the Sabbath – who for six days work hard for the Sabbath – who sit patiently on before ending the Sabbath – who call her an honor, delight, our Sabbath – who change their clothes, and dress for the Sabbath – who prepare themselves feast and drink for

---

bar Yoḥai and his son, hiding from the Romans, spent twelve years studying Torah together. When they emerged, they looked down on ordinary people who did not study Torah all day but were engaged in daily pursuits. As a result they were sentenced to a further year of exile. This time, when they emerged, they saw a man rushing home on the eve of Shabbat carrying two myrtle branches in honor of Shabbat. "See how precious are the commandments to Israel," said Rabbi Shimon to his son (*Shabbat* 33b).

כָּבוֹד וָעֹנֶג *Honor, delight.* The two positive duties in relation to Shabbat, based on a verse from Isaiah (58:13), "If you call the Sabbath a delight and the LORD's holy day honorable." Honoring means wearing special clothes; delight means preparing special meals.

הושענות לשבת

The ארון קודש *is opened but no* ספרי תורה *are taken out. The* קהל *does not walk around the* בימה.

קהל *then* שליח ציבור:

הוֹשַׁע נָא לְמַעַנְךָ אֱלֹהֵינוּ הוֹשַׁע נָא.

קהל *then* שליח ציבור:

הוֹשַׁע נָא לְמַעַנְךָ בּוֹרְאֵנוּ הוֹשַׁע נָא.

קהל *then* שליח ציבור:

הוֹשַׁע נָא לְמַעַנְךָ גּוֹאֲלֵנוּ הוֹשַׁע נָא.

קהל *then* שליח ציבור:

הוֹשַׁע נָא לְמַעַנְךָ דּוֹרְשֵׁנוּ הוֹשַׁע נָא.

הוֹשַׁע נָא

אֹם נְצוּרָה כְּבָבַת. בּוֹנֶנֶת בְּדָת נֶפֶשׁ מְשִׁיבַת. גּוֹמֶרֶת הִלְכוֹת שַׁבָּת. דּוֹרֶשֶׁת מַשְׂאַת שַׁבָּת. הַקּוֹבַעַת אַלְפַּיִם תְּחוּם שַׁבָּת. וּמְשִׁיבַת רֶגֶל מִשַּׁבָּת. זָכוֹר וְשָׁמוֹר מְקַיֶּמֶת בַּשַּׁבָּת. חָשָׁה לְמַהֵר בִּיאַת שַׁבָּת. טוֹרַחַת כָּל מִשְׁשָׁה לַשַּׁבָּת. יוֹשֶׁבֶת וּמְמַתֶּנֶת עַד כְּלוֹת שַׁבָּת. כָּבוֹד וָעֹנֶג קוֹרְאָה לַשַּׁבָּת. לְבוּשׁ וּכְסוּת מְחַלֶּפֶת בַּשַּׁבָּת. מַאֲכָל וּמִשְׁתֶּה מְכִינָה לַשַּׁבָּת.

אֹם נְצוּרָה *A people guarded.* The Four Kinds are not taken on Shabbat: this is one of several practices (including the blowing of the shofar on Rosh HaShana) not performed on Shabbat as a preventive decree against the possibility of carrying in a public domain. Accordingly, there is no *Hakafa* on Shabbat. Nonetheless the following *Hoshana* is recited. Its theme is Shabbat itself, the prohibition against carrying, and the care the Jewish people have taken to keep it and protect it.

אַלְפַּיִם *Two thousand.* This is the *teḥum*, the two thousand cubit limit of travel outside a town.

חָשָׁה לְמַהֵר *Speed to hasten.* The Talmud tells the story of how Rabbi Shimon

the Sabbath – laying a spread of sweet things on the Sabbath – holding three festive meals for the Sabbath – who break bread over two loaves on the Sabbath – distinguishing four domains on the Sabbath – who light the candles for the command, for the Sabbath – who sanctify the day on the Sabbath – who speak seven blessings [in the Amida] of the Sabbath – who read seven portions of Torah on the Sabbath – bring us into what is ours, the day that will be entirely Sabbath – Save us, please.

I and *HE*: save us, please.

כְּהוֹשַׁעְתָּ As You saved Adam, formed in Your hands, and protected him,
making the holy Sabbath his ransom, clemency – so, save us, please.

As You saved the people who remained distinct while longing for freedom –
in their thoughts already marking out the seventh day for rest –
so, save us, please.

As You saved the people You led and guided as Your flock,
and gave a Law at Mara, by the still waters – so, save us, please.

As You saved those who received Your gift in the Wilderness of Sin, the camp,
who were taught and collected two-fold bread on a Friday –
so, save us, please.

כְּהוֹשַׁעְתָּ אָדָם AS YOU SAVED ADAM
A poem composed by Rabbi Menachem ben Machir, a German scholar of the eleventh century who composed many liturgical poems. He lived through the massacre of Jewish communities in Germany during the First Crusade in 1096, and commemorated them in a series of *Seliḥot*. He inscribed his name as an acrostic at the end of the poem.

כְּהוֹשַׁעְתָּ אָדָם *As You saved Adam.* A reference to the tradition that the first humans, created on the sixth day, sinned by eating the forbidden fruit and were sent into exile from the Garden of Eden. However, God stayed execution of sentence by a day so that Adam and Eve were able to enjoy Shabbat in Eden.

דֵּעָה כִּוְּנוּ לָבוֹר *In their thoughts already marking out.* A midrashic tradition that Moses, while still a prince of Egypt, advised Pharaoh to let the people rest on the seventh day, to preserve their strength (*Shemot Raba* 1:28).

בְּמָרָה *At Mara.* It was there that the Shabbat was first given as a command to the Israelites (Ex. 15:25; Rashi ad loc.).

נֹעַם מְגָדִים מַנְעֶמֶת לַשַּׁבָּת. סְעוּדוֹת שָׁלֹשׁ מְקַיֶּמֶת בַּשַּׁבָּת. עַל שְׁתֵּי כִּכָּרוֹת בּוֹצַעַת בַּשַּׁבָּת. פּוֹרֶטֶת אַרְבַּע רְשֻׁיּוֹת שַׁבָּת. צִוּוּי הַדְלָקַת נֵר מַדְלֶקֶת בַּשַּׁבָּת. קִדּוּשׁ הַיּוֹם מְקַדֶּשֶׁת בַּשַּׁבָּת. רֶנֶן שֶׁבַע מְפַלֶּלֶת בַּשַּׁבָּת. שִׁבְעָה בַּדָּת קוֹרְאָה בַּשַּׁבָּת. תַּנְחִילֶנָּה לְיוֹם שֶׁכֻּלּוֹ שַׁבָּת. הוֹשַׁע נָא.

אֲנִי וָהוּ הוֹשִׁיעָה נָּא.

כְּהוֹשַׁעְתָּ אָדָם יְצִיר כַּפֶּיךָ לְגוֹנְנָה.
בְּשַׁבַּת קֹדֶשׁ הִמְצֵאתוֹ כֹּפֶר וַחֲנִינָה. כֵּן הוֹשַׁע נָא.

כְּהוֹשַׁעְתָּ גּוֹי מְצֻיָּן מְקַוִּים חֹפֶשׁ.
דֵּעָה כִּוְּנוּ לָבֹר שְׁבִיעִי לְנֹפֶשׁ. כֵּן הוֹשַׁע נָא.

כְּהוֹשַׁעְתָּ הָעָם נִהַגְתָּ כַּצֹּאן לְהַנְחוֹת.
וְחֹק שַׂמְתָּ בְּמָרָה עַל מֵי מְנוּחוֹת. כֵּן הוֹשַׁע נָא.

כְּהוֹשַׁעְתָּ זְבוּדֶיךָ בְּמִדְבַּר סִין בְּמַחֲנֶה.
חָכְמוּ וְלָקְטוּ בַּשִּׁשִּׁי לֶחֶם מִשְׁנֶה. כֵּן הוֹשַׁע נָא.

סְעוּדוֹת שָׁלֹשׁ *Three festive meals.* On weekdays it was customary to eat two meals. On Shabbat, in honor of the day, a third meal, *seuda shelishit*, was added.

שְׁתֵּי כִּכָּרוֹת *Two loaves.* In memory of the double portion of manna that fell on Friday so that the people would not have to gather manna on Shabbat.

אַרְבַּע רְשֻׁיּוֹת *Four domains.* Private, public, intermediary and exempt, the four categories of place in relation to the prohibition of carrying on Shabbat.

הַדְלָקַת נֵר *Light the candles.* The Shabbat candles.

שֶׁבַע מְפַלֶּלֶת *Speak seven blessings.* Each Amida on Shabbat consists of seven blessings.

תַּנְחִילֶנָּה *Bring us into what is ours.* Shabbat is a "foretaste of the world to come," a weekly dress rehearsal for the end of days, when there will be no more strife or hierarchies of power. Shabbat is a moment of paradise regained, and the end-of-history anticipated.

As You saved those who clung to You, who learned of their own mind to prepare for the Sabbath, / and [Moses] their shepherd blessed their strength and concurred – so, save us, please.

As You saved those who ate [manna] stored up on [their day of] delight, and it looked no different and its scent had not spoiled – so, save us, please.

As You saved those who learned every law of a journey on the Sabbath, who rested, stopped, and kept the boundaries of domain and encampment – so, save us, please.

As You saved those who could hear the fourth commandment at Sinai: both "Remember" and "Keep" to make the seventh day holy – so, save us, please.

As You saved those commanded to march seven times round Jericho, besieging her to strike until she fell on the Sabbath – so, save us, please.

As You saved Kohelet [Solomon] and his people in the eternal House, when they came to please You for seven days and seven – so, save us, please.

As You saved those who returned, rising up from Exile, redeemed, as they read Your Torah on this Festival, each day – so, save us, please.

As You saved those who rejoiced for You in the second House, renewed, in the Sanctuary where they took up the lulav all seven days – so, save us, please.

שִׁבְעָה וְשִׁבְעָה יָמִים *Seven days and seven.* The two weeks of celebration at the dedication of the Temple, the second of which coincided with Sukkot.

שָׁבִים *Those who returned.* A reference to the renewal of the covenant in the days of Ezra and Nehemiah. Ezra read the Torah to the people at a national assembly that began on Rosh HaShana. It was at this time that the people were reminded of the laws of Sukkot, which they performed with a devotion not seen since the days of Joshua (Neh. 8:12–18).

בְּבִנְיָן שֵׁנִי *The second House.* The second Temple, like the first, was consecrated on Sukkot (Ezra 3:4).

כְּהוֹשַׁעְתָּ טִפּוּלֶיךָ הוֹרוּ הַכָּנָה בְּמַדָּעָם.
יֹשֶׁר כֹּחָם, וְהוֹדָה לָמוֹ רוֹעָם. כֵּן הוֹשַׁע נָא.

כְּהוֹשַׁעְתָּ כִּלְכְּלוּ בְּעֹנֶג מָן הַמִּשְׁמָר.
לֹא הָפַךְ עֵינוֹ וְרֵיחוֹ לֹא נָמָר. כֵּן הוֹשַׁע נָא.

כְּהוֹשַׁעְתָּ מִשְׁפְּטֵי מַשְּׂאוֹת שַׁבָּת גָּמָרוּ.
נָחוּ וְשָׁבְתוּ, רְשֻׁיּוֹת וּתְחוּמִים שָׁמָרוּ. כֵּן הוֹשַׁע נָא.

כְּהוֹשַׁעְתָּ סִינַי הָשְׁמְעוּ בְּדִבּוּר רְבִיעִי.
עִנְיַן זָכוֹר וְשָׁמוֹר לְקַדֵּשׁ שְׁבִיעִי. כֵּן הוֹשַׁע נָא.

כְּהוֹשַׁעְתָּ פְּקִדוּ יְרִיחוֹ שֶׁבַע לְהַקֵּף.
צָרוּ עַד רְדְתָּהּ בַּשַּׁבָּת לְתַקֵּף. כֵּן הוֹשַׁע נָא.

כְּהוֹשַׁעְתָּ קֹהֶלֶת וְעַמּוֹ בְּבֵית עוֹלָמִים.
רִצּוּךָ בְּחָגְגָם שִׁבְעָה וְשִׁבְעָה יָמִים. כֵּן הוֹשַׁע נָא.

כְּהוֹשַׁעְתָּ שָׁבִים עוֹלֵי גוֹלָה לְפִדְיוֹם.
תּוֹרָתְךָ בְּקָרְאָם בֶּחָג יוֹם יוֹם. כֵּן הוֹשַׁע נָא.

כְּהוֹשַׁעְתָּ מְשַׂמְּחֶיךָ בְּבִנְיַן שֵׁנִי הַמְחֻדָּשׁ.
נוֹטְלִין לוּלָב כָּל שִׁבְעָה בַּמִּקְדָּשׁ. כֵּן הוֹשַׁע נָא.

זָכוֹר וְשָׁמוֹר *"Remember" and "keep".* The two different verbs introducing the command of Shabbat in the two versions of the Ten Commandments. According to tradition, they were said and heard simultaneously (*Shevuot* 20b).

יְרִיחוֹ *Jericho.* The city was circled by the Israelites once each day for six days and seven times on the seventh (Josh. 6:1–20), the model on which the processions in the Temple, and nowadays in the synagogue, were based.

קֹהֶלֶת *Kohelet.* King Solomon, called here by the name of his book, which we read during Sukkot.

As You saved those whose willow beating overrode the Sabbath,
who placed branches from Motza at the base of the Altar –
so, save us, please.

As You saved those who rejoiced with supple, long, high willows,
as they parted from the place calling "Praise to you, Altar!" –
so, save us, please.

As You saved those who gave thanks and who prayed and were true to their words, / all of them repeating "We are the LORD's and to Him our eyes are turned" – so, save us, please.

As You saved those circling [the Altar,] the wine-vat You carved out, with luscious willows, / as they sang out, "I and HE: save us, please" –
so, save us, please.

As You saved the eager legion [of priests], hastening to serve on the day of rest, / bringing a double Sabbath offering, burnt-offering and meal-offering – so, save us, please.

As You saved Your Levites, making them many on their platform,
singing "A psalm. A song for the Sabbath day" – so, save us, please.

As You saved those You comforted, always delighting in Your commands, and desired and delivered them, bringing them safe to respite and peace – so, save us, please.

As You saved the returning exiles of the tribes of Jacob,
so come back and return the exiles of the tents of Jacob –
and save us, please.

As You saved those who kept Your commandments and waited for salvation,
God of all salvation – save us, please.

I and HE: save us, please.

---

in a public domain. As the ceremony ended, they said, "Praise to you, Altar." According to R. Eliezer, they said, "We are the LORD's and to Him our eyes are turned" (Mishna *Sukka*, 4:5).

יְקֶב *The wine-vat.* A reference to the pit near the altar into which the wine libations flowed.

כְּהוֹשַׁעְתָּ חִבּוּט עֲרָבָה שַׁבָּת מַדְחִים.
מְרְבִיּוֹת מוֹצָא לִיסוֹד מִזְבֵּחַ מַנִּיחִים. כֵּן הוֹשַׁע נָא.

כְּהוֹשַׁעְתָּ בְּרַכּוֹת וַאֲרֻכּוֹת וּגְבוֹהוֹת מְעֻלָּסִים.
בִּפְטִירָתָן יֹפִי לְךָ מִזְבֵּחַ מְקֻלָּסִים. כֵּן הוֹשַׁע נָא.

כְּהוֹשַׁעְתָּ מוֹדִים וּמְיַחֲלִים וְלֹא מְשַׁנִּים.
כֻּלָּנוּ אָנוּ לְיָהּ וְעֵינֵינוּ לְיָהּ שׁוֹנִים. כֵּן הוֹשַׁע נָא.

כְּהוֹשַׁעְתָּ יֶקֶב מַחֲצָבֶיךָ סוֹבְבִים בִּרְנָנָה.
רוֹנְנִים אֲנִי וָהוּ הוֹשִׁיעָה נָּא. כֵּן הוֹשַׁע נָא.

כְּהוֹשַׁעְתָּ חֵיל זְרִיזִים מְשָׁרְתִים בִּמְנוּחָה.
קָרְבַּן שַׁבָּת כָּפוּל, עוֹלָה וּמִנְחָה. כֵּן הוֹשַׁע נָא.

כְּהוֹשַׁעְתָּ לְוִיֶּיךָ עַל דּוּכָנָם לְהַרְבַּת.
אוֹמְרִים מִזְמוֹר שִׁיר לְיוֹם הַשַּׁבָּת. כֵּן הוֹשַׁע נָא.

כְּהוֹשַׁעְתָּ נִחוּמֶיךָ בְּמִצְוֹתֶיךָ תָּמִיד יִשְׁתַּעַשְׁעוּן.
וּרְצֵם וְהַחֲלִיצֵם בְּשׁוּבָה וָנַחַת יִוָּשֵׁעוּן. כֵּן הוֹשַׁע נָא.

כְּהוֹשַׁעְתָּ שְׁבוּת שִׁבְטֵי יַעֲקֹב.
תָּשׁוּב וְתָשִׁיב שְׁבוּת אָהֳלֵי יַעֲקֹב. וְהוֹשִׁיעָה נָּא.

כְּהוֹשַׁעְתָּ שׁוֹמְרֵי מִצְוֹת וְחוֹכֵי יְשׁוּעוֹת.
אֵל לְמוֹשָׁעוֹת. וְהוֹשִׁיעָה נָּא.

אֲנִי וָהוּ הוֹשִׁיעָה נָּא.

חִבּוּט עֲרָבָה שַׁבָּת מַדְחִים *Whose willow beating overrode the Sabbath.* In Temple times, the willow, collected from Motza, a place near Jerusalem, was taken all seven days, culminating with an elaborate ceremony on Hoshana Raba. Because the ritual was performed by emissaries of the Beit Din, it was allowed to take place even on Shabbat, because there was no fear they would carry

הוֹשִׁיעָה Save Your people; bless Your legacy; tend them and carry them forever. Let these words with which I have pleaded with the LORD be close to the LORD our God day and night, that He may do justice for His servant, and justice for His people Israel, day after day; so that all the peoples of the earth will know that the LORD is God. There is no other. *Ps. 28* *1 Kings 8*

The Ark is closed.

FULL KADDISH

Some have the custom to include additional responses in Full Kaddish. They can be found in the version on page 1464.

Leader: יִתְגַּדַּל Magnified and sanctified may His great name be,
in the world He created by His will.
May He establish His kingdom
in your lifetime and in your days,
and in the lifetime of all the house of Israel,
swiftly and soon –
and say: Amen.

All: May His great name be blessed for ever and all time.

Leader: Blessed and praised, glorified and exalted,
raised and honored, uplifted and lauded
be the name of the Holy One, blessed be He,
beyond any blessing, song, praise and consolation
uttered in the world –
and say: Amen.

May the prayers and pleas of all Israel
be accepted by their Father in heaven –
and say: Amen.

May there be great peace from heaven,
and life for us and all Israel –
and say: Amen.

Bow, take three steps back, as if taking leave of the Divine Presence, then bow, first left, then right, then center, while saying:

May He who makes peace in His high places,
make peace for us and all Israel –
and say: Amen.

הוֹשִׁיעָה אֶת־עַמֶּךָ, וּבָרֵךְ אֶת־נַחֲלָתֶךָ, וּרְעֵם וְנַשְּׂאֵם עַד־הָעוֹלָם: וְיִהְיוּ תהלים כח
דְבָרַי אֵלֶּה, אֲשֶׁר הִתְחַנַּנְתִּי לִפְנֵי יהוה, קְרֹבִים אֶל־יהוה אֱלֹהֵינוּ יוֹמָם מלכים א׳ ח
וָלָיְלָה, לַעֲשׂוֹת מִשְׁפַּט עַבְדּוֹ וּמִשְׁפַּט עַמּוֹ יִשְׂרָאֵל, דְּבַר־יוֹם בְּיוֹמוֹ:
לְמַעַן דַּעַת כָּל־עַמֵּי הָאָרֶץ כִּי יהוה הוּא הָאֱלֹהִים, אֵין עוֹד:

The ארון קודש *is closed.*

קדיש שלם

Some have the custom to include additional responses in קדיש שלם.
They can be found in the version on page 1465.

ש״ץ: יִתְגַּדַּל וְיִתְקַדַּשׁ שְׁמֵהּ רַבָּא (קהל: אָמֵן)
בְּעָלְמָא דִּי בְרָא כִרְעוּתֵהּ
וְיַמְלִיךְ מַלְכוּתֵהּ
בְּחַיֵּיכוֹן וּבְיוֹמֵיכוֹן וּבְחַיֵּי דְכָל בֵּית יִשְׂרָאֵל
בַּעֲגָלָא וּבִזְמַן קָרִיב, וְאִמְרוּ אָמֵן. (קהל: אָמֵן)

קהל וש״ץ: יְהֵא שְׁמֵהּ רַבָּא מְבָרַךְ לְעָלַם וּלְעָלְמֵי עָלְמַיָּא.

ש״ץ: יִתְבָּרַךְ וְיִשְׁתַּבַּח וְיִתְפָּאַר
וְיִתְרוֹמַם וְיִתְנַשֵּׂא וְיִתְהַדָּר וְיִתְעַלֶּה וְיִתְהַלָּל
שְׁמֵהּ דְּקֻדְשָׁא בְּרִיךְ הוּא (קהל: בְּרִיךְ הוּא)
לְעֵלָּא מִן כָּל בִּרְכָתָא וְשִׁירָתָא, תֻּשְׁבְּחָתָא וְנֶחֱמָתָא
דַּאֲמִירָן בְּעָלְמָא, וְאִמְרוּ אָמֵן. (קהל: אָמֵן)

תִּתְקַבַּל צְלוֹתְהוֹן וּבָעוּתְהוֹן דְּכָל יִשְׂרָאֵל
קֳדָם אֲבוּהוֹן דִּי בִשְׁמַיָּא, וְאִמְרוּ אָמֵן. (קהל: אָמֵן)

יְהֵא שְׁלָמָא רַבָּא מִן שְׁמַיָּא
וְחַיִּים, עָלֵינוּ וְעַל כָּל יִשְׂרָאֵל, וְאִמְרוּ אָמֵן. (קהל: אָמֵן)

Bow, take three steps back, as if taking leave of the Divine Presence,
then bow, first left, then right, then center, while saying:

עֹשֶׂה שָׁלוֹם בִּמְרוֹמָיו
הוּא יַעֲשֶׂה שָׁלוֹם עָלֵינוּ וְעַל כָּל יִשְׂרָאֵל, וְאִמְרוּ אָמֵן. (קהל: אָמֵן)

אֵין כֵּאלֹהֵינוּ There is none like our God, none like our LORD,
none like our King, none like our Savior.
Who is like our God? Who is like our LORD?
Who is like our King? Who is like our Savior?
We will thank our God, we will thank our LORD,
we will thank our King, we will thank our Savior.
Blessed is our God, blessed is our LORD,
blessed is our King, blessed is our Savior.
You are our God, You are our LORD,
You are our King, You are our Savior.
You are He to whom our ancestors offered the fragrant incense.

פִּטּוּם הַקְּטֹרֶת The incense mixture consisted of balsam, onycha, galbanum and frankincense, each weighing seventy manehs; myrrh, cassia, spikenard and saffron, each weighing sixteen manehs; twelve manehs of costus, three of aromatic bark; nine of cinnamon; nine kabs of Carsina lye; three seahs and three kabs of Cyprus wine. If Cyprus wine was not available, old white wine might be used. A quarter of a kab of Sodom salt, and a minute amount of a smoke-raising herb. Rabbi Nathan says: Also a minute amount of Jordan amber. If one added honey to the mixture, he rendered it unfit for sacred use. If he omitted any one of its ingredients, he is guilty of a capital offense. *Keritot 6a*

Rabban Shimon ben Gamliel says: "Balsam" refers to the sap that drips from the balsam tree. The Carsina lye was used for bleaching the onycha to improve it. The Cyprus wine was used to soak the onycha in it to make it pungent. Though urine is suitable for this purpose, it is not brought into the Temple out of respect.

These were the psalms which the Levites used to recite in the Temple: *Mishna, Tamid 7*
On the first day of the week they used to say:
"The earth is the LORD's and all it contains, *Ps. 24*
the world and all who live in it."
On the second day they used to say:
"Great is the LORD and greatly to be praised *Ps. 48*
in the city of God, on His holy mountain."
On the third day they used to say:
"God stands in the divine assembly. *Ps. 82*
Among the judges He delivers judgment."
On the fourth day they used to say:
"God of retribution, LORD, God of retribution, appear." *Ps. 94*

אֵין כֵּאלֹהֵֽינוּ, אֵין כַּאדוֹנֵֽינוּ, אֵין כְּמַלְכֵּֽנוּ, אֵין כְּמוֹשִׁיעֵֽנוּ.
מִי כֵאלֹהֵֽינוּ, מִי כַאדוֹנֵֽינוּ, מִי כְמַלְכֵּֽנוּ, מִי כְמוֹשִׁיעֵֽנוּ.
נוֹדֶה לֵאלֹהֵֽינוּ, נוֹדֶה לַאדוֹנֵֽינוּ, נוֹדֶה לְמַלְכֵּֽנוּ, נוֹדֶה לְמוֹשִׁיעֵֽנוּ.
בָּרוּךְ אֱלֹהֵֽינוּ, בָּרוּךְ אֲדוֹנֵֽינוּ, בָּרוּךְ מַלְכֵּֽנוּ, בָּרוּךְ מוֹשִׁיעֵֽנוּ.
אַתָּה הוּא אֱלֹהֵֽינוּ, אַתָּה הוּא אֲדוֹנֵֽינוּ,
אַתָּה הוּא מַלְכֵּֽנוּ, אַתָּה הוּא מוֹשִׁיעֵֽנוּ.
אַתָּה הוּא שֶׁהִקְטִֽירוּ אֲבוֹתֵֽינוּ לְפָנֶֽיךָ אֶת קְטֹֽרֶת הַסַּמִּים.

פִּטּוּם הַקְּטֹֽרֶת. הַצֳּרִי, וְהַצִּפֹּֽרֶן, וְהַחֶלְבְּנָה, וְהַלְּבוֹנָה מִשְׁקַל שִׁבְעִים שִׁבְעִים מָנֶה, מֹר, וּקְצִיעָה, שִׁבֹּֽלֶת נֵרְדְּ, וְכַרְכֹּם מִשְׁקַל שִׁשָּׁה עָשָׂר שִׁשָּׁה עָשָׂר מָנֶה, הַקֹּשְׁטְ שְׁנֵים עָשָׂר, קִלּוּפָה שְׁלֹשָׁה, וְקִנָּמוֹן תִּשְׁעָה, בֹּרִית כַּרְשִׁינָה תִּשְׁעָה קַבִּין, יֵין קַפְרִיסִין סְאִין תְּלָת וְקַבִּין תְּלָתָא, וְאִם אֵין לוֹ יֵין קַפְרִיסִין, מֵבִיא חֲמַר חִוַּרְיָן עַתִּיק. מֶֽלַח סְדוֹמִית רֹֽבַע, מַעֲלֶה עָשָׁן כָּל שֶׁהוּא. רַבִּי נָתָן הַבַּבְלִי אוֹמֵר: אַף כִּפַּת הַיַּרְדֵּן כָּל שֶׁהוּא, וְאִם נָתַן בָּהּ דְּבַשׁ פְּסָלָהּ, וְאִם חִסַּר אַחַת מִכָּל סַמָּנֶֽיהָ, חַיָּב מִיתָה. כריתות ו.

רַבָּן שִׁמְעוֹן בֶּן גַּמְלִיאֵל אוֹמֵר: הַצֳּרִי אֵינוֹ אֶלָּא שְׂרָף הַנּוֹטֵף מֵעֲצֵי הַקְּטָף. בֹּרִית כַּרְשִׁינָה שֶׁשָּׁפִין בָּהּ אֶת הַצִּפֹּֽרֶן כְּדֵי שֶׁתְּהֵא נָאָה, יֵין קַפְרִיסִין שֶׁשּׁוֹרִין בּוֹ אֶת הַצִּפֹּֽרֶן כְּדֵי שֶׁתְּהֵא עַזָּה, וַהֲלֹא מֵי רַגְלַֽיִם יָפִין לָהּ, אֶלָּא שֶׁאֵין מַכְנִיסִין מֵי רַגְלַֽיִם בַּמִּקְדָּשׁ מִפְּנֵי הַכָּבוֹד.

הַשִּׁיר שֶׁהַלְוִיִּם הָיוּ אוֹמְרִים בְּבֵית הַמִּקְדָּשׁ: משנה תמיד ז

בַּיּוֹם הָרִאשׁוֹן הָיוּ אוֹמְרִים

לַיהוה הָאָֽרֶץ וּמְלוֹאָהּ, תֵּבֵל וְיֹֽשְׁבֵי בָהּ: תהלים כד

בַּשֵּׁנִי הָיוּ אוֹמְרִים

גָּדוֹל יהוה וּמְהֻלָּל מְאֹד, בְּעִיר אֱלֹהֵֽינוּ הַר־קָדְשׁוֹ: תהלים מח

בַּשְּׁלִישִׁי הָיוּ אוֹמְרִים

אֱלֹהִים נִצָּב בַּעֲדַת־אֵל, בְּקֶֽרֶב אֱלֹהִים יִשְׁפֹּט: תהלים פב

בָּרְבִיעִי הָיוּ אוֹמְרִים

אֵל־נְקָמוֹת יהוה, אֵל נְקָמוֹת הוֹפִֽיעַ: תהלים צד

On the fifth day they used to say:
"Sing for joy to God, our strength. Shout aloud to the God of Jacob." *Ps. 81*
On the sixth day they used to say:
"The LORD reigns: He is robed in majesty; *Ps. 93*
the LORD is robed, girded with strength;
the world is firmly established; it cannot be moved."
On the Sabbath they used to say:
"A psalm, a song for the Sabbath day" – *Ps. 92*
[meaning] a psalm and song for the time to come,
for the day which will be entirely Sabbath and rest for life everlasting.

It was taught in the Academy of Elijah: Whoever studies [Torah] laws every day *Megilla 28b*
is assured that he will be destined for the World to Come, as it is said, "The ways *Hab. 3*
of the world are His" – read not, "ways" [*halikhot*] but "laws" [*halakhot*].

Rabbi Elazar said in the name of Rabbi Ḥanina: The disciples of the sages *Berakhot 64a*
increase peace in the world, as it is said, "And all your children shall be taught *Is. 54*
of the LORD, and great shall be the peace of your children [*banayikh*]." Read
not *banayikh*, "your children," but *bonayikh*, "your builders." Those who love *Ps. 119*
Your Torah have great peace; there is no stumbling block for them. May there *Ps. 122*
be peace within your ramparts, prosperity in your palaces. For the sake of my
brothers and friends, I shall say, "Peace be within you." For the sake of the
House of the LORD our God, I will seek your good. ▸ May the LORD grant *Ps. 29*
strength to His people; may the LORD bless His people with peace.

THE RABBIS' KADDISH

The following prayer, said by mourners, requires the presence of a minyan.
A transliteration can be found on page 1466.

Mourner: יִתְגַּדַּל Magnified and sanctified may His great name be,
in the world He created by His will.
May He establish His kingdom in your lifetime
and in your days,
and in the lifetime of all the house of Israel,
swiftly and soon – and say: Amen.

All: May His great name be blessed for ever and all time.

Mourner: Blessed and praised, glorified and exalted,
raised and honored, uplifted and lauded
be the name of the Holy One,
blessed be He,

בַּחֲמִישִׁי הָיוּ אוֹמְרִים

הַרְנִינוּ לֵאלֹהִים עוּזֵּנוּ, הָרִיעוּ לֵאלֹהֵי יַעֲקֹב: תהלים פא

בַּשִּׁשִּׁי הָיוּ אוֹמְרִים

יהוה מָלָךְ גֵּאוּת לָבֵשׁ תהלים צג

לָבֵשׁ יהוה עֹז הִתְאַזָּר, אַף־תִּכּוֹן תֵּבֵל בַּל־תִּמּוֹט:

בַּשַּׁבָּת הָיוּ אוֹמְרִים

מִזְמוֹר שִׁיר לְיוֹם הַשַּׁבָּת: תהלים צב

מִזְמוֹר שִׁיר לֶעָתִיד לָבוֹא, לְיוֹם שֶׁכֻּלּוֹ שַׁבָּת וּמְנוּחָה לְחַיֵּי הָעוֹלָמִים.

תָּנָא דְבֵי אֵלִיָּהוּ: כָּל הַשּׁוֹנֶה הֲלָכוֹת בְּכָל יוֹם, מֻבְטָח לוֹ שֶׁהוּא בֶּן עוֹלָם מגילה כח:

הַבָּא, שֶׁנֶּאֱמַר, הֲלִיכוֹת עוֹלָם לוֹ: אַל תִּקְרֵי הֲלִיכוֹת אֶלָּא הֲלָכוֹת. חבקוק ג

אָמַר רַבִּי אֶלְעָזָר, אָמַר רַבִּי חֲנִינָא: תַּלְמִידֵי חֲכָמִים מַרְבִּים שָׁלוֹם בָּעוֹלָם, ברכות סד.

שֶׁנֶּאֱמַר, וְכָל־בָּנַיִךְ לִמּוּדֵי יהוה, וְרַב שְׁלוֹם בָּנָיִךְ: אַל תִּקְרֵי בָּנָיִךְ, אֶלָּא ישעיה נד

בּוֹנָיִךְ. שָׁלוֹם רָב לְאֹהֲבֵי תוֹרָתֶךָ, וְאֵין־לָמוֹ מִכְשׁוֹל: יְהִי־שָׁלוֹם בְּחֵילֵךְ, תהלים קיט תהלים קכב

שַׁלְוָה בְּאַרְמְנוֹתָיִךְ: לְמַעַן אַחַי וְרֵעָי אֲדַבְּרָה־נָּא שָׁלוֹם בָּךְ: לְמַעַן בֵּית־יהוה

אֱלֹהֵינוּ אֲבַקְשָׁה טוֹב לָךְ: ◂ יהוה עֹז לְעַמּוֹ יִתֵּן, יהוה יְבָרֵךְ אֶת־עַמּוֹ בַשָּׁלוֹם: תהלים כט

קדיש דרבנן

The following prayer, said by mourners, requires the presence of a מנין.
A transliteration can be found on page 1466.

אבל: **יִתְגַּדַּל וְיִתְקַדַּשׁ שְׁמֵהּ רַבָּא** (קהל: אָמֵן)

בְּעָלְמָא דִּי בְרָא כִרְעוּתֵהּ

וְיַמְלִיךְ מַלְכוּתֵהּ

בְּחַיֵּיכוֹן וּבְיוֹמֵיכוֹן וּבְחַיֵּי דְכָל בֵּית יִשְׂרָאֵל

בַּעֲגָלָא וּבִזְמַן קָרִיב, וְאִמְרוּ אָמֵן. (קהל: אָמֵן)

קהל ואבל: **יְהֵא שְׁמֵהּ רַבָּא מְבָרַךְ לְעָלַם וּלְעָלְמֵי עָלְמַיָּא.**

אבל: **יִתְבָּרַךְ וְיִשְׁתַּבַּח וְיִתְפָּאַר וְיִתְרוֹמַם וְיִתְנַשֵּׂא**

וְיִתְהַדָּר וְיִתְעַלֶּה וְיִתְהַלָּל

שְׁמֵהּ דְּקֻדְשָׁא בְּרִיךְ הוּא (קהל: בְּרִיךְ הוּא)

beyond any blessing,
song, praise and consolation
uttered in the world –
and say: Amen.

To Israel, to the teachers,
their disciples and their disciples' disciples,
and to all who engage
in the study of Torah,
in this (*in Israel add:* holy) place or elsewhere,
may there come to them and you great peace,
grace, kindness and compassion,
long life, ample sustenance
and deliverance, from their Father in Heaven –
and say: Amen.

May there be great peace from heaven,
and (good) life for us and all Israel –
and say: Amen.

Bow, take three steps back, as if taking leave of the Divine Presence, then bow, first left, then right, then center, while saying:

May He who makes peace in His high places,
in His compassion make peace
for us and all Israel –
and say: Amen.

Stand while saying Aleinu. Bow at ▾.

עָלֵינוּ It is our duty to praise the Master of all,
and ascribe greatness to the Author of creation,
who has not made us like the nations of the lands
nor placed us like the families of the earth;
who has not made our portion like theirs,
nor our destiny like all their multitudes.
(For they worship vanity and emptiness,
and pray to a god who cannot save.)

לְעֵלָּא מִן כָּל בִּרְכָתָא
וְשִׁירָתָא, תֻּשְׁבְּחָתָא וְנֶחֱמָתָא, דַּאֲמִירָן בְּעָלְמָא
וְאִמְרוּ אָמֵן. (קהל: אָמֵן)

עַל יִשְׂרָאֵל וְעַל רַבָּנָן
וְעַל תַּלְמִידֵיהוֹן וְעַל כָּל תַּלְמִידֵי תַלְמִידֵיהוֹן
וְעַל כָּל מָאן דְּעָסְקִין בְּאוֹרַיְתָא
דִּי בְּאַתְרָא (בארץ ישראל: קַדִּישָׁא) הָדֵין, וְדִי בְּכָל אֲתַר וַאֲתַר
יְהֵא לְהוֹן וּלְכוֹן שְׁלָמָא רַבָּא
חִנָּא וְחִסְדָּא, וְרַחֲמֵי, וְחַיֵּי אֲרִיכֵי, וּמְזוֹנֵי רְוִיחֵי
וּפֻרְקָנָא מִן קֳדָם אֲבוּהוֹן דִּי בִשְׁמַיָּא
וְאִמְרוּ אָמֵן. (קהל: אָמֵן)

יְהֵא שְׁלָמָא רַבָּא מִן שְׁמַיָּא
וְחַיִּים (טוֹבִים) עָלֵינוּ וְעַל כָּל יִשְׂרָאֵל
וְאִמְרוּ אָמֵן. (קהל: אָמֵן)

Bow, take three steps back, as if taking leave of the Divine Presence, then bow, first left, then right, then center, while saying:

עֹשֶׂה שָׁלוֹם בִּמְרוֹמָיו
הוּא יַעֲשֶׂה בְרַחֲמָיו שָׁלוֹם
עָלֵינוּ וְעַל כָּל יִשְׂרָאֵל
וְאִמְרוּ אָמֵן. (קהל: אָמֵן)

Stand while saying עָלֵינוּ*. Bow at* ▾.

עָלֵינוּ לְשַׁבֵּחַ לַאֲדוֹן הַכֹּל, לָתֵת גְּדֻלָּה לְיוֹצֵר בְּרֵאשִׁית
שֶׁלֹּא עָשָׂנוּ כְּגוֹיֵי הָאֲרָצוֹת, וְלֹא שָׂמָנוּ כְּמִשְׁפְּחוֹת הָאֲדָמָה
שֶׁלֹּא שָׂם חֶלְקֵנוּ כָּהֶם וְגוֹרָלֵנוּ כְּכָל הֲמוֹנָם.
(שֶׁהֵם מִשְׁתַּחֲוִים לְהֶבֶל וָרִיק וּמִתְפַּלְלִים אֶל אֵל לֹא יוֹשִׁיעַ.)

▾But we bow in worship
and thank the Supreme King of kings, the Holy One, blessed be He,
who extends the heavens and establishes the earth,
whose throne of glory is in the heavens above,
and whose power's Presence is in the highest of heights.
He is our God; there is no other.
Truly He is our King, there is none else,
as it is written in His Torah:
"You shall know and take to heart this day that the LORD is God, *Deut. 4*
in heaven above and on earth below. There is no other."

Therefore, we place our hope in You, LORD our God,
that we may soon see the glory of Your power,
when You will remove abominations from the earth,
and idols will be utterly destroyed,
when the world will be perfected
under the sovereignty of the Almighty,
when all humanity will call on Your name,
to turn all the earth's wicked toward You.
All the world's inhabitants will realize and know
that to You every knee must bow and every tongue swear loyalty.
Before You, LORD our God, they will kneel and bow down
and give honor to Your glorious name.
They will all accept the yoke of Your kingdom,
and You will reign over them soon and for ever.
For the kingdom is Yours,
and to all eternity You will reign in glory,
as it is written in Your Torah: "The LORD will reign for ever and ever." *Ex. 15*
▸ And it is said: "Then the LORD shall be King over all the earth; *Zech. 14*
on that day the LORD shall be One and His name One."

Some add:
Have no fear of sudden terror or of the ruin when it overtakes the wicked. *Prov. 3*
Devise your strategy, but it will be thwarted; propose your plan, *Is. 8*
but it will not stand, for God is with us.
When you grow old, I will still be the same. *Is. 46*
When your hair turns gray, I will still carry you.
I made you, I will bear you, I will carry you, and I will rescue you.

וַאֲנַחְנוּ כּוֹרְעִים וּמִשְׁתַּחֲוִים וּמוֹדִים
לִפְנֵי מֶלֶךְ מַלְכֵי הַמְּלָכִים, הַקָּדוֹשׁ בָּרוּךְ הוּא
שֶׁהוּא נוֹטֶה שָׁמַיִם וְיוֹסֵד אָרֶץ, וּמוֹשַׁב יְקָרוֹ בַּשָּׁמַיִם מִמַּעַל
וּשְׁכִינַת עֻזּוֹ בְּגָבְהֵי מְרוֹמִים.
הוּא אֱלֹהֵינוּ, אֵין עוֹד.
אֱמֶת מַלְכֵּנוּ, אֶפֶס זוּלָתוֹ, כַּכָּתוּב בְּתוֹרָתוֹ
וְיָדַעְתָּ הַיּוֹם וַהֲשֵׁבֹתָ אֶל־לְבָבֶךָ דברים ד
כִּי יהוה הוּא הָאֱלֹהִים בַּשָּׁמַיִם מִמַּעַל וְעַל־הָאָרֶץ מִתָּחַת
אֵין עוֹד:

עַל כֵּן נְקַוֶּה לְּךָ יהוה אֱלֹהֵינוּ, לִרְאוֹת מְהֵרָה בְּתִפְאֶרֶת עֻזֶּךָ
לְהַעֲבִיר גִּלּוּלִים מִן הָאָרֶץ, וְהָאֱלִילִים כָּרוֹת יִכָּרֵתוּן
לְתַקֵּן עוֹלָם בְּמַלְכוּת שַׁדַּי.
וְכָל בְּנֵי בָשָׂר יִקְרְאוּ בִשְׁמֶךָ לְהַפְנוֹת אֵלֶיךָ כָּל רִשְׁעֵי אָרֶץ.
יַכִּירוּ וְיֵדְעוּ כָּל יוֹשְׁבֵי תֵבֵל
כִּי לְךָ תִּכְרַע כָּל בֶּרֶךְ, תִּשָּׁבַע כָּל לָשׁוֹן.
לְפָנֶיךָ יהוה אֱלֹהֵינוּ יִכְרְעוּ וְיִפֹּלוּ, וְלִכְבוֹד שִׁמְךָ יְקָר יִתֵּנוּ
וִיקַבְּלוּ כֻלָּם אֶת עֹל מַלְכוּתֶךָ
וְתִמְלֹךְ עֲלֵיהֶם מְהֵרָה לְעוֹלָם וָעֶד.
כִּי הַמַּלְכוּת שֶׁלְּךָ הִיא וּלְעוֹלְמֵי עַד תִּמְלֹךְ בְּכָבוֹד
כַּכָּתוּב בְּתוֹרָתֶךָ, יהוה יִמְלֹךְ לְעֹלָם וָעֶד: שמות טו
וְנֶאֱמַר, וְהָיָה יהוה לְמֶלֶךְ עַל־כָּל־הָאָרֶץ זכריה יד
בַּיּוֹם הַהוּא יִהְיֶה יהוה אֶחָד וּשְׁמוֹ אֶחָד:

Some add:

אַל־תִּירָא מִפַּחַד פִּתְאֹם וּמִשֹּׁאַת רְשָׁעִים כִּי תָבֹא: משלי ג
עֻצוּ עֵצָה וְתֻפָר, דַּבְּרוּ דָבָר וְלֹא יָקוּם, כִּי עִמָּנוּ אֵל: ישעיה ח
וְעַד־זִקְנָה אֲנִי הוּא, וְעַד־שֵׂיבָה אֲנִי אֶסְבֹּל, אֲנִי עָשִׂיתִי וַאֲנִי אֶשָּׂא וַאֲנִי אֶסְבֹּל וַאֲמַלֵּט: ישעיה מו

MOURNER'S KADDISH

The following prayer, said by mourners, requires the presence of a minyan. A transliteration can be found on page 1467.

Mourner: יִתְגַּדַּל Magnified and sanctified may His great name be,
in the world He created by His will.
May He establish His kingdom
in your lifetime and in your days,
and in the lifetime of all the house of Israel,
swiftly and soon –
and say: Amen.

All: May His great name be blessed for ever and all time.

Mourner: Blessed and praised, glorified and exalted,
raised and honored, uplifted and lauded
be the name of the Holy One, blessed be He,
beyond any blessing, song, praise and consolation
uttered in the world –
and say: Amen.

May there be great peace from heaven,
and life for us and all Israel –
and say: Amen.

Bow, take three steps back, as if taking leave of the Divine Presence, then bow, first left, then right, then center, while saying:

May He who makes peace in His high places,
make peace for us and all Israel –
and say: Amen.

Many congregations say the Daily Psalm after the Song of Glory on the next page.

Today is the holy Sabbath,
on which the Levites used to say this psalm in the Temple:

מִזְמוֹר A psalm. A song for the Sabbath day. It is good to thank the LORD *Ps. 92*
and sing psalms to Your name, Most High – to tell of Your loving-kindness in the morning and Your faithfulness at night, to the music of the ten-stringed lyre and the melody of the harp. For You have made me rejoice by Your work, O LORD; I sing for joy at the deeds of Your hands.

קדיש יתום

The following prayer, said by mourners, requires the presence of a מנין.
A transliteration can be found on page 1467.

אבל: יִתְגַּדַּל וְיִתְקַדַּשׁ שְׁמֵהּ רַבָּא (קהל: אָמֵן)
בְּעָלְמָא דִּי בְרָא כִרְעוּתֵהּ
וְיַמְלִיךְ מַלְכוּתֵהּ
בְּחַיֵּיכוֹן וּבְיוֹמֵיכוֹן וּבְחַיֵּי דְכָל בֵּית יִשְׂרָאֵל
בַּעֲגָלָא וּבִזְמַן קָרִיב, וְאִמְרוּ אָמֵן. (קהל: אָמֵן)

קהל ואבל: יְהֵא שְׁמֵהּ רַבָּא מְבָרַךְ לְעָלַם וּלְעָלְמֵי עָלְמַיָּא.

אבל: יִתְבָּרַךְ וְיִשְׁתַּבַּח וְיִתְפָּאַר
וְיִתְרוֹמַם וְיִתְנַשֵּׂא וְיִתְהַדָּר וְיִתְעַלֶּה וְיִתְהַלָּל
שְׁמֵהּ דְּקֻדְשָׁא בְּרִיךְ הוּא (קהל: בְּרִיךְ הוּא)
לְעֵלָּא מִן כָּל בִּרְכָתָא וְשִׁירָתָא, תֻּשְׁבְּחָתָא וְנֶחֱמָתָא
דַּאֲמִירָן בְּעָלְמָא, וְאִמְרוּ אָמֵן. (קהל: אָמֵן)

יְהֵא שְׁלָמָא רַבָּא מִן שְׁמַיָּא
וְחַיִּים, עָלֵינוּ וְעַל כָּל יִשְׂרָאֵל, וְאִמְרוּ אָמֵן. (קהל: אָמֵן)

Bow, take three steps back, as if taking leave of the Divine Presence, then bow, first left, then right, then center, while saying:

עֹשֶׂה שָׁלוֹם בִּמְרוֹמָיו
הוּא יַעֲשֶׂה שָׁלוֹם עָלֵינוּ וְעַל כָּל יִשְׂרָאֵל, וְאִמְרוּ אָמֵן. (קהל: אָמֵן)

Many congregations say the שיר של יום *after* שיר הכבוד *on the next page.*

הַיּוֹם יוֹם שַׁבַּת קֹדֶשׁ, שֶׁבּוֹ הָיוּ הַלְוִיִּם אוֹמְרִים בְּבֵית הַמִּקְדָּשׁ:

מִזְמוֹר שִׁיר לְיוֹם הַשַּׁבָּת: טוֹב לְהֹדוֹת לַיהוה, וּלְזַמֵּר לְשִׁמְךָ עֶלְיוֹן: תהלים צב
לְהַגִּיד בַּבֹּקֶר חַסְדֶּךָ, וֶאֱמוּנָתְךָ בַּלֵּילוֹת: עֲלֵי־עָשׂוֹר וַעֲלֵי־נָבֶל,
עֲלֵי הִגָּיוֹן בְּכִנּוֹר: כִּי שִׂמַּחְתַּנִי יהוה בְּפָעֳלֶךָ, בְּמַעֲשֵׂי יָדֶיךָ אֲרַנֵּן:

How great are Your deeds, LORD, and how very deep Your thoughts. A boor cannot know, nor can a fool understand, that though the wicked spring up like grass and all evildoers flourish, it is only that they may be destroyed for ever. But You, LORD, are eternally exalted. For behold Your enemies, LORD, behold Your enemies will perish; all evildoers will be scattered. You have raised my pride like that of a wild ox; I am anointed with fresh oil. My eyes shall look in triumph on my adversaries; my ears shall hear the downfall of the wicked who rise against me. The righteous will flourish like a palm tree and grow tall like a cedar in Lebanon. Planted in the LORD's House, blossoming in our God's courtyards, ▸ they will still bear fruit in old age, and stay vigorous and fresh, proclaiming that the LORD is upright: He is my Rock, in whom there is no wrong.

Mourner's Kaddish (previous page)

לְדָוִד A psalm of David. The LORD is my light and my salvation – whom then shall I fear? The LORD is the stronghold of my life – of whom shall I be afraid? When evil men close in on me to devour my flesh, it is they, my enemies and foes, who stumble and fall. Should an army besiege me, my heart would not fear. Should war break out against me, still I would be confident. One thing I ask of the LORD, only this do I seek: to live in the House of the LORD all the days of my life, to gaze on the beauty of the LORD and worship in His Temple. For He will keep me safe in His pavilion on the day of trouble. He will hide me under the cover of His tent. He will set me high upon a rock. Now my head is high above my enemies who surround me. I will sacrifice in His tent with shouts of joy. I will sing and chant praises to the LORD. LORD, hear my voice when I call. Be gracious to me and answer me. On Your behalf my heart says, "Seek My face." Your face, LORD, will I seek. Do not hide Your face from me. Do not turn Your servant away in anger. You have been my help. Do not reject or forsake me, God, my Savior. Were my father and my mother to forsake me, the LORD would take me in. Teach me Your way, LORD, and lead me on a level path, because of my oppressors. Do not abandon me to the will of my foes, for false witnesses have risen against me, breathing violence. ▸ Were it not for my faith that I shall see the LORD's goodness in the land of the living. Hope in the LORD. Be strong and of good courage, and hope in the LORD! *Ps. 27*

Mourner's Kaddish (previous page)

מַה־גָּדְלוּ מַעֲשֶׂיךָ יהוה, מְאֹד עָמְקוּ מַחְשְׁבֹתֶיךָ: אִישׁ־בַּעַר לֹא יֵדָע, וּכְסִיל לֹא־יָבִין אֶת־זֹאת: בִּפְרֹחַ רְשָׁעִים כְּמוֹ־עֵשֶׂב, וַיָּצִיצוּ כָּל־פֹּעֲלֵי אָוֶן, לְהִשָּׁמְדָם עֲדֵי־עַד: וְאַתָּה מָרוֹם לְעֹלָם יהוה: כִּי הִנֵּה אֹיְבֶיךָ יהוה, כִּי־הִנֵּה אֹיְבֶיךָ יֹאבֵדוּ, יִתְפָּרְדוּ כָּל־פֹּעֲלֵי אָוֶן: וַתָּרֶם כִּרְאֵים קַרְנִי, בַּלֹּתִי בְּשֶׁמֶן רַעֲנָן: וַתַּבֵּט עֵינִי בְּשׁוּרָי, בַּקָּמִים עָלַי מְרֵעִים תִּשְׁמַעְנָה אָזְנָי: צַדִּיק כַּתָּמָר יִפְרָח, כְּאֶרֶז בַּלְּבָנוֹן יִשְׂגֶּה: שְׁתוּלִים בְּבֵית יהוה, בְּחַצְרוֹת אֱלֹהֵינוּ יַפְרִיחוּ: · עוֹד יְנוּבוּן בְּשֵׂיבָה, דְּשֵׁנִים וְרַעֲנַנִּים יִהְיוּ: לְהַגִּיד כִּי־יָשָׁר יהוה, צוּרִי, וְלֹא־עַוְלָתָה בּוֹ:

קדיש יתום (*previous page*)

לְדָוִד, יהוה אוֹרִי וְיִשְׁעִי, מִמִּי אִירָא, יהוה מָעוֹז־חַיַּי, מִמִּי אֶפְחָד: תהלים כז
בִּקְרֹב עָלַי מְרֵעִים לֶאֱכֹל אֶת־בְּשָׂרִי, צָרַי וְאֹיְבַי לִי, הֵמָּה כָשְׁלוּ וְנָפָלוּ: אִם־תַּחֲנֶה עָלַי מַחֲנֶה, לֹא־יִירָא לִבִּי, אִם־תָּקוּם עָלַי מִלְחָמָה, בְּזֹאת אֲנִי בוֹטֵחַ: אַחַת שָׁאַלְתִּי מֵאֵת־יהוה, אוֹתָהּ אֲבַקֵּשׁ, שִׁבְתִּי בְּבֵית־יהוה כָּל־יְמֵי חַיַּי, לַחֲזוֹת בְּנֹעַם־יהוה, וּלְבַקֵּר בְּהֵיכָלוֹ: כִּי יִצְפְּנֵנִי בְּסֻכֹּה בְּיוֹם רָעָה, יַסְתִּרֵנִי בְּסֵתֶר אָהֳלוֹ, בְּצוּר יְרוֹמְמֵנִי: וְעַתָּה יָרוּם רֹאשִׁי עַל אֹיְבַי סְבִיבוֹתַי, וְאֶזְבְּחָה בְאָהֳלוֹ זִבְחֵי תְרוּעָה, אָשִׁירָה וַאֲזַמְּרָה לַיהוה: שְׁמַע־יהוה קוֹלִי אֶקְרָא, וְחָנֵּנִי וַעֲנֵנִי: לְךָ אָמַר לִבִּי בַּקְּשׁוּ פָנָי, אֶת־פָּנֶיךָ יהוה אֲבַקֵּשׁ: אַל־תַּסְתֵּר פָּנֶיךָ מִמֶּנִּי, אַל תַּט־בְּאַף עַבְדֶּךָ, עֶזְרָתִי הָיִיתָ, אַל־תִּטְּשֵׁנִי וְאַל־תַּעַזְבֵנִי, אֱלֹהֵי יִשְׁעִי: כִּי־אָבִי וְאִמִּי עֲזָבוּנִי, וַיהוה יַאַסְפֵנִי: הוֹרֵנִי יהוה דַּרְכֶּךָ, וּנְחֵנִי בְּאֹרַח מִישׁוֹר, לְמַעַן שׁוֹרְרָי: אַל־תִּתְּנֵנִי בְּנֶפֶשׁ צָרָי, כִּי קָמוּ־בִי עֵדֵי־שֶׁקֶר, וִיפֵחַ חָמָס: · לוּלֵא הֶאֱמַנְתִּי לִרְאוֹת בְּטוּב־יהוה בְּאֶרֶץ חַיִּים: קַוֵּה אֶל־יהוה, חֲזַק וְיַאֲמֵץ לִבֶּךָ, וְקַוֵּה אֶל־יהוה:

קדיש יתום (*previous page*)

SONG OF GLORY

The Ark is opened and all stand.

Leader: I will sing sweet psalms and I will weave songs,
to You for whom my soul longs.

Cong: My soul yearns for the shelter of Your hand,
that all Your mystic secrets I might understand.

Leader: Whenever I speak of Your glory above,
my heart is yearning for Your love.

Cong: So Your glories I will proclaim,
and in songs of love give honor to Your name.

Leader: I will tell of Your glory though I have not seen You,
imagine and describe You, though I have not known You.

Cong: By the hand of Your prophets, through Your servants' mystery,
You gave a glimpse of Your wondrous majesty.

Leader: Recounting Your grandeur and Your glory,
of Your great deeds they told the story.

Cong: They depicted You, though not as You are,
but as You do: Your acts, Your power.

Leader: They represented You in many visions;
through them all You are One without divisions.

Cong: They saw You, now old, then young,
Your head with gray, with black hair hung.

Leader: Aged on the day of judgment, yet on the day of war,
a young warrior with mighty hands they saw.

Cong: Triumph like a helmet He wore on his head;
His right hand and holy arm to victory have led.

Leader: His curls are filled with dew drops of light,
His locks with fragments of the night.

Cong: He will glory in me, for He delights in me;
My diadem of beauty He shall be.

Leader: His head is like pure beaten gold;
Engraved on His brow, His sacred name behold.

Cong: For grace and glory, beauty and renown,
His people have adorned Him with a crown.

שיר הכבוד

The ארון קודש *is opened and all stand.*

ש״ץ: אַנְעִים זְמִירוֹת וְשִׁירִים אֶאֱרֹג, כִּי אֵלֶיךָ נַפְשִׁי תַעֲרֹג.
קהל: נַפְשִׁי חִמְּדָה בְּצֵל יָדֶךָ, לָדַעַת כָּל רָז סוֹדֶךָ.

ש״ץ: מִדֵּי דַבְּרִי בִּכְבוֹדֶךָ, הוֹמֶה לִבִּי אֶל דּוֹדֶיךָ.
קהל: עַל כֵּן אֲדַבֵּר בְּךָ נִכְבָּדוֹת, וְשִׁמְךָ אֲכַבֵּד בְּשִׁירֵי יְדִידוֹת.

ש״ץ: אֲסַפְּרָה כְבוֹדְךָ וְלֹא רְאִיתִיךָ, אֲדַמְּךָ אֲכַנְּךָ וְלֹא יְדַעְתִּיךָ.
קהל: בְּיַד נְבִיאֶיךָ בְּסוֹד עֲבָדֶיךָ, דִּמִּיתָ הֲדַר כְּבוֹד הוֹדֶךָ.

ש״ץ: גְּדֻלָּתְךָ וּגְבוּרָתֶךָ, כִּנּוּ לְתֹקֶף פְּעֻלָּתֶךָ.
קהל: דִּמּוּ אוֹתְךָ וְלֹא כְּפִי יֶשְׁךָ, וַיְשַׁוּוּךָ לְפִי מַעֲשֶׂיךָ.

ש״ץ: הִמְשִׁילוּךָ בְּרֹב חֶזְיוֹנוֹת, הִנְּךָ אֶחָד בְּכָל דִּמְיוֹנוֹת.
קהל: וַיֶּחֱזוּ בְךָ זִקְנָה וּבַחֲרוּת, וּשְׂעַר רֹאשְׁךָ בְּשֵׂיבָה וְשַׁחֲרוּת.

ש״ץ: זִקְנָה בְּיוֹם דִּין וּבַחֲרוּת בְּיוֹם קְרָב, כְּאִישׁ מִלְחָמוֹת יָדָיו לוֹ רָב.
קהל: חָבַשׁ כּוֹבַע יְשׁוּעָה בְּרֹאשׁוֹ, הוֹשִׁיעָה לּוֹ יְמִינוֹ וּזְרוֹעַ קָדְשׁוֹ.

ש״ץ: טַלְלֵי אוֹרוֹת רֹאשׁוֹ נִמְלָא, קְוֻצּוֹתָיו רְסִיסֵי לָיְלָה.
קהל: יִתְפָּאֵר בִּי כִּי חָפֵץ בִּי, וְהוּא יִהְיֶה לִּי לַעֲטֶרֶת צְבִי.

ש״ץ: כֶּתֶם טָהוֹר פָּז דְּמוּת רֹאשׁוֹ, וְחַק עַל מֵצַח כְּבוֹד שֵׁם קָדְשׁוֹ.
קהל: לְחֵן וּלְכָבוֹד צְבִי תִפְאָרָה, אֻמָּתוֹ לוֹ עִטְּרָה עֲטָרָה.

אַנְעִים זְמִירוֹת *Song of Glory.* Attributed to either Rabbi Yehuda HeḤasid (d. 1217) or his father Rabbi Shmuel, this hymn is structured as an alphabetical acrostic, with a (non-acrostic) four-line introduction and a three-line conclusion, followed by biblical verses. The poem, with great grace and depth, speaks about the limits of language in describing the experience of God. On the one hand, God – infinite, eternal, invisible – is beyond the reach of language. On the other, we can only address Him in and through language.

Leader: Like a youth's, His hair in locks unfurls;
Its black tresses flowing in curls.

Cong: Jerusalem, His splendor, is the dwelling place of right;
may He prize it as His highest delight.

Leader: Like a crown in His hand may His treasured people be,
a turban of beauty and of majesty.

Cong: He bore them, carried them, with a crown He adorned them.
They were precious in His sight, and He honored them.

Leader: His glory is on me; my glory is on Him.
He is near to me when I call to Him.

Cong: He is bright and rosy; red will be His dress,
when He comes from Edom, treading the winepress.

Leader: He showed the tefillin-knot to Moses, humble, wise,
when the LORD's likeness was before his eyes.

Cong: He delights in His people; the humble He does raise –
He glories in them; He sits enthroned upon their praise.

Leader: Your first word, Your call to every age, is true:
O seek the people who seek You.

Cong: My many songs please take and hear
and may my hymn of joy to You come near.

Leader: May my praise be a crown for Your head,
and like incense before You, the prayers I have said.

Cong: May a poor man's song be precious in Your eyes,
like a song sung over sacrifice.

Leader: To the One who sustains all, may my blessing take flight:
Creator, Life-Giver, God of right and might.

Cong: And when I offer blessing, to me Your head incline:
accepting it as spice, fragrant and fine.

Leader: May my prayer be to You sweet song.
For You my soul will always long.

The Ark is closed.

Yours, LORD, are the greatness and the power, the glory, the majesty and splendor, *1 Chr. 29*
for everything in heaven and earth is Yours. Yours, LORD, is the kingdom; You
are exalted as Head over all. ▸ Who can tell of the mighty acts of the LORD and *Ps. 106*
make all His praise be heard?

Mourner's Kaddish (page 934)

ש״ץ: מַחְלְפוֹת רֹאשׁוֹ כְּבִימֵי בְחוּרוֹת, קְוֻצּוֹתָיו תַּלְתַּלִּים שְׁחוֹרוֹת.
קהל: נְוֵה הַצֶּדֶק צְבִי תִפְאַרְתּוֹ, יַעֲלֶה נָּא עַל רֹאשׁ שִׂמְחָתוֹ.

ש״ץ: סְגֻלָּתוֹ תְּהִי בְיָדוֹ עֲטֶרֶת, וּצְנִיף מְלוּכָה צְבִי תִפְאֶרֶת.
קהל: עֲמוּסִים נְשָׂאָם, עֲטֶרֶת עִנְּדָם, מֵאֲשֶׁר יָקְרוּ בְעֵינָיו כִּבְּדָם.

ש״ץ: פְּאֵרוֹ עָלַי וּפְאֵרִי עָלָיו, וְקָרוֹב אֵלַי בְּקָרְאִי אֵלָיו.
קהל: צַח וְאָדֹם לִלְבוּשׁוֹ אָדֹם, פּוּרָה בְדָרְכוֹ בְּבוֹאוֹ מֵאֱדוֹם.

ש״ץ: קֶשֶׁר תְּפִלִּין הֶרְאָה לֶעָנָו, תְּמוּנַת יהוה לְנֶגֶד עֵינָיו.
קהל: רוֹצֶה בְעַמּוֹ עֲנָוִים יְפָאֵר, יוֹשֵׁב תְּהִלּוֹת בָּם לְהִתְפָּאֵר.

ש״ץ: רֹאשׁ דְּבָרְךָ אֱמֶת קוֹרֵא מֵרֹאשׁ דּוֹר וָדוֹר, עַם דּוֹרֶשְׁךָ דְּרֹשׁ.
קהל: שִׁית הֲמוֹן שִׁירַי נָא עָלֶיךָ, וְרִנָּתִי תִּקְרַב אֵלֶיךָ.

ש״ץ: תְּהִלָּתִי תְּהִי לְרֹאשְׁךָ עֲטֶרֶת, וּתְפִלָּתִי תִּכּוֹן קְטֹרֶת.
קהל: תִּיקַר שִׁירַת רָשׁ בְּעֵינֶיךָ, כַּשִּׁיר יוּשַׁר עַל קָרְבָּנֶיךָ.

ש״ץ: בִּרְכָתִי תַעֲלֶה לְרֹאשׁ מַשְׁבִּיר, מְחוֹלֵל וּמוֹלִיד, צַדִּיק כַּבִּיר.
קהל: וּבְבִרְכָתִי תְנַעֲנַע לִי רֹאשׁ, וְאוֹתָהּ קַח לְךָ כִּבְשָׂמִים רֹאשׁ.

ש״ץ: יֶעֱרַב נָא שִׂיחִי עָלֶיךָ, כִּי נַפְשִׁי תַעֲרֹג אֵלֶיךָ.

The ארון קודש *is closed.*

לְךָ יהוה הַגְּדֻלָּה וְהַגְּבוּרָה וְהַתִּפְאֶרֶת וְהַנֵּצַח וְהַהוֹד, כִּי־כֹל בַּשָּׁמַיִם דברי הימים א׳ כט
וּבָאָרֶץ, לְךָ יהוה הַמַּמְלָכָה וְהַמִּתְנַשֵּׂא לְכֹל לְרֹאשׁ: › מִי יְמַלֵּל גְּבוּרוֹת תהלים קו
יהוה, יַשְׁמִיעַ כָּל־תְּהִלָּתוֹ:

קדיש יתום (*page 935*)

Hence the various literary forms – metaphor, image, mystic vision – used by the prophets and poets and their successors to indicate, through words, that which lies beyond words. The images are many, but God is One.

In some communities the hymn is said each day. Many authorities, however, held that it was too sublime to be said daily, and limited its recital to Shabbat and Yom Tov.

LORD OF THE UNIVERSE,
who reigned before the birth of any thing –

When by His will all things were made
then was His name proclaimed King.

And when all things shall cease to be
He alone will reign in awe.

He was, He is, and He shall be
glorious for evermore.

He is One, there is none else,
alone, unique, beyond compare;

Without beginning, without end,
His might, His rule are everywhere.

He is my God; my Redeemer lives.
He is the Rock on whom I rely –

My banner and my safe retreat,
my cup, my portion when I cry.

Into His hand my soul I place,
when I awake and when I sleep.

The LORD is with me, I shall not fear;
body and soul from harm will He keep.

אֲדוֹן עוֹלָם

אֲשֶׁר מָלַךְ בְּטֶרֶם כָּל־יְצִיר נִבְרָא.
לְעֵת נַעֲשָׂה בְחֶפְצוֹ כֹּל אֲזַי מֶלֶךְ שְׁמוֹ נִקְרָא.
וְאַחֲרֵי כִּכְלוֹת הַכֹּל לְבַדּוֹ יִמְלֹךְ נוֹרָא.
וְהוּא הָיָה וְהוּא הֹוֶה וְהוּא יִהְיֶה בְּתִפְאָרָה.
וְהוּא אֶחָד וְאֵין שֵׁנִי לְהַמְשִׁיל לוֹ לְהַחְבִּירָה.
בְּלִי רֵאשִׁית בְּלִי תַכְלִית וְלוֹ הָעֹז וְהַמִּשְׂרָה.
וְהוּא אֵלִי וְחַי גּוֹאֲלִי וְצוּר חֶבְלִי בְּעֵת צָרָה.
וְהוּא נִסִּי וּמָנוֹס לִי מְנָת כּוֹסִי בְּיוֹם אֶקְרָא.
בְּיָדוֹ אַפְקִיד רוּחִי בְּעֵת אִישַׁן וְאָעִירָה.
וְעִם רוּחִי גְּוִיָּתִי יהוה לִי וְלֹא אִירָא.

Kiddush for Shabbat Morning

Some say:

אַתְקִינוּ Prepare the feast of perfect faith, joy of the holy King. Prepare the royal feast, this is the feast [mystically known as] "the Holy Ancient One" – and "the Small Face" and "the Field of Holy Apples" [mystical terms for aspects of the Divine] come to partake in the feast with it.

אֲסַדֵּר I will prepare the Sabbath morning feast, and invite to it "the Holy Ancient One." May His radiance shine on it, on the great Kiddush and goodly wine that gladdens the soul. May He send us His splendor; may we see His glory; may He reveal to us His whispered secrets. May He disclose to us the reason for the twelve loaves of bread, which are [the twelve combinations of the letters of] His name, and [the twelve sons of Jacob] the youngest patriarch. May we be united with the One above, who gives life to all; may our strength increase and [our prayers] reach [God's] head. Laborers in the field [of Torah] rejoice with speech and voice, speaking words sweet as honey. Before the Master of the Universe, reveal the meaning of, and give new interpretations to, matters veiled in mystery. To adorn the table with precious secrets, deep, esoteric, not widely to be shared. These words become sky; new heavens, and the sun then is the same. He will be lifted to a higher level, and [God] will take [Israel], from whom He had been separated, as His bride.

חַי יהוה The LORD lives; my Rock is blessed. My soul glories in the LORD. For the LORD gives light to my lamp; His radiance shines on my head. The LORD is my Shepherd, I shall not want. He leads me beside the still waters. He gives food to all flesh; He feeds me my daily bread. May it be Your will, You, my holy God, To prepare a table before me, to anoint my head with oil. Who will lay my rest before the LORD of peace, and grant that my children stay faithful, [blessed with] life and peace? May He send His angel before me, to accompany me on the way. I lift my face with a cup of salvation; my cup is filled to overflowing. My soul thirsts for God; may He fill my store with plenty. I lift my eyes to the sages, [celebrating Shabbat] like Hillel, not Shammai. Most delightful of days and eternity's years; awake, my soul, awake. Above my head let there shine as one, the lamp of the commandments and the Torah's light. Advance, LORD, to where I rest; You and Your mighty Ark. Please, God, take my blessing and strengthen the shield of Your seer.

מִזְמוֹר לְדָוִד A psalm of David. The LORD is my shepherd, I shall not want. He *Ps. 23*
makes me lie down in green pastures. He leads me beside the still waters. He refreshes my soul. He guides me in the paths of righteousness for His name's sake. Though I walk through the valley of the shadow of death, I will fear no evil, for You are with me; Your rod and Your staff, they comfort me. You set a table before me in the presence of my enemies; You anoint my head with oil; my cup is filled to overflowing. May goodness and kindness follow me all the days of my life, and may I live in the House of the LORD for evermore.

קידוש ליום שבת

Some say:

אַתְקִינוּ סְעוּדְתָא דִמְהֵימְנוּתָא שְׁלִימְתָא, חֶדְוְתָא דְמַלְכָּא קַדִּישָׁא. אַתְקִינוּ סְעוּדְתָא דְמַלְכָּא. דָּא הִיא סְעוּדְתָא דְעַתִּיקָא קַדִּישָׁא, וּזְעֵיר אַנְפִּין וַחֲקַל תַּפּוּחִין קַדִּישִׁין אָתַיִן לְסַעֲדָה בַּהֲדֵהּ.

אֲסַדֵּר לִסְעוּדְתָא בְּצַפְרָא דְשַׁבַּתָּא / וְאַזְמִין בַּהּ הַשְׁתָּא עַתִּיקָא קַדִּישָׁא.
נְהוֹרֵהּ יִשְׁרֵי בַהּ בְּקִדּוּשָׁא רַבָּה / וּמֵחַמְרָא טָבָא דְּבֵהּ תֶּחְדֵּי נַפְשָׁא.
יְשַׁדַּר לַן שְׁפְרֵהּ וְנֶחֱזֵי בִיקָרֵהּ / וְיַחֲוֵי לַן סִתְרֵהּ דְּמִתְאַמַר בִּלְחִישָׁה.
יְגַלֵּה לַן טַעֲמֵי דִּבִתְרֵיסַר נַהֲמֵי / דְּאִנּוּן אָת בִּשְׁמֵהּ כְּפִילָה וּקְלִישָׁא.
צְרוֹרָא דִלְעֵלָּא דְּבֵהּ חַיֵּי כֹלָּא / וְיִתְרַבֵּי חֵילָא וְתִסַּק עַד רֵישָׁא.
חֲדוּ חַצְדֵי חַקְלָא בְּדִבּוּר וּבְקָלָא / וּמַלְּלוּ מִלָּה מְתִיקָא כְּדֻבְשָׁא.
קֳדָם רִבּוֹן עָלְמִין בְּמִלִּין סְתִימִין / תְּגַלּוּן פִּתְגָּמִין וְתֵימְרוּן חִדּוּשָׁא.
לְעַטֵּר פָּתוֹרָא בְּרָזָא יַקִּירָא / עֲמִיקָא וּטְמִירָא וְלָאו מִלְּתָא אֱוְשָׁא.
וְאִלֵּין מִלַּיָּא יְהוֹן לִרְקִיעַיָּא / חֲדַתִּין וּשְׁמַיָּא בְּכֵן הַהוּא שִׁמְשָׁא.
רְבוּ יַתִּיר יִסְגֵּי לְעֵילָא מִן דַּרְגֵּהּ / וְיִסַּב בַּת זוּגֵהּ דַּהֲוַת פְּרִישָׁא.

חַי יהוה וּבָרוּךְ צוּרִי, בַּיהוה תִּתְהַלֵּל נַפְשִׁי, כִּי יהוה יָאִיר נֵרִי, בְּהִלּוֹ נֵרוֹ עֲלֵי רֹאשִׁי.
יהוה רוֹעִי לֹא אֶחְסָר, עַל מֵי מְנוּחוֹת יְנַהֲלֵנִי, נוֹתֵן לֶחֶם לְכָל בָּשָׂר, לֶחֶם חֻקִּי הַטְרִיפֵנִי.
יְהִי רָצוֹן מִלְּפָנֶיךָ, אַתָּה אֱלֹהֵי קְדוֹשִׁי, תַּעֲרֹךְ לְפָנַי שֻׁלְחָנֶךָ, תְּדַשֵּׁן בַּשֶּׁמֶן רֹאשִׁי.
מִי יִתֵּן מְנוּחָתִי, לִפְנֵי אֲדוֹן הַשָּׁלוֹם, וְהָיְתָה שְׁלֵמָה מִטָּתִי, הַחַיִּים וְהַשָּׁלוֹם.
יִשְׁלַח מַלְאָכוֹ לְפָנַי, לְלַוּוֹתִי לְוָיָה, בְּכוֹס יְשׁוּעוֹת אֶשָּׂא פָנַי, מְנָת כּוֹסִי רְוָיָה.
צָמְאָה נַפְשִׁי אֶל יהוה, יְמַלֵּא שֹׂבַע אֲסָמַי, אֶל הֶהָרִים אֶשָּׂא עֵינַי, כְּהִלֵּל וְלֹא כְשַׁמַּאי.
חֶדְוַת יָמִים וּשְׁנוֹת עוֹלָמִים, עוּרָה כְבוֹדִי עוּרָה, וְעַל רֹאשִׁי יִהְיוּ תַמִּים,
נֵר מִצְוָה וְאוֹר תּוֹרָה.
קוּמָה יהוה לִמְנוּחָתִי, אַתָּה וַאֲרוֹן עֻזֶּךָ, קַח נָא אֵל אֶת בִּרְכָתִי, וְהַחֲזֵק מָגֵן חוֹזֶךָ.

מִזְמוֹר לְדָוִד, יהוה רֹעִי לֹא אֶחְסָר: בִּנְאוֹת דֶּשֶׁא יַרְבִּיצֵנִי, עַל־מֵי מְנֻחוֹת תהלים כג
יְנַהֲלֵנִי: נַפְשִׁי יְשׁוֹבֵב, יַנְחֵנִי בְמַעְגְּלֵי־צֶדֶק לְמַעַן שְׁמוֹ: גַּם כִּי־אֵלֵךְ בְּגֵיא
צַלְמָוֶת לֹא־אִירָא רָע, כִּי־אַתָּה עִמָּדִי, שִׁבְטְךָ וּמִשְׁעַנְתֶּךָ הֵמָּה יְנַחֲמֻנִי:
תַּעֲרֹךְ לְפָנַי שֻׁלְחָן נֶגֶד צֹרְרָי, דִּשַּׁנְתָּ בַשֶּׁמֶן רֹאשִׁי, כּוֹסִי רְוָיָה: אַךְ טוֹב
וָחֶסֶד יִרְדְּפוּנִי כָּל־יְמֵי חַיָּי, וְשַׁבְתִּי בְּבֵית־יהוה לְאֹרֶךְ יָמִים:

SHABBAT MORNING KIDDUSH

Some say:

אִם־תָּשִׁיב If you keep your feet from breaking the Sabbath, and from pursuing your affairs on My holy day, if you call the Sabbath a delight, and the LORD's holy day honorable, and if you honor it by not going your own way or attending to your own affairs, or speaking idle words, then you will find joy in the LORD, and I will cause you to ride on the heights of the earth and to feast on the inheritance of your father Jacob, for the mouth of the LORD has spoken. *Is. 58*

Most begin Kiddush here.

וְשָׁמְרוּ The children of Israel must keep the Sabbath, *Ex. 31*
observing the Sabbath in every generation as an everlasting covenant.
It is a sign between Me and the children of Israel for ever,
for in six days the LORD made the heavens and the earth,
but on the seventh day He ceased work and refreshed Himself.

זָכוֹר Remember the Sabbath day to keep it holy. *Ex. 20*
Six days you shall labor and do all your work,
but the seventh day is a Sabbath of the LORD your God;
on it you shall not do any work – you, your son or daughter,
your male or female slave, or your cattle,
or the stranger within your gates.
For in six days the LORD made heaven and earth
and sea and all that is in them,
and rested on the seventh day;
therefore the LORD blessed the Sabbath day and declared it holy.

When saying Kiddush for others, add:
Please pay attention, my masters.

בָּרוּךְ Blessed are You, LORD our God, King of the Universe,
who creates the fruit of the vine.

If one is unable to sit in a sukka the following is not said.

בָּרוּךְ Blessed are You, LORD our God, King of the Universe,
who has made us holy through His commandments
and has commanded us to dwell in the sukka.

קידושא רבה

Some say:

אִם־תָּשִׁיב מִשַּׁבָּת רַגְלֶךָ עֲשׂוֹת חֲפָצֶךָ בְּיוֹם קָדְשִׁי, וְקָרָאתָ לַשַּׁבָּת ישעיה נח
עֹנֶג לִקְדוֹשׁ יהוה מְכֻבָּד, וְכִבַּדְתּוֹ מֵעֲשׂוֹת דְּרָכֶיךָ מִמְּצוֹא חֶפְצְךָ וְדַבֵּר
דָּבָר: אָז תִּתְעַנַּג עַל־יהוה, וְהִרְכַּבְתִּיךָ עַל־בָּמֳתֵי אָרֶץ, וְהַאֲכַלְתִּיךָ
נַחֲלַת יַעֲקֹב אָבִיךָ, כִּי פִּי יהוה דִּבֵּר:

Most begin קידוש *here.*

וְשָׁמְרוּ בְנֵי־יִשְׂרָאֵל אֶת־הַשַּׁבָּת שמות לא
לַעֲשׂוֹת אֶת־הַשַּׁבָּת לְדֹרֹתָם בְּרִית עוֹלָם:
בֵּינִי וּבֵין בְּנֵי יִשְׂרָאֵל אוֹת הִוא לְעֹלָם
כִּי־שֵׁשֶׁת יָמִים עָשָׂה יהוה אֶת־הַשָּׁמַיִם וְאֶת־הָאָרֶץ וּבַיּוֹם
הַשְּׁבִיעִי שָׁבַת וַיִּנָּפַשׁ:

זָכוֹר אֶת־יוֹם הַשַּׁבָּת לְקַדְּשׁוֹ: שמות כ
שֵׁשֶׁת יָמִים תַּעֲבֹד, וְעָשִׂיתָ כָּל־מְלַאכְתֶּךָ:
וְיוֹם הַשְּׁבִיעִי שַׁבָּת לַיהוה אֱלֹהֶיךָ
לֹא־תַעֲשֶׂה כָל־מְלָאכָה אַתָּה וּבִנְךָ וּבִתֶּךָ
עַבְדְּךָ וַאֲמָתְךָ וּבְהֶמְתֶּךָ, וְגֵרְךָ אֲשֶׁר בִּשְׁעָרֶיךָ:
כִּי שֵׁשֶׁת־יָמִים עָשָׂה יהוה אֶת־הַשָּׁמַיִם וְאֶת־הָאָרֶץ
אֶת־הַיָּם וְאֶת־כָּל־אֲשֶׁר־בָּם
וַיָּנַח בַּיּוֹם הַשְּׁבִיעִי, עַל־כֵּן בֵּרַךְ יהוה אֶת־יוֹם הַשַּׁבָּת וַיְקַדְּשֵׁהוּ:

When saying קידוש *for others, add:*

סַבְרִי מָרָנָן

בָּרוּךְ אַתָּה יהוה אֱלֹהֵינוּ מֶלֶךְ הָעוֹלָם בּוֹרֵא פְּרִי הַגָּפֶן.

If one is unable to sit in a סוכה *the following is not said.*

בָּרוּךְ אַתָּה יהוה אֱלֹהֵינוּ מֶלֶךְ הָעוֹלָם
אֲשֶׁר קִדְּשָׁנוּ בְּמִצְוֹתָיו וְצִוָּנוּ לֵישֵׁב בַּסֻּכָּה.

Minḥa for Shabbat

אַשְׁרֵי Happy are those who dwell in Your House; they shall continue to praise You, Selah! Ps. 84

Happy are the people for whom this is so; happy are the people whose God is the Lord. Ps. 144

A song of praise by David. Ps. 145

I will exalt You, my God, the King, and bless Your name for ever and all time. Every day I will bless You, and praise Your name for ever and all time. Great is the Lord and greatly to be praised; His greatness is unfathomable. One generation will praise Your works to the next, and tell of Your mighty deeds. On the glorious splendor of Your majesty I will meditate, and on the acts of Your wonders. They shall talk of the power of Your awesome deeds, and I will tell of Your greatness. They shall recite the record of Your great goodness, and sing with joy of Your righteousness. The Lord is gracious and compassionate, slow to anger and great in loving-kindness. The Lord is good to all, and His compassion extends to all His works. All Your works shall thank You, Lord, and Your devoted ones shall bless You. They shall talk of the glory of Your kingship, and speak of Your might. To make known to mankind His mighty deeds and the glorious majesty of His kingship. Your kingdom is an everlasting kingdom, and Your reign is for all generations. The Lord supports all who fall, and raises all who are bowed down. All raise their eyes to You in hope, and You give them their food in due season. You open Your hand, and satisfy every living thing with favor. The Lord is righteous in all His ways, and kind in all He does. The Lord is close to all who call on Him, to all who call on Him in truth. He fulfills the will of those who revere Him; He hears their cry and saves them. The Lord guards all who love Him, but all the wicked He will destroy. ▸ My mouth shall speak the praise of the Lord, and all creatures shall bless His holy name for ever and all time.

We will bless the Lord now and for ever. Halleluya! Ps. 115

מנחה לשבת

אַשְׁרֵי יוֹשְׁבֵי בֵיתֶךָ, עוֹד יְהַלְלְוּךָ סֶּלָה: תהלים פד
אַשְׁרֵי הָעָם שֶׁכָּכָה לּוֹ, אַשְׁרֵי הָעָם שֶׁיהוה אֱלֹהָיו: תהלים קמד
תְּהִלָּה לְדָוִד תהלים קמה

אֲרוֹמִמְךָ אֱלוֹהַי הַמֶּלֶךְ, וַאֲבָרְכָה שִׁמְךָ לְעוֹלָם וָעֶד:
בְּכָל־יוֹם אֲבָרְכֶךָּ, וַאֲהַלְלָה שִׁמְךָ לְעוֹלָם וָעֶד:
גָּדוֹל יהוה וּמְהֻלָּל מְאֹד, וְלִגְדֻלָּתוֹ אֵין חֵקֶר:
דּוֹר לְדוֹר יְשַׁבַּח מַעֲשֶׂיךָ, וּגְבוּרֹתֶיךָ יַגִּידוּ:
הֲדַר כְּבוֹד הוֹדֶךָ, וְדִבְרֵי נִפְלְאֹתֶיךָ אָשִׂיחָה:
וֶעֱזוּז נוֹרְאֹתֶיךָ יֹאמֵרוּ, וּגְדוּלָּתְךָ אֲסַפְּרֶנָּה:
זֵכֶר רַב־טוּבְךָ יַבִּיעוּ, וְצִדְקָתְךָ יְרַנֵּנוּ:
חַנּוּן וְרַחוּם יהוה, אֶרֶךְ אַפַּיִם וּגְדָל־חָסֶד:
טוֹב־יהוה לַכֹּל, וְרַחֲמָיו עַל־כָּל־מַעֲשָׂיו:
יוֹדְוּךָ יהוה כָּל־מַעֲשֶׂיךָ, וַחֲסִידֶיךָ יְבָרְכוּכָה:
כְּבוֹד מַלְכוּתְךָ יֹאמֵרוּ, וּגְבוּרָתְךָ יְדַבֵּרוּ:
לְהוֹדִיעַ לִבְנֵי הָאָדָם גְּבוּרֹתָיו, וּכְבוֹד הֲדַר מַלְכוּתוֹ:
מַלְכוּתְךָ מַלְכוּת כָּל־עֹלָמִים, וּמֶמְשַׁלְתְּךָ בְּכָל־דּוֹר וָדֹר:
סוֹמֵךְ יהוה לְכָל־הַנֹּפְלִים, וְזוֹקֵף לְכָל־הַכְּפוּפִים:
עֵינֵי־כֹל אֵלֶיךָ יְשַׂבֵּרוּ, וְאַתָּה נוֹתֵן־לָהֶם אֶת־אָכְלָם בְּעִתּוֹ:
פּוֹתֵחַ אֶת־יָדֶךָ, וּמַשְׂבִּיעַ לְכָל־חַי רָצוֹן:
צַדִּיק יהוה בְּכָל־דְּרָכָיו, וְחָסִיד בְּכָל־מַעֲשָׂיו:
קָרוֹב יהוה לְכָל־קֹרְאָיו, לְכֹל אֲשֶׁר יִקְרָאֻהוּ בֶאֱמֶת:
רְצוֹן־יְרֵאָיו יַעֲשֶׂה, וְאֶת־שַׁוְעָתָם יִשְׁמַע, וְיוֹשִׁיעֵם:
שׁוֹמֵר יהוה אֶת־כָּל־אֹהֲבָיו, וְאֵת כָּל־הָרְשָׁעִים יַשְׁמִיד:
◂ תְּהִלַּת יהוה יְדַבֶּר פִּי, וִיבָרֵךְ כָּל־בָּשָׂר שֵׁם קָדְשׁוֹ לְעוֹלָם וָעֶד:
וַאֲנַחְנוּ נְבָרֵךְ יָהּ מֵעַתָּה וְעַד־עוֹלָם, הַלְלוּיָהּ: תהלים קטו

וּבָא לְצִיּוֹן גּוֹאֵל "A redeemer will come to Zion, *Is. 59*
to those of Jacob who repent of their sins," declares the LORD.
"As for Me, this is My covenant with them," says the LORD.
"My spirit, that is on you, and My words I have placed in your mouth
will not depart from your mouth, or from the mouth of your children,
or from the mouth of their descendants from this time on and for
ever," says the LORD.

▸ You are the Holy One, enthroned on the praises of Israel. *Ps. 22*
And [the angels] call to one another, saying, ◂ "Holy, holy, holy *Is. 6*
is the LORD of hosts; the whole world is filled with His glory."
And they receive permission from one another, saying: *Targum Yonatan Is. 6*
"Holy in the highest heavens, home of His Presence; holy on earth,
the work of His strength; holy for ever and all time is the LORD of hosts;
the whole earth is full of His radiant glory."

▸ Then a wind lifted me up and I heard behind me the sound of a great *Ezek. 3*
noise, saying, ◂ "Blessed is the LORD's glory from His place."
Then a wind lifted me up and I heard behind me *Targum Yonatan Ezek. 3*
the sound of a great tempest of those who uttered praise, saying,
"Blessed is the LORD's glory from the place of the home of His Presence."

The LORD shall reign for ever and all time. *Ex. 15*
The LORD's kingdom is established for ever and all time. *Targum Onkelos Ex. 15*

יהוה LORD, God of Abraham, Isaac and Yisrael, our ancestors, may *1 Chr. 29*
You keep this for ever so that it forms the thoughts in Your people's
heart, and directs their heart toward You. He is compassionate. He *Ps. 78*
forgives iniquity and does not destroy. Repeatedly He suppresses His
anger, not rousing His full wrath. For You, my LORD, are good and *Ps. 86*
forgiving, abundantly kind to all who call on You. Your righteousness *Ps. 119*
is eternally righteous, and Your Torah is truth. Grant truth to Jacob, *Mic. 7*
loving-kindness to Abraham, as You promised our ancestors in ancient
times. Blessed is my LORD for day after day He burdens us [with His *Ps. 68*
blessings]; is our salvation, Selah! The LORD of hosts is with us; the *Ps. 46*
God of Jacob is our refuge, Selah! LORD of hosts, happy is the one who *Ps. 84*
trusts in You. LORD, save. May the King answer us on the day we call. *Ps. 20*

וּבָא לְצִיּוֹן גּוֹאֵל, וּלְשָׁבֵי פֶשַׁע בְּיַעֲקֹב, נְאֻם יהוה: ישעיה נט
וַאֲנִי זֹאת בְּרִיתִי אוֹתָם, אָמַר יהוה
רוּחִי אֲשֶׁר עָלֶיךָ וּדְבָרַי אֲשֶׁר־שַׂמְתִּי בְּפִיךָ
לֹא־יָמוּשׁוּ מִפִּיךָ וּמִפִּי זַרְעֲךָ וּמִפִּי זֶרַע זַרְעֲךָ
אָמַר יהוה, מֵעַתָּה וְעַד־עוֹלָם:

◂ וְאַתָּה קָדוֹשׁ יוֹשֵׁב תְּהִלּוֹת יִשְׂרָאֵל: וְקָרָא זֶה אֶל־זֶה וְאָמַר ◂ תהלים כב
קָדוֹשׁ, קָדוֹשׁ, קָדוֹשׁ, יהוה צְבָאוֹת, מְלֹא כָל־הָאָרֶץ כְּבוֹדוֹ: ישעיה ו
וּמְקַבְּלִין דֵּין מִן דֵּין וְאָמְרִין, קַדִּישׁ בִּשְׁמֵי מְרוֹמָא עִלָּאָה בֵּית שְׁכִינְתֵּהּ תרגום יונתן ישעיה ו
קַדִּישׁ עַל אַרְעָא עוֹבַד גְּבוּרְתֵּהּ, קַדִּישׁ לְעָלַם וּלְעָלְמֵי עָלְמַיָּא
יהוה צְבָאוֹת, מַלְיָא כָל אַרְעָא זִיו יְקָרֵהּ.

◂ וַתִּשָּׂאֵנִי רוּחַ, וָאֶשְׁמַע אַחֲרַי קוֹל רַעַשׁ גָּדוֹל ◂ יחזקאל ג
בָּרוּךְ כְּבוֹד־יהוה מִמְּקוֹמוֹ:
וּנְטָלַתְנִי רוּחָא, וּשְׁמָעִית בַּתְרַי קָל זִיעַ סַגִּיא, דִּמְשַׁבְּחִין וְאָמְרִין תרגום יונתן יחזקאל ג
בְּרִיךְ יְקָרָא דַיהוה מֵאֲתַר בֵּית שְׁכִינְתֵּהּ.

יהוה יִמְלֹךְ לְעֹלָם וָעֶד: שמות טו
יהוה מַלְכוּתֵהּ קָאֵם לְעָלַם וּלְעָלְמֵי עָלְמַיָּא. תרגום אונקלוס שמות טו

יהוה אֱלֹהֵי אַבְרָהָם יִצְחָק וְיִשְׂרָאֵל אֲבֹתֵינוּ, שָׁמְרָה־זֹּאת לְעוֹלָם דברי הימים א, כט
לְיֵצֶר מַחְשְׁבוֹת לְבַב עַמֶּךָ, וְהָכֵן לְבָבָם אֵלֶיךָ: וְהוּא רַחוּם יְכַפֵּר עָוֹן תהלים עח
וְלֹא־יַשְׁחִית, וְהִרְבָּה לְהָשִׁיב אַפּוֹ, וְלֹא־יָעִיר כָּל־חֲמָתוֹ: כִּי־אַתָּה תהלים פו
אֲדֹנָי טוֹב וְסַלָּח, וְרַב־חֶסֶד לְכָל־קֹרְאֶיךָ: צִדְקָתְךָ צֶדֶק לְעוֹלָם תהלים קיט
וְתוֹרָתְךָ אֱמֶת: תִּתֵּן אֱמֶת לְיַעֲקֹב, חֶסֶד לְאַבְרָהָם, אֲשֶׁר־נִשְׁבַּעְתָּ מיכה ז
לַאֲבֹתֵינוּ מִימֵי קֶדֶם: בָּרוּךְ אֲדֹנָי יוֹם יוֹם יַעֲמָס־לָנוּ, הָאֵל יְשׁוּעָתֵנוּ תהלים סח
סֶלָה: יהוה צְבָאוֹת עִמָּנוּ, מִשְׂגָּב לָנוּ אֱלֹהֵי יַעֲקֹב סֶלָה: יהוה צְבָאוֹת, תהלים מו תהלים פד
אַשְׁרֵי אָדָם בֹּטֵחַ בָּךְ: יהוה הוֹשִׁיעָה, הַמֶּלֶךְ יַעֲנֵנוּ בְיוֹם־קָרְאֵנוּ: תהלים כ

בָּרוּךְ Blessed is He, our God, who created us for His glory, separating us from those who go astray; who gave us the Torah of truth, planting within us eternal life. May He open our heart to His Torah, imbuing our heart with the love and awe of Him, that we may do His will and serve Him with a perfect heart, so that we neither toil in vain nor give birth to confusion.

יְהִי רָצוֹן May it be Your will, O Lord our God and God of our ancestors, that we keep Your laws in this world, and thus be worthy to live, see and inherit goodness and blessing in the Messianic Age and in the
life of the World to Come. So that my soul may sing to You and not *Ps. 30*
be silent. Lord, my God, for ever I will thank You. Blessed is the man *Jer. 17*
who trusts in the Lord, whose trust is in the Lord alone. Trust in the *Is. 26*
Lord for evermore, for God, the Lord, is an everlasting Rock. ▸ Those *Ps. 9*
who know Your name trust in You, for You, Lord, do not forsake those
who seek You. The Lord desired, for the sake of Israel's merit, to make *Is. 42*
the Torah great and glorious.

HALF KADDISH

Leader: יִתְגַּדַּל Magnified and sanctified
may His great name be,
in the world He created by His will.
May He establish His kingdom
in your lifetime and in your days,
and in the lifetime of all the house of Israel,
swiftly and soon –
and say: Amen.

All: May His great name be blessed for ever and all time.

Leader: Blessed and praised, glorified and exalted,
raised and honored, uplifted and lauded
be the name of the Holy One, blessed be He,
beyond any blessing,
song, praise and consolation
uttered in the world –
and say: Amen.

בָּרוּךְ הוּא אֱלֹהֵינוּ שֶׁבְּרָאָנוּ לִכְבוֹדוֹ, וְהִבְדִּילָנוּ מִן הַתּוֹעִים, וְנָתַן לָנוּ תּוֹרַת אֱמֶת, וְחַיֵּי עוֹלָם נָטַע בְּתוֹכֵנוּ. הוּא יִפְתַּח לִבֵּנוּ בְּתוֹרָתוֹ, וְיָשֵׂם בְּלִבֵּנוּ אַהֲבָתוֹ וְיִרְאָתוֹ וְלַעֲשׂוֹת רְצוֹנוֹ וּלְעָבְדוֹ בְּלֵבָב שָׁלֵם, לְמַעַן לֹא נִיגַע לָרִיק וְלֹא נֵלֵד לַבֶּהָלָה.

יְהִי רָצוֹן מִלְּפָנֶיךָ יהוה אֱלֹהֵינוּ וֵאלֹהֵי אֲבוֹתֵינוּ, שֶׁנִּשְׁמֹר חֻקֶּיךָ
בָּעוֹלָם הַזֶּה, וְנִזְכֶּה וְנִחְיֶה וְנִרְאֶה וְנִירַשׁ טוֹבָה וּבְרָכָה, לִשְׁנֵי יְמוֹת
הַמָּשִׁיחַ וּלְחַיֵּי הָעוֹלָם הַבָּא. לְמַעַן יְזַמֶּרְךָ כָבוֹד וְלֹא יִדֹּם, יהוה תהלים ל
אֱלֹהַי, לְעוֹלָם אוֹדֶךָּ: בָּרוּךְ הַגֶּבֶר אֲשֶׁר יִבְטַח בַּיהוה, וְהָיָה יהוה ירמיה יז
מִבְטַחוֹ: בִּטְחוּ בַיהוה עֲדֵי־עַד, כִּי בְּיָהּ יהוה צוּר עוֹלָמִים: ◂ וְיִבְטְחוּ ישעיה כו תהלים ט
בְךָ יוֹדְעֵי שְׁמֶךָ, כִּי לֹא־עָזַבְתָּ דֹרְשֶׁיךָ, יהוה: יהוה חָפֵץ לְמַעַן צִדְקוֹ, ישעיה מב
יַגְדִּיל תּוֹרָה וְיַאְדִּיר:

חצי קדיש

ש״ץ: יִתְגַּדַּל וְיִתְקַדַּשׁ שְׁמֵהּ רַבָּא (קהל: אָמֵן)
בְּעָלְמָא דִּי בְרָא כִרְעוּתֵהּ
וְיַמְלִיךְ מַלְכוּתֵהּ
בְּחַיֵּיכוֹן וּבְיוֹמֵיכוֹן וּבְחַיֵּי דְכָל בֵּית יִשְׂרָאֵל
בַּעֲגָלָא וּבִזְמַן קָרִיב, וְאִמְרוּ אָמֵן. (קהל: אָמֵן)

קהל וש״ץ: יְהֵא שְׁמֵהּ רַבָּא מְבָרַךְ לְעָלַם וּלְעָלְמֵי עָלְמַיָּא.

ש״ץ: יִתְבָּרַךְ וְיִשְׁתַּבַּח וְיִתְפָּאַר וְיִתְרוֹמַם וְיִתְנַשֵּׂא
וְיִתְהַדָּר וְיִתְעַלֶּה וְיִתְהַלָּל
שְׁמֵהּ דְּקֻדְשָׁא בְּרִיךְ הוּא (קהל: בְּרִיךְ הוּא)
לְעֵלָּא מִן כָּל בִּרְכָתָא וְשִׁירָתָא
תֻּשְׁבְּחָתָא וְנֶחֱמָתָא
דַּאֲמִירָן בְּעָלְמָא, וְאִמְרוּ אָמֵן. (קהל: אָמֵן)

וַאֲנִי As for me, may my prayer come to You, LORD, at a time of favor. O God, in Your great love, answer me with Your faithful salvation. *Ps. 69*

The Ark is opened and the congregation stands. All say:

וַיְהִי בִּנְסֹעַ Whenever the Ark set out, Moses would say, *Num. 10*
"Arise, LORD, and may Your enemies be scattered.
May those who hate You flee before You."
For the Torah shall come forth from Zion, *Is. 2*
and the word of the LORD from Jerusalem.
Blessed is He who in His Holiness
gave the Torah to His people Israel.

Blessed is the name of the Master of the Universe. Blessed is Your crown and Your place. May Your favor always be with Your people Israel. Show Your people the salvation of Your right hand in Your Temple. Grant us the gift of Your good light, and accept our prayers in mercy. May it be Your will to prolong our life in goodness. May I be counted among the righteous, so that You will have compassion on me and protect me and all that is mine and all that is Your people Israel's. You feed all; You sustain all; You rule over all; You rule over kings, for sovereignty is Yours. I am a servant of the Holy One, blessed be He, before whom and before whose glorious Torah I bow at all times. Not in man do I trust, nor on any angel do I rely, but on the God of heaven who is the God of truth, whose Torah is truth, whose prophets speak truth, and who abounds in acts of love and truth. ▸ In Him I trust, and to His holy and glorious name I offer praises. May it be Your will to open my heart to the Torah, and to fulfill the wishes of my heart and of the hearts of all Your people Israel for good, for life, and for peace. *Zohar, Vayak-hel*

The Leader takes the Torah scroll in his right arm, bows toward the Ark and says:

Magnify the LORD with me, and let us exalt His name together. *Ps. 34*

The Ark is closed. The Leader carries the Torah scroll to the bima and the congregation says:

לְךָ Yours, LORD, are the greatness and the power, the glory and the majesty and splendor, for everything in heaven and earth is Yours. Yours, LORD, is the kingdom; You are exalted as Head over all. *1 Chr. 29*

רוֹמְמוּ Exalt the LORD our God and bow to His footstool; He is holy. Exalt the LORD our God, and bow at His holy mountain, for holy is the LORD our God. *Ps. 99*

אַב הָרַחֲמִים May the Father of compassion have compassion on the people borne by Him. May He remember the covenant with the mighty [patriarchs], and deliver us from evil times. May He reproach the evil instinct in the people carried by Him, and graciously grant that we be an everlasting remnant. May He fulfill in good measure our requests for salvation and compassion.

וַאֲנִי תְפִלָּתִי־לְךָ יהוה, עֵת רָצוֹן, אֱלֹהִים בְּרָב־חַסְדֶּךָ תהלים סט
עֲנֵנִי בֶּאֱמֶת יִשְׁעֶךָ:

The ארון קודש *is opened and the* קהל *stands. All say:*

וַיְהִי בִּנְסֹעַ הָאָרֹן וַיֹּאמֶר מֹשֶׁה במדבר י
קוּמָה יהוה וְיָפֻצוּ אֹיְבֶיךָ וְיָנֻסוּ מְשַׂנְאֶיךָ מִפָּנֶיךָ:
כִּי מִצִּיּוֹן תֵּצֵא תוֹרָה וּדְבַר־יהוה מִירוּשָׁלָםִ: ישעיה ב
בָּרוּךְ שֶׁנָּתַן תּוֹרָה לְעַמּוֹ יִשְׂרָאֵל בִּקְדֻשָּׁתוֹ.

בְּרִיךְ שְׁמֵהּ דְּמָרֵא עָלְמָא, בְּרִיךְ כִּתְרָךְ וְאַתְרָךְ. יְהֵא רְעוּתָךְ עִם עַמָּךְ יִשְׂרָאֵל לְעָלַם, וּפֻרְקַן יְמִינָךְ אַחֲזִי לְעַמָּךְ בְּבֵית מַקְדְּשָׁךְ, וּלְאַמְטוּיֵי לַנָא מִטּוּב נְהוֹרָךְ, וּלְקַבֵּל צְלוֹתַנָא בְּרַחֲמִין. יְהֵא רַעֲוָא קֳדָמָךְ דְּתוֹרִיךְ לַן חַיִּין בְּטִיבוּ, וְלֶהֱוֵי אֲנָא פְקִידָא בְּגוֹ צַדִּיקַיָּא, לְמִרְחַם עָלַי וּלְמִנְטַר יָתִי וְיַת כָּל דִּי לִי וְדִי לְעַמָּךְ יִשְׂרָאֵל. אַנְתְּ הוּא זָן לְכֹלָּא וּמְפַרְנֵס לְכֹלָּא, אַנְתְּ הוּא שַׁלִּיט עַל כֹּלָּא, אַנְתְּ הוּא דְּשַׁלִּיט עַל מַלְכַיָּא, וּמַלְכוּתָא דִּילָךְ הִיא. אֲנָא עַבְדָּא דְקֻדְשָׁא בְּרִיךְ הוּא, דְּסָגֵדְנָא קַמֵּהּ וּמִקַּמֵּי דִּיקָר אוֹרַיְתֵהּ בְּכָל עִדָּן וְעִדָּן. לָא עַל אֱנָשׁ רָחִיצְנָא וְלָא עַל בַּר אֱלָהִין סָמִיכְנָא, אֶלָּא בֶּאֱלָהָא דִשְׁמַיָּא, דְּהוּא אֱלָהָא קְשׁוֹט, וְאוֹרַיְתֵהּ קְשׁוֹט, וּנְבִיאוֹהִי קְשׁוֹט, וּמַסְגֵּא לְמֶעְבַּד טַבְוָן וּקְשׁוֹט. ‹ בֵּהּ אֲנָא רָחִיץ, וְלִשְׁמֵהּ קַדִּישָׁא יַקִּירָא אֲנָא אֵמַר תֻּשְׁבְּחָן. יְהֵא רַעֲוָא קֳדָמָךְ דְּתִפְתַּח לִבַּאי בְּאוֹרַיְתָא, וְתַשְׁלִים מִשְׁאֲלִין דְּלִבַּאי וְלִבָּא דְכָל עַמָּךְ יִשְׂרָאֵל לְטָב וּלְחַיִּין וְלִשְׁלָם. זוהר ויקהל

The שליח ציבור *takes the* ספר תורה *in his right arm, bows toward the* ארון קודש *and says:*

גַּדְּלוּ לַיהוה אִתִּי וּנְרוֹמְמָה שְׁמוֹ יַחְדָּו: תהלים לד

The ארון קודש *is closed. The* שליח ציבור *carries the* ספר תורה *to the* בימה *and the* קהל *says:*

לְךָ יהוה הַגְּדֻלָּה וְהַגְּבוּרָה וְהַתִּפְאֶרֶת וְהַנֵּצַח וְהַהוֹד, כִּי־כֹל בַּשָּׁמַיִם וּבָאָרֶץ: לְךָ יהוה הַמַּמְלָכָה וְהַמִּתְנַשֵּׂא לְכֹל לְרֹאשׁ: דברי הימים א׳ כט

רוֹמְמוּ יהוה אֱלֹהֵינוּ וְהִשְׁתַּחֲווּ לַהֲדֹם רַגְלָיו, קָדוֹשׁ הוּא: רוֹמְמוּ יהוה אֱלֹהֵינוּ וְהִשְׁתַּחֲווּ לְהַר קָדְשׁוֹ, כִּי־קָדוֹשׁ יהוה אֱלֹהֵינוּ: תהלים צט

אַב הָרַחֲמִים הוּא יְרַחֵם עַם עֲמוּסִים, וְיִזְכֹּר בְּרִית אֵיתָנִים, וְיַצִּיל נַפְשׁוֹתֵינוּ מִן הַשָּׁעוֹת הָרָעוֹת, וְיִגְעַר בְּיֵצֶר הָרָע מִן הַנְּשׂוּאִים, וְיָחֹן אוֹתָנוּ לִפְלֵיטַת עוֹלָמִים, וִימַלֵּא מִשְׁאֲלוֹתֵינוּ בְּמִדָּה טוֹבָה יְשׁוּעָה וְרַחֲמִים.

The Torah scroll is placed on the bima and the Gabbai calls a Kohen to the Torah.

וְתִגָּלֶה May His kingship over us be soon revealed and made manifest. May He be gracious to our surviving remnant, the remnant of His people the house of Israel in grace, loving-kindness, compassion and favor, and let us say: Amen. Let us all render greatness to our God and give honor to the Torah. *Let the Kohen come forward. Arise (*name* son of *father's name*), the Kohen.

**If no Kohen is present, a Levi or Yisrael is called up as follows:*
/As there is no Kohen, arise (*name* son of *father's name*) in place of a Kohen./

Blessed is He who, in His holiness, gave the Torah to His people Israel.

The congregation followed by the Gabbai:
You who cling to the LORD your God are all alive today. *Deut. 4*

The Reader shows the oleh the section to be read.
The oleh touches the scroll at that place with the tzitzit
of his tallit or the fabric belt of the Torah scroll,
which he then kisses. Holding the handles of the scroll, he says:

Oleh: Bless the LORD, the blessed One.

Cong: Bless the LORD, the blessed One,
for ever and all time.

Oleh: Bless the LORD, the blessed One,
for ever and all time.

Blessed are You, LORD our God, King of the Universe,
who has chosen us from all peoples
and has given us His Torah.
Blessed are You, LORD,
Giver of the Torah.

After the reading, the oleh says:

Oleh: Blessed are You, LORD our God, King of the Universe,
who has given us the Torah of truth,
planting everlasting life in our midst.
Blessed are You, LORD,
Giver of the Torah.

The ספר תורה *is placed on the* שולחן *and the* גבאי *calls a* כהן *to the* תורה.

וְתִגָּלֶה וְתֵרָאֶה מַלְכוּתוֹ עָלֵינוּ בִּזְמַן קָרוֹב, וְיָחֹן פְּלֵיטָתֵנוּ וּפְלֵיטַת עַמּוֹ בֵּית יִשְׂרָאֵל לְחֵן וּלְחֶסֶד וּלְרַחֲמִים וּלְרָצוֹן וְנֹאמַר אָמֵן. הַכֹּל הָבוּ גֹדֶל לֵאלֹהֵינוּ וּתְנוּ כָבוֹד לַתּוֹרָה. *כֹּהֵן קְרַב, יַעֲמֹד (פלוני בֶּן פלוני) הַכֹּהֵן.

**If no* כהן *is present, a* לוי *or* ישראל *is called up as follows:*

/אֵין כָּאן כֹּהֵן, יַעֲמֹד (פלוני בֶּן פלוני) בִּמְקוֹם כֹּהֵן./

בָּרוּךְ שֶׁנָּתַן תּוֹרָה לְעַמּוֹ יִשְׂרָאֵל בִּקְדֻשָּׁתוֹ.

The קהל *followed by the* גבאי*:*

דברים ד וְאַתֶּם הַדְּבֵקִים בַּיהוה אֱלֹהֵיכֶם חַיִּים כֻּלְּכֶם הַיּוֹם:

The קורא *shows the* עולה *the section to be read.*
The עולה *touches the scroll at that place with the* ציצית *of his* טלית
or the gartel of the ספר תורה*, which he then kisses.*
Holding the handles of the scroll, he says:

עולה: בָּרְכוּ אֶת יהוה הַמְבֹרָךְ.

קהל: בָּרוּךְ יהוה הַמְבֹרָךְ לְעוֹלָם וָעֶד.

עולה: בָּרוּךְ יהוה הַמְבֹרָךְ לְעוֹלָם וָעֶד.

בָּרוּךְ אַתָּה יהוה, אֱלֹהֵינוּ מֶלֶךְ הָעוֹלָם
אֲשֶׁר בָּחַר בָּנוּ מִכָּל הָעַמִּים
וְנָתַן לָנוּ אֶת תּוֹרָתוֹ.
בָּרוּךְ אַתָּה יהוה, נוֹתֵן הַתּוֹרָה.

After the קריאת התורה*, the* עולה *says:*

עולה: בָּרוּךְ אַתָּה יהוה אֱלֹהֵינוּ מֶלֶךְ הָעוֹלָם
אֲשֶׁר נָתַן לָנוּ תּוֹרַת אֱמֶת
וְחַיֵּי עוֹלָם נָטַע בְּתוֹכֵנוּ.
בָּרוּךְ אַתָּה יהוה, נוֹתֵן הַתּוֹרָה.

On the first day of Sukkot if it falls on a Shabbat, on Shabbat Ḥol HaMo'ed and on Shemini Atzeret outside Israel this is portion is read. On Simḥat Torah in Israel, turn to the next page.

This is the blessing with which Moses, the man of God, blessed the children of Israel before he died. Moses said: "The LORD came to them from Sinai; He shone out from Seir. He appeared over the crest of Paran, and came, among myriad angels, at His right hand a law of fire, for them. And He embraces the tribes, their holy ones all in His hands; they are drawn after Your steps, and carry Your words. Moses gave us a Law, a heritage to the people of Jacob. There is a King in Yeshurun, as the heads of the people are gathered, the tribes of Israel together. *Deut. 33:1-*

"May Reuben live; let him not die, nor be left slight in number."

And this to Judah: he said, "Heed, LORD, the voice of Judah, and bring him home to his people. His arms alone need fight for him; You are his Support against his foes."

LEVI

To Levi he said, "Your tumim and urim are with Your devoted, the one You tested at Masa, and wrestled at Meriva; who said, of his father and mother: I have seen them not; who did not recognize his brothers, nor know his own sons, for he kept Your words, and guarded close Your covenant. They will teach Your laws to Jacob, and Your Torah to Israel. They will place before You the scent of incense, and offerings burnt on Your Altar. LORD, bless his strength, and receive the work of his hands. Those who rise against him – crush their bearing; all his enemies, until they rise no more."

To Benjamin he said, "Beloved of the LORD, he shall rest on Him in safety; and all through the day He shelters him, and rests upon his shoulders."

SHELISHI

To Joseph he said, "His land is blessed of the LORD, with the fruit of the skies, of rain, and of the deeps that bide below, and of the fruit of the sun's harvest, all the fruits of the moon's yield, of the heights of primeval mountains, of the fruit of the ancient hills, and the fruit of the world and its fullness – and the favor of that Presence at the Bush. May this come to the head of Joseph, to the crown of one raised above his brothers. His glory is that of a firstborn bull, his horns the grand horns of the oryx. With these he can gore nations; the ends of the earth together – yes, these are the myriads of Ephraim, the thousands of Manasseh."

Continue with Hagbaha on the next page.

On the first day of סוכות *if it falls on a* שבת*, on* שבת חול המועד *and on* שמני עצרת *outside* ארץ ישראל *this portion is read. On* שמחת תורה *in* ארץ ישראל*, turn to the next page.*

דברים לג:א–יז
וְזֹאת הַבְּרָכָה אֲשֶׁר בֵּרַךְ מֹשֶׁה אִישׁ הָאֱלֹהִים אֶת־בְּנֵי יִשְׂרָאֵל
לִפְנֵי מוֹתוֹ: וַיֹּאמַר יהוה מִסִּינַי בָּא וְזָרַח מִשֵּׂעִיר לָמוֹ הוֹפִיעַ
מֵהַר פָּארָן וְאָתָה מֵרִבְבֹת קֹדֶשׁ מִימִינוֹ אשדת לָמוֹ: אַף — אֵשׁ דָּת
חֹבֵב עַמִּים כָּל־קְדֹשָׁיו בְּיָדֶךָ וְהֵם תֻּכּוּ לְרַגְלֶךָ יִשָּׂא מִדַּבְּרֹתֶיךָ:
תּוֹרָה צִוָּה־לָנוּ מֹשֶׁה מוֹרָשָׁה קְהִלַּת יַעֲקֹב: וַיְהִי בִישֻׁרוּן מֶלֶךְ
בְּהִתְאַסֵּף רָאשֵׁי עָם יַחַד שִׁבְטֵי יִשְׂרָאֵל: יְחִי רְאוּבֵן וְאַל־יָמֹת
וִיהִי מְתָיו מִסְפָּר: וְזֹאת לִיהוּדָה וַיֹּאמַר שְׁמַע יהוה
קוֹל יְהוּדָה וְאֶל־עַמּוֹ תְּבִיאֶנּוּ יָדָיו רָב לוֹ וְעֵזֶר מִצָּרָיו תִּהְיֶה:
לוי — וּלְלֵוִי אָמַר תֻּמֶּיךָ וְאוּרֶיךָ לְאִישׁ חֲסִידֶךָ אֲשֶׁר נִסִּיתוֹ בְּמַסָּה
תְּרִיבֵהוּ עַל־מֵי מְרִיבָה: הָאֹמֵר לְאָבִיו וּלְאִמּוֹ לֹא רְאִיתִיו וְאֶת־
אֶחָיו לֹא הִכִּיר וְאֶת־בָּנָו לֹא יָדָע כִּי שָׁמְרוּ אִמְרָתֶךָ וּבְרִיתְךָ
יִנְצֹרוּ: יוֹרוּ מִשְׁפָּטֶיךָ לְיַעֲקֹב וְתוֹרָתְךָ לְיִשְׂרָאֵל יָשִׂימוּ קְטוֹרָה
בְּאַפֶּךָ וְכָלִיל עַל־מִזְבְּחֶךָ: בָּרֵךְ יהוה חֵילוֹ וּפֹעַל יָדָיו תִּרְצֶה
מְחַץ מָתְנַיִם קָמָיו וּמְשַׂנְאָיו מִן־יְקוּמוּן: לְבִנְיָמִן
אָמַר יְדִיד יהוה יִשְׁכֹּן לָבֶטַח עָלָיו חֹפֵף עָלָיו כָּל־הַיּוֹם וּבֵין
שלישי — כְּתֵפָיו שָׁכֵן: *וּלְיוֹסֵף אָמַר מְבֹרֶכֶת יהוה אַרְצוֹ
מִמֶּגֶד שָׁמַיִם מִטָּל וּמִתְּהוֹם רֹבֶצֶת תָּחַת: וּמִמֶּגֶד תְּבוּאֹת
שָׁמֶשׁ וּמִמֶּגֶד גֶּרֶשׁ יְרָחִים: וּמֵרֹאשׁ הַרְרֵי־קֶדֶם וּמִמֶּגֶד גִּבְעוֹת
עוֹלָם: וּמִמֶּגֶד אֶרֶץ וּמְלֹאָהּ וּרְצוֹן שֹׁכְנִי סְנֶה תָּבוֹאתָה לְרֹאשׁ
יוֹסֵף וּלְקָדְקֹד נְזִיר אֶחָיו: בְּכוֹר שׁוֹרוֹ הָדָר לוֹ וְקַרְנֵי רְאֵם קַרְנָיו
בָּהֶם עַמִּים יְנַגַּח יַחְדָּו אַפְסֵי־אָרֶץ וְהֵם רִבְבוֹת אֶפְרַיִם וְהֵם
אַלְפֵי מְנַשֶּׁה:

Continue with הגבהה *on the next page.*

On Simḥat Torah in Israel this portion is read:

In the beginning, God created heaven and earth. And the earth was desolate emptiness, and darkness over the deep; but the spirit of God moved over the waters. And God said: "Let there be light." Light came to be. And He saw that the light was good, and divided light from darkness. God named the light, "Day;" and the darkness He named, "Night." There was evening; then there was morning: one day. *Gen. 1:1–1*

LEVI God said: "Let there be a clear dome amid the waters, dividing water from water." And He shaped the dome, dividing the waters below the dome from the waters above it – and so it came to be. And God named that dome, "Sky." And there was evening; then there was morning: a second day.

SHELISH God said, "Let all the waters below the sky be gathered to one place; let dry ground be revealed." And so it came to be. And He named the dry ground, "Land;" and the gathering of waters He named "Seas." And God saw that it was good. He said, "Let the land sprout green plants that seed, and fruit trees, each bearing fruit with its own seeds in them, overspreading the land." And so it came to be. The land brought forth green, seeding plants, each with its own seeds, and trees bearing fruit, each with its own seeds in it. And God saw that it was good. There was evening; then there was morning: a third day.

HAGBAHA AND GELILA

The Torah scroll is lifted and the congregation says:

וְזֹאת הַתּוֹרָה This is the Torah that *Deut. 4*
Moses placed before the children of Israel,
at the LORD's commandment, by the hand of Moses. *Num. 9*

Some add: It is a tree of life to those who grasp it, *Prov. 3*
and those who uphold it are happy.
Its ways are ways of pleasantness, and all its paths are peace.
Long life is in its right hand; in its left, riches and honor.
It pleased the LORD for the sake of [Israel's] righteousness, *Is. 42*
to make the Torah great and glorious.

On שמחת תורה *in* ארץ ישראל *this portion is read:*

בראשית א:א–יג
בְּרֵאשִׁית בָּרָא אֱלֹהִים אֵת הַשָּׁמַיִם וְאֵת הָאָרֶץ: וְהָאָרֶץ הָיְתָה תֹהוּ וָבֹהוּ וְחֹשֶׁךְ עַל־פְּנֵי תְהוֹם וְרוּחַ אֱלֹהִים מְרַחֶפֶת עַל־פְּנֵי הַמָּיִם: וַיֹּאמֶר אֱלֹהִים יְהִי־אוֹר וַיְהִי־אוֹר: וַיַּרְא אֱלֹהִים אֶת־הָאוֹר כִּי־טוֹב וַיַּבְדֵּל אֱלֹהִים בֵּין הָאוֹר וּבֵין הַחֹשֶׁךְ: וַיִּקְרָא אֱלֹהִים ׀ לָאוֹר יוֹם וְלַחֹשֶׁךְ קָרָא לָיְלָה וַיְהִי־עֶרֶב וַיְהִי־בֹקֶר יוֹם אֶחָד:

לוי
וַיֹּאמֶר אֱלֹהִים יְהִי רָקִיעַ בְּתוֹךְ הַמָּיִם וִיהִי מַבְדִּיל בֵּין מַיִם לָמָיִם: וַיַּעַשׂ אֱלֹהִים אֶת־הָרָקִיעַ וַיַּבְדֵּל בֵּין הַמַּיִם אֲשֶׁר מִתַּחַת לָרָקִיעַ וּבֵין הַמַּיִם אֲשֶׁר מֵעַל לָרָקִיעַ וַיְהִי־כֵן: וַיִּקְרָא אֱלֹהִים לָרָקִיעַ שָׁמָיִם וַיְהִי־עֶרֶב וַיְהִי־בֹקֶר יוֹם שֵׁנִי:

ישראל
וַיֹּאמֶר אֱלֹהִים יִקָּווּ הַמַּיִם מִתַּחַת הַשָּׁמַיִם אֶל־מָקוֹם אֶחָד וְתֵרָאֶה הַיַּבָּשָׁה וַיְהִי־כֵן: וַיִּקְרָא אֱלֹהִים ׀ לַיַּבָּשָׁה אֶרֶץ וּלְמִקְוֵה הַמַּיִם קָרָא יַמִּים וַיַּרְא אֱלֹהִים כִּי־טוֹב: וַיֹּאמֶר אֱלֹהִים תַּדְשֵׁא הָאָרֶץ דֶּשֶׁא עֵשֶׂב מַזְרִיעַ זֶרַע עֵץ פְּרִי עֹשֶׂה פְּרִי לְמִינוֹ אֲשֶׁר זַרְעוֹ־בוֹ עַל־הָאָרֶץ וַיְהִי־כֵן: וַתּוֹצֵא הָאָרֶץ דֶּשֶׁא עֵשֶׂב מַזְרִיעַ זֶרַע לְמִינֵהוּ וְעֵץ עֹשֶׂה־פְּרִי אֲשֶׁר זַרְעוֹ־בוֹ לְמִינֵהוּ וַיַּרְא אֱלֹהִים כִּי־טוֹב: וַיְהִי־עֶרֶב וַיְהִי־בֹקֶר יוֹם שְׁלִישִׁי:

הגבהה וגלילה

The ספר תורה *is lifted and the* קהל *says:*

דברים ד
וְזֹאת הַתּוֹרָה אֲשֶׁר־שָׂם מֹשֶׁה לִפְנֵי בְּנֵי יִשְׂרָאֵל:

במדבר ט
עַל־פִּי יהוה בְּיַד מֹשֶׁה:

משלי ג
Some add עֵץ־חַיִּים הִיא לַמַּחֲזִיקִים בָּהּ וְתֹמְכֶיהָ מְאֻשָּׁר:
דְּרָכֶיהָ דַרְכֵי־נֹעַם וְכָל־נְתִיבוֹתֶיהָ שָׁלוֹם:
אֹרֶךְ יָמִים בִּימִינָהּ, בִּשְׂמֹאולָהּ עֹשֶׁר וְכָבוֹד:

ישעיה מב
יהוה חָפֵץ לְמַעַן צִדְקוֹ יַגְדִּיל תּוֹרָה וְיַאְדִּיר:

The Torah scroll is bound and covered.
The Ark is opened. The Leader takes the Torah scroll and says:

יְהַלְלוּ Let them praise the name of the LORD, *Ps. 148*
for His name alone is sublime.

The congregation responds:

הודו His majesty is above earth and heaven.
He has raised the horn of His people,
for the glory of all His devoted ones,
the children of Israel, the people close to Him.
Halleluya!

As the Torah scroll is returned to the Ark say:

לְדָוִד מִזְמוֹר A psalm of David. The earth is the LORD's and all it contains, *Ps. 24*
the world and all who live in it. For He founded it on the seas and established it on the streams. Who may climb the mountain of the LORD? Who may stand in His holy place? He who has clean hands and a pure heart, who has not taken My name in vain, or sworn deceitfully. He shall receive blessing from the LORD, and just reward from God, his salvation. This is a generation of those who seek Him, the descendants of Jacob who seek Your presence, Selah! Lift up your heads, O gates; be uplifted, eternal doors, so that the King of glory may enter. Who is the King of glory? It is the LORD, strong and mighty, the LORD mighty in battle. Lift up your heads, O gates; be uplifted, eternal doors, so that the King of glory may enter. Who is He, the King of glory? The LORD of hosts, He is the King of glory, Selah!

As the Torah scroll is placed into the Ark, say:

וּבְנֻחֹה יֹאמַר When the Ark came to rest, Moses would say:
"Return, O LORD, to the myriad thousands of Israel." *Num. 10*
Advance, LORD, to Your resting place, You and Your mighty Ark. *Ps. 132*
Your priests are clothed in righteousness,
and Your devoted ones sing in joy.
For the sake of Your servant David,
do not reject Your anointed one.

The ספר תורה is bound and covered.
The ארון קודש is opened. The שליח ציבור takes the ספר תורה and says:

תהלים קמח יְהַלְלוּ אֶת־שֵׁם יהוה, כִּי־נִשְׂגָּב שְׁמוֹ, לְבַדּוֹ

The קהל responds.

הוֹדוֹ עַל־אֶרֶץ וְשָׁמָיִם:
וַיָּרֶם קֶרֶן לְעַמּוֹ
תְּהִלָּה לְכָל־חֲסִידָיו
לִבְנֵי יִשְׂרָאֵל עַם קְרֹבוֹ
הַלְלוּיָהּ:

As the ספר תורה is returned to the ארון קודש, say:

תהלים כד לְדָוִד מִזְמוֹר, לַיהוה הָאָרֶץ וּמְלוֹאָהּ, תֵּבֵל וְיְשְׁבֵי בָהּ: כִּי־הוּא עַל־יַמִּים יְסָדָהּ, וְעַל־נְהָרוֹת יְכוֹנְנֶהָ: מִי־יַעֲלֶה בְהַר־יהוה, וּמִי־יָקוּם בִּמְקוֹם קָדְשׁוֹ: נְקִי כַפַּיִם וּבַר־לֵבָב, אֲשֶׁר לֹא־נָשָׂא לַשָּׁוְא נַפְשִׁי וְלֹא נִשְׁבַּע לְמִרְמָה: יִשָּׂא בְרָכָה מֵאֵת יהוה, וּצְדָקָה מֵאֱלֹהֵי יִשְׁעוֹ: זֶה דּוֹר דֹּרְשָׁו, מְבַקְשֵׁי פָנֶיךָ, יַעֲקֹב, סֶלָה: שְׂאוּ שְׁעָרִים רָאשֵׁיכֶם, וְהִנָּשְׂאוּ פִּתְחֵי עוֹלָם, וְיָבוֹא מֶלֶךְ הַכָּבוֹד: מִי זֶה מֶלֶךְ הַכָּבוֹד, יהוה עִזּוּז וְגִבּוֹר, יהוה גִּבּוֹר מִלְחָמָה: שְׂאוּ שְׁעָרִים רָאשֵׁיכֶם, וּשְׂאוּ פִּתְחֵי עוֹלָם, וְיָבֹא מֶלֶךְ הַכָּבוֹד: מִי הוּא זֶה מֶלֶךְ הַכָּבוֹד, יהוה צְבָאוֹת הוּא מֶלֶךְ הַכָּבוֹד, סֶלָה:

As the ספר תורה is placed into the ארון קודש, say:

במדבר י וּבְנֻחֹה יֹאמַר, שׁוּבָה יהוה רִבְבוֹת אַלְפֵי יִשְׂרָאֵל:
תהלים קלב קוּמָה יהוה לִמְנוּחָתֶךָ, אַתָּה וַאֲרוֹן עֻזֶּךָ:
כֹּהֲנֶיךָ יִלְבְּשׁוּ־צֶדֶק, וַחֲסִידֶיךָ יְרַנֵּנוּ:
בַּעֲבוּר דָּוִד עַבְדֶּךָ אַל־תָּשֵׁב פְּנֵי מְשִׁיחֶךָ:

For I give you good instruction; do not forsake My Torah. *Prov. 4*
It is a tree of life to those who grasp it, *Prov. 3*
and those who uphold it are happy.
Its ways are ways of pleasantness, and all its paths are peace.
▸ Turn us back, O LORD, to You, and we will return. *Lam. 5*
Renew our days as of old.

The Ark is closed.

HALF KADDISH

Leader: יִתְגַּדַּל Magnified and sanctified
may His great name be,
in the world He created by His will.
May He establish His kingdom
in your lifetime and in your days,
and in the lifetime of all the house of Israel,
swiftly and soon –
and say: Amen.

All: May His great name be blessed
for ever and all time.

Leader: Blessed and praised,
glorified and exalted,
raised and honored,
uplifted and lauded
be the name of the Holy One,
blessed be He,
beyond any blessing, song,
praise and consolation
uttered in the world –
and say: Amen.

On Yom Tov, continue with the Amida on page 578.

כִּי לֶקַח טוֹב נָתַתִּי לָכֶם, תּוֹרָתִי אַל־תַּעֲזֹבוּ: משלי ד

עֵץ־חַיִּים הִיא לַמַּחֲזִיקִים בָּהּ, וְתֹמְכֶיהָ מְאֻשָּׁר: משלי ג

דְּרָכֶיהָ דַרְכֵי־נֹעַם וְכָל־נְתִיבוֹתֶיהָ שָׁלוֹם:

◄ הֲשִׁיבֵנוּ יהוה אֵלֶיךָ וְנָשׁוּבָה, חַדֵּשׁ יָמֵינוּ כְּקֶדֶם: איכה ה

The ארון קודש *is closed.*

חצי קדיש

ש״ץ: יִתְגַּדַּל וְיִתְקַדַּשׁ שְׁמֵהּ רַבָּא (קהל: אָמֵן)

בְּעָלְמָא דִּי בְרָא כִרְעוּתֵהּ

וְיַמְלִיךְ מַלְכוּתֵהּ

בְּחַיֵּיכוֹן וּבְיוֹמֵיכוֹן, וּבְחַיֵּי דְכָל בֵּית יִשְׂרָאֵל

בַּעֲגָלָא וּבִזְמַן קָרִיב

וְאִמְרוּ אָמֵן. (קהל: אָמֵן)

קהל וש״ץ: יְהֵא שְׁמֵהּ רַבָּא מְבָרַךְ לְעָלַם וּלְעָלְמֵי עָלְמַיָּא.

ש״ץ: יִתְבָּרַךְ וְיִשְׁתַּבַּח וְיִתְפָּאַר וְיִתְרוֹמַם וְיִתְנַשֵּׂא

וְיִתְהַדָּר וְיִתְעַלֶּה וְיִתְהַלָּל

שְׁמֵהּ דְּקֻדְשָׁא בְּרִיךְ הוּא (קהל: בְּרִיךְ הוּא)

לְעֵלָּא מִן כָּל בִּרְכָתָא וְשִׁירָתָא

תֻּשְׁבְּחָתָא וְנֶחֱמָתָא

דַּאֲמִירָן בְּעָלְמָא

וְאִמְרוּ אָמֵן. (קהל: אָמֵן)

On יום טוב*, continue with the* עמידה *on page 579.*

AMIDA

The following prayer, until "in former years" on page 978, is said silently, standing with feet together. If there is a minyan, the Amida is repeated aloud by the Leader. Take three steps forward and at the points indicated by ▾, bend the knees at the first word, bow at the second, and stand straight before saying God's name.

When I proclaim the LORD's name, give glory to our God. *Deut. 32*
O LORD, open my lips, so that my mouth may declare Your praise. *Ps. 51*

PATRIARCHS

▾בָּרוּךְ▾ Blessed are You, LORD our God and God of our fathers,
God of Abraham, God of Isaac and God of Jacob;
the great, mighty and awesome God, God Most High,
who bestows acts of loving-kindness and creates all,
who remembers the loving-kindness of the fathers
and will bring a Redeemer
to their children's children
for the sake of His name, in love.
King, Helper, Savior, Shield:
▾Blessed are You, LORD,
Shield of Abraham.

DIVINE MIGHT

אַתָּה גִּבּוֹר You are eternally mighty, LORD.
You give life to the dead
and have great power to save.

In Israel:
He causes the dew to fall.

He sustains the living with loving-kindness,
and with great compassion revives the dead.
He supports the fallen, heals the sick,
sets captives free,
and keeps His faith with those who sleep in the dust.

עמידה

The following prayer, until קַדְמֹנִיּוֹת *on page 979, is said silently, standing with feet together. If there is a* מנין*, the* עמידה *is repeated aloud by the* שליח ציבור*. Take three steps forward and at the points indicated by* ּ*, bend the knees at the first word, bow at the second, and stand straight before saying God's name.*

כִּי שֵׁם יהוה אֶקְרָא, הָבוּ גֹדֶל לֵאלֹהֵינוּ: דברים לב

אֲדֹנָי, שְׂפָתַי תִּפְתָּח, וּפִי יַגִּיד תְּהִלָּתֶךָ: תהלים נא

אבות

בָּרוּךְ אַתָּה יהוה, אֱלֹהֵינוּ וֵאלֹהֵי אֲבוֹתֵינוּ
אֱלֹהֵי אַבְרָהָם, אֱלֹהֵי יִצְחָק, וֵאלֹהֵי יַעֲקֹב
הָאֵל הַגָּדוֹל הַגִּבּוֹר וְהַנּוֹרָא, אֵל עֶלְיוֹן
גּוֹמֵל חֲסָדִים טוֹבִים, וְקוֹנֵה הַכֹּל
וְזוֹכֵר חַסְדֵי אָבוֹת
וּמֵבִיא גוֹאֵל לִבְנֵי בְנֵיהֶם לְמַעַן שְׁמוֹ בְּאַהֲבָה.
מֶלֶךְ עוֹזֵר וּמוֹשִׁיעַ וּמָגֵן.
בָּרוּךְ אַתָּה יהוה, מָגֵן אַבְרָהָם.

גבורות

אַתָּה גִּבּוֹר לְעוֹלָם, אֲדֹנָי
מְחַיֵּה מֵתִים אַתָּה, רַב לְהוֹשִׁיעַ

In ארץ ישראל*:*

מוֹרִיד הַטָּל

מְכַלְכֵּל חַיִּים בְּחֶסֶד, מְחַיֵּה מֵתִים בְּרַחֲמִים רַבִּים
סוֹמֵךְ נוֹפְלִים, וְרוֹפֵא חוֹלִים
וּמַתִּיר אֲסוּרִים
וּמְקַיֵּם אֱמוּנָתוֹ לִישֵׁנֵי עָפָר.

Who is like You, Master of might,
and who can compare to You,
O King who brings death and gives life,
and makes salvation grow?
Faithful are You to revive the dead.
Blessed are You, LORD, who revives the dead.

When saying the Amida silently, continue with "You are holy" on the next page.

KEDUSHA

During the Leader's Repetition, the following is said standing with feet together, rising on the toes at the words indicated by ▴.

Cong. then Leader: נְקַדֵּשׁ We will sanctify Your name on earth,
as they sanctify it in the highest heavens,
as is written by Your prophet,
"And they [the angels] call to one another saying: *Is. 6*

Cong. then Leader: ▴Holy, ▴holy, ▴holy is the LORD of hosts;
the whole world is filled with His glory."
Those facing them say "Blessed –"

Cong. then Leader: ▴"Blessed is the LORD's glory from His place." *Ezek. 3*
And in Your holy Writings it is written thus:

Cong. then Leader: ▴"The LORD shall reign for ever. *Ps. 146*
He is your God, Zion,
from generation to generation, Halleluya!"

Leader: From generation to generation
we will declare Your greatness,
and we will proclaim Your holiness for evermore.
Your praise, our God,
shall not leave our mouth forever,
for You, God, are a great and holy King.
Blessed are You, LORD, the holy God.

The Leader continues with "You are one" on the next page.

מִי כָמְוֹךָ, בַּעַל גְּבוּרוֹת, וּמִי דּוֹמֶה לָּךְ
מֶלֶךְ, מֵמִית וּמְחַיֶּה וּמַצְמְיחַ יְשׁוּעָה.
וְנֶאֱמָן אַתָּה לְהַחֲיוֹת מֵתִים.
בָּרוּךְ אַתָּה יהוה, מְחַיֵּה הַמֵּתִים.

When saying the עמידה *silently, continue with* אַתָּה קָדוֹשׁ *on the next page.*

קדושה

During the חזרת הש״ץ*, the following is said standing with feet together, rising on the toes at the words indicated by* ˙.

קהל *then* ש״ץ: נְקַדֵּשׁ אֶת שִׁמְךָ בָּעוֹלָם
כְּשֵׁם שֶׁמַּקְדִּישִׁים אוֹתוֹ בִּשְׁמֵי מָרוֹם
כַּכָּתוּב עַל יַד נְבִיאֶךָ:
ישעיה ו וְקָרָא זֶה אֶל־זֶה וְאָמַר

קהל *then* ש״ץ: ˙קָדוֹשׁ, ˙קָדוֹשׁ, ˙קָדוֹשׁ, יהוה צְבָאוֹת
מְלֹא כָל־הָאָרֶץ כְּבוֹדוֹ:
לְעֻמָּתָם בָּרוּךְ יֹאמֵרוּ

יחזקאל ג קהל *then* ש״ץ: ˙בָּרוּךְ כְּבוֹד־יהוה מִמְּקוֹמוֹ:
וּבְדִבְרֵי קָדְשְׁךָ כָּתוּב לֵאמֹר

תהלים קמו קהל *then* ש״ץ: ˙יִמְלֹךְ יהוה לְעוֹלָם, אֱלֹהַיִךְ צִיּוֹן לְדֹר וָדֹר, הַלְלוּיָהּ:

ש״ץ: לְדוֹר וָדוֹר נַגִּיד גָּדְלֶךָ
וּלְנֵצַח נְצָחִים קְדֻשָּׁתְךָ נַקְדִּישׁ
וְשִׁבְחֲךָ אֱלֹהֵינוּ מִפִּינוּ לֹא יָמוּשׁ לְעוֹלָם וָעֶד
כִּי אֵל מֶלֶךְ גָּדוֹל וְקָדוֹשׁ אָתָּה.
בָּרוּךְ אַתָּה יהוה הָאֵל הַקָּדוֹשׁ.

The שליח ציבור *continues with* אַתָּה אֶחָד *on the next page.*

When saying the Amida silently, continue here:

HOLINESS

אַתָּה קָדוֹשׁ You are holy
and Your name is holy,
and holy ones praise You daily, Selah!
Blessed are You,
LORD, the holy God.

HOLINESS OF THE DAY

אַתָּה You are One, Your name is One;
and who is like Your people Israel,
a nation unique on earth?
Splendor of greatness and a crown of salvation
is the day of rest and holiness
You have given Your people.
Abraham will rejoice, Isaac will sing for joy,
Jacob and his children will find rest in it –
a rest of love and generosity,
a rest of truth and faith,
a rest of peace and tranquility, calm and trust;
a complete rest in which You find favor.
May Your children recognize and know
that their rest comes from You,
and that by their rest they sanctify Your name.

אֱלֹהֵינוּ Our God and God of our ancestors,
find favor in our rest.
Make us holy through Your commandments
and grant us our share in Your Torah.
Satisfy us with Your goodness,
grant us joy in Your salvation,
and purify our hearts to serve You in truth.

When saying the עמידה silently, continue here:

קדושת השם

אַתָּה קָדוֹשׁ וְשִׁמְךָ קָדוֹשׁ
וּקְדוֹשִׁים בְּכָל יוֹם יְהַלְלְוּךָ סֶּלָה.
בָּרוּךְ אַתָּה יהוה, הָאֵל הַקָּדוֹשׁ.

קדושת היום

אַתָּה אֶחָד וְשִׁמְךָ אֶחָד
וּמִי כְּעַמְּךָ יִשְׂרָאֵל גּוֹי אֶחָד בָּאָרֶץ.
תִּפְאֶרֶת גְּדֻלָּה וַעֲטֶרֶת יְשׁוּעָה
יוֹם מְנוּחָה וּקְדֻשָּׁה לְעַמְּךָ נָתָתָּ.
אַבְרָהָם יָגֵל, יִצְחָק יְרַנֵּן, יַעֲקֹב וּבָנָיו יָנְוּחוּ בוֹ
מְנוּחַת אַהֲבָה וּנְדָבָה
מְנוּחַת אֱמֶת וֶאֱמוּנָה
מְנוּחַת שָׁלוֹם וְשַׁלְוָה וְהַשְׁקֵט וָבֶטַח
מְנוּחָה שְׁלֵמָה שֶׁאַתָּה רוֹצֶה בָּהּ.
יַכִּירוּ בָנֶיךָ וְיֵדְעוּ
כִּי מֵאִתְּךָ הִיא מְנוּחָתָם
וְעַל מְנוּחָתָם יַקְדִּישׁוּ אֶת שְׁמֶךָ.

אֱלֹהֵינוּ וֵאלֹהֵי אֲבוֹתֵינוּ
רְצֵה בִמְנוּחָתֵנוּ
קַדְּשֵׁנוּ בְּמִצְוֹתֶיךָ וְתֵן חֶלְקֵנוּ בְּתוֹרָתֶךָ
שַׂבְּעֵנוּ מִטּוּבֶךָ וְשַׂמְּחֵנוּ בִּישׁוּעָתֶךָ
וְטַהֵר לִבֵּנוּ לְעָבְדְּךָ בֶּאֱמֶת.

In love and favor, LORD our God,
grant us as our heritage Your holy Sabbaths,
so that Israel who sanctify Your name may find rest on them.
Blessed are You, LORD,
who sanctifies the Sabbath.

TEMPLE SERVICE

רְצֵה Find favor, LORD our God,
in Your people Israel and their prayer.
Restore the service to Your most holy House,
and accept in love and favor
the fire-offerings of Israel and their prayer.
May the service of Your people Israel
always find favor with You.

אֱלֹהֵינוּ Our God and God of our ancestors,
may there rise, come, reach, appear, be favored, heard,
regarded and remembered before You,
our recollection and remembrance,
as well as the remembrance of our ancestors,
and of the Messiah son of David Your servant,
and of Jerusalem Your holy city,
and of all Your people the house of Israel –
for deliverance and well-being,
grace, loving-kindness and compassion,
life and peace,
on this day of the festival of Sukkot.
On it remember us, LORD our God, for good;
recollect us for blessing, and deliver us for life.
In accord with Your promise of salvation and compassion,
spare us and be gracious to us;
have compassion on us and deliver us,
for our eyes are turned to You
because You, God, are a gracious and compassionate King.

וְהַנְחִילֵנוּ יהוה אֱלֹהֵינוּ בְּאַהֲבָה וּבְרָצוֹן שַׁבְּתוֹת קָדְשֶׁךָ
וְיָנוּחוּ בָם יִשְׂרָאֵל מְקַדְּשֵׁי שְׁמֶךָ.
בָּרוּךְ אַתָּה יהוה, מְקַדֵּשׁ הַשַּׁבָּת.

עבודה

רְצֵה יהוה אֱלֹהֵינוּ בְּעַמְּךָ יִשְׂרָאֵל, וּבִתְפִלָּתָם
וְהָשֵׁב אֶת הָעֲבוֹדָה לִדְבִיר בֵּיתֶךָ
וְאִשֵּׁי יִשְׂרָאֵל וּתְפִלָּתָם בְּאַהֲבָה תְקַבֵּל בְּרָצוֹן
וּתְהִי לְרָצוֹן תָּמִיד עֲבוֹדַת יִשְׂרָאֵל עַמֶּךָ.

אֱלֹהֵינוּ וֵאלֹהֵי אֲבוֹתֵינוּ
יַעֲלֶה וְיָבוֹא וְיַגִּיעַ, וְיֵרָאֶה וְיֵרָצֶה וְיִשָּׁמַע
וְיִפָּקֵד וְיִזָּכֵר זִכְרוֹנֵנוּ וּפִקְדּוֹנֵנוּ
וְזִכְרוֹן אֲבוֹתֵינוּ
וְזִכְרוֹן מָשִׁיחַ בֶּן דָּוִד עַבְדֶּךָ
וְזִכְרוֹן יְרוּשָׁלַיִם עִיר קָדְשֶׁךָ
וְזִכְרוֹן כָּל עַמְּךָ בֵּית יִשְׂרָאֵל, לְפָנֶיךָ
לִפְלֵיטָה, לְטוֹבָה, לְחֵן וּלְחֶסֶד וּלְרַחֲמִים
לְחַיִּים וּלְשָׁלוֹם בְּיוֹם חַג הַסֻּכּוֹת הַזֶּה.
זָכְרֵנוּ יהוה אֱלֹהֵינוּ בּוֹ לְטוֹבָה
וּפָקְדֵנוּ בוֹ לִבְרָכָה
וְהוֹשִׁיעֵנוּ בוֹ לְחַיִּים.
וּבִדְבַר יְשׁוּעָה וְרַחֲמִים
חוּס וְחָנֵּנוּ, וְרַחֵם עָלֵינוּ וְהוֹשִׁיעֵנוּ
כִּי אֵלֶיךָ עֵינֵינוּ, כִּי אֵל מֶלֶךְ חַנּוּן וְרַחוּם אָתָּה.

וְתֶחֱזֶינָה And may our eyes witness
Your return to Zion in compassion.
Blessed are You, LORD, who restores His Presence to Zion.

THANKSGIVING

Bow at the first nine words.

▾מוֹדִים We give thanks to You,
for You are the LORD our God
and God of our ancestors
for ever and all time.
You are the Rock of our lives,
Shield of our salvation
from generation to generation.
We will thank You and
declare Your praise for our lives,
which are entrusted into Your hand;
for our souls,
which are placed in Your charge;
for Your miracles
which are with us every day;
and for Your wonders and favors
at all times, evening,
morning and midday.
You are good –
for Your compassion never fails.
You are compassionate –
for Your loving-kindnesses never cease.
We have always placed our hope in You.

During the Leader's Repetition, the congregation says quietly:

▾מוֹדִים We give thanks to You,
for You are the LORD our God
and God of our ancestors,
God of all flesh,
who formed us
and formed the universe.
Blessings and thanks
are due to Your great
and holy name for giving us
life and sustaining us.
May You continue
to give us life
and sustain us;
and may You gather our
exiles to Your holy courts,
to keep Your decrees,
do Your will and serve You
with a perfect heart,
for it is for us
to give You thanks.
Blessed be God to whom
thanksgiving is due.

וְעַל כֻּלָּם For all these things
may Your name be blessed and exalted, our King,
continually, for ever and all time.
Let all that lives thank You, Selah! and praise Your name in truth,
God, our Savior and Help, Selah!
▾Blessed are You, LORD, whose name is "the Good"
and to whom thanks are due.

וְתֶחֱזֶינָה עֵינֵינוּ בְּשׁוּבְךָ לְצִיּוֹן בְּרַחֲמִים.
בָּרוּךְ אַתָּה יהוה, הַמַּחֲזִיר שְׁכִינָתוֹ לְצִיּוֹן.

הודאה

Bow at the first five words.

ˈמוֹדִים אֲנַחְנוּ לָךְ
שָׁאַתָּה הוּא יהוה אֱלֹהֵינוּ
וֵאלֹהֵי אֲבוֹתֵינוּ לְעוֹלָם וָעֶד.
צוּר חַיֵּינוּ, מָגֵן יִשְׁעֵנוּ
אַתָּה הוּא לְדוֹר וָדוֹר.
נוֹדֶה לְּךָ וּנְסַפֵּר תְּהִלָּתֶךָ
עַל חַיֵּינוּ הַמְּסוּרִים בְּיָדֶךָ
וְעַל נִשְׁמוֹתֵינוּ הַפְּקוּדוֹת לָךְ
וְעַל נִסֶּיךָ שֶׁבְּכָל יוֹם עִמָּנוּ
וְעַל נִפְלְאוֹתֶיךָ וְטוֹבוֹתֶיךָ
שֶׁבְּכָל עֵת
עֶרֶב וָבֹקֶר וְצָהֳרָיִם.
הַטּוֹב, כִּי לֹא כָלוּ רַחֲמֶיךָ
וְהַמְרַחֵם, כִּי לֹא תַמּוּ חֲסָדֶיךָ
מֵעוֹלָם קִוִּינוּ לָךְ.

During the חזרת הש״ץ, *the* קהל *says quietly:*

ˈמוֹדִים אֲנַחְנוּ לָךְ
שָׁאַתָּה הוּא יהוה אֱלֹהֵינוּ
וֵאלֹהֵי אֲבוֹתֵינוּ
אֱלֹהֵי כָל בָּשָׂר
יוֹצְרֵנוּ, יוֹצֵר בְּרֵאשִׁית.
בְּרָכוֹת וְהוֹדָאוֹת
לְשִׁמְךָ הַגָּדוֹל וְהַקָּדוֹשׁ
עַל שֶׁהֶחֱיִיתָנוּ וְקִיַּמְתָּנוּ.
כֵּן תְּחַיֵּנוּ וּתְקַיְּמֵנוּ
וְתֶאֱסֹף גָּלֻיּוֹתֵינוּ
לְחַצְרוֹת קָדְשֶׁךָ
לִשְׁמֹר חֻקֶּיךָ
וְלַעֲשׂוֹת רְצוֹנֶךָ
וּלְעָבְדְּךָ בְּלֵבָב שָׁלֵם
עַל שֶׁאֲנַחְנוּ מוֹדִים לָךְ.
בָּרוּךְ אֵל הַהוֹדָאוֹת.

וְעַל כֻּלָּם יִתְבָּרַךְ וְיִתְרוֹמַם שִׁמְךָ מַלְכֵּנוּ תָּמִיד לְעוֹלָם וָעֶד.
וְכֹל הַחַיִּים יוֹדוּךָ סֶּלָה, וִיהַלְלוּ אֶת שִׁמְךָ בֶּאֱמֶת
הָאֵל יְשׁוּעָתֵנוּ וְעֶזְרָתֵנוּ סֶלָה.
ˈבָּרוּךְ אַתָּה יהוה, הַטּוֹב שִׁמְךָ וּלְךָ נָאֶה לְהוֹדוֹת.

PEACE

שָׁלוֹם רָב Grant great peace to Your people Israel for ever, for You are the sovereign LORD of all peace; and may it be good in Your eyes to bless Your people Israel at every time, at every hour, with Your peace.

In Israel:

שִׂים שָׁלוֹם Grant peace, goodness and blessing,
grace, loving-kindness and compassion
to us and all Israel Your people.
Bless us, our Father, all as one,
with the light of Your face,
for by the light of Your face
You have given us, LORD our God,
the Torah of life and love of kindness,
righteousness, blessing, compassion,
life and peace.
May it be good in Your eyes
to bless Your people Israel
at every time, in every hour,
with Your peace.

Blessed are You, LORD, who blesses His people Israel with peace.

The following verse concludes the Leader's Repetition of the Amida. Some also say it here as part of the silent Amida.

May the words of my mouth and the meditation of my heart *Ps. 19*
find favor before You, LORD, my Rock and Redeemer.

אֱלֹהַי My God, *Berakhot 17a*
guard my tongue from evil and my lips from deceitful speech.
To those who curse me, let my soul be silent;
may my soul be to all like the dust.
Open my heart to Your Torah
and let my soul pursue Your commandments.
As for all who plan evil against me,
swiftly thwart their counsel and frustrate their plans.
Act for the sake of Your name; act for the sake of Your right hand;
act for the sake of Your holiness; act for the sake of Your Torah.
That Your beloved ones may be delivered, *Ps. 60*
save with Your right hand and answer me.
May the words of my mouth and the meditation of my heart *Ps. 19*
find favor before You, LORD, my Rock and Redeemer.

Bow, take three steps back, then bow, first left, then right, then center, while saying:

May He who makes peace in His high places,
make peace for us and all Israel – and say: Amen.

ברכת שלום

שָׁלוֹם רָב עַל יִשְׂרָאֵל עַמְּךָ
תָּשִׂים לְעוֹלָם
כִּי אַתָּה הוּא
מֶלֶךְ אָדוֹן לְכָל הַשָּׁלוֹם.
וְטוֹב בְּעֵינֶיךָ
לְבָרֵךְ אֶת עַמְּךָ יִשְׂרָאֵל
בְּכָל עֵת וּבְכָל שָׁעָה
בִּשְׁלוֹמֶךָ.

In ארץ ישראל:

שִׂים שָׁלוֹם טוֹבָה וּבְרָכָה
חֵן וָחֶסֶד וְרַחֲמִים
עָלֵינוּ וְעַל כָּל יִשְׂרָאֵל עַמֶּךָ.
בָּרְכֵנוּ אָבִינוּ כֻּלָּנוּ כְּאֶחָד בְּאוֹר פָּנֶיךָ
כִּי בְאוֹר פָּנֶיךָ נָתַתָּ לָּנוּ יהוה אֱלֹהֵינוּ
תּוֹרַת חַיִּים וְאַהֲבַת חֶסֶד
וּצְדָקָה וּבְרָכָה וְרַחֲמִים וְחַיִּים וְשָׁלוֹם.
וְטוֹב בְּעֵינֶיךָ לְבָרֵךְ אֶת עַמְּךָ יִשְׂרָאֵל
בְּכָל עֵת וּבְכָל שָׁעָה בִּשְׁלוֹמֶךָ.

בָּרוּךְ אַתָּה יהוה, הַמְבָרֵךְ אֶת עַמּוֹ יִשְׂרָאֵל בַּשָּׁלוֹם.

The following verse concludes the חזרת הש״ץ.
Some also say it here as part of the silent עמידה.

יִהְיוּ לְרָצוֹן אִמְרֵי־פִי וְהֶגְיוֹן לִבִּי לְפָנֶיךָ, יהוה צוּרִי וְגֹאֲלִי: תהלים יט

אֱלֹהַי ברכות יז.
נְצֹר לְשׁוֹנִי מֵרָע וּשְׂפָתַי מִדַּבֵּר מִרְמָה
וְלִמְקַלְלַי נַפְשִׁי תִדֹּם, וְנַפְשִׁי כֶּעָפָר לַכֹּל תִּהְיֶה.
פְּתַח לִבִּי בְּתוֹרָתֶךָ, וּבְמִצְוֹתֶיךָ תִּרְדֹּף נַפְשִׁי.
וְכָל הַחוֹשְׁבִים עָלַי רָעָה
מְהֵרָה הָפֵר עֲצָתָם וְקַלְקֵל מַחֲשַׁבְתָּם.
עֲשֵׂה לְמַעַן שְׁמֶךָ, עֲשֵׂה לְמַעַן יְמִינֶךָ
עֲשֵׂה לְמַעַן קְדֻשָּׁתֶךָ, עֲשֵׂה לְמַעַן תּוֹרָתֶךָ.
לְמַעַן יֵחָלְצוּן יְדִידֶיךָ, הוֹשִׁיעָה יְמִינְךָ וַעֲנֵנִי: תהלים ס
יִהְיוּ לְרָצוֹן אִמְרֵי־פִי וְהֶגְיוֹן לִבִּי לְפָנֶיךָ, יהוה צוּרִי וְגֹאֲלִי: תהלים יט

Bow, take three steps back, then bow, first left, then right, then center, while saying:

עֹשֶׂה שָׁלוֹם בִּמְרוֹמָיו
הוּא יַעֲשֶׂה שָׁלוֹם עָלֵינוּ וְעַל כָּל יִשְׂרָאֵל, וְאִמְרוּ אָמֵן.

יְהִי רָצוֹן May it be Your will, LORD our God and God of our ancestors,
that the Temple be rebuilt speedily in our days, and grant us a share in Your Torah.
And there we will serve You with reverence,
as in the days of old and as in former years.
Then the offering of Judah and Jerusalem *Mal. 3*
will be pleasing to the LORD as in the days of old and as in former years.

FULL KADDISH

Some have the custom to include additional responses in Full Kaddish. They can be found in the version on page 1464.

Leader: יִתְגַּדַּל Magnified and sanctified may His great name be,
in the world He created by His will.
May He establish His kingdom
in your lifetime and in your days,
and in the lifetime of all the house of Israel,
swiftly and soon –
and say: Amen.

All: May His great name be blessed for ever and all time.

Leader: Blessed and praised, glorified and exalted,
raised and honored, uplifted and lauded be
the name of the Holy One,
blessed be He, beyond any blessing,
song, praise and consolation
uttered in the world –
and say: Amen.

May the prayers and pleas of all Israel
be accepted by their Father in heaven –
and say: Amen.

May there be great peace from heaven,
and life for us and all Israel –
and say: Amen.

Bow, take three steps back, as if taking leave of the Divine Presence, then bow, first left, then right, then center, while saying:

May He who makes peace in His high places,
make peace for us and all Israel –
and say: Amen.

יְהִי רָצוֹן מִלְּפָנֶיךָ יהוה אֱלֹהֵינוּ וֵאלֹהֵי אֲבוֹתֵינוּ
שֶׁיִּבָּנֶה בֵּית הַמִּקְדָּשׁ בִּמְהֵרָה בְיָמֵינוּ, וְתֵן חֶלְקֵנוּ בְּתוֹרָתֶךָ
וְשָׁם נַעֲבָדְךָ בְּיִרְאָה כִּימֵי עוֹלָם וּכְשָׁנִים קַדְמֹנִיּוֹת.
וְעָרְבָה לַיהוה מִנְחַת יְהוּדָה וִירוּשָׁלָםִ כִּימֵי עוֹלָם וּכְשָׁנִים קַדְמֹנִיּוֹת: מלאכי ג

קדיש שלם

Some have the custom to include additional responses in קדיש שלם.
They can be found in the version on page 1465.

ש״ץ: יִתְגַּדַּל וְיִתְקַדַּשׁ שְׁמֵהּ רַבָּא (קהל: אָמֵן)
בְּעָלְמָא דִּי בְרָא כִרְעוּתֵהּ
וְיַמְלִיךְ מַלְכוּתֵהּ
בְּחַיֵּיכוֹן וּבְיוֹמֵיכוֹן וּבְחַיֵּי דְכָל בֵּית יִשְׂרָאֵל
בַּעֲגָלָא וּבִזְמַן קָרִיב, וְאִמְרוּ אָמֵן. (קהל: אָמֵן)

קהל וש״ץ: יְהֵא שְׁמֵהּ רַבָּא מְבָרַךְ לְעָלַם וּלְעָלְמֵי עָלְמַיָּא.

ש״ץ: יִתְבָּרַךְ וְיִשְׁתַּבַּח וְיִתְפָּאַר
וְיִתְרוֹמַם וְיִתְנַשֵּׂא וְיִתְהַדָּר וְיִתְעַלֶּה וְיִתְהַלָּל
שְׁמֵהּ דְּקֻדְשָׁא בְּרִיךְ הוּא (קהל: בְּרִיךְ הוּא)
לְעֵלָּא מִן כָּל בִּרְכָתָא וְשִׁירָתָא, תֻּשְׁבְּחָתָא וְנֶחֱמָתָא
דַּאֲמִירָן בְּעָלְמָא, וְאִמְרוּ אָמֵן. (קהל: אָמֵן)

תִּתְקַבַּל צְלוֹתְהוֹן וּבָעוּתְהוֹן דְּכָל יִשְׂרָאֵל
קֳדָם אֲבוּהוֹן דִּי בִשְׁמַיָּא, וְאִמְרוּ אָמֵן. (קהל: אָמֵן)

יְהֵא שְׁלָמָא רַבָּא מִן שְׁמַיָּא
וְחַיִּים, עָלֵינוּ וְעַל כָּל יִשְׂרָאֵל, וְאִמְרוּ אָמֵן. (קהל: אָמֵן)

Bow, take three steps back, as if taking leave of the Divine Presence, then bow, first left, then right, then center, while saying:

עֹשֶׂה שָׁלוֹם בִּמְרוֹמָיו, הוּא יַעֲשֶׂה שָׁלוֹם
עָלֵינוּ וְעַל כָּל יִשְׂרָאֵל, וְאִמְרוּ אָמֵן. (קהל: אָמֵן)

Stand while saying Aleinu. Bow at ▾.

עָלֵינוּ It is our duty to praise the Master of all,
and ascribe greatness to the Author of creation,
who has not made us like the nations of the lands
nor placed us like the families of the earth;
who has not made our portion like theirs,
nor our destiny like all their multitudes.
(For they worship vanity and emptiness,
and pray to a god who cannot save.)
▾But we bow in worship
and thank the Supreme King of kings, the Holy One, blessed be He,
who extends the heavens and establishes the earth,
whose throne of glory is in the heavens above,
and whose power's Presence is in the highest of heights.
He is our God; there is no other.
Truly He is our King, there is none else, as it is written in His Torah:
"You shall know and take to heart this day that the Lord is God, *Deut. 4*
in heaven above and on earth below.
There is no other."

Therefore, we place our hope in You, Lord our God,
that we may soon see the glory of Your power,
when You will remove abominations from the earth,
and idols will be utterly destroyed,
when the world will be perfected
under the sovereignty of the Almighty,
when all humanity will call on Your name,
to turn all the earth's wicked toward You.
All the world's inhabitants will realize and know
that to You every knee must bow
and every tongue swear loyalty.
Before You, Lord our God, they will kneel and bow down
and give honor to Your glorious name.
They will all accept the yoke of Your kingdom,
and You will reign over them soon and for ever.
For the kingdom is Yours, and to all eternity You will reign in glory,
as it is written in Your Torah:
"The Lord will reign for ever and ever." *Ex. 15*

Stand while saying עָלֵינוּ*. Bow at* ˚.

עָלֵינוּ לְשַׁבֵּחַ לַאֲדוֹן הַכֹּל, לָתֵת גְּדֻלָּה לְיוֹצֵר בְּרֵאשִׁית
שֶׁלֹּא עָשָׂנוּ כְּגוֹיֵי הָאֲרָצוֹת, וְלֹא שָׂמָנוּ כְּמִשְׁפְּחוֹת הָאֲדָמָה
שֶׁלֹּא שָׂם חֶלְקֵנוּ כָּהֶם וְגוֹרָלֵנוּ כְּכָל הֲמוֹנָם.
(שֶׁהֵם מִשְׁתַּחֲוִים לְהֶבֶל וָרִיק וּמִתְפַּלְלִים אֶל אֵל לֹא יוֹשִׁיעַ.)
˚וַאֲנַחְנוּ כּוֹרְעִים וּמִשְׁתַּחֲוִים וּמוֹדִים
לִפְנֵי מֶלֶךְ מַלְכֵי הַמְּלָכִים, הַקָּדוֹשׁ בָּרוּךְ הוּא
שֶׁהוּא נוֹטֶה שָׁמַיִם וְיוֹסֵד אָרֶץ
וּמוֹשַׁב יְקָרוֹ בַּשָּׁמַיִם מִמַּעַל, וּשְׁכִינַת עֻזּוֹ בְּגָבְהֵי מְרוֹמִים.
הוּא אֱלֹהֵינוּ, אֵין עוֹד.
אֱמֶת מַלְכֵּנוּ, אֶפֶס זוּלָתוֹ, כַּכָּתוּב בְּתוֹרָתוֹ
דברים ד וְיָדַעְתָּ הַיּוֹם וַהֲשֵׁבֹתָ אֶל־לְבָבֶךָ
כִּי יהוה הוּא הָאֱלֹהִים בַּשָּׁמַיִם מִמַּעַל וְעַל־הָאָרֶץ מִתָּחַת
אֵין עוֹד:

עַל כֵּן נְקַוֶּה לְּךָ יהוה אֱלֹהֵינוּ, לִרְאוֹת מְהֵרָה בְּתִפְאֶרֶת עֻזֶּךָ
לְהַעֲבִיר גִּלּוּלִים מִן הָאָרֶץ, וְהָאֱלִילִים כָּרוֹת יִכָּרֵתוּן
לְתַקֵּן עוֹלָם בְּמַלְכוּת שַׁדַּי.
וְכָל בְּנֵי בָשָׂר יִקְרְאוּ בִשְׁמֶךָ לְהַפְנוֹת אֵלֶיךָ כָּל רִשְׁעֵי אָרֶץ.
יַכִּירוּ וְיֵדְעוּ כָּל יוֹשְׁבֵי תֵבֵל
כִּי לְךָ תִּכְרַע כָּל בֶּרֶךְ, תִּשָּׁבַע כָּל לָשׁוֹן.
לְפָנֶיךָ יהוה אֱלֹהֵינוּ יִכְרְעוּ וְיִפֹּלוּ
וְלִכְבוֹד שִׁמְךָ יְקָר יִתֵּנוּ
וִיקַבְּלוּ כֻלָּם אֶת עֹל מַלְכוּתֶךָ
וְתִמְלֹךְ עֲלֵיהֶם מְהֵרָה לְעוֹלָם וָעֶד.
כִּי הַמַּלְכוּת שֶׁלְּךָ הִיא וּלְעוֹלְמֵי עַד תִּמְלֹךְ בְּכָבוֹד
שמות טו כַּכָּתוּב בְּתוֹרָתֶךָ, יהוה יִמְלֹךְ לְעֹלָם וָעֶד:

▸ And it is said: "Then the LORD shall be King over all the earth; on that day the LORD shall be One and His name One." *Zech. 14*

Some add:

Have no fear of sudden terror or of the ruin when it overtakes the wicked. *Prov. 3*
Devise your strategy, but it will be thwarted; *Is. 8*
propose your plan, but it will not stand, for God is with us.
When you grow old, I will still be the same. *Is. 46*
When your hair turns gray, I will still carry you.
I made you, I will bear you, I will carry you, and I will rescue you.

MOURNER'S KADDISH

The following prayer, said by mourners, requires the presence of a minyan. A transliteration can be found on page 1467.

Mourner: יִתְגַּדַּל Magnified and sanctified may His great name be,
in the world He created by His will.
May He establish His kingdom in your lifetime
and in your days,
and in the lifetime of all the house of Israel,
swiftly and soon –
and say: Amen.

All: May His great name be blessed for ever and all time.

Mourner: Blessed and praised, glorified and exalted,
raised and honored, uplifted and lauded
be the name of the Holy One,
blessed be He,
beyond any blessing,
song, praise and consolation
uttered in the world –
and say: Amen.

May there be great peace from heaven,
and life for us and all Israel – and say: Amen.

Bow, take three steps back, as if taking leave of the Divine Presence, then bow, first left, then right, then center, while saying:

May He who makes peace in His high places,
make peace for us and all Israel –
and say: Amen.

◂ וְנֶאֱמַר, וְהָיָה יהוה לְמֶלֶךְ עַל־כָּל־הָאָרֶץ זכריה יד
בַּיּוֹם הַהוּא יִהְיֶה יהוה אֶחָד וּשְׁמוֹ אֶחָד:

Some add:

אַל־תִּירָא מִפַּחַד פִּתְאֹם וּמִשֹּׁאַת רְשָׁעִים כִּי תָבֹא: משלי ג
עֻצוּ עֵצָה וְתֻפָר, דַּבְּרוּ דָבָר וְלֹא יָקוּם, כִּי עִמָּנוּ אֵל: ישעיה ח
וְעַד־זִקְנָה אֲנִי הוּא, וְעַד־שֵׂיבָה אֲנִי אֶסְבֹּל, אֲנִי עָשִׂיתִי וַאֲנִי אֶשָּׂא וַאֲנִי אֶסְבֹּל וַאֲמַלֵּט: ישעיה מו

קדיש יתום

The following prayer, said by mourners, requires the presence of a מנין.
A transliteration can be found on page 1467.

אבל: יִתְגַּדַּל וְיִתְקַדַּשׁ שְׁמֵהּ רַבָּא (קהל: אָמֵן)
בְּעָלְמָא דִּי בְרָא כִרְעוּתֵהּ
וְיַמְלִיךְ מַלְכוּתֵהּ
בְּחַיֵּיכוֹן וּבְיוֹמֵיכוֹן וּבְחַיֵּי דְכָל בֵּית יִשְׂרָאֵל
בַּעֲגָלָא וּבִזְמַן קָרִיב, וְאִמְרוּ אָמֵן. (קהל: אָמֵן)

קהל ואבל: יְהֵא שְׁמֵהּ רַבָּא מְבָרַךְ לְעָלַם וּלְעָלְמֵי עָלְמַיָּא.

אבל: יִתְבָּרַךְ וְיִשְׁתַּבַּח וְיִתְפָּאַר
וְיִתְרוֹמַם וְיִתְנַשֵּׂא וְיִתְהַדָּר וְיִתְעַלֶּה וְיִתְהַלָּל
שְׁמֵהּ דְּקֻדְשָׁא בְּרִיךְ הוּא (קהל: בְּרִיךְ הוּא)
לְעֵלָּא מִן כָּל בִּרְכָתָא וְשִׁירָתָא, תֻּשְׁבְּחָתָא וְנֶחֱמָתָא
דַּאֲמִירָן בְּעָלְמָא, וְאִמְרוּ אָמֵן. (קהל: אָמֵן)

יְהֵא שְׁלָמָא רַבָּא מִן שְׁמַיָּא
וְחַיִּים, עָלֵינוּ וְעַל כָּל יִשְׂרָאֵל, וְאִמְרוּ אָמֵן. (קהל: אָמֵן)

Bow, take three steps back, as if taking leave of the Divine Presence, then bow, first left, then right, then center, while saying:

עֹשֶׂה שָׁלוֹם בִּמְרוֹמָיו
הוּא יַעֲשֶׂה שָׁלוֹם
עָלֵינוּ וְעַל כָּל יִשְׂרָאֵל, וְאִמְרוּ אָמֵן. (קהל: אָמֵן)

Hoshana Raba

REMOVING THE TORAH FROM THE ARK

אֵין־כָּמְוֹךָ There is none like You among the heavenly powers, Ps. 86
LORD, and there are no works like Yours.
Your kingdom is an eternal kingdom, Ps. 145
and Your dominion is for all generations.

The LORD is King, the LORD was King,
the LORD shall be King for ever and all time.
The LORD will give strength to His people; Ps. 29
the LORD will bless His people with peace.

Father of compassion,
favor Zion with Your goodness; Ps. 51
rebuild the walls of Jerusalem.
For we trust in You alone, King, God, high and exalted,
Master of worlds.

The Ark is opened and the congregation stands. All say:

וַיְהִי בִּנְסֹעַ Whenever the Ark set out, Moses would say, Num. 10
"Arise, LORD, and may Your enemies be scattered.
May those who hate You flee before You."
For the Torah shall come forth from Zion, Is. 2
and the word of the LORD from Jerusalem.
Blessed is He who in His Holiness
gave the Torah to His people Israel.

---

as King and Judge, deciding the fate of the world, the nation, and individuals for the coming year. This led to the insight of the *Zohar* (*Tzav* 3:31b), that the judgment that had been written on Rosh HaShana and sealed on Yom Kippur was not finalized until Hoshana Raba. Some said that just as Abraham belonged to the twenty-first generation of humanity beginning with Adam, so the twenty-first day of the new year was reserved, in his merit, as a day of grace for his descendants. The day became associated with the idea that this is the last moment when an appeal can be launched, and became, in its

הושענא רבה

הוצאת ספר תורה

אֵין־כָּמְוֹךָ בָאֱלֹהִים, אֲדֹנָי, וְאֵין כְּמַעֲשֶׂיךָ: תהלים פו
מַלְכוּתְךָ מַלְכוּת כָּל־עֹלָמִים, וּמֶמְשַׁלְתְּךָ בְּכָל־דּוֹר וָדֹר: תהלים קמה

יהוה מֶלֶךְ, יהוה מָלָךְ, יהוה יִמְלֹךְ לְעֹלָם וָעֶד.
יהוה עֹז לְעַמּוֹ יִתֵּן, יהוה יְבָרֵךְ אֶת־עַמּוֹ בַשָּׁלוֹם: תהלים כט

אַב הָרַחֲמִים
הֵיטִיבָה בִרְצוֹנְךָ אֶת־צִיּוֹן תִּבְנֶה חוֹמוֹת יְרוּשָׁלָםִ: תהלים נא
כִּי בְךָ לְבַד בָּטָחְנוּ, מֶלֶךְ אֵל רָם וְנִשָּׂא, אֲדוֹן עוֹלָמִים.

The ארון קודש *is opened and the* קהל *stands. All say:*

וַיְהִי בִּנְסֹעַ הָאָרֹן וַיֹּאמֶר מֹשֶׁה במדבר י
קוּמָה יהוה וְיָפֻצוּ אֹיְבֶיךָ וְיָנֻסוּ מְשַׂנְאֶיךָ מִפָּנֶיךָ:
כִּי מִצִּיּוֹן תֵּצֵא תוֹרָה וּדְבַר־יהוה מִירוּשָׁלָםִ: ישעיה ב
בָּרוּךְ שֶׁנָּתַן תּוֹרָה לְעַמּוֹ יִשְׂרָאֵל בִּקְדֻשָּׁתוֹ.

HOSHANA RABA

Hoshana Raba, the seventh day of Sukkot, brings to a culmination seven days that were a time of unique celebration in Jerusalem when the Temple stood. There were larger crowds that at any other time of the year, and the festivities associated with the water drawing bathed night-time Jerusalem with light and the sound of joyous song. On each of the previous days there had been a single procession around the altar, but on the seventh there were seven circuits, accompanied by many *Hoshanot*, litanies to which the crowds would respond with the word *Hoshana* – hence the name *Hoshana Raba*, "the Great Hoshana."

Not only was this the culmination of Sukkot, the festival of joy, but it also drew to a close the period that had begun on Rosh HaShana, reaching a climax on Yom Kippur: the days of judgment on which God metaphorically sits

The following (The Thirteen Attributes of Mercy) is said three times:

יהוה The LORD, the LORD, Ex. 34
compassionate and gracious God, slow to anger,
abounding in loving-kindness and truth,
extending loving-kindness to a thousand generations,
forgiving iniquity, rebellion and sin,
and absolving [the guilty who repent].

Master of the Universe, fulfill my requests for good. Satisfy my desire, grant my request, and pardon me for all my iniquities and all iniquities of the members of my household, with the pardon of loving-kindness and compassion. Purify us from our sins, our iniquities and our transgressions; remember us with a memory of favorable deeds before You and be mindful of us in salvation and compassion. Remember us for a good life, for peace, for livelihood and sustenance, for bread to eat and clothes to wear, for wealth, honor and length of days dedicated to Your Torah and its commandments. Grant us discernment and understanding that we may understand and discern its deep secrets. Send healing for all our pain, and bless all the work of our hands. Ordain for us decrees of good, salvation and consolation, and nullify all hard and harsh decrees against us. And may the hearts of the government, its advisers and ministers / *In Israel:* And may the hearts of our ministers and their advisers, / be favorable toward us. Amen. May this be Your will.

יִהְיוּ May the words of my mouth and the meditation of my heart find favor before You, LORD, my Rock and Redeemer. Ps. 19

Say the following verse three times:

וַאֲנִי As for me, may my prayer come to You, LORD, Ps. 69
at a time of favor. O God, in Your great love,
answer me with Your faithful salvation.

Yom Tov, since the day is like a festival in its own right, but also the Psalm of Thanksgiving (Ps. 100), normally not said on the Sabbath and festivals. The reason is that the Thanksgiving Offering was a private sacrifice offered by

The following (י״ג מידות הרחמים) *is said three times:*

שמות לד
יְהוָה, יְהוָה, אֵל רַחוּם וְחַנּוּן, אֶרֶךְ אַפַּיִם וְרַב־חֶסֶד וֶאֱמֶת: נֹצֵר חֶסֶד לָאֲלָפִים, נֹשֵׂא עָוֹן וָפֶשַׁע וְחַטָּאָה, וְנַקֵּה:

רִבּוֹנוֹ שֶׁל עוֹלָם, מַלֵּא מִשְׁאֲלוֹתַי לְטוֹבָה, וְהָפֵק רְצוֹנִי וְתֵן שְׁאֵלָתִי, וּמְחֹל לִי עַל כָּל עֲוֹנוֹתַי וְעַל כָּל עֲוֹנוֹת אַנְשֵׁי בֵיתִי, מְחִילָה בְּחֶסֶד מְחִילָה בְּרַחֲמִים, וְטַהֲרֵנוּ מֵחֲטָאֵינוּ וּמֵעֲוֹנוֹתֵינוּ וּמִפְּשָׁעֵינוּ, וְזָכְרֵנוּ בְּזִכָּרוֹן טוֹב לְפָנֶיךָ, וּפָקְדֵנוּ בִּפְקֻדַּת יְשׁוּעָה וְרַחֲמִים. וְזָכְרֵנוּ לְחַיִּים טוֹבִים וּלְשָׁלוֹם, וּפַרְנָסָה וְכַלְכָּלָה, וְלֶחֶם לֶאֱכֹל וּבֶגֶד לִלְבֹּשׁ, וְעֹשֶׁר וְכָבוֹד, וְאֹרֶךְ יָמִים לַהֲגוֹת בְּתוֹרָתֶךָ וּלְקַיֵּם מִצְוֹתֶיהָ, וְשֵׂכֶל וּבִינָה לְהָבִין וּלְהַשְׂכִּיל עִמְקֵי סוֹדוֹתֶיהָ. וְהָפֵק רְפוּאָה לְכָל מַכְאוֹבֵינוּ, וּבָרֵךְ כָּל מַעֲשֵׂה יָדֵינוּ, וּגְזֹר עָלֵינוּ גְּזֵרוֹת טוֹבוֹת יְשׁוּעוֹת וְנֶחָמוֹת, וּבַטֵּל מֵעָלֵינוּ כָּל גְּזֵרוֹת קָשׁוֹת וְרָעוֹת, וְתֵן בְּלֵב הַמַּלְכוּת וְיוֹעֲצֶיהָ וְשָׂרֶיהָ / בארץ ישראל: וְתֵן בְּלֵב שָׂרֵינוּ וְיוֹעֲצֵיהֶם/ עָלֵינוּ לְטוֹבָה. אָמֵן וְכֵן יְהִי רָצוֹן.

תהלים יט
יִהְיוּ לְרָצוֹן אִמְרֵי־פִי וְהֶגְיוֹן לִבִּי לְפָנֶיךָ, יְהוָה צוּרִי וְגֹאֲלִי:

Say the following verse three times:

תהלים סט
וַאֲנִי תְפִלָּתִי־לְךָ יְהוָה, עֵת רָצוֹן, אֱלֹהִים בְּרָב־חַסְדֶּךָ עֲנֵנִי בֶּאֱמֶת יִשְׁעֶךָ:

---

own right, a kind of minor Yom Kippur. Thus developed the custom for the leader of prayer (in some places, the congregation also) to wear a *Kittel*, as on the days of awe, and to use some of the melodies of those days. Some have the custom of wishing others a *Pitka tava* (in Yiddish, *Gut kvitel*), i.e., a good note, a favorable verdict.

Some have the custom, mentioned in the *Zohar*, of staying awake the whole night of Hoshana Raba, in study and prayer. A special set of readings was ordained for this night, known as the *Tikun Leil Hoshana Raba*, including the book of Deuteronomy (recited by the king on Sukkot after a sabbatical year) and the whole of the book of Psalms. Unusually, on Hoshana Raba in the morning service we say not only the extra psalms said on Shabbat and

בְּרִיךְ Blessed is the name of the Master of the Universe. Blessed is Your crown and Your place. May Your favor always be with Your people Israel. Show Your people the salvation of Your right hand in Your Temple. Grant us the gift of Your good light, and accept our prayers in mercy. May it be Your will to prolong our life in goodness. May I be counted among the righteous, so that You will have compassion on me and protect me and all that is mine and all that is Your people Israel's. You feed all; You sustain all; You rule over all; You rule over kings, for sovereignty is Yours. I am a servant of the Holy One, blessed be He, before whom and before whose glorious Torah I bow at all times. Not in man do I trust, nor on any angel do I rely, but on the God of heaven who is the God of truth, whose Torah is truth, whose prophets speak truth, and who abounds in acts of love and truth. ▸ In Him I trust, and to His holy and glorious name I offer praises. May it be Your will to open my heart to the Torah, and to fulfill the wishes of my heart and of the hearts of all Your people Israel for good, for life, and for peace. *Zohar, Vayak-hel*

Two Torah scrolls are removed from the Ark. The Leader takes one in his right arm and, followed by the congregation, says:

Listen, Israel: the LORD is our God, the LORD is One. *Deut. 6*

Leader then congregation:

One is our God; great is our Master;
holy and awesome is His name.

The Leader turns to face the Ark, bows and says:

Magnify the LORD with me,
and let us exalt His name together. *Ps. 34*

The Ark is closed. The Leader carries the Torah scroll to the bima and the congregation says:

לְךָ Yours, LORD, are the greatness and the power, the glory and the majesty and splendor, for everything in heaven and earth is Yours. Yours, LORD, is the kingdom; You are exalted as Head over all. *1 Chr. 29*

After the destruction of the Temple, when Rabban Yoḥanan ben Zakkai instituted that, in memory of the Temple, there should be circuits with the lulav and etrog throughout the seven days of the festival (with the exception of Shabbat), another rite that was performed daily in the Temple was

זוהר ויקהל בְּרִיךְ שְׁמֵהּ דְּמָרֵא עָלְמָא, בְּרִיךְ כִּתְרָךְ וְאַתְרָךְ. יְהֵא רְעוּתָךְ עִם עַמָּךְ יִשְׂרָאֵל לְעָלַם, וּפֻרְקַן יְמִינָךְ אַחֲזֵי לְעַמָּךְ בְּבֵית מַקְדְּשָׁךְ, וּלְאַמְטוּיֵי לַנָא מִטּוּב נְהוֹרָךְ, וּלְקַבֵּל צְלוֹתַנָא בְּרַחֲמִין. יְהֵא רַעֲוָא קֳדָמָךְ דְּתוֹרִיךְ לַן חַיִּין בְּטִיבוּ, וְלֶהֱוֵי אֲנָא פְקִידָא בְּגוֹ צַדִּיקַיָּא, לְמִרְחַם עֲלַי וּלְמִנְטַר יָתִי וְיַת כָּל דִּי לִי וְדִי לְעַמָּךְ יִשְׂרָאֵל. אַנְתְּ הוּא זָן לְכֹלָּא וּמְפַרְנֵס לְכֹלָּא, אַנְתְּ הוּא שַׁלִּיט עַל כֹּלָּא, אַנְתְּ הוּא דְּשַׁלִּיט עַל מַלְכַיָּא, וּמַלְכוּתָא דִּילָךְ הִיא. אֲנָא עַבְדָּא דְקֻדְשָׁא בְּרִיךְ הוּא, דְּסָגֵדְנָא קַמֵּהּ וּמִקַּמֵּי דִּיקַר אוֹרַיְתֵהּ בְּכָל עִדָּן וְעִדָּן. לָא עַל אֱנָשׁ רָחִיצְנָא וְלָא עַל בַּר אֱלָהִין סָמִיכְנָא, אֶלָּא בֶּאֱלָהָא דִשְׁמַיָּא, דְּהוּא אֱלָהָא קְשׁוֹט, וְאוֹרַיְתֵהּ קְשׁוֹט, וּנְבִיאוֹהִי קְשׁוֹט, וּמַסְגֵּא לְמֶעְבַּד טַבְוָן וּקְשׁוֹט. ◂ בֵּהּ אֲנָא רָחִיץ, וְלִשְׁמֵהּ קַדִּישָׁא יַקִּירָא אֲנָא אֵמַר תֻּשְׁבְּחָן. יְהֵא רַעֲוָא קֳדָמָךְ דְּתִפְתַּח לִבָּאִי בְּאוֹרַיְתָא, וְתַשְׁלִים מִשְׁאֲלִין דְּלִבָּאִי וְלִבָּא דְכָל עַמָּךְ יִשְׂרָאֵל לְטָב וּלְחַיִּין וְלִשְׁלָם.

Two ספרי תורה *are removed from the* ארון קודש. *The* שליח צבור *takes one in his right arm, and, followed by the* קהל, *says:*

דברים ו שְׁמַע יִשְׂרָאֵל, יהוה אֱלֹהֵינוּ, יהוה אֶחָד:

קהל *then* שליח ציבור:

אֶחָד אֱלֹהֵינוּ, גָּדוֹל אֲדוֹנֵינוּ, קָדוֹשׁ וְנוֹרָא שְׁמוֹ.

The שליח ציבור *turns to face the* ארון קודש, *bows and says:*

תהלים לד גַּדְּלוּ לַיהוה אִתִּי וּנְרוֹמְמָה שְׁמוֹ יַחְדָּו:

The ארון קודש *is closed. The* שליח ציבור *carries the* ספר תורה *to the* בימה *and the* קהל *says:*

דברי הימים א׳ כט לְךָ יהוה הַגְּדֻלָּה וְהַגְּבוּרָה וְהַתִּפְאֶרֶת וְהַנֵּצַח וְהַהוֹד, כִּי־כֹל בַּשָּׁמַיִם וּבָאָרֶץ, לְךָ יהוה הַמַּמְלָכָה וְהַמִּתְנַשֵּׂא לְכֹל לְרֹאשׁ:

---

individuals, not the nation as a whole. Private sacrifices were not offered on Shabbat and festivals, but they were permitted on Hoshana Raba. Since the day is not a full festival, *Nishmat* is not said.

רוֹמְמוּ Exalt the Lord our God and bow to His footstool; He is holy. *Ps. 99*
Exalt the Lord our God, and bow at His holy mountain, for holy is the Lord our God.

Over all may the name of the Supreme King of kings, the Holy One blessed be He, be magnified and sanctified, praised and glorified, exalted and extolled, in the worlds that He has created – this world and the World to Come – in accordance with His will, and the will of those who fear Him, and the will of the whole house of Israel. He is the Rock of worlds, Lord of all creatures, God of all souls, who dwells in the spacious heights and inhabits the high heavens of old. His holiness is over the Ḥayyot and over the throne of glory. Therefore may Your name, Lord our God, be sanctified among us in the sight
of all that lives. Let us sing before Him a new song, as it is written: "Sing to *Ps. 68*
God, make music for His name, extol Him who rides the clouds – the Lord is His name – and exult before Him." And may we see Him eye to eye when
He returns to His abode as it is written: "For they shall see eye to eye when *Is. 52*
the Lord returns to Zion." And it is said: "Then will the glory of the Lord *Is. 40*
be revealed, and all mankind together shall see that the mouth of the Lord has spoken."

Father of mercy, have compassion on the people borne by Him. May He remember the covenant with the mighty (patriarchs), and deliver us from evil times. May He reproach the evil instinct in the people by Him, and graciously grant that we be an eternal remnant. May He fulfill in good measure our requests for salvation and compassion.

---

departure, what would they say? "[It is] beautiful for you, altar; it is beautiful for you, altar". Rabbi Elazar said: "To the Lord and to you, altar; to the Lord and to you, altar".

As its performance during the week, so is its performance on Shabbat; except that they would gather [the branches] from [Shabbat] eve and place them in basins of gold so that they would not dry. Rabbi Yoḥanan ben Beroka says: They would bring palm branches to the Temple and place them on the ground at the sides of the altar, and that day was called: [The day of the] placing of palm branches. [*Sukka* 4:5–6. The law is not in accordance with this last view. Instead the day was known as "the day of the beating of the willow branches."]

Some even have the custom of throwing the beaten *arava* onto the ark, in memory of Temple times when people would rest willow branches against

תהלים צט רוֹמְמוּ יהוה אֱלֹהֵינוּ וְהִשְׁתַּחֲווּ לַהֲדֹם רַגְלָיו, קָדוֹשׁ הוּא: רוֹמְמוּ יהוה אֱלֹהֵינוּ וְהִשְׁתַּחֲווּ לְהַר קָדְשׁוֹ, כִּי־קָדוֹשׁ יהוה אֱלֹהֵינוּ:

עַל הַכֹּל יִתְגַּדַּל וְיִתְקַדַּשׁ וְיִשְׁתַּבַּח וְיִתְפָּאַר וְיִתְרוֹמַם וְיִתְנַשֵּׂא שְׁמוֹ שֶׁל מֶלֶךְ מַלְכֵי הַמְּלָכִים הַקָּדוֹשׁ בָּרוּךְ הוּא בָּעוֹלָמוֹת שֶׁבָּרָא, הָעוֹלָם הַזֶּה וְהָעוֹלָם הַבָּא, כִּרְצוֹנוֹ וְכִרְצוֹן יְרֵאָיו וְכִרְצוֹן כָּל בֵּית יִשְׂרָאֵל. צוּר הָעוֹלָמִים, אֲדוֹן כָּל הַבְּרִיּוֹת, אֱלוֹהַּ כָּל הַנְּפָשׁוֹת, הַיּוֹשֵׁב בְּמֶרְחֲבֵי מָרוֹם, הַשּׁוֹכֵן בִּשְׁמֵי שְׁמֵי קֶדֶם, קְדֻשָּׁתוֹ עַל הַחַיּוֹת, וּקְדֻשָּׁתוֹ עַל כִּסֵּא הַכָּבוֹד. וּבְכֵן יִתְקַדַּשׁ שִׁמְךָ בָּנוּ יהוה
תהלים סח אֱלֹהֵינוּ לְעֵינֵי כָּל חָי, וְנֹאמַר לְפָנָיו שִׁיר חָדָשׁ, כַּכָּתוּב: שִׁירוּ לֵאלֹהִים זַמְּרוּ
שְׁמוֹ, סֹלּוּ לָרֹכֵב בָּעֲרָבוֹת, בְּיָהּ שְׁמוֹ, וְעִלְזוּ לְפָנָיו: וְנִרְאֵהוּ עַיִן בְּעַיִן בְּשׁוּבוֹ
ישעיה נב אֶל נָוֵהוּ, כַּכָּתוּב: כִּי עַיִן בְּעַיִן יִרְאוּ בְּשׁוּב יהוה צִיּוֹן: וְנֶאֱמַר: וְנִגְלָה כְּבוֹד
ישעיה מ יהוה, וְרָאוּ כָל־בָּשָׂר יַחְדָּו כִּי פִּי יהוה דִּבֵּר:

אַב הָרַחֲמִים הוּא יְרַחֵם עַם עֲמוּסִים, וְיִזְכֹּר בְּרִית אֵיתָנִים, וְיַצִּיל נַפְשׁוֹתֵינוּ מִן הַשָּׁעוֹת הָרָעוֹת, וְיִגְעַר בְּיֵצֶר הָרָע מִן הַנְּשׂוּאִים, וְיָחֹן אוֹתָנוּ לִפְלֵיטַת עוֹלָמִים, וִימַלֵּא מִשְׁאֲלוֹתֵינוּ בְּמִדָּה טוֹבָה יְשׁוּעָה וְרַחֲמִים.

---

reserved for Hoshana Raba, namely the taking of the *arava*, a bundle of willow leaves, with which we process around the *Bima*, eventually beating them against the ground. Tradition ascribes this custom to the prophets of the Second Temple, Haggai, Zekharia, and Malachi. It is essentially an act designed to accompany the nation's prayer for rain – on which the produce of the next year, and thus the economy of the nation, depended. This is how the Mishna describes the rite:

> How is the mitzva of the willow branch [fulfilled]? There was a place below Jerusalem, and it was called Motza. They [would] descend there and gather willow branches from there. And they [would then] come and stand them upright at the sides of the altar, [and the tops of the branches would] be inclined over the top of the altar. They [then] sounded a *tekia*, sounded a *terua*, and sounded [another] *tekia*. Each day they [would] circle the altar one time and say: "Lord, please save us. Lord, please grant us success". Rabbi Yehuda says [that they would say]: *Ani vaho*, please save us. And on that day, they [would] circle the altar seven times. At the time of their

The Torah scroll is placed on the bima and the Gabbai calls a Kohen to the Torah.

וְיַעֲזֹר May He help, shield and save all who seek refuge in Him,
and let us say: Amen. Let us all render greatness to our God
and give honor to the Torah. *Let the Kohen come forward.
Arise (*name* son of *father's name*), the Kohen.

**If no Kohen is present, a Levi or Yisrael is called up as follows:*
/As there is no Kohen, arise (*name* son of *father's name*) in place of a Kohen./

Blessed is He who, in His holiness, gave the Torah to His people Israel.

The congregation followed by the Gabbai:

You who cling to the LORD your God are all alive today. *Deut. 4*

*The Reader shows the oleh the section to be read.
The oleh touches the scroll at that place with the tzitzit of his tallit, which
he then kisses. Holding the handles of the scroll, he says:*

Oleh: Bless the LORD, the blessed One.

Cong: Bless the LORD, the blessed One,
for ever and all time.

Oleh: Bless the LORD, the blessed One,
for ever and all time.

Blessed are You, LORD our God, King of the Universe,
who has chosen us from all peoples
and has given us His Torah.
Blessed are You, LORD, Giver of the Torah.

After the reading, the oleh says:

Oleh: Blessed are You, LORD our God, King of the Universe,
who has given us the Torah of truth,
planting everlasting life in our midst.
Blessed are You, LORD, Giver of the Torah.

"March in a festival procession with thick branches to the horns of the altar." Others save them until Pesaḥ, using them to light the fire on which matzot are baked, or on which leaven is burned.

The ספר תורה *is placed on the* שולחן *and the* גבאי *calls a* כהן *to the* תורה.

וְיַעֲזֹר וְיָגֵן וְיוֹשִׁיעַ לְכָל הַחוֹסִים בּוֹ, וְנֹאמַר אָמֵן. הַכֹּל הָבוּ גֹדֶל לֵאלֹהֵינוּ וּתְנוּ כָבוֹד לַתּוֹרָה. *כֹּהֵן קְרַב, יַעֲמֹד (פלוני בֶּן פלוני) הַכֹּהֵן.

**If no* כהן *is present, a* לוי *or* ישראל *is called up as follows:*

/אֵין כָּאן כֹּהֵן, יַעֲמֹד (פלוני בֶּן פלוני) בִּמְקוֹם כֹּהֵן./

בָּרוּךְ שֶׁנָּתַן תּוֹרָה לְעַמּוֹ יִשְׂרָאֵל בִּקְדֻשָּׁתוֹ.

The קהל *followed by the* גבאי:

וְאַתֶּם הַדְּבֵקִים בַּיהוה אֱלֹהֵיכֶם חַיִּים כֻּלְּכֶם הַיּוֹם: דברים ד

The קורא *shows the* עולה *the section to be read. The* עולה *touches the scroll at that place with the* ציצית *of his* טלית, *which he then kisses. Holding the handles of the scroll, he says:*

עולה: **בָּרְכוּ אֶת יהוה הַמְבֹרָךְ.**

קהל: בָּרוּךְ יהוה הַמְבֹרָךְ לְעוֹלָם וָעֶד.

עולה: **בָּרוּךְ יהוה הַמְבֹרָךְ לְעוֹלָם וָעֶד.**

בָּרוּךְ אַתָּה יהוה, אֱלֹהֵינוּ מֶלֶךְ הָעוֹלָם
אֲשֶׁר בָּחַר בָּנוּ מִכָּל הָעַמִּים
וְנָתַן לָנוּ אֶת תּוֹרָתוֹ.
בָּרוּךְ אַתָּה יהוה, נוֹתֵן הַתּוֹרָה.

After the קריאת התורה, *the* עולה *says:*

עולה: **בָּרוּךְ אַתָּה יהוה אֱלֹהֵינוּ מֶלֶךְ הָעוֹלָם**
אֲשֶׁר נָתַן לָנוּ תּוֹרַת אֱמֶת
וְחַיֵּי עוֹלָם נָטַע בְּתוֹכֵנוּ.
בָּרוּךְ אַתָּה יהוה, נוֹתֵן הַתּוֹרָה.

---

the altar, possibly hinted at in the line in Hallel (Ps. 118:27), "Bind the festival offering with thick cords to the altar," which could also be translated as,

One who has survived a situation of danger says:

Blessed are You, Lord our God, King of the Universe, who bestows good on the unworthy, who has bestowed on me much good.

The congregation responds:

Amen. May He who bestowed much good on you continue to bestow on you much good, Selah.

HOSHANA RABA

In Israel, the last three verses, "On the seventh day" through "its meal offering and its libation," are read for each of the four aliyot.°

On the fifth day, nine young bullocks, two rams, and fourteen unblemished yearling male lambs. And you shall perform their meal-offerings and their libations, for each of the bullocks, the rams and the lambs, in the proper quantities, according to the law. And likewise a male goat for atonement, as well as the regular daily offering and its meal offering and its libations. *Num. 29:26–34*

LEVI On the sixth day, eight young bullocks, two rams, and fourteen unblemished yearling male lambs. And you shall perform their meal-offerings and their libations, for each of the bullocks, the rams and the lambs, in the proper quantities, according to the law. And likewise a male goat for atonement, as well as the regular daily offering and its meal offering and its libations.

SHELISHI On the seventh day, seven young bullocks, two rams, and fourteen unblemished yearling male lambs. And you shall perform their meal-offerings and their libations, for each of the bullocks, the rams and the lambs, in the proper quantities, according to the law. And likewise a male goat for atonement, as well as the regular daily offering and its meal offering and its libation.

REVI'I On the sixth day, eight young bullocks, two rams, and fourteen unblemished yearling male lambs. And you shall perform their meal-offerings and their libations, for each of the bullocks, the rams and the lambs, in the proper quantities, according to the law. And likewise a male goat for atonement, as well as the regular daily offering and its meal offering and its libations.

°On the seventh day, seven young bullocks, two rams, and fourteen unblemished yearling male lambs. And you shall perform their meal-offerings and

One who has survived a situation of danger says:

בָּרוּךְ אַתָּה יהוה אֱלֹהֵינוּ מֶלֶךְ הָעוֹלָם
הַגּוֹמֵל לְחַיָּבִים טוֹבוֹת
שֶׁגְּמָלַנִי כָּל טוֹב.

The קהל *responds:*

אָמֵן. מִי שֶׁגְּמָלְךָ כָּל טוֹב הוּא יִגְמָלְךָ כָּל טוֹב, סֶלָה.

קריאה להושענא רבה

In ארץ ישראל*, the last three verses from* וּבַיּוֹם הַשְּׁבִיעִי *through* מִנְחָתָהּ וְנִסְכָּהּ *are read for each of the four* עליות.°

וּבַיּוֹם הַחֲמִישִׁי פָּרִים תִּשְׁעָה אֵילִם שְׁנָיִם כְּבָשִׂים בְּנֵי־שָׁנָה במדבר כט:כו–לד
אַרְבָּעָה עָשָׂר תְּמִימִם: וּמִנְחָתָם וְנִסְכֵּיהֶם לַפָּרִים לָאֵילִם
וְלַכְּבָשִׂים בְּמִסְפָּרָם כַּמִּשְׁפָּט: וּשְׂעִיר חַטָּאת אֶחָד מִלְּבַד
עֹלַת הַתָּמִיד וּמִנְחָתָהּ וְנִסְכָּהּ: ★וּבַיּוֹם הַשִּׁשִּׁי לוי
פָּרִים שְׁמֹנָה אֵילִם שְׁנָיִם כְּבָשִׂים בְּנֵי־שָׁנָה אַרְבָּעָה עָשָׂר
תְּמִימִם: וּמִנְחָתָם וְנִסְכֵּיהֶם לַפָּרִים לָאֵילִם וְלַכְּבָשִׂים בְּמִסְפָּרָם
כַּמִּשְׁפָּט: וּשְׂעִיר חַטָּאת אֶחָד מִלְּבַד עֹלַת הַתָּמִיד מִנְחָתָהּ
וּנְסָכֶיהָ: ★וּבַיּוֹם הַשְּׁבִיעִי פָּרִים שִׁבְעָה אֵילִם שְׁנָיִם שלישי
כְּבָשִׂים בְּנֵי־שָׁנָה אַרְבָּעָה עָשָׂר תְּמִימִם: וּמִנְחָתָם וְנִסְכֵּהֶם
לַפָּרִים לָאֵילִם וְלַכְּבָשִׂים בְּמִסְפָּרָם כְּמִשְׁפָּטָם: וּשְׂעִיר חַטָּאת
אֶחָד מִלְּבַד עֹלַת הַתָּמִיד מִנְחָתָהּ וְנִסְכָּהּ:

וּבַיּוֹם הַשִּׁשִּׁי פָּרִים שְׁמֹנָה אֵילִם שְׁנָיִם כְּבָשִׂים בְּנֵי־שָׁנָה אַרְבָּעָה רביעי
עָשָׂר תְּמִימִם: וּמִנְחָתָם וְנִסְכֵּיהֶם לַפָּרִים לָאֵילִם וְלַכְּבָשִׂים
בְּמִסְפָּרָם כַּמִּשְׁפָּט: וּשְׂעִיר חַטָּאת אֶחָד מִלְּבַד עֹלַת הַתָּמִיד
מִנְחָתָהּ וּנְסָכֶיהָ: °וּבַיּוֹם הַשְּׁבִיעִי פָּרִים שִׁבְעָה אֵילִם
שְׁנָיִם כְּבָשִׂים בְּנֵי־שָׁנָה אַרְבָּעָה עָשָׂר תְּמִימִם: וּמִנְחָתָם וְנִסְכֵּהֶם

their libations, for each of the bullocks, the rams and the lambs, in the proper quantities, according to the law. And likewise a male goat for atonement, as well as the regular daily offering and its meal offering and its libation.

HALF KADDISH

After the Reading of the Torah, the Reader says Half Kaddish:

Reader: יִתְגַּדַּל Magnified and sanctified may His great name be,
in the world He created by His will.
May He establish His kingdom
in your lifetime and in your days,
and in the lifetime of all the house of Israel,
swiftly and soon –
and say: Amen.

All: May His great name be blessed for ever and all time.

Reader: Blessed and praised, glorified and exalted,
raised and honored, uplifted and lauded
be the name of the Holy One, blessed be He,
beyond any blessing, song, praise and consolation
uttered in the world –
and say: Amen.

HAGBAHA AND GELILA

The Torah scroll is lifted and the congregation says:

וְזֹאת הַתּוֹרָה This is the Torah *Deut. 4*
that Moses placed before the children of Israel,
at the LORD's commandment, by the hand of Moses. *Num. 9*

Some add:

It is a tree of life to those who grasp it, *Prov. 3*
and those who uphold it are happy.
Its ways are ways of pleasantness, and all its paths are peace.
Long life is at its right hand; at its left, riches and honor.
It pleased the LORD for the sake of [Israel's] righteousness, *Is. 42*
to make the Torah great and glorious.

לְפָרִים לָאֵילִם וְלַכְּבָשִׂים בְּמִסְפָּרָם כַּמִּשְׁפָּט: וּשְׂעִיר חַטָּאת אֶחָד מִלְּבַד עֹלַת הַתָּמִיד מִנְחָתָהּ וְנִסְכָּהּ:

חצי קדיש

After קריאת התורה*, the* קורא *says* חצי קדיש*:*

קורא: יִתְגַּדַּל וְיִתְקַדַּשׁ שְׁמֵהּ רַבָּא (קהל: אָמֵן)
בְּעָלְמָא דִּי בְרָא כִרְעוּתֵהּ
וְיַמְלִיךְ מַלְכוּתֵהּ
בְּחַיֵּיכוֹן וּבְיוֹמֵיכוֹן וּבְחַיֵּי דְכָל בֵּית יִשְׂרָאֵל
בַּעֲגָלָא וּבִזְמַן קָרִיב, וְאִמְרוּ אָמֵן. (קהל: אָמֵן)

קהל וקורא: יְהֵא שְׁמֵהּ רַבָּא מְבָרַךְ לְעָלַם וּלְעָלְמֵי עָלְמַיָּא.

קורא: יִתְבָּרַךְ וְיִשְׁתַּבַּח וְיִתְפָּאַר וְיִתְרוֹמַם וְיִתְנַשֵּׂא
וְיִתְהַדָּר וְיִתְעַלֶּה וְיִתְהַלָּל
שְׁמֵהּ דְּקֻדְשָׁא בְּרִיךְ הוּא (קהל: בְּרִיךְ הוּא)
לְעֵלָּא מִן כָּל בִּרְכָתָא וְשִׁירָתָא
תֻּשְׁבְּחָתָא וְנֶחֱמָתָא
דַּאֲמִירָן בְּעָלְמָא, וְאִמְרוּ אָמֵן. (קהל: אָמֵן)

הגבהה וגלילה

The ספר תורה *is lifted and the* קהל *says:*

וְזֹאת הַתּוֹרָה אֲשֶׁר־שָׂם מֹשֶׁה לִפְנֵי בְּנֵי יִשְׂרָאֵל: דברים ד
עַל־פִּי יהוה בְּיַד מֹשֶׁה: במדבר ט

Some add עֵץ־חַיִּים הִיא לַמַּחֲזִיקִים בָּהּ וְתֹמְכֶיהָ מְאֻשָּׁר: משלי ג
דְּרָכֶיהָ דַרְכֵי־נֹעַם וְכָל־נְתִיבֹתֶיהָ שָׁלוֹם:
אֹרֶךְ יָמִים בִּימִינָהּ, בִּשְׂמֹאולָהּ עֹשֶׁר וְכָבוֹד:
יהוה חָפֵץ לְמַעַן צִדְקוֹ יַגְדִּיל תּוֹרָה וְיַאְדִּיר: ישעיה מב

RETURNING THE TORAH TO THE ARK

The Ark is opened. The Leader takes the Torah scroll and says:

יְהַלְלוּ Let them praise the name of the LORD, Ps. 148
for His name alone is sublime.

The congregation responds:

הוֹדוֹ His majesty is above earth and heaven.
He has raised the horn of His people,
for the glory of all His devoted ones,
the children of Israel, the people close to Him.
Halleluya!

As the Torah scroll is returned to the Ark, say:

לְדָוִד מִזְמוֹר A psalm of David. The earth is the LORD's and all it contains, Ps. 24
the world and all who live in it. For He founded it on the seas and established it on the streams. Who may climb the mountain of the LORD? Who may stand in His holy place? He who has clean hands and a pure heart, who has not taken My name in vain, or sworn deceitfully. He shall receive blessing from the LORD, and just reward from God, his salvation. This is a generation of those who seek Him, the descendants of Jacob who seek Your presence, Selah! Lift up your heads, O gates; be uplifted, eternal doors, so that the King of glory may enter. Who is the King of glory? It is the LORD, strong and mighty, the LORD mighty in battle. ▸ Lift up your heads, O gates; be uplifted, eternal doors, so that the King of glory may enter. Who is He, the King of glory? The LORD of hosts, He is the King of glory, Selah!

As the Torah scroll is placed into the Ark, say:

וּבְנֻחֹה יֹאמַר When the Ark came to rest, Moses would say: "Return, Num. 10
O LORD, to the myriad thousands of Israel." Advance, LORD, to Your Ps. 132
resting place, You and Your mighty Ark. Your priests are clothed in righteousness, and Your devoted ones sing in joy. For the sake of Your
servant David, do not reject Your anointed one. For I give you good Prov. 4
instruction; do not forsake My Torah. It is a tree of life to those who Prov. 3
grasp it, and those who uphold it are happy. Its ways are ways of pleas-
antness, and all its paths are peace. ▸ Turn us back, O LORD, to You, and Lam. 5
we will return. Renew our days as of old.

The Ark is closed.

הכנסת ספר תורה

The ארון קודש *is opened. The* שליח ציבור *takes the* ספר תורה *and says:*

יְהַלְלוּ אֶת־שֵׁם יהוה, כִּי נִשְׂגָּב־שְׁמוֹ, לְבַדּוֹ תהלים קמח

The קהל *responds:*

הוֹדוֹ עַל־אֶרֶץ וְשָׁמָיִם:
וַיָּרֶם קֶרֶן לְעַמּוֹ, תְּהִלָּה לְכָל־חֲסִידָיו
לִבְנֵי יִשְׂרָאֵל עַם קְרֹבוֹ, הַלְלוּיָהּ:

As the ספר תורה *is returned to the* ארון קודש*, say:*

לְדָוִד מִזְמוֹר, לַיהוה הָאָרֶץ וּמְלוֹאָהּ, תֵּבֵל וְיֽשְׁבֵי בָהּ: כִּי־הוּא עַל־ תהלים כד
יַמִּים יְסָדָהּ, וְעַל־נְהָרוֹת יְכוֹנְנֶהָ: מִי־יַעֲלֶה בְהַר־יהוה, וּמִי־יָקוּם
בִּמְקוֹם קָדְשׁוֹ: נְקִי כַפַּיִם וּבַר־לֵבָב, אֲשֶׁר לֹא־נָשָׂא לַשָּׁוְא נַפְשִׁי
וְלֹא נִשְׁבַּע לְמִרְמָה: יִשָּׂא בְרָכָה מֵאֵת יהוה, וּצְדָקָה מֵאֱלֹהֵי יִשְׁעוֹ:
זֶה דּוֹר דֹּרְשָׁו, מְבַקְשֵׁי פָנֶיךָ, יַעֲקֹב, סֶלָה: שְׂאוּ שְׁעָרִים רָאשֵׁיכֶם,
וְהִנָּשְׂאוּ פִּתְחֵי עוֹלָם, וְיָבוֹא מֶלֶךְ הַכָּבוֹד: מִי זֶה מֶלֶךְ הַכָּבוֹד, יהוה
עִזּוּז וְגִבּוֹר, יהוה גִּבּוֹר מִלְחָמָה: ‹ שְׂאוּ שְׁעָרִים רָאשֵׁיכֶם, וּשְׂאוּ
פִּתְחֵי עוֹלָם, וְיָבֹא מֶלֶךְ הַכָּבוֹד: מִי הוּא זֶה מֶלֶךְ הַכָּבוֹד, יהוה
צְבָאוֹת הוּא מֶלֶךְ הַכָּבוֹד, סֶלָה:

As the ספר תורה *is placed into the* ארון קודש*, say:*

וּבְנֻחֹה יֹאמַר, שׁוּבָה יהוה רִבְבוֹת אַלְפֵי יִשְׂרָאֵל: קוּמָה יהוה במדבר י תהלים קלב
לִמְנוּחָתֶךָ, אַתָּה וַאֲרוֹן עֻזֶּךָ: כֹּהֲנֶיךָ יִלְבְּשׁוּ־צֶדֶק, וַחֲסִידֶיךָ יְרַנֵּנוּ:
בַּעֲבוּר דָּוִד עַבְדֶּךָ אַל־תָּשֵׁב פְּנֵי מְשִׁיחֶךָ: כִּי לֶקַח טוֹב נָתַתִּי משלי ד
לָכֶם, תּוֹרָתִי אַל־תַּעֲזֹבוּ: עֵץ־חַיִּים הִיא לַמַּחֲזִיקִים בָּהּ, וְתֹמְכֶיהָ משלי ג
מְאֻשָּׁר: דְּרָכֶיהָ דַרְכֵי־נֹעַם וְכָל־נְתִיבוֹתֶיהָ שָׁלוֹם: ‹ הֲשִׁיבֵנוּ יהוה איכה ה
אֵלֶיךָ וְנָשׁוּבָ, חַדֵּשׁ יָמֵינוּ כְּקֶדֶם:

The ארון קודש *is closed.*

אַשְׁרֵי Happy are those who dwell in Your House; *Ps. 84*
they shall continue to praise You, Selah!
Happy are the people for whom this is so; *Ps. 144*
happy are the people whose God is the LORD.
A song of praise by David. *Ps. 145*

I will exalt You, my God, the King, and bless Your name for ever and all time. Every day I will bless You, and praise Your name for ever and all time. Great is the LORD and greatly to be praised; His greatness is unfathomable. One generation will praise Your works to the next, and tell of Your mighty deeds. On the glorious splendor of Your majesty I will meditate, and on the acts of Your wonders. They shall talk of the power of Your awesome deeds, and I will tell of Your greatness. They shall recite the record of Your great goodness, and sing with joy of Your righteousness. The LORD is gracious and compassionate, slow to anger and great in loving-kindness. The LORD is good to all, and His compassion extends to all His works. All Your works shall thank You, LORD, and Your devoted ones shall bless You. They shall talk of the glory of Your kingship, and speak of Your might. To make known to mankind His mighty deeds and the glorious majesty of His kingship. Your kingdom is an everlasting kingdom, and Your reign is for all generations. The LORD supports all who fall, and raises all who are bowed down. All raise their eyes to You in hope, and You give them their food in due season. You open Your hand, and satisfy every living thing with favor. The LORD is righteous in all His ways, and kind in all He does. The LORD is close to all who call on Him, to all who call on Him in truth. He fulfills the will of those who revere Him; He hears their cry and saves them. The LORD guards all who love Him, but all the wicked He will destroy. ▸ My mouth shall speak the praise of the LORD, and all creatures shall bless His holy name for ever and all time.

We will bless the LORD now and for ever. Halleluya! *Ps. 115*

אַשְׁרֵי יוֹשְׁבֵי בֵיתֶךָ, עוֹד יְהַלְלְוּךָ סֶּלָה: תהלים פד

אַשְׁרֵי הָעָם שֶׁכָּכָה לּוֹ, אַשְׁרֵי הָעָם שֶׁיהוה אֱלֹהָיו: תהלים קמד

תְּהִלָּה לְדָוִד תהלים קמה

אֲרוֹמִמְךָ אֱלוֹהַי הַמֶּלֶךְ, וַאֲבָרְכָה שִׁמְךָ לְעוֹלָם וָעֶד:

בְּכָל־יוֹם אֲבָרְכֶךָּ, וַאֲהַלְלָה שִׁמְךָ לְעוֹלָם וָעֶד:

גָּדוֹל יהוה וּמְהֻלָּל מְאֹד, וְלִגְדֻלָּתוֹ אֵין חֵקֶר:

דּוֹר לְדוֹר יְשַׁבַּח מַעֲשֶׂיךָ, וּגְבוּרֹתֶיךָ יַגִּידוּ:

הֲדַר כְּבוֹד הוֹדֶךָ, וְדִבְרֵי נִפְלְאֹתֶיךָ אָשִֽׂיחָה:

וֶעֱזוּז נוֹרְאֹתֶיךָ יֹאמֵרוּ, וּגְדוּלָּתְךָ אֲסַפְּרֶנָּה:

זֵכֶר רַב־טוּבְךָ יַבִּיעוּ, וְצִדְקָתְךָ יְרַנֵּנוּ:

חַנּוּן וְרַחוּם יהוה, אֶרֶךְ אַפַּיִם וּגְדָל־חָסֶד:

טוֹב־יהוה לַכֹּל, וְרַחֲמָיו עַל־כָּל־מַעֲשָׂיו:

יוֹדְוּךָ יהוה כָּל־מַעֲשֶׂיךָ, וַחֲסִידֶיךָ יְבָרְכוּכָה:

כְּבוֹד מַלְכוּתְךָ יֹאמֵרוּ, וּגְבוּרָתְךָ יְדַבֵּרוּ:

לְהוֹדִיעַ לִבְנֵי הָאָדָם גְּבוּרֹתָיו, וּכְבוֹד הֲדַר מַלְכוּתוֹ:

מַלְכוּתְךָ מַלְכוּת כָּל־עֹלָמִים, וּמֶמְשַׁלְתְּךָ בְּכָל־דּוֹר וָדֹר:

סוֹמֵךְ יהוה לְכָל־הַנֹּפְלִים, וְזוֹקֵף לְכָל־הַכְּפוּפִים:

עֵינֵי־כֹל אֵלֶיךָ יְשַׂבֵּרוּ, וְאַתָּה נוֹתֵן־לָהֶם אֶת־אָכְלָם בְּעִתּוֹ:

פּוֹתֵחַ אֶת־יָדֶךָ, וּמַשְׂבִּיעַ לְכָל־חַי רָצוֹן:

צַדִּיק יהוה בְּכָל־דְּרָכָיו, וְחָסִיד בְּכָל־מַעֲשָׂיו:

קָרוֹב יהוה לְכָל־קֹרְאָיו, לְכֹל אֲשֶׁר יִקְרָאֻהוּ בֶאֱמֶת:

רְצוֹן־יְרֵאָיו יַעֲשֶׂה, וְאֶת־שַׁוְעָתָם יִשְׁמַע, וְיוֹשִׁיעֵם:

שׁוֹמֵר יהוה אֶת־כָּל־אֹהֲבָיו, וְאֵת כָּל־הָרְשָׁעִים יַשְׁמִיד:

‹ תְּהִלַּת יהוה יְדַבֶּר פִּי, וִיבָרֵךְ כָּל־בָּשָׂר שֵׁם קָדְשׁוֹ לְעוֹלָם וָעֶד:

וַאֲנַחְנוּ נְבָרֵךְ יָהּ מֵעַתָּה וְעַד־עוֹלָם, הַלְלוּיָהּ: תהלים קטו

ובָא לְצִיּוֹן גּוֹאֵל "A redeemer will come to Zion, *Is. 59*
to those of Jacob who repent of their sins," declares the LORD.
"As for Me, this is My covenant with them," says the LORD.
"My spirit, that is on you, and My words I have placed in your mouth will not depart from your mouth, or from the mouth of your children, or from the mouth of their descendants from this time on and for ever," says the LORD.

▸ You are the Holy One, enthroned on the praises of Israel. *Ps. 22*
And [the angels] call to one another, saying, ◂ "Holy, holy, holy *Is. 6*
is the LORD of hosts; the whole world is filled with His glory."
And they receive permission from one another, saying: *Targum Yonatan Is. 6*
"Holy in the highest heavens, home of His Presence; holy on earth,
the work of His strength; holy for ever and all time is the LORD of hosts;
the whole earth is full of His radiant glory."

▸ Then a wind lifted me up and I heard behind me the sound of a great *Ezek. 3*
noise, saying, ◂ "Blessed is the LORD's glory from His place."
Then a wind lifted me up and I heard behind me *Targum Yonatan Ezek. 3*
the sound of a great tempest of those who uttered praise, saying,
"Blessed is the LORD's glory from the place of the home of His Presence."

The LORD shall reign for ever and all time. *Ex. 15*
The LORD's kingdom is established for ever and all time. *Targum Onkelos Ex. 15*

יהוה LORD, God of Abraham, Isaac and Yisrael, our ancestors, may *1 Chr. 29*
You keep this for ever so that it forms the thoughts in Your people's
heart, and directs their heart toward You. He is compassionate. He *Ps. 78*
forgives iniquity and does not destroy. Repeatedly He suppresses His
anger, not rousing His full wrath. For You, my LORD, are good and *Ps. 86*
forgiving, abundantly kind to all who call on You. Your righteousness *Ps. 119*
is eternally righteous, and Your Torah is truth. Grant truth to Jacob, *Mic. 7*
loving-kindness to Abraham, as You promised our ancestors in ancient
times. Blessed is my LORD for day after day He burdens us [with His *Ps. 68*
blessings]; is our salvation, Selah! The LORD of hosts is with us; the *Ps. 46*
God of Jacob is our refuge, Selah! LORD of hosts, happy is the one who *Ps. 84*
trusts in You. LORD, save. May the King answer us on the day we call. *Ps. 20*

וּבָא לְצִיּוֹן גּוֹאֵל, וּלְשָׁבֵי פֶשַׁע בְּיַעֲקֹב, נְאֻם יהוה: ישעיה נט
וַאֲנִי זֹאת בְּרִיתִי אוֹתָם, אָמַר יהוה
רוּחִי אֲשֶׁר עָלֶיךָ וּדְבָרַי אֲשֶׁר־שַׂמְתִּי בְּפִיךָ
לֹא־יָמְוּשׁוּ מִפִּיךָ וּמִפִּי זַרְעֲךָ וּמִפִּי זֶרַע זַרְעֲךָ
אָמַר יהוה, מֵעַתָּה וְעַד־עוֹלָם:

◂ וְאַתָּה קָדוֹשׁ יוֹשֵׁב תְּהִלּוֹת יִשְׂרָאֵל: וְקָרָא זֶה אֶל־זֶה וְאָמַר ◂ תהלים כב
קָדוֹשׁ, קָדוֹשׁ, קָדוֹשׁ, יהוה צְבָאוֹת, מְלֹא כָל־הָאָרֶץ כְּבוֹדוֹ: ישעיה ו
וּמְקַבְּלִין דֵּין מִן דֵּין וְאָמְרִין, קַדִּישׁ בִּשְׁמֵי מְרוֹמָא עִלָּאָה בֵּית שְׁכִינְתֵהּ תרגום יונתן ישעיה ו
קַדִּישׁ עַל אַרְעָא עוֹבַד גְּבוּרְתֵהּ, קַדִּישׁ לְעָלַם וּלְעָלְמֵי עָלְמַיָּא
יהוה צְבָאוֹת, מַלְיָא כָל אַרְעָא זִיו יְקָרֵהּ.

◂ וַתִּשָּׂאֵנִי רוּחַ, וָאֶשְׁמַע אַחֲרַי קוֹל רַעַשׁ גָּדוֹל ◂ יחזקאל ג
בָּרוּךְ כְּבוֹד־יהוה מִמְּקוֹמוֹ:
וּנְטָלַתְנִי רוּחָא, וּשְׁמָעִית בַּתְרַי קָל זִיעַ סַגִּיא, דִּמְשַׁבְּחִין וְאָמְרִין תרגום יונתן יחזקאל ג
בְּרִיךְ יְקָרָא דַיהוה מֵאֲתַר בֵּית שְׁכִינְתֵהּ.

יהוה יִמְלֹךְ לְעֹלָם וָעֶד: שמות טו
יהוה מַלְכוּתֵהּ קָאֵם לְעָלַם וּלְעָלְמֵי עָלְמַיָּא. תרגום אונקלוס שמות טו

יהוה אֱלֹהֵי אַבְרָהָם יִצְחָק וְיִשְׂרָאֵל אֲבֹתֵינוּ, שָׁמְרָה־זֹּאת לְעוֹלָם דברי הימים א, כט
לְיֵצֶר מַחְשְׁבוֹת לְבַב עַמֶּךָ, וְהָכֵן לְבָבָם אֵלֶיךָ: וְהוּא רַחוּם יְכַפֵּר עָוֹן תהלים עח
וְלֹא־יַשְׁחִית, וְהִרְבָּה לְהָשִׁיב אַפּוֹ, וְלֹא־יָעִיר כָּל־חֲמָתוֹ: כִּי־אַתָּה תהלים פו
אֲדֹנָי טוֹב וְסַלָּח, וְרַב־חֶסֶד לְכָל־קֹרְאֶיךָ: צִדְקָתְךָ צֶדֶק לְעוֹלָם תהלים קיט
וְתוֹרָתְךָ אֱמֶת: תִּתֵּן אֱמֶת לְיַעֲקֹב, חֶסֶד לְאַבְרָהָם, אֲשֶׁר־נִשְׁבַּעְתָּ מיכה ז
לַאֲבֹתֵינוּ מִימֵי קֶדֶם: בָּרוּךְ אֲדֹנָי יוֹם יוֹם יַעֲמָס־לָנוּ, הָאֵל יְשׁוּעָתֵנוּ תהלים סח
סֶלָה: יהוה צְבָאוֹת עִמָּנוּ, מִשְׂגָּב לָנוּ אֱלֹהֵי יַעֲקֹב סֶלָה: יהוה צְבָאוֹת, תהלים מו תהלים פד
אַשְׁרֵי אָדָם בֹּטֵחַ בָּךְ: יהוה הוֹשִׁיעָה, הַמֶּלֶךְ יַעֲנֵנוּ בְיוֹם־קָרְאֵנוּ: תהלים כ

בָּרוּךְ Blessed is He, our God, who created us for His glory, separating us from those who go astray; who gave us the Torah of truth, planting within us eternal life. May He open our heart to His Torah, imbuing our heart with the love and awe of Him, that we may do His will and serve Him with a perfect heart, so that we neither toil in vain nor give birth to confusion.

יְהִי רָצוֹן May it be Your will, O LORD our God and God of our ancestors, that we keep Your laws in this world, and thus be worthy to live, see and inherit goodness and blessing in the Messianic Age and in the life of the World to Come. So that my soul may sing to You and not *Ps. 30*
be silent. LORD, my God, for ever I will thank You. Blessed is the man *Jer. 17*
who trusts in the LORD, whose trust is in the LORD alone. Trust in the *Is. 26*
LORD for evermore, for God, the LORD, is an everlasting Rock. ▸ Those *Ps. 9*
who know Your name trust in You, for You, LORD, do not forsake those
who seek You. The LORD desired, for the sake of Israel's merit, to make *Is. 42*
the Torah great and glorious.

HALF KADDISH

Leader: יִתְגַּדַּל Magnified and sanctified
may His great name be,
in the world He created by His will.
May He establish His kingdom
in your lifetime and in your days,
and in the lifetime of all the house of Israel,
swiftly and soon –
and say: Amen.

All: May His great name be blessed for ever and all time.

Leader: Blessed and praised, glorified and exalted,
raised and honored, uplifted and lauded
be the name of the Holy One, blessed be He,
beyond any blessing,
song, praise and consolation
uttered in the world –
and say: Amen.

בָּרוּךְ הוּא אֱלֹהֵינוּ שֶׁבְּרָאָנוּ לִכְבוֹדוֹ, וְהִבְדִּילָנוּ מִן הַתּוֹעִים, וְנָתַן לָנוּ תּוֹרַת אֱמֶת, וְחַיֵּי עוֹלָם נָטַע בְּתוֹכֵנוּ. הוּא יִפְתַּח לִבֵּנוּ בְּתוֹרָתוֹ, וְיָשֵׂם בְּלִבֵּנוּ אַהֲבָתוֹ וְיִרְאָתוֹ וְלַעֲשׂוֹת רְצוֹנוֹ וּלְעָבְדוֹ בְּלֵבָב שָׁלֵם, לְמַעַן לֹא נִיגַע לָרִיק וְלֹא נֵלֵד לַבֶּהָלָה.

יְהִי רָצוֹן מִלְּפָנֶיךָ יהוה אֱלֹהֵינוּ וֵאלֹהֵי אֲבוֹתֵינוּ, שֶׁנִּשְׁמֹר חֻקֶּיךָ בָּעוֹלָם הַזֶּה, וְנִזְכֶּה וְנִחְיֶה וְנִרְאֶה וְנִירַשׁ טוֹבָה וּבְרָכָה, לִשְׁנֵי יְמוֹת
הַמָּשִׁיחַ וּלְחַיֵּי הָעוֹלָם הַבָּא. לְמַעַן יְזַמֶּרְךָ כָבוֹד וְלֹא יִדֹּם, יהוה תהלים ל
אֱלֹהַי, לְעוֹלָם אוֹדֶךָּ: בָּרוּךְ הַגֶּבֶר אֲשֶׁר יִבְטַח בַּיהוה, וְהָיָה יהוה ירמיה יז
מִבְטַחוֹ: בִּטְחוּ בַיהוה עֲדֵי־עַד, כִּי בְּיָהּ יהוה צוּר עוֹלָמִים: ‹ וְיִבְטְחוּ ישעיה כו תהלים ט
בְךָ יוֹדְעֵי שְׁמֶךָ, כִּי לֹא־עָזַבְתָּ דֹרְשֶׁיךָ, יהוה: יהוה חָפֵץ לְמַעַן צִדְקוֹ, ישעיה מב
יַגְדִּיל תּוֹרָה וְיַאְדִּיר:

חצי קדיש

ש״ץ: יִתְגַּדַּל וְיִתְקַדַּשׁ שְׁמֵהּ רַבָּא (קהל: אָמֵן)
בְּעָלְמָא דִּי בְרָא כִרְעוּתֵהּ
וְיַמְלִיךְ מַלְכוּתֵהּ
בְּחַיֵּיכוֹן וּבְיוֹמֵיכוֹן וּבְחַיֵּי דְכָל בֵּית יִשְׂרָאֵל
בַּעֲגָלָא וּבִזְמַן קָרִיב, וְאִמְרוּ אָמֵן. (קהל: אָמֵן)

קהל וש״ץ: יְהֵא שְׁמֵהּ רַבָּא מְבָרַךְ לְעָלַם וּלְעָלְמֵי עָלְמַיָּא.

ש״ץ: יִתְבָּרַךְ וְיִשְׁתַּבַּח וְיִתְפָּאַר וְיִתְרוֹמַם וְיִתְנַשֵּׂא
וְיִתְהַדָּר וְיִתְעַלֶּה וְיִתְהַלָּל
שְׁמֵהּ דְּקֻדְשָׁא בְּרִיךְ הוּא (קהל: בְּרִיךְ הוּא)
לְעֵלָּא מִן כָּל בִּרְכָתָא וְשִׁירָתָא
תֻּשְׁבְּחָתָא וְנֶחֱמָתָא
דַּאֲמִירָן בְּעָלְמָא, וְאִמְרוּ אָמֵן. (קהל: אָמֵן)

Musaf for Hoshana Raba

The following prayer, until "in former years" on page 1020, is said silently, standing with feet together. If there is a minyan, the Amida is repeated aloud by the Leader. Take three steps forward and at the points indicated by ▾, bend the knees at the first word, bow at the second, and stand straight before saying God's name.

When I proclaim the LORD's name, give glory to our God. *Deut. 32*
O LORD, open my lips, so that my mouth may declare Your praise. *Ps. 51*

PATRIARCHS

▾בָּרוּךְ▾ Blessed are You, LORD our God and God of our fathers,
God of Abraham, God of Isaac and God of Jacob;
the great, mighty and awesome God, God Most High,
who bestows acts of loving-kindness and creates all,
who remembers the loving-kindness of the fathers
and will bring a Redeemer to their children's children
for the sake of His name, in love.
King, Helper, Savior, Shield:
▾Blessed are You, LORD, Shield of Abraham.

DIVINE MIGHT

אַתָּה גִּבּוֹר You are eternally mighty, LORD.
You give life to the dead
and have great power to save.

In Israel:
He causes the dew to fall.

He sustains the living with loving-kindness,
and with great compassion revives the dead.
He supports the fallen, heals the sick, sets captives free,
and keeps His faith with those who sleep in the dust.
Who is like You, Master of might,
and who can compare to You,
O King who brings death and gives life,
and makes salvation grow?
Faithful are You to revive the dead.
Blessed are You, LORD, who revives the dead.

תפילת מוסף להושענא רבה

The following prayer, until קַדְמֹנִיּוֹת on page 1021, is said silently, standing with feet together. If there is a מנין, the עמידה is repeated aloud by the שליח ציבור. Take three steps forward and at the points indicated by ˚, bend the knees at the first word, bow at the second, and stand straight before saying God's name.

כִּי שֵׁם יהוה אֶקְרָא, הָבוּ גֹדֶל לֵאלֹהֵינוּ: דברים לב

אֲדֹנָי, שְׂפָתַי תִּפְתָּח, וּפִי יַגִּיד תְּהִלָּתֶךָ: תהלים נא

אבות

˚בָּרוּךְ אַתָּה יהוה, אֱלֹהֵינוּ וֵאלֹהֵי אֲבוֹתֵינוּ
אֱלֹהֵי אַבְרָהָם, אֱלֹהֵי יִצְחָק, וֵאלֹהֵי יַעֲקֹב
הָאֵל הַגָּדוֹל הַגִּבּוֹר וְהַנּוֹרָא, אֵל עֶלְיוֹן
גּוֹמֵל חֲסָדִים טוֹבִים, וְקוֹנֵה הַכֹּל, וְזוֹכֵר חַסְדֵי אָבוֹת
וּמֵבִיא גוֹאֵל לִבְנֵי בְנֵיהֶם לְמַעַן שְׁמוֹ בְּאַהֲבָה.
מֶלֶךְ עוֹזֵר וּמוֹשִׁיעַ וּמָגֵן.
˚בָּרוּךְ אַתָּה יהוה, מָגֵן אַבְרָהָם.

גבורות

אַתָּה גִּבּוֹר לְעוֹלָם, אֲדֹנָי
מְחַיֵּה מֵתִים אַתָּה, רַב לְהוֹשִׁיעַ

In ארץ ישראל:
מוֹרִיד הַטָּל

מְכַלְכֵּל חַיִּים בְּחֶסֶד, מְחַיֵּה מֵתִים בְּרַחֲמִים רַבִּים
סוֹמֵךְ נוֹפְלִים, וְרוֹפֵא חוֹלִים, וּמַתִּיר אֲסוּרִים
וּמְקַיֵּם אֱמוּנָתוֹ לִישֵׁנֵי עָפָר.
מִי כָמוֹךָ, בַּעַל גְּבוּרוֹת, וּמִי דּוֹמֶה לָּךְ
מֶלֶךְ, מֵמִית וּמְחַיֶּה וּמַצְמִיחַ יְשׁוּעָה.
וְנֶאֱמָן אַתָּה לְהַחֲיוֹת מֵתִים.
בָּרוּךְ אַתָּה יהוה, מְחַיֵּה הַמֵּתִים.

When saying the Amida silently, continue with "You are holy" on the next page.

KEDUSHA

The following is said standing with feet together, rising on the toes at the words indicated by ▴.

Cong. then Leader: נַעֲרִיצְךָ We will revere and sanctify You with the words uttered by the holy Seraphim who sanctify Your name in the Sanctuary; as is written by Your prophet:
"They call out to one another, saying: *Is. 6*

Cong. then Leader: ▴Holy, ▴holy, ▴holy is the LORD of hosts; the whole world is filled with His glory."
His glory fills the universe. His ministering angels ask each other, "Where is the place of His glory?"
Those facing them reply "Blessed –

Cong. then Leader: ▴"Blessed is the LORD's glory from His place." *Ezek. 3*
From His place may He turn with compassion and be gracious to the people who proclaim the unity of His name, morning and evening, every day, continually, twice each day reciting in love the Shema:

Cong. then Leader: "Listen, Israel, the LORD is our God, the LORD is One." *Deut. 6*
He is our God, He is our Father, He is our King, He is our Savior – and He, in His compassion, will let us hear a second time in the presence of all that lives, His promise "to be Your God. *Num. 15*
I am the LORD your God."

Cong. then Leader: Glorious is our Glorious One, LORD our Master, *Ps. 8*
and glorious is Your name throughout the earth.
Then the LORD shall be King over all the earth; *Zech. 14*
on that day the LORD shall be One and His name One.

Leader: And in Your holy Writings it is written:

Cong. then Leader: ▴"The LORD shall reign for ever. He is your God, Zion, *Ps. 146*
from generation to generation, Halleluya!"

Leader: From generation to generation we will declare Your greatness, and we will proclaim Your holiness for evermore.
Your praise, our God, shall not leave our mouth forever, for You, God, are a great and holy King.
Blessed are You, LORD, the holy God.

The Leader continues with "You have chosen us" on the next page.

When saying the עמידה *silently, continue with* אַתָּה קָדוֹשׁ *on the next page.*

קדושה

The following is said standing with feet together, rising on the toes at the words indicated by ^.

then קהל ש״ץ: נַעֲרִיצְךָ וְנַקְדִּישְׁךָ כְּסוֹד שִׂיחַ שַׂרְפֵי קֹדֶשׁ, הַמַּקְדִּישִׁים שִׁמְךָ
ישעיה ו בַּקֹּדֶשׁ, כַּכָּתוּב עַל יַד נְבִיאֶךָ: וְקָרָא זֶה אֶל־זֶה וְאָמַר

then קהל ש״ץ: ^קָדוֹשׁ, ^קָדוֹשׁ, ^קָדוֹשׁ, יהוה צְבָאוֹת, מְלֹא כָל הָאָרֶץ כְּבוֹדוֹ:
כְּבוֹדוֹ מָלֵא עוֹלָם, מְשָׁרְתָיו שׁוֹאֲלִים זֶה לָזֶה, אַיֵּה מְקוֹם
כְּבוֹדוֹ, לְעֻמָּתָם בָּרוּךְ יֹאמֵרוּ

יחזקאל ג *then* קהל ש״ץ: ^בָּרוּךְ כְּבוֹד־יהוה מִמְּקוֹמוֹ:
מִמְּקוֹמוֹ הוּא יִפֶן בְּרַחֲמִים, וְיָחֹן עַם הַמְיַחֲדִים שְׁמוֹ
עֶרֶב וָבֹקֶר בְּכָל יוֹם תָּמִיד, פַּעֲמַיִם בְּאַהֲבָה שְׁמַע אוֹמְרִים

דברים ו *then* קהל ש״ץ: שְׁמַע יִשְׂרָאֵל, יהוה אֱלֹהֵינוּ, יהוה אֶחָד:
הוּא אֱלֹהֵינוּ, הוּא אָבִינוּ, הוּא מַלְכֵּנוּ, הוּא מוֹשִׁיעֵנוּ
וְהוּא יַשְׁמִיעֵנוּ בְּרַחֲמָיו שֵׁנִית לְעֵינֵי כָּל חָי
במדבר טו לִהְיוֹת לָכֶם לֵאלֹהִים
אֲנִי יהוה אֱלֹהֵיכֶם:

תהלים ח *then* קהל ש״ץ: אַדִּיר אַדִּירֵנוּ, יהוה אֲדֹנֵינוּ, מָה־אַדִּיר שִׁמְךָ בְּכָל־הָאָרֶץ:
זכריה יד וְהָיָה יהוה לְמֶלֶךְ עַל־כָּל־הָאָרֶץ
בַּיּוֹם הַהוּא יִהְיֶה יהוה אֶחָד וּשְׁמוֹ אֶחָד:

ש״ץ: וּבְדִבְרֵי קָדְשְׁךָ כָּתוּב לֵאמֹר

תהלים קמו *then* קהל ש״ץ: ^יִמְלֹךְ יהוה לְעוֹלָם, אֱלֹהַיִךְ צִיּוֹן לְדֹר וָדֹר, הַלְלוּיָהּ:

ש״ץ: לְדוֹר וָדוֹר נַגִּיד גָּדְלֶךָ, וּלְנֵצַח נְצָחִים קְדֻשָּׁתְךָ נַקְדִּישׁ
וְשִׁבְחֲךָ אֱלֹהֵינוּ מִפִּינוּ לֹא יָמוּשׁ לְעוֹלָם וָעֶד
כִּי אֵל מֶלֶךְ גָּדוֹל וְקָדוֹשׁ אָתָּה.
בָּרוּךְ אַתָּה יהוה, הָאֵל הַקָּדוֹשׁ.

The שליח ציבור *continues with* אַתָּה בְחַרְתָּנוּ *on the next page.*

HOLINESS

אַתָּה קָדוֹשׁ You are holy and Your name is holy,
and holy ones praise You daily, Selah!
Blessed are You, LORD,
the holy God.

HOLINESS OF THE DAY

אַתָּה בְחַרְתָּנוּ You have chosen us
from among all peoples.
You have loved and favored us.
You have raised us above all tongues.
You have made us holy through Your commandments.
You have brought us near, our King, to Your service,
and have called us by Your great and holy name.

וַתִּתֶּן לָנוּ And You, LORD our God, have given us in love
festivals for rejoicing, holy days and seasons for joy,
this day of the festival of Sukkot, our time of rejoicing,
a holy assembly in memory of the exodus from Egypt.

וּמִפְּנֵי חֲטָאֵינוּ But because of our sins
we were exiled from our land
and driven far from our country.
We cannot go up to appear and bow before You,
and to perform our duties in Your chosen House,
the great and holy Temple that was called by Your name,
because of the hand that was stretched out
against Your Sanctuary.
May it be Your will,
LORD our God and God of our ancestors,
merciful King,
that You in Your abounding compassion may once more
have mercy on us and on Your Sanctuary,
rebuilding it swiftly and adding to its glory.

קדושת השם

אַתָּה קָדוֹשׁ וְשִׁמְךָ קָדוֹשׁ
וּקְדוֹשִׁים בְּכָל יוֹם יְהַלְלוּךָ סֶּלָה.
בָּרוּךְ אַתָּה יהוה, הָאֵל הַקָּדוֹשׁ.

קדושת היום

אַתָּה בְחַרְתָּנוּ מִכָּל הָעַמִּים
אָהַבְתָּ אוֹתָנוּ וְרָצִיתָ בָּנוּ
וְרוֹמַמְתָּנוּ מִכָּל הַלְּשׁוֹנוֹת
וְקִדַּשְׁתָּנוּ בְּמִצְוֹתֶיךָ
וְקֵרַבְתָּנוּ מַלְכֵּנוּ לַעֲבוֹדָתֶךָ
וְשִׁמְךָ הַגָּדוֹל וְהַקָּדוֹשׁ עָלֵינוּ קָרָאתָ.

וַתִּתֶּן לָנוּ יהוה אֱלֹהֵינוּ בְּאַהֲבָה
מוֹעֲדִים לְשִׂמְחָה, חַגִּים וּזְמַנִּים לְשָׂשׂוֹן
אֶת יוֹם חַג הַסֻּכּוֹת הַזֶּה, זְמַן שִׂמְחָתֵנוּ
מִקְרָא קֹדֶשׁ, זֵכֶר לִיצִיאַת מִצְרָיִם.

וּמִפְּנֵי חֲטָאֵינוּ גָּלִינוּ מֵאַרְצֵנוּ, וְנִתְרַחַקְנוּ מֵעַל אַדְמָתֵנוּ
וְאֵין אֲנַחְנוּ יְכוֹלִים לַעֲלוֹת וְלֵרָאוֹת וּלְהִשְׁתַּחֲווֹת לְפָנֶיךָ
וְלַעֲשׂוֹת חוֹבוֹתֵינוּ בְּבֵית בְּחִירָתֶךָ
בַּבַּיִת הַגָּדוֹל וְהַקָּדוֹשׁ שֶׁנִּקְרָא שִׁמְךָ עָלָיו
מִפְּנֵי הַיָּד שֶׁנִּשְׁתַּלְּחָה בְּמִקְדָּשֶׁךָ.
יְהִי רָצוֹן מִלְּפָנֶיךָ יהוה אֱלֹהֵינוּ וֵאלֹהֵי אֲבוֹתֵינוּ, מֶלֶךְ רַחֲמָן
שֶׁתָּשׁוּב וּתְרַחֵם עָלֵינוּ וְעַל מִקְדָּשְׁךָ בְּרַחֲמֶיךָ הָרַבִּים
וְתִבְנֵהוּ מְהֵרָה וּתְגַדֵּל כְּבוֹדוֹ.

Our Father, our King,
reveal the glory of Your kingdom to us swiftly.
Appear and be exalted over us in the sight of all that lives.
Bring back our scattered ones from among the nations,
and gather our dispersed people from the ends of the earth.
Lead us to Zion, Your city, in jubilation,
and to Jerusalem, home of Your Temple, with everlasting joy.
There we will prepare for You our obligatory offerings:
the regular daily offerings in their order
and the additional offerings according to their law.
And the additional offering of this day of the festival of Sukkot
we will prepare and offer before You in love,
in accord with Your will's commandment,
as You wrote for us in Your Torah
through Your servant Moses, by Your own word,
as it is said:

In Israel omit the following paragraph
and continue with "On the seventh day" below:

וּבַיּוֹם הַשִּׁשִּׁי On the sixth day you shall offer eight bullocks, two rams, fourteen yearling male lambs without blemish. And their meal-offerings and wine-libations as ordained: three-tenths of an ephah for each bull, two-tenths of an ephah for each ram, one-tenth of an ephah for each lamb, wine for the libations, a male goat for atonement, and two regular daily offerings according to their law. *Num. 29*

וּבַיּוֹם הַשְּׁבִיעִי On the seventh day you shall offer seven bullocks, two rams, fourteen yearling male lambs without blemish. And their meal-offerings and wine-libations as ordained: three-tenths of an ephah for each bull, two-tenths of an ephah for each ram, one-tenth of an ephah for each lamb, wine for the libations, a male goat for atonement, and two regular daily offerings according to their law. *Num. 29*

אָבִינוּ מַלְכֵּנוּ, גַּלֵּה כְּבוֹד מַלְכוּתְךָ עָלֵינוּ מְהֵרָה
וְהוֹפַע וְהִנָּשֵׂא עָלֵינוּ לְעֵינֵי כָּל חָי
וְקָרֵב פְּזוּרֵינוּ מִבֵּין הַגּוֹיִם
וּנְפוּצוֹתֵינוּ כַּנֵּס מִיַּרְכְּתֵי אָרֶץ.
וַהֲבִיאֵנוּ לְצִיּוֹן עִירְךָ בְּרִנָּה
וְלִירוּשָׁלַיִם בֵּית מִקְדָּשְׁךָ בְּשִׂמְחַת עוֹלָם
וְשָׁם נַעֲשֶׂה לְפָנֶיךָ אֶת קָרְבְּנוֹת חוֹבוֹתֵינוּ
תְּמִידִים כְּסִדְרָם וּמוּסָפִים כְּהִלְכָתָם
וְאֶת מוּסַף יוֹם חַג הַסֻּכּוֹת הַזֶּה
נַעֲשֶׂה וְנַקְרִיב לְפָנֶיךָ בְּאַהֲבָה כְּמִצְוַת רְצוֹנֶךָ
כְּמוֹ שֶׁכָּתַבְתָּ עָלֵינוּ בְּתוֹרָתֶךָ
עַל יְדֵי מֹשֶׁה עַבְדֶּךָ מִפִּי כְבוֹדֶךָ
כָּאָמוּר

In ארץ ישראל *omit the following paragraph and continue with* וּבַיּוֹם הַשְּׁבִיעִי *below:*

וּבַיּוֹם הַשִּׁשִּׁי, פָּרִים שְׁמֹנָה, אֵילִם שְׁנָיִם, כְּבָשִׂים בְּנֵי־שָׁנָה אַרְבָּעָה עָשָׂר, תְּמִימִם: וּמִנְחָתָם וְנִסְכֵּיהֶם כִּמְדֻבָּר, שְׁלֹשָׁה עֶשְׂרֹנִים לַפָּר, וּשְׁנֵי עֶשְׂרֹנִים לָאָיִל, וְעִשָּׂרוֹן לַכֶּבֶשׂ, וְיַיִן כְּנִסְכּוֹ, וְשָׂעִיר לְכַפֵּר, וּשְׁנֵי תְמִידִים כְּהִלְכָתָם. במדבר כט

וּבַיּוֹם הַשְּׁבִיעִי, פָּרִים שִׁבְעָה, אֵילִם שְׁנָיִם, כְּבָשִׂים בְּנֵי־שָׁנָה אַרְבָּעָה עָשָׂר, תְּמִימִם: וּמִנְחָתָם וְנִסְכֵּיהֶם כִּמְדֻבָּר, שְׁלֹשָׁה עֶשְׂרֹנִים לַפָּר, וּשְׁנֵי עֶשְׂרֹנִים לָאָיִל, וְעִשָּׂרוֹן לַכֶּבֶשׂ, וְיַיִן כְּנִסְכּוֹ, וְשָׂעִיר לְכַפֵּר, וּשְׁנֵי תְמִידִים כְּהִלְכָתָם. במדבר כט

אֱלֹהֵינוּ Our God and God of our ancestors,
merciful King, have compassion upon us.
You who are good and do good, respond to our call.
Return to us in Your abounding mercy
for the sake of our fathers who did Your will.
Rebuild Your Temple as at the beginning,
and establish Your Sanctuary on its site.
Let us witness its rebuilding and gladden us by its restoration.
Bring the priests back to their service,
the Levites to their song and music,
and the Israelites to their homes.

וְשָׁם נַעֲלֶה There we will go up and appear and bow before You
on the three pilgrimage festivals, as is written in Your Torah:
"Three times in the year all your males shall appear *Deut. 16*
before the LORD your God at the place He will choose:
on Pesaḥ, Shavuot and Sukkot.
They shall not appear before the LORD empty-handed.
Each shall bring such a gift as he can,
in proportion to the blessing
that the LORD your God grants you."

וְהַשִּׂיאֵנוּ Bestow on us, LORD our God,
the blessings of Your festivals
for good life and peace, joy and gladness,
as You desired and promised to bless us.
Make us holy through Your commandments
and grant us a share in Your Torah.
Satisfy us with Your goodness, gladden us with Your salvation,
and purify our hearts to serve You in truth.
Grant us as our heritage,
LORD our God with joy and gladness, Your holy festivals,
and may Israel, who sanctify Your name, rejoice in You.
Blessed are You, LORD, who sanctifies Israel and the festive seasons.

אֱלֹהֵינוּ וֵאלֹהֵי אֲבוֹתֵינוּ
מֶלֶךְ רַחֲמָן רַחֵם עָלֵינוּ, טוֹב וּמֵטִיב הִדָּרֶשׁ לָנוּ
שׁוּבָה אֵלֵינוּ בַּהֲמוֹן רַחֲמֶיךָ בִּגְלַל אָבוֹת שֶׁעָשׂוּ רְצוֹנֶךָ.
בְּנֵה בֵיתְךָ כְּבַתְּחִלָּה, וְכוֹנֵן מִקְדָּשְׁךָ עַל מְכוֹנוֹ
וְהַרְאֵנוּ בְּבִנְיָנוֹ, וְשַׂמְּחֵנוּ בְּתִקּוּנוֹ
וְהָשֵׁב כֹּהֲנִים לַעֲבוֹדָתָם, וּלְוִיִּם לְשִׁירָם וּלְזִמְרָם
וְהָשֵׁב יִשְׂרָאֵל לִנְוֵיהֶם.

וְשָׁם נַעֲלֶה וְנֵרָאֶה וְנִשְׁתַּחֲוֶה לְפָנֶיךָ בְּשָׁלֹשׁ פַּעֲמֵי רְגָלֵינוּ
כַּכָּתוּב בְּתוֹרָתֶךָ

דברים טז שָׁלוֹשׁ פְּעָמִים בַּשָּׁנָה יֵרָאֶה כָל־זְכוּרְךָ אֶת־פְּנֵי יהוה אֱלֹהֶיךָ
בַּמָּקוֹם אֲשֶׁר יִבְחָר
בְּחַג הַמַּצּוֹת, וּבְחַג הַשָּׁבֻעוֹת, וּבְחַג הַסֻּכּוֹת
וְלֹא יֵרָאֶה אֶת־פְּנֵי יהוה רֵיקָם:
אִישׁ כְּמַתְּנַת יָדוֹ, כְּבִרְכַּת יהוה אֱלֹהֶיךָ אֲשֶׁר נָתַן־לָךְ:

וְהַשִּׂיאֵנוּ יהוה אֱלֹהֵינוּ אֶת בִּרְכַּת מוֹעֲדֶיךָ
לְחַיִּים וּלְשָׁלוֹם, לְשִׂמְחָה וּלְשָׂשׂוֹן
כַּאֲשֶׁר רָצִיתָ וְאָמַרְתָּ לְבָרְכֵנוּ.
קַדְּשֵׁנוּ בְּמִצְוֹתֶיךָ, וְתֵן חֶלְקֵנוּ בְּתוֹרָתֶךָ
שַׂבְּעֵנוּ מִטּוּבֶךָ, וְשַׂמְּחֵנוּ בִּישׁוּעָתֶךָ
וְטַהֵר לִבֵּנוּ לְעָבְדְּךָ בֶּאֱמֶת.
וְהַנְחִילֵנוּ יהוה אֱלֹהֵינוּ בְּשִׂמְחָה וּבְשָׂשׂוֹן מוֹעֲדֵי קָדְשֶׁךָ
וְיִשְׂמְחוּ בְךָ יִשְׂרָאֵל מְקַדְּשֵׁי שְׁמֶךָ.
בָּרוּךְ אַתָּה יהוה, מְקַדֵּשׁ יִשְׂרָאֵל וְהַזְּמַנִּים.

TEMPLE SERVICE

רְצֵה Find favor, LORD our God, in Your people Israel
and their prayer.
Restore the service to Your most holy House,
and accept in love and favor
the fire-offerings of Israel and their prayer.
May the service of Your people Israel always find favor with You.
And may our eyes witness Your return to Zion in compassion.
Blessed are You, LORD, who restores His Presence to Zion.

THANKSGIVING

Bow at the first nine words.

מוֹדִים׳ We give thanks to You,
for You are the LORD our God
and God of our ancestors
for ever and all time.
You are the Rock of our lives,
Shield of our salvation
from generation to generation.
We will thank You and
declare Your praise for our lives,
which are entrusted into Your hand;
for our souls,
which are placed in Your charge;
for Your miracles
which are with us every day;
and for Your wonders and favors
at all times, evening,
morning and midday.
You are good –
for Your compassion never fails.
You are compassionate –
for Your loving-kindnesses never cease.
We have always placed our hope in You.

During the Leader's Repetition, the congregation says quietly:

מוֹדִים׳ We give thanks to You,
for You are the LORD our God
and God of our ancestors,
God of all flesh,
who formed us
and formed the universe.
Blessings and thanks
are due to Your great
and holy name for giving us
life and sustaining us.
May You continue
to give us life
and sustain us;
and may You gather our
exiles to Your holy courts,
to keep Your decrees,
do Your will and serve You
with a perfect heart,
for it is for us
to give You thanks.
Blessed be God to whom
thanksgiving is due.

עבודה

רְצֵה יהוה אֱלֹהֵינוּ בְּעַמְּךָ יִשְׂרָאֵל, וּבִתְפִלָּתָם
וְהָשֵׁב אֶת הָעֲבוֹדָה לִדְבִיר בֵּיתֶךָ
וְאִשֵּׁי יִשְׂרָאֵל וּתְפִלָּתָם בְּאַהֲבָה תְקַבֵּל בְּרָצוֹן
וּתְהִי לְרָצוֹן תָּמִיד עֲבוֹדַת יִשְׂרָאֵל עַמֶּךָ.
וְתֶחֱזֶינָה עֵינֵינוּ בְּשׁוּבְךָ לְצִיּוֹן בְּרַחֲמִים.
בָּרוּךְ אַתָּה יהוה, הַמַּחֲזִיר שְׁכִינָתוֹ לְצִיּוֹן.

הודאה

Bow at the first five words.

מוֹדִים אֲנַחְנוּ לָךְ
שָׁאַתָּה הוּא יהוה אֱלֹהֵינוּ
וֵאלֹהֵי אֲבוֹתֵינוּ לְעוֹלָם וָעֶד.
צוּר חַיֵּינוּ, מָגֵן יִשְׁעֵנוּ
אַתָּה הוּא לְדוֹר וָדוֹר.
נוֹדֶה לְּךָ וּנְסַפֵּר תְּהִלָּתֶךָ
עַל חַיֵּינוּ הַמְּסוּרִים בְּיָדֶךָ
וְעַל נִשְׁמוֹתֵינוּ הַפְּקוּדוֹת לָךְ
וְעַל נִסֶּיךָ שֶׁבְּכָל יוֹם עִמָּנוּ
וְעַל נִפְלְאוֹתֶיךָ וְטוֹבוֹתֶיךָ
שֶׁבְּכָל עֵת
עֶרֶב וָבֹקֶר וְצָהֳרָיִם.
הַטּוֹב, כִּי לֹא כָלוּ רַחֲמֶיךָ
וְהַמְרַחֵם, כִּי לֹא תַמּוּ חֲסָדֶיךָ
מֵעוֹלָם קִוִּינוּ לָךְ.

During the חזרת הש״ץ, *the* קהל *says quietly:*

מוֹדִים אֲנַחְנוּ לָךְ
שָׁאַתָּה הוּא יהוה אֱלֹהֵינוּ
וֵאלֹהֵי אֲבוֹתֵינוּ
אֱלֹהֵי כָל בָּשָׂר
יוֹצְרֵנוּ, יוֹצֵר בְּרֵאשִׁית.
בְּרָכוֹת וְהוֹדָאוֹת
לְשִׁמְךָ הַגָּדוֹל וְהַקָּדוֹשׁ
עַל שֶׁהֶחֱיִיתָנוּ וְקִיַּמְתָּנוּ.
כֵּן תְּחַיֵּנוּ וּתְקַיְּמֵנוּ
וְתֶאֱסֹף גָּלֻיּוֹתֵינוּ
לְחַצְרוֹת קָדְשֶׁךָ
לִשְׁמֹר חֻקֶּיךָ וְלַעֲשׂוֹת רְצוֹנֶךָ
וּלְעָבְדְּךָ בְּלֵבָב שָׁלֵם
עַל שֶׁאֲנַחְנוּ מוֹדִים לָךְ.
בָּרוּךְ אֵל הַהוֹדָאוֹת.

וְעַל כֻּלָּם For all these things
may Your name be blessed and exalted, our King,
continually, for ever and all time. Let all that lives thank You, Selah!
and praise Your name in truth, God, our Savior and Help, Selah!
▾Blessed are You, LORD, whose name is "the Good"
and to whom thanks are due.

For the blessing of the Kohanim in Israel, see page 1396.
The Leader says the following during the Repetition of the Musaf Amida.
It is also said in Israel when no Kohanim bless the congregation.

Our God and God of our fathers, bless us with the threefold blessing in the Torah, written by the hand of Moses Your servant and pronounced by Aaron and his sons the priests, Your holy people, as it is said:

May the LORD bless you and protect you. *Num. 6*
Cong: May it be Your will.
May the LORD make His face shine on you and be gracious to you.
Cong: May it be Your will.
May the LORD turn His face toward you, and grant you peace.
Cong: May it be Your will.

PEACE

שִׂים שָׁלוֹם Grant peace, goodness and blessing,
grace, loving-kindness and compassion
to us and all Israel Your people.
Bless us, our Father, all as one,
with the light of Your face,
for by the light of Your face You have given us, LORD our God,
the Torah of life and love of kindness,
righteousness, blessing, compassion, life and peace.
May it be good in Your eyes to bless Your people Israel
at every time, in every hour, with Your peace.
Blessed are You, LORD, who blesses His people Israel with peace.

The following verse concludes the Leader's Repetition of the Amida.
Some also say it here as part of the silent Amida.

May the words of my mouth and the meditation of my heart *Ps. 19*
find favor before You, LORD, my Rock and Redeemer.

וְעַל כֻּלָּם יִתְבָּרַךְ וְיִתְרוֹמַם שִׁמְךָ מַלְכֵּנוּ תָּמִיד לְעוֹלָם וָעֶד.
וְכֹל הַחַיִּים יוֹדְוּךָ סֶּלָה, וִיהַלְלוּ אֶת שִׁמְךָ בֶּאֱמֶת
הָאֵל יְשׁוּעָתֵנוּ וְעֶזְרָתֵנוּ סֶלָה.
ּבָּרוּךְ אַתָּה יהוה, הַטּוֹב שִׁמְךָ וּלְךָ נָאֶה לְהוֹדוֹת.

For the blessing of the כהנים *in* ארץ ישראל *see page 1397.*
The שליח ציבור *says the following during the* חזרת הש״ץ *of* מוסף.
It is also said in ארץ ישראל *when no* כהנים *bless the* קהל.

אֱלֹהֵינוּ וֵאלֹהֵי אֲבוֹתֵינוּ, בָּרְכֵנוּ בַּבְּרָכָה הַמְשֻׁלֶּשֶׁת בַּתּוֹרָה, הַכְּתוּבָה עַל יְדֵי מֹשֶׁה עַבְדֶּךָ, הָאֲמוּרָה מִפִּי אַהֲרֹן וּבָנָיו כֹּהֲנִים עַם קְדוֹשֶׁיךָ, כָּאָמוּר

יְבָרֶכְךָ יהוה וְיִשְׁמְרֶךָ: קהל: כֵּן יְהִי רָצוֹן — במדבר ו
יָאֵר יהוה פָּנָיו אֵלֶיךָ וִיחֻנֶּךָּ: קהל: כֵּן יְהִי רָצוֹן
יִשָּׂא יהוה פָּנָיו אֵלֶיךָ וְיָשֵׂם לְךָ שָׁלוֹם: קהל: כֵּן יְהִי רָצוֹן

שלום

שִׂים שָׁלוֹם טוֹבָה וּבְרָכָה
חֵן וָחֶסֶד וְרַחֲמִים עָלֵינוּ וְעַל כָּל יִשְׂרָאֵל עַמֶּךָ.
בָּרְכֵנוּ אָבִינוּ כֻּלָּנוּ כְּאֶחָד בְּאוֹר פָּנֶיךָ
כִּי בְאוֹר פָּנֶיךָ נָתַתָּ לָּנוּ יהוה אֱלֹהֵינוּ
תּוֹרַת חַיִּים וְאַהֲבַת חֶסֶד
וּצְדָקָה וּבְרָכָה וְרַחֲמִים וְחַיִּים וְשָׁלוֹם.
וְטוֹב בְּעֵינֶיךָ לְבָרֵךְ אֶת עַמְּךָ יִשְׂרָאֵל
בְּכָל עֵת וּבְכָל שָׁעָה בִּשְׁלוֹמֶךָ.
בָּרוּךְ אַתָּה יהוה, הַמְבָרֵךְ אֶת עַמּוֹ יִשְׂרָאֵל בַּשָּׁלוֹם.

The following verse concludes the חזרת הש״ץ.
Some also say it here as part of the silent עמידה.

יִהְיוּ לְרָצוֹן אִמְרֵי־פִי וְהֶגְיוֹן לִבִּי לְפָנֶיךָ, יהוה צוּרִי וְגֹאֲלִי: — תהלים יט

אֱלֹהַי My God, *Berakhot 17a*
guard my tongue from evil and my lips from deceitful speech.
To those who curse me, let my soul be silent;
may my soul be to all like the dust.
Open my heart to Your Torah
and let my soul pursue Your commandments.
As for all who plan evil against me,
swiftly thwart their counsel and frustrate their plans.
Act for the sake of Your name;
act for the sake of Your right hand;
act for the sake of Your holiness;
act for the sake of Your Torah.
That Your beloved ones may be delivered, *Ps. 60*
save with Your right hand and answer me.
May the words of my mouth and the meditation of my heart *Ps. 19*
find favor before You, LORD, my Rock and Redeemer.

Bow, take three steps back, then bow, first left, then right, then center, while saying:
May He who makes peace in His high places,
make peace for us and all Israel –
and say: Amen.

יְהִי רָצוֹן May it be Your will, LORD our God and God of our ancestors,
that the Temple be rebuilt speedily in our days,
and grant us a share in Your Torah.
And there we will serve You with reverence,
as in the days of old and as in former years.
Then the offering of Judah and Jerusalem *Mal. 3*
will be pleasing to the LORD
as in the days of old and as in former years.

The Leader repeats the Amida *(page 1006)*.

אֱלֹהַי ברכות יז.

נְצֹר לְשׁוֹנִי מֵרָע וּשְׂפָתַי מִדַּבֵּר מִרְמָה

וְלִמְקַלְלַי נַפְשִׁי תִדֹּם, וְנַפְשִׁי כֶּעָפָר לַכֹּל תִּהְיֶה.

פְּתַח לִבִּי בְּתוֹרָתֶךָ, וּבְמִצְוֹתֶיךָ תִּרְדֹּף נַפְשִׁי.

וְכָל הַחוֹשְׁבִים עָלַי רָעָה

מְהֵרָה הָפֵר עֲצָתָם וְקַלְקֵל מַחֲשַׁבְתָּם.

עֲשֵׂה לְמַעַן שְׁמֶךָ

עֲשֵׂה לְמַעַן יְמִינֶךָ

עֲשֵׂה לְמַעַן קְדֻשָּׁתֶךָ

עֲשֵׂה לְמַעַן תּוֹרָתֶךָ.

לְמַעַן יֵחָלְצוּן יְדִידֶיךָ, הוֹשִׁיעָה יְמִינְךָ וַעֲנֵנִי: תהלים ס

יִהְיוּ לְרָצוֹן אִמְרֵי־פִי וְהֶגְיוֹן לִבִּי לְפָנֶיךָ, יהוה צוּרִי וְגוֹאֲלִי: תהלים יט

Bow, take three steps back, then bow, first left, then right, then center, while saying:

עֹשֶׂה שָׁלוֹם בִּמְרוֹמָיו

הוּא יַעֲשֶׂה שָׁלוֹם עָלֵינוּ וְעַל כָּל יִשְׂרָאֵל

וְאִמְרוּ אָמֵן.

יְהִי רָצוֹן מִלְּפָנֶיךָ יהוה אֱלֹהֵינוּ וֵאלֹהֵי אֲבוֹתֵינוּ

שֶׁיִּבָּנֶה בֵּית הַמִּקְדָּשׁ בִּמְהֵרָה בְיָמֵינוּ

וְתֵן חֶלְקֵנוּ בְּתוֹרָתֶךָ

וְשָׁם נַעֲבָדְךָ בְּיִרְאָה כִּימֵי עוֹלָם וּכְשָׁנִים קַדְמֹנִיּוֹת.

וְעָרְבָה לַיהוה מִנְחַת יְהוּדָה וִירוּשָׁלָםִ כִּימֵי עוֹלָם וּכְשָׁנִים קַדְמֹנִיּוֹת: מלאכי ג

The Leader repeats the עמידה *(page 1007).*

HOSHANOT FOR HOSHANA RABA

It is the custom to leave the Ark open until the end of the Hoshanot. All of the Torah scrolls are held on the Bima. Members of the congregation who have a Lulav and Etrog circle the Bima seven times while the Hoshanot are read. After finishing the first circuit, say "For I said" and immediately proceed to make another circuit, saying "The Foundation Stone," etc.

Leader then congregation:

הוֹשַׁע נָא Save us, please for Your sake, our God, save us please.

Leader then congregation:

Save us, please for Your sake, our Creator, save us, please.

Leader then congregation:

Save us, please for Your sake, our Redeemer, save us, please.

Leader then congregation:

Save us, please for Your sake, You who seek us, save us, please.

Save us, please –

First Hakafa:

לְמַעַן אֲמִתָּךְ For the sake of Your truth – for the sake of Your covenant – for the sake of Your greatness and glory – for the sake of Your Law – for the sake of Your majesty – for the sake of Your promise – for the sake of Your remembrance – for the sake of Your love – for the sake of Your goodness – for the sake of Your Oneness – for the sake of Your honor – for the sake of Your wisdom – for the sake of Your kingship – for the sake of Your eternity – for the sake of Your mystery – for the sake of Your might – for the sake of Your splendor – for the sake of Your righteousness – for the sake of Your holiness – for the sake of Your great compassion – for the sake of Your Presence – for the sake of Your praise – Save us, please.

After circling the Bima the first time, say:

For I said, *Ps. 89*
the world is built by loving-kindness.

הושענות להושענא רבה

It is the custom to leave the ארון קודש *open until the end of the* הושענות. *All of the* ספרי תורה *are held on the* בימה. *Members of the* קהל *who have a* לולב *and* אתרוג *circle the* בימה *seven times while the* הושענות *are read. After finishing the first circuit, say* כִּי־אָמַרְתִּי *and immediately proceed to make another circuit, saying* אֶבֶן שְׁתִיָּה*, etc.*

then שליח ציבור :קהל

הוֹשַׁע נָא לְמַעַנְךָ אֱלֹהֵינוּ הוֹשַׁע נָא.

then שליח ציבור :קהל

הוֹשַׁע נָא לְמַעַנְךָ בּוֹרְאֵנוּ הוֹשַׁע נָא.

then שליח ציבור :קהל

הוֹשַׁע נָא לְמַעַנְךָ גּוֹאֲלֵנוּ הוֹשַׁע נָא.

then שליח ציבור :קהל

הוֹשַׁע נָא לְמַעַנְךָ דּוֹרְשֵׁנוּ הוֹשַׁע נָא.

הוֹשַׁע נָא

:הקפה *First*

לְמַעַן אֲמִתָּךְ. לְמַעַן בְּרִיתָךְ. לְמַעַן גָּדְלָךְ וְתִפְאַרְתָּךְ. לְמַעַן דָּתָךְ. לְמַעַן הוֹדָךְ. לְמַעַן וְעוּדָךְ. לְמַעַן זִכְרָךְ. לְמַעַן חַסְדָּךְ. לְמַעַן טוּבָךְ. לְמַעַן יִחוּדָךְ. לְמַעַן כְּבוֹדָךְ. לְמַעַן לִמּוּדָךְ. לְמַעַן מַלְכוּתָךְ. לְמַעַן נִצְחָךְ. לְמַעַן סוֹדָךְ. לְמַעַן עֻזָּךְ. לְמַעַן פְּאֵרָךְ. לְמַעַן צִדְקָתָךְ. לְמַעַן קְדֻשָּׁתָךְ. לְמַעַן רַחֲמֶיךָ הָרַבִּים. לְמַעַן שְׁכִינָתָךְ. לְמַעַן תְּהִלָּתָךְ. הוֹשַׁע נָא.

After circling the בימה *the first time, say:*

כִּי־אָמַרְתִּי עוֹלָם חֶסֶד יִבָּנֶה: תהלים פט

לְמַעַן אֲמִתָּךְ *For the sake of Your truth:* For commentary, see page 532.

Save us, please –

Second Hakafa:

אֶבֶן שְׁתִיָּה The Foundation Stone – the House You chose – the threshing-floor of Arnan – the hidden Shrine – Mount Moriah – where He shall be seen – Your glorious Sanctuary – where David camped – the best of Lebanon – the Beauty of Heights, Joy of all the earth – the Place of Perfect Beauty – the Lodge of Goodness – the Place of Your dwelling – the Shelter of Shalem – the tribes' Pilgrimage – the precious Cornerstone – shining Zion – the Holy of Holies – [the walls] lined with love – Residence of Your glory – the Hill toward which all mouths pray – Save us, please.

After circling the Bima the second time, say:

A strong arm is Yours, might is Yours; *Ps. 89*
Your hand holds its power, Your right hand raised.

Save us, please –

Third Hakafa:

אוֹם אֲנִי חוֹמָה "I am a wall," said the people – bright as the sun – exiled and reviled – fair like a date palm – killed on account of You – like sheep to the slaughter – dispersed among tormentors – wrapped in Your embrace, clinging to You – bearing Your yoke – the one to know Your Oneness – beaten down in exile – learning the awe of You – our faces scratched – given over to the violent – weighed down beneath Your burden – oppressed and in turmoil – redeemed by [Moses] Toviya – holy flock – the communities of Jacob – marked out with Your name – roaring, "Save us, please!" – leaning on You – Save us, please.

After circling the Bima the third time, say:

Grant truth to Jacob, loving-kindness to Abraham. *Mic. 7*

Save us, please –

Fourth Hakafa:

אָדוֹן הַמּוֹשִׁיעַ Master who saves – there is no one else – mighty, with great power to save – when I was brought low, He saved me – God who saves – who delivers and saves – save those who cry out to You – those who yet watch for

---

is the resurrection of the dead, and in which, starting on Shemini Atzeret, we will include reference to rain, which brings the barren land to life again.

גִּבּוֹר וְרַב לְהוֹשִׁיעַ *Mighty, with great power to save.* A key phrase from the second paragraph of the Amida. R. Joseph Albo comments that God's power is the

הוֹשַׁע נָא

Second הקפה:

אֶבֶן שְׁתִיָּה. בֵּית הַבְּחִירָה. גֹּרֶן אָרְנָן. דְּבִיר הַמֻּצְנָע. הַר הַמּוֹרִיָּה. וְהַר יֵרָאֶה. זְבוּל תִּפְאַרְתֶּךָ. חָנָה דָוִד. טוֹב הַלְּבָנוֹן. יְפֵה נוֹף מְשׂוֹשׂ כָּל הָאָרֶץ. כְּלִילַת יֹפִי. לִינַת הַצֶּדֶק. מָכוֹן לְשִׁבְתֶּךָ. נָוֶה שַׁאֲנָן. סֻכַּת שָׁלֵם. עֲלִיַּת שְׁבָטִים. פִּנַּת יִקְרַת. צִיּוֹן הַמְצֻיֶּנֶת. קֹדֶשׁ הַקֳּדָשִׁים. רָצוּף אַהֲבָה. שְׁכִינַת כְּבוֹדֶךָ. תֵּל תַּלְפִּיּוֹת. הוֹשַׁע נָא.

After circling the בימה *the second time, say:*

לְךָ זְרוֹעַ עִם־גְּבוּרָה, תָּעֹז יָדְךָ תָּרוּם יְמִינֶךָ: תהלים פט

הוֹשַׁע נָא

Third הקפה:

אוֹם אֲנִי חוֹמָה. בָּרָה כַּחַמָּה. גּוֹלָה וְסוּרָה. דָּמְתָה לְתָמָר. הַהֲרוּגָה עָלֶיךָ. וְנֶחְשֶׁבֶת כְּצֹאן טִבְחָה. זְרוּיָה בֵּין מַכְעִיסֶיהָ. חֲבוּקָה וּדְבוּקָה בָּךְ. טוֹעֶנֶת עֻלָּךְ. יְחִידָה לְיַחֲדָךְ. כְּבוּשָׁה בַגּוֹלָה. לוֹמֶדֶת יִרְאָתָךְ. מְרוּטַת לֶחִי. נְתוּנָה לְמַכִּים. סוֹבֶלֶת סִבְלָךְ. עֲנִיָּה סוֹעֲרָה. פְּדוּיַת טוֹבִיָּה. צֹאן קָדָשִׁים. קְהִלּוֹת יַעֲקֹב. רְשׁוּמִים בִּשְׁמֶךָ. שׁוֹאֲגִים הוֹשַׁע נָא. תְּמוּכִים עָלֶיךָ. הוֹשַׁע נָא.

After circling the בימה *the third time, say:*

תִּתֵּן אֱמֶת לְיַעֲקֹב, חֶסֶד לְאַבְרָהָם: מיכה ז

הוֹשַׁע נָא

Fourth הקפה:

אָדוֹן הַמּוֹשִׁיעַ. בִּלְתְּךָ אֵין לְהוֹשִׁיעַ. גִּבּוֹר וְרַב לְהוֹשִׁיעַ. דַּלּוֹתִי וְלִי יְהוֹשִׁיעַ. הָאֵל הַמּוֹשִׁיעַ. וּמַצִּיל וּמוֹשִׁיעַ. זוֹעֲקֶיךָ תּוֹשִׁיעַ. חוֹכֶיךָ הוֹשִׁיעַ.

אֶבֶן שְׁתִיָּה *The Foundation Stone:* For commentary, see page 535.

אוֹם אֲנִי חוֹמָה *I am a wall.* For commentary, see page 712.

אָדוֹן הַמּוֹשִׁיעַ MASTER WHO SAVES
This *Hoshana* is based on the second paragraph of the Amida, whose theme

You – nourish Your young lambs – make the harvest lavish – sprout every growing thing and save us – do not condemn this valley – make the good fruits sweet and save us – carry the clouds to us – shake down the raindrops – do not hold back the clouds – You who open Your hand and satisfy – relieve those who thirst for You – save those who call to You – save those You have loved – rescue those who rise to seek You – save Your innocent ones – Save us, please.

After circling the Bima the fourth time, say:

At Your hand, bliss for evermore. *Ps. 16*

Save us, please –

Fifth Hakafa:

אָדָם וּבְהֵמָה Man and beast – body, spirit and soul – muscle, bone, skin – likeness and image woven – glory reduced to mere breath – likened to beasts that fall silent – light and beauty and stature – renew the face of the land – planting trees on desolate ground – winepress and bounty of meadows – vineyard and sycamore fig – bring to the land renowned – mighty rain to scent spices – to recover a devastated place – to raise up the shrub – to make the delightful fruits robust – to make the land glorious with flowers – to soak the plants with rain – to make cool waters flow – to fill out the raindrops – to raise up the earth – the earth that is hung over nothingness – Save us, please.

After circling the Bima the fifth time, say:

LORD our Master, how majestic is Your name throughout the earth, *Ps. 8*
Your glory over all the heavens.

Save us, please –

Sixth Hakafa:

אֲדָמָה מֵאֶרֶר Save earth from cursedness – save cattle from miscarriage – save threshing floor from pest – save grain from burning – save wealth from

---

some of the same needs as animal and plant life. We may be spiritually and intellectually in "the image and likeness of God," but we are also "dust of the earth," mere mortals with biological needs. The landscape of Israel – fertile, yet often subject to drought – is peculiarly responsive to rain – at times barren, at others full of the colors and scents of luxuriant growth – scenes evoked in this prayer.

אֲדָמָה מֵאֶרֶר SAVE EARTH FROM CURSEDNESS
A litany of the many hazards that face farmers, threatening cattle or crops.

טְלָאֶיךָ תַּשְׂבִּיעַ. יְבוּל לְהַשְׁפִּיעַ. כָּל שִׂיחַ תַּדְשֵׁא וְתוֹשִׁיעַ. לְגֵיא בַּל תַּרְשִׁיעַ. מְגָדִים תַּמְתִּיק וְתוֹשִׁיעַ. נְשִׂיאִים לְהַסִּיעַ. שְׂעִירִים לְהָנִיעַ. עֲנָנִים מִלְּהַמְנִיעַ. פּוֹתֵחַ יָד וּמַשְׂבִּיעַ. צְמֵאֶיךָ תַּשְׂבִּיעַ. קוֹרְאֶיךָ תּוֹשִׁיעַ. רְחוּמֶיךָ תּוֹשִׁיעַ. שׁוֹחֲרֶיךָ הוֹשִׁיעַ. תְּמִימֶיךָ תּוֹשִׁיעַ. הוֹשַׁע נָא.

After circling the בימה *the fourth time, say:*

נְעִמוֹת בִּימִינְךָ נֶצַח: תהלים טז

הוֹשַׁע נָא

Fifth הקפה:

אָדָם וּבְהֵמָה. בָּשָׂר וְרוּחַ וּנְשָׁמָה. גִּיד וְעֶצֶם וְקָרְמָה. דְּמוּת וְצֶלֶם וְרִקְמָה. הוֹד לַהֶבֶל דָּמָה. וְנִמְשַׁל כַּבְּהֵמוֹת נִדְמָה. זִיו וְתֹאַר וְקוֹמָה. חִדּוּשׁ פְּנֵי אֲדָמָה. טִיעַת עֲצֵי נְשַׁמָּה. יְקָבִים וְקָמָה. כְּרָמִים וְשִׁקְמָה. לְתֵבֵל הַמְסֻיָּמָה. מְטָרוֹת עֹז לְסַמְּמָה. נְשִׁיָּה לְקַיְּמָה. שִׂיחִים לְקוֹמְמָה. עֲדָנִים לְעָצְמָה. פְּרָחִים לְהַעֲצִימָה. צְמָחִים לְגָשְׁמָה. קָרִים לְזָרְמָה. רְבִיבִים לְשַׁלְּמָה. שְׁתִיָּה לְרוֹמְמָה. תְּלוּיָה עַל בְּלִימָה. הוֹשַׁע נָא.

After circling the בימה *the fifth time, say:*

יהוה אֲדֹנֵינוּ מָה־אַדִּיר שִׁמְךָ בְּכָל־הָאָרֶץ תהלים ח
אֲשֶׁר־תְּנָה הוֹדְךָ עַל־הַשָּׁמָיִם:

הוֹשַׁע נָא

Sixth הקפה:

אֲדָמָה מֵאֶרֶר. בְּהֵמָה מִמְּשַׁכֶּלֶת. גֹּרֶן מִגָּזָם. דָּגָן מִדַּלֶּקֶת. הוֹן מִמְּאֵרָה.

---

opposite of man's: Humans have the power to kill, turning life into death; God alone has the power to turn death into life (*HaIkarim* 4:35).

טְלָאֶיךָ *Your young lambs.* "The Lord is my Shepherd," (Ps. 23:1); therefore we are His flock.

אָדָם וּבְהֵמָה MAN AND BEAST
A *Hoshana* speaking of all life's need for water. We are physical beings with

want – save sustenance from terror – save olive from windfall – save wheat from grasshopper – save food from vermin – save wine-vat from maggot – save vineyard from worm – save late harvest from locust – save bounty from crickets – save souls from horror – save abundance from insects – save herds from infirmity – save fruits from the gales – save flocks from destruction – save crops from the curse – save plenty from poverty – save the wheat-ears from leanness – save produce from pestilence – Save us, please.

After circling the Bima the sixth time, say:

The LORD is righteous in all His ways, *Ps. 145*
and kind in all He does.

Save us, please –

Seventh Hakafa:

לְמַעַן אֵיתָן For the sake of steadfast [Abraham], who was thrown into flames of fire –
for the sake of his son [Isaac] who was bound on the wood of the fire –
for the sake of the mighty [Jacob] who struggled with a prince of fire –
for the sake of the flags [of the tribes] You led in light and a cloud of fire –
for the sake of one who was raised up to the heights and rose, like an angel of fire –
for the sake of one who is to You like a deputy among erelim of fire –
for the sake of the gift of commandments made in fire –
for the sake of the curtained Tent [of Meeting] and its cloud of fire –
for the sake of that scene on the mountain, of Your coming down to it in fire –

לְמַעַן אֵיתָן FOR THE SAKE OF STEADFAST
A prayer for salvation in the merits of the great figures of the past, who were heroic in their faith despite the many trials they faced.

הַנִּזְרָק בְּלַהַב אֵשׁ *Who was thrown into flames.* According to tradition, Abraham was cast into a fiery furnace by Nimrod.

שַׂר אֵשׁ *A prince of fire.* The angel with whom Jacob wrestled at night (Gen. 34).

הָעֲלָה לַמָּרוֹם *Raised up to the heights.* Moses when he received the Torah.

כְּסֶגֶן *Like a deputy.* Aaron, the first high priest.

וְאֹכֶל מִמְּהוּמָה. זַיִת מִנֶּשֶׁל. חִטָּה מֵחָגָב. טֶרֶף מִגּוֹבַי. יֶקֶב מִיֶּלֶק. כֶּרֶם מִתּוֹלַעַת. לֶקֶשׁ מֵאַרְבֶּה. מֶגֶד מִצְּלָצַל. נֶפֶשׁ מִבֶּהָלָה. שֹׂבַע מִסָּלְעָם. עֲדָרִים מִדַּלּוּת. פֵּרוֹת מִשִּׁדָּפוֹן. צֹאן מִצְּמִיתוּת. קָצִיר מִקְּלָלָה. רֹב מֵרָזוֹן. שִׁבֹּלֶת מִצִּנָּמוֹן. תְּבוּאָה מֵחָסִיל. הוֹשַׁע נָא.

After circling the בימה *the sixth time, say:*

צַדִּיק יהוה בְּכָל־דְּרָכָיו, וְחָסִיד בְּכָל־מַעֲשָׂיו: תהלים קמה

הוֹשַׁע נָא

Seventh הקפה*:*

לְמַעַן אֵיתָן הַנִּזְרָק בְּלַהַב אֵשׁ.
לְמַעַן בֵּן הַנֶּעֱקַד עַל עֵצִים וָאֵשׁ.
לְמַעַן גִּבּוֹר הַנֶּאֱבַק עִם שַׂר אֵשׁ.
לְמַעַן דְּגָלִים נָחִיתָ בְּאוֹר וַעֲנַן אֵשׁ.
לְמַעַן הֹעֲלָה לַמָּרוֹם, וְנִתְעַלָּה כְּמַלְאֲכֵי אֵשׁ.
לְמַעַן וְהוּא לְךָ כְּסֶגֶן בְּאֶרְאֶלֵּי אֵשׁ.
לְמַעַן זֶבֶד דִּבְּרוֹת הַנִּתּוּנוֹת מֵאֵשׁ.
לְמַעַן חִפּוּי יְרִיעוֹת וַעֲנַן אֵשׁ.
לְמַעַן טֶכֶס הַר יָרַדְתָּ עָלָיו בָּאֵשׁ.

Israel, during much of the biblical era, was a nation of small farms and farmers. Sukkot is a time when, through the four kinds – the unprocessed products of nature – and through the Sukka itself, exposed to the elements, we are brought closure to nature than at other times of the year, reminding us of how vulnerable and fraught with risk agriculture and animal husbandry can be.

נֶפֶשׁ מִבֶּהָלָה *Save souls from horror.* The rest of the *Hoshana* is about animal and plant life. This, the sole exception, refers to the feelings of a farmer on seeing a crop ruined or animals infected (R. Herz Treves).

for the sake of the loveliness of that House You preferred above heavens of fire –
for the sake of [Moses] who yearned until the dying of the fire –
for the sake of [Aaron] who took a fire pan to quell a rage of fire –
for the sake of [Pinehas] who burned with a great jealousy, Your fire –
for the sake of [Joshua] who raised his hand and brought down stones of fire –
for the sake of [Samuel] who burned a milk lamb wholly in the fire –
for the sake of [David] who stood in the threshing floor and found favor again through fire –
for the sake of [Solomon] who spoke in the Courtyard and down came fire –
for the sake of Your messenger [Elijah] who rose and was raised up in a chariot with horses of fire –
for the sake of [Hananiah, Mishael and Azariah,] the holy ones flung into fire –
for the sake of [Daniel] who saw the thousands of myriad [angels], the rivers of fire –
for the sake of the desolate remains of Your city burnt up by fire –
for the sake of the past of these clans of Judah whom You shall make as a basin of fire – Save us, please.

After circling the Bima the seventh time, say:

לְךָ Yours, Lord, are the greatness and the power, *1 Chr. 29*
the glory and the majesty and splendor,
for everything in heaven and earth is Yours.
Yours, Lord, is the kingdom;
You are exalted as Head over all.
Then the Lord shall be King over all the earth; *Zech. 14*
on that day the Lord shall be One and His name One.
And in Your Torah it is written:
Listen, Israel: the Lord is our God, the Lord is One. *Deut. 6*
Blessed be the name of His glorious kingdom for ever and all time.

אַלּוּפֵי יְהוּדָה *These clans of Judah.* "On that day I will make the clans of Judah like a basin of fire in a woodpile, like a flaming torch among sheaves. They will consume all the surrounding peoples right and left, but Jerusalem will remain intact in her place" (Zech. 12:6).

לְמַעַן יְדִידוּת בֵּית אֲשֶׁר אָהַבְתָּ מִשְּׁמֵי אֵשׁ.
לְמַעַן כָּמַהּ עַד שָׁקְעָה הָאֵשׁ.
לְמַעַן לָקַח מַחְתַּת אֵשׁ וְהֵסִיר חֲרוֹן אֵשׁ.
לְמַעַן מְקַנֵּא קִנְאָה גְדוֹלָה בָּאֵשׁ.
לְמַעַן נָף יָדוֹ וְיָרְדוּ אַבְנֵי אֵשׁ.
לְמַעַן שָׂם טְלֵה חָלָב כְּלִיל אֵשׁ.
לְמַעַן עָמַד בַּגֹּרֶן וְנִתְרַצָּה בָּאֵשׁ.
לְמַעַן פִּלֵּל בָּעֲזָרָה וְיָרְדָה הָאֵשׁ.
לְמַעַן צִיר עָלָה וְנִתְעַלָּה בְּרֶכֶב וְסוּסֵי אֵשׁ.
לְמַעַן קְדוֹשִׁים מֻשְׁלָכִים בָּאֵשׁ.
לְמַעַן רִבּוֹ רִבְבָן חָז וְנַהֲרֵי אֵשׁ.
לְמַעַן שִׁמְמוֹת עִירָךְ הַשְּׂרוּפָה בָּאֵשׁ.
לְמַעַן תּוֹלְדוֹת אַלּוּפֵי יְהוּדָה, תָּשִׂים כְּכִיּוֹר אֵשׁ. הוֹשַׁע נָא.

After circling the בימה *the seventh time, say:*

לְךָ יהוה הַגְּדֻלָּה וְהַגְּבוּרָה וְהַתִּפְאֶרֶת וְהַנֵּצַח וְהַהוֹד דברי הימים א׳ כט
כִּי־כֹל בַּשָּׁמַיִם וּבָאָרֶץ
לְךָ יהוה הַמַּמְלָכָה וְהַמִּתְנַשֵּׂא לְכֹל לְרֹאשׁ:
וְהָיָה יהוה לְמֶלֶךְ עַל־כָּל־הָאָרֶץ זכריה יד
בַּיּוֹם הַהוּא יִהְיֶה יהוה אֶחָד וּשְׁמוֹ אֶחָד:
וּבְתוֹרָתְךָ כָּתוּב לֵאמֹר: שְׁמַע יִשְׂרָאֵל, יהוה אֱלֹהֵינוּ, יהוה אֶחָד: דברים ו
בָּרוּךְ שֵׁם כְּבוֹד מַלְכוּתוֹ לְעוֹלָם וָעֶד.

עַד שָׁקְעָה הָאֵשׁ *Until the dying of the fire.* A reference to Moses. The dying of the fire may mean, until the end of his life (at 120, "his sight had never dimmed, nor his strength evaded him" (Deut. 34:7), or until the fire of God's anger at the sin of the Golden Calf abated.

I and *HE*: save us, please.

כְּהוֹשַׁעְתָּ As You saved the mighty ones in Lud with You,
coming down for Your people's deliverance – save us, please.

As You saved nation and God together,
[the people] called for God's salvation – save us, please.

As You saved the crowding hosts,
and angelic hosts along with them – save us, please.

As You saved pure ones from the grip of slavery,
Gracious One; enslaved in cruel hands – save us, please.

As You saved those submerged between slices of the deep,
and brought Your own glory through it with them – save us, please.

As You saved the stem as they sang "And God saved" –
but the Deliverer reads it, "God was saved" – save us, please.

As You saved, and You said, "I took you out,"
but let it be pointed, "I was taken out with you" – save us, please.

As You saved those who encompassed the Altar,
bearing their willows to encircle the Altar – save us, please.

As You saved the Ark of wonders that was wronged,
tormenting Philistia with fury, and saving it – save us, please.

As You saved the communities You sent away to Babylon,
being sent too, for them, Your compassionate Self – save us, please.

As You saved the returning exiles of the tribes of Jacob,
so come back and return the exiles of the tents of Jacob –
and save us, please.

As You saved those who kept Your commandments and waited for
salvation, / God of all salvation – and save us, please.

אֲנִי וָהוֹ הוֹשִׁיעָה נָּא.

כְּהוֹשַׁעְתָּ אֵלִים בְּלוּד עִמָּךְ.
בְּצֵאתְךָ לְיֵשַׁע עַמָּךְ. כֵּן הוֹשַׁע נָא.

כְּהוֹשַׁעְתָּ גּוֹי וֵאלֹהִים.
דְּרוּשִׁים לְיֵשַׁע אֱלֹהִים. כֵּן הוֹשַׁע נָא.

כְּהוֹשַׁעְתָּ הֲמוֹן צְבָאוֹת.
וְעִמָּם מַלְאֲכֵי צְבָאוֹת. כֵּן הוֹשַׁע נָא.

כְּהוֹשַׁעְתָּ זַכִּים מִבֵּית עֲבָדִים.
חַנּוּן בְּיָדָם מַעֲבִידִים. כֵּן הוֹשַׁע נָא.

כְּהוֹשַׁעְתָּ טְבוּעִים בְּצוּל גְּזָרִים.
יְקָרְךָ עִמָּם מַעֲבִירִים. כֵּן הוֹשַׁע נָא.

כְּהוֹשַׁעְתָּ כַּנָּה מְשׁוֹרֶרֶת וַיּוֹשַׁע.
לְגוֹחָהּ מְצֻיֶּנֶת וַיִּוָּשַׁע. כֵּן הוֹשַׁע נָא.

כְּהוֹשַׁעְתָּ מַאֲמַר וְהוֹצֵאתִי אֶתְכֶם.
נָקוּב וְהוּצֵאתִי אִתְּכֶם. כֵּן הוֹשַׁע נָא.

כְּהוֹשַׁעְתָּ סוֹבְבֵי מִזְבֵּחַ.
עוֹמְסֵי עֲרָבָה לְהַקִּיף מִזְבֵּחַ. כֵּן הוֹשַׁע נָא.

כְּהוֹשַׁעְתָּ פִּלְאֵי אָרוֹן כְּהֻפְשַׁע.
צִעֵר פְּלֶשֶׁת בַּחֲרוֹן אַף, וְנוֹשַׁע. כֵּן הוֹשַׁע נָא.

כְּהוֹשַׁעְתָּ קְהִלּוֹת בָּבֶלָה שִׁלַּחְתָּ.
רַחוּם לְמַעֲנָם שֻׁלַּחְתָּ. כֵּן הוֹשַׁע נָא.

כְּהוֹשַׁעְתָּ שְׁבוּת שִׁבְטֵי יַעֲקֹב.
תָּשׁוּב וְתָשִׁיב שְׁבוּת אָהֳלֵי יַעֲקֹב. וְהוֹשִׁיעָה נָּא.

כְּהוֹשַׁעְתָּ שׁוֹמְרֵי מִצְוֹת וְחוֹכֵי יְשׁוּעוֹת.
אֵל לְמוֹשָׁעוֹת. וְהוֹשִׁיעָה נָּא.

I and *HE*: save us, please.

תְּתְּנֵנוּ לְשֵׁם Grant us name and honor; / return us to our home, our land; / raise us up, up above; / gather us to the House of prayer; / plant us as a tree on streams of water; / redeem us from infection and illness; / crown us with bridal love; / have us rejoice in the House of prayer; / lead us beside the still waters forever; / fill us with wisdom and insight; / clothe us with strength and dignity; / crown us with the finest crown; / guide us straight along a paved avenue; / set us down upon a straight pathway; / grace us with compassion and mercy; / remember us, "Who is this rising?" / save us, to the end, to Redemption; / have us glow with the splendor of the crowd; / bind us about You like a loincloth girt; / make us greater with Your great hand; / bring us to Your House in song, in jubilation; / make us majestic with salvation and joy; / strengthen us in Your relief and rescue; / sweep our hearts up in the building of Your city anew; / awaken us to Zion in her completion; / grant us the honor to see the city rebuilt on its hill; / set us down to pasture in happiness and joy; / strengthen us, God of Jacob, always –

Save us, please.

Leader then congregation:

Please: save us, please.

אָנָא Please – listen to the plea of those who hunger for Your rescue,
as they bring willows of the stream to delight You –
and save us, please.

בְּזִיו הֲמֻלָּה *With the splendor of the crowd.* A reference to Ezekiel's mystical vision when he heard the sound of the massed angels, "like the noise of a tumultuous crowd" (Ez. 1:24).

אָנָא אֵזֵן PLEASE LISTEN TO THE PLEA
A prelude to the point at which we put down the lulav and etrog and take up the bundle of willow.

אֲנִי וָהוּ הוֹשִׁיעָה נָּא.

תִּתְּנֵנוּ לְשֵׁם וְלִתְהִלָּה.
תְּשִׁיבֵנוּ אֶל הַחֶבֶל וְאֶל הַנַּחֲלָה.
תְּרוֹמְמֵנוּ לְמַעְלָה לְמָעְלָה.
תְּקַבְּצֵנוּ לְבֵית הַתְּפִלָּה.
תַּצִּיבֵנוּ כְּעֵץ עַל פַּלְגֵי מַיִם שְׁתוּלָה.
תִּפְדֵּנוּ מִכָּל נֶגַע וּמַחֲלָה.
תְּעַטְּרֵנוּ בְּאַהֲבָה כְּלוּלָה.
תְּשַׂמְּחֵנוּ בְּבֵית הַתְּפִלָּה.
תְּנַהֲלֵנוּ עַל מֵי מְנוּחוֹת סֶלָה.
תְּמַלְּאֵנוּ חָכְמָה וְשִׂכְלָה.
תַּלְבִּישֵׁנוּ עֹז וּגְדֻלָּה.
תַּכְתִּירֵנוּ בְּכֶתֶר כְּלוּלָה.
תְּיַשְּׁרֵנוּ בְּאֹרַח סְלוּלָה.
תִּטָּעֵנוּ בְּיֹשֶׁר מְסִלָּה.
תְּחָנֵּנוּ בְּרַחֲמִים וּבְחֶמְלָה.
תַּזְכִּירֵנוּ בְּמִי זֹאת עוֹלָה.
תּוֹשִׁיעֵנוּ לְקֵץ הַגְּאֻלָּה.
תְּהַדְּרֵנוּ בְּזִיו הַמֻּלָּה.
תַּדְבִּיקֵנוּ כְּאֵזוֹר חֲתוּלָה.
תְּגַדְּלֵנוּ בְּיָד הַגְּדוֹלָה.
תְּבִיאֵנוּ לְבֵיתְךָ בְּרִנָּה וְצָהֳלָה.
תְּאַדְּרֵנוּ בְּיֶשַׁע וְגִילָה.
תְּאַמְּצֵנוּ בְּרֶוַח וְהַצָּלָה.
תְּלַבְּבֵנוּ בְּבִנְיַן עִירְךָ כְּבַתְּחִלָּה.
תְּעוֹרְרֵנוּ לְצִיּוֹן בְּשִׁכְלוּלָהּ.
תְּזַכֵּנוּ בְּנִבְנְתָה הָעִיר עַל תִּלָּהּ.
תַּרְבִּיצֵנוּ בְּשָׂשׂוֹן וְגִילָה.
תְּחַזְּקֵנוּ אֱלֹהֵי יַעֲקֹב סֶלָה.

הוֹשַׁע נָא.

:קהל then שליח ציבור

אָנָּא, הוֹשִׁיעָה נָּא.

אָנָּא אֱזוֹן חִין תְּאֵבֵי יִשְׁעָךְ.
בְּעַרְבֵי נַחַל לְשַׁעְשְׁעָךְ. וְהוֹשִׁיעָה נָּא.

תִּתְּנֵנוּ לְשֵׁם וְלִתְהִלָּה GRANT US NAME AND HONOR
A prayer structured as a reverse acrostic, signed with the name of its author, R. Elazar (HaKalir). HaKalir was the supreme virtuoso of liturgical poetry, and author of the *Hoshanot*.

בְּמִי זֹאת עוֹלָה *Who is this rising?* A phrase from Song of Songs (8:5), a scene of love and closeness between God and His people.

Please – redeem this stem You planted,
as You sweep away Duma [the regime that rules us]–
and save us, please.

Please – look to the covenant You have sealed in us,
as You destroy the dark places of this earth –
and save us ,please.

Please – remember for our sake our father [Abraham] who knew You,
as You make Your love known to [the others] –
and save us ,please.

Please – as You perform miracles for the pure of heart,
make it known that these are Your own wonders –
and save us, please.

Please – You whose strength is immense, grant us Your salvation,
as You swore to our forefathers – and save us, please.

Please – answer the wishes of the people who entreat You,
like the prayer of [Isaac] bound on the Mountain of
Myrrh – and save us, please.

Please – strengthen [Israel,] the tamarisks You planted,
as You push aside oppressors – and save us, please.

Please – open for us Your treasuries of rain,
as from them You water arid land – and save us, please.

Please – when You shake the earth, lead those who call on You
to pasture in the best of Your meadows – and save us, please.

Please – lift the gates of Your [House] from their destruction,
as You raise the ruins each mouth prays towards –
and save us, please.

אֶרֶץ בְּרוֹעֲשָׁךְ *When You shake the earth.* A reference to the cosmic upheavals that will herald the end of days.

אָנָּא גְּאַל כַּנַּת נִטְעָךְ.
דּוּמָה בְּטַאטְאָךְ. וְהוֹשִׁיעָה נָּא.

אָנָּא הַבֵּט לַבְּרִית טִבְעָךְ.
וּמַחֲשַׁכֵּי אֶרֶץ בְּהַטְבִּיעָךְ. וְהוֹשִׁיעָה נָּא.

אָנָּא זְכָר לָנוּ אָב יְדָעָךְ.
חַסְדְּךָ לָמוֹ בְּהוֹדִיעָךְ. וְהוֹשִׁיעָה נָּא.

אָנָּא טְהוֹרֵי לֵב בְּהַפְלִיאָךְ.
יְוֻדַּע כִּי הוּא פִלְאָךְ. וְהוֹשִׁיעָה נָּא.

אָנָּא כַּבִּיר כֹּחַ תֶּן לָנוּ יִשְׁעָךְ.
לַאֲבוֹתֵינוּ כְּהִשָּׁבְעָךְ. וְהוֹשִׁיעָה נָּא.

אָנָּא מַלֵּא מִשְׁאֲלוֹת עַם מְשַׁוְּעָךְ.
נֶעֱקַד בְּהַר מוֹר כְּמוֹ שִׁוְּעָךְ. וְהוֹשִׁיעָה נָּא.

אָנָּא סַגֵּב אֶשְׁלֵי נִטְעָךְ.
עָרִיצִים בְּהָנִיעָךְ. וְהוֹשִׁיעָה נָּא.

אָנָּא פְּתַח לָנוּ אוֹצְרוֹת רִבְעָךְ.
צִיָּה מֵהֶם בְּהַרְבִּיעָךְ. וְהוֹשִׁיעָה נָּא.

אָנָּא קוֹרְאֶיךָ אֶרֶץ בְּרוֹעֲעָךְ.
רְעֵם בְּטוּב מִרְעָךְ. וְהוֹשִׁיעָה נָּא.

אָנָּא שְׁעָרֶיךָ תַּעַל מִמְּשׁוֹאָךְ.
תֵּל תַּלְפִּיּוֹת בְּהַשִּׂיאָךְ. וְהוֹשִׁיעָה נָּא.

דּוּמָה *Duma.* Edom (see Is. 21:11), which came to symbolize Rome.

יְוֻדַּע כִּי הוּא פִלְאָךְ *Make it known that these are Your own wonders.* When other nations are victorious, they take this as a tribute to themselves; when Israel is victorious, it attributes its successes to God.

Leader then congregation:

Please; God, please; save, please; save us, please.

אֵל נָא God, please; we have gone astray like lost sheep;
do not erase our name from Your book – save, please; save us, please.

God, please; tend the flock destined to slaughter,
raged against, killed in Your name – save, please; save us, please.

God, please; Your flock, the flock You tend,
Your creation, Your beloved – save, please; save us, please.

God, please; the poorest of the flock –
answer their prayer at a time of favor – save, please; save us, please.

God, please; those who raise their eyes to You –
may those who rise against You be as nothing beside them –
save, please; save us, please.

God, please; those who pour water out before You –
from the wellsprings of salvation, let them draw water –
save, please; save us, please.

God, please; let the redeemers go up to Zion,
leaning upon You, saved in Your name – save, please; save us, please.

God, please; Your clothes red with blood,
rage and shake away all those who betray –
save, please; save us, please.

God, please; surely remember,
those sold away for a letekh of grain, for a kor –
save, please; save us, please.

צֹאן הַהֲרֵגָה *Flock destined to slaughter.* A phrase from one of the end-time visions of Zechariah (11:4).

חֲמוּץ בְּגָדִים *Your clothes red with blood.* A reference to the battle that will precede the reign of peace, when, as it were, God Himself will take up arms in defense of His people.

בְּלֶתֶךְ וָכֹר *A letekh of grain, for a kor.* Two measures amounting to forty-five

קהל *then* שליח ציבור:

אָנָּא, אֵל נָא, הוֹשַׁע נָא וְהוֹשִׁיעָה נָּא.

אֵל נָא תָּעִינוּ כְּשֶׂה אוֹבֵד
שְׁמֵנוּ מִסִּפְרְךָ אַל תְּאַבֵּד — הוֹשַׁע נָא וְהוֹשִׁיעָה נָּא.

אֵל נָא רְעֵה אֶת צֹאן הַהֲרֵגָה
קְצוּפָה, וְעָלֶיךָ הֲרוּגָה — הוֹשַׁע נָא וְהוֹשִׁיעָה נָּא.

אֵל נָא צֹאנְךָ וְצֹאן מַרְעִיתֶךָ
פְּעֻלָּתְךָ וְרַעְיָתֶךָ — הוֹשַׁע נָא וְהוֹשִׁיעָה נָּא.

אֵל נָא עֲנִיֵּי הַצֹּאן
שִׂיחָם עֲנֵה בְּעֵת רָצוֹן — הוֹשַׁע נָא וְהוֹשִׁיעָה נָּא.

אֵל נָא נוֹשְׂאֵי לְךָ עַיִן
מִתְקוֹמְמֶיךָ יִהְיוּ כְּאַיִן — הוֹשַׁע נָא וְהוֹשִׁיעָה נָּא.

אֵל נָא לִמְנַסְּכֵי לְךָ מַיִם
כְּמִמַּעַיְנֵי הַיְשׁוּעָה
יִשְׁאֲבוּן מַיִם — הוֹשַׁע נָא וְהוֹשִׁיעָה נָּא.

אֵל נָא יַעֲלוּ לְצִיּוֹן מוֹשִׁיעִים
טְפוּלִים בְּךָ וּבְשִׁמְךָ נוֹשָׁעִים — הוֹשַׁע נָא וְהוֹשִׁיעָה נָּא.

אֵל נָא חֲמוּץ בְּגָדִים
זְעֹם לְנַעֵר כָּל בּוֹגְדִים — הוֹשַׁע נָא וְהוֹשִׁיעָה נָּא.

אֵל נָא וְזָכוֹר תִּזְכֹּר
הַנְּכוּרִים בְּלֶתֶךָ וָכֹר — הוֹשַׁע נָא וְהוֹשִׁיעָה נָּא.

אֵל נָא תָּעִינוּ GOD, PLEASE; WE HAVE GONE ASTRAY

תָּעִינוּ כְּשֶׂה אוֹבֵד *We have gone astray like lost sheep.* In exile, Israel has wandered without finding a safe home.

God, please; those who seek You with stems of willow,
hear their weeping from the highest heaven –
save, please; save us, please.

God, please; crown this year with blessing,
and hear my words as I pray, on the day of Hoshana –
save, please; save us, please.

Leader then congregation:

Please; God, please;
save, please; save us, please; You are our Father.

לְמַעַן For the sake of one perfect in his generation,
who escaped in his righteousness,
saved from the flood, when there came down a deluge of water –
the people that says "I am a wall" –
save, please: save us, please: You are our Father.

For the sake of one whole in all his doings, tested with ten trials,
who saw angels and said, "Please, bring a little water" –
the people shining like the sun –
save, please: save us, please: You are our Father.

For the sake of a tender, only child, young fruit borne to a man of a hundred,
who cried out, "Where is the lamb for the burnt offering?!"
Whose servants brought him news: "We have found water!" –
the people expelled and banished –
save, please: save us, please: You are our Father.

---

individuals in whose merit we ask God to send rain, in each case referring to an event in their lives connected with water.

תָּמִים בְּדוֹרוֹתָיו *One perfect in his generation.* Noah, who was saved from the flood.

שָׁלֵם בְּכָל מַעֲשִׂים *One whole in all his doings.* Abraham, who invited three passers-by to rest, wash, and eat, and brought them water (Gen. 18:4).

רַךְ וְיָחִיד *A tender, only child.* Isaac, whose servants found water in Beersheba (Gen. 26:32).

אֵל נָא דּוֹרְשֶׁיךָ בְּעַנְפֵי עֲרָבוֹת
גֹּעִים שְׁעֵה מֵעֲרָבוֹת הוֹשַׁע נָא וְהוֹשִׁיעָה נָּא.

אֵל נָא בָּרֵךְ בְּעִטּוּר שָׁנָה
אֲמָרַי רְצֵה בְּפִלּוּלִי
בְּיוֹם הוֹשַׁעְנָא הוֹשַׁע נָא וְהוֹשִׁיעָה נָּא.

קהל then שליח ציבור:

אָנָּא, אֵל נָא
הוֹשַׁע נָא וְהוֹשִׁיעָה נָּא, אָבִינוּ אָתָּה.

לְמַעַן תָּמִים בְּדוֹרוֹתָיו, הַנִּמְלָט בְּרֹב צִדְקוֹתָיו
מֻצָּל מִשֶּׁטֶף בְּבוֹא מַבּוּל מַיִם.
לְאֹם אֲנִי חוֹמָה הוֹשַׁע נָא וְהוֹשִׁיעָה נָּא, אָבִינוּ אָתָּה.

לְמַעַן שָׁלֵם בְּכָל מַעֲשִׂים, הַמְנֻסֶּה בַּעֲשָׂרָה נִסִּים
כְּשֶׁר מַלְאָכִים, נָם יֻקַּח נָא מְעַט מַיִם.
לְבָרָה כַּחַמָּה הוֹשַׁע נָא וְהוֹשִׁיעָה נָּא, אָבִינוּ אָתָּה.

לְמַעַן רַךְ וְיָחִיד נֶחֱנַט פְּרִי לְמֵאָה, זָעַק אַיֵּה הַשֶּׂה לְעֹלָה
בִּשְּׂרוּהוּ עֲבָדָיו מָצָאנוּ מַיִם.
לְגוֹלָה וְסוּרָה הוֹשַׁע נָא וְהוֹשִׁיעָה נָּא, אָבִינוּ אָתָּה.

---

se'ah, corresponding to the forty-five days between the exodus from Egypt and the arrival of the people at Mount Sinai.

בְּעַנְפֵי עֲרָבוֹת *Stems of willow.* A play on the word *Aravot*, which means "willow branches," but is also another name for Heaven (*Ḥagiga* 12b).

לְמַעַן תָּמִים FOR THE SAKE OF ONE PERFECT IN HIS GENERATION
A *Hoshana*, structured as a reverse acrostic, listing the many righteous

For the sake of one who came in first to bear blessing,
who gained a foe and waited for salvation by Your name;
who made goats fertile with branches, by troughs of water –
the people likened to a date palm –
save, please: save us, please: You are our Father.

For the sake of the one righteous enough to be chosen as Your priest,
serving You like a bridegroom adorned,
tested at Masa, by the Mei Meriva water –
the good mountain – save, please: save us, please: You are our Father.

For the sake of the one raised to be master of his brothers,
Judah who became the most powerful of brothers,
numerous as dust; his pail overflows with water –
not for us, but for Your sake –
save, please: save us, please: You are our Father.

For the sake of the humblest of men, the most faithful,
for whose righteous sake the manna fell,
pulled to be redeemer, drawn forth from the water –
this people, gazing out – save, please: save us, please: You are our Father.

For the sake of one You raised like angels of the heights, clad with the urim and tumim, commanded to come into the Temple with sanctified hands and feet, bathed in water –
this people sick with love –
save, please: save us, please: You are our Father.

For the sake of the prophetess who danced between the camps;
to whom the people on their yearning journey raised their eyes [to lead them]; for her sake it moved, it rose and it rested, the well of water –
the people of the goodly tents –
save, please: save us, please: You are our Father.

עָנָו מִכֹּל *The humblest of men.* Moses, given his name by Pharaoh's daughter, saying, "I have drawn him from the water" (Ex. 2:10).

כְּמַלְאֲכֵי מְרוֹמִים *Like angels of the heights.* Aaron, the first High Priest, who had to sanctify his hands and feet in water before performing his service in the Temple.

נְבִיאָה *The prophetess.* Miriam, in whose merit a well of water accompanied the Israelites during the wilderness years (*Ta'anit* 9a).

לְמַעַן קֹדֶם שְׂאֵת בְּרָכָה, הַנִּשְׁטָם וּלְשִׁמְךָ חִכָּה
מְיַחֵם בְּמַקְלוֹת בְּשִׁקְתוֹת הַמַּיִם.
לְדָמְתָה לְתָמָר הוֹשַׁע נָא וְהוֹשִׁיעָה נָּא, אָבִינוּ אָתָּה.

לְמַעַן צָדֵק הֱיוֹת לְךָ לְכֹהֵן, כְּחָתָן פְּאֵר יְכַהֵן
מְנֻסֶּה בְּמַסָּה בְּמֵי מְרִיבַת מַיִם.
לְהָהָר הַטּוֹב הוֹשַׁע נָא וְהוֹשִׁיעָה נָּא, אָבִינוּ אָתָּה.

לְמַעַן פְּאַר הֱיוֹת גְּבִיר לְאֶחָיו, יְהוּדָה אֲשֶׁר גָּבַר בְּאֶחָיו
מִסְפַּר רֹבַע מִדָּלְיָו יִזַּל מַיִם.
לֹא לָנוּ כִּי אִם לְמַעַנְךָ הוֹשַׁע נָא וְהוֹשִׁיעָה נָּא, אָבִינוּ אָתָּה.

לְמַעַן עָנָו מִכֹּל וְנֶאֱמָן, אֲשֶׁר בְּצִדְקוֹ כִּלְכֵּל הַמָּן
מָשׁוּךְ לְגוֹאֵל וּמָשׁוּי מִמַּיִם.
לְזֹאת הַנִּשְׁקָפָה הוֹשַׁע נָא וְהוֹשִׁיעָה נָּא, אָבִינוּ אָתָּה.

לְמַעַן שַׂמְתּוֹ כְּמַלְאֲכֵי מְרוֹמִים, הַלּוֹבֵשׁ אוּרִים וְתֻמִּים
מְצֻוֶּה לָבוֹא בַּמִּקְדָּשׁ בְּקִדּוּשׁ יָדַיִם וְרַגְלַיִם וּרְחִיצַת מַיִם.
לְחוֹלַת אַהֲבָה הוֹשַׁע נָא וְהוֹשִׁיעָה נָּא, אָבִינוּ אָתָּה.

לְמַעַן נְבִיאָה מְחוֹלַת מַחֲנַיִם, לִכְמֵהֵי לֵב הוּשְׂמָה עֵינַיִם
לְרַגְלָהּ רָצָה עֲלוֹת וָרֶדֶת בְּאֵר מַיִם.
לְטוֹבוּ אֹהָלָיו הוֹשַׁע נָא וְהוֹשִׁיעָה נָּא, אָבִינוּ אָתָּה.

קֹדֶם שְׂאֵת *One who came in first.* Jacob, who, while staying with Laban, brought flocks and herds to the water-troughs (Gen 30:38–39).

הֱיוֹת לְךָ לְכֹהֵן *Chosen as Your priest.* Levi, son of Jacob, whose descendants, Moses and Aaron, led the Israelites, and whose children, the Levites, did not join with the Israelites in complaining about the lack of water.

יְהוּדָה *Judah.* Ancestor of Israel's kings, who were anointed near a spring of water (*K'ritot* 5b).

For the sake of the servant who never left the Tent, over whom the holy
spirit rested, for whose sake the Jordan parted its water –
the people beautiful and shining –
save, please: save us, please: You are our Father.

For the sake of the one taught to read a sign of good things,
who cried out, "Where are the wonders now?"
But later wrung rain from the wool – a whole bowl full of water –
the bride of Lebanon –
save, please: save us, please: You are our Father.

For the sake of one who ground his enemies alone, dedicated from the womb
a Nazirite, from the hollow of a jawbone You brought him forth water –
for Your holy name's sake –
save, please: save us, please: You are our Father.

For the sake of those included in the army of Your war,
at whose hands You gave Your salvation,
marked out from the people as from their hands they lapped up water –
those who never betrayed –
save, please: save us, please: You are our Father.

For the sake of the good child growing more and more,
who never allowed himself to take from the people;
when the people repented he said, "Draw forth water!" –
the people, lovely as Jerusalem –
save, please: save us, please: You are our Father.

For the sake of one who laughed and danced in song,
who taught the Torah through any instrument of music,
who libated before You, though he longed to drink water –
those who placed their hope in You –
save, please: save us, please: You are our Father.

בְּלוּלֵי עֲשׂוֹת מִלְחַמְתֶּךָ *Included in the army.* Gideon's force of three hundred men, chosen by way they drank water from the river (Judges 7:6).

צוֹרְרִים דָּשׁ *One who ground his enemies alone.* Samson, for whom a miracle was wrought after he defeated the Philistines: a spring appeared so that he could drink water (Judges 15:19).

טוֹב *The good child.* Samuel, who led the people to repent, offering to God a libation of water (1 Sam. 7:6).

חַיָּךְ מְכַרְכֵּר *One who laughed and danced.* King David, who danced when the

לְמַעַן מְשָׁרֵת לֹא מָשׁ מֵאֹהֶל, וְרוּחַ הַקֹּדֶשׁ עָלָיו אֹהֵל
בְּעָבְרוֹ בַּיַּרְדֵּן נִכְרְתוּ הַמַּיִם.
לְיָפָה וּבָרָה הוֹשַׁע נָא וְהוֹשִׁיעָה נָּא, אָבִינוּ אָתָּה.

לְמַעַן לָמַד רְאוֹת לְטוֹבָה אוֹת, זָעַק אַיֵּה נִפְלָאוֹת
מִצָּה טַל מִגִּזָּה מְלֹא הַסֵּפֶל מַיִם.
לְכַלַּת לְבָנוֹן הוֹשַׁע נָא וְהוֹשִׁיעָה נָּא, אָבִינוּ אָתָּה.

לְמַעַן כְּלוּלֵי עֲשׂוֹת מִלְחַמְתֶּךָ, אֲשֶׁר בְּיָדָם תַּתָּה יְשׁוּעָתֶךָ
צְרוּפֵי מִגּוֹי בְּלָקְקָם בְּיָדָם מַיִם.
לְלֹא בָגְדוּ בָךְ הוֹשַׁע נָא וְהוֹשִׁיעָה נָּא, אָבִינוּ אָתָּה.

לְמַעַן יָחִיד צוֹרְרִים דָּשׁ, אֲשֶׁר מֵרֶחֶם לְנָזִיר הֻקְדָּשׁ
מִמַּכְתֵּשׁ לֶחִי הִבְקַעְתָּ לוֹ מַיִם.
לְמַעַן שֵׁם קָדְשֶׁךָ הוֹשַׁע נָא וְהוֹשִׁיעָה נָּא, אָבִינוּ אָתָּה.

לְמַעַן טוֹב הוֹלֵךְ וְגָדֵל, אֲשֶׁר מֵעֹשֶׁק עֵדָה חִדֵּל
בְּשׁוּב עָם מֵחֵטְא צִוָּה שְׁאֹב מַיִם.
לְנָאוָה כִּירוּשָׁלָיִם הוֹשַׁע נָא וְהוֹשִׁיעָה נָּא, אָבִינוּ אָתָּה.

לְמַעַן חִיךְ מְכַרְכֵּר בְּשִׁיר, הַמְלַמֵּד תּוֹרָה בְּכָל כְּלֵי שִׁיר
מְנַסֵּךְ לְפָנֶיךָ כְּתָאֵב שְׁתוֹת מַיִם.
לְשָׁמוּ בְךָ סִבְרָם הוֹשַׁע נָא וְהוֹשִׁיעָה נָּא, אָבִינוּ אָתָּה.

מְשָׁרֵת לֹא מָשׁ מֵאֹהֶל *The servant who never left the Tent.* Joshua, Moses' successor (see Ex. 33:11).

לָמַד רְאוֹת לְטוֹבָה אוֹת *Taught to read a sign of good things.* Gideon, leader of Israel in the days of the Judges, who asked God for a sign that the time was right to do battle against the Midianites. The sign was a fleece drenched overnight in dew (Judges 6:36-40).

For the sake of the pure one who went up in a storm cloud,
who was jealous for You and who turned back Your rage,
at whose word down came fire to lick the dust and water –
the people whose eyes are like pools –
save, please: save us, please: You are our Father.

For the sake of one who served his teacher truly,
and was assigned a double measure of his spirit.
When he called the musician to play, the pools were filled with water –
those who said "Who is like You?" –
save, please: save us, please: You are our Father.

For the sake of one who thought to do Your will,
who declared repentance to all Your flock;
then, when the blasphemer came, he stopped up all springs of water –
Zion, perfect beauty –
save, please: save us, please: You are our Father.

For the sake of those who sought You from the heart of Exile,
to whom Your secrets were revealed,
and not to be tainted [by meat and wine]
they asked for grains and water –
those who cry out to You from their distress –
save, please: save us, please: You are our Father.

For the sake of one who learned wisdom and insight,
the keen-minded scribe who set forth a pledge,
the one who made us wiser with words deep as oceans of water –
the [city that] flocked with people –
save, please: save us, please: You are our Father.

---

outside the city walls so that the enemy army would have nothing to drink (II Chron. 32:3–4).

דְּרָשׁוּךָ בְּתוֹךְ הַגּוֹלָה *Those who sought You from the heart of exile.* Daniel, Ḥananya, Misha'el and Azaria, who, in Nebuchadnezzar's court, refused to eat food and drink wine from the king's table, asking only for vegetables and water (Daniel 1:5–16).

סוֹפֵר מָהִיר *Keen-minded scribe.* Ezra, who taught Torah – often compared to water – to the people after the return from Babylon.

לְמַעַן זָךְ עָלָה בַּסְּעָרָה, הַמְקַנֵּא וּמֵשִׁיב עֶבְרָה
לִפְלוּלוֹ יָרְדָה אֵשׁ וְלִחֲכָה עָפָר וּמַיִם.
לְעֵינֶיהָ בְּרֵכוֹת הוֹשַׁע נָא וְהוֹשִׁיעָה נָּא, אָבִינוּ אָתָּה.

לְמַעַן וְשֵׁרֵת בֶּאֱמֶת לְרַבּוֹ, פִּי שְׁנַיִם בְּרוּחוֹ נֶאֱצַל בּוֹ
בְּקַחְתּוֹ מְנַגֵּן נִתְמַלְאוּ גֵּבִים מַיִם.
לְפָצוּ מִי כָמֹכָה הוֹשַׁע נָא וְהוֹשִׁיעָה נָּא, אָבִינוּ אָתָּה.

לְמַעַן הִרְהֵר עֲשׂוֹת רְצוֹנֶךָ, הַמַּכְרִיז תְּשׁוּבָה לְצֹאנֶךָ
אָז בְּבוֹא מְחָרֵף סָתַם עֵינוֹת מַיִם.
לְצִיּוֹן מִכְלַל יֹפִי הוֹשַׁע נָא וְהוֹשִׁיעָה נָּא, אָבִינוּ אָתָּה.

לְמַעַן דְּרָשׁוּךָ בְּתוֹךְ הַגּוֹלָה, וְסוֹדְךָ לָמוֹ נִגְלָה
בְּלִי לְהִתְגָּאֵל דָּרְשׁוּ זֵרְעוֹנִים וּמַיִם.
לְקוֹרְאֶיךָ בַּצָּר הוֹשַׁע נָא וְהוֹשִׁיעָה נָּא, אָבִינוּ אָתָּה.

לְמַעַן גְּמַר חָכְמָה וּבִינָה, סוֹפֵר מָהִיר מְפַלֵּשׁ אֲמָנָה
מַחְכִּימֵנוּ אֲמָרִים הַמְשׁוּלִים בְּרַחֲבֵי מַיִם.
לְרַבָּתִי עָם הוֹשַׁע נָא וְהוֹשִׁיעָה נָּא, אָבִינוּ אָתָּה.

---

ark was brought to Jerusalem, and whose warriors broke through enemy lines to bring him water. David offered this as a libation to God (II Sam. 23:15–16).

זָךְ *The pure one.* Elijah, who challenged the false prophets of Baal to a trial at Mount Carmel, when God sent fire to consume the sacrifice that the prophet has soaked with water (I Kings 18:33–38).

וְשֵׁרֵת בֶּאֱמֶת לְרַבּוֹ *One who served his teacher.* Elisha, disciple of Elijah, who on one occasion, when the armies of Israel, Judah, and Edom were parched, called for a harpist and communed with God, who then "filled the land with water" (II Kings 3:15–20).

הִרְהֵר עֲשׂוֹת רְצוֹנֶךָ *One who thought to do Your will.* King Hezekiah, who, during Sennacherib's siege of Jerusalem, closed the springs of water located

For the sake of those who come to You today with all their hearts,
who pour out their words without two minds,
who ask of You Your mighty torrents of water –
those who sang at the sea –
save, please: save us, please: You are our Father.

For the sake of those who say "May Your name be declared great" –
and they are Your inheritance, Your people;
who thirst for Your salvation as an arid land thirsts water –
those for whom You sought out a resting place –
save, please: save us, please: You are our Father.

Leader then congregation:

Save, please, God, please, save us, please.
Save, please, please forgive and grant us success, please.
Save us, God who is our Refuge.

Put down the Lulav and Etrog and pick up the Hoshanot.

תַּעֲנֶה Answer the faithful ones who pour out their hearts to You like water – and save us, please;
for the sake of [Abraham] who came through fire and water – and grant us success, please;
He gave the order and said, "Please, bring a little water" – save us, God our Refuge.

Answer the flagged tribes who went swift through the split sea – and save us, please;
for the sake of [Isaac who was] bound at the gate of heaven – and grant us success, please;
he who yet lived to return and to dig out wells of water – save us, God our Refuge.

---

willows – understood by the Talmud as a custom instituted by the prophets of the Second Temple – is that the willow, more than any other of the four kinds, signals the presence of water, and at this point our prayers for rain reach a crescendo.

תַּעֲנֶה אֱמוּנִים ANSWER THE FAITHFUL ONES
שׁוֹפְכִים לְךָ לֵב *Who pour out their hearts to You.* "Pour out your heart like water before the face of the LORD" (Lam. 2:19).

לְמַעַן בָּאֵי לְךָ הַיּוֹם בְּכָל לֵב, שׁוֹפְכִים לְךָ שִׂיחַ בְּלֹא לֵב וָלֵב
שׁוֹאֲלִים מִמְּךָ עֹז מִטְרוֹת מָיִם.
לְשׁוֹרְרוּ בַיָּם הוֹשַׁע נָא וְהוֹשִׁיעָה נָּא, אָבִינוּ אָתָּה.

לְמַעַן אוֹמְרֵי יִגְדַּל שְׁמֶךָ, וְהֵם נַחֲלָתְךָ וְעַמֶּךָ
צְמֵאִים לְיֶשְׁעֲךָ כְּאֶרֶץ עֲיֵפָה לַמָּיִם.
לְתוֹרָתְךָ לָמוֹ מְנוּחָה הוֹשַׁע נָא וְהוֹשִׁיעָה נָּא, אָבִינוּ אָתָּה.

קהל *then* שליח ציבור:

הוֹשַׁע נָא, אֵל נָא, אָנָּא הוֹשִׁיעָה נָּא.
הוֹשַׁע נָא, סְלַח נָא, וְהַצְלִיחָה נָא
וְהוֹשִׁיעֵנוּ אֵל מָעֻזֵּנוּ.

Put down the לולב *and* אתרוג *and pick up the* הושענות.

תַּעֲנֶה אֱמוּנִים שׁוֹפְכִים לְךָ לֵב כַּמַּיִם וְהוֹשִׁיעָה נָּא.
לְמַעַן בָּא בָאֵשׁ וּבַמַּיִם וְהַצְלִיחָה נָא.
גָּזַר וְנָם יֻקַּח נָא מְעַט מַיִם וְהוֹשִׁיעֵנוּ אֵל מָעֻזֵּנוּ.

תַּעֲנֶה דְגָלִים גָּזוּ גִּזְרֵי מַיִם וְהוֹשִׁיעָה נָּא.
לְמַעַן הַנֶּעֱקַד בְּשַׁעַר הַשָּׁמַיִם וְהַצְלִיחָה נָא.
וְשָׁב וְחָפַר בְּאֵרוֹת מַיִם וְהוֹשִׁיעֵנוּ אֵל מָעֻזֵּנוּ.

בְּלֹא לֵב וָלֵב *Without two minds.* A phrase from I Chronicles 12:34, meaning "an undivided heart."

צְמֵאִים לְיֶשְׁעֲךָ *Who thirst for Your salvation.* "I thirst for You, my whole being longs for You, in a dry and parched land where there is no water" (Ps. 63:2).

הוֹשַׁע נָא, אֵל נָא SAVE PLEASE, GOD, PLEASE
Most have the custom of setting down the Four Kinds at this point, and taking in their place the bundle of five willow branches, in commemoration of the procession with willows that took place in the Temple. The reason for the

Answer the pure ones encamped on the water – and save us, please;
for the sake of smooth-skinned [Jacob] who peeled branches by troughs of water – and grant us success, please;
he who heaved and rolled a rock from the well of water – save us, God our Refuge.

Answer the beloved ones, heirs to a Law likened to water – and save us, please;
for the sake of those [princes in the wilderness] whose staffs drew forth water – and grant us success, please;
to prepare for them and for their children – water – save us, God our Refuge.

Answer those who plead as in the wilderness for water – and save us, please;
for the sake of [Moses], trusted in Your household, who provided the people with water – and grant us success, please;
he hit the rock and out flowed water – save us, God our Refuge.

Answer those who sang in the wilderness, "Spring up, well of water!" – and save us, please;
for the sake of [Aaron,] commanded at the Mei Meriva water – and grant us success, please;
commanded to give those who thirsted, water – save us, God our Refuge.

Answer the holy ones who pour before You water – and save us, please;
for the sake of [David] father of song-makers who longed to drink water – and grant us success, please;
but who held back and poured before You water – save us, God our Refuge.

Answer those who come to beseech You with four species grown by water – and save us, please;
for the sake of the Hill of ruins all mouths pray towards, the source of water – and grant us success, please;
open up the earth and let the heavens rain down water – and save us, God our Refuge.

סֶלַע הָךְ *He hit the rock.* This is a reference to the incident shortly after the division of the Red Sea, when God told Moses to hit the rock (Ex. 17:6), not to the later incident when Moses hit the rock despite the fact that God had told him to speak to it (Num. 20:7–11).

תַּעֲנֶה עוֹנִים *Answer those who sang in the wilderness.* The song they sang, beginning "Spring up, well," toward the end of their journey through the wilderness (Num. 21:17–18).

תַּעֲנֶה זַכִּים חוֹנִים עֲלֵי מָיִם וְהוֹשִׁיעָה נָּא.
לְמַעַן חֵלֶק מְפַצֵּל מַקְלוֹת בְּשִׁקְתוֹת הַמָּיִם וְהַצְלִיחָה נָא.
טָעַן וְגָל אֶבֶן מִבְּאֵר מַיִם וְהוֹשִׁיעֵנוּ אֵל מָעֻזֵּנוּ.

תַּעֲנֶה יְדִידִים נוֹחֲלֵי דָת מְשׁוּלַת מַיִם וְהוֹשִׁיעָה נָּא.
לְמַעַן כָּרוּ בְּמִשְׁעֲנוֹתָם מַיִם וְהַצְלִיחָה נָא.
לְהָכִין לָמוֹ וּלְצֶאֱצָאֵימוֹ מַיִם וְהוֹשִׁיעֵנוּ אֵל מָעֻזֵּנוּ.

תַּעֲנֶה מִתְחַנְּנִים כְּבִישִׁימוֹן עֲלֵי מַיִם וְהוֹשִׁיעָה נָּא.
לְמַעַן נֶאֱמַן בַּיִת מַסְפִּיק לָעָם מַיִם וְהַצְלִיחָה נָא.
סֶלַע הָךְ וַיָּזוּבוּ מַיִם וְהוֹשִׁיעֵנוּ אֵל מָעֻזֵּנוּ.

תַּעֲנֶה עוֹנִים עֲלֵי בְאֵר מַיִם וְהוֹשִׁיעָה נָּא.
לְמַעַן פָּקַד בְּמֵי מְרִיבַת מַיִם וְהַצְלִיחָה נָא.
צְמֵאִים לְהַשְׁקוֹת מַיִם וְהוֹשִׁיעֵנוּ אֵל מָעֻזֵּנוּ.

תַּעֲנֶה קְדוֹשִׁים מְנַסְּכִים לְךָ מַיִם וְהוֹשִׁיעָה נָּא.
לְמַעַן רֹאשׁ מְשׁוֹרְרִים כְּתָאַב שְׁתוֹת מַיִם וְהַצְלִיחָה נָא.
שָׁב וְנָסַךְ לְךָ מַיִם וְהוֹשִׁיעֵנוּ אֵל מָעֻזֵּנוּ.

תַּעֲנֶה שׁוֹאֲלִים בְּרִבּוּעַ אֶשְׁלֵי מַיִם וְהוֹשִׁיעָה נָּא.
לְמַעַן תֵּל תַּלְפִּיּוֹת מוֹצָא מַיִם וְהַצְלִיחָה נָא.
תִּפְתַּח אֶרֶץ וְתַרְעִיף שָׁמַיִם וְהוֹשִׁיעֵנוּ אֵל מָעֻזֵּנוּ.

טָעַן וְגָל אֶבֶן *Who heaved and rolled a rock.* Jacob, who rolled away the heavy rock covering the well when Rachel came to water her flock (Gen. 29:10).

נוֹחֲלֵי דָת מְשׁוּלַת מַיִם *Heirs to a law likened to water.* "Let my teaching fall like rain and my words descend like the dew, like gentle rain on new grass, like showers on tender plants" (Deut. 32:2).

Leader then congregation:

Have compassion, please,
for the community of the people of Yeshurun;
forgive and pardon their iniquity,
and save us, God of our salvation.

אָז As the eyes of slaves are raised / to their masters' hands,
we come before You, judged, save us, God of our salvation.

Proud Masters of masters, / they have brought us to conflict;
they have trampled us; other masters have mastered us,
so save us, God of our salvation.

We have come today, pleading – / before You, Compassionate and Gracious One,
telling and repeating Your wondrous acts, now save us, God of our salvation.

Please do not dry up / what flowed with milk and honey;
heal the land's pain with clouds full of water and save us, God of our salvation.

Plant us in luscious land, / at the hand of the seven shepherds, the eight princes,
righteous, upright God of faithfulness, yes, save us, God of our salvation.

You forged a covenant with the land / for as long as the earth will be,
never to break it apart again, so save us, God of our salvation.

---

that the land is usually praised for its produce (grain and fruit) rather than for animal products, argued that "honey" here is that made from dates. A midrash, commenting on the phrase "His teeth are whiter than milk" says this refers to "wine" (Gen. 49:12, *Bereshit Raba* 98:10). Hence, he suggested, "milk" in this phrase is the biblical term for white wine.

שִׁבְעָה וּשְׁמוֹנָה *The seven ... the eight*: A reference to Micah 5:4, "We will raise against them seven shepherds, and eight princes." According to the Talmud (*Sukka* 52b) the seven shepherds are Adam, Seth and Methuselah on the right, David in the center, Abraham, Jacob and Moses on the left. The eight princes are Jesse, Saul, Samuel, Amos, Zephaniah, Hezekiah, Elijah and the Messiah.

כָּרַתָּ בְרִית לָאָרֶץ *You forged a covenant with the land.* God's promise after the Flood: "Never again will I curse the ground because of man.... And never again will I destroy all living creatures, as I have done" (Gen 8:21).

קהל then שליח ציבור:

רַחֵם נָא קְהַל עֲדַת יְשׁוּרוּן, סְלַח וּמְחַל עֲוֹנָם וְהוֹשִׁיעֵנוּ אֱלֹהֵי יִשְׁעֵנוּ.

אָז כְּעֵינֵי עֲבָדִים אֶל יַד אֲדוֹנִים
בָּאנוּ לְפָנֶיךָ נְדוֹנִים. וְהוֹשִׁיעֵנוּ אֱלֹהֵי יִשְׁעֵנוּ.

גֵּאֶה אֲדוֹנֵי הָאֲדוֹנִים, נִתְגָּרוּ בָנוּ מְדָנִים
דְּשׁוּנוּ וּבְעָלוּנוּ זוּלָתְךָ אֲדוֹנִים. וְהוֹשִׁיעֵנוּ אֱלֹהֵי יִשְׁעֵנוּ.

הֵן גַּשְׁנוּ הַיּוֹם בְּתַחֲנוּן, עָדֶיךָ רַחוּם וְחַנּוּן
וְסִפַּרְנוּ נִפְלְאוֹתֶיךָ בְּשִׁנּוּן. וְהוֹשִׁיעֵנוּ אֱלֹהֵי יִשְׁעֵנוּ.

זָבַת חָלָב וּדְבָשׁ, נָא אַל תִּיבָשׁ
חַשְׁרַת מַיִם כְּאֵבָה תֶּחְבָּשׁ. וְהוֹשִׁיעֵנוּ אֱלֹהֵי יִשְׁעֵנוּ.

טְעֵנוּ בַּשְּׁמֵנָה, בְּיַד שִׁבְעָה וּשְׁמוֹנָה
יָשָׁר צַדִּיק אֵל אֱמוּנָה. וְהוֹשִׁיעֵנוּ אֱלֹהֵי יִשְׁעֵנוּ.

כָּרַתָּ בְרִית לָאָרֶץ, עוֹד כָּל יְמֵי הָאָרֶץ
לְבִלְתִּי פְּרָץ בָּהּ פֶּרֶץ. וְהוֹשִׁיעֵנוּ אֱלֹהֵי יִשְׁעֵנוּ.

אָז כְּעֵינֵי עֲבָדִים AS THE EYES OF SLAVES

אָז *As.* In Temple times.

כְּעֵינֵי עֲבָדִים *As the eyes of slaves.* "As the eyes of slaves turn to their master's hand… so our eyes are turned to the LORD our God, awaiting His favor" (Ps. 123:2).

לְפָנֶיךָ נְדוֹנִים *Judged.* On Sukkot the rainfall of the world is judged for the coming year (Mishna, *Rosh HaShana* 1:2).

זָבַת חָלָב וּדְבָשׁ *Flowed with milk and honey.* The classic description of Israel, first used by God to Moses at the burning bush, and occurring twenty times in Tanakh. The Israeli scholar R. Reuben Margaliyot (1889–1971), noting

Those who plead with You for water / as willows thirst over streams of water –
remember for them the libation of water and save us, God of our salvation.

As they plead they carry with them / plants, held straight as they grow;
answer their prayer, their voice and save us, God of our salvation.

You who work salvations, / turn to hear their prayers,
and vindicate them, God of salvation, to save us, God of our salvation.

Listen to the voice of their crowds who come, / and open the earth, to bear fruit of salvation,
You who are great in saving, who desire no evil, save us, God of our salvation.

Open the gates of heaven, / and throw open Your treasury of good.
Save us, and do not press Your claims against us
but save us, God of our salvation.

Leader then congregation:

Open the gates of heaven,
and Your treasure-house of goodness – open for us.
Save us and do not extend judgment against us –
and save us, God of our salvation.

Leader then congregation:

The voice of the herald, he heralds and says –

אֹמֶן Your true salvation is coming; / the voice of my Beloved, here He is coming – heralding, saying. / A voice: He is coming with myriad [heavenly] legions, / coming to stand on the Mount of Olives – heralding, saying. / A voice: He is coming to sound the shofar, / as the mount is broken in half

---

אֹמֶן יֶשְׁעֲךָ YOUR TRUE SALVATION
An ecstatic anticipation of a future of peace and prosperity, bringing together phrases from the prophetic visions of Isaiah and Zechariah, alongside others drawn from Song of Songs. There are also references to the resurrection of the dead, an idea indissolubly linked, in Jewish prayer and thought, with the rain that brings life from the barren earth.

תַּחְתָּיו הַר יִבָּקַע *The mount is broken in half.* Drawn from Zechariah's prophecy, read as the *haftara* for the first day.

מִתְחַנְּנִים עֲלֵי מַיִם, כַּעֲרָבִים עַל יִבְלֵי מָיִם
נָא זְכָר לָמוֹ נִסּוּךְ הַמַּיִם. וְהוֹשִׁיעֵנוּ אֱלֹהֵי יִשְׁעֵנוּ.
שִׂיחִים בְּדֶרֶךְ מַטָּעָתָם, עוֹמְסִים בְּשַׁוְעָתָם
עֲנֵם בְּקוֹל פְּגִיעָתָם. וְהוֹשִׁיעֵנוּ אֱלֹהֵי יִשְׁעֵנוּ.
פּוֹעֵל יְשׁוּעוֹת, פְּנֵה לְפִלּוּלָם שְׁעוֹת
צַדִּיקֵם אֵל לְמוֹשָׁעוֹת. וְהוֹשִׁיעֵנוּ אֱלֹהֵי יִשְׁעֵנוּ.
קוֹל רִגְשָׁם תִּשַׁע, תִּפְתַּח אֶרֶץ וְיִפְרוּ יֶשַׁע
רַב לְהוֹשִׁיעַ וְלֹא חָפֵץ רֶשַׁע. וְהוֹשִׁיעֵנוּ אֱלֹהֵי יִשְׁעֵנוּ.

קהל *then* שליח ציבור:

שַׁעֲרֵי שָׁמַיִם פְּתַח
וְאוֹצָרְךָ הַטּוֹב לָנוּ תִפְתַּח.
תּוֹשִׁיעֵנוּ וְרִיב אַל תִּמְתַּח. וְהוֹשִׁיעֵנוּ אֱלֹהֵי יִשְׁעֵנוּ.

קהל *then* שליח ציבור:

קוֹל מְבַשֵּׂר מְבַשֵּׂר וְאוֹמֵר.

קוֹל אָמֵן יֶשְׁעֲךָ בָּא, קוֹל דּוֹדִי הִנֵּה זֶה בָּא. מְבַשֵּׂר וְאוֹמֵר.
קוֹל בָּא בְּרִבְבוֹת כִּתִּים, לַעֲמֹד עַל הַר הַזֵּיתִים. מְבַשֵּׂר וְאוֹמֵר.
קוֹל גִּשְׁתּוֹ בַּשּׁוֹפָר לִתְקַע, תַּחְתָּיו הַר יִבָּקַע. מְבַשֵּׂר וְאוֹמֵר.

כַּעֲרָבִים *As willows.* Taken from a beatific prophecy in Isaiah (44:3–4): "I will pour My spirit on your descendants, My blessing on your offspring; they will spring up among the grass, like willows on the riverbanks."

שַׁעֲרֵי שָׁמַיִם פְּתַח *Open the gates of heaven.* These lines, which originate here, were later taken and used in the Ne'ila service on Yom Kippur.

קוֹל מְבַשֵּׂר THE VOICE OF THE HERALD
Based on a messianic verse in Isaiah (52:7), "How beautiful on the mountains are the feet of the *herald* who proclaims peace, who *heralds* good tidings, who proclaim salvation, *and says* to Zion: Your God reigns!"

beneath Him – heralding, saying. / A voice: He knocks, He looks, He shines out, / and half the mount is moved from the east – heralding, saying. / A voice: He is fulfilling the words He spoke / and coming, and all His holy ones with Him – heralding, saying. / A voice: and for all who have come into this world, / the echo is heard in all the world – heralding, saying. / A voice: the children borne of His womb, / were born in a day like a child of his mother – heralding, saying. / A voice: she labored and bore – who is
this? / Who has heard of anything like this? – heralding, saying. / A voice: *Is. 66*
the Pure One who wrought all this – / and who has seen anything like this? – *Ibid.*
heralding, saying. / A voice: salvation, its time already set; / can the land give *Ibid.*
birth all in a day? – heralding, saying. / A voice: the One mighty above and
below, / can a nation be born all in one birth? – heralding, saying. / A voice: *Ibid.*
when the shining One redeems His people, / as evening falls, there shall be *Zech. 14*
light – heralding, saying. / A voice: saviors shall go up to Mount Zion: / for
Zion has labored and has given birth – heralding, saying. / A voice is heard *Is. 66*
throughout your borders: / "Broaden the spread of your tents!" – heralding, *Is. 54*
saying. / A voice: "Let your home extend as far as Damascus; / receive your sons and your daughters" – heralding, saying. / A voice: "Be joyful, dune flower of the coast; / for the [forebears] who slept in Hebron are awoken" –
heralding, saying. / A voice: "Turn to Me and be saved; / today, if you heed *Is. 45*
My voice" – heralding, saying. / A voice: a [savior] has grown up, Tzemaḥ his name, / and he is none other than David himself – heralding, saying. /
A voice: "Rise up, you who lie in the ashes; / awaken and sing, you who sleep *Is. 26*
in the dust" – heralding, saying. / A voice: the city flocking with people for
his crowning: / a tower of salvation, His own king – heralding, saying. / *II Sam. 22*
A voice to silence the names of the wicked; / dealing kindly with his anointed, *Ibid.*
David – heralding, saying. / A voice: grant salvation to an eternal people; / *Ibid.*
to David and his descendants forever – heralding, saying.

The Leader says three times, then the congregation repeats three times:

The voice of the herald, he heralds and says –

Beat the Hoshanot against a chair or the floor five times,
then say the following (see law 31):

הוֹשִׁיעָה Save Your people; bless Your legacy; *Ps. 28*
tend them and carry them forever.

(*Sukka* 43b), performed in the Temple on the seventh day of Sukkot. No blessing is said, since this act is a custom not a command (see *Sukka* 44b).

קוֹל דָּפַק וְהֵצִיץ וְזָרַח, וּמָשׁ חֲצִי הָהָר מִמִּזְרָח. מְבַשֵּׂר וְאוֹמֵר.
קוֹל הֵקִים מִלּוּל נְאֻמוֹ, וּבָא הוּא וְכָל קְדוֹשָׁיו עִמּוֹ. מְבַשֵּׂר וְאוֹמֵר.
קוֹל וּלְכָל בָּאֵי הָעוֹלָם, בַּת קוֹל יִשָּׁמַע בָּעוֹלָם. מְבַשֵּׂר וְאוֹמֵר.
קוֹל זֶרַע עֲמוּסֵי רַחְמוֹ, נוֹלְדוּ כְּיֶלֶד מִמְּעֵי אִמּוֹ. מְבַשֵּׂר וְאוֹמֵר.
קוֹל חָלָה וְיָלְדָה מִי זֹאת, מִי־שָׁמַע כָּזֹאת. מְבַשֵּׂר וְאוֹמֵר. ישעיה סו
קוֹל טָהוֹר פָּעַל כָּל אֵלֶּה, מִי רָאָה כָּאֵלֶּה. מְבַשֵּׂר וְאוֹמֵר. שם
קוֹל יֶשַׁע וּזְמַן הוּחַד, הֲיוּחַל אֶרֶץ בְּיוֹם אֶחָד. מְבַשֵּׂר וְאוֹמֵר. שם
קוֹל כַּבִּיר רוּם וָתַחַת, אִם־יִוָּלֵד גּוֹי פַּעַם אֶחָת. מְבַשֵּׂר וְאוֹמֵר. שם
קוֹל לְעֵת יִגְאַל עַמּוֹ נָאוֹר, וְהָיָה לְעֵת־עֶרֶב יִהְיֶה־אוֹר. מְבַשֵּׂר וְאוֹמֵר. זכריה יד
קוֹל מוֹשִׁיעִים יַעֲלוּ לְהַר צִיּוֹן, כִּי־חָלָה גַּם־יָלְדָה צִיּוֹן. מְבַשֵּׂר וְאוֹמֵר. ישעיה סו
קוֹל נִשְׁמַע בְּכָל גְּבוּלֵךְ, הַרְחִיבִי מְקוֹם אָהֳלֵךְ. מְבַשֵּׂר וְאוֹמֵר. ישעיה נד
קוֹל שִׂימִי עַד דַּמֶּשֶׂק מִשְׁכְּנוֹתַיִךְ, קַבְּלִי בָנַיִךְ וּבְנוֹתַיִךְ. מְבַשֵּׂר וְאוֹמֵר.
קוֹל עִלְזִי חֲבַצֶּלֶת הַשָּׁרוֹן, כִּי קָמוּ יְשֵׁנֵי חֶבְרוֹן. מְבַשֵּׂר וְאוֹמֵר.
קוֹל פְּנוּ אֵלַי וְהִוָּשְׁעוּ, הַיּוֹם אִם בְּקוֹלִי תִשְׁמָעוּ. מְבַשֵּׂר וְאוֹמֵר. ישעיה מה
קוֹל צֶמַח אִישׁ צֶמַח שְׁמוֹ, הוּא דָוִד בְּעַצְמוֹ. מְבַשֵּׂר וְאוֹמֵר.
קוֹל קוּמוּ כְּפוּשֵׁי עָפָר, הָקִיצוּ וְרַנְּנוּ שֹׁכְנֵי עָפָר. מְבַשֵּׂר וְאוֹמֵר. ישעיה כו
קוֹל רַבָּתִי עָם בְּהַמְלִיכוֹ, מִגְדּוֹל יְשׁוּעוֹת מַלְכּוֹ. מְבַשֵּׂר וְאוֹמֵר. שמואל ב׳ כב
קוֹל שֵׁם רְשָׁעִים לְהַאֲבִיד, עֹשֶׂה־חֶסֶד לִמְשִׁיחוֹ לְדָוִד. מְבַשֵּׂר וְאוֹמֵר. שם
קוֹל תְּנָה יְשׁוּעוֹת לְעַם עוֹלָם, לְדָוִד וּלְזַרְעוֹ עַד־עוֹלָם. מְבַשֵּׂר וְאוֹמֵר. שם

The שליח ציבור *says three times, then the* קהל *repeats three times:*

קוֹל מְבַשֵּׂר מְבַשֵּׂר וְאוֹמֵר.

Beat the הושענות *against a chair or the floor five times, then say the following (see law 31):*

תהלים כח הוֹשִׁיעָה אֶת־עַמֶּךָ, וּבָרֵךְ אֶת־נַחֲלָתֶךָ
וּרְעֵם וְנַשְּׂאֵם עַד־הָעוֹלָם:

חיבוט ערבות BEATING OF THE WILLOWS
This was a ceremony, mentioned in the *Tosefta* (*Sukka*, ch. 3) and the Talmud

Let these words with which I have pleaded with the LORD *1 Kings 8*
be close to the LORD our God day and night,
that they may do justice for His servant,
and justice for His people Israel, day after day;
so that all the peoples of the earth will know
that the LORD is God. There is no other.

The Torah scrolls are returned to the Ark, which is then closed.

May it be Your will, LORD our God, God of our ancestors, who chooses good prophets, and their good customs – to receive our prayers and our circlings with compassion and favor. Remember for us the merit of Your seven perfect ones, and remove the wall of iron that separates us from You, and hear our pleas, and seal us with a good judgment – You who suspends the world over nothingness. And seal us in the book of good life.

On this day, invest Your mighty Presence with the five sweetened powers – by means of the beating of the willows, the custom of Your holy prophets – and let love be awakened among them. Kiss us with the kisses of Your mouth, which sweetens all might and all judgments. Shine light upon Your mighty Presence, by the name *Yod-Heh-Vav*, which is the dew that is a dew of light. And from that place, emanate plenty to Your servant, who prays here before You; lengthen his life and forgive him his sins and iniquities and rebellions. And extend Your hand, Your right hand, to receive him in full repentance before You. Open Your treasury of good, to satisfy the yearning soul with water, as it is written, "The LORD will open His good treasury for You, open *Deut. 28* the heavens, to grant your land its rain in its right time, and to bless all the work of your hands:" Amen.

Kinds is dried up, it is invalid for use because, as it says in Psalm 115:17 "It is not the dead who praise the LORD" (Jerusalem Talmud, *Sukka* 3:1). Now, as this long sequence of sacred days draws to a close, we perform a powerfully symbolic act to declare this truth. Without water, there is no life. Without life, there is no song of praise to God. Without rain, we are like a cut willow that, under repeated blows of fate, sheds its leaves. Therefore, God, send rain, that the universe – life in all its forms – may sing Your praise.

וְיִהְיוּ דְבָרַי אֵלֶּה, אֲשֶׁר הִתְחַנַּנְתִּי לִפְנֵי יהוה מלכים א׳ ח
קְרֹבִים אֶל־יהוה אֱלֹהֵינוּ יוֹמָם וָלָיְלָה
לַעֲשׂוֹת מִשְׁפַּט עַבְדּוֹ וּמִשְׁפַּט עַמּוֹ יִשְׂרָאֵל, דְּבַר־יוֹם בְּיוֹמוֹ:
לְמַעַן דַּעַת כָּל־עַמֵּי הָאָרֶץ כִּי יהוה הוּא הָאֱלֹהִים, אֵין עוֹד:

The ספרי תורה *are returned to the* ארון קודש*, which is then closed.*

יְהִי רָצוֹן מִלְּפָנֶיךָ יהוה אֱלֹהֵינוּ וֵאלֹהֵי אֲבוֹתֵינוּ, הַבּוֹחֵר בִּנְבִיאִים טוֹבִים וּבְמִנְהֲגֵיהֶם הַטּוֹבִים, שֶׁתְּקַבֵּל בְּרַחֲמִים וּבְרָצוֹן אֶת תְּפִלָּתֵנוּ וְהַקָּפוֹתֵינוּ. וּזְכָר לָנוּ זְכוּת שִׁבְעַת תְּמִימֶיךָ, וְתָסִיר מְחִצַּת הַבַּרְזֶל הַמַּפְסֶקֶת בֵּינֵינוּ וּבֵינֶךָ, וְתַאֲזִין שַׁוְעָתֵנוּ, וְתֵיטִיב לָנוּ הַחֲתִימָה, תּוֹלֶה אֶרֶץ עַל בְּלִימָה, וְחָתְמֵנוּ בְּסֵפֶר חַיִּים טוֹבִים.

וְהַיּוֹם הַזֶּה תִּתֵּן בִּשְׁכִינַת עֻזָּךְ חָמֵשׁ גְּבוּרוֹת מְמֻתָּקוֹת, עַל יְדֵי חֲבִיטַת עֲרָבָה מִנְהַג נְבִיאֶיךָ הַקְּדוֹשִׁים, וְתִתְעוֹרֵר הָאַהֲבָה בֵּינֵיהֶם. וּתְנַשְּׁקֵנוּ מִנְּשִׁיקוֹת פִּיךָ, מְמַתֶּקֶת כָּל הַגְּבוּרוֹת וְכָל הַדִּינִין. וְתָאִיר לִשְׁכִינַת עֻזָּךְ בְּשֵׁם יו״ד הֵ״א וָא״ו שֶׁהוּא טַל אוֹרוֹת טַלֶּךָ, וּמִשָּׁם תַּשְׁפִּיעַ שֶׁפַע לְעַבְדְּךָ הַמִּתְפַּלֵּל לְפָנֶיךָ, שֶׁתַּאֲרִיךְ יָמָיו וְתִמְחַל לוֹ חֲטָאָיו וַעֲוֹנוֹתָיו וּפְשָׁעָיו. וְתִפְשֹׁט יְמִינְךָ וְיָדְךָ לְקַבְּלוֹ בִּתְשׁוּבָה שְׁלֵמָה לְפָנֶיךָ. וְאוֹצָרְךָ
הַטּוֹב תִּפְתַּח לְהַשְׂבִּיעַ מַיִם נֶפֶשׁ שׁוֹקֵקָה, כְּמוֹ שֶׁכָּתוּב: יִפְתַּח יהוה דברים כח
לְךָ אֶת־אוֹצָרוֹ הַטּוֹב אֶת־הַשָּׁמַיִם לָתֵת מְטַר־אַרְצְךָ בְּעִתּוֹ, וּלְבָרֵךְ אֵת כָּל־מַעֲשֵׂה יָדֶךָ: אָמֵן.

The custom to beat them five times is a mystical one, deriving from R. Isaac Luria.

Many explanations for the beating have been offered. The simplest is this: On Rosh HaShana and Yom Kippur we prayed for life: "Write us in the book of life." On Sukkot we have acknowledged that our life depends on the vitality of nature. In the Sukka, with its roof of leaves, we expose ourselves to the forces of nature. The Four Kinds are rare among mitzva objects in that they are natural: not processed or refined in any way. In these symbolic ways we acknowledge our dependence on God the Sustainer of nature, "the Force that through the green fuse drives the flower." The sages said that if any of the Four

FULL KADDISH

Some have the custom to include additional responses in Full Kaddish. *They can be found in the version on page 1464.*

Leader: יִתְגַּדַּל Magnified and sanctified may His great name be,
in the world He created by His will.
May He establish His kingdom
in your lifetime and in your days,
and in the lifetime of all the house of Israel,
swiftly and soon –
and say: Amen.

All: May His great name be blessed
for ever and all time.

Leader: Blessed and praised,
glorified and exalted,
raised and honored,
uplifted and lauded
be the name of the Holy One,
blessed be He,
beyond any blessing,
song, praise and consolation
uttered in the world –
and say: Amen.

May the prayers and pleas of all Israel
be accepted by their Father in heaven –
and say: Amen.

May there be great peace from heaven,
and life for us and all Israel –
and say: Amen.

Bow, take three steps back, as if taking leave of the Divine Presence, then bow, first left, then right, then center, while saying:

May He who makes peace in His high places,
make peace for us and all Israel –
and say: Amen.

קדיש שלם

Some have the custom to include additional responses in קדיש שלם.
They can be found in the version on page 1465.

ש״ץ: יִתְגַּדַּל וְיִתְקַדַּשׁ שְׁמֵהּ רַבָּא (קהל: אָמֵן)
בְּעָלְמָא דִּי בְרָא כִרְעוּתֵהּ
וְיַמְלִיךְ מַלְכוּתֵהּ
בְּחַיֵּיכוֹן וּבְיוֹמֵיכוֹן וּבְחַיֵּי דְכָל בֵּית יִשְׂרָאֵל
בַּעֲגָלָא וּבִזְמַן קָרִיב
וְאִמְרוּ אָמֵן. (קהל: אָמֵן)

קהל וש״ץ: יְהֵא שְׁמֵהּ רַבָּא מְבָרַךְ לְעָלַם וּלְעָלְמֵי עָלְמַיָּא.

ש״ץ: יִתְבָּרַךְ וְיִשְׁתַּבַּח וְיִתְפָּאַר
וְיִתְרוֹמַם וְיִתְנַשֵּׂא וְיִתְהַדָּר וְיִתְעַלֶּה וְיִתְהַלָּל
שְׁמֵהּ דְּקֻדְשָׁא בְּרִיךְ הוּא (קהל: בְּרִיךְ הוּא)
לְעֵלָּא מִן כָּל בִּרְכָתָא וְשִׁירָתָא, תֻּשְׁבְּחָתָא וְנֶחֱמָתָא
דַּאֲמִירָן בְּעָלְמָא
וְאִמְרוּ אָמֵן. (קהל: אָמֵן)

תִּתְקַבַּל צְלוֹתְהוֹן וּבָעוּתְהוֹן דְּכָל יִשְׂרָאֵל
קֳדָם אֲבוּהוֹן דִּי בִשְׁמַיָּא
וְאִמְרוּ אָמֵן. (קהל: אָמֵן)

יְהֵא שְׁלָמָא רַבָּא מִן שְׁמַיָּא
וְחַיִּים, עָלֵינוּ וְעַל כָּל יִשְׂרָאֵל
וְאִמְרוּ אָמֵן. (קהל: אָמֵן)

Bow, take three steps back, as if taking leave of the Divine Presence,
then bow, first left, then right, then center, while saying:

עֹשֶׂה שָׁלוֹם בִּמְרוֹמָיו
הוּא יַעֲשֶׂה שָׁלוֹם עָלֵינוּ וְעַל כָּל יִשְׂרָאֵל
וְאִמְרוּ אָמֵן. (קהל: אָמֵן)

אֵין כֵּאלֹהֵינוּ There is none like our God, none like our LORD,
none like our King, none like our Savior.
Who is like our God? Who is like our LORD?
Who is like our King? Who is like our Savior?
We will thank our God, we will thank our LORD,
we will thank our King, we will thank our Savior.
Blessed is our God, blessed is our LORD,
blessed is our King, blessed is our Savior.
You are our God, You are our LORD,
You are our King, You are our Savior.
You are He to whom our ancestors offered the fragrant incense.

פִּטּוּם הַקְּטֹרֶת The incense mixture consisted of balsam, onycha, galbanum and frankincense, each weighing seventy manehs; myrrh, cassia, spikenard and saffron, each weighing sixteen manehs; twelve manehs of costus, three of aromatic bark; nine of cinnamon; nine kabs of Carsina lye; three seahs and three kabs of Cyprus wine. If Cyprus wine was not available, old white wine might be used. A quarter of a kab of Sodom salt, and a minute amount of a smoke-raising herb. Rabbi Nathan says: Also a minute amount of Jordan amber. If one added honey to the mixture, he rendered it unfit for sacred use. If he omitted any one of its ingredients, he is guilty of a capital offense. *Keritot 6a*

Rabban Shimon ben Gamliel says: "Balsam" refers to the sap that drips from the balsam tree. The Carsina lye was used for bleaching the onycha to improve it. The Cyprus wine was used to soak the onycha in it to make it pungent. Though urine is suitable for this purpose, it is not brought into the Temple out of respect.

These were the psalms which the Levites used to recite in the Temple: *Mishna, Tamid 7*
On the first day of the week they used to say:
"The earth is the LORD's and all it contains, *Ps. 24*
the world and all who live in it."
On the second day they used to say:
"Great is the LORD and greatly to be praised *Ps. 48*
in the city of God, on His holy mountain."
On the third day they used to say:
"God stands in the divine assembly. *Ps. 82*
Among the judges He delivers judgment."
On the fourth day they used to say:
"God of retribution, LORD, God of retribution, appear." *Ps. 94*

אֵין כֵּאלֹהֵֽינוּ, אֵין כַּאדוֹנֵֽינוּ, אֵין כְּמַלְכֵּֽנוּ, אֵין כְּמוֹשִׁיעֵֽנוּ.
מִי כֵאלֹהֵֽינוּ, מִי כַאדוֹנֵֽינוּ, מִי כְמַלְכֵּֽנוּ, מִי כְמוֹשִׁיעֵֽנוּ.
נוֹדֶה לֵאלֹהֵֽינוּ, נוֹדֶה לַאדוֹנֵֽינוּ, נוֹדֶה לְמַלְכֵּֽנוּ, נוֹדֶה לְמוֹשִׁיעֵֽנוּ.
בָּרוּךְ אֱלֹהֵֽינוּ, בָּרוּךְ אֲדוֹנֵֽינוּ, בָּרוּךְ מַלְכֵּֽנוּ, בָּרוּךְ מוֹשִׁיעֵֽנוּ.
אַתָּה הוּא אֱלֹהֵֽינוּ, אַתָּה הוּא אֲדוֹנֵֽינוּ,
אַתָּה הוּא מַלְכֵּֽנוּ, אַתָּה הוּא מוֹשִׁיעֵֽנוּ.
אַתָּה הוּא שֶׁהִקְטִֽירוּ אֲבוֹתֵֽינוּ לְפָנֶֽיךָ אֶת קְטֹֽרֶת הַסַּמִּים.

פִּטּוּם הַקְּטֹֽרֶת. הַצֳּרִי, וְהַצִּפֹּֽרֶן, וְהַחֶלְבְּנָה, וְהַלְּבוֹנָה מִשְׁקַל שִׁבְעִים שִׁבְעִים מָנֶה, מֹר, וּקְצִיעָה, שִׁבֹּֽלֶת נֵרְדְּ, וְכַרְכֹּם מִשְׁקַל שִׁשָּׁה עָשָׂר שִׁשָּׁה עָשָׂר מָנֶה, הַקֹּשְׁטְ שְׁנֵים עָשָׂר, קִלּוּפָה שְׁלֹשָׁה, וְקִנָּמוֹן תִּשְׁעָה, בֹּרִית כַּרְשִׁינָה תִּשְׁעָה קַבִּין, יֵין קַפְרִיסִין סְאִין תְּלָת וְקַבִּין תְּלָתָא, וְאִם אֵין לוֹ יֵין קַפְרִיסִין, מֵבִיא חֲמַר חִוַּרְיָן עַתִּיק. מֶֽלַח סְדוֹמִית רֹֽבַע, מַעֲלֶה עָשָׁן כָּל שֶׁהוּא. רַבִּי נָתָן הַבַּבְלִי אוֹמֵר: אַף כִּפַּת הַיַּרְדֵּן כָּל שֶׁהוּא, וְאִם נָתַן בָּהּ דְּבַשׁ פְּסָלָהּ, וְאִם חִסַּר אֶחָד מִכָּל סַמָּנֶֽיהָ, חַיָּב מִיתָה. כריתות ו.

רַבָּן שִׁמְעוֹן בֶּן גַּמְלִיאֵל אוֹמֵר: הַצֳּרִי אֵינוֹ אֶלָּא שְׂרָף הַנּוֹטֵף מֵעֲצֵי הַקְּטָף. בֹּרִית כַּרְשִׁינָה שֶׁשָּׁפִין בָּהּ אֶת הַצִּפֹּֽרֶן כְּדֵי שֶׁתְּהֵא נָאָה, יֵין קַפְרִיסִין שֶׁשּׁוֹרִין בּוֹ אֶת הַצִּפֹּֽרֶן כְּדֵי שֶׁתְּהֵא עַזָּה, וַהֲלֹא מֵי רַגְלַֽיִם יָפִין לָהּ, אֶלָּא שֶׁאֵין מַכְנִיסִין מֵי רַגְלַֽיִם בַּמִּקְדָּשׁ מִפְּנֵי הַכָּבוֹד.

הַשִּׁיר שֶׁהַלְוִיִּם הָיוּ אוֹמְרִים בְּבֵית הַמִּקְדָּשׁ: משנה תמיד ז
בַּיּוֹם הָרִאשׁוֹן הָיוּ אוֹמְרִים
לַיהוה הָאָֽרֶץ וּמְלוֹאָהּ, תֵּבֵל וְיֽשְׁבֵי בָהּ: תהלים כד
בַּשֵּׁנִי הָיוּ אוֹמְרִים
גָּדוֹל יהוה וּמְהֻלָּל מְאֹד, בְּעִיר אֱלֹהֵֽינוּ הַר־קָדְשׁוֹ: תהלים מח
בַּשְּׁלִישִׁי הָיוּ אוֹמְרִים
אֱלֹהִים נִצָּב בַּעֲדַת־אֵל, בְּקֶֽרֶב אֱלֹהִים יִשְׁפֹּט: תהלים פב
בָּרְבִיעִי הָיוּ אוֹמְרִים
אֵל־נְקָמוֹת יהוה, אֵל נְקָמוֹת הוֹפִֽיעַ: תהלים צד

On the fifth day they used to say:
"Sing for joy to God, our strength. Shout aloud to the God of Jacob." *Ps. 81*
On the sixth day they used to say:
"The LORD reigns: He is robed in majesty; *Ps. 93*
the LORD is robed, girded with strength;
the world is firmly established; it cannot be moved."
On the Sabbath they used to say:
"A psalm, a song for the Sabbath day" – *Ps. 92*
[meaning] a psalm and song for the time to come,
for the day which will be entirely Sabbath and rest for life everlasting.

It was taught in the Academy of Elijah: Whoever studies [Torah] laws every day is assured that he will be destined for the World to Come, as it is said, "The ways of the world are His" – read not, "ways" [*halikhot*] but "laws" [*halakhot*]. *Megilla 28b* *Hab. 3*

Rabbi Elazar said in the name of Rabbi Ḥanina: The disciples of the sages increase peace in the world, as it is said, "And all your children shall be taught of the LORD, and great shall be the peace of your children [*banayikh*]." Read not *banayikh*, "your children," but *bonayikh*, "your builders." Those who love Your Torah have great peace; there is no stumbling block for them. May there be peace within your ramparts, prosperity in your palaces. For the sake of my brothers and friends, I shall say, "Peace be within you." For the sake of the House of the LORD our God, I will seek your good. ▸ May the LORD grant strength to His people; may the LORD bless His people with peace. *Berakhot 64a* *Is. 54* *Ps. 119* *Ps. 122* *Ps. 29*

THE RABBIS' KADDISH

The following prayer, said by mourners, requires the presence of a minyan. A transliteration can be found on page 1466.

Mourner: יִתְגַּדַּל Magnified and sanctified may His great name be,
in the world He created by His will.
May He establish His kingdom in your lifetime
and in your days,
and in the lifetime of all the house of Israel,
swiftly and soon – and say: Amen.

All: May His great name be blessed for ever and all time.

Mourner: Blessed and praised, glorified and exalted,
raised and honored, uplifted and lauded
be the name of the Holy One,
blessed be He,

בַּחֲמִישִׁי הָיוּ אוֹמְרִים

הַרְנִינוּ לֵאלֹהִים עוּזֵּנוּ, הָרִיעוּ לֵאלֹהֵי יַעֲקֹב: תהלים פא

בַּשִּׁשִּׁי הָיוּ אוֹמְרִים

יהוה מָלָךְ גֵּאוּת לָבֵשׁ תהלים צג

לָבֵשׁ יהוה עֹז הִתְאַזָּר, אַף־תִּכּוֹן תֵּבֵל בַּל־תִּמּוֹט:

בַּשַּׁבָּת הָיוּ אוֹמְרִים

מִזְמוֹר שִׁיר לְיוֹם הַשַּׁבָּת: תהלים צב

מִזְמוֹר שִׁיר לֶעָתִיד לָבוֹא, לְיוֹם שֶׁכֻּלּוֹ שַׁבָּת וּמְנוּחָה לְחַיֵּי הָעוֹלָמִים.

תָּנָא דְבֵי אֵלִיָּהוּ: כָּל הַשּׁוֹנֶה הֲלָכוֹת בְּכָל יוֹם, מֻבְטָח לוֹ שֶׁהוּא בֶּן עוֹלָם מגילה כח:
הַבָּא, שֶׁנֶּאֱמַר, הֲלִיכוֹת עוֹלָם לוֹ: אַל תִּקְרֵי הֲלִיכוֹת אֶלָּא הֲלָכוֹת. חבקוק ג

אָמַר רַבִּי אֶלְעָזָר, אָמַר רַבִּי חֲנִינָא: תַּלְמִידֵי חֲכָמִים מַרְבִּים שָׁלוֹם בָּעוֹלָם, ברכות סד.
שֶׁנֶּאֱמַר, וְכָל־בָּנַיִךְ לִמּוּדֵי יהוה, וְרַב שְׁלוֹם בָּנָיִךְ: אַל תִּקְרֵי בָּנָיִךְ, אֶלָּא ישעיה נד
בּוֹנָיִךְ. שָׁלוֹם רָב לְאֹהֲבֵי תוֹרָתֶךָ, וְאֵין־לָמוֹ מִכְשׁוֹל: יְהִי־שָׁלוֹם בְּחֵילֵךְ, תהלים קיט תהלים קכב
שַׁלְוָה בְּאַרְמְנוֹתָיִךְ: לְמַעַן אַחַי וְרֵעָי אֲדַבְּרָה־נָּא שָׁלוֹם בָּךְ: לְמַעַן בֵּית־יהוה
אֱלֹהֵינוּ אֲבַקְשָׁה טוֹב לָךְ: ◂ יהוה עֹז לְעַמּוֹ יִתֵּן, יהוה יְבָרֵךְ אֶת־עַמּוֹ בַשָּׁלוֹם: תהלים כט

קדיש דרבנן

The following prayer, said by mourners, requires the presence of a מנין.
A transliteration can be found on page 1466.

אבל: יִתְגַּדַּל וְיִתְקַדַּשׁ שְׁמֵהּ רַבָּא (קהל: אָמֵן)
בְּעָלְמָא דִּי בְרָא כִרְעוּתֵהּ
וְיַמְלִיךְ מַלְכוּתֵהּ
בְּחַיֵּיכוֹן וּבְיוֹמֵיכוֹן וּבְחַיֵּי דְכָל בֵּית יִשְׂרָאֵל
בַּעֲגָלָא וּבִזְמַן קָרִיב, וְאִמְרוּ אָמֵן. (קהל: אָמֵן)

קהל ואבל: יְהֵא שְׁמֵהּ רַבָּא מְבָרַךְ לְעָלַם וּלְעָלְמֵי עָלְמַיָּא.

אבל: יִתְבָּרַךְ וְיִשְׁתַּבַּח וְיִתְפָּאַר וְיִתְרוֹמַם וְיִתְנַשֵּׂא
וְיִתְהַדָּר וְיִתְעַלֶּה וְיִתְהַלָּל
שְׁמֵהּ דְּקֻדְשָׁא בְּרִיךְ הוּא (קהל: בְּרִיךְ הוּא)

beyond any blessing,
song, praise and consolation
uttered in the world –
and say: Amen.

To Israel, to the teachers,
their disciples and their disciples' disciples,
and to all who engage
in the study of Torah,
in this (*in Israel add:* holy) place or elsewhere,
may there come to them and you great peace,
grace, kindness and compassion,
long life, ample sustenance
and deliverance, from their Father in Heaven –
and say: Amen.

May there be great peace from heaven,
and (good) life for us and all Israel –
and say: Amen.

Bow, take three steps back, as if taking leave of the Divine Presence, then bow, first left, then right, then center, while saying:

May He who makes peace in His high places,
in His compassion make peace
for us and all Israel –
and say: Amen.

Stand while saying Aleinu. Bow at ▾.

עָלֵינוּ It is our duty to praise the Master of all,
and ascribe greatness to the Author of creation,
who has not made us like the nations of the lands
nor placed us like the families of the earth;
who has not made our portion like theirs,
nor our destiny like all their multitudes.
(For they worship vanity and emptiness,
and pray to a god who cannot save.)

לְעֵלָּא מִן כָּל בִּרְכָתָא
וְשִׁירָתָא, תֻּשְׁבְּחָתָא וְנֶחֱמָתָא, דַּאֲמִירָן בְּעָלְמָא
וְאִמְרוּ אָמֵן. (קהל: אָמֵן)

עַל יִשְׂרָאֵל וְעַל רַבָּנָן
וְעַל תַּלְמִידֵיהוֹן וְעַל כָּל תַּלְמִידֵי תַלְמִידֵיהוֹן
וְעַל כָּל מָאן דְּעָסְקִין בְּאוֹרַיְתָא
דִּי בְּאַתְרָא (בארץ ישראל: קַדִּישָׁא) הָדֵין, וְדִי בְּכָל אֲתַר וַאֲתַר
יְהֵא לְהוֹן וּלְכוֹן שְׁלָמָא רַבָּא
חִנָּא וְחִסְדָּא, וְרַחֲמֵי, וְחַיֵּי אֲרִיכֵי, וּמְזוֹנֵי רְוִיחֵי
וּפֻרְקָנָא מִן קֳדָם אֲבוּהוֹן דִּי בִשְׁמַיָּא
וְאִמְרוּ אָמֵן. (קהל: אָמֵן)

יְהֵא שְׁלָמָא רַבָּא מִן שְׁמַיָּא
וְחַיִּים (טוֹבִים) עָלֵינוּ וְעַל כָּל יִשְׂרָאֵל
וְאִמְרוּ אָמֵן. (קהל: אָמֵן)

Bow, take three steps back, as if taking leave of the Divine Presence, then bow, first left, then right, then center, while saying:

עֹשֶׂה שָׁלוֹם בִּמְרוֹמָיו
הוּא יַעֲשֶׂה בְרַחֲמָיו שָׁלוֹם
עָלֵינוּ וְעַל כָּל יִשְׂרָאֵל
וְאִמְרוּ אָמֵן. (קהל: אָמֵן)

Stand while saying עָלֵינוּ*. Bow at* ˅.

עָלֵינוּ לְשַׁבֵּחַ לַאֲדוֹן הַכֹּל, לָתֵת גְּדֻלָּה לְיוֹצֵר בְּרֵאשִׁית
שֶׁלֹּא עָשָׂנוּ כְּגוֹיֵי הָאֲרָצוֹת, וְלֹא שָׂמָנוּ כְּמִשְׁפְּחוֹת הָאֲדָמָה
שֶׁלֹּא שָׂם חֶלְקֵנוּ כָּהֶם וְגוֹרָלֵנוּ כְּכָל הֲמוֹנָם.
(שֶׁהֵם מִשְׁתַּחֲוִים לְהֶבֶל וָרִיק וּמִתְפַּלְלִים אֶל אֵל לֹא יוֹשִׁיעַ.)

▾But we bow in worship
and thank the Supreme King of kings, the Holy One, blessed be He,
who extends the heavens and establishes the earth,
whose throne of glory is in the heavens above,
and whose power's Presence is in the highest of heights.
He is our God; there is no other.
Truly He is our King, there is none else,
as it is written in His Torah:
"You shall know and take to heart this day that the LORD is God, *Deut. 4*
in heaven above and on earth below. There is no other."

Therefore, we place our hope in You, LORD our God,
that we may soon see the glory of Your power,
when You will remove abominations from the earth,
and idols will be utterly destroyed,
when the world will be perfected
under the sovereignty of the Almighty,
when all humanity will call on Your name,
to turn all the earth's wicked toward You.
All the world's inhabitants will realize and know
that to You every knee must bow and every tongue swear loyalty.
Before You, LORD our God, they will kneel and bow down
and give honor to Your glorious name.
They will all accept the yoke of Your kingdom,
and You will reign over them soon and for ever.
For the kingdom is Yours,
and to all eternity You will reign in glory,
as it is written in Your Torah: "The LORD will reign for ever and ever." *Ex. 15*
▸ And it is said: "Then the LORD shall be King over all the earth; *Zech. 14*
on that day the LORD shall be One and His name One."

Some add:
Have no fear of sudden terror or of the ruin when it overtakes the wicked. *Prov. 3*
Devise your strategy, but it will be thwarted; propose your plan, *Is. 8*
but it will not stand, for God is with us.
When you grow old, I will still be the same. *Is. 46*
When your hair turns gray, I will still carry you.
I made you, I will bear you, I will carry you, and I will rescue you.

וַאֲנַחְנוּ כּוֹרְעִים וּמִשְׁתַּחֲוִים וּמוֹדִים
לִפְנֵי מֶלֶךְ מַלְכֵי הַמְּלָכִים, הַקָּדוֹשׁ בָּרוּךְ הוּא
שֶׁהוּא נוֹטֶה שָׁמַיִם וְיוֹסֵד אָרֶץ, וּמוֹשַׁב יְקָרוֹ בַּשָּׁמַיִם מִמַּעַל
וּשְׁכִינַת עֻזּוֹ בְּגָבְהֵי מְרוֹמִים.
הוּא אֱלֹהֵינוּ, אֵין עוֹד.
אֱמֶת מַלְכֵּנוּ, אֶפֶס זוּלָתוֹ, כַּכָּתוּב בְּתוֹרָתוֹ
וְיָדַעְתָּ הַיּוֹם וַהֲשֵׁבֹתָ אֶל־לְבָבֶךָ דברים ד
כִּי יהוה הוּא הָאֱלֹהִים בַּשָּׁמַיִם מִמַּעַל וְעַל־הָאָרֶץ מִתָּחַת
אֵין עוֹד:

עַל כֵּן נְקַוֶּה לְּךָ יהוה אֱלֹהֵינוּ, לִרְאוֹת מְהֵרָה בְּתִפְאֶרֶת עֻזֶּךָ
לְהַעֲבִיר גִּלּוּלִים מִן הָאָרֶץ, וְהָאֱלִילִים כָּרוֹת יִכָּרֵתוּן
לְתַקֵּן עוֹלָם בְּמַלְכוּת שַׁדַּי.
וְכָל בְּנֵי בָשָׂר יִקְרְאוּ בִשְׁמֶךָ לְהַפְנוֹת אֵלֶיךָ כָּל רִשְׁעֵי אָרֶץ.
יַכִּירוּ וְיֵדְעוּ כָּל יוֹשְׁבֵי תֵבֵל
כִּי לְךָ תִּכְרַע כָּל בֶּרֶךְ, תִּשָּׁבַע כָּל לָשׁוֹן.
לְפָנֶיךָ יהוה אֱלֹהֵינוּ יִכְרְעוּ וְיִפֹּלוּ, וְלִכְבוֹד שִׁמְךָ יְקָר יִתֵּנוּ
וִיקַבְּלוּ כֻלָּם אֶת עֹל מַלְכוּתֶךָ
וְתִמְלֹךְ עֲלֵיהֶם מְהֵרָה לְעוֹלָם וָעֶד.
כִּי הַמַּלְכוּת שֶׁלְּךָ הִיא וּלְעוֹלְמֵי עַד תִּמְלֹךְ בְּכָבוֹד
כַּכָּתוּב בְּתוֹרָתֶךָ, יהוה יִמְלֹךְ לְעֹלָם וָעֶד: שמות טו
◂ וְנֶאֱמַר, וְהָיָה יהוה לְמֶלֶךְ עַל־כָּל־הָאָרֶץ זכריה יד
בַּיּוֹם הַהוּא יִהְיֶה יהוה אֶחָד וּשְׁמוֹ אֶחָד:

Some add:

אַל־תִּירָא מִפַּחַד פִּתְאֹם וּמִשֹּׁאַת רְשָׁעִים כִּי תָבֹא: משלי ג
עֻצוּ עֵצָה וְתֻפָר, דַּבְּרוּ דָבָר וְלֹא יָקוּם, כִּי עִמָּנוּ אֵל: ישעיה ח
וְעַד־זִקְנָה אֲנִי הוּא, וְעַד־שֵׂיבָה אֲנִי אֶסְבֹּל אֲנִי עָשִׂיתִי וַאֲנִי אֶשָּׂא וַאֲנִי אֶסְבֹּל וַאֲמַלֵּט: ישעיה מו

MOURNER'S KADDISH

The following prayer, said by mourners, requires the presence of a minyan. A transliteration can be found on page 1467.

Mourner: יִתְגַּדַּל Magnified and sanctified
may His great name be,
in the world He created by His will.
May He establish His kingdom
in your lifetime and in your days,
and in the lifetime of all the house of Israel,
swiftly and soon –
and say: Amen.

All: May His great name
be blessed for ever and all time.

Mourner: Blessed and praised,
glorified and exalted,
raised and honored,
uplifted and lauded
be the name of the Holy One,
blessed be He,
beyond any blessing,
song, praise and consolation
uttered in the world –
and say: Amen.

May there be great peace from heaven,
and life for us and all Israel –
and say: Amen.

Bow, take three steps back, as if taking leave of the Divine Presence, then bow, first left, then right, then center, while saying:

May He who makes peace in His high places,
make peace for us and all Israel –
and say: Amen.

קדיש יתום

The following prayer, said by mourners, requires the presence of a מנין.
A transliteration can be found on page 1467.

אבל: יִתְגַּדַּל וְיִתְקַדַּשׁ שְׁמֵהּ רַבָּא (קהל: אָמֵן)
בְּעָלְמָא דִּי בְרָא כִרְעוּתֵהּ
וְיַמְלִיךְ מַלְכוּתֵהּ
בְּחַיֵּיכוֹן וּבְיוֹמֵיכוֹן וּבְחַיֵּי דְכָל בֵּית יִשְׂרָאֵל
בַּעֲגָלָא וּבִזְמַן קָרִיב
וְאִמְרוּ אָמֵן. (קהל: אָמֵן)

קהל ואבל: יְהֵא שְׁמֵהּ רַבָּא מְבָרַךְ לְעָלַם וּלְעָלְמֵי עָלְמַיָּא.

אבל: יִתְבָּרַךְ וְיִשְׁתַּבַּח וְיִתְפָּאַר
וְיִתְרוֹמַם וְיִתְנַשֵּׂא וְיִתְהַדָּר וְיִתְעַלֶּה וְיִתְהַלָּל
שְׁמֵהּ דְּקֻדְשָׁא בְּרִיךְ הוּא (קהל: בְּרִיךְ הוּא)
לְעֵלָּא מִן כָּל בִּרְכָתָא
וְשִׁירָתָא, תֻּשְׁבְּחָתָא וְנֶחֱמָתָא
דַּאֲמִירָן בְּעָלְמָא
וְאִמְרוּ אָמֵן. (קהל: אָמֵן)

יְהֵא שְׁלָמָא רַבָּא מִן שְׁמַיָּא
וְחַיִּים, עָלֵינוּ וְעַל כָּל יִשְׂרָאֵל
וְאִמְרוּ אָמֵן. (קהל: אָמֵן)

Bow, take three steps back, as if taking leave of the Divine Presence,
then bow, first left, then right, then center, while saying:

עֹשֶׂה שָׁלוֹם בִּמְרוֹמָיו
הוּא יַעֲשֶׂה שָׁלוֹם עָלֵינוּ וְעַל כָּל יִשְׂרָאֵל
וְאִמְרוּ אָמֵן. (קהל: אָמֵן)

THE DAILY PSALM

One of the following psalms is said on the appropriate day of the week as indicated.

Sunday: Today is the first day of the week,
on which the Levites used to say this psalm in the Temple:

לְדָוִד מִזְמוֹר A psalm of David. The earth is the LORD's and all it contains, *Ps. 24*
the world and all who live in it. For He founded it on the seas and established it on the streams. Who may climb the mountain of the LORD? Who may stand in His holy place? He who has clean hands and a pure heart, who has not taken My name in vain or sworn deceitfully. He shall receive a blessing from the LORD, and just reward from the God of his salvation. This is a generation of those who seek Him, the descendants of Jacob who seek Your presence, Selah! Lift up your heads, O gates; be uplifted, eternal doors, so that the King of glory may enter. Who is the King of glory? It is the LORD, strong and mighty, the LORD mighty in battle. Lift up your heads, O gates; be uplifted, eternal doors, that the King of glory may enter. ▸ Who is He, the King of glory? The LORD of hosts, He is the King of glory, Selah!

Mourner's Kaddish (page 1076)

Monday: Today is the second day of the week,
on which the Levites used to say this psalm in the Temple:

שִׁיר מִזְמוֹר A song. A psalm of the sons of Koraḥ. Great is the LORD and *Ps. 48*
greatly to be praised in the city of God, on His holy mountain – beautiful in its heights, joy of all the earth, Mount Zion on its northern side, city of the great King. In its citadels God is known as a stronghold. See how the kings joined forces, advancing together. They saw, they were astounded, they panicked, they fled. There fear seized them, like the pains of a woman giving birth, like ships of Tarshish wrecked by an eastern wind. What we had heard, now we have seen, in the city of the LORD of hosts, in the city of our God. May God preserve it for ever, Selah! In the midst of Your Temple, God, we meditate on Your love. As is Your name, God, so is Your praise: it reaches to the ends of the earth. Your right hand is filled with righteousness. Let Mount Zion rejoice, let the towns of Judah be glad, because of Your judgments. Walk around Zion and encircle it. Count

שיר של יום

One of the following psalms is said on the appropriate day of the week as indicated.

Sunday הַיּוֹם יוֹם רִאשׁוֹן בְּשַׁבָּת, שֶׁבּוֹ הָיוּ הַלְוִיִּם אוֹמְרִים בְּבֵית הַמִּקְדָּשׁ:

תהלים כד לְדָוִד מִזְמוֹר, לַיהוה הָאָרֶץ וּמְלוֹאָהּ, תֵּבֵל וְיֹשְׁבֵי בָהּ: כִּי־הוּא עַל־
יַמִּים יְסָדָהּ, וְעַל־נְהָרוֹת יְכוֹנְנֶהָ: מִי־יַעֲלֶה בְהַר־יהוה, וּמִי־יָקוּם
בִּמְקוֹם קָדְשׁוֹ: נְקִי כַפַּיִם וּבַר־לֵבָב, אֲשֶׁר לֹא־נָשָׂא לַשָּׁוְא נַפְשִׁי, וְלֹא
נִשְׁבַּע לְמִרְמָה: יִשָּׂא בְרָכָה מֵאֵת יהוה, וּצְדָקָה מֵאֱלֹהֵי יִשְׁעוֹ: זֶה
דּוֹר דֹּרְשָׁו, מְבַקְשֵׁי פָנֶיךָ יַעֲקֹב סֶלָה: שְׂאוּ שְׁעָרִים רָאשֵׁיכֶם,
וְהִנָּשְׂאוּ פִּתְחֵי עוֹלָם, וְיָבוֹא מֶלֶךְ הַכָּבוֹד: מִי זֶה מֶלֶךְ הַכָּבוֹד,
יהוה עִזּוּז וְגִבּוֹר, יהוה גִּבּוֹר מִלְחָמָה: שְׂאוּ שְׁעָרִים רָאשֵׁיכֶם,
וּשְׂאוּ פִּתְחֵי עוֹלָם, וְיָבֹא מֶלֶךְ הַכָּבוֹד: ‹ מִי הוּא זֶה מֶלֶךְ הַכָּבוֹד,
יהוה צְבָאוֹת הוּא מֶלֶךְ הַכָּבוֹד סֶלָה:

קדיש יתום (page 1077)

Monday הַיּוֹם יוֹם שֵׁנִי בְּשַׁבָּת, שֶׁבּוֹ הָיוּ הַלְוִיִּם אוֹמְרִים בְּבֵית הַמִּקְדָּשׁ:

תהלים מח שִׁיר מִזְמוֹר לִבְנֵי־קֹרַח: גָּדוֹל יהוה וּמְהֻלָּל מְאֹד, בְּעִיר אֱלֹהֵינוּ, הַר־
קָדְשׁוֹ: יְפֵה נוֹף מְשׂוֹשׂ כָּל־הָאָרֶץ, הַר־צִיּוֹן יַרְכְּתֵי צָפוֹן, קִרְיַת מֶלֶךְ
רָב: אֱלֹהִים בְּאַרְמְנוֹתֶיהָ נוֹדַע לְמִשְׂגָּב: כִּי־הִנֵּה הַמְּלָכִים נוֹעֲדוּ,
עָבְרוּ יַחְדָּו: הֵמָּה רָאוּ כֵּן תָּמָהוּ, נִבְהֲלוּ נֶחְפָּזוּ: רְעָדָה אֲחָזָתַם שָׁם,
חִיל כַּיּוֹלֵדָה: בְּרוּחַ קָדִים תְּשַׁבֵּר אֳנִיּוֹת תַּרְשִׁישׁ: כַּאֲשֶׁר שָׁמַעְנוּ
כֵּן רָאִינוּ, בְּעִיר־יהוה צְבָאוֹת, בְּעִיר אֱלֹהֵינוּ, אֱלֹהִים יְכוֹנְנֶהָ עַד־
עוֹלָם סֶלָה: דִּמִּינוּ אֱלֹהִים חַסְדֶּךָ, בְּקֶרֶב הֵיכָלֶךָ: כְּשִׁמְךָ אֱלֹהִים כֵּן
תְּהִלָּתְךָ עַל־קַצְוֵי־אֶרֶץ, צֶדֶק מָלְאָה יְמִינֶךָ: יִשְׂמַח הַר־צִיּוֹן, תָּגֵלְנָה
בְּנוֹת יְהוּדָה, לְמַעַן מִשְׁפָּטֶיךָ: סֹבּוּ צִיּוֹן וְהַקִּיפוּהָ, סִפְרוּ מִגְדָּלֶיהָ:

its towers, note its strong walls, view its citadels, so that you may tell a future generation ▸ that this is God, our God, for ever and ever. He will guide us for evermore.

Mourner's Kaddish (on the next page)

Wednesday: Today is the fourth day of the week,
on which the Levites used to say this psalm in the Temple:

אֵל־נְקָמוֹת God of retribution, Lord, God of retribution, appear! Rise up, *Ps. 94*
Judge of the earth. Repay to the arrogant what they deserve. How long shall the wicked, Lord, how long shall the wicked triumph? They pour out insolent words. All the evildoers are full of boasting. They crush Your people, Lord, and oppress Your inheritance. They kill the widow and the stranger. They murder the orphaned. They say, "The Lord does not see. The God of Jacob pays no heed." Take heed, you most brutish people. You fools, when will you grow wise? Will He who implants the ear not hear? Will He who formed the eye not see? Will He who disciplines nations – He who teaches man knowledge – not punish? The Lord knows that the thoughts of man are a mere fleeting breath. Happy is the man whom You discipline, Lord, the one You instruct in Your Torah, giving him tranquility in days of trouble, until a pit is dug for the wicked. For the Lord will not forsake His people, nor abandon His heritage. Judgment shall again accord with justice, and all the upright in heart will follow it. Who will rise up for me against the wicked? Who will stand up for me against wrongdoers? Had the Lord not been my help, I would soon have dwelt in death's silence. When I thought my foot was slipping, Your loving-kindness, Lord, gave me support. When I was filled with anxiety, Your consolations soothed my soul. Can a corrupt throne be allied with You? Can injustice be framed into law? They join forces against the life of the righteous, and condemn the innocent to death. But the Lord is my stronghold, my God is the Rock of my refuge. He will bring back on them their wickedness, and destroy them for their evil deeds. The Lord our God will destroy them.

▸ Come, let us sing for joy to the Lord; let us shout aloud to the Rock of *Ps. 95*
our salvation. Let us greet Him with thanksgiving, shout aloud to Him with songs of praise. For the Lord is the great God, the King great above all powers.

Mourner's Kaddish (on the next page)

שִׁיתוּ לִבְּכֶם לְחֵילָה, פַּסְּגוּ אַרְמְנוֹתֶיהָ, לְמַעַן תְּסַפְּרוּ לְדוֹר אַחֲרוֹן:
› כִּי זֶה אֱלֹהִים אֱלֹהֵינוּ עוֹלָם וָעֶד, הוּא יְנַהֲגֵנוּ עַל־מוּת:

קדיש יתום (*on the next page*)

Wednesday הַיּוֹם יוֹם רְבִיעִי בְּשַׁבָּת, שֶׁבּוֹ הָיוּ הַלְוִיִּם אוֹמְרִים בְּבֵית הַמִּקְדָּשׁ:

אֵל־נְקָמוֹת יהוה, אֵל נְקָמוֹת הוֹפִיעַ: הִנָּשֵׂא שֹׁפֵט הָאָרֶץ, הָשֵׁב גְּמוּל עַל־גֵּאִים: עַד־מָתַי רְשָׁעִים, יהוה, עַד־מָתַי רְשָׁעִים יַעֲלֹזוּ: יַבִּיעוּ יְדַבְּרוּ עָתָק, יִתְאַמְּרוּ כָּל־פֹּעֲלֵי אָוֶן: עַמְּךָ יהוה יְדַכְּאוּ, וְנַחֲלָתְךָ יְעַנּוּ: אַלְמָנָה וְגֵר יַהֲרֹגוּ, וִיתוֹמִים יְרַצֵּחוּ: וַיֹּאמְרוּ לֹא יִרְאֶה־יָּהּ, וְלֹא־יָבִין אֱלֹהֵי יַעֲקֹב: בִּינוּ בֹּעֲרִים בָּעָם, וּכְסִילִים מָתַי תַּשְׂכִּילוּ: הֲנֹטַע אֹזֶן הֲלֹא יִשְׁמָע, אִם־יֹצֵר עַיִן הֲלֹא יַבִּיט: הֲיֹסֵר גּוֹיִם הֲלֹא יוֹכִיחַ, הַמְלַמֵּד אָדָם דָּעַת: יהוה יֹדֵעַ מַחְשְׁבוֹת אָדָם, כִּי־הֵמָּה הָבֶל: אַשְׁרֵי הַגֶּבֶר אֲשֶׁר־תְּיַסְּרֶנּוּ יָּהּ, וּמִתּוֹרָתְךָ תְלַמְּדֶנּוּ: לְהַשְׁקִיט לוֹ מִימֵי רָע, עַד יִכָּרֶה לָרָשָׁע שָׁחַת: כִּי לֹא־יִטֹּשׁ יהוה עַמּוֹ, וְנַחֲלָתוֹ לֹא יַעֲזֹב: כִּי־עַד־צֶדֶק יָשׁוּב מִשְׁפָּט, וְאַחֲרָיו כָּל־יִשְׁרֵי־לֵב: מִי־יָקוּם לִי עִם־מְרֵעִים, מִי־יִתְיַצֵּב לִי עִם־פֹּעֲלֵי אָוֶן: לוּלֵי יהוה עֶזְרָתָה לִּי, כִּמְעַט שָׁכְנָה דוּמָה נַפְשִׁי: אִם־אָמַרְתִּי מָטָה רַגְלִי, חַסְדְּךָ יהוה יִסְעָדֵנִי: בְּרֹב שַׂרְעַפַּי בְּקִרְבִּי, תַּנְחוּמֶיךָ יְשַׁעַשְׁעוּ נַפְשִׁי: הַיְחָבְרְךָ כִּסֵּא הַוּוֹת, יֹצֵר עָמָל עֲלֵי־חֹק: יָגוֹדּוּ עַל־נֶפֶשׁ צַדִּיק, וְדָם נָקִי יַרְשִׁיעוּ: וַיְהִי יהוה לִי לְמִשְׂגָּב, וֵאלֹהַי לְצוּר מַחְסִי: וַיָּשֶׁב עֲלֵיהֶם אֶת־אוֹנָם, וּבְרָעָתָם יַצְמִיתֵם, יַצְמִיתֵם יהוה אֱלֹהֵינוּ: תהלים צד

› לְכוּ נְרַנְּנָה לַיהוה, נָרִיעָה לְצוּר יִשְׁעֵנוּ: נְקַדְּמָה פָנָיו בְּתוֹדָה, בִּזְמִרוֹת נָרִיעַ לוֹ: כִּי אֵל גָּדוֹל יהוה, וּמֶלֶךְ גָּדוֹל עַל־כָּל־אֱלֹהִים: תהלים צה

קדיש יתום (*on the next page*)

Friday: Today is the sixth day of the week,
on which the Levites used to say this psalm in the Temple:

יהוה מָלָךְ The Lord reigns. He is robed in majesty. The Lord is robed, *Ps. 93*
girded with strength. The world is firmly established; it cannot be moved. Your throne stands firm as of old; You are eternal. Rivers lift up, Lord, rivers lift up their voice, rivers lift up their crashing waves. Mightier than the noise of many waters, than the mighty waves of the sea is the Lord on high. ▸ Your testimonies are very sure; holiness adorns Your House, Lord, for evermore.

Mourner's Kaddish on the next page.

MOURNER'S KADDISH

The following prayer, said by mourners, requires the presence of a minyan.
A transliteration can be found on page 1467.

Mourner: יִתְגַּדַּל Magnified and sanctified
may His great name be,
in the world He created by His will.
May He establish His kingdom
in your lifetime and in your days,
and in the lifetime of all the house of Israel,
swiftly and soon –
and say: Amen.

All: May His great name
be blessed for ever and all time.

Mourner: Blessed and praised,
glorified and exalted,
raised and honored,
uplifted and lauded
be the name of the Holy One, blessed be He,
beyond any blessing,
song, praise and consolation
uttered in the world –
and say: Amen.

Friday הַיּוֹם יוֹם שִׁשִּׁי בְּשַׁבָּת, שֶׁבּוֹ הָיוּ הַלְוִיִּם אוֹמְרִים בְּבֵית הַמִּקְדָּשׁ:

תהלים צג יהוה מָלָךְ, גֵּאוּת לָבֵשׁ, לָבֵשׁ יהוה עֹז הִתְאַזָּר, אַף־תִּכּוֹן תֵּבֵל בַּל־תִּמּוֹט: נָכוֹן כִּסְאֲךָ מֵאָז, מֵעוֹלָם אָתָּה: נָשְׂאוּ נְהָרוֹת יהוה, נָשְׂאוּ נְהָרוֹת קוֹלָם, יִשְׂאוּ נְהָרוֹת דָּכְיָם: מִקֹּלוֹת מַיִם רַבִּים, אַדִּירִים מִשְׁבְּרֵי־יָם, אַדִּיר בַּמָּרוֹם יהוה: › עֵדֹתֶיךָ נֶאֶמְנוּ מְאֹד, לְבֵיתְךָ נַאֲוָה־קֹּדֶשׁ, יהוה לְאֹרֶךְ יָמִים:

קדיש יתום

The following prayer, said by mourners, requires the presence of a מנין.
A transliteration can be found on page 1467.

אבל: יִתְגַּדַּל וְיִתְקַדַּשׁ שְׁמֵהּ רַבָּא (קהל: אָמֵן)
בְּעָלְמָא דִּי בְרָא כִרְעוּתֵהּ
וְיַמְלִיךְ מַלְכוּתֵהּ
בְּחַיֵּיכוֹן וּבְיוֹמֵיכוֹן וּבְחַיֵּי דְכָל בֵּית יִשְׂרָאֵל
בַּעֲגָלָא וּבִזְמַן קָרִיב
וְאִמְרוּ אָמֵן. (קהל: אָמֵן)

קהל ואבל: יְהֵא שְׁמֵהּ רַבָּא מְבָרַךְ לְעָלַם וּלְעָלְמֵי עָלְמַיָּא.

אבל: יִתְבָּרַךְ וְיִשְׁתַּבַּח וְיִתְפָּאַר
וְיִתְרוֹמַם וְיִתְנַשֵּׂא וְיִתְהַדָּר וְיִתְעַלֶּה וְיִתְהַלָּל
שְׁמֵהּ דְּקֻדְשָׁא בְּרִיךְ הוּא (קהל: בְּרִיךְ הוּא)
לְעֵלָּא מִן כָּל בִּרְכָתָא וְשִׁירָתָא
תֻּשְׁבְּחָתָא וְנֶחֱמָתָא
דַּאֲמִירָן בְּעָלְמָא
וְאִמְרוּ אָמֵן. (קהל: אָמֵן)

May there be great peace from heaven,
and life for us and all Israel –
and say: Amen.

Bow, take three steps back, as if taking leave of the Divine Presence, then bow, first left, then right, then center, while saying:

May He who makes peace in His high places,
make peace for us and all Israel –
and say: Amen.

לְדָוִד A psalm of David. The Lord is my light and my salvation – whom then shall I fear? The Lord is the stronghold of my life – of whom shall I be afraid? When evil men close in on me to devour my flesh, it is they, my enemies and foes, who stumble and fall. Should an army besiege me, my heart would not fear. Should war break out against me, still I would be confident. One thing I ask of the Lord, only this do I seek: to live in the House of the Lord all the days of my life, to gaze on the beauty of the Lord and worship in His Temple. For He will keep me safe in His pavilion on the day of trouble. He will hide me under the cover of His tent. He will set me high upon a rock. Now my head is high above my enemies who surround me. I will sacrifice in His tent with shouts of joy. I will sing and chant praises to the Lord. Lord, hear my voice when I call. Be gracious to me and answer me. On Your behalf my heart says, "Seek My face." Your face, Lord, will I seek. Do not hide Your face from me. Do not turn Your servant away in anger. You have been my help. Do not reject or forsake me, God, my Savior. Were my father and my mother to forsake me, the Lord would take me in. Teach me Your way, Lord, and lead me on a level path, because of my oppressors. Do not abandon me to the will of my foes, for false witnesses have risen against me, breathing violence. ▸ Were it not for my faith that I shall see the Lord's goodness in the land of the living. Hope in the Lord. Be strong and of good courage, and hope in the Lord! *Ps. 27*

Mourner's Kaddish (previous page)

יְהֵא שְׁלָמָא רַבָּא מִן שְׁמַיָּא
וְחַיִּים, עָלֵינוּ וְעַל כָּל יִשְׂרָאֵל
וְאִמְרוּ אָמֵן. (קהל: אָמֵן)

Bow, take three steps back, as if taking leave of the Divine Presence, then bow, first left, then right, then center, while saying:

עֹשֶׂה שָׁלוֹם בִּמְרוֹמָיו
הוּא יַעֲשֶׂה שָׁלוֹם עָלֵינוּ וְעַל כָּל יִשְׂרָאֵל
וְאִמְרוּ אָמֵן. (קהל: אָמֵן)

תהלים כז לְדָוִד, יהוה אוֹרִי וְיִשְׁעִי, מִמִּי אִירָא, יהוה מָעוֹז־חַיַּי, מִמִּי אֶפְחָד: בִּקְרֹב עָלַי מְרֵעִים לֶאֱכֹל אֶת־בְּשָׂרִי, צָרַי וְאֹיְבַי לִי, הֵמָּה כָשְׁלוּ וְנָפָלוּ: אִם־תַּחֲנֶה עָלַי מַחֲנֶה, לֹא־יִירָא לִבִּי, אִם־תָּקוּם עָלַי מִלְחָמָה, בְּזֹאת אֲנִי בוֹטֵחַ: אַחַת שָׁאַלְתִּי מֵאֵת־יהוה, אוֹתָהּ אֲבַקֵּשׁ, שִׁבְתִּי בְּבֵית־יהוה כָּל־יְמֵי חַיַּי, לַחֲזוֹת בְּנֹעַם־יהוה, וּלְבַקֵּר בְּהֵיכָלוֹ: כִּי יִצְפְּנֵנִי בְּסֻכֹּה בְּיוֹם רָעָה, יַסְתִּרֵנִי בְּסֵתֶר אָהֳלוֹ, בְּצוּר יְרוֹמְמֵנִי: וְעַתָּה יָרוּם רֹאשִׁי עַל אֹיְבַי סְבִיבוֹתַי, וְאֶזְבְּחָה בְאָהֳלוֹ זִבְחֵי תְרוּעָה, אָשִׁירָה וַאֲזַמְּרָה לַיהוה: שְׁמַע־יהוה קוֹלִי אֶקְרָא, וְחָנֵּנִי וַעֲנֵנִי: לְךָ אָמַר לִבִּי בַּקְּשׁוּ פָנָי, אֶת־פָּנֶיךָ יהוה אֲבַקֵּשׁ: אַל־תַּסְתֵּר פָּנֶיךָ מִמֶּנִּי, אַל תַּט־בְּאַף עַבְדֶּךָ, עֶזְרָתִי הָיִיתָ, אַל־תִּטְּשֵׁנִי וְאַל־תַּעַזְבֵנִי, אֱלֹהֵי יִשְׁעִי: כִּי־אָבִי וְאִמִּי עֲזָבוּנִי, וַיהוה יַאַסְפֵנִי: הוֹרֵנִי יהוה דַּרְכֶּךָ, וּנְחֵנִי בְּאֹרַח מִישׁוֹר, לְמַעַן שׁוֹרְרָי: אַל־תִּתְּנֵנִי בְּנֶפֶשׁ צָרָי, כִּי קָמוּ־בִי עֵדֵי־שֶׁקֶר, וִיפֵחַ חָמָס: ‹ לוּלֵא הֶאֱמַנְתִּי לִרְאוֹת בְּטוּב־יהוה בְּאֶרֶץ חַיִּים: קַוֵּה אֶל־יהוה, חֲזַק וְיַאֲמֵץ לִבֶּךָ, וְקַוֵּה אֶל־יהוה:

קדיש יתום (*previous page*)

Shemini Atzeret

REMOVING THE TORAH FROM THE ARK

אֵין־כָּמְוֹךָ There is none like You among the heavenly powers, Ps. 86
Lord, and there are no works like Yours.
Your kingdom is an eternal kingdom, Ps. 145
and Your dominion is for all generations.

The Lord is King, the Lord was King,
the Lord shall be King for ever and all time.
The Lord will give strength to His people; Ps. 29
the Lord will bless His people with peace.

Father of compassion,
favor Zion with Your goodness; rebuild the walls of Jerusalem. Ps. 51
For we trust in You alone, King, God, high and exalted, Master of worlds.

The Ark is opened and the congregation stands. All say:

וַיְהִי בִּנְסֹעַ Whenever the Ark set out, Moses would say, Num. 10
"Arise, Lord, and may Your enemies be scattered.
May those who hate You flee before You."
For the Torah shall come forth from Zion, Is. 2
and the word of the Lord from Jerusalem.
Blessed is He who in His Holiness gave the Torah to His people Israel.

On Shabbat, continue with "Blessed is the name" on the next page.

The following (The Thirteen Attributes of Mercy) is said three times:

יהוה The Lord, the Lord, compassionate and gracious God, Ex. 34
slow to anger, abounding in loving-kindness and truth,
extending loving-kindness to a thousand generations, forgiving iniquity,
rebellion and sin, and absolving [the guilty who repent].

Each individual says silently, inserting appropriate phrase/s in parentheses:

רִבּוֹנוֹ Master of the Universe, fulfill my heart's requests for good. Satisfy my desire, grant my request, and enable me (*name*, son/daughter of *father's name*), (and my wife/ husband, and my sons/daughters) and all the members of my household to do Your will with a perfect heart. Deliver us from the evil impulse, grant us our share in Your Torah, and make us worthy that Your Presence may rest upon us. Confer on us a spirit of wisdom and understanding, and may

שמיני עצרת

הוצאת ספר תורה

תהלים פו אֵין־כָּמְוֹךָ בָאֱלֹהִים, אֲדֹנָי, וְאֵין כְּמַעֲשֶׂיךָ:
תהלים קמה מַלְכוּתְךָ מַלְכוּת כָּל־עֹלָמִים, וּמֶמְשַׁלְתְּךָ בְּכָל־דּוֹר וָדֹר:

יהוה מֶלֶךְ, יהוה מָלָךְ, יהוה יִמְלֹךְ לְעֹלָם וָעֶד.
תהלים כט יהוה עֹז לְעַמּוֹ יִתֵּן, יהוה יְבָרֵךְ אֶת־עַמּוֹ בַשָּׁלוֹם:

תהלים נא אַב הָרַחֲמִים, הֵיטִיבָה בִרְצוֹנְךָ אֶת־צִיּוֹן תִּבְנֶה חוֹמוֹת יְרוּשָׁלָםִ:
כִּי בְךָ לְבַד בָּטָחְנוּ, מֶלֶךְ אֵל רָם וְנִשָּׂא, אֲדוֹן עוֹלָמִים.

The ארון קודש *is opened and the* קהל *stands. All say:*

במדבר י וַיְהִי בִּנְסֹעַ הָאָרֹן וַיֹּאמֶר מֹשֶׁה
קוּמָה יהוה וְיָפֻצוּ אֹיְבֶיךָ וְיָנֻסוּ מְשַׂנְאֶיךָ מִפָּנֶיךָ:
ישעיה ב כִּי מִצִּיּוֹן תֵּצֵא תוֹרָה וּדְבַר־יהוה מִירוּשָׁלָםִ:
בָּרוּךְ שֶׁנָּתַן תּוֹרָה לְעַמּוֹ יִשְׂרָאֵל בִּקְדֻשָּׁתוֹ.

On שבת*, continue with* בְּרִיךְ שְׁמֵהּ *on the next page.*

The following (י״ג מידות הרחמים) *is said three times:*

שמות לד יהוה, יהוה, אֵל רַחוּם וְחַנּוּן, אֶרֶךְ אַפַּיִם וְרַב־חֶסֶד וֶאֱמֶת:
נֹצֵר חֶסֶד לָאֲלָפִים, נֹשֵׂא עָוֹן וָפֶשַׁע וְחַטָּאָה, וְנַקֵּה:

Each individual says silently, inserting appropriate phrase/s in parentheses:

רִבּוֹנוֹ שֶׁל עוֹלָם, מַלֵּא מִשְׁאֲלוֹת לִבִּי לְטוֹבָה, וְהָפֵק רְצוֹנִי וְתֵן שְׁאֵלָתִי, וְזַכֵּה
לִי (פלוני/ת בֶּן/בַּת פלוני) (וְאִשְׁתִּי/בַּעֲלִי וּבָנַי וּבְנוֹתַי) וְכָל בְּנֵי בֵיתִי, לַעֲשׂוֹת
רְצוֹנְךָ בְּלֵבָב שָׁלֵם, וּמַלְּטֵנוּ מִיֵּצֶר הָרָע, וְתֵן חֶלְקֵנוּ בְּתוֹרָתֶךָ, וְזַכֵּנוּ שֶׁתִּשְׁרֶה
שְׁכִינָתְךָ עָלֵינוּ, וְהוֹפַע עָלֵינוּ רוּחַ חָכְמָה וּבִינָה. וְיִתְקַיֵּם בָּנוּ מִקְרָא שֶׁכָּתוּב:
ישעיה יא וְנָחָה עָלָיו רוּחַ יהוה, רוּחַ חָכְמָה וּבִינָה, רוּחַ עֵצָה וּגְבוּרָה, רוּחַ דַּעַת וְיִרְאַת
יהוה: וּבְכֵן יְהִי רָצוֹן מִלְּפָנֶיךָ יהוה אֱלֹהֵינוּ וֵאלֹהֵי אֲבוֹתֵינוּ, שֶׁתְּזַכֵּנוּ לַעֲשׂוֹת

there be fulfilled in us the verse: "The spirit of the LORD will rest upon him – a spirit of wisdom and understanding, a spirit of counsel and strength, a spirit of knowledge and reverence for the LORD." So too may it be Your will, LORD our God and God of our ancestors, that we be worthy to do deeds that are good in Your sight, and to walk before You in the ways of the upright. Make us holy through Your holiness, so that we may be worthy of a good and long life, and of the World to Come. Guard us from evil deeds and bad times that threaten to bring turmoil to the world. May loving-kindness surround one who trusts in the LORD. Amen. *Is. 11* *Ps. 32*

יִהְיוּ May the words of my mouth and the meditation of my heart find favor before You, LORD, my Rock and Redeemer. *Ps. 19*

Say the following verse three times:

וַאֲנִי As for me, may my prayer come to You, LORD,
at a time of favor. O God, in Your great love,
answer me with Your faithful salvation. *Ps. 69*

On all days continue:

בְּרִיךְ Blessed is the name of the Master of the Universe. Blessed is Your crown and Your place. May Your favor always be with Your people Israel. Show Your people the salvation of Your right hand in Your Temple. Grant us the gift of Your good light, and accept our prayers in mercy. May it be Your will to prolong our life in goodness. May I be counted among the righteous, so that You will have compassion on me and protect me and all that is mine and all that is Your people Israel's. You feed all; You sustain all; You rule over all; You rule over kings, for sovereignty is Yours. I am a servant of the Holy One, blessed be He, before whom and before whose glorious Torah I bow at all times. Not in man do I trust, nor on any angel do I rely, but on the God of heaven who is the God of truth, whose Torah is truth, whose prophets speak truth, and who abounds in acts of love and truth. ▸ In Him I trust, and to His holy and glorious name I offer praises. May it be Your will to open my heart to the Torah, and to fulfill the wishes of my heart and of the hearts of all Your people Israel for good, for life, and for peace. *Zohar, Vayak-hel*

Two Torah scrolls are removed from the Ark. The Leader takes one in his right arm and, followed by the congregation, says:

Listen, Israel: the LORD is our God, the LORD is One. *Deut. 6*

Leader then congregation:

One is our God; great is our Master; holy is His name.

The Leader turns to face the Ark, bows and says:

Magnify the LORD with me, and let us exalt His name together. *Ps. 34*

מַעֲשִׂים טוֹבִים בְּעֵינֶיךָ וְלָלֶכֶת בְּדַרְכֵי יְשָׁרִים לְפָנֶיךָ, וְקַדְּשֵׁנוּ בְּקְדֻשָּׁתֶךָ
כְּדֵי שֶׁנִּזְכֶּה לְחַיִּים טוֹבִים וַאֲרוּכִים וּלְחַיֵּי הָעוֹלָם הַבָּא, וְתִשְׁמְרֵנוּ מִמַּעֲשִׂים
רָעִים וּמִשָּׁעוֹת רָעוֹת הַמִּתְרַגְּשׁוֹת לָבוֹא לָעוֹלָם, וְהַבּוֹטֵחַ בַּיהוה חֶסֶד תהלים לב
יְסוֹבְבֶנּוּ: אָמֵן.

יִהְיוּ לְרָצוֹן אִמְרֵי־פִי וְהֶגְיוֹן לִבִּי לְפָנֶיךָ, יהוה צוּרִי וְגֹאֲלִי: תהלים יט

Say the following verse three times:

וַאֲנִי תְפִלָּתִי־לְךָ יהוה, עֵת רָצוֹן, אֱלֹהִים בְּרָב־חַסְדֶּךָ תהלים סט
עֲנֵנִי בֶּאֱמֶת יִשְׁעֶךָ:

On all days continue:

בְּרִיךְ שְׁמֵהּ דְּמָרֵא עָלְמָא, בְּרִיךְ כִּתְרָךְ וְאַתְרָךְ. יְהֵא רְעוּתָךְ עִם עַמָּךְ זוהר ויקהל
יִשְׂרָאֵל לְעָלַם, וּפֻרְקַן יְמִינָךְ אַחֲזֵי לְעַמָּךְ בְּבֵית מַקְדְּשָׁךְ, וּלְאַמְטוּיֵי לָנָא
מִטּוּב נְהוֹרָךְ, וּלְקַבֵּל צְלוֹתַנָא בְּרַחֲמִין. יְהֵא רַעֲוָא קֳדָמָךְ דְּתוֹרִיךְ לָן חַיִּין
בְּטִיבוּ, וְלֶהֱוֵי אֲנָא פְקִידָא בְּגוֹ צַדִּיקַיָּא, לְמִרְחַם עֲלַי וּלְמִנְטַר יָתִי וְיַת כָּל
דִּי לִי וְדִי לְעַמָּךְ יִשְׂרָאֵל. אַנְתְּ הוּא זָן לְכֹלָּא וּמְפַרְנֵס לְכֹלָּא, אַנְתְּ הוּא
שַׁלִּיט עַל כֹּלָּא, אַנְתְּ הוּא דְּשַׁלִּיט עַל מַלְכַיָּא, וּמַלְכוּתָא דִּילָךְ הִיא. אֲנָא
עַבְדָּא דְקֻדְשָׁא בְּרִיךְ הוּא, דְּסָגֵדְנָא קַמֵּהּ וּמִקַּמֵּי דִּיקַר אוֹרַיְתֵהּ בְּכָל עִדָּן
וְעִדָּן. לָא עַל אֱנָשׁ רָחִיצְנָא וְלָא עַל בַּר אֱלָהִין סָמִיכְנָא, אֶלָּא בֶּאֱלָהָא
דִשְׁמַיָּא, דְּהוּא אֱלָהָא קְשׁוֹט, וְאוֹרַיְתֵהּ קְשׁוֹט, וּנְבִיאוֹהִי קְשׁוֹט, וּמַסְגֵּא
לְמֶעְבַּד טַבְוָן וּקְשׁוֹט. • בֵּהּ אֲנָא רָחִיץ, וְלִשְׁמֵהּ קַדִּישָׁא יַקִּירָא אֲנָא אֵמַר
תֻּשְׁבְּחָן. יְהֵא רַעֲוָא קֳדָמָךְ דְּתִפְתַּח לִבַּאי בְּאוֹרַיְתָא, וְתַשְׁלִים מִשְׁאֲלִין
דְּלִבַּאי וְלִבָּא דְכָל עַמָּךְ יִשְׂרָאֵל לְטָב וּלְחַיִּין וְלִשְׁלָם.

Two ספרי תורה *are removed from the* ארון קודש*. The* שליח צבור *takes one in his right arm, and, followed by the* קהל*, says:*

שְׁמַע יִשְׂרָאֵל, יהוה אֱלֹהֵינוּ, יהוה אֶחָד: דברים ו

then שליח ציבור*:* קהל

אֶחָד אֱלֹהֵינוּ, גָּדוֹל אֲדוֹנֵינוּ, קָדוֹשׁ שְׁמוֹ.

The שליח ציבור *turns to face the* ארון קודש*, bows and says:*

גַּדְּלוּ לַיהוה אִתִּי וּנְרוֹמְמָה שְׁמוֹ יַחְדָּו: תהלים לד

The Ark is closed. The Leader carries the Torah scroll to the bima and the congregation says:

לְךָ Yours, LORD, are the greatness and the power, the glory and the majesty and splendor, for everything in heaven and earth is Yours. Yours, LORD, is the kingdom; You are exalted as Head over all. *I Chr. 29*

רוֹמְמוּ Exalt the LORD our God and bow to His footstool; He is holy. Exalt the LORD our God, and bow at His holy mountain, for holy is the LORD our God. *Ps. 99*

Over all may the name of the Supreme King of kings, the Holy One blessed be He, be magnified and sanctified, praised and glorified, exalted and extolled, in the worlds that He has created – this world and the World to Come – in accordance with His will, and the will of those who fear Him, and the will of the whole house of Israel. He is the Rock of worlds, LORD of all creatures, God of all souls, who dwells in the spacious heights and inhabits the high heavens of old. His holiness is over the Hayyot and over the throne of glory. Therefore may Your name, LORD our God, be sanctified among us in the sight of all that lives. Let us sing before Him a new song, as it is written: "Sing to God, make music for His name, extol Him who rides the clouds – the LORD is His name – and exult before Him." And may we see Him eye to eye when He returns to His abode as it is written: "For they shall see eye to eye when the LORD returns to Zion." And it is said: "Then will the glory of the LORD be revealed, and all mankind together shall see that the mouth of the LORD has spoken." *Ps. 68* *Is. 52* *Is. 40*

Father of mercy, have compassion on the people borne by Him. May He remember the covenant with the mighty (patriarchs), and deliver us from evil times. May He reproach the evil instinct in the people by Him, and graciously grant that we be an eternal remnant. May He fulfill in good measure our requests for salvation and compassion.

The Torah scroll is placed on the bima and the Gabbai calls a Kohen to the Torah.

וְיַעֲזֹר May He help, shield and save all who seek refuge in Him, and let us say: Amen. Let us all render greatness to our God and give honor to the Torah. *Let the Kohen come forward. Arise (*name* son of *father's name*), the Kohen.

**If no Kohen is present, a Levi or Yisrael is called up as follows:*

/As there is no Kohen, arise (*name* son of *father's name*) in place of a Kohen./

Blessed is He who, in His holiness, gave the Torah to His people Israel.

The congregation followed by the Gabbai:

You who cling to the LORD your God are all alive today. *Deut. 4*

The Torah portion is read.

The ארון קודש *is closed. The* שליח ציבור *carries the* ספר תורה *to the* בימה *and the* קהל *says:*

דברי הימים א׳ כט
לְךָ יהוה הַגְּדֻלָּה וְהַגְּבוּרָה וְהַתִּפְאֶרֶת וְהַנֵּצַח וְהַהוֹד, כִּי־כֹל בַּשָּׁמַיִם וּבָאָרֶץ, לְךָ יהוה הַמַּמְלָכָה וְהַמִּתְנַשֵּׂא לְכֹל לְרֹאשׁ:

תהלים צט
רוֹמְמוּ יהוה אֱלֹהֵינוּ וְהִשְׁתַּחֲווּ לַהֲדֹם רַגְלָיו, קָדוֹשׁ הוּא: רוֹמְמוּ יהוה אֱלֹהֵינוּ וְהִשְׁתַּחֲווּ לְהַר קָדְשׁוֹ, כִּי־קָדוֹשׁ יהוה אֱלֹהֵינוּ:

עַל הַכֹּל יִתְגַּדַּל וְיִתְקַדַּשׁ וְיִשְׁתַּבַּח וְיִתְפָּאַר וְיִתְרוֹמַם וְיִתְנַשֵּׂא שְׁמוֹ שֶׁל מֶלֶךְ
מַלְכֵי הַמְּלָכִים הַקָּדוֹשׁ בָּרוּךְ הוּא בָּעוֹלָמוֹת שֶׁבָּרָא, הָעוֹלָם הַזֶּה וְהָעוֹלָם הַבָּא,
כִּרְצוֹנוֹ וְכִרְצוֹן יְרֵאָיו וְכִרְצוֹן כָּל בֵּית יִשְׂרָאֵל. צוּר הָעוֹלָמִים, אֲדוֹן כָּל הַבְּרִיּוֹת,
אֱלוֹהַּ כָּל הַנְּפָשׁוֹת, הַיּוֹשֵׁב בְּמֶרְחֲבֵי מָרוֹם, הַשּׁוֹכֵן בִּשְׁמֵי שְׁמֵי קֶדֶם, קְדֻשָּׁתוֹ עַל
הַחַיּוֹת, וּקְדֻשָּׁתוֹ עַל כִּסֵּא הַכָּבוֹד. וּבְכֵן יִתְקַדַּשׁ שִׁמְךָ בָּנוּ יהוה אֱלֹהֵינוּ לְעֵינֵי
תהלים סח כָּל חָי, וְנֹאמַר לְפָנָיו שִׁיר חָדָשׁ, כַּכָּתוּב: שִׁירוּ לֵאלֹהִים זַמְּרוּ שְׁמוֹ, סֹלּוּ לָרֹכֵב
ישעיה נב בָּעֲרָבוֹת, בְּיָהּ שְׁמוֹ, וְעִלְזוּ לְפָנָיו: וְנִרְאֵהוּ עַיִן בְּעַיִן בְּשׁוּבוֹ אֶל נָוֵהוּ, כַּכָּתוּב: כִּי
ישעיה מ עַיִן בְּעַיִן יִרְאוּ בְּשׁוּב יהוה צִיּוֹן: וְנֶאֱמַר: וְנִגְלָה כְּבוֹד יהוה, וְרָאוּ כָל־בָּשָׂר יַחְדָּו
כִּי פִּי יהוה דִּבֵּר:

אַב הָרַחֲמִים הוּא יְרַחֵם עַם עֲמוּסִים, וְיִזְכֹּר בְּרִית אֵיתָנִים, וְיַצִּיל נַפְשׁוֹתֵינוּ מִן הַשָּׁעוֹת הָרָעוֹת, וְיִגְעַר בְּיֵצֶר הָרָע מִן הַנְּשׂוּאִים, וְיָחֹן אוֹתָנוּ לִפְלֵיטַת עוֹלָמִים, וִימַלֵּא מִשְׁאֲלוֹתֵינוּ בְּמִדָּה טוֹבָה יְשׁוּעָה וְרַחֲמִים.

The ספר תורה *is placed on the* שולחן *and the* גבאי *calls a* כהן *to the* תורה*.*

וְיַעֲזֹר וְיָגֵן וְיוֹשִׁיעַ לְכָל הַחוֹסִים בּוֹ, וְנֹאמַר אָמֵן. הַכֹּל הָבוּ גֹדֶל לֵאלֹהֵינוּ וּתְנוּ כָבוֹד לַתּוֹרָה. *כֹּהֵן קְרַב, יַעֲמֹד (פלוני בֶּן פלוני) הַכֹּהֵן.

**If no* כהן *is present, a* לוי *or* ישראל *is called up as follows:*

/אֵין כָּאן כֹּהֵן, יַעֲמֹד (פלוני בֶּן פלוני) בִּמְקוֹם כֹּהֵן./

בָּרוּךְ שֶׁנָּתַן תּוֹרָה לְעַמּוֹ יִשְׂרָאֵל בִּקְדֻשָּׁתוֹ.

The קהל *followed by the* גבאי*:*

דברים ד
וְאַתֶּם הַדְּבֵקִים בַּיהוה אֱלֹהֵיכֶם חַיִּים כֻּלְּכֶם הַיּוֹם:

The תורה *portion is read.*

The Reader shows the oleh the section to be read. The oleh touches the scroll at that place with the tzitzit of his tallit, which he then kisses. Holding the handles of the scroll, he says:

Oleh: Bless the LORD, the blessed One.

Cong: Bless the LORD, the blessed One,
for ever and all time.

Oleh: Bless the LORD, the blessed One,
for ever and all time.

Blessed are You, LORD our God,
King of the Universe,
who has chosen us from all peoples
and has given us His Torah.
Blessed are You, LORD, Giver of the Torah.

After the reading, the oleh says:

Oleh: Blessed are You, LORD our God,
King of the Universe,
who has given us the Torah of truth,
planting everlasting life in our midst.
Blessed are You, LORD, Giver of the Torah.

One who has survived a situation of danger, says:

Blessed are You, LORD our God, King of the Universe,
who bestows good on the unworthy,
who has bestowed on me much good.

The congregation responds:

Amen. May He who bestowed much good on you
continue to bestow on you much good, Selah.

After a Bar Mitzva boy has finished the Torah blessing, his father says aloud:

Blessed is He who has released me from the responsibility
for this child.

The קורא *shows the* עולה *the section to be read. The* עולה *touches the scroll at that place with the* ציצית *of his* טלית*, which he then kisses. Holding the handles of the scroll, he says:*

עולה: **בָּרְכוּ אֶת יהוה הַמְבֹרָךְ.**

קהל: בָּרוּךְ יהוה הַמְבֹרָךְ לְעוֹלָם וָעֶד.

עולה: **בָּרוּךְ יהוה הַמְבֹרָךְ לְעוֹלָם וָעֶד.**
בָּרוּךְ אַתָּה יהוה, אֱלֹהֵינוּ מֶלֶךְ הָעוֹלָם
אֲשֶׁר בָּחַר בָּנוּ מִכָּל הָעַמִּים
וְנָתַן לָנוּ אֶת תּוֹרָתוֹ.
בָּרוּךְ אַתָּה יהוה, נוֹתֵן הַתּוֹרָה.

After the קריאת התורה*, the* עולה *says:*

עולה: **בָּרוּךְ אַתָּה יהוה אֱלֹהֵינוּ מֶלֶךְ הָעוֹלָם**
אֲשֶׁר נָתַן לָנוּ תּוֹרַת אֱמֶת
וְחַיֵּי עוֹלָם נָטַע בְּתוֹכֵנוּ.
בָּרוּךְ אַתָּה יהוה, נוֹתֵן הַתּוֹרָה.

One who has survived a situation of danger, says:

בָּרוּךְ אַתָּה יהוה אֱלֹהֵינוּ מֶלֶךְ הָעוֹלָם
הַגּוֹמֵל לְחַיָּבִים טוֹבוֹת
שֶׁגְּמָלַנִי כָּל טוֹב.

The קהל *responds:*

אָמֵן. מִי שֶׁגְּמָלְךָ כָּל טוֹב
הוּא יִגְמָלְךָ כָּל טוֹב, סֶלָה.

After a בר מצוה *has finished the* תורה *blessing, his father says aloud:*

בָּרוּךְ שֶׁפְּטָרַנִי מֵעָנְשׁוֹ שֶׁלָּזֶה.

FOR AN OLEH

May He who blessed our fathers, Abraham, Isaac and Jacob, bless (*name*, son of *father's name*) who has been called up in honor of the All-Present, in honor of the Torah, and in honor of (*On Shabbat:* the Sabbath and in honor of) the festival. As a reward for this, may the Holy One, blessed be He, protect and deliver him from all trouble and distress, all infection and illness, and send blessing and success to all the work of his hands, and may he merit to go up to Jerusalem for the festivals, together with all Israel, his brethren, and let us say: Amen.

FOR A SICK MAN

May He who blessed our fathers, Abraham, Isaac and Jacob, Moses and Aaron, David and Solomon, bless and heal one who is ill, (*sick person's name*, son of *mother's name*), on whose behalf (*name of the one making the offering*) is making a contribution to charity. As a reward for this, may the Holy One, blessed be He, be filled with compassion for him, to restore his health, cure him, strengthen and revive him, sending him a swift and full recovery from heaven to all his 248 organs and 365 sinews, amongst the other sick ones in Israel, a healing of the spirit and a healing of the body – though on (*On Shabbat:* the Sabbath and) festivals it is forbidden to cry out, may healing be quick to come – now, swiftly and soon, and let us say: Amen.

FOR A SICK WOMAN

May He who blessed our fathers, Abraham, Isaac and Jacob, Moses and Aaron, David and Solomon, bless and heal one who is ill, (*sick person's name*, daughter of *mother's name*), on whose behalf (*name of the one making the offering*) is making a contribution to charity. As a reward for this, may the Holy One, blessed be He, be filled with compassion for her, to restore her health, cure her, strengthen and revive her, sending her a swift and full recovery from heaven to all her organs and sinews, amongst the other sick ones in Israel, a healing of the spirit and a healing of the body – though on (*On Shabbat:* the Sabbath and) festivals it is forbidden to cry out, may healing be quick to come – now, swiftly and soon, and let us say: Amen.

מי שברך לעולה לתורה

מִי שֶׁבֵּרַךְ אֲבוֹתֵינוּ אַבְרָהָם יִצְחָק וְיַעֲקֹב, הוּא יְבָרֵךְ אֶת (פלוני בֶּן פלוני), בַּעֲבוּר שֶׁעָלָה לִכְבוֹד הַמָּקוֹם וְלִכְבוֹד הַתּוֹרָה (בשבת: וְלִכְבוֹד הַשַּׁבָּת) וְלִכְבוֹד הָרֶגֶל. בִּשְׂכַר זֶה הַקָּדוֹשׁ בָּרוּךְ הוּא יִשְׁמְרֵהוּ וְיַצִּילֵהוּ מִכָּל צָרָה וְצוּקָה וּמִכָּל נֶגַע וּמַחֲלָה, וְיִשְׁלַח בְּרָכָה וְהַצְלָחָה בְּכָל מַעֲשֵׂה יָדָיו, וְיִזְכֶּה לַעֲלוֹת לָרֶגֶל עִם כָּל יִשְׂרָאֵל אֶחָיו, וְנֹאמַר אָמֵן.

מי שברך לחולֶה

מִי שֶׁבֵּרַךְ אֲבוֹתֵינוּ אַבְרָהָם יִצְחָק וְיַעֲקֹב, מֹשֶׁה וְאַהֲרֹן דָּוִד וּשְׁלֹמֹה הוּא יְבָרֵךְ וִירַפֵּא אֶת הַחוֹלֶה (פלוני בֶּן פלונית) בַּעֲבוּר שֶׁ(פלוני בֶּן פלוני) נוֹדֵר צְדָקָה בַּעֲבוּרוֹ. בִּשְׂכַר זֶה הַקָּדוֹשׁ בָּרוּךְ הוּא יִמָּלֵא רַחֲמִים עָלָיו לְהַחֲלִימוֹ וּלְרַפְּאתוֹ וּלְהַחֲזִיקוֹ וּלְהַחֲיוֹתוֹ וְיִשְׁלַח לוֹ מְהֵרָה רְפוּאָה שְׁלֵמָה מִן הַשָּׁמַיִם לִרְמַ״ח אֵבָרָיו וּשְׁסָ״ה גִּידָיו בְּתוֹךְ שְׁאָר חוֹלֵי יִשְׂרָאֵל, רְפוּאַת הַנֶּפֶשׁ וּרְפוּאַת הַגּוּף. יוֹם טוֹב הוּא מִלִּזְעֹק (בשבת: שַׁבָּת וְיוֹם טוֹב הֵם) וּרְפוּאָה קְרוֹבָה לָבוֹא, הַשְׁתָּא בַּעֲגָלָא וּבִזְמַן קָרִיב, וְנֹאמַר אָמֵן.

מי שברך לחולָה

מִי שֶׁבֵּרַךְ אֲבוֹתֵינוּ אַבְרָהָם יִצְחָק וְיַעֲקֹב, מֹשֶׁה וְאַהֲרֹן דָּוִד וּשְׁלֹמֹה הוּא יְבָרֵךְ וִירַפֵּא אֶת הַחוֹלָה (פלונית בַּת פלונית) בַּעֲבוּר שֶׁ(פלוני בֶּן פלוני) נוֹדֵר צְדָקָה בַּעֲבוּרָהּ. בִּשְׂכַר זֶה הַקָּדוֹשׁ בָּרוּךְ הוּא יִמָּלֵא רַחֲמִים עָלֶיהָ לְהַחֲלִימָהּ וּלְרַפְּאתָהּ וּלְהַחֲזִיקָהּ וּלְהַחֲיוֹתָהּ וְיִשְׁלַח לָהּ מְהֵרָה רְפוּאָה שְׁלֵמָה מִן הַשָּׁמַיִם לְכָל אֵבָרֶיהָ וּלְכָל גִּידֶיהָ בְּתוֹךְ שְׁאָר חוֹלֵי יִשְׂרָאֵל, רְפוּאַת הַנֶּפֶשׁ וּרְפוּאַת הַגּוּף. יוֹם טוֹב הוּא (בשבת: שַׁבָּת וְיוֹם טוֹב הֵם) מִלִּזְעֹק וּרְפוּאָה קְרוֹבָה לָבוֹא, הַשְׁתָּא בַּעֲגָלָא וּבִזְמַן קָרִיב, וְנֹאמַר אָמֵן.

ON THE BIRTH OF A SON

May He who blessed our fathers, Abraham, Isaac and Jacob, Moses and Aaron, David and Solomon, Sarah, Rebecca, Rachel and Leah, bless the woman (*name*, daughter of *father's name*) who has given birth, and her son who has been born to her as an auspicious sign. Her husband, the child's father, is making a contribution to charity. As a reward for this, may father and mother merit to bring the child into the covenant of Abraham and to a life of Torah, to the marriage canopy and to good deeds, and let us say: Amen.

ON THE BIRTH OF A DAUGHTER

May He who blessed our fathers, Abraham, Isaac and Jacob, Moses and Aaron, David and Solomon, Sarah, Rebecca, Rachel and Leah, bless the woman (*name*, daughter of *father's name*) who has given birth, and her daughter who has been born to her as an auspicious sign; and may her name be called in Israel (*baby's name*, daughter of *father's name*). Her husband, the child's father, is making a contribution to charity. As a reward for this, may father and mother merit to raise her to a life of Torah, to the marriage canopy, and to good deeds, and let us say: Amen.

FOR A BAR MITZVA

May He who blessed our fathers, Abraham, Isaac and Jacob, bless (*name*, son of *father's name*) who has completed thirteen years and attained the age of the commandments, who has been called to the Torah to give praise and thanks to God, may His name be blessed, for all the good He has bestowed on him. May the Holy One, blessed be He, protect and sustain him and direct his heart to be perfect with God, to walk in His ways and keep the commandments all the days of his life, and let us say: Amen.

FOR A BAT MITZVA

May He who blessed our fathers, Abraham, Isaac and Jacob, Sarah, Rebecca, Rachel and Leah, bless (*name*, daughter of *father's name*) who has completed twelve years and attained the age of the commandments, and gives praise and thanks to God, may His name be blessed, for all the good He has bestowed on her. May the Holy One, blessed be He, protect and sustain her and direct her heart to be perfect with God, to walk in His ways and keep the commandments all the days of her life, and let us say: Amen.

מי שברך ליולדת בן

מִי שֶׁבֵּרַךְ אֲבוֹתֵינוּ אַבְרָהָם יִצְחָק וְיַעֲקֹב, מֹשֶׁה וְאַהֲרֹן דָּוִד וּשְׁלֹמֹה, שָׂרָה רִבְקָה רָחֵל וְלֵאָה הוּא יְבָרֵךְ אֶת הָאִשָּׁה הַיּוֹלֶדֶת (פלונית בַּת פלוני) וְאֶת בְּנָהּ שֶׁנּוֹלַד לָהּ לְמַזָּל טוֹב בַּעֲבוּר שֶׁבַּעְלָהּ וְאָבִיו נוֹדֵר צְדָקָה בַּעֲדָם. בִּשְׂכַר זֶה יִזְכּוּ אָבִיו וְאִמּוֹ לְהַכְנִיסוֹ בִּבְרִיתוֹ שֶׁל אַבְרָהָם אָבִינוּ וּלְגַדְּלוֹ לְתוֹרָה וּלְחֻפָּה וּלְמַעֲשִׂים טוֹבִים, וְנֹאמַר אָמֵן.

מי שברך ליולדת בת

מִי שֶׁבֵּרַךְ אֲבוֹתֵינוּ אַבְרָהָם יִצְחָק וְיַעֲקֹב, מֹשֶׁה וְאַהֲרֹן דָּוִד וּשְׁלֹמֹה, שָׂרָה רִבְקָה רָחֵל וְלֵאָה הוּא יְבָרֵךְ אֶת הָאִשָּׁה הַיּוֹלֶדֶת (פלונית בַּת פלוני) וְאֶת בִּתָּהּ שֶׁנּוֹלְדָה לָהּ לְמַזָּל טוֹב וְיִקָּרֵא שְׁמָהּ בְּיִשְׂרָאֵל (פלונית בַּת פלוני), בַּעֲבוּר שֶׁבַּעְלָהּ וְאָבִיהָ נוֹדֵר צְדָקָה בַּעֲדָן. בִּשְׂכַר זֶה יִזְכּוּ אָבִיהָ וְאִמָּהּ לְגַדְּלָהּ לְתוֹרָה וּלְחֻפָּה וּלְמַעֲשִׂים טוֹבִים, וְנֹאמַר אָמֵן.

מי שברך לבר מצווה

מִי שֶׁבֵּרַךְ אֲבוֹתֵינוּ אַבְרָהָם יִצְחָק וְיַעֲקֹב הוּא יְבָרֵךְ אֶת (פלוני בֶּן פלוני) שֶׁמָּלְאוּ לוֹ שְׁלֹשׁ עֶשְׂרֵה שָׁנָה וְהִגִּיעַ לְמִצְוֹת, וְעָלָה לַתּוֹרָה, לָתֵת שֶׁבַח וְהוֹדָיָה לְהַשֵּׁם יִתְבָּרַךְ עַל כָּל הַטּוֹבָה שֶׁגָּמַל אִתּוֹ. יִשְׁמְרֵהוּ הַקָּדוֹשׁ בָּרוּךְ הוּא וִיחַיֵּהוּ, וִיכוֹנֵן אֶת לִבּוֹ לִהְיוֹת שָׁלֵם עִם יהוה וְלָלֶכֶת בִּדְרָכָיו וְלִשְׁמֹר מִצְוֹתָיו כָּל הַיָּמִים, וְנֹאמַר אָמֵן.

מי שברך לבת מצווה

מִי שֶׁבֵּרַךְ אֲבוֹתֵינוּ אַבְרָהָם יִצְחָק וְיַעֲקֹב, שָׂרָה רִבְקָה רָחֵל וְלֵאָה, הוּא יְבָרֵךְ אֶת (פלונית בַּת פלוני) שֶׁמָּלְאוּ לָהּ שְׁתֵּים עֶשְׂרֵה שָׁנָה וְהִגִּיעָה לְמִצְוֹת, וְנוֹתֶנֶת שֶׁבַח וְהוֹדָיָה לְהַשֵּׁם יִתְבָּרַךְ עַל כָּל הַטּוֹבָה שֶׁגָּמַל אִתָּהּ. יִשְׁמְרֶהָ הַקָּדוֹשׁ בָּרוּךְ הוּא וִיחַיֶּהָ, וִיכוֹנֵן אֶת לִבָּהּ לִהְיוֹת שָׁלֵם עִם יהוה וְלָלֶכֶת בִּדְרָכָיו וְלִשְׁמֹר מִצְוֹתָיו כָּל הַיָּמִים, וְנֹאמַר אָמֵן.

TORAH READING FOR SHEMINI ATZERET

Deut. 14:22–16:17

You must tithe all the produce of your grain, that which grows in the field, each year. You shall then eat it in the presence of the Lord your God, at the place He will choose as a dwelling place for His name; the tithes of your grain, wine and oil as well as the firstborn of your herd and flock, so that you might learn to hold the Lord your God in awe as long as you live. If the distance is very great for you, so that you cannot carry it all; if the place the Lord your God chooses as a dwelling place for His name is far away from you, and the Lord your God blesses you with plenty, then you may sell your produce for money and, holding that money in your hand, go to the place which the Lord your God will choose. You may purchase with that money anything you may wish for of the herd or flock, of wine or intoxicating drinks: anything your heart desires; and you shall eat there, in the presence of the Lord your God, and you and your household shall rejoice. As for the Levite who dwells within your gates – you shall not forsake him, for he does not have a portion or an inheritance among you.

---

festivals are times when people are to invite those at the margins of society: the widow, the orphan, the Levites who have no land of their own, the temporary residents, as well as slaves. No one is to be left out.

The preceding passages are also included – longer on Shabbat because of the two extra people called to the Torah on that day.

עַשֵּׂר תְּעַשֵּׂר *You must tithe.* This is the law of the second tithe. Unlike the first that was given to the Levites, this was taken by its owners to Jerusalem and eaten there, in the form of either the produce itself, or money for which it had been exchanged. This reminded the nation that its wealth came from God who was a constant presence in its midst. Maimonides adds that since people could not eat all the food themselves, they would naturally give part of it to others as charity. This strengthened "the bond of love and brotherhood" among the people as a whole: it reinforced civil society and the sense of national unity (*Guide for the Perplexed* 3:39).

קריאה לשמיני עצרת

דברים יד,כב–טז,יז

עַשֵּׂר תְּעַשֵּׂר אֵת כׇּל־תְּבוּאַת זַרְעֶךָ הַיֹּצֵא הַשָּׂדֶה שָׁנָה שָׁנָה׃
וְאָכַלְתָּ לִפְנֵי ׀ יהוה אֱלֹהֶיךָ בַּמָּקוֹם אֲשֶׁר־יִבְחַר לְשַׁכֵּן שְׁמוֹ
שָׁם מַעְשַׂר דְּגָנְךָ תִּירֹשְׁךָ וְיִצְהָרֶךָ וּבְכֹרֹת בְּקָרְךָ וְצֹאנֶךָ לְמַעַן
תִּלְמַד לְיִרְאָה אֶת־יהוה אֱלֹהֶיךָ כׇּל־הַיָּמִים׃ וְכִי־יִרְבֶּה מִמְּךָ
הַדֶּרֶךְ כִּי לֹא תוּכַל שְׂאֵתוֹ כִּי־יִרְחַק מִמְּךָ הַמָּקוֹם אֲשֶׁר יִבְחַר
יהוה אֱלֹהֶיךָ לָשׂוּם שְׁמוֹ שָׁם כִּי יְבָרֶכְךָ יהוה אֱלֹהֶיךָ׃ וְנָתַתָּה
בַּכָּסֶף וְצַרְתָּ הַכֶּסֶף בְּיָדְךָ וְהָלַכְתָּ אֶל־הַמָּקוֹם אֲשֶׁר יִבְחַר יהוה
אֱלֹהֶיךָ בּוֹ׃ וְנָתַתָּה הַכֶּסֶף בְּכֹל אֲשֶׁר־תְּאַוֶּה נַפְשְׁךָ בַּבָּקָר וּבַצֹּאן
וּבַיַּיִן וּבַשֵּׁכָר וּבְכֹל אֲשֶׁר תִּשְׁאָלְךָ נַפְשֶׁךָ וְאָכַלְתָּ שָּׁם לִפְנֵי יהוה
אֱלֹהֶיךָ וְשָׂמַחְתָּ אַתָּה וּבֵיתֶךָ׃ וְהַלֵּוִי אֲשֶׁר־בִּשְׁעָרֶיךָ לֹא תַעַזְבֶנּוּ

TORAH READING FOR SHEMINI ATZERET

The core of the reading for Shemini Atzeret is the passage dealing with the festivals in the book of Deuteronomy. The festivals are extensively described in three places in the Torah, in Leviticus (23), in Numbers (28–29), and here (Deut. 16). The sages explained that the first is to establish their order, the second to prescribe their sacrifices, and the third to explain them to the public (*Sifrei, Re'eh* 127).

Throughout Deuteronomy, Moses explains the laws to the people as a whole, reminding them of the historical background against which they are set, and the future of which they are the parameters. In the case of the festivals, Moses' presentation here has a strong emphasis on the seasons of the agricultural year: Pesaḥ is the festival of spring, the countdown to Shavuot begins "from when the sickle begins in the standing grain," and Sukkot is celebrated at the time when "you gather in from your threshing floor and your winepress." These are dimensions of the festivals the people have not yet experienced as desert nomads, but they will once they enter and make their home in the land which the Lord has blessed.

Moses also emphasizes the important dimension of social inclusion. The

At the end of every third year, you must take out all the tithes of your harvest from that year, and set them down within your gates. Then the Levite, who does not have a portion or an inheritance among you, along with the stranger and orphan and widow within your gates, shall come and eat and be satisfied; do this, so that the LORD your God might bless you in all that you do.

At the end of every seven years, you shall institute a release. And this is the manner of the release: every creditor shall let go of what he is entitled to from his debtor; he may not demand payment from his fellow or his kinsman, for a release has been proclaimed for [the honor of] the LORD. You may ask payment of a gentile, but any claim you hold against your kinsmen must be released. Nevertheless, you will not have paupers among you, for the LORD shall surely bless you in the land that He is giving you as a portion, to inherit it – but only if you heed the voice of the LORD your God, safeguarding and keeping all of the commandments I am commanding you today. For the LORD your God will bless you as He has promised you: you shall lend to many nations and you shall not borrow; you shall rule over many nations and shall not be ruled by others. (*Shabbat:* LEVI)

If there should be a poor person among you, one of your kinsmen in one of the cities in your land, which the LORD your God has given to you, you must not harden your heart and you must not close your hand to your impoverished kinsman. Rather, you must open your

---

We use our wealth to serve God when we ensure that those who have more than they need share their blessings with those who have less. In particular, we should ensure that no one in the nation God liberated from slavery is permanently enslaved, either by debt or poverty (the usual reason people sold themselves as slaves).

כִּי־יִהְיֶה בְךָ *If there should ... be among you.* This passage became, in the Talmud, the basis of the elaborate laws of *tzedaka*, one of the pillars of Jewish life, especially outside Israel where the agricultural laws that formed the basis of the Torah's welfare legislation were less applicable.

כִּי אֵין לוֹ חֵלֶק וְנַחֲלָה עִמָּךְ׃ מִקְצֵה ׀ שָׁלֹשׁ שָׁנִים
תּוֹצִיא אֶת־כָּל־מַעְשַׂר תְּבוּאָתְךָ בַּשָּׁנָה הַהִוא וְהִנַּחְתָּ בִּשְׁעָרֶיךָ׃
וּבָא הַלֵּוִי כִּי אֵין־לוֹ חֵלֶק וְנַחֲלָה עִמָּךְ וְהַגֵּר וְהַיָּתוֹם וְהָאַלְמָנָה
אֲשֶׁר בִּשְׁעָרֶיךָ וְאָכְלוּ וְשָׂבֵעוּ לְמַעַן יְבָרֶכְךָ יהוה אֱלֹהֶיךָ בְּכָל־
מַעֲשֵׂה יָדְךָ אֲשֶׁר תַּעֲשֶׂה׃ מִקֵּץ שֶׁבַע־שָׁנִים תַּעֲשֶׂה (בשבת לוי)
שְׁמִטָּה׃ וְזֶה דְּבַר הַשְּׁמִטָּה שָׁמוֹט כָּל־בַּעַל מַשֵּׁה יָדוֹ אֲשֶׁר
יַשֶּׁה בְּרֵעֵהוּ לֹא־יִגֹּשׂ אֶת־רֵעֵהוּ וְאֶת־אָחִיו כִּי־קָרָא שְׁמִטָּה
לַיהוה׃ אֶת־הַנָּכְרִי תִּגֹּשׂ וַאֲשֶׁר יִהְיֶה לְךָ אֶת־אָחִיךָ תַּשְׁמֵט
יָדֶךָ׃ אֶפֶס כִּי לֹא יִהְיֶה־בְּךָ אֶבְיוֹן כִּי־בָרֵךְ יְבָרֶכְךָ יהוה בָּאָרֶץ
אֲשֶׁר יהוה אֱלֹהֶיךָ נֹתֵן־לְךָ נַחֲלָה לְרִשְׁתָּהּ׃ רַק אִם־שָׁמוֹעַ
תִּשְׁמַע בְּקוֹל יהוה אֱלֹהֶיךָ לִשְׁמֹר לַעֲשׂוֹת אֶת־כָּל־הַמִּצְוָה
הַזֹּאת אֲשֶׁר אָנֹכִי מְצַוְּךָ הַיּוֹם׃ כִּי־יהוה אֱלֹהֶיךָ בֵּרַכְךָ כַּאֲשֶׁר
דִּבֶּר־לָךְ וְהַעֲבַטְתָּ גּוֹיִם רַבִּים וְאַתָּה לֹא תַעֲבֹט וּמָשַׁלְתָּ בְּגוֹיִם
רַבִּים וּבְךָ לֹא יִמְשֹׁלוּ׃ כִּי־יִהְיֶה בְךָ אֶבְיוֹן מֵאַחַד
אַחֶיךָ בְּאַחַד שְׁעָרֶיךָ בְּאַרְצְךָ אֲשֶׁר־יהוה אֱלֹהֶיךָ נֹתֵן לָךְ לֹא
תְאַמֵּץ אֶת־לְבָבְךָ וְלֹא תִקְפֹּץ אֶת־יָדְךָ מֵאָחִיךָ הָאֶבְיוֹן׃ כִּי־

מִקְצֵה שָׁלֹשׁ שָׁנִים *At the end of every third year.* On the third and sixth year of each septennial cycle, the second tithe, instead of being consumed by its owners in Jerusalem, is given locally to the poor. This, the *ma'aser ani,* "poor person's tithe," is part of the Torah's elaborate welfare system, designed to ensure that no one is left destitute or without the means of a dignified existence.

לְמַעַן יְבָרֶכְךָ יהוה אֱלֹהֶיךָ *So that the Lord your God might bless you.* God blesses those who are a source of blessing to others.

מִקֵּץ שֶׁבַע־שָׁנִים *At the end of every seven years.* The sequence here – second and poor person's tithe, and the release of debts and slaves in the seventh year – are ways in which we serve God *bekhol me'odekha,* "with all your wealth."

hand to him, making him a loan to tide him over his lack. Take care, lest evil thoughts enter your heart, saying: "The seventh year, the year of release draws near," causing you to treat your impoverished kinsman meanly, withholding loans from him; he might then call out to God because of you and it will be held against you as a sin. You must certainly give to him, and let your heart not be grudging when you give, for because of this deed, the LORD your God shall bless you in all that you do and in all of your endeavors. For there will never cease to be poor people in the land; and so I am commanding you: you must open your hand to your kinsman, to the poor and destitute in your land.

If your Hebrew kinsman or kinswoman is sold to you, he shall work for you for six years, and in the seventh year, you must release him from your service, free. When you set him free from your service you must not send him away empty-handed. You must give generously to him of your flock, your granary and your wine-vat with which the LORD your God has blessed you; so you shall give him. And you shall remember that you were once a slave in the land of Egypt and the LORD your God redeemed you; this is why, today, I command you thus. Should [the slave] say: "I would not leave your home;" because he is fond of you and of your household, and is happy living with you, then you shall take an awl and pierce his ear upon the door with it, and he shall then be your slave forever; the same should be done with your female slave. Do not feel it a hardship when you release him from your service, free; for he has served you for six years – twice a hired hand's work, and now the LORD your God will bless you in all that you do.

Every male firstborn that is delivered among your herd and your flock, you shall consecrate to the LORD your God: you may not perform work with the male firstborn of your oxen, nor shear the (*Shabbat:* SHELISH

---

izing about servitude, for servant and master alike. The gift is a humanizing gesture that marks a benign end to a less-than-benign episode.

פָּתֹחַ תִּפְתַּח אֶת־יָדְךָ לוֹ וְהַעֲבֵט תַּעֲבִיטֶנּוּ דֵּי מַחְסֹרוֹ אֲשֶׁר
יֶחְסַר לוֹ: הִשָּׁמֶר לְךָ פֶּן־יִהְיֶה דָבָר עִם־לְבָבְךָ בְלִיַּעַל לֵאמֹר
קָרְבָה שְׁנַת־הַשֶּׁבַע שְׁנַת הַשְּׁמִטָּה וְרָעָה עֵינְךָ בְּאָחִיךָ הָאֶבְיוֹן
וְלֹא תִתֵּן לוֹ וְקָרָא עָלֶיךָ אֶל־יהוה וְהָיָה בְךָ חֵטְא: נָתוֹן תִּתֵּן
לוֹ וְלֹא־יֵרַע לְבָבְךָ בְּתִתְּךָ לוֹ כִּי בִּגְלַל ׀ הַדָּבָר הַזֶּה יְבָרֶכְךָ יהוה
אֱלֹהֶיךָ בְּכָל־מַעֲשֶׂךָ וּבְכֹל מִשְׁלַח יָדֶךָ: כִּי לֹא־יֶחְדַּל אֶבְיוֹן
מִקֶּרֶב הָאָרֶץ עַל־כֵּן אָנֹכִי מְצַוְּךָ לֵאמֹר פָּתֹחַ תִּפְתַּח אֶת־
יָדְךָ לְאָחִיךָ לַעֲנִיֶּךָ וּלְאֶבְיֹנְךָ בְּאַרְצֶךָ: כִּי־יִמָּכֵר לְךָ
אָחִיךָ הָעִבְרִי אוֹ הָעִבְרִיָּה וַעֲבָדְךָ שֵׁשׁ שָׁנִים וּבַשָּׁנָה הַשְּׁבִיעִת
תְּשַׁלְּחֶנּוּ חָפְשִׁי מֵעִמָּךְ: וְכִי־תְשַׁלְּחֶנּוּ חָפְשִׁי מֵעִמָּךְ לֹא תְשַׁלְּחֶנּוּ
רֵיקָם: הַעֲנֵיק תַּעֲנִיק לוֹ מִצֹּאנְךָ וּמִגָּרְנְךָ וּמִיִּקְבֶךָ אֲשֶׁר בֵּרַכְךָ
יהוה אֱלֹהֶיךָ תִּתֶּן־לוֹ: וְזָכַרְתָּ כִּי עֶבֶד הָיִיתָ בְּאֶרֶץ מִצְרַיִם וַיִּפְדְּךָ
יהוה אֱלֹהֶיךָ עַל־כֵּן אָנֹכִי מְצַוְּךָ אֶת־הַדָּבָר הַזֶּה הַיּוֹם: וְהָיָה
כִּי־יֹאמַר אֵלֶיךָ לֹא אֵצֵא מֵעִמָּךְ כִּי אֲהֵבְךָ וְאֶת־בֵּיתֶךָ כִּי־טוֹב
לוֹ עִמָּךְ: וְלָקַחְתָּ אֶת־הַמַּרְצֵעַ וְנָתַתָּה בְאָזְנוֹ וּבַדֶּלֶת וְהָיָה לְךָ
עֶבֶד עוֹלָם וְאַף לַאֲמָתְךָ תַּעֲשֶׂה־כֵּן: לֹא־יִקְשֶׁה בְעֵינֶךָ בְּשַׁלֵּחֲךָ
אֹתוֹ חָפְשִׁי מֵעִמָּךְ כִּי מִשְׁנֶה שְׂכַר שָׂכִיר עֲבָדְךָ שֵׁשׁ שָׁנִים וּבֵרַכְךָ
יהוה אֱלֹהֶיךָ בְּכֹל אֲשֶׁר תַּעֲשֶׂה:

כָּל־הַבְּכוֹר אֲשֶׁר יִוָּלֵד בִּבְקָרְךָ וּבְצֹאנְךָ הַזָּכָר תַּקְדִּישׁ לַיהוה (בשבת שלישי)
אֱלֹהֶיךָ לֹא תַעֲבֹד בִּבְכֹר שׁוֹרֶךָ וְלֹא תָגֹז בְּכוֹר צֹאנֶךָ: לִפְנֵי

הַעֲנֵיק תַּעֲנִיק לוֹ *You must give generously to him.* There are three reasons for this law: first, to give the released slave the means to make a fresh start; second, to demonstrate your gratitude for the service he has given you; and third, to establish closure with goodwill. There is something profoundly dehuman-

male firstborn of your sheep. You shall eat them in the presence of the LORD your God each year, you and your household, in the place which the LORD will choose. If it is blemished: lame or blind, or with any other serious blemish, you may not offer it to the LORD your God. Eat it within your gates; [it may be eaten by] pure and impure alike, as the gazelle and as the hart. But its blood you may not eat; you must spill it on the ground like water.

LEVI (*Shabbat:* REVI'I) Remember the month of Spring: bring a Pesaḥ offering to the LORD your God, for in the month of Spring, the LORD your God took you out of Egypt at night. You shall bring a Pesaḥ offering to the LORD your God, sheep and cattle, at the place the LORD shall choose as a dwelling place for His name. You may not eat leaven with it; you must eat matzot, the bread of oppression, with it for seven days – for you left Egypt in great haste – so that you remember the day of your exodus from Egypt all the days of your life. SHELISH (*Shabbat:* ḤAMISHI) And no leaven shall be seen by you within all your borders for seven days, and none of the meat which you offer in the evening of the first day shall be allowed to remain until morning. You may not sacrifice the Pesaḥ offering in any one of your cities, which the LORD your God gives you. Only at the place which the LORD your God shall choose as a dwelling place for His name – that is where you should sacrifice the Pesaḥ offering in the evening, before sunset, in the season of your exodus from Egypt. You shall cook it and eat it in the place the LORD your God will choose, and in the morning you shall turn back and go to your abode. For six days, you shall eat matzot; the seventh day is a day of assembly for the LORD your God: on it, you may not perform work.

Israel, by which seven leap years are observed in the course of nineteen years.

לֶחֶם עֹנִי *Bread of oppression.* It is this phrase that defines matza as the taste of servitude, either because they were given it to eat in Egypt (being harder to digest than ordinary bread, it staved off hunger longer), or because, eating it

יְהוָה אֱלֹהֶיךָ תֹאכְלֶנּוּ שָׁנָה בְשָׁנָה בַּמָּקוֹם אֲשֶׁר־יִבְחַר יְהוָה
אַתָּה וּבֵיתֶךָ: וְכִי־יִהְיֶה בוֹ מוּם פִּסֵּחַ אוֹ עִוֵּר כֹּל מוּם רָע לֹא
תִזְבָּחֶנּוּ לַיהוָה אֱלֹהֶיךָ: בִּשְׁעָרֶיךָ תֹּאכְלֶנּוּ הַטָּמֵא וְהַטָּהוֹר
יַחְדָּו כַּצְּבִי וְכָאַיָּל: רַק אֶת־דָּמוֹ לֹא תֹאכֵל עַל־הָאָרֶץ תִּשְׁפְּכֶנּוּ
כַּמָּיִם:

לוי (בשבת רביעי) שָׁמוֹר אֶת־חֹדֶשׁ הָאָבִיב וְעָשִׂיתָ פֶּסַח לַיהוָה אֱלֹהֶיךָ כִּי בְּחֹדֶשׁ
הָאָבִיב הוֹצִיאֲךָ יְהוָה אֱלֹהֶיךָ מִמִּצְרַיִם לָיְלָה: וְזָבַחְתָּ פֶּסַח
לַיהוָה אֱלֹהֶיךָ צֹאן וּבָקָר בַּמָּקוֹם אֲשֶׁר יִבְחַר יְהוָה לְשַׁכֵּן שְׁמוֹ
שָׁם: לֹא־תֹאכַל עָלָיו חָמֵץ שִׁבְעַת יָמִים תֹּאכַל־עָלָיו מַצּוֹת
לֶחֶם עֹנִי כִּי בְחִפָּזוֹן יָצָאתָ מֵאֶרֶץ מִצְרַיִם לְמַעַן תִּזְכֹּר אֶת־יוֹם
שלישי (בשבת חמישי) צֵאתְךָ מֵאֶרֶץ מִצְרַיִם כֹּל יְמֵי חַיֶּיךָ: וְלֹא־יֵרָאֶה לְךָ שְׂאֹר בְּכָל־
גְּבֻלְךָ שִׁבְעַת יָמִים וְלֹא־יָלִין מִן־הַבָּשָׂר אֲשֶׁר תִּזְבַּח בָּעֶרֶב בַּיּוֹם
הָרִאשׁוֹן לַבֹּקֶר: לֹא תוּכַל לִזְבֹּחַ אֶת־הַפָּסַח בְּאַחַד שְׁעָרֶיךָ
אֲשֶׁר־יְהוָה אֱלֹהֶיךָ נֹתֵן לָךְ: כִּי אִם־אֶל־הַמָּקוֹם אֲשֶׁר־יִבְחַר
יְהוָה אֱלֹהֶיךָ לְשַׁכֵּן שְׁמוֹ שָׁם תִּזְבַּח אֶת־הַפֶּסַח בָּעָרֶב כְּבוֹא
הַשֶּׁמֶשׁ מוֹעֵד צֵאתְךָ מִמִּצְרָיִם: וּבִשַּׁלְתָּ וְאָכַלְתָּ בַּמָּקוֹם אֲשֶׁר
יִבְחַר יְהוָה אֱלֹהֶיךָ בּוֹ וּפָנִיתָ בַבֹּקֶר וְהָלַכְתָּ לְאֹהָלֶיךָ: שֵׁשֶׁת
יָמִים תֹּאכַל מַצּוֹת וּבַיּוֹם הַשְּׁבִיעִי עֲצֶרֶת לַיהוָה אֱלֹהֶיךָ לֹא

הָאָבִיב *Spring.* It is this requirement that Pesaḥ be celebrated in spring that necessitates the complex system by which the lunar calendar of Judaism is co-ordinated with the solar cycle of the seasons, by means of adding an extra month (a second Adar) from time to time. Originally this was done by decision of the Beit Din. Only a court in Israel has this power. So from the fourth century onward, when the centre of Jewish life had moved from Israel to Babylon, a fixed calendar was adopted on the authority of

Count for yourselves seven weeks; when the sickle begins to cut the standing grain, then shall you begin to count the seven weeks. And you shall celebrate a Festival of Weeks [Shavuot] for the LORD your God, bringing a free-will offering, as much as you can afford, according to the blessing the LORD your God has given you. And you shall rejoice in the presence of the LORD your God: you and your sons and daughters, your male and female slaves, and the Levite who dwells within your gates, along with the stranger and orphan and widow that are among you, at the place that the LORD your God shall choose as a dwelling place for His name. And you shall remember that you were once a slave in Egypt; keep and fulfill all of these statutes. REVI'I (*Shabbat:* SHISHI)

You shall celebrate a Festival of Booths [Sukkot] for yourselves for seven days, when you gather [your produce] into your granary and wine-vat. And you shall rejoice on your festival: you and your sons and daughters, your male and female slaves, and the Levite, the stranger and orphan and widow that dwell within your gates. You shall celebrate for seven days for the LORD your God in the place which the LORD shall choose, for the LORD your God shall bless you in all of your produce and all that you do; and you will be truly joyful. Three times in the year, all your males shall appear before the LORD your God at the place He will choose: on Pesaḥ, Shavuot and Sukkot. They shall not appear before the LORD empty-handed. Each shall bring such a gift as he can, in proportion to the blessing the LORD your God grants you. ḤAMISHI (*Shabbat:* SHEVI'I)

---

blessings. Note, however, that the word "rejoice" does not appear in the context of Pesaḥ, for it recalls two periods of suffering, the suffering inflicted on the Israelites by the Egyptians, and the subsequent suffering of the Egyptians themselves. Halakhically there is a mitzva of *simḥa* on Pesaḥ, but it comes on the first day(s) mixed with the taste of affliction and bitterness (matza and maror), and on the last with the memory of the Egyptians who died at the Red Sea, and as Proverbs 24:17 states, "Do not rejoice when your enemy falls" (*Yalkut Shimoni*, Emor, 654).

רביעי (בשבת שישי)

תַּעֲשֶׂה מְלָאכָה: שִׁבְעָה שָׁבֻעֹת תִּסְפָּר־לָךְ מֵהָחֵל
חֶרְמֵשׁ בַּקָּמָה תָּחֵל לִסְפֹּר שִׁבְעָה שָׁבֻעוֹת: וְעָשִׂיתָ חַג שָׁבֻעוֹת
לַיהוָה אֱלֹהֶיךָ מִסַּת נִדְבַת יָדְךָ אֲשֶׁר תִּתֵּן כַּאֲשֶׁר יְבָרֶכְךָ יְהוָה
אֱלֹהֶיךָ: וְשָׂמַחְתָּ לִפְנֵי ׀ יְהוָה אֱלֹהֶיךָ אַתָּה וּבִנְךָ וּבִתֶּךָ וְעַבְדְּךָ
וַאֲמָתֶךָ וְהַלֵּוִי אֲשֶׁר בִּשְׁעָרֶיךָ וְהַגֵּר וְהַיָּתוֹם וְהָאַלְמָנָה אֲשֶׁר
בְּקִרְבֶּךָ בַּמָּקוֹם אֲשֶׁר יִבְחַר יְהוָה אֱלֹהֶיךָ לְשַׁכֵּן שְׁמוֹ שָׁם:
וְזָכַרְתָּ כִּי־עֶבֶד הָיִיתָ בְּמִצְרָיִם וְשָׁמַרְתָּ וְעָשִׂיתָ אֶת־הַחֻקִּים
הָאֵלֶּה:

חמישי (בשבת שביעי)

חַג הַסֻּכֹּת תַּעֲשֶׂה לְךָ שִׁבְעַת יָמִים בְּאָסְפְּךָ מִגָּרְנְךָ וּמִיִּקְבֶךָ:
וְשָׂמַחְתָּ בְּחַגֶּךָ אַתָּה וּבִנְךָ וּבִתֶּךָ וְעַבְדְּךָ וַאֲמָתֶךָ וְהַלֵּוִי וְהַגֵּר
וְהַיָּתוֹם וְהָאַלְמָנָה אֲשֶׁר בִּשְׁעָרֶיךָ: שִׁבְעַת יָמִים תָּחֹג לַיהוָה
אֱלֹהֶיךָ בַּמָּקוֹם אֲשֶׁר־יִבְחַר יְהוָה כִּי יְבָרֶכְךָ יְהוָה אֱלֹהֶיךָ בְּכֹל־
תְּבוּאָתְךָ וּבְכֹל מַעֲשֵׂה יָדֶיךָ וְהָיִיתָ אַךְ שָׂמֵחַ: שָׁלוֹשׁ פְּעָמִים ׀
בַּשָּׁנָה יֵרָאֶה כָל־זְכוּרְךָ אֶת־פְּנֵי ׀ יְהוָה אֱלֹהֶיךָ בַּמָּקוֹם אֲשֶׁר
יִבְחָר בְּחַג הַמַּצּוֹת וּבְחַג הַשָּׁבֻעוֹת וּבְחַג הַסֻּכּוֹת וְלֹא יֵרָאֶה
אֶת־פְּנֵי יְהוָה רֵיקָם: אִישׁ כְּמַתְּנַת יָדוֹ כְּבִרְכַּת יְהוָה אֱלֹהֶיךָ
אֲשֶׁר נָתַן־לָךְ:

---

on their escape from Egypt, it served as a reminder of the slavery they were escaping from.

וְשָׂמַחְתָּ *You shall rejoice.* There is greater emphasis on rejoicing in Deuteronomy than elsewhere in the Torah. The root ש-מ-ח, "to rejoice," appears only once in each of the books of Genesis, Exodus, Leviticus and Numbers, but twelve times in Deuteronomy. The previous books have been about the long journey, begun by Abraham, toward the fulfillment of the Divine promises of children and a land. Deuteronomy is about the destination: a land where the people of the covenant can be free to pursue their vocation as a holy nation in a holy land, keeping God's law, sensing His presence and celebrating His

HALF KADDISH

Before Maftir is read, the second Sefer Torah is placed on the bima and the Reader says Half Kaddish:

Reader: יִתְגַּדַּל Magnified and sanctified
may His great name be,
in the world He created by His will.
May He establish His kingdom
in your lifetime and in your days,
and in the lifetime of all the house of Israel,
swiftly and soon –
and say: Amen.

All: May His great name be blessed for ever and all time.

Reader: Blessed and praised, glorified and exalted,
raised and honored, uplifted and lauded
be the name of the Holy One, blessed be He,
beyond any blessing,
song, praise and consolation
uttered in the world –
and say: Amen.

HAGBAHA AND GELILA

The first Torah scroll is lifted and the congregation says:

וְזֹאת הַתּוֹרָה This is the Torah *Deut. 4*
that Moses placed before the children of Israel,
at the LORD's commandment, by the hand of Moses. *Num. 9*

Some add: It is a tree of life to those who grasp it, *Prov. 3*
and those who uphold it are happy.
Its ways are ways of pleasantness, and all its paths are peace.
Long life is in its right hand; in its left, riches and honor.
It pleased the LORD for the sake of [Israel's] righteousness, *Is. 42*
to make the Torah great and glorious.

The first Torah scroll is bound and covered and the oleh for Maftir is called to the second Torah scroll.

חצי קדיש

Before מפטיר *is read, the second* ספר תורה *is placed on the* שולחן *and the* קורא *says* חצי קדיש:

קורא: יִתְגַּדַּל וְיִתְקַדַּשׁ שְׁמֵהּ רַבָּא (קהל: אָמֵן)
בְּעָלְמָא דִּי בְרָא כִרְעוּתֵהּ
וְיַמְלִיךְ מַלְכוּתֵהּ
בְּחַיֵּיכוֹן וּבְיוֹמֵיכוֹן וּבְחַיֵּי דְכָל בֵּית יִשְׂרָאֵל
בַּעֲגָלָא וּבִזְמַן קָרִיב
וְאִמְרוּ אָמֵן. (קהל: אָמֵן)

קהל וקורא: יְהֵא שְׁמֵהּ רַבָּא מְבָרַךְ לְעָלַם וּלְעָלְמֵי עָלְמַיָּא.

קורא: יִתְבָּרַךְ וְיִשְׁתַּבַּח וְיִתְפָּאַר וְיִתְרוֹמַם וְיִתְנַשֵּׂא
וְיִתְהַדָּר וְיִתְעַלֶּה וְיִתְהַלָּל
שְׁמֵהּ דְּקֻדְשָׁא בְּרִיךְ הוּא (קהל: בְּרִיךְ הוּא)
לְעֵלָּא מִן כָּל בִּרְכָתָא וְשִׁירָתָא
תֻּשְׁבְּחָתָא וְנֶחֱמָתָא
דַּאֲמִירָן בְּעָלְמָא
וְאִמְרוּ אָמֵן. (קהל: אָמֵן)

הגבהה וגלילה

The first ספר תורה *is lifted and the* קהל *says:*

וְזֹאת הַתּוֹרָה אֲשֶׁר־שָׂם מֹשֶׁה לִפְנֵי בְּנֵי יִשְׂרָאֵל: דברים ד
עַל־פִּי יהוה בְּיַד מֹשֶׁה: במדבר ט

Some add עֵץ־חַיִּים הִיא לַמַּחֲזִיקִים בָּהּ וְתֹמְכֶיהָ מְאֻשָּׁר: משלי ג
דְּרָכֶיהָ דַרְכֵי־נֹעַם וְכָל־נְתִיבוֹתֶיהָ שָׁלוֹם:
אֹרֶךְ יָמִים בִּימִינָהּ, בִּשְׂמֹאולָהּ עֹשֶׁר וְכָבוֹד:
יהוה חָפֵץ לְמַעַן צִדְקוֹ יַגְדִּיל תּוֹרָה וְיַאְדִּיר: ישעיה מב

The first ספר תורה *is bound and covered and the* עולה *for* מפטיר *is called to the second* ספר תורה.

MAFTIR

On the eighth day you shall hold an assembly; you shall do no laborious work. And you shall offer a burnt-offering, a fire-offering of pleasing odor to the LORD: one bullock, one ram, seven yearling male lambs without blemish. And for each of the bullock, the ram and the lambs, their meal-offerings and wine-libations, in the proper quantities, according to the law. And likewise a male goat for atonement, as well as the regular daily offering, its meal-offering and its libation. These are what you shall offer to the LORD at your appointed times, alongside the offerings you vow and your freewill-offerings: your burnt-offerings and meal-offerings, your wine-libations and your peace-offerings. And Moses told the children of Israel, all that the LORD had commanded to Moses. *Num. 29:35–30:1*

HAGBAHA AND GELILA

The second Torah scroll is lifted and the congregation says:

וְזֹאת הַתּוֹרָה This is the Torah *Deut. 4*
that Moses placed before the children of Israel,
at the LORD's commandment, by the hand of Moses. *Num. 9*

Some add: It is a tree of life to those who grasp it, *Prov. 3*
and those who uphold it are happy.
Its ways are ways of pleasantness, and all its paths are peace.
Long life is in its right hand; in its left, riches and honor.
It pleased the LORD for the sake of [Israel's] righteousness, *Is. 42*
to make the Torah great and glorious.

The second Torah scroll is bound and covered and the oleh for Maftir reads the Haftara.

BLESSING BEFORE READING THE HAFTARA

Before reading the Haftara, the person called up for Maftir says:

בָּרוּךְ Blessed are You, LORD our God, King of the Universe, who chose good prophets and was pleased with their words, spoken in truth. Blessed are You, LORD, who chose the Torah, His servant Moses, His people Israel, and the prophets of truth and righteousness.

מפטיר לשמיני עצרת

במדבר כט:לה–ל:א

בַּיּוֹם הַשְּׁמִינִי עֲצֶרֶת תִּהְיֶה לָכֶם כָּל־מְלֶאכֶת עֲבֹדָה לֹא תַעֲשׂוּ׃ וְהִקְרַבְתֶּם עֹלָה אִשֵּׁה רֵיחַ נִיחֹחַ לַיהוה פַּר אֶחָד אַיִל אֶחָד כְּבָשִׂים בְּנֵי־שָׁנָה שִׁבְעָה תְּמִימִם׃ מִנְחָתָם וְנִסְכֵּיהֶם לַפָּר לָאַיִל וְלַכְּבָשִׂים בְּמִסְפָּרָם כַּמִּשְׁפָּט׃ וּשְׂעִיר חַטָּאת אֶחָד מִלְּבַד עֹלַת הַתָּמִיד וּמִנְחָתָהּ וְנִסְכָּהּ׃ אֵלֶּה תַּעֲשׂוּ לַיהוה בְּמוֹעֲדֵיכֶם לְבַד מִנִּדְרֵיכֶם וְנִדְבֹתֵיכֶם לְעֹלֹתֵיכֶם וּלְמִנְחֹתֵיכֶם וּלְנִסְכֵּיכֶם וּלְשַׁלְמֵיכֶם׃ וַיֹּאמֶר מֹשֶׁה אֶל־בְּנֵי יִשְׂרָאֵל כְּכֹל אֲשֶׁר־צִוָּה יהוה אֶת־מֹשֶׁה׃

הגבהה וגלילה

The second ספר תורה *is lifted and the* קהל *says:*

וְזֹאת הַתּוֹרָה אֲשֶׁר־שָׂם מֹשֶׁה לִפְנֵי בְּנֵי יִשְׂרָאֵל׃ דברים ד

עַל־פִּי יהוה בְּיַד מֹשֶׁה׃ במדבר ט

Some add

עֵץ־חַיִּים הִיא לַמַּחֲזִיקִים בָּהּ וְתֹמְכֶיהָ מְאֻשָּׁר׃ משלי ג

דְּרָכֶיהָ דַרְכֵי־נֹעַם וְכָל־נְתִיבוֹתֶיהָ שָׁלוֹם׃

אֹרֶךְ יָמִים בִּימִינָהּ, בִּשְׂמֹאולָהּ עֹשֶׁר וְכָבוֹד׃

יהוה חָפֵץ לְמַעַן צִדְקוֹ יַגְדִּיל תּוֹרָה וְיַאְדִּיר׃ ישעיה מב

The second ספר תורה *is bound and covered and the* עולה *for* מפטיר *reads the* הפטרה.

ברכה קודם ההפטרה

Before reading the הפטרה*, the person called up for* מפטיר *says:*

בָּרוּךְ אַתָּה יהוה אֱלֹהֵינוּ מֶלֶךְ הָעוֹלָם אֲשֶׁר בָּחַר בִּנְבִיאִים טוֹבִים, וְרָצָה בְדִבְרֵיהֶם הַנֶּאֱמָרִים בֶּאֱמֶת. בָּרוּךְ אַתָּה יהוה, הַבּוֹחֵר בַּתּוֹרָה וּבְמֹשֶׁה עַבְדּוֹ וּבְיִשְׂרָאֵל עַמּוֹ וּבִנְבִיאֵי הָאֱמֶת וָצֶדֶק.

HAFTARA FOR SHEMINI ATZERET

When Solomon had finished uttering this prayer and this plea to the LORD, he rose up from before the altar of the LORD, and bowed down upon his knees, his palms outstretched towards the heavens. And he stood and blessed all the congregation of Israel, in a loud voice, saying: *I Kings. 8:54–9:1*

"Blessed be the LORD, who has granted rest to His people Israel just as He promised; no word of the good that the LORD promised through His servant has failed us. May the LORD our God be with us as He was with our ancestors; may He never leave us or forsake us. May He incline our hearts towards Him, that we follow in all His ways and keep His commands and all the statutes and laws with which He charged our ancestors. Let these words with which I have pleaded with the LORD be close to the LORD our God day and night, that He do justice for His servant, and justice for His people Israel, day after day; so that all the peoples of the earth will know

---

had done at the completion of the Sanctuary (Ex. 39:43; see also Lev. 9:23).

כְּכֹל אֲשֶׁר דִּבֵּר *As He promised.* "When you cross the Jordan and settle in the land that the LORD your God is allotting to you, and He grants you safety from all your enemies around you and you live in security, then you must bring everything that I command you to the site where the LORD your God will choose to establish His name" (Deut. 12: 10–11).

לְהַטּוֹת לְבָבֵנוּ *May He incline our hearts.* This is the essence of Jewish history as understood by priests, prophets, and kings alike. We are a nation and have a land only in virtue of the covenant. Therefore we must never forget its terms or fail to honor its responsibilities.

לְמַעַן דַּעַת כָּל־עַמֵּי הָאָרֶץ *So that all the peoples of the earth will know.* Another axiom of Jewish faith, that God, having chosen the children of Israel as His witnesses, has placed on us the responsibility of ensuring that we act in such a way as to bring the knowledge of Him to humanity as a whole. "I will insist that the Hebrews have done more to civilize men than any other nation. If I were an atheist, and believed in blind eternal fate, I should still believe that

הפטרה לשמיני עצרת

וַיְהִי ׀ כְּכַלּוֹת שְׁלֹמֹה לְהִתְפַּלֵּל אֶל־יהוה אֵת כָּל־הַתְּפִלָּה מלכים א׳
וְהַתְּחִנָּה הַזֹּאת קָם מִלִּפְנֵי מִזְבַּח יהוה מִכְּרֹעַ עַל־בִּרְכָּיו וְכַפָּיו ח:נד–ט:א
פְּרֻשׂוֹת הַשָּׁמָיִם׃ וַיַּעֲמֹד וַיְבָרֶךְ אֵת כָּל־קְהַל יִשְׂרָאֵל קוֹל גָּדוֹל
לֵאמֹר׃ בָּרוּךְ יהוה אֲשֶׁר נָתַן מְנוּחָה לְעַמּוֹ יִשְׂרָאֵל כְּכֹל אֲשֶׁר
דִּבֵּר לֹא־נָפַל דָּבָר אֶחָד מִכֹּל דְּבָרוֹ הַטּוֹב אֲשֶׁר דִּבֶּר בְּיַד מֹשֶׁה
עַבְדּוֹ׃ יְהִי יהוה אֱלֹהֵינוּ עִמָּנוּ כַּאֲשֶׁר הָיָה עִם־אֲבֹתֵינוּ אַל־
יַעַזְבֵנוּ וְאַל־יִטְּשֵׁנוּ׃ לְהַטּוֹת לְבָבֵנוּ אֵלָיו לָלֶכֶת בְּכָל־דְּרָכָיו
וְלִשְׁמֹר מִצְוֺתָיו וְחֻקָּיו וּמִשְׁפָּטָיו אֲשֶׁר צִוָּה אֶת־אֲבֹתֵינוּ׃ וְיִהְיוּ
דְבָרַי אֵלֶּה אֲשֶׁר הִתְחַנַּנְתִּי לִפְנֵי יהוה קְרֹבִים אֶל־יהוה אֱלֹהֵינוּ
יוֹמָם וָלָיְלָה לַעֲשׂוֹת ׀ מִשְׁפַּט עַבְדּוֹ וּמִשְׁפַּט עַמּוֹ יִשְׂרָאֵל דְּבַר־
יוֹם בְּיוֹמוֹ׃ לְמַעַן דַּעַת כָּל־עַמֵּי הָאָרֶץ כִּי יהוה הוּא הָאֱלֹהִים

HAFTARA: THE CONCLUSION OF THE DEDICATION OF THE TEMPLE

The *haftara* for Shemini Atzeret describes the end of the ceremony of the dedication of the Temple, conceived by David, and built under the direction of Solomon his son. The celebration lasted for two weeks, the first of which was the dedication itself, while the second took place on Sukkot. The sense of closure must have been immense. Sukkot reminded the people of the years when their ancestors wandered the desert without house or home. Now, some 480 years later (1 Kings 6:1), they had a land, a king, a capital city, Jerusalem, and finally a Temple, the visible home of the Divine Presence in the midst of the nation. They must have felt that the journey had been completed: they had arrived at their destination.

Solomon did what the great Jewish leaders of the biblical age always did at key moments in the life of the nation: he told the story of the people thus far, recalling its history, emphasizing the decisive role of God in the shape and outcome of events, His faithfulness to the covenant, and the way in which all His promises to the patriarchs and to Moses have come true. This is history through the eyes of faith, and it represents a profound moralization of politics.

שְׁלֹמֹה ... וַיְבָרֶךְ אֵת כָּל־קְהַל *Solomon ... blessed all the congregation.* As Moses

that the Lord is God. There is no other. And may your hearts be wholly with the Lord our God, to follow His statutes and to keep His commands as you do on this day."

Then the king and all of his people, Israel, brought offerings before the Lord. The peace offering that Solomon brought to the Lord consisted of twenty-two thousand heads of cattle and one hundred and twenty thousand sheep; and thus did the king and all the people of Israel dedicate the House of the Lord.

On that day, the king consecrated the center of the Courtyard before the House of the Lord, for there he prepared the burnt-offering, the meal-offering and fats of the peace-offerings; for the Brass Altar that stood before the Lord was too small to contain all the burnt-offerings and the meal-offerings and the fat of the peace-offerings. It was then that Solomon celebrated the Festival, and all of Israel his people with him, a vast congregation from all the land, from the border of Ḥamat to the river of Egypt, before the Lord our God for seven days and for seven days more, fourteen days all told.

And then, on the eighth day, Solomon sent the people on their way, and they blessed the king, going back to their tents happy and buoyant of heart over all the goodness that the Lord had performed for His servant, David, and for His people, Israel.

And so it was, when Solomon had finished building the House of the Lord and the palace of the king, all of Solomon's heart's desire, all that he had wished to do.

נַחַל מִצְרַיִם *The river of Egypt.* The southern boundary, identified by most scholars as Wadi El-Arish.

בַּיּוֹם הַשְּׁמִינִי *On the eighth day.* Shemini Atzeret, hence the choice of this passage as the *haftara* for this day. Solomon gave the people permission to leave. In fact, though, they held a farewell gathering on that day, and they left the day after, on 23 Tishrei (see II Chron. 7:9–10).

אֵין עוֹד׃ וְהָיָה לְבַבְכֶם שָׁלֵם עִם יהוה אֱלֹהֵינוּ לָלֶכֶת בְּחֻקָּיו וְלִשְׁמֹר מִצְוֺתָיו כַּיּוֹם הַזֶּה׃ וְהַמֶּלֶךְ וְכָל־יִשְׂרָאֵל עִמּוֹ זֹבְחִים זֶבַח לִפְנֵי יהוה׃ וַיִּזְבַּח שְׁלֹמֹה אֵת זֶבַח הַשְּׁלָמִים אֲשֶׁר זָבַח לַיהוה בָּקָר עֶשְׂרִים וּשְׁנַיִם אֶלֶף וְצֹאן מֵאָה וְעֶשְׂרִים אָלֶף וַיַּחְנְכוּ אֶת־בֵּית יהוה הַמֶּלֶךְ וְכָל־בְּנֵי יִשְׂרָאֵל׃ בַּיּוֹם הַהוּא קִדַּשׁ הַמֶּלֶךְ אֶת־תּוֹךְ הֶחָצֵר אֲשֶׁר לִפְנֵי בֵית־יהוה כִּי־עָשָׂה שָׁם אֶת־הָעֹלָה וְאֶת־הַמִּנְחָה וְאֵת חֶלְבֵי הַשְּׁלָמִים כִּי־מִזְבַּח הַנְּחֹשֶׁת אֲשֶׁר לִפְנֵי יהוה קָטֹן מֵהָכִיל אֶת־הָעֹלָה וְאֶת־הַמִּנְחָה וְאֵת חֶלְבֵי הַשְּׁלָמִים׃ וַיַּעַשׂ שְׁלֹמֹה בָעֵת־הַהִיא ׀ אֶת־הֶחָג וְכָל־יִשְׂרָאֵל עִמּוֹ קָהָל גָּדוֹל מִלְּבוֹא חֲמָת ׀ עַד־נַחַל מִצְרַיִם לִפְנֵי יהוה אֱלֹהֵינוּ שִׁבְעַת יָמִים וְשִׁבְעַת יָמִים אַרְבָּעָה עָשָׂר יוֹם׃ בַּיּוֹם הַשְּׁמִינִי שִׁלַּח אֶת־הָעָם וַיְבָרֲכוּ אֶת־הַמֶּלֶךְ וַיֵּלְכוּ לְאָהֳלֵיהֶם שְׂמֵחִים וְטוֹבֵי לֵב עַל כָּל־הַטּוֹבָה אֲשֶׁר עָשָׂה יהוה לְדָוִד עַבְדּוֹ וּלְיִשְׂרָאֵל עַמּוֹ׃

וַיְהִי כְּכַלּוֹת שְׁלֹמֹה לִבְנוֹת אֶת־בֵּית־יהוה וְאֶת־בֵּית הַמֶּלֶךְ וְאֵת כָּל־חֵשֶׁק שְׁלֹמֹה אֲשֶׁר חָפֵץ לַעֲשׂוֹת׃

---

fate had ordained the Jews to be the most essential instrument for civilizing the nations. If I were an atheist of the other sect, who believe or pretend to believe that all is ordered by chance, I should believe that chance had ordered the Jews to preserve and propagate to all mankind the doctrine of a supreme, intelligent, wise, almighty sovereign of the universe, which I believe to be the great essential principle of all morality, and consequently of all civilization." (John Adams, second President of the United States).

וְהַמֶּלֶךְ וְכָל־יִשְׂרָאֵל *The king and all of his people.* The massive number of sacrifices testifies to the size of the crowd there gathered.

מִלְּבוֹא חֲמָת *Border of Ḥamat.* Traditionally seen as the northern boundary of Israel (Num. 34:7–9).

BLESSINGS AFTER THE HAFTARA

After the Haftara, the person called up for Maftir says the following blessings:

בָּרוּךְ Blessed are You, Lord our God, King of the Universe, Rock of all worlds, righteous for all generations, the faithful God who says and does, speaks and fulfills, all of whose words are truth and righteousness. You are faithful, Lord our God, and faithful are Your words, not one of which returns unfulfilled, for You, God, are a faithful (and compassionate) King. Blessed are You, Lord, faithful in all His words.

רַחֵם Have compassion on Zion for it is the source of our life, and save the one grieved in spirit swiftly in our days. Blessed are You, Lord, who makes Zion rejoice in her children.

שַׂמְּחֵנוּ Grant us joy, Lord our God, through Elijah the prophet Your servant, and through the kingdom of the house of David Your anointed – may he soon come and make our hearts glad. May no stranger sit on his throne, and may others not continue to inherit his glory, for You promised him by Your holy name that his light would never be extinguished. Blessed are You, Lord, Shield of David.

On Shabbat, add the words in parentheses:

עַל הַתּוֹרָה For the Torah, for Divine worship, for the prophets (and for this Sabbath day), and for this day of the festival of Shemini Atzeret which You, Lord our God, have given us (for holiness and rest) for gladness and joy, for honor and glory – for all these we thank and bless You, Lord our God, and may Your name be blessed by the mouth of all that lives, continually, for ever and all time. Blessed are You, Lord, who sanctifies (the Sabbath and) Israel and the festive seasons.

On a weekday, the service continues with the various prayers for government on page 1114.

On Shabbat continue:

יְקוּם פֻּרְקָן May deliverance arise from heaven, bringing grace, love and compassion, long life, ample sustenance and heavenly help, physical

ברכות לאחר ההפטרה

After the הפטרה*, the person called up for* מפטיר *says the following blessings:*

בָּרוּךְ אַתָּה יהוה אֱלֹהֵינוּ מֶלֶךְ הָעוֹלָם, צוּר כָּל הָעוֹלָמִים, צַדִּיק בְּכָל הַדּוֹרוֹת, הָאֵל הַנֶּאֱמָן, הָאוֹמֵר וְעוֹשֶׂה, הַמְדַבֵּר וּמְקַיֵּם, שֶׁכָּל דְּבָרָיו אֱמֶת וָצֶדֶק. נֶאֱמָן אַתָּה הוּא יהוה אֱלֹהֵינוּ וְנֶאֱמָנִים דְּבָרֶיךָ, וְדָבָר אֶחָד מִדְּבָרֶיךָ אָחוֹר לֹא יָשׁוּב רֵיקָם, כִּי אֵל מֶלֶךְ נֶאֱמָן (וְרַחֲמָן) אָתָּה. בָּרוּךְ אַתָּה יהוה, הָאֵל הַנֶּאֱמָן בְּכָל דְּבָרָיו.

רַחֵם עַל צִיּוֹן כִּי הִיא בֵּית חַיֵּינוּ, וְלַעֲלוּבַת נֶפֶשׁ תּוֹשִׁיעַ בִּמְהֵרָה בְיָמֵינוּ. בָּרוּךְ אַתָּה יהוה, מְשַׂמֵּחַ צִיּוֹן בְּבָנֶיהָ.

שַׂמְּחֵנוּ יהוה אֱלֹהֵינוּ בְּאֵלִיָּהוּ הַנָּבִיא עַבְדֶּךָ, וּבְמַלְכוּת בֵּית דָּוִד מְשִׁיחֶךָ, בִּמְהֵרָה יָבוֹא וְיָגֵל לִבֵּנוּ. עַל כִּסְאוֹ לֹא יֵשֵׁב זָר, וְלֹא יִנְחֲלוּ עוֹד אֲחֵרִים אֶת כְּבוֹדוֹ, כִּי בְשֵׁם קָדְשְׁךָ נִשְׁבַּעְתָּ לּוֹ שֶׁלֹּא יִכְבֶּה נֵרוֹ לְעוֹלָם וָעֶד. בָּרוּךְ אַתָּה יהוה, מָגֵן דָּוִד.

On שבת*, add the words in parentheses:*

עַל הַתּוֹרָה וְעַל הָעֲבוֹדָה וְעַל הַנְּבִיאִים (וְעַל יוֹם הַשַּׁבָּת הַזֶּה), וְעַל יוֹם הַשְּׁמִינִי חַג הָעֲצֶרֶת הַזֶּה שֶׁנָּתַתָּ לָּנוּ יהוה אֱלֹהֵינוּ (לִקְדֻשָּׁה וְלִמְנוּחָה) לְשָׂשׂוֹן וּלְשִׂמְחָה, לְכָבוֹד וּלְתִפְאָרֶת. עַל הַכֹּל יהוה אֱלֹהֵינוּ אֲנַחְנוּ מוֹדִים לָךְ וּמְבָרְכִים אוֹתָךְ, יִתְבָּרַךְ שִׁמְךָ בְּפִי כָּל חַי תָּמִיד לְעוֹלָם וָעֶד. בָּרוּךְ אַתָּה יהוה, מְקַדֵּשׁ (הַשַּׁבָּת וְ)יִשְׂרָאֵל וְהַזְּמַנִּים.

On a weekday, the service continues with the various prayers for government on page 1115.

On שבת *continue:*

יְקוּם פֻּרְקָן מִן שְׁמַיָּא, חִנָּא וְחִסְדָּא וְרַחֲמֵי וְחַיֵּי אֲרִיכֵי וּמְזוֹנֵי רְוִיחֵי, וְסִיַּעְתָּא דִשְׁמַיָּא, וּבַרְיוּת גּוּפָא וּנְהוֹרָא מְעַלְיָא, זַרְעָא חַיָּא וְקַיָּמָא,

health and enlightenment of mind, living and thriving children who will neither interrupt nor cease from the words of the Torah – to our masters and teachers of the holy communities in the land of Israel and Babylon; to the leaders of assemblies and the leaders of communities in exile; to the heads of academies and to the judges in the gates; to all their disciples and their disciples' disciples, and to all who occupy themselves in study of the Torah. May the King of the Universe bless them, prolonging their lives, increasing their days, and adding to their years. May they be redeemed and delivered from all distress and illness. May our Master in heaven be their help at all times and seasons; and let us say: Amen.

יְקוּם פֻּרְקָן May deliverance arise from heaven, bringing grace, love and compassion, long life, ample sustenance and heavenly help, physical health and enlightenment of mind, living and thriving children who will neither interrupt nor cease from the words of the Torah – to all this holy congregation, great and small, women and children. May the King of the Universe bless you, prolonging your lives, increasing your days, and adding to your years. May you be redeemed and delivered from all distress and illness. May our Master in heaven be your help at all times and seasons; and let us say: Amen.

מִי שֶׁבֵּרַךְ May He who blessed our fathers, Abraham, Isaac and Jacob, bless all this holy congregation, together with all other holy congregations: them, their wives, their sons and daughters, and all that is theirs. May He bless those who unite to form synagogues for prayer and those who come there to pray; those who provide lamps for light and wine for Kiddush and Havdala, food for visitors and charity for the poor, and all who faithfully occupy themselves with the needs of the community. May the Holy One, blessed be He, give them their reward; may He remove from them all illness, grant them complete healing, and forgive all their sins. May He send blessing and success to all the work of their hands, together with all Israel their brethren; and let us say: Amen.

זַרְעָא דִּי לָא יִפְסֻק וְדִי לָא יִבְטֻל מִפִּתְגָּמֵי אוֹרַיְתָא, לְמָרָנָן וְרַבָּנָן חֲבוּרָתָא קַדִּישָׁתָא דִּי בְאַרְעָא דְיִשְׂרָאֵל וְדִי בְבָבֶל, לְרֵישֵׁי כַלָּה, וּלְרֵישֵׁי גַלְוָתָא, וּלְרֵישֵׁי מְתִיבָתָא, וּלְדַיָּנֵי דְבָבָא, לְכָל תַּלְמִידֵיהוֹן, וּלְכָל תַּלְמִידֵי תַלְמִידֵיהוֹן, וּלְכָל מָאן דְּעָסְקִין בְּאוֹרַיְתָא. מַלְכָּא דְעָלְמָא יְבָרֵךְ יָתְהוֹן, יַפֵּשׁ חַיֵּיהוֹן וְיַסְגֵּא יוֹמֵיהוֹן, וְיִתֵּן אַרְכָא לִשְׁנֵיהוֹן, וְיִתְפָּרְקוּן וְיִשְׁתֵּיזְבוּן מִן כָּל עָקָא וּמִן כָּל מַרְעִין בִּישִׁין. מָרַן דִּי בִשְׁמַיָּא יְהֵא בְסַעְדְּהוֹן כָּל זְמַן וְעִדָּן, וְנֹאמַר אָמֵן.

יְקוּם פֻּרְקָן מִן שְׁמַיָּא, חִנָּא וְחִסְדָּא וְרַחֲמֵי וְחַיֵּי אֲרִיכֵי וּמְזוֹנֵי רְוִיחֵי, וְסִיַּעְתָּא דִשְׁמַיָּא, וּבַרְיוּת גּוּפָא וּנְהוֹרָא מְעַלְּיָא, זַרְעָא חַיָּא וְקַיָּמָא, זַרְעָא דִּי לָא יִפְסֻק וְדִי לָא יִבְטֻל מִפִּתְגָּמֵי אוֹרַיְתָא, לְכָל קְהָלָא קַדִּישָׁא הָדֵין, רַבְרְבַיָּא עִם זְעֵרַיָּא, טַפְלָא וּנְשַׁיָּא. מַלְכָּא דְעָלְמָא יְבָרֵךְ יָתְכוֹן, יַפֵּשׁ חַיֵּיכוֹן וְיַסְגֵּא יוֹמֵיכוֹן, וְיִתֵּן אַרְכָא לִשְׁנֵיכוֹן, וְתִתְפָּרְקוּן וְתִשְׁתֵּיזְבוּן מִן כָּל עָקָא וּמִן כָּל מַרְעִין בִּישִׁין. מָרַן דִּי בִשְׁמַיָּא יְהֵא בְסַעְדְּכוֹן כָּל זְמַן וְעִדָּן, וְנֹאמַר אָמֵן.

מִי שֶׁבֵּרַךְ אֲבוֹתֵינוּ אַבְרָהָם יִצְחָק וְיַעֲקֹב, הוּא יְבָרֵךְ אֶת כָּל הַקָּהָל הַקָּדוֹשׁ הַזֶּה עִם כָּל קְהִלּוֹת הַקֹּדֶשׁ, הֵם וּנְשֵׁיהֶם וּבְנֵיהֶם וּבְנוֹתֵיהֶם וְכָל אֲשֶׁר לָהֶם, וּמִי שֶׁמְּיַחֲדִים בָּתֵּי כְנֵסִיּוֹת לִתְפִלָּה, וּמִי שֶׁבָּאִים בְּתוֹכָם לְהִתְפַּלֵּל, וּמִי שֶׁנּוֹתְנִים נֵר לַמָּאוֹר וְיַיִן לְקִדּוּשׁ וּלְהַבְדָּלָה וּפַת לָאוֹרְחִים וּצְדָקָה לָעֲנִיִּים, וְכָל מִי שֶׁעוֹסְקִים בְּצָרְכֵי צִבּוּר בֶּאֱמוּנָה. הַקָּדוֹשׁ בָּרוּךְ הוּא יְשַׁלֵּם שְׂכָרָם, וְיָסִיר מֵהֶם כָּל מַחֲלָה, וְיִרְפָּא לְכָל גּוּפָם, וְיִסְלַח לְכָל עֲוֹנָם, וְיִשְׁלַח בְּרָכָה וְהַצְלָחָה בְּכָל מַעֲשֵׂי יְדֵיהֶם עִם כָּל יִשְׂרָאֵל אֲחֵיהֶם, וְנֹאמַר אָמֵן.

The Prayer for the Welfare of the Canadian Government is on the next page.

PRAYER FOR THE WELFARE OF THE AMERICAN GOVERNMENT

The Leader says the following:

הַנּוֹתֵן תְּשׁוּעָה May He who gives salvation to kings and dominion to princes, whose kingdom is an everlasting kingdom, who delivers His servant David from the evil sword, who makes a way in the sea and a path through the mighty waters, bless and protect, guard and help, exalt, magnify and uplift the President, Vice President and all officials of this land. May the Supreme King of kings in His mercy put into their hearts and the hearts of all their counselors and officials, to deal kindly with us and all Israel. In their days and in ours, may Judah be saved and Israel dwell in safety, and may the Redeemer come to Zion. May this be His will, and let us say: Amen.

PRAYER FOR THE SAFETY OF THE AMERICAN MILITARY FORCES

The Leader says the following:

אַדִּיר בַּמָּרוֹם God on high who dwells in might, the King to whom peace belongs, look down from Your holy habitation and bless the soldiers of the American military forces who risk their lives for the sake of peace on earth. Be their shelter and stronghold, and let them not falter. Give them the strength and courage to thwart the plans of the enemy and end the rule of evil. May their enemies be scattered and their foes flee before them, and may they rejoice in Your salvation. Bring them back safely to their homes, as is written: "The LORD will guard you from all harm, He will guard your life. *Ps. 121* The LORD will guard your going and coming, now and for evermore." And may there be fulfilled for us the verse: "Nation shall not *Is. 2* lift up sword against nation, nor shall they learn war any more." Let all the inhabitants on earth know that sovereignty is Yours and Your name inspires awe over all You have created – and let us say: Amen.

The Prayer for the Welfare of the Canadian Government is on the next page.

תפילה לשלום המלכות (ארה״ב)

The שליח ציבור *says the following:*

הַנּוֹתֵן תְּשׁוּעָה לַמְּלָכִים וּמֶמְשָׁלָה לַנְּסִיכִים, מַלְכוּתוֹ מַלְכוּת כָּל עוֹלָמִים, הַפּוֹצֶה אֶת דָּוִד עַבְדּוֹ מֵחֶרֶב רָעָה, הַנּוֹתֵן בַּיָּם דֶּרֶךְ וּבְמַיִם עַזִּים נְתִיבָה, הוּא יְבָרֵךְ וְיִשְׁמֹר וְיִנְצֹר וְיַעֲזֹר וִירוֹמֵם וִיגַדֵּל וִינַשֵּׂא לְמַעְלָה אֶת הַנָּשִׂיא וְאֵת מִשְׁנֵהוּ וְאֶת כָּל שָׂרֵי הָאָרֶץ הַזֹּאת. מֶלֶךְ מַלְכֵי הַמְּלָכִים, בְּרַחֲמָיו יִתֵּן בְּלִבָּם וּבְלֵב כָּל יוֹעֲצֵיהֶם וְשָׂרֵיהֶם לַעֲשׂוֹת טוֹבָה עִמָּנוּ וְעִם כָּל יִשְׂרָאֵל. בִּימֵיהֶם וּבְיָמֵינוּ תִּוָּשַׁע יְהוּדָה, וְיִשְׂרָאֵל יִשְׁכֹּן לָבֶטַח, וּבָא לְצִיּוֹן גּוֹאֵל. וְכֵן יְהִי רָצוֹן, וְנֹאמַר אָמֵן.

תפילה לשלום חיילי צבא ארצות הברית

The שליח ציבור *says the following:*

אַדִּיר בַּמָּרוֹם שׁוֹכֵן בִּגְבוּרָה, מֶלֶךְ שֶׁהַשָּׁלוֹם שֶׁלּוֹ, הַשְׁקִיפָה מִמְּעוֹן קָדְשְׁךָ, וּבָרֵךְ אֶת חַיָּלֵי צְבָא אַרְצוֹת הַבְּרִית, הַמְחָרְפִים נַפְשָׁם בְּלֶכְתָּם לָשִׂים שָׁלוֹם בָּאָרֶץ. הֱיֵה נָא לָהֶם מַחֲסֶה וּמָעוֹז, וְאַל תִּתֵּן לַמּוֹט רַגְלָם, חַזֵּק יְדֵיהֶם וְאַמֵּץ רוּחָם לְהָפֵר עֲצַת אוֹיֵב וּלְהַעֲבִיר מֶמְשֶׁלֶת זָדוֹן, יָפוּצוּ אוֹיְבֵיהֶם וְיָנוּסוּ מְשַׂנְאֵיהֶם מִפָּנֵיהֶם, וְיִשְׂמְחוּ בִּישׁוּעָתֶךָ. הֲשִׁיבֵם בְּשָׁלוֹם אֶל בֵּיתָם, כַּכָּתוּב בְּדִבְרֵי קָדְשֶׁךָ:
יהוה יִשְׁמָרְךָ מִכָּל־רָע, יִשְׁמֹר אֶת־נַפְשֶׁךָ: יהוה יִשְׁמָר־צֵאתְךָ תהלים קכא
וּבוֹאֶךָ, מֵעַתָּה וְעַד־עוֹלָם: וְקַיֵּם בָּנוּ מִקְרָא שֶׁכָּתוּב: לֹא־יִשָּׂא גוֹי ישעיה ב
אֶל־גּוֹי חֶרֶב, וְלֹא־יִלְמְדוּ עוֹד מִלְחָמָה: וְיֵדְעוּ כָּל יוֹשְׁבֵי תֵבֵל כִּי לְךָ מְלוּכָה יָאֲתָה, וְשִׁמְךָ נוֹרָא עַל כָּל מַה שֶּׁבָּרָאתָ. וְנֹאמַר אָמֵן.

PRAYER FOR THE WELFARE OF THE CANADIAN GOVERNMENT

The Leader says the following:

הַנּוֹתֵן תְּשׁוּעָה May He who gives salvation to kings and dominion to princes, whose kingdom is an everlasting kingdom, who delivers His servant David from the evil sword, who makes a way in the sea and a path through the mighty waters, bless and protect, guard and help, exalt, magnify and uplift the Prime Minister and all the elected and appointed officials of Canada. May the Supreme King of kings in His mercy put into their hearts and the hearts of all their counselors and officials, to deal kindly with us and all Israel. In their days and in ours, may Judah be saved and Israel dwell in safety, and may the Redeemer come to Zion. May this be His will, and let us say: Amen.

PRAYER FOR THE SAFETY OF THE CANADIAN FORCES

The Leader says the following:

אַדִּיר בַּמָּרוֹם God on high who dwells in might, the King to whom peace belongs, look down from Your holy habitation and bless the soldiers of the Canadian Forces who risk their lives for the sake of peace on earth. Be their shelter and stronghold, and let them not falter. Give them the strength and courage to thwart the plans of the enemy and end the rule of evil. May their enemies be scattered and their foes flee before them, and may they rejoice in Your salvation. Bring them back safely to their homes, as is
written: "The LORD will guard you from all harm, He will guard *Ps. 121*
your life. The LORD will guard your going and coming, now and
for evermore." And may there be fulfilled for us the verse: "Nation *Is. 2*
shall not lift up sword against nation, nor shall they learn war any more." Let all the inhabitants on earth know that sovereignty is Yours and Your name inspires awe over all You have created – and let us say: Amen.

תפילה לשלום המלכות (קנדה)

The שליח ציבור *says the following:*

הַנּוֹתֵן תְּשׁוּעָה לַמְּלָכִים וּמֶמְשָׁלָה לַנְּסִיכִים, מַלְכוּתוֹ מַלְכוּת כָּל עוֹלָמִים, הַפּוֹצֶה אֶת דָּוִד עַבְדּוֹ מֵחֶרֶב רָעָה, הַנּוֹתֵן בַּיָּם דֶּרֶךְ וּבְמַיִם עַזִּים נְתִיבָה, הוּא יְבָרֵךְ וְיִשְׁמֹר וְיִנְצֹר וְיַעֲזֹר וִירוֹמֵם וִיגַדֵּל וִינַשֵּׂא לְמַעְלָה אֶת רֹאשׁ הַמֶּמְשָׁלָה וְאֶת כָּל שָׂרֵי הָאָרֶץ הַזֹּאת. מֶלֶךְ מַלְכֵי הַמְּלָכִים, בְּרַחֲמָיו יִתֵּן בְּלִבָּם וּבְלֵב כָּל יוֹעֲצֵיהֶם וְשָׂרֵיהֶם לַעֲשׂוֹת טוֹבָה עִמָּנוּ וְעִם כָּל יִשְׂרָאֵל. בִּימֵיהֶם וּבְיָמֵינוּ תִּוָּשַׁע יְהוּדָה, וְיִשְׂרָאֵל יִשְׁכֹּן לָבֶטַח, וּבָא לְצִיּוֹן גּוֹאֵל. וְכֵן יְהִי רָצוֹן, וְנֹאמַר אָמֵן.

תפילה לשלום חיילי צבא קנדה

The שליח ציבור *says the following:*

אַדִּיר בַּמָּרוֹם שׁוֹכֵן בִּגְבוּרָה, מֶלֶךְ שֶׁהַשָּׁלוֹם שֶׁלּוֹ, הַשְׁקִיפָה מִמְּעוֹן קָדְשְׁךָ, וּבָרֵךְ אֶת חַיָּלֵי צְבָא קָנָדָה, הַמְחָרְפִים נַפְשָׁם בְּלֶכְתָּם לָשִׂים שָׁלוֹם בָּאָרֶץ. הֱיֵה נָא לָהֶם מַחֲסֶה וּמָעוֹז, וְאַל תִּתֵּן לַמּוֹט רַגְלָם, חַזֵּק יְדֵיהֶם וְאַמֵּץ רוּחָם לְהָפֵר עֲצַת אוֹיֵב וּלְהַעֲבִיר מֶמְשֶׁלֶת זָדוֹן, יָפֽוּצוּ אוֹיְבֵיהֶם וְיָנֽוּסוּ מְשַׂנְאֵיהֶם מִפְּנֵיהֶם, וְיִשְׂמְחוּ בִּישׁוּעָתֶךָ. הֲשִׁיבֵם בְּשָׁלוֹם אֶל בֵּיתָם, כַּכָּתוּב
בְּדִבְרֵי קָדְשֶׁךָ: יהוה יִשְׁמָרְךָ מִכָּל־רָע, יִשְׁמֹר אֶת־נַפְשֶׁךָ: יהוה תהלים קכא
יִשְׁמָר־צֵאתְךָ וּבוֹאֶךָ, מֵעַתָּה וְעַד־עוֹלָם: וְקַיֵּם בָּנוּ מִקְרָא
שֶׁכָּתוּב: לֹא־יִשָּׂא גוֹי אֶל־גּוֹי חֶרֶב, וְלֹא־יִלְמְדוּ עוֹד מִלְחָמָה: ישעיה ב
וְיֵדְעוּ כָּל יוֹשְׁבֵי תֵבֵל כִּי לְךָ מְלוּכָה יָאֲתָה, וְשִׁמְךָ נוֹרָא עַל כָּל מַה שֶּׁבָּרָאתָ. וְנֹאמַר אָמֵן.

PRAYER FOR THE STATE OF ISRAEL

The Leader says the following prayer:

אָבִינוּ שֶׁבַּשָּׁמַיִם Heavenly Father, Israel's Rock and Redeemer, bless the State of Israel, the first flowering of our redemption. Shield it under the wings of Your loving-kindness and spread over it the Tabernacle of Your peace. Send Your light and truth to its leaders, ministers and counselors, and direct them with good counsel before You.

Strengthen the hands of the defenders of our Holy Land; grant them deliverance, our God, and crown them with the crown of victory. Grant peace in the land and everlasting joy to its inhabitants.

As for our brothers, the whole house of Israel, remember them in all the lands of our (*In Israel say:* their) dispersion, and swiftly lead us (*In Israel say:* them) upright to Zion Your city, and Jerusalem Your dwelling place, as is written in the Torah of Moses Your servant: "Even if you are scattered to the furthermost lands under the heavens, from there the LORD your God will gather you and take you back. The LORD your God will bring you to the land your ancestors possessed and you will possess it; and He will make you more prosperous and numerous than your ancestors. Then the LORD your God will open up your heart and the heart of your descendants, to love the LORD your God with all your heart and with all your soul, that you may live." *Deut. 30*

Unite our hearts to love and revere Your name and observe all the words of Your Torah, and swiftly send us Your righteous anointed one of the house of David, to redeem those who long for Your salvation.

Appear in Your glorious majesty over all the dwellers on earth, and let all who breathe declare: The LORD God of Israel is King and His kingship has dominion over all. Amen, Selah.

תפילה לשלום מדינת ישראל

The שליח ציבור *says the following prayer:*

אָבִינוּ שֶׁבַּשָּׁמַיִם, צוּר יִשְׂרָאֵל וְגוֹאֲלוֹ, בָּרֵךְ אֶת מְדִינַת יִשְׂרָאֵל, רֵאשִׁית צְמִיחַת גְּאֻלָּתֵנוּ. הָגֵן עָלֶיהָ בְּאֶבְרַת חַסְדֶּךָ וּפְרֹשׂ עָלֶיהָ סֻכַּת שְׁלוֹמֶךָ, וּשְׁלַח אוֹרְךָ וַאֲמִתְּךָ לְרָאשֶׁיהָ, שָׂרֶיהָ וְיוֹעֲצֶיהָ, וְתַקְּנֵם בְּעֵצָה טוֹבָה מִלְּפָנֶיךָ.

חַזֵּק אֶת יְדֵי מְגִנֵּי אֶרֶץ קָדְשֵׁנוּ, וְהַנְחִילֵם אֱלֹהֵינוּ יְשׁוּעָה וַעֲטֶרֶת נִצָּחוֹן תְּעַטְּרֵם, וְנָתַתָּ שָׁלוֹם בָּאָרֶץ וְשִׂמְחַת עוֹלָם לְיוֹשְׁבֶיהָ.

וְאֶת אַחֵינוּ כָּל בֵּית יִשְׂרָאֵל, פְּקָד נָא בְּכָל אַרְצוֹת פְּזוּרֵינוּ, וְתוֹלִיכֵנוּ / בארץ ישראל: פְּזוּרֵיהֶם, וְתוֹלִיכֵם/ מְהֵרָה קוֹמְמִיּוּת לְצִיּוֹן עִירֶךָ וְלִירוּשָׁלַיִם מִשְׁכַּן שְׁמֶךָ, כַּכָּתוּב בְּתוֹרַת מֹשֶׁה עַבְדֶּךָ:
אִם־יִהְיֶה נִדַּחֲךָ בִּקְצֵה הַשָּׁמָיִם, מִשָּׁם יְקַבֶּצְךָ יהוה אֱלֹהֶיךָ דברים ל
וּמִשָּׁם יִקָּחֶךָ: וֶהֱבִיאֲךָ יהוה אֱלֹהֶיךָ אֶל־הָאָרֶץ אֲשֶׁר־יָרְשׁוּ אֲבֹתֶיךָ וִירִשְׁתָּהּ, וְהֵיטִבְךָ וְהִרְבְּךָ מֵאֲבֹתֶיךָ: וּמָל יהוה אֱלֹהֶיךָ אֶת־לְבָבְךָ וְאֶת־לְבַב זַרְעֶךָ, לְאַהֲבָה אֶת־יהוה אֱלֹהֶיךָ בְּכָל־לְבָבְךָ וּבְכָל־נַפְשְׁךָ, לְמַעַן חַיֶּיךָ:

וְיַחֵד לְבָבֵנוּ לְאַהֲבָה וּלְיִרְאָה אֶת שְׁמֶךָ, וְלִשְׁמֹר אֶת כָּל דִּבְרֵי תוֹרָתֶךָ, וּשְׁלַח לָנוּ מְהֵרָה בֶּן דָּוִד מְשִׁיחַ צִדְקֶךָ, לִפְדּוֹת מְחַכֵּי קֵץ יְשׁוּעָתֶךָ.

וְהוֹפַע בַּהֲדַר גְּאוֹן עֻזֶּךָ עַל כָּל יוֹשְׁבֵי תֵּבֵל אַרְצֶךָ וְיֹאמַר כֹּל אֲשֶׁר נְשָׁמָה בְאַפּוֹ, יהוה אֱלֹהֵי יִשְׂרָאֵל מֶלֶךְ וּמַלְכוּתוֹ בַּכֹּל מָשָׁלָה, אָמֵן סֶלָה.

PRAYER FOR ISRAEL'S DEFENSE FORCES

The Leader says the following prayer:

מִי שֶׁבֵּרַךְ May He who blessed our ancestors, Abraham, Isaac and Jacob, bless the members of Israel's Defense Forces and its security services who stand guard over our land and the cities of our God from the Lebanese border to the Egyptian desert, from the Mediterranean sea to the approach of the Aravah, and wherever else they are, on land, in air and at sea. May the LORD make the enemies who rise against us be struck down before them. May the Holy One, blessed be He, protect and deliver them from all trouble and distress, affliction and illness, and send blessing and success to all the work of their hands. May He subdue our enemies under them and crown them with deliverance and victory. And may there be fulfilled in them the verse, "It is the LORD your God who goes with you to fight *Deut. 20*
for you against your enemies, to deliver you." And let us say: Amen.

PRAYER FOR THOSE BEING HELD IN CAPTIVITY

If Israeli soldiers or civilians are being held in captivity, the Leader says the following:

מִי שֶׁבֵּרַךְ May He who blessed our ancestors, Abraham, Isaac and Jacob, Joseph, Moses and Aaron, David and Solomon, bless, protect and guard the members of Israel's Defense Forces missing in action or held captive, and other captives among our brethren, the whole house of Israel, who are in distress or captivity, as we, the members of this holy congregation, pray on their behalf. May the Holy One, blessed be He, have compassion on them and bring them out from darkness and the shadow of death; may He break their bonds, deliver them from their distress, and bring them swiftly back to their families' embrace. Give *Ps. 107*
thanks to the LORD for His loving-kindness and for the wonders He does for the children of men; and may there be fulfilled in them the verse: "Those redeemed by the LORD will return; they will enter Zion *Is. 35*
with singing, and everlasting joy will crown their heads. Gladness and joy will overtake them, and sorrow and sighing will flee away." And let us say: Amen.

מי שברך לחיילי צה״ל

The שליח ציבור *says the following prayer:*

מִי שֶׁבֵּרַךְ אֲבוֹתֵינוּ אַבְרָהָם יִצְחָק וְיַעֲקֹב הוּא יְבָרֵךְ אֶת חַיָּלֵי צְבָא הַהֲגָנָה לְיִשְׂרָאֵל וְאַנְשֵׁי כֹּחוֹת הַבִּטָּחוֹן, הָעוֹמְדִים עַל מִשְׁמַר אַרְצֵנוּ וְעָרֵי אֱלֹהֵינוּ, מִגְּבוּל הַלְּבָנוֹן וְעַד מִדְבַּר מִצְרַיִם וּמִן הַיָּם הַגָּדוֹל עַד לְבוֹא הָעֲרָבָה וּבְכָל מָקוֹם שֶׁהֵם, בַּיַּבָּשָׁה, בָּאֲוִיר וּבַיָּם. יִתֵּן יהוה אֶת אוֹיְבֵינוּ הַקָּמִים עָלֵינוּ נִגָּפִים לִפְנֵיהֶם. הַקָּדוֹשׁ בָּרוּךְ הוּא יִשְׁמֹר וְיַצִּיל אֶת חַיָּלֵינוּ מִכָּל צָרָה וְצוּקָה וּמִכָּל נֶגַע וּמַחֲלָה, וְיִשְׁלַח בְּרָכָה וְהַצְלָחָה בְּכָל מַעֲשֵׂי יְדֵיהֶם. יַדְבֵּר שׂוֹנְאֵינוּ תַּחְתֵּיהֶם וִיעַטְּרֵם בְּכֶתֶר יְשׁוּעָה וּבַעֲטֶרֶת נִצָּחוֹן.
דברים כ וִיקֻיַּם בָּהֶם הַכָּתוּב: כִּי יהוה אֱלֹהֵיכֶם הַהֹלֵךְ עִמָּכֶם לְהִלָּחֵם לָכֶם עִם־אֹיְבֵיכֶם לְהוֹשִׁיעַ אֶתְכֶם: וְנֹאמַר אָמֵן.

מי שברך לשבויים

If Israeli soldiers or civilians are being held in captivity, the שליח ציבור *says the following:*

מִי שֶׁבֵּרַךְ אֲבוֹתֵינוּ אַבְרָהָם יִצְחָק וְיַעֲקֹב, יוֹסֵף מֹשֶׁה וְאַהֲרֹן, דָּוִד וּשְׁלֹמֹה, הוּא יְבָרֵךְ וְיִשְׁמֹר וְיִנְצֹר אֶת נֶעְדְּרֵי צְבָא הַהֲגָנָה לְיִשְׂרָאֵל וּשְׁבוּיָו, וְאֶת כָּל אַחֵינוּ הַנְּתוּנִים בְּצָרָה וּבְשִׁבְיָה, בַּעֲבוּר שֶׁכָּל הַקָּהָל הַקָּדוֹשׁ הַזֶּה מִתְפַּלֵּל בַּעֲבוּרָם. הַקָּדוֹשׁ בָּרוּךְ הוּא יִמָּלֵא רַחֲמִים עֲלֵיהֶם, וְיוֹצִיאֵם מֵחֹשֶׁךְ וְצַלְמָוֶת, וּמוֹסְרוֹתֵיהֶם יְנַתֵּק, וּמִמְּצוּקוֹתֵיהֶם יוֹשִׁיעֵם, וִישִׁיבֵם מְהֵרָה
תהלים קז לְחֵיק מִשְׁפְּחוֹתֵיהֶם. יוֹדוּ לַיהוה חַסְדּוֹ וְנִפְלְאוֹתָיו לִבְנֵי אָדָם:
ישעיה לה וִיקֻיַּם בָּהֶם מִקְרָא שֶׁכָּתוּב: וּפְדוּיֵי יהוה יְשֻׁבוּן, וּבָאוּ צִיּוֹן בְּרִנָּה, וְשִׂמְחַת עוֹלָם עַל־רֹאשָׁם, שָׂשׂוֹן וְשִׂמְחָה יַשִּׂיגוּ, וְנָסוּ יָגוֹן וַאֲנָחָה: וְנֹאמַר אָמֵן.

YIZKOR

On Shemini Atzeret (in Israel on Simḥat Torah), the Yizkor (memorial) service is said.
In some communities, those who have not been bereaved of a parent or close relative do not participate in the service, but leave the synagogue and return for "Father of compassion" on page 1128.

יהוה LORD, what is man that You care for him, a mortal that You notice him? *Ps. 144*
Man is like a fleeting breath, his days like a passing shadow.
In the morning he flourishes and grows; *Ps. 90*
in the evening he withers and dries up.
Teach us to number our days, that we may get a heart of wisdom.
Mark the blameless, note the upright, for the end of such a person is peace. *Ps. 37*
God will redeem my soul from the grave, for He will receive me, Selah. *Ps. 49*
My flesh and my heart may fail, *Ps. 73*
but God is the strength of my heart and my portion for ever.
The dust returns to the earth as it was, *Eccl. 12*
but the spirit returns to God who gave it.

---

for the sake of the future. This can be seen in the three cases in which the word *Yizkor* appears in connection with God in Genesis. God "remembered Noah" (8:1) and brought him out onto dry land. God "remembered Abraham" (19:29) and rescued his nephew Lot from the destruction of Sodom. God "remembered Rachel" (30:22) and gave her a child. In each case the act of remembering was for the sake of the future and of life.

Judaism gave two majestic ideas their greatest religious expression: *memory* and *hope*. Memory is our living connection to those who came before us. Hope is what we hand on to the generations yet to come. Those we remember live on in us: in words, gestures, a smile here, an act of kindness there, that we would not have done had that person not left their mark on our lives. That is what *Yizkor* is: memory as a religious act of thanksgiving for a life that was, and that still sends its echoes and reverberations into the life that is. For when Jews remember, they do so for the future, the place where, if we are faithful to it, the past never dies.

PRAYER FOR LIVING RELATIVES

Our Father in heaven: On this holy day, I give You thanks for my [father / mother / husband / wife / brother(s) / sister(s) / son(s) / daughter(s) / grandchild(ren)] who are with me in life, and for whose continued health and blessing I pray. Be with them, I pray You, in the days and months to come. Protect them from harm and distress, sickness and affliction, trouble

סדר הזכרת נשמות

On שמיני עצרת *(in* ארץ ישראל *on* שמחת תורה*), the* יזכור *(memorial) service is said.*
In some communities, those who have not been bereaved of a parent or close relative do not participate in the service, but leave the בית כנסת *and return for* אב הרחמים *on page 1129.*

יהוה מָה־אָדָם וַתֵּדָעֵהוּ, בֶּן־אֱנוֹשׁ וַתְּחַשְּׁבֵהוּ: תהלים קמד
אָדָם לַהֶבֶל דָּמָה, יָמָיו כְּצֵל עוֹבֵר:
בַּבֹּקֶר יָצִיץ וְחָלָף, לָעֶרֶב יְמוֹלֵל וְיָבֵשׁ: תהלים צ
לִמְנוֹת יָמֵינוּ כֵּן הוֹדַע, וְנָבִא לְבַב חָכְמָה:
שְׁמָר־תָּם וּרְאֵה יָשָׁר, כִּי־אַחֲרִית לְאִישׁ שָׁלוֹם: תהלים לז
אַךְ־אֱלֹהִים יִפְדֶּה נַפְשִׁי מִיַּד שְׁאוֹל, כִּי יִקָּחֵנִי סֶלָה: תהלים מט
כָּלָה שְׁאֵרִי וּלְבָבִי, צוּר־לְבָבִי וְחֶלְקִי אֱלֹהִים לְעוֹלָם: תהלים עג
וְיָשֹׁב הֶעָפָר עַל־הָאָרֶץ כְּשֶׁהָיָה, וְהָרְוּחַ תָּשׁוּב אֶל־הָאֱלֹהִים אֲשֶׁר נְתָנָהּ: קהלת יב

YIZKOR

From the eleventh century onward it has become customary to pray, at key moments in the year, for the souls of the departed. At first, this prayer was said only on Yom Kippur, but it was soon extended to the last days of the other festivals.

The formal name for this prayer is *Hazkarat Neshamot*, "the Remembrance of Souls," but it became popularly known as *Yizkor* because of the first word of the memorial prayer. Remembrance holds a special place in the Jewish soul. Jews were the first people to regard remembering as a religious duty. The verb "to remember" in one or other of its forms occurs 169 times in Tanakh.

At *Yizkor*, our memory reaches out to that of God. We ask Him to remember those of our family who are no longer here. We ask Him to look on the good we do, for it is because of their influence on us that we are in the synagogue; that we pray, and that we try to do good in this life. Hence it is a custom to donate a sum to charity at this time and dedicate it to the memory and merit of the departed ones. Nowadays, we also add prayers for the Jewish martyrs of the past and for the victims of the Holocaust, as well as those who went to their deaths defending the State of Israel, for we collectively are the guardians of their memory. A connection is thus made between the dead and the living. We remember them, and with God's help, their virtues live on in us. That is as much of immortality as we can know in the land of the living.

In Judaism we remember not just for the past but also, and especially,

יֹשֵׁב He who lives in the shelter of the Most High dwells in the shadow of the Almighty. I say of the LORD, my Refuge and Stronghold, my God in whom I trust, that He will save you from the fowler's snare and the deadly pestilence. With His pinions He will cover you, and beneath His wings you will find shelter; His faithfulness is an encircling shield. You need not fear terror by night, nor the arrow that flies by day; not the pestilence that stalks in darkness, nor the plague that ravages at noon. A thousand may fall at your side, ten thousand at your right hand, but it will not come near you. You will only look with your eyes and see the punishment of the wicked. Because you said, "the LORD is my Refuge," taking the Most High as your shelter, no harm will befall you, no plague will come near your tent, for He will command His angels about you, to guard you in all your ways. They will lift you in their hands, lest your foot stumble on a stone. You will tread on lions and vipers; you will trample on young lions and snakes. [God says:] "Because he loves Me, I will rescue him; I will protect him, because he acknowledges My name. When he calls on Me, I will answer him; I will be with him in distress, I will deliver him and bring him honor. With long life I will satisfy him and show him My salvation. With long life I will satisfy him and show him My salvation. *Ps. 91*

For one's father:

יִזְכֹּר May God remember the soul of my father, my teacher (*name* son of *father's name*) who has gone to his eternal home, and to this I pledge (without formal vow) to give charity on his behalf, that his soul may be bound in the bond of everlasting life together with the souls of Abraham, Isaac and Jacob, Sarah, Rebecca, Rachel and Leah, and all the other righteous men and women in the Garden of Eden, and let us say: Amen.

For one's mother:

יִזְכֹּר May God remember the soul of my mother, my teacher (*name* daughter of *father's name*) who has gone to her eternal home, and to this I pledge (without formal vow) to give charity on her behalf, that her soul may be bound in the bond of everlasting life together with the souls of Abraham, Isaac and Jacob, Sarah, Rebecca, Rachel and Leah, and all the other righteous men and women in the Garden of Eden, and let us say: Amen.

---

the words of my mouth and the meditation of my heart find favor before You, my Rock and Redeemer.

יֹשֵׁב בְּסֵתֶר עֶלְיוֹן, בְּצֵל שַׁדַּי יִתְלוֹנָן: אֹמַר לַיהוה מַחְסִי וּמְצוּדָתִי, תהלים צא
אֱלֹהַי אֶבְטַח־בּוֹ: כִּי הוּא יַצִּילְךָ מִפַּח יָקוּשׁ, מִדֶּבֶר הַוּוֹת: בְּאֶבְרָתוֹ
יָסֶךְ לָךְ, וְתַחַת־כְּנָפָיו תֶּחְסֶה, צִנָּה וְסֹחֵרָה אֲמִתּוֹ: לֹא־תִירָא מִפַּחַד
לָיְלָה, מֵחֵץ יָעוּף יוֹמָם: מִדֶּבֶר בָּאֹפֶל יַהֲלֹךְ, מִקֶּטֶב יָשׁוּד צָהֳרָיִם:
יִפֹּל מִצִּדְּךָ אֶלֶף, וּרְבָבָה מִימִינֶךָ, אֵלֶיךָ לֹא יִגָּשׁ: רַק בְּעֵינֶיךָ תַבִּיט,
וְשִׁלֻּמַת רְשָׁעִים תִּרְאֶה: כִּי־אַתָּה יהוה מַחְסִי, עֶלְיוֹן שַׂמְתָּ מְעוֹנֶךָ:
לֹא־תְאֻנֶּה אֵלֶיךָ רָעָה, וְנֶגַע לֹא־יִקְרַב בְּאָהֳלֶךָ: כִּי מַלְאָכָיו יְצַוֶּה־לָּךְ,
לִשְׁמָרְךָ בְּכָל־דְּרָכֶיךָ: עַל־כַּפַּיִם יִשָּׂאוּנְךָ, פֶּן־תִּגֹּף בָּאֶבֶן רַגְלֶךָ: עַל־
שַׁחַל וָפֶתֶן תִּדְרֹךְ, תִּרְמֹס כְּפִיר וְתַנִּין: כִּי בִי חָשַׁק וַאֲפַלְּטֵהוּ, אֲשַׂגְּבֵהוּ
כִּי־יָדַע שְׁמִי: יִקְרָאֵנִי וְאֶעֱנֵהוּ, עִמּוֹ־אָנֹכִי בְצָרָה, אֲחַלְּצֵהוּ וַאֲכַבְּדֵהוּ:
אֹרֶךְ יָמִים אַשְׂבִּיעֵהוּ, וְאַרְאֵהוּ בִּישׁוּעָתִי:
אֹרֶךְ יָמִים אַשְׂבִּיעֵהוּ, וְאַרְאֵהוּ בִּישׁוּעָתִי:

For one's father:

יִזְכֹּר אֱלֹהִים נִשְׁמַת אָבִי מוֹרִי (פלוני בֶּן פלוני) שֶׁהָלַךְ לְעוֹלָמוֹ, בַּעֲבוּר שֶׁבְּלִי נֶדֶר אֶתֵּן צְדָקָה בַּעֲדוֹ. בִּשְׂכַר זֶה תְּהֵא נַפְשׁוֹ צְרוּרָה בִּצְרוֹר הַחַיִּים עִם נִשְׁמוֹת אַבְרָהָם יִצְחָק וְיַעֲקֹב, שָׂרָה רִבְקָה רָחֵל וְלֵאָה, וְעִם שְׁאָר צַדִּיקִים וְצִדְקָנִיּוֹת שֶׁבְּגַן עֵדֶן, וְנֹאמַר אָמֵן.

For one's mother:

יִזְכֹּר אֱלֹהִים נִשְׁמַת אִמִּי מוֹרָתִי (פלונית בַּת פלוני) שֶׁהָלְכָה לְעוֹלָמָהּ, בַּעֲבוּר שֶׁבְּלִי נֶדֶר אֶתֵּן צְדָקָה בַּעֲדָהּ. בִּשְׂכַר זֶה תְּהֵא נַפְשָׁהּ צְרוּרָה בִּצְרוֹר הַחַיִּים עִם נִשְׁמוֹת אַבְרָהָם יִצְחָק וְיַעֲקֹב, שָׂרָה רִבְקָה רָחֵל וְלֵאָה, וְעִם שְׁאָר צַדִּיקִים וְצִדְקָנִיּוֹת שֶׁבְּגַן עֵדֶן, וְנֹאמַר אָמֵן.

---

and misfortune. Spread over them Your canopy of peace and may Your spirit live in the work of their hands. Prolong their days in goodness and happiness and may they and we have the privilege of seeing children and grandchildren occupying themselves with Torah and the life of the commandments. May

For a male close relative:

יִזְכֹּר May God remember the soul of (my grandfather / my uncle / my brother / my son / my husband) (*name* son of *father's name*) who has gone to his eternal home, and to this I pledge (without formal vow) to give charity on his behalf, that his soul may be bound in the bond of everlasting life together with the souls of Abraham, Isaac and Jacob, Sarah, Rebecca, Rachel and Leah, and all the other righteous men and women in the Garden of Eden, and let us say: Amen.

For a female close relative:

יִזְכֹּר May God remember the soul of (my grandmother / my aunt / my sister / my daughter / my wife) (*name* daughter of *father's name*) who has gone to her eternal home, and to this I pledge (without formal vow) to give charity on her behalf, that her soul may be bound in the bond of everlasting life together with the souls of Abraham, Isaac and Jacob, Sarah, Rebecca, Rachel and Leah, and all the other righteous men and women in the Garden of Eden, and let us say: Amen.

For a male relative:

אֵל מָלֵא רַחֲמִים God, full of mercy, who dwells on high, grant fitting rest on the wings of the Divine Presence, in the heights of the holy and the pure who shine like the radiance of heaven, to the soul of (*name* son of *father's name*) who has gone to his eternal home, and to this I pledge (without formal vow) to give charity in his memory, may his resting place be in the Garden of Eden. Therefore, Master of compassion, shelter him in the shadow of Your wings forever and bind his soul in the bond of everlasting life. The LORD is his heritage; may he rest in peace, and let us say: Amen.

For a female relative:

אֵל מָלֵא רַחֲמִים God, full of mercy, who dwells on high, grant fitting rest on the wings of the Divine Presence, in the heights of the holy and the pure who shine like the radiance of heaven, to the soul of (*name* daughter of *father's name*) who has gone to her eternal home, and to this I pledge (without formal vow) to give charity in her memory, may her resting place be in the Garden of Eden. Therefore, Master of compassion, shelter her in the shadow of Your wings forever and bind her soul in the bond of everlasting life. The LORD is her heritage; may she rest in peace, and let us say: Amen.

For a male close relative:

יִזְכֹּר אֱלֹהִים נִשְׁמַת (*my grandfather* זְקֵנִי / *my uncle* דּוֹדִי / *my brother* אָחִי / *my son* בְּנִי / *my husband* בַּעֲלִי) (פלוני בֶּן פלוני) שֶׁהָלַךְ לְעוֹלָמוֹ, בַּעֲבוּר שֶׁבְּלִי נֶדֶר אֶתֵּן צְדָקָה בַּעֲדוֹ. בִּשְׂכַר זֶה תְּהֵא נַפְשׁוֹ צְרוּרָה בִּצְרוֹר הַחַיִּים עִם נִשְׁמוֹת אַבְרָהָם יִצְחָק וְיַעֲקֹב, שָׂרָה רִבְקָה רָחֵל וְלֵאָה, וְעִם שְׁאָר צַדִּיקִים וְצִדְקָנִיּוֹת שֶׁבְּגַן עֵדֶן, וְנֹאמַר אָמֵן.

For a female close relative:

יִזְכֹּר אֱלֹהִים נִשְׁמַת (*my grandmother* זְקֵנָתִי / *my aunt* דּוֹדָתִי / *my sister* אֲחוֹתִי / *my daughter* בִּתִּי / *my wife* אִשְׁתִּי) (פלונית בַּת פלוני) שֶׁהָלְכָה לְעוֹלָמָהּ, בַּעֲבוּר שֶׁבְּלִי נֶדֶר אֶתֵּן צְדָקָה בַּעֲדָהּ. בִּשְׂכַר זֶה תְּהֵא נַפְשָׁהּ צְרוּרָה בִּצְרוֹר הַחַיִּים עִם נִשְׁמוֹת אַבְרָהָם יִצְחָק וְיַעֲקֹב, שָׂרָה רִבְקָה רָחֵל וְלֵאָה, וְעִם שְׁאָר צַדִּיקִים וְצִדְקָנִיּוֹת שֶׁבְּגַן עֵדֶן, וְנֹאמַר אָמֵן.

For a male relative:

אֵל מָלֵא רַחֲמִים, שׁוֹכֵן בַּמְּרוֹמִים, הַמְצֵא מְנוּחָה נְכוֹנָה עַל כַּנְפֵי הַשְּׁכִינָה, בְּמַעֲלוֹת קְדוֹשִׁים וּטְהוֹרִים, כְּזֹהַר הָרָקִיעַ מַזְהִירִים, לְנִשְׁמַת (פלוני בֶּן פלוני) שֶׁהָלַךְ לְעוֹלָמוֹ, בַּעֲבוּר שֶׁבְּלִי נֶדֶר אֶתֵּן צְדָקָה בְּעַד הַזְכָּרַת נִשְׁמָתוֹ, בְּגַן עֵדֶן תְּהֵא מְנוּחָתוֹ. לָכֵן, בַּעַל הָרַחֲמִים יַסְתִּירֵהוּ בְּסֵתֶר כְּנָפָיו לְעוֹלָמִים, וְיִצְרֹר בִּצְרוֹר הַחַיִּים אֶת נִשְׁמָתוֹ, יהוה הוּא נַחֲלָתוֹ, וְיָנוּחַ בְּשָׁלוֹם עַל מִשְׁכָּבוֹ, וְנֹאמַר אָמֵן.

For a female relative:

אֵל מָלֵא רַחֲמִים, שׁוֹכֵן בַּמְּרוֹמִים, הַמְצֵא מְנוּחָה נְכוֹנָה עַל כַּנְפֵי הַשְּׁכִינָה, בְּמַעֲלוֹת קְדוֹשִׁים וּטְהוֹרִים, כְּזֹהַר הָרָקִיעַ מַזְהִירִים, לְנִשְׁמַת (פלונית בַּת פלוני) שֶׁהָלְכָה לְעוֹלָמָהּ, בַּעֲבוּר שֶׁבְּלִי נֶדֶר אֶתֵּן צְדָקָה בְּעַד הַזְכָּרַת נִשְׁמָתָהּ, בְּגַן עֵדֶן תְּהֵא מְנוּחָתָהּ. לָכֵן, בַּעַל הָרַחֲמִים יַסְתִּירֶהָ בְּסֵתֶר כְּנָפָיו לְעוֹלָמִים, וְיִצְרֹר בִּצְרוֹר הַחַיִּים אֶת נִשְׁמָתָהּ, יהוה הוּא נַחֲלָתָהּ, וְתָנוּחַ בְּשָׁלוֹם עַל מִשְׁכָּבָהּ, וְנֹאמַר אָמֵן.

For martyrs:

יִזְכֹּר May God remember the soul of (*name*, son/daughter of *father's name*), and the souls of all my relatives, on my father's or mother's side, who were killed, murdered, slaughtered, burned, drowned or strangled for the sanctification of God's name, and to this I pledge (without formal vow) to give charity in their memory. May their souls be bound in the bond of everlasting life together with the souls of Abraham, Isaac and Jacob, Sarah, Rebecca, Rachel and Leah, and all the other righteous men and women in the Garden of Eden, and let us say: Amen.

For the Israeli soldiers:

אֵל מָלֵא רַחֲמִים God, full of mercy, who dwells on high, grant fitting rest on the wings of the Divine Presence, in the heights of the holy, the pure and the brave, who shine like the radiance of heaven, to the souls of the holy ones who fought in any of Israel's battles, in clandestine operations and in Israel's Defense Forces, who fell in battle and sacrificed their lives for the consecration of God's name, for the people and the land, and for this we pray for the ascent of their souls. Therefore, Master of compassion, shelter them in the shadow of Your wings forever, and bind their souls in the bond of everlasting life. The Lord is their heritage; may the Garden of Eden be their resting place, may they rest in peace, may their merit stand for all Israel, and may they receive their reward at the End of Days, and let us say: Amen.

For the Holocaust victims:

אֵל מָלֵא רַחֲמִים God, full of mercy, Justice of widows and Father of orphans, please do not be silent and hold Your peace for the blood of Israel that was shed like water. Grant fitting rest on the wings of the Divine Presence, in the heights of the holy and the pure who shine and radiate light like the radiance of heaven, to the souls of the millions of Jews, men, women and children, who were murdered, slaughtered, burned, strangled, and buried alive, in the lands touched by the German enemy and its followers. They were all holy and pure; among them were great scholars and righteous individuals, cedars of Lebanon and noble masters of Torah, may the Garden of Eden be their resting place. Therefore, Master of compassion, shelter them in the shadow of Your wings forever, and bind their souls in the bond of everlasting life. The Lord is their heritage; may they rest in peace, and let us say: Amen.

For martyrs:

יִזְכֹּר אֱלֹהִים נִשְׁמַת (*male* פלוני בֶּן פלוני / *female* פלונית בַּת פלוני) **וְנִשְׁמוֹת כָּל** קְרוֹבַי וּקְרוֹבוֹתַי, הֵן מִצַּד אָבִי הֵן מִצַּד אִמִּי, שֶׁהוּמְתוּ וְשֶׁנֶּהֶרְגוּ וְשֶׁנִּשְׁחֲטוּ וְשֶׁנִּשְׂרְפוּ וְשֶׁנִּטְבְּעוּ וְשֶׁנֶּחְנְקוּ עַל קִדּוּשׁ הַשֵּׁם, בַּעֲבוּר שֶׁבְּלִי נֶדֶר אֶתֵּן צְדָקָה בְּעַד הַזְכָּרַת נִשְׁמוֹתֵיהֶם. בִּשְׂכַר זֶה תִּהְיֶינָה נַפְשׁוֹתֵיהֶם צְרוּרוֹת בִּצְרוֹר הַחַיִּים עִם נִשְׁמוֹת אַבְרָהָם יִצְחָק וְיַעֲקֹב, שָׂרָה רִבְקָה רָחֵל וְלֵאָה, וְעִם שְׁאָר צַדִּיקִים וְצִדְקָנִיּוֹת שֶׁבְּגַן עֵדֶן, וְנֹאמַר אָמֵן.

For the Israeli soldiers:

אֵל מָלֵא רַחֲמִים, שׁוֹכֵן בַּמְּרוֹמִים, הַמְצֵא מְנוּחָה נְכוֹנָה עַל כַּנְפֵי הַשְּׁכִינָה, בְּמַעֲלוֹת קְדוֹשִׁים טְהוֹרִים וְגִבּוֹרִים, כְּזֹהַר הָרָקִיעַ מַזְהִירִים, לְנִשְׁמוֹת הַקְּדוֹשִׁים שֶׁנִּלְחֲמוּ בְּכָל מַעַרְכוֹת יִשְׂרָאֵל, בַּמַּחְתֶּרֶת וּבִצְבָא הַהֲגָנָה לְיִשְׂרָאֵל, וְשֶׁנָּפְלוּ בְּמִלְחַמְתָּם וּמָסְרוּ נַפְשָׁם עַל קְדֻשַּׁת הַשֵּׁם, הָעָם וְהָאָרֶץ, בַּעֲבוּר שֶׁאָנוּ מִתְפַּלְּלִים לְעִלּוּי נִשְׁמוֹתֵיהֶם. לָכֵן, בַּעַל הָרַחֲמִים יַסְתִּירֵם בְּסֵתֶר כְּנָפָיו לְעוֹלָמִים, וְיִצְרֹר בִּצְרוֹר הַחַיִּים אֶת נִשְׁמוֹתֵיהֶם, יהוה הוּא נַחֲלָתָם, בְּגַן עֵדֶן תְּהֵא מְנוּחָתָם, וְיָנוּחוּ בְשָׁלוֹם עַל מִשְׁכְּבוֹתֵיהֶם וְתַעֲמֹד לְכָל יִשְׂרָאֵל זְכוּתָם, וְיַעַמְדוּ לְגוֹרָלָם לְקֵץ הַיָּמִין, וְנֹאמַר אָמֵן.

For the Holocaust victims:

אֵל מָלֵא רַחֲמִים, דַּיַּן אַלְמָנוֹת וַאֲבִי יְתוֹמִים, אַל נָא תֶחֱשֶׁה וְתִתְאַפַּק לְדַם יִשְׂרָאֵל שֶׁנִּשְׁפַּךְ כַּמַּיִם. הַמְצֵא מְנוּחָה נְכוֹנָה עַל כַּנְפֵי הַשְּׁכִינָה, בְּמַעֲלוֹת קְדוֹשִׁים וּטְהוֹרִים, כְּזֹהַר הָרָקִיעַ מְאִירִים וּמַזְהִירִים, לְנִשְׁמוֹתֵיהֶם שֶׁל רִבְבוֹת אַלְפֵי יִשְׂרָאֵל, אֲנָשִׁים וְנָשִׁים, יְלָדִים וִילָדוֹת, שֶׁנֶּהֶרְגוּ וְנִשְׁחֲטוּ וְנִשְׂרְפוּ וְנֶחְנְקוּ וְנִקְבְּרוּ חַיִּים, בָּאֲרָצוֹת אֲשֶׁר נָגְעָה בָּהֶן יַד הַצּוֹרֵר הַגֶּרְמָנִי וּגְרוּרָיו. כֻּלָּם קְדוֹשִׁים וּטְהוֹרִים, וּבָהֶם גְּאוֹנִים וְצַדִּיקִים, אַרְזֵי הַלְּבָנוֹן אַדִּירֵי הַתּוֹרָה. בְּגַן עֵדֶן תְּהֵא מְנוּחָתָם. לָכֵן, בַּעַל הָרַחֲמִים יַסְתִּירֵם בְּסֵתֶר כְּנָפָיו לְעוֹלָמִים, וְיִצְרֹר בִּצְרוֹר הַחַיִּים אֶת נִשְׁמָתָם, יהוה הוּא נַחֲלָתָם, וְיָנוּחוּ בְשָׁלוֹם עַל מִשְׁכָּבָם, וְנֹאמַר אָמֵן.

Congregation and Leader:

אַב הָרַחֲמִים Father of compassion, who dwells on high: may He remember in His compassion the pious, the upright and the blameless – holy communities who sacrificed their lives for the sanctification of God's name. Lovely and pleasant in their lives, in death they were not parted. They were swifter than eagles and stronger than lions to do the will of their Maker and the desire of their Creator. O our God, remember them for good with the other righteous of the world, and may He exact retribution for the shed blood of His servants,
as it is written in the Torah of Moses, the man of God: "O nations, acclaim *Deut. 32*
His people, for He will avenge the blood of His servants, wreak vengeance on His foes, and make clean His people's land." And by Your servants, the
prophets, it is written: "I shall cleanse their blood which I have not yet *Joel 4*
cleansed, says the LORD who dwells in Zion." And in the holy Writings it says:
"Why should the nations say: Where is their God? Before our eyes, may those *Ps. 79*
nations know that You avenge the shed blood of Your servants." And it also
says: "For the Avenger of blood remembers them and does not forget the cry *Ps. 9*
of the afflicted." And it further says: "He will execute judgment among the *Ps. 110*
nations, filled with the dead, crushing rulers far and wide. From the brook by the wayside he will drink, then he will hold his head high."

In Israel some say the piyutim for Simhat Torah on page 1276.

אַשְׁרֵי Happy are those who dwell in Your House; *Ps. 84*
they shall continue to praise You, Selah!
Happy are the people for whom this is so; *Ps. 144*
happy are the people whose God is the LORD.
A song of praise by David. *Ps. 145*

I will exalt You, my God, the King, and bless Your name for ever and all time. Every day I will bless You, and praise Your name for ever and all time. Great is the LORD and greatly to be praised; His greatness is unfathomable. One generation will praise Your works to the next, and tell of Your mighty deeds. On the glorious splendor of Your majesty I will meditate, and on the acts of Your wonders. They shall talk of the power of Your awesome deeds, and I will tell of Your greatness. They shall recite the record of Your great goodness, and sing with

The שליח ציבור *and the* קהל:

אַב הָרַחֲמִים שׁוֹכֵן מְרוֹמִים, בְּרַחֲמָיו הָעֲצוּמִים הוּא יִפְקֹד בְּרַחֲמִים הַחֲסִידִים וְהַיְשָׁרִים וְהַתְּמִימִים, קְהִלּוֹת הַקֹּדֶשׁ שֶׁמָּסְרוּ נַפְשָׁם עַל קְדֻשַּׁת הַשֵּׁם, הַנֶּאֱהָבִים וְהַנְּעִימִים בְּחַיֵּיהֶם, וּבְמוֹתָם לֹא נִפְרָדוּ, מִנְּשָׁרִים קַלּוּ וּמֵאֲרָיוֹת גָּבֵרוּ לַעֲשׂוֹת רְצוֹן קוֹנָם וְחֵפֶץ צוּרָם. יִזְכְּרֵם אֱלֹהֵינוּ לְטוֹבָה עִם שְׁאָר צַדִּיקֵי עוֹלָם, וְיִנְקֹם לְעֵינֵינוּ נִקְמַת דַּם עֲבָדָיו
דברים לב הַשָּׁפוּךְ, כַּכָּתוּב בְּתוֹרַת מֹשֶׁה אִישׁ הָאֱלֹהִים, הַרְנִינוּ גוֹיִם עַמּוֹ, כִּי דַם־עֲבָדָיו יִקּוֹם, וְנָקָם יָשִׁיב לְצָרָיו, וְכִפֶּר אַדְמָתוֹ עַמּוֹ: וְעַל יְדֵי עֲבָדֶיךָ
יואל ד הַנְּבִיאִים כָּתוּב לֵאמֹר, וְנִקֵּיתִי, דָּמָם לֹא־נִקֵּיתִי, וַיהוה שֹׁכֵן בְּצִיּוֹן:
תהלים עט וּבְכִתְבֵי הַקֹּדֶשׁ נֶאֱמַר, לָמָּה יֹאמְרוּ הַגּוֹיִם אַיֵּה אֱלֹהֵיהֶם, יִוָּדַע בַּגּוֹיִם
תהלים ט לְעֵינֵינוּ נִקְמַת דַּם־עֲבָדֶיךָ הַשָּׁפוּךְ: וְאוֹמֵר, כִּי־דֹרֵשׁ דָּמִים אוֹתָם זָכָר, לֹא־שָׁכַח צַעֲקַת עֲנָוִים: וְאוֹמֵר, יָדִין בַּגּוֹיִם מָלֵא גְוִיּוֹת, מָחַץ רֹאשׁ
תהלים קי עַל־אֶרֶץ רַבָּה: מִנַּחַל בַּדֶּרֶךְ יִשְׁתֶּה, עַל־כֵּן יָרִים רֹאשׁ:

In ארץ ישראל *some say the piyutim for* שמחת תורה *on page 1277.*

תהלים פד אַשְׁרֵי יוֹשְׁבֵי בֵיתֶךָ, עוֹד יְהַלְלוּךָ סֶּלָה:
תהלים קמד אַשְׁרֵי הָעָם שֶׁכָּכָה לּוֹ, אַשְׁרֵי הָעָם שֶׁיהוה אֱלֹהָיו:
תהלים קמה תְּהִלָּה לְדָוִד

אֲרוֹמִמְךָ אֱלוֹהַי הַמֶּלֶךְ, וַאֲבָרְכָה שִׁמְךָ לְעוֹלָם וָעֶד:
בְּכָל־יוֹם אֲבָרְכֶךָּ, וַאֲהַלְלָה שִׁמְךָ לְעוֹלָם וָעֶד:
גָּדוֹל יהוה וּמְהֻלָּל מְאֹד, וְלִגְדֻלָּתוֹ אֵין חֵקֶר:
דּוֹר לְדוֹר יְשַׁבַּח מַעֲשֶׂיךָ, וּגְבוּרֹתֶיךָ יַגִּידוּ:
הֲדַר כְּבוֹד הוֹדֶךָ, וְדִבְרֵי נִפְלְאֹתֶיךָ אָשִׂיחָה:
וֶעֱזוּז נוֹרְאֹתֶיךָ יֹאמֵרוּ, וּגְדוּלָּתְךָ אֲסַפְּרֶנָּה:
זֵכֶר רַב־טוּבְךָ יַבִּיעוּ, וְצִדְקָתְךָ יְרַנֵּנוּ:
חַנּוּן וְרַחוּם יהוה, אֶרֶךְ אַפַּיִם וּגְדָל־חָסֶד:

joy of Your righteousness. The LORD is gracious and compassionate, slow to anger and great in loving-kindness. The LORD is good to all, and His compassion extends to all His works. All Your works shall thank You, LORD, and Your devoted ones shall bless You. They shall talk of the glory of Your kingship, and speak of Your might. To make known to mankind His mighty deeds and the glorious majesty of His kingship. Your kingdom is an everlasting kingdom, and Your reign is for all generations. The LORD supports all who fall, and raises all who are bowed down. All raise their eyes to You in hope, and You give them their food in due season. You open Your hand, and satisfy every living thing with favor. The LORD is righteous in all His ways, and kind in all He does. The LORD is close to all who call on Him, to all who call on Him in truth. He fulfills the will of those who revere Him; He hears their cry and saves them. The LORD guards all who love Him, but all the wicked He will destroy. ▸ My mouth shall speak the praise of the LORD, and all creatures shall bless His holy name for ever and all time.

We will bless the LORD now and for ever. Halleluya! Ps. 115

RETURNING THE TORAH TO THE ARK

The Ark is opened. All stand.
The Leader takes one of the Torah scrolls and says:

יְהַלְלוּ Let them praise the name of the LORD, Ps. 148
for His name alone is sublime.

The congregation responds:

הוֹדוֹ His majesty is above earth and heaven.
He has raised the horn of His people,
for the glory of all His devoted ones,
the children of Israel, the people close to Him.
Halleluya!

טוֹב־יהוה לַכֹּל, וְרַחֲמָיו עַל־כָּל־מַעֲשָׂיו:
יוֹדוּךָ יהוה כָּל־מַעֲשֶׂיךָ, וַחֲסִידֶיךָ יְבָרְכוּכָה:
כְּבוֹד מַלְכוּתְךָ יֹאמֵרוּ, וּגְבוּרָתְךָ יְדַבֵּרוּ:
לְהוֹדִיעַ לִבְנֵי הָאָדָם גְּבוּרֹתָיו, וּכְבוֹד הֲדַר מַלְכוּתוֹ:
מַלְכוּתְךָ מַלְכוּת כָּל־עֹלָמִים, וּמֶמְשַׁלְתְּךָ בְּכָל־דּוֹר וָדֹר:
סוֹמֵךְ יהוה לְכָל־הַנֹּפְלִים, וְזוֹקֵף לְכָל־הַכְּפוּפִים:
עֵינֵי־כֹל אֵלֶיךָ יְשַׂבֵּרוּ, וְאַתָּה נוֹתֵן־לָהֶם אֶת־אָכְלָם בְּעִתּוֹ:
פּוֹתֵחַ אֶת־יָדֶךָ, וּמַשְׂבִּיעַ לְכָל־חַי רָצוֹן:
צַדִּיק יהוה בְּכָל־דְּרָכָיו, וְחָסִיד בְּכָל־מַעֲשָׂיו:
קָרוֹב יהוה לְכָל־קֹרְאָיו, לְכֹל אֲשֶׁר יִקְרָאֻהוּ בֶאֱמֶת:
רְצוֹן־יְרֵאָיו יַעֲשֶׂה, וְאֶת־שַׁוְעָתָם יִשְׁמַע, וְיוֹשִׁיעֵם:
שׁוֹמֵר יהוה אֶת־כָּל־אֹהֲבָיו, וְאֵת כָּל־הָרְשָׁעִים יַשְׁמִיד:
◂ תְּהִלַּת יהוה יְדַבֶּר פִּי, וִיבָרֵךְ כָּל־בָּשָׂר שֵׁם קָדְשׁוֹ לְעוֹלָם וָעֶד:
תהלים קטו וַאֲנַחְנוּ נְבָרֵךְ יָהּ מֵעַתָּה וְעַד־עוֹלָם, הַלְלוּיָהּ:

הכנסת ספר תורה

The ארון קודש *is opened. All stand. The* שליח ציבור *takes one of the* ספרי תורה *and says:*

תהלים קמח יְהַלְלוּ אֶת־שֵׁם יהוה, כִּי־נִשְׂגָּב שְׁמוֹ, לְבַדּוֹ

The קהל *responds:*

הוֹדוֹ עַל־אֶרֶץ וְשָׁמָיִם:
וַיָּרֶם קֶרֶן לְעַמּוֹ
תְּהִלָּה לְכָל־חֲסִידָיו
לִבְנֵי יִשְׂרָאֵל עַם קְרֹבוֹ
הַלְלוּיָהּ:

While the Torah scrolls are being returned to the Ark, on a weekday the following is said. On Shabbat, Psalm 29, below, is said.

לְדָוִד מִזְמוֹר A psalm of David. The earth is the LORD's and all it contains, the world and all who live in it. For He founded it on the seas and established it on the streams. Who may climb the mountain of the LORD? Who may stand in His holy place? He who has clean hands and a pure heart, who has not taken My name in vain, or sworn deceitfully. He shall receive blessing from the LORD, and just reward from God, his salvation. This is a generation of those who seek Him, the descendants of Jacob who seek Your presence, Selah! Lift up your heads, O gates; be uplifted, eternal doors, so that the King of glory may enter. Who is the King of glory? It is the LORD, strong and mighty, the LORD mighty in battle. Lift up your heads, O gates; be uplifted, eternal doors, so that the King of glory may enter. ▸ Who is He, the King of glory? The LORD of hosts, He is the King of glory, Selah! *Ps. 24*

On Shabbat the following is said:

מִזְמוֹר לְדָוִד A psalm of David. Render to the LORD, you angelic powers, render to the LORD glory and might. Render to the LORD the glory due to His name. Bow to the LORD in the beauty of holiness. The LORD's voice echoes over the waters; the God of glory thunders; the LORD is over the mighty waters. The LORD's voice in power, the LORD's voice in beauty, the LORD's voice breaks cedars, the LORD shatters the cedars of Lebanon. He makes Lebanon skip like a calf, Sirion like a young wild ox. The LORD's voice cleaves flames of fire. The LORD's voice makes the desert quake, the LORD shakes the desert of Kadesh. The LORD's voice makes hinds calve and strips the forests bare, and in His temple all say: "Glory!" ▸ The LORD sat enthroned at the Flood, the LORD sits enthroned as King for ever. The LORD will give strength to His people; the LORD will bless His people with peace. *Ps. 29*

As the Torah scrolls are placed into the Ark, all say:

וּבְנֻחֹה יֹאמַר When the Ark came to rest, Moses would say:
"Return, O LORD, to the myriad thousands of Israel." *Num. 10*
Advance, LORD, to Your resting place, You and Your mighty Ark. *Ps. 132*

While the ספרי תורה *are being returned to the* ארון קודש*, on a weekday the following is said. On* שבת*, Psalm 29, below, is said.*

תהלים כד
לְדָוִד מִזְמוֹר, לַיהוה הָאָרֶץ וּמְלוֹאָהּ, תֵּבֵל וְיֹשְׁבֵי בָהּ: כִּי־הוּא עַל־יַמִּים יְסָדָהּ, וְעַל־נְהָרוֹת יְכוֹנְנֶהָ: מִי־יַעֲלֶה בְהַר־יהוה, וּמִי־יָקוּם בִּמְקוֹם קָדְשׁוֹ: נְקִי כַפַּיִם וּבַר־לֵבָב, אֲשֶׁר לֹא־נָשָׂא לַשָּׁוְא נַפְשִׁי וְלֹא נִשְׁבַּע לְמִרְמָה: יִשָּׂא בְרָכָה מֵאֵת יהוה, וּצְדָקָה מֵאֱלֹהֵי יִשְׁעוֹ: זֶה דּוֹר דֹּרְשָׁו, מְבַקְשֵׁי פָנֶיךָ, יַעֲקֹב, סֶלָה: שְׂאוּ שְׁעָרִים רָאשֵׁיכֶם, וְהִנָּשְׂאוּ פִּתְחֵי עוֹלָם, וְיָבוֹא מֶלֶךְ הַכָּבוֹד: מִי זֶה מֶלֶךְ הַכָּבוֹד, יהוה עִזּוּז וְגִבּוֹר, יהוה גִּבּוֹר מִלְחָמָה: שְׂאוּ שְׁעָרִים רָאשֵׁיכֶם, וּשְׂאוּ פִּתְחֵי עוֹלָם, וְיָבֹא מֶלֶךְ הַכָּבוֹד: ◂ מִי הוּא זֶה מֶלֶךְ הַכָּבוֹד, יהוה צְבָאוֹת הוּא מֶלֶךְ הַכָּבוֹד, סֶלָה:

On שבת *the following is said:*

תהלים כט
מִזְמוֹר לְדָוִד, הָבוּ לַיהוה בְּנֵי אֵלִים, הָבוּ לַיהוה כָּבוֹד וָעֹז: הָבוּ לַיהוה כְּבוֹד שְׁמוֹ, הִשְׁתַּחֲווּ לַיהוה בְּהַדְרַת־קֹדֶשׁ: קוֹל יהוה עַל־הַמָּיִם, אֵל־הַכָּבוֹד הִרְעִים, יהוה עַל־מַיִם רַבִּים: קוֹל־יהוה בַּכֹּחַ, קוֹל יהוה בֶּהָדָר: קוֹל יהוה שֹׁבֵר אֲרָזִים, וַיְשַׁבֵּר יהוה אֶת־אַרְזֵי הַלְּבָנוֹן: וַיַּרְקִידֵם כְּמוֹ־עֵגֶל, לְבָנוֹן וְשִׂרְיוֹן כְּמוֹ בֶן־רְאֵמִים: קוֹל־יהוה חֹצֵב לַהֲבוֹת אֵשׁ: קוֹל יהוה יָחִיל מִדְבָּר, יָחִיל יהוה מִדְבַּר קָדֵשׁ: קוֹל יהוה יְחוֹלֵל אַיָּלוֹת וַיֶּחֱשֹׂף יְעָרוֹת, וּבְהֵיכָלוֹ, כֻּלּוֹ אֹמֵר כָּבוֹד: ◂ יהוה לַמַּבּוּל יָשָׁב, וַיֵּשֶׁב יהוה מֶלֶךְ לְעוֹלָם: יהוה עֹז לְעַמּוֹ יִתֵּן, יהוה יְבָרֵךְ אֶת־עַמּוֹ בַשָּׁלוֹם:

As the ספרי תורה *are placed into the* ארון קודש*, all say:*

במדבר י
וּבְנֻחֹה יֹאמַר, שׁוּבָה יהוה רִבְבוֹת אַלְפֵי יִשְׂרָאֵל:

תהלים קלב
קוּמָה יהוה לִמְנוּחָתֶךָ, אַתָּה וַאֲרוֹן עֻזֶּךָ:

Your priests are clothed in righteousness,
and Your devoted ones sing in joy.
For the sake of Your servant David,
do not reject Your anointed one.
For I give you good instruction; do not forsake My Torah. *Prov. 4*
It is a tree of life to those who grasp it, *Prov. 3*
and those who uphold it are happy.
Its ways are ways of pleasantness, and all its paths are peace.
▸ Turn us back, O Lord, to You, and we will return. *Lam. 5*
Renew our days as of old.

The Ark is closed.

Congregations that say Prayer for Rain before the Amida, leave the Ark open, and continue with "Our God and God of our fathers" on page 1154.

HALF KADDISH

Leader: יִתְגַּדַּל Magnified and sanctified may His great name be,
in the world He created by His will.
May He establish His kingdom
in your lifetime and in your days,
and in the lifetime of all the house of Israel,
swiftly and soon –
and say: Amen.

All: May His great name be blessed for ever and all time.

Leader: Blessed and praised, glorified and exalted,
raised and honored,
uplifted and lauded
be the name of the Holy One,
blessed be He,
beyond any blessing, song,
praise and consolation
uttered in the world –
and say: Amen.

כֹּהֲנֶיךָ יִלְבְּשׁוּ־צֶדֶק, וַחֲסִידֶיךָ יְרַנֵּנוּ:
בַּעֲבוּר דָּוִד עַבְדֶּךָ אַל־תָּשֵׁב פְּנֵי מְשִׁיחֶךָ:
כִּי לֶקַח טוֹב נָתַתִּי לָכֶם, תּוֹרָתִי אַל־תַּעֲזֹבוּ: משלי ד
עֵץ־חַיִּים הִיא לַמַּחֲזִיקִים בָּהּ, וְתֹמְכֶיהָ מְאֻשָּׁר: משלי ג
דְּרָכֶיהָ דַרְכֵי־נֹעַם וְכָל־נְתִיבוֹתֶיהָ שָׁלוֹם:
◂ הֲשִׁיבֵנוּ יהוה אֵלֶיךָ וְנָשׁוּבָ, חַדֵּשׁ יָמֵינוּ כְּקֶדֶם: איכה ה

The ארון קודש *is closed.*

Congregations that say תפילת גשם *before the* עמידה*, leave the* ארון קודש *open, and continue with "*אֱלֹהֵינוּ וֵאלֹהֵי אֲבוֹתֵינוּ*" on page 1155.*

חצי קדיש

ש״ץ: יִתְגַּדַּל וְיִתְקַדַּשׁ שְׁמֵהּ רַבָּא (קהל: אָמֵן)
בְּעָלְמָא דִּי בְרָא כִרְעוּתֵהּ
וְיַמְלִיךְ מַלְכוּתֵהּ
בְּחַיֵּיכוֹן וּבְיוֹמֵיכוֹן וּבְחַיֵּי דְכָל בֵּית יִשְׂרָאֵל
בַּעֲגָלָא וּבִזְמַן קָרִיב
וְאִמְרוּ אָמֵן. (קהל: אָמֵן)

קהל וש״ץ: יְהֵא שְׁמֵהּ רַבָּא מְבָרַךְ לְעָלַם וּלְעָלְמֵי עָלְמַיָּא.

ש״ץ: יִתְבָּרַךְ וְיִשְׁתַּבַּח וְיִתְפָּאַר וְיִתְרוֹמַם וְיִתְנַשֵּׂא
וְיִתְהַדָּר וְיִתְעַלֶּה וְיִתְהַלָּל
שְׁמֵהּ דְּקֻדְשָׁא בְּרִיךְ הוּא (קהל: בְּרִיךְ הוּא)
לְעֵלָּא מִן כָּל בִּרְכָתָא וְשִׁירָתָא, תֻּשְׁבְּחָתָא וְנֶחֱמָתָא
דַּאֲמִירָן בְּעָלְמָא
וְאִמְרוּ אָמֵן. (קהל: אָמֵן)

Musaf for Shemini Atzeret

It is customary to announce that one adds "He makes the wind blow" in the Amida.

The following prayer, until "in former years" on page 1148, is said silently, standing with feet together. Take three steps forward and at the points indicated by ˚, bend the knees at the first word, bow at the second, and stand straight before saying God's name.

When I proclaim the LORD's name, give glory to our God. *Deut. 32*
O LORD, open my lips, so that my mouth may declare Your praise. *Ps. 51*

PATRIARCHS

˚בָּרוּךְ Blessed are You, LORD our God and God of our fathers,
God of Abraham, God of Isaac and God of Jacob;
the great, mighty and awesome God, God Most High,
who bestows acts of loving-kindness and creates all,
who remembers the loving-kindness of the fathers
and will bring a Redeemer
to their children's children
for the sake of His name, in love.
King, Helper, Savior, Shield:
˚Blessed are You, LORD, Shield of Abraham.

DIVINE MIGHT

אַתָּה גִּבּוֹר You are eternally mighty, LORD.
You give life to the dead
and have great power to save.

He makes the wind blow and the rain fall.

He sustains the living with loving-kindness,
and with great compassion revives the dead.
He supports the fallen,
heals the sick, sets captives free,
and keeps His faith with those who sleep in the dust.

מוסף לשמיני עצרת

It is customary to announce that one adds מַשִּׁיב הָרְוּחַ וּמוֹרִיד הַגֶּשֶׁם *in the Amida.*

The following prayer, until קַדְמֹנִיּוֹת *on page 1149, is said silently, standing with feet together. Take three steps forward and at the points indicated by* ', *bend the knees at the first word, bow at the second, and stand straight before saying God's name.*

כִּי שֵׁם יהוה אֶקְרָא, הָבוּ גֹדֶל לֵאלֹהֵינוּ: דברים לב
אֲדֹנָי, שְׂפָתַי תִּפְתָּח, וּפִי יַגִּיד תְּהִלָּתֶךָ: תהלים נא

אבות

'בָּרוּךְ אַתָּה יהוה, אֱלֹהֵינוּ וֵאלֹהֵי אֲבוֹתֵינוּ
אֱלֹהֵי אַבְרָהָם, אֱלֹהֵי יִצְחָק, וֵאלֹהֵי יַעֲקֹב
הָאֵל הַגָּדוֹל הַגִּבּוֹר וְהַנּוֹרָא, אֵל עֶלְיוֹן
גּוֹמֵל חֲסָדִים טוֹבִים, וְקוֹנֵה הַכֹּל
וְזוֹכֵר חַסְדֵי אָבוֹת
וּמֵבִיא גוֹאֵל לִבְנֵי בְנֵיהֶם לְמַעַן שְׁמוֹ בְּאַהֲבָה.
מֶלֶךְ עוֹזֵר וּמוֹשִׁיעַ וּמָגֵן.
'בָּרוּךְ אַתָּה יהוה, מָגֵן אַבְרָהָם.

גבורות

אַתָּה גִּבּוֹר לְעוֹלָם, אֲדֹנָי
מְחַיֵּה מֵתִים אַתָּה, רַב לְהוֹשִׁיעַ

מַשִּׁיב הָרְוּחַ וּמוֹרִיד הַגֶּשֶׁם

מְכַלְכֵּל חַיִּים בְּחֶסֶד, מְחַיֵּה מֵתִים בְּרַחֲמִים רַבִּים
סוֹמֵךְ נוֹפְלִים, וְרוֹפֵא חוֹלִים, וּמַתִּיר אֲסוּרִים
וּמְקַיֵּם אֱמוּנָתוֹ לִישֵׁנֵי עָפָר.

Who is like You, Master of might,
and who can compare to You,
O King who brings death and gives life,
and makes salvation grow?
Faithful are You to revive the dead.
Blessed are You, LORD,
who revives the dead.

HOLINESS

אַתָּה קָדוֹשׁ You are holy and Your name is holy,
and holy ones praise You daily, Selah!
Blessed are You, LORD,
the holy God.

HOLINESS OF THE DAY

אַתָּה בְחַרְתָּנוּ You have chosen us from among all peoples.
You have loved and favored us.
You have raised us above all tongues.
You have made us holy through Your commandments.
You have brought us near, our King, to Your service,
and have called us by Your great and holy name.

On Shabbat, add the words in parentheses:

וַתִּתֶּן לָנוּ And You, LORD our God, have given us in love
(Sabbaths for rest and) festivals for rejoicing,
holy days and seasons for joy,
(this Sabbath day and) this day of
the festival of the eighth day, Shemini Atzeret,
our time of rejoicing
(with love), a holy assembly
in memory of the exodus from Egypt.

מִי כָמוֹךָ, בַּעַל גְּבוּרוֹת
וּמִי דּוֹמֶה לָּךְ
מֶלֶךְ, מֵמִית וּמְחַיֶּה וּמַצְמִיחַ יְשׁוּעָה.
וְנֶאֱמָן אַתָּה לְהַחֲיוֹת מֵתִים.
בָּרוּךְ אַתָּה יהוה, מְחַיֵּה הַמֵּתִים.

קדושת השם

אַתָּה קָדוֹשׁ וְשִׁמְךָ קָדוֹשׁ
וּקְדוֹשִׁים בְּכָל יוֹם יְהַלְלוּךָ סֶּלָה.
בָּרוּךְ אַתָּה יהוה, הָאֵל הַקָּדוֹשׁ.

קדושת היום

אַתָּה בְחַרְתָּנוּ מִכָּל הָעַמִּים
אָהַבְתָּ אוֹתָנוּ וְרָצִיתָ בָּנוּ
וְרוֹמַמְתָּנוּ מִכָּל הַלְּשׁוֹנוֹת
וְקִדַּשְׁתָּנוּ בְּמִצְוֹתֶיךָ
וְקֵרַבְתָּנוּ מַלְכֵּנוּ לַעֲבוֹדָתֶךָ
וְשִׁמְךָ הַגָּדוֹל וְהַקָּדוֹשׁ עָלֵינוּ קָרָאתָ.

On שבת*, add the words in parentheses:*

וַתִּתֶּן לָנוּ יהוה אֱלֹהֵינוּ בְּאַהֲבָה
(שַׁבָּתוֹת לִמְנוּחָה וּ)מוֹעֲדִים לְשִׂמְחָה, חַגִּים וּזְמַנִּים לְשָׂשׂוֹן
אֶת יוֹם (הַשַּׁבָּת הַזֶּה וְאֶת יוֹם)
הַשְּׁמִינִי חַג הָעֲצֶרֶת הַזֶּה, זְמַן שִׂמְחָתֵנוּ
(בְּאַהֲבָה) מִקְרָא קֹדֶשׁ, זֵכֶר לִיצִיאַת מִצְרָיִם.

וּמִפְּנֵי חֲטָאֵינוּ But because of our sins
we were exiled from our land
and driven far from our country.
We cannot go up to appear and bow before You,
and to perform our duties in Your chosen House,
the great and holy Temple that was called by Your name,
because of the hand that was stretched out
against Your Sanctuary.
May it be Your will, Lord our God and God of our ancestors,
merciful King,
that You in Your abounding compassion may once more
have mercy on us and on Your Sanctuary,
rebuilding it swiftly and adding to its glory.
Our Father, our King,
reveal the glory of Your kingdom to us swiftly.
Appear and be exalted over us in the sight of all that lives.
Bring back our scattered ones from among the nations,
and gather our dispersed people from the ends of the earth.
Lead us to Zion, Your city, in jubilation,
and to Jerusalem, home of Your Temple,
with everlasting joy.
There we will prepare for You our obligatory offerings:
the regular daily offerings in their order
and the additional offerings according to their law.
And the additional offering(s of this Sabbath day and)
of this day of the festival of Shemini Atzeret.
we will prepare and offer before You in love,
in accord with Your will's commandment,
as You wrote for us in Your Torah
through Your servant Moses,
by Your own word,
as it is said:

וּמִפְּנֵי חֲטָאֵינוּ גָּלִינוּ מֵאַרְצֵנוּ, וְנִתְרַחַקְנוּ מֵעַל אַדְמָתֵנוּ
וְאֵין אֲנַחְנוּ יְכוֹלִים לַעֲלוֹת וְלֵרָאוֹת וּלְהִשְׁתַּחֲווֹת לְפָנֶיךָ
וְלַעֲשׂוֹת חוֹבוֹתֵינוּ בְּבֵית בְּחִירָתֶךָ
בַּבַּיִת הַגָּדוֹל וְהַקָּדוֹשׁ שֶׁנִּקְרָא שִׁמְךָ עָלָיו
מִפְּנֵי הַיָּד שֶׁנִּשְׁתַּלְּחָה בְּמִקְדָּשֶׁךָ.
יְהִי רָצוֹן מִלְּפָנֶיךָ יהוה אֱלֹהֵינוּ וֵאלֹהֵי אֲבוֹתֵינוּ
מֶלֶךְ רַחֲמָן
שֶׁתָּשׁוּב וּתְרַחֵם עָלֵינוּ וְעַל מִקְדָּשְׁךָ בְּרַחֲמֶיךָ הָרַבִּים
וְתִבְנֵהוּ מְהֵרָה וּתְגַדֵּל כְּבוֹדוֹ.
אָבִינוּ מַלְכֵּנוּ, גַּלֵּה כְּבוֹד מַלְכוּתְךָ עָלֵינוּ מְהֵרָה
וְהוֹפַע וְהִנָּשֵׂא עָלֵינוּ לְעֵינֵי כָּל חָי
וְקָרֵב פְּזוּרֵינוּ מִבֵּין הַגּוֹיִם
וּנְפוּצוֹתֵינוּ כַּנֵּס מִיַּרְכְּתֵי אָרֶץ.
וַהֲבִיאֵנוּ לְצִיּוֹן עִירְךָ בְּרִנָּה
וְלִירוּשָׁלַיִם בֵּית מִקְדָּשְׁךָ בְּשִׂמְחַת עוֹלָם
וְשָׁם נַעֲשֶׂה לְפָנֶיךָ אֶת קָרְבְּנוֹת חוֹבוֹתֵינוּ
תְּמִידִים כְּסִדְרָם וּמוּסָפִים כְּהִלְכָתָם
וְאֶת מוּסַף יוֹם / שבת: וְאֶת מוּסְפֵי יוֹם הַשַּׁבָּת הַזֶּה וְיוֹם/
הַשְּׁמִינִי חַג הָעֲצֶרֶת הַזֶּה.
נַעֲשֶׂה וְנַקְרִיב לְפָנֶיךָ בְּאַהֲבָה כְּמִצְוַת רְצוֹנֶךָ
כְּמוֹ שֶׁכָּתַבְתָּ עָלֵינוּ בְּתוֹרָתֶךָ
עַל יְדֵי מֹשֶׁה עַבְדֶּךָ
מִפִּי כְבוֹדֶךָ, כָּאָמוּר

On Shabbat:

וּבְיוֹם הַשַּׁבָּת On the Sabbath day, make an offering of two lambs a year old, without blemish, together with two-tenths of an ephah of fine flour mixed with oil as a meal-offering, and its appropriate libation. This is the burnt-offering for every Sabbath, in addition to the regular daily burnt-offering and its libation. *Num. 28*

בַּיּוֹם הַשְּׁמִינִי On the eighth day you shall hold an assembly; *Num. 29*
you shall do no laborious work.
And you shall offer a burnt-offering,
a fire-offering of pleasing odor to the LORD: one bullock,
one ram, seven yearling male lambs without blemish.

And their meal-offerings and wine-libations as ordained:
three-tenths of an ephah for each bull,
two-tenths of an ephah for each ram,
one-tenth of an ephah for each lamb,
wine for the libations, a male goat for atonement,
and two regular daily offerings according to their law.

On Shabbat:

יִשְׂמְחוּ Those who keep the Sabbath and call it a delight shall rejoice in Your kingship. The people who sanctify the seventh day shall all be satisfied and take delight in Your goodness, for You favored the seventh day and declared it holy. You called it "most desirable of days" in remembrance of Creation.

אֱלֹהֵינוּ Our God and God of our ancestors,
merciful King, have compassion upon us.
You who are good and do good, respond to our call.
Return to us in Your abounding mercy
for the sake of our fathers who did Your will.
Rebuild Your Temple as at the beginning,
and establish Your Sanctuary on its site.
Let us witness its rebuilding and gladden us by its restoration.
Bring the priests back to their service,
the Levites to their song and music,
and the Israelites to their homes.

On שבת:

וּבְיוֹם הַשַּׁבָּת, שְׁנֵי־כְבָשִׂים בְּנֵי־שָׁנָה תְּמִימִם וּשְׁנֵי עֶשְׂרֹנִים סֹלֶת מִנְחָה בְּלוּלָה בַשֶּׁמֶן וְנִסְכּוֹ: עֹלַת שַׁבַּת בְּשַׁבַּתּוֹ, עַל־עֹלַת הַתָּמִיד וְנִסְכָּהּ: במדבר כח

בַּיּוֹם הַשְּׁמִינִי, עֲצֶרֶת תִּהְיֶה לָכֶם במדבר כט
כָּל־מְלֶאכֶת עֲבֹדָה לֹא תַעֲשׂוּ:
וְהִקְרַבְתֶּם עֹלָה אִשֵּׁה רֵיחַ נִיחֹחַ לַיהוה
פַּר אֶחָד, אַיִל אֶחָד, כְּבָשִׂים בְּנֵי־שָׁנָה שִׁבְעָה, תְּמִימִם:

וּמִנְחָתָם וְנִסְכֵּיהֶם כִּמְדֻבָּר
שְׁלֹשָׁה עֶשְׂרֹנִים לַפָּר וּשְׁנֵי עֶשְׂרֹנִים לָאָיִל, וְעִשָּׂרוֹן לַכֶּבֶשׂ
וְיַיִן כְּנִסְכּוֹ, וְשָׂעִיר לְכַפֵּר, וּשְׁנֵי תְמִידִים כְּהִלְכָתָם.

On שבת:

יִשְׂמְחוּ בְמַלְכוּתְךָ שׁוֹמְרֵי שַׁבָּת וְקוֹרְאֵי עֹנֶג. עַם מְקַדְּשֵׁי שְׁבִיעִי כֻּלָּם יִשְׂבְּעוּ וְיִתְעַנְּגוּ מִטּוּבֶךָ, וּבַשְּׁבִיעִי רָצִיתָ בּוֹ וְקִדַּשְׁתּוֹ, חֶמְדַּת יָמִים אוֹתוֹ קָרָאתָ, זֵכֶר לְמַעֲשֵׂה בְרֵאשִׁית.

אֱלֹהֵינוּ וֵאלֹהֵי אֲבוֹתֵינוּ
מֶלֶךְ רַחֲמָן רַחֵם עָלֵינוּ, טוֹב וּמֵטִיב הִדָּרֶשׁ לָנוּ
שׁוּבָה אֵלֵינוּ בַּהֲמוֹן רַחֲמֶיךָ
בִּגְלַל אָבוֹת שֶׁעָשׂוּ רְצוֹנֶךָ.
בְּנֵה בֵיתְךָ כְּבַתְּחִלָּה, וְכוֹנֵן מִקְדָּשְׁךָ עַל מְכוֹנוֹ
וְהַרְאֵנוּ בְּבִנְיָנוֹ, וְשַׂמְּחֵנוּ בְּתִקּוּנוֹ
וְהָשֵׁב כֹּהֲנִים לַעֲבוֹדָתָם
וּלְוִיִּם לְשִׁירָם וּלְזִמְרָם
וְהָשֵׁב יִשְׂרָאֵל לִנְוֵיהֶם.

וְשָׁם נַעֲלֶה There we will go up and appear and bow before You
on the three pilgrimage festivals,
as is written in Your Torah:

"Three times in the year all your males shall appear *Deut. 16*
before the LORD your God at the place He will choose:
on Pesaḥ, Shavuot and Sukkot.
They shall not appear before the LORD empty-handed.
Each shall bring such a gift as he can,
in proportion to the blessing
that the LORD your God grants you."

On Shabbat add the words in parentheses:

וְהַשִּׂיאֵנוּ Bestow on us, LORD our God,
the blessing of Your festivals
for life and peace, joy and gladness,
as You desired and promised to bless us.
(Our God and God of our fathers, find favor in our rest.)
Make us holy through Your commandments
and grant us a share in Your Torah;
satisfy us with Your goodness,
gladden us with Your salvation,
and purify our hearts to serve You in truth.
And grant us a heritage, LORD our God, (with love and favor,)
with joy and gladness, Your holy (Sabbath and) festivals.
May Israel, who sanctify Your name, rejoice in You.
Blessed are You, LORD,
who sanctifies (the Sabbath and) Israel and the festive seasons.

TEMPLE SERVICE

רְצֵה Find favor, LORD our God,
in Your people Israel and their prayer.
Restore the service to Your most holy House,
and accept in love and favor
the fire-offerings of Israel and their prayer.
May the service of Your people Israel always find favor with You.

וְשָׁם נַעֲלֶה וְנֵרָאֶה וְנִשְׁתַּחֲוֶה לְפָנֶיךָ בְּשָׁלֹשׁ פַּעֲמֵי רְגָלֵינוּ
כַּכָּתוּב בְּתוֹרָתֶךָ
שָׁלוֹשׁ פְּעָמִים בַּשָּׁנָה יֵרָאֶה כָל־זְכוּרְךָ אֶת־פְּנֵי יהוה אֱלֹהֶיךָ דברים טז
בַּמָּקוֹם אֲשֶׁר יִבְחָר
בְּחַג הַמַּצּוֹת, וּבְחַג הַשָּׁבֻעוֹת, וּבְחַג הַסֻּכּוֹת
וְלֹא יֵרָאֶה אֶת־פְּנֵי יהוה רֵיקָם:
אִישׁ כְּמַתְּנַת יָדוֹ, כְּבִרְכַּת יהוה אֱלֹהֶיךָ אֲשֶׁר נָתַן־לָךְ:

On שבת add the words in parentheses:

וְהַשִּׂיאֵנוּ יהוה אֱלֹהֵינוּ אֶת בִּרְכַּת מוֹעֲדֶיךָ
לְחַיִּים וּלְשָׁלוֹם, לְשִׂמְחָה וּלְשָׂשׂוֹן
כַּאֲשֶׁר רָצִיתָ וְאָמַרְתָּ לְבָרְכֵנוּ.
(אֱלֹהֵינוּ וֵאלֹהֵי אֲבוֹתֵינוּ, רְצֵה בִמְנוּחָתֵנוּ)
קַדְּשֵׁנוּ בְּמִצְוֹתֶיךָ, וְתֵן חֶלְקֵנוּ בְּתוֹרָתֶךָ
שַׂבְּעֵנוּ מִטּוּבֶךָ, וְשַׂמְּחֵנוּ בִּישׁוּעָתֶךָ
וְטַהֵר לִבֵּנוּ לְעָבְדְּךָ בֶּאֱמֶת
וְהַנְחִילֵנוּ יהוה אֱלֹהֵינוּ (בְּאַהֲבָה וּבְרָצוֹן)
בְּשִׂמְחָה וּבְשָׂשׂוֹן (שַׁבָּת וּ) מוֹעֲדֵי קָדְשֶׁךָ
וְיִשְׂמְחוּ בְךָ יִשְׂרָאֵל מְקַדְּשֵׁי שְׁמֶךָ.
בָּרוּךְ אַתָּה יהוה, מְקַדֵּשׁ (הַשַּׁבָּת וְ) יִשְׂרָאֵל וְהַזְּמַנִּים.

עבודה

רְצֵה יהוה אֱלֹהֵינוּ בְּעַמְּךָ יִשְׂרָאֵל, וּבִתְפִלָּתָם
וְהָשֵׁב אֶת הָעֲבוֹדָה לִדְבִיר בֵּיתֶךָ
וְאִשֵּׁי יִשְׂרָאֵל וּתְפִלָּתָם בְּאַהֲבָה תְקַבֵּל בְּרָצוֹן
וּתְהִי לְרָצוֹן תָּמִיד עֲבוֹדַת יִשְׂרָאֵל עַמֶּךָ.

And may our eyes witness Your return to Zion in compassion.
Blessed are You, Lord, who restores His Presence to Zion.

THANKSGIVING

Bow at the first nine words.

מוֹדִים We give thanks to You,
for You are the Lord our God and God of our ancestors
for ever and all time.
You are the Rock of our lives,
Shield of our salvation from generation to generation.
We will thank You and declare Your praise for our lives,
which are entrusted into Your hand;
for our souls, which are placed in Your charge;
for Your miracles which are with us every day;
and for Your wonders and favors
at all times, evening, morning and midday.
You are good – for Your compassion never fails.
You are compassionate – for Your loving-kindnesses never cease.
We have always placed our hope in You.
For all these things may Your name be blessed and exalted,
our King, continually, for ever and all time.
Let all that lives thank You, Selah!
and praise Your name in truth, God, our Savior and Help, Selah!
Blessed are You, Lord, whose name is "the Good"
and to whom thanks are due.

PEACE

שִׂים שָׁלוֹם Grant peace, goodness and blessing,
grace, loving-kindness and compassion to us
and all Israel Your people.
Bless us, our Father, all as one, with the light of Your face,
for by the light of Your face You have given us,
Lord our God,
the Torah of life and love of kindness,
righteousness, blessing, compassion, life and peace.

וְתֶחֱזֶינָה עֵינֵינוּ בְּשׁוּבְךָ לְצִיּוֹן בְּרַחֲמִים.
בָּרוּךְ אַתָּה יהוה, הַמַּחֲזִיר שְׁכִינָתוֹ לְצִיּוֹן.

הודאה

Bow at the first five words.

מוֹדִים אֲנַחְנוּ לָךְ
שָׁאַתָּה הוּא יהוה אֱלֹהֵינוּ וֵאלֹהֵי אֲבוֹתֵינוּ לְעוֹלָם וָעֶד.
צוּר חַיֵּינוּ, מָגֵן יִשְׁעֵנוּ, אַתָּה הוּא לְדוֹר וָדוֹר.
נוֹדֶה לְּךָ וּנְסַפֵּר תְּהִלָּתֶךָ, עַל חַיֵּינוּ הַמְּסוּרִים בְּיָדֶךָ
וְעַל נִשְׁמוֹתֵינוּ הַפְּקוּדוֹת לָךְ, וְעַל נִסֶּיךָ שֶׁבְּכָל יוֹם עִמָּנוּ
וְעַל נִפְלְאוֹתֶיךָ וְטוֹבוֹתֶיךָ, שֶׁבְּכָל עֵת, עֶרֶב וָבֹקֶר וְצָהֳרָיִם.
הַטּוֹב, כִּי לֹא כָלוּ רַחֲמֶיךָ
וְהַמְרַחֵם, כִּי לֹא תַמּוּ חֲסָדֶיךָ
מֵעוֹלָם קִוִּינוּ לָךְ.
וְעַל כֻּלָּם יִתְבָּרַךְ וְיִתְרוֹמַם שִׁמְךָ מַלְכֵּנוּ תָּמִיד לְעוֹלָם וָעֶד.
וְכֹל הַחַיִּים יוֹדוּךָ סֶּלָה, וִיהַלְלוּ אֶת שִׁמְךָ בֶּאֱמֶת
הָאֵל יְשׁוּעָתֵנוּ וְעֶזְרָתֵנוּ סֶלָה.
בָּרוּךְ אַתָּה יהוה, הַטּוֹב שִׁמְךָ וּלְךָ נָאֶה לְהוֹדוֹת.

שלום

שִׂים שָׁלוֹם טוֹבָה וּבְרָכָה חֵן וָחֶסֶד וְרַחֲמִים
עָלֵינוּ וְעַל כָּל יִשְׂרָאֵל עַמֶּךָ.
בָּרְכֵנוּ אָבִינוּ כֻּלָּנוּ כְּאֶחָד בְּאוֹר פָּנֶיךָ
כִּי בְאוֹר פָּנֶיךָ נָתַתָּ לָּנוּ, יהוה אֱלֹהֵינוּ
תּוֹרַת חַיִּים וְאַהֲבַת חֶסֶד
וּצְדָקָה וּבְרָכָה וְרַחֲמִים וְחַיִּים וְשָׁלוֹם.

May it be good in Your eyes to bless Your people Israel
at every time, in every hour, with Your peace.
Blessed are You, LORD, who blesses His people Israel with peace.

Some say the following verse:
May the words of my mouth and the meditation of my heart find favor before You, LORD, my Rock and Redeemer. *Ps. 19*

אֱלֹהַי My God, *Berakhot 17a*
guard my tongue from evil and my lips from deceitful speech.
To those who curse me, let my soul be silent;
may my soul be to all like the dust.
Open my heart to Your Torah
and let my soul pursue Your commandments.
As for all who plan evil against me,
swiftly thwart their counsel and frustrate their plans.
Act for the sake of Your name;
act for the sake of Your right hand;
act for the sake of Your holiness;
act for the sake of Your Torah.
That Your beloved ones may be delivered, *Ps. 60*
save with Your right hand and answer me.
May the words of my mouth *Ps. 19*
and the meditation of my heart find favor before You,
LORD, my Rock and Redeemer.

Bow, take three steps back, then bow, first left, then right, then center, while saying:
May He who makes peace in His high places,
make peace for us and all Israel –
and say: Amen.

יְהִי רָצוֹן May it be Your will, LORD our God and God of our ancestors,
that the Temple be rebuilt speedily in our days,
and grant us a share in Your Torah.
And there we will serve You with reverence,
as in the days of old and as in former years.
Then the offering of Judah and Jerusalem *Mal. 3*
will be pleasing to the LORD as in the days of old and as in former years.

וְטוֹב בְּעֵינֶיךָ לְבָרֵךְ אֶת עַמְּךָ יִשְׂרָאֵל
בְּכָל עֵת וּבְכָל שָׁעָה בִּשְׁלוֹמֶךָ.
בָּרוּךְ אַתָּה יהוה, הַמְבָרֵךְ אֶת עַמּוֹ יִשְׂרָאֵל בַּשָּׁלוֹם.

Some say the following verse:

יִהְיוּ לְרָצוֹן אִמְרֵי־פִי וְהֶגְיוֹן לִבִּי לְפָנֶיךָ, יהוה צוּרִי וְגֹאֲלִי: תהלים יט

אֱלֹהַי ברכות יז.
נְצֹר לְשׁוֹנִי מֵרָע וּשְׂפָתַי מִדַּבֵּר מִרְמָה
וְלִמְקַלְלַי נַפְשִׁי תִדֹּם, וְנַפְשִׁי כֶּעָפָר לַכֹּל תִּהְיֶה.
פְּתַח לִבִּי בְּתוֹרָתֶךָ, וּבְמִצְוֹתֶיךָ תִּרְדֹּף נַפְשִׁי.
וְכָל הַחוֹשְׁבִים עָלַי רָעָה
מְהֵרָה הָפֵר עֲצָתָם וְקַלְקֵל מַחֲשַׁבְתָּם.
עֲשֵׂה לְמַעַן שְׁמֶךָ
עֲשֵׂה לְמַעַן יְמִינֶךָ
עֲשֵׂה לְמַעַן קְדֻשָּׁתֶךָ
עֲשֵׂה לְמַעַן תּוֹרָתֶךָ.
לְמַעַן יֵחָלְצוּן יְדִידֶיךָ, הוֹשִׁיעָה יְמִינְךָ וַעֲנֵנִי: תהלים ס
יִהְיוּ לְרָצוֹן אִמְרֵי־פִי וְהֶגְיוֹן לִבִּי לְפָנֶיךָ, יהוה צוּרִי וְגֹאֲלִי: תהלים יט

Bow, take three steps back, then bow, first left, then right, then center, while saying:

עֹשֶׂה שָׁלוֹם בִּמְרוֹמָיו
הוּא יַעֲשֶׂה שָׁלוֹם עָלֵינוּ וְעַל כָּל יִשְׂרָאֵל
וְאִמְרוּ אָמֵן.

יְהִי רָצוֹן מִלְּפָנֶיךָ יהוה אֱלֹהֵינוּ וֵאלֹהֵי אֲבוֹתֵינוּ
שֶׁיִּבָּנֶה בֵּית הַמִּקְדָּשׁ בִּמְהֵרָה בְיָמֵינוּ, וְתֵן חֶלְקֵנוּ בְּתוֹרָתֶךָ
וְשָׁם נַעֲבָדְךָ בְּיִרְאָה כִּימֵי עוֹלָם וּכְשָׁנִים קַדְמוֹנִיּוֹת.
וְעָרְבָה לַיהוה מִנְחַת יְהוּדָה וִירוּשָׁלָםִ כִּימֵי עוֹלָם וּכְשָׁנִים קַדְמֹנִיּוֹת: מלאכי ג

Leader's Repetition for Musaf Shemini Atzeret

On Shemini Atzeret, the Ark is opened at the Repetition of the Musaf Amida. All stand. If the Prayer for Rain was said before the silent Amida. Omit the paragraphs beginning "Af-bri" and "May He make", and the piyut "Remember the Patriarch".

The Leader takes three steps forward and at the points indicated by ▾, bends his knees at the first word, bows at the second, and stands straight before saying God's name.

When I proclaim the LORD's name, give glory to our God. *Deut. 32*
O LORD, open my lips, so that my mouth may declare Your praise. *Ps. 51*

PATRIARCHS

▾בָּרוּךְ▾ Blessed are You, LORD our God and God of our fathers,
God of Abraham, God of Isaac and God of Jacob;
the great, mighty and awesome God, God Most High,
who bestows acts of loving-kindness and creates all,
who remembers the loving-kindness of the fathers
and will bring a Redeemer to their children's children
for the sake of His name, in love.
King, Helper, Savior, Shield:

---

be said at the beginning of Sukkot, but since rainfall would interfere with the command to eat in the sukka, it was deferred to Shemini Atzeret. The liturgical poem that precedes the prayer was, like that for dew, composed by Elazar Kalir. The initial letter of each line spells out an alphabetical acrostic, and each line ends with the word "water." The six verses enumerate events related to water in six lives: those of the patriarchs, Abraham, Isaac and Jacob; the leaders of the Israelites in the wilderness, Moses and Aaron; and the people of Israel as a whole.

חזרת הש״ץ לשמיני עצרת

On שמיני עצרת, the ארון קודש is opened at חזרת הש״ץ of the מוסף עמידה. All stand. If תפילת גשם was said before the silent עמידה. Omit the paragraphs beginning אַף־בְּרִי and יַטְרִיחַ, and the piyut זְכוֹר אָב.

The שליח ציבור takes three steps forward and at the points indicated by ˚, bends his knees at the first word, bows at the second, and stands straight before saying God's name.

כִּי שֵׁם יהוה אֶקְרָא, הָבוּ גֹדֶל לֵאלֹהֵינוּ: דברים לב

אֲדֹנָי, שְׂפָתַי תִּפְתָּח, וּפִי יַגִּיד תְּהִלָּתֶךָ: תהלים נא

אבות

˚בָּרוּךְ אַתָּה יהוה, אֱלֹהֵינוּ וֵאלֹהֵי אֲבוֹתֵינוּ
אֱלֹהֵי אַבְרָהָם, אֱלֹהֵי יִצְחָק, וֵאלֹהֵי יַעֲקֹב
הָאֵל הַגָּדוֹל הַגִּבּוֹר וְהַנּוֹרָא, אֵל עֶלְיוֹן
גּוֹמֵל חֲסָדִים טוֹבִים, וְקוֹנֵה הַכֹּל
וְזוֹכֵר חַסְדֵי אָבוֹת
וּמֵבִיא גוֹאֵל לִבְנֵי בְנֵיהֶם לְמַעַן שְׁמוֹ בְּאַהֲבָה.
מֶלֶךְ עוֹזֵר וּמוֹשִׁיעַ וּמָגֵן.

PRAYER FOR RAIN

"At Sukkot they [the world] are judged for the water" (Mishna, *Rosh HaShana* 1:2). Israel is peculiarly dependent on rain, as Moses told the Israelites: "The land you are crossing the Jordan to take possession of is a land of mountains and valleys that drinks rain from heaven. It is a land the LORD your God cares for; the eyes of the LORD your God are continually on it from the beginning of the year to its end" (Deut. 11:11–12). Sukkot is the festival closest to the start of the rainy season. In theory, the prayer for rain should

The Leader says "Af-bri":

אַף־בְּרִי Af-bri is the name of the angel of rain,
Who overcasts [the sky],
forms clouds and precipitates them,
making them rain
Water to crown the valley with green.
May rain not be withheld from us
because of our unpaid debts.
May the merit of the faithful Patriarchs
protect their offspring who pray for rain.

▾Blessed are You,
LORD, Shield of Abraham.

DIVINE MIGHT

אַתָּה גִּבּוֹר You are eternally mighty, LORD.
You give life to the dead and have great power to save.

If the Prayer for Rain was said before the Amida (if said during the Leaders repetition it is not mentioned):

He makes the wind blow and the rain fall.

The Leader continues with "May He make" below and "Our God and God of our fathers" on the next page.

יַטְרִיחַ May He make him apportion due portions of rain,
Moistening the earth with drops pure as opal.
In the Torah You symbolized Your might by water.
Its drops refresh those in whom
was breathed the breath of life,
Reviving those who make mention of the powers of rain.

If added piyutim are said here, the Ark is closedand the Leader continues "אָפִיק מַעַן מְעָטָר" on page 1432.

personification of the two aspects of rain. At times it is fierce, like anger (*af*); at others it is gentle, healing (*bri*) the earth's thirst.

The שליח ציבור *says* אַף־בְּרִי*:*

אַף־בְּרִי אֻתַּת שֵׁם שַׂר מָטָר
לְהַעֲבִיב וּלְהַעֲנִין לְהָרִיק וּלְהַמְטַר
מַיִם אִבִּים בָּם גֵּיא לַעֲטַר
לְבַל יֵעָצְרוּ בְּנִשְׁיוֹן שְׁטָר
אֱמוּנִים גְּנוֹן בָּם, שׁוֹאֲלֵי מָטָר.

ּבָּרוּךְ אַתָּה יהוה, מָגֵן אַבְרָהָם.

גבורות

אַתָּה גִּבּוֹר לְעוֹלָם אֲדֹנָי
מְחַיֵּה מֵתִים אַתָּה, רַב לְהוֹשִׁיעַ

If תפילת גשם *was said before the* עמידה
(if said during חזרת הש״ץ *it is not mentioned):*

מַשִּׁיב הָרְוּחַ וּמוֹרִיד הַגֶּשֶׁם

The שליח ציבור *says* יַטְרִיחַ *below and* אֱלֹהֵינוּ וֵאלֹהֵי אֲבוֹתֵינוּ*, on the next page.*

יַטְרִיחַ לְפַלֵּג מִפֶּלֶג גֶּשֶׁם
לְמוֹגֵג פְּנֵי נֶשִׁי בְּצַחוּת לֶשֶׁם
מַיִם לְאַדְּרָךְ כִּנִּיתָ בְּרֶשֶׁם
לְהַרְגִּיעַ בְּרַעֲפָם לְנִפּוּחֵי נֶשֶׁם
לְהַחֲיוֹת מַזְכִּירִים גְּבוּרוֹת הַגֶּשֶׁם.

If added piyutim are said here, the ארון קודש *is closed and the* שליח ציבור *continues* אָפִיק מַעַן מְעֻטָר *on page 1432.*

אַף־בְּרִי *Af-bri is the name of the angel of rain.* Job 37:11 reads: "Even when it is clear [*af-bri*], He gives the dense clouds their load, and the clouds spread His mist abroad." Rashi interprets the phrase *Af-bri* as "the angel of rain," a

If the Prayer for Rain is said before the silent Amida, it begins here:

Our God and God of our fathers:

זְכוֹר Remember the Patriarch [Abraham]
who followed You like water.
You blessed him like a tree planted beside streams of water.
You shielded him and rescued him from fire and water.
You sought him because he sowed
[righteousness] by all waters.
Cong: For his sake do not withhold water.

זְכוֹר Remember [Isaac] whose birth was foretold
when [Abraham said] "Let there be brought some water." *Gen. 18*
You told his father to offer him, to shed his blood like water.
[Isaac], too, cared and poured out his soul like water.
When he dug, he discovered wells of water.
Cong: For his righteousness' sake grant abundant water.

זְכוֹר Remember [Jacob] who carried his staff
and crossed the Jordan's water.
With steadfast heart he rolled away the stone
from the well of water.
He wrestled with an angel composed of fire and water,
So You promised to be with him through fire and water.
Cong: For his sake do not withhold water.

חָפַר *When he dug.* Isaac reopened the wells Abraham had dug, which had been stopped up by the Philistines (Gen. 26:18).

וְגַל אֶבֶן מִפִּי בְאֵר מַיִם *He rolled away the stone from the well of water.* When Jacob arrived at Haran and saw Rachel coming to water the sheep, Jacob removed the stone covering the well (Gen. 29:10).

שַׂר בָּלוּל מֵאֵשׁ וּמִמַּיִם *An angel composed of fire and water.* the Talmud Yerushalmi (*Rosh HaShana* 2:4) describes the angel with whom Jacob wrestled as "half water, half fire."

If תפילת גשם *is said before the silent* עמידה*, it begins here:*

אֱלֹהֵינוּ וֵאלֹהֵי אֲבוֹתֵינוּ

זְכוֹר אָב נִמְשַׁךְ אַחֲרֶיךָ כַּמַּיִם
בֵּרַכְתּוֹ כְּעֵץ שָׁתוּל עַל פַּלְגֵי מַיִם
גְּנַנְתּוֹ, הִצַּלְתּוֹ מֵאֵשׁ וּמִמַּיִם
דְּרַשְׁתּוֹ בְּזָרְעוֹ עַל כָּל מָיִם.
קהל: בַּעֲבוּרוֹ אַל תִּמְנַע מָיִם.

זְכוֹר הַנּוֹלָד בִּבְשׂוֹרַת יֻקַּח־נָא מְעַט־מַיִם בראשית יח
וְשַׂחְתָּ לְהוֹרוֹ לְשָׁחֲטוֹ לִשְׁפֹּךְ דָּמוֹ כַּמַּיִם
זְהֵר גַּם הוּא לִשְׁפֹּךְ לֵב כַּמַּיִם
חָפַר וּמָצָא בְּאֵרוֹת מָיִם.
קהל: בְּצִדְקוֹ חֹן חַשְׁרַת מָיִם.

זְכוֹר טָעַן מַקְלוֹ וְעָבַר יַרְדֵּן מַיִם
יִחַד לֵב וְגָל אֶבֶן מִפִּי בְאֵר מַיִם
כְּנֶאֱבַק לוֹ שַׂר בָּלוּל מֵאֵשׁ וּמִמַּיִם
לָכֵן הִבְטַחְתּוֹ הֱיוֹת עִמּוֹ בָּאֵשׁ וּבַמָּיִם.
קהל: בַּעֲבוּרוֹ אַל תִּמְנַע מָיִם.

גְּנַנְתּוֹ, הִצַּלְתּוֹ מֵאֵשׁ וּמִמַּיִם *You shielded him and rescued him from fire and water.* According to rabbinic tradition, Abraham was cast into a fiery furnace by Nimrod and was saved by God (*Eiruvin* 53a; *Pesaḥim* 118a). Satan created a river to block Abraham's way on his journey to the binding of Isaac. Abraham walked undaunted into the water; when it came up to his neck, God rebuked Satan and the river vanished (*Tanḥuma, VaYera* 22).

זְכוֹר הַנּוֹלָד *Remember [Isaac] whose birth was foretold* when the three angels visited Abraham, and he urged them to stay, rest, eat and drink water (Gen. 18:4).

זְכוֹר Remember [Moses] who in a reed basket
was drawn out of the water.
They said: "He drew water for us, and gave the flock water."
When Your treasured people thirsted for water,
He struck the rock and out gushed water.
Cong: For his righteousness' sake grant abundant water.

זְכוֹר Remember [Aaron], chief officer of the Temple,
who immersed five times in water.
He went and washed his hands in the sanctifying water.
He called out and sprinkled blood,
purifying the people as if with water.
He kept apart from the people who were as unruly as water.
Cong: For his sake do not withhold water.

זְכוֹר Remember the twelve tribes
You brought through the divided water,
For whom You sweetened the bitterness of the water.
For Your sake their descendants' blood was spilled like water.
Turn to us, for troubles engulf our souls like water.
Cong: For their righteousness' sake grant abundant water.

Leader:

For You, Lord our God, make the wind blow and the rain fall.

Congregation then Leader, responsively:

For blessing, and not for curse. *Cong:* Amen.
For life, and not for death. *Cong:* Amen.
For plenty, and not for scarcity. *Cong:* Amen.

The Ark is closed.

The Leader continues the Repetition with "He sustains the living" on the next page. If the Prayer on Rain is said before the Amida, the Leader says Half Kaddish on page 1134 and the Musaf Amida is recited with the addition of "He makes the wind blow and the rain fall."

עַל הַסֶּלַע הָךְ *He struck the rock.* the reference is to Exodus 17:6, shortly after the crossing of the Reed Sea (and not to the later episode, Numbers, chapter 20, when God instructed Moses to speak to the rock).

טוֹבֵל חָמֵשׁ טְבִילוֹת בַּמַּיִם *Who immersed five times in water.* as part of the rites of Yom Kippur (Mishna, *Yoma* 3:3).

זְכוֹר מָשׁוּי בְּתֵבַת גֹּמֶא מִן הַמַּיִם
נָמוּ דָלֹה דָלָה וְהִשְׁקָה צֹאן מַיִם
סְגוּלֶיךָ עֵת צָמְאוּ לַמַּיִם
עַל הַסֶּלַע הָךְ, וַיֵּצְאוּ מָיִם.
קהל: בְּצִדְקוֹ חֹן חַשְׁרַת מָיִם.

זְכוֹר פְּקִיד שָׁתוֹת, טוֹבֵל חָמֵשׁ טְבִילוֹת בַּמַּיִם
צוֹעֶה וּמַרְחִיץ כַּפָּיו בְּקִדּוּשׁ מַיִם
קוֹרֵא וּמַזֶּה טָהֳרַת מַיִם
רֻחַק מֵעַם פַּחַז כַּמַּיִם.
קהל: בַּעֲבוּרוֹ אַל תִּמְנַע מָיִם.

זְכוֹר שְׁנֵים עָשָׂר שְׁבָטִים, שֶׁהֶעֱבַרְתָּ בְּגִזְרַת מַיִם
שֶׁהִמְתַּקְתָּ לָמוֹ מְרִירוּת מַיִם
תּוֹלְדוֹתָם נִשְׁפַּךְ דָּמָם עָלֶיךָ כַּמַּיִם
תֵּפֶן, כִּי נַפְשֵׁנוּ אָפְפוּ מָיִם.
קהל: בְּצִדְקָם חֹן חַשְׁרַת מָיִם.

שליח ציבור:

שָׁאַתָּה הוּא יהוה אֱלֹהֵינוּ, מַשִּׁיב הָרוּחַ וּמוֹרִיד הַגֶּשֶׁם

קהל then שליח ציבור, responsively:

לִבְרָכָה וְלֹא לִקְלָלָה קהל: אָמֵן
לְחַיִּים וְלֹא לְמָוֶת קהל: אָמֵן
לְשֹׂבַע וְלֹא לְרָזוֹן קהל: אָמֵן

The ארון קודש is closed.

The שליח ציבור continues the חזרת הש״ץ with מְכַלְכֵּל חַיִּים on the next page.
If תפילת הגשם is said before the עמידה, the שליח ציבור says חצי קדיש on page 1135
and the מוסף עמידה is recited with the addition of מַשִּׁיב הָרוּחַ וּמוֹרִיד הַגֶּשֶׁם.

נָמוּ דָלֹה דָלָה *They said: "He drew water for us".* the daughters of Jethro said this about Moses (Ex. 2:19).

He sustains the living with loving-kindness,
and with great compassion revives the dead.
He supports the fallen, heals the sick, sets captives free,
and keeps His faith with those who sleep in the dust.
Who is like You, Master of might,
and who can compare to You,
O King who brings death and gives life,
and makes salvation grow?
Faithful are You to revive the dead.
Blessed are You, LORD, who revives the dead.

KEDUSHA

The following is said standing with feet together, rising on the toes at the words indicated by ▴.

Cong. then Leader: נַעֲרִיצְךָ We will revere and sanctify You with the words uttered by the holy Seraphim who sanctify Your name in the Sanctuary; as is written by Your prophet:
"They call out to one another, saying: *Is. 6*

Cong. then Leader: ▴Holy, ▴holy, ▴holy is the LORD of hosts; the whole world is filled with His glory."
His glory fills the universe. His ministering angels ask each other, "Where is the place of His glory?" Those facing them say "Blessed –"

Cong. then Leader: "▴Blessed is the LORD's glory from His place." *Ezek. 3*
From His place may He turn with compassion and be gracious to the people who proclaim the unity of His name, morning and evening, every day, continually, twice each day reciting in love the Shema:

Cong. then Leader: "Listen, Israel, the LORD is our God, the LORD is One." *Deut. 6*
He is our God, He is our Father, He is our King, He is our Savior – and He, in His compassion, will let us hear a second time in the presence of all that lives, His promise
"to be your God. I am the LORD your God." *Num. 15*

מְכַלְכֵּל חַיִּים בְּחֶסֶד, מְחַיֵּה מֵתִים בְּרַחֲמִים רַבִּים
סוֹמֵךְ נוֹפְלִים, וְרוֹפֵא חוֹלִים, וּמַתִּיר אֲסוּרִים
וּמְקַיֵּם אֱמוּנָתוֹ לִישֵׁנֵי עָפָר.
מִי כָמְוֹךָ, בַּעַל גְּבוּרוֹת
וּמִי דּוֹמֶה לָּךְ
מֶלֶךְ, מֵמִית וּמְחַיֶּה וּמַצְמִיחַ יְשׁוּעָה.
וְנֶאֱמָן אַתָּה לְהַחֲיוֹת מֵתִים.
בָּרוּךְ אַתָּה יהוה, מְחַיֵּה הַמֵּתִים.

קדושה

The following is said standing with feet together, rising on the toes at the words indicated by ˄.

קהל then ש״ץ: נַעֲרִיצְךָ וְנַקְדִּישְׁךָ כְּסוֹד שִׂיחַ שַׂרְפֵי קֹדֶשׁ, הַמַּקְדִּישִׁים
שִׁמְךָ בַּקֹּדֶשׁ, כַּכָּתוּב עַל יַד נְבִיאֶךָ:
וְקָרָא זֶה אֶל־זֶה וְאָמַר ישעיה ו

קהל then ש״ץ: ˄קָדוֹשׁ, ˄קָדוֹשׁ, ˄קָדוֹשׁ, יהוה צְבָאוֹת, מְלֹא כָל־הָאָרֶץ
כְּבוֹדוֹ: כְּבוֹדוֹ מָלֵא עוֹלָם, מְשָׁרְתָיו שׁוֹאֲלִים זֶה לָזֶה,
אַיֵּה מְקוֹם כְּבוֹדוֹ לְעֻמָּתָם בָּרוּךְ יֹאמֵרוּ

קהל then ש״ץ: ˄בָּרוּךְ כְּבוֹד־יהוה מִמְּקוֹמוֹ: יחזקאל ג
מִמְּקוֹמוֹ הוּא יִפֶן בְּרַחֲמִים, וְיָחֹן עַם הַמְיַחֲדִים שְׁמוֹ, עֶרֶב
וָבְקֶר בְּכָל יוֹם תָּמִיד, פַּעֲמַיִם בְּאַהֲבָה שְׁמַע אוֹמְרִים

קהל then ש״ץ: שְׁמַע יִשְׂרָאֵל, יהוה אֱלֹהֵינוּ, יהוה אֶחָד: דברים ו
הוּא אֱלֹהֵינוּ, הוּא אָבִינוּ, הוּא מַלְכֵּנוּ, הוּא מוֹשִׁיעֵנוּ,
וְהוּא יַשְׁמִיעֵנוּ בְּרַחֲמָיו שֵׁנִית לְעֵינֵי כָּל חָי, לִהְיוֹת לָכֶם במדבר טו
לֵאלֹהִים, אֲנִי יהוה אֱלֹהֵיכֶם:

Cong. then Leader: Glorious is our Glorious One, LORD our Master, and glorious is Your name throughout the earth. Then the LORD shall be King over all the earth; on that day the LORD shall be One and His name One. *Ps. 8* *Zech. 14*

Leader: And in Your holy Writings it is written:

Cong. then Leader: "▲The LORD shall reign for ever. He is your God, Zion, from generation to generation, Halleluya!" *Ps. 146*

Leader: לְדוֹר וָדוֹר From generation to generation we will declare Your greatness, and we will proclaim Your holiness for evermore. Your praise, our God, shall not leave our mouth forever, for You, God, are a great and holy King. Blessed are You, LORD, the holy God.

HOLINESS OF THE DAY

אַתָּה בְחַרְתָּנוּ You have chosen us from among all peoples.
You have loved and favored us.
You have raised us above all tongues.
You have made us holy through Your commandments.
You have brought us near, our King, to Your service,
and have called us by Your great and holy name.

On Shabbat, add the words in parentheses:
וַתִּתֶּן לָנוּ And You, LORD our God, have given us in love
(Sabbaths for rest and) festivals for rejoicing,
holy days and seasons for joy, (this Sabbath day and) this day of:
the festival of the eighth day, Shemini Atzeret, our time of rejoicing
(with love), a holy assembly in memory of the exodus from Egypt.

וּמִפְּנֵי חֲטָאֵינוּ But because of our sins we were exiled from our land
and driven far from our country.
We cannot go up to appear and bow before You,
and to perform our duties in Your chosen House,
the great and holy Temple that was called by Your name,
because of the hand that was stretched out
against Your Sanctuary.

then קהל ש״ץ: אַדִּיר אַדִּירֵנוּ, יהוה אֲדֹנֵינוּ, מָה־אַדִּיר שִׁמְךָ בְּכָל־הָאָרֶץ: תהלים ח
וְהָיָה יהוה לְמֶלֶךְ עַל־כָּל־הָאָרֶץ, בַּיּוֹם הַהוּא יִהְיֶה יהוה זכריה יד
אֶחָד וּשְׁמוֹ אֶחָד:

ש״ץ: וּבְדִבְרֵי קָדְשְׁךָ כָּתוּב לֵאמֹר

then קהל ש״ץ: יִמְלֹךְ יהוה לְעוֹלָם, אֱלֹהַיִךְ צִיּוֹן לְדֹר וָדֹר, הַלְלוּיָהּ: תהלים קמו

ש״ץ: לְדוֹר וָדוֹר נַגִּיד גָּדְלֶךָ, וּלְנֵצַח נְצָחִים קְדֻשָּׁתְךָ נַקְדִּישׁ,
וְשִׁבְחֲךָ אֱלֹהֵינוּ מִפִּינוּ לֹא יָמוּשׁ לְעוֹלָם וָעֶד, כִּי אֵל מֶלֶךְ
גָּדוֹל וְקָדוֹשׁ אָתָּה. בָּרוּךְ אַתָּה יהוה, הָאֵל הַקָּדוֹשׁ.

קדושת היום

אַתָּה בְחַרְתָּנוּ מִכָּל הָעַמִּים
אָהַבְתָּ אוֹתָנוּ וְרָצִיתָ בָּנוּ, וְרוֹמַמְתָּנוּ מִכָּל הַלְּשׁוֹנוֹת
וְקִדַּשְׁתָּנוּ בְּמִצְוֹתֶיךָ, וְקֵרַבְתָּנוּ מַלְכֵּנוּ לַעֲבוֹדָתֶךָ
וְשִׁמְךָ הַגָּדוֹל וְהַקָּדוֹשׁ עָלֵינוּ קָרָאתָ.

On שבת, add the words in parentheses:

וַתִּתֶּן לָנוּ יהוה אֱלֹהֵינוּ בְּאַהֲבָה
(שַׁבָּתוֹת לִמְנוּחָה וּ)מוֹעֲדִים לְשִׂמְחָה, חַגִּים וּזְמַנִּים לְשָׂשׂוֹן
אֶת יוֹם (הַשַּׁבָּת הַזֶּה וְאֶת יוֹם) הַשְּׁמִינִי חַג הָעֲצֶרֶת הַזֶּה
זְמַן שִׂמְחָתֵנוּ, (בְּאַהֲבָה) מִקְרָא קֹדֶשׁ, זֵכֶר לִיצִיאַת מִצְרָיִם.

וּמִפְּנֵי חֲטָאֵינוּ גָּלִינוּ מֵאַרְצֵנוּ, וְנִתְרַחַקְנוּ מֵעַל אַדְמָתֵנוּ
וְאֵין אֲנַחְנוּ יְכוֹלִים לַעֲלוֹת וְלֵרָאוֹת וּלְהִשְׁתַּחֲווֹת לְפָנֶיךָ
וְלַעֲשׂוֹת חוֹבוֹתֵינוּ בְּבֵית בְּחִירָתֶךָ
בַּבַּיִת הַגָּדוֹל וְהַקָּדוֹשׁ שֶׁנִּקְרָא שִׁמְךָ עָלָיו
מִפְּנֵי הַיָּד שֶׁנִּשְׁתַּלְּחָה בְּמִקְדָּשֶׁךָ.

May it be Your will, LORD our God and God of our ancestors,
merciful King,
that You in Your abounding compassion may once more
have mercy on us and on Your Sanctuary,
rebuilding it swiftly and adding to its glory.
Our Father, our King, reveal the glory of Your kingdom to us swiftly.
Appear and be exalted over us in the sight of all that lives.
Bring back our scattered ones from among the nations,
and gather our dispersed people from the ends of the earth.

Lead us to Zion, Your city, in jubilation,
and to Jerusalem, home of Your Temple, with everlasting joy.
There we will prepare for You our obligatory offerings:
the regular daily offerings in their order
and the additional offerings according to their law.
And the additional offering(s of this Sabbath day and) of this day of
the festival of Shemini Atzeret.
we will prepare and offer before You in love,
in accord with Your will's commandment,
as You wrote for us in Your Torah
through Your servant Moses, by Your own word,
as it is said:

On Shabbat:

וּבְיוֹם הַשַּׁבָּת On the Sabbath day, make an offering of two lambs a year old, *Num. 28*
without blemish, together with two-tenths of an ephah of fine flour mixed with oil as a meal-offering, and its appropriate libation. This is the burnt-offering for every Sabbath, in addition to the regular daily burnt-offering and its libation.

בַּיּוֹם הַשְּׁמִינִי On the eighth day you shall hold an assembly; *Num. 29*
you shall do no laborious work.
And you shall offer a burnt-offering,
a fire-offering of pleasing odor to the LORD: one bullock,
one ram, seven yearling male lambs without blemish.

יְהִי רָצוֹן מִלְּפָנֶיךָ יהוה אֱלֹהֵינוּ וֵאלֹהֵי אֲבוֹתֵינוּ, מֶלֶךְ רַחֲמָן
שֶׁתָּשׁוּב וּתְרַחֵם עָלֵינוּ וְעַל מִקְדָּשְׁךָ בְּרַחֲמֶיךָ הָרַבִּים
וְתִבְנֵהוּ מְהֵרָה וּתְגַדֵּל כְּבוֹדוֹ.
אָבִינוּ מַלְכֵּנוּ, גַּלֵּה כְּבוֹד מַלְכוּתְךָ עָלֵינוּ מְהֵרָה
וְהוֹפַע וְהִנָּשֵׂא עָלֵינוּ לְעֵינֵי כָּל חָי
וְקָרֵב פְּזוּרֵינוּ מִבֵּין הַגּוֹיִם, וּנְפוּצוֹתֵינוּ כַּנֵּס מִיַּרְכְּתֵי אָרֶץ.

וַהֲבִיאֵנוּ לְצִיּוֹן עִירְךָ בְּרִנָּה
וְלִירוּשָׁלַיִם בֵּית מִקְדָּשְׁךָ בְּשִׂמְחַת עוֹלָם
וְשָׁם נַעֲשֶׂה לְפָנֶיךָ אֶת קָרְבְּנוֹת חוֹבוֹתֵינוּ
תְּמִידִים כְּסִדְרָם וּמוּסָפִים כְּהִלְכָתָם
וְאֶת מוּסַף יוֹם / שבת: וְאֶת מוּסְפֵי יוֹם הַשַּׁבָּת הַזֶּה וְיוֹם/
הַשְּׁמִינִי חַג הָעֲצֶרֶת הַזֶּה
נַעֲשֶׂה וְנַקְרִיב לְפָנֶיךָ בְּאַהֲבָה כְּמִצְוַת רְצוֹנֶךָ
כְּמוֹ שֶׁכָּתַבְתָּ עָלֵינוּ בְּתוֹרָתֶךָ
עַל יְדֵי מֹשֶׁה עַבְדֶּךָ מִפִּי כְבוֹדֶךָ, כָּאָמוּר

On שבת:

וּבְיוֹם הַשַּׁבָּת, שְׁנֵי־כְבָשִׂים בְּנֵי־שָׁנָה תְּמִימִם וּשְׁנֵי עֶשְׂרֹנִים סֹלֶת מִנְחָה בְּלוּלָה בַשֶּׁמֶן וְנִסְכּוֹ: עֹלַת שַׁבַּת בְּשַׁבַּתּוֹ, עַל־עֹלַת הַתָּמִיד וְנִסְכָּהּ: במדבר כח

בַּיּוֹם הַשְּׁמִינִי, עֲצֶרֶת תִּהְיֶה לָכֶם במדבר כט
כָּל־מְלֶאכֶת עֲבֹדָה לֹא תַעֲשׂוּ:
וְהִקְרַבְתֶּם עֹלָה אִשֵּׁה רֵיחַ נִיחֹחַ לַיהוה
פַּר אֶחָד, אַיִל אֶחָד, כְּבָשִׂים בְּנֵי־שָׁנָה שִׁבְעָה, תְּמִימִם:

And their meal-offerings and wine-libations as ordained:
three-tenths of an ephah for each bull,
two-tenths of an ephah for the ram,
one-tenth of an ephah for each lamb,
wine for the libations, a male goat for atonement,
and two regular daily offerings according to their law.

On Shabbat:

יִשְׂמְחוּ Those who keep the Sabbath and call it a delight shall rejoice in Your kingship. The people who sanctify the seventh day shall all be satisfied and take delight in Your goodness, for You favored the seventh day and declared it holy. You called it "most desirable of days" in remembrance of Creation.

אֱלֹהֵינוּ Our God and God of our ancestors,
merciful King, have compassion upon us.
You who are good and do good, respond to our call.
Return to us in Your abounding mercy
for the sake of our fathers who did Your will.
Rebuild Your Temple as at the beginning,
and establish Your Sanctuary on its site.
Let us witness its rebuilding and gladden us by its restoration.
Bring the priests back to their service,
the Levites to their song and music, and the Israelites to their homes.

וְשָׁם נַעֲלֶה There we will go up and appear and bow before You
on the three pilgrimage festivals, as is written in Your Torah:

"Three times in the year all your males shall appear *Deut. 16*
before the LORD your God at the place He will choose:
on Pesaḥ, Shavuot and Sukkot.
They shall not appear before the LORD empty-handed.
Each shall bring such a gift as he can, in proportion
to the blessing that the LORD your God grants you."

וּמִנְחָתָם וְנִסְכֵּיהֶם כִּמְדֻבָּר
שְׁלֹשָׁה עֶשְׂרֹנִים לַפָּר וּשְׁנֵי עֶשְׂרֹנִים לָאָיִל, וְעִשָּׂרוֹן לַכֶּבֶשׂ
וְיַיִן כְּנִסְכּוֹ, וְשָׂעִיר לְכַפֵּר, וּשְׁנֵי תְמִידִים כְּהִלְכָתָם.

On שבת*:*

יִשְׂמְחוּ בְמַלְכוּתְךָ שׁוֹמְרֵי שַׁבָּת וְקוֹרְאֵי עֹנֶג. עַם מְקַדְּשֵׁי שְׁבִיעִי
כֻּלָּם יִשְׂבְּעוּ וְיִתְעַנְּגוּ מִטּוּבֶךָ, וּבַשְּׁבִיעִי רָצִיתָ בּוֹ וְקִדַּשְׁתּוֹ, חֶמְדַּת
יָמִים אוֹתוֹ קָרָאתָ, זֵכֶר לְמַעֲשֵׂה בְרֵאשִׁית.

אֱלֹהֵינוּ וֵאלֹהֵי אֲבוֹתֵינוּ, מֶלֶךְ רַחֲמָן רַחֵם עָלֵינוּ
טוֹב וּמֵטִיב הִדָּרֶשׁ לָנוּ
שׁוּבָה אֵלֵינוּ בַּהֲמוֹן רַחֲמֶיךָ
בִּגְלַל אָבוֹת שֶׁעָשׂוּ רְצוֹנֶךָ.
בְּנֵה בֵיתְךָ כְּבַתְּחִלָּה וְכוֹנֵן מִקְדָּשְׁךָ עַל מְכוֹנוֹ
וְהַרְאֵנוּ בְּבִנְיָנוֹ, וְשַׂמְּחֵנוּ בְּתִקּוּנוֹ
וְהָשֵׁב כֹּהֲנִים לַעֲבוֹדָתָם, וּלְוִיִּם לְשִׁירָם וּלְזִמְרָם
וְהָשֵׁב יִשְׂרָאֵל לִנְוֵיהֶם.

וְשָׁם נַעֲלֶה וְנֵרָאֶה וְנִשְׁתַּחֲוֶה לְפָנֶיךָ בְּשָׁלֹשׁ פַּעֲמֵי רְגָלֵינוּ
כַּכָּתוּב בְּתוֹרָתֶךָ
שָׁלוֹשׁ פְּעָמִים בַּשָּׁנָה יֵרָאֶה כָל־זְכוּרְךָ אֶת־פְּנֵי יהוה אֱלֹהֶיךָ דברים טז
בַּמָּקוֹם אֲשֶׁר יִבְחָר
בְּחַג הַמַּצּוֹת, וּבְחַג הַשָּׁבֻעוֹת, וּבְחַג הַסֻּכּוֹת
וְלֹא יֵרָאֶה אֶת־פְּנֵי יהוה רֵיקָם:
אִישׁ כְּמַתְּנַת יָדוֹ, כְּבִרְכַּת יהוה אֱלֹהֶיךָ אֲשֶׁר נָתַן־לָךְ:

On Shabbat add the words in parentheses:

וְהַשִּׂיאֵנוּ Bestow on us, Lord our God,
the blessing of Your festivals
for life and peace, joy and gladness,
as You desired and promised to bless us.
(Our God and God of our fathers, find favor in our rest.)
Make us holy through Your commandments
and grant us a share in Your Torah;
satisfy us with Your goodness, gladden us with Your salvation,
and purify our hearts to serve You in truth.
And grant us a heritage, Lord our God, (with love and favor,)
with joy and gladness, Your holy (Sabbath and) festivals.
May Israel, who sanctify Your name, rejoice in You.
Blessed are You, Lord,
who sanctifies (the Sabbath and) Israel and the festive seasons.

TEMPLE SERVICE

רְצֵה Find favor, Lord our God, in Your people Israel
and their prayer.
Restore the service to Your most holy House,
and accept in love and favor the fire-offerings of Israel
and their prayer.
May the service of Your people Israel always find favor with You.

If Kohanim say the Priestly Blessing during the Leader's Repetition, the following is said (In Israel the formula on the next page is said); otherwise the Leader continues with "And may our eyes" on the next page.

All: וְתֶעֱרַב May our entreaty be as pleasing to You as a burnt-offering and sacrifice. Please, Compassionate One, in Your abounding mercy restore Your Presence to Zion, Your city, and the order of the Temple service to Jerusalem. And may our eyes witness Your return to Zion in compassion, there we may serve You with reverence as in the days of old and as in former years.

Leader: Blessed are You, Lord, for You alone do we serve with reverence.

The service continues with "We give thanks" on the next page.

On שבת *add the words in parentheses:*

וְהַשִּׂיאֵנוּ יהוה אֱלֹהֵינוּ אֶת בִּרְכַּת מוֹעֲדֶיךָ
לְחַיִּים וּלְשָׁלוֹם, לְשִׂמְחָה וּלְשָׂשׂוֹן
כַּאֲשֶׁר רָצִיתָ וְאָמַרְתָּ לְבָרְכֵנוּ.
(אֱלֹהֵינוּ וֵאלֹהֵי אֲבוֹתֵינוּ, רְצֵה בִמְנוּחָתֵנוּ)
קַדְּשֵׁנוּ בְּמִצְוֹתֶיךָ, וְתֵן חֶלְקֵנוּ בְּתוֹרָתֶךָ
שַׂבְּעֵנוּ מִטּוּבֶךָ, וְשַׂמְּחֵנוּ בִּישׁוּעָתֶךָ
וְטַהֵר לִבֵּנוּ לְעָבְדְּךָ בֶּאֱמֶת
וְהַנְחִילֵנוּ יהוה אֱלֹהֵינוּ (בְּאַהֲבָה וּבְרָצוֹן) בְּשִׂמְחָה וּבְשָׂשׂוֹן
(שַׁבָּת וּ)מוֹעֲדֵי קָדְשֶׁךָ וְיִשְׂמְחוּ בְךָ יִשְׂרָאֵל מְקַדְּשֵׁי שְׁמֶךָ.
בָּרוּךְ אַתָּה יהוה, מְקַדֵּשׁ (הַשַּׁבָּת וְ)יִשְׂרָאֵל וְהַזְּמַנִּים.

עבודה

רְצֵה יהוה אֱלֹהֵינוּ בְּעַמְּךָ יִשְׂרָאֵל, וּבִתְפִלָּתָם
וְהָשֵׁב אֶת הָעֲבוֹדָה לִדְבִיר בֵּיתֶךָ
וְאִשֵּׁי יִשְׂרָאֵל וּתְפִלָּתָם בְּאַהֲבָה תְקַבֵּל בְּרָצוֹן
וּתְהִי לְרָצוֹן תָּמִיד עֲבוֹדַת יִשְׂרָאֵל עַמֶּךָ.

If כהנים *say* ברכת כהנים *during* חזרת הש״ץ*,*
the following is said (In ארץ ישראל *the formula on the next page is said);*
otherwise the שליח ציבור *continues with* וְתֶחֱזֶינָה *on the next page.*

קהל וש״ץ: וְתֶעֱרַב עָלֶיךָ עֲתִירָתֵנוּ כְּעוֹלָה וּכְקָרְבָּן. אָנָּא רַחוּם, בְּרַחֲמֶיךָ הָרַבִּים הָשֵׁב שְׁכִינָתְךָ לְצִיּוֹן עִירֶךָ, וְסֵדֶר הָעֲבוֹדָה לִירוּשָׁלָיִם. וְתֶחֱזֶינָה עֵינֵינוּ בְּשׁוּבְךָ לְצִיּוֹן בְּרַחֲמִים. וְשָׁם נַעֲבָדְךָ בְּיִרְאָה כִּימֵי עוֹלָם וּכְשָׁנִים קַדְמוֹנִיּוֹת.

ש״ץ: בָּרוּךְ אַתָּה יהוה שֶׁאוֹתְךָ לְבַדְּךָ בְּיִרְאָה נַעֲבֹד.

The service continues with מוֹדִים *on the next page.*

In Israel the following formula is used instead:

All: וְתֶעֱרַב May our entreaty be as pleasing to You as a burnt-offering and sacrifice. Please, Compassionate One, in Your abounding mercy restore Your Presence to Zion, Your city, and the order of the Temple service to Jerusalem. That there we may serve You with reverence as in the days of old and as in former years.

When the Priestly Blessing is not said, and also in Israel, the Leader continues:

And may our eyes witness Your return to Zion in compassion. Blessed are You, LORD, who restores His Presence to Zion.

THANKSGIVING

Bow at the first nine words.

מוֹדִים We give thanks to You,
for You are the LORD our God
and God of our ancestors
for ever and all time.
You are the Rock of our lives,
Shield of our salvation
from generation to generation.
We will thank You and
declare Your praise for our lives,
which are entrusted into Your hand;
for our souls,
which are placed in Your charge;
for Your miracles
which are with us every day;
and for Your wonders and favors
at all times, evening,
morning and midday.
You are good –
for Your compassion never fails.
You are compassionate –
for Your loving-kindnesses never cease.
We have always placed our hope in You.

As the Leader recites Modim, the congregation says quietly:

מוֹדִים We give thanks to You,
for You are the LORD our God
and God of our ancestors,
God of all flesh,
who formed us
and formed the universe.
Blessings and thanks
are due to Your great
and holy name for giving us
life and sustaining us.
May You continue
to give us life
and sustain us;
and may You gather our
exiles to Your holy courts,
to keep Your decrees,
do Your will and serve You
with a perfect heart,
for it is for us
to give You thanks.
Blessed be God to whom
thanksgiving is due.

In ארץ ישראל *the following formula is used instead:*

קהל וש״ץ: וְתֶעֱרַב עָלֶיךָ עֲתִירָתֵנוּ כְּעוֹלָה וּכְקָרְבָּן. אָנָּא רַחוּם, בְּרַחֲמֶיךָ הָרַבִּים הָשֵׁב שְׁכִינָתְךָ לְצִיּוֹן עִירְךָ, וְסֵדֶר הָעֲבוֹדָה לִירוּשָׁלַיִם. וְשָׁם נַעֲבָדְךָ בְּיִרְאָה כִּימֵי עוֹלָם וּכְשָׁנִים קַדְמוֹנִיּוֹת.

When ברכת כהנים *is not said, and also in* ארץ ישראל*, the* שליח ציבור *continues:*

וְתֶחֱזֶינָה עֵינֵינוּ בְּשׁוּבְךָ לְצִיּוֹן בְּרַחֲמִים.
בָּרוּךְ אַתָּה יהוה, הַמַּחֲזִיר שְׁכִינָתוֹ לְצִיּוֹן.

הודאה

Bow at the first five words.

מוֹדִים אֲנַחְנוּ לָךְ
שָׁאַתָּה הוּא יהוה אֱלֹהֵינוּ
וֵאלֹהֵי אֲבוֹתֵינוּ לְעוֹלָם וָעֶד.
צוּר חַיֵּינוּ, מָגֵן יִשְׁעֵנוּ
אַתָּה הוּא לְדוֹר וָדוֹר.
נוֹדֶה לְּךָ וּנְסַפֵּר תְּהִלָּתֶךָ
עַל חַיֵּינוּ הַמְּסוּרִים בְּיָדֶךָ
וְעַל נִשְׁמוֹתֵינוּ הַפְּקוּדוֹת לָךְ
וְעַל נִסֶּיךָ שֶׁבְּכָל יוֹם עִמָּנוּ
וְעַל נִפְלְאוֹתֶיךָ וְטוֹבוֹתֶיךָ
שֶׁבְּכָל עֵת
עֶרֶב וָבֹקֶר וְצָהֳרָיִם.
הַטּוֹב, כִּי לֹא כָלוּ רַחֲמֶיךָ
וְהַמְרַחֵם, כִּי לֹא תַמּוּ חֲסָדֶיךָ
מֵעוֹלָם קִוִּינוּ לָךְ.

As the שליח ציבור *recites* מודים*, the* קהל *says quietly:*

מוֹדִים אֲנַחְנוּ לָךְ
שָׁאַתָּה הוּא יהוה אֱלֹהֵינוּ
וֵאלֹהֵי אֲבוֹתֵינוּ
אֱלֹהֵי כָל בָּשָׂר
יוֹצְרֵנוּ, יוֹצֵר בְּרֵאשִׁית.
בְּרָכוֹת וְהוֹדָאוֹת
לְשִׁמְךָ הַגָּדוֹל וְהַקָּדוֹשׁ
עַל שֶׁהֶחֱיִיתָנוּ וְקִיַּמְתָּנוּ.
כֵּן תְּחַיֵּנוּ וּתְקַיְּמֵנוּ
וְתֶאֱסֹף גָּלֻיּוֹתֵינוּ
לְחַצְרוֹת קָדְשֶׁךָ
לִשְׁמֹר חֻקֶּיךָ
וְלַעֲשׂוֹת רְצוֹנֶךָ וּלְעָבְדְּךָ
בְּלֵבָב שָׁלֵם
עַל שֶׁאֲנַחְנוּ מוֹדִים לָךְ.
בָּרוּךְ אֵל הַהוֹדָאוֹת.

וְעַל כֻּלָּם For all these things may Your name be
blessed and exalted, our King, continually, for ever and all time.
Let all that lives thank You, Selah!
and praise Your name in truth,
God, our Savior and Help, Selah!
▾Blessed are You, LORD, whose name is "the Good"
and to whom thanks are due.

BIRKAT KOHANIM

When the Priestly Blessing is not said, the Leader says the formula on page 1176.
The following supplication is recited quietly
while the Leader says "Let all that lives" above.

In some communities, the congregation says:

יְהִי רָצוֹן May it be Your will, LORD our God and God of our ancestors, that this blessing with which You have commanded to bless Your people Israel should be a complete blessing, with neither hindrance nor sin, now and forever.

The Kohanim say:

יְהִי רָצוֹן May it be Your will, LORD our God and God of our ancestors, that this blessing with which You have commanded us to bless Your people Israel should be a complete blessing, with neither hindrance nor sin, now and forever.

For the blessing of the Kohanim in Israel, see page 1396.
The following is recited quietly by the Leader:

אֱלֹהֵינוּ Our God and God of our fathers,
bless us with the threefold blessing in the Torah,
written by the hand of Moses Your servant
and pronounced by Aaron and his sons:

The Leader says aloud:

Kohanim!

In most places, the congregation responds:

Your holy people, as it said:

The Kohanim say the following blessing in unison:

בָּרוּךְ Blessed are You, LORD our God, King of the Universe,
who has made us holy with the holiness of Aaron,
and has commanded us to bless His people Israel with love.

וְעַל כֻּלָּם יִתְבָּרַךְ וְיִתְרוֹמַם שִׁמְךָ מַלְכֵּנוּ תָּמִיד לְעוֹלָם וָעֶד.
וְכֹל הַחַיִּים יוֹדְוּךָ סֶּלָה, וִיהַלְלוּ אֶת שִׁמְךָ בֶּאֱמֶת
הָאֵל יְשׁוּעָתֵנוּ וְעֶזְרָתֵנוּ סֶלָה.
ׂבָּרוּךְ אַתָּה יהוה, הַטּוֹב שִׁמְךָ וּלְךָ נָאֶה לְהוֹדוֹת.

ברכת כוהנים

When ברכת כהנים *is not said, the* שליח ציבור *says the formula on page 1177.*
The following supplication is recited quietly
while the שליח ציבור *says* וְכֹל הַחַיִּים *above.*

In some communities, the קהל *says:*

יְהִי רָצוֹן מִלְּפָנֶיךָ, יהוה אֱלֹהֵינוּ וֵאלֹהֵי אֲבוֹתֵינוּ, שֶׁתְּהֵא הַבְּרָכָה הַזֹּאת שֶׁצִּוִּיתָ לְבָרֵךְ אֶת עַמְּךָ יִשְׂרָאֵל בְּרָכָה שְׁלֵמָה, וְלֹא יִהְיֶה בָּהּ שׁוּם מִכְשׁוֹל וְעָוֹן מֵעַתָּה וְעַד עוֹלָם.

The כהנים *say:*

יְהִי רָצוֹן מִלְּפָנֶיךָ, יהוה אֱלֹהֵינוּ וֵאלֹהֵי אֲבוֹתֵינוּ, שֶׁתְּהֵא הַבְּרָכָה הַזֹּאת שֶׁצִּוִּיתָנוּ לְבָרֵךְ אֶת עַמְּךָ יִשְׂרָאֵל בְּרָכָה שְׁלֵמָה, וְלֹא יִהְיֶה בָּהּ שׁוּם מִכְשׁוֹל וְעָוֹן מֵעַתָּה וְעַד עוֹלָם.

For the blessing of the כהנים *in* ארץ ישראל *see page 1397.*
The following is recited quietly by the שליח ציבור*:*

אֱלֹהֵינוּ וֵאלֹהֵי אֲבוֹתֵינוּ
בָּרְכֵנוּ בַבְּרָכָה הַמְשֻׁלֶּשֶׁת בַּתּוֹרָה
הַכְּתוּבָה עַל יְדֵי מֹשֶׁה עַבְדֶּךָ
הָאֲמוּרָה מִפִּי אַהֲרֹן וּבָנָיו

The שליח ציבור *says aloud:*

כֹּהֲנִים

In most places, the קהל *responds:*

עַם קְדוֹשֶׁךָ, כָּאָמוּר:

The כהנים *say the following blessing in unison:*

בָּרוּךְ אַתָּה יהוה אֱלֹהֵינוּ מֶלֶךְ הָעוֹלָם, אֲשֶׁר קִדְּשָׁנוּ בִּקְדֻשָּׁתוֹ שֶׁל אַהֲרֹן, וְצִוָּנוּ לְבָרֵךְ אֶת עַמּוֹ יִשְׂרָאֵל בְּאַהֲבָה.

The first word in each sentence is said by the Leader, followed by the Kohanim. Some read silently the accompanying verses. One should remain silent and not look at the Kohanim while the blessings are being said.

May [He] bless you	May the LORD, Maker of heaven and earth, bless you from Zion.	*Ps. 134*
The LORD	LORD our Master, how majestic is Your name throughout the earth.	*Ps. 8*
And protect you.	Protect me, God, for in You I take refuge.	*Ps. 16*

Read the following silently while the Kohanim chant. Omit on Shabbat.

Master of the Universe, I am Yours and my dreams are Yours. I have dreamt a dream and I do not know what it means. May it be Your will, LORD my God and God of my fathers, that all my dreams be, for me and all Israel, for good, whether I have dreamt about myself, or about others, or others have dreamt about me. If they are good, strengthen and reinforce them, and may they be fulfilled in me and them like the dreams of the righteous Joseph. If, though, they need healing, heal them as You healed Hezekiah King of Judah from his illness, like Miriam the prophetess from her leprosy, like Na'aman from his leprosy, like the waters of Mara by Moses our teacher, and like the waters of Jericho by Elisha. And just as You turned the curses of Balaam the wicked from curse to blessing, so turn all my dreams about me and all Israel to good; protect me, be gracious to me and accept me. Amen.

May [He] make shine	May God be gracious to us and bless us; may He make His face shine upon us, Selah.	*Ps. 67*
The LORD	The LORD, the LORD, compassionate and gracious God, slow to anger, abounding in kindness and truth.	*Ex. 34*
His face	Turn to me and be gracious to me, for I am alone and afflicted.	*Ps. 25*
On you	To You, LORD, I lift up my soul.	*Ps. 25*
And be gracious to you.	As the eyes of slaves turn to their master's hand, or the eyes of a slave-girl to the hand of her mistress, so our eyes are turned to the LORD our God, awaiting His favor.	*Ps. 123*

Read the following silently while the Kohanim chant. Omit on Shabbat.

Master of the Universe, I am Yours and my dreams are Yours. I have dreamt a dream and I do not know what it means. May it be Your will, LORD my God and God of my fathers, that all my dreams be, for me and all Israel, for good, whether I have

The first word in each sentence is said by the שליח ציבור*, followed by the* כהנים*. Some read silently the accompanying verses. One should remain silent and not look at the* כהנים *while the blessings are being said.*

יְבָרֶכְךָ יְבָרֶכְךָ יהוה מִצִּיּוֹן, עֹשֵׂה שָׁמַיִם וָאָרֶץ: תהלים קלד

יהוה יהוה אֲדֹנֵינוּ, מָה־אַדִּיר שִׁמְךָ בְּכָל־הָאָרֶץ: תהלים ח

וְיִשְׁמְרֶךָ: שָׁמְרֵנִי אֵל, כִּי־חָסִיתִי בָךְ: תהלים טז

Read the following silently while the כהנים *chant. Omit on* שבת*.*

רִבּוֹנוֹ שֶׁל עוֹלָם, אֲנִי שֶׁלָּךְ וַחֲלוֹמוֹתַי שֶׁלָּךְ. חֲלוֹם חָלַמְתִּי וְאֵינִי יוֹדֵעַ מַה הוּא. יְהִי רָצוֹן מִלְּפָנֶיךָ, יהוה אֱלֹהַי וֵאלֹהֵי אֲבוֹתַי, שֶׁיִּהְיוּ כָּל חֲלוֹמוֹתַי עָלַי וְעַל כָּל יִשְׂרָאֵל לְטוֹבָה, בֵּין שֶׁחָלַמְתִּי עַל עַצְמִי, וּבֵין שֶׁחָלַמְתִּי עַל אֲחֵרִים, וּבֵין שֶׁחָלְמוּ אֲחֵרִים עָלָי. אִם טוֹבִים הֵם, חַזְּקֵם וְאַמְּצֵם, וְיִתְקַיְּמוּ בִי וּבָהֶם, כַּחֲלוֹמוֹתָיו שֶׁל יוֹסֵף הַצַּדִּיק. וְאִם צְרִיכִים רְפוּאָה, רְפָאֵם כְּחִזְקִיָּהוּ מֶלֶךְ יְהוּדָה מֵחָלְיוֹ, וּכְמִרְיָם הַנְּבִיאָה מִצָּרַעְתָּהּ, וּכְנַעֲמָן מִצָּרַעְתּוֹ, וּכְמֵי מָרָה עַל יְדֵי מֹשֶׁה רַבֵּנוּ, וּכְמֵי יְרִיחוֹ עַל יְדֵי אֱלִישָׁע. וּכְשֵׁם שֶׁהָפַכְתָּ אֶת קִלְלַת בִּלְעָם הָרָשָׁע מִקְּלָלָה לִבְרָכָה, כֵּן תַּהֲפֹךְ כָּל חֲלוֹמוֹתַי עָלַי וְעַל כָּל יִשְׂרָאֵל לְטוֹבָה, וְתִשְׁמְרֵנִי וּתְחָנֵּנִי וְתִרְצֵנִי. אָמֵן.

יָאֵר אֱלֹהִים יְחָנֵּנוּ וִיבָרְכֵנוּ, יָאֵר פָּנָיו אִתָּנוּ סֶלָה: תהלים סז

יהוה יהוה, יהוה, אֵל רַחוּם וְחַנּוּן, אֶרֶךְ אַפַּיִם וְרַב־חֶסֶד וֶאֱמֶת: שמות לד

פָּנָיו פְּנֵה־אֵלַי וְחָנֵּנִי, כִּי־יָחִיד וְעָנִי אָנִי: תהלים כה

אֵלֶיךָ אֵלֶיךָ יהוה נַפְשִׁי אֶשָּׂא: תהלים כה

וִיחֻנֶּךָּ: הִנֵּה כְעֵינֵי עֲבָדִים אֶל־יַד אֲדוֹנֵיהֶם תהלים קכג
כְּעֵינֵי שִׁפְחָה אֶל־יַד גְּבִרְתָּהּ, כֵּן עֵינֵינוּ אֶל־יהוה אֱלֹהֵינוּ
עַד שֶׁיְּחָנֵּנוּ:

Read the following silently while the כהנים *chant. Omit on* שבת*.*

רִבּוֹנוֹ שֶׁל עוֹלָם, אֲנִי שֶׁלָּךְ וַחֲלוֹמוֹתַי שֶׁלָּךְ. חֲלוֹם חָלַמְתִּי וְאֵינִי יוֹדֵעַ מַה הוּא. יְהִי רָצוֹן מִלְּפָנֶיךָ, יהוה אֱלֹהַי וֵאלֹהֵי אֲבוֹתַי, שֶׁיִּהְיוּ כָּל חֲלוֹמוֹתַי עָלַי וְעַל כָּל יִשְׂרָאֵל לְטוֹבָה, בֵּין שֶׁחָלַמְתִּי עַל עַצְמִי, וּבֵין שֶׁחָלַמְתִּי עַל אֲחֵרִים, וּבֵין שֶׁחָלְמוּ אֲחֵרִים עָלָי.

dreamt about myself, or about others, or others have dreamt about me. If they are good, strengthen and reinforce them, and may they be fulfilled in me and them like the dreams of the righteous Joseph. If, though, they need healing, heal them as You healed Hezekiah King of Judah from his illness, like Miriam the prophetess from her leprosy, like Na'aman from his leprosy, like the waters of Mara by Moses our teacher, and like the waters of Jericho by Elisha. And just as You turned the curses of Balaam the wicked from curse to blessing, so turn all my dreams about me and all Israel to good; protect me, be gracious to me and accept me. Amen.

May [He] turn	May he receive a blessing from the LORD and a just reward from the God of his salvation. And he will win grace and good favor in the eyes of God and man.	*Ps. 24* *Prov. 3*
The LORD	LORD, be gracious to us; we yearn for You. Be their strength every morning, our salvation in time of distress.	*Is. 33*
His face	Do not hide Your face from me in the day of my distress. Turn Your ear to me; on the day I call, swiftly answer me.	*Ps. 102*
Toward you	To You, enthroned in heaven, I lift my eyes.	*Ps. 123*
And give	They shall place My name on the children of Israel, and I will bless them.	*Num. 6*
You	Yours, LORD, are the greatness and the power, the glory, majesty and splendor, for everything in heaven and earth is Yours. Yours, LORD, is the kingdom; You are exalted as Head over all.	*1 Chr. 29*
Peace.	"Peace, peace, to those far and near," says the LORD, "and I will heal him."	*Is. 57*

Read the following silently while the Kohanim chant. Omit on Shabbat.

May it be Your will, LORD my God and God of my fathers, that You act for the sake of Your simple, sacred kindness and great compassion, and for the purity of Your great, mighty and awesome name of twenty-two letters derived from the verses of the priestly blessing spoken by Aaron and his sons, Your holy people. May You be close to me when I call to You. May You hear my prayer, plea and cry as You did the cry of Jacob Your perfect one who was called "a plain man." May You grant me and all the members of my household our food and sustenance, generously not meagerly, honestly not otherwise, with satisfaction not pain, from Your generous hand, just as You gave a portion of bread to eat and clothes to wear to Jacob our father who was called "a plain man." May we find love, grace, kindness and compassion in Your sight and in the eyes of all who see us. May my words in service to You be heard, as You

אִם טוֹבִים הֵם, חַזְּקֵם וְאַמְּצֵם, וְיִתְקַיְּמוּ בִי וּבָהֶם, כַּחֲלוֹמוֹתָיו שֶׁל יוֹסֵף הַצַּדִּיק. וְאִם צְרִיכִים רְפוּאָה, רְפָאֵם כְּחִזְקִיָּהוּ מֶלֶךְ יְהוּדָה מֵחָלְיוֹ, וּכְמִרְיָם הַנְּבִיאָה מִצָּרַעְתָּהּ, וּכְנַעֲמָן מִצָּרַעְתּוֹ, וּכְמֵי מָרָה עַל יְדֵי מֹשֶׁה רַבֵּנוּ, וּכְמֵי יְרִיחוֹ עַל יְדֵי אֱלִישָׁע. וּכְשֵׁם שֶׁהָפַכְתָּ אֶת קִלְלַת בִּלְעָם הָרָשָׁע מִקְּלָלָה לִבְרָכָה, כֵּן תַּהֲפֹךְ כָּל חֲלוֹמוֹתַי עָלַי וְעַל כָּל יִשְׂרָאֵל לְטוֹבָה, וְתִשְׁמְרֵנִי וּתְחָנֵּנִי וְתִרְצֵנִי. אָמֵן.

יִשָּׂא יִשָּׂא בְרָכָה מֵאֵת יהוה, וּצְדָקָה מֵאֱלֹהֵי יִשְׁעוֹ: תהלים כד
וּמְצָא־חֵן וְשֵׂכֶל־טוֹב בְּעֵינֵי אֱלֹהִים וְאָדָם: משלי ג

יהוה יהוה חָנֵּנוּ, לְךָ קִוִּינוּ, הֱיֵה זְרֹעָם לַבְּקָרִים ישעיה לג
אַף־יְשׁוּעָתֵנוּ בְּעֵת צָרָה:

פָּנָיו אַל־תַּסְתֵּר פָּנֶיךָ מִמֶּנִּי בְּיוֹם צַר לִי, הַטֵּה־אֵלַי אָזְנֶךָ תהלים קב
בְּיוֹם אֶקְרָא מַהֵר עֲנֵנִי:

אֵלֶיךָ אֵלֶיךָ נָשָׂאתִי אֶת־עֵינַי, הַיֹּשְׁבִי בַּשָּׁמָיִם: תהלים קכג

וְיָשֵׂם וְשָׂמוּ אֶת־שְׁמִי עַל־בְּנֵי יִשְׂרָאֵל, וַאֲנִי אֲבָרְכֵם: במדבר ו

לְךָ לְךָ יהוה הַגְּדֻלָּה וְהַגְּבוּרָה וְהַתִּפְאֶרֶת וְהַנֵּצַח וְהַהוֹד דברי הימים א׳ כט
כִּי־כֹל בַּשָּׁמַיִם וּבָאָרֶץ, לְךָ יהוה הַמַּמְלָכָה
וְהַמִּתְנַשֵּׂא לְכֹל לְרֹאשׁ:

שָׁלוֹם: שָׁלוֹם שָׁלוֹם לָרָחוֹק וְלַקָּרוֹב, אָמַר יהוה, וּרְפָאתִיו: ישעיה נז

Read the following silently while the כהנים *chant. Omit on* שבת*.*

יְהִי רָצוֹן מִלְּפָנֶיךָ, יהוה אֱלֹהַי וֵאלֹהֵי אֲבוֹתַי, שֶׁתַּעֲשֶׂה לְמַעַן קְדֻשַּׁת חֲסָדֶיךָ וְגֹדֶל רַחֲמֶיךָ הַפְּשׁוּטִים, וּלְמַעַן טָהֳרַת שִׁמְךָ הַגָּדוֹל הַגִּבּוֹר וְהַנּוֹרָא, בֶּן עֶשְׂרִים וּשְׁתַּיִם אוֹתִיּוֹת הַיּוֹצֵא מִפְּסוּקִים שֶׁל בִּרְכַּת כֹּהֲנִים הָאֲמוּרָה מִפִּי אַהֲרֹן וּבָנָיו עַם קְדוֹשֶׁךָ, שֶׁתִּהְיֶה קָרוֹב לִי בְּקָרְאִי לָךְ, וְתִשְׁמַע תְּפִלָּתִי נַאֲקָתִי וְאֶנְקָתִי תָּמִיד, כְּשֵׁם שֶׁשָּׁמַעְתָּ אֶנְקַת יַעֲקֹב תְּמִימֶךָ הַנִּקְרָא אִישׁ תָּם. וְתִתֶּן לִי וּלְכָל נַפְשׁוֹת בֵּיתִי מְזוֹנוֹתֵינוּ וּפַרְנָסָתֵנוּ בְּרֶוַח וְלֹא בְצִמְצוּם, בְּהֶתֵּר וְלֹא בְאִסּוּר, בְּנַחַת וְלֹא בְצַעַר, מִתַּחַת יָדְךָ הָרְחָבָה,

granted Joseph Your righteous one, at the time when he was robed by his father in a cloak of fine wool, that he find grace, kindness and compassion in Your sight and in the eyes of all who saw him. May You do wonders and miracles with me, and a sign for good. Grant me success in my paths, and set in my heart understanding that I may understand, discern and fulfill all the words of Your Torah's teachings and mysteries. Save me from errors and purify my thoughts and my heart to serve You and be in awe of You. Prolong my days (*add, where appropriate:* and those of my father, mother, wife, husband, son/s, and daughter/s) in joy and happiness, with much strength and peace. Amen, Selah.

The Leader continues with "Grant peace" below.

The congregation says:
אַדִּיר Majestic One on high who dwells in power: You are peace and Your name is peace. May it be Your will to bestow on us and on Your people the house of Israel, life and blessing as a safeguard for peace.

The Kohanim say:
רִבּוֹנוֹ Master of the Universe: we have done what You have decreed for us. So too may You deal with us as You have promised us. Look down from Your holy dwelling place, from heaven, and bless Your people Israel and the land You have given us as You promised on oath to our ancestors, a land flowing with milk and honey. *Deut. 26*

If the Priestly Blessing is not said, the following is said by the Leader:
Our God and God of our fathers, bless us with the threefold blessing in the Torah, written by the hand of Moses Your servant and pronounced by Aaron and his sons the priests, Your holy people, as it is said:

May the LORD bless you and protect you. *Num. 6*
Cong: May it be Your will.
May the LORD make His face shine on you and be gracious to you.
Cong: May it be Your will.
May the LORD turn His face toward you, and grant you peace.
Cong: May it be Your will.

PEACE

שִׂים שָׁלוֹם Grant peace, goodness and blessing,
grace, loving-kindness and compassion to us
and all Israel Your people.
Bless us, our Father, all as one, with the light of Your face,
for by the light of Your face You have given us, LORD our God,
the Torah of life and love of kindness,
righteousness, blessing, compassion, life and peace.

כְּשֵׁם שֶׁנָּתַתָּ פִּסַּת לֶחֶם לֶאֱכֹל וּבֶגֶד לִלְבֹּשׁ לְיַעֲקֹב אָבִינוּ הַנִּקְרָא אִישׁ תָּם. וְתִתְּנֵנוּ לְאַהֲבָה, לְחֵן וּלְחֶסֶד וּלְרַחֲמִים בְּעֵינֶיךָ וּבְעֵינֵי כָל רוֹאֵינוּ, וְיִהְיוּ דְבָרַי נִשְׁמָעִים לַעֲבוֹדָתֶךָ, כְּשֵׁם שֶׁנָּתַתָּ אֶת יוֹסֵף צַדִּיקֶךָ בְּשָׁעָה שֶׁהִלְבִּישׁוֹ אָבִיו כְּתֹנֶת פַּסִּים לְחֵן וּלְחֶסֶד וּלְרַחֲמִים בְּעֵינֶיךָ וּבְעֵינֵי כָל רוֹאָיו. וְתַעֲשֶׂה עִמִּי נִפְלָאוֹת וְנִסִּים, וּלְטוֹבָה אוֹת, וְתַצְלִיחֵנִי בִּדְרָכַי, וְתֵן בְּלִבִּי בִּינָה לְהָבִין וּלְהַשְׂכִּיל וּלְקַיֵּם אֶת כָּל דִּבְרֵי תַלְמוּד תּוֹרָתֶךָ וְסוֹדוֹתֶיהָ, וְתַצִּילֵנִי מִשְּׁגִיאוֹת, וּתְטַהֵר רַעְיוֹנַי וְלִבִּי לַעֲבוֹדָתֶךָ, וְתַאֲרִיךְ יָמַי (וִימֵי אָבִי וְאִמִּי / וְאִשְׁתִּי / וּבַעְלִי / וּבָנַי וּבְנוֹתַי) בְּטוֹב וּבִנְעִימוּת, בְּרֹב עֹז וְשָׁלוֹם, אָמֵן סֶלָה.

The שליח ציבור *continues with* שִׂים שָׁלוֹם *below.*

The קהל *says:*

אַדִּיר בַּמָּרוֹם שׁוֹכֵן בִּגְבוּרָה, אַתָּה שָׁלוֹם וְשִׁמְךָ שָׁלוֹם. יְהִי רָצוֹן שֶׁתָּשִׂים עָלֵינוּ וְעַל כָּל עַמְּךָ בֵּית יִשְׂרָאֵל חַיִּים וּבְרָכָה לְמִשְׁמֶרֶת שָׁלוֹם.

The כהנים *say:*

רִבּוֹנוֹ שֶׁל עוֹלָם, עָשִׂינוּ מַה שֶּׁגָּזַרְתָּ עָלֵינוּ, אַף אַתָּה
דברים כו עֲשֵׂה עִמָּנוּ כְּמוֹ שֶׁהִבְטַחְתָּנוּ. הַשְׁקִיפָה מִמְּעוֹן קָדְשְׁךָ מִן־הַשָּׁמַיִם, וּבָרֵךְ אֶת־עַמְּךָ אֶת־יִשְׂרָאֵל, וְאֵת הָאֲדָמָה אֲשֶׁר נָתַתָּה לָנוּ, כַּאֲשֶׁר נִשְׁבַּעְתָּ לַאֲבֹתֵינוּ, אֶרֶץ זָבַת חָלָב וּדְבָשׁ:

If ברכת כהנים *is not said, the following is said by the* שליח ציבור:

אֱלֹהֵינוּ וֵאלֹהֵי אֲבוֹתֵינוּ, בָּרְכֵנוּ בַּבְּרָכָה הַמְשֻׁלֶּשֶׁת בַּתּוֹרָה, הַכְּתוּבָה עַל יְדֵי מֹשֶׁה עַבְדֶּךָ, הָאֲמוּרָה מִפִּי אַהֲרֹן וּבָנָיו כֹּהֲנִים עַם קְדוֹשֶׁיךָ, כָּאָמוּר

במדבר ו יְבָרֶכְךָ יהוה וְיִשְׁמְרֶךָ: קהל: כֵּן יְהִי רָצוֹן
יָאֵר יהוה פָּנָיו אֵלֶיךָ וִיחֻנֶּךָּ: קהל: כֵּן יְהִי רָצוֹן
יִשָּׂא יהוה פָּנָיו אֵלֶיךָ וְיָשֵׂם לְךָ שָׁלוֹם: קהל: כֵּן יְהִי רָצוֹן

שלום

שִׂים שָׁלוֹם טוֹבָה וּבְרָכָה, חֵן וָחֶסֶד וְרַחֲמִים
עָלֵינוּ וְעַל כָּל יִשְׂרָאֵל עַמֶּךָ.
בָּרְכֵנוּ אָבִינוּ כֻּלָּנוּ כְּאֶחָד בְּאוֹר פָּנֶיךָ
כִּי בְאוֹר פָּנֶיךָ נָתַתָּ לָּנוּ, יהוה אֱלֹהֵינוּ
תּוֹרַת חַיִּים וְאַהֲבַת חֶסֶד
וּצְדָקָה וּבְרָכָה וְרַחֲמִים וְחַיִּים וְשָׁלוֹם.

May it be good in Your eyes to bless Your people Israel
at every time, in every hour, with Your peace.
Blessed are You, Lord, who blesses His people Israel with peace.

May the words of my mouth and the meditation of my heart Ps. 19
find favor before You, Lord, my Rock and Redeemer.

FULL KADDISH

Some have the custom to include additional responses in Full Kaddish. They can be found in the version on page 1464.

Leader: יִתְגַּדַּל Magnified and sanctified may His great name be,
in the world He created by His will.
May He establish His kingdom
in your lifetime and in your days,
and in the lifetime of all the house of Israel,
swiftly and soon –
and say: Amen.

All: May His great name be blessed for ever and all time.

Leader: Blessed and praised, glorified and exalted,
raised and honored, uplifted and lauded
be the name of the Holy One,
blessed be He, beyond any blessing,
song, praise and consolation uttered in the world –
and say: Amen.

May the prayers and pleas of all Israel
be accepted by their Father in heaven –
and say: Amen.

May there be great peace from heaven,
and life for us and all Israel –
and say: Amen.

Bow, take three steps back, as if taking leave of the Divine Presence, then bow, first left, then right, then center, while saying:

May He who makes peace in His high places,
make peace for us and all Israel –
and say: Amen.

וְטוֹב בְּעֵינֶיךָ לְבָרֵךְ אֶת עַמְּךָ יִשְׂרָאֵל
בְּכָל עֵת וּבְכָל שָׁעָה בִּשְׁלוֹמֶךָ.
בָּרוּךְ אַתָּה יהוה, הַמְבָרֵךְ אֶת עַמּוֹ יִשְׂרָאֵל בַּשָּׁלוֹם.

יִהְיוּ לְרָצוֹן אִמְרֵי־פִי וְהֶגְיוֹן לִבִּי לְפָנֶיךָ, יהוה צוּרִי וְגֹאֲלִי: תהלים יט

קדיש שלם

Some have the custom to include additional responses in קדיש שלם.
They can be found in the version on page 1465.

ש״ץ: יִתְגַּדַּל וְיִתְקַדַּשׁ שְׁמֵהּ רַבָּא (קהל: אָמֵן)
בְּעָלְמָא דִּי בְרָא כִרְעוּתֵהּ
וְיַמְלִיךְ מַלְכוּתֵהּ
בְּחַיֵּיכוֹן וּבְיוֹמֵיכוֹן וּבְחַיֵּי דְכָל בֵּית יִשְׂרָאֵל
בַּעֲגָלָא וּבִזְמַן קָרִיב, וְאִמְרוּ אָמֵן. (קהל: אָמֵן)

קהל וש״ץ: יְהֵא שְׁמֵהּ רַבָּא מְבָרַךְ לְעָלַם וּלְעָלְמֵי עָלְמַיָּא.

ש״ץ: יִתְבָּרַךְ וְיִשְׁתַּבַּח וְיִתְפָּאַר
וְיִתְרוֹמַם וְיִתְנַשֵּׂא וְיִתְהַדָּר וְיִתְעַלֶּה וְיִתְהַלָּל
שְׁמֵהּ דְּקֻדְשָׁא בְּרִיךְ הוּא (קהל: בְּרִיךְ הוּא)
לְעֵלָּא מִן כָּל בִּרְכָתָא וְשִׁירָתָא, תֻּשְׁבְּחָתָא וְנֶחֱמָתָא
דַּאֲמִירָן בְּעָלְמָא, וְאִמְרוּ אָמֵן. (קהל: אָמֵן)

תִּתְקַבַּל צְלוֹתְהוֹן וּבָעוּתְהוֹן דְּכָל יִשְׂרָאֵל
קֳדָם אֲבוּהוֹן דִּי בִשְׁמַיָּא, וְאִמְרוּ אָמֵן. (קהל: אָמֵן)

יְהֵא שְׁלָמָא רַבָּא מִן שְׁמַיָּא
וְחַיִּים, עָלֵינוּ וְעַל כָּל יִשְׂרָאֵל, וְאִמְרוּ אָמֵן. (קהל: אָמֵן)

Bow, take three steps back, as if taking leave of the Divine Presence, then bow, first left, then right, then center, while saying:

עֹשֶׂה שָׁלוֹם בִּמְרוֹמָיו, הוּא יַעֲשֶׂה שָׁלוֹם
עָלֵינוּ וְעַל כָּל יִשְׂרָאֵל, וְאִמְרוּ אָמֵן. (קהל: אָמֵן)

אֵין כֵּאלֹהֵינוּ There is none like our God, none like our LORD,
none like our King, none like our Savior.
Who is like our God? Who is like our LORD?
Who is like our King? Who is like our Savior?
We will thank our God, we will thank our LORD,
we will thank our King, we will thank our Savior.
Blessed is our God, blessed is our LORD,
blessed is our King, blessed is our Savior.
You are our God, You are our LORD,
You are our King, You are our Savior.
You are He to whom our ancestors offered the fragrant incense.

פִּטּוּם הַקְּטֹרֶת The incense mixture consisted of balsam, onycha, galbanum and frankincense, each weighing seventy manehs; myrrh, cassia, spikenard and saffron, each weighing sixteen manehs; twelve manehs of costus, three of aromatic bark; nine of cinnamon; nine kabs of Carsina lye; three seahs and three kabs of Cyprus wine. If Cyprus wine was not available, old white wine might be used. A quarter of a kab of Sodom salt, and a minute amount of a smoke-raising herb. Rabbi Nathan says: Also a minute amount of Jordan amber. If one added honey to the mixture, he rendered it unfit for sacred use. If he omitted any one of its ingredients, he is guilty of a capital offense. *Keritot 6a*

Rabban Shimon ben Gamliel says: "Balsam" refers to the sap that drips from the balsam tree. The Carsina lye was used for bleaching the onycha to improve it. The Cyprus wine was used to soak the onycha in it to make it pungent. Though urine is suitable for this purpose, it is not brought into the Temple out of respect.

These were the psalms which the Levites used to recite in the Temple: *Mishna, Tamid 7*
On the first day of the week they used to say: "The earth is the LORD's *Ps. 24*
and all it contains, the world and all who live in it."
On the second day they used to say: "Great is the LORD and *Ps. 48*
greatly to be praised in the city of God, on His holy mountain."
On the third day they used to say: "God stands in the divine assembly. *Ps. 82*
Among the judges He delivers judgment."
On the fourth day they used to say: "God of retribution, LORD, *Ps. 94*
God of retribution, appear."
On the fifth day they used to say: "Sing for joy to God, our strength. *Ps. 81*
Shout aloud to the God of Jacob."
On the sixth day they used to say: "The LORD reigns: He is robed in majesty; *Ps. 93*
the LORD is robed, girded with strength;
the world is firmly established; it cannot be moved."

אֵין כֵּאלֹהֵינוּ, אֵין כַּאדוֹנֵינוּ, אֵין כְּמַלְכֵּנוּ, אֵין כְּמוֹשִׁיעֵנוּ.
מִי כֵאלֹהֵינוּ, מִי כַאדוֹנֵינוּ, מִי כְמַלְכֵּנוּ, מִי כְמוֹשִׁיעֵנוּ.
נוֹדֶה לֵאלֹהֵינוּ, נוֹדֶה לַאדוֹנֵינוּ, נוֹדֶה לְמַלְכֵּנוּ, נוֹדֶה לְמוֹשִׁיעֵנוּ.
בָּרוּךְ אֱלֹהֵינוּ, בָּרוּךְ אֲדוֹנֵינוּ, בָּרוּךְ מַלְכֵּנוּ, בָּרוּךְ מוֹשִׁיעֵנוּ.
אַתָּה הוּא אֱלֹהֵינוּ, אַתָּה הוּא אֲדוֹנֵינוּ,
אַתָּה הוּא מַלְכֵּנוּ, אַתָּה הוּא מוֹשִׁיעֵנוּ.
אַתָּה הוּא שֶׁהִקְטִירוּ אֲבוֹתֵינוּ לְפָנֶיךָ אֶת קְטֹרֶת הַסַּמִּים.

כריתות ו. פִּטּוּם הַקְּטֹרֶת. הַצֳּרִי, וְהַצִּפֹּרֶן, וְהַחֶלְבְּנָה, וְהַלְּבוֹנָה מִשְׁקַל שִׁבְעִים שִׁבְעִים מָנֶה, מֹר, וּקְצִיעָה, שִׁבֹּלֶת נֵרְדְּ, וְכַרְכֹּם מִשְׁקַל שִׁשָּׁה עָשָׂר שִׁשָּׁה עָשָׂר מָנֶה, הַקֹּשְׁטְ שְׁנֵים עָשָׂר, קִלּוּפָה שְׁלֹשָׁה, וְקִנָּמוֹן תִּשְׁעָה, בֹּרִית כַּרְשִׁינָה תִּשְׁעָה קַבִּין, יֵין קַפְרִיסִין סְאִין תְּלָת וְקַבִּין תְּלָתָא, וְאִם אֵין לוֹ יֵין קַפְרִיסִין, מֵבִיא חֲמַר חִוַּרְיָן עַתִּיק. מֶלַח סְדוֹמִית רֹבַע, מַעֲלֶה עָשָׁן כָּל שֶׁהוּא. רַבִּי נָתָן הַבַּבְלִי אוֹמֵר: אַף כִּפַּת הַיַּרְדֵּן כָּל שֶׁהוּא, וְאִם נָתַן בָּהּ דְּבַשׁ פְּסָלָהּ, וְאִם חִסַּר אֶחָד מִכָּל סַמָּנֶיהָ, חַיָּב מִיתָה.

רַבָּן שִׁמְעוֹן בֶּן גַּמְלִיאֵל אוֹמֵר: הַצֳּרִי אֵינוֹ אֶלָּא שְׂרָף הַנּוֹטֵף מֵעֲצֵי הַקְּטָף. בֹּרִית כַּרְשִׁינָה שֶׁשָּׁפִין בָּהּ אֶת הַצִּפֹּרֶן כְּדֵי שֶׁתְּהֵא נָאָה, יֵין קַפְרִיסִין שֶׁשּׁוֹרִין בּוֹ אֶת הַצִּפֹּרֶן כְּדֵי שֶׁתְּהֵא עַזָּה, וַהֲלֹא מֵי רַגְלַיִם יָפִין לָהּ, אֶלָּא שֶׁאֵין מַכְנִיסִין מֵי רַגְלַיִם בַּמִּקְדָּשׁ מִפְּנֵי הַכָּבוֹד.

משנה תמיד ז הַשִּׁיר שֶׁהַלְוִיִּם הָיוּ אוֹמְרִים בְּבֵית הַמִּקְדָּשׁ:
תהלים כד בַּיּוֹם הָרִאשׁוֹן הָיוּ אוֹמְרִים, לַיהוה הָאָרֶץ וּמְלוֹאָהּ, תֵּבֵל וְיֹשְׁבֵי בָהּ:
תהלים מח בַּשֵּׁנִי הָיוּ אוֹמְרִים, גָּדוֹל יהוה וּמְהֻלָּל מְאֹד, בְּעִיר אֱלֹהֵינוּ הַר־קָדְשׁוֹ:
תהלים פב בַּשְּׁלִישִׁי הָיוּ אוֹמְרִים, אֱלֹהִים נִצָּב בַּעֲדַת־אֵל, בְּקֶרֶב אֱלֹהִים יִשְׁפֹּט:
תהלים צד בָּרְבִיעִי הָיוּ אוֹמְרִים, אֵל־נְקָמוֹת יהוה, אֵל נְקָמוֹת הוֹפִיעַ:
תהלים פא בַּחֲמִישִׁי הָיוּ אוֹמְרִים, הַרְנִינוּ לֵאלֹהִים עוּזֵּנוּ, הָרִיעוּ לֵאלֹהֵי יַעֲקֹב:
תהלים צג בַּשִּׁשִּׁי הָיוּ אוֹמְרִים, יהוה מָלָךְ גֵּאוּת לָבֵשׁ
לָבֵשׁ יהוה עֹז הִתְאַזָּר, אַף־תִּכּוֹן תֵּבֵל בַּל־תִּמּוֹט:

On the Sabbath they used to say: "A psalm, a song for the Sabbath day" – *Ps. 92*
[meaning] a psalm and song for the time to come,
for the day which will be entirely Sabbath and rest for life everlasting.

It was taught in the Academy of Elijah: Whoever studies [Torah] laws every day *Megilla 2*
is assured that he will be destined for the World to Come, as it is said, "The ways *Hab. 3*
of the world are His" – read not, "ways" [*halikhot*] but "laws" [*halakhot*].

Rabbi Elazar said in the name of Rabbi Ḥanina: The disciples of the sages increase *Berakhot 64a*
peace in the world, as it is said, "And all your children shall be taught of the LORD, *Is. 54*
and great shall be the peace of your children [*banayikh*]." Read not *banayikh*,
"your children," but *bonayikh*, "your builders." Those who love Your Torah have *Ps. 119*
great peace; there is no stumbling block for them. May there be peace within your *Ps. 122*
ramparts, prosperity in your palaces. For the sake of my brothers and friends, I
shall say, "Peace be within you." For the sake of the House of the LORD our God,
I will seek your good. ▸ May the LORD grant strength to His people; may the *Ps. 29*
LORD bless His people with peace.

THE RABBIS' KADDISH

The following prayer, said by mourners, requires the presence of a minyan.
A transliteration can be found on page 1466.

Mourner: יִתְגַּדַּל Magnified and sanctified
may His great name be,
in the world He created by His will.
May He establish His kingdom in your lifetime
and in your days,
and in the lifetime of all the house of Israel,
swiftly and soon –
and say: Amen.

All: May His great name be blessed for ever and all time.

Mourner: Blessed and praised, glorified and exalted,
raised and honored, uplifted and lauded
be the name of the Holy One, blessed be He,
beyond any blessing,
song, praise and consolation uttered in the world –
and say: Amen.

בַּשַּׁבָּת הָיוּ אוֹמְרִים, מִזְמוֹר שִׁיר לְיוֹם הַשַּׁבָּת: תהלים צב
מִזְמוֹר שִׁיר לֶעָתִיד לָבוֹא, לְיוֹם שֶׁכֻּלּוֹ שַׁבָּת וּמְנוּחָה לְחַיֵּי הָעוֹלָמִים.

תָּנָא דְבֵי אֵלִיָּהוּ: כָּל הַשּׁוֹנֶה הֲלָכוֹת בְּכָל יוֹם, מֻבְטָח לוֹ שֶׁהוּא בֶּן עוֹלָם מגילה כח:
הַבָּא, שֶׁנֶּאֱמַר, הֲלִיכוֹת עוֹלָם לוֹ: אַל תִּקְרֵי הֲלִיכוֹת אֶלָּא הֲלָכוֹת. חבקוק ג

אָמַר רַבִּי אֶלְעָזָר, אָמַר רַבִּי חֲנִינָא: תַּלְמִידֵי חֲכָמִים מַרְבִּים שָׁלוֹם בָּעוֹלָם, ברכות סד.
שֶׁנֶּאֱמַר, וְכָל־בָּנַיִךְ לִמּוּדֵי יהוה, וְרַב שְׁלוֹם בָּנָיִךְ: אַל תִּקְרֵי בָּנָיִךְ, אֶלָּא ישעיה נד
בּוֹנָיִךְ. שָׁלוֹם רָב לְאֹהֲבֵי תוֹרָתֶךָ, וְאֵין־לָמוֹ מִכְשׁוֹל: יְהִי־שָׁלוֹם בְּחֵילֵךְ, תהלים קיט תהלים קכב
שַׁלְוָה בְּאַרְמְנוֹתָיִךְ: לְמַעַן אַחַי וְרֵעָי אֲדַבְּרָה־נָּא שָׁלוֹם בָּךְ: לְמַעַן בֵּית־
יהוה אֱלֹהֵינוּ אֲבַקְשָׁה טוֹב לָךְ: ‹ יהוה עֹז לְעַמּוֹ יִתֵּן, יהוה יְבָרֵךְ אֶת־עַמּוֹ תהלים כט
בַשָּׁלוֹם:

קדיש דרבנן

The following prayer, said by mourners, requires the presence of a מנין.
A transliteration can be found on page 1466.

אבל: יִתְגַּדַּל וְיִתְקַדַּשׁ שְׁמֵהּ רַבָּא (קהל: אָמֵן)
בְּעָלְמָא דִּי בְרָא כִרְעוּתֵהּ
וְיַמְלִיךְ מַלְכוּתֵהּ
בְּחַיֵּיכוֹן וּבְיוֹמֵיכוֹן וּבְחַיֵּי דְכָל בֵּית יִשְׂרָאֵל
בַּעֲגָלָא וּבִזְמַן קָרִיב, וְאִמְרוּ אָמֵן. (קהל: אָמֵן)

קהל ואבל: יְהֵא שְׁמֵהּ רַבָּא מְבָרַךְ לְעָלַם וּלְעָלְמֵי עָלְמַיָּא.

אבל: יִתְבָּרַךְ וְיִשְׁתַּבַּח וְיִתְפָּאַר וְיִתְרוֹמַם וְיִתְנַשֵּׂא
וְיִתְהַדָּר וְיִתְעַלֶּה וְיִתְהַלָּל
שְׁמֵהּ דְּקֻדְשָׁא בְּרִיךְ הוּא (קהל: בְּרִיךְ הוּא)
לְעֵלָּא מִן כָּל בִּרְכָתָא וְשִׁירָתָא, תֻּשְׁבְּחָתָא וְנֶחֱמָתָא
דַּאֲמִירָן בְּעָלְמָא, וְאִמְרוּ אָמֵן. (קהל: אָמֵן)

To Israel, to the teachers,
their disciples and their disciples' disciples,
and to all who engage in the study of Torah,
in this (*in Israel add:* holy) place or elsewhere,
may there come to them and you great peace,
grace, kindness and compassion, long life, ample sustenance
and deliverance, from their Father in Heaven –
and say: Amen.

May there be great peace from heaven,
and (good) life for us and all Israel –
and say: Amen.

Bow, take three steps back, as if taking leave of the Divine Presence, then bow, first left, then right, then center, while saying:
May He who makes peace in His high places,
in His compassion make peace for us and all Israel –
and say: Amen.

Stand while saying Aleinu. Bow at ▾.

עָלֵינוּ It is our duty to praise the Master of all,
and ascribe greatness to the Author of creation,
who has not made us like the nations of the lands
nor placed us like the families of the earth;
who has not made our portion like theirs,
nor our destiny like all their multitudes.
(For they worship vanity and emptiness,
and pray to a god who cannot save.)
▾But we bow in worship
and thank the Supreme King of kings,
the Holy One, blessed be He,
who extends the heavens and establishes the earth,
whose throne of glory is in the heavens above,
and whose power's Presence is in the highest of heights.
He is our God; there is no other.

עַל יִשְׂרָאֵל וְעַל רַבָּנָן
וְעַל תַּלְמִידֵיהוֹן וְעַל כָּל תַּלְמִידֵי תַלְמִידֵיהוֹן
וְעַל כָּל מָאן דְּעָסְקִין בְּאוֹרַיְתָא
דִּי בְּאַתְרָא (בארץ ישראל: קַדִּישָׁא) הָדֵין, וְדִי בְּכָל אֲתַר וַאֲתַר
יְהֵא לְהוֹן וּלְכוֹן שְׁלָמָא רַבָּא
חִנָּא וְחִסְדָּא, וְרַחֲמֵי, וְחַיֵּי אֲרִיכֵי, וּמְזוֹנֵי רְוִיחֵי
וּפֻרְקָנָא מִן קֳדָם אֲבוּהוֹן דִּי בִשְׁמַיָּא, וְאִמְרוּ אָמֵן. (קהל: אָמֵן)
יְהֵא שְׁלָמָא רַבָּא מִן שְׁמַיָּא
וְחַיִּים (טוֹבִים) עָלֵינוּ וְעַל כָּל יִשְׂרָאֵל, וְאִמְרוּ אָמֵן. (קהל: אָמֵן)

Bow, take three steps back, as if taking leave of the Divine Presence, then bow, first left, then right, then center, while saying:

עֹשֶׂה שָׁלוֹם בִּמְרוֹמָיו
הוּא יַעֲשֶׂה בְרַחֲמָיו שָׁלוֹם
עָלֵינוּ וְעַל כָּל יִשְׂרָאֵל, וְאִמְרוּ אָמֵן. (קהל: אָמֵן)

Stand while saying עָלֵינוּ*. Bow at* ׳.

עָלֵינוּ לְשַׁבֵּחַ לַאֲדוֹן הַכֹּל, לָתֵת גְּדֻלָּה לְיוֹצֵר בְּרֵאשִׁית
שֶׁלֹּא עָשָׂנוּ כְּגוֹיֵי הָאֲרָצוֹת, וְלֹא שָׂמָנוּ כְּמִשְׁפְּחוֹת הָאֲדָמָה
שֶׁלֹּא שָׂם חֶלְקֵנוּ כָּהֶם וְגוֹרָלֵנוּ כְּכָל הֲמוֹנָם.
(שֶׁהֵם מִשְׁתַּחֲוִים לְהֶבֶל וָרִיק וּמִתְפַּלְלִים אֶל אֵל לֹא יוֹשִׁיעַ.)
׳וַאֲנַחְנוּ כּוֹרְעִים וּמִשְׁתַּחֲוִים וּמוֹדִים
לִפְנֵי מֶלֶךְ מַלְכֵי הַמְּלָכִים, הַקָּדוֹשׁ בָּרוּךְ הוּא
שֶׁהוּא נוֹטֶה שָׁמַיִם וְיוֹסֵד אָרֶץ
וּמוֹשַׁב יְקָרוֹ בַּשָּׁמַיִם מִמַּעַל
וּשְׁכִינַת עֻזּוֹ בְּגָבְהֵי מְרוֹמִים.
הוּא אֱלֹהֵינוּ, אֵין עוֹד.

Truly He is our King, there is none else,
as it is written in His Torah:
"You shall know and take to heart this day that the LORD is God, *Deut. 4*
in heaven above and on earth below.
There is no other."

Therefore, we place our hope in You, LORD our God,
that we may soon see the glory of Your power,
when You will remove abominations from the earth,
and idols will be utterly destroyed,
when the world will be perfected under
the sovereignty of the Almighty,
when all humanity will call on Your name,
to turn all the earth's wicked toward You.
All the world's inhabitants will realize and know
that to You every knee must bow
and every tongue swear loyalty.
Before You, LORD our God, they will kneel and bow down
and give honor to Your glorious name.
They will all accept the yoke of Your kingdom,
and You will reign over them soon and for ever.
For the kingdom is Yours,
and to all eternity You will reign in glory,
as it is written in Your Torah:
"The LORD will reign for ever and ever." *Ex. 15*
▸ And it is said:
"Then the LORD shall be King over all the earth; *Zech. 14*
on that day the LORD shall be One and His name One."

Some add:

Have no fear of sudden terror or of the ruin when it overtakes the wicked. *Prov. 3*
Devise your strategy, but it will be thwarted; *Is. 8*
propose your plan, but it will not stand, for God is with us.
When you grow old, I will still be the same. *Is. 46*
When your hair turns gray, I will still carry you.
I made you, I will bear you, I will carry you, and I will rescue you.

אֱמֶת מַלְכֵּנוּ, אֶפֶס זוּלָתוֹ, כַּכָּתוּב בְּתוֹרָתוֹ
וְיָדַעְתָּ הַיּוֹם וַהֲשֵׁבֹתָ אֶל־לְבָבֶךָ דברים ד
כִּי יהוה הוּא הָאֱלֹהִים בַּשָּׁמַיִם מִמַּעַל וְעַל־הָאָרֶץ מִתָּחַת
אֵין עוֹד:

עַל כֵּן נְקַוֶּה לְּךָ יהוה אֱלֹהֵינוּ, לִרְאוֹת מְהֵרָה בְּתִפְאֶרֶת עֻזֶּךָ
לְהַעֲבִיר גִּלּוּלִים מִן הָאָרֶץ
וְהָאֱלִילִים כָּרוֹת יִכָּרֵתוּן
לְתַקֵּן עוֹלָם בְּמַלְכוּת שַׁדַּי.
וְכָל בְּנֵי בָשָׂר יִקְרְאוּ בִשְׁמֶךָ לְהַפְנוֹת אֵלֶיךָ כָּל רִשְׁעֵי אָרֶץ.
יַכִּירוּ וְיֵדְעוּ כָּל יוֹשְׁבֵי תֵבֵל
כִּי לְךָ תִּכְרַע כָּל בֶּרֶךְ, תִּשָּׁבַע כָּל לָשׁוֹן.
לְפָנֶיךָ יהוה אֱלֹהֵינוּ יִכְרְעוּ וְיִפֹּלוּ
וְלִכְבוֹד שִׁמְךָ יְקָר יִתֵּנוּ
וִיקַבְּלוּ כֻלָּם אֶת עֹל מַלְכוּתֶךָ
וְתִמְלֹךְ עֲלֵיהֶם מְהֵרָה לְעוֹלָם וָעֶד.
כִּי הַמַּלְכוּת שֶׁלְּךָ הִיא וּלְעוֹלְמֵי עַד תִּמְלֹךְ בְּכָבוֹד
כַּכָּתוּב בְּתוֹרָתֶךָ
יהוה יִמְלֹךְ לְעֹלָם וָעֶד: שמות טו
◄ וְנֶאֱמַר, וְהָיָה יהוה לְמֶלֶךְ עַל־כָּל־הָאָרֶץ זכריה יד
בַּיּוֹם הַהוּא יִהְיֶה יהוה אֶחָד וּשְׁמוֹ אֶחָד:

Some add:

אַל־תִּירָא מִפַּחַד פִּתְאֹם וּמִשֹּׁאַת רְשָׁעִים כִּי תָבֹא: משלי ג
עֻצוּ עֵצָה וְתֻפָר, דַּבְּרוּ דָבָר וְלֹא יָקוּם, כִּי עִמָּנוּ אֵל: ישעיה ח
וְעַד־זִקְנָה אֲנִי הוּא, וְעַד־שֵׂיבָה אֲנִי אֶסְבֹּל ישעיה מו
אֲנִי עָשִׂיתִי וַאֲנִי אֶשָּׂא וַאֲנִי אֶסְבֹּל וַאֲמַלֵּט:

MOURNER'S KADDISH

The following prayer, said by mourners, requires the presence of a minyan. A transliteration can be found on page 1467.

Mourner: יִתְגַּדַּל Magnified and sanctified
may His great name be,
in the world He created by His will.
May He establish His kingdom
in your lifetime and in your days,
and in the lifetime of all the house of Israel,
swiftly and soon –
and say: Amen.

All: May His great name be blessed
for ever and all time.

Mourner: Blessed and praised,
glorified and exalted,
raised and honored,
uplifted and lauded
be the name of the Holy One,
blessed be He,
beyond any blessing, song,
praise and consolation
uttered in the world –
and say: Amen.

May there be great peace from heaven,
and life for us and all Israel –
and say: Amen.

Bow, take three steps back, as if taking leave of the Divine Presence, then bow, first left, then right, then center, while saying:

May He who makes peace in His high places,
make peace for us and all Israel –
and say: Amen.

קדיש יתום

The following prayer, said by mourners, requires the presence of a מנין.
A transliteration can be found on page 1467.

אבל: יִתְגַּדַּל וְיִתְקַדַּשׁ שְׁמֵהּ רַבָּא (קהל: אָמֵן)
בְּעָלְמָא דִּי בְרָא כִרְעוּתֵהּ
וְיַמְלִיךְ מַלְכוּתֵהּ
בְּחַיֵּיכוֹן וּבְיוֹמֵיכוֹן וּבְחַיֵּי דְכָל בֵּית יִשְׂרָאֵל
בַּעֲגָלָא וּבִזְמַן קָרִיב
וְאִמְרוּ אָמֵן. (קהל: אָמֵן)

קהל ואבל: יְהֵא שְׁמֵהּ רַבָּא מְבָרַךְ לְעָלַם וּלְעָלְמֵי עָלְמַיָּא.

אבל: יִתְבָּרַךְ וְיִשְׁתַּבַּח וְיִתְפָּאַר
וְיִתְרוֹמַם וְיִתְנַשֵּׂא וְיִתְהַדָּר וְיִתְעַלֶּה וְיִתְהַלָּל
שְׁמֵהּ דְּקֻדְשָׁא בְּרִיךְ הוּא (קהל: בְּרִיךְ הוּא)
לְעֵלָּא מִן כָּל בִּרְכָתָא וְשִׁירָתָא
תֻּשְׁבְּחָתָא וְנֶחֱמָתָא
דַּאֲמִירָן בְּעָלְמָא
וְאִמְרוּ אָמֵן. (קהל: אָמֵן)

יְהֵא שְׁלָמָא רַבָּא מִן שְׁמַיָּא
וְחַיִּים, עָלֵינוּ וְעַל כָּל יִשְׂרָאֵל
וְאִמְרוּ אָמֵן. (קהל: אָמֵן)

Bow, take three steps back, as if taking leave of the Divine Presence, then bow, first left, then right, then center, while saying:

עֹשֶׂה שָׁלוֹם בִּמְרוֹמָיו
הוּא יַעֲשֶׂה שָׁלוֹם עָלֵינוּ וְעַל כָּל יִשְׂרָאֵל
וְאִמְרוּ אָמֵן. (קהל: אָמֵן)

THE DAILY PSALM

One of the following psalms is said on the appropriate day of the week as indicated.
After the psalm, the Mourner's Kaddish is said.
Many congregations say the Daily Psalm after the Song of Glory, page 1198.

Monday: הַיּוֹם Today is the second day of the week,
on which the Levites used to say this psalm in the Temple:

שִׁיר מִזְמוֹר A song. A psalm of the sons of Koraḥ. Great is the LORD and greatly to be praised in the city of God, on His holy mountain – beautiful in its heights, joy of all the earth, Mount Zion on its northern side, city of the great King. In its citadels God is known as a stronghold. See how the kings joined forces, advancing together. They saw, they were astounded, they panicked, they fled. There fear seized them, like the pains of a woman giving birth, like ships of Tarshish wrecked by an eastern wind. What we had heard, now we have seen, in the city of the LORD of hosts, in the city of our God. May God preserve it for ever, Selah! In the midst of Your Temple, God, we meditate on Your love. As is Your name, God, so is Your praise: it reaches to the ends of the earth. Your right hand is filled with righteousness. Let Mount Zion rejoice, let the towns of Judah be glad, because of Your judgments. Walk around Zion and encircle it. Count its towers, note its strong walls, view its citadels, so that you may tell a future generation ▸ that this is God, our God, for ever and ever. He will guide us for evermore. *Ps. 48*

Mourner's Kaddish (page 1194)

Tuesday: הַיּוֹם Today is the third day of the week,
on which the Levites used to say this psalm in the Temple:

מִזְמוֹר לְאָסָף A psalm of Asaph. God stands in the Divine assembly. Among the judges He delivers judgment. How long will you judge unjustly, showing favor to the wicked? Selah. Do justice to the weak and the orphaned. Vindicate the poor and destitute. Rescue the weak and needy. Save them from the hand of the wicked. They do not know nor do they understand. They walk about in darkness while all the earth's foundations shake. I once said, "You are like gods, all of you are sons of the Most High." But you shall die like mere men, you will fall like any prince. ▸ Arise, O LORD, judge the earth, for all the nations are Your possession. *Ps. 82*

Mourner's Kaddish (page 1194)

שיר של יום

One of the following psalms is said on the appropriate day of the week as indicated.
After the psalm, קדיש יתום *is said.*
Many congregations say the שיר של יום *after the* שיר הכבוד*, page 1199.*

Monday הַיּוֹם יוֹם שֵׁנִי בְּשַׁבָּת, שֶׁבּוֹ הָיוּ הַלְוִיִּם אוֹמְרִים בְּבֵית הַמִּקְדָּשׁ:

שִׁיר מִזְמוֹר לִבְנֵי־קֹרַח: גָּדוֹל יהוה וּמְהֻלָּל מְאֹד, בְּעִיר אֱלֹהֵינוּ, הַר־קָדְשׁוֹ: יְפֵה נוֹף מְשׂוֹשׂ כָּל־הָאָרֶץ, הַר־צִיּוֹן יַרְכְּתֵי צָפוֹן, קִרְיַת מֶלֶךְ רָב: אֱלֹהִים בְּאַרְמְנוֹתֶיהָ נוֹדַע לְמִשְׂגָּב: כִּי־הִנֵּה הַמְּלָכִים נוֹעֲדוּ, עָבְרוּ יַחְדָּו: הֵמָּה רָאוּ כֵּן תָּמָהוּ, נִבְהֲלוּ נֶחְפָּזוּ: רְעָדָה אֲחָזָתַם שָׁם, חִיל כַּיּוֹלֵדָה: בְּרוּחַ קָדִים תְּשַׁבֵּר אֳנִיּוֹת תַּרְשִׁישׁ: כַּאֲשֶׁר שָׁמַעְנוּ כֵּן רָאִינוּ, בְּעִיר־יהוה צְבָאוֹת, בְּעִיר אֱלֹהֵינוּ, אֱלֹהִים יְכוֹנְנֶהָ עַד־עוֹלָם סֶלָה: דִּמִּינוּ אֱלֹהִים חַסְדֶּךָ, בְּקֶרֶב הֵיכָלֶךָ: כְּשִׁמְךָ אֱלֹהִים כֵּן תְּהִלָּתְךָ עַל־קַצְוֵי־אֶרֶץ, צֶדֶק מָלְאָה יְמִינֶךָ: יִשְׂמַח הַר־צִיּוֹן, תָּגֵלְנָה בְּנוֹת יְהוּדָה, לְמַעַן מִשְׁפָּטֶיךָ: סֹבּוּ צִיּוֹן וְהַקִּיפוּהָ, סִפְרוּ מִגְדָּלֶיהָ: שִׁיתוּ לִבְּכֶם לְחֵילָה, פַּסְּגוּ אַרְמְנוֹתֶיהָ, לְמַעַן תְּסַפְּרוּ לְדוֹר אַחֲרוֹן: ‹ כִּי זֶה אֱלֹהִים אֱלֹהֵינוּ עוֹלָם וָעֶד, הוּא יְנַהֲגֵנוּ עַל־מוּת: תהלים מח

קדיש יתום (*page 1195*)

Tuesday הַיּוֹם יוֹם שְׁלִישִׁי בְּשַׁבָּת, שֶׁבּוֹ הָיוּ הַלְוִיִּם אוֹמְרִים בְּבֵית הַמִּקְדָּשׁ:

מִזְמוֹר לְאָסָף, אֱלֹהִים נִצָּב בַּעֲדַת־אֵל, בְּקֶרֶב אֱלֹהִים יִשְׁפֹּט: עַד־מָתַי תִּשְׁפְּטוּ־עָוֶל, וּפְנֵי רְשָׁעִים תִּשְׂאוּ־סֶלָה: שִׁפְטוּ־דַל וְיָתוֹם, עָנִי וָרָשׁ הַצְדִּיקוּ: פַּלְּטוּ־דַל וְאֶבְיוֹן, מִיַּד רְשָׁעִים הַצִּילוּ: לֹא יָדְעוּ וְלֹא יָבִינוּ, בַּחֲשֵׁכָה יִתְהַלָּכוּ, יִמּוֹטוּ כָּל־מוֹסְדֵי אָרֶץ: אֲנִי־אָמַרְתִּי אֱלֹהִים אַתֶּם, וּבְנֵי עֶלְיוֹן כֻּלְּכֶם: אָכֵן כְּאָדָם תְּמוּתוּן, וּכְאַחַד הַשָּׂרִים תִּפֹּלוּ: ‹ קוּמָה אֱלֹהִים שָׁפְטָה הָאָרֶץ, כִּי־אַתָּה תִנְחַל בְּכָל־הַגּוֹיִם: תהלים פב

קדיש יתום (*page 1195*)

Thursday: הַיּוֹם Today is the fifth day of the week,
on which the Levites used to say this psalm in the Temple:

לַמְנַצֵּחַ For the conductor of music. On the Gittit. By Asaph. Sing for joy to God, our strength. Shout aloud to the God of Jacob. Raise a song, beat the drum, play the sweet harp and lyre. Sound the shofar on the new moon, on our feast day when the moon is hidden. For it is a statute for Israel, an ordinance of the God of Jacob. He established it as a testimony for Joseph when He went forth against the land of Egypt, where I heard a language that I did not know. I relieved his shoulder of the burden. His hands were freed from the builder's basket. In distress you called and I rescued you. I answered you from the secret place of thunder; I tested you at the waters of Meribah, Selah! Hear, My people, and I will warn you. Israel, if you would only listen to Me! Let there be no strange god among you. Do not bow down to an alien god. I am the LORD your God who brought you out of the land of Egypt. Open your mouth wide and I will fill it. But My people would not listen to Me. Israel would have none of Me. So I left them to their stubborn hearts, letting them follow their own devices. If only My people would listen to Me, if Israel would walk in My ways, I would soon subdue their enemies, and turn My hand against their foes. Those who hate the LORD would cower before Him and their doom would last for ever. ▸ He would feed Israel with the finest wheat – with honey from the rock I would satisfy you. *Ps. 81*

Mourner's Kaddish (on the next page)

Shabbat: הַיּוֹם Today is the holy Sabbath,
on which the Levites used to say this psalm in the Temple:

מִזְמוֹר A psalm. A song for the Sabbath day. It is good to thank the LORD and sing psalms to Your name, Most High – to tell of Your loving-kindness in the morning and Your faithfulness at night, to the music of the ten-stringed lyre and the melody of the harp. For You have made me rejoice by Your work, O LORD; I sing for joy at the deeds of Your hands. How great are Your deeds, LORD, and how very deep Your thoughts. A boor cannot know, nor can a fool understand, that though the wicked spring up like grass and all evildoers flourish, it is only that they may be destroyed for ever. But You, LORD, are eternally exalted. For behold Your enemies, LORD, behold Your enemies will perish; all evildoers will be scattered. You have raised my pride like that of a wild ox; I am anointed with fresh oil. My eyes shall look in triumph on my adversaries; my ears shall hear the downfall of the wicked who rise against me. The righteous will flourish like a palm tree and grow tall like a cedar in Lebanon. Planted in the LORD's House, blossoming in our God's courtyards, ▸ they will still bear fruit in old age, and stay vigorous and fresh, proclaiming that the LORD is upright: He is my Rock, in whom there is no wrong. *Ps. 92*

Thursday הַיּוֹם יוֹם חֲמִישִׁי בְּשַׁבָּת, שֶׁבּוֹ הָיוּ הַלְוִיִּם אוֹמְרִים בְּבֵית הַמִּקְדָּשׁ:

לַמְנַצֵּחַ עַל־הַגִּתִּית לְאָסָף: הַרְנִינוּ לֵאלֹהִים עוּזֵּנוּ, הָרִיעוּ לֵאלֹהֵי תהלים פא
יַעֲקֹב: שְׂאוּ־זִמְרָה וּתְנוּ־תֹף, כִּנּוֹר נָעִים עִם־נָבֶל: תִּקְעוּ בַחֹדֶשׁ שׁוֹפָר, בַּכֵּסֶה לְיוֹם חַגֵּנוּ: כִּי חֹק לְיִשְׂרָאֵל הוּא, מִשְׁפָּט לֵאלֹהֵי יַעֲקֹב: עֵדוּת בִּיהוֹסֵף שָׂמוֹ, בְּצֵאתוֹ עַל־אֶרֶץ מִצְרָיִם, שְׂפַת לֹא־יָדַעְתִּי אֶשְׁמָע: הֲסִירוֹתִי מִסֵּבֶל שִׁכְמוֹ, כַּפָּיו מִדּוּד תַּעֲבֹרְנָה: בַּצָּרָה קָרָאתָ וָאֲחַלְּצֶךָּ, אֶעֶנְךָ בְּסֵתֶר רַעַם, אֶבְחָנְךָ עַל־מֵי מְרִיבָה סֶלָה: שְׁמַע עַמִּי וְאָעִידָה בָּךְ, יִשְׂרָאֵל אִם־תִּשְׁמַע־לִי: לֹא־יִהְיֶה בְךָ אֵל זָר, וְלֹא תִשְׁתַּחֲוֶה לְאֵל נֵכָר: אָנֹכִי יהוה אֱלֹהֶיךָ, הַמַּעַלְךָ מֵאֶרֶץ מִצְרָיִם, הַרְחֶב־פִּיךָ וַאֲמַלְאֵהוּ: וְלֹא־שָׁמַע עַמִּי לְקוֹלִי, וְיִשְׂרָאֵל לֹא־אָבָה לִי: וָאֲשַׁלְּחֵהוּ בִּשְׁרִירוּת לִבָּם, יֵלְכוּ בְּמוֹעֲצוֹתֵיהֶם: לוּ עַמִּי שֹׁמֵעַ לִי, יִשְׂרָאֵל בִּדְרָכַי יְהַלֵּכוּ: כִּמְעַט אוֹיְבֵיהֶם אַכְנִיעַ, וְעַל־צָרֵיהֶם אָשִׁיב יָדִי: מְשַׂנְאֵי יהוה יְכַחֲשׁוּ־לוֹ, וִיהִי עִתָּם לְעוֹלָם: ‹ וַיַּאֲכִילֵהוּ מֵחֵלֶב חִטָּה, וּמִצּוּר, דְּבַשׁ אַשְׂבִּיעֶךָ:

קדיש יתום (*on the next page*)

שבת הַיּוֹם יוֹם שַׁבַּת קֹדֶשׁ, שֶׁבּוֹ הָיוּ הַלְוִיִּם אוֹמְרִים בְּבֵית הַמִּקְדָּשׁ:

מִזְמוֹר שִׁיר לְיוֹם הַשַּׁבָּת: טוֹב לְהֹדוֹת לַיהוה, וּלְזַמֵּר לְשִׁמְךָ עֶלְיוֹן: תהלים צב
לְהַגִּיד בַּבֹּקֶר חַסְדֶּךָ, וֶאֱמוּנָתְךָ בַּלֵּילוֹת: עֲלֵי־עָשׂוֹר וַעֲלֵי־נָבֶל, עֲלֵי הִגָּיוֹן בְּכִנּוֹר: כִּי שִׂמַּחְתַּנִי יהוה בְּפָעֳלֶךָ, בְּמַעֲשֵׂי יָדֶיךָ אֲרַנֵּן: מַה־גָּדְלוּ מַעֲשֶׂיךָ יהוה, מְאֹד עָמְקוּ מַחְשְׁבֹתֶיךָ: אִישׁ־בַּעַר לֹא יֵדָע, וּכְסִיל לֹא־יָבִין אֶת־זֹאת: בִּפְרֹחַ רְשָׁעִים כְּמוֹ עֵשֶׂב, וַיָּצִיצוּ כָּל־פֹּעֲלֵי אָוֶן, לְהִשָּׁמְדָם עֲדֵי־עַד: וְאַתָּה מָרוֹם לְעֹלָם יהוה: כִּי הִנֵּה אֹיְבֶיךָ יהוה, כִּי־הִנֵּה אֹיְבֶיךָ יֹאבֵדוּ, יִתְפָּרְדוּ כָּל־פֹּעֲלֵי אָוֶן: וַתָּרֶם כִּרְאֵים קַרְנִי, בַּלֹּתִי בְּשֶׁמֶן רַעֲנָן: וַתַּבֵּט עֵינִי בְּשׁוּרָי, בַּקָּמִים עָלַי מְרֵעִים תִּשְׁמַעְנָה אָזְנָי: צַדִּיק כַּתָּמָר יִפְרָח, כְּאֶרֶז בַּלְּבָנוֹן יִשְׂגֶּה: שְׁתוּלִים בְּבֵית יהוה, בְּחַצְרוֹת אֱלֹהֵינוּ יַפְרִיחוּ: ‹ עוֹד יְנוּבוּן בְּשֵׂיבָה, דְּשֵׁנִים וְרַעֲנַנִּים יִהְיוּ: לְהַגִּיד כִּי־יָשָׁר יהוה, צוּרִי, וְלֹא־עַוְלָתָה בּוֹ:

MOURNER'S KADDISH

The following prayer, said by mourners, requires the presence of a minyan.
A transliteration can be found on page 1467.

Mourner: יִתְגַּדַּל Magnified and sanctified
may His great name be,
in the world He created by His will.
May He establish His kingdom
in your lifetime and in your days,
and in the lifetime of all the house of Israel,
swiftly and soon –
and say: Amen.

All: May His great name be blessed
for ever and all time.

Mourner: Blessed and praised,
glorified and exalted,
raised and honored,
uplifted and lauded
be the name of the Holy One,
blessed be He,
beyond any blessing,
song, praise and consolation
uttered in the world –
and say: Amen.

May there be great peace from heaven,
and life for us and all Israel –
and say: Amen.

Bow, take three steps back, as if taking leave of the Divine Presence,
then bow, first left, then right, then center, while saying:

May He who makes peace in His high places,
make peace for us and all Israel –
and say: Amen.

קדיש יתום

The following prayer, said by mourners, requires the presence of a מנין.
A transliteration can be found on page 1467.

אבל: יִתְגַּדַּל וְיִתְקַדַּשׁ שְׁמֵהּ רַבָּא (קהל: אָמֵן)
בְּעָלְמָא דִּי בְרָא כִרְעוּתֵהּ
וְיַמְלִיךְ מַלְכוּתֵהּ
בְּחַיֵּיכוֹן וּבְיוֹמֵיכוֹן וּבְחַיֵּי דְכָל בֵּית יִשְׂרָאֵל
בַּעֲגָלָא וּבִזְמַן קָרִיב
וְאִמְרוּ אָמֵן. (קהל: אָמֵן)

קהל ואבל: יְהֵא שְׁמֵהּ רַבָּא מְבָרַךְ לְעָלַם וּלְעָלְמֵי עָלְמַיָּא.

אבל: יִתְבָּרַךְ וְיִשְׁתַּבַּח וְיִתְפָּאַר
וְיִתְרוֹמַם וְיִתְנַשֵּׂא וְיִתְהַדָּר וְיִתְעַלֶּה וְיִתְהַלָּל
שְׁמֵהּ דְּקֻדְשָׁא בְּרִיךְ הוּא (קהל: בְּרִיךְ הוּא)
לְעֵלָּא מִן כָּל בִּרְכָתָא וְשִׁירָתָא, תֻּשְׁבְּחָתָא וְנֶחֱמָתָא
דַּאֲמִירָן בְּעָלְמָא
וְאִמְרוּ אָמֵן. (קהל: אָמֵן)

יְהֵא שְׁלָמָא רַבָּא מִן שְׁמַיָּא
וְחַיִּים, עָלֵינוּ וְעַל כָּל יִשְׂרָאֵל
וְאִמְרוּ אָמֵן. (קהל: אָמֵן)

Bow, take three steps back, as if taking leave of the Divine Presence, then bow, first left, then right, then center, while saying:

עֹשֶׂה שָׁלוֹם בִּמְרוֹמָיו
הוּא יַעֲשֶׂה שָׁלוֹם עָלֵינוּ וְעַל כָּל יִשְׂרָאֵל
וְאִמְרוּ אָמֵן. (קהל: אָמֵן)

לְדָוִד A psalm of David. The LORD is my light and my salvation – whom then shall I fear? The LORD is the stronghold of my life – of whom shall I be afraid? When evil men close in on me to devour my flesh, it is they, my enemies and foes, who stumble and fall. Should an army besiege me, my heart would not fear. Should war break out against me, still I would be confident. One thing I ask of the LORD, only this do I seek: to live in the House of the LORD all the days of my life, to gaze on the beauty of the LORD and worship in His Temple. For He will keep me safe in His pavilion on the day of trouble. He will hide me under the cover of His tent. He will set me high upon a rock. Now my head is high above my enemies who surround me. I will sacrifice in His tent with shouts of joy. I will sing and chant praises to the LORD. LORD, hear my voice when I call. Be gracious to me and answer me. On Your behalf my heart says, "Seek My face." Your face, LORD, will I seek. Do not hide Your face from me. Do not turn Your servant away in anger. You have been my help. Do not reject or forsake me, God, my Savior. Were my father and my mother to forsake me, the LORD would take me in. Teach me Your way, LORD, and lead me on a level path, because of my oppressors. Do not abandon me to the will of my foes, for false witnesses have risen against me, breathing violence. ▸ Were it not for my faith that I shall see the LORD's goodness in the land of the living. Hope in the LORD. Be strong and of good courage, and hope in the LORD! *Ps. 27*

Mourner's Kaddish (previous page)

---

on the mountain to receive the second set of tablets (see Mishna Berura, *Oraḥ Ḥayyim* 581:2). Others continue to say it until the end of Sukkot, on the basis of the interpretation given by the sages: *The Lord is my light* on Rosh HaShana, *and my salvation* on Yom Kippur. *He will keep me safe in His pavilion* [*besukko*] refers to Sukkot (*Matte Ephraim* 581:6, *Shulḥan Arukh HaRav*). Our custom is to also say it (outside Israel) on Shemini Atzeret, because of the possibility that it may be the seventh day of Sukkot (Mishna Berura ad loc.).

תהלים כז

לְדָוִד, יהוה אוֹרִי וְיִשְׁעִי, מִמִּי אִירָא, יהוה מָעוֹז־חַיַּי, מִמִּי אֶפְחָד: בִּקְרֹב עָלַי מְרֵעִים לֶאֱכֹל אֶת־בְּשָׂרִי, צָרַי וְאֹיְבַי לִי, הֵמָּה כָשְׁלוּ וְנָפָלוּ: אִם־תַּחֲנֶה עָלַי מַחֲנֶה, לֹא־יִירָא לִבִּי, אִם־תָּקוּם עָלַי מִלְחָמָה, בְּזֹאת אֲנִי בוֹטֵחַ: אַחַת שָׁאַלְתִּי מֵאֵת־יהוה, אוֹתָהּ אֲבַקֵּשׁ, שִׁבְתִּי בְּבֵית־יהוה כָּל־יְמֵי חַיַּי, לַחֲזוֹת בְּנֹעַם־יהוה, וּלְבַקֵּר בְּהֵיכָלוֹ: כִּי יִצְפְּנֵנִי בְּסֻכֹּה בְּיוֹם רָעָה, יַסְתִּרֵנִי בְּסֵתֶר אָהֳלוֹ, בְּצוּר יְרוֹמְמֵנִי: וְעַתָּה יָרוּם רֹאשִׁי עַל אֹיְבַי סְבִיבוֹתַי, וְאֶזְבְּחָה בְאָהֳלוֹ זִבְחֵי תְרוּעָה, אָשִׁירָה וַאֲזַמְּרָה לַיהוה: שְׁמַע־יהוה קוֹלִי אֶקְרָא, וְחָנֵּנִי וַעֲנֵנִי: לְךָ אָמַר לִבִּי בַּקְּשׁוּ פָנָי, אֶת־פָּנֶיךָ יהוה אֲבַקֵּשׁ: אַל־תַּסְתֵּר פָּנֶיךָ מִמֶּנִּי, אַל תַּט־בְּאַף עַבְדֶּךָ, עֶזְרָתִי הָיִיתָ, אַל־תִּטְּשֵׁנִי וְאַל־תַּעַזְבֵנִי, אֱלֹהֵי יִשְׁעִי: כִּי־אָבִי וְאִמִּי עֲזָבוּנִי, וַיהוה יַאַסְפֵנִי: הוֹרֵנִי יהוה דַּרְכֶּךָ, וּנְחֵנִי בְּאֹרַח מִישׁוֹר, לְמַעַן שׁוֹרְרָי: אַל־תִּתְּנֵנִי בְּנֶפֶשׁ צָרָי, כִּי קָמוּ־בִי עֵדֵי־שֶׁקֶר, וִיפֵחַ חָמָס: ◂ לוּלֵא הֶאֱמַנְתִּי לִרְאוֹת בְּטוּב־יהוה בְּאֶרֶץ חַיִּים: קַוֵּה אֶל־יהוה, חֲזַק וְיַאֲמֵץ לִבֶּךָ, וְקַוֵּה אֶל־יהוה:

קדיש יתום (*previous page*)

PSALM 27.

As well as being one of the supreme expressions of faith, Psalm 27 contains thirteen mentions of the four-letter name of God, corresponding to the thirteen attributes of Divine compassion, and is thus particularly appropriate to the period of the year dedicated to Divine judgment and forgiveness. The custom is to begin saying it on the first day of Elul, but there was debate as to for how long it should be said. Some had a custom to say it only until Yom Kippur – corresponding to the forty days when Moses, having achieved forgiveness for the people after the sin of the Golden Calf, stayed

SONG OF GLORY

The Ark is opened and all stand.

Leader: I will sing sweet psalms and I will weave songs,
to You for whom my soul longs.

Cong: My soul yearns for the shelter of Your hand,
that all Your mystic secrets I might understand.

Leader: Whenever I speak of Your glory above,
my heart is yearning for Your love.

Cong: So Your glories I will proclaim,
and in songs of love give honor to Your name.

Leader: I will tell of Your glory though I have not seen You,
imagine and describe You, though I have not known You.

Cong: By the hand of Your prophets, through Your servants' mystery,
You gave a glimpse of Your wondrous majesty.

Leader: Recounting Your grandeur and Your glory,
of Your great deeds they told the story.

Cong: They depicted You, though not as You are,
but as You do: Your acts, Your power.

Leader: They represented You in many visions;
through them all You are One without divisions.

Cong: They saw You, now old, then young,
Your head with gray, with black hair hung.

Leader: Aged on the day of judgment, yet on the day of war,
a young warrior with mighty hands they saw.

Cong: Triumph like a helmet He wore on his head;
His right hand and holy arm to victory have led.

Leader: His curls are filled with dew drops of light,
His locks with fragments of the night.

Cong: He will glory in me, for He delights in me;
My diadem of beauty He shall be.

Leader: His head is like pure beaten gold;
Engraved on His brow, His sacred name behold.

Cong: For grace and glory, beauty and renown,
His people have adorned Him with a crown.

שיר הכבוד

The ארון קודש *is opened and all stand.*

ש״ץ: אַנְעִים זְמִירוֹת וְשִׁירִים אֶאֱרֹג, כִּי אֵלֶיךָ נַפְשִׁי תַעֲרֹג.
קהל: נַפְשִׁי חִמְּדָה בְּצֵל יָדֶךָ, לָדַעַת כָּל רָז סוֹדֶךָ.

ש״ץ: מִדֵּי דַבְּרִי בִּכְבוֹדֶךָ, הוֹמֶה לִבִּי אֶל דּוֹדֶיךָ.
קהל: עַל כֵּן אֲדַבֵּר בְּךָ נִכְבָּדוֹת, וְשִׁמְךָ אֲכַבֵּד בְּשִׁירֵי יְדִידוֹת.

ש״ץ: אֲסַפְּרָה כְבוֹדְךָ וְלֹא רְאִיתִיךָ, אֲדַמְּךָ אֲכַנְּךָ וְלֹא יְדַעְתִּיךָ.
קהל: בְּיַד נְבִיאֶיךָ בְּסוֹד עֲבָדֶיךָ, דִּמִּיתָ הֲדַר כְּבוֹד הוֹדֶךָ.

ש״ץ: גְּדֻלָּתְךָ וּגְבוּרָתֶךָ, כִּנּוּ לְתֹקֶף פְּעֻלָּתֶךָ.
קהל: דִּמּוּ אוֹתְךָ וְלֹא כְּפִי יֶשְׁךָ, וַיְשַׁוּוּךָ לְפִי מַעֲשֶׂיךָ.

ש״ץ: הִמְשִׁילוּךָ בְּרֹב חֶזְיוֹנוֹת, הִנְּךָ אֶחָד בְּכָל דִּמְיוֹנוֹת.
קהל: וַיֶּחֱזוּ בְךָ זִקְנָה וּבַחֲרוּת, וּשְׂעַר רֹאשְׁךָ בְּשֵׂיבָה וְשַׁחֲרוּת.

ש״ץ: זִקְנָה בְּיוֹם דִּין וּבַחֲרוּת בְּיוֹם קְרָב, כְּאִישׁ מִלְחָמוֹת יָדָיו לוֹ רָב.
קהל: חָבַשׁ כּוֹבַע יְשׁוּעָה בְּרֹאשׁוֹ, הוֹשִׁיעָה לּוֹ יְמִינוֹ וּזְרוֹעַ קָדְשׁוֹ.

ש״ץ: טַלְלֵי אוֹרוֹת רֹאשׁוֹ נִמְלָא, קְוֻצּוֹתָיו רְסִיסֵי לָיְלָה.
קהל: יִתְפָּאֵר בִּי כִּי חָפֵץ בִּי, וְהוּא יִהְיֶה לִּי לַעֲטֶרֶת צְבִי.

ש״ץ: כֶּתֶם טָהוֹר פָּז דְּמוּת רֹאשׁוֹ, וְחַק עַל מֵצַח כְּבוֹד שֵׁם קָדְשׁוֹ.
קהל: לְחֵן וּלְכָבוֹד צְבִי תִפְאָרָה, אֻמָּתוֹ לוֹ עִטְּרָה עֲטָרָה.

Leader: Like a youth's, His hair in locks unfurls;
Its black tresses flowing in curls.

Cong: Jerusalem, His splendor, is the dwelling place of right;
may He prize it as His highest delight.

Leader: Like a crown in His hand may His treasured people be,
a turban of beauty and of majesty.

Cong: He bore them, carried them, with a crown He adorned them.
They were precious in His sight, and He honored them.

Leader: His glory is on me; my glory is on Him.
He is near to me when I call to Him.

Cong: He is bright and rosy; red will be His dress,
when He comes from Edom, treading the winepress.

Leader: He showed the tefillin-knot to Moses, humble, wise,
when the Lord's likeness was before his eyes.

Cong: He delights in His people; the humble He does raise –
He glories in them; He sits enthroned upon their praise.

Leader: Your first word, Your call to every age, is true:
O seek the people who seek You.

Cong: My many songs please take and hear
and may my hymn of joy to You come near.

Leader: May my praise be a crown for Your head,
and like incense before You, the prayers I have said.

Cong: May a poor man's song be precious in Your eyes,
like a song sung over sacrifice.

Leader: To the One who sustains all, may my blessing take flight:
Creator, Life-Giver, God of right and might.

Cong: And when I offer blessing, to me Your head incline:
accepting it as spice, fragrant and fine.

Leader: May my prayer be to You sweet song.
For You my soul will always long.

The Ark is closed.

Yours, Lord, are the greatness and the power, *1 Chr. 29*
the glory, the majesty and splendor, for everything in heaven and earth is Yours.
Yours, Lord, is the kingdom; You are exalted as Head over all.
▸ Who can tell of the mighty acts of the Lord and make all His praise be heard? *Ps. 106*

ש״ץ: מַחְלְפוֹת רֹאשׁוֹ כְּבִימֵי בְחוּרוֹת, קְוֻצּוֹתָיו תַּלְתַּלִּים שְׁחוֹרוֹת.

קהל: נְוֵה הַצֶּדֶק צְבִי תִפְאַרְתּוֹ, יַעֲלֶה נָּא עַל רֹאשׁ שִׂמְחָתוֹ.

ש״ץ: סְגֻלָּתוֹ תְּהִי בְיָדוֹ עֲטֶרֶת, וּצְנִיף מְלוּכָה צְבִי תִפְאֶרֶת.

קהל: עֲמוּסִים נְשָׂאָם, עֲטֶרֶת עִנְּדָם, מֵאֲשֶׁר יָקְרוּ בְעֵינָיו כִּבְּדָם.

ש״ץ: פְּאֵרוֹ עָלַי וּפְאֵרִי עָלָיו, וְקָרוֹב אֵלַי בְּקָרְאִי אֵלָיו.

קהל: צַח וְאָדוֹם לִלְבוּשׁוֹ אָדֹם, פּוּרָה בְּדָרְכוֹ בְּבוֹאוֹ מֵאֱדוֹם.

ש״ץ: קֶשֶׁר תְּפִלִּין הֶרְאָה לֶעָנָו, תְּמוּנַת יהוה לְנֶגֶד עֵינָיו.

קהל: רוֹצֶה בְעַמּוֹ עֲנָוִים יְפָאֵר, יוֹשֵׁב תְּהִלּוֹת בָּם לְהִתְפָּאֵר.

ש״ץ: רֹאשׁ דְּבָרְךָ אֱמֶת קוֹרֵא מֵרֹאשׁ דּוֹר וָדוֹר, עַם דּוֹרֶשְׁךָ דְּרֹשׁ.

קהל: שִׁית הֲמוֹן שִׁירַי נָא עָלֶיךָ, וְרִנָּתִי תִּקְרַב אֵלֶיךָ.

ש״ץ: תְּהִלָּתִי תְּהִי לְרֹאשְׁךָ עֲטֶרֶת, וּתְפִלָּתִי תִּכּוֹן קְטֹרֶת.

קהל: תִּיקַר שִׁירַת רָשׁ בְּעֵינֶיךָ, כַּשִּׁיר יוּשַׁר עַל קָרְבָּנֶיךָ.

ש״ץ: בִּרְכָתִי תַעֲלֶה לְרֹאשׁ מַשְׁבִּיר, מְחוֹלֵל וּמוֹלִיד, צַדִּיק כַּבִּיר.

קהל: וּבְבִרְכָתִי תְנַעֲנַע לִי רֹאשׁ, וְאוֹתָהּ קַח לְךָ כִּבְשָׂמִים רֹאשׁ.

ש״ץ: יֶעֱרַב נָא שִׂיחִי עָלֶיךָ, כִּי נַפְשִׁי תַעֲרֹג אֵלֶיךָ.

The ארון קודש *is closed.*

לְךָ יהוה הַגְּדֻלָּה וְהַגְּבוּרָה וְהַתִּפְאֶרֶת וְהַנֵּצַח וְהַהוֹד (דברי הימים א׳ כט)
כִּי־כֹל בַּשָּׁמַיִם וּבָאָרֶץ
לְךָ יהוה הַמַּמְלָכָה וְהַמִּתְנַשֵּׂא לְכֹל לְרֹאשׁ:
◂ מִי יְמַלֵּל גְּבוּרוֹת יהוה, יַשְׁמִיעַ כָּל־תְּהִלָּתוֹ: (תהלים קו)

MOURNER'S KADDISH

The following prayer, said by mourners, requires the presence of a minyan.
A transliteration can be found on *page 1467.*

Mourner: יִתְגַּדַּל Magnified and sanctified
may His great name be,
in the world He created by His will.
May He establish His kingdom
in your lifetime and in your days,
and in the lifetime of all the house of Israel,
swiftly and soon –
and say: Amen.

All: May His great name be blessed
for ever and all time.

Mourner: Blessed and praised,
glorified and exalted,
raised and honored,
uplifted and lauded
be the name of the Holy One,
blessed be He,
beyond any blessing, song,
praise and consolation
uttered in the world –
and say: Amen.

May there be great peace from heaven,
and life for us and all Israel –
and say: Amen.

Bow, take three steps back, as if taking leave of the Divine Presence,
then bow, first left, then right, then center, while saying:

May He who makes peace in His high places,
make peace for us and all Israel –
and say: Amen.

קדיש יתום

The following prayer, said by mourners, requires the presence of a מנין*.*
A transliteration can be found on page 1467.

אבל: יִתְגַּדַּל וְיִתְקַדַּשׁ שְׁמֵהּ רַבָּא (קהל: אָמֵן)
בְּעָלְמָא דִּי בְרָא כִרְעוּתֵהּ
וְיַמְלִיךְ מַלְכוּתֵהּ
בְּחַיֵּיכוֹן וּבְיוֹמֵיכוֹן וּבְחַיֵּי דְכָל בֵּית יִשְׂרָאֵל
בַּעֲגָלָא וּבִזְמַן קָרִיב
וְאִמְרוּ אָמֵן. (קהל: אָמֵן)

קהל ואבל: יְהֵא שְׁמֵהּ רַבָּא מְבָרַךְ לְעָלַם וּלְעָלְמֵי עָלְמַיָּא.

אבל: יִתְבָּרַךְ וְיִשְׁתַּבַּח וְיִתְפָּאַר
וְיִתְרוֹמַם וְיִתְנַשֵּׂא וְיִתְהַדָּר וְיִתְעַלֶּה וְיִתְהַלָּל
שְׁמֵהּ דְּקֻדְשָׁא בְּרִיךְ הוּא (קהל: בְּרִיךְ הוּא)
לְעֵלָּא מִן כָּל בִּרְכָתָא וְשִׁירָתָא
תֻּשְׁבְּחָתָא וְנֶחֱמָתָא
דַּאֲמִירָן בְּעָלְמָא
וְאִמְרוּ אָמֵן. (קהל: אָמֵן)

יְהֵא שְׁלָמָא רַבָּא מִן שְׁמַיָּא
וְחַיִּים, עָלֵינוּ וְעַל כָּל יִשְׂרָאֵל
וְאִמְרוּ אָמֵן. (קהל: אָמֵן)

Bow, take three steps back, as if taking leave of the Divine Presence,
then bow, first left, then right, then center, while saying:

עֹשֶׂה שָׁלוֹם בִּמְרוֹמָיו
הוּא יַעֲשֶׂה שָׁלוֹם עָלֵינוּ וְעַל כָּל יִשְׂרָאֵל
וְאִמְרוּ אָמֵן. (קהל: אָמֵן)

Many congregations sing Adon Olam at this point.

LORD OF THE UNIVERSE,
who reigned before the birth of any thing –

When by His will all things were made
then was His name proclaimed King.

And when all things shall cease to be
He alone will reign in awe.

He was, He is, and He shall be
glorious for evermore.

He is One, there is none else,
alone, unique, beyond compare;

Without beginning, without end,
His might, His rule are everywhere.

He is my God; my Redeemer lives.
He is the Rock on whom I rely –

My banner and my safe retreat,
my cup, my portion when I cry.

Into His hand my soul I place,
when I awake and when I sleep.

The LORD is with me, I shall not fear;
body and soul from harm will He keep.

For Minha of Yom Tov, turn to page 572.

Many congregations sing אֲדוֹן עוֹלָם *at this point.*

אֲדוֹן עוֹלָם

אֲשֶׁר מָלַךְ בְּטֶרֶם כָּל־יְצִיר נִבְרָא.
לְעֵת נַעֲשָׂה בְחֶפְצוֹ כֹּל אֲזַי מֶלֶךְ שְׁמוֹ נִקְרָא.
וְאַחֲרֵי כִּכְלוֹת הַכֹּל לְבַדּוֹ יִמְלֹךְ נוֹרָא.
וְהוּא הָיָה וְהוּא הֹוֶה וְהוּא יִהְיֶה בְּתִפְאָרָה.
וְהוּא אֶחָד וְאֵין שֵׁנִי לְהַמְשִׁיל לוֹ לְהַחְבִּירָה.
בְּלִי רֵאשִׁית בְּלִי תַכְלִית וְלוֹ הָעֹז וְהַמִּשְׂרָה.
וְהוּא אֵלִי וְחַי גּוֹאֲלִי וְצוּר חֶבְלִי בְּעֵת צָרָה.
וְהוּא נִסִּי וּמָנוֹס לִי מְנָת כּוֹסִי בְּיוֹם אֶקְרָא.
בְּיָדוֹ אַפְקִיד רוּחִי בְּעֵת אִישַׁן וְאָעִירָה.
וְעִם רוּחִי גְּוִיָּתִי יהוה לִי וְלֹא אִירָא.

For מנחה *of* יום טוב*, turn to page 573.*

Simḥat Torah

HAKAFOT

At Shaḥarit of Simḥat Torah the following is said after Full Kaddish (page 424).

אַתָּה הָרְאֵתָ You have been shown [these things] so that you may know that the LORD is God; besides Him there is no other. *Deut. 4*

To the One who alone does great wonders, His loving-kindness is forever. *Ps. 136*

There is none like You among the heavenly powers, my LORD, and there are no works like Yours. *Ps. 86*

---

throughout the Jewish world. In Cairo in the twelfth century, for example, there were two communities, one following the Babylonian tradition, the other, that of Israel. Maimonides was strongly opposed to the idea that Jews were reading different sections of the Torah at any given time, and strongly urged the adoption of the annual reading (*Hilkhot Tefilla* 13:1). This indeed happened, though not in his lifetime. Benjamin of Tudela, the Jewish traveler who visited Cairo in 1170, reports that even while the different customs persisted, the members of both communities came together to celebrate the annual completion of the Torah, which he calls *Yom Simḥat Torah*, "the day of Rejoicing in the Torah."

Other customs rapidly followed. One was the practice of beginning the Torah anew immediately after the completion, so that the charge could never be leveled against the Jewish people that having reached the end of the Torah, they stopped, or even paused. Hence the reading of the beginning of Genesis immediately after the conclusion of Deuteronomy. The two honors, of being called to the ending and the beginning, were greatly prized, and soon became known by the name of *Ḥatan*, Bridegroom, *Ḥatan Torah* for the former, *Ḥatan Bereshit* for the latter. By the eleventh century the custom had already been established in many communities to call up every adult male to the Torah on the day. Shortly thereafter, we hear of the custom of collectively calling up *kol hane'arim*, "all the children." The practice of *Hakafot*, walking around the *Bima* seven times in procession holding the Torah scrolls, as was done with the Four Kinds on Hoshana Raba, came later, originating in the mystical circle around R. Yitzḥak Luria in Tzefat in the late sixteenth century, at roughly the same time and in the same place that the service known as Kabbalat Shabbat was born.

שמחת תורה

סדר הקפות

At שחרית *of* שמחת תורה*, the following is said after* קדיש שלם *(page 425).*

אַתָּה הׇרְאֵתָ לָדַעַת, כִּי יהוה הוּא הָאֱלֹהִים, אֵין עוֹד מִלְּבַדּוֹ: דברים ד
לְעֹשֵׂה נִפְלָאוֹת גְּדֹלוֹת לְבַדּוֹ, כִּי לְעוֹלָם חַסְדּוֹ: תהלים קלו
אֵין־כָּמְוֹךָ בָאֱלֹהִים, אֲדֹנָי, וְאֵין כְּמַעֲשֶׂיךָ: תהלים פו

SIMḤAT TORAH

For an essay on Simḥat Torah, see Introduction, page lxxviii.

Simḥat Torah as the name of the ninth day of Sukkot dates back to Babylon in the eighth or ninth century. It began as the convergence of two distinct customs. The first was the Torah reading of the day, namely the passage at the end of the Torah in which Moses blesses the tribes ("This is the blessing," Deut. 33:1). This had been chosen to parallel what was then the *haftara* (nowadays we say it on Shemini Atzeret) in which King Solomon blessed the people at the Temple dedication ceremony (1 Kings 8:55). Because of this, the day was initially known as *Yom Berakha*, "The Day of Blessing" (*Siddur Rav Sa'adia Gaon*).

The other was the long-established custom of making a festivity at the conclusion of the study of a text – an order of the Mishna, for example, or the conclusion of a Talmudic tractate (*Shabbat* 118b). This itself was based on the feast Solomon made when God blessed him with wisdom: "Then Solomon awoke – and realized [God had spoken to him in] a dream. He returned to Jerusalem, stood before the Ark of the LORD's Covenant, and sacrificed burnt offerings and fellowship offerings. Then he gave a feast for all his court" (1 Kings 3:15).

During the period of the Geonim, (seventh to eleventh centuries), the dispersion of Jews and the relative isolation of communities one from another meant that different localities had developed different customs. In particular, Babylonian Jewry had the custom of dividing the Torah into 54 portions, reading it in the course of a single year. In Israel some divided it into 155 portions and read it in a three-year cycle (*Megilla* 29b). Others divided it into 175 portions and read it in three-and-a-half years (*Soferim* 16:8).

The day on which the Torah readings were completed was already known as *Simḥat Torah* by the eighth century, but it was not yet the same day

May the LORD's glory be forever; may the LORD rejoice in His works. *Ps. 104*
May the LORD's name be blessed from now and forever. *Ps. 113*
May the LORD our God be with us as He was with our ancestors; *1 Kings 8*
may He never leave us or forsake us.
Say, "Save us, God our Savior; *1 Chr. 16*
gather and deliver us from the nations,
that we may give thanks to Your holy name,
that we may glory in Your praise."
The LORD is King, the LORD was King,
the LORD will be King for ever and all time.
The LORD will give strength to His people; *Ps. 29*
the LORD will bless His people with peace.
May our words find favor before the LORD of all.

The Ark is opened.

Whenever the Ark set out, Moses would say, *Num. 10*
"Arise, LORD, and may Your enemies be scattered;
may those who hate You flee before You."
Advance, LORD, to Your resting place, You and Your mighty Ark. *Ps. 132*
Your priests are clothed in righteousness,
and Your devoted ones sing for joy.
For the sake of Your servant David,
do not reject Your anointed one.

אַתָּה הָרְאֵתָ לָדַעַת *You have been shown... (Previous page).* The custom of reciting a long sequence of verses prior to taking out the scrolls from the ark is first mentioned in the *Maḥzor Vitry*, a work emanating from the school of Rashi in eleventh century France. These include not only the verses usually said on Shabbat or festivals on taking out the scrolls, but also others added in honor of the occasion.

יְהִי יהוה אֱלֹהֵינוּ עִמָּנוּ *May the Lord our God be with us.* Taken from Solomon's prayer at the dedication of the temple.

וְאִמְרוּ, הוֹשִׁיעֵנוּ *Say, "Save us".* From David's song of praise on bringing the Ark to Jerusalem.

תהלים קד
יְהִי כְבוֹד יהוה לְעוֹלָם, יִשְׂמַח יהוה בְּמַעֲשָׂיו:

תהלים קיג
יְהִי שֵׁם יהוה מְבֹרָךְ, מֵעַתָּה וְעַד־עוֹלָם:

מלכים א׳ ח
יְהִי יהוה אֱלֹהֵינוּ עִמָּנוּ, כַּאֲשֶׁר הָיָה עִם־אֲבֹתֵינוּ
אַל־יַעַזְבֵנוּ וְאַל־יִטְּשֵׁנוּ:

דברי הימים א׳ טז
וְאִמְרוּ, הוֹשִׁיעֵנוּ אֱלֹהֵי יִשְׁעֵנוּ, וְקַבְּצֵנוּ וְהַצִּילֵנוּ מִן־הַגּוֹיִם
לְהֹדוֹת לְשֵׁם קָדְשֶׁךָ, לְהִשְׁתַּבֵּחַ בִּתְהִלָּתֶךָ:
יהוה מֶלֶךְ, יהוה מָלָךְ, יהוה יִמְלֹךְ לְעֹלָם וָעֶד.

תהלים כט
יהוה עֹז לְעַמּוֹ יִתֵּן, יהוה יְבָרֵךְ אֶת־עַמּוֹ בַשָּׁלוֹם:
וְיִהְיוּ נָא אֲמָרֵינוּ לְרָצוֹן, לִפְנֵי אֲדוֹן כֹּל.

The ארון קודש *is opened.*

במדבר י
וַיְהִי בִּנְסֹעַ הָאָרֹן וַיֹּאמֶר מֹשֶׁה
קוּמָה יהוה וְיָפֻצוּ אֹיְבֶיךָ, וְיָנֻסוּ מְשַׂנְאֶיךָ מִפָּנֶיךָ:

תהלים קלב
קוּמָה יהוה לִמְנוּחָתֶךָ, אַתָּה וַאֲרוֹן עֻזֶּךָ:
כֹּהֲנֶיךָ יִלְבְּשׁוּ־צֶדֶק, וַחֲסִידֶיךָ יְרַנֵּנוּ:
בַּעֲבוּר דָּוִד עַבְדֶּךָ, אַל־תָּשֵׁב פְּנֵי מְשִׁיחֶךָ:

Simḥat Torah is one of the profoundest expressions of the Jewish spirit. The other festivals were either ordained by the Torah or, in the case of Purim and Ḥanukka, formally instituted to recall a saving event in Jewish history. Simḥat Torah, by contrast, emerged through a series of customs that rapidly spread throughout the Jewish world. It is what the mystics called אתערותא־דלתתא, an "awakening from below" – an initiative that emerged from the Jewish people itself. Through it we recapture some of the joy and exuberance that marked the Simḥat Beit HaSho'eva celebrations in Jerusalem in Temple times. More than that: we turn the day into a wedding, in which the Jewish people is the groom, and the Torah the bride. As the rabbis said, re-interpreting the verse, "Moses commanded us the Torah as the heritage of the congregation of Jacob" – Read not "heritage" [*morasha*] but "betrothed" [*me'orata*] (Deut. 33:4, *Berakhot* 57a). Never has a book been loved more.

In that day they will say, *Is. 25*
"This is our God; we trusted in Him, and He saved us.
This is the LORD, we trusted in Him;
let us rejoice and be glad in His salvation."
Your kingdom is an eternal kingdom, *Ps. 145*
and Your dominion is for all generations.
For the Torah shall come forth from Zion *Is. 2*
and the word of the LORD from Jerusalem.

Father of compassion, favor Zion with Your goodness; *Ps. 51*
rebuild the walls of Jerusalem.
For we trust in You alone, King, God, high and exalted, Master of worlds.

All the Torah scrolls are taken from the Ark.

First Hakafa

LORD, please save us. *Ps. 118*
LORD, please grant us success.
LORD, please answer us on the day we cry.

God of spirits, please save us.
Searcher of hearts, please grant us success.
Mighty Redeemer, answer us on the day we cry.

Some add: The LORD's Torah is perfect, refreshing the soul. *Ps. 19*
A psalm of David. Render to the LORD, you angelic powers, *Ps. 29*
render to the LORD glory and might.
Render to the LORD the glory due to His name.
Bow to the LORD in the beauty of holiness.
The LORD's voice echoes over the waters;
the God of glory thunders; the LORD is over the mighty waters.
For the conductor of music. With stringed instruments. *Ps. 67*
A psalm, a song.
May God be gracious to us and bless us.
May He make His face shine upon us, Selah.
Please, by the power of Your great right hand,
set the captive nation free.
For I said, the world is built by loving-kindness. *Ps. 89*

Said R. Menachem Mendel of Kotzk: "Three ways are open to a man who is in sorrow. He who stands on a normal rung weeps, he who stands higher is silent, but he who stands on the topmost rung converts his sorrow into song."

וְאָמַר בַּיּוֹם הַהוּא, הִנֵּה אֱלֹהֵינוּ זֶה קִוִּינוּ לוֹ, וְיוֹשִׁיעֵנוּ ישעיה כה
זֶה יהוה קִוִּינוּ לוֹ, נָגִילָה וְנִשְׂמְחָה בִּישׁוּעָתוֹ:
מַלְכוּתְךָ מַלְכוּת כָּל־עֹלָמִים, וּמֶמְשַׁלְתְּךָ בְּכָל־דּוֹר וָדֹר: תהלים קמה
כִּי מִצִּיּוֹן תֵּצֵא תוֹרָה, וּדְבַר־יהוה מִירוּשָׁלָםִ: ישעיה ב

אַב הָרַחֲמִים, הֵיטִיבָה בִרְצוֹנְךָ אֶת־צִיּוֹן, תִּבְנֶה חוֹמוֹת יְרוּשָׁלָםִ: תהלים נא
כִּי בְךָ לְבַד בָּטָחְנוּ, מֶלֶךְ אֵל רָם וְנִשָּׂא, אֲדוֹן עוֹלָמִים.

All the ספרי תורה *are taken from the* ארון קודש.

הקפה *First*

אָנָּא יהוה הוֹשִׁיעָה נָּא, אָנָּא יהוה הַצְלִיחָה נָא: תהלים קיח
אָנָּא יהוה עֲנֵנוּ בְיוֹם קָרְאֵנוּ.
אֱלֹהֵי הָרוּחוֹת הוֹשִׁיעָה נָּא, בּוֹחֵן לְבָבוֹת הַצְלִיחָה נָא
גּוֹאֵל חָזָק עֲנֵנוּ בְיוֹם קָרְאֵנוּ.

Some add תּוֹרַת יהוה תְּמִימָה, מְשִׁיבַת נָפֶשׁ תהלים יט
מִזְמוֹר לְדָוִד תהלים כט
הָבוּ לַיהוה בְּנֵי אֵלִים, הָבוּ לַיהוה כָּבוֹד וָעֹז:
הָבוּ לַיהוה כְּבוֹד שְׁמוֹ, הִשְׁתַּחֲווּ לַיהוה בְּהַדְרַת־קֹדֶשׁ:
קוֹל יהוה עַל־הַמָּיִם, אֵל־הַכָּבוֹד הִרְעִים
יהוה עַל־מַיִם רַבִּים:
לַמְנַצֵּחַ בִּנְגִינֹת, מִזְמוֹר שִׁיר: תהלים סז
אֱלֹהִים יְחָנֵּנוּ וִיבָרְכֵנוּ, יָאֵר פָּנָיו אִתָּנוּ סֶלָה:
אָנָּא, בְּכֹחַ גְּדֻלַּת יְמִינְךָ, תַּתִּיר צְרוּרָה.
כִּי־אָמַרְתִּי עוֹלָם חֶסֶד יִבָּנֶה: תהלים פט

The Baal Shem Tov told the following story: "Once a fiddler played so sweetly that all who heard him began to dance, and whoever came near enough to hear, joined in the dance. Then a deaf man who knew nothing of music happened along, and to him, all he saw seemed the action of madmen – senseless and in bad taste."

Second Hakafa

Speaker of righteousness, please save us.
Robed in majesty, please grant us success.
Ancient and loving One, answer us on the day we cry.

Some add: The LORD's testimony is faithful, making the simple wise. *Ps. 19*
The LORD's voice in power. *Ps. 29*
Then will Your name be known on earth, *Ps. 67*
Your salvation among the nations.
Accept Your people's prayer.
Strengthen us, purify us, You who are revered.
A strong arm is Yours, might is Yours; *Ps. 89*
Your hand holds its power, Your right hand raised.

Third Hakafa

Pure and right, please save us.
Gracious and compassionate, please grant us success.
He who is good and does good, answer us on the day we cry.

Some add: The LORD's precepts are just, gladdening the heart. *Ps. 19*
The LORD's voice in beauty. *Ps. 29*
Let the peoples praise You, God; let all peoples praise You. *Ps. 67*
Please, Mighty One, guard like the pupil of the eye
those who seek Your unity.
Grant truth to Jacob, loving-kindness to Abraham. *Mic. 7*

Fourth Hakafa

He who knows thoughts, please save us.
Mighty and resplendent, please grant us success.
Robed in righteousness, answer us on the day we cry.

Some add: The LORD's commandment is radiant, giving light to the eyes. *Ps. 19*
The LORD's voice breaks cedars, *Ps. 29*
the LORD shatters the cedars of Lebanon.
He makes Lebanon skip like a calf, Sirion like a young ox.
Let the nations rejoice and sing for joy, *Ps. 67*
for You judge the peoples with equity,
and guide the nations of the earth, Selah!
Bless them, cleanse them,
grant them the compassion of Your righteousness always.
Goodness is to be found at Your right hand always. *Ps. 16*

Second הקפה

דּוֹבֵר צְדָקוֹת הוֹשִׁיעָה נָּא, הָדוּר בִּלְבוּשׁוֹ הַצְלִיחָה נָא
וָתִיק וְחָסִיד עֲנֵנוּ בְּיוֹם קָרְאֵנוּ.

Some add עֵדוּת יהוה נֶאֱמָנָה, מַחְכִּימַת פֶּתִי: תהלים יט
קוֹל־יהוה בַּכֹּחַ תהלים כט
לָדַעַת בָּאָרֶץ דַּרְכֶּךָ, בְּכָל־גּוֹיִם יְשׁוּעָתֶךָ: תהלים סז
קַבֵּל רִנַּת עַמְּךָ, שַׂגְּבֵנוּ, טַהֲרֵנוּ, נוֹרָא.
לְךָ זְרוֹעַ עִם־גְּבוּרָה, תָּעֹז יָדְךָ תָּרוּם יְמִינֶךָ: תהלים פט

Third הקפה

זַךְ וְיָשָׁר הוֹשִׁיעָה נָּא, חַנּוּן וְרַחוּם הַצְלִיחָה נָא
טוֹב וּמֵטִיב עֲנֵנוּ בְּיוֹם קָרְאֵנוּ.

Some add פִּקּוּדֵי יהוה יְשָׁרִים, מְשַׂמְּחֵי־לֵב תהלים יט
קוֹל יהוה בֶּהָדָר: תהלים כט
יוֹדוּךָ עַמִּים אֱלֹהִים, יוֹדוּךָ עַמִּים כֻּלָּם: תהלים סז
נָא גִבּוֹר, דּוֹרְשֵׁי יִחוּדְךָ כְּבָבַת שָׁמְרֵם.
תִּתֵּן אֱמֶת לְיַעֲקֹב, חֶסֶד לְאַבְרָהָם: מיכה ז

Fourth הקפה

יוֹדֵעַ מַחֲשָׁבוֹת הוֹשִׁיעָה נָּא, כַּבִּיר כֹּחַ הַצְלִיחָה נָא
לוֹבֵשׁ צְדָקוֹת עֲנֵנוּ בְּיוֹם קָרְאֵנוּ.

Some add מִצְוַת יהוה בָּרָה, מְאִירַת עֵינָיִם: תהלים יט
קוֹל יהוה שֹׁבֵר אֲרָזִים, וַיְשַׁבֵּר יהוה אֶת־אַרְזֵי הַלְּבָנוֹן: תהלים כט
וַיַּרְקִידֵם כְּמוֹ־עֵגֶל, לְבָנוֹן וְשִׂרְיוֹן כְּמוֹ בֶן־רְאֵמִים:
יִשְׂמְחוּ וִירַנְּנוּ לְאֻמִּים, כִּי־תִשְׁפֹּט עַמִּים מִישֹׁר תהלים סז
וּלְאֻמִּים בָּאָרֶץ תַּנְחֵם סֶלָה:
בָּרְכֵם, טַהֲרֵם, רַחֲמֵי צִדְקָתְךָ תָּמִיד גָּמְלֵם.
נְעִמוֹת בִּימִינְךָ נֶצַח: תהלים טז

אֵין אַדִּיר There is none so majestic as the LORD,
and none so blessed as the son of Amram;
there is no greatness like the Torah,
and none to learn it out like Israel.

Of God's mouth, of God's mouth, shall Israel be blessed.

There is none so glorious as the LORD,
and none so venerable as the son of Amram;
there is none so worthy as the Torah,
nor any who delight in it like Israel.

Of God's mouth, of God's mouth, shall Israel be blessed.

There is none so pure as the LORD,
and none so upright as the son of Amram;
there is none so honored as the Torah,
and none who learn it quite like Israel.

Of God's mouth, of God's mouth, shall Israel be blessed.

There is no king like the LORD,
and no prophet like the son of Amram;
nothing is supported like the Torah,
and no one helps it like Israel.

Of God's mouth, of God's mouth, shall Israel be blessed.

There is no savior like the LORD,
and none so righteous as the son of Amram;
there is none so holy as the Torah,
and none who give voice to it like Israel.

Of God's mouth, of God's mouth, shall Israel be blessed.

There is no guardian like the LORD,
and none so whole as the son of Amram;
there is nothing so perfect as the Torah,
and none to support it quite like Israel.

Of God's mouth, of God's mouth, shall Israel be blessed.

---

joy its natural expression. At the end of his life, Moses gave the Israelites the last of the 613 commands – the command that each of us, in every generation,

אֵין אַדִּיר כַּיהוה וְאֵין בָּרוּךְ כְּבֶן עַמְרָם
אֵין גְּדוֹלָה כַּתּוֹרָה וְאֵין דּוֹרְשָׁהּ כְּיִשְׂרָאֵל
מִפִּי אֵל מִפִּי אֵל, יִתְבָּרַךְ יִשְׂרָאֵל

אֵין הָדוּר כַּיהוה וְאֵין וָתִיק כְּבֶן עַמְרָם
אֵין זַכָּאָה כַּתּוֹרָה וְאֵין חוֹמְדָהּ כְּיִשְׂרָאֵל
מִפִּי אֵל מִפִּי אֵל, יִתְבָּרַךְ יִשְׂרָאֵל

אֵין טָהוֹר כַּיהוה וְאֵין יָשָׁר כְּבֶן עַמְרָם
אֵין כְּבוּדָה כַּתּוֹרָה וְאֵין לוֹמְדָהּ כְּיִשְׂרָאֵל
מִפִּי אֵל מִפִּי אֵל, יִתְבָּרַךְ יִשְׂרָאֵל

אֵין מֶלֶךְ כַּיהוה וְאֵין נָבִיא כְּבֶן עַמְרָם
אֵין סְמוּכָה כַּתּוֹרָה וְאֵין עוֹזְרָהּ כְּיִשְׂרָאֵל
מִפִּי אֵל מִפִּי אֵל, יִתְבָּרַךְ יִשְׂרָאֵל

אֵין פּוֹדֶה כַּיהוה וְאֵין צַדִּיק כְּבֶן עַמְרָם
אֵין קְדוֹשָׁה כַּתּוֹרָה וְאֵין רוֹחֲשָׁהּ כְּיִשְׂרָאֵל
מִפִּי אֵל מִפִּי אֵל, יִתְבָּרַךְ יִשְׂרָאֵל

אֵין שׁוֹמֵר כַּיהוה וְאֵין שָׁלֵם כְּבֶן עַמְרָם
אֵין תְּמִימָה כַּתּוֹרָה וְאֵין תּוֹמְכָהּ כְּיִשְׂרָאֵל
מִפִּי אֵל מִפִּי אֵל, יִתְבָּרַךְ יִשְׂרָאֵל

R. Naḥman of Bratslav taught: Sometimes when people are joyous and dancing, they grab a man from outside the dancing circle, one who is sad and melancholy, and force him to join them in their dance. Thus it is with joy: when a person is happy, his own sadness and suffering stand off on the side. But it is a higher achievement to struggle and pursue that sadness, bringing it too into the joy, until it is transformed… you grab hold of this suffering, and force it to join with you in the rejoicing, just as in the parable.

When words take wing and break free of the gravitational pull of worldly desires, speech modulates into song. Music is the language of the soul, and

Fifth Hakafa

Eternal King, please save us.
Resplendent and mighty, please grant us success.
Supporter and Helper, answer us on the day we cry.

Some add: The fear of the LORD is pure, enduring for ever. *Ps. 19*
The LORD's voice cleaves flames of fire. *Ps. 29*
Let the peoples praise You, God; let all peoples praise You. *Ps. 67*
Mighty One, Holy One,
in Your great goodness guide Your congregation.
LORD our Master, how glorious is Your name throughout the earth, *Ps. 8*
setting Your splendor over the heavens.

Sixth Hakafa

Helper of the poor, please save us.
Redeemer and Rescuer, please grant us success.
Eternal Rock, answer us on the day we cry.

Some add: The LORD's judgments are true, altogether righteous. *Ps. 19*
The LORD's voice makes the desert quake, *Ps. 29*
the LORD shakes the desert of Kadesh.
The earth has yielded its harvest. May God, our God, bless us. *Ps. 67*
Only One, Exalted One,
turn to Your people, who proclaim Your holiness.
The LORD is righteous in all His ways, and kind in all He does. *Ps. 145*

Seventh Hakafa

Holy and awesome, please save us.
Compassionate and gracious, please grant us success.
Dweller in the heavens, answer us on the day we cry.

Supporter of the innocent, please save us.
Eternally powerful, please grant us success.
Perfect in His deeds, answer us on the day we cry.

---

teaching that it was not enough for the Jewish people to receive the Torah once only, from Moses himself. Rather, they had to make it new in each generation. The Torah was given once, but it must be received many times, as each of us, through our study and practice, strive to recapture the pristine voice heard at Sinai.

הקפה *Fifth*

מֶלֶךְ עוֹלָמִים הוֹשִׁיעָה נָּא, נָאוֹר וְאַדִּיר הַצְלִיחָה נָא
סוֹמֵךְ וְסוֹעֵד עֲנֵנוּ בְּיוֹם קָרְאֵנוּ.

Some add יִרְאַת יהוה טְהוֹרָה, עוֹמֶדֶת לָעַד תהלים יט
קוֹל־יהוה חֹצֵב לַהֲבוֹת אֵשׁ: תהלים כט
יוֹדוּךָ עַמִּים אֱלֹהִים, יוֹדוּךָ עַמִּים כֻּלָּם: תהלים סז
חֲסִין קָדוֹשׁ, בְּרֹב טוּבְךָ נַהֵל עֲדָתֶךָ.
יהוה אֲדֹנֵינוּ מָה־אַדִּיר שִׁמְךָ בְּכָל־הָאָרֶץ תהלים ח
אֲשֶׁר־תְּנָה הוֹדְךָ עַל־הַשָּׁמָיִם:

הקפה *Sixth*

עוֹזֵר דַּלִּים הוֹשִׁיעָה נָּא, פּוֹדֶה וּמַצִּיל הַצְלִיחָה נָא
צוּר עוֹלָמִים עֲנֵנוּ בְּיוֹם קָרְאֵנוּ.

Some add מִשְׁפְּטֵי־יהוה אֱמֶת, צָדְקוּ יַחְדָּו: תהלים יט
קוֹל יהוה יָחִיל מִדְבָּר, יָחִיל יהוה מִדְבַּר קָדֵשׁ: תהלים כט
אֶרֶץ נָתְנָה יְבוּלָהּ, יְבָרְכֵנוּ אֱלֹהִים אֱלֹהֵינוּ: תהלים סז
יָחִיד גֵּאֶה, לְעַמְּךָ פְּנֵה, זוֹכְרֵי קְדֻשָּׁתֶךָ.
צַדִּיק יהוה בְּכָל־דְּרָכָיו, וְחָסִיד בְּכָל־מַעֲשָׂיו: תהלים קמה

הקפה *Seventh*

קָדוֹשׁ וְנוֹרָא הוֹשִׁיעָה נָּא, רַחוּם וְחַנּוּן הַצְלִיחָה נָא
שׁוֹכֵן שְׁחָקִים עֲנֵנוּ בְּיוֹם קָרְאֵנוּ.
תּוֹמֵךְ תְּמִימִים הוֹשִׁיעָה נָּא, תַּקִּיף לָעַד הַצְלִיחָה נָא
תָּמִים בְּמַעֲשָׂיו עֲנֵנוּ בְּיוֹם קָרְאֵנוּ.

---

should write, or have a share in writing, a Sefer Torah, a scroll of the Mosaic books. Significantly at this point he used an unusual word to describe the Torah. He called it a *Shira*, a "Song" (Deut. 31:19). Why so? Moses was

Some add: More precious than gold, than much fine gold. *Ps. 19*
They are sweeter than honey, than honey from the comb.
The LORD's voice makes hinds calve and strips the forests bare, *Ps. 29*
and in His Temple all say: "Glory!"
The LORD sat enthroned at the Flood;
the LORD sits enthroned as King forever.
The LORD will give strength to His people;
the LORD will bless His people with peace.
God will bless us, and all the ends of the earth will fear Him. *Ps. 67*
Accept our plea and heed our cry,
You who know all secret thoughts.
Yours, LORD, are the greatness and the power, *1 Chr. 29*
the glory, majesty and splendor,
for everything in heaven and earth is Yours.
Yours, LORD, is the kingdom; You are exalted as Head over all.
Then the LORD shall be King over all the earth; *Zech. 14*
on that day the LORD shall be One and His name One.
And in Your Torah it is written:
Listen, Israel: the LORD is our God, the LORD is One. *Deut. 6*
Blessed be the name of His glorious kingdom for ever and all time.

יָבוֹא Majestic One, come quickly, / come, chosen God, in our times,
with Elijah bearing tidings; / let our righteous Messiah come, / the son of David to redeem us –

a day of joy, a day of song, a day of rejoicing, a day of happiness, – let it come.

Great One, come quickly, / come, unmistakable God, in our times,
with Elijah bearing tidings; / let our righteous Messiah come, / the son of David to redeem us –

a day of joy, a day of song, a day of rejoicing, a day of happiness, – let it come.

Glorious One, come quickly, / come, venerable God, in our times,
with Elijah bearing tidings; / let our righteous Messiah come, / the son of David to redeem us –

a day of joy, a day of song, a day of rejoicing, a day of happiness, – let it come.

---

harmony, as the Israelites did at the far shore of the Red Sea, because music is the sound of the soul taking flight, and at the level of the soul Jews enter the unity of the divine which transcends the oppositions of lower worlds.

Some add הַנֶּחֱמָדִים מִזָּהָב וּמִפַּז רָב, וּמְתוּקִים מִדְּבַשׁ וְנֹפֶת צוּפִים: תהלים יט
קוֹל יהוה יְחוֹלֵל אַיָּלוֹת וַיֶּחֱשֹׂף יְעָרוֹת, וּבְהֵיכָלוֹ, כֻּלּוֹ אֹמֵר כָּבוֹד: תהלים כט
יהוה לַמַּבּוּל יָשָׁב, וַיֵּשֶׁב יהוה מֶלֶךְ לְעוֹלָם:
יהוה עֹז לְעַמּוֹ יִתֵּן, יהוה יְבָרֵךְ אֶת־עַמּוֹ בַשָּׁלוֹם:
יְבָרְכֵנוּ אֱלֹהִים, וְיִירְאוּ אוֹתוֹ כָּל־אַפְסֵי־אָרֶץ: תהלים סז
שַׁוְעָתֵנוּ קַבֵּל וּשְׁמַע צַעֲקָתֵנוּ, יוֹדֵעַ תַּעֲלוּמוֹת.
לְךָ יהוה הַגְּדֻלָּה וְהַגְּבוּרָה וְהַתִּפְאֶרֶת וְהַנֵּצַח וְהַהוֹד דברי הימים א׳ כט
כִּי־כֹל בַּשָּׁמַיִם וּבָאָרֶץ
לְךָ יהוה הַמַּמְלָכָה וְהַמִּתְנַשֵּׂא לְכֹל לְרֹאשׁ:
וְהָיָה יהוה לְמֶלֶךְ עַל־כָּל־הָאָרֶץ זכריה יד
בַּיּוֹם הַהוּא יִהְיֶה יהוה אֶחָד וּשְׁמוֹ אֶחָד:
וּבְתוֹרָתְךָ כָּתוּב לֵאמֹר
שְׁמַע יִשְׂרָאֵל, יהוה אֱלֹהֵינוּ יהוה אֶחָד: דברים ו
בָּרוּךְ שֵׁם כְּבוֹד מַלְכוּתוֹ לְעוֹלָם וָעֶד.

יָבוֹא אַדִּיר בִּמְהֵרָה יָבוֹא בָּחוּר בְּיָמֵינוּ
יָבוֹא אֵלִיָּהוּ לְבַשְּׂרֵנוּ יָבוֹא מְשִׁיחַ צִדְקֵנוּ, בֶּן דָּוִד גּוֹאֲלֵנוּ
יוֹם גִּילָה, יוֹם רִנָּה, יוֹם דִּיצָה, יוֹם חֶדְוָה, יָבוֹא אֵלֵינוּ.

יָבוֹא גָּדוֹל בִּמְהֵרָה יָבוֹא דָּגוּל בְּיָמֵינוּ
יָבוֹא אֵלִיָּהוּ לְבַשְּׂרֵנוּ יָבוֹא מְשִׁיחַ צִדְקֵנוּ, בֶּן דָּוִד גּוֹאֲלֵנוּ
יוֹם גִּילָה, יוֹם רִנָּה, יוֹם דִּיצָה, יוֹם חֶדְוָה, יָבוֹא אֵלֵינוּ.

יָבוֹא הָדוּר בִּמְהֵרָה יָבוֹא וָתִיק בְּיָמֵינוּ
יָבוֹא אֵלִיָּהוּ לְבַשְּׂרֵנוּ יָבוֹא מְשִׁיחַ צִדְקֵנוּ, בֶּן דָּוִד גּוֹאֲלֵנוּ
יוֹם גִּילָה, יוֹם רִנָּה, יוֹם דִּיצָה, יוֹם חֶדְוָה, יָבוֹא אֵלֵינוּ.

The way it is endlessly renewed is through song, by investing it with emotion. The Torah is God's libretto, and we, the Jewish people, are His choir. Collectively we sing God's song. We are the performers of His choral symphony. And though, when Jews speak they often argue, when they sing, they sing in

Worthy One, come quickly, / come, our kind God, in our times,
with Elijah bearing tidings; / let our righteous Messiah come, / the son of David to redeem us –

a day of joy, a day of song, a day of rejoicing, a day of happiness, – let it come.

Pure One, come quickly, / come, upright God, in our times,
with Elijah bearing tidings; / let our righteous Messiah come, / the son of David to redeem us –

a day of joy, a day of song, a day of rejoicing, a day of happiness, – let it come.

Mighty One, come quickly, / come, learned God, in our times,
with Elijah bearing tidings; / let our righteous Messiah come, / the son of David to redeem us –

a day of joy, a day of song, a day of rejoicing, a day of happiness, – let it come.

Redeemer, come quickly, / come, awesome God, in our times
with Elijah bearing tidings; / let our righteous Messiah come, / the son of David to redeem us –

a day of joy, a day of song, a day of rejoicing, a day of happiness, – let it come.

Elevated One, come quickly, / come, strong God, in our times,
with Elijah bearing tidings; / let our righteous Messiah come, / the son of David to redeem us –

a day of joy, a day of song, a day of rejoicing, a day of happiness, – let it come.

Savior, come quickly, / come, righteous God, in our times,
with Elijah bearing tidings; / let our righteous Messiah come, / the son of David to redeem us –

a day of joy, a day of song, a day of rejoicing, a day of happiness, – let it come.

Holy One, come quickly, / come, compassionate God, in our times,
with Elijah bearing tidings; / let our righteous Messiah come, / the son of David to redeem us –

a day of joy, a day of song, a day of rejoicing, a day of happiness, – let it come.

Almighty One, come quickly, / come, powerful God, in our times,
with Elijah bearing tidings; / let our righteous Messiah come, / the son of David to redeem us –

a day of joy, a day of song, a day of rejoicing, a day of happiness, – let it come.

The Torah scrolls are returned to the Ark except for those used in the Torah Reading. The prevalent custom is to call up every adult male in the congregation. See law 52.

יָבוֹא זַכַּאי בִּמְהֵרָה יָבוֹא חָסִיד בְּיָמֵינוּ
יָבוֹא אֵלִיָּהוּ לְבַשְּׂרֵנוּ יָבוֹא מְשִׁיחַ צִדְקֵנוּ, בֶּן דָּוִד גֹּאֲלֵנוּ
יוֹם גִּילָה, יוֹם רִנָּה, יוֹם דִּיצָה, יוֹם חֶדְוָה, יָבוֹא אֵלֵינוּ.

יָבוֹא טָהוֹר בִּמְהֵרָה יָבוֹא יָשָׁר בְּיָמֵינוּ
יָבוֹא אֵלִיָּהוּ לְבַשְּׂרֵנוּ יָבוֹא מְשִׁיחַ צִדְקֵנוּ, בֶּן דָּוִד גֹּאֲלֵנוּ
יוֹם גִּילָה, יוֹם רִנָּה, יוֹם דִּיצָה, יוֹם חֶדְוָה, יָבוֹא אֵלֵינוּ.

יָבוֹא כַּבִּיר בִּמְהֵרָה יָבוֹא לָמוּד בְּיָמֵינוּ
יָבוֹא אֵלִיָּהוּ לְבַשְּׂרֵנוּ יָבוֹא מְשִׁיחַ צִדְקֵנוּ, בֶּן דָּוִד גֹּאֲלֵנוּ
יוֹם גִּילָה, יוֹם רִנָּה, יוֹם דִּיצָה, יוֹם חֶדְוָה, יָבוֹא אֵלֵינוּ.

יָבוֹא מוֹשִׁיעַ בִּמְהֵרָה יָבוֹא נוֹרָא בְּיָמֵינוּ
יָבוֹא אֵלִיָּהוּ לְבַשְּׂרֵנוּ יָבוֹא מְשִׁיחַ צִדְקֵנוּ, בֶּן דָּוִד גֹּאֲלֵנוּ
יוֹם גִּילָה, יוֹם רִנָּה, יוֹם דִּיצָה, יוֹם חֶדְוָה, יָבוֹא אֵלֵינוּ.

יָבוֹא סַגִּיב בִּמְהֵרָה יָבוֹא עִזּוּז בְּיָמֵינוּ
יָבוֹא אֵלִיָּהוּ לְבַשְּׂרֵנוּ יָבוֹא מְשִׁיחַ צִדְקֵנוּ, בֶּן דָּוִד גֹּאֲלֵנוּ
יוֹם גִּילָה, יוֹם רִנָּה, יוֹם דִּיצָה, יוֹם חֶדְוָה, יָבוֹא אֵלֵינוּ.

יָבוֹא פּוֹדֶה בִּמְהֵרָה יָבוֹא צַדִּיק בְּיָמֵינוּ
יָבוֹא אֵלִיָּהוּ לְבַשְּׂרֵנוּ יָבוֹא מְשִׁיחַ צִדְקֵנוּ, בֶּן דָּוִד גֹּאֲלֵנוּ
יוֹם גִּילָה, יוֹם רִנָּה, יוֹם דִּיצָה, יוֹם חֶדְוָה, יָבוֹא אֵלֵינוּ.

יָבוֹא קָדוֹשׁ בִּמְהֵרָה יָבוֹא רַחוּם בְּיָמֵינוּ
יָבוֹא אֵלִיָּהוּ לְבַשְּׂרֵנוּ יָבוֹא מְשִׁיחַ צִדְקֵנוּ, בֶּן דָּוִד גֹּאֲלֵנוּ
יוֹם גִּילָה, יוֹם רִנָּה, יוֹם דִּיצָה, יוֹם חֶדְוָה, יָבוֹא אֵלֵינוּ.

יָבוֹא שַׁדַּי בִּמְהֵרָה יָבוֹא תַּקִּיף בְּיָמֵינוּ
יָבוֹא אֵלִיָּהוּ לְבַשְּׂרֵנוּ יָבוֹא מְשִׁיחַ צִדְקֵנוּ, בֶּן דָּוִד גֹּאֲלֵנוּ
יוֹם גִּילָה, יוֹם רִנָּה, יוֹם דִּיצָה, יוֹם חֶדְוָה, יָבוֹא אֵלֵינוּ.

The ספרי תורה *are returned to the* ארון קודש *except for those used in the* קריאת התורה.
The prevalent custom is to call up every adult male in the congregation. See law 52.

Outside Israel, the service continues with "Listen, Israel" on the next page.
The following is said in Israel when Simhat Torah falls on a weekday.
On Shabbat in Israel, continue with "Blessed is the name" below.

The following (The Thirteen Attributes of Mercy) is said three times:

יהוה The LORD, the LORD, compassionate and gracious God, *Ex. 34*
slow to anger, abounding in loving-kindness and truth,
extending loving-kindness to a thousand generations,
forgiving iniquity, rebellion and sin,
and absolving [the guilty who repent].

Each individual says silently, inserting appropriate phrase/s in parentheses:

רִבּוֹנוֹ Master of the Universe, fulfill my heart's requests for good. Satisfy my desire, grant my request, and enable me (*name*, son/daughter of *father's name*), (and my wife/ husband, and my sons/daughters) and all the members of my household to do Your will with a perfect heart. Deliver us from the evil impulse, grant us our share in Your Torah, and make us worthy that Your Presence may rest upon us. Confer on us a spirit of wisdom and understanding, and may there be fulfilled in us the verse: "The spirit of the LORD will rest *Is. 11*
upon him – a spirit of wisdom and understanding, a spirit of counsel and strength, a spirit of knowledge and reverence for the LORD." So too may it be Your will, LORD our God and God of our ancestors, that we be worthy to do deeds that are good in Your sight, and to walk before You in the ways of the upright. Make us holy through Your holiness, so that we may be worthy of a good and long life, and of the World to Come. Guard us from evil deeds and bad times that threaten to bring turmoil to the world. May loving-kindness *Ps. 32*
surround one who trusts in the LORD. Amen.

יִהְיוּ May the words of my mouth and the meditation of my *Ps. 19*
heart find favor before You, LORD, my Rock and Redeemer.

Say the following verse three times:

וַאֲנִי As for me, may my prayer come to You, LORD, *Ps. 69*
at a time of favor. O God, in Your great love,
answer me with Your faithful salvation.

On Shabbat in Israel:

בְּרִיךְ Blessed is the name of the Master of the Universe. Blessed is Your crown *Zohar, Vayak-hel*
and Your place. May Your favor always be with Your people Israel. Show Your people the salvation of Your right hand in Your Temple. Grant us the gift of Your good light, and accept our prayers in mercy. May it be Your will to prolong our life in goodness. May I be counted among the righteous, so that You

Outside ארץ ישראל, *the service continues with* שְׁמַע יִשְׂרָאֵל *on the next page.*
The following is said in ארץ ישראל *when* שמחת תורה *falls on a weekday.*
On שבת *in* ארץ ישראל, *continue with* בְּרִיךְ שְׁמֵהּ *below.*

The following (י״ג מידות הרחמים) *is said three times:*

יהוה, יהוה, אֵל רַחוּם וְחַנּוּן, אֶרֶךְ אַפַּיִם וְרַב־חֶסֶד וֶאֱמֶת: שמות לד
נֹצֵר חֶסֶד לָאֲלָפִים, נֹשֵׂא עָוֹן וָפֶשַׁע וְחַטָּאָה, וְנַקֵּה:

Each individual says silently, inserting appropriate phrase/s in parentheses:

רִבּוֹנוֹ שֶׁל עוֹלָם, מַלֵּא מִשְׁאֲלוֹת לִבִּי לְטוֹבָה, וְהָפֵק רְצוֹנִי וְתֵן שְׁאֵלָתִי, וְזַכֵּה לִי (פלוני/ת בֶּן/בַּת פלוני) (וְאִשְׁתִּי/בַּעְלִי וּבָנַי וּבְנוֹתַי) וְכָל בְּנֵי בֵיתִי, לַעֲשׂוֹת רְצוֹנְךָ בְּלֵבָב שָׁלֵם, וּמַלְּטֵנוּ מִיֵּצֶר הָרָע, וְתֵן חֶלְקֵנוּ בְּתוֹרָתֶךָ, וְזַכֵּנוּ שֶׁתִּשְׁרֶה שְׁכִינָתְךָ עָלֵינוּ, וְהוֹפַע עָלֵינוּ רוּחַ חָכְמָה וּבִינָה. וְיִתְקַיֵּם
בָּנוּ מִקְרָא שֶׁכָּתוּב: וְנָחָה עָלָיו רוּחַ יהוה, רוּחַ חָכְמָה וּבִינָה, רוּחַ עֵצָה ישעיה יא
וּגְבוּרָה, רוּחַ דַּעַת וְיִרְאַת יהוה: וּבְכֵן יְהִי רָצוֹן מִלְּפָנֶיךָ יהוה אֱלֹהֵינוּ וֵאלֹהֵי אֲבוֹתֵינוּ, שֶׁתְּזַכֵּנוּ לַעֲשׂוֹת מַעֲשִׂים טוֹבִים בְּעֵינֶיךָ וְלָלֶכֶת בְּדַרְכֵי יְשָׁרִים לְפָנֶיךָ, וְקַדְּשֵׁנוּ בִּקְדֻשָּׁתֶךָ כְּדֵי שֶׁנִּזְכֶּה לְחַיִּים טוֹבִים וַאֲרוּכִים וּלְחַיֵּי הָעוֹלָם הַבָּא, וְתִשְׁמְרֵנוּ מִמַּעֲשִׂים רָעִים וּמִשָּׁעוֹת רָעוֹת הַמִּתְרַגְּשׁוֹת לָבוֹא לָעוֹלָם,
וְהַבּוֹטֵחַ בַּיהוה חֶסֶד יְסוֹבְבֶנּוּ: אָמֵן. תהלים לב

יִהְיוּ לְרָצוֹן אִמְרֵי־פִי וְהֶגְיוֹן לִבִּי לְפָנֶיךָ, יהוה צוּרִי וְגֹאֲלִי: תהלים יט

Say the following verse three times:

וַאֲנִי תְפִלָּתִי־לְךָ יהוה, עֵת רָצוֹן, אֱלֹהִים בְּרָב־חַסְדֶּךָ תהלים סט
עֲנֵנִי בֶּאֱמֶת יִשְׁעֶךָ:

On שבת *in* ארץ ישראל:

בְּרִיךְ שְׁמֵהּ דְּמָרֵא עָלְמָא, בְּרִיךְ כִּתְרָךְ וְאַתְרָךְ. יְהֵא רְעוּתָךְ עִם עַמָּךְ זוהר ויקהל
יִשְׂרָאֵל לְעָלַם, וּפֻרְקַן יְמִינָךְ אַחֲזֵי לְעַמָּךְ בְּבֵית מַקְדְּשָׁךְ, וּלְאַמְטוּיֵי לַנָא מִטּוּב נְהוֹרָךְ, וּלְקַבֵּל צְלוֹתָנָא בְּרַחֲמִין. יְהֵא רַעֲוָא קֳדָמָךְ דְּתוֹרִיךְ לַן חַיִּין בְּטִיבוּ, וְלֶהֱוֵי אֲנָא פְקִידָא בְּגוֹ צַדִּיקַיָּא, לְמִרְחַם עֲלַי וּלְמִנְטַר יָתִי וְיַת כָּל דִּי לִי וְדִי לְעַמָּךְ יִשְׂרָאֵל. אַנְתְּ הוּא זָן לְכֹלָּא וּמְפַרְנֵס לְכֹלָּא, אַנְתְּ הוּא

will have compassion on me and protect me and all that is mine and all that is Your people Israel's. You feed all; You sustain all; You rule over all; You rule over kings, for sovereignty is Yours. I am a servant of the Holy One, blessed be He, before whom and before whose glorious Torah I bow at all times. Not in man do I trust, nor on any angel do I rely, but on the God of heaven who is the God of truth, whose Torah is truth, whose prophets speak truth, and who abounds in acts of love and truth. ▸ In Him I trust, and to His holy and glorious name I offer praises. May it be Your will to open my heart to the Torah, and to fulfill the wishes of my heart and of the hearts of all Your people Israel for good, for life, and for peace.

Three Torah scrolls are removed from the Ark. The Leader takes one in his right arm and, followed by the congregation, says:

Listen, Israel: the LORD is our God, the LORD is One. *Deut. 6*

Leader then congregation:

One is our God; great is our Master; holy is His name.

The Leader turns to face the Ark, bows and says:

Magnify the LORD with me, and let us exalt His name together. *Ps. 34*

The Ark is closed. The Leader carries the Torah scroll to the bima and the congregation says:

לְךָ Yours, LORD, are the greatness and the power, the glory and the *1 Chr. 29*
majesty and splendor, for everything in heaven and earth is Yours. Yours, LORD, is the kingdom; You are exalted as Head over all.

רוֹמְמוּ Exalt the LORD our God and bow to His footstool; He is holy. *Ps. 99*
Exalt the LORD our God, and bow at His holy mountain, for holy is the LORD our God.

Over all may the name of the Supreme King of kings, the Holy One blessed be He, be magnified and sanctified, praised and glorified, exalted and extolled, in the worlds that He has created – this world and the World to Come – in accordance with His will, and the will of those who fear Him, and the will of the whole house of Israel. He is the Rock of worlds, LORD of all creatures, God of all souls, who dwells in the spacious heights and inhabits the high heavens of old. His holiness is over the Ḥayyot and over the throne of glory. Therefore may Your name, LORD our God, be sanctified among us in the sight of all that lives. Let us sing before Him a new song, as it is written: "Sing to God, make *Ps. 68*
music for His name, extol Him who rides the clouds – the LORD is His name – and exult before Him." And may we see Him eye to eye when He returns to

שַׁלִּיט עַל כֹּלָּא, אַנְתְּ הוּא דְשַׁלִּיט עַל מַלְכַיָּא, וּמַלְכוּתָא דִּילָךְ הִיא. אֲנָא עַבְדָּא דְקֻדְשָׁא בְּרִיךְ הוּא, דְּסָגֵדְנָא קַמֵּהּ וּמִקַּמֵּי דִּיקַר אוֹרַיְתֵהּ בְּכָל עִדָּן וְעִדָּן. לָא עַל אֱנָשׁ רָחִיצְנָא וְלָא עַל בַּר אֱלָהִין סָמִיכְנָא, אֶלָּא בֶּאֱלָהָא דִשְׁמַיָּא, דְּהוּא אֱלָהָא קְשׁוֹט, וְאוֹרַיְתֵהּ קְשׁוֹט, וּנְבִיאוֹהִי קְשׁוֹט, וּמַסְגֵּא לְמֶעְבַּד טַבְוָן וּקְשׁוֹט. ◂ בֵּהּ אֲנָא רָחִיץ, וְלִשְׁמֵהּ קַדִּישָׁא יַקִּירָא אֲנָא אֵמַר תֻּשְׁבְּחָן. יְהֵא רַעֲוָא קֳדָמָךְ דְּתִפְתַּח לִבַּאי בְּאוֹרַיְתָא, וְתַשְׁלִים מִשְׁאֲלִין דְּלִבַּאי וְלִבָּא דְכָל עַמָּךְ יִשְׂרָאֵל לְטָב וּלְחַיִּין וְלִשְׁלָם.

Three ספרי תורה *are removed from the* ארון קודש*. The* שליח צבור *takes one in his right arm, and, followed by the* קהל*, says:*

דברים ו — שְׁמַע יִשְׂרָאֵל, יהוה אֱלֹהֵינוּ, יהוה אֶחָד:

קהל *then* שליח ציבור*:*

אֶחָד אֱלֹהֵינוּ, גָּדוֹל אֲדוֹנֵינוּ, קָדוֹשׁ שְׁמוֹ.

The שליח ציבור *turns to face the* ארון קודש*, bows and says:*

תהלים לד — גַּדְּלוּ לַיהוה אִתִּי וּנְרוֹמְמָה שְׁמוֹ יַחְדָּו:

The ארון קודש *is closed. The* שליח ציבור *carries the* ספר תורה *to the* בימה *and the* קהל *says:*

לְךָ יהוה הַגְּדֻלָּה וְהַגְּבוּרָה וְהַתִּפְאֶרֶת וְהַנֵּצַח וְהַהוֹד, כִּי־כֹל בַּשָּׁמַיִם דברי הימים א׳ כט
וּבָאָרֶץ, לְךָ יהוה הַמַּמְלָכָה וְהַמִּתְנַשֵּׂא לְכֹל לְרֹאשׁ:

רוֹמְמוּ יהוה אֱלֹהֵינוּ וְהִשְׁתַּחֲווּ לַהֲדֹם רַגְלָיו, קָדוֹשׁ הוּא: רוֹמְמוּ תהלים צט
יהוה אֱלֹהֵינוּ וְהִשְׁתַּחֲווּ לְהַר קָדְשׁוֹ, כִּי־קָדוֹשׁ יהוה אֱלֹהֵינוּ:

עַל הַכֹּל יִתְגַּדַּל וְיִתְקַדַּשׁ וְיִשְׁתַּבַּח וְיִתְפָּאַר וְיִתְרוֹמַם וְיִתְנַשֵּׂא שְׁמוֹ שֶׁל מֶלֶךְ מַלְכֵי הַמְּלָכִים הַקָּדוֹשׁ בָּרוּךְ הוּא בָּעוֹלָמוֹת שֶׁבָּרָא, הָעוֹלָם הַזֶּה וְהָעוֹלָם הַבָּא, כִּרְצוֹנוֹ וְכִרְצוֹן יְרֵאָיו וְכִרְצוֹן כָּל בֵּית יִשְׂרָאֵל. צוּר הָעוֹלָמִים, אֲדוֹן כָּל הַבְּרִיּוֹת, אֱלוֹהַּ כָּל הַנְּפָשׁוֹת, הַיּוֹשֵׁב בְּמֶרְחֲבֵי מָרוֹם, הַשּׁוֹכֵן בִּשְׁמֵי שְׁמֵי קֶדֶם, קְדֻשָּׁתוֹ עַל הַחַיּוֹת, וּקְדֻשָּׁתוֹ עַל כִּסֵּא הַכָּבוֹד. וּבְכֵן יִתְקַדַּשׁ שִׁמְךָ בָּנוּ יהוה אֱלֹהֵינוּ לְעֵינֵי כָּל חָי, וְנֹאמַר לְפָנָיו שִׁיר חָדָשׁ, כַּכָּתוּב:
שִׁירוּ לֵאלֹהִים זַמְּרוּ שְׁמוֹ, סֹלּוּ לָרֹכֵב בָּעֲרָבוֹת, בְּיָהּ שְׁמוֹ, וְעִלְזוּ לְפָנָיו: תהלים סח

His abode as it is written: "For they shall see eye to eye when the LORD returns to Zion." And it is said: "Then will the glory of the LORD be revealed, and all mankind together shall see that the mouth of the LORD has spoken." *Is. 52* *Is. 40*

Father of mercy, have compassion on the people borne by Him. May He remember the covenant with the mighty (patriarchs), and deliver us from evil times. May He reproach the evil instinct in the people by Him, and graciously grant that we be an eternal remnant. May He fulfill in good measure our requests for salvation and compassion.

The Torah scroll is placed on the bima and the Gabbai calls a Kohen to the Torah.

וְיַעֲזֹר May He help, shield and save all who seek refuge in Him,
and let us say: Amen. Let us all render greatness to our God
and give honor to the Torah. *Let the Kohen come forward.
Arise (*name* son of *father's name*), the Kohen.

**If no Kohen is present, a Levi or Yisrael is called up as follows:*

/As there is no Kohen, arise (*name* son of *father's name*) in place of a Kohen./

Blessed is He who, in His holiness, gave the Torah to His people Israel.

The congregation followed by the Gabbai:

You who cling to the LORD your God are all alive today. *Deut. 4*

The Torah portion is read.

The Reader shows the oleh the section to be read. The oleh touches the scroll at that place with the tzitzit of his tallit, which he then kisses. Holding the handles of the scroll, he says:

Oleh: Bless the LORD, the blessed One.

Cong: Bless the LORD, the blessed One, for ever and all time.

Oleh: Bless the LORD, the blessed One,
for ever and all time.

Blessed are You, LORD our God, King of the Universe,
who has chosen us from all peoples
and has given us His Torah.
Blessed are You, LORD, Giver of the Torah.

After the reading, the oleh says:

Oleh: Blessed are You, LORD our God, King of the Universe,
who has given us the Torah of truth,
planting everlasting life in our midst.
Blessed are You, LORD, Giver of the Torah.

וְנִרְאֵהוּ עַיִן בְּעַיִן בְּשׁוּבוֹ אֶל נָוֵהוּ, כַּכָּתוּב: כִּי עַיִן בְּעַיִן יִרְאוּ בְּשׁוּב יהוה ישעיה נב
צִיּוֹן: וְנֶאֱמַר: וְנִגְלָה כְּבוֹד יהוה, וְרָאוּ כָל־בָּשָׂר יַחְדָּו כִּי פִּי יהוה דִּבֵּר: ישעיה מ

אַב הָרַחֲמִים הוּא יְרַחֵם עַם עֲמוּסִים, וְיִזְכֹּר בְּרִית אֵיתָנִים, וְיַצִּיל נַפְשׁוֹתֵינוּ מִן הַשָּׁעוֹת הָרָעוֹת, וְיִגְעַר בְּיֵצֶר הָרָע מִן הַנְּשׂוּאִים, וְיָחֹן אוֹתָנוּ לִפְלֵיטַת עוֹלָמִים, וִימַלֵּא מִשְׁאֲלוֹתֵינוּ בְּמִדָּה טוֹבָה יְשׁוּעָה וְרַחֲמִים.

The ספר תורה *is placed on the* שולחן *and the* גבאי *calls a* כהן *to the* תורה.

וְיַעֲזֹר וְיָגֵן וְיוֹשִׁיעַ לְכָל הַחוֹסִים בּוֹ, וְנֹאמַר אָמֵן. הַכֹּל הָבוּ גֹדֶל לֵאלֹהֵינוּ וּתְנוּ כָבוֹד לַתּוֹרָה. *כֹּהֵן קְרַב, יַעֲמֹד (פלוני בֶּן פלוני) הַכֹּהֵן.

**If no* כהן *is present, a* לוי *or* ישראל *is called up as follows:*

/אֵין כָּאן כֹּהֵן, יַעֲמֹד (פלוני בֶּן פלוני) בִּמְקוֹם כֹּהֵן./

בָּרוּךְ שֶׁנָּתַן תּוֹרָה לְעַמּוֹ יִשְׂרָאֵל בִּקְדֻשָּׁתוֹ.

The קהל *followed by the* גבאי:

וְאַתֶּם הַדְּבֵקִים בַּיהוה אֱלֹהֵיכֶם חַיִּים כֻּלְּכֶם הַיּוֹם: דברים ד

The תורה *portion is read.*

The קורא *shows the* עולה *the section to be read. The* עולה *touches the scroll at that place with the* ציצית *of his* טלית, *which he then kisses. Holding the handles of the scroll, he says:*

עולה: בָּרְכוּ אֶת יהוה הַמְבֹרָךְ.

קהל: בָּרוּךְ יהוה הַמְבֹרָךְ לְעוֹלָם וָעֶד.

עולה: בָּרוּךְ יהוה הַמְבֹרָךְ לְעוֹלָם וָעֶד.
בָּרוּךְ אַתָּה יהוה, אֱלֹהֵינוּ מֶלֶךְ הָעוֹלָם
אֲשֶׁר בָּחַר בָּנוּ מִכָּל הָעַמִּים וְנָתַן לָנוּ אֶת תּוֹרָתוֹ.
בָּרוּךְ אַתָּה יהוה, נוֹתֵן הַתּוֹרָה.

After the קריאת התורה, *the* עולה *says:*

עולה: בָּרוּךְ אַתָּה יהוה אֱלֹהֵינוּ מֶלֶךְ הָעוֹלָם
אֲשֶׁר נָתַן לָנוּ תּוֹרַת אֱמֶת וְחַיֵּי עוֹלָם נָטַע בְּתוֹכֵנוּ.
בָּרוּךְ אַתָּה יהוה, נוֹתֵן הַתּוֹרָה.

One who has survived a situation of danger, says:

Blessed are You, LORD our God, King of the Universe, who bestows good on the unworthy, who has bestowed on me much good.

The congregation responds:

Amen. May He who bestowed much good on you continue to bestow on you much good, Selah.

After a Bar Mitzva boy has finished the Torah blessing, his father says aloud:

Blessed is He who has released me from the responsibility for this child.

FOR AN OLEH

May He who blessed our fathers, Abraham, Isaac and Jacob, bless (*name*, son of *father's name*) who has been called up in honor of the All-Present, in honor of the Torah, and in honor of (*On Shabbat:* the Sabbath and in honor of) the festival. As a reward for this, may the Holy One, blessed be He, protect and deliver him from all trouble and distress, all infection and illness, and send blessing and success to all the work of his hands, and may he merit to go up to Jerusalem for the festivals, together with all Israel, his brethren, and let us say: Amen.

FOR AN OLEH (ABRIDGED)

In many congregations, where the custom is to call a large number of congregants to the Torah, the following shortened form may be said:

May He who blessed the fathers, bless the sons, and let us say: Amen.

FOR A SICK MAN

May He who blessed our fathers, Abraham, Isaac and Jacob, Moses and Aaron, David and Solomon, bless and heal one who is ill, (*sick person's name*, son of *mother's name*), on whose behalf (*name of the one making the offering*) is making a contribution to charity. As a reward for this, may the Holy One, blessed be He, be filled with compassion for him, to restore his health, cure him, strengthen and revive him, sending him a swift and full recovery from heaven to all his 248 organs and 365 sinews, amongst the other sick ones in Israel, a healing of the spirit and a healing of the body – though on (*On Shabbat:* the Sabbath and) festivals it is forbidden to cry out, may healing be quick to come – now, swiftly and soon, and let us say: Amen.

FOR A SICK WOMAN

May He who blessed our fathers, Abraham, Isaac and Jacob, Moses and Aaron, David and Solomon, bless and heal one who is ill, (*sick person's name*, daughter of *mother's name*), on whose behalf (*name of the one making the offering*) is making a contribution to charity. As a reward for this, may the Holy One, blessed be He, be filled with compassion for her, to restore her health, cure

One who has survived a situation of danger, says:

בָּרוּךְ אַתָּה יהוה אֱלֹהֵינוּ מֶלֶךְ הָעוֹלָם הַגּוֹמֵל לְחַיָּבִים טוֹבוֹת שֶׁגְּמָלַנִי כָּל טוֹב.

The קהל *responds:*

אָמֵן. מִי שֶׁגְּמָלְךָ כָּל טוֹב הוּא יִגְמָלְךָ כָּל טוֹב, סֶלָה.

After a בר מצווה *has finished the* תורה *blessing, his father says aloud:*

בָּרוּךְ שֶׁפְּטָרַנִי מֵעָנְשׁוֹ שֶׁלָּזֶה.

מי שברך לעולה לתורה

מִי שֶׁבֵּרַךְ אֲבוֹתֵינוּ אַבְרָהָם יִצְחָק וְיַעֲקֹב, הוּא יְבָרֵךְ אֶת (פלוני בֶּן פלוני), בַּעֲבוּר שֶׁעָלָה לִכְבוֹד הַמָּקוֹם וְלִכְבוֹד הַתּוֹרָה (בשבת: וְלִכְבוֹד הַשַּׁבָּת) וְלִכְבוֹד הָרֶגֶל. בִּשְׂכַר זֶה הַקָּדוֹשׁ בָּרוּךְ הוּא יִשְׁמְרֵהוּ וְיַצִּילֵהוּ מִכָּל צָרָה וְצוּקָה וּמִכָּל נֶגַע וּמַחֲלָה, וְיִשְׁלַח בְּרָכָה וְהַצְלָחָה בְּכָל מַעֲשֵׂה יָדָיו, וְיִזְכֶּה לַעֲלוֹת לָרֶגֶל עִם כָּל יִשְׂרָאֵל אֶחָיו, וְנֹאמַר אָמֵן.

מי שברך לעולה לתורה (מקוצר)

In many congregations, where the custom is to call a large number of congregants to the תורה, *the following shortened form may be said:*

מִי שֶׁבֵּרַךְ אֶת הָאָבוֹת, הוּא יְבָרֵךְ אֶת הַבָּנִים, וְנֹאמַר אָמֵן.

מי שברך לחולה

מִי שֶׁבֵּרַךְ אֲבוֹתֵינוּ אַבְרָהָם יִצְחָק וְיַעֲקֹב, מֹשֶׁה וְאַהֲרֹן דָּוִד וּשְׁלֹמֹה הוּא יְבָרֵךְ וִירַפֵּא אֶת הַחוֹלֶה (פלוני בֶּן פלונית) בַּעֲבוּר שֶׁ(פלוני בֶּן פלוני) נוֹדֵר צְדָקָה בַּעֲבוּרוֹ. בִּשְׂכַר זֶה הַקָּדוֹשׁ בָּרוּךְ הוּא יִמָּלֵא רַחֲמִים עָלָיו לְהַחֲלִימוֹ וּלְרַפֹּאתוֹ וּלְהַחֲזִיקוֹ וּלְהַחֲיוֹתוֹ וְיִשְׁלַח לוֹ מְהֵרָה רְפוּאָה שְׁלֵמָה מִן הַשָּׁמַיִם לִרְמַ״ח אֵבָרָיו וּשְׁסָ״ה גִּידָיו בְּתוֹךְ שְׁאָר חוֹלֵי יִשְׂרָאֵל, רְפוּאַת הַנֶּפֶשׁ וּרְפוּאַת הַגּוּף. יוֹם טוֹב הוּא מִלִּזְעֹק (בשבת: שַׁבָּת וְיוֹם טוֹב הֵם) וּרְפוּאָה קְרוֹבָה לָבוֹא, הַשְׁתָּא בַּעֲגָלָא וּבִזְמַן קָרִיב, וְנֹאמַר אָמֵן.

מי שברך לחולָה

מִי שֶׁבֵּרַךְ אֲבוֹתֵינוּ אַבְרָהָם יִצְחָק וְיַעֲקֹב, מֹשֶׁה וְאַהֲרֹן דָּוִד וּשְׁלֹמֹה הוּא יְבָרֵךְ וִירַפֵּא אֶת הַחוֹלָה (פלונית בַּת פלונית) בַּעֲבוּר שֶׁ(פלוני בֶּן פלוני) נוֹדֵר צְדָקָה בַּעֲבוּרָהּ. בִּשְׂכַר זֶה הַקָּדוֹשׁ בָּרוּךְ הוּא יִמָּלֵא רַחֲמִים עָלֶיהָ לְהַחֲלִימָהּ

her, strengthen and revive her, sending her a swift and full recovery from heaven to all her organs and sinews, amongst the other sick ones in Israel, a healing of the spirit and a healing of the body – though on (*On Shabbat:* the Sabbath and) festivals it is forbidden to cry out, may healing be quick to come – now, swiftly and soon, and let us say: Amen.

ON THE BIRTH OF A SON

May He who blessed our fathers, Abraham, Isaac and Jacob, Moses and Aaron, David and Solomon, Sarah, Rebecca, Rachel and Leah, bless the woman (*name,* daughter of *father's name*) who has given birth, and her son who has been born to her as an auspicious sign. Her husband, the child's father, is making a contribution to charity. As a reward for this, may father and mother merit to bring the child into the covenant of Abraham and to a life of Torah, to the marriage canopy and to good deeds, and let us say: Amen.

ON THE BIRTH OF A DAUGHTER

May He who blessed our fathers, Abraham, Isaac and Jacob, Moses and Aaron, David and Solomon, Sarah, Rebecca, Rachel and Leah, bless the woman (*name,* daughter of *father's name*) who has given birth, and her daughter who has been born to her as an auspicious sign; and may her name be called in Israel (*baby's name,* daughter of *father's name*). Her husband, the child's father, is making a contribution to charity. As a reward for this, may father and mother merit to raise her to a life of Torah, to the marriage canopy, and to good deeds, and let us say: Amen.

FOR A BAR MITZVA

May He who blessed our fathers, Abraham, Isaac and Jacob, bless (*name,* son of *father's name*) who has completed thirteen years and attained the age of the commandments, who has been called to the Torah to give praise and thanks to God, may His name be blessed, for all the good He has bestowed on him. May the Holy One, blessed be He, protect and sustain him and direct his heart to be perfect with God, to walk in His ways and keep the commandments all the days of his life, and let us say: Amen.

FOR A BAT MITZVA

May He who blessed our fathers, Abraham, Isaac and Jacob, Sarah, Rebecca, Rachel and Leah, bless (*name,* daughter of *father's name*) who has completed twelve years and attained the age of the commandments, and gives praise and thanks to God, may His name be blessed, for all the good He has bestowed on her. May the Holy One, blessed be He, protect and sustain her and direct her heart to be perfect with God, to walk in His ways and keep the commandments all the days of her life, and let us say: Amen.

וּלְרַפְּאֹתָהּ וּלְהַחֲזִיקָהּ וּלְהַחֲיוֹתָהּ וְיִשְׁלַח לָהּ מְהֵרָה רְפוּאָה שְׁלֵמָה מִן הַשָּׁמַיִם לְכָל אֵבָרֶיהָ וּלְכָל גִּידֶיהָ בְּתוֹךְ שְׁאָר חוֹלֵי יִשְׂרָאֵל, רְפוּאַת הַנֶּפֶשׁ וּרְפוּאַת הַגּוּף. יוֹם טוֹב הוּא (בשבת: שַׁבָּת וְיוֹם טוֹב הֵם) מִלִּזְעֹק וּרְפוּאָה קְרוֹבָה לָבוֹא, הַשְׁתָּא בַּעֲגָלָא וּבִזְמַן קָרִיב, וְנֹאמַר אָמֵן.

מי שברך ליולדת בן

מִי שֶׁבֵּרַךְ אֲבוֹתֵינוּ אַבְרָהָם יִצְחָק וְיַעֲקֹב, מֹשֶׁה וְאַהֲרֹן דָּוִד וּשְׁלֹמֹה, שָׂרָה רִבְקָה רָחֵל וְלֵאָה הוּא יְבָרֵךְ אֶת הָאִשָּׁה הַיּוֹלֶדֶת (פלונית בַּת פלוני) וְאֶת בְּנָהּ שֶׁנּוֹלַד לָהּ לְמַזָּל טוֹב בַּעֲבוּר שֶׁבַּעְלָהּ וְאָבִיו נוֹדֵר צְדָקָה בַּעֲדָם. בִּשְׂכַר זֶה יִזְכּוּ אָבִיו וְאִמּוֹ לְהַכְנִיסוֹ בִּבְרִיתוֹ שֶׁל אַבְרָהָם אָבִינוּ וּלְגַדְּלוֹ לְתוֹרָה וּלְחֻפָּה וּלְמַעֲשִׂים טוֹבִים, וְנֹאמַר אָמֵן.

מי שברך ליולדת בת

מִי שֶׁבֵּרַךְ אֲבוֹתֵינוּ אַבְרָהָם יִצְחָק וְיַעֲקֹב, מֹשֶׁה וְאַהֲרֹן דָּוִד וּשְׁלֹמֹה, שָׂרָה רִבְקָה רָחֵל וְלֵאָה הוּא יְבָרֵךְ אֶת הָאִשָּׁה הַיּוֹלֶדֶת (פלונית בַּת פלוני) וְאֶת בִּתָּהּ שֶׁנּוֹלְדָה לָהּ לְמַזָּל טוֹב וְיִקָּרֵא שְׁמָהּ בְּיִשְׂרָאֵל (פלונית בַּת פלוני), בַּעֲבוּר שֶׁבַּעְלָהּ וְאָבִיהָ נוֹדֵר צְדָקָה בַּעֲדָן. בִּשְׂכַר זֶה יִזְכּוּ אָבִיהָ וְאִמָּהּ לְגַדְּלָהּ לְתוֹרָה וּלְחֻפָּה וּלְמַעֲשִׂים טוֹבִים, וְנֹאמַר אָמֵן.

מי שברך לבר מצווה

מִי שֶׁבֵּרַךְ אֲבוֹתֵינוּ אַבְרָהָם יִצְחָק וְיַעֲקֹב הוּא יְבָרֵךְ אֶת (פלוני בֶּן פלוני) שֶׁמָּלְאוּ לוֹ שְׁלֹשׁ עֶשְׂרֵה שָׁנָה וְהִגִּיעַ לְמִצְוֹת, וְעָלָה לַתּוֹרָה, לָתֵת שֶׁבַח וְהוֹדָיָה לְהַשֵּׁם יִתְבָּרַךְ עַל כָּל הַטּוֹבָה שֶׁגָּמַל אִתּוֹ. יִשְׁמְרֵהוּ הַקָּדוֹשׁ בָּרוּךְ הוּא וִיחַיֵּהוּ, וִיכוֹנֵן אֶת לִבּוֹ לִהְיוֹת שָׁלֵם עִם יהוה וְלָלֶכֶת בִּדְרָכָיו וְלִשְׁמֹר מִצְוֹתָיו כָּל הַיָּמִים, וְנֹאמַר אָמֵן.

מי שברך לבת מצווה

מִי שֶׁבֵּרַךְ אֲבוֹתֵינוּ אַבְרָהָם יִצְחָק וְיַעֲקֹב, שָׂרָה רִבְקָה רָחֵל וְלֵאָה, הוּא יְבָרֵךְ אֶת (פלונית בַּת פלוני) שֶׁמָּלְאוּ לָהּ שְׁתֵּים עֶשְׂרֵה שָׁנָה וְהִגִּיעָה לְמִצְוֹת, וְנוֹתֶנֶת שֶׁבַח וְהוֹדָיָה לְהַשֵּׁם יִתְבָּרַךְ עַל כָּל הַטּוֹבָה שֶׁגָּמַל אִתָּהּ. יִשְׁמְרֶהָ הַקָּדוֹשׁ בָּרוּךְ הוּא וִיחַיֶּהָ, וִיכוֹנֵן אֶת לִבָּהּ לִהְיוֹת שָׁלֵם עִם יהוה וְלָלֶכֶת בִּדְרָכָיו וְלִשְׁמֹר מִצְוֹתָיו כָּל הַיָּמִים, וְנֹאמַר אָמֵן.

TORAH READING FOR SIMḤAT TORAH

In Israel, if Simḥat Torah falls on Shabbat, the first three verses of the reading for the Ḥatan Torah (page 1240), from "And He dispels every foe" through "traverse their high places," are read for Shishi.

This is the blessing with which Moses, the man of God, blessed the Deut. 33:1–26
children of Israel before he died. Moses said: "The LORD came to them from Sinai; He shone out from Seir. He appeared over the crest of Paran, and came, among myriad angels, at His right hand a law of fire, for them. And He embraces the tribes, their holy ones all in His hands; they are drawn after Your steps, and carry Your words. Moses gave us a Law, a heritage to the people of Jacob. There is a King in Yeshurun, as the heads of the people are gathered, the tribes of Israel together.

"May Reuben live; let him not die, nor be left slight in number."

And this to Judah: he said, "Heed, LORD, the voice of Judah, and bring him home to his people. His arms alone need fight for him; You are his Support against his foes."

To Levi he said, "Your Tumim and Urim are with Your devoted, the LEVI
one You tested at Masa, and wrestled at Meriva; who said, of his father and mother: I have seen them not; who did not recognize his brothers,

---

וַיְהִי בִישֻׁרוּן מֶלֶךְ *There is a King in Yeshurun.* Yeshurun is another name for Israel. The reference is to the assembly at Mount Sinai, when Israel became a kingdom of priests and a holy nation under the sovereignty of God.

יְחִי רְאוּבֵן וְאַל־יָמֹת *May Reuben live; let him not die.* The tribe of Reuben had chosen to live east of the Jordan, and were thus highly exposed to enemy attacks. Note the absence of Shimon from these blessings. Jacob, in his death-bed blessing, had already predicted that the tribes of Shimon and Levi would be scattered among the other tribes (Gen. 49:7). According to Joshua 19:1–9, Shimon's townships all lay within the territory of Judah. Thus their blessing is included in that of the tribe of Judah.

תֻּמֶּיךָ וְאוּרֶיךָ *Your Tumim and Urim.* Oracular devices held in the breastplate of the High Priest (Ex. 28:30).

הָאֹמֵר לְאָבִיו וּלְאִמּוֹ *Who said, of his father and mother.* The Levites rallied to the side of God in the aftermath of the sin of the Golden Calf (Ex. 32:26–29).

קריאה לשמחת תורה

In ארץ ישראל, *if* שמחת תורה *falls on* שבת, *the first three verses of the reading for the* חתן תורה *(page 1241), from* מְעֹנָה אֱלֹהֵי קֶדֶם *through* עַל־בָּמוֹתֵימוֹ תִדְרֹךְ, *are read for* שישי.

דברים לג:א–ח וְזֹאת הַבְּרָכָה אֲשֶׁר בֵּרַךְ מֹשֶׁה אִישׁ הָאֱלֹהִים אֶת־בְּנֵי יִשְׂרָאֵל
לִפְנֵי מוֹתוֹ: וַיֹּאמַר יהוה מִסִּינַי בָּא וְזָרַח מִשֵּׂעִיר לָמוֹ הוֹפִיעַ
מֵהַר פָּארָן וְאָתָה מֵרִבְבֹת קֹדֶשׁ מִימִינוֹ אשדת לָמוֹ: אַף אֵשׁ דָּת
חֹבֵב עַמִּים כָּל־קְדֹשָׁיו בְּיָדֶךָ וְהֵם תֻּכּוּ לְרַגְלֶךָ יִשָּׂא מִדַּבְּרֹתֶיךָ:
תּוֹרָה צִוָּה־לָנוּ מֹשֶׁה מוֹרָשָׁה קְהִלַּת יַעֲקֹב: וַיְהִי בִישֻׁרוּן מֶלֶךְ
בְּהִתְאַסֵּף רָאשֵׁי עָם יַחַד שִׁבְטֵי יִשְׂרָאֵל: יְחִי רְאוּבֵן וְאַל־
יָמֹת וִיהִי מְתָיו מִסְפָּר: וְזֹאת לִיהוּדָה וַיֹּאמַר שְׁמַע
יהוה קוֹל יְהוּדָה וְאֶל־עַמּוֹ תְּבִיאֶנּוּ יָדָיו רָב לוֹ וְעֵזֶר מִצָּרָיו
תִּהְיֶה:
לוי וּלְלֵוִי אָמַר תֻּמֶּיךָ וְאוּרֶיךָ לְאִישׁ חֲסִידֶךָ אֲשֶׁר נִסִּיתוֹ בְּמַסָּה
תְּרִיבֵהוּ עַל־מֵי מְרִיבָה: הָאֹמֵר לְאָבִיו וּלְאִמּוֹ לֹא רְאִיתִיו וְאֶת־

וְזֹאת הַבְּרָכָה *This is the blessing.* In one of the most intense convergences in Jewish time, this Torah reading brings together the last day in the life of Israel's greatest leader, the completion of the Torah, the last day of the "season of our joy," and the culmination of the long sequence of the holy days of the seventh month that began on Rosh HaShana. Appropriately, it consists of words of benediction. Following the precedent of Jacob on his deathbed (Gen. 49), Moses takes leave of the living by conferring on them his blessings.

צִוָּה־לָנוּ מֹשֶׁה *Moses gave us a law.* One of the basic principles of Jewish self-definition. The Torah is not the property of an elite. It is the heritage of every Jew. "There are three crowns in Israel. The crown of priesthood went to Aaron and his descendants. The crown of kingship went to David and his successors. But the crown of Torah lies in front of every Jew. Whoever wishes, let him come and take it." (Maimonides, Laws of Torah Study 3:1). This (along with "Hear O Israel") is one of the first lines Jewish parents are bidden to teach their children (Ibid., 1:6).

nor know his own sons, for he kept Your words, and guarded close Your covenant. They will teach Your laws to Jacob, and Your Torah to Israel. They will place before You the scent of incense, and offerings burnt on Your Altar. Lord, bless his strength, and receive the work of his hands. Those who rise against him – crush their bearing; all his enemies, until they rise no more."

To Benjamin he said, "Beloved of the Lord, he shall rest on Him in safety; and all through the day He shelters him, and rests between his shoulders."

To Joseph he said, "His land is blessed of the Lord, with the fruit of SHELISHI
the skies, of rain, and of the deeps that bide below, and of the fruit of the sun's harvest, all the fruits of the moon's yield, of the heights of primeval mountains, of the fruit of the ancient hills, and the fruit of the world and its fullness – and the favor of that Presence at the Bush. May this come to the head of Joseph, to the crown of one raised above his brothers. His glory is that of a firstborn bull, his horns the grand horns of the oryx. With these he can gore nations; the ends of the earth together – yes, these are the myriads of Ephraim, the thousands of Manasseh."

And to Zebulun he said, "Find happiness, Zebulun, in your journeys, REVI'I
and Issachar in your tents. Tribes shall be called to the mountain, to bring righteous offerings there. For they will draw of the plenty of oceans, and of the hidden, buried riches of the sands."

To Gad he said, "Blessed be the One who broadens Gad's borders; for he crouches like a lioness, to tear arm and head from his prey. He

---

אֶפְרַיִם ... מְנַשֶּׁה *Ephraim ... Manasseh*: The two children of Joseph, whom Jacob had blessed (Gen. 48:13–20).

זְבוּלֻן, וְיִשָּׂשכָר *Zebulun, Issachar.* Zebulun engaged in maritime trade. Jacob in his blessing said, "Zebulun will live by the seashore and become a haven for ships" (Gen. 49:13). The "tents" of Issachar may have referred to their occupation as farmers and shepherds. The sages understood it to mean, "houses of study" (Rashi ad. loc.).

אֶחָיו לֹא הִכִּיר וְאֶת־בָּנָו לֹא יָדָע כִּי שָׁמְרוּ אִמְרָתֶךָ וּבְרִיתְךָ
יִנְצֹרוּ׃ יוֹרוּ מִשְׁפָּטֶיךָ לְיַעֲקֹב וְתוֹרָתְךָ לְיִשְׂרָאֵל יָשִׂימוּ קְטוֹרָה
בְּאַפֶּךָ וְכָלִיל עַל־מִזְבְּחֶךָ׃ בָּרֵךְ יהוה חֵילוֹ וּפֹעַל יָדָיו תִּרְצֶה
מְחַץ מָתְנַיִם קָמָיו וּמְשַׂנְאָיו מִן־יְקוּמוּן׃ לְבִנְיָמִן
אָמַר יְדִיד יהוה יִשְׁכֹּן לָבֶטַח עָלָיו חֹפֵף עָלָיו כָּל־הַיּוֹם וּבֵין
כְּתֵפָיו שָׁכֵן׃ *וּלְיוֹסֵף אָמַר מְבֹרֶכֶת יהוה אַרְצוֹ שלישי
מִמֶּגֶד שָׁמַיִם מִטָּל וּמִתְּהוֹם רֹבֶצֶת תָּחַת׃ וּמִמֶּגֶד תְּבוּאֹת שָׁמֶשׁ
וּמִמֶּגֶד גֶּרֶשׁ יְרָחִים׃ וּמֵרֹאשׁ הַרְרֵי־קֶדֶם וּמִמֶּגֶד גִּבְעוֹת עוֹלָם׃
וּמִמֶּגֶד אֶרֶץ וּמְלֹאָהּ וּרְצוֹן שֹׁכְנִי סְנֶה תָּבוֹאתָה לְרֹאשׁ יוֹסֵף
וּלְקָדְקֹד נְזִיר אֶחָיו׃ בְּכוֹר שׁוֹרוֹ הָדָר לוֹ וְקַרְנֵי רְאֵם קַרְנָיו
בָּהֶם עַמִּים יְנַגַּח יַחְדָּו אַפְסֵי־אָרֶץ וְהֵם רִבְבוֹת אֶפְרַיִם וְהֵם
אַלְפֵי מְנַשֶּׁה׃ *וְלִזְבוּלֻן אָמַר שְׂמַח זְבוּלֻן בְּצֵאתֶךָ רביעי
וְיִשָּׂשכָר בְּאֹהָלֶיךָ׃ עַמִּים הַר־יִקְרָאוּ שָׁם יִזְבְּחוּ זִבְחֵי־צֶדֶק כִּי
שֶׁפַע יַמִּים יִינָקוּ וּשְׂפֻנֵי טְמוּנֵי חוֹל׃ וּלְגָד אָמַר בָּרוּךְ
מַרְחִיב גָּד כְּלָבִיא שָׁכֵן וְטָרַף זְרוֹעַ אַף־קָדְקֹד׃ וַיַּרְא רֵאשִׁית לוֹ

יוֹרוּ מִשְׁפָּטֶיךָ לְיַעֲקֹב *They will teach your laws to Jacob.* The priests and Levites had a special role as educators to the people (see Neh. 8:7–8). The prophet Malakhi says of the ideal priest: "True instruction was in his mouth and nothing false was found on his lips. He walked with me in peace and uprightness, and turned many from sin. For the lips of a priest guard knowledge, and men seek rulings from his mouth, for he is a messenger of the LORD of Hosts" (Mal. 2: 6–7).

וּבֵין כְּתֵפָיו *Between his shoulders.* A description of Jerusalem, set between hills (see Josh. 15:8).

מִמֶּגֶד שָׁמַיִם מִטָּל *With the fruit of the skies, of rain.* Reminiscent of Isaac's blessing, (Gen. 27:28).

שֹׁכְנִי סְנֶה *That Presence at the Bush.* A reference to Moses' first encounter with God at the burning bush (Ex. 3:2-5).

chose the first place for his own, for the grave of a law-giver hides there. He came with the heads of the people; he performed the LORD's righteousness, and dealt uprightly with Israel."

And to Dan he said, "Dan is a lion cub, leaping from Bashan." ḤAMISHI

And to Naftali he said, "Naftali is sated with favor; filled with the LORD's blessing: go and form your inheritance seaward and south."

To Asher he said, "Most blessed of sons is Asher – may he be beloved of his brothers; may his feet be steeped in oil. Your doors are locked with iron and bronze, and your strength is as long as your days.

"There is none like God, Yeshurun, riding the skies to help you, the heavens in His grandeur."

* THE CHILDREN'S ALIYA

In many congregations, the children participate in the last aliya before calling up the Ḥatan Torah. All the children gather on the Bima, a tallit is spread over them and they say the blessings aloud together with the Oleh. After the blessing which follows the Reading, the whole congregation sing together:

הַמַּלְאָךְ May the angel who rescued me from all harm, bless these boys. May they be called by my name and the names of my fathers Abraham and Isaac, and may they increase greatly on the earth. *Gen. 48*

Some add:

יְבָרֶכְךָ May the LORD bless you and protect you. *Num. 6*
May the LORD make His face shine on you and be gracious to you.
May the LORD turn His face toward you and grant you peace.

---

way of the LORD, doing righteousness and justice" (Gen. 18:19); and of the saying of the sages that "The world only exists for the breath of school children" (*Shabbat* 119b). Judaism is a child-centered faith, with education at its core.

הַמַּלְאָךְ הַגֹּאֵל אֹתִי *May the angel who redeems me.* The blessing given by Jacob to Joseph's children, Ephraim and Manasseh. Lord Jakobovits explained that this blessing was chosen over all others because it is the only instance in the Torah of a grandparent blessing grandchildren. Between parents and children there are sometimes tensions. The love between grandparents and grandchildren is less complicated, unconstrained.

כִּי־שָׁם חֶלְקַת מְחֹקֵק סָפוּן וַיֵּתֵא רָאשֵׁי עָם צִדְקַת יהוה עָשָׂה
וּמִשְׁפָּטָיו עִם־יִשְׂרָאֵל: *וּלְדָן אָמַר דָּן גּוּר אַרְיֵה חמישי*
יְזַנֵּק מִן־הַבָּשָׁן: וּלְנַפְתָּלִי אָמַר נַפְתָּלִי שְׂבַע רָצוֹן וּמָלֵא בִּרְכַּת
יהוה יָם וְדָרוֹם יְרָשָׁה: וּלְאָשֵׁר אָמַר בָּרוּךְ מִבָּנִים
אָשֵׁר יְהִי רְצוּי אֶחָיו וְטֹבֵל בַּשֶּׁמֶן רַגְלוֹ: בַּרְזֶל וּנְחֹשֶׁת מִנְעָלֶךָ
וּכְיָמֶיךָ דָּבְאֶךָ: אֵין כָּאֵל יְשֻׁרוּן רֹכֵב שָׁמַיִם בְּעֶזְרֶךָ וּבְגַאֲוָתוֹ
שְׁחָקִים:

*עלית כל הנערים

In many congregations, the children participate in the last עליה *before calling up the* חתן תורה*. All the children gather on the* בימה*, a* טלית *is spread over them and they say the blessings aloud together with the* עולה*. After the blessing which follows the Reading, the whole congregation sing together:*

הַמַּלְאָךְ הַגֹּאֵל אֹתִי מִכָּל־רָע יְבָרֵךְ אֶת־הַנְּעָרִים, וְיִקָּרֵא בָהֶם שְׁמִי וְשֵׁם בראשית מח
אֲבֹתַי אַבְרָהָם וְיִצְחָק, וְיִדְגּוּ לָרֹב בְּקֶרֶב הָאָרֶץ:

Some add:

במדבר ו
יְבָרֶכְךָ יהוה וְיִשְׁמְרֶךָ:
יָאֵר יהוה פָּנָיו אֵלֶיךָ וִיחֻנֶּךָּ:
יִשָּׂא יהוה פָּנָיו אֵלֶיךָ וְיָשֵׂם לְךָ שָׁלוֹם:

אָשֵׁר *Asher*. The name itself means "fruitful, prolific" (see Gen. 30:13). It also has the sense of "happiness, felicity."

THE CHILDREN'S ALIYA

The custom of calling up all the children on Simḥat Torah is an ancient one, going back at least to the time of Rashi in the eleventh century. It was done for educational reasons, to encourage children in their love of Torah. It is hard not to sense other echoes: of the national assembly held on Sukkot after the sabbatical year (*Hak-hel*, Deut. 31:12) in which the Torah specifies that children should be included; of the statement at the dawn of Jewish time, that Abraham was chosen to be the father of a new nation "so that he will instruct his children and his household after him to keep the

RESHUT FOR THE ḤATAN TORAH

The following is said by the Gabbai to call up the Ḥatan Torah to his aliya:

By leave of great, mighty and awesome God;
by leave of [the Torah] who is more precious than fine gold and pearls;
by leave of the holy and chosen Sanhedrin,
the leaders in Torah and heads of the academies,
and the elders and young men seated in their rows:
I shall open my mouth in poetry and song,
in thanks and praise to the One encircled in light,
who gives us life, sustains us, in pure awe,
who brings us to rejoice at this Simḥat Torah
that delights the heart and lights up the eyes,
gives life and richness, dignity and splendor,
brings happiness to those who walk the straight path of goodness,
lengthens life, heightens strength
of those who love and keep her with care, attentively,
those busy with her, who guard her in love and awe.
And so, from the Mighty One, it should be His will
that grace, kindness and life, crown and diadem, be given
to (*name* son of *father's name*), the one chosen to complete
the Torah.
Strengthen him, bless him, nurture him in the learning of Torah,
make him sought after, praised, included in the company of learners,
make him worthy, vital, honor him in the splendor of light,
make him strong, crown him,
teach him Torah and its way of thinking,

---

found in the *Maḥzor Vitry*, written by a student of Rashi in eleventh century France. In those days it was the custom to call bridegrooms to the Torah with a similar invocation, on the Shabbat after their wedding. Prefacing a religious act – as we do, for example, in the Grace after Meals if three men are present – with a request for *reshut*, permission, is a formal acknowledgment of the (often legally constituted) authority under which the act is taking place. Permission would be asked, first of God, then of the Torah, then of the local religious authorities, then of the congregation. This gave the act, in this case, the blessing, its gravitas as an official honor, one of the highest the community could bestow.

רשות לחתן תורה

The following is said by the גבאי *to call up the* חתן תורה *to his* עליה:

מֵרְשׁוּת הָאֵל הַגָּדוֹל הַגִּבּוֹר וְהַנּוֹרָא
וּמֵרְשׁוּת מִפָּז וּמִפְּנִינִים יְקָרָה
וּמֵרְשׁוּת סַנְהֶדְרִין הַקְּדוֹשָׁה וְהַבְּחוּרָה
וּמֵרְשׁוּת רָאשֵׁי יְשִׁיבוֹת וְאַלּוּפֵי תוֹרָה
וּמֵרְשׁוּת זְקֵנִים וּנְעָרִים יוֹשְׁבֵי שׁוּרָה
אֶפְתְּחָה פִּי בְּשִׁיר וּבְזִמְרָה
לְהוֹדוֹת לְהַלֵּל לְדָר בִּנְהוֹרָא
שֶׁהֶחֱיָנוּ וְקִיְּמָנוּ בְּיִרְאָתוֹ הַטְּהוֹרָה
וְהִגִּיעָנוּ לִשְׂמֹחַ בְּשִׂמְחַת הַתּוֹרָה
הַמְשַׂמַּחַת לֵב וְעֵינַיִם מְאִירָה
הַנּוֹתֶנֶת חַיִּים וְעֹשֶׁר וְכָבוֹד וְתִפְאָרָה
הַמְאַשֶּׁרֶת הוֹלְכִים בַּדֶּרֶךְ הַטּוֹבָה וְהַיְשָׁרָה
הַמַּאֲרֶכֶת יָמִים וּמוֹסֶפֶת גְּבוּרָה
לְאוֹהֲבֶיהָ וּלְשׁוֹמְרֶיהָ בְּצִוּוּי וְאַזְהָרָה
לְעוֹסְקֶיהָ וּלְנוֹצְרֶיהָ בְּאַהַב וּבְמוֹרָא.
וּבְכֵן יְהִי רָצוֹן מִלִּפְנֵי הַגְּבוּרָה
לָתֵת חֵן וָחֶסֶד וְחַיִּים וְנֵזֶר וַעֲטָרָה
לְרַבִּי (פלוני ב״ר פלוני) הַנִּבְחָר לְהַשְׁלִים הַתּוֹרָה
לְאַמְּצוֹ לְבָרְכוֹ לְגַדְּלוֹ בְּתַלְמוּד תּוֹרָה
לְדָרְשׁוֹ לְהַדְּרוֹ לְוַעֲדוֹ בַּחֲבוּרָה
לְזַכּוֹתוֹ לְחַיּוֹתוֹ לְטַכְּסוֹ בְּטֶכֶס אוֹרָה
לְיַשְּׁרוֹ לְכַלְּלוֹ לְלַמְּדוֹ לֶקַח וּסְבָרָה

RESHUT FOR THE ḤATAN TORAH

The custom of calling up the *Ḥatan Torah* with an elaborate invocation is first

protect him, elevate him, support him with direct assistance,
give him sustenance, make him refined
and righteous among Your created people,
bring him close, show him mercy, guard him from pain and precipice,
give him fortitude, sustain him, make him whole in broken spirit.
Stand, stand, stand (*name* son of *father's name*), groom to the Torah,
give honor to great, awesome God;
for this you shall merit from the awesome God
to see your children and grandchildren busy themselves in Torah
and fulfill the commandments amongst this beautiful, pure people;
and you shall be worthy of rejoicing in the joy of the Temple,
the Chosen House,
and your face should light up in righteousness like [the Presence of God
through] shining glass,
as Isaiah, filled with the spirit of wisdom and strength, prophesied:
Rejoice with Jerusalem, be happy with her, soon,
rejoice with her in joyfulness,
all you who grieved in pain and mourning.
Stand, stand, stand (*name* son of *father's name*), groom to the Torah;
by leave of this holy congregation,
complete the Torah.

Arise (*name* son of *father's name*), Ḥatan HaTorah.

Deut. 33:27–34:[illegible] *(On Shab[illegible]* SHISHI)

Your sanctuary the God of time immemorial, you rest in eternal arms. And He dispels every foe before you, saying: "Destroy." And Israel will rest in safety, untouched, the fountain of Jacob; in a land of grain and wine, its skies dripping with dew. Happy are you, Israel; who is like you, a people surviving through the LORD? He is the shield of your strength; the sword of your grandeur – your enemies may deny you, but you shall traverse their high places."*

On Shabb[illegible] Shishi en[illegible] here

אַשְׁרֶיךָ יִשְׂרָאֵל *Happy are you, Israel.* Moses' last words to the people he had led from slavery to freedom, through the wilderness, to the brink of the Promised Land. His message is moving and clear: If the people stay faithful to God, they will be safe from their enemies, and need have no fear. The real challenge will not be military but spiritual. So it was, so it is, so it will always be: Israel is summoned to be a small nation, made great not by its own power, but by

לְמַלְטוֹ לְנַשְּׂאוֹ לְסַעֲדוֹ בְּסַעַד בְּרוּרָה
לְעָדְנוֹ לְפַרְנְסוֹ לְצַדְּקוֹ בְּעַם נִבְרָא
לְקָרְבוֹ לְרַחֲמוֹ לְשָׁמְרוֹ מִכָּל צוּקָה וְצָרָה
לְתַקְּפוֹ לְתָמְכוֹ לְתוֹמְמוֹ בְּרוּחַ נִשְׁבָּרָה.
עֲמֹד עֲמֹד עֲמֹד רַבִּי (פלוני ב״ר פלוני) חֲתַן הַתּוֹרָה
וְתֵן כָּבוֹד לָאֵל גָּדוֹל וְנוֹרָא
וּבִשְׂכַר זֶה תִּזְכֶּה מֵאֵל נוֹרָא
לִרְאוֹת בָּנִים וּבְנֵי בָנִים עוֹסְקִים בַּתּוֹרָה
וּמְקַיְּמֵי מִצְוֹת בְּתוֹךְ עַם יָפָה וּבָרָה
וְתִזְכֶּה לִשְׂמֹחַ בְּשִׂמְחַת בֵּית הַבְּחִירָה
וּפָנֶיךָ לְהָאִיר בִּצְדָקָה כְּאִסְפַּקְלַרְיָא הַמְּאִירָה
כִּנְבָא יְשַׁעְיָהוּ מָלֵא רוּחַ עֵצָה וּגְבוּרָה
שִׂמְחוּ אֶת יְרוּשָׁלַיִם וְגִילוּ בָהּ מְהֵרָה
שִׂישׂוּ אִתָּהּ מָשׂוֹשׂ כָּל הַמִּתְאַבְּלִים בְּאֵבֶל וְצָרָה
עֲמֹד עֲמֹד רַבִּי (פלוני ב״ר פלוני) חֲתַן הַתּוֹרָה
מֵרְשׁוּת כָּל הַקָּהָל הַקָּדוֹשׁ הַזֶּה וְהַשְׁלֵם הַתּוֹרָה.

יַעֲמֹד רַבִּי (פלוני ב״ר פלוני) חֲתַן הַתּוֹרָה.

דברים לג: כז–לד:יב

בשבת שי ⋆מְעֹנָה אֱלֹהֵי קֶדֶם וּמִתַּחַת זְרֹעֹת עוֹלָם וַיְגָרֶשׁ מִפָּנֶיךָ אוֹיֵב
וַיֹּאמֶר הַשְׁמֵד: וַיִּשְׁכֹּן יִשְׂרָאֵל בֶּטַח בָּדָד עֵין יַעֲקֹב אֶל־אֶרֶץ
דָּגָן וְתִירוֹשׁ אַף־שָׁמָיו יַעַרְפוּ־טָל: אַשְׁרֶיךָ יִשְׂרָאֵל מִי כָמוֹךָ עַם
נוֹשַׁע בַּיהוָה מָגֵן עֶזְרֶךָ וַאֲשֶׁר־חֶרֶב גַּאֲוָתֶךָ וְיִכָּחֲשׁוּ אֹיְבֶיךָ לָךְ
בשבת עד כאן שי וְאַתָּה עַל־בָּמוֹתֵימוֹ תִדְרֹךְ:⋆ וַיַּעַל מֹשֶׁה מֵעַרְבֹת

זְרֹעֹת עוֹלָם *Eternal arms.* A poetic description of the way God would carry the people through the vicissitudes of history, if they stayed faithful to His covenant.

And Moses ascended from the Moab plains to Mount Nevo, to the very summit, looking out towards Jericho. And the LORD showed him all of the land, across Gilead to Dan; all of Naftali, and the lands of Ephraim and Manasseh, and all the domain of Judah to the far ocean, the Negev and the plain, the valley of Jericho, city of palms, and as far as Tzo'ar. And the LORD said to him, "This is the land I promised to Abraham, to Isaac and to Jacob, saying, 'I shall give this to your children.' Now I have let your eyes see it – but you shall not cross over there."

And there, in the land of Moab, Moses, the servant of the LORD, died at the word of the LORD. He buried him there in the valley, in the land of Moab, opposite Beit Peor, and no man knows his burial place to this day. Moses was a hundred and twenty years old when he died; his sight had never dimmed, nor his strength evaded him. And the children of Israel wept for Moses thirty days, there in the plains of Moab. Then the

---

וַיִּקְבֹּר *He buried.* The sages said that this is a reference to God. Hence their dictum that the Torah begins and ends with an act of living-kindness by God (see *Sota* 14a). It began with His clothing the naked (Adam and Eve prior to their departure from Eden, Gen. 3:21), and ends with His burying the dead.

וְלֹא־יָדַע אִישׁ אֶת־קְבֻרָתוֹ *No man knows his burial place.* To avoid the possibility of his grave becoming a shrine and place of pilgrimage. The greatest of humans is still a human, not a god or demigod. No religion has given a more elevated account of the human person, but none has insisted more categorically on the radical distinction between God and humankind. Even the greatest of human beings is unworthy of worship. That distinction belongs to God alone.

לֹא־כָהֲתָה עֵינוֹ וְלֹא־נָס לֵחֹה *His sight had never dimmed, nor his strength evaded him.* Moses' energy was unabated because his eye was undimmed, that is, he never lost the ideals of his youth. Despite the many setbacks he experienced, he did not allow himself to become disillusioned, or to give way to despair. His undimmed faith in the God he served, the people he led, and the mission to which he dedicated his life was the source of his ability to defeat entropy, the principle that all systems lose energy over time.

מוֹאָב אֶל־הַר נְבוֹ רֹאשׁ הַפִּסְגָּה אֲשֶׁר עַל־פְּנֵי יְרֵחוֹ וַיַּרְאֵהוּ יְהוָה
אֶת־כׇּל־הָאָרֶץ אֶת־הַגִּלְעָד עַד־דָּן: וְאֵת כׇּל־נַפְתָּלִי וְאֶת־אֶרֶץ
אֶפְרַיִם וּמְנַשֶּׁה וְאֵת כׇּל־אֶרֶץ יְהוּדָה עַד הַיָּם הָאַחֲרוֹן: וְאֶת־
הַנֶּגֶב וְאֶת־הַכִּכָּר בִּקְעַת יְרֵחוֹ עִיר הַתְּמָרִים עַד־צֹעַר: וַיֹּאמֶר
יְהוָה אֵלָיו זֹאת הָאָרֶץ אֲשֶׁר נִשְׁבַּעְתִּי לְאַבְרָהָם לְיִצְחָק וּלְיַעֲקֹב
לֵאמֹר לְזַרְעֲךָ אֶתְּנֶנָּה הֶרְאִיתִיךָ בְעֵינֶיךָ וְשָׁמָּה לֹא תַעֲבֹר: וַיָּמׇת
שָׁם מֹשֶׁה עֶבֶד־יְהוָה בְּאֶרֶץ מוֹאָב עַל־פִּי יְהוָה: וַיִּקְבֹּר אֹתוֹ
בַגַּי בְּאֶרֶץ מוֹאָב מוּל בֵּית פְּעוֹר וְלֹא־יָדַע אִישׁ אֶת־קְבֻרָתוֹ
עַד הַיּוֹם הַזֶּה: וּמֹשֶׁה בֶּן־מֵאָה וְעֶשְׂרִים שָׁנָה בְּמֹתוֹ לֹא־כָהֲתָה
עֵינוֹ וְלֹא־נָס לֵחֹה: וַיִּבְכּוּ בְנֵי יִשְׂרָאֵל אֶת־מֹשֶׁה בְּעַרְבֹת מוֹאָב

---

its fidelity to a Power greater than itself, larger than humankind, beyond the hazards of history and the winds of time.

THE DEATH OF MOSES

One of the most poignant moments in religious history. Moses, who had spent forty years leading the Israelites to the Promised Land, is told that he will not himself enter it: he will merely see it from afar. Thus he became the symbol both of the possibilities of a human life and of its limits. "It is not for you to complete the task," said Rabbi Tarfon, "but neither are you free to stand aside from it" (*Avot* 2:21). For each of us there is a Jordan we will not cross, a destination we will not reach, a fulfillment we will not see. Hence the importance, in Judaism, of handing the tradition on across the generations – through our children, as in the case of Aaron, or our disciples, as in the case of Moses.

עֶבֶד־ה׳ *The servant of God.* Moses' ultimate accolade was not that he was a leader of men, but that he was a servant of God: the basis of the concept of leadership as service (see *Horayot* 10a). Eighteen times in Tanakh Moses is given this simple accolade. The only other person to be so described (twice) was Joshua, his successor.

days of weeping ended, the days of mourning for Moses. And Joshua son of Nun was filled with a spirit of wisdom, Moses having pressed his hands upon him; and the children of Israel heeded him, and did as the LORD had commanded Moses.

No other prophet like Moses has ever risen up in Israel; one whom the LORD knew face to face. None was like him, with the signs and wonders the LORD sent him to perform in the land of Egypt; before Pharaoh and all his servants and all of his land. None like him with all the mighty power and all the great awe that he brought down, before the eyes of all Israel.

Be strong, be strong,
and let us strengthen one another.

HAGBAHA AND GELILA

The first Torah scroll is lifted and the congregation says:

וְזֹאת הַתּוֹרָה This is the Torah Deut. 4
that Moses placed before the children of Israel,
at the LORD's commandment, by the hand of Moses. Num. 9

Some add: It is a tree of life to those who grasp it, Prov. 3
and those who uphold it are happy.
Its ways are ways of pleasantness, and all its paths are peace.
Long life is in its right hand; in its left, riches and honor.
It pleased the LORD for the sake of [Israel's] righteousness, Is. 42
to make the Torah great and glorious.

The first Torah scroll is bound and covered and the Ḥatan Bereshit is called to the second Torah scroll.

---

children." There never was another Moses. There were other prophets but no other law-giver, no other voice-of-God-for-eternity.

חֲזַק חֲזַק וְנִתְחַזֵּק *Be strong, be strong, and let us strengthen one another.* Since the source of our strength is the Torah, as the reading of each book comes to an end, the congregation collectively rededicates itself to honor its words in our lives, thereby renewing our spiritual resilience.

שְׁלֹשִׁים יוֹם וַיִּתְּמוּ יְמֵי בְכִי אֵבֶל מֹשֶׁה: וִיהוֹשֻׁעַ בִּן־נוּן מָלֵא רוּחַ
חָכְמָה כִּי־סָמַךְ מֹשֶׁה אֶת־יָדָיו עָלָיו וַיִּשְׁמְעוּ אֵלָיו בְּנֵי־יִשְׂרָאֵל
וַיַּעֲשׂוּ כַּאֲשֶׁר צִוָּה יהוה אֶת־מֹשֶׁה: וְלֹא־קָם נָבִיא עוֹד בְּיִשְׂרָאֵל
כְּמֹשֶׁה אֲשֶׁר יְדָעוֹ יהוה פָּנִים אֶל־פָּנִים: לְכָל־הָאֹתֹת וְהַמּוֹפְתִים
אֲשֶׁר שְׁלָחוֹ יהוה לַעֲשׂוֹת בְּאֶרֶץ מִצְרָיִם לְפַרְעֹה וּלְכָל־עֲבָדָיו
וּלְכָל־אַרְצוֹ: וּלְכֹל הַיָּד הַחֲזָקָה וּלְכֹל הַמּוֹרָא הַגָּדוֹל אֲשֶׁר עָשָׂה
מֹשֶׁה לְעֵינֵי כָּל־יִשְׂרָאֵל:

חֲזַק חֲזַק וְנִתְחַזֵּק

הגבהה וגלילה

The first ספר תורה *is lifted and the* קהל *says:*

דברים ד וְזֹאת הַתּוֹרָה אֲשֶׁר־שָׂם מֹשֶׁה לִפְנֵי בְּנֵי יִשְׂרָאֵל:

במדבר ט עַל־פִּי יהוה בְּיַד מֹשֶׁה:

Some add

משלי ג עֵץ־חַיִּים הִיא לַמַּחֲזִיקִים בָּהּ וְתֹמְכֶיהָ מְאֻשָּׁר:
דְּרָכֶיהָ דַרְכֵי־נֹעַם וְכָל־נְתִיבוֹתֶיהָ שָׁלוֹם:
אֹרֶךְ יָמִים בִּימִינָהּ, בִּשְׂמֹאולָהּ עֹשֶׁר וְכָבוֹד:
ישעיה מב יהוה חָפֵץ לְמַעַן צִדְקוֹ יַגְדִּיל תּוֹרָה וְיַאְדִּיר:

The first ספר תורה *is bound and covered and the* חתן בראשית *is called to the second* ספר תורה.

וְלֹא־קָם נָבִיא עוֹד *No other prophet like Moses has ever risen.* Moses' greatness was his humility (Num. 12:3). It was his absence of self that allowed God's spirit to work through him, and his inability to speak (Ex. 4:10) that enabled God to place His words in his mouth. In a manuscript discovered after his death in 1778, Jean-Jacques Rousseau wrote: "The Jews provide us with an astonishing spectacle: the laws of Numa, Lycurgus, Solon are dead; the very much older laws of Moses are still alive. Athens, Sparta, Rome have perished and no longer have children left on earth; Zion, destroyed, has not lost its

RESHUT FOR THE ḤATAN BERESHIT

The following is said by the Gabbai to call up the Ḥatan Bereshit to his aliya:

By leave of the One higher than all poetry and blessing,
awesome above all praise and song,
wise-hearted, powerful, mighty,
Ruler of the world, Master of every creation;
and by leave of [the Torah], this King's daughter whose glory lies
concealed, within her, created first and hidden away,
for two thousand years,
pure, perfect, who restores the soul, returns it;
and with permission from Yeshurun – she is their legacy, given to be
kept and nurtured,
and the great leaders of Jacob – who learn to open her, to complete her,
the crowning splendor of the prince of the Beit Din
whose authority is great,
the rabbinical judges, who turn back conflict from her gate,
the academy heads, leaders of this dispersed exile.
And by leave of this righteous company, this joyous congregation,
elders and youths of each rank, together,
gathered, today, here, for Simḥat Torah,
collected to finish, and to begin again, with happiness and awe,
the one as beloved as on the day she was given in all her glory:
they delight in her, not as though old and past, but as new,
thirsty to drink in and enjoy her precious brilliance
for she makes the heart joyous, effaces sadness,
her comfort delights the soul of those who take pride in her,
who delve into the written and the spoken, the Mishna and the Gemara,

---

The Talmud (*Shabbat* 30a–b) says that King David asked God to tell him how long he would live. God replied that no one is allowed to know this. Then at least tell me, said David, on which day of the week I will die. God replied that he would die on Shabbat. At this David became distressed, since Shabbat is a day on which we are not permitted to conduct a funeral. He begged to be allowed to die on a Sunday, or a Friday, but both requests were denied. The Talmud then says that from then on, every Shabbat David engaged in uninterrupted study. When the designated day came, the angel of death was dispatched to bring David to heaven, but because "his mouth did not cease from study" the angel of death was powerless to take him. So the angel

רשות לחתן בראשית

The following is said by the גבאי *to call up the* חתן בראשית *to his* עליה:

מֵרְשׁוּת מְרוֹמָם עַל כָּל בְּרָכָה וְשִׁירָה
נוֹרָא עַל כָּל תְּהִלָּה וְזִמְרָה
חֲכַם לֵבָב וְאַמִּיץ כֹּחַ וּגְבוּרָה
מוֹשֵׁל עוֹלָם אֲדוֹן כָּל יְצִירָה
וּמֵרְשׁוּת כְּבוּדָּה בַּת מֶלֶךְ פְּנִימָה וַעֲצוּרָה
רֵאשִׁית קִנְיָנָהּ אַלְפַּיִם אֲצוּרָה
בָּרָה תְּמִימָה מְשִׁיבַת נֶפֶשׁ וּמַחֲזִירָה
יְשֻׁרוּן נִתְּנָה מוֹרָשָׁה לְעָבְדָהּ וּלְשָׁמְרָהּ
מְלַמְּדֶיהָ גְּאוֹנֵי יַעֲקֹב לְפָתְחָהּ וּלְסָגְרָהּ
כְּלִיל הוֹד נָשִׂיא מַרְבֶּה הַמִּשְׂרָה
יוֹשְׁבֵי מִדִּין מְשִׁיבֵי מִלְחָמָה שָׁעְרָה
רָאשֵׁי יְשִׁיבוֹת רָאשֵׁי גוֹלָה פְּזוּרָה
וּמֵרְשׁוּת חֲבוּרַת צֶדֶק עֵדָה זוֹ הַמְאֻשָּׁרָה
זְקֵנִים וּנְעָרִים יַחַד בְּכָל שׁוּרָה
קְבוּצִים פֹּה הַיּוֹם לְשִׂמְחַת תּוֹרָה
וְנֶעֱצָרִים לְסַיֵּם וּלְהָחֵל בְּגִיל וּבְמוֹרָא
אוֹתָהּ מְחַבְּבִים כְּיוֹם נְתִינָתָהּ בַּהֲדָרָהּ
מְסַלְסְלִים בָּהּ כַּחֲדָשָׁה וְלֹא כִּישָׁנָה שֶׁעָבְרָה
צְמֵאִים לָמֹץ וּלְהִתְעַנֵּג מִזִּיו יְקָרָהּ
בְּיַעַן מְשַׂמַּחַת לֵב וְעֶצֶב מְסִירָה
תַּנְחוּמֶיהָ יְשַׁעַשְׁעוּ נַפְשָׁם בָּהּ לְהִתְפָּאֲרָה
וְהוֹגִים בְּמִקְרָא וְהַגָּדָה בְּמִשְׁנָה וּגְמָרָא

TORAH READING FOR ḤATAN BERESHIT
This act of beginning the Torah reading anew exemplifies one of the most remarkable principles of Judaism: the idea of perpetual study.

who run to bring their little ones to the house of prayer,
and go out, do everything to keep her with care –
so, great is their reward from the Mighty One,
everlasting joy is upon their heads,
they long to see the Temple, the chosen house.
And so I have been appointed by the choice of us all
to elevate one man, from all the people among this company;
I found in him a wise heart for elucidating the Torah,
He seeks justice and kindness with integrity,
his heart has inspired him, awakening his spirit to giving –
he should be the first, foremost, to begin the Torah.
And now, arise (*name* son of *father's name*), stand, take courage,
come, present yourself, stand to my right and read out
the Beginning – created by the Rock for His glory
for which reason we immediately follow completion by beginning again
so the accusing angel will not be able to tell lies of this people.
Since you are the first to do this perfect commandment –
how great will be the goodness, how abundant your reward:
you who are so generous, may you have no constraint upon your giving;
from the blessing of your Creator, give, do not curb your hand,
for the one who honors the Torah with majesty
should be honored with healthy contentment.
So, quickly: stand, stand, stand (*name* son of *father's name*), groom to "In the beginning,"
with permission from this holy congregation, and bless awesome, mighty God –
quickly, all will answer after you: Amen.

Arise (*name* son of *father's name*), Ḥatan Bereshit.

---

devised a stratagem: he produced a noise in a nearby tree. David, curious to know who or what was making the noise, began climbing a ladder to see. The angel made one of the rungs break. David fell, and as he was falling, for a moment he stopped studying, and he died.

That story is a commentary on this unique point of the Jewish year, as we make the transition from the end of the Torah to a new beginning. The last letter of the Torah is the *lamed* of Yisrael, the first is the *beit* of Bereshit. When we join the end of the Torah to the beginning, the connection spells

רָצִים וּמְבִיאִים טַפָּם לְבֵית הָעֲתִירָה
הוֹלְכִים וְעוֹשִׂים לְהַזְהִירָה
לָכֵן גָּדוֹל שְׂכָרָם מֵאֵת הַגְּבוּרָה
עַל רֹאשָׁם שִׂמְחַת עוֹלָם קְשׁוּרָה
דָּאִים לִרְאוֹת בְּבֵית הַבְּחִירָה
וּבְכֵן נִסְמַכְתִּי דַּעַת כֻּלָּם לְבָרָרָה
בָּחוּר הֲרִימוֹתִי מֵעַם תּוֹךְ הַחֲבוּרָה
מְצָאתִיו לֵב נָבוֹן לְהַסְבִּירָה
צֶדֶק וְחֶסֶד רוֹדֵף בְּאֹרַח יְשָׁרָה
וּנְשָׂאוֹ לִבּוֹ וְנָדְבָה רוּחוֹ לְהִתְעוֹרְרָה
תְּחִלָּה וְרִאשׁוֹן הֱיוֹת לְהַתְחִיל הַתּוֹרָה.
וְעַתָּה קוּם רַבִּי (פלוני ב״ר פלוני) עֲמֹד לְהִתְאַזְּרָה
בֹּא וְהִתְיַצֵּב וַעֲמֹד לִימִינִי וּקְרָא
מַעֲשֵׂה בְרֵאשִׁית לִכְבוֹדוֹ צוּר בָּרָא
עַל זֹאת מַתְכִּיפִין הַתְחָלָה לְהַשְׁלָמָה בִּתְדִירָה
שָׂטָן שֶׁלֹּא יְרַגֵּל בְּעַם זוּ לְשַׁקְּרָה
יַעַן נַעֲשֵׂיתָ רִאשׁוֹן לְמִצְוָה גְמוּרָה
מָה רַב טוּבְךָ וּמַשְׂכֻּרְתְּךָ יְתֵרָה
טוֹב עַיִן תְּבֹרַךְ בְּנִדְבָתְךָ מִלְּעָצְרָה
וּמִבִּרְכַּת בּוֹרַאֲךָ תִּדּוֹר יָדְךָ מִלְּקַצְּרָה
בַּעֲבוּר שֶׁכָּל הַמְכַבֵּד תּוֹרָה בִּצְפִירָה
יְהֵא גּוּפוֹ מְכֻבָּד לְהִתְאַשְּׁרָה.
מַהֵר עֲמֹד עֲמֹד עֲמֹד רַבִּי (פלוני ב״ר פלוני) חֲתַן בְּרֵאשִׁית בָּרָא
מֵרְשׁוּת הַקָּהָל הַקָּדוֹשׁ הַזֶּה וּבָרֵךְ אֵל גָּדוֹל וְנוֹרָא
אָמֵן יַעֲנוּ אַחֲרֶיךָ הַכֹּל מְהֵרָה.

יַעֲמֹד רַבִּי (פלוני ב״ר פלוני) חֲתַן בְּרֵאשִׁית.

It is customary for the congregation to say aloud the passages marked by arrows, followed by the Reader.

In the beginning, God created heaven and earth. And the earth was desolate emptiness, and darkness over the deep; but the spirit of God moved over the waters. And God said: "Let there be light." Light came to be. And He saw that the light was good, and divided light from darkness. God named the light, "Day;" and the darkness He named, "Night." ▸ There was evening; then there was morning: one day. ◂ *Bereshit 1:1–2:3*

God said: "Let there be a clear dome amid the waters, dividing water from water." And He shaped the dome, dividing the waters below the dome from the waters above it – and so it came to be. And God named that dome, "Sky." ▸ And there was evening; then there was morning: a second day. ◂

God said, "Let all the waters below the sky be gathered to one place; let dry ground be revealed." And so it came to be. And He named the dry ground, "Land"; and the gathering of waters He named "Seas." And God saw that it was good. And God said, "Let the land sprout green plants that seed, and fruit trees, each bearing fruit with its own seeds in them, overspreading the land." And so it came to be. The land brought forth green, seeding plants, each with its own seeds, and trees bearing fruit, each with its own seeds in it. And God saw that it was good. ▸ There was evening; then there was morning: a third day. ◂

IN THE BEGINNING

This majestic opening sets out, for the first time, principles that were not only to shape Judaism, but eventually also to transform the imagination of the West. Genesis 1 represents the emancipation of the human understanding of the universe from mystery, magic and myth. All ancient religions had creation myths to explain why the world is as it is. Always they involved a multiplicity of gods, fighting and struggling among themselves for dominance. The opening chapter of the Torah represents a decisive break from that entire mindset. There is only one God, and it is His creative will alone that made the universe as it is. As sociologist Max Weber pointed out, the roots of Western rationality lie here.

However, the point of Genesis 1 is not to tell us *how* the world came into

It is customary for the קהל *to say aloud the passages marked by arrows, followed by the* קורא.

בראשית א:א–ב:ג

בְּרֵאשִׁית בָּרָא אֱלֹהִים אֵת הַשָּׁמַיִם וְאֵת הָאָרֶץ: וְהָאָרֶץ הָיְתָה
תֹהוּ וָבֹהוּ וְחֹשֶׁךְ עַל־פְּנֵי תְהוֹם וְרוּחַ אֱלֹהִים מְרַחֶפֶת עַל־פְּנֵי
הַמָּיִם: וַיֹּאמֶר אֱלֹהִים יְהִי־אוֹר וַיְהִי־אוֹר: וַיַּרְא אֱלֹהִים אֶת־
הָאוֹר כִּי־טוֹב וַיַּבְדֵּל אֱלֹהִים בֵּין הָאוֹר וּבֵין הַחֹשֶׁךְ: וַיִּקְרָא
אֱלֹהִים ׀ לָאוֹר יוֹם וְלַחֹשֶׁךְ קָרָא לָיְלָה ◂ וַיְהִי־עֶרֶב וַיְהִי־בֹקֶר
יוֹם אֶחָד: ◂
וַיֹּאמֶר אֱלֹהִים יְהִי רָקִיעַ בְּתוֹךְ הַמָּיִם וִיהִי מַבְדִּיל בֵּין מַיִם
לָמָיִם: וַיַּעַשׂ אֱלֹהִים אֶת־הָרָקִיעַ וַיַּבְדֵּל בֵּין הַמַּיִם אֲשֶׁר מִתַּחַת
לָרָקִיעַ וּבֵין הַמַּיִם אֲשֶׁר מֵעַל לָרָקִיעַ וַיְהִי־כֵן: וַיִּקְרָא אֱלֹהִים
לָרָקִיעַ שָׁמָיִם ◂ וַיְהִי־עֶרֶב וַיְהִי־בֹקֶר יוֹם שֵׁנִי: ◂
וַיֹּאמֶר אֱלֹהִים יִקָּווּ הַמַּיִם מִתַּחַת הַשָּׁמַיִם אֶל־מָקוֹם אֶחָד
וְתֵרָאֶה הַיַּבָּשָׁה וַיְהִי־כֵן: וַיִּקְרָא אֱלֹהִים ׀ לַיַּבָּשָׁה אֶרֶץ וּלְמִקְוֵה
הַמַּיִם קָרָא יַמִּים וַיַּרְא אֱלֹהִים כִּי־טוֹב: וַיֹּאמֶר אֱלֹהִים תַּדְשֵׁא
הָאָרֶץ דֶּשֶׁא עֵשֶׂב מַזְרִיעַ זֶרַע עֵץ פְּרִי עֹשֶׂה פְּרִי לְמִינוֹ אֲשֶׁר
זַרְעוֹ־בוֹ עַל־הָאָרֶץ וַיְהִי־כֵן: וַתּוֹצֵא הָאָרֶץ דֶּשֶׁא עֵשֶׂב מַזְרִיעַ
זֶרַע לְמִינֵהוּ וְעֵץ עֹשֶׂה־פְּרִי אֲשֶׁר זַרְעוֹ־בוֹ לְמִינֵהוּ וַיַּרְא אֱלֹהִים
כִּי־טוֹב: ◂ וַיְהִי־עֶרֶב וַיְהִי־בֹקֶר יוֹם שְׁלִישִׁי: ◂

---

the word *Lev*, "heart." The Talmudic story about David is less about the king than about the Jewish people. *So long as the Jewish people never stops studying, the Jewish heart will never stop beating.* Only Torah study is capable of defeating the angel of death. "You gave us a Torah of truth, thereby planting everlasting life in our midst," says the blessing after the reading of the Torah. The word of the Eternal is, this side of Heaven, our one taste of eternity.

God said, "Let there be lights in the dome of the sky, to divide day from night; let them mark out signs and seasons, days and years; and let them be lights in the dome of the sky to light up the land." Thus it came to be. God made the two great lights – the greater light to rule over the day, and the smaller light to rule over the night, and the stars. And He hung them in the dome of the sky, to light up the earth; to rule by day and by night, and to divide light from darkness; and God saw that it was good. ▸ There was evening; then there was morning: a fourth day. ◂

God said, "Let the water swarm with schools of living things; and let flying creatures fly across the land, against the dome of the sky. And God created the great sea beasts, and living things of all kinds that crawl and that swarm within the waters, and winged, flying creatures of all kinds; and He saw that it was good. God blessed them: "Be fruitful, grow numerous, fill the waters of the seas; and let the creatures that fly grow many on the land." ▸ There was evening; then there was morning: a fifth day.

God said, "Let the land bring forth living beings, cattle and creeping things and land animals of all kinds;" and so it came to be. He made land animals of all kinds, cattle of all kinds, and all the kinds of creature that crawl upon the earth; and God saw that it was good. And He said, "Let Us make man, in Our image, Our likeness, to rule the fish of the

---

articulation of fundamental moral principles that govern our understanding of the universe and our place within it. The first is that the world is *good* – the word chimes like a motif, no less than seven times. This in itself is a radical rejection of the view, widespread in the ancient world, and to some extent throughout history, that the physical world is bad, the arena of pain, suffering and injustice, from which we are liberated only by death and life-after-death.

Then there is the deep structure of the text itself. As modern commentators have noted, the pattern of seven – a universe created in seven days – lies not only on the surface, but is also replicated in less obvious ways throughout. So, for example, there are seven words in the first verse, fourteen in the second, thirty-five in the closing three verses describing the seventh day. The word *Elokim*, "God," appears thirty-five times, *eretz*, "earth," twenty-one times, and the passage as a whole contains 469 (7x67) words. There is an intimation here

וַיֹּאמֶר אֱלֹהִים יְהִי מְאֹרֹת בִּרְקִיעַ הַשָּׁמַיִם לְהַבְדִּיל בֵּין הַיּוֹם
וּבֵין הַלָּיְלָה וְהָיוּ לְאֹתֹת וּלְמוֹעֲדִים וּלְיָמִים וְשָׁנִים: וְהָיוּ לִמְאוֹרֹת
בִּרְקִיעַ הַשָּׁמַיִם לְהָאִיר עַל־הָאָרֶץ וַיְהִי־כֵן: וַיַּעַשׂ אֱלֹהִים
אֶת־שְׁנֵי הַמְּאֹרֹת הַגְּדֹלִים אֶת־הַמָּאוֹר הַגָּדֹל לְמֶמְשֶׁלֶת הַיּוֹם
וְאֶת־הַמָּאוֹר הַקָּטֹן לְמֶמְשֶׁלֶת הַלַּיְלָה וְאֵת הַכּוֹכָבִים: וַיִּתֵּן
אֹתָם אֱלֹהִים בִּרְקִיעַ הַשָּׁמָיִם לְהָאִיר עַל־הָאָרֶץ: וְלִמְשֹׁל בַּיּוֹם
וּבַלַּיְלָה וּלֲהַבְדִּיל בֵּין הָאוֹר וּבֵין הַחֹשֶׁךְ וַיַּרְא אֱלֹהִים כִּי־טוֹב:
• וַיְהִי־עֶרֶב וַיְהִי־בֹקֶר יוֹם רְבִיעִי: •
וַיֹּאמֶר אֱלֹהִים יִשְׁרְצוּ הַמַּיִם שֶׁרֶץ נֶפֶשׁ חַיָּה וְעוֹף יְעוֹפֵף עַל־
הָאָרֶץ עַל־פְּנֵי רְקִיעַ הַשָּׁמָיִם: וַיִּבְרָא אֱלֹהִים אֶת־הַתַּנִּינִם
הַגְּדֹלִים וְאֵת כָּל־נֶפֶשׁ הַחַיָּה ׀ הָרֹמֶשֶׂת אֲשֶׁר שָׁרְצוּ הַמַּיִם
לְמִינֵהֶם וְאֵת כָּל־עוֹף כָּנָף לְמִינֵהוּ וַיַּרְא אֱלֹהִים כִּי־טוֹב: וַיְבָרֶךְ
אֹתָם אֱלֹהִים לֵאמֹר פְּרוּ וּרְבוּ וּמִלְאוּ אֶת־הַמַּיִם בַּיַּמִּים וְהָעוֹף
יִרֶב בָּאָרֶץ: • וַיְהִי־עֶרֶב וַיְהִי־בֹקֶר יוֹם חֲמִישִׁי: •
וַיֹּאמֶר אֱלֹהִים תּוֹצֵא הָאָרֶץ נֶפֶשׁ חַיָּה לְמִינָהּ בְּהֵמָה וָרֶמֶשׂ
וְחַיְתוֹ־אֶרֶץ לְמִינָהּ וַיְהִי־כֵן: וַיַּעַשׂ אֱלֹהִים אֶת־חַיַּת הָאָרֶץ
לְמִינָהּ וְאֶת־הַבְּהֵמָה לְמִינָהּ וְאֵת כָּל־רֶמֶשׂ הָאֲדָמָה לְמִינֵהוּ
וַיַּרְא אֱלֹהִים כִּי־טוֹב: וַיֹּאמֶר אֱלֹהִים נַעֲשֶׂה אָדָם בְּצַלְמֵנוּ

---

being. It is neither science nor proto-science. We see this in the sheer brevity of the account, a mere thirty-four verses, less than a tenth of the space the Torah dedicates to the other creative act it describes, namely the Israelites' construction of the Sanctuary (Ex. 25–40). The Torah is telling us not *how* God created the world, but *that* God created the world. It did not merely happen. Behind the emergent order of the universe is a God who loves creativity and order.

The creation narrative is not a substitute for science, but rather the

sea and the flying creatures of the sky, cattle and all the animals of the land, and the crawling things that creep across the land." God created mankind in His image; in the image of God He created man; He created them male and female. And He blessed them: "Be fruitful, grow numerous; fill the earth and conquer it. Rule the fish of the sea and the flying creatures of the sky, and everything that creeps upon the earth." And God said, "I have given to you the green plants with their seeds that cover the land, and the trees that bear fruits with their seeds; these shall be yours to eat. And all the animals of the land, and all the flying creatures of the sky, and all that creeps upon the land that has a living spirit in it shall have all the green plants to eat." So it came to be. And God saw all that He had done – and it was very good. ▸ There was evening; then there was morning: the sixth day. ◂

▸ Then the heavens and the earth were completed, and all their array. With the seventh day, God completed the work He had done. He

---

is revolutionary about this idea is not that a human being could be in the image of God. That belief was commonplace in the ancient world: it is what rulers, emperors, pharaohs, and kings were imagined to be, a child of the gods or their chief intermediary. What was unprecedented was the idea that *every* human being, regardless of color, culture, class or caste, is in the image and likeness of God. The whole of the Torah's ethics and politics are already foreshadowed in this one verse.

It was to this that Rabbi Akiva was alluding when he said: "Beloved is man, for he was created in the image of God" (*Avot* 3:18). It is what the sages meant when they taught (Mishna, *Sanhedrin* 37a) that whoever destroys a life is as if he destroyed a universe, and whoever saves a life is as if he saved a universe, and that the first human was created alone so that no one would be able to say, my ancestor was greater than yours. The connection between this principle and the sanctity of human life is made explicit in the covenant with Noah: "Whoever sheds the blood of man, by man shall his blood be shed, for in the image of God He made man" (Gen. 9:6).

Finally, the Genesis creation narrative establishes the jurisprudential principle on which the entire Judaic structure of social ethics rests: that God, as Creator of the universe, owns the universe, and we, as its temporary residents, are bound by His sovereignty. Thus God rules, not by virtue of might, but of right.

כדמותנו וירדו בדגת הים ובעוף השמים ובבהמה ובכל־הארץ
ובכל־הרמש הרמש על־הארץ: ויברא אלהים ׀ את־האדם
בצלמו בצלם אלהים ברא אתו זכר ונקבה ברא אתם: ויברך
אתם אלהים ויאמר להם אלהים פרו ורבו ומלאו את־הארץ
וכבשה ורדו בדגת הים ובעוף השמים ובכל־חיה הרמשת על־
הארץ: ויאמר אלהים הנה נתתי לכם את־כל־עשב ׀ זרע זרע
אשר על־פני כל־הארץ ואת־כל־העץ אשר־בו פרי־עץ זרע
זרע לכם יהיה לאכלה: ולכל־חית הארץ ולכל־עוף השמים
ולכל ׀ רומש על־הארץ אשר־בו נפש חיה את־כל־ירק עשב
לאכלה ויהי־כן: וירא אלהים את־כל־אשר עשה והנה־טוב
מאד • ויהי־ערב ויהי־בקר יום הששי: •
• ויכלו השמים והארץ וכל־צבאם: ויכל אלהים ביום השביעי
מלאכתו אשר עשה וישבת ביום השביעי מכל־מלאכתו אשר

---

that the universe has a precisely calibrated mathematical structure at every level, from the microscopic to the cosmological.

The text is also designed to show that creation has an underlying order. For the first three days, God establishes a series of distinct domains from the undifferentiated void: On the first day, He separates light from darkness and day from night, on the second, the upper and lower waters, on the third, sea from dry land. For the next three days God furnishes each of the domains with the appropriate objects and life-forms: On the fourth day, the sun, moon and stars, on the fifth, birds and fish, on the sixth, animals and humankind.

The key verb, appearing five times, is ב-ד-ל, meaning "to distinguish, demarcate, separate." This will eventually become a key word relating to the priests: they will be charged with distinguishing between pure and impure, holy and mundane. There is a sacred ontology, a God-given structure to the universe whose integrity we are commanded to respect and preserve.

Then there is the single most transformative sentence in the religious history of humankind: "Let Us make man, in Our image, Our likeness." What

ceased on the seventh day from all the work He had done. God blessed the seventh day and declared it holy, because on it He ceased from all His work He had created to do. ◂

HALF KADDISH

Before Maftir is read, the third Sefer Torah is placed on the bima, next to the second Sefer Torah, and the Reader says Half Kaddish:

Reader: יִתְגַּדַּל Magnified and sanctified
may His great name be,
in the world He created by His will.
May He establish His kingdom
in your lifetime and in your days,
and in the lifetime of all the house of Israel,
swiftly and soon – and say: Amen.

All: May His great name be blessed for ever and all time.

Reader: Blessed and praised, glorified and exalted,
raised and honored, uplifted and lauded
be the name of the Holy One, blessed be He,
beyond any blessing, song, praise and consolation
uttered in the world – and say: Amen.

HAGBAHA AND GELILA

The second Torah scroll is lifted and the congregation says:

וְזֹאת הַתּוֹרָה This is the Torah *Deut. 4*
that Moses placed before the children of Israel,
at the LORD's commandment, by the hand of Moses. *Num. 9*

Some add: It is a tree of life to those who grasp it, *Prov. 3*
and those who uphold it are happy.
Its ways are ways of pleasantness, and all its paths are peace.
Long life is in its right hand; in its left, riches and honor.
It pleased the LORD for the sake of [Israel's] righteousness, *Is. 42*
to make the Torah great and glorious.

The second Torah scroll is bound and covered and the oleh for Maftir is called to the third Torah scroll.

עָשָׂה: וַיְבָרֶךְ אֱלֹהִים אֶת־יוֹם הַשְּׁבִיעִי וַיְקַדֵּשׁ אֹתוֹ כִּי בוֹ שָׁבַת מִכָּל־מְלַאכְתּוֹ אֲשֶׁר־בָּרָא אֱלֹהִים לַעֲשׂוֹת:

חצי קדיש

Before מפטיר *is read, the third* ספר תורה *is placed on the* שולחן*, next to the second* ספר תורה*, and the* קורא *says* חצי קדיש*:*

קורא: יִתְגַּדַּל וְיִתְקַדַּשׁ שְׁמֵהּ רַבָּא (קהל: אָמֵן)
בְּעָלְמָא דִּי בְרָא כִרְעוּתֵהּ
וְיַמְלִיךְ מַלְכוּתֵהּ
בְּחַיֵּיכוֹן וּבְיוֹמֵיכוֹן וּבְחַיֵּי דְכָל בֵּית יִשְׂרָאֵל
בַּעֲגָלָא וּבִזְמַן קָרִיב, וְאִמְרוּ אָמֵן. (קהל: אָמֵן)

קהל וקורא: יְהֵא שְׁמֵהּ רַבָּא מְבָרַךְ לְעָלַם וּלְעָלְמֵי עָלְמַיָּא.

קורא: יִתְבָּרַךְ וְיִשְׁתַּבַּח וְיִתְפָּאַר וְיִתְרוֹמַם וְיִתְנַשֵּׂא
וְיִתְהַדָּר וְיִתְעַלֶּה וְיִתְהַלָּל
שְׁמֵהּ דְּקֻדְשָׁא בְּרִיךְ הוּא (קהל: בְּרִיךְ הוּא)
לְעֵלָּא מִן כָּל בִּרְכָתָא וְשִׁירָתָא, תֻּשְׁבְּחָתָא וְנֶחֱמָתָא
דַּאֲמִירָן בְּעָלְמָא, וְאִמְרוּ אָמֵן. (קהל: אָמֵן)

הגבהה וגלילה

The second ספר תורה *is lifted and the* קהל *says:*

דברים ד וְזֹאת הַתּוֹרָה אֲשֶׁר־שָׂם מֹשֶׁה לִפְנֵי בְּנֵי יִשְׂרָאֵל:
במדבר ט עַל־פִּי יהוה בְּיַד מֹשֶׁה:

משלי ג *Some add* עֵץ־חַיִּים הִיא לַמַּחֲזִיקִים בָּהּ וְתֹמְכֶיהָ מְאֻשָּׁר:
דְּרָכֶיהָ דַרְכֵי־נֹעַם וְכָל־נְתִיבוֹתֶיהָ שָׁלוֹם:
אֹרֶךְ יָמִים בִּימִינָהּ, בִּשְׂמֹאולָהּ עֹשֶׁר וְכָבוֹד:
ישעיה מב יהוה חָפֵץ לְמַעַן צִדְקוֹ יַגְדִּיל תּוֹרָה וְיַאְדִּיר:

The second ספר תורה *is bound and covered and the* עולה *for* מפטיר *is called to the third* ספר תורה*.*

MAFTIR

On the eighth day, you shall hold an assembly: you shall do no laborious work. And you shall bring a burnt-offering, an offering consumed by fire, of pleasing aroma to the LORD: one bull, one ram, and seven yearling male lambs; they shall be without blemish. The meal-offerings and the libations for the bull, the ram and the lambs in their number shall be according to the ordinance, and one goat for a sin-offering; all of this aside from the regular daily burnt-offering with its meal-offering and its libation. You shall offer these to the LORD at your appointed festival-times, besides for your vows and your freewill-offerings, your burnt-offerings, your meal-offerings, your libations, and your peace-offerings. And Moses told the children of Israel, according to all that the LORD had commanded Moses. *Num. 29:35–30:1*

HAGBAHA AND GELILA

The third Torah scroll is lifted and the congregation says:

וְזֹאת הַתּוֹרָה This is the Torah *Deut. 4*
that Moses placed before the children of Israel,
at the LORD's commandment, by the hand of Moses. *Num. 9*

Some add: It is a tree of life to those who grasp it, *Prov. 3*
and those who uphold it are happy.
Its ways are ways of pleasantness, and all its paths are peace.
Long life is in its right hand; in its left, riches and honor.
It pleased the LORD for the sake of [Israel's] righteousness, *Is. 42*
to make the Torah great and glorious.

The third Torah scroll is bound and covered and the oleh for Maftir reads the Haftara.

BLESSING BEFORE READING THE HAFTARA

Before reading the Haftara, the person called up for Maftir says:

בָּרוּךְ Blessed are You, LORD our God, King of the Universe, who chose good prophets and was pleased with their words, spoken in truth. Blessed are You, LORD, who chose the Torah, His servant Moses, His people Israel, and the prophets of truth and righteousness.

Some congregations say the piyut אַשְׁרֶיךָ on page 1450.

מפטיר לשמחת תורה

במדבר כט:לה–ל:א
בַּיּוֹם הַשְּׁמִינִי עֲצֶרֶת תִּהְיֶה לָכֶם כָּל־מְלֶאכֶת עֲבֹדָה לֹא תַעֲשׂוּ: וְהִקְרַבְתֶּם עֹלָה אִשֵּׁה רֵיחַ נִיחֹחַ לַיהוה פַּר אֶחָד אַיִל אֶחָד כְּבָשִׂים בְּנֵי־שָׁנָה שִׁבְעָה תְּמִימִם: מִנְחָתָם וְנִסְכֵּיהֶם לַפָּר לָאַיִל וְלַכְּבָשִׂים בְּמִסְפָּרָם כַּמִּשְׁפָּט: וּשְׂעִיר חַטָּאת אֶחָד מִלְּבַד עֹלַת הַתָּמִיד וּמִנְחָתָהּ וְנִסְכָּהּ: אֵלֶּה תַּעֲשׂוּ לַיהוה בְּמוֹעֲדֵיכֶם לְבַד מִנִּדְרֵיכֶם וְנִדְבֹתֵיכֶם לְעֹלֹתֵיכֶם וּלְמִנְחֹתֵיכֶם וּלְנִסְכֵּיכֶם וּלְשַׁלְמֵיכֶם: וַיֹּאמֶר מֹשֶׁה אֶל־בְּנֵי יִשְׂרָאֵל כְּכֹל אֲשֶׁר־צִוָּה יהוה אֶת־מֹשֶׁה:

הגבהה וגלילה

The third ספר תורה *is lifted and the* קהל *says:*

דברים ד וְזֹאת הַתּוֹרָה אֲשֶׁר־שָׂם מֹשֶׁה לִפְנֵי בְּנֵי יִשְׂרָאֵל:

במדבר ט עַל־פִּי יהוה בְּיַד מֹשֶׁה:

Some add

משלי ג עֵץ־חַיִּים הִיא לַמַּחֲזִיקִים בָּהּ וְתֹמְכֶיהָ מְאֻשָּׁר:
דְּרָכֶיהָ דַרְכֵי־נֹעַם וְכָל־נְתִיבוֹתֶיהָ שָׁלוֹם:
אֹרֶךְ יָמִים בִּימִינָהּ, בִּשְׂמֹאולָהּ עֹשֶׁר וְכָבוֹד:
ישעיה מב יהוה חָפֵץ לְמַעַן צִדְקוֹ יַגְדִּיל תּוֹרָה וְיַאְדִּיר:

The third ספר תורה *is bound and covered and the* עולה *for* מפטיר *reads the* הפטרה.

ברכה קודם ההפטרה

Before reading the הפטרה*, the person called up for* מפטיר *says:*

בָּרוּךְ אַתָּה יהוה אֱלֹהֵינוּ מֶלֶךְ הָעוֹלָם אֲשֶׁר בָּחַר בִּנְבִיאִים טוֹבִים, וְרָצָה בְדִבְרֵיהֶם הַנֶּאֱמָרִים בֶּאֱמֶת. בָּרוּךְ אַתָּה יהוה, הַבּוֹחֵר בַּתּוֹרָה וּבְמֹשֶׁה עַבְדּוֹ וּבְיִשְׂרָאֵל עַמּוֹ וּבִנְבִיאֵי הָאֱמֶת וָצֶדֶק.

Some congregations say the piyut אַשְׁרֶיךָ *on page 1450.*

HAFTARA

Then, after the death of the Lord's servant, Moses, the Lord spoke *Josh. 1:1–18*
to Moses' disciple, Joshua son of Nun. "Moses, My servant, has died. Now come, you and all this people; rise up and cross this Jordan River to the land that I am giving them, giving to the children of Israel. Every place your feet should tread – I have given to you. This I told Moses: from the desert and the Lebanon, to the great river, the river Perat, all the land of the Hittites, and as far as the great ocean that lies towards the sunset; these shall be your borders. No man shall stand in your way all the days of your life; as I was with Moses, so shall I be with you. I shall not let go of you, nor shall I leave you. Be strong, be determined – for you shall endow this people with the land that I swore to give their ancestors. Only be very strong, be very determined, to keep all the Torah with which Moses My servant charged you. Be sure not to stray from it rightward or left; and then you shall be successful in every course you take. Let the Torah in this scroll never leave your lips; meditate upon it day and night, that you may keep and perform

---

a dramatic entry into both systems of time: cyclical as we move directly from the last word of the Torah to the first, ensuring that our cycle of Torah reading will be unbroken. Immediately thereafter, we take a decisive step into historical time, as Moses dies and his successor Joshua takes on the role of leadership. A new generation, and a new chapter in the Jewish story, begins, as the Israelites move from the desert to the land, from exile and exodus to homecoming, and from journey to destination.

רַק חֲזַק וֶאֱמַץ *Only be very strong, be very determined.* Dayan Yeḥezkel Abramsky noted that in the previous verse, speaking of the conquest of the land, God tells Joshua to be "strong and of good courage." Now, speaking of the religious challenge of remaining faithful to God's law, a far more emphatic form of words is used, signaling that the spiritual dimension of leadership demands greater strength and courage than the military or political dimension.

לֹא־יָמוּשׁ סֵפֶר הַתּוֹרָה הַזֶּה *Let the Torah in this scroll never leave your lips.* A command stated in the Torah in relation to a king (Deut. 17:18–20), thus conveying another fundamental rule of leadership: the heavier the responsibility, the greater the need for constant moral and spiritual guidance. A leader who

הפטרה

וַיְהִי אַחֲרֵי מוֹת מֹשֶׁה עֶבֶד יהוה וַיֹּאמֶר יהוה אֶל־יְהוֹשֻׁעַ יהושע א:א–יח
בִּן־נוּן מְשָׁרֵת מֹשֶׁה לֵאמֹר׃ מֹשֶׁה עַבְדִּי מֵת וְעַתָּה קוּם עֲבֹר
אֶת־הַיַּרְדֵּן הַזֶּה אַתָּה וְכָל־הָעָם הַזֶּה אֶל־הָאָרֶץ אֲשֶׁר אָנֹכִי
נֹתֵן לָהֶם לִבְנֵי יִשְׂרָאֵל׃ כָּל־מָקוֹם אֲשֶׁר תִּדְרֹךְ כַּף־רַגְלְכֶם
בּוֹ לָכֶם נְתַתִּיו כַּאֲשֶׁר דִּבַּרְתִּי אֶל־מֹשֶׁה׃ מֵהַמִּדְבָּר וְהַלְּבָנוֹן
הַזֶּה וְעַד־הַנָּהָר הַגָּדוֹל נְהַר־פְּרָת כֹּל אֶרֶץ הַחִתִּים וְעַד־הַיָּם
הַגָּדוֹל מְבוֹא הַשָּׁמֶשׁ יִהְיֶה גְּבוּלְכֶם׃ לֹא־יִתְיַצֵּב אִישׁ לְפָנֶיךָ
כֹּל יְמֵי חַיֶּיךָ כַּאֲשֶׁר הָיִיתִי עִם־מֹשֶׁה אֶהְיֶה עִמָּךְ לֹא אַרְפְּךָ
וְלֹא אֶעֶזְבֶךָּ׃ חֲזַק וֶאֱמָץ כִּי אַתָּה תַּנְחִיל אֶת־הָעָם הַזֶּה אֶת־
הָאָרֶץ אֲשֶׁר־נִשְׁבַּעְתִּי לַאֲבוֹתָם לָתֵת לָהֶם׃ רַק חֲזַק וֶאֱמַץ מְאֹד
לִשְׁמֹר לַעֲשׂוֹת כְּכָל־הַתּוֹרָה אֲשֶׁר צִוְּךָ מֹשֶׁה עַבְדִּי אַל־תָּסוּר
מִמֶּנּוּ יָמִין וּשְׂמֹאול לְמַעַן תַּשְׂכִּיל בְּכֹל אֲשֶׁר תֵּלֵךְ׃ לֹא־יָמוּשׁ
סֵפֶר הַתּוֹרָה הַזֶּה מִפִּיךָ וְהָגִיתָ בּוֹ יוֹמָם וָלַיְלָה לְמַעַן תִּשְׁמֹר

HAFTARA

There are, in Judaism, (at least) two conceptions of time: cyclical and historical. Cyclical time is time as it is in nature: in the succession of nights and days, the seasons, and the lifecycle. Historical time – held by many scholars to have been first conceived in the Hebrew Bible – is time as a narrative, with a beginning, middle, and end, or as a journey, with a starting-point and a destination. History in Judaism is an arena of change, as we come closer to, or drift further from, what R. Aaron Lichtenstein called "societal beatitude" – a world of justice, compassion and peace.

The three festivals, Pesaḥ, Shavuot, and Sukkot, all have this dual character. They are cyclical, seasonal, representing respectively spring, first fruits, and harvest. And they are also historical, commemorating first the exodus, then the revelation at Sinai, then the forty years of wandering without a permanent home.

On Simḥat Torah, after concluding the last of the Mosaic books, we make

all that is written there, for then shall all your ventures be fruitful; then shall you succeed. Know that I have charged you: be strong, be determined, do not be terrified and do not fear, for the LORD your God is with you wherever you go.

And Yehoshua charged the leaders of the people, saying, "Pass throughout the camp, commanding the people: 'Prepare yourselves provisions, for in three days' time you shall cross this Jordan river, to come into and to take possession of the land that the LORD your God is giving you as an inheritance.'"

And to the people of Reuben and Gad, and to half of the tribe of Manasseh, Joshua said, "Remember the words Moses the LORD's servant charged you with; the LORD your God will let you remain; He is giving you this land. The women and children among you, and your cattle, may settle now in this land that Moses gave you beyond the Jordan. But all your strong fighting men shall cross the river armed before your brothers, and help them, until the LORD has granted your brothers rest like yours, and they too shall inherit the land that the LORD has given them. And then shall you return to your own inheritance, which the LORD's servant Moses granted you, and take possession of it, here beyond the Jordan, towards the sunrise.

And they answered Joshua: "All that you charge us with, we shall fulfill, and wherever you send us we shall go. Just as we listened to Moses, so shall we listen to you. Only let the LORD your God be with you, as He used to be with Moses. If any man rebels against your word, and refuses to listen to your voice, to all that you charge us with – let that man die. Only be strong, be determined."

וְלָרְאוּבֵנִי וְלַגָּדִי *And to the people of Reuben and Gad.* A reminder of the agreement they made with Moses (Num. 32), that though they would settle on the east bank of the Jordan, they would first honor their commitment to lead the Israelites into battle against the Canaanites. Only when the land was conquered and settled would they return to their families.

כְּכֹל אֲשֶׁר־שָׁמַעְנוּ אֶל־מֹשֶׁה *Just as we listened to Moses.* The people give their

לַעֲשׂוֹת כְּכָל־הַכָּתוּב בּוֹ כִּי־אָז תַּצְלִיחַ אֶת־דְּרָכֶךָ וְאָז תַּשְׂכִּיל׃
הֲלוֹא צִוִּיתִיךָ חֲזַק וֶאֱמָץ אַל־תַּעֲרֹץ וְאַל־תֵּחָת כִּי עִמְּךָ יְהוָה
אֱלֹהֶיךָ בְּכֹל אֲשֶׁר תֵּלֵךְ׃ וַיְצַו יְהוֹשֻׁעַ אֶת־שֹׁטְרֵי
הָעָם לֵאמֹר׃ עִבְרוּ ׀ בְּקֶרֶב הַמַּחֲנֶה וְצַוּוּ אֶת־הָעָם לֵאמֹר הָכִינוּ
לָכֶם צֵידָה כִּי בְּעוֹד ׀ שְׁלֹשֶׁת יָמִים אַתֶּם עֹבְרִים אֶת־הַיַּרְדֵּן
הַזֶּה לָבוֹא לָרֶשֶׁת אֶת־הָאָרֶץ אֲשֶׁר יְהוָה אֱלֹהֵיכֶם נֹתֵן לָכֶם
לְרִשְׁתָּהּ׃ וְלָרֽאוּבֵנִי וְלַגָּדִי וְלַחֲצִי שֵׁבֶט הַמְנַשֶּׁה
אָמַר יְהוֹשֻׁעַ לֵאמֹר׃ זָכוֹר אֶת־הַדָּבָר אֲשֶׁר צִוָּה אֶתְכֶם מֹשֶׁה
עֶבֶד־יְהוָה לֵאמֹר יְהוָה אֱלֹהֵיכֶם מֵנִיחַ לָכֶם וְנָתַן לָכֶם אֶת־
הָאָרֶץ הַזֹּאת׃ נְשֵׁיכֶם טַפְּכֶם וּמִקְנֵיכֶם יֵשְׁבוּ בָּאָרֶץ אֲשֶׁר נָתַן
לָכֶם מֹשֶׁה בְּעֵבֶר הַיַּרְדֵּן וְאַתֶּם תַּעַבְרוּ חֲמֻשִׁים לִפְנֵי אֲחֵיכֶם
כֹּל גִּבּוֹרֵי הַחַיִל וַעֲזַרְתֶּם אוֹתָם׃ עַד אֲשֶׁר־יָנִיחַ יְהוָה ׀ לַאֲחֵיכֶם
כָּכֶם וְיָרְשׁוּ גַם־הֵמָּה אֶת־הָאָרֶץ אֲשֶׁר־יְהוָה אֱלֹהֵיכֶם נֹתֵן לָהֶם
וְשַׁבְתֶּם לְאֶרֶץ יְרֻשַּׁתְכֶם וִירִשְׁתֶּם אוֹתָהּ אֲשֶׁר ׀ נָתַן לָכֶם מֹשֶׁה
עֶבֶד יְהוָה בְּעֵבֶר הַיַּרְדֵּן מִזְרַח הַשָּׁמֶשׁ׃ וַיַּעֲנוּ אֶת־יְהוֹשֻׁעַ לֵאמֹר
כֹּל אֲשֶׁר־צִוִּיתָנוּ נַעֲשֶׂה וְאֶל־כָּל־אֲשֶׁר תִּשְׁלָחֵנוּ נֵלֵךְ׃ כְּכֹל אֲשֶׁר־
שָׁמַעְנוּ אֶל־מֹשֶׁה כֵּן נִשְׁמַע אֵלֶיךָ רַק יִהְיֶה יְהוָה אֱלֹהֶיךָ עִמָּךְ
כַּאֲשֶׁר הָיָה עִם־מֹשֶׁה׃ כָּל־אִישׁ אֲשֶׁר־יַמְרֶה אֶת־פִּיךָ וְלֹא־יִשְׁמַע
אֶת־דְּבָרֶיךָ לְכֹל אֲשֶׁר־תְּצַוֶּנּוּ יוּמָת רַק חֲזַק וֶאֱמָץ׃

---

guides people into the unmapped territory of the future needs, above all, an inner compass, to avoid the moral drift that is otherwise the fate of those who allow themselves to be merely reactive to events.

וְאַל־תֵּחָת *Do not be terrified.* Faith is the antidote to fear. "The LORD is my light and my salvation - whom then shall I fear?" (Ps. 27:1).

BLESSINGS AFTER THE HAFTARA

After the Haftara, the person called up for Maftir says the following blessings:

בָּרוּךְ Blessed are You, Lord our God, King of the Universe, Rock of all worlds, righteous for all generations, the faithful God who says and does, speaks and fulfills, all of whose words are truth and righteousness. You are faithful, Lord our God, and faithful are Your words, not one of which returns unfulfilled, for You, God, are a faithful (and compassionate) King. Blessed are You, Lord, faithful in all His words.

רַחֵם Have compassion on Zion for it is the source of our life, and save the one grieved in spirit swiftly in our days. Blessed are You, Lord, who makes Zion rejoice in her children.

שַׂמְּחֵנוּ Grant us joy, Lord our God, through Elijah the prophet Your servant, and through the kingdom of the house of David Your anointed – may he soon come and make our hearts glad. May no stranger sit on his throne, and may others not continue to inherit his glory, for You promised him by Your holy name that his light would never be extinguished. Blessed are You, Lord, Shield of David.

On Shabbat (in Israel), add the words in parentheses:

עַל הַתּוֹרָה For the Torah, for Divine worship, for the prophets (and for this Sabbath day), and for this day of the festival of Shemini Atzeret Festival of Matzot which You, Lord our God, have given us (for holiness and rest) for gladness and joy, for honor and glory – for all these we thank and bless You, Lord our God, and may Your name be blessed by the mouth of all that lives, continually, for ever and all time. Blessed are You, Lord, who sanctifies (the Sabbath and) Israel and the festive seasons.

The service continues with the various prayers for government on page 1268.
In Israel on Shabbat the service continues on the next page.

Independence, that leaders and governments derive their authority from the consent of the governed.

ברכות לאחר ההפטרה

After the הפטרה*, the person called up for* מפטיר *says the following blessings:*

בָּרוּךְ אַתָּה יהוה אֱלֹהֵינוּ מֶלֶךְ הָעוֹלָם, צוּר כָּל הָעוֹלָמִים, צַדִּיק בְּכָל הַדּוֹרוֹת, הָאֵל הַנֶּאֱמָן, הָאוֹמֵר וְעוֹשֶׂה, הַמְדַבֵּר וּמְקַיֵּם, שֶׁכָּל דְּבָרָיו אֱמֶת וָצֶדֶק. נֶאֱמָן אַתָּה הוּא יהוה אֱלֹהֵינוּ וְנֶאֱמָנִים דְּבָרֶיךָ, וְדָבָר אֶחָד מִדְּבָרֶיךָ אָחוֹר לֹא יָשׁוּב רֵיקָם, כִּי אֵל מֶלֶךְ נֶאֱמָן (וְרַחֲמָן) אָתָּה. בָּרוּךְ אַתָּה יהוה, הָאֵל הַנֶּאֱמָן בְּכָל דְּבָרָיו.

רַחֵם עַל צִיּוֹן כִּי הִיא בֵּית חַיֵּינוּ, וְלַעֲלוּבַת נֶפֶשׁ תּוֹשִׁיעַ בִּמְהֵרָה בְיָמֵינוּ. בָּרוּךְ אַתָּה יהוה, מְשַׂמֵּחַ צִיּוֹן בְּבָנֶיהָ.

שַׂמְּחֵנוּ יהוה אֱלֹהֵינוּ בְּאֵלִיָּהוּ הַנָּבִיא עַבְדֶּךָ, וּבְמַלְכוּת בֵּית דָּוִד מְשִׁיחֶךָ, בִּמְהֵרָה יָבוֹא וְיָגֵל לִבֵּנוּ. עַל כִּסְאוֹ לֹא יֵשֶׁב זָר, וְלֹא יִנְחֲלוּ עוֹד אֲחֵרִים אֶת כְּבוֹדוֹ, כִּי בְשֵׁם קָדְשְׁךָ נִשְׁבַּעְתָּ לוֹ שֶׁלֹּא יִכְבֶּה נֵרוֹ לְעוֹלָם וָעֶד. בָּרוּךְ אַתָּה יהוה, מָגֵן דָּוִד.

On שבת *(in* ארץ ישראל*), add the words in parentheses:*

עַל הַתּוֹרָה וְעַל הָעֲבוֹדָה וְעַל הַנְּבִיאִים (וְעַל יוֹם הַשַּׁבָּת הַזֶּה), וְעַל יוֹם הַשְּׁמִינִי חַג הָעֲצֶרֶת הַזֶּה, שֶׁנָּתַתָּ לָּנוּ יהוה אֱלֹהֵינוּ (לִקְדֻשָּׁה וְלִמְנוּחָה) לְשָׂשׂוֹן וּלְשִׂמְחָה, לְכָבוֹד וּלְתִפְאָרֶת. עַל הַכֹּל יהוה אֱלֹהֵינוּ אֲנַחְנוּ מוֹדִים לָךְ וּמְבָרְכִים אוֹתָךְ, יִתְבָּרַךְ שִׁמְךָ בְּפִי כָּל חַי תָּמִיד לְעוֹלָם וָעֶד. בָּרוּךְ אַתָּה יהוה, מְקַדֵּשׁ (הַשַּׁבָּת וְ)יִשְׂרָאֵל וְהַזְּמַנִּים.

The service continues with the various prayers for government on page 1269.
In ארץ ישראל *on* שבת *the service continues on the next page.*

---

consent and pledge their allegiance to Joshua as Moses' successor, an instance of a fundamental principle of Judaism, as of the American Declaration of

On Shabbat in Israel continue:

יְקוּם פֻּרְקָן May deliverance arise from heaven, bringing grace, love and compassion, long life, ample sustenance and heavenly help, physical health and enlightenment of mind, living and thriving children who will neither interrupt nor cease from the words of the Torah – to our masters and teachers of the holy communities in the land of Israel and Babylon; to the leaders of assemblies and the leaders of communities in exile; to the heads of academies and to the judges in the gates; to all their disciples and their disciples' disciples, and to all who occupy themselves in study of the Torah. May the King of the Universe bless them, prolonging their lives, increasing their days, and adding to their years. May they be redeemed and delivered from all distress and illness. May our Master in heaven be their help at all times and seasons; and let us say: Amen.

יְקוּם פֻּרְקָן May deliverance arise from heaven, bringing grace, love and compassion, long life, ample sustenance and heavenly help, physical health and enlightenment of mind, living and thriving children who will neither interrupt nor cease from the words of the Torah – to all this holy congregation, great and small, women and children. May the King of the Universe bless you, prolonging your lives, increasing your days, and adding to your years. May you be redeemed and delivered from all distress and illness. May our Master in heaven be your help at all times and seasons; and let us say: Amen.

מִי שֶׁבֵּרַךְ May He who blessed our fathers, Abraham, Isaac and Jacob, bless all this holy congregation, together with all other holy congregations: them, their wives, their sons and daughters, and all that is theirs. May He bless those who unite to form synagogues for prayer and those who come there to pray; those who provide lamps for light and wine for Kiddush and Havdala, food for visitors and charity for the poor, and all who faithfully occupy themselves with the needs of the community. May the Holy One, blessed be He, give them their reward; may He remove from them all illness, grant them complete healing, and forgive all their sins. May He send blessing and success to all the work of their hands, together with all Israel their brethren; and let us say: Amen.

On שבת *in* ארץ ישראל *continue:*

יְקוּם פֻּרְקָן מִן שְׁמַיָּא, חִנָּא וְחִסְדָּא וְרַחֲמֵי וְחַיֵּי אֲרִיכֵי וּמְזוֹנֵי רְוִיחֵי, וְסִיַּעְתָּא דִשְׁמַיָּא, וּבַרְיוּת גּוּפָא וּנְהוֹרָא מְעַלְיָא, זַרְעָא חַיָּא וְקַיָּמָא, זַרְעָא דִּי לָא יִפְסֻק וְדִי לָא יִבְטֻל מִפִּתְגָּמֵי אוֹרַיְתָא, לְמָרָנָן וְרַבָּנָן חֲבוּרָתָא קַדִּישָׁתָא דִּי בְאַרְעָא דְיִשְׂרָאֵל וְדִי בְּבָבֶל, לְרֵישֵׁי כַלָּה, וּלְרֵישֵׁי גַלְוָתָא, וּלְרֵישֵׁי מְתִיבָתָא, וּלְדַיָּנֵי דְבָבָא, לְכָל תַּלְמִידֵיהוֹן, וּלְכָל תַּלְמִידֵי תַלְמִידֵיהוֹן, וּלְכָל מָאן דְּעָסְקִין בְּאוֹרַיְתָא. מַלְכָּא דְעָלְמָא יְבָרֵךְ יָתְהוֹן, יַפֵּשׁ חַיֵּיהוֹן וְיַסְגֵּא יוֹמֵיהוֹן, וְיִתֵּן אַרְכָא לִשְׁנֵיהוֹן, וְיִתְפָּרְקוּן וְיִשְׁתֵּיזְבוּן מִן כָּל עָקָא וּמִן כָּל מַרְעִין בִּישִׁין. מָרַן דִּי בִשְׁמַיָּא יְהֵא בְסַעְדְּהוֹן כָּל זְמַן וְעִדָּן, וְנֹאמַר אָמֵן.

יְקוּם פֻּרְקָן מִן שְׁמַיָּא, חִנָּא וְחִסְדָּא וְרַחֲמֵי וְחַיֵּי אֲרִיכֵי וּמְזוֹנֵי רְוִיחֵי, וְסִיַּעְתָּא דִשְׁמַיָּא, וּבַרְיוּת גּוּפָא וּנְהוֹרָא מְעַלְיָא, זַרְעָא חַיָּא וְקַיָּמָא, זַרְעָא דִּי לָא יִפְסֻק וְדִי לָא יִבְטֻל מִפִּתְגָּמֵי אוֹרַיְתָא, לְכָל קְהָלָא קַדִּישָׁא הָדֵין, רַבְרְבַיָּא עִם זְעֵרַיָּא, טַפְלָא וּנְשַׁיָּא. מַלְכָּא דְעָלְמָא יְבָרֵךְ יָתְכוֹן, יַפֵּשׁ חַיֵּיכוֹן וְיַסְגֵּא יוֹמֵיכוֹן, וְיִתֵּן אַרְכָא לִשְׁנֵיכוֹן, וְתִתְפָּרְקוּן וְתִשְׁתֵּיזְבוּן מִן כָּל עָקָא וּמִן כָּל מַרְעִין בִּישִׁין. מָרַן דִּי בִשְׁמַיָּא יְהֵא בְסַעְדְּכוֹן כָּל זְמַן וְעִדָּן, וְנֹאמַר אָמֵן.

מִי שֶׁבֵּרַךְ אֲבוֹתֵינוּ אַבְרָהָם יִצְחָק וְיַעֲקֹב, הוּא יְבָרֵךְ אֶת כָּל הַקָּהָל הַקָּדוֹשׁ הַזֶּה עִם כָּל קְהִלּוֹת הַקֹּדֶשׁ, הֵם וּנְשֵׁיהֶם וּבְנֵיהֶם וּבְנוֹתֵיהֶם וְכָל אֲשֶׁר לָהֶם, וּמִי שֶׁמְּיַחֲדִים בָּתֵּי כְנֵסִיּוֹת לִתְפִלָּה, וּמִי שֶׁבָּאִים בְּתוֹכָם לְהִתְפַּלֵּל, וּמִי שֶׁנּוֹתְנִים נֵר לַמָּאוֹר וְיַיִן לְקִדּוּשׁ וּלְהַבְדָּלָה וּפַת לָאוֹרְחִים וּצְדָקָה לָעֲנִיִּים, וְכָל מִי שֶׁעוֹסְקִים בְּצָרְכֵי צִבּוּר בֶּאֱמוּנָה. הַקָּדוֹשׁ בָּרוּךְ הוּא יְשַׁלֵּם שְׂכָרָם, וְיָסִיר מֵהֶם כָּל מַחֲלָה, וְיִרְפָּא לְכָל גּוּפָם, וְיִסְלַח לְכָל עֲוֹנָם, וְיִשְׁלַח בְּרָכָה וְהַצְלָחָה בְּכָל מַעֲשֵׂי יְדֵיהֶם עִם כָּל יִשְׂרָאֵל אֲחֵיהֶם, וְנֹאמַר אָמֵן.

The Prayer for the Welfare of the Canadian Government is on the next page.

PRAYER FOR THE WELFARE OF THE AMERICAN GOVERNMENT

The Leader says the following:

הַנּוֹתֵן תְּשׁוּעָה May He who gives salvation to kings and dominion to princes, whose kingdom is an everlasting kingdom, who delivers His servant David from the evil sword, who makes a way in the sea and a path through the mighty waters, bless and protect, guard and help, exalt, magnify and uplift the President, Vice President and all officials of this land. May the Supreme King of kings in His mercy put into their hearts and the hearts of all their counselors and officials, to deal kindly with us and all Israel. In their days and in ours, may Judah be saved and Israel dwell in safety, and may the Redeemer come to Zion. May this be His will, and let us say: Amen.

PRAYER FOR THE SAFETY OF THE AMERICAN MILITARY FORCES

The Leader says the following:

אַדִּיר בַּמָּרוֹם God on high who dwells in might, the King to whom peace belongs, look down from Your holy habitation and bless the soldiers of the American military forces who risk their lives for the sake of peace on earth. Be their shelter and stronghold, and let them not falter. Give them the strength and courage to thwart the plans of the enemy and end the rule of evil. May their enemies be scattered and their foes flee before them, and may they rejoice in Your salvation. Bring them back safely to their homes, as is written:
"The LORD will guard you from all harm, He will guard your life. *Ps. 121*
The LORD will guard your going and coming, now and for evermore." And may there be fulfilled for us the verse: "Nation shall not *Is. 2*
lift up sword against nation, nor shall they learn war any more." Let all the inhabitants on earth know that sovereignty is Yours and Your name inspires awe over all You have created – and let us say: Amen.

The Prayer for the Welfare of the Canadian Government is on the next page.

תפילה לשלום המלכות (ארה״ב)

The שליח ציבור *says the following:*

הַנּוֹתֵן תְּשׁוּעָה לַמְּלָכִים וּמֶמְשָׁלָה לַנְּסִיכִים, מַלְכוּתוֹ מַלְכוּת כָּל עוֹלָמִים, הַפּוֹצֶה אֶת דָּוִד עַבְדּוֹ מֵחֶרֶב רָעָה, הַנּוֹתֵן בַּיָּם דֶּרֶךְ וּבְמַיִם עַזִּים נְתִיבָה, הוּא יְבָרֵךְ וְיִשְׁמֹר וְיִנְצֹר וְיַעֲזֹר וִירוֹמֵם וִיגַדֵּל וִינַשֵּׂא לְמַעְלָה אֶת הַנָּשִׂיא וְאֵת מִשְׁנֵהוּ וְאֶת כָּל שָׂרֵי הָאָרֶץ הַזֹּאת. מֶלֶךְ מַלְכֵי הַמְּלָכִים, בְּרַחֲמָיו יִתֵּן בְּלִבָּם וּבְלֵב כָּל יוֹעֲצֵיהֶם וְשָׂרֵיהֶם לַעֲשׂוֹת טוֹבָה עִמָּנוּ וְעִם כָּל יִשְׂרָאֵל. בִּימֵיהֶם וּבְיָמֵינוּ תִּוָּשַׁע יְהוּדָה, וְיִשְׂרָאֵל יִשְׁכֹּן לָבֶטַח, וּבָא לְצִיּוֹן גּוֹאֵל. וְכֵן יְהִי רָצוֹן, וְנֹאמַר אָמֵן.

תפילה לשלום חיילי צבא ארצות הברית

The שליח ציבור *says the following:*

אַדִּיר בַּמָּרוֹם שׁוֹכֵן בִּגְבוּרָה, מֶלֶךְ שֶׁהַשָּׁלוֹם שֶׁלּוֹ, הַשְׁקִיפָה מִמְּעוֹן קָדְשֶׁךָ, וּבָרֵךְ אֶת חַיָּלֵי צְבָא אַרְצוֹת הַבְּרִית, הַמְחָרְפִים נַפְשָׁם בְּלֶכְתָּם לָשִׂים שָׁלוֹם בָּאָרֶץ. הֱיֵה נָא לָהֶם מַחֲסֶה וּמָעוֹז, וְאַל תִּתֵּן לַמּוֹט רַגְלָם, חַזֵּק יְדֵיהֶם וְאַמֵּץ רוּחָם לְהָפֵר עֲצַת אוֹיֵב וּלְהַעֲבִיר מֶמְשֶׁלֶת זָדוֹן, יָפוּצוּ אוֹיְבֵיהֶם וְיָנוּסוּ מְשַׂנְאֵיהֶם מִפְּנֵיהֶם, וְיִשְׂמְחוּ בִּישׁוּעָתֶךָ. הֲשִׁיבֵם בְּשָׁלוֹם אֶל בֵּיתָם, כַּכָּתוּב בְּדִבְרֵי קָדְשֶׁךָ:
יהוה יִשְׁמָרְךָ מִכָּל־רָע, יִשְׁמֹר אֶת־נַפְשֶׁךָ: יהוה יִשְׁמָר־צֵאתְךָ תהלים קכא
וּבוֹאֶךָ, מֵעַתָּה וְעַד־עוֹלָם: וְקַיֵּם בָּנוּ מִקְרָא שֶׁכָּתוּב: לֹא־יִשָּׂא גוֹי ישעיה ב
אֶל־גּוֹי חֶרֶב, וְלֹא־יִלְמְדוּ עוֹד מִלְחָמָה: וְיֵדְעוּ כָּל יוֹשְׁבֵי תֵבֵל כִּי לְךָ מְלוּכָה יָאֲתָה, וְשִׁמְךָ נוֹרָא עַל כָּל מַה שֶּׁבָּרָאתָ. וְנֹאמַר אָמֵן.

PRAYER FOR THE WELFARE OF THE CANADIAN GOVERNMENT

The Leader says the following:

הַנּוֹתֵן תְּשׁוּעָה May He who gives salvation to kings and dominion to princes, whose kingdom is an everlasting kingdom, who delivers His servant David from the evil sword, who makes a way in the sea and a path through the mighty waters, bless and protect, guard and help, exalt, magnify and uplift the Prime Minister and all the elected and appointed officials of Canada. May the Supreme King of kings in His mercy put into their hearts and the hearts of all their counselors and officials, to deal kindly with us and all Israel. In their days and in ours, may Judah be saved and Israel dwell in safety, and may the Redeemer come to Zion. May this be His will, and let us say: Amen.

PRAYER FOR THE SAFETY OF THE CANADIAN FORCES

The Leader says the following:

אַדִּיר בַּמָּרוֹם God on high who dwells in might, the King to whom peace belongs, look down from Your holy habitation and bless the soldiers of the Canadian Forces who risk their lives for the sake of peace on earth. Be their shelter and stronghold, and let them not falter. Give them the strength and courage to thwart the plans of the enemy and end the rule of evil. May their enemies be scattered and their foes flee before them, and may they rejoice in Your salvation. Bring them back safely to their homes, as is
written: "The LORD will guard you from all harm, He will guard *Ps. 121*
your life. The LORD will guard your going and coming, now and
for evermore." And may there be fulfilled for us the verse: "Nation *Is. 2*
shall not lift up sword against nation, nor shall they learn war any more." Let all the inhabitants on earth know that sovereignty is Yours and Your name inspires awe over all You have created – and let us say: Amen.

תפילה לשלום המלכות (קנדה)

The שליח ציבור *says the following:*

הַנּוֹתֵן תְּשׁוּעָה לַמְּלָכִים וּמֶמְשָׁלָה לַנְּסִיכִים, מַלְכוּתוֹ מַלְכוּת כָּל עוֹלָמִים, הַפּוֹצֶה אֶת דָּוִד עַבְדּוֹ מֵחֶרֶב רָעָה, הַנּוֹתֵן בַּיָּם דֶּרֶךְ וּבְמַיִם עַזִּים נְתִיבָה, הוּא יְבָרֵךְ וְיִשְׁמֹר וְיִנְצֹר וְיַעֲזֹר וִירוֹמֵם וִיגַדֵּל וִינַשֵּׂא לְמַעְלָה אֶת רֹאשׁ הַמֶּמְשָׁלָה וְאֶת כָּל שָׂרֵי הָאָרֶץ הַזֹּאת. מֶלֶךְ מַלְכֵי הַמְּלָכִים, בְּרַחֲמָיו יִתֵּן בְּלִבָּם וּבְלֵב כָּל יוֹעֲצֵיהֶם וְשָׂרֵיהֶם לַעֲשׂוֹת טוֹבָה עִמָּנוּ וְעִם כָּל יִשְׂרָאֵל. בִּימֵיהֶם וּבְיָמֵינוּ תִּוָּשַׁע יְהוּדָה, וְיִשְׂרָאֵל יִשְׁכֹּן לָבֶטַח, וּבָא לְצִיּוֹן גּוֹאֵל. וְכֵן יְהִי רָצוֹן, וְנֹאמַר אָמֵן.

תפילה לשלום חיילי צבא קנדה

The שליח ציבור *says the following:*

אַדִּיר בַּמָּרוֹם שׁוֹכֵן בִּגְבוּרָה, מֶלֶךְ שֶׁהַשָּׁלוֹם שֶׁלּוֹ, הַשְׁקִיפָה מִמְּעוֹן קָדְשֶׁךָ, וּבָרֵךְ אֶת חַיָּלֵי צְבָא קָנָדָה, הַמְחָרְפִים נַפְשָׁם בְּלֶכְתָּם לָשִׂים שָׁלוֹם בָּאָרֶץ. הֱיֵה נָא לָהֶם מַחֲסֶה וּמָעוֹז, וְאַל תִּתֵּן לַמּוֹט רַגְלָם, חַזֵּק יְדֵיהֶם וְאַמֵּץ רוּחָם לְהָפֵר עֲצַת אוֹיֵב וּלְהַעֲבִיר מֶמְשֶׁלֶת זָדוֹן, יָפוּצוּ אוֹיְבֵיהֶם וְיָנוּסוּ מְשַׂנְאֵיהֶם מִפְּנֵיהֶם, וְיִשְׂמְחוּ בִּישׁוּעָתֶךָ. הֲשִׁיבֵם בְּשָׁלוֹם אֶל בֵּיתָם, כַּכָּתוּב
בְּדִבְרֵי קָדְשֶׁךָ: יהוה יִשְׁמָרְךָ מִכָּל־רָע, יִשְׁמֹר אֶת־נַפְשֶׁךָ: יהוה תהלים קכא
יִשְׁמָר־צֵאתְךָ וּבוֹאֶךָ, מֵעַתָּה וְעַד־עוֹלָם: וְקַיֵּם בָּנוּ מִקְרָא
שֶׁכָּתוּב: לֹא־יִשָּׂא גוֹי אֶל־גּוֹי חֶרֶב, וְלֹא־יִלְמְדוּ עוֹד מִלְחָמָה: ישעיה ב
וְיֵדְעוּ כָּל יוֹשְׁבֵי תֵבֵל כִּי לְךָ מְלוּכָה יָאֲתָה, וְשִׁמְךָ נוֹרָא עַל כָּל מַה שֶּׁבָּרָאתָ. וְנֹאמַר אָמֵן.

PRAYER FOR THE STATE OF ISRAEL

The Leader says the following prayer:

אָבִינוּ שֶׁבַּשָּׁמַיִם Heavenly Father, Israel's Rock and Redeemer, bless the State of Israel, the first flowering of our redemption. Shield it under the wings of Your loving-kindness and spread over it the Tabernacle of Your peace. Send Your light and truth to its leaders, ministers and counselors, and direct them with good counsel before You.

Strengthen the hands of the defenders of our Holy Land; grant them deliverance, our God, and crown them with the crown of victory. Grant peace in the land and everlasting joy to its inhabitants.

As for our brothers, the whole house of Israel, remember them in all the lands of our (*In Israel say:* their) dispersion, and swiftly lead us (*In Israel say:* them) upright to Zion Your city, and Jerusalem Your dwelling place, as is written in the Torah of Moses Your servant: "Even if you are scattered to the furthermost lands under the heavens, from there the LORD your God will gather you and take you back. The LORD your God will bring you to the land your ancestors possessed and you will possess it; and He will make you more prosperous and numerous than your ancestors. Then the LORD your God will open up your heart and the heart of your descendants, to love the LORD your God with all your heart and with all your soul, that you may live." *Deut. 30*

Unite our hearts to love and revere Your name and observe all the words of Your Torah, and swiftly send us Your righteous anointed one of the house of David, to redeem those who long for Your salvation.

Appear in Your glorious majesty over all the dwellers on earth, and let all who breathe declare: The LORD God of Israel is King and His kingship has dominion over all. Amen, Selah.

תפילה לשלום מדינת ישראל

The שליח ציבור *says the following prayer:*

אָבִינוּ שֶׁבַּשָּׁמַיִם, צוּר יִשְׂרָאֵל וְגוֹאֲלוֹ, בָּרֵךְ אֶת מְדִינַת יִשְׂרָאֵל, רֵאשִׁית צְמִיחַת גְּאֻלָּתֵנוּ. הָגֵן עָלֶיהָ בְּאֶבְרַת חַסְדֶּךָ וּפְרֹשׂ עָלֶיהָ סֻכַּת שְׁלוֹמֶךָ, וּשְׁלַח אוֹרְךָ וַאֲמִתְּךָ לְרָאשֶׁיהָ, שָׂרֶיהָ וְיוֹעֲצֶיהָ, וְתַקְּנֵם בְּעֵצָה טוֹבָה מִלְּפָנֶיךָ.

חַזֵּק אֶת יְדֵי מְגִנֵּי אֶרֶץ קָדְשֵׁנוּ, וְהַנְחִילֵם אֱלֹהֵינוּ יְשׁוּעָה וַעֲטֶרֶת נִצָּחוֹן תְּעַטְּרֵם, וְנָתַתָּ שָׁלוֹם בָּאָרֶץ וְשִׂמְחַת עוֹלָם לְיוֹשְׁבֶיהָ.

וְאֶת אַחֵינוּ כָּל בֵּית יִשְׂרָאֵל, פְּקָד נָא בְּכָל אַרְצוֹת פְּזוּרֵינוּ, וְתוֹלִיכֵנוּ /בארץ ישראל: פְּזוּרֵיהֶם, וְתוֹלִיכֵם/ מְהֵרָה קוֹמְמִיּוּת לְצִיּוֹן עִירֶךָ וְלִירוּשָׁלַיִם מִשְׁכַּן שְׁמֶךָ, כַּכָּתוּב בְּתוֹרַת מֹשֶׁה עַבְדֶּךָ:
דברים ל אִם־יִהְיֶה נִדַּחֲךָ בִּקְצֵה הַשָּׁמָיִם, מִשָּׁם יְקַבֶּצְךָ יהוה אֱלֹהֶיךָ וּמִשָּׁם יִקָּחֶךָ: וֶהֱבִיאֲךָ יהוה אֱלֹהֶיךָ אֶל־הָאָרֶץ אֲשֶׁר־יָרְשׁוּ אֲבֹתֶיךָ וִירִשְׁתָּהּ, וְהֵיטִבְךָ וְהִרְבְּךָ מֵאֲבֹתֶיךָ: וּמָל יהוה אֱלֹהֶיךָ אֶת־לְבָבְךָ וְאֶת־לְבַב זַרְעֶךָ, לְאַהֲבָה אֶת־יהוה אֱלֹהֶיךָ בְּכָל־לְבָבְךָ וּבְכָל־נַפְשְׁךָ, לְמַעַן חַיֶּיךָ:

וְיַחֵד לְבָבֵנוּ לְאַהֲבָה וּלְיִרְאָה אֶת שְׁמֶךָ, וְלִשְׁמֹר אֶת כָּל דִּבְרֵי תוֹרָתֶךָ, וּשְׁלַח לָנוּ מְהֵרָה בֶּן דָּוִד מְשִׁיחַ צִדְקֶךָ, לִפְדּוֹת מְחַכֵּי קֵץ יְשׁוּעָתֶךָ.

וְהוֹפַע בַּהֲדַר גְּאוֹן עֻזֶּךָ עַל כָּל יוֹשְׁבֵי תֵבֵל אַרְצֶךָ וְיֹאמַר כֹּל אֲשֶׁר נְשָׁמָה בְאַפּוֹ, יהוה אֱלֹהֵי יִשְׂרָאֵל מֶלֶךְ וּמַלְכוּתוֹ בַּכֹּל מָשָׁלָה, אָמֵן סֶלָה.

PRAYER FOR ISRAEL'S DEFENSE FORCES

The Leader says the following prayer:

מִי שֶׁבֵּרַךְ May He who blessed our ancestors, Abraham, Isaac and Jacob, bless the members of Israel's Defense Forces and its security services who stand guard over our land and the cities of our God from the Lebanese border to the Egyptian desert, from the Mediterranean sea to the approach of the Aravah, and wherever else they are, on land, in air and at sea. May the LORD make the enemies who rise against us be struck down before them. May the Holy One, blessed be He, protect and deliver them from all trouble and distress, affliction and illness, and send blessing and success to all the work of their hands. May He subdue our enemies under them and crown them with deliverance and victory. And may there be fulfilled in them the verse, "It is the LORD your God who goes with you to fight for you against your enemies, to deliver you." And let us say: Amen. *Deut. 20*

PRAYER FOR THOSE BEING HELD IN CAPTIVITY

If Israeli soldiers or civilians are being held in captivity, the Leader says the following:

מִי שֶׁבֵּרַךְ May He who blessed our ancestors, Abraham, Isaac and Jacob, Joseph, Moses and Aaron, David and Solomon, bless, protect and guard the members of Israel's Defense Forces missing in action or held captive, and other captives among our brethren, the whole house of Israel, who are in distress or captivity, as we, the members of this holy congregation, pray on their behalf. May the Holy One, blessed be He, have compassion on them and bring them out from darkness and the shadow of death; may He break their bonds, deliver them from their distress, and bring them swiftly back to their families' embrace. Give thanks to the LORD for His loving-kindness and for the wonders He does for the children of men; and may there be fulfilled in them the verse: "Those redeemed by the LORD will return; they will enter Zion with singing, and everlasting joy will crown their heads. Gladness and joy will overtake them, and sorrow and sighing will flee away." And let us say: Amen. *Ps. 107* *Is. 35*

In Israel on Simhat Torah, Yizkor is said (page 1124) and the service continues with Musaf for Shemini Atzeret.

מי שברך לחיילי צה״ל

The שליח ציבור *says the following prayer:*

מִי שֶׁבֵּרַךְ אֲבוֹתֵינוּ אַבְרָהָם יִצְחָק וְיַעֲקֹב הוּא יְבָרֵךְ אֶת חַיָּלֵי
צְבָא הַהֲגָנָה לְיִשְׂרָאֵל וְאַנְשֵׁי כֹּחוֹת הַבִּטָּחוֹן, הָעוֹמְדִים עַל מִשְׁמַר
אַרְצֵנוּ וְעָרֵי אֱלֹהֵינוּ, מִגְּבוּל הַלְּבָנוֹן וְעַד מִדְבַּר מִצְרַיִם וּמִן הַיָּם
הַגָּדוֹל עַד לְבוֹא הָעֲרָבָה וּבְכָל מָקוֹם שֶׁהֵם, בַּיַּבָּשָׁה, בָּאֲוִיר וּבַיָּם.
יִתֵּן יהוה אֶת אוֹיְבֵינוּ הַקָּמִים עָלֵינוּ נִגָּפִים לִפְנֵיהֶם. הַקָּדוֹשׁ בָּרוּךְ
הוּא יִשְׁמֹר וְיַצִּיל אֶת חַיָּלֵינוּ מִכָּל צָרָה וְצוּקָה וּמִכָּל נֶגַע וּמַחֲלָה,
וְיִשְׁלַח בְּרָכָה וְהַצְלָחָה בְּכָל מַעֲשֵׂי יְדֵיהֶם. יַדְבֵּר שׂוֹנְאֵינוּ תַּחְתֵּיהֶם
וִיעַטְּרֵם בְּכֶתֶר יְשׁוּעָה וּבַעֲטֶרֶת נִצָּחוֹן. וִיקֻיַּם בָּהֶם הַכָּתוּב: כִּי דברים כ
יהוה אֱלֹהֵיכֶם הַהֹלֵךְ עִמָּכֶם לְהִלָּחֵם לָכֶם עִם־אֹיְבֵיכֶם לְהוֹשִׁיעַ
אֶתְכֶם: וְנֹאמַר אָמֵן.

מי שברך לשבויים

If Israeli soldiers or civilians are being held in captivity, the שליח ציבור *says the following:*

מִי שֶׁבֵּרַךְ אֲבוֹתֵינוּ אַבְרָהָם יִצְחָק וְיַעֲקֹב, יוֹסֵף מֹשֶׁה וְאַהֲרֹן,
דָּוִד וּשְׁלֹמֹה, הוּא יְבָרֵךְ וְיִשְׁמֹר וְיִנְצֹר אֶת נֶעְדְּרֵי צְבָא הַהֲגָנָה
לְיִשְׂרָאֵל וּשְׁבוּיָו, וְאֶת כָּל אַחֵינוּ הַנְּתוּנִים בְּצָרָה וּבְשִׁבְיָה, בַּעֲבוּר
שֶׁכָּל הַקָּהָל הַקָּדוֹשׁ הַזֶּה מִתְפַּלֵּל בַּעֲבוּרָם. הַקָּדוֹשׁ בָּרוּךְ הוּא
יְמַלֵּא רַחֲמִים עֲלֵיהֶם, וְיוֹצִיאֵם מֵחֹשֶׁךְ וְצַלְמָוֶת, וּמוֹסְרוֹתֵיהֶם
יְנַתֵּק, וּמִמְּצוּקוֹתֵיהֶם יוֹשִׁיעֵם, וִישִׁיבֵם מְהֵרָה לְחֵיק מִשְׁפְּחוֹתֵיהֶם.
יוֹדוּ לַיהוה חַסְדּוֹ וְנִפְלְאוֹתָיו לִבְנֵי אָדָם: וִיקֻיַּם בָּהֶם מִקְרָא תהלים קז
שֶׁכָּתוּב: וּפְדוּיֵי יהוה יְשֻׁבוּן, וּבָאוּ צִיּוֹן בְּרִנָּה, וְשִׂמְחַת עוֹלָם ישעיה לה
עַל־רֹאשָׁם, שָׂשׂוֹן וְשִׂמְחָה יַשִּׂיגוּ, וְנָסוּ יָגוֹן וַאֲנָחָה: וְנֹאמַר אָמֵן.

In ארץ ישראל *on* שמחת תורה, יזכור *is said* *(page 1125)* *and the service continues with* מוסף *for* שמיני עצרת.

On Simhat Torah, some congregations add these piyutim before returning the Torah scrolls to the Ark. Congregations that omit the piyutim continue with "Lord my God" on page 1286.

אֲשֶׁר For the sake of the fathers, He made the children great; / and for them He gave them Torah.
Among Galgalim of spirit, the LORD was revealed, / and the hosts of angels, the heavenly thousands.
Mighty above proud men is the God of majesty, / and He called upon Moses to receive the stone tablets.
The whole world heard the words of God, / and the pillars that hold it shook.
He tipped the skies and descended; He rode upon a cherub, / soared on the wings of the wind.
Words emerged from fire / to be engraved upon stone.

As all the angels sang aloud / and a shofar sounded from the highest heavens.
The children of Esau were wrapped in trembling, / for the Presence of the LORD shone out from Seir.
The children of Ishmael slapped their palms in fear, / for the LORD appeared from Paran.

The LORD's right hand held the tablets by two handbreadths, / and two handbreadths were held in Moses' right hand,
for the length of the tablets was handbreadths six, / and two handbreadths separated hand from hand.

Go now, Moses, rejoice in your greatness, / for there is none like you among the prophets.
*Who else ascended to heaven, into the cloud, / and who else saw the image of our God?
(**Some substitute:* Moses ascended into the cloud, / and he saw the image of our God.)
Prince of princes was our teacher, Moses, / father of the wise and foremost of the prophets.
He closed the [Reed] Sea back in with his prayer; / and because of His messenger, God reined in His rage.

The LORD spoke and said to His people, / "I am the LORD your God, who brought you out of Egypt, redeemed you from the slave-house"; *Ex. 20*
and everyone opened their mouths and replied, / "The LORD will reign for ever and all time." *Ex. 15*

---

the scene in heaven when Moses ascended to receive the Torah, and then moves to Moses' reaction at being told he would die before the Israelites

On שמחת תורה*, some congregations add these piyutim before returning the* ספרי התורה *to the* ארון קודש*. Congregations that omit the piyutim continue with* יָהּ אֵלִי *on page 1287.*

אֲשֶׁר בִּגְלַל אָבוֹת בָּנִים גִּדֵּל / וּבַעֲבוּרָם תּוֹרָה נָתַן
בְּגַלְגַּלֵּי רוּחַ יהוה נִגְלָה / בְּמַלְאֲכֵי צְבָאוֹת, אַלְפֵי שִׁנְאָן
גִּבּוֹר עַל גֵּאִים, אֱלוֹהַּ אַדִּיר / קָרָא לְמֹשֶׁה לְקַבֵּל לוּחוֹת
דִּבְרֵי אֵל חַי שָׁמְעָה הָאָרֶץ / וְעַמּוּדֶיהָ יִתְפַּלָּצוּן
הִטָּה שָׁמַיִם וַיֵּרַד וַיִּרְכַּב עַל כְּרוּב / וַיֵּדֶא עַל כַּנְפֵי רוּחַ
וַיֵּצְאוּ דְּבָרִים מִתּוֹךְ הָאֵשׁ / וַיִּתְחוֹקְקוּ עַל לוּחוֹת הָאָבֶן.

זְמִירוֹת אָמְרוּ כָּל בְּנֵי אֱלֹהִים / שׁוֹפָר תָּקַע מִשְּׁמֵי מָרוֹם
חֲרָדָה לָבְשׁוּ כָּל בְּנֵי עֵשָׂו / כִּי מִשֵּׂעִיר יהוה זָרַח
טָפְחוּ כֻּלָּם בְּנֵי יִשְׁמָעֵאל / כִּי מִפָּארָן יהוה הוֹפִיעַ.

יְמִין יהוה טְפָחַיִם בַּלּוּחוֹת / וִימִין מֹשֶׁה טְפָחַיִם בַּלּוּחוֹת
כִּי אֹרֶךְ הַלּוּחוֹת שִׁשָּׁה טְפָחִים / טְפָחַיִם מְפֹרָשׁ בֵּין יָד לְיָד.

לְךָ מֹשֶׁה שְׂמַח בִּגְדֻלָּתֶךָ / כִּי אֵין כָּמוֹךָ בְּכָל הַנְּבִיאִים
מִי עָלָה שָׁמַיִם לְתוֹךְ הֶעָנָן / וּמִי רָאָה תְּמוּנַת אֱלֹהֵינוּ
(נ״א: מֹשֶׁה עָלָה בְּתוֹךְ הֶעָנָן / כִּי הוּא רָאָה תְּמוּנַת אֱלֹהֵינוּ)
נְשִׂיא נְשִׂיאִים הָיָה מֹשֶׁה רַבֵּנוּ / אָב לַחֲכָמִים וְרֹאשׁ לַנְּבִיאִים
סָגַר הַיָּם בִּתְפִלָּתוֹ / וְעַל יַד שְׁלוּחוֹ, חֲרוֹן אַף הֵשִׁיב.

עָנָה יהוה וְאָמַר לְעַמּוֹ /
שמות כ אָנֹכִי יהוה אֱלֹהֶיךָ, אֲשֶׁר הוֹצֵאתִיךָ מֵאֶרֶץ מִצְרָיִם:
וּמִבֵּית עֲבָדִים פְּדִיתִיךָ
שמות טו פָּתְחוּ כֻלָּם פִּיהֶם וְאָמְרוּ / יהוה יִמְלֹךְ לְעוֹלָם וָעֶד:

אֲשֶׁר בִּגְלַל אָבוֹת FOR THE SAKE OF THE FATHERS.
An ancient poem, written to be said at the conclusion of a cycle of Torah reading, but before the custom existed of doing so on the day we now call Simḥat Torah. Based on a series of midrashic traditions, it describes

Moses cried out, a great and bitter cry, / when the Holy One, blessed be He, told him, "Ascend and die upon the mountain."
He tore his clothes and raised his voice – / "Joshua son of Nun, take good care of my flock."
From the top of that mountain, Moses saw / the lands of the tribes who stood before him.
And there Moses, the servant of the LORD, died; / opposite Beit Peor, our God gathered him in.

Moses' prayer tore the heavens apart, / making the Rock answer His people in their time of anguish,
and never will his prayer return unanswered, / for Moses was a faithful shepherd to Israel.
Moses died: who will not die? / Our teacher, Moses, died at the word of the LORD.

Joshua, son of Nun, rose up after Moses, / and he too taught Torah to Israel.
Blessed are You, LORD, who chose righteous men,
and gave Your people, Israel, Torah at the hand of our teacher, Moses.

* * *

שִׂישׂוּ וְגִילוּ Sing out, celebrate, on Simḥat Torah, / and give honor to the Torah,
for better to trade in her than in any other riches; / for she is precious beyond gold and beyond pearls.

Let us sing out and celebrate this Torah,
for she is our strength and our light.

I shall praise my God and rejoice in Him; / and in Him shall I place my hope.
I glorify Him among the people close to Him; / in God my Rock I take my shelter.

Let us sing out and celebrate this Torah,
for she is our strength and our light.

שִׂישׂוּ וְגִילוּ SING OUT, CELEBRATE
A poem of later date, since it refers explicitly to Simḥat Torah, author unknown. The refrain that refers to Torah as "strength and light" is a reference to two midrashic traditions. One identifies the phrase "The LORD will give strength to His people" (Ps. 29:11) with the giving of the Torah (*Bemidbar Raba* 1:3), while another says that the five mentions of "light" in the first

צָעַק מֹשֶׁה צְעָקָה גְּדוֹלָה וּמָרָה
בְּשָׁעָה שֶׁאָמַר לוֹ הַקָּדוֹשׁ בָּרוּךְ הוּא, עֲלֵה וּמוּת בָּהָר
קָרַע בְּגָדָיו וְהֵרִים קוֹלוֹ / יְהוֹשֻׁעַ בִּן נוּן, שְׁמֹר נָא צֹאנִי
רָאָה מֹשֶׁה מֵרֹאשׁ הַפִּסְגָּה / נַחֲלַת שְׁבָטִים עוֹמְדִים לְפָנָיו
שָׁם מֵת מֹשֶׁה עֶבֶד יהוה / מוּל בֵּית פְּעוֹר אֲסָפוֹ אֱלֹהֵינוּ.

תְּפִלַּת מֹשֶׁה קָרַע רָקִיעַ / עָנָה צוּר לְעַמּוֹ בְּעֵת צָרָתָם
תְּפִלָּתוֹ לְעוֹלָם לֹא תָשׁוּב רֵיקָם / כִּי רוֹעֶה נֶאֱמָן הָיָה מֹשֶׁה לְיִשְׂרָאֵל
מֹשֶׁה מֵת, מִי לֹא יָמוּת / עַל פִּי יהוה מֵת מֹשֶׁה רַבֵּנוּ.

יְהוֹשֻׁעַ בִּן נוּן קָם אַחֲרֵי מֹשֶׁה / גַּם הוּא לִמֵּד תּוֹרָה לְיִשְׂרָאֵל
בָּרוּךְ אַתָּה יהוה, הַבּוֹחֵר בַּצַּדִּיקִים
וְנָתַן תּוֹרָה לְעַמּוֹ יִשְׂרָאֵל עַל יְדֵי מֹשֶׁה רַבֵּנוּ.

* * *

שִׂישׂוּ וְגִילוּ בְּשִׂמְחַת תּוֹרָה / וּתְנוּ כָבוֹד לַתּוֹרָה
כִּי טוֹב סַחְרָהּ מִכָּל סְחוֹרָה / מִפָּז וּמִפְּנִינִים יְקָרָה.
נָגִיל וְנָשִׂישׂ בְּזֹאת הַתּוֹרָה / כִּי הִיא לָנוּ עֹז וְאוֹרָה.

אֲהַלֵּל אֱלֹהַי וְאֶשְׂמְחָה בוֹ / וְאָשִׂימָה תִּקְוָתִי בּוֹ
אֲהוֹדֶנּוּ בְּסוֹד עַם קְרוֹבוֹ / אֱלֹהֵי צוּרִי, אֶחֱסֶה בּוֹ.
נָגִיל וְנָשִׂישׂ בְּזֹאת הַתּוֹרָה / כִּי הִיא לָנוּ עֹז וְאוֹרָה.

---

entered the Promised Land, and then to the death itself. The poet then tells how Moses' prayer on behalf of his people "rent the heavens," and that his intercession had a lasting effect. According to the Talmud, God taught Moses how to teach future generations to pray, promising that whenever they recited the Thirteen Attributes of Divine Mercy, their prayer would not return empty-handed (*Rosh HaShana* 17b). The poem ends by seeing Moses' death as an epitome of human mortality: "If Moses died, who shall not die?"

With all my heart I sing aloud Your might / and speak Your praises;
bring us back to Your House in the joy / of Your kindness and of Your truth.

Let us sing out and celebrate this Torah,
for she is our strength and our light.

Redeemer, bring quickly the herald of good things, / for You are a tower of goodness and strength.
The redeemed ones will thank You with joyful hearts – / Thank the LORD, for He is good. *Ps. 136*

Let us sing out and celebrate this Torah,
for she is our strength and our light.

Unmistakable One, redeem, please, our multitudes, / for there is none so holy as the LORD.
And those who seek You will give thanks to You, LORD – / Who can tell of the LORD's mighty acts? *Ps. 106*

Let us sing out and celebrate this Torah,
for she is our strength and our light.

Did He not choose us, in His great love, / calling us "My firstborn son"?
He made us splendid, glorious, with wisdom, / for His loving-kindness is ours forever.

Let us sing out and celebrate this Torah,
for she is our strength and our light.

* * *

הִתְקַבְּצוּ The angels gathered, one to another, / one to receive the other,
and said to one another, / "Who is this and which is he,
holding on to the Throne, / His cloud spread over him; *Job 26*

מִי עָלָה who ascended the heights,
who ascended the heights, / who ascended the heights
and brought might down from its hiding place?"

---

to the angels: "See what is written in the Torah: 'I am the LORD your God who brought you out of the land of Egypt.' Did you angels go down to Egypt? Were you enslaved? Do angels need the Ten Commandments to keep them from sin?" At this, the angels conceded that the Torah was indeed meant for humans on earth, not angels in Heaven.

בְּכָל עֵת אֲרַנֵּן גְּבוּרוֹתֶיךָ / וַאֲסַפֵּר תְּהִלָּתֶךָ
בְּשָׂשׂוֹן הֲשִׁיבֵנוּ לְבֵיתֶךָ / עַל חַסְדְּךָ וְעַל אֲמִתֶּךָ.
נָגִיל וְנָשִׂישׂ בְּזֹאת הַתּוֹרָה / כִּי הִיא לָנוּ עֹז וְאוֹרָה.

גּוֹאֵל הָחִישׁ מְבַשֵּׂר טוֹב / כִּי אַתָּה מִגְדַּל עֹז וָטוֹב
תהלים קלו גְּאוּלִים יְשַׁבְּחוּךָ בְּלֵב טוֹב / הוֹדוּ לַיהוה כִּי טוֹב.
נָגִיל וְנָשִׂישׂ בְּזֹאת הַתּוֹרָה / כִּי הִיא לָנוּ עֹז וְאוֹרָה.

דָּגוּל גְּאַל נָא אֶת הֲמוֹנָי / כִּי אֵין קָדוֹשׁ כַּיהוה
תהלים קו דּוֹרְשֶׁיךָ יוֹדוּךָ יהוה / מִי יְמַלֵּל גְּבוּרוֹת יהוה.
נָגִיל וְנָשִׂישׂ בְּזֹאת הַתּוֹרָה / כִּי הִיא לָנוּ עֹז וְאוֹרָה.

הֲלֹא בְּאַהֲבָתוֹ בָּחַר בָּנוּ / כִּי בְכוֹרִי קְרָאָנוּ
הוֹד וְהָדָר הֶחְכִּימָנוּ / כִּי לְעוֹלָם חַסְדּוֹ עִמָּנוּ.
נָגִיל וְנָשִׂישׂ בְּזֹאת הַתּוֹרָה / כִּי הִיא לָנוּ עֹז וְאוֹרָה.

* * *

הִתְקַבְּצוּ מַלְאָכִים זֶה אֶל זֶה / זֶה לְקָבֵל זֶה
וְאָמַר זֶה לָזֶה / מִי הוּא זֶה וְאֵיזֶה הוּא
איוב כו מְאַחֵז פְּנֵי־כִסֵּה, פַּרְשֵׁז עָלָיו עֲנָנוֹ:
מִי עָלָה לַמָּרוֹם / מִי עָלָה לַמָּרוֹם / מִי עָלָה לַמָּרוֹם
וּמִי הוֹרִיד עֹז מִבְטֶחָה

---

chapter of Genesis correspond to the Five Books of the Torah (*Bereshit Raba* 3:5).

הִתְקַבְּצוּ מַלְאָכִים *The angels gathered.* Based on a Talmudic passage (*Shabbat* 88b–89a) that states that when Moses ascended to Heaven to receive the Torah, the angels protested, saying to God, "Master of the universe, what business does one born of woman have in our midst? Are You about to give this precious heritage of Yours, that existed long before the universe was created, to mere flesh and blood?" God then told Moses to reply. Moses said

מֹשֶׁה Moses ascended the heights,
and brought might down from its hiding place;
Netanel ascended the heights, and brought might down from its hiding place;
Ḥever ascended the heights, and brought might down from its hiding place;
Avi Gedor ascended the heights,
and brought might down from its hiding place;
Avi Sokho ascended the heights,
and brought might down from its hiding place;
Yered ascended the heights, and brought might down from its hiding place;
Yekutiel ascended the heights, and brought might down from its hiding place;
Avi Zanoaḥ ascended the heights,
and brought might down from its hiding place;
Toviya ascended the heights, and brought might down from its hiding place;
Shemaya ascended the heights, and brought might down from its hiding place.

* * *

אָגִיל אֶשְׂמַח I shall sing out and celebrate at Simḥat Torah;
Tzemaḥ will come at Simḥat Torah.

* * *

תּוֹרָה The Torah is the tree of life;
all have life, / for with You is the wellspring of life.

* * *

אַבְרָהָם Abraham rejoiced at Simḥat Torah,
Isaac rejoiced at Simḥat Torah,
Jacob rejoiced at Simḥat Torah,
Moses rejoiced at Simḥat Torah,
Aaron rejoiced at Simḥat Torah,
David rejoiced at Simḥat Torah,
Solomon rejoiced at Simḥat Torah,
Tzemaḥ will come at Simḥat Torah.

* * *

אַבְרָהָם שָׂמַח *Abraham rejoiced.* Based on the tradition that the patriarchs kept the Torah before it was given (Mishna, *Kiddushin* 82a), itself based on the verse, "Abraham obeyed Me and kept My charge: My commandments, My laws and My teachings" (Gen. 26:5).

מֹשֶׁה עָלָה לַמָּרוֹם וְהוֹרִיד עֹז מִבְטֶחָה
נְתַנְאֵל עָלָה לַמָּרוֹם וְהוֹרִיד עֹז מִבְטֶחָה
חֶבֶר עָלָה לַמָּרוֹם וְהוֹרִיד עֹז מִבְטֶחָה
אֲבִי גְדוֹר עָלָה לַמָּרוֹם וְהוֹרִיד עֹז מִבְטֶחָה
אֲבִי סוֹכוֹ עָלָה לַמָּרוֹם וְהוֹרִיד עֹז מִבְטֶחָה
יֶרֶד עָלָה לַמָּרוֹם וְהוֹרִיד עֹז מִבְטֶחָה
יְקוּתִיאֵל עָלָה לַמָּרוֹם וְהוֹרִיד עֹז מִבְטֶחָה
אֲבִי זָנוֹחַ עָלָה לַמָּרוֹם וְהוֹרִיד עֹז מִבְטֶחָה
טוֹבִיָּה עָלָה לַמָּרוֹם וְהוֹרִיד עֹז מִבְטֶחָה
שְׁמַעְיָה עָלָה לַמָּרוֹם וְהוֹרִיד עֹז מִבְטֶחָה

* * *

אָגִיל וְאֶשְׂמַח בְּשִׂמְחַת תּוֹרָה
בּוֹא יָבוֹא צֶמַח בְּשִׂמְחַת תּוֹרָה.

* * *

תּוֹרָה הִיא עֵץ חַיִּים / לְכֻלָּם חַיִּים / כִּי עִמְּךָ מְקוֹר חַיִּים:

* * *

אַבְרָהָם שָׂמַח בְּשִׂמְחַת תּוֹרָה
יִצְחָק שָׂמַח בְּשִׂמְחַת תּוֹרָה
יַעֲקֹב שָׂמַח בְּשִׂמְחַת תּוֹרָה
מֹשֶׁה שָׂמַח בְּשִׂמְחַת תּוֹרָה
אַהֲרֹן שָׂמַח בְּשִׂמְחַת תּוֹרָה
דָּוִד שָׂמַח בְּשִׂמְחַת תּוֹרָה
שְׁלֹמֹה שָׂמַח בְּשִׂמְחַת תּוֹרָה
בּוֹא יָבוֹא צֶמַח בְּשִׂמְחַת תּוֹרָה.

* * *

How happy are you, Israel, / for God has chosen you,
and bequeathed you the Torah, / a gift from Sinai.

How happy are you, majestic ones of God, / how happy are you, Israel.
How happy are you, blessed ones of God, / how happy are you, Israel,
for God has chosen you.

How happy are those God has redeemed, / how happy are you, Israel.
How happy are those whom God has sought, / how happy are you, Israel.
for God has chosen you.

How happy are those God has made splendid, / how happy are you, Israel.
How happy are venerable ones of God, / how happy are you, Israel.
for God has chosen you.

How happy are those God keeps in mind, / how happy are you, Israel.
How happy are faithful followers of God, / how happy are you, Israel.
for God has chosen you.

How happy are pure ones of God, / how happy are you, Israel.
How happy are upright ones of God, / how happy are you, Israel.
for God has chosen you.

How happy are mighty ones of God, / how happy are you, Israel.
How happy are those who are taught of God, / how happy are you, Israel.
for God has chosen you.

How happy are those who praise God, / how happy are you, Israel.
How happy are cleansed ones of God, / how happy are you, Israel.
for God has chosen you.

How happy are treasured ones of God, / how happy are you, Israel.
How happy are those whom God has borne, / how happy are you, Israel.
for God has chosen you.

How happy are those whom God has saved, / how happy are you, Israel.
How happy are righteous ones of God, / how happy are you, Israel.
for God has chosen you.

How happy are holy ones of God, / how happy are you, Israel.
How happy are those for whom God has compassion,
how happy are you, Israel.
for God has chosen you.

How happy are those at peace with God, / how happy are you, Israel.
How happy are innocent ones of God, / how happy are you, Israel.
for God has chosen you.

In Israel continue with "Happy are those" on page 1128.

אַשְׁרֵיכֶם יִשְׂרָאֵל / אֲשֶׁר בָּחַר בָּכֶם אֵל / וְהִנְחִילְכֶם הַתּוֹרָה / מִסִּינַי מַתָּנָה.

אַשְׁרֵיכֶם אַדִּירֵי אֵל / אַשְׁרֵיכֶם יִשְׂרָאֵל
אַשְׁרֵיכֶם בְּרוּכֵי אֵל / אַשְׁרֵיכֶם יִשְׂרָאֵל / כִּי בָחַר בָּכֶם אֵל

אַשְׁרֵיכֶם גְּאוּלֵי אֵל / אַשְׁרֵיכֶם יִשְׂרָאֵל
אַשְׁרֵיכֶם דְּרוּשֵׁי אֵל / אַשְׁרֵיכֶם יִשְׂרָאֵל / כִּי בָחַר בָּכֶם אֵל

אַשְׁרֵיכֶם הֲדוּרֵי אֵל / אַשְׁרֵיכֶם יִשְׂרָאֵל
אַשְׁרֵיכֶם וָתִיקֵי אֵל / אַשְׁרֵיכֶם יִשְׂרָאֵל / כִּי בָחַר בָּכֶם אֵל

אַשְׁרֵיכֶם זְכוּרֵי אֵל / אַשְׁרֵיכֶם יִשְׂרָאֵל
אַשְׁרֵיכֶם חֲסִידֵי אֵל / אַשְׁרֵיכֶם יִשְׂרָאֵל / כִּי בָחַר בָּכֶם אֵל

אַשְׁרֵיכֶם טְהוֹרֵי אֵל / אַשְׁרֵיכֶם יִשְׂרָאֵל
אַשְׁרֵיכֶם יְשָׁרֵי אֵל / אַשְׁרֵיכֶם יִשְׂרָאֵל / כִּי בָחַר בָּכֶם אֵל

אַשְׁרֵיכֶם כַּבִּירֵי אֵל / אַשְׁרֵיכֶם יִשְׂרָאֵל
אַשְׁרֵיכֶם לִמּוּדֵי אֵל / אַשְׁרֵיכֶם יִשְׂרָאֵל / כִּי בָחַר בָּכֶם אֵל

אַשְׁרֵיכֶם מְהַלְלֵי אֵל / אַשְׁרֵיכֶם יִשְׂרָאֵל
אַשְׁרֵיכֶם נְקִיֵּי אֵל / אַשְׁרֵיכֶם יִשְׂרָאֵל / כִּי בָחַר בָּכֶם אֵל

אַשְׁרֵיכֶם סְגוּלֵי אֵל / אַשְׁרֵיכֶם יִשְׂרָאֵל
אַשְׁרֵיכֶם עֲמוּסֵי אֵל / אַשְׁרֵיכֶם יִשְׂרָאֵל / כִּי בָחַר בָּכֶם אֵל

אַשְׁרֵיכֶם פְּדוּיֵי אֵל / אַשְׁרֵיכֶם יִשְׂרָאֵל
אַשְׁרֵיכֶם צַדִּיקֵי אֵל / אַשְׁרֵיכֶם יִשְׂרָאֵל / כִּי בָחַר בָּכֶם אֵל

אַשְׁרֵיכֶם קְדוֹשֵׁי אֵל / אַשְׁרֵיכֶם יִשְׂרָאֵל
אַשְׁרֵיכֶם רְחוּמֵי אֵל / אַשְׁרֵיכֶם יִשְׂרָאֵל / כִּי בָחַר בָּכֶם אֵל

אַשְׁרֵיכֶם שְׁלוּמֵי אֵל / אַשְׁרֵיכֶם יִשְׂרָאֵל
אַשְׁרֵיכֶם תְּמִימֵי אֵל / אַשְׁרֵיכֶם יִשְׂרָאֵל / כִּי בָחַר בָּכֶם אֵל

In ארץ ישראל *continue with* אַשְׁרֵי *on page 1129.*

אַשְׁרֵיכֶם יִשְׂרָאֵל *Happy are you, Israel.* A threefold recapitulation of the phrase Moses used in his last words to the nation (Deut. 33:29).

יָהּ אֵלִי LORD my God and Redeemer, I will stand to greet You;
[God] who was and will be, was and is,
the land of every nation is Yours.

The thanksgiving-offering, burnt-offering, meal-offering, sin-offering, guilt-offering, peace-offering and inauguration-offering are all offerings to You. Remember the weary nation that has borne much, and bring it back to Your land. I will always praise You with "Happy are those who dwell in Your House."

Fine beyond fine, undecipherable, His understanding is unfathomable,
Awesome God who distinguishes between
good and evil with a single glance.

The thanksgiving-offering, burnt-offering, meal-offering, sin-offering, guilt-offering, peace-offering and inauguration-offering are all offerings to You. Remember the weary nation that has borne much, and bring it back to Your land. I will always praise You with "Happy are those who dwell in Your House."

LORD of hosts, with many wonders, He joined all His tent,
making all blossom in the ways of the heart:
the Rock, perfect is His work.

The thanksgiving-offering, burnt-offering, meal-offering, sin-offering, guilt-offering, peace-offering and inauguration-offering are all offerings to You. Remember the weary nation that has borne much, and bring it back to Your land. I will always praise You with "Happy are those who dwell in Your House."

---

the holiest name of God is that He is past, present and future, both in and beyond time.

דַּק עַל דַּק *Fine beyond fine.* The universe is finely tuned for the emergence of life, its delicately balanced mechanisms beyond the reach of human senses and understanding.

בְּאַחַת סְקִירָה *With a single glance.* There is no time-lag between an event and God's knowledge and judgment of it.

כָּל אָהֳלוֹ *All His tent.* A metaphor for the universe as a whole.

בִּנְתִיבוֹת לֵב *In the ways of the heart.* A mystical reference to thirty-two (the numerical value of *lev*, "heart") paths of wisdom with which the universe was created (*Sefer Yetzira*). God's name "*Elohim*" appears thirty-two times in Genesis 1.

יָהּ אֵלִי וְגוֹאֲלִי, אֶתְיַצְּבָה לִקְרָאתֶךָ
הָיָה וְיִהְיֶה, הָיָה וְהֹוֶה, כָּל גּוֹי אַדְמָתֶךָ.
וְתוֹדָה וְלָעוֹלָה וְלַמִּנְחָה וְלַחַטָּאת וְלָאָשָׁם
וְלַשְּׁלָמִים וְלַמִּלּוּאִים כָּל קָרְבָּנֶךָ.
זְכֹר נִלְאָה אֲשֶׁר נָשְׂאָה וְהָשִׁיבָה לְאַדְמָתֶךָ
סֶלָה אֲהַלְלֶךָּ בְּאַשְׁרֵי יוֹשְׁבֵי בֵיתֶךָ.

דַּק עַל דַּק, עַד אֵין נִבְדַּק, וְלִתְבוּנָתוֹ אֵין חֵקֶר
הָאֵל נוֹרָא, בְּאַחַת סְקִירָה, בֵּין טוֹב לְרַע יְבַקֵּר.
וְתוֹדָה וְלָעוֹלָה וְלַמִּנְחָה וְלַחַטָּאת וְלָאָשָׁם
וְלַשְּׁלָמִים וְלַמִּלּוּאִים כָּל קָרְבָּנֶךָ.
זְכֹר נִלְאָה אֲשֶׁר נָשְׂאָה וְהָשִׁיבָה לְאַדְמָתֶךָ
סֶלָה אֲהַלְלֶךָּ בְּאַשְׁרֵי יוֹשְׁבֵי בֵיתֶךָ.

אֲדוֹן צְבָאוֹת, בְּרֹב פְּלָאוֹת, חִבֵּר כָּל אֳהָלוֹ
בִּנְתִיבוֹת לֵב לִבְלֵב, הַצּוּר תָּמִים פָּעֳלוֹ.
וְתוֹדָה וְלָעוֹלָה וְלַמִּנְחָה וְלַחַטָּאת וְלָאָשָׁם
וְלַשְּׁלָמִים וְלַמִּלּוּאִים כָּל קָרְבָּנֶךָ.
זְכֹר נִלְאָה אֲשֶׁר נָשְׂאָה וְהָשִׁיבָה לְאַדְמָתֶךָ
סֶלָה אֲהַלְלֶךָּ בְּאַשְׁרֵי יוֹשְׁבֵי בֵיתֶךָ.

יָהּ אֵלִי *Lord my God.* A poem that originated in mystical circles, appearing for the first time in the Siddur of Rabbi Isaiah Horowitz (c. 1565–1630; known as *Shela*). It is a prelude, specific to the three pilgrimage festivals, to *Ashrei*, the first three words of which form its refrain. It expresses the sadness that we can no longer be present at the Temple bringing our offerings and rejoicing as our ancestors once did on these days when the nation came together in celebration. Some do not say it on Shabbat; some omit it on days when *Yizkor* is said, when our grief is specifically focused remembering the deceased.

הָיָה וְיִהְיֶה, הָיָה וְהֹוֶה *Who was and will be, was and is.* One of the senses of

אַשְׁרֵי Happy are those who dwell in Your House; *Ps. 84*
they shall continue to praise You, Selah!
Happy are the people for whom this is so; *Ps. 144*
happy are the people whose God is the LORD.
A song of praise by David. *Ps. 145*

I will exalt You, my God, the King, and bless Your name for ever and all time. Every day I will bless You, and praise Your name for ever and all time. Great is the LORD and greatly to be praised; His greatness is unfathomable. One generation will praise Your works to the next, and tell of Your mighty deeds. On the glorious splendor of Your majesty I will meditate, and on the acts of Your wonders. They shall talk of the power of Your awesome deeds, and I will tell of Your greatness. They shall recite the record of Your great goodness, and sing with joy of Your righteousness. The LORD is gracious and compassionate, slow to anger and great in loving-kindness. The LORD is good to all, and His compassion extends to all His works. All Your works shall thank You, LORD, and Your devoted ones shall bless You. They shall talk of the glory of Your kingship, and speak of Your might. To make known to mankind His mighty deeds and the glorious majesty of His kingship. Your kingdom is an everlasting kingdom, and Your reign is for all generations. The LORD supports all who fall, and raises all who are bowed down. All raise their eyes to You in hope, and You give them their food in due season. You open Your hand, and satisfy every living thing with favor. The LORD is righteous in all His ways, and kind in all He does. The LORD is close to all who call on Him, to all who call on Him in truth. He fulfills the will of those who revere Him; He hears their cry and saves them. The LORD guards all who love Him, but all the wicked He will destroy. ▸ My mouth shall speak the praise of the LORD, and all creatures shall bless His holy name for ever and all time.

We will bless the LORD now and for ever. Halleluya! *Ps. 115*

אַשְׁרֵי יוֹשְׁבֵי בֵיתֶךָ, עוֹד יְהַלְלְוּךָ סֶּלָה: תהלים פד
אַשְׁרֵי הָעָם שֶׁכָּכָה לּוֹ, אַשְׁרֵי הָעָם שֶׁיהוה אֱלֹהָיו: תהלים קמד
תְּהִלָּה לְדָוִד תהלים קמה

אֲרוֹמִמְךָ אֱלוֹהַי הַמֶּלֶךְ, וַאֲבָרְכָה שִׁמְךָ לְעוֹלָם וָעֶד:
בְּכָל־יוֹם אֲבָרְכֶךָּ, וַאֲהַלְלָה שִׁמְךָ לְעוֹלָם וָעֶד:
גָּדוֹל יהוה וּמְהֻלָּל מְאֹד, וְלִגְדֻלָּתוֹ אֵין חֵקֶר:
דּוֹר לְדוֹר יְשַׁבַּח מַעֲשֶׂיךָ, וּגְבוּרֹתֶיךָ יַגִּידוּ:
הֲדַר כְּבוֹד הוֹדֶךָ, וְדִבְרֵי נִפְלְאֹתֶיךָ אָשִׂיחָה:
וֶעֱזוּז נוֹרְאֹתֶיךָ יֹאמֵרוּ, וּגְדוּלָּתְךָ אֲסַפְּרֶנָּה:
זֵכֶר רַב־טוּבְךָ יַבִּיעוּ, וְצִדְקָתְךָ יְרַנֵּנוּ:
חַנּוּן וְרַחוּם יהוה, אֶרֶךְ אַפַּיִם וּגְדָל־חָסֶד:
טוֹב־יהוה לַכֹּל, וְרַחֲמָיו עַל־כָּל־מַעֲשָׂיו:
יוֹדְוּךָ יהוה כָּל־מַעֲשֶׂיךָ, וַחֲסִידֶיךָ יְבָרְכוּכָה:
כְּבוֹד מַלְכוּתְךָ יֹאמֵרוּ, וּגְבוּרָתְךָ יְדַבֵּרוּ:
לְהוֹדִיעַ לִבְנֵי הָאָדָם גְּבוּרֹתָיו, וּכְבוֹד הֲדַר מַלְכוּתוֹ:
מַלְכוּתְךָ מַלְכוּת כָּל־עֹלָמִים, וּמֶמְשַׁלְתְּךָ בְּכָל־דּוֹר וָדֹר:
סוֹמֵךְ יהוה לְכָל־הַנֹּפְלִים, וְזוֹקֵף לְכָל־הַכְּפוּפִים:
עֵינֵי־כֹל אֵלֶיךָ יְשַׂבֵּרוּ, וְאַתָּה נוֹתֵן־לָהֶם אֶת־אָכְלָם בְּעִתּוֹ:
פּוֹתֵחַ אֶת־יָדֶךָ, וּמַשְׂבִּיעַ לְכָל־חַי רָצוֹן:
צַדִּיק יהוה בְּכָל־דְּרָכָיו, וְחָסִיד בְּכָל־מַעֲשָׂיו:
קָרוֹב יהוה לְכָל־קֹרְאָיו, לְכֹל אֲשֶׁר יִקְרָאֻהוּ בֶאֱמֶת:
רְצוֹן־יְרֵאָיו יַעֲשֶׂה, וְאֶת־שַׁוְעָתָם יִשְׁמַע, וְיוֹשִׁיעֵם:
שׁוֹמֵר יהוה אֶת־כָּל־אֹהֲבָיו, וְאֵת כָּל־הָרְשָׁעִים יַשְׁמִיד:
◂ תְּהִלַּת יהוה יְדַבֶּר פִּי, וִיבָרֵךְ כָּל־בָּשָׂר שֵׁם קָדְשׁוֹ לְעוֹלָם וָעֶד:
וַאֲנַחְנוּ נְבָרֵךְ יָהּ מֵעַתָּה וְעַד־עוֹלָם, הַלְלוּיָהּ: תהלים קטו

RETURNING THE TORAH TO THE ARK

The Ark is opened. All stand.
The Leader takes one of the Torah scrolls and says:

יְהַלְלוּ Let them praise the name of the LORD, Ps. 148
for His name alone is sublime.

The congregation responds:

הוֹדוֹ His majesty is above earth and heaven.
He has raised the horn of His people,
for the glory of all His devoted ones,
the children of Israel, the people close to Him.
Halleluya!

While the Torah scrolls are being returned to the Ark, the following is said.

לְדָוִד מִזְמוֹר A psalm of David. The earth is the LORD's and all it contains, the world and all who live in it. For He founded it on the seas and established it on the streams. Who may climb the mountain of the LORD? Who may stand in His holy place? He who has clean hands and a pure heart, who has not taken My name in vain, or sworn deceitfully. He shall receive blessing from the LORD, and just reward from God, his salvation. This is a generation of those who seek Him, the descendants of Jacob who seek Your presence, Selah! Lift up your heads, O gates; be uplifted, eternal doors, so that the King of glory may enter. Who is the King of glory? It is the LORD, strong and mighty, the LORD mighty in battle. Lift up your heads, O gates; be uplifted, eternal doors, so that the King of glory may enter. ▸ Who is He, the King of glory? The LORD of hosts, He is the King of glory, Selah! Ps. 24

As the Torah scrolls are placed into the Ark, all say:

וּבְנֻחֹה יֹאמַר When the Ark came to rest, Moses would say:
"Return, O LORD, to the myriad thousands of Israel." Num. 10
Advance, LORD, to Your resting place, You and Your mighty Ark. Ps. 132

וּבְנֻחֹה יֹאמַר *When the Ark came to rest.* This is the verse that describes the occasions in the wilderness years when the Israelites encamped. As at the

הכנסת ספר תורה

The ארון קודש *is opened.*
All stand. The שליח ציבור *takes one of the* ספרי תורה *and says:*

תהלים קמח
יְהַלְלוּ אֶת־שֵׁם יהוה, כִּי־נִשְׂגָּב שְׁמוֹ, לְבַדּוֹ

The קהל *responds:*

הוֹדוֹ עַל־אֶרֶץ וְשָׁמָיִם:
וַיָּרֶם קֶרֶן לְעַמּוֹ, תְּהִלָּה לְכָל־חֲסִידָיו
לִבְנֵי יִשְׂרָאֵל עַם קְרֹבוֹ, הַלְלוּיָהּ:

While the ספרי תורה *are being returned to the* ארון קודש*, the following is said.*

תהלים כד
לְדָוִד מִזְמוֹר, לַיהוה הָאָרֶץ וּמְלוֹאָהּ, תֵּבֵל וְיֹשְׁבֵי בָהּ: כִּי־הוּא עַל־יַמִּים יְסָדָהּ, וְעַל־נְהָרוֹת יְכוֹנְנֶהָ: מִי־יַעֲלֶה בְהַר־יהוה, וּמִי־יָקוּם בִּמְקוֹם קָדְשׁוֹ: נְקִי כַפַּיִם וּבַר־לֵבָב, אֲשֶׁר לֹא־נָשָׂא לַשָּׁוְא נַפְשִׁי וְלֹא נִשְׁבַּע לְמִרְמָה: יִשָּׂא בְרָכָה מֵאֵת יהוה, וּצְדָקָה מֵאֱלֹהֵי יִשְׁעוֹ: זֶה דּוֹר דֹּרְשָׁו, מְבַקְשֵׁי פָנֶיךָ, יַעֲקֹב, סֶלָה: שְׂאוּ שְׁעָרִים רָאשֵׁיכֶם, וְהִנָּשְׂאוּ פִּתְחֵי עוֹלָם, וְיָבוֹא מֶלֶךְ הַכָּבוֹד: מִי זֶה מֶלֶךְ הַכָּבוֹד, יהוה עִזּוּז וְגִבּוֹר, יהוה גִּבּוֹר מִלְחָמָה: שְׂאוּ שְׁעָרִים רָאשֵׁיכֶם, וּשְׂאוּ פִּתְחֵי עוֹלָם, וְיָבֹא מֶלֶךְ הַכָּבוֹד: ‹ מִי הוּא זֶה מֶלֶךְ הַכָּבוֹד, יהוה צְבָאוֹת הוּא מֶלֶךְ הַכָּבוֹד, סֶלָה:

As the ספרי תורה *are placed into the* ארון קודש*, all say:*

במדבר י
וּבְנֻחֹה יֹאמַר, שׁוּבָה יהוה רִבְבוֹת אַלְפֵי יִשְׂרָאֵל:
תהלים קלב
קוּמָה יהוה לִמְנוּחָתֶךָ, אַתָּה וַאֲרוֹן עֻזֶּךָ:

לְדָוִד מִזְמוֹר *Psalm 24.* Associated with the occasion on which Solomon brought the Ark into the Temple. The reference to the opening of the gates – "Lift up your heads, O gates" – makes this an appropriate psalm to say as we open the doors of the Ark to receive the Torah scrolls.

Your priests are clothed in righteousness,
and Your devoted ones sing in joy.
For the sake of Your servant David,
do not reject Your anointed one.
For I give you good instruction; do not forsake My Torah. *Prov. 4*
It is a tree of life to those who grasp it, *Prov. 3*
and those who uphold it are happy.
Its ways are ways of pleasantness, and all its paths are peace.
▸ Turn us back, O LORD, to You, and we will return. *Lam. 5*
Renew our days as of old.

The Ark is closed.

HALF KADDISH

Leader: יִתְגַּדַּל Magnified and sanctified may His great name be,
in the world He created by His will.
May He establish His kingdom
in your lifetime and in your days,
and in the lifetime of all the house of Israel,
swiftly and soon – and say: Amen.

All: May His great name be blessed for ever and all time.

Leader: Blessed and praised, glorified and exalted,
raised and honored, uplifted and lauded
be the name of the Holy One, blessed be He,
beyond any blessing, song, praise and consolation
uttered in the world – and say: Amen.

---

mortality is to be found in how we live, not how long. In the union of divine word and human mind we become part of something beyond time, chance and change. The first humans may have lost paradise, but by giving us the Torah, God has given us access to it again.

חַדֵּשׁ יָמֵינוּ כְּקֶדֶם *Renew our days as of old.* A poignant verse taken from the book of Lamentations. In Judaism – the world's oldest monotheistic faith – the new is old, and the old remains new. The symbol of this constant renewal is the Torah, the word of the One beyond time.

כֹּהֲנֶיךָ יִלְבְּשׁוּ־צֶדֶק, וַחֲסִידֶיךָ יְרַנֵּנוּ:
בַּעֲבוּר דָּוִד עַבְדֶּךָ אַל־תָּשֵׁב פְּנֵי מְשִׁיחֶךָ:
כִּי לֶקַח טוֹב נָתַתִּי לָכֶם, תּוֹרָתִי אַל־תַּעֲזֹבוּ: משלי ד
עֵץ־חַיִּים הִיא לַמַּחֲזִיקִים בָּהּ, וְתֹמְכֶיהָ מְאֻשָּׁר: משלי ג
דְּרָכֶיהָ דַרְכֵי־נֹעַם וְכָל־נְתִיבוֹתֶיהָ שָׁלוֹם:
◂ הֲשִׁיבֵנוּ יהוה אֵלֶיךָ וְנָשׁוּבָה, חַדֵּשׁ יָמֵינוּ כְּקֶדֶם: איכה ה

The ארון קודש *is closed.*

חצי קדיש

ש״ץ: יִתְגַּדַּל וְיִתְקַדַּשׁ שְׁמֵהּ רַבָּא (קהל: אָמֵן)
בְּעָלְמָא דִּי בְרָא כִרְעוּתֵהּ
וְיַמְלִיךְ מַלְכוּתֵהּ
בְּחַיֵּיכוֹן וּבְיוֹמֵיכוֹן וּבְחַיֵּי דְכָל בֵּית יִשְׂרָאֵל
בַּעֲגָלָא וּבִזְמַן קָרִיב, וְאִמְרוּ אָמֵן. (קהל: אָמֵן)

קהל וש״ץ: יְהֵא שְׁמֵהּ רַבָּא מְבָרַךְ לְעָלַם וּלְעָלְמֵי עָלְמַיָּא.

ש״ץ: יִתְבָּרַךְ וְיִשְׁתַּבַּח וְיִתְפָּאַר וְיִתְרוֹמַם וְיִתְנַשֵּׂא
וְיִתְהַדָּר וְיִתְעַלֶּה וְיִתְהַלָּל
שְׁמֵהּ דְּקֻדְשָׁא בְּרִיךְ הוּא (קהל: בְּרִיךְ הוּא)
לְעֵלָּא מִן כָּל בִּרְכָתָא וְשִׁירָתָא, תֻּשְׁבְּחָתָא וְנֶחֱמָתָא
דַּאֲמִירָן בְּעָלְמָא, וְאִמְרוּ אָמֵן. (קהל: אָמֵן)

---

opening of the Ark, a ceremony in the present recalls the ancient past, when the Israelites carried the Ark, containing the Tablets, with them on all their journeys.

עֵץ־חַיִּים הִיא לַמַּחֲזִיקִים בָּהּ *It is a tree of life to those who grasp it.* The first humans were forbidden to eat from the Tree of Life "lest they live forever" (Gen. 3:22). In this fine instance of intertextuality the book of Proverbs tells us that im-

Musaf for Simḥat Torah

The following prayer, until "in former years" on page 1308, is said silently, standing with feet together. Take three steps forward and at the points indicated by ▾, bend the knees at the first word, bow at the second, and stand straight before saying God's name.

When I proclaim the LORD's name, give glory to our God. *Deut. 32*
O LORD, open my lips, so that my mouth may declare Your praise. *Ps. 51*

PATRIARCHS

▾בָּרוּךְ Blessed are You, LORD our God and God of our fathers,
God of Abraham, God of Isaac and God of Jacob;
the great, mighty and awesome God, God Most High,
who bestows acts of loving-kindness and creates all,
who remembers the loving-kindness of the fathers
and will bring a Redeemer to their children's children
for the sake of His name, in love.
King, Helper, Savior, Shield:
▾Blessed are You, LORD, Shield of Abraham.

DIVINE MIGHT

אַתָּה גִּבּוֹר You are eternally mighty, LORD.
You give life to the dead and have great power to save.

He makes the wind blow and the rain fall.

He sustains the living with loving-kindness,
and with great compassion revives the dead.
He supports the fallen, heals the sick,
sets captives free,
and keeps His faith with those who sleep in the dust.
Who is like You, Master of might,
and who can compare to You,
O King who brings death and gives life,
and makes salvation grow?
Faithful are You to revive the dead.
Blessed are You, LORD, who revives the dead.

מוסף לשמחת תורה

The following prayer, until קַדְמֹנִיּוֹת *on page 1309, is said silently, standing with feet together. Take three steps forward and at the points indicated by* ', *bend the knees at the first word, bow at the second, and stand straight before saying God's name.*

דברים לב כִּי שֵׁם יהוה אֶקְרָא, הָבוּ גֹדֶל לֵאלֹהֵינוּ:
תהלים נא אֲדֹנָי, שְׂפָתַי תִּפְתָּח, וּפִי יַגִּיד תְּהִלָּתֶךָ:

אבות

'בָּרוּךְ אַתָּה יהוה, אֱלֹהֵינוּ וֵאלֹהֵי אֲבוֹתֵינוּ
אֱלֹהֵי אַבְרָהָם, אֱלֹהֵי יִצְחָק, וֵאלֹהֵי יַעֲקֹב
הָאֵל הַגָּדוֹל הַגִּבּוֹר וְהַנּוֹרָא, אֵל עֶלְיוֹן
גּוֹמֵל חֲסָדִים טוֹבִים, וְקוֹנֵה הַכֹּל, וְזוֹכֵר חַסְדֵי אָבוֹת
וּמֵבִיא גוֹאֵל לִבְנֵי בְנֵיהֶם לְמַעַן שְׁמוֹ בְּאַהֲבָה.
מֶלֶךְ עוֹזֵר וּמוֹשִׁיעַ וּמָגֵן.
'בָּרוּךְ אַתָּה יהוה, מָגֵן אַבְרָהָם.

גבורות

אַתָּה גִּבּוֹר לְעוֹלָם אֲדֹנָי
מְחַיֵּה מֵתִים אַתָּה, רַב לְהוֹשִׁיעַ

מַשִּׁיב הָרוּחַ וּמוֹרִיד הַגֶּשֶׁם

מְכַלְכֵּל חַיִּים בְּחֶסֶד, מְחַיֵּה מֵתִים בְּרַחֲמִים רַבִּים
סוֹמֵךְ נוֹפְלִים, וְרוֹפֵא חוֹלִים, וּמַתִּיר אֲסוּרִים
וּמְקַיֵּם אֱמוּנָתוֹ לִישֵׁנֵי עָפָר.
מִי כָמְוֹךָ, בַּעַל גְּבוּרוֹת, וּמִי דּוֹמֶה לָּךְ
מֶלֶךְ, מֵמִית וּמְחַיֶּה וּמַצְמִיחַ יְשׁוּעָה.
וְנֶאֱמָן אַתָּה לְהַחֲיוֹת מֵתִים.
בָּרוּךְ אַתָּה יהוה, מְחַיֵּה הַמֵּתִים.

When saying the Amida silently, continue with "You are holy" on the next page.

KEDUSHA *During the Leader's Repetition, the following is said standing with feet together, rising on the toes at the words indicated by* ▴.

Cong. then Leader: נַעֲרִיצְךָ We will revere and sanctify You with the words uttered by the holy Seraphim who sanctify Your name in the Sanctuary;
as is written by Your prophet:
"They call out to one another, saying: *Is. 6*

Cong. then Leader: ▴Holy, ▴holy, ▴holy is the LORD of hosts;
the whole world is filled with His glory."
His glory fills the universe.
His ministering angels ask each other,
"Where is the place of His glory?"
Those facing them say "Blessed –"

Cong. then Leader: "▴Blessed is the LORD's glory from His place." *Ezek. 3*
From His place may He turn with compassion
and be gracious to the people who proclaim the unity
of His name, morning and evening, every day, continually,
twice each day reciting in love the Shema:

Cong. then Leader: "Listen, Israel, the LORD is our God, the LORD is One." *Deut. 6*
He is our God, He is our Father, He is our King,
He is our Savior – and He, in His compassion,
will let us hear a second time in the presence of all that lives,
His promise "to be your God. *Num. 15*
I am the LORD your God."

Cong. then Leader: Glorious is our Glorious One, LORD our Master, *Ps. 8*
and glorious is Your name throughout the earth.
Then the LORD shall be King over all the earth; *Zech. 14*
on that day the LORD shall be One and His name One.

Leader: And in Your holy Writings it is written:

Cong. then Leader: "▴The LORD shall reign for ever. *Ps. 146*
He is your God, Zion, from generation to generation, Halleluya!"

Leader: לְדוֹר וָדוֹר From generation to generation we will declare Your greatness, and we will proclaim Your holiness for evermore.
Your praise, our God, shall not leave our mouth forever,
for You, God, are a great and holy King.
Blessed are You, LORD, the holy God.

The Leader continues with "You have chosen us" on the next page.

When saying the עמידה silently, continue with אַתָּה קָדוֹשׁ on the next page.

קדושה

During the חזרת הש״ץ, the following is said standing with feet together, rising on the toes at the words indicated by ˄.

קהל *then* ש״ץ: נַעֲרִיצְךָ וְנַקְדִּישְׁךָ כְּסוֹד שִׂיחַ שַׂרְפֵי קֹדֶשׁ
הַמַּקְדִּישִׁים שִׁמְךָ בַּקֹּדֶשׁ, כַּכָּתוּב עַל יַד נְבִיאֶךָ:
וְקָרָא זֶה אֶל־זֶה וְאָמַר ישעיה ו

קהל *then* ש״ץ: ˄קָדוֹשׁ, ˄קָדוֹשׁ, ˄קָדוֹשׁ, יהוה צְבָאוֹת, מְלֹא כָל־הָאָרֶץ כְּבוֹדוֹ:
כְּבוֹדוֹ מָלֵא עוֹלָם, מְשָׁרְתָיו שׁוֹאֲלִים זֶה לָזֶה, אַיֵּה מְקוֹם כְּבוֹדוֹ
לְעֻמָּתָם בָּרוּךְ יֹאמֵרוּ

קהל *then* ש״ץ: ˄בָּרוּךְ כְּבוֹד־יהוה מִמְּקוֹמוֹ: יחזקאל ג
מִמְּקוֹמוֹ הוּא יִפֶן בְּרַחֲמִים, וְיָחֹן עַם הַמְיַחֲדִים שְׁמוֹ
עֶרֶב וָבֹקֶר בְּכָל יוֹם תָּמִיד, פַּעֲמַיִם בְּאַהֲבָה שְׁמַע אוֹמְרִים

קהל *then* ש״ץ: שְׁמַע יִשְׂרָאֵל, יהוה אֱלֹהֵינוּ, יהוה אֶחָד: דברים ו
הוּא אֱלֹהֵינוּ, הוּא אָבִינוּ, הוּא מַלְכֵּנוּ, הוּא מוֹשִׁיעֵנוּ
וְהוּא יַשְׁמִיעֵנוּ בְּרַחֲמָיו שֵׁנִית לְעֵינֵי כָּל חָי
לִהְיוֹת לָכֶם לֵאלֹהִים במדבר טו
אֲנִי יהוה אֱלֹהֵיכֶם:

קהל *then* ש״ץ: אַדִּיר אַדִּירֵנוּ, יהוה אֲדֹנֵינוּ, מָה־אַדִּיר שִׁמְךָ בְּכָל־הָאָרֶץ: תהלים ח
וְהָיָה יהוה לְמֶלֶךְ עַל־כָּל־הָאָרֶץ זכריה יד
בַּיּוֹם הַהוּא יִהְיֶה יהוה אֶחָד וּשְׁמוֹ אֶחָד:

ש״ץ: וּבְדִבְרֵי קָדְשְׁךָ כָּתוּב לֵאמֹר

קהל *then* ש״ץ: ˄יִמְלֹךְ יהוה לְעוֹלָם, אֱלֹהַיִךְ צִיּוֹן לְדֹר וָדֹר, הַלְלוּיָהּ: תהלים קמו

ש״ץ: לְדוֹר וָדוֹר נַגִּיד גָּדְלֶךָ, וּלְנֵצַח נְצָחִים קְדֻשָּׁתְךָ נַקְדִּישׁ
וְשִׁבְחֲךָ אֱלֹהֵינוּ מִפִּינוּ לֹא יָמוּשׁ לְעוֹלָם וָעֶד
כִּי אֵל מֶלֶךְ גָּדוֹל וְקָדוֹשׁ אָתָּה.
בָּרוּךְ אַתָּה יהוה, הָאֵל הַקָּדוֹשׁ.

The שליח ציבור continues with אַתָּה בְחַרְתָּנוּ on the next page.

HOLINESS

אַתָּה קָדוֹשׁ You are holy and Your name is holy,
and holy ones praise You daily, Selah!
Blessed are You, LORD, the holy God.

HOLINESS OF THE DAY

אַתָּה בְחַרְתָּנוּ You have chosen us from among all peoples.
You have loved and favored us.
You have raised us above all tongues.
You have made us holy through Your commandments.
You have brought us near, our King, to Your service,
and have called us by Your great and holy name.

וַתִּתֶּן לָנוּ And You, LORD our God, have given us in love
festivals for rejoicing,
holy days and seasons for joy,
this day of the festival of the eighth day,
Shemini Atzeret, our time of rejoicing, a holy assembly
in memory of the exodus from Egypt.

וּמִפְּנֵי חֲטָאֵינוּ But because of our sins we were exiled from our land
and driven far from our country.
We cannot go up to appear and bow before You,
and to perform our duties in Your chosen House,
the great and holy Temple that was called by Your name,
because of the hand that was stretched out against Your Sanctuary.
May it be Your will, LORD our God and God of our ancestors,
merciful King,
that You in Your abounding compassion may once more
have mercy on us and on Your Sanctuary,
rebuilding it swiftly and adding to its glory.
Our Father, our King,
reveal the glory of Your kingdom to us swiftly.
Appear and be exalted over us in the sight of all that lives.
Bring back our scattered ones from among the nations,
and gather our dispersed people from the ends of the earth.

קדושת השם

אַתָּה קָדוֹשׁ וְשִׁמְךָ קָדוֹשׁ, וּקְדוֹשִׁים בְּכָל יוֹם יְהַלְלוּךָ סֶּלָה.
בָּרוּךְ אַתָּה יהוה, הָאֵל הַקָּדוֹשׁ.

קדושת היום

אַתָּה בְחַרְתָּנוּ מִכָּל הָעַמִּים
אָהַבְתָּ אוֹתָנוּ וְרָצִיתָ בָּנוּ, וְרוֹמַמְתָּנוּ מִכָּל הַלְּשׁוֹנוֹת
וְקִדַּשְׁתָּנוּ בְּמִצְוֹתֶיךָ, וְקֵרַבְתָּנוּ מַלְכֵּנוּ לַעֲבוֹדָתֶךָ
וְשִׁמְךָ הַגָּדוֹל וְהַקָּדוֹשׁ עָלֵינוּ קָרָאתָ.

וַתִּתֶּן לָנוּ יהוה אֱלֹהֵינוּ בְּאַהֲבָה
מוֹעֲדִים לְשִׂמְחָה, חַגִּים וּזְמַנִּים לְשָׂשׂוֹן
אֶת יוֹם הַשְּׁמִינִי חַג הָעֲצֶרֶת הַזֶּה
זְמַן שִׂמְחָתֵנוּ, מִקְרָא קֹדֶשׁ
זֵכֶר לִיצִיאַת מִצְרָיִם.

וּמִפְּנֵי חֲטָאֵינוּ גָּלִינוּ מֵאַרְצֵנוּ, וְנִתְרַחַקְנוּ מֵעַל אַדְמָתֵנוּ
וְאֵין אֲנַחְנוּ יְכוֹלִים לַעֲלוֹת וְלֵרָאוֹת וּלְהִשְׁתַּחֲווֹת לְפָנֶיךָ
וְלַעֲשׂוֹת חוֹבוֹתֵינוּ בְּבֵית בְּחִירָתֶךָ
בַּבַּיִת הַגָּדוֹל וְהַקָּדוֹשׁ שֶׁנִּקְרָא שִׁמְךָ עָלָיו
מִפְּנֵי הַיָּד שֶׁנִּשְׁתַּלְּחָה בְּמִקְדָּשֶׁךָ.
יְהִי רָצוֹן מִלְּפָנֶיךָ יהוה אֱלֹהֵינוּ וֵאלֹהֵי אֲבוֹתֵינוּ, מֶלֶךְ רַחֲמָן
שֶׁתָּשׁוּב וּתְרַחֵם עָלֵינוּ וְעַל מִקְדָּשְׁךָ בְּרַחֲמֶיךָ הָרַבִּים
וְתִבְנֵהוּ מְהֵרָה וּתְגַדֵּל כְּבוֹדוֹ.
אָבִינוּ מַלְכֵּנוּ, גַּלֵּה כְּבוֹד מַלְכוּתְךָ עָלֵינוּ מְהֵרָה
וְהוֹפַע וְהִנָּשֵׂא עָלֵינוּ לְעֵינֵי כָּל חָי
וְקָרֵב פְּזוּרֵינוּ מִבֵּין הַגּוֹיִם, וּנְפוּצוֹתֵינוּ כַּנֵּס מִיַּרְכְּתֵי אָרֶץ.

Lead us to Zion, Your city, in jubilation,
and to Jerusalem, home of Your Temple, with everlasting joy.
There we will prepare for You our obligatory offerings:
the regular daily offerings in their order
and the additional offerings according to their law.
And the additional offering of this day
of the festival of Shemini Atzeret.
we will prepare and offer before You in love,
in accord with Your will's commandment,
as You wrote for us in Your Torah
through Your servant Moses, by Your own word, as it is said:

בַּיּוֹם הַשְּׁמִינִי On the eighth day you shall hold an assembly; *Num. 29*
you shall do no laborious work.
And you shall offer a burnt-offering,
a fire-offering of pleasing odor to the Lord:
one bullock, one ram, seven yearling male lambs without blemish.

And their meal-offerings and wine-libations as ordained:
three-tenths of an ephah for each bull,
two-tenths of an ephah for the ram,
one-tenth of an ephah for each lamb,
wine for the libations, a male goat for atonement,
and two regular daily offerings according to their law.

אֱלֹהֵינוּ Our God and God of our ancestors,
merciful King, have compassion upon us.
You who are good and do good, respond to our call.
Return to us in Your abounding mercy
for the sake of our fathers who did Your will.
Rebuild Your Temple as at the beginning,
and establish Your Sanctuary on its site.
Let us witness its rebuilding and gladden us by its restoration.
Bring the priests back to their service,
the Levites to their song and music,
and the Israelites to their homes.

וַהֲבִיאֵנוּ לְצִיּוֹן עִירְךָ בְּרִנָּה
וְלִירוּשָׁלַיִם בֵּית מִקְדָּשְׁךָ בְּשִׂמְחַת עוֹלָם
וְשָׁם נַעֲשֶׂה לְפָנֶיךָ אֶת קָרְבְּנוֹת חוֹבוֹתֵינוּ
תְּמִידִים כְּסִדְרָם וּמוּסָפִים כְּהִלְכָתָם
וְאֶת מוּסַף יוֹם הַשְּׁמִינִי חַג הָעֲצֶרֶת הַזֶּה
נַעֲשֶׂה וְנַקְרִיב לְפָנֶיךָ בְּאַהֲבָה כְּמִצְוַת רְצוֹנֶךָ
כְּמוֹ שֶׁכָּתַבְתָּ עָלֵינוּ בְּתוֹרָתֶךָ
עַל יְדֵי מֹשֶׁה עַבְדֶּךָ מִפִּי כְבוֹדֶךָ, כָּאָמוּר

בַּיּוֹם הַשְּׁמִינִי, עֲצֶרֶת תִּהְיֶה לָכֶם במדבר כט
כָּל־מְלֶאכֶת עֲבֹדָה לֹא תַעֲשׂוּ:
וְהִקְרַבְתֶּם עֹלָה אִשֵּׁה רֵיחַ נִיחֹחַ לַיהוה
פַּר אֶחָד, אַיִל אֶחָד
כְּבָשִׂים בְּנֵי־שָׁנָה שִׁבְעָה, תְּמִימִם:

וּמִנְחָתָם וְנִסְכֵּיהֶם כִּמְדֻבָּר
שְׁלֹשָׁה עֶשְׂרֹנִים לַפָּר וּשְׁנֵי עֶשְׂרֹנִים לָאָיִל, וְעִשָּׂרוֹן לַכֶּבֶשׂ
וְיַיִן כְּנִסְכּוֹ, וְשָׂעִיר לְכַפֵּר, וּשְׁנֵי תְמִידִים כְּהִלְכָתָם.

אֱלֹהֵינוּ וֵאלֹהֵי אֲבוֹתֵינוּ, מֶלֶךְ רַחֲמָן רַחֵם עָלֵינוּ
טוֹב וּמֵטִיב הִדָּרֶשׁ לָנוּ
שׁוּבָה אֵלֵינוּ בַּהֲמוֹן רַחֲמֶיךָ בִּגְלַל אָבוֹת שֶׁעָשׂוּ רְצוֹנֶךָ.
בְּנֵה בֵיתְךָ כְּבַתְּחִלָּה וְכוֹנֵן מִקְדָּשְׁךָ עַל מְכוֹנוֹ
וְהַרְאֵנוּ בְּבִנְיָנוֹ, וְשַׂמְּחֵנוּ בְּתִקּוּנוֹ
וְהָשֵׁב כֹּהֲנִים לַעֲבוֹדָתָם, וּלְוִיִּם לְשִׁירָם וּלְזִמְרָם
וְהָשֵׁב יִשְׂרָאֵל לִנְוֵיהֶם.

וְשָׁם נַעֲלֶה There we will go up and appear and bow before You on the three pilgrimage festivals, as is written in Your Torah:

"Three times in the year all your males shall appear *Deut. 16*
before the LORD your God
at the place He will choose:
on Pesaḥ, Shavuot and Sukkot.
They shall not appear before the LORD empty-handed.
Each shall bring such a gift as he can, in proportion
to the blessing that the LORD your God grants you."

וְהַשִּׂיאֵנוּ Bestow on us, LORD our God,
the blessing of Your festivals
for life and peace, joy and gladness,
as You desired and promised to bless us.
Make us holy through Your commandments
and grant us a share in Your Torah;
satisfy us with Your goodness,
gladden us with Your salvation,
and purify our hearts to serve You in truth.
And grant us a heritage, LORD our God,
with joy and gladness, Your holy festivals.
May Israel, who sanctify Your name, rejoice in You.
Blessed are You, LORD,
who sanctifies Israel and the festive seasons.

TEMPLE SERVICE

רְצֵה Find favor, LORD our God, in Your people Israel
and their prayer.
Restore the service to Your most holy House,
and accept in love and favor the fire-offerings of Israel
and their prayer.
May the service of Your people Israel
always find favor with You.

וְשָׁם נַעֲלֶה וְנֵרָאֶה וְנִשְׁתַּחֲוֶה לְפָנֶיךָ בְּשָׁלֹשׁ פַּעֲמֵי רְגָלֵינוּ
כַּכָּתוּב בְּתוֹרָתֶךָ

שָׁלוֹשׁ פְּעָמִים בַּשָּׁנָה יֵרָאֶה כָל־זְכוּרְךָ אֶת־פְּנֵי יהוה אֱלֹהֶיךָ דברים טז
בַּמָּקוֹם אֲשֶׁר יִבְחָר
בְּחַג הַמַּצּוֹת, וּבְחַג הַשָּׁבֻעוֹת, וּבְחַג הַסֻּכּוֹת
וְלֹא יֵרָאֶה אֶת־פְּנֵי יהוה רֵיקָם:
אִישׁ כְּמַתְּנַת יָדוֹ
כְּבִרְכַּת יהוה אֱלֹהֶיךָ אֲשֶׁר נָתַן־לָךְ:

וְהַשִּׂיאֵנוּ יהוה אֱלֹהֵינוּ אֶת בִּרְכַּת מוֹעֲדֶיךָ
לְחַיִּים וּלְשָׁלוֹם, לְשִׂמְחָה וּלְשָׂשׂוֹן
כַּאֲשֶׁר רָצִיתָ וְאָמַרְתָּ לְבָרְכֵנוּ.
קַדְּשֵׁנוּ בְּמִצְוֹתֶיךָ, וְתֵן חֶלְקֵנוּ בְּתוֹרָתֶךָ
שַׂבְּעֵנוּ מִטּוּבֶךָ, וְשַׂמְּחֵנוּ בִּישׁוּעָתֶךָ
וְטַהֵר לִבֵּנוּ לְעָבְדְּךָ בֶּאֱמֶת
וְהַנְחִילֵנוּ יהוה אֱלֹהֵינוּ בְּשִׂמְחָה וּבְשָׂשׂוֹן
מוֹעֲדֵי קָדְשֶׁךָ וְיִשְׂמְחוּ בְךָ יִשְׂרָאֵל מְקַדְּשֵׁי שְׁמֶךָ.
בָּרוּךְ אַתָּה יהוה, מְקַדֵּשׁ יִשְׂרָאֵל וְהַזְּמַנִּים.

עבודה

רְצֵה יהוה אֱלֹהֵינוּ בְּעַמְּךָ יִשְׂרָאֵל, וּבִתְפִלָּתָם
וְהָשֵׁב אֶת הָעֲבוֹדָה לִדְבִיר בֵּיתֶךָ
וְאִשֵּׁי יִשְׂרָאֵל וּתְפִלָּתָם בְּאַהֲבָה תְקַבֵּל בְּרָצוֹן
וּתְהִי לְרָצוֹן תָּמִיד עֲבוֹדַת יִשְׂרָאֵל עַמֶּךָ.

If Kohanim say the Priestly Blessing during the Leader's Repetition, *turn to page 1166.*

And may our eyes witness Your return to Zion in compassion.
Blessed are You, LORD, who restores His Presence to Zion.

THANKSGIVING

Bow at the first nine words.

מוֹדִים‎ We give thanks to You,
for You are the LORD our God
and God of our ancestors
for ever and all time.
You are the Rock of our lives,
Shield of our salvation
from generation to generation.
We will thank You and
declare Your praise for our lives,
which are entrusted into Your hand;
for our souls,
which are placed in Your charge;
for Your miracles
which are with us every day;
and for Your wonders and favors
at all times, evening,
morning and midday.
You are good –
for Your compassion never fails.
You are compassionate –
for Your loving-kindnesses never cease.
We have always placed our hope in You.

As the Leader recites Modim, the congregation says quietly:

מוֹדִים‎ We give thanks to You,
for You are the LORD our God
and God of our ancestors,
God of all flesh,
who formed us
and formed the universe.
Blessings and thanks
are due to Your great
and holy name for giving us
life and sustaining us.
May You continue
to give us life
and sustain us;
and may You gather our
exiles to Your holy courts,
to keep Your decrees,
do Your will and serve You
with a perfect heart,
for it is for us
to give You thanks.
Blessed be God to whom
thanksgiving is due.

וְעַל כֻּלָּם‎ For all these things may Your name be
blessed and exalted, our King, continually, for ever and all time.
Let all that lives thank You, Selah! and praise Your name in truth,
God, our Savior and Help, Selah!
Blessed are You, LORD, whose name is "the Good"
and to whom thanks are due.

If כהנים *say* ברכת כהנים *during* חזרת הש״ץ, *turn to page 1167.*

וְתֶחֱזֶינָה עֵינֵינוּ בְּשׁוּבְךָ לְצִיּוֹן בְּרַחֲמִים.
בָּרוּךְ אַתָּה יהוה, הַמַּחֲזִיר שְׁכִינָתוֹ לְצִיּוֹן.

הודאה

Bow at the first five words.

׳מוֹדִים אֲנַחְנוּ לָךְ
שָׁאַתָּה הוּא יהוה אֱלֹהֵינוּ
וֵאלֹהֵי אֲבוֹתֵינוּ לְעוֹלָם וָעֶד.
צוּר חַיֵּינוּ, מָגֵן יִשְׁעֵנוּ
אַתָּה הוּא לְדוֹר וָדוֹר.
נוֹדֶה לְּךָ וּנְסַפֵּר תְּהִלָּתֶךָ
עַל חַיֵּינוּ הַמְּסוּרִים בְּיָדֶךָ
וְעַל נִשְׁמוֹתֵינוּ הַפְּקוּדוֹת לָךְ
וְעַל נִסֶּיךָ שֶׁבְּכָל יוֹם עִמָּנוּ
וְעַל נִפְלְאוֹתֶיךָ וְטוֹבוֹתֶיךָ
שֶׁבְּכָל עֵת
עֶרֶב וָבֹקֶר וְצָהֳרָיִם.
הַטּוֹב, כִּי לֹא כָלוּ רַחֲמֶיךָ
וְהַמְרַחֵם, כִּי לֹא תַמּוּ חֲסָדֶיךָ
מֵעוֹלָם קִוִּינוּ לָךְ.

As the שליח ציבור *recites* מודים, *the* קהל *says quietly:*

׳מוֹדִים אֲנַחְנוּ לָךְ
שָׁאַתָּה הוּא יהוה אֱלֹהֵינוּ
וֵאלֹהֵי אֲבוֹתֵינוּ
אֱלֹהֵי כָל בָּשָׂר
יוֹצְרֵנוּ, יוֹצֵר בְּרֵאשִׁית.
בְּרָכוֹת וְהוֹדָאוֹת
לְשִׁמְךָ הַגָּדוֹל וְהַקָּדוֹשׁ
עַל שֶׁהֶחֱיִיתָנוּ וְקִיַּמְתָּנוּ.
כֵּן תְּחַיֵּנוּ וּתְקַיְּמֵנוּ
וְתֶאֱסֹף גָּלֻיּוֹתֵינוּ
לְחַצְרוֹת קָדְשֶׁךָ
לִשְׁמֹר חֻקֶּיךָ
וְלַעֲשׂוֹת רְצוֹנֶךָ וּלְעָבְדְּךָ
בְּלֵבָב שָׁלֵם
עַל שֶׁאֲנַחְנוּ מוֹדִים לָךְ.
בָּרוּךְ אֵל הַהוֹדָאוֹת.

וְעַל כֻּלָּם יִתְבָּרַךְ וְיִתְרוֹמַם שִׁמְךָ מַלְכֵּנוּ תָּמִיד לְעוֹלָם וָעֶד.
וְכֹל הַחַיִּים יוֹדְוּךָ סֶּלָה, וִיהַלְלוּ אֶת שִׁמְךָ בֶּאֱמֶת
הָאֵל יְשׁוּעָתֵנוּ וְעֶזְרָתֵנוּ סֶלָה.
׳בָּרוּךְ אַתָּה יהוה, הַטּוֹב שִׁמְךָ וּלְךָ נָאֶה לְהוֹדוֹת.

In most congregations, he Priestly Blessing is not said, and the Leader says the following:
Our God and God of our fathers, bless us with the threefold blessing in the Torah, written by the hand of Moses Your servant and pronounced by Aaron and his sons the priests, Your holy people, as it is said:

May the LORD bless you and protect you. *Num. 6*
Cong: May it be Your will.
May the LORD make His face shine on you and be gracious to you.
Cong: May it be Your will.
May the LORD turn His face toward you, and grant you peace.
Cong: May it be Your will.

PEACE

שִׂים שָׁלוֹם Grant peace, goodness and blessing,
grace, loving-kindness and compassion to us
and all Israel Your people.
Bless us, our Father, all as one, with the light of Your face,
for by the light of Your face You have given us, LORD our God,
the Torah of life and love of kindness,
righteousness, blessing, compassion, life and peace.
May it be good in Your eyes to bless Your people Israel
at every time, in every hour, with Your peace.
Blessed are You, LORD, who blesses His people Israel with peace.

The following verse concludes the Leader's Repetition of the Amida.
Some also say it here as part of the silent Amida.
May the words of my mouth and the meditation of my heart *Ps. 19*
find favor before You, LORD, my Rock and Redeemer.

אֱלֹהַי My God, *Berakhot 17a*
guard my tongue from evil and my lips from deceitful speech.
To those who curse me, let my soul be silent;
may my soul be to all like the dust.
Open my heart to Your Torah
and let my soul pursue Your commandments.
As for all who plan evil against me,
swiftly thwart their counsel and frustrate their plans.

In most congregations, ברכת כהנים *is not said, and the* שליח ציבור *says the following:*

אֱלֹהֵינוּ וֵאלֹהֵי אֲבוֹתֵינוּ, בָּרְכֵנוּ בַבְּרָכָה הַמְשֻׁלֶּשֶׁת בַּתּוֹרָה, הַכְּתוּבָה עַל יְדֵי מֹשֶׁה עַבְדֶּךָ, הָאֲמוּרָה מִפִּי אַהֲרֹן וּבָנָיו כֹּהֲנִים עַם קְדוֹשֶׁיךָ, כָּאָמוּר

במדבר ו יְבָרֶכְךָ יהוה וְיִשְׁמְרֶךָ: קהל: כֵּן יְהִי רָצוֹן
יָאֵר יהוה פָּנָיו אֵלֶיךָ וִיחֻנֶּךָּ: קהל: כֵּן יְהִי רָצוֹן
יִשָּׂא יהוה פָּנָיו אֵלֶיךָ וְיָשֵׂם לְךָ שָׁלוֹם: קהל: כֵּן יְהִי רָצוֹן

שלום

שִׂים שָׁלוֹם טוֹבָה וּבְרָכָה, חֵן וָחֶסֶד וְרַחֲמִים
עָלֵינוּ וְעַל כָּל יִשְׂרָאֵל עַמֶּךָ.
בָּרְכֵנוּ אָבִינוּ כֻּלָּנוּ כְּאֶחָד בְּאוֹר פָּנֶיךָ
כִּי בְאוֹר פָּנֶיךָ נָתַתָּ לָּנוּ, יהוה אֱלֹהֵינוּ
תּוֹרַת חַיִּים וְאַהֲבַת חֶסֶד
וּצְדָקָה וּבְרָכָה וְרַחֲמִים וְחַיִּים וְשָׁלוֹם.
וְטוֹב בְּעֵינֶיךָ לְבָרֵךְ אֶת עַמְּךָ יִשְׂרָאֵל
בְּכָל עֵת וּבְכָל שָׁעָה בִּשְׁלוֹמֶךָ.
בָּרוּךְ אַתָּה יהוה, הַמְבָרֵךְ אֶת עַמּוֹ יִשְׂרָאֵל בַּשָּׁלוֹם.

The following verse concludes the חזרת הש״ץ.
Some also say it here as part of the silent עמידה.

תהלים יט יִהְיוּ לְרָצוֹן אִמְרֵי־פִי וְהֶגְיוֹן לִבִּי לְפָנֶיךָ, יהוה צוּרִי וְגֹאֲלִי:

ברכות יז. אֱלֹהַי
נְצֹר לְשׁוֹנִי מֵרָע וּשְׂפָתַי מִדַּבֵּר מִרְמָה
וְלִמְקַלְלַי נַפְשִׁי תִדֹּם, וְנַפְשִׁי כֶּעָפָר לַכֹּל תִּהְיֶה.
פְּתַח לִבִּי בְּתוֹרָתֶךָ, וּבְמִצְוֹתֶיךָ תִּרְדֹּף נַפְשִׁי.
וְכָל הַחוֹשְׁבִים עָלַי רָעָה, מְהֵרָה הָפֵר עֲצָתָם וְקַלְקֵל מַחֲשַׁבְתָּם.

Act for the sake of Your name;
act for the sake of Your right hand;
act for the sake of Your holiness;
act for the sake of Your Torah.

That Your beloved ones may be delivered, *Ps. 60*
save with Your right hand and answer me.
May the words of my mouth *Ps. 19*
and the meditation of my heart find favor before You,
LORD, my Rock and Redeemer.

Bow, take three steps back, then bow, first left, then right, then center, while saying:

May He who makes peace in His high places,
make peace for us and all Israel –
and say: Amen.

יְהִי רָצוֹן May it be Your will, LORD our God and God of our ancestors,
that the Temple be rebuilt speedily in our days,
and grant us a share in Your Torah.
And there we will serve You with reverence,
as in the days of old and as in former years.
Then the offering of Judah and Jerusalem *Mal. 3*
will be pleasing to the LORD as in the days of old and as in former years.

עֲשֵׂה לְמַעַן שְׁמֶךָ
עֲשֵׂה לְמַעַן יְמִינֶךָ
עֲשֵׂה לְמַעַן קְדֻשָּׁתֶךָ
עֲשֵׂה לְמַעַן תּוֹרָתֶךָ.

לְמַעַן יֵחָלְצוּן יְדִידֶיךָ, הוֹשִׁיעָה יְמִינְךָ וַעֲנֵנִי: תהלים ס

יִהְיוּ לְרָצוֹן אִמְרֵי־פִי וְהֶגְיוֹן לִבִּי לְפָנֶיךָ, יהוה צוּרִי וְגֹאֲלִי: תהלים יט

Bow, take three steps back, then bow, first left, then right, then center, while saying:

עֹשֶׂה שָׁלוֹם בִּמְרוֹמָיו
הוּא יַעֲשֶׂה שָׁלוֹם עָלֵינוּ וְעַל כָּל יִשְׂרָאֵל
וְאִמְרוּ אָמֵן.

יְהִי רָצוֹן מִלְּפָנֶיךָ יהוה אֱלֹהֵינוּ וֵאלֹהֵי אֲבוֹתֵינוּ
שֶׁיִּבָּנֶה בֵּית הַמִּקְדָּשׁ בִּמְהֵרָה בְיָמֵינוּ
וְתֵן חֶלְקֵנוּ בְּתוֹרָתֶךָ
וְשָׁם נַעֲבָדְךָ בְּיִרְאָה כִּימֵי עוֹלָם וּכְשָׁנִים קַדְמֹנִיּוֹת.
וְעָרְבָה לַיהוה מִנְחַת יְהוּדָה וִירוּשָׁלָםִ כִּימֵי עוֹלָם וּכְשָׁנִים קַדְמֹנִיּוֹת: מלאכי ג

FULL KADDISH

Some have the custom to include additional responses in Full Kaddish. They can be found in the version on *page 1464.*

Leader: יִתְגַּדַּל Magnified and sanctified may His great name be,
in the world He created by His will.
May He establish His kingdom
in your lifetime and in your days,
and in the lifetime of all the house of Israel,
swiftly and soon –
and say: Amen.

All: May His great name be blessed
for ever and all time.

Leader: Blessed and praised,
glorified and exalted,
raised and honored,
uplifted and lauded
be the name of the Holy One,
blessed be He,
beyond any blessing,
song, praise and consolation
uttered in the world –
and say: Amen.

May the prayers and pleas of all Israel
be accepted by their Father in heaven –
and say: Amen.

May there be great peace from heaven,
and life for us and all Israel –
and say: Amen.

Bow, take three steps back, as if taking leave of the Divine Presence, then bow, first left, then right, then center, while saying:

May He who makes peace in His high places,
make peace for us and all Israel –
and say: Amen.

קדיש שלם

Some have the custom to include additional responses in קדיש שלם.
They can be found in the version on page 1465.

ש״ץ: יִתְגַּדַּל וְיִתְקַדַּשׁ שְׁמֵהּ רַבָּא (קהל: אָמֵן)
בְּעָלְמָא דִּי בְרָא כִרְעוּתֵהּ
וְיַמְלִיךְ מַלְכוּתֵהּ
בְּחַיֵּיכוֹן וּבְיוֹמֵיכוֹן וּבְחַיֵּי דְכָל בֵּית יִשְׂרָאֵל
בַּעֲגָלָא וּבִזְמַן קָרִיב
וְאִמְרוּ אָמֵן. (קהל: אָמֵן)

קהל וש״ץ: יְהֵא שְׁמֵהּ רַבָּא מְבָרַךְ לְעָלַם וּלְעָלְמֵי עָלְמַיָּא.

ש״ץ: יִתְבָּרַךְ וְיִשְׁתַּבַּח וְיִתְפָּאַר
וְיִתְרוֹמַם וְיִתְנַשֵּׂא וְיִתְהַדָּר וְיִתְעַלֶּה וְיִתְהַלָּל
שְׁמֵהּ דְּקֻדְשָׁא בְּרִיךְ הוּא (קהל: בְּרִיךְ הוּא)
לְעֵלָּא מִן כָּל בִּרְכָתָא וְשִׁירָתָא, תֻּשְׁבְּחָתָא וְנֶחֱמָתָא
דַּאֲמִירָן בְּעָלְמָא
וְאִמְרוּ אָמֵן. (קהל: אָמֵן)

תִּתְקַבַּל צְלוֹתְהוֹן וּבָעוּתְהוֹן דְּכָל יִשְׂרָאֵל
קֳדָם אֲבוּהוֹן דִּי בִשְׁמַיָּא
וְאִמְרוּ אָמֵן. (קהל: אָמֵן)

יְהֵא שְׁלָמָא רַבָּא מִן שְׁמַיָּא
וְחַיִּים, עָלֵינוּ וְעַל כָּל יִשְׂרָאֵל
וְאִמְרוּ אָמֵן. (קהל: אָמֵן)

Bow, take three steps back, as if taking leave of the Divine Presence, then bow, first left, then right, then center, while saying:

עֹשֶׂה שָׁלוֹם בִּמְרוֹמָיו
הוּא יַעֲשֶׂה שָׁלוֹם עָלֵינוּ וְעַל כָּל יִשְׂרָאֵל
וְאִמְרוּ אָמֵן. (קהל: אָמֵן)

אֵין כֵּאלֹהֵינוּ There is none like our God, none like our LORD,
none like our King, none like our Savior.
Who is like our God? Who is like our LORD?
Who is like our King? Who is like our Savior?
We will thank our God, we will thank our LORD,
we will thank our King, we will thank our Savior.
Blessed is our God, blessed is our LORD,
blessed is our King, blessed is our Savior.
You are our God, You are our LORD,
You are our King, You are our Savior.
You are He to whom our ancestors offered the fragrant incense.

פִּטּוּם הַקְּטֹרֶת The incense mixture consisted of balsam, onycha, galbanum and frankincense, each weighing seventy manehs; myrrh, cassia, spikenard and saffron, each weighing sixteen manehs; twelve manehs of costus, three of aromatic bark; nine of cinnamon; nine kabs of Carsina lye; three seahs and three kabs of Cyprus wine. If Cyprus wine was not available, old white wine might be used. A quarter of a kab of Sodom salt, and a minute amount of a smoke-raising herb. Rabbi Nathan says: Also a minute amount of Jordan amber. If one added honey to the mixture, he rendered it unfit for sacred use. If he omitted any one of its ingredients, he is guilty of a capital offense. *Keritot 6a*

Rabban Shimon ben Gamliel says: "Balsam" refers to the sap that drips from the balsam tree. The Carsina lye was used for bleaching the onycha to improve it. The Cyprus wine was used to soak the onycha in it to make it pungent. Though urine is suitable for this purpose, it is not brought into the Temple out of respect.

These were the psalms which the Levites used to recite in the Temple: *Mishna, Tamid 7*
On the first day of the week they used to say: "The earth is the LORD's *Ps. 24*
and all it contains, the world and all who live in it."
On the second day they used to say: "Great is the LORD and *Ps. 48*
greatly to be praised in the city of God, on His holy mountain."
On the third day they used to say: "God stands in the divine assembly. *Ps. 82*
Among the judges He delivers judgment."
On the fourth day they used to say: "God of retribution, LORD, *Ps. 94*
God of retribution, appear."
On the fifth day they used to say: "Sing for joy to God, our strength. *Ps. 81*
Shout aloud to the God of Jacob."
On the sixth day they used to say: "The LORD reigns: He is robed in majesty; *Ps. 93*
the LORD is robed, girded with strength;
the world is firmly established; it cannot be moved."

אֵין כֵּאלֹהֵינוּ, אֵין כַּאדוֹנֵינוּ, אֵין כְּמַלְכֵּנוּ, אֵין כְּמוֹשִׁיעֵנוּ.
מִי כֵאלֹהֵינוּ, מִי כַאדוֹנֵינוּ, מִי כְמַלְכֵּנוּ, מִי כְמוֹשִׁיעֵנוּ.
נוֹדֶה לֵאלֹהֵינוּ, נוֹדֶה לַאדוֹנֵינוּ, נוֹדֶה לְמַלְכֵּנוּ, נוֹדֶה לְמוֹשִׁיעֵנוּ.
בָּרוּךְ אֱלֹהֵינוּ, בָּרוּךְ אֲדוֹנֵינוּ, בָּרוּךְ מַלְכֵּנוּ, בָּרוּךְ מוֹשִׁיעֵנוּ.
אַתָּה הוּא אֱלֹהֵינוּ, אַתָּה הוּא אֲדוֹנֵינוּ,
אַתָּה הוּא מַלְכֵּנוּ, אַתָּה הוּא מוֹשִׁיעֵנוּ.
אַתָּה הוּא שֶׁהִקְטִירוּ אֲבוֹתֵינוּ לְפָנֶיךָ אֶת קְטֹרֶת הַסַּמִּים.

פִּטּוּם הַקְּטֹרֶת. הַצֳּרִי, וְהַצִּפֹּרֶן, וְהַחֶלְבְּנָה, וְהַלְּבוֹנָה מִשְׁקַל שִׁבְעִים שִׁבְעִים מָנֶה, מֹר, וּקְצִיעָה, שִׁבֹּלֶת נֵרְדְּ, וְכַרְכֹּם מִשְׁקַל שִׁשָּׁה עָשָׂר שִׁשָּׁה עָשָׂר מָנֶה, הַקֹּשְׁטְ שְׁנֵים עָשָׂר, קִלּוּפָה שְׁלֹשָׁה, וְקִנָּמוֹן תִּשְׁעָה, בֹּרִית כַּרְשִׁינָה תִּשְׁעָה קַבִּין, יֵין קַפְרִיסִין סְאִין תְּלָת וְקַבִּין תְּלָתָא, וְאִם אֵין לוֹ יֵין קַפְרִיסִין, מֵבִיא חֲמַר חִוַּרְיָן עַתִּיק. מֶלַח סְדוֹמִית רֹבַע, מַעֲלֶה עָשָׁן כָּל שֶׁהוּא. רַבִּי נָתָן הַבַּבְלִי אוֹמֵר: אַף כִּפַּת הַיַּרְדֵּן כָּל שֶׁהוּא, וְאִם נָתַן בָּהּ דְּבַשׁ פְּסָלָהּ, וְאִם חִסֵּר אֶחָד מִכָּל סַמָּנֶיהָ, חַיָּב מִיתָה. כריתות ו.

רַבָּן שִׁמְעוֹן בֶּן גַּמְלִיאֵל אוֹמֵר: הַצֳּרִי אֵינוֹ אֶלָּא שְׂרָף הַנּוֹטֵף מֵעֲצֵי הַקְּטָף. בֹּרִית כַּרְשִׁינָה שֶׁשָּׁפִין בָּהּ אֶת הַצִּפֹּרֶן כְּדֵי שֶׁתְּהֵא נָאָה, יֵין קַפְרִיסִין שֶׁשּׁוֹרִין בּוֹ אֶת הַצִּפֹּרֶן כְּדֵי שֶׁתְּהֵא עַזָּה, וַהֲלֹא מֵי רַגְלַיִם יָפִין לָהּ, אֶלָּא שֶׁאֵין מַכְנִיסִין מֵי רַגְלַיִם בַּמִּקְדָּשׁ מִפְּנֵי הַכָּבוֹד.

הַשִּׁיר שֶׁהַלְוִיִּם הָיוּ אוֹמְרִים בְּבֵית הַמִּקְדָּשׁ: משנה תמיד ז
בַּיּוֹם הָרִאשׁוֹן הָיוּ אוֹמְרִים, לַיהוה הָאָרֶץ וּמְלוֹאָהּ, תֵּבֵל וְיֹשְׁבֵי בָהּ: תהלים כד
בַּשֵּׁנִי הָיוּ אוֹמְרִים, גָּדוֹל יהוה וּמְהֻלָּל מְאֹד, בְּעִיר אֱלֹהֵינוּ הַר־קָדְשׁוֹ: תהלים מח
בַּשְּׁלִישִׁי הָיוּ אוֹמְרִים, אֱלֹהִים נִצָּב בַּעֲדַת־אֵל, בְּקֶרֶב אֱלֹהִים יִשְׁפֹּט: תהלים פב
בָּרְבִיעִי הָיוּ אוֹמְרִים, אֵל־נְקָמוֹת יהוה, אֵל נְקָמוֹת הוֹפִיעַ: תהלים צד
בַּחֲמִישִׁי הָיוּ אוֹמְרִים, הַרְנִינוּ לֵאלֹהִים עוּזֵּנוּ, הָרִיעוּ לֵאלֹהֵי יַעֲקֹב: תהלים פא
בַּשִּׁשִּׁי הָיוּ אוֹמְרִים, יהוה מָלָךְ גֵּאוּת לָבֵשׁ תהלים צג
לָבֵשׁ יהוה עֹז הִתְאַזָּר, אַף־תִּכּוֹן תֵּבֵל בַּל־תִּמּוֹט:

On the Sabbath they used to say: "A psalm, a song for the Sabbath day" – *Ps. 92*
[meaning] a psalm and song for the time to come,
for the day which will be entirely Sabbath and rest for life everlasting.

It was taught in the Academy of Elijah: Whoever studies [Torah] laws every day *Megilla 28*
is assured that he will be destined for the World to Come, as it is said, "The ways *Hab. 3*
of the world are His" – read not, "ways" [*halikhot*] but "laws" [*halakhot*].

Rabbi Elazar said in the name of Rabbi Ḥanina: The disciples of the sages increase *Berakhot 64a*
peace in the world, as it is said, "And all your children shall be taught of the LORD, *Is. 54*
and great shall be the peace of your children [*banayikh*]." Read not *banayikh*,
"your children," but *bonayikh*, "your builders." Those who love Your Torah have *Ps. 119*
great peace; there is no stumbling block for them. May there be peace within your *Ps. 122*
ramparts, prosperity in your palaces. For the sake of my brothers and friends, I
shall say, "Peace be within you." For the sake of the House of the LORD our God,
I will seek your good. ▸ May the LORD grant strength to His people; may the *Ps. 29*
LORD bless His people with peace.

THE RABBIS' KADDISH

The following prayer, said by mourners, requires the presence of a minyan.
A transliteration can be found on page 1466.

Mourner: יִתְגַּדַּל Magnified and sanctified
may His great name be,
in the world He created by His will.
May He establish His kingdom in your lifetime
and in your days,
and in the lifetime of all the house of Israel,
swiftly and soon –
and say: Amen.

All: May His great name be blessed for ever and all time.

Mourner: Blessed and praised, glorified and exalted,
raised and honored, uplifted and lauded
be the name of the Holy One, blessed be He,
beyond any blessing,
song, praise and consolation uttered in the world –
and say: Amen.

בַּשַּׁבָּת הָיוּ אוֹמְרִים, מִזְמוֹר שִׁיר לְיוֹם הַשַּׁבָּת: תהלים צב
מִזְמוֹר שִׁיר לֶעָתִיד לָבוֹא, לְיוֹם שֶׁכֻּלּוֹ שַׁבָּת וּמְנוּחָה לְחַיֵּי הָעוֹלָמִים.

תָּנָא דְבֵי אֵלִיָּהוּ: כָּל הַשּׁוֹנֶה הֲלָכוֹת בְּכָל יוֹם, מֻבְטָח לוֹ שֶׁהוּא בֶּן עוֹלָם מגילה כח:
הַבָּא, שֶׁנֶּאֱמַר, הֲלִיכוֹת עוֹלָם לוֹ: אַל תִּקְרֵי הֲלִיכוֹת אֶלָּא הֲלָכוֹת. חבקוק ג

אָמַר רַבִּי אֶלְעָזָר, אָמַר רַבִּי חֲנִינָא: תַּלְמִידֵי חֲכָמִים מַרְבִּים שָׁלוֹם בָּעוֹלָם, ברכות סד.
שֶׁנֶּאֱמַר, וְכָל־בָּנַיִךְ לִמּוּדֵי יהוה, וְרַב שְׁלוֹם בָּנָיִךְ: אַל תִּקְרֵי בָּנָיִךְ, אֶלָּא ישעיה נד
בּוֹנָיִךְ. שָׁלוֹם רָב לְאֹהֲבֵי תוֹרָתֶךָ, וְאֵין־לָמוֹ מִכְשׁוֹל: יְהִי־שָׁלוֹם בְּחֵילֵךְ, תהלים קיט תהלים קכב
שַׁלְוָה בְּאַרְמְנוֹתָיִךְ: לְמַעַן אַחַי וְרֵעָי אֲדַבְּרָה־נָּא שָׁלוֹם בָּךְ: לְמַעַן בֵּית־
יהוה אֱלֹהֵינוּ אֲבַקְשָׁה טוֹב לָךְ: ◂ יהוה עֹז לְעַמּוֹ יִתֵּן, יהוה יְבָרֵךְ אֶת־עַמּוֹ תהלים כט
בַשָּׁלוֹם:

קדיש דרבנן

The following prayer, said by mourners, requires the presence of a מנין*.*
A transliteration can be found on page 1466.

אבל: יִתְגַּדַּל וְיִתְקַדַּשׁ שְׁמֵהּ רַבָּא (קהל: אָמֵן)
בְּעָלְמָא דִּי בְרָא כִרְעוּתֵהּ
וְיַמְלִיךְ מַלְכוּתֵהּ
בְּחַיֵּיכוֹן וּבְיוֹמֵיכוֹן וּבְחַיֵּי דְכָל בֵּית יִשְׂרָאֵל
בַּעֲגָלָא וּבִזְמַן קָרִיב, וְאִמְרוּ אָמֵן. (קהל: אָמֵן)

קהל ואבל: יְהֵא שְׁמֵהּ רַבָּא מְבָרַךְ לְעָלַם וּלְעָלְמֵי עָלְמַיָּא.

אבל: יִתְבָּרַךְ וְיִשְׁתַּבַּח וְיִתְפָּאַר וְיִתְרוֹמַם וְיִתְנַשֵּׂא
וְיִתְהַדָּר וְיִתְעַלֶּה וְיִתְהַלָּל
שְׁמֵהּ דְּקֻדְשָׁא בְּרִיךְ הוּא (קהל: בְּרִיךְ הוּא)
לְעֵלָּא מִן כָּל בִּרְכָתָא וְשִׁירָתָא, תֻּשְׁבְּחָתָא וְנֶחֱמָתָא
דַּאֲמִירָן בְּעָלְמָא, וְאִמְרוּ אָמֵן. (קהל: אָמֵן)

To Israel, to the teachers,
their disciples and their disciples' disciples,
and to all who engage in the study of Torah,
in this (*in Israel add:* holy) place or elsewhere,
may there come to them and you great peace,
grace, kindness and compassion, long life, ample sustenance
and deliverance, from their Father in Heaven –
and say: Amen.

May there be great peace from heaven,
and (good) life for us and all Israel –
and say: Amen.

Bow, take three steps back, as if taking leave of the Divine Presence, then bow, first left, then right, then center, while saying:
May He who makes peace in His high places,
in His compassion make peace for us and all Israel –
and say: Amen.

Stand while saying Aleinu. Bow at ▾.
עָלֵינוּ It is our duty to praise the Master of all,
and ascribe greatness to the Author of creation,
who has not made us like the nations of the lands
nor placed us like the families of the earth;
who has not made our portion like theirs,
nor our destiny like all their multitudes.
(For they worship vanity and emptiness,
and pray to a god who cannot save.)
▾But we bow in worship
and thank the Supreme King of kings,
the Holy One, blessed be He,
who extends the heavens and establishes the earth,
whose throne of glory is in the heavens above,
and whose power's Presence is in the highest of heights.
He is our God; there is no other.

עַל יִשְׂרָאֵל וְעַל רַבָּנָן
וְעַל תַּלְמִידֵיהוֹן וְעַל כָּל תַּלְמִידֵי תַלְמִידֵיהוֹן
וְעַל כָּל מָאן דְּעָסְקִין בְּאוֹרַיְתָא
דִּי בְּאַתְרָא (בארץ ישראל: קַדִּישָׁא) הָדֵין, וְדִי בְּכָל אֲתַר וַאֲתַר
יְהֵא לְהוֹן וּלְכוֹן שְׁלָמָא רַבָּא
חִנָּא וְחִסְדָּא, וְרַחֲמֵי, וְחַיֵּי אֲרִיכֵי, וּמְזוֹנֵי רְוִיחֵי
וּפֻרְקָנָא מִן קֳדָם אֲבוּהוֹן דִּי בִשְׁמַיָּא, וְאִמְרוּ אָמֵן. (קהל: אָמֵן)
יְהֵא שְׁלָמָא רַבָּא מִן שְׁמַיָּא
וְחַיִּים (טוֹבִים) עָלֵינוּ וְעַל כָּל יִשְׂרָאֵל, וְאִמְרוּ אָמֵן. (קהל: אָמֵן)

Bow, take three steps back, as if taking leave of the Divine Presence, then bow, first left, then right, then center, while saying:

עֹשֶׂה שָׁלוֹם בִּמְרוֹמָיו
הוּא יַעֲשֶׂה בְרַחֲמָיו שָׁלוֹם
עָלֵינוּ וְעַל כָּל יִשְׂרָאֵל, וְאִמְרוּ אָמֵן. (קהל: אָמֵן)

Stand while saying עָלֵינוּ*. Bow at* ▾.

עָלֵינוּ לְשַׁבֵּחַ לַאֲדוֹן הַכֹּל, לָתֵת גְּדֻלָּה לְיוֹצֵר בְּרֵאשִׁית
שֶׁלֹּא עָשָׂנוּ כְּגוֹיֵי הָאֲרָצוֹת, וְלֹא שָׂמָנוּ כְּמִשְׁפְּחוֹת הָאֲדָמָה
שֶׁלֹּא שָׂם חֶלְקֵנוּ כָּהֶם וְגוֹרָלֵנוּ כְּכָל הֲמוֹנָם.
(שֶׁהֵם מִשְׁתַּחֲוִים לְהֶבֶל וָרִיק וּמִתְפַּלְלִים אֶל אֵל לֹא יוֹשִׁיעַ.)
▾וַאֲנַחְנוּ כּוֹרְעִים וּמִשְׁתַּחֲוִים וּמוֹדִים
לִפְנֵי מֶלֶךְ מַלְכֵי הַמְּלָכִים, הַקָּדוֹשׁ בָּרוּךְ הוּא
שֶׁהוּא נוֹטֶה שָׁמַיִם וְיוֹסֵד אָרֶץ
וּמוֹשַׁב יְקָרוֹ בַּשָּׁמַיִם מִמַּעַל
וּשְׁכִינַת עֻזּוֹ בְּגָבְהֵי מְרוֹמִים.
הוּא אֱלֹהֵינוּ, אֵין עוֹד.

Truly He is our King, there is none else,
as it is written in His Torah:
"You shall know and take to heart this day that the LORD is God, *Deut. 4*
in heaven above and on earth below.
There is no other."

Therefore, we place our hope in You, LORD our God,
that we may soon see the glory of Your power,
when You will remove abominations from the earth,
and idols will be utterly destroyed,
when the world will be perfected under
the sovereignty of the Almighty,
when all humanity will call on Your name,
to turn all the earth's wicked toward You.
All the world's inhabitants will realize and know
that to You every knee must bow
and every tongue swear loyalty.
Before You, LORD our God, they will kneel and bow down
and give honor to Your glorious name.
They will all accept the yoke of Your kingdom,
and You will reign over them soon and for ever.
For the kingdom is Yours,
and to all eternity You will reign in glory,
as it is written in Your Torah:
"The LORD will reign for ever and ever." *Ex. 15*
▸ And it is said:
"Then the LORD shall be King over all the earth; *Zech. 14*
on that day the LORD shall be One and His name One."

Some add:

Have no fear of sudden terror or of the ruin when it overtakes the wicked. *Prov. 3*
Devise your strategy, but it will be thwarted; *Is. 8*
propose your plan, but it will not stand, for God is with us.
When you grow old, I will still be the same. *Is. 46*
When your hair turns gray, I will still carry you.
I made you, I will bear you, I will carry you, and I will rescue you.

אֱמֶת מַלְכֵּנוּ, אֶפֶס זוּלָתוֹ, כַּכָּתוּב בְּתוֹרָתוֹ
וְיָדַעְתָּ הַיּוֹם וַהֲשֵׁבֹתָ אֶל־לְבָבֶךָ דברים ד
כִּי יהוה הוּא הָאֱלֹהִים בַּשָּׁמַיִם מִמַּעַל וְעַל־הָאָרֶץ מִתָּחַת
אֵין עוֹד:

עַל כֵּן נְקַוֶּה לְּךָ יהוה אֱלֹהֵינוּ, לִרְאוֹת מְהֵרָה בְּתִפְאֶרֶת עֻזֶּךָ
לְהַעֲבִיר גִּלּוּלִים מִן הָאָרֶץ
וְהָאֱלִילִים כָּרוֹת יִכָּרֵתוּן
לְתַקֵּן עוֹלָם בְּמַלְכוּת שַׁדַּי.
וְכָל בְּנֵי בָשָׂר יִקְרְאוּ בִשְׁמֶךָ לְהַפְנוֹת אֵלֶיךָ כָּל רִשְׁעֵי אָרֶץ.
יַכִּירוּ וְיֵדְעוּ כָּל יוֹשְׁבֵי תֵבֵל
כִּי לְךָ תִּכְרַע כָּל בֶּרֶךְ, תִּשָּׁבַע כָּל לָשׁוֹן.
לְפָנֶיךָ יהוה אֱלֹהֵינוּ יִכְרְעוּ וְיִפֹּלוּ
וְלִכְבוֹד שִׁמְךָ יְקָר יִתֵּנוּ
וִיקַבְּלוּ כֻלָּם אֶת עֹל מַלְכוּתֶךָ
וְתִמְלֹךְ עֲלֵיהֶם מְהֵרָה לְעוֹלָם וָעֶד.
כִּי הַמַּלְכוּת שֶׁלְּךָ הִיא וּלְעוֹלְמֵי עַד תִּמְלֹךְ בְּכָבוֹד
כַּכָּתוּב בְּתוֹרָתֶךָ
יהוה יִמְלֹךְ לְעֹלָם וָעֶד: שמות טו
◄ וְנֶאֱמַר, וְהָיָה יהוה לְמֶלֶךְ עַל־כָּל־הָאָרֶץ זכריה יד
בַּיּוֹם הַהוּא יִהְיֶה יהוה אֶחָד וּשְׁמוֹ אֶחָד:

Some add:

אַל־תִּירָא מִפַּחַד פִּתְאֹם וּמִשֹּׁאַת רְשָׁעִים כִּי תָבֹא: משלי ג
עֻצוּ עֵצָה וְתֻפָר, דַּבְּרוּ דָבָר וְלֹא יָקוּם, כִּי עִמָּנוּ אֵל: ישעיה ח
וְעַד־זִקְנָה אֲנִי הוּא, וְעַד־שֵׂיבָה אֲנִי אֶסְבֹּל ישעיה מו
אֲנִי עָשִׂיתִי וַאֲנִי אֶשָּׂא וַאֲנִי אֶסְבֹּל וַאֲמַלֵּט:

MOURNER'S KADDISH

The following prayer, said by mourners, requires the presence of a minyan. A transliteration can be found on page 1467.

Mourner: יִתְגַּדַּל Magnified and sanctified
may His great name be,
in the world He created by His will.
May He establish His kingdom
in your lifetime and in your days,
and in the lifetime of all the house of Israel,
swiftly and soon –
and say: Amen.

All: May His great name be blessed
for ever and all time.

Mourner: Blessed and praised,
glorified and exalted,
raised and honored,
uplifted and lauded
be the name of the Holy One,
blessed be He,
beyond any blessing, song,
praise and consolation
uttered in the world –
and say: Amen.

May there be great peace from heaven,
and life for us and all Israel –
and say: Amen.

Bow, take three steps back, as if taking leave of the Divine Presence, then bow, first left, then right, then center, while saying:

May He who makes peace in His high places,
make peace for us and all Israel –
and say: Amen.

קדיש יתום

The following prayer, said by mourners, requires the presence of a מנין*. A transliteration can be found on page 1467.*

אבל: יִתְגַּדַּל וְיִתְקַדַּשׁ שְׁמֵהּ רַבָּא (קהל: אָמֵן)
בְּעָלְמָא דִּי בְרָא כִרְעוּתֵהּ
וְיַמְלִיךְ מַלְכוּתֵהּ
בְּחַיֵּיכוֹן וּבְיוֹמֵיכוֹן וּבְחַיֵּי דְכָל בֵּית יִשְׂרָאֵל
בַּעֲגָלָא וּבִזְמַן קָרִיב
וְאִמְרוּ אָמֵן. (קהל: אָמֵן)

קהל ואבל: יְהֵא שְׁמֵהּ רַבָּא מְבָרַךְ לְעָלַם וּלְעָלְמֵי עָלְמַיָּא.

אבל: יִתְבָּרַךְ וְיִשְׁתַּבַּח וְיִתְפָּאַר
וְיִתְרוֹמַם וְיִתְנַשֵּׂא וְיִתְהַדָּר וְיִתְעַלֶּה וְיִתְהַלָּל
שְׁמֵהּ דְּקֻדְשָׁא בְּרִיךְ הוּא (קהל: בְּרִיךְ הוּא)
לְעֵלָּא מִן כָּל בִּרְכָתָא וְשִׁירָתָא
תֻּשְׁבְּחָתָא וְנֶחֱמָתָא
דַּאֲמִירָן בְּעָלְמָא
וְאִמְרוּ אָמֵן. (קהל: אָמֵן)

יְהֵא שְׁלָמָא רַבָּא מִן שְׁמַיָּא
וְחַיִּים, עָלֵינוּ וְעַל כָּל יִשְׂרָאֵל
וְאִמְרוּ אָמֵן. (קהל: אָמֵן)

Bow, take three steps back, as if taking leave of the Divine Presence, then bow, first left, then right, then center, while saying:

עֹשֶׂה שָׁלוֹם בִּמְרוֹמָיו
הוּא יַעֲשֶׂה שָׁלוֹם עָלֵינוּ וְעַל כָּל יִשְׂרָאֵל
וְאִמְרוּ אָמֵן. (קהל: אָמֵן)

THE DAILY PSALM

One of the following psalms is said on the appropriate day of the week as indicated.
After the psalm, the Mourner's Kaddish is said.
Many congregations say the Daily Psalm after the Song of Glory, page 1328.

Sunday: הַיּוֹם Today is the first day of the week,
on which the Levites used to say this psalm in the Temple:

לְדָוִד מִזְמוֹר A psalm of David. The earth is the LORD's and all it contains, the world and all who live in it. For He founded it on the seas and established it on the streams. Who may climb the mountain of the LORD? Who may stand in His holy place? He who has clean hands and a pure heart, who has not taken My name in vain or sworn deceitfully. He shall receive a blessing from the LORD, and just reward from the God of his salvation. This is a generation of those who seek Him, the descendants of Jacob who seek Your presence, Selah! Lift up your heads, O gates; be uplifted, eternal doors, so that the King of glory may enter. Who is the King of glory? It is the LORD, strong and mighty, the LORD mighty in battle. Lift up your heads, O gates; be uplifted, eternal doors, that the King of glory may enter. ▸ Who is He, the King of glory? The LORD of hosts, He is the King of glory, Selah! *Ps. 24*

Mourner's Kaddish (page 1326)

Tuesday: הַיּוֹם Today is the third day of the week,
on which the Levites used to say this psalm in the Temple:

מִזְמוֹר לְאָסָף A psalm of Asaph. God stands in the Divine assembly. Among the judges He delivers judgment. How long will you judge unjustly, showing favor to the wicked? Selah. Do justice to the weak and the orphaned. Vindicate the poor and destitute. Rescue the weak and needy. Save them from the hand of the wicked. They do not know nor do they understand. They walk about in darkness while all the earth's foundations shake. I once said, "You are like gods, all of you are sons of the Most High." But you shall die like mere men, you will fall like any prince. ▸ Arise, O LORD, judge the earth, for all the nations are Your possession. *Ps. 82*

Mourner's Kaddish (page 1326)

Wednesday: הַיּוֹם Today is the fourth day of the week,
on which the Levites used to say this psalm in the Temple:

אֵל־נְקָמוֹת God of retribution, LORD, God of retribution, appear! Rise up, Judge of the earth. Repay to the arrogant what they deserve. How long shall the wicked, LORD, how long shall the wicked triumph? They pour *Ps. 94*

שיר של יום

One of the following psalms is said on the appropriate day of the week as indicated.
After the psalm, קדיש יתום *is said.*
Many congregations say the שיר של יום *after the* שיר הכבוד*, page 1329.*

Sunday הַיּוֹם יוֹם רִאשׁוֹן בְּשַׁבָּת, שֶׁבּוֹ הָיוּ הַלְוִיִּם אוֹמְרִים בְּבֵית הַמִּקְדָּשׁ:

תהלים כד לְדָוִד מִזְמוֹר, לַיהוה הָאָרֶץ וּמְלוֹאָהּ, תֵּבֵל וְיֹשְׁבֵי בָהּ: כִּי־הוּא עַל־יַמִּים יְסָדָהּ, וְעַל־נְהָרוֹת יְכוֹנְנֶהָ: מִי־יַעֲלֶה בְהַר־יהוה, וּמִי־יָקוּם בִּמְקוֹם קָדְשׁוֹ: נְקִי כַפַּיִם וּבַר־לֵבָב, אֲשֶׁר לֹא־נָשָׂא לַשָּׁוְא נַפְשִׁי, וְלֹא נִשְׁבַּע לְמִרְמָה: יִשָּׂא בְרָכָה מֵאֵת יהוה, וּצְדָקָה מֵאֱלֹהֵי יִשְׁעוֹ: זֶה דּוֹר דֹּרְשָׁו, מְבַקְשֵׁי פָנֶיךָ יַעֲקֹב סֶלָה: שְׂאוּ שְׁעָרִים רָאשֵׁיכֶם, וְהִנָּשְׂאוּ פִּתְחֵי עוֹלָם, וְיָבוֹא מֶלֶךְ הַכָּבוֹד: מִי זֶה מֶלֶךְ הַכָּבוֹד, יהוה עִזּוּז וְגִבּוֹר, יהוה גִּבּוֹר מִלְחָמָה: שְׂאוּ שְׁעָרִים רָאשֵׁיכֶם, וּשְׂאוּ פִּתְחֵי עוֹלָם, וְיָבֹא מֶלֶךְ הַכָּבוֹד: ◂ מִי הוּא זֶה מֶלֶךְ הַכָּבוֹד, יהוה צְבָאוֹת הוּא מֶלֶךְ הַכָּבוֹד סֶלָה:

קדיש יתום (*page 1327*)

Tuesday הַיּוֹם יוֹם שְׁלִישִׁי בְּשַׁבָּת, שֶׁבּוֹ הָיוּ הַלְוִיִּם אוֹמְרִים בְּבֵית הַמִּקְדָּשׁ:

תהלים פב מִזְמוֹר לְאָסָף, אֱלֹהִים נִצָּב בַּעֲדַת־אֵל, בְּקֶרֶב אֱלֹהִים יִשְׁפֹּט: עַד־מָתַי תִּשְׁפְּטוּ־עָוֶל, וּפְנֵי רְשָׁעִים תִּשְׂאוּ־סֶלָה: שִׁפְטוּ־דַל וְיָתוֹם, עָנִי וָרָשׁ הַצְדִּיקוּ: פַּלְּטוּ־דַל וְאֶבְיוֹן, מִיַּד רְשָׁעִים הַצִּילוּ: לֹא יָדְעוּ וְלֹא יָבִינוּ, בַּחֲשֵׁכָה יִתְהַלָּכוּ, יִמּוֹטוּ כָּל־מוֹסְדֵי אָרֶץ: אֲנִי־אָמַרְתִּי אֱלֹהִים אַתֶּם, וּבְנֵי עֶלְיוֹן כֻּלְּכֶם: אָכֵן כְּאָדָם תְּמוּתוּן, וּכְאַחַד הַשָּׂרִים תִּפֹּלוּ: ◂ קוּמָה אֱלֹהִים שָׁפְטָה הָאָרֶץ, כִּי־אַתָּה תִנְחַל בְּכָל־הַגּוֹיִם:

קדיש יתום (*page 1327*)

Wednesday הַיּוֹם יוֹם רְבִיעִי בְּשַׁבָּת, שֶׁבּוֹ הָיוּ הַלְוִיִּם אוֹמְרִים בְּבֵית הַמִּקְדָּשׁ:

תהלים צד אֵל־נְקָמוֹת יהוה, אֵל נְקָמוֹת הוֹפִיעַ: הִנָּשֵׂא שֹׁפֵט הָאָרֶץ, הָשֵׁב גְּמוּל עַל־גֵּאִים: עַד־מָתַי רְשָׁעִים, יהוה, עַד־מָתַי רְשָׁעִים יַעֲלֹזוּ:

out insolent words. All the evildoers are full of boasting. They crush Your people, LORD, and oppress Your inheritance. They kill the widow and the stranger. They murder the orphaned. They say, "The LORD does not see. The God of Jacob pays no heed." Take heed, you most brutish people. You fools, when will you grow wise? Will He who implants the ear not hear? Will He who formed the eye not see? Will He who disciplines nations – He who teaches man knowledge – not punish? The LORD knows that the thoughts of man are a mere fleeting breath. Happy is the man whom You discipline, LORD, the one You instruct in Your Torah, giving him tranquility in days of trouble, until a pit is dug for the wicked. For the LORD will not forsake His people, nor abandon His heritage. Judgment shall again accord with justice, and all the upright in heart will follow it. Who will rise up for me against the wicked? Who will stand up for me against wrongdoers? Had the LORD not been my help, I would soon have dwelt in death's silence. When I thought my foot was slipping, Your loving-kindness, LORD, gave me support. When I was filled with anxiety, Your consolations soothed my soul. Can a corrupt throne be allied with You? Can injustice be framed into law? They join forces against the life of the righteous, and condemn the innocent to death. But the LORD is my stronghold, my God is the Rock of my refuge. He will bring back on them their wickedness, and destroy them for their evil deeds. The LORD our God will destroy them.

▸ Come, let us sing for joy to the LORD; let us shout aloud to the Rock of *Ps. 95*
our salvation. Let us greet Him with thanksgiving, shout aloud to Him with songs of praise. For the LORD is the great God, the King great above all powers.

Mourner's Kaddish (on the next page)

Friday: הַיּוֹם Today is the sixth day of the week,
on which the Levites used to say this psalm in the Temple:

יהוה מָלָךְ The LORD reigns. He is robed in majesty. The LORD is robed, *Ps. 93*
girded with strength. The world is firmly established; it cannot be moved. Your throne stands firm as of old; You are eternal. Rivers lift up, LORD, rivers lift up their voice, rivers lift up their crashing waves. Mightier than the noise of many waters, than the mighty waves of the sea is the LORD on high. ▸ Your testimonies are very sure; holiness adorns Your House, LORD, for evermore.

יַבִּיעוּ יְדַבְּרוּ עָתָק, יִתְאַמְּרוּ כָּל־פֹּעֲלֵי אָוֶן: עַמְּךָ יהוה יְדַכְּאוּ, וְנַחֲלָתְךָ יְעַנּוּ: אַלְמָנָה וְגֵר יַהֲרֹגוּ, וִיתוֹמִים יְרַצֵּחוּ: וַיֹּאמְרוּ לֹא יִרְאֶה־יָּהּ, וְלֹא־יָבִין אֱלֹהֵי יַעֲקֹב: בִּינוּ בֹּעֲרִים בָּעָם, וּכְסִילִים מָתַי תַּשְׂכִּילוּ: הֲנֹטַע אֹזֶן הֲלֹא יִשְׁמָע, אִם־יֹצֵר עַיִן הֲלֹא יַבִּיט: הֲיֹסֵר גּוֹיִם הֲלֹא יוֹכִיחַ, הַמְלַמֵּד אָדָם דָּעַת: יהוה יֹדֵעַ מַחְשְׁבוֹת אָדָם, כִּי־הֵמָּה הָבֶל: אַשְׁרֵי הַגֶּבֶר אֲשֶׁר־תְּיַסְּרֶנּוּ יָּהּ, וּמִתּוֹרָתְךָ תְלַמְּדֶנּוּ: לְהַשְׁקִיט לוֹ מִימֵי רָע, עַד יִכָּרֶה לָרָשָׁע שָׁחַת: כִּי לֹא־יִטֹּשׁ יהוה עַמּוֹ, וְנַחֲלָתוֹ לֹא יַעֲזֹב: כִּי־עַד־צֶדֶק יָשׁוּב מִשְׁפָּט, וְאַחֲרָיו כָּל־יִשְׁרֵי־לֵב: מִי־יָקוּם לִי עִם־מְרֵעִים, מִי־יִתְיַצֵּב לִי עִם־פֹּעֲלֵי אָוֶן: לוּלֵי יהוה עֶזְרָתָה לִּי, כִּמְעַט שָׁכְנָה דוּמָה נַפְשִׁי: אִם־אָמַרְתִּי מָטָה רַגְלִי, חַסְדְּךָ יהוה יִסְעָדֵנִי: בְּרֹב שַׂרְעַפַּי בְּקִרְבִּי, תַּנְחוּמֶיךָ יְשַׁעַשְׁעוּ נַפְשִׁי: הַיְחָבְרְךָ כִּסֵּא הַוּוֹת, יֹצֵר עָמָל עֲלֵי־חֹק: יָגוֹדּוּ עַל־נֶפֶשׁ צַדִּיק, וְדָם נָקִי יַרְשִׁיעוּ: וַיְהִי יהוה לִי לְמִשְׂגָּב, וֵאלֹהַי לְצוּר מַחְסִי: וַיָּשֶׁב עֲלֵיהֶם אֶת־אוֹנָם, וּבְרָעָתָם יַצְמִיתֵם, יַצְמִיתֵם יהוה אֱלֹהֵינוּ:

תהלים צה ‹ לְכוּ נְרַנְּנָה לַיהוה, נָרִיעָה לְצוּר יִשְׁעֵנוּ: נְקַדְּמָה פָנָיו בְּתוֹדָה, בִּזְמִרוֹת נָרִיעַ לוֹ: כִּי אֵל גָּדוֹל יהוה, וּמֶלֶךְ גָּדוֹל עַל־כָּל־אֱלֹהִים:

קדיש יתום (*on the next page*)

Friday הַיּוֹם יוֹם שִׁשִּׁי בְּשַׁבָּת, שֶׁבּוֹ הָיוּ הַלְוִיִּם אוֹמְרִים בְּבֵית הַמִּקְדָּשׁ:

תהלים צג יהוה מָלָךְ, גֵּאוּת לָבֵשׁ, לָבֵשׁ יהוה עֹז הִתְאַזָּר, אַף־תִּכּוֹן תֵּבֵל בַּל־תִּמּוֹט: נָכוֹן כִּסְאֲךָ מֵאָז, מֵעוֹלָם אָתָּה: נָשְׂאוּ נְהָרוֹת יהוה, נָשְׂאוּ נְהָרוֹת קוֹלָם, יִשְׂאוּ נְהָרוֹת דָּכְיָם: מִקֹּלוֹת מַיִם רַבִּים, אַדִּירִים מִשְׁבְּרֵי־יָם, אַדִּיר בַּמָּרוֹם יהוה: ‹ עֵדֹתֶיךָ נֶאֶמְנוּ מְאֹד, לְבֵיתְךָ נַאֲוָה־קֹדֶשׁ, יהוה לְאֹרֶךְ יָמִים:

MOURNER'S KADDISH

The following prayer, said by mourners, requires the presence of a minyan.
A transliteration can be found on page 1467.

Mourner: יִתְגַּדַּל Magnified and sanctified
may His great name be,
in the world He created by His will.
May He establish His kingdom
in your lifetime and in your days,
and in the lifetime of all the house of Israel,
swiftly and soon –
and say: Amen.

All: May His great name be blessed
for ever and all time.

Mourner: Blessed and praised,
glorified and exalted,
raised and honored,
uplifted and lauded
be the name of the Holy One,
blessed be He,
beyond any blessing,
song, praise and consolation
uttered in the world –
and say: Amen.

May there be great peace from heaven,
and life for us and all Israel –
and say: Amen.

Bow, take three steps back, as if taking leave of the Divine Presence,
then bow, first left, then right, then center, while saying:

May He who makes peace in His high places,
make peace for us and all Israel –
and say: Amen.

קדיש יתום

The following prayer, said by mourners, requires the presence of a מנין.
A transliteration can be found on page 1467.

אבל: יִתְגַּדַּל וְיִתְקַדַּשׁ שְׁמֵהּ רַבָּא (קהל: אָמֵן)
בְּעָלְמָא דִּי בְרָא כִרְעוּתֵהּ
וְיַמְלִיךְ מַלְכוּתֵהּ
בְּחַיֵּיכוֹן וּבְיוֹמֵיכוֹן וּבְחַיֵּי דְכָל בֵּית יִשְׂרָאֵל
בַּעֲגָלָא וּבִזְמַן קָרִיב
וְאִמְרוּ אָמֵן. (קהל: אָמֵן)

קהל ואבל: יְהֵא שְׁמֵהּ רַבָּא מְבָרַךְ לְעָלַם וּלְעָלְמֵי עָלְמַיָּא.

אבל: יִתְבָּרַךְ וְיִשְׁתַּבַּח וְיִתְפָּאַר
וְיִתְרוֹמַם וְיִתְנַשֵּׂא וְיִתְהַדָּר וְיִתְעַלֶּה וְיִתְהַלָּל
שְׁמֵהּ דְּקֻדְשָׁא בְּרִיךְ הוּא (קהל: בְּרִיךְ הוּא)
לְעֵלָּא מִן כָּל בִּרְכָתָא וְשִׁירָתָא, תֻּשְׁבְּחָתָא וְנֶחֱמָתָא
דַּאֲמִירָן בְּעָלְמָא
וְאִמְרוּ אָמֵן. (קהל: אָמֵן)

יְהֵא שְׁלָמָא רַבָּא מִן שְׁמַיָּא
וְחַיִּים, עָלֵינוּ וְעַל כָּל יִשְׂרָאֵל
וְאִמְרוּ אָמֵן. (קהל: אָמֵן)

Bow, take three steps back, as if taking leave of the Divine Presence, then bow, first left, then right, then center, while saying:

עֹשֶׂה שָׁלוֹם בִּמְרוֹמָיו
הוּא יַעֲשֶׂה שָׁלוֹם עָלֵינוּ וְעַל כָּל יִשְׂרָאֵל
וְאִמְרוּ אָמֵן. (קהל: אָמֵן)

SONG OF GLORY

The Ark is opened and all stand.

Leader: I will sing sweet psalms and I will weave songs,
to You for whom my soul longs.

Cong: My soul yearns for the shelter of Your hand,
that all Your mystic secrets I might understand.

Leader: Whenever I speak of Your glory above,
my heart is yearning for Your love.

Cong: So Your glories I will proclaim,
and in songs of love give honor to Your name.

Leader: I will tell of Your glory though I have not seen You,
imagine and describe You, though I have not known You.

Cong: By the hand of Your prophets, through Your servants' mystery,
You gave a glimpse of Your wondrous majesty.

Leader: Recounting Your grandeur and Your glory,
of Your great deeds they told the story.

Cong: They depicted You, though not as You are,
but as You do: Your acts, Your power.

Leader: They represented You in many visions;
through them all You are One without divisions.

Cong: They saw You, now old, then young,
Your head with gray, with black hair hung.

Leader: Aged on the day of judgment, yet on the day of war,
a young warrior with mighty hands they saw.

Cong: Triumph like a helmet He wore on his head;
His right hand and holy arm to victory have led.

Leader: His curls are filled with dew drops of light,
His locks with fragments of the night.

Cong: He will glory in me, for He delights in me;
My diadem of beauty He shall be.

Leader: His head is like pure beaten gold;
Engraved on His brow, His sacred name behold.

Cong: For grace and glory, beauty and renown,
His people have adorned Him with a crown.

שיר הכבוד

The ארון קודש *is opened and all stand.*

ש״ץ: אַנְעִים זְמִירוֹת וְשִׁירִים אֶאֱרֹג, כִּי אֵלֶיךָ נַפְשִׁי תַעֲרֹג.
קהל: נַפְשִׁי חִמְּדָה בְּצֵל יָדֶךָ, לָדַעַת כָּל רָז סוֹדֶךָ.

ש״ץ: מִדֵּי דַבְּרִי בִּכְבוֹדֶךָ, הוֹמֶה לִבִּי אֶל דּוֹדֶיךָ.
קהל: עַל כֵּן אֲדַבֵּר בְּךָ נִכְבָּדוֹת, וְשִׁמְךָ אֲכַבֵּד בְּשִׁירֵי יְדִידוֹת.

ש״ץ: אֲסַפְּרָה כְבוֹדְךָ וְלֹא רְאִיתִיךָ, אֲדַמְּךָ אֲכַנְּךָ וְלֹא יְדַעְתִּיךָ.
קהל: בְּיַד נְבִיאֶיךָ בְּסוֹד עֲבָדֶיךָ, דִּמִּיתָ הֲדַר כְּבוֹד הוֹדֶךָ.

ש״ץ: גְּדֻלָּתְךָ וּגְבוּרָתֶךָ, כִּנּוּ לְתֹקֶף פְּעֻלָּתֶךָ.
קהל: דִּמּוּ אוֹתְךָ וְלֹא כְּפִי יֶשְׁךָ, וַיְשַׁוּוּךָ לְפִי מַעֲשֶׂיךָ.

ש״ץ: הִמְשִׁילוּךָ בְּרֹב חֶזְיוֹנוֹת, הִנְּךָ אֶחָד בְּכָל דִּמְיוֹנוֹת.
קהל: וַיֶּחֱזוּ בְךָ זִקְנָה וּבַחֲרוּת, וּשְׂעַר רֹאשְׁךָ בְּשֵׂיבָה וְשַׁחֲרוּת.

ש״ץ: זִקְנָה בְּיוֹם דִּין וּבַחֲרוּת בְּיוֹם קְרָב, כְּאִישׁ מִלְחָמוֹת יָדָיו לוֹ רָב.
קהל: חָבַשׁ כּוֹבַע יְשׁוּעָה בְּרֹאשׁוֹ, הוֹשִׁיעָה לּוֹ יְמִינוֹ וּזְרוֹעַ קָדְשׁוֹ.

ש״ץ: טַלְלֵי אוֹרוֹת רֹאשׁוֹ נִמְלָא, קְוֻצּוֹתָיו רְסִיסֵי לָיְלָה.
קהל: יִתְפָּאֵר בִּי כִּי חָפֵץ בִּי, וְהוּא יִהְיֶה לִּי לַעֲטֶרֶת צְבִי.

ש״ץ: כֶּתֶם טָהוֹר פָּז דְּמוּת רֹאשׁוֹ, וְחַק עַל מֵצַח כְּבוֹד שֵׁם קָדְשׁוֹ.
קהל: לְחֵן וּלְכָבוֹד צְבִי תִפְאָרָה, אֻמָּתוֹ לוֹ עִטְּרָה עֲטָרָה.

Leader: Like a youth's, His hair in locks unfurls;
Its black tresses flowing in curls.

Cong: Jerusalem, His splendor, is the dwelling place of right;
may He prize it as His highest delight.

Leader: Like a crown in His hand may His treasured people be,
a turban of beauty and of majesty.

Cong: He bore them, carried them, with a crown He adorned them.
They were precious in His sight, and He honored them.

Leader: His glory is on me; my glory is on Him.
He is near to me when I call to Him.

Cong: He is bright and rosy; red will be His dress,
when He comes from Edom, treading the winepress.

Leader: He showed the tefillin-knot to Moses, humble, wise,
when the Lord's likeness was before his eyes.

Cong: He delights in His people; the humble He does raise –
He glories in them; He sits enthroned upon their praise.

Leader: Your first word, Your call to every age, is true:
O seek the people who seek You.

Cong: My many songs please take and hear
and may my hymn of joy to You come near.

Leader: May my praise be a crown for Your head,
and like incense before You, the prayers I have said.

Cong: May a poor man's song be precious in Your eyes,
like a song sung over sacrifice.

Leader: To the One who sustains all, may my blessing take flight:
Creator, Life-Giver, God of right and might.

Cong: And when I offer blessing, to me Your head incline:
accepting it as spice, fragrant and fine.

Leader: May my prayer be to You sweet song.
For You my soul will always long.

The Ark is closed.

Yours, Lord, are the greatness and the power, *I Chr. 29*
the glory, the majesty and splendor, for everything in heaven and earth is Yours.
Yours, Lord, is the kingdom; You are exalted as Head over all.
▸ Who can tell of the mighty acts of the Lord and make all His praise be heard? *Ps. 106*

ש״ץ: מַחְלְפוֹת רֹאשׁוֹ כְּבִימֵי בְחוּרוֹת, קְוֻצּוֹתָיו תַּלְתַּלִּים שְׁחוֹרוֹת.
קהל: נְוֵה הַצֶּדֶק צְבִי תִפְאַרְתּוֹ, יַעֲלֶה נָּא עַל רֹאשׁ שִׂמְחָתוֹ.

ש״ץ: סְגֻלָּתוֹ תְּהִי בְיָדוֹ עֲטֶרֶת, וּצְנִיף מְלוּכָה צְבִי תִפְאֶרֶת.
קהל: עֲמוּסִים נְשָׂאָם, עֲטֶרֶת עִנְּדָם, מֵאֲשֶׁר יָקְרוּ בְעֵינָיו כִּבְּדָם.

ש״ץ: פְּאֵרוֹ עָלַי וּפְאֵרִי עָלָיו, וְקָרוֹב אֵלַי בְּקָרְאִי אֵלָיו.
קהל: צַח וְאָדֹם לִלְבוּשׁוֹ אָדֹם, פּוּרָה בְדָרְכוֹ בְּבוֹאוֹ מֵאֱדוֹם.

ש״ץ: קֶשֶׁר תְּפִלִּין הֶרְאָה לֶעָנָו, תְּמוּנַת יהוה לְנֶגֶד עֵינָיו.
קהל: רוֹצֶה בְעַמּוֹ עֲנָוִים יְפָאֵר, יוֹשֵׁב תְּהִלּוֹת בָּם לְהִתְפָּאֵר.

ש״ץ: רֹאשׁ דְּבָרְךָ אֱמֶת קוֹרֵא מֵרֹאשׁ דּוֹר וָדוֹר, עַם דּוֹרֶשְׁךָ דְּרֹשׁ.
קהל: שִׁית הֲמוֹן שִׁירַי נָא עָלֶיךָ, וְרִנָּתִי תִּקְרַב אֵלֶיךָ.

ש״ץ: תְּהִלָּתִי תְּהִי לְרֹאשְׁךָ עֲטֶרֶת, וּתְפִלָּתִי תִּכּוֹן קְטֹרֶת.
קהל: תִּיקַר שִׁירַת רָשׁ בְּעֵינֶיךָ, כַּשִּׁיר יוּשַׁר עַל קָרְבָּנֶיךָ.

ש״ץ: בִּרְכָתִי תַעֲלֶה לְרֹאשׁ מַשְׁבִּיר, מְחוֹלֵל וּמוֹלִיד, צַדִּיק כַּבִּיר.
קהל: וּבְבִרְכָתִי תְנַעֲנַע לִי רֹאשׁ, וְאוֹתָהּ קַח לְךָ כִּבְשָׂמִים רֹאשׁ.

ש״ץ: יֶעֱרַב נָא שִׂיחִי עָלֶיךָ, כִּי נַפְשִׁי תַעֲרֹג אֵלֶיךָ.

The ארון קודש *is closed.*

דברי הימים א׳ כט
לְךָ יהוה הַגְּדֻלָּה וְהַגְּבוּרָה וְהַתִּפְאֶרֶת וְהַנֵּצַח וְהַהוֹד
כִּי־כֹל בַּשָּׁמַיִם וּבָאָרֶץ
לְךָ יהוה הַמַּמְלָכָה וְהַמִּתְנַשֵּׂא לְכֹל לְרֹאשׁ:
תהלים קו
◂ מִי יְמַלֵּל גְּבוּרוֹת יהוה, יַשְׁמִיעַ כָּל־תְּהִלָּתוֹ:

MOURNER'S KADDISH

The following prayer, said by mourners, requires the presence of a minyan. A transliteration can be found on page 1467.

Mourner: יִתְגַּדַּל Magnified and sanctified
may His great name be,
in the world He created by His will.
May He establish His kingdom
in your lifetime and in your days,
and in the lifetime of all the house of Israel,
swiftly and soon –
and say: Amen.

All: May His great name be blessed
for ever and all time.

Mourner: Blessed and praised,
glorified and exalted,
raised and honored,
uplifted and lauded
be the name of the Holy One,
blessed be He,
beyond any blessing, song,
praise and consolation
uttered in the world –
and say: Amen.

May there be great peace from heaven,
and life for us and all Israel –
and say: Amen.

Bow, take three steps back, as if taking leave of the Divine Presence, then bow, first left, then right, then center, while saying:

May He who makes peace in His high places,
make peace for us and all Israel –
and say: Amen.

קדיש יתום

The following prayer, said by mourners, requires the presence of a מנין.
A transliteration can be found on page 1467.

אבל: יִתְגַּדַּל וְיִתְקַדַּשׁ שְׁמֵהּ רַבָּא (קהל: אָמֵן)
בְּעָלְמָא דִּי בְרָא כִרְעוּתֵהּ
וְיַמְלִיךְ מַלְכוּתֵהּ
בְּחַיֵּיכוֹן וּבְיוֹמֵיכוֹן וּבְחַיֵּי דְכָל בֵּית יִשְׂרָאֵל
בַּעֲגָלָא וּבִזְמַן קָרִיב
וְאִמְרוּ אָמֵן. (קהל: אָמֵן)

קהל ואבל: יְהֵא שְׁמֵהּ רַבָּא מְבָרַךְ לְעָלַם וּלְעָלְמֵי עָלְמַיָּא.

אבל: יִתְבָּרַךְ וְיִשְׁתַּבַּח וְיִתְפָּאַר
וְיִתְרוֹמַם וְיִתְנַשֵּׂא וְיִתְהַדָּר וְיִתְעַלֶּה וְיִתְהַלָּל
שְׁמֵהּ דְּקֻדְשָׁא בְּרִיךְ הוּא (קהל: בְּרִיךְ הוּא)
לְעֵלָּא מִן כָּל בִּרְכָתָא וְשִׁירָתָא
תֻּשְׁבְּחָתָא וְנֶחֱמָתָא
דַּאֲמִירָן בְּעָלְמָא
וְאִמְרוּ אָמֵן. (קהל: אָמֵן)

יְהֵא שְׁלָמָא רַבָּא מִן שְׁמַיָּא
וְחַיִּים, עָלֵינוּ וְעַל כָּל יִשְׂרָאֵל
וְאִמְרוּ אָמֵן. (קהל: אָמֵן)

Bow, take three steps back, as if taking leave of the Divine Presence, then bow, first left, then right, then center, while saying:

עֹשֶׂה שָׁלוֹם בִּמְרוֹמָיו
הוּא יַעֲשֶׂה שָׁלוֹם עָלֵינוּ וְעַל כָּל יִשְׂרָאֵל
וְאִמְרוּ אָמֵן. (קהל: אָמֵן)

Many congregations sing Adon Olam at this point.

LORD OF THE UNIVERSE,
who reigned before the birth of any thing –

When by His will all things were made
then was His name proclaimed King.

And when all things shall cease to be
He alone will reign in awe.

He was, He is, and He shall be
glorious for evermore.

He is One, there is none else,
alone, unique, beyond compare;

Without beginning, without end,
His might, His rule are everywhere.

He is my God; my Redeemer lives.
He is the Rock on whom I rely –

My banner and my safe retreat,
my cup, my portion when I cry.

Into His hand my soul I place,
when I awake and when I sleep.

The LORD is with me, I shall not fear;
body and soul from harm will He keep.

For Minha of Yom Tov, turn to page 572.

Many congregations sing אֲדוֹן עוֹלָם *at this point.*

אֲדוֹן עוֹלָם

אֲשֶׁר מָלַךְ בְּטֶרֶם כָּל־יְצִיר נִבְרָא.
לְעֵת נַעֲשָׂה בְחֶפְצוֹ כֹּל אֲזַי מֶלֶךְ שְׁמוֹ נִקְרָא.
וְאַחֲרֵי כִּכְלוֹת הַכֹּל לְבַדּוֹ יִמְלֹךְ נוֹרָא.
וְהוּא הָיָה וְהוּא הֹוֶה וְהוּא יִהְיֶה בְּתִפְאָרָה.
וְהוּא אֶחָד וְאֵין שֵׁנִי לְהַמְשִׁיל לוֹ לְהַחְבִּירָה.
בְּלִי רֵאשִׁית בְּלִי תַכְלִית וְלוֹ הָעֹז וְהַמִּשְׂרָה.
וְהוּא אֵלִי וְחַי גּוֹאֲלִי וְצוּר חֶבְלִי בְּעֵת צָרָה.
וְהוּא נִסִּי וּמָנוֹס לִי מְנָת כּוֹסִי בְּיוֹם אֶקְרָא.
בְּיָדוֹ אַפְקִיד רוּחִי בְּעֵת אִישַׁן וְאָעִירָה.
וְעִם רוּחִי גְּוִיָּתִי יהוה לִי וְלֹא אִירָא.

For מנחה *of* יום טוב, *turn to page 573.*

Ma'ariv for Ḥol HaMo'ed and Motza'ei Yom Tov

וְהוּא רַחוּם He is compassionate. *Ps. 78*
He forgives iniquity and does not destroy.
Repeatedly He suppresses His anger,
not rousing His full wrath.
LORD, save! May the King, answer us on the day we call. *Ps. 20*

BLESSINGS OF THE SHEMA

The Leader says the following, bowing at "Bless," standing straight at "the LORD"; the congregation, followed by the Leader, responds, bowing at "Bless," standing straight at "the LORD":

Leader: BLESS
the LORD, the blessed One.

Congregation: Bless the LORD, the blessed One,
for ever and all time.

Leader: Bless the LORD, the blessed One,
for ever and all time.

בָּרוּךְ Blessed are You, LORD our God,
King of the Universe,
who by His word brings on evenings,
by His wisdom opens the gates of heaven,
with understanding makes time change
and the seasons rotate,
and by His will orders the stars in their constellations in the sky.

מעריב לחול המועד ולמוצאי יום טוב

וְהוּא רַחוּם, יְכַפֵּר עָוֹן וְלֹא־יַשְׁחִית תהלים עח
וְהִרְבָּה לְהָשִׁיב אַפּוֹ, וְלֹא־יָעִיר כָּל־חֲמָתוֹ:
יהוה הוֹשִׁיעָה, הַמֶּלֶךְ יַעֲנֵנוּ בְיוֹם־קָרְאֵנוּ: תהלים כ

קריאת שמע וברכותיה

The שליח ציבור *says the following, bowing at* בָּרְכוּ*, standing straight at* ה׳*; the* קהל*, followed by the* שליח ציבור*, responds, bowing at* בָּרוּךְ*, standing straight at* ה׳*:*

ש״ץ: בָּרְכוּ

אֶת יהוה הַמְבֹרָךְ.

קהל: בָּרוּךְ יהוה הַמְבֹרָךְ לְעוֹלָם וָעֶד.

ש״ץ: בָּרוּךְ יהוה הַמְבֹרָךְ לְעוֹלָם וָעֶד.

בָּרוּךְ אַתָּה יהוה אֱלֹהֵינוּ מֶלֶךְ הָעוֹלָם
אֲשֶׁר בִּדְבָרוֹ מַעֲרִיב עֲרָבִים
בְּחָכְמָה פּוֹתֵחַ שְׁעָרִים
וּבִתְבוּנָה מְשַׁנֶּה עִתִּים וּמַחֲלִיף אֶת הַזְּמַנִּים
וּמְסַדֵּר אֶת הַכּוֹכָבִים בְּמִשְׁמְרוֹתֵיהֶם בָּרָקִיעַ כִּרְצוֹנוֹ.

He creates day and night, rolling away the light before the darkness,
and darkness before the light.
▸ He makes the day pass and brings on night,
distinguishing day from night:
the LORD of hosts is His name.
May the living and forever enduring God rule over us for all time.
Blessed are You, LORD, who brings on evenings.

אַהֲבַת עוֹלָם With everlasting love
have You loved Your people, the house of Israel.
You have taught us Torah and commandments,
decrees and laws of justice.
Therefore, LORD our God, when we lie down and when we rise up
we will speak of Your decrees, rejoicing in the words of Your Torah
and Your commandments for ever.
▸ For they are our life and the length of our days;
on them will we meditate day and night.
May You never take away Your love from us.
Blessed are You, LORD, who loves His people Israel.

The Shema must be said with intense concentration.
When not with a minyan, say:
God, faithful King!

The following verse should be said aloud, while covering the eyes with the right hand:

Listen, Israel: the LORD is our God, the LORD is One.

Deut. 6

Quietly: Blessed be the name of His glorious kingdom for ever and all time.

וְאָהַבְתָּ Love the LORD your God with all your heart, with all your soul, and with all your might. These words which I command you today shall be on your heart. Teach them repeatedly to your children, speaking of them when you sit at home and when you travel on the way, when you lie down and when you rise. Bind them as a sign on your hand, and they shall be an emblem between your eyes. Write them on the doorposts of your house and gates. *Deut. 6*

בּוֹרֵא יוֹם וָלָיְלָה, גּוֹלֵל אוֹר מִפְּנֵי חֹשֶׁךְ וְחֹשֶׁךְ מִפְּנֵי אוֹר
◂ וּמַעֲבִיר יוֹם וּמֵבִיא לָיְלָה
וּמַבְדִּיל בֵּין יוֹם וּבֵין לָיְלָה
יהוה צְבָאוֹת שְׁמוֹ.
אֵל חַי וְקַיָּם תָּמִיד, יִמְלֹךְ עָלֵינוּ לְעוֹלָם וָעֶד.
בָּרוּךְ אַתָּה יהוה, הַמַּעֲרִיב עֲרָבִים.

אַהֲבַת עוֹלָם בֵּית יִשְׂרָאֵל עַמְּךָ אָהָבְתָּ
תּוֹרָה וּמִצְוֹת, חֻקִּים וּמִשְׁפָּטִים, אוֹתָנוּ לִמַּדְתָּ
עַל כֵּן יהוה אֱלֹהֵינוּ בְּשָׁכְבֵנוּ וּבְקוּמֵנוּ נָשִׂיחַ בְּחֻקֶּיךָ
וְנִשְׂמַח בְּדִבְרֵי תוֹרָתֶךָ וּבְמִצְוֹתֶיךָ לְעוֹלָם וָעֶד
◂ כִּי הֵם חַיֵּינוּ וְאֹרֶךְ יָמֵינוּ, וּבָהֶם נֶהְגֶּה יוֹמָם וָלָיְלָה.
וְאַהֲבָתְךָ אַל תָּסִיר מִמֶּנּוּ לְעוֹלָמִים.
בָּרוּךְ אַתָּה יהוה, אוֹהֵב עַמּוֹ יִשְׂרָאֵל.

The שמע *must be said with intense concentration.*
When not with a מנין*, say:*

אֵל מֶלֶךְ נֶאֱמָן

The following verse should be said aloud, while covering the eyes with the right hand:

דברים ו **שְׁמַע יִשְׂרָאֵל, יהוה אֱלֹהֵינוּ, יהוה ׀ אֶחָד:**

Quietly בָּרוּךְ שֵׁם כְּבוֹד מַלְכוּתוֹ לְעוֹלָם וָעֶד.

דברים ו וְאָהַבְתָּ אֵת יהוה אֱלֹהֶיךָ, בְּכָל־לְבָבְךָ וּבְכָל־נַפְשְׁךָ וּבְכָל־מְאֹדֶךָ:
וְהָיוּ הַדְּבָרִים הָאֵלֶּה, אֲשֶׁר אָנֹכִי מְצַוְּךָ הַיּוֹם, עַל־לְבָבֶךָ: וְשִׁנַּנְתָּם
לְבָנֶיךָ וְדִבַּרְתָּ בָּם, בְּשִׁבְתְּךָ בְּבֵיתֶךָ וּבְלֶכְתְּךָ בַדֶּרֶךְ, וּבְשָׁכְבְּךָ
וּבְקוּמֶךָ: וּקְשַׁרְתָּם לְאוֹת עַל־יָדֶךָ וְהָיוּ לְטֹטָפֹת בֵּין עֵינֶיךָ:
וּכְתַבְתָּם עַל־מְזֻזוֹת בֵּיתֶךָ וּבִשְׁעָרֶיךָ:

וְהָיָה If you indeed heed My commandments with which I charge *Deut. 11* you today, to love the LORD your God and worship Him with all your heart and with all your soul, I will give rain in your land in its season, the early and late rain; and you shall gather in your grain, wine and oil. I will give grass in your field for your cattle, and you shall eat and be satisfied. Be careful lest your heart be tempted and you go astray and worship other gods, bowing down to them. Then the LORD's anger will flare against you and He will close the heavens so that there will be no rain. The land will not yield its crops, and you will perish swiftly from the good land that the LORD is giving you. Therefore, set these, My words, on your heart and soul. Bind them as a sign on your hand, and they shall be an emblem between your eyes. Teach them to your children, speaking of them when you sit at home and when you travel on the way, when you lie down and when you rise. Write them on the doorposts of your house and gates, so that you and your children may live long in the land that the LORD swore to your ancestors to give them, for as long as the heavens are above the earth.

וַיֹּאמֶר The LORD spoke to Moses, saying: Speak to the Israelites *Num. 15* and tell them to make tassels on the corners of their garments for all generations. They shall attach to the tassel at each corner a thread of blue. This shall be your tassel, and you shall see it and remember all of the LORD's commandments and keep them, not straying after your heart and after your eyes, following your own sinful desires. Thus you will be reminded to keep all My commandments, and be holy to your God. I am the LORD your God, who brought you out of the land of Egypt to be your God. I am the LORD your God.

True –

The Leader repeats:

▸ The LORD your God is true –

דברים יא וְהָיָה אִם־שָׁמֹעַ תִּשְׁמְעוּ אֶל־מִצְוֺתַי אֲשֶׁר אָנֹכִי מְצַוֶּה אֶתְכֶם הַיּוֹם, לְאַהֲבָה אֶת־יהוה אֱלֹהֵיכֶם וּלְעָבְדוֹ, בְּכָל־לְבַבְכֶם וּבְכָל־נַפְשְׁכֶם: וְנָתַתִּי מְטַר־אַרְצְכֶם בְּעִתּוֹ, יוֹרֶה וּמַלְקוֹשׁ, וְאָסַפְתָּ דְגָנֶךָ וְתִירֹשְׁךָ וְיִצְהָרֶךָ: וְנָתַתִּי עֵשֶׂב בְּשָׂדְךָ לִבְהֶמְתֶּךָ, וְאָכַלְתָּ וְשָׂבָעְתָּ: הִשָּׁמְרוּ לָכֶם פֶּן־יִפְתֶּה לְבַבְכֶם, וְסַרְתֶּם וַעֲבַדְתֶּם אֱלֹהִים אֲחֵרִים וְהִשְׁתַּחֲוִיתֶם לָהֶם: וְחָרָה אַף־יהוה בָּכֶם, וְעָצַר אֶת־הַשָּׁמַיִם וְלֹא־יִהְיֶה מָטָר, וְהָאֲדָמָה לֹא תִתֵּן אֶת־יְבוּלָהּ, וַאֲבַדְתֶּם מְהֵרָה מֵעַל הָאָרֶץ הַטֹּבָה אֲשֶׁר יהוה נֹתֵן לָכֶם: וְשַׂמְתֶּם אֶת־דְּבָרַי אֵלֶּה עַל־לְבַבְכֶם וְעַל־נַפְשְׁכֶם, וּקְשַׁרְתֶּם אֹתָם לְאוֹת עַל־יֶדְכֶם, וְהָיוּ לְטוֹטָפֹת בֵּין עֵינֵיכֶם: וְלִמַּדְתֶּם אֹתָם אֶת־בְּנֵיכֶם לְדַבֵּר בָּם, בְּשִׁבְתְּךָ בְּבֵיתֶךָ וּבְלֶכְתְּךָ בַדֶּרֶךְ, וּבְשָׁכְבְּךָ וּבְקוּמֶךָ: וּכְתַבְתָּם עַל־מְזוּזוֹת בֵּיתֶךָ וּבִשְׁעָרֶיךָ: לְמַעַן יִרְבּוּ יְמֵיכֶם וִימֵי בְנֵיכֶם עַל הָאֲדָמָה אֲשֶׁר נִשְׁבַּע יהוה לַאֲבֹתֵיכֶם לָתֵת לָהֶם, כִּימֵי הַשָּׁמַיִם עַל־הָאָרֶץ:

במדבר טו וַיֹּאמֶר יהוה אֶל־מֹשֶׁה לֵּאמֹר: דַּבֵּר אֶל־בְּנֵי יִשְׂרָאֵל וְאָמַרְתָּ אֲלֵהֶם, וְעָשׂוּ לָהֶם צִיצִת עַל־כַּנְפֵי בִגְדֵיהֶם לְדֹרֹתָם, וְנָתְנוּ עַל־צִיצִת הַכָּנָף פְּתִיל תְּכֵלֶת: וְהָיָה לָכֶם לְצִיצִת, וּרְאִיתֶם אֹתוֹ וּזְכַרְתֶּם אֶת־כָּל־מִצְוֺת יהוה וַעֲשִׂיתֶם אֹתָם, וְלֹא תָתוּרוּ אַחֲרֵי לְבַבְכֶם וְאַחֲרֵי עֵינֵיכֶם, אֲשֶׁר־אַתֶּם זֹנִים אַחֲרֵיהֶם: לְמַעַן תִּזְכְּרוּ וַעֲשִׂיתֶם אֶת־כָּל־מִצְוֺתָי, וִהְיִיתֶם קְדֹשִׁים לֵאלֹהֵיכֶם: אֲנִי יהוה אֱלֹהֵיכֶם, אֲשֶׁר הוֹצֵאתִי אֶתְכֶם מֵאֶרֶץ מִצְרַיִם, לִהְיוֹת לָכֶם לֵאלֹהִים, אֲנִי יהוה אֱלֹהֵיכֶם:

אֱמֶת

The שליח ציבור *repeats:*

› יהוה אֱלֹהֵיכֶם אֱמֶת

וֶאֱמוּנָה – and faithful is all this,
and firmly established for us
that He is the LORD our God,
and there is none beside Him,
and that we, Israel, are His people.
He is our King, who redeems us from the hand of kings
and delivers us from the grasp of all tyrants.
He is our God, who on our behalf repays our foes
and brings just retribution on our mortal enemies;
who performs great deeds beyond understanding
and wonders beyond number;
who kept us alive, not letting our foot slip; *Ps. 66*
who led us on the high places of our enemies,
raising our pride above all our foes;
who did miracles for us
and brought vengeance against Pharaoh;
who performed signs and wonders
in the land of Ham's children;
who smote in His wrath all the firstborn of Egypt,
and brought out His people Israel from their midst
into everlasting freedom;
who led His children through the divided Reed Sea,
plunging their pursuers and enemies into the depths.
When His children saw His might,
they gave praise and thanks to His name,
▸ and willingly accepted His Sovereignty.
Moses and the children of Israel
then sang a song to You with great joy,
and they all exclaimed:

מִי־כָמֹכָה "Who is like You, LORD, among the mighty? *Ex. 15*
Who is like You, majestic in holiness,
awesome in praises, doing wonders?"

וֶאֱמוּנָה כָּל זֹאת וְקַיָּם עָלֵינוּ
כִּי הוּא יהוה אֱלֹהֵינוּ וְאֵין זוּלָתוֹ
וַאֲנַחְנוּ יִשְׂרָאֵל עַמּוֹ.
הַפּוֹדֵנוּ מִיַּד מְלָכִים
מַלְכֵּנוּ הַגּוֹאֲלֵנוּ מִכַּף כָּל הֶעָרִיצִים.
הָאֵל הַנִּפְרָע לָנוּ מִצָּרֵינוּ
וְהַמְשַׁלֵּם גְּמוּל לְכָל אוֹיְבֵי נַפְשֵׁנוּ.
הָעוֹשֶׂה גְדוֹלוֹת עַד אֵין חֵקֶר, וְנִפְלָאוֹת עַד אֵין מִסְפָּר
הַשָּׂם נַפְשֵׁנוּ בַּחַיִּים, וְלֹא־נָתַן לַמּוֹט רַגְלֵנוּ: תהלים סו
הַמַּדְרִיכֵנוּ עַל בָּמוֹת אוֹיְבֵינוּ
וַיָּרֶם קַרְנֵנוּ עַל כָּל שׂוֹנְאֵינוּ.
הָעוֹשֶׂה לָּנוּ נִסִּים וּנְקָמָה בְּפַרְעֹה
אוֹתוֹת וּמוֹפְתִים בְּאַדְמַת בְּנֵי חָם.
הַמַּכֶּה בְעֶבְרָתוֹ כָּל בְּכוֹרֵי מִצְרָיִם
וַיּוֹצֵא אֶת עַמּוֹ יִשְׂרָאֵל מִתּוֹכָם לְחֵרוּת עוֹלָם.
הַמַּעֲבִיר בָּנָיו בֵּין גִּזְרֵי יַם סוּף
אֶת רוֹדְפֵיהֶם וְאֶת שׂוֹנְאֵיהֶם בִּתְהוֹמוֹת טִבַּע
וְרָאוּ בָנָיו גְּבוּרָתוֹ, שִׁבְּחוּ וְהוֹדוּ לִשְׁמוֹ
◂ וּמַלְכוּתוֹ בְּרָצוֹן קִבְּלוּ עֲלֵיהֶם.
מֹשֶׁה וּבְנֵי יִשְׂרָאֵל, לְךָ עָנוּ שִׁירָה בְּשִׂמְחָה רַבָּה
וְאָמְרוּ כֻלָּם
מִי־כָמֹכָה בָּאֵלִם יהוה שמות טו
מִי כָּמֹכָה נֶאְדָּר בַּקֹּדֶשׁ
נוֹרָא תְהִלֹּת עֹשֵׂה פֶלֶא:

▸ Your children beheld Your majesty
as You parted the sea before Moses.
"This is my God!" they responded, and then said:
"The LORD shall reign for ever and ever." Ex. 15

▸ And it is said,
"For the LORD has redeemed Jacob Jer. 31
and rescued him from a power stronger than his own."
Blessed are You, LORD, who redeemed Israel.

הַשְׁכִּיבֵנוּ Help us lie down, O LORD our God, in peace,
and rise up, O our King, to life.
Spread over us Your canopy of peace.
Direct us with Your good counsel,
and save us for the sake of Your name.
Shield us and remove from us every enemy,
plague, sword, famine and sorrow.
Remove the adversary from before and behind us.
Shelter us in the shadow of Your wings,
for You, God, are our Guardian and Deliverer;
You, God, are a gracious and compassionate King.
▸ Guard our going out and our coming in,
for life and peace, from now and for ever.
Blessed are You, LORD, who guards His people Israel for ever.

In Israel the service continues with Half Kaddish on page 1348.

בָּרוּךְ Blessed be the LORD for ever. Amen and Amen. Ps. 89
Blessed from Zion be the LORD Ps. 135
who dwells in Jerusalem. Halleluya.
Blessed be the LORD, God of Israel, Ps. 72
who alone does wondrous things.
Blessed be His glorious name for ever,
and may the whole earth be filled with His glory.
Amen and Amen.

› מַלְכוּתְךָ רָאוּ בָנֶיךָ, בּוֹקֵעַ יָם לִפְנֵי מֹשֶׁה
זֶה אֵלִי עָנוּ, וְאָמְרוּ
יהוה יִמְלֹךְ לְעֹלָם וָעֶד: שמות טו

› וְנֶאֱמַר
כִּי־פָדָה יהוה אֶת־יַעֲקֹב ירמיה לא
וּגְאָלוֹ מִיַּד חָזָק מִמֶּנּוּ:
בָּרוּךְ אַתָּה יהוה, גָּאַל יִשְׂרָאֵל.

הַשְׁכִּיבֵנוּ יהוה אֱלֹהֵינוּ לְשָׁלוֹם
וְהַעֲמִידֵנוּ מַלְכֵּנוּ לְחַיִּים
וּפְרֹשׂ עָלֵינוּ סֻכַּת שְׁלוֹמֶךָ
וְתַקְּנֵנוּ בְּעֵצָה טוֹבָה מִלְּפָנֶיךָ
וְהוֹשִׁיעֵנוּ לְמַעַן שְׁמֶךָ.
וְהָגֵן בַּעֲדֵנוּ, וְהָסֵר מֵעָלֵינוּ אוֹיֵב, דֶּבֶר וְחֶרֶב וְרָעָב וְיָגוֹן
וְהָסֵר שָׂטָן מִלְּפָנֵינוּ וּמֵאַחֲרֵינוּ, וּבְצֵל כְּנָפֶיךָ תַּסְתִּירֵנוּ
כִּי אֵל שׁוֹמְרֵנוּ וּמַצִּילֵנוּ אָתָּה
כִּי אֵל מֶלֶךְ חַנּוּן וְרַחוּם אָתָּה.
› וּשְׁמֹר צֵאתֵנוּ וּבוֹאֵנוּ לְחַיִּים וּלְשָׁלוֹם מֵעַתָּה וְעַד עוֹלָם.
בָּרוּךְ אַתָּה יהוה, שׁוֹמֵר עַמּוֹ יִשְׂרָאֵל לָעַד.

In ארץ ישראל *the service continues with* חצי קדיש *on page 1349.*

בָּרוּךְ יהוה לְעוֹלָם, אָמֵן וְאָמֵן: תהלים פט
בָּרוּךְ יהוה מִצִּיּוֹן, שֹׁכֵן יְרוּשָׁלָםִ, הַלְלוּיָהּ: תהלים קלה
בָּרוּךְ יהוה אֱלֹהִים אֱלֹהֵי יִשְׂרָאֵל, עֹשֵׂה נִפְלָאוֹת לְבַדּוֹ: תהלים עב
וּבָרוּךְ שֵׁם כְּבוֹדוֹ לְעוֹלָם
וְיִמָּלֵא כְבוֹדוֹ אֶת־כׇּל־הָאָרֶץ, אָמֵן וְאָמֵן:

May the glory of the LORD endure for ever; *Ps. 104*
may the LORD rejoice in His works.
May the name of the LORD be blessed now and for all time. *Ps. 113*
For the sake of His great name *1 Sam. 12*
the LORD will not abandon His people,
for the LORD vowed to make you a people of His own.
When all the people saw [God's wonders] they fell on their faces *1 Kings 18*
and said: "The LORD, He is God; the LORD, He is God."
Then the LORD shall be King over all the earth; *Zech. 14*
on that day the LORD shall be One and His name One.
May Your love, LORD, be upon us, as we have put our hope in You. *Ps. 33*
Save us, LORD our God, gather us and deliver us from the nations, *Ps. 106*
to thank Your holy name, and glory in Your praise.
All the nations You made shall come and bow before You, LORD, *Ps. 86*
and pay honor to Your name,
for You are great and You perform wonders:
You alone are God.
We, Your people, the flock of Your pasture, will praise You for ever. *Ps. 79*
For all generations we will relate Your praise.

בָּרוּךְ Blessed is the LORD by day,
blessed is the LORD by night.
Blessed is the LORD when we lie down;
blessed is the LORD when we rise.
For in Your hand are the souls of the living and the dead,
[as it is written:] "In His hand is every living soul, *Job 12*
and the breath of all mankind."
Into Your hand I entrust my spirit: *Ps. 31*
You redeemed me, LORD, God of truth.
Our God in heaven, bring unity to Your name,
establish Your kingdom constantly
and reign over us for ever and all time.

יְהִי כְבוֹד יהוה לְעוֹלָם, יִשְׂמַח יהוה בְּמַעֲשָׂיו: תהלים קד

יְהִי שֵׁם יהוה מְבֹרָךְ מֵעַתָּה וְעַד־עוֹלָם: תהלים קיג

כִּי לֹא־יִטֹּשׁ יהוה אֶת־עַמּוֹ בַּעֲבוּר שְׁמוֹ הַגָּדוֹל שמואל א׳, י

כִּי הוֹאִיל יהוה לַעֲשׂוֹת אֶתְכֶם לוֹ לְעָם:

וַיַּרְא כָּל־הָעָם וַיִּפְּלוּ עַל־פְּנֵיהֶם מלכים א׳, יח

וַיֹּאמְרוּ, יהוה הוּא הָאֱלֹהִים, יהוה הוּא הָאֱלֹהִים:

וְהָיָה יהוה לְמֶלֶךְ עַל־כָּל־הָאָרֶץ זכריה יד

בַּיּוֹם הַהוּא יִהְיֶה יהוה אֶחָד וּשְׁמוֹ אֶחָד:

יְהִי־חַסְדְּךָ יהוה עָלֵינוּ, כַּאֲשֶׁר יִחַלְנוּ לָךְ: תהלים לג

הוֹשִׁיעֵנוּ יהוה אֱלֹהֵינוּ, וְקַבְּצֵנוּ מִן־הַגּוֹיִם תהלים קו

לְהוֹדוֹת לְשֵׁם קָדְשֶׁךָ, לְהִשְׁתַּבֵּחַ בִּתְהִלָּתֶךָ:

כָּל־גּוֹיִם אֲשֶׁר עָשִׂיתָ, יָבוֹאוּ וְיִשְׁתַּחֲווּ לְפָנֶיךָ, אֲדֹנָי תהלים פו

וִיכַבְּדוּ לִשְׁמֶךָ:

כִּי־גָדוֹל אַתָּה וְעֹשֵׂה נִפְלָאוֹת, אַתָּה אֱלֹהִים לְבַדֶּךָ:

וַאֲנַחְנוּ עַמְּךָ וְצֹאן מַרְעִיתֶךָ, נוֹדֶה לְּךָ לְעוֹלָם תהלים עט

לְדוֹר וָדֹר נְסַפֵּר תְּהִלָּתֶךָ:

בָּרוּךְ יהוה בַּיּוֹם, בָּרוּךְ יהוה בַּלָּיְלָה

בָּרוּךְ יהוה בְּשָׁכְבֵנוּ, בָּרוּךְ יהוה בְּקוּמֵנוּ.

כִּי בְיָדְךָ נַפְשׁוֹת הַחַיִּים וְהַמֵּתִים.

אֲשֶׁר בְּיָדוֹ נֶפֶשׁ כָּל־חָי, וְרוּחַ כָּל־בְּשַׂר־אִישׁ: איוב יב

בְּיָדְךָ אַפְקִיד רוּחִי, פָּדִיתָה אוֹתִי יהוה אֵל אֱמֶת: תהלים לא

אֱלֹהֵינוּ שֶׁבַּשָּׁמַיִם, יַחֵד שִׁמְךָ וְקַיֵּם מַלְכוּתְךָ תָּמִיד

וּמְלֹךְ עָלֵינוּ לְעוֹלָם וָעֶד.

יִרְאוּ May our eyes see, our hearts rejoice,
and our souls be glad in Your true salvation,
when Zion is told, "Your God reigns."
The LORD is King, the LORD was King,
the LORD will be King for ever and all time.
▸ For sovereignty is Yours,
and to all eternity You will reign in glory,
for we have no king but You.
Blessed are You, LORD,
the King who in His constant glory will reign over us
and all His creation for ever and all time.

HALF KADDISH

Leader: יִתְגַּדַּל Magnified and sanctified
may His great name be,
in the world He created by His will.
May He establish His kingdom
in your lifetime and in your days,
and in the lifetime of all the house of Israel,
swiftly and soon –
and say: Amen.

All: May His great name be blessed for ever and all time.

Leader: Blessed and praised, glorified and exalted,
raised and honored,
uplifted and lauded
be the name of the Holy One,
blessed be He,
beyond any blessing,
song, praise and consolation
uttered in the world –
and say: Amen.

יִרְאוּ עֵינֵינוּ וְיִשְׂמַח לִבֵּנוּ
וְתָגֵל נַפְשֵׁנוּ בִּישׁוּעָתְךָ בֶּאֱמֶת
בֶּאֱמֹר לְצִיּוֹן מָלַךְ אֱלֹהָיִךְ.
יהוה מֶלֶךְ, יהוה מָלָךְ, יהוה יִמְלֹךְ לְעֹלָם וָעֶד.
◂ כִּי הַמַּלְכוּת שֶׁלְּךָ הִיא, וּלְעוֹלְמֵי עַד תִּמְלֹךְ בְּכָבוֹד
כִּי אֵין לָנוּ מֶלֶךְ אֶלָּא אָתָּה.
בָּרוּךְ אַתָּה יהוה
הַמֶּלֶךְ בִּכְבוֹדוֹ תָּמִיד, יִמְלֹךְ עָלֵינוּ לְעוֹלָם וָעֶד
וְעַל כָּל מַעֲשָׂיו.

חצי קדיש

ש״ץ: יִתְגַּדַּל וְיִתְקַדַּשׁ שְׁמֵהּ רַבָּא (קהל: אָמֵן)
בְּעָלְמָא דִּי בְרָא כִרְעוּתֵהּ
וְיַמְלִיךְ מַלְכוּתֵהּ
בְּחַיֵּיכוֹן וּבְיוֹמֵיכוֹן וּבְחַיֵּי דְכָל בֵּית יִשְׂרָאֵל
בַּעֲגָלָא וּבִזְמַן קָרִיב
וְאִמְרוּ אָמֵן. (קהל: אָמֵן)

קהל וש״ץ: יְהֵא שְׁמֵהּ רַבָּא מְבָרַךְ לְעָלַם וּלְעָלְמֵי עָלְמַיָּא.

ש״ץ: יִתְבָּרַךְ וְיִשְׁתַּבַּח וְיִתְפָּאַר וְיִתְרוֹמַם וְיִתְנַשֵּׂא
וְיִתְהַדָּר וְיִתְעַלֶּה וְיִתְהַלָּל
שְׁמֵהּ דְּקֻדְשָׁא בְּרִיךְ הוּא (קהל: בְּרִיךְ הוּא)
לְעֵלָּא מִן כָּל בִּרְכָתָא וְשִׁירָתָא, תֻּשְׁבְּחָתָא וְנֶחֱמָתָא
דַּאֲמִירָן בְּעָלְמָא
וְאִמְרוּ אָמֵן. (קהל: אָמֵן)

THE AMIDA

The following prayer, until "in former years" on page 1364, is said silently, standing with feet together. Take three steps forward and at the points indicated by ▾, bend the knees at the first word, bow at the second, and stand straight before saying God's name.

O Lord, open my lips,
so that my mouth may declare Your praise. *Ps. 51*

PATRIARCHS

▾בָּרוּךְ▾ Blessed are You, Lord our God and God of our fathers,
God of Abraham, God of Isaac and God of Jacob;
the great, mighty and awesome God, God Most High,
who bestows acts of loving-kindness and creates all,
who remembers the loving-kindness of the fathers
and will bring a Redeemer to their children's children
for the sake of His name, in love.
King, Helper, Savior, Shield:
▾Blessed are You, Lord, Shield of Abraham.

DIVINE MIGHT

אַתָּה גִּבּוֹר You are eternally mighty, Lord.
You give life to the dead and have great power to save.

In Israel on Ḥol HaMo'ed:
He causes the dew to fall.

On Motza'ei Simḥat Torah:
He makes the wind blow and the rain fall.

He sustains the living with loving-kindness,
and with great compassion revives the dead.
He supports the fallen, heals the sick, sets captives free,
and keeps His faith with those who sleep in the dust.
Who is like You, Master of might,
and who can compare to You,
O King who brings death and gives life,
and makes salvation grow?
Faithful are You to revive the dead.
Blessed are You, Lord, who revives the dead.

עמידה

The following prayer, until קַדְמֹנִיּוֹת *on page 1365, is said silently, standing with feet together. Take three steps forward and at the points indicated by* ˅*, bend the knees at the first word, bow at the second, and stand straight before saying God's name.*

אֲדֹנָי, שְׂפָתַי תִּפְתָּח, וּפִי יַגִּיד תְּהִלָּתֶךָ׃ תהלים נא

אבות

˅בָּרוּךְ אַתָּה יהוה, אֱלֹהֵינוּ וֵאלֹהֵי אֲבוֹתֵינוּ
אֱלֹהֵי אַבְרָהָם, אֱלֹהֵי יִצְחָק, וֵאלֹהֵי יַעֲקֹב
הָאֵל הַגָּדוֹל הַגִּבּוֹר וְהַנּוֹרָא, אֵל עֶלְיוֹן
גּוֹמֵל חֲסָדִים טוֹבִים, וְקוֹנֵה הַכֹּל, וְזוֹכֵר חַסְדֵי אָבוֹת
וּמֵבִיא גוֹאֵל לִבְנֵי בְנֵיהֶם לְמַעַן שְׁמוֹ בְּאַהֲבָה.
מֶלֶךְ עוֹזֵר וּמוֹשִׁיעַ וּמָגֵן.
˅בָּרוּךְ אַתָּה יהוה, מָגֵן אַבְרָהָם.

גבורות

אַתָּה גִּבּוֹר לְעוֹלָם, אֲדֹנָי
מְחַיֵּה מֵתִים אַתָּה, רַב לְהוֹשִׁיעַ

In ארץ ישראל *on* חול המועד:

מוֹרִיד הַטָּל

On מוצאי שמחת תורה:

מַשִּׁיב הָרְוּחַ וּמוֹרִיד הַגֶּשֶׁם

מְכַלְכֵּל חַיִּים בְּחֶסֶד, מְחַיֵּה מֵתִים בְּרַחֲמִים רַבִּים
סוֹמֵךְ נוֹפְלִים, וְרוֹפֵא חוֹלִים, וּמַתִּיר אֲסוּרִים
וּמְקַיֵּם אֱמוּנָתוֹ לִישֵׁנֵי עָפָר.
מִי כָמְוֹךָ, בַּעַל גְּבוּרוֹת, וּמִי דּוֹמֶה לָּךְ
מֶלֶךְ, מֵמִית וּמְחַיֶּה וּמַצְמִיחַ יְשׁוּעָה.
וְנֶאֱמָן אַתָּה לְהַחֲיוֹת מֵתִים.
בָּרוּךְ אַתָּה יהוה, מְחַיֵּה הַמֵּתִים.

HOLINESS

אַתָּה קָדוֹשׁ You are holy and Your name is holy,
and holy ones praise You daily, Selah!
Blessed are You, Lord, the holy God.

KNOWLEDGE

אַתָּה חוֹנֵן You grace humanity with knowledge
and teach mortals understanding.

On Motza'ei Shabbat and Motza'ei Yom Tov say:

אַתָּה חוֹנַנְתָּנוּ You have graced us with the knowledge of Your Torah, and taught us to perform the statutes of Your will. You have distinguished, Lord our God, between sacred and profane, light and darkness, Israel and the nations, and between the seventh day and the six days of work. Our Father, our King, may the days approaching us bring peace; may we be free from all sin, cleansed from all iniquity, holding fast to our reverence of You. And

---

Grace us with the knowledge, understanding
and discernment that come from You.
Blessed are You, Lord, who graciously grants knowledge.

REPENTANCE

הֲשִׁיבֵנוּ Bring us back, our Father, to Your Torah.
Draw us near, our King, to Your service.
Lead us back to You in perfect repentance.
Blessed are You, Lord, who desires repentance.

FORGIVENESS

Strike the left side of the chest at °.

סְלַח לָנוּ Forgive us, our Father, for we have °sinned.
Pardon us, our King, for we have °transgressed;
for You pardon and forgive.
Blessed are You, Lord, the gracious One who repeatedly forgives.

קדושת השם

אַתָּה קָדוֹשׁ וְשִׁמְךָ קָדוֹשׁ
וּקְדוֹשִׁים בְּכָל יוֹם יְהַלְלְוּךָ סֶּלָה.
בָּרוּךְ אַתָּה יהוה, הָאֵל הַקָּדוֹשׁ.

דעת

אַתָּה חוֹנֵן לְאָדָם דַּעַת, וּמְלַמֵּד לֶאֱנוֹשׁ בִּינָה.

On מוצאי יום טוב *and* מוצאי שבת *say:*

אַתָּה חוֹנַנְתָּנוּ לְמַדַּע תּוֹרָתֶךָ, וַתְּלַמְּדֵנוּ לַעֲשׂוֹת חֻקֵּי רְצוֹנֶךָ, וַתַּבְדֵּל יהוה אֱלֹהֵינוּ בֵּין קֹדֶשׁ לְחוֹל, בֵּין אוֹר לְחְשֶׁךְ, בֵּין יִשְׂרָאֵל לָעַמִּים, בֵּין יוֹם הַשְּׁבִיעִי לְשֵׁשֶׁת יְמֵי הַמַּעֲשֶׂה. אָבִינוּ מַלְכֵּנוּ, הָחֵל עָלֵינוּ הַיָּמִים הַבָּאִים לִקְרָאתֵנוּ לְשָׁלוֹם, חֲשׂוּכִים מִכָּל חֵטְא וּמְנֻקִּים מִכָּל עָוֹן וּמְדֻבָּקִים בְּיִרְאָתֶךָ. וְ

חָנֵּנוּ מֵאִתְּךָ דֵּעָה בִּינָה וְהַשְׂכֵּל.
בָּרוּךְ אַתָּה יהוה, חוֹנֵן הַדָּעַת.

תשובה

הֲשִׁיבֵנוּ אָבִינוּ לְתוֹרָתֶךָ, וְקָרְבֵנוּ מַלְכֵּנוּ לַעֲבוֹדָתֶךָ
וְהַחֲזִירֵנוּ בִּתְשׁוּבָה שְׁלֵמָה לְפָנֶיךָ.
בָּרוּךְ אַתָּה יהוה, הָרוֹצֶה בִּתְשׁוּבָה.

סליחה

Strike the left side of the chest at °.

סְלַח לָנוּ אָבִינוּ כִּי °חָטָאנוּ
מְחַל לָנוּ מַלְכֵּנוּ כִּי °פָשָׁעְנוּ
כִּי מוֹחֵל וְסוֹלֵחַ אָתָּה.
בָּרוּךְ אַתָּה יהוה, חַנּוּן הַמַּרְבֶּה לִסְלְחַ.

REDEMPTION

רְאֵה Look on our affliction,
plead our cause,
and redeem us soon for Your name's sake,
for You are a powerful Redeemer.
Blessed are You, Lord,
the Redeemer of Israel.

HEALING

רְפָאֵנוּ Heal us, Lord, and we shall be healed.
Save us and we shall be saved,
for You are our praise.
Bring complete recovery for all our ailments,

The following prayer for a sick person may be said here:
May it be Your will, O Lord my God and God of my ancestors, that You speedily send a complete recovery from heaven, a healing of both soul and body, to the patient (*name*), son/daughter of (*mother's name*) among the other afflicted of Israel.

---

for You, God, King, are a faithful and compassionate Healer.
Blessed are You, Lord,
Healer of the sick of His people Israel.

PROSPERITY

בָּרֵךְ Bless this year for us, Lord our God,
and all its types of produce for good.
Grant blessing on the face of the earth,
and from its goodness satisfy us,
blessing our year as the best of years.
Blessed are You, Lord,
who blesses the years.

גאולה

רְאֵה בְעָנְיֵנוּ, וְרִיבָה רִיבֵנוּ
וּגְאָלֵנוּ מְהֵרָה לְמַעַן שְׁמֶךָ
כִּי גוֹאֵל חָזָק אָתָּה.
בָּרוּךְ אַתָּה יהוה, גּוֹאֵל יִשְׂרָאֵל.

רפואה

רְפָאֵנוּ יהוה וְנֵרָפֵא
הוֹשִׁיעֵנוּ וְנִוָּשֵׁעָה
כִּי תְהִלָּתֵנוּ אָתָּה
וְהַעֲלֵה רְפוּאָה שְׁלֵמָה לְכָל מַכּוֹתֵינוּ

The following prayer for a sick person may be said here:

יְהִי רָצוֹן מִלְּפָנֶיךָ יהוה אֱלֹהַי וֵאלֹהֵי אֲבוֹתַי, שֶׁתִּשְׁלַח מְהֵרָה רְפוּאָה שְׁלֵמָה מִן הַשָּׁמַיִם רְפוּאַת הַנֶּפֶשׁ וּרְפוּאַת הַגּוּף לַחוֹלֶה/לַחוֹלָה *name of patient* בֶּן/בַּת *mother's name* בְּתוֹךְ שְׁאָר חוֹלֵי יִשְׂרָאֵל.

כִּי אֵל מֶלֶךְ רוֹפֵא נֶאֱמָן וְרַחֲמָן אָתָּה.
בָּרוּךְ אַתָּה יהוה, רוֹפֵא חוֹלֵי עַמּוֹ יִשְׂרָאֵל.

ברכת השנים

בָּרֵךְ עָלֵינוּ יהוה אֱלֹהֵינוּ אֶת הַשָּׁנָה הַזֹּאת
וְאֶת כָּל מִינֵי תְבוּאָתָהּ, לְטוֹבָה
וְתֵן בְּרָכָה עַל פְּנֵי הָאֲדָמָה
וְשַׂבְּעֵנוּ מִטּוּבָהּ
וּבָרֵךְ שְׁנָתֵנוּ כַּשָּׁנִים הַטּוֹבוֹת.
בָּרוּךְ אַתָּה יהוה, מְבָרֵךְ הַשָּׁנִים.

INGATHERING OF EXILES

תְּקַע Sound the great shofar for our freedom,
raise high the banner to gather our exiles,
and gather us together from the four quarters of the earth.
Blessed are You, LORD,
who gathers the dispersed of His people Israel.

JUSTICE

הָשִׁיבָה Restore our judges as at first,
and our counselors as at the beginning,
and remove from us sorrow and sighing.
May You alone, LORD, reign over us
with loving-kindness and compassion,
and vindicate us in justice.
Blessed are You, LORD,
the King who loves righteousness and justice.

AGAINST INFORMERS

וְלַמַּלְשִׁינִים For the slanderers
let there be no hope,
and may all wickedness perish in an instant.
May all Your people's enemies swiftly be cut down.
May You swiftly uproot,
crush, cast down and humble the arrogant
swiftly in our days.
Blessed are You, LORD,
who destroys enemies and humbles the arrogant.

THE RIGHTEOUS

עַל הַצַּדִּיקִים To the righteous, the pious,
the elders of Your people the house of Israel,
the remnant of their scholars,
the righteous converts, and to us,
may Your compassion be aroused, LORD our God.

קבוץ גלויות

תְּקַע בְּשׁוֹפָר גָּדוֹל לְחֵרוּתֵֽנוּ
וְשָׂא נֵס לְקַבֵּץ גָּלֻיּוֹתֵֽינוּ
וְקַבְּצֵֽנוּ יַֽחַד מֵאַרְבַּע כַּנְפוֹת הָאָֽרֶץ.
בָּרוּךְ אַתָּה יהוה, מְקַבֵּץ נִדְחֵי עַמּוֹ יִשְׂרָאֵל.

השבת המשפט

הָשִֽׁיבָה שׁוֹפְטֵֽינוּ כְּבָרִאשׁוֹנָה, וְיוֹעֲצֵֽינוּ כְּבַתְּחִלָּה
וְהָסֵר מִמֶּֽנּוּ יָגוֹן וַאֲנָחָה
וּמְלֹךְ עָלֵֽינוּ אַתָּה יהוה לְבַדְּךָ בְּחֶֽסֶד וּבְרַחֲמִים
וְצַדְּקֵֽנוּ בַּמִּשְׁפָּט.
בָּרוּךְ אַתָּה יהוה, מֶֽלֶךְ אוֹהֵב צְדָקָה וּמִשְׁפָּט.

ברכת המינים

וְלַמַּלְשִׁינִים אַל תְּהִי תִקְוָה, וְכָל הָרִשְׁעָה כְּרֶֽגַע תֹּאבֵד
וְכָל אוֹיְבֵי עַמְּךָ מְהֵרָה יִכָּרֵֽתוּ
וְהַזֵּדִים מְהֵרָה
תְעַקֵּר וּתְשַׁבֵּר וּתְמַגֵּר וְתַכְנִֽיעַ
בִּמְהֵרָה בְיָמֵֽינוּ.
בָּרוּךְ אַתָּה יהוה, שׁוֹבֵר אוֹיְבִים וּמַכְנִֽיעַ זֵדִים.

על הצדיקים

עַל הַצַּדִּיקִים וְעַל הַחֲסִידִים
וְעַל זִקְנֵי עַמְּךָ בֵּית יִשְׂרָאֵל, וְעַל פְּלֵיטַת סוֹפְרֵיהֶם
וְעַל גֵּרֵי הַצֶּֽדֶק, וְעָלֵֽינוּ
יֶהֱמוּ רַחֲמֶֽיךָ יהוה אֱלֹהֵֽינוּ

Grant a good reward to all
who sincerely trust in Your name.
Set our lot with them,
so that we may never be ashamed,
for in You we trust.
Blessed are You, LORD,
who is the support and trust of the righteous.

REBUILDING JERUSALEM

וְלִירוּשָׁלַיִם To Jerusalem, Your city,
may You return in compassion,
and may You dwell in it as You promised.
May You rebuild it rapidly in our days
as an everlasting structure,
and install within it soon the throne of David.
Blessed are You, LORD,
who builds Jerusalem.

KINGDOM OF DAVID

אֶת צֶמַח May the offshoot of Your servant David soon flower,
and may his pride be raised high by Your salvation,
for we wait for Your salvation all day.
Blessed are You, LORD,
who makes the glory of salvation flourish.

RESPONSE TO PRAYER

שְׁמַע קוֹלֵנוּ Listen to our voice, LORD our God.
Spare us and have compassion on us,
and in compassion and favor accept our prayer,
for You, God, listen to prayers and pleas.
Do not turn us away, O our King,
empty-handed from Your presence,
for You listen with compassion to the prayer of Your people Israel.
Blessed are You, LORD, who listens to prayer.

וְתֵן שָׂכָר טוֹב לְכָל הַבּוֹטְחִים בְּשִׁמְךָ בֶּאֱמֶת
וְשִׂים חֶלְקֵנוּ עִמָּהֶם
וּלְעוֹלָם לֹא נֵבוֹשׁ כִּי בְךָ בָּטָחְנוּ.
בָּרוּךְ אַתָּה יהוה, מִשְׁעָן וּמִבְטָח לַצַּדִּיקִים.

בניין ירושלים

וְלִירוּשָׁלַיִם עִירְךָ בְּרַחֲמִים תָּשׁוּב
וְתִשְׁכֹּן בְּתוֹכָהּ כַּאֲשֶׁר דִּבַּרְתָּ
וּבְנֵה אוֹתָהּ בְּקָרוֹב בְּיָמֵינוּ בִּנְיַן עוֹלָם
וְכִסֵּא דָוִד מְהֵרָה לְתוֹכָהּ תָּכִין.
בָּרוּךְ אַתָּה יהוה, בּוֹנֵה יְרוּשָׁלָיִם.

משיח בן דוד

אֶת צֶמַח דָּוִד עַבְדְּךָ מְהֵרָה תַצְמִיחַ
וְקַרְנוֹ תָּרוּם בִּישׁוּעָתֶךָ
כִּי לִישׁוּעָתְךָ קִוִּינוּ כָּל הַיּוֹם.
בָּרוּךְ אַתָּה יהוה, מַצְמִיחַ קֶרֶן יְשׁוּעָה.

שומע תפלה

שְׁמַע קוֹלֵנוּ יהוה אֱלֹהֵינוּ
חוּס וְרַחֵם עָלֵינוּ
וְקַבֵּל בְּרַחֲמִים וּבְרָצוֹן אֶת תְּפִלָּתֵנוּ
כִּי אֵל שׁוֹמֵעַ תְּפִלּוֹת וְתַחֲנוּנִים אָתָּה
וּמִלְּפָנֶיךָ מַלְכֵּנוּ רֵיקָם אַל תְּשִׁיבֵנוּ
כִּי אַתָּה שׁוֹמֵעַ תְּפִלַּת עַמְּךָ יִשְׂרָאֵל בְּרַחֲמִים.
בָּרוּךְ אַתָּה יהוה, שׁוֹמֵעַ תְּפִלָּה.

TEMPLE SERVICE

רְצֵה Find favor, LORD our God,
in Your people Israel and their prayer.
Restore the service to Your most holy House,
and accept in love and favor
the fire-offerings of Israel and their prayer.
May the service of Your people Israel always find favor with You.

On Motza'ei Simḥat Torah, continue with "And may our eyes" below.

On Ḥol HaMo'ed, say:

אֱלֹהֵינוּ Our God and God of our ancestors,
may there rise, come, reach, appear, be favored, heard,
regarded and remembered before You,
our recollection and remembrance,
as well as the remembrance of our ancestors,
and of the Messiah son of David Your servant,
and of Jerusalem Your holy city,
and of all Your people the house of Israel –
for deliverance and well-being,
grace, loving-kindness and compassion, life and peace,
on this day of the festival of Sukkot.
On it remember us, LORD our God, for good;
recollect us for blessing, and deliver us for life.
In accord with Your promise of salvation and compassion,
spare us and be gracious to us;
have compassion on us and deliver us,
for our eyes are turned to You because You, God,
are a gracious and compassionate King.

וְתֶחֱזֶינָה And may our eyes witness
Your return to Zion in compassion.
Blessed are You, LORD,
who restores His Presence to Zion.

עבודה

רְצֵה יהוה אֱלֹהֵינוּ בְּעַמְּךָ יִשְׂרָאֵל, וּבִתְפִלָּתָם
וְהָשֵׁב אֶת הָעֲבוֹדָה לִדְבִיר בֵּיתֶךָ
וְאִשֵּׁי יִשְׂרָאֵל וּתְפִלָּתָם בְּאַהֲבָה תְקַבֵּל בְּרָצוֹן
וּתְהִי לְרָצוֹן תָּמִיד עֲבוֹדַת יִשְׂרָאֵל עַמֶּךָ.

On מוצאי שמחת תורה*, continue with* וְתֶחֱזֶינָה *below.*

On חול המועד*, say:*

אֱלֹהֵינוּ וֵאלֹהֵי אֲבוֹתֵינוּ
יַעֲלֶה וְיָבוֹא וְיַגִּיעַ, וְיֵרָאֶה וְיֵרָצֶה וְיִשָּׁמַע
וְיִפָּקֵד וְיִזָּכֵר זִכְרוֹנֵנוּ וּפִקְדוֹנֵנוּ
וְזִכְרוֹן אֲבוֹתֵינוּ
וְזִכְרוֹן מָשִׁיחַ בֶּן דָּוִד עַבְדֶּךָ
וְזִכְרוֹן יְרוּשָׁלַיִם עִיר קָדְשֶׁךָ
וְזִכְרוֹן כָּל עַמְּךָ בֵּית יִשְׂרָאֵל, לְפָנֶיךָ
לִפְלֵיטָה, לְטוֹבָה, לְחֵן וּלְחֶסֶד וּלְרַחֲמִים, לְחַיִּים וּלְשָׁלוֹם
בְּיוֹם חַג הַסֻּכּוֹת הַזֶּה.
זָכְרֵנוּ יהוה אֱלֹהֵינוּ בּוֹ לְטוֹבָה, וּפָקְדֵנוּ בוֹ לִבְרָכָה
וְהוֹשִׁיעֵנוּ בוֹ לְחַיִּים.
וּבִדְבַר יְשׁוּעָה וְרַחֲמִים
חוּס וְחָנֵּנוּ, וְרַחֵם עָלֵינוּ וְהוֹשִׁיעֵנוּ
כִּי אֵלֶיךָ עֵינֵינוּ, כִּי אֵל מֶלֶךְ חַנּוּן וְרַחוּם אָתָּה.

וְתֶחֱזֶינָה עֵינֵינוּ בְּשׁוּבְךָ לְצִיּוֹן בְּרַחֲמִים.
בָּרוּךְ אַתָּה יהוה, הַמַּחֲזִיר שְׁכִינָתוֹ לְצִיּוֹן.

THANKSGIVING

Bow at the first nine words.

מוֹדִים We give thanks to You,
for You are the LORD our God and God of our ancestors
for ever and all time.
You are the Rock of our lives,
Shield of our salvation from generation to generation.
We will thank You and declare Your praise for our lives,
which are entrusted into Your hand;
for our souls, which are placed in Your charge;
for Your miracles which are with us every day;
and for Your wonders and favors at all times,
evening, morning and midday.
You are good – for Your compassion never fails.
You are compassionate –
for Your loving-kindnesses never cease.
We have always placed our hope in You.
For all these things may Your name be blessed and exalted, our King, continually, for ever and all time.
Let all that lives thank You, Selah!
and praise Your name in truth,
God, our Savior and Help, Selah!
Blessed are You, LORD, whose name is "the Good"
and to whom thanks are due.

PEACE

שָׁלוֹם רָב Grant great peace to Your people Israel for ever,
for You are the sovereign LORD of all peace;
and may it be good in Your eyes to bless Your people Israel
at every time, at every hour, with Your peace.
Blessed are You,
LORD, who blesses His people Israel with peace.

הודאה

Bow at the first five words.

מוֹדִים אֲנַחְנוּ לָךְ
שָׁאַתָּה הוּא יהוה אֱלֹהֵינוּ וֵאלֹהֵי אֲבוֹתֵינוּ לְעוֹלָם וָעֶד.
צוּר חַיֵּינוּ, מָגֵן יִשְׁעֵנוּ אַתָּה הוּא לְדוֹר וָדוֹר.
נוֹדֶה לְּךָ וּנְסַפֵּר תְּהִלָּתֶךָ
עַל חַיֵּינוּ הַמְּסוּרִים בְּיָדֶךָ
וְעַל נִשְׁמוֹתֵינוּ הַפְּקוּדוֹת לָךְ
וְעַל נִסֶּיךָ שֶׁבְּכָל יוֹם עִמָּנוּ
וְעַל נִפְלְאוֹתֶיךָ וְטוֹבוֹתֶיךָ
שֶׁבְּכָל עֵת, עֶרֶב וָבֹקֶר וְצָהֳרָיִם.
הַטּוֹב, כִּי לֹא כָלוּ רַחֲמֶיךָ
וְהַמְרַחֵם, כִּי לֹא תַמּוּ חֲסָדֶיךָ מֵעוֹלָם קִוִּינוּ לָךְ.
וְעַל כֻּלָּם יִתְבָּרַךְ וְיִתְרוֹמַם שִׁמְךָ מַלְכֵּנוּ תָּמִיד לְעוֹלָם וָעֶד.
וְכֹל הַחַיִּים יוֹדוּךָ סֶּלָה, וִיהַלְלוּ אֶת שִׁמְךָ בֶּאֱמֶת
הָאֵל יְשׁוּעָתֵנוּ וְעֶזְרָתֵנוּ סֶלָה.
בָּרוּךְ אַתָּה יהוה, הַטּוֹב שִׁמְךָ וּלְךָ נָאֶה לְהוֹדוֹת.

ברכת שלום

שָׁלוֹם רָב עַל יִשְׂרָאֵל עַמְּךָ תָּשִׂים לְעוֹלָם
כִּי אַתָּה הוּא מֶלֶךְ אָדוֹן לְכָל הַשָּׁלוֹם.
וְטוֹב בְּעֵינֶיךָ לְבָרֵךְ אֶת עַמְּךָ יִשְׂרָאֵל
בְּכָל עֵת וּבְכָל שָׁעָה בִּשְׁלוֹמֶךָ.
בָּרוּךְ אַתָּה יהוה, הַמְבָרֵךְ אֶת עַמּוֹ יִשְׂרָאֵל בַּשָּׁלוֹם.

Some say the following verse:
May the words of my mouth and the meditation of my heart find favor before You, LORD, my Rock and Redeemer. *Ps. 19*

אֱלֹהַי My God, *Berakhot 17a*
guard my tongue from evil and my lips from deceitful speech.
To those who curse me, let my soul be silent;
may my soul be to all like the dust.
Open my heart to Your Torah
and let my soul pursue Your commandments.
As for all who plan evil against me,
swiftly thwart their counsel and frustrate their plans.
Act for the sake of Your name;
act for the sake of Your right hand;
act for the sake of Your holiness;
act for the sake of Your Torah.
That Your beloved ones may be delivered, *Ps. 60*
save with Your right hand and answer me.
May the words of my mouth *Ps. 19*
and the meditation of my heart find favor before You,
LORD, my Rock and Redeemer.

Bow, take three steps back, then bow, first left, then right, then center, while saying:
May He who makes peace in His high places,
make peace for us and all Israel –
and say: Amen.

יְהִי רָצוֹן May it be Your will, LORD our God and God of our ancestors,
that the Temple be rebuilt speedily in our days,
and grant us a share in Your Torah.
And there we will serve You with reverence,
as in the days of old and as in former years.
Then the offering of Judah and Jerusalem *Mal. 3*
will be pleasing to the LORD as in the days of old and as in former years.

In Israel, if Motza'ei Simḥat Torah falls on Motza'ei Shabbat, the Leader continues with Half Kaddish and "May the pleasantness" on the next page.
On other evenings the Leader says Full Kaddish on page 1370.

Some say the following verse:

יִהְיוּ לְרָצוֹן אִמְרֵי־פִי וְהֶגְיוֹן לִבִּי לְפָנֶיךָ, יהוה צוּרִי וְגֹאֲלִי: תהלים יט

אֱלֹהַי ברכות יז.

נְצֹר לְשׁוֹנִי מֵרָע וּשְׂפָתַי מִדַּבֵּר מִרְמָה

וְלִמְקַלְלַי נַפְשִׁי תִדֹּם, וְנַפְשִׁי כֶּעָפָר לַכֹּל תִּהְיֶה.

פְּתַח לִבִּי בְּתוֹרָתֶךָ, וּבְמִצְוֹתֶיךָ תִּרְדֹּף נַפְשִׁי.

וְכָל הַחוֹשְׁבִים עָלַי רָעָה

מְהֵרָה הָפֵר עֲצָתָם וְקַלְקֵל מַחֲשַׁבְתָּם.

עֲשֵׂה לְמַעַן שְׁמֶךָ

עֲשֵׂה לְמַעַן יְמִינֶךָ

עֲשֵׂה לְמַעַן קְדֻשָּׁתֶךָ

עֲשֵׂה לְמַעַן תּוֹרָתֶךָ.

לְמַעַן יֵחָלְצוּן יְדִידֶיךָ, הוֹשִׁיעָה יְמִינְךָ וַעֲנֵנִי: תהלים ס

יִהְיוּ לְרָצוֹן אִמְרֵי־פִי וְהֶגְיוֹן לִבִּי לְפָנֶיךָ, יהוה צוּרִי וְגֹאֲלִי: תהלים יט

Bow, take three steps back, then bow, first left, then right, then center, while saying:

עֹשֶׂה שָׁלוֹם בִּמְרוֹמָיו

הוּא יַעֲשֶׂה שָׁלוֹם עָלֵינוּ וְעַל כָּל יִשְׂרָאֵל

וְאִמְרוּ אָמֵן.

יְהִי רָצוֹן מִלְּפָנֶיךָ יהוה אֱלֹהֵינוּ וֵאלֹהֵי אֲבוֹתֵינוּ

שֶׁיִּבָּנֶה בֵּית הַמִּקְדָּשׁ בִּמְהֵרָה בְיָמֵינוּ, וְתֵן חֶלְקֵנוּ בְּתוֹרָתֶךָ

וְשָׁם נַעֲבָדְךָ בְּיִרְאָה כִּימֵי עוֹלָם וּכְשָׁנִים קַדְמוֹנִיּוֹת.

וְעָרְבָה לַיהוה מִנְחַת יְהוּדָה וִירוּשָׁלָיִם כִּימֵי עוֹלָם וּכְשָׁנִים קַדְמוֹנִיּוֹת: מלאכי ג

In ארץ ישראל*, if* מוצאי שמחת תורה *falls on* מוצאי שבת*, the* שליח ציבור *continues with* חצי קדיש *and* וִיהִי נֹעַם *on the next page.*

On other evenings the שליח ציבור *says* קדיש שלם *on page 1371.*

HALF KADDISH

Leader: יִתְגַּדַּל Magnified and sanctified may His great name be,
in the world He created by His will.
May He establish His kingdom
in your lifetime and in your days,
and in the lifetime of all the house of Israel,
swiftly and soon – and say: Amen.

All: May His great name be blessed for ever and all time.

Leader: Blessed and praised, glorified and exalted,
raised and honored, uplifted and lauded be
the name of the Holy One,
blessed be He, beyond any blessing,
song, praise and consolation
uttered in the world – and say: Amen.

וִיהִי נֹעַם May the pleasantness of the LORD our God be upon us. Establish *Ps. 90*
for us the work of our hands, O establish the work of our hands.

יֹשֵׁב He who lives in the shelter of the Most High dwells in the shadow of *Ps. 91*
the Almighty. I say of the LORD, my Refuge and Stronghold, my God in whom I trust, that He will save you from the fowler's snare and the deadly pestilence. With His pinions He will cover you, and beneath His wings you will find shelter; His faithfulness is an encircling shield. You need not fear terror by night, nor the arrow that flies by day; not the pestilence that stalks in darkness, nor the plague that ravages at noon. A thousand may fall at your side, ten thousand at your right hand, but it will not come near you. You will only look with your eyes and see the punishment of the wicked. Because you said, "The LORD is my Refuge," taking the Most High as your shelter, no harm will befall you, no plague come near your tent, for He will command His angels about you, to guard you in all your ways. They will lift you in their hands, lest your foot stumble on a stone. You will tread on lions and vipers; you will trample on young lions and snakes. [God says:] "Because he loves Me, I will rescue him; I will protect him, because he acknowledges My name. When he calls on Me, I will answer him; I will be with him in distress, I will deliver him and bring him honor.
▸ With long life I will satisfy him and show him My salvation.
With long life I will satisfy him and show him My salvation.

חצי קדיש

ש״ץ: יִתְגַּדַּל וְיִתְקַדַּשׁ שְׁמֵהּ רַבָּא (קהל: אָמֵן)
בְּעָלְמָא דִּי בְרָא כִרְעוּתֵהּ
וְיַמְלִיךְ מַלְכוּתֵהּ
בְּחַיֵּיכוֹן וּבְיוֹמֵיכוֹן וּבְחַיֵּי דְכָל בֵּית יִשְׂרָאֵל
בַּעֲגָלָא וּבִזְמַן קָרִיב, וְאִמְרוּ אָמֵן. (קהל: אָמֵן)

קהל וש״ץ: יְהֵא שְׁמֵהּ רַבָּא מְבָרַךְ לְעָלַם וּלְעָלְמֵי עָלְמַיָּא.

ש״ץ: יִתְבָּרַךְ וְיִשְׁתַּבַּח וְיִתְפָּאַר וְיִתְרוֹמַם וְיִתְנַשֵּׂא
וְיִתְהַדָּר וְיִתְעַלֶּה וְיִתְהַלָּל
שְׁמֵהּ דְּקֻדְשָׁא בְּרִיךְ הוּא (קהל: בְּרִיךְ הוּא)
לְעֵלָּא מִן כָּל בִּרְכָתָא וְשִׁירָתָא, תֻּשְׁבְּחָתָא וְנֶחֱמָתָא
דַּאֲמִירָן בְּעָלְמָא, וְאִמְרוּ אָמֵן. (קהל: אָמֵן)

תהלים צ וִיהִי נֹעַם אֲדֹנָי אֱלֹהֵינוּ עָלֵינוּ וּמַעֲשֵׂה יָדֵינוּ כּוֹנְנָה עָלֵינוּ וּמַעֲשֵׂה יָדֵינוּ
כּוֹנְנֵהוּ:

תהלים צא יֹשֵׁב בְּסֵתֶר עֶלְיוֹן, בְּצֵל שַׁדַּי יִתְלוֹנָן: אֹמַר לַיהוה מַחְסִי וּמְצוּדָתִי,
אֱלֹהַי אֶבְטַח־בּוֹ: כִּי הוּא יַצִּילְךָ מִפַּח יָקוּשׁ, מִדֶּבֶר הַוּוֹת: בְּאֶבְרָתוֹ
יָסֶךְ לָךְ, וְתַחַת־כְּנָפָיו תֶּחְסֶה, צִנָּה וְסֹחֵרָה אֲמִתּוֹ: לֹא־תִירָא מִפַּחַד
לָיְלָה, מֵחֵץ יָעוּף יוֹמָם: מִדֶּבֶר בָּאֹפֶל יַהֲלֹךְ, מִקֶּטֶב יָשׁוּד צָהֳרָיִם:
יִפֹּל מִצִּדְּךָ אֶלֶף, וּרְבָבָה מִימִינֶךָ, אֵלֶיךָ לֹא יִגָּשׁ: רַק בְּעֵינֶיךָ תַבִּיט,
וְשִׁלֻּמַת רְשָׁעִים תִּרְאֶה: כִּי־אַתָּה יהוה מַחְסִי, עֶלְיוֹן שַׂמְתָּ מְעוֹנֶךָ:
לֹא־תְאֻנֶּה אֵלֶיךָ רָעָה, וְנֶגַע לֹא־יִקְרַב בְּאָהֳלֶךָ: כִּי מַלְאָכָיו יְצַוֶּה־לָּךְ,
לִשְׁמָרְךָ בְּכָל־דְּרָכֶיךָ: עַל־כַּפַּיִם יִשָּׂאוּנְךָ, פֶּן־תִּגֹּף בָּאֶבֶן רַגְלֶךָ: עַל־
שַׁחַל וָפֶתֶן תִּדְרֹךְ, תִּרְמֹס כְּפִיר וְתַנִּין: כִּי בִי חָשַׁק וַאֲפַלְּטֵהוּ, אֲשַׂגְּבֵהוּ
כִּי־יָדַע שְׁמִי: יִקְרָאֵנִי וְאֶעֱנֵהוּ, עִמּוֹ אָנֹכִי בְצָרָה, אֲחַלְּצֵהוּ וַאֲכַבְּדֵהוּ:
◂ אֹרֶךְ יָמִים אַשְׂבִּיעֵהוּ, וְאַרְאֵהוּ בִּישׁוּעָתִי:
אֹרֶךְ יָמִים אַשְׂבִּיעֵהוּ, וְאַרְאֵהוּ בִּישׁוּעָתִי:

▸ You are the Holy One, enthroned on the praises of Israel. *Ps. 22*
And [the angels] call to one another, saying, "Holy, holy, holy *Is. 6*
is the LORD of hosts; the whole world is filled with His glory."
And they receive permission from one another, saying: "Holy in the highest heavens, home of His Presence; holy on earth, the work of His strength; holy for ever and all time is the LORD of hosts; the whole earth is full of His radiant glory." *Targum Yonatan Is. 6*

▸ Then a wind lifted me up and I heard behind me the sound of a great noise, saying, "Blessed is the LORD's glory from His place." *Ezek. 3*
Then a wind lifted me up and I heard behind me the sound of a great tempest of those who uttered praise, saying, "Blessed is the LORD's glory from the place of the home of His Presence." *Targum Yonatan Ezek. 3*

The LORD shall reign for ever and all time. *Ex. 15*
The LORD's kingdom is established for ever and all time. *Targum Onkelos E*

יהוה LORD, God of Abraham, Isaac and Yisrael, our ancestors, may You keep this for ever so that it forms the thoughts in Your people's heart, and directs their heart toward You. He is compassionate. He forgives iniquity and does not destroy. Repeatedly He suppresses His anger, not rousing His full wrath. For You, my LORD, are good and forgiving, abundantly kind to all who call on You. Your righteousness is eternally righteous, and Your Torah is truth. Grant truth to Jacob, loving-kindness to Abraham, as You promised our ancestors in ancient times. Blessed is my LORD for day after day He burdens us [with His blessings]; God is our salvation, Selah! The LORD of hosts is with us; the God of Jacob is our refuge, Selah! LORD of hosts, happy is the one who trusts in You. LORD, save! May the King answer us on the day we call. *1 Chr. 29; Ps. 78; Ps. 86; Ps. 119; Mic. 7; Ps. 68; Ps. 46; Ps. 84; Ps. 20*

בָּרוּךְ Blessed is He, our God, who created us for His glory, separating us from those who go astray; who gave us the Torah of truth, planting within us eternal life. May He open our heart to His Torah, imbuing our heart with the love and awe of Him, that we may do His will and serve Him with a perfect heart, so that we neither toil in vain nor give birth to confusion.

יְהִי רָצוֹן May it be Your will, O LORD our God and God of our ancestors, that we keep Your laws in this world, and thus be worthy to live, see and inherit goodness and blessing in the Messianic Age and in the life of the World to Come. So that my soul may sing to You and not be silent. LORD, my God, for ever I will thank You. Blessed is the man who trusts in the LORD, whose trust is in the LORD alone. Trust in the LORD for evermore, *Ps. 30; Jer. 17; Is. 26*

◂ וְאַתָּה קָדוֹשׁ יוֹשֵׁב תְּהִלּוֹת יִשְׂרָאֵל: וְקָרָא זֶה אֶל־זֶה וְאָמַר קָדוֹשׁ, תהלים כב ישעיה ו
קָדוֹשׁ, קָדוֹשׁ, יהוה צְבָאוֹת, מְלֹא כָל־הָאָרֶץ כְּבוֹדוֹ:

וּמְקַבְּלִין דֵּין מִן דֵּין וְאָמְרִין, קַדִּישׁ בִּשְׁמֵי מְרוֹמָא עִלָּאָה בֵּית שְׁכִינְתֵּהּ, קַדִּישׁ תרגום יונתן ישעיה ו
עַל אַרְעָא עוֹבַד גְּבוּרְתֵּהּ, קַדִּישׁ לְעָלַם וּלְעָלְמֵי עָלְמַיָּא יהוה צְבָאוֹת, מַלְיָא
כָּל אַרְעָא זִיו יְקָרֵהּ.

◂ וַתִּשָּׂאֵנִי רוּחַ, וָאֶשְׁמַע אַחֲרַי קוֹל רַעַשׁ גָּדוֹל, בָּרוּךְ כְּבוֹד־יהוה מִמְּקוֹמוֹ: יחזקאל ג
וּנְטָלַתְנִי רוּחָא, וּשְׁמָעִית בַּתְרַי קָל זִיעַ סַגִּיא, דִּמְשַׁבְּחִין וְאָמְרִין, בְּרִיךְ יְקָרָא תרגום יונתן יחזקאל ג
דַּיהוה מֵאֲתַר בֵּית שְׁכִינְתֵּהּ.

יהוה יִמְלֹךְ לְעֹלָם וָעֶד: שמות טו
יהוה מַלְכוּתֵהּ קָאֵם לְעָלַם וּלְעָלְמֵי עָלְמַיָּא. תרגום אונקלוס שמות טו

יהוה אֱלֹהֵי אַבְרָהָם יִצְחָק וְיִשְׂרָאֵל אֲבֹתֵינוּ, שָׁמְרָה־זֹּאת לְעוֹלָם לְיֵצֶר דברי הימים א׳ כט
מַחְשְׁבוֹת לְבַב עַמֶּךָ, וְהָכֵן לְבָבָם אֵלֶיךָ: וְהוּא רַחוּם יְכַפֵּר עָוֹן וְלֹא־ תהלים עח
יַשְׁחִית, וְהִרְבָּה לְהָשִׁיב אַפּוֹ, וְלֹא־יָעִיר כָּל־חֲמָתוֹ: כִּי־אַתָּה אֲדֹנָי טוֹב תהלים פו
וְסַלָּח, וְרַב־חֶסֶד לְכָל־קֹרְאֶיךָ: צִדְקָתְךָ צֶדֶק לְעוֹלָם וְתוֹרָתְךָ אֱמֶת: תהלים קיט
תִּתֵּן אֱמֶת לְיַעֲקֹב, חֶסֶד לְאַבְרָהָם, אֲשֶׁר־נִשְׁבַּעְתָּ לַאֲבֹתֵינוּ מִימֵי קֶדֶם: מיכה ז
בָּרוּךְ אֲדֹנָי יוֹם יוֹם יַעֲמָס־לָנוּ, הָאֵל יְשׁוּעָתֵנוּ סֶלָה: יהוה צְבָאוֹת עִמָּנוּ, תהלים סח תהלים מו
מִשְׂגָּב לָנוּ אֱלֹהֵי יַעֲקֹב סֶלָה: יהוה צְבָאוֹת, אַשְׁרֵי אָדָם בֹּטֵחַ בָּךְ: יהוה תהלים פד תהלים כ
הוֹשִׁיעָה, הַמֶּלֶךְ יַעֲנֵנוּ בְיוֹם־קָרְאֵנוּ:

בָּרוּךְ הוּא אֱלֹהֵינוּ שֶׁבְּרָאָנוּ לִכְבוֹדוֹ, וְהִבְדִּילָנוּ מִן הַתּוֹעִים, וְנָתַן לָנוּ תּוֹרַת אֱמֶת, וְחַיֵּי עוֹלָם נָטַע בְּתוֹכֵנוּ. הוּא יִפְתַּח לִבֵּנוּ בְּתוֹרָתוֹ, וְיָשֵׂם בְּלִבֵּנוּ אַהֲבָתוֹ וְיִרְאָתוֹ וְלַעֲשׂוֹת רְצוֹנוֹ וּלְעָבְדוֹ בְּלֵבָב שָׁלֵם, לְמַעַן לֹא נִיגַע לָרִיק וְלֹא נֵלֵד לַבֶּהָלָה.

יְהִי רָצוֹן מִלְּפָנֶיךָ יהוה אֱלֹהֵינוּ וֵאלֹהֵי אֲבוֹתֵינוּ, שֶׁנִּשְׁמֹר חֻקֶּיךָ בָּעוֹלָם הַזֶּה, וְנִזְכֶּה וְנִחְיֶה וְנִרְאֶה וְנִירַשׁ טוֹבָה וּבְרָכָה, לִשְׁנֵי יְמוֹת הַמָּשִׁיחַ וּלְחַיֵּי
הָעוֹלָם הַבָּא. לְמַעַן יְזַמֶּרְךָ כָבוֹד וְלֹא יִדֹּם, יהוה אֱלֹהַי, לְעוֹלָם אוֹדֶךָּ: תהלים ל
בָּרוּךְ הַגֶּבֶר אֲשֶׁר יִבְטַח בַּיהוה, וְהָיָה יהוה מִבְטַחוֹ: בִּטְחוּ בַיהוה עֲדֵי־ ישעיה כו ירמיה יז

for God, the Lord, is an everlasting Rock. ▸ Those who know Your name Ps. 9
trust in You, for You, Lord, do not forsake those who seek You. The Lord Is. 42
desired, for the sake of Israel's merit, to make the Torah great and glorious.

FULL KADDISH

Some have the custom to include additional responses in Full Kaddish.
They can be found in the version on page 1464.

Leader: יִתְגַּדַּל Magnified and sanctified may His great name be,
in the world He created by His will.
May He establish His kingdom in your lifetime
and in your days, and in the lifetime
of all the house of Israel,
swiftly and soon –
and say: Amen.

All: May His great name be blessed for ever and all time.

Leader: Blessed and praised, glorified and exalted,
raised and honored, uplifted and lauded be
the name of the Holy One, blessed be He,
beyond any blessing, song, praise and consolation
uttered in the world –
and say: Amen.

May the prayers and pleas of all Israel
be accepted by their Father in heaven –
and say: Amen.

May there be great peace from heaven,
and life for us and all Israel –
and say: Amen.

Bow, take three steps back, as if taking leave of the Divine Presence,
then bow, first left, then right, then center, while saying:

May He who makes peace in His high places,
make peace for us and all Israel –
and say: Amen.

On Motza'ei Yom Tov which is not Motza'ei Shabbat, continue with Havdala on page 1378.
On Motza'ei Shabbat, continue "May God give you" on the next page.
On a weekday, the service continues with Aleinu on page 1378.

עַד, כִּי בְּיָהּ יהוה צוּר עוֹלָמִים: ◂ וְיִבְטְחוּ בְךָ יוֹדְעֵי שְׁמֶךָ, כִּי לֹא־עָזַבְתָּ תהלים ט
דֹרְשֶׁיךָ, יהוה: יהוה חָפֵץ לְמַעַן צִדְקוֹ, יַגְדִּיל תּוֹרָה וְיַאְדִּיר: ישעיה מב

קדיש שלם

Some have the custom to include additional responses in קדיש שלם*.*
They can be found in the version on page 1465.

ש״ץ: יִתְגַּדַּל וְיִתְקַדַּשׁ שְׁמֵהּ רַבָּא (קהל: אָמֵן)
בְּעָלְמָא דִּי בְרָא כִרְעוּתֵהּ
וְיַמְלִיךְ מַלְכוּתֵהּ
בְּחַיֵּיכוֹן וּבְיוֹמֵיכוֹן וּבְחַיֵּי דְכָל בֵּית יִשְׂרָאֵל
בַּעֲגָלָא וּבִזְמַן קָרִיב, וְאִמְרוּ אָמֵן. (קהל: אָמֵן)

קהל וש״ץ: יְהֵא שְׁמֵהּ רַבָּא מְבָרַךְ לְעָלַם וּלְעָלְמֵי עָלְמַיָּא.

ש״ץ: יִתְבָּרַךְ וְיִשְׁתַּבַּח וְיִתְפָּאַר
וְיִתְרוֹמַם וְיִתְנַשֵּׂא וְיִתְהַדָּר וְיִתְעַלֶּה וְיִתְהַלָּל
שְׁמֵהּ דְּקֻדְשָׁא בְּרִיךְ הוּא (קהל: בְּרִיךְ הוּא)
לְעֵלָּא מִן כָּל בִּרְכָתָא וְשִׁירָתָא, תֻּשְׁבְּחָתָא וְנֶחֱמָתָא
דַּאֲמִירָן בְּעָלְמָא, וְאִמְרוּ אָמֵן. (קהל: אָמֵן)

תִּתְקַבַּל צְלוֹתְהוֹן וּבָעוּתְהוֹן דְּכָל יִשְׂרָאֵל
קֳדָם אֲבוּהוֹן דִּי בִשְׁמַיָּא, וְאִמְרוּ אָמֵן. (קהל: אָמֵן)

יְהֵא שְׁלָמָא רַבָּא מִן שְׁמַיָּא
וְחַיִּים, עָלֵינוּ וְעַל כָּל יִשְׂרָאֵל, וְאִמְרוּ אָמֵן. (קהל: אָמֵן)

Bow, take three steps back, as if taking leave of the Divine Presence, then bow, first left, then right, then center, while saying:

עֹשֶׂה שָׁלוֹם בִּמְרוֹמָיו, הוּא יַעֲשֶׂה שָׁלוֹם
עָלֵינוּ וְעַל כָּל יִשְׂרָאֵל, וְאִמְרוּ אָמֵן. (קהל: אָמֵן)

On מוצאי יום טוב *which is not* מוצאי שבת*, continue with* הבדלה *on page 1379.*
On מוצאי שבת*, continue* וְיִתֶּן־לְךָ *on the next page.*
On a weekday, the service continues with עָלֵינוּ *on page 1379.*

BIBLICAL VERSES OF BLESSING

וְיִתֶּן־לְךָ May God give you dew from heaven and the richness of the earth, and Gen. 27
corn and wine in plenty. May peoples serve you and nations bow down to you.
Be lord over your brothers, and may your mother's sons bow down to you. A
curse on those who curse you, but a blessing on those who bless you.

וְאֵל שַׁדַּי May God Almighty bless you; may He make you fruitful and numerous Gen. 28
until you become an assembly of peoples. May He give you and your descendants
the blessing of Abraham, that you may possess the land where you are now staying,
the land God gave to Abraham. This comes from the God of your father – may Gen. 49
He help you – and from the Almighty – may He bless you with blessings of the
heaven above and the blessings of the deep that lies below, the blessings of breast
and womb. The blessings of your father surpass the blessings of my fathers to the
bounds of the endless hills. May they rest on the head of Joseph, on the brow of
the prince among his brothers. He will love you and bless you and increase your Deut. 7
numbers. He will bless the fruit of your womb and the fruit of your land: your
corn, your wine and oil, the calves of your herds and the lambs of your flocks,
in the land He swore to your fathers to give you. You will be blessed more than
any other people. None of your men or women will be childless, nor any of your
livestock without young. The Lord will keep you free from any disease. He will
not inflict on you the terrible diseases you knew in Egypt, but He will inflict them
on those who hate you.

הַמַּלְאָךְ May the angel who rescued me from all harm, bless these boys. May Gen. 48
they be called by my name and the names of my fathers Abraham and Isaac,
and may they increase greatly on the earth. The Lord your God has increased Deut. 1
your numbers so that today you are as many as the stars in the sky. May the
Lord, God of your fathers, increase you a thousand times, and bless you as
He promised you.

בָּרוּךְ You will be blessed in the city, and blessed in the field. You will be blessed Deut. 28
when you come in, and blessed when you go out. Your basket and your kneading
trough will be blessed. The fruit of your womb will be blessed, and the crops of
your land, and the young of your livestock, the calves of your herds and the lambs
of your flocks. The Lord will send a blessing on your barns, and on everything
you put your hand to. The Lord your God will bless you in the land He is giving
you. The Lord will open for you the heavens, the storehouse of His bounty, to
send rain on your land in season, and to bless all the work of your hands. You
will lend to many nations but will borrow from none. For the Lord your God Deut. 15
will bless you as He has promised: you will lend to many nations but will borrow
from none. You will rule over many nations, but none will rule over you. Happy Deut. 33

פסוקי ברכה

וְיִתֶּן־לְךָ הָאֱלֹהִים מִטַּל הַשָּׁמַיִם וּמִשְׁמַנֵּי הָאָרֶץ, וְרֹב דָּגָן וְתִירֹשׁ: יַעַבְדוּךָ בראשית כז
עַמִּים וְיִשְׁתַּחֲוֻ לְךָ לְאֻמִּים, הֱוֵה גְבִיר לְאַחֶיךָ וְיִשְׁתַּחֲווּ לְךָ בְּנֵי אִמֶּךָ,
אֹרְרֶיךָ אָרוּר וּמְבָרְכֶיךָ בָּרוּךְ:

וְאֵל שַׁדַּי יְבָרֵךְ אֹתְךָ וְיַפְרְךָ וְיַרְבֶּךָ, וְהָיִיתָ לִקְהַל עַמִּים: וְיִתֶּן־לְךָ אֶת־ בראשית כח
בִּרְכַּת אַבְרָהָם, לְךָ וּלְזַרְעֲךָ אִתָּךְ, לְרִשְׁתְּךָ אֶת־אֶרֶץ מְגֻרֶיךָ אֲשֶׁר־נָתַן
אֱלֹהִים לְאַבְרָהָם: מֵאֵל אָבִיךָ וְיַעְזְרֶךָּ וְאֵת שַׁדַּי וִיבָרְכֶךָּ, בִּרְכֹת שָׁמַיִם בראשית מט
מֵעָל בִּרְכֹת תְּהוֹם רֹבֶצֶת תָּחַת, בִּרְכֹת שָׁדַיִם וָרָחַם: בִּרְכֹת אָבִיךָ גָּבְרוּ
עַל־בִּרְכֹת הוֹרַי עַד־תַּאֲוַת גִּבְעֹת עוֹלָם, תִּהְיֶיןָ לְרֹאשׁ יוֹסֵף וּלְקָדְקֹד
נְזִיר אֶחָיו: וַאֲהֵבְךָ וּבֵרַכְךָ וְהִרְבֶּךָ, וּבֵרַךְ פְּרִי־בִטְנְךָ וּפְרִי־אַדְמָתֶךָ, דְּגָנְךָ דברים ז
וְתִירֹשְׁךָ וְיִצְהָרֶךָ, שְׁגַר־אֲלָפֶיךָ וְעַשְׁתְּרֹת צֹאנֶךָ, עַל הָאֲדָמָה אֲשֶׁר־נִשְׁבַּע
לַאֲבֹתֶיךָ לָתֶת לָךְ: בָּרוּךְ תִּהְיֶה מִכָּל־הָעַמִּים, לֹא־יִהְיֶה בְךָ עָקָר וַעֲקָרָה
וּבִבְהֶמְתֶּךָ: וְהֵסִיר יהוה מִמְּךָ כָּל־חֹלִי, וְכָל־מַדְוֵי מִצְרַיִם הָרָעִים אֲשֶׁר
יָדַעְתָּ, לֹא יְשִׂימָם בָּךְ, וּנְתָנָם בְּכָל־שֹׂנְאֶיךָ:

הַמַּלְאָךְ הַגֹּאֵל אֹתִי מִכָּל־רָע יְבָרֵךְ אֶת־הַנְּעָרִים, וְיִקָּרֵא בָהֶם שְׁמִי וְשֵׁם בראשית מח
אֲבֹתַי אַבְרָהָם וְיִצְחָק, וְיִדְגּוּ לָרֹב בְּקֶרֶב הָאָרֶץ: יהוה אֱלֹהֵיכֶם הִרְבָּה דברים א
אֶתְכֶם, וְהִנְּכֶם הַיּוֹם כְּכוֹכְבֵי הַשָּׁמַיִם לָרֹב: יהוה אֱלֹהֵי אֲבוֹתֵיכֶם יֹסֵף
עֲלֵיכֶם כָּכֶם אֶלֶף פְּעָמִים, וִיבָרֵךְ אֶתְכֶם כַּאֲשֶׁר דִּבֶּר לָכֶם:

בָּרוּךְ אַתָּה בָּעִיר, וּבָרוּךְ אַתָּה בַּשָּׂדֶה: בָּרוּךְ אַתָּה בְּבֹאֶךָ, וּבָרוּךְ אַתָּה דברים כח
בְּצֵאתֶךָ: בָּרוּךְ טַנְאֲךָ וּמִשְׁאַרְתֶּךָ: בָּרוּךְ פְּרִי־בִטְנְךָ וּפְרִי אַדְמָתְךָ וּפְרִי
בְהֶמְתֶּךָ, שְׁגַר אֲלָפֶיךָ וְעַשְׁתְּרוֹת צֹאנֶךָ: יְצַו יהוה אִתְּךָ אֶת־הַבְּרָכָה
בַּאֲסָמֶיךָ וּבְכֹל מִשְׁלַח יָדֶךָ, וּבֵרַכְךָ בָּאָרֶץ אֲשֶׁר־יהוה אֱלֹהֶיךָ נֹתֵן לָךְ:
יִפְתַּח יהוה לְךָ אֶת־אוֹצָרוֹ הַטּוֹב אֶת־הַשָּׁמַיִם, לָתֵת מְטַר־אַרְצְךָ בְּעִתּוֹ,
וּלְבָרֵךְ אֵת כָּל־מַעֲשֵׂה יָדֶךָ, וְהִלְוִיתָ גּוֹיִם רַבִּים וְאַתָּה לֹא תִלְוֶה: כִּי־יהוה דברים טו
אֱלֹהֶיךָ בֵּרַכְךָ כַּאֲשֶׁר דִּבֶּר־לָךְ, וְהַעֲבַטְתָּ גּוֹיִם רַבִּים וְאַתָּה לֹא תַעֲבֹט,
וּמָשַׁלְתָּ בְּגוֹיִם רַבִּים וּבְךָ לֹא יִמְשֹׁלוּ: אַשְׁרֶיךָ יִשְׂרָאֵל, מִי כָמוֹךָ, עַם דברים לג

are you, Israel! Who is like you, a people saved by the Lord? He is your Shield
and Helper and your glorious Sword. Your enemies will cower before you, and
you will tread on their high places.

מָחִיתִי I have wiped away your transgressions like a cloud, your sins like the morn- *Is. 44*
ing mist. Return to Me for I have redeemed you. Sing for joy, O heavens, for the
Lord has done this; shout aloud, you depths of the earth; burst into song, you
mountains, you forests and all your trees, for the Lord has redeemed Jacob, and
will glory in Israel. Our Redeemer, the Lord of hosts is His name, the Holy One *Is. 47*
of Israel.

יִשְׂרָאֵל Israel is saved by the Lord with everlasting salvation. You will never be *Is. 45*
ashamed or disgraced to time everlasting. You will eat your fill and praise the *Joel 2*
name of the Lord your God, who has worked wonders for you. Never again
shall My people be shamed. Then you will know that I am in the midst of Israel,
that I am the Lord your God, and there is no other. Never again will My people
be shamed. You will go out in joy and be led out in peace. The mountains and *Is. 55*
hills will burst into song before you, and all the trees of the field will clap their
hands. Behold, God is my salvation, I will trust and not be afraid. The Lord, the *Is. 12*
Lord, is my strength and my song. He has become my salvation. With joy you
will draw water from the springs of salvation. On that day you will say, "Thank
the Lord, proclaim His name, make His deeds known among the nations."
Declare that His name is exalted. Sing to the Lord, for He has done glorious
things; let this be known throughout the world. Shout aloud and sing for joy,
you who dwell in Zion, for great in your midst is the Holy One of Israel. On that *Is. 25*
day they will say, "See, this is our God; we set our hope in Him and He saved us.
This is the Lord in whom we hoped; let us rejoice and be glad in His salvation."

בֵּית Come, house of Jacob: let us walk in the light of the Lord. He will be the *Is. 2* *Is. 32*
sure foundation of your times; a rich store of salvation, wisdom and knowl-
edge – the fear of the Lord is a person's treasure. In everything he did, David *I Sam. 18*
was successful, for the Lord was with him.

פָּדָה He redeemed my soul in peace from the battle waged against me, for the *Ps. 55*
sake of the many who were with me. The people said to Saul, "Shall Jonathan *I Sam. 14*
die – he who has brought about this great deliverance in Israel? Heaven forbid!
As surely as the Lord lives, not a hair of his head shall fall to the ground, for he
did this today with God's help." So the people rescued Jonathan and he did not
die. Those redeemed by the Lord shall return; they will enter Zion singing; *Is. 35*
everlasting joy will crown their heads. Gladness and joy will overtake them, and
sorrow and sighing will flee away.

נוֹשַׁע בַּיהוה, מָגֵן עֶזְרֶךָ וַאֲשֶׁר־חֶרֶב גַּאֲוָתֶךָ, וְיִכָּחֲשׁוּ אֹיְבֶיךָ לָךְ, וְאַתָּה
עַל־בָּמוֹתֵימוֹ תִדְרֹךְ:

מָחִיתִי כָעָב פְּשָׁעֶיךָ וְכֶעָנָן חַטֹּאותֶיךָ, שׁוּבָה אֵלַי כִּי גְאַלְתִּיךָ: רָנּוּ שָׁמַיִם ישעיה מד
כִּי־עָשָׂה יהוה, הָרִיעוּ תַּחְתִּיּוֹת אָרֶץ, פִּצְחוּ הָרִים רִנָּה, יַעַר וְכָל־עֵץ בּוֹ,
כִּי־גָאַל יהוה יַעֲקֹב וּבְיִשְׂרָאֵל יִתְפָּאָר: גֹּאֲלֵנוּ, יהוה צְבָאוֹת שְׁמוֹ, קְדוֹשׁ ישעיה מז
יִשְׂרָאֵל:

יִשְׂרָאֵל נוֹשַׁע בַּיהוה תְּשׁוּעַת עוֹלָמִים, לֹא־תֵבֹשׁוּ וְלֹא־תִכָּלְמוּ עַד־עוֹלְמֵי ישעיה מה
עַד: וַאֲכַלְתֶּם אָכוֹל וְשָׂבוֹעַ, וְהִלַּלְתֶּם אֶת־שֵׁם יהוה אֱלֹהֵיכֶם אֲשֶׁר־עָשָׂה יואל ב
עִמָּכֶם לְהַפְלִיא, וְלֹא־יֵבֹשׁוּ עַמִּי לְעוֹלָם: וִידַעְתֶּם כִּי בְקֶרֶב יִשְׂרָאֵל
אָנִי, וַאֲנִי יהוה אֱלֹהֵיכֶם וְאֵין עוֹד, וְלֹא־יֵבֹשׁוּ עַמִּי לְעוֹלָם: כִּי־בְשִׂמְחָה ישעיה נה
תֵצֵאוּ וּבְשָׁלוֹם תּוּבָלוּן, הֶהָרִים וְהַגְּבָעוֹת יִפְצְחוּ לִפְנֵיכֶם רִנָּה, וְכָל־עֲצֵי
הַשָּׂדֶה יִמְחֲאוּ־כָף: הִנֵּה אֵל יְשׁוּעָתִי אֶבְטַח, וְלֹא אֶפְחָד, כִּי־עָזִּי וְזִמְרָת ישעיה יב
יָהּ יהוה, וַיְהִי־לִי לִישׁוּעָה: וּשְׁאַבְתֶּם־מַיִם בְּשָׂשׂוֹן, מִמַּעַיְנֵי הַיְשׁוּעָה:
וַאֲמַרְתֶּם בַּיּוֹם הַהוּא, הוֹדוּ לַיהוה קִרְאוּ בִשְׁמוֹ, הוֹדִיעוּ בָעַמִּים עֲלִילֹתָיו,
הַזְכִּירוּ כִּי נִשְׂגָּב שְׁמוֹ: זַמְּרוּ יהוה כִּי גֵאוּת עָשָׂה, מוּדַעַת זֹאת בְּכָל־
הָאָרֶץ: צַהֲלִי וָרֹנִּי יוֹשֶׁבֶת צִיּוֹן, כִּי־גָדוֹל בְּקִרְבֵּךְ קְדוֹשׁ יִשְׂרָאֵל: וְאָמַר ישעיה כה
בַּיּוֹם הַהוּא, הִנֵּה אֱלֹהֵינוּ זֶה קִוִּינוּ לוֹ וְיוֹשִׁיעֵנוּ, זֶה יהוה קִוִּינוּ לוֹ, נָגִילָה
וְנִשְׂמְחָה בִּישׁוּעָתוֹ:

בֵּית יַעֲקֹב לְכוּ וְנֵלְכָה בְּאוֹר יהוה: וְהָיָה אֱמוּנַת עִתֶּיךָ, חֹסֶן יְשׁוּעֹת ישעיה ב / ישעיה לב
חָכְמַת וָדָעַת, יִרְאַת יהוה הִיא אוֹצָרוֹ: וַיְהִי דָוִד לְכָל־דְּרָכָו מַשְׂכִּיל, שמואל א׳ יד
וַיהוה עִמּוֹ:

פָּדָה בְשָׁלוֹם נַפְשִׁי מִקְּרָב־לִי, כִּי־בְרַבִּים הָיוּ עִמָּדִי: וַיֹּאמֶר הָעָם אֶל־ תהלים נה / שמואל א׳ יד
שָׁאוּל, הֲיוֹנָתָן יָמוּת אֲשֶׁר עָשָׂה הַיְשׁוּעָה הַגְּדוֹלָה הַזֹּאת בְּיִשְׂרָאֵל,
חָלִילָה, חַי־יהוה אִם־יִפֹּל מִשַּׂעֲרַת רֹאשׁוֹ אַרְצָה, כִּי־עִם־אֱלֹהִים עָשָׂה
הַיּוֹם הַזֶּה, וַיִּפְדּוּ הָעָם אֶת־יוֹנָתָן וְלֹא־מֵת: וּפְדוּיֵי יהוה יְשֻׁבוּן וּבָאוּ צִיּוֹן ישעיה לה
בְּרִנָּה, וְשִׂמְחַת עוֹלָם עַל־רֹאשָׁם, שָׂשׂוֹן וְשִׂמְחָה יַשִּׂיגוּ, וְנָסוּ יָגוֹן וַאֲנָחָה:

הָפַכְתָּ You have turned my sorrow into dancing. You have removed my sackcloth *Ps. 30*
and clothed me with joy. The LORD your God refused to listen to Balaam; in- *Deut. 23*
stead the LORD your God turned the curse into a blessing, for the LORD your
God loves you. Then maidens will dance and be glad; so too will young men and *Jer. 31*
old together; I will turn their mourning into gladness; I will give them comfort
and joy instead of sorrow.

בּוֹרֵא I create the speech of lips: Peace, peace to those far and near, says the LORD, *Is. 57*
and I will heal them. Then the spirit came upon Amasai, chief of the captains, *1 Chr. 12*
and he said: "We are yours, David! We are with you, son of Jesse! Peace, peace to
you, and peace to those who help you; for your God will help you." Then David
received them and made them leaders of his troop. And you shall say: "To life! *1 Sam. 25*
Peace be to you, peace to your household, and peace to all that is yours!" The *Ps. 29*
LORD will give strength to His people; the LORD will bless His people with peace.

אָמַר Rabbi Yoḥanan said: Wherever you find the greatness of the Holy One, *Megilla 31*
blessed be He, there you find His humility. This is written in the Torah, repeated
in the Prophets, and stated a third time in the Writings. It is written in the
Torah: "For the LORD your God is God of gods and LORD of lords, the great, *Deut. 10*
mighty and awe-inspiring God, who shows no favoritism and accepts no bribe."
Immediately afterwards it is written, "He upholds the cause of the orphan and
widow, and loves the stranger, giving him food and clothing." It is repeated in the
Prophets, as it says: "So says the High and Exalted One, who lives for ever and *Is. 57*
whose name is Holy: I live in a high and holy place, but also with the contrite
and lowly in spirit, to revive the spirit of the lowly, and to revive the heart of the
contrite." It is stated a third time in the Writings: "Sing to God, make music for *Ps. 68*
His name, extol Him who rides the clouds – the LORD is His name – and exult
before Him." Immediately afterwards it is written: "Father of the orphans and
Justice of widows, is God in His holy habitation."

יְהִי May the LORD our God be with us, as He was with our ancestors. May He *1 Kings 8*
never abandon us or forsake us. You who cleave to the LORD your God are all alive *Deut. 4*
this day. For the LORD will comfort Zion, He will comfort all her ruins; He will *Is. 51*
make her wilderness like Eden, and her desert like a garden of the LORD. Joy and
gladness will be found there, thanksgiving and the sound of singing. It pleased the *Is. 42*
LORD for the sake of [Israel's] righteousness to make the Torah great and glorious.

שִׁיר הַמַּעֲלוֹת A song of ascents. Happy are all who fear the LORD, who walk in His *Ps. 128*
ways. When you eat the fruit of your labor, happy and fortunate are you. Your wife shall be like a fruitful vine within your house; your sons like olive saplings around your table. So shall the man who fears the LORD be blessed. May the LORD bless you from Zion; may you see the good of Jerusalem all the days of your life; and may you live to see your children's children. Peace be on Israel!

תהלים ל הָפַכְתָּ מִסְפְּדִי לְמָחוֹל לִי, פִּתַּחְתָּ שַׂקִּי, וַתְּאַזְּרֵנִי שִׂמְחָה: וְלֹא־אָבָה יהוה
דברים כג אֱלֹהֶיךָ לִשְׁמֹעַ אֶל־בִּלְעָם, וַיַּהֲפֹךְ יהוה אֱלֹהֶיךָ לְּךָ אֶת־הַקְּלָלָה לִבְרָכָה,
ירמיה לא כִּי אֲהֵבְךָ יהוה אֱלֹהֶיךָ: אָז תִּשְׂמַח בְּתוּלָה בְּמָחוֹל, וּבַחֻרִים וּזְקֵנִים יַחְדָּו,
וְהָפַכְתִּי אֶבְלָם לְשָׂשׂוֹן, וְנִחַמְתִּים, וְשִׂמַּחְתִּים מִיגוֹנָם:

ישעיה נז בּוֹרֵא נִיב שְׂפָתָיִם, שָׁלוֹם שָׁלוֹם לָרָחוֹק וְלַקָּרוֹב אָמַר יהוה, וּרְפָאתִיו: וְרוּחַ
דברי הימים א׳ יב לָבְשָׁה אֶת־עֲמָשַׂי רֹאשׁ הַשָּׁלִישִׁים, לְךָ דָוִיד וְעִמְּךָ בֶן־יִשַׁי, שָׁלוֹם שָׁלוֹם
לְךָ וְשָׁלוֹם לְעֹזְרֶךָ, כִּי עֲזָרְךָ אֱלֹהֶיךָ, וַיְקַבְּלֵם דָּוִיד וַיִּתְּנֵם בְּרָאשֵׁי הַגְּדוּד:
שמואל א׳ כ וַאֲמַרְתֶּם כֹּה לֶחָי, וְאַתָּה שָׁלוֹם וּבֵיתְךָ שָׁלוֹם וְכֹל אֲשֶׁר־לְךָ שָׁלוֹם: יהוה
תהלים כט עֹז לְעַמּוֹ יִתֵּן, יהוה יְבָרֵךְ אֶת־עַמּוֹ בַשָּׁלוֹם:

מגילה לא. אָמַר רַבִּי יוֹחָנָן: בְּכָל מָקוֹם שֶׁאַתָּה מוֹצֵא גְּדֻלָּתוֹ שֶׁל הַקָּדוֹשׁ בָּרוּךְ
הוּא, שָׁם אַתָּה מוֹצֵא עַנְוְתָנוּתוֹ. דָּבָר זֶה כָּתוּב בַּתּוֹרָה, וְשָׁנוּי בַּנְּבִיאִים,
דברים י וּמְשֻׁלָּשׁ בַּכְּתוּבִים. כָּתוּב בַּתּוֹרָה: כִּי יהוה אֱלֹהֵיכֶם הוּא אֱלֹהֵי הָאֱלֹהִים
וַאֲדֹנֵי הָאֲדֹנִים, הָאֵל הַגָּדֹל הַגִּבֹּר וְהַנּוֹרָא, אֲשֶׁר לֹא־יִשָּׂא פָנִים וְלֹא יִקַּח
שֹׁחַד: וּכְתִיב בָּתְרֵהּ: עֹשֶׂה מִשְׁפַּט יָתוֹם וְאַלְמָנָה, וְאֹהֵב גֵּר לָתֶת לוֹ לֶחֶם
ישעיה נז וְשִׂמְלָה: שָׁנוּי בַּנְּבִיאִים, דִּכְתִיב: כִּי כֹה אָמַר רָם וְנִשָּׂא שֹׁכֵן עַד וְקָדוֹשׁ
שְׁמוֹ, מָרוֹם וְקָדוֹשׁ אֶשְׁכּוֹן, וְאֶת־דַּכָּא וּשְׁפַל־רוּחַ, לְהַחֲיוֹת רוּחַ שְׁפָלִים
תהלים סח וּלְהַחֲיוֹת לֵב נִדְכָּאִים: מְשֻׁלָּשׁ בַּכְּתוּבִים, דִּכְתִיב: שִׁירוּ לֵאלֹהִים, זַמְּרוּ
שְׁמוֹ, סֹלּוּ לָרֹכֵב בָּעֲרָבוֹת בְּיָהּ שְׁמוֹ, וְעִלְזוּ לְפָנָיו: וּכְתִיב בָּתְרֵהּ: אֲבִי
יְתוֹמִים וְדַיַּן אַלְמָנוֹת, אֱלֹהִים בִּמְעוֹן קָדְשׁוֹ:

מלכים א׳ ח יְהִי יהוה אֱלֹהֵינוּ עִמָּנוּ כַּאֲשֶׁר הָיָה עִם־אֲבֹתֵינוּ, אַל־יַעַזְבֵנוּ וְאַל־יִטְּשֵׁנוּ:
דברים ד וְאַתֶּם הַדְּבֵקִים בַּיהוה אֱלֹהֵיכֶם, חַיִּים כֻּלְּכֶם הַיּוֹם: כִּי־נִחַם יהוה צִיּוֹן, נִחַם
ישעיה נא כָּל־חָרְבֹתֶיהָ, וַיָּשֶׂם מִדְבָּרָהּ כְּעֵדֶן וְעַרְבָתָהּ כְּגַן־יהוה, שָׂשׂוֹן וְשִׂמְחָה יִמָּצֵא
ישעיה מב בָהּ, תּוֹדָה וְקוֹל זִמְרָה: יהוה חָפֵץ לְמַעַן צִדְקוֹ, יַגְדִּיל תּוֹרָה וְיַאְדִּיר:

תהלים קכח שִׁיר הַמַּעֲלוֹת, אַשְׁרֵי כָּל־יְרֵא יהוה, הַהֹלֵךְ בִּדְרָכָיו: יְגִיעַ כַּפֶּיךָ כִּי תֹאכֵל,
אַשְׁרֶיךָ וְטוֹב לָךְ: אֶשְׁתְּךָ כְּגֶפֶן פֹּרִיָּה בְּיַרְכְּתֵי בֵיתֶךָ, בָּנֶיךָ כִּשְׁתִלֵי זֵיתִים,
סָבִיב לְשֻׁלְחָנֶךָ: הִנֵּה כִי־כֵן יְבֹרַךְ גָּבֶר יְרֵא יהוה: יְבָרֶכְךָ יהוה מִצִּיּוֹן, וּרְאֵה
בְּטוּב יְרוּשָׁלָםִ, כֹּל יְמֵי חַיֶּיךָ: וּרְאֵה־בָנִים לְבָנֶיךָ, שָׁלוֹם עַל־יִשְׂרָאֵל:

HAVDALA IN THE SYNAGOGUE

Some say the full Havdala on page 1386.
On Motza'ei Yom Tov that is not on Motza'ei Shabbat, the blessings for the spices and flame are omitted.

The Leader takes the cup of wine in his right hand, and says:
Please pay attention, my masters.

Blessed are You, Lord our God, King of the Universe,
who creates the fruit of the vine.

Holding the spice box, the Leader says:

Blessed are You, Lord our God, King of the Universe,
who creates the various spices.

The Leader smells the spices and puts the spice box down.
He lifts his hands toward the flame of the Havdala candle, and says:

Blessed are You, Lord our God, King of the Universe,
who creates the lights of fire.

He lifts the cup of wine in his right hand, and says:

Blessed are You, Lord our God, King of the Universe,
who distinguishes between sacred and secular,
between light and darkness,
between Israel and the nations,
between the seventh day and the six days of work.
Blessed are You, Lord, who distinguishes between sacred and secular.

On Ḥol HaMo'ed the following blessing is added if the Havdala is said in a sukka.

בָּרוּךְ Blessed are You, Lord our God, King of the Universe,
who has made us holy though His commandments,
and has commanded us to dwell in the sukka.

Stand while saying Aleinu. Bow at ▾.

עָלֵינוּ It is our duty to praise the Master of all,
and ascribe greatness to the Author of creation,
who has not made us like the nations of the lands
nor placed us like the families of the earth;
who has not made our portion like theirs,
nor our destiny like all their multitudes.
(For they worship vanity and emptiness,
and pray to a god who cannot save.)

הבדלה בבית הכנסת

Some say the full הבדלה *on page 1387.*
On מוצאי שבת *that is not on* מוצאי יום טוב*,*
the blessings for the spices and flame are omitted.

The שליח ציבור *takes the cup of wine in his right hand, and says:*

סַבְרִי מָרָנָן

בָּרוּךְ אַתָּה יהוה אֱלֹהֵינוּ מֶלֶךְ הָעוֹלָם, בּוֹרֵא פְּרִי הַגָּפֶן.

Holding the spice box, the שליח ציבור *says:*

בָּרוּךְ אַתָּה יהוה אֱלֹהֵינוּ מֶלֶךְ הָעוֹלָם, בּוֹרֵא מִינֵי בְשָׂמִים.

The שליח ציבור *smells the spices and puts the spice box down.*
He lifts his hands toward the flame of the הבדלה *candle, and says:*

בָּרוּךְ אַתָּה יהוה אֱלֹהֵינוּ מֶלֶךְ הָעוֹלָם, בּוֹרֵא מְאוֹרֵי הָאֵשׁ.

He lifts the cup of wine in his right hand, and says:

בָּרוּךְ אַתָּה יהוה אֱלֹהֵינוּ מֶלֶךְ הָעוֹלָם
הַמַּבְדִּיל בֵּין קֹדֶשׁ לְחֹל, בֵּין אוֹר לְחֹשֶׁךְ
בֵּין יִשְׂרָאֵל לָעַמִּים
בֵּין יוֹם הַשְּׁבִיעִי לְשֵׁשֶׁת יְמֵי הַמַּעֲשֶׂה.
בָּרוּךְ אַתָּה יהוה, הַמַּבְדִּיל בֵּין קֹדֶשׁ לְחֹל.

On חול המועד *the following blessing is added if the* הבדלה *is said in a* סוכה*.*

בָּרוּךְ אַתָּה יהוה אֱלֹהֵינוּ מֶלֶךְ הָעוֹלָם
אֲשֶׁר קִדְּשָׁנוּ בְּמִצְוֹתָיו וְצִוָּנוּ לֵישֵׁב בַּסֻּכָּה.

Stand while saying עָלֵינוּ*. Bow at* ▾*.*

עָלֵינוּ לְשַׁבֵּחַ לַאֲדוֹן הַכֹּל, לָתֵת גְּדֻלָּה לְיוֹצֵר בְּרֵאשִׁית
שֶׁלֹּא עָשָׂנוּ כְּגוֹיֵי הָאֲרָצוֹת, וְלֹא שָׂמָנוּ כְּמִשְׁפְּחוֹת הָאֲדָמָה
שֶׁלֹּא שָׂם חֶלְקֵנוּ כָּהֶם וְגוֹרָלֵנוּ כְּכָל הֲמוֹנָם.
(שֶׁהֵם מִשְׁתַּחֲוִים לְהֶבֶל וָרִיק וּמִתְפַּלְלִים אֶל אֵל לֹא יוֹשִׁיעַ.)

ˀBut we bow in worship and thank the Supreme King of kings,
the Holy One, blessed be He,
who extends the heavens and establishes the earth,
whose throne of glory is in the heavens above,
and whose power's Presence is in the highest of heights.
He is our God; there is no other.
Truly He is our King, there is none else, as it is written in His Torah:
"You shall know and take to heart this day that the LORD is God, *Deut. 4*
in heaven above and on earth below.
There is no other."

Therefore, we place our hope in You, LORD our God,
that we may soon see the glory of Your power,
when You will remove abominations from the earth,
and idols will be utterly destroyed,
when the world will be perfected under the sovereignty of the Almighty,
when all humanity will call on Your name,
to turn all the earth's wicked toward You.
All the world's inhabitants will realize and know
that to You every knee must bow and every tongue swear loyalty.
Before You, LORD our God, they will kneel and bow down
and give honor to Your glorious name.
They will all accept the yoke of Your kingdom,
and You will reign over them soon and for ever.
For the kingdom is Yours, and to all eternity You will reign in glory,
as it is written in Your Torah:
"The LORD will reign for ever and ever." *Ex. 15*
▸ And it is said: "Then the LORD shall be King over all the earth; *Zech. 14*
on that day the LORD shall be One and His name One."

Some add:
Have no fear of sudden terror or of the ruin when it overtakes the wicked. *Prov. 3*
Devise your strategy, but it will be thwarted; propose your plan, *Is. 8*
but it will not stand, for God is with us.
When you grow old, I will still be the same. *Is. 46*
When your hair turns gray, I will still carry you.
I made you, I will bear you,
I will carry you, and I will rescue you.

וַאֲנַחְנוּ כּוֹרְעִים וּמִשְׁתַּחֲוִים וּמוֹדִים
לִפְנֵי מֶלֶךְ מַלְכֵי הַמְּלָכִים, הַקָּדוֹשׁ בָּרוּךְ הוּא
שֶׁהוּא נוֹטֶה שָׁמַיִם וְיוֹסֵד אָרֶץ, וּמוֹשַׁב יְקָרוֹ בַּשָּׁמַיִם מִמַּעַל
וּשְׁכִינַת עֻזּוֹ בְּגָבְהֵי מְרוֹמִים.
הוּא אֱלֹהֵינוּ, אֵין עוֹד.
אֱמֶת מַלְכֵּנוּ, אֶפֶס זוּלָתוֹ, כַּכָּתוּב בְּתוֹרָתוֹ
וְיָדַעְתָּ הַיּוֹם וַהֲשֵׁבֹתָ אֶל־לְבָבֶךָ דברים ד
כִּי יהוה הוּא הָאֱלֹהִים בַּשָּׁמַיִם מִמַּעַל וְעַל־הָאָרֶץ מִתָּחַת
אֵין עוֹד:

עַל כֵּן נְקַוֶּה לְּךָ יהוה אֱלֹהֵינוּ, לִרְאוֹת מְהֵרָה בְּתִפְאֶרֶת עֻזֶּךָ
לְהַעֲבִיר גִּלּוּלִים מִן הָאָרֶץ, וְהָאֱלִילִים כָּרוֹת יִכָּרֵתוּן
לְתַקֵּן עוֹלָם בְּמַלְכוּת שַׁדַּי.
וְכָל בְּנֵי בָשָׂר יִקְרְאוּ בִשְׁמֶךָ לְהַפְנוֹת אֵלֶיךָ כָּל רִשְׁעֵי אָרֶץ.
יַכִּירוּ וְיֵדְעוּ כָּל יוֹשְׁבֵי תֵבֵל
כִּי לְךָ תִּכְרַע כָּל בֶּרֶךְ, תִּשָּׁבַע כָּל לָשׁוֹן.
לְפָנֶיךָ יהוה אֱלֹהֵינוּ יִכְרְעוּ וְיִפֹּלוּ, וְלִכְבוֹד שִׁמְךָ יְקָר יִתֵּנוּ
וִיקַבְּלוּ כֻלָּם אֶת עֹל מַלְכוּתֶךָ וְתִמְלֹךְ עֲלֵיהֶם מְהֵרָה לְעוֹלָם וָעֶד.
כִּי הַמַּלְכוּת שֶׁלְּךָ הִיא וּלְעוֹלְמֵי עַד תִּמְלֹךְ בְּכָבוֹד
כַּכָּתוּב בְּתוֹרָתֶךָ, יהוה יִמְלֹךְ לְעֹלָם וָעֶד: שמות טו
► וְנֶאֱמַר, וְהָיָה יהוה לְמֶלֶךְ עַל־כָּל־הָאָרֶץ זכריה יד
בַּיּוֹם הַהוּא יִהְיֶה יהוה אֶחָד וּשְׁמוֹ אֶחָד:

Some add:

אַל־תִּירָא מִפַּחַד פִּתְאֹם וּמִשֹּׁאַת רְשָׁעִים כִּי תָבֹא: משלי ג
עֻצוּ עֵצָה וְתֻפָר, דַּבְּרוּ דָבָר וְלֹא יָקוּם, כִּי עִמָּנוּ אֵל: ישעיה ח
וְעַד־זִקְנָה אֲנִי הוּא, וְעַד־שֵׂיבָה אֲנִי אֶסְבֹּל ישעיה מו
אֲנִי עָשִׂיתִי וַאֲנִי אֶשָּׂא וַאֲנִי אֶסְבֹּל וַאֲמַלֵּט:

MOURNER'S KADDISH

The following prayer, said by mourners, requires the presence of a minyan. *A transliteration can be found on page 1467.*

Mourner: יִתְגַּדַּל Magnified and sanctified
may His great name be,
in the world He created by His will.
May He establish His kingdom
in your lifetime and in your days,
and in the lifetime of all the house of Israel,
swiftly and soon –
and say: Amen.

All: May His great name be blessed
for ever and all time.

Mourner: Blessed and praised,
glorified and exalted,
raised and honored,
uplifted and lauded
be the name of the Holy One,
blessed be He,
beyond any blessing,
song, praise and consolation
uttered in the world –
and say: Amen.

May there be great peace from heaven,
and life for us and all Israel –
and say: Amen.

Bow, take three steps back, as if taking leave of the Divine Presence, then bow, first left, then right, then center, while saying:

May He who makes peace in His high places,
make peace for us and all Israel –
and say: Amen.

קדיש יתום

The following prayer, said by mourners, requires the presence of a מנין.
A transliteration can be found on page 1467.

אבל: יִתְגַּדַּל וְיִתְקַדַּשׁ שְׁמֵהּ רַבָּא (קהל: אָמֵן)
בְּעָלְמָא דִּי בְרָא כִרְעוּתֵהּ
וְיַמְלִיךְ מַלְכוּתֵהּ
בְּחַיֵּיכוֹן וּבְיוֹמֵיכוֹן וּבְחַיֵּי דְכָל בֵּית יִשְׂרָאֵל
בַּעֲגָלָא וּבִזְמַן קָרִיב
וְאִמְרוּ אָמֵן. (קהל: אָמֵן)

קהל ואבל: יְהֵא שְׁמֵהּ רַבָּא מְבָרַךְ לְעָלַם וּלְעָלְמֵי עָלְמַיָּא.

אבל: יִתְבָּרַךְ וְיִשְׁתַּבַּח וְיִתְפָּאַר
וְיִתְרוֹמַם וְיִתְנַשֵּׂא וְיִתְהַדָּר וְיִתְעַלֶּה וְיִתְהַלָּל
שְׁמֵהּ דְּקֻדְשָׁא בְּרִיךְ הוּא (קהל: בְּרִיךְ הוּא)
לְעֵלָּא מִן כָּל בִּרְכָתָא וְשִׁירָתָא
תֻּשְׁבְּחָתָא וְנֶחֱמָתָא
דַּאֲמִירָן בְּעָלְמָא
וְאִמְרוּ אָמֵן. (קהל: אָמֵן)

יְהֵא שְׁלָמָא רַבָּא מִן שְׁמַיָּא
וְחַיִּים, עָלֵינוּ וְעַל כָּל יִשְׂרָאֵל
וְאִמְרוּ אָמֵן. (קהל: אָמֵן)

Bow, take three steps back, as if taking leave of the Divine Presence, then bow, first left, then right, then center, while saying:

עֹשֶׂה שָׁלוֹם בִּמְרוֹמָיו
הוּא יַעֲשֶׂה שָׁלוֹם עָלֵינוּ וְעַל כָּל יִשְׂרָאֵל
וְאִמְרוּ אָמֵן. (קהל: אָמֵן)

On Ḥol HaMo'ed the following psalm is said:

לְדָוִד A psalm of David. The LORD is my light and my salvation – whom then shall I fear? The LORD is the stronghold of my life – of whom shall I be afraid? When evil men close in on me to devour my flesh, it is they, my enemies and foes, who stumble and fall. Should an army besiege me, my heart would not fear. Should war break out against me, still I would be confident. One thing I ask of the LORD, only this do I seek: to live in the House of the LORD all the days of my life, to gaze on the beauty of the LORD and worship in His Temple. For He will keep me safe in His pavilion on the day of trouble. He will hide me under the cover of His tent. He will set me high upon a rock. Now my head is high above my enemies who surround me. I will sacrifice in His tent with shouts of joy. I will sing and chant praises to the LORD. LORD, hear my voice when I call. Be gracious to me and answer me. On Your behalf my heart says, "Seek My face." Your face, LORD, will I seek. Do not hide Your face from me. Do not turn Your servant away in anger. You have been my help. Do not reject or forsake me, God, my Savior. Were my father and my mother to forsake me, the LORD would take me in. Teach me Your way, LORD, and lead me on a level path, because of my oppressors. Do not abandon me to the will of my foes, for false witnesses have risen against me, breathing violence. ▸ Were it not for my faith that I shall see the LORD's goodness in the land of the living. Hope in the LORD. Be strong and of good courage, and hope in the LORD! *Ps. 27*

Mourner's Kaddish (on previous page)

On חול המועד *the following psalm is said:*

לְדָוִד, יהוה אוֹרִי וְיִשְׁעִי, מִמִּי אִירָא, יהוה מָעוֹז־חַיַּי, מִמִּי אֶפְחָד: תהלים כז
בִּקְרֹב עָלַי מְרֵעִים לֶאֱכֹל אֶת־בְּשָׂרִי, צָרַי וְאֹיְבַי לִי, הֵמָּה כָשְׁלוּ
וְנָפָלוּ: אִם־תַּחֲנֶה עָלַי מַחֲנֶה, לֹא־יִירָא לִבִּי, אִם־תָּקוּם עָלַי
מִלְחָמָה, בְּזֹאת אֲנִי בוֹטֵחַ: אַחַת שָׁאַלְתִּי מֵאֵת־יהוה, אוֹתָהּ
אֲבַקֵּשׁ, שִׁבְתִּי בְּבֵית־יהוה כָּל־יְמֵי חַיַּי, לַחֲזוֹת בְּנֹעַם־יהוה, וּלְבַקֵּר
בְּהֵיכָלוֹ: כִּי יִצְפְּנֵנִי בְּסֻכֹּה בְּיוֹם רָעָה, יַסְתִּרֵנִי בְּסֵתֶר אָהֳלוֹ, בְּצוּר
יְרוֹמְמֵנִי: וְעַתָּה יָרוּם רֹאשִׁי עַל אֹיְבַי סְבִיבוֹתַי, וְאֶזְבְּחָה בְאָהֳלוֹ
זִבְחֵי תְרוּעָה, אָשִׁירָה וַאֲזַמְּרָה לַיהוה: שְׁמַע־יהוה קוֹלִי אֶקְרָא,
וְחָנֵּנִי וַעֲנֵנִי: לְךָ אָמַר לִבִּי בַּקְּשׁוּ פָנָי, אֶת־פָּנֶיךָ יהוה אֲבַקֵּשׁ:
אַל־תַּסְתֵּר פָּנֶיךָ מִמֶּנִּי, אַל תַּט־בְּאַף עַבְדֶּךָ, עֶזְרָתִי הָיִיתָ, אַל־
תִּטְּשֵׁנִי וְאַל־תַּעַזְבֵנִי, אֱלֹהֵי יִשְׁעִי: כִּי־אָבִי וְאִמִּי עֲזָבוּנִי, וַיהוה
יַאַסְפֵנִי: הוֹרֵנִי יהוה דַּרְכֶּךָ, וּנְחֵנִי בְּאֹרַח מִישׁוֹר, לְמַעַן שׁוֹרְרָי:
אַל־תִּתְּנֵנִי בְּנֶפֶשׁ צָרָי, כִּי קָמוּ־בִי עֵדֵי־שֶׁקֶר, וִיפֵחַ חָמָס: ◂ לוּלֵא
הֶאֱמַנְתִּי לִרְאוֹת בְּטוּב־יהוה בְּאֶרֶץ חַיִּים: קַוֵּה אֶל־יהוה, חֲזַק
וְיַאֲמֵץ לִבֶּךָ, וְקַוֵּה אֶל־יהוה:

קדיש יתום (*on previous page*)

HAVDALA AT HOME

On Motza'ei Yom Tov that is not on Motza'ei Shabbat, the first paragraph and the blessings for the spices and flame are omitted.

Taking a cup of wine in the right hand, say:

הִנֵּה Behold, God is my salvation. I will trust and not be afraid. The LORD, the Is. 12
LORD, is my strength and my song. He has become my salvation. With joy
you will draw water from the springs of salvation. Salvation is the LORD's; on Ps. 3
Your people is Your blessing, Selah. The LORD of hosts is with us, the God of Ps. 46
Jacob is our stronghold, Selah. LORD of hosts: happy is the one who trusts Ps. 84
in You. LORD, save! May the King answer us on the day we call. For the Jews Ps. 20 Esther 8
there was light and gladness, joy and honor – so may it be for us. I will lift Ps. 116
the cup of salvation and call on the name of the LORD.

When making Havdala for others, add:
Please pay attention, my masters.

Blessed are You, LORD our God, King of the Universe,
who creates the fruit of the vine.

If Havdala is made on beer, substitute:

Blessed are You, LORD our God, King of the Universe,
by whose word all things came to be.

Hold the spice box and say:

Blessed are You, LORD our God, King of the Universe,
who creates the various spices.

Smell the spices and put the spice box down.
Lift the hands toward the flame of the Havdala candle and say:

Blessed are You, LORD our God, King of the Universe,
who creates the lights of fire.

Holding the cup of wine again in the right hand, say:

בָּרוּךְ Blessed are You, LORD our God, King of the Universe, who distinguishes between sacred and secular, between light and darkness, between Israel and the nations, between the seventh day and the six days of work. Blessed are You, LORD, who distinguishes between sacred and secular.

On Ḥol HaMo'ed the following blessing is added if Havdala is said in a sukka.

בָּרוּךְ Blessed are You, LORD our God, King of the Universe,
who has made us holy though His commandments,
and has commanded us to dwell in the sukka.

סדר הבדלה בבית

On מוצאי יום טוב *that is not on* מוצאי שבת*, the first paragraph and the blessings for the spices and flame are omitted.*
Taking a cup of wine in the right hand, say:

הִנֵּה אֵל יְשׁוּעָתִי אֶבְטַח, וְלֹא אֶפְחָד, כִּי־עָזִּי וְזִמְרָת יָהּ יהוה, וַיְהִי־לִי ישעיה יב
לִישׁוּעָה: וּשְׁאַבְתֶּם־מַיִם בְּשָׂשׂוֹן, מִמַּעַיְנֵי הַיְשׁוּעָה: לַיהוה הַיְשׁוּעָה, תהלים ג
עַל־עַמְּךָ בִרְכָתֶךָ סֶּלָה: יהוה צְבָאוֹת עִמָּנוּ, מִשְׂגָּב לָנוּ אֱלֹהֵי יַעֲקֹב תהלים מו
סֶלָה: יהוה צְבָאוֹת, אַשְׁרֵי אָדָם בֹּטֵחַ בָּךְ: יהוה הוֹשִׁיעָה, הַמֶּלֶךְ יַעֲנֵנוּ תהלים פד תהלים כ
בְיוֹם־קָרְאֵנוּ: לַיְּהוּדִים הָיְתָה אוֹרָה וְשִׂמְחָה וְשָׂשֹׂן וִיקָר: כֵּן תִּהְיֶה לָּנוּ. אסתר ח
כּוֹס־יְשׁוּעוֹת אֶשָּׂא, וּבְשֵׁם יהוה אֶקְרָא: תהלים קטז

When making הבדלה *for others, add:*

סַבְרִי מָרָנָן

בָּרוּךְ אַתָּה יהוה אֱלֹהֵינוּ מֶלֶךְ הָעוֹלָם, בּוֹרֵא פְּרִי הַגָּפֶן.

If הבדלה *is made on beer, substitute:*

בָּרוּךְ אַתָּה יהוה אֱלֹהֵינוּ מֶלֶךְ הָעוֹלָם, שֶׁהַכֹּל נִהְיָה בִּדְבָרוֹ.

Hold the spice box and say:

בָּרוּךְ אַתָּה יהוה אֱלֹהֵינוּ מֶלֶךְ הָעוֹלָם, בּוֹרֵא מִינֵי בְשָׂמִים.

Smell the spices and put the spice box down.
Lift the hands toward the flame of the הבדלה *candle and say:*

בָּרוּךְ אַתָּה יהוה אֱלֹהֵינוּ מֶלֶךְ הָעוֹלָם, בּוֹרֵא מְאוֹרֵי הָאֵשׁ.

Holding the cup of wine again in the right hand, say:

בָּרוּךְ אַתָּה יהוה אֱלֹהֵינוּ מֶלֶךְ הָעוֹלָם, הַמַּבְדִּיל בֵּין קֹדֶשׁ לְחֹל, בֵּין אוֹר לְחֹשֶׁךְ, בֵּין יִשְׂרָאֵל לָעַמִּים, בֵּין יוֹם הַשְּׁבִיעִי לְשֵׁשֶׁת יְמֵי הַמַּעֲשֶׂה.
בָּרוּךְ אַתָּה יהוה, הַמַּבְדִּיל בֵּין קֹדֶשׁ לְחֹל.

On חול המועד *the following blessing is added if* הבדלה *is said in a* סוכה*.*

בָּרוּךְ אַתָּה יהוה אֱלֹהֵינוּ מֶלֶךְ הָעוֹלָם
אֲשֶׁר קִדְּשָׁנוּ בְּמִצְוֹתָיו וְצִוָּנוּ לֵישֵׁב בַּסֻּכָּה.

הַמַּבְדִּיל He who distinguishes between sacred and secular,
may He forgive our sins.
May He multiply our offspring and wealth like the sand,
and like the stars at night.

The day has passed like a palm tree's shadow;
I call on God to fulfill what the watchman said: *Is. 21*
"Morning comes, though now it is night."

Your righteousness is as high as Mount Tabor.
May You pass high over my sins.
[Let them be] like yesterday when it has passed, *Ps. 90*
like a watch in the night.

The time of offerings has passed. Would that I might rest.
I am weary with my sighing, every night I drench [with tears]. *Ps. 6*

Hear my voice; let it not be cast aside. Open for me the lofty gate.
My head is filled with the dew of dawn, *Song. 5*
my hair with raindrops of the night.

Heed my prayer, revered and awesome God.
When I cry, grant me deliverance at twilight, *Prov. 7*
as the day fades, or in the darkness of the night.

I call to You, LORD: Save me. Make known to me the path of life.
Rescue me from misery before day turns to night.

Cleanse the defilement of my deeds, lest those who torment me say,
"Where is the God who made me, *Job 35*
who gives cause for songs in the night?"

We are in Your hands like clay:
please forgive our sins, light and grave.
Day to day they pour forth speech, *Ps. 19*
and night to night [they communicate knowledge].

הַמַּבְדִּיל בֵּין קֹדֶשׁ לְחֹל, חַטֹּאתֵינוּ הוּא יִמְחֹל
זַרְעֵנוּ וְכַסְפֵּנוּ יַרְבֶּה כַחוֹל וְכַכּוֹכָבִים בַּלָּיְלָה.

יוֹם פָּנָה כְּצֵל תֹּמֶר, אֶקְרָא לָאֵל עָלַי גּוֹמֵר
אָמַר שֹׁמֵר, אָתָא בֹקֶר וְגַם־לָיְלָה: ישעיה כא

צִדְקָתְךָ כְּהַר תָּבוֹר, עַל חֲטָאַי עָבוֹר תַּעֲבֹר
כְּיוֹם אֶתְמוֹל כִּי יַעֲבֹר, וְאַשְׁמוּרָה בַלָּיְלָה: תהלים צ

חָלְפָה עוֹנַת מִנְחָתִי, מִי יִתֵּן מְנוּחָתִי
יָגַעְתִּי בְאַנְחָתִי, אַשְׂחֶה בְכָל־לָיְלָה: תהלים ו

קוֹלִי בַּל יֻנְטַל, פְּתַח לִי שַׁעַר הַמְנֻטָּל
שֶׁרֹּאשִׁי נִמְלָא טָל, קְוֻצּוֹתַי רְסִיסֵי לָיְלָה: שיר השירים ה

הֵעָתֵר נוֹרָא וְאָיֹם, אֲשַׁוֵּעַ, תְּנָה פִדְיוֹם
בְּנֶשֶׁף־בְּעֶרֶב יוֹם, בְּאִישׁוֹן לָיְלָה: משלי ז

קְרָאתִיךָ יָהּ, הוֹשִׁיעֵנִי, אֹרַח חַיִּים תּוֹדִיעֵנִי
מִדַּלָּה תְבַצְּעֵנִי, מִיּוֹם עַד לָיְלָה.

טַהֵר טִנּוּף מַעֲשַׂי, פֶּן יֹאמְרוּ מַכְעִיסַי
אַיֵּה אֱלוֹהַּ עֹשָׂי, נֹתֵן זְמִרוֹת בַּלָּיְלָה: איוב לה

נַחְנוּ בְיָדְךָ כַּחֹמֶר, סְלַח נָא עַל קַל וָחֹמֶר
יוֹם לְיוֹם יַבִּיעַ אֹמֶר, וְלַיְלָה לְלָיְלָה: תהלים יט

BRIT MILA

When the baby is brought in, all stand and say:

Blessed is he who comes.

The mohel (in some congregations, all) say (in Israel omit):

וַיְדַבֵּר The LORD spoke to Moses, saying: Pinehas the son of Elazar, the son of Aaron the priest, turned back My rage from the children of Israel, when he was zealous for Me among them, and I did not annihilate the children of Israel in My own zeal. And so tell him, that I now give him My covenant for peace. *Num. 25*

The following verses, through "LORD, please, grant us success," are only said in Israel.

Mohel: Happy are those You choose and bring near to dwell in Your courts. *Ps. 65*

All: May we be sated with the goodness of Your House,
Your holy Temple.

The father takes the baby in his hands and says quietly:

אִם אֶשְׁכָּחֵךְ If I forget you, Jerusalem, may my right hand forget its skill. May my tongue cling to the roof of my mouth, if I do not remember you, if I do not set Jerusalem above my highest joy. *Ps. 137*

The father says aloud, followed by the congregation:

Listen, Israel: the LORD is our God, the LORD is One. *Deut. 6*

The Mohel, followed by the congregation,
recites each of the following three phrases twice:

The LORD is King, the LORD was King,
the LORD shall be King for ever and all time.
LORD, please, save us. *Ps. 118*
LORD, please, grant us success.

The baby is placed on Eliyahu's seat, and the Mohel says:

This is the throne of Elijah the prophet, may he be remembered for good.

The Mohel continues:

לִישׁוּעָתְךָ For Your salvation I wait, O LORD. I await Your deliverance, *Gen. 49* *Ps. 119*
LORD, and I observe Your commandments. Elijah, angel of the covenant,
behold: yours is before you. Stand at my right hand and be close to me.
I await Your deliverance, LORD. I rejoice in Your word like one who finds *Ibid.*
much spoil. Those who love Your Torah have great peace, and there is

סדר ברית מילה

When the baby is brought in, all stand and say:

בָּרוּךְ הַבָּא.

The מוהל *(in some congregations, all) say (in* ארץ ישראל *omit):*

במדבר כה וַיְדַבֵּר יהוה אֶל־מֹשֶׁה לֵּאמֹר: פִּינְחָס בֶּן־אֶלְעָזָר בֶּן־אַהֲרֹן הַכֹּהֵן הֵשִׁיב אֶת־חֲמָתִי מֵעַל בְּנֵי־יִשְׂרָאֵל, בְּקַנְאוֹ אֶת־קִנְאָתִי בְּתוֹכָם, וְלֹא־כִלִּיתִי אֶת־בְּנֵי־יִשְׂרָאֵל בְּקִנְאָתִי: לָכֵן אֱמֹר, הִנְנִי נֹתֵן לוֹ אֶת־בְּרִיתִי שָׁלוֹם:

The following verses, through אָנָּא יהוה הַצְלִיחָה נָא *are only said in Israel.*

תהלים סה המוהל: אַשְׁרֵי תִּבְחַר וּתְקָרֵב, יִשְׁכֹּן חֲצֵרֶיךָ

הקהל: נִשְׂבְּעָה בְּטוּב בֵּיתֶךָ, קְדֹשׁ הֵיכָלֶךָ:

The father takes the baby in his hands and says quietly:

תהלים קלז אִם־אֶשְׁכָּחֵךְ יְרוּשָׁלָםִ, תִּשְׁכַּח יְמִינִי: תִּדְבַּק לְשׁוֹנִי לְחִכִּי אִם־לֹא אֶזְכְּרֵכִי, אִם־לֹא אַעֲלֶה אֶת־יְרוּשָׁלָםִ עַל רֹאשׁ שִׂמְחָתִי:

The father says aloud, followed by the קהל:

דברים ו שְׁמַע יִשְׂרָאֵל, יהוה אֱלֹהֵינוּ, יהוה אֶחָד:

The מוהל *repeats each of the following three phrases twice, followed by the* קהל:

יהוה מֶלֶךְ, יהוה מָלָךְ, יהוה יִמְלֹךְ לְעוֹלָם וָעֶד.

תהלים קיח אָנָּא יהוה הוֹשִׁיעָה נָּא

אָנָּא יהוה הַצְלִיחָה נָא:

The baby is placed on the כסא של אליהו*, and the* מוהל *says:*

זֶה הַכִּסֵּא שֶׁל אֵלִיָּהוּ הַנָּבִיא זָכוּר לַטּוֹב.

The מוהל *continues:*

בראשית מט / תהלים קיט לִישׁוּעָתְךָ קִוִּיתִי יהוה: שִׂבַּרְתִּי לִישׁוּעָתְךָ יהוה, וּמִצְוֹתֶיךָ עָשִׂיתִי: אֵלִיָּהוּ מַלְאַךְ הַבְּרִית, הִנֵּה שֶׁלְּךָ לְפָנֶיךָ, עֲמֹד עַל יְמִינִי וְסָמְכֵנִי.

תהלים קיט שִׂבַּרְתִּי לִישׁוּעָתְךָ יהוה: שָׂשׂ אָנֹכִי עַל־אִמְרָתֶךָ, כְּמוֹצֵא שָׁלָל רָב:

no stumbling block before them. Happy are those You choose and bring Ps. 65
near to dwell in Your courts.

All respond:

May we be sated with the goodness of Your House, Your holy Temple.

The baby is placed on the knees of the Sandak, and the Mohel says:

בָּרוּךְ Blessed are You, Lord our God, King of the Universe,
who has made us holy through His commandments,
and has commanded us concerning circumcision.

Immediately after the circumcision, the father says:

בָּרוּךְ Blessed are You, Lord our God, King of the Universe,
who has made us holy through His commandments,
and has commanded us to bring him [our son]
into the covenant of Abraham, our father.

In Israel the father adds (some outside Israel add it as well):

בָּרוּךְ Blessed are You, Lord our God, King of the Universe,
who has given us life, sustained us, and brought us to this time.

All respond:

אָמֵן Amen. Just as he has entered into the covenant,
so may he enter into Torah, marriage and good deeds.

---

the covenant of Abraham, our father – a separate blessing, referring not to the circumcision itself, but what it is a sign of – namely entry into the life of the covenant, under the sheltering wings of the Divine Presence (*Arukh HaShulḥan, Yoreh De'ah* 365:2); (3) *Who made the beloved one* [*Isaac*] *holy from the womb* – a blessing of acknowledgment. Isaac was the first child to have a circumcision at the age of eight days. He was consecrated before birth, Abraham having been told that it would be Isaac who would continue the covenant (Gen. 17:19–21).

כְּשֵׁם שֶׁנִּכְנַס לַבְּרִית *Just as he has entered into the covenant.* Mentioned already in early rabbinic sources as the response of those present. The three phrases refer to the duties of a parent to a child: (1) to teach him Torah; (2) to ensure that he marries; and (3) to train him to do good deeds, as the Torah says in the case of Abraham: "For I have singled him out so that he may instruct his children and his posterity to keep the way of the Lord by doing what is just and right" (Gen. 18:19).

שָׁלוֹם רָב לְאֹהֲבֵי תוֹרָתֶךָ, וְאֵין־לָמוֹ מִכְשׁוֹל: אַשְׁרֵי תִּבְחַר וּתְקָרֵב, יִשְׁכֹּן חֲצֵרֶיךָ תהלים סה

All respond:

נִשְׂבְּעָה בְּטוּב בֵּיתֶךָ, קְדֹשׁ הֵיכָלֶךָ:

The baby is placed on the knees of the סנדק*, and the* מוהל *says:*

בָּרוּךְ אַתָּה יהוה אֱלֹהֵינוּ מֶלֶךְ הָעוֹלָם
אֲשֶׁר קִדְּשָׁנוּ בְּמִצְוֹתָיו, וְצִוָּנוּ עַל הַמִּילָה.

Immediately after the circumcision, the father says:

בָּרוּךְ אַתָּה יהוה אֱלֹהֵינוּ מֶלֶךְ הָעוֹלָם, אֲשֶׁר קִדְּשָׁנוּ
בְּמִצְוֹתָיו, וְצִוָּנוּ לְהַכְנִיסוֹ בִּבְרִיתוֹ שֶׁל אַבְרָהָם אָבִינוּ.

In ארץ ישראל *the father adds (some in* חוץ לארץ *add it as well):*

בָּרוּךְ אַתָּה יהוה אֱלֹהֵינוּ מֶלֶךְ הָעוֹלָם
שֶׁהֶחֱיָנוּ וְקִיְּמָנוּ וְהִגִּיעָנוּ לַזְּמַן הַזֶּה.

All respond:

אָמֵן. כְּשֵׁם שֶׁנִּכְנַס לַבְּרִית
כֵּן יִכָּנֵס לְתוֹרָה וּלְחֻפָּה וּלְמַעֲשִׂים טוֹבִים.

SERVICE AT A CIRCUMCISION

Since the days of Abraham (Gen. 17:4–14), circumcision has been the sign, for Jewish males, of the covenant between God and His people. Despite the fact that the law was restated by Moses (Lev. 12:3), it remains known as the "Covenant of Abraham." The ceremony – always performed on the eighth day, even on Shabbat, unless there are medical reasons for delay – marks the entry of the child into the covenant of Jewish fate and destiny. The duty of circumcision devolves, in principle, on the father of the child; in practice it is performed only by a qualified *mohel.*

בָּרוּךְ *Blessed are You.* There are three blessings to be said at a circumcision: (1) *And has commanded us concerning circumcision* – a blessing over the commandment itself, the "about" formula signaling that the *mohel* is performing the commandment on behalf of the father; (2) *To bring him [our son] into*

After the circumcision has been completed, the Mohel (or another honoree) takes a cup of wine and says:

בָּרוּךְ Blessed are You, LORD our God, King of the Universe, who creates the fruit of the vine.

בָּרוּךְ Blessed are You, LORD our God, King of the Universe, who made the beloved one [Isaac] holy from the womb, marked the decree of circumcision in his flesh, and gave his descendants the seal and sign of the holy covenant. As a reward for this, the Living God, our Portion, our Rock, did order deliverance from destruction for the beloved of our flesh, for the sake of His covenant that He set in our flesh. Blessed are You, LORD, who establishes the covenant.

אֱלֹהֵינוּ Our God and God of our fathers, preserve this child to his father and mother, and let his name be called in Israel (*baby's name* son of *father's name*). May the father rejoice in the issue of his body, and the mother
be glad with the fruit of her womb, as is written, "May your father and *Prov. 23*
mother rejoice, and she who bore you be glad." And it is said, "Then I
passed by you and saw you downtrodden in your blood, and I said to you: *Ezek. 16*
In your blood, live; and I said to you: In your blood, live."

וְנֶאֱמַר And it is said, "He remembered His covenant for ever; the word *Ps. 105*
He ordained for a thousand generations; the covenant He made with Abraham and gave on oath to Isaac, confirming it as a statute for Jacob, an everlasting covenant for Israel." And it is said, "And Abraham circumcised
his son Isaac at the age of eight days, as God had commanded him." Thank *Ps. 118*
the LORD for He is good; His loning-kindness is for ever. *Gen. 21*

All respond:

Thank the LORD for He is good; His loving-kindness is for ever.

The Mohel (or honoree) continues:

May this child (*baby's name* son of *father's name*) become great. Just as he has entered into the covenant, so may he enter into Torah, marriage and good deeds.

The Sandak also drinks some of the wine; some drops are given to the baby. The cup is then sent to the mother, who also drinks from it.

All say Aleinu on page 1378, and Mourner's Kaddish on page 1382 is said.

After the circumcision has been completed, the מוהל *(or another honoree), takes a cup of wine and says:*

בָּרוּךְ אַתָּה יהוה אֱלֹהֵינוּ מֶלֶךְ הָעוֹלָם, בּוֹרֵא פְּרִי הַגָּפֶן.

בָּרוּךְ אַתָּה יהוה אֱלֹהֵינוּ מֶלֶךְ הָעוֹלָם, אֲשֶׁר קִדַּשׁ יְדִיד מִבֶּטֶן, וְחֹק בִּשְׁאֵרוֹ שָׂם, וְצֶאֱצָאָיו חָתַם בְּאוֹת בְּרִית קֹדֶשׁ. עַל כֵּן בִּשְׂכַר זֹאת, אֵל חַי חֶלְקֵנוּ צוּרֵנוּ צַוֵּה לְהַצִּיל יְדִידוּת שְׁאֵרֵנוּ מִשַּׁחַת, לְמַעַן בְּרִיתוֹ אֲשֶׁר שָׂם בִּבְשָׂרֵנוּ. בָּרוּךְ אַתָּה יהוה, כּוֹרֵת הַבְּרִית.

אֱלֹהֵינוּ וֵאלֹהֵי אֲבוֹתֵינוּ, קַיֵּם אֶת הַיֶּלֶד הַזֶּה לְאָבִיו וּלְאִמּוֹ, וְיִקָּרֵא
שְׁמוֹ בְּיִשְׂרָאֵל (פלוני בֶּן פלוני). יִשְׂמַח הָאָב בְּיוֹצֵא חֲלָצָיו וְתָגֵל אִמּוֹ
בִּפְרִי בִטְנָהּ, כַּכָּתוּב: יִשְׂמַח־אָבִיךָ וְאִמֶּךָ, וְתָגֵל יוֹלַדְתֶּךָ: וְנֶאֱמַר: משלי כג
וָאֶעֱבֹר עָלַיִךְ וָאֶרְאֵךְ מִתְבּוֹסֶסֶת בְּדָמָיִךְ, וָאֹמַר לָךְ בְּדָמַיִךְ חֲיִי, יחזקאל טז
וָאֹמַר לָךְ בְּדָמַיִךְ חֲיִי:

וְנֶאֱמַר: זָכַר לְעוֹלָם בְּרִיתוֹ, דָּבָר צִוָּה לְאֶלֶף דּוֹר: אֲשֶׁר כָּרַת אֶת־ תהלים קה
אַבְרָהָם, וּשְׁבוּעָתוֹ לְיִשְׂחָק: וַיַּעֲמִידֶהָ לְיַעֲקֹב לְחֹק, לְיִשְׂרָאֵל
בְּרִית עוֹלָם: וְנֶאֱמַר: וַיָּמָל אַבְרָהָם אֶת־יִצְחָק בְּנוֹ בֶּן־שְׁמֹנַת יָמִים, בראשית כא
כַּאֲשֶׁר צִוָּה אֹתוֹ אֱלֹהִים: הוֹדוּ לַיהוה כִּי־טוֹב, כִּי לְעוֹלָם חַסְדּוֹ: תהלים קיח

All respond:

הוֹדוּ לַיהוה כִּי־טוֹב, כִּי לְעוֹלָם חַסְדּוֹ:

The מוהל *(or honoree) continues:*

(פלוני בֶּן פלוני) זֶה הַקָּטָן גָּדוֹל יִהְיֶה, כְּשֵׁם שֶׁנִּכְנַס לַבְּרִית, כֵּן יִכָּנֵס לְתוֹרָה וּלְחֻפָּה וּלְמַעֲשִׂים טוֹבִים.

The סנדק *also drinks some of the wine; some drops are given to the baby. The cup is then sent to the mother, who also drinks from it.*

All say עָלֵינוּ*, on page 1379, and* קדיש יתום *on page 1383 is said.*

BIRKAT KOHANIM IN ISRAEL

In Israel, the following is said by the Leader during the Repetition of the Amida when Kohanim bless the congregation. If there is more than one Kohen, a member of the congregation calls:

Kohanim!

The Kohanim respond:

Blessed are You, Lord our God, King of the Universe, who has made us holy with the holiness of Aaron, and has commanded us to bless His people Israel with love.

The Leader calls word by word, followed by the Kohanim:

יְבָרֶכְךָ May the Lord bless you and protect you. (*Cong:* Amen.) *Num. 6*
May the Lord make His face shine on you
and be gracious to you. (*Cong:* Amen.)
May the Lord turn His face toward you,
and grant you peace. (*Cong:* Amen.)

The congregation says:

אַדִּיר Majestic One on high who dwells in power: You are peace and Your name is peace. May it be Your will to bestow on us and on Your people the house of Israel, life and blessing as a safeguard for peace.

The Kohanim say:

רִבּוֹנוֹ Master of the Universe: we have done what You have decreed for us. So too may You deal with us as You have promised us. Look down from Your holy dwelling place, from heaven, and bless Your people Israel and the land You have given us as You promised on oath to our ancestors, a land flowing with milk and honey. *Deut. 26*

The Leader continues:

שִׂים שָׁלוֹם Grant peace, goodness and blessing, grace, loving-kindness and compassion to us and all Israel Your people. Bless us, our Father, all as one, with the light of Your face, for by the light of Your face You have given us, Lord our God, the Torah of life and love of kindness, righteousness, blessing, compassion, life and peace. May it be good in Your eyes to bless Your people Israel at every time, in every hour, with Your peace. Blessed are You, Lord, who blesses His people Israel with peace.

The following verse concludes the Leader's Repetition of the Amida.

May the words of my mouth and the meditation of my heart *Ps. 19*
find favor before You, Lord, my Rock and Redeemer.

On the first day of Sukkot, Shaharit continues with the Blessing on Taking the Lulav on page 404; Musaf continues with Hoshanot on page 530. On Ḥol HaMo'ed, Shaḥarit continues with the Blessing on Taking the Lulav on page 658; Musaf continues with Hoshanot on page 710. On Shabbat Ḥol HaMo'ed, Shaḥarit continues with Hallel on page 802; Musaf continues with Hoshanot on page 916. On Hoshana Raba, Shaḥarit continues with the Blessing on Taking the Lulav on page 658; Musaf continues with Hoshanot on page 1022. On Shemini Atzeret, Shaḥarit continues with Hallel on page 408; Musaf continues with Full Kaddish on page 1178.

ברכת כהנים בארץ ישראל

In ארץ ישראל*, the following is said by the* שליח ציבור *during the* חורת הש״ץ *when* כהנים *say* ברכת כהנים*. If there is more than one* כהן*, a member of the* קהל *calls:*

כֹּהֲנִים

The כהנים *respond:*

בָּרוּךְ אַתָּה יהוה אֱלֹהֵינוּ מֶלֶךְ הָעוֹלָם, אֲשֶׁר קִדְּשָׁנוּ בִּקְדֻשָּׁתוֹ שֶׁל אַהֲרֹן
וְצִוָּנוּ לְבָרֵךְ אֶת עַמּוֹ יִשְׂרָאֵל בְּאַהֲבָה.

The שליח ציבור *calls word by word, followed by the* כהנים*:*

במדבר ו יְבָרֶכְךָ יהוה וְיִשְׁמְרֶךָ: קהל: אָמֵן
יָאֵר יהוה פָּנָיו אֵלֶיךָ וִיחֻנֶּךָּ: קהל: אָמֵן
יִשָּׂא יהוה פָּנָיו אֵלֶיךָ וְיָשֵׂם לְךָ שָׁלוֹם: קהל: אָמֵן

The קהל *says:*

אַדִּיר בַּמָּרוֹם שׁוֹכֵן בִּגְבוּרָה, אַתָּה שָׁלוֹם וְשִׁמְךָ שָׁלוֹם. יְהִי רָצוֹן שֶׁתָּשִׂים עָלֵינוּ וְעַל כָּל עַמְּךָ בֵּית יִשְׂרָאֵל חַיִּים וּבְרָכָה לְמִשְׁמֶרֶת שָׁלוֹם.

The כהנים *say:*

רִבּוֹנוֹ שֶׁל עוֹלָם, עָשִׂינוּ מַה שֶּׁגָּזַרְתָּ עָלֵינוּ, אַף אַתָּה עֲשֵׂה עִמָּנוּ כְּמוֹ שֶׁהִבְטַחְתָּנוּ. הַשְׁקִיפָה מִמְּעוֹן קָדְשְׁךָ מִן־הַשָּׁמַיִם, וּבָרֵךְ אֶת־עַמְּךָ אֶת־יִשְׂרָאֵל, וְאֵת הָאֲדָמָה אֲשֶׁר נָתַתָּה לָנוּ, כַּאֲשֶׁר נִשְׁבַּעְתָּ לַאֲבֹתֵינוּ, אֶרֶץ זָבַת חָלָב וּדְבָשׁ: דברים כו

The שליח ציבור *continues:*

שִׂים שָׁלוֹם טוֹבָה וּבְרָכָה, חֵן וָחֶסֶד וְרַחֲמִים עָלֵינוּ וְעַל כָּל יִשְׂרָאֵל עַמֶּךָ. בָּרְכֵנוּ אָבִינוּ כֻּלָּנוּ כְּאֶחָד בְּאוֹר פָּנֶיךָ, כִּי בְאוֹר פָּנֶיךָ נָתַתָּ לָּנוּ יהוה אֱלֹהֵינוּ, תּוֹרַת חַיִּים וְאַהֲבַת חֶסֶד, וּצְדָקָה וּבְרָכָה וְרַחֲמִים וְחַיִּים וְשָׁלוֹם. וְטוֹב בְּעֵינֶיךָ לְבָרֵךְ אֶת עַמְּךָ יִשְׂרָאֵל, בְּכָל עֵת וּבְכָל שָׁעָה בִּשְׁלוֹמֶךָ. בָּרוּךְ אַתָּה יהוה, הַמְבָרֵךְ אֶת עַמּוֹ יִשְׂרָאֵל בַּשָּׁלוֹם.

The following verse concludes the חורת הש״ץ.

תהלים יט יִהְיוּ לְרָצוֹן אִמְרֵי־פִי וְהֶגְיוֹן לִבִּי לְפָנֶיךָ, יהוה צוּרִי וְגֹאֲלִי:

On the first day of סוכות*,* שחרית *continues with* סדר נטילת לולב *on page 405;* מוסף *continues with* הושענות *on page 531. On* חול המועד*,* שחרית *continues with* סדר נטילת לולב *on page 659;* הלל *continues with* הושענות *on page 711. On* שבת חול המועד*,* שחרית *continues with* הושענות *on page 803;* מוסף *continues with* הושענות *on page 917. On* הושענא רבה*,* שחרית *continues with* סדר נטילת לולב *on page 659;* מוסף *continues with* הושענות *on page 1023. On* שמיני עצרת*,* שחרית *continues with* הלל *on page 409;* מוסף *continues with* קדיש שלם *on page 1179.*

פיוטים נוספים

ADDITIONAL PIYUTIM

יוצר ליום טוב ראשון של סוכות

שחרית *is said up to and including* בָּרְכוּ *(page 363).*

בָּרוּךְ אַתָּה יהוה אֱלֹהֵינוּ מֶלֶךְ הָעוֹלָם
יוֹצֵר אוֹר וּבוֹרֵא חֹשֶׁךְ
עֹשֶׂה שָׁלוֹם וּבוֹרֵא אֶת הַכֹּל.

אוֹר עוֹלָם בְּאוֹצַר חַיִּים, אוֹרוֹת מֵאֹפֶל אָמַר וַיֶּהִי.

יוצר

אַכְתִּיר זֵר תְּהִלָּה / לְנוֹרָא עֲלִילָה / בְּמִי זֹאת עוֹלָה.
בְּאֶדֶר רְנָנִים אֶעֱלֹסָה / כְּנַף רְנָנִים נֶעֱלָסָה / לְמֶלֶךְ רָם וְנִשָּׂא.
גַּדְתִּי אַרְבַּע / בְּמִסְפַּר רֹבַע / לְחָן עַל אַרְבַּע.

אֲסַלֵּד בְּשֶׁבַח וְתוֹדָה / בְּתוֹךְ קָהָל וְעֵדָה
בְּלָקְחִי לוּלָב וַאֲגֻדָּה / קָדוֹשׁ.

דְּרֹשׁ בְּמוֹ צֶדֶק / לְשָׁפְטָם בְּצֶדֶק / דִּינָם לְהוֹצִיא לְצֶדֶק.
הַלֵּל בָּם אֶפְצֶה / וּמְלִיצַי יִרְצֶה / וְכַזָּהָב אֵצֵא.
וְרוֹבֵץ בַּפֶּתַח יֵבוֹשׁ / וְחֵטְא בְּצוּל תִּכְבֹּשׁ / קְרָאתִיךָ, אַל אֵבוֹשׁ.
זֵכֶר סִכּוּךְ לְדוֹרוֹת / לָהֶם לְהוֹרוֹת / לְסַכֵּךְ וּלְקָרוֹת.
חֲסוֹת בְּצֵל סֻכָּה / כְּחֹק נְסוּכָה / שִׁבְעָה לְהִסְתּוֹכְכָה.
טִלּוּל עֲנָנִים אֶזְכְּרָה / בְּכָל דּוֹר וָדוֹר אַזְכִּירָה / לְחַסְדֵי דָוִיד זָכְרָה.
יָקֵם סֻכָּתוֹ / וְתִכּוֹן מַלְכוּתוֹ / וְתָרֶב גְּדֻלָּתוֹ.
כִּימֵי עוֹלָם / וּמַלְכוּתוֹ עַד הָעוֹלָם / לְדָוִד וּלְזַרְעוֹ עַד עוֹלָם.
לְדוֹר וָדוֹר תִּמְלֹךְ / וְהוּא עֲדֵי עַד יִמְלֹךְ / מֶלֶךְ מַמְלִיךְ מֶלֶךְ.
מְהֵרָה לְהַצְמִיחַ זַרְעוֹ / עַל עַם מְשׁוּעוֹ / לַעֲבֹר עַל פִּשְׁעוֹ.
נֶחֱזֶה בְּעֻזָּךְ / בְּשׁוּבְךָ לְגַן אֱגוֹזָךְ / וְעַיִן בְּעַיִן נֶחֱזָךְ.
סֻכָּתְךָ עֲלֵיהֶם תִּמְתַּח / וּבְצֵל לְקוּחֶיךָ יִמְתַּח / וְלֹא יַכֵּם מְרִתָּה.

עֵצִים בְּנָטְלָם אַרְבָּעָה / לִמְזוּזַת רְבוּעָה / לִזּוֹכֵר בְּרִית שְׁבוּעָה.
פְּרִי עֵץ הָדָר / אֶקַּח לַנֶּאְדָּר / כִּי כְבוֹדוֹ הוֹד וְהָדָר.
צֶמַח תָּמָר / אֶשָּׂא לְהַאֲמֵר / לְכֻלּוֹ כָבוֹד אוֹמֵר.
קִיחַת עֲנַף עֵץ עָבוֹת / אֶאֱסֹר בַּעֲבוֹת / לְמַבִּיט בְּרִית אָבוֹת.
רַעֲנַנֵּי עֲרָבָה / כְּצִמְחֵי רְבָבָה / לְדָגוּל מֵרְבָבָה.
שְׁתוּלִים בַּחֲצֵרוֹת / בָּם יוּפְדוּ מִצָּרוֹת / כִּבְזֵכֶר חֲצוֹצְרוֹת.
תְּכוּנִים לְכַפָּרָה / לְסוֹרְרָה כְּפָרָה / בְּלִי צֵאת חֲפוּרָה
מִפְּנֵי קָדוֹשׁ.

*Continue with "*הַמֵּאִיר לָאָרֶץ*" on page 365 (on* שבת*, with "*הַכֹּל יוֹדוּךָ*" on page 367) to "*מְלֹא כָל־הָאָרֶץ כְּבוֹדוֹ*" on page 373.*

אופן לשני ימי סוכות

אַאֲמִיר אוֹתְךָ סֶלָה / בְּהוֹד וְהָדָר וּתְהִלָּה
גּוֹאֵל, הַצְמִיחַ גְּאֻלָּה / דְּרֹשׁ אֲיֻמָּתְךָ לְשֵׁם וְלִתְהִלָּה.

הַצָּגִים לְפָנֶיךָ בְּשִׂמְחָה / וּבְלוּלְבֵיהֶם אוֹתְךָ לְשַׁמְּחָה
זוֹעֲקִים לְפָנֶיךָ שִׂיחָה / חֲמֹל עֲלֵיהֶם, הוֹשִׁיעָה וְהַצְלִיחָה.

טוֹב, בְּרַחֲמֶיךָ הָרַבִּים / יְקַר עֲדַת אֲהוּבִים
כּוֹרְעִים וּמִשְׁתַּחֲוִים [וּמוֹדִים] בְּאֲהָבִים / לְשַׁעַר בַּת רַבִּים.

מַחֲמַדָּם תֵּן לָהֶם / נָא שְׂמַח עִמָּהֶם
שָׂא נָא חַטֹּאתֵיהֶם / עֲבֹר עַל פִּשְׁעֵיהֶם.

פּוֹצְחִים הַלֵּל וְתוֹדוֹת / צוּר הַיּוֹדֵעַ עֲתִידוֹת
קוֹל לְהַשְׁמִיעַ אוֹתָם לַחֲדוֹת / רַחֵם בְּנָשְׂאָם אֲגֻדּוֹת.

שׁוֹקְדִים, וְאוֹתְךָ מַקְדִּישִׁים / שִׁבְחֲךָ בְּפִיהֶם רוֹחֲשִׁים
תּוֹקְפִים (נ״א: תּוֹבְעִים) בָּרוּךְ וְלוֹחֲשִׁים / תּוֹמְכִים כְּאֵילֵי תַרְשִׁישִׁים.

וְהַחַיּוֹת יְשׁוֹרֵרוּ / וּכְרוּבִים יְפָאֵרוּ
וּשְׂרָפִים יָרֹנּוּ / וְאֶרְאֶלִּים יְבָרֵכוּ
פְּנֵי כָל חַיָּה וְאוֹפָן וּכְרוּב לְעֻמַּת שְׂרָפִים
לְעֻמָּתָם מְשַׁבְּחִים וְאוֹמְרִים

All say aloud:

יחזקאל ג בָּרוּךְ כְּבוֹד־יהוה מִמְּקוֹמוֹ:

Continue with "לָאֵל בָּרוּךְ" on page 375 to "אֵין אֱלֹהִים זוּלָתֶךָ" on page 385.

זולת

אָנָּא הוֹשִׁיעָה נָּא / בְּנֵי עֲפַר מִי מָנָה
גּוֹאֵל הַצְלִיחָה נָּא / דּוֹרְשֶׁיךָ בְּכָל עוֹנָה.

הָקֵם סֻכַּת דָּוִד הַנּוֹפֶלֶת / וּבַל תְּהִי עוֹד מְשֻׁפֶּלֶת
זְכֹר אֲיֻמָּה הַנִּקְהֶלֶת / חוֹפְפָה (נ״א: חוֹפֶפֶת) וּבְצִלְּךָ נֶאֱהֶלֶת.

טוֹב, הַצְמַח שִׂמְחָתָם / יָהּ, כַּפֵּר אַשְׁמָתָם
כַּלֵּה עַתָּה אַנְחוֹתָם / לְמַעַנְךָ חִישׁ פְּדוּתָם.

מַלֵּא מִשְׁאֲלוֹת לִבָּם / נוֹאֲקִים אֵלֶיךָ בְּכָל לְבָבָם
סָמְכֵם וְרִיב רִיבָם / עַתָּה תִּשְׁכֹּן בְּקִרְבָּם.

פָּנֶה תִפְנֶה לְפָאֳרָם / צוּר, אֱמֹר לְעָזְרָם
קוֹמֵם בֵּית הֲדָרָם / רְאוֹתָם פִּתְאוֹם שִׁבְרָם.

שָׁלֵם מְהֵרָה תִּבָּנֶה
שְׁלֵמֶיךָ בְּכֵן תַּעֲנֶה
תַּכֶּה אוֹיְבֵינוּ כְּמַכַּת בְּכוֹרִים, וְתַעֲנֶה
תִּקְרָעֵם כִּקְרִיעַת יַם סוּף, וְנִקְרָאֲךָ וְתַעֲנֶה.

Continue with "עֶזְרַת אֲבוֹתֵינוּ" on page 385.

קרובה ליו״ט ראשון של סוכות

The שליח ציבור *takes three steps forward and at the points indicated by* °*,*
bends his knees at the first word, bows at the second, and
stands straight before saying God's name.

אֲדֹנָי, שְׂפָתַי תִּפְתָּח, וּפִי יַגִּיד תְּהִלָּתֶךָ: תהלים נא

אבות

°בָּרוּךְ אַתָּה יהוה, אֱלֹהֵינוּ וֵאלֹהֵי אֲבוֹתֵינוּ
אֱלֹהֵי אַבְרָהָם, אֱלֹהֵי יִצְחָק, וֵאלֹהֵי יַעֲקֹב
הָאֵל הַגָּדוֹל הַגִּבּוֹר וְהַנּוֹרָא, אֵל עֶלְיוֹן
גּוֹמֵל חֲסָדִים טוֹבִים, וְקֹנֵה הַכֹּל
וְזוֹכֵר חַסְדֵי אָבוֹת
וּמֵבִיא גוֹאֵל לִבְנֵי בְנֵיהֶם לְמַעַן שְׁמוֹ בְּאַהֲבָה.
מֶלֶךְ עוֹזֵר וּמוֹשִׁיעַ וּמָגֵן.

The רשויות *(prefatory prayers, asking permission to commence)*
*consist only of the standard opening "*מִסּוֹד חֲכָמִים...*".*

מִסּוֹד חֲכָמִים וּנְבוֹנִים
וּמִלֶּמֶד דַּעַת מְבִינִים
אֶפְתְּחָה פִּי בְּשִׁיר וּבִרְנָנִים
לְהוֹדוֹת וּלְהַלֵּל פְּנֵי שׁוֹכֵן מְעוֹנִים

מגן

אֲיֻמָּתִי בְּחִיל כִּפּוּר / בְּעוּתָה בְּחֶשְׁבּוֹן הַסִּפּוּר
גֻּלְּתִי כְּהִצְדַּק פּוּר / דּוֹלֵק כְּנִמְצָא חָפוּר.

הֶדְרָאוּ מְתֵי הוֹלְלִים / וְצָמְתוּ לְרֶגֶב חֲלָלִים
זַכִּים כְּיָצְאוּ מְהַלְלִים / חָלִים וְשָׁרִים כְּחוֹלְלִים.

טִיעַת עֲצֵי עֵשֶׂב / יִשְׂאוּ הַיּוֹם מִזְבֵּחַ לְהָסֵב
כְּתֵשֶׁר יְפַלְּסוּ בְּמֵסַב / לְהֵרָצוֹת בְּשׁוֹר וָכֶשֶׂב.

בָּךְ אָגִילָה וְאֶשְׂמְחָה / בְּרִנָּה וְשִׂמְחָה
בְּאֵם הַבָּנִים שְׂמֵחָה / גּוֹנְנֵנוּ בִּפְדוּת צָמְחָה.

בָּרוּךְ אַתָּה יהוה, מָגֵן אַבְרָהָם.

גבורות

אַתָּה גִּבּוֹר לְעוֹלָם, אֲדֹנָי
מְחַיֵּה מֵתִים אַתָּה, רַב לְהוֹשִׁיעַ

In ארץ ישראל:
מוֹרִיד הַטָּל

מְכַלְכֵּל חַיִּים בְּחֶסֶד, מְחַיֵּה מֵתִים בְּרַחֲמִים רַבִּים
סוֹמֵךְ נוֹפְלִים, וְרוֹפֵא חוֹלִים, וּמַתִּיר אֲסוּרִים
וּמְקַיֵּם אֱמוּנָתוֹ לִישֵׁנֵי עָפָר.
מִי כָמְוֹךָ, בַּעַל גְּבוּרוֹת, וּמִי דְּוֹמֶה לָּךְ
מֶלֶךְ, מֵמִית וּמְחַיֶּה וּמַצְמִיחַ יְשׁוּעָה.
וְנֶאֱמָן אַתָּה לְהַחֲיוֹת מֵתִים.

מחיה

מְאַלְּמֵי מְגָדִים אַרְבָּעָה / מְשַׁמְּרֵי סֻכָּה שִׁבְעָה
נוֹסְכֵי נֶזֶל שִׁבְעָה / נַהֲלֵם נְעִימוֹת שִׁבְעָה.

שִׂיחִים בְּדֶרֶךְ מַטָּעָתָם / סוֹלְלִים סְכוּת שַׁוְעָתָם
עֲלֵי קָרִים נְטִיעָתָם / עֲלוֹת בָּמוֹ מִטְּבִיעָתָם.

פְּאוּרִים לְשֵׁם יוֹם / פְּאֵר בָּם לְאָיֹם
צִוּוּי קִיּוּמָם הַיּוֹם / צַחְצוּחַ בְּזֶה רִאשׁוֹן יוֹם.

בָּךְ אָגִילָה וְאֶשְׂמְחָה / בְּגִילָה וְשִׂמְחָה
בְּאֵם הַבָּנִים שְׂמֵחָה / טְלוּלִים בִּתְחִיָּה אֲשֶׁר צָמְחָה.

(נ״א: תַּעֲלֵנוּ מִכַּנְפוֹת הָאָרֶץ / וְנָגִילָה בִּמְשׂוֹשׂ כָּל הָאָרֶץ
וְאַחֲרֶיךָ מָשְׁכֵנוּ לָרֶץ / וּבְטַל תְּחִי תְּעוֹרֵר יְשֵׁנֵי אֶרֶץ.)

בָּרוּךְ אַתָּה יהוה, מְחַיֵּה הַמֵּתִים.

משלש

קֹשֶׁט שְׁעִינַת עֵץ / לְעוֹמְסֵי פְּרִי עֵץ
זְכֹר נָא לְהִוָּעֵץ / וּתְשׁוּעָה בְּרֹב יוֹעֵץ.

רִבְבוֹת סָע סֻכּוֹתָה / בְּלוּד צִקְּנָם הִסְכַּתָּה
בְּנֶשֶׁק לְרֹאשָׁם סַכּוֹתָה / וּמֵאֶנֶף לַהֲקָם חָשַׁכְתָּ.

שִׁבְעָה עַנְנֵי מֶשִׁי סִבַּבְתָּם / בְּעֲנִינַת פָּרֵשׂ סִכַּכְתָּם
תָּעוּ כְּחֵדֶק מִמְּסוּכָתָם / בְּכֵן רְשָׁפָה סֻכָּתָם.

תּוֹלְדוֹת שָׂעִיר תְּאַבִּיד / גְּבִיר לְבִלְתִּי לְהַעֲבִיד
תְּאַפְּדֵנוּ כְּאָז רְבִיד / בְּקוֹמְמְךָ סֻכַּת דָּוִד.

The קהל *aloud, followed by the* שליח ציבור*:*

תהלים קמו יִמְלֹךְ יהוה לְעוֹלָם, אֱלֹהַיִךְ צִיּוֹן לְדֹר וָדֹר, הַלְלוּיָהּ:
תהלים כב וְאַתָּה קָדוֹשׁ, יוֹשֵׁב תְּהִלּוֹת יִשְׂרָאֵל:
אֵל נָא.

אֲנוֹבֵב בְּפֶה וְלָשׁוֹן / הַלֵּל בְּיוֹם רִאשׁוֹן
לְהַעֲרִיץ לְאֵל אַחֲרוֹן וְרִאשׁוֹן / קָדוֹשׁ.

שַׂגִּיא כֹּחַ לֹא נִמְצֵאתָ / לְהַצְדִּיק עַם זוּ כְּחָפַצְתָּ
בְּכֵן בְּאֵלֶּה נִרְצֵיתָ / קָדוֹשׁ.

אֶקְחָה פְּרִי עֵץ הָדָר / בְּכָל שָׁנָה בְּתָדִר / מָקוֹם שֶׁהוּא מִתְהַדֵּר
לְהַלֵּל בּוֹ בְּהָדָר / לָעַט הוֹד וְהָדָר / עֲלֵי שִׁבְעָה דָּר
עִזּוּז בַּקֹּדֶשׁ נֶאְדָּר / וּמִכָּל יְצִיר מְאֻדָּר / וְחָפֵץ זוּ לְהַדָּר.

אֲנוֹבֵב בְּפֶה וְלָשׁוֹן / הַלֵּל בְּיוֹם רִאשׁוֹן
לְהַעֲרִיץ לְאֵל אַחֲרוֹן וְרִאשׁוֹן / קָדוֹשׁ.

זִמּוּן תֹּמֶר כַּף / אֶקְחָה הַיּוֹם בְּכַף / בָּם לְצוּר אִכַּף
רָחַצְתִּי בְנִקָּיוֹן כַּפּוֹת / עֲמֹס בְּמוֹ כַפּוֹת / אַף וָאֶנֶף לִכְפּוֹת
בְּלוּלָב שׁוֹד חֲמָסִים / אֵיךְ אֶפְרֹט מַעֲשִׂים / פְּנֵי מַקְדִּיחַ הֲמָסִים.

שַׂגִּיא כֹּחַ לֹא נִמְצֵאתָ / לְהַצְדִּיק עַם זוּ כְּחָפַצְתָּ
בְּכֵן בְּאֵלֶּה נִרְצֵיתָ / קָדוֹשׁ.

יְפִי שְׁלוֹשׁ הֲדַסִּים / בְּהוֹד טַעַם אִשִּׁים / לְצָג בֵּין הַהֲדַסִּים
רְעוּלִים וְגַם מְתוּקִים / אֲשֵׁוֶּה כְּחֹק מְצוּקִים / לְחִכּוֹ מַמְתַקִּים
בְּעַנְפֵי עֵץ עָבוֹת / שְׁעוּרִים לְבֵית אָבוֹת / אֶאֱסֹר חַג בַּעֲבוֹת.

אֲנוֹבֵב בְּפֶה וְלָשׁוֹן / הַלֵּל בְּיוֹם רִאשׁוֹן
לְהַעֲרִיץ לְאֵל אַחֲרוֹן וְרִאשׁוֹן / קָדוֹשׁ.

יֹשֶׁר פְּאֵר עַרְבוֹת / בָּמוֹ עֹז לְהַרְבּוֹת / לְרוֹכֵב בָּעֲרָבוֹת
קְצוּבוֹת בַּדֵּי שְׂתָיִם / כְּמוֹ עֲפִיפוֹת שְׂפָתַיִם / וּמְצָעוֹת בֵּינָתַיִם
יְעוּרוֹת בְּאִבֵּי הַנַּחַל / לְהַעֲרִיב בָּם מַחַל / לְיַעֲרֵי רְתוּמֵי גַּחַל.

שַׂגִּיא כֹּחַ לֹא נִמְצֵאתָ / לְהַצְדִּיק עַם זוּ כְּחָפַצְתָּ
בְּכֵן בְּאֵלֶּה נִרְצֵיתָ / קָדוֹשׁ.

לְכָל עֵץ תְּעַב / וּבְאַרְבַּעַת אֵלֶּה תָּאַב / לְהַלְלוֹ בָם כְּאָב
יַחַד בָּם לְהַלֵּל / שִׁבְעָה כְּבֵית הִלֵּל / בַּיּוֹם וְלֹא בַלֵּיל
רוֹנְנִים מֵלִיץ בַּעֲדֵנוּ / לְהָחִישׁ נָא לְסַעֲדֵנוּ / עַתָּה לְקִרְיַת מוֹעֲדֵנוּ.

אֲנוֹבֵב בְּפֶה וְלָשׁוֹן / הַלֵּל בְּיוֹם רִאשׁוֹן
לְהַעֲרִיץ לְאֵל אַחֲרוֹן וְרִאשׁוֹן / קָדוֹשׁ.

וּבְכֵן, וַיְהִי בְשָׁלֵם סֻכּוֹ: תהלים עו

אָז הָיְתָה חֲנַיַּת סֻכּוֹ בְּתַלְתַּלֵּי תֹּקֶף בְּשִׁנְאַנֵּי שֶׁקֶט
בְּרֶכֶב רִבּוֹתַיִם בִּקְדוֹשֵׁי קֶדֶם בְּסַפִּיר וְסֻכּוֹת.
וְחָן בְּשָׁלֵם סֻכּוֹ בִּצְנוּעֵי צֶדֶק בִּפְאֵר פָּרֹכֶת
בַּעֲבוֹדַת עֶרֶךְ בְּסֻכַּת סְגֻלָּה וְהִיא סֻכָּתוֹ.
אָז הָיְתָה חֲנַיַּת סֻכּוֹ בְּנוֹצְצֵי נֹגַהּ בְּמַלְאֲכֵי מָרוֹם
בְּלַהַט לוֹהֲטִים בְּכַנְפֵי כְרוּבִים בְּסַפִּיר וְסֻכּוֹת.
וְחָן בְּשָׁלֵם סֻכּוֹ בִּידִידוּת יַעַר בְּטִירַת טָהֳרָה
בְּחֻפַּת חֶדְוָה בְּזֵר זְמִירַת זְבוּל וְהִיא סֻכָּתוֹ.
אָז הָיְתָה חֲנַיַּת סֻכּוֹ בְּוֹעוּדֵי וַעַד בְּהוֹגֵי הֲמֻלָּה
בִּדְמָמָה דַקָּה בְּדוֹהֲרֵי דוֹלְקִים בְּסַפִּיר וְסֻכּוֹת.
וְחָן בְּשָׁלֵם סֻכּוֹ בִּגְלוּמֵי גֵיא בְּבֵית בְּחִירָתוֹ
בְּאֹהֶל אִוּוּיוֹ בְּאֶדֶר אַפַּדְנוֹ וְהִיא סֻכָּתוֹ.

All:

וּבְכֵן לְךָ תַעֲלֶה קְדֻשָּׁה, כִּי אַתָּה קְדוֹשׁ יִשְׂרָאֵל וּמוֹשִׁיעַ.

Some congregations say the piyut אֶקְחָה *before* קדושה.
Many congregations omit it, and those who do so
*continue with "*נְקַדֵּשׁ אֶת שִׁמְךָ*" on page 391.*

סילוק

אֶקְחָה בָּרִאשׁוֹן / לְאַחֲרוֹן וְרִאשׁוֹן
פְּרִי עֵץ הָדָר / לְבַקֹּדֶשׁ נֶאְדָּר

כַּפּוֹת תָּמָר / לְצַדִּיק כַּתָּמָר
עַנְפֵי הֲדַסִּים / לְצָג בֵּין הַהֲדַסִּים
טַרְפֵּי עֲרָבוֹת / לְרוֹכֵב בָּעֲרָבוֹת

בָּמוֹ לְהַלֵּל / בְּזֶמֶר וְהַלֵּל / בַּיּוֹם וְלֹא בַלֵּיל / לְאֵין לְפָנָיו לֵיל
בְּלוּלָב אֶחָד / וְאֶתְרוֹג אֶחָד / לַיהוה אֶחָד / וּשְׁמוֹ אֶחָד
בַּעֲרָבוֹת שְׁתַּיִם / כְּאִמָּהוֹת שְׁתַּיִם / וְכִמְעוֹפְפוֹת שְׁתַּיִם
בַּעֲבוֹת שְׁלֹשָׁה / כְּאָבוֹת שְׁלֹשָׁה / וּכְמַקְדִּישֵׁי שְׁלֹשָׁה
בַּאֲגֻדּוֹת אַרְבַּע / כְּגְבָעוֹת אַרְבַּע / וּכְחַיּוֹת אַרְבַּע / וּכְנָפַיִם אַרְבַּע
בְּשְׂמָחוֹת שֶׁבַע / כִּימֵי שֶׁבַע
בַּחֲגִיגַת שְׁמוֹנָה / כְּמִילַת שְׁמוֹנָה.

בְּהָדָר לְהַזְכִּיר הַדּוּר זִקְנָה / בְּכַפּוֹת לְהַזְכִּיר לְמֵחִים נִקְנָה
בַּעֲבוֹת לְהַזְכִּיר תָּם, חַיֵּי עַד קָנָה / בַּעֲרָבָה לְהַזְכִּיר אָח לְעֶבֶד הַקְּנָה.

בְּהָדָר לַחְשֹׁב בְּלוּיַת עֶדְנָה / בְּכַפּוֹת לַחְשֹׁב מְשׁוּלַּת שׁוֹשַׁנָּה
בַּעֲבוֹת לַחְשֹׁב יְחוּמַת דִּינָה / בַּעֲרָבָה לַחְשֹׁב בְּאָחוֹת מְקַנְּאָה.

בְּהָדָר לְהַמְשִׁיל מַפְלִיא עֲגָלָה / בְּכַפּוֹת לְהַמְשִׁיל אַגַּן סְגֻלָּה
בַּעֲבוֹת לְהַמְשִׁיל שׁוּרַת דְּגוּלָה / בַּעֲרָבָה לְהַמְשִׁיל מְחוֹקְקֵי מְגִלָּה.

בְּהָדָר לְכַפֵּר סַרְעַפֵּי לֵב / בְּכַפּוֹת לְכַפֵּר שְׁזָרָה מוּל לֵב
בַּעֲבוֹת לְכַפֵּר סִקּוּר עַיִן וָלֵב / בַּעֲרָבָה לְכַפֵּר נִבּוּל פֶּה עִם לֵב.

בְּהָדָר לְכַנּוֹת שְׁלֵמִים תְּמִימִים / בְּכַפּוֹת לְכַנּוֹת בַּעֲלֵי מַעֲשִׂים נְעִימִים
בַּעֲבוֹת לְכַנּוֹת יְשָׁרִים, בְּמִצְוֹת חֲתוּמִים / בַּעֲרָבָה לְכַנּוֹת בְּשִׁמְצָה כְּתוּמִים.

וּכְמוֹ בְּעֵץ הָדָר, רֵיחַ וְטַעַם / כֵּן בְּעַם זוּ, בַּעֲלֵי מִצְוֹת וְדֵעַ נֹעַם
וּכְמוֹ בְּכַף תֹּמֶר, טַעַם וְלֹא רֵיחַ / כֵּן בְּעַם זוּ, בַּעֲלֵי מִצְוֹת בְּלֹא דַת רֵיחַ
וּכְמוֹ בַּעֲבוֹת, רֵיחַ וְטַעַם מַר / כֵּן בֵּינֵימוֹ הוֹגֵי דָת וְחִכָּם מַר
וּכְמוֹ עֲרָבָה, בְּלִי טַעַם וָרֵיחַ / כֵּן בֵּינֵימוֹ עִקְּשִׁים אֲטוּמִים מִלְּהָרִיחַ

וּכְמוֹ עֵץ פְּרִי עָלֵי סָרָק מְחוֹפְפִים / כֵּן יְשָׁרִים עָלֵי רְשָׁעִים מְחוֹפְפִים
וּכְמוֹ הֵם אֲגוּדִים אֵלֶּה בְּאֵלֶּה / וּלְכַפֵּר אֵלֶּה עַל אֵלֶּה
לַעֲשׂוֹת אֵלֶּה כְּאֵלֶּה / לְהַנְעִים זְמִירוֹת אֵלֶּה / לְמִי בָרָא אֵלֶּה.

לְמַלֵּל לְהַלֵּל / לְכַלֵּל לְחוֹלֵל
לְאַשֵּׁר לְיַשֵּׁר / לְהַכְשֵׁר לְהַתְשֵׁר
לְבָרֵר לְשׁוֹרֵר / לְאַדֵּר לְהַדֵּר
לְגַבֵּר לְדַבֵּר / לְהַאֲמֵר לְזַמֵּר
לְחַנֵּן לְרַנֵּן / לְשַׁנֵּן לְהַרְנֵן
לְקַלֵּס לְעַלֵּס / לְנַצֵּחַ לְפַצֵּחַ
לְהַעֲלִיץ וּלְהַעֲרִיץ / לְהַרְגִּישׁ לְהַקְדִּישׁ

כְּשִׁיר עִירִין / כְּשִׁירַת קַדִּישִׁין
כְּזֶמֶר חַשְׁמַלָּה / כְּזִמְרַת הֲמֻלָּה
כְּפְאֵר אֵלִים / כְּתִפְאֶרֶת אֶרְאֶלִּים
כַּהֲדַר זִקִּים / כְּהַדְרַת בְּרָקִים
כְּנֹעַם גְּלִילִים / כִּנְעִימַת גַּלְגַּלִּים
כְּנִגּוּן רוֹבִים / כִּנְגִינַת כְּרוּבִים
כְּרֶנֶן אוֹפַנִּים / כְּרִנְנַת מְרֻבְּעֵי פָנִים
כְּחִדּוּשׁ בְּרָקִים / כְּמִתְחַדְּשִׁים לַבְּקָרִים
כְּקִדּוּשׁ עָפִים / כִּקְדֻשַּׁת עוֹפְפִים
כְּרֶגֶשׁ מְעוֹפְפִים / כְּרִגְשַׁת מְתוֹפְפִים
כְּשִׁנּוּן צְפוּפִים / כְּהֶגֶה מְצַפְצְפִים
כְּרַעַשׁ סִפִּים / כְּמַעֲמַד שְׂרָפִים

כְּמַחֲנוֹת קְדוֹשִׁים / לַקָּדוֹשׁ מַקְדִּישִׁים / וּקְדֻשָּׁה מְשַׁלְּשִׁים

Continue with "כַּכָּתוּב עַל יַד נְבִיאֶךָ" on page 391.

יוצר ליום טוב שני של סוכות

שחרית *is said up to and including* בָּרְכוּ *(page 363).*

בָּרוּךְ אַתָּה יהוה אֱלֹהֵינוּ מֶלֶךְ הָעוֹלָם
יוֹצֵר אוֹר וּבוֹרֵא חֹשֶׁךְ
עֹשֶׂה שָׁלוֹם וּבוֹרֵא אֶת הַכֹּל.

אוֹר עוֹלָם בְּאוֹצַר חַיִּים, אוֹרוֹת מֵאֹפֶל אָמַר וַיֶּהִי.

יוצר

אַאֲמִיץ לְנוֹרָא וְאָיֹם / בְּהִסְתּוֹפְפִי לְפָנָיו אֶמְצָא פִּדְיוֹם
אַךְ בַּחֲמִשָּׁה עָשָׂר יוֹם: ויקרא כג
בְּלָקְחִי כַּף תָּמָר, וּשְׁלֹשֶׁת מִינֵי קְבוּעִי / בָּם אֲהַלֵּל לְאוֹרִי וְיִשְׁעִי
בַּחֹדֶשׁ הַשְּׁבִיעִי
גֵּאוּת אַלְבִּישׁ לְדָר בַּמְּרוֹמִים / לְהַלְלוֹ בְּמַרְבִּיּוֹת, שְׁלֵמִים וְלֹא קְטוּמִים /
תָּחֹגּוּ אֶת־חַג־יהוה שִׁבְעַת יָמִים: שם

אֲהַלֵּל בְּפֶה וְלָשׁוֹן / לְשׁוֹמֵעַ קוֹל לַחֲשׁוֹן
כְּנָם, וּלְקַחְתֶּם לָכֶם בַּיּוֹם הָרִאשׁוֹן: / קָדוֹשׁ. שם

דָּגוּל מִקּוֹלוֹת מַיִם נֶאְדָּר / אַאַפְּדֶנּוּ הוֹד וְהָדָר / בִּפְרִי עֵץ הָדָר.
הַמְּרוֹמָם בִּקְהַל עַם נְצוּרִים / בְּהִלּוּל וּפְאֵר אוֹתוֹ מַכְתִּירִים
בְּכַפּוֹת תְּמָרִים.
וְיָרִיק רֹב בְּרָכוֹת מֵאֲרֻבּוֹת / לְאוֹם מְהַלְלוֹ מִסַּרְעַף וּמִקְּרָבוֹת
וַעֲנַף עֵץ עָבוֹת.
זְכִיּוֹת יִכְרָעוּ וְעָוֹן יִמְחַל / מִלְּהִכָּווֹת בְּשַׁלְהֶבֶת רִשְׁפֵּי גַּחַל
תּוֹמְכֵי עַרְבֵי נָחַל.
חֶדְוַת רַב תִּמְצְאוּ בְּלַהֲקַתְכֶם / חֲסוּנִים בְּצִוּוּי דַּת מַלְכְּכֶם
וּשְׂמַחְתֶּם לִפְנֵי יהוה אֱלֹהֵיכֶם: ויקרא כג

טָרְחֲכֶם יָפִיק לֵילוֹת וְיָמִים / גְּאוֹן נוֹגְשֵׂיכֶם יְגַדַּע וְיִדַּמִּים
לְבַל תֵּעָנְשׁוּ בַּחֲגִיגַת שִׁבְעַת יָמִים.
יַסְכִּית פִּלּוּלִי, וְיַאֲזִין הֶגְיוֹנִי / וִיקַבֵּל כְּקָרְבָּן רַחַשׁ עִנְיָנִי
וְחַגֹּתֶם אֹתוֹ חַג לַיהוה: שם
כִּשְׁרוֹן כֹּחַ יַחֲלִיף לַשּׁוֹשַׁנָּה / חוֹגֶגֶת וְסוֹכֶכֶת, וְעוֹצֶרֶת בְּרִנָּה
שִׁבְעַת יָמִים בַּשָּׁנָה: שם
לְעֵת יָסִיר סֵבֶל מֵעַל שִׁכְמֵיכֶם / תָּרֹנּוּ וְתָחֹגּוּ בְּקִרְיַת מוֹעֲדֵיכֶם
חֻקַּת עוֹלָם לְדוֹרֹתֵיכֶם: שם
מַשְׂגִּיחַ מֵחֶרֶךְ תְּהַלְלוּ בְּאִיּוּמִים / מַנְעִימִים קוֹל, וְלֹא דוֹמִים
בַּסֻּכֹּת תֵּשְׁבוּ שִׁבְעַת יָמִים: שם
נְדִיבֵי עַמִּים, סוֹדְרֵי עֲרָכוֹת / בְּאֶבְרָתוֹ לָעַד יָהוּ סְכוּכוֹת
כָּל־הָאֶזְרָח בְּיִשְׂרָאֵל יֵשְׁבוּ בַּסֻּכֹּת: שם
סֹלּוּ בְּהִלּוּל לְשׁוֹכֵן בֵּינֵיכֶם / וְתָנוּחוּ בְּהַשְׁקֵט כָּל יְמֵיכֶם
לְמַעַן יֵדְעוּ דֹרֹתֵיכֶם: שם
עֶלְיוֹן הוֹדִיעַ פְּלָאָיו עַל יַד גּוֹאֵל / עֲמוּסָיו סִכֵּךְ בַּעֲנָנִים כְּהוֹאֵל
כִּי בַסֻּכּוֹת הוֹשַׁבְתִּי אֶת־בְּנֵי יִשְׂרָאֵל: שם
פָּקַדְתִּי עַמִּי לָחֹן שִׁירִים / מִשְׁפָּטָם לְהוֹצִיא כָאוֹר וְכַצָּהֳרָיִם
בְּהוֹצִיאִי אוֹתָם מֵאֶרֶץ מִצְרָיִם: שם
צִקּוּן צַעֲקַתְכֶם הִסְכַּתִּי בְּאָזְנַי / וּפְדוּת שָׁלַחְתִּי לְכָל הֲמוֹנַי
וַיְדַבֵּר מֹשֶׁה אֶת־מֹעֲדֵי יהוה: שם
קָרָא דוֹרוֹת, חַי עוֹלָמִים / צִוָּה לְעַם שְׁמוֹ מַנְעִימִים
חַג הַסֻּכֹּת תַּעֲשֶׂה לְךָ שִׁבְעַת יָמִים: דברים טז
רָם, מִמְּעוֹנְךָ הַסֵּךְ מַקְהֵלוֹתֶיךָ / לְרַחֵם וּלְהוֹשִׁיעַ כָּל לַהֲקוֹתֶיךָ
וְשָׂמַחְתָּ בְּחַגֶּךָ, אַתָּה וּבִנְךָ וּבִתֶּךָ: שם
שׁוֹדֵד עוֹד בַּל יְבַהֲלֶךָ / לָתֵת תִּקְוָה לִפְזוּרֵי כְּמֵהֶיךָ
שִׁבְעַת יָמִים תָּחֹג לַיהוה אֱלֹהֶיךָ: שם
תְּאֵבֵי יִשְׁעוֹ, לַחֲזוֹת כְּבוֹדוֹ / לְהִתְעַשֵּׁרוּ מִשֶּׁלּוֹ, וְהַכֹּל בְּיָדוֹ
אִישׁ כְּמַתְּנַת יָדוֹ: דברים טז

תּוֹמְכֵי סַנְסִנֵּי דְשָׁאִים / מִשָּׂטָן וּמִמַּשְׁחִית, יְהוּ חֲבוּאִים
שם לַחֲזוֹת וּלְהַסְכִּית בִּבְשׂוֹרוֹת טוֹבוֹת, לָכֵן הִנֵּה־יָמִים בָּאִים:

אֲהַלֵּל בְּפֶה וְלָשׁוֹן / לְשׁוֹמֵעַ קוֹל לַחֲשׁוֹן
ויקרא כג כְּנָם, וּלְקַחְתֶּם לָכֶם בַּיּוֹם הָרִאשׁוֹן: / קָדוֹשׁ.

Continue with "הַמֵּאִיר לָאָרֶץ" on page 365 to "מְלֹא כָל־הָאָרֶץ כְּבוֹדוֹ" on page 373.

זולת

אָנָּא תֶּרֶב עֲלִיצוּתֶיךָ / לְקוֹוֵי יְשׁוּעָתֶךָ
בָּאִים לְאַמֵּץ תְּהִלָּתֶךָ / בְּוַעַד בֵּית דְּגִילָתֶךָ
גּוֹדְדֵם לְבֵית בְּחִירָתֶךָ / יֶשַׁע לְרֹאשָׁם בְּתִתֶּךָ
דְּלֵם מִכְּשֶׁל תִּגְרָתֶךָ / וּתְסוֹכְכֵם בְּגִין אֶבְרָתֶךָ.

הוֹשֵׁב עַל מִשְׁפָּטוֹ אַרְמוֹן / אֲשֶׁר שַׁתָּה יְלֵל יְשִׁימוֹן
וְכַנֵּס נִדְחֵי הֲמוֹן / זֶרַע תָּם פִּצֵּל לַח לוּז וְעַרְמוֹן
זֵדֵי רֶשַׁע עֵקֶר אַדְמוֹן / יְבוֹאוּם שְׁכוֹל וְאַלְמוֹן
חֲנוּנֶיךָ הוֹגֵי אָמוֹן / תִּטָּעֵם בְּהַר חֶרְמוֹן.

טוֹעֲנֵי עֻלְּךָ עַל גַּבָּם / יָהּ הַשְׁרֵה שְׁכִינָתְךָ בְּקִרְבָּם
יַעֲלוּ לָחֹג לְבֵית נָוָם / בְּהִכּוֹנֵן עִיר מוֹשָׁבָם
כֹּחַ וְלָאֵל תְּשַׂגְּבָם / צוּר עֻזָּם וּמִשְׂגַּבָּם
לֹא לָנֶצַח תְּרִיבָם / כִּי עָלֶיךָ מַשְׁלִיכִים יְהָבָם.

מִקְדָּשְׁךָ הַשָּׁמֵם / כִּימֵי עוֹלָם תְּרוֹמֵם
נֶצַח לְבַל יִשְׁתּוֹמֵם / תֵּת שִׁקּוּץ שׁוֹמֵם
סֻכַּת דָּוִד קוֹמֵם / וּפוֹרְצֵי גְּדֵרָהּ הַשְׁמֵם
עוּרָה כִּנּוֹרִי הַדּוֹמֵם / וְנִימָיו עוֹד בַּל תְּנַמֵּם.

פִּנַּת מִגְדַּל עֵדֶר / עֲפֵלָה כְּשַׁחֲרוּרֵי קֵדָר
צְפֵה לְהַדְרָה בְּהֶדֶר / הֱיוֹת סוּגָה וְגָדֵר
קִנְיַן צֹאן דֵּיר / אֲשֶׁר נִזְרָה כִּבְמַעְדֵּר
רְעֵה לְהַשְׁמֵן וּלְהִפָּדֵר / כְּבַקָּרַת רוֹעֶה עֶדֶר.

שַׁעַר בַּת רַבִּים / מְקוֹם תְּמוּרוֹת וּכְרוּבִים
תְּחַטְּבוּ בַּחֲטוּבִים / בְּמִסְגְּרוֹת וּשְׁלַבִּים
תְּחַדֵּשׁ שִׁירִים עֲרֵבִים / בְּפֶה מַשְׁכִּימִים וּמַעֲרִיבִים
תִּפְדֵּנוּ בְּאֹמֶץ וְשִׁגּוּבִים / כְּאָז פְּדִיתָ דַּיֵּי רְהָבִים.

Continue with "עֶזְרַת אֲבוֹתֵינוּ" on page 385.

קרובה ליו״ט שני של סוכות

The שליח ציבור *takes three steps forward and at the points indicated by* ▾*, bends his knees at the first word, bows at the second, and stands straight before saying God's name.*

אֲדֹנָי, שְׂפָתַי תִּפְתָּח, וּפִי יַגִּיד תְּהִלָּתֶךָ: תהלים נא

אבות

▾בָּרוּךְ ▾אַתָּה יהוה, אֱלֹהֵינוּ וֵאלֹהֵי אֲבוֹתֵינוּ
אֱלֹהֵי אַבְרָהָם, אֱלֹהֵי יִצְחָק, וֵאלֹהֵי יַעֲקֹב
הָאֵל הַגָּדוֹל הַגִּבּוֹר וְהַנּוֹרָא, אֵל עֶלְיוֹן
גּוֹמֵל חֲסָדִים טוֹבִים, וְקוֹנֵה הַכֹּל
וְזוֹכֵר חַסְדֵי אָבוֹת
וּמֵבִיא גוֹאֵל לִבְנֵי בְנֵיהֶם לְמַעַן שְׁמוֹ בְּאַהֲבָה.
מֶלֶךְ עוֹזֵר וּמוֹשִׁיעַ וּמָגֵן.

מִסּוֹד חֲכָמִים וּנְבוֹנִים
וּמִלֶּמֶד דַּעַת מְבִינִים
אֶפְתְּחָה פִּי בְּשִׁיר וּבִרְנָנִים
לְהוֹדוֹת וּלְהַלֵּל פְּנֵי שׁוֹכֵן מְעוֹנִים

מגן

אֶרְחַץ בְּנִקָּיוֹן כַּפּוֹת / בְּלִי חָמָס, קַחַת סִנְסוּן כַּפּוֹת
גְּמוּנֵי פָז לֶאֱגֹד וְלִכְפּוֹת / דִּשְׁאֵי אֲשָׁלִים, בָּם אַף לִכְפּוֹת.

הֵן מִבְּעָשׂוֹר חֻקְקִי לְחַיִּים / וְהוֹדִיעַנִי אֹרַח חַיִּים
זַעַם מֵאָז תַּרְשִׁישׁ וְאִיִּים / חָרָה אַפּוֹ בָּם מִהְיוֹת חַיִּים.

טְרָחִי נָשָׂא, וְשָׁת לִי סְלִיחָה / יָצְתָה בַּת קוֹל, לֵךְ אֱכֹל בְּשִׂמְחָה
כְּאַרְבַּעַת יוֹם שַׁת גְּבוּל שִׂיחָה / לְבַל לְעָרֵב שִׂמְחָה בְּשִׂמְחָה.

מוֹעֵד רְאִיַּת חֲגִיגַת אָסֵף / נִתְמַךְ בְּחֶלְשִׁי לְחוֹגְגֵי בְּכֶסֶף
סֻכָּה וּפוּר נֶזֶל, לְהַעֲדִיף לִי בְּתֹסֶף / עֲנָנַי, קְחוּ מוּסָרִי וְאַל כָּסֶף.

פְּרָחִים כְּנָטְעָם, אֶעֱמְסָה לְאָיֹם / צַחוֹת לְצַחְצֵחַ, מְצֹא בָם פִּדְיוֹם
קִיחָתָם בְּדָמִים, יָכְשְׁרוּ לְשֵׁם אָיֹם / רְאוּיִים לְהִנָּטֵל בְּזֶה רִאשׁוֹן יוֹם.

שִׁמְךָ מְשֻׁתָּף בִּשְׁמֵנוּ / שָׁקַדְתָּ מִכִּפּוּר מְחוֹת אֲשָׁמֵנוּ
תְּסוֹכְכֵנוּ וְאַל תַּאֲשִׁימֵנוּ / תְּגוֹנְנֵנוּ וּתְרוֹמְמֵנוּ, עַד מָרוֹם שִׂימֵנוּ.

ׄבָּרוּךְ אַתָּה יהוה, מָגֵן אַבְרָהָם.

גבורות

אַתָּה גִּבּוֹר לְעוֹלָם, אֲדֹנָי
מְחַיֵּה מֵתִים אַתָּה, רַב לְהוֹשִׁיעַ

In ארץ ישראל:
מוֹרִיד הַטָּל

מְכַלְכֵּל חַיִּים בְּחֶסֶד, מְחַיֵּה מֵתִים בְּרַחֲמִים רַבִּים
סוֹמֵךְ נוֹפְלִים, וְרוֹפֵא חוֹלִים, וּמַתִּיר אֲסוּרִים
וּמְקַיֵּם אֱמוּנָתוֹ לִישֵׁנֵי עָפָר.
מִי כָמְוֹךָ, בַּעַל גְּבוּרוֹת
וּמִי דּוֹמֶה לָּךְ
מֶלֶךְ, מֵמִית וּמְחַיֶּה וּמַצְמִיחַ יְשׁוּעָה.
וְנֶאֱמָן אַתָּה לְהַחֲיוֹת מֵתִים.

מחיה

תְּשׁוּרַת שַׁי אֲלָפִים שִׁבְעִים / שִׁלַּמְתִּי בְּזֶה רֶגֶל עֲלֵי אֹם שִׁבְעִים
רָצִיתָ שַׁיִּים שְׁמוֹנָה וְתִשְׁעִים / קָלַע בָּם תּוֹכָחוֹת שְׁמוֹנֶה וְתִשְׁעִים.

צֵרַפְתִּי אֵלֶּה בְּאֵלֶּה בְּאָסִיף / פְּדוּת וְגִילָה לִי לְהוֹסִיף
עֹז וִישׁוּעָה לִי תּוֹסִיף / סִכּוּךְ נֶשֶׁק זְרוֹעַ לְהַחְשִׂיף.

נוֹצְרֵי כַּדָּת יְמֵי חֲגִיגָתוֹ / מְלוֹן סֻכַּת עוֹר תְּהֵא הַשָּׂגָתוֹ
לִקְשׁוֹר לִוְיַת צִלְצַל דָּגָתוֹ / כְּגִבּוֹרֵי כֹחַ, חֲזוֹת אֲפִיקֵי גַאֲוָתוֹ.

יוֹשֵׁב בְּסֻכָּה תְּמוּר נְוֵה אָהֳלוֹ / טִלּוּל עֲצֵי עֵדֶן יַאֲהִילוֹ
חֹם יוֹם הַבָּא, בְּבוֹא לְהַבְהִילוֹ / זְכוּתוֹ תָּלִיץ סֻכָּה לְנַהֲלוֹ.

וְשֹׂבַע שְׂמָחוֹת מְדֻשָּׁנָה / הֲלֹא בְּעֵדָה שָׂבֹעַ מִשְּׁאָנָנָה
דָּגוּל לְהַנְזִיר שִׁבְעָה שׁוֹשַׁנָּה / גָּזַר לְחוֹגְגָהּ שִׁבְעָה בַּשָּׁנָה.

הַמִּזְבֵּחַ בְּכַפּוֹת וּבַעֲרָבוֹת
בָּאתִי לְסוֹבְבֶנְהוּ בָּם הֱיוֹת עֲרֵבוֹת (נ״א: בְּשִׂיחוֹת עֲרֵבוֹת)
אֲנִי וְהוּא (נ״א: וָהוֹ) הוֹשִׁיעָה נָּא, בְּנִיב לְהַרְבּוֹת
אוֹרוֹת טַל לְהַחֲיוֹת יוֹנֵי אֲרֻבּוֹת.

בָּרוּךְ אַתָּה יהוה, מְחַיֵּה הַמֵּתִים.

משלש

אוּוֵי סֻכַּת דָּוִד הַנּוֹפֶלֶת / תָּקִים, לְבַל תְּהִי עוֹד מֻשְׁפֶּלֶת
בְּמִדּוֹתֶיהָ נוֹסֶבֶת וּמְכֻפֶּלֶת / שְׁלֹשִׁים וְשִׁשָּׁה, כְּמוֹ שֶׁהָיְתָה מִתְכַּפֶּלֶת.

גֹּרֶן שֶׁהָיְתָה בְּאֹרֶךְ חֲמֵשׁ מֵאוֹת / רְחָבָה עַל חֲמֵשׁ מֵאוֹת
דּוֹד יִנְטֶה קַו שְׁלֹשֶׁת אַלְפֵי אַמּוֹת / קְצוּבָה עַל שְׁלֹשֶׁת אַלְפֵי אַמּוֹת.

הַסְּכוּכָה בֶּעָנָן צֵל יוֹמָם / צְלָלֶיהָ מְסַכְּכִים כְּלֵיל צֵל יוֹמָם
וְעַם אֲשֶׁר עַתָּה סֻכָּה בְּקַיְּמָם / פֶּרַח יַפְרְחוּ בָּהּ בְּסִיּוּמָם.

זָרִים יֶאֱתָיוּ לִשְׁמָהּ בְּחֹסֶף / עֲשׂוֹת חֲגִיגָה, לְהִשְׁתַּחֲווֹת בְּכֹסֶף
חַרְבוֹנֵי קַיִץ יְלַהֲטוּם לְשַׁסֵּף / סְגוּרִים בְּמַסְגֵּר עַל חֲמִשִּׁים כֶּסֶף.

טָסִים וְעָפִים בִּקְצוֹת יְקָרֶיהָ / נִסְכָּכִים בְּשֶׁבַע, קְרֹא מִקְרָאֶיהָ
יֵאָגְדוּ מִמֶּרְחָק כָּל קְרוּאֶיהָ
כְּתוֹרִים (נ״א: כְּתוּרִים) לִמְכוֹן הַר צִיּוֹן וּמִקְרָאֶיהָ (נ״א: וְעַל מִקְרָאֶיהָ).

The שליח ציבור *aloud, followed by the* קהל:

יִמְלֹךְ יהוה לְעוֹלָם, אֱלֹהַיִךְ צִיּוֹן לְדֹר וָדֹר, הַלְלוּיָהּ: תהלים קמו

וְאַתָּה קָדוֹשׁ, יוֹשֵׁב תְּהִלּוֹת יִשְׂרָאֵל: תהלים כב

אֵל נָא.

בַּל תְּהִי מִצְוַת סֻכָּה בְּעֵינֶיךָ קַלָּה
כִּי כָל מִצְוַת דָּת כְּחֻקּוֹתֶיהָ שְׁקוּלָה
הַמְעֻזָּקָה וְהַמְסֻקָּלָה
סֹלּוּ מְסִלָּה בְּסִלְסוּלֶיהָ מְסֻקָּלָה
כִּי לְכָל שׁוֹמְרֶיהָ לֹא יֶאֱרַע תְּקָלָה
וְכָל בּוֹגְדֶיהָ, לֶעָתִיד לָבֹא לְקַח מֵהֶם קְלָלָה
בְּלַהַט הַיּוֹם הַבָּא, קְלוֹנָם מַקְלָה
וְחוֹסֶיהָ מְרוּעָה (נ"א: לְצֶדֶק מַכְרִיעָה) / וּבָם מִתְרוֹעֲעָה
לְסוֹכְכָם מֵרָעָה / אוֹתָם לְהָרִעָה
בְּסֻכַּת יְרִיעָה / לִהְיוֹת רוֹעָה
שְׁאֵתָהּ בְּטוּב מִרְעָה / אֶתְנַנֶּה לִפְרָעָה
בְּסֻכַּת חַי וְקַיָּם, נוֹרָא וּמָרוֹם וְקָדוֹשׁ.

לְסוֹכְכֵי לְמָסְכֵי / לְנָסְכֵי בְּנִסְכֵּי
בִּנְסִיכַת קָדוֹשׁ.

לְחַדְּשֵׁי רִאשׁוֹן כְּמֵרִאשׁוֹן / לִנְצוּרֵי כְּאִישׁוֹן
אֲהַלֵּל בְּלָשׁוֹן / לְמָרוֹם וְקָדוֹשׁ.

אָמְנָם מִצְוָה גּוֹרֶרֶת מִצְוֹת
בְּזֹאת אֲשֶׁר בְּאִבֶּיהָ תּוֹרוֹת קְצוּבוֹת
גְּזֵרוֹת חֻבְּרוּ לָהּ לְצַוּוֹת.
לְסוֹכְכֵי לְמָסְכֵי / לְנָסְכֵי בְּנִסְכֵּי
בִּנְסִיכַת קָדוֹשׁ.

דֹּרַשׁ יוֹם זֶה לְיַחֲסוֹ רִאשׁוֹן
הוּא חֲמִשָּׁה עָשָׂר וְהֻנְקַב רִאשׁוֹן
וּכְדֵי לְבַשְּׂרֵנוּ כִּי מָחַל רִאשׁוֹן.

לְחַדְּשִׁי רִאשׁוֹן כְּמֵרִאשׁוֹן / לִנְצוּרֵי כְּאִישׁוֹן
אֲהַלֵּל בְּלָשׁוֹן / לְמָרוֹם וְקָדוֹשׁ.

זִכְרוּ סוֹף שָׁנָה וְהוּא תְּחִלַּת שָׁנָה
חַג הָאָסִיף תְּקוּפַת הַשָּׁנָה
טוֹב יָדִין בּוֹ נִזְלֵי שָׁנָה.

לְסוֹכְכֵי לְמָסְכִּי / לְנָסְכֵי בְּנִסְכִּי
בִּנְסִיכַת קָדוֹשׁ.

יִקְחוּ לִשְׁמוֹ אַרְבַּעַת מִינִים
כְּלוּלִים, בְּחוּרִים וּמְזֻמָּנִים
לְהַלֵּל בָּם כִּבְעֻגָב וּבְמִנִּים.

לְחַדְּשִׁי רִאשׁוֹן כְּמֵרִאשׁוֹן / לִנְצוּרֵי כְּאִישׁוֹן
אֲהַלֵּל בְּלָשׁוֹן / לְמָרוֹם וְקָדוֹשׁ.

מֵהוֹד הָדָר הַמְּהֻדָּר
נֶאְדָּר וְנֶהְדָּר בַּהֲדָרוֹ לְהַדֵּר
סוֹד אֶדֶר יְקָר, בְּכֶתֶם פָּז לְאַדֵּר.

לְסוֹכְכֵי לְמָסְכִּי / לְנָסְכֵי בְּנִסְכִּי
בִּנְסִיכַת קָדוֹשׁ.

עֲנַף עֵץ עָבֹת חֲפוּת מִבַּחוּץ
פּוֹנוֹת לְכַוֵּן לֵב מִבַּיִת וּמִחוּץ
צָפוּי לְכַפֵּר בְּעַד לֵב שָׁחוּץ.

לְחַדְּשִׁי רִאשׁוֹן כְּמֵרִאשׁוֹן / לִנְצוּרֵי כְּאִישׁוֹן
אֲהַלֵּל בְּלָשׁוֹן / לְמָרוֹם וְקָדוֹשׁ.

קִיחַת לוּלָב וְעַרְבֵי נְחָלִים
רְגִילִים עֲנוֹת בָּם שִׁיר הִלּוּלִים
שְׁקוּלִים הֵם כְּבִמְחוֹל חֲלִילִים.

לְסוֹכְכֵי לְמָסְכֵי / לְנָסְכֵי בְּנִסְכֵּי
בִּנְסִיכַת קָדוֹשׁ.

תְּפִיסַת שְׁלֹשָׁה הֲדַסִּים וּשְׁתֵּי עֲרָבוֹת
שִׁיר לְהַסְלִיל לְרוֹכֵב בָּעֲרָבוֹת
אֶתְרוֹג וְכַף תָּמָר יְחִידִים מִלְּמַעֵט וּמִלְּהַרְבּוֹת.

לְחַדְּשֵׁי רִאשׁוֹן כְּמֵרִאשׁוֹן / לִנְצוּרֵי כְּאִישׁוֹן
אֲהַלֵּל בְּלָשׁוֹן / לְמָרוֹם וְקָדוֹשׁ.

All:

וּבְכֵן, וּלְךָ תַעֲלֶה קְדֻשָּׁה, כִּי אַתָּה קְדוֹשׁ יִשְׂרָאֵל וּמוֹשִׁיעַ.

Some congregations say the piyut כִּי אֶקַּח *before* קדושה.
Many congregation omit it, and continue with "נְקַדֵּשׁ אֶת שִׁמְךָ" *on page 391.*

סילוק

כִּי אֶקַּח מוֹעֵד / לָבֹא לְקֵץ וּלְמוֹעֵד
כְּמֵאָז לְדַבֵּר מֵאֹהֶל מוֹעֵד / לֵישֵׁב בְּהַר הַמּוֹעֵד
בְּיַרְכְּתֵי צָפוֹן, בְּקִרְיַת מוֹעֵד / קְדוֹשִׁים בְּתוֹכָהּ לְוַעֵד
לְמוֹעֵד מוֹעֲדִים וַחֲצִי מוֹעֵד / לְהִתְהַלֵּךְ בְּתוֹכָם וּלְהִוָּעֵד
לְהוֹשִׁיבָם בָּאֳהָלִים כִּימֵי מוֹעֵד / וְעָנְתָה הַשִּׁירָה הַזֹּאת לְפָנָיו לְעֵד
וְסֻכָּה תִּהְיֶה לְצֵל יוֹמָם, לָעַד / כְּמֵלִיץ מַגִּיד יֹשֶׁר, טוֹב תָּעַד
עַל כָּל שֶׁקִּיֵּם מִצְוַת סֻכָּה לְהָעֵד / וְכָל שֶׁשְּׁמָרָהּ, יָבֹא וְיָעֵד
וְאָנֹכִי הַיּוֹדֵעַ וָעֵד.

כִּי עַמִּי קִיְּמוּ מִצְוֹתֶיהָ / בְּמִדּוֹתֶיהָ וּבְקִצְבוֹתֶיהָ
בְּאַמּוֹתֶיהָ וּבִמְחִצּוֹתֶיהָ / בְּדָפְנוֹתֶיהָ וּבְמַצְּבוֹתֶיהָ
בִּסְכוּכֶיהָ וּבְצִלְלוֹתֶיהָ / בְּבִיאוֹתֶיהָ וּבִיצִיאוֹתֶיהָ

בִּגְדְרוֹתֶיהָ וּבִפְרְצוֹתֶיהָ / בַּחֲגִיגוֹתֶיהָ וּבַעֲלִיצוֹתֶיהָ
וְזָר לֹא יִהְיֶה בְּמוֹצָאוֹתֶיהָ / וְנֵכָר לֹא יַעֲבֹר בְּתוֹצְאוֹתֶיהָ
וְעָרֵל לֹא יְשַׁתֵּף בִּמְחִצּוֹתֶיהָ / וְגוֹי לֹא יִרְמֹס חֲצֵרוֹתֶיהָ
וּלְאֹם לֹא יֶעֱרַב בְּחוּצוֹתֶיהָ / כִּי אִם עֲמוּסַי, נוֹצְרֵי מִצְוֹתֶיהָ (נ״א: עֵדוֹתֶיהָ)
וְגַם לֹא יָפֵרוּ מוֹעֲצוֹתֶיהָ / בְּלֵב שָׁלֵם יָשׁוּבוּ בִּקְצוֹתֶיהָ
[וּבְנֶפֶשׁ טוֹבָה יָבוֹאוּ חֲצֵרוֹתֶיהָ]
עַתָּה יָבוֹאוּ עַמִּי לִקְצוֹתֶיהָ
כְּמוֹ הֵם לְבָדָם דִּגְלוּ מִשְׁבְּצוֹתֶיהָ / כֵּן בָּדָד יִשְׁכְּנוּ בְּרְבִיצוֹתֶיהָ
לָתֵת לָמוֹ שְׂכַר מְרוּצוֹתֶיהָ / לְקֵץ סֻכַּת אֵל לְרַצּוֹתֶיהָ
לְעֵת חִלּוּק אַרְצוֹתֶיהָ / בְּאֹרֶךְ מִפְּאַת קָדִים לִקְצוֹתֶיהָ
וְעַד יָם אוֹקְיָנוֹס לְמִצְוֹתֶיהָ / בְּרֹחַב שִׁבְעִים וַחֲמִשָּׁה מִיל חֲרִיצוֹתֶיהָ
כְּשׁוּרוֹת הַכֶּרֶם, לְחַבְּרָם לְתוֹצְאוֹתֶיהָ
גְּבוּל כָּל שֵׁבֶט וָשֵׁבֶט כָּךְ יַעֲלוּ בִּנְפִיצוֹתֶיהָ.

וְאָז בַּת קוֹל תֵּצֵא בָּאָרֶץ הַזֹּאת / עַל הַר גָּבֹהַּ לְבַשֵּׂר בְּשׂוֹרָה זֹאת
כָּל שֶׁקִּיֵּם מִצְוָה זֹאת / יָבוֹא בְּנֹעַם צוּרוֹ חֲזוֹת
לִשְׁקֹד דְּלָתוֹת וְלִשְׁמֹר מְזוּזוֹת / לְהַבִּיט וְלָשׁוּר נֵס עַל זֹאת
יְשׁוּעוֹת עַלִּיזוֹת / עַל כָּל כָּבוֹד חֻפּוֹת מְזוּזוֹת
חֻפּוֹת בְּחֻפּוֹת בְּחֻלְיוֹת אֲחוּזוֹת / עַד כִּסֵּא כָבוֹד מְאֻחָזוֹת
לְיוֹשֵׁב עַל כִּסֵּא, בְּיָפְיוֹ חֲזוֹת / בְּמַחֲזוֹת הַמְצֻחְצָחוֹת בְּתֵשַׁע מַחֲזוֹת
וְכָל אֲשֶׁר תָּדִיר לַעֲשׂוֹת זֹאת / יִזְכֶּה לְהֵאָמֵר לוֹ כָּזֹאת
אַשְׁרֵי אֱנוֹשׁ יַעֲשֶׂה זֹּאת / יֵחָשֵׁב לוֹ כְּשָׁמַר כָּל הַתּוֹרָה הַזֹּאת
וּמִי שָׁמַע כָּזֹאת / וּמִיהוּ הָיְתָה זֹאת
וַאֲחַשְּׁבָה לָדַעַת זֹאת / וְהִיא נִפְלָאת בְּעֵינַי, זֹאת
עַד אָבוֹא לְיוֹשְׁבֵי פְּרָזוֹת / וְאֶשְׁאֲלָה לְזִקְנֵי מִי זֹאת
מָה אֶתְנַן עִם שׁוֹמְרֵי מִצְוַת סֻכָּה זֹאת
וְהֵם יְשִׁיבוּנִי תְּשׁוּבוֹת עַזּוֹת / וְיַרְאוּנִי צְפוּנוֹת גְּנוּזוֹת
רַב טוּב הַצָּפוּן בְּבֵית גְּנָזוֹת / לְבַעֲלֵי סֻכָּה, יָהוּ נִבְזָזוֹת.

וּמֵחַיִל אֶל חַיִל יִצְעָדוּ / וּמִסֻּכָּה לְסֻכָּה יִוָּעֵדוּ
וּמֵאֹהֶל אֶל אֹהֶל יוּעָדוּ / בְּסֻכָּה אֲשֶׁר יִצָּמֵדוּ
בְּסֻכַּת שָׁלֵם יִצְמָדוּ / בְּסֻכַּת עֲמָקִים יְמַדֵּדוּ
בְּסֻכַּת צִלְצַל יְעַדְּדוּ / בְּסֻכַּת סְבִיבָיו יְחַדֵּדוּ
בְּסֻכַּת מַלְכָּם יִתְוַעֲדוּ / בְּסֻכַּת צְפוּנוֹ יְאַחֲדוּ
בְּסֻכַּת נְאוֹת דֶּשֶׁא יְבַדֵּדוּ / בְּסֻכַּת מֵי מְנוּחוֹת יְכַבֵּדוּ
בְּסֻכַּת עֵץ חַיִּים יִתְיַסֵּדוּ / בְּסֻכַּת שֶׁתַּחְתָּיו יְסַעֲדוּ
בְּסֻכַּת צְלָלוֹתָיו, בְּחִיל יְסַלֵּדוּ
בְּמַעֲלוֹתָיו, אֵל יְיַחֲדוּ / בַּעֲרָבוֹתָיו זַר יְאַפֵּדוּ
בִּרְחוֹבוֹתָיו יִתְרַפֵּדוּ / וְשִׁעוּר תְּפִיסוֹתָיו יְמַדֵּדוּ.

חֲמֵשׁ מֵאוֹת שָׁנָה, הֲלִיכוֹתָיו עֲלוֹת / עֳבִי כָּרְתוֹ [עִקָּרוֹ] בְּזֶה קַו לְהַעֲלוֹת
אֲבָל מִנְיַן עֲנָפָיו אֵין בְּמִדָּה לְהַעֲלוֹת / וְעַל יוּבַל שָׁרָשָׁיו פְּעוּלוֹת
וְכָל מֵי בְרֵאשִׁית מִמֶּנּוּ נִפְעָלוֹת / וּפְלָגִים נִפְלָגִים לְכָל תְּעָלוֹת
וְשֶׁבַע כִּתֵּי קֹדֶשׁ הַמְּעֻלּוֹת / תַּחַת סֻכַּת נוֹפוֹ מִתְעַלּוֹת
וּמִתַּחְתֵּיהֶם שְׁלֹשִׁים מַעֲלוֹת / מִסְתּוֹפְפִים בְּצִלָּם בְּשִׁיר הַמַּעֲלוֹת
וְעַל גַּבָּם שִׁשִּׁים מַעֲלוֹת / זוֹ לְמַעְלָה מִזּוֹ עוֹלוֹת
וְעַד כִּסֵּא הַכָּבוֹד טָסוֹת וְעוֹלוֹת / בְּשִׂיחַ נְעִימוֹת שִׁיר לַמַּעֲלוֹת.

וְכָל אֶחָד וְאֶחָד לְפִי כְבוֹדוֹ / בְּכָבוֹד וְהָדָר יִתֵּן הוֹדוֹ
בְּזִיו שְׁכִינָה יְיַחֲדוֹ / בְּמַרְאֵה פָנִים יְכַבְּדוֹ
בַּעֲשָׂרָה לְבוּשִׁים לְאַפְּדוֹ / בְּרִקְמָה וְעָתִיק לְרַפְּדוֹ
כְּמַרְאֵה הַקֶּשֶׁת לְחַסְּדוֹ / כְּמַרְאֵה הַנֹּגַהּ לְנָגְדוֹ
כְּצֵאת הַשֶּׁמֶשׁ בְּעוֹדוֹ / אֲשֶׁר בּוֹ צִדְקוֹ יְעִידוֹ
וּלְפִי הָרָשׁוּם בִּכְתַב יָדוֹ / וּלְפִי מַעֲשָׂיו וּמַעְבָּדוֹ
יְשַׁלְּמוֹ פְּעֻלָּה כְּמַעְבָּדוֹ.

יֵשׁ מִמֵּאָה אַמָּה קוֹמָתָם / כְּתַבְנִית הֵיכָל וְקָמָתָם
יֵשׁ מִמָּאתַיִם וּשְׁלֹשׁ מֵאוֹת תְּקוּמָתָם / [כֵּן] וְעַד תְּשַׁע מֵאוֹת הֲקָמָתָם

וּלְפִי שִׁעוּר תְּקוּמָתָם / כֵּן תְּהֵא בָּאָרֶץ מַמְלַכְתָּם
יֵשׁ מֵהֶם, מְלֹא הָעוֹלָם מַהֲלָכְתָּם / וּמִסּוֹף הָעוֹלָם וְעַד סוֹפוֹ הֲלִיכָתָם
יֵשׁ מִשִּׁשָּׁה עָשָׂר עוֹלָמוֹת מַלְכוּתָם
וְיֵשׁ מִשְּׁלֹשׁ מֵאוֹת וַעֲשָׂרָה מֶמְשַׁלְתָּם
וְיֵשׁ מִשְּׁלֹשׁ מֵאוֹת וּשְׁלֹשִׁים וּשְׁלֹשָׁה שְׁלִיחוּתָם
וְשָׁלוֹם גָּדוֹל יֵשׁ בֵּינוֹתָם / וְשִׂנְאָה אֵין בְּמַחֲנוֹתָם
וְתַחֲרוּת אֵין בְּמַחְצָתָם / וְאֵיבָה אֵין בַּהֲלִיכָתָם
וּפַלְגּוּת אֵין בְּחֻפָּתָם / וְקִנְאָה אֵין בְּמִשְׁכְּנוֹתָם
וְשֵׁנָה אֵין בִּרְפִידָתָם / וּתְנוּמָה אֵין בִּרְבִיצָתָם
וְאָסוֹן אֵין בִּמְגוּרָתָם / וְדִמְעָה אֵין בְּעַפְעַפּוֹתָם
וְצָרָה אֵין בְּמַחְשְׁבוֹתָם / וְצוּקָה אֵין בְּטוּחוֹתָם
וְיֵצֶר רַע אֵין בְּלִבּוֹתָם / וְרַע עַיִן אֵין בְּדִירָתָם
וּמִיתָה אֵין בִּמְדוּרָתָם / וּמַחֲלָה אֵין בִּגְוִיָּתָם
שָׂשִׂים כָּל אֶחָד וְאֶחָד בְּנַחֲלָתָם / שְׂמֵחִים בְּמִפְעֲלוֹתָם
גָּלִים בִּירֻשָּׁתָם / רוֹנְנִים בְּפוּר חֶלְקָם
עוֹלְצִים בְּאָרְחוֹתָם / חָדִים אֶת אֵל בְּחֶדְוָתָם.

וְהוּא יִתְהַלֵּךְ בְּתוֹכָם / עִמּוֹ לְסַכּוֹ לְמָשְׁכָם
בַּעֲבוֹתוֹת אַהֲבָה לְהַמְשִׁיכָם / בְּאֶבְרָתוֹ לְסוֹכְכָם
תַּחַת כְּנָפָיו לְסַכְּכָם / בְּסֵתֶר אָהֳלוֹ לְמָסְכָם
בֵּינוֹ לְבֵין מְשָׁרְתָיו לְתַוְּכָם.

וְיָנִיחַ רוֹכֵב עֲרָבוֹת / וְיִחַן בְּתוֹךְ מַעֲלוֹת עֲרָבוֹת
בְּצֶדֶק קִיחַת שְׁתֵּי עֲרָבוֹת / וְאָתָה מֵרִבְבוֹת אַלְפֵי רְבָבוֹת
לַעֲמֹד בֵּין הֲדַסֵּי עָבוֹת / בְּצֶדֶק שְׁלֹשֶׁת אָבוֹת.

וְיָרוּם כִּסֵּא מְיֻחָד / וְיֵשֵׁב עִם זִקְנֵי גּוֹי אֶחָד
אוֹגְדֵי לוּלָב אֶחָד / וּמַעֲמִיתִים בָּם אֶתְרוֹג אֶחָד.

יָחִיד כְּשֶׁבָּרָא עוֹלָמוֹ / וְכִלְּלוֹ בְּמִינִים בְּעִצּוּמוֹ
שְׁנַיִם שְׁנַיִם כְּנְאֻמוֹ.
כְּשֶׁיָּצַר לִוְיָתָן וְזוּגָתוֹ / כֵּן עָשׁ זִיז שָׂדַי וְהוֹרָתוֹ
וּמִרְעֵהוּ אֶלֶף הָרִים וְאִשְׁתּוֹ.
לְשַׂחֵק בָּם צִנֵּן הַזְּכָרִים בְּלֹהוּקִים / וְהַנְּקֵבוֹת הָרַג בְּבִתּוּקִים
וּמְלָחָם לֶעָתִיד לָבֹא לַצַּדִּיקִים.
מוֹעֲדִים בְּגַן עֵדֶן בִּמְסִבָּה / וַיהוה עַל רֹאשָׁם לְטוֹבָה
וְהַמֶּלֶךְ הַמָּשִׁיחַ וְשַׂר הַצָּבָא.
נִכְנָסִין כָּל הָאֻמּוֹת לָדִין / פְּנֵי יוֹשֵׁב עַל כִּסֵּא דִין
בְּצֶדֶק אוֹתָם יָדִין.
סֵדֶר מִצְוֹתֶיךָ תֵּן לָנוּ וּנְקַיְּמָה / וְנִזְכֶּה עִם אֵלּוּ בְּנֶחָמָה
שַׂגִּיא כֹּחַ שׁוֹכֵן רוּמָה.
עֶלְיוֹן הַשּׁוֹפֵט כֹּל בֶּאֱמוּנָה / יַשְׁמִיעַ לָהֶם בִּתְבוּנָה
יֵשׁ לִי מִצְוָה קְטַנָּה.
פֵּרוּשׁ סֻכָּה וּשְׁאֵלֶיהָ / אַרְבַּע דְּפָנוֹת וְצֵל עָלֶיהָ
לֹא תִרְחֲקוּ מֵאֵלֶיהָ.
צְלָלִים לַעֲשׂוֹת יַעֲטוּ / וְחַמָּה קָדְחָה עֲלֵיהֶם וְלִהֲטוּ
וּבְאָהֳלֵיהֶם יְבַעֲטוּ.
קָדוֹשׁ יִשְׁפֹּךְ עֲלֵיהֶם חֵמָה / וְיַפִּילֵם בְּגֵיהִנֹּם בְּלִי רְחִימָה
בְּמַדְרֵגָה הַתַּחְתּוֹנָה בִּמְהוּמָה.
רָם רוֹכֵב עֲרָבוֹת / הִזְהִירָנוּ מִצְוֹת עֲרָבוֹת
וְתַחַן לְפָנָיו לְהַרְבּוֹת.
שָׁם יֶחֱזוּ וְיֵבוֹשׁוּ קִנְאַת עָם / אַף אֵשׁ צָרֶיךָ תֹאכְלֵם בְּמַסָּעָם
בְּאַבְנֵי אֶלְגָּבִישׁ אֵשׁ וְגָפְרִית וָזַעַם.
תַּקִּיף יְחַיֵּינוּ מִיּוֹמַיִם / הוֹד וְהָדָר תּוֹדִיעַ בְּכִפְלַיִם
כְּהַיּוֹם הַזֶּה בִּירוּשָׁלַיִם / קָדוֹשׁ.

Continue with "מְלֹא כָל־הָאָרֶץ כְּבוֹדוֹ" *on page 367 to* "הַכֹּל יוֹדוּךָ" *on page 373.*

אופן

יְרוּצְצוּ כִּבְרָקִים / יִשְׁתַּפְּכוּ כִּמְזָרְקִים / יְסַפְּרוּ לִפְרָקִים
יָעוּשׁוּ אִישׁ בְּאָחִיו, וְלֹא נֵזֶק. וְהַחַיּוֹת רָצוֹא וָשׁוֹב, כְּמַרְאֵה הַבָּזָק: יחזקאל א

צָגִים בְּמִשְׁמָרוֹת / צֹהַר וְאַשְׁמוּרוֹת / צִלְצוּלָם זְמִירוֹת
צָהַל קוֹל יָרִיעוּ, הוֹלֵךְ וְחָזָק. וְהַחַיּוֹת רָצוֹא וָשׁוֹב, כְּמַרְאֵה הַבָּזָק:

חַשְׁמַלֵּי מֶרְכָּבָה / חֲשָׁשָׁם לֹא כָבָה / חָשִׁים בְּלִי עַכָּבָה
חֲרֵדִים וּמְזִיעִים, בְּצוּק מַיִם יָזֵק. וְהַחַיּוֹת רָצוֹא וָשׁוֹב, כְּמַרְאֵה הַבָּזָק:

קַפְצִיאֵל הַשָּׂר / קוֹלוֹת יְבַשֵּׂר / קֶשֶׁת לֹא יֶחְסַר
קָרֵב לְהִסְתַּכֵּל, יָרֵא פֶּן יִתְנַזֵּק. וְהַחַיּוֹת רָצוֹא וָשׁוֹב, כְּמַרְאֵה הַבָּזָק:

הֲמוֹנֵי לְגְיוֹן / קוֹבְעִים הִגָּיוֹן / טוֹבְלִים בְּרִגְיוֹן
נוֹגְנִים בְּהֶקְדֵּשׁ גַּן נָעוּל וּמְעֻזָּק. וְהַחַיּוֹת רָצוֹא וָשׁוֹב, כְּמַרְאֵה הַבָּזָק:

וְהַחַיּוֹת יְשׁוֹרֵרוּ / וּכְרוּבִים יְפָאֵרוּ
וּשְׂרָפִים יָרֹנּוּ / וְאֶרְאֶלִּים יְבָרֵכוּ
פְּנֵי כָל חַיָּה וְאוֹפָן וּכְרוּב לְעֻמַּת שְׂרָפִים
לְעֻמָּתָם מְשַׁבְּחִים וְאוֹמְרִים

All say aloud:

יחזקאל ג בָּרוּךְ כְּבוֹד־יהוה מִמְּקוֹמוֹ:

Continue with "לָאֵל בָּרוּךְ" on page 375 to "אֵין אֱלֹהִים זוּלָתֶךָ" on page 385.

זולת

יָפָה וּבָרָה, כְּרוּדָה לְגֵיא פַּתְרוּסִים
יָהִיר חֲסַר לֵב הִכְבִּיד עֹל בְּשִׁנּוּסִים
צָרְחָה וְקָבְלָה לְמַעְתִּיק פְּלוּסִים
פָּקַד לָהּ סַרְסוּר לְהוֹצִיאָהּ בְּנִסִּים.

הִקְשָׁה עֲקַלָּתוֹן לְשַׁלֵּחַ [אִם־] עֲמוּסָה
הֵטִיחַ דְּבָרִים כְּמֻטָּל בַּעֲרִיסָה
וּפָץ מִי יהוה לְהַצִּיל אֲרוּסָה
וּבְסֵפֶר דָּתוֹתַי אֵין שְׁמוֹ בְּטַכְסִיסָה.

וֶהֱשִׁיבוֹ שָׁלִישׁ בְּשֵׁם דָּר מְעוֹנִים
הִתְיַצֵּב וְהָכֵן לָךְ מוּל נֶגֶף אֲבָנִים
דָּם וּצְפַרְדְּעִים, עֵדִים נְכוֹנִים
וַחֲיָלִים קְטַנִּים הַמְכֻנִּים כִּנִּים.

דִּבֵּר וְהִשְׁלִים מַכּוֹת עֲשָׂרָה
וְהוֹצִיאָהּ בְּתֻפִּים מֵאֲפֵלָה לְאוֹרָה
וְהִכָּה עוֹיְנֶיהָ מַכָּה כְּעוּרָה
וְהִנְחִילָהּ קְדוּמָה אַלְפַּיִם כְּתוּרָה.

הוֹשִׁיבָהּ בַּסֻּכָּה בְּאֶרֶץ מִדְבָּרִים
וְהִכְנִיסָהּ לְחֻפָּה בְּחַדְרֵי חֲדָרִים
וַעֲנַף עֵץ עָבוֹת וּפְרִי עֵץ הֲדָרִים
וְעַרְבֵי נְחָלִים וְכַפּוֹת תְּמָרִים.

חִדְּשָׁה שִׁיר וָזֶמֶר, רְנָנוֹת וּרְנָנִים
זְכוּת אָבוֹת וּבָנִים יְמַלְּטֵם מֵאֲנוּנִים
כְּנִרְאָה בַּיָּם וּטְבִיעַת גְּאוֹנִים
חֲנֻנָּה מִמָּרוֹם, עוֹזֵר אָבוֹת וּבָנִים.

Continue with "עֶזְרַת אֲבוֹתֵינוּ" on page 385.

יוצר לשמיני עצרת

שחרית is said up to and including בָּרְכוּ *(page 363).*

בָּרוּךְ אַתָּה יהוה אֱלֹהֵינוּ מֶלֶךְ הָעוֹלָם
יוֹצֵר אוֹר וּבוֹרֵא חֹשֶׁךְ
עֹשֶׂה שָׁלוֹם וּבוֹרֵא אֶת הַכֹּל.

אוֹר עוֹלָם בְּאוֹצַר חַיִּים, אוֹרוֹת מֵאֹפֶל אָמַר וַיֶּהִי.

יוצר

אֹם כְּאִישׁוֹן נִנְצֶרֶת / חֲשֹׂךְ אוֹתָהּ מִבַּצֹּרֶת / בַּיּוֹם הַשְּׁמִינִי עֲצֶרֶת.
בָּאָה בְּתַחֲנוּן לְפָנֶיךָ / לְחַלּוֹת אֶת פָּנֶיךָ / בִּיטָה וּפְקַח עֵינֶיךָ.
גַּלֵּה לָהּ יוֹמָךְ / וַחֲמֹל עַל עַמָּךְ / וְשִׂמְחָה יַשִּׂיגוּ מֵעִמָּךְ.

בַּיּוֹם הַשְּׁמִינִי / שְׂמָחוֹת הַזְמִינִי / וּסְכוֹת נָא מַעֲנִי / קָדוֹשׁ.

דּוֹרְשִׁים בְּתַכְלִית מוֹעֲדָם / גִּשְׁמֵי נְדָבוֹת בְּמַעֲמָדָם / צְפֵה נָא לְעוֹדְדָם.
הַשְׁקִיפָה עֲלֵיהֶם מִמְּרוֹמִים / וּזְכֹר שְׁלֹשֶׁת קְדוּמִים
וְהִמָּלֵא עַל צֶאֱצָאֵימוֹ רַחֲמִים.
וְאִם עִקְּלוּ בְּרֶשַׁע / חוּסָה וַעֲבֹר עַל פֶּשַׁע / וְהַצְמַח לָמוֹ יֶשַׁע.
זוֹעֲקִים אֵלֶיךָ בְּכָל לֵב / הָרוֹפֵא לִשְׁבוּרֵי לֵב / כּוֹנֵן מְקוֹם עַיִן וָלֵב.
חֶטְאָם תְּנָאֹם לְכַפֵּר / וּבְרִית אַל תָּפֵר / בִּזְכוּת אִמְרֵי שָׁפֶר.
טוֹב הַשּׁוֹכֵן רוּמָה / חִישׁ קֵץ נֶחָמָה / וְעוֹרֵר יְשֵׁנֵי אֲדָמָה.
יָהּ שׁוֹכֵן עֲלִיּוֹת / וְרַב הָעֲלִילִיּוֹת / עַתָּה כַּנֵּס גָּלִיּוֹת.
כָּל שׂוֹטְנִים לְהַאֲבִיד / וְאוֹהֲבֶיךָ שְׂמָחוֹת לְהַרְבִּיד
בְּמַלְכוּת מָשִׁיחַ בֶּן דָּוִד.
לְמַעְלָה לְמַעְלָה לְרוֹמֵם / בֵּית מִקְדָּשְׁךָ הַשָּׁמֵם / צָרִים מְנוֹ לְהַדְמֵם.
מְהַלְלִים לְךָ בַּחֲגִיגָתָם / שׁוּר קְהַל עֲדָתָם / וּשְׁמַע קוֹל זַעֲקָתָם.
נֶגְדְּךָ בְּתַחַן עוֹמְדִים / וְעַל דַּלְתוֹתֶיךָ שׁוֹקְדִים / וְאוֹתְךָ בְּהַתְמֵד מְיַחֲדִים.
שִׂיחָם לְפָנֶיךָ יֶעֱרַב / וְחָשְׁבֵם מִיּוֹם קְרָב / וּמִמְּחִתָּה כִּי לֹא תִקְרָב.

עַטְּרֵם רֹב בְּרָכוֹת / וְחַיִּים אֲרֻכּוֹת / עֲדֵי עַד מַאֲרִיכוֹת.
פְּתַח לָמוֹ אוֹצָרֶיךָ / וְקַיֵּם עָלֵימוֹ אֲמָרֶךָ / וְאַל יֵבֹשׁוּ מִשִּׂבְרֶךָ.
צִקּוּן לַחֲשָׁם תִּשְׁמַע / וְקוֹל מְבַשֵּׂר לְהַשְׁמַע / טוֹבוֹת וְנֶחָמוֹת בְּמַשְׁמָע.
קוֹלוֹת אַרְבָּעָה לְהַחִישָׁה / וּלְעֶזְרָתֵנוּ חוּשָׁה / וְצוֹרְרֵינוּ תַּכְחִישָׁה.
רָם עַל רָמִים / שַׂמַּח נֶפֶשׁ עֲגוּמִים / בְּבָנוּי כְּמוֹ רָמִים.
שִׁבְחֲךָ בְּפִימוֹ מְתַנִּים / וְגָדְלְךָ בְּלִבָּם מְשַׁנְּנִים / וְיִחוּדְךָ בְּכָל יוֹם עוֹנִים.
תּוֹקְפִים וְהוֹדָיָה רוֹחֲשִׁים / רוֹעֲשִׁים וְלוֹחֲשִׁים
וְאוֹתְךָ מַעֲרִיצִים וּמַקְדִּישִׁים / קָדוֹשׁ

Continue with "הַמֵּאִיר לָאָרֶץ" on page 365 (on שבת, with "הַכֹּל יוֹדוּךָ" on page 367) to "מְלֹא כָל־הָאָרֶץ כְּבוֹדוֹ" on page 373.

אופן

אֶרְאֶלִּים וּמַלְאָכִים / מַקְדִּישִׁים וּמְבָרְכִים — לְמֶלֶךְ מַלְכֵי הַמְּלָכִים
מוּכָנִים וַעֲרוּכִים / בְּכַנְפֵיהֶם סוֹכְכִים
יוֹם יוֹם מַמְלִיכִים — לְמֶלֶךְ מַלְכֵי הַמְּלָכִים
תַּקִּיפֵי שְׂרָפִים / תִּשְׁבָּחוֹת מְיַפִּים — לְמֶלֶךְ מַלְכֵי הַמְּלָכִים
יְקָר אַלְפֵי אֲלָפִים / וְרִבֵּי רִבְבָן צְפוּפִים
רָאשֵׁיהֶם כּוֹפְפִים — לְמֶלֶךְ מַלְכֵי הַמְּלָכִים
בְּחוּרֵי מֶרְכָּבָה / מְרַנְּנִים בְּאַהֲבָה — לְמֶלֶךְ מַלְכֵי הַמְּלָכִים
יִדּוֹן יְצָבָא / בְּהוֹד שִׁירָה עֲרֵבָה
לְשׁוֹרֵר בְּחִבָּה — לְמֶלֶךְ מַלְכֵי הַמְּלָכִים
רִגְיוֹן הַנָּהָר / מְאֹד חָשׁ וְיִמַהֵר — לְמֶלֶךְ מַלְכֵי הַמְּלָכִים
בּוֹ לְהַטְהֵר / חַשְׁמַלֵּי זֹהַר
בְּחִדּוּשׁ שִׁיר לְהַגְהֵר — לְמֶלֶךְ מַלְכֵי הַמְּלָכִים
יְשׁוֹרֵר מִיכָאֵל / וִיזַמֵּר גַּבְרִיאֵל — לְמֶלֶךְ מַלְכֵי הַמְּלָכִים
שׁוֹאֵג קְמוּאֵל / וְגוֹעֶה רְפָאֵל
וּמְהַדֵּר הֲדַרְנִיאֵל — לְמֶלֶךְ מַלְכֵי הַמְּלָכִים
פּוֹחֵד סַנְדַּלְפוֹן / לְצַד דִּפָּן יִדְפֹּן — לְמֶלֶךְ מַלְכֵי הַמְּלָכִים

טַעֲמֵי חִין יְחַפֵּן / וְכֶתֶר מֵהֶם לִסְפֹּן
וּמַשְׁבִּיעַ לְאוֹפָן   עַל רֹאשׁ מֶלֶךְ מַלְכֵי הַמְּלָכִים
יְקַדֵּשׁ גְּלִיצוּר / הַמְגַלֶּה טַעֲמֵי צוּר   מִפִּי מֶלֶךְ מַלְכֵי הַמְּלָכִים
הַמַּשְׁמִיעַ לְכָל יְצוּר / שְׁנַת שֹׂבַע וּבָצוּר
וְכָל דְּבַר הָאָצוּר   בִּרְצוֹן מֶלֶךְ מַלְכֵי הַמְּלָכִים
חַיּוֹת אַרְבַּעְתָּן / מְשַׁלְּשׁוֹת קְדֻשָּׁתָן   לְמֶלֶךְ מַלְכֵי הַמְּלָכִים
זוֹעוֹת מֵאֵימָתָן / קוֹפְצוֹת בְּנַהֲמָתָן
קוֹרְאוֹת לְעֻמָּתָן   לְמֶלֶךְ מַלְכֵי הַמְּלָכִים

וְהַחַיּוֹת יְשׁוֹרֵרוּ / וּכְרוּבִים יְפָאֵרוּ
וּשְׂרָפִים יָרֹנּוּ / וְאֶרְאֶלִּים יְבָרֵכוּ
פְּנֵי כָל חַיָּה וְאוֹפָן וּכְרוּב לְעֻמַּת שְׂרָפִים
לְעֻמָּתָם מְשַׁבְּחִים וְאוֹמְרִים

All say aloud:

יחזקאל ג   בָּרוּךְ כְּבוֹד־יהוה מִמְּקוֹמוֹ:

*Continue with "*לָאֵל בָּרוּךְ*" on page 375 to "*אֵין אֱלֹהִים זוּלָתֶךָ*" on page 385.*

זולת

אֱמוּנִים אֲשֶׁר נֶאֱסָפוּ / בְּרָכוֹת נִכְסָפוּ
גַּם קוֹמָתָם כָּפָפוּ / דְּבַר חִנּוּנָם הֶעֱדִיפוּ.
הוֹבִילָם לְאָהֳלֵיהֶם לְשָׁלוֹם / וַיִּמְצְאוּ שָׁם שָׁלוֹם
זֶרַע הַשָּׁלוֹם / חִסְּנָם בְּצֶדֶק וְשָׁלוֹם.
טוֹבוֹת לְכַלְּלָם / יָקָר לְהַלְּלָם
כָּבוֹד לְהַנְחִילָם / לְמַעְלָה לְעֵלָּם.
מַלֵּא מִשְׁאֲלוֹתָם / נְהֹג בְּשִׂמְחָתָם
שַׂמַּח עֲדָתָם / עוֹרֵר פְּדוּתָם.

פְּנֵה לְחָנְנָם / צַמֵּת מְעַנָּם
קַבֵּל מַעֲנָם / רוֹמֵם הֲמוֹנָם.
שְׁמֹר הֲדוּרִים / שַׁכַּח אֲרוּרִים
תַּכֶּה אוֹיְבֵינוּ כְּמַכַּת בְּכוֹרִים
וּנְהַלֶּלְךָ כְּעַל קְרִיעַת גְּזָרִים.

Continue with "עֶזְרַת אֲבוֹתֵינוּ" on page 385.

תפילת גשם מלאה

רשות

אָפִיק מַעַן מְעֻטָּר / בְּיוֹם הַמְעֻטָּר
אֶעֱרֹךְ שׁוּעַ וְלֹא אֶפְטַר / בְּנִיב הַמְּפֻטָּר
בְּקֵץ הַמְנֻטָּר / שְׁאוֹנוֹ הָנְטָר
בְּמוּסָפֵי לַעֲטַר / תְּפִלַּת מָטָר.

גִּילַת פַּעֲמַיִם / שׁוֹשׁ יוֹם מִיּוֹמַיִם
גַּל לִי מִשָּׁמַיִם / בְּשַׁאֲלִי בּוֹ מַיִם
דַּלְתֵי שָׁמַיִם / אֲשֶׁר מוּל שַׁעַר הַמַּיִם
דּוֹד יִפְתַּח מִשָּׁמַיִם / בְּשָׁפְכִי לוֹ לֵב כַּמַּיִם.

הֲגִיגִי בַּל יַדְמִים / בְּצַע אֲשֵׁמִים
הָלְבְּנוּ בְּכִפּוּר אֲשָׁמִים / וְשׁוֹטֵן מַה יַּשְׁמִים
וְאִמְרֵי רְשׁוּמִים / בְּעָרְכָם נִרְשָׁמִים
וְדִיתִי עִם שָׁמִים / לְהַזְכִּיר גְּבוּרוֹת גְּשָׁמִים.

זַעַק מִמֵּצַר / אֶקְרָא בְּכָל צַר
זֶה יַרְחִיב לִי בַּצַּר / שׁוּעַ אֲשֶׁר לֹא בְצָר
חֹזֶק יָד לֹא תִקְצַר / מִפְתְּחַ אוֹצָר
חֵטְא אִם עָצַר / יָפֶן בְּעַם נֶעֱצָר.

טְעָמִים אֲחַבֵּר / חֲיָלִים לְגַבֵּר
טִפֵּי נִתּוּרִים אֲדַבֵּר / וְלֹא כְמִתְגַּבֵּר
יוֹרוּנִי מָה אֲדַבֵּר / פְּנֵי תֵבָה כְּעוֹבֵר
יַרְשׁוּנִי בְּעָדָם לְהַסְבֵּר / כִּי עֵת לַחֲשׁוֹת וְעֵת לְדַבֵּר.

כֹּרַע בֶּרֶךְ לְהַבְרִיךְ / בָּמוֹת לְהַדְרִיךְ
כִּוּוּן חִין לְהַעֲרִיךְ / בְּעַד עַם מַעֲרִיךְ
לַחֲבשׁ וּלְהַאֲרִיךְ / חַרְבוֹן חֹרֶב מַפְרִיךְ
לְדַבֵּר גְּבוּרוֹת אַאֲרִיךְ / כִּי עֵת לְקַצֵּר וְעֵת לְהַאֲרִיךְ.

מַמַּטַע דָּרְבוֹנוֹת / אָבִינָה תְּבוּנוֹת
מֵעַם בִּינוֹת / אֲדַבֵּר נְכוֹנוֹת
נְאָקוֹת מְכֻוָּנוֹת / לְהַמְטִיר גֵּיא וְלִבְנוֹת
נְשַׁמּוֹת לְכוֹנְנוֹת / בְּרַבּוֹת בָּנוֹת.

שְׂעִירִים לְהַרְבִּיב / חֲזִיזִים לְהַעֲבִיב
שִׂיחִים לְהַאֲבִיב / עַד זְמַן אָבִיב
עֲדָנִים לְהַנְבִּיב / מִקְּדִיחַת שְׁבִיב
עָבִים לְהַלְבִּיב / רַוּוֹת עַם חָבִיב.

פָּנִים לִי יִשָּׂא / בְּצִיגָתִי פְּנֵי כְנִיסָה
פֹּעַל בְּעֶשֶׂר נִסָּה / יִזְכֹּר לִי לְחוּסָה
צוּר רָם וְנִשָּׂא / אֵלָיו עַיִן אֶשָּׂא
צְבָאָיו לוֹ אֲגַיְּסָה / וְלֹא בְּרוּחַ גַּסָּה.

קוֹלִי יֶעֱרַב / רִנָּתִי לְפָנָיו תִּקְרַב
קַמְתִּי כְּבַקְּרָב / חָגוּר כְּלֵי קְרָב
רְשׁוּת צָעִיר וָרַב / אֶטֹּל טֶרֶם אֶקְרַב
רַחַשׁ אֲבַשֵּׂר וְיֶעֱרַב / צֶדֶק בְּקָהָל רָב.

שָׁלִיחַ לְמִסְתּוֹפְפִים / צִיר לַאֲסוּפִים
שִׁבְעַת יְמֵי חַג אוֹסְפִים / וְנִסּוּךְ הַמַּיִם חוֹסְפִים
שְׁמִינִי מוֹסִיפִים / וּבוֹ נֶאֱסָפִים
שַׁוְעַת מַיִם מְחַסְּפִים / בְּחִין מוּסָפִים.

תְּפוּצֶינָה עֵינוֹת מַיִם / בָּרְחֹבוֹת פַּלְגֵי מָיִם
תִּמְשַׁכְנָה בְּטוּחוֹת לְפֶה מַיִם / לְהִתְגַּבֵּר כְּנַחֲלֵי מָיִם
תִּזְכֹּר לִי אֲתוּי נַהֲרַיִם / מִשּׁוּב אֲחוֹרַיִם
תְּעַנְּנֵי עֲדֵי אֶפְרַיִם / בְּשָׁפְכִי שִׂיחוֹת צָהֳרָיִם.

אַקְשְׁטָה כֶּסֶל וָקֶרֶב לְהַבִּיעַ בְּעַד מַיִם
אֹזֶם לְפִי מְעַט גַּעַת בְּלַחְלוּחַ מְלֶאכֶת מַיִם
אֲחַסְּפָה מֵעַיִן מַעַשׂ מִפְעַל מַיִם
אֶת פְּנֵי מֵבִין לְהַשְׁמִיעַ גְּבוּרוֹת מָיִם.

בְּגָבְהֵי שָׁמַיִם אָצַר אָסְמֵי מַיִם
בְּתַחְתִּיּוֹת אֶרֶץ הֶחְבִּיא תְּהוֹמוֹת מַיִם
בָּם הֵחֵל, וְכָל חוּג אֶרֶץ וְשָׁמַיִם
בָּם הִרְקִיעַ הֲדוֹם וְקֵרָה שָׁמָיִם.

גַּם בְּטֶרֶם יוּצְרוּ פְּתוּכֵי אֵשׁ וּמַיִם
גָּמַר וְכִלֵּל כֹּל, בְּמִשּׁוּלַת מַיִם
גָּרָה אֶצְלוֹ אָמוֹן, לְשַׁעֲשְׁעוֹ יוֹמַיִם
גְּנָזָהּ, פְּעָל אִתּוֹ עוֹלָמוֹת שְׁנָיִם.

דָּרַךְ וְהִשְׁתָּה שָׁתוֹת כְּמַשְׁתִּיַּת מַיִם
דַּעַת כִּי כֹל הוּשְׁתָה מִשְׁתִיַּת מַיִם
דִּבֵּר וְהֶעֱרִיךְ תָּפְתָּה מִשְׁלִיגַת מַיִם
דָּרַשׁ וְנָטַע שָׁתוּל עַל פַּלְגֵי מָיִם.

הִצְפִּין לַיְשָׁרִים אֱמוּנַת יוֹמַיִם
הֶעֱבִיר תְּשַׁע מֵאוֹת וְשִׁבְעִים וְאַרְבָּעָה דוֹרוֹת כְּבְשֶׁטֶף מַיִם
הֵכִין שִׁבְעָה בְּרֹאוֹת עַד לֹא שָׁמַיִם
הִשְׁרָה בָּם שְׁכִינָה, קֶדֶם דַּר שָׁמָיִם.

וְנָכוֹן מֵאָז, צָר כֵּס וַיְחַסּוּ שָׁמַיִם
וּבְסָסוֹ עַל רוּחַ מְרַחֶפֶת עַל פְּנֵי הַמַּיִם
וּכְצָר מַעֲשֵׂה בְרֵאשִׁית וּמָדַד בְּשָׁעֳלוֹ מַיִם
וְעָדוֹ בֵּין חַשְׁרַת מַיִם לְחֶשְׁכַת מָיִם.

זְמַן לוֹ לַעֲמֹס גַּבּוֹת מְלֵאוֹת עֵינָיִם
זִיו מִסְפַּר רְבַע פָּנִים חֲמִשִּׁים וְשֵׁשׁ וּמָאתַיִם
זוֹעוֹת מִמַּשָּׂא וְרוֹעֲשׁוֹת מִקּוֹלוֹת מַיִם
זְבוּדִים אִתָּם כְּרוּב וְאוֹפַן וְגַלְגַּל מָיִם.

חֵיל שַׂרְפֵי מַעַל כְּתַרְשִׁישׁ מַיִם
חֲקוּקִים וְנִשְׁעָרִים בְּאֹרֶךְ עִמְקֵי מַיִם
חֶצְיָם בְּרִיַּת אֵשׁ וְחֶצְיָם יְצִירַת מַיִם
חוֹצְצִים, תֵּת מְחִיצָה בֵּין אֵשׁ וּבֵין מָיִם.

טָסִים וּמְעוֹפְפִים בְּכַנְפֵי אֵשׁ וּמַיִם
טוֹבְעִים בִּנְהַר דִּינוּר נֶגֶד כְּנַחֲלֵי מַיִם
טִכֵּס אוֹצְרוֹת שֶׁלֶג וָאֵשׁ וּבָרָד מַיִם
טְמוּנִים לְסַעֲרַת חֵמָה, לְצַלְמוֹנַת מָיִם.

יָזַם וְאָצַר לְחַיִּים, פֶּלֶג מָלֵא מַיִם
יָעַץ לְפַלֵּג מֶנּוּ לִפְלַגּוֹת מַיִם
יָהּ, כְּבָט בְּכָל פֹּעַל, כִּי אֵין חַיּוּת בְּלִי מַיִם
יִשֵּׁר תֵּת מַתְּנַת חִנָּם לָעוֹלָם מָיִם.

כְּפָץ תֵּת מֵאָז יִשּׁוּב דָּת לַמַּיִם
כָּל לְהַשְׁקוֹת נֶשִׁי מִתַּחְתִּית מַיִם
כְּשָׁר בְּבַעֲלֵי זְרוֹעַ כִּי יֶחְמְסוּ מַיִם
כֵּוֵן וְשָׁב לְשׁוֹקְקָהּ מֵאוֹצַר שָׁמָיִם.

לְמַעַל לָרָקִיעַ עָשׁ כִּבְרֵכַת מַיִם
לִנְטוֹת עָלֶיהָ כִּפָּה מַזַּעַת מֵחַמַּת מַיִם
לְהַטִּיף מִמֶּנָּה מִגַּרַע נִטְפֵי מַיִם
לַהֲלֹךְ מַהֲלַךְ כַּמָּה בְּלִי עֵרוּב מָיִם.

מַרְאֵה הַקֶּשֶׁת כַּעֲשָׁשִׁית בַּמַּיִם
מֻנָּה כֹּל יָבִינוּ כֹּחַ מוֹדֵד מַיִם
מַרְאָה כָּל מַרְאֶה וּמַרְאָה בְּמַרְאִית מַיִם
מוֹדַעַת לְגֵיא אוֹת בְּרִית, בְּלִי טוֹבַעַת מָיִם.

נוֹצֵץ בָּרָק בְּבֶהָל, לְהַבְרִיק כְּמֶהַת מַיִם
נוֹהֵם בְּרַעַשׁ וְקוֹל רַעַם מַרְעִים עַל הַמַּיִם
נְשִׂיאִים וְרוּחוֹת מַקְדִּימִים לְמֹדּוֹ מַיִם
נִרְאִים כְּעוֹלִים מִמַּיִם וְשָׁבִים אֶל הַמָּיִם.

שָׂם מִשְׁקָל לָרוּחַ, בּוֹ לְפַלֵּס מַיִם
סִיֵּם לְפִי כָל אֶרֶץ, מַה לְהַגְרִיל מַיִם
סִפֵּק וּמַד בְּמִדָּה, תִּכֵּן מִדַּת מַיִם
סִדֵּר לְשֵׁבֶט לָאָרֶץ לְחֶסֶד לְהַמְצִיא מָיִם.

עָב וְחָזִיז וְנָשִׂיא וְאֵד וַעֲנַן מַיִם
עָרַךְ בָּם שְׂאֵת מַשָּׂא מֵעִמּוּס מַיִם
עָפִים וְדָאִים עַל פְּנֵי רְקִיעַ הַשָּׁמַיִם
עוֹמְדִים צְרוּרִים עַד יֻרְשׁוּ לְהָרִיק מָיִם.

פַּחַד שְׂעִירִים מִשְׁתַּעֲרִים בְּהַרְעִיפָם מַיִם
פּוֹתְחִים, כְּנֹס כַּנֵּד שְׁתִיַּת מַיִם
פּוֹרְחִים לְהַמְתִּיק בְּשַׁחַק תַּמְלוּחִית מַיִם
פּוֹנִים שׁוּב לָלֶכֶת אֶל מְקוֹם הַמַּיִם.

צְבָאוֹת רְבִיבִים הַמַּרְבִּיבִים מַיִם
צוֹמְחִים כַּעֲרָבִים עַל יִבְלֵי מַיִם
צִיָּה מְמוֹגְגִים בְּנַחַת זִילַת מַיִם
צִחְיוֹן חַרְבוֹן קַיִץ, לְהַשְׂבִּיעַ שֹׂבַע מָיִם.

קַו מְבַדֵּל, אֲשֶׁר הִבְדִּילוּ מִמַּיִם
קִצְבָּם תָּלוּי בְּאֹמֶר, לְהַפְרוֹת מְטַר מַיִם
קוֹל צִנּוֹרוֹת כִּי יַזְחִילוּ מֵהֶם מַיִם
קוֹלוֹת יִתְּנוּ תְּהוֹמוֹת, שְׁעוֹת לְצִמְאוֹן מָיִם.

רוֹעֲשִׁים וּמַרְעִישִׁים קוֹל, מִקּוֹלוֹת מַיִם
רוֹגְשִׁים וְנוֹשְׂאִים קוֹל לְאַדִּיר קוֹלוֹ עַל הַמַּיִם
רֶנֶן מַרְעִימִים לְמַרְעִים עַל רֹב מַיִם
רְדִתָּם כֹּל, יָשִׁירוּ שִׁיר לְמוֹדֵד מָיִם.

שֶׁבַח כִּנּוּי שֵׁם כִּנָּה בְּשֵׁם מַיִם
שִׁתֵּף בְּשֵׁם אַדִּיר אַדִּירִים לְמַיִם
שָׁת מַעֲטֶה לְבוּשׁוֹ מַחֲזֶה שֶׁלֶג מַיִם
שַׁוֶּה קוֹל הוֹדוֹ כְּקוֹל רִבּוּי מָיִם.

תִּכֵּן וְכָל וּמַד וְגָזַר וְדָלָה מַיִם
תֵּת לְכָל גַּיְא וְגַיְא מַעְיָן לִשְׁתּוֹת מַיִם
תִּרְגֵּל מֵעֵדֶן נָהָר יוּבַל מַיִם
תִּוְּכוֹ לְהִפָּרֵד לְרִבּוּעַ רָאשֵׁי מָיִם.

תִּכְּנָם לָאֶרֶץ וְחוּצוֹת לַחֲצוֹת מַיִם
אִמֵּן לְכָל אֶחָד וְאֶחָד מַה יִּתְּנוּ מָיִם
שָׁקַל לְרֹאשׁ עַפְרוֹת תֵּבֵל לְבַד פַּלְגֵי מַיִם
לִמְטַר הַשָּׁמַיִם תִּשְׁתֶּה מָּיִם
רְצוֹת לָהּ שָׁלוֹם בִּירִידַת מַיִם
עֹמֶק וְתָלוּל, גָּלוּי וְחָבוּי כְּאַחַת שָׁתוֹת מָיִם
קֶרַח וּכְפוֹר וְשֶׁלֶג וְנֹזֵל מַיִם
זִמְּנוּ לָהּ לְשׁוֹקְקָהּ בְּכָל מִינֵי מָיִם

צוֹפָה בָהּ עַיִן, לְהַתְמִידָהּ בְּמַיִם
רֵאשִׁית וְעַד אַחֲרִית, דְּרוּשָׁה רַוּוֹת מַיִם
פֶּשַׁע אִם הָעֲצַם, וְנִגְזַר עֲצִירַת מַיִם
בְּתַחַן וָפֶלֶל יְפַתּוּ מִגֶּרַע נִטְפֵי מַיִם
עַיִן יִשְׂאוּ לָרוֹכֵב בְּעֶזְרָם שָׁמַיִם
יְשֵׁנִים הֱיוֹת בְּמִצְעָ, וְהוּא מַסְפִּיק לָמוֹ מַיִם
שִׂיחַ מֵהַיּוֹם נֶעֱצָרִים לְהַזְכִּיר בְּשִׂיחָם מַיִם
רוֹגְשִׁים בְּסוֹף שִׁבְעָה לְצַיֵּן בְּמוּסַף מַיִם
נִסּוּךְ מְנַסְּכִים שְׁלֹשֶׁת לֻגֵּי מַיִם
בָּם לַעֲרֹךְ כְּסֵדֶר שְׁלֹשֶׁת רְבִיעִיּוֹת מַיִם
מִמַּעַל לְהַרְבִּיעַ זְכִרוֹת רֶבַע מַיִם
יַעַל בְּכֶפֶל מִתַּחַת פְּרִית נִקְבוֹת מַיִם
לִיפַתַּח אֶרֶץ, וְיִפְרוּ יֶשַׁע מְטַר מַיִם
קוֹרְאִים זֶה לָזֶה עַד יַשִּׁיקוּ מַיִם לְמַיִם
כַּאֲשֶׁר יֵרֵד הַגֶּשֶׁם וְהַשֶּׁלֶג מִן הַשָּׁמַיִם
לְצִמָּאוֹן יְשַׁעֲשְׁעוּהוּ עֲיָנוֹת וּתְהוֹמוֹת מַיִם
יַחַד דָּגַת וְקַשְׂקֶשֶׂת הַגְּדֵלִים בַּהֲמוֹן מַיִם
יִתְאַוּוּ לְרִדְתּוֹ גְּמוֹת מֶנּוּ מְעַט מַיִם
טְרוּחֵי שְׁחִין וּכְאֵב וְחוֹלֵי מֵעַיִם
רוֹגְעִים וּמִתְרַוְּחִים בְּאִוּוּי קָרַת מַיִם
חַיֵּי כָּל נֶשִׁי מְסַרְתָּ בְּמַזָּלוֹת שָׁמַיִם
מְמֻנִּים עַל כָּל אֶרֶץ אֵיךְ לְפַרְנְסָהּ מַיִם
זָבַת חָלָב וּדְבָשׁ, אֶרֶץ נַחֲלֵי מַיִם
קִדַּשְׁתָּ לְשִׁמְךָ, אוֹתָהּ לְמוֹגְגָהּ מַיִם
וְאַתָּה בְּיָדְךָ תַּתָּה מַפְתֵּחַ מְטַר מַיִם
רְשׁוּת אֵין לְהִנָּתֵן בִּלְעָדֶיךָ, לִפְתֹּחַ אוֹצַר מַיִם
הָקֵם דְּבָרְךָ הַטּוֹב, תֵּת בְּשֶׁפַע מַיִם
יַחַד לְרָצוֹן לְנֶדֶב, לְטֹהַר לְהָנִיף מַיִם

דֵּי אַרְבָּעִים סְאָה מְשַׁעֵר מִקְוֵה מַיִם
תְּמִימֶיךָ אֵיךְ בּוֹ יִטְהָרוּ, אִם אֵין בּוֹ שִׁעוּר מָיִם
גְּשָׁמִים שִׁבְעָה מִשִּׁבְעָה רְקִיעֵי מַיִם
שֶׁבַע אֲרָצוֹת שֶׁבַע וְשִׁבְעַת עַמּוּדֵי מָיִם
בְּצוּר חוֹגְגִים שִׁבְעָה וְנֶעֱצָרִים עֲדֵי מַיִם
פִּלּוּלָם קְשֹׁב בְּשָׁפְכָם לְךָ לֵב כַּמַּיִם
אָדוֹן, הַשְׁקִיפָה מִמְּעוֹן קָדְשְׁךָ מִן־הַשָּׁמַיִם: דברים כו
רֵעֶיךָ לְנַהֵל בְּרֶבֶץ כְּעַל מַבּוּעֵי מָיִם.

יִפְתַּח	אֶרֶץ לְיֶשַׁע / לִשְׁבֹּר מַטֵּה רֶשַׁע
מַיִם	אִם כִּזְּבוּ בְּפֶשַׁע / זְכֹר נָם, יֻקַּח נָא מְעַט מַיִם, וְתִשַּׁע.
כִּי	אֲרֻבּוֹת שְׁמֵי עֶרֶץ / עַד אָבִיב יִפָּתְחוּ בְּלִי פֶּרֶץ
מַיִם	אֵד לְהַעֲלוֹת בְּמֶרֶץ / טֶרֶם יִהְיֶה בָּאָרֶץ: בראשית ב
יהוה	בְּיָדוֹ מַפְתֵּחַ / זוּלָתוֹ בְּלִי יִפָּתֵחַ
מַיִם	בְּצוּל יַרְתִּיחַ / חָגוּר בְּנֵי עָקוּד לְפַתֵּחַ.
כַּאֲשֶׁר	בֹּחַן וְשָׁפַךְ לֵב כַּמַּיִם / יְחַיּוּ טְלָאָיו מִיּוֹמַיִם
מַיִם	בְּאֵר חָפַר פַּעֲמַיִם / לְקוֹל תִּתּוֹ הֲמוֹן מַיִם בַּשָּׁמַיִם: ירמיה י
לְךָ	גָּשִׁים וְשַׁוְעַ מַרְהִיטִים / לְהָקֵר חֹרֶב לְהָטִים
מַיִם	גַּבֵּר כַּמֶּרְהָטִים / בְּחִין פִּצֵּל בָּרְהָטִים.
יֵרֵד	גֶּשֶׁם לְנִדְשָׁאִים / לְעַדֵּן זִיו עַיִן לְךָ נוֹשְׂאִים
מַיִם	גְּנוּזִים וְנִשָּׂאִים / לַשְׂאוֹתָם מַעֲלֶה נְשִׂיאִים.
אֶת	דְּרוּשָׁה מֵרֹאשׁ / תָּמִיד אוֹתָהּ דְּרֹשׁ
מַיִם	דָּגָן וְתִירוֹשׁ / יְרַוּוּ בְּשִׂיחַ בְּכוֹר רֹאשׁ.
הַגֶּשֶׁם	דְּשָׁאִים יְרַעֲנֵן / וְשׁוֹר וּמְרִיא בּוֹ יְחֻנַּן
מַיִם	דְּלֵה לְעָב מְעֻנָּן / בְּאוֹת קֶשֶׁת עֲנִינַת עָנָן.

אוֹצָרוֹ הַמָּלֵא / מְזֵעַת כִּפַּת דֹּק מִתְמַלֵּא
מַיִם הַמְצַיַּת מֵי מָלֵא / לְגֵיא מְעַקְּרֵי שׁוֹר תְּמַלֵּא.
וְהַשֶּׁלֶג הַקְּפֵא לְנִלְקֶשֶׁת / לְרָשׁוּ בַּשְּׁלִישִׁי מִתְבַּקֶּשֶׁת
מַיִם הַזֵּל לְמִתְנַקֶּשֶׁת / בְּהוֹד נֹגַהּ מַרְאֵה הַקֶּשֶׁת.

הַטּוֹב וְהַנָּעִים / שְׁעֵה זֶמֶר נָעִים
מַיִם וְקוֹל מְזַעְזְעִים / בְּמֵי מְרִיבָה לֹא תַזְעִים.
מִן וְדוּי תְּאוֹמִים וְרֵעִים / תִּתְרַצֶּה בְּשִׂיחַ הַנָּעִים
מַיִם וַעֵד לְזוֹרְעִים / בְּקוֹל גַּלְגַּל הַמַּרְעִים.

אֶת זְמַן חָבוּי גֹּפֶר / הָגְבְּלוּ גְּבוּלוֹת בַּסֵּפֶר
מַיִם זִילַת שֶׁפֶר / לְמַדֵּד אַדְמַת גּוּר עֹפֶר.
הַשָּׁמַיִם זַעַק לְקַבֵּל / חֹם בְּתַמּוּז מִלְּחַבֵּל
מַיִם זֹרְמוּ לְתַבֵּל / בְּשֵׁשֶׁת מִינֵי תֵּבֵל.

הַשָּׁמַיִם חַשְׁרַת כְּבָדָה / חֲשֹׁר לְרוּחַ נִשְׁבָּרָה
מַיִם חַזֵּז בִּגְבוּרָה / לִמְבִינֵי עִתֵּי בָּרָה.
וְשָׁמָּה חֶלְקָם בַּחַיִּים / כְּסַרְטָן גָּדֵל בְּמַיִם חַיִּים
מַיִם חֲשׂוּפִים וּבְקַו חֲצוּיִים / הוֹצֵא מִבֵּית מַיִם חַיִּים.

לָתֵת טַעַם וָנֹפֶשׁ / לְהוֹצִיא אֲסִירִים לְחֹפֶשׁ
מַיִם טְבִיעַת רֶפֶשׁ / בַּל יַבְעִיתוּ מְחָרֵף נֶפֶשׁ.
לֹא טַרְחוּת כְּמַבּוּלוֹת / וְלֹא בְּחֹרֶב אָב מַחְבִּילוֹת
מַיִם טְמוּנִים בְּתַחְבּוּלוֹת / חֲשֹׂף לְהַצִּיב כָּל גְּבוּלוֹת.

מְטַר יוֹרֶה לִירוֹת / שָׂדוֹת וִיעָרוֹת
מַיִם יִמָּלְאוּ יְאוֹרוֹת / לִמְגוֹדְדֵי גְּדוּד שְׁיָרוֹת.
יָשׁוּב יִפְרֶה הַר וְגִבְעָה / יִרְבַּץ כְּאַרְיֵה עֲלֵי תְבוּעָה
מַיִם יְשַׁלְּשׁוּ רְבִיעָה / לְהִפָּרֵד לְרָאשִׁים אַרְבָּעָה.

אַרְצְךָ כִּוּוּן הֲדוֹם רֶגֶל / וְלֹא נִשְׁקֵית כְּגַן בְּרֶגֶל
מַיִם כְּזִנּוּק אֱגֶל / יְזַנְּקוּ בָּשָׁן בִּמְנוֹחַ עֵגֶל.
כִּי כֹל בַּשְּׁקִי יָשִׁישׁ / בְּאָסְפָם בָּר בֶּאֱלוּל, בְּטִלּוּל רְסִיס
מַיִם כְּרָמִים לְהַעֲסִיס / בִּנְטִיפֵי חָלָב וְעָסִיס.

בְּעִתּוֹ לְהַרְעִים רַעַם / בְּנַחַת וְלֹא בְזַעַם
מַיִם לָתֵת טַעַם / בְּאַדְמַת מַשְׁפִּיר אִמְרֵי נֹעַם.
אִם לְשֵׁבֶט לְאֶרֶץ נִשְׁלָחִים / לְהַעֲלִיץ בְּתוּלָה בְּאִבֵּי שְׁלָחִים
מַיִם לִפְלָגִים נִשְׁלָחִים / לְשַׂמֵּחַ עִיר אֱלֹהִים.

וּלְבָרֵךְ מִמֶּגֶד יְרָחִים / בְּעִדּוּן תְּנוּב פְּרָחִים
מַיִם מֵעָבִים מַטְרִיחִים / וּמַעֲדַנֵּי מֶלֶךְ מַאֲרִיחִים.
הִרְוָה מְזוֹנִים וְנָטַר / בְּיֶרַח אֵיתָנִים לְהַתִּיר קְטַר
מַיִם מֵעַתָּה בַּל יֶאְטַר / לְהַרְעִיף שְׂעִירֵי מָטָר.

אֶת נִיב מַזְכִּירֵי שֶׁוַע / שְׁעֵה בְּנִסּוּךְ שֶׁבַע
מַיִם נַחַל לְשֹׂבַע / לְקַרְנֵי רְאֵם לְשַׁלֵּשׁ רֶבַע.
אֶת נִטְעֵי חֲמַת כֶּמֶשׁ / תַּטְרִים לֶאֱסֹף בָּר, בְּפִלּוּס גֹּמֶשׁ
מַיִם נֵזֶל בִּנְטִיפֵי אֶמֶשׁ / וּכְאוֹר בֹּקֶר יִזְרַח־שָׁמֶשׁ: שמואל ב׳ כג

כָּל שִׂיחִים בּוֹ יְאֻשָּׁרוּ / יִתְרוֹעֲעוּ אַף יָשִׁירוּ
מַיִם שְׂעִירִים יַחְשֹׁרוּ / וְאַדְמַת רֹדֵם יַעֲשִׁירוּ.
הָאָרֶץ סוֹקְרִים כִּבְרַק אֵשׁ / פֶּן כְּמַבּוּל בּוּל תִּתְבַּיֵּשׁ
מַיִם סַפֵּק מִלְּבַיֵּשׁ / נוֹאֲמִים, אָב לַמָּטָר הֲיֵשׁ.

מַעֲשֵׂה עִקּוּשׁ כָּל בְּרִיָּה / לֹא יַעַצְרוּ מִגֵּיא פּוֹרִיָּה
מַיִם עֲמָקִים יַעַטְפוּ פִּרְיָהּ / בְּזֵכֶר עֲנֻיַּת מוֹרִיָּה.
וְהוֹלִידָהּ עָב חִתּוּל בָּשְׁתָּהּ / כְּבִמְקוֹם עַקְרָב בְּלִי לְשִׁיתָהּ
מַיִם עֶרֶף רֵאשִׁיתָהּ / הַמְטֵר לְעוֹבְרִים שָׁמָּה לְרִשְׁתָּהּ.

יָדְךָ פְּתַח בִּזְרוֹעַ חָשׂוּף / לִפְתֹּחַ אוֹצַר אָסוּף
מַיִם פְּקֹד לְצִיָּה כָּסוּף / בְּזֵכֶר עֲנִיַּת יַם סוּף.
וְהַצְמִיחָהּ פֵּרוֹת בְּמֵי שֶׁלֶג / בִּימֵי חֲנֻכָּה לְהָצִין מֶלֶג
מַיִם פְּנוֹת אַרְצָה בְּלִי פֶלֶג / מְדַק לְהוֹרִיד גֶּשֶׁם וָשֶׁלֶג.

וְהִלְוִיתָ צְבָאֶיךָ רְסִיסֵי אֵגֶל / בְּנַחַת נַהֵל מַעְגָּל
מַיִם צַק בְּקוֹל גַּלְגַּל / בְּזֵכֶר עֲנִיַּת גִּלְגָּל.
וְנָתַן צֹאנְךָ סוֹעַרְךָ בְּמֶרֶץ / קֶשֶׁת לְהֵרָאוֹת, לְחַיֵּל אֶרֶץ
מַיִם צְרוּרִים לְמִטְרוֹת עֶרֶץ / תַּתִּיר לֵאמֹר לַשֶּׁלֶג, הֱוֵא אָרֶץ.

גּוֹיִם קָצְפוּ מִמֵּי הַקְּצָפָה / כְּנִפְתְּחוּ אֲרֻבּוֹת לְהָצִיפָה
מַיִם קָרִים בְּלִי חֲצִיפָה / בְּזֵכֶר עֲנִיַּת מִצְפָּה.
זֶרַע קֹדֶשׁ מַטָּעָתוֹ / מָכְפֶּלֶת לְהָכִין מַרְעִיתוֹ
מַיִם קַלִּים מִלְּהַבְעִיתוֹ / צַו לָתֵת מְטַר אַרְצְךָ בְּעִתּוֹ.

רַבִּים רְנָנוֹת בְּיַשְׁבִי / הִרְבֵּיתִי לְךָ לְהַקְשִׁיבִי
מַיִם רַוֵּה לְהַשְׁאִיבִי / בְּזֵכֶר עֲנִיַּת תִּשְׁבִּי.
לַזּוֹרֵעַ רְאֵה שִׂיחַ נִדְכּוֹ / כִּבְדֵי רוֹבֵץ לְהַשְׁדִּיכוֹ
מַיִם רַבֵּה כְּגַהֵר דַּכּוֹ / כְּקָדְרוּ עַד כֹּה וְעַד כֹּה.

וְאַתָּה שְׁעֵה נִיב שְׂפָתַי / הַמַּזְכִּירִים מֵאֵימָתַי
מַיִם שׁוֹקֵק עֲמוּתַי / בְּזֵכֶר עֲנִיַּת בֶּן אֲמִתַּי.
וְלֶחֶם שָׁמֵן וְדָשֵׁן לְרֵשֶׁם / בִּדְלִי שְׁבָט יְצַחְצֵחַ כְּלֶשֶׁם
מַיִם שַׁפַּע לִנְפוּחֵי נֶשֶׁם / וְיִמָּלְאוּ הֶעָבִים גֶּשֶׁם.

לֹא תִלְוֶה מְלַפְתֵּחַ כָּל סָגוּר / לַעֲנוֹת מְצַפְצְפִים כְּעָגוּר
מַיִם תָּרִיק לְכָל מָגוּר / בְּזֵכֶר עֲנִיַּת גּוּר וְאָגוּר.
לֶאֱכֹל תְּלוּת לְךָ עֵינַיִם / לְאַדְּרוֹ וּלְהַדְּגוֹ מִמֶּגֶד שָׁמַיִם
מַיִם תֵּן לְהַחֲיוֹת כִּמְיוּמַיִם / אֶרֶץ נַחֲלֵי מָיִם: דברים ח

Continue with אֱלֹהֵינוּ וֵאלֹהֵי אֲבוֹתֵינוּ *on page 1155*

רשות לנשמת לשמחת תורה

שחרית *is said up to the end of* פסוקי דזמרה *(page 351).*

נִשְׁמַת מְלַמְּדֵי מוֹרָשָׁה, נִקְרָאִים בְּנֵי חֹפֶשׁ
תְּנַצֵּחַ נוֹטֵעַ לְחַיֵּי עוֹלָם וְנֶפֶשׁ
תוֹרַת יהוה תְּמִימָה מְשִׁיבַת נָפֶשׁ: תהלים יט

נִשְׁמַת חַכְמֵי חֶמְדָּה, בִּגְבוּרָה וְלֹא בַשְּׁתִי: קהלת י
תַּמְלִיךְ מוֹרֶה וְשִׂים רְפוּאָתִי
עֵדוּת יהוה נֶאֱמָנָה, מַחְכִּימַת פֶּתִי: תהלים יט

נִשְׁמַת בְּנֵי בִינָה, מִתְעַנְּגִים מִטּוּב הַלֵּב
תַּרְגִּישׁ רָזֵי דָרֵי הַלֵּב
פִּקּוּדֵי יהוה יְשָׁרִים מְשַׂמְּחֵי־לֵב: שם

נִשְׁמַת בָּנִים נְבוֹנִים בְּשִׁקּוּל וְהַכְרֵעַ מֹאזְנַיִם
תְּיַשֵּׁר יְפִי חִקּוּר וְתִקּוּן אָזְנַיִם
מִצְוַת יהוה בָּרָה, מְאִירַת עֵינָיִם: שם

נִשְׁמַת מְבִינֵי מַדָּע תּוֹרָה בְּלִבָּם לְמִסְעָד
תְּכַבֵּד כּוֹנֵן אֲשׁוּרֵימוֹ, לֹא תִמְעַד
יִרְאַת יהוה טְהוֹרָה, עוֹמֶדֶת לָעַד: שם

נִשְׁמַת יְדִידִים, יָדָם זַיֵּן פִּיפִיּוֹת חֲדָיו
תָּרֹן רוֹמְמוֹת סִלְסוּל עֹז מַחֲמַדָּיו
מִשְׁפְּטֵי־יהוה אֱמֶת, צָדְקוּ יַחְדָּו: שם

[נִשְׁמַת וְעוֹדִים בְּאַרְצוֹת שְׁבִיָּם
שְׂרִידֶיךָ, פְּזוּרֶיךָ, יְרוֹמְמוּךָ בְּעֵת תְּשִׁיבֵם לִצְבִי עֶדְיָם
בְּאוֹמְרִים, אִלּוּ פִינוּ מָלֵא שִׁירָה כַּיָּם]

*Continue with "*נִשְׁמַת*" on page 353.*

יוצר לשמחת תורה

In some congregations, the following is said after בָּרְכוּ *(page 363):*

בָּרוּךְ אַתָּה יהוה אֱלֹהֵינוּ מֶלֶךְ הָעוֹלָם
יוֹצֵר אוֹר וּבוֹרֵא חֹשֶׁךְ
עֹשֶׂה שָׁלוֹם וּבוֹרֵא אֶת הַכֹּל.

אוֹר עוֹלָם בְּאוֹצַר חַיִּים, אוֹרוֹת מֵאֹפֶל אָמַר וַיֶּהִי.

יוצר

אַשְׁרֵי הָעָם שֶׁלּוֹ כָּכָה / מֵאֱלֹהָיו וְגוֹאֲלוֹ יִשָּׂא בְּרָכָה
מִתְבָּרֵךְ בָּאָרֶץ וּבַשָּׁמַיִם נֶעֱרָכָה — וְזֹאת הַבְּרָכָה: דברים לג

בִּפְנוֹת עָנָו לָנוּחַ שְׁכִיבָה / הִזְהִיר אֲמָרָיו לְאַלְפֵי רְבָבָה
שְׁמֹר דָּת בִּזְרוֹעַ כְּתוּבָה — וַיֹּאמַר, יהוה מִסִּינַי בָּא:

גּוֹאֵל חָזַר בְּכָל אֻמִּים / וּמְצָאָם כֻּלָּם בַּעֲלֵי מוּמִים
הִפִּיל חֲבָלִים לוֹ בַּנְּעִימִים — אַף חֹבֵב עַמִּים:

דּוֹדִים מַקְדִּימִים לְנִשְׁמַע נַעֲשֶׂה / הֵשִׁיבוּ זֹאת בַּל תִּמָּשֶׁה
בֹּקֶר וָעֶרֶב לֹא נִנָּשֶׁה — תּוֹרָה צִוָּה־לָנוּ מֹשֶׁה:

הִכְתַּר אָדוֹן כֶּתֶר לְהִמָּלֵךְ / יַהַב עַם אֵלָיו בְּהִשְׁתַּלֵּךְ
רַנְּנוּ כָּל גּוֹי וָפֶלֶךְ — וַיְהִי בִישֻׁרוּן מֶלֶךְ:

וּמִיַּד מָחָה כָּעָב אֲשָׁמוֹת / כְּנָאָה לְמֶלֶךְ בְּיוֹם רוֹמֵמוֹת
שְׂאֵת וָיֶתֶר יְהִי לִתְקוּמוֹת — יְחִי רְאוּבֵן וְאַל־יָמֹת:

זֶבֶד טוֹב וְנָעִים כְּנֶאֱמַר / שֶׁבֶת אַחִים יַחַד כְּהִתְאַמֵּר
מִצָּרִימוֹ הֱיוֹת לָמוֹ מִשְׁמָר — וְזֹאת לִיהוּדָה, וַיֹּאמַר:

חֲסִידְךָ אִישׁ נוֹצֵר מַאֲמָרֶךָ / נִסִּיתוֹ בְּמַסָּה, וַיֶּאֱמַן דְּבָרֶךָ
וּלְעוֹלָם שָׁרֵת בְּבֵית דְּבִירֶךָ — וּלְלֵוִי אָמַר, תֻּמֶּיךָ וְאוּרֶיךָ:

טוֹב בְּשַׁעַר הַמַּחֲנֶה בְּקוּמוֹ / מִי לַיהוה אֵלַי כְּנָאֳמוֹ
אָסְפוּ חֲסִידָיו כְּאֶחָד לְעֻמּוֹ — הָאֹמֵר לְאָבִיו וּלְאִמּוֹ:

יְמַלֵּא פִּימוֹ תְּהִלָּתְךָ נְקֹב / שִׁירֶיךָ בְּאַדְמַת נֵכָר מִקֹּב
לְהַסְלִיל אֹרַח וּלְיַשֵּׁר עָקֹב — יוֹרוּ מִשְׁפָּטֶיךָ לְיַעֲקֹב:

כְּקֶדֶם מִבֵּן בְּכוֹר בְּהַבְדִּלוֹ / קֹדֶשׁ קָדָשִׁים הֱיוֹת גּוֹרָלוֹ
בְּכִפְלַיִם כֵּן עוֹד לְאֵילוֹ — בָּרֵךְ יהוה חֵילוֹ:

לִשְׁכֹּן בֵּין כְּתֵפֵי גְאוֹנִי / מְקוֹם שִׁירוֹת לְוִיֵּי וְכֹהֲנַי
רֹחַב אָהֳלַי וִירִיעוֹת מִשְׁכָּנַי — לְבִנְיָמִן אָמַר, יְדִיד יהוה:

מִבִּרְכֹת שָׁמַיִם וְתַחַת נִסְמֶכֶת / בִּרְכֹת שָׁדַיִם וָרַחַם מִתְבָּרֶכֶת
אַרְצוֹ מִכֹּל הֱיוֹת נֶעֱרֶכֶת — וּלְיוֹסֵף אָמַר, מְבֹרֶכֶת:

נָא חַסְדּוֹ לֹא יָמֵשׁ / חָשַׂךְ עַצְמוֹ, זָרָה מִלְּשַׁמֵּשׁ
בְּטוּב כָּל גְּבוּלוֹ יִתְגַּמֵּשׁ — וּמִמֶּגֶד תְּבוּאֹת שָׁמֶשׁ:

סָמוּךְ יֵצֶר מֵהַחֵוֶר וְהָאָדֹם / פִּזּוּ זְרוֹעָיו מִזָּהָב אָדֹם
שָׁלוֹם יִצֹּר מְרַחֲמוֹ מִקֶּדֶם — וּמֵרֹאשׁ הַרְרֵי־קֶדֶם:

עַל קָדְקֹד גֻּלְגֹּלֶת נָאָה / בִּרְכַּת כָּל טוּב תָּבוֹאָה
לְהַשְׁפִּיעַ שֶׁפַע כָּל תְּבוּאָה — וּמִמֶּגֶד אֶרֶץ וּמְלֹאָהּ:

פִּי שְׁנַיִם בְּנַחֲלַת חַבְלוֹ / תַּחַת מְחַלֵּל יְצוּעַ מְחוֹלְלוֹ
וְעַד נְחֹל בְּחֵלֶשׁ גּוֹרָלוֹ — בְּכוֹר שׁוֹרוֹ הָדָר לוֹ:

צִידוֹן יַרְכָתוֹ לְהַרְבּוֹת צֶמַח / מִמֵּבִין עִתִּים לִלְחֹם קֶמַח
מֵאֵת זֶה זֶה יִשְׂמַח — וְלִזְבוּלֻן אָמַר, שְׂמַח:

קִנְיַן חִלָּזוֹן סָפוּן חִבּוּאוֹ / בַּל יוֹעִיל לִמְכַסֶּה מַשָּׂאוֹ
יִזְבְּחוּ זִבְחֵי צֶדֶק וְיֵירָאוּ — עַמִּים הַר־יִקְרָאוּ:

רֵאשִׁית רָאָה לוֹ, וַיֵּאָגֵד / שֶׁשָּׁם חֶלְקַת מְחוֹקֵק יֵאָגֵד
גְּדוּד יְגוּדֶנּוּ בְּבוֹא גָּד — וּלְגָד אָמַר, בָּרוּךְ מַרְחִיב גָּד:

שָׁכֵן לַמְּצַד בִּרְאוֹת חֵילוֹ / הַקָּטֹן לְמֵאָה וְלָאֶלֶף גְּדוֹלוֹ
דָּלָם בְּרֹאשׁ גְּדוּדֵי חֵילוֹ — וַיַּרְא רֵאשִׁית לוֹ:

תַּנִּין עֲלֵי דֶרֶךְ הֱיֵה / שְׁפִיפוֹן עֲלֵי אֹרַח חֱיֵה
בְּצָרָיו נִלְחַם בְּשֵׁם אֶהְיֶה   וּלְדָן אָמַר, דָּן גּוּר אַרְיֵה:

שָׂבֵעַ וְדָשֵׁן בִּפְנִימִי וְחִיצוֹן / יָם וְדָרוֹם יִירַשׁ בְּעֶלְצוֹן
תִּלְבֹּשֶׁת כָּרִים לְבוּשׁ הַצֹּאן   וּלְנַפְתָּלִי אָמַר, נַפְתָּלִי שְׂבַע רָצוֹן:

מְטַבֵּל בַּשֶּׁמֶן רַגְלוֹ בְּאֹשֶׁר / רְצוּי אֶחָיו הָיָה בְּכֹשֶׁר
וּמַעֲדַנֵּי מֶלֶךְ נוֹתֵן מֵעֹשֶׁר   וּלְאָשֵׁר אָמַר, בָּרוּךְ מִבָּנִים אָשֵׁר:

וּכְיָמֶיךָ דָּבְאֲךָ בְּחֹזֶק חֲיָלֶיךָ / תִּדְרֹךְ עַל בָּמָתֵי גּוֹעֲלֶיךָ
רַגְלְךָ בַּל תִּגֹּף לְהַכְשִׁילֶךָ   בַּרְזֶל וּנְחֹשֶׁת מִנְעָלֶךָ:

אַדִּיר בּוֹרֵא שַׁחֲקֵי שִׁפְרוֹן / רוֹקַע הָאָרֶץ כִּנְסֵי מֵחָרוֹן
הַעֵינֵי כֹל אֵלֶיךָ יְשַׂבֵּרוּן   אֵין כָּאֵל יְשֻׁרוּן:

לְהַבְדִּיל בֵּין מַיִם לְמַיִם, וּלְבוֹדְדֵם / הִתְוִיךְ רָקִיעַ בֵּינָם, וַיַּפְרִידֵם
אֶל מְקוֹמָם הִקְוָם וַיְמַדְּדֵם   מְעֹנָה אֱלֹהֵי קֶדֶם:

יְקַר שְׁנֵי מְאוֹרוֹת חִדֵּד / חַיָּה הִשְׁרִיץ וְצִפּוֹר נִבְדַּד
מְרֻקָּם בְּצֶלֶם צָר לְהִתְעוֹדֵד   וַיִּשְׁכֹּן יִשְׂרָאֵל בֶּטַח בָּדָד:

יָהּ שָׁבַת מִמִּפְעָל כְּהוֹאֵל / וַיְקַדֵּשׁ שְׁבִיעִי כְּכָתַב יְקוּתִיאֵל
נִשָּׂא וַיְאַשֵּׁר עַמּוֹ אֵל   אַשְׁרֶיךָ יִשְׂרָאֵל:

Continue with "הַמֵּאִיר לָאָרֶץ" on page 365 to "מְלֹא כָל־הָאָרֶץ כְּבוֹדוֹ" on page 373.

אופן

אַשְׁרֶיךָ   אֹם קָדוֹשׁ, בְּהַקְדִּישְׁךָ הַשֵּׁם
יִשְׂרָאֵל   נוֹשֵׁק חָתוּם בְּכִסְאוֹ בְּלֶשֶׁם
מִי   יָחִיד בִּלְתְּךָ, מַאֲמִירְךָ בְּרֶשֶׁם
כָּמוֹךָ   מֵאֵין בָּאָרֶץ מַאֲרִיכְךָ בְּנֶשֶׁם.

עַם   נַחֲלָתוֹ קָשַׁר בִּתְפִלַּת זְרוֹעוֹ
נוֹשַׁע   מוֹשִׁיעַ בְּהוֹשִׁיעוֹ כְּאָב וְזַרְעוֹ
בַּיהוה   בָּטוּחַ חֲקָקוֹ בְּכַפּוֹ לְהַכְרִיעוֹ
מָגֵן   נֶצַח בַּעֲדוֹ שְׂכָרוֹ בְּפָרְעוֹ.

עֻזֶּךָ אָבִיךָ גִּיל יָגִיל בָּךְ
וַאֲשֶׁר בְּתוֹרַת מֹשֶׁה שָׂמַח לִבָּךְ
חֶרֶב בְּיָדְךָ, פִּיפִיּוֹת רַבִּים בְּהַעֲלִיבָךְ
גַּאֲוָתֶךָ לְוִיּוֹת עֲבוֹתוֹת אַהֲבָה יַשְׁלִיבָךְ.

וְיִכָּחֲשׁוּ בְּרֹב עֻזּוֹ אַנְשֵׁי רִיבוֹת
אוֹיְבֶיךָ יְבִיאוּךָ לְהַר קָדְשׁוֹ תִּקְרוֹבוֹת
לָךְ יוֹסִיפוּ לְכַבֵּד בְּמִנְחוֹת עֲרֵבוֹת
וְאַתָּה הָחֵל לְסַלְסֵל לָרוֹכֵב בָּעֲרָבוֹת.

עַל כִּסֵּא מְנֻשָּׂא בִּשְׁמֵי מְתֻלָּל
בָּמוֹתֵימוֹ מְנָה זִיו נוֹצְצִים כְּקָלָל
תִּדְרֹךְ יֹשֶׁר אֳרְחוֹתָיו בְּיֹפִי מִכְלָל
וְאַתָּה תָּגִיל בַּיהוה, בִּקְדוֹשׁ יִשְׂרָאֵל תִּתְהַלָּל: ישעיה מא

אֶשְׁנַבֵּי שְׁחָקִים / נִרְאִים כְּנִרְתֵּקִים
וְכִרְאִי מוּצָקִים / נֹעַם שִׁיר מַמְתִּיקִים.
קָדוֹשׁ, קָדוֹשׁ, קָדוֹשׁ, יהוה צְבָאוֹת: ישעיה ו

מַרְאֵה הַקֶּשֶׁת / כְּאֵשׁ צְבוּעָה מְאֻשֶּׁשֶׁת
דְּמוּת מִינִים שְׁלֹשֶׁת / לְזוֹכֵר הַבְּרִית מְקֻדֶּשֶׁת.
קָדוֹשׁ, קָדוֹשׁ, קָדוֹשׁ, יהוה צְבָאוֹת:

תַּקִּיף מְטַטְרוֹן שַׂר / הַנֶּהְפָּךְ לְאֵשׁ מִבָּשָׂר
מְלַמֵּד מוּסָר / לְיַלְדֵי אוֹר נִמְסָר.
קָדוֹשׁ, קָדוֹשׁ, קָדוֹשׁ, יהוה צְבָאוֹת:

יְפֵיפִיָּה שַׂר הַתּוֹרָה / הַחוֹפֵן אֵשׁ שְׁחוֹרָה
לִקְשֹׁר עֲטָרָה / לְאוֹתִיּוֹת הַתּוֹרָה.
קָדוֹשׁ, קָדוֹשׁ, קָדוֹשׁ, יהוה צְבָאוֹת:

יְסוֹד עוֹלָמוֹ / הַנִּקְרָא צַדִּיק שְׁמוֹ
בְּהִגָּיוֹן נְאֻמוֹ / הוּא הַמַּרְעִישׁ עוֹלָמוֹ.
קָדוֹשׁ, קָדוֹשׁ, קָדוֹשׁ, יהוה צְבָאוֹת:

חַדְרֵי תֵימָן / כְּסִיל וְעָשׁ הַמְזֻמָּן
הָאֵל הַנֶּאֱמָן / לְהַקְדִּישׁוֹ מְיַשְּׁבִין טַעֲמָן.
קָדוֹשׁ, קָדוֹשׁ, קָדוֹשׁ, יהוה צְבָאוֹת:

יְפִי קַרְקְסֵי אֵשׁ / הַחֲתוּמִין בְּטַבַּעַת אֵשׁ
לְאֵשׁ אוֹכְלָה אֵשׁ / בְּשִׁלּוּשׁ קְדֻשּׁוֹת לְהָאֵשׁ.
קָדוֹשׁ, קָדוֹשׁ, קָדוֹשׁ, יהוה צְבָאוֹת:

וְהַחַיּוֹת יְשׁוֹרֵרוּ / וּכְרוּבִים יְפָאֵרוּ
וּשְׂרָפִים יָרֹנּוּ / וְאֶרְאֶלִּים יְבָרֵכוּ
פְּנֵי כָל חַיָּה וְאוֹפָן וּכְרוּב לְעֻמַּת שְׂרָפִים
לְעֻמָּתָם מְשַׁבְּחִים וְאוֹמְרִים

All say aloud:

יחזקאל ג
בָּרוּךְ כְּבוֹד־יהוה מִמְּקוֹמוֹ:

Continue with "לְאֵל בָּרוּךְ" on page 375 to "אֵין אֱלֹהִים זוּלָתֶךָ" on page 385.

זולת

אָז בִּקְשֹׁב עָנָו, עֲלֵה אֶל הַר הָעֲבָרִים
בְּדַעְתּוֹ חִשֵּׁב כַּעֲלִיַּת סִין בְּהִדּוּרִים
גְּזֵרַת דָּת חֲדָשָׁה וּפִקּוּדִים יְשָׁרִים
דּוֹד יֵשׁ לוֹ לִתֵּן לְמִשְׁבְּעִים בְּחוּרִים.

הָעֵת קָשַׁב, וּמֻת בָּהָר אֲשֶׁר אַתָּה עוֹלֶה
וַי וַי צָוַח בְּפֶה מָלֵא
זוֹ עֲלִיָּה, יְרִידָה הִיא לְהִתְכַּלֶּה
חַנּוּן, אֶעְבְּרָה נָּא וְאֶרְאֶה הָהָר הַטּוֹב וְהַמְעֻלֶּה.

טָהוֹר עֲנָהוּ, רַב לָךְ, אַל תּוֹסֶף דַּבֵּר
יְהוֹשֻׁעַ מְשָׁרֶתְךָ, הִגִּיעַ זְמַן הֱיוֹת חָבֵר
כִּי הַמַּלְכוּת בַּחֲבֶרְתָּהּ כִּמְלֹא נִימָא לֹא תִתְחַבֵּר
לְהַר נְבוֹ תַּעֲלֶה וְשָׁם תָּמוּת, וּבַגַּי תִּקָּבֵר.

מֹשֶׁה כְּיָדַע כִּי גְזֵרָה עָלָיו נִגְזָרָה
נָם לַאֲדוֹן כֹּל, הוֹדַע חוֹבָתִי לְיָפָה וּבָרָה
סְגָלִים פֶּן יֹאמְרוּ, בְּסֵתֶר עָבַר עֲבֵרָה
עַל כֵּן לֹא עֲנָהוּ אָיֹם וְנוֹרָא.

פּוֹדֶה הֱשִׁיבוֹ, עַל אֲשֶׁר מְעַלְתֶּם בִּי בְּמֵי מְרִיבָה
צַעֲקַת שַׁוְעַתְכֶם לָכֵן לְפָנַי לֹא בָא
קְנִיסָה זוֹ עֲלֵיכֶם לָכֵן נִקְנְסָה וְנִקְצָבָה
רָשׁוּם יֵרָשֵׁם וְיִכָּתֵב בְּדַת נֶפֶשׁ מְשִׁיבָה.

שִׁבְטֵי יְשֻׁרוּן קִבֵּץ וְנִחַת
תְּמִימַי, תִּפְדּוּנִי מֵרֶדֶת שַׁחַת
מַר צָרְחוּ כֻּלָּם, וְצָוְחוּ כְּאַחַת
שֶׁאֵין פִּדְיוֹן וְכֹפֶר בִּכְלוּם חֵפֶץ וּדְבַר תּוֹכָחַת.

הִשְׁלִים נַפְשׁוֹ מִיָּד לְמִיתַת נְשִׁיקָה
בִּרְאוֹתוֹ כִּי אֵין הַצָּלָה בִּתְפִלָּה וּצְעָקָה
שְׁמָעוּנִי אַחַי וְרֵעַי, עִסְקוּ בְּדָת חֲשׁוּקָה
וְאַל תְּהִי זֹאת לָכֶם לְמִכְשׁוֹל וּלְפוּקָה.

חֲיָלָיו בְּכוּהוּ שְׁלֹשִׁים יָמִים
זוֹכְרִים צִדְקַת מִשְׁפָּטָיו אֲשֶׁר עִמָּם הִתְמִים
קָפַץ וְדִלֵּג כַּאֲרִי לִפְדוֹתָם מִבֵּין עֲנָמִים
וְהַיָּם בָּקַע לִפְנֵיהֶם, וַיַּמְלִיכוּ מַלְכָּם לְעוֹלָמִים.

Continue with "עֶזְרַת אֲבוֹתֵינוּ" on page 385.

פיוט לאחר קריאת התורה לשמחת תורה

The following piyut, is said before the reading of the הפטרה.

אַשְׁרֶיךָ הַר הָעֲבָרִים   עַל הֶהָרִים הַגְּבוֹהִים
יַעַן בְּךָ מִבְחַר קְבָרִים   הַקֶּבֶר אִישׁ הָאֱלֹהִים.

בִּלְבָבִי לַבָּה, וְכַף אַךְ   עַל מוֹת צִיר נֶאֱמָן אֲשֶׁר לֹא
קָם כָּמְוֹהוּ עוֹד, וּמַלְאַךְ   נִרְאָה מִתּוֹךְ הַסְּנֶה לוֹ
בּוֹעֵר בָּאֵשׁ הַסְּנֶה, אַךְ   לֹא נֶאְכָל עַצְמוֹ וְחֵילוֹ

וַיּוֹאֶל עֵינָיו לְהָרִים   וַיִּקְרָא אֵלָיו אֱלֹהִים
הִסְתִּיר פָּנָיו הַיְקָרִים   מֵהַבִּיט אֶל הָאֱלֹהִים.

רַב מוֹפְתָיו אַךְ בֶּאֱמוּנָה   אֵל חַי עִצְּמוֹ בְּעָצְמָה
הוּא הִנְחִיל דָּת נֶאֱמָנָה   דָּת מְלֵאָה דַּעַת וְחָכְמָה
כַּבֵּד הוֹרֶיךָ, וְאַל נָא   תִּשְׁאַל אֵיךְ הָיָה וְכַמָּה

הַנִּפְלָאִים הַזְּכוּרִים   לָמָּה יִקְצֹף הָאֱלֹהִים
הַדּוֹבְרִים עָלָיו שְׁקָרִים   לֹא הֶאֱמִינוּ בֵּאלֹהִים.

הוּא הוֹרִיד לוּחוֹת שְׁתַּיִם   וּבְעֵת תַּעֲנִיתִי בְּמַעֲלִי
אַרְבָּעִים יוֹם פַּעֲמַיִם   לֹא אָכַל לֶחֶם בְּשֶׁלִּי
אֵיךְ אֹכַל לֶחֶם, וּמַיִם   אֶשְׁתֶּה, כִּי נֶאְסַף פְּלִילִי

שֶׁפֵּרֵשׁ לִי סוֹד אֲמָרִים   שֶׁאָמַר לוֹ הָאֱלֹהִים
וּבְמוֹתוֹ בֵּרַךְ יְשָׁרִים   וַיְבָרֶךְ אֹתָם אֱלֹהִים.

מַה נִּכְבָּד מִקְרָא וּמִדְרָשׁ   דָּת הָיְתָה אָמוֹן בְּשַׁחַק
הוֹרִישָׁהּ עָנָו, וְיָרַשׁ   דּוֹר מִדּוֹר קָרוֹב לְמֶרְחָק
וִיסוֹד הַשֵּׁם הַמְפֹרָשׁ   עַל סֵפֶר, אֵלֶּה שְׁמוֹת חָק

וַיִּקְרָא סוֹד הַסְּפָרִים   וַיְדַבֵּר אִתּוֹ אֱלֹהִים
דִּבֵּר אֵלֶּה הַדְּבָרִים   וּבְרֵאשִׁית בָּרָא אֱלֹהִים.

Continue with the blessing before the הפטרה *on page 1259.*

הלכות תפילה

HALAKHA GUIDE

GUIDE TO SUKKOT

EREV SUKKOT (14TH OF TISHREI)

1 The construction and decoration of the sukka should be completed before Sukkot begins. Likewise, the myrtle (*hadasim*) and willow (*aravot*) should be bound to the lulav before the holiday begins [שו״ע או״ח, תרנא: א].

2 When Sukkot falls on Thursday and Friday, each household must prepare an *Eiruv Tavshilin* (page 5); this makes it permissible to prepare food on Friday for the Shabbat meals [שו״ע או״ח, תקכז].

FIRST DAYS OF SUKKOT (15TH–16TH OF TISHREI)

3 Candle lighting: Two blessings are said: (1) לְהַדְלִיק נֵר שֶׁל יוֹם טוֹב and (2) שֶׁהֶחֱיָנוּ. When Sukkot eve falls on Friday night, the conclusion of the first blessing is: לְהַדְלִיק נֵר שֶׁל שַׁבָּת וְשֶׁל יוֹם טוֹב (page 5).

4 Ma'ariv: for Shabbat and Yom Tov (page 45). Many congregations say the special verse for Yom Tov (וַיְדַבֵּר מֹשֶׁה on page 59), before saying the Amida for Yom Tov. This is followed by Full Kaddish, *Aleinu*, Mourner's Kaddish, Psalm 27 and Mourner's Kaddish. It is customary to conclude with the singing of Adon Olam or Yigdal.

5 When Sukkot eve falls on Friday night, Ma'ariv for Shabbat is preceded by the last two psalms of Kabbalat Shabbat: מִזְמוֹר שִׁיר לְיוֹם הַשַּׁבָּת and יהוה מָלָךְ, גֵּאוּת לָבֵשׁ (page 41). בַּמֶּה מַדְלִיקִין is omitted. וְשָׁמְרוּ (page 59) precedes the Yom Tov Amida,

which is said with additions for Shabbat. After the Amida, the congregation says וַיְכֻלּוּ הַשָּׁמַיִם, and the *Shaliah Tzibbur* says the abbreviated Repetition of the Amida as is customary on Shabbat eve [שו״ע או״ח, תרמב: א].

6 When the eve of the second day falls on Motza'ei Shabbat, the congregation adds the paragraph וַתּוֹדִיעֵנוּ in the middle section of the Amida.

7 Upon returning home, one enters the sukka. Some say a special meditation (page 181). When saying the Kiddush for Yom Tov on the first night, the blessing לֵישֵׁב בַּסֻּכָּה ("to dwell in the sukka") precedes the blessing שֶׁהֶחֱיָנוּ. On the second night, the blessing שֶׁהֶחֱיָנוּ is said prior to the blessing לֵישֵׁב בַּסֻּכָּה [שו״ע או״ח, תרסא: א]; some say the blessings in the same order as on the first night. [משנ״ב, שם: ב] When Sukkot eve falls on Friday night, Kiddush is said with additions for Shabbat. When the second night of Sukkot falls on Motza'ei Shabbat, the two blessings for Havdala are inserted prior to the blessing שֶׁהֶחֱיָנוּ; thus the order of blessings is: wine, Kiddush, flame, Havdala, שֶׁהֶחֱיָנוּ, sukka (pages 189–191) [שו״ע או״ח, תרמג: א]. In *Birkat HaMazon*, one adds יַעֲלֶה וְיָבוֹא (page 203).

8 Shaharit: for Shabbat and Yom Tov (page 307). The *Shaliah Tzibbur* for Shaharit begins from the words הָאֵל בְּתַעֲצוּמוֹת עֻזֶּךָ (page 357). After *Barekhu*, the congregation says הַמֵּאִיר לָאָרֶץ or, if it is also Shabbat, הַכֹּל יוֹדוּךָ. The Amida for Yom Tov is said (page 389); if also Shabbat, one says the additions for Shabbat.

9 After the *Shaliah Tzibbur* repeats the Amida, the congregation takes the lulav and says the blessing עַל נְטִילַת לוּלָב. On the first day the lulav is taken, the blessing שֶׁהֶחֱיָנוּ is also said (page 407). On Shabbat, one does not take the lulav [שו״ע או״ח, תרמד: א; שם, תרנח: א-ב]. Hallel is said, and some congregations say *Hoshanot* after Hallel. This is followed by Full Kaddish and taking the Torah from the Ark. Some congregations precede taking the Torah from the Ark with the Daily Psalm and Psalm 27, followed by the Mourner's Kaddish. Most congregations say the "Thirteen Attributes of Mercy" and a special supplication (page 429), except on Shabbat.

10 Torah Reading: first day and second day – page 441. Maftir and Haftarot – pages 453–463 [שו״ע או״ח, תרנט: א, תרסב: ג].

11 The Haftara is followed by (*Yekum Purkan* on Shabbat, then) the prayers for the government and the State of Israel. The *Shaliah Tzibbur* says יָהּ אֵלִי וְגוֹאֲלִי (page 479) (except when Sukkot falls on Shabbat), the congregation says *Ashrei*, and the Torah scrolls are returned to the Ark. The *Shaliah Tzibbur* says Half Kaddish.

12 Musaf: for Festivals (page 489). If also Shabbat, one says the additions for Shabbat. During the Repetition of the Amida, the Kohanim say *Birkat Kohanim*. After the Repetition, the congregation takes the lulav, the Ark is opened and one

Torah scroll is taken out. The *Shaliaḥ Tzibbur* leads the congregation in saying the *Hoshanot*, while making a circuit around the *bima* (page 531) [שו״ע או״ח, תרס:א]. On Shabbat, the Ark is opened, and the special *Hoshanot* for Shabbat, אֹם נְצוּרָה and כְּהוֹשַׁעְתָּ אָדָם (page 537), are said [שו״ע, שם:ג]. The Torah scroll is returned to the Ark, and the *Shaliaḥ Tzibbur* says Full Kaddish. This is followed by *Ein Keloheinu*, the Rabbis' Kaddish, *Aleinu*, Mourner's Kaddish, the Daily Psalm, Psalm 27, Mourner's Kaddish, *Anim Zemirot*, Mourner's Kaddish and Adon Olam.

13 Minḥa: for Shabbat and Yom Tov. When Sukkot falls on Shabbat, the Torah is taken from the Ark and the beginning of וְזֹאת הַבְּרָכָה (page 959) is read. After returning the Torah to the Ark, the *Shaliaḥ Tzibbur* says Half Kaddish, and the congregation says the Amida for Yom Tov (page 579), with additions for Shabbat.

ḤOL HAMO'ED SUKKOT

14 During Shaḥarit, Minḥa and Ma'ariv, יַעֲלֶה וְיָבוֹא is added to the seventeenth blessing of the Amida (רְצֵה). It is also added during *Birkat HaMazon* (page 203) [שו״ע או״ח, תצ:ב].

15 The traditional Ashkenazi practice is to wear tefillin during Shaḥarit until the recitation of Hallel. However, some congregations follow the Sephardi custom, in which tefillin are not worn on Ḥol HaMo'ed; this is also the practice in Israel [שו״ע ורמ״א או״ח, לא:ב].

16 First Evening of Ḥol HaMo'ed: Ma'ariv for weekdays (page 1337). אַתָּה חוֹנַנְתָּנוּ is added in the fourth blessing of the Amida. Havdala is said in the sukka (unless Ḥol HaMo'ed begins on Friday night). No blessing is made over spices or a flame (unless Ḥol HaMo'ed begins on Saturday night), but one says the blessing לֵישֵׁב בַּסֻּכָּה before drinking (page 1387).

17 Shaḥarit: for weekdays. After the *Shaliaḥ Tzibbur* repeats the Amida, the congregation takes the lulav and says the blessing עַל נְטִילַת לוּלָב [שו״ע או״ח, תרסב:א]. Hallel is said, and some congregations say *Hoshanot* after Hallel instead of after Musaf. This is followed by Full Kaddish.

18 Torah Reading: Pages 675–681. Four men are called up. Each day's reading is nine verses long. For each of the first three *aliyot*, one reads three verses. The fourth *oleh* goes back to the beginning and reads the first six verses a second time [רמ״א או״ח, תרסג:א].

19 After the Torah reading, Half Kaddish is said, the Torah is returned to the Ark, and *Ashrei* and וּבָא לְצִיּוֹן are said. The *Shaliaḥ Tzibbur* then says Half Kaddish.

20 Musaf: for Festivals (page 693). The *Kedusha* for weekdays is said; no *Birkat Kohanim* is said. After the Repetition of the Amida, the congregation takes the lulav, the Ark is opened and one Torah scroll is taken out. The *Shaliaḥ Tzibbur* leads the congregation in saying the *Hoshanot* of the day (see table on page 711), while making a circuit around the *bima*. The Torah scroll is returned to the Ark, and the *Shaliaḥ Tzibbur* says Full Kaddish. This is followed by *Aleinu* (page 721), and the conclusion of the weekday service.

SHABBAT ḤOL HAMO'ED SUKKOT

21 Ma'ariv for Shabbat is preceded by Psalms 92 and 93: מִזְמוֹר שִׁיר לְיוֹם הַשַּׁבָּת and יהוה מָלָךְ, גֵּאוּת לָבֵשׁ (page 741). בַּמֶּה מַדְלִיקִין is not said. The Amida for Shabbat is said with the addition of יַעֲלֶה וְיָבוֹא [שו״ע או״ח, תרסג: ב].

22 Shaḥarit: for Shabbat (page 307). The Amida for Shabbat is said with the addition of יַעֲלֶה וְיָבוֹא [שם]. Hallel is said, and some congregations say *Hoshanot* after Hallel instead of after Musaf. This is followed by Full Kaddish, the reading of *Kohelet* and Mourner's Kaddish [רמ״א או״ח, תצ: ט].

23 Torah Reading: page 863. Maftir: Reading for the fourth *aliya* of the appropriate day (pages 873–875). Haftara: page 875 [שו״ע או״ח, תרסג: ג]. In the concluding blessing after the Haftara, one says מְקַדֵּשׁ הַשַּׁבָּת וְיִשְׂרָאֵל וְהַזְּמַנִּים [משנ״ב, שם: ט].

24 The Haftara is followed by (*Yekum Purkan* on Shabbat, then) the prayers for the government and the State of Israel. *Ashrei* is said and the Torah scrolls are returned to the Ark. The *Shaliaḥ Tzibbur* says Half Kaddish.

25 Musaf: for Festivals, with additions for Shabbat (page 899). However, אַדִּיר אַדִּירֵנוּ is not added to *Kedusha*, and *Birkat Kohanim* is not said. After the Repetition of the Amida, the Ark is opened, no Torah scroll is taken out, and the special *Hoshanot* for Shabbat, אֹם נְצוּרָה and כְּהוֹשַׁעְתָּ אָדָם (page 917), are said. The Ark is closed, and the *Shaliaḥ Tzibbur* says Full Kaddish. This is followed by *Ein Keloheinu* (page 927) and the conclusion of Musaf, as for Shabbat.

26 Minḥa: for Shabbat (page 949). The Torah is taken from the Ark and the beginning of וְזֹאת הַבְּרָכָה (page 959) is read. After returning the Torah to the Ark, the

Shaliaḥ Tzibbur says Half Kaddish, and the congregation says the Amida for Shabbat with the addition of יַעֲלֶה וְיָבוֹא.

27 Motza'ei Shabbat: Ma'ariv for Motza'ei Shabbat is said. After the Amida, וִיהִי נֹעַם is omitted, and the *Shaliaḥ Tzibbur* says Full Kaddish. וְיִתֶּן־לְךָ (page 1373) is said [רמ״א או״ח, רצה: ט].

HOSHANA RABA (21ST OF TISHREI)

28 Shaḥarit: It is customary for the *Shaliaḥ Tzibbur* to wear a *kittel*. *Pesukei DeZimra* for Shabbat and Yom Tov is said, including Psalm 100 (מִזְמוֹר לְתוֹדָה, page 319). After אָז יָשִׁיר־מֹשֶׁה (page 347), prayers continue with Shaḥarit for weekdays (page 621) [שו״ע ורמ״א או״ח, תרסד: א]. Some have the custom to open the Ark after *Yishtabaḥ*, and say Psalm 130 responsively (some say Psalm 130 before *Yishtabaḥ*). After the *Shaliaḥ Tzibbur* repeats the Amida, the congregation takes the lulav and says the blessing עַל נְטִילַת לוּלָב. Hallel is said, and some congregations say *Hoshanot* after Hallel instead of after Musaf. This is followed Full Kaddish.

29 While the Torah is taken from the Ark, the congregation says *Ein Kamokha* (page 985) [רמ״א, שם]. Most congregations say the "Thirteen Attributes of Mercy" and a special supplication (page 987). Torah Reading: page 995. Some have the custom to read in the melody of *Yamim Nora'im*.

30 After the Torah reading, Half Kaddish is said, the Torah is returned to the Ark, and *Ashrei* and וּבָא לְצִיּוֹן are said. The *Shaliaḥ Tzibbur* says Half Kaddish.

31 Musaf: for Festivals (page 1007). It is customary for the *Shaliaḥ Tzibbur* to wear a *kittel* [רמ״א, שם]. The *Kedusha* for Yom Tov is said, but *Birkat Kohanim* is not. After the Repetition of the Amida, the congregation takes the lulav, the Ark is opened and seven Torah scrolls are taken out to the *bima*. Many congregations have the custom of taking out all the Torah scrolls [רמ״א או״ח, תרס: א]. The *Shaliaḥ Tzibbur* leads the congregation in saying the *Hoshanot* while making seven circuits around the *bima* (page 1023) [רמ״א או״ח, תרסד: א]. These are followed by special *piyutim* asking for rain. Then five willow branches (*aravot*) are taken and beaten five times before the Torah scrolls are returned to the Ark (page 1057). Some have the custom of beating the *aravot* after the *Shaliaḥ Tzibbur* says the Full Kaddish [רמ״א, שם: ז]. This is followed by *Ein Keloheinu*, Rabbis' Kaddish, *Aleinu*, Mourner's Kaddish, the Daily Psalm, Psalm 27 and Mourner's Kaddish.

SHEMINI ATZERET (22ND OF TISHREI)

32 Candle lighting: Two blessings are said: (1) לְהַדְלִיק נֵר שֶׁל יוֹם טוֹב, and (2) שֶׁהֶחֱיָנוּ. When Shemini Atzeret eve falls on Friday night, the conclusion of the first blessing is: לְהַדְלִיק נֵר שֶׁל שַׁבָּת וְשֶׁל יוֹם טוֹב.

33 Ma'ariv: for Shabbat and Yom Tov. Many congregations say the special verse for Yom Tov (וַיְדַבֵּר מֹשֶׁה on page 59), before saying the Amida for Yom Tov. This is followed by Full Kaddish, *Aleinu*, Mourner's Kaddish, Psalm 27 and Mourner's Kaddish. It is customary to conclude with the singing of Adon Olam or Yigdal.

34 When Shemini Atzeret eve falls on Friday night, Ma'ariv is preceded by the last two psalms of Kabbalat Shabbat: מִזְמוֹר שִׁיר לְיוֹם הַשַּׁבָּת and יהוה מָלָךְ, גֵּאוּת לָבֵשׁ (page 41). בַּמֶּה מַדְלִיקִין is omitted. וְשָׁמְרוּ (page 59) precedes the Yom Tov Amida, which is said with additions for Shabbat. After the Amida, the congregation says וַיְכֻלּוּ הַשָּׁמַיִם, and the *Shaliaḥ Tzibbur* says the abbreviated Repetition of the Amida as is customary on Shabbat eve.

35 When Shemini Atzeret eve falls on Friday night, Kiddush for Yom Tov is said with additions for Shabbat.

36 Outside Israel the traditional Ashkenazi practice is to sit in the sukka on Shemini Atzeret, without saying the blessing לֵישֵׁב בַּסֻּכָּה [שו״ע או״ח, תרסח:א]. However, some follow the Ḥasidic custom, according to which Kiddush is said in the sukka on Shemini Atzeret eve, while the rest of the meals are eaten in the house.

37 Shaḥarit: for Shabbat and Yom Tov (page 307). The *Shaliaḥ Tzibbur* for Shaḥarit begins from the words הָאֵל בְּתַעֲצוּמוֹת עֻזֶּךָ (page 357). After *Barekhu*, the congregation says הַמֵּאִיר לָאָרֶץ or, if it is also Shabbat, הַכֹּל יוֹדוּךָ. The Amida for Yom Tov is said (page 389); if also Shabbat, one says the additions for Shabbat. The Repetition of the Amida is followed by Hallel and Full Kaddish. On Shabbat, *Kohelet* is read, followed by the Mourner's Kaddish.

38 While the Torah is taken from the Ark, most congregations say the "Thirteen Attributes of Mercy" and a special supplication (page 1081), except on Shabbat.

39 Torah Reading: page 1093. Maftir and Haftara: page 1105 [שו״ע או״ח, תרסח:ב].

40 The Haftara is followed by (*Yekum Purkan* on Shabbat, then) the prayers for the government and the State of Israel, *Yizkor* (page 1123), and אַב הָרַחֲמִים [משנ״ב, שם:טו]. The congregation says *Ashrei* (page 1129), and the Torah scrolls are returned to the Ark. The *Shaliaḥ Tzibbur* says Half Kaddish.

41 Musaf for Festivals (page 1137) is said. If also Shabbat, one says the additions

for Shabbat. It is customary for the *Shaliaḥ Tzibbur* to wear a *kittel*. In most congregations, the announcement to begin saying מַשִּׁיב הָרְוּחַ וּמוֹרִיד הַגֶּשֶׁם precedes the silent recitation of the Amida [רמ״א או״ח, קיד:ב]. The Repetition of the Amida begins with the opening of the Ark, and the *Shaliaḥ Tzibbur* says the Prayer for Rain (page 1153). The Kohanim say *Birkat Kohanim*. After the Repetition, the service continues with Full Kaddish, and the conclusion of the service is as for Shabbat and Yom Tov (page 1181).

▸ LAWS OF מַשִּׁיב הָרְוּחַ

42 One begins saying מַשִּׁיב הָרְוּחַ in Musaf of Shemini Atzeret and continues until Musaf of the first day of Pesaḥ [שו״ע או״ח, קיד:א].

43 If one forgets to say מַשִּׁיב הָרְוּחַ in its proper place but realizes before beginning the words of the blessing מְחַיֵּה הַמֵּתִים, one should immediately say מַשִּׁיב הָרְוּחַ and continue with the rest of the blessing. If one realizes the omission immediately after completing the blessing מְחַיֵּה הַמֵּתִים, one should say מַשִּׁיב הָרְוּחַ and continue with the following blessing. If one realizes the omission after beginning the words אַתָּה קָדוֹשׁ, one must repeat the Amida from the beginning [שו״ע או״ח, קיד:ו].

44 If one forgets to say מַשִּׁיב הָרְוּחַ but says מוֹרִיד הַטָּל (as is the custom in Israel, and that of *Nusaḥ Sepharad*, in the spring and summer months), one need not repeat the Amida [שו״ע או״ח, קיד:ה]. If there is doubt whether one said מַשִּׁיב הָרְוּחַ, the presumption is as follows: within the first thirty days from *Shemini Atzeret*, one should assume that one forgot to say מַשִּׁיב הָרְוּחַ. After thirty days, one should assume that one said מַשִּׁיב הָרְוּחַ [שו״ע או״ח, קיד:ח].

45 Minḥa: for Shabbat and Yom Tov. When Shemini Atzeret falls on Shabbat, the Torah is taken from the Ark and the beginning of וְזֹאת הַבְּרָכָה (page 959) is read. After returning the Torah to the Ark, the *Shaliaḥ Tzibbur* says Half Kaddish, and the congregation says the Amida for Yom Tov (page 579).

SIMḤAT TORAH (23RD OF TISHREI)

46 Candle lighting: Two blessings are said: (1) לְהַדְלִיק נֵר שֶׁל יוֹם טוֹב, and (2) שֶׁהֶחֱיָנוּ.

47 Ma'ariv: as for Shabbat and Yom Tov. Many congregations say the special verse for Yom Tov (וַיְדַבֵּר מֹשֶׁה on page 59), before saying the Amida for Yom Tov. If Shemini Atzeret fell on Shabbat, the congregation adds the paragraph וַתּוֹדִיעֵנוּ in the middle section of the Amida.

48 After Full Kaddish, the verses of אַתָּה הׇרְאֵתָ are said responsively (page 93). The ark is opened, all of the Torah scrolls are taken from the Ark, and the seven *Hakafot* are performed amid joyous singing and dancing. After completion of seven *Hakafot*, all of the Torah scrolls except one are returned to the Ark. The *Shaliaḥ Tzibbur* takes the remaining scroll, and leads the congregation in saying שְׁמַע יִשְׂרָאֵל and the rest of the ceremony for taking the Torah from the Ark (page 105) [רמ״א או״ח, תרסט: א].

49 Torah reading: Customs differ. Most congregations read the beginning of וְזֹאת הַבְּרָכָה (page 109) and three (in some congregations, five) are called up. It is customary for the Reader to use the melody of *Yamim Nora'im*. After the completion of the reading, the Torah is returned to the Ark (page 113). This is followed by *Aleinu* (page 83), and Mourner's Kaddish. It is customary to conclude with the singing of Adon Olam or Yigdal.

50 Kiddush for Yom Tov (page 189) is said. If Shemini Atzeret fell on Shabbat, the two blessings for Havdala (page 191) are inserted prior to the blessing שֶׁהֶחֱיָנוּ.

51 Shaḥarit: for Shabbat and Yom Tov. The *Shaliaḥ Tzibbur* for Shaḥarit begins from the words הָאֵל בְּתַעֲצוּמוֹת עֻזֶּךָ. After *Barekhu*, the congregation says הַמֵּאִיר לָאָרֶץ. The Amida for Yom Tov is said (page 389). During the Repetition of the Amida, the Kohanim say *Birkat Kohanim*. This is followed by Hallel and Full Kaddish. The Ark is opened and the verses of אַתָּה הׇרְאֵתָ (page 1207) are said responsively. All of the Torah scrolls are taken from the Ark, and the seven *Hakafot* are performed amid joyous singing and dancing.

52 Torah Reading: pages 1233–1259. The Torah reading is repeated, in cycles of five *aliyot*, until all males over thirteen have received an *aliya* [רמ״א או״ח, תרסט: א]. It is customary for children under 13 years to participate in an *aliya*, known as *Kol HaNe'arim*, in which multiple tallitot are spread to form a canopy over the children and the *oleh*. This is followed by the calling up of the *Ḥatan Torah*, for whom the final verses of the Torah are read. After the completion of the reading, it is customary that *Hagbaha* is performed with arms crossed, so that when the Torah is raised and the arms uncrossed, the lettering on the scroll faces outward toward the congregation. A second scroll is opened; the *Ḥatan Bereshit* is called up and the first verses of *Bereshit* are read [שו״ע ורמ״א או״ח, תרסט: א]. It is customary to pause in the reading for the congregation to read aloud וַיְהִי־עֶרֶב וַיְהִי בֹקֶר for each day of Creation, and to read aloud the last three verses, starting with וַיְכֻלּוּ הַשָּׁמַיִם. This is followed by Half Kaddish. A third scroll is opened for Maftir. The Haftara is the beginning of the book of Joshua (page 1261) [שם].

53 After the Haftara, the prayers for the government and the State of Israel are

said. The congregation says *Ashrei,* and the Torah scrolls are returned to the Ark. The *Shaliaḥ Tzibbur* says Half Kaddish.

54 Musaf: for Festivals (page 1295). The Kohanim do not say *Birkat Kohanim,* because they are assumed to have drunk alcohol. The Repetition of the Amida is followed by Full Kaddish, and the conclusion of the service is as for Shabbat and Yom Tov (page 1313).

55 Minḥa: for Shabbat and Yom Tov.

MOTZA'EI SUKKOT (24TH OF TISHREI)

56 Ma'ariv: for weekdays. In the fourth blessing of the Amida, the paragraph of אַתָּה חוֹנַנְתָּנוּ is said (page 1353). Havdala is said over a cup of wine or grape juice; no blessing is made over spices or a flame [שו״ע או״ח, תרא: א].

A HALAKHIC GUIDE TO PRAYER FOR VISITORS TO ISRAEL

General Rules
Public vs. Private Conduct

57 For halakhic purposes, the definition of "visitor" is one who intends to return to his place of origin within one year [משנ״ב, קיז: ה]. Unmarried students may be considered visitors as long as they are supported by their parents [שו״ת אגרות משה או״ח ח״ב, קא].

58 In general, a visitor to Israel should continue to follow his or her customs in private. In public, however, one should avoid conduct that deviates from local practice [שו״ע או״ח, תסח: ד; משנ״ב, שם: יד]. Hence, a visitor to Israel should generally pray in accordance with his non-Israeli customs. This rule is limited, however, to one's private prayers.

59 If one is serving as *Shaliaḥ Tzibbur*, one is required to pray in accordance with the local Israeli custom. This includes, for example, repeating the Amida according to Israeli practice: saying מוֹרִיד הַטָּל in the summer, and saying שִׂים שָׁלוֹם during Minḥa on Shabbat (pages 589 and 977). This also includes saying *Ein Keloheinu* at the end of weekday Shaḥarit (page 737).

60 If one is serving as *Shaliaḥ Tzibbur* for Musaf on Yom Tov in a congregation of Israelis, in the silent Amida one should say the *Korbanot* as said outside Israel, but when repeating the Amida, say them following the Israeli practice [יום טוב שני כהלכתו, א (בשם שערי יצחק)].

61 Even if one is not serving as *Shaliaḥ Tzibbur*, a visitor praying with Israelis should say the following prayers, because of their public nature, following local Israeli custom:

a *Birkat Kohanim* is said daily in Shaḥarit and Musaf.

b In the Rabbis' Kaddish, the word קַדִּישָׁא is added after the words דִּי בְאַתְרָא.

Laws of Tefillin on Ḥol HaMo'ed

62 The custom in Israel is not to put on tefillin on Ḥol HaMo'ed. One whose custom is to put on tefillin on Ḥol HaMo'ed may, when visiting Israel, put on tefillin in private, but should not do so when praying with a congregation [שו״ת אגרות משה או״ח ח״ד, קה: ה].

Laws of Second Day Yom Tov – יום טוב שני של גלויות

63 Most authorities require a visitor to Israel to celebrate two days of Yom Tov [משנ״ב, תצו: יג]. Some hold that one should not publicly celebrate the second day, but say the festival prayers in private [שם]. Others permit organizing a public service for visitors on the second day of Yom Tov, and this has become the accepted practice. If, however, there are fewer than ten visitors, they should pray privately, rather than recruit Israeli residents to complete a *minyan* [אשי ישראל, טו: יח (בשם רש״ז אויערבאך)].

64 Some authorities rule that a visitor to Israel should celebrate only one day of Yom Tov, but, on the next day (Yom Tov outside Israel, but either Ḥol HaMo'ed or *Isru Ḥag* in Israel), one should abstain from labor and perform the **מצוות עשה דאורייתא** associated with Yom Tov [עיר הקודש והמקדש ח״ג, פ: יא]:

- **a** On the second day of Sukkot, one says Ḥol HaMo'ed prayers rather than those of Yom Tov, but refrains from performing any labor.
- **b** On the day after Shemini Atzeret (Simḥat Torah outside Israel, *Isru Ḥag* in Israel), one abstains from labor, but says weekday prayers (putting on tefillin in the morning).

65 Some authorities rule that a visitor to Israel should celebrate only one day of Yom Tov. According to this view, the visitor should follow local Israeli practice without deviation [שו״ת חכם צבי, קסז].

66 On a day when *Yizkor* is said in Israel, a visitor should not join, but should say *Yizkor* the following day with a *minyan* of visitors. If such a *minyan* will not be available, some rule that one should join with the Israelis [שו״ת רבבות אפרים ח״א, שמב: ב]; others rule that *Yizkor* be said in private the following day [שו״ת בצל החכמה ח״ד, קכ: א].

FULL KADDISH

Leader: יִתְגַּדַּל Magnified and sanctified
may His great name be,
in the world He created by His will.
May He establish His kingdom
in your lifetime and in your days,
and in the lifetime of all the house of Israel,
swiftly and soon –
and say: Amen.

All: May His great name be blessed for ever and all time.

Leader: Blessed and praised, glorified and exalted,
raised and honored, uplifted and lauded be
the name of the Holy One, blessed be He,
beyond any blessing,
song, praise and consolation
uttered in the world –
and say: Amen.

(*All:* In compassion and favor accept our prayer.)

May the prayers and pleas of all Israel
be accepted by their Father in heaven –
and say: Amen.

(*All:* May the name of the LORD be blessed from now and for ever.) *Ps. 113*

May there be great peace from heaven,
and life for us and all Israel –
and say: Amen.

(*All:* My help comes from the LORD, Maker of heaven and earth.) *Ps. 113*

Bow, take three steps back, as if taking leave of the Divine Presence, then bow, first left, then right, then center, while saying:
May He who makes peace in His high places,
make peace for us and all Israel –
and say: Amen.

קדיש שלם

ש״ץ: יִתְגַּדַּל וְיִתְקַדַּשׁ שְׁמֵהּ רַבָּא (קהל: אָמֵן)
בְּעָלְמָא דִּי בְרָא כִרְעוּתֵהּ
וְיַמְלִיךְ מַלְכוּתֵהּ
בְּחַיֵּיכוֹן וּבְיוֹמֵיכוֹן וּבְחַיֵּי דְכָל בֵּית יִשְׂרָאֵל
בַּעֲגָלָא וּבִזְמַן קָרִיב, וְאִמְרוּ אָמֵן. (קהל: אָמֵן)

קהל וש״ץ: יְהֵא שְׁמֵהּ רַבָּא מְבָרַךְ לְעָלַם וּלְעָלְמֵי עָלְמַיָּא.

ש״ץ: יִתְבָּרַךְ וְיִשְׁתַּבַּח וְיִתְפָּאַר וְיִתְרוֹמַם וְיִתְנַשֵּׂא
וְיִתְהַדָּר וְיִתְעַלֶּה וְיִתְהַלָּל
שְׁמֵהּ דְּקֻדְשָׁא בְּרִיךְ הוּא (קהל: בְּרִיךְ הוּא)
לְעֵלָּא מִן כָּל בִּרְכָתָא וְשִׁירָתָא, תֻּשְׁבְּחָתָא וְנֶחֱמָתָא
דַּאֲמִירָן בְּעָלְמָא, וְאִמְרוּ אָמֵן. (קהל: אָמֵן)
(קהל: קַבֵּל בְּרַחֲמִים וּבְרָצוֹן אֶת תְּפִלָּתֵנוּ)

תִּתְקַבַּל צְלוֹתְהוֹן וּבָעוּתְהוֹן דְּכָל יִשְׂרָאֵל
קֳדָם אֲבוּהוֹן דִּי בִשְׁמַיָּא, וְאִמְרוּ אָמֵן. (קהל: אָמֵן)
(קהל: יְהִי שֵׁם יהוה מְבֹרָךְ מֵעַתָּה וְעַד־עוֹלָם:) תהלים קיג

יְהֵא שְׁלָמָא רַבָּא מִן שְׁמַיָּא
וְחַיִּים, עָלֵינוּ וְעַל כָּל יִשְׂרָאֵל, וְאִמְרוּ אָמֵן. (קהל: אָמֵן)
(קהל: עֶזְרִי מֵעִם יהוה, עֹשֵׂה שָׁמַיִם וָאָרֶץ:) תהלים קכא

Bow, take three steps back, as if taking leave of the Divine Presence, then bow, first left, then right, then center, while saying:

עֹשֶׂה שָׁלוֹם בִּמְרוֹמָיו
הוּא יַעֲשֶׂה שָׁלוֹם
עָלֵינוּ וְעַל כָּל יִשְׂרָאֵל, וְאִמְרוּ אָמֵן. (קהל: אָמֵן)

RABBIS' KADDISH

Mourner: Yitgadal ve-yitkadash shemeh raba. (*Cong:* Amen)
Be-alema di vera khir'uteh,
ve-yamlikh malkhuteh,
be-ḥayyeikhon, uv-yomeikhon, uv-ḥayyei de-khol beit Yisrael,
ba-agala uvi-zman kariv,
ve-imru Amen. (*Cong:* Amen)

All: Yeheh shemeh raba mevarakh le'alam ul-alemei alemaya.

Mourner: Yitbarakh ve-yishtabaḥ ve-yitpa'ar ve-yitromam ve-yitnaseh
ve-yit-hadar ve-yit'aleh ve-yit-hallal
shemeh dekudsha, berikh hu. (*Cong:* Berikh hu)
Le-ela lmin kol birkhata ve-shirata,
tushbeḥata ve-neḥemata,
da-amiran be-alema,
ve-imru, Amen. (*Cong:* Amen)

Al Yisrael, ve-al rabanan,
ve-al talmideihon, ve-al kol talmidei talmideihon,
ve-al kol man de-asekin be-oraita
di be-atra (*In Israel:* kadisha) ha-dein ve-di be-khol atar va-atar,
yeheh lehon ul-khon shelama raba,
ḥina ve-ḥisda, ve-raḥamei,
ve-ḥayyei arikhei, um-zonei re-viḥei,
u-furkana min kodam avuhon di vish-maya,
ve-imru Amen. (*Cong:* Amen)

Yeheh shelama raba min shemaya
ve-ḥayyim (tovim) aleinu ve-al kol Yisrael,
ve-imru Amen. (*Cong:* Amen)

Bow, take three steps back, as if taking leave of the Divine Presence, then bow, first left, then right, then center, while saying:

Oseh shalom bim-romav,
hu ya'aseh ve-raḥamav shalom aleinu, ve-al kol Yisrael,
ve-imru Amen. (*Cong:* Amen)

MOURNER'S KADDISH

Mourner: Yitgadal ve-yitkadash shemeh raba. (*Cong:* Amen)
Be-alema di vera khir'uteh,
ve yamlikh malkhuteh,
be ḥayyeikhon, uv-yomeikhon, uv-ḥayyei de-khol beit Yisrael,
ba-agala uvi-zman kariv,
ve-imru Amen. (*Cong:* Amen)

All: Yeheh shemeh raba mevarakh le'alam ul-alemei alemaya.

Mourner: Yitbarakh ve-yishtabaḥ ve-yitpa'ar ve-yitromam ve-yitnaseh
ve-yit-hadar ve-yit'aleh ve-yit-hallal
shemeh dekudsha, berikh hu. (*Cong:* Berikh hu)
Le-ela min kol birkhata ve-shirata,
tushbeḥata ve-neḥemata,
da-amiran be-alema,
ve-imru, Amen. (*Cong:* Amen)

Yeheh shelama raba min shemaya
ve-ḥayyim aleinu ve-al kol Yisrael,
ve-imru Amen. (*Cong:* Amen)

Bow, take three steps back, as if taking leave of the Divine Presence, then bow, first left, then right, then center, while saying:

Oseh shalom bim-romav,
hu ya'aseh shalom aleinu, ve-al kol Yisrael,
ve-imru Amen. (*Cong:* Amen)

קורֵן ירושלים